Compact Oxford Dictionary and Thesaurus

THIRD EDITION

Edited by
Maurice Waite
Sara Hawker

OXFORD
UNIVERSITY PRESS

Great Clarendon Street, Oxford OX2 6DP

Oxford University Press is a department of the University of Oxford.
It furthers the University's objective of excellence in research, scholarship,
and education by publishing worldwide in

Oxford New York

Auckland Cape Town Dar es Salaam Hong Kong Karachi
Kuala Lumpur Madrid Melbourne Mexico City Nairobi
New Delhi Shanghai Taipei Toronto

With offices in

Argentina Austria Brazil Chile Czech Republic France Greece
Guatemala Hungary Italy Japan Poland Portugal Singapore
South Korea Switzerland Thailand Turkey Ukraine Vietnam

Oxford is a registered trade mark of Oxford University Press
in the UK and in certain other countries

British Library Cataloguing in Publication Data

Data available

Library of Congress Cataloging in Publication Data

Data available

ISBN 978-0-19-955847-6

10 9 8 7 6 5 4 3

Typeset in Frutiger and Parable
by Asiatype Inc.
Printed and bound in China
through Asia Pacific Offset

5956320342760783

Contents

Preface

The *Compact Oxford Dictionary and Thesaurus* is an invaluable combined reference tool for anyone who wants to enrich their vocabulary and increase their command of the English language. It aims to provide a wide variety of information about language and the core vocabulary of current English in a conveniently sized volume and a readily accessible format. In this new edition, you only have to look at one entry to find both what a word means and a range of synonyms for it.

The dictionary is adapted from the *Colour Oxford English Dictionary* and is based on our analysis of the two billion words of real English, taken from books, newspapers, magazines, and the Internet, which are contained in the Oxford English Corpus. It focuses on clear explanations of meaning together with extra help on the spelling, pronunciation, grammar, or usage of words which often cause difficulty. Individual notes give clear guidance on confusable words (such as *accept* and *except*, or *flaunt* and *flout*), points of good English (for example, whether to say 'different from' or 'different to'), and tricky spellings (like *Mediterranean*, *skilful*, and *weird*). Information is presented in clear, concise language, avoiding the use of difficult or technical terms wherever possible. The pronunciations use a simple respelling system which makes them very easy to understand.

The 8,000 boxed synonym sections are derived from the *Colour Oxford Thesaurus* and work just like a thesaurus to help you to express yourself more accurately and in more interesting and varied ways. By listing groups of words that have similar meanings to each other, they offer a choice of alternative words that can be used in place of one that you already have in mind. They can provide the answer when a word is on the tip of your tongue, as well as expanding your vocabulary or helping to solve crossword puzzles and many other word games. Antonyms (words with opposite meanings) are also provided in many entries.

The new Wordfinder section in the middle of the book contains hundreds of lists of words covering a wide range of subjects, from types of pasta and breeds of dog to organs of the body and parts of a car, all organized into thematic groups such as Food, Society, and Technology to make them interesting to browse, with a handy index at the start to help you go straight to the information you need.

Guide to the dictionary and thesaurus

1. Structure of entries

Here are examples of the major types of information in entries:

part of speech
(word class)

headword

absurd ▸ adjective completely unreasonable
or inappropriate.

words that can be used as alternatives to the headword

SYNONYMS **irrational**, illogical,
inappropriate, ridiculous, ludicrous,
farcical, comical, stupid, foolish, silly,
pointless, senseless, preposterous; informal
crazy, cockeyed; Brit. informal **barmy**, daft.
ANTONYMS reasonable, sensible.

geographical label showing where the following synonym(s) are used
(see section 2)

words meaning the opposite of the headword; most have entries of their own, where a wider choice will be found

derivatives
(words formed from the headword)

□ **absurdity** noun **absurdly** adverb.

ace ▸ noun **1** a playing card with a single spot
on it, the highest card in its suit in most
games. **2** informal a person who is very good
at a particular activity. **3** Tennis a service
that an opponent is unable to return.
▸ adjective informal very good.

subject label

numbered sense of the headword

acquit ▸ verb (acquits, acquitting, acquitted)
1 formally state that someone is not guilty
of a criminal charge. **2** (**acquit yourself**)
behave or perform in a particular way.

verb inflections
(forms)

SYNONYMS **1** *the jury acquitted her* **clear**,
exonerate, find innocent, absolve,
discharge, free, release; informal let
off (the hook). **2** *the boys acquitted
themselves well* **behave**, conduct
yourself, perform, act.
ANTONYMS convict.

□ **acquittal** noun.

pronunciation
(for selected words)

aesthetic /ess-thet-ik/ (US spelling
esthetic) ▸ adjective **1** concerned with
beauty. **2** having a pleasant appearance.
▸ noun a set of principles behind the work of
an artist or artistic movement.
□ **aesthetically** adverb.

variant (alternative) spelling

ain't ▸ short form informal **1** am not; are not; is
not. **2** has not; have not.

label showing the situation in which the word is used
(see section 2 for explanations)

note giving help with using the headword

! Do not use **ain't** when writing or speaking
in a formal situation.

air ▸ noun **1** the invisible mixture of gases surrounding the earth. **2** the open space above the surface of the earth. **3** (**an air of**) an impression of. **4** (**airs**) a pretentious or condescending way of behaving. **5** a tune.

> SYNONYMS **1 breeze**, draught, wind, gust/puff of wind. **2** *an air of defiance* **look**, appearance, impression, aspect, manner, tone, feel, atmosphere, mood.

▸ verb **1** express an opinion or complaint publicly. **2** broadcast a programme on radio or television. **3** expose something to fresh or warm air.

> SYNONYMS **1** *a chance to air your views* **express,** voice, make public, articulate, state, declare. **2** *the room needs airing* **ventilate,** freshen, refresh, cool.

■ **air conditioning** a system that cools the air in a building or vehicle. **air force** the branch of the armed forces concerned with fighting in the air. **air gun** a gun which uses compressed air to fire pellets. **on the air** being broadcast on radio or television. □ **airing** noun.

airplane ▸ noun N. Amer. a plane.

alibi /a-li-by/ ▸ noun (plural **alibis**) a piece of evidence that a person was somewhere else when a crime was committed.

alight¹ ▸ verb **1** get off a train or bus. **2** (of a bird) land on something.

alight² ▸ adverb & adjective **1** on fire. **2** shining brightly.

> SYNONYMS *the stable was alight* **burning,** ablaze, on fire, in flames, blazing.

amuck ➡ AMOK.

attach ▸ verb **1** fasten; join. **2** believe that something has significance or importance. **3** (**be attached to**) be working with a group of people. **4** (**attached to**) very fond of.

> SYNONYMS **1** *a weight is attached to the cord* **fasten,** fix, join, secure, stick. **2** *they attach importance to research* **ascribe,** assign, attribute, accredit, impute. **3** *the medical officer attached to HQ* **assign,** appoint, allocate, second. **4** (**attached to**) *she's very attached to him* **fond of,** devoted to, keen on; informal mad about.
> ANTONYMS detach.

□ **attachable** adjective.

✔ **-ch**, not **-tch**: atta**ch**.

2. Labels

Most of the words and senses in the dictionary and thesaurus are part of standard English. Some words, however, are appropriate only to certain situations (such as an informal conversation) or are found only in certain contexts (for example, in poetry or in official documents). Where this is the case a label (or a combination of labels) is used.

Register labels

Register labels refer to a particular level of use in language. They show that a term is informal, formal, old-fashioned, or technical, and so on.

- **formal:** normally used only in writing, especially in official documents (e.g. *dwelling* or *deceased*)

- **informal:** normally used only in speaking, or in informal writing or email (e.g. *gawp* or *barmy*)

- **dated:** no longer used by most people (e.g. *gramophone*)

- **old use:** not in ordinary use today, though sometimes used to give an old-fashioned effect and also found in the literature of the past (e.g. *farewell* or *maiden*)

- **historical:** only used today to refer to things that are no longer part of modern life (e.g. *blunderbuss* or *doublet*)

- **literary:** found only or mainly in poems, plays, and novels (e.g. *flaxen* or *serpent*)

- **technical:** normally used only in technical language (e.g. *node* or *fluvial*)

- **humorous:** used to sound amusing or playful (e.g. *underwhelmed*)

- **dialect:** used only in certain local regions of the UK (e.g. *aye* or *bide*)

- **disapproving:** meant to convey a low opinion or to insult someone (e.g. *pleb*)

- **offensive:** likely to cause offence, whether you mean to or not

Geographical labels

English is spoken throughout the world. While most of the words used in standard British English will be the same as those used in other varieties, there are some words which are only found in one type of English. For example, the normal American word for a lift is **elevator**. If a word or phrase has the geographical label Brit. in this book, it is used in standard British English but not in American English, although it may be found in other varieties such as Australian English. The labels US and N. Amer., on the other hand, mean that the word or phrase is typically American and is not standard in British English, though it may be found elsewhere.

Subject labels

Subject labels are used to show that a word or sense is connected with a particular subject or specialist activity such as Music, Computing, or Rugby.

3. Cross references

A cross reference is a pointer to another entry, where full information on a word will be found. An arrow (as in **caftan** ▶ **KAFTAN**) will take you to a different spelling, while an equals sign (as in **groundnut** = **PEANUT**) will take you to a different word that means the same.

4. Pronunciations

Pronunciations are given for words which might cause difficulty, but not for everyday words which are assumed to be familiar to everyone (such as **table** or **happy**). The part of the pronunciation printed in **bold** is the syllable that is stressed when the word is spoken, as in **dulcet** /**dul**-sit/.

List of Symbols

Vowels	Examples	Vowels	Examples	Vowels	Examples
a	as in **cat**	ew	as in **few**	oy	as in **boy**
ah	as in **calm**	i	as in **pin**	u	as in **cup**
air	as in **hair**	I	as in **eye**	uh	as in **along**
ar	as in **bar**	o	as in **top**	uu	as in **book**
aw	as in **law**	oh	as in **most**	y	as in **cry**
ay	as in **say**	oi	as in **join**	yoo	as in **unit**
e	as in **bed**	oo	as in **soon**	yoor	as in **Europe**
ee	as in **meet**	oor	as in **poor**	yr	as in **fire**
eer	as in **beer**	or	as in **corn**		
er	as in **her**	ow	as in **cow**		

Consonants	Examples	Consonants	Examples	Consonants	Examples
b	as in **bat**	l	as in **leg**	t	as in **top**
ch	as in **chin**	m	as in **man**	th	as in **thin**
d	as in **day**	n	as in **not**	*th*	as in **this**
f	as in **fat**	ng	as in **sing, finger**	v	as in **van**
g	as in **get**	nk	as in **thank**	w	as in **will**
h	as in **hat**	p	as in **pen**	y	as in **yes**
j	as in **jam**	r	as in **red**	z	as in **zebra**
k	as in **king**	s	as in **sit**	*zh*	as in **vision**
kh	as in **loch**	sh	as in **shop**		

Note on trademarks and proprietary status

This dictionary includes some words which have, or are asserted to have, proprietary status as trademarks or otherwise. Their inclusion does not imply that they have acquired for legal purposes a non-proprietary or general significance, nor any other judgement concerning their legal status. In cases where the editorial staff have some evidence that a word has proprietary status this is indicated in the entry for that word by the label trademark, but no judgement concerning the legal status of such words is made or implied thereby.

Aa

A (or **a**) ▶ noun (plural **As** or **A's**) the first letter of the alphabet.
▶ abbreviation **1** ampere(s). **2** (Å) angstroms.
■ **A level** (in the UK except Scotland) the higher of the two main levels of the GCE exam.

a ▶ determiner **1** used when mentioning someone or something for the first time; the indefinite article. **2** one single. **3** per.

AA ▶ abbreviation **1** Alcoholics Anonymous. **2** Automobile Association.

aardvark /ard-vark/ ▶ noun an African animal with a long snout, that eats ants and termites.

aback ▶ adverb (**be taken aback**) be shocked or surprised.

abacus /ab-uh-kuhss/ ▶ noun (plural **abacuses**) a frame with rows of wires along which you slide beads, used for counting.

abaft ▶ adverb & preposition at the back of or behind a ship.

abandon ▶ verb **1** leave a place or person permanently. **2** give up a practice completely. **3** (**abandon yourself to**) give in to a desire.

> SYNONYMS **1** *he abandoned his wife* **desert,** leave, turn your back on, cast aside, finish with, jilt, throw over; informal walk/run out on, dump, ditch; literary forsake. **2** *she had abandoned painting* **give up,** stop, have done with; informal pack in, quit; Brit. informal jack in. **3** *they abandoned the car* **leave (behind),** vacate, dump, quit, evacuate, discard, jettison. **4** *the party abandoned those policies* **renounce,** relinquish, dispense with, discard, give up, drop; informal ditch, scrap, junk; formal forswear.
> ANTONYMS keep, continue, retain.

▶ noun complete lack of self-consciousness or self-control.

> SYNONYMS *with reckless abandon* **uninhibitedness,** recklessness, lack of restraint, lack of inhibition.
> ANTONYMS self-control.

□ **abandonment** noun.

abase ▶ verb (**abases, abasing, abased**) (**abase yourself**) behave in a very humble way.

□ **abasement** noun.

abashed ▶ adjective embarrassed or ashamed.

abate ▶ verb (**abates, abating, abated**) become less severe or widespread.

> SYNONYMS *the storm had abated* **subside,** die down/away/out, lessen, ease (off), let up, decrease, diminish, fade, weaken.
> ANTONYMS intensify.

abatement ▶ noun the action of abating.

> SYNONYMS **1** *the storm still rages with no sign of abatement* **subsiding,** dying down/away/out, lessening, easing (off), let-up. **2** *noise abatement* **reduction,** control.

abattoir /ab-uh-twar/ ▶ noun Brit. a slaughterhouse.

abbess ▶ noun a woman who is the head of an abbey of nuns.

abbey ▶ noun (plural **abbeys**) a building occupied by a community of monks or nuns.

abbot ▶ noun a man who is the head of an abbey of monks.

abbreviate ▶ verb (**abbreviates, abbreviating, abbreviated**) shorten a word or phrase.

> SYNONYMS **shorten,** reduce, cut, contract, condense, compress, abridge.
> ANTONYMS lengthen, expand.

abbreviation ▶ noun a shortened form of a word or phrase.

> SYNONYMS **short form,** contraction, acronym, initialism.

ABC ▶ noun **1** the alphabet. **2** the basic facts of a subject.

abdicate ▶ verb (**abdicates, abdicating, abdicated**) **1** give up being king or queen. **2** fail to carry out a duty.

> SYNONYMS **resign,** retire, stand down, step down, renounce the throne.

□ **abdication** noun.

abdomen /ab-duh-muhn/ ▶ noun **1** the part of the body that contains the organs used for digestion and reproduction. **2** the rear part of the body of an insect, spider, or crustacean.

a

SYNONYMS **stomach,** belly, gut, middle; informal **tummy,** guts; Austral. informal **bingy.**

abdominal ▸ adjective relating to the abdomen.

SYNONYMS **gastric,** intestinal, stomach, duodenal, visceral, coeliac, ventral.

abduct ▸ verb take someone away, especially by force.

SYNONYMS **kidnap,** carry off, seize, capture, run away/off with; informal snatch.

▫ **abduction** noun **abductor** noun.

aberrant /uh-**berr**-uhnt/ ▸ adjective not normal or acceptable.

aberration /a-buh-**ray**-sh'n/ ▸ noun **1** an action or event which is not normal or acceptable. **2** an unexpected silly mistake.

SYNONYMS **anomaly,** deviation, abnormality, irregularity, variation, freak, oddity, peculiarity, curiosity, mistake.

abet ▸ verb (**abets, abetting, abetted**) encourage or help someone to do something wrong.

abeyance /uh-**bay**-uhnss/ ▸ noun (**in or into abeyance**) temporarily not occurring or in use.

abhor /uhb-**hor**/ ▸ verb (**abhors, abhorring, abhorred**) feel strong hatred for.

SYNONYMS **hate,** detest, loathe, despise, regard with disgust, shudder at; formal abominate.
ANTONYMS love, admire.

abhorrent ▸ adjective disgusting or hateful.

SYNONYMS **hateful,** detestable, loathsome, abominable, repellent, repugnant, repulsive, revolting, disgusting, horrible, horrid, horrifying, awful, heinous.
ANTONYMS admirable.

▫ **abhorrence** noun.

abide ▸ verb (**abides, abiding, abided**) **1** (**abide by**) accept or obey a rule or decision. **2** (**cannot abide**) dislike very much. **3** (of a feeling or memory) last for a long time.

SYNONYMS **1** I can't abide smoke **stand,** bear; Brit. informal stick. **2** one memory will abide **continue,** remain, survive, last, persist, live on.

abiding ▸ adjective lasting a long time.

SYNONYMS **enduring,** lasting, everlasting, perpetual, eternal, unending, permanent.
ANTONYMS short-lived, ephemeral.

ability ▸ noun (plural **abilities**) **1** the power or capacity to do something. **2** skill or talent.

SYNONYMS **1** the ability to read **capacity,** capability, power, faculty, facility, wherewithal, means. **2** leadership ability **talent,** skill, aptitude, expertise, savoir faire, prowess, accomplishment, competence, proficiency, flair, gift, knack, genius; informal know-how.
ANTONYMS inability.

abject /**ab**-jekt/ ▸ adjective **1** very unpleasant and humiliating. **2** completely without pride or dignity.
▫ **abjectly** adverb.

abjure /uhb-**joor**/ ▸ verb (**abjures, abjuring, abjured**) formal swear that you will give up a belief or claim.

ablaze ▸ adjective burning fiercely.

able ▸ adjective (**abler, ablest**) **1** having the power, skill, or means to do something. **2** skilful and capable.

SYNONYMS **1** able to resume his duties **capable of,** competent to, up to, fit to, in a position to, allowed to, free to. **2** an able student **intelligent,** clever, talented, skilful, skilled, accomplished, gifted, proficient, apt, adroit, adept, capable, competent.
ANTONYMS incompetent, incapable.

■ **able-bodied** physically fit and healthy.
▫ **ably** adverb.

ablutions /uh-**bloo**-shuhnz/ ▸ plural noun the act of washing yourself.

abnegation /ab-ni-**gay**-sh'n/ ▸ noun formal the giving up of something wanted or valuable.
▫ **abnegate** verb.

abnormal ▸ adjective different from what is usual or expected in a bad or worrying way.

SYNONYMS **unusual,** uncommon, atypical, untypical, unrepresentative, irregular, anomalous, deviant, aberrant, freak, strange, odd, peculiar, bizarre, weird, unnatural, perverted, twisted, warped; informal funny, freaky, kinky.
ANTONYMS normal, typical, common.

▫ **abnormally** adverb.

abnormality ▸ noun **1** the state of being abnormal. **2** a feature or event which is not normal.

SYNONYMS **oddity,** strangeness, irregularity, anomaly, deviation, aberration, deformity, defect, malformation.
ANTONYMS normality.

aboard ▸ adverb & preposition on or into a ship, train, or other vehicle.

abode ▸ noun a house or home.

abolish ▸ verb put an end to a custom or law.

SYNONYMS **put an end to,** get rid of, scrap, cancel, end, remove, dissolve, stop, ban;

informal **do away with, ditch.**
ANTONYMS retain, create.

abolition ▶ noun the abolishing of a custom or law.

> SYNONYMS **scrapping,** ending, cancellation, dissolution, removal.
> ANTONYMS retention, creation.

abolitionist ▶ noun a person who supports the abolition of a custom or law.

abominable ▶ adjective **1** very unpleasant and causing disgust. **2** informal very bad.

> SYNONYMS **loathsome,** detestable, hateful, obnoxious, despicable, contemptible, disgusting, revolting, repellent, repulsive, repugnant, abhorrent, reprehensible, atrocious, foul, vile, wretched, horrible, awful, dreadful, appalling, nauseating; informal terrible, shocking, God-awful; Brit. informal beastly.
> ANTONYMS good, admirable.

■ **Abominable Snowman** = YETI.
□ **abominably** adverb.

abominate ▶ verb (**abominates, abominating, abominated**) feel strong hatred for.

abomination ▶ noun **1** something that you hate or find disgusting. **2** a feeling of hatred.

aboriginal ▶ adjective **1** existing in a country from the earliest times. **2** (**Aboriginal**) having to do with the Australian Aborigines.
▶ noun (**Aboriginal**) an Australian Aborigine.

Aborigine /ab-uh-**ri**-ji-nee/ ▶ noun a member of one of the original peoples of Australia.

abort ▶ verb **1** end a pregnancy early to stop the baby from developing and being born. **2** undergo a natural abortion. **3** end something early because of a problem or fault.

> SYNONYMS **1 miscarry,** have a miscarriage, terminate. **2** the crew aborted the take-off **halt,** stop, end, call off, abandon, discontinue, terminate, arrest; informal pull the plug on.

abortion ▶ noun **1** the deliberate ending of a human pregnancy. **2** the natural ending of a pregnancy before the fetus is able to survive on its own.

> SYNONYMS **termination,** miscarriage.

abortionist ▶ noun disapproving a person who carries out abortions.

abortive ▶ adjective failing to achieve the intended result; unsuccessful.

> SYNONYMS **unsuccessful,** failed, vain, ineffective, ineffectual, unproductive.
> ANTONYMS successful, fruitful.

abound ▶ verb **1** exist in large numbers or amounts. **2** (**abound in** or **with**) have a large number or amount of something.

> SYNONYMS **1** cafes abound in the narrow streets **be plentiful,** be abundant, be numerous, be thick on the ground; informal grow on trees, be two/ten a penny. **2** a stream which abounded with trout **be full of,** overflow with, teem with, be packed with, be crowded with; informal be stuffed with, be chock-a-block with.

about ▶ preposition on the subject of.

> SYNONYMS a book about Greece **regarding,** concerning, referring to, with regard to, with respect to, relating to, on, touching on, dealing with, on the subject of.

▶ adverb **1** here and there within a particular area. **2** approximately.

> SYNONYMS **1** there were babies crawling about **around,** here and there, to and fro, back and forth, in all directions. **2** he was about somewhere **near,** nearby, around, hereabouts, in the vicinity, in the neighbourhood. **3** about £15,000 **approximately,** roughly, around, in the region of, circa, of the order of, or so, or thereabouts, more or less; Brit. getting on for; N. Amer. informal in the ballpark of.

■ **about-turn** Brit. **1** Military a turn made so as to face the opposite direction. **2** a complete change of opinion or attitude.

above ▶ preposition & adverb **1** at a higher level than. **2** rather or more than. **3** (in printed writing) mentioned earlier.

> SYNONYMS **1** a tiny window above the door **over,** higher (up) than, on top of, on. **2** in the darkness above, something moved **overhead,** on/at the top, high up, on high, up above, (up) in the sky. **3** those above the Colonel **superior to,** senior to, over, higher (up) than, more powerful than, in charge of, commanding.
> ANTONYMS below.

■ **above board** lawful and honest.

abracadabra ▶ exclamation a word said by magicians when performing a trick.

abrade ▶ verb (**abrades, abrading, abraded**) scrape or wear away.

abrasion /uh-**bray**-zh'n/ ▶ noun **1** the process of scraping or wearing away. **2** an area of scraped skin.

> SYNONYMS **1** the metal is resistant to abrasion **erosion,** wearing away/down. **2** he had abrasions to his forehead **graze,** cut, scrape, scratch, gash, laceration.

abrasive /uh-**bray**-siv/ ▶ adjective **1** able to polish or clean a surface by rubbing or grinding. **2** harsh or unkind.

SYNONYMS **1** *abrasive kitchen cleaners* **rough,** coarse, harsh, scratchy. **2** *her abrasive manner* **curt,** brusque, sharp, harsh, rough.
ANTONYMS gentle, friendly.

□ **abrasively** adverb.

abreast ▸ adverb **1** side by side and facing the same way. **2** (**abreast of**) up to date with.

abridge ▸ verb (**abridges, abridging, abridged**) shorten a book or film.

SYNONYMS **shorten,** cut (down), edit, abbreviate, condense, compress, truncate, prune, summarize, precis; (**abridged**) concise.
ANTONYMS extend.

□ **abridgement** noun.

abroad ▸ adverb **1** in or to a foreign country or countries. **2** felt or talked about by many people.

SYNONYMS **overseas,** out of the country, to/in foreign parts, to/in a foreign country/land.

abrogate /ab-ruh-gayt/ ▸ verb (**abrogates, abrogating, abrogated**) formal cancel or do away with a law or agreement.
□ **abrogation** noun.

abrupt ▸ adjective **1** sudden and unexpected. **2** brief to the point of rudeness.

SYNONYMS **1** *an abrupt halt* **sudden,** rapid, quick, unexpected, unanticipated, unforeseen, precipitate. **2** *an abrupt manner* **curt,** brusque, blunt, short, rude, sharp, terse, brisk, unceremonious.
ANTONYMS gradual, gentle.

□ **abruptly** adverb **abruptness** noun.

abscess ▸ noun a swelling that contains pus.

✔ Remember the **s** and **c**: ab**sc**ess.

abscond /uhb-**skond**/ ▸ verb leave quickly and secretly to escape from custody or avoid arrest.

abseil /**ab**-sayl/ ▸ verb Brit. climb down a rock face using a rope wrapped round the body and fixed at a higher point.

absence ▸ noun **1** the state of being away from a place or person. **2** (**absence of**) the lack of.

SYNONYMS **1** *his absence from the office* **non-attendance,** absenteeism, truancy, leave, holiday, vacation, sabbatical. **2** *the absence of activity* **lack,** want, non-existence, unavailability, scarcity, shortage, dearth.
ANTONYMS presence.

absent ▸ adjective /**ab**-s'nt/ **1** not present. **2** not paying attention.

SYNONYMS **1** *she was absent from work* **away,** off, out, elsewhere, off duty,

on holiday, on leave; informal AWOL. **2** *symptoms were absent* **non-existent,** lacking, missing. **3** *an absent look* **distracted,** preoccupied, inattentive, vague, absorbed, dreamy, faraway, blank, empty, vacant.
ANTONYMS present, attentive, alert.

▸ verb /uhb-**sent**/ (**absent yourself**) go away.
□ **absently** adverb.

absentee ▸ noun a person who is absent.

absenteeism ▸ noun frequent absence from work or school without good reason.

absent-minded ▸ adjective forgetful, or not paying attention.

SYNONYMS **forgetful,** distracted, scatterbrained, preoccupied, inattentive; informal with a mind/memory like a sieve.

absinthe /**ab**-sinth/ ▸ noun a green aniseed-flavoured liqueur.

absolute ▸ adjective **1** complete; total. **2** having unlimited power. **3** not related or compared to anything else.

SYNONYMS **1** *absolute silence* | *an absolute disgrace* **complete,** total, utter, out-and-out, outright, perfect, pure, thorough, unqualified, unreserved, downright, unmitigated, sheer. **2** *absolute power* **unlimited,** unrestricted, unrestrained, infinite, total, supreme, unconditional. **3** *an absolute ruler* **autocratic,** dictatorial, all-powerful, omnipotent, supreme.
ANTONYMS partial, qualified, limited, democratic.

■ **absolute zero** the lowest temperature theoretically possible (-273.15°C).

absolutely ▸ adverb completely.

SYNONYMS **completely,** totally, utterly, perfectly, entirely, wholly, fully, quite, thoroughly, unreservedly, definitely, certainly, unquestionably, undoubtedly, without (a) doubt, without question, in every way/respect, one hundred per cent.
ANTONYMS partially.

absolution ▸ noun formal forgiveness of a person's sins.

absolutism ▸ noun the principle that the government or ruler should have unlimited power.
□ **absolutist** noun & adjective.

absolve /uhb-**zolv**/ ▸ verb (**absolves, absolving, absolved**) formally declare that someone is free from guilt, blame, or sin.

absorb ▸ verb **1** soak up liquid or another substance. **2** take in information. **3** take over something less powerful. **4** use up time or resources. **5** reduce the effect or strength of sound or an impact. **6** hold someone's attention.

a

SYNONYMS **1** *a material which absorbs water* **soak up,** suck up, draw up/in, take up/in, mop up. **2** *she was absorbed in her book* **engross,** captivate, occupy, preoccupy, engage, rivet, grip, hold, immerse, involve, enthral, spellbind, fascinate.

absorbent ▸ adjective able to soak up liquid easily.

SYNONYMS **spongy,** sponge-like, porous, permeable.

□ **absorbency** noun.

absorbing ▸ adjective very interesting.

SYNONYMS **fascinating,** interesting, captivating, gripping, engrossing, compelling, compulsive, enthralling, riveting, spellbinding; informal unputdownable.
ANTONYMS boring.

absorption ▸ noun the process of absorbing, or of being absorbed.

SYNONYMS **1** *the absorption of water* **soaking up,** sucking up. **2** *her total absorption in the music* **involvement,** immersion, raptness, preoccupation, captivation, fascination, enthralment.

abstain ▸ verb **1** (**abstain from**) stop yourself from doing something pleasant. **2** formally choose not to vote.

SYNONYMS **1** *he abstained from wine* **refrain,** desist, forbear, give up, renounce, avoid, eschew, forgo, go/do without, refuse, decline; informal cut out. **2** *one member abstained* **not vote,** decline to vote.

abstemious /uhb-**stee**-mi-uhss/ ▸ adjective not letting yourself have much food, alcohol, or enjoyment.

SYNONYMS **moderate,** restrained, temperate, self-disciplined, self-restrained, sober, austere, ascetic, puritanical, spartan.
ANTONYMS self-indulgent.

abstention /uhb-**sten**-sh'n/ ▸ noun **1** a deliberate decision not to vote. **2** abstinence.

abstinence /**ab**-sti-nuhnss/ ▸ noun the avoidance of something enjoyable, such as food or alcohol.

SYNONYMS **self-denial,** self-restraint, teetotalism, temperance, sobriety, abstemiousness.

□ **abstinent** adjective.

abstract ▸ adjective /**ab**-strakt/ **1** having to do with ideas or qualities rather than physical or concrete things. **2** (of art) using colour and shapes to create an effect rather than attempting to represent real life accurately.

SYNONYMS *abstract concepts* **theoretical,** conceptual, intellectual, metaphysical, philosophical, academic.
ANTONYMS actual, concrete.

▸ verb /uhb-**strakt**/ take out or remove.
▸ noun /**ab**-strakt/ a summary of a book or article.

SYNONYMS *an abstract of her speech* **summary,** synopsis, precis, résumé, outline; N. Amer. wrap-up.

□ **abstractly** adverb.

abstracted ▸ adjective not paying attention to what is happening; preoccupied.
□ **abstractedly** adverb.

abstraction ▸ noun **1** the quality of being abstract. **2** something which exists only as an idea. **3** the state of being preoccupied.

abstruse /uhb-**strooss**/ ▸ adjective difficult to understand.

SYNONYMS **obscure,** arcane, esoteric, rarefied, recondite, difficult, hard, cryptic, over/above your head, incomprehensible, unfathomable, impenetrable.

absurd ▸ adjective completely unreasonable or inappropriate.

SYNONYMS **irrational,** illogical, inappropriate, ridiculous, ludicrous, farcical, comical, stupid, foolish, silly, pointless, senseless, preposterous; informal crazy, cockeyed; Brit. informal barmy, daft.
ANTONYMS reasonable, sensible.

□ **absurdity** noun **absurdly** adverb.

abundance ▸ noun a very large quantity or amount of something.

SYNONYMS **plenty,** plethora, profusion, exuberance, riot, superabundance.
ANTONYMS lack, scarcity.

abundant ▸ adjective **1** existing in large quantities or amounts; plentiful. **2** (**abundant in**) having plenty of.

SYNONYMS **plentiful,** copious, ample, profuse, large, huge, great, bumper, prolific, overflowing, teeming, superabundant; informal galore.
ANTONYMS scarce, sparse.

□ **abundantly** adverb.

abuse ▸ verb /uh-**byooz**/ (**abuses, abusing, abused**) **1** use something wrongly or badly. **2** treat someone cruelly or violently. **3** speak to someone in an insulting way.

SYNONYMS **1** *the judge abused his power* **misuse,** exploit, take advantage of. **2** *he was accused of abusing women* **mistreat,** maltreat, ill-treat, molest, beat, sexually abuse, interfere with. **3** *the referee was abused by players* **insult,** be rude to, swear at, shout at.

▸ noun /uh-**byooss**/ **1** the wrong or harmful

a

use of something. **2** cruel and violent treatment. **3** insulting language.

> SYNONYMS **1** *the abuse of power* **misuse,** exploitation. **2** *the abuse of women* **mistreatment,** maltreatment, ill-treatment, molestation, beating, sexual abuse. **3** *torrents of abuse* **insults,** expletives, swear words, swearing, name-calling, invective.

□ **abuser** noun.

abusive ▶ adjective **1** very insulting. **2** involving cruelty and violence.

> SYNONYMS **1** *abusive language* **insulting,** rude, offensive, derogatory, slanderous, libellous. **2** *an abusive husband* **violent,** brutal, cruel, harsh, oppressive. ANTONYMS polite, kind.

□ **abusively** adverb.

abut /uh-**but**/ ▶ verb (**abuts, abutting, abutted**) be next to or touching.

abysmal /uh-**biz**-m'l/ ▶ adjective very bad; terrible.

> SYNONYMS **terrible,** dreadful, awful, frightful, atrocious, disgraceful, lamentable; informal rotten, appalling, pathetic, pitiful, woeful, useless, lousy, dire, poxy, the pits; Brit. informal chronic, shocking.

□ **abysmally** adverb.

abyss /uh-**biss**/ ▶ noun a very deep hole.

AC ▶ abbreviation alternating current.

acacia /uh-**kay**-shuh/ ▶ noun a tree or shrub with yellow or white flowers.

academia /a-kuh-**dee**-mi-uh/ ▶ noun the world of higher education.

academic ▶ adjective **1** having to do with education or study. **2** not related to a real situation; theoretical.

> SYNONYMS **1** *an academic institution* **educational,** scholastic. **2** *his academic turn of mind* **scholarly,** learned, literary, intellectual, bookish, studious. **3** *only of academic interest* **theoretical,** hypothetical, notional, speculative, conjectural, irrelevant, beside the point.

▶ noun a teacher or scholar in a university or college.

> SYNONYMS *a group of academics* **scholar,** intellectual, don, professor, man/woman of letters, thinker; informal egghead; Brit. informal boffin.

□ **academically** adverb.

academy ▶ noun (plural **academies**) **1** a place where people study or are trained in a particular field. **2** a society of scholars, artists, or scientists.

> SYNONYMS **educational institution,** school, college, university, institute.

■ **Academy Award** an Oscar.

acanthus /uh-**kan**-thuhss/ ▶ noun a plant or shrub with spiny leaves.

a cappella /a kuh-**pel**-luh/ ▶ adjective & adverb (of music) sung without instrumental accompaniment.

accede /uhk-**seed**/ ▶ verb (**accedes, acceding, acceded**) (usu. **accede to**) formal **1** agree to a demand or request. **2** take up a role or position: *accede to the throne.*

accelerate ▶ verb (**accelerates, accelerating, accelerated**) **1** begin to move more quickly. **2** begin to happen more quickly.

> SYNONYMS **1** *the car accelerated* **speed up,** go faster, gain momentum, increase speed, pick up speed, gather speed. **2** *sunlight accelerates growth* **hasten,** quicken, speed up, further, advance, expedite; informal crank up. ANTONYMS decelerate, delay.

acceleration ▶ noun the action of moving or happening more quickly.

> SYNONYMS **speeding up,** quickening, hastening.

accelerator ▶ noun **1** a foot pedal which controls the speed of a vehicle. **2** Physics a machine that makes charged particles move at high speeds.

accent ▶ noun /**ak**-suhnt/ **1** a way of pronouncing a language. **2** an emphasis given to a syllable, word, or musical note. **3** a mark on a letter or word that shows how a sound is pronounced or stressed. **4** a particular emphasis.

> SYNONYMS **1** *a Scottish accent* **pronunciation,** intonation, enunciation, articulation, inflection. **2** *the accent is on comfort* **emphasis,** stress, priority, importance, prominence.

▶ verb /ak-**sent**/ **1** (**accented**) spoken with a particular accent. **2** stress or emphasize.

accentuate /uhk-**sen**-tyuu-ayt/ ▶ verb (**accentuates, accentuating, accentuated**) make a feature more noticeable.
□ **accentuation** noun.

accept ▶ verb **1** agree to receive or do something that is offered or suggested. **2** believe that something said is true or correct. **3** admit responsibility for something. **4** come to terms with something unwelcome.

> SYNONYMS **1** *he accepted a pen as a present* **receive,** take, get, obtain, acquire, pick up. **2** *just accept what you're told* **go along with,** believe, respect, abide by, defer to, put up with, give in to, resign yourself to; informal buy, swallow. ANTONYMS refuse, reject.

> ❗ Don't confuse **accept** with **except**, which means 'not including'.

acceptable ▸ adjective **1** able to be accepted. **2** good enough; adequate.

> SYNONYMS **satisfactory,** adequate, reasonable, fair, good enough, sufficient, tolerable, passable.
> ANTONYMS unacceptable.

□ **acceptability** noun **acceptably** adverb.

acceptance ▸ noun the action or fact of accepting.

> SYNONYMS **1** *the acceptance of an award* **receipt,** receiving, taking. **2** *his acceptance of her ideas* **respect,** acknowledgement, belief, toleration, consent, agreement, assent, compliance, acquiescence.

accepted ▸ adjective believed to be true or correct.

> SYNONYMS **recognized,** acknowledged, established, traditional, orthodox, agreed, approved, customary, normal, standard.
> ANTONYMS unorthodox.

access ▸ noun **1** a way of approaching or entering a place. **2** the right or opportunity to use something or see someone.

> SYNONYMS **1** *the building has a side access* **entrance,** entry, approach, path, drive, way in. **2** *they were denied access to the stadium* **admission,** admittance, entry.

▸ verb **1** approach or enter a place. **2** obtain information stored in a computer.

accessible ▸ adjective **1** able to be reached or used. **2** friendly and easy to talk to. **3** easily understood or enjoyed.

> SYNONYMS **1** **approachable,** attainable, reachable, obtainable, available; informal get-at-able. **2** **understandable,** comprehensible, intelligible.

□ **accessibility** noun **accessibly** adverb.

accession ▸ noun **1** the gaining of an important position or rank. **2** a new item added to a library or museum collection.

accessory ▸ noun (plural **accessories**) **1** a thing which can be added to or worn with something else to make it more useful or attractive. **2** Law a person who helps someone commit a crime without taking part in it.

> SYNONYMS **1** *a car accessory* **extra,** add-on, addition, supplement, attachment. **2** *an accessory to murder* **accomplice,** abetter, collaborator, co-conspirator, henchman, associate.

accident ▸ noun **1** something harmful that happens unexpectedly or without being intended. **2** an incident that happens by chance or without apparent cause.

> SYNONYMS **1** *an accident at work* **mishap,** misadventure, disaster,

tragedy, catastrophe, calamity. **2** *a road accident* **crash,** collision, smash, bump, derailment; N. Amer. wreck; informal smash-up, pile-up; Brit. informal shunt. **3** *we met by accident* **chance,** fate, fortune, luck, good luck, fluke, coincidence.

accidental ▸ adjective happening by chance.

> SYNONYMS **1** *accidental death* **chance,** coincidental, unexpected, incidental, fortuitous, serendipitous. **2** *accidental damage* **unintentional,** unintended, unplanned, inadvertent, unwitting.
> ANTONYMS predictable, intentional.

□ **accidentally** adverb.

acclaim ▸ verb praise enthusiastically and publicly.

> SYNONYMS *the booklet has been acclaimed by teachers* **praise,** applaud, cheer, commend, approve, welcome, hail.
> ANTONYMS criticize.

▸ noun enthusiastic public praise.

> SYNONYMS *she has won widespread acclaim* **praise,** applause, tributes, approval, admiration, congratulations, commendation.
> ANTONYMS criticism.

acclamation ▸ noun enthusiastic approval or praise.

acclimatize (or **acclimatise**) ▸ verb (**acclimatizes, acclimatizing, acclimatized**) get used to a new climate or conditions.

> SYNONYMS **adjust,** adapt, get used, familiarize yourself, find your feet, get your bearings; N. Amer. acclimate.

□ **acclimatization** noun.

accolade /ak-kuh-layd/ ▸ noun something given as a special honour or as a reward for excellence.

accommodate ▸ verb (**accommodates, accommodating, accommodated**) **1** provide a room or rooms for someone, or space for something. **2** adapt to or fit in with.

> SYNONYMS **1** *refugees were accommodated in army camps* **lodge,** house, put up, billet, board. **2** *the cottages accommodate six people* **hold,** take, have room for, sleep, seat. **3** *we tried to accommodate her* **help,** assist, oblige, cater for, fit in with, satisfy.

> ✔ double **c,** double **m:** ac**c**o**mm**odate.

accommodating ▸ adjective willing to fit in with someone's wishes.

> SYNONYMS **obliging,** cooperative, helpful, amenable, hospitable, flexible.

accommodation ▸ noun a room or building where someone may live or stay.

> SYNONYMS **housing,** homes, lodging(s), (living) quarters, rooms, billet, shelter,

a

a roof over your head; informal digs, pad; formal residence, dwelling.

accompaniment ▸ noun 1 a musical part which accompanies an instrument, voice, or group. 2 something that adds to or improves something else.

SYNONYMS 1 *a musical accompaniment* **backing,** support, background, soundtrack. 2 *the wine makes a superb accompaniment to cheese* **complement,** addition, adjunct, accessory, companion.

accompany ▸ verb (accompanies, accompanying, accompanied) 1 go somewhere with someone. 2 be present or happen at the same time as. 3 play musical backing for an instrument or voice.

SYNONYMS 1 *the driver accompanied her to the door* **go with,** travel with, keep someone company, partner, escort, show, see, usher, conduct. 2 *an illness accompanied by nausea* **go along with,** occur with, go together with, attend, be linked with. 3 *he accompanied the choir on the piano* **back,** play along with, support.

□ **accompanist** noun.

accomplice ▸ noun a person who helps another commit a crime.

SYNONYMS **partner in crime,** abetter, accessory, collaborator, co-conspirator, henchman, associate.

accomplish ▸ verb achieve or complete something successfully.

SYNONYMS **achieve,** succeed in, realize, attain, manage, bring off, carry through, execute, effect, perform, complete.

accomplished ▸ adjective highly trained or skilled.

SYNONYMS **expert,** skilled, skilful, masterly, virtuoso, master, consummate, talented, gifted, able, capable; informal mean, nifty, crack, ace.

accomplishment ▸ noun 1 an activity that you can do well. 2 something that has been achieved successfully. 3 the successful achievement of a task.

SYNONYMS 1 *a remarkable accomplishment* **achievement,** success, act, deed, exploit, effort, feat, coup. 2 *her many accomplishments* **talent,** skill, gift, ability.

accord ▸ verb 1 give power or recognition to. 2 (**accord with**) be consistent or in agreement with.

SYNONYMS 1 *the national assembly accorded him more power* **give,** grant, present, award, confer on, bestow on. 2 *his views accorded with mine* **correspond,** agree, tally, match, concur,

be in harmony, be in tune. ANTONYMS withhold, disagree, differ.

▸ noun 1 agreement in opinion or feeling. 2 an official agreement or treaty.

SYNONYMS 1 *a peace accord* **pact,** treaty, agreement, settlement, deal, entente, protocol. 2 *the two sides failed to reach accord* **agreement,** consensus, unanimity, harmony. ANTONYMS disagreement.

■ **of your own accord** willingly.

accordance ▸ noun (**in accordance with**) in a way that fits in with.

according ▸ adverb (**according to**) 1 as stated by. 2 in a way that corresponds to.

accordingly ▸ adverb 1 appropriately. 2 therefore.

accordion ▸ noun a musical instrument that you play by stretching and squeezing it with your hands and pressing buttons or keys.
□ **accordionist** noun.

accost ▸ verb approach someone and speak to them, often in a rude or aggressive way.

account ▸ noun 1 a description of an event. 2 a record of money that has been spent and received. 3 an arrangement by which you can keep money in a bank or buy things from a business on credit. 4 importance.

SYNONYMS 1 *his account of the incident* **description,** report, version, story, statement, explanation, tale, chronicle, history, record, log. 2 *the firm's accounts* **financial record,** ledger, balance sheet, financial statement; (**accounts**) books. 3 *his background is of no account* **importance,** import, significance, consequence, value.

▸ verb consider in a particular way.
■ **account for 1** supply or make up an amount. 2 give an explanation of. **on account of** because of. **on no account** under no circumstances. **take account of** take into consideration.

accountability ▸ noun the state of being accountable.

SYNONYMS **responsibility,** liability, answerability.

accountable ▸ adjective expected to explain your actions or decisions.

SYNONYMS **responsible,** liable, answerable, to blame.

accountant ▸ noun a person who keeps or inspects financial accounts.
□ **accountancy** noun.

accoutrement /uh-**koo**-truh-muhnt/ (US spelling **accouterment**) ▸ noun an extra item of clothing or equipment.

accredit ▸ verb (**accredits, accrediting, accredited**) **1** (**accredit something to**) give someone the credit for something. **2** give official authorization to.
□ **accreditation** noun.

accretion ▸ noun **1** growth or increase by a gradual build-up. **2** something formed or added gradually.

accrue ▸ verb (**accrues, accruing, accrued**) **1** (of money) be received in regular or increasing amounts. **2** collect or receive payments or benefits.
□ **accrual** noun.

accumulate ▸ verb (**accumulates, accumulating, accumulated**) **1** gather together a number or quantity of. **2** increase.

> SYNONYMS **gather,** collect, amass, stockpile, pile up, build up, store (up), hoard, lay in/up, increase, accrue, run up. ANTONYMS disperse.

□ **accumulative** adjective.

> ✔ two **c**s, one **m**: ac**c**u**m**ulate.

accumulation ▸ noun a mass or quantity of something that has gathered or been acquired gradually.

> SYNONYMS **mass,** build-up, pile, collection, stock, store, stockpile, hoard.

accumulator ▸ noun Brit. **1** a large rechargeable electric battery. **2** a bet placed on a series of events, the winnings from each being placed on the next.

accuracy ▸ noun the state of being accurate.

> SYNONYMS **correctness,** precision, exactness, fidelity, truth, truthfulness, authenticity, realism.

accurate ▸ adjective **1** correct in all details. **2** reaching an intended target.

> SYNONYMS **1** *accurate information* **correct,** precise, exact, right, factual, literal, faithful, true, truthful, on the mark, authentic, realistic; Brit. informal spot on, bang on; N. Amer. informal on the money, on the button. **2** *an accurate shot* **well aimed,** on target, unerring, deadly, true.

□ **accurately** adverb.

accursed /uh-**ker**-sid, uh-**kerst**/ ▸ adjective literary under a curse.

accusation ▸ noun a claim that someone has done something illegal or wrong.

> SYNONYMS **allegation,** charge, indictment, impeachment, claim, assertion, imputation.

accusative ▸ noun Grammar (in some languages) the case used for the object of a verb.

accuse ▸ verb (**accuses, accusing, accused**) (often **accuse someone of**) claim that someone has done something wrong or illegal.

> SYNONYMS **1** *four people were accused of assault* **charge with,** indict for, impeach for. **2** *you accused the companies of causing job losses* **blame for,** hold responsible for, condemn for, criticize for, denounce for; informal point the finger at. ANTONYMS absolve, exonerate.

□ **accusatory** adjective **accuser** noun.

accustom ▸ verb **1** (**accustom someone/thing to**) make someone or something used to. **2** (**be accustomed to**) be used to.

> SYNONYMS **adapt,** adjust, acclimatize, habituate, familiarize, become reconciled; get used to, come to terms with, learn to live with; N. Amer. acclimate.

accustomed ▸ adjective usual or habitual.

> SYNONYMS **customary,** established, habitual, usual, normal, regular, routine.

AC/DC ▸ adjective alternating current/direct current.

ace ▸ noun **1** a playing card with a single spot on it, the highest card in its suit in most games. **2** informal a person who is very good at a particular activity. **3** Tennis a service that an opponent is unable to return.
▸ adjective informal very good.

acerbic /uh-**ser**-bik/ ▸ adjective sharp and direct.
□ **acerbically** adverb **acerbity** noun.

acetate /**a**-si-tayt/ ▸ noun **1** a kind of chemical compound made from acetic acid. **2** fibre or plastic made of cellulose acetate.

acetic acid /uh-**see**-tik/ ▸ noun the acid that gives vinegar its taste.

acetone /**a**-si-tohn/ ▸ noun a colourless liquid used as a solvent.

acetylene /uh-**set**-i-leen/ ▸ noun a gas which burns with a bright flame, used in welding.

ache ▸ noun a continuous or long-lasting dull pain.

> SYNONYMS **pain,** twinge, pang, soreness, tenderness, irritation, discomfort, burning, cramp.

▸ verb (**aches, aching, ached**) **1** suffer from an ache. **2** (**ache for** or **to do**) want very much to have or do something.

> SYNONYMS *my legs were aching* **hurt,** be sore, be painful, be tender, burn, be in pain.

□ **achy** adjective.

achieve ▸ verb (**achieves, achieving, achieved**) manage to do something by effort, skill, or courage.

a

SYNONYMS **attain,** reach, realize, bring off, pull off, accomplish, carry through, fulfil, complete; informal **wrap up, swing.**

□ **achievable** adjective **achiever** noun.

✔ The usual rule is **i** before **e** except after **c**: ach**ie**ve.

achievement ▸ noun **1** a thing that is achieved. **2** the process of achieving something.

SYNONYMS **1** *the achievement of high growth* **attainment,** realization, accomplishment, fulfilment, implementation, completion. **2** *they were proud of their achievement* **feat,** exploit, triumph, coup, accomplishment, act, action, deed, effort, work, handiwork.

Achilles heel /uh-**kil**-leez/ ▸ noun a weak point.

Achilles tendon ▸ noun the tendon connecting calf muscles to the heel.

acid ▸ noun **1** a substance that turns litmus red, neutralizes alkalis, and dissolves some metals. **2** informal the drug LSD.
▸ adjective **1** sharp-tasting or sour. **2** (of a remark) bitter or cutting.

SYNONYMS **1** *an acid flavour* **sour,** acidic, tart, sharp, vinegary. **2** *acid remarks* **sharp,** sharp-tongued, sarcastic, scathing, cutting, biting, stinging, caustic; informal **bitchy, catty.**
ANTONYMS alkali, sweet, kind.

■ **acid rain** rainfall that has been made acidic by pollution. **acid test** a decisive test of something.
□ **acidic** adjective **acidity** noun **acidly** adverb.

acidify ▸ verb (**acidifies, acidifying, acidified**) make or become acid.

acknowledge ▸ verb (**acknowledges, acknowledging, acknowledged**) **1** accept that something exists or is true. **2** confirm that you have received something. **3** greet someone with words or gestures.

SYNONYMS **1** *he acknowledges his unfitness for the role* **admit,** accept, grant, allow, concede, confess, recognize. **2** *he did not acknowledge Colin* **greet,** salute, address, nod to, wave to, say hello to. **3** *few people acknowledged my letters* **answer,** reply to, respond to.
ANTONYMS reject, deny, ignore.

acknowledgement (or **acknowledgment**)
▸ noun **1** the action of acknowledging. **2** something done or given as thanks to someone. **3** a mention of someone in a book thanking them for work they have done.

acme /**ak**-mi/ ▸ noun the highest point of achievement or excellence.

acne ▸ noun a skin condition causing red pimples.

acolyte /**ak**-uh-lyt/ ▸ noun an assistant or follower.

acorn ▸ noun the fruit of the oak tree, a smooth oval nut in a cup-like base.

acoustic ▸ adjective **1** having to do with sound or hearing. **2** not electrically amplified.
▸ noun (**acoustics**) **1** the aspects of a room or building that affect how well it transmits sound. **2** the branch of physics concerned with sound.
□ **acoustically** adverb.

acquaint ▸ verb **1** (**acquaint someone with**) make someone aware of or familiar with. **2** (**be acquainted with**) know someone personally.

SYNONYMS **familiarize,** make aware of, inform of, advise of; informal **fill in on, clue in on.**

✔ **Acquaint, acquiesce, acquire, acquit,** and words related to them have a **c** before the **qu**: ac**qu**aint.

acquaintance ▸ noun **1** familiarity with someone or something. **2** a person you know slightly.

SYNONYMS **1** *a business acquaintance* **contact,** associate, colleague. **2** *my acquaintance with George* **association,** relationship. **3** *some acquaintance with the language* **familiarity with,** knowledge of, experience of, awareness of, understanding of, grasp of.

acquiesce /**ak**-wi-**ess**/ ▸ verb (**acquiesces, acquiescing, acquiesced**) accept something without protest.

acquiescent ▸ adjective ready to accept or do something without protest.
□ **acquiescence** noun.

acquire ▸ verb (**acquires, acquiring, acquired**) **1** buy or obtain an article. **2** learn or develop a skill or quality.

SYNONYMS **get,** obtain, come by, receive, collect, gain, buy, earn, win, come into, secure, pick up; informal **get your hands on, get hold of, land, bag, score.**
ANTONYMS lose.

acquisition ▸ noun **1** something that you have recently obtained. **2** the action of obtaining or learning something.

SYNONYMS **1** *a new acquisition* **purchase,** addition, investment, possession; informal **buy. 2** *the acquisition of funds* **obtaining,** collection, gaining, earning, winning, securing.

acquisitive ▸ adjective too interested in gaining money or material things.

acquit ▸ verb (**acquits, acquitting, acquitted**) **1** formally state that someone is not guilty of a criminal charge. **2** (**acquit yourself**) behave or perform in a particular way.

SYNONYMS **1** *the jury acquitted her* **clear,** exonerate, find innocent, absolve, discharge, free, release; informal let off (the hook). **2** *the boys acquitted themselves well* **behave,** conduct yourself, perform, act.
ANTONYMS convict.

□ **acquittal** noun.

acre ▸ noun a unit of land area equal to 4,840 square yards (0.405 hectare).
□ **acreage** noun.

acrid ▸ adjective unpleasantly bitter or sharp.

acrimonious ▸ adjective angry and bitter.
□ **acrimoniously** adverb.

acrimony ▸ noun feelings of anger and bitterness.

acrobat ▸ noun an entertainer who performs spectacular gymnastic feats.

acrobatic ▸ adjective involving or performing spectacular gymnastic feats.
▸ noun (**acrobatics**) spectacular gymnastic feats.
□ **acrobatically** adverb.

acronym /ak-ruh-nim/ ▸ noun a word formed from the first letters of other words (e.g. *Aids*).

acropolis ▸ noun (in an ancient Greek city) a fortress built on high ground.

across ▸ preposition & adverb from one side to the other of something.
■ **across the board** applying to all.

acrostic /uh-kross-tik/ ▸ noun a poem or puzzle in which certain letters in each line form a word or words.

acrylic ▸ adjective (of paint, fabric, etc.) made using **acrylic acid** (an organic acid).

act ▸ verb **1** do something. **2** have a particular effect. **3** behave in a particular way. **4** (**act as**) perform the function of. **5** (**acting**) temporarily doing the duties of another person. **6** perform a role in a play or film.

SYNONYMS **1** *the Government must act* **take action,** take steps, take measures, move. **2** *Alison began to act oddly* **behave,** conduct yourself, react. **3** *I'll act as lookout* **function,** work, serve, operate. **4** (**acting**) *the acting commander* **temporary,** interim, caretaker, pro tem, provisional, stopgap; N. Amer. informal pinch-hitting. **5** *he acted in a film* **perform,** play, appear.

▸ noun **1** a thing done. **2** a law passed formally by a parliament. **3** a pretence. **4** a main division of a play, ballet, or opera. **5** a set performance, or a performing group.

SYNONYMS **1** *acts of kindness* **deed,** action, gesture, feat, exploit. **2** *the act will raise taxes* **law,** decree, statute, bill, edict, ruling, order. **3** *a comedy act*

performance, turn, routine, number, sketch. **4** *it was all an act* **pretence,** show, front, facade, masquerade, charade, pose; informal a put-on.

■ **act of God** an event caused by natural forces beyond human control.

actinium ▸ noun a rare radioactive metallic element.

action ▸ noun **1** the process of doing something to achieve an aim. **2** a thing done. **3** the effect of something such as a chemical. **4** a lawsuit. **5** fighting in a battle or war. **6** the way in which something works or moves.

SYNONYMS **1** *their actions are inexcusable* **deed,** act, undertaking, exploit, behaviour, conduct, activity. **2** *the need for local action* **measures,** steps, activism, campaigning, pressure. **3** *the action of hormones* **operation,** working, effect, influence, process, power. **4** *he died in action* **battle,** combat, hostilities, fighting, active service. **5** *a civil action* **lawsuit,** suit, case, prosecution, litigation, proceedings.

▸ verb deal with a particular matter.

actionable ▸ adjective giving someone grounds to take legal action.

activate ▸ verb (**activates, activating, activated**) make something start working.

SYNONYMS **start (up),** switch on, turn on, set going, trigger (off), set off, energize.
ANTONYMS switch off.

□ **activation** noun.

active ▸ adjective **1** moving about often or energetically. **2** regularly taking part in something. **3** working; functioning. **4** (of a volcano) erupting or having erupted in historical times. **5** Grammar (of a verb) having as its subject the person or thing doing the action (e.g. *she loved him* as opposed to the passive form *he was loved*).

SYNONYMS **1** *she kept active* **busy,** mobile, lively, vigorous; informal on the go, full of beans. **2** *an active member of the union* **hard-working,** industrious, tireless, energetic. **3** *the watermill was active until 1960* **working,** operative, functioning, operational, in action, in operation, in force; informal (up and) running.
ANTONYMS listless, inactive.

■ **active service** military service in wartime.
□ **actively** adverb.

activist ▸ noun a person who campaigns for political or social change.
□ **activism** noun.

activity ▸ noun (plural **activities**) **1** a condition in which things are happening or being done. **2** busy or energetic action or movement. **3** an action, especially one done for interest or pleasure.

a

SYNONYMS **1** *there was a lot of activity* **action,** bustle, movement, life; informal toing and froing, comings and goings. **2** *a leisure activity* **pursuit,** occupation, hobby, pastime, recreation, diversion, venture, undertaking, enterprise, project, scheme.
ANTONYMS inactivity.

actor ▸ noun a person whose profession is acting.

SYNONYMS **performer,** player, thespian, star, starlet; Brit. informal luvvy.

actress ▸ noun a female actor.

actual ▸ adjective existing in fact or reality.

SYNONYMS **real,** true, genuine, authentic, confirmed, definite, hard, concrete; informal real live.
ANTONYMS imaginary.

actuality ▸ noun (plural **actualities**) actual reality or fact.

actualize (or **actualise**) ▸ verb (**actualizes, actualizing, actualized**) make something real or actual.

actually ▸ adverb in truth; in reality.

SYNONYMS **really,** in (actual) fact, in point of fact, as a matter of fact, in reality, in truth, if truth be told, to tell the truth.

actuary ▸ noun (plural **actuaries**) a person who calculates insurance risks.
□ **actuarial** adjective.

actuate ▸ verb **1** cause a machine to function. **2** motivate someone to act in a particular way.

acuity /uh-**kyoo**-i-ti/ ▸ noun sharpness of thought, vision, or hearing.

acumen /ak-yoo-muhn/ ▸ noun the ability to make good judgements and take quick decisions.

acupuncture ▸ noun a medical treatment in which very thin needles are inserted into the skin.
□ **acupuncturist** noun.

acute ▸ adjective **1** (of something bad) very serious. **2** intelligent and shrewd. **3** (of a physical sense or faculty) highly developed. **4** (of an angle) less than 90°.

SYNONYMS **1** *acute food shortages* **severe,** dire, terrible, grave, serious, desperate. **2** *acute pain* **excruciating,** sharp, severe, stabbing, agonizing, racking, searing. **3** *his acute mind* **quick,** astute, shrewd, sharp, keen, penetrating, razor-sharp, quick-witted, agile, nimble, intelligent, canny, discerning, perceptive.
ANTONYMS mild, dull.

■ **acute accent** a mark (´) placed over certain letters in some languages to show pronunciation (e.g. in *fiancée*).

□ **acutely** adverb **acuteness** noun.

AD ▸ abbreviation used to indicate that a date comes a particular number of years after the traditional date of Jesus's birth.
ORIGIN short for *Anno Domini* ('in the year of our Lord' in Latin).

❗ If a date is written in figures, AD should be placed **before** the numerals, e.g. AD 375, but when the date is spelled out, AD should be placed after it, as in *the third century* AD.

adage /**ad**-ij/ ▸ noun a popular saying expressing something that most people accept as true.

adagio /uh-**dah**-ji-oh/ ▸ noun (plural **adagios**) a piece of music to be played in slow time.

adamant ▸ adjective refusing to be persuaded or to change your mind.

SYNONYMS **unshakeable,** unwavering, unswerving, immovable, resolute, resolved, determined, firm, dead set.

□ **adamantly** adverb.

Adam's apple ▸ noun a projection at the front of the neck, more prominent in men than women.

adapt ▸ verb **1** make something suitable for a new use or purpose. **2** become adjusted to new conditions.

SYNONYMS **1** *the policy can be adapted* **modify,** alter, change, adjust, remodel, reorganize, customize, tailor; informal tweak. **2** *he adapts well to new surroundings* **adjust,** conform, acclimatize, accommodate.

adaptable ▸ adjective able to adjust to, or be altered for, new conditions or uses.
□ **adaptability** noun **adaptably** adverb.

adaptation (or **adaption**) ▸ noun **1** the process of adapting. **2** a film or play adapted from a written work.

adaptor (or **adapter**) ▸ noun **1** a device for connecting pieces of equipment. **2** Brit. a device for connecting several electric plugs to one socket.

add ▸ verb **1** put something together with something else. **2** put together two or more numbers or amounts to find their total value. **3** (**add up**) increase in amount or number. **4** say as a further remark. **5** (**add up**) informal make sense.

SYNONYMS **1** *the porch was added later* **attach,** append, tack on, join on. **2** *they added the figures up* **total,** count (up), reckon up, tally; Brit. tot up.
ANTONYMS subtract.

addendum /uh-**den**-duhm/ ▸ noun (plural **addenda**) an extra item added at the end of a book or other publication.

adder ▸ noun a poisonous snake with a dark zigzag pattern on its back.

addict ▸ noun a person who is addicted to something.

SYNONYMS **1** *a heroin addict* **abuser**; informal **junkie, druggy, -head, freak**; N. Amer. informal **hophead. 2** *skiing addicts* **enthusiast,** fan, lover, devotee, aficionado; informal buff, freak, nut, fanatic.

addicted ▸ adjective (usu. **addicted to**) **1** physically dependent on a particular substance. **2** very keen on a particular interest or activity.

SYNONYMS **dependent,** obsessed, fixated, fanatical, passionate, a slave to; informal hooked.

addiction ▸ noun the condition of being addicted to something.

SYNONYMS **dependency,** dependence, habit, obsession, infatuation, passion, love, mania, enslavement.

addictive ▸ adjective (of a substance or activity) causing someone to become addicted to it.

SYNONYMS **habit-forming,** compulsive; Brit. informal moreish.

addition ▸ noun **1** the action of adding. **2** a person or thing that is added.

SYNONYMS **1** *the addition of extra rooms* **adding,** inclusion, incorporation, introduction. **2** *a useful addition* **add-on,** extra, adjunct, appendage, supplement, rider. ANTONYMS subtraction, removal, essential.

additional ▸ adjective added; extra.

SYNONYMS **extra,** added, supplementary, further, more, spare, other, new, fresh.

additionally ▸ adverb as an extra factor or circumstance.

SYNONYMS **also,** in addition, besides, too, as well, on top (of that), furthermore, moreover, into the bargain, to boot, to say nothing of.

additive ▸ noun a substance added to improve or preserve something.

addled ▸ adjective **1** humorous confused or puzzled. **2** (of an egg) rotten.

address ▸ noun **1** the details of where a building is or where someone lives. **2** a string of characters identifying a destination for email messages. **3** a formal speech.

SYNONYMS **1** *officers called at the address* **house,** flat, apartment, home; formal residence, dwelling. **2** *his address to Parliament* **speech,** lecture, talk, presentation, dissertation, sermon.

▸ verb **1** write a name and address on an envelope or parcel. **2** make a speech or remark to. **3** think about a task and begin to deal with it.

SYNONYMS *he addressed his audience* **speak to,** talk to, give a talk to, make a speech to, hold forth to.

✔ two **d**s: add**ress**.

adduce ▸ verb (**adduces, adducing, adduced**) formal refer to something as evidence.

adenoids /ad-uh-noydz/ ▸ plural noun a mass of tissue between the back of the nose and the throat.

adept ▸ adjective /uh-**dept**, **ad**-ept/ very skilled or able.

SYNONYMS **expert,** proficient, accomplished, skilful, practised, masterly, consummate. ANTONYMS inept.

▸ noun /**ad**-ept/ an adept person.
□ **adeptly** adverb.

adequate ▸ adjective satisfactory or acceptable; good enough.

SYNONYMS **1** *adequate financial resources* **sufficient,** enough. **2** *an adequate service* **satisfactory,** acceptable, passable, reasonable, tolerable, fair, average, not bad, all right, middling; informal OK. ANTONYMS insufficient, inadequate.

□ **adequacy** noun **adequately** adverb.

adhere ▸ verb (**adheres, adhering, adhered**) (**adhere to**) **1** stick firmly to. **2** follow or observe.

SYNONYMS **1 stick,** cling, bond, hold. **2 abide by,** stick to, hold to, comply with, conform to, follow, obey, heed, observe, respect, uphold, fulfil.

□ **adherence** noun.

adherent ▸ noun a person who supports a particular party, person, or set of ideas.
▸ adjective sticking firmly to an object or surface.

adhesion ▸ noun the process of adhering.

adhesive ▸ noun a substance used to stick things together.
▸ adjective sticky.

ad hoc ▸ adjective & adverb created or done for a particular purpose only.

adieu /uh-**dyoo**/ ▸ exclamation old use goodbye.

Adi Granth /ah-di **grunt**/ ▸ noun the main sacred scripture of Sikhism.

ad infinitum /ad in-fi-**ny**-tuhm/ ▸ adverb endlessly; forever.

adjacent /uh-**jay**-s'nt/ ▸ adjective near or next to something else.

SYNONYMS **adjoining,** neighbouring, next-door, abutting.

adjective ▸ noun Grammar a word used to describe a noun or to make its meaning

a

clearer, such as *sweet* or *red*.
□ **adjectival** adjective.

adjoin ▸ verb be next to and joined with.

adjoining ▸ adjective next-door or connected.

> SYNONYMS **connecting**, connected, interconnecting, bordering, abutting, attached, adjacent, neighbouring, next-door.

adjourn /uh-**jern**/ ▸ verb 1 break off a meeting until later. 2 postpone a decision.

> SYNONYMS 1 *the hearing was adjourned* **suspend**, break off, discontinue, interrupt, recess. 2 *sentencing was adjourned until June 9* **postpone**, put off/back, defer, delay, hold over.

□ **adjournment** noun.

adjudge ▸ verb (**adjudges, adjudging, adjudged**) (of a law court or judge) formally decide.

adjudicate /uh-**joo**-di-kayt/ ▸ verb (**adjudicates, adjudicating, adjudicated**) 1 make a formal judgement. 2 judge a competition.
□ **adjudication** noun **adjudicator** noun.

adjunct ▸ noun an additional part or thing.

adjure ▸ verb (**adjures, adjuring, adjured**) formal urge someone to do something.

adjust ▸ verb 1 alter something slightly. 2 become used to a new situation. 3 decide the amount to be paid when settling an insurance claim.

> SYNONYMS 1 *he adjusted the brakes* **modify**, alter, regulate, tune, fine-tune, balance, tailor, customize, rearrange, change, reshape; informal tweak.
> 2 *Kate had adjusted to her new life* **adapt**, become accustomed, get used, accommodate, acclimatize, habituate yourself, assimilate, come to terms with, blend in with, fit in with; N. Amer. acclimate.

□ **adjustment** noun.

adjustable ▸ adjective able to be adjusted.

> SYNONYMS **alterable**, adaptable, modifiable, variable, multiway, versatile.

adjutant /a-juu-tuhnt/ ▸ noun a military officer who helps a senior officer with administrative work.

ad-lib ▸ verb (**ad-libs, ad-libbing, ad-libbed**) speak or perform in public without preparing first.
▸ noun an unprepared remark or speech.

administer ▸ verb (**administers, administering, administered**) 1 organize or put into effect. 2 give out or apply a drug or remedy.

> SYNONYMS 1 *the union is administered by an executive* **manage**, direct, control,

operate, regulate, coordinate, conduct, handle, run, organize, govern, steer.
> 2 *the crew administered first aid* **dispense**, issue, give out, provide, apply, offer, distribute, deliver, hand out, deal out, dole out.

administrate ▸ verb (**administrates, administrating, administrated**) manage the affairs of a business or organization.

administration ▸ noun 1 the running of a business or system. 2 the action of giving out or applying something. 3 the government in power.

> SYNONYMS 1 *the administration of the company* **management**, direction, control, conduct, operation, running, coordination, governance, supervision, regulation. 2 *the Labour administration* **government**, regime, executive, cabinet, authority, directorate, council, leadership, management, term of office, incumbency.

administrative ▸ adjective relating to the running of a business or other organization.

> SYNONYMS **managerial**, executive, operational, organizational, supervisory, directorial, governmental, regulatory.

administrator ▸ noun a person who administers a business or other organization.

> SYNONYMS **manager**, director, executive, controller, official, coordinator, supervisor.

admirable /**ad**-mi-ruh-b'l/ ▸ adjective deserving respect and approval.

> SYNONYMS **commendable**, praiseworthy, laudable, creditable, exemplary, worthy, deserving, respectable, worthwhile, good, sterling, fine.
> ANTONYMS deplorable.

□ **admirably** adverb.

admiral ▸ noun 1 the most senior commander of a fleet or navy. 2 a naval officer of the second most senior rank.

admiration ▸ noun respect and warm approval.

> SYNONYMS **respect**, approval, appreciation, (high) regard, esteem, recognition.
> ANTONYMS scorn.

admire ▸ verb (**admires, admiring, admired**) 1 respect or approve of. 2 look at with pleasure.

> SYNONYMS 1 *I admire your courage* **respect**, think highly of, hold in high regard, rate highly, esteem, prize, approve of. 2 *Simon had admired her for a long time* **adore**, love, worship, be

taken with, be attracted to; informal carry a torch for, have a thing about.
ANTONYMS despise.

admirer ▸ noun someone who feels respect or approval for someone or something.

SYNONYMS **fan,** devotee, enthusiast, aficionado, supporter, adherent, follower, disciple.

admissible ▸ adjective acceptable or valid.

admission ▸ noun **1** the process of being allowed into a place. **2** a confession.

SYNONYMS **1** *an admission of liability* **confession,** acknowledgement, acceptance, concession, disclosure, divulgence. **2** *free admission* **admittance,** entry, entrance, access, entrée, acceptance, initiation.

admit ▸ verb (admits, admitting, admitted) **1** confess that something is true or is the case. **2** allow someone to enter a place. **3** accept that something is valid.

SYNONYMS **1** *Paul admitted that he was angry* **confess,** acknowledge, concede, grant, accept, allow, reveal, disclose, divulge. **2** *he admitted the offence* **confess (to),** plead guilty to, own up to. **3** *he was admitted to the college* **let in,** accept, receive, initiate, take on.
ANTONYMS deny, exclude.

admittance ▸ noun the process of entering, or of being allowed to enter.

SYNONYMS **entry,** admission, entrance, access, entrée.
ANTONYMS exclusion.

admonish ▸ verb firmly tell someone off.
□ admonition noun admonitory adjective.

ad nauseam /ad **naw**-zi-am/ ▸ adverb to an annoying or boring extent.

ado ▸ noun trouble; fuss.

adobe /uh-**doh**-bi/ ▸ noun a kind of clay used to make sun-dried bricks.

adolescence ▸ noun the adolescent period of a person's life.

SYNONYMS **teenage years,** teens, youth, later childhood.

adolescent ▸ adjective in the process of developing from a child into an adult.

SYNONYMS **teenage,** young, immature, childish, juvenile, infantile, puerile; informal teen.
ANTONYMS mature.

▸ noun an adolescent boy or girl.

SYNONYMS **teenager,** youth, juvenile; informal teen, teeny-bopper.

Adonis /uh-**doh**-nis/ ▸ noun a very handsome young man.

adopt ▸ verb **1** legally take someone else's child and bring it up as your own. **2** choose an option or course of action.

SYNONYMS **take on,** embrace, take up, espouse, assume, follow, choose, endorse, approve.
ANTONYMS abandon.
□ adoption noun.

adoptive ▸ adjective (of a parent) having adopted a child.

adorable ▸ adjective very lovable or charming.
□ adorably adverb.

adore ▸ verb (adores, adoring, adored) love deeply.

SYNONYMS **love,** be devoted to, dote on, cherish, treasure, prize, think the world of, admire, look up to, revere, worship.
ANTONYMS hate.
□ adoration noun.

adorn ▸ verb make more attractive; decorate.

SYNONYMS **decorate,** embellish, array, ornament, enhance.
ANTONYMS disfigure.
□ adornment noun.

adrenal /uh-**dree**-nuhl/ ▸ adjective having to do with the adrenal glands, a pair of glands above the kidneys.

adrenalin (or adrenaline /uh-**dre**-nuh-lin/) ▸ noun a hormone produced by the adrenal glands in response to stress, that makes the body's natural processes work more quickly.

adrift ▸ adjective & adverb **1** (of a boat) drifting without control. **2** no longer fixed in position.

SYNONYMS **1** *adrift in a strange country* **lost,** off course, drifting, disorientated, confused, (all) at sea, rootless, unsettled. **2** *the hook has come adrift* **loose,** free, detached, unsecured, unfastened.

adroit ▸ adjective clever or skilful.
□ adroitly adverb.

adulation ▸ noun excessive admiration.
□ adulatory adjective.

adult ▸ noun a person who is fully grown and developed.
▸ adjective **1** fully grown and developed. **2** suitable for or typical of adults.

SYNONYMS **1** *an adult woman* **mature,** grown-up, fully grown, fully developed, of age. **2** *an adult movie* **(sexually) explicit,** pornographic, obscene, dirty, erotic, sexy; informal porn, porno, naughty, blue, X-rated.
□ adulthood noun.

adulterate ▸ verb (adulterates, adulterating, adulterated) make something

a

worse in quality by adding another substance.
□ **adulteration** noun.

adulterer ▶ noun (feminine **adulteress**) a person who has committed adultery.

adultery ▶ noun sex between a married person and a person who is not their husband or wife.
□ **adulterous** adjective.

adumbrate /ad-um-brayt/ ▶ verb (**adumbrates, adumbrating, adumbrated**) formal give a faint or general idea of.

advance ▶ verb (**advances, advancing, advanced**) 1 move forwards. 2 put forward a theory or suggestion. 3 hand over payment to someone as a loan or before it is due.

> SYNONYMS 1 *the battalion advanced rapidly* **move forward**, press on, push on, attack, make progress, make headway, gain ground. 2 *the move advanced his career* **promote**, further, forward, help, aid, assist, boost. 3 *technology has advanced* **progress**, develop, evolve, make strides, move forward (in leaps and bounds), move on. 4 *a relative advanced him some money* **lend**, loan, put up, come up with; Brit. informal sub.
> ANTONYMS retreat, hinder, regress.

▶ noun 1 a forward movement. 2 a development or improvement. 3 an amount of money advanced. 4 an approach made with the aim of beginning a sexual or romantic relationship.

> SYNONYMS 1 *the army's advance* **progress**, (forward) movement, attack. 2 *a significant medical advance* **breakthrough**, development, step forward, (quantum) leap.

▶ adjective done, sent, or supplied beforehand.

> SYNONYMS *advance warning* **early**, prior.

advanced ▶ adjective 1 far on in progress or life. 2 complex; not basic.

> SYNONYMS 1 *advanced manufacturing techniques* **state-of-the-art**, modern, up to date, up to the minute, cutting-edge, new, the latest, pioneering, innovative, sophisticated. 2 *an advanced course* **higher-level**, higher, tertiary.
> ANTONYMS primitive, elementary.

■ **advanced level** an A level.

advancement ▶ noun 1 the process of helping a cause or plan to develop or succeed. 2 the raising of a person to a higher rank or status. 3 a development or improvement.

advantage ▶ noun 1 something that puts you in a good position. 2 Tennis a score marking a point between deuce and winning the game.

> SYNONYMS 1 *they have the advantage* **upper hand**, edge, lead, sway, whip hand, superiority, dominance, supremacy. 2 *the advantage of belonging to a union* **benefit**, value, good/strong point, asset, plus, bonus, boon, blessing, virtue, profit, good.
> ANTONYMS disadvantage.

■ **take advantage of 1** make unfair use of someone. 2 make good use of an opportunity.

advantageous ▶ adjective good or useful in a particular situation.

> SYNONYMS 1 *an advantageous position* **superior**, dominant, powerful, fortunate, lucky, favourable. 2 *the arrangement is advantageous to both sides* **beneficial**, of benefit, helpful, of assistance, useful, of value, profitable, in someone's interests.
> ANTONYMS disadvantageous.

advent ▶ noun 1 the arrival of an important person or thing. 2 (**Advent**) (in Christian belief) the coming or second coming of Jesus. 3 (**Advent**) the time leading up to Christmas.

adventitious /ad-vuhn-**ti**-shuhss/ ▶ adjective formal happening by chance.

adventure ▶ noun 1 an unusual, exciting, and daring experience. 2 excitement resulting from danger or risk.

> SYNONYMS 1 *her adventures in Italy* **exploit**, escapade, undertaking, experience, incident. 2 *in search of adventure* **excitement**, thrills, action, stimulation, risk, danger.

adventurer ▶ noun 1 a person willing to take risks or do dishonest things for personal gain. 2 a person who looks for adventure.

adventurous ▶ adjective 1 involving new or daring methods or experiences. 2 willing to take risks and try new things.

> SYNONYMS 1 *an adventurous traveller* **daring**, intrepid, bold, fearless, brave; informal gutsy. 2 *adventurous activities* **risky**, dangerous, perilous, hazardous, exciting.
> ANTONYMS cautious, safe, predictable.

□ **adventurously** adverb.

adverb ▶ noun Grammar a word that gives more information about an adjective, verb, or other adverb (e.g. *gently*, *very*).
□ **adverbial** adjective.

adversarial /ad-ver-**sair**-i-uhl/ ▶ adjective having to do with conflict or opposition.

adversary /ad-ver-suh-ri/ ▶ noun (plural **adversaries**) an opponent or enemy.

> SYNONYMS **opponent**, rival, enemy, antagonist, challenger, contender,

competitor, opposition, competition; literary foe.
ANTONYMS ally, supporter.

adverse ▶ adjective harmful or unfavourable.

SYNONYMS **1** *adverse weather* **unfavourable**, inclement, bad, poor, untoward. **2** *the drug's adverse side effects* **harmful**, dangerous, injurious, detrimental. **3** *an adverse response* **hostile**, unfavourable, antagonistic, unfriendly, negative.
ANTONYMS favourable, auspicious, beneficial.

☐ **adversely** adverb.

❗ Don't confuse **adverse** with **averse**, which means 'strongly disliking or opposed to', as in *I am not averse to helping out.*

adversity ▶ noun (plural **adversities**) a difficult or unpleasant situation.

advert ▶ noun Brit. informal an advertisement.

advertise ▶ verb (**advertises**, **advertising**, **advertised**) **1** describe a product, service, or event in a publication or on television or radio in order to increase sales. **2** try to fill a job vacancy by publishing details of it. **3** make a fact known.

SYNONYMS **publicize**, make public, announce, broadcast, proclaim, trumpet, promote; informal push, plug, hype; N. Amer. informal ballyhoo, flack.

☐ **advertiser** noun.

advertisement ▶ noun a notice or display advertising something.

SYNONYMS **announcement**, commercial, promotion, blurb, write-up; informal ad, push, plug, puff; Brit. informal advert.

advice ▶ noun guidance or recommendations about what someone should do in the future.

SYNONYMS **guidance**, counselling, counsel, help, direction, recommendations, guidelines, suggestions, hints, tips, pointers.

❗ Don't confuse the noun **advice** and the verb **advise**.

advisable ▶ adjective sensible; to be recommended.
☐ **advisability** noun.

advise ▶ verb (**advises**, **advising**, **advised**) **1** recommend that someone should do something. **2** tell someone about a fact or situation.

SYNONYMS **1** *her grandmother advised her about marriage* **counsel**, give guidance, guide, offer suggestions, give hints/tips/pointers. **2** *he advised caution* **recommend**, advocate, suggest,

urge. **3** *you will be advised of our decision* **inform**, notify, give notice, apprise, warn.

advised ▶ adjective behaving as someone would recommend; sensible.
☐ **advisedly** adverb.

adviser (or **advisor**) ▶ noun a person who gives advice.

SYNONYMS **counsellor**, aide, mentor, guide, consultant, confidant, confidante, guru.

advisory ▶ adjective having the power to make recommendations but not to make sure that they are carried out.

advocaat /ad-vuh-kah/ ▶ noun a liqueur made with eggs, sugar, and brandy.

advocate ▶ noun /ad-vuh-kuht/ **1** a person who publicly supports or recommends a cause or policy. **2** a person who argues a case on someone else's behalf. **3** Scottish a barrister.

SYNONYMS **champion**, upholder, supporter, backer, promoter, proponent, campaigner, lobbyist; N. Amer. booster.
ANTONYMS critic.

▶ verb /ad-vuh-kayt/ (**advocates**, **advocating**, **advocated**) publicly recommend or support.

SYNONYMS **recommend**, champion, uphold, support, back, promote, campaign for, urge, subscribe to, speak for, argue for, lobby for.
ANTONYMS oppose, advise against.

☐ **advocacy** noun.

adze /adz/ (US spelling **adz**) ▶ noun a tool like an axe, with an arched blade.

aegis /ee-jiss/ ▶ noun the protection, backing, or support of someone.

aeon /ee-on/ (US spelling **eon**) ▶ noun a very long period of time.

aerate ▶ verb bring air into something.
☐ **aeration** noun.

aerial ▶ noun a wire, rod, etc. that sends out or receives radio or television signals.
▶ adjective **1** existing or taking place in the air. **2** involving the use of aircraft.

aerie US spelling of EYRIE.

aerobatics ▶ noun exciting and daring flying performed for display.
☐ **aerobatic** adjective.

aerobic /air-oh-bik/ ▶ adjective (of exercise) intended to increase the amount of oxygen you breathe in and make it move around the body more quickly.
☐ **aerobically** adverb.

aerobics ▶ noun exercises intended to strengthen the heart and lungs.

aerodrome ▶ noun Brit. an airfield.

aerodynamic ▶ adjective **1** relating to aerodynamics. **2** having a shape which

a

moves through the air quickly.
▸ noun (aerodynamics) the science concerned with the movement of objects through the air.
  □ aerodynamically adverb.

aerofoil ▸ noun Brit. a curved structure, such as a wing, designed to give an aircraft lift.

aeronautics ▸ noun the study or practice of travel through the air.
  □ aeronautical adjective.

aeroplane ▸ noun Brit. a powered flying vehicle with fixed wings.

aerosol ▸ noun a substance sealed in a container under pressure and released as a fine spray.

aerospace ▸ noun the technology and industry concerned with flight.

aesthete /eess-theet/ (US spelling esthete) ▸ noun a person who appreciates art and beauty.

aesthetic /ess-thet-ik/ (US spelling esthetic) ▸ adjective 1 concerned with beauty. 2 having a pleasant appearance.
▸ noun a set of principles behind the work of an artist or artistic movement.
  □ aesthetically adverb.

aesthetics (US spelling esthetics) ▸ noun 1 a set of principles concerned with beauty. 2 the branch of philosophy which deals with questions of beauty and artistic taste.

afar ▸ adverb at or to a distance.

affable ▸ adjective good-natured and friendly.
  □ affability noun affably adverb.

affair ▸ noun 1 an event or series of events. 2 a matter that is a particular person's responsibility. 3 a love affair. 4 (affairs) matters of public interest and importance.

SYNONYMS 1 *it was a strange affair* event, incident, episode, case, matter, business. 2 *what you do is your affair* business, concern, matter, responsibility; Brit. informal lookout. 3 (affairs) *financial affairs* transactions, activities, dealings, undertakings, ventures, business. 4 *his affair with Anthea was over* relationship, romance, fling, dalliance, liaison, involvement, amour; informal hanky-panky; Brit. informal carry-on.

affect ▸ verb 1 make a difference to. 2 make someone feel sadness, pity, etc. 3 pretend to have a particular feeling. 4 wear something or behave in a particular way in an attempt to impress people.

SYNONYMS 1 *this affected our decision* influence, have an effect on, have an impact on, act on, change, alter, modify. 2 *he was visibly affected by the experience* move, touch, hit (hard), make an impression on, upset, trouble, distress, disturb, shake (up). 3 *he affected an air*

of boredom put on, assume, take on, adopt, feign.

❗ Don't confuse **affect** and **effect**. **Affect** chiefly means 'make a difference to', as in *the changes will affect everyone*. **Effect** is chiefly a noun meaning 'a result', as in *the effects of ageing*.

affectation ▸ noun behaviour that is designed to impress people.

SYNONYMS **pretension**, pretentiousness, affectedness, artificiality, posturing, airs (and graces); Brit. informal side.

affected ▸ adjective designed to impress people.
  □ affectedly adverb.

affection ▸ noun a feeling of fondness or liking.

SYNONYMS **fondness**, love, liking, tenderness, warmth, devotion, caring, attachment, friendship.

affectionate ▸ adjective readily showing affection.

SYNONYMS **fond**, loving, adoring, devoted, caring, tender, warm, friendly, demonstrative; informal touchy-feely, lovey-dovey.
ANTONYMS cold.

  □ affectionately adverb.

affidavit /af-fi-day-vit/ ▸ noun a written statement that a person swears is true and that can be used as evidence in a law court.

affiliate ▸ verb /uh-fil-i-ayt/ (affiliates, affiliating, affiliated) officially link a person or group to an organization.

SYNONYMS **associate**, unite, combine, join (up), join forces, link up, ally, align, amalgamate, merge.

▸ noun /uh-fil-i-uht/ an affiliated person or group.
  □ affiliation noun.

affinity ▸ noun (plural affinities) 1 a natural liking or understanding. 2 a close relationship between people or things with similar qualities.

SYNONYMS **empathy**, rapport, sympathy, accord, harmony, similarity, relationship, bond, closeness, understanding; informal chemistry.
ANTONYMS aversion, dislike, dissimilarity.

affirm ▸ verb state firmly or publicly.

SYNONYMS **declare**, state, assert, proclaim, pronounce, attest, swear.
ANTONYMS deny.

  □ affirmation noun.

affirmative ▸ adjective agreeing with a statement, or consenting to a request.

SYNONYMS **positive,** assenting, consenting, approving, favourable.
ANTONYMS negative.

□ **affirmatively** adverb.

affix ▶ verb /uh-**fiks**/ attach or fasten something to something else.
▶ noun /**af**-fiks/ Grammar a prefix or suffix.

afflict ▶ verb cause pain or suffering to.

SYNONYMS **trouble,** burden, distress, beset, harass, worry, oppress, torment, plague.

□ **affliction** noun.

affluent ▶ adjective wealthy; rich.

SYNONYMS **wealthy,** rich, prosperous, well off, well-to-do, of means; informal well heeled, rolling in it, made of money, loaded.
ANTONYMS poor.

□ **affluence** noun.

afford ▶ verb **1** have enough money or time for. **2** provide an opportunity or facility.

SYNONYMS **1** *I can't afford a new car* **pay for,** find the money for, run to, stretch to, stand, manage. **2** *can you afford the time?* **spare,** allow yourself. **3** *the terrace affords beautiful views* **give,** offer, supply, provide, furnish, yield.

□ **affordable** adjective.

affray ▶ noun Law, dated a breach of the peace by fighting in a public place.

affront ▶ noun an action or remark that offends someone.
▶ verb offend someone.

Afghan /af-gan/ ▶ noun a person from Afghanistan.
▶ adjective relating to Afghanistan.

aficionado /uh-fi-shuh-**nah**-doh/ ▶ noun (plural **aficionados**) a person who knows a lot about an activity or subject and is very keen on it.

afield ▶ adverb to or at a distance.

aflame ▶ adjective in flames.

afloat ▶ adjective & adverb **1** floating in water. **2** out of debt or difficulty.

afoot ▶ adverb & adjective happening; in preparation or progress.

aforementioned ▶ adjective previously mentioned.

afraid ▶ adjective feeling fear.

SYNONYMS **1** *they ran away because they were afraid* **frightened,** scared, terrified, fearful, nervous, petrified, intimidated, cowardly, faint-hearted; informal scared stiff; N. Amer. informal spooked. **2** *don't be afraid to ask awkward questions* **reluctant,** hesitant, unwilling, slow, shy. **3** *I'm afraid I'm late* **sorry.**
ANTONYMS brave, confident, glad.

afresh ▶ adverb in a new or different way.

African ▶ noun a person from Africa.
▶ adjective relating to Africa or Africans.

Afrikaans /af-ri-**kahns**/ ▶ noun a language of southern Africa that developed from Dutch.

Afrikaner /af-ri-**kah**-ner/ ▶ noun an Afrikaans-speaking white person in South Africa.

aft ▶ adverb & adjective at or towards the rear of a ship or an aircraft.

after ▶ preposition **1** in the time following an event or another period of time. **2** next to and following in order or importance. **3** behind. **4** trying to find or get. **5** in reference to.

SYNONYMS **following,** subsequent to, at the end of, in the wake of.

▶ conjunction & adverb in the time following an event.
■ **after-effect** an effect that happens some time after its cause.

afterbirth ▶ noun the placenta and other material that passes out of the mother's womb after a birth.

afterlife ▶ noun life after death.

aftermath ▶ noun the situation that exists as a result of an unpleasant or disastrous event.

SYNONYMS **consequences,** after-effects, results, repercussions, upshot.

afternoon ▶ noun the time from noon or lunchtime to evening.

aftershave ▶ noun a scented liquid for men to apply to their skin after shaving.

afterthought ▶ noun something that is thought of or added later.

afterwards (US spelling **afterward**) ▶ adverb at a later or future time.

SYNONYMS **later,** later on, subsequently, then, next, after this/that, in due course.

again ▶ adverb **1** once more. **2** returning to a previous position or condition. **3** in addition.

SYNONYMS **once more,** another time, afresh, anew.

against ▶ preposition **1** in opposition to. **2** in resistance to. **3** in contrast to. **4** in or into contact with.

SYNONYMS **1** *most delegates were against the motion* **opposed to,** in opposition to, hostile to, antagonistic towards, unsympathetic to, at odds with, in disagreement with; informal anti, agin. **2** *swimming against the tide* **counter to,** contrary to, in the opposite direction to, resisting. **3** *she leaned against the wall* **touching,** in contact with, up against,

abutting, on.
ANTONYMS in favour of, with.

agape ▶ adjective (of a person's mouth) wide open.

agate /ag-uht/ ▶ noun an ornamental stone marked with bands of colour.

agave /uh-gay-vi, uh-gah-vi/ ▶ noun an American plant with narrow spiny leaves.

age ▶ noun 1 the length of time that a person or thing has existed. 2 a particular stage in someone's life. 3 old age. 4 a distinct period of history.

SYNONYMS 1 *her hearing deteriorated with age* **old age,** maturity, advancing years, elderliness, seniority. 2 *the Elizabethan age* **era,** epoch, period, time.

▶ verb (**ages, ageing** or **aging, aged**) grow old or older.

SYNONYMS 1 *Cabernet Sauvignon ages well* **mature,** mellow, ripen, soften, season, weather. 2 *the experience has aged her* **make old,** wear out, weather. 3 *she has aged a lot* **grow old,** decline, wither, fade.

■ **age of consent** the age at which a person can legally have sex. **come of age** be legally recognized as an adult.

aged ▶ adjective 1 /ayjd/ of a specified age. 2 /ay-jid/ old.

ageism ▶ noun prejudice or discrimination on the grounds of a person's age.
□ **ageist** adjective & noun.

ageless ▶ adjective not ageing or appearing to age.

agency ▶ noun 1 an organization providing a particular service. 2 action or intervention.

SYNONYMS **business,** organization, company, firm, office, bureau.

agenda ▶ noun 1 a list of items to be discussed at a meeting. 2 a list of matters to be dealt with.

SYNONYMS **programme,** schedule, to-do list, timetable, plan.

agent ▶ noun 1 a person who provides a particular service. 2 a spy. 3 a person or thing that takes an active role or produces a particular effect.

SYNONYMS 1 *the sale was arranged through an agent* **representative,** intermediary, negotiator, go-between, proxy, broker, emissary, envoy, spokesperson; informal rep. 2 *a CIA agent* **spy,** secret agent, operative, mole; N. Amer. informal spook, G-man.

agent provocateur /a-zhon pruh-vo-kuh-ter/ ▶ noun (plural **agents provocateurs** /a-zhon pruh-vo-kuh-ter/) a person who tempts suspected criminals to commit a crime and therefore be convicted.

agglomeration ▶ noun a mass or collection of things.

aggrandize (or **aggrandise**) ▶ verb (**aggrandizes, aggrandizing, aggrandized**) make more powerful, important, or impressive.
□ **aggrandizement** noun.

aggravate ▶ verb (**aggravates, aggravating, aggravated**) 1 make worse. 2 informal annoy or exasperate.

SYNONYMS 1 *the new law could aggravate the situation* **worsen,** make worse, exacerbate, inflame, compound. 2 *you'll only aggravate him!* **annoy,** antagonize, irritate, exasperate, nettle, provoke, get on someone's nerves; Brit. rub up the wrong way; informal needle, hack off, get someone's goat, get up someone's nose; Brit. informal **wind up;** N. Amer. informal tick off.
ANTONYMS alleviate, improve, placate.

□ **aggravation** noun.

aggregate ▶ noun /ag-gri-guht/ 1 a whole formed by combining several different elements. 2 the total score of a player or team in a fixture that is made up of more than one game or round.

SYNONYMS **total,** sum, grand total, combined score.

▶ adjective /ag-gri-guht/ formed by combining many separate items.
▶ verb /ag-gri-gayt/ (**aggregates, aggregating, aggregated**) combine into a whole.

aggression ▶ noun hostile or violent behaviour or attitudes.

SYNONYMS 1 *an act of aggression* **hostility,** belligerence, force, violence, attack. 2 *he played with unceasing aggression* **confidence,** self-confidence, boldness, determination, forcefulness, vigour, energy, dynamism, commitment.

aggressive ▶ adjective 1 very angry or hostile. 2 too forceful.

SYNONYMS 1 *aggressive behaviour* **violent,** confrontational, antagonistic, pugnacious. 2 *aggressive foreign policy* **warmongering,** warlike, warring, belligerent, bellicose, hawkish, militaristic, expansionist; informal gung-ho. 3 *an aggressive promotional drive* **assertive,** forceful, vigorous, energetic, dynamic, audacious; informal in-your-face, feisty.
ANTONYMS peaceable, peaceful, laid-back.

□ **aggressively** adverb.

✔ double **g,** double **s:** aggressive.

aggressor ▶ noun a person or country that attacks another without being provoked.

aggrieved ▶ adjective resentful because you feel you have been treated unfairly.

aghast /uh-gahst/ ▶ adjective filled with horror or shock.

a

agile ▶ adjective **1** able to move quickly and easily. **2** able to think quickly and intelligently.

SYNONYMS **1** *she was as agile as a monkey* **nimble,** lithe, supple, acrobatic. **2** *an agile mind* **alert,** sharp, acute, shrewd, astute, perceptive, quick.
ANTONYMS stiff, clumsy, dull.

□ **agilely** adverb **agility** noun.

agitate ▶ verb (**agitates, agitating, agitated**) **1** make someone troubled or nervous. **2** try to arouse public concern about an issue. **3** stir or shake a liquid.

SYNONYMS **1** *any mention of Clare agitates my grandmother* **upset,** fluster, ruffle, disconcert, unnerve, disquiet, disturb, distress, unsettle; informal rattle, faze. **2** *agitate the solution* **shake,** whisk, beat, stir.

□ **agitation** noun.

agitator ▶ noun a person who urges other people to protest or rebel.

AGM ▶ abbreviation Brit. annual general meeting.

agnostic ▶ noun a person who believes it is impossible to know whether or not God exists.
□ **agnosticism** noun.

ago ▶ adverb before the present.

agog ▶ adjective very eager to hear or see something.

agonize (or **agonise**) ▶ verb (**agonizes, agonizing, agonized**) worry about something very much.

agonizing ▶ adjective causing great pain.

SYNONYMS **excruciating,** painful, acute, harrowing, torturous.

agony ▶ noun (plural **agonies**) extreme suffering.

SYNONYMS **suffering,** torture, pain, torment, anguish.

■ **agony column** Brit. informal a column in a newspaper or magazine offering advice on readers' personal problems.

agoraphobia /ag-uh-ruh-**foh**-bi-uh/ ▶ noun abnormal fear of open or public places.
□ **agoraphobic** adjective & noun.

agrarian /uh-**grair**-i-uhn/ ▶ adjective having to do with agriculture.

agree ▶ verb (**agrees, agreeing, agreed**) **1** have the same opinion about something. **2** (**agree to**) say that you will do something that has been suggested by someone else. **3** (**agree with**) be consistent with. **4** (**agree with**) be good for.

SYNONYMS **1** *I agree with you* **concur,** see eye to eye, be in sympathy, be as one, be unanimous. **2** *they agreed to a ceasefire* **consent,** assent, acquiesce; formal accede.

3 *the plan and the drawing do not agree* **match (up),** correspond, conform, coincide, fit, tally, be consistent; informal square. **4** *they agreed a price* **settle,** decide on, arrive at, negotiate, shake hands on.
ANTONYMS differ, reject, contradict.

agreeable ▶ adjective **1** pleasant. **2** willing to agree to something. **3** acceptable.

SYNONYMS **1** *an agreeable atmosphere* **pleasant,** pleasing, enjoyable, pleasurable, nice, appealing, relaxing, friendly, congenial. **2** *an agreeable man* **likeable,** amiable, affable, pleasant, nice, friendly, good-natured, sociable, genial. **3** *we should get together, if you're agreeable* **willing,** amenable, in agreement.
ANTONYMS unpleasant.

□ **agreeably** adverb.

agreement ▶ noun **1** the state of sharing the same opinion or feeling. **2** an arrangement that has been made between people.

SYNONYMS **1** *all heads nodded in agreement* **accord,** concurrence, consensus, assent, acceptance, consent, acquiescence. **2** *an agreement on imports* **contract,** treaty, pact, accord, settlement, understanding, bargain. **3** *there is some agreement between the two datasets* **correspondence,** consistency, compatibility, accord, similarity, resemblance, likeness.
ANTONYMS discord, dissimilarity.

agricultural ▶ adjective relating to agriculture.

SYNONYMS **farm,** farming, agrarian, rural, rustic, countryside.
ANTONYMS urban.

□ **agriculturally** adverb.

agriculture ▶ noun the science or practice of farming.

SYNONYMS **farming,** cultivation, husbandry, agribusiness, agronomy.

agronomy ▶ noun the scientific study of the relationship between crop production and the environment.
□ **agronomist** noun.

aground ▶ adjective & adverb (of a ship) touching the bottom in shallow water.

ague /**ay**-gyoo/ ▶ noun old use malaria or some other illness involving fever and shivering.

ahead ▶ adverb **1** further forward. **2** in the lead.

ahoy ▶ exclamation a call used by people in ships or boats to attract attention.

aid ▶ noun **1** help or support. **2** food or money given to a country in need of help.

a

SYNONYMS **1** *with the aid of his colleagues* **assistance**, support, help, backing, cooperation. **2** *humanitarian aid* **relief**, assistance, support, subsidy, funding, donations, grants; historical alms.
ANTONYMS hindrance.

▶ verb give help to.

SYNONYMS **help**, assist, support, encourage, further, boost, promote, facilitate.
ANTONYMS hinder.

aide /ayd/ ▶ noun an assistant to a political leader.

SYNONYMS **assistant**, helper, adviser, supporter, right-hand man/woman, adjutant, deputy, second (in command), lieutenant.

Aids ▶ noun a disease, caused by the HIV virus and transmitted in body fluids, which breaks down the sufferer's natural defences against infection.
ORIGIN short for *acquired immune deficiency syndrome*.

aikido /I-**kee**-doh/ ▶ noun a Japanese martial art.

ail ▶ verb old use cause someone to suffer or have problems.

aileron /**ayl**-uh-ron/ ▶ noun a hinged part of an aircraft's wing, used to control the aircraft's balance.

ailing ▶ adjective in bad health.

SYNONYMS **1** *his ailing mother* **ill**, sick, sickly, poorly, weak, in poor/bad health, infirm. **2** *the country's ailing economy* **failing**, weak, poor, tottering, fragile, unstable.
ANTONYMS healthy.

ailment ▶ noun a minor illness.

SYNONYMS **illness**, disease, disorder, affliction, malady, complaint, infirmity; informal bug, virus.

aim ▶ verb **1** point a weapon, camera, etc. at a target. **2** try to achieve something.

SYNONYMS **1** *he aimed the rifle* **point**, direct, train, sight, line up. **2** *she aimed at the target* **take aim**, fix on, zero in on, draw a bead on. **3** *this food is aimed at children* **target**, intend, direct, design, tailor, market, pitch. **4** *we aim to give you good service* **intend**, mean, hope, want, plan, propose.

▶ noun **1** a purpose or intention. **2** the aiming of a weapon or missile.

SYNONYMS *our aim is to develop top gymnasts* **objective**, object, goal, end, target, design, desire, intention, intent, plan, purpose, ambition, aspiration, wish, dream, hope.

aimless ▶ adjective having no direction or purpose.

SYNONYMS **purposeless**, directionless, undirected, random.
ANTONYMS purposeful.

☐ **aimlessly** adverb.

ain't ▶ short form informal **1** am not; are not; is not. **2** has not; have not.

❗ Do not use **ain't** when writing or speaking in a formal situation.

air ▶ noun **1** the invisible mixture of gases surrounding the earth. **2** the open space above the surface of the earth. **3** (**an air of**) an impression of. **4** (**airs**) a pretentious or condescending way of behaving. **5** a tune.

SYNONYMS **1 breeze**, draught, wind, gust/puff of wind. **2** *an air of defiance* **look**, appearance, impression, aspect, manner, tone, feel, atmosphere, mood.

▶ verb **1** express an opinion or complaint publicly. **2** broadcast a programme on radio or television. **3** expose something to fresh or warm air.

SYNONYMS **1** *a chance to air your views* **express**, voice, make public, articulate, state, declare. **2** *the room needs airing* **ventilate**, freshen, refresh, cool.

■ **air conditioning** a system that cools the air in a building or vehicle. **air force** the branch of the armed forces concerned with fighting in the air. **air gun** a gun which uses compressed air to fire pellets. **on the air** being broadcast on radio or television.
☐ **airing** noun.

airbase ▶ noun a base for military aircraft.

airborne ▶ adjective **1** carried or spread through the air. **2** (of an aircraft) in the air; flying.

airbrush ▶ noun a device for spraying paint by means of compressed air.
▶ verb paint a picture or alter a photograph with an airbrush.

aircraft ▶ noun (plural **aircraft**) a plane, helicopter, or other machine that can fly.
☐ **aircraft carrier** a large warship from which aircraft can operate.

Airedale ▶ noun a large black-and-tan breed of terrier with a rough coat.

airfield ▶ noun an area of ground where aircraft can take off and land.

airless ▶ adjective stuffy; not ventilated.

SYNONYMS **stuffy**, close, stifling, suffocating, oppressive, unventilated.
ANTONYMS airy.

airlift ▶ noun an act of transporting supplies by aircraft.

airline ▶ noun a company that provides regular flights for the public to use.

airliner ▶ noun a large passenger aircraft.

airlock ▶ noun **1** a bubble of air that stops the flow in a pump or pipe. **2** a compartment which allows people to move between areas that are at different pressures.

airmail ▶ noun a system of transporting mail overseas by air.

airman ▶ noun (plural **airmen**) a pilot or crew member in a military aircraft.

airplane ▶ noun N. Amer. a plane.

airport ▶ noun an area consisting of a set of runways and buildings where non-military aircraft can take off and land.

airship ▶ noun a large aircraft filled with gas which is lighter than air.

airspace ▶ noun the part of the air above a particular country.

airstrip ▶ noun a strip of ground where aircraft can take off and land.

airtight ▶ adjective **1** not allowing air to escape or pass through. **2** unable to be proved false.

airwaves ▶ plural noun the radio frequencies used for broadcasting.

airway ▶ noun **1** the passage by which air reaches the lungs. **2** a recognized route followed by aircraft.

airworthy ▶ adjective (of an aircraft) safe to fly.

airy ▶ adjective (**airier**, **airiest**) **1** spacious and having plenty of fresh air. **2** showing that you feel something is not worth serious consideration.

> SYNONYMS **spacious**, uncluttered, light, bright, well ventilated, fresh.
> ANTONYMS poky, stuffy.

□ **airily** adverb.

airy-fairy ▶ adjective informal vague and unrealistic or impractical.

aisle (*rhymes with* mile) ▶ noun a passage between rows of seats in a public building, aircraft, or train or between shelves in a shop.

> SYNONYMS **passage**, passageway, lane, path, gangway, walkway.

ajar ▶ adverb & adjective (of a door or window) slightly open.

aka ▶ abbreviation also known as.

akimbo /uh-**kim**-boh/ ▶ adverb with hands on the hips and elbows turned outwards.

akin ▶ adjective similar in nature or type.

> SYNONYMS **similar**, related, close, near, comparable, equivalent, connected, alike, analogous.
> ANTONYMS unlike.

alabaster /**al**-uh-bass-ter/ ▶ noun a white, semi-transparent mineral that is carved into ornaments.

à la carte /a la kart/ ▶ adjective & adverb (of a menu) offering dishes that are separately priced, rather than part of a set meal.

alacrity ▶ noun great eagerness or enthusiasm.

alarm ▶ noun **1** anxiety or fear caused by being aware of danger. **2** a warning of danger. **3** a sound or device that gives a warning of danger.

> SYNONYMS **1** *the girl spun round in alarm* **fear**, anxiety, apprehension, distress, agitation, consternation, fright, panic. **2** *a fire alarm* **warning**, danger signal, siren, bell, detector, sensor.
> ANTONYMS calmness, composure.

▶ verb **1** frighten or disturb. **2** (**be alarmed**) (of a car or building) be fitted with an alarm.

> SYNONYMS *the news alarmed her* **frighten**, scare, panic, unnerve, distress, agitate, upset, disconcert, shock, disturb; informal rattle, spook; Brit. informal put the wind up.
> ANTONYMS reassure.

■ **alarm clock** a clock set to sound at a particular time to wake you up.

alarming ▶ adjective making someone feel anxiety or fear.

> SYNONYMS **frightening**, unnerving, shocking, worrying, upsetting, disconcerting, disturbing; informal scary.
> ANTONYMS reassuring.

alarmist ▶ noun a person who exaggerates a danger and causes unnecessary alarm.

alas ▶ exclamation literary or humorous an expression of grief, pity, or concern.

albatross /**al**-buh-tross/ ▶ noun (plural **albatrosses**) a very large white seabird with long, narrow wings.

albeit /awl-**bee**-it/ ▶ conjunction though.

albino /al-**bee**-noh/ ▶ noun (plural **albinos**) a person or animal born with white skin and hair and pink eyes.

album ▶ noun **1** a blank book for displaying photographs, stamps, etc. **2** a collection of musical recordings issued as a single item.

albumen /**al**-byuu-muhn/ ▶ noun egg white.

alchemy /**al**-kuh-mi/ ▶ noun a medieval form of chemistry that was chiefly concerned with trying to convert ordinary metals into gold.
□ **alchemical** adjective **alchemist** noun.

alcohol ▶ noun **1** drinks containing a colourless liquid that can make people drunk, such as wine, beer, and spirits. **2** this liquid.

alcoholic ▶ adjective relating to alcohol.

> SYNONYMS **intoxicating**, strong, hard, stiff, fermented, brewed, distilled.

▶ noun a person suffering from alcoholism.

> SYNONYMS **drunkard**, dipsomaniac, drunk, heavy drinker, problem drinker,

a

alcohol-abuser; informal boozer, alky, dipso, soak, wino; Austral./NZ informal hophead.

alcoholism ▶ noun addiction to alcoholic drink.

alcopop ▶ noun Brit. informal a ready-mixed fizzy drink containing alcohol.

alcove ▶ noun a recess in the wall of a room.

alder ▶ noun a tree of the birch family, which produces catkins.

alderman ▶ noun (plural **aldermen**) chiefly historical a member of a council below the rank of mayor.

ale ▶ noun chiefly Brit. beer, especially bitter.

alert ▶ adjective 1 quick to notice and respond to danger or change. 2 quick-thinking; intelligent.

> SYNONYMS **1** *an alert sentry* **vigilant**, watchful, attentive, observant, wide awake, on the lookout, on your guard/toes; informal keeping your eyes open/peeled. **2** *mentally alert* **quick-witted**, sharp, bright, quick, perceptive, on your toes; informal on the ball, quick on the uptake, all there, with it.
> ANTONYMS inattentive, dull.

▶ noun 1 a watchful state. 2 a warning of danger.

> SYNONYMS **1** *a state of alert* **vigilance**, watchfulness, attentiveness, alertness. **2** *a flood alert* **warning**, notification, notice, siren, alarm, signal.

▶ verb warn someone of a danger or problem.

> SYNONYMS *police were alerted* **warn**, notify, forewarn, put someone on their guard; informal tip off.

□ **alertly** adverb **alertness** noun.

alfalfa /al-**fal**-fuh/ ▶ noun a plant with bluish flowers, used as food for animals.

alfresco /al-**fress**-koh/ ▶ adverb & adjective in the open air.

algae /**al**-jee, **al**-gee/ ▶ plural noun simple plants that do not have true stems, roots, and leaves, such as seaweed.

algebra /**al**-ji-bruh/ ▶ noun the branch of mathematics in which letters and other symbols are used to represent numbers and quantities.

□ **algebraic** /al-ji-**bray**-ik/ adjective.

Algerian ▶ noun a person from Algeria. ▶ adjective relating to Algeria.

algorithm /**al**-guh-ri-*th*'m/ ▶ noun a process or set of rules used in calculations.

alias /**ay**-li-uhss/ ▶ adverb also known as. ▶ noun a false identity.

alibi /**a**-li-by/ ▶ noun (plural **alibis**) a piece of evidence that a person was somewhere else when a crime was committed.

alien ▶ adjective 1 belonging to a foreign country. 2 unfamiliar and unappealing.

3 from another world.

> SYNONYMS **foreign**, unfamiliar, unknown, peculiar, exotic, strange.
> ANTONYMS native, familiar.

▶ noun 1 a foreigner. 2 a being from another world.

> SYNONYMS **1** *an illegal alien* **foreigner**, non-native, immigrant, émigré, stranger. **2** *the alien's spaceship crashed* **extraterrestrial**, ET; informal little green man.

alienate ▶ verb (**alienates, alienating, alienated**) 1 make someone feel isolated. 2 lose the support or sympathy of.

> SYNONYMS **isolate**, distance, estrange, cut off, turn away, drive apart, set at variance/odds, drive a wedge between.

alienation ▶ noun the state or experience of being alienated.

> SYNONYMS **isolation**, detachment, estrangement, separation.

alight¹ ▶ verb 1 get off a train or bus. 2 (of a bird) land on something.

alight² ▶ adverb & adjective 1 on fire. 2 shining brightly.

> SYNONYMS *the stable was alight* **burning**, ablaze, on fire, in flames, blazing.

align ▶ verb 1 place something in a straight line or in the right position in relation to other things. 2 (**align yourself with**) be on the side of.

> SYNONYMS **1** *the desks are aligned with the wall* **line up**, straighten, even up, arrange, coordinate. **2** *he aligned himself with the workers* **ally**, affiliate, associate, side, join forces, team up, band together, throw in your lot.

□ **alignment** noun.

alike ▶ adjective similar.

> SYNONYMS *all the doors looked alike* **similar**, (much) the same, indistinguishable, identical, uniform, interchangeable; informal much of a muchness.
> ANTONYMS different.

▶ adverb in a similar way.

> SYNONYMS *great minds think alike* **similarly**, the same, correspondingly, analogously, identically.
> ANTONYMS differently.

alimentary canal ▶ noun the passage along which food passes through the body.

alimony /**a**-li-muh-ni/ ▶ noun chiefly N. Amer. financial support for a husband or wife after separation or divorce.

alive ▶ adjective 1 living; not dead. 2 continuing in existence or use. 3 alert and active. 4 (**alive with**) full of. 5 (**alive**

to) aware of and willing to respond to.

SYNONYMS **1** *the synagogue has kept the Jewish faith alive* **active**, in existence, functioning, in operation, operative, on the map. **2** *teachers need to be alive to their pupils' needs* **alert**, awake, aware, conscious, mindful, heedful, sensitive, familiar.
ANTONYMS dead, unaware.

alkali /al-kuh-ly/ ▸ noun (plural **alkalis**) a substance whose chemical properties include turning litmus blue and neutralizing acids.
□ **alkaline** adjective.

all ▸ determiner **1** the whole quantity or extent of. **2** any whatever. **3** the greatest possible.
▸ pronoun everything or everyone.
▸ adverb **1** completely. **2** indicating an equal score: *one–all*.
■ **all and sundry** everyone. **the all clear** a signal that danger is over. **all in** informal exhausted. **all out** trying as hard as you can. **all-rounder** Brit. a person with a wide range of skills. **all told** in total. **on all fours** on hands and knees.

Allah /al-luh/ ▸ noun the Arabic name of God.

allay /uh-lay/ ▸ verb reduce or end fear, concern, or difficulty.

SYNONYMS **reduce**, diminish, decrease, lessen, alleviate, ease, relieve, soothe, soften, calm.
ANTONYMS increase, intensify.

allegation ▸ noun a claim that someone has done something illegal or wrong.

SYNONYMS **claim**, assertion, charge, accusation, contention.

allege ▸ verb (**alleges**, **alleging**, **alleged**) claim that someone has done something illegal or wrong.

SYNONYMS **claim**, assert, charge, accuse, contend.

alleged ▸ adjective said, without proof, to have happened or have an undesirable quality.

SYNONYMS **reported**, supposed, so-called, claimed, professed, purported, ostensible, unproven.
ANTONYMS confirmed.

□ **allegedly** adverb.

allegiance ▸ noun loyalty to a person, group, or cause.

SYNONYMS **loyalty**, faithfulness, fidelity, obedience, adherence, devotion.
ANTONYMS disloyalty, treachery.

allegory ▸ noun (plural **allegories**) a story, poem, or picture which contains a hidden meaning.

□ **allegorical** adjective.

allegro /uh-lay-groh/ ▸ noun (plural **allegros**) a piece of music that is to be played at a brisk speed.

alleluia ➡ HALLELUJAH.

allergen ▸ noun a substance that causes an allergic reaction.

allergic ▸ adjective **1** caused by an allergy. **2** having an allergy.

allergy ▸ noun (plural **allergies**) a medical condition that makes you feel ill when you eat or come into contact with a particular substance.

alleviate ▸ verb (**alleviates**, **alleviating**, **alleviated**) make a pain or problem less severe.

SYNONYMS **ease**, relieve, take the edge off, deaden, dull, lessen, reduce, moderate, allay, soothe, help, soften.
ANTONYMS aggravate.

□ **alleviation** noun.

alley ▸ noun (plural **alleys**) **1** (also **alleyway**) a narrow passageway between or behind buildings. **2** a path in a park or garden. **3** a long, narrow area in which skittles and bowling are played.

SYNONYMS **passage**, passageway, alleyway, backstreet, lane, path, pathway, walk.

alliance ▸ noun **1** the state of being joined or associated. **2** an agreement made between countries or organizations to work together. **3** a relationship or connection.

SYNONYMS **association**, union, league, confederation, federation, coalition, marriage, cooperation.

allied ▸ adjective **1** joined by an alliance. **2** (**Allied**) relating to Britain and its allies in the First and Second World Wars. **3** (**allied to** or **with**) combined with.

SYNONYMS **associated**, united, related, connected, interconnected, linked, cooperating, in league, affiliated, combined, coupled, married.
ANTONYMS unrelated, independent.

alligator ▸ noun a large reptile similar to a crocodile.

alliteration ▸ noun the occurrence of the same letter or sound at the beginning of words that are next to or close to each other.
□ **alliterative** adjective.

allocate ▸ verb (**allocates**, **allocating**, **allocated**) assign or give to.

SYNONYMS **allot**, assign, set aside, earmark, consign, distribute, apportion, share out, dole out, give out.

allocation ▸ noun **1** the action of allocating something. **2** an amount of a resource given to someone.

a

SYNONYMS 1 *the efficient allocation of resources* **allotment**, assignment, distribution, sharing out, doling out, giving out. **2** *our annual allocation of funds* **allowance**, allotment, consignment, quota, share, ration; informal cut; Brit. informal whack.

allot ▸ verb (allots, allotting, allotted) give or share out something.

allotment ▸ noun **1** Brit. a small plot of rented land for growing vegetables or flowers. **2** the action of allotting something, or an amount of something allotted to someone.

allow ▸ verb **1** let someone do something. **2** (allow for) take into consideration. **3** provide or set aside. **4** admit that something is true.

SYNONYMS 1 *the police allowed him to go home* **permit**, let, enable, authorize, give leave, license, entitle, consent to, assent to, acquiesce in, agree to, approve; informal give the go-ahead to, give the thumbs up to, OK, give the green light to; formal accede to. **2** *allow an hour or so for driving* **set aside**, allocate, allot, earmark, designate, reserve.
ANTONYMS prevent, forbid.

□ **allowable** adjective.

! Don't confuse **allowed**, meaning 'permitted', with **aloud**, meaning 'out loud'.

allowance ▸ noun **1** the amount of something that is allowed. **2** a sum of money paid regularly to a person. **3** Brit. an amount of money that can be earned free of tax.

SYNONYMS 1 *your baggage allowance* **allocation**, quota, ration, share, ration, grant, limit. **2** *her father gave her an allowance* **payment**, pocket money, contribution, grant, handout, subsidy, maintenance.

▪ **make allowances for 1** take into consideration. **2** treat someone less harshly because they are in difficult circumstances.

alloy ▸ noun /**al**-loy/ **1** a mixture of two or more metals. **2** an inferior metal mixed with a precious one.
▸ verb /uh-**loy**/ mix metals to make an alloy.

all right ▸ adjective **1** satisfactory; acceptable. **2** allowed.

SYNONYMS 1 *the tea was all right* **satisfactory**, acceptable, adequate, passable, reasonable; informal so-so, OK. **2** *are you all right?* **unhurt**, uninjured, unharmed, in one piece, safe (and sound), alive and well; informal OK. **3** *it's all right for you to go* **permissible**, permitted, allowed, acceptable, legal, lawful, authorized, approved, in order; informal OK, legit, cool.
ANTONYMS unsatisfactory, hurt, forbidden.

▸ adverb fairly well.

SYNONYMS *the system works all right* **satisfactorily**, adequately, fairly well, passably, acceptably, reasonably, well, fine; informal OK.
ANTONYMS unsatisfactorily.

✔ Use the spelling **all right** rather than **alright**.

allspice ▸ noun the dried fruit of a Caribbean tree, used as a spice in cookery.

allude ▸ verb (alludes, alluding, alluded) (allude to) **1** mention in passing. **2** hint at.

allure ▸ noun the quality of being very attractive or appealing.

alluring ▸ adjective very attractive or tempting.
□ **alluringly** adverb.

allusion ▸ noun an indirect reference to something.
□ **allusive** adjective.

alluvial ▸ adjective made of clay, silt, and sand that is left by flood water.

ally /**al**-ly/ ▸ noun (plural **allies**) **1** a person, organization, or country that cooperates with another. **2** (the Allies) the countries that fought with Britain in the First and Second World Wars.

SYNONYMS *a political ally* **associate**, colleague, friend, confederate, partner, supporter.
ANTONYMS enemy, opponent.

▸ verb /uh-**ly**/ (allies, allying, allied) **1** (ally something to or with) combine one resource with another in a way that benefits both. **2** (ally yourself with) side with.

SYNONYMS *the Catholic powers allied with Philip II* **unite**, combine, join (up), join forces, band together, team up, collaborate, side, align yourself.
ANTONYMS split.

alma mater /al-muh **mah**-ter, **may**-ter/ ▸ noun the school, college, or university that a person once attended.

almanac (or almanack /**al**-muh-nak/) ▸ noun **1** a calendar that gives important dates and also information about the sun, moon, tides, etc. **2** a book published yearly and containing useful information for that year.

almighty ▸ adjective **1** having unlimited or very great power. **2** informal enormous.
▸ noun (the Almighty) God.

almond ▸ noun an oval nut with a woody shell, growing on a tree found in warm climates.

almost ▶ adverb very nearly.

> SYNONYMS **nearly,** (just) about,
> practically, virtually, all but, as good as,
> close to, not quite; informal pretty nearly/
> much/well; literary well-nigh, nigh on.

alms /ahmz/ ▶ plural noun (in the past)
money or goods given to the poor.

almshouse ▶ noun (in the past) a house
built for poor people to live in.

aloe /a-loh/ ▶ noun a tropical plant with
succulent leaves, whose bitter juice is used
in medicine.

aloe vera /veer-uh/ ▶ noun a jelly-like
substance obtained from a kind of aloe,
used to soothe the skin.

aloft ▶ adjective & adverb up in or into the air.

alone ▶ adjective & adverb **1** on your own.
2 isolated and lonely. **3** only; exclusively.

> SYNONYMS **1** *she was alone in the house*
> **by yourself,** on your own, solitary,
> single, solo; Brit. informal on your tod.
> **2** *he travelled alone* **by yourself,** on
> your own, solo, singly, independently,
> unaccompanied, apart, without help.
> **3** *she felt terribly alone* **lonely,** isolated,
> deserted, abandoned, friendless.
> ANTONYMS accompanied, loved.

along ▶ preposition & adverb **1** moving on a
surface in a constant direction. **2** extending
on a surface in a horizontal line. **3** in
company with other people.

alongside ▶ preposition **1** close to the side
of; next to. **2** at the same time as.

aloof ▶ adjective not friendly or showing an
interest in other people.
□ **aloofness** noun.

alopecia /a-luh-**pee**-shuh/ ▶ noun abnormal
loss of hair.

aloud ▶ adverb not silently; out loud.

> ! Don't confuse **aloud**, meaning 'out loud',
> with **allowed**, meaning 'permitted'.

alp ▶ noun **1** a high mountain. **2** (**the Alps**)
a high range of mountains in Switzerland
and adjoining countries.

alpaca /al-**pak**-uh/ ▶ noun (plural **alpaca** or
alpacas) a long-haired South American
animal related to the llama.

alpha ▶ noun the first letter of the Greek
alphabet (Α, α).
▶ adjective referring to the dominant animal
or person in a group: *the alpha male.*

alphabet ▶ noun a set of letters or symbols
used to represent the basic speech sounds
of a language.

alphabetical ▶ adjective in the order of the
letters of the alphabet.
□ **alphabetically** adverb.

alpine ▶ adjective **1** relating to or found on
high mountains. **2** (**Alpine**) relating to

the Alps.

already ▶ adverb **1** before the time in
question. **2** as surprisingly soon or early
as this.

alright = ALL RIGHT.

Alsatian ▶ noun Brit. a German shepherd dog.

also ▶ adverb in addition.

> SYNONYMS **too,** as well, besides, in
> addition, additionally, furthermore,
> further, moreover, into the bargain, on
> top (of that), what's more, to boot.

■ **also-ran** a loser in a race or contest.

altar ▶ noun **1** the table in a Christian church
at which bread and wine are made sacred.
2 a table or block on which offerings are
made to a god or goddess.

alter ▶ verb make or become different;
change.

> SYNONYMS **1** *Eliot was persuaded to
> alter the passage* **change,** adjust, adapt,
> amend, modify, revise, rework, redo,
> transform; informal tweak. **2** *the situation
> has altered* **change,** become different,
> undergo a (sea) change, evolve, move on.
> ANTONYMS preserve, stay the same.

□ **alteration** noun.

altercation ▶ noun a noisy argument or
disagreement.

alter ego /awl-ter ee-goh/ ▶ noun **1** another
side to a person's normal personality. **2** a
close friend who is very like yourself.

alternate ▶ verb /**awl**-ter-nayt/ (**alternates,
alternating, alternated**) **1** (of two things or
people) repeatedly follow one another in
turn. **2** keep changing between two states.

> SYNONYMS **1** *rows of trees alternate with
> dense shrub* **be interspersed,** follow one
> another, take turns, take it in turns,
> oscillate, see-saw. **2** *we could alternate
> the two groups* **rotate,** swap, exchange,
> interchange.

▶ adjective /**awl**-ter-nuht/ **1** every other. **2** (of
two things) each following and succeeded
by the other in a regular pattern.

> SYNONYMS **1** *she attended on alternate
> days* **every other,** every second,
> alternating. **2** *alternate posts and trees*
> **alternating,** sequential, rotating, by
> turns.

■ **alternating current** electric current that
reverses direction many times a second.
□ **alternately** adverb **alternation** noun.

alternative ▶ adjective **1** (of one or more
things) available as another possibility.
2 different from what is usual or
traditional: *alternative therapy.*

> SYNONYMS **1** *an alternative route*
> **different,** other, second, substitute,
> replacement, standby, emergency,
> reserve, backup, auxiliary, fallback;

a

N. Amer. **alternate**. **2** *an alternative lifestyle* **unorthodox**, unconventional, nonconformist, radical, revolutionary, avant-garde; informal offbeat, way-out.

▶ noun one of two or more available possibilities.

> SYNONYMS *we have no alternative* (**other**) **option**, (other) choice, substitute, replacement.

□ **alternatively** adverb.

alternator ▶ noun a dynamo that generates an alternating current.

although ▶ conjunction **1** in spite of the fact that. **2** but.

altimeter /al-ti-mee-ter/ ▶ noun an instrument which indicates the altitude that has been reached.

altitude ▶ noun the height of an object or point above sea level or ground level.

alto ▶ noun (plural **altos**) the highest adult male or lowest female singing voice.

altogether ▶ adverb **1** completely. **2** in total. **3** on the whole.

> SYNONYMS **1** *he wasn't altogether happy* **completely**, totally, entirely, absolutely, wholly, fully, thoroughly, utterly, perfectly, one hundred per cent, in all respects. **2** *we have five offices altogether* **in all**, all told, in total.

altruism /al-troo-iz'm/ ▶ noun unselfish concern for other people.
□ **altruist** noun **altruistic** adjective.

alum /al-uhm/ ▶ noun a compound of aluminium and potassium, used in dyeing and in making leather.

aluminium /al-yoo-**min**-i-uhm/ (US spelling **aluminum** /uh-**loo**-mi-nuhm/) ▶ noun a lightweight silvery-grey metal.

alumnus /uh-**lum**-nuhss/ ▶ noun (plural **alumni** /uh-**lum**-ny/) a former student of a particular school, college, or university.

alveolus /al-vee-**oh**-luhss/ ▶ noun (plural **alveoli** /al-vee-**oh**-lee/) any of the many tiny air sacs in the lungs.
□ **alveolar** adjective.

always ▶ adverb **1** at all times. **2** forever. **3** repeatedly. **4** failing all else.

> SYNONYMS **1** *he's always late* **every time**, all the time, without fail, consistently, invariably, regularly, habitually, unfailingly. **2** *she's always complaining* **continually**, continuously, constantly, forever, all the time, day and night; informal 24-7. **3** *the place will always be dear to me* **forever**, for good, for evermore, for ever and ever, until the end of time, eternally.
> ANTONYMS never, seldom, sometimes.

Alzheimer's disease /**alts**-hy-merz/ ▶ noun a disease of the brain which can affect older people, causing memory loss and confusion.

AM ▶ abbreviation amplitude modulation.

am 1st person singular present of **BE**.

a.m. ▶ abbreviation before noon.
ORIGIN short for Latin *ante meridiem*.

amalgam ▶ noun **1** a mixture or blend of things. **2** an alloy of mercury with another metal.

amalgamate ▶ verb (**amalgamates, amalgamating, amalgamated**) combine two or more things to form one organization or structure.

> SYNONYMS **combine**, merge, unite, join, fuse, blend, meld.
> ANTONYMS separate.

□ **amalgamation** noun.

amanuensis /uh-man-yoo-en-siss/ ▶ noun (plural **amanuenses** /uh-man-yoo-en-seez/) a person who helps a writer with their work.

amass ▶ verb build up over time.

> SYNONYMS **gather**, collect, assemble, accumulate, stockpile, hoard.
> ANTONYMS disperse.

amateur ▶ noun **1** a person who takes part in a sport or other activity without being paid. **2** a person who is not skilled at an activity.

> SYNONYMS **1** *the crew were all amateurs* **non-professional**, non-specialist, layman, layperson, dilettante, dabbler. **2** *what a bunch of amateurs* **incompetent**, bungler; Brit. informal bodger, cowboy, clown.
> ANTONYMS professional, expert.

▶ adjective **1** non-professional. **2** not skilful.

> SYNONYMS **non-professional**, unpaid, non-specialist, lay, dilettante.

□ **amateurism** noun.

> ✔ **eur**, not **uer**: amat**eur**.

amateurish ▶ adjective not done or made very well; unskilful.

> SYNONYMS **incompetent**, inept, inexpert, amateur, clumsy, bumbling; Brit. informal bodged.

amatory /am-uh-tuh-ri/ ▶ adjective having to do with love or desire.

amaze ▶ verb (**amazes, amazing, amazed**) make someone feel very surprised.

> SYNONYMS **astonish**, astound, surprise, stun, stagger, nonplus, shock, startle, stop someone in their tracks, leave open-mouthed, dumbfound; informal bowl over, flabbergast; Brit. informal knock for six; (**amazed**) thunderstruck, at a loss for words, speechless; Brit. informal gobsmacked.

amazement ▸ noun a feeling of great surprise.

> synonyms **astonishment**, surprise, shock, speechlessness, awe, wonder.

amazing ▸ adjective very surprising.

> synonyms **astonishing**, astounding, surprising, stunning, staggering, breathtaking, awesome, awe-inspiring, sensational, remarkable, spectacular, stupendous, phenomenal, extraordinary, incredible, unbelievable; informal mind-blowing; literary wondrous.

□ **amazingly** adverb.

Amazon ▸ noun 1 a member of a legendary race of female warriors. 2 a very tall, strong woman.

□ **Amazonian** adjective.

ambassador ▸ noun 1 a person sent by a state as its permanent representative in a foreign country. 2 a person who represents or promotes a particular activity.

> synonyms **envoy**, emissary, representative, diplomat, minister, consul, attaché.

amber ▸ noun 1 a hard, clear yellowish substance used in jewellery. 2 a yellowish colour.

ambergris /**am**-ber-greess/ ▸ noun a wax-like substance produced by sperm whales, used in making perfume.

ambidextrous /am-bi-**deks**-truhss/ ▸ adjective able to use the right and left hands equally well.

ambience (or **ambiance**) ▸ noun the character and atmosphere of a place.

ambient ▸ adjective 1 relating to the surroundings of something. 2 (of music) quiet and relaxing.

ambiguity ▸ noun (plural **ambiguities**) the quality of having more than one possible meaning.

ambiguous ▸ adjective 1 having more than one possible meaning. 2 not clear or decided.

> synonyms **vague**, unclear, ambivalent, equivocal, inconclusive, enigmatic, cryptic.
> antonyms clear.

□ **ambiguously** adverb.

ambit ▸ noun the scope or extent of something.

ambition ▸ noun 1 a strong desire to do or achieve something. 2 desire for success, wealth, or fame.

> synonyms **1** *young people with ambition* **drive**, determination, enterprise, initiative, eagerness, motivation, a sense of purpose; informal get-up-and-go. **2** *her ambition was to become a model*

aspiration, desire, dream, intention, goal, aim, objective, plan.

ambitious ▸ adjective 1 having or showing determination to succeed. 2 intended to reach a high standard and therefore difficult to achieve.

> synonyms **1** *an ambitious politician* **aspiring**, determined, motivated, energetic, committed, purposeful, power-hungry; informal go-ahead, go-getting. **2** *an ambitious task* **challenging**, exacting, demanding, formidable, difficult, hard, tough.
> antonyms laid-back, easy.

□ **ambitiously** adverb.

ambivalent /am-**biv**-uh-luhnt/ ▸ adjective having mixed feelings about something or someone.

□ **ambivalence** noun **ambivalently** adverb.

amble ▸ verb (**ambles, ambling, ambled**) walk at a leisurely pace.
▸ noun a leisurely walk.

ambrosia ▸ noun 1 Greek Roman Mythology the food of the gods. 2 something very pleasing to taste or smell.

ambulance ▸ noun a vehicle for taking sick or injured people to and from hospital.

ambulatory ▸ adjective relating to walking, or able to walk or move.

ambush ▸ noun a surprise attack by people lying in wait in a hidden position.
▸ verb make a surprise attack on someone from a hidden position.

> synonyms **surprise**, waylay, trap, ensnare, attack, jump on, pounce on; N. Amer. bushwhack.

ameba US spelling of AMOEBA.

ameliorate /uh-**mee**-li-uh-rayt/ ▸ verb (**ameliorates, ameliorating, ameliorated**) formal make something better.

amen /ah-**men**, ay-**men**/ ▸ exclamation a word said at the end of a prayer or hymn, meaning 'so be it'.

amenable /uh-**meen**-uh-b'l/ ▸ adjective 1 willing to be persuaded. 2 (**amenable to**) able to be affected by.

amend ▸ verb change or make minor improvements to.

> synonyms **revise**, alter, change, modify, adapt, adjust, edit, rewrite, redraft, rephrase, reword.

amendment ▸ noun a minor change or improvement.

amends ▸ plural noun (**make amends**) make up for a wrongdoing.

amenity ▸ noun (plural **amenities**) a useful or desirable feature of a place.

> synonyms **facility**, service, resource, convenience, comfort.

American ► adjective relating to the United States or to the continents of America.
► noun a person from the United States or any of the countries of North, South, or Central America.
■ **American football** a kind of football played with an oval ball on a field marked with parallel lines. **American Indian** a member of one of the original peoples of America.

americium /am-uh-**riss**-i-uhm/ ► noun a radioactive metallic element.

amethyst /am-uh-thist/ ► noun a violet or purple precious stone.

amiable ► adjective friendly and pleasant.
□ **amiability** noun **amiably** adverb.

amicable ► adjective friendly and without disagreement.
□ **amicably** adverb.

amid (or **amidst**) ► preposition in the middle of.

amidships ► adverb & adjective in the middle of a ship.

amino acid /uh-**mee**-noh/ ► noun any of the natural substances which combine to form proteins.

amir → **EMIR**.

amiss ► adjective not quite right; inappropriate.
■ **take something amiss** be offended by something.

amity ► noun formal friendly relations between people or countries.

ammeter ► noun an instrument for measuring electric current.

ammo ► noun informal ammunition.

ammonia ► noun a colourless, strong-smelling gas which can be used to make a cleaning fluid.

ammonite ► noun an extinct sea creature with a spiral shell.

ammunition ► noun **1** a supply of bullets and shells. **2** points used to support your case in an argument.

amnesia /am-**nee**-zi-uh/ ► noun loss of memory.
□ **amnesiac** adjective & noun.

amnesty ► noun (plural **amnesties**) **1** a pardon given to people who have committed an offence against the government. **2** a period during which people who admit to committing an offence are not punished.

> SYNONYMS **pardon**, reprieve, forgiveness, release, discharge; informal let-off.

amniocentesis /am-ni-oh-sen-**tee**-siss/ ► noun (plural **amniocenteses** /am-ni-oh-sen-**tee**-seez/) a medical procedure in which a sample of amniotic fluid is taken to check for possible abnormalities in the unborn baby.

amniotic fluid ► noun the fluid surrounding an unborn baby in the womb.

amoeba /uh-**mee**-buh/ (US spelling **ameba**) ► noun (plural **amoebas** or **amoebae** /uh-**mee**-bee/) a microscopic creature that is made up of a single cell and can change its shape.

amok /uh-**mok**/ (or **amuck** /uh-**muk**/) ► adverb (**run amok**) behave in an uncontrolled way.

among (or **amongst**) ► preposition **1** surrounded by. **2** included or occurring in. **3** shared by; between.

amoral /ay-**mo**-ruhl/ ► adjective not concerned with doing what is right.
□ **amorality** noun.

amorous ► adjective showing or feeling sexual desire.
□ **amorously** adverb.

amorphous /uh-**mor**-fuhss/ ► adjective without a clear shape or form.

amortize (or **amortise**) ► verb (**amortizes**, **amortizing**, **amortized**) gradually pay off a debt.

amount ► noun **1** the total number, size, or value of something. **2** a quantity.

> SYNONYMS **quantity**, number, total, aggregate, sum, quota, size, mass, weight, volume.

► verb (**amount to**) **1** add up to. **2** be the same as.

ampere /am-**pair**/ ► noun a basic unit of electric current.

ampersand /**am**-per-sand/ ► noun the sign &, which means *and*.

amphetamine /am-**fet**-uh-meen/ ► noun a drug used as a stimulant.

amphibian ► noun an animal such as a frog or toad, which lives in the water when young and on the land as an adult.
□ **amphibious** adjective.

amphitheatre (US spelling **amphitheater**) ► noun a round building without a roof, in which tiers of seats surround a central space used for performing plays or for sports.

amphora /**am**-for-uh/ ► noun (plural **amphorae** /**am**-for-ee/ or **amphoras**) a tall ancient Greek or Roman jar with two handles and a narrow neck.

ample ► adjective **1** enough or more than enough; plentiful. **2** large.

> SYNONYMS **1** *there is ample time for discussion* **enough**, sufficient, adequate, plenty of, more than enough. **2** *an ample supply of wine* **plentiful**, abundant, copious, profuse, lavish, liberal, generous; informal galore. **3** *his ample tunic* **spacious**, full, capacious, roomy, voluminous, loose-fitting, baggy, sloppy. ANTONYMS insufficient, meagre, tight.

□ **amply** adverb.

amplifier ▶ noun a device that makes sounds or radio signals louder.

amplify ▶ verb (amplifies, amplifying, amplified) **1** increase the strength of a sound or an electrical signal. **2** explain something in more detail.
☐ **amplification** noun.

amplitude ▶ noun **1** the maximum amount by which a vibration such as an alternating current varies from its average level. **2** great size, range, or extent.

ampoule ▶ noun a small glass capsule containing liquid used in giving an injection.

amputate ▶ verb (amputates, amputating, amputated) cut off a limb in a surgical operation.
☐ **amputation** noun.

amputee ▶ noun a person who has had a limb amputated.

amuck → AMOK.

amulet ▶ noun a small piece of jewellery worn as protection against evil.

amuse ▶ verb (amuses, amusing, amused) **1** make someone laugh or smile. **2** give someone something enjoyable to do.

> SYNONYMS **1** *her annoyance simply amused him* **make someone laugh,** entertain, delight, divert, cheer (up), please, charm, tickle; informal crack up; Brit. informal crease up. **2** *he amused himself by writing poetry* **occupy,** engage, busy, absorb, engross, entertain.
> ANTONYMS bore.

amusement ▶ noun **1** the feeling that you have when something is funny. **2** a game or activity that provides entertainment and pleasure.

> SYNONYMS **1** *the cause of much amusement* **mirth,** merriment, hilarity, glee, delight. **2** *I read the book for amusement* **entertainment,** pleasure, leisure, relaxation, fun, enjoyment, interest. **3** *a range of amusements* **activity,** entertainment, diversion, pastime, recreation, game, sport.

amusing ▶ adjective causing laughter and providing entertainment.

> SYNONYMS **funny,** comical, humorous, light-hearted, jocular, witty, droll, entertaining, diverting; informal rib-tickling.
> ANTONYMS solemn, boring.

an ▶ determiner the form of the indefinite article 'a' used before words beginning with a vowel sound.

anabolic steroid /an-uh-**bol**-ik/ ▶ noun a synthetic hormone used to build up muscle.

anachronism /uh-**nak**-ruh-ni-z'm/ ▶ noun **1** something which seems to belong to another time. **2** something which is wrongly placed in a particular period.
☐ **anachronistic** adjective.

anaconda /an-uh-**kon**-duh/ ▶ noun a very large snake of the boa family, found in South America.

anaemia /uh-**nee**-mi-uh/ (US spelling anemia) ▶ noun a shortage of red cells or haemoglobin in the blood, making a person pale and tired.
☐ **anaemic** adjective.

anaesthetic /an-iss-**thet**-ik/ (US spelling anesthetic) ▶ noun a drug or gas that stops you feeling pain.

anaesthetize (or anaesthetise /uh-**neess**-thuh-tyz/) (US spelling anesthetize) ▶ verb (anaesthetizes, anaesthetizing, anaesthetized) give an anaesthetic to.
☐ **anaesthetist** noun.

anagram ▶ noun a word or phrase formed by rearranging the letters of another.

anal /**ay**-nuhl/ ▶ adjective having to do with the anus.

analgesic /an-uhl-**jee**-zik/ ▶ noun a pain-relieving drug.

analogous /uh-**nal**-uh-guhss/ ▶ adjective similar to and able to be compared with something else.

analogue /**an**-uh-log/ (US spelling analog) ▶ adjective using a variable physical effect, such as voltage or the position of a pointer, to represent information, rather than a digital display.
▶ noun something that is similar to and can be compared with something else.

analogy /uh-**nal**-uh-ji/ ▶ noun (plural analogies) a way of explaining something by comparing it to something else.

> SYNONYMS **similarity,** parallel, correspondence, likeness, resemblance, correlation, relation, comparison.
> ANTONYMS dissimilarity.

☐ **analogical** adjective.

analyse (US spelling analyze) ▶ verb (analyses, analysing, analysed) **1** examine something in detail to explain it or to find out its structure or composition. **2** psychoanalyse someone.

> SYNONYMS **examine,** inspect, survey, study, scrutinize, investigate, probe, explore, evaluate.

analysis /uh-**nal**-i-siss/ ▶ noun (plural analyses /uh-**nal**-i-seez/) **1** a detailed examination of the elements or structure of something. **2** psychoanalysis.

> SYNONYMS **examination,** inspection, study, scrutiny, investigation, exploration, evaluation.

analyst ▶ noun a person who carries out analysis.

analytical (or **analytic**) ▶ adjective using analysis.

> SYNONYMS **systematic**, logical, scientific, methodical, precise, meticulous, rigorous, investigative, enquiring.
> ANTONYMS unsystematic.

☐ **analytically** adverb.

anarchic /uh-**nar**-kik/ ▶ adjective not controlled or governed by any rules or principles.

anarchist ▶ noun a person who believes that all government and laws should be abolished.

☐ **anarchism** noun **anarchistic** adjective.

anarchy ▶ noun 1 a situation in which no rules or principles are being followed and there is complete disorder. 2 a society with no government.

> SYNONYMS **lawlessness**, disorder, chaos, pandemonium, riot, revolution.
> ANTONYMS government, order.

anathema /uh-**na**-thuh-muh/ ▶ noun something that you hate.

anatomy ▶ noun (plural **anatomies**) 1 the scientific study of the structure of the human body. 2 the structure of a person, animal, or plant. 3 a detailed examination or analysis.

> SYNONYMS **structure**, make-up, composition, constitution, form, body, physique.

☐ **anatomical** adjective **anatomically** adverb **anatomist** noun.

ancestor ▶ noun 1 a person from whom you are descended. 2 something from which a later species or version has developed.

> SYNONYMS **forefather**, forebear, predecessor, antecedent, progenitor, parent, grandparent.
> ANTONYMS descendant.

ancestral /an-**sess**-truhl/ ▶ adjective inherited from your ancestors.

ancestry ▶ noun (plural **ancestries**) your ancestors or ethnic origins.

anchor ▶ noun a heavy object that is attached to a boat by a rope or chain and is dropped to the sea bed to stop the boat from drifting.
▶ verb 1 hold with an anchor. 2 secure or fix firmly in position.

anchorage ▶ noun a place where ships may anchor safely.

anchorite /ang-kuh-ryt/ ▶ noun (in the past) a person who lived alone for religious reasons.

anchorman (or **anchorwoman**) ▶ noun (plural **anchormen** or **anchorwomen**) a person who presents a live television or radio programme.

anchovy /an-**chuh**-vi/ ▶ noun (plural **anchovies**) a small fish of the herring family, with a strong flavour.

ancien régime /on-si-an ray-z**heem**/ ▶ noun (plural **anciens régimes** /on-si-an ray-z**heem**/) a political or social system that has been replaced by a more modern one.

ancient ▶ adjective 1 belonging to the very distant past. 2 very old.

> SYNONYMS 1 *ancient civilizations* **early**, prehistoric, primeval, primordial, primitive. 2 *an ancient custom* **old**, age-old, archaic, antediluvian, time-honoured. 3 *I feel positively ancient* **antiquated**, decrepit, antediluvian, geriatric; informal out of the ark; Brit. informal past its/your sell-by date.
> ANTONYMS recent, contemporary, young.

▶ noun (**the ancients**) the people of ancient times.

ancillary ▶ adjective 1 providing support. 2 additional; extra.

and ▶ conjunction 1 used to connect words, clauses, or sentences. 2 (connecting two numbers) plus.

andante /an-**dan**-tay/ ▶ adverb & adjective Music at a moderately slow pace.

androgynous /an-**dro**-ji-nuhss/ ▶ adjective partly male and partly female.
☐ **androgyny** noun.

android /**an**-droyd/ ▶ noun (in science fiction) a robot with a human appearance.

anecdotal /an-ik-**doh**-t'l/ ▶ adjective (of a story) not backed up by facts.

anecdote /**an**-ik-doht/ ▶ noun a short entertaining story about a real incident or person.

> SYNONYMS **story**, tale, urban myth, narrative, reminiscence; informal yarn.

anemia US spelling of ANAEMIA.

anemometer ▶ noun an instrument for measuring the speed of the wind.

anemone /uh-**nem**-uh-ni/ ▶ noun a plant with brightly coloured flowers.

anesthetic US spelling of ANAESTHETIC.

aneurysm (or **aneurism**) /**an**-yuu-ri-z'm/ ▶ noun a swelling of the wall of an artery.

anew ▶ adverb 1 in a new or different way. 2 once more; again.

angel ▶ noun 1 a messenger of God, pictured as being of human form but with wings. 2 a very beautiful or good person.

angelic ▶ adjective very beautiful or innocent.

> SYNONYMS **innocent**, pure, virtuous, saintly, cherubic, adorable.

angelica /an-**jel**-li-kuh/ ▶ noun a plant whose stalks are preserved in sugar and used in cake decoration.

anger ▶ noun a strong feeling of extreme displeasure.

> SYNONYMS **annoyance**, vexation, temper, indignation, rage, fury, wrath, outrage.
> ANTONYMS pleasure, good humour.

▶ verb (**angers**, **angering**, **angered**) make someone angry.

> SYNONYMS **annoy**, irk, vex, enrage, incense, infuriate, rile, outrage.
> ANTONYMS pacify, placate.

angina /an-**jy**-nuh/ (or **angina pectoris** /**pek**-tuh-riss/) ▶ noun severe pain in the chest caused by an inadequate supply of blood to the heart.

angle¹ ▶ noun **1** the space between two lines or surfaces that meet. **2** a position from which something is viewed. **3** a way of thinking about something.

> SYNONYMS **1** *an angle of 33°* **gradient**, slope, slant, inclination. **2** *right in the angle of the roof* **corner**, point, fork, nook, crook, edge. **3** *consider the problem from a different angle* **perspective**, point of view, viewpoint, standpoint, position, aspect, slant, direction, approach, tack.

▶ verb (**angles**, **angling**, **angled**) **1** place something in a slanting position. **2** present information from a particular point of view.

> SYNONYMS *Anna angled her camera upwards* **tilt**, slant, twist, swivel, lean, tip, turn.

angle² ▶ verb (**angles**, **angling**, **angled**) **1** fish with a rod and line. **2** try to get something without asking for it directly.
   □ **angler** noun.

Anglican ▶ adjective relating to the Church of England.
▶ noun a member of the Church of England.
   □ **Anglicanism** noun.

anglicize (or **anglicise**) ▶ verb (**anglicizes**, **anglicizing**, **anglicized**) make something English.
   □ **anglicization** noun.

Anglophile ▶ noun a person who admires England or Britain.

Anglo-Saxon ▶ noun **1** a person living in England between the 5th century and the Norman Conquest, whose ancestors came from north and west Europe. **2** the Old English language.

Angolan ▶ noun a person from Angola, a country in SW Africa.
▶ adjective relating to Angola.

angora /ang-**gor**-uh/ ▶ noun **1** a breed of cat, goat, or rabbit with long, soft hair. **2** fabric made from the hair of the angora goat or rabbit.

angostura /ang-guh-**styoor**-uh/ ▶ noun the bitter bark of a South American tree, used as a flavouring.

angry ▶ adjective (**angrier**, **angriest**) **1** feeling or showing anger. **2** (of a wound or sore) red and swollen.

> SYNONYMS **furious**, irate, vexed, irked, enraged, seething, infuriated, in a temper, fuming, outraged, cross; informal (hopping) mad, up in arms, foaming at the mouth, steamed up, in a paddy; Brit. informal shirty; N. Amer. informal sore, teed off, ticked off; Austral./NZ informal ropeable, snaky.
> ANTONYMS pleased, good-humoured.

   □ **angrily** adverb.

angst ▶ noun a strong feeling of anxiety about life in general.

angstrom /ang-**struhm**/ ▶ noun a unit of length equal to one hundred-millionth of a centimetre.

anguish ▶ noun severe pain or suffering.

> SYNONYMS **agony**, pain, torment, torture, suffering, distress, woe, misery, sorrow, heartache.
> ANTONYMS happiness.

   □ **anguished** adjective.

angular /ang-**gyuu**-ler/ ▶ adjective **1** having angles or sharp corners. **2** (of a person) lean and bony. **3** placed or directed at an angle.
   □ **angularity** noun.

animal ▶ noun **1** a living being that can move about of its own accord and has specialized sense organs and nervous system. **2** a mammal, as opposed to a bird, reptile, fish, or insect.

> SYNONYMS **1** **creature**, beast, (living) thing; (**animals**) wildlife, fauna. **2** *the man was an animal* **beast**, brute, monster, devil, fiend; informal swine, bastard, pig.

▶ adjective **1** having to do with animals. **2** physical rather than spiritual or intellectual.
   □ **animality** noun.

animate ▶ verb /**an**-i-mayt/ (**animates**, **animating**, **animated**) **1** bring life or energy to. **2** make drawings or models into an animated film.

> SYNONYMS *the forces animating community life* **enliven**, energize, invigorate, liven up, inspire, fire, rouse, excite, move.
> ANTONYMS depress.

▶ adjective /**an**-i-muht/ living.

> SYNONYMS *an animate being* **living**, alive, live, breathing, sentient.
> ANTONYMS inanimate.

   □ **animator** noun.

animated ▶ adjective **1** lively. **2** (of a film) made using animation.

> SYNONYMS **lively**, spirited, energetic, full of life, excited, enthusiastic, eager, alive, vigorous, vibrant, vivacious, exuberant,

a

ebullient, bouncy, bubbly, perky; informal bright-eyed and bushy-tailed, full of beans, bright and breezy, chirpy, chipper.
ANTONYMS lethargic, lifeless.

□ **animatedly** adverb.

animation ▶ noun **1** liveliness. **2** the technique of filming a sequence of drawings or positions of models to give the appearance of movement. **3** the creation of moving images by means of a computer.

animism /an-i-mi-z'm/ ▶ noun the belief that all things in nature have a soul.
□ **animist** noun.

animosity ▶ noun (plural **animosities**) hatred or strong dislike.

SYNONYMS **hostility,** antipathy, antagonism, enmity, resentment, ill feeling/will, bad blood.
ANTONYMS goodwill, friendship.

animus ▶ noun hatred or dislike.

anion /an-I-uhn/ ▶ noun an ion with a negative charge.

aniseed ▶ noun the seed of the anise plant, used as a flavouring.

ankle ▶ noun the joint connecting the foot with the leg.

anklet ▶ noun a chain or band worn round the ankle.

annals ▶ plural noun a historical record of events made year by year.

anneal /uh-neel/ ▶ verb heat metal or glass and allow it to cool slowly, so as to toughen it.

annex ▶ verb /an-neks/ **1** take possession of another country's land. **2** add something as an extra part.
▶ noun (also **annexe**) /an-neks/ (plural **annexes**) **1** a building attached or near to a main building. **2** an addition to a document.
□ **annexation** noun.

annihilate /uh-ny-i-layt/ ▶ verb (annihilates, annihilating, annihilated) destroy completely.

SYNONYMS **destroy,** obliterate, eradicate, wipe out, wipe off the face of the earth; informal rub out, snuff out.
ANTONYMS create.

□ **annihilation** noun.

anniversary ▶ noun (plural **anniversaries**) the date on which an event took place in a previous year.

annotate ▶ verb (annotates, annotating, annotated) add explanatory notes to.
□ **annotation** noun.

announce ▶ verb (announces, announcing, announced) **1** make a public statement about. **2** be a sign of.

SYNONYMS **make public,** make known, report, declare, state, give out, publicize, broadcast, publish, advertise, circulate, proclaim, release.

□ **announcer** noun.

announcement ▶ noun a public statement.

SYNONYMS **1** an announcement by the Minister **statement,** declaration, proclamation, pronouncement, bulletin, communiqué; N. Amer. advisory. **2** the announcement of the decision **declaration,** notification, reporting, publishing, broadcasting.

annoy ▶ verb make someone slightly angry.

SYNONYMS **irritate,** bother, vex, make cross, exasperate, irk, anger, antagonize, nettle; Brit. rub up the wrong way; informal aggravate, peeve, miff, rile, needle, get (to), bug, hack off; Brit. informal wind up, nark, get on someone's wick; N. Amer. informal tee off, tick off, burn up, rankle, gravel.
ANTONYMS please, gratify.

annoyance ▶ noun the feeling or state of being annoyed.

SYNONYMS **irritation,** exasperation, vexation, indignation, anger, displeasure, chagrin.

annual ▶ adjective **1** happening once a year. **2** calculated over or covering a year. **3** (of a plant) living for a year or less.

SYNONYMS **yearly,** once-a-year, year-long, twelve-month.

▶ noun a book published once a year.

annually ▶ adverb every year.

SYNONYMS **yearly,** once a year, each year, every year, per annum.

annuity /uh-nyoo-i-ti/ ▶ noun (plural **annuities**) a fixed sum of money paid to someone each year.

annul /uh-nul/ ▶ verb (annuls, annulling, annulled) declare a law, marriage, or other legal contract to be no longer valid.

SYNONYMS **declare invalid,** declare null and void, nullify, invalidate, void, repeal, revoke.
ANTONYMS restore, enact.

□ **annulment** noun.

annular /an-yuu-ler/ ▶ adjective technical ring-shaped.

Annunciation ▶ noun (the Annunciation) (in Christian belief) the announcement by the angel Gabriel to the Virgin Mary that she was to be the mother of Jesus.

anode /an-ohd/ ▶ noun an electrode with a positive charge.

anodized (or **anodised**) ▶ adjective (of metal) coated with a protective layer by the action of an electric current.

anodyne ▶ adjective not likely to cause offence or disagreement.

▸ **noun** a painkilling drug.

anoint ▸ **verb** dab or smear water or oil on someone as part of a religious ceremony.

anomalous ▸ **adjective** differing from what is standard or normal.

anomaly /uh-**nom**-uh-li/ ▸ **noun** (plural **anomalies**) something that is different from what is normal or expected.

> SYNONYMS **oddity**, peculiarity, abnormality, irregularity, inconsistency, aberration, quirk.

anon ▸ **adverb** old use soon; shortly.

anonymous ▸ **adjective** 1 having a name that is not publicly known. 2 having no outstanding or individual features.

> SYNONYMS 1 *an anonymous donor* **unnamed,** nameless, unidentified, unknown, incognito. 2 *an anonymous letter* **unsigned,** unattributed.
> ANTONYMS known.

□ **anonymity** noun **anonymously** adverb.

anorak ▸ **noun** a waterproof jacket with a hood.

anorexia (or **anorexia nervosa**) ▸ **noun** a disorder in which a person refuses to eat because they are afraid of becoming fat.
□ **anorexic** adjective & noun.

another ▸ **determiner & pronoun** 1 one more. 2 different from the one already mentioned.

answer ▸ **noun** 1 something said or written in reaction to a question or statement. 2 the solution to a problem.

> SYNONYMS 1 *her answer was unequivocal* **reply,** response, rejoinder, reaction, retort, riposte; informal comeback. 2 *the answer to this problem* **solution,** remedy, way out, explanation.
> ANTONYMS question.

▸ **verb** (**answers, answering, answered**) 1 give an answer. 2 (**answer back**) give a cheeky reply. 3 (**answer to**) have to explain your actions or decisions to someone. 4 (**answer for**) be responsible for the things you do. 5 meet a need.

> SYNONYMS *Steve was about to answer* **reply,** respond, rejoin, retort, riposte.

■ **answering machine** a machine which gives a pre-recorded reply to a telephone call and can record a message from the caller.

answerable ▸ **adjective** 1 (**answerable to**) having to explain to someone why you have done the things you have done. 2 (**answerable for**) responsible for something.

ant ▸ **noun** a small insect that lives with many others in an organized group.

antacid /an-**tass**-id/ ▸ **adjective** (of a medicine) reducing excess acid in the stomach.

antagonism /an-**tag**-uh-ni-z'm/ ▸ **noun** the expression of hostile feelings.

antagonist ▸ **noun** an opponent or enemy.

antagonistic ▸ **adjective** showing or feeling hostility.

> SYNONYMS **hostile,** opposed, antipathetic, ill-disposed, resistant, in disagreement; informal anti.
> ANTONYMS pro.

antagonize (or **antagonise**) ▸ **verb** (**antagonizes, antagonizing, antagonized**) make someone feel hostile.

> SYNONYMS **provoke,** intimidate, alienate, anger, annoy.
> ANTONYMS pacify, disarm.

Antarctic ▸ **adjective** relating to the region surrounding the South Pole.

> ✔ Remember the **c** after the **r**: Antar**c**tic.

anteater ▸ **noun** an animal with a long snout and sticky tongue, that feeds on ants and termites.

antecedent ▸ **noun** 1 a thing that exists or comes before another. 2 (**antecedents**) a person's ancestors. ▸ **adjective** coming before in time or order.

antechamber ▸ **noun** an anteroom.

antedate ▸ **verb** (**antedates, antedating, antedated**) come or exist before something else.

antediluvian /an-ti-di-**loo**-vi-uhn/ ▸ **adjective** 1 very old-fashioned. 2 belonging to the time before the biblical Flood.

antelope ▸ **noun** a swift deer-like animal found in Africa and Asia.

antenatal ▸ **adjective** Brit. before birth; during pregnancy.

antenna /an-**ten**-nuh/ ▸ **noun** 1 (plural **antennae** /an-**ten**-nee/) each of a pair of long, thin feelers on the heads of some insects and shellfish. 2 (plural **antennae** or **antennas**) an aerial.

anterior ▸ **adjective** at or near the front.

anteroom ▸ **noun** a small room leading to a more important one.

anthem ▸ **noun** 1 a song chosen by a country to express patriotic feelings. 2 a musical setting of a religious work that is sung by a choir during a church service.

> SYNONYMS **hymn,** song, chorale, chant, psalm, canticle.

anther ▸ **noun** the part of a flower's stamen that contains the pollen.

anthill ▸ **noun** a mound of earth made by ants when they build a nest.

anthology ▸ **noun** (plural **anthologies**) a collection of poems or other pieces of writing or music.

a

anthracite ▶ noun hard coal that burns without producing much flame and smoke.

anthrax ▶ noun a serious disease of sheep and cattle, that can be passed to humans.

anthropoid ▶ adjective having to do with apes that resemble human beings in form, such as gorillas or chimpanzees.

anthropology ▶ noun the study of human origins, societies, and cultures.
□ **anthropological** adjective **anthropologist** noun.

anthropomorphic /an-thruh-puh-**mor**-fik/ ▶ adjective treating a god, animal, or object as if they were human.

antibiotic ▶ noun a medicine that kills bacteria.

antibody ▶ noun (plural **antibodies**) a protein produced in the blood to react against harmful substances.

Antichrist ▶ noun an enemy of Christ that some people believe will appear before the end of the world.

anticipate ▶ verb (**anticipates, anticipating, anticipated**) **1** be aware of and prepared for a future event. **2** look forward to. **3** do something earlier than someone else.

SYNONYMS **1** *the police did not anticipate trouble* **expect**, foresee, predict, be prepared for, bargain on, reckon on; N. Amer. informal figure on. **2** *we eagerly anticipated his arrival* **look forward to**, await, long for, can't wait for.

□ **anticipatory** adjective.

anticipation ▶ noun the action of anticipating something.

SYNONYMS **expectation**, expectancy, prediction, hope, excitement, suspense.

anticlimax ▶ noun a disappointing end to an exciting series of events.

SYNONYMS **let-down**, disappointment, comedown, non-event, disillusionment; Brit. damp squib; informal washout.

□ **anticlimactic** adjective.

anticlockwise ▶ adverb & adjective Brit. in the opposite direction to the way in which a clock's hands move round.

antics ▶ plural noun silly or amusing behaviour.

SYNONYMS **capers**, pranks, larks, high jinks, skylarking, horseplay, clowning; Brit. informal monkey tricks.

anticyclone ▶ noun an area of high atmospheric pressure around which air slowly circulates, usually resulting in calm, fine weather.

antidote ▶ noun a medicine taken to undo the effect of a poison.

SYNONYMS **remedy**, cure, solution, countermeasure, corrective.

antifreeze ▶ noun a liquid added to water to prevent it from freezing, used in car radiators.

antigen /an-ti-jen/ ▶ noun a harmful substance which causes the body to produce antibodies.

anti-hero ▶ noun a central character in a story, film, or play who is either ordinary or unpleasant.

antihistamine ▶ noun a drug that is used in treating allergies.

antimacassar /an-ti-muh-**kass**-er/ ▶ noun a decorative piece of cloth put over the back of a chair to protect it from grease and dirt.

antimatter ▶ noun Physics matter consisting of particles with the same mass as those of normal matter but opposite electric or magnetic properties.

antimony /an-ti-muh-ni/ ▶ noun a brittle silvery-white metallic element.

antipasto /an-ti-**pas**-toh/ ▶ noun (plural **antipasti** /an-ti-**pas**-ti/) (in Italian cooking) a small savoury first course of a meal.

antipathy /an-**ti**-puh-thi/ ▶ noun (plural **antipathies**) a strong feeling of dislike.

SYNONYMS **hostility**, antagonism, animosity, aversion, animus, distaste, hatred, abhorrence, loathing. ANTONYMS affinity, liking.

□ **antipathetic** adjective.

antiperspirant ▶ noun a substance applied to the skin to prevent or reduce sweating.

antiphonal ▶ adjective sung or recited alternately by two groups.

Antipodes /an-ti-puh-deez/ ▶ plural noun (**the Antipodes**) Australia and New Zealand.
□ **Antipodean** adjective & noun.

antiquarian /an-ti-**kwair**-i-uhn/ ▶ adjective relating to the collection or study of antiques or rare books.

antiquated ▶ adjective very old-fashioned or out of date.

SYNONYMS **outdated**, outmoded, outworn, behind the times, old-fashioned, anachronistic; informal out of the ark; N. Amer. informal horse-and-buggy, clunky. ANTONYMS modern, up to date.

antique ▶ noun an object or piece of furniture that is valuable because of its age.

SYNONYMS **collector's item**, museum piece, period piece, bygone, antiquity.

▶ adjective having value because of its age.

SYNONYMS *antique furniture* **antiquarian**, old, collectable, vintage, classic. ANTONYMS modern.

antiquity ▶ noun (plural **antiquities**) **1** the distant past. **2** an object from the distant past.

anti-Semitism ▶ noun hostility to or prejudice against Jews.
◻ **anti-Semite** noun **anti-Semitic** adjective.

antiseptic ▶ adjective preventing the growth of germs that cause disease or infection.
▶ noun an antiseptic substance.

antisocial ▶ adjective **1** behaving in a way that is unacceptable or annoying to other people. **2** not wanting to mix with other people.

> SYNONYMS **1** antisocial behaviour **objectionable,** offensive, unacceptable, disruptive, rowdy. **2** I'm feeling a bit antisocial **unsociable,** unfriendly, uncommunicative, reclusive.
> ANTONYMS acceptable, sociable.

antithesis /an-**ti**-thuh-siss/ ▶ noun (plural **antitheses** /an-**ti**-thuh-seez/) **1** a person or thing that is the direct opposite of another. **2** the putting together of contrasting ideas or words to produce an effect in writing or speaking.

antithetical /an-ti-**thet**-i-k'l/ ▶ adjective opposed to each other.

antler ▶ noun each of a pair of branched horns on the head of an adult male deer.

antonym /**an**-tuh-nim/ ▶ noun a word opposite in meaning to another.

anus /**ay**-nuhss/ ▶ noun the opening through which solid waste matter leaves the body.

anvil ▶ noun an iron block on which metal is hammered and shaped.

anxiety ▶ noun (plural **anxieties**) an anxious feeling or state.

> SYNONYMS **worry,** concern, apprehension, unease, fear, disquiet, doubts, nervousness, nerves; informal butterflies (in your stomach), the jitters, collywobbles.
> ANTONYMS confidence.

anxious ▶ adjective **1** feeling worried or nervous. **2** very eager.

> SYNONYMS **1** I'm anxious about her **worried,** concerned, apprehensive, fearful, uneasy, disturbed, fretful, agitated, nervous, on edge, worked up, jumpy; informal uptight, with butterflies in your stomach, jittery, twitchy; N. Amer. informal antsy, squirrelly, in a twit; Austral./NZ informal toey. **2** she was anxious for news **eager,** keen, itching, impatient.
> ANTONYMS confident, unconcerned.

◻ **anxiously** adverb.

any ▶ determiner & pronoun **1** one or some, no matter how much or how many. **2** whichever or whatever you choose.
▶ adverb at all.

anybody ▶ pronoun anyone.

anyhow ▶ adverb **1** anyway. **2** in a careless or haphazard way.

anyone ▶ pronoun any person or people.

anything ▶ pronoun a thing of any kind.

anyway ▶ adverb **1** said to emphasize something just said or to change the subject. **2** nevertheless.

anywhere ▶ adverb in or to any place.
▶ pronoun any place.

aorta /ay-**or**-tuh/ ▶ noun the main artery supplying blood from the heart to the rest of the body.

apace ▶ adverb quickly.

Apache /uh-**pa**-chi/ ▶ noun (plural **Apache** or **Apaches**) a member of an American Indian people living in New Mexico and Arizona.

apart ▶ adverb **1** separated by a distance. **2** into pieces.
■ **apart from 1** except for. **2** as well as.

apartheid /uh-**par**-tayt/ ▶ noun the official system of racial segregation formerly in force in South Africa.

apartment ▶ noun **1** a flat. **2** (**apartments**) a private set of rooms in a large house.

> SYNONYMS **1** a rented apartment **flat,** suite, penthouse; Austral. home unit; N. Amer. informal crib. **2** the royal apartments **suite (of rooms),** rooms, quarters, accommodation.

> ✔ only one **p**: a**p**artment.

apathetic ▶ adjective not interested or enthusiastic.

> SYNONYMS **uninterested,** indifferent, unconcerned, unmoved, uninvolved, unemotional, lukewarm, lethargic; informal couldn't-care-less.
> ANTONYMS interested, enthusiastic, involved.

apathy ▶ noun general lack of interest or enthusiasm.

> SYNONYMS **indifference,** lack of interest, lack of enthusiasm, lack of concern, lack of involvement, unconcern, lethargy.
> ANTONYMS enthusiasm, interest, concern.

apatosaurus /uh-pa-tuh-**sor**-uhss/ ▶ noun a huge plant-eating dinosaur with a long neck and tail; a brontosaurus.

ape ▶ noun an animal related to the monkeys but with no tail, such as a chimpanzee or gorilla.
▶ verb (**apes, aping, aped**) imitate someone.

aperitif /uh-pe-ri-**teef**/ ▶ noun an alcoholic drink taken before a meal.

aperture ▶ noun **1** an opening, hole, or gap. **2** the variable opening by which light enters a camera.

> SYNONYMS **opening,** hole, gap, slit, slot, vent, crevice, chink, crack; technical orifice.

apex /**ay**-peks/ ▶ noun (plural **apexes** or **apices** /**ay**-pi-seez/) the top or highest point of something.

a

aphid /ay-fid/ ▸ noun a small insect that feeds on the sap of plants.

aphorism ▸ noun a short clever phrase which makes a true point.

aphrodisiac /af-ruh-**diz**-i-ak/ ▸ noun a food, drink, or drug that makes people want to have sex.

apiary /**ay**-pee-uh-ri/ ▸ noun (plural **apiaries**) a place where bees are kept.

apiece ▸ adverb for or by each one.

aplenty ▸ adjective in large amounts.

aplomb /uh-**plom**/ ▸ noun calm self-confidence.

apocalypse ▸ noun a terrible event in which everything is destroyed.

apocalyptic /uh-po-kuh-**lip**-tik/ ▸ adjective having to do with or resembling the destruction of the world.

apocryphal ▸ adjective (of a story or piece of information) widely known but unlikely to be true.

apogee /ap-uh-jee/ ▸ noun **1** the highest point reached. **2** the point in the orbit of the moon or a satellite at which it is furthest from the earth.

apolitical ▸ adjective not interested or involved in politics.

apologetic ▸ adjective showing that you are sorry for making a mistake or doing something wrong.

> SYNONYMS **sorry,** regretful, contrite, remorseful, penitent, repentant. ANTONYMS unrepentant.

◻ **apologetically** adverb.

apologia /ap-uh-**loh**-ji-uh/ ▸ noun a formal defence of opinions or actions.

apologist ▸ noun a person who defends something controversial.

apologize (or apologise) ▸ verb (**apologizes, apologizing, apologized**) say that you are sorry for making a mistake or doing something wrong.

> SYNONYMS **say sorry,** express regret, ask forgiveness, ask for pardon, eat humble pie.

apology ▸ noun (plural **apologies**) **1** a statement in which someone apologizes for a mistake made or for harm done. **2** (an apology for) a very bad example of.

> SYNONYMS **regrets,** expression of regret.

apoplectic /a-puh-**plek**-tik/ ▸ adjective **1** very angry. **2** old use relating to apoplexy (a stroke).

apoplexy /a-puh-plek-si/ ▸ noun (plural **apoplexies**) old use a stroke.

apostasy /uh-**poss**-tuh-si/ ▸ noun the abandoning of a belief or principle.

apostate /a-puh-stayt/ ▸ noun a person who abandons a belief or principle.

apostle ▸ noun **1** (**Apostle**) each of the twelve chief disciples of Jesus. **2** a person who strongly supports a policy, cause, etc.

apostrophe /uh-**poss**-truh-fi/ ▸ noun a punctuation mark (') used to show that something belongs to someone or to show that letters or numbers have been missed out.

apothecary /uh-**poth**-uh-kuh-ri/ ▸ noun (plural **apothecaries**) old use a person who prepared and sold medicines.

apotheosis /uh-po-thi-**oh**-siss/ ▸ noun (plural **apotheoses** /uh-po-thi-**oh**-seez/) the highest level in the development of something.

appal (US spelling appall) ▸ verb (**appals, appalling, appalled**) make someone feel horror and dismay.

> SYNONYMS **horrify,** shock, dismay, distress, outrage, scandalize, disgust, revolt, sicken, nauseate, offend, make someone's blood run cold.

appalling ▸ adjective shockingly bad.

> SYNONYMS **1** *an appalling crime* **horrific,** shocking, horrible, terrible, awful, dreadful, ghastly, hideous, horrendous, frightful, atrocious, abominable, outrageous. **2** *your schoolwork is appalling* **dreadful,** terrible, atrocious, deplorable, hopeless, lamentable; informal rotten, crummy, woeful, useless, lousy, abysmal, dire; Brit. informal chronic, shocking.

◻ **appallingly** adverb.

apparatus ▸ noun (plural **apparatuses**) the equipment needed for a particular activity or task.

> SYNONYMS **1** *laboratory apparatus* **equipment,** gear, tackle, mechanism, appliance, device. **2** *the apparatus of government* **system,** machinery, framework, structure, organization.

apparel /uh-**pa**-ruhl/ ▸ noun formal clothing.

apparent ▸ adjective **1** clearly seen or understood; obvious. **2** seeming real, but not necessarily so.

> SYNONYMS **1** *their relief was all too apparent* **evident,** plain, obvious, clear, manifest, visible, discernible, unmistakable. **2** *his apparent lack of concern* **seeming,** ostensible, outward, superficial. ANTONYMS unclear, real.

> ✔ **-ent**, not **-ant**: apparent.

apparently ▸ adverb as far as one knows or can see.

> SYNONYMS **seemingly,** evidently, ostensibly, outwardly.

apparition ▸ noun a remarkable thing making a sudden appearance, especially a ghost.

appeal ▸ verb 1 ask earnestly or formally for something. 2 be attractive or interesting. 3 ask a higher court of law to reverse the decision of a lower court.

> SYNONYMS **1 ask,** request, call, plead, entreat, beg, implore. **2 attract,** interest, fascinate, please, tempt, lure, draw; informal float someone's boat.

▸ noun 1 an act of appealing. 2 the quality of being attractive or interesting.

> SYNONYMS **1** *an appeal for help* **plea,** request, entreaty, cry, call. **2** *the cultural appeal of the island* **attraction,** allure, charm, fascination, magnetism, pull.

appealing ▸ adjective attractive or interesting.

> SYNONYMS **attractive,** engaging, alluring, enchanting, captivating, bewitching, fascinating, tempting, enticing, irresistible, charming; Brit. informal tasty.
> ANTONYMS disagreeable, off-putting.

□ **appealingly** adverb.

appear ▸ verb 1 come into view or start to exist. 2 seem. 3 present yourself as a performer or in a law court.

> SYNONYMS **1 become visible,** come into view/sight, materialize. **2** *differences were beginning to appear* **be revealed,** emerge, surface, manifest itself, become apparent/evident, come to light, arrive, arise, crop up, show up. **3** *they appeared completely devoted* **seem,** look, give the impression of being, come across as, strike someone as.
> ANTONYMS vanish.

appearance ▸ noun 1 the way that someone or something looks or seems. 2 an act of appearing.

> SYNONYMS **1** *her dishevelled appearance* **look,** air, aspect, looks, mien, expression, behaviour. **2** *an appearance of respectability* **impression,** air, (outward) show, semblance, illusion, facade, front, pretence. **3** *the appearance of these symptoms* **occurrence,** manifestation, emergence, arrival, development, materialization.

appease ▸ verb (appeases, appeasing, appeased) make someone calm or less hostile by agreeing to their demands.

> SYNONYMS **placate,** conciliate, pacify, mollify, reconcile, win over; informal sweeten.
> ANTONYMS provoke, inflame.

□ **appeasement** noun.

appellation ▸ noun formal a name or title.

append ▸ verb add something to the end of a document.

appendage ▸ noun a thing that is attached to something larger or more important.

appendicitis ▸ noun inflammation of the appendix.

appendix ▸ noun (plural **appendices** or **appendixes**) 1 a small tube of tissue attached to the lower end of the large intestine. 2 a section of additional information at the end of a book.

> SYNONYMS **supplement,** addendum, postscript, codicil, coda, epilogue, afterword, tailpiece.

appertain ▸ verb (appertain to) formal relate to.

appetite ▸ noun 1 a natural desire and physical need for food. 2 a liking or desire for something.

> SYNONYMS **1 hunger,** taste, palate. **2** *my appetite for learning* **desire,** liking, hunger, thirst, longing, yearning, passion, enthusiasm, keenness, eagerness; informal yen.

appetizer (or appetiser) ▸ noun a small dish of food or a drink taken before a meal to stimulate the appetite.

appetizing (or appetising) ▸ adjective stimulating the appetite.

applaud ▸ verb 1 show approval by clapping. 2 say that you approve of or admire something.

> SYNONYMS **1** *the audience applauded* **clap,** give a standing ovation, put your hands together; informal give someone a big hand. **2** *police have applauded the decision* **praise,** commend, salute, welcome, celebrate, approve of.
> ANTONYMS boo, criticize.

applause ▸ noun clapping.

> SYNONYMS **clapping,** (standing) ovation, cheering.

apple ▸ noun a round fruit with green or red skin and crisp flesh.
■ **the apple of your eye** a person who you are very fond and proud of.

appliance ▸ noun an electrically operated machine for use in the home.

> SYNONYMS **device,** machine, instrument, gadget, contraption, apparatus, mechanism, contrivance, labour-saving device; informal gizmo.

applicable ▸ adjective relevant to someone or something.

> SYNONYMS **relevant,** appropriate, pertinent, apposite, material, fitting, suitable, apt.
> ANTONYMS inappropriate, irrelevant.

□ **applicability** noun.

applicant ▸ noun a person who applies for something.

SYNONYMS **candidate,** interviewee, contender, entrant, claimant, petitioner, prospective student/employee, job-seeker.

application ▸ noun **1** a formal request to an authority. **2** the action of applying something. **3** practical use or relevance. **4** continued effort.

SYNONYMS **1** *an application for an overdraft* **request,** appeal, petition, approach, claim, demand. **2** *the application of anti-inflation policies* **implementation,** use, exercise, employment, execution, enactment. **3** *the job requires a great deal of application* **hard work,** diligence, industry, effort, commitment, dedication, devotion, perseverance, persistence, concentration.

applicator ▸ noun a device for putting something into or on to something.

applied ▸ adjective (of a subject of study) used in a practical way.

appliqué /uh-**plee**-kay/ ▸ noun decorative needlework in which fabric shapes are fixed on to a background.

apply ▸ verb (applies, applying, applied) **1** make a formal request for something. **2** bring into operation or use. **3** be relevant. **4** put a substance on a surface. **5** (apply yourself) concentrate on what you are doing.

SYNONYMS **1** *300 people applied for the job* **bid,** put in, try, audition, seek, solicit, claim, request, ask, petition. **2** *the Act did not apply to Scotland* **be relevant,** pertain, relate, concern, affect, involve, cover, touch, deal with, have a bearing on. **3** *countries apply their own national rules* **implement,** put into practice, introduce. **4** *she applied some ointment* **put on,** rub in/on, work in, spread, smear on, slap on. **5** *steady pressure should be applied* **exert,** administer, use, exercise, employ, utilize, bring to bear.

appoint ▸ verb **1** give someone a job or role. **2** decide on a time for something.

SYNONYMS **nominate,** name, designate, install, commission, engage, co-opt, select, choose, elect, vote in. ANTONYMS reject.

appointed ▸ adjective **1** (of a time or place) prearranged. **2** furnished or equipped.

SYNONYMS **1** *at the appointed time* **prearranged,** arranged, scheduled, specified, agreed, designated, allotted, set, fixed. **2** *a well appointed room* **furnished,** decorated, fitted out, supplied.

appointment ▸ noun **1** an arrangement to meet. **2** the appointing of someone to a job.

3 (appointments) furniture or fittings.

SYNONYMS **1** *a six o'clock appointment* **meeting,** engagement, interview, consultation, session. **2** *the appointment of directors* **nomination,** naming, designation, installation, commissioning, engagement, co-option, selection, choosing, election. **3** *he held an appointment at the university* **job,** post, position, situation, place, office.

apportion ▸ verb share out.
□ **apportionment** noun.

apposite ▸ adjective appropriate.

appraisal ▸ noun **1** an assessment of the quality or value of something. **2** a formal assessment of an employee's performance.

SYNONYMS **assessment,** evaluation, estimation, judgement, summing-up, consideration.

appraise ▸ verb (appraises, appraising, appraised) assess the quality or value of someone or something.

appreciable ▸ adjective large or important enough to be noticed.
□ **appreciably** adverb.

appreciate ▸ verb (appreciates, appreciating, appreciated) **1** recognize the value of something. **2** understand a situation fully. **3** be grateful for. **4** rise in value or price.

SYNONYMS **1** *I'm not appreciated here* **value,** admire, respect, think highly of, think much of, be grateful for, be glad of. **2** *we appreciate the problems* **recognize,** realize, know, be aware of, be conscious of, be sensitive to, understand, sympathize with. **3** *a home will appreciate in value* **increase,** gain, grow, rise, go up, soar.
ANTONYMS disparage, depreciate, decrease.

appreciation ▸ noun **1** recognition of the value of something. **2** gratitude for something. **3** a piece of writing in which the qualities of a person or their work are discussed. **4** an increase in value.

SYNONYMS **1** *her appreciation of literature* **knowledge,** awareness, enjoyment, love, feeling, discrimination, sensitivity. **2** *he showed his appreciation* **gratitude,** thanks, gratefulness. **3** *an appreciation of the value of teamwork* **acknowledgement,** recognition, realization, knowledge, awareness, consciousness, understanding. **4** *an appreciation of the professor's work* **review,** critique, criticism, analysis, assessment, evaluation, judgement; Brit. informal crit. **5** *the appreciation of the euro against the pound* **increase,** gain, growth, rise, inflation, escalation.

ANTONYMS ingratitude, unawareness, depreciation, decrease.

appreciative ▸ adjective feeling or showing gratitude or pleasure.

SYNONYMS **1** *we are appreciative of all your efforts* **grateful,** thankful, obliged, indebted. **2** *an appreciative audience* **admiring,** enthusiastic, approving, complimentary.
ANTONYMS ungrateful, disparaging.

□ **appreciatively** adverb.

apprehend ▸ verb **1** arrest someone for doing something wrong. **2** understand something.

apprehension ▸ noun **1** a feeling of worry or fear about what might happen. **2** the action of arresting someone.

SYNONYMS **1** *he was filled with apprehension* **anxiety,** worry, unease, nervousness, nerves, misgivings, disquiet, concern, trepidation. **2** *the apprehension of a criminal* **arrest,** capture, seizure, detention.
ANTONYMS confidence.

apprehensive ▸ adjective worried or afraid about what might happen.

SYNONYMS **anxious,** worried, uneasy, nervous, concerned, agitated.
ANTONYMS confident.

□ **apprehensively** adverb.

apprentice ▸ noun a person learning a skilled trade from an employer.

SYNONYMS **trainee,** learner, probationer, novice, beginner, starter, pupil, student; N. Amer. **tenderfoot;** informal **rookie;** N. Amer. informal **greenhorn.**
ANTONYMS veteran, master, expert.

▸ verb (**be apprenticed**) be employed as an apprentice.
□ **apprenticeship** noun.

apprise ▸ verb (**apprises, apprising, apprised**) (**apprise someone of**) make someone aware of.

approach ▸ verb **1** come near to. **2** go to someone with a proposal or request. **3** deal with something in a certain way.

SYNONYMS **1** *she approached the altar* **move towards,** near, come near, close in on, close with, gain on. **2** *she approached him about a pay rise* **speak to,** talk to, sound out, make a proposal to, proposition. **3** *he approached the problem in the best way* **tackle,** address, manage, set about, go about, start work on.
ANTONYMS leave.

▸ noun **1** a way of dealing with something. **2** a proposal or request. **3** the action of approaching. **4** a way leading to a place.

SYNONYMS **1** *the traditional British approach* **method,** procedure, technique, modus operandi, style, way, strategy, tactic, system, means, line of action. **2** *he considered an approach to the High Court* **proposal,** submission, application, appeal, plea, request. **3** *the dog barked at the approach of any intruder* **advance,** arrival, appearance. **4** *the approach to the castle* **driveway,** drive, road, path, entry, way.

approachable ▸ adjective **1** friendly and easy to talk to. **2** able to be reached from a particular direction.

SYNONYMS **1** *students found the staff approachable* **friendly,** welcoming, pleasant, agreeable, sympathetic, congenial. **2** *the island is approachable by boat* **accessible,** reachable, attainable; informal get-at-able.
ANTONYMS aloof, inaccessible.

approbation ▸ noun approval.

appropriate ▸ adjective /uh-**proh**-pri-uht/ suitable or right in the circumstances.

SYNONYMS *this isn't the appropriate time* **suitable,** proper, fitting, apt, right, convenient, opportune, relevant, apposite.
ANTONYMS inappropriate.

▸ verb /uh-**proh**-pri-ayt/ (**appropriates, appropriating, appropriated**) **1** take something for your own use without permission. **2** set money aside for a special purpose.

SYNONYMS *the barons appropriated church lands* **seize,** commandeer, expropriate, usurp, take over, hijack, steal; informal swipe, rip off, nab; Brit. informal pinch, nick.

□ **appropriately** adverb **appropriation** noun.

approval ▸ noun **1** a feeling that someone or something is good or acceptable. **2** official permission or agreement.

SYNONYMS **1** *Lily looked at him with approval* **favour,** liking, appreciation, admiration, regard, esteem, respect. **2** *their proposals went to the ministry for approval* **acceptance,** agreement, consent, assent, permission, rubber stamp, sanction, blessing, endorsement, ratification, authorization; informal the go-ahead, the green light, the OK, the thumbs up.
ANTONYMS disapproval, refusal.

approve ▸ verb (**approves, approving, approved**) **1** feel that something is good or acceptable. **2** officially accept something as satisfactory.

SYNONYMS **agree to,** accept, consent to, assent to, give your blessing to, bless, ratify, sanction, endorse, authorize,

a

validate, pass; informal give the go-ahead to, give the green light to, give the OK to, give the thumbs-up to.
ANTONYMS refuse.

approximate ▸ adjective /uh-**prok**-si-muht/ almost but not completely accurate.

> SYNONYMS **estimated**, rough, imprecise, inexact, broad, loose; N. Amer. informal ballpark.
> ANTONYMS precise.

▸ verb /uh-**prok**-si-mayt/ (**approximates, approximating, approximated**) come close or be similar to.
□ **approximation** noun.

approximately ▸ adverb not exactly; nearly.

> SYNONYMS **roughly**, about, around, circa, round about, more or less, nearly, almost, approaching; Brit. getting on for; informal pushing; N. Amer. informal in the ballpark of.
> ANTONYMS precisely.

appurtenances /uh-**per**-ti-nuhn-siz/ ▸ plural noun the things you need for a particular activity.

après-ski /ap-ray **skee**/ ▸ noun parties and entertainments which take place after a day's skiing.

apricot ▸ noun an orange-yellow fruit resembling a small peach.

April ▸ noun the fourth month of the year.

a priori /ay pry-**or**-I/ ▸ adjective & adverb using facts that are known to be true in order to decide what an unknown effect or result will be.

apron ▸ noun **1** a garment tied over the front of clothes to keep them clean. **2** an area on an airfield used for manoeuvring or parking aircraft. **3** a strip of stage extending in front of the curtain.

apropos /a-pruh-**poh**/ ▸ preposition (apropos of) with reference to.

apse ▸ noun a recess with a domed or arched roof at the end of a church.

apt ▸ adjective **1** suitable for the occasion; appropriate. **2** (**apt to**) tending to. **3** quick to learn.

> SYNONYMS **1** *a very apt description* **suitable**, fitting, appropriate, relevant, apposite; Brit. informal spot on. **2** *they are apt to be a bit slipshod* **inclined**, given, likely, liable, prone. **3** *an apt pupil* **bright**, quick, clever, sharp, smart, able, gifted, talented.
> ANTONYMS inappropriate, unlikely, slow.

□ **aptly** adverb.

aptitude ▸ noun a natural ability.

aqualung ▸ noun a piece of equipment worn by divers to enable them to breathe underwater.

aquamarine ▸ noun **1** a bluish-green precious stone. **2** a light bluish-green colour.

aquaplane ▸ verb (**aquaplanes, aquaplaning, aquaplaned**) (of a vehicle) slide uncontrollably on a wet surface.

aquarium ▸ noun (plural **aquaria** or **aquariums**) a water-filled glass tank in which fish and other water creatures are kept.

Aquarius /uh-**kwair**-i-uhss/ ▸ noun a sign of the zodiac (the Water Carrier), 21 January–20 February.

aquatic /uh-**kwat**-ik/ ▸ adjective **1** relating to water. **2** living in or near water.

aqueduct /**ak**-wuh-dukt/ ▸ noun a long channel or bridge-like structure for carrying water across country.

aqueous /**ay**-kwee-uhss/ ▸ adjective relating to or containing water.

aquiline /**ak**-wi-lyn/ ▸ adjective **1** (of a person's nose) curved like an eagle's beak. **2** like an eagle.

Arab ▸ noun a member of a people inhabiting much of the Middle East and North Africa.
□ **Arabian** noun & adjective.

arabesque ▸ noun **1** a ballet position in which one leg is extended horizontally backwards and the arms are outstretched. **2** an ornamental design of intertwined flowing lines.

Arabic ▸ noun the language of the Arabs, written from right to left.
▸ adjective relating to the Arabs or Arabic.
■ **Arabic numeral** any of the numerals 0, 1, 2, 3, 4, 5, 6, 7, 8, and 9.

arable ▸ adjective (of land) able to be used for growing crops.

arachnid /uh-**rak**-nid/ ▸ noun a creature of a class including spiders, scorpions, mites, and ticks.

arachnophobia /uh-rak-nuh-**foh**-bi-uh/ ▸ noun extreme fear of spiders.

Aran ▸ adjective (of knitted clothes) having a pattern involving thick raised stitches and large diamond designs.

arbiter /**ar**-bi-ter/ ▸ noun **1** a person who settles a dispute. **2** a person who has influence in a particular area.

arbitrary ▸ adjective **1** not seeming to be based on any plan or system. **2** (of power) used without restraint.

> SYNONYMS **random**, unpredictable, capricious, subjective, whimsical, wanton, motiveless, irrational, groundless, unjustified.
> ANTONYMS reasoned, democratic.

□ **arbitrarily** adverb.

arbitrate ▸ verb (**arbitrates, arbitrating, arbitrated**) act as an arbitrator to settle a dispute.

a

arbitration ▸ noun the use of an arbitrator to settle a dispute.

> SYNONYMS **adjudication**, judgement, mediation, conciliation, intervention.

arbitrator ▸ noun a person or organization appointed to settle a dispute.

> SYNONYMS **adjudicator**, arbiter, judge, referee, umpire, mediator, go-between.

arboreal /ar-**bor**-i-uhl/ ▸ adjective **1** living in trees. **2** relating to trees.

arboretum /ar-buh-**ree**-tuhm/ ▸ noun (plural **arboretums** or **arboreta**) a garden in which trees are grown for study and display to the public.

arbour (US spelling **arbor**) ▸ noun a shady place in a garden, with a canopy of trees or climbing plants.

arc ▸ noun **1** a curve forming part of the circumference of a circle. **2** a curving movement through the air. **3** a glowing electrical discharge between two points.

> SYNONYMS **curve**, arch, bow, curl, crescent, semicircle, half-moon.

▸ verb (**arcs**, **arcing**, **arced**) move in an arc.

arcade ▸ noun **1** a series of arches supporting a roof or wall. **2** a covered walk with shops along the sides.

Arcadian ▸ adjective literary having to do with a perfect country scene or way of life.

arcane ▸ adjective secret and mysterious.

arch¹ ▸ noun **1** a curved structure spanning an opening or supporting the weight of a bridge or roof. **2** the inner side of the foot.

> SYNONYMS *a stone arch* **archway**, vault, span.

▸ verb form an arch.

> SYNONYMS *she arched her eyebrows* **curve**, arc, bend, bow, crook, hunch.

arch² ▸ adjective suggesting in a playful way that you know more than you are revealing.
□ **archly** adverb.

archaeology (US spelling **archeology**) ▸ noun the study of ancient history through the examination of objects, structures, and materials dug up from old sites.
□ **archaeological** adjective **archaeologist** noun.

archaic /ar-**kay**-ik/ ▸ adjective **1** very old or old-fashioned. **2** belonging to an earlier period.
□ **archaism** noun.

archangel /**ark**-ayn-j'l/ ▸ noun an angel of high rank.

archbishop ▸ noun a bishop of the highest rank.

archdeacon ▸ noun a senior Christian priest.

arch-enemy ▸ noun a chief enemy.

archer ▸ noun a person who shoots with a bow and arrows.

□ **archery** noun.

archetype /**ar**-ki-typ/ ▸ noun **1** a very typical example. **2** an original model which others follow.
□ **archetypal** adjective.

archipelago /ar-ki-**pel**-uh-goh/ ▸ noun (plural **archipelagos** or **archipelagoes**) a group of many islands and the sea surrounding them.

architect ▸ noun **1** a person who designs buildings. **2** the person responsible for something: *the architect of the reforms*.

> SYNONYMS **designer**, planner, originator, author, creator, founder, inventor.

architecture ▸ noun **1** the design and construction of buildings. **2** the complex structure of something.

> SYNONYMS **1** *modern architecture* **building**, planning, design, construction. **2** *computer architecture* **structure**, construction, organization, layout, design, build, make-up; informal set-up.

□ **architectural** adjective.

architrave /**ar**-ki-trayv/ ▸ noun **1** (in classical architecture) a beam resting across the tops of columns. **2** the frame around a doorway or window.

archive /**ar**-kyv/ ▸ noun **1** a collection of historical documents or records. **2** a complete record of the data in a computer system.

> SYNONYMS **1** *the family archives* **records**, papers, documents, files, annals, chronicles, history. **2** *the National Sound Archive* **record office**, registry, repository, museum, library.

▸ verb (**archives**, **archiving**, **archived**) put something in an archive.

> SYNONYMS *the videos are archived for future use* **file**, log, catalogue, document, record, register, store.

□ **archival** adjective.

archivist /**ar**-ki-vist/ ▸ noun a person who is in charge of archives of historical material.

archway ▸ noun a curved structure forming a passage or entrance.

Arctic ▸ adjective relating to the regions around the North Pole.

> ✔ Remember the first **c**: Ar**c**tic.

ardent ▸ adjective **1** feeling passionate about something. **2** old use burning; glowing.

> SYNONYMS **passionate**, fervent, zealous, wholehearted, intense, enthusiastic, keen, eager, avid, committed, dedicated.
> ANTONYMS apathetic.

□ **ardently** adverb.

ardour (US spelling **ardor**) ▸ noun passionate feelings.

arduous ▸ adjective difficult and tiring.

SYNONYMS **tough,** difficult, hard, heavy, laborious, onerous, taxing, strenuous, back-breaking, demanding, challenging, punishing, gruelling; informal killing; Brit. informal knackering.
ANTONYMS easy.

□ **arduously** adverb.

are 2nd person singular present and 1st, 2nd, and 3rd person plural present of BE.

❗ Don't confuse **are** with **our**.

area ▸ noun **1** a part of a place, object, or surface. **2** the extent or measurement of a surface. **3** a subject or range of activity.

SYNONYMS **1** an inner-city area **district,** zone, region, sector, quarter, locality, neighbourhood; informal neck of the woods; Brit. informal **manor**; N. Amer. informal turf. **2** the dining area **space,** section, part, place, room. **3** specific areas of knowledge **field,** sphere, realm, domain, sector, province, territory.

arena ▸ noun **1** a level area surrounded by seating, in which sports and other events are held. **2** an area of activity.

SYNONYMS **1** an ice-hockey arena **stadium,** amphitheatre, ground, field, ring, rink, pitch, court; N. Amer. informal bowl, park. **2** the political arena **scene,** sphere, realm, province, domain, forum, territory, world.

aren't ▸ short form **1** are not. **2** am not (only in questions).

areola /uh-ree-uh-luh/ ▸ noun (plural **areolae** /uh-**ree**-uh-lee/) the circular area of darker skin surrounding a human nipple.

Argentinian (or **Argentine**) ▸ noun a person from Argentina.
▸ adjective relating to Argentina.

argon ▸ noun an inert gaseous element, present in small amounts in the air.

argot /ar-goh/ ▸ noun the jargon or slang of a particular group.

arguable ▸ adjective able to be argued or disagreed with.
□ **arguably** adverb.

argue ▸ verb (**argues, arguing, argued**) **1** discuss something in a serious or angry way with someone who disagrees with you. **2** make statements in support of an action or opinion.

SYNONYMS **1** the children are always arguing **quarrel,** disagree, dispute, row, squabble, bicker, have words, cross swords. **2** they argued that the government was to blame **claim,** maintain, insist, contend, assert, hold, reason, allege.

argument ▸ noun **1** a serious or angry discussion between people who disagree with each other. **2** a set of reasons given in support of an action or opinion.

SYNONYMS **1** he had an argument with Tony **quarrel,** disagreement, squabble, dispute, altercation; informal slanging match; Brit. informal row, barney. **2** an argument for the existence of God **reasoning,** justification, explanation, case, defence, vindication, evidence, reasons, grounds.

✔ There is no **e** in the middle: **argu**ment, not **argue**-.

argumentative ▸ adjective tending to argue.

aria /ah-ri-uh/ ▸ noun a song for a solo voice in an opera.

arid ▸ adjective **1** very dry because having little or no rain. **2** dull and boring.
□ **aridity** noun.

Aries /**air**-eez/ ▸ noun a sign of the zodiac (the Ram), 20 March–20 April.

arise ▸ verb (**arises, arising, arose**; past participle **arisen**) **1** start to exist or be noticed. **2** (**arise from** or **out of**) happen as a result of. **3** formal stand up.

SYNONYMS **1** many problems arose **come about,** happen, occur, come into being, emerge, crop up, come to light, become apparent, appear, turn up, surface, spring up. **2** injuries arising from defective products **result,** stem, originate, proceed, follow, ensue, be caused by.

aristocracy ▸ noun (plural **aristocracies**) the highest social class, consisting of people whose families hold a title such as *Lord* or *Duke*.

aristocrat ▸ noun a member of the aristocracy.

SYNONYMS **nobleman,** noblewoman, lord, lady, peer (of the realm), patrician; informal aristo; Brit. informal toff, nob.
ANTONYMS commoner.

aristocratic ▸ adjective relating to or typical of the aristocracy.

SYNONYMS **noble,** titled, upper-class, blue-blooded, high-born; informal upper crust, top drawer; Brit. informal posh.
ANTONYMS common.

arithmetic ▸ noun the use of numbers in counting and calculation.
□ **arithmetical** adjective **arithmetically** adverb.

ark ▸ noun **1** (in the Bible) the ship built by Noah to save two of every kind of animal from the Flood. **2** a chest or cupboard in a synagogue in which the holy scrolls are kept. **3** (**Ark of the Covenant**) the chest which contained the laws of the ancient Israelites.

arm¹ ▸ noun **1** each of the two upper limbs of the human body from the shoulder to the hand. **2** a side part of a chair supporting a sitter's arm. **3** a strip of water or land. **4** a branch or division of a company or organization.

arm² ▸ verb **1** supply with weapons. **2** provide with essential equipment or information. **3** make a bomb ready to explode.

> SYNONYMS **equip**, provide, supply, furnish, issue, fit out.

armada ▸ noun a fleet of warships.

armadillo ▸ noun (plural **armadillos**) an insect-eating animal of Central and South America, with a body covered in bony plates.

Armageddon /ar-muh-ged-duhn/ ▸ noun **1** (in the Bible) the final battle between good and evil before the Last Judgement. **2** a terrible war with a catastrophic ending.

armament ▸ noun **1** (also **armaments**) military weapons and equipment. **2** the equipping of military forces.

> SYNONYMS **arms,** weapons, weaponry, firearms, guns, ordnance, artillery, munitions, materiel.

armature ▸ noun **1** the rotating coil of a dynamo or electric motor. **2** a piece of iron placed across the poles of a magnet to preserve its power.

armchair ▸ noun a comfortable chair with padded sides on which to rest your arms.

armed ▸ adjective carrying a weapon.
  ■ **armed forces** a country's army, navy, and air force.

Armenian ▸ noun a person from Armenia.
▸ adjective relating to Armenia.

armistice /ar-miss-tiss/ ▸ noun an agreement to stop fighting.

armorial ▸ adjective relating to coats of arms.

armour (US spelling **armor**) ▸ noun **1** metal coverings worn in the past to protect the body in battle. **2** (also **armour plate**) the tough metal layer covering a military vehicle or ship.

armoured ▸ adjective covered with armour.

> SYNONYMS **armour-plated,** steel-plated, ironclad, bulletproof, bombproof, reinforced, toughened.

armourer (US spelling **armorer**) ▸ noun a person who makes, supplies, or looks after weapons or armour.

armoury (US spelling **armory**) ▸ noun (plural **armouries**) a store of arms.

armpit ▸ noun a hollow under the arm at the shoulder.

arms ▸ plural noun **1** guns and other weapons.

2 the emblems on a coat of arms.

> SYNONYMS **weapons,** weaponry, firearms, guns, ordnance, artillery, armaments, munitions.

  ■ **up in arms** protesting strongly.

army ▸ noun (plural **armies**) **1** a military force that fights on land. **2** a large number of people or things.

> SYNONYMS **1 armed force,** military force, land force(s), military, soldiery, infantry, militia, troops, soldiers. **2** *an army of ants* **crowd,** swarm, horde, mob, gang, throng, mass, flock, herd, pack.

aroma ▸ noun a pleasant smell.

> SYNONYMS **smell,** odour, fragrance, scent, perfume, bouquet, nose.

aromatherapy ▸ noun the use of aromatic oils for healing or to give pleasant feelings.
  □ **aromatherapist** noun.

aromatic ▸ adjective having a pleasant and distinctive smell.

> SYNONYMS **fragrant,** scented, perfumed, fragranced.

arose past of ARISE.

around ▸ adverb & preposition **1** on every side of something. **2** in or to many places throughout an area.

> SYNONYMS *the hills around the city* **surrounding,** enclosing, on all sides of.

▸ adverb **1** so as to face in the opposite direction. **2** about; approximately. **3** available or present.

> SYNONYMS *around three miles* **approximately,** about, round about, circa, roughly, more or less, nearly, almost, approaching; Brit. getting on for; N. Amer. informal in the ballpark of.
> ANTONYMS precisely.

arouse ▸ verb (**arouses, arousing, aroused**) **1** bring about a feeling or response in someone. **2** excite someone sexually. **3** awaken someone from sleep.

> SYNONYMS **1** *they had aroused suspicion* **provoke,** trigger, stir up, kindle, engender, cause. **2** *his ability to arouse the masses* **stir up,** whip up, rouse, galvanize, electrify, stimulate, inspire, fire up, inflame, agitate, incite. **3** *she was aroused from sleep* **wake (up),** awaken, bring to/round, rouse.
> ANTONYMS allay, pacify.

  □ **arousal** noun.

arpeggio /ar-pej-i-oh/ ▸ noun (plural **arpeggios**) the notes of a musical chord played in rapid succession.

arraign /uh-rayn/ ▸ verb call someone before a court to answer a criminal charge.
  □ **arraignment** noun.

arrange ▸ verb (**arranges, arranging, arranged**) **1** put tidily or in a particular order. **2** organize or plan. **3** adapt a piece of music for performance.

> SYNONYMS **1** *she arranged the flowers in a vase* **set out**, order, lay out, position, present, display, exhibit, group, sort, organize. **2** *they hoped to arrange a meeting* **organize**, fix (up), plan, schedule, contrive, determine, agree. **3** *he arranged the piece for a full orchestra* **adapt**, set, score, orchestrate.

□ **arranger** noun.

arrangement ▸ noun **1** a plan for a future event. **2** something made up of things arranged in a particular way. **3** an arranged piece of music.

> SYNONYMS **1** *the arrangement of the furniture* **positioning**, presentation, grouping, organization, alignment. **2** *the arrangements for my trip* **preparation**, plan, provision, planning. **3** *we had an arrangement* **agreement**, deal, understanding, bargain, settlement, pact. **4** *an arrangement of Beethoven's symphonies* **adaptation**, orchestration, scoring, interpretation.

arrant /a-ruhnt/ ▸ adjective complete; absolute: *arrant nonsense.*

array ▸ noun **1** an impressive display or range. **2** an ordered arrangement of troops. **3** literary elaborate clothing.

> SYNONYMS **range**, collection, selection, assortment, variety, arrangement, line-up, display, exhibition.

▸ verb **1** (**be arrayed**) be displayed or arranged in a neat or impressive way. **2** (**be arrayed in**) be dressed in.

> SYNONYMS **arrange**, assemble, group, order, range, place, position, set out, lay out, spread out, display, exhibit.

arrears ▸ plural noun money owed that should already have been paid.
■ **in arrears 1** behind with paying money that is owed. **2** (of wages or rent) paid at the end of each period of work or occupation.

arrest ▸ verb **1** seize someone and take them into custody. **2** stop the progress of something.

> SYNONYMS **1** *police arrested him for murder* **detain**, apprehend, seize, capture, take into custody; informal pick up, pull in, collar; Brit. informal nick. **2** *the spread of the disease can be arrested* **stop**, halt, check, block, curb, prevent, obstruct.
> ANTONYMS release, start.

▸ noun **1** the action of arresting someone. **2** a sudden stop.

> SYNONYMS **detention**, apprehension, seizure, capture.

arresting ▸ adjective attracting attention.

> SYNONYMS **striking**, eye-catching, conspicuous, impressive, imposing, spectacular, dramatic, breathtaking, stunning, awe-inspiring.
> ANTONYMS inconspicuous.

arrival ▸ noun **1** the process of arriving somewhere. **2** a person or thing that has just arrived.

> SYNONYMS **1** *they awaited Ruth's arrival* **coming**, appearance, entrance, entry, approach. **2** *the arrival of democracy* **emergence**, appearance, advent, coming, dawn, onset.
> ANTONYMS departure, end.

arrive ▸ verb (**arrives, arriving, arrived**) **1** reach a destination. **2** (of a particular moment) come about. **3** (**arrive at**) reach a conclusion or decision.

> SYNONYMS **1** *more police arrived* **come**, turn up, get here/there, make it, appear; informal show (up), roll in/up, blow in. **2** *virtual reality had arrived* **emerge**, appear, surface, dawn, be born, come into being, arise.
> ANTONYMS depart, leave.

arrogant ▸ adjective behaving in an unpleasant way because you think that you are better than other people.

> SYNONYMS **haughty**, conceited, self-important, cocky, supercilious, condescending, full of yourself, overbearing, proud; informal high and mighty, too big for your boots.
> ANTONYMS modest.

□ **arrogance** noun **arrogantly** adverb.

arrogate /a-ruh-gayt/ ▸ verb (**arrogates, arrogating, arrogated**) formal take or claim something that you have no right to.

arrow ▸ noun **1** a stick with a sharp point, shot from a bow. **2** a symbol resembling this, used to show direction or position.

arrowroot ▸ noun a starch obtained from a plant and used as a thickener in cookery.

arsenal ▸ noun a store of weapons and ammunition.

arsenic ▸ noun a brittle grey element from which a highly poisonous white powder is obtained.

arson ▸ noun the criminal act of deliberately setting fire to property.
□ **arsonist** noun.

art ▸ noun **1** the expression of creative skill in a visual form such as painting or sculpture. **2** paintings, drawings, and sculpture as a whole. **3** (**the arts**) creative activities such as painting, music, and drama. **4** (**arts**) subjects of study concerned with human culture. **5** a skill.

> SYNONYMS **1** *he studied art* **fine art,** design, artwork, aesthetics. **2** *the art of writing* **skill,** craft, technique, knack, aptitude, talent, flair, mastery, expertise.

artefact /**ar**-ti-fakt/ (US spelling **artifact**) ▸ noun a useful or decorative man-made object.

artery ▸ noun (plural **arteries**) **1** any of the tubes through which blood flows from the heart around the body. **2** an important transport route.
□ **arterial** adjective.

artesian well /ar-**tee**-zh'n/ ▸ noun a well in which water comes to the surface through natural pressure.

artful ▸ adjective clever in a cunning way.
□ **artfully** adverb.

arthritis /ar-**thry**-tiss/ ▸ noun painful inflammation and stiffness of the joints.
□ **arthritic** /ar-**thri**-tik/ adjective & noun.

arthropod /**ar**-thruh-pod/ ▸ noun an animal with a body that is divided into segments, such as an insect, spider, crab, etc.

artichoke ▸ noun a vegetable consisting of the unopened flower head of a thistle-like plant.

article ▸ noun **1** a particular object. **2** a piece of writing in a newspaper or magazine. **3** an item in a legal document. **4** (**articles**) a period of training in a company as a solicitor, accountant, etc.

> SYNONYMS **1** *household articles* **object,** thing, item, piece, artefact, device, implement. **2** *an article in The Times* **report,** account, story, essay, feature, item, piece (of writing), column, commentary. **3** *the crucial article of the treaty* **clause,** section, paragraph, head, point, item.

▸ verb (**be articled**) (of a solicitor, accountant, etc.) be employed as a trainee.

articulate ▸ adjective /ar-**tik**-yuu-luht/ **1** fluent and clear in speech. **2** having joints or jointed segments.

> SYNONYMS *an articulate speaker* **eloquent,** fluent, effective, persuasive, lucid, expressive, silver-tongued.
> ANTONYMS unintelligible.

▸ verb /ar-**tik**-yuu-layt/ (**articulates, articulating, articulated**) **1** pronounce words distinctly. **2** clearly express an idea or feeling. **3** (**articulated**) having sections connected by a flexible joint or joints.

> SYNONYMS *they were unable to articulate their emotions* **express,** voice, vocalize, put in words, communicate, state.

□ **articulacy** noun **articulately** adverb **articulation** noun.

artifact US spelling of **ARTEFACT**.

artifice ▸ noun the clever use of tricks to deceive someone.

artificer ▸ noun a person skilled in making or planning things.

artificial ▸ adjective **1** made as a copy of something natural. **2** not sincere.

> SYNONYMS **1** *artificial flowers* **synthetic,** fake, imitation, mock, ersatz, man-made, manufactured, plastic; informal pretend. **2** *an artificial smile* **insincere,** feigned, false, unnatural, contrived, put-on, forced, laboured, hollow; informal pretend, phoney.
> ANTONYMS natural, genuine.

■ **artificial insemination** the injection of semen through a syringe into the vagina or womb. **artificial intelligence** the performance by computers of tasks that normally need human intelligence. **artificial respiration** the forcing of air into and out of a person's lungs to make them begin breathing again.
□ **artificiality** noun **artificially** adverb.

artillery ▸ noun **1** large guns used in warfare on land. **2** a branch of the armed forces that uses artillery.

artisan ▸ noun a skilled worker who makes things by hand.

artist ▸ noun **1** a person who paints or draws. **2** a person who practises or performs any of the creative arts.

artiste /ar-**teest**/ ▸ noun a professional singer or dancer.

artistic ▸ adjective **1** having creative skill. **2** having to do with art or artists.

> SYNONYMS **1** *he's very artistic* **creative,** imaginative, inventive, expressive, sensitive, perceptive, discerning. **2** *artistic dances* **aesthetic,** beautiful, stylish, ornamental, graceful, subtle, expressive.
> ANTONYMS unimaginative.

□ **artistically** adverb.

artistry ▸ noun creative skill or ability.

artless ▸ adjective straightforward and sincere.
□ **artlessly** adverb.

artwork ▸ noun illustrations to be included in a publication.

arty (US spelling **artsy**) ▸ adjective informal displaying an obvious interest in the arts.
□ **artiness** noun.

arum lily /**air**-uhm/ ▸ noun a tall lily-like African plant.

Aryan /**air**-i-uhn/ ▸ noun **1** a member of an ancient people of Europe and Asia. **2** (in Nazi thinking) a white person not of Jewish descent.
▸ adjective relating to Aryans.

as ▸ adverb used in comparisons to refer to extent or amount.
▸ conjunction 1 while. 2 in the way that. 3 because. 4 even though.
▸ preposition 1 in the role of; being. 2 while; when.

asap ▸ abbreviation as soon as possible.

asbestos ▸ noun a fibrous grey-white mineral that does not burn.

asbestosis /az-bes-**toh**-sis/ ▸ noun a serious lung disease caused by breathing asbestos dust.

ASBO ▸ abbreviation Brit. antisocial behaviour order.

ascend ▸ verb go up; climb or rise.

ascendant ▸ adjective 1 rising in power or status. 2 (of a planet or sign of the zodiac) just above the eastern horizon.
□ ascendancy noun.

ascension ▸ noun 1 the action of reaching a higher position or status. 2 (**the Ascension**) the ascent of Jesus into heaven after the Resurrection.

ascent ▸ noun 1 the action of going up. 2 an upward slope.

SYNONYMS 1 *the ascent of the Matterhorn* climbing, scaling, conquest. 2 *the ascent grew steeper* slope, incline, gradient.
ANTONYMS descent, drop.

ascertain /ass-er-**tayn**/ ▸ verb find something out for certain.

SYNONYMS **find out,** discover, get to know, work out, make out, fathom (out), learn, deduce, divine, establish, determine; informal figure out.

□ ascertainable adjective.

ascetic /uh-**set**-ik/ ▸ adjective choosing to live without pleasures and luxuries.
▸ noun an ascetic person.
□ asceticism noun.

ascorbic acid /uh-**skor**-bik/ ▸ noun vitamin C.

ascribe ▸ verb (**ascribes, ascribing, ascribed**) (**ascribe something to**) say or believe that something is caused by.
□ ascription noun.

aseptic /ay-**sep**-tik/ ▸ adjective free from germs.

asexual ▸ adjective 1 without sex or sexual organs. 2 not having sexual feelings.
□ asexually adverb.

ash¹ ▸ noun 1 the powder remaining after something has been burned. 2 (**ashes**) the remains of a human body after cremation.

ash² ▸ noun a tree with winged fruits and hard pale wood.

ashamed ▸ adjective feeling embarrassed or guilty.

SYNONYMS 1 *she felt ashamed that she had hit him* sorry, shamefaced, sheepish,

guilty, contrite, remorseful, regretful, mortified, humiliated. 2 *he was ashamed to admit it* reluctant, loath, unwilling, afraid, embarrassed.
ANTONYMS proud, pleased.

ashen ▸ adjective very pale from shock, fear, or illness.

ashlar ▸ noun large, thin slabs of stone used as the surface layer of a wall.

ashore ▸ adverb to or on the shore or land.

ashram /**ash**-ruhm/ ▸ noun a Hindu religious retreat or community.

ashtray ▸ noun a small container for tobacco ash and cigarette ends.

Asian ▸ noun a person from Asia, or whose family originally came from Asia.
▸ adjective relating to Asia.

Asiatic ▸ adjective relating to Asia.

aside ▸ adverb 1 to one side; out of the way. 2 in reserve.
▸ noun 1 an actor's remark spoken to the audience. 2 a remark not directly related to the subject being discussed.

asinine /**ass**-i-nyn/ ▸ adjective very foolish.

ask ▸ verb 1 say something so as to get an answer or some information. 2 say that you want someone to do, give, or allow something. 3 (**ask for**) say that you want to speak to. 4 expect something of someone. 5 invite someone to a social occasion.

SYNONYMS 1 *he asked what time we opened* enquire, want to know, question, interrogate, quiz. 2 *they'll ask a few questions* put (forward), pose, raise, submit. 3 *do ask for advice* request, demand, seek, solicit, apply, petition, call, appeal.
ANTONYMS answer.

askance /uh-**skanss**/ ▸ adverb with a suspicious or disapproving look.

askew /uh-**skyoo**/ ▸ adverb & adjective not straight or level.

aslant ▸ adverb & preposition at a slant or crossing something at a slant.

asleep ▸ adjective & adverb 1 in or into a state of sleep. 2 (of a limb) numb.

SYNONYMS **sleeping,** napping, dozing, drowsing; informal snoozing, dead to the world; humorous in the land of Nod.
ANTONYMS awake.

asp ▸ noun a small viper.

asparagus /uh-**spa**-ruh-guhss/ ▸ noun a vegetable consisting of the tender young shoots of a tall plant.

aspartame /uh-**spah**-taym/ ▸ noun a low-calorie artificial sweetener.

aspect ▸ noun 1 a particular part or feature of something. 2 a particular appearance or quality. **3** the side of a building facing a particular direction.

> SYNONYMS **1** *every aspect of life* **feature,** facet, side, characteristic, particular, detail. **2** *from every aspect* **point of view,** position, standpoint, viewpoint, perspective, angle, slant. **3** *his face had a sinister aspect* **appearance,** look, air, mien, demeanour, expression.

aspen ▶ noun a poplar tree with small rounded leaves.

asperity /uh-**spe**-ri-ti/ ▶ noun harshness in the way you speak to or treat someone.

aspersion /uh-**sper**-sh'n/ ▶ noun (**cast aspersions on**) attack someone's character or reputation.

asphalt /**ass**-falt/ ▶ noun a tar-like substance used in surfacing roads or roofs.

asphyxia /uh-**sfik**-si-uh/ ▶ noun a condition in which someone cannot get enough oxygen and becomes unconscious or dies.

asphyxiate ▶ verb (**asphyxiates, asphyxiating, asphyxiated**) die or cause to die from lack of oxygen.
□ **asphyxiation** noun.

aspic ▶ noun a savoury jelly made with meat stock.

aspidistra /ass-pi-**diss**-truh/ ▶ noun a plant with broad tapering leaves.

aspirant ▶ noun a person with ambitions to do or be something.

aspiration ▶ noun a hope or ambition.

> SYNONYMS **desire,** hope, dream, wish, longing, yearning, aim, ambition, expectation, goal, target.

□ **aspirational** adjective.

aspire ▶ verb (**aspires, aspiring, aspired**) have a strong desire to achieve or become something.

> SYNONYMS *she aspired to be a writer* **desire,** aim for, hope for, dream of, long for, yearn for, set your heart on, wish for, want, seek, set your sights on.

aspirin ▶ noun (plural **aspirin** or **aspirins**) a medicine used to relieve pain and reduce fever and inflammation.

aspiring ▶ adjective ambitious to be or do something.

> SYNONYMS **would-be,** hopeful, budding, potential, prospective; informal wannabe.

ass ▶ noun **1** a donkey or related small wild horse. **2** informal a stupid person.

assail ▶ verb **1** attack someone violently. **2** (of an unpleasant feeling) come over someone strongly.

assailant ▶ noun an attacker.

assassin ▶ noun a person who assassinates someone.

> SYNONYMS **murderer,** killer, gunman, executioner; informal hit man.

assassinate ▶ verb (**assassinates, assassinating, assassinated**) murder a political or religious leader.

> SYNONYMS **murder,** kill, eliminate, liquidate, execute; N. Amer. terminate; informal hit.

□ **assassination** noun.

assault ▶ noun **1** a violent attack. **2** a determined attempt.

> SYNONYMS **1** *he was charged with assault* **violence,** battery; Brit. grievous bodily harm, GBH, actual bodily harm, ABH. **2** *an assault on the city* **attack,** strike, onslaught, offensive, charge, push, thrust, raid.

▶ verb make an assault on.

> SYNONYMS *he assaulted a police officer* **attack,** hit, strike, beat up, thump; informal wallop, belt, clobber, lay into, rough up; Austral. informal quilt.

■ **assault course** Brit. an obstacle course used for training soldiers.

assay ▶ noun the testing of a metal to see how pure it is.
▶ verb test a metal.

assegai /**ass**-uh-gy/ ▶ noun (plural **assegais**) an iron-tipped spear used by southern African peoples.

assemblage ▶ noun **1** a collection or gathering of things or people. **2** something made of pieces fitted together.

assemble ▶ verb (**assembles, assembling, assembled**) **1** come or bring together. **2** construct something by fitting parts together.

> SYNONYMS **1** *a crowd had assembled* **gather,** collect, get together, congregate, convene, meet, muster, rally. **2** *he assembled the suspects* **bring/call together,** gather, collect, round up, marshal, muster. **3** *how to assemble the kite* **construct,** build, erect, set up, put together, connect.
> ANTONYMS disperse, dismantle.

assembly ▶ noun (plural **assemblies**) **1** a group of people gathered together. **2** a group of people with powers to make decisions and laws. **3** the action of fitting the parts of something together.

> SYNONYMS **1** *an assembly of dockers* **gathering,** meeting, congregation, convention, council, rally, group, crowd; informal get-together. **2** *car assembly* **construction,** manufacture, building, fabrication, erection.

■ **assembly line** a series of workers and machines in a factory along which identical products pass to be assembled in stages.

assent ▸ noun approval or agreement.
▸ verb agree to a request or suggestion.

assert ▸ verb **1** confidently state that something is true. **2** (**assert yourself**) be confident and forceful.

> SYNONYMS **1** *she asserts that hysteria is universal* **declare,** maintain, contend, argue, claim, insist. **2** *you should assert your rights* **insist on,** stand up for, uphold, defend, press/push for.

assertion ▸ noun a confident and forceful statement.

> SYNONYMS **declaration,** contention, statement, claim, opinion, protestation.

assertive ▸ adjective speaking and doing things in a confident and forceful way.

> SYNONYMS **confident,** self-confident, bold, decisive, forceful, insistent, determined, commanding, pushy; informal feisty.
> ANTONYMS timid.

□ **assertively** adverb **assertiveness** noun.

assess ▸ verb make a judgement about the value or quality of something.

> SYNONYMS **1** *the committee's power is hard to assess* **evaluate,** judge, gauge, rate, estimate, appraise, weigh up; informal size up. **2** *the damage was assessed at £5 billion* **value,** calculate, work out, determine, cost, price, estimate.

□ **assessor** noun.

assessment ▸ noun the action of assessing someone or something.

> SYNONYMS **1** *a teacher's assessment of the pupil's abilities* **evaluation,** judgement, rating, estimation, appraisal, opinion. **2** *some assessments valued the estate at £2 million* **valuation,** calculation, costing, pricing, estimate.

asset ▸ noun **1** a useful or valuable thing or person. **2** (**assets**) property owned by a person or company.

> SYNONYMS **1** **benefit,** advantage, blessing, good/strong point, strength, forte, virtue, recommendation, attraction, resource. **2** (**assets**) **property,** resources, estate, holdings, funds, valuables, possessions, effects, belongings.
> ANTONYMS liability.

assiduous /uh-**sid**-yoo-uhss/ ▸ adjective showing great care and thoroughness.
□ **assiduity** noun **assiduously** adverb.

assign ▸ verb give someone a task or duty.

> SYNONYMS **1** *a young doctor was assigned the task* **allocate,** allot, give, set, charge with, entrust with. **2** *she was assigned to a new post* **appoint,** promote, delegate, nominate, commission, post, co-opt; Military detail. **3** *we assign*

large sums of money to travel budgets **earmark,** designate, set aside, reserve, appropriate, allot, allocate, apportion.

assignation ▸ noun a secret meeting, especially between lovers.

> SYNONYMS **rendezvous,** date, appointment, meeting.

assignment ▸ noun a piece of work that someone has been asked to do.

> SYNONYMS **task,** job, duty, mission, errand, undertaking, exercise, project, homework.

assimilate ▸ verb (**assimilates, assimilating, assimilated**) **1** take in and understand information. **2** absorb people or ideas into a society or culture.
□ **assimilation** noun.

assist ▸ verb help someone.

> SYNONYMS **1** **help,** aid, lend a (helping) hand to, support, back (up), work with. **2** *the aim was to assist cashflow* **facilitate,** aid, ease, promote, boost, speed, benefit, encourage, further.
> ANTONYMS hinder.

assistance ▸ noun help or support.

> SYNONYMS **help,** aid, a (helping) hand, support, backing, reinforcement.
> ANTONYMS hindrance.

assistant ▸ noun a person employed to help someone more senior.

> SYNONYMS **helper,** aide, deputy, second (in command), number two, right-hand man/woman, PA, mate, auxiliary, attendant; informal sidekick, gofer; Brit. informal dogsbody, skivvy.

assize /uh-**syz**/ (or **assizes**) ▸ noun historical a court which sat at intervals in each county of England and Wales.

associate ▸ verb (**associates, associating, associated**) **1** (**associate something with**) mentally connect something with something else. **2** (**associate with**) frequently meet or have dealings with. **3** (**associate yourself with**) be involved with.

> SYNONYMS **1** *the colours that we associate with fire* **link,** connect, relate, bracket, identify, equate. **2** *I was forced to associate with them* **mix,** keep company, mingle, socialize, go around, have dealings; informal hobnob, hang out/around/round.
> ANTONYMS avoid.

▸ noun a work partner or colleague.

> SYNONYMS *a business associate* **partner,** colleague, co-worker, workmate, collaborator, comrade, ally; informal crony.

▸ adjective **1** connected with an organization. **2** belonging to an association but not having full membership.

associated ▸ adjective related or connected.

> SYNONYMS **related,** connected, linked, similar, corresponding, attendant, accompanying, incidental.
> ANTONYMS unrelated.

association ▸ noun 1 a group of people organized for a joint purpose. 2 a connection or link.

> SYNONYMS 1 *a trade association* **alliance,** consortium, coalition, union, league, guild, syndicate, federation, confederation, cooperative, partnership. 2 *the association between man and environment* **relationship,** relation, interrelation, connection, interconnection, link, bond, interdependence.

■ Association Football soccer.

assonance /ass-uh-nuhnss/ ▸ noun a rhyming of vowel sounds.

assorted ▸ adjective made up of various sorts.

> SYNONYMS **various,** miscellaneous, mixed, varied, diverse, different, sundry.
> ANTONYMS uniform.

assortment ▸ noun a varied collection.

> SYNONYMS **variety,** mixture, array, mix, miscellany, selection, medley.

assuage /uh-swayj/ ▸ verb (assuages, assuaging, assuaged) 1 make an unpleasant feeling less strong. 2 relieve thirst or an appetite or desire.

assume ▸ verb (assumes, assuming, assumed) 1 think that something must be true but have no proof. 2 take responsibility or control. 3 begin to have. 4 pretend to have or feel.

> SYNONYMS 1 *I assumed he wanted me to keep the book* **presume,** suppose, take it (as given), take for granted, take as read, conclude, infer, think, fancy, believe, understand, gather; N. Amer. figure. 2 *he assumed a Southern accent* **affect,** adopt, put on. 3 *they are to assume more responsibility* **accept,** shoulder, bear, undertake, take on/up. 4 *he assumed control of their finances* **seize,** take (over), appropriate, wrest, usurp.
> ANTONYMS know, drop, give up.

assumed ▸ adjective pretended; false.

> SYNONYMS **false,** fictitious, fake, bogus, invented, made-up; informal pretend, phoney.
> ANTONYMS genuine.

assumption ▸ noun 1 a feeling that something must be true. 2 the taking on of responsibility or control.

> SYNONYMS **presumption,** supposition, inference, conjecture, belief.
> ANTONYMS knowledge.

assurance ▸ noun 1 something said to make someone feel confident about something. 2 self-confidence. 3 Brit. life insurance.

> SYNONYMS 1 *you have my assurance* **promise,** word (of honour), pledge, vow, oath, undertaking, guarantee, commitment. 2 *her calm assurance* **confidence,** self-confidence, self-assurance, self-possession, nerve, poise; informal cool. 3 *life assurance* **insurance,** indemnity, protection, security, cover.
> ANTONYMS self-doubt, nervousness.

assure ▸ verb (assures, assuring, assured) 1 make someone feel confident about something. 2 make certain. 3 Brit. insure a person's life.

> SYNONYMS 1 *we must assure him of our loyal support* **reassure,** convince, satisfy, persuade. 2 *I assure you all is well* **promise,** guarantee, swear, confirm, certify, vow. 3 *he wants to assure a favourable vote* **ensure,** secure, guarantee, seal, clinch; informal sew up.
> ANTONYMS avoid.

assured ▸ adjective 1 confident in yourself and your abilities. 2 certain; guaranteed.

> SYNONYMS 1 *an assured performance* **confident,** self-confident, self-assured, self-possessed, poised, composed, imperturbable, unruffled; informal unflappable, together. 2 *an assured supply of weapons* **guaranteed,** certain, sure, secure, reliable, dependable; informal sure-fire.
> ANTONYMS nervous, uncertain.

□ **assuredly** adverb.

astatine /ass-tuh-teen/ ▸ noun a radioactive chemical element.

aster ▸ noun a plant of the daisy family, with pink or purple flowers.

asterisk ▸ noun a symbol (*) used as a pointer to a note.

> ✔ aster**isk**, not **-x** (Astérix is a character in a cartoon strip).

astern ▸ adverb behind or towards the rear of a ship or aircraft.

asteroid /ass-tuh-royd/ ▸ noun a small rocky planet orbiting the sun.

asthma /ass-muh/ ▸ noun a medical condition that causes difficulty in breathing.
□ **asthmatic** adjective & noun.

astigmatism /uh-stig-muh-ti-z'm/ ▸ noun a fault in the shape of the eye which prevents clear vision.

a

astir ▸ adjective **1** in a state of excited movement. **2** awake and out of bed.

astonish ▸ verb surprise someone very much.

> SYNONYMS **amaze**, astound, stagger, startle, stun, confound, dumbfound, nonplus, take aback, leave open-mouthed; informal flabbergast, bowl over; Brit. informal knock for six.

□ **astonishment** noun.

astonishing ▸ adjective extremely surprising.

> SYNONYMS **amazing**, astounding, staggering, surprising, breathtaking, remarkable, extraordinary, incredible, unbelievable, phenomenal; informal mind-boggling.
> ANTONYMS unremarkable.

astound ▸ verb shock or surprise someone very much.

> SYNONYMS **amaze**, astonish, stagger, surprise, startle, stun, confound, dumbfound, take aback, leave open-mouthed; informal flabbergast, bowl over; Brit. informal knock for six.

astounding ▸ adjective surprisingly impressive or notable.

> SYNONYMS **amazing**, astonishing, staggering, surprising, breathtaking, remarkable, extraordinary, incredible, unbelievable, phenomenal; informal mind-boggling.
> ANTONYMS unremarkable.

astrakhan /ass-truh-**kan**/ ▸ noun the dark curly fleece of young lambs from central Asia, used to make coats and hats.

astral ▸ adjective relating to the stars.

astray ▸ adverb away from the correct course.

astride ▸ preposition & adverb with a leg on each side of.
▸ adverb (of a person's legs) apart.

astringent /uh-**strin**-juhnt/ ▸ adjective **1** causing body tissue to contract. **2** sharp or severe.
▸ noun an astringent lotion.
□ **astringency** noun.

astrolabe /ass-truh-layb/ ▸ noun an instrument formerly used in navigation and for measuring the altitude of the stars.

astrology ▸ noun the study of the supposed influence of the stars and planets on human affairs.
□ **astrologer** noun **astrological** adjective.

astronaut ▸ noun a person trained to travel in a spacecraft.

astronomical ▸ adjective **1** relating to astronomy. **2** informal very large.
□ **astronomic** adjective **astronomically** adverb.

astronomy ▸ noun the scientific study of stars, planets, and the universe.
□ **astronomer** noun.

astrophysics ▸ noun the study of the physical nature of stars and planets.
□ **astrophysicist** noun.

astute /uh-**styoot**/ ▸ adjective good at making accurate judgements.

> SYNONYMS **shrewd**, sharp, acute, quick, clever, intelligent, bright, smart, canny, perceptive; informal quick on the uptake.
> ANTONYMS stupid.

□ **astutely** adverb.

asunder ▸ adverb apart or into pieces.

asylum ▸ noun **1** protection from danger. **2** protection given to someone who has fled their country for political reasons. **3** dated an institution for people who are mentally ill.

> SYNONYMS *political asylum* **refuge**, sanctuary, shelter, protection, immunity, a safe haven.

asymmetrical ▸ adjective not symmetrical.
□ **asymmetric** adjective.

asymmetry ▸ noun (plural **asymmetries**) lack of symmetry.

at ▸ preposition used to express. **1** location, arrival, or time. **2** a value, rate, or point on a scale. **3** a state or condition. **4** direction towards. **5** the means by which something is done.

atavistic /at-uh-**viss**-tik/ ▸ adjective inherited from the earliest human beings.
□ **atavism** noun.

ate past of EAT.

atelier /uh-**tel**-i-ay/ ▸ noun a workshop or studio.

atheism /**ay**-thi-iz'm/ ▸ noun the belief that God does not exist.
□ **atheist** noun **atheistic** adjective.

athlete ▸ noun **1** a person who is good at sports. **2** a person who competes in track and field events.
■ **athlete's foot** a form of ringworm infection affecting the feet.

athletic ▸ adjective **1** fit and good at sport. **2** relating to athletics.

> SYNONYMS **muscular**, fit, strapping, well built, strong, sturdy, powerful, brawny, burly.
> ANTONYMS puny.

▸ noun (**athletics**) Brit. the sport of competing in track and field events.
□ **athletically** adverb **athleticism** noun.

athwart ▸ preposition across from side to side.

Atlantic ▸ adjective having to do with the Atlantic Ocean.

atlas ▸ noun a book of maps or charts.

atmosphere ▶ noun **1** the gases surrounding the earth or another planet. **2** the quality of the air in a place. **3** an overall tone or mood. **4** a unit of pressure equal to the pressure of the atmosphere at sea level.

SYNONYMS **1** air, sky; literary the heavens. **2** *a relaxed atmosphere* spirit, ambience, air, mood, feel, feeling, character, tone, aura, quality; informal vibe.

atmospheric ▶ adjective **1** relating to the atmosphere of a planet. **2** creating a distinctive mood.
▶ noun (**atmospherics**) electrical disturbances in the atmosphere.

atoll ▶ noun a ring-shaped coral reef or chain of islands.

atom ▶ noun **1** the smallest particle of a chemical element that can exist. **2** a very small amount.
■ **atom bomb** (or **atomic bomb**) a bomb whose explosive power comes from the fission (splitting) of the nuclei of atoms.

atomic ▶ adjective **1** relating to an atom or atoms. **2** relating to nuclear energy or weapons.

atomize (or **atomise**) ▶ verb (**atomizes, atomizing, atomized**) convert something into very fine particles or droplets.
□ **atomizer** noun.

atonal /ay-toh-n'l/ ▶ adjective not written in any musical key.

atone ▶ verb (**atones, atoning, atoned**) (**atone for**) do something to show you are sorry for something that happened in the past.
□ **atonement** noun.

atrium /ay-tri-uhm/ ▶ noun (plural **atria** /ay-tri-uh/ or **atriums**) **1** a central hall rising through several storeys. **2** an open central court in an ancient Roman house. **3** each of the two upper cavities of the heart.

atrocious ▶ adjective **1** horrifyingly wicked. **2** very bad or unpleasant.

SYNONYMS **1** *atrocious cruelties* wicked, cruel, brutal, barbaric, vicious, monstrous, vile, inhuman, fiendish. **2** *the weather was atrocious* appalling, dreadful, terrible, miserable; informal abysmal, dire, rotten, lousy; Brit. informal shocking.
ANTONYMS admirable, superb.

□ **atrociously** adverb.

atrocity ▶ noun (plural **atrocities**) a very wicked or cruel act.

SYNONYMS **1** *a number of atrocities* outrage, horror, violation, abuse, massacre. **2** *scenes of hardship and atrocity* wickedness, cruelty, brutality, barbarity, viciousness, savagery, inhumanity.
ANTONYMS humanity.

atrophy /a-truh-fi/ ▶ verb (**atrophies, atrophying, atrophied**) (of a part of the body) waste away.
▶ noun the condition or process of atrophying.

attach ▶ verb **1** fasten; join. **2** believe that something has significance or importance. **3** (**be attached to**) be working with a group of people. **4** (**attached to**) very fond of.

SYNONYMS **1** *a weight is attached to the cord* fasten, fix, join, secure, stick. **2** *they attach importance to research* ascribe, assign, attribute, accredit, impute. **3** *the medical officer attached to HQ* assign, appoint, allocate, second. **4** (**attached to**) *she's very attached to him* fond of, devoted to, keen on; informal mad about.
ANTONYMS detach.

□ **attachable** adjective.

✔ **-ch**, not **-tch**: atta**ch**.

attaché /uh-tash-ay/ ▶ noun a person on an ambassador's staff.
■ **attaché case** a small, flat briefcase for carrying documents.

attachment ▶ noun **1** an extra part that is attached to something. **2** a computer file sent with an email.

SYNONYMS **1** *a strong attachment to his mother* bond, closeness, devotion, loyalty, fondness for, love for, affection for, feeling for, sympathy for. **2** *the shower had a massage attachment* accessory, fitting, extension, add-on.

attack ▶ verb **1** violently hurt or attempt to hurt. **2** have a harmful effect on. **3** fiercely criticize. **4** tackle something with determination. **5** (in sport) try to score goals or points.

SYNONYMS **1** *Chris was brutally attacked* assault, beat up, set upon, mug; N. Amer. beat up on; informal work over, rough up; Brit. informal duff up. **2** *the French attacked the fort* strike at, assault, charge, pounce on, raid, storm. **3** *the clergy attacked government policies* criticize, censure, condemn, disparage; informal knock, slam, lay into; Brit. informal slate, slag off, rubbish.
ANTONYMS defend, praise.

▶ noun **1** an instance of attacking. **2** a sudden period of illness.

SYNONYMS **1** *an attack on their home* assault, onslaught, offensive, strike, blitz, raid, charge, invasion. **2** *an attack on his leadership* criticism, censure, condemnation, disparagement; Brit. informal slating. **3** *an asthmatic attack* fit, seizure, spasm, convulsion, paroxysm, bout, episode.
ANTONYMS defence, praise.

a

attacker ▸ noun a person who attacks someone or something.

> SYNONYMS **assailant**, assaulter, mugger, aggressor, raider, invader.
> ANTONYMS defender, victim.

attain ▸ verb **1** succeed in doing. **2** reach.

> SYNONYMS **achieve**, accomplish, reach, obtain, gain, secure, get, win, earn, realize, fulfil; informal clinch, bag, wrap up.

□ **attainable** adjective.

attainment ▸ noun **1** the achieving of something. **2** an achievement.

attar /at-tar/ ▸ noun a sweet-smelling oil made from rose petals.

attempt ▸ verb make an effort to do something.

> SYNONYMS *I attempted to answer the question* **try**, strive, aim, venture, endeavour, seek, have a go.

▸ noun an effort to do something.

> SYNONYMS *an attempt to reach the summit* **try**, effort, endeavour, venture, bid, go; informal crack, shot, stab.

attend ▸ verb **1** be present at or go regularly to. **2** (**attend to**) deal with or pay attention to. **3** happen at the same time as or as a result of. **4** escort and help someone.

> SYNONYMS **1** *they attended a carol service* **be present at**, sit in on, take part in, appear at, turn up at, visit, go to; informal show up at. **2** *the children were not attending* **pay attention**, listen, be attentive, concentrate.
> ANTONYMS miss, take no notice.

attendance ▸ noun **1** the action of attending. **2** the number of people present.

> SYNONYMS **1** *you requested the attendance of a doctor* **presence**, appearance, attention. **2** *their gig attendances grew* **audience**, turnout, house, gate, crowd; Austral. informal muster.
> ANTONYMS absence.

attendant ▸ noun **1** a person employed to help people in a public place. **2** an assistant to an important person.

> SYNONYMS *a royal attendant* **assistant**, aide, companion, steward, equerry, escort, servant, retainer, valet, maid.

▸ adjective accompanying.

> SYNONYMS *new discoveries and the attendant excitement* **accompanying**, associated, related, connected, resulting, consequent.

attention ▸ noun **1** special care, notice, or consideration. **2** (**attentions**) things done to help someone or to express sexual interest. **3** a straight standing position taken by soldiers.

> SYNONYMS **1** *the issue needs further attention* **consideration**, contemplation, deliberation, thought, study, observation, mind, investigation, action. **2** *he tried to attract the attention of a policeman* **awareness**, notice, scrutiny, eye, gaze. **3** *medical attention* **care**, treatment, relief, aid, assistance.

attentive ▸ adjective **1** paying close attention. **2** considerate and helpful.

> SYNONYMS **1** *an attentive pupil* **alert**, perceptive, observant, acute, aware, heedful, focused, studious, diligent, conscientious, earnest. **2** *the most attentive of husbands* **considerate**, conscientious, thoughtful, kind, caring, solicitous, understanding, sympathetic.
> ANTONYMS inattentive.

□ **attentively** adverb.

attenuate ▸ verb (**attenuates, attenuating, attenuated**) **1** make something weaker. **2** make something thin or thinner. □ **attenuation** noun.

attest ▸ verb **1** provide or act as clear evidence of something. **2** declare something to be true. □ **attestation** noun.

attic ▸ noun a space or room inside the roof of a building.

> SYNONYMS **loft**, roof space, garret.

attire formal ▸ noun clothes of a particular kind.
▸ verb (**be attired**) be wearing clothes of a particular kind.

attitude ▸ noun **1** a way of thinking. **2** a position of the body. **3** informal self-confident or aggressive behaviour.

> SYNONYMS **1** *you seem ambivalent in your attitude* **view**, viewpoint, outlook, perspective, stance, standpoint, position, approach, opinion. **2** *an attitude of prayer* **position**, posture, pose, stance.

attitudinize (or **attitudinise**) /at-ti-tyoo-di-nyz/ ▸ verb (**attitudinizes, attitudinizing, attitudinized**) adopt an attitude just for effect.

attorney /uh-ter-ni/ ▸ noun (plural **attorneys**) **1** a person who is appointed to act for someone else in legal matters. **2** chiefly US a lawyer.

attract ▸ verb **1** draw someone in by offering something interesting or appealing. **2** cause a particular reaction. **3** draw something closer by an unseen force.

> SYNONYMS **1** *he was attracted by her smile* **entice**, appeal to, tempt, lure, allure, charm, win, woo, captivate; informal turn on. **2** *electrical equipment attracts dust*

draw, pull, suck.
ANTONYMS repel, put off.

attraction ▶ noun **1** the action or power of attracting. **2** something interesting or appealing.

> SYNONYMS **1** *she had lost her attraction* **appeal,** attractiveness, pull, desirability, fascination, allure, charisma, charm. **2** *the town's attractions* **entertainment,** activity, diversion, amenity, service. **3** *magnetic attraction* **pull,** draw, force. ANTONYMS repulsion.

attractive ▶ adjective **1** very pleasing to look at. **2** arousing interest.

> SYNONYMS **1** **good-looking,** beautiful, pretty, handsome, lovely, stunning, striking, arresting, gorgeous, prepossessing, fetching; Scottish & N. English bonny; informal drop-dead gorgeous; Brit. informal fit; N. Amer. informal cute; Austral./NZ informal spunky. **2** *an attractive career* **appealing,** inviting, tempting, pleasing, interesting.
> ANTONYMS unattractive, ugly, uninviting.

□ **attractively** adverb **attractiveness** noun.

attribute ▶ verb /uh-**trib**-yoot/ (**attributes, attributing, attributed**) (**attribute something to**) say or believe that something is the result of or belongs to.

> SYNONYMS *they attributed their success to him* **ascribe,** assign, accredit, credit, put down, chalk up, pin on.

▶ noun /**at**-tri-byoot/ a quality or feature.

> SYNONYMS *the attributes of a top player* **quality,** characteristic, trait, feature, element, aspect, property, sign, hallmark, mark.

□ **attributable** adjective **attribution** noun.

attrition ▶ noun gradual wearing down through prolonged attack, pressure, or friction.

attune ▶ verb (**be attuned**) be receptive to and able to understand someone or something.

atypical ▶ adjective not typical.

aubergine /**oh**-ber-zheen/ ▶ noun a large vegetable with purple skin.

aubretia (or **aubrietia**) /aw-**bree**-shuh/ ▶ noun a plant with purple, pink, or white flowers.

auburn ▶ noun a reddish-brown colour.

auction ▶ noun a public sale in which each item is sold to the person who offers most for it.
▶ verb sell something at an auction.

auctioneer ▶ noun a person who conducts auctions.

audacious ▶ adjective very confident and daring.

□ **audaciously** adverb **audacity** noun.

audible ▶ adjective able to be heard.

> SYNONYMS **perceptible,** discernible, detectable, clear, distinct.
> ANTONYMS inaudible, faint.

□ **audibility** noun **audibly** adverb.

audience ▶ noun **1** the people gathered to see or listen to a play, concert, film, etc. **2** a formal interview with a person in authority.

> SYNONYMS **1** *the audience applauded* **spectators, listeners,** viewers, onlookers, crowd, throng, gallery, congregation, turnout. **2** *an audience with the Pope* **meeting,** interview, consultation, conference, hearing, reception.

audio tape ▶ noun magnetic tape on which sound can be recorded.

audit ▶ noun an official inspection of an organization's accounts.
▶ verb (**audits, auditing, audited**) inspect the accounts of.
□ **auditor** noun.

audition ▶ noun an interview for an actor, singer, etc. in which they give a practical demonstration of their skill.
▶ verb assess or be assessed by an audition.

auditorium ▶ noun (plural **auditoriums** or **auditoria**) the part of a theatre or hall in which the audience sits.

auditory ▶ adjective relating to hearing.

au fait /oh **fay**/ ▶ adjective (**au fait with**) completely familiar with.

auger /**aw**-ger/ ▶ noun a tool for boring holes.

aught ▶ pronoun old use anything at all.

augment ▶ verb increase the amount or value of.

> SYNONYMS **increase,** add to, supplement, enhance, build up, raise, up, hike up, enlarge, swell, expand, extend; informal jack up.
> ANTONYMS decrease, reduce.

□ **augmentation** noun.

augur /**aw**-ger/ ▶ verb be a sign of a likely outcome.

augury /**aw**-gyoo-ri/ ▶ noun (plural **auguries**) a sign of what will happen in the future.

August ▶ noun the eighth month of the year.

august /aw-**gust**/ ▶ adjective inspiring respect and admiration.

> SYNONYMS **distinguished,** respected, eminent, venerable, illustrious, prestigious, renowned, celebrated, honoured, acclaimed, esteemed.
> ANTONYMS lowly, obscure, disreputable.

auk ▶ noun a black and white seabird.

a

a

aunt ▶ noun the sister of your father or mother or the wife of your uncle.

au pair /oh **pair**/ ▶ noun a foreign girl employed to look after children and help with housework.

aura /**aw**-ruh/ ▶ noun (plural **auras**) the distinctive feeling that seems to surround a particular place or person.

> SYNONYMS **atmosphere**, ambience, air, quality, character, mood, feeling; informal vibe.

aural /**aw**-ruhl/ ▶ adjective having to do with the ear or hearing.
□ **aurally** adverb.

aureole /**aw**-ri-ohl/ ▶ noun a circle of light around the sun or moon.

au revoir /aw ruh-**vwar**/ ▶ exclamation goodbye.

aurora borealis /aw-**raw**-ruh bo-ri-**ay**-liss/ ▶ noun streamers of light sometimes seen in the sky near the North Pole; the Northern Lights.

auspice /**awss**-piss/ ▶ noun (**under the auspices of**) with the support or protection of.

auspicious /aw-**spi**-shuhss/ ▶ adjective suggesting that there is a good chance of success.

> SYNONYMS **favourable**, promising, encouraging, fortunate, opportune, timely, advantageous, good.
> ANTONYMS inauspicious, unfavourable.

□ **auspiciously** adverb.

Aussie informal ▶ noun (plural **Aussies**) an Australian.
▶ adjective Australian.

austere ▶ adjective **1** without luxuries or decoration; very simple and plain. **2** severe or strict in appearance or behaviour.

> SYNONYMS **1** an austere man **severe**, stern, strict, harsh, dour, grim, cold, frosty, unfriendly. **2** an austere life **spartan**, frugal, ascetic, puritanical, abstemious, strict, simple, hard. **3** an austere building **plain**, simple, basic, functional, unadorned, bleak, bare, clinical.
> ANTONYMS easy-going, friendly, luxurious, extravagant, ornate.

□ **austerely** adverb **austerity** noun.

Australasian ▶ adjective relating to Australasia, a region made up of Australia, New Zealand, and neighbouring islands.

Australian ▶ noun a person from Australia.
▶ adjective relating to Australia.

Austrian ▶ noun a person from Austria.
▶ adjective relating to Austria.

authentic ▶ adjective known to be real; genuine.

> SYNONYMS **1** an authentic document **genuine**, real, bona fide, true, legitimate; informal pukka, kosher; Austral./NZ informal dinkum. **2** an authentic depiction of the situation **accurate**, factual, true, truthful, reliable, trustworthy, honest, faithful.
> ANTONYMS fake, inaccurate, unreliable.

□ **authentically** adverb **authenticity** noun.

authenticate ▶ verb (**authenticates**, **authenticating**, **authenticated**) prove or show that something is authentic.

> SYNONYMS **verify**, validate, prove, substantiate, corroborate, confirm, support, back up.
> ANTONYMS disprove.

□ **authentication** noun.

author ▶ noun **1** a writer of a book or article. **2** the inventor of something.

> SYNONYMS **1** modern Canadian authors **writer**, novelist, poet, playwright, columnist, reporter, wordsmith; informal scribe, scribbler. **2** the author of the peace plan **creator**, originator, founder, father, architect, designer, producer.

□ **authorship** noun.

authoritarian ▶ adjective demanding strict obedience of authority and rules.

> SYNONYMS **strict**, autocratic, dictatorial, despotic, tyrannical, domineering, imperious, illiberal, undemocratic; informal bossy.
> ANTONYMS democratic, liberal.

▶ noun an authoritarian person.

> SYNONYMS **disciplinarian**, autocrat, dictator, despot, tyrant.
> ANTONYMS democrat, liberal.

authoritative ▶ adjective **1** true or accurate and so able to be trusted. **2** commanding and self-confident. **3** official.

> SYNONYMS **1** authoritative information **reliable**, dependable, trustworthy, accurate, authentic, valid. **2** the authoritative edition **definitive**, most reliable, best, authorized, approved. **3** his authoritative manner **commanding**, masterful, assertive, self-assured, self-confident.
> ANTONYMS unreliable, timid.

□ **authoritatively** adverb.

authority ▶ noun (plural **authorities**) **1** the power to give orders and make people obey you. **2** a person or organization that has official power. **3** recognized knowledge or expertise. **4** a person or book that is trusted as a source of knowledge.

> SYNONYMS **1** a rebellion against those in authority **power**, command, control, charge, dominance, jurisdiction, rule; informal clout. **2** the authority to arrest drug

traffickers **right,** authorization, power, mandate, prerogative, licence. **3** _the money was spent without parliamentary authority_ **permission,** authorization, consent, sanction, assent, agreement, approval, clearance; _informal_ the go-ahead. **4** _the authorities_ **officials,** officialdom, government, administration, establishment, police; _informal_ the powers that be. **5** _an authority on coins_ **expert,** specialist, professional, master, connoisseur, pundit, doyen(ne), guru.
ANTONYMS amateur, ignoramus.

authorize (or authorise) ▶ verb (**authorizes, authorizing, authorized**) give official permission for.

SYNONYMS **1** _they authorized further action_ **permit,** sanction, allow, approve, consent to, assent to; _informal_ give the go-ahead to, OK. **2** _the troops were authorized to fire_ **empower,** give authority, mandate, commission, entitle.
ANTONYMS forbid.

☐ **authorization** noun.

authorized ▶ adjective officially permitted.

SYNONYMS **approved,** sanctioned, accredited, recognized, licensed, certified, official, legal, legitimate.
ANTONYMS unauthorized, unofficial.

autism ▶ noun a mental condition in which a person has great difficulty in communicating with other people.
☐ **autistic** adjective.

autobiography ▶ noun (plural **autobiographies**) an account of a person's life written by that person.
☐ **autobiographical** adjective.

autocracy /aw-tok-ruh-si/ ▶ noun (plural **autocracies**) a system of government in which one person has total power.

autocrat ▶ noun **1** a ruler who has total power. **2** a person who expects obedience.
☐ **autocratic** adjective.

autogiro (or autogyro) ▶ noun (plural **autogiros**) a type of aircraft that is powered by a propeller and has rotating horizontal blades like a helicopter.

autograph ▶ noun a celebrity's signature written for an admirer.
▶ verb write an autograph on something.

automate ▶ verb (**automates, automating, automated**) convert a process or machine so that it can operate automatically.
☐ **automation** noun.

automatic ▶ adjective **1** operating by itself without human control. **2** (of a gun) able to fire continuously until the bullets run out. **3** done without conscious thought. **4** (of a punishment) applied without question because of a fixed rule.

SYNONYMS **1** _automatic garage doors_ **mechanized,** powered, mechanical, automated, computerized, electronic, robotic. **2** _an automatic reaction_ **instinctive,** involuntary, unconscious, reflex, knee-jerk, subconscious, spontaneous, impulsive, unthinking, mechanical; _informal_ gut. **3** _the automatic choice_ **inevitable,** unavoidable, inescapable, only possible.
ANTONYMS manual, conscious, deliberate.

■ **automatic pilot** a device for keeping an aircraft on course without the pilot having to control it.
☐ **automatically** adverb.

automaton /aw-tom-uh-tuhn/ ▶ noun (plural **automata** /aw-tom-uh-tuh/ or **automatons**) a mechanical device that looks like a human being.

automobile ▶ noun N. Amer. a car.

automotive ▶ adjective having to do with motor vehicles.

autonomous /aw-ton-uh-muhss/ ▶ adjective self-governing or independent.

SYNONYMS **self-governing,** independent, sovereign, free.
ANTONYMS dependent, repressed.

☐ **autonomously** adverb.

autonomy ▶ noun **1** self-government. **2** freedom of action.

SYNONYMS **self-government,** self-rule, home rule, self-determination, independence, sovereignty, freedom.
ANTONYMS dependence, repression.

autopsy /aw-top-si/ ▶ noun (plural **autopsies**) an examination of a dead body to discover the cause of death.

autumn ▶ noun chiefly Brit. the season after summer and before winter.
☐ **autumnal** adjective.

auxiliary ▶ adjective providing extra help and support.

SYNONYMS **additional,** supplementary, extra, reserve, backup, emergency, fallback, second.
ANTONYMS primary, regular.

▶ noun (plural **auxiliaries**) an auxiliary person or thing.
■ **auxiliary verb** a verb such as _be_, _do_, and _have_, which is used to form tenses of other verbs.

avail ▶ verb (**avail yourself of**) formal use or take advantage of.
▶ noun use or benefit.

available ▶ adjective **1** able to be used or obtained. **2** not occupied.

SYNONYMS **1** _refreshments will be available_ **obtainable,** accessible, to/at hand, to be had, on sale, untaken, unsold; _informal_ up

for grabs, on tap. **2** *I'll see if he's available*
free, unoccupied, on duty, contactable.
ANTONYMS unavailable, taken, busy.

□ **availability** noun.

avalanche /av-uh-lahnsh/ ▸ noun **1** a mass
of snow and ice falling rapidly down a
mountainside. **2** an overwhelming amount
of something.

SYNONYMS *an avalanche of enquiries*
barrage, flood, deluge, torrent, wave.
ANTONYMS trickle.

avant-garde /a-von gard/ ▸ adjective (in
the arts) new and experimental.

SYNONYMS **experimental,** modern,
cutting-edge, progressive, unorthodox,
unconventional; informal edgy, offbeat,
way-out.
ANTONYMS conservative, established.

avarice /av-uh-riss/ ▸ noun extreme greed
for money or material things.

SYNONYMS **greed,** acquisitiveness,
covetousness, materialism.
ANTONYMS generosity.

avaricious ▸ adjective very greedy for
money or material things.

avatar /av-uh-tar/ ▸ noun (in Hinduism) a
god or goddess appearing in physical form
on earth.

avenge ▸ verb (**avenges, avenging,**
avenged) repay something bad that has
been done to you by harming the person
who did it.
□ **avenger** noun.

avenue ▸ noun **1** a broad road or path. **2** a
way of making progress towards achieving
something.

aver /uh-ver/ ▸ verb (**avers, averring,**
averred) formal declare that something is
the case.

average ▸ noun **1** the result obtained by
adding several amounts together and
then dividing the total by the number of
amounts. **2** a usual amount or level.

SYNONYMS *the national average* **mean,**
median, mode, norm, standard, rule, par.

▸ adjective **1** being an average. **2** usual or
ordinary.

SYNONYMS **1** *the average temperature*
mean, median, modal. **2** *a woman of*
average height **ordinary,** standard,
normal, typical, regular.
ANTONYMS abnormal, unusual.

▸ verb (**averages, averaging, averaged**)
1 amount to a particular figure as an
average. **2** calculate the average of several
amounts.

averse ▸ adjective (**averse to**) strongly
disliking or opposed to.

SYNONYMS **opposed,** hostile, antagonistic,
resistant, disinclined, reluctant, loath;
informal anti.
ANTONYMS keen.

❗ Don't confuse **averse** with **adverse**, which
means 'harmful or unfavourable'.

aversion ▸ noun a strong dislike.

SYNONYMS **dislike,** hatred, loathing,
abhorrence, distaste, antipathy, hostility,
reluctance, disinclination.
ANTONYMS liking.

avert ▸ verb **1** turn away your eyes.
2 prevent something unpleasant
happening.

SYNONYMS **1** *she averted her gaze* **turn**
aside, turn away, shift, redirect. **2** *an*
attempt to avert political chaos **prevent,**
avoid, stave off, ward off, head off,
forestall.
ANTONYMS bring about, allow.

avian /ay-vi-uhn/ ▸ adjective having to do
with birds.

aviary ▸ noun (plural **aviaries**) a large
enclosure for keeping birds in.

aviation ▸ noun the activity of operating
and flying aircraft.

aviator ▸ noun dated a pilot.

avid ▸ adjective very interested or
enthusiastic.

SYNONYMS **keen,** eager, enthusiastic,
ardent, passionate, zealous, devoted.
ANTONYMS apathetic.

□ **avidly** adverb.

avionics ▸ plural noun electronics used in
aviation.

avocado ▸ noun (plural **avocados**) a pear-
shaped fruit with pale green flesh and a
large stone.

avocet /av-uh-set/ ▸ noun a wading bird
with long legs and an upturned bill.

avoid ▸ verb **1** keep away from, or stop
yourself from doing. **2** prevent something
from happening. **3** manage not to collide
with.

SYNONYMS **1** *I avoid situations that cause*
me stress **keep away from,** steer clear
of, give a wide berth to. **2** *he avoids*
responsibility **evade,** dodge, sidestep,
escape, run away from; informal duck,
wriggle out of, get out of. **3** *book early to*
avoid disappointment **prevent,** preclude,
stave off, forestall, head off, ward off.
4 *he should avoid drinking alcohol* **refrain**
from, abstain from, desist from, steer
clear of.
ANTONYMS confront, face up to, seek out,
cause, allow, continue, insist on.

□ **avoidable** adjective **avoidance** noun.

avoirdupois /av-war-dyoo-**pwah**/ ▸ noun the system of weights based on a pound of 16 ounces.

avow ▸ verb openly state or confess.
□ **avowed** adjective.

avuncular /uh-**vung**-kyuu-ler/ ▸ adjective kind and friendly towards a younger person.

await ▸ verb wait for.

SYNONYMS **1** *Peter was awaiting news* **wait for,** expect, look forward to, anticipate. **2** *many dangers await them* **be in store for,** lie ahead of, lie in wait for, be waiting for, be round the corner.

awake ▸ verb (**awakes, awaking, awoke;** past participle **awoken**) **1** stop sleeping. **2** make or become active again.

SYNONYMS *she awoke early* **wake up,** wake, awaken, waken, stir, come to, come round, rouse, call.

▸ adjective not asleep.

SYNONYMS **1** *she was still awake* **sleepless,** wide awake, restless, insomniac. **2** *too few are awake to the dangers* **aware of,** conscious of, mindful of, alert to. ANTONYMS asleep, oblivious.

awaken ▸ verb **1** awake. **2** stir up a feeling.

SYNONYMS **1** See **AWAKE** (verb). **2** *he had awakened strong emotions in her* **arouse,** bring out, trigger, stir up, stimulate, kindle, revive. ANTONYMS suppress.

award ▸ verb give an official prize or reward to.

SYNONYMS *the society awarded him a medal* **give,** grant, accord, confer on, bestow on, present to, decorate with.

▸ noun **1** an official prize or reward. **2** the action of awarding.

SYNONYMS **1** *an award for long service* **prize,** trophy, medal, decoration, reward; informal gong. **2** *an award of £1,500* **grant,** scholarship, endowment; Brit. bursary.

aware ▸ adjective (usu. **aware of** or **that**) knowing about a situation or fact.

SYNONYMS **1** *she is aware of the dangers* **conscious of,** mindful of, informed about, acquainted with, familiar with, alive to, alert to; informal wise to, in the know about. **2** *environmentally aware* **sensitive,** enlightened, knowledgeable, (well) informed; informal clued up; Brit. informal switched-on. ANTONYMS unaware, ignorant.

awareness ▸ noun the quality of being aware.

SYNONYMS **consciousness,** recognition, realization, perception, understanding, grasp, appreciation, knowledge, familiarity.

awash ▸ adjective covered or flooded with water.

away ▸ adverb **1** to or at a distance. **2** into a place for storage. **3** out of existence. **4** constantly or continuously.

SYNONYMS *we'll be away for two weeks* **elsewhere,** abroad, gone, off, out, absent, on holiday, on vacation.

▸ adjective (of a sports match) played at the opponents' ground.

awe ▸ noun a feeling of great respect mixed with fear.

SYNONYMS **wonder,** wonderment, admiration, reverence, respect, fear, dread.

▸ verb (**awes, awing, awed**) fill someone with awe.

awesome ▸ adjective **1** inspiring awe. **2** informal excellent.

SYNONYMS **breathtaking,** awe-inspiring, magnificent, amazing, stunning, staggering, imposing, formidable, intimidating; informal mind-boggling, mind-blowing, brilliant. ANTONYMS unimpressive.

□ **awesomely** adverb.

awful ▸ adjective **1** very bad or unpleasant. **2** used to emphasize something: *an awful lot.*

SYNONYMS **1** *the place smelled awful* **disgusting,** terrible, dreadful, ghastly, horrible, vile, foul, revolting, repulsive, repugnant, sickening, nauseating; informal gross; Brit. informal beastly. **2** *an awful book* **dreadful,** terrible, frightful, atrocious, lamentable; informal crummy, pathetic, rotten, woeful, lousy, appalling, abysmal, dismal, dire; Brit. informal rubbish. **3** *an awful accident* **serious,** bad, terrible, dreadful, shocking. **4** *I feel awful* **ill,** unwell, sick, nauseous; Brit. off colour, poorly; Brit. informal grotty, ropy; Scottish informal wabbit, peely-wally; Austral./NZ informal crook. ANTONYMS delightful, excellent, well.

awfully ▸ adverb **1** informal very or very much. **2** very badly.

SYNONYMS **1** *an awfully nice man* **very,** extremely, really, immensely, exceedingly, thoroughly, dreadfully, terrifically, terribly, exceptionally, remarkably, extraordinarily; N. English right; informal seriously, majorly; Brit. informal jolly, dead, well; N. Amer. informal real, mighty, awful; informal, dated frightfully. **2** *we played awfully* **terribly,** dreadfully, atrociously, appallingly; informal abysmally, pitifully, diabolically.

a

awhile ▸ adverb for a short time.

awkward ▸ adjective **1** hard to do or deal with. **2** causing or feeling embarrassment. **3** inconvenient. **4** clumsy.

> SYNONYMS **1** *the box was awkward to carry* **difficult**, tricky, cumbersome, unwieldy; Brit. informal fiddly. **2** *you're being really awkward* **unreasonable**, uncooperative, unhelpful, difficult, obstructive, contrary, obstinate; Brit. informal bloody-minded, bolshie; N. Amer. informal balky. **3** *an awkward time* **inconvenient**, inappropriate, inopportune, difficult. **4** *he put her in a very awkward position* **embarrassing**, uncomfortable, unenviable, delicate, tricky, problematic, troublesome, humiliating, compromising; informal sticky. **5** *she felt awkward when alone with him* **uncomfortable**, uneasy, tense, nervous, edgy, self-conscious, embarrassed. **6** *his awkward movements* **clumsy**, ungainly, uncoordinated, graceless, inelegant, gauche, gawky, stiff, unskilful, inept, blundering; informal ham-fisted, cack-handed; Brit. informal all (fingers and) thumbs.
> ANTONYMS easy, amenable, convenient, at ease, graceful, dexterous.

□ **awkwardly** adverb.

awl ▸ noun a small pointed tool used for making holes.

awning ▸ noun a sheet of canvas on a frame, used for shelter.

awoke past of AWAKE.

awoken past participle of AWAKE.

AWOL /ay-wol/ ▸ adjective (**go AWOL**) informal go missing.
ORIGIN short for *absent without official leave*, a military expression.

awry /uh-ry/ ▸ adverb & adjective away from the expected course or position.

axe (US spelling **ax**) ▸ noun a tool with a heavy blade, used for chopping wood.

> SYNONYMS **hatchet**, chopper, cleaver, adze.

▸ verb (**axes**, **axing**, **axed**) suddenly and ruthlessly cancel or dismiss.

> SYNONYMS **1** *the show was axed* **cancel**, withdraw, drop, scrap, cut, discontinue, end; informal ditch, dump, pull the plug on. **2** *500 staff were axed* **dismiss**, make redundant, lay off, get rid of; informal sack, fire.
> ANTONYMS start, launch, recruit.

■ **have an axe to grind** have a private reason for doing something.

axiom /ak-si-uhm/ ▸ noun a statement regarded as being obviously true.
□ **axiomatic** adjective.

axis /ak-sis/ ▸ noun (plural **axes** /ak-seez/) **1** an imaginary line around which an object or shape rotates. **2** a fixed line against which points on a graph are measured. **3** (**the Axis**) Germany and its allies in the Second World War.

axle ▸ noun a rod passing through the centre of a wheel or group of wheels.

> SYNONYMS **shaft**, spindle, rod.

ayatollah /I-uh-tol-luh/ ▸ noun a religious leader in Iran.

aye (*rhymes with* my) ▸ exclamation old use or dialect yes.

azalea /uh-zay-li-uh/ ▸ noun a shrub with brightly coloured flowers.

Azerbaijani /a-zer-by-jah-ni/ ▸ noun (plural **Azerbaijanis**) a person from Azerbaijan.
▸ adjective relating to Azerbaijan.

azimuth /az-i-muhth/ ▸ noun Astronomy the direction of a star measured horizontally as an angle from due north or south.

Aztec ▸ noun a member of an American Indian people that ruled Mexico before the Spanish conquest.

azure /az-yuur/ ▸ noun a bright blue colour like a cloudless sky.

Bb

B (or **b**) ▸ noun (plural **Bs** or **B's**) the second letter of the alphabet.

B. & B. ▸ abbreviation bed and breakfast.

BA ▸ abbreviation Bachelor of Arts.

baa ▸ verb (**baas**, **baaing**, **baaed**) (of a sheep or lamb) bleat.

babble ▸ verb talk quickly in a silly or confused way.

> SYNONYMS **prattle**, rattle on, gabble, chatter, jabber, twitter, burble, blather; informal yatter, blabber, jaw, gas, shoot your mouth off; Brit. informal witter, rabbit, chunter, natter, waffle.

▸ noun silly or confused talk.

babe ▸ noun **1** literary a baby. **2** informal an attractive young woman.

babel /bay-b'l/ ▸ noun a confused noise made by many people speaking together.

baboon ▸ noun a large monkey with a long snout and a pink rump.

baby ▸ noun (plural **babies**) **1** a child or animal that has recently been born. **2** a timid or childish person.

> SYNONYMS **infant**, newborn, child; Scottish & N. English bairn; technical neonate; informal sprog, tot; literary babe.

▸ adjective small or very young.

> SYNONYMS *baby carrots* **miniature**, mini, little, toy, pocket, midget, dwarf; Scottish wee; N. Amer. vest-pocket; informal teeny, teensy, tiddly, bite-sized; Brit. informal titchy; N. Amer. informal little-bitty.
> ANTONYMS large.

▸ verb (**babies**, **babying**, **babied**) treat someone too protectively.
□ **babyhood** noun.

babyish ▸ adjective childish and immature.

> SYNONYMS **childish**, infantile, juvenile, puerile, immature.
> ANTONYMS mature.

babysit ▸ verb (**babysits**, **babysitting**, **babysat**) look after a child or children while the parents are out.
□ **babysitter** noun.

baccalaureate /ba-kuh-lor-i-uht/ ▸ noun an exam taken in some countries to qualify for higher education.

baccarat /bak-kuh-rah/ ▸ noun a gambling card game.

bacchanalian /bak-kuh-**nay**-li-uhn/ ▸ adjective (of a party or celebration) drunken and wild.

bachelor ▸ noun **1** a man who has never been married. **2** a person who holds a first degree from a university.

bacillus /buh-**sil**-luhss/ ▸ noun (plural **bacilli** /buh-**sil**-lee/) a type of bacterium.

back ▸ noun **1** the rear surface of a person's body, or the upper part of an animal's body. **2** the side or part of something that is furthest from the front. **3** a defending player in a team game.

> SYNONYMS **1** spine, backbone, spinal column, vertebral column. **2** *the back of the house* rear; Nautical stern. **3** *the back of the queue* end, tail end, rear end; N. Amer. tag end. **4** *the back of a postcard* reverse, other side, underside; informal flip side.
> ANTONYMS front, bow, head, face.

▸ adverb **1** in the opposite direction from the one in which you are facing or travelling. **2** so as to return to an earlier or normal position or state. **3** into the past. **4** in return.

> SYNONYMS **1** *he pushed his chair back* backwards, behind you, to your rear, rearwards, away. **2** *a few months back* ago, earlier, previously, before.
> ANTONYMS forward, ahead.

▸ adjective **1** at or towards the back. **2** in a remote or less important position. **3** relating to the past.

> SYNONYMS **1** *the back seats* rear, rearmost, hind, hindmost, posterior. **2** *a back copy* past, old, previous, earlier.
> ANTONYMS front, future.

▸ verb **1** give support to. **2** walk or drive backwards. **3** bet money on a person or animal to win a race or contest. **4** (**back on to**) (of a building) have its back facing or next to. **5** cover the back of an object. **6** provide musical backing for a singer or musician.

b

SYNONYMS **1** *companies backed the scheme generously* **sponsor,** finance, fund, subsidize, underwrite; informal pick up the bill for. **2** *most people backed the idea* **support,** endorse, sanction, approve of, give your blessing to, smile on, favour, advocate, promote, champion; informal throw your weight behind. **3** *he backed the horse at 33–1* **bet on,** gamble on, stake money on. **4** *he backed away* **reverse,** draw back, step back, pull back, retreat, withdraw.
ANTONYMS oppose, advance.

■ **the back of beyond** a very remote place. **back down** give in. **back off** stop opposing someone. **back out** withdraw from something you have promised to do. **back-pedal** go back on something previously said. **back someone/thing up 1** support someone or something. **2** Computing make a spare copy of data or a disk. **put someone's back up** annoy someone.

backbencher ▶ noun an MP who does not hold a government or opposition post.

backbiting ▶ noun spiteful talk about a person who is not present.

backbone ▶ noun **1** the spine. **2** strength of character.

backchat ▶ noun Brit. informal rude or cheeky remarks.

backdate ▶ verb (backdates, backdating, backdated) Brit. make something valid from an earlier date.

backdrop ▶ noun **1** a painted cloth hung at the back of a theatre stage as part of the scenery. **2** the setting or background for a scene or event.

backer ▶ noun a person or organization that supports someone or something, especially financially.

SYNONYMS **1** *our financial backers* **sponsor,** investor, underwriter, financier, patron, benefactor; informal angel. **2** *the backers of the proposition* **supporter,** defender, advocate, promoter; N. Amer. booster.

backfire ▶ verb (backfires, backfiring, backfired) **1** (of an engine) make a banging sound as a result of fuel igniting wrongly. **2** produce the opposite effect to what was intended.

SYNONYMS *Bernard's plan backfired on him* **rebound,** boomerang, come back, fail; informal blow up in someone's face.

backgammon ▶ noun a board game played with counters and a dice.

background ▶ noun **1** the part of a scene or picture behind the main figures. **2** information or circumstances that influence or explain something. **3** a person's education, experience, and early life.

SYNONYMS **1** *a background of trees* **backdrop,** backcloth, surrounding(s), setting, scene. **2** *students from different backgrounds* **social circumstances,** family circumstances, environment, class, culture, tradition. **3** *her nursing background* **experience,** record, history, past, training, education.
ANTONYMS foreground.

backhand ▶ noun (in tennis and similar games) a stroke played with the back of the hand facing in the direction of the stroke.

backhanded ▶ adjective expressed in a way that is indirect or has more than one meaning: *a backhanded compliment.*

backhander ▶ noun **1** a backhand stroke or blow. **2** Brit. informal a bribe.

backing ▶ noun **1** support. **2** a layer of material that forms or strengthens the back of something. **3** music or singing accompanying a pop singer.

SYNONYMS **1** *he has the backing of his colleagues* **support,** endorsement, approval, blessing. **2** *financial backing* **sponsorship,** finance, funding, subsidy, patronage.

backlash ▶ noun an angry reaction by a large number of people.

SYNONYMS **adverse reaction,** counterblast, repercussion, comeback, retaliation, reprisal.

backlog ▶ noun a build-up of things needing to be dealt with.

backpack ▶ noun a rucksack.
▶ verb travel carrying your belongings in a rucksack.
□ **backpacker** noun.

backside ▶ noun informal a person's bottom.

backslapping ▶ noun the offering of hearty congratulations or praise.

backsliding ▶ noun a return to bad behaviour after an attempt to improve.

backstage ▶ adverb & adjective behind the stage in a theatre.

backstreet ▶ noun a less important street in a town or city.

backstroke ▶ noun a swimming stroke in which you lie on your back and lift your arms out of the water in a backward circular movement.

backtrack ▶ verb **1** retrace your steps. **2** change your opinion to the opposite of what it was.

backup ▶ noun **1** support. **2** a person or thing kept ready to be used when needed.

SYNONYMS *troops will provide backup* **help,** support, assistance, aid, reserve, reinforcements.

▶ adjective kept ready to be used when needed.

SYNONYMS *a backup supply* **reserve,** spare, substitute, replacement, standby, fallback, emergency.

backward ▸ adjective **1** directed towards the back. **2** having made less progress than is normal or expected.

SYNONYMS **1** *a backward look* **rearward,** towards the rear, behind you, reverse. **2** *the decision was a backward step* **retrograde,** regressive, for the worse, in the wrong direction, downhill, negative. **3** *economically backward* **underdeveloped,** undeveloped, primitive. **4** *he was not backward in displaying his talents* **hesitant,** reticent, reluctant, shy, diffident, timid. ANTONYMS forward, progressive, advanced, confident.

▸ adverb (also **backwards**) **1** towards the back, or back towards the starting point. **2** opposite to the usual direction or order.

SYNONYMS **towards the rear,** rearwards, behind you. ANTONYMS forwards.

backwash ▸ noun waves flowing outwards behind a ship.

backwater ▸ noun **1** a stretch of stagnant water on a river. **2** a place where change happens very slowly.

backwoods ▸ plural noun a remote area or region.

bacon ▸ noun salted or smoked meat from the back or sides of a pig.

bacteria ▸ plural noun (sing. **bacterium**) a group of microscopic organisms, many kinds of which can cause disease. □ **bacterial** adjective.

❗ **Bacteria** is actually a plural (the singular is **bacterium**), and should always be used with a plural verb, e.g. *the bacteria were multiplying.*

bad ▸ adjective (**worse, worst**) **1** low in quality; well below standard. **2** unpleasant. **3** severe; serious. **4** wicked or evil. **5** (**bad for**) harmful to. **6** injured, ill, or diseased. **7** (of food) decayed.

SYNONYMS **1** *bad workmanship* **unsatisfactory,** substandard, poor, inferior, second-rate, second-class, inadequate, deficient, imperfect, defective, faulty, shoddy, negligent; informal crummy, rotten, pathetic, useless, woeful, lousy; Brit. informal duff, rubbish. **2** *the alcohol had a bad effect* **harmful,** damaging, detrimental, injurious, hurtful, destructive. **3** *the bad guys* **wicked,** evil, sinful, criminal, immoral, corrupt; informal crooked, bent. **4** *you bad girl!* **naughty,** badly behaved, disobedient, wayward, wilful, defiant, unruly, undisciplined.

5 *bad news* **unpleasant,** disagreeable, unwelcome, unfavourable, unfortunate, grim, distressing, gloomy. **6** *a bad time to arrive* **unfavourable,** inauspicious, inopportune, unfortunate, disadvantageous, inappropriate, unsuitable. **7** *a bad accident* **serious,** severe, grave, critical, acute. **8** *the meat's bad* **rotten,** off, decayed, putrid, rancid, curdled, sour, mouldy. **9** *a bad knee* **injured,** wounded, diseased; Brit. informal gammy, knackered; Austral./NZ informal crook. ANTONYMS good, quality, beneficial, virtuous, well behaved, welcome, favourable, slight, fresh, healthy.

□ **badness** noun.

bade past of BID².

badge ▸ noun a small flat object that a person pins to their clothing to show that they belong to an organization, have a particular rank, etc.

SYNONYMS **1** **brooch,** pin, emblem, crest, insignia; N. Amer. button. **2** *a badge of success* **sign,** symbol, indication, signal, mark, hallmark, trademark.

badger ▸ noun an animal with a black and white striped head which lives underground and is active at night. ▸ verb (**badgers, badgering, badgered**) pester someone to do something.

SYNONYMS **pester,** harass, hound, harry, nag, bother, go on at; informal hassle, bug.

badinage /bad-i-nahzh/ ▸ noun witty conversation.

badlands ▸ plural noun land where plants or crops will not grow.

badly ▸ adverb (**worse, worst**) **1** in a way that is not acceptable or satisfactory. **2** severely; seriously. **3** very much.

SYNONYMS **1** *the job had been badly done* **poorly,** unsatisfactorily, inadequately, incorrectly, faultily, defectively, shoddily, amateurishly, carelessly, negligently, incompetently, inexpertly. **2** *try not to think badly of me* **unfavourably,** ill, critically, disapprovingly. **3** *stop behaving badly* **naughtily,** disobediently, wilfully, mischievously. **4** *he had been badly treated* **cruelly,** wickedly, unkindly, harshly, shamefully, unfairly, unjustly, wrongly. **5** *it turned out badly* **unfavourably,** unsuccessfully, adversely, unfortunately. **6** *some of the victims are badly hurt* **severely,** seriously, gravely, acutely, critically. ANTONYMS well, properly, humanely, fairly, favourably, slightly.

■ **badly off** poor.

badminton ▸ noun a game in which the players hit a shuttlecock across a high net with rackets.

bad-tempered ▸ adjective easily angered or annoyed.

> synonyms **irritable**, irascible, tetchy, testy, grumpy, grouchy, crotchety, in a (bad) mood, cantankerous, curmudgeonly, ill-tempered, ill-humoured, peevish, cross, fractious, pettish, crabby; informal snappish, on a short fuse; Brit. informal shirty, stroppy, ratty; N. Amer. informal cranky, ornery; Austral./NZ informal snaky.
> antonyms good-humoured, affable.

baffle ▸ verb (**baffles**, **baffling**, **baffled**) make someone feel puzzled.

> synonyms **puzzle**, perplex, bewilder, mystify, confuse; informal flummox, stump, beat, fox.
> antonyms enlighten.

▸ noun a device for controlling the flow of sound, light, gas, or fluid.
□ **bafflement** noun.

bag ▸ noun **1** a flexible container with an opening at the top. **2** (**bags**) loose folds of skin under a person's eyes. **3** (**bags of**) Brit. informal plenty of. **4** informal an unpleasant or unattractive woman.

> synonyms **suitcase**, case, valise, holdall, grip.

▸ verb (**bags**, **bagging**, **bagged**) **1** put something in a bag. **2** manage to catch an animal. **3** informal manage to get.

> synonyms **1** *locals bagged the most fish* **catch**, land, capture, trap, net, snare. **2** *he bagged seven medals* **get**, secure, obtain, acquire, pick up, win, achieve; informal land, net.

bagatelle ▸ noun **1** a game in which you hit small balls into numbered holes on a board. **2** something unimportant or of little value.

bagel /bay-g'l/ ▸ noun a ring-shaped bread roll with a heavy texture.

baggage ▸ noun luggage packed with belongings for travelling.

> synonyms **luggage**, suitcases, cases, bags.

baggy ▸ adjective (**baggier**, **baggiest**) loose and hanging in folds.

> synonyms **loose**, roomy, generously cut, sloppy, full, voluminous.
> antonyms tight.

bagpipe (or **bagpipes**) ▸ noun a musical instrument with pipes that are sounded by wind squeezed from a bag.
□ **bagpiper** noun.

baguette /ba-get/ ▸ noun a long, narrow French loaf of bread.

bail¹ ▸ noun **1** the release of an accused person on condition that a sum of money is left with the court, which will be returned as long as the person attends their trial.

2 money paid to release an accused person.

> synonyms *he was released on bail* **surety**, security, indemnity, bond, guarantee, pledge.

▸ verb release an accused person on payment of bail.

bail² ▸ noun Cricket either of the two small pieces of wood that rest on the stumps.

bail³ (or Brit. **bale**) ▸ verb **1** scoop water out of a ship or boat. **2** (**bail out**) make an emergency jump out of an aircraft, using a parachute. **3** (**bail someone out**) rescue someone who is in difficulties.

bailey ▸ noun (plural **baileys**) the outer wall of a castle.

bailiff ▸ noun a person who delivers writs and seizes the property of people who owe money for rent.

bailiwick ▸ noun **1** a district over which a bailiff has authority. **2** a person's area of activity or interest.

bairn ▸ noun Scottish N. English a child.

bait ▸ noun food put on a hook or in a trap to attract fish or other animals.

> synonyms *was she the bait to lure him into a trap?* **enticement**, lure, decoy, snare, trap, inducement, siren, carrot, attraction; informal come-on.

▸ verb **1** taunt or tease. **2** (**baiting**) the activity of setting dogs on an animal that is trapped or tied up. **3** put bait on a hook or in a trap.

> synonyms *he was baited at school* **taunt**, tease, goad, pick on, torment, persecute; informal needle; Brit. informal wind up.

baize ▸ noun a thick green material used for covering billiard tables.

bake ▸ verb (**bakes**, **baking**, **baked**) **1** cook food in an oven. **2** heat something to dry or harden it. **3** (**baking**) informal (of weather) very hot.
■ **baking soda** sodium bicarbonate.

baker ▸ noun a person whose job is making bread and cakes.
■ **baker's dozen** a group of thirteen.
□ **bakery** noun (plural **bakeries**).

baksheesh ▸ noun (in India and some other eastern countries) money given as charity, a tip, or a bribe.

balaclava /ba-luh-klah-vuh/ ▸ noun a close-fitting woollen hat covering the head and neck except for the face.

balalaika /ba-luh-ly-kuh/ ▸ noun a Russian musical instrument like a guitar, with a triangular body.

balance ▸ noun **1** a state in which weight is evenly distributed, so that a person or object does not wobble or fall over. **2** a situation in which different parts are in the right proportions. **3** a piece of equipment for weighing. **4** an amount that is the difference between money received and money spent in an account. **5** an amount still owed when part of a debt has been paid.

SYNONYMS **1** *I tripped and lost my balance* **stability,** equilibrium, steadiness, footing. **2** *political balance in broadcasting* **fairness,** justice, impartiality, parity, equity, evenness, uniformity, comparability. **3** *the balance of the rent* **remainder,** outstanding amount, rest, residue, difference. ANTONYMS instability, bias.

▸ verb (**balances, balancing, balanced**) **1** put your body, or an object, in a steady position. **2** compare the value of one thing with another. **3** give equal importance to two or more things.

SYNONYMS **1** *she balanced the book on her head* **steady,** stabilize, poise, level. **2** *he balanced his radical remarks with more familiar declarations* **counterbalance,** balance out, offset, counteract, compensate for, make up for. **3** *their income and expenditure do not balance* **correspond,** agree, tally, match up, coincide. **4** *you need to balance cost against benefit* **weigh (up),** compare, evaluate, consider, assess.

■ **balance of payments** the difference between payments into and out of a country over a period. **balance sheet** a written statement of what a business owns and what it owes.

balcony ▸ noun (plural **balconies**) **1** a platform with a railing or low wall, projecting from the outside of a building. **2** the highest level of seats in a theatre or cinema.

bald ▸ adjective **1** having no hair on the head. **2** (of a tyre) having the tread worn away. **3** plain or blunt.

SYNONYMS **1** *a bald head* **hairless,** smooth, shaven, depilated. **2** *a bald statement* **plain,** simple, direct, blunt, unadorned, unvarnished; informal upfront. ANTONYMS hairy, vague.

□ **baldly** adverb **baldness** noun.

balderdash ▸ noun nonsense.

balding ▸ adjective going bald.

bale¹ ▸ noun a large bundle of paper, hay, or cloth.
▸ verb (**bales, baling, baled**) make paper, hay, or cloth into bales.

bale² ➡ BAIL³.

baleen /buh-**leen**/ ▸ noun whalebone.

baleful ▸ adjective threatening to cause harm.
□ **balefully** adverb.

balk US spelling of BAULK.

Balkan ▸ adjective relating to countries on the peninsula of SE Europe surrounded by the Adriatic, Ionian, Aegean, and the Black Seas.

ball¹ ▸ noun **1** a rounded object that is kicked, thrown, or hit in a game. **2** a single throw or kick of the ball in a game. **3** a rounded part or thing.

SYNONYMS **sphere,** globe, orb, globule, spheroid.

▸ verb squeeze or form something into a ball.
■ **ball bearing 1** a ring of small metal balls which separate moving parts to reduce rubbing. **2** one of these balls.

ball² ▸ noun a formal gathering for dancing and meeting people.

ballad ▸ noun **1** a poem or song telling a story. **2** a slow, sentimental song.

ballast ▸ noun **1** a heavy substance carried by a ship or hot-air balloon to keep it stable. **2** stones used to form the base of a railway track or road.

ballcock ▸ noun a valve which automatically tops up a cistern when liquid is drawn from it.

ballerina ▸ noun a female ballet dancer.

ballet ▸ noun an artistic form of dancing performed to music, using set steps and gestures.
□ **balletic** adjective.

ballistic /buh-**liss**-tik/ ▸ adjective having to do with the flight of missiles, bullets, or similar objects.
■ **ballistic missile** a missile which is fired into the air and falls on to its target.

balloon ▸ noun **1** a small rubber bag which is blown up and used as a toy or decoration. **2** (also **hot-air balloon**) a large bag filled with hot air or gas to make it rise in the air, with a basket for passengers attached to it. **3** a rounded outline in which the words of characters in a cartoon are written.
▸ verb **1** swell outwards. **2** increase quickly. **3** (**ballooning**) travelling by hot-air balloon.

ballot ▸ noun **1** a way of voting on something secretly by putting paper slips in a box. **2** (**the ballot**) the total number of votes recorded.

SYNONYMS **vote,** poll, election, referendum, show of hands, plebiscite.

▸ verb (**ballots, balloting, balloted**) ask people to vote secretly about something.

ballpark ▸ noun N. Amer. a baseball ground.
▸ adjective informal approximate: *a ballpark figure.*

ballpoint pen ▸ noun a pen with a tiny ball as its writing point.

ballroom ▸ noun a large room for formal dancing.
■ **ballroom dancing** formal dancing for couples.

ballyhoo ▸ noun informal a lot of fuss.

b

balm ▸ noun **1** a sweet-smelling ointment used to heal or soothe the skin. **2** something that soothes or heals.

balmy ▸ adjective (**balmier, balmiest**) (of the weather) pleasantly warm.

baloney ▸ noun informal nonsense.

balsa /bawl-suh/ ▸ noun very lightweight wood from a tropical American tree, used for making models.

balsam ▸ noun a scented substance obtained from some trees and shrubs, used in perfumes and medicines.

balti ▸ noun (plural **baltis**) a spicy Pakistani dish that is cooked in a small two-handled pan.

Baltic ▸ adjective relating to the Baltic Sea or the countries on its eastern shores.

baluster ▸ noun a short pillar forming part of a series supporting a rail.

balustrade ▸ noun a railing supported by balusters.

bamboo ▸ noun a giant tropical grass with hollow woody stems.

bamboozle ▸ verb (**bamboozles, bamboozling, bamboozled**) informal cheat or deceive.

ban ▸ verb (**bans, banning, banned**) **1** officially forbid something. **2** forbid someone to do something.

> SYNONYMS **1** *smoking was banned* **prohibit,** forbid, veto, proscribe, outlaw, make illegal, bar. **2** *Gary was banned from the playground* **exclude,** bar, banish, expel, eject, evict, drive out, force out; informal kick out.
> ANTONYMS permit, admit.

▸ noun an official order forbidding something.

> SYNONYMS **1** *a ban on smoking* **prohibition,** veto, bar, proscription, moratorium, injunction. **2** *a ban from league football* **exclusion,** bar, banishment, expulsion, ejection, eviction.
> ANTONYMS permission, admission.

banal /buh-**nahl**/ ▸ adjective boring through being too ordinary and predictable.

> SYNONYMS **unoriginal,** unimaginative, trite, hackneyed, clichéd, commonplace, stereotyped, overused, stale, boring, obvious; informal corny.
> ANTONYMS original.

□ **banality** noun (plural **banalities**) **banally** adverb.

banana ▸ noun a long curved fruit of a tropical tree, with yellow skin.

band¹ ▸ noun **1** a flat, thin strip or loop of material used for fastening, strengthening, or decoration. **2** a stripe or strip that is different from its surroundings.

> SYNONYMS *a band round his wrist* **loop,** wristband, headband, ring, hoop, circlet, belt, sash, girdle, strap, strip, tape, circle.

□ **banded** adjective.

band² ▸ noun **1** a small group of musicians and singers who play pop, jazz, or rock music. **2** a group of musicians who play brass, wind, or percussion instruments. **3** a group of people with the same aim or a shared feature.

> SYNONYMS **1** *the band played on* **group,** pop group, ensemble, orchestra; informal combo. **2** *a band of robbers* **gang,** group, mob, pack, troop, troupe, company, set, party, crew, body, team; informal bunch.

▸ verb form a group with other people.

bandage ▸ noun a strip of material tied round a wound or an injury.

> SYNONYMS **dressing,** covering, plaster, compress, gauze, lint.

▸ verb (**bandages, bandaging, bandaged**) tie a bandage round.

> SYNONYMS *she bandaged my knee* **bind,** dress, cover, strap (up).

bandanna ▸ noun a square of cloth tied round the head or neck.

bandit ▸ noun a member of a gang of armed robbers.

> SYNONYMS **robber,** thief, raider, mugger, pirate, outlaw, hijacker, looter, gangster; literary brigand; historical rustler, highwayman.

□ **banditry** noun.

bandolier /ban-duh-**leer**/ ▸ noun a belt with loops or pockets for carrying bullets, worn over the shoulder.

bandstand ▸ noun a covered outdoor platform for a band to play on.

bandwagon ▸ noun an activity or cause that has suddenly become fashionable or popular.

bandwidth ▸ noun **1** a range of frequencies used in telecommunications. **2** the ability of a computer network to transmit signals.

bandy¹ ▸ adjective (**bandier, bandiest**) (of a person's legs) curved outwards so that the knees are wide apart.

bandy² ▸ verb (**bandies, bandying, bandied**) use an idea or word frequently in casual talk. ■ **bandy words** exchange angry remarks.

bane ▸ noun a cause of great distress or annoyance.

bang ▸ noun **1** a sudden loud noise. **2** a sudden painful blow.

> SYNONYMS **1** *the door slammed with a bang* **thud,** thump, bump, crack, crash, smack, boom, blast, clap, report, explosion. **2** *a bang on the head* **blow,**

knock, thump, bump, hit, smack, crack; informal bash, whack.

▶ **verb 1** hit or put down forcefully and noisily. **2** make a bang.

SYNONYMS **1** *he banged the table with his fist* **hit,** strike, beat, thump, hammer, knock, rap, pound, thud, punch, bump, smack, crack, slap, slam; informal bash, whack, clobber, clout, wallop. **2** *fireworks banged in the air* **thud,** thump, bump, crack, crash, boom, pound, explode, detonate, burst, blow up.

▶ **adverb** Brit. informal exactly: *bang on time.*

banger ▶ **noun** Brit. informal **1** a sausage. **2** an old car. **3** a loud explosive firework.

Bangladeshi ▶ **noun** (plural **Bangladeshis**) a person from Bangladesh.
▶ **adjective** relating to Bangladesh.

bangle ▶ **noun** a bracelet of rigid material worn loosely on the wrist.

banish ▶ **verb 1** make someone leave a place as a punishment. **2** get rid of; drive away.

SYNONYMS **1** *he was banished for his crime* **exile,** expel, deport, eject, repatriate, transport, extradite, evict, throw out, exclude, shut out, ban. **2** *he tried to banish his fear* **dispel,** dismiss, disperse, scatter, dissipate, drive away, chase away, shut out.
ANTONYMS admit, cause, induce.

□ **banishment** noun.

banister (or **bannister**) ▶ **noun 1** the upright posts and handrail at the side of a staircase. **2** a single upright post at the side of a staircase.

banjo ▶ **noun** (plural **banjos** or **banjoes**) a musical instrument like a guitar, with a circular body.

bank¹ ▶ **noun 1** the land alongside a river or lake. **2** a long, high slope, mound, or mass. **3** a set of similar things grouped together in rows.

SYNONYMS **1** *the banks of Lake Michigan* **edge,** shore, side, embankment, levee, margin, verge, brink. **2** *a grassy bank* **slope,** rise, incline, gradient, ramp, mound, pile, heap, ridge, hillock, knoll, bar, shoal, mass, drift. **3** *a bank of switches* **array,** row, line, tier, group, series.

▶ **verb 1** form into a bank. **2** (of an aircraft) tilt sideways in making a turn.

SYNONYMS **1** *they banked up the earth* **pile up,** heap up, stack up, amass. **2** *the aircraft banked* **tilt,** lean, tip, slant, incline, angle, list, camber, pitch.
ANTONYMS level, spread out, level out.

bank² ▶ **noun 1** an organization that makes loans and keeps customers' money for them. **2** a stock or supply of something.

3 a site or container where you can leave something for recycling.

SYNONYMS **store,** reserve, stock, stockpile, supply, pool, fund, cache, hoard, deposit.

▶ **verb 1** put money in a bank. **2** have an account at a bank. **3** (**bank on**) rely on.

SYNONYMS *I banked the money* **deposit,** pay in, save.
ANTONYMS withdraw.

■ **bank holiday** Brit. a public holiday, when banks are officially closed. **break the bank** informal cost more than you can afford.
□ **banker** noun **banking** noun.

bankable ▶ **adjective** certain to bring profit and success.

banknote ▶ **noun** a piece of paper money.

bankroll ▶ **verb** informal give money to.
▶ **noun** N. Amer. a roll of banknotes.

bankrupt ▶ **adjective** officially declared not to have the money to pay your debts.

SYNONYMS **insolvent,** ruined; Brit. in administration, in receivership; informal bust, broke, belly up, wiped out.
ANTONYMS solvent.

▶ **noun** a bankrupt person.
▶ **verb** make someone bankrupt.
□ **bankruptcy** noun (plural **bankruptcies**).

banner ▶ **noun** a long strip of cloth with a slogan or design, hung up or carried on poles.

SYNONYMS **1** *students waved banners* **placard,** sign, poster, notice. **2** *banners fluttered above the troops* **flag,** standard, ensign, colour(s), pennant, banderole.

bannister ➡ BANISTER.

banns ▶ **plural noun** an announcement of an intended marriage read out in a church.

banquet ▶ **noun** an elaborate formal meal for many people.

SYNONYMS **feast,** dinner; informal spread, blowout; Brit. informal nosh-up, slap-up meal.
ANTONYMS snack.

▶ **verb** (**banquets, banqueting, banqueted**) attend a banquet.

banshee ▶ **noun** (in Irish legend) a female spirit whose wailing warns of a death.

bantam ▶ **noun** a kind of small chicken.

banter ▶ **noun** friendly teasing.
▶ **verb** (**banters, bantering, bantered**) make friendly teasing remarks.

banyan ▶ **noun** an Indian fig tree with spreading branches from which roots grow downwards to the ground and form new trunks.

baobab /bay-oh-bab/ ▶ **noun** a short African tree with a very thick trunk.

bap ▶ **noun** Brit. a soft, round, flattish bread roll.

baptism ▶ **noun** the Christian ceremony of sprinkling a person with water or dipping

b

them in it to show that they have entered the Church.

■ **baptism of fire** a difficult new experience.

□ **baptismal** adjective.

Baptist ▶ noun a member of a Christian group believing that only adults, not babies, should be baptized.

baptize (or **baptise**) ▶ verb (**baptizes, baptizing, baptized**) **1** perform the baptism ceremony on someone. **2** give someone a name or nickname.

SYNONYMS **1** *he was baptized as a baby* **christen. 2** *they were baptized into the church* **admit**, initiate, enrol, recruit. **3** *he was baptized Enoch* **name**, call, dub.

bar ▶ noun **1** a long rigid piece of wood, metal, etc. **2** a counter, room, or place where alcohol is served. **3** something that stops or delays progress. **4** any of the short units into which a piece of music is divided. **5** (**the bar**) the place in a courtroom where an accused person stands during a trial. **6** (**the Bar**) the profession of barrister. **7** Brit. a metal strip added to a medal as an additional honour.

SYNONYMS **1** *an iron bar* **rod**, stick, pole, batten, shaft, rail, spar, strut, crosspiece, beam. **2** *a bar of chocolate* **block**, slab, cake, tablet, wedge, ingot. **3** *your drinks are on the bar* **counter**, table, buffet. **4** *she had a drink in a bar* **inn**, tavern, hostelry; Brit. pub, public house; Brit. informal local, boozer. **5** *a bar to promotion* **obstacle**, impediment, hindrance, obstruction, block, hurdle, barrier. ANTONYMS aid.

▶ verb (**bars, barring, barred**) **1** fasten with a bar or bars. **2** forbid or prevent.

SYNONYMS **1** *they have barred the door* **bolt**, lock, fasten, secure, block, barricade, obstruct. **2** *I was barred from entering* **prohibit**, debar, preclude, forbid, ban, exclude, obstruct, prevent, hinder, block. ANTONYMS open, admit, allow.

▶ preposition except for.

■ **bar code** a row of printed stripes identifying a product and its price, able to be read by a computer.

barb ▶ noun **1** the backward-pointing part of a fish hook, the tip of an arrow, etc. **2** a spiteful remark.

barbarian ▶ noun **1** (in ancient times) a person who did not belong to the Greek, Roman, or Christian civilizations. **2** a very uncivilized or cruel person.

SYNONYMS **1** *the city was besieged by barbarians* **savage**, heathen. **2** *you arrogant barbarian!* **brute**, beast,

philistine, boor, yahoo, oaf, lout; Brit. informal yob.

barbaric ▶ adjective **1** savagely cruel. **2** not cultured or civilized.

SYNONYMS **1** *barbaric crimes* **cruel**, brutal, barbarous, brutish, savage, vicious, wicked, ruthless, vile, inhuman. **2** *barbaric cultures* **uncultured**, uncivilized, barbarian, philistine, boorish, loutish; Brit. informal yobbish. ANTONYMS civilized.

barbarism ▶ noun **1** great cruelty. **2** an uncivilized or primitive state.

□ **barbarity** noun (plural **barbarities**).

barbarous ▶ adjective **1** very cruel. **2** uncivilized or uncultured.

barbecue ▶ noun **1** an outdoor meal at which food is grilled over a charcoal fire. **2** a grill used at a barbecue.

▶ verb (**barbecues, barbecuing, barbecued**) cook food on a barbecue.

barbed ▶ adjective **1** having a barb or barbs. **2** (of a remark) spiteful.

□ **barbed wire** wire with clusters of short, sharp spikes along it.

barbel ▶ noun **1** a long, thin growth hanging from the mouth or snout of some fish. **2** a freshwater fish with barbels.

barbell ▶ noun a long metal bar with discs of different weights attached at each end, used for weightlifting.

barber ▶ noun a person whose job is cutting men's hair and shaving or trimming their beards.

barbican ▶ noun a double tower above a gate or drawbridge of a castle.

barbiturate ▶ noun a kind of drug used as a sedative.

bard ▶ noun old use a poet.

bare ▶ adjective **1** not wearing clothes. **2** without the usual covering or contents. **3** without detail; basic. **4** only just enough.

SYNONYMS **1** *he was bare to the waist* **naked**, unclothed, undressed, uncovered, stripped, with nothing on, nude; informal without a stitch on, in the altogether; Brit. informal starkers; Scottish informal in the scud; N. Amer. informal buck naked. **2** *the room was bare* **empty**, unfurnished, clear, undecorated, unadorned. **3** *the bare facts* **basic**, essential, fundamental, plain, straightforward, simple, unembellished, pure, stark, bald, cold, hard. ANTONYMS dressed, furnished, decorated, embellished.

▶ verb (**bares, baring, bared**) uncover or reveal.

□ **bareness** noun.

bareback ▶ adverb & adjective on a horse without a saddle.

barefaced ▶ adjective done openly and without shame.

barefoot (or **barefooted**) ▸ adjective wearing nothing on your feet.

barely ▸ adverb only just; almost not.

> SYNONYMS **hardly**, scarcely, only just, narrowly, by the skin of your teeth, by a hair's breadth; informal by a whisker; Brit. informal at a push.
> ANTONYMS easily.

bargain ▸ noun **1** an agreement made between people to do something for each other. **2** a thing sold at a low price.

> SYNONYMS **1** *I'll make a bargain with you* **agreement**, arrangement, understanding, deal, contract, pact. **2** *this binder is a bargain at £1.98* **good value**; informal good buy, cheap buy, snip, steal, giveaway.
> ANTONYMS rip-off.

▸ verb **1** discuss the terms of an agreement. **2** (**bargain for** or **on**) expect.

> SYNONYMS **haggle**, negotiate, discuss terms, deal, barter.

■ **into the bargain** as well.

> ✔ Remember the second **a**: bar**gain**.

barge ▸ noun a long flat-bottomed boat for carrying goods on canals and rivers.
▸ verb (**barges**, **barging**, **barged**) **1** move forcefully or roughly. **2** (**barge in**) burst in on someone rudely.

baritone ▸ noun a man's singing voice between tenor and bass.

barium ▸ noun a chemical element that is a soft white metal.

bark[1] ▸ noun the sharp sudden cry of a dog, fox, or seal.
▸ verb **1** give a bark. **2** say a command or question suddenly or fiercely. **3** (**barking**) Brit. informal completely mad.

> SYNONYMS **1** *the dog barked* **woof**, yap. **2** *'Okay, outside!' he barked* **shout**, snap, bawl, yell, roar, bellow, thunder; informal holler.
> ANTONYMS whisper.

bark[2] ▸ noun the tough outer covering of the trunk and branches of a tree.

> SYNONYMS *the bark of a tree* **rind**, skin, peel, covering.

▸ verb scrape the skin off your shin by accidentally hitting it.

barley ▸ noun a type of cereal plant with a bristly head.
■ **barley sugar** an orange sweet made of boiled sugar.

barmaid ▸ noun a woman who serves drinks in a bar or pub.

barman ▸ noun (plural **barmen**) a man who serves drinks in a bar or pub.

bar mitzvah /bar mits-vuh/ ▸ noun a religious ceremony in which a Jewish boy aged 13 takes on the responsibilities of an adult.

barmy ▸ adjective (**barmier**, **barmiest**) Brit. informal mad.

barn ▸ noun a large farm building used for storing hay or grain or keeping livestock.
■ **barn dance** a party with country dancing.

barnacle ▸ noun a small shellfish which fixes itself to things.

barnstorming ▸ adjective done in a very showy, energetic way.

barnyard ▸ noun N. Amer. a farmyard.

barometer ▸ noun an instrument that measures the pressure of the atmosphere, used to forecast the weather.

baron ▸ noun **1** a man belonging to the lowest rank of the British nobility. **2** (in the Middle Ages) a man who held lands or property granted to him by the king or queen or a lord. **3** a powerful person in business or industry.
□ **baronial** adjective.

baroness ▸ noun **1** the wife or widow of a baron. **2** a woman holding the rank of baron.

baronet ▸ noun a man who holds a title below that of baron.

baroque /buh-**rok**/ ▸ adjective in a highly decorated style of European architecture, art, and music popular during the 17th and 18th centuries.

barque /bark/ ▸ noun **1** a sailing ship with three masts. **2** literary a boat.

barrack ▸ verb Brit. shout loud insulting comments at a performer or speaker.

barracks ▸ plural noun a building or set of buildings for soldiers to live in.

> SYNONYMS **garrison**, camp, encampment, depot, billet, quarters, fort, cantonment.

barracuda /ba-ruh-**koo**-duh/ ▸ noun (plural **barracuda** or **barracudas**) a large predatory fish found in tropical seas.

barrage ▸ noun **1** a continuous attack by heavy guns. **2** an overwhelming number of questions or complaints. **3** a barrier placed across a river to control the water level.

> SYNONYMS **1** *an artillery barrage* **bombardment**, gunfire, shelling, salvo, volley, fusillade; historical broadside.
> **2** *a barrage of criticism* **deluge**, stream, storm, torrent, onslaught, flood, spate, tide, avalanche, hail, blaze. **3** *a barrage across the river* **dam**, barrier, weir, dyke, embankment, wall.

barrel ▸ noun **1** a large cylindrical container bulging out in the middle and with flat ends. **2** a tube forming part of a gun, pen, etc.

> SYNONYMS **cask**, keg, butt, vat, tun, drum, hogshead, firkin.

b

■ **barrel organ** a small organ that plays a tune when you turn a handle.

barren ▸ adjective **1** (of land) not good enough to produce plants or crops. **2** unable to produce children or young animals. **3** bleak.

> SYNONYMS **unproductive,** infertile, unfruitful, sterile, arid, desert.
> ANTONYMS fertile.

barrette /ba-ret/ ▸ noun a hairslide.

barricade ▸ noun a makeshift barrier used to block a road or entrance.

> SYNONYMS *a barricade across the street* **barrier,** roadblock, blockade, obstacle, obstruction.

▸ verb (**barricades, barricading, barricaded**) block or defend with a barricade.

> SYNONYMS *they barricaded the building* **seal up,** close up, block off, shut off/up, defend, protect, fortify, occupy.

barrier ▸ noun something that stops people entering a place or making progress.

> SYNONYMS **1 fence,** railing, barricade, hurdle, bar, blockade, roadblock. **2** *a barrier to international trade* **obstacle,** obstruction, hurdle, stumbling block, bar, impediment, hindrance, curb.

barring ▸ preposition except for; if not for.

barrister ▸ noun Brit. a lawyer qualified to argue a case in court.

barrow¹ ▸ noun Brit. a two-wheeled cart pushed by hand and used by street traders.

barrow² ▸ noun a mound of earth built over a grave in ancient times.

bartender ▸ noun a person serving drinks at a bar.

barter ▸ verb (**barters, bartering, bartered**) exchange goods or services for other goods or services.

> SYNONYMS **1** *they bartered grain for salt* **trade,** swap, exchange, sell. **2** *you can barter for souvenirs* **haggle,** bargain, negotiate, deal.

▸ noun trade by bartering.

basalt /ba-sawlt/ ▸ noun a dark volcanic rock.

base¹ ▸ noun **1** the lowest or supporting part of something. **2** the main place where a person works or stays. **3** a centre of operations: *a military base.* **4** a main element to which others are added. **5** Chemistry a substance able to react with an acid to form a salt and water. **6** Baseball each of the four points that you must reach in turn to score a run.

> SYNONYMS **1** *the base of the tower* **foundation,** bottom, foot, support, stand, pedestal, plinth. **2** *the system uses existing technology as its base* **basis,** foundation, bedrock, starting

point, source, origin, root(s), core, key component. **3** *the troops returned to their base* **headquarters,** camp, site, station, settlement, post, centre.
> ANTONYMS top.

▸ verb (**bases, basing, based**) **1** (**base something on**) use something as the foundation for something else. **2** station someone or something at a particular base.

> SYNONYMS **1** *he based his idea on a movie* **found,** build, construct, form, ground; (**be based on**) derive from, spring from, stem from, depend on. **2** *the company was based in London* **locate,** situate, position, install, station, site.

base² ▸ adjective **1** bad or immoral. **2** old use of low social class.

> SYNONYMS *base motives* **sordid,** ignoble, low, mean, immoral, unscrupulous, unprincipled, dishonest, dishonourable, shameful.
> ANTONYMS noble.

■ **base metal** a common non-precious metal.

baseball ▸ noun a game played with a bat and ball on a diamond-shaped circuit of four bases, which a batsman must run around to score.

■ **baseball cap** a cotton cap with a large peak.

baseless ▸ adjective not based on fact; untrue.

baseline ▸ noun **1** a starting point for comparisons. **2** (in tennis, volleyball, etc.) the line marking each end of a court.

basement ▸ noun a room or floor below ground level.

bases plural of BASE¹ and BASIS.

bash informal ▸ verb hit hard and violently. ▸ noun **1** a heavy blow. **2** a party. **3** Brit. an attempt.

bashful ▸ adjective shy and easily embarrassed.

> SYNONYMS **shy,** reserved, diffident, inhibited, retiring, reticent, reluctant, shrinking, timid, nervous.
> ANTONYMS bold, confident.

□ **bashfully** adverb.

basic ▸ adjective **1** forming an essential foundation; fundamental. **2** of the simplest or lowest kind or standard.

> SYNONYMS **1** *basic human rights* **fundamental,** essential, vital, primary, principal, cardinal, elementary, intrinsic, central, pivotal, critical, key, focal. **2** *basic cooking facilities* **plain,** simple, unsophisticated, straightforward, adequate, spartan, stark, severe, austere, limited, meagre, rudimentary, patchy, sketchy, minimal, crude, makeshift; informal bog-standard.

ANTONYMS secondary, unimportant, elaborate.

basically ▸ adverb **1** in the most fundamental respects. **2** used to sum up a complex situation: *I basically did the same thing every day.*

> SYNONYMS **fundamentally,** essentially, first and foremost, primarily, at heart, at bottom, intrinsically, inherently, principally, chiefly, above all, mostly, mainly, on the whole, by and large; informal at the end of the day.

basics ▸ plural noun essential facts or principles.

> SYNONYMS **fundamentals,** essentials, first principles, foundations, preliminaries, groundwork, essence, basis, core; informal nitty-gritty, brass tacks, nuts and bolts, ABC.

basil ▸ noun a herb used in cooking.

basilica /buh-**zil**-i-kuh/ ▸ noun a large church or hall with two rows of columns inside and a curved end with a dome.

basilisk /**baz**-i-lisk/ ▸ noun a mythical reptile that could kill people by looking at or breathing on them.

basin ▸ noun **1** a large bowl or open container for holding liquid. **2** a circular valley. **3** an area drained by a river. **4** an enclosed area of water for mooring boats.

> SYNONYMS **bowl,** dish, pan.

basis ▸ noun (plural **bases** /**bay**-seez/) **1** the foundation of a theory or process. **2** the reasons why something is done.

> SYNONYMS **1** *the basis of his method* **foundation,** support, base, reasoning, rationale, defence, reason, grounds, justification. **2** *the basis of discussion* **starting point,** base, point of departure, beginning, premise, fundamental point/principle, cornerstone, core, heart. **3** *on a part-time basis* **footing,** condition, status, position, arrangement.

bask ▸ verb **1** lie in the sun for pleasure. **2** (bask in) take great pleasure in.

> SYNONYMS **laze,** lie, lounge, relax, sprawl, loll.

basket ▸ noun **1** a container for carrying things, made from strips of cane or wire. **2** a net fixed on a hoop, used as the goal in basketball.

basketball ▸ noun a team game in which goals are scored by throwing a ball through a hoop.

basmati rice /baz-**mah**-ti/ ▸ noun a kind of long-grain Indian rice.

Basque /bask, bahsk/ ▸ noun **1** a member of a people living in the western Pyrenees in France and Spain. **2** the language of the Basques.

bass¹ /bayss/ ▸ noun **1** the lowest adult male singing voice. **2** a bass guitar or double bass. **3** the deep, low-frequency part of sound. ▫ bassist noun.

bass² /bass/ ▸ noun (plural **bass** or **basses**) a fish related to the perch, used for food.

basset hound ▸ noun a breed of hunting dog with a long body, short legs, and long, drooping ears.

bassoon ▸ noun a large low-pitched woodwind instrument. ▫ bassoonist noun.

bastard ▸ noun **1** old use a person who was born when their parents were not married. **2** informal a nasty person.

bastardize (or bastardise) ▸ verb (bastardizes, bastardizing, bastardized) make something less good by adding new elements.

baste ▸ verb (bastes, basting, basted) pour fat or juices over meat while it cooks.

bastion ▸ noun **1** a part of a fortified building that sticks out. **2** something that protects or preserves particular principles or activities.

bat¹ ▸ noun a piece of wood with a handle and a solid surface, used in sports for hitting the ball.
▸ verb (bats, batting, batted) **1** (in sport) take the role of hitting rather than throwing the ball. **2** hit with the flat of your hand.
■ off your own bat Brit. informal of your own accord.

bat² ▸ noun **1** a flying animal that is active at night. **2** (old bat) informal an unpleasant woman.

bat³ ▸ verb (bats, batting, batted) flutter your eyelashes.

batch ▸ noun a quantity of goods produced or dispatched at one time.

> SYNONYMS **group,** quantity, lot, bunch, cluster, raft, set, collection, bundle, pack, consignment, shipment.

bated ▸ adjective (with bated breath) in great suspense.

> ✔ This expression has nothing to do with bait: ba**te**d, not ba**i**ted.

bath ▸ noun **1** a large tub that you fill with water and sit or lie in to wash your body. **2** an act of washing yourself in a bath. **3** (also baths) Brit. a building containing a public swimming pool or washing facilities.
▸ verb Brit. wash in a bath.

bathe ▸ verb (bathes, bathing, bathed) **1** wash by putting your body in water. **2** Brit. have a swim. **3** soak or wipe gently with liquid.

> SYNONYMS **1** *I bathed in the pool* **swim,** take a dip. **2** *they bathed his wounds*

b

clean, wash, rinse, wet, soak. **3** *the room was bathed in light* **flood**, cover, envelop, fill, wash, pervade, suffuse.

▶ noun Brit. a swim.
□ **bather** noun.

bathos /bay-thoss/ ▶ noun (in literature) a change from a serious mood to something trivial.

bathroom ▶ noun **1** a room containing a bath and usually also a washbasin and toilet. **2** N. Amer. a room containing a toilet.

batik /ba-**teek**/ ▶ noun a method of producing coloured designs on cloth using wax to cover the areas not to be dyed.

baton ▶ noun **1** a thin stick used to conduct an orchestra or choir. **2** a short stick passed from runner to runner in a relay race. **3** a police officer's truncheon.

SYNONYMS **1** *the conductor's baton* **stick**, rod, staff, wand. **2** *police batons* **truncheon**, club, cudgel, stick, mace, shillelagh; N. Amer. nightstick, blackjack; Brit. informal cosh.

batsman ▶ noun (plural **batsmen**) a player who bats in cricket.

battalion ▶ noun an army unit forming part of a brigade.

batten ▶ noun a long wooden or metal strip used for strengthening or securing something.
■ **batten down the hatches** prepare for a crisis.

batter¹ ▶ verb (**batters, battering, battered**) hit repeatedly with hard blows.

SYNONYMS **beat up**, hit repeatedly, pummel, pound, rain blows on, buffet, belabour, thrash; informal knock about/ around, lay into, do over.

batter² ▶ noun a mixture of flour, egg, and milk or water, used for making pancakes or coating food before frying.

battery ▶ noun (plural **batteries**) **1** a device containing one or more electrical cells, used as a source of power. **2** an extensive series: *a battery of tests.* **3** Brit. a series of small cages for keeping chickens in artificial conditions. **4** Law an unlawful physical attack on another person.

battle ▶ noun **1** a prolonged fight between organized armed forces. **2** a long and difficult struggle or conflict.

SYNONYMS **1** *he was killed in the battle* **fight**, engagement, armed conflict, clash, struggle, skirmish, fray, war, campaign, crusade, warfare, combat, action, hostilities; informal scrap, dogfight, shoot-out. **2** *a legal battle* **conflict**, clash, struggle, disagreement, argument, dispute.
ANTONYMS peace.

▶ verb (**battles, battling, battled**) fight or struggle with determination.

SYNONYMS **fight**, combat, contend with, resist, withstand, stand up to, confront, war, feud, struggle, strive, work.

battleaxe ▶ noun **1** a large axe used in ancient warfare. **2** informal an aggressive older woman.

battledress ▶ noun clothing worn by soldiers for fighting.

battlefield ▶ noun the piece of ground where a battle is fought.

SYNONYMS **battleground**, field of battle, field of operations, combat zone, lines, front, theatre of war.

battlement ▶ noun a wall at the top of a castle with gaps for firing through.

battleship ▶ noun a heavily armoured warship with large guns.

batty ▶ adjective (**battier, battiest**) informal mad.

bauble ▶ noun a small, showy trinket or decoration.

baulk /bawlk/ (US spelling **balk**) ▶ verb **1** (**baulk at**) hesitate to accept an idea. **2** prevent from getting or doing something.

bauxite ▶ noun a clay-like rock from which aluminium is obtained.

bawdy ▶ adjective (**bawdier, bawdiest**) referring to sex in an amusing way.

bawl ▶ verb **1** shout out noisily. **2** cry noisily.

SYNONYMS **1** *'Come on!' he bawled* **shout**, yell, roar, bellow, screech, scream, shriek, bark, thunder; informal yammer, holler. **2** *the children continued to bawl* **cry**, sob, weep, wail, whine, howl; Scottish informal greet.
ANTONYMS whisper.

▶ noun a loud shout.

bay¹ ▶ noun an area of sea and coast forming a broad curve.

SYNONYMS *ships were anchored in the bay* **cove**, inlet, gulf, sound, bight, basin, fjord.

bay² ▶ noun a Mediterranean shrub whose leaves are used in cookery.

bay³ ▶ noun **1** a window area that sticks out from a wall. **2** an area for a particular purpose: *a loading bay.*

SYNONYMS *there was a bay let into the wall* **alcove**, recess, niche, nook, opening, inglenook.

■ **bay window** a window sticking out from a wall.

bay⁴ ▶ adjective (of a horse) mainly reddish-brown in colour.

bay⁵ ▶ verb (of a dog) bark or howl loudly.
■ **at bay** trapped or cornered. **hold** (or **keep**) **someone/thing at bay** prevent

someone or something from approaching
or having an effect.

bayonet ▸ noun a long blade fixed to a rifle
for hand-to-hand fighting.
▸ verb (**bayonets**, **bayoneting**, **bayoneted**)
stab someone with a bayonet.

bazaar ▸ noun **1** a market in a Middle Eastern
country. **2** a sale of goods to raise funds.

> SYNONYMS **1** *a Turkish bazaar* **market**,
> marketplace, souk, mart. **2** *the church
> bazaar* **fête**, fair, fund-raiser, charity
> event; Brit. jumble sale, bring-and-buy
> sale, car boot sale; N. Amer. tag sale.

bazooka ▸ noun a short-range rocket
launcher used against tanks.

BBC ▸ abbreviation British Broadcasting
Corporation.

BC ▸ abbreviation before Christ (used to show
that a date is before the traditional date of
Jesus's birth).

> ❗ Write BC **after** the numerals, as in *72 BC.*

be ▸ verb (singular present **am**; **are**; **is**; plural present
are; 1st and 3rd singular past **was**; 2nd singular past
and plural past **were**; present participle **being**; past
participle **been**) **1** exist; be present. **2** happen.
3 have the specified state, nature, or role.
4 come, go, or visit.
▸ auxiliary verb **1** used with a present participle
to form continuous tenses. **2** used with a
past participle to form the passive voice.
3 used to show something that is due to,
may, or should happen.

beach ▸ noun a shore of sand or pebbles at
the edge of the sea.

> SYNONYMS **sands**, seaside, seashore, coast;
> literary strand.

▸ verb bring something on to a beach from
the water.

> SYNONYMS *they beached the boat* **land**,
> ground, strand, run ashore.

beachcomber ▸ noun a person who
searches beaches for valuable things.

beacon ▸ noun **1** a fire lit on the top of a hill
as a signal. **2** a light acting as a signal for
ships or aircraft.

> SYNONYMS **signal**, light, fire, danger
> signal, bonfire, lighthouse.

bead ▸ noun **1** a small piece of glass, stone,
etc., threaded with others to make a
necklace. **2** a drop of a liquid on a surface.

> SYNONYMS **1** *a string of beads* **ball**, pellet,
> pill, globule, sphere, spheroid, orb,
> round; (**beads**) necklace, rosary, chaplet.
> **2** *beads of sweat* **droplet**, drop, drip,
> blob, pearl, dot.

□ **beaded** adjective.

beadle ▸ noun Brit. **1** an official of a church,
college, etc. **2** historical a parish officer who

dealt with minor offenders.

beady ▸ adjective (of a person's eyes) small,
round, and observant.

beagle ▸ noun a small short-legged breed
of hound.

beak ▸ noun a bird's hard projecting jaws.

beaker ▸ noun Brit. **1** a tall plastic cup.
2 a cylindrical glass container used in
laboratories.

> SYNONYMS **cup**, tumbler, glass, mug,
> drinking vessel.

beam ▸ noun **1** a long piece of timber or
metal used as a support in building. **2** a
narrow length of timber for balancing on in
gymnastics. **3** a ray of light or particles. **4** a
wide, happy smile. **5** the width of a ship.

> SYNONYMS **1** *an oak beam* **plank**, timber,
> joist, rafter, lintel, spar, girder, support.
> **2** *a beam of light* **ray**, shaft, stream,
> streak, flash, gleam, glint. **3** *the beam on
> her face* **grin**, smile.
> ANTONYMS frown.

▸ verb **1** transmit a radio signal. **2** shine
brightly. **3** smile broadly.

> SYNONYMS **1** *the signal is beamed out*
> **broadcast**, transmit, relay, disseminate,
> direct, send, aim. **2** *the sun beamed down*
> **shine**, radiate, glare, gleam. **3** *he beamed
> broadly* **grin**, smile, smirk.
> ANTONYMS frown.

bean ▸ noun **1** an edible seed growing in
long pods on certain plants. **2** the hard seed
of a coffee or cocoa plant.
■ **full of beans** informal in high spirits.

beanbag ▸ noun **1** a small bag filled with
dried beans and used in children's games.
2 a large cushion filled with polystyrene
beads, used as a seat.

bear¹ ▸ verb (**bears**, **bearing**, **bore**; past participle
borne) **1** carry. **2** have a particular quality
or visible mark. **3** support a weight. **4** (**bear
yourself**) behave in a particular way.
5 tolerate. **6** give birth to a child. **7** (of
a tree or plant) produce fruit or flowers.
8 turn and go in a particular direction.

> SYNONYMS **1** *she was bearing a box* **carry**,
> bring, transport, move, convey, take,
> fetch; informal tote. **2** *the bag bore my
> name* **display**, be marked with, show,
> carry, exhibit. **3** *will it bear his weight?*
> **support**, withstand, sustain, stand,
> take, carry, hold up, cope with, handle.
> **4** *she bore no grudge* **harbour**, foster,
> entertain, cherish, nurse. **5** *I can't bear
> sport* **endure**, tolerate, put up with,
> stand, abide, countenance, stomach;
> informal hack, swallow; Brit. informal stick,
> wear, be doing with; formal brook. **6** *she
> bore a son* **give birth to**, bring forth,
> deliver, have, produce, spawn. **7** *a shrub*

b

that bears berries **produce,** yield, give, provide, supply.

■ **bear down on** approach someone in a determined or threatening way. **bear something in mind** remember and take something into account. **bear something out** support or confirm something. **bear up** remain cheerful in difficult circumstances. **bear with** be patient with.
□ **bearable** adjective **bearably** adverb.

bear² ▸ noun a large, heavy animal with thick fur.

beard ▸ noun a growth of hair on a man's chin and lower cheeks.
▸ verb boldly confront or challenge an important or powerful person.
□ **bearded** adjective.

bearer ▸ noun a person or thing that carries something.

SYNONYMS **1** *a lantern-bearer* **carrier,** porter. **2** *the bearer of bad news* **bringer,** messenger, agent, conveyor, emissary.

bearing ▸ noun **1** a person's way of standing, moving, or behaving. **2** relevance. **3** (**bearings**) a part of a machine that allows one part to rotate or move in contact with another. **4** direction or position in relation to a fixed point. **5** (**your bearings**) awareness of where you are.

SYNONYMS **1** *a man of military bearing* **posture,** stance, carriage, gait; Brit. deportment. **2** *a rather regal bearing* **demeanour,** manner, air, aspect, attitude, style. **3** *this has no bearing on the matter* **relevance,** pertinence, connection, import, significance. **4** *a bearing of 015°* **direction,** orientation, course, trajectory, heading, tack, path. **5** (**bearings**) **orientation,** sense of direction, whereabouts, location, position.
ANTONYMS irrelevance.

bearskin ▸ noun a tall black fur cap worn on ceremonial occasions by some British troops.

beast ▸ noun **1** an animal, especially a large or dangerous mammal. **2** a very cruel or wicked person.

SYNONYMS **1** *the beasts of the forest* **animal,** creature, brute; N. Amer. informal critter. **2** *he is a cruel beast* **monster,** brute, savage, barbarian, animal, swine, ogre, fiend, sadist, demon, devil.

■ **beast of burden** an animal used for carrying loads.

beastly ▸ adjective Brit. informal very unpleasant.
□ **beastliness** noun.

beat ▸ verb (**beats, beating, beat**; past participle **beaten**) **1** hit someone repeatedly and violently. **2** hit something repeatedly to flatten it or make a noise. **3** defeat or be better than. **4** informal baffle someone. **5** (of the heart) throb. **6** (of a bird) move its wings up and down. **7** stir cooking ingredients vigorously.

SYNONYMS **1** hit, strike, batter, thump, bang, hammer, punch, knock, thrash, pound, pummel, slap, rain blows on, assault; informal wallop, belt, bash, whack, clout, clobber. **2** *her heart was still beating* **throb,** pulse, pulsate, pump, palpitate, pound, thump, thud, hammer, drum. **3** *the eagle beat its wings* **flap,** flutter, thrash, wave, vibrate. **4** *beat the cream into the mixture* **whisk,** mix, blend, whip. **5** *the team they need to beat* **defeat,** conquer, vanquish, trounce, rout, overpower, overcome; informal lick, thrash, whip. **6** *he beat the record* **exceed,** surpass, better, improve on, eclipse, transcend, top, trump, cap.

▸ noun **1** an act of beating. **2** the main rhythm, or a unit of rhythm, in music or poetry. **3** a brief pause. **4** an area patrolled by a police officer.

SYNONYMS **1** *the song has a good beat* **rhythm,** pulse, metre, time, measure, cadence, stress, accent. **2** *the beat of hooves* **pounding,** banging, thumping, thudding, hammering, crashing. **3** *the beat of her heart* **pulse,** pulsation, vibration, throb, palpitation, reverberation, pounding, thump, thud, hammering, drumming. **4** *a policeman on his beat* **circuit,** round, route, path.

▸ adjective informal completely exhausted.
■ **beat about the bush** discuss something without coming to the point. **beat it** informal leave. **beat someone up** hit or kick someone repeatedly. **off the beaten track** isolated.

beatific /bee-uh-**tif**-ik/ ▸ adjective feeling or expressing blissful happiness.
□ **beatifically** adverb.

beatify /bi-**at**-i-fy/ ▸ verb (**beatifies, beatifying, beatified**) state officially that a dead person is very holy (the first step towards making them a saint).

beatitude /bi-**at**-i-tyood/ ▸ noun very great happiness or blessedness.

beatnik ▸ noun a young person in the 1950s and early 1960s who rejected conventional society.

beau /boh/ ▸ noun (plural **beaux** or **beaus** /bohz, boh/) dated a young woman's boyfriend.

Beaujolais /**boh**-zhuh-lay/ ▸ noun a light red wine from the Beaujolais district of France.

beauteous ▸ adjective literary beautiful.

beautician ▸ noun a person whose job is to give beauty treatments.

b

beautiful ▶ adjective **1** very pleasing to the senses. **2** of a very high standard; excellent.

SYNONYMS **attractive**, pretty, handsome, good-looking, fetching, lovely, charming, graceful, elegant, appealing, winsome, ravishing, gorgeous, stunning, glamorous; Scottish & N. English **bonny**; informal tasty, knockout, drop-dead gorgeous; Brit. informal **smashing**; N. Amer. informal cute, foxy; Austral./NZ informal beaut, spunky. ANTONYMS ugly.

☐ **beautifully** adverb.

✔ Remember the **u** before the **t**: bea**u**tiful.

beautify ▶ verb (**beautifies, beautifying, beautified**) make someone or something look more attractive.

beauty ▶ noun (plural **beauties**) **1** the quality of being very pleasing to the senses. **2** a beautiful woman. **3** an excellent example of something. **4** an attractive feature or advantage.

SYNONYMS **1 attractiveness**, prettiness, good looks, loveliness, appeal, winsomeness, charm, grace, elegance, exquisiteness, glamour; Scottish & N. English bonniness. **2** *she is a beauty* **belle**, vision, goddess, picture, Venus; informal babe, looker, lovely, stunner, knockout, bombshell, bit of all right. ANTONYMS ugliness, hag, boot.

beaver ▶ noun (plural **beaver** or **beavers**) a large rodent that lives partly in water.
▶ verb (**beavers, beavering, beavered**) (**beaver away**) informal work hard.

bebop /**bee**-bop/ ▶ noun a type of jazz with complex rhythms.

becalmed ▶ adjective (of a sailing ship) unable to move because there is no wind.

because ▶ conjunction for the reason that; since.

SYNONYMS **since**, as, seeing that, in view of the fact that, in that.

béchamel /**bay**-shuh-mel/ ▶ noun a rich white sauce flavoured with herbs and other seasonings.

beck ▶ noun (**at someone's beck and call**) always having to be ready to obey someone's orders.

beckon ▶ verb **1** make a movement encouraging someone to approach or follow. **2** seem appealing.

SYNONYMS **1** *the guard beckoned to Benny* **gesture**, signal, wave, gesticulate, motion. **2** *the countryside beckons you* **entice**, invite, tempt, lure, charm, attract, draw, call.

become ▶ verb (**becomes, becoming, became**; past participle **become**) **1** begin to be. **2** turn into. **3** (**become of**) happen to. **4** suit or be appropriate to.

SYNONYMS **1** *she became rich* **grow**, get, turn, come to be, get to be. **2** *he became a tyrant* **turn into**, change into, transform into, be converted into. **3** *he became Foreign Secretary* **be appointed**, be assigned as, be nominated, be elected. **4** *the dress becomes her* **suit**, flatter, look good on, set off; informal do something for.

becoming ▶ adjective (of clothing) looking good on someone.

SYNONYMS **flattering**, fetching, attractive, pretty, elegant, handsome, well-chosen, stylish, fashionable, tasteful.

becquerel /**bek**-kuh-rel/ ▶ noun a unit of radioactivity.

bed ▶ noun **1** a piece of furniture for sleeping on. **2** an area of ground where flowers and shrubs are grown. **3** a flat base.

SYNONYMS **1 couch**, berth, billet, cot; informal the sack. **2** *a flower bed* **patch**, plot, border, strip. **3** *built on a bed of stones* **base**, foundation, footing, support, basis.

▶ verb (**beds, bedding, bedded**) **1** (**bed down**) sleep in a place where you do not usually sleep. **2** (**bed something in**) fix something firmly.

SYNONYMS *the tiles are bedded in mortar* **embed**, set, fix, insert, inlay, implant, bury, plant.

bedclothes ▶ plural noun coverings for a bed, such as sheets and blankets.

bedding ▶ noun **1** bedclothes. **2** straw for animals to sleep on.

bedevil ▶ verb (**bedevils, bedevilling, bedevilled**; US spelling **bedevils, bedeviling, bedeviled**) cause continual trouble to.

bedlam ▶ noun a scene of great confusion and noise.

Bedouin /**bed**-oo-in/ ▶ noun (plural **Bedouin**) an Arab living as a nomad in the desert.

bedpan ▶ noun a container used as a toilet by a bedridden patient.

bedraggled ▶ adjective untidy.

SYNONYMS **dishevelled**, disordered, untidy, unkempt, tousled; N. Amer. informal mussed. ANTONYMS neat.

bedridden ▶ adjective unable to get out of bed because of illness or old age.

bedrock ▶ noun **1** a layer of solid rock under soil. **2** the central principles on which something is based.

bedroom ▶ noun a room for sleeping in.

bedsit (or **bedsitter**) ▶ noun Brit. a rented room consisting of a combined bedroom and living room, with cooking facilities.

b

bedsore ▸ noun a sore caused by lying in bed in one position for a long time.

bedspread ▸ noun a decorative cloth used to cover a bed.

bedstead ▸ noun the framework of a bed.

bee ▸ noun a winged insect which collects nectar and pollen from flowers and makes wax and honey.

beech ▸ noun a large tree with grey bark and pale wood.

beef ▸ noun the flesh of a cow, bull, or ox, used as food.
▸ verb (**beef something up**) informal make something stronger or larger.

beefburger ▸ noun a fried or grilled cake of minced beef eaten in a bun.

beefy ▸ adjective (**beefier, beefiest**) informal muscular or strong.

beehive ▸ noun a structure in which bees are kept.

beeline ▸ noun (**make a beeline for**) hurry straight to.

Beelzebub /bi-el-zi-bub/ ▸ noun the Devil.

been past participle of **BE**.

beep ▸ noun a short, high-pitched sound made by electronic equipment or the horn of a vehicle.
▸ verb produce a beep.

beer ▸ noun an alcoholic drink made from fermented malt flavoured with hops.

beeswax ▸ noun wax produced by bees to make honeycombs, used for wood polishes and candles.

beet ▸ noun a plant with a fleshy root, grown as food and for making into sugar.

beetle ▸ noun an insect with hard, shiny covers over its wings.

beetroot ▸ noun Brit. the edible dark-red root of a kind of beet.

befall ▸ verb (**befalls, befalling, befell**; past participle **befallen**) literary (of something bad) happen to someone.

befit ▸ verb (**befits, befitting, befitted**) be appropriate for.
□ **befitting** adjective.

before ▸ preposition, conjunction, & adverb 1 during the time preceding. 2 in front of. 3 rather than.

SYNONYMS 1 *he dressed up before going out* **prior to**, previous to, earlier than, preparatory to, in advance of, ahead of, pre-.... 2 *he appeared before the judge* **in front of**, in the presence of. 3 *death before dishonour* **in preference to**, rather than, sooner than.
ANTONYMS after.

beforehand ▸ adverb in advance.

SYNONYMS **in advance**, in readiness, ahead of time, before, before now/then,

earlier (on), previously, already, sooner.
ANTONYMS afterwards.

befriend ▸ verb become a friend to.

befuddled ▸ adjective confused.

beg ▸ verb (**begs, begging, begged**) 1 humbly ask someone for something. 2 ask for food or money as charity.

SYNONYMS 1 *he begged on the streets* **ask for money**, seek charity; informal sponge, cadge, scrounge, bum. 2 *we begged for mercy* **plead for**, request, ask for, appeal for, call for, sue for, solicit, seek. 3 *he begged her not to go* **implore**, entreat, plead with, appeal to, pray to, call on, petition; literary beseech.

■ **beg the question** 1 (of a fact or action) invite a question or point that has not been dealt with. 2 assume that something is true without discussing it. **go begging** be available because other people do not want it.

beget /bi-get/ ▸ verb (**begets, begetting, begot** or **begat**; past participle **begotten**) old use 1 cause something. 2 become the father of a child.

beggar ▸ noun 1 a person who lives by begging for food or money. 2 informal a particular type of person: *lucky beggar!*

SYNONYMS **tramp**, vagrant, vagabond, mendicant; N. Amer. hobo; informal scrounger, sponger, cadger, freeloader; Brit. informal dosser; N. Amer. informal bum; Austral./NZ informal bagman.

■ **beggar belief** be too extraordinary to be believed.
□ **beggarly** adjective.

begin ▸ verb (**begins, beginning, began**; past participle **begun**) 1 carry out or experience the first part of an action or activity. 2 come into being. 3 have a particular starting point. 4 (**begin on**) set to work on.

SYNONYMS 1 *we began work* **start**, commence, set about, go about, embark on, launch into, get down to, take up, initiate, set in motion, get going, get off the ground, lead off, institute, inaugurate, open; informal get cracking on, kick off. 2 *when did the illness begin?* **appear**, arise, become apparent, spring up, crop up, turn up, come into existence, originate, start, commence, develop.
ANTONYMS finish, end, disappear.

beginner ▸ noun a person just starting to learn a skill or take part in an activity.

SYNONYMS **novice**, learner, starter, (raw) recruit, newcomer, tyro, fresher, probationer; N. Amer. tenderfoot; informal rookie, new kid (on the block), newie; N. Amer. informal greenhorn.
ANTONYMS expert, veteran.

b

beginning ▸ noun **1** the time or place at which something begins. **2** the first or earliest part.

SYNONYMS **1** *the beginning of socialism* **start**, commencement, creation, birth, inception, conception, origination, origin, genesis, emergence, rise, dawn, launch, onset, outset, day one; informal kick-off. **2** *the beginning of the article* **opening**, start, commencement, first part, introduction, preamble.
ANTONYMS end, conclusion.

begonia /bi-**goh**-ni-uh/ ▸ noun a plant with brightly coloured flowers.

begrudge ▸ verb **1** feel envious that someone possesses something. **2** give something resentfully.

beguile ▸ verb charm or trick.

behalf ▸ noun (**on behalf of** or **on someone's behalf**) **1** in the interests of a particular person, group, or principle. **2** as a representative of.

behave ▸ verb **1** act in a certain way. **2** (also **behave yourself**) act in a polite or proper way.

SYNONYMS **1** *she behaved badly* **act**, conduct yourself, acquit yourself. **2** *the children behaved themselves* **act correctly**, be good, be well behaved, conduct yourself well.
ANTONYMS misbehave.

behaved ▸ adjective acting in a certain way: *a well-behaved child.*

behaviour (US spelling **behavior**) ▸ noun the way in which someone or something behaves.

SYNONYMS **1** *his behaviour was inexcusable* **conduct**, actions, doings, manners, ways, deportment, bearing, etiquette. **2** *the behaviour of these organisms* **functioning**, action, performance, operation, working, reaction, response.

□ **behavioural** adjective.

behead ▸ verb execute someone by cutting off their head.

behemoth /bi-**hee**-moth/ ▸ noun a huge creature, or a very large organization.

behest /bi-**hest**/ ▸ noun (**at someone's behest**) in response to someone's order.

behind ▸ preposition & adverb **1** at or to the back or far side of. **2** further back than other members of a group. **3** in support of. **4** responsible for an event or plan. **5** late in doing something.

SYNONYMS **1** *he hid behind a tree* **at the back/rear of,** beyond, on the far/other side of; N. Amer. in back of. **2** *a guard ran behind him* **after,** following, at the back/rear of, hard on the heels of, in the wake of. **3** *a man followed behind* **after,** afterwards, at the back/end, in

the rear. **4** *I looked behind* **over your shoulder,** towards the back/rear, backwards. **5** *you are behind the rest of the class* **less advanced than,** slower than, weaker than. **6** *he was behind the bombings* **responsible for,** at the bottom of, the cause of, the perpetrator of, the organizer of, to blame for, guilty of. **7** *they have the nation behind them* **supporting,** backing, for, on the side of, in agreement with; informal rooting for. **8** *we're behind, so don't stop* **running late,** behind schedule, behindhand, not on time. **9** *he was behind with his subscription* **in arrears,** overdue, late, unpunctual, behindhand.
ANTONYMS in front of, ahead of, against, in front, ahead, in advance.

behold ▸ verb (**beholds, beholding, beheld**) old use see or look at.

beholden ▸ adjective (**beholden to**) owing something to someone because they have done you a favour.

behove ▸ verb (**it behoves someone to do**) formal it is right or appropriate for someone to do.

beige ▸ noun a pale sandy colour.

being ▸ noun **1** existence. **2** the nature of a person. **3** a living creature.

SYNONYMS **1** *she is warmed by his very being* **existence,** living, life, reality, lifeblood, vital force. **2** *God is alive in the being of man* **soul,** spirit, nature, essence, psyche, heart, bosom, breast. **3** *an enlightened being* **creature,** life form, organism, living thing, individual, person, human.

bejewelled (US spelling **bejeweled**) ▸ adjective decorated with jewels.

belated ▸ adjective coming late or too late.

SYNONYMS **late,** overdue, behindhand, delayed, tardy, unpunctual.
ANTONYMS early, punctual.

□ **belatedly** adverb.

belay /bi-**lay**/ ▸ verb fix a rope round a rock, pin, or other object to secure it.

belch ▸ verb **1** noisily expel wind from the stomach through the mouth. **2** give out smoke or flames with great force.
▸ noun an act of belching.

beleaguered ▸ adjective **1** in difficulties. **2** under siege.

SYNONYMS **1** *a beleaguered government* **troubled,** harassed, hard-pressed, in difficulties, under pressure, in a tight corner; informal up against it. **2** *the beleaguered garrison* **besieged,** blockaded, surrounded, encircled, hemmed in, under attack.

belfry ▸ noun (plural **belfries**) the place in a bell tower or steeple which contains the bells.

Belgian ▸ noun a person from Belgium.
▸ adjective relating to Belgium.

belie ▸ verb (**belies**, **belying**, **belied**) **1** fail to give a true idea of. **2** show that something is not true.

belief ▸ noun **1** a feeling that something exists or is true. **2** a firmly held opinion. **3** (**belief in**) trust or confidence in. **4** religious faith.

> SYNONYMS **1** *it's my belief that age is irrelevant* **opinion,** view, conviction, judgement, thinking, idea, theory.
> **2** *belief in God* **faith,** trust, reliance, confidence, credence. **3** *traditional beliefs* **ideology,** principle, ethic, tenet, doctrine, teaching, dogma, creed, credo.
> ANTONYMS disbelief, doubt.

believe ▸ verb (**believes**, **believing**, **believed**) **1** accept that something is true or someone is telling the truth. **2** (**believe in**) have faith that something is true or exists. **3** think or suppose. **4** have a religious faith.

> SYNONYMS **1** *I don't believe you* **trust,** have confidence in, consider honest, consider truthful. **2** *do you believe that story?* **accept,** be convinced by, give credence to, credit, trust, put confidence in; informal swallow, buy, go for. **3** *I believe he worked for you* **think,** be of the opinion that, have an idea that, imagine, assume, presume, take it, understand, gather; informal reckon, figure.
> ANTONYMS doubt.

□ **believable** adjective.

> ✔ **i** before **e** except after **c**: bel**ie**ve.

believer ▸ noun **1** a person who believes in the truth or existence or something. **2** a person who follows a particular religion.

> SYNONYMS **disciple,** follower, supporter, adherent, devotee, upholder, worshipper.
> ANTONYMS infidel, sceptic.

belittle ▸ verb (**belittles**, **belittling**, **belittled**) dismiss as unimportant.

> SYNONYMS **disparage,** denigrate, run down, deprecate, play down, trivialize, minimize; informal do down, pooh-pooh.
> ANTONYMS praise, magnify.

Belizean (or **Belizian**) /be-**leez**-i-uhn/
▸ noun a person from Belize, a country in Central America.
▸ adjective relating to Belize.

bell ▸ noun **1** a deep metal cup held upside down, that sounds a clear musical note when struck. **2** a device that buzzes or rings to give a signal.
■ **ring a bell** informal sound vaguely familiar.

belladonna ▸ noun **1** deadly nightshade. **2** a drug made from deadly nightshade.

belle ▸ noun a beautiful woman.

bellicose ▸ adjective aggressive and ready to fight.

belligerence ▸ noun aggressive or warlike behaviour.

belligerent ▸ adjective **1** hostile and aggressive. **2** taking part in a war or conflict.

> SYNONYMS **1** *a belligerent stare* **hostile,** aggressive, threatening, antagonistic, pugnacious, bellicose, truculent, confrontational, contentious, militant, combative; informal spoiling for a fight; Brit. informal stroppy, bolshie; N. Amer. informal scrappy. **2** *the belligerent states* **warring,** combatant, fighting, battling.
> ANTONYMS peaceable, neutral.

□ **belligerently** adverb.

bellow ▸ verb **1** give a deep roar of pain or anger. **2** shout or sing very loudly.

> SYNONYMS **roar,** shout, bawl, thunder, boom, bark, yell, shriek, howl, scream; informal holler.
> ANTONYMS whisper.

▸ noun a deep shout or noise.

bellows ▸ plural noun a device consisting of a bag with two handles, used for blowing air into a fire.

belly ▸ noun (plural **bellies**) **1** the front part of the body below the ribs, containing the stomach and bowels. **2** a person's stomach.

> SYNONYMS **stomach,** abdomen, paunch, middle, midriff, girth; informal tummy, gut, insides.

bellyache informal ▸ noun a stomach pain.
▸ verb complain noisily or often.

bellyflop ▸ noun informal a dive into water in which you land flat on your front.

belong ▸ verb **1** (**belong to**) be the property of. **2** (**belong to**) be a member of. **3** be rightly put into a particular position or class. **4** feel at ease in a particular place or situation.

> SYNONYMS **1** *the house belongs to his mother* **be owned by,** be the property of, be held by, be in the hands of. **2** *I belong to a union* **be a member of,** be in, be affiliated to, be allied to, be associated with. **3** *the garden belongs to the flat* **be part of,** be attached to, go with. **4** *she doesn't belong here* **fit in,** be suited to; informal go, click.

belongings ▸ plural noun a person's movable possessions.

> SYNONYMS **possessions,** effects, worldly goods, chattels, property; informal gear, tackle, kit, things, stuff, bits and pieces; Brit. informal clobber.

beloved ▸ adjective dearly loved.

SYNONYMS *her beloved brother* **darling**, dear, precious, adored, cherished, treasured, prized, valued, idolized.
ANTONYMS hated.

▶ noun a dearly loved person.

SYNONYMS *he watched his beloved* **sweetheart**, love, darling, dearest, lover, girlfriend, boyfriend; informal steady, baby, angel, honey, pet.

below ▶ preposition & adverb 1 at a lower level than. 2 (in printed writing) mentioned further down.

SYNONYMS 1 *the water rushed below them* **beneath**, under, underneath, lower than. 2 *I could see what was happening below* **further down**, lower down, underneath, beneath. 3 *the sum is below average* **less than**, lower than, under, not as much as, smaller than. 4 *a captain is below a major* **lower than**, under, inferior to, subordinate to. 5 *the statements below* **underneath**, following, further on, at a later point.
ANTONYMS above, over, more than.

belt ▶ noun 1 a strip of leather or fabric worn round the waist. 2 a continuous band in machinery that connects two wheels. 3 a strip or encircling area.

SYNONYMS 1 **sash**, girdle, band, strap, cummerbund. 2 *the commuter belt* **region**, strip, stretch, zone, area, district, sector, territory.

▶ verb 1 fasten with a belt. 2 hit very hard. 3 (**belt something out**) informal sing or play something loudly. 4 (**belt up**) Brit. informal be quiet.

■ **below the belt** against the rules; unfair.

belying present participle of BELIE.

bemoan ▶ verb express sadness or regret about something.

bemused ▶ adjective confused or bewildered.

SYNONYMS **bewildered**, confused, puzzled, perplexed, baffled, mystified, nonplussed, dumbfounded, at sea, at a loss; informal flummoxed, bamboozled, fazed.

□ **bemusement** noun.

bench ▶ noun 1 a long seat for more than one person. 2 a long table for working at in a workshop or laboratory. 3 (**the bench**) the office of judge or magistrate. 4 (**the bench**) a seat at the side of a sports field for coaches and reserve players.

SYNONYMS 1 *he sat on a bench* **seat**, form, pew, stall, settle. 2 *a laboratory bench* **workbench**, worktop, counter.

benchmark ▶ noun a standard against which things may be compared.

SYNONYMS **standard**, point of reference, guide, guideline, norm, touchstone, yardstick, barometer, model, gauge, criterion, specification.

bend ▶ verb (**bends, bending, bent**) 1 change from being straight; make or become curved or angled. 2 lean or curve the body downwards. 3 change a rule to suit yourself.

SYNONYMS 1 *the frames can be bent to fit your face* **curve**, crook, flex, angle, hook, bow, arch, buckle, warp, contort, distort, deform, twist. 2 *the highway bent to the left* **turn**, curve, incline, swing, veer, fork, change course, curl, loop. 3 *he bent down to tie his shoe* **stoop**, bow, crouch, hunch, lean down/over.
ANTONYMS straighten.

▶ noun 1 a place where something bends; a curve or turn. 2 (**the bends**) decompression sickness.

SYNONYMS *a bend in the road* **curve**, turn, corner, kink, angle, arc, twist.
ANTONYMS straight.

■ **round the bend** informal mad.

beneath ▶ preposition 1 extending or directly under. 2 of lower status or worth than.

SYNONYMS 1 *we sat beneath the trees* **under**, underneath, below, at the foot of, at the bottom of, lower than. 2 *the rank beneath theirs* **inferior to**, below, lower than, subordinate to. 3 *such an attitude was beneath her* **unworthy of**, unbecoming to, degrading to.
ANTONYMS above.

▶ adverb extending or directly underneath.

SYNONYMS *sand with rock beneath* **underneath**, below, further down, lower down.
ANTONYMS above.

benediction ▶ noun the speaking of a blessing.

benefactor ▶ noun a person who gives money or other help.

SYNONYMS **patron**, supporter, backer, sponsor, donor, contributor, subscriber; informal angel.

benefice /**ben**-i-fiss/ ▶ noun an arrangement by which a Christian priest is paid and given accommodation for being in charge of a parish.

beneficent /bi-**nef**-i-suhnt/ ▶ adjective doing or resulting in good.
□ **beneficence** noun.

beneficial ▶ adjective having a good effect.

SYNONYMS **advantageous**, favourable, helpful, useful, of assistance, valuable,

profitable, rewarding, gainful.
ANTONYMS disadvantageous.

□ **beneficially** adverb.

beneficiary ▶ noun (plural **beneficiaries**) a person who benefits from something, especially a trust or will.

> SYNONYMS **recipient**, payee, heir, heiress, inheritor.

benefit ▶ noun **1** advantage or profit. **2** payment made by the state to someone in need: *unemployment benefit*. **3** a public performance to raise money for a charity.

> SYNONYMS **1** *for the benefit of others* **good**, sake, welfare, well-being, advantage, comfort, ease, convenience, help, aid, assistance, service. **2** *the benefits of working for a large firm* **advantage**, profit, plus point, boon, blessing, reward; informal perk. **3** *state benefit* **social security payment**, welfare, charity; informal the dole; Scottish informal the broo.
> ANTONYMS detriment, disadvantage.

▶ verb (**benefits, benefiting, benefited** or **benefitting, benefitted**) **1** get an advantage; profit. **2** bring advantage to.

> SYNONYMS **1** *the deal benefited them both* **be advantageous to**, be beneficial to, profit, do good to, be of service to, serve, be useful to, be helpful to, aid. **2** *they may benefit from drugs* **profit**, gain, reap reward, make the most of, exploit, turn to your advantage, put to good use.
> ANTONYMS disadvantage, harm, suffer.

> ✔ There is usually a single **t** in **benefited** and **benefiting**; the spellings with **tt** are commoner in American English.

benevolent ▶ adjective **1** well meaning and kindly. **2** (of an organization) charitable rather than profit-making.

> SYNONYMS **kind**, kindly, kind-hearted, good-natured, compassionate, caring, altruistic, humanitarian, philanthropic.
> ANTONYMS unkind.

□ **benevolence** noun.

Bengali /ben-gaw-li/ ▶ noun (plural **Bengalis**) **1** a person from Bengal in the Indian subcontinent. **2** the language of Bangladesh and West Bengal.
▶ adjective relating to Bengal.

benighted ▶ adjective ignorant or primitive.

benign /bi-nyn/ ▶ adjective **1** cheerful and kindly. **2** favourable; not harmful. **3** (of a tumour) not malignant.

> SYNONYMS **1** *a benign grandfatherly role* **kindly**, kind, warm-hearted, good-natured, friendly, genial, tender-hearted, gentle, sympathetic, compassionate, caring, well disposed, benevolent. **2** *a*

benign climate **mild**, temperate, gentle, balmy, soft, pleasant, favourable, healthy. **3** *a benign tumour* **harmless**, non-malignant, non-cancerous.
ANTONYMS unkind, unhealthy, hostile, malignant.

Beninese /ben-i-neez/ ▶ noun a person from Benin, a country in West Africa.
▶ adjective relating to Benin.

bent past and past participle of BEND.
▶ adjective **1** Brit. informal dishonest or corrupt. **2** (**bent on**) determined to do.

> SYNONYMS **1 twisted**, crooked, warped, contorted, deformed, misshapen, out of shape, bowed, arched, curved, angled, hooked, kinked; N. Amer. informal pretzeled. **2** *a mob bent on violence* **intent**, determined, set, insistent, resolved.
> ANTONYMS straight.

▶ noun a natural talent.

> SYNONYMS *an artistic bent* **inclination**, leaning, tendency, talent, gift, flair, aptitude, facility, skill.

benzene ▶ noun a liquid present in coal tar and petroleum.

bequeath ▶ verb **1** leave property to someone by a will. **2** hand down or pass on.

> SYNONYMS **leave**, will, hand down, pass on, entrust, make over, grant, transfer, give, bestow on, confer on.

bequest ▶ noun **1** something that is left to someone by a will. **2** the action of bequeathing.

> SYNONYMS **legacy**, estate, inheritance, endowment, settlement.

berate ▶ verb (**berates, berating, berated**) angrily scold or criticize.

bereave ▶ verb (**be bereaved**) be deprived of a close relation or friend through their death.

bereavement ▶ noun an instance of being bereaved.

> SYNONYMS **death in the family**, loss, passing (away), demise.

bereft ▶ adjective **1** (**bereft of**) deprived of; without. **2** lonely and abandoned.

beret /be-ray/ ▶ noun a flat round cap of felt or cloth.

bergamot /ber-guh-mot/ ▶ noun an oily substance found in some oranges, used as a flavouring.

beriberi ▶ noun a disease caused by a lack of vitamin B_1.

berk ▶ noun Brit. informal a stupid person.

berkelium ▶ noun a radioactive metallic element.

berry ▶ noun (plural **berries**) a small, juicy round fruit without a stone.

berserk ▶ adjective out of control; wild and frenzied.

SYNONYMS **mad**, crazy, insane, out of your mind, hysterical, frenzied, crazed, demented, maniacal, manic, frantic, raving, wild, out of control, amok, on the rampage; informal off your head, off the deep end, ape, bananas, bonkers; Brit. informal spare; N. Amer. informal postal.

berth ▶ noun **1** a place in a harbour where a boat can stay. **2** a bunk on a ship or train.

SYNONYMS **1** *the vessel left its berth* **mooring**, dock, pier, jetty, quay. **2** *a 4-berth cabin* **bunk**, bed, cot, couch, hammock.

▶ verb moor a boat in a berth.

SYNONYMS *the ship berthed in London* **dock**, moor, land, tie up, make fast.

■ **give a wide berth to** stay well away from.

beryl ▶ noun a transparent pale green, blue, or yellow gemstone.

beryllium /buh-**ril**-li-uhm/ ▶ noun a hard, grey, lightweight metallic element.

beseech ▶ verb (beseeches, beseeching, besought or beseeched) ask in a pleading way.

beset ▶ verb (besets, besetting, beset) continually trouble or worry.

beside ▶ preposition **1** at the side of. **2** compared with. **3** (also **besides**) as well as.

SYNONYMS **1** **alongside**, by/at the side of, next to, parallel to, abreast of, adjacent to, next door to, neighbouring. **2** *who did you ask besides Mary?* **in addition to**, as well as, over and above, on top of, apart from, other than, aside from, not counting, excluding, leaving aside; N. Amer. informal outside of.

▶ adverb (**besides**) as well.

SYNONYMS **1** *there's a lot more besides* **in addition**, as well, too, also, into the bargain, on top of that, to boot. **2** *besides, he's a man* **furthermore**, moreover, further; informal what's more.

■ **beside yourself** frantic with worry.

besiege ▶ verb (besieges, besieging, besieged) **1** surround a place so that no one can come or go. **2** overwhelm someone with requests or complaints.

SYNONYMS **1** *the army besieged Leith* **lay siege to**, beleaguer, blockade. **2** *he was besieged by fans* **surround**, mob, harass, pester, badger. **3** *we were besieged with requests* **overwhelm**, bombard, inundate, deluge, flood, swamp, snow under.

✔ Remember, **i** before **e** except after **c**: bes**ie**ge.

besmirch ▶ verb damage someone's reputation.

besom /bee-zuhm/ ▶ noun a broom made of twigs tied round a stick.

besotted ▶ adjective so much in love that you stop acting sensibly.

bespoke ▶ adjective Brit. made to a customer's requirements.

best ▶ adjective **1** of the highest quality. **2** most suitable or sensible.

SYNONYMS **1** *the best hotel in Paris* **finest**, premier, greatest, top, foremost, leading, pre-eminent, supreme, superlative, unrivalled, second to none, without equal, unsurpassed, unparalleled, unbeatable, optimum, ultimate, incomparable, record-breaking; informal star, number-one, a cut above the rest, top-drawer. **2** *do whatever you think best* **most advantageous**, most useful, most suitable, most fitting, most appropriate, most advisable.
ANTONYMS worst.

▶ adverb **1** to the highest degree; most. **2** most suitably or sensibly.

SYNONYMS **1** *the best-dressed man* **to the highest standard**, in the best way. **2** *the food he liked best* **most**, to the highest/greatest degree. **3** *this is best done at home* **most appropriately**, most suitably, most fittingly, most usefully, most advantageously, most sensibly, most prudently, most wisely.
ANTONYMS worst, least.

▶ noun (**the best**) something which is of the highest quality.

SYNONYMS *only the best will do* **finest**, choicest, top, cream, choice, prime, elite, crème de la crème, flower, jewel in the crown; informal tops, pick of the bunch.
ANTONYMS worst.

■ **best man** a male friend or relative who helps a bridegroom at his wedding. **best-seller** a book or other product that sells in very large numbers. **make the best of** get what advantage you can from.

bestial ▶ adjective savagely cruel.

bestiality ▶ noun **1** savagely cruel behaviour. **2** sex between a person and an animal.

bestir ▶ verb (bestirs, bestirring, bestirred) (**bestir yourself**) make yourself start to do something.

bestow ▶ verb give an honour, right, or gift.

SYNONYMS **confer on**, grant, accord, afford, endow someone with, present, award, give, donate, entrust with, vouchsafe.

bestride ▶ verb (bestrides, bestriding, bestrode; past participle bestridden) put a leg on either side of.

b

bet ▶ verb (bets, betting, bet or betted)
1 risk money against someone else's on the basis of the outcome of an unpredictable event such as a race. **2** informal feel sure.

> SYNONYMS **1** *he bet £10 on the favourite* **wager,** gamble, stake, risk, venture, hazard, chance; Brit. informal punt, have a flutter. **2** *I bet it was your idea* **be certain,** be sure, be convinced, be confident, expect, predict, guess.

▶ noun an act of betting or the money betted.

> SYNONYMS **1** *a £20 bet* **wager,** gamble, stake, ante; Brit. informal punt, flutter. **2** *your best bet is to go early* **option,** choice, alternative, course of action, plan.

beta /bee-tuh/ ▶ noun the second letter of the Greek alphabet (B, β).
■ **beta blocker** a drug used to treat high blood pressure and angina.

bête noire /bet nwar/ ▶ noun (plural **bêtes noires** /bet **nwar**/) a person or thing that you greatly dislike.

betide ▶ verb (betide, betiding, betided) literary happen or happen to.

betimes ▶ adverb in good time; early.

betoken ▶ verb be a sign of.

betray ▶ verb **1** harm someone or something by giving information to an enemy. **2** be disloyal to someone. **3** reveal a secret without meaning to.

> SYNONYMS **1** *he betrayed his own brother* **be disloyal to,** be unfaithful to, break faith with, play someone false, inform on/against, give away, denounce, sell out, stab in the back; informal split on, rat on, stitch up, do the dirty on, sell down the river; Brit. informal grass on, shop, sneak on; N. Amer. informal rat out, drop a/the dime on, finger; Austral./NZ informal dob in, point the bone at. **2** *he betrayed a secret* **reveal,** disclose, divulge, tell, give away, leak, bring out into the open.
> ANTONYMS be loyal to, keep.

betrayal ▶ noun the act of betraying.

> SYNONYMS **disloyalty,** treachery, bad faith, breach of faith, breach of trust, faithlessness, duplicity, deception, double-dealing, stab in the back, double-cross, sell-out.
> ANTONYMS loyalty.

betrothed ▶ adjective engaged to be married.
□ **betrothal** noun.

better ▶ adjective **1** of a higher standard or quality. **2** partly or fully recovered from illness or injury.

> SYNONYMS **1** *better facilities* **superior,** finer, of higher quality, preferable; informal a cut above, streets ahead, head and shoulders above, ahead of the

pack/field. **2** *there couldn't be a better time* **more advantageous,** more suitable, more fitting, more appropriate, more useful, more valuable, more desirable. **3** *are you better?* **healthier,** fitter, stronger, well again, cured, healed, recovered, recovering, on the road to recovery, on the mend.
> ANTONYMS worse, inferior.

▶ adverb **1** in a more satisfactory way. **2** to a greater degree; more.

> SYNONYMS **1** *I played better today* **to a higher standard,** in a superior way, more effectively. **2** *this may suit you better* **more,** to a greater degree/extent. **3** *the money could be better spent* **more wisely,** more sensibly, more suitably, more fittingly, more advantageously, more usefully.

▶ noun (**your betters**) people who have greater ability or are more important than you.
▶ verb **1** improve on something. **2** (**better yourself**) improve your social position.

> SYNONYMS **1** *he bettered the record* **surpass,** improve on, beat, exceed, top, cap, trump, eclipse. **2** *refugees who want to better their lot* **improve,** ameliorate, raise, advance, further, lift, upgrade, enhance.
> ANTONYMS worsen.

■ **better off** having more money or being in a more desirable situation. **get the better of** defeat.

betterment ▶ noun improvement.

between ▶ preposition & adverb **1** at, into, or across the space separating two things. **2** in the period separating two points in time. **3** indicating a connection or relationship. **4** shared by two or more people or things.

> SYNONYMS **1** *Philip stood between his parents* **in the middle of,** with one on either side, among; archaic betwixt. **2** *the bond between her and her mother* **connecting,** linking, joining, uniting, allying.

betwixt ▶ preposition & adverb old use between.

bevel ▶ noun an edge cut at an angle in wood or glass.
▶ verb (**bevels, bevelling, bevelled**; US spelling **bevels, beveling, beveled**) cut the edge of wood or glass at an angle.

beverage ▶ noun a drink.

bevy ▶ noun (plural **bevies**) a large group.

bewail ▶ verb be very sorry or sad about.

beware ▶ verb be aware of danger.

> SYNONYMS **watch out,** look out, mind out, be alert, keep your eyes open/peeled, keep an eye out, take care, be careful, be cautious, watch your step, guard against.

bewilder ▶ verb (bewilders, bewildering, bewildered) puzzle or confuse.

> SYNONYMS **baffle,** mystify, bemuse, perplex, puzzle, confuse; informal flummox, faze, stump, beat.
> ANTONYMS enlighten.

□ **bewilderment** noun.

bewitch ▶ verb **1** put a magic spell on. **2** attract and delight.

beyond ▶ preposition & adverb **1** at or to the further side of. **2** outside the range or limits of. **3** happening or continuing after. **4** except.

> SYNONYMS **1** *beyond the trees* **on the far side of,** on the other side of, further away than, behind, past, after. **2** *beyond six o'clock* **later than,** past, after. **3** *inflation beyond 10 per cent* **greater than,** more than, exceeding, in excess of, above, upwards of. **4** *little beyond food was provided* **apart from,** except, other than, besides; informal outside of; formal save.

bhaji /bah-ji/ ▶ noun (plural **bhajis**) an Indian dish of vegetables fried in batter.

biannual ▶ adjective happening twice a year. □ **biannually** adverb.

bias ▶ noun **1** a feeling for or against a person or thing that is not based on reason. **2** a direction diagonal to the grain of a fabric.

> SYNONYMS *he accused the media of bias* **prejudice,** partiality, favouritism, unfairness, one-sidedness, discrimination, leaning, tendency, inclination.
> ANTONYMS impartiality.

biased ▶ adjective having a bias; prejudiced.

> SYNONYMS **prejudiced,** partial, partisan, one-sided, bigoted, discriminatory, distorted, warped, twisted, skewed.
> ANTONYMS impartial.

bib ▶ noun **1** a piece of cloth or plastic fastened under a baby's chin to protect its clothes when it is being fed. **2** the part of an apron or pair of dungarees that covers the chest.

Bible ▶ noun the book containing the writings of the Christian Church. □ **biblical** adjective.

bibliography ▶ noun (plural **bibliographies**) a list of books on a particular subject. □ **bibliographer** noun **bibliographic** adjective.

bibliophile /bib-li-oh-fyl/ ▶ noun a person who collects books.

bibulous ▶ adjective fond of drinking alcohol.

bicameral ▶ adjective (of a parliament) having two separate parts.

bicarbonate of soda ▶ noun a soluble white powder used in fizzy drinks and in baking.

bicentenary ▶ noun (plural **bicentenaries**) a two-hundredth anniversary. □ **bicentennial** noun & adjective.

biceps /by-seps/ ▶ noun (plural **biceps**) a large muscle in the upper arm which flexes the arm and forearm.

bicker ▶ verb (bickers, bickering, bickered) argue about unimportant things.

bicycle ▶ noun a two-wheeled vehicle that you ride by pushing the pedals with your feet.
▶ verb (bicycles, bicycling, bicycled) ride a bicycle.

bid[1] ▶ verb (bids, bidding, bid) **1** offer a price for something. **2** (bid for) offer to do work for a stated price. **3** (bid for) try to get.

> SYNONYMS *United bid £1 million for the striker* **offer,** put up, tender, proffer, propose.

▶ noun an act of bidding.

> SYNONYMS **1** *a bid of £3,000* **offer,** tender, proposal. **2** *a bid to cut crime* **attempt,** effort, endeavour, try; informal crack, go, shot, stab.

bid[2] ▶ verb (bids, bidding, bid or bade; past participle **bid**) **1** say a greeting. **2** old use command.

biddable ▶ adjective obedient.

bidding ▶ noun ordering or requesting someone to do something.

> SYNONYMS **command,** order, direction, instruction, decree, injunction, demand, beck and call, request.

biddy ▶ noun (plural **biddies**) informal an old woman.

bide ▶ verb (bides, biding, bided) old use or dialect stay in a place.
■ **bide your time** wait patiently for an opportunity to do something.

bidet /bee-day/ ▶ noun a low basin that you sit on to wash your bottom.

biennial ▶ adjective **1** taking place every other year. **2** (of a plant) living for two years.

bier /beer/ ▶ noun a platform on which a coffin or dead body is placed before burial.

bifocal ▶ adjective (of a lens) made in two sections, one for distant and one for close vision.
▶ noun (**bifocals**) a pair of glasses with bifocal lenses.

big ▶ adjective (bigger, biggest) **1** large in size, amount, or extent. **2** very important or serious. **3** informal (of a brother or sister) older.

> SYNONYMS **1** *a big building* **large,** sizeable, substantial, great, huge, immense, enormous, extensive, colossal, massive,

b

b

vast, gigantic, giant, spacious; informal jumbo, whopping, thumping, bumper, mega; Brit. informal whacking, ginormous; formal commodious. **2** *a big man* **well built**, sturdy, brawny, burly, broad-shouldered, muscular, bulky, hulking, strapping, hefty, tall, huge, fat, stout; informal hunky, beefy. **3** *my big brother* **grown-up**, adult, mature, grown, elder, older. **4** *a big decision* **important**, significant, major, momentous, weighty, far-reaching, key, vital, crucial. **5** *that was big of you* **generous**, kind, kindly, caring, compassionate, loving.
ANTONYMS small, little, younger, minor, mean.

■ **Big Bang** the rapid expansion of dense matter which is thought to have started the formation of the universe. **big-headed** conceited. **big top** the main tent in a circus.

bigamy ▶ noun the crime of marrying someone when you are already married to someone else.
□ **bigamist** noun **bigamous** adjective.

bigot /big-uht/ ▶ noun a prejudiced and intolerant person.
□ **bigotry** noun.

bigoted ▶ adjective unreasonably intolerant.
SYNONYMS **prejudiced**, biased, partial, one-sided, sectarian, discriminatory, opinionated, dogmatic, intolerant, narrow-minded, blinkered, illiberal.
ANTONYMS open-minded.

bigwig ▶ noun informal an important person.
bijou /bee-zhoo/ ▶ adjective small and elegant.
bike informal ▶ noun a bicycle or motorcycle.
▶ verb (**bikes, biking, biked**) ride a bicycle or motorcycle.
□ **biker** noun.
bikini ▶ noun (plural **bikinis**) a woman's two-piece swimsuit.
bilateral ▶ adjective involving two countries or groups of people.
bilberry ▶ noun (plural **bilberries**) a small blue edible berry.
bile ▶ noun **1** a bitter fluid which is produced by the liver and helps digestion. **2** anger.
bilge ▶ noun the bottom of a ship's hull.
bilingual ▶ adjective **1** speaking two languages fluently. **2** expressed in two languages.
bilious ▶ adjective feeling sick.
bilk ▶ verb informal cheat someone.
bill¹ ▶ noun **1** a note saying how much a person owes for something. **2** a written proposal for a new law, presented to parliament for discussion. **3** a programme of entertainment at a theatre or cinema. **4** an advertising poster. **5** N. Amer. a banknote.

SYNONYMS **1** *a bill for £6* **invoice**, account, statement, list of charges; humorous the damage; N. Amer. check; N. Amer. informal tab. **2** *a parliamentary bill* **draft law**, proposal, measure. **3** *she was top of the bill* **programme**, line-up; N. Amer. playbill. **4** *a $10 bill* **banknote**, note; US informal greenback. **5** *he had been posting bills* **poster**, advertisement, notice, announcement, flyer, leaflet, handbill; informal ad; Brit. informal advert.

▶ verb **1** send someone a bill saying what they owe. **2** list someone in a programme of entertainment. **3** (**bill someone/thing as**) describe someone or something as.

SYNONYMS **1** *please bill me for the work* **invoice**, charge, debit. **2** *the concert went ahead as billed* **advertise**, announce, schedule, programme, timetable; N. Amer. slate. **3** *he was billed as the new Sean Connery* **describe**, call, style, label, dub, promote, talk up; informal hype.

■ **fit the bill** be suitable.
bill² ▶ noun a bird's beak.
billabong ▶ noun Austral. a stretch of a river forming a backwater or stagnant pool.
billboard ▶ noun a large board for displaying advertising posters.
billet ▶ noun a private house where soldiers live temporarily.
▶ verb (**be billeted**) (of a soldier) stay in a particular place.
billet-doux /bil-li-doo/ ▶ noun (plural **billets-doux** /bil-li-dooz/) a love letter.
billhook ▶ noun a tool with a curved blade, used for pruning.
billiards ▶ noun a game played on a table with pockets at the sides and corners, into which balls are struck with a cue.
billion ▶ cardinal number (plural **billions** or (with another word or number) **billion**) a thousand million; 1,000,000,000.
□ **billionth** ordinal number.
billionaire ▶ noun a person owning money and property worth at least a billion pounds or dollars.
billow ▶ verb **1** (of smoke, cloud, or steam) roll outward. **2** fill with air and swell out.

SYNONYMS **1** *smoke billowed from the chimney* **swirl**, spiral, roll, undulate, eddy, pour, flow. **2** *her dress billowed around her* **puff up/out**, balloon (out), swell, fill (out).

▶ noun **1** a large rolling mass of cloud, smoke, or steam. **2** literary a large sea wave.

SYNONYMS *billows of smoke* **cloud**, mass.

billy (or **billycan**) ▶ noun (plural **billies**) Brit. a metal cooking pot with a lid and handle, used in camping.
billy goat ▶ noun a male goat.

bimbo ▸ noun (plural **bimbos**) informal an attractive but unintelligent young woman.

bin Brit. ▸ noun **1** a container for rubbish. **2** a large storage container.
▸ verb (**bins, binning, binned**) throw away.

binary /by-nuh-ri/ ▸ adjective **1** composed of or involving two things. **2** relating to a system of numbers which has two as its base and uses only the digits 0 and 1.

bind ▸ verb (**binds, binding, bound**) **1** firmly tie, wrap, or fasten. **2** hold together in a united group or mass. **3** (**be bound by**) be hampered or restricted by. **4** require someone to do something by law or because of a contract. **5** (**bind someone over**) (of a court of law) require someone to do something. **6** enclose the pages of a book in a cover. **7** trim the edge of a piece of material with a fabric strip.

> SYNONYMS **1** they bound her hands **tie up,** fasten together, secure, make fast, attach, rope, lash, tether. **2** Shelley bound up the wound **bandage,** dress, cover, wrap, strap up, tape up. **3** the edges are bound in a contrasting colour **trim,** hem, edge, border, fringe. See also BOUND³ (adjective).
> ANTONYMS untie.

▸ noun informal an annoying or difficult situation.

binder ▸ noun **1** a cover for holding loose papers together. **2** a machine that binds grain into sheaves. **3** a person who binds books.
□ **bindery** noun (plural **binderies**).

bindi ▸ noun (plural **bindis**) a decorative mark worn in the middle of the forehead by some Indian women.

binding ▸ noun **1** a strong covering holding the pages of a book together. **2** fabric in a strip, used for binding the edges of material.
▸ adjective (of an agreement) legally compelling someone to do what is stated.

> SYNONYMS **irrevocable,** unalterable, inescapable, unbreakable, contractual, compulsory, obligatory, mandatory, incumbent.

bindweed ▸ noun a plant that twines itself round things.

binge informal ▸ noun a short period of uncontrolled eating or drinking.

> SYNONYMS **bout,** spell, fling, spree, orgy, drinking bout; informal bender, session; Scottish informal skite; N. Amer. informal jag, toot.

▸ verb (**binges, bingeing, binged**) eat or drink in an uncontrolled way.

bingo ▸ noun a game in which players mark off on a card numbers called at random, the winner being the first to mark off all their numbers.

binocular ▸ adjective for or using both eyes.

▸ noun (**binoculars**) an instrument with a separate lens for each eye, for viewing distant objects.

biochemistry ▸ noun the study of the chemical processes that take place within living things.
□ **biochemical** adjective **biochemist** noun.

biodegradable ▸ adjective able to be decomposed by bacteria or other living things.

biodiversity ▸ noun the variety of plant and animal life in the world or in a particular environment.

biography ▸ noun (plural **biographies**) an account of a person's life written by someone else.
□ **biographer** noun **biographical** adjective.

biological ▸ adjective **1** relating to biology or living things. **2** (of a parent or child) related by blood. **3** relating to the use of germs as a weapon in war. **4** (of a detergent) containing enzymes.
□ **biologically** adverb.

biology ▸ noun the scientific study of the life and structure of plants and animals.
□ **biologist** noun.

bionic ▸ adjective **1** (of an artificial body part) electronically powered. **2** informal having superhuman powers.

biopsy ▸ noun (plural **biopsies**) an examination of tissue taken from the body, to discover the presence or cause of a disease.

biorhythm ▸ noun a recurring cycle in the functioning of an animal or plant.

biosphere ▸ noun the parts of the earth in which plants and animals live.

bioterrorism ▸ noun the use of harmful organisms such as viruses or bacteria as weapons of terrorism.

bipartite ▸ adjective involving two separate groups or parties.

biped /by-ped/ ▸ noun an animal that walks on two feet.

biplane ▸ noun an early type of aircraft with two pairs of wings, one above the other.

bipolar ▸ adjective having two poles or outer limits.

birch ▸ noun **1** a slender tree with thin peeling bark. **2** (**the birch**) (in the past) the punishment of being beaten with a bundle of birch twigs.

bird ▸ noun **1** an animal with feathers, wings, and a beak, that lays eggs and is usually able to fly. **2** Brit. informal a young woman or girlfriend.
■ **bird of prey** (plural **birds of prey**) a bird that eats small animals or birds, such as an eagle or hawk. **bird's-eye view** a view of something from high above.

b

birdie ► noun (plural **birdies**) Golf a score of one stroke under par at a hole.

biro ► noun (plural **biros**) Brit. trademark a ballpoint pen.

birth ► noun **1** the process by which a baby or other young animal comes out of its mother's body. **2** the beginning of something. **3** a person's family origins.

> SYNONYMS **1 childbirth,** delivery, nativity. **2** *the birth of science* **beginning(s),** emergence, genesis, dawn, dawning, rise, start. **3** *he is of noble birth* **ancestry,** lineage, blood, descent, parentage, family, extraction, origin, stock. ANTONYMS death, end.

■ **birth control** the use of contraceptives to prevent unwanted pregnancies. **give birth** produce a baby or young animal.

birthday ► noun the day in each year which is the same as the day on which a person was born.

birthmark ► noun an unusual mark on the body which is there from birth.

birthright ► noun **1** a right or privilege that a person inherits. **2** a basic right belonging to all human beings.

biscuit ► noun **1** Brit. a small, flat, crisp cake. **2** a light brown colour.

> ✔ Don't forget the **u**: biscuit.

bisect ► verb divide into two parts.

bisexual ► adjective **1** sexually attracted to both men and women. **2** Biology having both male and female organs.
► noun a bisexual person.
□ **bisexuality** noun.

bishop ► noun (in the Christian Church) a senior minister who is in charge of a diocese (a district).

bismuth ► noun a brittle reddish-grey metallic element resembling lead.

bison ► noun (plural **bison**) a wild ox with a humped back and shaggy hair.

bistro /bee-stroh/ ► noun (plural **bistros**) a small, inexpensive restaurant.

bit¹ ► noun **1** a small piece or quantity. **2** (**a bit**) a short time or distance. **3** (**a bit**) rather; slightly.

> SYNONYMS **piece,** portion, section, part, chunk, lump, hunk, fragment, scrap, shred, crumb, grain, speck, spot, drop, pinch, dash, morsel, mouthful, bite, sample, iota, jot, whit, atom, particle, trace, touch, suggestion, hint, tinge; informal smidgen, tad.
> ANTONYMS lot.

■ **bit part** a small acting role in a play or a film.

bit² ► noun **1** a metal mouthpiece attached to a bridle, used to control a horse. **2** a tool or piece for boring or drilling.

bit³ ► noun Computing the smallest unit of information, expressed as either a 0 or 1.

bitch ► noun **1** a female dog. **2** informal a spiteful or unpleasant woman.
► verb informal say spiteful things about someone.

bitchy ► adjective (**bitchier, bitchiest**) informal spiteful.
□ **bitchiness** noun.

bite ► verb (**bites, biting, bit;** past participle **bitten**) **1** cut into something with your teeth. **2** (of a tool, tyre, etc.) grip a surface. **3** take effect in an unwelcome way.

> SYNONYMS **1 chew,** sink your teeth into, munch, crunch, champ. **2** *my boots failed to bite* **grip,** hold, get a purchase. **3** *the measures begin to bite* **take effect,** work, act, have results.

► noun **1** an act of biting or a piece bitten off. **2** informal a quick snack. **3** a feeling of cold in the air.

> SYNONYMS **1** *he took a bite at his sandwich* **chew,** munch, nibble, gnaw, nip, snap. **2** *he ate it in two bites* **mouthful,** piece, bit, morsel. **3** *the appetizer had a fiery bite* **piquancy,** pungency, spiciness, tang, zest; informal kick, punch, zing.

■ **bite the bullet** make yourself do something that is difficult or unpleasant.

biting ► adjective **1** (of a wind) painfully cold. **2** (of something said) cruel.

> SYNONYMS **1** *the biting wind* **freezing,** icy, arctic, bitter, piercing, penetrating, raw. **2** *biting comments* **vicious,** harsh, cruel, savage, cutting, sharp, bitter, scathing, caustic, acid, acrimonious, spiteful, venomous; informal bitchy, catty.
> ANTONYMS mild, pleasant, warm.

bitter ► adjective **1** having a sharp or sour taste or smell; not sweet. **2** feeling or causing resentment or unhappiness. **3** (of a conflict) intense and full of hatred. **4** very cold.

> SYNONYMS **1** *bitter coffee* **sharp,** acid, acrid, tart, sour, vinegary. **2** *a bitter row* **acrimonious,** hostile, angry, rancorous, spiteful, vicious, vitriolic, savage, ferocious, nasty. **3** *a bitter woman* **resentful,** embittered, aggrieved, spiteful, jaundiced, sullen, sour. **4** *a bitter wind* **freezing,** icy, arctic, biting, piercing, penetrating, raw.
> ANTONYMS pleasant, sweet, amicable, magnanimous, content, mild, warm.

► noun **1** Brit. bitter-tasting beer that is strongly flavoured with hops. **2** (**bitters**) bitter alcoholic spirits used in cocktails.
□ **bitterly** adverb.

bittern ► noun a wading bird with a very loud call.

bitterness ▸ noun the quality of state of being bitter.

> SYNONYMS **1** *the bitterness of the medicine* **sharpness,** acidity, tartness, sourness. **2** *there was no bitterness between them* **acrimony,** hostility, anger, antipathy, antagonism, enmity, animus, friction, rancour, vitriol, venom, nastiness, bad blood. **3** *his bitterness grew* **resentment,** rancour, indignation, grudge, spite, sullenness, sourness, pique.
> ANTONYMS sweetness, pleasantness, goodwill, magnanimity, contentment.

bittersweet ▸ adjective **1** sweet with a bitter aftertaste. **2** bringing pleasure mixed with sadness.

bitty ▸ adjective (**bittier, bittiest**) Brit. informal made up of small unrelated parts.

bitumen ▸ noun a black sticky substance obtained from oil, used for covering roads and roofs.
> □ **bituminous** adjective.

bivalve ▸ noun a creature that has a shell divided into two parts, such as an oyster or mussel.

bivouac ▸ noun a makeshift open-air camp without tents.
▸ verb (**bivouacs, bivouacking, bivouacked**) stay overnight in such a camp.

bizarre ▸ adjective very strange or unusual.

> SYNONYMS **strange,** peculiar, odd, funny, fantastic, curious, outlandish, eccentric, unconventional, unorthodox; informal weird, wacky, oddball, way out, freaky; N. Amer. informal wacko.
> ANTONYMS normal.

> □ **bizarrely** adverb.

> ✔ one **z**, double **rr**: bizarre.

blab ▸ verb (**blabs, blabbing, blabbed**) informal give away a secret.

blabber ▸ verb (**blabbers, blabbering, blabbered**) informal talk in a silly or annoying way.

black ▸ adjective **1** of the very darkest colour. **2** relating to people who have dark-coloured skin. **3** (of coffee or tea) without milk. **4** indicating that bad or unwelcome things are likely to happen. **5** (of a joke) making something bad or unwelcome seem funny. **6** full of anger or hatred.

> SYNONYMS **1** *a black horse* **dark,** pitch-black, jet-black, ebony, inky. **2** *the blackest day of the war* **tragic,** dark, disastrous, calamitous, catastrophic, cataclysmic, fateful. **3** *Mary was in a black mood* **miserable,** unhappy, sad, wretched, heartbroken, grief-stricken, sorrowful, anguished, desolate, despairing, disconsolate, downcast, dejected, gloomy; informal blue. **4** *black*
> *humour* **macabre,** cynical, unhealthy, ghoulish, weird, morbid, gruesome; informal sick.
> ANTONYMS white, bright, happy.

▸ noun **1** black colour. **2** a black person.
▸ verb **1** make something black. **2** (**black out**) faint. **3** (**black something out**) make a building dark by switching off lights and covering windows.
■ **black belt** a black belt awarded to an expert in judo, karate, and other martial arts. **black box** a machine that records what is happening to the controls in an aircraft during a flight. **black eye** an area of bruising around the eye. **black hole** an area in space where gravity is so strong that nothing, not even light, can escape. **black ice** a transparent coating of ice on a road. **black magic** magic in which evil spirits are called on. **black market** the illegal trade in goods that are officially controlled or hard to obtain. **black pudding** a pork sausage containing dried pig's blood. **black sheep** a person who is considered bad or embarrassing by the rest of their family. **black spot** a place that is dangerous or where problems arise. **black widow** a very poisonous American spider with a black body and red markings. **in the black** not owing any money.
□ **blackness** noun.

blackball ▸ verb prevent someone from joining a club.

blackberry ▸ noun (plural **blackberries**) a soft purple-black fruit that grows on a prickly bush.

blackbird ▸ noun a bird with black feathers and a yellow beak.

blackboard ▸ noun a board with a black surface for writing on with chalk.

blackcurrant ▸ noun a small round edible purple-black berry.

blacken ▸ verb **1** make or become black. **2** damage someone's reputation.

blackfly ▸ noun (plural **blackflies**) a small black fly which eats the young shoots of plants.

blackguard /blag-gerd/ ▸ noun dated a man who is dishonest or treats other people badly.

blackhead ▸ noun a lump of oily matter blocking a pore in the skin.

blackleg ▸ noun Brit. disapproving a person who continues working when other workers are on strike.

blacklist ▸ noun a list of people who cannot be trusted or who are out of favour.
▸ verb put someone on a blacklist.

> SYNONYMS **boycott,** ostracize, avoid, embargo, ignore, refuse to employ.

blackmail ▸ noun **1** the demanding of money from someone in return for not giving away secret information about them. **2** the use of threats or other pressure to influence someone.

SYNONYMS *he was accused of blackmail* **extortion,** demanding money with menaces, threats, intimidation.

▶ verb use blackmail on someone.

SYNONYMS **1** *he was blackmailing the murderer* **extort money from,** threaten, hold to ransom, intimidate. **2** *she blackmailed me into working for her* **coerce,** pressure, force, dragoon; informal lean on, twist someone's arm.

blackout ▶ noun **1** a period when all lights must be switched off or covered during an enemy air raid. **2** a sudden failure of electric lights. **3** a short loss of consciousness. **4** an official restriction on the publishing of news.

blacksmith ▶ noun a person who makes and repairs things made of iron.

blackthorn ▶ noun a thorny bush that has blue-black fruits (called sloes).

bladder ▶ noun a bag-like organ in the abdomen in which urine collects before it is passed from the body.

blade ▶ noun **1** the flat cutting edge of a knife or other tool or weapon. **2** the broad flat part of an oar, leaf, or other object. **3** a long, narrow leaf of grass.

blag ▶ verb (**blags, blagging, blagged**) Brit. informal get something by clever talk or lying. □ **blagger** noun.

blame ▶ verb (**blames, blaming, blamed**) say that someone is responsible for something bad.

SYNONYMS **1** *he always blames others* **hold responsible,** hold accountable, condemn, accuse, find/consider guilty. **2** *they blame youth crime on unemployment* **attribute to,** ascribe to, impute to, lay at the door of, put down to; informal pin.
ANTONYMS absolve.

▶ noun responsibility for something bad.

SYNONYMS *he was cleared of all blame* **responsibility,** guilt, accountability, liability, culpability, fault.

□ **blameworthy** adjective.

blameless ▶ adjective having done nothing bad; innocent.

SYNONYMS **innocent,** guiltless, above reproach, unimpeachable, in the clear, exemplary; informal squeaky clean.
ANTONYMS blameworthy.

blanch ▶ verb **1** become white or pale. **2** prepare vegetables by putting them briefly in boiling water.

blancmange /bluh-**monzh**/ ▶ noun Brit. a dessert like a milky jelly, made with cornflour and milk.

bland ▶ adjective **1** not having any interesting features or qualities. **2** showing no emotion or excitement.

SYNONYMS **1** *a bland film* **uninteresting,** dull, boring, tedious, monotonous, ordinary, run-of-the-mill, drab, dreary, unexciting, lacklustre, flat, stale, trite. **2** *bland food* **tasteless,** flavourless, plain, insipid, weak, watery, thin, wishy-washy.
ANTONYMS interesting, tangy.

blandishments ▶ plural noun nice things said to someone in order to persuade them to do something.

blank ▶ adjective **1** not marked or decorated. **2** not understanding or reacting.

SYNONYMS **1** *a blank sheet of paper* **empty,** unmarked, unused, clear, free, bare, clean, plain. **2** *a blank face* **expressionless,** deadpan, wooden, stony, impassive, glazed, fixed, lifeless, inscrutable.
ANTONYMS full, marked, expressive.

▶ noun **1** a space in a form left to be filled in. **2** a state in which you cannot understand or remember something. **3** a gun cartridge containing gunpowder but no bullet.

SYNONYMS *fill in the blanks* **space,** gap.

▶ verb **1** (**blank something out**) hide or block out something. **2** Brit. informal deliberately ignore someone.
■ **blank verse** poetry that has a regular rhythm but does not rhyme.
□ **blankly** adverb **blankness** noun.

blanket ▶ noun **1** a large piece of woollen material used as a warm covering. **2** a thick mass or layer.

SYNONYMS *a blanket of cloud* **covering,** layer, coating, carpet, cloak, mantle, veil, pall, shroud.

▶ verb (**blankets, blanketing, blanketed**) cover with a thick layer.

SYNONYMS *snow blanketed the mountains* **cover,** coat, carpet, cloak, shroud, swathe, envelop.

blare ▶ verb (**blares, blaring, blared**) make a loud, harsh sound.
▶ noun a loud, harsh sound.

blarney ▶ noun talk that is friendly and charming but may not be truthful.

blasé /**blah**-zay/ ▶ adjective not impressed by something because you have experienced it often before.

blaspheme ▶ verb (**blasphemes, blaspheming, blasphemed**) speak rudely about God or use the name of God as a swear word.
□ **blasphemous** adjective **blasphemy** noun (plural **blasphemies**).

blast ▶ noun **1** an explosion, or the rush of compressed air spreading outwards from it. **2** a strong gust of wind. **3** a single loud note of a horn or whistle.

> SYNONYMS **1** *the blast from the bomb* **shock wave**, pressure wave. **2** *Friday's blast killed two people* **explosion**, detonation, discharge, burst. **3** *a blast of cold air* **gust**, rush, gale, squall, flurry. **4** *the shrill blast of the trumpets* **blare**, wail, roar, screech, shriek, hoot, honk, beep.

▶ verb **1** blow something up with explosives. **2** (**blast off**) (of a rocket or spacecraft) take off. **3** produce loud music or noise.

> SYNONYMS **1** *bombers were blasting airfields* **blow up**, bomb, blow (to pieces), dynamite, explode. **2** *guns were blasting away* **fire**, shoot, blaze, let fly, discharge. **3** *he blasted his horn* **honk**, beep, toot, sound. **4** *radios blasting out pop music* **blare**, boom, roar, thunder, bellow, pump, shriek, screech.

■ **blast furnace** a furnace for extracting metal from ore, using blasts of hot compressed air.

blatant ▶ adjective done in an open and unashamed way.

> SYNONYMS **flagrant**, glaring, obvious, undisguised, open, shameless, barefaced, unashamed, brazen.
> ANTONYMS inconspicuous, shamefaced.

□ **blatancy** noun **blatantly** adverb.

> ✔ **-ant**, not **-ent**: blat**ant**.

blather ▶ verb (**blathers, blathering, blathered**) talk without making much sense.
▶ noun rambling talk.

blaze ▶ noun **1** a very large or fierce fire. **2** a very bright light or display of colour. **3** a conspicuous display or outburst of something: *a blaze of publicity.* **4** a white stripe down the face of a horse.

> SYNONYMS **1** **fire**, flames, conflagration, inferno, holocaust. **2** *a blaze of light* **glare**, flash, burst, flare, streak, radiance, brilliance, beam, glitter.

▶ verb (**blazes, blazing, blazed**) **1** burn or shine fiercely or brightly. **2** shoot repeatedly or wildly.

> SYNONYMS **1** *the fire blazed merrily* **burn**, be alight, be on fire, be in flames. **2** *headlights blazed* **shine**, flash, flare, glare, gleam, glitter, glisten. **3** *soldiers blazed away* **fire**, shoot, blast, let fly.

■ **blaze a trail 1** mark out a path. **2** be the first to do something.

blazer ▶ noun **1** a jacket worn by schoolchildren or sports players as part of a uniform. **2** a man's smart jacket.

blazon /blay-zuhn/ ▶ verb display or proclaim something in a way that catches people's attention.

bleach ▶ verb lighten something by using a chemical or leaving it in sunlight.

> SYNONYMS **turn white**, whiten, turn pale, blanch, lighten, fade.
> ANTONYMS darken.

▶ noun a chemical used to remove stains and also to sterilize drains, sinks, etc.

bleak ▶ adjective **1** bare and exposed to the weather. **2** dreary and unwelcoming. **3** (of a situation) not hopeful.

> SYNONYMS **1** *a bleak landscape* **bare**, exposed, desolate, stark, desert, lunar, open, empty, windswept. **2** *the future is bleak* **unpromising**, unfavourable, dim, gloomy, black, grim, discouraging, disheartening, depressing.
> ANTONYMS lush, promising.

□ **bleakly** adverb **bleakness** noun.

bleary ▶ adjective (**blearier, bleariest**) (of the eyes) tired and not focusing properly.

> SYNONYMS **blurry**, unfocused, fogged, clouded, misty, watery.
> ANTONYMS clear.

□ **blearily** adverb.

bleat ▶ verb **1** (of a sheep or goat) make a weak, wavering cry. **2** speak or complain in a weak or silly way.
▶ noun a bleating sound.

bleed ▶ verb (**bleeds, bleeding, bled**) **1** lose blood from the body. **2** informal drain someone of money or resources. **3** (of dye or colour) seep into an adjoining colour or area. **4** allow fluid or gas to escape from a closed system through a valve. **5** (in the past) take blood from someone as a medical treatment.
▶ noun an instance of bleeding.

bleep ▶ noun a short, high-pitched sound made by an electronic device.
▶ verb make a bleep.
□ **bleeper** noun.

blemish ▶ noun a small mark or flaw.
▶ verb spoil the appearance of.

blench ▶ verb flinch suddenly out of fear or pain.

blend ▶ verb **1** mix and combine one thing with something else. **2** (**blend in**) become unnoticeable.

> SYNONYMS **1** *blend the ingredients until smooth* **mix**, mingle, combine, merge, amalgamate, stir, whisk, fold in. **2** *the new buildings blend with the older ones* **harmonize**, go (well), fit (in), be in tune, be compatible, coordinate, match, complement, suit.

▶ noun a mixture.

> SYNONYMS *a blend of bananas and ginger* **mixture**, mix, combination, compound, amalgam, fusion, alloy.

b

blender ▸ noun an electric device for liquidizing or chopping food.

bless ▸ verb 1 make something holy by saying a prayer over it. 2 ask God to protect a person or thing. 3 (**be blessed with**) have or be given something that is desired.

> SYNONYMS 1 *the Cardinal blessed the memorial plaque* **consecrate,** sanctify, dedicate to God, make holy; formal hallow. 2 *the gods blessed us with magical voices* **endow,** bestow, furnish, give, favour, confer on. 3 *the government refused to bless the undertaking* **sanction,** consent to, endorse, agree to, approve, back, support; informal give the green light to, OK.
> ANTONYMS curse, trouble, oppose.

blessed /**bless**-id, blest/ ▸ adjective 1 holy and protected by God. 2 bringing welcome pleasure or relief.

> SYNONYMS **holy,** sacred, hallowed, consecrated, sanctified, ordained, canonized, beatified.
> ANTONYMS cursed.

□ **blessedly** adverb.

blessing ▸ noun 1 God's approval and protection, or a prayer asking for this. 2 something for which you are very grateful. 3 a person's approval or support.

> SYNONYMS 1 *a blessing from the priest* **benediction,** dedication, consecration, grace, invocation, intercession. 2 *she gave the plan her blessing* **sanction,** endorsement, approval, consent, assent, agreement, backing, support; informal the green light, OK. 3 *it was a blessing they didn't have far to go* **advantage,** godsend, boon, benefit, help, bonus, plus, stroke of luck, windfall.
> ANTONYMS condemnation, affliction.

blew past of BLOW¹.

blight ▸ noun 1 a plant disease caused by fungi. 2 a thing that spoils or damages something.

> SYNONYMS 1 *potato blight* **disease,** canker, infestation, fungus, mildew, mould. 2 *the blight of aircraft noise* **curse,** scourge, affliction, plague, menace, misfortune, bane, trouble, nuisance, pest.
> ANTONYMS blessing.

▸ verb spoil or damage something.

> SYNONYMS *scandal blighted his career* **ruin,** wreck, spoil, mar, frustrate, disrupt, undo, scotch, destroy, shatter, devastate, demolish; informal mess up, foul up, put paid to, put the kibosh on, stymie; Brit. informal scupper.

blighter ▸ noun Brit. informal an annoying or unfortunate person.

blind ▸ adjective 1 not able to see. 2 done without being able to see or without certain information. 3 without awareness or judgement. 4 concealed, closed, or blocked off: *a blind alley.*

> SYNONYMS 1 **sightless,** unsighted, visually impaired, unseeing. 2 *blind acceptance of conventional opinion* **uncritical,** unreasoned, unthinking, unquestioning, mindless, undiscerning, indiscriminate. 3 *she was blind to the realities of her position* **unaware of,** oblivious to, ignorant of, unmindful of, heedless of, insensible to, indifferent to.
> ANTONYMS sighted, discerning, mindful.

▸ verb 1 make someone blind. 2 stop someone thinking clearly or sensibly. 3 (**blind someone with**) confuse someone by presenting them with something hard to understand.

▸ noun a screen for a window.

> SYNONYMS *a window blind* **screen,** shade, sunshade, curtain, awning, canopy, louvre, jalousie, shutter.

■ **blind date** a meeting with a person you have not met before, arranged in the hope of starting a romantic relationship. **blind man's buff** a game in which a player tries to catch people while wearing a blindfold. **blind spot 1** an area where someone's view is obstructed. **2** an inability to understand something. **turn a blind eye** pretend not to notice.

□ **blindness** noun.

blindfold ▸ noun a piece of cloth covering someone's eyes, so that they cannot see.

▸ verb cover someone's eyes with a blindfold.

blinding ▸ adjective 1 (of light) very bright. 2 (of pain) very severe.

□ **blindingly** adverb.

blindly ▸ adverb 1 in a blind way. 2 without foresight or reason.

> SYNONYMS 1 *he ran blindly upstairs* **impetuously,** impulsively, recklessly, heedlessly. 2 *they blindly followed US policy* **uncritically,** unquestioningly, unthinkingly, mindlessly, indiscriminately.
> ANTONYMS cautiously, critically.

bling-bling (or **bling**) ▸ noun informal showy, expensive clothes and jewellery.

blink ▸ verb 1 shut and open the eyes quickly. 2 (of a light) flash on and off.

▸ noun an act of blinking.

■ **on the blink** informal no longer working properly.

blinkered ▸ adjective having a limited point of view.

blinkers ▸ plural noun a pair of flaps used to prevent a horse from seeing sideways.

blip ▸ noun **1** a short, high-pitched sound made by an electronic device. **2** a small flashing point of light on a radar screen. **3** a temporary change in a situation or process that is generally steady.
▸ verb (**blips**, **blipping**, **blipped**) make a blip.

bliss ▸ noun perfect happiness.

SYNONYMS **joy,** happiness, pleasure, delight, ecstasy, elation, rapture, euphoria.
ANTONYMS misery.

blissful ▸ adjective full of joy and happiness.
□ **blissfully** adverb.

blister ▸ noun **1** a small bubble on the skin filled with watery liquid. **2** a similar bubble on a surface.
▸ verb (**blisters**, **blistering**, **blistered**) form blisters.

blistering ▸ adjective **1** (of heat) very strong. **2** very fierce or forceful.

blithe /bly*th*/ ▸ adjective **1** without thought or care. **2** very happy.
□ **blithely** adverb.

blithering ▸ adjective informal thoroughly stupid.

blitz ▸ noun **1** a sudden fierce military attack. **2** informal a sudden and concentrated effort.

SYNONYMS **bombing,** air raid, air strike, bombardment, barrage, attack, assault.

▸ verb make a sudden fierce attack on.

blizzard ▸ noun a snowstorm with high winds.

bloated ▸ adjective swollen with liquid or gas.

SYNONYMS **swollen,** distended, bulging, inflated, dilated.
ANTONYMS shrunken.

bloater ▸ noun a salted and smoked herring.

blob ▸ noun **1** a drop of a thick or sticky liquid. **2** a roundish mass or shape.

SYNONYMS **1** *a blob of cold gravy* **drop,** droplet, globule, bead, bubble. **2** *a blob of ink* **spot,** dab, blotch, blot, dot, smudge; informal splodge.

bloc ▸ noun a group of allied countries with similar political systems.

SYNONYMS **group,** alliance, coalition, federation, confederation, league, union, axis, association.

block ▸ noun **1** a large solid piece of material. **2** Brit. a large building divided into flats or offices. **3** a group of buildings with streets on all four sides. **4** an obstacle.

SYNONYMS **1** *a block of cheese* **chunk,** hunk, lump, wedge, cube, brick, slab, piece. **2** *an apartment block* **building,** complex, structure, development. **3** *a block to development* **obstacle,** bar, barrier, impediment, hindrance, check, hurdle.
ANTONYMS aid.

▸ verb **1** prevent movement or flow in something. **2** prevent the progress of something.

SYNONYMS **1** *weeds can block ditches* **clog,** stop up, choke, plug, bung up, obstruct, gum up, dam up, congest, jam. **2** *picket lines blocked access to the factory* **hinder,** hamper, obstruct, impede, inhibit, halt, stop, bar, check, prevent, fend off, hold off, repel.
ANTONYMS clear, aid, allow.

■ **block capitals** plain capital letters.

blockade ▸ noun a blocking of the way in or out of a place to prevent people or goods from entering or leaving it.
▸ verb (**blockades**, **blockading**, **blockaded**) block the way in or out of a place.

blockage ▸ noun an obstruction.

SYNONYMS **obstruction,** stoppage, block, jam, congestion.

blockbuster ▸ noun informal a film or book that is very successful.

blog ▸ noun a weblog.
▸ verb (**blogs**, **blogging**, **blogged**) regularly update a weblog.
□ **blogger** noun.

bloke ▸ noun Brit. informal a man.

blonde ▸ adjective (also **blond**) **1** (of hair) pale yellow. **2** having pale yellow hair.

SYNONYMS **fair,** light, yellow, flaxen, golden.
ANTONYMS dark.

▸ noun a woman with blonde hair.

blood ▸ noun **1** the red liquid that flows through the arteries and veins. **2** family background: *she must have Irish blood.*

SYNONYMS **1** **lifeblood,** gore, vital fluid. **2** *a woman of noble blood* **ancestry,** lineage, descent, parentage, family, birth, extraction, origin, stock.

▸ verb give someone their first experience of an activity.
■ **blood-curdling** horrifying. **blood pressure** the pressure created by blood as it moves around the body. **blood poisoning** a serious illness that occurs when harmful bacteria have infected the blood. **blood sport** a sport involving the hunting or killing of animals. **blood vessel** a vein, artery, or capillary carrying blood through the body. **new** (or **fresh**) **blood** people who join a group and give it new ideas.

bloodbath ▸ noun an event in which many people are violently killed.

bloodhound ▸ noun a large hound used for following scents.

bloodless ▸ adjective **1** without violence or killing. **2** (of the skin) drained of colour. **3** lacking emotion or vitality.

b

bloodletting ▶ noun **1** violent conflict. **2** (in the past) the removal of some of a patient's blood, as a medical treatment.

bloodshed ▶ noun the killing or wounding of people.

> SYNONYMS **slaughter**, massacre, killing, wounding, carnage, butchery, bloodletting, bloodbath.

bloodshot ▶ adjective (of the eyes) having tiny red blood vessels visible in the whites.

bloodstock ▶ noun thoroughbred horses.

bloodstream ▶ noun the blood circulating through the body.

bloodthirsty ▶ adjective (**bloodthirstier**, **bloodthirstiest**) taking pleasure in killing and violence.

> SYNONYMS **murderous**, homicidal, violent, vicious, barbarous, barbaric, savage, brutal, cut-throat.

bloody ▶ adjective (**bloodier**, **bloodiest**) **1** covered with or containing blood. **2** involving violence or cruelty.

> SYNONYMS **1** *his hands were all bloody* **bloodstained**, blood-soaked, gory, bleeding. **2** *a bloody civil war* **vicious**, ferocious, savage, fierce, brutal, cruel, murderous, gory.
> ANTONYMS clean, bloodless.

▶ verb (**bloodies**, **bloodying**, **bloodied**) cover or stain with blood.
■ **bloody-minded** Brit. informal deliberately unhelpful.

bloom ▶ verb **1** produce flowers; be in flower. **2** be healthy and happy.

> SYNONYMS **1** *the geraniums bloomed* **flower**, blossom, open, mature. **2** *the children bloomed in the Devonshire air* **flourish**, thrive, prosper, progress, burgeon; informal be in the pink.
> ANTONYMS wither, fade, decline.

▶ noun **1** a flower. **2** a state or period of blooming. **3** a healthy glow in a person's complexion. **4** a powdery coating on the surface of some fruit.

bloomers ▶ plural noun **1** women's baggy knee-length knickers. **2** historical women's loose-fitting trousers.

blossom ▶ noun a flower or a mass of flowers on a tree.

> SYNONYMS *pink blossoms* **flower**, bloom, bud.

▶ verb **1** produce blossom. **2** become strong and healthy.

> SYNONYMS **1** *the snowdrops have blossomed* **bloom**, flower, open, mature. **2** *the whole region had blossomed* **develop**, grow, mature, progress, evolve, burgeon, flourish, thrive, prosper,

bloom.
ANTONYMS wither, fade, decline.

blot ▶ noun **1** a spot of ink. **2** a thing that spoils something good.

> SYNONYMS **1** *an ink blot* **patch**, dab, smudge, blotch, mark, dot, spot; Brit. informal splodge. **2** *the only blot on a clean campaign* **blemish**, taint, stain, blight, flaw, fault. **3** *a blot on the landscape* **eyesore**, monstrosity, carbuncle, mess; informal sight.

▶ verb (**blots**, **blotting**, **blotted**) **1** dry something with an absorbent material. **2** mark or spoil. **3** (**blot something out**) hide something.
■ **blotting paper** absorbent paper used for drying ink when writing. **blot your copybook** Brit. spoil your good reputation.

blotch ▶ noun an irregular mark.
▶ verb mark something with blotches.
□ **blotchy** adjective.

blotter ▶ noun a pad of blotting paper.

blouse ▶ noun a woman's top that is similar to a shirt.

blouson /bloo-zon/ ▶ noun a short loose-fitting jacket.

blow[1] ▶ verb (**blows**, **blowing**, **blew**; past participle **blown**) **1** (of the wind) move. **2** send out air through pursed lips. **3** force air into an instrument through the mouth. **4** sound a horn. **5** break something open with explosives. **6** burst through pressure or overheating. **7** informal spend money recklessly. **8** informal waste an opportunity.

> SYNONYMS **1** *the icy wind blew around us* **gust**, puff, flurry, blast, roar, bluster, rush, storm. **2** *his ship was blown on to the rocks* **sweep**, carry, toss, drive, push, force. **3** *leaves blew across the road* **drift**, flutter, waft, float, glide, whirl, move. **4** *he blew a smoke ring* **exhale**, puff. **5** *he blew a trumpet* **sound**, blast, toot, play, pipe, trumpet.

▶ noun an act of blowing.
■ **blow-dry** style the hair while drying it with a hand-held dryer. **blow hot and cold** keep changing your mind. **blow over** (of trouble) fade away. **blow up** explode. **blow something up 1** make something explode. **2** inflate something.

blow[2] ▶ noun **1** a powerful stroke with a hand or weapon. **2** a sudden shock or disappointment.

> SYNONYMS **1** *a blow on the head* **knock**, bang, hit, punch, thump, smack, crack, rap; informal whack, bash, clout, wallop. **2** *losing his wife must have been a blow* **upset**, disaster, setback, misfortune, disappointment, calamity, catastrophe, thunderbolt, bombshell, shock, surprise, jolt.

b

blowfly ▸ noun (plural **blowflies**) a large fly which lays its eggs in meat.

blowhole ▸ noun the nostril of a whale or dolphin on the top of its head.

blowout ▸ noun the release of air or gas from a tyre, oil well, etc.

blowsy (or **blowzy**) (*rhymes with* drowsy) ▸ adjective (of a woman) plump and untidy.

blowtorch (or **blowlamp**) ▸ noun a portable device producing a hot flame, used to burn off paint.

blowy ▸ adjective windy or windswept.

blub ▸ verb (**blubs**, **blubbing**, **blubbed**) informal cry noisily.

blubber[1] ▸ noun the fat of whales and seals.
□ **blubbery** adjective.

blubber[2] ▸ verb (**blubbers**, **blubbering**, **blubbered**) informal cry noisily.

bludgeon ▸ noun a thick, heavy stick used as a weapon.
▸ verb **1** hit someone with a thick, heavy stick. **2** bully someone into doing something.

blue ▸ adjective (**bluer**, **bluest**) **1** of the colour of the sky on a sunny day. **2** informal sad or depressed. **3** informal indecent or pornographic.

SYNONYMS sky-blue, azure, cobalt, sapphire, navy, ultramarine, aquamarine, cyan.

▸ noun a blue colour.
■ **blue-blooded** from a royal or aristocratic family. **blue cheese** cheese having veins of mould in it. **blue-chip** (of an investment) safe and reliable. **blue-collar** relating to manual work. **out of the blue** unexpectedly.

bluebell ▸ noun a woodland plant with clusters of blue bell-shaped flowers.

blueberry ▸ noun (plural **blueberries**) a blue-black berry that grows on a North American bush.

bluebottle ▸ noun a large fly with a bluish body.

blueprint ▸ noun **1** a technical drawing or plan. **2** a model or prototype.

SYNONYMS **1** *blueprints of the aircraft* **plan,** design, diagram, drawing, sketch, layout. **2** *a blueprint for similar measures in other countries* **model,** plan, template, pattern, example, guide, prototype, pilot.

blues ▸ noun **1** slow, sad music of black American origin. **2** (**the blues**) informal feelings of sadness or depression.
□ **bluesy** adjective.

bluestocking ▸ noun a serious intellectual woman.

bluff[1] ▸ noun a pretence that you know or can do something when this is not true.

SYNONYMS *this offer was denounced as a bluff* **trick,** deception, fraud, ruse,

pretence, sham, fake, hoax, charade; informal put-on.
▸ verb pretend in this way.

SYNONYMS **1** *they are bluffing to hide their guilt* **pretend,** sham, fake, feign, lie, hoax, pose. **2** *I managed to bluff the board into believing me* **deceive,** delude, mislead, trick, fool, hoodwink, dupe, hoax; informal con, kid, have on.

■ **call someone's bluff** challenge someone to do something, in the belief that they will not be able to.

bluff[2] ▸ adjective frank and direct in a good-natured way.

SYNONYMS *a bluff man* **plain-spoken,** straightforward, blunt, direct, no-nonsense, frank, open, candid, forthright, unequivocal; informal upfront. ANTONYMS guarded, secretive.

bluff[3] ▸ noun a steep cliff or bank.

bluish (or **blueish**) ▸ adjective having a blue tinge.

blunder ▸ noun a clumsy mistake.

SYNONYMS *he shook his head at his blunder* **mistake,** error, gaffe, slip, oversight, faux pas; informal slip-up, boo-boo; Brit. informal clanger, boob; N. Amer. informal blooper.

▸ verb (**blunders**, **blundering**, **blundered**) **1** make a blunder. **2** move clumsily or as if unable to see.

SYNONYMS **1** *the government admitted it had blundered* **make a mistake,** err, miscalculate, bungle, trip up; informal slip up, screw up, blow it, goof; Brit. informal boob. **2** *she blundered down the steps* **stumble,** lurch, stagger, flounder, grope.

blunderbuss ▸ noun historical a gun with a short, wide barrel.

blunt ▸ adjective **1** not having a sharp edge or point. **2** frank and direct.

SYNONYMS **1** *a blunt knife* **dull,** worn. **2** *the leaf is broad with a blunt tip* **rounded,** flat, stubby. **3** *a blunt message* **straightforward,** frank, plain-spoken, candid, direct, bluff, forthright, unequivocal, brusque, abrupt, curt, bald, brutal, harsh, stark; informal upfront. ANTONYMS sharp, pointed, subtle.

▸ verb make or become blunt.

SYNONYMS *age hasn't blunted my passion for life* **dull,** deaden, dampen, numb, take the edge off, weaken, allay, diminish, lessen.
ANTONYMS intensify.

□ **bluntly** adverb.

blur ▸ verb (**blurs**, **blurring**, **blurred**) make or become unclear or less distinct.

b

SYNONYMS **1** *she felt tears blur her vision* **cloud**, fog, obscure, dim, make hazy, make fuzzy, soften, dull, numb, deaden, mute. **2** *the digits on the screen blurred* **become fuzzy**, become dim, become hazy, become vague.
ANTONYMS sharpen, focus.

▶ noun something that cannot be seen, heard, or remembered clearly.

SYNONYMS *a blur on the horizon* **indistinct shape**, smudge, haze, cloud, mist.

□ **blurry** adjective.

blurb ▶ noun a short description written to promote a book, film, or other product.

blurred ▶ adjective (of vision or an image) without sharp edges to objects.

SYNONYMS **indistinct**, fuzzy, hazy, misty, foggy, faint, unclear, vague, indefinite, unfocused.
ANTONYMS sharp, clear.

blurt ▶ verb (**blurt something out**) say something suddenly and without thinking.

SYNONYMS *she blurted out the truth* **burst out with**, exclaim, call out, divulge, disclose, reveal, betray, let slip, give away; informal blab, let on, spill the beans.

blush ▶ verb become red in the face from shyness or embarrassment.

SYNONYMS *Joan blushed at the compliment* **redden**, go pink, go red, flush, colour, burn up.

▶ noun a reddening of the face from shyness or embarrassment.

SYNONYMS *the darkness hid her blush* **flush**, rosiness, redness, pinkness, bloom, high colour, glow.

blusher ▶ noun a cosmetic used to give a reddish tinge to the cheeks.

bluster ▶ verb (**blusters, blustering, blustered**) **1** talk loudly or aggressively but without having any effect. **2** (of wind or rain) blow or beat fiercely and noisily.

▶ noun loud and aggressive talk that does not have much effect.

blustery ▶ adjective (of weather) marked by strong winds.

SYNONYMS **stormy**, gusty, blowy, windy, squally, wild.
ANTONYMS calm.

boa ▶ noun **1** a large snake which winds itself round and crushes its prey. **2** a long, thin scarf of feathers or fur.

boar ▶ noun (plural **boar** or **boars**) **1** (also **wild boar**) a wild pig with tusks. **2** a male pig.

board ▶ noun **1** a long, narrow, flat piece of wood used in building. **2** a rectangular piece of stiff material used as a surface for a particular purpose. **3** the people who control and direct an organization. **4** regular meals provided in return for payment.

SYNONYMS **1** *a wooden board* **plank**, beam, panel, slat, batten, timber. **2** *the board of directors* **committee**, council, panel, directorate, commission.

▶ verb **1** get on a ship, aircraft, or other passenger vehicle. **2** (**board something up** or **over**) seal something in with pieces of wood. **3** have a bedroom and receive meals in return for payment. **4** (of a pupil) live in school during term time.

SYNONYMS **1** *he boarded the aircraft* **get on**, go aboard, enter, mount, ascend, embark, catch. **2** *a number of students boarded with them* **lodge**, live, reside, stay, be housed; N. Amer. room; informal put up.

■ **board game** a game in which counters are moved around a board. **boarding house** a private house providing rooms and meals for paying guests. **boarding school** a school in which the pupils live during term time. **go by the board** (of a plan or principle) be rejected or abandoned. **on board** on or in a ship, aircraft, or other vehicle.

boarder ▶ noun a pupil who lives in school during term time.

boardroom ▶ noun a room in which a board of directors regularly meets.

boast ▶ verb **1** talk about yourself with too much pride. **2** (of a place or organization) have something as an impressive feature.

SYNONYMS **1** *his mother had been boasting about him* **brag**, crow, swagger, swank, gloat, show off; informal talk big, lay it on thick; Austral./NZ informal skite. **2** *the hotel boasts a fine restaurant* **have**, possess, own, enjoy, pride yourself/itself on, offer.
ANTONYMS hush up.

▶ noun an act of boasting.

SYNONYMS **1** *the government's main boast seemed undone* **brag**, exaggeration, overstatement; informal swank; Austral./NZ informal skite. **2** *the hall is the boast of the county* **pride**, joy, pride and joy, apple of someone's eye, wonder, delight.

boastful ▶ adjective showing too much pride in yourself.

SYNONYMS **bragging**, swaggering, bumptious, puffed up, full of yourself, cocky, conceited, arrogant; informal swanky, big-headed.
ANTONYMS modest.

□ **boastfully** adverb.

boat ▶ noun a vehicle that travels on water and is smaller than a ship.

■ **be in the same boat** informal be in the same difficult situation as other people.

boater ▶ noun a flat-topped straw hat with a brim.

boathouse ▶ noun a shed at the edge of a river or lake in which boats are kept.

boatswain /boh-s'n/ ▶ noun an officer in charge of equipment and the crew on a ship.

bob¹ ▶ verb (**bobs, bobbing, bobbed**) **1** make a quick, short movement up and down. **2** curtsy briefly.

> SYNONYMS **move up and down,** bounce, toss, skip, dance, wobble, jiggle, joggle, jolt, jerk.

▶ noun a bobbing movement.

bob² ▶ noun a short hairstyle that hangs evenly all round.
▶ verb (**bobs, bobbing, bobbed**) cut hair in a bob.

bob³ ▶ noun (plural **bob**) Brit. informal, dated a shilling (five pence).

bobbin ▶ noun a reel for holding thread.

bobble ▶ noun a small ball made of strands of wool.

bobby ▶ noun (plural **bobbies**) Brit. informal, dated a police officer.

bobsleigh ▶ noun a sledge used for racing down an ice-covered run.

bode ▶ verb (**bodes, boding, boded**) (**bode well** or **ill**) be a sign of a good or bad outcome.

bodge ▶ verb (**bodges, bodging, bodged**) Brit. informal make or repair something badly or clumsily.

bodice ▶ noun **1** the part of a dress above the waist. **2** a woman's sleeveless undergarment.

bodily ▶ adjective relating to the body.

> SYNONYMS *bodily sensations* **physical,** corporeal, corporal, mortal, material, tangible, concrete, real, actual. ANTONYMS spiritual, mental.

▶ adverb by taking hold of a person's body with force.

> SYNONYMS *he hauled her bodily from the van* **forcefully,** forcibly, violently, completely, entirely.

bodkin ▶ noun a thick needle with a blunt, rounded end.

body ▶ noun (plural **bodies**) **1** a person's or animal's physical structure. **2** the main part of the body, apart from the head and limbs. **3** the main or central part of something. **4** a mass or collection. **5** a group of people organized for a particular purpose. **6** Brit. a woman's stretchy garment for the upper body.

> SYNONYMS **1** *the human body* **figure,** frame, form, physique, anatomy, skeleton. **2** *he was hit by shrapnel in the head and body* **torso,** trunk. **3** *the*

bodies were put in the fire **corpse,** carcass, skeleton, remains; informal stiff; Medicine cadaver. **4** *the body of the article* **main part,** core, heart, hub. **5** *the representative body of the employers* **association,** organization, assembly, delegation, committee, executive, company, society, corporation, group.

■ **body language** the showing of your feelings through the way in which you move or hold your body.

bodybuilder ▶ noun a person who enlarges their muscles through exercise.

bodyguard ▶ noun a person paid to protect someone rich or famous.

bodywork ▶ noun the metal outer shell of a vehicle.

Boer (*rhymes with* more *or* mower) ▶ noun a member of the Dutch people who settled in southern Africa.

boffin ▶ noun Brit. informal a scientist.

bog ▶ noun an area of soft, wet ground.

> SYNONYMS **marsh,** swamp, mire, quagmire, morass, slough, fen, wetland.

▶ verb (**be/get bogged down**) be prevented from making progress.
□ **boggy** adjective.

bogey (or **bogy**) ▶ noun (plural **bogeys**) **1** an evil spirit. **2** a cause of fear or alarm.

bogeyman (or **bogyman**) ▶ noun (plural **bogeymen**) an evil spirit.

boggle ▶ verb (**boggles, boggling, boggled**) informal **1** be astonished or baffled. **2** (**boggle at**) hesitate to do.

bogie /boh-gi/ ▶ noun (plural **bogies**) a supporting frame with wheels, fitted beneath the end of a railway vehicle.

bogus ▶ adjective not genuine or true.

> SYNONYMS **fake,** spurious, false, fraudulent, sham, counterfeit, forged, feigned; informal phoney, pretend. ANTONYMS genuine.

Bohemian ▶ noun an artistic and unconventional person.
▶ adjective unconventional.

boil¹ ▶ verb **1** (of a liquid) reach a temperature where it bubbles and turns to vapour. **2** cook food in boiling water. **3** (**boil down to**) amount to.

> SYNONYMS *the soup is boiling* **simmer,** bubble, stew, seethe, froth, foam.

▶ noun the process of boiling.

boil² ▶ noun an inflamed pus-filled swelling on the skin.

> SYNONYMS *a boil on her neck* **swelling,** spot, pimple, blister, gathering, pustule, carbuncle, abscess.

boiler ▶ noun a device for heating water.
■ **boiler suit** Brit. a pair of overalls worn for dirty work.

b

boiling ▸ adjective **1** (of a liquid) at or near the temperature at which it boils. **2** informal very hot.

boisterous ▸ adjective lively and high-spirited.

> SYNONYMS **lively**, animated, exuberant, spirited, noisy, loud, rowdy, unruly, wild, uproarious, unrestrained, uninhibited, uncontrolled, rough, disorderly, riotous; informal rumbustious. ANTONYMS restrained.

□ **boisterously** adverb.

bold ▸ adjective **1** brave and confident. **2** (of a colour or design) strong or vivid. **3** (of printed words or letters) in thick, dark type.

> SYNONYMS **1** *bold adventurers* **daring**, intrepid, brave, courageous, valiant, fearless, dauntless, audacious, daredevil, adventurous, heroic, plucky; informal gutsy, spunky. **2** *a bold pattern* **striking**, vivid, bright, strong, eye-catching, prominent, gaudy, lurid, garish. ANTONYMS timid, pale, faint.

□ **boldly** adverb **boldness** noun.

bole ▸ noun a tree trunk.

bolero ▸ noun (plural **boleros**) **1** /buh-**lair**-oh/ a Spanish dance. **2** /**bol**-uh-roh/ a woman's short open jacket.

Bolivian ▸ noun a person from Bolivia. ▸ adjective relating to Bolivia.

boll ▸ noun the rounded seed capsule of plants such as cotton or flax.

bollard ▸ noun **1** Brit. a short post used to prevent traffic from entering an area. **2** a short post on a ship or quayside for securing a rope.

Bolshevik ▸ noun a member of the group which seized power in the Russian Revolution of 1917.
□ **Bolshevism** noun.

bolshie (or **bolshy**) ▸ adjective Brit. informal bad-tempered and uncooperative.

bolster ▸ noun a long, firm pillow. ▸ verb (**bolsters**, **bolstering**, **bolstered**) support or strengthen.

> SYNONYMS **strengthen**, reinforce, boost, fortify, support, buoy up, shore up, maintain, help, augment, increase. ANTONYMS undermine.

bolt ▸ noun **1** a heavy metal pin with a head that screws into a nut, used to fasten things together. **2** a bar that slides into a socket to fasten a door or window. **3** a short, heavy arrow shot from a crossbow. **4** a flash of lightning. **5** a roll of fabric.

> SYNONYMS **1** *the bolt on the door* **bar**, lock, catch, latch, fastener. **2** *nuts and bolts* **pin**, rivet, peg, screw.

▸ verb **1** fasten with a bolt. **2** run away suddenly. **3** eat food quickly. **4** (of a plant)

grow quickly upwards and stop flowering as seeds develop.

> SYNONYMS **1** *he bolted the door* **lock**, bar, latch, fasten, secure. **2** *the lid was bolted down* **pin**, rivet, peg, screw, fasten, fix. **3** *Anna bolted from the room* **dash**, dart, run, sprint, hurtle, rush, fly, shoot; informal tear, scoot, leg it. **4** *he bolted his breakfast* **gobble**, gulp, wolf, guzzle, devour; informal demolish, polish off, shovel down; N. Amer. informal scarf, snarf.

■ **bolt-hole** a place to escape to and hide in. **bolt upright** with the back very straight. **make a bolt for** run suddenly towards.

bomb ▸ noun **1** a device designed to explode and cause damage. **2** (**the bomb**) nuclear weapons. **3** (**a bomb**) Brit. informal a large sum of money.

> SYNONYMS **explosive**, incendiary (device), missile, projectile.

▸ verb **1** attack with a bomb or bombs. **2** Brit. informal move very quickly. **3** informal fail badly.

> SYNONYMS *their headquarters were bombed* **blow up**, blast, shell, blitz, strafe, pound, bombard, attack, assault, destroy, demolish.

bombard ▸ verb **1** attack continuously with bombs or other missiles. **2** direct a continuous flow of questions or information at.

> SYNONYMS **1** *gun batteries bombarded the islands* **shell**, pound, blitz, strafe, bomb, batter, blast, pelt. **2** *we were bombarded with information* **swamp**, inundate, flood, deluge, snow under, overwhelm.

□ **bombardment** noun.

bombardier /bom-buh-**deer**/ ▸ noun **1** a rank of non-commissioned officer in some artillery regiments. **2** a member of a bomber crew in the US air force who is responsible for releasing the bombs.

bombast ▸ noun language that sounds impressive but has little meaning.
□ **bombastic** adjective.

bomber ▸ noun **1** an aircraft designed for dropping bombs. **2** a person who plants bombs.

bombshell ▸ noun **1** a great surprise or shock. **2** informal a very attractive woman.

bona fide /boh-nuh fy-di/ ▸ adjective genuine; real.

bonanza ▸ noun **1** a situation creating wealth or success. **2** a large amount of something desirable.

> SYNONYMS **windfall**, godsend, blessing, bonus, stroke of luck; informal jackpot.

bonbon ▸ noun a sweet.

bond ▸ noun **1** a thing used to tie or fasten things together. **2** (**bonds**) ropes or

chains used to hold someone prisoner.
3 an instinct or feeling that draws people together. **4** a legally binding agreement. **5** a certificate issued by a government or public company promising to repay money lent to it at a fixed rate of interest and at a particular time.

> SYNONYMS **1** *the women forged a close bond* **friendship,** relationship, fellowship, partnership, association, affiliation, alliance, attachment. **2** *I've broken my bond* **promise,** pledge, vow, oath, word (of honour), guarantee, assurance, agreement, contract, pact, deal.

▶ **verb 1** join or be joined securely to something else. **2** feel connected to someone.

> SYNONYMS *the extensions are bonded to your hair* **join,** fasten, fix, affix, attach, secure, bind, stick, fuse.

bondage ▶ **noun 1** the state of being a slave or of having no freedom. **2** sexual activity that involves the tying up of one partner.

bone ▶ **noun 1** any of the pieces of hard material that make up the skeleton in vertebrates. **2** the hard material of which bones are made.
▶ **verb** (**bones, boning, boned**) remove the bones from meat or fish before cooking.
■ **bone china** white porcelain that contains a mineral obtained from bone. **bone dry** completely dry. **bone idle** very lazy. **bone of contention** something argued about. **close to the bone 1** (of a remark) accurate to the point of making you feel uncomfortable. **2** (of a joke or story) rather rude. **have a bone to pick with** informal have reason to quarrel with someone or to tell them off. **make no bones about** be direct in stating or dealing with.
□ **boneless** adjective.

bonemeal ▶ **noun** ground bones used as a fertilizer.

bonfire ▶ **noun** an open-air fire lit to burn rubbish or as a celebration.

bongo ▶ **noun** (plural **bongos**) each of a pair of small drums that are held between the knees.

bonhomie /bon-uh-mee/ ▶ **noun** good-natured friendliness.

bonkers ▶ **adjective** informal mad.

bonnet ▶ **noun 1** a woman's or child's hat tied under the chin. **2** Brit. the hinged metal cover over the engine of a vehicle.

bonny (or **bonnie**) ▶ **adjective** (**bonnier, bonniest**) chiefly Scottish N. English attractive and healthy-looking.

bonsai /bon-sy/ ▶ **noun** the art of growing miniature ornamental trees.

bonus ▶ **noun 1** a sum of money added to a person's wages for good performance. **2** an unexpected extra benefit.

> SYNONYMS **1** *the extra work's a real bonus* **extra,** plus, benefit, advantage, boon, blessing, godsend, stroke of luck, attraction. **2** *she's on a good salary and she gets a bonus* **gratuity,** handout, gift, present, reward, prize, incentive; informal perk, sweetener.
> ANTONYMS disadvantage.

bon voyage /bon voy-**yah**zh/ ▶ **exclamation** have a good journey.

bony ▶ **adjective** (**bonier, boniest**)
1 containing or resembling bones. **2** so thin that the bones can be seen.

> SYNONYMS **skinny,** thin, lean, gaunt, spare, skin and bone, skeletal, emaciated, underweight.
> ANTONYMS plump.

boo ▶ **exclamation 1** said suddenly to surprise someone. **2** said to show disapproval or contempt.
▶ **verb** (**boos, booing, booed**) say 'boo' to show disapproval or contempt.

boob Brit. informal ▶ **noun** an embarrassing mistake.
▶ **verb** make an embarrassing mistake.

booby ▶ **noun** (plural **boobies**) informal a stupid person.
■ **booby prize** a prize given to someone who comes last in a contest. **booby trap** an object containing a hidden explosive device.

boogie ▶ **verb** (**boogies, boogieing, boogied**) informal dance to pop music.

book ▶ **noun 1** a written or printed work consisting of pages fastened together along one side and bound in covers. **2** a main division of a literary work or of the Bible. **3** (**books**) a record of financial transactions.

> SYNONYMS **1** *he published his first book in 1610* **volume,** tome, publication, title, novel, treatise, manual. **2** *he scribbled in his book* **notepad,** notebook, pad, exercise book, logbook, ledger, journal, diary; Brit. jotter, pocketbook; N. Amer. scratch pad.

▶ **verb 1** reserve accommodation or a ticket. **2** (**book in**) register your arrival at a hotel. **3** engage a performer or guest for an event. **4** (**be booked up**) have all places or dates reserved. **5** make an official note of the name of someone who has broken a law or rule.

> SYNONYMS **1** *she booked a table at the restaurant* **reserve,** prearrange, order; informal bag. **2** *we booked a number of events in the Festival* **arrange,** programme, schedule, timetable, line up, lay on; N. Amer. slate.

bookcase ▶ **noun** a cabinet containing shelves on which books are kept.

b

bookend ▸ noun a support placed at the end of a row of books to keep them upright.

bookie ▸ noun (plural **bookies**) informal a bookmaker.

bookish ▸ adjective very interested in reading and studying.

bookkeeping ▸ noun the keeping of records of financial transactions.

booklet ▸ noun a small, thin book with paper covers.

SYNONYMS **pamphlet**, brochure, leaflet, tract; N. Amer. folder, mailer.

bookmaker ▸ noun a person who takes bets and pays out winnings.

bookmark ▸ noun **1** a strip of leather or card used to mark a place in a book. **2** a record of the address of a computer file, Internet page, etc., enabling a user to return to it quickly.
▸ verb record the address of a computer file, Internet page, etc.

bookworm ▸ noun informal a person who loves reading.

boom¹ ▸ noun **1** a deep, loud sound. **2** a period of fast economic growth.

SYNONYMS **1** *the boom of the waves on the rocks* **roar**, rumble, thunder, crashing, drumming, pounding, echoing, resonance, reverberation. **2** *an unprecedented boom in sales* **increase**, growth, advance, boost, escalation, improvement, upsurge, upturn. ANTONYMS slump.

▸ verb **1** make a deep, loud sound. **2** experience fast economic growth.

SYNONYMS **1** *thunder boomed overhead* **roar**, rumble, thunder, crash, roll, clap, explode, bang, resound, blare, echo, resonate, reverberate. **2** *a voice boomed at her* **shout**, yell, bellow, roar, thunder, bawl; informal holler. **3** *the market continued to boom* **flourish**, thrive, prosper, burgeon, progress, improve, pick up, expand. ANTONYMS whisper, slump.

boom² ▸ noun **1** a movable pole to which the bottom of a sail is attached. **2** a movable arm carrying a microphone or film camera. **3** a beam used to form a barrier across the mouth of a harbour.

boomerang ▸ noun a curved flat piece of wood that follows a circle through the air and returns to you when you throw it.

boon ▸ noun a very helpful thing.

boor ▸ noun a rough and bad-mannered person.

boorish ▸ adjective rough and ill-mannered.

SYNONYMS **coarse**, uncouth, rude, vulgar, uncivilized, unrefined, rough, thuggish, loutish, Neanderthal; Brit. informal yobbish;

Austral. informal ocker. ANTONYMS refined.

boost ▸ verb help or encourage.

SYNONYMS *they used advertising to boost sales* **increase**, raise, escalate, improve, strengthen, inflate, push up, promote, advance, foster, stimulate, encourage, facilitate, help, assist, aid; informal hike, bump up. ANTONYMS decrease.

▸ noun a source of help or encouragement.

SYNONYMS **1** *a boost to their morale* **uplift**, lift, spur, encouragement, help, inspiration, stimulus, fillip; informal shot in the arm. **2** *a boost in sales* **increase**, expansion, upturn, upsurge, rise, escalation, improvement, advance, growth, boom; informal hike. ANTONYMS decrease.

booster ▸ noun **1** a dose of a vaccine that increases or renews the effect of an earlier one. **2** the part of a rocket or spacecraft used to give acceleration after lift-off.

boot ▸ noun **1** an item of footwear covering the foot and the ankle or lower leg. **2** Brit. a space at the back of a car for carrying luggage. **3** informal a hard kick. **4** (**the boot**) informal dismissal from a job.
▸ verb **1** informal kick someone hard. **2** (**boot someone out**) informal force someone to leave. **3** start a computer and make it ready to operate.

SYNONYMS **kick**, punt, tap, propel, drive, knock.

■ **to boot** as well.

bootee (or **bootie**) ▸ noun **1** a baby's woollen shoe. **2** a woman's short boot.

booth ▸ noun **1** an enclosed compartment that gives you privacy when telephoning, voting, etc. **2** a small temporary structure used for selling goods or staging shows at a market or fair.

SYNONYMS **1** *booths for different traders* **stall**, stand, kiosk. **2** *a phone booth* **cubicle**, kiosk, box, enclosure, cabin.

bootleg ▸ adjective made or distributed illegally.
□ **bootlegger** noun **bootlegging** noun.

booty ▸ noun valuable stolen goods.

SYNONYMS **loot**, plunder, haul, spoils, ill-gotten gains, pickings; informal swag.

booze informal ▸ noun alcoholic drink.
▸ verb (**boozes**, **boozing**, **boozed**) drink a lot of alcohol.
□ **boozer** noun **boozy** adjective.

bop informal ▸ noun a dance to pop music.
▸ verb (**bops**, **bopping**, **bopped**) dance to pop music.
□ **bopper** noun.

boracic ▸ adjective having to do with boric acid.

borage ▸ noun a plant with bright blue flowers and hairy leaves.

borax ▸ noun a white mineral used in making glass.

Bordeaux /bor-**doh**/ ▸ noun a wine from the Bordeaux region of France.

border ▸ noun 1 a boundary between two countries or areas. 2 a decorative band around the edge of something. 3 a strip of ground along the edge of a lawn where flowers or shrubs are planted.

> SYNONYMS 1 *the border of a medieval manuscript* edge, margin, perimeter, circumference, periphery, rim, fringe, verge, sides. 2 *the French border* frontier, boundary, borderline, perimeter.

▸ verb (**borders**, **bordering**, **bordered**) 1 form a border around or along. 2 (of a country or area) be next to. 3 (**border on**) come near to.

> SYNONYMS 1 *the fields were bordered by hedges* surround, enclose, encircle, edge, fringe, bound, flank. 2 *the straps are bordered with gold braid* edge, fringe, hem, trim, pipe, finish. 3 *the forest bordered Broadmoor* adjoin, abut, be next to, be adjacent to, touch.

borderline ▸ noun a boundary.
▸ adjective on the boundary between two qualities or categories.

bore¹ ▸ verb (**bores**, **boring**, **bored**) make a hole in something with a drill or other tool.

> SYNONYMS *bore a hole* drill, pierce, perforate, puncture, punch, tunnel, burrow, mine, dig, gouge, sink.

▸ noun the hollow part inside a gun barrel or other tube.

bore² ▸ noun a dull person or activity.

> SYNONYMS *you can be such a bore* tedious person/thing, tiresome person/thing, bother, nuisance, pest, annoyance, trial, thorn in your flesh/side; informal drag, pain (in the neck), headache, hassle.

▸ verb (**bores**, **boring**, **bored**) make someone feel tired and unenthusiastic by being dull.

> SYNONYMS *the television news bored Philip* weary, pall on, tire, fatigue, send to sleep, leave cold; informal turn off.
> ANTONYMS interest.

bore³ past of BEAR¹.

bored ▸ adjective feeling tired and unenthusiastic because you have nothing interesting to do.

> ❗ Use **bored by** or **bored with** rather than **bored of**.

boredom ▸ noun the state of feeling bored.

> SYNONYMS tedium, ennui, apathy, weariness, dullness, monotony, repetitiveness, flatness, dreariness.
> ANTONYMS interest, excitement.

borehole ▸ noun a deep hole in the ground made to find water or oil.

boric acid ▸ noun a substance made from boron, used as an antiseptic.

boring ▸ adjective not interesting; tedious.

> SYNONYMS tedious, dull, dreary, monotonous, repetitive, uneventful, unimaginative, characterless, featureless, colourless, lifeless, uninteresting, unexciting, lacklustre, humdrum, mind-numbing, soul-destroying, wearisome, tiresome; informal deadly; Brit. informal samey; N. Amer. informal dullsville.
> ANTONYMS interesting, exciting.

born ▸ adjective 1 having come out of your mother's body; having started life. 2 having a particular natural ability: *a born engineer*. 3 (**born of**) existing as a result of a situation or feeling.
∎ **born-again** newly converted to Christianity or some other cause.

> ❗ Don't confuse **born** with **borne**, which is the past participle of **bear** and means 'carried'.

borne past participle of BEAR¹.

Bornean /bor-ni-uhn/ ▸ noun a person from Borneo.
▸ adjective relating to Borneo.

boron ▸ noun a chemical element used in making alloy steel and in nuclear reactors.

borough ▸ noun 1 Brit. a town with a corporation and privileges granted by a royal charter. 2 a part of London or New York City which has its own local council.

borrow ▸ verb take and use something belonging to someone else with the intention of returning it.

> SYNONYMS 1 *we borrowed a lot of money* loan, lease, hire; informal cadge, scrounge, bum, touch someone for; N. Amer. informal mooch; Austral./NZ informal bludge. 2 *adventurous chefs borrow foreign techniques* adopt, take on, acquire, embrace.
> ANTONYMS lend.

borscht (or **borsch**) /borsht, borsh/ ▸ noun a Russian or Polish soup made with beetroot.

borstal ▸ noun Brit. historical a type of prison for young offenders.

Bosnian /boz-ni-uhn/ ▸ noun a person from Bosnia.
▸ adjective relating to Bosnia.

bosom ▸ noun 1 a woman's breast or chest. 2 loving care: *he went home to the bosom of his family*.
▸ adjective (of a friend) very close.

b

boss[1] informal ▸ noun a person who is in charge of other people at work.

> SYNONYMS *the boss of a large company* **head,** chief, principal, director, president, chief executive, chair, manager, supervisor, foreman, overseer, controller, employer, owner, proprietor; Brit. informal **gaffer, governor;** N. Amer. informal **head honcho.**

▸ verb tell someone what to do in an arrogant or annoying way.

> SYNONYMS *you have no right to boss me about* **order about/around,** dictate to, bully, push around/about, call the shots, lay down the law; informal **bulldoze, walk all over, railroad.**

boss[2] ▸ noun a knob at the centre of a shield, propeller, or similar object.

bossa nova /bos-suh **noh**-vuh/ ▸ noun a dance like the samba, from Brazil.

boss-eyed ▸ adjective Brit. informal cross-eyed.

bossy ▸ adjective (**bossier, bossiest**) tending to tell people what to do in an arrogant or annoying way.

> SYNONYMS **domineering,** pushy, overbearing, imperious, officious, authoritarian, dictatorial; informal **high and mighty.**
> ANTONYMS submissive.

▫ **bossiness** noun.

bosun (or **bo'sun**) /**boh**-suhn/ = BOATSWAIN.

botany ▸ noun the scientific study of plants.
▫ **botanical** (or **botanic**) adjective **botanist** noun.

botch ▸ verb informal do something badly or carelessly.

both ▸ determiner & pronoun two people or things, considered together.
▸ adverb applying to each of two alternatives.

bother ▸ verb (**bothers, bothering, bothered**) **1** take the trouble to do something. **2** annoy, worry, or upset someone. **3** (**bother with** or **about**) feel concern about or interest in.

> SYNONYMS **1** *no one bothered her* **disturb,** trouble, inconvenience, pester, badger, harass, molest, plague; informal **hassle, bug;** N. English informal **mither;** N. Amer. informal **ride. 2** *the incident was too small to bother about* **mind,** care, worry, concern yourself, trouble yourself. **3** *there was something bothering him* **worry,** trouble, concern, perturb, disturb, disquiet; informal **rattle.**

▸ noun **1** trouble and fuss. **2** (**a bother**) a cause of trouble or fuss.

> SYNONYMS **1** *I don't want to put you to any bother* **trouble,** effort, exertion, inconvenience, fuss, pains; informal **hassle. 2** *the food was such a bother to cook* **nuisance,** pest, palaver, rigmarole, job,

trial, bind, bore, drag, inconvenience, trouble; informal **hassle, headache, pain** (in the neck). **3** *a spot of bother in the public bar* **disorder,** fighting, trouble, disturbance, commotion, uproar; informal **hoo-ha, aggro, argy-bargy, kerfuffle.**

bothersome ▸ adjective troublesome.

Botswanan ▸ noun a person from Botswana, a country in southern Africa.
▸ adjective relating to Botswana.

bottle ▸ noun **1** a container with a narrow neck, used for storing liquids. **2** Brit. informal courage.
▸ verb (**bottles, bottling, bottled**) **1** place in bottles for storage. **2** (**bottle something up**) hide your feelings.
■ **bottle green** dark green.

bottleneck ▸ noun a narrow section of road where the flow of traffic is restricted.

bottom ▸ noun **1** the lowest or furthest point or part of something. **2** the lowest position in a competition or ranking. **3** a person's buttocks. **4** (also **bottoms**) the lower half of a two-piece garment.

> SYNONYMS **1** *the bottom of the stairs* **foot,** lowest part, base, foundation. **2** *the bottom of the car* **underside,** underneath, undersurface, underbelly. **3** *the bottom of Lake Ontario* **floor,** bed, depths. **4** *the bottom of his garden* **farthest point,** far end, extremity. **5** *I've got a tattoo on my bottom* **buttocks,** rear (end), rump, seat; informal **behind,** backside; Brit. informal **bum, botty, jacksie;** N. Amer. informal **butt, fanny;** humorous **posterior.**
> ANTONYMS top, surface.

▸ adjective in the lowest or furthest position.

> SYNONYMS *she sat on the bottom step* **lowest,** last, bottommost.
> ANTONYMS top.

▸ verb (**bottom out**) (of a situation) reach the lowest point before becoming stable or improving.
■ **get to the bottom of** find an explanation for. **the bottom line** informal the most important factor.
▫ **bottomless** adjective.

botulism /bot-yuu-li-z'm/ ▸ noun a dangerous form of food poisoning.

boudoir /boo-dwar/ ▸ noun a woman's bedroom or small private room.

bouffant /boo-fon/ ▸ adjective (of hair) styled so as to stand out from the head in a rounded shape.

bougainvillea /boo-guhn-**vil**-li-uh/ ▸ noun a tropical climbing plant with brightly coloured flower-like leaves (called bracts).

bough ▸ noun a large branch.

bought past and past participle of BUY.

b

! Don't confuse **bought** with **brought**, which is the past of **bring**.

boulder ▶ noun a large rock.

boulevard /boo-luh-vard/ ▶ noun a wide street.

bounce ▶ verb (**bounces**, **bouncing**, **bounced**) **1** move quickly up or away from a surface after hitting it. **2** move or jump up and down repeatedly. **3** informal (of a cheque) be returned by a bank when there is not enough money in an account for it to be paid.

SYNONYMS **1** *the ball bounced* **rebound**, spring back, ricochet; N. Amer. carom. **2** *William bounced down the stairs* **bound**, leap, jump, spring, bob, hop, skip, gambol, trip, prance.

▶ noun **1** an act of bouncing. **2** lively confidence.

SYNONYMS **1** *the pitch's uneven bounce* **springiness**, resilience, elasticity, give. **2** *she had lost her bounce* **vitality**, vigour, energy, vivacity, liveliness, animation, sparkle, verve, spirit; informal get-up-and-go, pep, zing.

bouncer ▶ noun a person employed by a nightclub to control or keep out troublemakers.

bouncy ▶ adjective (**bouncier**, **bounciest**) **1** able to bounce, or making something bounce. **2** confident and lively.

bound¹ ▶ verb move with long, leaping strides.

SYNONYMS *Louis came bounding down the stairs* **leap**, jump, spring, vault, bounce, hop, skip, dance, prance, gambol, gallop.

▶ noun a leaping movement.

bound² ▶ verb **1** form the boundary of. **2** restrict.

SYNONYMS **1** *corporate freedom is bounded by law* **limit**, restrict, confine, circumscribe, demarcate, delimit. **2** *the heath is bounded by a hedge* **enclose**, surround, encircle, circle, border, close in/off, hem in. **3** *the garden was bounded by Mill Lane* **border**, adjoin, abut, be next to, be adjacent to.

▶ noun a boundary or restriction.
■ **out of bounds 1** (in sport) beyond the field of play. **2** beyond where you are allowed to go.

bound³ past and past participle of BIND.
▶ adjective **1** restricted to or by a place or situation: *his job kept him city-bound.* **2** going towards somewhere: *a train bound for Edinburgh.* **3** (**bound to**) certain to be, do, or have.

SYNONYMS **1** *he raised his bound ankles* **tied**, restrained, fixed, fastened, secured. **2** *she seemed bound to win* **certain**, sure, very likely, destined. **3** *bound by the Official Secrets Act* **constrained**, obliged, compelled, required, obligated. **4** *religion and morality are bound up with one another* **connected**, linked, tied, united, allied, interdependent.
ANTONYMS free, unlikely, independent.

boundary ▶ noun (plural **boundaries**) a line marking the limits of an area.

SYNONYMS **1** *the boundary between Israel and Jordan* **border**, frontier, borderline, partition. **2** *the boundary between art and advertising* **dividing line**, division, borderline, cut-off point. **3** *the boundary of his estate* **limits**, confines, bounds, margins, edges, fringes, border, periphery, perimeter.

bounder ▶ noun Brit. informal, dated a man who is dishonest or treats other people badly.

boundless ▶ adjective unlimited.

bounteous ▶ adjective old use given or giving generously.

bountiful ▶ adjective **1** existing in large quantities. **2** giving generously.

bounty ▶ noun (plural **bounties**) **1** literary generosity, or something given in generous amounts. **2** a reward paid for killing or capturing someone.

bouquet /boo-kay, boh-kay/ ▶ noun **1** a bunch of flowers. **2** the pleasant smell of a particular wine or perfume.

SYNONYMS **1** *her bridal bouquet* **posy**, nosegay, spray, corsage, buttonhole, garland, wreath, arrangement. **2** *the Chardonnay has a fine bouquet* **aroma**, nose, smell, fragrance, perfume, scent, odour.

bourbon /ber-buhn/ ▶ noun an American whisky made from maize and rye.

bourgeois /boor-zhwah/ ▶ adjective having to do with the middle class, especially in being concerned with wealth and social status.

SYNONYMS **middle-class**, conservative, conformist, conventional, propertied, provincial, suburban, small-town.
ANTONYMS proletarian.

bourgeoisie /boor-zhwah-zee/ ▶ noun the middle class.

bout ▶ noun **1** a short period of great activity, or of illness. **2** a wrestling or boxing match.

SYNONYMS **1** *a bout of exercise* **spell**, period, stretch, stint, session, burst, flurry, spurt. **2** *a coughing bout* **attack**, fit, spasm. **3** *he is fighting only his fifth bout* **contest**, fight, match, round, competition, meeting, encounter.

boutique /boo-teek/ ▶ noun a small shop selling fashionable clothes.

b

bovine /boh-vyn/ ▸ adjective **1** having to do with cattle. **2** rather slow and stupid.

bow[1] (*rhymes with* toe) ▸ noun **1** a knot tied with two loops and two loose ends. **2** a weapon for shooting arrows, consisting of a string held taut by a strip of bent wood. **3** a rod with horsehair stretched along its length, used for playing some stringed instruments.
■ **bow-legged** having legs that curve outwards at the knee. **bow tie** a man's tie that is tied in a bow.

bow[2] (*rhymes with* cow) ▸ verb **1** bend the head and upper body as a sign of respect. **2** bend with age or under a heavy weight. **3** give in to pressure. **4** (**bow out**) withdraw from an activity.

> SYNONYMS **1** *the officers bowed* **nod**, bend, stoop, bob, curtsy, kneel, genuflect. **2** *the mast quivered and bowed* **bend**, buckle, curve, flex, deform. **3** *the government bowed to foreign pressure* **give in**, submit, yield, surrender, succumb, capitulate.

▸ noun an act of bowing.

> SYNONYMS *a perfunctory bow* **nod**, bob, obeisance, curtsy, genuflection.

■ **bow and scrape** try too hard to please someone.

bow[3] (*rhymes with* cow) (or **bows**) ▸ noun the front end of a ship.

> SYNONYMS *the bow of the tanker* **prow**, front, stem, nose, head.

bowdlerize (or **bowdlerise**) /bowd-luh-ryz/ ▸ verb (**bowdlerizes**, **bowdlerizing**, **bowdlerized**) remove parts of a written work that might shock or offend people.

bowel ▸ noun **1** (also **bowels**) the intestine. **2** (**bowels**) the innermost parts of something.

> SYNONYMS **1** *a disorder of the bowels* **intestines**, entrails, viscera, innards, digestive system; Medicine gut; informal guts, insides. **2** *the bowels of the ship* **interior**, inside, core, belly, depths, recesses; informal innards.

■ **bowel movement** an act of emptying waste matter from the bowels.

bower ▸ noun a pleasant shady place under trees.

bowl[1] ▸ noun **1** a round, deep dish or basin. **2** a rounded, hollow part of an object.

> SYNONYMS **dish**, basin, pot, crock, vessel, receptacle.

bowl[2] ▸ verb **1** roll a round object along the ground. **2** Cricket (of a bowler) throw the ball towards the wicket. **3** Brit. move along rapidly and smoothly.

> SYNONYMS *he bowled a hundred or so balls* **throw**, pitch, hurl, toss, lob, fling, roll, launch, propel; informal chuck, sling, bung.

▸ noun a heavy ball used in bowls or tenpin bowling.

■ **bowl someone over 1** knock someone down. **2** informal surprise or impress someone very much.

bowler[1] ▸ noun **1** Cricket a member of the fielding side who bowls. **2** a player at bowls or tenpin bowling.

bowler[2] ▸ noun a man's hard black felt hat that is rounded at the top and has a rim.

bowling ▸ noun bowls, tenpin bowling, or skittles.

bowls ▸ noun a game played with wooden balls called bowls, in which you roll your bowl as close as possible to a small white ball (the jack).

box[1] ▸ noun **1** a square or rectangular container with a lid. **2** an enclosed area reserved for a group of people in a theatre or sports ground. **3** (**the box**) informal television.

> SYNONYMS **1** **carton**, pack, packet, case, crate, chest, coffer, casket. **2** *a telephone box* **booth**, cubicle, compartment, kiosk, cabin, hut.

▸ verb **1** put something in a box. **2** (**box someone in**) restrict or confine someone.

> SYNONYMS *Muriel boxed up his clothes* **pack**, package, parcel, encase, bundle, crate.

■ **box number** a number identifying an advertisement in a newspaper, used as an address for replies. **box office** the place at a theatre or cinema where tickets are sold. **box room** Brit. a small room used for storage.

box[2] ▸ verb take part in boxing.

> SYNONYMS *he began boxing professionally* **fight**, prizefight, spar, battle, brawl; informal scrap.

▸ noun a slap on the side of a person's head.
■ **box someone's ears** slap someone on both sides of the head.

box[3] ▸ noun a shrub with small, round glossy leaves.

boxer ▸ noun **1** a person who boxes as a sport. **2** a breed of dog with a smooth brown coat and a flattened face.

> SYNONYMS **fighter**, pugilist, prizefighter; informal bruiser, scrapper.

■ **boxer shorts** men's underpants that look like shorts.

boxing ▸ noun a sport in which contestants fight each other wearing big padded gloves.

Boxing Day ▸ noun Brit. a public holiday on the day after Christmas Day.

boxy ▸ adjective **1** roughly square in shape. **2** (of a room or space) cramped.

boy ▸ noun a male child or youth.

SYNONYMS **lad,** youth, young man, stripling; Scottish & N. English laddie; derogatory brat. See also CHILD.

□ boyhood noun boyish adjective.

boycott ▸ verb **1** refuse to have dealings with. **2** refuse to buy goods as a protest.

SYNONYMS *they boycotted the election* **shun,** snub, spurn, avoid, abstain from, reject, veto.
ANTONYMS support.

▸ noun an act of boycotting someone or something.

SYNONYMS *a boycott on the use of tropical timbers* **ban,** veto, embargo, prohibition, sanction, restriction, avoidance, rejection.

boyfriend ▸ noun a person's regular male companion in a romantic or sexual relationship.

SYNONYMS **lover,** sweetheart, beloved, darling, partner; informal fella, flame, fancy man; N. Amer. informal squeeze.

bra ▸ noun a woman's undergarment worn to support the breasts.

brace ▸ noun **1** a part that strengthens or supports something. **2** (**braces**) Brit. a pair of straps that pass over the shoulders and fasten to the top of trousers to hold them up. **3** a wire device used to straighten the teeth. **4** (plural **brace**) a pair. **5** (also **brace and bit**) a drilling tool with a crank handle and a socket to hold a bit.

SYNONYMS *the aquarium is supported by wooden braces* **prop,** strut, stay, support, bracket.

▸ verb (**braces, bracing, braced**) **1** make something stronger or firmer with a brace. **2** press your body firmly against something to stay balanced. **3** (**brace yourself**) prepare for something difficult or unpleasant.

SYNONYMS **1** *the plane's wing is braced by rods* **support,** shore up, prop up, hold up, buttress, reinforce. **2** *he braced his hand on the railing* **steady,** secure, stabilize, poise, fix. **3** *brace yourself for disappointment* **prepare,** get ready, gear up, nerve, steel, fortify; informal psych yourself up.

bracelet ▸ noun an ornamental band or chain worn on the wrist or arm.

bracing ▸ adjective refreshing; making you feel full of energy.

SYNONYMS **invigorating,** refreshing, stimulating, energizing, exhilarating, restorative, rejuvenating.

bracken ▸ noun a tall fern.

bracket ▸ noun **1** each of a pair of marks ( ) [ ] ( ) ‹ › used to enclose words or figures. **2** a category of similar people or things. **3** a right-angled support that sticks out from a wall.

SYNONYMS **1** *each speaker is fixed on a bracket* **support,** prop, stay, batten, rest, mounting, rack, frame. **2** *a higher tax bracket* **group,** category, grade, classification, division.

▸ verb (**brackets, bracketing, bracketed**) **1** enclose in brackets. **2** place in the same category.

brackish ▸ adjective (of water) slightly salty.

bract ▸ noun a leaf with a flower in the angle where it meets the stem.

brag ▸ verb (**brags, bragging, bragged**) speak boastfully.

SYNONYMS **boast,** crow, swagger, swank, bluster, gloat, show off, blow your own trumpet, sing your own praises; informal talk big.

▸ noun a simplified form of the card game poker.

braggart /brag-gert/ ▸ noun a boastful person.

braid ▸ noun **1** threads woven into a decorative band. **2** a length of hair made up of strands plaited together.

▸ verb **1** form hair into a braid. **2** trim something with braid.

Braille ▸ noun a written language for blind people, using raised dots.

brain ▸ noun **1** an organ contained in the skull that controls thought and feeling and is the centre of the nervous system. **2** intellectual ability. **3** (**the brains**) informal the main organizer within a group.

SYNONYMS **intelligence,** intellect, brainpower, cleverness, wit(s), reasoning, wisdom, judgement, understanding, sense; informal nous, grey matter; N. Amer. informal smarts.

▸ verb informal hit someone hard on the head.

brainchild ▸ noun informal an idea or invention thought up by a particular person.

brainless ▸ adjective very stupid.

brainstorm ▸ noun Brit. informal a moment in which you are suddenly unable to think clearly.

▸ verb hold a group discussion to solve a problem or produce new ideas.

brainwash ▸ verb force someone to accept an idea or belief by putting pressure on them or repeating the same thing over and over again.

brainwave ▸ noun **1** an electrical impulse in the brain. **2** informal a sudden clever idea.

brainy ▸ adjective (**brainier, brainiest**) informal intelligent.

braise ▸ verb (braises, braising, braised) fry food lightly and then stew it slowly in a closed container.

brake ▸ noun a device for slowing or stopping a moving vehicle.

> SYNONYMS **curb**, check, restraint, constraint, control, limit.
> ANTONYMS accelerator.

▸ verb (brakes, braking, braked) slow or stop a vehicle with a brake.

> SYNONYMS **slow (down)**, decelerate, reduce speed.
> ANTONYMS accelerate.

> ❗ Don't confuse **brake** with **break** which mainly means 'separate into pieces' or 'a pause or short rest'.

bramble ▸ noun 1 a blackberry bush or similar prickly shrub. 2 Brit. the fruit of the blackberry.

bran ▸ noun pieces of the outer husk left when grain is made into flour.

branch ▸ noun 1 a part of a tree which grows out from the trunk. 2 a river, road, or railway extending out from a main one. 3 a division of a larger group.

> SYNONYMS 1 *the branches of a tree* **bough**, limb, arm, offshoot, twig. 2 *the judicial branch of government* **division**, subdivision, section, subsection, department, unit, sector, wing. 3 *the corporation's New York branch* **office**, bureau, agency, subsidiary.

▸ verb 1 divide into one or more branches. 2 (**branch out**) start doing a different sort of activity.

> SYNONYMS 1 *the place where the road branches* **fork**, divide, split, bifurcate. 2 *narrow paths branched off the road* **diverge**, deviate, split off, fan out, radiate.

brand ▸ noun 1 a type of product made by a company under a particular name. 2 (also **brand name**) a name given to a product by its maker. 3 a mark burned on farm animals with a piece of hot metal. 4 a piece of smouldering wood.

> SYNONYMS 1 *a new brand of margarine* **make**, line, label, marque, trade name, trademark, proprietary name. 2 *her particular brand of humour* **type**, kind, sort, variety, class, category, genre, style, ilk; N. Amer. stripe.

▸ verb 1 mark with a piece of hot metal. 2 mark someone out as being bad in a particular way. 3 give a brand name to.

> SYNONYMS 1 *the letter M was branded on each animal* **mark**, stamp, burn, sear. 2 *the scene was branded on her brain* **engrave**, stamp, etch, imprint.

3 *the media branded us as communists* **stigmatize**, mark out, denounce, discredit, vilify, label.

■ **brand new** completely new.

brandish ▸ verb wave something as a threat or in anger or excitement.

> SYNONYMS **flourish**, wave, shake, wield, swing, swish.

brandy ▸ noun (plural **brandies**) a strong alcoholic drink made from wine or fermented fruit juice.

brash ▸ adjective confident in a rather rude or aggressive way.

> SYNONYMS 1 *a brash man* **self-assertive**, pushy, cocky, self-confident, arrogant, bold, audacious, brazen. 2 *brash colours* **garish**, gaudy, loud, flamboyant, showy, tasteless; informal flashy, tacky.
> ANTONYMS meek, subdued.

▫ **brashly** adverb **brashness** noun.

brass ▸ noun 1 a yellowish metal made by mixing copper and zinc. 2 (also **horse brass**) Brit. a flat brass ornament for a horse's harness. 3 Brit. a brass plate fixed in a church in memory of someone. 4 brass wind instruments forming a section of an orchestra.

■ **brass band** a group of musicians playing brass instruments. **top brass** informal people in authority.

brasserie /brass-uh-ri/ ▸ noun (plural **brasseries**) an inexpensive French or French-style restaurant.

brassica /brass-ik-uh/ ▸ noun a plant of a family that includes cabbages and swedes.

brassiere /braz-i-er/ ▸ noun a bra.

brassy ▸ adjective (**brassier, brassiest**) 1 resembling brass in colour. 2 unpleasantly bright or showy. 3 harsh or blaring like a brass instrument.

brat ▸ noun informal a badly behaved child.

bravado ▸ noun confidence or a show of confidence that is intended to impress.

brave ▸ adjective willing to do something that is dangerous or frightening; not afraid.

> SYNONYMS **courageous**, intrepid, bold, plucky, heroic, fearless, daring, audacious, dauntless, valiant; informal game, gutsy.
> ANTONYMS cowardly.

▸ noun dated an American Indian warrior.

▸ verb (**braves, braving, braved**) face or deal with something frightening or unpleasant.

> SYNONYMS *fans braved freezing temperatures* **endure**, put up with, bear, withstand, weather, suffer, face, confront, defy.
> ANTONYMS succumb to.

▫ **bravely** adverb.

bravery ▸ noun courageous behaviour or character.

SYNONYMS **courage**, boldness, heroism, intrepidity, nerve, daring, fearlessness, audacity, pluck, valour; informal guts; Brit. informal bottle; N. Amer. informal moxie.

bravo ▸ exclamation shouted to express approval for a performer.

bravura /bruh-**vyoor**-uh/ ▸ noun **1** great skill; brilliance. **2** the display of great daring.

brawl ▸ noun a noisy fight or quarrel.

SYNONYMS **fight**, skirmish, scuffle, tussle, fray, melee, fracas, fisticuffs; informal scrap, set-to; Brit. informal punch-up.

▸ verb take part in a brawl.

brawn ▸ noun physical strength.

brawny ▸ adjective physically strong; muscular.

SYNONYMS **strong**, muscular, muscly, well built, powerful, strapping, burly, sturdy; informal beefy, hulking. ANTONYMS puny, weak.

bray ▸ verb (of a donkey) make a loud, harsh cry.

▸ noun the loud, harsh cry of a donkey.

brazen ▸ adjective not caring if other people think you are behaving badly; shameless.

▸ verb (**brazen it out**) endure an awkward situation without seeming ashamed or embarrassed.
□ **brazenly** adverb.

brazier /**bray**-zi-er/ ▸ noun a portable heater holding lighted coals.

Brazilian ▸ noun a person from Brazil.
▸ adjective relating to Brazil.

brazil nut ▸ noun the large three-sided nut of a South American forest tree.

breach ▸ verb **1** make a hole in; break through. **2** break a rule or agreement.

SYNONYMS **1** the river breached its banks **break (through)**, burst, rupture. **2** the changes breached union rules **break**, contravene, violate, infringe, defy, disobey, flout.

▸ noun **1** a gap made in a wall or barrier. **2** an act that breaks a rule or agreement. **3** a quarrel or disagreement.

SYNONYMS **1** a breach of the regulations **contravention**, violation, infringement, infraction, transgression. **2** a breach in the sea wall **break**, rupture, split, crack, fracture, opening, gap, hole, fissure. ANTONYMS observance.

■ **step into the breach** replace someone who is suddenly unable to do a job.

bread ▸ noun **1** food made of flour, water, and yeast mixed together and baked. **2** informal money.

■ **bread and butter** a person's main source of income.

breadcrumb ▸ noun a very small fragment of bread.

breaded ▸ adjective (of food) coated with breadcrumbs and fried.

breadline ▸ noun (**on the breadline**) Brit. very poor.

breadth ▸ noun **1** the distance from side to side of something. **2** wide range.

SYNONYMS **1** a breadth of 100 metres **width**, broadness, thickness, span, diameter. **2** the breadth of his knowledge **range**, extent, scope, depth, reach, compass, scale.

breadwinner ▸ noun a person who supports their family with the money they earn.

break ▸ verb (**breaks**, **breaking**, **broke**; past participle **broken**) **1** separate into pieces as a result of a blow or strain. **2** stop working. **3** interrupt a sequence or course. **4** fail to obey a rule or agreement. **5** beat a record. **6** work out a code. **7** make a rush or dash. **8** soften a fall. **9** suddenly become public. **10** (of a person's voice) falter and change tone. **11** (of a teenage boy's voice) become deeper. **12** (of the weather) change suddenly.

SYNONYMS **1** **shatter**, smash, crack, snap, fracture, fragment, splinter, split, burst; informal bust. **2** the coffee machine has broken **stop working**, break down, give out, go wrong, malfunction, crash; informal go kaput, conk out; Brit. informal pack up. **3** traders who break the law **violate**, contravene, infringe, breach, defy, flout, disobey. **4** the film broke box-office records **beat**, surpass, exceed, better, cap, top, outdo, outstrip. **5** he tried to break the news gently **reveal**, disclose, divulge, impart, tell, announce, release. ANTONYMS repair, obey.

▸ noun **1** a pause or gap. **2** a short rest. **3** an instance of breaking, or the point where something is broken. **4** a sudden rush or dash. **5** informal a chance. **6** Tennis the winning of a game against an opponent's serve. **7** Snooker Billiards a continuous series of successful shots. **8** a short solo in music.

SYNONYMS **1** the magazine has been published without a break since 1950 **stop**, interruption, interval, gap, disruption, stoppage, cessation. **2** let's have a break **rest**, respite, recess, pause, interval, intermission; informal breather, time out. **3** a break in the wall **gap**, opening, space, hole, breach, chink, crack, fracture, fissure, tear, split.

■ **break away** escape. **break down 1** stop working. **2** lose control of your emotions when upset. **break in** force your way into a building. **break something in** make a horse used to being ridden. **break off** stop suddenly. **break out 1** (of something unwelcome) start suddenly. **2** escape. **break up 1** (of a gathering) end. **2** (of a couple) end a relationship. **3** end a school term. **break wind** release gas from the anus. □ **breakable** adjective.

breakage ▸ noun the action of breaking something.

breakaway ▸ noun **1** a major change from something established. **2** (in sport) a sudden attack or forward movement.

breakdown ▸ noun **1** a failure or collapse. **2** a careful analysis of costs or figures.

> SYNONYMS **1** *the breakdown of the negotiations* **failure**, collapse, disintegration, foundering. **2** *she suffered a breakdown* **nervous breakdown**, collapse. **3** *a breakdown of the computer system* **malfunction**, failure, crash. **4** *a breakdown of the figures* **analysis**, itemization, classification, examination, investigation, explanation.

breaker ▸ noun **1** a heavy sea wave that breaks on the shore. **2** a person who breaks up old machinery.

breakfast ▸ noun the first meal of the day. ▸ verb eat breakfast.

break-in ▸ noun an act of forcing your way into a building to steal something.

> SYNONYMS **burglary**, robbery, theft, raid, breaking and entering; informal smash-and-grab.

breakneck ▸ adjective dangerously fast.

breakthrough ▸ noun a sudden important development or success.

> SYNONYMS **advance**, development, step forward, success, improvement, discovery, innovation, revolution. ANTONYMS setback.

breakwater ▸ noun a barrier built out into the sea to protect a coast or harbour from waves.

bream ▸ noun (plural **bream**) a greenish-bronze freshwater fish.

breast ▸ noun **1** either of the two soft organs on a woman's chest which produce milk when she has had a baby. **2** a person's or animal's chest.

> SYNONYMS **1** *the curve of her breasts* **bosom(s)**, bust; informal boobs, knockers. **2** *her heart was hammering in her breast* **chest**, bosom, front.

▸ verb **1** reach the top of a hill. **2** move forwards while pushing against something.

breastbone ▸ noun a bone running down the centre of the chest and connecting the ribs.

breastfeed ▸ verb (**breastfeeds, breastfeeding, breastfed**) feed a baby with milk from the breast.

breastplate ▸ noun a piece of armour covering the chest.

breaststroke ▸ noun a swimming stroke in which you push your arms forwards and then sweep them back while kicking your legs out.

breath ▸ noun **1** air taken into or sent out of the lungs. **2** an instance of breathing in or out. **3** a slight movement of air. **4** a sign or hint.

> SYNONYMS **inhalation**, gulp of air, puff, gasp, exhalation; Medicine respiration.

□ **breathable** adjective.

breathalyser (US spelling **Breathalyzer** trademark) ▸ noun a device for measuring the amount of alcohol in a driver's breath. □ **breathalyse** (US spelling **breathalyze**) verb.

breathe ▸ verb (**breathes, breathing, breathed**) **1** take air into the lungs and send it out again. **2** say quietly. **3** let air or moisture in or out.

> SYNONYMS **1** *she breathed deeply* **inhale**, exhale, respire, draw breath, puff, pant, blow, gasp, wheeze; Medicine inspire, expire. **2** *'Together at last,' she breathed* **whisper**, murmur, purr, sigh.

breather ▸ noun informal a brief pause for rest.

breathless ▸ adjective **1** gasping for breath. **2** feeling or causing great excitement.

> SYNONYMS **1** *Will arrived breathless* **out of breath**, panting, puffing, gasping, wheezing, winded; informal out of puff. **2** *the crowd were breathless with anticipation* **eager**, agog, open-mouthed, excited, on the edge of your seat, on tenterhooks.

□ **breathlessly** adverb.

breathtaking ▸ adjective astonishing or awe-inspiring.

> SYNONYMS **spectacular**, magnificent, awe-inspiring, awesome, astonishing, amazing, stunning, thrilling; informal sensational, out of this world. ANTONYMS run-of-the-mill.

□ **breathtakingly** adverb.

breathy ▸ adjective (of speech or singing) having a noticeable sound of breathing.

breech ▸ noun the back part of a rifle or gun barrel.

breech birth ▸ noun a birth in which the baby's buttocks or feet are delivered first.

breeches ▸ plural noun short trousers fastened just below the knee.

breed ▸ verb (**breeds, breeding, bred**) **1** (of animals) mate and then produce young.

2 keep animals for the young that they produce. **3** produce or cause.

> SYNONYMS **1** *elephants breed readily in captivity* **reproduce,** produce offspring, procreate, multiply, mate. **2** *she was born and bred in the village* **bring up,** rear, raise, nurture. **3** *the political system bred discontent* **cause,** produce, bring about, give rise to, arouse, stir up, generate, foster.
> ANTONYMS stifle.

▶ noun a particular type of domestic or farm animal that has been specially developed.

> SYNONYMS **1** *a breed of cow* **variety,** stock, strain, race, species. **2** *a new breed of journalist* **type,** kind, sort, variety, class, genre, generation.

□ **breeder** noun.

breeding ▶ noun upper-class good manners.

> SYNONYMS **(good) manners,** gentility, refinement, cultivation, polish, urbanity; informal **class.**

breeze ▶ noun a gentle wind.

> SYNONYMS **gentle wind,** puff of air, gust, draught; literary zephyr.

▶ verb (**breezes, breezing, breezed**) informal come or go casually.

breeze block ▶ noun Brit. a lightweight building brick made from sand, cement, and pieces of partly burnt coal or wood.

breezy ▶ adjective (**breezier, breeziest**) **1** pleasantly windy. **2** relaxed and cheerfully brisk.

> SYNONYMS **1** *a breezy day* **windy,** fresh, brisk, blowy, blustery, gusty. **2** *his breezy manner* **jaunty,** cheerful, cheery, brisk, carefree, easy, casual, relaxed, informal, light-hearted; informal **upbeat.**

brethren ▶ plural noun **1** old-fashioned plural of BROTHER. **2** fellow Christians or members of group.

Breton /bre-tuhn/ ▶ noun **1** a person from Brittany. **2** the language of Brittany.

breve (*rhymes with* sleeve) ▶ noun Music a note twice as long as a semibreve.

brevity ▶ noun **1** economical and exact use of words. **2** the fact of lasting a short time.

brew ▶ verb **1** make beer. **2** make tea or coffee by mixing it with hot water. **3** begin to develop.

> SYNONYMS **1** *this beer is brewed in Frankfurt* **ferment,** make. **2** *I'll brew some tea* **prepare,** infuse, make; Brit. informal **mash. 3** *there's trouble brewing* **develop,** loom, be imminent, be on the horizon, be in the offing, be just around the corner.

▶ noun something brewed.

> SYNONYMS **1** *home brew* **beer,** ale. **2** *a hot reviving brew* **drink,** beverage. **3** *a rich*

brew of myths and distortion **mixture,** mix, blend, combination, amalgam, cocktail.

□ **brewer** noun.

brewery ▶ noun (plural **breweries**) a place where beer is made.

briar (or **brier**) ▶ noun a prickly shrub.

bribe ▶ verb (**bribes, bribing, bribed**) pay someone to do something dishonest that helps you.

> SYNONYMS *they tried to bribe the police* **buy off,** pay off, suborn; informal **grease someone's palm, keep someone sweet, square;** Brit. informal **nobble.**

▶ noun an amount of money offered in an attempt to bribe someone.

> SYNONYMS *he accepted a bribe* **inducement;** informal **backhander, pay-off, kickback, sweetener.**

bribery ▶ noun giving or offering a bribe.

> SYNONYMS **corruption;** N. Amer. **payola;** informal **palm-greasing, graft, hush money.**

bric-a-brac ▶ noun various objects of little value.

brick ▶ noun a small rectangular block of fired clay, used in building.

▶ verb (**brick something up**) block or enclose something with a wall of bricks.

brickbat ▶ noun a critical remark.

bricklayer ▶ noun a person whose job is to build structures with bricks.

bridal ▶ adjective relating to a bride or a newly married couple.

bride ▶ noun a woman at the time of her wedding.

bridegroom ▶ noun a man at the time of his wedding.

bridesmaid ▶ noun a girl or woman who accompanies a bride at her wedding.

bridge ▶ noun **1** a structure that allows people or vehicles to cross a river, road, etc. **2** the platform on a ship where the captain and officers stand. **3** the upper bony part of a person's nose. **4** the part on a stringed instrument over which the strings are stretched. **5** a card game played by two teams of two players.

▶ verb (**bridges, bridging, bridged**) be or make a bridge over.

bridgehead ▶ noun a strong position gained by an army inside enemy territory.

bridle ▶ noun the harness used to control a horse.

▶ verb (**bridles, bridling, bridled**) **1** put a bridle on. **2** show resentment or anger.

bridleway ▶ noun Brit. a path along which horse riders have right of way.

brief ▶ adjective **1** lasting a short time. **2** using few words. **3** (of clothing) not covering much of the body.

b

SYNONYMS **1** *a brief account* **concise,** succinct, short, pithy, compact, thumbnail, potted. **2** *a brief visit* **short,** flying, fleeting, hasty, hurried, quick, cursory, perfunctory, temporary, short-lived.
ANTONYMS lengthy.

▸ noun Brit. **1** a set of instructions about a task. **2** a summary of the facts in a case given to a barrister to argue in court. **3** informal a solicitor or barrister.

SYNONYMS **1** *my brief is to reorganize the project* **instructions,** directions, directive, remit, mandate. **2** *a barrister's brief* **case,** summary, argument, contention, dossier.

▸ verb give someone information to prepare them for a task.

SYNONYMS *employees were briefed about the decision* **inform,** tell, update, notify, advise, prepare, prime, instruct; informal fill in, put in the picture.

briefcase ▸ noun a flat rectangular case for carrying documents.

briefing ▸ noun a meeting for giving information or instructions.

SYNONYMS **1** *a press briefing* **conference,** meeting, interview. **2** *this briefing explains the systems* **information,** rundown, guidance, instructions, directions, guidelines.

briefly ▸ adverb **1** for a short time. **2** in a few words.

SYNONYMS **1** *Henry paused briefly* **momentarily,** temporarily, fleetingly. **2** *tell me as briefly as you can* **concisely,** succinctly. **3** *briefly, the plot is as follows* **in short,** in brief, in a word, in a nutshell, in essence.

briefs ▸ plural noun short, close-fitting underpants.

SYNONYMS **underpants,** pants, knickers, bikini briefs; N. Amer. shorts; informal panties; Brit. informal kecks.

brier → BRIAR.

brig ▸ noun a sailing ship with two masts.

brigade ▸ noun **1** a large army unit, forming part of a division. **2** disapproving a particular group of people: *the anti-smoking brigade.*

SYNONYMS **squad,** team, group, band, party, crew, force, outfit.

brigadier /bri-guh-**deer**/ ▸ noun a rank of officer in the British army, above colonel.

brigand /**brig**-uhnd/ ▸ noun a member of a gang of bandits.

bright ▸ adjective **1** giving out light, or filled with light. **2** (of colour) strong and eye-catching. **3** intelligent and quick-witted.

4 (of sound) clear and high-pitched. **5** cheerfully lively. **6** (of prospects) good.

SYNONYMS **1** *the bright surface of the metal* **shining,** brilliant, dazzling, glaring, sparkling, flashing, glittering, gleaming, glowing, luminous, shiny, glossy. **2** *a bright morning* **sunny,** cloudless, clear, fair, fine. **3** *bright colours* **vivid,** brilliant, intense, strong, vibrant, bold, gaudy, lurid, garish. **4** *a bright young graduate* **clever,** intelligent, quick-witted, smart, canny, astute, perceptive, ingenious; informal brainy.
ANTONYMS dull, cloudy, dark, stupid.

◻ **brightly** adverb **brightness** noun.

brighten ▸ verb make or become brighter or more cheerful.

SYNONYMS **1** *sunshine brightened the room* **illuminate,** light up, lighten. **2** *the sky brightened* **become lighter,** grow brighter, lighten. **3** *Sarah brightened up* **cheer up,** perk up, rally, feel heartened; informal buck up.

brilliance ▸ noun **1** intense brightness of light. **2** great cleverness or talent.

SYNONYMS **1** *the brilliance of the sunshine* **brightness,** vividness, intensity, sparkle, glitter, blaze, luminosity, radiance. **2** *a philosopher of great brilliance* **genius,** intelligence, talent, ability, prowess, skill, expertise, aptitude, flair, wisdom, intellect. **3** *the brilliance of Paris* **splendour,** magnificence, grandeur, resplendence, glory.
ANTONYMS dullness, stupidity, simplicity, lowliness.

brilliant ▸ adjective **1** (of light or colour) very bright or vivid. **2** very clever or talented. **3** Brit. informal very good; marvellous.

SYNONYMS **1** *a shaft of brilliant light* **bright,** shining, blazing, dazzling, vivid, intense, glaring, luminous, radiant. **2** *a brilliant student* **clever,** bright, intelligent, smart, able, talented, gifted, skilful, astute; informal brainy. **3** *his brilliant career* **superb,** glorious, illustrious, impressive, remarkable, exceptional.
ANTONYMS dim, stupid, undistinguished.

◻ **brilliantly** adverb.

brim ▸ noun **1** the projecting edge around the bottom of a hat. **2** the lip of a cup, bowl, etc.

▸ verb (**brims, brimming, brimmed**) be full to the point of overflowing.

brimstone ▸ noun old use sulphur.

brindle (or **brindled**) ▸ adjective (of an animal) brownish with streaks of grey or black.

brine ▸ noun water which contains dissolved salt.

bring ▸ verb (**brings, bringing, brought**) **1** take someone or something to a place. **2** cause to be in a particular position or state. **3** cause someone to receive something. **4** (**bring yourself to do**) force yourself to do something unpleasant. **5** begin legal action.

SYNONYMS **1** *he brought over a tray* **fetch**, carry, bear, take, convey, transport, shift. **2** *Philip brought his bride to his mansion* **escort**, conduct, guide, lead. **3** *the wind brought rain* **cause**, produce, create, generate, precipitate, occasion, provoke, lead to, give rise to, result in.

■ **bring something about** cause something to happen. **bring something off** achieve something successfully. **bring something on** cause something unpleasant to develop. **bring something out 1** produce and launch a new product. **2** emphasize a feature. **bring someone round 1** make someone conscious again. **2** persuade someone to agree to something. **bring someone/thing up 1** look after a child until it is an adult. **2** mention something in order to discuss it. □ **bringer** noun.

brink ▸ noun **1** the edge of land before a steep slope or an area of water. **2** the stage just before a new situation.

SYNONYMS **1** *the brink of the crater* **edge**, verge, margin, rim, lip, border, boundary. **2** *two countries on the brink of war* **verge**, threshold, point, edge.

brinkmanship ▸ noun the practice of continuing with a dangerous course of action to the limits of safety before stopping.

briny ▸ adjective salty.
▸ noun (**the briny**) Brit. informal the sea.

brio /bree-oh/ ▸ noun energy or liveliness.

brioche /bree-osh/ ▸ noun a soft, sweet French roll.

brisk ▸ adjective **1** quick, active, or energetic. **2** (of a person's manner) practical and efficient.

SYNONYMS **1** *a brisk pace* **quick**, rapid, fast, swift, speedy, hurried, energetic, lively; informal nippy. **2** *his tone became brisk* **no-nonsense**, businesslike, decisive, brusque, abrupt, short, sharp, curt, blunt, terse; informal snappy. ANTONYMS leisurely.

□ **briskly** adverb.

brisket ▸ noun meat from the chest of a cow.

bristle ▸ noun a short, stiff hair.

SYNONYMS **1** *the bristles on his chin* **hair**, whisker; (**bristles**) stubble, five o'clock

shadow. **2** *a hedgehog's bristles* **spine**, prickle, quill, barb.

▸ verb (**bristles, bristling, bristled**) **1** (of hair or fur) stand upright away from the skin. **2** react angrily or defensively. **3** (**bristle with**) be covered with.

SYNONYMS **1** *the hair on the back of his neck bristled* **rise**, stand up, stand on end. **2** *she bristled at his tone* **take offence**, bridle, take umbrage, be offended. **3** *the roof bristled with antennae* **be crowded**, be full, be packed, be jammed, be covered, overflow; informal be thick, be chock-full.

□ **bristly** adjective.

British ▸ adjective relating to Great Britain.

Briton ▸ noun a British person.

brittle ▸ adjective **1** hard but likely to break easily. **2** sharp or artificial: *a brittle laugh.*

SYNONYMS **breakable**, fragile, crisp, crumbly, friable, delicate. ANTONYMS flexible, solid.

broach ▸ verb **1** raise a subject for discussion. **2** pierce a container.

SYNONYMS **bring up**, raise, introduce, mention, touch on, air.

broad ▸ adjective **1** larger than usual from side to side; wide. **2** large in area or range. **3** without detail; general. **4** (of a hint) clear and unmistakable. **5** (of an accent) very strong.

SYNONYMS **1** *a broad expanse of prairie* **wide**, extensive, vast, immense, great, spacious, expansive, sizeable, sweeping. **2** *a broad range of opportunities* **comprehensive**, inclusive, extensive, wide, all-embracing, unlimited. **3** *this report gives a broad outline* **general**, non-specific, rough, approximate, basic, loose, vague. ANTONYMS narrow, limited, detailed.

▸ noun N. Amer. informal a woman.
■ **broad bean** a large flat green bean.
□ **broadly** adverb.

broadband ▸ noun a telecommunications technique which uses a wide range of frequencies, enabling messages to be sent at the same time.

broadcast ▸ verb (**broadcasts, broadcasting, broadcast**; past participle **broadcast** or **broadcasted**) **1** transmit on radio or television. **2** tell to a lot of people.

SYNONYMS **1** *the show will be broadcast worldwide* **transmit**, relay, air, beam, show, televise, screen. **2** *the result was broadcast far and wide* **report**, announce, publicize, advertise, make public, proclaim, spread, circulate.

▸ noun a radio or television programme.

b

SYNONYMS *a live broadcast* **transmission,** programme, show, telecast, production, screening.

□ **broadcaster** noun.

broaden ▸ verb make or become broader.

SYNONYMS **1** *her smile broadened* **widen,** expand, stretch (out), spread. **2** *the government tried to broaden its political base* **expand,** enlarge, extend, widen, swell, increase, add to, develop.
ANTONYMS narrow, restrict.

broadleaved (or **broadleaf**) ▸ adjective having fairly wide flat leaves.

broad-minded ▸ adjective not easily shocked; tolerant.

SYNONYMS **liberal,** tolerant, freethinking, indulgent, progressive, permissive, unshockable, unprejudiced, unbiased.
ANTONYMS intolerant.

broadsheet ▸ noun a newspaper printed on large sheets of paper.

broadside ▸ noun **1** a fierce verbal or written criticism. **2** historical a firing of all the guns from one side of a warship.

broadsword ▸ noun a sword with a wide blade.

brocade ▸ noun a rich fabric woven with a raised pattern.

broccoli /brok-kuh-li/ ▸ noun a vegetable with heads of small green or purplish flower buds.

✔ two **c**s, one **l**: bro**cc**oli.

brochure /broh-sher/ ▸ noun a booklet or magazine containing information about a product or service.

SYNONYMS **booklet,** prospectus, catalogue, pamphlet, leaflet, circular, mailshot; N. Amer. folder.

brogue ▸ noun **1** a strong outdoor shoe with perforated patterns in the leather. **2** a strong regional accent.

broil ▸ verb N. Amer. cook meat or fish using direct heat.

broke past of BREAK.
▸ adjective informal having no money.

broken past participle of BREAK. ▸ adjective (of a language) spoken hesitantly and with many mistakes.

SYNONYMS **1 smashed,** shattered, fragmented, splintered, crushed, snapped, in bits, in pieces, cracked, split, fractured; informal in smithereens. **2** *his video's broken* **faulty,** damaged, defective, not working, malfunctioning, out of order, broken down, down; informal kaput, bust, acting up; Brit. informal knackered. **3** *a night of broken sleep* **interrupted,** disturbed, fitful, disrupted,

discontinuous, intermittent. **4** *she spoke in broken English* **halting,** hesitating, disjointed, faltering, imperfect.
ANTONYMS whole, working, uninterrupted, fluent, perfect.

■ **broken home** a family in which the parents are divorced or separated.

broker ▸ noun a person who buys and sells things for other people.

SYNONYMS **dealer,** agent, middleman, intermediary, mediator, factor, liaison, stockbroker.

▸ verb arrange a deal or plan.

SYNONYMS **arrange,** organize, orchestrate, work out, settle, clinch, negotiate, mediate.

bromide ▸ noun a compound of bromine, used in medicine.

bromine ▸ noun a dark red liquid chemical element.

bronchial ▸ adjective relating to the tubes leading to the lungs.

bronchitis /brong-ky-tiss/ ▸ noun inflammation of the tubes that lead to the lungs.

bronco ▸ noun (plural **broncos**) a wild or half-tamed horse of the western US.

brontosaurus former term for APATOSAURUS.

bronze ▸ noun **1** a yellowish-brown metal made by mixing copper and tin. **2** a yellowish-brown colour. **3** (also **bronze medal**) a medal given for third place in a competition.
▸ verb (**bronzes, bronzing, bronzed**) **1** give something a bronze surface. **2** make someone suntanned.
■ **Bronze Age** an ancient period when weapons and tools were made of bronze, following the Stone Age.

brooch ▸ noun an ornament fastened to clothing with a hinged pin.

brood ▸ noun a family of young animals born or hatched at one time.

SYNONYMS *she looked after her brood well* **offspring,** young, family, litter, clutch, progeny.

▸ verb **1** think deeply about an unpleasant subject. **2** (**brooding**) appearing mysterious or menacing. **3** (of a bird) sit on eggs to hatch them.

SYNONYMS *he does brood a lot* **think,** ponder, contemplate, meditate, ruminate, muse, worry, fret, agonize.

broody ▸ adjective (**broodier, broodiest**) **1** (of a hen) wanting to hatch eggs. **2** informal (of a woman) having a strong desire to have a baby. **3** thoughtful and unhappy.

brook¹ ▸ noun a small stream.

SYNONYMS **stream,** rill; N. English beck; Scottish & N. English **burn;** N. Amer. & Austral./NZ creek.

brook² ▶ verb formal tolerate.

broom ▶ noun **1** a long-handled brush used for sweeping. **2** a shrub with yellow flowers.

broomstick ▶ noun a brush with twigs at one end and a long handle, on which witches are said to fly.

Bros ▶ abbreviation brothers.

broth ▶ noun thin soup or stock, sometimes with chunks of meat or vegetables.

brothel ▶ noun a house where men visit prostitutes.

brother ▶ noun **1** a man or boy in relation to other children of his parents. **2** a male colleague or friend. **3** (plural **brothers** or **brethren**) a male fellow Christian or member of a religious order.
■ **brother-in-law** (plural **brothers-in-law**) **1** the brother of a person's wife or husband. **2** the husband of a person's sister or sister-in-law.

brotherhood ▶ noun **1** the relationship between brothers. **2** a feeling of friendliness and understanding between people. **3** a group of people linked by a shared interest.

brotherly ▶ adjective relating to or like a brother; affectionate.

SYNONYMS **fraternal,** friendly, comradely, affectionate, amicable, kind, devoted, loyal.

brought past and past participle of **BRING**.

❗ Don't confuse **brought** with **bought**, which is the past of **buy**.

brouhaha ▶ noun a noisy and overexcited reaction.

brow ▶ noun **1** a person's forehead. **2** an eyebrow. **3** the highest point of a hill.

SYNONYMS **1** forehead, temple. **2** the brow of the hill **summit,** peak, top, crest, crown, head, pinnacle, apex.

browbeat ▶ verb (**browbeats, browbeating, browbeat;** past participle **browbeaten**) bully someone with aggressive or threatening words.

brown ▶ adjective **1** of a colour produced by mixing red, yellow, and blue. **2** dark-skinned or suntanned.

SYNONYMS **1** brown eyes hazel, chocolate, coffee, brunette, sepia, mahogany, tan, café au lait, caramel, chestnut. **2** his face was brown from the sun **tanned,** suntanned, bronzed.

▶ noun a brown colour.
▶ verb **1** make or become brown by

cooking. **2** (**be browned off**) Brit. informal be dissatisfied.

SYNONYMS the grill browns food evenly **grill,** toast, singe, sear, barbecue, sauté.

brownfield ▶ adjective Brit. (of a piece of land) having had buildings on it already.

Brownie ▶ noun (plural **Brownies**) **1** a member of the junior branch of the Guides Association. **2** (**brownie**) a small square of rich chocolate cake. **3** (**brownie**) a kind elf believed to do people's housework secretly.

browse ▶ verb (**browses, browsing, browsed**) **1** read or look at something in a leisurely way. **2** look at information on a computer. **3** (of an animal) feed on leaves, twigs, etc.

SYNONYMS **look round**/**over,** scan, skim, glance, peruse, thumb, leaf, flick, dip into.

▶ noun an act of browsing.

browser ▶ noun **1** a person or animal that browses. **2** a computer program for navigating the World Wide Web.

bruise ▶ noun **1** an area of discoloured skin on the body, caused by a blow. **2** a damaged area on a fruit or vegetable.

SYNONYMS a bruise on her forehead **contusion,** bump, swelling, lump, mark, injury, welt.

▶ verb (**bruises, bruising, bruised**) make a bruise appear on.

SYNONYMS **1** her face was badly bruised **contuse,** injure, mark, discolour, make black and blue. **2** every one of the apples is bruised **mark,** discolour, blemish, damage, spoil.

bruiser ▶ noun informal a tough, aggressive person.

brunch ▶ noun a late morning meal eaten instead of breakfast and lunch.

brunette ▶ noun a woman or girl with dark brown hair.

brunt ▶ noun the chief impact of something bad.

brush¹ ▶ noun **1** an object with a handle and a block of bristles, hair, or wire. **2** an act of brushing. **3** a slight, brief touch. **4** a brief encounter with something bad. **5** the bushy tail of a fox.

SYNONYMS **1** a dustpan and brush **broom,** sweeper, besom, whisk. **2** he gave the seat a brush with his hand **clean,** sweep, wipe, dust. **3** a brush with the law **encounter,** clash, confrontation, conflict, altercation, incident; informal run-in, to-do; Brit. informal spot of bother.

▶ verb **1** clean, smooth, or apply with a brush. **2** touch lightly. **3** (**brush someone/thing off**) dismiss someone or something abruptly. **4** (**brush something up**) work to improve a skill you have not used for a long time.

> SYNONYMS **1** *he spent his day brushing the floors* **sweep,** clean, buff, polish, scrub. **2** *she brushed her hair* **groom,** comb, neaten, tidy, smooth, arrange, curry. **3** *she felt his lips brush her cheek* **touch,** stroke, caress, skim, sweep, graze, contact, kiss.

brush² ▶ noun undergrowth, small trees, and shrubs.

> SYNONYMS **undergrowth,** scrub, brushwood, shrubs, bushes; N. Amer. underbrush, chaparral.

brushwood ▶ noun undergrowth, twigs, and small branches.

brusque /bruusk/ ▶ adjective rather rude and abrupt.

> SYNONYMS **curt,** abrupt, blunt, short, sharp, brisk, peremptory, gruff.
> ANTONYMS polite.

□ **brusquely** adverb.

Brussels sprout ▶ noun a small green vegetable, the bud of a variety of cabbage.

brutal ▶ adjective **1** savagely violent. **2** not attempting to hide something unpleasant: *brutal honesty.*

> SYNONYMS **1** *a brutal attack* **savage,** cruel, vicious, ferocious, barbaric, wicked, murderous, bloodthirsty, cold-blooded, callous, heartless, merciless, sadistic. **2** *brutal honesty* **harsh,** unforgiving, pitiless, frank, blunt, tough, hard, bleak, disagreeable.
> ANTONYMS gentle, kind.

□ **brutality** noun **brutally** adverb.

brutalize (or **brutalise**) ▶ verb (**brutalizes, brutalizing, brutalized**) **1** make someone cruel or violent by frequently exposing them to violence. **2** treat someone in a violent way.

brute ▶ noun a violent or savage person, or a large and uncontrollable animal.
▶ adjective involving physical strength rather than reasoning: *brute force.*
□ **brutish** adjective.

BSE ▶ abbreviation bovine spongiform encephalopathy, a fatal brain disease in cattle.

BST ▶ abbreviation British Summer Time.

bubble ▶ noun **1** a thin ball of liquid enclosing a gas. **2** a ball filled with gas in a liquid or a material such as glass. **3** a transparent dome.
▶ verb (**bubbles, bubbling, bubbled**) **1** (of a liquid) contain rising bubbles of gas. **2** (**bubble with**) be filled with.

bubblegum ▶ noun chewing gum that can be blown into bubbles.

bubbly ▶ adjective (**bubblier, bubbliest**) **1** containing bubbles. **2** cheerful and high-spirited.

> SYNONYMS **1** *bubbly water* **fizzy,** sparkling, effervescent, gassy, aerated, carbonated, frothy, foamy. **2** *she was bubbly and full of life* **vivacious,** animated, ebullient, lively, high-spirited, bouncy, merry, happy, cheerful, sunny; informal chirpy.
> ANTONYMS still, listless.

▶ noun informal champagne.

bubonic plague ▶ noun a form of plague passed on by rat fleas.

buccaneer ▶ noun **1** historical a pirate. **2** a recklessly adventurous person.
□ **buccaneering** adjective.

buck¹ ▶ noun **1** the male of some animals, e.g. deer and rabbits. **2** a vertical jump performed by a horse. **3** old use a fashionable young man.
▶ verb **1** (of a horse) perform a buck. **2** go against something: *don't try to buck the system.* **3** (**buck up** or **buck someone up**) informal become or make someone more cheerful.
■ **buck teeth** teeth that stick out.

buck² ▶ noun N. Amer. Austral./NZ informal a dollar.

buck³ ▶ noun an object placed in front of a poker player whose turn it is to deal.
■ **pass the buck** informal shift responsibility to someone else.

bucket ▶ noun **1** an open container with a handle, used to carry liquids. **2** (**buckets**) informal large quantities.
▶ verb (**buckets, bucketing, bucketed**) (**bucket down**) Brit. informal rain very heavily.

buckle ▶ noun a flat frame with a hinged pin, used as a fastener.

> SYNONYMS *a belt buckle* **clasp,** clip, catch, hasp, fastener.

▶ verb (**buckles, buckling, buckled**) **1** fasten with a buckle. **2** bend and give way under pressure. **3** (**buckle down**) tackle a task with determination.

> SYNONYMS **1** *he buckled the belt round his waist* **fasten,** do up, hook, secure, clasp, clip. **2** *the front axle buckled* **bend,** warp, twist, distort, contort, deform, crumple, collapse, give way.
> ANTONYMS unbuckle, straighten.

buckwheat ▶ noun a grain used for flour or animal feed.

bucolic /byoo-kol-ik/ ▶ adjective relating to country life.

bud ▶ noun a growth on a plant which develops into a leaf, flower, or shoot.
▶ verb (**buds, budding, budded**) form a bud or buds.

Buddhism /buud-di-z'm/ ▶ noun a religion based on the teachings of Buddha (real name Siddartha Gautama, c.563–c.460 BC).
□ **Buddhist** noun & adjective.

budding ▸ adjective beginning and showing signs of promise.

SYNONYMS **promising,** up-and-coming, rising, in the making, aspiring, future, fledgling, developing.

buddleia /bud-li-uh/ ▸ noun a shrub with clusters of lilac, white, or yellow flowers.

buddy ▸ noun (plural **buddies**) informal, chiefly N. Amer. a close friend.

budge ▸ verb (**budges, budging, budged**) **1** move very slightly. **2** change an opinion.

SYNONYMS **1** *the horses wouldn't budge* **move,** shift, stir, go. **2** *I couldn't budge the door* **dislodge,** shift, move, stir, reposition.

budgerigar ▸ noun a small Australian parakeet.

budget ▸ noun **1** an estimate of income and spending for a set period of time. **2** the amount of money needed or available for a purpose. **3** (**Budget**) a regular estimate of national income and spending put forward by a finance minister.

SYNONYMS **1** *your budget for the week* **financial plan,** forecast. **2** *the defence budget* **allowance,** allocation, quota, funds, resources, capital.

▸ verb (**budgets, budgeting, budgeted**) plan to spend a particular amount of money.

SYNONYMS *we have to budget £7,000 for the work* **allocate,** allot, allow, earmark, designate, set aside.

▸ adjective inexpensive.
□ **budgetary** adjective.

budgie ▸ noun a budgerigar.

buff[1] ▸ noun a yellowish-beige colour.
▸ verb polish something with a soft cloth.

SYNONYMS *he buffed the glass* **polish,** burnish, shine, smooth, rub.

■ **in the buff** informal naked.

buff[2] ▸ noun informal a person who knows a lot about a particular subject.

SYNONYMS *a film buff* **enthusiast,** fan, devotee, lover, admirer, expert, aficionado, authority; informal freak, nut, addict.

buffalo ▸ noun (plural **buffalo** or **buffaloes**) **1** a heavily built wild ox with backward-curving horns. **2** the North American bison.

buffer ▸ noun **1** (**buffers**) Brit. shock absorbers at the end of a railway track or on a railway vehicle. **2** a person or thing that lessens the impact of harmful effects.

SYNONYMS **cushion,** bulwark, shield, barrier, guard, safeguard.

buffet[1] /boo-fay, buf-fay/ ▸ noun **1** a meal made up of several dishes from which you serve yourself. **2** a counter at which snacks are sold.

SYNONYMS **1** *a sumptuous buffet* **cold table,** self-service meal, smorgasbord. **2** *a station buffet* **cafe,** cafeteria, snack bar, canteen, restaurant.

buffet[2] /buf-fit/ ▸ verb (**buffets, buffeting, buffeted**) (especially of wind or waves) strike repeatedly.

SYNONYMS *rough seas buffeted the coast* **batter,** pound, lash, strike, hit.

buffoon ▸ noun a ridiculous but amusing person.
□ **buffoonery** noun.

bug ▸ noun **1** a small insect. **2** informal a germ, or an illness caused by one. **3** informal an enthusiasm for something: *the sailing bug.* **4** a microphone used for secret recording. **5** an error in a computer program or system.

SYNONYMS **1** *a stomach bug* **illness,** disease, sickness, disorder, upset, ailment, infection, virus; Brit. informal lurgy. **2** *bugs were crawling everywhere* **insect,** minibeast; informal creepy-crawly, beastie. **3** *the bug planted on his phone* **listening device,** hidden microphone, wire, wiretap, tap. **4** *the program developed a bug* **fault,** error, defect, flaw, virus; informal glitch, gremlin.

▸ verb (**bugs, bugging, bugged**) **1** hide a microphone in a room or telephone. **2** informal annoy someone.

SYNONYMS *her conversations were bugged* **eavesdrop on,** spy on, tap, monitor.

bugbear ▸ noun something that causes anxiety or irritation.

buggery ▸ noun anal sex.

buggy ▸ noun (plural **buggies**) **1** a kind of pushchair. **2** a small motor vehicle with an open top. **3** historical a light horse-drawn vehicle.

bugle ▸ noun a brass instrument like a small trumpet.
□ **bugler** noun.

build ▸ verb (**builds, building, built**) **1** make something by putting parts together. **2** (**build up**) increase over time. **3** (**build on**) use as a basis for further development.

SYNONYMS **construct,** erect, put up, assemble, make, create, fashion, model, shape.
ANTONYMS demolish, dismantle.

▸ noun the size or form of someone or something.

SYNONYMS *a man of slim build* **physique,** frame, body, figure, form, shape, stature, proportions; informal vital statistics.

□ **builder** noun.

building ▸ noun **1** a structure with a roof and walls. **2** the process or trade of building houses and other structures.

b

SYNONYMS **structure,** construction, edifice, erection, property, premises, establishment.

■ **building society** Brit. a financial organization which pays interest on members' investments and lends money for mortgages.

build-up ▶ noun **1** a gradual increase. **2** a period of preparation before an event.

SYNONYMS **increase,** growth, expansion, enlargement, escalation, accumulation, development.

built past and past participle of **BUILD.**
▶ adjective of a particular physical build.
■ **built-in** included as part of a larger structure. **built-up** covered by many buildings.

bulb ▶ noun **1** the rounded base of the stem of some plants, from which the roots grow. **2** (also **light bulb**) a glass ball filled with gas, which provides light when an electric current is passed through it.

bulbous ▶ adjective **1** round or bulging in shape. **2** (of a plant) growing from a bulb.

SYNONYMS **bulging,** round, fat, rotund, swollen, distended, bloated.

Bulgarian ▶ noun **1** a person from Bulgaria. **2** the language of Bulgaria.
▶ adjective relating to Bulgaria.

bulge ▶ noun a rounded swelling on a flat surface.

SYNONYMS *a bulge under his jacket* **swelling,** bump, lump, hump, protrusion.

▶ verb (**bulges, bulging, bulged**) **1** swell or stick out unnaturally. **2** (**bulge with**) be full of.

SYNONYMS *the veins in his neck bulged* **swell,** stick out, project, protrude, stand out, puff out, balloon (out), fill out, distend.

bulimia /buu-**lim**-mi-uh/ ▶ noun a disorder marked by bouts of overeating, followed by fasting or vomiting.
□ **bulimic** adjective & noun.

bulk ▶ noun **1** the mass or size of something large. **2** the greater part of something. **3** a large mass or shape.

SYNONYMS **1** *the sheer bulk of the bags* **size,** volume, dimensions, proportions, mass, scale. **2** *the bulk of entrants were British* **majority,** mass, generality, main part, lion's share, preponderance.
ANTONYMS minority.

▶ adjective large in quantity.
■ **in bulk** (of goods) in large quantities.

bulkhead ▶ noun an internal wall or barrier in a ship or aircraft.

bulky ▶ adjective (**bulkier, bulkiest**) large and unwieldy.

SYNONYMS **unwieldy,** cumbersome, unmanageable, awkward, ponderous, outsize, oversized; informal hulking.
ANTONYMS manageable, handy.

bull[1] ▶ noun **1** an adult male animal of the cattle group. **2** a large male animal, e.g. a whale or elephant.
■ **take the bull by the horns** deal decisively with a difficult situation.

bull[2] ▶ noun an order or announcement issued by the Pope.

bulldog ▶ noun a breed of dog with a flat wrinkled face and a broad chest.

bulldoze ▶ verb (**bulldozes, bulldozing, bulldozed**) clear or destroy with a bulldozer.

bulldozer ▶ noun a tractor with a broad curved blade at the front for clearing ground.

bullet ▶ noun a small piece of metal fired from a gun.

SYNONYMS **ball,** shot, pellet; informal slug; (**bullets**) lead.

bulletin ▶ noun **1** a short official statement or summary of news. **2** a regular newsletter or report.

SYNONYMS **1** *a news bulletin* **report,** dispatch, story, flash, statement, announcement, message, communication, communiqué. **2** *the society's monthly bulletin* **newsletter,** news-sheet, proceedings, newspaper, magazine, gazette, review.

■ **bulletin board** a site on a computer system where any user can read or write messages.

bullfighting ▶ noun the sport of tormenting and killing bulls as a public entertainment.
□ **bullfight** noun **bullfighter** noun.

bullfinch ▶ noun a finch (songbird) with a reddish breast.

bullfrog ▶ noun a very large frog with a deep croak.

bullion ▶ noun gold or silver in bulk before being made into coins.

bullish ▶ adjective aggressively confident.

bullock ▶ noun a castrated bull.

bullring ▶ noun an arena where bullfights are held.

bullseye ▶ noun the centre of the target in sports such as archery and darts.

bully ▶ noun (plural **bullies**) a person who frightens or persecutes weaker people.

SYNONYMS *the school bully* **persecutor,** oppressor, tyrant, tormentor, intimidator, bully boy, thug.

▶ verb (**bullies, bullying, bullied**) frighten or persecute a weaker person.

SYNONYMS **1** *the others bully him* **persecute,** oppress, tyrannize, browbeat, intimidate, dominate; informal push around/about. **2** *she was bullied into helping* **coerce,** pressure, press, push, prod, browbeat, dragoon, strong-arm; informal bulldoze, railroad, lean on.

bulrush (or **bullrush**) ▶ noun a tall reed-like waterside plant.

bulwark /buul-werk/ ▶ noun **1** a defensive wall. **2** a person or thing that acts as a defence. **3** an extension of a ship's sides above deck level.

bum[1] ▶ noun Brit. informal a person's bottom.

bum[2] N. Amer. informal ▶ noun **1** a homeless person or beggar. **2** a lazy or worthless person.
▶ verb (**bums, bumming, bummed**) **1** get something by asking or begging. **2** (**bum around**) laze around.
▶ adjective bad.

bumble ▶ verb (**bumbles, bumbling, bumbled**) act or speak in an awkward or confused way.

bumblebee ▶ noun a large hairy bee with a loud hum.

bumf (or **bumph**) ▶ noun Brit. informal printed information.

bump ▶ noun **1** a light blow or collision. **2** a hump or projection on a level surface.

SYNONYMS **1** *I landed with a bump* **jolt,** crash, smash, smack, crack, bang, thud, thump; informal whack, wallop. **2** *I was woken by a bump* **bang,** crack, boom, clang, knock, thud, thump, clunk, crash, smash. **3** *a bump in the road* **hump,** lump, ridge, bulge, knob. **4** *a bump on his head* **swelling,** lump, bulge, injury, contusion.

▶ verb **1** knock or run into with a jolt. **2** move with a lot of jolting. **3** (**bump into**) meet by chance. **4** (**bump someone off**) informal murder someone. **5** (**bump something up**) informal increase something.

SYNONYMS **1** *cars bumped into each other* **hit,** crash, smash, slam, bang, knock, run, plough, ram, collide with, strike; N. Amer. impact. **2** *a cart bumping along the road* **bounce,** jolt, jerk, rattle, shake.

bumper ▶ noun a bar fixed across the front or back of a vehicle to reduce damage in a collision.
▶ adjective exceptionally large or successful.

SYNONYMS **exceptional,** large, abundant, rich, bountiful, good, plentiful, record, successful; informal whopping.
ANTONYMS meagre.

bumpkin ▶ noun an unsophisticated person from the countryside.

bumptious ▶ adjective irritatingly confident and self-important.

bumpy ▶ adjective (**bumpier, bumpiest**) uneven; full of bumps or jolts.

SYNONYMS **1** *a bumpy road* **uneven,** rough, rutted, pitted, potholed, lumpy, rocky. **2** *a bumpy ride* **bouncy,** rough, uncomfortable, jolting, lurching, jerky, jarring, bone-shaking.
ANTONYMS smooth.

bun ▶ noun **1** a small cake or bread roll. **2** a tight coil of hair at the back of the head.

bunch ▶ noun **1** a number of things grouped or held together. **2** informal a group of people.

SYNONYMS **1** *a bunch of flowers* **bouquet,** posy, nosegay, spray, wreath, garland. **2** *a bunch of keys* **cluster,** clump, knot, group.

▶ verb collect or form into a bunch.

SYNONYMS *the runners bunched up behind him* **cluster,** huddle, gather, congregate, collect, amass, group, crowd.
ANTONYMS scatter.

bundle ▶ noun a group of things tied or wrapped up together.

SYNONYMS *a bundle of clothes* **bunch,** roll, clump, wad, parcel, sheaf, bale, pile, stack, heap, mass; informal load, wodge.

▶ verb (**bundles, bundling, bundled**) **1** tie or roll up in a bundle. **2** (**be bundled up**) be dressed in a lot of warm clothes. **3** informal push or carry forcibly.

SYNONYMS **1** *she bundled up her things* **tie,** pack, parcel, wrap, swathe, roll, fold, bind. **2** *he was bundled into a van* **push,** shove, thrust, throw, propel, jostle, manhandle.

bunfight ▶ noun Brit. humorous a grand party or other large social event.

bung ▶ noun a stopper for a hole in a container.
▶ verb **1** (**bung something up**) block something up. **2** Brit. informal put or throw something somewhere casually or carelessly.

bungalow ▶ noun a house with only one storey.

bungee jumping ▶ noun the sport of jumping from a high place to which you are attached with a long elastic cord tied to your ankles.

bungle ▶ verb (**bungles, bungling, bungled**) fail in performing a task.

SYNONYMS **mishandle,** mismanage, mess up, spoil, ruin; informal blow, botch, fluff, make a hash of, screw up; Brit. informal make a pig's ear of, cock up; N. Amer. informal goof up.
ANTONYMS carry off.

▶ noun a mistake or failure.
□ **bungler** noun.

b

bungling ▸ adjective tending to make many mistakes.

SYNONYMS **incompetent**, blundering, amateurish, inept, unskilful, clumsy, awkward, bumbling; informal ham-fisted, cack-handed.
ANTONYMS competent.

bunion ▸ noun a painful swelling on the big toe.

bunk¹ ▸ noun a narrow shelf-like bed.

bunk² ▸ verb (**bunk off**) Brit. informal play truant from school.
■ **do a bunk** leave hurriedly.

bunker ▸ noun **1** a large container for storing fuel. **2** an underground shelter for use in wartime. **3** a hollow filled with sand on a golf course.

bunkum ▸ noun informal, dated nonsense.

bunny ▸ noun (plural **bunnies**) informal a rabbit.

Bunsen burner ▸ noun a small gas burner used in laboratories.

bunting¹ ▸ noun a small bird with brown streaked feathers.

bunting² ▸ noun flags and streamers used as decorations.

buoy ▸ noun an anchored float used to mark an area of water.

SYNONYMS **float**, marker, beacon.

▸ verb (**be buoyed** or **buoyed up**) be cheered up and made more confident.

✔ The **u** comes before the **o** in b**uo**y and b**uo**yant.

buoyant ▸ adjective **1** able to keep afloat. **2** cheerful and optimistic.

SYNONYMS **1** a buoyant substance **floating**, floatable. **2** a buoyant mood **cheerful**, cheery, happy, light-hearted, carefree, joyful, bubbly, bouncy, sunny; informal upbeat.
ANTONYMS gloomy.

□ **buoyancy** noun.

burble ▸ verb (**burbles, burbling, burbled**) **1** make a continuous murmuring noise. **2** speak for a long time in a way that is hard to understand.
▸ noun a continuous murmuring noise.

burden ▸ noun **1** a heavy load. **2** something that causes hardship, worry, or grief. **3** the main responsibility for a task.

SYNONYMS a financial burden **responsibility**, onus, obligation, liability, trouble, care, problem, worry, strain.

▸ verb **1** load heavily. **2** cause someone worry, hardship, or grief.

SYNONYMS avoid burdening them with guilt **oppress**, trouble, worry, weigh down, harass, upset, distress, haunt, afflict.

burdensome ▸ adjective causing worry or difficulty.

burdock ▸ noun a plant with large leaves and prickly flowers.

bureau /byoor-oh/ ▸ noun (plural **bureaux** or **bureaus**) **1** Brit. a writing desk with a sloping top. **2** N. Amer. a chest of drawers. **3** an office for carrying out particular business. **4** a government department.

SYNONYMS **1** an oak bureau **desk**, writing table, secretaire. **2** the intelligence bureau **department**, agency, office, division, branch, section, station, unit.

bureaucracy /byuu-rok-ruh-si/ ▸ noun (plural **bureaucracies**) **1** administrative procedures that are too complicated. **2** a system of government in which most decisions are taken by state officials.

SYNONYMS **1** the ranks of the bureaucracy **civil service**, government, administration, establishment, system, powers that be, authorities. **2** unnecessary bureaucracy **red tape**, rules and regulations, protocol, officialdom, paperwork.

bureaucrat ▸ noun a government official, especially one who follows guidelines rigidly.
□ **bureaucratic** adjective.

burgeon ▸ verb grow or increase rapidly.

SYNONYMS **grow**, increase, rocket, mushroom, expand, escalate, swell, boom, flourish, thrive, prosper.

burger ▸ noun a hamburger.

burgher /ber-guh/ ▸ noun old use a citizen of a town or city.

burglar ▸ noun a person who burgles a building.

SYNONYMS **housebreaker**, robber, thief, raider, looter, cat burglar.

burglary ▸ noun (plural **burglaries**) the action of burgling a building.

SYNONYMS **1** a sentence for burglary **housebreaking**, breaking and entering, theft, stealing, robbery, larceny, looting, pillaging. **2** a series of burglaries **break-in**, theft, robbery, raid; informal smash-and-grab; N. Amer. informal heist.

burgle ▸ verb (**burgles, burgling, burgled**) go into a building illegally to steal its contents.

SYNONYMS **rob**, loot, steal from, pillage.

burgundy /ber-guhn-di/ ▸ noun (plural **burgundies**) **1** a red wine from Burgundy in France. **2** a deep red colour.

burial ▸ noun the burying of a dead body.

SYNONYMS **funeral,** interment, committal, inhumation, entombment. ANTONYMS exhumation.

burlesque /ber-lesk/ ▸ noun **1** a comically exaggerated imitation of something. **2** N. Amer. a variety show.

burly ▸ adjective (**burlier, burliest**) (of a man) large and strong.

SYNONYMS **strapping,** well built, strong, muscular, muscly, hefty, sturdy, brawny; informal hunky, beefy. ANTONYMS puny.

burn[1] ▸ verb (**burns, burning, burned** or chiefly Brit. **burnt**) **1** (of a fire) produce flames and heat while using up a fuel. **2** harm or damage by fire. **3** (**be burning with**) experience a very strong desire or emotion. **4** (**burn out**) become exhausted through working too hard. **5** produce a CD by copying from an original or master copy.

SYNONYMS **1** *the coal was burning* **be on fire,** be alight, blaze, go up (in smoke), be in flames, smoulder, glow. **2** *he burned the letters* **set fire to,** set alight, set light to, kindle, ignite, touch off, incinerate, cremate; informal torch. **3** *I burned my dress with the iron* **scorch,** singe, sear, char, blacken, brand.

▸ noun an injury caused by burning.
■ **burn your boats** (or **bridges**) do something which makes turning back impossible.

burn[2] ▸ noun Scottish a small stream.

burner ▸ noun a part of a cooker, lamp, etc. that produces a flame.
■ **on the back burner** given a low priority.

burning ▸ adjective **1** very hot. **2** deeply felt. **3** important and urgent.

SYNONYMS **1** *burning coals* **on fire,** blazing, flaming, fiery, glowing, red-hot, smouldering. **2** *a burning desire* **intense,** passionate, deep-seated, profound, strong, ardent, fervent, urgent, fierce, consuming. **3** *burning issues* **important,** crucial, critical, vital, essential, pivotal, urgent, pressing, compelling.

burnish ▸ verb polish something by rubbing it.

burnout ▸ noun physical or mental collapse.

burp informal ▸ verb belch.
▸ noun a belch.

burr ▸ noun **1** a strong pronunciation of the letter *r*. **2** a prickly seed case or flower head that clings to clothing and animal fur.

burrow ▸ noun a hole or tunnel dug by a small animal to live in.

SYNONYMS *a rabbit's burrow* **warren,** tunnel, hole, dugout, lair, set, den, earth.

▸ verb **1** make a burrow. **2** hide underneath or search inside something.

SYNONYMS *rabbits burrowed among the roots* **tunnel,** dig, excavate, mine, bore, channel.

bursar ▸ noun a person who manages the financial affairs of a college or school.

bursary ▸ noun (plural **bursaries**) Brit. a grant for studying.

burst ▸ verb (**bursts, bursting, burst**) **1** break suddenly and violently apart. **2** (**be bursting**) be very full. **3** move or be opened suddenly and forcibly. **4** (**be bursting with**) feel full of an emotion. **5** (**burst out** or **into**) suddenly do something as a result of strong emotion.

SYNONYMS **1** *one balloon burst* **split** (**open**), rupture, break, tear. **2** *a shell burst* **explode,** blow up, detonate, go off. **3** *smoke burst through the hole* **gush,** erupt, surge, rush, stream, flow, pour, spurt, jet. **4** *he burst into the room* **charge,** plunge, barge, plough, hurtle, career, rush, dash, tear.

▸ noun **1** an instance of bursting. **2** a sudden brief outbreak. **3** a period of continuous effort.

SYNONYMS **1** *a burst in the tyre* **rupture,** puncture, breach, split, blowout. **2** *mortar bursts* **explosion,** detonation, blast, eruption, bang. **3** *a burst of gunfire* **volley,** salvo, barrage, hail, rain. **4** *a burst of activity* **outbreak,** eruption, flare-up, blaze, attack, fit, rush, storm, surge, spurt.

bury ▸ verb (**buries, burying, buried**) **1** place or hide something underground. **2** make something disappear or be hidden. **3** (**bury yourself**) involve yourself deeply in something.

SYNONYMS **1** *the dead were buried* **inter,** lay to rest, entomb. **2** *she buried her face in her hands* **hide,** conceal, cover, enfold, cup, sink. **3** *the bullet buried itself in the wood* **embed,** sink, implant, submerge, lodge. ANTONYMS exhume.

bus ▸ noun (plural **buses;** US also **busses**) a large motor vehicle that carries customers along a fixed route.
▸ verb (**buses, busing, bused** or **busses, bussing, bussed**) transport or travel in a bus.
■ **a busman's holiday** leisure time spent doing the same thing that you do at work.

busby ▸ noun (plural **busbies**) a tall fur hat worn by certain military regiments.

bush ▸ noun **1** a shrub or clump of shrubs. **2** (**the bush**) (in Australia and Africa) wild or uncultivated country.

SYNONYMS **1** *a rose bush* **shrub,** thicket; (**bushes**) undergrowth, shrubbery. **2** *the bush* **wilds,** wilderness, backwoods;

N. Amer. backcountry; Austral./NZ outback, backblocks; N. Amer. informal boondocks.

bushbaby ▸ noun (plural **bushbabies**) a small African animal with very large eyes.

bushel ▸ noun **1** Brit. a measure of capacity equal to 8 gallons (36.4 litres). **2** US a measure of capacity equal to 64 US pints (35.2 litres).

bushy ▸ adjective (**bushier**, **bushiest**) **1** growing thickly. **2** covered with bushes.

SYNONYMS **thick**, shaggy, curly, fuzzy, bristly, fluffy, woolly.
ANTONYMS sleek, wispy.

business ▸ noun **1** a person's regular occupation. **2** commercial activity. **3** a commercial organization. **4** work to be done or things to be attended to. **5** a person's concern: *it's none of your business.*

SYNONYMS **1** *she has to smile in her business* **work**, occupation, profession, career, employment, job, position.
2 *who do you do business with?* **trade**, commerce, dealing, traffic, dealings, transactions, negotiations. **3** *her own business* **firm**, company, concern, enterprise, venture, organization, operation, undertaking; informal outfit.
4 *none of your business* **concern**, affair, responsibility, duty. **5** *an odd business* **affair**, matter, case, circumstance, situation, event, incident.

✔ Remember the **i**: business.

businesslike ▸ adjective efficient and practical.

businessman (or **businesswoman**) ▸ noun (plural **businessmen** or **businesswomen**) a person who works in business.

SYNONYMS **executive**, entrepreneur, industrialist, merchant, dealer, trader, manufacturer, tycoon, employer, broker, buyer, seller, tradesman, retailer, supplier.

busk ▸ verb play music in the street in the hope of being given money by passers-by.
□ **busker** noun.

bust¹ ▸ noun **1** a woman's breasts. **2** a sculpture of a person's head, shoulders, and chest.

SYNONYMS **1** *her large bust* **bosom**, breasts, chest; informal boobs, knockers; N. Amer. informal bazooms. **2** *a bust of Caesar* **sculpture**, carving, effigy, statue, head and shoulders.

bust² informal ▸ verb (**busts**, **busting**, **busted** or **bust**) **1** break, split, or burst. **2** chiefly N. Amer. raid or search a building, or arrest someone.
▸ noun **1** a period of economic difficulty. **2** a police raid.

▸ adjective **1** Brit. damaged; broken. **2** bankrupt.
■ **bust-up** a serious quarrel or fight.

bustard ▸ noun a large fast-running bird with speckled feathers.

bustle¹ ▸ verb (**bustles**, **bustling**, **bustled**) **1** move energetically or noisily. **2** (of a place) be full of activity.

SYNONYMS *people bustled about* **rush**, dash, hurry, scurry, scuttle, scamper, scramble; informal scoot, beetle, buzz.

▸ noun excited activity and movement.

SYNONYMS *the bustle of the market* **activity**, action, liveliness, excitement, tumult, commotion, hubbub, whirl; informal toing and froing.

bustle² ▸ noun a pad or frame formerly worn by women under a skirt to puff it out behind.

bustling ▸ adjective full of activity.

SYNONYMS **busy**, crowded, swarming, teeming, humming, buzzing, hectic, lively.
ANTONYMS leisurely, deserted.

busy ▸ adjective (**busier**, **busiest**) **1** having a lot to do. **2** occupied with an activity. **3** crowded or full of activity.

SYNONYMS **1** *they are very busy at the moment* **hard at work**, involved, rushed off your feet, hard-pressed, on the job; informal on the go, hard at it; Brit. informal on the hop. **2** *I'm sorry, she is busy* **unavailable**, engaged, occupied, absorbed, engrossed, immersed, preoccupied, working; informal tied up.
3 *a busy day* **hectic**, active, lively, full, eventful, energetic, tiring.
ANTONYMS idle, free, quiet.

▸ verb (**busies**, **busying**, **busied**) (**busy yourself**) keep yourself occupied.

SYNONYMS *he busied himself with paperwork* **occupy**, involve, engage, concern, absorb, engross, immerse, distract, divert.

□ **busily** adverb.

busybody ▸ noun (plural **busybodies**) an interfering or nosy person.

but ▸ conjunction **1** nevertheless. **2** on the contrary. **3** other than; otherwise than. **4** old use without it being the case that.

SYNONYMS **1** *he stumbled but didn't fall* **however**, nevertheless, nonetheless, even so, yet, still. **2** *I am clean but you aren't* **whereas**, conversely.

▸ preposition except; apart from.

SYNONYMS *everyone but him* **except (for)**, apart from, other than, besides, aside from, with the exception of, bar.

▸ adverb only.
■ **but for 1** except for. **2** if it were not for.

butane /byoo-tayn/ ▸ noun a flammable gas present in petroleum and natural gas and used as a fuel.

butch ▸ adjective informal aggressively masculine.

butcher ▸ noun **1** a person who cuts up and sells meat as a trade. **2** a person who kills animals for food. **3** a person who kills brutally.
▸ verb (**butchers, butchering, butchered**) **1** kill or cut up an animal for food. **2** kill someone brutally.
□ **butchery** noun.

butler ▸ noun the chief male servant of a house.

butt¹ ▸ verb **1** hit with the head or horns. **2** (**butt in**) interrupt a conversation.

> SYNONYMS *she butted him* **ram,** headbutt, bump, poke, prod, push, shove, thrust.

▸ noun a rough push with the head.

butt² ▸ noun **1** an object of criticism or ridicule. **2** a target in archery or shooting.

> SYNONYMS *the butt of a joke* **target,** victim, object, dupe, laughing stock.

butt³ ▸ noun **1** the thicker end of a tool or a weapon. **2** the stub of a cigar or a cigarette. **3** N. Amer. informal a person's bottom.

> SYNONYMS **1** *the butt of a gun* **stock,** end, handle, hilt, haft. **2** *a cigarette butt* **stub,** end, stump; informal fag end, dog end.

▸ verb meet end to end.

> SYNONYMS *the shop butts up against the house* **adjoin,** abut, be next to, be adjacent to, border (on), neighbour.

butt⁴ ▸ noun a cask used for wine, beer, or water.

butter ▸ noun a pale yellow fatty substance made by churning cream.
▸ verb (**butters, buttering, buttered**) **1** spread with butter. **2** (**butter someone up**) informal flatter someone.
■ **butter bean** Brit. a large flat edible bean.

buttercream ▸ noun a mixture of butter and icing sugar used to ice cakes.

buttercup ▸ noun a plant with small bright yellow flowers.

butterfly ▸ noun (plural **butterflies**) **1** an insect with two pairs of large wings, which feeds on nectar. **2** (**butterflies**) informal a fluttering sensation in the stomach when you are nervous. **3** a stroke in swimming in which you raise both arms out of the water together.

buttermilk ▸ noun the slightly sour liquid left after butter has been churned.

butterscotch ▸ noun a sweet made with butter and brown sugar.

buttery ▸ adjective containing, resembling, or covered with butter.

▸ noun (plural **butteries**) Brit. a room in a college where food is sold to students.

buttock ▸ noun either of the two round fleshy parts of the human body that form the bottom.

> SYNONYMS (**buttocks**) **bottom,** rear (end), rump, seat; informal behind, backside; Brit. informal bum, botty, jacksie; N. Amer. informal butt, fanny; humorous posterior.

button ▸ noun **1** a small disc sewn on to a garment to fasten it by being pushed through a buttonhole. **2** a knob on a piece of equipment which is pressed to operate it.
▸ verb fasten a garment with buttons.

buttonhole ▸ noun **1** a slit in a piece of clothing through which a button is pushed to fasten it. **2** Brit. a flower worn in a buttonhole of a lapel.
▸ verb (**buttonholes, buttonholing, buttonholed**) informal stop someone and hold them in conversation.

buttress ▸ noun **1** a projecting support built against a wall. **2** a projecting part of a hill or mountain.
▸ verb support or strengthen.

buxom ▸ adjective (of a woman) attractively plump and large-breasted.

buy ▸ verb (**buys, buying, bought**) **1** get something in return for payment. **2** informal accept that something is true.

> SYNONYMS *they bought a new house* **purchase,** acquire, obtain, get, pick up, snap up, invest in; informal get hold of, score.
> ANTONYMS sell.

▸ noun informal something that has been bought.

> SYNONYMS *a good buy* **purchase,** deal, bargain, investment, acquisition.

■ **buy someone out** pay someone to give up a share in something.

buyer ▸ noun a person who buys something.

> SYNONYMS **purchaser,** customer, consumer, shopper, investor; (**buyers**) clientele, patronage, market.

buzz ▸ noun **1** a low continuous humming sound. **2** the sound of a buzzer or telephone. **3** an atmosphere of excitement and activity. **4** informal a thrill.

> SYNONYMS **1** *the buzz of the bees* **hum,** murmur, drone. **2** *an insistent buzz from her control panel* **tone,** purr, ring, warble, note, beep, alarm, warning.

▸ verb **1** make a humming sound. **2** call someone with a buzzer. **3** move quickly. **4** (**buzz off**) informal go away. **5** have an air of excitement or activity.

buzzard ▸ noun a large bird of prey.

buzzer ▸ noun an electrical device that makes a buzzing noise to attract attention.

buzzword ▸ noun informal a technical word or phrase that has become fashionable.

by ▸ preposition **1** through the action of. **2** indicating an amount or the size of a margin. **3** indicating the end of a time period. **4** beside. **5** past and beyond. **6** during. **7** according to.

> SYNONYMS **1** *I broke it by forcing the lid* **through,** as a result of, because of, by dint of, by means of, with the help of, by virtue of. **2** *be there by midday* **no later than,** in good time for, before. **3** *a house by the lake* **next to,** beside, alongside, by/at the side of, adjacent to.

▸ adverb so as to go past.

> SYNONYMS *people hurried by* **past,** on, along.

■ **by and by** before long. **by the by** in passing. **by and large** on the whole.

bye[1] ▸ noun **1** the moving of a competitor straight to the next round of a competition because they have no opponent. **2** Cricket a run scored from a ball that passes the batsman without being hit.

bye[2] ▸ exclamation informal goodbye.

by-election ▸ noun Brit. an election held during a government's term of office to fill a vacant seat.

bygone ▸ adjective belonging to an earlier time.

■ **let bygones be bygones** decide to forget past disagreements.

by-law (or **bye-law**) ▸ noun **1** Brit. a rule made by a local authority. **2** a rule made by a company or society.

byline ▸ noun **1** a line in a newspaper naming the writer of an article. **2** (in soccer) the part of the goal line to either side of the goal.

bypass ▸ noun **1** a road passing round a town. **2** an operation to help the circulation of blood by directing it through a new passage.

> SYNONYMS **ring road,** detour, diversion, alternative route; Brit. relief road.

▸ verb go past or round.

> SYNONYMS **1** *bypass the farm* **go round,** go past, make a detour round, avoid. **2** *the system had been bypassed* **ignore,** sidestep, avoid, evade, escape, elude, skirt, dodge, circumvent, get round, go over the head of, pass over; informal short-circuit, duck.

by-product ▸ noun **1** a product produced in the process of making something else. **2** an unintended but unavoidable secondary result.

> SYNONYMS **spin-off,** consequence, result, corollary, side effect, ramification, repercussion, fallout; fruits; Brit. knock-on effect.

byre ▸ noun Brit. a cowshed.

bystander ▸ noun a person who is present at an event but does not take part.

> SYNONYMS **onlooker,** passer-by, observer, spectator, eyewitness.

byte ▸ noun a unit of information stored in a computer, equal to eight bits.

byway ▸ noun a minor road or path.

byword ▸ noun **1** a notable example of something. **2** a saying.

Byzantine /bɪ-**zan**-tyn/ ▸ adjective **1** relating to Byzantium (now Istanbul) or the Eastern Orthodox Church. **2** very complicated and detailed.

Cc

C (or **c**) ▸ noun (plural **Cs** or **C's**) **1** the third letter of the alphabet. **2** the Roman numeral for 100.
▸ abbreviation **1** Celsius or centigrade. **2** (©) copyright. **3** (c) cents. **4** (c or ca.) circa. **5** (c.) century or centuries.

cab ▸ noun **1** a taxi. **2** the driver's compartment in a truck, bus, or train.

> SYNONYMS **taxi,** taxi cab; Brit. minicab, hackney carriage; N. Amer. hack.

cabal /kuh-**bal**/ ▸ noun a secret political group.

cabaret /**kab**-uh-ray/ ▸ noun entertainment held in a nightclub or restaurant while the audience sit at tables.

cabbage ▸ noun a vegetable with thick green or purple leaves.

caber /**kay**-ber/ ▸ noun a tree trunk used in the Scottish Highland sport of tossing the caber.

cabin ▸ noun **1** a private compartment on a ship. **2** the passenger compartment in an aircraft. **3** a small wooden shelter or house.

> SYNONYMS **1** *a ship's cabin* **berth,** stateroom, compartment. **2** *a cabin by the lake* **hut,** log cabin, shanty, shack, chalet; Scottish bothy; N. Amer. cabana.

cabinet ▸ noun **1** a cupboard with drawers or shelves for storing things. **2** a piece of furniture enclosing a radio, speaker, etc. **3** (**Cabinet**) a committee of senior government ministers.

> SYNONYMS **cupboard,** bureau, chest of drawers.

cabinetmaker ▸ noun a person who makes fine wooden furniture as a job.

cable ▸ noun **1** a thick rope of wire or fibre. **2** a wire for transmitting electricity or telecommunication signals.

> SYNONYMS **1** *a thick cable moored the ship* **rope,** cord, line; Nautical hawser; N. Amer. choker. **2** *electric cables* **wire,** lead, cord, power line; Brit. flex.

■ **cable car** a small carriage that hangs from a moving cable and travels up and down the side of a mountain. **cable television**

a system in which programmes are transmitted by cable.

caboodle ▸ noun (**the whole caboodle**) informal the whole number of people or things in question.

caboose /kuh-**booss**/ ▸ noun N. Amer. a guards' van on a goods train.

cabriolet /**kab**-ri-oh-lay/ ▸ noun **1** a car with a roof that folds down. **2** a horse-drawn carriage with a hood.

cacao /kuh-**kah**-oh/ ▸ noun the seeds of a tropical American tree, from which cocoa and chocolate are made.

cache /kash/ ▸ noun a hidden store of things.

> SYNONYMS **hoard,** store, stockpile, stock, supply, reserve, arsenal; informal stash.

cachet /ka-**shay**/ ▸ noun the state of being respected or admired; prestige.

cackle ▸ verb (**cackles, cackling, cackled**) **1** laugh noisily. **2** (of a hen) make a noisy clucking cry.
▸ noun a noisy cry or laugh.

cacophony /kuh-**koff**-uh-ni/ ▸ noun (plural **cacophonies**) a mixture of loud and unpleasant sounds.
□ **cacophonous** adjective.

cactus /**kak**-tuhss/ ▸ noun (plural **cacti** /**kak**-ty/ or **cactuses**) a plant with a thick fleshy stem that has spines but no leaves.

cad ▸ noun dated or humorous a man who is dishonest or treats other people badly.
□ **caddish** adjective.

cadaver /kuh-**da**-ver/ ▸ noun Medicine a dead body.

cadaverous ▸ adjective very pale and thin.

caddie (or **caddy**) ▸ noun (plural **caddies**) a person who carries a golfer's clubs.
▸ verb (**caddies, caddying, caddied**) work as a caddie.

caddy ▸ noun (plural **caddies**) a small storage container.

cadence /**kay**-duhnss/ ▸ noun **1** the rise and fall in pitch of the voice. **2** the close of a musical phrase.

cadenza /kuh-**den**-zuh/ ▸ noun a difficult solo passage in a piece of music.

cadet ▸ noun a young trainee in the armed services or police.

cadge ▸ verb (cadges, cadging, cadged) informal ask for or get something without paying or working for it.

cadmium /kad-mi-uhm/ ▸ noun a silvery-white metallic element.

cadre /kah-der/ ▸ noun a small group of people trained for a particular purpose or at the centre of a political organization.

Caesar /see-zer/ ▸ noun a title of Roman emperors.

> ✔ -ae-, not -ea-: Caesar.

Caesarean (or Caesarean section) /si-**zair**-i-uhn/ ▸ noun an operation for delivering a child by cutting through the wall of the mother's abdomen.

caesium /see-zi-uhm/ (US spelling cesium) ▸ noun a soft, silvery metallic element.

cafe /ka-fay/ ▸ noun a small restaurant selling light meals and drinks.

> SYNONYMS **snack bar,** cafeteria, coffee bar/shop, tea room/shop, bistro, brasserie; N. Amer. diner, lunchroom.

cafeteria /ka-fuh-**teer**-i-uh/ ▸ noun a self-service restaurant.

> SYNONYMS **self-service restaurant,** canteen, cafe, buffet, refectory, mess hall.

cafetière /ka-fuh-**tyair**/ ▸ noun a coffee pot containing a plunger to push the grounds to the bottom.

caffeine /**kaf**-feen/ ▸ noun a stimulating substance found in tea and coffee.

caftan ➡ KAFTAN.

cage ▸ noun a structure of bars or wires used for confining animals.

> SYNONYMS *the lion's cage* **enclosure,** pen, pound, coop, hutch, birdcage, aviary.

▸ verb (cages, caging, caged) confine an animal in a cage.

> SYNONYMS *they were caged up like animals* **confine,** shut in/up, pen, coop up, enclose.

cagey ▸ adjective informal cautiously reluctant to speak.

> SYNONYMS **secretive,** guarded, tight-lipped, reticent, evasive; informal playing your cards close to your chest.
> ANTONYMS open.

□ **cagily** adverb.

cagoule /kuh-**gool**/ ▸ noun Brit. a lightweight hooded waterproof jacket.

cahoots /kuh-**hoots**/ ▸ plural noun (in cahoots) informal making secret plans together.

caiman /**kay**-muhn/ ▸ noun a tropical American reptile similar to an alligator.

cairn ▸ noun a mound of rough stones built as a memorial or landmark.

cajole /kuh-**johl**/ ▸ verb (cajoles, cajoling, cajoled) persuade someone to do something by flattering them.

> SYNONYMS **persuade,** wheedle, coax, talk into, prevail on; informal sweet-talk, soft-soap.

cake ▸ noun **1** an item of soft sweet food made from baking a mixture of flour, fat, eggs, and sugar. **2** a flat round item of savoury food.

> SYNONYMS **1** *cream cakes* **bun,** pastry, gateau, slice. **2** *a cake of soap* **bar,** tablet, block, slab, lump, wedge.

▸ verb (cakes, caking, caked) (of a thick or sticky substance) cover and become encrusted on something.

> SYNONYMS *boots caked with mud* **coat,** encrust, plaster, cover.

calabrese /kal-uh-**breez**/ ▸ noun a bright green variety of broccoli.

calamine /**kal**-uh-myn/ ▸ noun a pink powder used to make a soothing lotion or ointment.

calamity ▸ noun (plural calamities) an event causing great and sudden damage or distress.
□ **calamitous** adjective.

calcified /**kal**-si-fyd/ ▸ adjective hardened by the addition of calcium salts.

calcium ▸ noun a soft grey metallic substance.
■ **calcium carbonate** a white compound found as chalk, limestone, and marble.

calculate ▸ verb (calculates, calculating, calculated) **1** work out a number or amount using mathematics. **2** intend an action to have a particular effect.

> SYNONYMS **1** *the interest is calculated daily* **compute,** work out, reckon, figure, add up/together, count up, tally, total; Brit. tot up. **2** *his words were calculated to wound her* **intend,** mean, design.

□ **calculable** adjective.

calculated ▸ adjective done with awareness of the likely effect.

> SYNONYMS **deliberate,** premeditated, planned, pre-planned, preconceived, intentional, intended.
> ANTONYMS unintentional, rash.

calculating ▸ adjective craftily planning things so as to benefit yourself.

> SYNONYMS **cunning,** crafty, wily, sly, scheming, devious, disingenuous.
> ANTONYMS ingenuous, innocent.

calculation ▸ noun **1** a count or assessment done using mathematics. **2** an assessment of the risks or effects of a course of action.

> SYNONYMS **1** *the calculation of the overall cost* **computation**, reckoning, adding up, counting up, working out, figuring; Brit. totting up. **2** *political calculations* **assessment**, judgement, forecast, projection, prediction.

calculator ▸ noun a small electronic device used for making mathematical calculations.

calculus /kal-kyuu-luhss/ ▸ noun the branch of mathematics concerned with problems involving rates of change.

caldron US spelling of CAULDRON.

calendar ▸ noun **1** a chart showing the days, weeks, and months of a particular year. **2** a system by which the beginning and end of a year are fixed. **3** a list of special days or events.

> SYNONYMS *my social calendar* **schedule**, programme, diary, timetable, agenda.

calf¹ ▸ noun (plural **calves**) **1** a young cow or bull. **2** the young of some other large animals, e.g. elephants.

calf² ▸ noun (plural **calves**) the fleshy part at the back of a person's leg below the knee.

calibrate ▸ verb (**calibrates**, **calibrating**, **calibrated**) **1** mark a gauge or instrument with units of measurement. **2** compare the readings of an instrument with those of a standard.
□ **calibration** noun.

calibre (US spelling **caliber**) ▸ noun **1** the diameter of the inside of a gun barrel, or of a bullet or shell. **2** a person's quality or ability.

> SYNONYMS **1** *a man of his calibre* **quality**, merit, distinction, stature, excellence, ability, expertise, talent, capability. **2** *rugby of this calibre* **standard**, level, quality. **3** *the calibre of a gun* **bore**, diameter, gauge.

calico ▸ noun (plural **calicoes** or US **calicos**) **1** Brit. a type of plain white cotton cloth. **2** N. Amer. printed cotton fabric.

californium ▸ noun a radioactive metallic element that is produced artificially.

caliper (or **calliper**) ▸ noun **1** (also **calipers**) a measuring instrument with two hinged legs. **2** a metal support for a person's leg.

caliph /kay-lif/ ▸ noun (in the past) the chief Muslim ruler.

calk US spelling of CAULK.

call ▸ verb **1** shout to someone to attract their attention or ask them to come somewhere. **2** telephone someone. **3** (of a bird or animal) make its characteristic cry. **4** pay a brief visit. **5** name or describe

someone or something. **6** predict the result of a vote or contest.

> SYNONYMS **1** *'Wait for me!' she called* **cry out**, shout, yell, sing out, chant, exclaim; informal holler. **2** *Mum called me in the morning* **wake (up)**, awaken, rouse; Brit. informal knock up. **3** *I'll call you tomorrow* **phone**, telephone, give someone a call; Brit. ring (up), give someone a ring; informal call up; Brit. informal give someone a bell, get someone on the blower; N. Amer. informal get someone on the horn. **4** *Rose called a taxi* **summon**, send for, order. **5** *he called at Ashgrove Cottage* **pay a visit to**, visit, call/drop/look in on, drop/stop by, pop into, nip over to. **6** *the prime minister called a meeting* **convene**, summon, assemble. **7** *they called their daughter Hannah* **name**, christen, baptize, designate, style, term, dub. **8** *I would call him a friend* **describe as**, regard as, look on as, think of as, consider to be.

▸ noun **1** an act of calling someone. **2** an act of telephoning someone. **3** the cry of a bird or animal. **4** a brief visit. **5** (**call for**) demand or need for.

> SYNONYMS **1** *I heard calls from the auditorium* **cry**, shout, yell, chant, exclamation; informal holler. **2** *the call of the barn owl* **cry**, song. **3** *I'll give you a call tomorrow* **phone call**, telephone call; Brit. ring; informal buzz; Brit. informal bell. **4** *a call for party unity* **appeal**, request, plea. **5** *there's no call for that kind of language* **need**, necessity, reason, justification, excuse. **6** *there's no call for expensive wine here* **demand**, desire, market. **7** *the call of the Cairngorms* **attraction**, appeal, lure, allure, pull, draw.

■ **call centre** an office in which large numbers of telephone calls are handled for an organization. **call for** require. **call something off** cancel something. **call on** turn to for help. **call the shots** (or **tune**) be in charge of how something should be done. **call someone up** summon someone to serve in the army or to play in a team.
□ **caller** noun.

calligraphy /kuh-**lig**-ruh-fi/ ▸ noun decorative handwriting.
□ **calligrapher** noun **calligraphic** adjective.

calling ▸ noun **1** a profession or occupation. **2** a strong feeling that you are suitable for a particular occupation; a vocation.

> SYNONYMS **profession**, occupation, vocation, career.

callisthenics /kal-liss-**then**-iks/ (US spelling **calisthenics**) ▸ plural noun gymnastic exercises.

callous ▸ adjective insensitive and cruel.

c

SYNONYMS **heartless,** unfeeling, uncaring, cold, cold-hearted, hard, as hard as nails, hard-hearted, insensitive, unsympathetic.
ANTONYMS kind, compassionate.

□ **callously** adverb.

callow ▸ adjective young and inexperienced.

callus (or **callous**) ▸ noun an area of thickened and hardened skin.

calm ▸ adjective **1** not nervous, angry, or excited. **2** peaceful and undisturbed.

SYNONYMS **1** *she seemed very calm* **relaxed,** serene, tranquil, unruffled, unperturbed, unflustered, untroubled, unexcitable, unemotional, phlegmatic, composed; informal unflappable, laid-back. **2** *the night was calm* **windless,** still, quiet, tranquil, smooth.
ANTONYMS excited, nervous, stormy.

▸ noun a calm state or period.

SYNONYMS **1** *his usual calm deserted him* **composure,** coolness, calmness, self-possession, sangfroid, serenity, tranquillity; informal cool, unflappability. **2** *calm prevailed* **tranquillity,** stillness, quiet, peace.

▸ verb (often **calm down** or **calm someone down**) become or make someone calm.
□ **calmly** adverb **calmness** noun.

calorie ▸ noun (plural **calories**) **1** a unit for measuring how much energy food will produce. **2** a unit of heat.

calorific ▸ adjective relating to the amount of energy contained in food or fuel.

calumny /**ka**-luhm-ni/ ▸ noun (plural **calumnies**) formal the making of false and damaging statements about someone.

calve ▸ verb (**calves, calving, calved**) give birth to a calf.

calves plural of CALF¹, CALF².

calypso ▸ noun (plural **calypsos**) a kind of West Indian song with improvised words on a topical theme.

calyx /**kay**-liks/ ▸ noun (plural **calyces** /**kay**-li-seez/ or **calyxes**) the ring of small leaves (sepals) which form a layer around the bud of a flower.

cam ▸ noun **1** a projecting part on a wheel or shaft, which comes into contact with another part while rotating and makes it move. **2** a camshaft.

camaraderie /kam-uh-**rah**-duh-ri/ ▸ noun trust and friendship between people.

camber ▸ noun a slightly curved shape of a horizontal surface such as a road.

Cambodian /kam-**boh**-di-uhn/ ▸ noun a person from Cambodia.
▸ adjective relating to Cambodia.

cambric ▸ noun a lightweight white linen or cotton fabric.

camcorder ▸ noun a portable combined video camera and video recorder.

came past tense of COME.

camel ▸ noun a large long-necked animal with either one or two humps on its back.

camellia /kuh-**mee**-li-uh/ ▸ noun an evergreen shrub with bright flowers and shiny leaves.

cameo ▸ noun (plural **cameos**) **1** a piece of jewellery consisting of a carving of a head against a differently coloured background. **2** a short piece of writing giving a good description of a person or thing. **3** a small part played by a well-known actor.

camera ▸ noun a device for taking photographs or recording moving images.
■ **in camera** Law in a judge's private rooms, without the press and public being present.

Cameroonian ▸ noun a person from Cameroon, a country in West Africa.
▸ adjective relating to Cameroon.

camisole ▸ noun a woman's loose-fitting undergarment for the upper body.

camomile (or **chamomile**) /**kam**-uh-myl/ ▸ noun a plant with white and yellow flowers, used in herbal preparations.

camouflage /**kam**-uh-flahzh/ ▸ noun **1** the painting or covering of soldiers and military equipment to make them blend in with their surroundings. **2** clothing or materials used for this purpose. **3** the natural appearance of an animal which allows it to blend in with its surroundings.

SYNONYMS *the stripes act as camouflage* **disguise,** mask, screen, cover, cloak, front, facade, blind, concealment, subterfuge.

▸ verb (**camouflages, camouflaging, camouflaged**) disguise using camouflage.

SYNONYMS *I used cement to camouflage the hole* **disguise,** hide, conceal, mask, screen, cover (up).

camp¹ ▸ noun **1** a place where soldiers, refugees, etc. live temporarily in tents, huts, or cabins. **2** a complex of buildings for holidaymakers. **3** the supporters of a particular party or set of beliefs.

SYNONYMS **1** *an army camp* **campsite,** encampment, camping ground, bivouac, base, settlement. **2** *the liberal and conservative camps* **faction,** wing, group, lobby, caucus, bloc.

▸ verb live in a tent while on holiday.
■ **camp bed** Brit. a folding portable bed. **camp follower** a person who associates with a group without being a full member.
□ **camper** noun.

camp² informal ▸ adjective **1** (of a man) effeminate in an exaggerated way.

2 deliberately exaggerated and theatrical in style.

■ **camp it up** behave in a camp way.

campaign ▸ noun **1** a series of military operations in a particular area. **2** an organized course of action to achieve a goal.

> SYNONYMS **1** *Napoleon's Russian campaign* **operation(s)**, manoeuvre(s), offensive, attack, war, battle, crusade. **2** *the campaign to reduce vehicle emissions* **effort**, drive, push, struggle, movement, crusade, operation, strategy.

▸ verb work towards a goal.

> SYNONYMS *they are campaigning for political reform* **fight**, battle, push, press, strive, struggle, lobby, agitate.

□ **campaigner** noun.

campanile /kam-puh-**nee**-lay/ ▸ noun a bell tower.

campanology /kam-puh-**nol**-uh-ji/ ▸ noun the art of bell-ringing.

campanula ▸ noun a plant with blue, purple, or white bell-shaped flowers.

campfire ▸ noun an open-air fire in a camp.

camphor ▸ noun a strong-smelling white substance, used in medicine and in insect repellents.

campion ▸ noun a plant with pink or white flowers.

campus ▸ noun (plural **campuses**) the grounds and buildings of a university or college.

camshaft ▸ noun a shaft with one or more cams attached to it.

can[1] ▸ modal verb (3rd singular present **can**; past **could**) **1** be able to. **2** be allowed to.

> ❗ When you're asking to be allowed to do something, it is more polite to say **may** rather than **can** (*may we leave now?* rather than *can we leave now?*).

can[2] ▸ noun a cylindrical metal container.
▸ verb (**cans**, **canning**, **canned**) preserve food in a can.

■ **a can of worms** a complicated matter that will prove difficult to manage.

Canadian ▸ noun a person from Canada.
▸ adjective relating to Canada.

canal ▸ noun **1** a water-filled channel made for boats to travel on or to convey water to fields. **2** a passage in a plant or animal carrying food, liquid, or air.

canapé /**kan**-uh-pay/ ▸ noun a small piece of bread or pastry with a savoury topping.

canard /ka-**nard**/ ▸ noun a false rumour or story.

canary ▸ noun (plural **canaries**) a small bright yellow bird with a tuneful song.

canasta /kuh-**nass**-tuh/ ▸ noun a card game using two packs and usually played by two pairs of partners.

cancan ▸ noun a lively, high-kicking stage dance.

cancel ▸ verb (**cancels**, **cancelling**, **cancelled**; US spelling **cancels**, **canceling**, **canceled**) **1** decide that a planned event will not take place. **2** withdraw from or end an arrangement. **3** (**cancel something out**) (of one thing) have an equal but opposite effect on another thing. **4** mark a stamp, ticket, etc. to show that it has been used.

> SYNONYMS **1** *the match was cancelled* **call off**, abandon, scrap, drop, axe; informal scrub; N. Amer. informal redline. **2** *his visa has been cancelled* **annul**, invalidate, declare null and void, void, revoke, rescind, retract, withdraw. **3** **neutralize**, negate, nullify, wipe out, balance (out), make up for, compensate for, offset.
> ANTONYMS arrange, confirm, reinstate, issue.

□ **cancellation** noun.

Cancer ▸ noun a sign of the zodiac (the Crab), 21 June–22 July.

cancer ▸ noun **1** a disease caused by an uncontrolled growth of abnormal cells in a part of the body. **2** a tumour. **3** something evil or destructive that is hard to contain or destroy.

> SYNONYMS **(malignant) growth**, tumour.

□ **cancerous** adjective.

candela /kan-**dee**-luh/ ▸ noun the basic unit of luminous intensity.

candelabrum /kan-di-**lah**-bruhm/ ▸ noun (plural **candelabra** /kan-di-**lah**-bruh/) a large branched holder for several candles or lamps.

candid ▸ adjective truthful and straightforward; frank.

> SYNONYMS **frank**, forthright, direct, blunt, open, honest, truthful, sincere; informal upfront; N. Amer. informal on the up and up.
> ANTONYMS guarded.

□ **candidly** adverb.

candidate ▸ noun **1** a person who applies for a job or is nominated for election. **2** Brit. a person taking an exam.

> SYNONYMS **applicant**, contender, competitor, entrant, claimant, nominee, interviewee, examinee, possible; Brit. informal runner.

□ **candidacy** noun.

candied ▸ adjective (of fruit) preserved in a sugar syrup.

candle ▸ noun a stick of wax with a central wick which is lit to produce light as it burns.

candlestick ▸ noun a support or holder for a candle.

candlewick ▸ noun a thick, soft cotton fabric with a tufted pattern.

candour (US spelling candor) ▸ noun the quality of being open and honest.

candy ▸ noun (plural candies) N. Amer. sweets.

candyfloss ▸ noun Brit. a mass of pink or white fluffy spun sugar wrapped round a stick.

cane ▸ noun 1 the hollow stem of tall reeds, grasses, etc. 2 a length of cane used as a walking stick, for beating someone, etc.
▸ verb (canes, caning, caned) beat someone with a cane as a punishment.

canine /kay-nyn/ ▸ adjective relating to or resembling a dog.
▸ noun a pointed tooth next to the incisors.

canister ▸ noun a round or cylindrical container.

canker ▸ noun 1 a disease of trees and plants. 2 a condition in animals that causes open sores.

cannabis ▸ noun a drug made from the hemp plant.

canned ▸ adjective preserved in a sealed can.

cannelloni /kan-nuh-loh-ni/ ▸ plural noun rolls of pasta stuffed with a meat or vegetable mixture and cooked in a cheese sauce.

cannery ▸ noun (plural canneries) a factory where food is canned.

cannibal ▸ noun a person who eats the flesh of human beings.
◻ cannibalism noun cannibalistic adjective.

cannibalize (or cannibalise) ▸ verb (cannibalizes, cannibalizing, cannibalized) use a machine as a source of spare parts for others.

cannon ▸ noun (plural cannon or cannons) 1 a large, heavy gun formerly used in warfare. 2 an automatic heavy gun that fires shells from an aircraft or tank.
▸ verb (cannons, cannoning, cannoned) (cannon into or off) chiefly Brit. collide with.
■ cannon fodder soldiers seen merely as a resource to be used up in war.

cannonade /kan-nuh-nayd/ ▸ noun a period of continuous heavy gunfire.

cannonball ▸ noun a metal or stone ball fired from a cannon.

cannot ▸ short form can not.

canny ▸ adjective (cannier, canniest) shrewd, especially in financial matters.

SYNONYMS **shrewd**, astute, smart, sharp, discerning, discriminating, perceptive. ANTONYMS foolish.

◻ cannily adverb.

canoe ▸ noun a narrow boat with pointed ends, propelled with a paddle.

SYNONYMS **kayak**, dugout, outrigger.

▸ verb (canoes, canoeing, canoed) travel in a canoe.
◻ canoeist noun.

canon ▸ noun 1 a general rule or principle by which something is judged. 2 a Church decree or law. 3 the works of a particular author or artist that are recognized as genuine. 4 a list of literary works considered as being of the highest quality. 5 a member of the clergy on the staff of a cathedral. 6 a piece of music in which a theme is taken up by two or more parts that overlap.
■ canon law the laws of the Christian Church.

canonical /kuh-non-i-k'l/ ▸ adjective 1 accepted as authentic or as a standard. 2 according to the laws of the Christian Church.

canonize (or canonise) ▸ verb (canonizes, canonizing, canonized) officially declare a dead person to be a saint.
◻ canonization noun.

canoodle ▸ verb (canoodles, canoodling, canoodled) informal kiss and cuddle lovingly.

canopy ▸ noun (plural canopies) 1 a cloth covering over a throne or bed. 2 a roof-like covering or shelter. 3 the expanding, umbrella-like part of a parachute.

SYNONYMS **awning**, shade, sunshade, covering.

◻ canopied adjective.

cant[1] (*rhymes with* rant) ▸ noun 1 insincere talk about moral or religious matters. 2 disapproving the language typical of a particular group.

cant[2] (*rhymes with* rant) ▸ verb tilt or slope.
▸ noun a slope or tilt.

can't ▸ short form cannot.

cantaloupe /kan-tuh-loop/ ▸ noun a small melon with orange flesh.

cantankerous ▸ adjective bad-tempered and uncooperative.

cantata /kan-tah-tuh/ ▸ noun a musical work for accompanied solo voices and chorus.

canteen ▸ noun 1 a restaurant in a workplace, school, or college. 2 Brit. a case containing a set of cutlery. 3 a small water bottle used by soldiers or campers.

canter ▸ noun a pace of a horse between a trot and a gallop.
▸ verb (canters, cantering, cantered) move at this pace.

canticle ▸ noun a hymn or chant forming part of a church service.

cantilever ▸ noun a long beam or girder fixed at only one end, used for supporting a bridge.

◻ **cantilevered** adjective.

canto /kan-toh/ ▸ noun (plural **cantos**) a division of a long poem.

canton ▸ noun a political or administrative subdivision of a country, especially in Switzerland.

canvas ▸ noun (plural **canvases** or **canvasses**) **1** a strong, coarse cloth used to make sails, tents, etc. **2** an oil painting on canvas.

canvass ▸ verb **1** visit someone to ask for their vote in an election. **2** question someone to find out their opinion.

> SYNONYMS **1** *he's canvassing for the Green Party* **campaign,** electioneer. **2** *they promised to canvass all members* **poll,** question, survey, interview, consult.

◻ **canvasser** noun.

canyon ▸ noun a deep gorge.

> SYNONYMS **ravine,** gorge, gully, chasm, abyss, gulf; N. Amer. gulch, coulee.

cap ▸ noun **1** a soft flat hat with a peak. **2** Brit. a cap awarded to members of a national sports team. **3** a lid or cover. **4** an upper limit on spending or borrowing. **5** a small amount of explosive powder in a case that explodes when you hit it. **6** a contraceptive diaphragm.

> SYNONYMS **1** *a white plastic cap* **lid,** top, stopper, cork, bung; N. Amer. stopple. **2** *a cap on spending* **limit,** ceiling, curb, check.

▸ verb (**caps, capping, capped**) **1** put a cap on. **2** be a fitting end to. **3** put a limit on. **4** (**be capped**) Brit. be chosen as a member of a national sports team.

> SYNONYMS **1** *mountains capped with snow* **top,** crown, cover, coat, tip. **2** *budgets will be capped* **limit,** restrict, curb, control, peg.

■ **cap in hand** humbly asking for a favour.

capability ▸ noun (plural **capabilities**) the power or ability to do something.

> SYNONYMS **ability,** capacity, power, potential, competence, aptitude, faculty, skill, talent, flair; informal know-how. ANTONYMS inability.

capable ▸ adjective **1** (**capable of**) having the ability to do something. **2** able to achieve what you need to do; competent.

> SYNONYMS **able,** competent, effective, proficient, accomplished, experienced, skilful, talented, gifted; informal useful. ANTONYMS incompetent.

◻ **capably** adverb.

capacious ▸ adjective having a lot of space inside; roomy.

capacitance ▸ noun the ability to store electric charge.

capacitor ▸ noun a device used to store electric charge.

capacity ▸ noun (plural **capacities**) **1** the maximum amount that something can contain or produce. **2** the ability or power to do something. **3** a role or position.

> SYNONYMS **1** *the capacity of the freezer* **volume,** size, dimensions, measurements, proportions. **2** *his capacity to inspire trust.* See CAPABILITY. **3** *in his capacity as Commander-in-Chief* **role,** function, position, post, job, office.

cape¹ ▸ noun a short cloak.

> SYNONYMS *a woollen cape* **cloak,** mantle, poncho.

cape² ▸ noun a piece of land that sticks out into the sea.

> SYNONYMS *the ship rounded the cape* **headland,** promontory, point, head, horn, mull, peninsula.

caper¹ ▸ verb (**capers, capering, capered**) skip or dance about in a lively or playful way.
▸ noun informal a light-hearted or dishonest activity.

caper² ▸ noun the flower bud of a shrub, pickled and used in cooking.

capillarity ▸ noun capillary action.

capillary /kuh-**pil**-luh-ri/ ▸ noun (plural **capillaries**) **1** a very small blood vessel. **2** a tube with a very narrow diameter.
■ **capillary action** the force which acts on a liquid in a narrow tube to push it up or down.

capital ▸ noun **1** the most important city or town of a country or region. **2** wealth that is owned or invested, lent, or borrowed. **3** a capital letter. **4** the top part of a pillar.

> SYNONYMS **money,** finance(s), funds, cash, wherewithal, means, assets, wealth, resources.

▸ adjective informal, dated excellent.
■ **capital letter** a large size of letter used to begin sentences and names. **capital offence** an offence that is punished by death. **capital punishment** the punishment of a crime by death. **make capital out of** use to your own advantage.

capitalism ▸ noun a system in which a country's trade and industry are controlled by private owners for profit.

> SYNONYMS **private enterprise,** free enterprise, the free market, private ownership. ANTONYMS communism.

◻ **capitalist** noun & adjective.

capitalize (or **capitalise**) ▸ verb (**capitalizes, capitalizing, capitalized**) **1** (**capitalize on**) take advantage of. **2** convert into or

c

provide with financial capital. **3** write in capital letters or with a capital first letter.

> SYNONYMS *Wales failed to capitalize on their early lead* **take advantage of**, profit from, make the most of, exploit, develop; informal cash in on.

□ **capitalization** noun.

capitation ▶ noun the payment of a fee or grant to a doctor, school, etc., the amount of which depends on the number of pupils, patients, etc. that are involved.

capitulate ▶ verb (**capitulates**, **capitulating**, **capitulated**) give in to an opponent.

> SYNONYMS **surrender**, give in, yield, concede defeat, give up (the struggle), submit, lay down your arms, throw in the towel/sponge.
> ANTONYMS resist, hold out.

□ **capitulation** noun.

capon /**kay**-puhn/ ▶ noun a male chicken that has been fattened up for eating.

cappuccino /kap-puh-**chee**-noh/ ▶ noun (plural **cappuccinos**) coffee made with milk that has been frothed up with pressurized steam.

caprice /kuh-**preess**/ ▶ noun a sudden change of mood or behaviour.

capricious /kuh-**pri**-shuhss/ ▶ adjective having sudden changes of mood.

> SYNONYMS **fickle**, volatile, unpredictable, temperamental, erratic, wayward, whimsical, flighty, faddish.
> ANTONYMS consistent.

□ **capriciously** adverb.

Capricorn ▶ noun a sign of the zodiac (the Goat), 21 December–20 January.

capsicum ▶ noun (plural **capsicums**) a sweet pepper or chilli pepper.

capsize ▶ verb (**capsizes**, **capsizing**, **capsized**) (of a boat) overturn in the water.

capstan ▶ noun a broad revolving cylinder for winding a heavy rope or cable.

capsule ▶ noun **1** a small gelatin container with a dose of medicine inside, swallowed whole. **2** a small case or compartment.

> SYNONYMS **1** *he swallowed a capsule* **pill**, tablet, lozenge, pastille; informal tab. **2** *a space capsule* **module**, craft, probe.

captain ▶ noun **1** the person in command of a ship or commercial aircraft. **2** the rank of naval officer above commander. **3** the rank of army officer above lieutenant. **4** the leader of a team.

> SYNONYMS **1** *the ship's captain* **commander**, master; informal skipper. **2** *the team captain* **leader**, head, chief; informal boss, skipper.

▶ verb be the captain of.

□ **captaincy** noun.

caption ▶ noun **1** a title or explanation accompanying an illustration or cartoon. **2** a piece of writing appearing as part of a film or television broadcast.

> SYNONYMS **title**, heading, legend, description.

▶ verb provide a caption for.

captivate ▶ verb (**captivates**, **captivating**, **captivated**) attract and hold the interest of; charm.

> SYNONYMS **enthral**, charm, enchant, bewitch, fascinate, beguile, entrance, delight, attract, allure.
> ANTONYMS repel, bore.

□ **captivation** noun.

captive ▶ noun a person who has been captured.

> SYNONYMS **prisoner**, convict, detainee, hostage, prisoner of war, internee.

▶ adjective unable to escape.

> SYNONYMS **confined**, caged, incarcerated, locked up, jailed, imprisoned, interned, detained.
> ANTONYMS free.

captivity ▶ noun the state of being captive.

> SYNONYMS **imprisonment**, incarceration, confinement, detention, internment.
> ANTONYMS freedom.

captor ▶ noun a person who captures another.

capture ▶ verb (**captures**, **capturing**, **captured**) **1** take prisoner, or forcibly get possession of. **2** record accurately in words or pictures. **3** cause data to be stored in a computer.

> SYNONYMS **1** *Mark Dawes was captured in Moscow* **catch**, apprehend, seize, arrest. **2** *guerrillas have captured several towns* **occupy**, invade, conquer, seize, take.
> ANTONYMS release, abandon, liberate.

▶ noun the action of capturing.

> SYNONYMS *he tried to avoid capture* **arrest**, seizure.

capybara /ka-pi-**bah**-ruh/ ▶ noun (plural **capybara** or **capybaras**) a large South American rodent.

car ▶ noun **1** a powered road vehicle designed to carry a small number of people. **2** a railway carriage or wagon.

> SYNONYMS **1** *he drove up in his car* **motor**, motor car, automobile; informal wheels; N. Amer. informal auto. **2** *the dining car* **carriage**, coach; Brit. saloon.

■ **car park** Brit. an area or building where cars may be left temporarily.

carafe /kuh-**raf**/ ▶ noun a wide-necked glass bottle for serving wine.

caramel ▸ noun **1** sugar or syrup heated until it turns brown. **2** soft toffee made with sugar and butter.

carapace /ka-ruh-payss/ ▸ noun the hard upper shell of a tortoise, lobster, etc.

carat /ka-ruht/ ▸ noun **1** a unit of weight for precious stones and pearls. **2** a measure of the purity of gold.

caravan ▸ noun **1** a vehicle equipped for living in, designed to be towed by a car or a horse. **2** historical a group of people travelling together across a desert.

caraway ▸ noun a plant whose seeds are used as a spice.

carbide ▸ noun a compound of carbon with a metal or other element.

carbine ▸ noun a light automatic rifle.

carbohydrate ▸ noun a substance (e.g. sugar and starch) containing carbon, hydrogen, and oxygen, found in food and used to give energy.

carbolic (or **carbolic acid**) ▸ noun a kind of disinfectant.

carbon ▸ noun a chemical element with two main pure forms (diamond and graphite), found in all organic compounds.
■ **carbon copy 1** a copy made with carbon paper. **2** a person or thing identical to another. **carbon dating** a method of finding out how old something is by measuring the amount of radioactive carbon-14 in it. **carbon dioxide** a gas produced by people and animals breathing out, and also by burning carbon, which is absorbed by plants in photosynthesis. **carbon monoxide** a poisonous gas formed when carbon is not completely burned. **carbon paper** thin paper coated with carbon, used for making a copy of a document.

carbonaceous ▸ adjective consisting of or containing carbon or its compounds.

carbonate ▸ noun a compound containing carbon and oxygen together with a metal.

carbonated ▸ adjective (of a drink) fizzy because it contains small bubbles of carbon dioxide.

carbonic acid ▸ noun a very weak acid formed from carbon dioxide and water.

carborundum ▸ noun a very hard black substance used for grinding and polishing.

carbuncle ▸ noun **1** a large abscess or boil in the skin. **2** a polished red gem.

carburettor (US spelling **carburetor**) ▸ noun a device in an engine that mixes the fuel with air.

carcass (or **carcase**) ▸ noun the dead body of an animal.

> synonyms **corpse**, dead body, remains; Medicine cadaver; informal stiff.

carcinogen /kar-sin-uh-juhn/ ▸ noun a substance that can cause cancer.
□ **carcinogenic** adjective.

carcinoma /kar-si-noh-muh/ ▸ noun (plural **carcinomas**) a cancer of the skin or of the internal organs.

card[1] ▸ noun **1** thick, stiff paper or thin cardboard. **2** a piece of card printed with information, greetings, etc. **3** a small rectangular piece of plastic used for obtaining money from a bank or paying for goods. **4** a playing card. **5** (**cards**) a game played with playing cards.
■ **card sharp** a person who cheats at cards. **on the cards** possible or likely.

card[2] ▸ verb disentangle the fibres of raw wool by combing it with a sharp-toothed instrument.

cardamom ▸ noun the seed and pods of a SE Asian plant, used as a spice.

cardboard ▸ noun thin board made from paper pulp.

cardiac ▸ adjective having to do with the heart.

cardigan ▸ noun a sweater with buttons down the front.

cardinal ▸ noun an important Roman Catholic priest, having the power to elect the Pope.
▸ adjective most important; chief.
■ **cardinal number** a number expressing quantity (one, two, three, etc.).

cardiograph ▸ noun an instrument for recording heart movements.

cardiology ▸ noun the branch of medicine concerned with the heart.

cardiovascular ▸ adjective having to do with the heart and blood vessels.

care ▸ noun **1** special attention or effort made to avoid damage, risk, or error. **2** the process of looking after and protecting someone or something. **3** a cause for anxiety, or a worried feeling. **4** the responsibility of a local authority to look after children, rather than their parents.

> synonyms **1** *the care of the child* safe keeping, supervision, custody, charge, protection, responsibility, guardianship. **2** *she chose her words with care* discretion, caution, sensitivity, thought, regard, consideration. **3** *the cares of the day* worry, anxiety, trouble, concern, stress, pressure, strain.
> antonyms neglect, carelessness.

▸ verb (**cares**, **caring**, **cared**) **1** feel concern or interest. **2** feel affection or liking. **3** (**care for** or **to do**) like to have or be willing to do. **4** (**care for**) look after.

> synonyms *the teachers didn't care about our work* be concerned, worry

(yourself), trouble/concern yourself, bother, mind, be interested; informal give a damn/hoot.

■ **care of** at the address of someone who will look after or pass on mail. **take care of** look after or deal with.

careen /kuh-**reen**/ ▸ verb (of a ship) tilt to one side.

career ▸ noun an occupation which is undertaken for a long period of a person's life.

> SYNONYMS *a business career* **profession,** occupation, vocation, calling, life's work, employment.

▸ verb (**careers, careering, careered**) move very fast and in an uncontrolled way.

> SYNONYMS *they careered down the hill* **hurtle,** rush, shoot, race, speed, charge, hare, fly; informal belt, tear; Brit. informal bucket.

careerist ▸ noun a person whose only concern is to make progress in their career. □ **careerism** noun.

carefree ▸ adjective free from anxiety or responsibility.

> SYNONYMS **unworried,** untroubled, blithe, nonchalant, happy-go-lucky, free and easy, easy-going, relaxed; informal laid-back. ANTONYMS troubled.

careful ▸ adjective **1** taking care to avoid harm; cautious. **2** showing a lot of thought and attention.

> SYNONYMS **1** *be careful when you go up the stairs* **cautious,** alert, attentive, watchful, vigilant, wary, on your guard, circumspect. **2** *careful with money* **prudent,** thrifty, economical, sparing, frugal. **3** *careful consideration of the facts* **attentive,** conscientious, painstaking, meticulous, diligent, assiduous, scrupulous, methodical. ANTONYMS careless, extravagant, casual.

□ **carefully** adverb **carefulness** noun.

careless ▸ adjective not giving enough attention to avoiding harm or mistakes.

> SYNONYMS **1** *careless motorists* **inattentive,** negligent, heedless, irresponsible, impetuous, reckless. **2** *careless work* **shoddy,** slapdash, slipshod, scrappy, slovenly, sloppy, negligent, lax, slack, disorganized, hasty, hurried. **3** *a careless remark* **thoughtless,** insensitive, indiscreet, unguarded, incautious, inadvertent. ANTONYMS careful, attentive, meticulous, deliberate, calculated.

□ **carelessly** adverb **carelessness** noun.

carer ▸ noun someone who looks after a sick, elderly, or disabled person.

caress ▸ verb touch or stroke gently or lovingly.

> SYNONYMS **stroke,** touch, fondle, brush, feel, skim.

▸ noun a gentle or loving touch.

caretaker ▸ noun a person employed to look after a public building.

> SYNONYMS **janitor,** attendant, porter, custodian, concierge; N. Amer. superintendent.

▸ adjective doing a job temporarily.

> SYNONYMS *the caretaker manager* **temporary,** acting, provisional, substitute, interim, stand-in, fill-in, stopgap; N. Amer. informal pinch-hitting. ANTONYMS permanent.

careworn ▸ adjective showing signs of prolonged worry.

cargo ▸ noun (plural **cargoes** or **cargos**) goods carried on a ship, aircraft, etc.

> SYNONYMS **freight,** load, haul, consignment, delivery, shipment, goods, merchandise.

Caribbean /ka-rib-**bee**-uhn/ ▸ adjective relating to the Caribbean Sea and its islands.

> ✔ one **r** and two **b**s: Cari**bb**ean.

caribou /**ka**-ri-boo/ ▸ noun (plural **caribou**) N. Amer. a reindeer.

caricature /**ka**-ri-kuh-tyoor/ ▸ noun a picture in which a person's distinctive features are amusingly exaggerated.

▸ verb (**caricatures, caricaturing, caricatured**) make a caricature of.

caries /**kair**-eez/ ▸ noun decay of a tooth or bone.

carjacking ▸ noun the action of stealing a car after attacking its driver or forcing them to abandon it.

carmine /**kar**-myn/ ▸ noun a vivid crimson colour.

carnage /**kar**-nij/ ▸ noun the killing of a large number of people.

> SYNONYMS **slaughter,** massacre, murder, butchery, bloodbath, bloodletting, holocaust.

carnal ▸ adjective relating to sexual needs and activities. □ **carnality** noun.

carnation ▸ noun a plant with pink, white, or red flowers.

carnelian /kar-**nee**-li-uhn/ ▸ noun a dull red or pink semi-precious stone.

carnival ▸ noun a festival involving processions, music, and dancing.

SYNONYMS **festival,** fiesta, fête, fair, gala, Mardi Gras.

carnivore /**kar**-ni-vor/ ▶ noun an animal that eats meat.

carnivorous /kar-**niv**-uh-ruhss/ ▶ adjective eating a diet of meat.

carob ▶ noun a substitute for chocolate made from the pod of an Arabian tree.

carol ▶ noun a religious song associated with Christmas.
▶ verb (**carols, carolling, carolled;** US spelling **carols, caroling, caroled**) **1** sing carols in the streets. **2** sing or say happily.

carotene ▶ noun an orange or red substance found in carrots and other plants, important in the formation of vitamin A.

carotid artery /kuh-**rot**-id/ ▶ noun either of two main arteries carrying blood to the head.

carouse /kuh-**rowz**/ ▶ verb (**carouses, carousing, caroused**) drink alcohol and enjoy yourself with other people in a noisy, lively way.

carousel ▶ noun **1** a merry-go-round at a fair. **2** a rotating device for baggage collection at an airport.

carp[1] ▶ noun (plural **carp**) an edible freshwater fish.

carp[2] ▶ verb complain or find fault.

SYNONYMS **complain,** find fault, quibble, grumble, grouse, whine; informal nit-pick, gripe, moan, bitch, whinge.
ANTONYMS praise.

carpal ▶ adjective relating to the bones in the wrist.

carpel ▶ noun the female reproductive organ of a flower.

carpenter ▶ noun a person who makes objects and structures out of wood.

SYNONYMS **woodworker,** joiner, cabinetmaker; Brit. informal chippy.

☐ **carpentry** noun.

carpet ▶ noun **1** a floor covering made from thick woven fabric. **2** a thick or soft layer of something.
▶ verb (**carpets, carpeting, carpeted**) **1** cover with a carpet. **2** informal tell someone off severely.
■ **carpet-bomb** bomb an area intensively.

carpetbagger ▶ noun informal, disapproving a politician who tries to get elected in an area where they have no local connections.

carport ▶ noun an open-sided shelter for a parked car.

carriage ▶ noun **1** a four-wheeled horse-drawn vehicle for passengers. **2** a passenger vehicle in a train. **3** the carrying of goods from one place to another. **4** a person's way of standing or moving. **5** a wheeled support for moving a gun.

SYNONYMS **1** a railway carriage **coach,** car; Brit. saloon. **2** a horse and carriage **wagon,** coach. **3** an erect carriage **posture,** bearing, gait; Brit. deportment.

■ **carriage clock** a portable clock with a handle on top.

carriageway ▶ noun **1** each of the two sides of a dual carriageway or motorway. **2** the part of a road intended for vehicles.

carrier ▶ noun **1** a person or thing that carries or holds something. **2** a company that transports goods or people for payment.
■ **carrier bag** a plastic or paper bag with handles. **carrier pigeon** a homing pigeon trained to carry messages.

carrion ▶ noun the decaying flesh of dead animals.

carrot ▶ noun **1** a tapering orange root vegetable. **2** something tempting offered as a means of persuasion.

carry ▶ verb (**carries, carrying, carried**) **1** move or take from one place to another. **2** support the weight of. **3** take on or accept responsibility or blame. **4** have a particular feature or result. **5** approve a proposal by a majority of votes. **6** publish or broadcast something. **7** (of a sound or voice) travel a long way. **8** (**carry yourself**) stand and move in a particular way. **9** be pregnant with.

SYNONYMS **1** she carried the box into the kitchen **convey,** transfer, transport, move, take, bring, bear, fetch; informal cart, hump, lug. **2** satellites carry the signal over the Atlantic **transmit,** conduct, relay, communicate, convey, beam, send. **3** a resolution was carried **approve,** pass, accept, endorse, ratify. **4** his voice carried across the quay **be audible,** travel, reach, be heard.
ANTONYMS reject.

■ **be** (or **get**) **carried away** lose self-control. **carry the can** informal take responsibility for a mistake. **carry something off** succeed in doing something. **carry on 1** continue with something. **2** informal have a love affair. **carry-on** informal **1** a fuss. **2** (also **carryings-on**) improper behaviour. **carry something out** perform a task. **carry something through** manage to complete something.

carrycot ▶ noun a baby's small portable cot.

cart ▶ noun **1** an open horse-drawn vehicle for carrying goods or people. **2** a shallow open container on wheels, pulled or pushed by hand.
▶ verb **1** carry in a cart or similar vehicle. **2** informal carry a heavy object with difficulty.

carte blanche /kart blahnsh/ ▸ noun complete freedom to act as you wish.

cartel /kar-tel/ ▸ noun an association of manufacturers or suppliers formed to keep prices high.

carthorse ▸ noun a large, strong horse suitable for heavy work.

cartilage /kar-ti-lij/ ▸ noun firm, flexible tissue which covers the ends of joints and forms structures such as the external ear.
□ **cartilaginous** adjective.

cartography /kar-tog-ruh-fi/ ▸ noun the science or practice of drawing maps.
□ **cartographer** noun **cartographic** adjective.

carton ▸ noun a light cardboard box or container.

SYNONYMS **box,** package, cardboard box, case, container, pack, packet.

cartoon ▸ noun 1 a humorous drawing in a newspaper or magazine. 2 (also **cartoon strip**) a sequence of cartoon drawings that tell a story. 3 a film made from a sequence of drawings, using animation techniques to give the appearance of movement. 4 a full-size drawing made as a preliminary design for a work of art.

SYNONYMS 1 *a cartoon of the Prime Minister* **caricature,** parody, lampoon, satire; informal take-off, send-up. 2 *he was reading cartoons* **comic strip,** comic, graphic novel. 3 *we watched Yogi Bear cartoons* **cartoon film,** animated film, animation.

□ **cartoonist** noun.

cartridge ▸ noun 1 a container holding film, ink, etc., designed to be inserted into a mechanism such as a camera or printer. 2 a casing containing explosives and a bullet or shot for a gun.

SYNONYMS **cassette,** magazine, canister, case, container.

■ **cartridge paper** thick paper for drawing on.

cartwheel ▸ noun a sideways somersault performed with the arms and legs extended.
▸ verb perform cartwheels.

carve ▸ verb (**carves, carving, carved**) 1 cut into a hard material to produce an object or design. 2 cut cooked meat into slices for eating. 3 (**carve something out**) develop a career, reputation, etc. through great effort. 4 (**carve something up**) divide something up ruthlessly.

SYNONYMS 1 *he carved horn handles* **sculpt,** cut, hew, whittle, chisel, shape, fashion. 2 *I carved my initials on the tree* **engrave,** incise, score, cut. 3 *he carved the roast chicken* **slice,** cut up, chop.

carvery ▸ noun (plural **carveries**) a restaurant where cooked joints of meat are carved as required.

carving ▸ noun an object or design carved from wood or stone.

Casanova /ka-suh-noh-vuh/ ▸ noun a man known for seducing many women.

casbah ➡ KASBAH.

cascade ▸ noun 1 a small waterfall. 2 a mass of something falling or hanging down.
▸ verb (**cascades, cascading, cascaded**) pour downwards in large quantities.

case¹ ▸ noun 1 an instance of something happening. 2 an incident being investigated by the police. 3 a legal action decided in a court of law. 4 a set of facts or arguments supporting one side of a debate or lawsuit. 5 a person or problem being given the attention of a doctor, social worker, etc. 6 Grammar a form of a noun, adjective, or pronoun expressing the relationship of the word to others in the sentence.

SYNONYMS 1 *a classic case of overreaction* **instance,** example, occurrence, occasion, demonstration, illustration. 2 *is that the case?* **situation,** position, state of affairs, circumstances, conditions, facts; Brit. state of play; informal score. 3 *the officers on the case* **assignment,** job, project, investigation, exercise. 4 *he lost his case* **lawsuit,** legal action, trial, legal proceedings, litigation. 5 *the case against animal testing* **argument,** defence, justification, vindication, exposition, thesis.

■ **in case** so as to allow for the possibility of something happening.

case² ▸ noun 1 a container or protective covering. 2 a suitcase. 3 a box containing twelve bottles of wine.

SYNONYMS 1 *a cigarette case* **container,** box, canister, holder. 2 *a seed case* **casing,** cover, sheath, envelope, sleeve, jacket, shell. 3 *she threw some clothes into a case* **suitcase,** travel bag, valise; (**cases**) luggage, baggage. 4 *a glass display case* **cabinet,** cupboard.

▸ verb (**cases, casing, cased**) 1 enclose in a case. 2 informal examine a place before robbing it.

casein /kay-seen/ ▸ noun the main protein in milk and cheese.

casement ▸ noun a window hinged at the side so that it opens like a door.

cash ▸ noun 1 money in coins or notes. 2 money available for use.

SYNONYMS 1 *a wallet stuffed with cash* **money,** currency, bank notes, coins, change; N. Amer. bills; informal dough, loot; Brit. informal dosh, brass; N. Amer.

informal dinero. **2** *a lack of cash* **finance,** money, resources, funds, assets, means, wherewithal.

▶ verb **1** give or receive notes or coins for a cheque or money order. **2** (**cash something in**) convert an insurance policy, savings account, etc. into money. **3** (**cash in on**) informal take advantage of.

■ **cash crop** a crop produced for sale rather than for use by the grower. **cash flow** the total amount of money passing into and out of a business. **cash register** a machine used in shops for adding up and recording the amount of each sale and storing the money received.

cashew ▶ noun an edible kidney-shaped nut.

cashier ▶ noun a person responsible for paying out and receiving money in a shop, bank, etc.

SYNONYMS **clerk,** teller, banker, treasurer, bursar, purser.

▶ verb (**cashiers, cashiering, cashiered**) dismiss someone from the armed forces.

cashmere ▶ noun fine, soft wool from a breed of Himalayan goat.

casing ▶ noun a cover that protects or encloses something.

casino ▶ noun (plural **casinos**) a public building or room for gambling.

cask ▶ noun a large barrel for storing alcoholic drinks.

casket ▶ noun **1** a small ornamental box or chest for holding valuable objects. **2** chiefly N. Amer. a coffin.

cassava /kuh-**sah**-vuh/ ▶ noun the root of a tropical American tree, used as food.

casserole ▶ noun **1** a large dish with a lid, used for cooking food slowly in an oven. **2** a kind of stew cooked slowly in an oven.

▶ verb (**casseroles, casseroling, casseroled**) cook food in a casserole.

cassette ▶ noun a sealed plastic case containing audio tape, videotape, film, etc., designed to be inserted into a player or camera.

cassock ▶ noun a long garment worn by Christian priests and members of church choirs.

cassowary /**kass**-uh-wuh-ri/ ▶ noun (plural **cassowaries**) a very large bird that cannot fly, found in New Guinea.

cast ▶ verb (**casts, casting, cast**) **1** throw forcefully. **2** make light or shadow appear on a surface. **3** direct your eyes or thoughts. **4** give a vote. **5** make a magic spell take effect. **6** throw a fishing line out into the water. **7** shed or discard. **8** shape metal by pouring it into a mould while molten. **9** give a part to an actor, or allocate parts in a play or film.

SYNONYMS **1** *he cast the stone into the stream* **throw,** toss, fling, pitch, hurl, lob; informal chuck, sling, bung. **2** *she cast a fearful glance over her shoulder* **direct,** shoot, throw, fling, send. **3** *each citizen cast a vote* **register,** record, enter, file. **4** *the fire cast a soft light* **emit,** give off, throw, send out, radiate. **5** *printing type was cast by hand* **mould,** fashion, form, shape, forge.

▶ noun **1** the actors taking part in a play or film. **2** (also **casting**) an object made by casting metal. **3** a bandage stiffened with plaster of Paris to support and protect a broken limb. **4** the appearance or character of a person or thing. **5** a slight squint.

SYNONYMS **1** *a cast of his hand* **mould,** die, matrix, shape, casting, model. **2** *the cast of 'Hamlet'* **actors,** performers, players, company, troupe, dramatis personae, characters.

■ **cast about** (or **around** or **round**) search far and wide. **casting vote** an extra vote used by a chairperson to decide an issue when votes on each side are equal. **cast iron** a hard alloy of iron and carbon which can be cast in a mould. **cast off** release a boat or ship from its moorings. **cast-off** abandoned or discarded.

castanets ▶ plural noun a pair of small curved pieces of wood, clicked together by the fingers to accompany Spanish dancing.

castaway ▶ noun a person who has been shipwrecked in an isolated place.

caste ▶ noun each of the classes of Hindu society.

SYNONYMS **class,** rank, level, order, stratum, echelon, status.

castellated ▶ adjective having battlements.

castigate ▶ verb (**castigates, castigating, castigated**) tell someone off severely.
□ **castigation** noun.

castle ▶ noun **1** a large fortified building of the medieval period. **2** Chess a rook.

SYNONYMS **fortress,** fort, stronghold, fortification, keep, citadel, palace, chateau, tower.

■ **castles in the air** dreams or plans that will never be achieved.

castor (or **caster**) ▶ noun **1** a small swivelling wheel fixed to the legs or base of a piece of furniture. **2** a small container with holes in the top, used for sprinkling salt, sugar, etc.

■ **castor oil** oil from the seeds of an African shrub, used as a laxative. **castor sugar** white sugar in fine granules.

castrate ▶ verb (**castrates, castrating, castrated**) **1** remove the testicles of. **2** make something less powerful or strong.

□ **castration** noun.

casual ▶ adjective **1** relaxed and unconcerned. **2** done without enough attention or proper planning. **3** occasional or temporary: *casual work*. **4** happening by chance; accidental. **5** (of clothes) informal.

SYNONYMS **1** *a casual attitude to life* **unconcerned,** uncaring, indifferent, lackadaisical, nonchalant, offhand, flippant, easy-going, free and easy, blithe, carefree, devil-may-care; informal laid-back. **2** *a casual remark* **offhand,** spontaneous, unthinking, unconsidered, impromptu, throwaway, unguarded; informal off-the-cuff. **3** *a casual glance* **cursory,** perfunctory, superficial, passing, fleeting. **4** *a casual acquaintance* **slight,** superficial. **5** *casual work* **temporary,** freelance, irregular, occasional. **6** *a casual meeting changed his life* **chance,** accidental, unplanned, unintended, unexpected, unforeseen. **7** *a casual shirt* **informal,** leisure, everyday; informal sporty. **8** *the inn's casual atmosphere* **relaxed,** friendly, informal, easy-going, free and easy; informal laid-back. ANTONYMS serious, premeditated, careful, good, permanent, planned, formal.

□ **casually** adverb.

casualty ▶ noun (plural **casualties**) **1** a person killed or injured in a war or accident. **2** a person or thing badly affected by an event or situation.

SYNONYMS **victim,** sufferer, fatality, death, loss, wounded person, injured person.

casuistry /kazh-oo-iss-tri/ ▶ noun the use of clever but false reasoning.

cat ▶ noun **1** a small furry animal kept as a pet. **2** a wild animal related to this, such as a lion or tiger.

SYNONYMS **feline,** tomcat, tom, kitten; informal pussy (cat), puss, kitty; Brit. informal moggie, mog.

■ **cat burglar** a thief who enters a building by climbing to an upper storey. **cat's paw** a person used by another to carry out an unpleasant task. **the cat's whiskers** informal an excellent person or thing. **let the cat out of the bag** reveal a secret by mistake.

cataclysm /kat-uh-kli-z'm/ ▶ noun a violent upheaval or disaster.
□ **cataclysmic** adjective.

catacomb /kat-uh-koom/ ▶ noun an underground cemetery consisting of tunnels with recesses for tombs.

catafalque /kat-uh-falk/ ▶ noun a decorated wooden framework used to support a coffin.

catalepsy /kat-uh-lep-si/ ▶ noun a condition in which a person becomes unconscious

and goes rigid.

catalogue (US spelling **catalog**) ▶ noun **1** a list of items arranged in order. **2** a publication containing details of items for sale. **3** a series of bad things: *a catalogue of failures*.

SYNONYMS *a library catalogue* **directory,** register, index, list, listing, record, schedule, archive, inventory.

▶ verb (**catalogues, cataloguing, catalogued;** US spelling **catalogs, cataloging, cataloged**) list in a catalogue.

SYNONYMS *the collection is fully catalogued* **classify,** categorize, index, list, archive, record, itemize.

catalyse /kat-uh-lyz/ (US spelling **catalyze**) ▶ verb (**catalyses, catalysing, catalysed**) cause or speed up a reaction by acting as a catalyst.

catalysis /kuh-tal-i-siss/ ▶ noun the speeding up of a chemical reaction by a catalyst.
□ **catalytic** /kat-uh-lit-ik/ adjective.

catalyst /kat-uh-list/ ▶ noun **1** a substance that increases the rate of a chemical reaction while remaining unchanged itself. **2** a person or thing that causes something to happen.

catalytic converter ▶ noun a device in a motor vehicle which converts pollutant exhaust gases into less harmful ones.

catamaran /kat-uh-muh-ran/ ▶ noun a boat with twin parallel hulls.

catapult ▶ noun **1** a forked stick with elastic fastened to the two prongs, used for shooting small stones. **2** a device for launching a glider or aircraft.
▶ verb **1** throw forcefully. **2** move suddenly or very fast.

cataract ▶ noun **1** a large waterfall. **2** a condition in which the lens of the eye becomes cloudy, resulting in blurred vision.

catarrh /kuh-tar/ ▶ noun excessive mucus in the nose or throat.

catastrophe /kuh-tass-truh-fi/ ▶ noun a sudden event that causes great damage or suffering.

SYNONYMS **disaster,** calamity, cataclysm, ruin, tragedy, fiasco, debacle.

□ **catastrophic** adjective **catastrophically** adverb.

catatonia /kat-uh-toh-ni-uh/ ▶ noun a condition in which a person experiences both periods of near unconsciousness and periods of overactivity.
□ **catatonic** adjective.

catcall ▶ noun a shrill whistle or shout of mockery or disapproval.
▶ verb make a catcall.

C

catch ▸ verb (**catches, catching, caught**)
1 seize and hold something moving.
2 capture a person or animal. **3** be in time to get on a vehicle or to see a person or event. **4** entangle or become entangled.
5 surprise someone in the act of doing something wrong or embarrassing. **6** (**be caught in**) unexpectedly find yourself in an unwelcome situation. **7** see, hear, or understand. **8** hit or strike. **9** become infected with an illness.

> SYNONYMS **1** *he caught the ball* **seize,** grab, snatch, grasp, grip, clutch, intercept, trap, receive, get. **2** *we've caught the thief* **capture,** seize, apprehend, arrest, take prisoner, trap, snare, net; informal nab, collar; Brit. informal nick. **3** *her heel caught in a hole* **become trapped,** become entangled, snag, jam, wedge, lodge, get stuck. **4** *they were caught siphoning petrol* **discover,** find, come across, stumble on, chance on, surprise. **5** *he caught malaria* **contract,** go/come down with, be taken ill with, develop, pick up.
> ANTONYMS drop, miss, release.

▸ noun **1** an act of catching. **2** a device for fastening a door, window, etc. **3** a hidden problem. **4** a break in a person's voice caused by emotion. **5** an amount of fish caught.

> SYNONYMS **1** *he inspected the catch* **haul,** net, bag, yield. **2** *he slipped the catch* **latch,** lock, fastener, clasp, hasp. **3** *there must be a catch* **snag,** disadvantage, drawback, stumbling block, hitch, complication, problem, trap, trick.

■ **catch on** informal **1** become popular.
2 understand. **catch someone out** discover that someone has done something wrong. **catch-22** a difficult situation from which there is no escape because it involves conditions which conflict with each other. **catch up** do tasks which you should have done earlier. **catch someone up** succeed in reaching a person ahead of you.

catching ▸ adjective (of a disease) infectious.

> SYNONYMS **infectious,** contagious, communicable; dated infective.
> ANTONYMS non-infectious.

catchment area ▸ noun **1** the area from which a hospital's patients or a school's pupils are drawn. **2** the area from which rainfall flows into a river, lake, or reservoir.

catchphrase ▸ noun a well-known sentence or phrase.

catchword ▸ noun a word or phrase frequently used to sum something up.

catchy ▸ adjective (**catchier, catchiest**) (of a tune or phrase) appealing and easy to remember.

> SYNONYMS **memorable,** unforgettable, haunting, appealing, popular.
> ANTONYMS forgettable.

catechism /kat-i-ki-z'm/ ▸ noun a summary of the principles of Christian religion in the form of questions and answers, used for teaching.

categorical ▸ adjective completely clear and direct.

> SYNONYMS **unqualified,** unconditional, unequivocal, absolute, explicit, unambiguous, definite, direct, emphatic, positive, out-and-out.
> ANTONYMS qualified, equivocal.

□ **categorically** adverb.

categorize (or **categorise**) ▸ verb (**categorizes, categorizing, categorized**) place in a category.
□ **categorization** noun.

category ▸ noun (plural **categories**) a class or group of people or things with shared characteristics.

> SYNONYMS **class,** classification, group, grouping, bracket, heading, set, type, sort, kind, grade, order, rank.

cater ▸ verb **1** (**cater for**) Brit. provide food and drink at a social event. **2** (**cater for**) provide someone with what is needed.
3 (**cater to**) satisfy a need or demand.
□ **caterer** noun.

caterpillar ▸ noun a creature like a small worm with legs, which develops into a butterfly or moth.

caterwaul /kat-er-wawl/ ▸ verb make a shrill howling or wailing noise.

catfish ▸ noun (plural **catfish** or **catfishes**) a fish with whisker-like growths round its mouth.

catgut ▸ noun material used for the strings of musical instruments, made of the dried intestines of sheep or horses.

catharsis /kuh-thar-siss/ ▸ noun the process of releasing strong but pent-up emotions in such a way as to free yourself of them.
□ **cathartic** adjective.

cathedral ▸ noun the most important church of a diocese (district).

Catherine wheel ▸ noun Brit. a firework in the form of a spinning coil.

catheter /kath-i-ter/ ▸ noun a tube that is inserted into a body cavity to drain fluid.

cathode /kath-ohd/ ▸ noun an electrode with a negative charge.
■ **cathode ray tube** a tube in which beams of electrons produce a luminous image on a screen, as in a television.

catholic ▸ adjective **1** including a wide variety of things. **2** (**Catholic**) Roman Catholic.

c

▶ noun (**Catholic**) a Roman Catholic.
◻ **Catholicism** noun.

cation /kat-I-uhn/ ▶ noun an ion with a positive charge.

catkin ▶ noun a spike of small, soft flowers hanging from trees such as willow and hazel.

catnap ▶ noun a short sleep during the day.

catseye ▶ noun Brit. trademark each of a series of reflective studs marking the lanes or edges of a road.

catsuit ▶ noun a woman's close-fitting one-piece garment with trouser legs.

cattery ▶ noun (plural **catteries**) a place where pet cats are kept while their owners are away.

cattle ▶ plural noun cows, bulls, and oxen.

SYNONYMS **cows**, oxen, herd, livestock.

catty ▶ adjective (**cattier**, **cattiest**) spiteful.

catwalk ▶ noun **1** a narrow platform along which models walk to display clothes. **2** a narrow raised walkway.

Caucasian ▶ adjective **1** relating to peoples from Europe, western Asia, and parts of India and North Africa. **2** white-skinned.
▶ noun a Caucasian person.

caucus /kaw-kuhss/ ▶ noun (plural **caucuses**) **1** a meeting of a policymaking group of a political party. **2** a group of people within a larger organization who have similar interests.

caught past and past participle of **CATCH**.

caul (*rhymes with* ball) ▶ noun a membrane that encloses an unborn baby in the womb.

cauldron (US spelling **caldron**) ▶ noun a large metal cooking pot.

cauliflower ▶ noun a vegetable with a large white edible flower head.

caulk (US spelling **calk**) ▶ noun a waterproof substance used to fill cracks and seal joins.

causal ▶ adjective relating to or being a cause.
◻ **causally** adverb **causality** noun.

causation ▶ noun the process of causing an effect.
◻ **causative** adjective.

cause ▶ noun **1** a person or thing that produces an effect. **2** a good reason for thinking or doing something. **3** a principle or movement.

SYNONYMS **1** *the cause of the fire* **source**, root, origin, beginning(s), starting point, originator, author, creator, agent. **2** *there is no cause for alarm* **reason**, grounds, justification, call, need, necessity, occasion, excuse. **3** *the cause of human rights | a good cause* **principle**, ideal, belief, conviction, object, aim, objective, purpose, charity.

▶ verb (**causes**, **causing**, **caused**) make something happen.

SYNONYMS *this disease can cause blindness* **bring about**, give rise to, lead to, result in, create, produce, generate, engender, spawn, bring on, precipitate, prompt, provoke, trigger, make happen, induce, inspire, promote, foster.

causeway ▶ noun a raised road or track across low or wet ground.

caustic ▶ adjective **1** able to burn through or wear away something by chemical action. **2** sarcastic in a hurtful way.
■ **caustic soda** sodium hydroxide, used in industrial processes, such as soap-making.
◻ **caustically** adverb.

cauterize (or **cauterise**) ▶ verb (**cauterizes**, **cauterizing**, **cauterized**) burn the area round a wound to stop bleeding or prevent infection.

caution ▶ noun **1** care taken to avoid danger or mistakes. **2** a warning to the public. **3** Brit. an official or legal warning given to someone who has committed a minor offence.

SYNONYMS **1** *proceed with caution* **care**, attention, alertness, circumspection, discretion, prudence. **2** *a first offender may receive a caution* **warning**, admonishment, injunction, reprimand, rebuke; informal telling-off, dressing-down; Brit. informal ticking-off.

▶ verb **1** warn or advise someone. **2** give someone a legal caution.

SYNONYMS **1** *advisers cautioned against tax increases* **advise**, warn, counsel, urge. **2** *he was cautioned by the police* **warn**, admonish, reprimand; informal tell off; Brit. informal tick off.

cautionary ▶ adjective acting as a warning.

cautious ▶ adjective taking care to avoid possible problems or dangers.

SYNONYMS **careful**, attentive, alert, judicious, circumspect, prudent, tentative, guarded.
ANTONYMS reckless.

◻ **cautiously** adverb.

cavalcade ▶ noun a procession of vehicles or people on horseback.

cavalier ▶ noun (**Cavalier**) a supporter of King Charles I in the English Civil War.
▶ adjective showing a lack of proper concern.

cavalry ▶ noun (plural **cavalries**) (in the past) the part of the army that fought on horseback.
◻ **cavalryman** noun.

cave ▶ noun a large natural hollow in the side of a hill or cliff, or underground.

> SYNONYMS **cavern,** grotto, pothole, chamber, gallery, hollow.

▶ verb (**caves, caving, caved**) **1** (**cave in**) give way or collapse. **2** (**cave in**) give in to demands. **3** (**caving**) the exploring of caves as a sport.

caveat /ka-vi-at/ ▶ noun a warning.

cavern ▶ noun a large cave.

cavernous /ka-ver-nuhss/ ▶ adjective huge, spacious, or gloomy.

caviar (or **caviare**) /ka-vi-ar/ ▶ noun the pickled roe of the sturgeon (a large fish).

cavil /ka-vuhl/ ▶ verb (**cavils, cavilling, cavilled**; US spelling **cavils, caviling, caviled**) make unnecessary complaints.
▶ noun an unnecessary complaint.

cavity ▶ noun (plural **cavities**) **1** a hollow space inside something solid. **2** a decayed part of a tooth.

> SYNONYMS **space,** chamber, hollow, hole, pocket, gap, crater, pit.

cavort ▶ verb jump or dance around excitedly.

caw ▶ verb make a harsh cry.

cayenne /kay-en/ ▶ noun a hot-tasting red powder made from dried chillies.

CBE ▶ abbreviation Commander of the Order of the British Empire.

cc (or **c.c.**) ▶ abbreviation **1** carbon copy. **2** cubic centimetres.

CCTV ▶ abbreviation closed-circuit television.

CD ▶ abbreviation compact disc.

CD-ROM ▶ abbreviation a compact disc storing large amounts of information, used in a computer (*ROM* stands for 'read-only memory').

CDT ▶ abbreviation craft, design, and technology (as a school subject).

cease ▶ verb (**ceases, ceasing, ceased**) come or bring to an end; stop.

> SYNONYMS **come/bring to an end,** come/bring to a halt, end, halt, stop, conclude, terminate, finish, wind up, discontinue, suspend, break off.
> ANTONYMS start, continue.

ceasefire ▶ noun a temporary period during a conflict when fighting stops.

ceaseless ▶ adjective not stopping.
□ **ceaselessly** adverb.

cedar ▶ noun a tall evergreen tree with sweet-smelling wood.

cede ▶ verb (**cedes, ceding, ceded**) give up power or territory.

cedilla /si-dil-luh/ ▶ noun a mark ( ) written under the letter *c* to show that it is pronounced like an *s* (e.g. *soupçon*).

ceilidh /kay-li/ ▶ noun a party with Scottish or Irish folk music and dancing.

ceiling ▶ noun **1** the top surface of a room. **2** a top limit set on prices, wages, or spending.

> ✔ **i** before **e** except after **c**: ce**i**ling.

celandine ▶ noun a wild plant with small yellow flowers.

celebrate ▶ verb (**celebrates, celebrating, celebrated**) **1** mark an important occasion by doing something special. **2** honour or praise someone publicly. **3** perform a religious ceremony.

> SYNONYMS **1** *they were celebrating their wedding anniversary* **commemorate,** observe, mark, keep, honour, remember. **2** *let's all celebrate!* **enjoy yourself,** make merry, have fun, have a good time, have a party; N. Amer. step out; informal party, whoop it up, have a ball. **3** (**celebrated**) **acclaimed,** admired, highly rated, esteemed, exalted, vaunted, eminent, great, distinguished, prestigious, illustrious, notable. **4** *the priest celebrated mass* **perform,** observe, officiate at, preside at.

□ **celebratory** adjective.

celebration ▶ noun **1** the action of celebrating. **2** a social gathering held to celebrate something.

> SYNONYMS **1** *the celebration of his 50th birthday* **commemoration,** observance, marking, keeping. **2** *a cause for celebration* **merrymaking,** jollification, revelry, revels, festivities; informal partying. **3** *the celebration of the Eucharist* **performance,** observance, officiation, solemnization. **4** *a birthday celebration* **party,** function, gathering, festivities, festival, fête, carnival, jamboree; informal do, bash, rave; Brit. informal rave-up.

celebrity ▶ noun (plural **celebrities**) **1** a famous person. **2** the state of being famous.

> SYNONYMS **1** *his celebrity grew* **fame,** prominence, renown, stardom, popularity, distinction, prestige, stature, repute, reputation. **2** *a sporting celebrity* **famous person,** VIP, personality, big name, household name, star, superstar; informal celeb, megastar.
> ANTONYMS obscurity, nonentity.

celeriac /suh-lair-i-ak/ ▶ noun a vegetable with a large edible root.

celerity /si-le-ri-ti/ ▶ noun old use speed of movement.

celery ▸ noun a vegetable with crisp juicy stalks.

celestial ▸ adjective **1** relating to heaven. **2** relating to the sky or outer space.

celibate /sel-i-buht/ ▸ adjective not married or in a sexual relationship.
□ **celibacy** noun.

cell ▸ noun **1** a small room for a prisoner, monk, or nun. **2** the smallest unit of a living thing. **3** a small political group that is part of a larger organization. **4** a device for producing electricity by chemical action or light.

> SYNONYMS **1** *a prison cell* **room,** cubicle, chamber, dungeon, compartment, lock-up. **2** *terrorist cells* **unit,** squad, detachment, group.

cellar ▸ noun **1** a room below ground level, used for storage. **2** a stock of wine.

> SYNONYMS **basement,** vault, crypt.

cello /chel-loh/ ▸ noun (plural **cellos**) an instrument like a large violin, held upright on the floor between the legs of the seated player.
□ **cellist** noun.

cellophane ▸ noun trademark a thin transparent wrapping material.

cellphone ▸ noun a mobile phone.

cellular ▸ adjective **1** relating to or made up of cells. **2** (of a mobile phone system) using a number of short-range radio stations to cover the area it serves.

cellulite ▸ noun fat that builds up under the skin, causing a dimpled effect.

celluloid ▸ noun a kind of transparent plastic formerly used for cinema film.

cellulose ▸ noun a substance found in all plant tissues, used in making paint, plastics, and fibres.

Celsius /sel-si-uhss/ ▸ noun a scale of temperature on which water freezes at 0° and boils at 100°.

Celt /kelt/ ▸ noun a member of a people who lived in Britain and elsewhere in Europe before the Romans arrived.

Celtic /kel-tik/ ▸ noun a group of languages including Irish, Scottish Gaelic, and Welsh.
▸ adjective relating to Celtic languages or to the Celts.

cement ▸ noun a powdery substance made by heating lime and clay, used in making mortar and concrete.

> SYNONYMS **adhesive,** glue, fixative, gum, paste; N. Amer. **mucilage;** N. Amer. informal stickum.

▸ verb **1** fix with cement. **2** make something stronger.

cemetery ▸ noun (plural **cemeteries**) a large burial ground.

> SYNONYMS **graveyard,** churchyard, burial ground, necropolis, garden of remembrance, mass grave; Scottish kirkyard.

> ✔ **-tery,** not **-try** or **-tary**: ceme**tery**.

cenotaph ▸ noun a monument built to honour soldiers killed in a war.

censer ▸ noun a container in which incense is burnt.

censor ▸ noun a person who examines films, books, or documents and bans unacceptable parts.
▸ verb ban unacceptable parts of a film, book, or document.

> SYNONYMS *letters home were censored* **cut,** edit, expurgate, sanitize, clean up, ban, delete.

□ **censorship** noun.

censorious /sen-sor-i-uhss/ ▸ adjective very critical.

censure ▸ verb (**censures, censuring, censured**) criticize strongly.

> SYNONYMS *he was censured for his conduct* **condemn,** criticize, attack, reprimand, rebuke, admonish, upbraid, reproach. ANTONYMS defend, praise.

▸ noun strong disapproval or criticism.

> SYNONYMS *a note of censure* **condemnation,** criticism, attack, reprimand, rebuke, admonishment, reproof, disapproval, reproach. ANTONYMS approval, praise.

census ▸ noun (plural **censuses**) an official count of a population.

cent ▸ noun a unit of money equal to one hundredth of a dollar, euro, or other decimal currency unit.

centaur ▸ noun (in Greek mythology) a creature with a man's head, arms, and upper body and a horse's lower body and legs.

centenarian /sen-ti-nair-i-uhn/ ▸ noun a person who has reached one hundred years of age.

centenary /sen-tee-nuh-ri/ ▸ noun (plural **centenaries**) Brit. the hundredth anniversary of an event.

centennial ▸ adjective relating to a hundredth anniversary.
▸ noun a hundredth anniversary.

center US spelling of CENTRE.

centigrade ▸ adjective measured by the Celsius scale of temperature.

centilitre (US spelling **centiliter**) ▸ noun a metric unit equal to one hundredth of a litre.

centime /son-teem/ ▸ noun a unit of money equal to one hundredth of a franc.

centimetre (US spelling **centimeter**) ▸ noun a metric unit equal to one hundredth of a metre.

centipede ▸ noun an insect-like creature with a long, thin body and many legs.

central ▸ adjective **1** in or near the centre. **2** very important.

> SYNONYMS **1** *occupying a central position* **middle,** centre, halfway, midway, mid. **2** *central London* **inner,** innermost, middle, mid. **3** *their central campaign issue* **main,** chief, principal, primary, foremost, key, crucial, vital, essential, basic, fundamental, core; informal number-one.
> ANTONYMS side, extreme, outer, subordinate.

■ **central heating** heating conducted from a boiler through pipes and radiators. **central nervous system** the system of nerve tissues in the brain and spinal cord in vertebrates.
□ **centrally** adverb.

centralize (or **centralise**) ▸ verb (**centralizes, centralizing, centralized**) bring under the control of a central authority.

> SYNONYMS **concentrate,** consolidate, amalgamate, condense, unify, focus.
> ANTONYMS devolve.

□ **centralization** noun.

centre (US spelling **center**) ▸ noun **1** a point in the middle of something. **2** a place where a particular activity takes place. **3** a point from which something spreads or to which something is directed.

> SYNONYMS *the centre of the town* **middle,** nucleus, heart, core, hub.
> ANTONYMS edge.

▸ verb (**centres, centring, centred;** US spelling **centers, centering, centered**) **1** place in the centre. **2** (**centre on** or **around**) have as a main concern or theme.

> SYNONYMS *the story centres on a doctor* **focus,** concentrate, pivot, revolve, be based.

■ **centre back** (or **centre half**) (in soccer) a defender who plays in the middle of the field. **centre forward** (in soccer) an attacker who plays in the middle of the field. **centre of gravity** the central point in an object, around which its mass is evenly distributed.

centrefold ▸ noun the two middle pages of a magazine, usually containing a special feature.

centrepiece ▸ noun an item that is designed to have people's attention focused on it.

centrifugal force ▸ noun a force which appears to cause something travelling round a central point to fly outwards from its circular path.

centurion ▸ noun a commander of one hundred men in the army of ancient Rome.

century ▸ noun (plural **centuries**) **1** a period of one hundred years. **2** a batsman's score of a hundred runs in cricket. **3** a unit of a hundred men in the army of ancient Rome.

ceramic ▸ adjective made of fired clay.
▸ noun (**ceramics**) the art of making ceramic articles.

cereal ▸ noun **1** a grass producing an edible grain, such as wheat, oats, maize, or rye. **2** a breakfast food made from the grain of cereals.

cerebellum /se-ri-bel-luhm/ ▸ noun (plural **cerebellums** or **cerebella**) the part of the brain at the back of the skull.

cerebral /se-ri-bruhl, suh-ree-bruhl/ ▸ adjective **1** relating to the brain. **2** intellectual rather than emotional or physical.
■ **cerebral palsy** a condition in which a person has difficulty in controlling their muscles.

cerebrum /se-ri-bruhm/ ▸ noun (plural **cerebra**) the main part of the brain, in the front of the skull.

ceremonial ▸ adjective relating to or used in ceremonies.

> SYNONYMS **formal,** official, state, public, ritual, ritualistic, stately, solemn.
> ANTONYMS informal.

□ **ceremonially** adverb.

ceremonious ▸ adjective done in a formal and grand way.
□ **ceremoniously** adverb.

ceremony ▸ noun (plural **ceremonies**) a formal occasion during which a set of special acts are performed.

> SYNONYMS **1** *a wedding ceremony* **rite,** ritual, observance, service, event, function, formality. **2** *the new Queen was proclaimed with due ceremony* **pomp,** protocol, formalities, niceties, decorum, etiquette.

■ **stand on ceremony** behave formally.

cerise /suh-reess/ ▸ noun a light pinkish-red colour.

cerium /seer-i-uhm/ ▸ noun a silvery-white metallic element.

certain ▸ adjective **1** able to be relied on to happen or be the case. **2** completely sure about something. **3** specific but not directly named or stated.

> SYNONYMS **1** *I'm certain he's guilty* **sure,** confident, positive, convinced,

in no doubt, satisfied. **2** *it is certain that more changes are in the offing* **unquestionable,** sure, definite, beyond question, indubitable, undeniable, indisputable. **3** *they are certain to win* **sure,** bound, destined. **4** *certain defeat* **inevitable,** assured, unavoidable, inescapable, inexorable. **5** *there is no certain cure for this* **reliable,** dependable, foolproof, guaranteed, sure, infallible; informal sure-fire.
ANTONYMS doubtful, unlikely, possible.

▶ pronoun some but not all.

certainly ▶ adverb **1** without doubt; definitely. **2** yes.

SYNONYMS **definitely,** surely, assuredly, unquestionably, beyond/without question, undoubtedly, without doubt, indubitably, undeniably, irrefutably, indisputably.
ANTONYMS possibly.

certainty ▶ noun (plural **certainties**) **1** the state of being certain. **2** a fact that is true or an event that is definitely going to take place.

SYNONYMS **1** *she knew with certainty that it was true* **confidence,** sureness, conviction, assurance. **2** *he accepted defeat as a certainty* **inevitability,** foregone conclusion; informal sure thing; Brit. informal (dead) cert.
ANTONYMS doubt, possibility.

certifiable ▶ adjective able or needing to be officially declared insane.

certificate ▶ noun **1** an official document recording a particular fact, event, or achievement. **2** an official classification given to a cinema film, saying which age group it is suitable for.

SYNONYMS **guarantee,** document, authorization, authentication, accreditation, credentials, testimonial.

☐ **certification** noun.

certify ▶ verb (**certifies, certifying, certified**) **1** declare or confirm in a certificate or other official document. **2** officially declare someone insane.

SYNONYMS **1** *the aircraft was certified as airworthy* **verify,** guarantee, attest, validate, confirm, endorse. **2** *a certified hospital* **accredit,** recognize, license, authorize, approve.

certitude ▶ noun a feeling of complete certainty.

cervical /ser-**vi**-k'l, ser-**vy**-k'l/ ▶ adjective relating to the cervix.
■ **cervical smear** a specimen of cells taken from the neck of the womb and examined for signs of cancer.

cervix /ser-viks/ ▶ noun (plural **cervices** /ser-vi-seez/) the narrow neck-like passage between the lower end of the womb and the vagina.

Cesarean US spelling of CAESAREAN.

cesium US spelling of CAESIUM.

cessation ▶ noun the stopping of something.

SYNONYMS **end,** termination, halt, finish, stoppage, conclusion, winding up, pause, suspension.
ANTONYMS start, resumption.

cession ▶ noun the giving up of rights or territory by a state.

cesspool (or **cesspit**) ▶ noun an underground tank or covered pit where sewage is collected.

cetacean /si-**tay**-sh'n/ ▶ noun the name in zoology for a whale or dolphin.

cf. ▶ abbreviation compare with.
ORIGIN short for Latin *confer*, meaning 'compare'.

CFC ▶ abbreviation chlorofluorocarbon, a gas used in fridges and aerosols that is harmful to the ozone layer.

CFE ▶ abbreviation College of Further Education.

Chablis /**shab**-lee/ ▶ noun a dry white French wine.

Chadian /**chad**-i-uhn/ ▶ noun a person from Chad, a country in central Africa.
▶ adjective relating to Chad.

chador /**chah**-dor/ ▶ noun a piece of dark cloth worn by Muslim women around the head and upper body.

chafe ▶ verb (**chafes, chafing, chafed**) **1** make something sore or worn by rubbing against it. **2** rub a part of the body to warm it. **3** become impatient because of restrictions.

chaff[1] ▶ noun husks of grain that have been separated from the seed.

chaff[2] ▶ verb tease someone.

chaffinch ▶ noun a small finch (songbird) with a pink breast.

chagrin /sha-**grin**/ ▶ noun a feeling of disappointment or annoyance.
▶ verb (**be chagrined**) feel disappointed or annoyed.

chain ▶ noun **1** a series of connected metal links. **2** a connected series, set, or sequence.

SYNONYMS **1** *he was held in chains* **fetters,** shackles, irons, manacles, handcuffs; informal cuffs, bracelets. **2** *a chain of events* **series,** succession, string, sequence, train, course.

▶ verb fasten or restrain with a chain.

SYNONYMS *she chained her bicycle to the railings* **secure,** fasten, tie, tether, hitch, restrain, shackle, fetter, manacle, handcuff.

■ **chain mail** armour made of small metal rings linked together. **chain reaction** a series of events, each caused by the previous one. **chain-smoke** smoke cigarettes one after the other. **chain store** each of a series of shops owned by one firm.

chainsaw ▶ noun a power-driven saw with teeth set on a moving chain.

chair ▶ noun 1 a seat for one person, with a back and four legs. 2 a person in charge of a meeting or an organization. 3 a post as professor.
▶ verb be in charge of a meeting.

chairlift ▶ noun a lift for carrying skiers up and down a mountain, consisting of a series of chairs hung from a moving cable.

chairman (or **chairwoman**) ▶ noun (plural **chairmen** or **chairwomen**) a person in charge of a meeting or organization.

SYNONYMS **chair,** chairperson, president, chief executive, leader, master of ceremonies, MC.

chairperson ▶ noun a person in charge of a meeting.

chaise longue /shayz longg/ ▶ noun (plural **chaises longues** /shayz longg/) a sofa with a backrest at only one end.

chalet /**sha**-lay/ ▶ noun 1 a wooden house with overhanging eaves, found in the Swiss Alps. 2 a wooden cabin used by holidaymakers.

chalice /**cha**-liss/ ▶ noun a large cup or glass for wine.

chalk ▶ noun 1 a soft white limestone. 2 a similar substance made into sticks and used for drawing or writing.
▶ verb draw or write with chalk.
■ **by a long chalk** by far. **chalk something up** achieve something noteworthy.
□ **chalkiness** noun **chalky** adjective.

challenge ▶ noun 1 an interesting but difficult task or situation. 2 an invitation to someone to take part in a contest or to prove something.

SYNONYMS 1 *he accepted the challenge* **dare,** provocation, offer. 2 *a challenge to his leadership* **opposition,** confrontation, stand, dispute, test. 3 *it was proving quite a challenge* **problem,** difficult task, test, trial.
ANTONYMS cinch.

▶ verb (**challenges, challenging, challenged**) 1 raise doubt as to whether something is true or genuine. 2 call on someone to fight or do something difficult. 3 (of a guard) call on someone to prove their identity.

SYNONYMS 1 *we challenged their statistics* **question,** dispute, take issue with, call into question. 2 *he challenged me to deny it* **dare,** defy, invite, throw down the gauntlet to. 3 *changes that would challenge them* **test,** tax, strain, make demands on, stretch.
□ **challenger** noun.

challenging ▶ adjective testing your abilities in an interesting way.

SYNONYMS **demanding,** testing, taxing, exacting.
ANTONYMS easy.

chamber ▶ noun 1 a large room used for formal or public events. 2 each of the houses of a parliament. 3 (**chambers**) rooms used by a barrister. 4 old use a bedroom. 5 a hollow space inside something. 6 the part of a gun bore that contains the explosive.
■ **chamber music** classical music played by a small group of musicians. **chamber pot** a bowl kept in a bedroom and used as a toilet.

chamberlain ▶ noun (in the past) a person who looked after the household of a king or queen, or a noble.

chambermaid ▶ noun a woman who cleans rooms in a hotel.

chameleon /kuh-**mee**-li-uhn/ ▶ noun a small lizard that is able to change colour to fit in with its surroundings.

chamfer /**cham**-fer/ ▶ verb (**chamfers, chamfering, chamfered**) (in carpentry) cut an angled edge on a piece of wood.

chamois /**sham**-wah/ ▶ noun (plural **chamois** /**sham**-wah, **sham**-wahz/) an antelope that lives in the mountains of southern Europe.
■ **chamois leather** /**sham**-mi/ very soft leather made from the skin of sheep, goats, or deer.

chamomile ➡ CAMOMILE.

champ ▶ verb munch noisily.
■ **champ at the bit** be very impatient.

champagne /sham-**payn**/ ▶ noun a white sparkling wine from the Champagne region of France.

champion ▶ noun 1 a person who has won a contest. 2 a person who argues or fights for a cause.

SYNONYMS 1 *the world champion* **winner,** title-holder, gold medallist, prizewinner; informal champ, number one. 2 *a champion of change* **advocate,** proponent, promoter, supporter, defender, upholder, backer; N. Amer. booster.

▶ verb argue or fight in support of a cause.

SYNONYMS *championing the rights of tribal peoples* **advocate,** promote, defend, uphold, support, espouse, stand up for, campaign for, lobby for, fight for.
ANTONYMS oppose.

▶ **adjective** informal or dialect excellent.

championship ▶ **noun** a competition for the position of champion.

chance ▶ **noun 1** (also **chances**) a possibility of something happening. **2** an opportunity. **3** the way that things happen without any obvious plan or cause: *they met by chance.*

SYNONYMS **1** *there was a chance he might be released* **possibility,** prospect, probability, likelihood, risk, threat, danger. **2** *I gave her a chance to answer* **opportunity,** opening, occasion, window; N. Amer. & Austral./NZ show; Brit. informal look-in. **3** *Nigel took an awful chance* **risk,** gamble, leap in the dark. **4** *pure chance* **accident,** coincidence, fate, destiny, providence, happenstance, good fortune, luck, fluke.
ANTONYMS certainty.

▶ **verb** (**chances, chancing, chanced**) **1** happen to do something. **2** informal do something even though it is risky.
▶ **adjective** happening without any intention or obvious cause.

SYNONYMS *a chance discovery* **accidental,** fortuitous, fluky, coincidental.
ANTONYMS planned.

■ **on the off chance** just in case.

chancel /**chahn**-s'l/ ▶ **noun** the part of a church near the altar, where the choir sits.

chancellor ▶ **noun 1** a senior state or legal official. **2** (**Chancellor**) the head of the government in some European countries.
■ **Chancellor of the Exchequer** (in the UK) the government minister in charge of the country's finances.

chancer ▶ **noun** informal a person who makes the most of any opportunity.

chancy ▶ **adjective** (**chancier, chanciest**) informal uncertain and risky.

chandelier /shan-duh-**leer**/ ▶ **noun** an ornamental hanging light with holders for several candles or light bulbs.

chandler ▶ **noun** a person who buys and sells supplies and equipment for ships and boats.
□ **chandlery** noun.

change ▶ **verb** (**changes, changing, changed**) **1** make or become different. **2** exchange one thing for something else. **3** (**change over**) move from one system or situation to another. **4** exchange a sum of money for the same sum in a different currency or different units.

SYNONYMS **1** *this could change Britain |* *things have changed* **alter,** make/become different, adjust, adapt, amend, modify, revise, vary, transform, metamorphose, evolve. **2** *he's changed his job* **exchange,** substitute, swap, switch, replace, alternate.
ANTONYMS preserve, keep.

▶ **noun 1** a process through which something becomes different. **2** money returned as the balance of the amount paid or given in exchange for the same amount in larger units. **3** coins as opposed to banknotes. **4** a clean set of clothes.

SYNONYMS **1** *a change of plan* **alteration,** modification, variation, revision, amendment, adjustment, adaptation, metamorphosis, transformation, evolution. **2** *a change of government* **replacement,** exchange, substitution, swap, switch.

■ **change hands** pass to a different owner.

changeable ▶ **adjective 1** likely to change in an unpredictable way. **2** able to be changed.

changeling ▶ **noun** a child believed to have been left by fairies in exchange for the parents' real child.

changeover ▶ **noun** a change from one system or situation to another.

channel ▶ **noun 1** a band of frequencies used in radio and television broadcasting. **2** a means of communication. **3** a wide stretch of water joining two seas. **4** a passage along which liquid flows. **5** a passage that boats can pass through in a stretch of water. **6** an electric circuit which acts as a path for a signal.

SYNONYMS **1** *the English Channel* **strait(s),** sound, narrows, passage. **2** *the water ran down a channel* **duct,** gutter, conduit, trough, sluice, drain. **3** *a channel of communication* **means,** medium, instrument, mechanism, agency, vehicle, route, avenue.

▶ **verb** (**channels, channelling, channelled;** US spelling **channels, channeling, channeled**) **1** direct something towards a particular purpose. **2** pass along or through a particular channel.

SYNONYMS *many countries channel their aid through charities* **convey,** transmit, conduct, direct, relay, pass on, transfer.

chant ▶ **noun 1** a repeated rhythmic phrase that is called out or sung to music. **2** a tune to which the words of psalms are fitted by singing several syllables or words to the same note.

SYNONYMS **shout,** cry, call, slogan, chorus, refrain.

▶ verb say, shout, or sing in a chant.

> SYNONYMS **shout,** chorus, repeat, call.

Chanukkah ➞ Hanukkah.

chaos /**kay**-oss/ ▶ noun complete confusion and disorder.

> SYNONYMS **disorder,** disorganization, confusion, mayhem, bedlam, pandemonium, havoc, turmoil, anarchy, lawlessness; Brit. a shambles; informal all hell broken loose.
> ANTONYMS order.

chaotic /kay-**ot**-ik/ ▶ adjective in a state of complete confusion and disorder.

> SYNONYMS **disorderly,** disorganized, in confusion, in turmoil, topsy-turvy, anarchic, lawless; Brit. informal shambolic.

□ **chaotically** adverb.

chap ▶ noun informal a man or boy.

> SYNONYMS **man,** boy, individual, character; informal fellow, guy, geezer; Brit. informal bloke, lad; N. Amer. informal dude, hombre.

chapatti /chuh-**pah**-ti/ ▶ noun (plural **chapattis**) (in Indian cookery) a flat round piece of unleavened bread.

chapel ▶ noun **1** a small building or room used for prayers. **2** a part of a large church with its own altar.

chaperone /**shap**-uh-rohn/ ▶ noun **1** a person who accompanies and looks after another person or group of people. **2** dated an older woman in charge of an unmarried girl at social occasions.
▶ verb (**chaperones, chaperoning, chaperoned**) go with and look after.

chaplain ▶ noun a minister of the church attached to a chapel in an institution or military unit, or a private house.
□ **chaplaincy** noun.

chapped ▶ adjective (of the skin) cracked and sore through exposure to cold weather.

chapter ▶ noun **1** a main division of a book. **2** a particular period in history or in a person's life. **3** the group of people in charge of a cathedral or other religious community. **4** chiefly N. Amer. a local branch of a society.

> SYNONYMS **1** *the first chapter of the book* **section,** part, division, topic, stage, episode. **2** *a new chapter in our history* **period,** phase, page, stage, epoch, era.

char[1] ▶ verb (**chars, charring, charred**) partially burn something so as to blacken the surface.

char[2] ▶ noun informal a woman employed as a cleaner in a private house.

char[3] ▶ noun informal tea.

character ▶ noun **1** the particular qualities that make a person or thing an individual and different from others. **2** strong personal qualities such as courage and determination. **3** a person's good reputation. **4** a person in a novel, play, or film. **5** informal an eccentric or amusing person. **6** a printed or written letter or symbol.

> SYNONYMS **1** *a forceful character* | *the character of a town* **personality,** nature, quality, disposition, temperament, mentality, make-up, spirit, identity, tone, feel. **2** *a woman of character* **integrity,** honour, moral strength/fibre, strength, backbone, resolve, grit, will power; informal guts; Brit. informal bottle. **3** *a stain on his character* **reputation,** (good) name, standing, position, status. **4** *a bit of a character* **eccentric,** oddity, crank, original, individualist, madcap, nonconformist; informal oddball. **5** *a boorish character* **person,** man, woman, soul, creature, individual, customer; informal cookie; Brit. informal bod, guy. **6** *written in Cyrillic characters* **letter,** figure, symbol, mark, device, sign, hieroglyph.

□ **characterful** adjective **characterless** adjective.

characteristic ▶ noun a quality typical of a person or thing.

> SYNONYMS *interesting characteristics* **attribute,** feature, quality, property, trait, aspect, idiosyncrasy, peculiarity, quirk.

▶ adjective typical of a particular person or thing.

> SYNONYMS *his characteristic eloquence* **typical,** usual, normal, distinctive, representative, particular, special, peculiar, idiosyncratic.
> ANTONYMS abnormal.

□ **characteristically** adverb.

characterize (or **characterise**)
▶ verb (**characterizes, characterizing, characterized**) **1** describe the character of. **2** be typical of.

> SYNONYMS **1** *the period was characterized by scientific advancement* **distinguish,** mark, typify, set apart. **2** *the women are characterized as prophets of doom* **portray,** depict, present, represent, describe, categorize, class, brand.

□ **characterization** noun.

charade /shuh-**rahd**/ ▶ noun **1** a pretence that something is true when it is clearly not. **2** (**charades**) a game of guessing a word or phrase from clues that are acted out.

> SYNONYMS **pretence,** act, masquerade, show, facade, pantomime, farce, travesty, mockery, parody.

charcoal ▸ noun **1** a form of carbon obtained when wood is burned slowly with little air. **2** a dark grey colour.

chard ▸ noun a vegetable with large leaves and thick leaf stalks.

Chardonnay ▸ noun a type of white wine.

charge ▸ verb (**charges, charging, charged**) **1** ask an amount as a price. **2** formally accuse someone of something. **3** rush forward in an attack. **4** (**charge someone with**) give someone a task or responsibility. **5** store electrical energy in a battery. **6** load or fill a container, gun, etc. **7** fill with an emotion or quality: *the air was charged with menace.*

> SYNONYMS **1** *he didn't charge much* **ask,** demand, bill, invoice. **2** *two men were charged with murder* **accuse,** indict, arraign, prosecute, try, put on trial; N. Amer. impeach. **3** *they charged him with reforming the system* **entrust,** burden, encumber, saddle, tax. **4** *the cavalry charged the tanks* **attack,** storm, assault, assail, descend on; informal lay into, tear into. **5** *we charged into the crowd* **rush,** storm, stampede, push, plough, launch yourself, go headlong; informal steam; N. Amer. informal barrel. **6** *charge your glasses!* **fill (up),** top up, load (up), arm.

▸ noun **1** a price asked. **2** a formal accusation. **3** responsibility for the care or control of a person or thing. **4** a person or thing handed over to someone's care. **5** a headlong rush forward. **6** the electricity naturally existing in a substance. **7** energy stored chemically in a battery. **8** a quantity of explosive needed to fire a gun.

> SYNONYMS **1** *all customers pay a charge* **fee,** payment, price, rate, tariff, fare, levy. **2** *he pleaded guilty to the charge* **accusation,** allegation, indictment, arraignment; N. Amer. impeachment. **3** *an infantry charge* **attack,** assault, offensive, onslaught, drive, push. **4** *the child was in her charge* **care,** protection, safe keeping, control, custody, hands.

■ **charge card** a kind of credit card issued by a large shop.
□ **chargeable** adjective.

chargé d'affaires /shar-zhay da-**fair**/ ▸ noun (plural **chargés d'affaires** /shar-zhay da-**fair**/) **1** an ambassador's deputy. **2** the diplomatic representative in a country to which an ambassador has not been sent.

charger ▸ noun **1** a device for charging a battery. **2** a strong horse formerly ridden by a knight or mounted soldier.

chargrill ▸ verb grill food quickly at a very high heat.

chariot ▸ noun a two-wheeled horse-drawn vehicle, used in ancient warfare and racing.
□ **charioteer** noun.

charisma /kuh-**riz**-muh/ ▸ noun attractiveness that inspires admiration or enthusiasm in other people.

> SYNONYMS **charm,** presence, (force of) personality, strength of character, (animal) magnetism, appeal, allure.

charismatic ▸ adjective having charisma.

> SYNONYMS **charming,** magnetic, compelling, inspiring, captivating, mesmerizing, appealing, alluring, glamorous.

charitable ▸ adjective **1** relating to help given to people in need. **2** showing kindness and understanding when judging other people.

> SYNONYMS **1** *charitable activities* **philanthropic,** humanitarian, altruistic, benevolent, non-profit-making. **2** *charitable people* **generous,** open-handed, munificent. **3** *he was charitable in his judgements* **magnanimous,** generous, liberal, tolerant, sympathetic, understanding, lenient, indulgent, forgiving.
> ANTONYMS commercial, mean, harsh.

□ **charitably** adverb.

charity ▸ noun (plural **charities**) **1** an organization set up to help people in need. **2** the giving of money or other help to people in need. **3** kindness and understanding shown when judging other people.

> SYNONYMS **1** *an AIDS charity* **voluntary organization,** charitable institution, fund, trust, foundation. **2** *we don't need charity* **aid,** financial assistance, welfare, relief, donations, handouts, gifts, largesse; historical alms. **3** *his actions are motivated by charity* **philanthropy,** humanitarianism, altruism, public-spiritedness, social conscience, benevolence. **4** *show a bit of charity* **goodwill,** compassion, consideration, concern, kindness, sympathy, indulgence, tolerance, leniency.
> ANTONYMS business, misanthropy, intolerance.

charlatan /shar-luh-tuhn/ ▸ noun a person who claims to have skills or knowledge that they do not really have.

charleston ▸ noun a lively dance of the 1920s.

charm ▸ noun **1** the power or quality of delighting or fascinating other people. **2** a small ornament worn on a necklace or bracelet. **3** an object or saying believed to have magic power.

> SYNONYMS **1** *people were captivated by her charm* **appeal,** attraction, fascination, beauty, loveliness, allure,

seductiveness, magnetism, charisma; informal pulling power. **2** *magical charms* **spell,** incantation, formula; N. Amer. mojo, hex. **3** *a lucky charm* **talisman,** trinket, amulet, mascot, fetish.

▶ verb **1** make someone feel great pleasure or delight. **2** use your charm in order to influence someone. **3** (**charmed**) unusually lucky as if protected by magic.

> SYNONYMS **1** *he charmed them with his singing* **delight,** please, win (over), attract, captivate, lure, fascinate, enchant, beguile. **2** *he charmed his mother into agreeing* **coax,** cajole, wheedle; informal sweet-talk, soft-soap.

□ **charmer** noun **charmless** adjective.

charming ▶ adjective **1** delightful; attractive. **2** very likeable.

> SYNONYMS **delightful,** pleasing, endearing, lovely, adorable, appealing, attractive, good-looking, alluring, winning, fetching, captivating, enchanting, entrancing.
> ANTONYMS repulsive.

□ **charmingly** adverb.

charnel house ▶ noun a place formerly used for keeping dead bodies and bones in.

chart ▶ noun **1** a sheet of paper on which information is displayed in the form of a table, graph, or diagram. **2** a map used for navigation by sea or air. **3** (**the charts**) a weekly listing of the current best-selling pop records.

> SYNONYMS *check your ideal weight on the chart* **graph,** table, diagram, plan, map; Computing graphic.

▶ verb **1** make a map of. **2** follow progress or record something on a chart.

> SYNONYMS **1** *the changes were charted accurately* **plot,** tabulate, graph, record, register, represent. **2** *the book charted his progress* **follow,** trace, outline, describe, detail, record, document.

charter ▶ noun **1** an official document stating that a ruler or government allows an institution to exist and setting out its rights. **2** a document listing and describing the functions of an organization. **3** the hiring of an aircraft, ship, or vehicle.

> SYNONYMS **1** *a Royal charter* **authority,** authorization, sanction, dispensation, permit, licence, warrant. **2** *the UN Charter* **constitution,** code, principles.

▶ verb **1** hire an aircraft, ship, or vehicle. **2** grant a charter to an institution.

> SYNONYMS *they chartered a bus* **hire,** lease, rent, book.

■ **charter flight** a flight by an aircraft that has been hired for a specific journey.

chartered ▶ adjective (of an accountant, engineer, etc.) qualified as a member of a professional institution that has a royal charter.

chary /chair-i/ ▶ adjective (**charier, chariest**) cautious about doing something.

chase[1] ▶ verb (**chases, chasing, chased**) **1** go after someone in order to catch them. **2** rush or hurry. **3** try to make contact with or get hold of.

> SYNONYMS **1** *the dogs chased the fox* **pursue,** run after, follow, hunt, track, trail; informal tail. **2** *she chased away the donkeys* **drive,** send, scare; informal send packing. **3** *she chased away all thoughts of him* **dispel,** banish, dismiss, drive away, shut out, put out of your mind.

▶ noun **1** an act of chasing. **2** (**the chase**) hunting as a sport.

> SYNONYMS *they gave up the chase* **pursuit,** hunt, trail.

chase[2] ▶ verb (**chases, chasing, chased**) engrave metal.

chaser ▶ noun informal a strong alcoholic drink taken after a weaker one.

chasm /ka-z'm/ ▶ noun **1** a deep crack in the earth. **2** a very big difference between two people or their opinions.

chassis /sha-si/ ▶ noun (plural **chassis** /sha-siz/) the framework forming the base of a vehicle.

chaste ▶ adjective **1** having sex only with your husband or wife, or not at all. **2** not expressing sexual interest; demure and modest.

□ **chastely** adverb.

chasten /chay-s'n/ ▶ verb make someone feel subdued and less confident about something.

chastise ▶ verb (**chastises, chastising, chastised**) tell someone off in a very strict way.

chastity ▶ noun the practice of having sex only with your husband or wife, or not at all.

chasuble /chaz-yuu-b'l/ ▶ noun a long sleeveless garment worn by a priest over other robes.

chat ▶ verb (**chats, chatting, chatted**) **1** talk informally. **2** (**chat someone up**) informal talk flirtatiously to someone.

> SYNONYMS *they chatted with the guests* **talk,** gossip; informal gas, jaw, chew the rag/fat; Brit. informal natter, have a chinwag; N. Amer. informal shoot the breeze/bull; Austral./NZ informal mag.

▶ noun an informal conversation.

C

SYNONYMS *I popped in for a chat* **talk,** conversation, gossip; informal **jaw, gas, confab;** Brit. informal **natter, chinwag.**

■ **chat room** an area on the Internet where users can communicate.

chateau /sha-toh/ ▶ noun (plural **chateaux** or **chateaus** /sha-toh, sha-tohz/) a large French country house or castle.

chattel /chat-t'l/ ▶ noun a personal possession.

chatter ▶ verb (**chatters, chattering, chattered**) **1** talk informally about unimportant things. **2** (of a person's teeth) click together continuously from cold or fear.

SYNONYMS *they chattered excitedly* **prattle,** chat, gossip, jabber, babble; informal **yatter;** Brit. informal **natter, chunter, rabbit on.**

▶ noun informal or unimportant talk.

SYNONYMS *she tired him with her chatter* **prattle,** chat, gossip, patter, jabber, babble; informal **chit-chat, yattering;** Brit. informal **nattering, chuntering, rabbiting on.**

chatterbox ▶ noun informal a person who likes to chatter.

chatty ▶ adjective inclined to chat.

SYNONYMS **talkative,** communicative, effusive, gossipy, loquacious, voluble; informal **mouthy, gabby.**
ANTONYMS taciturn.

chauffeur ▶ noun a person who is employed to drive someone around in a car.
▶ verb be a driver for someone.

chauvinism /shoh-vin-iz'm/ ▶ noun **1** a strong and unreasonable belief that your own country or group is better than others. **2** the belief held by some men that men are superior to women.
□ **chauvinist** adjective & noun **chauvinistic** adjective.

cheap ▶ adjective **1** low in price, or charging low prices. **2** low in price and of bad quality. **3** having no value because achieved in a bad way.

SYNONYMS **1** *cheap tickets* **inexpensive,** low-priced, low-cost, economical, competitive, affordable, reasonable, budget, economy, bargain, cut-price, reduced, discounted; informal **dirt cheap. 2** *plain without looking cheap* **poor-quality,** second-rate, substandard, inferior, vulgar, shoddy, trashy, tawdry, cheap and nasty; informal **rubbishy, cheapo, junky, tacky, kitsch;** Brit. informal **naff, duff, ropy, grotty;** N. Amer. informal **two-bit, dime-store. 3** *a cheap remark* **despicable,** contemptible, immoral,

unscrupulous, unprincipled, cynical.
ANTONYMS expensive, superior, kind.

□ **cheaply** adverb **cheapness** noun.

cheapen ▶ verb lower the quality or value of something.

cheapskate ▶ noun informal a person who hates to spend money.

cheat ▶ verb **1** act dishonestly or unfairly to gain an advantage. **2** deprive someone of something by tricking them.

SYNONYMS **swindle,** defraud, deceive, trick, dupe, hoodwink, double-cross, gull; informal **diddle, rip off, con, pull a fast one on;** N. Amer. informal **sucker, goldbrick;** Austral. informal **rort.**

▶ noun a person who cheats.

SYNONYMS **swindler,** fraudster, confidence trickster, double-dealer, double-crosser, fraud, fake, charlatan; informal **con artist;** N. Amer. informal **bunco artist, gold brick;** Austral. informal **shicer.**

check¹ ▶ verb **1** examine the accuracy, quality, or condition of. **2** make sure that something is the case. **3** stop or slow the progress of.

SYNONYMS **1** *troops checked all vehicles* **examine,** inspect, look at/over, scrutinize, study, investigate, probe, look into, enquire into; informal **check out, give something a/the once-over. 2** *he checked that the gun was cocked* **make sure,** confirm, verify. **3** *two defeats checked their progress* **halt,** stop, arrest, bar, obstruct, foil, thwart, curb, block.

▶ noun **1** an act of checking accuracy, quality, or condition. **2** a control or restraint. **3** Chess a position in which a king is directly threatened. **4** N. Amer. the bill in a restaurant.

SYNONYMS **1** *a check of the records* **examination,** inspection, scrutiny, perusal, study, investigation, test, check-up; informal **once-over. 2** *a check on the abuse of authority* **control,** restraint, constraint, curb, limitation.

■ **check in** register at a hotel or airport. **check out** pay your hotel bill before leaving. **check something out** find out about something. **check-up** an examination by a doctor or dentist. **check up on** investigate. **in check** under control.

check² ▶ noun a pattern of small squares.
▶ adjective (also **checked**) having a pattern of small squares.

check³ US spelling of **CHEQUE**.

checker US spelling of **CHEQUER**.

checklist ▶ noun a list of items to be considered or things to be done.

checkmate Chess ▸ noun a position of check from which a king cannot escape.
▸ verb put a king into checkmate.

checkout ▸ noun a point at which goods are paid for in a supermarket or large shop.

checkpoint ▸ noun a barrier where security checks are carried out on travellers.

Cheddar ▸ noun a kind of firm, smooth cheese.

cheek ▸ noun 1 the area on either side of the face below the eye. 2 either of the buttocks. 3 rude or disrespectful behaviour.

> SYNONYMS impudence, impertinence, insolence, rudeness, disrespect; informal brass neck, lip, mouth, chutzpah; Brit. informal backchat; N. Amer. informal sass, nerviness, back talk.
> ANTONYMS respect, politeness.

▸ verb informal speak to someone rudely or disrespectfully.
■ **cheek by jowl** close together. **turn the other cheek** stop yourself from fighting back.

cheekbone ▸ noun the rounded bone below the eye.

cheeky ▸ adjective (**cheekier, cheekiest**) showing a cheerful lack of respect.

> SYNONYMS impudent, impertinent, insolent, rude, disrespectful; informal brass-necked, lippy, mouthy, fresh; N. Amer. informal sassy, nervy.
> ANTONYMS respectful, polite.

□ **cheekily** adverb.

cheep ▸ noun a squeaky cry made by a young bird.
▸ verb make a cheep.

cheer ▸ verb 1 shout for joy or in praise or encouragement. 2 praise or encourage a person or group. 3 (**cheer up** or **cheer someone up**) become or make someone less miserable. 4 give comfort to someone.

> SYNONYMS 1 they cheered their team **applaud,** hail, salute, shout for, clap, put your hands together for; informal holler for, give someone a big hand; N. Amer. informal ballyhoo. 2 the bad weather did little to cheer me **raise/lift someone's spirits,** brighten, buoy up, hearten, gladden, perk up, encourage; informal buck up.
> ANTONYMS boo, depress.

▸ noun 1 a shout of joy, encouragement, or praise. 2 (also **good cheer**) cheerfulness; optimism.

> SYNONYMS the cheers of the crowd **hurrah,** hurray, whoop, bravo, shout; (**cheers**) acclaim, applause, ovation.
> ANTONYMS boo.

cheerful ▸ adjective 1 noticeably happy and optimistic. 2 bright and pleasant.

> SYNONYMS 1 he arrived looking cheerful **happy,** jolly, merry, bright, sunny, joyful, in good/high spirits, buoyant, cheery, animated, smiling, good-humoured; informal chipper, chirpy, full of beans. 2 a cheerful room **pleasant,** attractive, agreeable, bright, sunny, friendly, welcoming.
> ANTONYMS sad, gloomy.

□ **cheerfully** adverb **cheerfulness** noun.

cheerleader ▸ noun (in North America) a girl belonging to a group that performs organized chanting and dancing at sports events.

cheerless ▸ adjective gloomy; depressing.

cheers ▸ exclamation informal 1 said before having an alcoholic drink with other people. 2 said to express thanks or on parting.

cheery ▸ adjective (**cheerier, cheeriest**) happy and optimistic.
□ **cheerily** adverb.

cheese¹ ▸ noun a food made from the pressed curds of milk.
■ **cheese-paring** very careful about spending money; mean.

cheese² ▸ verb (**be cheesed off**) informal be irritated or bored.

cheeseburger ▸ noun a beefburger with a slice of cheese on it, served in a bread roll.

cheesecake ▸ noun a rich, sweet tart having a thick topping made with cream cheese.

cheesecloth ▸ noun thin, loosely woven cotton cloth.

cheesy ▸ adjective (**cheesier, cheesiest**) 1 like cheese. 2 informal sentimental or of bad quality.

cheetah ▸ noun a large spotted cat that can run very fast, found in Africa and parts of Asia.

chef ▸ noun a professional cook in a restaurant or hotel.

chef-d'œuvre /shay **derv**-ruh/ ▸ noun (plural **chefs-d'œuvre** /shay **derv**-ruh/) a masterpiece.

chemical ▸ adjective relating to chemistry or chemicals.
▸ noun a substance which has been artificially prepared or purified.
□ **chemically** adverb.

chemise /shuh-**meez**/ ▸ noun a woman's loose-fitting dress, nightdress, or petticoat.

chemist ▸ noun 1 a person who is authorized to give out or sell medicines. 2 a shop where medicines, toiletries, and cosmetics are sold. 3 a person who studies chemistry.

> SYNONYMS **pharmacist,** dispenser; N. Amer. druggist; archaic apothecary.

chemistry ▸ noun 1 the branch of science concerned with the nature of substances and how they react with each other. 2 attraction or interaction between two people.

chemotherapy ▸ noun the treatment of cancer with drugs.

chenille /shuh-**neel**/ ▸ noun a fabric with a thick velvety pile.

cheque (US spelling **check**) ▸ noun a written order to a bank to pay a stated sum from an account to a named person.
■ **cheque card** a card issued by a bank to guarantee payment of a customer's cheques.

chequer (US spelling **checker**) ▸ noun 1 (**chequers**) a pattern of alternately coloured squares. 2 (**checkers**) N. Amer. the game of draughts.

chequered ▸ adjective 1 divided into or marked with chequers. 2 having successful and unsuccessful periods: *a chequered career*.

cherish ▸ verb 1 protect and care for someone lovingly. 2 keep a thought or memory in your mind.

> SYNONYMS 1 *a woman he could cherish* **adore,** love, dote on, be devoted to, revere, think the world of, care for, look after, protect, keep safe. 2 *I cherish her letters* **treasure,** prize, hold dear. 3 *they cherished dreams of glory* **harbour,** entertain, nurse, cling to, foster.
> ANTONYMS hate, disdain.

Cherokee ▸ noun (plural **Cherokee** or **Cherokees**) a member of an American Indian people formerly living in much of the southern US.

cheroot /shuh-**root**/ ▸ noun a cigar with both ends open.

cherry ▸ noun (plural **cherries**) 1 a small, round red fruit with a stone. 2 a bright red colour.

cherub ▸ noun 1 (plural **cherubim** or **cherubs**) a type of angel, shown in art as a plump child with wings. 2 (plural **cherubs**) a beautiful or innocent-looking child. □ **cherubic** adjective /chuh-**roo**-bik/.

chervil ▸ noun a herb with an aniseed flavour.

chess ▸ noun a board game for two players, the object of which is to put the opponent's king under a direct attack, leading to checkmate.

chest ▸ noun 1 the front of a person's body between the neck and the stomach. 2 a large, strong box for storing or transporting things.

> SYNONYMS 1 *a wound in the chest* **breast,** upper body, torso, trunk, front. 2 *an*

oak chest **box,** case, casket, crate, trunk, coffer, strongbox.

■ **chest of drawers** a piece of furniture fitted with a set of drawers.

chesterfield ▸ noun a sofa with a back of the same height as the arms.

chestnut ▸ noun 1 an edible nut with a glossy brown shell. 2 a deep reddish-brown colour. 3 (**old chestnut**) a joke, story, or subject that has become boring through being repeated too often.

chesty ▸ adjective informal having a lot of catarrh in the lungs.

chevron ▸ noun a V-shaped line or stripe, worn on the sleeve of a military uniform to show rank or length of service.

chew ▸ verb 1 grind food with the teeth to make it easier to swallow. 2 (**chew something over**) discuss or consider something at length.

> SYNONYMS **munch,** champ, chomp, crunch, gnaw, bite, masticate.

▸ noun a sweet meant for chewing.
■ **chewing gum** flavoured gum for chewing.

chewy ▸ adjective needing a lot of chewing.

Chianti /ki-**an**-ti/ ▸ noun a red Italian wine produced in Tuscany.

chic /sheek/ ▸ adjective (**chicer, chicest**) smart and fashionable.

> SYNONYMS **stylish,** smart, elegant, sophisticated, fashionable; informal trendy; Brit. informal swish; N. Amer. informal kicky, tony.
> ANTONYMS unfashionable.

chicane /shi-**kayn**/ ▸ noun a sharp double bend in a motor-racing track.

chicanery ▸ noun the use of cunning tricks to get what you want.

chick ▸ noun 1 a newly hatched young bird. 2 informal a young woman.

chicken ▸ noun 1 a large domestic bird kept for its eggs or meat. 2 informal a coward.
▸ adjective informal cowardly.
▸ verb (**chicken out**) informal be too scared to do something.

chickenpox ▸ noun a disease causing itchy inflamed pimples.

chickpea ▸ noun a yellowish seed eaten as a vegetable.

chickweed ▸ noun a small white-flowered plant that grows as a garden weed.

chicory ▸ noun (plural **chicories**) a plant whose leaves are eaten and whose root can be used instead of coffee.

chide ▸ verb (**chides, chiding, chided**) tell someone off.

chief ▸ noun a leader or ruler.

SYNONYMS **1** *a Highland chief* **leader,** chieftain, head, ruler, master, commander. **2** *the chief of the central bank* **head,** chief executive, chief executive officer, president, chairman, chairwoman, principal, governor, director, manager; informal boss, (head) honcho; Brit. informal gaffer, guv'nor.

▸ adjective **1** having the highest rank or authority. **2** most important.

SYNONYMS **1** *the chief rabbi* **head,** leading, principal, premier, highest, supreme, arch. **2** *their chief aim* **main,** principal, primary, prime, first, cardinal, central, key, crucial, essential; informal number-one.
ANTONYMS subordinate, minor.

chiefly ▸ adverb mainly; mostly.

SYNONYMS **mainly,** in the main, primarily, principally, predominantly, mostly, for the most part, usually, typically, commonly, generally, on the whole, largely.

chieftain ▸ noun the leader of a people or clan.

chiffon ▸ noun a light, see-through fabric.

chignon /**sheen**-yon/ ▸ noun a knot or coil of hair arranged on the back of a woman's head.

chihuahua /chi-**wah**-wuh/ ▸ noun a very small breed of dog with smooth hair.

chilblain ▸ noun a painful, itchy swelling on a hand or foot caused by exposure to cold.

child ▸ noun (plural **children**) **1** a young human being below the age of full physical development. **2** a son or daughter of any age.

SYNONYMS **youngster,** baby, infant, toddler, minor, juvenile, junior, descendant; Scottish & N. English **bairn;** informal kid, kiddie, nipper, tiny, tot; derogatory brat.

□ **childless** adjective.

childbirth ▸ noun the process of giving birth to a baby.

SYNONYMS **labour,** delivery, birthing; archaic confinement.

childhood ▸ noun the period when someone is a child.

SYNONYMS **youth,** early years/life, infancy, babyhood, boyhood, girlhood, minority.
ANTONYMS adulthood.

childish ▸ adjective **1** silly and immature. **2** like a child.

SYNONYMS *childish behaviour* **immature,** babyish, infantile, juvenile, puerile, silly.
ANTONYMS mature.

childlike ▸ adjective (of an adult) innocent and unsuspecting like a child.

SYNONYMS *childlike curiosity* **youthful,** innocent, unsophisticated, naive, trusting, artless, unaffected, uninhibited, natural, spontaneous.
ANTONYMS adult.

childminder ▸ noun Brit. a person who is paid to look after other people's children.

Chilean /chil-i-uhn/ ▸ noun a person from Chile.
▸ adjective relating to Chile.

chill ▸ noun **1** an unpleasant feeling of coldness. **2** a feverish cold.

SYNONYMS **1** *a chill in the air* **coldness,** chilliness, coolness, nip. **2** *he had a chill* **cold,** dose of flu, fever. **3** *a chill ran down my spine* **shiver,** frisson.
ANTONYMS warmth.

▸ verb **1** make cold. **2** frighten or horrify. **3** (usu. **chill out**) informal relax.

SYNONYMS *his quiet tone chilled Ruth* **scare,** frighten, petrify, terrify, alarm, make someone's blood run cold; informal scare the pants off; Brit. informal put the wind up.
ANTONYMS warm.

▸ adjective unpleasantly cold.

SYNONYMS *a chill wind* **cold,** chilly, cool, fresh, wintry, frosty, icy, arctic, bitter, freezing; informal nippy; Brit. informal parky.

chilli (US spelling **chili**) ▸ noun (plural **chillies**) a small hot-tasting pepper, used in cookery and as a spice.
■ **chilli con carne** a stew of minced beef and beans flavoured with chilli.

chilly ▸ adjective (**chillier, chilliest**) **1** too cold to be comfortable. **2** unfriendly.

SYNONYMS **1** *the weather had turned chilly* **cold,** cool, crisp, fresh, wintry, frosty, icy; informal nippy; Brit. informal parky. **2** *a chilly reception* **unfriendly,** unwelcoming, cold, cool, frosty; informal stand-offish.
ANTONYMS warm.

chime ▸ noun **1** a tuneful ringing sound. **2** a bell, bar, or tube used in a set to produce chimes when struck.
▸ verb (**chimes, chiming, chimed**) **1** (of a bell or clock) make a tuneful ringing sound. **2** (**chime in**) interrupt a conversation with a remark.

chimera (or **chimaera**) /ky-**meer**-uh/ ▸ noun **1** (in Greek mythology) a female monster with a lion's head, a goat's body, and a snake's tail. **2** an unrealistic hope or dream.

chimerical /ky-merr-i-k'l/ ▸ adjective not real or possible.

chimney ▸ noun (plural **chimneys**) a pipe or channel which takes smoke and gases up from a fire or furnace.
■ **chimney breast** the part of an inside wall that surrounds a chimney.

chimpanzee ▸ noun an ape native to west and central Africa.

chin ▸ noun the part of the face below the mouth.

china ▸ noun **1** a delicate white ceramic material. **2** household objects made from china.

SYNONYMS **crockery**, dishes, plates, cups and saucers, tableware, porcelain, dinnerware, dinner service, tea service.

chinchilla /chin-chil-luh/ ▸ noun a small South American rodent with soft grey fur and a long bushy tail.

Chinese ▸ noun (plural **Chinese**) **1** the language of China. **2** a person from China.
▸ adjective relating to China.

chink¹ ▸ noun **1** a narrow opening or crack. **2** a beam of light entering through a chink.

SYNONYMS *a chink in the curtains* **gap**, crack, space, hole, aperture, fissure, cranny, cleft, split, slit.

chink² ▸ verb make a high-pitched ringing sound.
▸ noun a high-pitched ringing sound.

chinos /chee-nohz/ ▸ plural noun casual trousers made from a smooth cotton fabric.

chintz ▸ noun patterned cotton fabric with a glazed finish, used for curtains and upholstery.

chintzy ▸ adjective **1** like chintz. **2** colourful but fussy and tasteless.

chip ▸ noun **1** a small piece cut or broken off from something hard. **2** Brit. a long, thin piece of deep-fried potato. **3** (also **potato chip**) chiefly N. Amer. a potato crisp. **4** a microchip. **5** a counter used in some gambling games to represent money.

SYNONYMS **1** *wood chips* **fragment**, sliver, splinter, shaving, shard, flake. **2** *a chip in the glass* **nick**, crack, scratch. **3** *gambling chips* **counter**, token; N. Amer. check.

▸ verb (**chips, chipping, chipped**) **1** cut or break off a small piece from something hard. **2** (**chip away**) gradually make something smaller or weaker. **3** (**chip in**) add a contribution.

SYNONYMS **1** *the teacup was chipped* **nick**, crack, scratch. **2** *chip off the old plaster* **cut**, hack, chisel, carve, hew, whittle.

■ **a chip on your shoulder** informal a long-held feeling of resentment.

chipboard ▸ noun a building material made from chips of wood pressed and stuck together.

chipmunk ▸ noun a burrowing squirrel with light and dark stripes running down the body.

chipolata ▸ noun Brit. a small, thin sausage.

chipping ▸ noun a small fragment of stone, wood, or similar material.

chiropody /ki-rop-uh-di/ ▸ noun care and treatment of the feet.
□ **chiropodist** noun.

chiropractic /ky-roh-prak-tik/ ▸ noun a system of complementary medicine based on the manipulation of the joints, especially those of the spinal column.
□ **chiropractor** noun.

chirp ▸ verb (of a small bird) make a short, high-pitched sound.
▸ noun a chirping sound.

chirpy ▸ adjective (**chirpier, chirpiest**) informal cheerful and lively.

chirrup ▸ verb (**chirrups, chirruping, chirruped**) chirp.
▸ noun a chirping sound.

chisel ▸ noun a hand tool with a narrow blade, used with a hammer to cut or shape wood, stone, or metal.
▸ verb (**chisels, chiselling, chiselled**; US spelling **chisels, chiseling, chiseled**) **1** cut or shape something with a chisel. **2** (**chiselled**) (of a man's facial features) clear and strong.

chit ▸ noun a short note recording a sum of money owed.

chivalrous ▸ adjective acting in a polite and charming way towards women.
□ **chivalrously** adverb.

chivalry ▸ noun **1** an honourable code of behaviour which knights in medieval times were expected to follow. **2** polite behaviour by a man towards women.

chives ▸ plural noun a plant with long, thin leaves that are used as a herb.

chivvy ▸ verb (**chivvies, chivvying, chivvied**) keep telling someone to do something.

chloride ▸ noun a compound of chlorine with another substance.

chlorinate ▸ verb (**chlorinates, chlorinating, chlorinated**) treat water with chlorine.
□ **chlorination** noun.

chlorine /klor-een/ ▸ noun a chemical element in the form of a green gas, sometimes added to water as a disinfectant.

chlorofluorocarbon ➡ CFC.

chloroform ▸ noun a liquid used to dissolve things and formerly as an anaesthetic.

chlorophyll /klo-ruh-fil/ ▸ noun a green pigment in plants which allows them to absorb sunlight and use it in photosynthesis.

chock ▶ noun a wedge or block placed against a wheel to prevent it from moving. ■ **chock-a-block** crammed full.

chocolate ▶ noun **1** a dark brown sweet food from roasted cacao seeds. **2** a drink made by mixing milk or water with powdered chocolate.

choice ▶ noun **1** an act of choosing. **2** the right or ability to choose. **3** a range from which to choose. **4** something that has been chosen.

> SYNONYMS **1** *freedom of choice* **selection**, choosing, picking, pick, preference, decision, say, vote. **2** *you have no other choice* **option**, alternative, course of action. **3** *an extensive choice* **range**, variety, selection, assortment.

▶ adjective of very good quality.

> SYNONYMS *choice plums* **superior**, first-class, first-rate, prime, premier, grade A, best, finest, select, quality, top, top-quality, high-grade, prize; informal A1, top-notch.
> ANTONYMS inferior.

choir ▶ noun **1** an organized group of singers. **2** the part of a church between the altar and the nave, used by the choir.

choirboy ▶ noun a boy who sings in a church choir.

choke ▶ verb (**chokes, choking, choked**) **1** prevent someone from breathing by blocking their throat or depriving them of air. **2** have trouble breathing. **3** (**be choked with**) be blocked or filled with.

> SYNONYMS **1** *Christopher started to choke* **gag**, retch, cough, fight for breath. **2** *she had been choked to death* **suffocate**, asphyxiate, smother, stifle, strangle, throttle; informal strangulate. **3** *the guttering was choked with leaves* **clog (up)**, bung up, stop up, block, obstruct.

▶ noun a valve used to reduce the amount of air in the fuel mixture of a petrol engine.

choker ▶ noun a close-fitting necklace.

cholera /kol-uh-ruh/ ▶ noun an infectious disease causing severe vomiting and diarrhoea.

choleric /ko-luh-rik/ ▶ adjective literary bad-tempered.

cholesterol /kuh-**less**-tuh-rol/ ▶ noun a substance in the body which is believed to cause disease of the arteries when there is too much of it in the blood.

chomp ▶ verb munch or chew food noisily.

choose ▶ verb (**chooses, choosing, chose**; past participle **chosen**) pick something out as being the closest to what you want or need.

> SYNONYMS **1** *we chose a quiet country hotel* **select**, pick (out), opt for, plump for, settle on, prefer, decide on, fix on, elect, adopt. **2** *I'll stay as long as I choose* **wish**, want, desire, please, like.

choosy ▶ adjective (**choosier, choosiest**) informal very careful in making a choice.

chop ▶ verb (**chops, chopping, chopped**) **1** cut something into pieces with a knife or axe. **2** hit with a short downward stroke.

> SYNONYMS **cut (up)**, cube, dice, hew, split, fell; N. Amer. hash.

▶ noun **1** a thick slice of meat cut from or including the rib bone. **2** a downward cutting movement. **3** (**the chop**) Brit. informal the cancellation or end of something. ■ **chop and change** Brit. informal keep changing your mind.

chopper ▶ noun **1** a short axe with a large blade. **2** informal a helicopter.

choppy ▶ adjective (of the sea) having many small waves.

chopstick ▶ noun each of a pair of thin sticks used by the Chinese and Japanese to eat with.

chop suey ▶ noun a Chinese-style dish of meat with bean sprouts, bamboo shoots, and onions.

choral ▶ adjective sung by a choir or chorus.

chorale ▶ noun a simple, stately hymn tune.

chord ▶ noun a group of three or more musical notes sounded together in harmony.

> ❗ Don't confuse **chord** with **cord**, which means 'thin string or rope'.

chore ▶ noun a boring or routine job or task.

> SYNONYMS **task**, job, duty, errand, burden; informal hassle.

choreograph /ko-ri-uh-grahf/ ▶ verb compose the sequence of steps for a ballet or dance routine. □ **choreographer** noun **choreography** noun.

chorister ▶ noun a member of a church choir.

chortle ▶ verb (**chortles, chortling, chortled**) chuckle happily.

chorus ▶ noun (plural **choruses**) **1** a part of a song which is repeated after each verse. **2** a group of singers or dancers performing together in a supporting role in an opera, musical, etc. **3** something said at the same time by many people.

▶ verb (**choruses, chorusing, chorused**) (of a group of people) say the same thing at the same time.

chose past of CHOOSE.

chosen past participle of CHOOSE.

choux pastry /shoo/ ▶ noun very light pastry made with egg.

chowder ▸ noun a rich soup containing fish, clams, or corn.

chow mein /chow **mayn**/ ▸ noun a Chinese-style dish of fried noodles served with shredded meat or seafood and vegetables.

Christ ▸ noun the title given to Jesus.

christen ▸ verb give a name to a baby while it is being baptized.

> SYNONYMS **1** *she was christened Sara* **baptize**, name, give the name of, call. **2** *a group who were christened 'The Magic Circle'* **call**, name, dub, style, term, label, nickname.

Christian ▸ adjective based on or believing in Christianity.
▸ noun a person who believes in Christianity.
■ **Christian name** a person's first name.

Christianity ▸ noun the religion based on the life and teaching of Jesus.

Christmas ▸ noun (plural **Christmases**) the annual Christian festival celebrating the birth of Jesus, held on 25 December.
■ **Christmas tree** an evergreen tree decorated with lights and ornaments at Christmas.

chromatic ▸ adjective **1** Music using notes that do not belong to the key in which the passage is written. **2** Music going up or down by semitones. **3** relating to or produced by colour.

chrome ▸ noun a hard, bright metal coating made from chromium.

chromium ▸ noun a hard white metallic element.

chromosome ▸ noun a thread-like structure found in the nuclei of most living cells, carrying genetic information in the form of genes.

chronic ▸ adjective **1** (of an illness or problem) lasting for a long time. **2** having a long-lasting illness or bad habit. **3** Brit. informal very bad.
□ **chronically** adverb.

chronicle ▸ noun a record of historical events made in the order in which they happened.

> SYNONYMS *a chronicle of the region's past* **record**, account, history, annals, archive(s), log, diary, journal.

▸ verb (**chronicles**, **chronicling**, **chronicled**) record a series of events in detail.

> SYNONYMS *the events have been chronicled* **record**, write down, set down, document, report.

□ **chronicler** noun.

chronological ▸ adjective (of a record of events) starting with the earliest and following the order in which they happened.

□ **chronologically** adverb.

chronology /kruh-**nol**-uh-ji/ ▸ noun (plural **chronologies**) the arrangement of events or dates in the order in which they happened.

chronometer ▸ noun an instrument for measuring time.

chrysalis /**kriss**-uh-liss/ ▸ noun (plural **chrysalises**) a butterfly or moth when it is changing from a larva to the adult form, inside a hard case.

chrysanthemum /kri-**san**-thi-muhm/ ▸ noun (plural **chrysanthemums**) a garden plant with brightly coloured flowers.

chub ▸ noun a thick-bodied river fish.

chubby ▸ adjective (**chubbier**, **chubbiest**) plump and rounded.

> SYNONYMS **plump**, tubby, flabby, rotund, portly, chunky; Brit. informal podgy; N. Amer. informal zaftig, corn-fed.
> ANTONYMS skinny.

chuck¹ ▸ verb informal throw something carelessly or casually.

> SYNONYMS **1** *he chucked the letter on to the table* **throw**, toss, fling, hurl, pitch, cast, lob; informal sling, bung; Austral. informal hoy; NZ informal bish. **2** *I chucked the rubbish* **throw away/out**, discard, dispose of, get rid of, dump, bin, jettison; informal ditch, junk; N. Amer. informal trash. **3** *I've chucked my job* **give up**, leave, resign from; informal quit, pack in; Brit. informal jack in. **4** *Mary chucked him for another guy* **leave**, finish with, break off with, jilt; informal dump, ditch, give someone the elbow; Brit. informal give someone the push.

chuck² ▸ verb touch someone playfully under the chin.

chuckle ▸ verb (**chuckles**, **chuckling**, **chuckled**) laugh quietly.

> SYNONYMS **laugh**, chortle, giggle, titter, snigger.

▸ noun a quiet laugh.

chuff ▸ verb (of a steam engine) move with a regular puffing sound.

chuffed ▸ adjective Brit. informal very pleased.

chug ▸ verb (**chugs**, **chugging**, **chugged**) (of a vehicle) move slowly with a loud, regular sound.

chum ▸ noun informal a close friend.

> SYNONYMS **friend**, companion, playmate, classmate, schoolmate, workmate; informal pal, crony; Brit. informal mate; N. Amer. informal buddy.
> ANTONYMS enemy, stranger.

□ **chummy** adjective.

chump ▸ noun informal a silly person.

chunk ▸ noun a thick, solid piece.

SYNONYMS **lump,** hunk, wedge, block, slab, square, nugget, brick, cube; informal wodge; N. Amer. informal gob.

□ **chunky** adjective.

church ▸ noun **1** a building where Christians go to worship. **2** (**Church**) a particular Christian organization. **3** (**the Church**) people within the Christian faith.

churchyard ▸ noun an enclosed area surrounding a church.

churlish ▸ adjective unfriendly and rude.

SYNONYMS **rude,** ill-mannered, discourteous, impolite, inconsiderate, surly, sullen.
ANTONYMS polite.

□ **churlishly** adverb.

churn ▸ noun **1** a machine for making butter by shaking milk or cream. **2** a large metal milk can.
▸ verb **1** (of liquid) move about vigorously. **2** (**churn something out**) produce something in large quantities and without much thought. **3** shake milk or cream in a churn to produce butter.

SYNONYMS **disturb,** stir up, agitate, beat.

chute ▸ noun **1** a sloping channel for moving things to a lower level. **2** a slide into a swimming pool.

chutney ▸ noun (plural **chutneys**) a spicy sauce made of fruits or vegetables with vinegar, spices, and sugar.

chutzpah /**khuuts**-puh/ ▸ noun informal extreme self-confidence.

CIA ▸ abbreviation (in the US) Central Intelligence Agency.

ciabatta /chuh-**bah**-tuh/ ▸ noun a flat Italian bread made with olive oil.

cicada /si-**kah**-duh/ ▸ noun an insect which makes a shrill droning noise.

CID ▸ abbreviation Criminal Investigation Department.

cider ▸ noun an alcoholic drink made from apple juice.

cigar ▸ noun a cylinder of tobacco rolled in tobacco leaves for smoking.

cigarette ▸ noun a cylinder of finely cut tobacco rolled in paper for smoking.

cilium /**sil**-i-uhm/ ▸ noun (plural **cilia** /**sil**-i-uh/) a microscopic hair-like structure, found on the surface of certain cells.

cinch ▸ noun informal **1** a very easy task. **2** a certainty.

cinder ▸ noun a piece of partly burnt coal or wood.

cine ▸ adjective relating to or used for the making of films.

cinema ▸ noun Brit. **1** a place where films are shown. **2** the production of films as an art or industry.

SYNONYMS **1** *the local cinema* **the movies,** the pictures; N. Amer. movie theatre/house; informal the flicks. **2** *British cinema* **films,** film, movies, pictures, motion pictures.

cinematic ▸ adjective relating to the cinema, or like a film.

cinematography ▸ noun the skilled use of the camera in film-making.
□ **cinematographer** noun.

cinnamon ▸ noun a spice made from the bark of an Asian tree.

cipher (or **cypher**) ▸ noun **1** a code. **2** a key to a code. **3** an unimportant person or thing.

circa /**ser**-kuh/ ▸ preposition approximately.

SYNONYMS **approximately,** (round) about, around, in the region of, roughly, something like, or so, or thereabouts, more or less; informal as near as dammit; N. Amer. informal in the ballpark of.
ANTONYMS exactly.

circadian /ser-**kay**-di-uhn/ ▸ adjective relating to processes in the body that happen regularly every twenty-four hours.

circle ▸ noun **1** a round flat shape whose edge is at the same distance from the centre all the way round. **2** a group of people with shared interests, friends, etc. **3** Brit. a curved upper tier of seats in a theatre.

SYNONYMS **1** *a circle of gold stars* **ring,** band, hoop, circlet, halo, disc. **2** *her circle of friends* **group,** set, crowd, band, company, clique, coterie, club, society; informal gang, bunch.

▸ verb (**circles, circling, circled**) **1** move or be placed all the way round. **2** draw a line round.

SYNONYMS **1** *seagulls circled above* **wheel,** revolve, rotate, whirl, spiral. **2** *satellites circling the earth* **go round,** travel round, circumnavigate, orbit. **3** *the abbey was circled by a wall* **surround,** encircle, ring, enclose.

circuit ▸ noun **1** a roughly circular line, route, or movement. **2** Brit. a track used for motor racing. **3** a system of components forming a complete path for an electric current. **4** a series of sports events or entertainments.

SYNONYMS **1** *two circuits of the track* **lap,** turn, round, circle. **2** *a racing circuit* **track,** racetrack, course, route, stadium.

circuitous /ser-**kyoo**-i-tuhss/ ▸ adjective (of a route) long and indirect.

circuitry ▸ noun (plural **circuitries**) a system of electric circuits.

circular ▸ adjective **1** having the form of a circle. **2** (of a letter or advertisement) for distribution to a large number of people.

> SYNONYMS *a circular room* **round,** ring-shaped.

▸ noun a circular letter or advertisement.

> SYNONYMS **leaflet,** pamphlet, handbill, flyer, advertisement, notice.

circulate ▸ verb (**circulates, circulating, circulated**) **1** move continuously through a system or area. **2** pass from place to place or person to person.

> SYNONYMS **1** *the news was widely circulated* **spread,** communicate, disseminate, make known, make public, broadcast, publicize, distribute. **2** *they circulated among the guests* **socialize,** mingle, mix, wander, stroll.

circulation ▸ noun **1** movement through a system or area. **2** the continuous movement of blood round the body. **3** the spreading or passing of something from one person or place to another. **4** the number of copies of a newspaper or magazine sold.

circumcise ▸ verb (**circumcises, circumcising, circumcised**) **1** cut off a boy's or man's foreskin. **2** cut off a girl's or woman's clitoris.
□ **circumcision** noun.

circumference ▸ noun **1** the boundary which encloses a circle. **2** the distance around something.

circumflex ▸ noun a mark (^) placed over a vowel in some languages to show a change in its sound.

circumlocution ▸ noun a way of saying something which uses more words than are necessary.

circumnavigate ▸ verb (**circumnavigates, circumnavigating, circumnavigated**) sail all the way around.
□ **circumnavigation** noun.

circumscribe ▸ verb (**circumscribes, circumscribing, circumscribed**) restrict the freedom or power of.

circumspect ▸ adjective not wanting to take risks; cautious.

circumstance ▸ noun **1** a fact or condition that is connected with an event or action. **2** things that happen that are beyond your control. **3** (**circumstances**) the practical things that affect a person's life.

> SYNONYMS (**circumstances**) **situation,** conditions, state of affairs, position, the lie of the land, (turn of) events, factors, facts, background, environment, context.

circumstantial ▸ adjective (of evidence) consisting of facts that make something seem likely but do not prove it.
□ **circumstantially** adverb.

circumvent /ser-kuhm-**vent**/ ▸ verb find a way of avoiding a problem or obstacle.

circus ▸ noun (plural **circuses**) a travelling group of entertainers, including acrobats, clowns, and people who perform with trained animals.

cirrhosis /si-roh-siss/ ▸ noun a disease of the liver.

cirrus /si-ruhss/ ▸ noun (plural **cirri** /si-ry/) cloud forming wispy streaks high in the sky.

CIS ▸ abbreviation Commonwealth of Independent States.

cistern ▸ noun a tank connected to a toilet, in which the water used for flushing it is stored.

citadel ▸ noun a fortress protecting or overlooking a city.

citation ▸ noun **1** a quotation from a book or author. **2** an official mention of someone who has done something deserving praise.

cite ▸ verb (**cites, citing, cited**) quote a book or author as evidence for an argument.

> SYNONYMS **1** *cite the passage in full* **quote,** reproduce, excerpt. **2** *he cited the case of Leigh v. Gladstone* **refer to,** allude to, instance, specify, mention, name.

citizen ▸ noun **1** a person who is legally recognized as being a member of a country. **2** an inhabitant of a town or city.

> SYNONYMS **1** *a British citizen* **subject,** national, passport holder. **2** *the citizens of Edinburgh* **inhabitant,** resident, native, townsman, townswoman, taxpayer, people; formal denizen.

□ **citizenship** noun.

citric acid ▸ noun a sharp-tasting acid present in the juice of lemons and other sour fruits.

citrus ▸ noun (plural **citruses**) a fruit of a group that includes the lemon, lime, orange, and grapefruit.

city ▸ noun (plural **cities**) **1** a large town, in particular (Brit.) a town that has been created a city by charter, usually containing a cathedral. **2** (**the City**) the part of London that is a centre of finance and business.

> SYNONYMS **town,** municipality, metropolis, conurbation, urban area; Scottish **burgh;** informal **big smoke;** N. Amer. informal **burg.**

■ **city state** a city that forms an independent state.

civet /siv-it/ ▸ noun **1** a cat native to Africa and Asia. **2** a strong perfume obtained from the civet.

civic ▸ adjective having to do with a city or town.

> SYNONYMS **municipal,** city, town, urban, metropolitan, public, community.

civil ▸ adjective **1** relating to the lives of ordinary people rather than to military or church matters. **2** (of a court) dealing with personal legal matters rather than criminal offences. **3** polite.

> SYNONYMS **1** *a civil marriage* **secular,** non-religious, lay. **2** *civil aviation* **non-military,** civilian. **3** *he behaved in a civil manner* **polite,** courteous, well mannered, gentlemanly, chivalrous, ladylike.
> ANTONYMS religious, military, rude.

■ **civil engineer** an engineer who designs roads, bridges, dams, etc. **civil liberties** a person's rights to freedom of action and speech (while staying within the law). **civil servant** a person who works in the civil service. **civil service** the departments that carry out the work of the government. **civil war** a war between groups of people within the same country.
□ **civilly** adverb.

civilian ▸ noun a person who is not a member of the armed services or the police force.
▸ adjective relating to a civilian.

civility ▸ noun (plural **civilities**) polite behaviour or speech.

civilization (or **civilisation**) ▸ noun **1** an advanced stage of human development in which people in a society behave well towards each other and share a common culture. **2** the society, culture, and way of life of a particular area or period.

> SYNONYMS **1** *a higher stage of civilization* **human development,** advancement, progress, enlightenment, culture, refinement, sophistication. **2** *ancient civilizations* **culture,** society, nation, people.

civilize (or **civilise**) ▸ verb (**civilizes, civilizing, civilized**) **1** bring a person or group to an advanced stage of social development. **2** (**civilized**) polite and good-mannered.

> SYNONYMS **1** **enlighten,** improve, educate, instruct, refine, cultivate, socialize. **2** (**civilized**) *civilized society* **advanced,** developed, sophisticated, enlightened, educated, cultured, cultivated. **3** (**civilized**) *civilized behaviour* **polite,** courteous, well mannered, civil, refined, polished.

CJD ▸ abbreviation Creutzfeldt–Jakob disease, a fatal disease affecting the brain, possibly linked to BSE.

cl ▸ abbreviation centilitre.

clack ▸ verb make a sharp sound like that of one hard object hitting another.
▸ noun a clacking sound.

clad ▸ adjective **1** clothed. **2** fitted with cladding.

cladding ▸ noun a protective or insulating covering or coating.

claim ▸ verb **1** say that something is true although you are not able to prove it. **2** request something that you believe you have a right to. **3** cause the loss of someone's life. **4** ask for money under the terms of an insurance policy. **5** call for someone's attention.

> SYNONYMS **1** *he claimed that she was lying* **assert,** declare, profess, protest, maintain, insist, contend, allege. **2** *you can claim compensation* **request,** ask for, apply for, demand.

▸ noun **1** a statement that something is true. **2** a statement requesting something that you believe you have a right to. **3** a request for compensation under the terms of an insurance policy.

> SYNONYMS **1** *her claim that she was robbed* **assertion,** declaration, profession, protestation, insistence, contention, allegation. **2** *a claim for damages* **application,** request, demand.

□ **claimant** noun.

clairvoyant ▸ noun a person who claims that they are able to see into the future or communicate mentally with people who are dead or far away.
▸ adjective able to see into the future.
□ **clairvoyance** noun.

clam ▸ noun a large shellfish with a hinged shell.
▸ verb (**clams, clamming, clammed**) (**clam up**) informal suddenly stop talking about something.

clamber ▸ verb (**clambers, clambering, clambered**) climb or move using your hands and feet.

clammy ▸ adjective (**clammier, clammiest**) **1** unpleasantly damp and sticky. **2** (of air) cold and damp.

clamour (US spelling **clamor**) ▸ noun **1** a loud and confused noise. **2** a loud protest or demand.

> SYNONYMS **noise,** din, racket, rumpus, uproar, shouting, commotion, hubbub; informal **hullabaloo**; Brit. informal **row.**

▸ verb shout or demand something loudly.
□ **clamorous** adjective.

c

clamp ▶ noun **1** a brace, band, or clasp for holding something tightly. **2** a device attached to the wheel of an illegally parked car to prevent it being driven away.
▶ verb **1** fasten or hold with a clamp. **2** (**clamp down**) suppress or prevent something. **3** fit a wheel clamp to a car.

> SYNONYMS **fasten**, secure, fix, attach, clench, grip, hold, press, clasp, screw, bolt.

clan ▶ noun a group of families, especially in the Scottish Highlands.

> SYNONYMS **family**, house, dynasty, tribe.

clandestine /klan-dess-tin/ ▶ adjective done secretly.
□ **clandestinely** adverb.

clang ▶ noun a loud metallic sound.
▶ verb make a clang.

clank ▶ noun a sharp sound like that of pieces of metal being struck together.
▶ verb make a clank.

clannish ▶ adjective (of a group) tending to exclude people from outside the group.

clap ▶ verb (**claps, clapping, clapped**) **1** bring the palms of your hands together loudly and repeatedly to show that you approve of something. **2** slap someone encouragingly on the back. **3** suddenly place a hand over a part of your face as a gesture of dismay.

> SYNONYMS *the audience clapped* **applaud**, give someone a round of applause, put your hands together; informal give someone a (big) hand; N. Amer. informal give it up.

▶ noun **1** an act of clapping. **2** a sudden loud sound of thunder.

> SYNONYMS **1** *everybody gave him a clap* **round of applause**, handclap; informal hand. **2** *a clap of thunder* **crack**, peal, crash, bang, boom.

■ **clapped-out** Brit. informal worn out from age or heavy use.

clapper ▶ noun the moving part inside a bell.

clapperboard ▶ noun a pair of hinged boards that are struck together at the beginning of filming so that the picture and sound can be matched.

claret /kla-ruht/ ▶ noun a red wine from Bordeaux in France.

clarify ▶ verb (**clarifies, clarifying, clarified**) **1** make something easier to understand. **2** melt butter to separate out the impurities.

> SYNONYMS **make clear**, shed/throw light on, illuminate, elucidate, explain, interpret, spell out, clear up.
> ANTONYMS confuse.

□ **clarification** noun.

clarinet ▶ noun a woodwind instrument with holes that are stopped by keys.
□ **clarinettist** (US spelling **clarinetist**) noun.

clarion /kla-ri-uhn/ ▶ noun historical a war trumpet.
■ **clarion call** a loud, clear call for action.

clarity ▶ noun **1** the quality of being clear and easily understood. **2** transparency or purity.

> SYNONYMS **1** *the clarity of his explanation* **lucidity**, precision, coherence, transparency, simplicity. **2** *the clarity of the image* **sharpness**, clearness, crispness, definition. **3** *the clarity of the water* **transparency**, clearness, limpidity, translucence.
> ANTONYMS vagueness, blurriness, cloudiness.

clash ▶ verb **1** come into violent conflict. **2** disagree or be at odds. **3** (of colours) look unpleasant together. **4** (of events) happen inconveniently at the same time. **5** strike metal objects together, producing a loud harsh sound.

> SYNONYMS **1** *protesters clashed with police* **fight**, battle, confront, skirmish, contend, come to blows. **2** *the prime minister clashed with union leaders* **disagree**, differ, wrangle, dispute, cross swords, lock horns, be at loggerheads. **3** *the dates clash* **conflict**, coincide, overlap. **4** *she clashed the cymbals together* **bang**, strike, clang, crash.

▶ noun an act or sound of clashing.

> SYNONYMS **1** *clashes between armed gangs* **fight**, battle, confrontation, skirmish, engagement, encounter, conflict. **2** *clashes in parliament* **argument**, altercation, confrontation, quarrel, disagreement, dispute; informal run-in, slanging match. **3** *the clash of cymbals* **crash**, clang, bang.

clasp ▶ verb **1** grasp tightly with your hand. **2** place your arms tightly around. **3** fasten with a clasp.

> SYNONYMS *Ruth clasped him to her* **grasp**, grip, clutch, hold, squeeze, seize, grab, embrace, hug.

▶ noun **1** a device with interlocking parts used for fastening. **2** an act of clasping.

> SYNONYMS **1** *a gold clasp* **fastener**, catch, clip, pin, buckle. **2** *his tight clasp* **grasp**, grip, squeeze, embrace, hug.

■ **clasp knife** a knife with a blade that folds into the handle.

class ▶ noun **1** a set or category of things that have something in common. **2** the division of people into different groups according to their social status. **3** a group of people of the same social status. **4** a group of students or pupils who are taught together. **5** a school or college lesson. **6** informal impressive stylishness.

SYNONYMS **1** *a new class of drug* **kind,** sort, type, variety, genre, category, grade, rating, classification. **2** *mixing with people of her own class* **group,** grouping, rank, stratum, level, echelon, status, caste.

▶ verb place something in a particular category.

SYNONYMS *the 12-seater is classed as a commercial vehicle* **classify,** categorize, group, grade, order, rate, bracket, designate, label, rank.

□ **classless** adjective.

classic ▶ adjective **1** judged over a period of time to be of the highest quality. **2** typical.

SYNONYMS **1** *the classic work on the subject* **definitive,** authoritative, outstanding, first-rate, first-class, best, finest, excellent, superior, masterly. **2** *a classic example of Norman design* **typical,** archetypal, quintessential, model, representative, perfect, prime, textbook. **3** *a classic look* **timeless,** traditional, simple, elegant, understated. ANTONYMS insignificant, second-rate, atypical, ephemeral.

▶ noun (**Classics**) the study of ancient Greek and Latin language and culture.

SYNONYMS *a classic of the genre* **definitive example,** model, epitome, paradigm, exemplar, masterpiece.

classical ▶ adjective **1** relating to the literature, art, or culture of ancient Greece and Rome. **2** representing the highest standard within a long-established form. **3** (of music) written in the tradition of formal European music. □ **classically** adverb.

classicism ▶ noun the use of a simple and elegant style characteristic of the art, architecture, or literature of ancient Greece and Rome.

classicist ▶ noun a person who studies Classics.

classification ▶ noun **1** the arrangement of things in categories. **2** a category into which something is put.

SYNONYMS **categorization,** classifying, grouping, grading, ranking, organization, sorting, codification.

classified ▶ adjective **1** (of newspaper or magazine advertisements) organized in categories. **2** (of information or documents) officially secret.

classify ▶ verb (**classifies, classifying, classified**) **1** arrange things in groups according to features that they have in

common. **2** put in a particular class or category.

SYNONYMS **categorize,** group, grade, rank, order, organize, sort, type, codify, bracket.

classroom ▶ noun a room in which a class of pupils or students is taught.

classy ▶ adjective (**classier, classiest**) informal stylish and sophisticated.

SYNONYMS **stylish,** high-class, superior, exclusive, chic, elegant, smart, sophisticated; Brit. upmarket; N. Amer. high-toned; informal posh, ritzy, plush, swanky; Brit. informal swish.

clatter ▶ noun a loud rattling sound like that of hard objects hitting each other.
▶ verb (**clatters, clattering, clattered**) make a clatter.

clause ▶ noun **1** a group of words that includes a subject and a verb and forms part of a sentence. **2** a part of a treaty, bill, or contract.

SYNONYMS **section,** paragraph, article, passage, subsection, chapter, condition, proviso, rider.

claustrophobia /kloss-truh-**foh**-bi-uh/
▶ noun an extreme fear of being in a small or enclosed space.
□ **claustrophobic** adjective.

clavichord ▶ noun a small early keyboard instrument.

clavicle ▶ noun the collarbone.

claw ▶ noun **1** each of the horny nails on the feet of birds, lizards, and some mammals. **2** the pincer of a shellfish.

SYNONYMS **1** *a bird's claw* **talon,** nail. **2** *a crab's claw* **pincer,** nipper.

▶ verb scratch or tear at something with the claws or fingernails.

SYNONYMS *her fingers clawed his shoulders* **scratch,** lacerate, tear, rip, scrape, dig into.

clay ▶ noun sticky earth that can be moulded when wet and baked to make bricks and pottery.

clean ▶ adjective **1** free from dirt or harmful substances. **2** not yet used or marked. **3** not obscene. **4** having no record of offences or crimes. **5** (of an action) smoothly and skilfully done.

SYNONYMS **1** *keep the wound clean* **washed,** scrubbed, cleansed, cleaned, laundered, spotless, unstained, unsullied, unblemished, immaculate, pristine, disinfected, sterilized, sterile, aseptic, decontaminated. **2** *a clean sheet of paper* **blank,** empty, clear, plain, unused, new, pristine, fresh, unmarked.

3 *clean air* **pure,** clear, fresh, unpolluted, uncontaminated.
ANTONYMS dirty, polluted, used.

▶ verb make something free from dirt or harmful substances.

> SYNONYMS *Dad cleaned the windows* **wash,** cleanse, wipe, sponge, scrub, mop, rinse, scour, swab, shampoo, launder, dry-clean.
> ANTONYMS dirty.

▶ noun an act of cleaning.
■ **clean-cut** (of a person) clean and neat. **clean-shaven** (of a man) without a beard or moustache. **come clean** informal fully confess something.
□ **cleaner** noun **cleanly** adverb.

cleanliness /klen-li-nuhss/ ▶ noun the quality of being clean.

cleanse /klenz/ ▶ verb (**cleanses, cleansing, cleansed**) make something thoroughly clean or pure.

> SYNONYMS **1** *the wound was cleansed* **clean (up),** wash, bathe, rinse, disinfect. **2** *cleansing the environment of traces of lead* **rid,** clear, free, purify, purge.

□ **cleanser** noun.

clear ▶ adjective **1** easy to see, hear, or understand. **2** leaving or feeling no doubt. **3** transparent. **4** free of obstructions or unwanted objects. **5** (of a period of time) free of commitments. **6** free from disease or guilt. **7** (**clear of**) not touching.

> SYNONYMS **1** *clear instructions* **understandable,** comprehensible, intelligible, plain, uncomplicated, explicit, lucid, coherent, simple, straightforward, unambiguous, clear-cut. **2** *a clear case of harassment* **obvious,** evident, plain, sure, definite, unmistakable, manifest, indisputable, unambiguous, patent, incontrovertible, visible, conspicuous, overt, blatant, glaring. **3** *clear water* **transparent,** limpid, translucent, crystal clear. **4** *a clear sky* **bright,** cloudless, unclouded, blue, sunny, starry. **5** *the road was clear* **unobstructed,** passable, open, unrestricted, unhindered.
> ANTONYMS vague, disputed, cloudy, obstructed.

▶ verb **1** make or become clear. **2** get past or over something safely or without touching it. **3** show or state that someone is innocent. **4** give official approval to. **5** make people leave a place. **6** (of a cheque) be paid into someone's account.

> SYNONYMS **1** *the smoke had cleared* **disappear,** go away, stop, die away, fade, wear off, lift, settle, evaporate, dissipate, decrease, lessen, shift. **2** *they cleared the table* **empty,** unload, strip. **3** *clearing*

drains **unblock,** unstop. **4** *staff cleared the building* **evacuate,** empty, leave. **5** *Karen cleared the dirty plates* **remove,** take away, carry away, tidy away/up. **6** *I cleared the bar at my first attempt* **go over,** pass over, sail over, jump (over), vault (over), leap (over). **7** *he was cleared by the court* **acquit,** declare innocent, find not guilty, absolve, exonerate; informal let off (the hook).

■ **clear off** informal go away. **clear up 1** (of an illness) become cured. **2** stop raining. **clear something up 1** tidy something. **2** solve or explain a mystery or misunderstanding. **in the clear** no longer in danger or under suspicion.

clearance ▶ noun **1** the action of clearing. **2** official permission for something to take place. **3** clear space allowed for a thing to move past or under another.

> SYNONYMS **1** *slum clearance* **removal,** clearing, demolition. **2** *you must have Home Office clearance* **authorization,** permission, consent, approval, leave, sanction, licence, dispensation; informal the go-ahead. **3** *there is plenty of clearance* **space,** room (to spare), headroom, margin, leeway.

clear-cut ▶ adjective sharply defined; easy to see or understand.

> SYNONYMS **definite,** distinct, precise, specific, explicit, unambiguous, unequivocal, black and white.
> ANTONYMS vague.

clearing ▶ noun an open space in a wood or forest.

clearly ▶ adverb **1** in a clear way. **2** without doubt; obviously.

> SYNONYMS **1** *write clearly* **intelligibly,** plainly, distinctly, comprehensibly, legibly, audibly. **2** *clearly, substantial changes are needed* **obviously,** evidently, patently, unquestionably, undoubtedly, without doubt, plainly, undeniably.

clearway ▶ noun Brit. a main road other than a motorway on which vehicles are not allowed to stop.

cleat ▶ noun **1** a projection to which a rope may be attached. **2** a projecting wedge on a tool, the sole of a boot, etc., to prevent it slipping.

cleavage ▶ noun **1** the space between a woman's breasts. **2** a sharp difference or division between people.

cleave[1] ▶ verb (**cleaves, cleaving, clove** or **cleft** or **cleaved**; past participle **cloven** or **cleft** or **cleaved**) divide or split in two.

cleave[2] ▶ verb (**cleaves, cleaving, cleaved**) (**cleave to**) literary stick to something.

cleaver ▸ noun a tool with a broad, heavy blade, used for chopping meat.

clef ▸ noun Music a symbol placed next to the notes on a stave, to show their pitch.

cleft past and past participle of CLEAVE¹.
▸ adjective split or divided into two.
▸ noun a split or indentation.

> SYNONYMS **split,** crack, fissure, crevice.

■ **cleft lip** an upper lip with an abnormal split in the centre. **cleft palate** a split in the roof of the mouth.

clematis /klem-uh-tiss/ ▸ noun an ornamental climbing plant.

clemency ▸ noun kind or merciful treatment.

clement ▸ adjective (of weather) mild.

clementine ▸ noun a small citrus fruit with bright orange-red skin.

clench ▸ verb 1 close your fist or hold your teeth or muscles together tightly in response to stress or anger. 2 grasp something tightly.

> SYNONYMS **grip,** grasp, grab, clutch, clasp, clamp, hold tightly, seize, squeeze.

clerestory /kleer-stor-i/ ▸ noun (plural **clerestories**) a row of windows in the upper part of the wall of a church or other large building.

clergy /kler-ji/ ▸ noun (plural **clergies**) the priests and ministers of a religion, especially those of the Christian Church.

clergyman (or **clergywoman**) ▸ noun (plural **clergymen** or **clergywomen**) a Christian priest or minister.

> SYNONYMS **priest,** cleric, minister, preacher, chaplain, padre, father, pastor, vicar, rector, parson, curate; Scottish kirkman.

cleric ▸ noun a priest or religious leader.

clerical ▸ adjective 1 relating to the normal work of an office clerk. 2 relating to the priests and ministers of the Christian Church.

clerk ▸ noun 1 a person employed in an office or bank to keep records or accounts and do other routine work. 2 a person in charge of the records of a local council or court.

clever ▸ adjective (**cleverer, cleverest**) 1 quick to understand and learn. 2 skilled at doing something.

> SYNONYMS 1 **intelligent,** bright, smart, astute, quick-witted, shrewd, talented, gifted, capable, able, competent; informal brainy. 2 *a clever scheme* **ingenious,** canny, cunning, crafty, artful, slick, neat. 3 *she was clever with her hands* **skilful,** dexterous, adroit, adept, deft, nimble, handy, skilled, talented, gifted.
> ANTONYMS stupid.

□ **cleverly** adverb **cleverness** noun.

cliché /klee-shay/ ▸ noun a phrase or idea that has been used too much and is no longer fresh or interesting.

> SYNONYMS **platitude,** hackneyed phrase, commonplace, banality, truism, stock phrase; informal old chestnut.

□ **clichéd** adjective.

click ▸ noun a short, sharp sound as of two hard objects coming into contact.
▸ verb 1 make a click. 2 move or become secured with a click. 3 Computing press a mouse button. 4 informal become suddenly clear or understood.

client ▸ noun a person who uses the services of a professional person or organization.

> SYNONYMS **customer,** buyer, purchaser, shopper, patient, patron; Brit. informal punter.

clientele /klee-on-**tel**/ ▸ noun the clients or customers of a shop, restaurant, or professional service.

cliff ▸ noun a steep rock face at the edge of the sea.

> SYNONYMS **precipice,** rock face, crag, bluff, ridge, escarpment, scar, scarp.

cliffhanger ▸ noun a situation in a story which is exciting because you do not know what is going to happen next.

climacteric /kly-**mak**-tuh-rik/ ▸ noun the period in a person's life when their fertility has started to decline.

climactic /kly-**mak**-tik/ ▸ adjective forming an exciting climax.

climate ▸ noun 1 the general weather conditions in an area over a long period. 2 a general attitude or feeling among people.

> SYNONYMS 1 *a mild climate* **(weather) conditions,** weather. 2 *the political climate* **atmosphere,** mood, spirit, ethos, feeling, ambience, environment.

□ **climatic** adjective.

climax ▸ noun 1 the most intense, exciting, or important point of something. 2 an orgasm.

> SYNONYMS *the climax of his career* **peak,** pinnacle, height, high point, top, zenith, culmination.
> ANTONYMS anticlimax, nadir.

▸ verb reach a climax.

climb ▸ verb 1 go or come up to a higher position. 2 go up a hill, rock face, etc. 3 move somewhere, especially with effort or difficulty. 4 increase in value or amount.

> SYNONYMS 1 *we climbed the hill* **ascend,** mount, scale, scramble up, clamber up,

shin up, conquer. **2** *the plane climbed* **rise**, ascend, go up, gain height, soar, rocket. **3** *the road climbs steeply* **slope (upwards)**, rise, go uphill, incline. ANTONYMS descend.

▶ **noun 1** an act of climbing. **2** a route up a mountain or cliff.
■ **climb down** admit that you are wrong about something.
□ **climber** noun.

clime ▶ **noun** literary a place considered in terms of its climate: *sunnier climes*.

clinch ▶ **verb 1** settle a contract or contest. **2** settle something that has been uncertain or undecided.

SYNONYMS **1** *he clinched the deal* **secure**, settle, conclude, close, confirm, seal, finalize; informal sew up. **2** *these findings clinched the matter* **settle**, decide, determine, resolve. **3** *they clinched the title* **win**, secure.
ANTONYMS lose.

▶ **noun 1** a tight hold in a fight or struggle. **2** informal a tight embrace.

cling ▶ **verb** (**clings**, **clinging**, **clung**) (**cling to** or **on to**) **1** hold on tightly to. **2** stick to. **3** be unwilling to give up a belief or hope. **4** be emotionally dependent on.

SYNONYMS *rice grains cling together* **stick**, adhere, hold.

■ **cling film** Brit. thin plastic film used to wrap or cover food.
□ **clingy** adjective.

clinic ▶ **noun** a place where medical treatment or advice is given.

clinical ▶ **adjective 1** relating to the observation and treatment of patients. **2** (of a place) very clean and plain. **3** efficient and showing no emotion.

SYNONYMS **1** *he seemed so clinical* **detached**, impersonal, dispassionate, indifferent, uninvolved, distant, remote, aloof, cold. **2** *the room was very clinical* **plain**, stark, austere, spartan, bleak, bare, functional, basic, institutional.
ANTONYMS emotional, luxurious.

□ **clinically** adverb.

clink ▶ **noun** a sharp ringing sound.
▶ **verb** make a clink.

clinker ▶ **noun** the stony remains from burnt coal or from a furnace.

clip¹ ▶ **noun 1** a flexible or spring-loaded device for holding objects together or in place. **2** a piece of jewellery that is fastened to a garment with a clip.

SYNONYMS *the clip on his briefcase* **fastener**, clasp, hasp, catch, hook, buckle, lock.

▶ **verb** (**clips**, **clipping**, **clipped**) fasten with a clip.

SYNONYMS *he clipped the pages together* **fasten**, attach, fix, join, pin, staple, tack.

clip² ▶ **verb** (**clips**, **clipping**, **clipped**) **1** cut or trim with shears or scissors. **2** trim the hair or wool of an animal. **3** hit quickly or lightly.

SYNONYMS **1** *I clipped the hedge* **trim**, prune, cut, snip, crop, shear, lop. **2** *his lorry clipped a van* **hit**, strike, graze, glance off, nudge, scrape.

▶ **noun 1** an act of clipping. **2** a short sequence taken from a film or broadcast. **3** informal a quick or light blow.

SYNONYMS *a film clip* **extract**, excerpt, snippet, fragment, trailer.

clipboard ▶ **noun** a board with a clip at the top, for holding papers and writing on.

clipped ▶ **adjective** (of speech) having short, sharp vowel sounds and clear pronunciation.

clipper ▶ **noun 1** (**clippers**) an instrument for clipping. **2** (in the past) a type of fast sailing ship.

clipping ▶ **noun 1** a small piece trimmed from something. **2** an article cut from a newspaper or magazine.

clique (*rhymes with* seek) ▶ **noun** a small group of people who do not allow other people to join them.
□ **cliquey** adjective.

clitoris /kli-tuh-riss/ ▶ **noun** the small sensitive organ just in front of the vagina.

cloak ▶ **noun** an outer garment that hangs loosely from the shoulders to the knees or ankles.

SYNONYMS **1** *the cloak over his shoulders* **cape**, robe, wrap, mantle. **2** *a cloak of secrecy* **cover**, veil, mantle, shroud, screen, blanket.

▶ **verb** cover or hide something.

SYNONYMS *a peak cloaked in mist* **conceal**, hide, cover, veil, shroud, mask, obscure, cloud, envelop, swathe, surround.

■ **cloak-and-dagger** involving secret activities.

cloakroom ▶ **noun 1** a room where coats and bags may be left. **2** Brit. a room that contains a toilet.

clobber informal ▶ **verb** (**clobbers**, **clobbering**, **clobbered**) hit someone hard.
▶ **noun** Brit. clothing and personal belongings.

cloche /klosh/ ▶ **noun 1** a small cover for protecting young or tender plants. **2** a woman's close-fitting bell-shaped hat.

clock ▶ **noun 1** an instrument that indicates the time. **2** informal a measuring device resembling a clock, such as a speedometer.
▶ **verb** informal **1** reach a particular speed or distance. **2** (**clock in** or **out** or Brit. **on** or **off**)

register the time you are arriving at or leaving work. **3** (**clock something up**) reach a total.

clockwise ▶ adverb & adjective in the direction of the movement of the hands of a clock.

clockwork ▶ noun a mechanism which has a spring and a system of interlocking wheels, used to make a mechanical clock or other device work.
■ **like clockwork** very smoothly and easily.

clod ▶ noun **1** a lump of earth. **2** informal a stupid person.

clodhopper ▶ noun informal **1** a large, heavy shoe. **2** a clumsy person.

clog ▶ noun a shoe with a thick wooden sole.
▶ verb (**clogs, clogging, clogged**) (often **clog something up**) block something up.

> SYNONYMS **block,** obstruct, congest, jam, choke, bung up, plug, stop up.

cloister ▶ noun a covered passage round an open courtyard in a convent, monastery, cathedral, etc.

cloistered ▶ adjective **1** having a cloister. **2** protected from the outside world.

clomp ▶ verb walk with a heavy tread.
▶ noun the sound of a heavy tread.

clone ▶ noun an animal or plant created from the cells of another, to which it is genetically identical.
▶ verb (**clones, cloning, cloned**) **1** create something as a clone. **2** make an identical copy of something.

close¹ (*rhymes with* dose) ▶ adjective **1** only a short distance away or apart in space or time. **2** (of a connection or likeness) strong. **3** (of two people) very affectionate and friendly. **4** (of observation or examination) done in a careful and thorough way.

> SYNONYMS **1** *the town is close to Leeds* **near,** nearby, adjacent, neighbouring, adjoining, abutting, at hand. **2** *a very close match* **even,** neck and neck. **3** *close friends* **intimate,** dear, bosom, close-knit, inseparable, devoted, faithful, special, firm. **4** *a close resemblance* **noticeable,** marked, distinct, pronounced, strong. **5** *a close examination* **careful,** detailed, thorough, minute, searching, painstaking, meticulous, rigorous. **6** *the weather was close* **humid,** muggy, stuffy, airless, heavy, sticky, sultry, stifling.
> ANTONYMS far, distant, one-sided, slight, cursory, fresh.

▶ adverb so as to be very near; with very little space between.
▶ noun Brit. a street of houses that is closed at one end.

■ **close-knit** (of a group of people) united by strong relationships. **at close quarters** (or **range**) from a position close to someone or something. **close shave** (or **close call**) informal a narrow escape from danger or disaster. **close-up** a photograph or sequence in a film that is taken from a very short distance.
□ **closely** adverb.

close² (*rhymes with* nose) ▶ verb (**closes, closing, closed**) **1** move something so as to cover an opening. **2** (also **close something up**) bring two parts of something together. **3** (**close on** or **in on**) gradually surround or get nearer to. **4** (**close around** or **over**) encircle and hold. **5** come or bring something to an end. **6** finish speaking or writing. **7** (often **close down**) stop trading or working. **8** bring a deal or arrangement to a conclusion.

> SYNONYMS **1** *she closed the door* **shut,** pull to, push to, slam. **2** *close the hole* **block,** stop up, plug, seal, bung up, clog up, choke, obstruct. **3** *he closed the meeting* **end,** conclude, finish, terminate, wind up. **4** *the factory is to close* **shut down,** close down, cease production, cease trading, be wound up, go out of business; informal fold, go to the wall, go bust. **5** *he closed a deal* **clinch,** settle, secure, seal, confirm, pull off, conclude, finalize; informal wrap up.
> ANTONYMS open, start.

▶ noun the end of an event or of a period of time or activity.

> SYNONYMS *the close of the talks* **end,** finish, conclusion.
> ANTONYMS beginning.

■ **close season** (or **closed season**) a period in the year when fishing or hunting is officially forbidden, or when a sport is not played.

closed ▶ adjective **1** not open or allowing people to go in. **2** not communicating with or influenced by other people.
■ **closed-circuit television** a television system used to watch people within a building, shopping centre, etc. **closed shop** a place of work where all employees must belong to a particular trade union.

closet ▶ noun chiefly N. Amer. **1** a tall cupboard or wardrobe. **2** a small room.
▶ verb (**closets, closeting, closeted**) shut yourself in a private room.
■ **in** (or **out of**) **the closet** not open (or open) about being homosexual.

close-up ▶ noun a photograph or film sequence taken at close range.

closure ▶ noun **1** the closing of something. **2** a feeling that an upsetting experience has been resolved.

clot ▸ noun 1 a lump that is formed when a thick liquid substance dries or becomes thicker. 2 *Brit. informal* a stupid person.
▸ verb (**clots, clotting, clotted**) form into clots.
■ **clotted cream** thick cream obtained by heating and cooling milk slowly.

cloth ▸ noun (plural **cloths**) 1 fabric made from a soft fibre such as wool or cotton. 2 a piece of cloth used for a particular purpose. 3 (**the cloth**) ministers of the Church.

> SYNONYMS 1 *a maker of cloth* **fabric**, material, textile(s). 2 *a cloth to wipe the table* **rag**, wipe, duster, flannel; *Austral.* washer.

clothe ▸ verb (**clothes, clothing, clothed**) 1 provide with clothes. 2 (**be clothed in**) be dressed in.

> SYNONYMS **dress**, attire, robe, garb, costume, swathe, deck (out), turn out, fit out, rig (out); *informal* get up.

clothes ▸ plural noun things worn to cover the body.

> SYNONYMS **clothing**, garments, attire, garb, dress, wear, costume, wardrobe; *informal* gear, togs; *Brit. informal* clobber; *N. Amer. informal* threads.

■ **clothes horse** a frame on which washed clothes are hung to dry.

clothing ▸ noun clothes.

> SYNONYMS See **CLOTHES.**

cloud ▸ noun 1 a mass of vapour floating in the atmosphere. 2 a mass of smoke, dust, etc. in the air. 3 a state or cause of gloom or anxiety.

> SYNONYMS *a cloud of exhaust smoke* **mass**, billow, pall, mantle, blanket.

▸ verb 1 (**cloud over**) (of the sky) become full of clouds. 2 become less clear. 3 (of someone's face or eyes) show sadness, anxiety, or anger.

> SYNONYMS *anger clouded my judgement* **confuse**, muddle, obscure.

■ **cloud cuckoo land** a state of unrealistic fantasy. **on cloud nine** very happy. **under a cloud** out of favour or suspected of having done wrong.
□ **cloudless** adjective.

cloudburst ▸ noun a sudden fall of very heavy rain.

cloudy ▸ adjective 1 covered with clouds. 2 (of a liquid) not clear or transparent.

> SYNONYMS 1 *a cloudy sky* **overcast**, dark, grey, black, leaden, murky, gloomy, sunless, starless. 2 *cloudy water* **murky**, muddy, milky, dirty, turbid.
> ANTONYMS clear, sunny.

clout *informal* ▸ noun 1 a heavy blow. 2 influence or power.

▸ verb hit someone hard.

clove¹ ▸ noun the dried flower bud of a tropical tree, used as a spice.

clove² ▸ noun any of the segments making up a bulb of garlic.

clove³ past of **CLEAVE¹.**

■ **clove hitch** a knot used to fasten a rope to a spar or another rope.

cloven past participle of **CLEAVE¹.**

■ **cloven hoof** the divided hoof of animals such as cattle, sheep, and deer.

clover ▸ noun a plant with white or pink flowers and a leaf with three lobes.

■ **in clover** in ease and luxury.

clown ▸ noun 1 an entertainer who does silly things to make people laugh. 2 a playful or silly person.

> SYNONYMS 1 *the class clown* **joker**, comedian, comic, wag, wit, jester, buffoon. 2 *bureaucratic clowns* **fool**, idiot, dolt, ass, ignoramus; *informal* moron, numbskull, halfwit, fathead; *Brit. informal* prat, berk, twit, twerp.

▸ verb 1 perform as a clown. 2 behave in a funny or silly way.

> SYNONYMS *Harvey clowned around* **fool around/about**, play the fool, play about/around, monkey about/around, joke; *informal* mess about/around, lark (about/around); *Brit. informal* muck about/around.

□ **clownish** adjective.

cloying ▸ adjective 1 too sweet and making you feel slightly sick. 2 too sentimental.

club¹ ▸ noun 1 a group of people who meet regularly for a particular activity. 2 a place where members can relax, eat meals, or stay overnight. 3 a nightclub with dance music.

> SYNONYMS 1 *a canoeing club* **society**, association, group, circle, league, guild, union. 2 *the city has great clubs* **nightclub**, bar; *informal* disco. 3 *the top club in the league* **team**, squad, side.

▸ verb (**clubs, clubbing, clubbed**) 1 (**club together**) combine with other people to do something. 2 *informal* go out to nightclubs.
□ **clubber** noun.

club² ▸ noun 1 a heavy stick used as a weapon. 2 a heavy stick with a thick head, used to hit the ball in golf. 3 (**clubs**) one of the four suits in a pack of playing cards, represented by a design of three black clover leaves on a short stem.

> SYNONYMS *a wooden club* **stick**, cudgel, truncheon, bludgeon, baton, mace, bat; *N. Amer.* blackjack, nightstick; *Brit. informal* cosh.

▸ verb (**clubs, clubbing, clubbed**) beat someone with a heavy stick.

SYNONYMS *he was clubbed with an iron bar* **hit,** beat, strike, cudgel, bludgeon, batter; informal clout, clobber; Brit. informal cosh.

■ **club foot** a deformed foot which is twisted so that the sole cannot be placed flat on the ground.

clubhouse ▶ noun a building having a bar and other facilities for club members.

cluck ▶ verb (of a hen) make a short, throaty sound.
▶ noun the short, throaty sound made by a hen.

clue ▶ noun a fact or piece of evidence that helps to clear up a mystery or solve a problem.

SYNONYMS **hint,** indication, sign, signal, pointer, lead, tip, evidence.

■ **not have a clue** informal have no idea about something. **clued up** informal well informed.

clueless ▶ adjective not able to understand or do something.

clump ▶ noun 1 a small group of trees or plants growing closely together. 2 a mass or lump of something. 3 the sound of a heavy tread.

SYNONYMS 1 *a clump of trees* **cluster,** thicket, group, bunch. 2 *a clump of earth* **lump,** clod, mass, chunk.

▶ verb 1 form into a clump or mass. 2 walk heavily.

clumpy ▶ adjective (of shoes or boots) thick and heavy.

clumsy ▶ adjective (clumsier, clumsiest) 1 awkward and badly coordinated. 2 tactless.

SYNONYMS 1 *she was terribly clumsy* **awkward,** uncoordinated, ungainly, graceless, lumbering, inelegant, inept, unskilful, accident-prone, all fingers and thumbs; informal cack-handed, ham-fisted, butterfingered; N. Amer. informal klutzy. 2 *a clumsy contraption* **unwieldy,** cumbersome, bulky, awkward.
ANTONYMS graceful, handy.

□ **clumsily** adverb **clumsiness** noun.

clung past and past participle of CLING.

clunk ▶ noun a dull, heavy sound.
▶ verb make a clunk.

cluster ▶ noun a group of similar things placed or occurring closely together.

SYNONYMS *clusters of berries* **bunch,** clump, mass, knot, group, clutch, huddle, crowd.

▶ verb (**cluster, clustering, clustered**) form a cluster.

SYNONYMS *they clustered around the television* **congregate,** gather, collect, group, assemble, huddle, crowd.

clutch¹ ▶ verb grasp something tightly.

SYNONYMS **grip,** grasp, clasp, cling to, hang on to, clench, hold, grab, snatch.

▶ noun 1 a tight grasp. 2 (**clutches**) power and control. 3 a mechanism in a vehicle that connects the engine with the axle and wheels.

clutch² ▶ noun 1 a group of eggs fertilized at the same time and laid in a single session. 2 a group of chicks hatched from the same clutch of eggs.

clutter ▶ verb (**clutters, cluttering, cluttered**) cover or fill with an untidy assortment of things.

SYNONYMS **litter,** mess up, be strewn, be scattered, cover, bury.

▶ noun things lying about untidily.

SYNONYMS **disorder,** chaos, disarray, untidiness, mess, confusion, litter, rubbish, junk.

cm ▶ abbreviation centimetres.

Co. ▶ abbreviation 1 company. 2 county.

co- ▶ prefix joint; mutual; together with another or others: *coexist* | *co-star*.

c/o ▶ abbreviation care of.

coach¹ ▶ noun 1 Brit. a comfortable single-decker bus used for longer journeys. 2 a railway carriage. 3 a large horse-drawn carriage.

SYNONYMS 1 *a journey by coach* **bus.** 2 *a railway coach* **carriage,** wagon; N. Amer. car.

coach² ▶ noun 1 a person who trains someone in a sport. 2 a person who gives private lessons in a subject.

SYNONYMS *a football coach* **instructor,** trainer, teacher, tutor, mentor, guru.

▶ verb give private lessons or training to someone.

SYNONYMS *he coached Richard in maths* **instruct,** teach, tutor, school, educate, drill, train.

coagulate /koh-ag-yoo-layt/ ▶ verb (**coagulates, coagulating, coagulated**) (of a liquid) thicken or become solid.
□ **coagulant** noun **coagulation** noun.

coal ▶ noun a black rock used as fuel, consisting mainly of carbon formed from the remains of ancient plants.
■ **coal tar** a thick black liquid produced when gas is made from coal.

coalesce /koh-uh-**less**/ ▶ verb (**coalesces, coalescing, coalesced**) come or bring together to form a single mass or whole.

C

coalface ▸ noun an exposed surface of coal in a mine.

coalfield ▸ noun a large area where there is a lot of coal underground.

coalition /koh-uh-**li**-sh'n/ ▸ noun a government made up of two political parties who have agreed to work together.

SYNONYMS **alliance,** union, partnership, bloc, federation, league, association, confederation, consortium, syndicate, amalgamation, merger.

coarse ▸ adjective 1 having a rough texture. 2 consisting of large grains or particles. 3 rude or vulgar.

SYNONYMS 1 *coarse blankets* **rough,** scratchy, prickly, wiry, harsh. 2 *coarse manners* **uncouth,** oafish, loutish, boorish, rude, impolite, ill-mannered, vulgar, common, rough. 3 *a coarse remark* **vulgar,** crude, rude, off colour, lewd, smutty, indelicate.
ANTONYMS soft, refined, polite.

■ **coarse fish** Brit. any freshwater fish other than salmon and trout.
□ **coarsely** adverb.

❗ Don't confuse **coarse** with **course,** which means 'a direction', as in *the plane changed course.*

coarsen ▸ verb make or become coarse.

coast ▸ noun a stretch of land next to or near the sea.

SYNONYMS *the west coast* **shore,** coastline, seashore, seaboard, shoreline, seaside.

▸ verb 1 move easily without using power. 2 do something without making much effort.

SYNONYMS *the car coasted down a hill* **freewheel,** cruise, taxi, drift, glide, sail.

■ **the coast is clear** there is no danger of being seen or caught.
□ **coastal** adjective.

coaster ▸ noun 1 a small mat for a glass. 2 a ship that sails along the coast from port to port.

coastguard ▸ noun an organization or person that keeps watch over coastal waters.

coastline ▸ noun the shape or appearance of the land along a coast.

coat ▸ noun 1 a full-length outer garment with sleeves. 2 an animal's covering of fur or hair. 3 an outer layer or covering. 4 a single layer of paint.

SYNONYMS 1 *a dog's coat* **fur,** hair, wool, fleece, hide, pelt, skin. 2 *a coat of paint* **layer,** covering, coating, skin, film, deposit.

▸ verb form or provide with a layer or covering.

SYNONYMS *the tube was coated with wax* **cover,** surface, plate, spread, daub, smear, plaster.

■ **coat of arms** a design used as a special symbol of a family, city, or organization.

coating ▸ noun a thin layer or covering.

coax ▸ verb 1 gently persuade someone to do something. 2 gently guide or move something.

SYNONYMS **persuade,** wheedle, cajole, get round, inveigle, manoeuvre; informal sweet-talk, soft-soap, twist someone's arm.

coaxial /koh-**ak**-si-uhl/ ▸ adjective (of a cable) having two wires, one wrapped round the other but separated by insulation.

cob ▸ noun 1 Brit. a loaf of bread. 2 the central part of an ear of maize. 3 (also **cobnut**) a hazelnut or filbert. 4 a sturdily built horse.

cobalt ▸ noun a silvery-white metallic element.

cobber ▸ noun Austral./NZ informal a companion or friend.

cobble¹ (or **cobblestone**) ▸ noun a small round stone used to cover road surfaces.
□ **cobbled** adjective.

cobble² ▸ verb (**cobbles, cobbling, cobbled**) (**cobble something together**) make up something roughly from materials that happen to be available.

cobbler ▸ noun 1 a person whose job is mending shoes. 2 chiefly N. Amer. a fruit pie with a cake-like crust.

cobra ▸ noun a highly poisonous snake native to Africa and Asia.

cobweb ▸ noun a spider's web.

cocaine ▸ noun an addictive drug made from the leaves of a tropical plant.

coccyx /**kok**-siks/ ▸ noun (plural **coccyges** /**kok**-si-jeez/ or **coccyxes**) a small triangular bone at the base of the spine.

cochineal /koch-i-**neel**/ ▸ noun a bright red dye used for colouring food.

cochlea /**kok**-li-uh/ ▸ noun (plural **cochleae** /**kok**-li-ee/) the spiral cavity of the inner ear.

cock ▸ noun a male chicken or game bird.
▸ verb 1 tilt or bend something in a particular direction. 2 raise the firing lever of a gun to make it ready to shoot. 3 (**cock something up**) Brit. informal spoil something by doing it badly.
■ **cock-a-hoop** very pleased. **cock and bull story** a very unlikely story.

cockade ▸ noun a rosette or knot of ribbons worn on a hat as part of a uniform.

cockatiel /kok-uh-**teel**/ ▶ noun a small Australian parrot with a crest.

cockatoo ▶ noun a kind of parrot with a crest.

cockcrow ▶ noun literary dawn.

cockerel ▶ noun a young cock.

cocker spaniel ▶ noun a small breed of spaniel with a silky coat.

cockeyed ▶ adjective informal **1** crooked. **2** stupid and impractical.

cockle ▶ noun an edible shellfish with a ribbed shell.

cockney ▶ noun (plural **cockneys**) **1** a person who was born in the East End of London. **2** the dialect or accent used in this area.

cockpit ▶ noun **1** a compartment for the pilot and crew in an aircraft or spacecraft. **2** the driver's compartment in a racing car.

cockroach ▶ noun a beetle-like insect with long antennae and legs.

cocksure ▶ adjective arrogantly confident.

cocktail ▶ noun **1** an alcoholic drink consisting of a spirit mixed with other ingredients. **2** a mixture.

cocky ▶ adjective (**cockier**, **cockiest**) too self-confident.

> SYNONYMS **arrogant**, conceited, overconfident, swollen-headed, self-important, egotistical, presumptuous, boastful.
> ANTONYMS modest.

□ **cockily** adverb **cockiness** noun.

cocoa ▶ noun a drink made from powdered cacao seeds, mixed with hot milk.

coconut ▶ noun **1** the large brown seed of a kind of palm tree, consisting of a woody husk lined with edible white flesh. **2** the white flesh of a coconut.
■ **coconut shy** a sideshow at a fair, in which you throw balls at a coconut and win it if you knock it off a stand.

> ✔ just **-o-**, not **-oa-**: coc**o**nut.

cocoon ▶ noun **1** a silky case spun by the larva of many insects, which protects it while it is turning into an adult. **2** something that envelops you in a protective or comforting way.
▶ verb wrap in a cocoon.

cod ▶ noun (plural **cod**) a large sea fish used for food.
■ **cod liver oil** oil obtained from the liver of cod, rich in vitamins D and A.

coda /**koh**-duh/ ▶ noun an extra passage marking the end of a piece of music.

coddle ▶ verb (**coddles**, **coddling**, **coddled**) give someone too much care and attention.

code ▶ noun **1** a system of words, figures, or symbols used to represent others secretly or briefly. **2** (also **dialling code**) a sequence of numbers dialled to connect a telephone line with another exchange. **3** instructions for a computer program. **4** a set of laws or rules.

> SYNONYMS **1** *a secret code* **cipher**. **2** *a strict social code* **convention**, etiquette, protocol, ethic. **3** *the penal code* **law(s)**, rules, regulations, constitution, system.

▶ verb (**codes**, **coding**, **coded**) **1** convert into a code. **2** (**coded**) expressed in an indirect way.

codeine /**koh**-deen/ ▶ noun a painkilling drug obtained from morphine.

codex ▶ noun (plural **codices** /**koh**-di-seez/ or **codexes**) an ancient manuscript in the form of a book.

codger ▶ noun informal an elderly man.

codicil /**koh**-di-sil/ ▶ noun a part added to a will that explains or alters an earlier part.

codify /**koh**-di-fy/ ▶ verb (**codifies**, **codifying**, **codified**) arrange a set of rules as a formal code.
□ **codification** noun.

codpiece ▶ noun (in the past) a pouch worn by a man over his trousers, covering the groin.

codswallop ▶ noun Brit. informal nonsense.

co-education ▶ noun the teaching of boys and girls together in the same schools.
□ **co-educational** adjective.

coefficient ▶ noun **1** Maths a quantity which is placed before another which it multiplies (e.g. 4 in $4x^2$). **2** Physics a multiplier or factor that measures some property.

coerce /**koh**-erss/ ▶ verb (**coerces**, **coercing**, **coerced**) force someone to do something.

> SYNONYMS **pressure**, press, push, constrain, force, compel, oblige, browbeat, bully, threaten, intimidate, dragoon, twist someone's arm; informal railroad, steamroller, lean on.

□ **coercion** noun **coercive** adjective.

coexist ▶ verb **1** exist at the same time or in the same place. **2** be together in harmony.
□ **coexistence** noun.

C. of E. ▶ abbreviation Church of England.

coffee ▶ noun a hot drink made from the seeds of a tropical shrub.
■ **coffee table** a small low table for putting cups, books, etc. on.

coffer ▶ noun a small chest for holding money or valuable items.

coffin ▶ noun a long box in which a dead body is buried or cremated.

cog ▶ noun **1** (also **cogwheel**) a wheel or bar with projections on its edge, which transfers motion by engaging with

c

projections on another wheel or bar. **2** a projection on a cog.

cogent /**koh**-juhnt/ ▶ adjective (of an argument) clear, logical, and convincing.
□ **cogency** noun **cogently** adverb.

cogitate /**koj**-i-tayt/ ▶ verb (**cogitates, cogitating, cogitated**) formal think carefully about something.
□ **cogitation** noun.

cognac /**kon**-yak/ ▶ noun brandy made in Cognac in western France.

cognition /kog-**ni**-sh'n/ ▶ noun the process of gaining knowledge through thought, experience, and the senses.
□ **cognitive** adjective.

cognizance (or **cognisance**) /kog-ni-zuhnss/ ▶ noun formal knowledge or awareness.
□ **cognizant** adjective.

cognoscenti /kog-nuh-**shen**-ti/ ▶ plural noun people who are well informed about a particular subject.

cohabit ▶ verb (**cohabits, cohabiting, cohabited**) live together and have a sexual relationship without being married.
□ **cohabitation** noun.

cohere ▶ verb (**coheres, cohering, cohered**) hold firmly together; form a whole.

coherent ▶ adjective **1** (of an argument or theory) logical and consistent. **2** able to speak clearly and logically.

SYNONYMS **logical,** reasoned, rational, sound, cogent, consistent, lucid, articulate, intelligible.
ANTONYMS muddled.

□ **coherence** noun **coherently** adverb.

cohesion /koh-**hee**-zh'n/ ▶ noun the fact of holding firmly together.

cohesive ▶ adjective holding or making something hold together.

cohort /**koh**-hort/ ▶ noun **1** a large group of people. **2** an ancient Roman military unit equal to one tenth of a legion.

coif ▶ noun /koyf/ a close-fitting cap worn by nuns under a veil.
▶ verb /kwahf, kwof/ (**coifs, coiffing, coiffed**) arrange someone's hair.

coiffure /kwah-**fyoor**/ ▶ noun a person's hairstyle.
□ **coiffured** adjective.

coil ▶ noun **1** a length of something wound in loops. **2** a contraceptive in the form of a small coil, fitted into the womb.
▶ verb arrange or form something into a coil.

SYNONYMS **wind,** loop, twist, curl, spiral, twine, wrap.

coin ▶ noun a flat disc or piece of metal used as money.

▶ verb **1** invent a new word or phrase. **2** make coins by stamping metal.

SYNONYMS **invent,** create, make up, conceive, originate, think up, dream up.

coinage ▶ noun **1** coins of a particular type. **2** a newly invented word or phrase.

coincide ▶ verb (**coincides, coinciding, coincided**) **1** happen at the same time or place. **2** be the same or similar; tally.

SYNONYMS **1** *the events coincided* **occur simultaneously,** happen together, co-occur, coexist. **2** *their interests do not always coincide* **tally,** correspond, agree, accord, match up, be compatible, dovetail, mesh; informal square.
ANTONYMS differ.

coincidence ▶ noun **1** a remarkable instance of things happening at the same time by chance. **2** the fact of things being the same or similar.

SYNONYMS **accident,** chance, providence, happenstance, fate, luck, fortune, fluke.

coincidental ▶ adjective resulting from a coincidence.

SYNONYMS **accidental,** chance, fluky, random, fortuitous.

□ **coincidentally** adverb.

coitus /**koh**-i-tuhss/ ▶ noun technical sexual intercourse.
□ **coital** adjective.

coke[1] ▶ noun a solid fuel made by heating coal in the absence of air.

coke[2] ▶ noun informal cocaine.

colander ▶ noun a bowl with holes in it, used to strain off liquid from food.

cold ▶ adjective **1** at a low temperature. **2** not feeling or showing emotion. **3** (of a colour) containing a lot of blue or grey and giving no impression of warmth. **4** (of a scent or trail) no longer fresh and easy to follow. **5** without preparation; unawares.

SYNONYMS **1** *a cold day* **chilly,** chill, cool, freezing, icy, wintry, frosty, bitter, raw; informal **nippy;** Brit. informal parky. **2** *a cold reception* **unfriendly,** inhospitable, unwelcoming, cool, frigid, frosty, distant, formal, stiff.
ANTONYMS hot, warm.

▶ noun **1** cold weather. **2** an infection causing a streaming nose and sneezing.
■ **cold-blooded 1** (of reptiles and fish) having a body that is the same temperature as the surrounding air. **2** heartless and cruel. **the cold shoulder** deliberately unfriendly behaviour. **cold sore** an inflamed blister near the mouth, caused by a virus. **cold snap** a brief period of cold weather. **cold turkey** unpleasant feelings experienced by someone who has suddenly

stopped taking a drug to which they are addicted. **cold war** a state of hostility between the Soviet Union and its allies and the Western powers after the Second World War. **get cold feet** lose your nerve. **in cold blood** deliberately cruel.
□ **coldly** adverb **coldness** noun.

coleslaw ▸ noun a dish of shredded raw cabbage and carrots mixed with mayonnaise.

colic ▸ noun severe pain in the abdomen caused by wind or an obstruction in the intestines.
□ **colicky** adjective.

collaborate ▸ verb (**collaborates, collaborating, collaborated**) **1** work together on an activity. **2** cooperate with your country's enemy.

> SYNONYMS **1** *they collaborated on the project* **cooperate,** join forces, work together, combine, pool resources, club together. **2** *they collaborated with the enemy* **fraternize,** conspire, collude, cooperate, consort.

□ **collaboration** noun **collaborative** adjective.

collaborator ▸ noun a person who collaborates.

> SYNONYMS **1** *his collaborator on the book* **co-worker,** partner, associate, colleague, confederate, assistant. **2** *a wartime collaborator* **sympathizer,** traitor, quisling, fifth columnist.

collage /kol-lah*z*h/ ▸ noun a form of art in which various materials are arranged and stuck to a backing.

collagen ▸ noun a protein found in skin and bone.

collapse ▸ verb (**collapses, collapsing, collapsed**) **1** suddenly fall down or give way. **2** fail and come to a sudden end.

> SYNONYMS **1** *the roof collapsed* **cave in,** fall in, subside, fall down, give (way), crumple, crumble, disintegrate. **2** *he collapsed last night* **faint,** pass out, black out, lose consciousness. **3** *she collapsed in tears* **break down,** go to pieces, be overcome; informal crack up. **4** *peace talks collapsed* **break down,** fail, fall through, fold, founder; informal flop, fizzle out.

▸ noun **1** the falling down or giving way of a structure. **2** a sudden failure.

> SYNONYMS **1** *the collapse of the roof* **cave-in,** disintegration. **2** *the collapse of the talks* **breakdown,** failure.

collapsible ▸ adjective able to be folded down.

collar ▸ noun **1** a band of material around the neck of a shirt or other garment. **2** a band put around the neck of a dog or cat.
▸ verb informal seize someone.

collarbone ▸ noun either of the pair of bones joining the breastbone to the shoulder blades.

collate ▸ verb (**collates, collating, collated**) collect and combine documents or information.
□ **collation** noun.

collateral ▸ noun something that you promise to give to someone if you cannot repay a loan.
▸ adjective additional but less important; secondary.

colleague ▸ noun a person that you work with.

> SYNONYMS **co-worker,** fellow worker, workmate, teammate, associate, partner, collaborator, ally, confederate.

collect ▸ verb **1** bring or gather things together. **2** come together and form a group. **3** go somewhere to fetch someone or something. **4** buy or find and keep items of a particular kind as a hobby.

> SYNONYMS **1** *he collected up the rubbish* **gather,** accumulate, assemble, amass, stockpile, pile up, heap up, store (up), hoard, save. **2** *a crowd soon collected* **gather,** assemble, meet, muster, congregate, convene, converge. **3** *I must collect the children* **fetch,** pick up, go/come and get, call for, meet. ANTONYMS distribute, disperse, deliver.

□ **collectable** (or **collectible**) adjective **collector** noun.

collected ▸ adjective **1** calm. **2** brought together in one volume or edition.

> SYNONYMS **calm,** cool, self-possessed, self-controlled, composed, poised, serene, tranquil, relaxed; informal laid-back. ANTONYMS excited, hysterical.

collection ▸ noun **1** the action of collecting. **2** a group of things that have been collected. **3** a time when mail is picked up from a postbox, or when rubbish is taken away.

> SYNONYMS **1** *a collection of stolen items* **hoard,** pile, heap, stock, store, stockpile, accumulation, reserve, supply, bank, pool, fund; informal stash. **2** *a collection of shoppers* **group,** crowd, body, gathering, knot, cluster. **3** *a collection of short stories* **anthology,** selection, compendium, compilation, miscellany. **4** *a collection for famine relief* **appeal;** informal whip-round.

collective ▸ adjective **1** done by or belonging to all the members of a group. **2** taken as a whole.

> SYNONYMS **common,** shared, joint, combined, mutual, communal, pooled,

c

united, allied, cooperative, collaborative.
ANTONYMS individual.

▶ noun a small business or project owned by all the people who work for it.

■ **collective noun** a noun that refers to a group of people or things (e.g. *staff* or *herd*).

☐ **collectively** adverb.

college ▶ noun **1** a place providing higher education or specialized training.
2 (in Britain) any of the independent institutions into which some universities are separated.

collegiate /kuh-lee-ji-uht/ ▶ adjective **1** having to do with a college or college students. **2** (of a university) composed of different colleges.

collide ▶ verb (collides, colliding, collided) move or bump into something.

SYNONYMS **crash**, hit, strike, run into, bump into.

collie ▶ noun (plural collies) a breed of sheepdog with long hair.

collier ▶ noun a coal miner.

colliery ▶ noun (plural collieries) a coal mine.

collision ▶ noun an instance when two or more things collide.

SYNONYMS **crash**, accident, smash; N. Amer. wreck; informal pile-up; Brit. informal shunt.

colloquial /kuh-loh-kwi-uhl/ ▶ adjective (of language) used in ordinary conversation.

SYNONYMS **informal**, conversational, everyday, familiar, popular, casual, idiomatic, slangy, vernacular.
ANTONYMS formal.

☐ **colloquialism** noun **colloquially** adverb.

colloquy /kol-luh-kwi/ ▶ noun (plural colloquies) formal a conference or conversation.

collude ▶ verb (colludes, colluding, colluded) make a secret plan with someone to do something illegal or dishonest.
☐ **collusion** noun.

collywobbles ▶ plural noun informal anxiety or nervousness.

cologne /kuh-lohn/ ▶ noun a type of light perfume.

Colombian ▶ noun a person from Colombia.
▶ adjective relating to Colombia.

colon¹ ▶ noun a punctuation mark (:) used before a list of items, a quotation, or an expansion or explanation.

colon² ▶ noun the main part of the large intestine, which leads to the rectum.
☐ **colonic** adjective.

colonel /ker-nuhl/ ▶ noun a rank of officer in the army and in the US air force, above a lieutenant colonel.

colonial ▶ adjective having to do with a colony or with colonialism.
▶ noun a person who lives in a colony.

colonialism ▶ noun the practice of gaining control over other countries and occupying them with settlers.
☐ **colonialist** noun & adjective.

colonist ▶ noun an inhabitant of a colony.

colonize (or colonise) ▶ verb (colonizes, colonizing, colonized) **1** make a colony in. **2** take over a place for your own use.

SYNONYMS **settle (in)**, people, populate, occupy, take over, invade.

☐ **colonization** noun.

colonnade ▶ noun a row of evenly spaced columns supporting a roof.

colony ▶ noun (plural colonies) **1** a country or area under the control of another country and occupied by settlers from that country. **2** a group of people of one nationality or race living in a foreign place. **3** a place where a group of people with a common interest live together. **4** a community of animals or plants living close together.

SYNONYMS **territory**, dependency, protectorate, satellite, settlement, outpost, province.

coloration (or colouration) ▶ noun the colours and markings of a plant or animal.

colossal ▶ adjective very large.

SYNONYMS **huge**, massive, enormous, gigantic, giant, mammoth, vast, immense, monumental, mountainous; informal monster, whopping, humongous; Brit. informal ginormous.
ANTONYMS tiny.

☐ **colossally** adverb.

colossus /kuh-loss-uhss/ ▶ noun (plural colossi /kuh-loss-I/) a person or thing that is very important or large in size.

colostomy /kuh-loss-tuh-mi/ ▶ noun (plural colostomies) a surgical operation in which the colon is shortened and the cut end is moved to a new opening made in the wall of the abdomen.

colour (US spelling color) ▶ noun **1** an object's property of producing different sensations on the eye as a result of the way it reflects or gives out light. **2** one of the parts into which light can be separated. **3** the use of all colours in photography or television. **4** the natural colouring of the skin as an indication of someone's race. **5** redness of the complexion. **6** interest and excitement.

SYNONYMS **1** *the lights changed colour* **hue**, shade, tint, tone, coloration. **2** *oil colour* **paint**, pigment, colourant, dye, stain.

▶ verb **1** change the colour of something.
2 blush. **3** influence something.

> SYNONYMS **1** *the wood was coloured blue*
> **tint,** dye, stain, tinge. **2** *the experience*
> *coloured her outlook* **influence,** affect,
> taint, warp, skew, distort.

■ **colour-blind** not able to see certain
colours.

coloured (US spelling **colored**) ▶ adjective
1 having a colour or colours. **2** offensive not
having white skin. **3** (in South Africa)
having parents who are of different races.
▶ noun **1** offensive a non-white person. **2** (in
South Africa) a person with parents of
different races.

colourful (US spelling **colorful**) ▶ adjective
1 having many or varied colours. **2** lively
and exciting; vivid.

> SYNONYMS **1** *a colourful picture* **brightly**
> **coloured,** vivid, vibrant, brilliant,
> radiant, gaudy, garish, multicoloured;
> informal jazzy. **2** *a colourful account* **vivid,**
> graphic, lively, animated, dramatic,
> fascinating, interesting, stimulating,
> scintillating, evocative.
> ANTONYMS drab, plain, boring.

□ **colourfully** adverb.

colouring (US spelling **coloring**) ▶ noun
1 the process or art of applying colour.
2 visual appearance in terms of colour. **3** a
substance used to colour something.

colourist (US spelling **colorist**) ▶ noun an
artist or designer who uses colour in a
special or skilful way.

colourless (US spelling **colorless**)
▶ adjective **1** without colour. **2** without
character or interest; dull.

colt ▶ noun a young male horse.

coltish ▶ adjective energetic but awkward in
movement or behaviour.

columbine ▶ noun a plant with purplish-
blue flowers.

column ▶ noun **1** an upright pillar
supporting a structure or standing alone as
a monument. **2** a line of people or vehicles
moving in the same direction. **3** a vertical
division of a page or piece of writing. **4** a
regular section of a newspaper or magazine
on a particular subject or by a particular
person.

> SYNONYMS **1** *arches supported by massive*
> *columns* **pillar,** post, support, upright,
> pier, pile. **2** *a column in the paper* **article,**
> piece, feature. **3** *we walked in a column*
> **line,** file, queue, procession, convoy;
> informal crocodile.

columnist ▶ noun a journalist who writes a
column in a newspaper or magazine.

coma ▶ noun a state of long-lasting deep
unconsciousness.

Comanche /kuh-**man**-chi/ ▶ noun (plural
Comanche or **Comanches**) a member of an
American Indian people of the south-
western US.

comatose ▶ adjective in a coma.

comb ▶ noun **1** an object with a row
of narrow teeth, used for smoothing
and neatening the hair. **2** a device for
separating and smoothing the fibres of raw
wool or cotton. **3** the red fleshy crest on the
head of a chicken.
▶ verb **1** neaten the hair with a comb. **2** search
systematically through something.
3 prepare wool or cotton for manufacture
with a comb.

> SYNONYMS **1** *she combed her hair* **groom,**
> brush, untangle, smooth, straighten,
> neaten, tidy, arrange. **2** *police combed*
> *the area* **search,** scour, explore, sweep.

combat ▶ noun fighting, especially between
armed forces.

> SYNONYMS *he was killed in combat* **battle,**
> fighting, action, hostilities, conflict, war,
> warfare.

▶ verb (**combats, combating, combated** or
combats, combatting, combatted) take
action to prevent something undesirable.

> SYNONYMS *they tried to combat the disease*
> **fight,** battle, tackle, attack, counter,
> resist.

combatant ▶ noun a person or group that is
fighting a battle or war.

combative ▶ adjective ready or eager to
fight or argue.

combe /koom/ ▶ noun Brit. a short valley or
hollow on a hillside or coastline.

combination ▶ noun **1** something that is
made up of distinct parts. **2** the action of
combining different things.

> SYNONYMS **mixture,** mix, blend, fusion,
> amalgamation, amalgam, merger,
> marriage, synthesis.

■ **combination lock** a lock that is opened
using a sequence of letters or numbers.

combine ▶ verb /kuhm-**byn**/ (**combines,**
combining, combined) **1** join or mix
together. **2** join together to do something.

> SYNONYMS **1** *he combines comedy with*
> *tragedy* **mix,** blend, fuse, amalgamate,
> integrate, merge, marry. **2** *teachers*
> *combined to tackle the problem* **unite,**
> collaborate, join forces, get together,
> team up.

▶ noun /**kom**-byn/ a group acting together for
a commercial purpose.
■ **combine harvester** a farming machine
that cuts a crop and separates out the grain
in one process.

combust ▸ verb catch fire or burn.
□ **combustion** noun.

combustible ▸ adjective able to catch fire and burn easily.

come ▸ verb (**comes, coming, came;** past participle **come**) **1** move towards or into a place near to the speaker. **2** arrive. **3** happen; take place. **4** have or achieve a certain position. **5** be sold or available in a particular form. **6** (**coming**) likely to be successful in the future.

SYNONYMS **1** *come and listen* **approach,** advance, draw close/closer, draw near/nearer. **2** (**coming**) *the coming election* **forthcoming,** imminent, impending, approaching. **3** (**coming**) *the coming of spring* **approach,** advance, advent, arrival, appearance, emergence. **4** *they came last night* **arrive,** get here/there, make it, appear, turn up, materialize; informal show (up), roll up. **5** *they came to a stream* **reach,** arrive at, get to, come across, run across, happen on, chance on, come upon, stumble on, end up at; informal wind up at. **6** *she comes from Belgium* **be from,** be a native of, hail from, live in, reside in. **7** *attacks came without warning* **happen,** occur, take place, come about, fall, crop up.
ANTONYMS go, leave.

■ **come about** happen. **come across 1** give a particular impression. **2** meet or find by chance. **come by** manage to get. **come into** inherit. **come off** succeed. **come on 1** (of a state or condition) begin. **2** (also **come upon**) meet or find by chance. **come out 1** (of a fact) become known. **2** declare publicly that you are homosexual. **come round** Brit. **1** recover consciousness. **2** be converted to another person's opinion. **come to 1** recover consciousness. **2** (of an expense) amount to. **come up** happen.

comeback ▸ noun **1** a return to fame or popularity. **2** informal a quick reply to a remark.

SYNONYMS **return,** recovery, resurgence, rally, upturn; Brit. fightback.

comedian ▸ noun (feminine **comedienne**) an entertainer whose act is intended to make people laugh.

SYNONYMS **1** *a famous comedian* **comic,** comedienne, funny man/woman, humorist, stand-up; N. Amer. tummler. **2** *Dad was such a comedian* **joker,** wit, wag, comic, clown; informal laugh, hoot.

comedown ▸ noun informal **1** a loss of status or importance. **2** a feeling of disappointment or depression.

comedy ▸ noun (plural **comedies**) **1** a film, play, or other entertainment intended to make people laugh. **2** a light-hearted play in which the characters find happiness after experiencing difficult situations.

SYNONYMS *the comedy in their work* **humour,** fun, hilarity, funny side, laughs, jokes.
ANTONYMS tragedy.

comely /kum-li/ ▸ adjective old use pleasant to look at.

comestibles ▸ plural noun formal items of food.

comet ▸ noun a mass of ice and dust with a long tail, moving around the solar system.

comeuppance ▸ noun (**get your comeuppance**) informal get the punishment or fate that you deserve.

comfort ▸ noun **1** a pleasant state of ease and relaxation. **2** (**comforts**) things that contribute to comfort. **3** consolation for unhappiness or anxiety.

SYNONYMS **1** *travel in comfort* **ease,** repose, luxury, prosperity. **2** *words of comfort* **consolation,** condolence, sympathy, commiseration, support, reassurance, cheer.
ANTONYMS discomfort.

▸ verb make someone less unhappy.

SYNONYMS *a friend tried to comfort her* **console,** support, reassure, soothe, calm, cheer, hearten.
ANTONYMS distress, depress.

□ **comforter** noun.

comfortable ▸ adjective **1** giving or enjoying physical comfort. **2** free from financial worry. **3** (of a victory) easily achieved.

SYNONYMS **1** *a comfortable lifestyle* **pleasant,** affluent, well-to-do, luxurious, opulent. **2** *a comfortable room* **cosy,** snug, warm, pleasant, agreeable, homely; informal comfy. **3** *comfortable clothes* **loose,** casual; informal comfy.
ANTONYMS hard, spartan, restricting.

□ **comfortably** adverb.

comfrey /kum-fri/ ▸ noun (plural **comfreys**) a plant with clusters of purplish or white flowers.

comfy ▸ adjective (**comfier, comfiest**) informal comfortable.

comic ▸ adjective **1** making people laugh; amusing. **2** having to do with comedy.

SYNONYMS **humorous,** funny, amusing, hilarious, comical, zany, witty.
ANTONYMS serious.

▸ noun **1** a comedian. **2** a children's magazine that contains comic strips.

SYNONYMS **comedian,** comedienne, funny man/woman, humorist, wit, joker.

■ **comic strip** a sequence of drawings that tell an amusing story.

comical ▸ adjective causing laughter, especially through being ridiculous.

SYNONYMS **1** *he could be quite comical* **funny,** humorous, droll, witty, amusing, entertaining; informal wacky. **2** *they look comical in those suits* **silly,** absurd, ridiculous, laughable, ludicrous, preposterous, foolish; informal crazy.
ANTONYMS serious, sensible.

☐ **comically** adverb.

comma ▸ noun a punctuation mark (,) showing a pause between parts of a sentence or separating items in a list.

command ▸ verb **1** give an order. **2** be in charge of a military unit.

SYNONYMS **1** *he commanded his men to retreat* **order,** tell, direct, instruct, call on, require. **2** *Jones commanded a tank squadron* **be in charge of,** be in command of, head, lead, control, direct, manage, supervise, oversee; informal head up.

▸ noun **1** an order. **2** authority. **3** a group of officers in control of a particular group or operation. **4** the ability to use or control something. **5** an instruction which makes a computer carry out one of its basic functions.

SYNONYMS **1** *officers shouted commands* **order,** instruction, direction. **2** *he had 160 men under his command* **authority,** control, charge, power, direction, dominion, guidance, leadership, rule, government, management, supervision, jurisdiction. **3** *a brilliant command of English* **knowledge,** mastery, grasp, comprehension, understanding.

commandant ▸ noun an officer in charge of a force or institution.

commandeer ▸ verb (**commandeers, commandeering, commandeered**) officially take possession of something for military purposes.

commander ▸ noun **1** a person in command. **2** the rank of naval officer below captain.

SYNONYMS **leader,** head, chief, overseer, director, controller; informal boss, skipper, head honcho; Brit. informal gaffer, guv'nor.

■ **commander-in-chief** (plural **commanders-in-chief**) an officer in charge of all of the armed forces of a country.

commanding ▸ adjective **1** having or showing authority. **2** having greater strength.

SYNONYMS **dominant,** controlling, superior, powerful, advantageous, favourable.
ANTONYMS disadvantageous, weak.

commandment ▸ noun a divine rule, especially one of the Ten Commandments.

commando ▸ noun (plural **commandos**) a soldier trained for carrying out raids.

commemorate ▸ verb (**commemorates, commemorating, commemorated**) honour the memory of.

SYNONYMS **celebrate,** remember, recognize, acknowledge, observe, mark, pay tribute to, pay homage to, honour, salute.

☐ **commemoration** noun **commemorative** adjective.

✔ The first **m** is double, but not the second: co**mm**e**m**orate.

commence ▸ verb (**commences, commencing, commenced**) begin.

SYNONYMS **begin,** inaugurate, start, initiate, launch into, open, get the ball rolling, get going, get under way, get off the ground, set about, embark on; informal kick off.
ANTONYMS conclude.

commencement ▸ noun the beginning of something.

commend ▸ verb **1** praise formally or officially. **2** recommend someone or something.

SYNONYMS **1** *we should commend him* **praise,** compliment, congratulate, applaud, salute, honour, sing the praises of, pay tribute to. **2** *I commend her to you without reservation* **recommend,** endorse, vouch for, speak for, support, back.
ANTONYMS criticize.

☐ **commendation** noun.

commendable ▸ adjective deserving praise.

SYNONYMS **admirable,** praiseworthy, creditable, laudable, meritorious, exemplary, honourable, respectable.
ANTONYMS reprehensible.

☐ **commendably** adverb.

commensurable ▸ adjective formal able to be measured by the same standard.

commensurate ▸ adjective (often **commensurate with**) matching something else in size, value, etc.

comment ▸ noun **1** a remark expressing an opinion or reaction. **2** discussion of an issue or event.

SYNONYMS **1** *their comments on her appearance* **remark,** observation, statement, pronouncement, judgement, reflection, opinion, view. **2** *a great deal of comment* **discussion,** debate, interest. **3** *a comment in the margin* **note,** annotation, commentary, footnote, gloss, explanation.

▸ verb express an opinion or reaction.

SYNONYMS **1** *they commented on the food* **remark on**, speak about, talk about, discuss, mention. **2** *'It will soon be night,' he commented* **remark**, observe, say, state, note, point out.

commentary ▸ noun (plural **commentaries**) **1** a broadcast account of a sports match or other event as it happens. **2** the expression of opinions about an event or situation. **3** a set of explanatory notes on a written work.

SYNONYMS **1** *the test match commentary* **narration**, description, report, review, voice-over. **2** *textual commentary* **explanation**, elucidation, interpretation, analysis, assessment, review, criticism, notes, comments.

commentate ▸ verb (**commentates, commentating, commentated**) give a commentary on an event.

commentator ▸ noun **1** a person who commentates. **2** a person who comments.

SYNONYMS **1** *a sports commentator* **reporter**, narrator, journalist, newscaster. **2** *a political commentator* **analyst**, pundit, critic, columnist, leader-writer, opinion-former, monitor, observer.

commerce ▸ noun the activity of buying and selling; trade.

SYNONYMS **trade**, trading, business, dealing, buying and selling, traffic, trafficking.

commercial ▸ adjective **1** concerned with commerce. **2** making or intended to make a profit.

SYNONYMS **1** *a vessel built for commercial purposes* **trade**, trading, business, mercantile, sales. **2** *a commercial organization* **profit-making**, materialistic, mercenary. ANTONYMS non-profit-making.

▸ noun a television or radio advertisement. □ **commercially** adverb.

commercialism ▸ noun emphasis on making as much profit as possible.

commercialize (or **commercialise**) ▸ verb (**commercializes, commercializing, commercialized**) manage something in a way designed to make a profit. □ **commercialization** noun.

commiserate ▸ verb (**commiserates, commiserating, commiserated**) express sympathy or pity; sympathize. □ **commiseration** noun.

commissar ▸ noun an official of the Communist Party responsible for political education.

commission ▸ noun **1** an instruction, command, or duty. **2** a formal request

for something to be produced. **3** a group of people given official authority to do something. **4** payment made to someone for selling goods or services. **5** the position of officer in the armed forces.

SYNONYMS **1** *the dealer's commission* **percentage**, share, premium, fee, bonus, royalty; informal cut, rake-off, slice; Brit. informal whack. **2** *a commission to design a monument* **contract**, engagement, assignment, booking, job. **3** *an independent commission* **committee**, board, council, panel, body.

▸ verb **1** order something to be made or produced. **2** bring something into working order. **3** (**commissioned**) having the rank of a military officer.

SYNONYMS **1** *he was commissioned to paint a portrait* **engage**, contract, book, employ, hire, recruit, take on, retain, appoint. **2** *they commissioned a sculpture* **order**.

■ **out of commission** not in working order.

commissionaire ▸ noun Brit. a uniformed door attendant at a hotel, theatre, etc.

commissioner ▸ noun **1** a member of an official commission. **2** a representative of the highest authority in an area.

commit ▸ verb (**commits, committing, committed**) **1** do something wrong or bad. **2** set aside something for a particular use. **3** (**commit yourself**) say that you will definitely do something. **4** put something in a safe place. **5** send someone to prison or a psychiatric hospital.

SYNONYMS **1** *he committed a murder* **carry out**, do, perpetrate, engage in, execute, accomplish, be responsible for; informal pull off. **2** *she was committed to their care* **entrust**, consign, assign, deliver, hand over. **3** *the judge committed him to prison* **consign**, send, confine.

commitment ▸ noun **1** the time, work, and loyalty that someone devotes to a cause, activity, or job. **2** a promise. **3** an engagement or duty that limits your freedom of action.

SYNONYMS **1** *the pressure of his commitments* **responsibility**, obligation, duty, liability, engagement, tie. **2** *her commitment to her students* **dedication**, devotion, allegiance, loyalty. **3** *he made a commitment* **promise**, vow, pledge, undertaking.

✔ There's a single **t** in the middle: commi**t**ment.

committal ▸ noun the sending of someone to prison or a psychiatric hospital, or for trial.

committed ▸ adjective devoting a lot of time and hard work to a cause, activity, or job.

> SYNONYMS **devoted,** dedicated, staunch, loyal, faithful, devout, firm, steadfast, unwavering, passionate, ardent, sworn. ANTONYMS apathetic.

committee ▸ noun a group of people appointed for a particular function by a larger group.

> ✔ double **m**, double **t**: committee.

commode ▸ noun a piece of furniture containing a concealed chamber pot.

commodious ▸ adjective formal roomy and comfortable.

commodity ▸ noun (plural **commodities**) **1** a raw material or agricultural product that can be bought and sold. **2** something useful or valuable.

commodore ▸ noun **1** the naval rank above captain. **2** the president of a yacht club.

common ▸ adjective (**commoner, commonest**) **1** happening, found, or done often; not rare. **2** without special qualities or position; ordinary. **3** of the most familiar type. **4** shared by two or more people or things. **5** belonging to or affecting the whole of a community. **6** Brit. not well mannered or tasteful, in a way supposedly typical of lower-class people.

> SYNONYMS **1** *a common occurrence* **frequent,** regular, everyday, normal, usual, ordinary, familiar, standard, commonplace. **2** *a common belief* **widespread,** general, universal, popular, mainstream, prevalent, rife, established, conventional, accepted. **3** *the common people* **ordinary,** normal, average, unexceptional, typical, simple. **4** *the common good* **collective,** communal, shared, community, public, popular, general. **5** *she's so common* **uncouth,** vulgar, coarse, rough, uncivilized, unsophisticated, unrefined, inferior, plebeian; informal plebby. ANTONYMS unusual, rare, individual, refined.

▸ noun **1** a piece of open land for the public to use. **2** (**the Commons**) the House of Commons.
■ **common denominator 1** Maths a number that can be divided exactly by all the numbers below the line in a set of fractions. **2** a feature shared by all members of a group. **the common market** the European Union. **common noun** a noun referring to a class of things (e.g. *plant, sea*) as opposed to a particular person or thing. **common or garden** Brit. informal of the usual or ordinary type. **common room** a room in a school or college for students

or staff to use outside teaching hours. **in common** shared.
  □ **commonly** adverb.

commoner ▸ noun an ordinary person as opposed to an aristocrat.

commonplace ▸ adjective ordinary.

> SYNONYMS See **common** (sense 1 of the adjective).

▸ noun a remark that is not new or interesting.

common sense ▸ noun good sense and judgement in practical matters.

> SYNONYMS **good sense,** native wit, good judgement, level-headedness, prudence, wisdom; informal horse sense, nous; Brit. informal common; N. Amer. informal smarts. ANTONYMS stupidity.

commonsensical ▸ adjective having common sense.

commonwealth ▸ noun **1** (**the Commonwealth**) an association consisting of the UK together with countries that used to be part of the British Empire. **2** an independent state or community.

commotion ▸ noun a state of confused and noisy disturbance.

> SYNONYMS **disturbance,** uproar, disorder, confusion, rumpus, fuss, furore, hue and cry, stir, storm, chaos, havoc, pandemonium.

communal ▸ adjective shared or done by all members of a community.

> SYNONYMS **1** *a communal kitchen* **shared,** joint, common. **2** *they farm on a communal basis* **collective,** cooperative, community. ANTONYMS private, individual.

  □ **communally** adverb.

commune[1] /kom-myoon/ ▸ noun a group of people living together and sharing possessions.

commune[2] /kuh-myoon/ ▸ verb (**communes, communing, communed**) (**commune with**) share your intimate thoughts or feelings with.

communicable ▸ adjective (of a disease) able to be passed on to other people.

communicant ▸ noun a person who receives Holy Communion.

communicate ▸ verb (**communicates, communicating, communicated**) **1** share or exchange information or ideas. **2** pass on or convey an emotion, disease, etc. **3** (**communicating**) (of two rooms) having a connecting door.

> SYNONYMS **1** *they communicate daily* **liaise,** be in touch, be in contact, have dealings, talk, speak. **2** *he communicated*

the news to his boss **convey,** tell, relay, transmit, impart, pass on, report, recount, relate. **3** *the disease is communicated easily* **transmit,** spread, transfer, pass on.

communication ▸ noun **1** the action of communicating. **2** a letter or message. **3** (**communications**) means of sending information or travelling.

SYNONYMS **1** *there was no communication between them* **contact,** dealings, relations, connection, correspondence, dialogue, conversation. **2** *an official communication* **message,** statement, announcement, report, dispatch, bulletin, disclosure, communiqué, letter, correspondence.

communicative ▸ adjective willing or eager to talk or pass on information.

SYNONYMS **forthcoming,** expansive, expressive, unreserved, vocal, outgoing, frank, open, candid, talkative, chatty. ANTONYMS uncommunicative.

communion ▸ noun **1** the sharing of intimate thoughts and feelings. **2** (also **Holy Communion**) the service of Christian worship at which bread and wine are made holy and shared; the Eucharist.

communiqué /kuh-myoo-ni-kay/ ▸ noun an official announcement or statement.

communism ▸ noun **1** a political system in which all property is owned by the community. **2** a system of this kind based on Marxism.

communist ▸ adjective & noun relating to communism; an adherent of communism.

SYNONYMS **collectivist,** Bolshevik, Marxist, Maoist, Soviet; informal, derogatory Commie, red.

community ▸ noun (plural **communities**) **1** a group of people living together in one place or having the same religion, race, etc. **2** (**the community**) the people of an area or country considered as a group.

SYNONYMS **society,** population, populace, people, public, residents, inhabitants, citizens.

■ **community service** socially useful work that an offender is sentenced to do instead of going to prison.

commute ▸ verb (**commutes, commuting, commuted**) **1** regularly travel some distance between your home and place of work. **2** reduce a sentence given to an offender to a less severe one.
□ **commuter** noun.

compact¹ ▸ adjective /kuhm-**pakt**/ **1** closely and neatly packed together; dense. **2** having all the necessary parts fitted into

a small space.

SYNONYMS **1** *extremely compact rugs* **dense,** tightly packed, compressed, thick, tight, firm, solid. **2** *a very compact phone* **neat,** small, handy, petite. **3** *her tale is compact and readable* **concise,** succinct, condensed, brief, pithy, to the point, short and sweet; informal snappy. ANTONYMS loose, bulky, lengthy.

▸ verb /kuhm-**pakt**/ press something together into a small space.

SYNONYMS *the rubbish is then compacted* **compress,** condense, pack down, tamp (down), flatten.

▸ noun /**kom**-pakt/ a small case containing face powder, a mirror, and a powder puff.
■ **compact disc** a small disc on which music or other digital information is stored.

compact² /**kom**-pakt/ ▸ noun a formal agreement between two or more parties.

SYNONYMS *the warring states signed a compact* **treaty,** pact, accord, agreement, contract, bargain, deal, settlement.

companion ▸ noun **1** a person that you spend time or travel with. **2** each of a pair of things intended to match each other, or that can be used together.

SYNONYMS **comrade,** fellow ..., partner, associate, escort, compatriot, confederate, friend; informal pal, chum, crony; Brit. informal mate; N. Amer. informal buddy.

□ **companionship** noun.

companionable ▸ adjective friendly and sociable.
□ **companionably** adverb.

company ▸ noun (plural **companies**) **1** a commercial business. **2** the fact of being with other people. **3** a guest or guests. **4** a number of people gathered together. **5** a unit of soldiers. **6** a group of actors, singers, or dancers who perform together.

SYNONYMS **1** *an oil company* **firm,** business, corporation, establishment, agency, office, house, institution, concern, enterprise, consortium, syndicate; informal outfit. **2** *I enjoy his company* **companionship,** fellowship, society, presence. **3** *a company of infantry* **unit,** section, detachment, corps, squad, platoon.

comparable ▸ adjective similar to someone or something else and able to be compared.

SYNONYMS **1** *comparable incomes* **similar,** close, near, approximate, equivalent, proportionate. **2** *nobody is comparable with him* **equal to,** as good as, in the same league as, on a level with, a match for. ANTONYMS incomparable.

□ **comparably** adverb.

comparative ▶ adjective **1** measured or judged by comparing one thing with another. **2** involving comparison between two or more subjects. **3** (of an adjective or adverb) expressing a higher degree of a quality, but not the highest possible (e.g. *braver*).
□ **comparatively** adverb.

> ✔ compar**ative**, not **-itive**.

compare ▶ verb (**compares**, **comparing**, **compared**) **1** (often **compare something to** or **with**) estimate or measure the ways in which one person or thing is similar to or unlike another. **2** (**compare something to**) point out the ways in which one person or thing is similar to another. **3** (usu. **compare with**) be similar to another thing or person.

> SYNONYMS **1** *we compared the two portraits* **contrast**, balance, set against, weigh up. **2** *he was compared to Wagner* **liken**, equate, class with, bracket with. **3** *the porcelain compares with Dresden china* **be as good as**, be comparable to, bear comparison with, be the equal of, match up to, be on a par with, be in the same league as, come close to, rival.

comparison ▶ noun **1** the action of comparing. **2** the quality of being similar.

> SYNONYMS *there's no comparison between them* **resemblance**, likeness, similarity, correspondence.

compartment ▶ noun a separate section of a structure or container.

> SYNONYMS **bay**, locker, recess, alcove, cell, cubicle, pod, pigeonhole, cubbyhole.

compartmentalize (or **compartmentalise**) ▶ verb (**compartmentalizes**, **compartmentalizing**, **compartmentalized**) divide into categories or sections.

compass ▶ noun **1** an instrument containing a pointer which shows the direction of magnetic north. **2** (also **compasses**) an instrument for drawing circles, consisting of two arms linked by a movable joint. **3** range or scope.

> SYNONYMS **scope**, range, extent, reach, span, breadth, ambit, limits, parameters, bounds.

compassion ▶ noun sympathetic pity and concern for the sufferings of other people.

> SYNONYMS **sympathy**, empathy, understanding, fellow feeling, pity, care, concern, sensitivity, kindness.
> ANTONYMS indifference, cruelty.

compassionate ▶ adjective feeling or showing compassion.

> SYNONYMS **sympathetic**, understanding, pitying, caring, sensitive, warm, loving, kind.
> ANTONYMS unsympathetic, uncaring.

□ **compassionately** adverb.

compatible ▶ adjective **1** able to exist or be used together. **2** (of two people) able to have a good relationship; well suited. **3** (usu. **compatible with**) consistent or in keeping.

> SYNONYMS **well matched**, (well) suited, like-minded, in tune, in harmony, in keeping, consistent, consonant; informal on the same wavelength.
> ANTONYMS incompatible.

□ **compatibility** noun.

> ✔ compat**ible**, not **-able**.

compatriot ▶ noun a person from the same country; a fellow citizen.

compel ▶ verb (**compels**, **compelling**, **compelled**) **1** force someone to do something. **2** make something happen.

> SYNONYMS **force**, pressure, coerce, dragoon, press, push, oblige, require, make; informal lean on, railroad, put the screws on.

compelling ▶ adjective powerfully gaining people's attention or admiration.

> SYNONYMS **1** *a compelling performance* **enthralling**, captivating, gripping, riveting, spellbinding, mesmerizing, absorbing. **2** *a compelling argument* **convincing**, persuasive, cogent, irresistible, powerful, strong.
> ANTONYMS boring, weak.

□ **compellingly** adverb.

compendium ▶ noun (plural **compendiums** or **compendia**) **1** a collection of information about a subject. **2** a collection of similar items.

compensate ▶ verb (**compensates**, **compensating**, **compensated**) **1** give someone something to reduce or balance the bad effect of loss, suffering, or injury. **2** (**compensate for**) reduce or balance something bad by having an opposite force or effect.

> SYNONYMS **1** *we agreed to compensate him for his loss* **recompense**, repay, pay back, reimburse, remunerate, indemnify. **2** *his flair compensated for his faults* **balance (out)**, counterbalance, counteract, offset, make up for, cancel out.

□ **compensatory** adjective.

compensation ▶ noun **1** something given to compensate for loss, suffering, or injury. **2** something that compensates for something bad.

c

SYNONYMS **recompense**, repayment, reimbursement, remuneration, redress, amends, damages; N. Amer. informal **comp.**

compère /kom-pair/ Brit. ▶ noun a person who introduces the different acts that are performing in one show.
▶ verb (**compères, compèring, compèred**) act as a compère for.

compete ▶ verb (**competes, competing, competed**) try to gain or win something by defeating other people.

SYNONYMS **1** *they competed in a tennis tournament* **take part,** participate, be a contestant, play, enter, go in for. **2** *they had to compete with other firms* **contend,** vie, battle, jockey, go head to head, pit yourself against, challenge, take on.

competence ▶ noun **1** the ability to do something well. **2** the state of being adequate.

SYNONYMS **1** *my technical competence* **ability,** capability, proficiency, accomplishment, expertise, skill, prowess; informal **know-how. 2** *the competence of the system* **adequacy,** suitability, fitness.
ANTONYMS incompetence, inadequacy.

competent ▶ adjective **1** having the necessary skill or knowledge to do something successfully. **2** satisfactory, though not outstanding.

SYNONYMS **1** *a competent carpenter* **able,** capable, proficient, adept, accomplished, skilful, skilled, expert. **2** *she spoke competent French* **satisfactory,** acceptable, adequate, passable, reasonable, tolerable, fair, average, not bad, all right, middling; informal **OK.**
ANTONYMS incompetent, inadequate.

□ **competently** adverb.

competition ▶ noun **1** the activity of competing against other people. **2** an event or contest in which people compete. **3** the person or people that you are competing against.

SYNONYMS **1** *Stephanie won the competition* **contest,** tournament, championship. **2** *I'm not interested in competition* **rivalry,** competitiveness, conflict; informal **keeping up with the Joneses. 3** *we must stay ahead of the competition* **opposition,** rivals, other side, field, enemy; informal **other guy.**

competitive ▶ adjective **1** involving competition. **2** strongly wanting to be more successful than other people. **3** as good as or better than others of a similar nature.

SYNONYMS **1** *a competitive player* **ambitious,** zealous, keen, combative, aggressive; informal **go-ahead. 2** *a highly*

competitive industry **ruthless,** aggressive, fierce, cut-throat; informal **dog-eat-dog. 3** *competitive prices* **reasonable,** moderate, keen, low, cheap, budget, bargain, rock-bottom, bargain-basement.
ANTONYMS apathetic, exorbitant.

□ **competitively** adverb.

competitor ▶ noun **1** a person who takes part in a sports contest. **2** an organization that competes with others in business.

SYNONYMS **1** *the competitors in the race* **contestant,** contender, challenger, participant, entrant, player. **2** *our European competitors* **rival,** challenger, opponent, competition, opposition.
ANTONYMS partner, teammate, ally.

compilation ▶ noun **1** a book, record, etc. compiled from different sources. **2** the process of compiling something.

compile ▶ verb (**compiles, compiling, compiled**) produce a book, record, etc. by bringing together material from different sources.

SYNONYMS **assemble,** put together, make up, collate, compose, organize, arrange, gather, collect.

□ **compiler** noun.

complacency ▶ noun smug self-satisfaction.

SYNONYMS **smugness,** self-satisfaction, self-congratulation, self-regard.

complacent ▶ adjective smugly satisfied with yourself.

SYNONYMS **smug,** self-satisfied, self-congratulatory, resting on your laurels.

□ **complacently** adverb.

complain ▶ verb **1** express dissatisfaction or annoyance. **2** (**complain of**) state that you are suffering from a particular symptom.

SYNONYMS **protest,** grumble, whine, bleat, carp, cavil, grouse, make a fuss, object, find fault; informal **whinge, gripe, moan, bitch.**

complainant ▶ noun Law a plaintiff.

complaint ▶ noun **1** an act of complaining. **2** a reason to be dissatisfied. **3** a minor illness or medical condition.

SYNONYMS **1** *they lodged a complaint* **protest,** objection, grievance, grouse, grumble, criticism; informal **gripe, whinge. 2** *a kidney complaint* **disorder,** disease, illness, sickness, ailment, infection, condition, problem, upset, trouble.

complaisant /kuhm-**play**-z'nt/ ▶ adjective willing to please other people or to accept their behaviour without protest.

complement ▶ noun /kom-pli-muhnt/ **1** a thing that contributes extra features to something else so as to improve it. **2** the number or quantity that makes something complete. **3** Grammar a word or words used with a verb to complete the meaning (e.g. *happy* in *we are happy*).

> SYNONYMS **1** *the perfect complement to the food* **accompaniment,** companion, addition, supplement, accessory, finishing touch. **2** *a full complement of lifeboats* **amount,** contingent, capacity, allowance, quota.
> ANTONYMS contrast.

▶ verb /**kom**-pli-ment/ add to something in a way that improves it.

> SYNONYMS *this sauce complements the dessert* **accompany,** go with, round off, set off, suit, harmonize with, enhance, complete.
> ANTONYMS contrast with.

❗ Don't confuse **complement** and **compliment**. **Complement** means 'add to something in a way that improves it', while **compliment** means 'politely congratulate or praise'.

complementary ▶ adjective combining so as to form a complete whole or to improve each other's qualities.

> SYNONYMS **harmonious,** compatible, corresponding, matching, reciprocal.
> ANTONYMS incompatible.

▫ **complementary medicine** medical therapy that is not part of scientific medicine, e.g. acupuncture.

complete ▶ adjective **1** having all the necessary parts. **2** having run its course; finished. **3** to the greatest extent or degree; total. **4** skilled at every aspect of an activity.

> SYNONYMS **1** *the complete text* **entire,** whole, full, total, uncut, unabridged, unexpurgated. **2** *their research was complete* **finished,** ended, concluded, completed; informal wrapped up, sewn up. **3** *a complete fool* **absolute,** utter, out-and-out, total, downright, prize, perfect, unqualified, unmitigated, sheer; N. Amer. full-bore.
> ANTONYMS partial, unfinished.

▶ verb (**completes, completing, completed**) **1** finish making or doing something. **2** make something complete. **3** write the required information on a form.

> SYNONYMS **1** *he had to complete his training* **finish,** end, conclude, finalize, wind up; informal wrap up. **2** *the outfit was completed with a veil* **finish off,** round off, top off, crown, cap. **3** *complete the application form* **fill in/out,** answer.

▫ **completion** noun.

completely ▶ adverb totally.

> SYNONYMS **totally,** entirely, wholly, thoroughly, fully, utterly, absolutely, perfectly, downright.

complex ▶ adjective **1** consisting of many different and connected parts. **2** not easy to understand; complicated.

> SYNONYMS **1** *a complex structure* **compound,** composite, multiplex. **2** *a complex situation* **complicated,** involved, intricate, convoluted, elaborate, difficult; Brit. informal fiddly.
> ANTONYMS simple.

▶ noun **1** a group of similar buildings or facilities on the same site. **2** a network of linked things. **3** a group of subconscious ideas or feelings that influence a person's mental state or behaviour.

> SYNONYMS **1** *a complex of roads* **network,** system, nexus, web. **2** *he had a complex about losing his hair* **obsession,** fixation, preoccupation, neurosis; informal hang-up, thing.

▫ **complexity** noun (plural **complexities**).

complexion ▶ noun **1** the natural condition of the skin of a person's face. **2** the general character of something.

> SYNONYMS **1** *a pale complexion* **skin,** skin colour/tone, colouring. **2** *governments of all complexions* **kind,** nature, character, colour, persuasion, outlook.

compliance ▶ noun the action of complying.

compliant ▶ adjective **1** meeting rules or standards. **2** too ready to do what other people want.

complicate ▶ verb (**complicates, complicating, complicated**) make something less easy to understand or deal with.

> SYNONYMS **make (more) difficult,** make complicated, mix up, confuse, muddle, compound.
> ANTONYMS simplify.

complicated ▶ adjective **1** consisting of many connected elements; intricate. **2** involving many different and confusing aspects.

> SYNONYMS **1** *a complicated stereo system* **compound,** composite, multiplex. **2** *a long and complicated saga* **involved,** intricate, complex, convoluted, elaborate, difficult; Brit. informal fiddly.
> ANTONYMS simple, straightforward.

complication ▶ noun **1** a circumstance that complicates something; a difficulty. **2** an involved or confused state. **3** an extra disease or condition which makes an existing one worse.

> SYNONYMS **difficulty,** problem, obstacle, hurdle, stumbling block, snag, catch,

hitch; Brit. spanner in the works; informal headache.

complicit ▸ adjective involved with other people in an unlawful activity.

complicity ▸ noun involvement with other people in an unlawful activity.

compliment ▸ noun /kom-pli-muhnt/ **1** a remark that expresses praise or admiration. **2** (**compliments**) formal greetings.

> SYNONYMS *an unexpected compliment* **tribute,** accolade, commendation, pat on the back; (**compliments**) praise, acclaim, admiration, flattery, congratulations.
> ANTONYMS criticism, insult.

▸ verb /kom-pli-ment/ politely congratulate or praise.

> SYNONYMS *they complimented him on his performance* **praise,** pay tribute to, flatter, commend, acclaim, applaud, salute, congratulate.
> ANTONYMS criticize.

> ❗ Don't confuse **compliment** and **complement**: see the note at **COMPLEMENT**.

complimentary ▸ adjective **1** praising or approving. **2** given free of charge.

> SYNONYMS **1** *complimentary remarks* **flattering,** appreciative, congratulatory, admiring, approving, favourable, glowing. **2** *complimentary tickets* **free (of charge),** gratis, donated, courtesy; informal on the house.
> ANTONYMS critical.

comply ▸ verb (**complies, complying, complied**) (**comply with**) **1** do what someone wants or tells you to do. **2** meet specified standards.

> SYNONYMS **obey,** observe, abide by, adhere to, conform to, follow, respect, go along with.
> ANTONYMS disobey.

component ▸ noun a part of a larger whole.

> SYNONYMS **part,** piece, bit, element, constituent, ingredient, unit, module.

comport ▸ verb (**comport yourself**) formal behave in a particular way.

compose ▸ verb (**composes, composing, composed**) **1** make up a whole. **2** create a work of art, especially music or poetry. **3** arrange in an orderly or artistic way.

> SYNONYMS **1** *a poem composed by Shelley* **write,** devise, make up, think up, produce, invent, pen, author. **2** *how to compose a photograph* **organize,** arrange, construct, set out. **3** *the congress is composed of ten senators* **make up,** constitute, form, comprise.

☐ **composer** noun.

composed ▸ adjective calm and in control of your feelings.

> SYNONYMS **calm,** collected, cool (as a cucumber), self-possessed, poised, serene, relaxed, at ease, unruffled, unperturbed; informal unflappable, together, laid-back.
> ANTONYMS excited.

composite /kom-puh-zit/ ▸ adjective made up of several parts.
▸ noun a thing made up of several parts.

composition ▸ noun **1** the way in which something is made up. **2** a work of music, literature, or art. **3** an essay written by a school pupil. **4** the action of composing.

> SYNONYMS **1** *the composition of the council* **make-up,** constitution, configuration, structure, formation, anatomy, organization. **2** *a literary composition* **work (of art),** creation, opus, piece. **3** *the composition of a poem* **writing,** creation, formulation, compilation. **4** *a school composition* **essay,** paper, study, piece of writing; N. Amer. theme. **5** *the composition of the painting* **arrangement,** layout, proportions, balance, symmetry.

compositor ▸ noun a person who arranges type or keys material for printing.

compos mentis /kom-poss men-tiss/ ▸ adjective having full control of your mind.

compost ▸ noun decayed organic material added to soil as a fertilizer.

composure ▸ noun the state of being calm and self-controlled.

compote /kom-poht/ ▸ noun fruit preserved or cooked in syrup.

compound¹ ▸ noun /kom-pownd/ **1** a thing made up of two or more separate elements. **2** a substance formed from two or more elements chemically united in fixed proportions.

> SYNONYMS *a compound of two materials* **amalgam,** blend, mixture, mix, alloy.

▸ adjective /kom-pownd/ made up or consisting of several parts.

> SYNONYMS *a compound substance* **composite,** complex, multiple.
> ANTONYMS simple.

▸ verb /kuhm-pownd/ **1** make up a whole from several elements. **2** make something bad worse.

> SYNONYMS **1** *soap compounded with disinfectant* **mix,** combine, blend. **2** *his illness compounds their problems* **aggravate,** exacerbate, worsen, add to, augment, intensify, heighten, increase.
> ANTONYMS separate, alleviate.

■ **compound fracture** an injury in which a broken bone pierces the skin.

compound² /kom-pownd/ ▸ noun a large open area enclosed by a fence.

comprehend ▸ verb understand something.

> SYNONYMS **understand**, grasp, see, take in, follow, make sense of, fathom; informal work out, figure out, get.

comprehensible ▸ adjective able to be understood.

> SYNONYMS **intelligible**, understandable, accessible, self-explanatory, clear, plain, straightforward.
> ANTONYMS opaque.

comprehension ▸ noun 1 the action of understanding. 2 the ability to understand.

> SYNONYMS **understanding**, grasp, mastery, conception, knowledge, awareness.
> ANTONYMS ignorance.

comprehensive ▸ adjective 1 including or dealing with all or nearly all aspects of something. 2 Brit. (of secondary education) in which children of all abilities are educated in one school. 3 (of a victory or defeat) by a large margin.

> SYNONYMS **inclusive**, all-inclusive, complete, thorough, full, extensive, all-embracing, blanket, exhaustive, detailed, sweeping, wholesale, broad, wide-ranging.
> ANTONYMS limited.

▸ noun Brit. a comprehensive school.
□ **comprehensively** adverb.

compress ▸ verb /kuhm-press/ 1 flatten by pressure; force into less space. 2 squeeze or press two things together. 3 alter the form of computer data so that it takes up less space on a disk or magnetic tape.

> SYNONYMS 1 *it is coconut compressed into a slab* **squeeze**, press, squash, crush, compact. 2 *the material has been compressed into 17 pages* **shorten**, abridge, condense, abbreviate, contract, telescope, summarize, precis.
> ANTONYMS expand, pad out.

▸ noun /kom-press/ an absorbent pad pressed on to part of the body to relieve inflammation or stop bleeding.
□ **compression** noun.

compressor ▸ noun a machine used to supply air at increased pressure.

comprise ▸ verb (**comprises**, **comprising**, **comprised**) 1 be made up of; consist of. 2 (also **be comprised of**) make up a whole.

> SYNONYMS 1 *the country comprises twenty states* **consist of**, be made up of, be composed of, contain. 2 *this breed comprises half the herd* **make up**, constitute, form, account for.

compromise ▸ noun 1 an agreement reached by each side giving way on some points. 2 something that is midway between different or conflicting elements: *a compromise between price and quality of output.*

> SYNONYMS *they reached a compromise* **agreement**, understanding, settlement, terms, deal, trade-off, bargain, middle ground.
> ANTONYMS intransigence.

▸ verb (**compromises**, **compromising**, **compromised**) 1 give way on some points in order to settle a dispute. 2 accept something that is less good than you would like. 3 cause someone danger or embarrassment by behaving in an indiscreet or reckless way.

> SYNONYMS 1 *we compromised* **meet each other halfway**, come to an understanding, make a deal, make concessions, find a happy medium, strike a balance. 2 *his actions could compromise his reputation* **undermine**, weaken, damage, harm, jeopardize, prejudice.

comptroller /kuhn-**troh**-ler, komp-**troh**-ler/ ▸ noun a person in charge of the financial affairs of an organization.

compulsion ▸ noun 1 pressure to do something. 2 an irresistible urge to do something.

> SYNONYMS 1 *he is under no compulsion to go* **obligation**, pressure, coercion. 2 *a compulsion to tell the truth* **urge**, impulse, need, desire, drive, obsession, fixation, addiction.

compulsive ▸ adjective 1 done because of an irresistible urge. 2 unable to stop yourself doing something. 3 irresistibly exciting.

> SYNONYMS 1 *a compulsive desire* **irresistible**, uncontrollable, compelling, overwhelming. 2 *compulsive eating* **obsessive**, obsessional, addictive, uncontrollable. 3 *a compulsive liar* **inveterate**, chronic, incorrigible, incurable, hopeless, persistent, habitual; informal pathological. 4 *it's compulsive viewing* **fascinating**, compelling, gripping, riveting, engrossing, enthralling, captivating.

□ **compulsively** adverb.

compulsory ▸ adjective required by law or a rule; obligatory.

> SYNONYMS **obligatory**, mandatory, required, requisite, necessary, binding, enforced, prescribed.
> ANTONYMS optional.

compunction ▸ noun a feeling of guilt about doing something wrong.

computation ▸ noun 1 mathematical calculation. 2 the use of computers.
□ **computational** adjective.

compute ▸ verb (**computes, computing, computed**) calculate a figure or amount.

> SYNONYMS **calculate,** work out, reckon, determine, evaluate, add up, total.

computer ▸ noun an electronic device capable of storing and processing information according to a set of instructions.
□ **computing** noun.

computerize (or **computerise**)
▸ verb (**computerizes, computerizing, computerized**) convert to a system controlled by or stored on computer.

comrade ▸ noun 1 (among men) a person who shares your activities or is a fellow member of an organization. 2 a fellow soldier.

> SYNONYMS **companion,** friend, colleague, associate, partner, ally; Brit. informal mate; N. Amer. informal buddy.

□ **comradeship** noun.

con¹ informal ▸ verb (**cons, conning, conned**) deceive someone into doing or believing something.
▸ noun a deception of this kind.
■ **con man** a man who cheats people after gaining their trust.

con² ▸ noun (usu. in **pros and cons**) a disadvantage of or argument against something.

concatenation ▸ noun a series of interconnected things.

concave ▸ adjective having an outline or surface that curves inwards.
□ **concavity** noun.

conceal ▸ verb 1 stop someone or something being seen. 2 keep something secret.

> SYNONYMS 1 *clouds concealed the sun* **hide,** screen, cover, obscure, block out, blot out, mask. 2 *he concealed his true feelings* **keep secret,** hide, disguise, mask, veil, bottle up; informal keep a/the lid on.
> ANTONYMS reveal, confess.

□ **concealment** noun.

concede ▸ verb (**concedes, conceding, conceded**) 1 finally admit that something is true. 2 give up a possession, advantage, or right. 3 admit defeat in a match or contest. 4 fail to prevent an opponent scoring a goal or point.

> SYNONYMS 1 *I had to concede that I'd overreacted* **admit,** acknowledge, accept, allow, grant, recognize, own, confess,

agree. 2 *he eventually conceded the title* **surrender,** yield, give up, relinquish, hand over.
> ANTONYMS deny, retain.

conceit ▸ noun 1 too much pride in yourself. 2 an artistic effect. 3 a complicated metaphor.

> SYNONYMS **vanity,** pride, arrogance, egotism, self-importance, narcissism, self-admiration.
> ANTONYMS humility.

conceited ▸ adjective too proud of yourself.

> SYNONYMS **vain,** proud, arrogant, egotistic, self-satisfied, self-important, narcissistic, full of yourself; informal big-headed, stuck-up.

conceivable ▸ adjective able to be imagined or understood.
□ **conceivably** adverb.

conceive ▸ verb (**conceives, conceiving, conceived**) 1 become pregnant with a child. 2 form an idea in your mind.

> SYNONYMS 1 *the project was conceived in 1977* **think up,** think of, dream up, devise, formulate, design, create, develop. 2 *I could hardly conceive what it must be like* **imagine,** envisage, visualize, picture, grasp, appreciate.

> ✔ **i** before **e** except after **c**: conc**ei**ve.

concentrate ▸ verb (**concentrates, concentrating, concentrated**) 1 focus all your attention on something. 2 gather together in numbers or a mass at one point.

> SYNONYMS 1 *the government concentrated its efforts on staying in power* **focus,** direct, centre. 2 *she concentrated on the film* **focus on,** pay attention to, keep your mind on, be absorbed in, be engrossed in, be immersed in. 3 *troops concentrated on the horizon* **collect,** gather, congregate, converge, mass, rally.
> ANTONYMS disperse.

▸ noun a concentrated substance or solution.

concentrated ▸ adjective 1 achieved by focussing all your attention on something. 2 (of a solution) strong.

> SYNONYMS 1 *a concentrated effort* **strenuous,** concerted, intensive, all-out, intense. 2 *a concentrated solution* **condensed,** reduced, undiluted, strong.
> ANTONYMS half-hearted, diluted.

concentration ▸ noun 1 the action or power of concentrating. 2 a close gathering of people or things. 3 the amount of a particular substance in a solution or mixture.

> SYNONYMS **close attention,** attentiveness, application, single-mindedness,

absorption.
ANTONYMS inattention.

■ **concentration camp** a camp for holding political prisoners.

concentric ▶ adjective (of circles or arcs) sharing the same centre.

concept ▶ noun an abstract idea.

SYNONYMS **idea,** notion, conception, abstraction, theory, hypothesis.

conception ▶ noun **1** the conceiving of a child. **2** the forming of a plan or idea. **3** an idea or concept. **4** ability to imagine or understand.

SYNONYMS **1** *the fertility treatment resulted in conception* **pregnancy,** fertilization, impregnation, insemination. **2** *the product's conception* **inception,** genesis, origination, creation, invention, beginning, origin. **3** *his original conception* **plan,** idea, notion, scheme, project, proposal, intention, aim.

conceptual ▶ adjective having to do with concepts.
□ **conceptually** adverb.

conceptualize (or **conceptualise**)
▶ verb (**conceptualizes, conceptualizing, conceptualized**) form an idea of something in your mind.

concern ▶ verb **1** relate to; be about. **2** affect or involve. **3** make someone worried.

SYNONYMS **1** *the report concerns the war* **be about,** deal with, cover, relate to, pertain to. **2** *that doesn't concern you* **affect,** involve, be relevant to, apply to, have a bearing on, impact on. **3** *one thing still concerns me* **worry,** disturb, trouble, bother, perturb, unsettle.

▶ noun **1** worry; anxiety. **2** a matter of interest or importance. **3** a business.

SYNONYMS **1** *a voice full of concern* **anxiety,** worry, disquiet, apprehensiveness, unease, misgiving. **2** *his concern for others* **care,** consideration, solicitude, sympathy. **3** *housing is the concern of the council* **responsibility,** business, affair, duty, job; informal bailiwick; Brit. informal lookout. **4** *issues of concern to women* **interest,** importance, relevance, significance. **5** *a publishing concern* **firm,** business, company, enterprise, operation, corporation; informal outfit.
ANTONYMS indifference.

concerned ▶ adjective **1** worried. **2** involved.

SYNONYMS **1** *her mother looked concerned* **worried,** anxious, upset, troubled, uneasy, bothered. **2** *all concerned*

parties **interested,** involved, affected, implicated.
ANTONYMS unconcerned.

concerning ▶ preposition about.

SYNONYMS **about,** regarding, relating to, with reference to, referring to, with regard to, as regards, touching, in connection with, re, apropos.

concert ▶ noun a musical performance given in public.
■ **in concert** acting together.

concerted ▶ adjective **1** jointly arranged or carried out. **2** done in a determined way.

concertina ▶ noun a small musical instrument which you play by stretching and squeezing it and pressing buttons.
▶ verb (**concertinas, concertinaing, concertinaed**) compress in folds like those of a concertina.

concerto /kuhn-cher-toh/ ▶ noun (plural **concertos** or **concerti** /kuhn-cher-ti/) a musical work for an orchestra and one or more solo instruments.

concession ▶ noun **1** something done or given up in order to settle a dispute. **2** a reduction allowed in the price of something. **3** the right to use land or other property for a particular purpose. **4** a stall, bar, or small shop selling things within a larger business or shop.

SYNONYMS **1** *the government made several concessions* **compromise,** accommodation, trade-off, sop. **2** *tax concessions* **reduction,** cut, discount, deduction, rebate; informal break. **3** *a logging concession* **right,** privilege, licence, permit, franchise, warrant.

□ **concessionary** adjective.

conch ▶ noun (plural **conches**) a shellfish with a spiral shell.

concierge /kon-si-airzh/ ▶ noun (especially in France) a resident caretaker of a block of flats or small hotel.

conciliate ▶ verb (**conciliates, conciliating, conciliated**) **1** make someone calm and content. **2** try to bring the two sides in a dispute together.
□ **conciliation** noun **conciliatory** adjective.

concise ▶ adjective giving a lot of information clearly and in few words.

SYNONYMS **succinct,** pithy, brief, abridged, condensed, abbreviated, compact, potted.
ANTONYMS lengthy.

□ **concisely** adverb **concision** noun.

conclave ▶ noun a private meeting.

conclude ▶ verb (**concludes, concluding, concluded**) **1** bring or come to an end. **2** arrive at an opinion by reasoning.

c

3 formally settle or arrange a treaty or agreement.

> SYNONYMS **1** *the meeting concluded at ten* **finish,** end, draw to a close, stop, cease. **2** *he concluded the press conference* **bring to an end,** close, wind up, terminate; informal wrap up. **3** *an attempt to conclude a deal* **settle,** clinch, finalize, tie up. **4** *I concluded that he was rather unpleasant* **deduce,** infer, gather, judge, decide, surmise; N. Amer. figure.
> ANTONYMS begin.

conclusion ▸ noun **1** an end or finish. **2** the summing up of an argument or written work. **3** a decision reached by reasoning.

> SYNONYMS **1** *the conclusion of his speech* **end,** ending, finish, close. **2** *the conclusion of a trade agreement* **settlement,** clinching, completion, arrangement. **3** *his conclusions have been verified* **deduction,** inference, interpretation, judgement, verdict.
> ANTONYMS beginning.

conclusive ▸ adjective decisive or convincing.
□ **conclusively** adverb.

concoct ▸ verb **1** make a dish by combining ingredients. **2** think up a story or plan.
□ **concoction** noun.

concomitant /kuhn-**kom**-i-tuhnt/
▸ adjective formal naturally accompanying or connected with something else.

concord ▸ noun literary agreement; harmony.

concordance ▸ noun an alphabetical list of the important words in a written work.

concordat /kuhn-**kor**-dat/ ▸ noun an agreement or treaty.

concourse ▸ noun a large open area inside or in front of a public building.

concrete ▸ noun a building material made from gravel, sand, cement, and water.
▸ adjective **1** existing in a physical form; not abstract. **2** definite: *concrete proof.*

> SYNONYMS **1** *concrete objects* **solid,** material, real, physical, tangible. **2** *concrete proof* **definite,** specific, firm, positive, conclusive, precise.
> ANTONYMS abstract, imaginary.

▸ verb (**concretes, concreting, concreted**) cover with concrete.

concretion ▸ noun a hard solid mass.

concubine /**kong**-kyuu-byn/ ▸ noun (in some societies, especially in the past) a woman who lives with a man but has lower status than his wife or wives.

concur ▸ verb (**concurs, concurring, concurred**) (often **concur with**) agree.

concurrent ▸ adjective existing or happening at the same time.

□ **concurrently** adverb.

concussion ▸ noun temporary unconsciousness or confusion caused by a blow on the head.
□ **concussed** adjective.

condemn ▸ verb **1** express complete disapproval of someone or something. **2** (usu. **condemn someone to**) sentence someone to a punishment. **3** (**condemn someone to**) force someone to endure something unpleasant. **4** officially declare something to be unfit for use.

> SYNONYMS **1** *he condemned the suspended players* **censure,** criticize, denounce; informal slam; Brit. informal slate, slag off. **2** *his illness condemned him to a lonely life* **doom,** destine, damn, sentence.
> ANTONYMS praise.

condemnation ▸ noun complete disapproval.

> SYNONYMS **censure,** criticism, denunciation; informal flak, a bad press.
> ANTONYMS praise, approval.

condensation ▸ noun **1** water from humid air collecting as droplets on a cold surface. **2** the conversion of a vapour or gas to a liquid.

condense ▸ verb (**condenses, condensing, condensed**) **1** change from a gas or vapour to a liquid. **2** make a liquid thicker or more concentrated. **3** express a piece of writing or a speech in fewer words.

> SYNONYMS **abridge,** compress, summarize, shorten, cut, abbreviate, edit.
> ANTONYMS expand.

■ **condensed milk** milk that has been thickened and sweetened.

condescend ▸ verb **1** behave as if you were better than someone else. **2** do something even though you think it is beneath your dignity. **3** (**condescending**) behaving as if you are better than other people.

condescension ▸ noun a patronizing attitude or way of behaving.

condiment ▸ noun something such as salt or mustard that is added to food to bring out its flavour.

condition ▸ noun **1** the state that someone or something is in as regards appearance, fitness, or working order. **2** (**conditions**) circumstances that affect the way something works or exists. **3** a situation that must exist before something else is possible. **4** an illness or medical problem.

> SYNONYMS **1** *check the condition of your wiring* **state,** shape, order; Brit. informal nick. **2** *they lived in appalling conditions* **circumstances,** surroundings, environment, situation. **3** *she was in*

tip-top condition **fitness,** health, form, shape. **4** *a liver condition* **disorder,** problem, complaint, illness, disease. **5** *a condition of employment* **stipulation,** constraint, prerequisite, precondition, requirement, term, proviso.

▸ **verb 1** train or influence someone to behave in a certain way. **2 (be conditioned by)** be influenced or determined by. **3** bring something into a good condition.

SYNONYMS *our minds are conditioned by habit* **train,** teach, educate, guide, accustom, adapt, habituate, mould.

conditional ▸ **adjective 1** depending on one or more conditions being fulfilled. **2** Grammar expressing something that must happen or be true before something else can happen or be true.

SYNONYMS **qualified,** dependent, contingent, with reservations, limited, provisional, provisory.

◻ **conditionally** adverb.

conditioner ▸ **noun** a liquid added when washing hair or clothing, to make them softer.

condo = CONDOMINIUM.

condolence ▸ **noun** an expression of sympathy.

condom ▸ **noun** a rubber sheath that a man wears on his penis during sex to stop the woman getting pregnant or to protect against infection.

condominium /kon-duh-**min**-i-uhm/ ▸ **noun** (plural **condominiums**) N. Amer. a building containing a number of individually owned flats.

condone ▸ **verb** (**condones, condoning, condoned**) accept or forgive an offence or wrong.

SYNONYMS **disregard,** accept, allow, let pass, turn a blind eye to, overlook, forget, forgive, pardon, excuse. ANTONYMS condemn.

condor ▸ **noun** a very large South American vulture.

conducive ▸ **adjective** (**conducive to**) contributing or helping towards.

conduct ▸ **noun** /kon-dukt/ **1** the way in which a person behaves. **2** management or direction.

SYNONYMS **1** *they complained about her conduct* **behaviour,** actions, deeds, doings, exploits. **2** *the conduct of the elections* **management,** running, direction, control, supervision, regulation, administration, organization, coordination, handling.

▸ **verb** /kuhn-**dukt**/ **1** organize and carry out. **2** direct the performance of a piece of music. **3** guide or lead someone to a place. **4** (**conduct yourself**) behave in a particular way. **5** transmit heat or electricity directly through a substance.

SYNONYMS **1** *the election was conducted lawfully* **manage,** direct, run, administer, organize, coordinate, orchestrate, handle, carry out/on. **2** *he was conducted through the corridors* **escort,** guide, lead, usher, steer. **3** *aluminium conducts heat* **transmit,** convey, carry, channel.

◻ **conduction** noun.

condtuctance ▸ **noun** the degree to which a material conducts electricity.

conductive ▸ **adjective** conducting heat or electricity.
◻ **conductivity** noun.

conductor ▸ **noun 1** a person who conducts musicians. **2** a material or device that conducts heat or electricity. **3** a person who collects fares on a bus.

conduit /kon-dwit, kon-dyuu-it/ ▸ **noun 1** a channel for moving water from one place to another. **2** a tube protecting electric wiring.

cone ▸ **noun 1** an object which tapers from a circular base to a point. **2** the hard, dry fruit of a pine or fir tree.

coney ▸ **noun** (plural **coneys**) a rabbit.

confection ▸ **noun 1** an elaborate sweet dish. **2** something put together in an elaborate or complicated way.

confectionery ▸ **noun** (plural **confectioneries**) sweets and chocolates.

✔ The ending is **-ery,** not **-ary**: confection**ery**.

confederacy ▸ **noun** (plural **confederacies**) **1** an alliance of states or groups. **2 (the Confederacy)** the Confederate states of the US.

confederate ▸ **adjective** /kuhn-**fed**-uh-ruht/ **1** joined by an agreement or treaty. **2 (Confederate)** having to do with the southern states which separated from the US in 1860–1.
▸ **verb** /kuhn-**fed**-uh-rayt/ (**confederates, confederating, confederated**) unite in an alliance.

confederation ▸ **noun** an alliance of states or groups.

confer ▸ **verb** (**confers, conferring, conferred**) **1** formally give a title, benefit, or right to someone. **2** have discussions.

SYNONYMS **1** *she conferred a knighthood on him* **bestow on,** present to, grant to, award to, decorate with. **2** *she went to confer with her colleagues* **consult,** talk, speak, converse, have a chat, deliberate.

◻ **conferment** noun.

conference ▸ noun a formal meeting to discuss something.

SYNONYMS **meeting,** congress, convention, seminar, discussion, council, forum, summit.

confess ▸ verb **1** admit that you have done something criminal or wrong. **2** acknowledge something reluctantly. **3** formally declare your sins to a priest.

SYNONYMS **1** *he confessed that he had done it* **admit,** acknowledge, reveal, disclose, divulge, own up; informal come clean. **2** *they could not make him confess* **own up,** plead guilty, accept the blame; informal come clean. **3** *I confess I don't know* **acknowledge,** admit, concede, grant, allow, own.
ANTONYMS deny.

confession ▸ noun **1** an act of confessing. **2** formal declaration of your sins to a priest.

confessional ▸ noun **1** an enclosed box in a church, in which a priest sits to hear confessions. **2** a confession.

confessor ▸ noun a priest who hears confessions.

confetti ▸ noun small pieces of coloured paper traditionally thrown over a bride and groom after a marriage ceremony.

confidant ▸ noun (feminine **confidante**) a person you trust and confide in.

confide ▸ verb (**confides, confiding, confided**) (often **confide in**) tell someone about a secret or private matter.

SYNONYMS **reveal,** disclose, divulge, impart, declare, vouchsafe, tell, confess.

confidence ▸ noun **1** faith in someone or something. **2** a positive feeling gained from a belief in your own ability to do things well. **3** a feeling of certainty about something.

SYNONYMS **1** *I have little confidence in these figures* **trust,** belief, faith, credence. **2** *she's brimming with confidence* **self-assurance,** self-confidence, self-possession, assertiveness, self-belief, conviction.
ANTONYMS distrust, doubt.

■ **confidence trick** an act of cheating someone after gaining their trust. **in confidence** as a secret.

confident ▸ adjective **1** feeling confidence in yourself. **2** feeling certain about something.

SYNONYMS **1** *we are confident that business will improve* **sure,** certain, positive, convinced, in no doubt, satisfied. **2** *a confident girl* **self-assured,**

assured, self-confident, positive, assertive, self-possessed.

□ **confidently** adverb.

confidential ▸ adjective intended to be kept secret.

SYNONYMS **private,** personal, intimate, quiet, secret, sensitive, classified, restricted; informal hush-hush.

□ **confidentiality** noun **confidentially** adverb.

configuration ▸ noun a particular arrangement of parts.

configure ▸ verb (**configures, configuring, configured**) **1** arrange or set up in a particular way. **2** arrange a computer system so that it is able to do a particular task.

confine ▸ verb /kuhn-**fyn**/ (**confines, confining, confined**) **1** (**confine someone/ thing to**) keep someone or something within certain limits. **2** (**be confined to**) be unable to leave a place due to illness or disability.

SYNONYMS **1** *they were confined in the house* **enclose,** incarcerate, imprison, intern, hold captive, cage, lock up, coop up. **2** *he confined his remarks to the weather* **restrict,** limit.

▸ noun (**confines**) /**kon**-fynz/ limits, boundaries, or restrictions.

confined ▸ adjective (of a space) small and enclosed.

confinement ▸ noun **1** the state of being confined. **2** dated the time around which a woman gives birth to a baby.

confirm ▸ verb **1** state or establish that something is definitely true or correct. **2** make something definite or valid. **3** (**be confirmed**) go through the religious ceremony of confirmation.

SYNONYMS **1** *records confirm the latest evidence* **corroborate,** verify, prove, substantiate, justify, vindicate, bear out. **2** *he confirmed that help was on the way* **affirm,** reaffirm, assert, assure someone, repeat. **3** *his appointment was confirmed by the President* **ratify,** approve, endorse, validate, sanction, authorize.
ANTONYMS contradict, deny.

confirmation ▸ noun **1** the action of confirming. **2** the ceremony at which a baptized person is admitted as a full member of the Christian Church.

confirmed ▸ adjective firmly established in a habit, belief, etc.

confiscate ▸ verb (**confiscates, confiscating, confiscated**) officially take or seize someone's property.

SYNONYMS **impound,** seize, commandeer, requisition, appropriate, expropriate,

sequester.
ANTONYMS return.

conflagration ▸ noun a large and destructive fire.

conflate ▸ verb (**conflates**, **conflating**, **conflated**) combine into one.
□ **conflation** noun.

conflict ▸ noun /kon-flikt/ **1** a serious disagreement. **2** a long-lasting armed struggle. **3** a difference of opinions, principles, etc.

SYNONYMS **1** *industrial conflicts* **dispute**, quarrel, squabble, disagreement, clash, feud, discord, friction, strife, antagonism, hostility. **2** *the Vietnam conflict* **war**, campaign, fighting, engagement, struggle, hostilities, warfare, combat. **3** *a conflict between work and home life* **clash**, incompatibility, friction, mismatch, variance, contradiction.
ANTONYMS agreement, peace, harmony.

▸ verb /kuhn-**flikt**/ (of opinions, stories, etc.) disagree or be different.

SYNONYMS **1** *their interests sometimes conflict* **clash**, be incompatible, be at odds, differ, diverge, disagree, collide. **2** (**conflicting**) *there are conflicting views on this* **contradictory**, incompatible, inconsistent, irreconcilable, contrary, opposite, opposing, clashing.
ANTONYMS agree.

confluence ▸ noun the junction of two rivers.

conform ▸ verb (often **conform to**) **1** obey a rule. **2** behave in an expected or conventional way. **3** be similar in form or type.

SYNONYMS **1** *visitors have to conform to our rules* **comply with**, abide by, obey, observe, follow, keep to, stick to, adhere to, uphold, heed, accept, go along with. **2** *they refuse to conform* **fit in**, behave (yourself), toe the line, obey the rules; informal play by the rules.
ANTONYMS flout, rebel.

□ **conformity** noun.

conformist ▸ noun a person who behaves in an expected or conventional way.

confound ▸ verb **1** surprise or bewilder someone. **2** prove a person, theory, or expectation wrong. **3** (**confounded**) informal, dated used to express annoyance.

SYNONYMS **baffle**, bewilder, mystify, bemuse, perplex, puzzle, confuse, dumbfound, throw; informal flabbergast, flummox.

confront ▸ verb **1** meet an enemy or opponent face to face. **2** face up to and deal with a problem. **3** make someone face up to

a problem.

SYNONYMS **1** *Martin confronted the burglar* **challenge**, square up to, face (up to), come face to face with, meet, accost, stand up to, tackle. **2** *the problems that confront us* **face**, plague, bother, trouble, beset, threaten. **3** *they must confront these issues* **tackle**, address, face, get to grips with, grapple with. **4** *she confronted him with the evidence* **present**, face.
ANTONYMS evade.

confrontation ▸ noun a situation of angry disagreement or hostility.

SYNONYMS **conflict**, clash, fight, battle, encounter, head-to-head; informal set-to, run-in, dust-up, showdown.

□ **confrontational** adjective.

confuse ▸ verb (**confuses**, **confusing**, **confused**) **1** make someone bewildered or puzzled. **2** make something less easy to understand. **3** mistake one thing or person for another.

SYNONYMS **1** *don't confuse students with too much detail* **bewilder**, baffle, mystify, bemuse, perplex, puzzle, nonplus; informal flummox, faze. **2** (**confusing**) *all this detail is very confusing* **puzzling**, baffling, perplexing, bewildering, mystifying, ambiguous, misleading, inconsistent, contradictory. **3** *the authors have confused the issue* **complicate**, muddle, blur, obscure, cloud. **4** *some confuse strokes with heart attacks* **mix up**, muddle up, mistake for.
ANTONYMS enlighten, simplify.

confused ▸ adjective **1** bewildered. **2** difficult to understand or distinguish.

SYNONYMS **1** *they are confused about what is going on* **puzzled**, bemused, bewildered, perplexed, baffled, mystified; informal flummoxed. **2** *her confused elderly mother* **disorientated**, bewildered, muddled, addled, befuddled, demented, senile. **3** *a confused recollection* **vague**, unclear, indistinct, imprecise, blurred, hazy, dim. **4** *a confused mass of bones* **disorderly**, disorganized, untidy, jumbled, mixed up, chaotic, topsy-turvy, tangled; informal higgledy-piggledy; Brit. informal shambolic.
ANTONYMS clear, lucid, precise, neat.

confusion ▸ noun **1** uncertainty or bewilderment. **2** a situation of panic or disorder. **3** the mistaking of one person or thing for another.

SYNONYMS **1** *there is confusion about the new system* **uncertainty**, doubt, ignorance. **2** *she stared in confusion* **bewilderment**, bafflement, perplexity, puzzlement, befuddlement. **3** *her life*

was in utter confusion **disorder**, disarray, chaos, mayhem, turmoil, muddle, mess; informal **shambles**.
ANTONYMS certainty, order.

confute ▶ verb (**confutes, confuting, confuted**) formal prove a person or argument to be wrong.

conga ▶ noun a Latin American dance performed by people in single file.

congeal /kuhn-**jeel**/ ▶ verb become semi-solid.

congenial /kuhn-**jee**-ni-uhl/ ▶ adjective suited or pleasing to your tastes.

SYNONYMS **1** *very congenial people* **sociable**, convivial, hospitable, genial, personable, agreeable, friendly, amiable. **2** *a congenial environment* **pleasant**, agreeable, enjoyable, pleasurable, relaxing, welcoming, hospitable, favourable.
ANTONYMS unsociable, unpleasant.

□ **congeniality** noun.

congenital /kuhn-**jen**-i-t'l/ ▶ adjective **1** (of a disease or abnormality) present from birth. **2** having a particular characteristic as part of your character: *a congenital liar*.
□ **congenitally** adverb.

conger eel /**kong**-ger/ ▶ noun a large eel found in coastal waters.

congested ▶ adjective **1** so crowded that it is difficult to move freely. **2** abnormally full of blood. **3** blocked with mucus.

SYNONYMS **blocked**, clogged, choked, jammed, obstructed, crowded, overcrowded, overflowing, packed; informal **snarled up, gridlocked**.
ANTONYMS clear.

□ **congestion** noun.

conglomerate ▶ noun /kuhn-**glom**-muh-ruht/ **1** a large corporation formed by the merging of separate firms. **2** something consisting of a number of different and distinct things.
□ **conglomeration** noun.

Congolese /kong-guh-**leez**/ ▶ noun (plural **Congolese**) a person from the Congo or the Democratic Republic of Congo (formerly Zaire).
▶ adjective relating to the Congo or the Democratic Republic of Congo.

congratulate ▶ verb (**congratulates, congratulating, congratulated**) **1** tell someone that you are pleased at their success or good fortune. **2** (**congratulate yourself**) think that you are fortunate or clever.

SYNONYMS **compliment**, wish someone happiness, pay tribute to, pat on the back, take your hat off to, praise,

applaud, salute, honour.
ANTONYMS criticize.

□ **congratulatory** adjective.

congratulation ▶ noun **1** (**congratulations**) good wishes given to someone who has had success or good fortune. **2** the action of congratulating someone.

SYNONYMS (**congratulations**) **best wishes**, compliments, greetings, felicitations.

congregate ▶ verb (**congregates, congregating, congregated**) gather into a crowd or mass.

SYNONYMS **assemble**, gather, collect, come together, convene, rally, muster, meet, cluster, group.
ANTONYMS disperse.

congregation ▶ noun **1** a group of people assembled for religious worship. **2** a gathering or collection of people or things.

congress ▶ noun **1** a formal meeting or series of meetings between representatives of different groups. **2** (**Congress**) (in the US and some other countries) the group of people elected to pass laws.
□ **congressional** adjective.

congruent /kong-**groo**-uhnt/ ▶ adjective **1** in agreement or harmony. **2** Geometry (of figures) identical in form.
□ **congruence** noun.

conical ▶ adjective shaped like a cone.

conifer ▶ noun a tree that produces hard dry fruit (**cones**) and evergreen needle-like leaves.
□ **coniferous** adjective.

conjecture ▶ noun an opinion based on incomplete information; a guess.
▶ verb (**conjectures, conjecturing, conjectured**) form a conjecture; guess.
□ **conjectural** adjective.

conjoin ▶ verb formal join; combine.

conjugal /**kon**-juu-g'l/ ▶ adjective having to do with marriage.

conjugate /**kon**-juu-gayt/ ▶ verb (**conjugates, conjugating, conjugated**) Grammar give the different forms of a verb.
□ **conjugation** noun.

conjunction ▶ noun **1** a word used to connect words or clauses (e.g. *and, if*). **2** an instance of two or more things happening at the same time or being in the same place.

conjunctivitis /kuhn-jungk-ti-**vy**-tiss/ ▶ noun inflammation of the eye.

conjure ▶ verb (**conjures, conjuring, conjured**) (usu. **conjure something up**) **1** make something appear by magic, or as if by magic. **2** make something appear as an image in your mind.

SYNONYMS **1** *he conjured a cigarette out of the air* **produce**, magic, summon. **2** *the* *picture that his words conjured up* **bring to mind,** call to mind, evoke, summon up, suggest.

conjuring ▶ noun entertainment in the form of seemingly magical tricks.
□ **conjuror** (or **conjurer**) noun.

conk informal ▶ verb (**conk out**) **1** (of a machine) break down. **2** faint or go to sleep.
▶ noun a person's nose.

conker ▶ noun Brit. the dark brown nut of a horse chestnut tree.

connect ▶ verb **1** join or bring together; link. **2** (**be connected**) be related in some way.

SYNONYMS **1** *electrodes were connected to the device* **attach,** join, fasten, fix, link, hook (up), secure, hitch, stick. **2** *customs connected with Easter* **associate,** link, couple, identify, relate to.
ANTONYMS detach.

connection (or Brit. **connexion**) ▶ noun **1** a link or relationship. **2** the action of linking one thing with another. **3** (**connections**) influential people that you know or are related to. **4** a train, bus, etc. that you can catch to continue a journey.

SYNONYMS **1** *the connection between commerce and art* **link,** relationship, relation, interconnection, interdependence, association, bond, tie, tie-in, correspondence. **2** *he has the right connections* **contact,** friend, acquaintance, ally, colleague, associate, relation.

connective ▶ adjective connecting one thing to another.
▶ noun a word or phrase that links parts of a sentence.

connive /kuh-**nyv**/ ▶ verb (**connives, conniving, connived**) **1** (**connive at** or **in**) secretly allow something wrong to be done. **2** (often **connive with**) conspire to do something wrong.
□ **connivance** noun.

connoisseur /kon-nuh-**ser**/ ▶ noun a person with great knowledge and appreciation of something.

connotation ▶ noun an idea or feeling that is suggested by a word in addition to its main meaning.

connote ▶ verb (**connotes, connoting, connoted**) (of a word) suggest something in addition to its main meaning.

connubial /kuh-**nyoo**-bi-uhl/ ▶ adjective having to do with marriage.

conquer ▶ verb (**conquers, conquering, conquered**) **1** take control of a country or its people by military force. **2** successfully overcome a problem.

SYNONYMS **1** *the Franks conquered the Visigoths* **defeat,** beat, vanquish, triumph over, overcome, overwhelm, overpower, overthrow, subdue, subjugate. **2** *Peru was conquered by Spain* **seize,** take (over), appropriate, capture, occupy, invade, annex, overrun. **3** *the first men to conquer Mount Everest* **climb,** ascend, scale. **4** *the way to conquer fear* **overcome,** get the better of, control, master, deal with, cope with, rise above; informal lick.
ANTONYMS lose to, lose, give in to.
□ **conqueror** noun.

conquest ▶ noun **1** the action of conquering. **2** a place that has been conquered. **3** a person whose affection you have won.

SYNONYMS **1** *the conquest of the Aztecs* **defeat,** overthrow, subjugation. **2** *their conquest of the territory* **seizure,** takeover, capture, occupation, invasion, annexation. **3** *the conquest of Everest* **ascent,** climbing.

conscience ▶ noun a person's moral sense of right and wrong.

SYNONYMS **sense of right and wrong,** morals, standards, values, principles, ethics, beliefs, scruples, qualms.

conscientious /kon-shi-**en**-shuhss/ ▶ adjective careful and thorough in carrying out your work or duty.

SYNONYMS **diligent,** industrious, punctilious, painstaking, dedicated, careful, meticulous, thorough, attentive, hard-working, rigorous, scrupulous, religious.
ANTONYMS casual.

■ **conscientious objector** a person who refuses to serve in the armed forces for moral reasons.
□ **conscientiously** adverb.

conscious ▶ adjective **1** aware of and responding to your surroundings. **2** (usu. **conscious of**) aware. **3** deliberate; intentional.

SYNONYMS **1** *the patient was conscious* **aware,** awake; informal with us. **2** *a conscious decision* **deliberate,** purposeful, knowing, considered, calculated, wilful, premeditated.
ANTONYMS unaware, unconscious.
□ **consciously** adverb **consciousness** noun.

conscript ▶ verb /kuhn-**skript**/ call someone up for compulsory military service.
▶ noun /**kon**-skript/ a person who has been conscripted.
□ **conscription** noun.

consecrate ▶ verb (**consecrates, consecrating, consecrated**) **1** make or declare something holy. **2** officially make someone a bishop.

☐ **consecration** noun.

consecutive ▶ adjective following one after another in unbroken sequence.

SYNONYMS **successive,** succeeding, in succession, running, in a row, straight; informal on the trot.

☐ **consecutively** adverb.

consensual ▶ adjective relating to or involving consent or consensus.

consensus ▶ noun general agreement.

SYNONYMS **1** *there was consensus among delegates* **agreement,** unanimity, harmony, accord, unity, solidarity. **2** *the consensus was that they should act* **general opinion,** common view. ANTONYMS disagreement.

✔ con**sen**sus, not **-cen-**.

consent ▶ noun permission or agreement.

SYNONYMS *the consent of all members* **agreement,** assent, acceptance, approval, permission, authorization, sanction; informal go-ahead, green light, OK. ANTONYMS dissent.

▶ verb **1** give permission. **2** agree to do something.

SYNONYMS *she consented to surgery* **agree,** assent, submit, allow, sanction, approve, go along with. ANTONYMS forbid, refuse.

consequence ▶ noun **1** a result or effect. **2** importance or relevance.

SYNONYMS **1** *a consequence of inflation* **result,** upshot, outcome, effect, repercussion, ramification, product, end result. **2** *the past is of no consequence* **importance,** import, significance, account, value, concern. ANTONYMS cause.

consequent ▶ adjective following as a consequence.

consequently ▶ adverb as a result.

SYNONYMS **as a result,** as a consequence, so, thus, therefore, accordingly, hence, for this/that reason, because of this/that.

conservation ▶ noun **1** preservation or restoration of the natural environment. **2** preservation of historical sites and objects. **3** careful use of a resource.

SYNONYMS **preservation,** protection, safe keeping, husbandry, upkeep, maintenance, repair, restoration.

☐ **conservationist** noun.

conservative ▶ adjective **1** opposed to change and holding traditional values. **2** (in politics) favouring free enterprise

and private ownership. **3** (**Conservative**) relating to the Conservative Party, a British right-wing political party favouring free enterprise and private ownership. **4** (of an estimate) deliberately low for the sake of caution.

SYNONYMS **1** *the conservative wing of the party* **right-wing,** reactionary, traditionalist. **2** *the conservative trade-union movement* **traditionalist,** old-fashioned, dyed-in-the-wool, hidebound, unadventurous, reactionary, set in your ways; informal stick in the mud. **3** *a conservative suit* **conventional,** sober, modest, sensible, restrained; informal square. ANTONYMS socialist, radical, ostentatious.

▶ noun **1** a conservative person. **2** (**Conservative**) a supporter or member of the Conservative Party.

☐ **conservatism** noun **conservatively** adverb.

conservatory ▶ noun (plural **conservatories**) Brit. a room with a glass roof and walls, attached to a house.

conserve /kuhn-**serv**/ ▶ verb (**conserves, conserving, conserved**) protect something from being harmed or overused.

SYNONYMS *fossil fuel should be conserved* **preserve,** protect, save, safeguard, keep, look after, sustain, husband. ANTONYMS squander.

▶ noun /kuhn-**serv, kon**-serv/ fruit jam.

consider ▶ verb (**considers, considering, considered**) **1** think carefully about. **2** believe or think. **3** take into account when making a judgement.

SYNONYMS **1** *Isabel considered her choices* **think about,** contemplate, reflect on, mull over, ponder, deliberate on, chew over, meditate on, ruminate on, evaluate, weigh up, appraise, take account of, bear in mind; informal size up. **2** *I consider him irresponsible* **deem,** think, believe, judge, rate, count, find, regard as, hold to be, reckon to be, view as, see as. **3** *he considered the painting* **look at,** contemplate, observe, regard, survey, examine, inspect.

considerable ▶ adjective great in size, amount, or importance.

SYNONYMS **sizeable,** substantial, appreciable, significant, plentiful, goodly; informal tidy. ANTONYMS paltry.

considerably ▶ adverb to a large extent.

SYNONYMS **greatly,** (very) much, a great deal, a lot, lots, significantly, substantially, appreciably, markedly, noticeably; informal plenty.

considerate ▸ adjective careful not to harm or inconvenience other people.

> SYNONYMS **attentive**, thoughtful, solicitous, kind, unselfish, caring, polite, sensitive.

□ **considerately** adverb.

consideration ▸ noun **1** careful thought. **2** a fact taken into account when making a decision. **3** thoughtfulness towards other people.

> SYNONYMS **1** *your case needs careful consideration* **thought**, deliberation, reflection, contemplation, examination, inspection, scrutiny, analysis, discussion, attention. **2** *his health is the prime consideration* **factor**, issue, matter, concern, aspect, feature. **3** *firms should show more consideration* **attentiveness**, concern, care, thoughtfulness, solicitude, understanding, respect, sensitivity.

considering ▸ preposition & conjunction taking something into account.

> SYNONYMS **bearing in mind**, taking into consideration, taking into account, in view of, in the light of.

consign ▸ verb **1** deliver something to someone. **2** (**consign someone/thing to**) put someone or something in a place so as to be rid of them.

consignment ▸ noun a batch of goods that are delivered.

consist ▸ verb **1** (**consist of**) be composed or made up of. **2** (**consist in**) have as an essential feature.

> SYNONYMS *the crew consists of five men* **be composed of**, be made up of, be formed of, comprise, include, contain.

consistency ▸ noun (plural **consistencies**) **1** the state of being consistent. **2** the thickness of a liquid or semi-liquid substance.

consistent ▸ adjective **1** always behaving in the same way; unchanging. **2** (usu. **consistent with**) in agreement.

> SYNONYMS **1** *consistent opinion-poll evidence* **constant**, regular, uniform, steady, stable, even, unchanging. **2** *her injuries were consistent with a knife attack* **compatible**, in tune, in line, corresponding to, conforming to. ANTONYMS irregular, incompatible.

□ **consistently** adverb.

consolation ▸ noun **1** comfort received after a loss or disappointment. **2** a source of such comfort.

> SYNONYMS **comfort**, solace, sympathy, pity, commiseration, relief, encouragement, reassurance.

■ **consolation prize** a prize given to a competitor who just fails to win.

console[1] /kuhn-**sohl**/ ▸ verb (**consoles, consoling, consoled**) comfort someone who is unhappy or disappointed about something.

> SYNONYMS **comfort**, sympathize with, commiserate with, show compassion for, help, support, cheer (up), hearten, encourage, reassure, soothe. ANTONYMS upset.

console[2] /**kon**-sohl/ ▸ noun **1** a panel or unit containing a set of controls. **2** a small machine for playing computerized video games.

consolidate ▸ verb (**consolidates, consolidating, consolidated**) **1** make stronger or more solid. **2** combine into a single unit.

> SYNONYMS **1** *we consolidated our position in the market* **strengthen**, secure, stabilize, reinforce, fortify. **2** *consolidate the results into an action plan* **combine**, unite, merge, integrate, amalgamate, fuse, synthesize.

□ **consolidation** noun.

consommé /kuhn-**som**-may/ ▸ noun a clear soup made with concentrated stock.

consonance ▸ noun formal agreement or compatibility.

consonant ▸ noun a letter of the alphabet representing a sound in which the breath is completely or partly obstructed.
▸ adjective (**consonant with**) formal in agreement or harmony with.

consort formal ▸ noun /**kon**-sort/ a wife, husband, or companion.
▸ verb /kuhn-**sort**/ (**consort with**) habitually associate with.

consortium ▸ noun (plural **consortia** or **consortiums**) an association of several companies.

conspicuous /kuhn-**spik**-yoo-uhss/ ▸ adjective **1** clearly visible. **2** attracting notice.

> SYNONYMS **obvious**, evident, apparent, visible, noticeable, clear, plain, marked, patent, blatant. ANTONYMS inconspicuous.

□ **conspicuously** adverb.

conspiracy ▸ noun (plural **conspiracies**) a secret plan by a group to do something unlawful or harmful.

> SYNONYMS **plot**, scheme, intrigue, plan, collusion, ploy.

conspire ▸ verb (**conspires, conspiring, conspired**) **1** jointly make secret plans to commit a wrongful act. **2** (of

C

circumstances) seem to be working together to bring about something bad.

synonyms **1** *they admitted conspiring to steal cars* **plot**, scheme, intrigue, manoeuvre, plan. **2** *circumstances conspired against them* **combine**, unite, join forces, work together.

◻ **conspirator** noun **conspiratorial** adjective.

constable ▸ noun Brit. a police officer of the lowest rank.

constabulary /kuhn-**stab**-yuu-luh-ri/ ▸ noun (plural **constabularies**) Brit. a police force.

constant ▸ adjective **1** occurring continuously. **2** remaining the same. **3** faithful and dependable.

synonyms **1** *constant noise* **continuous**, persistent, sustained, ceaseless, unceasing, perpetual, incessant, never-ending, eternal, endless, non-stop. **2** *a constant speed* **consistent**, regular, steady, uniform, even, invariable, unvarying, unchanging. **3** *a constant friend* **faithful**, loyal, devoted, true, fast, firm, unswerving.
antonyms intermittent, variable, fickle.

▸ noun **1** an unchanging situation. **2** Maths Physics a number or quantity that does not change its value.
◻ **constancy** noun **constantly** adverb.

constellation ▸ noun a group of stars forming a recognized pattern.

consternation ▸ noun anxiety or dismay.

constipated ▸ adjective suffering from constipation.

constipation ▸ noun difficulty in emptying the bowels.

constituency ▸ noun (plural **constituencies**) chiefly Brit. an area that elects a representative to a parliament.

constituent ▸ adjective being a part of a whole.
▸ noun **1** a member of a constituency. **2** a part of a whole.

constitute ▸ verb (**constitutes, constituting, constituted**) **1** be a part of a whole. **2** be equivalent to. **3** establish by law.

synonyms **1** *farmers constituted 10 per cent of the population* **comprise**, make up, form, account for. **2** *this constitutes a breach of copyright* **amount to**, be tantamount to, be equivalent to, represent. **3** *the courts were constituted in 1875* **establish**, inaugurate, found, create, set up.

constitution ▸ noun **1** a set of principles according to which a state or organization is governed. **2** the composition or formation of something. **3** a person's physical or mental state.

synonyms **1** *the chemical constitution of the dye* **composition**, make-up, structure, construction, arrangement, configuration, formation, anatomy. **2** *she has the constitution of an ox* **health**, condition, strength, stamina, build, physique.

constitutional ▸ adjective **1** relating or according to a constitution. **2** relating to a person's physical or mental state.
▸ noun dated a walk taken regularly so as to stay healthy.
◻ **constitutionally** adverb.

constrain ▸ verb **1** force someone to do something. **2** (**constrained**) appearing forced or unnatural. **3** severely restrict or limit.

constraint ▸ noun a limitation or restriction.

synonyms **1** *financial constraints* **restriction**, limitation, curb, check, restraint, control. **2** *they were able to talk without constraint* **inhibition**, uneasiness, embarrassment, self-consciousness, awkwardness.
antonyms freedom, ease.

constrict ▸ verb **1** make or become narrower; tighten. **2** stop someone moving or acting freely.

synonyms **narrow**, tighten, compress, contract, squeeze, strangle.
antonyms expand, dilate.

◻ **constriction** noun.

constrictor ▸ noun a snake that kills by squeezing and choking its prey.

construct ▸ verb /kuhn-**strukt**/ build or put together.

synonyms **1** *a bridge constructed by the army* **build**, erect, put up, set up, assemble, fabricate. **2** *he constructed a faultless argument* **create**, formulate, form, put together, devise, compose, work out, frame.
antonyms demolish.

▸ noun /**kon**-strukt/ an idea or theory containing various elements.

construction ▸ noun **1** the process of constructing something. **2** a building or other structure. **3** an interpretation of something.

synonyms **1** *the station was a spectacular construction* **structure**, building, edifice, work. **2** *you put such a sordid construction on it* **interpretation**, explanation, analysis, reading, meaning; informal take.

constructive ▸ adjective having a useful and helpful effect.

synonyms **useful**, helpful, productive, positive, practical, valuable, profitable,

worthwhile.
ANTONYMS unhelpful.

□ **constructively** adverb.

construe ► verb (construes, construing, construed) interpret something in a particular way.

consul ► noun **1** an official who is based in a foreign city and protects their country's citizens and interests there. **2** (in ancient Rome) each of two elected officials who ruled the republic jointly for a year.
□ **consular** adjective.

consulate ► noun the place where a consul works.

consult ► verb **1** try to get advice or information from. **2** ask someone for permission or approval.

SYNONYMS **1** *you need to consult a solicitor* **seek advice from,** ask, call (on), turn to; informal pick someone's brains. **2** *the government must consult with interested parties* **confer,** talk things over, communicate, deliberate, compare notes. **3** *she consulted her diary* **refer to,** look at, check.

□ **consultative** adjective.

consultancy ► noun (plural consultancies) a company that gives expert advice in a particular field.

consultant ► noun **1** a person who provides expert advice professionally. **2** Brit. a senior hospital doctor.

SYNONYMS **adviser,** expert, specialist, authority.

consultation ► noun the process or an act of consulting.

SYNONYMS **1** *the need for further consultation with industry* **discussion,** dialogue, debate, negotiation, deliberation. **2** *a 30-minute consultation* **meeting,** talk, discussion, interview, examination, audience, hearing.

consume ► verb (consumes, consuming, consumed) **1** eat or drink. **2** use up. **3** (of a fire) completely destroy. **4** (of a feeling) absorb someone wholly.

SYNONYMS **1** *vast amounts of food and drink were consumed* **eat,** devour, swallow, gobble up, wolf down, guzzle, drink. **2** *natural resources are being consumed at an alarming rate* **use (up),** expend, deplete, exhaust, spend. **3** *the fire consumed fifty houses* **destroy,** demolish, lay waste, raze, devastate, gut, ruin, wreck. **4** *Carolyn was consumed with guilt* **eat up,** devour, grip, overwhelm, absorb, obsess, preoccupy.

consumer ► noun a person who buys a product or uses a service.

SYNONYMS **buyer,** purchaser, customer, shopper, user.

consumerism ► noun the preoccupation of society with buying goods.
□ **consumerist** adjective.

consummate ► verb /kon-syuu-mayt/ (consummates, consummating, consummated) **1** make a marriage or relationship complete by having sex. **2** complete a transaction.
► adjective /kuhn-**sum**-muht, **kon**-sum-muht/ showing great skill and flair.
□ **consummation** noun.

consumption ► noun **1** the process of consuming, or an amount consumed. **2** dated tuberculosis.
□ **consumptive** adjective dated.

contact ► noun **1** physical touching. **2** communicating or meeting. **3** a person whom you can ask for information or help. **4** a connection for an electric current to pass from one thing to another.

SYNONYMS **1** *have you had any contact with him?* **communication,** correspondence, connection, relations, dealings, touch. **2** *he had many contacts in Germany* **connection,** link, acquaintance, associate, friend.

► verb get in touch with.

SYNONYMS *he should contact the police* **get in touch with,** communicate with, approach, notify, speak to, write to, come forward; informal get hold of.

■ **contact lens** a plastic lens placed on the surface of the eye to help you see better.

contagion ► noun the passing of a disease from one person to another by close contact.

contagious ► adjective **1** (of a disease) spread by contact between people. **2** having a contagious disease.

contain ► verb **1** have or hold something inside. **2** control or restrain. **3** prevent a problem from becoming worse.

SYNONYMS **1** *the boat contained four people* **hold,** carry, enclose, accommodate. **2** *the archive contains much unpublished material* **include,** comprise, incorporate, involve, consist of, be made up of, be composed of. **3** *he must contain his anger* **restrain,** control, curb, rein in, suppress, stifle, swallow, bottle up, keep in check.
ANTONYMS vent.

container ► noun **1** a box or similar object for holding something. **2** a large metal box for transporting goods.

SYNONYMS **receptacle,** vessel, holder, repository.

containment ▸ noun the keeping of something harmful under control.

contaminate ▸ verb (**contaminates, contaminating, contaminated**) make something dirty or poisonous by allowing it to come into contact with harmful substances.

SYNONYMS **pollute,** taint, poison, stain, adulterate, defile, debase, corrupt. ANTONYMS purify.

☐ **contamination** noun.

contemplate ▸ verb (**contemplates, contemplating, contemplated**) 1 look at thoughtfully. 2 think about. 3 think deeply and at length.

SYNONYMS 1 *she contemplated her image in the mirror* **look at,** gaze at, stare at, view, regard, examine, inspect, observe, survey, study, eye. 2 *he contemplated his fate* **think about,** ponder, reflect on, consider, mull over, muse on, dwell on, deliberate over, meditate on, ruminate on, chew over. 3 *he was contemplating legal action* **consider,** think about, have in mind, intend, plan, propose.

☐ **contemplation** noun **contemplative** adjective.

contemporaneous /kuhn-tem-puh-**ray**-ni-uhss/ ▸ adjective existing at or happening in the same period of time.

contemporary ▸ adjective 1 living or happening at the same time. 2 belonging to or happening in the present. 3 modern in style.

SYNONYMS 1 *contemporary sources* **of the time,** contemporaneous, concurrent, coexisting. 2 *contemporary society* **modern,** present-day, present, current. 3 *a very contemporary design* **modern,** up to date, up to the minute, fashionable, recent; informal trendy. ANTONYMS older, newer, former, old-fashioned.

▸ noun (plural **contemporaries**) a person living or working in the same period as another.

✔ contem**porary**, not -**pory**.

contempt ▸ noun 1 the feeling that someone or something is worthless. 2 (also **contempt of court**) the offence of disobeying or being disrespectful to a court of law.

SYNONYMS **scorn,** disdain, derision, disgust, disrespect. ANTONYMS respect.

contemptible ▸ adjective deserving contempt. ☐ **contemptibly** adverb.

contemptuous ▸ adjective showing contempt.

SYNONYMS **scornful,** disdainful, derisive, mocking, sneering, scoffing, condescending, dismissive. ANTONYMS respectful.

☐ **contemptuously** adverb.

contend ▸ verb 1 (**contend with** or **against**) struggle to deal with a difficulty. 2 (**contend for**) struggle to achieve. 3 put forward a view in an argument.

SYNONYMS 1 *three groups were contending for power* **compete,** vie, battle, tussle, struggle, jostle, strive. 2 *he contends that the judge was wrong* **assert,** maintain, hold, claim, argue, insist, allege.

☐ **contender** noun.

content¹ /kuhn-**tent**/ ▸ adjective peacefully happy or satisfied.

SYNONYMS *she seemed content with life* **satisfied,** contented, pleased, fulfilled, happy, glad, at ease. ANTONYMS dissatisfied.

▸ verb satisfy or please.

SYNONYMS *her reply seemed to content him* **satisfy,** comfort, gratify, gladden, please, soothe, placate, appease, mollify.

▸ noun a state of happiness or satisfaction. ☐ **contentment** noun.

content² /**kon**-tent/ ▸ noun 1 (**contents**) the things that are contained in something. 2 the amount of a particular thing occurring in a substance. 3 (**contents**) a list of chapters given at the front of a book or magazine. 4 the material in a piece of writing, as opposed to its form or style.

SYNONYMS 1 *foods with a high fibre content* **amount,** proportion, level. 2 (**contents**) *the contents of a vegetarian sausage* **constituents,** ingredients, components. 3 *the content of the essay* **subject matter,** theme, argument, thesis, message, substance, material, ideas.

contented ▸ adjective happy or satisfied.

SYNONYMS See **CONTENT¹** (adjective).

☐ **contentedly** adverb.

contention ▸ noun 1 heated disagreement. 2 a point of view that is expressed. ■ **in contention** having a good chance of success in a contest.

contentious ▸ adjective causing disagreement or controversy; controversial.

SYNONYMS 1 *a contentious issue* **controversial,** debatable, disputed, open to debate, moot, vexed. 2 *contentious people* **quarrelsome,** argumentative, confrontational; Brit. informal stroppy.

contest ▸ noun /**kon**-test/ an event in which people compete to see who is the best.

SYNONYMS **1** *a boxing contest* **competition**, match, tournament, game, bout. **2** *the contest for the party leadership* **fight**, battle, tussle, struggle, competition, race.

▶ verb /kuhn-**test**/ **1** take part in a competition or election. **2** challenge or dispute a decision or theory.

SYNONYMS **1** *he intended to contest the seat* **compete for**, contend for, vie for, fight for. **2** *a system where parties contest elections* **compete in**, take part in, fight, enter. **3** *we contested the decision* **oppose**, challenge, take issue with, question, call into question, object to. ANTONYMS accept.

contestant ▶ noun a person who takes part in a contest.

SYNONYMS **competitor**, participant, player, contender, candidate, entrant.

context ▶ noun **1** the circumstances surrounding an event, statement, or idea. **2** the parts that come immediately before and after a word or passage and make its meaning clearer.

SYNONYMS **circumstances**, conditions, frame of reference, factors, state of affairs, situation, background, scene, setting.

□ **contextual** adjective.

contiguous /kuhn-**tig**-yoo-uhss/ ▶ adjective sharing a border.

continent[1] ▶ noun **1** any of the world's main continuous expanses of land (Europe, Asia, Africa, North and South America, Australia, Antarctica). **2** (**the Continent**) the mainland of Europe as distinct from the British Isles.

continent[2] ▶ adjective **1** able to control movements of the bowels and bladder. **2** restrained; self-disciplined.
□ **continence** noun.

continental ▶ adjective **1** forming or belonging to a continent. **2** coming from or like mainland Europe.
▶ noun a person from mainland Europe.
■ **continental breakfast** a light breakfast of coffee and bread rolls.

contingency ▶ noun (plural **contingencies**) a future event which may happen but cannot be predicted with certainty.

SYNONYMS **eventuality**, possibility, chance event, incident, occurrence, accident, emergency.

contingent ▶ noun a group of people with a common feature, forming part of a larger group.
▶ adjective **1** (**contingent on**) dependent on. **2** depending on chance.

continual ▶ adjective happening constantly or often, with intervals in between: *he met with continual delays.*

SYNONYMS **1** *continual breakdowns* **frequent**, repeated, constant, recurrent, recurring, regular. **2** *continual pain* **constant**, continuous, unremitting, unrelenting, chronic, uninterrupted, unbroken. ANTONYMS occasional, temporary.

□ **continually** adverb.

❗ Note that **continual** and **continuous** don't mean exactly the same thing.

continuation ▶ noun **1** the action of continuing. **2** a part that is attached to something else and is an extension of it.

continue ▶ verb (**continues**, **continuing**, **continued**) **1** keep doing something; carry on with. **2** keep existing or happening. **3** carry on travelling in the same direction. **4** start doing something again.

SYNONYMS **1** *he was unable to continue with his job* **carry on**, proceed, pursue, go on, keep on, persist, persevere, keep at; informal stick at. **2** *discussions continued throughout the year* **go on**, carry on, last, extend, run on, drag on. **3** *we are keen to continue this relationship* **maintain**, keep up, sustain, keep going, keep alive, preserve. **4** *his willingness to continue in office* **remain**, stay, carry on, keep going. **5** *we continued our conversation after supper* **resume**, pick up, take up, carry on with, return to, revisit. ANTONYMS stop, break off, leave.

continuity ▶ noun (plural **continuities**) **1** the fact of not stopping or changing. **2** an unbroken connection or line of development. **3** organization of a film or television programme so that the plot makes sense and clothing, scenery, etc. remain the same in different scenes.

continuous ▶ adjective forming an unbroken whole or sequence without interruptions or exceptions: *a day of continuous rain.*

SYNONYMS **continual**, persistent, sustained, ceaseless, unceasing, perpetual, incessant, never-ending, eternal, endless, non-stop. ANTONYMS intermittent.

□ **continuously** adverb.

continuum /kuhn-**tin**-yoo-uhm/ ▶ noun (plural **continua**) a continuous sequence in which the elements change gradually.

contort ▶ verb twist or bend something out of its normal shape.

SYNONYMS **twist**, bend out of shape, distort, misshape, warp, buckle, deform.

□ **contortion** noun.

c

contortionist ▸ noun an entertainer who twists and bends their body into unnatural positions.

contour ▸ noun 1 an outline of the shape or form of something. 2 (also **contour line**) a line on a map joining points of equal height.
□ **contoured** adjective.

contraband ▸ noun goods that have been imported or exported illegally.

contraception ▸ noun the use of contraceptives.

contraceptive ▸ noun a device or drug used to prevent a woman becoming pregnant.
▸ adjective preventing a woman becoming pregnant.

contract ▸ noun /**kon**-trakt/ 1 an official, legally binding agreement. 2 informal an arrangement for someone to be murdered by a hired killer.

SYNONYMS *a legally binding contract* **agreement**, arrangement, commitment, settlement, understanding, compact, covenant, deal, bargain.

▸ verb /kuhn-**trakt**/ 1 make or become smaller. 2 become shorter and tighter. 3 shorten a word or phrase. 4 make a formal and legally binding agreement to do something. 5 catch or develop a disease.

SYNONYMS 1 *the market began to contract* **shrink**, diminish, reduce, decrease, dwindle, decline. 2 *her stomach muscles contracted* **tighten**, tense, flex, constrict, draw in. 3 *the company was contracted to build the stadium* **engage**, take on, hire, commission, employ. 4 *she contracted German measles* **catch**, pick up, come/go down with, develop.
ANTONYMS expand, relax, lengthen.

□ **contractual** adjective.

contraction ▸ noun 1 the process of contracting. 2 a shortening of the muscles of the womb happening at intervals during childbirth. 3 a shortened form of a word or words.

SYNONYMS 1 *the contraction of the industry* **shrinking**, shrinkage, decline, decrease, diminution, dwindling. 2 *the contraction of muscles* **tightening**, tensing, flexing. 3 *'goodbye' is a contraction of 'God be with you'* **abbreviation**, short form, shortening.
ANTONYMS expansion, relaxation, lengthening.

contractor ▸ noun a person or firm that undertakes to provide materials or labour for a job.

contradict ▸ verb deny the truth of a statement made by someone by saying the opposite.

SYNONYMS 1 *he contradicted the government's account* **deny**, refute, rebut, dispute, challenge, counter. 2 *nobody dared contradict him* **argue with**, go against, challenge, oppose.
ANTONYMS confirm, agree with.

contradiction ▸ noun 1 a combination of statements, ideas, or features which are opposed to one another. 2 saying the opposite to something already said.

SYNONYMS 1 *the contradiction between his faith and his lifestyle* **conflict**, clash, disagreement, inconsistency, mismatch. 2 *a contradiction of his statement* **denial**, refutation, rebuttal, countering.
ANTONYMS agreement, confirmation.

contradictory ▸ adjective 1 inconsistent with or opposing each other. 2 containing inconsistent elements.

SYNONYMS **inconsistent**, incompatible, irreconcilable, opposed, opposite, contrary, conflicting, at variance.

contradistinction ▸ noun distinction made by contrasting two things.

contraflow ▸ noun Brit. an arrangement by which the lanes of a dual carriageway normally carrying traffic in one direction become two-directional.

contralto /kuhn-**tral**-toh/ ▸ noun (plural **contraltos**) the lowest female singing voice.

contraption ▸ noun a machine or device that appears strange or unnecessarily complicated.

contrapuntal /kon-truh-**pun**-t'l/ ▸ adjective Music relating to or in counterpoint.

contrariwise ▸ adverb in the opposite way.

contrary /**kon**-truh-ri/ ▸ adjective 1 opposite in nature, direction, or meaning. 2 (of two or more statements, beliefs, etc.) opposed to one another. 3 /kuhn-**trair**-i/deliberately inclined to do the opposite of what is expected or wanted.

SYNONYMS 1 *contrary views* **opposite**, opposing, contradictory, clashing, conflicting, antithetical, incompatible, irreconcilable. 2 *she was sulky and contrary* **perverse**, awkward, difficult, uncooperative, obstinate, pig-headed, intractable; Brit. informal bloody-minded, stroppy; N. Amer. informal balky.
ANTONYMS compatible, accommodating.

▸ noun (**the contrary**) the opposite.

SYNONYMS *in fact, the contrary is true* **opposite**, reverse, converse, antithesis.

□ **contrariness** noun.

contrast ▸ noun /**kon**-trahst/ 1 the state of being noticeably different from something else. 2 a thing or person noticeably different from another. 3 the amount of difference between tones in a television picture, photograph, etc.

> SYNONYMS **1** *the contrast between rural and urban trends* **difference,** dissimilarity, disparity, divergence, variance, distinction, comparison. **2** *Jane was a complete contrast to Sarah* **opposite,** antithesis, foil, complement.
> ANTONYMS similarity.

▸ verb /kuhn-**trahst**/ **1** be noticeably different. **2** compare two things to emphasize their differences.

> SYNONYMS **1** *a view which contrasts with his earlier opinion* **differ,** be at variance, be contrary, conflict, be at odds, disagree, clash. **2** *people contrasted her with her sister* **compare,** juxtapose, measure, distinguish, differentiate.
> ANTONYMS resemble, liken.

contravene ▸ verb (**contravenes, contravening, contravened**) **1** do something that breaks a law, treaty, etc. **2** conflict with a right, principle, etc.
□ **contravention** noun.

contretemps /**kon**-truh-ton/ ▸ noun (plural **contretemps** /**kon**-truh-tonz/) a minor disagreement.

contribute ▸ verb (**contributes, contributing, contributed**) **1** give something in order to help an undertaking or effort. **2** (**contribute to**) help to cause or bring about.

> SYNONYMS **give,** donate, put up, grant, provide, supply; informal chip in; Brit. informal stump up.

contribution ▸ noun something contributed.

> SYNONYMS **gift,** donation, offering, present, handout, grant, subsidy.

contributor ▸ noun a person who contributes something.

> SYNONYMS **donor,** benefactor, supporter, backer, patron, sponsor.

contributory ▸ adjective **1** playing a part in bringing something about. **2** (of a pension or insurance scheme) operated by means of a fund into which people pay.

contrite ▸ adjective sorry for something that you have done.
□ **contritely** adverb **contrition** noun.

contrivance ▸ noun **1** a clever device or scheme. **2** the action of contriving something.

contrive ▸ verb (**contrives, contriving, contrived**) **1** plan or achieve something in a clever or skilful way. **2** manage to do something foolish.

> SYNONYMS **1** *they contrived a plan* **create,** engineer, manufacture, devise, concoct,

construct, fabricate, hatch. **2** *Lomax contrived to bump into him* **manage,** find a way, engineer a way, arrange, succeed in.
> ANTONYMS fail.

contrived ▸ adjective deliberately created and seeming artificial; not natural or spontaneous.

> SYNONYMS **forced,** strained, laboured, overdone, unnatural, artificial, false, affected.
> ANTONYMS natural.

control ▸ noun **1** the power to influence people's behaviour or the course of events. **2** the restriction of something: *crime control.* **3** a way of regulating or limiting something: *controls on local spending.* **4** a person or thing used as a standard of comparison for checking the results of a survey or experiment.

> SYNONYMS **1** *China retained control over the region* **power,** authority, command, dominance, sway, management, direction, leadership, rule, government, sovereignty, supremacy. **2** *strict import controls* **limit,** limitation, restriction, restraint, check, curb, regulation. **3** *her control deserted her* **self-control,** self-restraint, composure, calm; informal cool.

▸ verb (**controls, controlling, controlled**) **1** have control or command of. **2** limit or regulate.

> SYNONYMS **1** *one family controlled the company* **run,** manage, direct, preside over, supervise, command, rule, govern, lead, dominate. **2** *she struggled to control her temper* **restrain,** keep in check, curb, hold back, suppress, repress. **3** *public spending was controlled* **limit,** restrict, curb, cap.

■ **control tower** a tall building at an airport from which the movements of aircraft are controlled.
□ **controllable** adjective **controller** noun.

controversial ▸ adjective causing or likely to cause controversy.

> SYNONYMS **disputed,** contentious, moot, debatable, arguable, vexed.

□ **controversially** adverb.

controversy /**kon**-truh ver si, kuhn-**trov**-er-si/ ▸ noun (plural **controversies**) debate or disagreement about a subject which arouses strong opinions.

> SYNONYMS **dispute,** disagreement, argument, debate, contention, quarrel, war of words, storm; Brit. informal row.

contumely /kon-**tyoom**-li/ ▸ noun (plural **contumelies**) old use insulting language or treatment.

contusion ▸ noun a bruise.

conundrum /kuh-**nun**-druhm/ ▶ noun (plural **conundrums**) **1** a difficult problem or question. **2** a riddle.

conurbation /kon-er-**bay**-sh'n/ ▶ noun an area consisting of several towns merging together or with a city.

convalesce ▶ verb (**convalesces**, **convalescing**, **convalesced**) gradually get better after an illness or injury.

convalescent ▶ adjective recovering from an illness or injury.
□ **convalescence** noun.

convection ▶ noun the process by which heat moves through a gas or liquid as the warmer part rises and the cooler part sinks.

convector ▶ noun a heater that circulates warm air by convection.

convene ▶ verb (**convenes**, **convening**, **convened**) **1** call people together for a meeting. **2** come together for a meeting.

SYNONYMS **1** *he convened a secret meeting* **summon**, call, order. **2** *the committee convened for its final session* **assemble**, gather, meet, come together; formal foregather.
ANTONYMS disperse.

□ **convener** (or **convenor**) noun.

convenience ▶ noun **1** freedom from effort or difficulty. **2** a useful or helpful device or situation. **3** Brit. a public toilet.

SYNONYMS **1** *the convenience of the arrangement* **advantage**, benefit, expedience, suitability. **2** *for convenience, the handset is wall-mounted* **ease of use**, usefulness, utility, accessibility, availability.
ANTONYMS inconvenience.

convenient ▶ adjective **1** fitting in well with a person's needs, activities, and plans. **2** involving little trouble or effort.

SYNONYMS **1** *a convenient time* **suitable**, favourable, advantageous, appropriate, opportune, timely, expedient. **2** *a convenient shop* **nearby**, handy, well situated, practical, useful, accessible.
ANTONYMS inconvenient.

□ **conveniently** adverb.

convent ▶ noun a building where nuns live together.

convention ▶ noun **1** a way in which something is usually done. **2** socially acceptable behaviour. **3** a large meeting or conference. **4** an agreement between countries.

SYNONYMS **1** *social conventions* **custom**, usage, practice, tradition, etiquette, protocol. **2** *a convention signed by 74 countries* **agreement**, accord, protocol, pact, treaty. **3** *the party's biennial*

convention **conference**, meeting, congress, assembly, gathering.

conventional ▶ adjective **1** based on or following what is generally done. **2** not individual or adventurous. **3** (of weapons or power) non-nuclear.

SYNONYMS **1** *conventional wisdom* **orthodox**, traditional, established, accepted, received, prevailing. **2** *a conventional railway* **normal**, standard, regular, ordinary, usual, traditional, typical. **3** *a very conventional woman* **conservative**, traditional, conformist, old-fashioned; informal square, stick-in-the-mud. **4** *a conventional piece of work* **unoriginal**, formulaic, predictable, unadventurous.
ANTONYMS unorthodox, unconventional, original.

□ **conventionally** adverb.

converge ▶ verb (**converges**, **converging**, **converged**) **1** come together from different directions. **2** (**converge on**) come from different directions and meet at.

SYNONYMS *here the lines converge* **meet**, intersect, cross, connect, link up, join, merge.
ANTONYMS diverge.

□ **convergent** adjective.

conversant ▶ adjective (**conversant with**) familiar with or knowledgeable about.

conversation ▶ noun an informal talk between two or more people.

SYNONYMS **discussion**, talk, chat, gossip, tête-à-tête, exchange, dialogue; Brit. informal chinwag, natter.

□ **conversational** adjective **conversationalist** noun.

converse¹ /kuhn-**verss**/ ▶ verb (**converses**, **conversing**, **conversed**) hold a conversation.

converse² /kon-verss/ ▶ noun something that is the opposite of another.
▶ adjective opposite.
□ **conversely** adverb.

conversion ▶ noun **1** the action of converting. **2** Brit. a building that has been converted to a new purpose. **3** Rugby a successful kick at goal after a try.

SYNONYMS **1** *the conversion of waste into energy* **change**, transformation, metamorphosis. **2** *the conversion of the building* **adaptation**, alteration, modification, redevelopment.

convert ▶ verb /kuhn-**vert**/ **1** change the form, character, or function of something. **2** change money or units into others of a different kind. **3** adapt a building for a new purpose. **4** change your religious faith.

SYNONYMS **1** *plants convert the sun's energy into chemical energy* **change**, turn, transform, metamorphose. **2** *the factory was converted into flats* **adapt**, turn, change, alter, modify, redevelop. **3** *they sought to convert sinners* **win over**, claim, redeem, save, reform, re-educate, proselytize, evangelize.

▸ noun /**kon**-vert/ a person who has changed their religious faith.

convertible ▸ adjective **1** able to be converted. **2** (of a car) having a folding or detachable roof.
▸ noun a convertible car.

convex ▸ adjective having an outline or surface that curves outwards.

convey ▸ verb **1** transport or carry to a place. **2** communicate an idea or feeling.

SYNONYMS **1** *taxis conveyed guests to the station* **transport**, carry, bring, take, fetch, move. **2** *he conveyed the information to me* **communicate**, pass on, impart, relate, relay, transmit, send. **3** *it's impossible to convey how I felt* **express**, communicate, get across/over, put across/over, indicate.

conveyance ▸ noun **1** the action of conveying. **2** formal a means of transport. **3** the legal process of transferring property from one owner to another.
□ **conveyancing** noun.

conveyor belt ▸ noun a continuous moving band used for transporting objects from one place to another.

convict ▸ verb /kuhn-**vikt**/ officially declare that someone is guilty of a criminal offence.

SYNONYMS **find guilty**, sentence.
ANTONYMS acquit.

▸ noun /**kon**-vikt/ a person in prison after being convicted of a criminal offence.

SYNONYMS **prisoner**, inmate, criminal, offender, felon; informal jailbird, con, (old) lag.

conviction ▸ noun **1** an instance of being convicted of a criminal offence. **2** a firmly held belief or opinion. **3** the quality of showing that you believe strongly in what you are saying or doing.

SYNONYMS **1** *his political convictions* **beliefs**, opinions, views, persuasion, ideals, position, stance, values. **2** *she spoke with conviction* **assurance**, confidence, certainty.
ANTONYMS diffidence.

convince ▸ verb (**convinces**, **convincing**, **convinced**) **1** cause someone to believe firmly that something is true. **2** persuade someone to do something.

SYNONYMS **1** *he convinced me that I was wrong* **assure**, persuade, satisfy, prove to. **2** *I convinced her to marry me* **persuade**, induce, prevail on, talk into, talk round, win over, coax, cajole, inveigle.

convincing ▸ adjective **1** able to convince someone. **2** (of a victory or a winner) leaving no margin of doubt.

SYNONYMS **1** *a convincing argument* **persuasive**, powerful, strong, forceful, compelling, cogent, plausible, irresistible, telling. **2** *a convincing 5–0 win* **resounding**, emphatic, decisive, conclusive.
ANTONYMS unconvincing, narrow.

□ **convincingly** adverb.

convivial ▸ adjective **1** (of an atmosphere or event) friendly and lively. **2** (of a person) cheerfully sociable.
□ **conviviality** noun.

convoluted ▸ adjective **1** (of an argument or account) very complex. **2** folded or twisted in an elaborate way.

convolution ▸ noun **1** a coil or twist. **2** (**convolutions**) something complex and difficult to follow.

convoy ▸ noun a group of ships or vehicles travelling together under armed protection.

convulse ▸ verb (**convulses**, **convulsing**, **convulsed**) **1** suffer convulsions. **2** (**be convulsed**) make sudden, uncontrollable movements because of emotion, laughter, etc.
□ **convulsive** adjective.

convulsion ▸ noun **1** a sudden, irregular movement of the body caused by muscles contracting uncontrollably. **2** (**convulsions**) uncontrollable laughter. **3** a violent upheaval.

coo ▸ verb (**coos**, **cooing**, **cooed**) **1** (of a pigeon or dove) make a soft murmuring sound. **2** speak in a soft, gentle voice.
▸ noun a cooing sound.

cook ▸ verb **1** prepare food or a meal by heating the ingredients. **2** (of food) be heated so as to become edible. **3** informal alter accounts dishonestly. **4** (**cook something up**) informal invent a story or plan.
▸ noun a person who cooks.

cooker ▸ noun Brit. an appliance for cooking food.

cookery ▸ noun the practice or skill of preparing and cooking food.

cookie ▸ noun (plural **cookies**) **1** N. Amer. a sweet biscuit. **2** informal a person of a particular kind: *she's a tough cookie.*

cool ▸ adjective **1** fairly cold. **2** stopping you from becoming too hot. **3** unfriendly or unenthusiastic. **4** not anxious or excited. **5** informal fashionably attractive or impressive. **6** informal excellent.

> SYNONYMS **1** *a cool breeze* **chilly,** chill, cold, bracing, brisk, crisp, fresh; informal **nippy;** Brit. informal **parky.** **2** *a cool response to the suggestion* **unenthusiastic,** lukewarm, tepid, indifferent, uninterested, apathetic. **3** *David seemed distinctly cool* **unfriendly,** distant, remote, aloof, cold, chilly, frosty, unwelcoming; informal **stand-offish. 4** *his ability to keep cool in a crisis* **calm,** collected, composed, self-possessed, poised, serene, relaxed, at ease, unruffled, unperturbed; informal **unflappable, together, laid-back.** ANTONYMS warm, enthusiastic, friendly, excited.

▶ **noun** the state of being calm and self-controlled.

> SYNONYMS **1** *the cool of the evening* **chill,** chilliness, coldness, coolness. **2** *Ken lost his cool* **self-control,** control, composure, self-possession, calmness, aplomb, poise. ANTONYMS warmth.

▶ **verb** (**cools, cooling, cooled**) make or become cool.

> SYNONYMS *cool the sauce in the fridge* **chill,** refrigerate, freeze. ANTONYMS warm.

▫ **cooler** noun **coolly** adverb **coolness** noun.

coolant ▶ **noun** a fluid used to cool an engine or other device.

coolie ▶ **noun** (plural **coolies**) dated an unskilled labourer in an Asian country.

coon ▶ **noun** N. Amer. a raccoon.

coop ▶ **noun** a cage or pen for poultry.
▶ **verb** (**coop someone/thing up**) confine a person or animal in a small space.

cooper ▶ **noun** a person who makes or repairs casks and barrels.

cooperate (or **co-operate**) ▶ **verb** (**cooperates, cooperating, cooperated**) **1** work together towards the same end. **2** do what someone wants.

> SYNONYMS **1** *police and social services cooperated* **collaborate,** work together, pull together, join forces, team up, unite, combine, pool resources. **2** *he was happy to cooperate* **assist,** help, lend a hand, be of service, do your bit; informal **play ball.**

cooperation (or **co-operation**) ▶ **noun** the action of cooperating.

> SYNONYMS **1** *cooperation between management and workers* **collaboration,** joint action, combined effort, teamwork, give and take, compromise. **2** *thank you for your cooperation* **assistance,** help.

cooperative (or **co-operative**) ▶ **adjective** **1** involving cooperation. **2** willing to help. **3** (of a business) owned and run jointly by its members.

> SYNONYMS **1** *a cooperative effort* **collaborative,** collective, combined, joint, shared, united, concerted. **2** *pleasant and cooperative staff* **helpful,** eager to help, obliging, accommodating, willing.

▶ **noun** a cooperative organization.
▫ **cooperatively** adverb.

co-opt ▶ **verb 1** appoint someone as a member of a committee or other body. **2** adopt an idea or policy for your own use.

coordinate (or **co-ordinate**) ▶ **verb** /koh-or-di-nayt/ (**coordinates, coordinating, coordinated**) **1** bring the different elements of something together so that it works well. **2** (**coordinate with**) negotiate with other people to work together effectively. **3** (of different things) match or look attractive together.

> SYNONYMS **organize,** arrange, order, synchronize, bring together, orchestrate.

▶ **noun** /koh-or-di-nuht/ Maths each of a group of numbers used to indicate the position of a point, line, or plane.
▫ **coordinator** noun.

coordination (or **co-ordination**) ▶ **noun** **1** the process of coordinating. **2** the ability to move different parts of the body smoothly and at the same time.

coot ▶ **noun** a waterbird with black feathers and a white bill.

cop informal ▶ **noun** a police officer.
▶ **verb** (**cops, copping, copped**) **1** arrest an offender. **2** receive or experience something unwelcome. **3** (**cop out**) avoid doing something that you ought to do. ■ **cop it** Brit. get into trouble. **not much cop** Brit. not very good.

cope¹ ▶ **verb** (**copes, coping, coped**) deal effectively with something difficult.

> SYNONYMS **1** *she couldn't cope on her own* **manage,** survive, look after yourself, fend for yourself, shift for yourself, get by/through, hold your own. **2** *his inability to cope with the situation* **deal with,** handle, manage, address, face (up to), confront, tackle, get to grips with.

cope² ▶ **noun** a long cloak worn by a priest on ceremonial occasions.

copier ▶ **noun** a machine that makes exact copies of something.

co-pilot ▶ **noun** a second pilot in an aircraft.

coping ▶ **noun** the top line of bricks or stones in a wall.

copious ▶ **adjective** in large amounts; plentiful.

□ **copiously** adverb.

copper¹ ▸ noun **1** a reddish-brown metal. **2** (**coppers**) Brit. coins made of copper or bronze. **3** a reddish-brown colour.
■ **copper-bottomed** Brit. thoroughly reliable.

copper² ▸ noun Brit. informal a police officer.

copperplate ▸ noun an elaborate style of handwriting.

coppice ▸ noun an area of woodland in which the trees or shrubs are periodically cut back to ground level.

copse ▸ noun a small group of trees.

copulate ▸ verb (**copulates, copulating, copulated**) mate or have sex.
□ **copulation** noun.

copy ▸ noun (plural **copies**) **1** a thing made to be similar or identical to another. **2** a single example of a particular book, record, etc. **3** material for a newspaper or magazine article.

> SYNONYMS **1** *a copy of the report* **duplicate**, facsimile, photocopy; trademark Xerox. **2** *a copy of a sketch by Leonardo da Vinci* **replica**, reproduction, imitation, likeness, forgery, fake, counterfeit.

▸ verb (**copies, copying, copied**) **1** make a copy of. **2** imitate the behaviour or style of.

> SYNONYMS **1** *each form had to be copied* **duplicate**, photocopy, xerox, photostat, reproduce. **2** *portraits copied from originals* **reproduce**, replicate, forge, fake, counterfeit. **3** *their sound was copied by a lot of jazz players* **imitate**, reproduce, emulate, mimic; informal rip off.

■ **copy-edit** check that written material is consistent and accurate.
□ **copyist** noun.

copyright ▸ noun the exclusive right to publish, perform, film, or record literary, artistic, or musical material.

copywriter ▸ noun a person who writes advertisements or publicity material.

coquette /ko-**ket**/ ▸ noun a flirtatious woman.
□ **coquetry** noun **coquettish** adjective.

coracle /**ko**-ruh-k'l/ ▸ noun a small round boat made of wickerwork covered with a watertight material.

coral ▸ noun **1** a hard substance found in warm seas which consists of the skeletons of small animals living together as a stationary group. **2** a pinkish-red colour.

cor anglais /kor ong-**glay**/ ▸ noun (plural **cors anglais** /kor **ong**-glay/) a woodwind instrument of the oboe family.

corbel ▸ noun a projection jutting out from a wall to support a structure above it.

cord ▸ noun **1** thin string or rope made from several twisted strands. **2** an electric flex. **3** corduroy. **4** (**cords**) trousers made of corduroy.

> SYNONYMS **string**, thread, line, rope, cable, wire, twine, yarn.

□ **cordless** adjective.

> ❗ Don't confuse **cord** with **chord**, which means 'a group of musical notes'.

cordial ▸ adjective **1** warm and friendly. **2** sincere.
▸ noun **1** Brit. a sweet fruit-flavoured drink, sold in concentrated form. **2** chiefly N. Amer. a liqueur.
□ **cordiality** noun **cordially** adverb.

cordite ▸ noun a kind of explosive.

cordon ▸ noun a line or circle of police, soldiers, or guards forming a barrier.

> SYNONYMS **barrier**, line, chain, ring, circle.

▸ verb (**cordon something off**) close somewhere off by means of a cordon.

cordon bleu /kor-don **bler**/ ▸ adjective Cookery of the highest class.

corduroy /**kor**-duh-roy/ ▸ noun a thick cotton fabric with velvety ridges.

core ▸ noun **1** the tough central part of a fruit. **2** the central or most important part of something.

> SYNONYMS **1** *the earth's core* **centre**, interior, middle, nucleus. **2** *the core of the argument* **heart**, nucleus, nub, kernel, meat, essence, crux, pith, substance; informal nitty-gritty.
> ANTONYMS edge, periphery.

▸ verb (**cores, coring, cored**) remove the core from a fruit.

co-respondent ▸ noun a person named in a divorce case as having committed adultery with the respondent.

corgi ▸ noun (plural **corgis**) a breed of dog with short legs and a pointed face.

coriander /ko-ri-**an**-der/ ▸ noun a plant used as a herb in cookery.

cork ▸ noun **1** a light, soft brown substance obtained from the bark of a tree. **2** a bottle stopper made of cork.
▸ verb **1** seal a bottle with a cork. **2** (**corked**) (of wine) spoilt by a faulty cork.

corker ▸ noun informal an excellent person or thing.
□ **corking** adjective.

corkscrew ▸ noun a device used for pulling corks from bottles.
▸ verb move or twist in a spiral.

corm ▸ noun an underground part of certain plants.

cormorant /kor-muh-ruhnt/ ▸ noun a diving seabird with a long hooked bill and black feathers.

corn¹ ▸ noun 1 Brit. the chief cereal crop of a district (in England, wheat). 2 N. Amer. Austral./NZ maize.

■ **corn on the cob** maize cooked and eaten straight from the cob.

corn² ▸ noun a painful area of thickened skin on the toes or foot.

cornea ▸ noun the transparent layer forming the front of the eye.

corned beef ▸ noun beef preserved with salt, often sold in tins.

corner ▸ noun 1 a place or angle where two or more sides or edges meet. 2 a place where two streets meet. 3 a secluded or remote area. 4 a difficult or awkward position. 5 Soccer a free kick taken by the attacking side from a corner of the field.

SYNONYMS 1 *the cart lurched round the corner* **bend**, curve, turn, junction; Brit. hairpin bend. 2 *a charming corner of Italy* **district**, region, area, quarter; informal neck of the woods.

▸ verb (**corners, cornering, cornered**) 1 force someone into a place or situation from which it is hard to escape. 2 go round a bend in a road. 3 control the trade in a particular type of goods.

SYNONYMS 1 *he was eventually cornered by police dogs* **surround**, trap, hem in, pen in, cut off. 2 *crime syndicates have cornered the stolen car market* **gain control of**, take over, dominate, monopolize, capture; informal sew up.

cornerstone ▸ noun 1 a vital part. 2 a stone that forms the base of a corner of a building.

cornet ▸ noun 1 a brass instrument resembling a trumpet but shorter and wider. 2 Brit. a cone-shaped wafer for holding ice cream.

cornflour ▸ noun Brit. ground maize flour, used for thickening sauces.

cornflower ▸ noun a plant with deep blue flowers.

cornice /kor-niss/ ▸ noun a decorative border round the wall of a room just below the ceiling.

cornucopia /kor-nyuu-koh-pi-uh/ ▸ noun a plentiful supply of good things.

corny ▸ adjective (**cornier, corniest**) informal sentimental or unoriginal.

corolla /kuh-rol-luh/ ▸ noun the petals of a flower.

corollary /kuh-rol-luh-ri/ ▸ noun (plural **corollaries**) 1 a direct consequence or result. 2 a logical conclusion.

corona /kuh-roh-nuh/ ▸ noun (plural **coronae** /kuh-roh-nee/) 1 the gases surrounding the sun or a star. 2 a small circle of light around the sun or moon.

coronary /ko-ruh-nuh-ri/ ▸ adjective having to do with the heart, in particular with the arteries which supply it with blood.

▸ noun (plural **coronaries**) (also **coronary thrombosis**) a blockage of the flow of blood to the heart.

coronation ▸ noun the ceremony of crowning a king or queen.

coroner ▸ noun an official who holds inquests into violent, sudden, or suspicious deaths.

coronet ▸ noun 1 a small or simple crown. 2 a decorative band put around the head.

corpora plural of **CORPUS**.

corporal¹ ▸ noun a rank of officer in the army, below sergeant.

corporal² ▸ adjective relating to the human body.

■ **corporal punishment** physical punishment, such as caning.

corporate ▸ adjective 1 relating to a business corporation. 2 relating to or shared by all members of a group.

corporation ▸ noun 1 a large company, or a group of companies acting as a single unit. 2 Brit. a group of people elected to govern a city, town, or borough.

SYNONYMS **company**, firm, business, concern, operation, conglomerate, group, chain, multinational.

corporeal /kor-por-i-uhl/ ▸ adjective relating to a person's body; physical rather than spiritual.

corps /kor/ ▸ noun (plural **corps** /korz/) 1 a large unit of an army. 2 a branch of an army with a particular kind of work. 3 a group of people involved in a particular activity.

corpse ▸ noun a dead body.

SYNONYMS **dead body**, carcass, remains; informal stiff; Medicine cadaver.

corpulent /kor-pyuu-luhnt/ ▸ adjective (of a person) fat.

□ **corpulence** noun.

corpus /kor-puhss/ ▸ noun (plural **corpora** /kor-puh-ruh/ or **corpuses**) a collection of written works.

corpuscle /kor-pus-s'l/ ▸ noun a red or white blood cell.

corral /kuh-rahl/ ▸ noun N. Amer. a pen for animals on a farm or ranch.

▸ verb (**corrals, corralling, corralled**) 1 N. Amer. drive animals into a corral. 2 gather a group together.

correct ▸ adjective **1** free from mistakes; true or right. **2** following accepted social standards.

SYNONYMS **1** *the correct answer* **right**, accurate, exact, true, perfect. **2** *correct behaviour* **proper**, right, decent, respectable, decorous, suitable, appropriate, accepted.
ANTONYMS wrong, improper.

▸ verb **1** put something right. **2** mark the mistakes in a piece of writing. **3** tell someone that they are wrong.

SYNONYMS *correct any mistakes* **rectify**, right, put right, set right, amend, remedy, repair, reform, cure.

□ **correctness** noun.

correction ▸ noun **1** the process of correcting. **2** a change that corrects a mistake or inaccuracy.

SYNONYMS **rectification**, righting, amendment, repair, remedy, cure.

corrective ▸ adjective designed to put something right.

correctly ▸ adverb in a correct way.

SYNONYMS **1** *the questions were answered correctly* **accurately**, right, perfectly, exactly, precisely. **2** *she behaved correctly at all times* **properly**, decorously, with decorum, decently, fittingly, appropriately, well.
ANTONYMS wrongly, improperly.

correlate ▸ verb (**correlates, correlating, correlated**) place things together so that one thing depends on another and vice versa.

correlation ▸ noun **1** a situation in which one thing depends on another and vice versa. **2** the process of correlating two or more things.

correspond ▸ verb **1** match or agree almost exactly. **2** be similar or the same. **3** communicate by exchanging letters.

SYNONYMS **1** *the setting corresponds with the number on the dial* **be consistent**, correlate, agree, accord, coincide, tally, tie in, match; informal square. **2** (**corresponding**) *a rank corresponding to a British sergeant* **equivalent**, related, parallel, matching, comparable, analogous. **3** *Debbie and I corresponded for years* **exchange letters**, write, communicate.

correspondence ▸ noun **1** letters sent or received. **2** a close connection or similarity.

SYNONYMS **1** *there is some correspondence between the two variables* **parallel**, correlation, agreement, consistency, conformity, similarity, resemblance, comparability. **2** *his private* *correspondence* **letters**, messages, mail, post, communication.

■ **correspondence course** a course of study in which student and tutors communicate by post.

✔ The ending is **-ence**, not **-ance**: correspond**ence**.

correspondent ▸ noun **1** a journalist who reports on a particular subject. **2** a person who writes letters.

SYNONYMS **reporter**, journalist, columnist, writer, contributor, commentator.

corridor ▸ noun **1** a passage in a building or train, with doors leading into rooms or compartments. **2** a strip of land linking two other areas.

✔ **-dor**, not **-door**: corri**dor**.

corroborate ▸ verb (**corroborates, corroborating, corroborated**) confirm or give support to a statement or theory.
□ **corroboration** noun.

corrode ▸ verb (**corrodes, corroding, corroded**) **1** slowly wear away a hard material by the action of a chemical. **2** gradually weaken or destroy.

corrosion ▸ noun the process of corroding, or damage caused by it.

corrosive ▸ adjective tending to cause corrosion.

corrugated ▸ adjective shaped into alternate ridges and grooves.
□ **corrugation** noun.

corrupt ▸ adjective **1** willing to act dishonestly in return for money or other reward. **2** evil or immoral. **3** (of a written work or computer data) unreliable because of mistakes or alterations.

SYNONYMS **1** *a corrupt official | corrupt practices* **dishonest**, unscrupulous, criminal, fraudulent, illegal, unlawful; informal **crooked**; Brit. informal **bent**. **2** *he is utterly corrupt* **immoral**, depraved, degenerate, debauched, vice-ridden, perverted, dissolute.
ANTONYMS honest, ethical, pure.

▸ verb make corrupt.

SYNONYMS **deprave**, pervert, lead astray, debauch, defile, pollute, sully.

□ **corruptly** adverb.

corruption ▸ noun **1** dishonest or illegal behaviour. **2** the action of corrupting.

SYNONYMS **1** *political corruption* **dishonesty**, unscrupulousness, double-dealing, fraud, misconduct, bribery, venality; N. Amer. **payola**; informal **graft**, sleaze. **2** *his fall into corruption* **immorality**, depravity, vice, degeneracy,

perversion, debauchery, wickedness, evil, sin.
ANTONYMS honesty, morality, purity.

corsage /kor-**sah**zh/ ▸ noun a small bunch of flowers worn pinned to a woman's clothes.

corset ▸ noun a tight-fitting undergarment worn to shape a woman's figure or to support a person's back.

cortège /kor-**tezh**/ ▸ noun a funeral procession.

cortex /**kor**-teks/ ▸ noun (plural **cortices** /**kor**-ti-seez/) the outer layer of an organ or structure, especially the outer layer of the brain.

cortisone ▸ noun a hormone used to treat inflammation and allergies.

coruscating /**ko**-ruh-skay-ting/ ▸ adjective literary flashing or sparkling.

corvette /kor-**vet**/ ▸ noun a small warship designed for escorting convoys.

cos ▸ abbreviation cosine.

cosh ▸ noun a thick, heavy stick or bar used as a weapon.
▸ verb hit someone on the head with a cosh.

cosine /**koh**-syn/ ▸ noun Maths (in a right-angled triangle) the ratio of the side next to a particular acute angle to the longest side.

cosmetic ▸ adjective **1** (of treatment) intended to improve a person's appearance. **2** improving something only outwardly.

SYNONYMS **superficial**, surface, skin-deep, outward, external.
ANTONYMS fundamental.

▸ noun (**cosmetics**) substances put on the face and body to make them more attractive.

cosmic ▸ adjective relating to the universe.

cosmonaut ▸ noun a Russian astronaut.

cosmopolitan ▸ adjective **1** made up of people from many different countries and cultures. **2** familiar with many different countries.

SYNONYMS **1** the student body has a cosmopolitan character **multicultural**, multiracial, international, worldwide, global. **2** a very cosmopolitan chap **sophisticated**, cultivated, cultured, worldly, suave, urbane.

cosmos ▸ noun the universe.

Cossack /**koss**-ak/ ▸ noun a member of a people of Russia and Ukraine famous for being good riders.

cosset ▸ verb (**cossets, cosseting, cosseted**) look after and protect someone in a way that is too indulgent.

cost ▸ verb (**costs, costing, cost**) **1** be able to be bought or done for a specific price.

2 involve the loss of. **3** (**costs, costing, costed**) estimate the cost of work that needs to be done.

SYNONYMS **1** the chair costs £186 **be priced at**, sell for, be valued at, fetch, come to, amount to; informal set someone back, go for. **2** the proposal has not yet been costed **price**, value, put a price/value/figure on.

▸ noun **1** an amount given or required as payment. **2** the effort or loss necessary to achieve something. **3** (**costs**) legal expenses.

SYNONYMS **1** the cost of the equipment **price**, fee, tariff, fare, toll, levy, charge, payment, value, rate, outlay; humorous damage. **2** the human cost of the conflict **sacrifice**, loss, toll, harm, damage, price. **3** (**costs**) we need to cover our costs **expenses**, outgoings, overheads, expenditure, spend, outlay.

■ **cost-effective** effective or productive in relation to its cost.

co-star ▸ noun a performer in a film or play appearing with another or others of equal importance.
▸ verb **1** appear as a co-star. **2** (of a film or play) include someone as a co-star.

Costa Rican ▸ noun a person from Costa Rica.
▸ adjective relating to Costa Rica.

costermonger ▸ noun dated a person who sells fruit and vegetables in the street.

costly ▸ adjective (**costlier, costliest**) **1** expensive. **2** causing suffering, loss, or disadvantage.

SYNONYMS **1** costly machinery **expensive**, dear, high-cost, overpriced; informal steep, pricey. **2** a costly mistake **catastrophic**, disastrous, calamitous, ruinous, damaging, harmful, deleterious.
ANTONYMS cheap.

◻ **costliness** noun.

costume ▸ noun **1** a set of clothes in a style typical of a particular country or historical period. **2** a set of clothes worn by an actor or performer for a role.

SYNONYMS **clothes**, garments, outfit, ensemble, dress, clothing, attire, garb, uniform, livery; formal apparel.

■ **costume jewellery** jewellery made with inexpensive materials or imitation gems.

costumier /koss-**tyoo**-mi-er/ ▸ noun a person who makes or supplies theatrical or fancy-dress costumes.

cosy (US spelling **cozy**) ▸ adjective (**cosier, cosiest**) **1** comfortable, warm, and secure. **2** not difficult or demanding.

SYNONYMS **1** a cosy country cottage **snug**, comfortable, warm, homely, welcoming, safe, sheltered, secure; informal comfy. **2** *a cosy chat* **intimate**, relaxed, informal, friendly.

▶ noun (plural **cosies**) a cover to keep a teapot or a boiled egg hot.
☐ **cosily** adverb **cosiness** noun.

cot ▶ noun a small bed with high barred sides for a baby or very young child.
■ **cot death** the unexplained death of a baby in its sleep.

coterie /koh-tuh-ri/ ▶ noun (plural **coteries**) a small, close-knit group of people.

cottage ▶ noun a small house in the country.

synonyms **lodge**, chalet, cabin, shack, shanty; in Russia **dacha**; Scottish **bothy**; Austral. informal **weekender**.

■ **cottage cheese** soft, lumpy white cheese.

cotter pin ▶ noun a metal pin used to fasten two parts of a mechanism together.

cotton ▶ noun **1** soft white fibres surrounding the seeds of a plant that grows in warm climates. **2** cloth or thread made from these fibres.
▶ verb (**cotton on**) informal begin to understand.
■ **cotton wool** fluffy soft material used for cleaning the skin or a wound.

cotyledon /ko-ti-**lee**-duhn/ ▶ noun the first leaf that grows from a seed.

couch ▶ noun a long padded piece of furniture for sitting or lying on.
▶ verb (**couch something in**) express something in language of a particular style.
■ **couch potato** informal a person who watches a lot of television.

couchette /koo-**shet**/ ▶ noun a bed or bunk on a train, converted from a seat or folded down from a wall.

cougar /koo-ger/ ▶ noun N. Amer. a puma.

cough ▶ verb **1** send out air from the lungs with a sudden sharp sound. **2** (**cough something up**) informal reluctantly give money or information.

synonyms *he coughed loudly* **hack**, hawk, bark, clear your throat.

▶ noun **1** an act of coughing. **2** an illness of the throat or lungs causing coughing.

synonyms *a loud cough* **bark**, hack; informal frog in your throat.

could ▶ modal verb past of **can**[1].

couldn't ▶ short form could not.

coulomb /koo-lom/ ▶ noun a unit of electric charge.

council ▶ noun **1** a group of people that meet regularly to discuss or organize something. **2** a group of people elected to manage the affairs of a city, county, or district.

synonyms **1** *the town council* **authority**, government, administration, executive,

chamber, assembly; Brit. corporation. **2** *the Schools Council* **committee**, board, commission, assembly, panel, synod.

■ **council house** a house owned by a local council and rented to tenants. **council tax** (in the UK) a tax charged on households by local authorities.

councillor ▶ noun a member of a council.

❗ Note the difference between **councillor** and **counsellor**.

counsel ▶ noun **1** advice. **2** (plural **counsel**) a barrister or other lawyer involved in a case.

synonyms **1** *his wise counsel* **advice**, guidance, counselling, recommendations, suggestions, direction. **2** *the counsel for the defence* **barrister**, lawyer; Scottish **advocate**; N. Amer. attorney, counselor(-at-law).

▶ verb (**counsels**, **counselling**, **counselled**; US spelling **counsels**, **counseling**, **counseled**)
1 advise or recommend. **2** give professional help and advice to someone with psychological or personal problems.

synonyms *he counselled the team to withdraw* **advise**, recommend, advocate, encourage, warn, caution, guide.

counsellor (US spelling **counselor**) ▶ noun a person trained to give advice on personal or psychological problems.

count[1] ▶ verb **1** find the total number of. **2** recite numbers in ascending order. **3** take into account. **4** regard as being: *people she counted as her friends*. **5** be important. **6** (**count on**) rely on. **7** (**count someone in** or **out**) include (or not include) someone in an activity.

synonyms **1** *she counted the money again* **add up**, reckon up, total, tally, calculate, compute; Brit. tot up. **2** *250 employees, not counting overseas staff* **include**, take into account/consideration, take account of, allow for. **3** *I count it a privilege to be asked* **consider**, think, feel, regard, look on as, view as, hold to be, judge, deem. **4** *it's your mother's feelings that count* **matter**, be important, be of consequence, be significant, signify, carry weight, rate.

▶ noun **1** an act of counting. **2** a total found by counting. **3** a point to be discussed or considered. **4** Law each of the charges against an accused person.
■ **out for the count 1** Boxing defeated by being knocked to the ground and unable to get up within ten seconds. **2** informal unconscious or asleep.

count[2] ▶ noun a foreign nobleman.

countdown ▶ noun an act of counting backwards to zero.

countenance ▸ noun a person's face or expression.
▸ verb (**countenances, countenancing, countenanced**) tolerate or allow.

counter[1] ▸ noun **1** a long flat surface over which goods are sold or served or across which business is conducted with customers. **2** a small disc used in board games or to represent a coin. **3** a person or thing that counts something.
■ **under the counter** bought or sold secretly and illegally.

counter[2] ▸ verb (**counters, countering, countered**) **1** argue against or reply to. **2** try to stop or prevent.

> SYNONYMS **1** *workers countered accusations of dishonesty with claims of oppression* **respond to,** parry, hit back at, answer. **2** *the second argument is more difficult to counter* **oppose,** dispute, argue against/with, contradict, challenge, contest. ANTONYMS support.

▸ adverb (**counter to**) **1** in the opposite direction to. **2** in opposition to.

counteract ▸ verb do something to reduce or prevent the bad effects of.

counter-attack ▸ noun an attack made in response to an attack.
▸ verb attack in response.

counterbalance ▸ noun **1** a weight that balances another. **2** something that has an equal but opposite effect to something else.
▸ verb (**counterbalances, counterbalancing, counterbalanced**) have an equal but opposite effect on.

counter-espionage ▸ noun activities designed to prevent spying by an enemy.

counterfeit /kown-ter-fit/ ▸ adjective made in exact imitation of something valuable so as to deceive or cheat people.
▸ noun a forgery.
▸ verb imitate something dishonestly.

counterfoil ▸ noun the part of a cheque, ticket, etc. that you keep when you give the other part up.

countermand ▸ verb cancel an order.

countermeasure ▸ noun something done to deal with a danger or threat.

counterpane ▸ noun dated a bedspread.

counterpart ▸ noun a person or thing that corresponds to another.

> SYNONYMS **equivalent,** opposite number, peer, equal, parallel, complement, analogue, match, twin, mate, fellow.

counterpoint ▸ noun **1** the playing of two or more tunes at the same time. **2** a tune played at the same time as another.

counterproductive ▸ adjective having the opposite effect to the one intended.

countersign ▸ verb sign a document that has already been signed by another person.

countersink ▸ verb (**countersinks, countersinking, countersunk**) insert a screw or bolt so that the head lies flat with the surface.

countertenor ▸ noun the highest male adult singing voice.

counterterrorism ▸ noun political or military activities designed to prevent terrorism.

countervailing ▸ adjective having an equal but opposite effect.

countess ▸ noun **1** the wife or widow of a count or earl. **2** a woman holding the rank of count or earl.

counting ▸ preposition taking account of; including.

countless ▸ adjective too many to be counted; very many.

> SYNONYMS **innumerable,** numerous, untold, legion, numberless, limitless, incalculable; informal umpteen; N. Amer. informal gazillions of.
> ANTONYMS few.

countrified ▸ adjective characteristic of the country or country life.

country ▸ noun (plural **countries**) **1** a nation with its own government. **2** areas outside large towns and cities. **3** an area of land with particular physical features: *hilly country*.

> SYNONYMS **1** *foreign countries* **nation,** state, kingdom, realm, land, territory, province. **2** *the country took to the streets* **people,** public, population, populace, citizens, nation; Brit. informal Joe Public. **3** *thickly forested country* **terrain,** land, territory, landscape, countryside, scenery, surroundings, environment. **4** *she hated living in the country* **countryside,** provinces, rural areas, backwoods, hinterland; Austral./NZ outback, bush, back country; informal sticks.

■ **country music** (or **country and western**) a kind of popular music from country areas of the southern US.

countryside ▸ noun land and scenery outside towns and cities.

> SYNONYMS See COUNTRY (sense 3), COUNTRY (sense 4).

county ▸ noun (plural **counties**) each of the main areas into which some countries are divided for the purposes of local government.

SYNONYMS shire, province, territory, region, district, area.

■ **county town** the main town of a county, where its council is based.

coup /koo/ ► noun (plural **coups** /kooz/)
1 (also **coup d'état** /koo day-**tah**/) a sudden violent seizing of power from a government. **2** a successful move or action.

SYNONYMS **1** *a violent military coup* **takeover,** coup d'état, overthrow, palace revolution, rebellion, uprising. **2** *a major publishing coup* **success,** triumph, feat, masterstroke, accomplishment, achievement, scoop.

coupe /koo-pay, koop/ ► noun a sports car with a fixed roof and a sloping rear.

couple ► noun **1** two individuals of the same sort considered together. **2** two people who are married or in a romantic or sexual relationship. **3** informal an unspecified small number.

SYNONYMS **1** *a couple of girls* **pair,** duo, twosome, two, brace. **2** *a honeymoon couple* **husband and wife,** twosome, partners, lovers; informal item.

► verb (**couples, coupling, coupled**) **1** connect or combine. **2** have sex.

SYNONYMS **1** *hope is coupled with a sense of loss* **combine,** accompany, mix, incorporate, ally, add to. **2** *a cable is coupled to one of the wheels* **connect,** attach, join, fasten, fix, link, secure, hook (up).
ANTONYMS detach.

couplet ► noun a pair of rhyming lines of poetry one after another.

coupling ► noun a device for connecting railway vehicles or parts of machinery together.

coupon ► noun **1** a voucher that gives you the right to claim a discount or buy something. **2** a form that can be sent off to ask for information or to enter a competition.

SYNONYMS **voucher,** token, ticket, slip; N. Amer. informal **rain check.**

courage ► noun **1** the ability to do something frightening; bravery. **2** strength when faced with pain or grief.

SYNONYMS **bravery,** pluck, valour, fearlessness, nerve, daring, audacity, boldness, grit, heroism, gallantry; informal guts; Brit. informal bottle.
ANTONYMS cowardice.

courageous ► adjective having courage; brave.

SYNONYMS **brave,** plucky, fearless, intrepid, valiant, heroic, undaunted,

dauntless; informal gutsy, have-a-go.
ANTONYMS cowardly.

□ **courageously** adverb.

courgette /koor-**zhet**/ ► noun Brit. a long, thin vegetable with green skin.

courier ► noun **1** a person employed to deliver goods or documents quickly. **2** a person employed to guide and help a group of tourists.

course ► noun **1** a direction that is taken or intended. **2** the way in which something progresses or develops. **3** (also **course of action**) a way of dealing with a situation. **4** a dish forming one of the stages of a meal. **5** a series of lectures or lessons in a particular subject. **6** a series of repeated treatments or doses of a drug. **7** an area prepared for racing, golf, or another sport.

SYNONYMS **1** *the island was not far off our course* **route,** way, track, path, line, trail, trajectory, bearing, heading. **2** *the best course to adopt* **procedure,** plan (of action), course of action, practice, approach, technique, policy, strategy, tactic. **3** *a waterlogged course* **racecourse,** racetrack, track. **4** *a French course* **programme/course of study,** curriculum, syllabus, classes, lectures, studies. **5** *a course of antibiotics* **programme,** series, sequence, system, schedule, regime.

► verb (**courses, coursing, coursed**) **1** (of liquid) flow. **2** (**coursing**) the activity of hunting animals, especially hares, with greyhounds.

SYNONYMS *tears coursed down her cheeks* **flow,** pour, stream, run, rush, gush, cascade, flood, roll.

■ **of course 1** as expected. **2** certainly; yes.

❗ Don't confuse **course** with **coarse,** which means 'having a rough texture'.

court ► noun **1** the judge, jury, and lawyers who sit and hear legal cases. **2** the place where a law court meets. **3** an area marked out for ball games such as tennis. **4** a courtyard. **5** the home, advisers, and staff of a king or queen.

SYNONYMS **1** *the court found him guilty* **court of law,** law court, bench, bar, tribunal, assizes. **2** *the King's court* **household,** retinue, entourage, train, courtiers, attendants.

► verb **1** try to win someone's support. **2** behave in a way that might lead to something bad happening. **3** dated try to win the love of someone you want to marry.

SYNONYMS **1** *he was courting a girl from the village* **woo,** go out with, date, go steady with. **2** *an editor who was courted by politicians* **cultivate,** flatter, curry favour with, wine and dine; informal butter up. **3** *he was courting public attention* **seek,** pursue, go after, strive for, solicit. **4** *he's often courted controversy* **risk,** invite, attract, bring on yourself.

■ **court shoe** a woman's plain shoe with a low-cut upper and no fastening. **hold court** be the centre of attention.

courteous /ker-ti-uhss/ ▸ adjective polite and considerate.

> SYNONYMS **polite,** well mannered, civil, respectful, well behaved, gracious, obliging, considerate.
> ANTONYMS rude.

□ **courteously** adverb.

courtesan /kor-ti-**zan**/ ▸ noun a prostitute with wealthy clients.

courtesy /**ker**-tuh-si/ ▸ noun (plural **courtesies**) **1** polite and considerate behaviour. **2** a polite speech or action.

> SYNONYMS **politeness,** good manners, civility, respect, grace, consideration, thought.

■ **courtesy of** given or allowed by.

courtier /kor-ti-er/ ▸ noun a companion or adviser of a king or queen.

courtly ▸ adjective (**courtlier, courtliest**) very dignified and polite.

court martial ▸ noun (plural **courts martial**) a court for trying people accused of breaking military law.
▸ verb (**court-martial**) (**court-martials, court-martialling, court-martialled**) try someone in a court martial.

courtship ▸ noun **1** a period during which a couple develop a romantic relationship. **2** the process of trying to win someone's love or support.

courtyard ▸ noun an open area enclosed by walls or buildings.

couscous /**kuuss**-kuuss/ ▸ noun a North African dish of steamed or soaked semolina.

cousin ▸ noun (also **first cousin**) a child of your uncle or aunt.
■ **second cousin** a child of your mother's or father's first cousin.

couture /koo-**tyoor**/ ▸ noun the design and making of fashionable clothes, especially for a particular customer.

couturier /koo-**tyoo**-ri-ay/ ▸ noun a person who designs couture clothes.

cove ▸ noun a small sheltered bay.

> SYNONYMS **bay,** inlet, fjord.

coven /**kuv**-uhn/ ▸ noun a group of witches who meet regularly.

covenant /**kuv**-uh-nuhnt/ ▸ noun **1** a formal agreement. **2** an agreement to make

regular payments to a charity.

cover ▸ verb (**covers, covering, covered**) **1** put something over or in front of a person or thing so as to protect or hide them. **2** spread or extend over an area. **3** deal with a subject. **4** travel a particular distance. **5** (of money) be enough to pay for something. **6** (of insurance) protect against a loss or accident. **7** (**cover something up**) try to hide or deny a mistake or crime. **8** (**cover for**) temporarily take over someone's job. **9** perform a cover version of a song.

> SYNONYMS **1** *she covered her face with a towel* **protect,** shield, shelter, hide, conceal, mask. **2** *his car was covered in mud* **cake,** coat, encrust, plaster, smother. **3** *snow covered the fields* **blanket,** carpet, coat, shroud, smother. **4** *a course covering all aspects of the business* **deal with,** consider, take in, include, involve, incorporate, embrace.
> ANTONYMS reveal.

▸ noun **1** something that covers or protects. **2** a thick protective outer part or page of a book or magazine. **3** shelter. **4** a means of hiding an illegal or secret activity. **5** protection by insurance. **6** (also **cover version**) a performance of a song previously recorded by a different artist.

> SYNONYMS **1** *a protective cover* **covering,** sleeve, wrapping, wrapper, envelope, sheath, housing, jacket, casing, cowling, canopy. **2** *a manhole cover* **lid,** top, cap. **3** *a book cover* **binding,** jacket, dust jacket, dust cover, wrapper. **4** *a thick cover of snow* **coating,** coat, covering, layer, carpet, blanket, film, sheet, veneer, crust, skin, cloak, mantle, veil, pall, shroud. **5** *panicking onlookers ran for cover* **shelter,** protection, refuge, sanctuary.

■ **break cover** suddenly leave shelter when being chased. **cover charge** a charge per person added to the bill in a restaurant. **covering letter** a letter sent with a document or parcel to explain what it is. **cover-up** an attempt to hide a mistake or crime.

coverage ▸ noun the extent to which something is covered.

coverlet ▸ noun a bedspread.

covert ▸ adjective /**kuv**-ert, **koh**-vert/ not done openly; secret.
▸ noun /**kuv**-ert/ an area of bushes and undergrowth where game birds and animals can hide.
□ **covertly** adverb.

covet /**kuv**-it/ ▸ verb (**covets, coveting, coveted**) long to possess something belonging to someone else.
□ **covetous** adjective.

covey /kuv-i/ ▶ noun (plural **coveys**) a small flock of game birds.

cow[1] ▶ noun **1** a mature female animal of a domesticated breed of ox. **2** the female of certain other large animals. **3** informal a nasty woman.

cow[2] ▶ verb frighten someone so much that they do what you want.

coward ▶ noun a person who is too scared to do dangerous or unpleasant things.

SYNONYMS **mouse,** baby; informal chicken, scaredy-cat, yellow-belly, sissy; Brit. informal big girl's blouse; N. Amer. informal pantywaist, pussy; Austral./NZ informal sook. ANTONYMS hero.

cowardice ▶ noun lack of bravery.

cowardly ▶ adjective lacking bravery.

SYNONYMS **faint-hearted,** lily-livered, spineless, craven, timid, timorous, fearful; informal yellow, chicken, gutless, yellow-bellied. ANTONYMS brave.

cowboy ▶ noun **1** a man on horseback who herds cattle in the western US. **2** informal a dishonest or unqualified tradesman.

cower ▶ verb (**cowers, cowering, cowered**) crouch down or shrink back in fear.

SYNONYMS **cringe,** shrink, flinch, crouch, blench.

cowl ▶ noun **1** a large, loose hood forming part of a monk's garment. **2** a hood-shaped covering for a chimney or ventilation shaft.

cowling ▶ noun a removable cover for a vehicle or aircraft engine.

cowrie ▶ noun (plural **cowries**) a shellfish whose glossy shell has a long, narrow opening.

cowslip ▶ noun a wild plant with clusters of yellow flowers.

cox ▶ noun the person who steers a rowing boat.

coxcomb ▶ noun old use a vain and conceited man.

coxswain /kok-suhn/ = cox.

coy ▶ adjective (**coyer, coyest**) **1** pretending to be shy or modest. **2** reluctant to give details about something.

SYNONYMS **demure,** shy, modest, bashful, diffident, self-effacing, shrinking. ANTONYMS brazen.

□ **coyly** adverb.

coyote /koy-**oh**-ti/ ▶ noun (plural **coyote** or **coyotes**) a wolf-like wild dog found in North America.

coypu /koy-poo/ ▶ noun (plural **coypus**) a large South American rodent resembling a beaver.

cozy US spelling of cosy.

crab ▶ noun a sea creature with a broad shell and five pairs of legs.
  ■ **crab apple** a small, sour kind of apple.

crabbed ▶ adjective **1** (of writing) hard to read or understand. **2** bad-tempered.

crabby ▶ adjective (**crabbier, crabbiest**) informal bad-tempered.

crack ▶ noun **1** a narrow opening between two parts of something which has split or been broken. **2** a sudden sharp noise. **3** a sharp blow. **4** informal a joke. **5** informal an attempt to do something. **6** (also **crack cocaine**) a very strong form of cocaine.

SYNONYMS **1** *a crack in the glass* **split,** break, chip, fracture, rupture. **2** *a crack between two rocks* **space,** gap, crevice, fissure, cleft, cranny, chink. **3** *the crack of a rifle* **bang,** report, explosion, detonation, clap, crash. **4** *a crack on the head* **blow,** bang, hit, knock, rap, bump, smack, slap; informal bash, whack, clout.

▶ verb **1** break without dividing into separate parts. **2** give way under pressure or strain. **3** make a sudden sharp sound. **4** hit hard. **5** (of a person's voice) suddenly change in pitch. **6** informal solve or decipher.

SYNONYMS **1** *the glass cracked in the heat* **break,** split, fracture, rupture, snap. **2** *he finally cracked* **break down,** give way, cave in, go to pieces, give in, yield, succumb. **3** *she cracked him across the forehead* **hit,** strike, smack, slap, beat, thump, knock, rap; informal bash, whack, clobber, clout, clip. **4** *the code proved hard to crack* **decipher,** interpret, decode, break, solve.

▶ adjective very good or skilful: *a crack shot.*
  ■ **crack down on** informal deal severely with. **crack of dawn** daybreak. **crack a joke** tell a joke. **crack up** informal **1** suffer an emotional breakdown. **2** (**be cracked up to be**) be said to be.

crackdown ▶ noun a series of severe measures against undesirable or illegal behaviour.

cracker ▶ noun **1** a paper cylinder which makes a sharp noise and releases a small toy when it is pulled apart. **2** a firework that explodes with a crack. **3** a thin, dry biscuit. **4** informal a very good example of something.

crackers (or **cracked**) ▶ adjective informal mad.

cracking ▶ adjective informal **1** excellent. **2** fast: *a cracking pace.*

crackle ▶ verb (**crackles, crackling, crackled**) make a series of slight cracking noises.
▶ noun a crackling sound.
  □ **crackly** adjective.

crackling ▶ noun the crisp fatty skin of roast pork.

c

crackpot ▸ noun informal an eccentric or foolish person.

cradle ▸ noun 1 a baby's bed on rockers. 2 a place or period in which something originates or flourishes: *the cradle of civilization.* 3 a supporting framework.

SYNONYMS 1 *the baby's cradle* **crib**, Moses basket, cot, carrycot. 2 *the cradle of democracy* **birthplace**, fount, fountainhead, source, spring, origin.

▸ verb (**cradles, cradling, cradled**) hold gently and protectively.

SYNONYMS *she cradled his head in her arms* **hold**, support, cushion, pillow, nurse, rest.

craft ▸ noun 1 an activity involving skill in making things by hand. 2 skill in carrying out work. 3 (**crafts**) things made by hand. 4 (plural **craft**) a boat, ship, or aircraft. 5 skill in deceiving people.

SYNONYMS 1 *the historian's craft* **activity**, occupation, trade, profession, work, line of work, job. 2 *she used craft and diplomacy* **cunning**, craftiness, guile, wiliness, artfulness, deviousness, slyness, artfulness, trickery, duplicity, dishonesty, deceit, deceitfulness, deception, intrigue, subterfuge, wiles, ploys, ruses, schemes, tricks. 3 *a sailing craft* **vessel**, ship, boat, aircraft, spacecraft.

▸ verb make something skilfully.

craftsman ▸ noun (plural **craftsmen**) a worker who is skilled in a particular craft.

SYNONYMS **artisan**, artist, skilled worker, technician, expert, master.
□ **craftsmanship** noun.

crafty ▸ adjective (**craftier, craftiest**) clever at deceiving people; cunning.

SYNONYMS **cunning**, wily, sly, artful, devious, tricky, scheming, calculating, shrewd, canny, dishonest, deceitful. ANTONYMS open, honest.
□ **craftily** adverb.

crag ▸ noun a steep or rugged cliff or rock face.
□ **craggy** adjective.

cram ▸ verb (**crams, cramming, crammed**) 1 force too many people or things into a space. 2 fill something to the point of overflowing. 3 study hard just before an exam.

SYNONYMS 1 *wardrobes crammed with clothes* **fill**, stuff, pack, jam, fill to overflowing, overload, crowd, throng. 2 *they all crammed into the car* **crowd**, pack, pile, squash. 3 *he crammed his clothes into a suitcase* **push**, thrust, shove, force, ram, jam, stuff, pack, pile, squash, squeeze. 4 *most of the students are*

cramming for exams **revise**; informal swot, mug up, bone up.

crammer ▸ noun a college that prepares students for exams.

cramp ▸ noun 1 pain caused by a muscle or muscles tightening. 2 a tool for clamping two objects together.

SYNONYMS *stomach cramps* **spasm**, pain, shooting pain, twinge, pang, convulsion.

▸ verb restrict the development of.

SYNONYMS *tighter rules will cramp economic growth* **hinder**, impede, inhibit, hamper, constrain, hamstring, interfere with, restrict, limit, slow.

cramped ▸ adjective 1 uncomfortably small or crowded. 2 (of handwriting) small and difficult to read.

SYNONYMS 1 *cramped accommodation* **poky**, uncomfortable, confined, restricted, constricted, small, tiny, narrow, crowded, congested. 2 *cramped handwriting* **small**, crabbed, illegible, unreadable, indecipherable.
ANTONYMS spacious, flamboyant.

crampon ▸ noun a spiked plate fixed to a boot for climbing on ice or rock.

cranberry ▸ noun (plural **cranberries**) a small sour-tasting red berry.

crane ▸ noun 1 a tall machine used for moving heavy objects by suspending them from a projecting arm. 2 a wading bird with long legs and a long neck.
▸ verb (**cranes, craning, craned**) stretch out your neck to see something.
■ **crane fly** a flying insect with very long legs.

cranium /kray-ni-uhm/ ▸ noun (plural **craniums** or **crania** /kray-ni-uh/) the part of the skull that encloses the brain.
□ **cranial** adjective.

crank ▸ noun 1 a part of an axle or shaft that is bent at right angles, turned to produce motion. 2 an eccentric person.
▸ verb 1 start an engine by turning a crankshaft. 2 (**crank something up**) informal make something more intense. 3 (**crank something out**) informal produce something regularly and routinely.

crankshaft ▸ noun a shaft driven by a crank.

cranky ▸ adjective (**crankier, crankiest**) informal 1 strange or eccentric. 2 bad-tempered.

cranny ▸ noun (plural **crannies**) a small, narrow space or opening.

crape ▸ noun black silk, formerly used for mourning clothes.

craps ▸ noun a North American gambling game played with two dice.

crash ▸ verb 1 (of a vehicle) collide violently with an obstacle or another vehicle. 2 (of an aircraft) fall from the sky and hit the land or sea. **3** move or fall with a sudden loud noise. **4** (of shares) fall suddenly in value. **5** Computing fail suddenly. **6** (also **crash out**) informal fall deeply asleep. **7** (**crashing**) informal complete; total: *a crashing bore.*

SYNONYMS **1** *the car crashed into a tree* **smash into,** collide with, be in collision with, hit, strike, ram, cannon into, plough into, meet head-on; N. Amer. impact. **2** *he crashed his car* **smash,** wreck; Brit. write off; N. Amer. informal total. **3** *a tree crashed to the ground* **fall,** drop, plummet, plunge, sink, dive, tumble. **4** *his company crashed* **collapse,** fold, fail, go under, go bankrupt; informal go bust, go to the wall.

▸ noun **1** an instance of crashing. **2** a sudden loud, deep noise.

SYNONYMS **1** *a crash on the motorway* **accident,** collision, smash; N. Amer. wreck; informal pile-up; Brit. informal shunt. **2** *a loud crash* **bang,** smash, smack, crack, bump, thud. **3** *the crash of her company* **collapse,** failure, liquidation, bankruptcy.

▸ adjective rapid and concentrated: *a crash course in Italian.*
■ **crash helmet** a helmet worn by a motorcyclist to protect the head. **crash-land** (of an aircraft) land roughly in an emergency.

crass ▸ adjective very thoughtless and stupid.
□ **crassly** adverb.

crate ▸ noun **1** a wooden case for transporting goods. **2** a square container divided into individual units for holding bottles.

SYNONYMS **packing case,** chest, tea chest, box, container.

crater ▸ noun a large hollow caused by an explosion or impact or forming the mouth of a volcano.

SYNONYMS **hollow,** bowl, basin, hole, cavity, depression, dip; Geology caldera.

cravat /kruh-**vat**/ ▸ noun a strip of fabric worn by men round the neck and tucked inside a shirt.

crave ▸ verb (**craves, craving, craved**) **1** feel a very strong desire for. **2** old use ask for.

SYNONYMS **long for,** yearn for, hanker after, desire, want, hunger for, thirst for, pine for; informal be dying for.

craven ▸ adjective cowardly.

craving ▸ noun a very strong desire for something.

SYNONYMS **longing,** yearning, desire, hankering, hunger, thirst, appetite.

craw ▸ noun dated the part of a bird's throat where food is prepared for digestion.

crawl ▸ verb **1** move forward on the hands and knees or with the body close to the ground. **2** move very slowly along. **3** (**be crawling with**) be unpleasantly covered or crowded with. **4** feel an unpleasant sensation like that of something moving over the skin. **5** informal be too friendly or obedient in order to make someone like you.

SYNONYMS **1** *they crawled under the table* **creep,** worm your way, go on all fours, wriggle, slither, squirm. **2** *I'm not crawling to him* **grovel,** kowtow, pander, toady, bow and scrape, fawn; informal suck up, lick someone's boots.

▸ noun **1** an act of crawling. **2** a very slow rate of movement. **3** a swimming stroke involving alternate overarm movements and rapid kicks of the legs.

crayfish ▸ noun (plural **crayfish** or **crayfishes**) a shellfish like a small lobster.

crayon ▸ noun a stick of coloured chalk or wax, used for drawing.
▸ verb draw with a crayon or crayons.

craze ▸ noun a widespread but short-lived enthusiasm for something.

SYNONYMS **fad,** fashion, trend, vogue, enthusiasm, mania, passion, rage; informal thing.

crazed ▸ adjective **1** behaving in a wild or mad way. **2** covered with fine cracks.

crazy ▸ adjective (**crazier, craziest**) **1** mad. **2** (usu. **crazy about**) informal very enthusiastic about or fond of. **3** foolish or ridiculous.

SYNONYMS **1** *a crazy old man* **mad,** insane, out of your mind, deranged, demented, crazed, lunatic, unbalanced, unhinged; informal mental, off your head, round the bend; Brit. informal barmy, crackers, barking (mad), potty, round the twist. **2** *a crazy idea* **stupid,** foolish, idiotic, silly, absurd, ridiculous, ludicrous, preposterous; informal cockeyed; Brit. informal barmy, daft. **3** *he's crazy about her* **passionate,** very keen, enamoured, infatuated, smitten, enthusiastic, fanatical; informal wild, mad, nuts; Brit. informal potty.
ANTONYMS sane, sensible, apathetic.

■ **crazy paving** paving made of irregular pieces of flat stone.
□ **crazily** adverb **craziness** noun.

creak ▸ verb make a harsh, high sound.
▸ noun a creaking sound.
□ **creaky** adjective.

cream ▸ noun **1** the thick fatty liquid which rises to the top when milk is left to stand. **2** a food containing cream or having a creamy texture. **3** a thick liquid substance that is applied to the skin. **4** the very best of a group. **5** a very pale yellow or off-white colour.

> SYNONYMS **1** *skin cream* **lotion,** ointment, moisturizer, cosmetic, salve, rub. **2** *the cream of the world's photographers* **best,** finest, pick, flower, crème de la crème, elite.
> ANTONYMS dregs.

▸ verb **1** mash a cooked vegetable with milk or cream. **2** (**cream someone/thing off**) take away the best of a group.
 ■ **cream cheese** a soft, rich kind of cheese.

creamy ▸ adjective resembling or containing a lot of cream.

> SYNONYMS **smooth,** thick, velvety, rich, buttery.
> ANTONYMS lumpy.

crease ▸ noun **1** a line or ridge produced on paper or cloth by folding or pressing it. **2** Cricket any of a number of lines marked on the pitch.

> SYNONYMS **1** *trousers with creases* **fold,** line, ridge, furrow, groove, corrugation. **2** *creases at the corners of her eyes* **wrinkle,** line, crinkle, pucker, crow's foot.

▸ verb (**creases, creasing, creased**) make creases in.

> SYNONYMS *her skirt was creased* **crumple,** wrinkle, crinkle, line, scrunch up, rumple.

create ▸ verb (**creates, creating, created**) **1** bring into existence. **2** cause something to happen. **3** informal make a fuss; complain.

> SYNONYMS **1** *she has created a work of stunning originality* **produce,** generate, bring into being, make, fashion, build, construct. **2** *regular socializing creates a good team spirit* **bring about,** give rise to, lead to, result in, cause, breed, generate, engender, produce. **3** *the governments planned to create a free-trade zone* **establish,** found, initiate, institute, constitute, inaugurate, launch, set up. **4** *she was created a life peer* **appoint,** make.
> ANTONYMS destroy, abolish.

creation ▸ noun **1** the action of creating. **2** a thing which has been made or invented. **3** (**Creation**) literary the universe.

> SYNONYMS **1** *the creation of a government* **establishment,** formation, foundation, initiation, institution, inauguration, constitution, setting up. **2** *the whole of creation* **the world,** the universe, the cosmos, nature, the natural world. **3** *Dickens's literary creations* **work,** work of art, production, opus, achievement,

concoction, invention; informal brainchild.
> ANTONYMS abolition, destruction.

creative ▸ adjective involving the use of the imagination in order to create something.

> SYNONYMS **inventive,** imaginative, innovative, experimental, original, artistic, inspired, visionary.
> ANTONYMS unimaginative.

□ **creatively** adverb.

creativity ▸ noun the quality of being creative.

> SYNONYMS **inventiveness,** imagination, innovation, originality, artistry, inspiration, vision.

creator ▸ noun **1** a person or thing that creates. **2** (**the Creator**) God.

> SYNONYMS **maker,** producer, author, designer, deviser, originator, inventor, architect.

creature ▸ noun a living being, in particular an animal rather than a person.

> SYNONYMS **animal,** beast, brute, living thing, living being; N. Amer. informal critter.

■ **creature comforts** things that make life comfortable.

crèche /kresh/ ▸ noun a place where babies and young children are looked after while their parents are at work.

credence /kree-duhnss/ ▸ noun belief that something is true.

credential /kri-den-sh'l/ ▸ noun **1** a qualification, achievement, or quality used to indicate how suitable a person is for something. **2** (**credentials**) documents that prove a person's identity or qualifications.

> SYNONYMS **1** *a biologist with impeccable credentials* **suitability,** eligibility, attributes, qualifications, record, experience, background. **2** *examine the credentials of all callers* **documents,** identity papers, ID, passport, testimonial, reference, certification.

credibility ▸ noun the quality of being trusted or believable.

> SYNONYMS **plausibility,** believability, credence, trustworthiness, reliability, dependability, integrity.

credible ▸ adjective able to be believed; convincing.

> SYNONYMS **believable,** plausible, conceivable, persuasive, convincing, tenable, probable, possible, feasible, reasonable.

□ **credibly** adverb.

! Don't confuse **credible** with **creditable**: **credible** means 'believable or convincing', whereas **creditable** means 'deserving recognition and praise'.

credit ▶ noun **1** the system of doing business by trusting that a customer will pay at a later date for goods or services supplied. **2** public recognition or praise given for an achievement or quality. **3** (**a credit to**) a source of pride to. **4** (**credits**) a list of the people who worked on a film or television programme, displayed at the end. **5** a unit of study counting towards a degree or diploma. **6** an entry in an account recording an amount received.

SYNONYMS *he got the credit for the work* **praise**, commendation, acclaim, acknowledgement, recognition, kudos, glory, respect, appreciation.

▶ verb (**credits, crediting, credited**) **1** (**credit someone with**) feel that someone is responsible for something good. **2** believe something surprising. **3** add an amount of money to an account.

SYNONYMS *you wouldn't credit it!* **believe**, accept, give credence to, trust, have faith in.

■ **be in credit** (of an account) have money in it. **credit card** a plastic card that allows you to buy things and pay for them later.

creditable ▶ adjective deserving recognition and praise.
□ **creditably** adverb.

creditor ▶ noun a person or company to whom money is owed.

credo /**kree**-doh, **kray**-doh/ ▶ noun (plural **credos**) a statement of a person's beliefs or aims.

credulous ▶ adjective too ready to believe things.
□ **credulity** noun.

creed ▶ noun **1** a system of religious belief; a faith. **2** a set of beliefs or principles.

SYNONYMS **1** *people of many creeds* **faith**, religion, belief, religious persuasion. **2** *his political creed* **beliefs**, principles, articles of faith, ideology, credo.

creek ▶ noun **1** a narrow stretch of water running inland from the coast. **2** N. Amer. Austral./NZ a stream or small river.

SYNONYMS **inlet**, bay, estuary, fjord; Scottish firth.

■ **up the creek** informal in severe difficulty.

creel ▶ noun a large basket for carrying fish.

creep ▶ verb (**creeps, creeping, crept**) **1** move slowly and cautiously. **2** progress or develop gradually.

SYNONYMS **tiptoe**, steal, sneak, slink, edge, inch, skulk, prowl.

▶ noun informal a person who is insincerely friendly or respectful.

■ **give you the creeps** make you feel disgust or fear.

creeper ▶ noun a plant that grows along the ground or another surface.

creepy ▶ adjective (**creepier, creepiest**) informal causing an unpleasant feeling of fear or unease.

SYNONYMS **frightening**, eerie, disturbing, sinister, weird, menacing, threatening; informal spooky, scary.

cremate ▶ verb (**cremates, cremating, cremated**) dispose of a dead body by burning it.
□ **cremation** noun.

crematorium /kre-muh-**tor**-i-uhm/ ▶ noun (plural **crematoria** or **crematoriums**) a building where dead people are cremated.

crème de la crème /krem duh la **krem**/ ▶ noun the best person or thing of a particular kind.

crenellations ▶ plural noun battlements.
□ **crenellated** adjective.

Creole /**kree**-ohl/ ▶ noun **1** (in the Caribbean) a person of mixed European and black descent. **2** a descendant of French settlers in the southern US. **3** a combination of a European language and an African language.

creosote /**kree**-uh-soht/ ▶ noun a dark brown oil painted on to wood to preserve it.

crêpe (or **crepe**) /krayp/ ▶ noun **1** a light, thin fabric with a wrinkled surface. **2** hard-wearing wrinkled rubber used for the soles of shoes. **3** /krayp, krep/ a thin pancake.
■ **crêpe paper** thin, crinkled paper.

crept past and past participle of CREEP.

crepuscular /kri-**puss**-kyuu-ler/ ▶ adjective literary resembling twilight; dim and shadowy.

crescendo /kri-**shen**-doh/ ▶ noun (plural **crescendos** or **crescendi** /kri-**shen**-di/) **1** a gradual increase in loudness in a piece of music. **2** a climax.

crescent ▶ noun a narrow curved shape tapering to a point at each end.

cress ▶ noun a plant with hot-tasting leaves.

crest ▶ noun **1** a tuft or growth of feathers, fur, or skin on the head of a bird or animal. **2** a plume of feathers on a helmet. **3** the top of a ridge, wave, etc. **4** a distinctive design in heraldry representing a family or organization.

SYNONYMS **1** *the bird's crest* **tuft**, comb, plume, crown. **2** *the crest of the hill* **summit**, peak, top, ridge, pinnacle, brow, crown, apex. **3** *the Duke's crest* **insignia**, emblem, coat of arms, arms, badge, device, regalia.

▶ verb reach the top of.
☐ **crested** adjective.

crestfallen ▶ adjective sad and disappointed.

cretin ▶ noun a stupid person.
☐ **cretinous** adjective.

crevasse /kri-vass/ ▶ noun a deep open crack in a glacier.

crevice ▶ noun a narrow opening or crack in a rock or wall.

SYNONYMS **crack,** fissure, cleft, chink, cranny, slit, split.

crew[1] ▶ noun **1** a group of people who work on a ship, aircraft, or train. **2** the members of a crew other than the officers. **3** a group of people who work together: *a film crew.*

SYNONYMS **1** *the ship's crew* **company,** complement, sailors, hands. **2** *a film crew* **team,** squad, company, unit, party, gang.

▶ verb act as a member of a crew.
■ **crew cut** a very short haircut for men and boys. **crew neck** a close-fitting round neckline.

crew[2] past of CROW[2].

crib ▶ noun **1** chiefly N. Amer. a child's cot. **2** informal a list of answers or other information used, for example, by students to cheat in a test. **3** the card game cribbage.
▶ verb (**cribs, cribbing, cribbed**) informal copy something dishonestly.

cribbage ▶ noun a card game for two players.

crick ▶ noun a painful stiff feeling in the neck or back.
▶ verb twist or strain the neck or back.

cricket[1] ▶ noun a team game played with a bat, ball, and wickets.
☐ **cricketer** noun.

cricket[2] ▶ noun an insect like a grasshopper, the male of which produces a shrill chirping sound.

cried past and past participle of CRY.

crime ▶ noun **1** an action that is against the law. **2** illegal actions as a whole. **3** something disgraceful or very unfair.

SYNONYMS **1** *kidnapping is a serious crime* **offence,** unlawful act, illegal act, felony, violation, misdemeanour. **2** *the increase in crime* **lawbreaking,** delinquency, wrongdoing, criminality, misconduct, illegality, villainy, vice.

criminal ▶ noun a person who has committed a crime.

SYNONYMS *a convicted criminal* **lawbreaker,** offender, villain, delinquent, felon, culprit; informal **crook;** Austral./NZ informal **crim.**

▶ adjective **1** relating to crime or a crime. **2** informal disgraceful or very unfair.

SYNONYMS **1** *criminal conduct* **unlawful,** illegal, illicit, lawless, delinquent, corrupt; informal **crooked;** Brit. informal **bent.** **2** *a criminal waste of money* **deplorable,** shameful, reprehensible, disgraceful, inexcusable, outrageous, scandalous.
ANTONYMS lawful, reasonable.

☐ **criminality** noun **criminally** adverb.

crimp ▶ verb press into small folds or ridges.

crimson ▶ noun a deep red colour.

cringe ▶ verb (**cringes, cringing, cringed**) **1** shrink back or cower in fear. **2** have a sudden feeling of embarrassment or disgust.

crinkle ▶ verb (**crinkle, crinkling, crinkled**) form small creases or wrinkles.
▶ noun a small crease or wrinkle.
☐ **crinkly** adjective.

crinoline /krin-uh-lin/ ▶ noun a petticoat stiffened with hoops, formerly worn to make a long skirt stand out.

cripple ▶ noun old use or offensive a person who is unable to walk or move properly because they are disabled or injured.
▶ verb (**cripples, crippling, crippled**) **1** make someone unable to move or walk properly. **2** severely damage or weaken.

SYNONYMS **1** *the accident crippled her* **disable,** paralyse, immobilize, incapacitate, handicap. **2** (**crippled**) *a poor crippled child* **disabled,** paralysed, incapacitated, (physically) handicapped, lame, immobilized, bedridden, confined to a wheelchair; euphemistic physically challenged. **3** *the company had been crippled by the recession* **damage,** weaken, hamper, paralyse, ruin, destroy, wipe out, bring to a standstill, put out of action, put out of business.
ANTONYMS assist.

crisis ▶ noun (plural **crises**) **1** a time of severe difficulty or danger. **2** a time when a difficult decision must be made.

SYNONYMS **1** *the current economic crisis* **emergency,** disaster, catastrophe, calamity, meltdown, predicament, plight, dire straits. **2** *the situation had reached a crisis* **critical point,** turning point, crossroads, head, moment of truth; informal **crunch.**

crisp ▶ adjective **1** firm, dry, and brittle. **2** (of the weather) cool and fresh. **3** brisk and decisive.

SYNONYMS **1** *crisp bacon* **crunchy,** crispy, brittle, breakable, dry. **2** *a crisp autumn day* **invigorating,** brisk, fresh, refreshing, exhilarating. **3** *crisp white*

bedlinen **smooth,** fresh, ironed, starched.
ANTONYMS soft, sultry, crumpled.

▶ noun a thin, crisp slice of deep-fried potato.
□ **crisply** adverb **crispy** adjective.

crispbread ▶ noun a thin, crisp biscuit made from rye or wheat.

criss-cross ▶ adjective with a pattern of crossing lines.
▶ verb **1** form a criss-cross pattern on. **2** repeatedly go back and forth around a place.

criterion /kry-**teer**-i-uhn/ ▶ noun (plural **criteria** /kry-**teer**-i-uh/) a standard by which something may be judged.

> SYNONYMS **standard,** measure, gauge, test, benchmark, yardstick, touchstone, barometer.

> ❗ The singular form is **criterion** and the plural form is **criteria**. It's wrong to use **criteria** as a singular: say *further criteria need to be considered* not *a further criteria needs to be considered*.

critic ▶ noun **1** a person who finds fault with someone or something. **2** a person who assesses literary or artistic works.

> SYNONYMS **1** *critics of the government* **detractor,** attacker, fault-finder; informal knocker. **2** *a literary critic* **reviewer,** commentator, analyst, judge, pundit, expert.

critical ▶ adjective **1** expressing disapproving comments. **2** assessing a literary or artistic work. **3** very important in terms of the success or failure of something. **4** at a point of danger or crisis.

> SYNONYMS **1** *a highly critical report* **disapproving,** disparaging, scathing, fault-finding, judgemental, negative, unfavourable, censorious; informal nit-picking, picky. **2** *the situation is critical* **serious,** grave, precarious, touch-and-go, in the balance, desperate, dire, acute, life-and-death. **3** *the choice of materials is critical* **crucial,** vital, essential, all-important, paramount, fundamental, key, pivotal.
> ANTONYMS complimentary, safe, unimportant.

□ **critically** adverb.

criticism ▶ noun **1** expression of disapproval. **2** the assessment of literary or artistic works.

> SYNONYMS **1** *she was stung by his criticism* **fault-finding,** censure, condemnation, disapproval, disparagement; informal flak, a bad press, panning; Brit. informal stick. **2** *literary criticism* **evaluation,** assessment, appraisal, appreciation, analysis, critique, judgement,

commentary.
ANTONYMS praise.

criticize (or **criticise**) ▶ verb (**criticizes, criticizing, criticized**) **1** express disapproval of. **2** assess a literary or artistic work.

> SYNONYMS **find fault with,** censure, condemn, attack, disparage, denigrate, run down; informal knock, pan, pull to pieces; Brit. informal slag off, slate, rubbish; N. Amer. informal pummel, trash; Austral./NZ informal bag.
> ANTONYMS praise.

critique /kri-**teek**/ ▶ noun a critical assessment.

croak ▶ noun a deep, hoarse sound, like that made by a frog.
▶ verb make a croak.
□ **croaky** adjective.

Croatian /kroh-**ay**-sh'n/ ▶ noun (also **Croat** /**kroh**-at/) **1** a person from Croatia. **2** the language of Croatia.
▶ adjective relating to Croatia or Croatian.

crochet /**kroh**-shay/ ▶ noun a craft in which yarn is made into fabric with a hooked needle.
▶ verb (**crochets, crocheting, crocheted**) make an article by means of crochet.

crock[1] ▶ noun informal a feeble and useless old person.

crock[2] ▶ noun an earthenware pot or jar.

crockery ▶ noun plates, dishes, cups, etc. made of earthenware or china.

crocodile ▶ noun **1** a large reptile with long jaws, a long tail, and a thick skin. **2** Brit. informal a line of schoolchildren walking in pairs.
■ **crocodile tears** insincere tears or sorrow.

crocus ▶ noun (plural **crocuses**) a small plant with bright yellow, purple, or white flowers.

croft ▶ noun a small rented farm in Scotland or northern England.
□ **crofter** noun.

croissant /**krwass**-on/ ▶ noun a flaky crescent-shaped bread roll.

crone ▶ noun an ugly old woman.

crony ▶ noun (plural **cronies**) informal a close friend or companion.

crook ▶ noun **1** a shepherd's or bishop's hooked staff. **2** a bend at a person's elbow. **3** informal a criminal or dishonest person.

> SYNONYMS See **CRIMINAL** (noun).

▶ verb bend a finger or leg.

crooked ▶ adjective **1** bent or twisted out of shape or position. **2** informal dishonest or illegal.

> SYNONYMS **1** *narrow, crooked streets* **winding,** twisting, zigzag, meandering,

tortuous, serpentine. **2** *a crooked spine* **bent,** twisted, misshapen, deformed, malformed, contorted, warped, bowed, distorted. **3** *the picture over the bed looked crooked* **lopsided,** askew, awry, off-centre, out of true, at an angle, slanting, squint; Scottish agley; Brit. informal skew-whiff, wonky. **4** *a crooked deal* **dishonest,** criminal, illegal, unlawful, nefarious, fraudulent, corrupt; informal shady; Brit. informal bent.
ANTONYMS straight, legal, honest.

croon ▶ verb hum, sing, or speak in a soft, low voice.
□ **crooner** noun.

crop ▶ noun **1** a plant grown in large quantities, especially as food. **2** an amount of a crop harvested at one time. **3** a very short hairstyle. **4** a pouch in a bird's throat where food is stored or prepared for digestion. **5** a short flexible whip used by horse riders.

> SYNONYMS *some farmers lost their entire crop* **harvest,** yield, fruits, produce, vintage.

▶ verb (**crops, cropping, cropped**) **1** cut something very short. **2** (of an animal) bite off and eat the tops of plants. **3** (**crop up**) appear or happen unexpectedly.

> SYNONYMS **1** *she's had her hair cropped* **cut,** clip, trim, shear, shave, lop off, chop off, hack off, dock. **2** *a flock of sheep were cropping the turf* **graze on,** browse on, feed on, nibble, eat.

cropper ▶ noun (**come a cropper**) informal fall or fail heavily.

croquet /kroh-kay/ ▶ noun a game in which wooden balls are hit through hoops with a mallet.

croquette /kroh-ket/ ▶ noun a small cake or roll of vegetables, meat, or fish, fried in breadcrumbs.

cross ▶ noun **1** a mark, object, or shape formed by two short intersecting lines or pieces (+ or ×). **2** a medal or monument shaped like a cross. **3** (**the Cross**) the wooden cross on which Jesus was crucified. **4** an animal or plant resulting from cross-breeding. **5** a mixture of two things.

> SYNONYMS **1** *we all have our crosses to bear* **burden,** trouble, worry, trial, affliction, curse, misfortune, woe; informal hassle, headache. **2** *a cross between a yak and a cow* **mixture,** blend, combination, amalgam, hybrid, cross-breed, mongrel.

▶ verb **1** go or extend across or to the other side of. **2** pass in an opposite or different direction. **3** place crosswise. **4** draw a line or lines across. **5** Brit. mark a cheque with a pair of parallel lines to indicate that it must be paid into a named bank account. **6** Soccer

pass the ball across the field towards the centre. **7** oppose or stand in the way of. **8** make an animal breed with another of a different species.

> SYNONYMS **1** *they crossed the hills on foot* **travel across,** traverse, negotiate, navigate, cover. **2** *the two roads cross* **intersect,** meet, join, connect. **3** *no one dared cross him* **oppose,** resist, defy, obstruct, contradict, argue with, stand up to. **4** *the breed was crossed with Friesian* **hybridize,** cross-breed, interbreed, cross-fertilize, cross-pollinate.

▶ adjective annoyed.

> SYNONYMS *Jane was getting cross* **angry,** annoyed, irate, irritated, in a bad mood, put out; informal hot under the collar, peeved; Brit. informal shirty, ratty; N. Amer. informal sore, ticked off; Austral./NZ informal ropeable, snaky.
ANTONYMS pleased.

■ **at cross purposes** misunderstanding or having different aims from one another. **cross-breed** produce an animal or plant by making two different species, breeds, or varieties breed. **cross-check** check figures or information by using a different source or method. **cross-country 1** across fields or countryside. **2** across a region or country. **cross-dressing** the wearing of clothes usually worn by the opposite sex. **cross-examine** question a witness called by the other party in a court of law. **cross-eyed** having one or both eyes turned inwards towards the nose. **cross-fertilize** fertilize a plant using pollen from another plant of the same species. **cross something off** remove an item from a list. **cross something out** remove a word or phrase by drawing a line through it. **cross-question** question in great detail. **cross reference** a reference to another written work, or part of one, given to provide further information. **cross section 1** a surface exposed by making a straight cut through a solid object at right angles to its length. **2** a sample of a larger group. **cross swords** have an argument or dispute.
□ **crossly** adverb.

crossbar ▶ noun **1** a horizontal bar between the two upright posts of a football goal. **2** a bar between the handlebars and saddle on a bicycle.

crossbow ▶ noun a bow with a mechanism for drawing and releasing the string.

crossfire ▶ noun gunfire from two or more directions passing through the same area.

cross-hatch ▶ verb shade an area with many intersecting parallel lines.

crossing ▶ noun **1** a place where roads or railway lines cross. **2** a place to cross a street or railway line.

crossroads ▸ noun a place where two or more roads cross each other.

crosswise (or **crossways**) ▸ adverb **1** in the form of a cross. **2** diagonally.

crossword ▸ noun a puzzle in which words crossing each other vertically and horizontally are written as answers to clues.

crotch ▸ noun the part of the human body between the legs.

crotchet ▸ noun a musical note that lasts half as long as a minim.

crotchety ▸ adjective irritable.

crouch ▸ verb bend the knees and bring the upper body forward and down.

> SYNONYMS **squat,** bend (down), hunker down, hunch over, stoop, duck, cower.

▸ noun a crouching position.

croup¹ /kroop/ ▸ noun an illness of children, with coughing and breathing difficulties.

croup² /kroop/ ▸ noun a horse's hindquarters.

croupier /kroo-pi-ay, kroo-pi-er/ ▸ noun the person in charge of a gambling table in a casino.

crouton /kroo-ton/ ▸ noun a small piece of fried or toasted bread served with soup.

crow¹ ▸ noun a large black bird with a harsh call.
■ **as the crow flies** in a straight line across country. **crow's feet** wrinkles at the outer corner of a person's eye. **crow's-nest** a platform at the top of a ship's mast to watch from.

crow² ▸ verb (**crows, crowing, crowed** or **crew**) **1** (of a cock) make its loud, shrill cry. **2** boastfully express pride or triumph.

> SYNONYMS **boast,** brag, blow your own trumpet, swagger, swank, gloat.

▸ noun the cry of a cock.

crowbar ▸ noun an iron bar with a flattened end, used as a lever.

crowd ▸ noun **1** a large number of people gathered together. **2** informal a group of people with a shared quality.

> SYNONYMS **1** *a crowd gathered* **throng,** horde, mass, multitude, host, army, swarm, mob, rabble; informal gaggle. **2** *they're a nice crowd* **group,** set, circle, clique; informal gang, bunch, crew, lot. **3** *the final attracted a capacity crowd* **audience,** spectators, listeners, viewers, house, turnout, attendance, gate, congregation.

▸ verb **1** fill a space almost completely. **2** move or come together as a crowd. **3** move or stand too close to.

> SYNONYMS **1** *reporters crowded round her* **cluster,** flock, swarm, mill, throng, huddle, gather, assemble, congregate, converge. **2** (**crowded**) **packed,** full, filled to capacity, full to bursting, congested, overflowing, teeming, swarming, thronged, populous, overpopulated, busy; informal jam-packed, stuffed, chock-a-block, chock-full, bursting at the seams, full to the gunwales, wall-to-wall, mobbed; Austral./NZ informal chocker. **3** *the guests crowded into the dining room* **surge,** throng, push, jostle, elbow your way, squeeze, pile, cram.

crown ▸ noun **1** a circular headdress worn by a king or queen. **2** (**the Crown**) the reigning king or queen. **3** a wreath of leaves or flowers worn as an emblem of victory. **4** an award gained by a victory. **5** the top or highest part of something. **6** an artificial replacement or covering for the upper part of a tooth. **7** a former British coin worth five shillings (25 pence).

> SYNONYMS **1** *the royal crown* **coronet,** diadem, tiara, circlet. **2** *loyal servants of the Crown* **monarch,** sovereign, king, queen, emperor, empress, monarchy, royalty. **3** *the crown of the hill* **top,** crest, summit, peak, pinnacle, tip, brow, apex.

▸ verb **1** place a crown on the head of someone to declare them to be king or queen. **2** rest on or form the top of.

> SYNONYMS **1** *the building is crowned by a balustrade* **top,** cap, tip, head, surmount. **2** *a teaching post at Harvard crowned his career* **round off,** cap, be the climax of, be the culmination of, top off, complete.

crozier /kroh-zi-er/ ▸ noun a hooked staff carried by a bishop.

crucial ▸ adjective very important, especially in terms of the success or failure of something.

> SYNONYMS **1** *negotiations were at a crucial stage* **pivotal,** critical, key, decisive, life-and-death. **2** *confidentiality is crucial* **all-important,** of the utmost importance, of the essence, critical, paramount, essential, vital.
> ANTONYMS insignificant, unimportant.

□ **crucially** adverb.

crucible ▸ noun a container in which metals or other substances may be melted or heated.

crucifix ▸ noun a small cross with a figure of Jesus on it.

crucifixion ▸ noun **1** the execution of a person by crucifying them. **2** (**the Crucifixion**) the crucifixion of Jesus.

cruciform ▸ adjective having the shape of a cross.

crucify ▸ verb (crucifies, crucifying, crucified) **1** kill someone by nailing or tying them to a cross. **2** informal criticize someone severely.

crude ▸ adjective **1** in a natural state; not yet processed. **2** rough or simple. **3** coarse or vulgar.

> SYNONYMS **1** *crude oil* **unrefined,** unpurified, unprocessed, untreated, coarse, raw, natural. **2** *a crude barricade* **primitive,** simple, basic, homespun, rudimentary, rough and ready, improvised. **3** *crude jokes* **vulgar,** rude, dirty, naughty, smutty, indecent, obscene, coarse; informal blue.
> ANTONYMS refined, sophisticated, clean.

☐ **crudely** adverb **crudity** noun.

cruel ▸ adjective (**crueller, cruellest** or **crueler, cruelest**) **1** taking pleasure in the suffering of other people. **2** causing suffering or pain.

> SYNONYMS **1** *a cruel man* **brutal,** savage, inhuman, barbaric, vicious, sadistic, monstrous, callous, ruthless, merciless, heartless, unkind, inhumane. **2** *her death was a cruel blow* **harsh,** severe, bitter, heartbreaking, heart-rending, painful, agonizing, traumatic.
> ANTONYMS compassionate.

☐ **cruelly** adverb.

cruelty ▸ noun (plural **cruelties**) cruel behaviour or treatment.

> SYNONYMS **brutality,** savagery, inhumanity, barbarity, viciousness, sadism, callousness, ruthlessness.

cruet ▸ noun a small container or set of containers for salt, pepper, oil, or vinegar.

cruise ▸ verb (cruises, cruising, cruised) **1** move slowly around without a definite destination. **2** travel smoothly at a moderate speed.

> SYNONYMS **1** *she cruised across the Atlantic* **sail,** voyage. **2** *a taxi cruised past* **drive slowly,** drift, sail; informal mosey, tootle; Brit. informal pootle.

▸ noun a voyage on a ship taken as a holiday.

> SYNONYMS *a cruise down the Nile* (**boat**) **trip,** voyage, sail.

cruiser ▸ noun **1** a large, fast warship. **2** a yacht or motorboat with passenger accommodation.

crumb ▸ noun **1** a small fragment of bread, cake, or biscuit. **2** a very small amount.

> SYNONYMS **fragment,** bit, morsel, particle, speck, scrap, shred, atom, trace, mite, jot, ounce; informal smidgen, tad.

crumble ▸ verb (crumbles, crumbling, crumbled) **1** break or fall apart into small fragments. **2** gradually decline or fall apart.

> SYNONYMS **1** *the plaster was crumbling* **disintegrate,** fall apart, fall to pieces, collapse, decompose, break up, decay, become dilapidated. **2** *crumble the cheese with your fingers* **break up,** crush, fragment. **3** *party unity began to crumble* **collapse,** deteriorate, degenerate, fail.

▸ noun Brit. a baked pudding made with fruit and a crumbly topping.
☐ **crumbly** adjective.

crummy ▸ adjective (**crummier, crummiest**) informal bad or unpleasant.

crumpet ▸ noun **1** a soft, flat cake with an open texture, eaten toasted and buttered. **2** Brit. informal sexually attractive women.

crumple ▸ verb (crumples, crumpling, crumpled) **1** crease something by crushing it. **2** collapse.

> SYNONYMS **1** *she crumpled the note in her fist* **crush,** scrunch up, screw up, squash, squeeze. **2** *his trousers were dirty and crumpled* **crease,** wrinkle, crinkle, rumple. **3** *her resistance crumpled* **collapse,** give way, cave in, go to pieces, break down, crumble.
> ANTONYMS flatten out, iron, hold.

crunch ▸ verb **1** crush something hard or brittle with the teeth. **2** move with a noisy grinding sound.

> SYNONYMS **munch,** chomp, champ, bite into, crush, grind, break, smash.

▸ noun **1** a crunching sound. **2** (**the crunch**) informal the crucial point of a situation.
☐ **crunchy** adjective.

crusade ▸ noun **1** (**the Crusades**) a series of medieval military expeditions made by Europeans against Muslims in the Middle East. **2** an energetic organized campaign.

> SYNONYMS *a crusade against crime* **campaign,** drive, push, movement, effort, struggle, battle, war, offensive.

▸ verb (crusades, crusading, crusaded) take part in a crusade.

> SYNONYMS *he has crusaded for hopeless causes* **campaign,** fight, battle, strive, struggle, agitate, lobby.

☐ **crusader** noun.

crush ▸ verb **1** squash, crease, or break up something by pressing it. **2** defeat completely.

> SYNONYMS **1** *essential oils are released when the herbs are crushed* **squash,** squeeze, press, pulp, mash, mangle, pulverize. **2** *your dress will get crushed* **crease,** crumple, rumple, wrinkle, scrunch up. **3** *crush the biscuits with a rolling pin* **pulverize,** pound, grind, break up, smash, crumble. **4** *the new regime crushed all opposition* **suppress,**

put down, quell, stamp out, repress, subdue, extinguish. **5** *Alan was crushed by her words* **demoralize**, deflate, flatten, squash, devastate, shatter, mortify, humiliate.
ANTONYMS allow, promote, encourage.

▸ noun **1** a crowd of people pressed closely together. **2** informal a strong, short-lived feeling of love for someone.

SYNONYMS *the crush of people* **crowd**, throng, horde, swarm, press, mob.

crust ▸ noun **1** the tough outer part of a loaf of bread. **2** a hardened layer, coating, or deposit. **3** the outermost layer of the earth. **4** a layer of pastry covering a pie.

SYNONYMS **covering**, layer, coating, surface, topping, sheet, film, skin, shell, scab.

▸ verb form into a crust, or cover with a crust.

crustacean /kruss-**tay**-sh'n/ ▸ noun a hard-shelled creature such as a crab or lobster, usually living in water.

crusty ▸ adjective (**crustier**, **crustiest**) **1** having or consisting of a crust. **2** easily irritated.

crutch ▸ noun **1** a long stick with a bar at the top, used as a support by a lame person. **2** a person's crotch.

crux ▸ noun (**the crux**) the most important point that is being discussed.

cry ▸ verb (**cries**, **crying**, **cried**) **1** shed tears. **2** shout or scream loudly. **3** (of an animal) make a distinctive call. **4** (**cry out for**) demand or need. **5** (**cry off**) informal fail to keep to an arrangement.

SYNONYMS **1** *Mandy started to cry* **weep**, shed tears, sob, wail, snivel, whimper; Scottish greet; informal blub, blubber; Brit. informal grizzle. **2** *'Wait!' he cried* **call**, shout, exclaim, sing out, yell, bawl, bellow, roar; informal holler.
ANTONYMS laugh, whisper.

▸ noun (plural **cries**) **1** a period of shedding tears. **2** a loud shout or scream. **3** an animal's distinctive call.

SYNONYMS **call**, shout, exclamation, yell, bawl, bellow, roar; informal holler.

■ **a crying shame** a very unfortunate situation.

cryogenics /kry-uh-**jen**-iks/ ▸ noun the branch of physics concerned with very low temperatures.
□ **cryogenic** adjective.

crypt ▸ noun an underground room beneath a church, used as a chapel or burial place.

cryptic ▸ adjective mysterious or obscure in meaning.
□ **cryptically** adverb.

crystal ▸ noun **1** a transparent mineral, especially quartz. **2** a piece of a solid substance that is formed naturally and has flat sides arranged symmetrically. **3** very clear glass.
■ **crystal ball** a globe of glass or crystal, used for predicting the future.

crystalline ▸ adjective **1** resembling a crystal. **2** literary very clear.

crystallize (or **crystallise**) ▸ verb (**crystallizes**, **crystallizing**, **crystallized**) **1** form crystals. **2** become definite and clear. **3** (**crystallized**) (of fruit) coated with and preserved in sugar.

cu. ▸ abbreviation cubic.

cub ▸ noun **1** the young of a fox, bear, lion, or other meat-eating mammal. **2** (also **Cub Scout**) a member of the junior branch of the Scout Association.

Cuban ▸ noun a person from Cuba.
▸ adjective relating to Cuba.

cubbyhole ▸ noun a small enclosed space or room.

cube ▸ noun **1** a three-dimensional shape with six equal square faces. **2** the result obtained when a number is multiplied by itself twice.
▸ verb **1** cut food into small cubes. **2** find the cube of a number.
■ **cube root** the number which produces a given number when cubed.

cubic ▸ adjective **1** having the shape of a cube. **2** involving the cube of a quantity: *a cubic metre*.

cubicle ▸ noun a small area of a room that is separated off for privacy.

cubism ▸ noun a style of painting featuring regular lines and shapes.
□ **cubist** noun & adjective.

cubit ▸ noun an ancient measure of length, approximately equal to the length of a forearm.

cuckoo ▸ noun a bird known for laying its eggs in the nests of other birds.
▸ adjective informal crazy.

cucumber ▸ noun a long green fruit with watery flesh, eaten in salads.

cud ▸ noun (usu. in **chew the cud**) partly digested food that cows and similar animals bring back from the first stomach to the mouth for further chewing.

cuddle ▸ verb (**cuddles**, **cuddling**, **cuddled**) **1** hold closely and lovingly in your arms. **2** (often **cuddle up to**) lie or sit close.

SYNONYMS **1** *she picked up the baby and cuddled her* **hug**, embrace, clasp, hold in your arms. **2** *the pair were kissing and cuddling* **embrace**, hug, caress, pet, fondle; informal canoodle, smooch. **3** *I cuddled up to him* **snuggle**, nestle, curl, nuzzle.

▶ noun an affectionate hug.

cuddly ▶ adjective (**cuddlier**, **cuddliest**) pleasantly soft or plump.

cudgel ▶ noun a short, thick stick used as a weapon.

SYNONYMS **club**, truncheon, bludgeon, baton, shillelagh, mace; N. Amer. blackjack, nightstick; Brit. informal cosh.

▶ verb (**cudgels**, **cudgelling**, **cudgelled**; US spelling **cudgels**, **cudgeling**, **cudgeled**) beat with a cudgel.

SYNONYMS **club**, bludgeon, beat, batter, bash; Brit. informal cosh.

cue¹ ▶ noun 1 a signal to an actor to enter or to begin their speech or performance. 2 a signal or prompt for action.

SYNONYMS **signal**, sign, indication, prompt, reminder.

▶ verb (**cues**, **cueing** or **cuing**, **cued**) 1 give a cue to. 2 set a piece of audio or video equipment to play a particular part of a recording.

cue² ▶ noun a long rod for hitting the ball in snooker, billiards, or pool.

cuff¹ ▶ noun 1 the end part of a sleeve, where the material of the sleeve is turned back or a separate band is sewn on. 2 chiefly N. Amer. a trouser turn-up.

■ **off the cuff** informal without preparation.

cuff² ▶ verb hit with an open hand.
▶ noun a blow with an open hand.

cufflink ▶ noun a device for fastening together the sides of a shirt cuff.

cuisine /kwi-**zeen**/ ▶ noun a particular style of cooking.

cul-de-sac /**kul**-duh-sak/ ▶ noun (plural **cul-de-sacs**) a street or passage closed at one end.

culinary ▶ adjective having to do with cooking.

cull ▶ verb 1 kill a selected number of a certain kind of animal to reduce its population. 2 choose a few things from a wide range.
▶ noun a selective killing of a certain kind of animal.

culminate ▶ verb (**culminates**, **culminating**, **culminated**) reach a climax or point of highest development.

SYNONYMS **come to a climax**, come to a head, climax, end, finish, conclude, build up to, lead up to.

□ **culmination** noun.

culottes /kyuu-**lots**/ ▶ plural noun women's wide-legged knee-length trousers.

culpable ▶ adjective deserving blame.

SYNONYMS **to blame**, guilty, at fault, in the wrong, answerable, accountable,

responsible.
ANTONYMS innocent.

□ **culpability** noun.

culprit ▶ noun the person responsible for an offence.

SYNONYMS **guilty party**, offender, wrongdoer, miscreant, criminal, lawbreaker, felon, delinquent; informal baddy, crook.

cult ▶ noun 1 a system of religious worship directed towards a particular person or object. 2 a small, unconventional religious group. 3 something popular or fashionable among a particular group of people.

SYNONYMS 1 *a religious cult* **sect**, group, movement. 2 *the cult of youth in Hollywood* **obsession**, fixation, idolization, devotion, worship, veneration.

cultivate ▶ verb (**cultivates**, **cultivating**, **cultivated**) 1 prepare and use land for crops or gardening. 2 grow plants or crops. 3 try to develop or gain a particular quality. 4 try to win the friendship or support of. 5 (**cultivated**) well educated and having good taste.

SYNONYMS 1 *the peasants cultivated the land* **farm**, work, till, plough, dig. 2 *they cultivated basic food crops* **grow**, raise, rear, tend, plant, sow. 3 *Tessa tried to cultivate her* **woo**, court, curry favour with, ingratiate yourself with; informal get in someone's good books. 4 *he wants to cultivate his mind* **improve**, better, refine, educate, develop, enrich. 5 (**cultivated**) See **CULTURED**.

□ **cultivation** noun **cultivator** noun.

cultural ▶ adjective 1 relating to the culture of a society. 2 relating to the arts and intellectual achievements.

SYNONYMS 1 *cultural differences* **social**, lifestyle, sociological, anthropological, racial, ethnic. 2 *cultural achievements* **aesthetic**, artistic, intellectual, educational, civilizing.

□ **culturally** adverb.

culture ▶ noun 1 the arts, customs, and institutions of a nation, people, or group. 2 the arts and intellectual achievements regarded as a whole. 3 a refined understanding or appreciation of culture. 4 a preparation of cells or bacteria grown for medical or scientific study.

SYNONYMS 1 *a lover of culture* **the arts**, high art. 2 *a man of culture* **education**, cultivation, enlightenment, discernment, discrimination, taste, refinement, sophistication. 3 *Afro-Caribbean culture* **civilization**, society, way of life, lifestyle, customs, traditions, heritage, values. **4** *a corporate culture of greed and envy* **philosophy,** ethic, outlook, approach, rationale.

cultured ▶ adjective **1** well educated and having good taste. **2** (of a pearl) formed round a foreign body inserted into an oyster.

> SYNONYMS **cultivated,** artistic, enlightened, civilized, educated, well read, learned, discerning, discriminating, refined, sophisticated; informal arty.
> ANTONYMS ignorant.

culvert ▶ noun a tunnel carrying a stream or open drain under a road or railway.

cum ▶ preposition combined with.

cumbersome ▶ adjective **1** difficult to carry or use because of its size or weight. **2** complicated and time-consuming.

cumin /**kyoo**-min/ ▶ noun the seeds of a plant, used as a spice.

cummerbund ▶ noun a sash worn round the waist as part of a man's formal evening suit.

cumulative ▶ adjective increasing by successive additions.
□ **cumulatively** adverb.

cumulus /**kyoo**-myuu-luhss/ ▶ noun (plural **cumuli** /**kyoo**-myuu-lee/) a type of cloud that forms rounded masses heaped on a flat base.

cuneiform /**kyoo**-ni-form/ ▶ adjective (of ancient writing systems) using wedge-shaped characters.

cunning ▶ adjective **1** skilled at deceiving people. **2** skilful or clever.

> SYNONYMS **1** *a cunning scheme* **crafty,** wily, artful, devious, sly, scheming, canny, dishonest, deceitful. **2** *a cunning plan* **clever,** ingenious, imaginative, enterprising, inventive, creative, original, inspired, brilliant.
> ANTONYMS open, honest, stupid.

▶ noun craftiness.

> SYNONYMS **1** *his political cunning* **guile,** craftiness, deviousness, trickery, duplicity. **2** *it took cunning just to survive* **ingenuity,** imagination, inventiveness, enterprise, creativity, brilliance.

□ **cunningly** adverb.

cup ▶ noun **1** a small bowl-shaped drinking container with a handle. **2** a trophy in the shape of a cup on a stem, awarded as a prize in a sports contest. **3** a sports contest in which the winner is awarded a cup. **4** either of the two parts of a bra shaped to contain one breast.

▶ verb (**cups, cupping, cupped**) **1** form your hand or hands into the curved shape of a cup. **2** place your curved hand or hands

around.

cupboard ▶ noun a piece of furniture, or a recess in a wall with a door, used for storage.
■ **cupboard love** affection shown to someone in order to obtain something.

Cupid ▶ noun **1** the Roman god of love. **2** (also **cupid**) a picture or statue of a naked winged child carrying a bow.

cupidity ▶ noun greed for money or possessions.

cupola ▶ noun a rounded dome that forms or decorates a roof.

cur ▶ noun an aggressive mongrel dog.

curate ▶ noun a priest who assists a parish priest.

curative ▶ adjective able to cure disease.

curator ▶ noun a keeper of a museum or other collection.

> SYNONYMS **custodian,** keeper, conservator, guardian, caretaker.

curb ▶ verb control or put a limit on.

> SYNONYMS *a plan to curb consumer spending* **restrain,** hold back, keep in check, control, rein in, contain; informal keep a lid on.

▶ noun **1** a control or limit on something. **2** a type of bit with a strap or chain which passes under a horse's lower jaw. **3** US spelling of **KERB**.

> SYNONYMS *a curb on imports* **restraint,** restriction, check, brake, rein, control, limit.

curd (or **curds**) ▶ noun a soft, white substance formed when milk coagulates.

curdle ▶ verb (**curdles, curdling, curdled**) form curds or lumps.

cure ▶ verb (**cures, curing, cured**) **1** make a person who is ill well again. **2** end a disease, condition, or problem by treatment or appropriate action. **3** preserve meat, fish, etc. by salting, drying, or smoking.

> SYNONYMS **1** *he was cured of the disease* **heal,** restore to health, make well/better. **2** *economic equality cannot cure all social ills* **rectify,** remedy, put/set right, right, fix, mend, repair, solve, sort out, eliminate, end. **3** *some farmers cured their own bacon* **preserve,** smoke, salt, dry, pickle.

▶ noun **1** something that cures; a remedy. **2** the healing of a person who is ill.

> SYNONYMS *a cure for cancer* **remedy,** medicine, medication, antidote, treatment, therapy.

□ **curable** adjective.

curfew ▶ noun **1** a regulation requiring people to remain indoors between specific

c

hours of the night. **2** the time at which a curfew begins.

curie ▸ noun (plural **curies**) a unit of radioactivity.

curio ▸ noun (plural **curios**) an object that is interesting because it is rare or unusual.

curiosity ▸ noun (plural **curiosities**) **1** a strong desire to know or learn something. **2** an unusual or interesting object or fact.

> SYNONYMS **1** *his evasiveness roused my curiosity* interest, inquisitiveness, attention, prying; informal nosiness. **2** *the shop is full of curiosities* oddity, curio, novelty, rarity.

curious ▸ adjective **1** eager to know or learn something. **2** strange; unusual.

> SYNONYMS **1** *she was curious to know what had happened* intrigued, interested, eager, inquisitive. **2** *her curious behaviour* strange, odd, peculiar, funny, unusual, bizarre, weird, eccentric, extraordinary, abnormal, anomalous.
> ANTONYMS uninterested, normal.

◻ **curiously** adverb.

curium ▸ noun a radioactive metallic element that is produced artificially.

curl ▸ verb form a curved or spiral shape.

> SYNONYMS **1** *smoke curled up from his cigarette* spiral, coil, wreathe, twirl, swirl, wind, curve, twist (and turn), snake, corkscrew. **2** *Ruth curled her arms around his neck* wind, twine, entwine, wrap.

▸ noun something in the shape of a spiral or coil.

> SYNONYMS **1** *the tangled curls of her hair* ringlet, corkscrew, kink, lock. **2** *a curl of smoke* spiral, coil, twirl, swirl, twist, corkscrew.

curler ▸ noun a roller or clasp around which you wrap hair to curl it.

curlew /ker-lyoo/ ▸ noun (plural **curlew** or **curlews**) a large wading bird with a long curved bill.

curling ▸ noun a game played on ice, in which you slide large circular flat stones towards a mark.

curly ▸ adjective having curls.

> SYNONYMS **wavy**, curling, curled, frizzy, kinky, corkscrew.
> ANTONYMS straight.

curmudgeon ▸ noun a bad-tempered person.
◻ **curmudgeonly** adjective.

currant ▸ noun a dried fruit made from a small seedless variety of grape.

currency ▸ noun (plural **currencies**) **1** a system of money used in a country. **2** the state or period of being current.

> SYNONYMS **1** *foreign currency* money, legal tender, cash, banknotes, notes, coins; N. Amer. bills. **2** *a term which has gained new currency* popularity, circulation, exposure, acceptance, prevalence.

current ▸ adjective **1** happening or being used or done now. **2** in common or general use.

> SYNONYMS **1** *current events* contemporary, present-day, modern, topical, live, burning. **2** *the idea is still current* prevalent, common, accepted, in circulation, popular, widespread. **3** *a current driving licence* valid, usable, up to date. **4** *the current prime minister* incumbent, present, in office, in power, reigning.
> ANTONYMS past, out of date, former.

▸ noun **1** a flow of water or air in a particular direction. **2** a flow of electrically charged particles.

> SYNONYMS **1** *a current of air* flow, stream, draught, jet, tide. **2** *the current of human life* course, progress, progression, flow, tide, movement.

■ **current account** Brit. a bank or building society account from which you may withdraw money at any time.
◻ **currently** adverb.

> ❗ Don't confuse **current** with **currant**, which means 'a dried grape'.

curriculum ▸ noun (plural **curricula** or **curriculums**) the subjects that make up a course of study in a school or college.
■ **curriculum vitae** /**vee**-ty/ a written account of a person's qualifications and previous jobs, sent with a job application.
◻ **curricular** adjective.

curry[1] ▸ noun (plural **curries**) an Indian dish of meat, vegetables, or fish, cooked in a hot, spicy sauce.

curry[2] ▸ verb (**curry favour**) try to win someone's approval by flattering them and being very helpful.

curry comb ▸ noun a hand-held rubber device used for grooming horses.

curse ▸ noun **1** an appeal to a supernatural power to harm someone or something. **2** a cause of harm or misery. **3** an offensive word or phrase used to express anger or annoyance.

> SYNONYMS **1** *she'd put a curse on him* jinx; N. Amer. hex. **2** *the curse of unemployment* affliction, burden, misery, ordeal, evil, scourge. **3** *muffled curses* swear word, expletive, oath, profanity, four-letter word, dirty word, obscenity; informal cuss word.

▶ verb (**curses, cursing, cursed**) **1** use a curse against. **2** (**be cursed with**) continuously suffer from or be affected by. **3** say offensive words; swear.

> SYNONYMS **1** *she was cursed with feelings of inadequacy* **afflict,** trouble, plague, bedevil. **2** *he cursed loudly* **swear,** take the Lord's name in vain; informal **cuss,** turn the air blue, eff and blind.

cursor ▶ noun a mark on a computer screen identifying the point where typing or other input will take effect.

> ✔ **-or** at the end, not **-er**: curs**or**.

cursory ▶ adjective hasty and therefore not thorough.

> SYNONYMS **brief,** hasty, hurried, rapid, passing, perfunctory, desultory, casual. ANTONYMS thorough.

□ **cursorily** adverb.

curt ▶ adjective (of a person's speech) rudely brief.

> SYNONYMS **terse,** brusque, abrupt, clipped, blunt, short, sharp. ANTONYMS expansive.

□ **curtly** adverb.

curtail ▶ verb cut short or restrict.

> SYNONYMS **1** *policies designed to curtail spending* **reduce,** cut, cut down, decrease, trim, restrict, limit, curb, rein in/back; informal **slash. 2** *his visit was curtailed* **shorten,** cut short, truncate. ANTONYMS increase, extend.

□ **curtailment** noun.

curtain ▶ noun a piece of material hung up to form a screen at a window or between the stage and the audience in a theatre.
▶ verb provide or screen something with a curtain or curtains.
■ **curtain call** the appearance of a performer on stage after a performance to acknowledge applause. **curtain-raiser** an event happening just before a longer or more important one.

curtsy (or **curtsey**) ▶ noun (plural **curtsies** or **curtseys**) a woman's or girl's respectful greeting, made by bending the knees with one foot in front of the other.
▶ verb (**curtsies, curtsying, curtsied** or **curtseys, curtseying, curtseyed**) perform a curtsy.

curvaceous ▶ adjective having an attractively curved shape.

curvature ▶ noun the fact of being curved; a curved shape.

curve ▶ noun a line which gradually turns from a straight course.

> SYNONYMS *the curves of the river* **bend,** turn, loop, arc, arch, bow, curvature.

▶ verb (**curves, curving, curved**) form a curve.

> SYNONYMS **1** *the road curved back on itself* **bend,** turn, loop, wind, meander, snake, arc, arch. **2** (**curved**) **bent,** arched, bowed, rounded, crescent.

□ **curvy** adjective.

cushion ▶ noun **1** a bag of cloth stuffed with soft material, used to provide comfort when sitting. **2** something that gives protection against impact or something unpleasant. **3** the inner sides of a billiard table.

> SYNONYMS *a cushion against inflation* **protection,** buffer, shield, defence, bulwark.

▶ verb **1** soften the effect of an impact on. **2** lessen the bad effects of.

> SYNONYMS **1** *residents are cushioned from the outside world* **protect,** shield, shelter, cocoon. **2** *to cushion the blow, pensions were increased* **soften,** lessen, diminish, mitigate, alleviate, take the edge off, dull, deaden.

cushy ▶ adjective (**cushier, cushiest**) informal easy and undemanding.

cusp ▶ noun **1** a pointed end where two curves meet. **2** a point in between two different states.

custard ▶ noun **1** a sweet sauce made with milk and eggs, or milk and flavoured cornflour. **2** a baked dessert made from eggs and milk.

custodian ▶ noun a person responsible for looking after something.

custody ▶ noun **1** protective care. **2** imprisonment.

> SYNONYMS *custody of the child* **care,** guardianship, charge, supervision, safe keeping, responsibility, protection.

□ **custodial** adjective.

custom ▶ noun **1** a traditional way of behaving or doing something. **2** regular dealings with a shop or business by customers.

> SYNONYMS **1** *his unfamiliarity with local customs* **tradition,** practice, usage, way, convention, formality, ritual, mores. **2** *it was his custom to sleep in a chair* **habit,** practice, routine, way; formal **wont.**

■ **custom-built** (or **custom-made**) made to a particular customer's order.

customary ▶ adjective usual or habitual.

> SYNONYMS **usual,** traditional, normal, conventional, habitual, familiar, accepted, accustomed, routine, established, time-honoured, prevailing. ANTONYMS unusual.

□ **customarily** adverb.

customer ▶ noun **1** a person who buys goods or services from a shop or business. **2** a person or thing that you have to deal with: *a tough customer.*

SYNONYMS **consumer,** buyer, purchaser, patron, client, shopper; Brit. informal punter.

customize (or customise) ▶ verb (**customizes, customizing, customized**) modify something to suit a person or task.

customs ▶ plural noun **1** charges made by a government on imported goods. **2** the official department that administers and collects customs charges.

cut ▶ verb (**cuts, cutting, cut**) **1** make an opening or wound with something sharp. **2** shorten, divide, or remove with something sharp. **3** make or design a garment in a particular way. **4** reduce the amount or quantity of. **5** go across or through an area. **6** stop filming or recording. **7** divide a pack of playing cards by lifting a portion from the top.

SYNONYMS **1** *he cut his finger* **gash,** slash, lacerate, slit, wound, scratch, graze, nick. **2** *cut the pepper into small pieces* **slice,** chop, dice, cube, carve; N. Amer. hash. **3** *the name had been cut into the stone* **carve,** engrave, incise, etch, score, chisel, whittle. **4** *the government will cut expenditure* **reduce,** cut back/down on, decrease, lessen, mark down, discount, lower; informal slash. **5** *the text has been substantially cut* **shorten,** abridge, condense, abbreviate, truncate, edit, censor. **6** *you need to cut ten lines per page* **delete,** remove, take out, excise.

▶ noun **1** a wound or opening resulting from cutting. **2** a reduction. **3** the style in which a garment or a person's hair is cut. **4** a piece of meat cut from a carcass. **5** informal a share of profits. **6** a version of a film after editing.

SYNONYMS **1** *a cut on his jaw* **gash,** slash, laceration, incision, wound, scratch, graze, nick. **2** *a cut of beef* **piece,** joint, fillet, section. **3** *they want their cut* **share,** portion, quota, percentage; informal slice (of the cake). **4** *a cut in interest rates* **reduction,** cutback, decrease, lessening; N. Amer. rollback. **5** *the cut of his jacket* **style,** design, line, fit.

■ **cut and dried** already decided. **cut and thrust** a competitive atmosphere or environment. **cut corners** do something badly to save time or money. **cut glass** glass with decorative patterns cut into it. **cut in 1** interrupt. **2** pull in too closely in front of another vehicle. **3** (of a machine) begin operating automatically. **cut the mustard** informal reach the required standard. **cut no ice** informal have no influence or effect. **cut someone/thing off 1** make it impossible to reach a place. **2** deprive someone of a supply. **3** break a telephone connection with someone. **cut out** (of an engine) suddenly stop operating. **cut someone out** exclude someone. **cut-throat** ruthless and fierce.

cutaneous /kyoo-tay-ni-uhss/ ▶ adjective having to do with the skin.

cutback ▶ noun a reduction.

SYNONYMS **reduction,** cut, decrease, economy, saving; N. Amer. rollback. ANTONYMS increase.

cute ▶ adjective **1** charmingly pretty; sweet. **2** N. Amer. informal clever; shrewd.

SYNONYMS **endearing,** adorable, lovable, sweet, lovely, appealing, engaging, delightful, dear; informal twee; Brit. informal dinky. ANTONYMS hateful, ugly.

□ **cutely** adverb.

cuticle /kyoo-ti-k'l/ ▶ noun the dead skin at the base of a fingernail or toenail.

cutlass ▶ noun a short sword with a slightly curved blade, formerly used by sailors.

cutlery ▶ noun knives, forks, and spoons used for eating or serving food.

cutlet ▶ noun **1** a lamb or veal chop from just behind the neck. **2** a flat cake of minced meat, nuts, etc., covered in breadcrumbs and fried.

cutter ▶ noun **1** a person or thing that cuts. **2** a light, fast patrol boat or sailing boat.

cutting ▶ noun **1** an article cut from a newspaper. **2** a piece cut from a plant to grow a new one. **3** a way dug through higher ground for a railway, road, etc.

SYNONYMS *a newspaper cutting* **clipping,** article, piece, column, paragraph.

▶ adjective hurtful: *a cutting remark.*

SYNONYMS *a cutting remark* **hurtful,** wounding, barbed, scathing, caustic, sarcastic, snide, spiteful, malicious, cruel; informal bitchy; Brit. informal sarky; N. Amer. informal snarky. ANTONYMS friendly, warm.

■ **the cutting edge** the most advanced or modern stage; the forefront.

cuttlefish ▶ noun (plural **cuttlefish** or **cuttlefishes**) a sea creature resembling a squid.

CV ▶ abbreviation curriculum vitae.

cwt ▶ abbreviation hundredweight.

cyan /sy-uhn/ ▶ noun a greenish-blue colour.

cyanide ▶ noun a highly poisonous compound containing a metal combined with carbon and nitrogen atoms.

cybercafe ▶ noun a cafe with computers on which customers can access the Internet, send emails, etc.

cybernetics ▸ noun the science of communications and control in machines (e.g. computers) and living things (e.g. by the nervous system).
□ **cybernetic** adjective.

cyberspace ▸ noun the hypothetical place in which communication over computer networks takes place.

cyclamen /**sik**-luh-muhn/ ▸ noun a plant having pink, red, or white flowers with backward-curving petals.

cycle ▸ noun 1 a series of events that are regularly repeated in the same order. 2 a complete sequence of changes associated with something recurring such as an alternating electric current. 3 a series of musical or literary works composed around a particular theme. 4 a bicycle.

> SYNONYMS 1 *the cycle of birth, death, and rebirth* circle, round, pattern, rhythm, loop. 2 *a cycle of three plays* series, set, sequence, succession, run.

▸ verb (**cycles, cycling, cycled**) ride a bicycle.
□ **cyclist** noun.

cyclic /**syk**-lik, **sik**-lik/ (or **cyclical**) ▸ adjective happening in cycles.

cyclone ▸ noun 1 a system of winds rotating inwards to an area of low atmospheric pressure. 2 a violent tropical storm.
□ **cyclonic** adjective.

cygnet /**sig**-nit/ ▸ noun a young swan.

cylinder ▸ noun 1 a three-dimensional shape with straight parallel sides and circular or oval ends. 2 a chamber in which a piston moves in an engine.
□ **cylindrical** adjective.

cymbal ▸ noun a musical instrument consisting of a round brass plate which is either struck against another one or hit with a stick.

cynic ▸ noun 1 a person who believes that people always act from selfish motives. 2 a person who raises doubts about something.

> SYNONYMS **sceptic,** doubter, doubting Thomas, pessimist, prophet of doom.
> ANTONYMS idealist, optimist.

□ **cynicism** noun.

cynical ▸ adjective 1 believing that people always act from selfish motives. 2 doubtful or sneering. 3 concerned only with your own interests.

> SYNONYMS **sceptical,** doubtful, distrustful, suspicious, disbelieving, pessimistic, negative, world-weary, disillusioned, disenchanted, jaundiced.
> ANTONYMS idealistic, optimistic.

□ **cynically** adverb.

cypher ➡ CIPHER.

cypress ▸ noun an evergreen coniferous tree with small dark leaves.

Cypriot ▸ noun a person from Cyprus.
▸ adjective relating to Cyprus.

Cyrillic /si-**ril**-lik/ ▸ noun the alphabet used for Russian and related languages.

cyst /sist/ ▸ noun an abnormal cavity in the body which contains fluid.

cystic ▸ adjective 1 having to do with cysts. 2 relating to the bladder or the gall bladder.
■ **cystic fibrosis** an inherited disease which causes too much mucus to be produced and often leads to blockage of tubes in the body.

cystitis /si-**sty**-tiss/ ▸ noun inflammation of the bladder.

cytology /sy-**tol**-uh-ji/ ▸ noun the scientific study of plant and animal cells.
□ **cytological** adjective **cytologist** noun.

cytoplasm ▸ noun the material of a living cell, excluding the nucleus.

czar, etc. ➡ TSAR etc.

Czech /chek/ ▸ noun 1 a person from the Czech Republic or (formerly) Czechoslovakia. 2 the language spoken in the Czech Republic.

C

Dd

d

D (or d) ▶ noun (plural **Ds** or **D's**) **1** the fourth letter of the alphabet. **2** the Roman numeral for 500.
▶ abbreviation (**d**) (before decimal currency was brought in) penny or pence.

'd ▶ short form **1** had. **2** would.

DA ▶ abbreviation (in the US) district attorney.

dab ▶ verb (**dabs, dabbing, dabbed**) **1** press lightly with something absorbent. **2** apply with light, quick strokes.

> synonyms *she dabbed disinfectant on the cut* **pat,** press, touch, swab, daub, wipe.

▶ noun a small amount of something applied lightly.

> synonyms *a dab of glue* **drop,** spot, smear, splash, bit.

■ **dab hand** Brit. informal a person who is very good at something.

dabble ▶ verb (**dabbles, dabbling, dabbled**) **1** gently move your hands or feet around in water. **2** take part in an activity in a casual way.

> synonyms **toy with,** dip into, flirt with, tinker with, play with.

□ **dabbler** noun.

dace ▶ noun (plural **dace**) a small freshwater fish related to the carp.

dachshund ▶ noun a breed of dog with a long body and very short legs.

dad (or **daddy**) ▶ noun (plural **dads** or **daddies**) informal your father.

daddy-long-legs ▶ noun Brit. informal a crane fly.

dado /**day**-doh/ ▶ noun (plural **dados**) the lower part of the wall of a room, when it is decorated differently from the upper part.

daffodil ▶ noun a plant that has bright yellow flowers with a long trumpet-shaped centre.

daft ▶ adjective informal silly; foolish.

> synonyms **1** *a daft idea* **absurd,** preposterous, ridiculous, ludicrous, idiotic, stupid, foolish; informal crazy; Brit. informal barmy. **2** *he's really daft* **stupid,** idiotic, empty-headed, unhinged, insane, mad; informal thick, dim, dopey; Brit. informal barmy, crackers. **3** *she's daft about him* **infatuated,** smitten, besotted; informal crazy, mad, nuts; Brit. informal potty. antonyms sensible, sane.

dagger ▶ noun a short pointed knife, used as a weapon.

daguerreotype /duh-**ger**-ruh-typ/ ▶ noun an early kind of photograph produced using a silver-coated plate.

dahlia /**day**-li-uh/ ▶ noun a garden plant with brightly coloured flowers.

daily ▶ adjective done, happening, or produced every day or every weekday.

> synonyms *a daily event* **everyday,** day-to-day.

▶ adverb every day.

> synonyms *the museum is open daily* **every day,** once a day, day after day.

dainty ▶ adjective (**daintier, daintiest**) delicately small and pretty.

> synonyms **1** *a dainty china cup* **delicate,** fine, elegant, exquisite. **2** *a dainty eater* **fastidious,** fussy, particular; informal choosy, picky; Brit. informal faddy. antonyms unwieldy, undiscriminating.

▶ noun (plural **dainties**) a small, tasty item of food.
□ **daintily** adverb.

dairy ▶ noun (plural **dairies**) a building where milk and milk products are produced.
▶ adjective **1** made from milk. **2** involved in milk production.

dais /**day**-iss/ ▶ noun a low platform that supports a throne, or that people stand on to make a speech.

daisy ▶ noun (plural **daisies**) a small plant that has flowers with a yellow centre and white petals.

dale ▶ noun (in northern England) a valley.

dalliance ▶ noun a casual relationship.

dally ▶ verb (**dallies, dallying, dallied**) **1** do something in a leisurely way. **2** (**dally with**) have a casual relationship with.

Dalmatian /dal-**may**-sh'n/ ▶ noun a breed of large dog with short white hair and dark spots.

dam[1] ▸ noun a barrier constructed across a river to hold back water.

> SYNONYMS **barrage,** barrier, wall, embankment, barricade, obstruction.

▸ verb (**dams, damming, dammed**) build a dam across.

> SYNONYMS **block (up),** obstruct, bung up, close, hold back.

dam[2] ▸ noun the female parent of an animal.

damage ▸ noun **1** physical harm that makes something less valuable or effective. **2** harmful effects. **3** (**damages**) money paid to compensate for a loss or injury.

> SYNONYMS **1** *did the thieves do any damage?* **harm,** destruction, vandalism, injury, ruin, devastation. **2** (**damages**) **compensation,** recompense, restitution, redress, reparation(s); N. Amer. informal comp.

▸ verb (**damages, damaging, damaged**) cause harm to.

> SYNONYMS **1** *the parcel had been damaged* **harm,** injure, deface, spoil, impair, vandalize, ruin, destroy, wreck; N. Amer. informal trash. **2** (**damaging**) **harmful,** detrimental, injurious, hurtful, destructive, ruinous, deleterious.
> ANTONYMS repair.

damask ▸ noun a rich, heavy fabric with a pattern woven into it.

dame ▸ noun **1** (**Dame**) (in the UK) the title of a woman awarded a knighthood, equivalent to *Sir*. **2** N. Amer. informal a woman. **3** Brit. a comic female character in pantomime, played by a man.

damn ▸ verb **1** (**be damned**) (in Christian belief) be condemned by God to eternal punishment in hell. **2** harshly condemn. **3** curse.

> SYNONYMS **1 condemn,** censure, criticize, attack, denounce. **2** (**damning**) **incriminating,** implicating, damaging, condemnatory, conclusive, irrefutable.
> ANTONYMS bless, praise.

damnable /dam-nuh-b'l/ ▸ adjective very bad or unpleasant.

damnation ▸ noun the fate of being condemned to eternal punishment in hell.

damned ▸ adjective said to emphasize anger or frustration.

damp ▸ adjective slightly wet.

> SYNONYMS *her hair was damp* **moist,** humid, muggy, clammy, sweaty, dank, wet, rainy, drizzly, showery, misty, foggy, dewy.
> ANTONYMS dry.

▸ noun moisture in the air, on a surface, or in a solid substance.

> SYNONYMS *the damp in the air* **moisture,** liquid, wet, wetness, dampness, humidity.
> ANTONYMS dryness.

▸ verb **1** make something damp. **2** (**damp something down**) control a feeling or situation.
 ■ **damp course** a layer of waterproof material in a wall near the ground, to prevent rising damp. **damp squib** Brit. something that turns out to be a lot less impressive than expected.

dampen ▸ verb **1** make something damp. **2** make a feeling or reaction less strong or intense.

> SYNONYMS **1** *the rain dampened her face* **moisten,** damp, wet, soak. **2** *nothing could dampen her enthusiasm* **lessen,** decrease, diminish, reduce, moderate, cool, suppress, stifle, inhibit.
> ANTONYMS dry, heighten.

damper ▸ noun **1** a pad for silencing a piano string. **2** a movable metal plate for controlling the air flow in a chimney.
 ■ **put a damper on** informal make something less enjoyable or lively.

damsel ▸ noun old use a young unmarried woman.

damson ▸ noun a small purple-black fruit resembling a plum.

dance ▸ verb (**dances, dancing, danced**) **1** move rhythmically to music. **2** move in a quick and lively way.

> SYNONYMS **1** *he danced with her* **trip,** sway, twirl, whirl, pirouette, gyrate; informal bop, trip the light fantastic; N. Amer. informal get down. **2** *the girls danced round me* **caper,** cavort, frolic, skip, prance, gambol, leap, hop, bounce.

▸ noun **1** a series of steps and movements performed to music. **2** a social gathering at which people dance.

> SYNONYMS *the school dance* **ball;** N. Amer. prom, hoedown; informal disco, rave, hop, bop.

 □ **dancer** noun.

dandelion ▸ noun a weed with large bright yellow flowers.

dander ▸ noun (**get your dander up**) informal lose your temper.

dandle ▸ verb (**dandles, dandling, dandled**) gently bounce a young child on your knees or in your arms.

dandruff ▸ noun flakes of dead skin on a person's scalp and in the hair.

dandy ▸ noun (plural **dandies**) a man who is too concerned with looking stylish and fashionable.

▸ adjective (**dandier, dandiest**) N. Amer. informal excellent.
 □ **dandified** adjective.

Dane ▸ noun a person from Denmark.

d

danger ▸ noun **1** the possibility of suffering harm or of experiencing something unpleasant. **2** a cause of harm.

> SYNONYMS **1** *an element of danger* **peril,** hazard, risk, jeopardy. **2** *he is a danger to society* **menace,** hazard, threat, risk. **3** *a serious danger of fire* **possibility,** chance, risk, probability, likelihood.
> ANTONYMS safety.

dangerous ▸ adjective likely to cause harm or injury.

> SYNONYMS **1** *a dangerous animal* **menacing,** threatening, treacherous. **2** *dangerous wiring* **hazardous,** perilous, risky, unsafe, unpredictable, precarious, insecure; informal dicey, hairy; Brit. informal dodgy.
> ANTONYMS harmless, safe.

□ **dangerously** adverb.

dangle ▸ verb (**dangles, dangling, dangled**) **1** hang or swing freely. **2** offer something to someone to persuade them to do something.

> SYNONYMS **1** *a chain dangled from his belt* **hang,** swing, droop, wave, trail, stream. **2** *he dangled the keys* **wave,** swing, jiggle, brandish, flourish.

Danish ▸ adjective relating to Denmark or the Danes.
▸ noun the language of Denmark.

dank ▸ adjective damp and cold.

> SYNONYMS **damp,** musty, chilly, clammy.
> ANTONYMS dry.

dapper ▸ adjective (of a man) neat in appearance; smart.

> SYNONYMS **smart,** spruce, trim, debonair, neat, well dressed, elegant; informal snappy, natty; N. Amer. informal spiffy, fly.
> ANTONYMS scruffy.

dapple ▸ verb (**dapples, dappling, dappled**) mark with patches of colour or of light and shadow.
■ **dapple grey** (of a horse) grey with darker ring-shaped markings.

dare ▸ verb (**dares, daring, dared**) **1** have the courage to do something. **2** challenge someone to do something.

> SYNONYMS **1** *nobody dared to say a word* **be brave enough,** have the courage, venture, have the nerve, risk, take the liberty of; N. Amer. take a flyer; informal stick your neck out. **2** *she dared him to go* **challenge,** defy, invite, bid, provoke, goad.

▸ noun a challenge to do something brave or risky.

> SYNONYMS *she accepted the dare* **challenge,** invitation, wager, bet.

daredevil ▸ noun a person who enjoys doing dangerous things.

daring ▸ adjective willing to do dangerous or risky things.

> SYNONYMS *a daring attack* **bold,** audacious, intrepid, fearless, brave, heroic, dashing; informal gutsy.
> ANTONYMS cowardly, timid.

▸ noun the courage to do dangerous or risky things.

> SYNONYMS *his sheer daring* **boldness,** audacity, temerity, fearlessness, bravery, courage, pluck; informal nerve, guts; Brit. informal bottle; N. Amer. informal moxie.
> ANTONYMS cowardice.

□ **daringly** adverb.

dark ▸ adjective **1** with little or no light. **2** of a deep colour. **3** depressing or gloomy. **4** evil; wicked. **5** mysterious: *a dark secret.*

> SYNONYMS **1** *a dark night* **dingy,** gloomy, shadowy, murky, poorly lit, grey, inky, black. **2** *dark hair* **brunette,** dark brown, sable, jet-black, ebony. **3** *dark skin* **swarthy,** dusky, olive, black, ebony. **4** *dark thoughts* **gloomy,** dismal, negative, downbeat, bleak, grim, fatalistic, black. **5** *a dark look* **angry,** forbidding, threatening, ominous, moody, brooding, sullen, scowling, glowering. **6** *dark deeds* **evil,** wicked, sinful, bad, iniquitous, ungodly, vile, foul, monstrous; informal dirty, crooked, shady.
> ANTONYMS bright, light, blonde, pale, white, happy, friendly, good.

▸ noun **1** (**the dark**) the absence of light. **2** nightfall.

> SYNONYMS *walking in the dark* **night,** night-time, darkness, nightfall, blackout.
> ANTONYMS light, day.

■ **the Dark Ages** the period *c.*500–1100 in Europe, seen as lacking culture or learning. **dark horse** a person about whom little is known. **in the dark** knowing nothing about a situation or matter. **a shot in the dark** a wild guess.
□ **darkly** adverb.

darken ▸ verb **1** make or become darker. **2** become unhappy or angry.

> SYNONYMS **grow dark,** make dark, blacken, grow dim, cloud over, lour.
> ANTONYMS lighten.

darkness ▸ noun **1** the absence of light. **2** night.

> SYNONYMS **1** *lights shone in the darkness* **dark,** blackness, gloom, dimness, murk, shadow, shade. **2** *darkness fell* **night,** night-time, dark. **3** *the forces of darkness* **evil,** wickedness, sin, ungodliness, the Devil.

darkroom ▸ noun a darkened room for developing photographs.

darling ▸ noun **1** an affectionate form of address. **2** a lovable person.

> SYNONYMS **1** *good night, darling* **dear**, dearest, love, sweetheart, beloved; informal honey, angel, pet, sweetie, baby, poppet. **2** *the darling of the media* **favourite**, idol, hero, heroine; Brit. informal blue-eyed boy/girl.
> ANTONYMS bugbear, villain.

▸ adjective **1** much loved. **2** charming.

> SYNONYMS **1** *his darling wife* **dear**, dearest, precious, beloved. **2** *a darling little hat* **adorable**, charming, cute, sweet, enchanting, dear, delightful; Scottish & N. English bonny.
> ANTONYMS ugly.

darn¹ ▸ verb mend a hole in a knitted garment by weaving yarn across it.

darn² (or **darned**) ▸ adjective informal another way of saying DAMNED.

dart ▸ noun **1** a small pointed missile fired as a weapon or thrown in the game of darts. **2** (**darts**) an indoor game in which you throw darts at a circular board marked with numbers. **3** a sudden rapid movement. **4** a tapered tuck stitched into a garment to make it fit better.
▸ verb move suddenly or rapidly.

> SYNONYMS **1** *Karl darted across the road* **dash**, rush, tear, shoot, sprint, bound, scurry, scamper; informal scoot, whip. **2** *he darted a glance at her* **direct**, cast, throw, shoot, send, flash.

dash ▸ verb **1** run or travel in a great hurry. **2** hit or throw with great force. **3** destroy: *his hopes were dashed*. **4** (**dash something off**) write something hurriedly.

> SYNONYMS **1** *he dashed home* **rush**, race, run, sprint, career, charge, shoot, hurtle, hare, fly, speed, zoom; informal tear, belt; Brit. informal bomb; N. Amer. informal barrel. **2** *he dashed the glass to the ground* **hurl**, smash, fling, slam, throw, toss, cast; informal chuck, sling; N. Amer. informal peg. **3** *her hopes were dashed* **shatter**, destroy, wreck, ruin, demolish, scotch, frustrate, thwart; informal put paid to; Brit. informal scupper.
> ANTONYMS dawdle, raise.

▸ noun **1** an act of dashing. **2** a small amount added to something. **3** a horizontal stroke in writing (—).

> SYNONYMS **1** *a dash for the door* **rush**, race, run, sprint, bolt, dart, leap, charge, bound. **2** *a dash of salt* **pinch**, touch, sprinkle, taste, spot, drop, dab, splash; informal smidgen, tad. **3** *he led off with such dash* **verve**, style, flamboyance, gusto, zest, elan, flair, vigour, panache; informal pizzazz, oomph.

dashboard ▸ noun the panel of instruments and controls facing the driver of a vehicle.

dashing ▸ adjective (of a man) attractive, stylish, and confident.

> SYNONYMS **1** *a dashing pilot* **debonair**, devil-may-care, raffish, flamboyant, swashbuckling. **2** *he looked very dashing* **stylish**, smart, elegant, dapper, spruce, trim, debonair; informal natty; N. Amer. informal spiffy.

dastardly /**dass**-terd-li/ ▸ adjective old use wicked and cruel.

data ▸ noun **1** facts, statistics, or other information. **2** information stored by a computer.

> SYNONYMS **facts**, figures, statistics, details, particulars, information.

> ❗ **Data** is the plural of the Latin word **datum**. Scientists use it as a plural noun, taking a plural verb (as in *the data were classified*). In everyday use, however, **data** is usually treated as a singular noun with a singular verb (as in *here is the data*).

database ▸ noun a set of data held in a computer.

date¹ ▸ noun **1** the day of the month or year as specified by a number. **2** a day or year when a particular event happened or will happen. **3** a social or romantic appointment. **4** a musical or theatrical performance.

> SYNONYMS **1** *at a later date* **day**, occasion, time, year, age, period, era, epoch. **2** *a lunch date* **appointment**, meeting, engagement, rendezvous, commitment. **3** *a date for tonight* **partner**, escort, girlfriend, boyfriend.

▸ verb (**dates**, **dating**, **dated**) **1** mark something with a date. **2** establish the date when something existed or was made. **3** (**date from** or **back to**) have existed since a particular time in the past. **4** informal go on a date or regular dates with.

> SYNONYMS **1** *the best films don't date* **age**, grow old, become dated, show its age, be of its time. **2** **assign a date to**, put a date on. **3** *he's dating Jill* **go out with**, take out, go with, see; informal go steady with.

∎ **to date** until now.
□ **datable** (or **dateable**) adjective.

date² ▸ noun the sweet, dark brown, oval fruit of a palm tree.

dated ▸ adjective old-fashioned.

> SYNONYMS **old-fashioned**, outdated, outmoded, unfashionable, passé, behind the times, archaic, obsolete, antiquated; informal old hat, out of the ark.
> ANTONYMS modern.

dative ▸ noun Grammar (in Latin, Greek, German, etc.) the case of nouns and pronouns that indicates an indirect object or the person or thing affected by a verb.

datum ▶ noun (plural **data**) a piece of information.

daub ▶ verb smear something with a thick substance.
▶ noun **1** plaster, clay, or a similar substance, used in building. **2** a smear of a thick substance.

daughter ▶ noun **1** a girl or woman in relation to her parents. **2** a female descendant.
■ **daughter-in-law** (plural **daughters-in-law**) the wife of a person's son.

daunt ▶ verb make someone feel nervous or discouraged.

daunting ▶ adjective seeming difficult to deal with: *they faced a daunting task*.

> SYNONYMS **intimidating**, forbidding, challenging, formidable, unnerving, disconcerting, discouraging, disheartening, demoralizing, dismaying, scary, frightening, alarming.
> ANTONYMS inviting, reassuring.

dauntless ▶ adjective brave and determined.

dauphin /doh-fan/ ▶ noun (in the past) the eldest son of the King of France.

davit ▶ noun a small crane on a ship.

dawdle ▶ verb (**dawdles**, **dawdling**, **dawdled**) move slowly; take your time.

> SYNONYMS **1** *they dawdled over breakfast* **linger**, take your time, be slow, waste time, dally; informal dilly-dally. **2** *Ruth dawdled home* **amble**, stroll, trail, dally, move at a snail's pace; informal mosey, tootle; Brit. informal pootle.
> ANTONYMS hurry.

dawn ▶ noun **1** the first appearance of light in the sky in the morning. **2** the beginning of something new.

> SYNONYMS **1** *we got up at dawn* **daybreak**, sunrise, first light, daylight, cockcrow, first thing; N. Amer. sunup. **2** *the dawn of civilization* **beginning**, start, birth, inception, genesis, emergence, advent, appearance, arrival, rise, origin.
> ANTONYMS dusk, end.

▶ verb **1** (of a day) begin. **2** come into existence. **3** (**dawn on**) (of a fact) become clear to.

> SYNONYMS **1** *Thursday dawned crisp and sunny* **begin**, break, arrive, emerge. **2** *a bright new future has dawned* **begin**, start, commence, be born, appear, arrive, emerge, arise, rise, unfold, develop. **3** *the reality dawned on him* **become evident**, register, cross someone's mind, suggest itself, occur, come, strike, hit.
> ANTONYMS end.

■ **dawn chorus** the early-morning singing of birds.

day ▶ noun **1** a period of twenty-four hours, reckoned from midnight to midnight. **2** the time between sunrise and sunset. **3** (usu. **days**) a particular period of the past. **4** (**the day**) the present time or the time in question.

> SYNONYMS **1** *I stayed for a day* **twenty-four hours**. **2** *enjoy the beach during the day* **daytime**, daylight, waking hours. **3** *the leading architect of the day* **period**, time, date, age, era, generation.
> ANTONYMS night.

■ **call it a day** decide to stop doing something.

daybreak ▶ noun dawn.

daydream ▶ noun a series of pleasant thoughts that distract your attention from the present.
▶ verb have a daydream.

daylight ▶ noun **1** the natural light of the day. **2** dawn.
■ **daylight robbery** Brit. informal the fact of charging far too much for something.

daze ▶ verb make someone unable to think or react properly.

> SYNONYMS *she was dazed by the revelations* **dumbfound**, stupefy, stun, shock, stagger, bewilder, take aback, nonplus; informal flabbergast; Brit. informal knock for six.

▶ noun a state of stunned confusion or bewilderment.

> SYNONYMS *she is in a daze* **stupor**, trance, haze, spin, whirl, muddle, jumble.

□ **dazed** adjective.

dazzle ▶ verb (**dazzles**, **dazzling**, **dazzled**) **1** (of a bright light) blind someone temporarily. **2** amaze someone by being very impressive.

> SYNONYMS **1** *she was dazzled by the headlights* **blind**, confuse, disorient. **2** *I was dazzled by the exhibition* **overwhelm**, overcome, impress, move, stir, touch, awe, overawe; informal bowl over, blow away, knock out.

▶ noun blinding brightness.
□ **dazzling** adjective.

dB ▶ abbreviation decibels.

DC ▶ abbreviation **1** direct current. **2** District of Columbia.

DDT ▶ noun a compound used as an insecticide (now banned in many countries).

deacon /dee-kuhn/ ▶ noun **1** a Christian minister just below the rank of priest. **2** (in some Protestant Churches) a person who helps a minister but is not a member of the clergy.
□ **deaconess** noun.

deactivate ▶ verb (**deactivates**, **deactivating**, **deactivated**) stop equipment from working by disconnecting or destroying it.

dead ▶ adjective **1** no longer alive. **2** (of a part of the body) numb. **3** showing no emotion. **4** without activity or excitement. **5** complete: *dead silence*.

> SYNONYMS **1** *my parents are dead* **passed on/away**, departed, late, lost, perished, fallen, killed, lifeless, extinct; informal six feet under, pushing up daisies; formal deceased. **2** *a dead issue/language* **obsolete**, extinct, defunct, disused, abandoned, superseded, vanished, archaic, ancient. **3** *the phone was dead* **not working**, out of order, inoperative, inactive, broken, defective; informal kaput, conked out, on the blink, bust; Brit. informal knackered. **4** *a dead town* **boring**, uninteresting, unexciting, uninspiring, dull, flat, quiet, sleepy, slow, lifeless; informal one-horse; N. Amer. informal dullsville. ANTONYMS alive, live, living, working, lively.

▶ adverb **1** absolutely, exactly, or directly: *you're dead right*. **2** Brit. informal very.

> SYNONYMS **1** *he was dead serious* **completely**, absolutely, totally, utterly, deadly, perfectly, entirely, quite, thoroughly. **2** *flares were seen dead ahead* **directly**, exactly, precisely, immediately, right, straight, due.

■ **dead end** a road or passage that is closed at one end. **dead heat** a result in a race in which two or more competitors finish at exactly the same time. **dead loss** a useless person or thing. **dead reckoning** a way of finding out your position by estimating the direction and distance travelled. **dead ringer** informal a person or thing very like another.

deadbeat ▶ noun informal a lazy or aimless person.

deaden ▶ verb **1** make a noise or sensation less strong or intense. **2** make something numb.

deadhead ▶ verb remove dead flower heads from a plant.

deadline ▶ noun the time or date by which you have to complete something.

> SYNONYMS **time limit**, finishing date, target date, cut-off point.

deadlock ▶ noun **1** a situation in which no one can make any progress. **2** Brit. a lock operated by a key.

> SYNONYMS **stalemate**, impasse, checkmate, stand-off, standstill, gridlock.

▶ verb (**be deadlocked**) be unable to make any progress.

deadly ▶ adjective (**deadlier**, **deadliest**) **1** causing or able to cause death. **2** (of a

voice, glance, etc.) filled with hate. **3** very accurate or effective. **4** informal very boring.

> SYNONYMS **1** *these drugs can be deadly* **fatal**, lethal, mortal, life-threatening, noxious, toxic, poisonous. **2** *deadly enemies* **mortal**, irreconcilable, implacable, bitter, sworn. **3** *his aim is deadly* **unerring**, unfailing, perfect, true, accurate; Brit. informal spot on. ANTONYMS harmless, inaccurate.

▶ adverb very: *she was deadly serious*.
■ **deadly nightshade** a plant with purple flowers and poisonous black berries.

deadpan ▶ adjective not showing any emotion; expressionless.

deadweight ▶ noun **1** the weight of a motionless person or thing. **2** the total weight which a ship can carry.

deaf ▶ adjective **1** unable to hear. **2** (**deaf to**) unwilling to listen to.
■ **deaf mute** offensive a person who is deaf and unable to speak.
□ **deafness** noun.

deafen ▶ verb make someone deaf.

deafening ▶ adjective very loud.

> SYNONYMS **ear-splitting**, thunderous, crashing, uproarious, almighty, booming. ANTONYMS low, soft.

□ **deafeningly** adverb.

deal¹ ▶ verb (**deals**, **dealing**, **dealt**) **1** (**deal something out**) distribute something. **2** buy and sell a product commercially. **3** buy and sell illegal drugs. **4** give out cards to players of a card game.

> SYNONYMS **1** *the article deals with advances in biochemistry* **concern**, be about, have to do with, discuss, consider, cover, tackle, explore, investigate, examine. **2** *the company deals in high-tech goods* **trade in**, buy and sell, purvey, supply, market, traffic in. **3** *the cards were dealt* **distribute**, give out, share out, divide out, hand out, pass out, pass round, dispense, allocate.

▶ noun **1** an agreement between two or more people or groups. **2** a particular form of treatment received.

> SYNONYMS *completion of the deal* **agreement**, understanding, pact, bargain, covenant, contract, treaty, arrangement, compromise, settlement, terms.

■ **deal with 1** do business with. **2** do things to put a problem right. **3** cope with. **4** have something as a subject. **a good** (or **great**) **deal** a lot.

deal² ▶ noun fir or pine wood.

dealer ▶ noun **1** a person who buys and sells goods. **2** a person who buys and sells shares directly (rather than as a broker or agent). **3** a player who deals cards in a card game.

SYNONYMS **trader,** merchant, salesman/woman, seller, vendor, purveyor, pedlar, distributor, supplier, shopkeeper, retailer, wholesaler, tradesman, tradesperson; Brit. stockist.

dean ▸ noun **1** the head of a cathedral's governing body. **2** the head of a university department or medical school.

dear ▸ adjective **1** much loved. **2** used in the polite introduction to a letter. **3** expensive.

SYNONYMS **1** *a dear friend* **beloved,** precious, close, intimate, bosom. **2** *her pictures were too dear to part with* **precious,** treasured, valued, prized, cherished, special. **3** *such a dear man* **endearing,** adorable, lovable, appealing, engaging, charming, captivating, lovely, delightful, sweet, darling. **4** *rather dear meals* **expensive,** costly, high-priced, overpriced, exorbitant, extortionate; Brit. over the odds; informal pricey.
ANTONYMS disagreeable, cheap.

▸ noun a lovable person.

SYNONYMS *don't worry, my dear* **darling,** dearest, love, beloved, sweetheart, precious; informal sweetie, sugar, honey, baby, pet, poppet.

dearly ▸ adverb **1** very much. **2** at great cost.

SYNONYMS *I love him dearly* **very much,** a great deal, greatly, deeply, profoundly.

dearth ▸ noun a lack of something.

SYNONYMS **lack,** scarcity, shortage, shortfall, deficiency, insufficiency, inadequacy, absence.
ANTONYMS surfeit.

death ▸ noun **1** an instance of a person or an animal dying. **2** the end of life; the state of being dead. **3** the end of something.

SYNONYMS **1** *her father's death* **dying,** demise, end, passing, loss of life; formal decease. **2** *the death of their dream* **end,** finish, termination, extinction, extinguishing, collapse, destruction.
ANTONYMS life, birth, start.

■ **at death's door** so ill that you may die. **death knell** an event that signals the end of something. **death penalty** punishment by being executed. **death row** a block of cells for prisoners who have been sentenced to death. **death-watch beetle** a beetle that makes a ticking sound which people used to think was an omen of death.

deathly ▸ adjective suggesting death: *a deathly hush.*

SYNONYMS **deathlike,** ghostly, ghastly, ashen, white, pale, pallid.

debacle /day-**bah**-k'l/ ▸ noun an utter failure or disaster.

SYNONYMS **fiasco,** failure, catastrophe, disaster.

debar ▸ verb (**debars, debarring, debarred**) officially prevent someone from doing something.

debase ▸ verb (**debases, debasing, debased**) make something worse in quality, value, or character.
□ **debasement** noun.

debatable ▸ adjective open to discussion or argument.

debate ▸ noun **1** a formal discussion in which people present opposing arguments. **2** an argument.

SYNONYMS *a debate on the reforms* **discussion,** argument, dispute, talks.

▸ verb (**debates, debating, debated**) **1** discuss or argue about. **2** consider a possible course of action.

SYNONYMS **1** *MPs will debate our future* **discuss,** talk over/through, talk about, thrash out, argue, dispute. **2** *he debated whether to call her* **consider,** think over/about, chew over, mull over, weigh up, ponder, deliberate.

debauched ▸ adjective indulging in a lot of pleasures in a way considered to be immoral.
□ **debauchery** noun.

debenture /di-**ben**-cher/ ▸ noun Brit. a certificate issued by a company confirming that it has borrowed money on which interest is being paid.

debilitate /di-**bil**-i-tayt/ ▸ verb (**debilitates, debilitating, debilitated**) severely weaken.

debility ▸ noun (plural **debilities**) physical weakness.

debit ▸ noun **1** an entry in an account recording a sum owed. **2** a payment that has been made or that is owed.
▸ verb (**debits, debiting, debited**) (of a bank) remove money from a customer's account.
■ **debit card** a card that lets you take money from your bank account electronically when buying something.

debonair ▸ adjective (of a man) confident, stylish, and charming.

debrief ▸ verb question someone in detail about a mission they have completed.

debris /**deb**-ree/ ▸ noun **1** scattered items or pieces of rubbish. **2** loose broken pieces of rock.

SYNONYMS **ruins,** remains, rubble, wreckage, detritus, refuse, rubbish, waste, scrap, flotsam and jetsam.

debt ▸ noun **1** a sum of money owed. **2** a situation where you owe someone money. **3** gratitude for a favour or service.

SYNONYMS **1** *he couldn't pay his debts* **bill,** account, dues, arrears, charges.

2 *his debt to the author* indebtedness, obligation, gratitude, appreciation.

debtor ▶ noun a person who owes money.

debug ▶ verb (**debugs, debugging, debugged**) remove errors from computer hardware or software.

debunk ▶ verb show that something believed in by many people is false or exaggerated.

debut /**day**-byoo/ ▶ noun a person's first appearance in a role.
▶ verb make a debut.

debutant /**deb**-yoo-ton(t)/ ▶ noun a person making a debut.

debutante /**deb**-yoo-tont/ ▶ noun a young upper-class woman making her first appearance in society.

decade ▶ noun a period of ten years.

decadent ▶ adjective **1** immoral and interested only in pleasure. **2** luxuriously self-indulgent.
□ **decadence** noun **decadently** adverb.

decaffeinated ▶ adjective (of tea or coffee) having had most or all of its caffeine removed.

decagon ▶ noun a figure with ten straight sides and angles.

decahedron /de-kuh-**hee**-druhn/ ▶ noun (plural **decahedra** or **decahedrons**) a solid figure with ten sides.

decamp ▶ verb depart suddenly or secretly.

decant /di-**kant**/ ▶ verb pour liquid from one container into another.

decanter ▶ noun a glass container with a stopper, for wine or spirits.

decapitate ▶ verb (**decapitates, decapitating, decapitated**) cut off the head of.
□ **decapitation** noun.

decathlon /di-**kath**-luhn/ ▶ noun an athletic event in which each competitor takes part in the same ten events.
□ **decathlete** noun.

decay ▶ verb **1** (of plant or animal material) rot. **2** become weaker or less good.

SYNONYMS **1** *the corpses had decayed* decompose, rot, putrefy, go bad, go off, spoil, fester, perish. **2** *the cities continue to decay* deteriorate, degenerate, decline, go downhill, slump, slide, go to rack and ruin, go to seed; informal go to the dogs.

▶ noun **1** the state or process of decaying. **2** rotten matter or tissue.

SYNONYMS **1** *signs of decay* decomposition, putrefaction, rot. **2** *the decay of American values* deterioration, degeneration, decline, weakening, crumbling, disintegration, collapse.

decease ▶ noun formal or Law death.

deceased formal or Law ▶ noun (**the deceased**) the recently dead person in question.
▶ adjective recently dead.

deceit ▶ noun behaviour intended to make someone believe something that is not true.

SYNONYMS **deception**, deceitfulness, duplicity, double-dealing, lies, fraud, cheating, trickery.
ANTONYMS honesty.

deceitful ▶ adjective deliberately deceiving other people.

SYNONYMS **dishonest**, untruthful, insincere, false, disingenuous, untrustworthy, unscrupulous, unprincipled, two-faced, duplicitous, fraudulent, double-dealing; informal sneaky, tricky, crooked; Brit. informal bent.
ANTONYMS honest.

□ **deceitfully** adverb.

deceive ▶ verb (**deceives, deceiving, deceived**) **1** deliberately make someone believe something that is not true. **2** (of a thing) give a mistaken impression.

SYNONYMS **trick**, cheat, defraud, swindle, hoodwink, hoax, dupe, take in, mislead, delude, fool; informal con, pull the wool over someone's eyes; N. Amer. informal sucker, goldbrick; Austral. informal rort.

□ **deceiver** noun.

✔ **i** before **e** except after **c**: dec**ei**ve.

decelerate ▶ verb (**decelerates, decelerating, decelerated**) slow down.
□ **deceleration** noun.

December ▶ noun the twelfth month of the year.

decency ▶ noun (plural **decencies**) **1** decent behaviour. **2** (**decencies**) standards of acceptable behaviour.

SYNONYMS **1** *standards of taste and decency* propriety, decorum, good taste, respectability, morality, virtue, modesty. **2** *he didn't have the decency to tell me* courtesy, politeness, good manners, civility, consideration, thoughtfulness.

decennial /di-**sen**-i-uhl/ ▶ adjective happening every ten years.

decent ▶ adjective **1** having good moral standards. **2** of an acceptable quality. **3** Brit. informal kind or generous.

SYNONYMS **1** *a decent burial* proper, correct, right, appropriate, suitable, respectable, decorous, modest, seemly, accepted; informal pukka. **2** *a job with decent pay* satisfactory, reasonable, fair, acceptable, adequate, sufficient, not bad, all right, tolerable, passable,

d

suitable; informal OK. **3** *a very decent chap* **kind,** generous, thoughtful, considerate, obliging, courteous, polite, well mannered, neighbourly, hospitable, pleasant, agreeable, amiable.
ANTONYMS indecent, unsatisfactory, unpleasant.
□ **decently** adverb.

decentralize (or **decentralise**)
▶ verb (**decentralizes, decentralizing, decentralized**) transfer authority from central to local government.
□ **decentralization** noun.

deception ▶ noun **1** the action of deceiving. **2** a thing that deceives.

SYNONYMS **1** *they obtained money by deception* **deceit,** duplicity, double-dealing, fraud, cheating, trickery, guile, bluff, lying, pretence, treachery. **2** *it was all a deception* **trick,** sham, fraud, pretence, hoax, ruse, scheme, dodge, cheat, swindle; informal con, set-up, scam.

deceptive ▶ adjective giving a false impression.

SYNONYMS **misleading,** confusing, illusory, distorted, ambiguous.

□ **deceptively** adverb.

decibel /dess-i-bel/ ▶ noun a unit for measuring the loudness of a sound or the power of an electrical signal.

decide ▶ verb (**decides, deciding, decided**) **1** think about something and make a judgement or decision. **2** settle an issue or contest.

SYNONYMS **1** *she decided to become a writer* **resolve,** determine, make up your mind, choose, opt, plan, aim, intend, have in mind, set your sights on. **2** *research to decide a variety of questions* **settle,** resolve, determine, work out, answer; informal sort out. **3** *the court is to decide the case* **adjudicate,** arbitrate, judge, pronounce on, give a verdict on, rule on.

decided ▶ adjective definite; clear.
decidedly ▶ adverb clearly; undoubtedly.

SYNONYMS **distinctly,** clearly, markedly, obviously, noticeably, unmistakably, patently, manifestly, definitely, positively.

decider ▶ noun a contest that settles the winner of a series of contests.

deciduous ▶ adjective (of a tree or shrub) shedding its leaves annually.

decimal ▶ adjective having to do with a system of numbers based on the number ten.
▶ noun a fractional number in the decimal system, written with figures either side of a full point.

■ **decimal place** the position of a digit to the right of a decimal point. **decimal point** a full point placed after the figure representing units in a decimal fraction.

decimate ▶ verb (**decimates, decimating, decimated**) **1** kill or destroy a large proportion of. **2** drastically reduce in strength.
□ **decimation** noun.

decipher ▶ verb (**deciphers, deciphering, deciphered**) **1** convert something from code into normal language. **2** succeed in understanding something that is hard to interpret.

decision ▶ noun **1** a choice or judgement made after considering something. **2** the ability to decide things quickly.

SYNONYMS **1** *they came to a decision* **resolution,** conclusion, settlement, choice, option, selection. **2** *the judge's decision* **verdict,** finding, ruling, judgement, adjudication, sentence.

decisive ▶ adjective **1** having great importance for the outcome of a situation. **2** able to make decisions quickly.

SYNONYMS **1** *the decisive factor* **deciding,** conclusive, determining, key, pivotal, critical, crucial. **2** *a decisive man* **resolute,** firm, strong-minded, strong-willed, determined, purposeful.
ANTONYMS indecisive.

□ **decisively** adverb **decisiveness** noun.

deck ▶ noun **1** a floor of a ship. **2** a floor or platform. **3** chiefly N. Amer. a pack of cards. **4** a player or recorder for discs or tapes.
▶ verb decorate something.

deckchair ▶ noun a folding chair with a wooden frame and a canvas seat.

decking ▶ noun material used in making a deck.

declaim ▶ verb speak or recite in a dramatic or passionate way.

declamation ▶ noun the action of declaiming something.
□ **declamatory** adjective.

declaration ▶ noun **1** a formal statement or announcement. **2** the action of declaring.

SYNONYMS **1** *they issued a declaration* **announcement,** statement, communication, pronouncement, proclamation; N. Amer. advisory. **2** *a declaration of faith* **assertion,** profession, affirmation, acknowledgement, revelation, disclosure, confirmation, testimony, avowal, protestation.

declare ▶ verb (**declares, declaring, declared**) **1** announce something solemnly or officially. **2** (**declare yourself**) reveal your intentions or identity. **3** acknowledge that you have income or goods on which tax or duty should be paid. **4** Cricket voluntarily close an innings before all the players have batted.

> SYNONYMS **1** *she declared her political principles* **announce,** proclaim, state, reveal, air, voice, articulate, express, vent, set forth, publicize, broadcast. **2** *he declared that they were guilty* **assert,** profess, affirm, maintain, state, contend, argue, insist.

declassify ▸ verb (**declassifies, declassifying, declassified**) officially declare information or documents to be no longer secret.

declension ▸ noun Grammar the changes in the form of a noun, pronoun, or adjective that identify its case, number, and gender.

decline ▸ verb (**declines, declining, declined**) **1** become smaller, weaker, or worse. **2** politely refuse. **3** Grammar form a word according to its case, number, and gender.

> SYNONYMS **1** *she declined all invitations* **turn down,** reject, brush aside, refuse, rebuff, spurn, repulse, dismiss, pass up, say no; informal give something a miss. **2** *the number of traders has declined* **decrease,** reduce, lessen, diminish, dwindle, contract, shrink, fall off, tail off, drop, fall, go down. **3** *standards steadily declined* **deteriorate,** degenerate, decay, crumble, collapse, slump, slip, slide, go downhill, worsen; informal go to the dogs.
> ANTONYMS accept, increase, rise, improve.

▸ noun a gradual loss of strength, numbers, or value.

> SYNONYMS **1** *a decline in profits* **reduction,** decrease, downturn, downswing, diminution, ebb, drop, slump, plunge. **2** *habitat decline* **deterioration,** degeneration, degradation, shrinkage, erosion.
> ANTONYMS rise, improvement.

declivity /di-**kliv**-i-ti/ ▸ noun (plural **declivities**) formal a downward slope.

decode ▸ verb (**decodes, decoding, decoded**) convert a coded message into understandable language.
□ **decoder** noun.

décolletage /day-kol-i-**tah**zh/ ▸ noun a low neckline on a woman's dress or top.

décolleté /day **kol**-tay/ ▸ adjective having a low neckline.

decommission ▸ verb take a nuclear reactor or weapon out of use and make it safe.

decompose ▸ verb (**decomposes, decomposing, decomposed**) decay; rot.
□ **decomposition** noun.

decompress ▸ verb **1** reduce the pressure on. **2** expand compressed computer data to its normal size.

decompression ▸ noun **1** reduction in air pressure. **2** the decompressing of computer data.
■ **decompression sickness** a serious condition that results when a deep-sea diver surfaces too quickly.

decongestant ▸ noun a medicine used to relieve a blocked nose.

deconstruct ▸ verb reduce something to its basic elements in order to interpret it in a different way.
□ **deconstruction** noun.

decontaminate ▸ verb (**decontaminates, decontaminating, decontaminated**) remove dangerous substances from.
□ **decontamination** noun.

decor /**day**-kor/ ▸ noun the furnishing and decoration of a room.

> SYNONYMS **decoration,** furnishing, colour scheme.

decorate ▸ verb (**decorates, decorating, decorated**) **1** make something more attractive by adding extra items. **2** apply paint or wallpaper to the walls of a room or house. **3** give someone an award or medal.

> SYNONYMS **1** *the door was decorated with a wreath* **ornament,** adorn, trim, embellish, garnish, furnish, enhance. **2** *he started to decorate his home* **paint, wallpaper,** paper, refurbish, renovate, redecorate; informal do up, give something a facelift, give something a makeover. **3** *he was decorated for courage* **give a medal to,** honour, cite, reward.

decoration ▸ noun **1** the process or art of decorating. **2** a decorative object or pattern. **3** the way in which something is decorated. **4** a medal or award given as an honour.

> SYNONYMS **1** *a ceiling with rich decoration* **ornamentation,** adornment, trimming, embellishment, beautification. **2** *a Christmas tree decoration* **ornament,** bauble, trinket, knick-knack. **3** *a decoration won on the battlefield* **medal,** award, prize; Brit. informal gong.

decorative ▸ adjective **1** making something look more attractive. **2** having to do with decoration.

> SYNONYMS **ornamental,** fancy, ornate, attractive, pretty, showy.
> ANTONYMS functional.

□ **decoratively** adverb.

decorator ▸ noun a person who decorates, in particular (Brit.) a person whose job is to paint interior walls or hang wallpaper.

decorous ▸ adjective in good taste; polite and restrained.
□ **decorously** adverb.

decorum /di-**kor**-uhm/ ▸ noun polite and socially acceptable behaviour.

decoy ▸ noun **1** a real or imitation bird or animal, used by hunters to lure game. **2** a person or thing used to mislead or lure someone into a trap.
▸ verb lure by means of a decoy.

decrease ▸ verb (**decreases, decreasing, decreased**) make or become smaller or fewer.

> synonyms **1** *pollution levels decreased* **lessen,** reduce, drop, diminish, decline, dwindle, fall off, plummet, plunge. **2** *decrease the amount of fat in your body* **reduce,** lessen, lower, cut, deplete, minimize; informal slash.
> antonyms increase.

▸ noun the process of decreasing, or the amount by which something decreases.

> synonyms *a decrease in crime* **reduction,** drop, decline, downturn, cut, cutback, diminution.
> antonyms increase.

decree ▸ noun **1** an official order that has the force of law. **2** a judgement of certain law courts.

> synonyms **1** *a presidential decree* **order,** command, commandment, edict, proclamation, law, statute, act. **2** *a court decree* **judgement,** verdict, adjudication, finding, ruling, decision.

▸ verb (**decrees, decreeing, decreed**) order something officially.

> synonyms *he decreed that a stadium should be built* **order,** direct, command, rule, dictate, pronounce, proclaim, ordain.

decrepit ▸ adjective worn out or ruined because of age or neglect.
□ **decrepitude** noun.

decriminalize (or **decriminalise**) ▸ verb (**decriminalizes, decriminalizing, decriminalized**) change the law to make something no longer illegal.
□ **decriminalization** noun.

decry ▸ verb (**decries, decrying, decried**) publicly declare something to be wrong or bad.

decrypt ▸ verb convert a coded or unclear message into understandable language.

dedicate ▸ verb (**dedicates, dedicating, dedicated**) **1** give time or effort to a particular subject, task, or purpose. **2** address a book to someone as a sign of respect or affection.

> synonyms **1** *she dedicated her life to the sick* **devote,** commit, pledge, give (up), sacrifice, set aside. **2** *the book is dedicated to his wife* **inscribe,** address, offer. **3** *a chapel dedicated to St Jude* **devote,** assign, bless, consecrate, sanctify.

dedicated ▸ adjective **1** devoting a lot of time and attention to a particular task

or subject. **2** exclusively given over to a particular purpose.

> synonyms **1** *a dedicated supporter* **committed,** devoted, staunch, firm, steadfast, loyal, faithful. **2** *a dedicated rail link* **specialized,** custom-built, customized, purpose-built, exclusive.
> antonyms half-hearted, general-purpose.

dedication ▸ noun **1** devotion to a particular task or subject. **2** the action of dedicating. **3** the words with which a book is dedicated to someone.

> synonyms **1** *sport requires dedication* **commitment,** devotion, loyalty, allegiance, application, resolve, conscientiousness, perseverance, persistence. **2** *the book has a dedication to his wife* **inscription,** message.
> antonyms apathy.

deduce ▸ verb (**deduces, deducing, deduced**) reach a conclusion by thinking about the information or evidence that is available.

deduct ▸ verb take an amount away from a total.

> synonyms **subtract,** take away, take off, debit, dock, stop; informal knock off.
> antonyms add.

□ **deductible** adjective.

deduction ▸ noun **1** the action of deducting something. **2** an amount that is or may be deducted. **3** the process of deducing something.

> synonyms **1** *the deduction of tax* **subtraction,** removal, debit. **2** *gross pay, before deductions* **stoppage,** tax, expenses, rebate, discount, concession. **3** *she was right in her deduction* **conclusion,** inference, supposition, hypothesis, assumption, presumption, suspicion.

□ **deductive** adjective.

deed ▸ noun **1** something that is done deliberately. **2** (usu. **deeds**) a legal document.

> synonyms **1** *heroic deeds* **act,** action, feat, exploit, achievement, accomplishment, endeavour. **2** *mortgage deeds* **document,** contract, instrument.

■ **deed poll** Law a legal deed made by one party only.

deem ▸ verb formal consider in a particular way.

deep ▸ adjective **1** extending far down or in from the top or surface. **2** extending a specified distance from the top or surface. **3** (of sound) not shrill. **4** (of colour) dark. **5** very intense or extreme: *he was in deep trouble.* **6** difficult to understand. **7** (in ball games) far down or across the field.

SYNONYMS **1** *a deep ravine* **cavernous**, yawning, gaping, huge, extensive, bottomless, fathomless. **2** *deep affection* **intense**, heartfelt, wholehearted, deep-seated, sincere, genuine, earnest, enthusiastic, great. **3** *a deep sleep* **sound**, heavy. **4** *a deep thinker* **profound**, serious, intelligent, intellectual, learned, wise, scholarly. **5** *he was deep in concentration* **rapt**, absorbed, engrossed, preoccupied, immersed, lost, gripped. **6** *a deep mystery* **obscure**, complex, mysterious, unfathomable, opaque, abstruse, esoteric, enigmatic. **7** *his deep voice* **low-pitched**, low, bass, rich, resonant, booming, sonorous. **8** *a deep red* **dark**, intense, rich, strong, vivid. ANTONYMS shallow, superficial, light, high, shrill.

▶ noun (**the deep**) literary the sea.
■ **deep freeze** (or **deep freezer**) a freezer. **deep-fry** fry food in enough fat or oil to cover it completely.

deepen ▶ verb make or become deep or deeper.

SYNONYMS **1** *his love for her had deepened* **grow**, increase, intensify, strengthen; informal step up. **2** *they deepened the hole* **dig out**, dig deeper, excavate.

deeply ▶ adverb profoundly: *he was deeply hurt by the allegation.*

SYNONYMS **profoundly**, greatly, enormously, extremely, strongly, intensely, keenly, acutely, thoroughly, completely, entirely, seriously, gravely; informal majorly.

deer ▶ noun (plural **deer**) a grazing animal with hooves, the male of which usually has antlers.

deerstalker ▶ noun a soft cloth cap, with peaks in front and behind and ear flaps which can be tied together over the top.

deface ▶ verb (**defaces**, **defacing**, **defaced**) spoil the surface or appearance of.

de facto /day **fak**-toh/ ▶ adjective & adverb existing or happening in fact, whether it is supposed to or not.

defame ▶ verb (**defames**, **defaming**, **defamed**) damage the good reputation of.
□ **defamation** noun **defamatory** adjective.

default ▶ noun **1** failure to do something that is required by law. **2** an option adopted by a computer program or other mechanism when no alternative is specified.
▶ verb **1** fail to do something that is required by law. **2** (**default to**) go back automatically to a default option.
■ **by default** because there is no opposition or positive action.
□ **defaulter** noun.

defeat ▶ verb **1** win a victory against; beat. **2** prevent someone from achieving an aim.

3 reject or block a proposal or motion.

SYNONYMS **1** *the army which defeated the Scots* **beat**, conquer, win against, triumph over, get the better of, vanquish, rout, trounce, overcome, overpower; informal lick, thrash. **2** *this defeats the original point of the plan* **thwart**, frustrate, foil, ruin, scotch, derail; informal put paid to, stymie; Brit. informal scupper.

▶ noun an instance of defeating or of being defeated.

SYNONYMS *a crippling defeat* **loss**, conquest, rout; informal thrashing, hiding, drubbing, licking.
ANTONYMS victory.

defeatist ▶ noun a person who gives in to difficulty or failure too easily.
□ **defeatism** noun.

defecate /**def**-uh-kayt/ ▶ verb expel waste matter from the bowels.
□ **defecation** noun.

defect¹ /**dee**-fekt/ ▶ noun a fault or imperfection.

SYNONYMS *he spotted a defect in my work* **fault**, flaw, imperfection, deficiency, deformity, blemish, mistake, error.

defect² /di-**fekt**/ ▶ verb abandon your country or cause in favour of an opposing one.
□ **defection** noun **defector** noun.

defective ▶ adjective not perfect; faulty.

SYNONYMS **faulty**, flawed, imperfect, unsound, inoperative, malfunctioning, out of order, broken; informal on the blink; Brit. informal duff.
ANTONYMS perfect, working, intact.

defence (US spelling **defense**) ▶ noun **1** the action of defending something. **2** something that protects a building, country, etc. against attack. **3** an attempt to justify something. **4** the case presented by the person being accused or sued in a lawsuit. **5** (**the defence**) the lawyer or lawyers acting for the person being accused or sued in a lawsuit. **6** (in sport) the action of defending the goal or wicket, or the players who perform this role.

SYNONYMS **1** *the defence of the fortress* **protection**, guarding, security, fortification, resistance. **2** *more spending on defence* **armaments**, weapons, weaponry, arms, the military, the armed forces. **3** *the prisoner's defence* **justification**, vindication, explanation, mitigation, excuse, alibi, denial, rebuttal, plea, pleading, argument, case.
ANTONYMS attack, prosecution.

defenceless (US spelling **defenseless**) ▶ adjective completely vulnerable.

defend ▶ verb **1** protect from harm or danger. **2** argue in support of the person

d

being accused or sued in a lawsuit.
3 attempt to justify. **4** compete to hold on
to a title or seat in a contest or election.
5 (in sport) protect your goal or wicket
rather than attempt to score against your
opponents.

> SYNONYMS **1** *a fort built to defend Ireland*
> **protect,** guard, safeguard, secure, shield,
> fortify, watch over. **2** *he defended his
> policy* **justify,** vindicate, explain, argue
> for, support, back, stand by, make a case
> for, stick up for.
> ANTONYMS attack, criticize.

defendant ▸ noun a person sued or accused
in a court of law.

defender ▸ noun a person who defends
someone or something.

> SYNONYMS **1** *defenders of the environment*
> **protector,** guardian, guard, custodian.
> **2** *a defender of colonialism* **supporter,**
> upholder, backer, champion, advocate,
> apologist.

defensible ▸ adjective **1** able to be justified
by argument. **2** able to be protected.

defensive ▸ adjective **1** used or intended to
defend or protect. **2** very anxious to defend
yourself against criticism.

> SYNONYMS **1** *troops in defensive positions*
> **defending,** protective, guarding. **2** *a
> defensive response* **self-justifying,**
> oversensitive, prickly, paranoid,
> neurotic; informal twitchy.

□ **defensively** adverb **defensiveness** noun.

defer¹ ▸ verb (**defers, deferring, deferred**)
put something off to a later time.

> SYNONYMS **postpone,** put off, delay, hold
> over/off, put back, shelve, suspend;
> N. Amer. table; informal put on ice, put on the
> back burner.

□ **deferment** noun **deferral** noun.

defer² ▸ verb (**defers, deferring, deferred**)
(**defer to**) give in to or agree to accept.

deference ▸ noun polite respect.

deferential ▸ adjective polite and
respectful.
□ **deferentially** adverb.

defiance ▸ noun open refusal to obey
someone or something.

> SYNONYMS **resistance,** opposition,
> non-compliance, disobedience,
> insubordination, rebellion, disregard,
> contempt, insolence.
> ANTONYMS obedience.

defiant ▸ adjective openly refusing to obey
someone or something.

> SYNONYMS **disobedient,** resistant,
> obstinate, uncooperative, non-compliant,
> recalcitrant, insubordinate; Brit. informal

stroppy, bolshie.
ANTONYMS cooperative.

□ **defiantly** adverb.

deficiency ▸ noun (plural **deficiencies**) **1** a
lack or shortage of something. **2** a failing
or shortcoming.

> SYNONYMS **1** *a vitamin deficiency* **lack,**
> insufficiency, shortage, inadequacy,
> deficit, shortfall, scarcity, dearth. **2** *the
> team's big deficiency* **defect,** fault,
> flaw, failing, weakness, shortcoming,
> limitation.
> ANTONYMS surplus, sufficiency, strength.

deficient ▸ adjective **1** not having enough
of a particular quality or ingredient.
2 inadequate in amount or quantity.

deficit ▸ noun **1** the amount by which a
total falls short of that required. **2** the
amount by which money spent is greater
than money earned in a particular period
of time.

> SYNONYMS **shortfall,** deficiency, shortage,
> debt, arrears, loss.
> ANTONYMS surplus.

defile¹ ▸ verb (**defiles, defiling, defiled**)
1 make dirty. **2** treat something sacred
with disrespect.
□ **defilement** noun.

defile² ▸ noun a narrow steep-sided gorge or
mountain pass.

define ▸ verb (**defines, defining, defined**)
1 describe the exact nature or scope of.
2 give the meaning of a word or phrase.
3 mark out the limits or outline of.
□ **definable** adjective.

definite ▸ adjective **1** clearly stated or
decided. **2** (of a person) certain about
something. **3** known to be true or real.
4 having exact and measurable physical
limits.

> SYNONYMS **specific,** explicit, express,
> precise, exact, clear, clear-cut,
> unambiguous, certain, sure, positive,
> conclusive, decisive, firm, unequivocal,
> unmistakable, proven, decided, marked,
> distinct, identifiable.
> ANTONYMS vague, ambiguous,
> indeterminate.

■ **the definite article** Grammar the word *the.*

> ✔ **-ite**, not **-ate**: defin**ite**.

definitely ▸ adverb without doubt: *that is
definitely the best.*

> SYNONYMS **certainly,** surely, for sure,
> unquestionably, without doubt,
> undoubtedly, undeniably, clearly,
> positively, absolutely, unmistakably.

definition ▸ noun **1** a statement of the exact
meaning of a word or the nature or scope
of something. **2** the degree of sharpness in

outline of an object or image.

> SYNONYMS **1** *the definition of 'intelligence'* **meaning,** sense, interpretation, explanation, description. **2** *the definition of the picture* **clarity,** sharpness, focus, crispness, resolution.

definitive ▸ adjective **1** (of a conclusion or agreement) final and not able to be changed. **2** (of a written work) the most accurate of its kind.

> SYNONYMS **1** *a definitive decision* **conclusive,** final, unqualified, absolute, categorical, positive, definite. **2** *the definitive guide* **authoritative,** best, ultimate, classic, standard, recognized, accepted, exhaustive.
> ANTONYMS provisional, average.

□ **definitively** adverb.

deflate ▸ verb (**deflates, deflating, deflated**) **1** let air or gas out of a tyre, balloon, etc. **2** make someone feel suddenly depressed. **3** reduce price levels in an economy.

deflation ▸ noun **1** the action of deflating something. **2** reduction of the general level of prices in an economy.
□ **deflationary** adjective.

deflect ▸ verb **1** turn something aside from a straight course. **2** make someone change their mind about doing something.

> SYNONYMS **divert,** turn away, draw away, distract, fend off, parry, stave off.

□ **deflection** noun.

deflower ▸ verb literary have sex with a woman who is a virgin.

defoliate ▸ verb (**defoliates, defoliating, defoliated**) remove the leaves from trees or plants.
□ **defoliant** noun **defoliation** noun.

deforest ▸ verb clear an area of trees.
□ **deforestation** noun.

deform ▸ verb change or spoil the usual shape of.
□ **deformed** adjective.

deformity ▸ noun (plural **deformities**) **1** a deformed part. **2** the state of being deformed.

defraud ▸ verb illegally obtain money from someone by deception.

> SYNONYMS **swindle,** cheat, rob, deceive, dupe, hoodwink, double-cross, trick; informal con, do, sting, diddle, rip off, shaft, pull a fast one on, put one over on, sell a pup to; N. Amer. informal sucker, snooker, stiff; Austral. informal pull a swifty on.

defray ▸ verb provide money to pay a cost.

defrock ▸ verb remove the official status of a Christian priest.

defrost ▸ verb **1** remove ice from something. **2** thaw frozen food.

deft ▸ adjective quick and neatly skilful.
□ **deftly** adverb **deftness** noun.

defunct ▸ adjective no longer existing or functioning.

defuse ▸ verb (**defuses, defusing, defused**) **1** make a situation less tense or difficult. **2** remove the fuse from an explosive device to prevent it from exploding.

> ❗ Don't confuse **defuse** with **diffuse**, which means 'spread over a wide area'.

defy ▸ verb (**defies, defying, defied**) **1** openly resist or refuse to obey. **2** challenge someone to do or prove something.

> SYNONYMS **disobey,** flout, disregard, ignore, break, violate, contravene, breach, challenge, confront.
> ANTONYMS obey.

degenerate ▸ verb /di-**jenn**-uh-rayt/ (**degenerates, degenerating, degenerated**) deteriorate physically or morally; get worse.

> SYNONYMS *their quality of life had degenerated* **deteriorate,** decline, slip, slide, go downhill; informal go to the dogs.
> ANTONYMS improve.

▸ adjective /di-**jenn**-uh-ruht/ having very low moral standards.

> SYNONYMS *her degenerate brother* **corrupt,** perverted, decadent, dissolute, dissipated, debauched, immoral, unprincipled, disreputable.
> ANTONYMS upright, pure.

▸ noun /di-**jenn**-uh-ruht/ a person with very low moral standards.
□ **degeneracy** noun **degeneration** noun.

degenerative ▸ adjective (of a disease) becoming progressively worse.

degrade ▸ verb (**degrades, degrading, degraded**) **1** cause someone to lose dignity or self-respect. **2** make worse in character or quality. **3** make something break down or deteriorate chemically.

> SYNONYMS **demean,** debase, humiliate, humble, belittle, mortify, dehumanize, brutalize.
> ANTONYMS dignify.

□ **degradable** adjective **degradation** noun.

degree ▸ noun **1** the amount, level, or extent to which something happens or is present. **2** a unit for measuring angles, equivalent to one ninetieth of a right angle. **3** a stage in a scale, e.g. of temperature or hardness. **4** a qualification awarded to someone who has successfully completed a course at a university.

> SYNONYMS **level,** standard, grade, stage, mark, amount, extent, measure, intensity, strength, proportion.

dehumanize (or **dehumanise**)
▸ verb (**dehumanizes, dehumanizing,**

dehumanized) remove the positive human qualities from.

dehumidify ▸ verb (dehumidifies, dehumidifying, dehumidified) remove moisture from the air or a gas.
□ **dehumidifier** noun.

dehydrate ▸ verb (dehydrates, dehydrating, dehydrated) **1** make someone lose a lot of water from their body. **2** remove water from food to preserve it.
□ **dehydration** noun.

de-ice ▸ verb (de-ices, de-icing, de-iced) remove ice from.
□ **de-icer** noun.

deify /day-i-fy/ ▸ verb (deifies, deifying, deified) treat or worship someone as a god.
□ **deification** noun.

deign ▸ verb (deign to do) do something that you think you are too important to do.

deity /day-i-ti/ ▸ noun (plural deities) a god or goddess.

déjà vu /day-zhah voo/ ▸ noun a feeling of having already experienced the present situation.

dejected ▸ adjective sad and in low spirits.

SYNONYMS **downcast,** downhearted, despondent, disconsolate, dispirited, crestfallen, disheartened, depressed; informal down in the mouth, down in the dumps.
ANTONYMS cheerful.

□ **dejection** noun.

dekko ▸ noun Brit. informal a quick look.

delay ▸ verb **1** make someone late or slow. **2** hesitate or be slow. **3** put off or postpone.

SYNONYMS **1** we were delayed by the traffic **detain,** hold up, make late, slow up/down, bog down, hinder, hamper, impede, obstruct. **2** don't delay **linger,** drag your feet, hold back, dawdle, waste time, stall, hesitate, dither, shilly-shally; informal dilly-dally. **3** he may delay the cut in interest rates **postpone,** put off, defer, hold over, adjourn, reschedule.
ANTONYMS assist, hurry, advance.

▸ noun the period or length of time that someone or something is delayed.

SYNONYMS **1** drivers will face lengthy delays **hold-up,** wait, interruption, stoppage. **2** the delay of his trial **postponement,** deferral, adjournment.

delectable ▸ adjective lovely, delightful, or delicious.
□ **delectably** adverb.

delectation /dee-lek-**tay**-sh'n/ ▸ noun formal pleasure and delight.

delegate ▸ noun /**del**-i-guht/ **1** a person sent to represent other people. **2** a member of a committee.

SYNONYMS trade union delegates **representative,** envoy, emissary, commissioner, agent, deputy.

▸ verb /**del**-i-gayt/ (delegates, delegating, delegated) **1** give a task or responsibility to someone else, especially someone more junior. **2** authorize someone to act as a representative.

SYNONYMS she must delegate routine tasks **assign,** entrust, pass on, hand on/over, turn over, devolve.

delegation ▸ noun **1** a group of delegates. **2** the process of delegating something.

SYNONYMS **1** the delegation from South Africa **deputation,** mission, commission, contingent, legation. **2** the delegation of tasks to others **assignment,** entrusting, devolution.

delete ▸ verb (deletes, deleting, deleted) cross out or remove something written or printed or stored in a computer's memory.

SYNONYMS **remove,** cut (out), take out, edit out, excise, cancel, cross out, strike out, obliterate, rub out, erase.
ANTONYMS add.

□ **deletion** noun.

deleterious /de-li-**tee**-ri-uhss/ ▸ adjective formal causing harm or damage.

deli ▸ noun (plural delis) informal a delicatessen.

deliberate ▸ adjective /di-**lib**-uh-ruht/ **1** done on purpose; intentional. **2** careful and unhurried.

SYNONYMS **1** a deliberate attempt to provoke him **intentional,** calculated, conscious, intended, planned, wilful, premeditated. **2** small, deliberate steps **careful,** cautious, measured, regular, even, steady. **3** a deliberate worker **methodical,** systematic, careful, painstaking, meticulous, thorough.
ANTONYMS accidental, hasty, careless.

▸ verb /di-**lib**-uh-rayt/ (deliberates, deliberating, deliberated) think about something carefully and for a long time.

SYNONYMS she deliberated on his words **think about/over,** ponder, consider, contemplate, reflect on, muse on, meditate on, ruminate on, mull over; N. Amer. think on.

deliberately ▸ adverb **1** consciously and intentionally. **2** carefully and unhurriedly.

SYNONYMS **1** he deliberately hurt me **intentionally,** on purpose, purposely, by design, knowingly, wittingly, consciously, wilfully. **2** he walked deliberately down the aisle **carefully,** cautiously, slowly, steadily, evenly.

deliberation ▸ noun **1** long and careful consideration. **2** slow and careful movement or thought.

> SYNONYMS **thought,** consideration, reflection, contemplation, discussion.

deliberative ▶ adjective having to do with consideration or discussion.

delicacy ▶ noun (plural **delicacies**) **1** intricate or fragile texture or structure. **2** discretion and tact. **3** a tasty, expensive food.

> SYNONYMS **1** *the delicacy of the fabric* **fineness,** delicateness, fragility, thinness, lightness, flimsiness. **2** *the delicacy of the situation* **difficulty,** trickiness, sensitivity, ticklishness, awkwardness. **3** *treat this matter with delicacy* **care,** sensitivity, tact, discretion, diplomacy, subtlety. **4** *an Australian delicacy* **treat,** luxury, speciality.

delicate ▶ adjective **1** attractively light and intricate in texture or structure. **2** easily broken or damaged. **3** tending to become ill easily. **4** needing or showing careful handling: *a delicate issue.* **5** (of colour or flavour) subtle and pleasant.

> SYNONYMS **1** *delicate embroidery* **fine,** intricate, dainty. **2** *a delicate shade of blue* **subtle,** soft, muted, pastel, pale, light. **3** *delicate china cups* **fragile,** frail. **4** *his wife is very delicate* **sickly,** unhealthy, frail, feeble, weak. **5** *a delicate issue* **difficult,** tricky, sensitive, ticklish, awkward, touchy, embarrassing; informal sticky, dicey. **6** *the matter required delicate handling* **careful,** sensitive, tactful, diplomatic, discreet, kid-glove, subtle.
> ANTONYMS coarse, lurid, strong, robust, clumsy.

□ **delicately** adverb.

delicatessen ▶ noun a shop selling unusual or foreign prepared foods.

delicious ▶ adjective having a very pleasant taste or smell.

> SYNONYMS **delectable,** mouth-watering, appetizing, tasty, flavoursome; informal scrumptious, scrummy, yummy; N. Amer. informal nummy.
> ANTONYMS unpalatable.

□ **deliciously** adverb.

delight ▶ verb **1** please someone very much. **2** (delight in) take great pleasure in.

> SYNONYMS *her manners delighted him* **charm,** enchant, captivate, entrance, thrill, entertain, amuse, divert; informal send, tickle pink, bowl over.
> ANTONYMS dismay, disgust.

▶ noun great pleasure, or something that causes it.

> SYNONYMS *she squealed with delight* **pleasure,** happiness, joy, glee,

excitement, amusement, bliss.
> ANTONYMS displeasure.

delighted ▶ adjective very pleased.

> SYNONYMS **pleased,** glad, happy, thrilled, overjoyed, ecstatic, elated, on cloud nine, walking on air, in seventh heaven, jumping for joy; enchanted, charmed; amused, diverted; gleeful, cock-a-hoop; informal over the moon, tickled pink, as pleased as Punch, on top of the world, as happy as Larry; Brit. informal chuffed; N. English informal made up; Austral. informal wrapped.

□ **delightedly** adverb.

delightful ▶ adjective causing delight; very pleasing.

> SYNONYMS **1** *a delightful evening* **lovely,** enjoyable, amusing, entertaining. **2** *the delightful Sally* **charming,** enchanting, captivating, bewitching, appealing, sweet, endearing, cute.

□ **delightfully** adverb.

delineate /di-**lin**-i-ayt/ ▶ verb (**delineates, delineating, delineated**) describe or indicate something precisely.
□ **delineation** noun.

delinquency ▶ noun (plural **delinquencies**) minor crime.

delinquent ▶ adjective tending to commit crime.
▶ noun a delinquent person.

deliquesce /de-li-**kwess**/ ▶ verb (**deliquesces, deliquescing, deliquesced**) (of a solid) become liquid by absorbing moisture.
□ **deliquescence** noun **deliquescent** adjective.

delirious ▶ adjective **1** suffering from delirium. **2** very excited or happy.
□ **deliriously** adverb.

> ✔ Note there's an **i**, not an **e**, in the middle: delirious.

delirium ▶ noun a disturbed state of mind in which a person becomes very restless, has illusions, and is unable to think clearly.

deliver ▶ verb **1** bring something and hand it over to the person who is supposed to receive it. **2** provide something promised or expected. **3** give a speech. **4** launch or aim a blow or attack. **5** save or set free. **6** assist in the birth of a baby. **7** give birth to a baby.

> SYNONYMS **1** *the parcel was delivered to his house* **bring,** take, convey, carry, transport, send, distribute, dispatch, ship. **2** *the court delivered its verdict* **state,** utter, give, read, broadcast, pronounce, announce, declare, proclaim, hand down, return. **3** *she delivered a blow to his head* **administer,** deal, inflict, give; informal land.

d

deliverance ▸ noun the process of being rescued or set free.

delivery ▸ noun (plural **deliveries**) **1** the action of delivering something. **2** the process of giving birth. **3** an act of throwing or bowling a ball.

SYNONYMS **1** *the delivery of the goods* **conveyance**, carriage, transportation, transport, distribution, dispatch, shipping. **2** *we get several deliveries a day* **consignment**, load, shipment. **3** *her delivery was stilted* **speech**, pronunciation, enunciation, articulation, elocution.

dell ▸ noun literary a small valley.

delphinium /del-fin-i-uhm/ ▸ noun (plural **delphiniums**) a garden plant that has tall spikes of blue flowers.

delta ▸ noun **1** an area of land where the mouth of a river has split into several channels. **2** the fourth letter of the Greek alphabet (Δ, δ).

delude ▸ verb (**deludes**, **deluding**, **deluded**) persuade someone to believe something that is not true.

deluge ▸ noun **1** a severe flood or very heavy fall of rain. **2** a great quantity of something arriving at the same time: *a deluge of complaints*.
▸ verb (**deluges**, **deluging**, **deluged**) **1** overwhelm someone with a great quantity of something. **2** flood a place.

delusion ▸ noun a mistaken belief or impression.

SYNONYMS **misapprehension**, misconception, false impression, misunderstanding, mistake, error, misconstruction, illusion, fantasy, fancy.

□ **delusional** adjective.

de luxe /di luks/ ▸ adjective of a higher quality than usual.

delve ▸ verb (**delves**, **delving**, **delved**) **1** reach inside a container and search for something. **2** research something very thoroughly.

demagnetize (or **demagnetise**) ▸ verb (**demagnetizes**, **demagnetizing**, **demagnetized**) stop something being magnetic.

demagogue /dem-uh-gog/ ▸ noun a political leader who appeals to people's desires and prejudices rather than using reasoned arguments.

demand ▸ noun **1** a very firm request for something. **2** (**demands**) tasks or requirements that are urgent or difficult. **3** the desire of consumers for a particular product or service.

SYNONYMS **1** *I gave in to her demands* **request**, call, command, order, dictate. **2** *the demands of a young family*

requirement, need, claim, commitment, imposition. **3** *the big demand for such toys* **market**, call, appetite, desire.
▸ verb **1** ask very firmly. **2** insist on having. **3** require; need.

SYNONYMS **1** *workers demanded wage increases* **call for**, ask for, request, push for, seek, claim. **2** *Harvey demanded that I tell him the truth* **order**, command, enjoin, require, insist. **3** *'Where is she?' he demanded* **ask**, enquire. **4** *an activity demanding detailed knowledge* **require**, need, necessitate, call for, involve, entail. **5** *they demanded complete anonymity* **insist on**, stipulate, expect, look for.

∎ **in demand** wanted by many people.

demanding ▸ adjective needing a lot of skill or effort.

SYNONYMS **1** *a demanding task* **difficult**, challenging, taxing, exacting, tough, hard, onerous, formidable, arduous, gruelling, back-breaking, punishing. **2** *a demanding child* **nagging**, trying, tiresome, hard to please.
ANTONYMS easy.

demarcate /dee-mar-kayt/ ▸ verb (**demarcates**, **demarcating**, **demarcated**) set the boundaries of.
□ **demarcation** noun.

dematerialize (or **dematerialise**) ▸ verb (**dematerializes**, **dematerializing**, **dematerialized**) stop being physically present.

demean ▸ verb make someone lose dignity or respect.

demeaning ▸ adjective causing someone to lose dignity or respect.

SYNONYMS **degrading**, humiliating, shameful, undignified, menial; informal infra dig.

demeanour (US spelling **demeanor**) ▸ noun the way a person behaves or looks.

demented ▸ adjective **1** suffering from dementia. **2** informal wild and irrational.

dementia /di-men-shuh/ ▸ noun a disorder in which a person is unable to remember things or think clearly.

demerara sugar /dem-uh-rair-uh/ ▸ noun a type of light brown sugar.

demerit ▸ noun a fault or disadvantage.

demesne /di-mayn/ ▸ noun (in the past) land attached to a manor.

demigod ▸ noun a being that is partly a god and partly a human.

demilitarize (or **demilitarise**) ▸ verb (**demilitarizes**, **demilitarizing**, **demilitarized**) remove all military forces from an area.
□ **demilitarization** noun.

demi-monde /de-mi-**mond**/ ► noun a group of people on the fringes of respectable society.

demise /di-**myz**/ ► noun **1** a person's death. **2** the end or failure of something.

> SYNONYMS **1** *her tragic demise* **death,** dying, passing, end. **2** *the demise of the Ottoman Empire* **end,** break-up, disintegration, fall, downfall, collapse, overthrow.
> ANTONYMS birth.

demo ► noun (plural **demos**) informal **1** a political demonstration. **2** a tape or disc containing a demonstration of a performer's music or a piece of software.

demob ► verb (**demobs, demobbing, demobbed**) Brit. informal demobilize.

demobilize (or **demobilise**) ► verb (**demobilizes, demobilizing, demobilized**) take troops out of active service.
□ **demobilization** noun.

democracy /di-**mok**-ruh-si/ ► noun (plural **democracies**) **1** a form of government in which the people can vote for representatives to govern the state on their behalf. **2** a state governed in this way.

democrat ► noun **1** a supporter of democracy. **2** (**Democrat**) (in the US) a member of the Democratic Party.

democratic ► adjective **1** relating to or supporting democracy. **2** based on the principle that everyone in society is equal. **3** (**Democratic**) (in the US) relating to or supporting the Democratic Party.

> SYNONYMS **elected,** representative, parliamentary, popular, egalitarian, self-governing.
> □ **democratically** adverb.

democratize (or **democratise**) ► verb (**democratizes, democratizing, democratized**) introduce a democratic system or democratic ideas to.
□ **democratization** noun.

demography ► noun the study of changes in human populations using records of the numbers of births, deaths, etc. in a particular area.
□ **demographic** adjective.

demolish /di-**mol**-ish/ ► verb **1** knock down a building. **2** show that a theory is completely wrong. **3** humorous eat up food quickly.

> SYNONYMS **1** *they demolished a block of flats* **knock down,** pull down, tear down, destroy, flatten, raze to the ground, dismantle, level, bulldoze, blow up. **2** *he demolished her credibility* **destroy,** ruin, wreck, overturn, explode, drive a coach and horses through; informal shoot full of holes.
> ANTONYMS build, strengthen.

□ **demolition** noun.

demon ► noun an evil spirit or devil.
► adjective very forceful or skilful: *a demon cook*.

demoniac /di-**moh**-ni-ak/ (or **demoniacal** /dee-muh-**ny**-u-k'l/) ► adjective demonic.

demonic /di-**mon**-ik/ ► adjective having to do with demons or evil spirits.
□ **demonically** adverb.

demonize (or **demonise**) ► verb (**demonizes, demonizing, demonized**) portray someone as wicked and threatening.

demonstrable ► adjective clearly apparent or able to be proved.
□ **demonstrably** adverb.

demonstrate ► verb (**demonstrates, demonstrating, demonstrated**) **1** clearly show that something exists or is true. **2** show and explain how something works. **3** express a feeling or quality by your actions. **4** take part in a public demonstration.

> SYNONYMS **1** *his findings demonstrate that boys commit more crimes* **show,** indicate, establish, prove, confirm, verify. **2** *she demonstrated various drawing techniques* **show,** display, present, illustrate, exemplify. **3** *his work demonstrated an analytical ability* **reveal,** manifest, indicate, signify, signal, denote, show, display, exhibit. **4** *they demonstrated against the Government* **protest,** march, parade, picket, strike.

□ **demonstrator** noun.

demonstration ► noun **1** the action of demonstrating. **2** a public meeting or march expressing an opinion on an issue.

> SYNONYMS **1** *a demonstration of carving* **exhibition,** presentation, display. **2** *his paintings are a demonstration of his talent* **manifestation,** indication, sign, mark, proof, testimony. **3** *an anti-racism demonstration* **protest,** march, rally, mass lobby, sit-in, sit-down strike; informal demo.

demonstrative /di-**mon**-struh-tiv/ ► adjective **1** tending to show your feelings openly. **2** demonstrating something.
□ **demonstratively** adverb.

demoralize (or **demoralise**) ► verb (**demoralizes, demoralizing, demoralized**) make someone lose confidence or hope.
□ **demoralization** noun.

demoralized ► adjective having lost confidence or hope.

> SYNONYMS **dispirited,** disheartened, downhearted, dejected, downcast, low, depressed, dismayed, daunted, discouraged.

demote ► verb (**demotes, demoting, demoted**) move someone to a less senior position.

□ **demotion** noun.

demotivate ▶ verb make someone less eager to work or make an effort.

demur /di-**mer**/ ▶ verb (**demurs, demurring, demurred**) show reluctance.
■ **without demur** without objecting or hesitating.
□ **demurral** noun.

demure ▶ adjective (of a woman) reserved, modest, and shy.

> SYNONYMS **modest,** reserved, shy, unassuming, decorous, decent, proper.
> ANTONYMS brazen.

□ **demurely** adverb.

demystify ▶ verb (**demystifies, demystifying, demystified**) make a subject less difficult to understand.

den ▶ noun **1** a wild animal's lair or home. **2** informal a person's private room. **3** a place where people meet to do something immoral or forbidden: *an opium den.*

> SYNONYMS **1** *the wolves' den* **lair,** burrow, hole, shelter, hiding place, hideout. **2** *sulking in his den* **study,** studio, workshop, retreat, sanctuary, hideaway; informal hidey-hole.

denationalize (or **denationalise**) ▶ verb (**denationalizes, denationalizing, denationalized**) transfer an industry or business from public to private ownership.

denial ▶ noun **1** a statement that something is not true. **2** the refusal to acknowledge or accept something unpleasant: *he's still in denial.*

> SYNONYMS **1** *the reports met with a denial* **contradiction,** rebuttal, repudiation, refutation, disclaimer. **2** *the denial of insurance to certain people* **refusal,** withholding.

denier /**den**-yer/ ▶ noun a unit for measuring the fineness of nylon or silk.

denigrate ▶ verb (**denigrates, denigrating, denigrated**) criticize someone unfairly.
□ **denigration** noun.

denim ▶ noun **1** a hard-wearing cotton fabric. **2** (**denims**) jeans or other clothes made of denim.

denizen /**den**-i-zuhn/ ▶ noun formal an inhabitant or occupant.

denominate ▶ verb (**denominates, denominating, denominated**) formal call; name.

denomination ▶ noun **1** a recognized branch of a Church or religion. **2** the face value of a banknote, coin, postage stamp, etc. **3** formal a name or designation.

> SYNONYMS **1** *a Christian denomination* **religious group,** sect, cult, movement, persuasion, order, creed, school,

church. **2** *banknotes in a number of denominations* **value,** unit, size.

□ **denominational** adjective.

denominator ▶ noun Maths the number below the line in a fraction, for example 4 in ¼.

denote ▶ verb (**denotes, denoting, denoted**) **1** be a sign of. **2** (of a word) have something as a main meaning.

> SYNONYMS **indicate,** be a mark of, signify, signal, designate, symbolize, represent.

denouement /day-**noo**-mon/ ▶ noun the final part of a play, film, or story, in which matters are explained or settled.

denounce ▶ verb (**denounces, denouncing, denounced**) publicly declare that someone is wrong or evil.

> SYNONYMS **1** *the pope denounced his critics* **condemn,** attack, censure, decry, stigmatize, deprecate, disparage, revile, damn. **2** *he was denounced as a traitor* **expose,** betray, inform on, incriminate, implicate, cite, accuse.
> ANTONYMS praise.

dense ▶ adjective **1** containing many people or things crowded closely together. **2** having a thick or closely packed texture. **3** informal stupid.

> SYNONYMS **1** *a dense forest* **thick,** crowded, compact, solid, tight, overgrown, impenetrable, impassable. **2** *dense smoke* **thick,** heavy, opaque, murky. **3** *they were dense enough to believe me* **stupid,** brainless, foolish, slow, simple-minded, empty-headed, idiotic; informal thick, dim; Brit. informal daft.
> ANTONYMS sparse, thin, clever.

□ **densely** adverb.

density ▶ noun (plural **densities**) **1** the degree to which something is dense. **2** the quantity of people or things in a given area.

dent ▶ noun a slight hollow in a surface made by a blow or pressure.

> SYNONYMS *a dent in his car* **knock,** indentation, dint, depression, hollow, crater, pit; N. Amer. informal ding.

▶ verb **1** mark with a dent. **2** have a bad effect on.

> SYNONYMS *Jamie dented his car* **knock,** dint, mark; N. Amer. informal ding.

dental ▶ adjective relating to the teeth or to dentistry.

dentine /**den**-teen/ ▶ noun the hard, bony tissue that teeth are made of.

dentist ▶ noun a person who is qualified to treat the diseases and conditions that affect the teeth and gums.
□ **dentistry** noun.

denture /**den**-cher/ ▶ noun a removable plate or frame fitted with one or more false teeth.

denude ▶ verb (**denudes, denuding, denuded**) make something bare or empty.

denunciation ▶ noun the action of denouncing.

deny ▶ verb (**denies, denying, denied**) **1** state that something is not true. **2** refuse to admit something. **3** refuse to give someone a thing that they want. **4** (**deny yourself**) go without something you want.

> SYNONYMS **1** *the report was denied by witnesses* **contradict,** rebut, repudiate, refute, challenge, contest. **2** *he denied the request* **refuse,** turn down, reject, rebuff, decline, veto, dismiss; informal give the thumbs down to.
> ANTONYMS confirm, allow, accept.

deodorant ▶ noun a substance which prevents unpleasant bodily odours.

deodorize (or **deodorise**) ▶ verb (**deodorizes, deodorizing, deodorized**) prevent an unpleasant smell in.

depart ▶ verb **1** leave; go away. **2** (**depart from**) do something different from the usual or accepted thing.

> SYNONYMS **1** *James departed after lunch* **leave,** go away, withdraw, absent yourself, quit, exit, decamp, retreat, retire, make off; informal make tracks, take off, split; Brit. informal sling your hook. **2** *the budget departed from the norm* **deviate,** diverge, digress, stray, veer, differ, vary.
> ANTONYMS arrive, stick to.

departed ▶ adjective deceased; dead.

department ▶ noun **1** a division of a business, government, or other large organization. **2** an administrative district in some countries, e.g. France. **3** informal a person's area of special knowledge or responsibility.

> SYNONYMS **division,** section, sector, unit, branch, wing, office, bureau, agency, ministry.

■ **department store** a large shop that stocks many types of goods in different departments.
□ **departmental** adjective **departmentally** adverb.

departure ▶ noun **1** the action of leaving. **2** a change from the usual way of doing something.

> SYNONYMS **1** *he tried to delay her departure* **leaving,** going, leave-taking, withdrawal, exit. **2** *a departure from normality* **deviation,** divergence, digression, shift, variation. **3** *an exciting departure for film-makers* **change,** innovation, novelty.

depend ▶ verb (**depend on**) **1** be determined by. **2** rely on.

> SYNONYMS **1** *her career depends on this reference* **be dependent on,** hinge on, hang on, rest on, rely on. **2** *my family depends on me* **rely on,** lean on, count on, bank on, trust (in), pin your hopes on.

dependable ▶ adjective trustworthy and reliable.
□ **dependability** noun **dependably** adverb.

dependant (or **dependent**) ▶ noun a person who relies on another for financial support.

> ✔ The noun can be spelled **dependant** or **dependent**. The adjective is always spelled **dependent**.

dependency ▶ noun (plural **dependencies**) **1** a country or province controlled by another. **2** the state of being dependent.

dependent ▶ adjective **1** (**dependent on**) determined by. **2** relying on someone or something for support. **3** (**dependent on**) unable to do without.

> SYNONYMS **1** *she is dependent on drugs* **addicted,** reliant; informal hooked. **2** *he is ill and dependent* **reliant,** needy, helpless, infirm, invalid, incapable, debilitated, disabled.
> ANTONYMS independent.

▶ noun ➡ DEPENDANT.
□ **dependence** noun **dependently** adverb.

depict ▶ verb **1** represent something by a drawing, painting, or other art form. **2** portray in words.

> SYNONYMS **1** *the painting depicts the Last Supper* **portray,** show, represent, picture, illustrate, reproduce, render. **2** *the process depicted by Darwin's theory* **describe,** detail, relate, present, set forth, set out, outline.

□ **depiction** noun.

depilate /**dep**-i-layt/ ▶ verb (**depilates, depilating, depilated**) remove the hair from.
□ **depilation** noun **depilatory** adjective.

deplete ▶ verb (**depletes, depleting, depleted**) reduce the number or quantity of.

> SYNONYMS **reduce,** decrease, diminish, exhaust, use up, consume, expend, drain, empty.
> ANTONYMS augment.

□ **depletion** noun.

deplorable ▶ adjective shockingly bad.
□ **deplorably** adverb.

deplore ▶ verb (**deplores, deploring, deplored**) strongly disapprove of.

> SYNONYMS **1** *we deplore violence* **abhor,** find unacceptable, frown on, disapprove of, take a dim view of, take exception

to, condemn, denounce. **2** *he deplored their lack of flair* **regret,** lament, mourn, bemoan, bewail, complain about, grieve over, sigh over.
ANTONYMS applaud, rejoice at.

deploy ▸ verb **1** bring or move forces into position for military action. **2** use a resource or quality effectively.

SYNONYMS **1** *forces were deployed at strategic points* **position,** station, post, place, install, locate, base. **2** *she deployed all her skills* **use,** utilize, employ, take advantage of, exploit, call on.

□ **deployment** noun.

depopulate ▸ verb (**depopulates, depopulating, depopulated**) greatly reduce the population of a place.
□ **depopulation** noun.

deport ▸ verb expel a foreigner or immigrant from a country.

SYNONYMS **expel,** banish, extradite, repatriate.
ANTONYMS admit.

□ **deportation** noun **deportee** noun.

deportment ▸ noun **1** the way a person stands and walks. **2** N. Amer. a person's behaviour or manners.

depose ▸ verb (**deposes, deposing, deposed**) remove someone from office suddenly and forcefully.

SYNONYMS **overthrow,** unseat, dethrone, topple, remove, supplant, displace, oust.

deposit ▸ noun **1** a sum of money placed in an account. **2** a payment made as a first instalment in buying something. **3** a returnable sum paid when renting something, to cover possible loss or damage. **4** a layer of a substance that has built up.

SYNONYMS **1** *a thick deposit of ash* **layer,** covering, coating, blanket, accumulation, sediment. **2** *a copper deposit* **seam,** vein, lode, layer, stratum, bed. **3** *they paid a deposit* **down payment,** advance payment, prepayment, instalment, retainer, security.

▸ verb (**deposits, depositing, deposited**) **1** put something down in a particular place. **2** store something somewhere for safekeeping. **3** pay a sum as a deposit. **4** lay down a layer of a substance.

SYNONYMS **1** *she deposited her books on the table* **put down,** place, set down, unload, rest, drop; informal dump, park, plonk; N. Amer. informal plunk. **2** *the silt deposited by flood water* **leave (behind),** precipitate, dump, wash up, cast up. **3** *the gold was deposited at the bank* **lodge,** bank, house, store, stow.

deposition ▸ noun **1** the action of deposing

someone from office. **2** Law a sworn statement to be used as evidence in a court of law. **3** the action of depositing.

depository ▸ noun (plural **depositories**) a place where things are stored.

depot /dep-oh/ ▸ noun **1** a place where large quantities of goods are stored. **2** a place where vehicles are kept and maintained. **3** N. Amer. /dee-poh/ a railway or bus station.

SYNONYMS **1** *an arms depot* **storehouse,** warehouse, store, repository, depository, cache, arsenal, armoury, dump. **2** *the bus depot* **terminal,** terminus, station, garage, headquarters, base.

deprave ▸ verb (**depraves, depraving, depraved**) make someone morally bad; corrupt someone.

depravity /di-prav-i-ti/ ▸ noun immoral behaviour or character.

deprecate /dep-ri-kayt/ ▸ verb (**deprecates, deprecating, deprecated**) express disapproval of.
□ **deprecation** noun.

depreciate /di-pree-shi-ayt/ ▸ verb (**depreciates, depreciating, depreciated**) **1** decrease in value over a period of time. **2** dismiss something as being unimportant.
□ **depreciation** noun.

depredations ▸ plural noun acts that cause harm or damage.

depress ▸ verb **1** make someone feel very unhappy. **2** make something less active. **3** push or pull down.

SYNONYMS **1** *the news depressed him* **sadden,** dispirit, cast down, get down, dishearten, demoralize, crush, weigh down on. **2** *new economic policies depressed sales* **slow down,** weaken, impair, inhibit, restrict. **3** *imports will depress farm prices* **reduce,** lower, cut, cheapen, discount, deflate, diminish, depreciate, devalue. **4** *depress each key in turn* **press,** push, hold down, tap.
ANTONYMS cheer, boost, raise, lift.

depressant ▸ noun a drug or other substance that slows down the natural processes of the body.

depressed ▸ adjective **1** feeling very unhappy and without hope. **2** suffering the damaging effects of an economic slump.

SYNONYMS **1** *he felt lonely and depressed* **sad,** unhappy, miserable, gloomy, dejected, downhearted, downcast, down, despondent, dispirited, low, morose, dismal, desolate; informal blue, down in the dumps, down in the mouth. **2** *a depressed economy* **weak,** inactive, flat, slow, slack, sluggish, stagnant. **3** *a depressed area* **poverty-stricken,** poor, disadvantaged, deprived, needy,

distressed, run down.
ANTONYMS cheerful, strong, prosperous.

depressing ▸ adjective making someone feel very unhappy.

> SYNONYMS **dismal,** sad, unhappy, sombre, gloomy, grave, bleak, black, melancholy, dreary, grim, cheerless.

depression ▸ noun **1** a mental state in which a person has feelings of great unhappiness and hopelessness. **2** a long and severe slump in an economy or market. **3** the action of depressing. **4** a sunken or hollow place. **5** an area of low pressure which may bring rain.

> SYNONYMS **1** *she ate to ease her depression* **unhappiness,** sadness, melancholy, melancholia, misery, sorrow, gloom, despondency, low spirits. **2** *an economic depression* **recession,** slump, decline, downturn. **3** *a depression in the ground* **hollow,** indentation, dent, cavity, dip, pit, crater, basin, bowl.

depressive ▸ adjective tending to cause or feel depression.

deprivation /dep-ri-**vay**-sh'n/ ▸ noun **1** hardship resulting from not having enough of the things necessary for life. **2** the action of depriving someone of something.

> SYNONYMS **1** *unemployment and deprivation* **poverty,** impoverishment, privation, hardship, destitution, need, want. **2** *deprivation of political rights* **dispossession,** withholding, withdrawal, removal, seizure.
> ANTONYMS prosperity, granting.

deprive ▸ verb (deprives, depriving, deprived) prevent someone from having or using something.

> SYNONYMS **dispossess,** strip, divest, relieve, rob, cheat out of.

deprived ▸ adjective not having enough of the things necessary for life.

> SYNONYMS **disadvantaged,** underprivileged, poverty-stricken, impoverished, poor, destitute, needy.
> ANTONYMS privileged.

Dept ▸ abbreviation Department.

depth ▸ noun **1** the distance from the top or surface down, or from front to back. **2** complex or meaningful thought. **3** extensive and detailed study. **4** strength of emotion. **5** (**the depths**) the deepest, lowest, or innermost part of something.

> SYNONYMS **1** *the depth of the caves* **deepness,** drop, height. **2** *the depth of his knowledge* **extent,** range, scope, breadth, width. **3** *her lack of depth* **profundity,** wisdom, understanding, intelligence, discernment, penetration, insight,

awareness. **4** *depth of colour* **intensity,** richness, vividness, strength, brilliance.
ANTONYMS triviality.

■ **depth charge** a device designed to explode under water, used for attacking submarines.

deputation ▸ noun a group of people who are sent to do something on behalf of a larger group.

depute ▸ verb (deputes, deputing, deputed) instruct someone to do something that you are responsible for.

deputize (or **deputise**) ▸ verb (deputizes, deputizing, deputized) temporarily act on behalf of someone else.

deputy ▸ noun (plural **deputies**) a person appointed to do the work of a more senior person in that person's absence.

> SYNONYMS **second in command,** number two, assistant, aide, proxy, stand-in, replacement, substitute, representative, reserve.

derail ▸ verb **1** make a train leave the tracks. **2** prevent a process from following its intended course.
□ **derailment** noun.

deranged ▸ adjective mad; insane.
□ **derangement** noun.

derby /**dar**-bi/ ▸ noun (plural **derbies**) a sports match between two rival teams from the same area.

deregulate ▸ verb (deregulates, deregulating, deregulated) remove regulations or restrictions from.
□ **deregulation** noun.

derelict /**de**-ri-likt/ ▸ adjective in a very bad condition as a result of disuse and neglect.

> SYNONYMS *a derelict building* **dilapidated,** ramshackle, run down, tumbledown, in ruins, falling down, disused, abandoned, deserted.

▸ noun a person without a home, job, or property.

> SYNONYMS *the derelicts who survive on the streets* **tramp,** vagrant, down and out, homeless person, drifter, beggar, outcast; informal dosser, bag lady.

dereliction ▸ noun **1** an abandoned and run-down state. **2** (usu. **dereliction of duty**) shameful failure to do something you are supposed to do.

deride ▸ verb (derides, deriding, derided) express contempt for; ridicule.

de rigueur /duh ri-**ger**/ ▸ adjective necessary if you want to be accepted socially.

derision ▸ noun scornful ridicule or mockery.

d

SYNONYMS **mockery,** ridicule, jeers, sneers, taunts, disdain, disparagement, denigration, insults.

derisive /di-**ry**-siv/ ▸ adjective expressing contempt or ridicule.
□ derisively adverb.

derisory /di-**ry**-suh-ri/ ▸ adjective
1 ridiculously small or inadequate.
2 expressing contempt or ridicule; derisive.

derivation ▸ noun **1** the obtaining of something from a source. **2** the formation of a word from another word.

derivative ▸ adjective imitating the work of another artist, writer, etc.; not original.
▸ noun something which comes from or is based on another source.

derive ▸ verb (derives, deriving, derived) **1** (derive something from) obtain something from a source. **2** (derive from) originate or develop from.

dermatitis /der-muh-**ty**-tiss/ ▸ noun inflammation of the skin as a result of irritation or an allergic reaction.

dermatology ▸ noun the branch of medicine concerned with skin disorders.
□ dermatological adjective dermatologist noun.

derogatory /di-**rog**-uh-tri/ ▸ adjective critical or disrespectful.

SYNONYMS **disparaging,** disrespectful, demeaning, critical, pejorative, negative, unfavourable, uncomplimentary, unflattering, insulting, defamatory, slanderous, libellous.
ANTONYMS complimentary.

derrick ▸ noun **1** a type of crane. **2** the framework over an oil well for holding the drilling machinery.

derring-do ▸ noun old use heroic actions.

dervish ▸ noun a member of a Muslim religious group, some orders of which are known for their wild rituals.

descant /**dess**-kant/ ▸ noun an independent melody sung or played above a basic melody.

descend ▸ verb **1** move down or downwards. **2** slope or lead downwards. **3** (descend to) do something very shameful. **4** (descend on) make a sudden attack on or unwelcome visit to. **5** (be descended from) have a particular person as an ancestor.

SYNONYMS **1** *the plane started descending* **go down,** come down, drop, fall, sink, dive, plummet, plunge, nosedive. **2** *she descended the stairs* **climb down,** go down, come down, shin down, slide down. **3** *the road descends to a village* **slope,** dip, slant, go down, fall away. **4** *she saw Leo descend from the bus* **alight,** disembark, get down, get off,

dismount.
ANTONYMS climb, board.

descendant ▸ noun a person who is descended from a particular ancestor.

✔ The correct spelling of the noun **descendant** is with **-ant**, not **-ent**, at the end.

descent ▸ noun **1** an act of descending. **2** a downward slope. **3** a person's origin or nationality.

SYNONYMS **1** *the plane began its descent* **dive,** drop, fall, plunge, nosedive. **2** *a steep descent* **slope,** incline, dip, drop, gradient. **3** *his descent into alcoholism* **decline,** slide, fall, degeneration, deterioration. **4** *she is of Italian descent* **ancestry,** parentage, ancestors, family, extraction, origin, derivation, birth, lineage, stock, blood, roots, origins.

describe ▸ verb (describes, describing, described) **1** give a detailed account of something in words. **2** mark out or draw a shape.

SYNONYMS **1** *he described his experiences* **report,** recount, relate, narrate, tell of, set out, detail, give a rundown of. **2** *she described him as a pathetic figure* **portray,** depict, paint, define, characterize, call, label, class, brand. **3** *the pen described a circle* **mark out,** delineate, outline, trace, draw.

description ▸ noun **1** a spoken or written account. **2** the process of describing. **3** a sort, kind, or class: *people of any description.*

SYNONYMS **1** *a description of my travels* **account,** report, narrative, story, portrayal, portrait, sketch, details. **2** *the description of oil as 'black gold'* **designation,** labelling, naming, dubbing, characterization, definition, classification, branding. **3** *vehicles of every description* **sort,** variety, kind, type.

descriptive ▸ adjective describing something, especially in a vivid style.
□ descriptively adverb.

descry ▸ verb (descries, descrying, descried) literary catch sight of.

desecrate /**dess**-i-krayt/ ▸ verb (desecrates, desecrating, desecrated) damage something sacred or treat it with great disrespect.
□ desecration noun.

desegregate ▸ verb (desegregates, desegregating, desegregated) end a policy by which people of different races are kept separate.
□ desegregation noun.

deselect ▸ verb Brit. (of a local branch of a political party) reject an existing MP as a candidate in a forthcoming election.
□ deselection noun.

desensitize (or **desensitise**) ▸ **verb** (**desensitizes, desensitizing, desensitized**) make less sensitive.

desert¹ /di-**zert**/ ▸ **verb 1** leave someone without help or support. **2** leave a place, making it seem empty. **3** illegally leave the armed forces.

> SYNONYMS **1** *his wife deserted him* **abandon,** leave, jilt, leave high and dry, leave in the lurch, leave behind, strand, maroon; informal walk/run out on, dump, ditch; literary forsake. **2** (**deserted**) *a deserted village* **empty,** uninhabited, unoccupied, abandoned, evacuated, desolate, lonely, godforsaken. **3** *soldiers deserted in droves* **abscond,** defect, run away, decamp, flee, turn tail, take French leave; Military go AWOL.

■ **desert island** an uninhabited tropical island.
□ **deserter** noun **desertion** noun.

desert² /**dez**-ert/ ▸ **noun** an empty, waterless area of land with very few plants.

> SYNONYMS *an African desert* **wasteland,** wastes, wilderness, dust bowl.

> ❗ Don't confuse **desert** (a waterless area) with **dessert** (the sweet course)

deserts /di-**zerts**/ ▸ **plural noun** (**get your just deserts**) get the reward or punishment that you deserve.

deserve ▸ **verb** (**deserves, deserving, deserved**) do something worthy of a particular reward or punishment.

> SYNONYMS **merit,** earn, warrant, rate, justify, be worthy of, be entitled to.

deserved ▸ **adjective** well earned: *his deserved success.*

> SYNONYMS **well earned,** merited, warranted, justified, rightful, due, fitting, just, proper.

□ **deservedly** adverb.

deserving ▸ **adjective** worthy of being treated well or helped.

> SYNONYMS *a deserving cause* **worthy,** commendable, praiseworthy, admirable, estimable, creditable.

déshabillé /day-za-**bee**-yay/ ▸ **noun** the state of being only partly clothed.

desiccate ▸ **verb** (**desiccates, desiccating, desiccated**) remove the moisture from.
□ **desiccation** noun.

design ▸ **noun 1** a plan or drawing produced before something is made. **2** the production of such plans or drawings. **3** purpose or deliberate planning. **4** a decorative pattern.

> SYNONYMS **1** *a design for the offices* **plan,** blueprint, drawing, sketch, outline, map, plot, diagram, draft. **2** *a Celtic design* **pattern,** motif, device, style, theme, layout.

▸ **verb 1** produce a design for. **2** (**be designed**) be intended for a purpose.

> SYNONYMS **1** *they designed a new engine* **invent,** create, think up, come up with, devise, formulate, conceive; informal dream up. **2** *this paper is designed to provoke discussion* **intend,** aim, mean.

■ **have designs on** aim to obtain.

designate ▸ verb /**dez**-ig-nayt/ (**designates, designating, designated**) **1** officially give a particular status or name to. **2** appoint someone to a job or position.

> SYNONYMS **1** *some firms designate a press officer* **appoint,** nominate, delegate, select, choose, pick, elect, name, identify, assign. **2** *the rivers are designated 'Sites of Special Scientific Interest'* **classify,** class, label, tag, name, call, term, dub.

▸ **adjective** /**dez**-ig-nuht/ appointed to a position but not yet having taken it up: *the Director designate.*

designation ▸ **noun 1** the action of designating. **2** an official title or description.

designer ▸ **noun** a person who designs things.
▸ **adjective** made by a famous fashion designer: *designer jeans.*

desirable ▸ **adjective 1** wished for as being attractive, useful, or necessary. **2** (of a person) sexually attractive.

> SYNONYMS **1** *a desirable location* **attractive,** sought-after, in demand, popular, enviable; informal to die for, must-have. **2** *it is desirable that they should meet* **advantageous,** advisable, wise, sensible, recommended, beneficial, preferable. **3** *a very desirable woman* (**sexually**) **attractive,** beautiful, pretty, appealing, seductive, alluring, irresistible; informal sexy.
> ANTONYMS unattractive, unwise, ugly.

□ **desirability** noun.

desire ▸ **noun** a strong feeling of wanting to have something or wishing for something to happen.

> SYNONYMS **1** *a desire to see the world* **wish,** want, aspiration, yearning, longing, craving, hankering, hunger; informal yen, itch. **2** *his eyes glittered with desire* **lust,** passion, sensuality, sexuality, libido, lasciviousness, lechery.

▸ **verb** (**desires, desiring, desired**) **1** strongly wish for or want. **2** find someone attractive.

> SYNONYMS *they desired peace* **want,** wish for, long for, yearn for, crave, hanker after, be desperate for, be bent on, covet, aspire to.

desirous ▸ adjective (desirous of or to do) wanting a particular thing.

desist ▸ verb stop doing something.

desk ▸ noun **1** a piece of furniture with a flat or sloping surface for writing on. **2** a counter in a hotel, bank, etc.

desktop ▸ noun **1** a computer suitable to be used at a desk. **2** the area of a computer screen that you can work in.

desolate ▸ adjective **1** (of a place) bleak and empty. **2** very unhappy.

> SYNONYMS **1** *desolate moorlands* **bleak,** stark, bare, dismal, grim, wild, inhospitable, deserted, uninhabited, godforsaken, abandoned, empty, isolated, remote. **2** *she is desolate* **miserable,** despondent, depressed, disconsolate, devastated, despairing, inconsolable.
> ANTONYMS populous, joyful.

▸ verb (be desolated) be very unhappy.
□ **desolation** noun.

despair ▸ noun the complete loss or absence of hope.

> SYNONYMS **desperation,** anguish, unhappiness, despondency, depression, misery, wretchedness, hopelessness.
> ANTONYMS hope, joy.

▸ verb lose hope, or be without hope.

> SYNONYMS **lose hope,** give up, lose heart, be discouraged, be despondent, be demoralized.

> ✔ des-, not dis-: despair.

despatch → DISPATCH.

desperado /dess-puh-**rah**-doh/ ▸ noun (plural **desperadoes** or **desperados**) a reckless and dangerous criminal.

desperate ▸ adjective **1** feeling, showing, or involving despair. **2** done when everything else has failed. **3** very serious: *a desperate shortage.* **4** needing or wanting something very much.

> SYNONYMS **1** *a desperate look* **despairing,** hopeless, anguished, distressed, wretched, desolate, forlorn, distraught, at your wits' end, at the end of your tether. **2** *a desperate attempt to escape* **last-ditch,** last-gasp, eleventh-hour, do-or-die, final, frantic, frenzied, wild. **3** *a desperate shortage of teachers* **grave,** serious, critical, acute, urgent, pressing, drastic, extreme.

□ **desperately** adverb.

> ✔ desperate, not -parate.

desperation ▸ noun a state of despair.

> SYNONYMS **hopelessness,** despair, distress, anguish, agony, torment, misery.

despicable ▸ adjective deserving hatred and contempt.
□ **despicably** adverb.

despise ▸ verb (despise, despising, despised) hate or feel disgusted by.

> SYNONYMS **detest,** hate, loathe, abhor, deplore, scorn, disdain, deride, sneer at, revile, spurn, shun.
> ANTONYMS adore, respect.

despite ▸ preposition in spite of.

> SYNONYMS **in spite of,** notwithstanding, regardless of, in the face of, in the teeth of, undeterred by, for all, even with.

despoil ▸ verb literary steal valuable possessions from a place.

despondent ▸ adjective very sad and without much hope.
□ **despondency** noun **despondently** adverb.

despot /**dess**-pot/ ▸ noun a ruler with unlimited power.
□ **despotic** adjective **despotism** noun.

dessert /di-**zert**/ ▸ noun the sweet course eaten at the end of a meal.

> ❗ Don't confuse **dessert** (the sweet course) with **desert** (a waterless area)

dessertspoon ▸ noun a spoon smaller than a tablespoon and larger than a teaspoon.

destabilize (or destabilise) ▸ verb (destabilizes, destabilizing, destabilized) make a country or government less stable.

destination ▸ noun the place to which someone or something is going or being sent.

destine ▸ verb **1** (be destined for or to) be intended for a particular purpose, or certain to do or be a particular thing. **2** (be destined for) be on the way to a particular place.

> SYNONYMS **1** *he is destined to lead a troubled life* **fated,** ordained, predestined, doomed, meant, intended. **2** *computers destined for Pakistan* **heading,** bound, en route, scheduled, headed.

destiny ▸ noun (plural **destinies**) **1** the things that will happen to a person. **2** the hidden power believed to control what will happen in the future.

> SYNONYMS **1** *master of his own destiny* **future,** fate, fortune, doom, lot. **2** *she was sent by destiny* **fate,** providence, God, the stars, luck, fortune, chance, karma.

destitute ▸ adjective very poor and without a home or other things necessary for life.
□ **destitution** noun.

destroy ▸ verb **1** make something stop existing by damaging or attacking it. **2** kill a sick or unwanted animal using a humane method.

d

SYNONYMS **1** *their offices were destroyed by bombing* **demolish,** knock down, level, raze to the ground, fell, blow up. **2** *traffic would destroy the conservation area* **spoil,** ruin, wreck, blight, devastate, wreak havoc on. **3** *the horse had to be destroyed* **kill,** put down, put to sleep, slaughter, cull. **4** *we had to destroy the enemy* **annihilate,** wipe out, obliterate, eliminate, eradicate, liquidate, exterminate; informal take out; N. Amer. informal waste.
ANTONYMS build, preserve, spare.

destroyer ▸ noun **1** a person or thing that destroys. **2** a small, fast warship.

destruction ▸ noun the destroying of something.

SYNONYMS **1** *the destruction caused by allied bombers* **devastation,** carnage, ruin, chaos, wreckage. **2** *the destruction of the countryside* **wrecking,** ruining, annihilation, obliteration, elimination, eradication, devastation. **3** *the destruction of cattle* **killing,** slaughter, putting down, extermination, culling.
ANTONYMS preservation.

destructive ▸ adjective **1** causing destruction. **2** negative and unhelpful.

SYNONYMS **devastating,** ruinous, damaging, harmful, detrimental, injurious, hurtful, deleterious.

□ **destructively** adverb.

desultory /dez-uhl-tuh-ri/ ▸ adjective lacking enthusiasm or a definite plan.
□ **desultorily** adverb.

detach ▸ verb **1** remove something that is attached to something larger. **2** (**be detached**) Military be sent on a mission.

SYNONYMS **disconnect,** separate, unfasten, disengage, uncouple, isolate, remove, loose, unhitch, unhook, free, pull off, cut off, break off, split off, sever.
ANTONYMS attach, join.

□ **detachable** adjective.

✔ **-ach,** not **-atch:** det**ach**.

detached ▸ adjective **1** separate or disconnected. **2** not involved or interested; aloof.

SYNONYMS **1** *a detached collar* **disconnected,** separated, separate, unfastened, disengaged, uncoupled, isolated, loosened, unhitched, unhooked, free, severed, cut off. **2** *a detached observer* **dispassionate,** disinterested, objective, outside, neutral, unbiased, impartial.

detachment ▸ noun **1** a feeling of being uninvolved or aloof. **2** a group of troops, ships, etc. sent away on a mission.

SYNONYMS **1** *she looked on with detachment* **objectivity,** dispassion, disinterest, neutrality, impartiality. **2** *a detachment of soldiers* **unit,** squad, detail, troop, contingent, task force, party, platoon.

detail ▸ noun **1** a small individual item or fact. **2** small items or facts as a group: *attention to detail.* **3** a small part of a picture reproduced separately. **4** a small group of troops or police officers given a special duty.

SYNONYMS **1** *the picture is correct in every detail* **particular,** respect, feature, characteristic, specific, aspect, fact, point, element. **2** *that's just a detail* **triviality,** technicality, nicety, fine point. **3** *a guard detail* **unit,** detachment, squad, troop, contingent, outfit, task force, party, platoon.

▸ verb **1** describe something item by item. **2** instruct someone to undertake a particular task.

SYNONYMS *the report details our objections* **describe,** relate, catalogue, list, spell out, itemize, identify, specify.

detailed ▸ adjective having many details.

SYNONYMS **comprehensive,** full, complete, thorough, exhaustive, all-inclusive, elaborate, minute, precise, itemized, blow-by-blow.
ANTONYMS general.

detain ▸ verb **1** keep someone back. **2** keep someone in custody.

SYNONYMS **1** *don't let me detain you* **delay,** hold up, make late, keep, slow up/down, hinder. **2** *they were detained for questioning* **hold,** take into custody, confine, imprison, intern, arrest, apprehend, seize; informal pick up; Brit. informal nick.
ANTONYMS release.

detainee ▸ noun a person who is kept in custody.

detect ▸ verb **1** discover or notice that something is present. **2** discover or investigate a crime or criminal.

SYNONYMS **1** *I detected a note of urgency in her voice* **notice,** perceive, discern, become aware of, note, make out, spot, recognize, identify, catch, sense. **2** *they are responsible for detecting fraud* **discover,** uncover, turn up, unearth, dig up, root out, expose. **3** *the hackers were detected* **catch,** hunt down, track down, find out, expose, reveal, unmask, smoke out.

□ **detectable** adjective **detection** noun.

detective ▸ noun a person whose job is investigating crimes.

SYNONYMS investigator, police officer; informal private eye, sleuth; N. Amer. informal gumshoe.

detector ▸ noun a device designed to detect that something, e.g. smoke or gas, is present.

détente /day-**tont**/ ▸ noun the easing of hostility or strained relations between countries.

detention ▸ noun **1** the state of being kept in custody. **2** the punishment of being kept in school after hours.

SYNONYMS custody, imprisonment, incarceration, internment, captivity, remand, arrest, quarantine. **ANTONYMS** release.

deter ▸ verb (deters, deterring, deterred) **1** make someone decide not to do something because they are afraid of the consequences. **2** prevent something happening.

SYNONYMS 1 *the high cost deterred many* **discourage,** dissuade, put off, scare off, dishearten, demoralize, daunt, intimidate. **2** *the presence of a caretaker deters crime* **prevent,** stop, avert, stave off, ward off. **ANTONYMS** encourage.

detergent ▸ noun a chemical substance used for removing dirt and grease.

deteriorate ▸ verb (deteriorates, deteriorating, deteriorated) become gradually worse.

SYNONYMS worsen, decline, degenerate, fail, go downhill, wane. **ANTONYMS** improve.

☐ deterioration noun.

determination ▸ noun **1** persistence in continuing to do something even when it is difficult. **2** the process of establishing something exactly.

SYNONYMS resolution, resolve, will power, strength of character, dedication, single-mindedness, perseverance, persistence, tenacity, staying power, doggedness; informal guts.

determine ▸ verb **1** make something develop in a particular way or be of a particular type. **2** discover the facts about something by research or calculation. **3** firmly decide.

SYNONYMS 1 *chromosomes determine the sex of the embryo* **control,** decide, regulate, direct, dictate, govern. **2** *he determined to sell up* **resolve,** decide, make up your mind, choose, elect, opt. **3** *the rent shall be determined by an accountant* **specify,** set, fix, decide on, settle, establish, ordain, prescribe, decree. **4** *determine the composition of*

the fibres **ascertain,** find out, discover, learn, establish, calculate, work out; informal figure out.

determined ▸ adjective persisting in doing something even when it is difficult; resolute.

SYNONYMS resolute, purposeful, adamant, single-minded, unswerving, unwavering, persevering, persistent, tenacious, dedicated, dogged. **ANTONYMS** irresolute.

☐ determinedly adverb.

determiner ▸ noun **1** a person or thing that determines. **2** Grammar a word that comes before a noun to show how the noun is being used, e.g. *a, the, every.*

deterrent ▸ noun a thing that deters or is intended to deter.

SYNONYMS disincentive, discouragement, damper, curb, check, restraint, inhibition. **ANTONYMS** incentive.

☐ deterrence noun.

detest ▸ verb feel strong dislike for.

SYNONYMS hate, abhor, loathe, regard with disgust, be unable to bear, have an aversion to, find intolerable, disdain, despise. **ANTONYMS** love.

☐ detestable adjective detestation noun.

dethrone ▸ verb (dethrones, dethroning, dethroned) remove a ruler from power.

detonate ▸ verb (detonates, detonating, detonated) explode, or make something explode.
☐ detonation noun.

detonator ▸ noun a device used to detonate an explosive.

detour ▸ noun a long or roundabout route taken to avoid something or to visit something along the way.

detoxify ▸ verb (detoxifies, detoxifying, detoxified) remove poisonous substances from.

detract ▸ verb (detract from) make something seem less valuable or impressive.

detractor ▸ noun a person who is critical about someone or something.

detriment ▸ noun harm or damage.
☐ detrimental adjective detrimentally adverb.

detritus /di-**try**-tuhss/ ▸ noun debris or waste material.

deuce /dyooss/ ▸ noun **1** Tennis the score of 40 all in a game, at which two consecutive points are needed to win the game. **2** (the deuce) informal said instead of 'devil' when making an exclamation.

Deutschmark /**doych**-mark/ ▸ noun the former basic unit of money in Germany.

devalue ▸ verb (devalues, devaluing, devalued) **1** make something seem less important than it is. **2** reduce the value of a currency in relation to other currencies. □ **devaluation** noun.

devastate ▸ verb (devastates, devastating, devastated) **1** destroy or ruin. **2** (**be devastated**) be overwhelmed with shock or grief.

> SYNONYMS **1** *the city was devastated by an earthquake* **destroy,** ruin, wreck, lay waste, ravage, demolish, raze to the ground, level, flatten. **2** *he was devastated by the news* **shatter,** shock, stun, daze, dumbfound, traumatize, distress; informal knock sideways; Brit. informal knock for six.

devastating ▸ adjective **1** highly destructive. **2** very distressing. **3** informal very impressive or attractive.
□ **devastatingly** adverb.

devastation ▸ noun the fact of being devastated.

> SYNONYMS **destruction,** ruin, desolation, wreckage, ruins.

develop ▸ verb (develops, developing, developed) **1** make or become larger or more advanced. **2** start to exist; come into being. **3** start to experience or possess something. **4** convert land to a new purpose. **5** treat a photographic film with chemicals to make a visible image.

> SYNONYMS **1** *the industry developed rapidly* **grow,** expand, spread, advance, progress, evolve, mature. **2** *a plan was developed* **initiate,** instigate, set in motion, originate, invent, form. **3** *children should develop their talents* **expand,** augment, broaden, supplement, reinforce, enhance, refine, improve, polish, perfect. **4** *a row developed* **start,** begin, emerge, erupt, break out, arise, break, unfold.
> ANTONYMS shrink, regress.

□ **developer** noun.

> ✔ There is no **e** at the end: deve**lop**.

development ▸ noun **1** the action of developing. **2** a new product or idea. **3** a new stage in a changing situation. **4** an area of land with new buildings on it.

> SYNONYMS **1** *the development of the firm* **evolution,** growth, expansion, enlargement, spread, progress. **2** *there have been a number of developments* **event,** change, circumstance, incident, occurrence. **3** *a housing development* **estate,** complex, site.

□ **developmental** adjective.

deviant ▸ adjective different from what is considered normal.

▸ noun disapproving a deviant person.
□ **deviance** noun.

deviate ▸ verb (deviates, deviating, deviated) depart from an established course or from normal standards.

> SYNONYMS **diverge,** digress, drift, stray, veer, swerve, get sidetracked, branch off, differ, vary.

□ **deviation** noun.

device ▸ noun **1** a piece of equipment made for a particular purpose. **2** a plan or method with a particular aim. **3** an emblem or design.

> SYNONYMS **1** *a device for measuring pressure* **implement,** gadget, utensil, tool, appliance, apparatus, instrument, machine, mechanism, contrivance, contraption; informal gizmo. **2** *an ingenious legal device* **ploy,** tactic, move, stratagem, scheme, plot, trick, ruse, manoeuvre.

■ **leave someone to their own devices** leave someone to do as they wish.

devil ▸ noun **1** (**the Devil**) (in Christian and Jewish belief) the most powerful spirit of evil. **2** an evil spirit. **3** a very wicked or cruel person. **4** informal a person of a particular sort: *the poor devil.*

> SYNONYMS **1** *God and the Devil* **Satan,** Beelzebub, Lucifer, the Prince of Darkness; informal Old Nick. **2** *they drove out the devils* **evil spirit,** demon, fiend. **3** *he was a devil* **brute,** beast, monster, fiend, villain, sadist, barbarian, ogre.

■ **devil-may-care** cheerful and reckless. **devil's advocate** a person who expresses an opinion that they do not really hold in order to provoke discussion.

devilish ▸ adjective **1** like a devil in evil and cruelty. **2** mischievous. **3** very difficult to deal with.
□ **devilishly** adverb.

devilment ▸ noun mischievous behaviour.

devilry ▸ noun **1** wicked activity. **2** mischievous behaviour.

devious ▸ adjective **1** behaving in a cunning way to get what you want. **2** (of a route or journey) indirect.

> SYNONYMS **1** *the devious ways in which they bent the rules* **underhand,** dishonest, crafty, cunning, conniving, scheming, sneaky, furtive; informal crooked, shady; Brit. informal dodgy. **2** *a devious route* **circuitous,** roundabout, indirect, meandering, tortuous.
> ANTONYMS open, honest, direct.

□ **deviously** adverb **deviousness** noun.

devise ▸ verb (devises, devising, devised) plan or invent a complex procedure or device.

> SYNONYMS **conceive,** think up, dream up, work out, formulate, concoct, hatch,

d

contrive, design, invent, coin; informal cook up.

devoid ▸ adjective (**devoid of**) entirely without.

SYNONYMS *her voice was devoid of emotion* **empty of,** free of, bereft of, lacking, deficient in, without, wanting in; informal **minus.**

devolution ▸ noun the transfer of power by central government to local or regional governments.

devolve ▸ verb (**devolves, devolving, devolved**) **1** transfer power to a lower level. **2** (**devolve on** or **to**) (of duties or responsibility) pass to.

devote ▸ verb (**devotes, devoting, devoted**) (**devote something to**) give time or resources to.

SYNONYMS **dedicate,** allocate, assign, allot, commit, give (over), consign, pledge, set aside, earmark, reserve.

devoted ▸ adjective very loving or loyal.

SYNONYMS **dedicated,** committed, devout, loyal, faithful, true, staunch, steadfast, fond, loving.

□ **devotedly** adverb.

devotee /dev-oh-**tee**/ ▸ noun **1** a person who is very enthusiastic about someone or something. **2** a follower of a particular religion or god.

SYNONYMS **enthusiast,** fan, lover, aficionado, admirer, supporter, disciple; informal **buff,** freak, nut, fanatic.

devotion ▸ noun **1** great love or loyalty. **2** religious worship. **3** (**devotions**) prayers or other religious practices.

SYNONYMS **1** *wifely devotion* **loyalty,** fidelity, commitment, allegiance, dedication, fondness, love, care. **2** *a life of devotion* **piety,** spirituality, godliness, holiness, sanctity.

□ **devotional** adjective.

devour ▸ verb **1** eat something greedily. **2** (of a force) destroy something completely. **3** read something quickly and eagerly.

SYNONYMS **1** *he devoured his meal* **gobble,** guzzle, gulp down, bolt, wolf; informal **polish off;** Brit. informal **scoff. 2** *flames devoured the house* **consume,** engulf, envelop.

devout ▸ adjective **1** deeply religious. **2** earnestly sincere: *a devout hope.*

SYNONYMS **dedicated,** devoted, committed, loyal, sincere, fervent, pious, reverent, God-fearing, dutiful, churchgoing.

□ **devoutly** adverb.

dew ▸ noun tiny drops of moisture that form on cool surfaces at night, when water vapour in the air condenses.
□ **dewy** adjective.

dewlap ▸ noun a fold of loose skin hanging from the neck or throat of an animal or bird.

dexterity ▸ noun skill in performing tasks.

dexterous (or **dextrous**) ▸ adjective showing skill, especially with the hands.
□ **dexterously** adverb.

dextrose ▸ noun a form of glucose.

dhoti /**doh**-ti/ ▸ noun (plural **dhotis**) a long piece of cloth tied around the waist, worn by some Hindu men.

diabetes /dy-uh-**bee**-teez/ ▸ noun an illness in which the body cannot absorb sugar and starch properly because it does not have enough of the hormone insulin.

diabetic ▸ adjective having to do with diabetes.
▸ noun a person with diabetes.

diabolical ▸ adjective **1** (also **diabolic**) relating to or like the Devil. **2** informal very bad.
□ **diabolically** adverb.

diadem ▸ noun a crown.

diagnose ▸ verb (**diagnoses, diagnosing, diagnosed**) identify which illness or problem a person is suffering from by examining the symptoms.

SYNONYMS **identify,** determine, distinguish, recognize, interpret, detect, pinpoint.

□ **diagnostic** adjective.

diagnosis ▸ noun (plural **diagnoses**) the identification of which illness or problem a person is suffering from by examining the symptoms.

SYNONYMS **1** *the diagnosis of coeliac disease* **identification,** detection, recognition, determination, discovery, pinpointing. **2** *the results confirmed his diagnosis* **opinion,** judgement, verdict, conclusion.

diagonal ▸ adjective **1** (of a straight line) joining opposite corners of a rectangle, square, or other figure. **2** straight and at an angle; slanting.

SYNONYMS **crosswise,** crossways, slanting, slanted, oblique, angled, cornerways, cornerwise.

▸ noun a diagonal line.
□ **diagonally** adverb.

diagram ▸ noun a simplified drawing showing the appearance or structure of something.

SYNONYMS **drawing,** representation, plan, outline, figure, chart, graph.

□ **diagrammatic** adjective.

dial ▸ noun 1 a disc marked to show the time or to indicate a measurement. 2 a disc with numbered holes on a telephone, turned to make a call. 3 a disc turned to choose a setting on a radio, cooker, etc.
▸ verb (**dials, dialling, dialled**; US spelling **dials, dialing, dialed**) call a telephone number by turning a dial or pressing numbered keys.

dialect ▸ noun a form of a language used in a particular region or by a particular social group.
□ **dialectal** adjective.

dialectic (or **dialectics**) ▸ noun a way of discovering whether ideas are true by discussion and logical argument.
□ **dialectical** adjective.

dialogue (US spelling **dialog**) ▸ noun 1 conversation between two or more people in a book, play, or film. 2 a discussion intended to explore a subject or solve a problem.

SYNONYMS **conversation,** talk, discussion, chat, tête-à-tête, exchange, debate, conference, consultation; informal confab.

dialysis /dy-**al**-i-siss/ ▸ noun the use of a machine to purify the blood of a person whose kidneys do not work properly.

diamanté /dy-uh-**mon**-tay/ ▸ adjective decorated with glass that is cut to look like diamonds.

diameter ▸ noun a straight line passing from side to side through the centre of a circle or sphere.

diametrical ▸ adjective 1 complete: *the diametrical opposite.* 2 having to do with a diameter.
□ **diametrically** adverb.

diamond ▸ noun 1 a clear precious stone, the hardest naturally occurring substance. 2 a figure with four straight sides of equal length forming two opposite acute angles and two opposite obtuse angles.
■ **diamond jubilee** the sixtieth anniversary of a notable event. **diamond wedding** Brit. the sixtieth anniversary of a wedding.

diaper /**dy**-uh-per/ ▸ noun N. Amer. a baby's nappy.

diaphanous /dy-**af**-uh-nuhss/ ▸ adjective light, delicate, and semi-transparent.

diaphragm /**dy**-uh-fram/ ▸ noun 1 a layer of muscle between the lungs and the stomach. 2 a piece of flexible material in mechanical or sound systems. 3 a thin rubber or plastic contraceptive device worn over the cervix.

diarist ▸ noun a person who writes a diary.

diarrhoea /dy-uh-**ree**-uh/ (US spelling **diarrhea**) ▸ noun a condition in which a person has frequent liquid bowel movements.

✔ two **r**s, and **-hoea** at the end: dia**rrhoea**.

diary ▸ noun (plural **diaries**) a book in which you keep a daily record of events and experiences, or note down future appointments.

SYNONYMS 1 *he put the date in his diary* **appointment book,** engagement book, personal organizer; trademark Filofax. 2 *her World War II diaries* **journal,** memoir, chronicle, log, logbook, history, annal, record; N. Amer. daybook.

diastole /dy-**ass**-tuh-li/ ▸ noun the stage of the heartbeat when the heart muscle relaxes and the chambers fill with blood.
□ **diastolic** /dy-uh-**stol**-ik/ adjective.

diatonic /dy-uh-**ton**-ik/ ▸ adjective Music involving only the notes of the appropriate major or minor scale.

diatribe /**dy**-uh-tryb/ ▸ noun a speech or piece of writing forcefully attacking someone.

dice ▸ noun (plural **dice**) a small cube whose sides are marked with one to six spots, used in games of chance.
▸ verb (**dices, dicing, diced**) 1 cut food into small cubes. 2 (**dice with**) take great risks with: *dicing with death.*

dicey ▸ adjective (**dicier, diciest**) informal difficult or risky.

dichotomy /dy-**kot**-uh-mi/ ▸ noun (plural **dichotomies**) a separation or contrast between two things.

dicky ▸ adjective Brit. informal not strong, healthy, or working properly.

dictate ▸ verb /dik-**tayt**/ (**dictates, dictating, dictated**) 1 give orders with great authority. 2 control or influence. 3 speak words for someone else to type or write down.

SYNONYMS 1 *his attempts to dictate policy* **prescribe,** lay down, impose, set down, order, command, decree, ordain, direct. 2 *choice is often dictated by availability* **determine,** control, govern, decide, influence, affect.

▸ noun /**dik**-tayt/ an order or principle that must be obeyed.
□ **dictation** noun.

dictator ▸ noun a ruler who has total power over a country.

SYNONYMS **autocrat,** despot, tyrant, absolute ruler.
ANTONYMS democrat.

dictatorial ▸ adjective like or typical of a dictator.

SYNONYMS **domineering,** autocratic, authoritarian, oppressive, imperious, overweening, overbearing, peremptory; informal bossy, high-handed.

d

d

dictatorship ▸ noun **1** government by a dictator. **2** a country governed by a dictator.

diction ▸ noun **1** the choice and use of words in speech or writing. **2** a person's way of pronouncing words.

dictionary ▸ noun (plural **dictionaries**) a book that lists the words of a language and gives their meaning, or their equivalent in a different language.

> SYNONYMS **lexicon**, glossary, vocabulary.

dictum ▸ noun (plural **dicta** or **dictums**) **1** a formal announcement made by someone in authority. **2** a short statement that expresses a general principle.

did past of **DO**.

didactic ▸ adjective intended to teach or give moral instruction.
□ **didactically** adverb.

diddle ▸ verb (**diddles, diddling, diddled**) informal cheat or swindle.

didgeridoo ▸ noun an Australian Aboriginal musical instrument in the form of a long wooden tube, which produces a deep sound when blown.

didn't ▸ short form did not.

die¹ ▸ verb (**dies, dying, died**) **1** stop living. **2** (**die out**) become extinct. **3** become less loud or strong. **4** (**be dying for** or **to do**) informal be very eager to have or do.

> SYNONYMS **1** *her father died last year* **pass away**, pass on, perish; informal give up the ghost, kick the bucket, croak; Brit. informal snuff it, peg out; N. Amer. informal buy the farm. **2** *the wind had died* **lessen**, subside, drop, ease (off), let up, moderate, abate, fade, peter out, wane, ebb. **3** *the engine died* **fail**, cut out, give out, break down, stop; informal conk out, go kaput; Brit. informal pack up.
> ANTONYMS live, intensify.

die² ▸ noun **1** a dice. **2** (plural **dies**) a device for cutting or moulding metal or for stamping a design on to coins or medals.
■ **die-cast** formed by pouring molten metal into a mould.

diehard ▸ noun a person who stubbornly continues to support something in spite of opposition or changing circumstances.

diesel /dee-zuhl/ ▸ noun **1** a type of engine in which heat produced by compressing air is used to ignite the fuel. **2** a form of petroleum used as fuel in diesel engines.

diet ▸ noun **1** the kinds of food that a person or animal usually eats. **2** a limited range or amount of food, eaten in order to lose weight or for medical reasons.

> SYNONYMS **1** *a healthy diet* **food**, nutrition, eating habits. **2** *she's on a diet* **dietary regime**, regimen, restricted diet, fast, abstinence.
> ANTONYMS binge.

▸ verb (**diets, dieting, dieted**) keep to a special diet in order to lose weight.

> SYNONYMS *I began dieting again* **be on a diet**, slim, lose weight, watch your weight; N. Amer. reduce; N. Amer. informal slenderize.
> ANTONYMS binge.

dietary /dy-uh-tri/ ▸ adjective **1** having to do with diets or dieting. **2** provided by the food you eat.

dietitian (or **dietician**) ▸ noun an expert on diet and nutrition.

differ ▸ verb (**differs, differing, differed**) **1** be different. **2** disagree.

> SYNONYMS **1** *the second set of data differed from the first* **contrast with**, be different to, vary from, deviate from, conflict with, run counter to, be at odds with, contradict. **2** *the two sides differed over this issue* **disagree**, conflict, be at variance/odds, be in dispute, not see eye to eye.
> ANTONYMS resemble, agree.

difference ▸ noun **1** a way in which people or things are unlike each other. **2** a disagreement or dispute. **3** what is left when one number or amount is subtracted from another.

> SYNONYMS **1** *the difference between the two sets of data* **dissimilarity**, contrast, distinction, differentiation, variance, variation, divergence, disparity, contradiction. **2** *we've had our differences* **disagreement**, difference of opinion, dispute, argument, quarrel; Brit. informal row. **3** *I'll pay the difference* **balance**, remainder, rest.
> ANTONYMS similarity.

different ▸ adjective **1** not the same as another or each other. **2** separate. **3** informal new and unusual.

> SYNONYMS **1** *people with different lifestyles* **dissimilar**, unlike, contrasting, differing, varying, disparate, poles apart, incompatible, mismatched; informal like chalk and cheese. **2** *suddenly everything in her life was different* **changed**, altered, transformed, new, unfamiliar, unknown, strange. **3** *two different occasions* **distinct**, separate, individual, independent. **4** *try something different* **unusual**, out of the ordinary, unfamiliar, novel, new, fresh, original, unconventional, exotic.
> ANTONYMS similar, normal, related, ordinary.

□ **differently** adverb.

❗ Say **different from**, not **different to** in British English; **different than** is American.

differential /dif-fuh-**ren**-sh'l/ ▶ adjective involving a difference.
▶ noun 1 Brit. a difference in wages between industries or between categories of worker. 2 Maths a minute difference between successive values of a variable. 3 a gear that allows a vehicle's wheels to revolve at different speeds when going around corners.

differentiate /dif-fuh-**ren**-shi-ayt/
▶ verb (**differentiates**, **differentiating**, **differentiated**) 1 recognize things as being different from each other; distinguish. 2 make things appear different from each other.
□ **differentiation** noun.

difficult ▶ adjective 1 needing a lot of effort or skill to do or understand; hard. 2 causing or involving problems. 3 not easy to please or satisfy; awkward.

SYNONYMS 1 *a very difficult job* laborious, strenuous, arduous, hard, tough, demanding, punishing, gruelling, back-breaking, exhausting, tiring; informal hellish, killing, no picnic. 2 *a difficult problem* hard, complicated, beyond you, puzzling, baffling, problematic, thorny, ticklish. 3 *a difficult child* troublesome, tiresome, trying, exasperating, awkward, demanding, contrary, uncooperative, fussy.
ANTONYMS easy, simple, cooperative, accommodating.

difficulty ▶ noun (plural **difficulties**) 1 the state of being difficult. 2 a difficult or dangerous situation; a problem.

SYNONYMS 1 *the difficulty of balancing motherhood with a career* strain, trouble, problems, struggle, laboriousness, arduousness; informal hassle, stress. 2 *practical difficulties* problem, complication, snag, hitch, obstacle, hurdle, stumbling block; Brit. spanner in the works; informal headache. 3 *Charles got into difficulties* trouble, predicament, plight, hard times.
ANTONYMS ease.

diffident ▶ adjective not having much self-confidence.
□ **diffidence** noun **diffidently** adverb.

diffract ▶ verb cause a beam of light to be spread out as a result of passing through a narrow opening or across an edge.
□ **diffraction** noun.

diffuse ▶ verb /dif-**fyooz**/ (**diffuses**, **diffusing**, **diffused**) 1 spread over a wide area. 2 (of a gas or liquid) become mingled with a substance.
▶ adjective /dif-**fyooss**/ 1 spread out over a large area; not concentrated. 2 not clearly or concisely expressed.
□ **diffusely** adverb **diffusion** noun.

❗ Don't confuse **diffuse** with **defuse**, which means 'make a situation less tense or difficult' or 'remove the fuse from'.

dig ▶ verb (**digs**, **digging**, **dug**) 1 cut into earth in order to turn it over or move it. 2 remove or produce something by digging. 3 push or poke sharply. 4 (**dig into** or **through**) search or rummage in. 5 (**dig something out** or **up**) discover facts. 6 (**dig in**) start eating heartily. 7 informal, dated like.

SYNONYMS 1 *she began to dig the soil* turn over, work, break up. 2 *he dug a hole* excavate, dig out, quarry, hollow out, scoop out, bore, burrow, mine. 3 *Winnie dug her elbow into his ribs* poke, prod, jab, stab, shove, ram, push, thrust, drive, stick. 4 *he'd been digging into my past* delve, probe, search, enquire, look, investigate, research.

▶ noun 1 an act of digging. 2 an investigation of a site by archaeologists. 3 a sharp push or poke. 4 informal a critical remark. 5 (**digs**) informal temporary accommodation.

SYNONYMS 1 *a dig in the ribs* poke, prod, jab, stab, shove, push. 2 *they're always making digs at each other* snide remark, cutting remark, jibe, taunt, sneer, insult; informal wisecrack, put-down.

□ **digger** noun.

digest ▶ verb /dy-**jest**/ 1 break down food in the stomach and intestines so that it can be absorbed by the body. 2 reflect on and absorb information.

SYNONYMS *Liz digested this information* assimilate, absorb, take in, understand, comprehend, grasp.

▶ noun /**dy**-jest/ a summary or collection of material or information.

SYNONYMS *a digest of their findings* summary, synopsis, abstract, precis, résumé, summation.

□ **digestible** adjective.

digestion ▶ noun 1 the process of digesting food. 2 a person's ability to digest food.

digestive ▶ adjective relating to the digestion of food.
▶ noun Brit. a semi-sweet biscuit made with wholemeal flour.

digit ▶ noun 1 any of the numerals from 0 to 9. 2 a finger or thumb.

digital ▶ adjective 1 having to do with information represented as a series of binary digits, as in a computer. 2 having to do with computer technology. 3 (of a clock or watch) showing the time by displaying numbers electronically, rather than having a clock face. 4 having to do with a finger or fingers.
□ **digitally** adverb.

digitize (or **digitise**) ▶ verb (**digitizes**, **digitizing**, **digitized**) convert pictures or sound into a digital form.

d

dignified ▸ adjective having or showing dignity.

SYNONYMS **stately,** noble, majestic, distinguished, regal, imposing, impressive, grand, solemn, formal, ceremonious, decorous, sedate.

dignify ▸ verb (**dignifies, dignifying, dignified**) make something impressive or worthy of respect.

dignitary /dig-ni-tuh-ri/ ▸ noun (plural **dignitaries**) a very important or high-ranking person.

dignity ▸ noun (plural **dignities**) **1** the quality of being worthy of respect. **2** a calm or serious manner. **3** pride in yourself.

SYNONYMS **1** *the dignity of the Crown* **stateliness,** nobility, majesty, impressiveness, grandeur, magnificence, ceremoniousness, formality, decorum, propriety, respectability, worthiness, integrity, solemnity, gravitas. **2** *little regard for human dignity* **self-respect,** pride, self-esteem, self-worth.
ANTONYMS informality.

digress ▸ verb temporarily leave the main subject in speech or writing.
□ **digression** noun.

dike → DYKE.

diktat /dik-tat/ ▸ noun an order given by someone in power.

dilapidated ▸ adjective old and in bad condition.
□ **dilapidation** noun.

✔ **dil-**, not **del-**: **dil**apidated.

dilate ▸ verb (**dilates, dilating, dilated**) become wider, larger, or more open.
□ **dilation** noun.

dilatory /di-luh-tri/ ▸ adjective **1** slow to act. **2** intended to cause delay.

dilemma /di-lem-muh, dy-lem-muh/ ▸ noun a difficult situation in which you have to make a choice between alternatives.

SYNONYMS **quandary,** predicament, catch-22, vicious circle, plight, conflict; informal fix, tight spot/corner; (**in a dilemma**) between the devil and the deep blue sea, between a rock and a hard place.

dilettante /di-li-**tan**-ti/ ▸ noun (plural **dilettanti** or **dilettantes**) a person who does or studies something for enjoyment but does not take it very seriously.

diligent ▸ adjective showing care and effort in a task or duty.
□ **diligence** noun **diligently** adverb.

dill ▸ noun a herb used in cookery and medicine.

dilly-dally ▸ verb (**dilly-dallies, dilly-dallying, dilly-dallied**) informal be slow or indecisive.

dilute ▸ verb (**dilutes, diluting, diluted**) **1** make a liquid thinner or weaker by adding water or other liquid. **2** weaken something by modifying it or adding other elements.

SYNONYMS **1** *strong bleach can be diluted with water* **make weaker,** water down, thin, doctor, adulterate; informal cut. **2** *the original plans have been diluted* **weaken,** moderate, tone down, water down, compromise.
ANTONYMS concentrate, beef up.

▸ adjective (of a liquid) diluted; weak.
□ **dilution** noun.

dim ▸ adjective (**dimmer, dimmest**) **1** not bright or well lit. **2** not clearly seen or remembered. **3** not able to see clearly. **4** informal stupid.

SYNONYMS **1** *the dim light* **faint,** weak, feeble, soft, pale, dull, subdued, muted. **2** *long dim corridors* **dark,** badly lit, dingy, dismal, gloomy, murky. **3** *a dim figure* **indistinct,** ill-defined, vague, shadowy, nebulous, blurred, fuzzy. **4** *dim memories* **vague,** imprecise, imperfect, unclear, indistinct, sketchy, hazy. **5** *I'm awfully dim.* See STUPID (sense 1).
ANTONYMS bright, distinct, clear.

▸ verb (**dims, dimming, dimmed**) make or become dim.

SYNONYMS **1** *the lights were dimmed* **turn down,** lower, soften, subdue. **2** *memories have dimmed* **fade,** dwindle, dull.
ANTONYMS brighten.

■ **take a dim view of** disapprove of.
□ **dimly** adverb **dimness** noun.

dime ▸ noun N. Amer. a ten-cent coin.

dimension ▸ noun **1** a measure of how long, broad, high, etc. something is. **2** an aspect or feature.

SYNONYMS **1** *the dimensions of the room* **size,** measurements, proportions, extent, length, width, breadth, depth. **2** *the cultural dimensions of the problem* **aspect,** feature, element, angle, facet, side.

□ **dimensional** adjective.

diminish ▸ verb make or become smaller, weaker, or less.

SYNONYMS **1** *the pain will gradually diminish* **decrease,** lessen, decline, reduce, subside, dwindle, fade, slacken off, let up. **2** *new legislation diminished the courts' authority* **reduce,** decrease, lessen, curtail, cut, limit, curb.
ANTONYMS increase.

diminution ▸ noun a reduction.

diminutive ▸ adjective very or unusually small.
▸ noun a shortened form of a person's name.

dimmer ▸ noun a device for varying the brightness of an electric light.

dimple ▸ noun a small hollow formed in the cheeks when you smile.
□ **dimpled** adjective.

dimwit ▸ noun informal a stupid person.
□ **dim-witted** adjective.

din ▸ noun a prolonged loud and unpleasant noise.

> SYNONYMS **noise,** racket, rumpus, cacophony, hubbub, uproar, commotion, clangour, clatter, clamour; informal hullabaloo; Brit. informal row.
> ANTONYMS silence.

▸ verb (**dins, dinning, dinned**) (**din something into**) teach something to someone by constantly repeating it.

dine ▸ verb (**dines, dining, dined**) eat dinner.

> SYNONYMS **eat,** have dinner, have lunch; dated sup.

diner ▸ noun 1 a person who dines. 2 a carriage providing meals on a train. 3 N. Amer. a small, cheap restaurant.

dinghy /ding-gi, ding-i/ ▸ noun (plural **dinghies**) 1 a small open boat with a mast and sails. 2 a small inflatable rubber boat.

dingo /ding-goh/ ▸ noun (plural **dingoes** or **dingos**) a wild or semi-domesticated Australian dog.

dingy /din-ji/ ▸ adjective (**dingier, dingiest**) gloomy and drab.
□ **dinginess** noun.

dinky ▸ adjective (**dinkier, dinkiest**) Brit. informal attractively small and neat.

dinner ▸ noun 1 the main meal of the day, eaten either around midday or in the evening. 2 a formal evening meal.

> SYNONYMS **main meal,** lunch, evening meal, supper, feast, banquet; Brit. tea.

□ **dinner jacket** a black or white jacket worn by men for formal evening occasions.

dinosaur ▸ noun an extinct reptile that lived millions of years ago, some kinds of which were very large.

dint ▸ noun a dent.
■ **by dint of** by means of.

diocese /dy-uh-siss/ ▸ noun (plural **dioceses** /dy-uh-seez, dy-uh-seez-iz/) a district under the control of a bishop in the Christian Church.

diode ▸ noun an electrical device that has two terminals and allows current to flow in one direction only.

dioxide ▸ noun an oxide with two atoms of oxygen to one of a metal or other element.

dip ▸ verb (**dips, dipping, dipped**) 1 (**dip something in** or **into**) put or lower something briefly in or into. 2 sink, drop, or slope downwards. 3 (of a level or amount) temporarily become lower

or smaller. 4 lower something briefly. 5 (**dip into**) reach into a container to take something out.

> SYNONYMS 1 *he dipped a rag in the water* **immerse,** submerge, plunge, dunk, bathe, sink. 2 *the sun dipped below the horizon* **sink,** set, drop, fall, descend. 3 *the president's popularity has dipped* **decrease,** fall, drop, fall off, decline, diminish, dwindle, slump, plummet, plunge. 4 *the road dipped* **slope down,** descend, go down, drop (away), fall away.
> ANTONYMS rise, increase.

▸ noun 1 an act of dipping. 2 a thick sauce in which you dip pieces of food before eating them. 3 a brief swim. 4 a brief downward slope followed by an upward one.

> SYNONYMS 1 *a dip in the pool* **swim,** bathe, paddle. 2 *the hedge at the bottom of the dip* **slope,** incline, decline, descent, hollow, depression, basin. 3 *a dip in sales* **decrease,** fall, drop, downturn, decline, falling-off, slump, reduction.

diphtheria /dip-theer-i-uh/ ▸ noun a serious illness that causes inflammation of the mucous membranes, especially in the throat.

diphthong /dif-thong, dip-thong/ ▸ noun a sound formed by the combination of two vowels in a single syllable (as in *coin*).

diploma ▸ noun a certificate awarded to someone who has successfully completed a course of study.

diplomacy ▸ noun 1 the management of relations between countries. 2 skill and tact in dealing with people.

> SYNONYMS 1 *diplomacy failed to win them independence* **statesmanship,** statecraft, negotiation(s), discussion(s), talks. 2 *Jack's quiet diplomacy* **tact,** tactfulness, sensitivity, discretion.

diplomat ▸ noun an official who represents a country abroad.

> SYNONYMS **ambassador,** attaché, consul, chargé d'affaires, envoy, emissary.

diplomatic ▸ adjective 1 having to do with diplomacy. 2 tactful.

> SYNONYMS **tactful,** sensitive, subtle, delicate, polite, discreet, judicious, politic.
> ANTONYMS tactless.

□ **diplomatically** adverb.

dipper ▸ noun 1 a bird that dives into fast-flowing streams to feed. 2 a ladle.

dipsomania /dip-suh-may-ni-uh/ ▸ noun alcoholism.
□ **dipsomaniac** noun.

dipstick ▸ noun a rod for measuring the depth of a liquid.

dire ▶ adjective **1** very serious or urgent. **2** informal of very bad quality.

SYNONYMS **terrible,** dreadful, appalling, frightful, awful, grim, sore, alarming, acute, grave, serious, urgent, pressing, wretched, desperate, parlous.

direct ▶ adjective **1** going from one place to another without changing direction or stopping. **2** with nothing or no one in between. **3** saying exactly what you mean; frank. **4** clear and explicit.

SYNONYMS **1** *the most direct route* **straight,** short, quick. **2** *a direct flight* **non-stop,** through, unbroken, uninterrupted. **3** *he is very direct* **frank,** candid, straightforward, open, blunt, plain-spoken, outspoken, forthright, no-nonsense, matter-of-fact; informal upfront.

▶ adverb in a direct way or by a direct route.
▶ verb **1** aim something towards. **2** tell or show someone the way. **3** control the operations of. **4** supervise the production of a film, play, etc. **5** give an order to.

SYNONYMS **1** *an economic elite directed the nation's affairs* **manage,** govern, run, administer, control, conduct, handle, be in charge of, preside over, lead, head, rule. **2** *was that remark directed at me?* **aim,** target, address to, intend for, mean for, design for. **3** *a man in uniform directed them to the hall* **give directions,** show the way, point someone in the direction of. **4** *the judge directed the jury to return a not guilty verdict* **instruct,** tell, command, order, require.

■ **direct current** an electric current that flows in one direction only. **direct debit** Brit. an arrangement by which a bank transfers money from your account to pay a particular person or organization. **direct speech** the actual words of a speaker quoted in writing.

direction ▶ noun **1** a course along which someone or something moves, or which leads to a destination. **2** a point to or from which someone or something moves or faces. **3** the directing or managing of people. **4** (**directions**) instructions on how to reach a destination or how to do something.

SYNONYMS **1** *a northerly direction* **way,** route, course, line, bearing, orientation. **2** *his direction of the project* **running,** management, administration, conduct, handling, supervision, superintendence, command, rule, leadership. **3** *explicit directions about nursing care* **instruction,** order, command, rule, regulation, requirement.

□ **directional** adjective.

directive ▶ noun an official instruction.

SYNONYMS **instruction,** direction, command, order, injunction, decree, dictum, edict.

directly ▶ adverb **1** in a direct way. **2** exactly in a particular position: *the house directly opposite.* **3** immediately.

SYNONYMS **1** *they flew directly to New York* **straight,** as the crow flies. **2** *directly after breakfast* **immediately,** right (away), straight (away), without delay, promptly. **3** *the houses directly opposite* **exactly,** right, immediately, diametrically; informal bang. **4** *she spoke simply and directly* **frankly,** candidly, openly, bluntly, forthrightly, without beating around the bush.

▶ conjunction Brit. as soon as.

director ▶ noun **1** a person who is in charge of an organization or activity. **2** a member of the board which manages a business. **3** a person responsible for directing a film, play, etc.

SYNONYMS **manager,** head, chief, principal, leader, governor, president, chair, chief executive; informal boss, gaffer.

■ **director general** (plural **directors general**) the chief executive of a large organization. □ **directorial** adjective.

directory ▶ noun (plural **directories**) a book that lists individuals or organizations and gives their addresses, telephone numbers, etc.

dirge ▶ noun **1** a piece of music expressing sadness for someone's death. **2** a slow, boring song or piece of music.

dirigible /di-rij-i-b'l/ ▶ noun an airship.

dirk ▶ noun a kind of short dagger formerly carried by Scottish Highlanders.

dirt ▶ noun **1** a substance that makes something dirty. **2** soil or earth. **3** informal scandalous or damaging information about someone.

SYNONYMS **1** *his face was streaked with dirt* **grime,** filth, muck, dust, mud; Brit. informal gunge. **2** *a dirt road* **earth,** soil, clay, ground.

dirty ▶ adjective (**dirtier, dirtiest**) **1** covered or marked with mud, dust, grease, etc.; not clean. **2** obscene. **3** unfair or dishonest.

SYNONYMS **1** *a dirty sweatshirt | dirty water* **soiled,** grimy, grubby, filthy, mucky, stained, unwashed, greasy, muddy, dusty, polluted, contaminated, foul, unhygienic; Brit. informal manky, grotty. **2** *a dirty joke* **obscene,** indecent, rude, naughty, vulgar, smutty, coarse, crude, filthy, off colour, pornographic, explicit, X-rated; informal blue; euphemistic adult. **3** *a dirty look* **malevolent,** hostile, black,

angry, disapproving.
ANTONYMS clean, friendly.

▸ verb (dirties, dirtying, dirtied) make something dirty.

> SYNONYMS *the dog had dirtied her dress* **soil**, stain, muddy, blacken, mess (up), mark, spatter, smudge, smear, splatter, sully, pollute, foul.
> ANTONYMS clean.

■ **dirty look** informal a look expressing disapproval, disgust, or anger.

disability ▸ noun (plural disabilities) **1** a physical or mental condition that restricts your movements, senses, or activities. **2** a disadvantage or handicap.

> SYNONYMS **handicap**, incapacity, impairment, infirmity, defect, abnormality, condition, disorder, affliction.

disable ▸ verb (disables, disabling, disabled) **1** cause someone to be disabled. **2** put something out of action.

> SYNONYMS **1** *an injury that could disable somebody for life* **incapacitate**, put out of action, debilitate, handicap, cripple, lame, maim, immobilize, paralyse. **2** *the bomb squad disabled the device* **deactivate**, defuse, disarm, make safe.

□ **disablement** noun.

disabled ▸ adjective having a disability.

> SYNONYMS **handicapped**, incapacitated, infirm, crippled, lame, paralysed, immobilized, bedridden; euphemistic physically challenged, differently abled.
> ANTONYMS able-bodied.

disabuse ▸ verb (disabuses, disabusing, disabused) (disabuse someone of) persuade someone that an idea or belief is mistaken.

disadvantage ▸ noun something that causes a problem or reduces the chances of success.

> SYNONYMS **1** *that's the disadvantage of this scheme* **drawback**, snag, downside, fly in the ointment, catch, nuisance, handicap, trouble; informal minus. **2** *she did nothing to his disadvantage* **detriment**, prejudice, harm, loss, hurt.
> ANTONYMS advantage.

▸ verb (disadvantages, disadvantaging, disadvantaged) **1** put someone in an unfavourable position. **2** (disadvantaged) having less money and fewer opportunities than most people.
□ **disadvantageous** adjective.

disaffected ▸ adjective unhappy with the people in authority or with the organization you belong to, and no longer willing to support them.
□ **disaffection** noun.

disagree ▸ verb (disagrees, disagreeing, disagreed) **1** have a different opinion. **2** be inconsistent. **3** (disagree with) make someone slightly unwell.

> SYNONYMS **1** *no one disagreed with him* **be of a different opinion**, not see eye to eye, take issue, challenge, contradict, differ, dissent, be in dispute, clash. **2** *their accounts disagree* **differ**, be dissimilar, be different, be at variance/ odds, vary, contradict each other, conflict. **3** *the spicy food disagreed with her* **make ill**, make unwell, sicken, upset.
> ANTONYMS agree.

disagreeable ▸ adjective **1** unpleasant. **2** bad-tempered.

disagreement ▸ noun the state of disagreeing.

> SYNONYMS **dissent**, difference of opinion, controversy, discord, division, dispute, quarrel.
> ANTONYMS agreement.

disallow ▸ verb declare to be invalid.

disappear ▸ verb **1** stop being visible. **2** cease to exist.

> SYNONYMS **1** *the mist had disappeared* **vanish**, be lost to view/sight, recede, fade away, melt away, clear. **2** *this way of life has disappeared* **die out**, cease to exist, end, go, pass away, pass into oblivion, perish, vanish.
> ANTONYMS materialize, arise.

□ **disappearance** noun.

> ✔ one **s**, two **p**s: di**s**a**pp**ear.

disappoint ▸ verb **1** make someone sad or upset through failing to fulfil their hopes or expectations. **2** prevent hopes or expectations being fulfilled.

> SYNONYMS **let down**, fail, dissatisfy, upset, dismay, sadden, disenchant, disillusion, shatter someone's illusions.
> ANTONYMS delight.

> ✔ one **s**, two **p**s: di**s**a**pp**oint.

disappointed ▸ adjective sad or displeased because your hopes have not been realized.

> SYNONYMS **upset**, saddened, let down, displeased, dissatisfied, disheartened, downhearted, discouraged, crestfallen, disenchanted, disillusioned; informal choked, cut up; Brit. informal gutted, as sick as a parrot.
> ANTONYMS delighted.

disappointment ▸ noun **1** sadness felt when hopes or expectations are not fulfilled. **2** a person or thing that causes disappointment.

> SYNONYMS **1** *she tried to hide her disappointment* **sadness**, sorrow, regret,

dismay, displeasure, dissatisfaction, disenchantment, disillusionment. **2** *the trip was a disappointment* **let-down**, non-event, anticlimax; Brit. damp squib; informal washout.
ANTONYMS delight, pleasant surprise.

disapprobation ▸ noun strong disapproval.

disapproval ▸ noun the feeling that someone or something is bad or immoral.

> SYNONYMS **disfavour**, objection, dislike, dissatisfaction, distaste, displeasure, criticism, censure, condemnation, denunciation.
> ANTONYMS approval.

disapprove ▸ verb (disapproves, disapproving, disapproved) feel that someone or something is bad or immoral.

> SYNONYMS *he strongly disapproved of smoking* **object to**, take exception to, dislike, take a dim view of, look askance at, frown on, be against, deplore, censure, condemn, denounce.

disarm ▸ verb **1** take a weapon or weapons away from someone. **2** (of a country) reduce the size of its armed forces or give up its weapons. **3** win over a hostile or suspicious person, especially through being charming. **4** remove the fuse from a bomb.

> SYNONYMS **1** *the militia refused to disarm* **lay down your arms**, demobilize, disband, demilitarize. **2** *police disarmed the bomb* **defuse**, disable, deactivate, make safe. **3** *the warmth in his voice disarmed her* **win over**, charm, persuade, soothe, mollify, appease, placate. **4** (disarming) **winning**, charming, irresistible, persuasive, soothing, conciliatory, mollifying.
> ANTONYMS arm, antagonize.

disarmament ▸ noun the reduction or withdrawal of military forces and weapons.

> SYNONYMS **demilitarization**, demobilization, disbandment, decommissioning, arms reduction, arms limitation.
> ANTONYMS arming.

disarrange ▸ verb (disarranges, disarranging, disarranged) make something untidy or disordered.

disarray ▸ noun disorder or confusion.

> SYNONYMS **disorder**, confusion, chaos, untidiness, disorganization, a mess, a muddle, a shambles.
> ANTONYMS tidiness.

disassemble ▸ verb (disassembles, disassembling, disassembled) take to pieces.

disassociate = DISSOCIATE.

disaster ▸ noun **1** a sudden accident or

natural event that causes great damage or loss of life. **2** a sudden misfortune.

> SYNONYMS **1** *a railway disaster* **catastrophe**, calamity, cataclysm, tragedy, act of God, accident. **2** *a string of personal disasters* **misfortune**, mishap, misadventure, setback, reversal, stroke of bad luck, blow. **3** *the film was a disaster* **failure**, fiasco, catastrophe; informal flop, washout, dead loss.
> ANTONYMS success.

disastrous ▸ adjective **1** causing great damage. **2** informal very unsuccessful.

> SYNONYMS **catastrophic**, calamitous, cataclysmic, tragic, devastating, ruinous, terrible, awful.

☐ **disastrously** adverb.

> ✔ no **e**: disa**stro**us, not **-erous**.

disavow ▸ verb deny that you are responsible for or in favour of something.
☐ **disavowal** noun.

disband ▸ verb (of an organized group) break up.

disbar ▸ verb (disbars, disbarring, disbarred) stop a barrister from working as a lawyer.

disbelief ▸ noun **1** inability or refusal to accept that something is true or real. **2** lack of faith.

> SYNONYMS **incredulity**, incredulousness, scepticism, doubt, cynicism, suspicion, distrust, mistrust.
> ANTONYMS belief.

disbelieve ▸ verb (disbelieves, disbelieving, disbelieved) be unable to believe.

disburse ▸ verb (disburses, disbursing, disbursed) pay out money from a fund.
☐ **disbursement** noun.

disc (US spelling disk) ▸ noun **1** a flat, thin, round object. **2** (disk) a device on which computer data is stored. **3** a layer of cartilage that separates vertebrae in the spine. **4** a compact disc or record.
■ **disc jockey** a DJ.

discard ▸ verb /diss-kard/ get rid of something useless or unwanted.

> SYNONYMS **dispose of**, throw away/out, get rid of, toss out, jettison, dispense with, scrap, reject, drop; informal ditch, bin, junk; Brit. informal get shot of; N. Amer. informal trash.
> ANTONYMS keep.

▸ noun /diss-kard/ something that has been discarded.

discern /di-sern/ ▸ verb **1** recognize or be aware of. **2** see or hear something with difficulty.
☐ **discernible** adjective.

discerning ▸ adjective having or showing good judgement.

☐ **discernment** noun.

discharge ▶ verb (**discharges, discharging, discharged**) **1** dismiss or allow to leave. **2** send out a liquid, gas, or other substance. **3** fire a gun or missile. **4** fulfil a responsibility.

SYNONYMS **1** *he was discharged from service* **dismiss,** eject, expel, throw out, make redundant, release, let go; Military cashier; informal sack, fire. **2** *he was discharged from prison* **release,** free, let out. **3** *oil is routinely discharged from ships* **release,** eject, let out, pour out, give off, dump. **4** *he accidentally discharged a pistol* **fire,** shoot, let off, set off, loose off, trigger, launch. **5** *the ferry was discharging passengers* **unload,** offload, put off, remove. **6** *they discharged their duties efficiently* **carry out,** perform, execute, conduct, fulfil, complete. ANTONYMS recruit, imprison, take on.

▶ noun **1** the action of discharging. **2** a substance that has been discharged.

SYNONYMS **1** *his discharge from the service* **dismissal,** release, removal, ejection, expulsion; Military cashiering; informal the sack, the boot. **2** *her discharge from prison* **release**. **3** *a discharge of diesel oil into the river* **leak,** leakage, emission, release, outflow. **4** *a watery discharge from the eyes* **emission,** secretion, excretion, suppuration, pus. **5** *the discharge of their duties* **carrying out,** performance, execution, conduct, fulfilment, accomplishment, completion.

disciple /di-sy-puhl/ ▶ noun **1** a person who followed Jesus during his life, especially one of the twelve Apostles. **2** a follower of a teacher, leader, or philosophy.

SYNONYMS **follower,** adherent, believer, admirer, devotee, acolyte, apostle, supporter, advocate.

disciplinarian ▶ noun a person who enforces firm discipline.

disciplinary ▶ adjective having to do with discipline.

discipline ▶ noun **1** the training of people to obey rules or a code of behaviour. **2** controlled behaviour resulting from such training. **3** a branch of academic study.

SYNONYMS **1** *parental discipline* **control,** regulation, direction, order, authority, strictness. **2** *he maintained discipline among his men* **good behaviour,** order, control, obedience. **3** *sociology is a fairly new discipline* **field (of study),** branch of knowledge, subject, area, speciality.

▶ verb (**disciplines, disciplining, disciplined**) **1** train someone to be obedient or self-controlled. **2** formally punish someone for an offence. **3** (**disciplined**) behaving in a controlled way.

SYNONYMS **1** *she had disciplined herself to ignore the pain* **train,** drill, teach, school, coach. **2** *he was disciplined by the management* **punish,** penalize, bring to book, reprimand, rebuke; Brit. informal carpet.

✔ There's a **c** in the middle: disc**i**pline.

disclaim ▶ verb refuse to acknowledge that you are responsible for or interested in something.

disclaimer ▶ noun a statement disclaiming responsibility for something.

disclose ▶ verb (**discloses, disclosing, disclosed**) **1** make new or secret information known. **2** allow to be seen.

SYNONYMS **1** *the information must not be disclosed* **reveal,** make known, divulge, tell, impart, communicate, pass on, release, make public, broadcast, publish. **2** *surgery disclosed a growth* **uncover,** reveal, show, bring to light. ANTONYMS keep secret, conceal.

disclosure ▶ noun **1** the disclosing of information. **2** a secret that is disclosed.

disco ▶ noun (plural **discos**) a club or party at which people dance to pop music.

discolour (US spelling **discolor**) ▶ verb make something stained or unattractive in colour.
☐ **discoloration** (or **discolouration**) noun.

discomfit /diss-**kum**-fit/ ▶ verb (**discomfits, discomfiting, discomfited**) make someone uneasy or embarrassed.
☐ **discomfiture** noun.

discomfort ▶ noun **1** slight pain. **2** slight anxiety or embarrassment.

SYNONYMS **1** *discomfort caused by indigestion* **pain,** aches and pains, soreness, aching, twinge, pang, throb, cramp. **2** *the discomforts of life at sea* **inconvenience,** difficulty, problem, trial, tribulation, hardship. **3** *Thomas noticed her discomfort* **embarrassment,** discomfiture, unease, awkwardness, discomposure, confusion, nervousness, distress, anxiety.

▶ verb cause someone discomfort.

discompose ▶ verb (**discomposes, discomposing, discomposed**) make someone feel worried or disturbed.

disconcert ▶ verb make someone feel worried, confused, or uneasy.

disconnect ▶ verb **1** break the connection between two things. **2** detach an electrical device from a power supply.
☐ **disconnection** noun.

disconsolate ▶ adjective very unhappy and unable to be consoled.

discontent ▶ noun a feeling of unhappiness or dissatisfaction.

SYNONYMS **dissatisfaction**, disaffection, grievances, unhappiness, displeasure, resentment, envy, restlessness, unrest, unease.
ANTONYMS satisfaction.

☐ **discontentment** noun.

discontented ▸ adjective unhappy or dissatisfied, especially with your own situation.

SYNONYMS **dissatisfied**, disgruntled, disaffected, unhappy, aggrieved, displeased, resentful, envious, restless, frustrated; informal fed up.
ANTONYMS satisfied.

discontinue ▸ verb (discontinues, discontinuing, discontinued) stop doing, providing, or making.
☐ **discontinuation** noun.

discontinuous ▸ adjective having intervals or gaps; not continuous.
☐ **discontinuity** noun.

discord ▸ noun 1 lack of agreement or harmony. 2 lack of harmony between musical notes sounding together.

discordant ▸ adjective 1 not in harmony or agreement. 2 (of a sound or sounds) harsh and unpleasant.

discotheque /diss-kuh-tek/ = DISCO.

discount ▸ noun an amount by which the usual cost of something is reduced.

SYNONYMS *a 10 per cent discount* **reduction**, deduction, markdown, price cut, concession, rebate.

▸ verb 1 reduce the usual price of something. 2 decide not to believe something because you think it is unlikely.

SYNONYMS **1** *the price is heavily discounted* **reduce**, mark down, cut, lower; informal knock down. **2** *I discounted the rumours* **disregard**, pay no attention to, take no notice of, dismiss, ignore, overlook; informal pooh-pooh.
ANTONYMS increase, believe.

discourage ▸ verb (discourages, discouraging, discouraged) 1 cause someone to lose confidence or enthusiasm. 2 try to persuade someone not to do something.

SYNONYMS **1** *we want to discourage children from smoking* **dissuade**, deter, put off, talk out of. **2** *she was discouraged by his hostile tone* **dishearten**, dispirit, demoralize, disappoint, put off, unnerve, daunt, intimidate. **3** *he sought to discourage further speculation* **prevent**, deter, stop, avert, inhibit, curb.
ANTONYMS encourage.

☐ **discouragement** noun.

discourse ▸ noun 1 written or spoken communication or debate. 2 a formal

discussion of a topic.
▸ verb (discourses, discoursing, discoursed) speak or write about something with authority.

discourteous ▸ adjective rude and without consideration for other people.

discourtesy ▸ noun (plural discourtesies) behaviour that is rude and inconsiderate.

discover ▸ verb (discovers, discovering, discovered) 1 find something unexpectedly or in the course of a search. 2 gain knowledge about, or become aware of. 3 be the first to find or observe something.

SYNONYMS **1** *firemen discovered a body* **find**, locate, come across/upon, stumble on, chance on, uncover, unearth, turn up. **2** *I discovered the truth* **find out**, learn, realize, ascertain, work out, recognize; informal figure out; Brit. informal twig.

discovery ▸ noun (plural discoveries) 1 the action of discovering. 2 a person or thing discovered.

SYNONYMS **1** *the discovery of the body* **finding**, location, uncovering, unearthing. **2** *the discovery that she was pregnant* **realization**, recognition, revelation, disclosure. **3** *he failed to take out a patent on his discoveries* **find**, finding, breakthrough, innovation.

discredit ▸ verb (discredits, discrediting, discredited) 1 make someone seem less trustworthy or honourable. 2 make something seem false or unreliable.

SYNONYMS **1** *an attempt to discredit him* **bring into disrepute**, disgrace, dishonour, blacken the name of, put/show in a bad light, compromise, smear, tarnish; N. Amer. slur. **2** *that theory has been discredited* **disprove**, invalidate, explode, refute; informal debunk.
ANTONYMS honour, prove.

▸ noun damage to someone's reputation.

SYNONYMS *to his discredit* **dishonour**, disgrace, shame, humiliation, ignominy.
ANTONYMS honour, glory.

discreditable ▸ adjective causing damage to someone's reputation; shameful.

discreet ▸ adjective careful not to attract attention or give offence.

SYNONYMS **tactful**, circumspect, diplomatic, judicious, sensitive, careful, cautious, strategic.

☐ **discreetly** adverb.

❗ Don't confuse **discreet** with **discrete**, which means 'separate'.

discrepancy ▸ noun (plural discrepancies) a difference between things that should be the same.

SYNONYMS **difference,** disparity, variation, deviation, divergence, disagreement, inconsistency, mismatch, conflict.
ANTONYMS correspondence.

discrete ▸ adjective separate and distinct.

discretion ▸ noun **1** the quality of being discreet. **2** the freedom to decide what should be done in a particular situation.

SYNONYMS **1** *you can rely on his discretion* **tact,** diplomacy, delicacy, sensitivity, good sense, prudence, circumspection. **2** *at the discretion of the council* **choice,** option, preference, disposition, pleasure, will, inclination.
ANTONYMS tactlessness.

discretionary ▸ adjective done or used according to the judgement of a particular person.

discriminate ▸ verb (discriminates, discriminating, discriminated) **1** recognize a difference between one thing and another. **2** treat people unfairly on the grounds of race, sex, or age.

SYNONYMS **1** *he cannot discriminate between fact and opinion* **differentiate,** distinguish, draw a distinction, tell the difference, tell apart, separate. **2** *policies that discriminate against women* **be biased,** be prejudiced, treat differently, treat unfairly, put at a disadvantage, victimize, pick on.

discriminating ▸ adjective having or showing good taste or judgement.

SYNONYMS **discerning,** perceptive, judicious, selective, tasteful, refined, sensitive, cultivated, cultured.
ANTONYMS indiscriminate.

discrimination ▸ noun **1** unfair treatment of people on the grounds of race, sex, or age. **2** recognition of the difference between one thing and another. **3** good judgement or taste.

SYNONYMS **1** *racial discrimination* **prejudice,** bias, bigotry, intolerance, favouritism, partisanship. **2** *a man with no discrimination* **discernment,** judgement, perceptiveness, (good) taste, refinement, sensitivity, cultivation.
ANTONYMS impartiality.

discriminatory ▸ adjective showing discrimination or prejudice.

discursive ▸ adjective (of writing) moving from subject to subject.

discus ▸ noun (plural **discuses**) a heavy disc thrown in athletic contests.

discuss ▸ verb **1** talk about something in order to reach a decision. **2** talk or write about a topic in detail.

SYNONYMS **1** *I discussed the matter with my wife* **talk over,** talk about, talk through, debate, confer about. **2** *chapter three discusses this topic* **examine,** explore, study, analyse, go into, deal with, consider, tackle.

discussion ▸ noun **1** conversation or debate about something. **2** a detailed treatment of a topic in writing.

SYNONYMS **1** *a long discussion with her husband* **conversation,** talk, dialogue, conference, debate, exchange of views, consultation, deliberation; informal confab. **2** *see Chapter 7 for a detailed discussion* **examination,** exploration, study, analysis, treatment, consideration.

disdain ▸ noun the feeling that someone or something does not deserve respect.

SYNONYMS *she looked at him with disdain* **contempt,** scorn, derision, disrespect, condescension, superciliousness, hauteur, haughtiness.
ANTONYMS respect.

▸ verb treat with disdain.

SYNONYMS *she disdained exhibitionism* **scorn,** deride, regard with contempt, sneer at, look down your nose at, look down on, despise.
ANTONYMS value.

□ **disdainful** adjective **disdainfully** adverb.

disease ▸ noun an illness in a human, animal, or plant.

SYNONYMS **illness,** sickness, ill health, infection, ailment, malady, disorder, condition, problem; informal bug, virus; Brit. informal lurgy.
ANTONYMS health.

diseased ▸ adjective suffering from disease.

SYNONYMS **unhealthy,** ill, sick, unwell, ailing, infected, septic, rotten, bad.
ANTONYMS healthy.

disembark ▸ verb leave a ship, aircraft, or train.
□ **disembarkation** noun.

disembodied ▸ adjective **1** separated from the body, or existing without a body. **2** (of a sound) not having any obvious physical source.

disembowel ▸ verb (disembowels, disembowelling, disembowelled; US spelling disembowels, disemboweling, disemboweled) cut open and remove the internal organs of.

disempower ▸ verb (disempowers, disempowering, disempowered) make someone less powerful or confident.

disenchant ▸ verb make someone disillusioned.
□ **disenchantment** noun.

d

disenfranchise ▸ verb (disenfranchises, disenfranchising, disenfranchised)
1 deprive someone of the right to vote.
2 deprive someone of a right or privilege.

disengage ▸ verb (disengages, disengaging, disengaged) **1** release or detach. **2** remove troops from an area of conflict.
□ **disengagement** noun.

disentangle ▸ verb (disentangles, disentangling, disentangled) stop something being tangled.

disestablish ▸ verb end the official status of a national Church.

disfavour (US spelling **disfavor**) ▸ noun disapproval or dislike.

disfigure ▸ verb (disfigures, disfiguring, disfigured) spoil the appearance of.
□ **disfigurement** noun.

disgorge ▸ verb (disgorges, disgorging, disgorged) **1** cause something to pour out.
2 bring up food from the stomach.

disgrace ▸ noun **1** the loss of other people's respect as the result of behaving badly. **2** a shamefully bad person or thing.

> SYNONYMS **1** *he brought disgrace on the family* **dishonour,** shame, discredit, ignominy, disrepute, infamy, scandal, stigma, humiliation, loss of face. **2** *the unemployment figures are a disgrace* **scandal,** discredit, reproach, stain, blemish, blot, outrage, affront.
> ANTONYMS honour, credit.

▸ verb (**disgraces, disgracing, disgraced**) bring disgrace to.

> SYNONYMS *you have disgraced the family name* **shame,** bring shame on, dishonour, discredit, stigmatize, taint, sully, tarnish, stain, blacken.
> ANTONYMS honour.

disgraceful ▸ adjective shockingly unacceptable.

> SYNONYMS **shameful,** scandalous, contemptible, dishonourable, discreditable, disreputable, reprehensible, blameworthy, unworthy, ignoble.
> ANTONYMS admirable.

□ **disgracefully** adverb.

disgruntled ▸ adjective angry or dissatisfied.

> SYNONYMS **dissatisfied,** discontented, aggrieved, resentful, displeased, unhappy, disappointed, annoyed; informal hacked off, browned off; Brit. informal cheesed off, narked; N. Amer. informal sore, ticked off.
> ANTONYMS contented.

□ **disgruntlement** noun.

disguise ▸ verb (disguises, disguising, disguised) **1** change the appearance of someone or something so they cannot be recognized. **2** hide a feeling or situation.

> SYNONYMS **camouflage,** conceal, hide, cover up, mask, screen, veil, paper over.
> ANTONYMS expose.

▸ noun **1** a way of disguising yourself. **2** the state of being disguised.

disgust ▸ noun a strong feeling that something is unpleasant, offensive, or unacceptable.

> SYNONYMS **1** *the sight filled her with disgust* **revulsion,** repugnance, aversion, distaste, abhorrence, loathing, hatred. **2** *the audience walked out in disgust* **disapproval,** displeasure, indignation, annoyance, anger, fury, outrage, contempt, resentment.
> ANTONYMS delight.

▸ verb give someone a feeling of disgust.

> SYNONYMS **1** *they were disgusted by the violence* **revolt,** repel, repulse, sicken, horrify, appal, turn someone's stomach; N. Amer. informal gross out. **2** *Toby's behaviour disgusted her* **displease,** dissatisfy, arouse the disapproval of, annoy, anger, outrage, scandalize, offend, affront, dismay.
> ANTONYMS delight.

disgusting ▸ adjective causing disgust.

> SYNONYMS **1** *the food was disgusting* **revolting,** repulsive, sickening, nauseating, stomach-turning, off-putting; N. Amer. vomitous; informal sick-making. **2** *I find racism disgusting* **outrageous,** objectionable, abhorrent, repellent, loathsome, offensive, appalling, shocking, horrifying, scandalous, monstrous, detestable; informal gross, sick.
> ANTONYMS delightful.

dish ▸ noun **1** a shallow container for cooking or serving food. **2** (**the dishes**) all the crockery and utensils used for a meal. **3** a particular kind of food. **4** a shallow concave object. **5** informal an attractive person.

> SYNONYMS **1** *a china dish* **bowl,** plate, platter, salver, pot. **2** *vegetarian dishes* **recipe,** meal, course, fare.

▸ verb (**dish something out or up**) put food on to plates before a meal.

disharmony ▸ noun lack of harmony.

dishearten ▸ verb make someone lose determination or confidence.

dishevelled (US spelling **disheveled**)
▸ adjective untidy in appearance.

dishonest ▸ adjective not honest, trustworthy, or sincere.

> SYNONYMS **fraudulent,** cheating, underhand, devious, treacherous, unfair, dirty, criminal, illegal, unlawful, false, untruthful, deceitful, lying; informal

crooked, shady, sharp; Brit. informal bent; Austral./NZ informal shonky.
ANTONYMS honest.

☐ **dishonestly** adverb **dishonesty** noun.

dishonour (US spelling **dishonor**) ▸ noun shame or disgrace.
▸ verb **1** bring shame or disgrace to. **2** fail to keep an agreement.

dishonourable (US spelling **dishonorable**) ▸ adjective bringing shame or disgrace.

dishwasher ▸ noun a machine for washing dishes automatically.

dishy ▸ adjective (**dishier**, **dishiest**) informal good-looking.

disillusion ▸ verb make someone realize that a belief they hold is mistaken or unrealistic.
▸ noun disappointment caused by discovering that your beliefs are mistaken or unrealistic.
☐ **disillusionment** noun.

disincentive ▸ noun a factor that discourages someone from doing a particular thing.

disinclination ▸ noun a reluctance to do something.

disinclined ▸ adjective reluctant; unwilling.

disinfect ▸ verb clean with a disinfectant in order to destroy bacteria.
☐ **disinfection** noun.

disinfectant ▸ noun a chemical liquid that destroys bacteria.

disinformation ▸ noun information which is intended to mislead people.

disingenuous ▸ adjective not sincere, especially in pretending ignorance about something.

disinherit ▸ verb (**disinherits**, **disinheriting**, **disinherited**) prevent a person from inheriting something.

disintegrate ▸ verb (**disintegrates**, **disintegrating**, **disintegrated**) break up into small parts as a result of impact or decay.

SYNONYMS **break up,** crumble, break apart, fall apart, fall to pieces, collapse, fragment, shatter, splinter.

☐ **disintegration** noun.

disinter /diss-in-**ter**/ ▸ verb (**disinters**, **disinterring**, **disinterred**) dig up something buried.

disinterest ▸ noun **1** impartiality. **2** lack of interest.

disinterested ▸ adjective not influenced by personal feelings; impartial.

SYNONYMS *disinterested advice* **unbiased,** unprejudiced, impartial, neutral, detached, objective, dispassionate.

❗ Don't confuse **disinterested** and **uninterested**. **Disinterested** means 'impartial', while **uninterested** means 'not interested'.

disjointed ▸ adjective not having a logical sequence or clear connection; disconnected.

disjunction ▸ noun a difference or lack of agreement between things that you might expect to be the same.

disk → DISC.
■ **disk drive** a device which allows a computer to read from and write on to computer disks.

diskette ▸ noun a floppy disk.

dislike ▸ verb (**dislikes**, **disliking**, **disliked**) find someone or something unpleasant or offensive.

SYNONYMS *a man she had always disliked* **find distasteful,** regard with distaste, be averse to, have an aversion to, hate, disapprove of, object to, take exception to.
ANTONYMS like.

▸ noun **1** a feeling that someone or something is unpleasant or offensive. **2** a person or thing that you dislike.

SYNONYMS *she viewed the other woman with dislike* **distaste,** aversion, disfavour, antipathy, disgust, abhorrence, hatred.
ANTONYMS liking.

dislocate ▸ verb (**dislocates**, **dislocating**, **dislocated**) **1** put a bone out of its proper position in a joint. **2** stop something from working properly; disrupt.
☐ **dislocation** noun.

dislodge ▸ verb (**dislodges**, **dislodging**, **dislodged**) remove something from its position.

disloyal ▸ adjective not loyal or faithful.
☐ **disloyalty** noun.

dismal ▸ adjective **1** causing or showing gloom or depression. **2** informal disgracefully bad.

SYNONYMS **1** *a dismal look* **gloomy,** glum, melancholy, morose, doleful, woebegone, forlorn, dejected, downcast. **2** *dismal weather* **dim,** dingy, dark, gloomy, dreary, drab, dull.
ANTONYMS cheerful, bright.

☐ **dismally** adverb.

dismantle ▸ verb (**dismantles**, **dismantling**, **dismantled**) take something to pieces.

SYNONYMS **take apart,** take to pieces/bits, pull to pieces, disassemble, break up, strip (down).
ANTONYMS build.

dismay ▸ noun a feeling of unhappiness and discouragement.

SYNONYMS *to his dismay* **alarm,** distress, concern, surprise, consternation, disquiet.
ANTONYMS pleasure, relief.

▶ **verb** cause someone to feel dismay.

> SYNONYMS *he was dismayed by the answer*
> **concern,** distress, disturb, worry, alarm,
> disconcert, take aback, unnerve, unsettle.
> ANTONYMS encourage, please.

dismember ▶ **verb** (**dismembers,**
dismembering, dismembered) **1** tear or cut
the limbs from. **2** divide up a territory or
organization.
□ **dismemberment** noun.

dismiss ▶ **verb 1** order or allow someone to
leave. **2** order an employee to leave a job.
3 treat something as not being worthy of
serious consideration. **4** refuse to allow
a legal case to continue. **5** Cricket end the
innings of a batsman or side.

> SYNONYMS **1** *the president dismissed five*
> *ministers* **give someone their notice,**
> discharge, lay off, make redundant;
> informal sack, fire. **2** *the guards were*
> *dismissed* **send away,** let go, release.
> **3** *don't dismiss the idea so lightly* **reject,**
> deny, repudiate, spurn. **4** *she dismissed*
> *the thought* **banish,** set aside, put out of
> your mind.
> ANTONYMS appoint, keep on, entertain,
> dwell on.

□ **dismissal** noun.

dismissive ▶ **adjective** showing that you
feel something is not worth serious
consideration.
□ **dismissively** adverb.

dismount ▶ **verb** get off a horse or bicycle.

disobedient ▶ **adjective** failing or refusing
to be obedient.

> SYNONYMS **naughty,** insubordinate,
> defiant, unruly, wayward, badly
> behaved, delinquent, rebellious,
> mutinous, troublesome, wilful.
> ANTONYMS obedient.

□ **disobedience** noun.

disobey ▶ **verb** fail or refuse to obey.

> SYNONYMS **defy,** go against, flout,
> contravene, infringe, transgress, violate,
> disregard, ignore, pay no heed to.

disorder ▶ **noun 1** untidiness or
disorganization. **2** the breakdown of
peaceful and law-abiding behaviour. **3** an
illness or disease.

> SYNONYMS **1** *he hates disorder* **untidiness,**
> mess, disarray, chaos, confusion, clutter,
> jumble, a muddle, a shambles. **2** *incidents*
> *of public disorder* **unrest,** disturbance,
> turmoil, mayhem, violence, fighting,
> fracas, rioting, lawlessness, anarchy,
> breach of the peace. **3** *a blood disorder*
> **disease,** infection, complaint, condition,
> affliction, malady, sickness, illness,
> ailment.
> ANTONYMS order, tidiness, peace.

□ **disordered** adjective.

disorderly ▶ **adjective 1** involving a
breakdown of peaceful behaviour. **2** untidy
or disorganized.

> SYNONYMS **1** *a disorderly desk* **untidy,**
> disorganized, messy, cluttered, in
> disarray; informal like a bomb's hit it,
> higgledy-piggledy; Brit. informal shambolic.
> **2** *disorderly behaviour* **unruly,** riotous,
> disruptive, troublesome, lawless.
> ANTONYMS tidy, peaceful.

disorganized (or **disorganised**) ▶ **adjective**
1 not well planned and controlled. **2** not
able to plan your activities efficiently.
□ **disorganization** noun.

disorientate (or **disorient**) ▶ **verb**
(**disorientates, disorientating,**
disorientated) make someone lose their
bearings or feel confused.
□ **disorientation** noun.

disown ▶ **verb** show or decide that you no
longer want to have anything to do with
someone.

disparage /diss-pa-rij/ ▶ **verb** (**disparages,**
disparaging, disparaged) speak critically or
negatively about.

disparate /**diss**-puh-ruht/ ▶ **adjective 1** very
different from one another. **2** containing
elements that are very different from one
another.

disparity ▶ **noun** (plural **disparities**) a great
difference.

dispassionate ▶ **adjective** not influenced
by strong feelings; impartial.
□ **dispassionately** adverb.

dispatch (or **despatch**) ▶ **verb 1** send to
a destination, especially for a particular
purpose. **2** send a letter or parcel
somewhere. **3** deal with a task or problem
quickly and efficiently. **4** kill a person or
animal.

> SYNONYMS **1** *all the messages were*
> *dispatched* **send (off),** post, mail,
> forward. **2** *the business was dispatched*
> *in the morning* **deal with,** finish,
> conclude, settle, discharge, perform.
> **3** *the good guy dispatched a host of*
> *villains* **kill,** put to death, massacre, wipe
> out, exterminate, eliminate, murder,
> assassinate, execute.

▶ **noun 1** the action of dispatching. **2** a report
on the latest situation in state or military
affairs. **3** speed and efficiency.

> SYNONYMS *the latest dispatch from the*
> *front* **message,** report, communication,
> communiqué, bulletin, statement, letter,
> news, intelligence.

dispel ▶ **verb** (**dispels, dispelling, dispelled**)
make a doubt, feeling, or belief disappear.

> SYNONYMS **banish,** drive away/off, chase
> away, scatter, eliminate, dismiss, allay,

ease, quell.
ANTONYMS form, give rise to.

dispensable ▸ adjective able to be replaced or done without.

dispensary ▸ noun (plural **dispensaries**) a room where medicines are prepared and provided.

dispensation ▸ noun **1** special permission not to obey a rule. **2** the religious system of a particular time. **3** the action of dispensing.

dispense ▸ verb (**dispenses, dispensing, dispensed**) **1** distribute something to a number of people. **2** (of a chemist) prepare and supply medicine according to a prescription. **3** (**dispense with**) get rid of or manage without.

> SYNONYMS **1** *servants dispensed the drinks* **distribute,** pass round, hand out, dole out, dish out, share out. **2** *the soldiers dispensed summary justice* **administer,** deliver, issue, deal out, mete out. **3** *dispensing medicines* **prepare,** make up, supply, provide.

□ **dispenser** noun.

disperse ▸ verb (**disperses, dispersing, dispersed**) **1** move apart and go in different directions. **2** (of gas, smoke, etc.) thin out and eventually disappear.

> SYNONYMS **1** *the crowd began to disperse | police dispersed the demonstrators* **break up,** split up, disband, scatter, leave, go their separate ways, drive away/off, chase away. **2** *the fog finally dispersed* **dissipate,** dissolve, melt away, fade away, clear, lift. **3** *the seeds are dispersed by birds* **scatter,** distribute, spread, disseminate.
> ANTONYMS assemble, form, gather.

□ **dispersal** noun **dispersion** noun.

dispirited ▸ adjective discouraged or depressed.
□ **dispiriting** adjective.

displace ▸ verb (**displaces, displacing, displaced**) **1** move something from its proper or usual position. **2** take over the position or role of. **3** force someone to leave their home.

> SYNONYMS **1** *roof tiles were displaced by gales* **dislodge,** dislocate, move out of place/position, shift. **2** *English displaced the local language* **replace,** take the place of, supplant, supersede.
> ANTONYMS replace.

displacement ▸ noun **1** the action of displacing something, or the amount by which something is displaced. **2** the volume or weight of water displaced by a floating ship, used as a measure of the ship's size.

display ▸ verb **1** put something on show in

a noticeable and attractive way. **2** show a quality or feeling. **3** show data or an image on a screen.

> SYNONYMS **1** *the Crown Jewels are displayed in London* **exhibit,** show, arrange, array, present, lay out, set out. **2** *the play displays his many theatrical talents* **show off,** parade, highlight, reveal, showcase. **3** *she displayed a vein of sharp humour* **manifest,** show evidence of, reveal, demonstrate, show.
> ANTONYMS conceal.

▸ noun **1** a performance, show, or event for public entertainment. **2** the displaying of a quality or feeling. **3** a collection of objects being displayed. **4** the data or image shown on a screen.

> SYNONYMS **1** *a display of dolls* **exhibition,** exposition, array, arrangement, presentation, demonstration, spectacle, show, parade. **2** *his display of concern* **manifestation,** expression, show, proof, demonstration, evidence.

displease ▸ verb (**displeases, displeasing, displeased**) annoy or upset.

> SYNONYMS **annoy,** irritate, anger, incense, irk, vex, nettle, put out, upset, exasperate.

displeasure ▸ noun annoyance or dissatisfaction.

disport ▸ verb (**disport yourself**) old use enjoy yourself in an unrestrained way.

disposable ▸ adjective **1** intended to be used once and then thrown away. **2** (of money) available to be used.

disposal ▸ noun the action of disposing of something.
■ **at your disposal** available to be used whenever or however you wish.

dispose ▸ verb (**disposes, disposing, disposed**) **1** (**dispose of**) get rid of. **2** (**be disposed to**) be inclined to do or think something. **3** (**disposed**) having a particular attitude: *they were favourably disposed towards him.* **4** arrange something in a particular position.

> SYNONYMS *a more sanitary way to dispose of waste* **throw away/out,** get rid of, discard, jettison, scrap; informal dump, junk, ditch, chuck out/away; Brit. informal get shot of; N. Amer. informal trash.

disposition ▸ noun **1** the natural qualities of a person's character. **2** an inclination or tendency. **3** the way in which something is arranged.

> SYNONYMS **1** *a nervous disposition* **temperament,** nature, character, constitution, make-up, mentality. **2** *the disposition of the troops* **arrangement,** positioning, placement, configuration, set-up, line-up, layout.

dispossess ▸ verb deprive someone of a possession.
□ **dispossession** noun.

disproportionate ▸ adjective too large or too small in comparison with something else.
□ **disproportionately** adverb.

disprove ▸ verb (**disproves, disproving, disproved**) prove something to be false.

SYNONYMS **refute**, prove false, rebut, debunk, give the lie to, demolish; informal shoot full of holes, blow out of the water.

disputation ▸ noun debate or argument.

disputatious ▸ adjective fond of arguing.

dispute ▸ verb (**disputes, disputing, disputed**) **1** argue about. **2** question whether something is true or valid. **3** compete for.

SYNONYMS **1** *George disputed with him* **debate**, discuss, exchange views, quarrel, argue, disagree, clash, fall out, wrangle, bicker, squabble. **2** *they disputed his proposals* **challenge**, contest, question, call into question, quibble over, contradict, argue about, disagree with, take issue with.
ANTONYMS accept.

▸ noun an argument or disagreement.

SYNONYMS **1** *a subject of dispute* **debate**, discussion, argument, controversy, disagreement, dissent, conflict. **2** *they have settled their dispute* **quarrel**, argument, altercation, squabble, falling-out, disagreement, difference of opinion, clash; Brit. informal row.
ANTONYMS agreement.

□ **disputable** adjective.

disqualify ▸ verb (**disqualifies, disqualifying, disqualified**) prevent someone performing an activity or taking an office because they have broken a rule or are not suitable.
□ **disqualification** noun.

disquiet ▸ noun a feeling of anxiety.
□ **disquieting** adjective.

disquisition ▸ noun a long or complex discussion of a topic.

disregard ▸ verb pay no attention to.

SYNONYMS *Annie disregarded the remark* **ignore**, take no notice of, pay no attention to, discount, overlook, turn a blind eye to, shut your eyes to, gloss over, brush off/aside, shrug off.
ANTONYMS heed.

▸ noun the action of disregarding something.

SYNONYMS *blithe disregard for the rules* **indifference**, non-observance, inattention, heedlessness, neglect,

contempt.
ANTONYMS attention.

disrepair ▸ noun (**in disrepair**) in a bad condition as a result of being neglected.

disreputable ▸ adjective not respectable in appearance or character.

disrepute ▸ noun the state of having a bad reputation.

disrespect ▸ noun lack of respect or courtesy.
□ **disrespectful** adjective **disrespectfully** adverb.

disrobe ▸ verb (**disrobes, disrobing, disrobed**) take off your clothes.

disrupt ▸ verb interrupt or disturb an activity or process.

SYNONYMS **interrupt**, disturb, interfere with, play havoc with, upset, unsettle, obstruct, impede, hold up, delay.
□ **disruption** noun.

disruptive ▸ adjective causing disruption.

SYNONYMS **troublesome**, disturbing, upsetting, unsettling, unruly, badly behaved, rowdy, disorderly, undisciplined, unmanageable, uncontrollable, uncooperative.
ANTONYMS well behaved.

dissatisfaction ▸ noun lack of satisfaction.

SYNONYMS **discontent**, disaffection, disquiet, unhappiness, disappointment, disgruntlement, displeasure, vexation, annoyance, irritation.

dissatisfied ▸ adjective not content or happy.

SYNONYMS **discontented**, disappointed, disaffected, displeased, disgruntled, aggrieved, unhappy.
ANTONYMS contented.

dissect ▸ verb **1** cut up the dead body of a person or animal to study its internal parts. **2** analyse in great detail.
□ **dissection** noun.

✔ **Dissect** has a double **s**.

dissemble ▸ verb (**dissembles, dissembling, dissembled**) hide or disguise your motives or feelings.

disseminate ▸ verb (**disseminates, disseminating, disseminated**) spread information widely.
□ **dissemination** noun.

dissension ▸ noun disagreement that causes trouble within a group.

dissent ▸ verb **1** express disagreement with a widely held view. **2** disagree with the doctrine of an established Church. **3** (in sport) disagree with the referee's decision.

SYNONYMS **disagree**, differ, demur, be at variance/odds, take issue, protest, object.
ANTONYMS agree, conform.

► noun disagreement with a widely held view.

SYNONYMS **disagreement,** difference of opinion, argument, dispute, resistance, objection, protest, opposition.
ANTONYMS agreement, conformity.

□ **dissenter** noun.

dissertation ► noun a long essay, especially one written for a university degree.

disservice ► noun a harmful action.

dissident ► noun a person who opposes official policy.

SYNONYMS **dissenter,** objector, protester, rebel, revolutionary, subversive, agitator, refusenik.
ANTONYMS conformist.

► adjective opposing official policy.

SYNONYMS **dissenting,** opposing, objecting, protesting, rebellious, revolutionary, subversive, nonconformist.
ANTONYMS conformist.

□ **dissidence** noun.

dissimilar ► adjective not similar; different.
□ **dissimilarity** noun.

dissimulate ► verb (**dissimulates, dissimulating, dissimulated**) hide or disguise your thoughts or feelings.
□ **dissimulation** noun.

dissipate ► verb (**dissipates, dissipating, dissipated**) **1** disappear or disperse. **2** waste money, energy, or resources. **3** (**dissipated**) indulging too much in alcohol and other physical pleasures.
□ **dissipation** noun.

dissociate ► verb (**dissociates, dissociating, dissociated**) **1** disconnect or separate. **2** (**dissociate yourself from**) say publicly that you are not connected with.

SYNONYMS **separate,** detach, disconnect, sever, cut off, divorce, isolate, alienate.
ANTONYMS relate.

□ **dissociation** noun.

dissolute ► adjective indulging too much in physical pleasures.

dissolution ► noun **1** the formal closing down or ending of an official body or agreement. **2** the action of dissolving or decomposing.

dissolve ► verb (**dissolves, dissolving, dissolved**) **1** (of a solid) mix with a liquid and form a solution. **2** close down or end an assembly or agreement. **3** (**dissolve into** or **in**) give way to strong emotion.

SYNONYMS **1** *sugar dissolves in water* **break down,** liquefy, melt, deliquesce, disintegrate. **2** *the crowd dissolved* **disperse,** disband, break up, scatter. **3** *the assembly was dissolved* **disband,** bring to an end, end, terminate, discontinue, close down, wind up/down,

suspend, adjourn. **4** *their marriage was dissolved* **annul,** nullify, void, invalidate, revoke.

dissonant ► adjective without harmony; discordant.
□ **dissonance** noun.

dissuade ► verb (**dissuades, dissuading, dissuaded**) persuade or advise someone not to do something.

SYNONYMS **discourage,** deter, prevent, divert, stop, talk out of, persuade against, advise against, argue out of.
ANTONYMS encourage.

□ **dissuasion** noun.

distaff /diss-tahf/ ► noun a stick or spindle on to which wool or flax is wound for spinning.
■ **distaff side** the female side of a family.

distance ► noun **1** the length of the space between two points. **2** the state of being distant. **3** a far-off point or place. **4** the full length or time of a race.

SYNONYMS **1** *they measured the distance* **interval,** space, span, gap, extent, length, range, reach. **2** *a mix of warmth and distance* **aloofness,** remoteness, detachment, unfriendliness, reserve, reticence, formality; informal stand-offishness.
ANTONYMS proximity, friendliness.

► verb (**distances, distancing, distanced**) (**distance yourself**) become less friendly or supportive.

distant ► adjective **1** far away in space or time. **2** at a specified distance. **3** far apart in terms of resemblance or relationship. **4** aloof or reserved.

SYNONYMS **1** *distant parts of the world* **faraway,** far-off, far-flung, remote, out of the way, outlying. **2** *the distant past* **remote,** bygone, ancient, prehistoric. **3** *a distant memory* **vague,** faint, dim, indistinct, sketchy, hazy. **4** *father was always very distant* **aloof,** reserved, remote, detached, unapproachable, unfriendly; informal stand-offish. **5** *a distant look in his eyes* **distracted,** absent, faraway, detached, vague.
ANTONYMS near, recent, clear, close, friendly, alert.

□ **distantly** adverb.

distaste ► noun the feeling that something is unpleasant or offensive.

distasteful ► adjective unpleasant or disliked.
□ **distastefully** adverb.

distemper ► noun **1** a kind of paint used on walls. **2** a disease of dogs, causing fever and coughing.

distend ► verb swell because of internal pressure.
□ **distension** noun.

distil (US spelling **distill**) ▸ verb (**distils**, **distilling**, **distilled**) **1** purify a liquid by heating it until it vaporizes, then condensing the vapour and collecting the resulting liquid. **2** make alcoholic spirits such as whisky in this way. **3** extract the most important aspects of.
◻ **distiller** noun **distillation** noun.

distillery ▸ noun (plural **distilleries**) a factory that makes alcoholic spirits.

distinct ▸ adjective **1** recognizably different. **2** able to be perceived clearly by the senses.

SYNONYMS **1** *two distinct categories* **discrete,** separate, different, unconnected, distinctive, contrasting. **2** *the tail has distinct black tips* **clear,** well defined, unmistakable, easily distinguishable, recognizable, visible, obvious, pronounced, prominent, striking.
ANTONYMS overlapping, similar, indefinite.

distinction ▸ noun **1** a noticeable difference. **2** outstanding excellence. **3** a special honour or recognition.

SYNONYMS **1** *distinctions that we observed* **difference,** contrast, variation, division, differentiation, discrepancy. **2** *a painter of distinction* **merit,** worth, greatness, excellence, quality, repute, renown. **3** *he had served with distinction* **honour,** credit, excellence, merit.
ANTONYMS similarity, mediocrity, dishonour.

distinctive ▸ adjective characteristic of a person or thing and distinguishing them from others.

SYNONYMS **distinguishing,** characteristic, typical, individual, particular, peculiar, unique, exclusive, special.
ANTONYMS common.

◻ **distinctively** adverb.

distinctly ▸ adverb recognizably.

SYNONYMS **1** *there's something distinctly odd about him* **decidedly,** markedly, definitely, unmistakably, manifestly, patently. **2** *Laura spoke quite distinctly* **clearly,** plainly, intelligibly, audibly.

distinguish ▸ verb **1** recognize the difference between two people or things. **2** manage to see or hear. **3** be a characteristic that makes two people or things different. **4** (**distinguish yourself**) do something very well.

SYNONYMS **1** *he can distinguish reality from fantasy* **differentiate,** tell apart, discriminate between, tell the difference between. **2** *he could distinguish shapes in the dark* **discern,** see, perceive, make out, detect, recognize, identify. **3** *this is what distinguishes history from other disciplines*

separate, set apart, make distinctive, make different, single out, mark off.

◻ **distinguishable** adjective.

distinguished ▸ adjective **1** successful and greatly respected. **2** having a dignified appearance.

SYNONYMS **eminent,** famous, renowned, prominent, well known, esteemed, respected, illustrious, acclaimed, celebrated.
ANTONYMS unknown, obscure.

distort ▸ verb **1** pull or twist out of shape. **2** give a misleading account of.

SYNONYMS **1** **twist,** warp, contort, buckle, deform, malform, misshapen, disfigure. **2** **misrepresent,** pervert, twist, falsify, misreport, misstate, garble, bias, prejudice.

◻ **distortion** noun.

distract ▸ verb **1** prevent someone from giving their full attention to something. **2** take attention away from something.

SYNONYMS **divert,** sidetrack, draw away, lead astray, disturb, put off.

distracted ▸ adjective unable to concentrate on something.

SYNONYMS **preoccupied,** inattentive, vague, abstracted, absent-minded, faraway, in a world of your own, troubled, harassed, worried; informal miles away, not with it.
ANTONYMS attentive.

distraction ▸ noun **1** a thing that distracts someone's attention. **2** something that provides entertainment. **3** the state of being distracted.

SYNONYMS **1** *a distraction from the real issues* **diversion,** interruption, disturbance, interference. **2** *frivolous distractions* **amusement,** entertainment, diversion, recreation, pastime, leisure pursuit.

distraught ▸ adjective very worried and upset.

SYNONYMS **distressed,** frantic, fraught, overcome, overwrought, beside yourself, out of your mind, desperate, hysterical, worked up, at your wits' end; informal in a state.
ANTONYMS calm.

distress ▸ noun **1** extreme unhappiness, pain, or suffering. **2** the state of a ship or aircraft when in danger or difficulty.

SYNONYMS **1** *she concealed her distress* **anguish,** suffering, pain, agony, torment, heartache, heartbreak, sorrow, sadness, unhappiness. **2** *a ship in distress* **danger,** peril, difficulty, trouble, jeopardy, risk.
ANTONYMS happiness, safety.

▸ verb cause distress to.

> SYNONYMS *he was distressed by the trial* **upset,** pain, trouble, worry, perturb, disturb, disquiet, agitate, torment.
> ANTONYMS comfort.

distribute ▸ verb (**distributes, distributing, distributed**) **1** hand or share out to a number of people. **2** (**be distributed**) be spread over an area. **3** supply goods to retailers.

> SYNONYMS **1** *the proceeds were distributed among his creditors* **give out,** deal out, dole out, dish out, hand out/round, share out, divide out/up, parcel out. **2** *the newsletter is distributed free* **circulate,** issue, deliver, disseminate, publish.
> ANTONYMS gather in, pool.

distribution ▸ noun **1** the action of distributing. **2** the way in which something is distributed.

> SYNONYMS **1** *the distribution of aid* **giving out,** dealing out, doling out, handing out/round, issuing, allocation, sharing out, dividing up/out, parcelling out. **2** *centres of food distribution* **supply,** delivery, dispersal, transportation.
> ANTONYMS gathering in, pooling, collection.

distributor ▸ noun **1** a company that supplies goods to retailers. **2** a device in a petrol engine for passing electric current to each spark plug in turn.

district ▸ noun a particular area of a town or region.

> SYNONYMS **area,** region, quarter, sector, zone, territory, locality, neighbourhood, community.

distrust ▸ noun lack of trust.

> SYNONYMS *distrust of Soviet intentions* **mistrust,** suspicion, wariness, chariness, scepticism, doubt, cynicism, misgivings, qualms.
> ANTONYMS trust.

▸ verb have little trust in.

> SYNONYMS *the Army distrusted the peace process* **mistrust,** be suspicious of, be wary of, be chary of, regard with suspicion, suspect, be sceptical of, doubt, be unsure of/about, have misgivings about.
> ANTONYMS trust.

□ **distrustful** adjective.

disturb ▸ verb **1** interrupt the sleep, relaxation, or privacy of. **2** move something from its normal position. **3** make someone anxious. **4** (**disturbed**) having emotional or mental problems.

> SYNONYMS **1** *somewhere where we won't be disturbed* **interrupt,** intrude on, butt in on, barge in on, distract,

disrupt, bother, trouble, pester, harass. **2** (**disturbed**) *disturbed sleep* **disrupted,** interrupted, fitful, intermittent, broken. **3** *don't disturb his papers* **move,** rearrange, mix up, interfere with, mess up, muddle. **4** *he wasn't disturbed by the allegations* **perturb,** trouble, concern, worry, upset, fluster, disconcert, dismay, alarm, distress, unsettle. **5** (**disturbed**) *disturbed children* **troubled,** distressed, upset, distraught, unbalanced, unstable, disordered, dysfunctional, maladjusted, neurotic, unhinged; informal screwed up.
> ANTONYMS calm, reassure.

disturbance ▸ noun **1** the interruption of a normal or settled condition. **2** a riot or other breakdown of peaceful behaviour.

> SYNONYMS **1** *a disturbance to local residents* **disruption,** distraction, interference, inconvenience, upset, annoyance, irritation, intrusion. **2** *disturbances in the town centre* **riot,** fracas, brawl, street fight, free-for-all, commotion, disorder.
> ANTONYMS order.

disunited ▸ adjective not united.
□ **disunity** noun.

disuse ▸ noun the state of not being used; neglect.
□ **disused** adjective.

ditch ▸ noun a narrow channel dug to hold or carry water.

> SYNONYMS **trench,** trough, channel, dyke, drain, gutter, gully, watercourse.

▸ verb **1** informal abandon or get rid of. **2** (of an aircraft) come down in a forced landing on the sea.

dither ▸ verb (**dithers, dithering, dithered**) be indecisive.

ditto ▸ noun **1** the same thing again (used in lists). **2** a symbol consisting of two apostrophes (") placed under the item to be repeated.

ditty ▸ noun (plural **ditties**) a short, simple song.

diuretic /dy-uh-ret-ik/ ▸ adjective (of a drug) making you pass more urine.

diurnal /dy-er-n'l/ ▸ adjective **1** relating to or during the daytime. **2** daily.

diva /dee-vuh/ ▸ noun a famous female opera singer.

Divali → DIWALI.

divan ▸ noun **1** a bed consisting of a base and mattress but no headboard. **2** a long, low sofa without a back or arms.

dive ▸ verb (**dives, diving, dived**; US past and past participle also **dove** /dohv/) **1** plunge head first into water. **2** (of a submarine or swimmer) go under water. **3** plunge steeply downwards through the air. **4** move quickly or suddenly in a downward direction or under cover.

d

SYNONYMS **1** *they dived into the clear water* | *the plane was diving towards the ground* **plunge,** nosedive, jump, plummet, fall, drop, pitch. **2** *they dived for cover* **leap,** jump, lunge, throw/fling yourself, go headlong, duck.

▸ noun **1** an act of diving. **2** *informal* a disreputable nightclub or bar.

SYNONYMS **1** *a dive into the pool* **plunge,** nosedive, jump, fall, drop, swoop. **2** *a sideways dive* **lunge,** spring, jump, leap.

■ **dive-bomb** bomb a target while diving steeply in an aircraft.

diver ▸ noun **1** a person who dives under water. **2** a large diving waterbird.

diverge ▸ verb (**diverges, diverging, diverged**) **1** (of a route or line) separate from another route or line and go in a different direction. **2** be different.

SYNONYMS **1** *the two roads diverged* **separate,** part, fork, divide, split, bifurcate, go in different directions. **2** *areas where our views diverge* **differ,** be different, be dissimilar, disagree, be at variance/odds, conflict, clash. ANTONYMS converge, agree.

□ **divergence** noun **divergent** adjective.

diverse ▸ adjective widely varied.

SYNONYMS **various,** sundry, varied, varying, miscellaneous, assorted, mixed, diversified, divergent, different, differing, distinct, unlike, dissimilar. ANTONYMS similar.

diversify ▸ verb (**diversifies, diversifying, diversified**) **1** make or become more varied. **2** (of a company) expand its range of products or area of operation. □ **diversification** noun.

diversion ▸ noun **1** the action of diverting something from its course. **2** *Brit.* an alternative route used when a road is closed. **3** something intended to distract attention. **4** a pastime or other pleasant activity.

SYNONYMS **1** *the diversion of the river* **re-routing,** redirection, deflection, deviation, divergence. **2** *traffic diversions* **detour,** deviation, alternative route. **3** *the noise created a diversion* **distraction,** disturbance, smokescreen; *informal* red herring. **4** *a city full of diversions* **entertainment,** amusement, pastime, delight, fun, recreation, pleasure.

□ **diversionary** adjective.

diversity ▸ noun (plural **diversities**) **1** the state of being varied. **2** a range of different things.

SYNONYMS **variety,** miscellany, assortment, mixture, mix, range, array, multiplicity, variation, diverseness, difference. ANTONYMS uniformity.

divert ▸ verb **1** change the direction or course of. **2** distract a person or their attention. **3** amuse or entertain.

SYNONYMS **1** *a plan to divert Siberia's rivers* **re-route,** redirect, change the course of, deflect, channel. **2** *he diverted her from her studies* **distract,** sidetrack, disturb, draw away, put off. **3** *the story diverted them* **amuse,** entertain, distract, delight, enchant, interest, fascinate, absorb, engross, rivet, grip.

divest ▸ verb **1** (**divest someone/thing of**) deprive someone or something of. **2** (**divest yourself of**) remove or get rid of.

divide ▸ verb (**divides, dividing, divided**) **1** separate into parts. **2** share out. **3** cause disagreement between people or groups. **4** form a boundary between. **5** find how many times one number contains another.

SYNONYMS **1** *he divided his kingdom into four* **split (up),** cut up, carve up, dissect, bisect, halve, quarter. **2** *a curtain divided her cabin from the galley* **separate,** segregate, partition, screen off, section off, split off. **3** *the stairs divide at the mezzanine* **diverge,** separate, part, branch (off), fork, split (in two). **4** *Jack divided the cash* **share out,** ration out, parcel out, deal out, dole out, dish out, distribute. **5** *he aimed to divide his opponents* **disunite,** drive apart, drive a wedge between, break up, split (up), separate, isolate, alienate. ANTONYMS unify, converge, collect, unite.

▸ noun a difference or disagreement between two groups.

dividend ▸ noun **1** a sum of money that is divided among a number of people, such as the part of a company's profits paid to its shareholders. **2** (**dividends**) benefits.

divider ▸ noun **1** a screen that divides a room into separate parts. **2** (**dividers**) a measuring compass.

divination ▸ noun the use of supernatural means to find out about the future or the unknown.

divine¹ ▸ adjective **1** having to do with God or a god. **2** *informal* excellent.

SYNONYMS **1** *a divine being* **godly,** angelic, heavenly, celestial, holy. **2** *divine worship* **religious,** holy, sacred, sanctified, consecrated, blessed, devotional. ANTONYMS mortal, infernal.

□ **divinely** adverb.

divine² ▸ verb (**divines, divining, divined**) **1** discover by guesswork or intuition. **2** have supernatural insight into the future.

SYNONYMS *Fergus divined how afraid she was* **guess**, surmise, deduce, infer, discern, discover, perceive; informal figure (out); Brit. informal suss.
□ **diviner** noun.

divinity ▸ noun (plural **divinities**) **1** the state of being divine. **2** a god or goddess. **3** the study of religion; theology.

divisible ▸ adjective **1** capable of being divided. **2** (of a number) containing another number a number of times without a remainder.

division ▸ noun **1** the action of dividing, or the state of being divided. **2** each of the parts into which something is divided. **3** a major section of an organization. **4** a number of sports teams or competitors grouped to compete against each other. **5** a partition.

SYNONYMS **1** *the division of the island* | *cell division* **dividing (up)**, breaking up, break-up, carving up, splitting, dissection, partitioning, separation, segregation. **2** *the division of his estates* **sharing out**, dividing up, parcelling out, dishing out, allocation, allotment, splitting up, carving up. **3** *the division between nomadic and urban cultures* **dividing line**, divide, boundary, border, demarcation line, gap, gulf. **4** *each class is split into nine divisions* **section**, subsection, subdivision, category, class, group, grouping, set. **5** *an independent division of the executive* **department**, branch, arm, wing. **6** *the causes of social division* **disunity**, disunion, conflict, discord, disagreement, alienation, isolation.
ANTONYMS unification, unity.

■ **division sign** the sign ÷, placed between two numbers showing that the first is to be divided by the second, as in $6 ÷ 3 = 2$.
□ **divisional** adjective.

divisive ▸ adjective causing disagreement or hostility between people.

divorce ▸ noun the legal ending of a marriage.

SYNONYMS **1** *she wants a divorce* **dissolution**, annulment, decree nisi, separation. **2** *a growing divorce between the church and people* **separation**, division, split, disunity, alienation, schism, gulf.
ANTONYMS unity.

▸ verb (**divorces**, **divorcing**, **divorced**) **1** legally end your marriage with. **2** (**divorce something from**) separate something from.

SYNONYMS **1** *her parents have divorced* **split up**, get a divorce, separate, end your marriage. **2** *religion cannot be divorced from morality* **separate**, divide, detach, isolate, alienate, set apart, cut off.

divorcee ▸ noun a divorced person.

divot /di-vuht/ ▸ noun a piece of turf cut out of the ground.

divulge ▸ verb (**divulges**, **divulging**, **divulged**) reveal information.

SYNONYMS **disclose**, reveal, tell, communicate, pass on, publish, give away, let slip.
ANTONYMS conceal.

Diwali (or **Divali**) /di-wah-li/ ▸ noun a Hindu festival at which lights, candles, etc. are lit, held in October and November.

DIY ▸ abbreviation Brit. do it yourself.

dizzy ▸ adjective (**dizzier**, **dizziest**) having a sensation of spinning around and losing your balance.

SYNONYMS **giddy**, light-headed, faint, unsteady, shaky, muzzy, wobbly; informal woozy.

▸ verb (**dizzies**, **dizzying**, **dizzied**) make unsteady or confused.
□ **dizzily** adverb **dizziness** noun.

DJ ▸ noun a person who introduces and plays recorded pop music on radio or at a club.

DNA ▸ noun a substance carrying genetic information that is found in the cells of nearly all animals and plants.
ORIGIN short for *deoxyribonucleic acid.*

do ▸ verb (**does**, **doing**, **did**; past participle **done**) **1** carry out or complete an action, duty, or task. **2** have a specified amount of success: *the team did well.* **3** make or provide something. **4** have a particular result or effect on. **5** work at for a living or take as a subject of study. **6** be suitable or acceptable. **7** informal swindle someone.

SYNONYMS **1** *she does most of the work* **carry out**, undertake, discharge, execute, perform, accomplish, achieve, bring about, engineer; informal pull off. **2** *they can do as they please* **act**, behave, conduct yourself. **3** *regular coffee will do* **suffice**, be adequate, be satisfactory, fill/fit the bill, serve. **4** *a portrait I am doing* **make**, create, produce, work on, design, manufacture.

▸ auxiliary verb **1** used before a verb in questions and negative statements. **2** used to refer back to a verb already mentioned. **3** used in commands, or to give emphasis to a verb.

▸ noun (plural **dos** or **do's**) Brit. informal a party or other social event.
■ **do away with** informal put an end to or kill. **do something up 1** fasten or wrap something. **2** informal renovate or redecorate a room or building.

Dobermann (or **Dobermann pinscher**) /doh-ber-muhn, pin-sher/ ▸ noun a large breed of dog with strong jaws.

docile ▸ adjective quiet and easy to control.
□ **docilely** adverb **docility** noun.

d

dock¹ ▸ noun an enclosed area of water in a port for loading, unloading, and repairing ships.

> SYNONYMS *his boat was moored at the dock* **harbour,** marina, port, wharf, quay, pier, jetty, landing stage.

▸ verb **1** (of a ship) come into a dock. **2** (of a spacecraft) join with a space station or another spacecraft in space.

> SYNONYMS *the ship docked* **moor,** berth, put in, tie up, anchor.

dock² ▸ noun the enclosure in a criminal court for a person on trial.

dock³ ▸ noun a weed with broad leaves.

dock⁴ ▸ verb **1** take away money from a person's wages before they are paid. **2** cut short an animal's tail.

docker ▸ noun a person employed in a port to load and unload ships.

docket ▸ noun Brit. a document accompanying a batch of goods that lists its contents, shows that duty has been paid, etc.

dockyard ▸ noun an area with docks and equipment for repairing and building ships.

doctor ▸ noun **1** a person who is qualified to practise medicine. **2** (Doctor) a person who holds the highest university degree.

> SYNONYMS **physician,** medical practitioner, general practitioner, GP, clinician, consultant; informal doc, medic.

▸ verb **1** change something in order to deceive people. **2** add a harmful or strong ingredient to food or drink. **3** Brit. remove the sexual organs of an animal.

> SYNONYMS **1** *he doctored Stephen's drink* **adulterate,** tamper with, lace; informal spike. **2** *the reports have been doctored* **falsify,** tamper with, interfere with, alter, change, forge, fake; Brit. informal fiddle.

doctoral ▸ adjective relating to a doctorate.

doctorate ▸ noun the highest degree awarded by a university.

doctrinaire ▸ adjective very strict in applying beliefs or principles.

doctrine /dok-trin/ ▸ noun a set of beliefs or principles held by a religious or political group.

> SYNONYMS **creed,** credo, dogma, belief, teaching, ideology, tenet, maxim, canon, principle.

□ **doctrinal** /dok-try-n'l/ adjective.

document ▸ noun a piece of written, printed, or electronic material that provides information or evidence.

> SYNONYMS *a legal document* **paper,** certificate, deed, form, contract, agreement, report, record.

▸ verb record something in written or other form.

> SYNONYMS *its history is well documented* **record,** register, report, log, chronicle, authenticate, verify.

documentary ▸ noun (plural **documentaries**) a film or television or radio programme giving a factual report, using film, photographs, and sound recordings of real events.

▸ adjective consisting of documents: *documentary evidence.*

documentation ▸ noun documents providing official information, evidence, or instructions.

dodder ▸ verb be slow and unsteady. □ **doddery** adjective.

doddle ▸ noun Brit. informal a very easy task.

dodecagon /doh-**dek**-uh-guhn/ ▸ noun a figure with twelve straight sides and angles.

dodecahedron /doh-dek-uh-**hee**-druhn/ ▸ noun (plural **dodecahedra** or **dodecahedrons**) a three-dimensional shape with twelve faces.

dodge ▸ verb (**dodges, dodging, dodged**) **1** avoid something by a sudden quick movement. **2** avoid something in a cunning or dishonest way.

> SYNONYMS **1** *he could easily dodge the two coppers* **elude,** evade, avoid, escape, run away from, lose, shake (off); informal give someone the slip. **2** *the minister tried to dodge the debate* **avoid,** evade, get out of, back out of, sidestep; informal duck, wriggle out of. **3** *she dodged into a telephone booth* **dart,** bolt, dive, slip.

▸ noun an act of avoiding something.

> SYNONYMS *a clever dodge | a tax dodge* **ruse,** ploy, scheme, tactic, stratagem, subterfuge, trick, hoax, cheat, deception, fraud; informal scam; Brit. informal wheeze; Austral. informal lurk, rort.

□ **dodger** noun.

dodgem ▸ noun a small electric car driven at a funfair with the aim of bumping other such cars.

dodgy ▸ adjective Brit. informal **1** dishonest. **2** risky. **3** not good or reliable.

dodo ▸ noun (plural **dodos** or **dodoes**) a large extinct bird that could not fly, formerly found on Mauritius.

doe ▸ noun **1** a female deer or reindeer. **2** the female of some other animals, such as a rabbit or hare.

does 3rd person singular present of **DO**.

doesn't ▸ short form does not.

doff ▸ verb remove your hat when greeting someone.

dog ▸ noun **1** a four-legged meat-eating animal, kept as a pet or used for work or hunting. **2** any member of the dog family, such as the wolf or fox. **3** the male of an animal of the dog family.

SYNONYMS **hound,** canine, man's best friend; informal pooch, mutt; Austral. informal bitzer.

▸ verb (**dogs, dogging, dogged**) **1** follow someone closely and persistently. **2** cause continual trouble for.

SYNONYMS *the scheme was dogged by bad weather* **plague,** beset, bedevil, blight, trouble.

■ **a dog in the manger** a person who stops other people having things that they do not need themselves. **dog collar** informal a white upright collar worn by Christian priests. **dog-eared** (of a book) having the corners of the pages curled or folded over from constant use. **dog-end** informal a cigarette end. **dog-leg** a sharp bend. **go to the dogs** informal get much worse.

doge /dohj/ ▸ noun (in the past) the chief magistrate of Venice or Genoa.

dogfight ▸ noun a close combat between military aircraft.

dogfish ▸ noun (plural **dogfish** or **dogfishes**) a small shark with a long tail.

dogged /dog-gid/ ▸ adjective very persistent.

SYNONYMS **tenacious,** determined, resolute, stubborn, obstinate, purposeful, persistent, persevering, single-minded, tireless.
ANTONYMS half-hearted, tentative.

□ **doggedly** adverb.

doggerel ▸ noun badly written verse.

doggo ▸ adverb (**lie doggo**) informal hide by keeping still and quiet.

doggy-paddle ▸ noun a simple swimming stroke like that of a dog.

doghouse ▸ noun N. Amer. a dog's kennel.
■ **in the doghouse** informal in disgrace.

dogma ▸ noun a firm set of principles.

dogmatic ▸ adjective firmly putting forward your own opinions and not willing to accept those of other people.

SYNONYMS **opinionated,** assertive, insistent, emphatic, adamant, doctrinaire, authoritarian, imperious, dictatorial, uncompromising.

□ **dogmatically** adverb.

dogsbody ▸ noun (plural **dogsbodies**) Brit. informal a person who is given boring tasks that no one else wants to do.

doily ▸ noun (plural **doilies**) a small decorative mat made of lace or paper.

doings ▸ plural noun a person's actions or activities.

doldrums ▸ plural noun (**the doldrums**) a state of being inactive or feeling depressed.

dole ▸ noun Brit. informal money paid by the state to unemployed people.
▸ verb (**doles, doling, doled**) (**dole something out**) distribute something.

SYNONYMS *waitresses doled out plates of chicken* **distribute,** share out, divide up, allocate, deal out, dispense, hand out, give out, dish up.

doleful ▸ adjective sad or depressing.
□ **dolefully** adverb.

doll ▸ noun a small model of a human figure, used as a child's toy.
▸ verb (**be dolled up**) informal be dressed in smart or fancy clothes.

dollar ▸ noun the chief unit of money in the US, Canada, Australia, and some other countries.

dollop informal ▸ noun a shapeless mass or lump.
▸ verb (**dollops, dolloping, dolloped**) casually add or serve out a mass of something.

dolmen ▸ noun a prehistoric tomb with a large flat stone laid on upright ones.

dolomite /dol-uh-myt/ ▸ noun a mineral or rock that consists of a carbonate of calcium and magnesium.

dolour /dol-er/ (US spelling dolor) ▸ noun literary great sorrow or distress.
□ **dolorous** adjective.

dolphin ▸ noun a small whale with a beak-like snout and a curved fin on the back.

dolphinarium ▸ noun (plural **dolphinariums** or **dolphinaria**) an aquarium in which dolphins are kept and trained for public entertainment.

dolt ▸ noun a stupid person.

domain ▸ noun **1** an area controlled by a ruler or government. **2** an area of activity or knowledge. **3** a set of websites whose addresses end with the same group of letters.

SYNONYMS **1** *they extended their domain* **realm,** kingdom, empire, dominion, province, territory, land. **2** *the domain of art* **field,** area, sphere, discipline, province, world.

dome ▸ noun **1** a rounded roof with a circular base. **2** a stadium or other building with a rounded roof.
□ **domed** adjective.

domestic ▸ adjective **1** relating to a home or family. **2** for use in the home. **3** (of an animal) tame and kept by humans. **4** existing or occurring within a country; not foreign.

SYNONYMS **1** *domestic commitments* **family,** home, household. **2** *she was not* at all *domestic* **domesticated,** homely, home-loving. **3** *small domestic animals* **tame,** pet, domesticated, household. **4** *the domestic car industry* **national,** state, home, internal.

□ **domestically** adverb.

domesticate ▸ verb (**domesticates, domesticating, domesticated**) tame an animal and keep it as a pet or on a farm.
□ **domestication** noun.

domesticity ▸ noun home life.

domicile /dom-i-syl/ formal or Law ▸ noun **1** the country in which a person lives permanently. **2** a person's home.
▸ verb (**be domiciled**) be living in a particular country or place.

dominant ▸ adjective **1** most important, powerful, or influential. **2** (of a gene) appearing in offspring even if a contrary gene is also inherited.

SYNONYMS **1** *the dominant classes* **ruling,** governing, controlling, presiding, commanding. **2** *he has a dominant personality* **assertive,** authoritative, forceful, domineering, commanding, controlling, pushy. **3** *the dominant issues in psychology* **main,** principal, prime, chief, primary, central, key, crucial, core.
ANTONYMS subservient, subsidiary.

□ **dominance** noun **dominantly** adverb.

dominate ▸ verb (**dominates, dominating, dominated**) **1** have a very strong influence over. **2** be the most important or noticeable person or thing in.

SYNONYMS **1** *the Russians dominated Iran in the nineteenth century* **control,** influence, command, be in charge of, rule, govern, direct. **2** *the village is dominated by the viaduct* **overlook,** command, tower above/over, loom over.

domination ▸ noun the state of dominating.

SYNONYMS **control,** power, command, authority, dominion, rule, supremacy, superiority, ascendancy, sway.

domineering ▸ adjective arrogantly trying to control other people.

dominion ▸ noun **1** supreme power or control. **2** the territory of a ruler or government.

domino ▸ noun (plural **dominoes**) any of twenty-eight small oblong pieces marked with 0–6 pips in each half, used in the game of dominoes.

don¹ ▸ noun a university teacher.

don² ▸ verb (**dons, donning, donned**) put on an item of clothing.

SYNONYMS **put on,** get dressed in, dress (yourself) in, get into, slip into/on, change into.

donate ▸ verb (**donates, donating, donated**) give something to a charity or other good cause.

SYNONYMS **give,** contribute, gift, subscribe, grant, present, endow.

donation ▸ noun something given to a charity or other good cause.

SYNONYMS **gift,** contribution, subscription, present, handout, grant, offering.

done past participle of **DO.**
▸ adjective **1** cooked thoroughly. **2** no longer happening or existing. **3** informal socially acceptable: *the done thing.*

doner kebab /doh-ner, don-er/ ▸ noun a Turkish dish of spiced lamb cooked on a spit and served in slices.

donkey ▸ noun (plural **donkeys**) a domesticated animal of the horse family with long ears and a braying call.
■ **donkey jacket** Brit. a heavy jacket with a patch of waterproof material across the shoulders. **donkey's years** informal a very long time.

donor ▸ noun a person who donates something.

SYNONYMS **giver,** contributor, benefactor, benefactress, subscriber, supporter, backer, patron, sponsor.
ANTONYMS beneficiary.

don't ▸ short form do not.

donut US spelling of **DOUGHNUT.**

doodle ▸ verb (**doodles, doodling, doodled**) scribble absent-mindedly.
▸ noun a drawing made absent-mindedly.

doom ▸ noun death, destruction, or another terrible fate.

SYNONYMS *prepare to meet your doom* **destruction,** downfall, ruin, extinction, annihilation, death, nemesis.

▸ verb (**be doomed**) be fated to fail or be destroyed.

SYNONYMS **1** (doomed) **ill-fated,** ill-starred, cursed, jinxed, damned. **2** (doomed) *they were doomed to die* **destine,** fate, predestine, preordain, mean, condemn, sentence.

doomsday ▸ noun **1** the last day of the world's existence. **2** (in religious belief) the day of the Last Judgement.

door ▸ noun a movable barrier at the entrance to a building, room, vehicle, etc.
■ **out of doors** in or into the open air.

doorman ▸ noun (plural **doormen**) a man who is on duty at the entrance to a large building.

doormat ▸ noun **1** a mat placed in a doorway for wiping your shoes. **2** informal a person who lets other people control them.

d

doorstep ▶ noun a step leading up to the outer door of a house.

doorstop ▶ noun an object that keeps a door open or in place.

doorway ▶ noun an entrance with a door.

dope ▶ noun 1 informal an illegal drug, especially cannabis. 2 a drug used to improve the performance of an athlete, racehorse, or greyhound. 3 informal a stupid person.
▶ verb (dopes, doping, doped) give a drug to.

SYNONYMS 1 *the horse was doped* **drug**, tamper with, interfere with, sedate; Brit. informal nobble. 2 *they doped his drink* **add drugs to**, tamper with, adulterate, lace; informal spike, doctor.

dopey (or **dopy**) ▶ adjective informal 1 in a semi-conscious state from sleepiness or a drug. 2 stupid.

doppelgänger /dop-puhl-gang-er/ ▶ noun a ghost or double of a living person.

Doppler effect ▶ noun an apparent change in the frequency of sound or light waves as the source and the observer move towards or away from each other.

dormant ▶ adjective 1 (of an animal) in a deep sleep. 2 (of a plant or bud) alive but not growing. 3 (of a volcano) temporarily inactive.
□ **dormancy** noun.

dormer window ▶ noun a window set vertically into a sloping roof.

dormitory ▶ noun (plural **dormitories**) a bedroom for a number of people in an institution.
▶ adjective (of a town) from which people travel to work in a nearby city.

dormouse ▶ noun (plural **dormice**) a small mouse-like rodent with a bushy tail.

dorsal ▶ adjective relating to the upper side or back.

dose ▶ noun 1 a quantity of a medicine taken at one time. 2 an amount of radiation absorbed at one time.

SYNONYMS *a dose of medicine* **measure**, portion, draught, dosage.

▶ verb (doses, dosing, dosed) give a dose of medicine to.

SYNONYMS *he dosed himself with vitamins* **drug**, fill (up), pump, prime, load, stuff, cram.

□ **dosage** noun.

dosh ▶ noun Brit. informal money.

doss ▶ verb Brit. informal 1 sleep in an uncomfortable place or without a proper bed. 2 spend time in a lazy or aimless way.
□ **dosser** noun.

dossier /doss-i-er, doss-i-ay/ ▶ noun a collection of documents about a person or subject.

dot ▶ noun a small round mark or spot.

SYNONYMS *a pattern of dots* **spot**, speck, fleck, speckle, full stop, decimal point.

▶ verb (dots, dotting, dotted) 1 mark with a dot or dots. 2 cover an area with a scattering of something.

SYNONYMS 1 *spots of rain dotted his shirt* **spot**, fleck, mark, spatter. 2 *restaurants are dotted around the site* **scatter**, pepper, sprinkle, strew, spread.

■ **dot-com** a company that carries out its business on the Internet. **on the dot** informal exactly on time.

dotage /doh-tij/ ▶ noun the period of life in which a person is old and weak.

dote ▶ verb (dotes, doting, doted) (**dote on**) love someone very much, ignoring their faults.

SYNONYMS *his grandmother dotes on him* **adore**, love dearly, be devoted to, idolize, treasure, cherish, worship.

dotty ▶ adjective Brit. informal slightly mad or eccentric.

double ▶ adjective 1 consisting of two equal, identical, or similar parts or things. 2 having twice the usual size, quantity, or strength. 3 designed to be used by two people. 4 having two different roles or meanings.

SYNONYMS *a double garage* **dual**, duplex, twin, binary, duplicate, coupled, matching, twofold, in pairs.
ANTONYMS single.

▶ adverb twice the amount or quantity.
▶ noun 1 a thing which is twice as large as usual or is made up of two parts. 2 a person who looks exactly like another. 3 (**doubles**) a game involving sides made up of two players.

SYNONYMS *it must be her double* **lookalike**, twin, clone, duplicate, exact likeness, replica, copy, facsimile, Doppelgänger; informal spitting image, dead ringer.

▶ verb (doubles, doubling, doubled) 1 make or become double. 2 fold or bend over on itself. 3 (**double up**) curl up with pain or laughter. 4 (**double as**) be used in or play a different role.

■ **at the double** very fast. **double agent** an agent who pretends to act as a spy for one country while in fact acting for its enemy. **double back** go back in the direction you have come from. **double-barrelled** Brit. (of a surname) having two parts joined by a hyphen. **double bass** the largest and lowest-pitched instrument of the violin family. **double-breasted** (of a jacket or coat) having a large overlap at the front and two rows of buttons. **double chin** a roll of flesh below a person's chin. **double cream** Brit. thick cream

d

with a high fat content. **double-cross** betray or deceive a person that you are supposed to be helping. **double-dealing** deceitful behaviour. **double-decker** a bus with two floors. **double Dutch** Brit. informal language that is hard to understand. **double glazing** windows having two layers of glass with a space between them. **double-jointed** (of a person) having unusually flexible joints. **double standard** a rule or principle applied unfairly in different ways to different people. **double take** a second reaction to something unexpected, immediately after your first one.
□ **doubly** adverb.

double entendre /doo-b'l on-**ton**-druh/ ▶ noun (plural **double entendres** /doo-b'l on-**ton**-druh/) a word or phrase with two meanings, one of which is usually rude.

doublet ▶ noun historical a man's short close-fitting padded jacket.

doubloon /dub-**loon**/ ▶ noun historical a Spanish gold coin.

doubt ▶ noun a feeling of uncertainty.

SYNONYMS **1** *there was some doubt as to the caller's identity* **uncertainty,** confusion, controversy. **2** *a weak leader racked by doubt* **indecision,** hesitation, uncertainty, insecurity, hesitancy, vacillation. **3** *there is doubt about their motives* **scepticism,** distrust, mistrust, suspicion, cynicism, wariness, reservations, misgivings, suspicions. ANTONYMS certainty, conviction, trust.

▶ verb **1** feel uncertain about something. **2** disbelieve or mistrust someone.

SYNONYMS *they doubted my story* **disbelieve,** distrust, mistrust, suspect, be suspicious of, have misgivings about. ANTONYMS trust.

■ **no doubt** certainly; probably.

doubtful ▶ adjective **1** feeling uncertain. **2** causing uncertainty. **3** not likely or probable.

SYNONYMS **1** *I was doubtful about going* **hesitant,** in doubt, unsure, uncertain, in two minds, in a quandary, in a dilemma. **2** *it is doubtful whether he will come* **in doubt,** uncertain, open to question, unsure, debatable, up in the air. **3** *the whole trip is looking rather doubtful* **unlikely,** improbable. **4** *they are doubtful of the methods used* **distrustful,** mistrustful, suspicious, wary, chary, leery, sceptical. **5** *this decision is of doubtful validity* **questionable,** arguable, debatable, controversial, contentious. ANTONYMS confident, certain, probable, trusting.

□ **doubtfully** adverb.

doubtless ▶ adverb very probably.

SYNONYMS **undoubtedly,** no doubt, unquestionably, indisputably, undeniably, certainly, surely, of course.

douche /doosh/ ▶ noun a jet of water applied to part of the body.

dough ▶ noun **1** a thick mixture of flour and liquid, for baking into bread or pastry. **2** informal money.
□ **doughy** adjective.

doughnut (US spelling donut) ▶ noun a small fried cake or ring of sweetened dough.

doughty /**dow**-ti/ ▶ adjective old use brave and determined.

dour /doo-er, dow-er/ ▶ adjective very severe, stern, or gloomy.

douse ▶ verb (douses, dousing, doused) **1** drench with liquid. **2** extinguish a fire.

SYNONYMS **1** *a mob doused the thieves with petrol* **drench,** soak, saturate, wet. **2** *a guard doused the flames* **extinguish,** put out, quench, smother.

dove[1] /duv/ ▶ noun **1** a bird with a cooing voice, very similar to a pigeon. **2** (in politics) a person who is in favour of a policy of peace and negotiation.

dove[2] US past and past participle of DIVE.

dovecote (or dovecot) /**duv**-kot/ ▶ noun a shelter with nest holes for domesticated pigeons.

dovetail ▶ verb fit together neatly.
▶ noun a wedge-shaped joint formed by interlocking two pieces of wood.

dowager /**dow**-uh-jer/ ▶ noun **1** a widow who holds a title that belonged to her late husband. **2** a dignified elderly woman.

dowdy ▶ adjective unfashionable and dull in appearance.

dowel ▶ noun a peg used to hold together parts of a structure.

down[1] ▶ adverb **1** towards, in, or at a lower place, position, or level. **2** to a smaller amount or size. **3** in or into a weaker or worse position or condition. **4** away from a central place or the north. **5** from an earlier to a later point in time or order. **6** in or into writing. **7** (of a computer system) out of action.
▶ preposition **1** from a higher to a lower point of. **2** at or to a point further along the course of.
▶ adjective **1** directed or moving downwards. **2** unhappy or depressed.
▶ verb informal drink something quickly.
■ **down and out** homeless and without money. **down at heel** shabby because of a lack of money. **down payment** an initial payment made when buying something on credit. **down-to-earth** practical and realistic. **down under** informal Australia and New Zealand.

down[2] ▸ noun fine, soft feathers or hairs.

downbeat ▸ adjective **1** gloomy. **2** relaxed and low-key.

downcast ▸ adjective **1** (of eyes) looking downwards. **2** unhappy; discouraged.

downer ▸ noun informal **1** a tranquillizing or depressant drug. **2** a depressing experience.

downfall ▸ noun a loss of power, wealth, or status.

> SYNONYMS **ruin,** ruination, undoing, defeat, overthrow, destruction, annihilation, end, collapse, fall, crash, failure.
> ANTONYMS rise.

downgrade ▸ verb (**downgrades, downgrading, downgraded**) bring someone down to a lower rank or level of importance.

> SYNONYMS **demote,** reduce, relegate.
> ANTONYMS promote.

downhearted ▸ adjective unhappy; discouraged.

downhill ▸ adverb & adjective **1** towards the bottom of a slope. **2** into a steadily worsening situation.

download ▸ verb copy data from one computer system to another.
▸ noun data that has been downloaded.

downmarket ▸ adjective chiefly Brit. cheap and of low quality.

downplay ▸ verb make something appear less important than it really is.

downpour ▸ noun a heavy fall of rain.

downright ▸ adjective utter; complete.

> SYNONYMS *downright lies* **complete,** total, absolute, utter, thorough, out-and-out, outright, sheer, arrant, pure.

▸ adverb extremely.

> SYNONYMS *that's downright dangerous* **thoroughly,** utterly, positively, profoundly, really, completely, totally, entirely.

downs ▸ noun gently rolling hills.

downshift ▸ verb change to a job or way of life that is simpler and less stressful.

downside ▸ noun the negative aspect of something.

Down's syndrome ▸ noun a medical condition in which a person is born with physical abnormalities and an intellectual ability that is lower than average.

downstairs ▸ adverb & adjective on or to a lower floor.

downstream (or **downriver**) ▸ adverb in the direction in which a stream or river flows.

downtown ▸ adjective & adverb chiefly N. Amer. in, to, or towards the central or main business area of a city.

downtrodden ▸ adjective treated badly by those in power.

downward ▸ adjective & adverb towards a lower point or level.
▫ **downwards** adverb.

downwind ▸ adverb in the direction in which the wind is blowing.

downy ▸ adjective covered with fine soft hair or feathers.

dowry ▸ noun (plural **dowries**) property or money brought by a bride to her husband on their marriage.

dowse ▸ verb (**dowses, dowsing, dowsed**) search for underground water or minerals with a pointer which is supposedly moved by unseen influences.

doyen /doy-yen/ ▸ noun (feminine **doyenne** /doy-**yen**/) the most respected or prominent person in a field.

doze ▸ verb (**dozes, dozing, dozed**) sleep lightly.
▸ noun a short, light sleep.
▫ **dozy** adjective.

dozen ▸ noun **1** (plural **dozen**) a group or set of twelve. **2** (**dozens**) a lot.

DPhil ▸ abbreviation Doctor of Philosophy.

Dr ▸ abbreviation Doctor.

drab ▸ adjective (**drabber, drabbest**) dull and uninteresting.

> SYNONYMS **1** *a drab interior* **colourless,** grey, dull, washed out, dingy, dreary, dismal, cheerless, gloomy, sombre. **2** *a drab existence* **uninteresting,** dull, boring, tedious, monotonous, dry, dreary.
> ANTONYMS bright, cheerful, interesting.

▫ **drabness** noun.

drachma /drak-muh/ ▸ noun (plural **drachmas** or **drachmae** /drak-mee/) the former basic unit of money in Greece.

draconian /druh-koh-ni-uhn/ ▸ adjective (of laws) very harsh and severe.

draft ▸ noun **1** a rough early version of a piece of writing. **2** a written order requesting a bank to pay a specific sum of money. **3** (**the draft**) US compulsory recruitment for military service. **4** US spelling of DRAUGHT.

> SYNONYMS **1** *the first draft of his speech* **version,** sketch, attempt, effort, outline, plan. **2** *a banker's draft* **cheque,** order, money order, bill of exchange.

▸ verb **1** prepare a rough version of a piece of writing. **2** select someone for a particular purpose. **3** (**be drafted**) US recruit someone for compulsory military service.

drafty US spelling of DRAUGHTY.

drag ▸ verb (**drags, dragging, dragged**) **1** pull along forcefully, roughly, or with difficulty. **2** trail along the ground. **3** (of time) pass slowly. **4** (**drag something out**)

d

make something last longer than necessary. **5** move an image across a computer screen using a mouse. **6** search the bottom of an area of water with hooks or nets.

> SYNONYMS *she dragged the chair backwards* **haul**, pull, tug, heave, lug, draw, trail.

▶ noun **1** informal a boring or annoying person or thing. **2** a person or thing that makes progress difficult. **3** informal an act of inhaling smoke from a cigarette. **4** the force exerted by air or water to slow down a moving object.

> SYNONYMS **1** *work can be a drag* **bore**, nuisance, bother, trouble, pest, annoyance, trial; informal pain (in the neck), bind, headache, hassle. **2** *the drag from the parachute* **pull**, resistance, tug.

■ **drag race** a short race between two cars from a standstill. **in drag** (of a man) wearing women's clothes.

dragnet ▶ noun a net drawn through water or across ground to trap fish or game.

dragon ▶ noun a mythical monster that can breathe out fire.

dragonfly ▶ noun (plural **dragonflies**) an insect with a long body and two pairs of large transparent wings.

dragoon ▶ noun a member of any of several British cavalry regiments.
▶ verb force someone into doing something.

drain ▶ verb **1** make something empty or dry by removing the liquid from it. **2** (of liquid) run off or out. **3** make someone feel weak or tired. **4** use up a resource. **5** drink the entire contents of a glass or cup.

> SYNONYMS **1** *a valve for draining the tank* **empty (out)**, void, clear (out), evacuate, unload. **2** *drain off any surplus liquid* **draw off**, extract, siphon off, pour out, pour off, bleed, tap, filter, discharge. **3** *the water drained away to the sea* **flow**, pour, trickle, stream, run, rush, gush, flood, surge, leak, ooze, seep, dribble. **4** *more people would just drain our resources* **use up**, exhaust, deplete, consume, expend, get through, sap, milk, bleed. **5** *he drained his drink* **drink (up/down)**, gulp (down), guzzle, quaff, swallow, finish off, toss off; informal sink, down, swig, swill (down), knock back.
> ANTONYMS fill.

▶ noun **1** a channel or pipe for carrying off rainwater or liquid waste. **2** a thing that uses up a resource or strength.

> SYNONYMS **1** *the drain filled with water* **sewer**, channel, ditch, culvert, duct, pipe, gutter. **2** *a drain on the battery* **strain**, pressure, burden, load, demand.

■ **draining board** Brit. a surface next to a sink, on which crockery is left after it has been washed.

□ **drainage** noun.

drainpipe ▶ noun **1** a pipe for carrying off rainwater from a building. **2** (**drainpipes**) trousers with very narrow legs.

drake ▶ noun a male duck.

dram ▶ noun a small drink of spirits.

drama ▶ noun **1** a play. **2** plays as a literary form. **3** an exciting series of events.

> SYNONYMS **1** *a television drama* **play**, show, piece, theatrical work, stage show, dramatization. **2** *he is studying drama* **acting**, the theatre, the stage, dramatic art, stagecraft, dramaturgy. **3** *she liked to create a drama* **incident**, scene, spectacle, crisis, disturbance, row, commotion, excitement, thrill, sensation, dramatics, theatrics, histrionics.

dramatic ▶ adjective **1** relating to drama. **2** sudden and striking. **3** exciting or impressive.

> SYNONYMS **1** *dramatic art* **theatrical**, thespian, stage, dramaturgical. **2** *a dramatic increase* **considerable**, substantial, significant, remarkable, extraordinary, exceptional, phenomenal. **3** *there were dramatic scenes in the city* **exciting**, stirring, action-packed, sensational, spectacular, startling, unexpected, tense, gripping, riveting, thrilling, hair-raising, lively. **4** *dramatic headlands* **striking**, impressive, imposing, spectacular, breathtaking, dazzling, sensational, awesome, awe-inspiring, remarkable. **5** *a dramatic gesture* **exaggerated**, theatrical, ostentatious, actressy, stagy, showy, melodramatic.
> ANTONYMS insignificant, boring, unremarkable, unimposing, restrained.

▶ noun (**dramatics**) the practice of acting in and presenting plays.
□ **dramatically** adverb.

dramatist ▶ noun a person who writes plays.

dramatize (or **dramatise**) ▶ verb (**dramatizes, dramatizing, dramatized**) **1** present a novel or story as a play. **2** make something seem more exciting or serious than it really is.

> SYNONYMS **1** *the novel was dramatized for television* **turn into a play/film**, adapt (for the stage/screen). **2** *the tabloids dramatized the event* **exaggerate**, overdo, overstate, hyperbolize, magnify, amplify, inflate, sensationalize, embroider, colour, aggrandize, embellish, elaborate; informal blow up (out of all proportion).

□ **dramatization** noun.

drank past of DRINK.

drape ▶ verb (**drapes, draping, draped**) **1** arrange cloth or clothing loosely on or round something. **2** rest part of your body on something in a relaxed way.

> SYNONYMS **wrap**, cover, envelop, shroud, wind, swathe, festoon, hang.

▶ noun (**drapes**) N. Amer. long curtains.

draper ▶ noun Brit. dated a person who sells fabrics.

drapery ▶ noun (plural **draperies**) curtains or fabric hanging in loose folds.

drastic ▶ adjective having a strong or far-reaching effect.

> SYNONYMS **extreme**, serious, desperate, radical, far-reaching, momentous, substantial.
> ANTONYMS moderate.

◻ **drastically** adverb.

draught (US spelling **draft**) ▶ noun **1** a current of cool air indoors. **2** an act of drinking or breathing in. **3** old use a quantity of a medicinal liquid. **4** the depth of water needed to float a particular ship. **5** (**draughts**) Brit. a game played on a chequered board.

> SYNONYMS **1** *the draught made Robin shiver* **current of air,** wind, breeze, gust, puff, waft. **2** *a draught of beer* **gulp,** drink, swallow, mouthful; informal swig.

▶ verb = **DRAFT**.
▶ adjective **1** (of beer) served from a cask. **2** (of an animal) used for pulling heavy loads.

draughtsman ▶ noun (plural **draughtsmen**) **1** a person who makes detailed technical plans or drawings. **2** an artist skilled in drawing.

draughty (US spelling **drafty**) ▶ adjective uncomfortable because of draughts of cold air.

draw ▶ verb (**draws, drawing, drew**; past participle **drawn**) **1** produce a picture or diagram by making lines and marks on paper. **2** pull or drag a vehicle. **3** move in a particular direction. **4** pull curtains shut or open. **5** arrive at a point in time. **6** take from a container or source. **7** be the cause of a particular response. **8** attract people to a place or an event. **9** persuade someone to reveal something. **10** reach a conclusion. **11** finish a contest or game with an even score. **12** take in a breath.

> SYNONYMS **1** *he drew the house* **sketch,** outline, rough out, illustrate, render, represent, trace, portray, depict. **2** *she drew her chair in to the table* **pull,** haul, drag, tug, heave, lug, tow; informal yank. **3** *the train drew into the station* **move,** go, come, proceed, progress, pass, drive, inch, roll, glide, cruise, sweep. **4** *he drew his gun* **pull out,** take out, produce, fish out, extract, withdraw, unsheathe. **5** *she drew huge audiences* **attract,** win,

capture, catch, engage, lure, entice, bring in.

▶ noun **1** a game or match that ends with the scores even. **2** an act of choosing names at random for prizes, sports fixtures, etc. **3** a person or thing that is very attractive or interesting. **4** an act of inhaling smoke from a cigarette.

> SYNONYMS **1** *the match ended in a draw* **tie,** dead heat, stalemate. **2** *she won the Christmas draw* **raffle,** lottery, sweepstake, sweep, tombola, ballot. **3** *the draw of central London* **attraction,** lure, allure, pull, appeal, temptation, charm, fascination.

■ **draw the line at** refuse to do or tolerate. **draw something out** make something last longer. **draw up** (of a vehicle) come to a halt. **draw something up** prepare a plan or document.

> ❗ Don't confuse **draw** with **drawer**, which means 'a sliding storage compartment'.

drawback ▶ noun a disadvantage or problem.

> SYNONYMS **disadvantage**, snag, downside, stumbling block, catch, hitch, pitfall, fly in the ointment, weak spot/point, weakness, imperfection; informal minus.
> ANTONYMS benefit.

drawbridge ▶ noun a bridge which is hinged at one end so that it can be raised.

drawer ▶ noun **1** a compartment for storage that slides horizontally in and out of a desk or chest. **2** (**drawers**) dated knickers or underpants. **3** a person who draws something.

drawing ▶ noun a picture or diagram made with a pencil, pen, or crayon.

> SYNONYMS **sketch**, picture, illustration, representation, portrayal, depiction, diagram, outline.

■ **drawing pin** Brit. a short flat-headed pin for fastening paper to a surface. **drawing room** a sitting room.

drawl ▶ verb speak in a slow, lazy way with long vowel sounds.
▶ noun a drawling accent.

drawn past participle of **DRAW**.
▶ adjective looking strained from illness or exhaustion.

drawstring ▶ noun a string in the seam of a garment or bag, which can be pulled to tighten or close it.

dray ▶ noun a low truck or cart for delivering barrels or other loads.

dread ▶ verb think about something with great fear or anxiety.

> SYNONYMS *I used to dread going to school* **fear,** be afraid of, worry about, be

anxious about, shudder at the thought of.
ANTONYMS look forward to.

▶ noun great fear or anxiety.

SYNONYMS *she was filled with dread* **fear**, apprehension, trepidation, anxiety, panic, alarm, terror, disquiet, unease.
ANTONYMS confidence.

dreadful ▶ adjective **1** very bad or serious. **2** used for emphasis: *he's a dreadful flirt.*

SYNONYMS **1** *a dreadful accident* **terrible**, frightful, horrible, grim, awful, horrifying, shocking, distressing, appalling, harrowing, ghastly, fearful, horrendous, tragic. **2** *a dreadful meal* **very bad,** frightful, shocking, awful, abysmal, atrocious, disgraceful, deplorable; informal woeful, rotten, lousy, ropy; Brit. informal duff, rubbish. **3** *you're a dreadful flirt* **outrageous**, shocking, real, awful, terrible, inordinate, incorrigible, quite a.
ANTONYMS pleasant, wonderful, excellent, no.

□ **dreadfully** adverb.

dreadlocks ▶ plural noun a Rastafarian hairstyle in which the hair is twisted into tight braids or ringlets.

dream ▶ noun **1** a series of images and feelings that happen in your mind while you are asleep. **2** an ambition or wish. **3** informal a wonderful or perfect person or thing.

SYNONYMS **1** *she went around in a dream* **daydream**, reverie, trance, daze, stupor. **2** *he realized his childhood dream* **ambition**, aspiration, hope, goal, aim, objective, intention, desire, wish, daydream, fantasy. **3** *he's an absolute dream* **delight**, joy, marvel, wonder, gem, treasure, beauty, vision.
ANTONYMS alertness, nightmare, horror.

▶ verb (**dreams, dreaming, dreamed** or **dreamt** /dremt/) **1** experience dreams during sleep. **2** have daydreams. **3** think of something as possible. **4** (**dream something up**) imagine or invent something.

SYNONYMS **1** *I dreamed of making the Olympic team* **fantasize**, daydream, wish, hope, long, yearn, hanker. **2** *she's always dreaming* **daydream**, be in a trance, be lost in thought, be preoccupied, be abstracted, stare into space, be in cloud cuckoo land.

□ **dreamer** noun.

dreamy ▶ adjective **1** tending to daydream. **2** having a magical or pleasantly unreal quality.
□ **dreamily** adverb.

dreary ▶ adjective (**drearier, dreariest**) dull, bleak, and depressing.

SYNONYMS **dull**, uninteresting, tedious, boring, unexciting, unstimulating, uninspiring, soul-destroying, monotonous, uneventful.
ANTONYMS exciting.

□ **drearily** adverb **dreariness** noun.

dredge ▶ verb (**dredges, dredging, dredged**) **1** use a machine to scoop out mud and objects from the bed of a river, canal, etc. **2** (**dredge something up**) mention something unpleasant that people have forgotten.
□ **dredger** noun.

dregs ▶ plural noun **1** the last remaining amount of a liquid left in a cup, bottle, etc. together with any sediment. **2** the most worthless parts: *the dregs of society.*

drench ▶ verb wet thoroughly; soak.

SYNONYMS **soak**, saturate, wet through, douse, steep, flood, drown.

dress ▶ verb **1** (also **get dressed**) put on your clothes. **2** put clothes on someone. **3** clean or apply a dressing to a wound. **4** prepare food for cooking or eating. **5** decorate or arrange in an artistic or attractive way.

SYNONYMS **1** *he dressed quickly* **put on clothes,** clothe yourself, get dressed. **2** *she was dressed in a suit* **clothe**, attire, deck out; informal get up. **3** *she enjoyed dressing the tree* **decorate**, trim, adorn, arrange, prepare. **4** *they dressed his wounds* **bandage**, cover, bind, wrap.
ANTONYMS undress.

▶ noun **1** a woman's garment that covers the body and extends down over the legs. **2** clothing of a particular kind.

SYNONYMS **1** *a long blue dress* **frock**, gown, robe, shift. **2** *full evening dress* **clothes**, clothing, garments, attire, costume, outfit; informal get-up; Brit. informal clobber.

■ **dress rehearsal** a final rehearsal in which costumes are worn and things are done as if it is a real performance. **dress up** dress in smart clothes or in a special costume.

dressage /dress-ahzh/ ▶ noun the training of a horse to perform a series of precise movements at the rider's command.

dresser ▶ noun a sideboard with shelves above it.

dressing ▶ noun **1** a sauce for salads, usually consisting of oil and vinegar with flavourings. **2** a piece of material placed on a wound to protect it.

■ **dressing-down** informal a severe telling-off or reprimand. **dressing gown** a long, loose garment worn after getting out of bed. **dressing room** a room in which performers change their clothes. **dressing table** a table with a mirror, used while dressing or putting on make-up.

dressmaker ▸ noun a person who makes women's clothes.
□ **dressmaking** noun.

dressy ▸ adjective (**dressier, dressiest**) (of clothes) smart or formal.

drew past of DRAW.

dribble ▸ verb (**dribbles, dribbling, dribbled**) **1** (of a liquid) fall slowly in drops or a thin stream. **2** let saliva run from the mouth. **3** (in sport) take the ball forward with slight touches.

> SYNONYMS **1** *the baby started to dribble* **drool,** slaver, slobber. **2** *rainwater dribbled down her face* **trickle,** drip, roll, run, drizzle, ooze, seep, leak.

▸ noun a thin stream of liquid.

dribs and drabs ▸ plural noun (**in dribs and drabs**) informal in small amounts over a period of time.

dried past and past participle of DRY.

drier¹ ➡ DRYER.

drier² comparative of DRY.

drift ▸ verb **1** be carried slowly by a current of air or water. **2** walk or move slowly or casually. **3** (of snow, leaves, etc.) be blown into heaps by the wind.

> SYNONYMS **1** *his raft drifted down the river* **be carried,** be borne, float, bob, glide, coast, waft. **2** *the guests drifted away* **wander,** meander, stray, stroll, dawdle, float, roam. **3** *don't allow your attention to drift* **stray,** digress, wander, deviate, be diverted. **4** *snow drifted over the path* **pile up,** bank up, heap up, accumulate, gather, amass.

▸ noun **1** a continuous slow movement from one place to another. **2** the general meaning of someone's remarks. **3** a large mass of snow, leaves, etc. piled up by the wind.

> SYNONYMS **1** *a drift from the country to urban areas* **movement,** shift, flow, transfer, gravitation. **2** *he caught the drift of her thoughts* **gist,** meaning, sense, significance, thrust, import, tenor, intention, direction. **3** *a drift of deep snow* **pile,** heap, bank, mound, mass, accumulation.

drifter ▸ noun a person who moves from place to place, with no fixed home or job.

driftwood ▸ noun pieces of wood floating on the sea or washed ashore.

drill ▸ noun **1** a tool or machine used for boring holes. **2** training in military exercises. **3** (**the drill**) informal the correct procedure. **4** a machine for sowing seed in rows.

> SYNONYMS **1** *military drill* **training,** instruction, coaching, teaching, (physical) exercises; informal square-bashing. **2** *Estelle knew the drill*

procedure, routine, practice, programme, schedule, method, system.

▸ verb **1** bore a hole with a drill. **2** give someone military training or other strict instruction.

> SYNONYMS **1** *drill the piece of wood* **bore,** pierce, puncture, perforate. **2** *a sergeant drilling new recruits* **train,** instruct, coach, teach, discipline, exercise.

drily (or **dryly**) ▸ adverb in a matter-of-fact or ironically humorous way.

drink ▸ verb (**drinks, drinking, drank;** past participle **drunk**) **1** take a liquid into the mouth and swallow it. **2** drink alcohol.

> SYNONYMS **1** *she drank her coffee* **swallow,** gulp (down), quaff, guzzle, imbibe, sip, drain; informal swig, down, knock back. **2** *he never drank* **drink alcohol,** tipple, indulge, carouse; informal hit the bottle, booze; Brit. informal bevvy.

▸ noun **1** a liquid for drinking. **2** a quantity of liquid swallowed at one time. **3** alcohol, or an alcoholic drink.

> SYNONYMS **1** *cocoa is a nice drink* **beverage,** liquid refreshment; Brit. informal bevvy. **2** *she turned to drink* **alcohol,** intoxicating liquor, spirits; informal booze, the hard stuff, the bottle, grog. **3** *she took a drink of wine* **swallow,** gulp, mouthful, draught, sip; informal swig, slug.

■ **drink-driving** Brit. the crime of driving a vehicle after drinking too much alcohol.
□ **drinkable** adjective **drinker** noun.

drip ▸ verb (**drips, dripping, dripped**) fall in small drops of liquid.

> SYNONYMS **1** *there was a tap dripping* **dribble,** leak. **2** *sweat dripped from his chin* **drop,** dribble, trickle, run, splash, sprinkle, leak.

▸ noun **1** a small drop of a liquid. **2** a device which slowly passes a liquid substance into a patient's body through a vein. **3** informal a weak person.

> SYNONYMS *a bucket caught the drips* **drop,** dribble, spot, trickle, splash.

■ **drip-feed** give a patient liquid nourishment through a drip.
□ **drippy** adjective.

dripping ▸ noun Brit. fat that has dripped from roasting meat.

▸ adjective very wet.

drive ▸ verb (**drives, driving, drove;** past participle **driven**) **1** operate a motor vehicle. **2** take someone somewhere in a motor vehicle. **3** make someone or something move in a particular direction. **4** make someone behave in a particular way. **5** provide energy to make an engine or machine work.

SYNONYMS **1** *I can't drive a car* **operate,** handle, manage, pilot, steer, work. **2** *he drove to the police station* **go by car,** motor. **3** *I'll drive you to the airport* **run,** chauffeur, give someone a lift, take, ferry, transport, convey. **4** *the engine drives the front wheels* **power,** propel, move, push. **5** *he drove a nail into the boot* **hammer,** screw, ram, sink, plunge, thrust, knock. **6** *she was driven to crime* **force,** compel, prompt, precipitate, oblige, coerce, pressure, spur, prod.

▶ noun **1** a journey in a car. **2** (also **driveway**) a short private road leading to a house. **3** a natural urge. **4** an organized effort to achieve something. **5** determination and ambition.

SYNONYMS **1** *an afternoon drive* **excursion,** outing, trip, jaunt, tour, ride, run, journey; informal spin. **2** *she lacked the drive to succeed* **motivation,** ambition, single-mindedness, willpower, dedication, doggedness, tenacity, enthusiasm, zeal, commitment, energy, vigour; informal get-up-and-go. **3** *an anti-corruption drive* **campaign,** crusade, movement, effort, push, initiative.

□ **driver** noun.

drivel /driv-uhl/ ▶ noun nonsense.

drizzle ▶ noun light rain falling in fine drops.
▶ verb (**it drizzles, it is drizzling, it drizzled**) rain lightly.
□ **drizzly** adjective.

droll /drohl/ ▶ adjective amusing in a strange or unusual way.

dromedary /drom-i-duh-ri/ ▶ noun (plural **dromedaries**) a kind of camel with one hump.

drone ▶ verb (**drones, droning, droned**)
1 make a low continuous humming sound.
2 talk for a long time in a boring way.
▶ noun **1** a low continuous humming sound.
2 a male bee which does no work but can fertilize a queen.

drool ▶ verb (**drools, drooling, drooled**)
1 drop saliva uncontrollably from the mouth. **2** (often **drool over**) informal show great pleasure or desire.

droop ▶ verb bend, hang, or sag downwards limply or wearily.

SYNONYMS **hang down,** wilt, dangle, sag, flop, sink, slump, drop.

droopy ▶ adjective (**droopier, droopiest**)
1 hanging down limply. **2** not having much strength or spirit.

drop ▶ verb (**drops, dropping, dropped**)
1 fall, or let something fall. **2** make or become lower or less. **3** abandon a course of action. **4** (often **drop someone/thing off**) set down or unload a passenger or goods. **5** (in sport) lose a point or match.

SYNONYMS **1** *Eric dropped the box* **let fall,** let go of, lose your grip on, release. **2** *a plane dropped out of the sky* **fall,** descend, plunge, plummet, dive, sink, dip, tumble. **3** *the exchange rate dropped* **decrease,** lessen, reduce, fall, decline, dwindle, sink, slump. **4** *let's drop this pretence* **abandon,** give up, discontinue, finish with, renounce, reject, forgo, relinquish, dispense with, leave out; informal dump, pack in, quit.
ANTONYMS rise, increase, keep.

▶ noun **1** a small round or pear-shaped amount of liquid. **2** a small drink. **3** an abrupt fall or slope. **4** a type of sweet.

SYNONYMS **1** *a drop of water* **droplet,** blob, globule, bead. **2** *it needs a drop of oil* **small amount,** little, bit, dash, spot, dribble, sprinkle, trickle, splash, mouthful; informal smidgen, tad. **3** *a small drop in profits* **decrease,** reduction, decline, fall-off, downturn, slump. **4** *I walked to the edge of the drop* **cliff,** precipice, slope, descent, incline.
ANTONYMS flood, increase.

■ **drop kick** a kick made by dropping a ball and kicking it as it bounces. **drop off** fall asleep. **drop out 1** stop taking part in something. **2** start living an alternative lifestyle.

droplet ▶ noun a very small drop of a liquid.

dropout ▶ noun a person who has started living an alternative lifestyle, or abandoned a course of study.

droppings ▶ plural noun the excrement of animals.

dross ▶ noun rubbish.

drought /drowt/ ▶ noun a very long period of abnormally low rainfall.

drove[1] past of **DRIVE**.

drove[2] ▶ noun **1** a flock of animals being moved along. **2** a large number of people doing the same thing.

drown ▶ verb **1** die through taking water into the lungs, or kill someone in this way. **2** flood an area. **3** (usu. **drown something out**) make something impossible to hear by being much louder.

drowsy ▶ adjective (**drowsier, drowsiest**) sleepy.
□ **drowsily** adverb **drowsiness** noun.

drub ▶ verb (**drubs, drubbing, drubbed**) beat repeatedly.
□ **drubbing** noun.

drudge ▶ noun a person who is made to do hard or dull work.

drudgery ▶ noun hard or dull work.

drug ▶ noun **1** a substance used as a medicine. **2** an illegal substance taken for the effects it has on the body.

SYNONYMS **1** *drugs prescribed by doctors* **medicine,** medication, remedy, cure, antidote. **2** *she was under the influence of drugs* **narcotic,** stimulant, hallucinogen; informal dope, gear.

▶ verb (**drugs, drugging, drugged**) make a person or animal unconscious or sleepy by giving them a drug.

SYNONYMS **1** *he was drugged* **anaesthetize,** poison, knock out; informal dope. **2** *she drugged his coffee* **tamper with,** lace, poison; informal dope, spike, doctor.

drugstore ▶ noun N. Amer. a shop which sells medicines and also cosmetics and other articles.

Druid /droo-id/ ▶ noun a priest in the ancient Celtic religion.

drum ▶ noun **1** a percussion instrument which you play by hitting it with sticks or the hands. **2** a cylindrical object or part.

SYNONYMS *a drum of radioactive waste* **canister,** barrel, cylinder, tank, bin, can.

▶ verb (**drums, drumming, drummed**) **1** play on a drum. **2** make a continuous rhythmic noise. **3** (**drum something into**) teach something to someone by constantly repeating it. **4** (**drum something up**) try hard to get support or business.

SYNONYMS **1** *she drummed her fingers on the desk* **tap,** beat, rap, thud, thump, tattoo, thrum. **2** *the rules were drummed into us at school* **instil,** drive, din, hammer, drill, implant, ingrain, inculcate.

■ **drum and bass** a type of dance music consisting largely of electronic drums and bass.
□ **drummer** noun.

drumstick ▶ noun **1** a stick used for beating a drum. **2** the lower joint of the leg of a cooked chicken.

drunk past participle of **DRINK**.
▶ adjective having drunk so much alcohol that you cannot think or speak clearly.

SYNONYMS **intoxicated,** inebriated, drunken, tipsy, under the influence; informal tight, merry, plastered, sloshed, pickled, tanked (up), ratted; Brit. informal legless, paralytic, Brahms and Liszt, trolleyed, tiddly; N. Amer. informal loaded, trashed, sauced.
ANTONYMS sober.

▶ noun a person who is drunk or who often drinks too much.

SYNONYMS **drunkard,** inebriate; informal boozer, soak, wino, alky.
ANTONYMS teetotaller.

drunkard ▶ noun a person who is often drunk.

drunken ▶ adjective **1** drunk. **2** caused by or showing the effects of drink.
□ **drunkenly** adverb **drunkenness** noun.

drupe ▶ noun Botany a fruit with a central stone, e.g. a plum or olive.

dry ▶ adjective (**drier, driest**) **1** free from moisture. **2** dull and serious. **3** (of humour) subtle and expressed in a matter-of-fact way. **4** (of wine) not sweet.

SYNONYMS **1** *the dry desert* **arid,** parched, waterless, dehydrated, desiccated, withered, shrivelled, wizened. **2** *a dry debate* **dull,** uninteresting, boring, unexciting, tedious, dreary, monotonous, unimaginative, sterile; informal deadly. **3** *a dry sense of humour* **wry,** subtle, laconic, ironic, sardonic, sarcastic, cynical.
ANTONYMS wet, moist, interesting, lively, broad.

▶ verb (**dries, drying, dried**) **1** make or become dry. **2** preserve something by evaporating the moisture. **3** (**dry up**) (of a supply) decrease and stop.

SYNONYMS **1** *the sun dried the ground* **parch,** scorch, bake, sear, dehydrate, desiccate, wither, shrivel. **2** *he dried the dishes* **wipe,** towel, rub dry, drain.
ANTONYMS wet, moisten.

■ **dry-clean** clean a garment with a chemical rather than by washing it. **dry rot** a fungus that causes wood to decay. **dry run** a rehearsal.
□ **dryness** noun.

dryer (or **drier**) ▶ noun a machine or device for drying something.

dryly → **DRILY**.

drystone ▶ adjective Brit. (of a stone wall) built without using mortar.

dual ▶ adjective consisting of two parts or aspects.

SYNONYMS **double,** twofold, duplex, binary, twin, matching, paired, coupled.
ANTONYMS single.

■ **dual carriageway** Brit. a road with two or more lanes in each direction.

dualism ▶ noun **1** division into two contrasted aspects, such as good and evil. **2** duality.
□ **dualist** noun & adjective.

duality ▶ noun (plural **dualities**) the state of having two parts or aspects.

dub¹ ▶ verb (**dubs, dubbing, dubbed**) **1** give an unofficial name to. **2** knight someone by touching their shoulder with a sword in a special ceremony.

SYNONYMS **name,** call, nickname, label, christen, term, tag.

dub² ▶ verb (**dubs, dubbing, dubbed**) **1** give a film a soundtrack in a different language from the original. **2** add sound effects or music to a film or recording.

d

d

dubbin ▶ noun Brit. a grease used for softening and waterproofing leather.

dubious ▶ adjective **1** hesitating or doubting. **2** probably not honest. **3** of uncertain quality or value.

> SYNONYMS **1** *I was rather dubious about the idea* **doubtful,** uncertain, unsure, hesitant, sceptical, suspicious; informal iffy. **2** *a dubious businessman* **suspicious,** suspect, untrustworthy, unreliable, questionable; informal shady; Brit. informal dodgy.
> ANTONYMS certain, trustworthy.

□ **dubiously** adverb.

ducal /dyoo-k'l/ ▶ adjective relating to a duke or dukedom.

ducat /**duk**-uht/ ▶ noun a gold coin formerly used in Europe.

duchess ▶ noun **1** the wife or widow of a duke. **2** a woman holding a rank equivalent to duke.

duchy ▶ noun (plural **duchies**) the territory of a duke or duchess.

duck¹ ▶ noun (plural **duck** or **ducks**) **1** a waterbird with a broad blunt bill, short legs, and webbed feet. **2** a female duck.
■ **duck-billed platypus** ➡ PLATYPUS.

duck² ▶ verb **1** lower yourself quickly to avoid being hit or seen. **2** push someone under water. **3** informal avoid an unwelcome duty.

> SYNONYMS **1** *he ducked behind the wall* **bob down,** bend down, stoop, crouch, squat, hunch down, hunker down. **2** *they cannot duck the issue forever* **shirk,** dodge, evade, avoid, elude, escape, sidestep.

duck³ ▶ noun Cricket a batsman's score of nought.

duckboards ▶ plural noun wooden slats joined together to form a path over muddy ground.

duckling ▶ noun a young duck.

duct ▶ noun **1** a tube or passageway for air, cables, etc. **2** a tube in the body through which fluid passes.

> SYNONYMS **tube,** channel, canal, vessel, conduit, pipe, outlet, inlet, flue, shaft, vent.

ductile ▶ adjective (of a metal) able to be drawn out into a thin wire.

dud informal ▶ noun a thing that fails to work properly.
▶ adjective failing to work properly.

dude ▶ noun N. Amer. informal a man.

dudgeon ▶ noun deep resentment.

due ▶ adjective **1** expected at a certain time. **2** owing; needing to be paid or given. **3** (of a person) owed or deserving something. **4** proper or adequate.

> SYNONYMS **1** *their fees were due* **owing,** owed, payable, outstanding, overdue, unpaid, unsettled. **2** *the chancellor's statement is due today* **expected,** anticipated, scheduled for, awaited, required. **3** *a little respect is due* **deserved,** merited, warranted, justified, owing, appropriate, fitting, right, rightful, proper. **4** *he drove without due care* **proper,** correct, suitable, appropriate, adequate, sufficient.

▶ noun **1** (**someone's due** or **dues**) what someone deserves or is owed. **2** (**dues**) fees.

> SYNONYMS *members have paid their dues* **fee,** subscription, charge, payment, contribution, levy.

▶ adverb directly: *head due south*.

> SYNONYMS *due north* **directly,** straight, exactly, precisely, dead.

■ **due to 1** caused by. **2** because of.

duel ▶ noun **1** historical a contest with deadly weapons between two people to settle a point of honour. **2** a contest between two parties.

> SYNONYMS **1** *he was killed in a duel* **single combat,** fight, confrontation, head-to-head; informal shoot-out. **2** *a snooker duel* **contest,** match, game, meet, encounter, clash.

▶ verb (**duels, duelling, duelled;** US spelling **duels, dueling, dueled**) fight a duel.
□ **duellist** (US spelling **duelist**) noun.

duet ▶ noun **1** a performance by two singers or musicians. **2** a piece of music for two performers.

duff Brit. informal ▶ adjective of very bad quality; useless.
▶ verb (**duff someone up**) beat someone up.

duffel bag (or **duffle bag**) ▶ noun a cylinder-shaped canvas bag closed by a drawstring.

duffel coat (or **duffle coat**) ▶ noun a hooded coat made of a rough woollen material.

duffer ▶ noun informal an incompetent or stupid person.

dug¹ past and past participle of DIG.

dug² ▶ noun the udder, teat, or nipple of a female animal.

dugout ▶ noun **1** a trench that is roofed over as a shelter for troops. **2** a low shelter at the side of a sports field for a team's coaches and substitutes. **3** a canoe made from a hollowed-out tree trunk.

duke ▶ noun **1** the highest rank of nobleman in Britain and certain other countries. **2** historical (in parts of Europe) a male ruler of a small independent state.
□ **dukedom** noun.

dulcet /**dul**-sit/ ▶ adjective (of a sound) sweet and soothing.

dulcimer /dul-si-mer/ ► noun a musical instrument which you play by hitting the strings with small hammers.

dull ► adjective **1** not very interesting. **2** not vivid or bright. **3** (of the weather) overcast. **4** slow to understand.

> SYNONYMS **1** *a dull novel* **uninteresting,** boring, tedious, monotonous, unimaginative, uneventful, characterless, featureless, colourless, lifeless, unexciting, uninspiring, flat, bland, stodgy, dreary; informal deadly; N. Amer. informal dullsville. **2** *a dull morning* **overcast,** cloudy, gloomy, dark, dismal, dreary, sombre, grey, murky, sunless. **3** *dull colours* **drab,** dreary, sombre, dark, subdued, muted. **4** *a dull sound* **muffled,** muted, quiet, soft, faint, indistinct, stifled. **5** *the chisel became dull* **blunt,** worn. **6** *a rather dull child* **unintelligent,** stupid, slow, brainless, mindless, foolish, idiotic; informal dense, dim, half-witted, thick.
> ANTONYMS interesting, bright, resonant, sharp, clever.

► verb make or become dull.

> SYNONYMS *the pain was dulled by drugs* **lessen,** decrease, diminish, reduce, dampen, blunt, deaden, allay, ease.
> ANTONYMS intensify.

□ **dullness** noun **dully** adverb.

dullard ► noun a slow or stupid person.

duly ► adverb in the proper or expected way.

> SYNONYMS **1** *the document was duly signed* **properly,** correctly, appropriately, suitably, fittingly. **2** *he duly arrived to collect Alice* **at the right time,** on time, punctually.

dumb ► adjective **1** offensive unable to speak; not having the power of speech. **2** temporarily unable or unwilling to speak. **3** N. Amer. informal stupid.

> SYNONYMS **1** *she stood dumb while he shouted* **mute,** speechless, tongue-tied, silent, at a loss for words. **2** *he is not as dumb as you'd think* **stupid,** unintelligent, ignorant, dense, brainless, foolish, slow, dull, simple; informal thick, dim; Brit. informal daft.
> ANTONYMS talkative, clever.

► verb (**dumb something down**) informal make something less intellectually challenging.

■ **dumb-bell** a short bar with a weight at each end, used for exercise. **dumb waiter** a small lift for carrying food and crockery between floors.

dumbfounded ► adjective greatly astonished.

dumbstruck ► adjective so shocked or surprised that you cannot speak.

dumdum bullet ► noun a kind of soft-nosed bullet that expands on impact.

dummy ► noun (plural **dummies**) **1** a model of a human being. **2** an object designed to resemble and take the place of the real one. **3** Brit. a rubber or plastic teat for a baby to suck on. **4** (in sport) a movement made to deceive an opponent into thinking that you are about to kick or pass the ball. **5** informal a stupid person.

> SYNONYMS *a shop-window dummy* **mannequin,** model, figure.

► adjective not real, and intended to deceive someone.

> SYNONYMS *a dummy attack* **simulated,** practice, trial, mock, make-believe; informal pretend.
> ANTONYMS real.

■ **dummy run** a practice or trial.

dump ► noun **1** a place where rubbish or waste is left. **2** a temporary store of weapons or military provisions. **3** informal an unpleasant or boring place.

> SYNONYMS **1** *take the rubbish to the dump* **tip,** rubbish dump, dumping ground, recycling centre. **2** *the house is a dump* **hovel,** slum; informal hole, pigsty.

► verb **1** get rid of something unwanted. **2** put down something carelessly. **3** informal abandon someone.

> SYNONYMS **1** *they will dump asbestos at the site* **dispose of,** get rid of, throw away/out, discard, bin, jettison; informal ditch, junk. **2** *he dumped his bag on the table* **put down,** set down, deposit, place, shove, unload, drop, throw down; informal stick, park, plonk; Brit. informal bung.

dumpling ► noun a small savoury ball of dough boiled in water or in a stew.

dumps ► plural noun (**down in the dumps**) informal depressed or unhappy.

dumpy ► adjective short and stout.

dun ► noun a dull greyish-brown colour.

dunce ► noun a person who is slow at learning.

dune ► noun a mound or ridge of sand formed by the wind.

> SYNONYMS **bank,** mound, hillock, hummock, knoll, ridge, heap, drift.

dung ► noun manure.

dungarees /dung-guh-reez/ ► noun a garment consisting of trousers held up by straps over the shoulders.

dungeon ► noun a strong underground prison cell.

dunk ► verb **1** dip food into a drink or soup before eating it. **2** put something in water.

dunnock ► noun a small bird with a grey head and a reddish-brown back.

duo ▸ noun (plural **duos**) **1** a pair of people or things, especially in music or entertainment. **2** Music a duet.

duodenum /dyoo-uh-**dee**-nuhm/ ▸ noun (plural **duodenums**) the first part of the small intestine immediately beyond the stomach.

dupe ▸ verb (**dupes, duping, duped**) deceive; trick.
▸ noun a person who is tricked or deceived.

duple /**dyoo**-p'l/ ▸ adjective Music (of rhythm) based on two main beats to the bar.

duplex /**dyoo**-pleks/ N. Amer. ▸ noun **1** a building divided into two flats. **2** a flat on two floors.

duplicate ▸ adjective /**dyoo**-pli-kuht/ **1** exactly like something else. **2** having two corresponding parts.

> SYNONYMS *duplicate keys* **matching,** identical, twin, corresponding, equivalent.

▸ noun /**dyoo**-pli-kuht/ each of two or more identical things.

> SYNONYMS *a duplicate of the invoice* **copy,** photocopy, facsimile, reprint, replica, reproduction, clone; trademark Xerox, photostat.

▸ verb /**dyoo**-pli-kayt/ (**duplicates, duplicating, duplicated**) **1** make or be an exact copy of. **2** multiply by two. **3** do something again unnecessarily.

> SYNONYMS **1** *she will duplicate the newsletter* **copy,** photocopy, photostat, xerox, reproduce, replicate, reprint, run off. **2** *a feat difficult to duplicate* **repeat,** do again, redo, replicate.

□ **duplication** noun **duplicator** noun.

duplicity /dyoo-**pli**-si-ti/ ▸ noun deceitful behaviour.
□ **duplicitous** adjective.

durable ▸ adjective **1** hard-wearing. **2** (of goods) not for immediate consumption and so able to be kept.

> SYNONYMS **1** *durable carpets* **hard-wearing,** wear-resistant, heavy-duty, tough, long-lasting, strong, sturdy, robust. **2** *a durable peace* **lasting,** long-lasting, long-term, enduring, persistent, abiding, permanent, undying, everlasting.
> ANTONYMS delicate, short-lived.

□ **durability** noun.

duration ▸ noun the time during which something continues.

> SYNONYMS **length,** time, period, term, span, extent, stretch.

duress ▸ noun threats or violence used to force a person to do something.

during ▸ preposition **1** throughout the course of. **2** at a particular point in the course of.

dusk ▸ noun the darker stage of twilight.

> SYNONYMS **twilight,** nightfall, sunset, sundown, evening, close of day, semi-darkness, gloom; literary gloaming.
> ANTONYMS dawn.

dusky ▸ adjective dark, or darkish in colour.

dust ▸ noun fine, dry powder, especially tiny particles of earth, sand, etc.

> SYNONYMS *the desk was covered in dust* **dirt,** grime, grit, powder, particles.

▸ verb **1** remove dust from the surface of. **2** cover lightly with a powdered substance.

> SYNONYMS **1** *she dusted her mantelpiece* **wipe,** clean, brush, sweep. **2** *dust the cake with icing sugar* **sprinkle,** scatter, powder, dredge, sift, cover.

■ **dust-up** informal a fight.

dustbin ▸ noun Brit. a large container for household rubbish.

dustcart ▸ noun Brit. a vehicle used for collecting household rubbish.

duster ▸ noun a cloth for dusting furniture.

dustman ▸ noun (plural **dustmen**) Brit. a man employed to remove rubbish from dustbins.

dustpan ▸ noun a hand-held container into which you sweep dust and waste.

dusty ▸ adjective covered with or resembling dust.

> SYNONYMS **1** *the floor was dusty* **dirty,** grimy, grubby, mucky, unswept. **2** *dusty sandstone* **powdery,** crumbly, chalky, granular, soft, gritty.
> ANTONYMS clean, hard, smooth.

Dutch ▸ adjective relating to the Netherlands or its language.
▸ noun the language of the Netherlands.
■ **Dutch courage** confidence gained from drinking alcohol. **go Dutch** share the cost of a meal equally.

dutiable ▸ adjective on which duty needs to be paid.

dutiful ▸ adjective carrying out all your obligations; doing your duty.
□ **dutifully** adverb.

> SYNONYMS **conscientious,** responsible, dedicated, devoted, attentive, obedient, respectful.
> ANTONYMS remiss.

duty ▸ noun (plural **duties**) **1** a moral or legal obligation. **2** a person's regular work, or a task required as part of their job. **3** a charge made when some goods are imported, exported, or sold.

> SYNONYMS **1** *a misguided sense of duty* **responsibility,** obligation, commitment, allegiance, loyalty. **2** *it was his duty to attend the king* **job,** task, assignment, mission, function, role. **3** *the duty was*

raised on alcohol **tax,** levy, tariff, excise, toll, rate.

■ **duty-bound** morally or legally obliged. **duty-free** not requiring duty to be paid.

duvet /**dyoo**-vay, **doo**-vay/ ▸ noun chiefly Brit. a thick quilt used instead of an upper sheet and blankets.

DVD ▸ abbreviation digital versatile disc.

dwarf ▸ noun (plural **dwarfs** or **dwarves**) **1** a member of a mythical race of short human-like creatures. **2** a person who is unusually small.

SYNONYMS **1** *the wizard captured the dwarf* **gnome,** goblin, hobgoblin, troll, imp, elf, brownie, leprechaun. **2 small person,** person of restricted growth, midget, pygmy.

▸ verb make something seem small in comparison.

SYNONYMS **1** *the buildings dwarf the trees* **dominate,** tower over, loom over, overshadow. **2** *her progress was dwarfed by her sister's success* **overshadow,** outshine, surpass, exceed, outclass, outstrip, outdo, top.

▸ adjective unusually small.

SYNONYMS *dwarf conifers* **miniature,** toy, pocket, baby, pygmy; informal mini. ANTONYMS giant.

dwell ▸ verb (**dwells, dwelling,** past and past participle **dwelt** or **dwelled**) **1** formal live in or at a place. **2** (**dwell on**) think about something at length.

SYNONYMS **live,** reside, be housed, lodge.

dwelling ▸ noun formal a house or home.

dwindle ▸ verb (**dwindles, dwindling, dwindled**) gradually become smaller or weaker.

SYNONYMS **diminish,** decrease, reduce, lessen, shrink, wane. ANTONYMS increase.

dye ▸ noun a substance used to colour something.

SYNONYMS *a blue dye* **colouring,** dyestuff, pigment, tint, stain, wash.

▸ verb (**dyes, dyeing, dyed**) make something a particular colour with dye.

SYNONYMS *the gloves were dyed* **colour,** tint, pigment, stain, wash.

■ **dyed in the wool** having firm beliefs that never change.

dying present participle of DIE[1].

SYNONYMS **1** *his dying aunt* **terminally ill,** at death's door, on your deathbed, fading fast, not long for this world. **2** *a dying art form* **declining,** vanishing, fading, waning; informal on the way out. **3** *her dying words* **final,** last. ANTONYMS thriving, first.

dyke (or **dike**) ▸ noun **1** a barrier built to prevent flooding from the sea. **2** a ditch or water-filled channel. **3** informal a lesbian.

dynamic ▸ adjective **1** full of energy, enthusiasm, and new ideas. **2** (of a process or system) constantly changing and developing. **3** Physics relating to forces that produce motion.

SYNONYMS **energetic,** spirited, active, lively, vigorous, forceful, high-powered, aggressive, enterprising; informal go-getting, go-ahead. ANTONYMS lackadaisical.

□ **dynamically** adverb.

dynamics ▸ plural noun **1** the study of the forces involved in movement. **2** forces which stimulate change. **3** the varying levels of sound in a musical performance.

dynamism ▸ noun the quality of being full of energy, enthusiasm, and new ideas.

dynamite ▸ noun a kind of high explosive. ▸ verb (**dynamites, dynamiting, dynamited**) blow up something with dynamite.

dynamo ▸ noun (plural **dynamos**) a machine for converting mechanical energy into electrical energy.

dynasty /di-**nuh**-sti/ ▸ noun (plural **dynasties**) a series of rulers or powerful people who belong to the same family.

SYNONYMS **family,** house, line, lineage, regime, empire.

dysentery /**diss**-uhn-tri/ ▸ noun a disease of the intestines which results in severe diarrhoea.

dysfunctional ▸ adjective **1** not operating properly. **2** unable to deal with normal social relations.

dyslexia /diss-**lek**-si-uh/ ▸ noun a disorder involving difficulty in learning to read words and letters.

□ **dyslexic** adjective & noun.

dyspepsia ▸ noun indigestion.

dyspeptic ▸ adjective **1** suffering from indigestion. **2** irritable.

Ee

e

E (or **e**) ▸ noun **1** (plural **Es** or **E's**) the fifth letter of the alphabet. **2** (€) euro or euros.
▸ abbreviation **1** East or Eastern. **2** informal the drug Ecstasy.
■ **E-number** Brit. a code number starting with the letter E, given to food additives according to European Union instructions.

e- ▸ prefix referring to the use of electronic communication in order to send information, do business, etc., especially through the Internet: *e-commerce*.

each ▸ determiner & pronoun every one of two or more people or things, regarded separately.
▸ adverb to, for, or by every one of a group.

> SYNONYMS *they gave a tenner each* **apiece,** per person, per head, per capita.

eager ▸ adjective very much wanting to do or have something.

> SYNONYMS **1** *small eager faces* **keen,** enthusiastic, avid, ardent, highly motivated, committed, earnest. **2** *we were eager for news* **anxious,** impatient, longing, yearning, wishing, hoping; informal itching, dying.
> ANTONYMS apathetic.

□ **eagerly** adverb.

eagle ▸ noun a large bird of prey with long, broad wings.
■ **eagle-eyed** very observant.

ear ▸ noun **1** the organ of hearing in humans and animals. **2** an ability to recognize and appreciate music or language. **3** the spike of seeds at the top of the stalk of a cereal plant.
■ **within** (or **out of**) **earshot** near enough (or too far away) to be heard.

earache ▸ noun pain inside the ear.

eardrum ▸ noun a membrane in the ear which vibrates in response to sound waves.

earl ▸ noun a British nobleman ranking above a viscount.
□ **earldom** noun.

early ▸ adjective (**earlier**, **earliest**)
1 happening or done before the expected time. **2** happening at the beginning of a particular period.

> SYNONYMS **1** *an early death* **untimely,** premature, unseasonable. **2** *an early response* **prompt,** timely, quick, speedy. **3** *early copies of the book* **advance,** initial, preliminary, first. **4** *early man* **primitive,** ancient, prehistoric, primeval.
> ANTONYMS late, timely, modern.

▸ adverb **1** before the expected time. **2** at the beginning of a particular period.

> SYNONYMS **1** *she was widowed very early* **prematurely,** before the usual time, too soon, ahead of schedule. **2** *get your application in early* **in advance,** in good time, ahead of schedule, with time to spare, before the last moment.
> ANTONYMS late.

earmark ▸ verb choose or set aside for a particular purpose.

> SYNONYMS **set aside,** keep (back), reserve, designate, assign, allocate.

earmuffs ▸ plural noun a pair of fabric coverings worn over the ears to protect them from cold or noise.

earn ▸ verb **1** be given money in return for work or services. **2** gain a reward for hard work or good qualities.

> SYNONYMS **1** *they earned £20,000* **be paid,** take home, gross, receive, get, make, collect, bring in; informal pocket, bank. **2** *he has earned their trust* **deserve,** merit, warrant, justify, be worthy of, gain, win, secure, obtain.
> ANTONYMS lose.

□ **earner** noun.

earnest ▸ adjective very serious.

> SYNONYMS **1** *he is dreadfully earnest* **serious,** solemn, grave, sober, humourless, staid, intense. **2** *earnest prayer* **devout,** heartfelt, wholehearted, sincere, impassioned, fervent, intense.
> ANTONYMS frivolous, half-hearted.

■ **in earnest** sincere and serious about your intentions.
□ **earnestly** adverb.

earnings ▸ plural noun money or income earned.

SYNONYMS **income,** pay, wages, salary, stipend, remuneration, fees, revenue, yield, profit, takings, proceeds.

earphones ▸ plural noun devices worn on the ears to listen to radio, recorded sound, etc.

earpiece ▸ noun the part of a telephone or other device that is held to or put inside the ear during use.

earplug ▸ noun a piece of wax, cotton wool, etc., placed in the ear as protection against noise or water.

earring ▸ noun a piece of jewellery worn on the lobe or edge of the ear.

earth ▸ noun 1 (also **Earth**) the planet on which we live. 2 the ground. 3 soil. 4 Brit. a wire that connects an electrical circuit to the ground and makes it safe. 5 the underground lair of a badger or fox.

SYNONYMS **1** *the moon orbits the earth* **world,** globe, planet. **2** *a trembling of the earth* **land,** ground, terra firma, floor. **3** *he ploughed the earth* **soil,** clay, dust, dirt, loam, ground, turf.

▸ verb Brit. connect an electrical device to earth.

earthen ▸ adjective made of earth or baked clay.

earthenware ▸ noun pottery made of fired clay.

earthling ▸ noun (in science fiction) a person from the earth.

earthly ▸ adjective 1 having to do with the earth or human life. 2 remotely possible: *no earthly reason.*

SYNONYMS **worldly,** temporal, mortal, human, material, carnal, fleshly, bodily, physical, corporeal, sensual.
ANTONYMS extraterrestrial, heavenly.

earthquake ▸ noun a sudden violent shaking of the ground, caused by movements within the earth's crust.

earthwork ▸ noun a large man-made bank of soil.

earthworm ▸ noun a burrowing worm that lives in the soil.

earthy ▸ adjective (**earthier, earthiest**) 1 like soil. 2 direct and unembarrassed about sexual subjects or bodily functions.

earwig ▸ noun a small insect with a pair of pincers at its rear end.

ease ▸ noun 1 lack of difficulty or effort. 2 freedom from problems.

SYNONYMS **1** *he defeated them all with ease* **effortlessness,** no trouble, simplicity. **2** *his ease of manner* **naturalness,** casualness, informality, composure, nonchalance, insouciance. **3** *a life of ease* **affluence,** wealth, prosperity, luxury, plenty, comfort,

enjoyment, well-being.
ANTONYMS difficulty, formality, hardship.

▸ verb (**eases, easing, eased**) 1 make or become less serious or severe. 2 move carefully or gradually.

SYNONYMS **1** *the alcohol eased his pain* **relieve,** alleviate, soothe, moderate, dull, deaden, numb. **2** *the rain eased off* **let up,** abate, subside, die down, slacken off, diminish, lessen. **3** *work helped to ease her mind* **calm,** quieten, pacify, soothe, comfort, console. **4** *he eased out the cork* **slide,** slip, squeeze, guide, manoeuvre, inch, edge.
ANTONYMS aggravate, intensify, unsettle.

easel ▸ noun a wooden frame on legs used by artists for holding the picture they are working on.

easily ▸ adverb 1 without difficulty. 2 without doubt.

SYNONYMS **1** *he won easily* **effortlessly,** comfortably, simply, without difficulty, readily, without a hitch. **2** *that's easily the best* **undoubtedly,** without doubt, without question, without difficulty, undeniably, definitely, certainly, obviously, by far.

east ▸ noun 1 the direction in which the sun rises. 2 the eastern part of a place.
▸ adjective & adverb 1 towards or facing the east. 2 (of a wind) blowing from the east.
□ **eastward** adjective & adverb **eastwards** adverb.

Easter ▸ noun the Christian festival celebrating the resurrection of Jesus.
■ **Easter egg** a chocolate egg given as a gift at Easter.

easterly ▸ adjective & adverb 1 facing or moving towards the east. 2 (of a wind) blowing from the east.

eastern ▸ adjective 1 situated in or facing the east. 2 (**Eastern**) having to do with the part of the world to the east of Europe.

easterner ▸ noun a person from the east of a region.

easy ▸ adjective (**easier, easiest**) 1 able to be done without great effort. 2 free from worry or problems.

SYNONYMS **1** *the task was very easy* **uncomplicated,** undemanding, effortless, painless, trouble-free, simple, straightforward, elementary, plain sailing; informal a piece of cake, child's play, a cinch. **2** *an easy target* **vulnerable,** susceptible, defenceless, naive, gullible, trusting. **3** *Vic's easy manner* **natural,** casual, informal, unceremonious, unreserved, unaffected, easy-going, amiable, affable, genial, good-humoured, carefree, nonchalant, unconcerned; informal laid-back. **4** *an easy life* **quiet,** tranquil, serene, peaceful,

e

untroubled, contented, relaxed, comfortable, secure, safe; informal cushy. **5** *an easy pace* **leisurely,** unhurried, comfortable, undemanding, easy-going, gentle, sedate, moderate, steady.
ANTONYMS difficult, formal, hard, demanding.

■ **easy chair** a comfortable armchair.
easy-going having a relaxed and tolerant attitude.

eat ▶ verb (**eats, eating, ate**; past participle **eaten**) **1** put food into the mouth and chew and swallow it. **2** (**eat something away**) gradually wear away or destroy something. **3** (**eat something up**) use resources in very large quantities.

SYNONYMS **1** *we ate a hearty breakfast* **consume,** devour, swallow, partake of, munch, chomp; informal tuck into, put away. **2** *we ate at a local restaurant* **have a meal,** feed, snack, breakfast, lunch, dine; informal graze.

■ **eat your words** admit that what you previously said was wrong.
□ **eatable** adjective.

eatery ▶ noun (plural **eateries**) informal a cafe or restaurant.

eau de cologne /oh duh kuh-**lohn**/ = COLOGNE.

eaves ▶ plural noun the part of a roof that meets or overhangs the walls of a building.

eavesdrop ▶ verb (**eavesdrops, eavesdropping, eavesdropped**) secretly listen to a conversation.

ebb ▶ noun the movement of the tide out to sea.
▶ verb **1** (of the tide) move away from the land. **2** (**ebb away**) gradually become less or weaker.

SYNONYMS **1** *the tide ebbed* **recede,** go out, retreat. **2** *his courage began to ebb* **diminish,** dwindle, wane, fade (away), peter out, decline, flag.
ANTONYMS flow, increase.

■ **at a low ebb** in a weakened or depressed state.

ebony ▶ noun **1** heavy dark wood from a tree of tropical and warm regions. **2** a very dark brown or black colour.

ebullient /i-**bul**-yuhnt/ ▶ adjective cheerful and full of energy.
□ **ebullience** noun.

EC ▶ abbreviation European Community.

eccentric ▶ adjective unconventional and slightly strange.

SYNONYMS *eccentric behaviour* **unconventional,** abnormal, anomalous, odd, strange, peculiar, weird, bizarre, outlandish, idiosyncratic, quirky; informal oddball, kooky, cranky.
ANTONYMS conventional.

▶ noun an eccentric person.

SYNONYMS *he was something of an eccentric* **oddity,** free spirit, misfit; informal oddball, weirdo.

□ **eccentrically** adverb **eccentricity** noun.
ecclesiastical /i-klee-zi-**ass**-ti-k'l/
▶ adjective relating to the Christian Church or its clergy.

echelon /**esh**-uh-lon/ ▶ noun a level or rank in an organization, profession, or society.

echo ▶ noun (plural **echoes**) **1** a sound caused by the reflection of sound waves from a surface back to the listener. **2** a reflected radio or radar beam.

SYNONYMS *a faint echo of my shout* **reverberation,** reflection, ringing, repetition, repeat.

▶ verb (**echoes, echoing, echoed**) **1** (of a sound) reverberate or be repeated after the original sound has stopped. **2** repeat someone's words or opinions.

SYNONYMS **1** *his laughter echoed round the room* **reverberate,** resonate, resound, reflect, ring, vibrate. **2** *Bill echoed Rex's words* **repeat,** restate, reiterate, imitate, parrot, mimic, reproduce, recite.

□ **echoey** adjective.

eclair /i-**klair**, ay-**klair**/ ▶ noun a cake of light pastry filled with cream and topped with chocolate icing.

éclat /ay-**klah**/ ▶ noun a notably brilliant or successful effect.

eclectic ▶ adjective taking ideas from a wide range of sources.

eclipse ▶ noun **1** an occasion when one planet, the moon, etc. passes between another and the observer, or in front of a planet's source of light. **2** a sudden loss of significance or power.
▶ verb (**eclipses, eclipsing, eclipsed**) **1** (of a planet, the moon, etc.) obscure the light coming from or shining on another. **2** make less significant or powerful.

SYNONYMS **outshine,** overshadow, surpass, exceed, outclass, outstrip, outdo, transcend.

eco-friendly ▶ adjective not harmful to the environment.

ecology ▶ noun the study of how animals and plants relate to one another and to their surroundings.
□ **ecological** adjective **ecologically** adverb **ecologist** noun.

economic ▶ adjective **1** relating to economics or the economy of a country or region. **2** profitable, or concerned with profitability.

SYNONYMS **1** *economic reform* **financial,** monetary, budgetary, fiscal, commercial. **2** *the firm cannot remain economic*

profitable, moneymaking, lucrative, remunerative, fruitful, productive.
ANTONYMS unprofitable.

economical ▶ adjective **1** giving good value in relation to the resources used or money spent. **2** careful in the use of resources or money.

SYNONYMS **1** *an economical car* **cheap,** inexpensive, low-cost, budget, economy, cut-price, bargain. **2** *a very economical shopper* **thrifty,** provident, prudent, sensible, frugal.
ANTONYMS expensive, spendthrift.

□ **economically** adverb.

economics ▶ plural noun the study of the production, consumption, and transfer of wealth.

economist ▶ noun an expert in economics.

economize (or **economise**) ▶ verb (**economizes, economizing, economized**) spend less; be economical.

SYNONYMS **save (money),** cut costs, cut back, make cutbacks, retrench, scrimp.

economy ▶ noun (plural **economies**) **1** the state of a country or region in terms of the production and consumption of goods and services and the supply of money. **2** careful management of resources. **3** a financial saving.

SYNONYMS **1** *the nation's economy* **wealth,** financial resources, financial system, financial management. **2** *one can combine good living with economy* **thrift,** thriftiness, prudence, careful budgeting, saving, restraint, frugality.
ANTONYMS extravagance.

ecosystem ▶ noun all the plants and animals of a particular area considered in terms of how they interact with their environment.

ecstasy ▶ noun (plural **ecstasies**) **1** an overwhelming feeling of great happiness. **2** (**Ecstasy**) an illegal drug that produces feelings of excitement and happiness.

SYNONYMS **rapture,** bliss, joy, elation, euphoria, rhapsodies.
ANTONYMS misery.

✔ no **x**: there is a **-cs-** at the beginning and an **s** at the end: e**cs**ta**s**y.

ecstatic ▶ adjective very happy or enthusiastic.

SYNONYMS **enraptured,** elated, euphoric, rapturous, joyful, overjoyed, blissful; informal over the moon, on top of the world.

□ **ecstatically** adverb.

ectoplasm ▶ noun a substance that is thought by some people to come out of the body of a medium during a seance.

Ecuadorean (or **Ecuadorian**) /ek-wuh-**dor**-i-uhn/ ▶ noun a person from Ecuador.
▶ adjective relating to Ecuador.

ecumenical ▶ adjective **1** representing a number of different Christian Churches. **2** wishing for the world's Christian Churches to be united.

eczema /eks-muh/ ▶ noun a condition in which patches of skin become rough and inflamed.

eddy ▶ noun (plural **eddies**) a circular movement of water causing a small whirlpool.

SYNONYMS *eddies at the river's edge* **swirl,** whirlpool, vortex.

▶ verb (**eddies, eddying, eddied**) (of water, air, etc.) move in a circular way.

SYNONYMS *the snow eddied around her* **swirl,** whirl, spiral, wind, twist.

edelweiss /ay-duhl-vyss/ ▶ noun a mountain plant with small flowers.

edema US spelling of OEDEMA.

Eden ▶ noun **1** (also **Garden of Eden**) the place where Adam and Eve lived in the story of the Creation in the Bible. **2** a place of happiness or unspoilt beauty.

edge ▶ noun **1** the outside limit of an object, area, or surface. **2** the sharpened side of a blade. **3** the line along which two surfaces meet. **4** a slight advantage over close rivals.

SYNONYMS **1** *the edge of the lake* **border,** boundary, extremity, fringe, margin, side, lip, rim, brim, brink, verge, perimeter. **2** *she had an edge in her voice* **sharpness,** severity, bite, sting, sarcasm, malice, spite, venom. **3** *they have an edge over their rivals* **advantage,** lead, head start, the whip hand, the upper hand, dominance.
ANTONYMS middle, kindness, disadvantage.

▶ verb (**edges, edging, edged**) **1** provide with an edge. **2** move slowly and carefully.

SYNONYMS **1** *poplars edged the orchard* **border,** fringe, skirt, surround, enclose, encircle, bound. **2** *a frock edged with lace* **trim,** decorate, finish, border, fringe. **3** *he edged closer to the fire* **creep,** inch, work your way, ease yourself, sidle, steal.
ANTONYMS stride.

■ **on edge** tense or irritable.

edgeways (or **edgewise**) ▶ adverb with the edge uppermost or towards the viewer.
■ **get a word in edgeways** manage to break into a conversation.

edgy ▶ adjective (**edgier, edgiest**) tense, nervous, or irritable.

edible ▶ adjective fit to be eaten.

edict /ee-dikt/ ▶ noun an official order or announcement.

edifice /ed-i-fiss/ ▶ noun formal a large, impressive building.

edify /ed-i-fy/ ▶ verb (edifies, edifying, edified) teach someone something that is educational or morally improving.
□ **edification** noun.

edit ▶ verb (edits, editing, edited) 1 prepare written material for publication by correcting or shortening it. 2 prepare material for a recording or broadcast. 3 be editor of a newspaper or magazine.

SYNONYMS **correct,** check, copy-edit, improve, polish, modify, adapt, revise, rewrite, reword, shorten, condense, cut, abridge.

edition ▶ noun 1 a particular form of a published written work. 2 the total number of copies of a book, newspaper, etc. that are issued. 3 a particular example of a regular programme or broadcast.

SYNONYMS **issue,** number, volume, printing, impression, publication, programme, version.

editor ▶ noun 1 a person who is in charge of a newspaper or magazine. 2 a person who prepares material for publication or broadcasting.

editorial ▶ adjective relating to the editing of material.
▶ noun a newspaper article giving the editor's opinion.

educate ▶ verb (educates, educating, educated) train or instruct someone to improve their mind or character.

SYNONYMS 1 **teach,** school, tutor, instruct, coach, train, inform, enlighten. 2 (**educated**) **informed,** literate, schooled, tutored, well read, learned, knowledgeable, enlightened, intellectual, academic, erudite, scholarly, cultivated, cultured.

education ▶ noun 1 the process of teaching or learning. 2 the theory and practice of teaching. 3 training in a particular subject.

SYNONYMS 1 *the education of young children* **teaching,** schooling, tuition, tutoring, instruction, coaching, training, guidance, enlightenment. 2 *a woman of some education* **learning,** knowledge, literacy, scholarship, enlightenment.

educational ▶ adjective 1 relating to education. 2 serving to educate.

SYNONYMS 1 *an educational establishment* **academic,** scholastic, learning, teaching, pedagogic. 2 *an educational experience* **instructive,** instructional, educative, informative, illuminating, enlightening; formal edifying.

□ **educationally** adverb.

Edwardian /ed-wor-di-uhn/ ▶ adjective relating to the reign of King Edward VII (1901–10).

EEC ▶ abbreviation European Economic Community.

eel ▶ noun a snake-like fish with a slender body.

eerie ▶ adjective (eerier, eeriest) strange and frightening.

SYNONYMS **uncanny,** sinister, ghostly, unnatural, unearthly, supernatural, other-worldly, strange, abnormal, weird, freakish; informal creepy, scary, spooky.

□ **eerily** adverb.

efface ▶ verb (effaces, effacing, effaced) 1 rub off a mark from a surface. 2 make something disappear. 3 (**efface yourself**) make yourself appear unimportant.

effect ▶ noun 1 a change that something causes in something else; a result. 2 operation or effectiveness. 3 the extent to which something succeeds. 4 (**effects**) personal belongings. 5 (**effects**) the lighting, sound, or scenery used in a play or film.

SYNONYMS 1 *the effect of these changes* **result,** consequence, upshot, outcome, repercussions, end result, aftermath. 2 *the effect of the drug* **impact,** action, effectiveness, power, potency, strength, success. 3 *the dead man's effects* **belongings,** possessions, worldly goods, chattels, property; informal things, stuff; Brit. informal clobber.
ANTONYMS cause.

▶ verb make something happen.

SYNONYMS *they effected many changes* **achieve,** accomplish, carry out, manage, bring off, execute, conduct, engineer, perform, do, cause, bring about, produce.

■ **in effect** in practice, even if not formally acknowledged.

❗ Don't confuse **effect** and **affect**. **Effect** chiefly means 'a result', while **affect** is a verb whose main meaning is 'make a difference to'.

effective ▶ adjective 1 producing a desired or intended result; successful. 2 (of a law or policy) in operation. 3 existing in fact, though not formally acknowledged as such.

SYNONYMS 1 *an effective treatment* **successful,** effectual, potent, powerful, helpful, beneficial, advantageous, valuable, useful. 2 *an effective argument* **convincing,** compelling, strong, forceful, persuasive, plausible, credible, logical, reasonable, cogent. 3 *the new law will be effective from next week* **operative,** in force, in effect, valid, official, legal, binding. 4 *Korea was under effective Japanese control* **virtual,** practical, essential, actual.

ANTONYMS ineffective, weak, invalid, theoretical.

□ **effectively** adverb **effectiveness** noun.

effectual ▸ adjective producing the intended result; effective.

effeminate ▸ adjective disapproving (of a man) looking, behaving, or sounding like a woman.

□ **effeminacy** noun.

effervescent /ef-fuh-**ve**-suhnt/ ▸ adjective **1** (of a liquid) giving off bubbles; fizzy. **2** lively and enthusiastic.

□ **effervesce** verb **effervescence** noun.

effete /i-**feet**/ ▸ adjective **1** weak; feeble. **2** (of a man) effeminate.

efficacious /ef-fi-**kay**-shuhss/ ▸ adjective formal effective.

efficacy /**ef**-fi-kuh-si/ ▸ noun formal effectiveness.

efficiency ▸ noun the quality of being efficient.

> SYNONYMS **1** *we need reforms to bring efficiency* **economy**, productivity, cost-effectiveness, organization, order, orderliness, regulation. **2** *I compliment you on your efficiency* **competence**, capability, ability, proficiency, expertise, skill, effectiveness.
> ANTONYMS inefficiency, incompetence.

efficient ▸ adjective working well with no waste of money or effort.

> SYNONYMS **1** *efficient techniques* **economic**, productive, effective, cost-effective, streamlined, organized, methodical, systematic, orderly. **2** *an efficient secretary* **competent**, capable, able, proficient, skilful, skilled, effective, productive, organized, businesslike.
> ANTONYMS inefficient, incompetent.

□ **efficiently** adverb.

effigy /**ef**-fi-ji/ ▸ noun (plural **effigies**) a sculpture or statue of a person.

effluent ▸ noun liquid waste or sewage that flows into a river or the sea.

effluvium /i-**floo**-vi-uhm/ ▸ noun (plural **effluvia** /i-**floo**-vi-uh/) an unpleasant or harmful smell.

effort ▸ noun **1** a determined attempt to do something. **2** the physical or mental energy needed to do something.

> SYNONYMS **1** *an effort to work together* **attempt**, try, endeavour; informal shot, stab, bash. **2** *a fine effort* **achievement**, accomplishment, feat, undertaking, enterprise, work, result, outcome. **3** *the job requires little effort* **exertion**, energy, work, application; informal elbow grease; Brit. informal graft.

effortless ▸ adjective done or achieved without effort; natural and easy.

□ **effortlessly** adverb.

effrontery /i-**frun**-tuh-ri/ ▸ noun rude and disrespectful behaviour.

effusion ▸ noun an act of talking or writing in an unrestrained way.

effusive ▸ adjective expressing pleasure or approval in a warm and emotional way.

□ **effusively** adverb.

e.g. ▸ abbreviation for example.

ORIGIN short for Latin *exempli gratia*, meaning 'for the sake of example'.

egalitarian /i-gal-i-**tair**-i-uhn/ ▸ adjective believing that all people are equal and deserve equal rights and opportunities.

▸ noun an egalitarian person.

□ **egalitarianism** noun.

egg[1] ▸ noun **1** a small oval or round object laid by a female bird, reptile, fish, etc., and containing a cell which can develop into a new creature. **2** a female reproductive cell; an ovum.

egg[2] ▸ verb (**egg someone on**) urge someone to do something foolish.

egghead ▸ noun informal a very intelligent and hard-working person.

eggplant ▸ noun N. Amer. an aubergine.

ego /**ee**-goh/ ▸ noun (plural **egos**) **1** a person's sense of their own value and importance. **2** the part of the mind that is responsible for a person's sense of who they are.

egocentric ▸ adjective self-centred.

egomania ▸ noun an obsessive concern with yourself.

egotism (or **egoism**) ▸ noun the quality of being very conceited or self-absorbed.

□ **egotist** (or **egoist**) noun **egotistical** (or **egoistical**) adjective.

egregious /i-**gree**-juhss/ ▸ adjective formal very bad.

egress /**ee**-gress/ ▸ noun formal **1** the action of going out of a place. **2** a way out.

egret /**ee**-grit/ ▸ noun a kind of heron with white feathers.

Egyptian ▸ noun **1** a person from Egypt. **2** the language used in ancient Egypt.

▸ adjective relating to Egypt.

Egyptology ▸ noun the study of the language, history, and culture of ancient Egypt.

□ **Egyptologist** noun.

Eid (or **Id**) /eed/ ▸ noun **1** the Muslim festival marking the end of the fast of Ramadan. **2** the Muslim festival marking the end of the annual pilgrimage to Mecca.

eider /**I**-der/ ▸ noun (plural **eider** or **eiders**) a black and white duck that lives in northern countries.

eiderdown ▸ noun Brit. a quilt filled with down or another soft material.

eight ▸ cardinal number **1** one more than seven; 8. (Roman numeral: **viii** or **VIII**.) **2** a rowing boat with eight oars.

eighteen ▸ cardinal number one more than seventeen; 18. (Roman numeral: **xviii** or **XVIII**.)
□ **eighteenth** ordinal number.

eighth ▸ ordinal number **1** at number eight in a sequence; 8th. **2** (an eighth or one eighth) each of eight equal parts of something.

> ✔ There are two **h**s: eig**h**th.

eighty ▸ cardinal number (plural **eighties**) ten less than ninety; 80. (Roman numeral: **lxxx** or **LXXX**.)
□ **eightieth** ordinal number.

eisteddfod /I-ste*th*-vod/ ▸ noun a Welsh festival with music and poetry competitions.

either ▸ conjunction & adverb **1** used before the first of two alternatives specified. **2** used to indicate a similarity or link with a statement just made. **3** for that matter; moreover.
▸ determiner & pronoun **1** one or the other of two people or things. **2** each of two.

ejaculate ▸ verb (**ejaculates, ejaculating, ejaculated**) **1** (of a man or male animal) eject semen from the penis at the moment of orgasm. **2** dated say something suddenly.
□ **ejaculation** noun.

eject ▸ verb **1** force or throw out violently or suddenly. **2** force someone to leave a place. **3** (of a pilot) escape from an aircraft by means of an ejection seat.

> SYNONYMS **1** *the volcano ejected ash* **emit,** spew out, discharge, give off, send out, belch, vent. **2** *they were ejected from the hall* **expel,** throw out, remove, oust, evict, banish; informal kick out. **3** *the pilot had time to eject* **bail out,** escape.
> ANTONYMS take in, admit.

■ **ejection seat** (or **ejector seat**) a seat that can throw the pilot out of the aircraft in an emergency.
□ **ejection** noun.

eke ▸ verb (**ekes, eking, eked**) (**eke something out**) **1** make a supply of something last a long time. **2** make a living with difficulty.

elaborate ▸ adjective /i-**lab**-uh-ruht/ involving many carefully arranged parts or details; complicated.

> SYNONYMS **1** *an elaborate plan* **complicated,** complex, intricate, involved, detailed. **2** *an elaborate plasterwork ceiling* **ornate,** decorated, embellished, adorned, ornamented, fancy, fussy, busy.
> ANTONYMS simple, plain.

▸ verb /i-**lab**-uh-rayt/ (**elaborates, elaborating, elaborated**) develop something in more detail.

> SYNONYMS *both sides refused to elaborate on their reasons* **expand on,** enlarge

on, add to, flesh out, develop, fill out, amplify.
□ **elaborately** adverb **elaboration** noun.

elan /ay-**lan**/ ▸ noun energy and stylishness.

elapse ▸ verb (**elapses, elapsing, elapsed**) (of time) pass.

elastic ▸ adjective **1** able to go back to its normal shape after being stretched or squeezed. **2** flexible.

> SYNONYMS **1** *elastic material* **stretchy,** elasticated, springy, flexible, pliable, supple. **2** *an elastic concept of nationality* **adaptable,** flexible, adjustable, accommodating, variable, fluid, versatile.
> ANTONYMS rigid.

▸ noun cord or fabric which returns to its original length or shape after being stretched.
■ **elastic band** a rubber band.
□ **elasticity** noun.

elasticated ▸ adjective Brit. (of a garment or part of a garment) made elastic with rubber thread or tape.

elated ▸ adjective very happy and excited.

elation ▸ noun great happiness and excitement.

elbow ▸ noun the joint between the forearm and the upper arm.
▸ verb push someone with your elbow.
■ **elbow grease** informal hard work in cleaning something.

elder¹ ▸ adjective older.

> SYNONYMS *his elder brother* **older,** senior, big.

▸ noun **1** (your elder) a person who is older than you are. **2** a leader or senior figure in a tribe.

> SYNONYMS *the church elders* **leader,** patriarch, father.

elder² ▸ noun a small tree or shrub with white flowers and bluish-black or red berries (**elderberries**).

elderly ▸ adjective old or ageing.

> SYNONYMS **aged,** old, ageing, long in the tooth, grey-haired, in your dotage; informal getting on, over the hill.
> ANTONYMS youthful.

eldest ▸ adjective oldest.

elect ▸ verb **1** choose someone to hold a position by voting for them. **2** choose to do something.

> SYNONYMS **1** *a new president was elected* **vote in,** vote for, return, cast your vote for, choose, pick, select. **2** *she elected to stay behind* **choose,** decide, opt, prefer, vote.

▸ adjective elected to a position but not yet in office: *the President-Elect.*

election ▸ noun **1** a procedure by which a person is elected. **2** the action of electing.

> SYNONYMS **ballot,** vote, poll; Brit. by-election; US primary.

electioneering ▸ noun the action of campaigning to be elected.

elective ▸ adjective **1** using or chosen by election. **2** (of study, treatment, etc.) chosen; not compulsory.

elector ▸ noun a person who has the right to vote in an election.

electoral ▸ adjective relating to elections or electors.
■ **electoral roll** (or **electoral register**) an official list of the people in a district who are entitled to vote in an election.

electorate ▸ noun the people who are entitled to vote in an election.

electric ▸ adjective **1** of, worked by, or producing electricity. **2** very exciting.

> SYNONYMS *the atmosphere was electric* **exciting,** charged, electrifying, thrilling, dramatic, dynamic, stimulating, galvanizing.

▸ noun (**electrics**) Brit. the system of electric wiring in a house or vehicle.
■ **electric chair** a chair in which convicted criminals are executed by electrocution. **electric shock** a sudden discharge of electricity through a part of the body.

electrical ▸ adjective concerned with, operating by, or producing electricity.
□ **electrically** adverb.

electrician ▸ noun a person who installs and maintains electrical equipment.

electricity ▸ noun **1** a form of energy resulting from charged particles. **2** the supply of electric current to a building for heating, lighting, etc.

electrify ▸ verb (**electrifies, electrifying, electrified**) **1** charge something with electricity. **2** convert something to use electrical power. **3** (**electrifying**) very exciting.

> SYNONYMS **excite,** thrill, stimulate, arouse, rouse, inspire, stir (up), exhilarate, galvanize, fire (with enthusiasm), fire someone's imagination, invigorate, animate; N. Amer. light a fire under.

electroconvulsive ▸ adjective (of therapy for mental illness) using electric shocks applied to the brain.

electrocute ▸ verb (**electrocutes, electrocuting, electrocuted**) injure or kill by electric shock.
□ **electrocution** noun.

electrode ▸ noun a conductor through which electricity enters or leaves something.

electrolysis /i-lek-**trol**-i-siss/ ▸ noun **1** the separation of a liquid into its chemical parts by passing an electric current through it. **2** the removal of hair roots or small blemishes on the skin by means of an electric current.

electrolyte ▸ noun a liquid or gel that an electric current can pass through, e.g. in a battery.

electromagnet ▸ noun a metal core made into a magnet by passing electric current through a surrounding coil.

electromagnetic ▸ adjective relating to electric currents and magnetic fields.
□ **electromagnetism** noun.

electromotive ▸ adjective tending to produce an electric current.

electron ▸ noun Physics a subatomic particle with a negative charge, found in all atoms.
■ **electron microscope** a powerful microscope using electron beams instead of light.

electronic ▸ adjective **1** having parts such as microchips and transistors that control and direct electric currents. **2** relating to electrons or electronics. **3** carried out by means of a computer.
■ **electronic mail** email.
□ **electronically** adverb.

electronics ▸ plural noun **1** the use or study of electronic devices. **2** the study of the behaviour and movement of electrons. **3** circuits or devices using transistors, microchips, etc.

electroplate ▸ verb (**electroplates, electroplating, electroplated**) coat a metal object with another metal using electrolysis.

elegance ▸ noun the quality of being elegant.

> SYNONYMS **1** *he was attracted by her elegance* **style,** grace, taste, sophistication, refinement, dignity, poise. **2** *the elegance of the idea* **neatness,** simplicity.

elegant ▸ adjective attractive, graceful, and stylish.

> SYNONYMS **1** *an elegant black outfit* **stylish,** graceful, tasteful, sophisticated, classic, chic, smart, poised, cultivated, polished, cultured. **2** *an elegant solution* **neat,** simple.
> ANTONYMS inelegant.

□ **elegantly** adverb.

elegiac /el-i-**jy**-uhk/ ▸ adjective expressing sadness, especially about the past or a person who has died.

elegy /**el**-i-ji/ ▸ noun (plural **elegies**) a poem expressing sadness, especially for a person who has died.

element ▸ noun **1** a basic part of something. **2** each of more than one hundred

e

substances that cannot be changed or broken down. **3** any of the four substances (earth, water, air, and fire) which were formerly believed to make up all matter. **4** a trace. **5** a distinct group within a larger group. **6** (**the elements**) weather conditions such as rain, wind, and cold. **7** a part in an electric device through which an electric current is passed to provide heat.

> SYNONYMS **1** *an essential element of the local community* **component**, constituent, part, section, portion, piece, segment, aspect, factor, feature, facet, ingredient, strand, detail, member. **2** *there is an element of truth in this stereotype* **trace**, touch, hint, smattering, soupçon. **3** (**elements**) *I braved the elements* **weather**, climate, weather conditions.

elemental ▶ adjective **1** fundamental. **2** having to do with or like the primitive forces of nature.

elementary ▶ adjective **1** relating to the most basic aspects of a subject. **2** straightforward and uncomplicated.

> SYNONYMS **1** *an elementary astronomy course* **basic**, rudimentary, preparatory, introductory. **2** *a lot of the work is elementary* **easy**, simple, straightforward, uncomplicated, undemanding, painless, child's play, plain sailing; informal a piece of cake.
> ANTONYMS advanced, difficult.

elephant ▶ noun (plural **elephant** or **elephants**) a very large animal with a trunk, long curved tusks, and large ears, found in Africa and Asia.

elephantine /el-i-fan-tyn/ ▶ adjective resembling an elephant.

elevate ▶ verb (**elevates, elevating, elevated**) **1** lift to a higher position. **2** raise to a higher level or status.

> SYNONYMS **1** *we need a breeze to elevate the kite* **raise**, lift (up), raise up/aloft, hoist, hike up, haul up. **2** *he was elevated to Secretary of State* **promote**, upgrade, move up, raise; informal kick upstairs.
> ANTONYMS lower, demote.

elevated ▶ adjective of a high intellectual or moral level.

> SYNONYMS **1** *an elevated motorway* **raised**, overhead, in the air, high up. **2** *elevated language* **lofty**, grand, exalted, fine, sublime, inflated, pompous, bombastic. **3** *his elevated status* **high**, high-ranking, lofty, exalted, grand, noble.
> ANTONYMS sunken, everyday, lowly.

elevation ▶ noun **1** the action of elevating. **2** height above a given level, especially sea level. **3** the angle of something with the horizontal.

elevator ▶ noun N. Amer. a lift in a building.

eleven ▶ cardinal number **1** one more than ten; 11. (Roman numeral: **xi** or **XI**.) **2** a sports team of eleven players.
■ **the eleventh hour** the latest possible moment.
□ **eleventh** ordinal number.

elevenses ▶ plural noun Brit. informal a mid-morning snack.

elf ▶ noun (plural **elves**) (in folk tales) a creature resembling a small human figure with pointed ears.

elfin ▶ adjective (of a person) small and delicate.

elicit /i-**liss**-it/ ▶ verb (**elicits, eliciting, elicited**) produce or draw out a response or reaction.

> SYNONYMS **obtain**, draw out, extract, bring out, evoke, induce, prompt, generate, trigger, provoke.

elide /i-**lyd**/ ▶ verb (**elides, eliding, elided**) **1** omit a sound or syllable when speaking. **2** join together.

eligible ▶ adjective **1** meeting the conditions to do or receive something. **2** desirable as a husband or wife.

> SYNONYMS **1** *those eligible to vote* **entitled**, permitted, allowed, qualified, able. **2** *an eligible bachelor* **desirable**, suitable, available, single, unmarried, unattached.
> □ **eligibility** noun.

eliminate ▶ verb (**eliminates, eliminating, eliminated**) **1** completely remove or get rid of. **2** exclude someone from a competition by beating them.

> SYNONYMS **1** *a policy that would eliminate inflation* **remove**, get rid of, put an end to, do away with, end, stop, eradicate, destroy, stamp out. **2** *he was eliminated from the title race* **knock out**, exclude, rule out, disqualify.
> □ **elimination** noun.

elision /i-**li**-zh'n/ ▶ noun the omission of a sound or syllable in speech.

elite /i-**leet**/ ▶ noun a group of people regarded as the best in a particular society or organization.

> SYNONYMS **best**, pick, cream, crème de la crème, flower, high society, beautiful people, aristocracy, ruling class.
> ANTONYMS dregs.

elitism ▶ noun **1** the belief that a society should be run by an elite. **2** the superior attitude associated with an elite.
□ **elitist** adjective & noun.

elixir /i-**lik**-seer/ ▶ noun a drink believed to make people live for ever or have other magical effects.

Elizabethan ▶ adjective relating to the reign of Queen Elizabeth I (1558–1603).

elk ▸ noun (plural **elk** or **elks**) a kind of large deer.

ellipse ▸ noun a regular oval shape.

ellipsis /i-**lip**-siss/ ▸ noun (plural **ellipses** /i-**lip**-seez/) **1** the omission of words from speech or writing. **2** a set of dots indicating such an omission.

elliptical ▸ adjective **1** (of speech or writing) having a word or words deliberately left out. **2** (also **elliptic**) having the shape of an ellipse.

elm ▸ noun a tall tree with rough leaves.

elocution ▸ noun the skill of speaking clearly.

elongate ▸ verb (**elongates**, **elongating**, **elongated**) make or become longer.
□ **elongation** noun.

elope ▸ verb (**elopes**, **eloping**, **eloped**) run away secretly to get married.

eloquence ▸ noun fluent or persuasive speaking or writing.

eloquent ▸ adjective **1** fluent or persuasive in speech or writing. **2** clearly expressive.

> SYNONYMS **articulate**, fluent, expressive, persuasive, well expressed, effective, lucid, vivid.
> ANTONYMS inarticulate.

□ **eloquently** adverb.

else ▸ adverb **1** in addition. **2** different; instead.
■ **or else** if not; otherwise.

elsewhere ▸ adverb in, at, or to some other place or other places.

elucidate ▸ verb (**elucidates**, **elucidating**, **elucidated**) make clear; explain.
□ **elucidation** noun.

elude ▸ verb (**eludes**, **eluding**, **eluded**) **1** cleverly escape from or avoid. **2** fail to be understood or achieved by.

elusive ▸ adjective difficult to find, catch, or achieve.

> SYNONYMS **1** *her elusive husband* **difficult to find**, slippery. **2** *an elusive quality* **indefinable**, intangible, impalpable, fugitive, fleeting, transitory, ambiguous.

elver ▸ noun a young eel.

elves plural of ELF.

Elysian /i-**liz**-i-uhn/ ▸ adjective relating to or like paradise.

emaciated /i-**may**-si-ay-tid/ ▸ adjective abnormally thin and weak.
□ **emaciation** noun.

email (or **e-mail**) ▸ noun the sending of electronic messages from one computer user to another via a network, or a message sent in this way.
▸ verb send someone a message using email.

emanate /**em**-uh-nayt/ ▸ verb (**emanates**, **emanating**, **emanated**) **1** (**emanate from**) come out from a place or source. **2** give out

a feeling or quality.
□ **emanation** noun.

emancipate ▸ verb (**emancipates**, **emancipating**, **emancipated**) **1** set free from restrictions. **2** free from slavery.
□ **emancipation** noun.

emasculate ▸ verb (**emasculates**, **emasculating**, **emasculated**) **1** make weaker or less effective. **2** deprive a man of his male role or identity.
□ **emasculation** noun.

embalm ▸ verb treat a dead body to preserve it from decay.

embankment ▸ noun **1** a wall or bank built to prevent flooding by a river. **2** a bank of earth or stone built to carry a road or railway over an area of low ground.

embargo /em-**bar**-goh/ ▸ noun (plural **embargoes**) an official ban, especially on trade with a particular country.

> SYNONYMS *an embargo on oil sales* **ban,** bar, prohibition, stoppage, veto, moratorium, restriction, block, boycott.

▸ verb (**embargoes**, **embargoing**, **embargoed**) put an embargo on.

> SYNONYMS *arms sales were embargoed* **ban,** bar, prohibit, stop, outlaw, blacklist, restrict, block, boycott.
> ANTONYMS allow.

embark ▸ verb **1** go on board a ship or aircraft. **2** (**embark on**) begin a new project or course of action.

> SYNONYMS **board (ship)**, go on board, go aboard; informal hop on, jump on.
> ANTONYMS disembark.

□ **embarkation** noun.

embarrass ▸ verb make someone feel awkward or ashamed.

> SYNONYMS **1** **humiliate**, shame, put someone to shame, abash, mortify, fluster, discomfit; informal show up. **2** (**embarrassed**) **humiliated**, mortified, red-faced, blushing, abashed, shamed, ashamed, shamefaced, self-conscious, uncomfortable, discomfited, disconcerted, flustered; informal with egg on your face. **3** (**embarrassing**) **humiliating**, shameful, mortifying, ignominious, awkward, uncomfortable, compromising; discomfiting; informal cringeworthy, cringe-making, toe-curling.

> ✔ double **r**, double **s**: embar**r**a**ss**.

embarrassment ▸ noun a feeling of shame or awkwardness.

> SYNONYMS **1** *he was scarlet with embarrassment* **humiliation**, mortification, shame, shamefacedness, awkwardness, self-consciousness, discomfort, discomfiture. **2** *his current*

financial embarrassment **difficulty,** predicament, plight, problem, mess; informal **bind, pickle, fix.**

embassy ▸ noun (plural **embassies**) the official residence or offices of an ambassador.

embattled ▸ adjective **1** facing a lot of difficulties. **2** surrounded by enemy forces.

embed (or **imbed**) ▸ verb (**embeds, embedding, embedded**) fix something firmly in a surrounding mass.

embellish ▸ verb **1** make more attractive; decorate. **2** add extra details to a story.

ember ▸ noun a piece of burning wood or coal in a dying fire.

embezzle ▸ verb (**embezzles, embezzling, embezzled**) steal money that you have been given responsibility for.
□ **embezzlement** noun.

embittered ▸ adjective angry or resentful.

emblazon /im-**blay**-zuhn/ ▸ verb display a design on something in a very noticeable way.

emblem ▸ noun a design or symbol as a badge of a nation, organization, or family.

SYNONYMS **symbol,** representation, token, image, figure, mark, sign, crest, badge, device, insignia, coat of arms, shield, logo, trademark.

emblematic ▸ adjective representing a particular quality or idea.

embody ▸ verb (**embodies, embodying, embodied**) **1** give a tangible or visible form to an idea or quality. **2** include or contain.

SYNONYMS **1** *Gradgrind embodies the spirit of industrial capitalism* **personify,** manifest, symbolize, represent, express, epitomize, stand for, typify, exemplify. **2** *the changes embodied in the Act* **incorporate,** include, contain.

□ **embodiment** noun.

embolden ▸ verb make someone braver or more confident.

embolism /em-buh-li-z'm/ ▸ noun obstruction of an artery by a clot of blood or an air bubble.

emboss ▸ verb carve a raised design on.

embrace ▸ verb (**embraces, embracing, embraced**) **1** hold someone closely in your arms. **2** include or contain. **3** willingly accept or support a belief or change.

SYNONYMS **1** *he embraced her warmly* **hug,** take/hold in your arms, hold, cuddle, clasp to your bosom, squeeze, clutch, enfold. **2** *most western European countries have embraced the concept* **welcome,** welcome with open arms, accept, take on board, take up, take to your heart, adopt, espouse. **3** *the faculty embraces a wide range of disciplines*

include, take in, comprise, contain, incorporate, encompass, cover, subsume.

▸ noun an act of embracing.

SYNONYMS *a fond embrace* **hug,** cuddle, squeeze, clinch, caress.

embrocation ▸ noun a liquid medication rubbed on the body to relieve pain from strains.

embroider ▸ verb (**embroiders, embroidering, embroidered**) **1** sew decorative needlework patterns on. **2** add false or exaggerated details to.

embroidery ▸ noun (plural **embroideries**) **1** the art of embroidering. **2** embroidered cloth.

embroil ▸ verb (**embroil someone in**) involve someone in a conflict or difficult situation.

embryo /em-bri-oh/ ▸ noun (plural **embryos**) an unborn or unhatched baby or animal in the early stages of development.

embryonic ▸ adjective **1** relating to an embryo. **2** in a very early stage of development.

emend ▸ verb correct and revise a piece of writing.

emerald ▸ noun **1** a green precious stone. **2** a bright green colour.

emerge ▸ verb (**emerges, emerging, emerged**) **1** become gradually visible. **2** (of facts) become known. **3** recover from a difficult situation or experience.

SYNONYMS **1** *a policeman emerged from the alley* **come out,** appear, come into view, become visible, surface, materialize, issue, come forth. **2** *several unexpected facts emerged* **become known,** become apparent, be revealed, come to light, come out, turn up, transpire, unfold, turn out, prove to be the case.

emergence ▸ noun the process of emerging.

SYNONYMS **appearance,** arrival, coming, materialization, advent, inception, dawn, birth, origination, start, development.

emergency ▸ noun (plural **emergencies**) a serious and unexpected situation requiring immediate action.

SYNONYMS *a military emergency* **crisis,** disaster, catastrophe, calamity, plight; informal **panic stations.**

▸ adjective **1** arising from an emergency. **2** used in an emergency.

SYNONYMS **1** *an emergency meeting* **urgent,** crisis, extraordinary. **2** *emergency supplies* **reserve,** standby, backup, fallback.

emergent ▶ adjective new and still developing.

emeritus /i-**me**-ri-tuhss/ ▶ adjective having retired but allowed to keep a title as an honour: *an emeritus professor*.

emery board ▶ noun a strip of thin wood or card coated with a rough material and used as a nail file.

emetic /i-**met**-ik/ ▶ adjective causing vomiting.

emigrant ▶ noun a person who emigrates.

emigrate ▶ verb (**emigrates, emigrating, emigrated**) leave your own country and settle permanently in another.

SYNONYMS **move abroad,** move overseas, leave your country, migrate, relocate, resettle.
ANTONYMS immigrate.

☐ **emigration** noun.

émigré /**em**-i-gray/ ▶ noun a person who has emigrated.

eminence ▶ noun 1 the quality of being very famous and respected in a particular area of activity. 2 an important or distinguished person.

eminent ▶ adjective 1 very famous and respected; distinguished. 2 outstanding or obvious.

SYNONYMS **illustrious,** distinguished, renowned, esteemed, pre-eminent, notable, noted, noteworthy, great, prestigious, important, outstanding, celebrated, prominent, well known, acclaimed, exalted.
ANTONYMS unknown.

☐ **eminently** adverb.

emir /e-**meer**/ (or **amir** /uh-**meer**/) ▶ noun a title of some Muslim rulers.

emissary /**em**-i-suh-ri/ ▶ noun (plural **emissaries**) a person sent as a diplomatic representative on a mission.

emission ▶ noun 1 the action of emitting. 2 a substance which is emitted.

SYNONYMS **discharge,** release, outpouring, outflow, outrush, leak.

emit ▶ verb (**emits, emitting, emitted**) 1 give out light, heat, gas, etc. 2 make a sound.

SYNONYMS 1 *hydrocarbons emitted from vehicle exhausts* **discharge,** release, give out/off, pour out, radiate, leak, ooze, disgorge, eject, belch, spew out, exude. 2 *he emitted a loud cry* **utter,** voice, let out, produce, give vent to, come out with.
ANTONYMS absorb, stifle.

emollient /i-**mol**-li-uhnt/ ▶ adjective 1 softening or soothing the skin. 2 attempting to avoid conflict; calming.
☐ **emollience** noun.

emolument /i-**mol**-yuu-muhnt/ ▶ noun formal a salary or fee.

emotion ▶ noun 1 a strong feeling, such as joy or anger. 2 instinctive feeling as opposed to reasoning.

SYNONYMS 1 *she was good at hiding her emotions* **feeling,** sentiment, reaction, response, instinct, intuition, heart. 2 *overcome by emotion, she turned away* **passion,** strength of feeling.

emotional ▶ adjective 1 relating to the emotions. 2 arousing or showing emotion.

SYNONYMS 1 *an emotional young man* **passionate,** hot-blooded, ardent, fervent, excitable, temperamental, demonstrative. 2 *he paid an emotional tribute to his wife* **poignant,** moving, touching, affecting, powerful, stirring, emotive, impassioned, dramatic; informal tear-jerking.
ANTONYMS cold, clinical.

☐ **emotionally** adverb.

emotive ▶ adjective arousing strong feeling.

empathize (or **empathise**) ▶ verb (**empathizes, empathizing, empathized**) understand and share the feelings of someone else.

empathy ▶ noun the ability to understand and share the feelings of someone else.

emperor ▶ noun the ruler of an empire.

emphasis /**em**-fuh-siss/ ▶ noun (plural **emphases** /**em**-fuh-seez/) 1 special importance or value given to something. 2 stress put on a word or words in speaking.

SYNONYMS 1 *the curriculum gave more emphasis to reading and writing* **prominence,** importance, significance, value, stress, weight, accent, attention, priority. 2 *the emphasis is on the word 'little'* **stress,** accent, weight, beat.

emphasize (or **emphasise**) ▶ verb (**emphasizes, emphasizing, emphasized**) give special importance or prominence to.

SYNONYMS **stress,** underline, highlight, focus attention on, point up, lay stress on, draw attention to, spotlight, foreground.
ANTONYMS understate.

emphatic ▶ adjective 1 showing or giving emphasis. 2 definite and clear.

SYNONYMS **forceful,** firm, vehement, wholehearted, energetic, vigorous, direct, insistent, certain, definite, out-and-out, decided, categorical, unqualified, unconditional, unequivocal, unambiguous, absolute, explicit, downright, outright, clear.
ANTONYMS hesitant.

☐ **emphatically** adverb.

e

emphysema /em-fi-**see**-muh/ ▶ noun a condition that affects the lungs, causing breathlessness.

empire ▶ noun **1** a large group of countries under a single authority or ruler. **2** a large commercial organization under the control of one person or group.

> synonyms **1** *the Ottoman Empire* **kingdom,** realm, domain, territory, commonwealth, power. **2** *a worldwide shipping empire* **business,** firm, company, corporation, multinational, conglomerate, group, consortium, operation.

empirical ▶ adjective based on observation or experience rather than theory or logic. □ **empirically** adverb **empiricism** noun **empiricist** noun.

emplacement ▶ noun a structure or platform where a gun is placed for firing.

employ ▶ verb **1** give work to someone and pay them for it. **2** make use of. **3** keep someone occupied.

> synonyms **1** *she employed a chauffeur* **hire,** engage, recruit, take on, sign up, appoint, retain. **2** *Sam was employed in carving a stone figure* **occupy,** engage, involve, keep busy, tie up. **3** (**employed**) **working,** in work, in employment, holding down a job, earning, salaried, waged. **4** *the team employed subtle psychological tactics* **use,** utilize, make use of, apply, exercise, practise, put into practice, exert, bring into play, bring to bear, draw on, resort to, turn to, have recourse to.
> antonyms dismiss.

employee ▶ noun a person who is employed by a company or individual.

> synonyms **worker,** member of staff, blue-collar worker, white-collar worker, workman, labourer, (hired) hand; (**employees**) personnel, staff, workforce.

employer ▶ noun a company or individual that employs people.

employment ▶ noun **1** the state of having paid work. **2** a person's work or profession.

> synonyms **work,** labour, service, job, post, position, situation, occupation, profession, trade, business, line of work.

emporium /em-**por**-i-uhm/ ▶ noun (plural **emporia** or **emporiums**) a large store selling a wide variety of goods.

empower ▶ verb (**empowers, empowering, empowered**) **1** give authority or power to. **2** give strength and confidence to.

> synonyms **1** *the act empowered Henry to punish heretics* **authorize,** entitle, permit, allow, license, enable. **2** *movements to empower the poor* **emancipate,**

unshackle, set free, liberate, enfranchise.
> antonyms forbid.

□ **empowerment** noun.

empress ▶ noun **1** a female emperor. **2** the wife or widow of an emperor.

empty ▶ adjective (**emptier, emptiest**) **1** containing nothing; not filled or occupied. **2** (of words or gestures) having no real meaning: *empty promises.*

> synonyms **1** *an empty house* **vacant,** unoccupied, uninhabited, bare, clear, free. **2** *an empty threat* **meaningless,** hollow, idle, vain, futile, worthless, useless, ineffectual. **3** *without her my life is empty* **futile,** pointless, purposeless, worthless, meaningless, valueless, of no value, aimless, senseless.
> antonyms full, occupied, serious, worthwhile.

▶ verb (**empties, emptying, emptied**) **1** make or become empty. **2** (of a river) flow into the sea or a lake.

> synonyms **1** *I emptied the dishwasher* **unload,** unpack, clear, evacuate, drain. **2** *he emptied out the contents of the case* **remove,** take out, extract, tip out, pour out.
> antonyms fill, replace.

□ **emptiness** noun.

emu ▶ noun a large Australian bird which is unable to fly, similar to an ostrich.

emulate ▶ verb (**emulates, emulating, emulated**) try to do as well as or be better than.

> synonyms **imitate,** copy, mirror, echo, follow, model yourself on, take a leaf out of someone's book.

□ **emulation** noun.

emulsify ▶ verb (**emulsifies, emulsifying, emulsified**) combine two liquids into a smooth mixture.
□ **emulsifier** noun.

emulsion ▶ noun **1** a mixture of two liquids in which particles of one are evenly distributed in the other. **2** a type of paint for walls and ceilings. **3** a light-sensitive coating for photographic film.

enable ▶ verb (**enables, enabling, enabled**) **1** provide with the ability or means to do something. **2** make something possible.

> synonyms **allow,** permit, let, equip, empower, make able, fit, authorize, entitle, qualify.
> antonyms prevent.

enact ▶ verb **1** pass a law. **2** act out a role or play.

> synonyms **1** *the government enacted an environmental protection bill* **make law,** pass, approve, ratify, validate, sanction, authorize. **2** *they are to enact a nativity*

play **act out,** perform, appear in, stage, mount, put on, present.
ANTONYMS repeal.

☐ **enactment** noun.

enamel ▸ noun **1** a coloured glassy substance applied to metal, glass, or pottery for decoration or protection. **2** the hard substance that covers the crown of a tooth. **3** a paint that dries to give a hard coat.
▸ verb (**enamels, enamelling, enamelled;** US spelling **enamels, enameling, enameled**) coat or decorate with enamel.

enamour (US spelling **enamor**) ▸ verb (**be enamoured of** or **with**) be filled with love or admiration for.

en bloc /on **blok**/ ▸ adverb all together, or all at once.

encamp ▸ verb settle in or set up a camp.

encampment ▸ noun a place where a camp is set up.

encapsulate ▸ verb (**encapsulates, encapsulating, encapsulated**) summarize clearly and in few words.

encase ▸ verb (**encases, encasing, encased**) enclose or cover in a case.

encephalitis /en-sef-uh-ly-tiss/ ▸ noun inflammation of the brain.

enchant ▸ verb **1** delight; charm. **2** put under a spell.
☐ **enchanter** noun **enchantment** noun **enchantress** noun.

enchanting ▸ adjective delightfully charming or attractive.

SYNONYMS **captivating,** charming, delightful, adorable, lovely, attractive, appealing, engaging, fetching, irresistible, fascinating.

enchilada /en-chi-**lah**-duh/ ▸ noun a tortilla filled with meat or cheese and served with chilli sauce.

encircle ▸ verb (**encircles, encircling, encircled**) form a circle around.

enclave /en-**klayv**/ ▸ noun a small area of one country's territory which is surrounded by another country.

enclose ▸ verb (**encloses, enclosing, enclosed**) **1** surround or close off on all sides. **2** put a document or object in an envelope along with a letter.

SYNONYMS **1** *tall trees enclosed the garden* **surround,** circle, ring, encircle, bound, close in, wall in. **2** *please enclose a stamped addressed envelope* **include,** insert, put in, send.

enclosure ▸ noun **1** an enclosed area. **2** a document or object put in an envelope along with a letter.

SYNONYMS **compound,** pen, fold, stockade, ring, paddock, yard, run, coop; N. Amer. corral.

encode ▸ verb (**encodes, encoding, encoded**) convert into a coded form.

encompass ▸ verb **1** include a wide range of things. **2** surround or cover.

SYNONYMS **include,** cover, embrace, incorporate, take in, contain, comprise, involve, deal with.

encore /**ong**-kor/ ▸ noun a short extra performance given at the end of a concert in response to calls by the audience.

encounter ▸ verb (**encounters, encountering, encountered**) unexpectedly meet or be faced with.

SYNONYMS **1** *we encountered a slight problem* **experience,** run into, meet, come up against, face, be faced with, confront, suffer. **2** *I encountered a girl I used to know* **meet,** run into, come across/upon, stumble across/on, chance on, happen on; informal bump into.
▸ noun **1** an unexpected or casual meeting. **2** a confrontation.

SYNONYMS **1** *an unexpected encounter* **meeting,** chance meeting. **2** *a violent encounter between police and demonstrators* **battle,** fight, clash, scuffle, confrontation, struggle; informal run-in, scrap.

encourage ▸ verb (**encourages, encouraging, encouraged**) **1** give support, confidence, or hope to. **2** help the development of.

SYNONYMS **1** *the players were encouraged by the crowd* **hearten,** cheer, buoy up, uplift, inspire, motivate, spur on, stir, fire up, stimulate, embolden; informal buck up. **2** *she encouraged him to go* **persuade,** coax, urge, press, push, pressure, prod. **3** *the Government was keen to encourage local businesses* **support,** back, promote, further, foster, nurture, cultivate, strengthen, stimulate.
ANTONYMS discourage, dissuade, hinder.

☐ **encouraging** adjective.

encouragement ▸ noun **1** the action of encouraging someone to do something. **2** something that encourages someone to do something.

SYNONYMS **1** *she needed a bit of encouragement* **support,** cheering up, inspiration, motivation, stimulation, morale-boosting. **2** *they required no encouragement to get back to work* **persuasion,** coaxing, urging, prodding, prompting, inducement, incentive, carrot. **3** *the encouragement of foreign investment* **support,** backing, sponsorship, promotion, furtherance, fostering, nurture, cultivation, stimulation.

encroach ▸ verb **1** (**encroach on**) gradually intrude on a person's territory, rights, etc. **2** gradually advance beyond expected or acceptable limits.
□ **encroachment** noun.

encrust ▸ verb cover with a hard crust.

encrypt ▸ verb convert into code.
□ **encryption** noun.

encumber ▸ verb (**encumbers, encumbering, encumbered**) prevent someone from moving or acting freely.

encumbrance ▸ noun a thing that prevents someone from moving or acting freely.

encyclopedia (or **encyclopaedia**) ▸ noun a book or set of books giving information on many subjects.
□ **encyclopedic** adjective.

end ▸ noun **1** the final part of something. **2** the furthest or most extreme part. **3** the stopping of a state or situation. **4** a person's death or downfall. **5** a goal or desired result.

> SYNONYMS **1** *the end of the novel* **conclusion**, termination, ending, finish, close, resolution, climax, finale, culmination, denouement. **2** *the end of the road* **extremity**, limit, edge, border, boundary, periphery, point, tip, head, top, bottom. **3** *wealth is not an end in itself* **aim**, goal, purpose, objective, object, target, intention, aspiration, wish, desire, ambition.
> ANTONYMS beginning, means.

▸ verb **1** come or bring to an end. **2** (**end in**) have a particular result. **3** (**end up**) eventually reach or come to a particular state or place.

> SYNONYMS **1** *the show ended with a wedding scene* **finish**, conclude, terminate, close, stop, cease, culminate, climax. **2** *she ended their relationship* **break off**, call off, bring to an end, put an end to, stop, finish, terminate, discontinue, cancel.
> ANTONYMS begin.

■ **make ends meet** earn just enough money to live on.

endanger ▸ verb (**endangers, endangering, endangered**) put in danger.

> SYNONYMS **jeopardize**, risk, put at risk, put in danger, be a danger to, threaten, compromise, imperil.
> ANTONYMS safeguard.

endangered ▸ adjective in danger of extinction.

endear ▸ verb (**endear someone to**) make someone popular with or liked by.

endearing ▸ adjective inspiring affection; lovable.

> SYNONYMS **charming**, appealing, attractive, engaging, winning, captivating, enchanting, cute, sweet, delightful, lovely.

□ **endearingly** adverb.

endearment ▸ noun **1** a word or phrase expressing affection. **2** love or affection.

endeavour (US spelling **endeavor**) ▸ verb try hard to achieve something.

> SYNONYMS *the company endeavoured to expand* **try**, attempt, seek, strive, struggle, labour, toil, work.

▸ noun **1** an attempt to achieve something. **2** concentrated hard work and effort.

> SYNONYMS **1** *an endeavour to build a more buoyant economy* **attempt**, try, bid, effort. **2** *an extremely unwise endeavour* **undertaking**, enterprise, venture, exercise, activity, exploit, deed, act, action, move.

endemic /en-**dem**-ik/ ▸ adjective **1** (of a disease or condition) regularly found among particular people or in a certain area. **2** (of a plant or animal) native to a certain area.

ending ▸ noun an end or final part.

> SYNONYMS **end**, finish, close, conclusion, resolution, summing-up, denouement, finale.
> ANTONYMS beginning.

endive /en-dyv, en-div/ ▸ noun a plant with bitter leaves, eaten in salads.

endless ▸ adjective having or seeming to have no end or limit.

> SYNONYMS **1** *a woman with endless energy* **unlimited**, limitless, infinite, inexhaustible, boundless, unbounded, ceaseless, unending, everlasting, constant, continuous, interminable, unfailing, perpetual, eternal. **2** *we played endless games* **countless**, innumerable, numerous, a multitude of; informal umpteen, no end of; literary myriad.
> ANTONYMS limited, few.

□ **endlessly** adverb.

endocrine /en-duh-kryn/ ▸ adjective (of a gland) secreting hormones or other products directly into the blood.

endorphin /en-**dor**-fin/ ▸ noun a painkilling substance within the brain and nervous system.

endorse ▸ verb (**endorses, endorsing, endorsed**) **1** publicly state that you approve of something. **2** sign a cheque on the back so that it can be paid into an account. **3** Brit. mark details of a driving offence on a driving licence.

> SYNONYMS **support**, back, agree with, approve (of), favour, subscribe to,

recommend, champion, uphold, sanction.
ANTONYMS oppose.

endorsement ▸ noun a declaration of approval.

> SYNONYMS **support,** backing, approval, seal of approval, agreement, recommendation, patronage, sanction.

endow ▸ verb **1** give someone your property, or leave it to them in your will. **2** donate a large sum of money to an institution, from which they will be able to receive a regular income. **3** (**be endowed with**) have as a natural quality or characteristic.

> SYNONYMS **1** *Henry II endowed the hospital* **finance,** fund, pay for, subsidize, sponsor. **2** *he was endowed with great strength* **provide,** supply, furnish, equip, favour, bless, grace.

endowment ▸ noun **1** property or a regular income that has been given or left to a person or an institution. **2** a quality or ability that you are born with.

> SYNONYMS **gift,** present, grant, funding, award, donation, contribution, subsidy, sponsorship, bequest, legacy.

■ **endowment mortgage** Brit. a mortgage linked to an insurance policy, in which the sum received when the policy matures is used to pay back the money borrowed.

endpaper ▸ noun a sheet of paper at the beginning or end of a book, fixed to the inside of the cover.

endurance ▸ noun the ability to do or cope with something painful or difficult for a long time.

> SYNONYMS **1** *she pushed him beyond endurance* **toleration,** tolerance, forbearance, patience, acceptance, resignation, stoicism. **2** *an endurance test* **resistance,** durability, permanence, longevity, strength, toughness, stamina, staying power, fortitude.

endure ▸ verb (**endures, enduring, endured**) **1** experience and be able to cope with prolonged pain or difficulty. **2** last for a long time.

> SYNONYMS **1** *he endured much pain* **undergo,** go through, live through, experience, cope with, deal with, face, suffer, tolerate, put up with, brave, bear, withstand. **2** *our love will endure* **last,** live, live on, go on, survive, abide, continue, persist, remain.
> ANTONYMS fade.

enema /en-i-muh/ ▸ noun a process in which liquid is injected into the rectum to clean it out.

enemy ▸ noun (plural **enemies**) **1** a person who is hostile to you. **2** (**the enemy**) a

country that your own is fighting in a war.

> SYNONYMS **opponent,** adversary, rival, antagonist, combatant, challenger, competitor, opposition, competition, the other side; literary foe.
> ANTONYMS friend, ally.

energetic ▸ adjective having a lot of energy.

> SYNONYMS **1** *an energetic woman* **active,** lively, dynamic, spirited, animated, bouncy, bubbly, sprightly, tireless, indefatigable, enthusiastic; informal full of beans. **2** *energetic exercises* **vigorous,** strenuous, brisk, hard, arduous, demanding, taxing, tough, rigorous. **3** *an energetic advertising campaign* **forceful,** vigorous, aggressive, hard-hitting, high-powered, all-out, determined, bold, intensive; informal in-your-face.
> ANTONYMS lethargic, gentle, half-hearted.

□ **energetically** adverb.

energize (or **energise**) ▸ verb (**energizes, energizing, energized**) give energy and enthusiasm to.

energy ▸ noun (plural **energies**) **1** the strength and vitality that you need in order to be active. **2** (**energies**) a person's physical and mental powers. **3** power obtained from physical or chemical resources to provide light and heat or to work machines.

> SYNONYMS **vitality,** vigour, strength, stamina, animation, spirit, verve, enthusiasm, zest, exuberance, dynamism, drive; informal punch, bounce, oomph, go, get-up-and-go.

enervate /en-er-vayt/ ▸ verb (**enervates, enervating, enervated**) cause someone to feel drained of energy.

enfant terrible /on-fon te-ree-bluh/ ▸ noun (plural **enfants terribles** /on-fon te-ree-bluh/) a person who is known for behaving in an unconventional or controversial way.

enfeeble ▸ verb (**enfeebles, enfeebling, enfeebled**) make someone weak.

enfold ▸ verb envelop someone.

enforce ▸ verb (**enforces, enforcing, enforced**) **1** make sure a law or rule is obeyed. **2** force something to happen.

> SYNONYMS **1** *the sheriff enforced the law* **impose,** apply, administer, carry out, implement, bring to bear, put into effect. **2** *they cannot enforce cooperation* **force,** compel, coerce, exact.

□ **enforceable** adjective **enforcement** noun **enforcer** noun.

enfranchise ▸ verb (**enfranchises, enfranchising, enfranchised**) **1** give a person or group the right to vote. **2** historical free a slave.
□ **enfranchisement** noun.

engage ▸ verb (engages, engaging, engaged) **1** attract or involve someone's interest or attention. **2** (**engage in** or **with**) become involved in. **3** employ or hire someone. **4** move a part of a machine or engine into position.

SYNONYMS **1** *tasks which engage children's interest* **capture**, catch, arrest, grab, draw, attract, gain, hold, grip, absorb, occupy. **2** *he engaged a secretary* **employ**, hire, recruit, take on, enrol, appoint. **3** *the chance to engage in a wide range of pursuits* **participate in**, join in, take part in, partake in/of, enter into, embark on. **4** *infantry units engaged the enemy* **attack**, fall on, take on, clash with, encounter, meet, fight, do battle with. ANTONYMS lose, dismiss.

engaged ▸ adjective **1** occupied. **2** Brit. (of a telephone line) unavailable because already in use. **3** having formally agreed to get married.

engagement ▸ noun **1** a formal agreement to get married. **2** an appointment. **3** the state of being involved in something. **4** fighting between armed forces.

SYNONYMS **1** *a business engagement* **appointment**, meeting, arrangement, commitment, date, assignation, rendezvous. **2** *Britain's engagement in open trading* **participation**, involvement. **3** *the first engagement of the war* **battle**, fight, clash, confrontation, encounter, conflict, skirmish, action, hostilities.

engaging ▸ adjective charming and attractive.

SYNONYMS **charming**, attractive, appealing, pleasing, pleasant, agreeable, likeable, lovable, sweet, winning, fetching; Scottish & N. English **bonny**. ANTONYMS unappealing.

□ **engagingly** adverb.

engender ▸ verb (engenders, engendering, engendered) give rise to.

engine ▸ noun **1** a machine with moving parts that converts power into motion. **2** a railway locomotive.

SYNONYMS **motor**, generator, machine, turbine.

engineer ▸ noun **1** a person who is qualified in engineering. **2** a person who maintains or controls an engine or machine.

SYNONYMS **1** *a structural engineer* **designer**, planner, builder. **2** *a repair engineer* **mechanic**, repairer, technician, maintenance man, operator, driver, controller.

▸ verb (engineers, engineering, engineered) **1** design and build. **2** arrange for something to happen.

SYNONYMS *he engineered a takeover deal* **bring about**, arrange, pull off, bring off, contrive, manoeuvre, negotiate, organize, plan, mastermind.

engineering ▸ noun the study of the design, building, and use of engines, machines, and structures.

English ▸ noun the language of England, used in many varieties throughout the world.
▸ adjective relating to England.

engorged ▸ adjective swollen.

engrained ➙ INGRAINED.

engrave ▸ verb (engraves, engraving, engraved) **1** carve words or a design on a hard surface or object. **2** (**be engraved on** or **in**) be fixed in a person's mind. □ **engraver** noun.

engraving ▸ noun **1** a print made from an engraved plate or block. **2** the process of engraving.

SYNONYMS **etching**, print, plate, picture, illustration, inscription.

engross /in-grohss/ ▸ verb (often be engrossed in) absorb all of someone's attention.

engulf ▸ verb (of a natural force) sweep over someone or something and completely surround or cover them.

SYNONYMS **swamp**, inundate, flood, deluge, immerse, swallow up, submerge, bury, envelop, overwhelm.

enhance ▸ verb (enhances, enhancing, enhanced) increase the quality, value, or extent of something.

SYNONYMS **improve**, add to, strengthen, boost, increase, intensify, heighten, magnify, amplify, inflate, build up, supplement, augment. ANTONYMS diminish.

□ **enhancement** noun.

enigma ▸ noun a mysterious or puzzling person or thing.
□ **enigmatic** adjective **enigmatically** adverb.

enjoin ▸ verb instruct or urge someone to do something.

enjoy ▸ verb **1** get pleasure from. **2** (**enjoy yourself**) have a good time. **3** have and benefit from.

SYNONYMS **1** *he enjoys playing the piano* **like**, be fond of, take pleasure in, be keen on, delight in, relish, revel in, adore, lap up, savour, luxuriate in, bask in; informal get a thrill out of. **2** *she had always enjoyed good health* **benefit from**, be blessed with, be favoured with, be endowed with, possess, own, boast. ANTONYMS dislike, lack.

enjoyable ▸ adjective giving pleasure.

SYNONYMS **entertaining,** amusing, delightful, pleasant, congenial, convivial, agreeable, pleasurable, satisfying.
ANTONYMS disagreeable.

☐ **enjoyably** adverb.

enjoyment ▸ noun taking pleasure in something.

SYNONYMS **pleasure,** fun, entertainment, amusement, recreation, relaxation, happiness, merriment, joy, satisfaction, liking.

enlarge ▸ verb (enlarges, enlarging, enlarged) **1** make or become bigger. **2** (enlarge on) speak or write about something in greater detail.

SYNONYMS **1** *they enlarged the scope of their research* **extend,** expand, grow, add to, amplify, augment, magnify, build up, stretch, widen, broaden, lengthen, elongate, deepen, thicken. **2** *the lymph glands had enlarged* **swell,** distend, bloat, bulge, dilate, blow up, puff up.
ANTONYMS reduce, shrink.

enlargement ▸ noun **1** the state of being enlarged. **2** a photograph that is larger than the original negative or than an earlier print.

enlighten ▸ verb **1** give someone greater knowledge and understanding. **2** (enlightened) well informed and able to make good judgements.

SYNONYMS **1** **inform,** tell, make aware, open someone's eyes, illuminate; informal put someone in the picture. **2** (enlightened) **informed,** aware, sophisticated, liberal, open-minded, broad-minded, educated, knowledgeable, civilized, refined, cultured.

enlightenment ▸ noun the gaining of knowledge and understanding.

SYNONYMS **insight,** understanding, awareness, education, learning, knowledge, illumination, awakening, instruction, teaching, open-mindedness, broad-mindedness, culture, refinement, cultivation, civilization.

enlist ▸ verb **1** join the armed services. **2** ask for someone's help in doing something.

SYNONYMS **1** *he enlisted in the Royal Engineers* **join up,** enrol, sign up, volunteer, register. **2** *he was enlisted in the army* **recruit,** call up, enrol, sign up, conscript, mobilize; US draft. **3** *he enlisted the help of a friend* **obtain,** engage, secure, win, get.
ANTONYMS discharge, demobilize.

☐ **enlistment** noun.

enliven ▸ verb **1** make something more interesting. **2** make someone more cheerful or animated.

en masse /on mass/ ▸ adverb all together.
enmesh ▸ verb (be enmeshed in) be involved in a complicated situation.
enmity ▸ noun (plural enmities) hostility.
ennoble ▸ verb (ennobles, ennobling, ennobled) give greater dignity to.
ennui /on-wee/ ▸ noun a feeling of listlessness, boredom, and dissatisfaction.
enormity ▸ noun (plural enormities) **1** (the enormity of) the extreme seriousness of something bad. **2** great size or scale. **3** a serious crime or sin.

SYNONYMS **1** *the enormity of his crimes* **wickedness,** vileness, heinousness, baseness, depravity, outrageousness. **2** *the enormity of the task* **immensity,** hugeness, size, extent, magnitude.

enormous ▸ adjective very large.

SYNONYMS **huge,** vast, immense, gigantic, giant, massive, colossal, mammoth, tremendous, extensive, mighty, monumental, mountainous; informal mega, monster, whopping; Brit. informal ginormous.
ANTONYMS tiny.

☐ **enormously** adverb.

enough ▸ determiner & pronoun as much or as many as is necessary or desirable.

SYNONYMS **1** *they had enough food* **sufficient,** adequate, ample, abundant, the necessary; informal plenty of. **2** *there's enough for everyone* **sufficient,** plenty, an adequate amount, as much as necessary, a sufficiency, an ample supply, your fill.
ANTONYMS insufficient.

▸ adverb **1** to the required degree. **2** to a moderate degree.

enquire ▸ verb (enquires, enquiring, enquired) **1** ask for information. **2** (enquire after) ask how someone is. **3** (enquire into) investigate.

SYNONYMS **1** *I enquired about training courses* **ask,** make enquiries. **2** *the commission is to enquire into the payments* **investigate,** probe, look into, research, examine, explore, delve into; informal check out.

enquiry ▸ noun (plural enquiries) **1** an act of asking for information. **2** an official investigation.

SYNONYMS **1** *telephone enquiries* **question,** query. **2** *an enquiry into alleged security leaks* **investigation,** probe, examination, exploration, inquest, hearing.

enrage ▸ verb (enrages, enraging, enraged) make someone very angry.

SYNONYMS **1** **anger,** infuriate, incense, madden, inflame, antagonize, provoke;

e

informal **drive mad/crazy, make someone see red, make someone's blood boil.** **2 (enraged) furious,** infuriated, irate, incensed, raging, incandescent, fuming, seething, beside yourself; informal mad, livid, foaming at the mouth.
ANTONYMS placate.

enrapture ▶ verb (**enraptures, enrapturing, enraptured**) make someone feel great pleasure or joy.

enrich ▶ verb **1** improve the quality or value of. **2** improve something by adding an extra item or ingredient.

SYNONYMS **enhance,** improve, better, add to, augment, supplement, complement, refine.
ANTONYMS spoil.

□ **enrichment** noun.

enrol (US spelling **enroll**) ▶ verb (**enrols, enrolling, enrolled**) officially register or recruit someone as a member or student.

SYNONYMS **1** *they both enrolled for the course* **register,** sign on/up, put your name down, apply, volunteer, enter, join. **2** *280 new members were enrolled* **accept,** admit, take on, sign on/up, recruit, engage.

□ **enrolment** noun.

en route /on **root**/ ▶ adverb on the way.

ensconce ▶ verb (**ensconces, ensconcing, ensconced**) establish in a comfortable, safe, or secret place.

ensemble /on-**som**-buhl/ ▶ noun **1** a group of musicians, actors, or dancers who perform together. **2** a group of items viewed as a whole.

SYNONYMS **1** *a Bulgarian folk ensemble* **group,** band, company, troupe, cast, chorus, corps; informal combo. **2** *the buildings present a charming provincial ensemble* **whole,** unit, body, set, collection, combination, composite, package. **3** *a pink and black ensemble* **outfit,** costume, suit; informal get-up.

enshrine ▶ verb (**enshrines, enshrining, enshrined**) preserve a right, tradition, or idea in a form that ensures it will be respected.

enshroud ▶ verb completely envelop something and hide it from view.

ensign ▶ noun a ship's flag.

enslave ▶ verb (**enslaves, enslaving, enslaved**) **1** make someone a slave. **2** make someone dependent on something.
□ **enslavement** noun.

ensnare ▶ verb (**ensnares, ensnaring, ensnared**) **1** catch an animal in a trap. **2** keep someone in a situation from which they cannot escape.

ensue ▶ verb (**ensues, ensuing, ensued**) happen afterwards or as a result.

SYNONYMS **result,** follow, develop, succeed, emerge, arise, proceed, stem.

en suite /on **sweet**/ ▶ adjective & adverb Brit. (of a bathroom) leading directly off a bedroom.

ensure ▶ verb (**ensures, ensuring, ensured**) **1** make certain that something will turn out in a particular way. **2** (**ensure against**) make sure that a problem does not happen.

SYNONYMS **1** *ensure that the surface is completely clean* **make sure,** make certain, see to it, check, confirm, establish, verify. **2** *legislation to ensure equal opportunities for all* **secure,** guarantee, assure, certify.

entail ▶ verb involve something as an inevitable part or result.

SYNONYMS **involve,** necessitate, require, need, demand, call for, mean, imply, cause, give rise to, occasion.

entangle ▶ verb (**entangles, entangling, entangled**) **1** cause something to become tangled. **2** involve someone in complicated circumstances.
□ **entanglement** noun.

entente /on-**tont**/ (or **entente cordiale** /on-tont kor-di-**ahl**/) ▶ noun a friendly understanding between people or countries.

enter ▶ verb (**enters, entering, entered**) **1** come or go into. **2** (often **enter into**) begin to be involved in or do. **3** join an institution or profession. **4** register as a participant in a competition or contest. **5** (**enter into**) undertake to be bound by an agreement. **6** record information in a book, computer, etc.

SYNONYMS **1** *police entered the house* **go into,** come into, get into, set foot in, gain access to. **2** *a bullet entered his chest* **penetrate,** pierce, puncture, perforate. **3** *they entered the Army at eighteen* **join,** enrol in/for, enlist in, volunteer for, sign up for. **4** *she entered a cookery competition* **go in for,** register for, enrol for, sign on/up for, compete in, take part in, participate in. **5** *the cashier entered the details in a ledger* **record,** write, put down, take down, note, jot down, register, log. **6** *please enter your password* **key (in),** type (in), tap in.
ANTONYMS leave.

enterprise ▶ noun **1** a business or company. **2** a large project. **3** the ability to think of and set up new projects.

SYNONYMS **1** *a joint enterprise* **undertaking,** endeavour, venture, exercise, activity, operation, task, business, project, scheme. **2** *a woman with enterprise* **initiative,** resourcefulness, imagination, ingenuity,

inventiveness, originality, creativity.
3 *a profit-making enterprise* **business,** company, firm, venture, organization, operation, concern, establishment; informal **outfit.**

enterprising ▶ adjective having the ability to think of and set up new projects.

> SYNONYMS **resourceful,** entrepreneurial, imaginative, ingenious, inventive, creative, adventurous; informal go-ahead.
> ANTONYMS unimaginative.

entertain ▶ verb **1** provide someone with interest or amusement. **2** receive someone as a guest and provide them with food and drink. **3** give consideration to.

> SYNONYMS **1** *he wrote stories to entertain them* **amuse,** please, charm, cheer, interest, engage, occupy. **2** *he entertains foreign visitors* **receive,** play host/hostess to, invite (round/over), throw a party for, wine and dine, feed. **3** *I would never entertain such an idea* **consider,** contemplate, think of, hear of, countenance.
> ANTONYMS bore, reject.

□ **entertainer** noun.

entertaining ▶ adjective providing amusement or enjoyment.
□ **entertainingly** adverb.

entertainment ▶ noun **1** the action of entertaining. **2** an event or activity designed to entertain other people.

> SYNONYMS **amusement,** pleasure, leisure, recreation, relaxation, fun, enjoyment, interest.

enthral (US spelling **enthrall**) ▶ verb (**enthrals, enthralling, enthralled**) fascinate someone and hold their attention.

> ✔ one **l** in **enthral** and **enthrals,** two in **enthralled** and **enthralling.**

enthrone ▶ verb (**enthrones, enthroning, enthroned**) mark the new reign of a king or queen by a ceremony in which they sit on a throne.
□ **enthronement** noun.

enthuse ▶ verb (**enthuses, enthusing, enthused**) **1** express enthusiasm about something. **2** make someone enthusiastic.

enthusiasm ▶ noun excited interest in and enjoyment of something.

> SYNONYMS **keenness,** eagerness, passion, fervour, zeal, zest, gusto, energy, vigour, fire, spirit, interest, commitment, devotion; informal get-up-and-go.
> ANTONYMS apathy.

enthusiast ▶ noun a person who is very interested in a particular activity.

> SYNONYMS **fan,** devotee, supporter, follower, aficionado, lover, admirer; informal **buff.**

enthusiastic ▶ adjective feeling very interested in and happy about something.

> SYNONYMS **keen,** eager, avid, ardent, fervent, passionate, zealous, excited, wholehearted, committed, devoted, fanatical, earnest.
> ANTONYMS apathetic.

□ **enthusiastically** adverb.

entice ▶ verb (**entices, enticing, enticed**) attract someone by offering them something desirable.

> SYNONYMS **tempt,** lure, attract, appeal to, invite, persuade, beguile, coax, woo, lead on, seduce; informal sweet-talk.

□ **enticingly** adverb.

entire ▶ adjective with no part left out; whole.

> SYNONYMS **whole,** complete, total, full.

entirely ▶ adverb wholly; completely.

> SYNONYMS **1** *that's entirely out of the question* **absolutely,** completely, totally, wholly, utterly, quite, altogether, thoroughly. **2** *a gift entirely for charitable purposes* **solely,** only, exclusively, purely, merely, just, alone.

entirety ▶ noun (**the entirety**) the whole.
■ **in its entirety** as a whole.

entitle ▶ verb (**entitles, entitling, entitled**) **1** give someone a right to do or have something. **2** give a title to a book, play, etc.

> SYNONYMS **1** *this pass entitles you to visit the museum* **qualify,** make eligible, authorize, allow, permit, enable, empower. **2** *a chapter entitled 'Comedy and Tragedy'* **name,** title, call, label, designate, dub.

□ **entitlement** noun.

entity ▶ noun (plural **entities**) a thing which exists independently.

> SYNONYMS **being,** creature, individual, organism, life form, body, object, article, thing.

entomb ▶ verb **1** place someone in a tomb. **2** bury or completely cover.

entomology ▶ noun the study of insects.
□ **entomological** adjective **entomologist** noun.

entourage /on-toor-ahzh/ ▶ noun a group of people who accompany and assist an important person.

entrails ▶ plural noun a person's or animal's intestines or internal organs.

entrance¹ /en-truhnss/ ▶ noun **1** a door or passageway into a place. **2** an act of entering. **3** the right or opportunity to go into a place.

> SYNONYMS **1** *the main entrance* **entry,** way in, access, approach, door, portal, gate, opening, mouth, foyer, lobby, porch; N. Amer. entryway. **2** *the entrance of Mrs Knight* **appearance,** arrival, entry, coming. **3** *he was refused entrance* **admission,** admittance, (right of) entry, entrée, access.
> ANTONYMS exit, departure.

entrance² /in-**trahnss**/ ▸ verb (**entrances, entrancing, entranced**) **1** fill someone with wonder and delight. **2** cast a spell on.

> SYNONYMS *I was entranced by her beauty* **enchant,** bewitch, beguile, captivate, mesmerize, hypnotize, spellbind, transfix, enthral, engross, absorb, fascinate, stun, electrify, charm, delight; informal bowl over, knock out.

entrant ▸ noun a person who joins or takes part in something.

> SYNONYMS **competitor,** contestant, contender, participant, candidate, applicant.

entrap ▸ verb (**entraps, entrapping, entrapped**) **1** catch a person or animal in a trap. **2** trick someone into committing a crime in order to have them prosecuted.
□ **entrapment** noun.

entreat ▸ verb ask someone earnestly or anxiously to do something.

entreaty ▸ noun (plural **entreaties**) an earnest request.

entrecôte /**on**-truh-koht/ ▸ noun a steak cut off a sirloin of beef.

entrée /**on**-tray/ ▸ noun **1** the main course of a meal. **2** Brit. a dish served between the first and main courses at a formal dinner. **3** the right to enter a place or social group.

entrench ▸ verb **1** establish a military force in fortified positions. **2** (**be entrenched**) be so firmly established that change is difficult.
□ **entrenchment** noun.

entrepreneur /**on**-truh-pruh-**ner**/ ▸ noun a person who is successful in setting up businesses.
□ **entrepreneurial** /**on**-truh-pruh-**ner**-i-uhl/ adjective.

entropy ▸ noun Physics a quantity expressing how much of a system's thermal energy is not available for conversion into mechanical work.

entrust ▸ verb make someone responsible for doing or looking after something.

> SYNONYMS **1** *he was entrusted with the task* **charge,** give someone the responsibility for, present. **2** *the powers entrusted to the Home Secretary* **assign,**

confer on, bestow on, vest in, delegate, give, grant, vouchsafe.

entry ▸ noun (plural **entries**) **1** an act of entering. **2** a door or passageway into a place. **3** the right or opportunity to enter. **4** an item included in a list, reference book, etc.

> SYNONYMS **1** *my moment of entry* **appearance,** arrival, entrance, coming. **2** *the entry to the flats* **entrance,** way in, access, approach, door, portal, gate, entrance hall, foyer, lobby; N. Amer. entryway. **3** *he was refused entry* **admission,** admittance, entrance, access. **4** *entries in the cash book* **item,** record, note, memo, memorandum. **5** *data entry* **recording,** archiving, logging, documentation, capture. **6** *we must pick a winner from the entries* **submission,** entry form, application.
> ANTONYMS departure, exit.

entwine ▸ verb (**entwines, entwining, entwined**) wind or twist together.

enumerate ▸ verb (**enumerates, enumerating, enumerated**) mention a number of things one by one.
□ **enumeration** noun.

enunciate ▸ verb (**enunciates, enunciating, enunciated**) **1** say or pronounce clearly. **2** set something out clearly and precisely.
□ **enunciation** noun.

envelop /in-**vel**-uhp/ ▸ verb (**envelops, enveloping, enveloped**) wrap up, cover, or surround completely.

> SYNONYMS **surround,** cover, enfold, engulf, encircle, cocoon, sheathe, swathe, enclose, cloak, veil, shroud.

> ✔ Unlike the noun *envelope,* the verb **envelop** has no **e** on the end.

envelope /**en**-vuh-lohp/ ▸ noun a flat paper container with a flap, used to enclose a letter or document.

enviable ▸ adjective offering something desirable.
□ **enviably** adverb.

envious ▸ adjective feeling discontented because you want something that someone else has.
□ **enviously** adverb.

environment ▸ noun **1** the surroundings in which a person, animal, or plant lives or operates. **2** (**the environment**) the natural world.

> SYNONYMS **1** *the hospital environment* **situation,** setting, milieu, background, backdrop, context, conditions, ambience, atmosphere. **2** *the impact of pesticides on the environment* **the natural world,** nature, the earth, the ecosystem, the

biosphere, Mother Nature, wildlife, flora and fauna, the countryside.

□ **environmental** adjective **environmentally** adverb.

✔ Remember the **n**: enviro**n**ment.

environmentalist ▸ noun a person who is concerned with the protection of the environment.

SYNONYMS **conservationist**, ecologist, nature-lover, green; informal eco-warrior, tree-hugger.

□ **environmentalism** noun.

environs ▸ plural noun the surrounding area or district.

envisage /in-**viz**-ij/ ▸ verb (**envisages**, **envisaging**, **envisaged**) **1** see something as a possibility. **2** form a mental picture of.

SYNONYMS **1** *it was envisaged that the hospital would open soon* **foresee**, predict, forecast, anticipate, expect, think likely. **2** *I cannot envisage what the future holds* **imagine**, contemplate, picture, conceive of, think of.

envoy ▸ noun a messenger or representative.

SYNONYMS **ambassador**, emissary, diplomat, representative, delegate, spokesperson, agent, intermediary, mediator; informal go-between.

envy ▸ noun (plural **envies**) **1** a feeling of wanting something that belongs to someone else. **2** (**the envy of**) a thing that is wanted by other people.

SYNONYMS *feelings of envy* **jealousy**, covetousness, resentment, bitterness.

▸ verb (**envies**, **envying**, **envied**) wish that you had the same possessions or opportunities as someone.

SYNONYMS **1** *I admired and envied her* **be envious of,** be jealous of, be resentful of. **2** *we envied her lifestyle* **covet**, desire, aspire to, wish for, want, long for, yearn for, hanker after, crave.

enzyme /en-zym/ ▸ noun a substance produced by an animal or plant which helps a chemical change happen without being changed itself.

eon US spelling of AEON.

epaulette /ep-uh-**let**/ (US spelling **epaulet**) ▸ noun a flap attached to the shoulder of a coat or jacket.

ephemera /i-**fem**-uh-ruh, i-**feem**-uh-ruh/ ▸ plural noun things that people use or are interested in for only a short time.

ephemeral ▸ adjective lasting only for a short time.

epic ▸ noun **1** a long poem about the actions of great men or women or about a nation's history. **2** a long film or book dealing with

a long period of time.
▸ adjective **1** having to do with an epic. **2** great and impressive in scale or character.

epicene /e-pi-**seen**/ ▸ adjective having both male and female characteristics or no characteristics of either sex.

epicentre (US spelling **epicenter**) ▸ noun the point on the earth's surface where the effects of an earthquake are felt most strongly.

epicure ▸ noun a person who enjoys and is interested in good food and drink.
□ **epicurean** noun & adjective.

epidemic ▸ noun a situation in which a large number of people have caught the same infectious disease.

SYNONYMS **1** *an epidemic of typhoid* **outbreak**, plague, pandemic. **2** *a joyriding epidemic* **spate**, rash, wave, eruption, plague, outbreak, craze, upsurge.

epidermis ▸ noun **1** the surface layer of an animal's skin, on top of the dermis. **2** the outer layer of tissue in a plant.
□ **epidermal** adjective.

epidural ▸ noun an anaesthetic injected into the space around the spinal cord, especially during childbirth.

epiglottis ▸ noun a flap of cartilage in the throat that descends during swallowing to cover the opening of the windpipe.

epigram ▸ noun **1** a concise and witty saying. **2** a short witty poem.
□ **epigrammatic** adjective.

epigraph ▸ noun **1** an inscription on a building, statue, or coin. **2** a short quotation introducing a book or chapter.

epilepsy ▸ noun a disorder of the nervous system that causes convulsions and loss of consciousness.
□ **epileptic** adjective & noun.

epilogue (US spelling **epilog**) ▸ noun a section at the end of a book or play which comments on what has happened.

epiphany ▸ noun (plural **epiphanies**) **1** (**Epiphany**) (in the Bible) the time when the Magi visited the baby Jesus in Bethlehem. **2** a sudden and inspiring revelation.

episcopacy /i-**piss**-kuh-puh-si/ ▸ noun (plural **episcopacies**) **1** government of a Church by bishops. **2** (**the episcopacy**) the bishops of a region or Church as a group.

episcopal /i-**piss**-kuh-puhl/ ▸ adjective having to do with a bishop or bishops.

episcopalian /i-piss-kuh-**pay**-li-uhn/ ▸ adjective having to do with the government of a Church by bishops.
▸ noun a supporter of this type of Church government.

episode ▸ noun **1** an event or group of events happening as part of a sequence.

2 each of the separate parts into which a serialized story or programme is divided.

SYNONYMS **1** *the best episode of his career* **incident,** event, occurrence, chapter, experience, occasion, interlude, adventure, exploit. **2** *the final episode of the series* **instalment,** chapter, passage, part, portion, section, programme, show. **3** *an episode of illness* **period,** spell, bout, attack, phase; informal dose.

episodic ▸ adjective **1** made up of a series of separate events. **2** happening at irregular intervals.

epistemology /i-piss-ti-**mol**-uh-ji/ ▸ noun the branch of philosophy that deals with knowledge.

epistle /i-**piss**-uhl/ ▸ noun **1** formal a letter. **2** (**Epistle**) a book of the New Testament in the form of a letter from an Apostle.

epistolary ▸ adjective **1** relating to the writing of letters. **2** (of a literary work) in the form of letters.

epitaph ▸ noun words written in memory of a person who has died.

epithet ▸ noun a word or phrase describing someone or something's character or most important quality.

epitome /i-**pit**-uh-mi/ ▸ noun (**the epitome of**) a perfect example of something.

epitomize (or **epitomise**) ▸ verb (**epitomizes, epitomizing, epitomized**) be a perfect example of.

epoch /**ee**-pok/ ▸ noun a long and distinct period of time.

eponym /**ep**-uh-nim/ ▸ noun **1** a person after whom something is named. **2** a word or phrase based on someone's name.

eponymous /i-**pon**-i-muhss/ ▸ adjective **1** (of a person) giving their name to something. **2** (of a thing) named after a particular person.

equable /**ek**-wuh-b'l/ ▸ adjective **1** calm and even-tempered. **2** (of a climate) not changing very much.
□ **equably** adverb.

equal ▸ adjective **1** the same in quantity, size, value, or status. **2** evenly balanced. **3** (**equal to**) able to face a challenge.

SYNONYMS **1** *lines of equal length* **identical,** uniform, alike, like, the same, matching, equivalent, corresponding. **2** *equal treatment before the law* **impartial,** non-partisan, fair, just, equitable, unprejudiced, non-discriminatory. **3** *an equal contest* **evenly matched,** even, balanced, level; informal level pegging, neck and neck.
ANTONYMS different, discriminatory.

▸ noun a person or thing that is equal to another.

SYNONYMS *they did not treat him as their equal* **equivalent,** peer, fellow, like, counterpart, match, parallel.

▸ verb (**equals, equalling, equalled;** US spelling **equals, equaling, equaled**) **1** be equal to. **2** be as good as.

SYNONYMS **1** *two plus two equals four* **be equal to,** be equivalent to, be the same as, come to, amount to, make, total, add up to. **2** *he equalled the world record* **match,** reach, parallel, be level with.

□ **equally** adverb.

equality ▸ noun the state of having the same rights, opportunities, or advantages as others.

SYNONYMS **fairness,** equal rights, equal opportunities, impartiality, even-handedness, justice.

equalize (or **equalise**) ▸ verb (**equalizes, equalizing, equalized**) **1** make things equal. **2** level the score in a match by scoring a goal.
□ **equalization** noun **equalizer** noun.

equanimity /ek-wuh-**nim**-i-ti/ ▸ noun calmness of temper.

equate ▸ verb (**equates, equating, equated**) consider one thing as equal to another.

SYNONYMS **1** *he equates criticism with treachery* **identify,** compare, bracket, class, associate, connect, link, relate. **2** *moves to equate supply and demand* **equalize,** balance, even out/up, level, square, tally, match.

equation ▸ noun **1** the process of equating one thing with another. **2** Maths a statement that the values of two mathematical expressions are equal (indicated by the sign =). **3** Chemistry a formula representing the changes which happen in a chemical reaction.

equator ▸ noun an imaginary line around the earth at an equal distance from the two poles, dividing the earth into northern and southern hemispheres.

equatorial ▸ adjective having to do with the equator.

equerry /**ek**-wuh-ri/ ▸ noun (plural **equerries**) a male officer of the British royal household who acts as an attendant to a member of the royal family.

equestrian /i-**kwess**-tri-uhn/ ▸ adjective relating to horse riding.
▸ noun a person on horseback.

equestrianism ▸ noun the skill or sport of horse riding.

equidistant ▸ adjective at equal distances.

equilateral ▸ adjective having all its sides of the same length.

equilibrium ▸ noun (plural **equilibria**) **1** a state in which opposing forces are balanced. **2** the state of being physically balanced. **3** a calm state of mind.

SYNONYMS **balance,** stability, poise, symmetry, harmony.
ANTONYMS imbalance.

equine ▸ adjective **1** relating to horses. **2** resembling a horse.

equinoctial ▸ adjective **1** having to do with the equinox. **2** at or near the equator.

equinox ▸ noun the time or date (twice each year, about 22 September and 20 March) when day and night are of equal length.

equip ▸ verb (**equips, equipping, equipped**) **1** supply someone with the things they need for a particular activity. **2** prepare someone for a situation or task.

SYNONYMS **1** *the boat was equipped with a flare gun* **provide,** furnish, supply, issue, kit out, stock, provision, arm. **2** *the course will equip them for the workplace* **prepare,** qualify, ready, suit, train.

equipment ▸ noun the items needed for a particular activity.

SYNONYMS **apparatus,** paraphernalia, tools, utensils, implements, hardware, gadgetry, things; informal stuff, gear.

equitable ▸ adjective fair and impartial.
□ **equitably** adverb.

equity ▸ noun (plural **equities**) **1** the quality of being fair and impartial. **2** the value of the shares issued by a company. **3** the value of a mortgaged property after all charges and debts have been paid.

equivalent ▸ adjective (often **equivalent to**) **1** equal in value, amount, function, meaning, etc. **2** having the same effect.

SYNONYMS *a degree or equivalent qualification* **comparable,** corresponding, commensurate, similar, parallel, analogous.

▸ noun a person or thing that is equivalent to another.

SYNONYMS *Denmark's equivalent of the Daily Mirror* **counterpart,** parallel, alternative, analogue, twin, opposite number.

□ **equivalence** noun.

equivocal /i-kwiv-uh-k'l/ ▸ adjective (of words or intentions) not clear because they can be interpreted in more than one way.
□ **equivocally** adverb.

equivocate /i-kwiv-uh-kayt/ ▸ verb (**equivocates, equivocating, equivocated**) use language that can be interpreted in more than one way in order to hide the truth or avoid committing yourself.
□ **equivocation** noun.

era ▸ noun a long and distinct period of history.

SYNONYMS **age,** epoch, period, time, date, day, generation.

eradicate ▸ verb (**eradicates, eradicating, eradicated**) remove or destroy completely.

SYNONYMS **eliminate,** get rid of, remove, obliterate, extinguish, exterminate, destroy, annihilate, kill, wipe out.

□ **eradication** noun.

erase ▸ verb (**erases, erasing, erased**) **1** rub out something written in pencil. **2** remove all traces of something.

SYNONYMS **1** *they erased his name* **delete,** rub out, wipe off, blank out, expunge, excise, remove, obliterate. **2** *the data had been erased* **wipe,** kill, delete, record over, format.

eraser ▸ noun a piece of rubber or plastic used to rub out something written in pencil.

erbium ▸ noun a soft silvery-white metallic element.

ere /air/ ▸ preposition & conjunction old use before (in time).

erect ▸ adjective **1** rigidly upright. **2** (of the penis) enlarged and stiffened.

SYNONYMS **upright,** straight, vertical, perpendicular, standing (on end), bristling, stiff.
ANTONYMS bent, flat.

▸ verb **1** put up a structure or object. **2** create or establish something.

SYNONYMS **build,** construct, put up, assemble, put together, fabricate, raise.
ANTONYMS demolish, dismantle, lower.

erectile ▸ adjective able to become erect.

erection ▸ noun **1** the action of erecting a structure or object. **2** a building or other upright structure. **3** an erect state of the penis.

ergo /er-goh/ ▸ adverb therefore.

ergonomics /er-guh-nom-iks/ ▸ noun the study of people's efficiency in their working environment.
□ **ergonomic** adjective.

Eritrean /e-ri-tray-uhn/ ▸ noun a person from the independent state of Eritrea in NE Africa.
▸ adjective relating to Eritrea.

ermine /er-min/ ▸ noun (plural **ermine** or **ermines**) **1** a stoat. **2** the white winter fur of the stoat.

erode ▸ verb (**erodes, eroding, eroded**) **1** gradually wear away. **2** gradually destroy.

SYNONYMS **wear away/down,** abrade, grind down, crumble, weather, undermine, weaken, deteriorate, destroy.

erogenous /i-roj-i-nuhss/ ▸ adjective (of a part of the body) giving pleasure in a sexual way when it is touched.

erosion ▶ noun the process of eroding.

> SYNONYMS **wearing away,** abrasion, attrition, weathering, dissolution, deterioration, disintegration, destruction.

erotic ▶ adjective having to do with sexual desire or excitement.

> SYNONYMS **sexually arousing,** sexually stimulating, titillating, suggestive, pornographic, sexually explicit; informal blue, X-rated; euphemistic adult.

□ **erotically** adverb.

erotica ▶ noun literature or art that is intended to make people feel sexually excited.

eroticism ▶ noun **1** the use of images that are intended to be sexually exciting. **2** sexual desire or excitement.

err ▶ verb **1** make a mistake. **2** do wrong.

errand ▶ noun a short journey made to deliver or collect something.

> SYNONYMS **task,** job, chore, assignment, mission.

errant ▶ adjective **1** doing something wrong or unacceptable. **2** old use travelling in search of adventure.

erratic ▶ adjective happening, moving, or acting in an irregular or uneven way.

> SYNONYMS **unpredictable,** inconsistent, changeable, variable, inconstant, irregular, fitful, unstable, varying, fluctuating, unreliable.
> ANTONYMS consistent.

□ **erratically** adverb.

erratum /e-**rah**-tuhm/ ▶ noun (plural **errata**) a mistake in a book or printed document.

erroneous ▶ adjective incorrect.
□ **erroneously** adverb.

error ▶ noun **1** a mistake. **2** the state of being wrong.

> SYNONYMS **mistake,** inaccuracy, miscalculation, blunder, slip, oversight, misconception, delusion, misprint; Brit. informal boob.

ersatz ▶ adjective (of a product) artificial and not as good as the real thing.

erstwhile ▶ adjective former.

erudite ▶ adjective having or showing knowledge gained from reading and study.
□ **erudition** noun.

erupt ▶ verb **1** (of a volcano) become active and eject lava, ash, and gases. **2** break out suddenly. **3** show or express your feelings in a sudden and noisy way. **4** (of a spot, rash, etc.) suddenly appear on the skin.

> SYNONYMS **1** the volcano erupted **give out lava,** become active, explode. **2** fighting erupted **break out,** flare up, start.

eruption ▶ noun an instance of erupting.

> SYNONYMS **1** a volcanic eruption **discharge,** explosion, lava flow, pyroclastic flow. **2** an eruption of violence **outbreak,** flare-up, upsurge, outburst, explosion, wave, spate.

erythrocyte /i-**rith**-ruh-syt/ ▶ noun technical a red blood cell.

escalate ▶ verb (**escalates, escalating, escalated**) **1** increase rapidly. **2** become more serious.

> SYNONYMS **1** prices have escalated **increase rapidly,** soar, rocket, shoot up, spiral; informal go through the roof. **2** the dispute escalated **grow,** develop, mushroom, increase, heighten, intensify, accelerate.
> ANTONYMS plunge, subside.

□ **escalation** noun.

escalator ▶ noun a moving staircase consisting of a circulating belt of steps driven by a motor.

escalope /i-**ska**-luhp/ ▶ noun a thin slice of meat coated in breadcrumbs and fried.

escapade ▶ noun an adventure.

escape ▶ verb (**escapes, escaping, escaped**) **1** break free from captivity or control. **2** succeed in avoiding something bad. **3** fail to be noticed or remembered by.

> SYNONYMS **1** he escaped from prison **run away/off,** get out, break out, break free, bolt, make your getaway, slip away; Brit. informal do a runner. **2** he escaped his pursuers **get away from,** elude, avoid, dodge, shake off; informal give someone the slip. **3** they escaped injury **avoid,** evade, elude, cheat, sidestep, circumvent, steer clear of, shirk. **4** lethal gas escaped **leak (out),** spill (out), seep (out), discharge, flow (out), pour (out).

▶ noun **1** an act of escaping. **2** a means of escaping.

> SYNONYMS **1** his escape from prison **getaway,** breakout, flight. **2** a gas escape **leak,** spill, seepage, discharge, outflow, outpouring.

□ **escapee** noun **escaper** noun.

escapism ▶ noun the habit of doing enjoyable things to stop you thinking about unpleasant realities.
□ **escapist** noun & adjective.

escapologist /ess-kuh-**pol**-uh-jist/ ▶ noun an entertainer whose act consists of breaking free from ropes and chains.
□ **escapology** noun.

escarpment ▶ noun a long, steep slope at the edge of an area of high land.

eschew /iss-**choo**/ ▶ verb deliberately avoid doing or having something.

escort ▶ noun **1** a person, vehicle, or group

accompanying someone to protect or honour them. **2** a person who accompanies a member of the opposite sex to a social event.

SYNONYMS *a police escort* **guard,** bodyguard, protector, minder, attendant, chaperone, entourage, retinue, protection, convoy.

▶ verb accompany someone as an escort.

SYNONYMS **1** *he was escorted home by the police* **conduct,** accompany, guide, usher, shepherd, take. **2** *he escorted her in to dinner* **accompany,** partner, take, bring.

escudo /ess-**kyoo**-doh/ ▶ noun (plural **escudos**) the former basic unit of money in Portugal.

escutcheon /i-sku-chuhn/ ▶ noun a shield on which a coat of arms is depicted.

Eskimo ▶ noun (plural **Eskimo** or **Eskimos**) a member of a people inhabiting northern Canada, Alaska, Greenland, and eastern Siberia.

❗ Many of the peoples traditionally called **Eskimos** now prefer to call themselves **Inuit**.

esophagus US spelling of OESOPHAGUS.

esoteric /e-suh-**te**-rik, ee-suh-**te**-rik/ ▶ adjective intended for or understood by only a small number of people with a specialized knowledge.

ESP ▶ abbreviation extrasensory perception.

espadrille /ess-puh-**dril**/ ▶ noun a light canvas shoe with a plaited fibre sole.

espalier /i-**spal**-yer/ ▶ noun a fruit tree or shrub whose branches are trained to grow flat against a wall.

especial ▶ adjective **1** special. **2** for or belonging chiefly to one person or thing.

especially ▶ adverb **1** in particular. **2** to a great extent.

SYNONYMS **1** *work poured in, especially from Kent* **mainly,** mostly, chiefly, particularly, principally, largely, primarily. **2** *a committee formed especially for the purpose* **expressly,** specially, specifically, exclusively, just, particularly, explicitly. **3** *he is especially talented* **exceptionally,** particularly, specially, unusually, extraordinarily, uncommonly, uniquely, remarkably, outstandingly; informal seriously, majorly.

espionage /ess-pi-uh-nahzh/ ▶ noun the practice of spying.

esplanade /ess-pluh-**nayd**/ ▶ noun a long, open, level area where people may walk for pleasure.

espouse /i-**spowz**/ ▶ verb (**espouses, espousing, espoused**) support or choose a particular belief or way of doing things.
◻ **espousal** noun.

espresso /ess-**press**-oh/ ▶ noun (plural

espressos) strong black coffee made by forcing steam through ground coffee beans.

✔ **Espresso** is an Italian word (from *caffè espresso,* meaning 'pressed out coffee') and should be spelled the Italian way, with an **s,** not an **x**.

esprit de corps /e-spree duh **kor**/ ▶ noun a feeling of pride and loyalty that unites the members of a group.

espy ▶ verb (**espies, espying, espied**) literary catch sight of.

Esq. ▶ abbreviation Esquire.

Esquire /i-**skwy**-er/ ▶ noun Brit. a polite title placed after a man's name when no other title is used.

essay ▶ noun **1** a piece of writing on a particular subject. **2** formal an attempt.

SYNONYMS **article,** composition, paper, dissertation, thesis, discourse, study, assignment, treatise, piece, feature; N. Amer. theme.

▶ verb formal attempt to do something.
◻ **essayist** noun.

essence ▶ noun **1** the quality which is most important in making something what it is. **2** an extract obtained from a plant or other substance and used for flavouring or scent.

SYNONYMS **1** *the very essence of economics* **nature,** heart, core, substance, basis, principle, quintessence, soul, spirit, reality; informal nitty-gritty. **2** *essence of ginger* **extract,** concentrate, elixir, juice, oil.

essential ▶ adjective **1** absolutely necessary. **2** relating to the most important part or basic nature of something.

SYNONYMS **1** *it is essential to remove the paint* **crucial,** key, vital, indispensable, all-important, critical, imperative. **2** *the essential simplicity of his style* **basic,** inherent, fundamental, quintessential, intrinsic, underlying, characteristic, innate, primary.
ANTONYMS unimportant, incidental.

▶ noun **1** a thing that is absolutely necessary. **2** (**essentials**) things that are part of the basic nature of something.

SYNONYMS **1** *an essential for broadcasters* **necessity,** prerequisite; informal must. **2** *the essentials of the job* **fundamentals,** basics, rudiments, first principles, foundations, essence, basis, core, kernel, crux; informal nitty-gritty, nuts and bolts.

■ **essential oil** a natural oil extracted from a plant.
◻ **essentially** adverb.

establish ▶ verb **1** set something up on a firm or permanent basis. **2** make someone or something accepted, recognized, or respected by other people. **3** show something to be true.

> SYNONYMS **1** *they established an office in Moscow* **set up,** start, initiate, institute, found, create, inaugurate. **2** *evidence to establish his guilt* **prove,** demonstrate, show, indicate, determine, confirm.

establishment ▸ noun **1** the action of establishing something. **2** a business, public institution, or household. **3** (**the Establishment**) the group in society who have control over policy and resist change.

> SYNONYMS **1** *the establishment of a democracy* **foundation,** institution, formation, inception, creation, installation, inauguration. **2** *a dressmaking establishment* **business,** firm, company, concern, enterprise, venture, organization, operation; informal **outfit**. **3** *educational establishments* **institution,** place, premises, institute. **4** *they dare to poke fun at the Establishment* **the authorities,** the powers that be, the system, the ruling class.

estate ▸ noun **1** a property consisting of a large house with grounds. **2** Brit. a group of modern houses, or of buildings used by businesses. **3** a property where crops such as coffee or grapes are grown. **4** all the money and property owned by a person at the time of their death.

> SYNONYMS **1** *the Balmoral estate* **property,** grounds, garden(s), park, parkland, land(s), territory. **2** *a housing estate* **area,** development, complex; Scottish **scheme**. **3** *a coffee estate* **plantation,** farm, holding, forest, vineyard; N. Amer. **ranch**. **4** *he left an estate worth £610,000* **assets,** capital, wealth, riches, holdings, fortune, property, effects, possessions, belongings.

■ **estate agent** a person who sells or rents out houses or flats for clients. **estate car** Brit. a car with a large storage area behind the seats and an extra door at the rear.

esteem ▸ noun respect and admiration.

> SYNONYMS *she was held in high esteem* **respect,** admiration, acclaim, appreciation, recognition, honour, reverence, estimation, regard.

▸ verb respect and admire someone.

> SYNONYMS *such ceramics are highly esteemed* **respect,** admire, value, regard, appreciate, like, prize, treasure, revere.

ester ▸ noun Chemistry an organic compound formed by a reaction between an acid and an alcohol.

esthetic US spelling of AESTHETIC.

estimable ▸ adjective deserving respect and admiration.

estimate ▸ verb /ess-ti-mayt/ (**estimates, estimating, estimated**) roughly calculate the value, number, or amount of something.

> SYNONYMS **1** *estimate the cost* **calculate roughly,** approximate, guess, evaluate, judge. **2** *we estimate it to be worth £50,000* **consider,** believe, reckon, deem, judge, rate.

▸ noun /ess-ti-muht/ **1** a rough calculation. **2** a written statement giving the likely price that will be charged for work. **3** an opinion.

> SYNONYMS *an estimate of the cost* **rough calculation,** approximation, estimation, guess, costing, quotation, valuation, evaluation; informal **guesstimate**.

□ **estimation** noun.

Estonian ▸ noun a person from Estonia.
▸ adjective relating to Estonia.

estranged ▸ adjective **1** no longer friendly or in contact with someone. **2** (of someone's husband or wife) no longer living with them.
□ **estrangement** noun.

estrogen US spelling of OESTROGEN.

estuary ▸ noun (plural **estuaries**) the mouth of a large river where it becomes affected by tides.

et al. ▸ abbreviation and others.
ORIGIN Latin, short for *et alii*.

etc. ▸ abbreviation et cetera.

et cetera (or **etcetera**) /et set-uh-ruh/
▸ adverb and other similar things; and so on.

etch ▸ verb **1** engrave metal, glass, or stone by applying a coating, drawing on it with a needle, and then covering the surface with acid to attack the exposed parts. **2** cut words or a design on a surface. **3** (**be etched on** or **in**) be fixed permanently in someone's mind.

> SYNONYMS **engrave,** carve, inscribe, incise, score, mark, scratch, scrape.

etching ▸ noun **1** the process of etching. **2** a print produced by etching.

> SYNONYMS **engraving,** print, plate.

eternal ▸ adjective lasting or existing forever.

> SYNONYMS **1** *eternal happiness* **everlasting,** never-ending, endless, perpetual, undying, immortal, abiding, permanent, enduring. **2** *eternal vigilance* **constant,** continual, continuous, perpetual, sustained, uninterrupted, unbroken, non-stop, round-the-clock.
> ANTONYMS transient, intermittent.

□ **eternally** adverb.

eternity ▸ noun (plural **eternities**) **1** unending time. **2** (**an eternity**) informal an undesirably long period of time.

SYNONYMS **1** *the memory will remain for eternity* **ever,** all time, perpetuity. **2** *I waited an eternity for you* **a long time,** an age, ages, a lifetime, hours, years, forever.

ethane ▸ noun a flammable gas present in petroleum and natural gas.

ether /ee-ther/ ▸ noun **1** a highly flammable liquid used as an anaesthetic and a solvent. **2** literary the upper regions of the air.

ethereal /i-theer-i-uhl/ ▸ adjective **1** very delicate and light. **2** heavenly or spiritual.

ethic ▸ noun **1** (also **ethics**) a set of principles concerning right and wrong and how people should behave. **2** (**ethics**) the branch of philosophy concerned with moral principles.

SYNONYMS (**ethics**) **morals,** morality, values, principles, ideals, standards (of behaviour).

ethical ▸ adjective **1** having to do with principles about right and wrong. **2** morally correct.

SYNONYMS **1** *an ethical dilemma* **moral.** **2** *ethical investment* **morally correct,** right-minded, principled, good, moral, just, honourable, fair.
ANTONYMS unethical.

□ **ethically** adverb.

Ethiopian ▸ noun a person from Ethiopia. ▸ adjective relating to Ethiopia.

ethnic ▸ adjective **1** having to do with people from the same national or cultural background. **2** referring to a person's origins rather than their present nationality. **3** belonging to a non-Western cultural tradition.

SYNONYMS **racial,** race-related, national, cultural, folk, tribal, ethnological.

■ **ethnic cleansing** the removal or killing of members of one ethnic or religious group in an area by those of another. **ethnic minority** a group which has a different ethnic origin from the main population. □ **ethnically** adverb **ethnicity** noun.

ethnology ▸ noun the study of different peoples and the relationships between them. □ **ethnological** adjective **ethnologist** noun.

ethos /ee-thoss/ ▸ noun the characteristic spirit of a culture, period, etc.

ethyl /eth-yl/ ▸ noun Chemistry a radical obtained from ethane, present in alcohol and ether.

etiolated /ee-ti-uh-lay-tid/ ▸ adjective (of a plant) pale and weak as a result of a lack of light.

etiquette ▸ noun the rules of polite or correct behaviour in a society.

etymology ▸ noun (plural **etymologies**)

an account of the origins and the developments in meaning of a word. □ **etymological** adjective.

EU ▸ abbreviation European Union.

eucalyptus /yoo-kuh-**lip**-tuhss/ ▸ noun (plural **eucalyptuses**) an evergreen Australasian tree whose leaves produce a strong-smelling oil.

Eucharist /yoo-kuh-rist/ ▸ noun **1** the Christian ceremony commemorating the Last Supper, in which consecrated bread and wine are consumed. **2** the consecrated bread and wine used in this ceremony.

eugenics /yoo-jen-iks/ ▸ noun the study of ways to increase the occurrence of desirable characteristics in a population by choosing which people become parents.

eulogize (or **eulogise**) /yoo-luh-jyz/ ▸ verb (**eulogizes, eulogizing, eulogized**) praise highly.

eulogy /yoo-luh-ji/ ▸ noun (plural **eulogies**) a speech or piece of writing that praises someone or something highly.

eunuch /yoo-nuhk/ ▸ noun a man who has had his testicles removed.

euphemism /yoo-fuh-mi-z'm/ ▸ noun a less direct word used instead of one that is blunt or offensive. □ **euphemistic** adjective **euphemistically** adverb.

euphonious /yoo-foh-ni-uhss/ ▸ adjective sounding pleasant. □ **euphoniously** adverb.

euphonium /yoo-foh-ni-uhm/ ▸ noun a brass musical instrument like a small tuba.

euphony /yoo-fuh-ni/ ▸ noun (plural **euphonies**) the quality of sounding pleasant.

euphoria /yoo-for-i-uh/ ▸ noun a feeling of great happiness.

SYNONYMS **elation,** happiness, joy, delight, glee, excitement, exhilaration, jubilation, exultation, ecstasy, bliss, rapture.
ANTONYMS misery.

□ **euphoric** adjective.

Eurasian ▸ adjective **1** of mixed European and Asian parentage. **2** relating to Eurasia (the land mass of Europe and Asia together).

eureka /yoo-ree-kuh/ ▸ exclamation a cry of joy or satisfaction when you discover something.

euro ▸ noun the basic unit of money in fifteen states of the European Union.

European ▸ noun **1** a person from Europe. **2** a person who is of European parentage. ▸ adjective having to do with Europe or the European Union.
■ **European Union** an economic and political association of certain European countries.

e

europium ▸ noun a soft silvery-white metallic element.

Eustachian tube /yoo-**stay**-sh'n/ ▸ noun a narrow passage leading from the throat to the middle ear.

euthanasia /yoo-thuh-**nay**-zi-uh/ ▸ noun the painless killing of a patient suffering from an incurable disease.

evacuate ▸ verb (evacuates, evacuating, evacuated) **1** remove someone from a place of danger to a safer place. **2** leave a dangerous place. **3** empty the bowels.

> SYNONYMS **1** *local residents were evacuated* **remove,** move out, take away. **2** *they evacuated the building* **leave,** vacate, abandon, move out of, quit, withdraw from, retreat from, flee. **3** *police evacuated the area* **clear,** empty.

□ **evacuation** noun.

evacuee ▸ noun a person who is evacuated from a place of danger.

evade ▸ verb (evades, evading, evaded) **1** escape or avoid. **2** avoid giving a direct answer to a question.

> SYNONYMS **1** *they evaded the guards* **elude,** avoid, dodge, escape (from), steer clear of, sidestep, lose, leave behind, shake off; informal give someone the slip. **2** *he evaded the question* **avoid,** dodge, sidestep, bypass, skirt round; informal duck.
> ANTONYMS confront.

evaluate ▸ verb (evaluates, evaluating, evaluated) form an idea of the amount or value of.

> SYNONYMS **assess,** judge, gauge, rate, estimate, appraise, weigh up; informal size up.

□ **evaluation** noun.

evanescent /ev-uh-**ness**-uhnt/ ▸ adjective soon passing out of existence; fleeting.
□ **evanescence** noun.

evangelical ▸ adjective **1** having to do with a tradition within Protestant Christianity which emphasizes the authority of the Bible and salvation through personal faith in Jesus. **2** having to do with the teaching of the gospel or Christianity. **3** showing passionate support for something.
▸ noun a member of the evangelical tradition in the Christian Church.
□ **evangelicalism** noun.

evangelist ▸ noun **1** a person who sets out to convert other people to Christianity. **2** the writer of one of the four Gospels. **3** a passionate supporter of something.
□ **evangelism** noun **evangelistic** adjective.

evangelize (or evangelise) ▸ verb (evangelizes, evangelizing, evangelized) **1** set out to convert people to Christianity. **2** preach the gospel.

evaporate ▸ verb (evaporates, evaporating, evaporated) **1** turn from liquid into vapour. **2** cease to exist.

> SYNONYMS **1** *the water evaporated* **vaporize,** dry up. **2** *the feeling has evaporated* **end,** pass (away), fizzle out, peter out, wear off, vanish, fade, disappear, melt away.
> ANTONYMS condense, materialize.

■ **evaporated milk** thick sweetened milk from which some of the liquid has been evaporated.
□ **evaporation** noun.

evasion ▸ noun the action of avoiding something.

evasive ▸ adjective **1** avoiding committing yourself or revealing things about yourself. **2** (of an action) intended to avoid or escape something.

> SYNONYMS **equivocal,** prevaricating, elusive, ambiguous, non-committal, vague, unclear, oblique.

□ **evasively** adverb.

eve ▸ noun **1** the day or period of time immediately before an event or occasion. **2** evening.

even¹ ▸ adjective **1** flat and smooth; level. **2** equal in number, amount, or value. **3** regular. **4** equally balanced. **5** placid; calm. **6** (of a number) able to be divided by two without a remainder.

> SYNONYMS **1** *an even surface* **flat,** smooth, uniform, level, plane. **2** *an even temperature* **uniform,** constant, steady, stable, consistent, unvarying, unchanging, regular. **3** *the score was even* **level,** drawn, tied, all square, neck and neck; Brit. level pegging; informal even-steven(s).
> ANTONYMS bumpy, irregular, unequal.

▸ verb (evens, evening, evened) make or become even.
▸ adverb used for emphasis: *he knows even less than I do.*
■ **even-handed** fair and impartial.
□ **evenly** adverb **evenness** noun.

even² ▸ noun old use evening.

evening ▸ noun the period of time at the end of the day.

> SYNONYMS **dusk,** twilight, nightfall, sunset, sundown, night.

evensong ▸ noun a Christian service of evening prayers, psalms, and hymns.

event ▸ noun **1** a thing that happens or takes place. **2** a public or social occasion. **3** each of several contests making up a sports competition.

> SYNONYMS **1** *an annual event* **occurrence,** happening, incident, affair, occasion, phenomenon, function, gathering; informal

do. **2** *a team event* **competition,** contest, tournament, match, fixture, race, game, sport, discipline.

eventful ▸ adjective marked by interesting or exciting events.

> SYNONYMS **busy,** action-packed, full, lively, active, hectic.
> ANTONYMS dull.

eventual ▸ adjective occurring at the end of or resulting from a process or period of time.

> SYNONYMS **final,** ultimate, resulting, ensuing, consequent, subsequent.

eventuality ▸ noun (plural **eventualities**) a possible event or outcome.

eventually ▸ adverb in the end, especially after a delay, dispute, or problem.

> SYNONYMS **in the end,** in due course, by and by, in time, after a time, finally, at last, ultimately, in the long run, at the end of the day, one day, some day, sometime, sooner or later.

ever ▸ adverb **1** at any time. **2** used for emphasis in comparisons and questions: *better than ever.* **3** always. **4** increasingly.

> SYNONYMS **1** *the best I've ever done* **at any time,** at any point, on any occasion, under any circumstances, on any account, until now. **2** *he was ever the optimist* **always,** forever, eternally. **3** *an ever increasing rate of crime* **continually,** constantly, always, endlessly, perpetually, incessantly.

evergreen ▸ adjective (of a plant) having green leaves throughout the year.

everlasting ▸ adjective lasting forever or a very long time.

> SYNONYMS **eternal,** endless, never-ending, perpetual, undying, abiding, enduring, infinite.
> ANTONYMS transient, occasional.

☐ **everlastingly** adverb.

evermore ▸ adverb always; forever.

every ▸ determiner **1** used to refer to all the individual members of a set without exception. **2** used to indicate how often something happens: *every thirty minutes.* **3** all possible: *every effort was made.*

> SYNONYMS **1** *he exercised every day* **each,** each and every, every single. **2** *we make every effort to satisfy our clients* **all possible,** the utmost.
> ANTONYMS no.

everybody ▸ pronoun every person.

> SYNONYMS **everyone,** every person, each person, all, one and all, all and sundry, the whole world, the public.
> ANTONYMS nobody.

everyday ▸ adjective **1** daily. **2** happening regularly. **3** commonplace.

> SYNONYMS **1** *the everyday demands of a baby* **daily,** day-to-day, ongoing. **2** *everyday drugs like aspirin* **commonplace,** ordinary, common, usual, regular, familiar, conventional, routine, run-of-the-mill, standard, stock, household, domestic; Brit. common or garden.
> ANTONYMS unusual.

everyone ▸ pronoun every person.

> SYNONYMS See **EVERYBODY**.

everything ▸ pronoun **1** all things, or all the things of a group. **2** the most important thing.

> SYNONYMS **every single thing,** each thing, the (whole) lot, all; informal the works.
> ANTONYMS nothing.

everywhere ▸ adverb **1** in or to all places. **2** in many places.

> SYNONYMS **all over,** all around, in every nook and cranny, far and wide, near and far, high and low, (here, there, and everywhere), the world over, worldwide; informal all over the place; Brit. informal all over the shop; N. Amer. informal all over the map.
> ANTONYMS nowhere.

evict ▸ verb legally force someone to leave a property.
☐ **eviction** noun.

evidence ▸ noun **1** information indicating whether something is true or valid. **2** information used to establish facts in a legal investigation.

> SYNONYMS **1** *evidence of his infidelity* **proof,** confirmation, verification, substantiation, corroboration. **2** *the court accepted her evidence* **testimony,** witness statement, declaration, submission; Law deposition, affidavit. **3** *evidence of a struggle* **signs,** indications, marks, traces, suggestions, hints.

▸ verb (**evidences, evidencing, evidenced**) be or show evidence of.
■ **in evidence** noticeable.

evident ▸ adjective easily seen or understood; obvious.

> SYNONYMS **obvious,** apparent, noticeable, conspicuous, visible, discernible, clear, plain, manifest, patent; informal as clear as day.

evidently ▸ adverb **1** in a way that is clearly seen or understood. **2** it would seem that.

> SYNONYMS **1** *he was evidently upset* **obviously,** clearly, plainly, unmistakably, manifestly, patently.

e

2 *evidently, she believed him* **seemingly,** apparently, as far as one can tell, from all appearances, on the face of it, it seems, it appears.

evil ▶ adjective **1** deeply immoral and wicked. **2** very unpleasant.

SYNONYMS **1** *an evil deed* **wicked,** bad, wrong, immoral, sinful, vile, iniquitous, villainous, vicious, malicious, malevolent, demonic, diabolical, fiendish, dark, monstrous. **2** *an evil spirit* **harmful,** bad, malign. **3** *evil weather* **unpleasant,** disagreeable, nasty, horrible, foul, filthy, vile.
ANTONYMS good, benign, pleasant.

▶ noun **1** extreme wickedness. **2** something harmful or undesirable.

SYNONYMS **1** *the evil in our midst* **wickedness,** badness, wrongdoing, sin, sinfulness, immorality, vice, iniquity, corruption, villainy. **2** *nothing but evil will result* **harm,** pain, misery, sorrow, suffering, trouble, disaster, misfortune, woe.
ANTONYMS good.

□ **evilly** adverb.

evince ▶ verb (**evinces, evincing, evinced**) formal reveal the presence of.

eviscerate /i-viss-uh-rayt/ ▶ verb (**eviscerates, eviscerating, eviscerated**) formal remove the intestines of.
□ **evisceration** noun.

evocative ▶ adjective bringing strong images, memories, or feelings to mind.

evoke ▶ verb (**evokes, evoking, evoked**) **1** bring a feeling or memory into someone's mind. **2** obtain a response.

SYNONYMS **bring to mind,** put one in mind of, conjure up, summon (up), invoke, elicit, induce, kindle, awaken, arouse.

□ **evocation** noun.

evolution ▶ noun **1** the process by which different kinds of animals and plants develop from earlier forms. **2** gradual development.

SYNONYMS **1** *his interest in evolution* **natural selection,** Darwinism, adaptation, development. **2** *the evolution of Bolshevism* **development,** progress, rise, expansion, growth.

□ **evolutionary** adjective.

evolve ▶ verb (**evolves, evolving, evolved**) **1** develop gradually. **2** (of an animal or plant) develop and change over many generations by evolution.

SYNONYMS **develop,** progress, advance, grow, expand, spread.

ewe ▶ noun a female sheep.

ewer /yoo-er/ ▶ noun a large jug with a wide mouth.

ex ▶ noun informal a former husband, wife, boyfriend, or girlfriend.
▶ prefix (**ex-**) **1** out: *exclude.* **2** former: *ex-husband.*

exacerbate ▶ verb (**exacerbates, exacerbating, exacerbated**) make something that is already bad worse.
□ **exacerbation** noun.

exact ▶ adjective **1** precise. **2** accurate in all details.

SYNONYMS **1** *an exact description* **precise,** accurate, correct, faithful, close, true, literal, strict, perfect. **2** *an exact record keeper* **careful,** meticulous, painstaking, punctilious, conscientious, scrupulous.
ANTONYMS inaccurate, careless.

▶ verb **1** demand and obtain something from someone. **2** take revenge on someone.

SYNONYMS **1** *he exacted certain promises* **demand,** require, impose, extract, compel, force, wring. **2** *they exacted a terrible vengeance on him* **inflict,** impose, administer, mete out, wreak.

□ **exactness** noun.

exacting ▶ adjective (of a task) making you concentrate or work very hard.

SYNONYMS **demanding,** stringent, testing, challenging, arduous, laborious, taxing, gruelling, punishing, hard, tough.
ANTONYMS easy, easy-going.

exactitude ▶ noun the quality of being exact.

exactly ▶ adverb **1** in an exact way. **2** used to agree with what has just been said.

SYNONYMS **1** *it's exactly as I expected* **precisely,** entirely, absolutely, completely, totally, just, quite, in every respect. **2** *write it out exactly* **accurately,** precisely, unerringly, faultlessly, perfectly, faithfully.

exaggerate ▶ verb (**exaggerates, exaggerating, exaggerated**) make something seem larger, more important, etc. than it really is.

SYNONYMS **overstate,** overemphasize, overestimate, inflate, embellish, embroider, elaborate, overplay, dramatize; Brit. informal blow out of all proportion.
ANTONYMS understate.

□ **exaggeration** noun.

✔ two **g**s: exa**gg**erate.

exalt ▶ verb **1** praise someone or something highly. **2** give someone or something a higher rank or status.

exaltation ▶ noun **1** extreme happiness. **2** the action of exalting.

exalted ▶ adjective **1** having high rank or status. **2** very grand or noble; high-flown.

exam ▸ noun an examination in a subject or skill.

examination ▸ noun **1** a detailed inspection. **2** a formal test of knowledge or ability in a subject or skill. **3** the action of examining.

SYNONYMS **1** *artefacts spread out for examination* **scrutiny,** inspection, perusal, study, investigation, consideration, analysis. **2** *a medical examination* **inspection,** check-up, assessment, appraisal, test, scan. **3** *a school examination* **test,** exam, assessment; N. Amer. quiz.

examine ▸ verb (**examines, examining, examined**) **1** inspect something closely. **2** (of a doctor or dentist) look closely at a part of a person's body to detect any problems. **3** test someone's knowledge or ability.

SYNONYMS **1** *they examined the bank records* **inspect,** scrutinize, investigate, look at, study, appraise, analyse, review, survey; informal check out. **2** *students were examined after a year* **test,** quiz, question, assess, appraise.

□ **examinee** noun **examiner** noun.

example ▸ noun **1** a thing that is typical of or represents a particular group. **2** something that shows or supports a general rule. **3** a person or thing seen in terms of how suitable they are to be copied.

SYNONYMS **1** *a fine example of Chinese porcelain* **specimen,** sample, instance, case, illustration. **2** *we must follow their example* **precedent,** lead, model, pattern, ideal, standard. **3** *he was hanged as an example to others* **warning,** lesson, deterrent, disincentive.

exasperate ▸ verb (**exasperates, exasperating, exasperated**) irritate someone very much.
□ **exasperation** noun.

excavate ▸ verb (**excavates, excavating, excavated**) **1** make a hole by digging. **2** carefully remove earth from an area in order to find buried remains. **3** dig material out of the ground.

SYNONYMS **unearth,** dig up, uncover, reveal, disinter, exhume, dig out, quarry, mine.

□ **excavation** noun.

exceed ▸ verb **1** be greater in number or size than. **2** go beyond a set limit. **3** go beyond what is expected.

SYNONYMS **be more than,** be greater than, be over, go beyond, top, surpass.

exceedingly ▸ adverb extremely.

excel ▸ verb (**excels, excelling, excelled**) **1** be very good at something. **2** (**excel yourself**) do something exceptionally well.

SYNONYMS **shine,** be excellent, be outstanding, be skilful, be talented, stand out, be second to none.

excellence ▸ noun the quality of being excellent.

SYNONYMS **distinction,** quality, superiority, brilliance, greatness, calibre, eminence.

Excellency ▸ noun (plural **Excellencies**) (**His, Your,** etc. **Excellency**) a form of address for certain high officials of state or of the Roman Catholic Church.

excellent ▸ adjective very good; outstanding.

SYNONYMS **very good,** superb, outstanding, exceptional, marvellous, wonderful, splendid; informal terrific, fantastic.
ANTONYMS inferior.

□ **excellently** adverb.

except ▸ preposition not including.

SYNONYMS **excluding,** not including, excepting, except for, omitting, not counting, but, besides, apart from, aside from, barring, bar, other than; informal outside of.
ANTONYMS including.

▸ conjunction used before a statement that forms an exception to one just made.
▸ verb exclude.

✔ Don't forget the **c** in **except** and related words. Also, don't confuse **except** and **accept,** which means 'agree to receive or do something'.

excepting ▸ preposition except for.

exception ▸ noun a person or thing that is excluded or that does not follow a rule.

SYNONYMS **anomaly,** irregularity, deviation, special case, peculiarity, abnormality, oddity.

■ **take exception to** object strongly to.

exceptionable ▸ adjective formal causing disapproval or offence.

exceptional ▸ adjective **1** unusual; not typical. **2** unusually good.

SYNONYMS **1** *the drought was exceptional* **unusual,** abnormal, atypical, out of the ordinary, rare, unprecedented, unexpected, surprising. **2** *her exceptional ability* **outstanding,** extraordinary, remarkable, special, phenomenal, prodigious.
ANTONYMS normal, average.

□ **exceptionally** adverb.

excerpt ▸ noun a short extract from a film or piece of music or writing.

e

SYNONYMS **extract,** part, section, piece, portion, snippet, clip, citation, quotation, quote, line, passage, fragment.

excess ▶ noun **1** an amount that is too much. **2** (**excesses**) extreme or outrageous behaviour. **3** Brit. a part of an insurance claim to be paid by the person insured.

SYNONYMS **1** *an excess of calcium* **surplus,** surfeit, over-abundance, superabundance, superfluity, glut. **2** *the excess is turned into fat* **extra,** surplus, remainder, rest, residue. **3** *a life of excess* **overindulgence,** intemperance, immoderation, profligacy, extravagance, self-indulgence.
ANTONYMS lack, restraint.

▶ adjective going beyond an allowed or desirable amount.

SYNONYMS *excess oil* **surplus,** superfluous, redundant, unwanted, unneeded, excessive, extra.

excessive ▶ adjective more than is necessary, normal, or desirable.

SYNONYMS **1** *excessive alcohol consumption* **immoderate,** intemperate, overindulgent, unrestrained, uncontrolled, extravagant. **2** *the cost is excessive* **exorbitant,** extortionate, unreasonable, outrageous, uncalled for, inordinate, unwarranted, disproportionate; informal over the top.

□ **excessively** adverb.

exchange ▶ noun **1** an act of giving something and receiving something else in return. **2** a short conversation or argument. **3** the changing of money to its equivalent in another currency. **4** a building used for financial trading. **5** a set of equipment that connects telephone lines during a call.

SYNONYMS **1** *the exchange of ideas* **interchange,** trade, trading, swapping, traffic, trafficking. **2** *a brief exchange* **conversation,** dialogue, chat, talk, discussion.

▶ verb (**exchanges, exchanging, exchanged**) give something and receive something else in return.

SYNONYMS *we exchanged shirts* **trade,** swap, switch, change.

■ **exchange rate** the value at which one currency may be exchanged for another.

exchequer ▶ noun **1** a royal or national treasury. **2** (**Exchequer**) Brit. the account at the Bank of England into which public money is paid.

excise[1] /ek-syz/ ▶ noun a tax charged on certain goods, such as alcohol.

excise[2] /ik-syz/ ▶ verb (**excises, excising, excised**) **1** cut something out surgically. **2** remove a section from a written work or

piece of music.
□ **excision** noun.

excitable ▶ adjective easily excited.
□ **excitability** noun **excitably** adverb.

excite ▶ verb (**excites, exciting, excited**) **1** make someone feel very enthusiastic and eager. **2** make someone feel sexually aroused. **3** give rise to. **4** increase the energy or activity in a physical or biological system.

SYNONYMS **1** *the prospect of a holiday excited me* **thrill,** exhilarate, animate, enliven, rouse, stir, stimulate, galvanize. **2** *his clothes excited envy* **provoke,** stir up, rouse, arouse, kindle, trigger, spark off, incite, cause.
ANTONYMS bore.

□ **excitation** noun.

✔ Don't forget the **c**: ex**c**ite.

excitement ▶ noun **1** a feeling of great enthusiasm and eagerness. **2** something that arouses such a feeling. **3** sexual arousal.

SYNONYMS **1** *the excitement of seeing a leopard in the wild* **thrill,** pleasure, delight, joy; informal buzz. **2** *excitement in her eyes* **exhilaration,** elation, animation, enthusiasm, eagerness, anticipation.

exciting ▶ adjective causing great enthusiasm and eagerness.

SYNONYMS **thrilling,** exhilarating, stirring, rousing, stimulating, intoxicating, electrifying, invigorating, gripping, compelling, powerful, dramatic.

□ **excitingly** adverb.

exclaim ▶ verb cry out suddenly.

SYNONYMS **cry out,** declare, proclaim, blurt out, call out, shout, yell.

exclamation ▶ noun a sudden cry or remark.
■ **exclamation mark** a punctuation mark (!) indicating an exclamation.
□ **exclamatory** adjective.

exclude ▶ verb (**excludes, excluding, excluded**) **1** choose not to include something in what you are counting or considering. **2** prevent someone from being a part of something.

SYNONYMS **1** *women were excluded from the club* **keep out,** deny access to, shut out, bar, ban, prohibit. **2** *the clause excluded any judicial review* **rule out,** preclude. **3** *the price excludes postage* **be exclusive of,** not include.
ANTONYMS admit, include, allow for.

exclusion ▶ noun the process of excluding, or the state of being excluded.

exclusive ▶ adjective **1** restricted to the

person, group, or area concerned. **2** high-quality and expensive. **3** not including other things. **4** not published or broadcast elsewhere.

synonyms **1** *an exclusive club* **select,** chic, high-class, elite, fashionable, stylish, elegant, premier; Brit. upmarket; informal posh, classy; Brit. informal swish. **2** *a room for your exclusive use* **sole,** unshared, unique, individual, personal, private. **3** *prices exclusive of VAT* **not including,** excluding, leaving out, omitting, excepting.
antonyms shared, inclusive.

▸ **noun** a story or film that has not been published or broadcast elsewhere.
□ **exclusively** adverb **exclusivity** noun.

excommunicate ▸ verb (**excommunicates, excommunicating, excommunicated**) officially bar someone from membership of the Christian Church.
□ **excommunication** noun.

excoriate ▸ verb (**excoriates, excoriating, excoriated**) **1** formal criticize someone severely. **2** Medicine damage or remove part of the surface of the skin.
□ **excoriation** noun.

excrement ▸ noun waste material passed from the body through the bowels.

excrescence ▸ noun an abnormal growth or lump on a part of the body or a plant.

excreta ▸ noun waste material that is passed out of the body.

excrete ▸ verb (**excretes, excreting, excreted**) pass waste material from the body.
□ **excretion** noun **excretory** adjective.

excruciating ▸ adjective **1** very painful. **2** very embarrassing, awkward, or boring.
□ **excruciatingly** adverb.

exculpate /eks-kul-payt/ ▸ verb (**exculpates, exculpating, exculpated**) formal say that someone is not guilty of doing something wrong.
□ **exculpation** noun.

excursion ▸ noun a short journey or trip taken for pleasure.

synonyms **outing,** trip, jaunt, expedition, journey, tour, day trip, day out, drive, run; informal spin.

excuse ▸ verb /ik-**skyooz**/ (**excuses, excusing, excused**) **1** give reasons why something that someone has done wrong may be justified. **2** forgive someone for something they have done wrong. **3** allow someone to not do something that is usually required. **4** allow someone to leave a room or meeting.

synonyms **1** *please excuse me* **forgive,** pardon. **2** *such conduct cannot be excused* **justify,** defend, condone, forgive, overlook, disregard, ignore, tolerate,

explain, mitigate. **3** *she was excused from her duties* **let off,** release, relieve, exempt, absolve, free.
antonyms punish, blame, condemn.

▸ **noun** /ik-**skyooss**/ **1** a reason put forward to justify a fault or wrongdoing. **2** something said to conceal the real reason for an action. **3** informal a very bad example of something.

synonyms **1** *that's no excuse for stealing* **justification,** defence, reason, explanation, mitigating circumstances, mitigation. **2** *an excuse to get away* **pretext,** pretence; Brit. get-out; informal story, alibi.

□ **excusable** adjective.

ex-directory ▸ adjective Brit. not listed in a telephone directory at your own request.

execrable /ek-si-kruh-b'l/ ▸ adjective very bad or unpleasant.

execrate /ek-si-krayt/ ▸ verb (**execrates, execrating, execrated**) feel or express great hatred for.
□ **execration** noun.

execute ▸ verb (**executes, executing, executed**) **1** carry out a plan, order, etc. **2** carry out an activity or manoeuvre. **3** kill a condemned person as a legal punishment.

synonyms **1** *he executed a series of financial deals* **carry out,** accomplish, bring off/about, implement, achieve, complete, engineer; informal pull off. **2** *he was finally executed* **put to death,** kill, hang, behead, electrocute, shoot.

execution ▸ noun **1** the carrying out of something. **2** the killing of a person who has been condemned to death.

synonyms **1** *the execution of the plan* **implementation,** carrying out, performance, accomplishment, bringing off/about, attainment, realization. **2** *public execution* **killing,** capital punishment, the death penalty.

executioner ▸ noun an official who executes condemned criminals.

executive ▸ noun **1** a senior manager in a business. **2** a group of people who run an organization or business. **3** (**the executive**) the branch of a government responsible for putting plans, actions, or laws into effect.

synonyms **1** *the company's chief executive* **director,** manager, senior official, administrator; informal boss, exec, suit. **2** *the future role of the executive* **administration,** management, directorate, government, authority.

▸ **adjective** having the power to put plans, actions, or laws into effect.

synonyms *executive powers* **administrative,** managerial, decision-

e

making, law-making, governing, controlling.

executor /ig-**zek**-yuu-ter/ ▸ noun a person appointed by someone to carry out the terms of their will.

exegesis /ek-si-**jee**-siss/ ▸ noun (plural **exegeses** /ek-si-**jee**-seez/) an explanation or interpretation of a written work.

exemplar /ig-**zem**-pler/ ▸ noun a person or thing that is a good or typical example of something.

exemplary ▸ adjective 1 giving a good example to other people. 2 (of a punishment) acting as a warning.

> SYNONYMS **perfect**, ideal, model, faultless, flawless, impeccable, irreproachable.
> ANTONYMS deplorable.

exemplify ▸ verb (**exemplifies**, **exemplifying**, **exemplified**) be or give a typical example of.

> SYNONYMS **typify**, epitomize, be an example of, be representative of, symbolize, illustrate, demonstrate.

□ **exemplification** noun.

exempt ▸ adjective not having to do or pay something that other people have to do or pay.

> SYNONYMS **free**, not liable, not subject, immune, excepted, excused, absolved.
> ANTONYMS subject to.

▸ verb make someone exempt.

> SYNONYMS **excuse**, free, release, exclude, grant immunity, spare, absolve; informal let off.
> ANTONYMS oblige.

exemption ▸ noun the state of being exempt.

> SYNONYMS **immunity**, exception, dispensation, indemnity, exclusion, freedom, release, relief, absolution.

exercise ▸ noun 1 physical activity done to stay healthy or become stronger. 2 a set of movements, activities, or questions that test your ability or help you practise a skill. 3 an activity carried out for a specific purpose. 4 the putting into practice of a power or right.

> SYNONYMS 1 *exercise improves your heart* **physical activity**, a workout, working out, movement, training. 2 *translation exercises* **task**, piece of work, problem, assignment, practice. 3 *a military exercise* **manoeuvre**, operation, deployment.

▸ verb (**exercises**, **exercising**, **exercised**) 1 use or apply a power or right. 2 do physical exercise. 3 worry or puzzle someone.

> SYNONYMS 1 *she exercised every day* **work out**, do exercises, train. 2 *he must*

learn to exercise patience **use**, employ, make use of, utilize, practise, apply. 3 *the problem continued to exercise him* **concern**, occupy, worry, trouble, bother, disturb, prey on someone's mind.

■ **exercise book** Brit. a booklet with blank pages for students to write in.

exert ▸ verb 1 use a force, influence, or quality to make something happen. 2 (**exert yourself**) make a physical or mental effort.

> SYNONYMS **bring to bear**, apply, use, utilize, deploy.

□ **exertion** noun.

exeunt /**ek**-si-uhnt/ ▸ verb (in a play) a stage direction telling actors to leave the stage.

exfoliate ▸ verb (**exfoliates**, **exfoliating**, **exfoliated**) wash or rub the skin with a grainy substance to remove dead cells. □ **exfoliation** noun.

exhale ▸ verb (**exhales**, **exhaling**, **exhaled**) 1 breathe out. 2 give off vapour or fumes. □ **exhalation** noun.

exhaust ▸ verb 1 tire someone out. 2 use up all of something. 3 talk about a subject so thoroughly that there is nothing left to say.

> SYNONYMS 1 *the effort had exhausted him* **tire out**, wear out, overtire, fatigue, weary, drain; informal take it out of you, shatter; Brit. informal knacker; N. Amer. informal poop, tucker out. 2 *the country has exhausted its reserves* **use up**, get through, consume, finish, deplete, spend, empty, drain; informal blow.
> ANTONYMS invigorate, replenish.

▸ noun 1 waste gases that are expelled from the engine of a car or other machine. 2 the system through which these gases are expelled.
□ **exhaustible** adjective.

exhaustion ▸ noun the state of being exhausted.

> SYNONYMS **tiredness**, overtiredness, fatigue, weariness.

exhaustive ▸ adjective thoroughly covering all aspects of something. □ **exhaustively** adverb.

exhibit ▸ verb 1 display an item in an art gallery or museum. 2 show a particular quality.

> SYNONYMS 1 *the paintings were exhibited in Glasgow* **display**, show, put on display, unveil, present. 2 *Luke exhibited signs of jealousy* **show**, reveal, display, manifest, indicate, demonstrate, express.

▸ noun 1 an object or collection on display in an art gallery or museum. 2 an object produced in a court of law as evidence.

SYNONYMS *an exhibit at the British Museum* **item,** piece, artefact, display, collection.

□ **exhibitor** noun.

exhibition ▸ noun 1 a public display of items in an art gallery or museum. 2 a display or demonstration of a skill or quality.

SYNONYMS 1 *a photography exhibition* **display,** show, showing, presentation, exposition. 2 *a convincing exhibition of concern* **display,** show, demonstration, manifestation, expression.

exhibitionism ▸ noun behaviour that is intended to make people notice you.
□ **exhibitionist** noun.

exhilarate ▸ verb (**exhilarates, exhilarating, exhilarated**) make someone feel very happy and full of energy.

SYNONYMS (**exhilarating**) **thrilling,** exciting, invigorating, stimulating, intoxicating, electrifying.

□ **exhilaration** noun.

✔ The middle is **-lar-,** not **-ler-:** exhi**lar**ate.

exhort ▸ verb strongly urge someone to do something.
□ **exhortation** noun.

exhume ▸ verb (**exhumes, exhuming, exhumed**) dig out from the ground something that has been buried.
□ **exhumation** noun.

exigency /ek-si-juhn-si/ ▸ noun (plural **exigencies**) formal an urgent need.

exigent /ek-si-juhnt/ ▸ adjective formal needing urgent action; pressing.

exiguous /eg-zig-yoo-uhss/ ▸ adjective formal very small.

exile ▸ noun 1 the state of being forbidden to live or spend time in your own country. 2 a person who lives in exile.

SYNONYMS 1 *his exile from his homeland* **banishment,** expulsion, deportation, eviction, isolation. 2 *political exiles* **expatriate,** émigré, deportee, displaced person, refugee.

▸ verb (**exiles, exiling, exiled**) expel and bar someone from their own country.

exist ▸ verb 1 be present in a place or situation. 2 live.

SYNONYMS 1 *animals that existed long ago* **live,** be alive, be, be present. 2 *the liberal climate that now exists* **prevail,** occur, be found, be in existence, be the case. 3 *she had to exist on a low income* **survive,** subsist, live, support yourself, manage, make do, get by, scrape by, make ends meet.

existence ▸ noun 1 the fact or state of existing. 2 a way of living: *a rural existence.*

SYNONYMS 1 *the industry's continued existence* **survival,** continuation. 2 *her suburban existence* **way of life,** life, lifestyle, situation.

✔ **-ence,** not **-ance:** exist**ence.**

existential /eg-zi-sten-sh'l/ ▸ adjective 1 having to do with existence. 2 Philosophy concerned with existentialism.

existentialism ▸ noun a theory in philosophy which says that people are free individuals, responsible for their own actions.
□ **existentialist** noun & adjective.

exit ▸ noun 1 a way out of a place. 2 an act of leaving.

SYNONYMS 1 *a fire exit* **way out,** door, escape route, egress. 2 *take the second exit* **turning,** turn-off, junction. 3 *his sudden exit* **departure,** leaving, withdrawal, going, retreat, flight, exodus, escape.
ANTONYMS entrance, arrival.

▸ verb (**exits, exiting, exited**) go out of or leave a place.

SYNONYMS *the doctor had just exited* **leave,** go out, depart, withdraw, retreat.
ANTONYMS enter.

■ **exit poll** an opinion poll in which people leaving a polling station are asked how they voted.

exocrine /ek-soh-kryn/ ▸ adjective (of a gland) secreting hormones or other products through ducts rather than directly into the blood.

exodus ▸ noun a mass departure of people.

exonerate /ig-zon-uh-rayt/ ▸ verb (**exonerates, exonerating, exonerated**) officially state that someone has not done something wrong or illegal.
□ **exoneration** noun.

exorbitant ▸ adjective (of an amount charged) unreasonably high.
□ **exorbitantly** adverb.

✔ no **h:** ex**or**bitant.

exorcize (or **exorcise**) ▸ verb (**exorcizes, exorcizing, exorcizes**) drive an evil spirit from a person or place.
□ **exorcism** noun **exorcist** noun.

exotic ▸ adjective 1 coming from or characteristic of a distant foreign country. 2 strikingly colourful or unusual.

SYNONYMS 1 *exotic birds* **foreign,** non-native, alien, tropical. 2 *exotic places* **foreign,** faraway, far-off, far-flung, distant. 3 *Linda's exotic appearance* **striking,** colourful, eye-catching, unusual, unconventional, extravagant, outlandish.
ANTONYMS native, nearby, conventional.

□ **exotically** adverb **exoticism** noun.

expand ▸ verb **1** make or become larger or more extensive. **2** (**expand on**) give a fuller account of.

> SYNONYMS **1** *metals expand when heated* **enlarge**, increase in size, swell, lengthen, stretch, spread, thicken, fill out. **2** *the company is expanding* **grow**, enlarge, increase in size, extend, augment, broaden, widen, develop, diversify, build up, branch out, spread.
> ANTONYMS contract.

□ **expandable** adjective.

expanse ▸ noun a wide continuous area of something.

expansion ▸ noun the action of becoming larger.

> SYNONYMS **1** *expansion and contraction* **enlargement**, swelling, lengthening, elongation, stretching, thickening. **2** *the expansion of the company* **growth**, increase in size, enlargement, extension, development, diversification, spread.
> ANTONYMS contraction.

expansive ▸ adjective **1** covering a wide area. **2** relaxed, friendly, and communicative.

□ **expansively** adverb.

expat = EXPATRIATE.

expatiate /ek-spay-shi-ayt/ ▸ verb (**expatiates, expatiating, expatiated**) (**expatiate on**) speak or write in detail about something.

expatriate ▸ noun /eks-pat-ri-uht/ a person who lives outside their own country.

expect ▸ verb **1** think something is likely to happen. **2** think someone is likely to do or be something. **3** believe that someone will arrive soon. **4** assume or demand that someone will do something because it is their duty or responsibility. **5** (**be expecting**) informal be pregnant.

> SYNONYMS **1** *I expect she'll be late* **suppose**, presume, imagine, assume, surmise; informal guess, reckon; N. Amer. informal figure. **2** *a 10 per cent rise was expected* **anticipate**, envisage, await, look for, hope for, look forward to, contemplate, bargain for/on, predict, forecast. **3** *we expect total loyalty* **require**, ask for, call for, want, insist on, demand.

expectancy ▸ noun (plural **expectancies**) the belief or hope that something will happen.

expectant ▸ adjective **1** believing or hoping that something is about to happen. **2** (of a woman) pregnant.

□ **expectantly** adverb.

expectation ▸ noun **1** belief that something will happen or be the case. **2** a thing that is expected to happen.

> SYNONYMS **1** *her expectations were unrealistic* **supposition**, assumption, presumption, conjecture, calculation, prediction, hope. **2** *tense with expectation* **anticipation**, expectancy, eagerness, excitement, suspense.

expectorant ▸ noun a medicine which helps to bring up phlegm from the air passages, used to treat a cough.

expectorate ▸ verb (**expectorates, expectorating, expectorated**) cough or spit out phlegm from the throat or lungs.

expedient /ik-spee-di-uhnt/ ▸ adjective **1** useful or helpful for a particular purpose. **2** useful in achieving something, rather than morally correct.
▸ noun a means of achieving something.
□ **expediency** (or **expedience**) noun.

expedite /eks-pi-dyt/ ▸ verb (**expedites, expediting, expedited**) make something happen more quickly.

expedition ▸ noun a journey with a particular purpose, made by a group of people.

> SYNONYMS **journey**, voyage, tour, safari, trek, mission, quest, hike, trip.

□ **expeditionary** adjective.

expeditious /eks-pi-di-shuhss/ ▸ adjective quick and efficient.
□ **expeditiously** adverb.

expel ▸ verb (**expels, expelling, expelled**) **1** force someone to leave a school, organization, or place. **2** force something out.

> SYNONYMS **throw out**, bar, ban, debar, drum out, banish, exile, deport, evict; informal chuck out.
> ANTONYMS admit.

expend ▸ verb spend or use up a resource.

expendable ▸ adjective able to be sacrificed in order to gain or achieve something.

expenditure ▸ noun **1** the action of spending money. **2** the amount of money spent.

expense ▸ noun **1** the amount something costs. **2** something on which money must be spent. **3** (**expenses**) money spent in doing a particular thing. **4** (**expenses**) money paid for meals, fares, etc. by an employee in the course of their work, which they can claim back from their employer.

> SYNONYMS **cost**, expenditure, spending, outlay, outgoings, payment, price, charge, fees, overheads, tariff, bill.
> ANTONYMS income, profit.

expensive ▸ adjective costing a lot of money.

> SYNONYMS **costly**, dear, high-priced, overpriced, exorbitant, extortionate;

informal steep, stiff, pricey.
ANTONYMS cheap.

□ **expensively** adverb.

experience ▸ noun **1** the fact of being present at or taking part in something. **2** knowledge or skill gained over time. **3** an event which affects you in some way.

> SYNONYMS **1** *qualifications and experience* **skill,** practical knowledge, understanding, background, track record, history; informal know-how. **2** *an enjoyable experience* **incident,** occurrence, event, happening, episode, adventure. **3** *his first experience of business* **involvement in,** participation in, contact with, acquaintance with, exposure to.

▸ verb (**experiences, experiencing, experienced**) **1** be present at or be affected by something. **2** feel an emotion.

> SYNONYMS *they experience daily harassment* **undergo,** go through, encounter, face, meet, come across, come up against.

experienced ▸ adjective having gained a lot of knowledge or skill in a job or activity over time.

> SYNONYMS **knowledgeable,** skilful, skilled, expert, proficient, trained, competent, capable, seasoned, practised, mature, veteran.
> ANTONYMS inexperienced.

experiment ▸ noun **1** a scientific procedure carried out to make a discovery, test a theory, or demonstrate a fact. **2** a new course of action that you try out without being sure of the outcome.

> SYNONYMS *the calculations were confirmed by experiment* **test,** investigation, trial, examination, observation, research, assessment, evaluation, appraisal, analysis, study.

▸ verb **1** perform a scientific experiment. **2** try out new things.

> SYNONYMS *they experimented with new ideas* **carry out experiments,** test, trial, try out, assess, appraise, evaluate.

□ **experimentation** noun.

experimental ▸ adjective **1** based on a new idea and not yet fully tested. **2** having to do with scientific experiments. **3** (of art, music, etc.) new and unconventional.

> SYNONYMS **1** *the experimental stage* **exploratory,** investigational, trial, test, pilot, speculative, tentative, preliminary. **2** *experimental music* **new,** innovative, creative, radical, avant-garde, alternative, unorthodox, unconventional, cutting-edge.

□ **experimentally** adverb.

expert ▸ noun a person who has great knowledge or skill in a particular field.

> SYNONYMS **specialist,** authority, pundit, maestro, virtuoso, master, wizard, connoisseur, aficionado; informal ace, pro, hotshot; Brit. informal dab hand; N. Amer. informal maven.
> ANTONYMS amateur.

▸ adjective having or involving great knowledge or skill.

> SYNONYMS **skilful,** skilled, adept, accomplished, experienced, practised, knowledgeable, talented, masterly, virtuoso; informal ace, crack, mean.
> ANTONYMS incompetent.

□ **expertly** adverb.

expertise ▸ noun great skill or knowledge in a particular field.

> SYNONYMS **skill,** prowess, proficiency, competence, knowledge, ability, aptitude, capability; informal know-how.

expiate /ek-spi-ayt/ ▸ verb (**expiates, expiating, expiated**) do something to make up for having done something wrong.
□ **expiation** noun.

expire ▸ verb (**expires, expiring, expired**) **1** (of a document or agreement) cease to be valid. **2** (of a period of time) come to an end. **3** (of a person) die. **4** breathe out air from the lungs.

> SYNONYMS **1** *my contract has expired* **run out,** become invalid, become void, lapse, end, finish, stop, terminate. **2** *the spot where he expired* **die,** pass away, breathe your last; informal kick the bucket, croak; Brit. informal snuff it, peg out; N. Amer. informal buy the farm.

expiry ▸ noun the end of the period for which something is valid.

explain ▸ verb **1** describe something in a way that makes it easy to understand. **2** give a reason for something. **3** (**explain yourself**) say why you are doing something in order to justify or excuse it.

> SYNONYMS **1** *he explained the procedure* **describe,** make clear, spell out, put into words, define, elucidate, expound, clarify, throw light on. **2** *that could explain his behaviour* **account for,** give a reason for, excuse.

explanation ▸ noun **1** a statement or description that makes something clear. **2** a justification or excuse.

> SYNONYMS **1** *an explanation of his theory* **clarification,** description, statement, interpretation, definition, commentary. **2** *I owe you an explanation* **account,** reason, justification, answer, excuse, defence, vindication.

e

explanatory ▶ adjective giving the reason for something, or making something clear.

expletive /ik-**splee**-tiv/ ▶ noun a swear word.

explicable ▶ adjective able to be explained.

explicit ▶ adjective 1 clear, detailed, and easy to understand. 2 showing or describing sexual activity openly and clearly.

SYNONYMS 1 *explicit instructions* **clear,** plain, straightforward, crystal clear, precise, exact, specific, unequivocal, unambiguous, detailed. 2 *sexually explicit material* **graphic,** candid, full-frontal, uncensored.
ANTONYMS vague, tasteful, decent.

□ **explicitly** adverb.

explode ▶ verb (**explodes, exploding, exploded**) 1 burst or shatter violently as a result of the release of internal energy. 2 show sudden violent emotion. 3 increase suddenly in number or extent. 4 show a belief to be false.

SYNONYMS 1 *a bomb has exploded* **blow up,** detonate, go off, burst, erupt. 2 *exploding an atomic device* **detonate,** set off, let off, discharge. 3 *he just exploded* **lose your temper,** blow up; informal fly off the handle, hit the roof, blow your top; Brit. informal go spare; N. Amer. informal blow your lid/stack. 4 *the city's exploding population* **increase rapidly,** mushroom, snowball, escalate, burgeon, rocket. 5 *exploding the myths about men* **disprove,** refute, rebut, repudiate, debunk, give the lie to; informal shoot full of holes, blow out of the water.
ANTONYMS shrink.

exploit ▶ verb /ik-**sployt**/ 1 make use of someone unfairly. 2 make good use of a resource.

SYNONYMS 1 *exploiting the workers* **take advantage of,** abuse, impose on, treat unfairly, misuse, ill-treat; informal walk (all) over. 2 *we should exploit this opportunity* **utilize,** make use of, turn/put to good use, make the most of, capitalize on, benefit from; informal cash in on.

▶ noun /**ek**-sployt/ a daring act.

SYNONYMS *his exploits brought him notoriety* **feat,** deed, act, adventure, stunt, escapade, achievement.

□ **exploitative** adjective.

exploitation ▶ noun the action of exploiting someone or something.

SYNONYMS **taking advantage,** abuse, misuse, ill-treatment, unfair treatment, oppression.

exploration ▶ noun the action of exploring.

SYNONYMS **investigation,** study, survey, research, inspection, examination, scrutiny, observation.

explore ▶ verb (**explores, exploring, explored**) 1 travel through an unfamiliar area in order to learn about it. 2 examine or discuss something in detail. 3 investigate.

SYNONYMS 1 *exploring Iceland* **travel through,** tour, survey, scout, reconnoitre. 2 *they explored the possibilities* **investigate,** look into, consider, examine, research, survey, scrutinize, study, review; informal check out.

□ **exploratory** adjective **explorer** noun.

explosion ▶ noun an instance of exploding.

SYNONYMS 1 *Ed heard the explosion* **detonation,** eruption, bang, blast, boom. 2 *an explosion of anger* **outburst,** flare-up, outbreak, eruption, storm, rush, surge, fit, paroxysm. 3 *a population explosion* **sudden increase,** mushrooming, snowballing, escalation, multiplication, burgeoning, rocketing.

explosive ▶ adjective 1 able or likely to explode. 2 likely to cause anger or controversy. 3 (of an increase) sudden and dramatic.

SYNONYMS 1 *explosive gases* **volatile,** inflammable, flammable, combustible, incendiary. 2 *Marco's explosive temper* **fiery,** stormy, violent, volatile, passionate, tempestuous, turbulent, touchy, irascible. 3 *an explosive situation* **tense,** highly charged, overwrought, dangerous, perilous, hazardous, sensitive, delicate, unstable, volatile.
ANTONYMS inert, cool, stable.

▶ noun a substance which can be made to explode.

SYNONYMS *stocks of explosives* **bomb,** charge, incendiary (device).

□ **explosively** adverb.

exponent /ik-**spoh**-nuhnt/ ▶ noun 1 a promoter of an idea or theory. 2 a person who does a particular thing skilfully. 3 Maths a raised figure beside a number indicating how many times that number is to be multiplied by itself (e.g. ^{3} in $2^3 = 2 \times 2 \times 2$).

exponential /eks-puh-**nen**-sh'l/ ▶ adjective 1 (of an increase) becoming more and more rapid. 2 Maths having to do with a mathematical exponent.
□ **exponentially** adverb.

export ▶ verb /ik-**sport**/ send goods or services to another country for sale.
▶ noun /**ek**-sport/ 1 the exporting of goods or services. 2 an exported item.
□ **exportation** noun **exporter** noun.

expose ▶ verb (**exposes, exposing, exposed**)

1 uncover something and make it visible.
2 show the true nature of someone or
something. **3** (**exposed**) not protected
from the weather. **4** (**expose someone to**)
make someone vulnerable to. **5** subject
photographic film to light. **6** (**expose
yourself**) show your sexual organs in
public.

SYNONYMS **1** *at low tide the rocks are
exposed* reveal, uncover, lay bare. **2** *he
was exposed to radiation* lay open,
subject, put at risk of, put in jeopardy
of, leave unprotected from. **3** *they were
exposed to new ideas* introduce to,
bring into contact with, make aware of,
familiarize with, acquaint with. **4** *he was
exposed as a liar* uncover, reveal, unveil,
unmask, detect, find out, denounce,
condemn; informal blow the whistle on.
ANTONYMS cover, protect from, insulate
from, protect.

exposé /ik-**spoh**-zay/ ▸ noun a report in the
news revealing shocking information about
someone.
exposition ▸ noun **1** a careful setting out
of the facts or ideas involved in something.
2 an exhibition. **3** Music the part of a
movement in which the main themes are
first presented.
expostulate ▸ verb (**expostulates**,
expostulating, **expostulated**) express strong
disapproval or disagreement.
□ **expostulation** noun.
exposure ▸ noun **1** the state of being
exposed to something harmful. **2** a physical
condition resulting from being exposed
to severe weather conditions. **3** the
revealing of the true facts about someone
or something. **4** the fact of being discussed
or mentioned on television, in newspapers,
etc. **5** the quantity of light reaching a
photographic film.

SYNONYMS **1** *suffering from exposure*
frostbite, cold, hypothermia. **2** *the
exposure of a banking fraud* uncovering,
revelation, disclosure, unveiling,
unmasking, discovery, detection. **3** *we're
getting a lot of exposure* publicity,
advertising, public attention, media
interest; informal hype.

expound ▸ verb set out and explain the
facts or ideas involved in something.
express[1] ▸ verb **1** show by words or actions
what you are thinking or feeling. **2** squeeze
out liquid or air.

SYNONYMS communicate, convey,
indicate, show, demonstrate, reveal, put
across/over, get across/over, articulate,
put into words, voice, give voice to, state,
air, give vent to.

express[2] ▸ adjective operating or delivered
very quickly.

SYNONYMS **rapid**, swift, fast, high-speed,
non-stop, direct.
ANTONYMS slow.

▸ adverb by express train or delivery service.
▸ noun **1** a train that travels quickly and stops
at few stations. **2** a special delivery service.
express[3] ▸ adjective **1** stated very clearly.
2 excluding anything else.

SYNONYMS **1** *it was his express wish*
explicit, clear, direct, plain, distinct,
unambiguous, categorical. **2** *his express
purpose was to do aid work* sole, specific,
particular, special, specified.
ANTONYMS vague, implied.

□ **expressly** adverb.
expression ▸ noun **1** the action of
expressing. **2** the look on someone's face.
3 a word or phrase expressing an idea.
4 Maths a collection of symbols expressing
a quantity.

SYNONYMS **1** *the free expression of their
views* utterance, uttering, voicing,
declaration, articulation. **2** *an expression
of sympathy* indication, demonstration,
show, exhibition, token, communication,
illustration. **3** *a sad expression* look,
appearance, air, manner, countenance.
4 *a well-known expression* idiom, phrase,
term, proverb, saying, adage, maxim.
5 *put more expression into it* emotion,
feeling, spirit, passion, intensity, style.

□ **expressionless** adjective.

expressionism ▸ noun a style in art, music,
or drama in which the artist or writer
shows the inner world of emotion rather
than external reality.
□ **expressionist** noun & adjective.
expressive ▸ adjective clearly showing
thoughts or feelings.

SYNONYMS **1** *an expressive shrug* eloquent,
meaningful, demonstrative, suggestive.
2 *an expressive song* emotional,
passionate, poignant, moving, stirring,
emotionally charged.
ANTONYMS undemonstrative,
inexpressive.

□ **expressively** adverb **expressiveness** noun.
expropriate ▸ verb (**expropriates**,
expropriating, **expropriated**) (of the state
or an authority) take property from its
owner.
□ **expropriation** noun.
expulsion ▸ noun the action of expelling.

SYNONYMS **1** *expulsion from the party*
removal, debarment, dismissal,
exclusion, ejection, banishment,
eviction. **2** *the expulsion of waste*
discharge, ejection, excretion, voiding,
evacuation, elimination, passing.
ANTONYMS admission.

expunge /ik-**spunj**/ ▸ verb (**expunges**, **expunging**, **expunged**) remove something completely.

expurgate /**eks**-per-gayt/ ▸ verb (**expurgates**, **expurgating**, **expurgated**) remove unsuitable material from a written work.
□ **expurgation** noun.

exquisite ▸ adjective **1** very beautiful and delicate. **2** showing great sensitivity or refinement. **3** strongly felt.

SYNONYMS **1** *exquisite antiques* **beautiful**, lovely, elegant, fine, delicate, fragile, dainty, subtle. **2** *exquisite taste* **discriminating**, discerning, sensitive, fastidious, refined.

□ **exquisitely** adverb.

extant ▸ adjective still in existence.

extempore /ik-**stem**-puh-ri/ ▸ adjective & adverb spoken or done without preparation.

extemporize (or **extemporise**) ▸ verb (**extemporizes**, **extemporizing**, **extemporized**) make something up as you go along.

extend ▸ verb **1** make something larger in area. **2** make something last longer. **3** occupy a particular area or continue for a particular distance. **4** stretch out a part of your body. **5** offer something to someone.

SYNONYMS **1** *we've extended the kitchen* **expand**, enlarge, increase, lengthen, widen, broaden. **2** *the garden extends to the road* **continue**, carry on, stretch, reach. **3** *we have extended our range* **widen**, expand, broaden, augment, supplement, increase, add to, enhance, develop. **4** *extending the life of parliament* **prolong**, lengthen, increase, stretch out, protract, spin out, string out. **5** *he extended a hand* **hold out**, reach out, hold forth, stretch out, offer, give, proffer. **6** *we wish to extend our thanks* **offer**, proffer, give, accord.
ANTONYMS reduce, shorten, withdraw.

■ **extended family** a family group consisting of parents and children and close relatives living nearby.
□ **extendable** (or **extendible**) adjective **extensible** adjective.

extension ▸ noun **1** the action of extending something. **2** a part added to a building to make it bigger. **3** an additional period of time. **4** an extra telephone on the same line as the main one.

SYNONYMS **1** *they are planning an extension* **addition**, add-on, adjunct, annex, wing. **2** *an extension of our knowledge* **expansion**, increase, enlargement, widening, broadening, deepening, augmentation, enhancement, development, growth. **3** *an extension of opening hours* **prolongation**, lengthening, increase.
ANTONYMS restriction, shortening.

■ **extension lead** a length of electric cable which can be plugged into a socket and has another socket on the end.

extensive ▸ adjective **1** covering a large area. **2** large in amount or scale.

SYNONYMS **1** *extensive grounds* **large**, sizeable, substantial, considerable, ample, great, vast. **2** *extensive knowledge* **comprehensive**, thorough, exhaustive, broad, wide, wide-ranging, catholic.

□ **extensively** adverb.

extensor ▸ noun a muscle which makes a part of the body extend.

extent ▸ noun **1** the area covered by something. **2** size or scale. **3** the degree to which something is the case.

SYNONYMS **1** *two acres in extent* **area**, size, expanse, length, proportions, dimensions. **2** *the full extent of her illness* **degree**, scale, level, magnitude, scope, size, reach, range.

extenuating /ik-**sten**-yoo-ay-ting/ ▸ adjective serving to make an offence less serious by partially excusing it: *extenuating circumstances.*
□ **extenuation** noun.

exterior ▸ adjective having to do with the outside of something.

SYNONYMS *the exterior surface* **outer**, outside, outermost, outward, external.
ANTONYMS interior.

▸ noun the outer surface or structure of something.

SYNONYMS *a beautiful exterior* **outside**, external surface, outward appearance, facade.
ANTONYMS interior.

exterminate ▸ verb (**exterminates**, **exterminating**, **exterminated**) destroy something completely.
□ **extermination** noun **exterminator** noun.

external ▸ adjective **1** having to do with the outside of something. **2** coming from outside an organization or situation. **3** having to do with another country or institution.

SYNONYMS **1** *an external wall* **outer**, outside, outermost, outward, exterior. **2** *an external examiner* **outside**, independent, visiting.
ANTONYMS internal.

□ **externally** adverb.

externalize (or **externalise**) ▸ verb (**externalizes**, **externalizing**, **externalized**) express a thought or feeling in words or actions.

extinct ▸ adjective **1** no longer in existence. **2** (of a volcano) not having erupted in

e

recorded history.

SYNONYMS **1** *an extinct species* **vanished,** lost, gone, died out, wiped out, destroyed. **2** *an extinct volcano* **inactive.** ANTONYMS living, dormant.

extinction ▸ noun the process of becoming extinct.

SYNONYMS **dying out,** disappearance, vanishing, extermination, destruction, elimination, eradication, annihilation.

extinguish ▸ verb **1** put out a fire or light. **2** put an end to.

SYNONYMS **douse,** put out, quench, stamp out, smother, snuff out, stub out.

□ **extinguisher** noun.

extirpate /**ek**-ster-payt/ ▸ verb (**extirpates, extirpating, extirpated**) search out and destroy something completely.
□ **extirpation** noun.

extol ▸ verb (**extols, extolling, extolled**) praise enthusiastically.

extort ▸ verb obtain something by force, threats, or other unfair means.

SYNONYMS **extract,** exact, wring, wrest, screw, squeeze.

□ **extortion** noun.

extortionate ▸ adjective (of a price) much too high.

SYNONYMS **exorbitant,** excessive, outrageous, unreasonable, prohibitive, inflated; Brit. over the odds; informal over the top, daylight robbery.

□ **extortionately** adverb.

extra ▸ adjective added to an existing or usual amount or number.

SYNONYMS **additional,** more, added, supplementary, further, auxiliary, ancillary, subsidiary, secondary.

▸ adverb **1** to a greater extent than usual. **2** in addition.

SYNONYMS **exceptionally,** particularly, specially, especially, extremely.

▸ noun **1** an additional item, for which an extra charge is made. **2** a person employed to take part in a crowd scene in a film or play.

SYNONYMS **addition,** supplement, bonus, adjunct, addendum, add-on.

▸ prefix (**extra-**) outside; beyond: *extramarital.*

extract ▸ verb /ik-**strakt**/ **1** remove something with care or effort. **2** obtain something from someone unwilling to give it. **3** separate out a substance by a special method.

SYNONYMS **1** *he extracted the cassette* **take out,** draw out, pull out, remove, withdraw, release, extricate. **2** *they extracted a confession* **wrest,** exact, wring, screw, squeeze, obtain by force,

extort. **3** *the roots are crushed to extract the juice* **squeeze out,** press out, obtain. ANTONYMS insert.

▸ noun /**ek**-strakt/ **1** a short passage taken from a written work, film, or piece of music. **2** an extracted substance.

SYNONYMS **1** *an extract from his article* **excerpt,** passage, citation, quotation. **2** *an extract of ginseng* **distillation,** distillate, concentrate, essence, juice.

■ **extractor fan** a device that removes steam and smells from a room.

extraction ▸ noun **1** the action of extracting. **2** the ethnic origin of someone's family.

extradite /**ek**-struh-dyt/ ▸ verb (**extradites, extraditing, extradited**) hand over a person accused or convicted of committing a crime in a foreign state to the legal authority of that state.
□ **extradition** noun.

extramarital ▸ adjective happening outside marriage.

extramural ▸ adjective Brit. (of a course of study) for people who are not full-time members of an educational establishment.

extraneous /ik-**stray**-ni-uhss/ ▸ adjective **1** unrelated to the subject being dealt with. **2** of external origin.

extraordinaire /ek-struh-or-di-**nair**/ ▸ adjective outstanding in a particular capacity: *she was a gardener extraordinaire.*

extraordinary ▸ adjective **1** very unusual or remarkable. **2** (of a meeting) held for a particular reason rather than being one of a regular series.

SYNONYMS **1** *an extraordinary coincidence* **remarkable,** exceptional, amazing, astonishing, astounding, sensational, stunning, incredible, unbelievable, phenomenal; informal fantastic.
2 *extraordinary speed* **very great,** tremendous, enormous, immense, prodigious, stupendous, monumental.
ANTONYMS unremarkable, tiny.

□ **extraordinarily** adverb.

✔ The beginning is **extra-,** not just **extr-: extra**ordinary.

extrapolate /ik-**strap**-uh-layt/ ▸ verb (**extrapolates, extrapolating, extrapolated**) use a fact or conclusion that is valid for one situation and apply it to a larger or different one.
□ **extrapolation** noun.

extrasensory perception ▸ noun the supposed ability to perceive things by means other than the known senses, e.g. by telepathy.

extra terrestrial ▸ adjective having to do with things that come from beyond the earth or its atmosphere.
▸ noun a fictional being from outer space.

extravagant ▸ adjective **1** spending or using more than is necessary or more than you can afford. **2** very expensive. **3** going beyond what is reasonable.

SYNONYMS **1** *an extravagant lifestyle* **spendthrift,** profligate, wasteful, prodigal, lavish. **2** *extravagant praise* **excessive,** immoderate, exaggerated, gushing, unrestrained, effusive, fulsome. **3** *decorated in an extravagant style* **ornate,** elaborate, fancy, over-elaborate, ostentatious, exaggerated; informal flashy.
ANTONYMS thrifty, moderate, plain.

☐ **extravagance** noun **extravagantly** adverb.

extravaganza ▸ noun an elaborate and spectacular entertainment.

extreme ▸ adjective **1** to the highest degree. **2** highly unusual. **3** very severe or serious. **4** not moderate. **5** furthest from the centre or a given point.

SYNONYMS **1** *extreme danger* **utmost,** (very) great, greatest (possible), maximum, great, acute, enormous, severe, serious. **2** *extreme measures* **drastic,** serious, desperate, dire, radical, far-reaching, draconian; Brit. swingeing. **3** *extreme views* **radical,** extremist, immoderate, fanatical, revolutionary, subversive, militant. **4** *extreme sports* **dangerous,** hazardous, risky, high-risk, adventurous; informal white-knuckle. **5** *the extreme north-west* **furthest,** farthest, utmost, remotest, ultra-.
ANTONYMS slight, moderate, safe, near.

▸ noun **1** either of two abstract things that are as different from each other as possible. **2** the most extreme degree.

SYNONYMS *the two extremes* **opposite,** antithesis, side of the coin, (opposite) pole, limit, extremity, contrast.

extremely ▸ adverb to an extreme degree; very much.

SYNONYMS **very,** exceptionally, especially, extraordinarily, tremendously, immensely, hugely, supremely, highly, mightily; informal awfully, terribly, seriously; Brit. informal jolly; N. Amer. informal mighty.
ANTONYMS slightly.

extremist ▸ noun a person who holds extreme political or religious views.

SYNONYMS **fanatic,** radical, zealot, fundamentalist, hardliner, militant, activist.
ANTONYMS moderate.

☐ **extremism** noun.

extremity ▸ noun (plural **extremities**) **1** the furthest point or limit. **2** (**extremities**) a person's hands and feet. **3** extreme hardship.

extricate ▸ verb (**extricates, extricating, extricated**) **1** free someone from a difficult situation. **2** free something that is trapped.

extrinsic ▸ adjective coming from outside; not part of something's basic nature.

extrovert ▸ noun an outgoing, lively person. ▸ adjective outgoing and lively.

✔ extro-, not extra-: extrovert.

extrude ▸ verb (**extrudes, extruding, extruded**) thrust or force something out.

exuberant ▸ adjective **1** lively and cheerful. **2** growing thickly.
☐ **exuberance** noun **exuberantly** adverb.

exude ▸ verb (**exudes, exuding, exuded**) **1** send out or give off a liquid or smell slowly and steadily. **2** display an emotion or quality strongly and openly.

exult ▸ verb show or feel triumphant joy.
☐ **exultant** adjective **exultantly** adverb **exultation** noun.

eye ▸ noun **1** the organ of sight in humans and animals. **2** the small hole in a needle through which the thread is passed. **3** a small metal loop into which a hook is fitted as a fastener on a garment. **4** a person's opinion or feelings. **5** the calm region at the centre of a storm. **6** a dark spot on a potato from which a new shoot grows.
▸ verb (**eyes, eyeing** or **eying, eyed**) look at closely or with interest.

SYNONYMS **look at,** observe, view, gaze at, stare at, regard, contemplate, survey, scrutinize, consider, glance at, watch; informal check out, size up; N. Amer. informal eyeball.

■ **see eye to eye** be in complete agreement.

eyeball ▸ noun the round part of the eye of a vertebrate, within the eyelids.

eyebrow ▸ noun the strip of hair growing on the ridge above a person's eye socket.

eyeglass ▸ noun a single lens for correcting eyesight.

eyelash ▸ noun each of the short hairs growing on the edges of the eyelids.

eyelet ▸ noun a small round hole with a metal ring around it, for threading a lace or cord through.

eyelid ▸ noun each of the upper and lower folds of skin which cover the eye when it is closed.

eyeliner ▸ noun a cosmetic applied as a line round the eyes.

eyeshadow ▸ noun a cosmetic applied to the skin around the eyes.

eyesight ▸ noun a person's ability to see.

eyesore ▸ noun a thing that is very ugly.

eyewitness ▸ noun a person who has seen something happen.

eyrie /eer-i, I-ri/ (US spelling **aerie**) ▸ noun a large nest of a bird of prey.

Ff

F (or **f**) ▶ noun (plural **Fs** or **F's**) the sixth letter of the alphabet.
▶ abbreviation Fahrenheit.

FA ▶ abbreviation Football Association.

fable ▶ noun **1** a short story, often about animals, which teaches about right and wrong behaviour. **2** a story about mythical characters or events.

SYNONYMS **parable**, allegory, myth, legend, story.

fabled ▶ adjective **1** famous. **2** described in myths and legends.

fabric ▶ noun **1** cloth. **2** the walls, floor, and roof of a building. **3** the basic structure of a system or organization.

SYNONYMS **1** *the finest fabrics* **cloth**, material, textile. **2** *the fabric of society* **structure**, construction, make-up, organization, framework, essence.

fabricate ▶ verb (**fabricates, fabricating, fabricated**) **1** make up facts that are not true. **2** make an industrial product.
◻ **fabrication** noun.

fabulous ▶ adjective **1** great; extraordinary. **2** informal wonderful. **3** existing in myths and legends.

SYNONYMS **1** *fabulous salaries* **stupendous**, prodigious, phenomenal, exceptional, fantastic, breathtaking, staggering, unthinkable, unimaginable, incredible, undreamed of. **2** *we had a fabulous time.* See **EXCELLENT**.

◻ **fabulously** adverb.

facade /fuh-**sahd**/ ▶ noun **1** the front of a building. **2** a misleading outward appearance.

SYNONYMS **1** *a half-timbered facade* **front**, frontage, face, elevation, exterior, outside. **2** *a facade of bonhomie* **show**, front, appearance, pretence, simulation, affectation, act, charade, mask, veneer.

face ▶ noun **1** the front part of the head from the forehead to the chin. **2** an expression on someone's face. **3** the surface of a thing. **4** a vertical or sloping side of a mountain or cliff. **5** an aspect of something.

SYNONYMS **1** *a beautiful face* **countenance**, physiognomy, features, profile. **2** *her face grew sad* **expression**, look, appearance, countenance. **3** *he made a face* **grimace**, scowl, wince, frown, pout. **4** *a cube has six faces* **side**, aspect, surface, plane, facet, wall, elevation.

▶ verb (**faces, facing, faced**) **1** be positioned with the face or front towards something. **2** confront and deal with. **3** have a difficulty ahead of you. **4** cover the surface of something with a layer of material.

SYNONYMS **1** *the hotel faces the sea* **look out on,** front on to, look towards, look over/across, overlook, be opposite (to). **2** *you'll have to face the truth* **accept**, get used to, adjust to, learn to live with, cope with, deal with, come to terms with, become resigned to. **3** *the problems facing our police force* **beset**, worry, trouble, confront, torment, plague, bedevil. **4** *he faced the challenge* **brave**, face up to, encounter, meet (head-on), confront. **5** *a wall faced with flint* **cover**, clad, veneer, surface, dress, laminate, coat, line.

■ **face pack** Brit. a cream or gel spread over the face to improve the skin. **face the music** be confronted with the unpleasant results of your actions. **face value 1** the value stated on a coin or postage stamp. **2** the value that something seems to have before you look at it closely. **lose** (or **save**) **face** suffer (or avoid) humiliation.

facecloth ▶ noun a small towelling cloth for washing your face.

faceless ▶ adjective without character or individuality; impersonal.

facelift ▶ noun an operation to remove wrinkles in the face by tightening the skin.

SYNONYMS **renovation**, redecoration, refurbishment, revamp, makeover.

facet ▶ noun **1** one of the sides of a cut gemstone. **2** an aspect of something.

SYNONYMS **aspect**, feature, side, dimension, strand, component, element.

◻ **faceted** adjective.

facetious /fuh-see-shuhss/ ▸ adjective trying to be funny or clever about something that should be treated seriously. □ **facetiously** adverb.

facia ➡ FASCIA.

facial ▸ adjective having to do with the face. ▸ noun a beauty treatment for the face. □ **facially** adverb.

facile /fa-syl/ ▸ adjective 1 produced without careful thought. 2 too simple, or too easily achieved.

facilitate ▸ verb (facilitates, facilitating, facilitated) make something possible or easier.

> SYNONYMS **make easy/easier,** ease, make possible, smooth the way for, enable, assist, help (along), aid, promote, hasten, speed up.
> ANTONYMS impede.

□ **facilitation** noun **facilitator** noun.

facility ▸ noun (plural **facilities**) 1 a building, service, or piece of equipment provided for a particular purpose. 2 a natural ability to do something well and easily.

> SYNONYMS **1** *car-parking facilities* **provision,** space, means, equipment. **2** *the camera has a zoom facility* **feature,** setting, mode, option. **3** *a wealth of local facilities* **amenity,** resource, service. **4** *a medical facility* **establishment,** centre, station, location, premises, site, post, base.

facing ▸ noun 1 a strip of material sewn inside the neck, armhole, etc. of a piece of clothing to strengthen it. 2 an outer layer covering the surface of a wall.

facsimile /fak-sim-i-li/ ▸ noun an exact copy of written or printed material.

fact ▸ noun 1 a thing that is definitely the case. 2 (**facts**) information used as evidence or as part of a report.

> SYNONYMS **1** *a fact we cannot ignore* **reality,** actuality, certainty, truth, verity, gospel. **2** *every fact was double-checked* **detail,** particular, finding, point, factor, feature, characteristic, aspect; (**facts**) information, data.
> ANTONYMS lie, fiction.

■ **the facts of life** information explaining things relating to sex.

faction ▸ noun a small group within a larger one.

> SYNONYMS **1** *a faction of the Liberal Party* **clique,** coterie, caucus, bloc, camp, group, grouping, splinter group. **2** *the council was split by faction* **infighting,** dissent, dispute, discord, strife, conflict, friction, argument, disagreement, disunity, schism.
> ANTONYMS agreement, unity.

□ **factional** adjective.

factious /fak-shuhss/ ▸ adjective having opposing views.

factitious /fak-ti-shuhss/ ▸ adjective made up; not genuine.

factor ▸ noun 1 a circumstance, fact, or influence that helps to bring about a result. 2 Maths a number by which a larger number can be divided exactly. 3 the amount by which something increases or decreases. 4 any of a number of substances in the blood which are involved in clotting.

> SYNONYMS **element,** part, component, ingredient, strand, constituent, feature, facet, aspect, characteristic, consideration, influence, circumstance.

▸ verb (**factor something in** or **out**) consider (or ignore) something when making a decision.

factory ▸ noun (plural **factories**) a building where goods are made or assembled in large numbers.

> SYNONYMS **works,** plant, yard, mill, facility, workshop, shop.

■ **factory farming** the rearing of poultry, pigs, or cattle indoors under strictly controlled conditions.

factotum /fak-toh-tuhm/ ▸ noun (plural **factotums**) an employee who does all kinds of jobs.

factual ▸ adjective based on or concerned with facts.

> SYNONYMS **truthful,** true, accurate, authentic, historical, genuine, true-to-life, correct, exact.
> ANTONYMS fictitious.

□ **factually** adverb.

faculty ▸ noun (plural **faculties**) 1 a basic mental or physical power. 2 a talent. 3 a department or group of related departments in a university.

> SYNONYMS **1** *the faculty of speech* **power,** capability, capacity, facility; (**faculties**) senses, wits, reason, intelligence. **2** *the arts faculty* **department,** school.

fad ▸ noun 1 a craze. 2 a fussy like or dislike of something.

> SYNONYMS **craze,** vogue, trend, fashion, mode, mania, rage.

□ **faddish** adjective **faddy** adjective.

fade ▸ verb (**fades, fading, faded**) 1 gradually grow faint and disappear. 2 lose colour. 3 (**fade something in** or **out**) make a film or video image or sound more or less clear or loud.

> SYNONYMS **1** *the paintwork has faded* **become pale,** become bleached, become washed out, lose colour, discolour. **2** *sunlight had faded the picture* **bleach,**

wash out, make pale, blanch. **3** *the afternoon light began to fade* (**grow**) **dim,** grow faint, fail, dwindle, die away, wane, disappear, vanish, decline, melt away. **4** *Communism was fading away* **decline,** die out, diminish, decay, crumble, collapse, fail.
ANTONYMS brighten, grow.

faeces /fee-seez/ (US spelling **feces**) ▸ plural noun waste matter passed out of the body from the bowels.
□ **faecal** /fee-k'l/ adjective.

fag[1] ▸ noun Brit. informal a cigarette.

fag[2] Brit. informal ▸ noun **1** a tiring or boring task. **2** a junior schoolboy at a public school who does minor chores for an older one.

faggot ▸ noun **1** Brit. a ball of seasoned chopped liver which is baked or fried. **2** a bundle of sticks bound together as fuel.

Fahrenheit /fa-ruhn-hyt/ ▸ noun a scale of temperature on which water freezes at 32° and boils at 212°.

fail ▸ verb **1** not succeed in achieving something. **2** be unable to meet the standards set by a test. **3** not do something that you should have done. **4** stop working properly. **5** become weaker or less good. **6** let someone down.

SYNONYMS **1** *the scheme had failed* **be unsuccessful,** fall through, fall flat, collapse, founder, backfire, miscarry, come unstuck; informal flop, bomb. **2** *he failed his examination* **be unsuccessful in,** not make the grade; informal flunk. **3** *his friends had failed him* **let down,** disappoint, desert, abandon, betray, be disloyal to. **4** *the ventilation system has failed* **break (down),** stop working, cut out, crash, malfunction, go wrong; informal conk out; Brit. informal pack up. **5** *Ceri's health was failing* **deteriorate,** degenerate, decline, fade. **6** *900 businesses are failing a week* **collapse,** crash, go under, go bankrupt, cease trading, be wound up; informal fold, go bust.
ANTONYMS succeed, pass, work, improve, thrive.

▸ noun a mark which is not high enough to pass an exam.
■ **fail-safe 1** (of machinery) going back to a safe condition if it is faulty. **2** unlikely or unable to fail. **without fail** whatever happens.

failing ▸ noun a weakness in a person's character.

SYNONYMS **fault,** shortcoming, weakness, imperfection, deficiency, defect, flaw, frailty.
ANTONYMS strength.

▸ preposition if not.

failure ▸ noun **1** lack of success. **2** an unsuccessful person or thing. **3** a situation in which something stops working properly. **4** an instance of not doing something that is expected.

SYNONYMS **1** *the failure of the escape attempt* **lack of success,** defeat, collapse, foundering. **2** *the scheme had been a failure* **fiasco,** debacle, catastrophe, disaster; informal flop, washout, dead loss. **3** *she was a failure* **loser,** underachiever, ne'er-do-well, disappointment; informal no-hoper. **4** *a failure on my part* **negligence,** dereliction, omission, oversight. **5** *the failure of the heating system* **breaking down,** breakdown, malfunction, crash. **6** *company failures* **collapse,** crash, bankruptcy, insolvency, liquidation, closure.
ANTONYMS success.

faint ▸ adjective **1** not clearly seen, heard, or smelt. **2** slight: *a faint chance.* **3** close to losing consciousness.

SYNONYMS **1** *a faint mark* **indistinct,** vague, unclear, indefinite, ill-defined, imperceptible, pale, light, faded. **2** *a faint cry* **quiet,** muted, muffled, stifled, feeble, weak, low, soft, gentle. **3** *a faint possibility* **slight,** slender, slim, small, tiny, remote, vague. **4** *I suddenly felt faint* **dizzy,** giddy, light-headed, unsteady; informal woozy.
ANTONYMS clear, loud, strong.

▸ verb briefly lose consciousness.

SYNONYMS *he nearly fainted* **pass out,** lose consciousness, black out, keel over, swoon.

▸ noun a sudden loss of consciousness.

SYNONYMS *a dead faint* **blackout,** fainting fit, loss of consciousness, coma, swoon.
■ **faint-hearted** timid.

faintly ▸ adverb **1** indistinctly. **2** very slightly.

SYNONYMS **1** *Maria called his name faintly* **indistinctly,** softly, gently, weakly, in a whisper. **2** *he looked faintly bewildered* **slightly,** vaguely, somewhat, quite, fairly, rather, a little, a bit, a touch, a tad, a shade.
ANTONYMS loudly, extremely.

fair[1] ▸ adjective **1** treating people equally. **2** reasonable or appropriate. **3** quite large in size or amount. **4** quite good. **5** (of hair or complexion) light; blonde. **6** (of weather) fine and dry. **7** old use beautiful.

SYNONYMS **1** *the courts were generally fair* **just,** equitable, honest, impartial, unbiased, unprejudiced, neutral, even-handed. **2** *fair weather* **fine,** dry, bright, clear, sunny, cloudless. **3** *fair hair* **blond(e),** yellow, golden, flaxen, light. **4** *fair skin* **pale,** light, pink, white,

creamy. **5** *a fair achievement* **reasonable**, passable, tolerable, satisfactory, acceptable, respectable, decent, all right, good enough, pretty good.
ANTONYMS unfair, inclement, dark, poor.

■ **fair game** a person or thing that people feel they can criticize or exploit. **fair-weather friend** a person who stops being a friend when you have problems.

fair² ▸ noun **1** a gathering of sideshows and amusements for public entertainment. **2** an event held to promote or sell goods: *an antiques fair*.

SYNONYMS **1** *a country fair* **fête**, gala, festival, carnival. **2** *an antiques fair* **market**, bazaar, exchange, sale. **3** *an art fair* **exhibition**, display, show, exposition.

fairground ▸ noun an outdoor area where a fair is held.

fairing ▸ noun a structure added to make a vehicle, boat, or aircraft more streamlined.

fairly ▸ adverb **1** in a fair way. **2** to some extent; quite.

SYNONYMS **1** *we were treated fairly* **justly**, equitably, impartially, without bias, without prejudice, even-handedly, equally. **2** *in fairly good condition* **reasonably**, passably, tolerably, adequately, moderately, quite, relatively, comparatively; informal pretty. **3** *he fairly hauled her along the street* **positively**, really, simply, actually, absolutely.
ANTONYMS unfairly.

fairway ▸ noun the part of a golf course between a tee and a green.

fairy ▸ noun (plural **fairies**) a small imaginary being that has magical powers.

SYNONYMS **sprite**, pixie, elf, imp, brownie, puck, leprechaun.

■ **fairy godmother** a female character in fairy stories who brings good fortune to the hero or heroine. **fairy lights** small electric lights used to decorate a Christmas tree. **fairy tale** (or **fairy story**) **1** a children's story about magical beings and lands. **2** a lie.

fait accompli /fayt uh-**kom**-pli/ ▸ noun something that has been done and cannot be changed.

faith ▸ noun **1** complete trust or confidence. **2** belief in a religion. **3** a system of religious belief.

SYNONYMS **1** *our faith in him* **trust**, belief, confidence, conviction, reliance. **2** *she died for her faith* **religion**, belief, creed, church, persuasion, ideology, doctrine.
ANTONYMS mistrust.

■ **faith healing** healing achieved by religious faith, rather than by medical

treatment.

faithful ▸ adjective **1** remaining loyal and committed. **2** accurate; true to the facts.

SYNONYMS **1** *his faithful assistant* **loyal**, constant, true, devoted, staunch, steadfast, dedicated, committed, trusty, dependable, reliable. **2** *a faithful copy* **accurate**, precise, exact, true, strict, realistic, authentic.
ANTONYMS disloyal, inaccurate.

▸ noun (**the faithful**) the people who believe in a particular religion.
□ **faithfully** adverb.

faithless ▸ adjective unable to be trusted; disloyal.

fake ▸ adjective not genuine.

SYNONYMS **1** *fake banknotes* **counterfeit**, forged, fraudulent, sham, pirated, false, bogus; informal phoney, dud. **2** *fake diamonds* **imitation**, artificial, synthetic, simulated, reproduction, replica, ersatz, man-made, dummy, false, mock; informal pretend. **3** *a fake accent* **feigned**, faked, put-on, assumed, invented, affected.
ANTONYMS genuine, real, authentic.

▸ noun a person or thing that is not genuine.

SYNONYMS **1** *the sculpture was a fake* **forgery**, counterfeit, copy, pirated copy, sham, fraud, hoax, imitation; informal phoney, rip-off. **2** *that doctor is a fake* **charlatan**, quack, sham, fraud, impostor; informal phoney.

▸ verb (**fakes**, **faking**, **faked**) **1** make a copy or imitation of something in order to deceive. **2** pretend to have an emotion or illness.

SYNONYMS **1** *the certificate was faked* **forge**, counterfeit, falsify, copy, pirate. **2** *he faked a yawn* **feign**, pretend, simulate, put on, affect.

fakir /fay-keer/ ▸ noun a Muslim or Hindu holy man who lives by asking people for money or food.

falcon ▸ noun a fast-flying bird of prey with long pointed wings.

falconry ▸ noun the keeping and training of birds of prey.
□ **falconer** noun.

fall ▸ verb (**falls**, **falling**, **fell**; past participle **fallen**) **1** move downwards quickly and without control. **2** collapse to the ground. **3** slope down. **4** become less or lower. **5** become. **6** happen; come about. **7** (of someone's face) show dismay. **8** be captured or defeated.

SYNONYMS **1** *bombs began to fall* **drop**, descend, plummet, plunge, sink, dive, tumble, cascade. **2** *he tripped and fell* **topple over**, tumble over, fall down/over, collapse. **3** *the water level began to fall* **subside**, recede, drop, retreat, fall away, go down, sink. **4** *inflation will fall* **decrease,** decline, diminish, fall off, drop off, lessen, dwindle, plummet, plunge, slump, sink. **5** *those who fell in the war* **die,** perish, lose your life, be killed, be slain, be lost; informal bite the dust, buy it. **6** *the town fell to the barbarians* **surrender,** yield, submit, give in, capitulate, succumb, be taken, be overwhelmed. **7** *Easter falls on 23rd April* **occur,** take place, happen, come about. ANTONYMS rise.

▶ noun **1** an act of falling. **2** a thing which falls or has fallen. **3** (**falls**) a waterfall. **4** a drop in size or number. **5** a defeat or downfall. **6** N. Amer. autumn.

SYNONYMS **1** *an accidental fall* **tumble,** trip, spill, topple. **2** *a fall in sales* **decline,** fall-off, drop, decrease, cut, dip, reduction, slump; informal crash. **3** *the fall of the Roman Empire* **downfall,** collapse, failure, decline, destruction, overthrow, demise. **4** *the fall of Berlin* **surrender,** capitulation, yielding, submission, defeat. **5** *a steep fall down to the ocean* **descent,** slope, slant. ANTONYMS rise.

■ **fall back** retreat. **fall back on** turn to something for help. **fall for** informal **1** fall in love with. **2** be tricked by. **fall foul of** come into conflict with. **fall guy** informal a person who is blamed for something that is not their fault. **fall out** have an argument. **fall short** fail to reach a required standard. **fall through** fail to happen or be completed.

fallacious /fuh-**lay**-shuhss/ ▶ adjective based on a mistaken belief.

fallacy /**fal**-luh-si/ ▶ noun (plural **fallacies**) **1** a mistaken belief. **2** a false or misleading argument.

fallback ▶ noun an alternative plan for use in an emergency.

fallible /**fal**-li-b'l/ ▶ adjective capable of making mistakes.
□ **fallibility** noun.

Fallopian tube /fuh-**loh**-pi-uhn/ ▶ noun either of a pair of tubes along which eggs travel from the ovaries to the uterus of a female mammal.

fallout ▶ noun **1** radioactive particles that are spread over a wide area after a nuclear explosion. **2** the bad effects of a situation.

fallow ▶ adjective (of farmland) ploughed but left for a period without being planted with crops.

fallow deer ▶ noun a small deer that has a white-spotted reddish-brown coat in summer.

false ▶ adjective **1** not correct or true; wrong. **2** fake; artificial. **3** based on something that is not true or correct: *a false sense of security.* **4** disloyal.

SYNONYMS **1** *a false report* **incorrect,** untrue, wrong, inaccurate, untruthful, fictitious, fabricated, invented, made up, trumped up, counterfeit, forged, fraudulent. **2** *a false friend* **disloyal,** faithless, unfaithful, untrue, inconstant, treacherous, double-crossing, deceitful, dishonest, duplicitous. **3** *false pearls* **fake,** artificial, imitation, synthetic, simulated, reproduction, replica, ersatz, man-made, dummy, mock; informal pretend. ANTONYMS correct, faithful, genuine.

■ **false alarm** a warning given about something that does not happen. **false pretences** behaviour intended to deceive.
□ **falsely** adverb **falsity** noun.

falsehood ▶ noun **1** the state of being untrue. **2** a lie.

falsetto /fawl-**set**-toh/ ▶ noun (plural **falsettos**) a high-pitched voice used by male singers.

falsify ▶ verb (**falsifies, falsifying, falsified**) alter something in order to mislead people.
□ **falsification** noun.

falter ▶ verb (**falters, faltering, faltered**) **1** lose momentum. **2** move or speak hesitantly.

SYNONYMS **hesitate,** delay, drag your feet, stall, waver, vacillate, be indecisive, be irresolute; Brit. hum and haw; informal sit on the fence.

fame ▶ noun the state of being famous.

SYNONYMS **renown,** celebrity, stardom, popularity, prominence, distinction, esteem, eminence, repute. ANTONYMS obscurity.

famed ▶ adjective famous; well known.

familial /fuh-**mil**-i-uhl/ ▶ adjective having to do with a family.

familiar ▶ adjective **1** well known. **2** frequently encountered; common. **3** (**familiar with**) having a good knowledge of. **4** friendly or informal.

SYNONYMS **1** *a familiar task* **well known,** recognized, accustomed, everyday, day-to-day, habitual, customary, routine. **2** *are you familiar with the subject?* **acquainted,** conversant, versed, knowledgeable, well informed, au fait; informal well up on. **3** *he is too familiar with the teachers* **overfamiliar,** presumptuous, disrespectful, forward, bold, impudent, impertinent. ANTONYMS unfamiliar, formal.

▶ noun a spirit believed to accompany a witch.
□ **familiarly** adverb.

✔ **Familiar** is spelled with only one **l**.

familiarity ▶ noun **1** significant knowledge of something. **2** relaxed friendliness. **3** inappropriate informality.

SYNONYMS **1** *a familiarity with politics* **acquaintance with,** awareness of, knowledge of, experience of, insight into, understanding of, comprehension of. **2** *our familiarity allows us to tease each other* **closeness,** intimacy, friendliness, friendship. **3** *she was affronted by his familiarity* **overfamiliarity,** presumption, forwardness, boldness, cheek, impudence, impertinence, disrespect.

familiarize (or **familiarise**) ▶ verb (**familiarizes, familiarizing, familiarized**) (**familiarize someone with**) give someone knowledge of something.
□ **familiarization** noun.

family ▶ noun (plural **families**) **1** a group of parents and their children. **2** a group of people related by marriage or through having the same ancestors. **3** the children of a person or couple. **4** a group of things that are alike in some way. **5** a group of related plants or animals.

SYNONYMS **1** *I met his family* **relatives,** relations, (next of) kin, clan, tribe; informal folks. **2** *she is married with a family* **children,** little ones, youngsters; informal kids. **3** *the cat family* **species,** order, class, genus, phylum.

▶ adjective designed to be suitable for children as well as adults.
■ **family name** a surname. **family planning** control of the number of children in a family by using contraceptives. **family tree** a diagram showing the relationship between people in a family.

famine ▶ noun a period when there is a severe shortage of food in a region.

SYNONYMS **1** *a nation threatened by famine* **food shortage,** hunger, starvation, malnutrition. **2** *the cotton famine* **shortage,** scarcity, lack, dearth, deficiency, insufficiency, shortfall, drought.
ANTONYMS plenty.

famished ▶ adjective informal very hungry.

famous ▶ adjective **1** known about by many people. **2** informal very good or impressive.

SYNONYMS **well known,** prominent, famed, popular, renowned, noted, eminent, distinguished, celebrated.
ANTONYMS unknown.

□ **famously** adverb.

fan¹ ▶ noun **1** a device which uses rotating blades to create a current of air. **2** a semicircular object that you wave to cool yourself.
▶ verb (**fans, fanning, fanned**) **1** make a current of air blow towards. **2** make a belief or emotion stronger. **3** (**fan out**) spread out from a central point.
■ **fan belt** a belt driving the fan that cools the radiator of a motor vehicle.

fan² ▶ noun a person who is very interested in a sport, celebrity, etc.

SYNONYMS **enthusiast,** devotee, admirer, lover, supporter, follower, disciple, adherent; informal buff.

fanatic ▶ noun a person who is too enthusiastic about something.

SYNONYMS **extremist,** militant, dogmatist, bigot, zealot, radical, diehard; informal maniac.

□ **fanatical** adjective **fanatically** adverb **fanaticism** noun.

fancier ▶ noun a person who keeps or breeds a particular type of animal: *a pigeon fancier.*

fanciful ▶ adjective **1** existing only in the imagination. **2** very unusual or creative.
□ **fancifully** adverb.

fancy ▶ verb (**fancies, fancying, fancied**) **1** Brit. informal want or want to do. **2** Brit. informal find someone attractive. **3** imagine; think.

SYNONYMS **1** *I fancied a change of scene* **wish for,** want, desire, long for, yearn for, crave, thirst for, hanker after, dream of, covet. **2** *she fancied him* **be attracted to,** find attractive, be infatuated with, be taken with; informal have a crush on, carry a torch for. **3** *I fancied I could see lights* **imagine,** believe, think, be under the impression; informal reckon.

▶ adjective (**fancier, fanciest**) elaborate or highly decorated.

SYNONYMS *fancy clothes* **elaborate,** ornate, ornamental, decorative, embellished, intricate, ostentatious, showy, flamboyant, lavish, expensive; informal flashy, snazzy, posh, classy; Brit. informal swish.
ANTONYMS plain.

▶ noun (plural **fancies**) **1** a brief feeling of attraction. **2** the ability to imagine things. **3** a belief or idea that may not be true.

SYNONYMS **1** *a passing fancy* **whim,** foible, urge, whimsy, fascination, fad, craze, enthusiasm, passion, caprice. **2** *a flight of fancy* **fantasy,** dreaming, imagination, delusion, creativity.

■ **fancy dress** an unusual costume or disguise worn at a party. **fancy-free** not in a serious relationship. **take a fancy to** become fond of.
□ **fanciness** noun.

fandango /fan-**dang**-goh/ ▶ noun (plural **fandangoes** or **fandangos**) a lively Spanish dance for two people.

fanfare ▶ noun a short tune played on brass instruments to announce someone or something.

fang ▶ noun **1** a long, pointed tooth of a dog or wolf. **2** a tooth with which a snake injects poison.

fanlight ▸ noun a small semicircular window over a door or window.

fantasia /fan-**tay**-zi-uh/ ▸ noun a piece of music that does not follow a conventional form, or one based on several familiar tunes.

fantasize (or fantasise) ▸ verb (fantasizes, fantasizing, fantasized) daydream about something that you would like to do, or that you would like to happen.

fantastic ▸ adjective 1 hard to believe. 2 strange or exotic. 3 informal very good or large.

SYNONYMS 1 *a fantastic notion* **fanciful**, extravagant, extraordinary, irrational, wild, absurd, far-fetched, unthinkable, implausible, improbable, unlikely; informal crazy. 2 *fantastic shapes* **strange**, weird, bizarre, outlandish, grotesque, surreal, exotic. 3 *a fantastic car* **marvellous**, wonderful, sensational, outstanding, superb, excellent; informal terrific, fabulous; Brit. informal brilliant; Austral./NZ informal bonzer.
ANTONYMS rational, ordinary, indifferent.

□ **fantastical** adjective **fantastically** adverb.

fantasy ▸ noun (plural **fantasies**) 1 the imagining of things that do not exist in reality. 2 an imagined situation or event that is desirable but unlikely to happen. 3 a type of fiction that involves magic and adventure.

SYNONYMS 1 *a mix of fantasy and realism* **imagination**, fancy, invention, make-believe, creativity, vision, daydreaming, reverie. 2 *his fantasy about being famous* **dream**, daydream, pipe dream, fanciful notion, wish, fond hope, delusion; informal pie in the sky.
ANTONYMS realism.

fanzine ▸ noun a magazine for fans of a particular performer, team, etc.

FAQ ▸ abbreviation Computing frequently asked questions.

far ▸ adverb (**further**, **furthest** or **farther**, **farthest**) 1 at, to, or by a great distance in space or time. 2 by a great deal.

SYNONYMS 1 *far from the palace* **a long way**, a great distance, a good way, afar. 2 *her charm far outweighs any flaws* **much**, considerably, markedly, greatly, significantly, substantially, appreciably, by a long way, by a mile, easily.
ANTONYMS near, barely.

▸ adjective 1 distant in space or time. 2 extreme.

SYNONYMS 1 *far places* **distant**, faraway, far-off, remote, out of the way, far-flung, outlying. 2 *the far side* **further**, opposite.
ANTONYMS near.

■ **far-fetched** exaggerated or unlikely.

far-flung spread out; scattered. **the Far East** China, Japan, and other countries of east Asia. **far-off** distant in space or time.

farad ▸ noun the basic unit of electrical capacitance.

faraway ▸ adjective 1 remote or distant. 2 lost in thought; dreamy.

farce ▸ noun 1 a comedy based on situations which are ridiculous and improbable. 2 an absurd event.

SYNONYMS **mockery**, travesty, parody, sham, pretence, charade, joke; informal shambles.
ANTONYMS tragedy.

farcical ▸ adjective absurd or ridiculous. □ **farcically** adverb.

fare ▸ noun 1 the money which a passenger pays to travel on public transport. 2 a range of food.

SYNONYMS 1 *we paid the fare* **price**, cost, charge, fee, toll, tariff. 2 *they eat simple fare* **food**, meals, cooking, cuisine.

▸ verb (**fares**, **faring**, **fared**) get on in a particular situation: *the party fared badly in the elections*.

SYNONYMS *how are you faring?* **get on**, get along, cope, manage, do, survive; informal make out.

farewell ▸ exclamation old use goodbye.

SYNONYMS *farewell, Patrick!* **goodbye**, so long, adieu, au revoir, ciao; informal bye, cheerio, see you (later); Brit. informal ta-ta, cheers.

▸ noun an act of leaving.

SYNONYMS *an emotional farewell* **goodbye**, adieu, leave-taking, parting, departure, send-off.

farinaceous /fa-ri-**nay**-shuhss/ ▸ adjective containing or like starch.

farm ▸ noun 1 an area of land and buildings used for growing crops and rearing animals. 2 a farmhouse.
▸ verb 1 make a living by growing crops or keeping animals. 2 (**farm something out**) give work to other people to do.

farmer ▸ noun a person who owns or manages a farm.

farmhouse ▸ noun a house attached to a farm.

farming ▸ noun the activity of running a farm.

SYNONYMS **agriculture**, cultivation, husbandry; Brit. crofting.

farmstead ▸ noun a farm and its buildings.

farmyard ▸ noun a yard or enclosure surrounded by farm buildings.

farrago /fuh-**rah**-goh/ ▸ noun (plural **farragos** or **farragoes**) a confused mixture.

farrier ▶ noun a person who shoes horses.

farrow ▶ noun a litter of pigs.
▶ verb (of a sow) give birth to piglets.

farther → FURTHER.

farthest → FURTHEST.

farthing ▶ noun a former UK coin, worth a quarter of an old penny.

fascia (or Brit. **facia**) /fay-shuh/ ▶ noun **1** a board covering the ends of rafters or other fittings. **2** Brit. a board above the entrance of a shop, displaying the shop's name. **3** the dashboard of a motor vehicle. **4** a detachable cover for the front of a mobile phone.

fascinate ▶ verb (**fascinates**, **fascinating**, **fascinated**) interest or charm someone greatly.

SYNONYMS (**fascinating**) **interesting**, captivating, engrossing, absorbing, enchanting, enthralling, spellbinding, riveting, engaging, compelling, compulsive, gripping, charming, attractive, intriguing, diverting, entertaining.

✔ Spell **fascinate** and **fascination** with an **s** before the **c**.

fascination ▶ noun the state of being fascinated by someone or something.

SYNONYMS **interest**, preoccupation, passion, obsession, compulsion, allure, lure, charm, attraction, appeal, pull, draw.

fascism /fash-i-z'm/ ▶ noun **1** a right-wing system of government with extreme nationalistic beliefs. **2** an attitude which is very intolerant or right-wing.
□ **fascist** noun & adjective.

fashion ▶ noun **1** a popular style of clothes, way of behaving, etc. **2** a way of doing something.

SYNONYMS **1** *the fashion for tight clothes* **vogue**, trend, craze, rage, mania, fad, style, look, convention; informal thing. **2** *the world of fashion* **clothes**, clothing design, couture; informal the rag trade. **3** *in a sensible fashion* **manner**, way, method, style, approach.

▶ verb make or shape something.

SYNONYMS *fashioned from clay* **construct**, build, make, manufacture, cast, shape, form, mould, sculpt, forge, hew, carve.

fashionable ▶ adjective in a style that is currently popular.

SYNONYMS **in vogue**, in fashion, popular, up to date, up to the minute, modern, all the rage, trendsetting, stylish, chic; informal trendy, classy, cool; N. Amer. informal tony.
ANTONYMS unfashionable.

□ **fashionably** adverb.

fast¹ ▶ adjective **1** moving or capable of moving very quickly. **2** taking place quickly. **3** (of a clock or watch) ahead of the correct time. **4** firmly fixed or attached. **5** (of a dye) not fading.

SYNONYMS **1** *a fast pace* **speedy**, quick, swift, rapid, high-speed, accelerated, express, blistering, breakneck, hasty, hurried; informal nippy, scorching, supersonic; Brit. informal cracking. **2** *make the rope fast* **secure**, fastened, tight, firm, closed, shut, immovable. **3** *fast friends* **loyal**, devoted, faithful, firm, steadfast, staunch, true, boon, bosom, inseparable.
ANTONYMS slow, loose, temporary.

▶ adverb **1** quickly. **2** firmly or securely.

SYNONYMS **1** *she drove fast* **quickly**, rapidly, swiftly, speedily, briskly, at full tilt, hastily, hurriedly, in a hurry; informal double quick, nippily; N. Amer. informal lickety-split. **2** *his wheels were stuck fast* **securely**, firmly, tight. **3** *he's fast asleep* **deeply**, sound, completely.
ANTONYMS slowly, loosely, lightly.

fast² ▶ verb go without food or drink.

SYNONYMS *we must fast and pray* **eat nothing**, refrain from eating, go without food, go hungry, starve yourself, go on hunger strike.
ANTONYMS eat.

▶ noun a period of fasting.

SYNONYMS *a five-day fast* **period of fasting**, period of abstinence, hunger strike, diet.
ANTONYMS feast.

fasten ▶ verb **1** close or do up securely. **2** fix or hold in place. **3** (**fasten on**) pick out and concentrate on.

SYNONYMS **1** *he fastened the door* **bolt**, lock, secure, make fast, chain, seal. **2** *they fastened splints to his leg* **attach**, fix, affix, clip, pin, tack, stick, join. **3** *he fastened his horse to a tree* **tie (up)**, tether, hitch, truss, fetter, lash, anchor, strap, rope.
ANTONYMS unlock, remove, untie.

□ **fastener** noun **fastening** noun.

fastidious /fa-stid-i-uhss/ ▶ adjective **1** paying a lot of attention to detail. **2** very concerned about cleanliness.
□ **fastidiously** adverb.

fastness ▶ noun **1** a place that is secure and well protected. **2** the ability of a dye to keep its colour.

fat ▶ noun **1** an oily substance found in animals. **2** a substance used in cooking made from the fat of animals, or from plants.

SYNONYMS **1** *whale fat* **blubber,** fatty tissue, adipose tissue, cellulite. **2** *eggs in sizzling fat* **oil,** grease, lard, suet, butter, margarine.

▶ adjective (**fatter, fattest**) **1** having a lot of fat. **2** informal large; substantial.

SYNONYMS **1** *a fat man* **obese,** overweight, plump, stout, chubby, portly, flabby, paunchy, pot-bellied, corpulent; informal tubby; Brit. informal podgy. **2** *fat bacon* **fatty,** greasy, oily. **3** *a fat book* **thick,** big, chunky, substantial, long.
ANTONYMS thin, slim, lean.

■ **fat cat** disapproving a wealthy and powerful businessperson.
□ **fatness** noun.

fatal ▶ adjective **1** causing death. **2** leading to disaster.

SYNONYMS **1** *a fatal disease* **deadly,** lethal, mortal, death-dealing, terminal, incurable, untreatable, inoperable. **2** *a fatal mistake* **disastrous,** devastating, ruinous, catastrophic, calamitous, dire.
ANTONYMS harmless, beneficial.

□ **fatally** adverb.

fatalism ▶ noun the belief that all events are decided in advance by a supernatural power.
□ **fatalist** noun **fatalistic** adjective.

fatality ▶ noun (plural **fatalities**) a death occurring in a war, or caused by an accident or disease.

fate ▶ noun **1** a supernatural power believed to control all events. **2** the things that will inevitably happen to someone or something.

SYNONYMS **1** *what has fate in store for me?* **destiny,** providence, the stars, chance, luck, serendipity, fortune. **2** *my fate was in their hands* **future,** destiny, outcome, end, lot. **3** *a similar fate would befall Harris* **death,** demise, end, sentence.

▶ verb (**be fated**) be destined to happen in a particular way.

SYNONYMS *she was fated to face the same problem* **predestine,** preordain, destine, mean, doom.

fateful ▶ adjective having important, often unpleasant, consequences.

father ▶ noun **1** a male parent. **2** an important figure in the early history of something. **3** literary a male ancestor. **4** a priest. **5** (**the Father**) God.

SYNONYMS **1** informal **dad,** daddy, pop, pa, old man. **2** *the father of democracy* **originator,** initiator, founder, inventor, creator, author, architect.

▶ verb (**fathers, fathering, fathered**) be the father of.

SYNONYMS **sire,** spawn, breed, give life to.

■ **father-in-law** (plural **fathers-in-law**) the father of a person's husband or wife.
□ **fatherhood** noun.

fatherland ▶ noun a person's native country.

fatherly ▶ adjective protective and affectionate.

fathom ▶ noun a measure of the depth of water, equal to six feet (1.8 metres).
▶ verb understand after a lot of thought.

fatigue ▶ noun **1** great tiredness. **2** weakness in metals caused by repeated stress. **3** (**fatigues**) loose-fitting clothing worn by soldiers.

SYNONYMS **tiredness,** weariness, exhaustion.
ANTONYMS energy.

▶ verb (**fatigues, fatiguing, fatigued**) make someone very tired.

SYNONYMS **tire out,** exhaust, wear out, drain, weary, overtire; informal knock out, take it out of; Brit. informal knacker.
ANTONYMS invigorate.

fatten ▶ verb make or become fat or fatter.

fatty ▶ adjective (**fattier, fattiest**) containing a lot of fat.

SYNONYMS **greasy,** fat, oily, creamy, rich.
ANTONYMS lean.

fatuity /fuh-tyoo-i-ti/ ▶ noun **1** a silly remark. **2** foolishness.

fatuous ▶ adjective silly and pointless.
□ **fatuously** adverb.

fatwa /fat-wah/ ▶ noun a ruling on a point of Islamic law given by a recognized authority.

faucet /faw-sit/ ▶ noun N. Amer. a tap.

fault ▶ noun **1** a defect or mistake. **2** responsibility for an accident or unfortunate event. **3** (in tennis) a service that is against the rules. **4** a break in the layers of rock of the earth's crust.

SYNONYMS **1** *he has his faults* **defect,** failing, imperfection, flaw, blemish, shortcoming, weakness, vice. **2** *engineers have located the fault* **defect,** flaw, imperfection, bug, error, mistake, inaccuracy; informal glitch. **3** *it was not my fault* **responsibility,** liability, culpability, guilt.
ANTONYMS strength.

▶ verb find a defect or mistake in someone or something.

SYNONYMS *you can't fault their commitment* **find fault with,** criticize, attack, condemn; informal knock; Brit. informal slag off.

□ **faultless** adjective.

faulty ▶ adjective (**faultier**, **faultiest**) having faults.

SYNONYMS **1** *a faulty electric blanket* **malfunctioning**, broken, damaged, defective, not working, out of order; informal on the blink, acting up; Brit. informal playing up. **2** *her logic is faulty* **defective**, flawed, unsound, inaccurate, incorrect, erroneous, wrong.
ANTONYMS working, sound.

faun ▶ noun (in Roman mythology) a god of woods and fields, with a human body and a goat's horns, ears, legs, and tail.

fauna ▶ noun the animals of a particular region or period.

faux pas /foh **pah**/ ▶ noun (plural **faux pas**) a mistake which causes embarrassment in a social situation.

favour (US spelling **favor**) ▶ noun **1** approval or liking. **2** a kind or helpful act. **3** special treatment of one person or group.

SYNONYMS **1** *will you do me a favour?* **good turn**, service, good deed, act of kindness, courtesy. **2** *she looked on him with favour* **approval**, approbation, goodwill, kindness, benevolence.
ANTONYMS disservice, disapproval.

▶ verb **1** view or treat with favour. **2** work to the advantage of. **3** (**favour someone with**) give someone something they wish for.

SYNONYMS **1** *the party favours electoral reform* **advocate**, recommend, approve of, be in favour of, support, back, champion, campaign for, press for, lobby for, promote; informal push for. **2** *Robyn favours loose clothes* **prefer**, go for, choose, opt for, select, pick, plump for. **3** *Father always favoured George* **prefer**, be biased towards, indulge, like more/better. **4** *the conditions favoured the other team* **benefit**, be to the advantage of, help, assist, aid, be of service to.
ANTONYMS oppose, dislike, hinder.

■ **in favour of 1** to be replaced by. **2** in support of.

favourable (US spelling **favorable**)
▶ adjective **1** expressing approval or consent. **2** advantageous or helpful.

SYNONYMS **1** *a favourable review* **approving**, positive, complimentary, full of praise, flattering, glowing, enthusiastic, kind, good; informal rave. **2** *conditions are favourable* **advantageous**, beneficial, in your favour, good, right, suitable, appropriate, auspicious, promising, encouraging. **3** *a favourable reply* **positive**, affirmative, assenting, approving, encouraging, reassuring.
ANTONYMS critical, disadvantageous, negative.

□ **favourably** adverb.

favourite (US spelling **favorite**) ▶ adjective preferred to all other people or things of the same kind.

SYNONYMS **favoured**, preferred, chosen, choice, best-loved, dearest, pet.

▶ noun **1** a favourite person or thing. **2** the competitor thought most likely to win.

SYNONYMS **first choice**, pick, preference, pet, darling, the apple of your eye; informal golden boy, teacher's pet; Brit. informal blue-eyed boy/girl; N. Amer. informal fair-haired boy/girl.

favouritism (US spelling **favoritism**) ▶ noun the unfair favouring of one person or group.

fawn[1] ▶ noun **1** a young deer. **2** a light brown colour.

fawn[2] ▶ verb try to please someone by flattering them and being too attentive.

fax ▶ noun **1** a copy of a document which has been scanned and transmitted electronically. **2** a machine for transmitting and receiving faxes.
▶ verb send a document by fax.

faze ▶ verb (**fazes**, **fazing**, **fazed**) informal shock or confuse.

FBI ▶ abbreviation (in the US) Federal Bureau of Investigation.

FC ▶ abbreviation Football Club.

fealty /**fee**-uhl-ti/ ▶ noun (in the feudal system) the loyalty sworn to a lord by a person who served him or worked for him.

fear ▶ noun **1** an unpleasant emotion caused by the threat of danger. **2** the likelihood of something unwelcome happening.

SYNONYMS **1** *she felt fear at entering the house* **terror**, fright, fearfulness, horror, alarm, panic, trepidation, dread, anxiety, angst, apprehension, nervousness. **2** *a fear of heights* **phobia**, aversion, antipathy, dread, nightmare, horror, terror; informal hang-up.

▶ verb **1** be afraid of. **2** (**fear for**) be anxious about.

SYNONYMS **1** *she feared her husband* **be afraid of**, be fearful of, be scared of, be apprehensive of, dread, live in fear of, be terrified of. **2** *I fear you may be right* **suspect**, be afraid, have a sneaking suspicion, be inclined to think, have a hunch.

fearful ▶ adjective **1** feeling afraid. **2** causing fear. **3** informal very great.

SYNONYMS **1** *they are fearful of being overheard* **afraid**, scared, frightened, scared stiff, scared to death, terrified, petrified, nervous, apprehensive, uneasy, anxious, timid; informal jittery. **2** *a fearful accident* **terrible**, dreadful, awful,

appalling, frightful, ghastly, horrific, horrible, shocking, gruesome.
ANTONYMS unafraid.
□ **fearfully** adverb.

fearless ▸ adjective having no fear; brave.

SYNONYMS **brave,** courageous, bold, audacious, intrepid, valiant, plucky, heroic, daring, unafraid; informal gutsy.
ANTONYMS timid, cowardly.

□ **fearlessly** adverb.

fearsome ▸ adjective very impressive and frightening.

feasible ▸ adjective 1 able to be done easily. 2 likely.

SYNONYMS **practicable,** practical, workable, achievable, attainable, realizable, viable, realistic, possible; informal doable.
ANTONYMS impracticable.

□ **feasibility** noun **feasibly** adverb.

❗ Some people say **feasible** should not be used to mean 'likely', but this sense has been in the language for centuries and is generally considered to be acceptable.

feast ▸ noun 1 a large meal marking a special occasion. 2 an annual religious celebration.

SYNONYMS *a wedding feast* **banquet,** dinner, treat; informal spread; Brit. informal beanfeast, slap-up meal.

▸ verb 1 have a feast. 2 (**feast on**) eat large quantities of.

SYNONYMS *they feasted on lobster* **gorge,** dine, binge; (**feast on**) devour, consume, partake of, eat your fill of; informal stuff your face with, pig out.

feat ▸ noun an achievement requiring great courage, skill, or strength.

SYNONYMS **achievement,** accomplishment, coup, triumph, undertaking, enterprise, venture, exploit, operation, exercise, endeavour, effort.

feather ▸ noun any of the structures growing from a bird's skin, consisting of a hollow shaft fringed with fine strands.

SYNONYMS **plume,** quill; (**feathers**) plumage, down.

▸ verb (**feathers, feathering, feathered**) turn an oar so that the blade passes through the air edgeways.
■ **a feather in your cap** an achievement to be proud of. **feather your nest** make money dishonestly.
□ **feathery** adjective.

feature ▸ noun 1 a distinctive element or aspect. 2 a part of the face. 3 a special article in a newspaper or magazine. 4 (also **feature film**) the main film showing at a cinema.

SYNONYMS 1 *a feature of Indian music* **characteristic,** attribute, quality, property, trait, hallmark, aspect, facet, factor, ingredient, component, element. 2 *her delicate features* **face,** countenance, physiognomy; informal mug; Brit. informal mush, phizog. 3 *she made a feature of her sculptures* **centrepiece,** special attraction, highlight, focal point, focus, conversation piece. 4 *a series of short features* **article,** piece, item, report, story, column.

▸ verb (**features, featuring, featured**) 1 have as a feature. 2 have an important part in something.

SYNONYMS 1 *Radio 3 is featuring a week of live concerts* **present,** promote, make a feature of, spotlight, highlight, showcase, foreground. 2 *she is to feature in a new movie* **star,** appear, participate.

□ **featureless** adjective.

febrile /fee-bryl/ ▸ adjective 1 having the symptoms of a fever. 2 overactive and excitable.

February /feb-yuu-ri, feb-ruu-uh-ri/ ▸ noun (plural **Februaries**) the second month of the year.

✔ **-ruary**, not **-uary**: February.

feces US spelling of FAECES.

feckless ▸ adjective irresponsible and without strength of character.

fecund ▸ adjective very fertile.
□ **fecundity** noun.

fed past and past participle of FEED.
■ **fed up** informal annoyed or bored.

federal ▸ adjective 1 having a system of government in which several states unite under a central authority. 2 having to do with the central government of a federation. 3 (**Federal**) US historical having to do with the Northern States in the Civil War.
□ **federalism** noun **federalist** noun & adjective **federally** adverb.

federate ▸ verb (**federates, federating, federated**) join as a federation.

federation ▸ noun 1 a group of states united under a central authority in which individual states keep control of their internal affairs. 2 a group organized like a federation.

SYNONYMS **confederation,** confederacy, association, league, alliance, coalition, union, syndicate, guild, consortium.

fedora /fi-dor-uh/ ▸ noun a soft felt hat with a curled brim.

fee ▸ noun 1 a payment given for professional advice or services. 2 a sum paid to be allowed to do something.

SYNONYMS **payment**, wage, salary, price, charge, bill, tariff, rate; (**fees**) remuneration, dues, earnings, pay; formal emolument.

feeble ▸ adjective (**feebler**, **feeblest**) **1** weak. **2** not convincing or effective.

SYNONYMS **1** *old and feeble* **weak**, weakened, debilitated, enfeebled, frail, decrepit, infirm, delicate, sickly, ailing, unwell, poorly. **2** *a feeble argument* **ineffective**, unconvincing, implausible, unsatisfactory, poor, weak, flimsy, lame. **3** *he's too feeble to stand up to her* **cowardly**, faint-hearted, spineless, timid, timorous, fearful, unassertive, weak, ineffectual; informal sissy, chicken; Brit. informal wet. **4** *a feeble light* **faint**, dim, weak, pale, soft, subdued, muted. ANTONYMS strong, well, brave.

□ **feebleness** noun **feebly** adverb.

feed ▸ verb (**feeds**, **feeding**, **fed**) **1** give food to. **2** provide enough food for. **3** (of an animal or baby) eat. **4** supply with material or information. **5** pass something gradually through a confined space.

SYNONYMS **1** *a large family to feed* **cater for**, provide for, cook for, dine, nourish. **2** *cows feeding* **eat**, graze, browse, crop. **3** *she fed secrets to the Russians* **supply**, provide, give, deliver, furnish, issue, leak.

▸ noun **1** an act of feeding. **2** food for domestic animals.

SYNONYMS *animal feed* **fodder**, food, provender.

feedback ▸ noun **1** comments made in response to something you have done. **2** the return of part of the output of an amplifier to its input, causing a whistling sound.

feeder ▸ noun **1** a thing that feeds or supplies something. **2** a minor route that links outlying areas with the main route.

feel ▸ verb (**feels**, **feeling**, **felt**) **1** be aware of, examine, or search by touch. **2** give a particular sensation when touched. **3** experience an emotion or sensation. **4** be affected by. **5** have a belief or opinion.

SYNONYMS **1** *she felt the fabric* **touch**, stroke, caress, fondle, finger, paw, handle. **2** *she felt a breeze on her back* **perceive**, sense, detect, discern, notice, be aware of, be conscious of. **3** *he will not feel any pain* **experience**, undergo, go through, bear, endure, suffer. **4** *he felt his way towards the door* **grope**, fumble, scrabble. **5** *he feels that he should go* **believe**, think, consider it right, be of the opinion, hold, maintain, judge; informal reckon, figure.

▸ noun **1** an act of feeling. **2** the sense of

touch. **3** a sensation or impression. **4** (a **feel for**) a sensitive appreciation of.

SYNONYMS **1** *the feel of the paper* **texture**, finish, touch, consistency. **2** *the feel of the house* **atmosphere**, ambience, aura, mood, feeling, air, impression, spirit; informal vibes. **3** *a feel for languages* **aptitude**, knack, flair, bent, talent, gift, ability.

feeler ▸ noun **1** an organ used by certain animals for testing things by touch. **2** a cautious proposal intended to find out someone's opinion.

feeling ▸ noun **1** an emotional state or reaction. **2** (**feelings**) the emotional side of a person's character. **3** strong emotion. **4** the ability to feel. **5** the sensation of touching or being touched. **6** a belief or opinion. **7** (**feeling for**) an understanding of.

SYNONYMS **1** *a feeling of nausea* **sensation**, sense. **2** *I had a feeling I would win* (**sneaking**) **suspicion**, notion, inkling, hunch, intuition, funny feeling, fancy, idea. **3** *the strength of her feeling* **love**, affection, fondness, tenderness, warmth, emotion, passion, desire. **4** *public feeling* **mood**, (tide of) opinion, attitude, sentiment, emotion, belief, views, consensus. **5** *show some feeling* **compassion**, sympathy, empathy, fellow feeling, concern, pity, sorrow, commiseration. **6** *he had hurt her feelings* **sensibilities**, sensitivities, self-esteem, pride. **7** *my feeling is that it is true* **opinion**, belief, view, impression, intuition, instinct, hunch, estimation, guess. **8** *a feeling of peace* **atmosphere**, ambience, aura, air, mood, impression, spirit; informal vibes. **9** *a remarkable feeling for language* **aptitude**, knack, flair, bent, talent, feel, gift, ability.

feet plural of **FOOT**.

feign ▸ verb pretend to feel or have.

feint /faynt/ ▸ noun a movement made to deceive an opponent, especially in boxing or fencing.
▸ verb make a feint.

feisty /fy-sti/ ▸ adjective (**feistier**, **feistiest**) lively and spirited.

feldspar (or **felspar**) ▸ noun a mineral that forms igneous rocks.

felicitations ▸ plural noun formal congratulations.

felicitous /fuh-li-si-tuhss/ ▸ adjective well chosen or appropriate.

felicity ▸ noun (plural **felicities**) **1** great happiness. **2** the ability to express yourself in an appropriate way. **3** a pleasing feature of an artistic work.

feline ▸ adjective having to do with a cat or cats.
▸ noun a cat or other animal of the cat family.

fell[1] past of FALL.

fell[2] ▶ verb **1** cut down a tree. **2** knock someone down.

> SYNONYMS **1** *the dead trees had to be felled* **cut down,** chop down, hack down, saw down, clear. **2** *she felled him with one punch* **knock down,** knock to the ground, floor, strike down, knock out; informal deck, flatten, lay out.

fell[3] ▶ noun a hill or stretch of high moorland in northern England.

fellow ▶ noun **1** a man or boy. **2** a person in the same situation as you. **3** a thing of the same kind as another. **4** a member of a learned society. **5** Brit. a senior member of certain universities or colleges.

> SYNONYMS **1** *he's a decent sort of fellow* **man,** boy, person, individual, character; informal guy, lad; Brit. informal chap, bloke; N. Amer. informal dude. **2** *he exchanged glances with his fellows* **companion,** friend, comrade, partner, associate, co-worker, colleague; informal pal, buddy; Brit. informal mate.

▶ adjective in the same situation: *a fellow sufferer.*

fellowship ▶ noun **1** friendship between people who share an interest. **2** a group of people who share an interest. **3** the position of a fellow of a college or society.

> SYNONYMS **1** *a community bound together in fellowship* **companionship,** comradeship, camaraderie, friendship, sociability, solidarity. **2** *the church fellowship* **association,** organization, society, club, league, union, guild, alliance, fraternity, brotherhood.

felon ▶ noun a person who has committed a felony.
□ **felonious** /fi-**loh**-ni-uhss/ adjective.

felony /**fe**-luh-ni/ ▶ noun (plural **felonies**) (in the US and formerly also in English Law) a serious crime.

felspar = FELDSPAR.

felt[1] ▶ noun cloth made from wool that has been rolled and pressed.
■ **felt-tip pen** a pen with a writing point made of felt or tightly packed fibres.

felt[2] past and past participle of FEEL.

female ▶ adjective **1** of the sex that can give birth to offspring or produce eggs. **2** having to do with women. **3** (of a plant or flower) having a pistil but no stamens. **4** (of a fitting) having a hollow so that a corresponding part can be inserted.
▶ noun a female person, animal, or plant.

feminine ▶ adjective **1** having qualities associated with women. **2** female. **3** Grammar (of nouns and adjectives in some languages) having a gender regarded as female.

> SYNONYMS **womanly,** ladylike, soft, gentle, tender, delicate, pretty.
> ANTONYMS masculine.

□ **femininity** noun.

feminism ▶ noun a movement or theory that supports the rights of women.
□ **feminist** noun & adjective.

feminize (or feminise) ▶ verb (**feminizes, feminizing, feminized**) make more feminine or female.

femme fatale /fam fuh-**tahl**/ ▶ noun (plural **femmes fatales** /fam fuh-**tahl**/) an attractive and seductive woman.

femur /**fee**-mer/ ▶ noun (plural **femurs** or **femora** /**fem**-uh-ruh/) the bone of the thigh.
□ **femoral** adjective.

fen ▶ noun a low and marshy or frequently flooded area of land.

fence ▶ noun **1** a barrier made of wire or wood that encloses an area of land. **2** an obstacle for horses to jump over in a competition. **3** informal a person who buys and resells stolen goods.

> SYNONYMS **barrier,** paling, railing, enclosure, barricade, stockade.

▶ verb (**fences, fencing, fenced**) **1** surround or protect with a fence. **2** take part in the sport of fencing.

> SYNONYMS **1** *they fenced off the meadow* **enclose,** surround, encircle. **2** *he fenced in his chickens* **confine,** pen in, coop up, shut in/up, enclose, surround; N. Amer. corral.

■ **sit on the fence** avoid making a decision.
□ **fencer** noun.

fencing ▶ noun **1** the sport of fighting with blunted swords. **2** fences or material for making fences.

fend ▶ verb **1** (**fend for yourself**) look after yourself without help from other people. **2** (**fend someone/thing off**) defend yourself from an attack or attacker.

> SYNONYMS *she tried to fend him off* **ward off,** head off, stave off, hold off, repel, repulse, resist, fight off.

fender ▶ noun **1** a low frame around a fireplace to stop coals from falling out. **2** a soft object that is hung over the side of a ship to protect it from collisions. **3** N. Amer. the mudguard or area around the wheel of a vehicle.

feng shui /feng shoo-i, fung **shway**/ ▶ noun an ancient Chinese system of designing buildings and arranging objects in rooms to achieve a good flow of energy and so bring happiness or good luck.

fennel ▸ noun a plant whose leaves and seeds are used as a herb and whose bulb is eaten as a vegetable.

feral ▸ adjective **1** (of an animal) wild, especially after having been tame or kept as a pet. **2** savage or fierce.

ferment ▸ verb /fer-**ment**/ **1** undergo a chemical change by the action of yeast or bacteria. **2** stir up disorder.
▸ noun /**fer**-ment/ a state of widespread unrest or excitement.
☐ **fermentation** noun.

fermium ▸ noun an unstable radioactive element that is produced artificially.

fern ▸ noun (plural **fern** or **ferns**) a plant which has feathery fronds and no flowers.

ferocious ▸ adjective very fierce or violent.

SYNONYMS **1** *ferocious animals* **fierce,** savage, wild, predatory, ravening, aggressive, dangerous. **2** *a ferocious attack* **brutal,** vicious, violent, bloody, barbaric, savage, frenzied.
ANTONYMS gentle, mild.

☐ **ferociously** adverb.

ferocity ▸ noun the state of being ferocious.

ferret ▸ noun a small, fierce animal with a long thin body, used for catching rabbits.
▸ verb (**ferrets, ferreting, ferreted**) **1** search among a lot of things. **2** (**ferret something out**) discover something by searching thoroughly. **3** (**ferreting**) hunting with ferrets.

Ferris wheel ▸ noun a fairground ride consisting of a large upright revolving wheel.

ferrous ▸ adjective (of a metal) containing iron.

ferrule ▸ noun a metal cap which protects the end of a stick or umbrella.

ferry ▸ noun (plural **ferries**) a boat or ship that transports passengers and goods as a regular service.
▸ verb (**ferries, ferrying, ferried**) carry by ferry or other transport.

SYNONYMS **transport,** convey, carry, run, ship, shuttle.

fertile ▸ adjective **1** (of soil or land) producing a lot of plants or crops. **2** (of a person, animal, or plant) able to produce offspring or seeds. **3** producing a lot of good results or ideas.

SYNONYMS **1** *the soil is fertile* **productive,** fruitful, fecund, rich, lush. **2** *a fertile imagination* **creative,** inventive, innovative, visionary, original, ingenious, prolific.
ANTONYMS barren, uncreative.

☐ **fertility** noun.

fertilize (or **fertilise**) ▸ verb (**fertilizes, fertilizing, fertilized**) **1** introduce sperm or pollen into an egg or plant so that a new individual develops. **2** add fertilizer to soil.
☐ **fertilization** noun.

fertilizer (or **fertiliser**) ▸ noun a chemical or natural substance added to soil to make it more fertile.

SYNONYMS **plant food,** dressing, manure, muck, compost.

fervent ▸ adjective showing strong or passionate feeling.
☐ **fervently** adverb.

fervid ▸ adjective fervent.

fervour (US spelling **fervor**) ▸ noun strong or passionate feeling.

festal ▸ adjective relating to a festival.

fester ▸ verb (**festers, festering, festered**) **1** (of a wound or sore) become septic. **2** become rotten. **3** become worse or more strongly felt.

festival ▸ noun **1** a time when people celebrate a special occasion. **2** an organized series of concerts, films, etc.

SYNONYMS **celebration,** festivity, fête, fair, gala, carnival, fiesta, jamboree, feast day, holiday, holy day.

festive ▸ adjective relating to a period of celebration.

SYNONYMS **jolly,** merry, joyous, joyful, happy, jovial, light-hearted, cheerful, jubilant, celebratory, holiday, carnival.

festivity ▸ noun (plural **festivities**) **1** joyful celebration. **2** (**festivities**) activities or events celebrating a special occasion.

festoon ▸ verb decorate with chains of flowers, ribbons, etc.
▸ noun a decorative chain of flowers, ribbons, etc.

feta /**fe**-tuh/ ▸ noun a salty Greek cheese made from the milk of sheep or goats.

fetal (or Brit. **foetal**) ▸ adjective relating to a fetus.

fetch ▸ verb **1** go for something and bring it back. **2** be sold for a particular price. **3** (**fetching**) attractive.

SYNONYMS **1** *he went to fetch a doctor* **go and get,** go for, call for, summon, pick up, collect, bring, carry, convey, transport. **2** *the land could fetch millions* **sell for,** bring in, raise, realize, yield, make, command; informal go for. **3** (**fetching**) **attractive,** appealing, sweet, pretty, lovely, delightful, charming, captivating, enchanting; Scottish & N. English bonny; Brit. informal fit.

fete (or **fête**) /fayt/ ▸ noun Brit. an outdoor event to raise funds for a special purpose.
▸ verb (**fetes, feting, feted**) praise or entertain someone lavishly.

fetid (or **foetid**) ▸ adjective smelling very unpleasant.

f

fetish ▸ noun 1 a form of sexual desire in which pleasure is gained from a particular object or part of the body. 2 an object worshipped for its supposed magical powers.
  □ **fetishism** noun **fetishist** noun.

fetlock ▸ noun a joint of a horse's leg between the knee and the hoof.

fetter ▸ verb (**fetters, fettering, fettered**) 1 limit the freedom of. 2 restrain with chains or shackles.
  ▸ noun 1 (**fetters**) restraints or controls. 2 a chain placed around a prisoner's ankles.

fettle ▸ noun condition.

fettuccine /fet-tuh-**chee**-ni/ ▸ plural noun pasta made in long flat strips.

fetus (or Brit. **foetus**) ▸ noun (plural **fetuses**) an unborn baby of a mammal.

feud ▸ noun a long and bitter dispute.

> SYNONYMS *a long-standing feud* **vendetta,** conflict, quarrel, row, rivalry, hostility, strife.

  ▸ verb take part in a feud.

> SYNONYMS *feuding families* **quarrel,** fight, clash, argue, squabble, dispute.

feudal ▸ adjective having to do with feudalism.

feudalism ▸ noun the social system in medieval Europe, in which people worked and fought for a nobleman in return for land.

fever ▸ noun 1 an abnormally high body temperature. 2 a state of nervous excitement.

> SYNONYMS 1 *he developed fever* **feverishness,** high temperature; Medicine pyrexia; informal temperature. 2 *World Cup fever* **excitement,** mania, frenzy, agitation, passion.

  □ **feverish** adjective.

fevered ▸ adjective 1 having a fever. 2 nervously excited.

few ▸ determiner, pronoun, & adjective 1 (**a few**) a small number of; some. 2 not many.

> SYNONYMS *police are revealing few details* **not many,** hardly any, scarcely any, a small number of, a handful of, a couple of, one or two.
> ANTONYMS many.

  ▸ noun (**the few**) a select minority.

> ❗ Make sure you distinguish between **fewer** and **less**. Use **fewer** with plural nouns, as in *there were fewer tourists this year*; use **less** with nouns referring to things that can't be counted, as in *there is less blossom on this tree*. It's wrong to use **less** with a plural noun (as in *there were less tourists*).

fey ▸ adjective seeming vague or mysterious and unaware of the realities of life.

fez ▸ noun (plural **fezzes**) a conical red hat with a flat top, worn by men in some Muslim countries.

ff. ▸ abbreviation following pages.

fiancé /fi-on-say/ ▸ noun (feminine **fiancée** /fi-on-say/) a person to whom you are engaged to be married.

fiasco ▸ noun (plural **fiascos**) a ridiculous or humiliating failure.

> SYNONYMS **failure,** disaster, catastrophe, debacle, farce, mess; informal flop, washout, shambles; Brit. informal cock-up; N. Amer. informal snafu; Austral./NZ informal fizzer.
> ANTONYMS success.

fiat /fee-at/ ▸ noun an official order.

fib ▸ noun a trivial lie.
  ▸ verb (**fibs, fibbing, fibbed**) tell a fib.
  □ **fibber** noun.

fibre (US spelling **fiber**) ▸ noun 1 each of the thin threads which form plant or animal tissue, cloth, or minerals. 2 a material made from fibres. 3 the part of some foods that is difficult to digest and which helps food to pass through the body. 4 strength of character.

> SYNONYMS **thread,** strand, filament, wisp, yarn.

  ■ **fibre optics** the use of glass fibres to send information in the form of light.
  □ **fibrous** adjective.

fibreboard (US spelling **fiberboard**) ▸ noun a building material made of compressed wood fibres.

fibreglass (US spelling **fiberglass**) ▸ noun 1 a strong plastic material containing glass fibres. 2 a material made from woven glass fibres.

fibrillate ▸ verb (**fibrillates, fibrillating, fibrillated**) (of a muscle, especially in the heart) twitch irregularly.
  □ **fibrillation** noun.

fibroid ▸ noun a lump consisting of mass of fibrous tissues, usually developing in a woman's womb.

fibula /fib-yuu-luh/ ▸ noun (plural **fibulae** /fib-yuu-lee/ or **fibulas**) the outer of the two bones between the knee and the ankle.

fickle ▸ adjective changeable in your loyalties.

> SYNONYMS **capricious,** flighty, giddy, changeable, volatile, mercurial, erratic, unpredictable, unreliable, unsteady.
> ANTONYMS constant.

fiction ▸ noun 1 literature describing imaginary events and people. 2 something that is invented and not true.

> SYNONYMS 1 *the traditions of British fiction* **novels,** stories, literature, creative writing. 2 *this is an absolute fiction* **fabrication,** invention, lie, fib, tall story,

untruth, falsehood, fantasy, nonsense.
ANTONYMS non-fiction, fact.

□ **fictional** adjective.

fictionalize (or **fictionalise**) ▸ verb
(**fictionalizes, fictionalizing, fictionalized**)
make into a fictional story.

fictitious /fik-**tish**-uhss/ ▸ adjective
imaginary or invented; not real.

SYNONYMS **false**, fake, fabricated, bogus,
spurious, assumed, affected, adopted,
invented, made up; informal pretend,
phoney.
ANTONYMS genuine.

fiddle ▸ noun informal **1** a violin. **2** something
done dishonestly in order to obtain money.

SYNONYMS a VAT fiddle **fraud**, swindle,
confidence trick; informal racket, scam.

▸ verb (**fiddles, fiddling, fiddled**) **1** touch or
move something restlessly or nervously.
2 informal change the details of something
dishonestly.

SYNONYMS **1** he fiddled with a beer mat
fidget, play, toy, finger, handle. **2** he
fiddled with the dials **adjust**, tinker,
play about/around, fool about/around,
meddle, interfere, tamper; informal tweak,
mess about/around; Brit. informal muck
about/around. **3** fiddling the figures
falsify, manipulate, massage, rig, distort,
misrepresent, doctor, tamper with,
interfere with; informal fix, cook (the
books).

■ **play second fiddle** take a less important
role.
□ **fiddler** noun.

fiddly ▸ adjective Brit. complicated and
awkward to do or use.

fidelity ▸ noun **1** faithfulness to a person
or belief. **2** the accuracy with which
something is copied or reproduced.

SYNONYMS **1** fidelity to her husband
faithfulness, loyalty, constancy,
allegiance, commitment, devotion. **2** the
fidelity of the reproduction **accuracy**,
exactness, precision, correctness,
strictness, closeness, authenticity.
ANTONYMS disloyalty, inaccuracy.

fidget ▸ verb (**fidgets, fidgeting, fidgeted**)
make small movements because you are
nervous or impatient.
▸ noun a person who fidgets.
□ **fidgety** adjective.

fief /feef/ ▸ noun historical a piece of land held
under the feudal system.
□ **fiefdom** noun.

field ▸ noun **1** an enclosed area of land for
growing crops or keeping animals. **2** a
piece of land used for a sport or game. **3** a
subject of study or area of activity. **4** an
area within which a force has an effect: a

magnetic field. **5** (**the field**) all the people
taking part in a contest or sport.

SYNONYMS **1** a large ploughed field
meadow, pasture, paddock, grassland.
2 a football field **pitch,** ground; Brit. informal
park. **3** the field of biotechnology **area,**
sphere, discipline, province, department,
domain, territory, branch, subject. **4** your
field of vision **scope,** range, sweep, reach,
extent. **5** she is well ahead of the field
competitors, entrants, competition,
applicants, candidates, runners.

▸ verb **1** Cricket Baseball attempt to catch or stop
the ball after it has been hit. **2** try to deal
with something. **3** choose someone to play
in a game or to stand in an election.

SYNONYMS **1** she fielded the ball **catch,**
stop, retrieve, return, throw back.
2 fielding a great team **send out,** play,
put up, assemble, offer. **3** he fielded some
awkward questions **deal with,** handle,
cope with, answer, reply to, respond to.

■ **field day** a good opportunity to do
something. **field events** athletic sports
other than races. **field marshal** the highest
rank of officer in the British army. **field
sports** hunting, shooting, and fishing. **play
the field** informal have a series of casual
sexual relationships.
□ **fielder** noun.

fiend ▸ noun **1** an evil spirit. **2** a very wicked
or cruel person. **3** informal a person who is
very enthusiastic about something: an
exercise fiend.

fiendish ▸ adjective **1** very cruel or
unpleasant. **2** informal very difficult.
□ **fiendishly** adverb.

fierce ▸ adjective **1** violent or aggressive.
2 strong or powerful.

SYNONYMS **1** a fierce black mastiff
ferocious, savage, vicious, aggressive.
2 fierce competition **aggressive**, cut-
throat, keen, intense, strong, relentless.
3 fierce jealousy **intense**, powerful,
vehement, passionate, impassioned,
fervent, ardent. **4** a fierce wind
powerful, strong, violent, forceful,
stormy, howling, raging, tempestuous.
ANTONYMS gentle, mild.

□ **fiercely** adverb **fierceness** noun.

✔ **i** before **e** except after **c**: fie**rc**e.

fiery ▸ adjective (**fierier, fieriest**) **1** consisting
of or resembling fire. **2** quick-tempered or
passionate.

SYNONYMS **1** a fiery blast **burning**,
blazing, flaming, on fire, ablaze. **2** a fiery
red **bright**, brilliant, vivid, intense, rich.
3 her fiery spirit **passionate**, impassioned,
excitable, spirited, quick-tempered,
volatile, explosive, impetuous.

fiesta ▶ noun (in Spanish-speaking countries) a religious festival.

fife ▶ noun a small, high-pitched flute used in military bands.

fifteen ▶ cardinal number one more than fourteen; 15. (Roman numeral: **xv** or **XV**.)
□ **fifteenth** ordinal number.

fifth ▶ ordinal number **1** being number five in a sequence; 5th. **2** (**a fifth** or **one fifth**) each of five equal parts of something.
■ **fifth column** a group within a country at war who are working for its enemies.

fifty ▶ cardinal number (plural **fifties**) ten less than sixty; 50. (Roman numeral: **l** or **L**.)
■ **fifty-fifty** with equal shares or chances.
□ **fiftieth** ordinal number.

fig ▶ noun a soft, sweet fruit with many small seeds.

fight ▶ verb (**fights, fighting, fought**) **1** take part in a violent struggle involving physical force. **2** (**fight someone off**) defend yourself against an attacker. **3** struggle to overcome or prevent.

> SYNONYMS **1** *two men were fighting* **brawl,** exchange blows, scuffle, grapple, wrestle; informal scrap; Brit. informal **have a punch-up;** N. Amer. informal **rough-house;** Austral./NZ informal stoush. **2** *he fought in Vietnam* **do battle,** serve your country, go to war, take up arms, engage, meet, clash, skirmish. **3** *a war fought for freedom* **wage,** engage in, conduct, prosecute, undertake. **4** *they are always fighting* **quarrel,** argue, row, bicker, squabble, fall out; informal scrap. **5** *fighting against injustice* **campaign,** strive, battle, struggle, contend, crusade, agitate, lobby, push, press. **6** *they will fight the decision* **oppose,** contest, confront, challenge, appeal against, combat, dispute. **7** *Don fought the urge to cry* **repress,** restrain, suppress, stifle, smother, hold back, fight back, keep in check, curb, choke back; informal keep the lid on, cork up.

▶ noun a period of fighting.

> SYNONYMS **1** *a fight outside a club* **brawl,** scuffle, disturbance, fisticuffs, fracas, melee, skirmish, clash; informal scrap, dust-up; Brit. informal **punch-up;** N. Amer. informal rough house; Austral./NZ informal stoush. **2** *a heavyweight boxing match* **boxing match,** bout, match, contest. **3** *the fight against terrorism* **battle,** engagement, conflict, struggle, war, campaign, crusade, action, hostilities. **4** *a fight with my girlfriend* **argument,** quarrel, squabble, row, wrangle, disagreement, falling-out, dispute; informal tiff, spat, scrap; Brit. informal barney, ding-dong. **5** *their fight for control of the company* **struggle,** battle, campaign, push, effort. **6** *she had no fight left in her* **will,** resistance,

spirit, pluck, grit, strength, backbone, determination, resolution, resolve.

■ **fighting chance** a possibility of succeeding if you make an effort. **fighting fit** in very good health. **fight shy of** be unwilling to do or accept.

fighter ▶ noun **1** a person or animal that fights. **2** a fast military aircraft designed for attacking other aircraft.

> SYNONYMS **1** *a guerrilla fighter* **soldier,** fighting man/woman, warrior, combatant, serviceman, servicewoman; (**fighters**) troops, personnel, militia. **2** *the fighter was knocked to the ground* **boxer,** pugilist, prizefighter, wrestler.

figment ▶ noun a thing that exists only in the imagination.

figurative ▶ adjective **1** not using words in their literal sense; metaphorical. **2** (of art) representing things as they appear in real life.
□ **figuratively** adverb.

figure ▶ noun **1** a number or numerical symbol. **2** the shape of a person's body, especially that of a woman. **3** an important or distinctive person. **4** a shape defined by one or more lines. **5** a diagram or drawing.

> SYNONYMS **1** *the figure for April* **statistic,** number, quantity, amount, level, total, sum; (**figures**) data, statistics, information. **2** *the second figure was 9* **digit,** numeral, character, symbol. **3** *he can't put a figure on it* **price,** cost, amount, value, valuation. **4** *her petite figure* **shape,** outline, form, silhouette, proportions, physique, build, frame. **5** *a figure of authority* **person,** personage, individual, character, personality, celebrity. **6** *geometrical figures* **shape,** pattern, design, motif. **7** *figure 1 shows an ignition circuit* **diagram,** illustration, drawing, picture, plate.

▶ verb (**figures, figuring, figured**) **1** play a significant part. **2** (**figure something out**) informal understand something. **3** N. Amer. informal think; consider.

> SYNONYMS *he figures in many myths* **feature,** appear, be featured, be mentioned, be referred to.

■ **figure of speech** a word or phrase used in a way different from its usual sense. **figure skating** ice skating in set patterns.

figurehead ▶ noun **1** a leader without real power. **2** a wooden statue of a person at the front of a sailing ship.

figurine ▶ noun a small statue of a human form.

Fijian /fee-jee-uhn/ ▶ noun a person from Fiji. ▶ adjective relating to Fiji.

filament ▶ noun **1** a long, thin thread-like piece of something. **2** a metal wire in a light bulb, which glows when an electric current is passed through it.

filbert ▸ noun a type of hazelnut.

filch ▸ verb informal steal something.

file¹ ▸ noun **1** a folder or box for keeping loose papers together. **2** a collection of computer data stored under a single name. **3** a line of people or things one behind another.

> SYNONYMS **1** *he opened the file* **folder**, portfolio, binder. **2** *we have files on all of you* **dossier**, document, record, report, data, information, documentation, archives.

▸ verb (**files, filing, filed**) **1** place in a file. **2** officially present a legal document, application, etc. so that it can be dealt with. **3** walk one behind the other.

> SYNONYMS **1** *file the documents correctly* **categorize**, classify, organize, put in order, order, arrange, catalogue, store, archive. **2** *two women have filed a civil suit* **bring**, press, lodge.

file² ▸ noun a tool with a roughened surface, used for smoothing or shaping.

▸ verb (**files, filing, filed**) smooth or shape with a file.

> SYNONYMS *she filed her nails* **smooth**, buff, rub down, polish, shape, scrape, abrade, rasp, manicure.

filial ▸ adjective having to do with a son or daughter.

filibuster ▸ noun (in parliament) a very long speech made to prevent the passing of a new law.

filigree ▸ noun delicate ornamental work of thin wire.

filings ▸ plural noun small particles rubbed off by a file.

Filipino ▸ noun (plural **Filipinos**; feminine **Filipina**, plural **Filipinas**) **1** a person from the Philippines. **2** the national language of the Philippines.

▸ adjective relating to the Philippines or to Filipinos.

fill ▸ verb **1** make or become full. **2** block up a hole or gap. **3** appoint a person to a vacant post. **4** hold a particular position or role.

> SYNONYMS **1** *he filled a bowl* **fill up**, top up, charge. **2** *guests filled the room* **crowd into**, throng, pack (into), occupy, squeeze into, cram (into). **3** *he began filling his shelves* **stock**, pack, load, supply, replenish. **4** *fill all the holes with putty* **block up**, stop (up), plug, seal, caulk. **5** *the perfume filled the room* **pervade**, permeate, suffuse, penetrate, infuse. **6** *the person who fills this vacancy* **occupy**, hold, take up.
> ANTONYMS empty, clear, leave.

▸ noun (**your fill**) as much as you want or can bear.

■ **fill in** act as a substitute. **fill something in** complete a form. **fill someone in** give someone information.

filler ▸ noun something used to fill a hole or gap, or to increase bulk.

fillet ▸ noun **1** a piece of meat without bones. **2** a piece of fish with the bones taken out. **3** a decorative band or ribbon worn round the head.

▸ verb (**fillets, filleting, filleted**) take the bones out of a piece of fish.

filling ▸ noun a quantity or piece of material used to fill something.

> SYNONYMS *filling for cushions* **stuffing**, padding, wadding, filler, contents.

▸ adjective (of food) giving you a pleasantly full feeling.

> SYNONYMS *a filling meal* **substantial**, hearty, ample, satisfying, square, heavy, stodgy.

fillip ▸ noun a stimulus or boost.

filly ▸ noun (plural **fillies**) **1** a young female horse. **2** humorous a lively girl or young woman.

film ▸ noun **1** a thin flexible strip coated with light-sensitive material, used in a camera to make photographs or motion pictures. **2** a story or event recorded by a camera and shown in a cinema or on television. **3** material in the form of a very thin flexible sheet. **4** a thin layer of something on a surface.

> SYNONYMS **1** *a film of sweat* **layer**, coat, coating, covering, cover, skin, patina, tissue. **2** *Emma was watching a film* **movie**, picture, feature film, motion picture, video, DVD. **3** *she would like to work in film* **cinema**, movies, the pictures, films, the silver screen, the big screen.

▸ verb make a film of; record on film.

> SYNONYMS **1** *he filmed the next scene* **photograph**, record on film, shoot, capture on film, video. **2** *his eyes had filmed over* **cloud**, mist, haze, blur.

filmy ▸ adjective (**filmier, filmiest**) thin and almost transparent.

filter ▸ noun **1** a device or substance that lets liquid or gas pass through but holds back solid particles. **2** a screen, plate, or layer that absorbs some of the light passing through it. **3** Brit. (at a junction) a set of lights that lets vehicles turn but stops traffic waiting to go straight ahead.

> SYNONYMS *a carbon filter* **strainer**, sifter, sieve, gauze, mesh, net.

▸ verb (**filters, filtering, filtered**) **1** pass through a filter. **2** move gradually in or out of somewhere.

SYNONYMS **1** *the farmers filter the water* **sieve,** strain, sift, clarify, purify, refine, treat. **2** *the rain had filtered through her jacket* **seep,** percolate, leak, trickle, ooze, leach.

filth ▸ noun **1** disgusting dirt. **2** obscene and offensive language or material.

filthy ▸ adjective (**filthier, filthiest**) **1** disgustingly dirty. **2** obscene and offensive. **3** informal very unpleasant.

SYNONYMS **1** *the room was filthy* **dirty,** mucky, grimy, foul, squalid, sordid, soiled, stained, polluted, contaminated, unwashed. **2** *filthy jokes* **obscene,** rude, vulgar, dirty, smutty, improper, coarse, bawdy, lewd; informal blue. **3** *he was in a filthy mood* **bad,** foul, irritable, grumpy, grouchy, cross; informal snappy; Brit. informal shirty, stroppy; N. Amer. informal cranky, ornery.
ANTONYMS clean, pleasant.

filtrate ▸ noun a liquid which has passed through a filter.

filtration ▸ noun the action of passing something through a filter.

fin ▸ noun **1** a flattened projection on the body of a fish or whale, used for swimming and balancing. **2** an underwater swimmer's flipper. **3** a projection on an aircraft, rocket, etc., for making it more stable.

final ▸ adjective **1** coming at the end; last. **2** allowing no further doubt or dispute.

SYNONYMS **1** *the final year of study* **last,** closing, concluding, finishing, end, ultimate, eventual. **2** *their decisions are final* **irrevocable,** unalterable, absolute, conclusive, irrefutable, incontrovertible, indisputable, unchallengeable, binding.
ANTONYMS first, provisional.

▸ noun **1** the last game in a tournament, which will decide the overall winner. **2** (**finals**) Brit. a series of exams at the end of a degree course.

finale /fi-nah-li/ ▸ noun the last part of a piece of music or entertainment.

SYNONYMS **climax,** culmination, end, ending, finish, close, conclusion, termination, denouement.
ANTONYMS opening.

finalist ▸ noun a person or team competing in a final.

finality ▸ noun the fact or quality of being final.

finalize (or **finalise**) ▸ verb (**finalizes, finalizing, finalized**) complete or agree on the last part of a plan, agreement, etc.

finally ▸ adverb **1** after a long time and much difficulty or delay. **2** as a final item or stage in a series.

SYNONYMS **1** *she finally got married* **eventually,** ultimately, in the end, after a long time, at (long) last, in the long run, in the fullness of time. **2** *finally, attach the ribbon* **lastly,** last, in conclusion. **3** *this should finally dispel that myth* **conclusively,** irrevocably, decisively, definitively, for ever, for good, once and for all.

finance ▸ noun **1** the management of large amounts of money by governments or large companies. **2** money to support an enterprise. **3** (**finances**) the money held by a state, organization, or person.

SYNONYMS **1** *he knows about finance* **financial affairs,** money matters, economics, commerce, business, investment. **2** *short-term finance* **funds,** money, capital, cash, resources, assets, reserves, funding.

▸ verb (**finances, financing, financed**) provide funding for.

SYNONYMS *a project financed by grants* **fund,** pay for, back, capitalize, endow, subsidize, invest in, sponsor; N. Amer. informal bankroll.

financial ▸ adjective relating to finance.

SYNONYMS **monetary,** money, economic, pecuniary, fiscal, banking, commercial, business, investment.

□ **financially** adverb.

financier ▸ noun a person who manages money for large organizations.

finch ▸ noun a small bird with a short, stubby bill.

find ▸ verb (**finds, finding, found**) **1** discover by chance or by searching. **2** discover that something is the case. **3** work out or confirm by research or calculation. **4** (of a law court) officially declare that a defendant is guilty or not guilty.

SYNONYMS **1** *I found the book I wanted* **locate,** spot, pinpoint, unearth, obtain, search out, track down, root out, come across/upon, run across/into, chance on, happen on, stumble on, encounter; informal bump into. **2** *they found a cure for rabies* **discover,** invent, come up with, hit on. **3** *you'll find that it's a lively area* **discover,** become aware, realize, observe, notice, note, learn. **4** *I find this strange* **consider,** think, feel to be, look on as, view as, see as, judge, deem, regard as. **5** *he was found guilty* **judge,** deem, rule, declare, pronounce.
ANTONYMS lose.

▸ noun a valuable or interesting discovery.

SYNONYMS **1** *an archaeological find* **discovery,** acquisition. **2** *this table is a* *real find* **bargain,** godsend, boon, catch, asset; informal good buy.

■ **find someone/thing out 1** discover information. **2** discover that someone has lied or been dishonest.
□ **finder** noun.

finding ▸ noun a conclusion reached as a result of an enquiry or trial.

fine¹ ▸ adjective **1** of very high quality. **2** satisfactory. **3** in good health and feeling well. **4** (of the weather) bright and clear. **5** (of a thread, strand, or hair) thin. **6** consisting of small particles. **7** delicate or complex. **8** difficult to distinguish or describe accurately.

SYNONYMS **1** *fine wines* **good,** choice, select, prime, quality, special, superior, of distinction, premium, classic, vintage. **2** *a fine piece of work* **excellent,** first-class, first-rate, great, exceptional, outstanding, splendid, magnificent, exquisite, superb, wonderful, superlative; informal A1, top-notch. **3** *a fine fellow* **worthy,** admirable, praiseworthy, laudable, upright, upstanding, respectable. **4** *that's fine, but it's not enough* **all right,** acceptable, suitable, good (enough), passable, satisfactory, adequate, reasonable, tolerable; informal OK. **5** *I feel fine* **good,** well, healthy, all right, (fighting) fit, blooming, thriving, in good shape/condition; informal OK, great, in the pink. **6** *a fine day* **fair,** dry, bright, clear, sunny, cloudless. **7** *fine clothes* **elegant,** stylish, expensive, smart, chic, fashionable, fancy, sumptuous, lavish, opulent; informal flashy. **8** *a fine mind* **keen,** quick, alert, sharp, bright, brilliant, astute, clever, intelligent. **9** *fine china* **delicate,** dainty, thin, light, fragile. **10** *fine hair* **thin,** light, delicate, wispy, flyaway. **11** *a fine point* **sharp,** keen, acute, sharp, razor-sharp. **12** *fine material* **sheer,** light, lightweight, thin, flimsy, diaphanous, filmy, see-through. **13** *fine sand* **fine-grained,** powdery, dusty, ground, crushed. **14** *fine details* **intricate,** delicate, detailed, elaborate, meticulous. **15** *a fine distinction* **subtle,** ultra-fine, nice, hair-splitting.
ANTONYMS everyday, poor, contemptible, ill, dull, wet, coarse.

■ **fine art** art such as painting or sculpture.
fine-tune make small adjustments to.
with a fine-tooth comb (or **fine-toothed comb**) with a very thorough search or examination.
□ **finely** adverb **fineness** noun.

fine² ▸ noun a sum of money that has to be paid as a punishment.

SYNONYMS *heavy fines* **financial penalty,** forfeit, damages, sanction, fee, excess charge.

▸ verb (**fines, fining, fined**) make a person, company, etc. pay a fine.

finery ▸ noun smart, colourful clothes or decoration.

finesse /fi-**ness**/ ▸ noun **1** elegant or delicate skill. **2** subtle skill in handling people or situations.

finger ▸ noun **1** each of the four long, thin parts attached to either hand (or five, if the thumb is included). **2** an object shaped like a finger. **3** an amount of alcohol in a glass equivalent to the width of a finger.

SYNONYMS **digit.**

▸ verb (**fingers, fingering, fingered**) touch or feel with the fingers.

SYNONYMS *she fingered her brooch* **touch,** feel, handle, stroke, rub, caress, fondle, toy with, play (about/around) with, fiddle with.

fingerboard ▸ noun a flat strip on the neck of a stringed instrument, against which you press the strings.

fingering ▸ noun a way of using the fingers to play a musical instrument.

fingernail ▸ noun the nail on the upper surface of the tip of each finger.

fingerprint ▸ noun a mark made on a surface by a person's fingertip, which can be used to identify the person.
▸ verb record the fingerprints of.

finial /**fin**-i-uhl/ ▸ noun a decorative part at the top of a roof, wall, or other structure.

finicky ▸ adjective fussy and hard to please.

finish ▸ verb **1** bring or come to an end. **2** (**finish with**) have nothing more to do with. **3** reach the end of a race or other competition. **4** (**finish someone off**) kill or completely defeat someone. **5** give an article an attractive surface appearance.

SYNONYMS **1** *Pam finished her work* **complete,** end, conclude, terminate, wind up, round off; informal wrap up, sew up, polish off. **2** *Hitch finished his dinner* **consume,** eat, devour, drink, finish off, polish off, gulp (down), use (up), exhaust, empty, drain, get through; informal down. **3** *the programme has finished* **end,** come to an end, stop, conclude, come to a close, cease. **4** *finished in a black lacquer* **coat,** surface, texture.
ANTONYMS start.

▸ noun **1** an end or final stage. **2** the place at which a race or competition ends. **3** the way in which a manufactured article is finished.

SYNONYMS **1** *the finish of filming* **end,** ending, completion, conclusion, close, termination, finale, denouement. **2** *a shiny finish* **surface,** texture, coating,

covering, lacquer, glaze, veneer, gloss, patina, sheen, lustre.
ANTONYMS start.

■ **finishing school** a college where girls are taught how to behave in fashionable society.
□ **finisher** noun.

finite /fy-nyt/ ▸ adjective limited in size or extent.

Finn ▸ noun a person from Finland.

Finnish ▸ noun the language of the Finns.
▸ adjective relating to Finland or the Finns.

fiord → FJORD.

fir ▸ noun an evergreen coniferous tree with needle-shaped leaves.

fire ▸ noun **1** the light, heat, and smoke produced when something burns. **2** an occasion in which a building is damaged or destroyed by a fire. **3** wood or coal that is burning for heating or cooking. **4** a heater for a room that uses electricity or gas as fuel. **5** passionate emotion or enthusiasm. **6** the firing of guns.

SYNONYMS **1** *a fire broke out* **blaze,** conflagration, inferno, flames, burning, combustion. **2** *he lacked fire* **dynamism,** energy, vigour, animation, vitality, exuberance, zest, elan, passion, zeal, spirit, verve, vivacity, enthusiasm; informal go, get-up-and-go, oomph. **3** *machine-gun fire* **gunfire,** firing, shooting, bombardment, shelling, volley, salvo, hail.

▸ verb (**fires, firing, fired**) **1** send a bullet, shell, etc. from a gun or other weapon. **2** direct a rapid series of questions or statements towards someone. **3** informal dismiss an employee from a job. **4** supply a furnace or power station with fuel. **5** stimulate. **6** bake or dry pottery or bricks in a kiln. **7** old use set fire to.

SYNONYMS **1** *howitzers firing shells* **launch,** shoot, discharge, let fly with. **2** *someone fired a gun* **shoot,** discharge, let off, set off. **3** *he was fired* **dismiss,** discharge, give someone their notice, lay off, let go; informal sack. **4** *the story fired my imagination* **stimulate,** stir up, excite, awaken, rouse, inflame, animate, inspire, motivate.

■ **fire brigade** Brit. a team of people employed to put out fires. **fire door** a strong door for preventing the spread of fire. **fire drill** a practice of the emergency procedures to be used in case of fire. **fire engine** a vehicle carrying firefighters and their equipment. **fire escape** a staircase or ladder for escaping from a burning building. **fire extinguisher** a device that sprays a jet of liquid, foam, or gas to put out a fire. **the firing line 1** the front line of troops in a battle. **2** a situation where you are likely to be criticized. **firing squad** a group of soldiers ordered to shoot a condemned person.

firearm ▸ noun a rifle, pistol, or other portable gun.

fireball ▸ noun a ball of flames.

firebomb ▸ noun a bomb intended to cause a fire.

firebrand ▸ noun a person who passionately supports a particular cause.

firebreak ▸ noun a strip of open space cleared in a forest to stop a fire from spreading.

firecracker ▸ noun a firework that makes a loud bang.

firefighter ▸ noun a person whose job is to put out fires.

firefly ▸ noun (plural **fireflies**) a kind of beetle which glows in the dark.

fireguard ▸ noun a protective screen or grid in front of an open fire.

fireman ▸ noun (plural **firemen**) a male firefighter.

fireplace ▸ noun a space at the base of a chimney for lighting a fire.

firepower ▸ noun the destructive capacity of guns, missiles, or forces.

fireproof ▸ adjective able to withstand fire or great heat.

firestorm ▸ noun a very fierce fire fanned by strong currents of air.

firewall ▸ noun a part of a computer system that prevents people from seeing the information stored in it unless they are authorized to do so.

firewood ▸ noun wood that is burnt as fuel.

firework ▸ noun **1** a device consisting of a small container of chemicals that produces spectacular effects and explosions when it is lit. **2** (**fireworks**) an outburst of anger or a display of skill.

firm¹ ▸ adjective **1** not giving way under pressure. **2** solidly in place and stable. **3** having steady power or strength. **4** showing determination and strength of character. **5** fixed or definite.

SYNONYMS **1** *the ground is fairly firm* **hard,** solid, unyielding, resistant, compacted, compressed, dense, stiff, rigid, set. **2** *firm foundations* **secure,** stable, steady, strong, fixed, fast, tight, immovable, rooted, stationary, motionless. **3** *I was very firm | a firm supporter* **resolute,** determined, decided, resolved, steadfast, adamant, emphatic, insistent, single-minded, wholehearted, unfaltering, unwavering, unflinching, unswerving, unbending, committed. **4** *firm friends* **close,** good, boon, intimate, inseparable, dear, special, constant, devoted, loving, faithful, long-standing, steady, steadfast.

f

5 *firm plans* **definite,** fixed, settled, decided, cut-and-dried, established, confirmed, agreed.
ANTONYMS soft, unstable, irresolute, indefinite.

▸ verb make firm.
□ **firmly** adverb **firmness** noun.

firm² ▸ noun a business organization.

SYNONYMS *an accountancy firm* **business,** company, concern, enterprise, organization, corporation, conglomerate, office, bureau, agency, consortium; informal outfit, operation.

firmament ▸ noun literary the heavens; the sky.

first ▸ ordinal number **1** coming before all others in time, order, or importance. **2** before doing something else. **3** Brit. a place in the top grade in an exam for a degree. **4** informal something that has never happened or been done before.

SYNONYMS **1** *the first chapter* **earliest,** initial, opening, introductory. **2** *first principles* **fundamental,** basic, rudimentary, primary, key, cardinal, central, chief, vital, essential. **3** *our first priority* **foremost,** principal, highest, greatest, paramount, top, main, overriding, central, core; informal number-one. **4** *first prize* **top,** best, prime, premier, winner's, winning. **5** *that's a first* **novelty,** innovation, departure, break with tradition.
ANTONYMS last.

■ **first aid** emergency medical help given to a sick or injured person. **first class 1** the best accommodation in a train, ship, etc. **2** very good. **first-degree** (of burns) causing only reddening of the skin. **first-hand** from the original source or personal experience; direct. **first lady** the wife of the President of the United States. **first name** a name given to someone when they are born or baptized. **first-rate** very good.
□ **firstly** adverb.

firstborn ▸ noun the first child to be born to someone.

firth ▸ noun a narrow channel of the sea that runs inland.

fiscal ▸ adjective relating to the income received by a government, especially from taxes.
□ **fiscally** adverb.

fish ▸ noun (plural **fish** or **fishes**) **1** a cold-blooded animal with a backbone, gills and fins, living in water. **2** the flesh of fish as food.

▸ verb **1** try to catch fish. **2** (**fish something out**) take something out of water or a container. **3** (**fish for**) search or feel for something hidden. **4** (**fish for**) try to get something: *fishing for compliments.*

SYNONYMS **1** *some people were fishing in the lake* **go fishing,** angle, trawl. **2** *she fished for her purse* **search,** delve, look, hunt, grope, fumble, ferret, rummage.

fisherman ▸ noun (plural **fishermen**) a person who catches fish for a living or as a sport.

fishery ▸ noun (plural **fisheries**) a place where fish are reared for food, or caught in large quantities.

fisheye lens ▸ noun a highly curved lens for a camera, covering a very wide angle of view.

fishmonger ▸ noun a person who sells fish for food.

fishnet ▸ noun an open mesh fabric resembling a fishing net.

fishwife ▸ noun (plural **fishwives**) a woman with a loud, coarse voice.

fishy ▸ adjective (**fishier, fishiest**) **1** resembling fish. **2** informal causing feelings of doubt or suspicion.

fissile ▸ adjective **1** able to undergo nuclear fission. **2** (of rock) easily split.

fission ▸ noun **1** the action of splitting into two or more parts. **2** a reaction in which an atomic nucleus splits in two, releasing a great deal of energy. **3** reproduction by means of a cell dividing into two or more new cells.

fissure ▸ noun a long, narrow crack.

fist ▸ noun a person's hand when the fingers are bent in towards the palm and held there tightly.
□ **fistful** noun.

fisticuffs ▸ plural noun fighting with the fists.

fit¹ ▸ adjective (**fitter, fittest**) **1** of a suitable quality, standard, or type. **2** in good health.

SYNONYMS **1** *a fit subject for a book* **suitable,** appropriate, suited, apposite, fitting, good enough, apt, -worthy. **2** *not fit to look after children* **competent,** able, capable, ready, prepared, equipped. **3** *tanned and fit* **healthy,** well, in good health, in (good) shape, in trim, in good condition, fighting fit, athletic, muscular, strapping, strong, robust, hale and hearty.
ANTONYMS unsuitable, incapable, unfit.

▸ verb (**fits, fitting, fitted**) **1** be the right shape and size for. **2** be able to occupy a particular position or space. **3** fix into place. **4** provide with a part or attachment; equip. **5** be in harmony with; match. **6** (**fit in**) be well suited.

SYNONYMS **1** *having carpets fitted* **lay,** install, put in, position, place, fix, arrange. **2** *cameras fitted with autofocus* **equip,** provide, supply, fit out, furnish. **3** *they fitted the slabs together* **join,** connect, piece together, attach, unite, link. **4** *a sentence that fits his crime* **be appropriate to,** suit, match, correspond to, tally with, go with, accord with. **5** *an MSc fits you for a scientific career* **qualify,** prepare, make ready, train.

▸ **noun** the way in which something fits.
□ **fitter** noun.

fit² ▸ **noun 1** a sudden attack when a person makes violent, uncontrolled movements. **2** a sudden attack of coughing, fainting, etc. **3** a sudden burst of strong feeling.

> SYNONYMS **1** *an epileptic fit* **convulsion,** spasm, paroxysm, seizure, attack. **2** *a fit of the giggles* **outbreak,** outburst, attack, bout, spell. **3** *mum would have a fit* **tantrum,** frenzy; informal paddy, heart attack; N. Amer. informal blowout.

▸ **verb** (**fits, fitting, fitted**) have a fit or convulsion.
■ **in fits and starts** with irregular bursts of activity.

fitful ▸ **adjective** not steady or continuous.
□ **fitfully** adverb.

fitment ▸ **noun** Brit. a fixed item of furniture or piece of equipment.

fitness ▸ **noun 1** the condition of being physically fit and healthy. **2** the quality of being suitable for a particular role or task.

> SYNONYMS **1** *polo requires tremendous fitness* **good health,** strength, robustness, vigour, athleticism, toughness, stamina. **2** *his fitness for active service* **suitability,** capability, competence, ability, aptitude, readiness, preparedness.

fitted ▸ **adjective** made to fill a space or to cover something closely.

fitting ▸ **noun 1** a small part attached to furniture or equipment. **2** (**fittings**) items which are fixed in a building but can be removed when the owner moves. **3** a time when someone tries on an item of clothing that is being made or altered.

> SYNONYMS **1** *a light fitting* **attachment,** part, piece, component, accessory, apparatus. **2** *bathroom fittings* **furnishings,** furniture, fixtures, fitments, equipment.

▸ **adjective** appropriate.

> SYNONYMS *a fitting conclusion* **apt,** appropriate, suitable, apposite, fit, proper, right, seemly, correct.
> ANTONYMS unsuitable.

□ **fittingly** adverb.

five ▸ **cardinal number** one more than four; 5. (Roman numeral: **v** or **V**.)

▸ **noun** (**fives**) a game in which a ball is hit with a gloved hand or a bat against a wall.

fiver ▸ **noun** Brit. informal a five-pound note.

fix ▸ **verb 1** attach or position securely. **2** mend or repair. **3** decide or settle

on. **4** make arrangements for. **5** make something unchanging or permanent. **6** informal dishonestly influence the outcome of.

> SYNONYMS **1** *signs were fixed to lamp posts* **fasten,** attach, affix, secure, connect, couple, link, install, stick, glue, pin, nail, screw, bolt, clamp, clip. **2** *his words are fixed in my memory* **stick,** lodge, embed. **3** *his eyes were fixed on the ground* **focus,** direct, level, point, train. **4** *he fixed my car* **repair,** mend, put right, get working, restore. **5** *Jim fixed it for us to see the show* **arrange,** organize, contrive, manage, engineer; informal swing, wangle. **6** *Laura was fixing her hair* **arrange,** put in order, adjust, style, groom, comb, brush; informal do. **7** *I'll fix supper* **prepare,** cook, make, get; informal rustle up; Brit. informal knock up. **8** *let's fix a date* **decide on,** select, choose, settle, set, arrange, establish, allot, designate, name, appoint, specify. **9** (**fixed**) *at a fixed price* **predetermined,** set, established, arranged, specified, decided, agreed, determined, confirmed, prescribed, definite, defined, explicit, precise. **10** *the fight was fixed* **rig,** tamper with, skew, influence; informal fiddle.
> ANTONYMS remove.

▸ **noun** informal **1** a difficult or awkward situation. **2** a dose of an addictive drug. **3** an act of fixing something.

> SYNONYMS **1** *they are in a bit of a fix* **predicament,** plight, difficulty, awkward situation, corner, tight spot, mess; informal pickle, jam, hole, scrape, bind. **2** *the result was a fix* **fraud,** swindle, trick, charade, sham; informal set-up, fiddle.

□ **fixer** noun.

fixate ▸ **verb** (**fixates, fixating, fixated**) (**fixate on** or **be fixated on**) be obsessed with.

fixation ▸ **noun** an obsessive interest in someone or something.

fixative ▸ **noun** a substance used to fix or protect something.

fixity ▸ **noun** the state of being unchanging or permanent.

fixture ▸ **noun 1** a piece of equipment or furniture which is fixed in position. **2** (**fixtures**) articles attached to a house that normally remain in place when the owner moves. **3** Brit. a sports event arranged to take place on a particular date.

fizz ▸ **verb** make a hissing sound, like gas escaping in bubbles from a liquid.

> SYNONYMS *the mixture fizzed like mad* **bubble,** sparkle, effervesce, froth.

▸ **noun** the sound of fizzing or the quality of being fizzy.

SYNONYMS 1 *the fizz in champagne* **bubbles,** sparkle, fizziness, effervescence, gassiness, froth. **2** *the fizz of the static* **crackle,** buzz, hiss, white noise.

fizzle ▸ verb (fizzles, fizzling, fizzled) **1** make a weak hissing sound. **2** (**fizzle out**) end or fail in a weak or disappointing way.

fizzy ▸ adjective (fizzier, fizziest) (of a drink) containing bubbles of gas.

SYNONYMS sparkling, effervescent, carbonated, gassy, bubbly, frothy. **ANTONYMS** still, flat.

fjord (or **fiord**) /fyord, fee-ord/ ▸ noun a long, narrow inlet of the sea between high cliffs, especially in Norway.

fl. ▸ abbreviation fluid.

flab ▸ noun informal excess fat on a person's body.

flabbergasted ▸ adjective informal very surprised.

flabby ▸ adjective (flabbier, flabbiest) (of a part of a person's body) fat and floppy. □ **flabbiness** noun.

flaccid /flass-id/ ▸ adjective soft and limp. □ **flaccidity** noun.

flack → **FLAK.**

flag¹ ▸ noun a piece of cloth that is attached to a pole or rope and used as a symbol of a country or organization or as a signal.

SYNONYMS *the Irish flag* **banner,** standard, ensign, pennant, streamer, colours; Brit. pendant.

▸ verb (flags, flagging, flagged) **1** mark something as needing attention. **2** (**flag someone down**) signal to a driver to stop.

flag² (or **flagstone**) ▸ noun a flat stone slab used for paving.

flag³ ▸ verb (flags, flagging, flagged) become tired or less enthusiastic.

SYNONYMS 1 *they were flagging towards the finish* **tire,** grow tired, weaken, grow weak, wilt, droop. **2** *my energy flags in the afternoon* **fade,** decline, wane, ebb, diminish, decrease, lessen, dwindle. **ANTONYMS** revive.

flagellate /fla-juh-layt/ ▸ verb whip someone as a form of religious punishment or for sexual pleasure. □ **flagellation** noun.

flagon ▸ noun a large bottle or jug for wine, cider, or beer.

flagpole (or **flagstaff**) ▸ noun a pole used for flying a flag.

flagrant /flay-gruhnt/ ▸ adjective very obvious and unashamed.

SYNONYMS blatant, glaring, obvious, conspicuous, barefaced, shameless, brazen, undisguised.

□ **flagrantly** adverb.

flagship ▸ noun **1** the ship in a fleet which carries the admiral in command. **2** the best or most important thing owned or produced by an organization.

flail ▸ verb **1** swing something wildly. **2** (**flail around** or **about**) move around in an uncontrolled way.
▸ noun a tool or machine that is swung to separate grains of wheat from the husks.

flair ▸ noun **1** a natural ability or talent. **2** stylishness.

SYNONYMS 1 *a flair for publicity* **aptitude,** talent, gift, instinct, ability, facility, knack, skill. **2** *she dressed with flair* **style,** elegance, panache, dash, elan, poise, taste; informal class.

❗ Don't confuse **flair** with **flare**, which means 'burn' or 'gradually become wider'.

flak (or **flack**) ▸ noun **1** anti-aircraft fire. **2** strong criticism.

flake ▸ noun a small, flat, very thin piece of something.

SYNONYMS *a flake of paint* **sliver,** wafer, shaving, paring, chip, fragment, scrap, shred.

▸ verb (flakes, flaking, flaked) **1** come away from a surface in flakes. **2** separate into flakes. **3** (**flake out**) informal fall asleep or drop from exhaustion.

SYNONYMS *the paint was flaking off* **peel** (**off**), chip, blister, come off.

□ **flaky** adjective.

flambé /flom-bay/ ▸ verb (flambés, flambéing, flambéed) cover food with spirits and set it on fire briefly.

flamboyant ▸ adjective **1** very confident and lively. **2** brightly coloured or highly decorated.

SYNONYMS 1 *her flamboyant personality* **ostentatious,** exuberant, confident, lively, animated, vibrant, vivacious. **2** *a flamboyant cravat* **colourful,** bright, vibrant, vivid, dazzling, bold, showy, gaudy, garish, loud; informal jazzy, flashy. **ANTONYMS** restrained.

□ **flamboyance** noun **flamboyantly** adverb.

flame ▸ noun **1** a glowing stream of burning gas produced by something on fire. **2** a brilliant orange-red colour. **3** informal a lover.

SYNONYMS 1 *a sheet of flames* **fire,** blaze, conflagration, inferno. **2** *an old flame* **sweetheart,** boyfriend, girlfriend, lover, partner.

▸ verb (flames, flaming, flamed) **1** give off flames. **2** set on fire. **3** (of a strong emotion) appear suddenly and fiercely. **4** informal send insulting email messages to.

flamenco ▸ noun a lively style of Spanish guitar music accompanied by singing and dancing.

flamingo ▸ noun (plural **flamingos** or **flamingoes**) a wading bird with mainly pink or red feathers and a long neck and legs.

flammable ▸ adjective easily set on fire.

flan ▸ noun a baked dish consisting of an open pastry case with a savoury or sweet filling.

flange ▸ noun a projecting flat rim for strengthening an object or attaching it to something.
□ **flanged** adjective.

flank ▸ noun **1** the side of the body between the ribs and the hip. **2** the side of something such as a mountain. **3** the left or right side of a group of people.

> SYNONYMS **1** *the horse's flanks* **side,** haunch, quarter, thigh. **2** *the southern flank of the Eighth Army* **side,** wing, sector, face, aspect.

▸ verb be on the side of.

> SYNONYMS *the garden is flanked by two rivers* **edge,** bound, line, border, fringe.

flannel ▸ noun **1** a kind of soft woollen or cotton fabric. **2** (**flannels**) men's trousers made of woollen flannel. **3** Brit. a small piece of towelling for washing yourself. **4** Brit. informal talk that does not have much meaning, used to avoid a difficult subject.

flannelette ▸ noun a soft cotton fabric resembling flannel.

flap ▸ verb (**flaps, flapping, flapped**) **1** move up and down or from side to side. **2** Brit. informal be very anxious; panic.

> SYNONYMS **1** *the mallards flapped their wings* **beat,** flutter, agitate, vibrate, wag, thrash, flail. **2** *the flag flapped in the breeze* **flutter,** wave, fly, blow, swing, ripple, stir.

▸ noun **1** a flat piece of paper, cloth, or metal that is attached to one side of something and covers an opening. **2** a movable section of an aircraft wing, used to control upward movement. **3** a flapping movement. **4** informal a panic.

> SYNONYMS **1** *a few flaps of its wing* **beat,** stroke, flutter, movement. **2** *in a flap* **panic,** fluster; informal state, stew, tizzy; N. Amer. informal twit.

flapjack ▸ noun **1** Brit. a soft biscuit made from oats and butter. **2** N. Amer. a pancake.

flapper ▸ noun informal a fashionable young woman of the 1920s.

flare ▸ noun **1** a sudden brief burst of flame or light. **2** a device that produces a very bright flame as a signal or marker. **3** (**flares**) trousers whose legs widen from the knees down.

> SYNONYMS **1** *the flare of the match* **blaze,** flame, flash, burst, flicker. **2** *a flare set off by the crew* **signal,** beacon, rocket, light, torch, maroon.

▸ verb (**flares, flaring, flared**) **1** burn or shine suddenly and strongly. **2** (usu. **flare up**) suddenly become intense or violent. **3** gradually become wider at one end.

> SYNONYMS **1** *the match flared* **blaze,** flash, flare up, flame, burn, flicker. **2** *her nostrils flared* **spread,** splay, broaden, widen, dilate.

> ! Don't confuse **flare** with **flair**, which means 'a natural ability or talent'.

flash ▸ verb **1** shine with a bright but brief or irregular light. **2** move quickly. **3** display words or images briefly or repeatedly. **4** informal display something in an obvious way to impress people. **5** informal (of a man) show his genitals in public.

> SYNONYMS **1** *a torch flashed* **shine,** flare, blaze, gleam, glint, sparkle, burn, blink, wink, flicker, shimmer, twinkle, glimmer, glisten. **2** *flashing his money about* **show off,** flaunt, flourish, display, parade. **3** *racing cars flashed past* **zoom,** streak, tear, shoot, dash, dart, fly, whistle, hurtle, rush, bolt, race, speed, career; informal belt, zap; Brit. informal bomb, bucket; N. Amer. informal barrel.

▸ noun **1** a sudden brief burst of bright light. **2** a camera attachment that produces a flash of light, for taking photographs in bad light. **3** a sudden or brief occurrence. **4** Brit. a coloured patch on a uniform, used to identify a regiment, country, etc.

> SYNONYMS *a flash of light* **flare,** blaze, burst, gleam, glint, sparkle, flicker, shimmer, twinkle, glimmer.

▸ adjective informal stylish or expensive in a showy way.
■ **flash flood** a sudden local flood resulting from very heavy rainfall. **flash in the pan** a sudden but brief success.
□ **flasher** noun.

flashback ▸ noun **1** a scene in a film or novel set in a time earlier than the main story. **2** a sudden vivid memory of a past event.

flashgun ▸ noun a device which gives a brief flash of intense light, used for taking photographs in bad light.

flashing ▸ noun a strip of metal used to seal the join of a roof with another surface.

flashlight ▸ noun **1** an electric torch with a strong beam. **2** a flashgun.

flashpoint ▸ noun a point or place at which anger or violence flares up.

flashy ▸ adjective (**flashier, flashiest**) attractive in a showy or cheap way.

SYNONYMS **ostentatious,** flamboyant, showy, conspicuous, extravagant, expensive, vulgar, tasteless, brash, garish, loud, gaudy; informal snazzy, fancy, swanky, flash, glitzy.
ANTONYMS understated.

flask ▸ noun **1** a bottle with a narrow neck. **2** Brit. a container that keeps a substance hot or cold by means of a double wall that encloses a vacuum.

flat¹ ▸ adjective (**flatter, flattest**) **1** having a level and even surface. **2** not sloping; horizontal. **3** with a level surface and little height or depth. **4** not lively or interesting. **5** (of a sparkling drink) no longer fizzy. **6** (of something inflated) having lost its air. **7** Brit. (of a battery) having used up its charge. **8** (of a charge or price) fixed. **9** definite and firm. **10** (of a musical sound) below the proper pitch. **11** (of a note or key) lower by a semitone than a stated note or key.

SYNONYMS **1** a flat roof **level,** horizontal. **2** the sea was flat **calm,** still, glassy, smooth, placid, like a millpond. **3** plane the wood completely flat **smooth,** even, plane. **4** a flat wooden box **shallow,** low, low-sided. **5** his voice was flat **monotonous,** toneless, droning, boring, dull, tedious, uninteresting, unexciting. **6** the market was flat **slow,** inactive, sluggish, slack, quiet, depressed. **7** a flat battery **run down,** dead, used up, expired. **8** a flat tyre **deflated,** punctured, burst, blown. **9** a flat fee **fixed,** set, invariable, regular, constant. **10** a flat denial **outright,** direct, absolute, definite, positive, straight, plain, explicit.
ANTONYMS sloping, vertical, rough, uneven, curved, tall, animated, lively, charged, new, inflated, variable, equivocal.

▸ adverb **1** in or to a horizontal position. **2** informal completely; absolutely. **3** below the proper pitch of a musical sound.

SYNONYMS she lay flat on the floor **stretched out,** outstretched, spreadeagled, sprawling, prone, prostrate.

▸ noun **1** the flat part of something. **2** (**flats**) low, level ground near water. **3** informal a flat tyre. **4** (**the Flat**) Brit. flat racing. **5** a musical note that is a semitone lower than the named note, shown by the sign ♭.
■ **flat feet** feet with arches that are lower than usual. **flat out** as fast or as hard as possible. **flat race** a horse race over a course with no jumps.
□ **flatly** adverb **flatness** noun.

flat² ▸ noun Brit. a set of rooms on one floor forming an individual home within a larger building.

SYNONYMS a two-bedroom flat **apartment,** suite, penthouse, rooms.

flatfish ▸ noun (plural **flatfish** or **flatfishes**) a sea fish, such as a plaice, that has both eyes on the upper side of its flattened body.

flatmate ▸ noun Brit. a person that you share a flat with.

flatten ▸ verb make or become flat or flatter.

SYNONYMS **1** Tom flattened the crumpled paper **make/become flat,** even out, smooth out, level. **2** the cows flattened the grass **squash,** compress, press down, crush, compact, trample. **3** tornadoes can flatten buildings in seconds **demolish,** raze (to the ground), tear down, knock down, destroy, wreck, devastate.
ANTONYMS crumple, raise, build.

flatter ▸ verb (**flatters, flattering, flattered**) **1** compliment someone too much or in an insincere way. **2** (**be flattered**) feel honoured and pleased. **3** make someone appear attractive.

SYNONYMS **1** it amused him to flatter her **compliment,** praise, express admiration for, fawn on, humour, wheedle, blarney; informal sweet-talk, soft-soap, butter up, play up to. **2** I was flattered to be asked **honour,** gratify, please, delight; informal tickle pink. **3** a hairstyle that flattered her **suit,** become, look good on, go well with; informal do something for.
ANTONYMS insult, offend.

flattering ▸ adjective **1** full of praise and compliments. **2** pleasing or gratifying. **3** enhancing someone's appearance.

SYNONYMS **1** flattering remarks **complimentary,** praising, favourable, admiring, appreciative, fulsome, honeyed, obsequious, ingratiating, sycophantic. **2** it was very flattering to be nominated **pleasing,** gratifying, an honour. **3** her most flattering dress **becoming,** enhancing.
ANTONYMS unflattering.

flattery ▸ noun excessive or insincere praise.

SYNONYMS **praise,** adulation, compliments, blandishments, honeyed words, fawning, blarney; informal sweet talk, soft soap, buttering up, toadying.

flatulent ▸ adjective suffering from a build-up of gas in the intestines or stomach.
□ **flatulence** noun.

flatworm ▸ noun a type of worm with a simple flattened body.

flaunt ▸ verb display proudly or obviously.

SYNONYMS **show off**, display, make a great show of, put on show/display, parade, draw attention to, brag about, crow about, vaunt; informal flash.

❗ Don't confuse **flaunt** with **flout**, which means 'ignore a rule'.

flautist ▶ noun a flute player.

flavour (US spelling **flavor**) ▶ noun **1** the distinctive taste of a food or drink. **2** a particular quality.

SYNONYMS **1** *the flavour of basil* **taste**, savour, tang, smack. **2** *salami can give extra flavour* **flavouring**, seasoning, taste, tang, relish, bite, piquancy, spice. **3** *a strong international flavour* **character**, quality, feel, feeling, ambience, atmosphere, air, mood, tone, spirit. **4** *this excerpt will give you a flavour of the report* **impression**, suggestion, hint, taste.

▶ verb give flavour to.

SYNONYMS *spices for flavouring food* **season**, spice (up), add piquancy to, ginger up, enrich, infuse.

◻ **flavouring** noun **flavourless** adjective.

flaw ▶ noun **1** a mark or fault that spoils something. **2** a weakness or mistake.

SYNONYMS **defect**, blemish, fault, imperfection, deficiency, weakness, weak spot/point, failing; Computing bug; informal glitch.
ANTONYMS strength.

◻ **flawless** adjective.

flawed ▶ adjective spoilt or weakened.

SYNONYMS **1** *a flawed mirror* **faulty**, defective, unsound, imperfect, blemished, broken, cracked, scratched; Brit. informal duff. **2** *the findings were flawed* **unsound**, distorted, inaccurate, incorrect, erroneous, fallacious.
ANTONYMS flawless.

flax ▶ noun a blue-flowered plant that is grown for its seed (linseed) and for its stalks, from which thread is made.

flaxen ▶ adjective literary (of hair) pale yellow.

flay ▶ verb **1** strip the skin from a body. **2** whip or beat very harshly.

flea ▶ noun a small wingless jumping insect which feeds on the blood of mammals and birds.
■ **flea market** a street market selling second-hand goods.

fleapit ▶ noun Brit. informal a run-down cinema.

flock ▶ noun **1** a very small patch of colour or light. **2** a very small piece of something.
▶ verb mark or dot with flecks.

fledged /flejd/ ▶ adjective (of a young bird) having developed wing feathers that are

large enough for it to fly.

fledgling (or **fledgeling**) ▶ noun a young bird that has just learned to fly.

flee ▶ verb (**flees, fleeing, fled**) run away.

SYNONYMS **run (away/off)**, run for it, make off, take off, take to your heels, make a break for it, bolt, beat a (hasty) retreat, make a quick exit, escape; informal beat it, clear off/out, skedaddle, scram; Brit. informal scarper; N. Amer. informal light out; Austral./NZ informal shoot through.

fleece ▶ noun **1** the wool coat of a sheep. **2** a soft, warm fabric with a pile, or a jacket made from this.
▶ verb (**fleeces, fleecing, fleeced**) informal swindle someone.
◻ **fleecy** adjective.

fleet[1] ▶ noun **1** a group of ships travelling together. **2** a group of vehicles or aircraft with the same owner.

SYNONYMS **navy**, naval force, (naval) task force, armada, flotilla, squadron, convoy.

fleet[2] ▶ adjective literary fast in movement.

fleeting ▶ adjective lasting for a very short time.

SYNONYMS **brief**, short-lived, quick, momentary, cursory, transient, ephemeral, passing, transitory.
ANTONYMS lasting.

◻ **fleetingly** adverb.

Flemish ▶ noun **1** (**the Flemish**) the people of Flanders, a region divided between Belgium, France, and the Netherlands. **2** the form of the Dutch language spoken in Flanders.
▶ adjective relating to Flanders or the Flemish.

flesh ▶ noun **1** the soft substance in the body consisting of muscle and fat. **2** the edible part of a fruit or vegetable. **3** (**the flesh**) the physical aspects and needs of the body.

SYNONYMS **1** *his smooth, white flesh* **tissue**, skin, body, muscle, fat. **2** *strip the flesh from the bone* **meat**, muscle. **3** *a fruit with juicy flesh* **pulp**, marrow, meat. **4** *the pleasures of the flesh* **the body**, human nature, physicality, sensuality, sexuality.

▶ verb (**flesh something out**) make something more detailed.
■ **in the flesh** in person.

fleshly ▶ adjective relating to the body and its needs.

fleshpots ▶ plural noun humorous places with a lot of nightlife and lively entertainment.

fleshy ▶ adjective (**fleshier, fleshiest**) **1** plump. **2** soft and thick.

fleur-de-lis (or **fleur-de-lys**) /fler-duh-**lee**/ ▶ noun (plural **fleurs-de-lis** /fler-duh-**lee**/) a design showing a lily made up of three petals bound together at the bottom.

flew past of FLY[1].

flex ▸ verb **1** bend a limb or joint. **2** tighten a muscle.
▸ noun Brit. a cable for carrying electric current to an appliance.

flexibility ▸ noun the quality of being flexible.

> SYNONYMS **1** the flexibility of wood **pliability,** suppleness, elasticity, stretchiness, springiness, spring, resilience, bounce; informal give. **2** the flexibility of an endowment loan **adaptability,** adjustability, versatility, open-endedness, freedom, latitude. **3** the flexibility shown by the local authority **willingness to compromise,** accommodation, give and take, amenability, cooperation, tolerance. ANTONYMS rigidity, inflexibility, intransigence.

flexible ▸ adjective **1** able to bend easily without breaking. **2** able to adapt to different circumstances.

> SYNONYMS **1** flexible tubing **bendy,** pliable, supple, pliant, plastic, elastic, stretchy, springy, resilient, bouncy. **2** a flexible arrangement **adaptable,** adjustable, variable, versatile, open-ended, open. **3** the need to be flexible towards tenants **accommodating,** amenable, willing to compromise, cooperative, tolerant. ANTONYMS rigid, inflexible, intransigent.

□ **flexibly** adverb.

flexitime ▸ noun a system that lets you vary your working hours.

flexor ▸ noun a muscle which makes a part of the body bend.

flick ▸ verb **1** hit or remove with a quick light movement. **2** make a sudden quick movement. **3** (**flick through**) look quickly through a book, magazine, etc.

> SYNONYMS **1** he flicked the switch **click,** snap, flip, jerk, throw. **2** the horse flicked its tail **swish,** twitch, wave, wag, waggle, shake.

▸ noun **1** a sudden quick movement. **2** informal a cinema film.

> SYNONYMS a flick of the wrist **jerk,** snap, flip, whisk.

■ **flick knife** Brit. a knife with a blade that springs out from the handle when you press a button.

flicker ▸ verb (**flickers, flickering, flickered**) **1** shine or burn unsteadily. **2** appear briefly. **3** make small, quick movements.

> SYNONYMS **1** the lights flickered **glimmer,** flare, dance, gutter, twinkle, sparkle, wink, flash. **2** his eyelids flickered **flutter,**

quiver, tremble, shiver, shudder, jerk, twitch.

▸ noun **1** a flickering movement or light. **2** a brief occurrence of a feeling.

flier ➠ FLYER.

flight ▸ noun **1** the action of flying. **2** a journey made in an aircraft or in space. **3** the path of something through the air. **4** the action of running away. **5** a group of birds or aircraft flying together. **6** a series of steps between floors or levels. **7** the tail of an arrow or dart.

> SYNONYMS **1** the history of flight **aviation,** flying, air transport, aeronautics. **2** a flight to Rome **plane trip/journey,** air trip/journey, service. **3** the flight of the ball **trajectory,** path (through the air), track, orbit. **4** a flight of birds **flock,** swarm, cloud, throng. **5** his headlong flight from home **escape,** getaway, hasty departure, exit, exodus, breakout, bolt, disappearance; Brit. informal flit.

■ **flight deck 1** the cockpit of a large aircraft. **2** the deck of an aircraft carrier. **flight of fancy** a very imaginative idea or story.
□ **flightless** adjective.

flighty ▸ adjective unreliable and uninterested in serious things.

flimsy ▸ adjective (**flimsier, flimsiest**) **1** weak and fragile. **2** (of clothing) light and thin. **3** unconvincing: a flimsy excuse.

> SYNONYMS **1** a flimsy building **insubstantial,** fragile, frail, rickety, ramshackle, makeshift, jerry-built, shoddy. **2** a flimsy dress **thin,** light, fine, filmy, floaty, diaphanous, sheer, delicate, gossamer, gauzy. **3** flimsy evidence **weak,** feeble, poor, inadequate, insufficient, thin, unsubstantial, unconvincing, implausible. ANTONYMS sturdy, thick, sound.

flinch ▸ verb **1** make a quick, nervous movement as a reaction to fear or pain. **2** (**flinch from**) avoid something because you are scared or anxious.

> SYNONYMS **1** he flinched at the noise **wince,** start, shudder, quiver, jerk. **2** he never flinched from his duty **shrink from,** recoil from, shy away from, dodge, evade, avoid, duck, baulk at.

fling ▸ verb (**flings, flinging, flung**) throw or move forcefully.

> SYNONYMS he flung the axe into the river **throw,** hurl, toss, sling, launch, pitch, lob; informal chuck, heave.

▸ noun **1** a short period of enjoyment or wild behaviour. **2** a short sexual relationship.

> SYNONYMS **1** a birthday fling **good time,** party, spree, fun and games; informal

binge, bash, night on the town. **2** *she had a brief fling with him* **affair,** love affair, relationship, romance, liaison, entanglement, involvement.

flint ▸ noun **1** a hard grey rock. **2** a piece of flint or a metal alloy, used to produce a spark in a cigarette lighter.

flintlock ▸ noun an old-fashioned type of gun fired by a spark from a flint.

flip ▸ verb (**flips, flipping, flipped**) **1** turn over with a quick, smooth movement. **2** move or throw with a sudden sharp movement. **3** informal suddenly become very angry or lose your self-control.
▸ noun a flipping action or movement.
▸ adjective not serious or respectful; flippant.
■ **flip-flop** a light sandal with a thong that passes between the big and second toes. **flip side** informal the reverse and less welcome aspect of a situation.

flippant ▸ adjective not properly serious or respectful.

> SYNONYMS **frivolous,** facetious, tongue-in-cheek, disrespectful, irreverent, cheeky; informal **flip,** saucy; N. Amer. informal sassy.
> ANTONYMS serious, respectful.

□ **flippancy** noun **flippantly** adverb.

flipper ▸ noun **1** a broad, flat limb used for swimming by sea creatures such as turtles. **2** a flat rubber attachment worn on each foot for swimming underwater.

flirt ▸ verb **1** behave as if you are trying to attract someone sexually, but without serious intentions. **2** (**flirt with**) show a casual interest in. **3** (**flirt with**) deliberately risk danger or death.
▸ noun a person who likes to flirt.

> SYNONYMS *Anna was quite a flirt* **tease,** coquette, heartbreaker.

□ **flirtation** noun **flirty** adjective.

flirtatious ▸ adjective liking to flirt.

flit ▸ verb (**flits, flitting, flitted**) move quickly and lightly.

flitter ▸ verb move quickly here and there.

float ▸ verb **1** rest on the surface of a liquid without sinking. **2** move or be held up in a liquid or the air. **3** put forward a suggestion. **4** (**floating**) not having fixed opinions. **5** (**floating**) not living in a fixed location. **6** put shares in a company on sale for the first time.

> SYNONYMS **1** *oil floats on water* **stay afloat,** stay on the surface, be buoyant, be buoyed up. **2** *the balloon floated in the air* **hover,** levitate, be suspended, hang, defy gravity. **3** *a cloud floated across the moon* **drift,** glide, sail, slip, slide, waft. **4** (**floating**) *floating voters* **uncommitted,** undecided, undeclared, wavering; informal sitting on the fence.

5 (**floating**) *a floating population* **unsettled,** transient, temporary, migrant, wandering, nomadic, migratory, itinerant. **6** *the company was floated on the Stock Exchange* **launch,** offer, sell, introduce.
> ANTONYMS sink, drop, rush, take private.

▸ noun **1** a lightweight object designed to float on water. **2** a vehicle that carries a display in a procession. **3** Brit. a sum of money available for minor expenses.
□ **floaty** adjective.

floatation ➠ FLOTATION.

flock¹ ▸ noun **1** a number of birds, sheep, or goats together. **2** (**a flock** or **flocks**) a large number or crowd. **3** a Christian congregation.

> SYNONYMS **1** *a flock of sheep* **herd,** drove. **2** *a flock of birds* **flight,** swarm, cloud, gaggle, skein.

▸ verb gather or move in a flock.

> SYNONYMS **1** *people flocked around her* **gather,** collect, congregate, assemble, converge, mass, crowd, throng, cluster, swarm. **2** *tourists flock to the place* **stream,** go in large numbers, swarm, crowd, troop.

flock² ▸ noun **1** a soft material for stuffing cushions and quilts. **2** powdered wool or cloth, used to give a raised pattern on wallpaper.

floe ▸ noun a sheet of floating ice.

flog ▸ verb (**flogs, flogging, flogged**) **1** beat with a whip or stick as a punishment. **2** Brit. informal sell.

> SYNONYMS **whip,** thrash, lash, scourge, birch, cane, beat.

flood ▸ noun **1** an overflow of a large amount of water over dry land. **2** an overwhelming quantity or amount. **3** the rising of the tide.

> SYNONYMS **1** *a severe flood* **inundation,** deluge, torrent, overflow, flash flood; Brit. spate. **2** *a flood of tears* **gush,** outpouring, torrent, rush, stream, surge, cascade. **3** *a flood of complaints* **succession,** series, string, barrage, volley, battery, avalanche, torrent, stream, storm.
> ANTONYMS trickle.

▸ verb **1** cover with water in a flood. **2** (of a river) overflow its banks. **3** arrive in very large numbers.

> SYNONYMS **1** *the town was flooded* **inundate,** swamp, deluge, immerse, submerge, drown, engulf. **2** *the river could flood* **overflow,** burst its banks, brim over, run over. **3** *cheap goods flooding the market* **glut,** swamp, saturate. **4** *refugees flooded in* **pour,**

stream, flow, surge, swarm, pile, crowd. ANTONYMS drain, starve, trickle.

■ **flood plain** an area of low ground next to a river that is regularly flooded. **flood tide** an incoming tide.

floodgate ▶ noun **1** a gate that can be opened or closed to control a flow of water. **2** (**floodgates**) controls that hold back something powerful.

floodlight ▶ noun a large, powerful lamp used to light up a sports ground.
▶ verb (**floodlights, floodlighting, floodlit**) light up with floodlights.

floor ▶ noun **1** the lower surface of a room. **2** a storey of a building. **3** the bottom of the sea, a cave, etc. **4** (**the floor**) the part of a parliament or other law-making assembly in which members sit and from which they speak.

SYNONYMS **1** *he sat on the floor* **ground,** flooring. **2** *the second floor* **storey,** level, deck, tier, stage.

▶ verb informal **1** knock someone to the ground. **2** surprise or confuse someone.

SYNONYMS **1** *he floored his attacker* **knock down,** knock over, fell; informal deck, lay out. **2** *the question floored him* **baffle,** defeat, confound, perplex, puzzle, disconcert; informal throw, beat, stump; N. Amer. informal buffalo.

■ **floor show** an entertainment presented on the floor of a nightclub or restaurant. □ **floored** adjective.

floorboard ▶ noun a long plank making up part of a wooden floor.

floozy (or **floozie**) ▶ noun (plural **floozies**) informal a girl or woman who has many sexual partners.

flop ▶ verb (**flops, flopping, flopped**) **1** hang or swing loosely. **2** sit or lie down heavily. **3** informal fail totally.

SYNONYMS **1** *he flopped into a chair* **collapse,** slump, crumple, sink, drop. **2** *his hair flopped over his eyes* **hang (down),** dangle, droop, sag, loll. **3** *the play flopped* **be unsuccessful,** fail, fall flat, founder; informal bomb; N. Amer. informal tank.
ANTONYMS spring, succeed.

▶ noun **1** a heavy and clumsy fall. **2** informal a total failure.

SYNONYMS *the play was a flop* **failure,** disaster, fiasco, debacle, catastrophe; Brit. damp squib; informal washout, also-ran; N. Amer. informal clinker.
ANTONYMS success.

floppy ▶ adjective not firm or rigid.

SYNONYMS **limp,** flaccid, slack, flabby, relaxed, drooping, droopy, loose,

flowing.
ANTONYMS erect, stiff.

■ **floppy disk** a flexible disk used for storing computer data.

flora ▶ noun the plants of a particular area or period.

floral ▶ adjective having to do with flowers.

floret ▶ noun **1** each of the small flowers making up a flower head. **2** each of the flowering stems making up a head of cauliflower or broccoli.

florid ▶ adjective **1** having a red or flushed complexion. **2** too elaborate.

florin ▶ noun a former British coin worth two shillings (ten pence).

florist ▶ noun a person who sells cut flowers.

floss ▶ noun **1** (also **dental floss**) soft thread used to clean between the teeth. **2** silk thread used in embroidery.
▶ verb clean between the teeth with dental floss.

flotation (or **floatation**) ▶ noun **1** the action of floating. **2** the offering of a company's shares for sale for the first time.

flotilla ▶ noun a small fleet of ships or boats.

flotsam ▶ noun wreckage found floating on the sea.

flounce ▶ verb (**flounces, flouncing, flounced**) move in an angry or impatient way.
▶ noun **1** an exaggerated action expressing annoyance or impatience. **2** a wide strip of material sewn to a skirt or dress.

flounder[1] ▶ verb (**flounders, floundering, floundered**) **1** stagger clumsily in mud or water. **2** have trouble doing or understanding something.

SYNONYMS **1** *floundering in the water* **struggle,** thrash, flail, twist and turn, splash, stagger, stumble, reel, lurch, blunder. **2** *she floundered, not knowing what to say* **struggle,** be out of your depth, be confused; informal scratch your head, be flummoxed, be fazed, be floored.

flounder[2] ▶ noun a small flatfish.

flour ▶ noun a powder produced by grinding grain, used to make bread, cakes, and pastry.
□ **floury** adjective.

flourish ▶ verb **1** grow or develop well; thrive. **2** be successful. **3** wave something about in a noticeable way.

SYNONYMS **1** *ferns flourish in the shade* **grow,** thrive, prosper, do well, burgeon, increase, multiply, proliferate, run riot. **2** *the arts flourished* **thrive,** prosper, bloom, be in good health, be vigorous, be in its heyday, make progress, advance, expand; informal go places. **3** *he flourished*

a *sword* **brandish,** wave, shake, wield, swing, display, show off.
ANTONYMS die, wither, decline.

▶ noun 1 a dramatic or exaggerated movement or gesture. 2 a decorative flowing curve in handwriting. 3 a fanfare played by brass instruments.

flout ▶ verb openly fail to follow a rule, law, or custom.

SYNONYMS **defy,** refuse to obey, disobey, break, violate, fail to comply with, fail to observe, contravene, infringe, breach, commit a breach of, transgress against, ignore, disregard; informal cock a snook at.
ANTONYMS observe.

❗ Don't confuse **flout** with **flaunt,** which means 'display proudly or obviously'.

flow ▶ verb 1 move steadily and continuously in a current or stream. 2 hang loosely and elegantly.

SYNONYMS 1 *the water flowed down the channel* **pour,** run, course, circulate, stream, swirl, surge, sweep, gush, cascade, roll, rush, trickle, seep, ooze, dribble. 2 *many questions flow from today's announcement* **result,** proceed, arise, follow, ensue, stem, originate, emanate, spring.

▶ noun a steady, continuous stream.

SYNONYMS *a good flow of water* **movement,** motion, current, circulation, stream, swirl, surge, gush, rush, spate, tide, trickle, ooze.

■ **flow chart** a diagram that shows the sequence of stages making up a complex process.

flower ▶ noun 1 the part of a plant from which the seed or fruit develops, usually having brightly coloured petals. 2 (**the flower of**) the best of a group.

SYNONYMS **bloom,** blossom.

▶ verb (**flowers, flowering, flowered**) 1 produce flowers. 2 develop fully and well.

SYNONYMS **bloom,** blossom.

flowerpot ▶ noun a container for growing plants in.

flowery ▶ adjective 1 full of or decorated with flowers. 2 (of speech or writing) elaborate.

flown past participle of FLY¹.

flu ▶ noun influenza or any similar, milder infection.

fluctuate ▶ verb (**fluctuates, fluctuating, fluctuated**) rise and fall irregularly in number or amount.

SYNONYMS **vary,** change, shift, alter, waver, swing, oscillate, alternate, rise and fall.

□ **fluctuation** noun.

flue ▶ noun a pipe that takes smoke and gases away from a chimney, heater, etc.

fluent ▶ adjective 1 able to use a language in a clear and natural way. 2 smoothly graceful and easy.

SYNONYMS **articulate,** eloquent, silver-tongued, communicative, natural, effortless.
ANTONYMS inarticulate.

□ **fluency** noun **fluently** adverb.

fluff ▶ noun 1 soft fibres gathered in small, light clumps. 2 the soft fur or feathers of a young animal or bird.
▶ verb 1 (**fluff something up**) make something fuller and softer by shaking or patting it. 2 informal fail to do something properly.

fluffy ▶ adjective (**fluffier, fluffiest**) 1 covered with fluff. 2 (of food) light in texture.

flugelhorn /floo-guhl-horn/ ▶ noun a brass musical instrument like a cornet but with a broader tone.

fluid ▶ noun a liquid or gas.

SYNONYMS *the fluid seeps up the tube* **liquid,** solution, liquor, gas, vapour.
ANTONYMS solid.

▶ adjective 1 able to flow easily. 2 not fixed or stable: *a fluid situation.* 3 graceful.

SYNONYMS 1 *a fluid substance* **free-flowing,** runny, liquid, liquefied, melted, molten, gaseous. 2 *he stood up in one fluid movement* **smooth,** fluent, flowing, effortless, easy, continuous, graceful, elegant.
ANTONYMS solid, jerky.

■ **fluid ounce** Brit. one twentieth of a pint (approximately 0.028 litre).
□ **fluidity** noun **fluidly** adverb.

fluke ▶ noun something lucky that happens by chance.
□ **fluky** adjective.

flume ▶ noun 1 an artificial channel for carrying water. 2 a water slide at a swimming pool or amusement park.

flummery ▶ noun (plural **flummeries**) empty talk or compliments.

flummox ▶ verb informal baffle someone completely.

flung past and past participle of FLING.

flunk ▶ verb informal, chiefly N. Amer. fail an exam.

flunkey (or **flunky**) ▶ noun (plural **flunkeys** or **flunkies**) 1 a uniformed male servant. 2 a person who does menial tasks for someone else.

fluoresce ▶ verb (**fluoresces, fluorescing, fluoresced**) shine or glow brightly.

fluorescent /fluu-uh-ress-uhnt/ ▸ adjective **1** giving off bright light when exposed to radiation such as ultraviolet light. **2** vividly colourful.
□ **fluorescence** noun.

> ✔ **fluor-**, not **flour-**: **fluor**escent.

fluoridate ▸ verb (**fluoridates, fluoridating, fluoridated**) add fluoride to a water supply.
□ **fluoridation** noun.

fluoride /floo-uh-ryd, flor-yd/ ▸ noun a compound of fluorine that is added to water supplies or toothpaste to reduce tooth decay.

fluorine /floo-uh-reen, flor-een/ ▸ noun a poisonous pale yellow gas.

fluorite /floo-uh-ryt, flor-yt/ ▸ noun a mineral found in the form of crystals.

fluorspar /floo-uh-spar, flor-spar/ = FLUORITE.

flurry ▸ noun (plural **flurries**) **1** a small swirling mass of snow, leaves, etc. moved by a gust of wind. **2** a sudden short period of activity or excitement. **3** a number of things arriving suddenly and at the same time.

> SYNONYMS **1** *a flurry of snow* **swirl**, whirl, eddy, shower, gust. **2** *a flurry of activity* **burst**, outbreak, spurt, fit, spell, bout, rash, eruption.
> ANTONYMS dearth.

flush[1] ▸ verb **1** (of a person's skin or face) become red and hot. **2** (**be flushed with**) be very pleased by. **3** clean something by passing large quantities of water through it. **4** force a person or animal out into the open.

> SYNONYMS **1** *she flushed in embarrassment* **blush**, redden, go pink, go red, go crimson, go scarlet, colour (up). **2** *flushing toxins from the body* **rinse**, wash, sluice, swill, cleanse, clean; Brit. informal sloosh. **3** *they flushed out the snipers* **drive**, chase, force, dislodge, expel.
> ANTONYMS pale.

▸ noun **1** a reddening of the face or skin. **2** a sudden rush of strong emotion. **3** a period of freshness and energy: *the first flush of youth*. **4** an act of flushing.

> SYNONYMS *a flush crept over her face* **blush**, colour, rosiness, pinkness, ruddiness, bloom.
> ANTONYMS pallor.

flush[2] ▸ adjective **1** completely level with another surface. **2** informal having plenty of money.

flush[3] ▸ noun (in poker) a hand of cards all of the same suit.

fluster ▸ noun an agitated and confused state.

flustered ▸ adjective agitated and confused.

flute ▸ noun **1** a high-pitched wind instrument that you hold sideways and play by blowing across a hole at one end. **2** a tall, narrow wine glass.

fluted ▸ adjective decorated with a series of gently rounded grooves.

flutter ▸ verb (**flutters, fluttering, fluttered**) **1** fly unsteadily by flapping the wings quickly and lightly. **2** move or fall with a light trembling motion. **3** (of a pulse or heartbeat) beat feebly or irregularly.

> SYNONYMS **1** *butterflies fluttered around* **flit**, hover, dance. **2** *a tern was fluttering its wings* **flap**, beat, quiver, agitate, vibrate. **3** *she fluttered her eyelashes* **flicker**, bat. **4** *flags fluttered* **flap**, wave, ripple, undulate, quiver, fly. **5** *her heart fluttered* **beat irregularly**, palpitate, miss/skip a beat, quiver.

▸ noun **1** a state of nervous excitement. **2** Brit. informal a small bet.
□ **fluttery** adjective.

fluvial /floo-vi-uhl/ ▸ adjective technical having to do with a river.

flux ▸ noun **1** continuous change. **2** a flow.

fly[1] ▸ verb (**flies, flying, flew**; past participle **flown**) **1** (of a winged creature or aircraft) move through the air. **2** control the flight of an aircraft. **3** move quickly through the air. **4** go or move quickly. **5** (of a flag) be displayed on a flagpole. **6** (**fly at**) attack. **7** old use run away.

> SYNONYMS **1** *a bird flew overhead* **wing**, glide, soar, wheel, take wing, take to the air. **2** *they flew to Paris* **travel by plane/air**, jet. **3** *we flew in supplies* **transport (by plane/air)**, airlift, lift, jet, drop, parachute. **4** *he can fly a plane* **pilot**, operate, control, manoeuvre, steer. **5** *the ship was flying a French flag* **display**, show, exhibit. **6** *flags flew in the town* **flutter**, flap, wave. **7** *doesn't time fly?* **go quickly**, fly by/past, pass swiftly, rush past.

▸ noun (plural **flies**) **1** (Brit. also **flies**) an opening at the crotch of a pair of trousers, closed with a zip or buttons. **2** a flap of material covering the opening of a tent. **3** (**the flies**) the space over the stage in a theatre.
■ **fly-by-night** unreliable or untrustworthy. **fly-post** Brit. put up advertising posters without permission. **flying saucer** a disc-shaped flying spacecraft supposedly piloted by aliens. **flying squad** a division of a police force which is capable of reaching an incident quickly. **flying start** a good beginning that gives an advantage over competitors. **fly in the face of** do the opposite of what is usual or expected. **fly off the handle** informal lose your temper. **with flying colours** with distinction.

fly² ▸ noun (plural **flies**) **1** a flying insect with transparent wings. **2** an artificial fly used as a fishing bait.
■ **a fly in the ointment** a small irritation that spoils the enjoyment of something. **a fly on the wall** an unnoticed observer.

fly³ ▸ adjective (**flyer**, **flyest**) Brit. informal knowing and clever.

flyaway ▸ adjective (of hair) fine and difficult to control.

flyblown ▸ adjective contaminated by contact with flies.

flycatcher ▸ noun a small bird that catches flying insects.

flyer (or **flier**) ▸ noun **1** a person or thing that flies. **2** a small printed advertisement.

flyleaf ▸ noun (plural **flyleaves**) a blank page at the beginning or end of a book.

flyover ▸ noun Brit. a bridge carrying one road or railway line over another.

flysheet ▸ noun Brit. a cover over a tent for keeping the rain out.

flywheel ▸ noun a heavy revolving wheel in a machine that helps it to work smoothly.

FM ▸ abbreviation frequency modulation.

foal ▸ noun a young horse or related animal.
▸ verb give birth to a foal.

foam ▸ noun **1** a mass of small bubbles formed on the surface of liquid. **2** a liquid substance containing many small bubbles. **3** a lightweight form of rubber or plastic that is full of small holes.

SYNONYMS *the foam on the waves* **froth**, spume, surf, spray, fizz, effervescence, bubbles, head, lather, suds.

▸ verb form or produce foam.

SYNONYMS *the water foamed* **froth**, fizz, effervesce, bubble, lather, ferment, boil, seethe.

□ **foamy** adjective.

fob¹ ▸ noun **1** a chain attached to a watch for carrying in a pocket. **2** a tab on a key ring.

fob² ▸ verb (**fobs**, **fobbing**, **fobbed**) **1** (**fob someone off**) try to deceive someone into accepting excuses or something inferior. **2** (**fob something off on**) give something inferior to.

focaccia /fuh-**kach**-uh/ ▸ noun a type of flat Italian bread made with olive oil.

focal ▸ adjective relating to a focus.
■ **focal point 1** the point at which rays or waves of light, sound, etc. meet, or from which they seem to come. **2** the centre of interest or activity.

fo'c's'le ➡ FORECASTLE.

focus /**foh**-kuhss/ ▸ noun (plural **focuses** or **foci** /**foh**-sy/) **1** the centre of interest or activity. **2** the state of having or producing a clear image: *his face is out of focus*. **3** the point at which an object must be situated

for a lens or mirror to produce a clear image of it. **4** a focal point.

SYNONYMS **1** *a focus of community life* **centre**, focal point, central point, centre of attention, hub, pivot, nucleus, heart, cornerstone, linchpin. **2** *the main focus of this chapter* **subject**, theme, concern, subject matter, topic, point, essence, gist.

▸ verb (**focuses**, **focusing** or **focussing**, **focused** or **focussed**) **1** adapt to the amount of light available and become able to see clearly. **2** (**focus on**) pay particular attention to. **3** adjust the focus of a telescope, camera, etc. **4** (of rays or waves) meet at a single point.

SYNONYMS *he focused his binoculars on the tower* **bring into focus**, aim, point, turn.

■ **focus group** a group of people brought together to give their opinions of a new product, political campaign, etc.

fodder ▸ noun **1** food for cattle and other livestock. **2** a person or thing viewed only as material to satisfy a particular need.

foe ▸ noun an enemy or opponent.

foetid ➡ FETID.

foetus ➡ FETUS.

fog ▸ noun a thick cloud of water droplets which is difficult to see through.

SYNONYMS **mist**, smog, murk, haze; informal pea-souper.

▸ verb (**fogs**, **fogging**, **fogged**) **1** become covered with steam. **2** confuse.

fogey ▸ noun (plural **fogeys** or **fogies**) a very old-fashioned or conservative person.

foggy ▸ adjective (**foggier**, **foggiest**) **1** full of fog. **2** confused or unclear.

foghorn ▸ noun a device that makes a loud, deep sound as a warning to ships in fog.

foible ▸ noun a slight peculiarity in a person's character or habits.

foil¹ ▸ verb **1** prevent something from happening. **2** stop someone from doing something.

SYNONYMS *the escape attempt was foiled* **thwart**, frustrate, stop, defeat, block, prevent, obstruct, hinder, snooker, scotch; informal put paid to; Brit. informal scupper.
ANTONYMS assist.

foil² ▸ noun **1** metal in the form of a thin flexible sheet. **2** a person or thing that contrasts with and so emphasizes the qualities of another.

SYNONYMS *the wine was a perfect foil to pasta* **contrast**, complement, antithesis.

foil³ ▸ noun a light, blunt-edged fencing sword.

foist ▸ verb (**foist someone/thing on**) make someone accept an unwelcome person or thing.

fold¹ ▸ verb **1** bend something over on itself so that one part of it covers another. **2** be able to be folded into a flatter shape. **3** clasp someone in your arms. **4** informal (of a company) stop trading as a result of financial problems. **5** (**fold something in** or **into**) mix one ingredient gently with another.

> SYNONYMS **1** *I folded the cloth* **double**, crease, turn, bend, tuck, pleat. **2** *the firm folded last year* **fail**, collapse, founder, go bankrupt, cease trading, be wound up, be shut (down); informal crash, go bust, go under, go to the wall, go belly up.

▸ noun **1** a folded part. **2** a line or crease produced by folding.

> SYNONYMS *there was a fold in the paper* **crease**, knife-edge, wrinkle, crinkle, pucker, furrow, pleat.

fold² ▸ noun **1** a pen or enclosure for livestock. **2** (**the fold**) a group or community.

folder ▸ noun a folding cover or wallet for storing loose papers.

foliage ▸ noun the leaves of plants.

folic acid ▸ noun a vitamin found especially in green vegetables, liver, and kidney.

folio /foh-li-oh/ ▸ noun (plural **folios**) **1** a sheet of paper folded once to form four pages of a book. **2** a large-sized book made up of such sheets.

folk ▸ plural noun **1** (also **folks**) informal people in general. **2** (**your folks**) informal, chiefly N. Amer. your family. **3** (also **folk music**) traditional music whose composer is unknown, passed on through performances.

> SYNONYMS **1** *the local folk* **people**, individuals, (men, women, and children), (living) souls, citizenry, inhabitants, residents, populace, population. **2** *my folks live in Hull* **relatives**, relations, family, people; informal peeps.

■ **folk tale** a traditional story passed on by word of mouth.

folklore ▸ noun the traditional stories and customs of a community.

folksy ▸ adjective traditional and homely.

follicle ▸ noun one of the small holes in the skin that hair grows out of.

follow ▸ verb **1** go after or move along behind. **2** go along a route. **3** come after in time or order. **4** be a result or consequence. **5** act according to advice or an instruction. **6** understand or pay attention to. **7** (**follow something through**) continue an action or task to its end. **8** (**follow something up**) pursue something further.

> SYNONYMS **1** *we'll let the others follow* **come behind**, come after, go behind, go after, walk behind. **2** *people who follow the band around* **accompany**, go along with, go around with, travel with, escort, attend; informal tag along with. **3** *the police followed her everywhere* **shadow**, trail, stalk, track; informal tail. **4** *follow the instructions* **obey**, comply with, conform to, adhere to, stick to, keep to, act in accordance with, abide by, observe. **5** *I couldn't follow what he said* **understand**, comprehend, take in, grasp, fathom, see; informal make head or tail of, figure out; Brit. informal suss out. **6** *he follows Manchester United* **be a fan of**, be a supporter of, support, watch, keep up with.
> ANTONYMS lead, flout, misunderstand.

■ **follow suit** do the same as someone else.

follower ▸ noun **1** a supporter, fan, or disciple. **2** a person who follows.

> SYNONYMS **1** *a follower of Christ* **disciple**, apostle, defender, champion, believer, worshipper. **2** *followers of Scottish football* **fan**, enthusiast, admirer, devotee, lover, supporter, adherent.
> ANTONYMS leader, opponent.

following ▸ preposition coming after or as a result of.

▸ noun a group of supporters.

> SYNONYMS *his devoted following* **admirers**, supporters, backers, fans, adherents, devotees, public, audience.
> ANTONYMS opposition.

▸ adjective **1** next in time or order. **2** about to be mentioned.

> SYNONYMS **1** *the following day* **next**, ensuing, succeeding, subsequent. **2** *the following questions* **below**, underneath, these.
> ANTONYMS preceding, above.

folly ▸ noun (plural **follies**) **1** foolishness. **2** a foolish act. **3** an ornamental building with no practical purpose.

> SYNONYMS **foolishness**, foolhardiness, stupidity, idiocy, lunacy, madness, rashness, recklessness, irresponsibility.
> ANTONYMS wisdom.

foment /foh-ment/ ▸ verb stir up revolution or conflict.

fond ▸ adjective **1** (**fond of**) having a liking or affection for. **2** affectionate. **3** hoped for but unlikely to be fulfilled.

> SYNONYMS **1** *she was fond of dancing* **keen on**, partial to, enthusiastic about, attached to, attracted to; informal into. **2** *his fond father* **adoring**, devoted, doting, loving, caring, affectionate. **3** *a fond hope* **unrealistic**, naive, foolish,

over-optimistic, absurd, vain.
ANTONYMS indifferent, uncaring, realistic.

□ **fondly** adverb **fondness** noun.

fondant ▸ noun a thick paste made of sugar and water, used in making sweets and icing cakes.

fondle ▸ verb (**fondles, fondling, fondled**) stroke or caress lovingly or in a sexual way.

SYNONYMS **caress,** stroke, pat, pet, finger, tickle, play with.

fondue ▸ noun a dish in which you dip small pieces of food into melted cheese or a hot sauce.

font ▸ noun **1** a large stone bowl in a church for the water used in baptizing people. **2** (Brit. also **fount**) a set of printed letters of a particular size and design.

fontanelle (US spelling **fontanel**) ▸ noun a soft area between the bones of the skull in a baby or fetus.

food ▸ noun any substance that people or animals eat to stay alive.

SYNONYMS **nourishment,** sustenance, nutriment, fare, cooking, cuisine, foodstuffs, refreshments, meals, provisions, rations; informal eats, grub.

■ **food chain** a series of creatures in which each depends on the next as a source of food. **food for thought** something that makes you think carefully about an issue. **food poisoning** illness caused by food contaminated by bacteria.

foodstuff ▸ noun a substance that can be eaten as food.

fool[1] ▸ noun **1** a person who behaves in a silly or stupid way. **2** historical a jester or clown.

SYNONYMS **1** *acting like a fool* **idiot,** ass, halfwit, blockhead, dunce, simpleton; informal nincompoop, clod, dimwit, dummy, fathead, numbskull; Brit. informal nitwit, twit, clot, berk, prat, pillock, wally, dork, twerp, charlie; Scottish informal nyaff, balloon; N. Amer. informal schmuck, turkey; Austral./NZ informal drongo, nong, galah, boofhead. **2** *she made a fool of me* **laughing stock,** dupe, gull; informal stooge, sucker, mug, fall guy; N. Amer. informal sap. ANTONYMS genius.

▸ verb **1** trick or deceive. **2** (**fool about** or **around**) act in a joking or silly way.

SYNONYMS **1** *he'd been fooled* **deceive,** trick, hoax, dupe, take in, mislead, delude, hoodwink, bluff, gull; informal bamboozle, take for a ride, have on; N. Amer. informal sucker; Austral. informal pull a swifty on. **2** *I'm not fooling, I promise* **pretend,** make believe, put on an act,

act, sham, fake, joke, jest; informal kid; Brit. informal have someone on.

■ **fool's gold** a yellowish mineral that can be mistaken for gold. **fool's paradise** a happy state that is based on ignoring possible trouble.

fool[2] ▸ noun Brit. a cold dessert made of puréed fruit and cream or custard.

foolhardy ▸ adjective recklessly daring.

foolish ▸ adjective silly or stupid.

SYNONYMS **stupid,** idiotic, mindless, unintelligent, thoughtless, imprudent, unwise, ill-advised, rash, reckless, foolhardy; informal dumb, dim, dim-witted, half-witted, thick, hare-brained; Brit. informal barmy, daft; Scottish & N. English informal glaikit; N. Amer. informal dumb-ass, chowderheaded. ANTONYMS sensible, wise.

□ **foolishly** adverb **foolishness** noun.

foolproof ▸ adjective incapable of going wrong or being wrongly used.

foolscap ▸ noun Brit. a size of paper, about 330 × 200 (or 400) mm.

foot ▸ noun (plural **feet**) **1** the part of the leg below the ankle, on which a person walks. **2** the bottom of something vertical. **3** the end of a bed. **4** a unit of length equal to 12 inches (30.48 cm). **5** a group of syllables making up a basic unit of rhythm in poetry.
▸ verb informal pay a bill.
■ **foot-and-mouth disease** a disease of cattle and sheep, causing ulcers on the hoofs and around the mouth.

footage ▸ noun a length of film made for cinema or television.

football ▸ noun **1** a team game involving kicking a ball, in particular (in the UK) soccer or (in the US) American football. **2** a large inflated ball used in football.
□ **footballer** noun.

footbridge ▸ noun a bridge for pedestrians.

footfall ▸ noun the sound of a footstep or footsteps.

foothill ▸ noun a low hill at the base of a mountain.

foothold ▸ noun **1** a place where you can put a foot down securely while climbing. **2** a secure position from which to make further progress.

footing ▸ noun **1** a secure grip with the feet. **2** the basis on which something is established or operates.

SYNONYMS **1** *a solid financial footing* **basis,** base, foundation. **2** *on an equal footing* **standing,** status, position, condition, arrangement, basis, relationship, terms.

footlights ▸ plural noun a row of spotlights along the front of a stage at the level of the actors' feet.

footling ▸ adjective unimportant and irritating.

footloose ▸ adjective free to do as you please.

footman ▸ noun (plural **footmen**) a servant who lets in visitors and serves food at the table.

footnote ▸ noun an additional piece of information printed at the bottom of a page.

footpad ▸ noun (in the past) a highwayman who operated on foot.

footpath ▸ noun a path for people to walk along.

footprint ▸ noun the mark left by a foot or shoe on the ground.

footsore ▸ adjective having sore feet from walking.

footstep ▸ noun a step taken in walking.

footstool ▸ noun a low stool for resting the feet on when sitting.

fop ▸ noun a man who is too concerned with his clothes and appearance.
□ **foppish** adjective.

for ▸ preposition **1** affecting or relating to. **2** in favour of. **3** on behalf of. **4** because of. **5** so as to get, have, or do. **6** in place of. **7** in exchange for. **8** in the direction of. **9** over a distance or during a period. **10** so as to happen at.
▸ conjunction literary because.

fora plural of FORUM.

forage ▸ verb (**forages, foraging, foraged**) search for food.
▸ noun food for horses and cattle.

foray ▸ noun **1** a sudden attack or move into enemy territory. **2** a brief but spirited attempt to become involved in a new activity.

forbear[1] /for-**bair**/ ▸ verb (**forbears, forbearing, forbore**; past participle **forborne**) stop yourself from doing something.

forbear[2] /for-**bair**/ ➡ FOREBEAR.

forbearance ▸ noun patient self-control.

forbearing ▸ adjective patient and self-controlled.

forbid ▸ verb (**forbids, forbidding, forbade** or **forbad**; past participle **forbidden**) **1** refuse to allow something. **2** order someone not to do something.

SYNONYMS **prohibit,** ban, outlaw, make illegal, veto, proscribe, embargo, bar, debar, rule out.
ANTONYMS permit.

forbidding ▸ adjective appearing unfriendly or threatening.

SYNONYMS **threatening,** ominous, menacing, sinister, brooding, daunting.
ANTONYMS inviting.

□ **forbiddingly** adverb.

force ▸ noun **1** physical strength or energy that makes something move. **2** violence used to obtain or achieve something. **3** effect or influence. **4** a person or thing that has influence. **5** an organized group of soldiers, police, or workers. **6** (**the forces**) Brit. the army, navy, and air force.

SYNONYMS **1** *he pushed with all his force* **strength,** power, energy, might, effort. **2** *they used force to achieve their aims* **coercion,** compulsion, constraint, duress, pressure, oppression, harassment, intimidation, violence; informal arm-twisting. **3** *the force of the argument* **power,** weight, effectiveness, validity, strength, significance, influence, authority; informal punch. **4** *a peacekeeping force* **body,** group, outfit, party, team, detachment, unit, squad.

▸ verb (**forces, forcing, forced**) **1** make someone do something against their will. **2** use physical strength to move something. **3** achieve something by making an effort: *he forced a smile.* **4** (**force something on**) impose something on.

SYNONYMS **1** *he was forced to pay* **compel,** coerce, make, constrain, oblige, impel, drive, pressure, press-gang, bully; informal lean on, twist someone's arm. **2** *the door had to be forced* **break open,** knock/smash/break down, kick in. **3** *water was forced through a hole* **propel,** push, thrust, shove, drive, press, pump. **4** (**forced**) *a forced smile* **strained,** unnatural, artificial, false, feigned, simulated, contrived, laboured, affected, hollow; informal phoney, pretend, put on. **5** (**forced**) *forced repatriation* **enforced,** compulsory, obligatory, mandatory, involuntary, imposed, required.

■ **force-feed** force someone to eat food. **in force 1** in great strength or numbers. **2** (of a law or rule) in effect.

forceful ▸ adjective powerful and confident.

SYNONYMS **1** *a forceful personality* **dynamic,** energetic, assertive, authoritative, vigorous, powerful, strong, pushy; informal in-your-face, go-ahead, feisty. **2** *a forceful argument* **convincing,** cogent, compelling, strong, powerful, persuasive, coherent.
ANTONYMS weak, submissive, unconvincing.

□ **forcefully** adverb.

forcemeat ▸ noun chopped meat or vegetables used as a stuffing.

forceps /for-seps/ ▸ plural noun a pair of pincers used in surgery.

forcible ▸ adjective done by force.
□ **forcibly** adverb.

ford ▸ noun a shallow place in a river or stream where it can be crossed.
▸ verb cross a river or stream at a ford.

fore ▸ adjective found or placed in front.
▸ noun the front part of something.
▸ combining form (fore-) **1** in front. **2** in advance. **3** coming before: *forefather*.
▸ exclamation called out as a warning to people in the path of a golf ball.

forearm¹ ▸ noun the part of a person's arm from the elbow to the wrist or the fingertips.

forearm² ▸ verb (be forearmed) be prepared in advance for danger or attack.

forebear (or forbear) ▸ noun an ancestor.

foreboding ▸ noun a feeling that something bad will happen.

forecast ▸ verb (forecasts, forecasting, forecast or forecasted) predict what will happen in the future.

> SYNONYMS *they forecast record profits* **predict,** prophesy, foretell, foresee.

▸ noun a prediction.

> SYNONYMS *a gloomy forecast* **prediction,** prophecy, prognostication, prognosis.

□ forecaster noun.

forecastle (or fo'c's'le) /fohk-suhl/ ▸ noun the front part of a ship below the deck.

foreclose ▸ verb (forecloses, foreclosing, foreclosed) take possession of a property because the occupant has not kept up their mortgage payments.
□ foreclosure noun.

forecourt ▸ noun **1** an open area in front of a large building or petrol station. **2** Tennis the part of the court between the service line and the net.

forefather ▸ noun an ancestor.

forefinger ▸ noun the finger next to the thumb.

forefoot ▸ noun (plural forefeet) each of the two front feet of a four-footed animal.

forefront ▸ noun the leading position.

forego¹ → FORGO.

forego² ▸ verb (foregoes, foregoing, forewent; past participle foregone) old use come before in place or time.
■ foregone conclusion a result that can be easily predicted.

foregoing ▸ adjective previously mentioned.

foreground ▸ noun **1** the part of a view or image nearest to the observer. **2** the most important position.

forehand ▸ noun (in tennis and similar games) a stroke played with the palm of the hand facing in the direction of the stroke.

forehead ▸ noun the part of the face above the eyebrows.

foreign ▸ adjective **1** having to do with a country or language other than your own. **2** coming from outside. **3** (foreign to) not familiar to or typical of.

> SYNONYMS **alien,** overseas, non-native, imported, distant, external, far-off, exotic, strange.
> ANTONYMS domestic, native.

■ foreign body a small piece of material that has entered the body from outside.

> ✔ -eign, not -iegn: for**eign**.

foreigner ▸ noun **1** a person from a foreign country. **2** informal a stranger.

> SYNONYMS **alien,** non-native, stranger, outsider, immigrant, settler, newcomer, incomer.
> ANTONYMS native, national.

foreknowledge ▸ noun awareness of something before it happens.

foreleg ▸ noun either of the front legs of a four-legged animal.

forelimb ▸ noun either of an animal's front limbs.

forelock ▸ noun a lock of hair growing just above the forehead.

foreman ▸ noun (plural foremen) **1** a worker who supervises other workers. **2** (in a law court) a person who is head of a jury.

foremast ▸ noun the mast of a ship nearest the bow.

foremost ▸ adjective highest in rank, importance, or position.

> SYNONYMS **leading,** principal, premier, prime, top, greatest, best, supreme, pre-eminent, outstanding, most important, most notable; N. Amer. ranking; informal number-one.
> ANTONYMS minor.

▸ adverb in the first place.

forename ▸ noun a person's first name.

forensic /fuh-ren-sik/ ▸ adjective **1** having to do with the use of scientific methods in investigating crime. **2** having to do with courts of law.

foreplay ▸ noun activities such as kissing and touching that people may engage in before having sex.

forerunner ▸ noun a person or thing which exists before another comes or is developed.

foresee ▸ verb (foresees, foreseeing, foresaw; past participle foreseen) be aware of something before it happens; predict.

> SYNONYMS **anticipate,** expect, envisage, predict, forecast, foretell, prophesy.

□ foreseeable adjective.

foreshadow ▸ verb be a warning or indication of a future event.

foreshore ▸ noun the part of a shore between the highest and lowest levels reached by the sea.

foreshorten ▸ verb **1** portray something as being closer or shallower than it really is. **2** end something before the usual or intended time.

foresight ▸ noun the ability to predict future events and needs.

foreskin ▸ noun the roll of skin covering the end of the penis.

forest ▸ noun **1** a large area covered thickly with trees and plants. **2** a large number of tangled or upright objects.
□ **forested** adjective.

forestall ▸ verb prevent or delay something by taking action in advance.

forestry ▸ noun the science or practice of planting and taking care of forests.
□ **forester** noun.

foretaste ▸ noun a sample of something that is to come.

foretell ▸ verb (**foretells, foretelling, foretold**) predict.

SYNONYMS **predict**, forecast, prophesy, foresee, anticipate, envisage, warn of.

forethought ▸ noun careful consideration of what will be necessary or may happen in the future.

forever ▸ adverb **1** (also **for ever**) for all future time. **2** a very long time. **3** continually.

SYNONYMS **1** *their love would last forever* **for always,** evermore, for ever and ever, for good, for all time, until the end of time, eternally; N. Amer. forevermore; informal until the cows come home. **2** *he was forever banging into things* **always,** continually, constantly, perpetually, incessantly, endlessly, persistently, repeatedly, regularly; informal 24-7.
ANTONYMS never, occasionally.

forewarn ▸ verb warn in advance.

forewent past of FOREGO¹, FOREGO².

foreword ▸ noun a short introduction to a book.

forfeit /for-fit/ ▸ verb (**forfeits, forfeiting, forfeited**) lose property or a right as a punishment for doing wrong.

SYNONYMS **lose,** be deprived of, surrender, relinquish, sacrifice, give up, renounce, forgo.
ANTONYMS retain.

▸ noun a punishment for doing wrong.

SYNONYMS **penalty,** sanction, punishment, penance, fine, confiscation, loss, forfeiture, surrender.

forge¹ ▸ verb (**forges, forging, forged**) **1** shape a metal object by heating and hammering it. **2** create something through effort. **3** produce a copy of a banknote, signature, etc. to deceive people.

SYNONYMS **1** *he forged a huge sword* **hammer out,** beat out, fashion. **2** *they forged a partnership* **build,** construct, form, create, establish, set up. **3** *he forged her signature* **fake,** falsify, counterfeit, copy, imitate; informal pirate. **4** (**forged**) **fake,** false, counterfeit, imitation, copied, pirate, bogus; informal phoney, dud.

▸ noun **1** a blacksmith's workshop. **2** a furnace for melting or refining metal.
□ **forger** noun.

forge² ▸ verb (**forges, forging, forged**) **1** move forward gradually or steadily. **2** (**forge ahead**) make progress.

forgery ▸ noun **1** the action of forging a banknote, work of art, etc. **2** a forged or copied item.

SYNONYMS *the painting was a forgery* **fake,** counterfeit, fraud, imitation, replica, copy, pirate copy; informal phoney.

forget ▸ verb (**forgets, forgetting, forgot;** past participle **forgotten** or chiefly US **forgot**) **1** be unable to remember. **2** fail to remember to do something. **3** stop thinking of. **4** (**forget yourself**) behave in an inappropriate or unacceptable way.

SYNONYMS **1** *he forgot where he was* **fail to remember,** be unable to remember. **2** *I never forget my briefcase* **leave behind,** fail to take/bring, travel/leave home without. **3** *I forgot to close the door* **neglect,** fail, omit.
ANTONYMS remember.

■ **forget-me-not** a plant with light blue flowers.
□ **forgettable** adjective.

forgetful ▸ adjective tending to forget things.
□ **forgetfully** adverb.

forgive ▸ verb (**forgives, forgiving, forgave;** past participle **forgiven**) **1** stop feeling angry or resentful towards a person who has done something hurtful or wrong. **2** excuse an offence or mistake.

SYNONYMS **1** *she would not forgive him* **pardon,** excuse, exonerate, absolve. **2** *you must forgive his rude conduct* **excuse,** overlook, disregard, ignore, make allowances for, turn a blind eye to, condone, indulge, tolerate.
ANTONYMS blame, resent.

□ **forgivable** adjective.

forgiveness ▸ noun the action of forgiving, or the state of being forgiven.

SYNONYMS **pardon,** absolution, exoneration, indulgence, clemency,

mercy, reprieve, amnesty; informal let-off.
ᴀɴᴛᴏɴʏᴍꜱ mercilessness, punishment.

forgo (or **forego**) ▶ verb (**forgoes, forgoing, forwent**; past participle **forgone**) go without something that you want.

fork ▶ noun **1** an object with two or more prongs used for lifting or holding food. **2** a similar-shaped farm or garden tool used for digging or lifting. **3** the point where a road, river, etc. divides into two parts. **4** either of two such parts.
▶ verb **1** divide into two parts. **2** take one route or the other at a fork. **3** dig or lift with a fork. **4** (**fork something out**) informal pay money.

> ꜱʏɴᴏɴʏᴍꜱ **split**, branch, divide, separate, part, diverge, go in different directions, bifurcate.

forked ▶ adjective **1** having a divided or fork-shaped end. **2** in the shape of a zigzag.

forklift truck ▶ noun a vehicle with a device on the front for lifting and carrying heavy loads.

forlorn /fer-**lorn**/ ▶ adjective **1** pitifully sad and lonely. **2** unlikely to succeed or be fulfilled: *a forlorn hope*.
□ **forlornly** adverb.

form ▶ noun **1** the shape or arrangement of something. **2** a particular way in which a thing exists. **3** a type. **4** a printed document with blank spaces for information to be filled in. **5** the current standard of play of a sports player or team. **6** a person's mood and state of health. **7** the way something is usually done. **8** Brit. a class or year in a school.

> ꜱʏɴᴏɴʏᴍꜱ **1** *the form of the landscape* **shape,** configuration, formation, structure, construction, arrangement, appearance, exterior, outline, format, layout, design. **2** *the human form* **body,** shape, figure, frame, physique, anatomy; informal vital statistics. **3** *the infection takes different forms* **manifestation,** appearance, embodiment, incarnation, semblance, shape, guise. **4** *sponsorship is a form of advertising* **kind,** sort, type, class, category, variety, genre, brand, style. **5** *you have to fill in a form* **questionnaire,** document, coupon, slip. **6** *what form is your daughter in?* **class,** year; N. Amer. grade. **7** *in good form* **condition,** fettle, shape, health; Brit. informal nick.

▶ verb **1** create something by shaping material or bringing together parts. **2** go to make up. **3** establish or develop.

> ꜱʏɴᴏɴʏᴍꜱ **1** *formed from mild steel* **make,** construct, build, manufacture, fabricate, assemble, put together, create, fashion, shape. **2** *he formed a plan* **formulate,** devise, conceive, work out, think up, lay, draw up, put together, produce, fashion, concoct, forge, hatch; informal dream up. **3** *they formed a company* **set up,** establish, found, launch, create, institute, start, inaugurate. **4** *a mist was forming* **materialize,** come into being/existence, emerge, develop, take shape, gather, accumulate, collect, amass. **5** *his men formed themselves into a line* **arrange,** draw up, line up, assemble, organize, sort, order. **6** *these parts form an integrated whole* **comprise,** make, make up, constitute, compose, add up to.
> ᴀɴᴛᴏɴʏᴍꜱ dissolve, disappear.

□ **formless** adjective.

formal ▶ adjective **1** suitable for or referring to official or important occasions. **2** officially recognized. **3** arranged in a regular way, according to an exact plan.

> ꜱʏɴᴏɴʏᴍꜱ **1** *a formal dinner* **ceremonial,** ritualistic, ritual, conventional, traditional, stately, solemn, elaborate. **2** *a very formal manner* **aloof,** reserved, remote, detached, unapproachable, stiff, stuffy, ceremonious, correct, proper; informal stand-offish. **3** *formal permission* **official,** legal, authorized, approved, certified, endorsed, sanctioned, licensed, recognized.
> ᴀɴᴛᴏɴʏᴍꜱ informal, friendly, casual, colloquial, unofficial.

□ **formally** adverb.

formaldehyde /for-**mal**-di-hyd/ ▶ noun a strong-smelling gas mixed with water and used as a preservative and disinfectant.

formalin /for-muh-lin/ ▶ noun a solution of formaldehyde in water.

formality ▶ noun (plural **formalities**) **1** a thing done to follow rules or usual customs. **2** correct and formal behaviour. **3** (a **formality**) a thing done or happening as a matter of course.

> ꜱʏɴᴏɴʏᴍꜱ **1** *the formality of the occasion* **ceremony,** ritual, protocol, decorum, solemnity. **2** *his formality was off-putting* **aloofness,** reserve, remoteness, detachment, unapproachability, stiffness, stuffiness, correctness; informal stand-offishness. **3** *we keep the formalities to a minimum* **official procedure,** bureaucracy, red tape, paperwork. **4** *the interview is just a formality* **routine,** routine practice, normal procedure.
> ᴀɴᴛᴏɴʏᴍꜱ informality, friendliness.

formalize (or **formalise**) ▶ verb (**formalizes, formalizing, formalized**) make an arrangement official.

format ▶ noun **1** the way in which something is arranged or presented. **2** the shape, size, and presentation of a book, document, etc.

f

f

SYNONYMS **design,** style, appearance, look, form, shape, size, arrangement, plan, structure, scheme, composition, configuration.

▶ verb (**formats, formatting, formatted**) give something a particular format.

formation ▶ noun **1** the action of forming. **2** something that has been formed. **3** a particular structure or arrangement.

SYNONYMS **1** *the formation of the island* **emergence,** genesis, development, evolution, shaping, origin. **2** *the formation of a new government* **establishment,** setting up, institution, foundation, creation, inauguration. **3** *fighters flying in a V formation* **configuration,** arrangement, grouping, pattern, array, alignment, order.
ANTONYMS destruction, disappearance, dissolution.

formative ▶ adjective having a strong influence in the way something is formed.

former[1] ▶ adjective **1** having been previously: *her former boyfriend.* **2** in the past. **3** (**the former**) referring to the first of two things mentioned.

SYNONYMS **1** *the former bishop* **one-time,** erstwhile, sometime, ex-, previous, preceding, earlier, prior, last. **2** *in former times* **earlier,** old, past, bygone, olden, long ago, gone by, long past, of old. **3** *the former view* **first-mentioned,** first.
ANTONYMS future, current, latter.

former[2] ▶ noun **1** a person or thing that forms something. **2** Brit. a person in a particular school year.

formerly ▶ adverb in the past.

SYNONYMS **previously,** earlier, before, until now/then, once, once upon a time, at one time, in the past.

Formica ▶ noun trademark a hard plastic material used for worktops, cupboard doors, etc.

formic acid ▶ noun an acid present in the fluid produced by some ants.

formidable ▶ adjective frightening or intimidating through being very large, powerful, or capable.

SYNONYMS **1** *a formidable beast* **intimidating,** forbidding, alarming, frightening, awesome, fearsome, threatening. **2** *a formidable pianist* **accomplished,** masterly, virtuoso, expert, impressive, powerful, terrific, superb; informal tremendous, nifty, crack, ace, wizard, magic, mean, wicked, deadly.
ANTONYMS pleasant-looking, comforting, poor.

□ **formidably** adverb.

formula ▶ noun (plural **formulae** /for-myuu-lee/ or **formulas**) **1** a mathematical relationship or rule expressed in symbols. **2** a set of chemical symbols showing what elements are present in a compound. **3** a method for achieving something. **4** a fixed form of words used in particular situations. **5** a list of ingredients with which something is made. **6** a powder based milky drink for babies.

SYNONYMS **1** *a legal formula* **form of words,** set expression, phrase, saying. **2** *a peace formula* **recipe,** prescription, blueprint, plan, policy, method, procedure.

formulaic /for-myuu-**lay**-ik/ ▶ adjective **1** containing a set form of words. **2** made by closely following a rule or style.

formulate ▶ verb (**formulates, formulating, formulated**) **1** create or prepare something methodically. **2** express an idea clearly and briefly.

SYNONYMS **1** *the miners formulated a plan* **devise,** conceive, work out, think up, lay, draw up, form, concoct, contrive, forge, hatch, prepare, develop. **2** *how Marx formulated his question* **express,** phrase, word, define, specify, put into words, frame, couch, put, articulate, say.

□ **formulation** noun.

fornicate ▶ verb (**fornicates, fornicating, fornicated**) formal have sex with someone you are not married to.
□ **fornication** noun **fornicator** noun.

forsake ▶ verb (**forsakes, forsaking, forsook**; past participle **forsaken**) literary **1** abandon. **2** give up.

forsooth ▶ adverb old use indeed.

forswear ▶ verb (**forswears, forswearing, forswore**; past participle **forsworn**) formal agree to give up or do without.

forsythia ▶ noun a shrub with bright yellow flowers.

fort ▶ noun a building constructed to defend a place against attack.

SYNONYMS **fortress,** castle, citadel, bunker, stronghold, fortification, bastion.

■ **hold the fort** be responsible for something while a person is away.

forte /for-tay/ ▶ noun a thing for which someone has a particular talent.

SYNONYMS **strength,** strong point, speciality, strong suit, talent, skill, gift; informal thing.
ANTONYMS weakness.

forth ▶ adverb old use **1** forwards or into view. **2** onwards in time.

forthcoming ▶ adjective **1** about to happen or appear. **2** made available when required. **3** willing to reveal information.

SYNONYMS **1** *forthcoming events* **coming,** upcoming, approaching, imminent, impending, future. **2** *no reply was forthcoming* **available,** on offer, offered. **3** *he was not very forthcoming* **communicative,** talkative, chatty, expansive, expressive, frank, open, candid.
ANTONYMS past, current, unavailable, uncommunicative.

forthright ▸ adjective direct and outspoken.

forthwith ▸ adverb without delay.

fortify ▸ verb (fortifies, fortifying, fortified) **1** strengthen a place to protect it against attack. **2** give strength or energy to. **3** add alcohol or vitamins to food or drink.

SYNONYMS **1** *measures to fortify the building* **strengthen,** secure, barricade, protect. **2** *I'll have a drink to fortify me* **invigorate,** strengthen, energize, enliven, animate, vitalize; informal pep up, buck up.
ANTONYMS weaken, sedate, subdue.

◻ **fortification** noun.

fortissimo /for-**tiss**-i-moh/ ▸ adverb & adjective Music very loud or loudly.

fortitude ▸ noun courage and strength when facing pain or trouble.

SYNONYMS **courage,** bravery, endurance, resilience, mettle, strength of character, backbone, grit; informal guts; Brit. informal bottle.
ANTONYMS faint-heartedness.

fortnight ▸ noun Brit. a period of two weeks.

fortnightly Brit. ▸ adjective & adverb happening or produced every two weeks.

fortress ▸ noun a building or town which has been strengthened against attack.

SYNONYMS **fort,** castle, citadel, bunker, stronghold, fortification.

fortuitous /for-**tyoo**-i-tuhss/ ▸ adjective **1** happening by chance. **2** lucky.
◻ **fortuitously** adverb.

fortunate ▸ adjective **1** involving good luck. **2** advantageous or favourable.

SYNONYMS **1** *he was fortunate enough to survive* **lucky,** favoured, blessed, blessed with good luck, in luck; Brit. informal jammy. **2** *in a fortunate position* **favourable,** advantageous, happy.
ANTONYMS unfortunate, unfavourable.

fortunately ▸ adverb it is fortunate that.

SYNONYMS **luckily,** by good luck, by good fortune, as luck would have it, happily, mercifully, thankfully.

fortune ▸ noun **1** chance or luck as it affects human affairs. **2** (fortunes) the success or failure of a person or undertaking. **3** a large amount of money or property.

SYNONYMS **1** *fortune favoured him* **chance,** accident, coincidence, serendipity, destiny, providence; N. Amer. happenstance. **2** *a change of fortune* **luck,** fate, destiny, predestination, the stars, karma, lot. **3** *an upswing in Sheffield's fortunes* **circumstances,** state of affairs, condition, position, situation. **4** *he made his fortune in steel* **wealth,** money, riches, assets, resources, means, possessions, property, estate.

forty ▸ cardinal number (plural **forties**) ten less than fifty; 40. (Roman numeral: **xl** or **XL**.)
■ **forty winks** informal a short daytime sleep.
◻ **fortieth** ordinal number.

✔ **for-**, not **four-**: **forty**.

forum ▸ noun (plural **forums**) **1** a meeting or opportunity for exchanging views. **2** (plural **fora**) (in ancient Roman cities) a square or marketplace used for public business.

SYNONYMS **meeting,** assembly, gathering, rally, conference, seminar, convention, symposium.

forward ▸ adverb & adjective **1** in the direction that you are facing or travelling. **2** towards a successful end. **3** ahead in time. **4** in or near the front of a ship or aircraft.

SYNONYMS **1** *the traffic moved forward* **ahead,** forwards, onwards, onward, on, further. **2** *the winner stepped forward* **towards the front,** out, forth, into view, up. **3** *a forward movement* **onward,** advancing. **4** *the Red Army's forward bridgehead* **front,** advance, foremost, leading. **5** *from that day forward* **onward,** onwards, on, forth, for ever. **6** *forward planning* **future,** forward-looking, for the future, anticipatory.
ANTONYMS backwards, backward, rear.

▸ adjective behaving in a way that is too confident or friendly.

SYNONYMS *the girls were very forward* **bold,** brazen, cheeky, shameless, familiar, overfamiliar, presumptuous; informal fresh.
ANTONYMS shy.

▸ noun an attacking player in sport.
▸ verb send a letter, especially on to a further destination.

SYNONYMS **1** *my mother forwarded your letter* **send on,** post on, redirect, readdress, pass on. **2** *the goods were forwarded by sea* **send,** dispatch, transmit, carry, convey, deliver, ship.

◻ **forwards** adverb.

forwent past of FORGO.

fossil ▸ noun the remains of a prehistoric plant or animal that have become hardened into rock.
■ **fossil fuel** a fuel such as coal or gas that is formed from the remains of animals and plants.

fossilize (or **fossilise**) ▸ verb (**fossilizes, fossilizing, fossilized**) preserve an animal or plant so that it becomes a fossil.
□ **fossilization** noun.

foster ▸ verb (**fosters, fostering, fostered**) 1 encourage the development of. 2 bring up a child that is not your own by birth.

SYNONYMS 1 *he fostered the arts* **encourage,** promote, further, nurture, help, aid, assist, support, back. 2 *they fostered two children* **bring up,** rear, raise, care for, take care of, look after, provide for.
ANTONYMS suppress, neglect.

fought past and past participle of FIGHT.

foul ▸ adjective 1 having a disgusting smell or taste. 2 very unpleasant. 3 wicked or obscene. 4 polluted.

SYNONYMS 1 *a foul smell* **disgusting,** revolting, repulsive, repugnant, abhorrent, loathsome, offensive, sickening, nauseating; informal ghastly, gruesome, gross. 2 *foul drinking water* **contaminated,** polluted, infected, tainted, impure, filthy, dirty, unclean. 3 *foul language* **vulgar,** crude, coarse, filthy, dirty, obscene, indecent, naughty, offensive; informal blue.
ANTONYMS pleasant, clean.

▸ noun (in sport) a piece of play that is not allowed by the rules.
▸ verb 1 make foul or dirty. 2 (in sport) commit a foul against. 3 (**foul something up**) make a mistake with something. 4 make a cable or anchor become entangled or jammed.

SYNONYMS 1 *the river had been fouled* **dirty,** pollute, contaminate, poison, taint. 2 *the trawler had fouled its nets* **tangle up,** entangle, snarl, catch, entwine.
ANTONYMS clean up, disentangle.

■ **foul-mouthed** using bad language. **foul play** 1 unfair play in sport. 2 criminal or violent activity.
□ **foully** adverb.

found[1] past and past participle of FIND.

found[2] ▸ verb 1 establish an institution or organization. 2 (**be founded on**) be based on a particular concept.

SYNONYMS **establish,** set up, start, begin, get going, institute, inaugurate, launch.
ANTONYMS dissolve.

found[3] ▸ verb melt and mould metal to make an object.

foundation ▸ noun 1 the lowest part of a building, which supports the weight. 2 an underlying basis or reason. 3 an institution or organization. 4 the action of founding something. 5 a cream or powder applied to the face as a base for other make-up.

SYNONYMS 1 *the foundations of the wall* **footing,** foot, base, substructure, underpinning. 2 *there was no foundation for the claim* **justification,** grounds, evidence, basis. 3 *an educational foundation* **endowed institution,** charitable body, funding agency.

founder[1] ▸ noun a person who founds an institution or settlement.

SYNONYMS *the founder of modern physics* **originator,** creator, (founding) father, architect, developer, pioneer, author, inventor, mastermind.

founder[2] ▸ verb (**founders, foundering, foundered**) 1 (of a plan or undertaking) fail; come to nothing. 2 (of a ship) fill with water and sink.

SYNONYMS 1 *the scheme foundered* **fail,** be unsuccessful, fall flat, fall through, collapse, backfire, meet with disaster; informal flop, bomb. 2 *the ship foundered* **sink,** go to the bottom, go down, be lost at sea.
ANTONYMS succeed, be raised.

foundling ▸ noun a child that has been abandoned by its parents and is discovered and cared for by other people.

foundry ▸ noun (plural **foundries**) a workshop or factory for casting metal.

fount ▸ noun 1 a source of a desirable quality. 2 literary a spring or fountain. 3 ➡ FONT.

fountain ▸ noun 1 a decorative structure in a pool or lake from which a jet of water is pumped into the air. 2 literary a natural spring of water.

SYNONYMS 1 *a fountain of water* **jet,** spray, spout, spurt, cascade, water feature. 2 *a fountain of knowledge* **source,** fount, well, reservoir, fund, mine.

■ **fountain pen** a pen with a container from which ink flows to the nib.

fountainhead ▸ noun an original source of something.

four ▸ cardinal number 1 one more than three; 4. (Roman numeral: **iv** or **IV**.) 2 Cricket a hit that reaches the boundary after first hitting the ground, scoring four runs.
■ **four-poster bed** a bed with a post at each corner holding up a canopy. **four-square** having a square shape and solid appearance.

foursome ▸ noun a group of four people.

fourteen ▸ cardinal number one more than thirteen; 14. (Roman numeral: **xiv** or **XIV**.)
□ **fourteenth** ordinal number.

fourth ▸ ordinal number **1** number four in a sequence; 4th. **2** (**a fourth** or **one fourth**) a quarter.
□ **fourthly** adverb.

fowl ▸ noun (plural **fowl** or **fowls**) **1** a bird kept for its eggs or meat, such as a chicken or turkey. **2** birds as a group.

fox ▸ noun an animal with a pointed muzzle, bushy tail, and a reddish coat.
▸ verb informal baffle or deceive.

foxglove ▸ noun a tall plant with spikes of flowers shaped like the fingers of gloves.

foxhole ▸ noun a hole in the ground used by troops as a shelter against the enemy or as a place to fire from.

foxhound ▸ noun a breed of dog trained to hunt foxes in packs.

foxtrot ▸ noun a ballroom dance which involves switching between slow and quick steps.

foxy ▸ adjective (**foxier**, **foxiest**) **1** like a fox. **2** crafty or sly.

foyer /foy-ay/ ▸ noun a large entrance hall in a hotel or theatre.

SYNONYMS **entrance hall,** hallway, entry, porch, reception area, atrium, concourse, lobby, anteroom; N. Amer. entryway.

fracas /fra-kah/ ▸ noun (plural **fracas** /fra-kah, fra-kahz/) a noisy disturbance or quarrel.

fraction ▸ noun **1** a number that is not a whole number (e.g. ½, 0.5). **2** a very small part or amount.

SYNONYMS **1** *a fraction of the population* **tiny part,** fragment, snippet, snatch. **2** *he moved a fraction closer* **tiny amount,** little, bit, touch, soupçon, trifle, mite, shade, jot; informal smidgen, tad.
ANTONYMS whole.

fractional ▸ adjective **1** having to do with a fraction. **2** very small in amount.
□ **fractionally** adverb.

fractious ▸ adjective **1** bad-tempered. **2** difficult to control.

fracture ▸ noun **1** a crack or break. **2** the cracking or breaking of a hard object or material.

SYNONYMS **break,** crack, split, rupture, fissure.

▸ verb (**fractures**, **fracturing**, **fractured**) **1** break. **2** (of a group) break up.

SYNONYMS **break,** crack, split, rupture, snap, shatter, fragment, splinter.

fragile ▸ adjective **1** easily broken or damaged. **2** (of a person) delicate and vulnerable.

SYNONYMS **1** *fragile vases* **breakable,** delicate, brittle, flimsy, dainty, fine. **2** *the fragile ceasefire* **tenuous,** shaky, insecure, vulnerable, flimsy. **3** *she is*

still very fragile **weak,** delicate, frail, debilitated, ill, unwell, poorly, sickly.
ANTONYMS sturdy, durable, robust.
□ **fragility** noun.

fragment ▸ noun /frag-muhnt/ a small part that has broken off or come from something larger.

SYNONYMS **1** *meteorite fragments* **piece,** bit, particle, speck, chip, shard, sliver, splinter, flake. **2** *a fragment of conversation* **snatch,** snippet, scrap, bit.

▸ verb /frag-ment/ break into fragments.

SYNONYMS *explosions caused the chalk to fragment* **break up,** crack open, shatter, splinter, fracture, disintegrate, fall to pieces, fall apart.
□ **fragmentary** adjective **fragmentation** noun.

fragrance ▸ noun **1** a pleasant, sweet smell. **2** a perfume or aftershave.

SYNONYMS **1** *the fragrance of spring flowers* **sweet smell,** scent, perfume, bouquet, aroma, nose. **2** *a daring new fragrance* **perfume,** scent, eau de toilette.

fragrant ▸ adjective having a pleasant, sweet smell.

SYNONYMS **sweet-scented,** sweet-smelling, scented, perfumed, aromatic.
ANTONYMS smelly.

frail ▸ adjective **1** weak and delicate. **2** easily damaged or broken.

SYNONYMS **1** *a frail old lady* **weak,** delicate, feeble, infirm, ill, unwell, sickly, poorly. **2** *a frail structure* **fragile,** easily damaged, delicate, flimsy, insubstantial, unsteady, unstable, rickety.
ANTONYMS strong, robust.

frailty ▸ noun (plural **frailties**) the condition of being frail; weakness.

frame ▸ noun **1** a rigid structure surrounding a picture, door, etc. or giving support to a building or vehicle. **2** the structure of a person's body. **3** a single picture in a series forming a cinema or video film. **4** a single game of snooker.

SYNONYMS **1** *a tubular metal frame* **framework,** structure, substructure, skeleton, casing, chassis, shell. **2** *his tall, slender frame* **body,** figure, form, shape, physique, anatomy, build.

▸ verb (**frames**, **framing**, **framed**) **1** put a picture in a frame. **2** create or develop a plan or system. **3** informal produce false evidence against someone to make them appear guilty of a crime.

SYNONYMS **1** *he had the picture framed* **mount,** set in a frame. **2** *those who frame the regulations* **formulate,** draw up, draft, shape, compose, put together, form, devise.

■ **frame of mind** a particular mood.

framework ▶ noun a supporting or underlying structure.

> SYNONYMS **1** *a metal framework* **frame,** structure, skeleton, chassis, support, scaffolding. **2** *the framework of society* **structure,** shape, fabric, order, scheme, system, organization, anatomy; informal make-up.

franc ▶ noun the basic unit of money of Switzerland and some other countries, and formerly also of France, Belgium, and Luxembourg.

franchise ▶ noun **1** a licence allowing a person or company to use or sell certain products. **2** a business that has been given a franchise. **3** the right to vote in elections.

frank¹ ▶ adjective **1** honest and direct. **2** open or undisguised.

> SYNONYMS **1** *he was quite frank with me* **candid,** direct, forthright, plain, straight, to the point, matter-of-fact, open, honest; informal upfront. **2** *she looked at Sam with frank admiration* **open,** undisguised, unconcealed, naked, unmistakable, clear, obvious, transparent, patent, evident.
> ANTONYMS evasive, disguised.

□ **frankness** noun.

frank² ▶ verb stamp a mark on a letter or parcel to indicate that postage has been paid or does not need to be paid.

frankfurter ▶ noun a seasoned smoked sausage made of beef and pork.

frankincense ▶ noun a kind of sweet-smelling gum that is burnt as incense.

frankly ▶ adverb **1** in an honest and direct way. **2** to be frank.

> SYNONYMS **1** *he stated the case quite frankly* **candidly,** directly, plainly, straightforwardly, forthrightly, openly, honestly, without beating about the bush, bluntly. **2** *frankly, I'm not interested* **to be frank,** to be honest, to tell the truth, in all honesty.

frantic ▶ adjective **1** agitated because of fear, anxiety, etc. **2** done in a hurried and chaotic way.

> SYNONYMS **panic-stricken,** panicky, beside yourself, at your wits' end, distraught, overwrought, worked up, frenzied, frenetic, fraught, feverish, desperate; informal in a state, tearing your hair out; Brit. informal having kittens, in a flat spin.
> ANTONYMS calm.

□ **frantically** adverb.

fraternal ▶ adjective **1** brotherly. **2** having to do with a fraternity.

fraternity ▶ noun (plural **fraternities**) **1** a group of people sharing a common profession or interests. **2** N. Amer. a male students' society in a university or college. **3** friendship and support within a group.

> SYNONYMS **1** *a spirit of fraternity* **brotherhood,** fellowship, kinship, friendship, mutual support, solidarity, community. **2** *the teaching fraternity* **profession,** community, trade, set, circle. **3** *a college fraternity* **society,** club, association, group.

fraternize (or **fraternise**) ▶ verb (**fraternizes, fraternizing, fraternized**) be on friendly terms.
□ **fraternization** noun.

fratricide ▶ noun **1** the killing by someone of their brother or sister. **2** the accidental killing of your own forces in war.

fraud ▶ noun **1** the crime of deceiving someone in order to get money or goods. **2** a person who deceives other people by claiming to be something they are not.

> SYNONYMS **1** *he was arrested for fraud* **deception,** sharp practice, cheating, swindling, trickery, embezzlement, deceit, double-dealing, chicanery. **2** *social security frauds* **swindle,** racket, deception, trick, cheat, hoax; informal scam, con, rip-off, sting, fiddle; N. Amer. informal hustle. **3** *they exposed him as a fraud* **impostor,** fake, sham, charlatan, swindler, fraudster, confidence trickster; informal phoney.

fraudster ▶ noun a person who commits fraud.

fraudulent ▶ adjective **1** involving fraud. **2** deceitful or dishonest.

> SYNONYMS **dishonest,** cheating, swindling, corrupt, criminal, deceitful, double-dealing, duplicitous; informal crooked, shady, dirty; Brit. informal bent, dodgy; Austral./NZ informal shonky.
> ANTONYMS honest.

□ **fraudulently** adverb.

fraught ▶ adjective **1** (**fraught with**) filled with something undesirable. **2** causing or feeling anxiety or stress.

fray¹ ▶ verb **1** (of a fabric or rope) unravel or become worn at the edge. **2** (of a person's nerves or temper) show the effects of strain.

> SYNONYMS **1** (**frayed**) *a frayed collar* **worn,** threadbare, tattered, ragged, the worse for wear; informal tatty; N. Amer. informal raggedy. **2** (**frayed**) *his frayed nerves* **strained,** fraught, tense, edgy, stressed.

fray² ▶ noun (the fray) **1** a battle or fight. **2** a very competitive situation.

frazzle ▶ noun (a frazzle) informal **1** an exhausted state. **2** a charred or burnt state.
□ **frazzled** adjective.

freak ▶ noun **1** informal a person who is obsessed with a particular interest: *a fitness freak.* **2** a very unusual and unexpected event. **3** a person, animal, or plant with a physical abnormality.

> SYNONYMS **1** *a genetically engineered freak* **aberration,** abnormality, oddity, monster, monstrosity, mutant, chimera. **2** *the accident was a freak* **anomaly,** aberration, rarity, oddity, one-off, fluke, twist of fate. **3** *a bunch of freaks* **oddity,** eccentric, misfit, crank; informal oddball, weirdo, nut; Brit. informal nutter; N. Amer. informal wacko, kook. **4** *a fitness freak* **enthusiast,** fan, devotee, lover, aficionado; informal nut, fanatic, addict, maniac.

▶ verb (**freak out**) informal behave in a wild, excited, or shocked way.
□ **freakish** adjective **freaky** adjective.

freckle ▶ noun a small light brown spot on the skin.
□ **freckled** adjective **freckly** adjective.

free ▶ adjective (**freer, freest**) **1** not under the control of someone else. **2** not confined, obstructed, or fixed. **3** not being used. **4** (**free of** or **from**) not affected by. **5** given or available without charge. **6** (**free with**) giving something generously.

> SYNONYMS **1** *admission is free* **free of charge,** without charge, for nothing, complimentary, gratis; informal for free, on the house. **2** *free of any pressures* **without,** unencumbered by, unaffected by, clear of, rid of, exempt from, not liable to, safe from, immune to, excused. **3** *I'm free this afternoon* **unoccupied,** not busy, available, off duty, off work, on holiday, on leave, at leisure, with time to spare. **4** *bathroom's free* **vacant,** empty, available, unoccupied, not in use. **5** *a free nation* **independent,** self-governing, self-determining, sovereign, autonomous, democratic. **6** *the killer is still free* **on the loose,** at liberty, at large, loose, unrestrained. **7** *you are free to leave* **able,** in a position, allowed, permitted. **8** *the free flow of water* **unobstructed,** unimpeded, unrestricted, unhampered, clear, open. **9** *she was free with her money* **generous,** liberal, open-handed, unstinting.
> ANTONYMS chargeable, busy, occupied, captive, confined, obstructed, mean.

▶ adverb without cost or payment.
▶ verb (**frees, freeing, freed**) make free.

> SYNONYMS **1** *the hostages were freed* **release,** set free, let go, liberate, set loose, untie. **2** *victims were freed by firefighters* **extricate,** release, get out, cut free, pull free, rescue.
> ANTONYMS confine, trap.

■ **free enterprise** a system in which private businesses compete with each other. **free fall** unrestricted downward movement under the force of gravity. **free-for-all** a disorganized situation in which everyone may take part. **free-form** not in a regular or formal structure. **a free hand** freedom to do exactly what you want. **free house** Brit. a pub not controlled by a brewery. **free kick** (in soccer and rugby) an unopposed kick of the ball awarded when the opposition have broken the rules. **the free market** a system in which prices are determined by unrestricted competition between privately owned businesses. **free-range** referring to farming in which animals are kept in natural conditions where they can move around freely. **free-standing** not supported by another structure. **free trade** unrestricted international trade without taxes or regulations on imports and exports. **free will** the power to act according to your own wishes. **free verse** poetry that does not rhyme or have a regular rhythm.

freebie ▶ noun informal a thing given free of charge.

freedom ▶ noun **1** the right to act or speak freely. **2** the state of not being a prisoner or slave. **3** (**freedom from**) not being affected by something undesirable. **4** unrestricted use of something. **5** Brit. a special honour given to someone by a city.

> SYNONYMS **1** *a desperate bid for freedom* **liberty,** liberation, release, deliverance. **2** *the fight for freedom* **independence,** self-government, self-determination, self-rule, home rule, sovereignty, autonomy, democracy. **3** *freedom from political accountability* **exemption,** immunity, dispensation, impunity. **4** *patients have more freedom to choose who treats them* **right,** entitlement, privilege, prerogative, discretion, latitude, elbow room, licence, free rein, a free hand, carte blanche.
> ANTONYMS captivity, subjection, liability, obligation.

freehand ▶ adjective & adverb drawn by hand without a ruler or other aid.

freehold ▶ noun permanent ownership of land or property with the freedom to sell it whenever you want.
□ **freeholder** noun.

freelance ▶ adjective self-employed and working for different companies on particular assignments.

▶ noun (also **freelancer**) a freelance worker.
▶ verb (**freelances, freelancing, freelanced**) work as a freelance.

freeloader ▶ noun informal a person who takes advantage of other people's generosity.

freely ▶ adverb **1** not under someone else's control. **2** without restriction or restraint. **3** willingly and readily.

> SYNONYMS **1** *may I speak freely?* **openly,** candidly, frankly, directly, without beating about the bush, without mincing your words. **2** *they gave their time and labour freely* **voluntarily,** willingly, readily, of your own accord, of your own free will, without being told to.

freeman ▶ noun (plural **freemen**) **1** Brit. a person who has been given the freedom of a city. **2** historical a person who was not a slave or serf.

Freemason ▶ noun a member of an organization whose members help each other and hold secret ceremonies.
□ **Freemasonry** noun.

freesia /free-zhuh/ ▶ noun a plant with sweet-smelling, colourful flowers.

freestyle ▶ adjective (of a contest or sport) having few restrictions on the technique that competitors use.

freethinker ▶ noun a person who questions or rejects accepted opinions.

freeway ▶ noun N. Amer. a dual-carriageway main road.

freewheel ▶ verb ride a bicycle without using the pedals.

freeze ▶ verb (**freezes, freezing, froze**; past participle **frozen**) **1** (of a liquid) turn into a solid as a result of extreme cold. **2** become blocked or rigid with ice. **3** be very cold. **4** preserve something by storing it at a very low temperature. **5** suddenly become motionless with fear, shock, etc. **6** (of a computer screen) suddenly become locked. **7** keep or hold at a fixed level.

> SYNONYMS **1** *the stream had frozen* **ice over,** ice up, solidify. **2** *she froze in horror* **stop dead in your tracks,** stand (stock) still, go rigid, become motionless, become paralysed. **3** *the prices of basic foodstuffs were frozen* **fix,** hold, peg, set, limit, restrict, cap.
> ANTONYMS thaw.

▶ noun **1** an act of freezing. **2** a period of very cold weather.
■ **freeze-dry** preserve something by rapidly freezing it and then drying it in a vacuum. **freeze-frame** the stopping of a film or videotape to obtain a single still image.

freezer ▶ noun a refrigerated cabinet or room for preserving food at very low temperatures.

freezing ▶ adjective **1** having a temperature below 0°C. **2** very cold.

> SYNONYMS **1** *a freezing wind* **icy,** bitter, chill, frosty, glacial, arctic, wintry, subzero, raw, biting. **2** *you must be freezing* **frozen,** numb with cold, chilled to the bone/marrow.
> ANTONYMS balmy, hot.

freight ▶ noun goods transported by truck, train, ship, or aircraft.

> SYNONYMS **goods,** cargo, merchandise.

▶ verb transport goods by truck, train, etc.

freighter ▶ noun a large ship or aircraft designed to carry freight.

French ▶ adjective having to do with France or its language.
▶ noun the language of France, also used in parts of Belgium, Switzerland, Canada, etc.
■ **French dressing** a salad dressing of vinegar, oil, and seasonings. **French fries** chiefly N. Amer. chips. **French horn** a brass instrument with a coiled tube and a wide opening at the end. **French kiss** a kiss with contact between tongues. **French polish** a kind of polish used on wood to give it a very glossy finish. **French windows** glazed doors in an outside wall.

frenetic ▶ adjective fast and energetic in a rather wild and uncontrolled way.
□ **frenetically** adverb.

frenzied ▶ adjective wildly excited or uncontrolled.

> SYNONYMS **frantic,** wild, frenetic, hectic, feverish, fevered, mad, crazed, manic, furious, uncontrolled.
> ANTONYMS calm.

□ **frenziedly** adverb.

frenzy ▶ noun (plural **frenzies**) a state of uncontrolled excitement or wild behaviour.

> SYNONYMS **hysteria,** madness, mania, delirium, wild excitement, fever, lather, passion, panic, fury, rage.

frequency ▶ noun (plural **frequencies**) **1** the rate at which something happens. **2** the state of being frequent. **3** the number of cycles per second of a sound, light, or radio wave. **4** the particular waveband at which radio signals are transmitted.

frequent ▶ adjective /free-kwuhnt/ **1** happening or done many times at short intervals. **2** doing something often.

> SYNONYMS *frequent complaints* **recurrent,** recurring, repeated, periodic, continual, habitual, regular, successive, numerous, several.
> ANTONYMS occasional.

▶ verb /fri-kwent/ visit a place often.

> SYNONYMS *he frequented chic clubs* **visit,** patronize, spend time in, visit regularly,

haunt; informal hang out at.
ANTONYMS avoid.

frequently ▸ adverb at frequent intervals.

> SYNONYMS **often,** all the time, habitually, regularly, customarily, routinely, again and again, repeatedly, recurrently, continually; N. Amer. oftentimes.
> ANTONYMS infrequently.

fresco ▸ noun (plural **frescoes** or **frescos**) a painting that is done on wet plaster on a wall or ceiling.

fresh ▸ adjective **1** new or different. **2** (of food) recently made or obtained. **3** recently created and not faded. **4** pleasantly clean and cool: *fresh air.* **5** (of the wind) cool and fairly strong. **6** (of water) not salty. **7** full of energy. **8** informal too familiar with someone.

> SYNONYMS **1** *a fresh approach* **new,** modern, original, novel, different, innovative. **2** *fresh food* **recently made,** just picked, crisp, raw, natural, unprocessed. **3** *feeling fresh after a sleep* **refreshed,** rested, restored, energetic, vigorous, invigorated, lively, sprightly, bright, alert, bouncing, perky; informal full of beans, bright-eyed and bushy-tailed. **4** *a fresh breeze* **strong,** brisk, bracing, invigorating, chilly, cool; informal nippy; Brit. informal parky. **5** *the night air was fresh* **cool,** crisp, refreshing, invigorating, pure, clean, clear. **6** *he's getting too fresh* **impudent,** impertinent, insolent, presumptuous, forward, cheeky, disrespectful, rude; informal mouthy, saucy, lippy; N. Amer. informal sassy.
> ANTONYMS stale, old, used, cooked, preserved, processed, tired, light, warm, sultry, respectful.

□ **freshly** adverb **freshness** noun.

freshen ▸ verb **1** make or become fresh. **2** (**freshen up**) wash and tidy yourself.

fresher ▸ noun Brit. a first-year student at college or university.

freshman ▸ noun (plural **freshmen**) a first-year student at university or (N. Amer.) at high school.

fret¹ ▸ verb (**frets, fretting, fretted**) be anxious and restless.

> SYNONYMS **worry,** be anxious, distress yourself, upset yourself, concern yourself, agonize, lose sleep.

fret² ▸ noun each of the ridges on the neck of guitars and similar instruments.

fretful ▸ adjective anxious and restless.
□ **fretfully** adverb.

fretwork ▸ noun decorative designs cut into in wood.

friable /fry-uh-b'l/ ▸ adjective easily crumbled.

friar ▸ noun a member of certain religious orders of men.

friary ▸ noun (plural **friaries**) a building or community occupied by friars.

fricassée /fri-kuh-say, fri-kuh-see/ ▸ noun a dish of stewed or fried pieces of meat served in a thick white sauce.

friction ▸ noun **1** the resistance that one surface or object encounters when moving over another. **2** the action of one surface or object rubbing against another. **3** conflict or disagreement.

> SYNONYMS **1** *lubrication reduces friction* **rubbing,** chafing, grating, rasping, scraping, resistance, drag, abrasion. **2** *friction between father and son* **discord,** disagreement, dissension, dispute, conflict, hostility, animosity, antipathy, antagonism, resentment, acrimony, bitterness, bad feeling.
> ANTONYMS harmony.

Friday ▸ noun the day of the week before Saturday and following Thursday.

fridge ▸ noun an appliance in which food and drink are stored at a low temperature.

fried past and past participle of **FRY¹**.

friend ▸ noun **1** a person that you know well and like. **2** a supporter of a cause or organization. **3** (**Friend**) a Quaker.

> SYNONYMS **companion,** comrade, confidant, confidante, familiar, intimate, soul mate, playmate, playfellow, ally, associate; informal pal, chum; Brit. informal mate; N. Amer. informal buddy, amigo, compadre, homeboy.
> ANTONYMS enemy.

□ **friendless** adjective.

> ✔ **-ie-,** not **-ei-**: friend.

friendly ▸ adjective (**friendlier, friendliest**) **1** treating someone as a friend; on good terms. **2** kind and pleasant. **3** not harmful to a particular thing: *environment-friendly.*

> SYNONYMS **1** *a friendly woman* **amiable,** companionable, sociable, gregarious, comradely, neighbourly, hospitable, easy to get on with, affable, genial, cordial, warm, affectionate, convivial; Scottish couthy; informal chummy, pally; Brit. informal matey; N. Amer. informal buddy-buddy. **2** *friendly conversation* **amicable,** cordial, pleasant, easy, relaxed, casual, informal, unceremonious, close, intimate, familiar.
> ANTONYMS unfriendly, hostile.

▸ noun (plural **friendlies**) Brit. a game not forming part of a serious competition.
□ **friendliness** noun.

friendship ▸ noun **1** the state of being friends. **2** a relationship between friends.

> SYNONYMS **1** *ties of friendship* **friendliness,** affection, camaraderie,

comradeship, companionship, fellowship, closeness, affinity, unity, intimacy. **2** *lasting friendships* **relationship**, attachment, association, bond, tie, link, union.
ANTONYMS hostility.

frieze ▸ noun a broad horizontal band of sculpted or painted decoration.

frigate ▸ noun a kind of fast warship.

fright ▸ noun **1** a sudden strong feeling of fear. **2** a shock.

SYNONYMS **1** *she was paralysed with fright* **fear**, terror, horror, alarm, panic, dread, trepidation, dismay, nervousness. **2** *the experience gave everyone a fright* **scare**, shock, surprise, turn, jolt, start.
ANTONYMS pleasant surprise.

frighten ▸ verb make someone afraid.

SYNONYMS **scare**, startle, alarm, terrify, petrify, shock, chill, panic, unnerve, intimidate; informal **spook**; Brit. informal put the wind up.
ANTONYMS reassure.

□ **frightening** adjective **frighteningly** adverb.

frightful ▸ adjective **1** very unpleasant, serious, or shocking. **2** informal terrible; awful.

SYNONYMS **horrible**, horrific, ghastly, horrendous, awful, dreadful, terrible, nasty; informal **horrid**.

□ **frightfully** adverb.

frigid /frij-id/ ▸ adjective **1** literary very cold. **2** disapproving (of a woman) not interested in sex.
□ **frigidity** noun.

frill ▸ noun **1** a decorative strip of gathered or pleated cloth attached to the edge of clothing or material. **2** (**frills**) unnecessary extra features.
□ **frilled** adjective **frilly** adjective.

fringe ▸ noun **1** a decorative border of threads or tassels attached to the edge of clothing or material. **2** Brit. a part of someone's hair that hangs over the forehead. **3** the outer part of an area, group, etc.

SYNONYMS **1** *blue curtains with a yellow fringe* **edging**, border, trimming, frill, flounce, ruffle. **2** *the city's northern fringe* **edge**, border, margin, extremity, perimeter, periphery, rim, limits, outskirts.
ANTONYMS middle.

▸ adjective not part of the mainstream: *fringe theatre*.

SYNONYMS *fringe theatre* **alternative**, avant-garde, experimental, innovative, left-field, radical, off-Broadway.
ANTONYMS mainstream.

▸ verb (**fringes**, **fringing**, **fringed**) add a fringe to something.

■ **fringe benefit** something extra given to someone as well as wages.

frippery ▸ noun (plural **fripperies**) showy or unnecessary decoration.

frisbee ▸ noun trademark a plastic disc that you skim through the air as an outdoor game.

frisk ▸ verb **1** pass your hands over someone in a search for hidden weapons or drugs. **2** skip or move playfully.
▸ noun a playful skip or leap.

frisky ▸ adjective (**friskier**, **friskiest**) playful and full of energy.

frisson /free-son/ ▸ noun a sudden shiver of excitement.

fritillary /fri-til-luh-ri/ ▸ noun (plural **fritillaries**) **1** a plant with hanging bell-like flowers. **2** a butterfly with orange-brown wings.

fritter¹ ▸ verb (**fritters**, **frittering**, **frittered**) (**fritter something away**) waste time or money on unimportant matters.

fritter² ▸ noun a piece of food that is coated in batter and deep-fried.

frivolous ▸ adjective **1** not having any serious purpose or value. **2** (of a person) not treating things seriously.

SYNONYMS **flippant**, glib, facetious, joking, jokey, light-hearted, fatuous, inane; informal **flip**.
ANTONYMS serious.

□ **frivolity** noun **frivolously** adverb.

frizz ▸ verb (of hair) form into a mass of tight curls.
▸ noun a mass of tightly curled hair.
□ **frizzy** adjective.

frock ▸ noun **1** a dress. **2** a loose outer garment, worn by priests.
■ **frock coat** a man's long, double-breasted coat, worn on formal occasions.

frog ▸ noun an amphibian with a short body, very long hind legs for leaping, and no tail.
■ **have a frog in your throat** informal be hoarse.

frogman ▸ noun (plural **frogmen**) a diver equipped with a rubber suit, flippers, and breathing equipment.

frogmarch ▸ verb force someone to walk forward by holding their arms from behind.

frogspawn ▸ noun a mass of frogs' eggs surrounded by transparent jelly.

frolic ▸ verb (**frolics**, **frolicking**, **frolicked**) play or move about in a cheerful and lively way.
▸ noun a playful action or movement.

frolicsome ▸ adjective lively and playful.

from ▸ preposition **1** indicating the point at which a journey, process, or action starts.

2 indicating the source of something. **3** indicating separation, removal, or prevention. **4** indicating a cause. **5** indicating a difference.

fromage frais /from-ahzh fray/ ▸ noun a type of smooth, soft cheese.

frond ▸ noun the leaf of a palm, fern, or similar plant.

front ▸ noun **1** the part of an object that faces forwards or that is normally seen first. **2** the position directly ahead. **3** the furthest position that an army has reached. **4** a particular situation or area of activity. **5** (in weather forecasting) the forward edge of an advancing mass of air. **6** a false appearance or way of behaving. **7** a person or organization that is a cover for secret or illegal activities. **8** a very confident manner.

SYNONYMS **1** *the front of the boat* **fore**, foremost part, forepart, nose, head, bow, prow, foreground. **2** *a shop front* **frontage**, face, facing, facade, window. **3** *the front of the queue* **head**, beginning, start, top, lead. **4** *a brave front* **appearance**, air, face, manner, exterior, veneer, (outward) show, act, pretence. **5** *the shop was a front for his real business* **cover**, blind, disguise, facade, mask, cloak, screen, smokescreen, camouflage. ANTONYMS back.

▸ adjective having to do with the front.

SYNONYMS **leading**, lead, first, foremost. ANTONYMS back, last.

▸ verb **1** have the front facing towards. **2** be at the front of. **3** (**be fronted with**) have the front covered with. **4** be the leader or presenter of.
■ **the front line** the part of an army that is closest to the enemy. **front runner** the leader in a competition.

frontage ▸ noun **1** the front of a building. **2** a strip of land next to a street or waterway.

frontal ▸ adjective having to do with the front.
□ **frontally** adverb.

frontier ▸ noun **1** a border separating two countries. **2** the furthest part of land that has been settled. **3** the limit of what is known about a subject or area of activity.

SYNONYMS **border**, boundary, borderline, dividing line, perimeter, limit, edge.

frontispiece ▸ noun an illustration facing the title page of a book.

frontman ▸ noun (plural **frontmen**) a person who represents an illegal organization to make it seem respectable.

frost ▸ noun **1** white ice crystals that form on surfaces when the temperature falls below freezing. **2** a period of cold weather when frost forms.

frostbite ▸ noun injury to parts of the body caused by exposure to extreme cold.
□ **frostbitten** adjective.

frosted ▸ adjective **1** covered with frost. **2** (of glass) having a semi-transparent textured surface. **3** N. Amer. (of a cake) covered with icing.

frosting ▸ noun N. Amer. icing.

frosty ▸ adjective (**frostier**, **frostiest**) **1** (of the weather) very cold with frost forming on surfaces. **2** cold and unfriendly.

SYNONYMS **1** *a frosty morning* **cold**, freezing, frozen, icy, bitter, chill, wintry, arctic; informal nippy; Brit. informal parky. **2** *a frosty reception* **unfriendly**, cold, frigid, icy, glacial, inhospitable, unwelcoming, forbidding, hostile, stony. ANTONYMS warm, friendly.

□ **frostily** adverb.

froth ▸ noun **1** a mass of small bubbles in liquid. **2** appealing but trivial ideas or activities.
▸ verb produce or contain froth.
□ **frothy** adjective.

frown ▸ verb **1** make an angry or worried expression by bringing your eyebrows together so that lines appear on your forehead. **2** (**frown on**) disapprove of.

SYNONYMS **scowl**, glower, glare, lour, make a face, look daggers, give someone a black look, knit your brows; informal give someone a dirty look. ANTONYMS smile.

▸ noun a frowning expression.

frowsty ▸ adjective Brit. warm and stuffy.

frowzy (or **frowsy**) ▸ adjective scruffy and neglected in appearance.

froze past of FREEZE.

frozen past participle of FREEZE.

fructose /fruk-tohz/ ▸ noun a kind of sugar found in honey and fruit.

frugal /froo-g'l/ ▸ adjective **1** careful in the use of money or food. **2** (of a meal) plain and cheap.
□ **frugality** noun **frugally** adverb.

fruit ▸ noun **1** a fleshy part of a plant that contains seed and can be eaten as food. **2** Botany the part of a plant in which seeds develop, e.g. an acorn. **3** the result of work or activity.
▸ verb produce fruit.
■ **fruit machine** Brit. a coin-operated gambling machine.

fruiterer ▸ noun a person who sells fruit.

fruitful ▸ adjective **1** producing a lot of fruit. **2** producing good results.

SYNONYMS **productive**, constructive, useful, worthwhile, helpful, beneficial, valuable, rewarding, profitable,

advantageous.
ANTONYMS barren, futile.
□ **fruitfully** adverb **fruitfulness** noun.

fruition /fruu-i-sh'n/ ▸ noun the fulfilment of a plan or project.

fruitless ▸ adjective failing to achieve the desired results.
□ **fruitlessly** adverb.

fruity ▸ adjective (**fruitier**, **fruitiest**) **1** having to do with fruit. **2** (of someone's voice) mellow, deep, and rich.

frump ▸ noun an unattractive woman who wears unfashionable clothes.
□ **frumpy** adjective.

frustrate ▸ verb (**frustrates**, **frustrating**, **frustrated**) **1** prevent a plan or action from succeeding. **2** prevent someone from doing or achieving something. **3** make someone feel dissatisfied or unfulfilled.

SYNONYMS **1** *his plans were frustrated* **thwart**, defeat, foil, block, stop, counter, spoil, check, forestall, scotch, derail, snooker; informal stymie; Brit. informal scupper. **2** *the delays frustrated him* **exasperate**, infuriate, discourage, dishearten, disappoint.
ANTONYMS further, satisfy.

□ **frustrating** adjective.

frustration ▸ noun **1** the feeling of being upset or annoyed as a result of being unable to do something. **2** the prevention of the success of something.

SYNONYMS **1** *he clenched his fists in frustration* **exasperation**, annoyance, anger, vexation, irritation, disappointment, dissatisfaction. **2** *the frustration of his plans* **thwarting**, defeat, prevention, foiling, blocking, spoiling, forestalling, derailment, obstruction.

fry[1] ▸ verb (**fries**, **frying**, **fried**) cook in hot fat or oil.
▸ noun (**fries**) French fries; chips.
■ **frying pan** a shallow pan used for frying food.
□ **fryer** (or **frier**) noun.

fry[2] ▸ plural noun young fish.

ft ▸ abbreviation foot or feet.

fuchsia /fyoo-shuh/ ▸ noun a shrub with drooping purplish-red flowers.

fuddled ▸ adjective not able to think clearly.

fuddy-duddy ▸ noun (plural **fuddy-duddies**) informal a person who is very old-fashioned and pompous.

fudge ▸ noun **1** a soft sweet made from sugar, butter, and milk or cream. **2** an attempt to present an issue in a vague way.
▸ verb (**fudges**, **fudging**, **fudged**) present something in a vague or deceptive way.

SYNONYMS **evade**, avoid, dodge, skirt, duck, gloss over, cloud, hedge, beat about the bush, equivocate.

fuel ▸ noun **1** material such as coal, gas, or oil that is burned to produce heat or power. **2** something that stirs up argument or strong emotion.
▸ verb (**fuels**, **fuelling**, **fuelled**; US spelling **fuels**, **fueling**, **fueled**) **1** supply or power with fuel. **2** stir up strong feeling.

SYNONYMS **1** *power stations fuelled by coal* **power**, fire, drive, run. **2** *the rumours fuelled people's anxiety* **fan**, feed, stoke up, inflame, intensify, stimulate, encourage, provoke, incite, sustain.

■ **fuel injection** the direct introduction of fuel into the cylinders of an engine.

fug ▸ noun Brit. informal a warm, stuffy atmosphere.

fugitive /fyoo-ji-tiv/ ▸ noun a person who has escaped from captivity or is in hiding.

SYNONYMS **escapee**, runaway, deserter, absconder, refugee.

fugue /fyoog/ ▸ noun a piece of music in which a short melody is introduced and then successively taken up by other instruments or voices.

führer (or **fuehrer**) /fyoo-ruh/ ▸ noun the title that Hitler held as leader of Germany.

fulcrum /fuul-kruhm/ ▸ noun the point on which a lever turns or is supported.

fulfil (US spelling **fulfill**) ▸ verb (**fulfils**, **fulfilling**, **fulfilled**) **1** do or achieve something that was desired, promised, or predicted. **2** meet a requirement. **3** (**fulfil yourself**) fully develop your abilities.

SYNONYMS **1** *he fulfilled a lifelong ambition* **achieve**, attain, realize, make happen, succeed in, bring to completion, bring to fruition, satisfy. **2** *she failed to fulfil her duties* **carry out**, perform, accomplish, execute, do, discharge, conduct. **3** *they fulfilled the criteria* **meet**, satisfy, comply with, conform to, fill, answer. **4** (**fulfilled**) *a fulfilled life* **satisfied**, content, contented, happy, pleased, at peace.

□ **fulfilment** noun.

full ▸ adjective **1** holding as much or as many as possible. **2** (**full of**) having a large number or quantity of. **3** (also **full up**) filled to capacity. **4** complete: *full details.* **5** plump or rounded. **6** (of flavour, sound, or colour) strong or rich.

SYNONYMS **1** *her glass was full* **filled**, brimming, brimful, packed, loaded, crammed, crowded, bursting, overflowing, congested; informal jam-packed, wall-to-wall, chock-a-block, chock-full, awash. **2** *I'm full* **replete**,

full up, satisfied, sated, satiated; informal stuffed. **3** *a full life* **eventful**, interesting, exciting, lively, action-packed, busy, active. **4** *a full list of facilities* **comprehensive**, thorough, exhaustive, all-inclusive, all-encompassing, all-embracing, in-depth, complete, entire, whole, unabridged, uncut. **5** *at full speed* **maximum**, top. **6** *a full figure* **plump**, rounded, buxom, shapely, ample, curvaceous, voluptuous; informal busty, curvy, well endowed; N. Amer. informal zaftig. **7** *a full skirt* **loose-fitting**, loose, baggy, voluminous, roomy, capacious, billowing.
ANTONYMS empty, hungry, uneventful, selective, low, thin, tight.

▶ adverb straight; directly.
■ **full back** (in soccer and similar sports) a defender who plays at the side of the pitch. **full-blooded** wholehearted and enthusiastic. **full-blown** fully developed. **full board** Brit. accommodation at a hotel or guest house which includes all meals. **full-bodied** rich and satisfying in flavour or sound. **full-frontal** fully exposing the front of the body. **full house 1** a theatre that is filled to capacity. **2** a poker hand with three of a kind and a pair. **3** a winning card at bingo. **full moon** the moon when its whole disc is illuminated. **full-scale 1** (of a model or plan) of the same size as the thing represented. **2** complete and thorough. **full stop** a punctuation mark (.) used at the end of a sentence or abbreviation. **full time** the end of a sports match. **full-time** working for the whole of the available time.
□ **fullness** (or **fulness**) noun.

fuller ▶ noun historical a person whose job was treating cloth to make it thicker.

fully ▶ adverb **1** completely. **2** no less or fewer than.

SYNONYMS **completely**, entirely, wholly, totally, perfectly, quite, altogether, thoroughly, in all respects, (up) to the hilt.
ANTONYMS partly, nearly.

■ **fully fledged** Brit. completely developed or established.

fulminate ▶ verb (fulminates, fulminating, fulminated) protest strongly.
□ **fulmination** noun.

fulsome ▶ adjective **1** too flattering or complimentary. **2** of large size or quantity.
□ **fulsomely** adverb.

fumble ▶ verb (fumbles, fumbling, fumbled) **1** use the hands clumsily while doing something. **2** deal with something clumsily. **3** fail to catch a ball cleanly.

SYNONYMS **grope**, fish, scrabble, feel.

▶ noun an act of fumbling.

fume ▶ noun a gas or vapour that smells strongly or is dangerous to breathe in.

SYNONYMS *toxic fumes* **smoke**, vapour, gas, exhaust, pollution.

▶ verb (fumes, fuming, fumed) **1** send out fumes. **2** be very angry.

SYNONYMS *Ella was fuming at his arrogance* **be furious**, seethe, be livid, be incensed, boil, be beside yourself, spit; informal foam at the mouth, see red.

fumigate ▶ verb (fumigates, fumigating, fumigated) disinfect an area using chemical fumes.

SYNONYMS **disinfect**, purify, sterilize, sanitize, decontaminate, cleanse, clean out.
ANTONYMS soil.

□ **fumigation** noun.

fun ▶ noun **1** light-hearted pleasure, or something that provides it. **2** playfulness.

SYNONYMS **1** *I joined in with the fun* **enjoyment**, entertainment, amusement, pleasure, jollification, merrymaking, recreation, leisure, relaxation, a good time; informal living it up, a ball. **2** *she's full of fun* **merriment**, cheerfulness, jollity, joviality, high spirits, mirth, laughter, hilarity, light-heartedness, levity. **3** *he became a figure of fun* **ridicule**, derision, mockery, scorn, contempt.
ANTONYMS boredom, misery, respect.

▶ adjective informal amusing, entertaining, or enjoyable.

SYNONYMS *a fun evening* **enjoyable**, entertaining, amusing, pleasurable, pleasant, agreeable, convivial.

■ **make fun of** laugh at in a mocking way.

function ▶ noun **1** a purpose or natural activity of a person or thing. **2** a large social event. **3** a basic task of a computer. **4** Maths a quantity whose value depends on the varying values of others.

SYNONYMS **1** *the main function of the machine* **purpose**, task, use, role. **2** *my function was to train the recruits* **responsibility**, duty, role, province, activity, assignment, task, job, mission. **3** *a function attended by local dignitaries* **social event**, party, social occasion, affair, gathering, reception, soirée; N. Amer. levee; informal do, bash.

▶ verb **1** work or operate. **2** (**function as**) fulfil the purpose of.

SYNONYMS **1** *the system had ceased to function* **work**, go, run, be in working/running order, operate. **2** *the museum functions as an education centre* **act**, serve, operate, perform, do duty.

functional ▶ adjective **1** having to do with a function. **2** designed to be practical and useful. **3** working or operating.

SYNONYMS **1** *a small functional kitchen* **practical**, useful, utilitarian, workaday, serviceable, no-frills. **2** *the machine is now fully functional* **working**, in working order, functioning, in service, in use, going, running, operative; informal up and running.

□ **functionality** noun **functionally** adverb.

functionary ▸ noun (plural **functionaries**) an official.

fund ▸ noun **1** a sum of money saved or made available for a purpose. **2** (**funds**) financial resources. **3** a large stock.

SYNONYMS **1** *an emergency fund* **collection**, kitty, reserve, pool, purse, savings, coffers. **2** *short of funds* **money**, cash, wealth, means, assets, resources, savings, capital, reserves, the wherewithal; informal dosh; Brit. informal lolly.

▸ verb provide money for.

SYNONYMS *we were funded by the Treasury* **finance**, pay for, back, capitalize, subsidize, endow, invest in, sponsor; N. Amer. informal bankroll.

fundamental ▸ adjective of basic importance.

SYNONYMS **basic**, underlying, core, rudimentary, root, primary, prime, cardinal, principal, chief, key, central, vital, essential. ANTONYMS secondary, incidental.

▸ noun a basic rule or principle.

fundamentalism ▸ noun strict following of the basic teachings of a religion.
□ **fundamentalist** noun & adjective.

fundamentally ▸ adverb in central or primary respects.

SYNONYMS **essentially**, in essence, basically, at heart, at bottom, deep down, profoundly, primarily, above all.

funeral ▸ noun a ceremony in which a dead person is buried or cremated.

SYNONYMS **burial**, interment, entombment, committal, laying to rest, cremation.

■ **funeral director** an undertaker.

funerary /fyoo-nuh-ruh-ri/ ▸ adjective having to do with a funeral or other rites in which dead people are remembered.

funereal /fyoo-neer-i-uhl/ ▸ adjective solemn, in a way appropriate to a funeral.

funfair ▸ noun Brit. a fair consisting of rides, sideshows, etc.

fungicide /fun-ji-syd, fung-gi-syd/ ▸ noun a chemical that destroys fungus.

fungus ▸ noun (plural **fungi** /fung-gy/) an organism, such as a mushroom, that has no leaves or flowers and grows on plants or decaying vegetable matter and reproduces by spores.
□ **fungal** adjective.

funicular railway /fyuu-nik-yuu-ler/ ▸ noun a railway on a steep slope which is operated by cable.

funk[1] ▸ noun a style of popular dance music with a strong rhythm.

funk[2] ▸ noun informal a state of panic or anxiety.

funky ▸ adjective (**funkier**, **funkiest**) informal **1** (of music) having a strong dance rhythm. **2** modern and stylish.

funnel ▸ noun **1** an object that is wide at the top and narrow at the bottom, used for guiding liquid or powder into a small opening. **2** a chimney on a ship or steam engine.
▸ verb (**funnels**, **funnelling**, **funnelled**; US spelling **funnels**, **funneling**, **funneled**) guide through a funnel or narrow space.

funny ▸ adjective (**funnier**, **funniest**) **1** causing laughter or amusement. **2** strange; odd. **3** suspicious or illegal. **4** informal slightly unwell.

SYNONYMS **1** *a very funny film* **amusing**, humorous, witty, comic, comical, hilarious, hysterical, riotous, uproarious, farcical; informal rib-tickling, priceless. **2** *a funny coincidence* **strange**, peculiar, odd, weird, bizarre, curious, freakish, quirky, unusual. **3** *there's something funny about him* **suspicious**, suspect, dubious, untrustworthy, questionable; informal fishy; Brit. informal dodgy. ANTONYMS unfunny, serious, unsurprising, trustworthy.

■ **funny bone** informal the part of the elbow over which a very sensitive nerve passes.
□ **funnily** adverb.

fur ▸ noun **1** the short, soft hair of certain animals. **2** the skin of an animal with fur on it, or a coat made from this. **3** Brit. a coating formed by hard water on the inside surface of a pipe, kettle, etc.
□ **furred** adjective.

furbelow ▸ noun **1** a strip of gathered or pleated material sewn on a skirt or petticoat. **2** (**furbelows**) showy decorations or ornaments.

furious ▸ adjective **1** very angry. **2** with great energy or speed.

SYNONYMS **1** *he was furious when we told him* **very angry**, enraged, infuriated, irate, incensed, fuming, ranting, raving, seething, beside yourself, outraged; informal hopping mad, wild, livid. **2** *a furious debate* **fierce**, heated, passionate, fiery, tumultuous, turbulent, tempestuous, violent, stormy, acrimonious. ANTONYMS pleased, calm.

□ **furiously** adverb.

furl ▸ verb roll or fold up neatly.

furlong ▶ noun an eighth of a mile, 220 yards.

furlough /**fer**-loh/ ▶ noun a time when you have permission to be away from your work or duties.

furnace ▶ noun 1 an enclosed space for heating material to very high temperatures. 2 a very hot place.

furnish ▶ verb 1 provide a room or building with furniture and fittings. 2 supply or provide.

> SYNONYMS 1 *the bedrooms are elegantly furnished* fit out, appoint, equip; Brit. informal do out. 2 *they furnished us with waterproofs* supply, provide, equip, issue, kit out; informal fix up.

furnishings ▶ noun furniture and fittings in a room or building.

furniture ▶ noun the movable articles that make a room or building suitable for living or working in.

furore /fyoo-**ror**-i/ (US spelling **furor** /fyoo-**ror**/) ▶ noun an outbreak of public anger or excitement.

> SYNONYMS **commotion,** uproar, outcry, fuss, upset, brouhaha, stir; informal to-do, hoo-ha, hullabaloo.

furrier ▶ noun a person who deals in clothes made of fur.

furrow ▶ noun 1 a long, narrow trench made in the ground by a plough. 2 a deep wrinkle on a person's face.
▶ verb make a furrow in.

furry ▶ adjective (**furrier, furriest**) covered with or like fur.

further ▶ adverb (also **farther**) 1 at, to, or by a greater distance. 2 at or to a more advanced stage. 3 in addition.

> SYNONYMS *further, it gave him an alibi.* See **FURTHERMORE.**

▶ adjective 1 (also **farther**) more distant in space. 2 additional.

> SYNONYMS *further information* **additional,** more, extra, supplementary, new, fresh.
> ANTONYMS existing.

▶ verb (**furthers, furthering, furthered**) help the progress of.

> SYNONYMS *attempts to further his career* **promote,** advance, forward, develop, facilitate, aid, assist, help, boost, encourage.
> ANTONYMS impede.

■ **further education** Brit. education below degree level for people older than school age.

furtherance ▶ noun the process of helping something to develop or succeed.

furthermore ▶ adverb in addition.

> SYNONYMS **moreover,** further, what's more, also, additionally, in addition, besides, as well, too, on top of that, into the bargain.

furthest (or **farthest**) ▶ adverb & adjective at or to the greatest distance.

> SYNONYMS **most distant,** remotest, farthest, furthermost, farthermost, outer, outermost, extreme.
> ANTONYMS nearest.

furtive ▶ adjective secretively trying to avoid being noticed.

> SYNONYMS **surreptitious,** secretive, secret, clandestine, hidden, covert, conspiratorial, cloak-and-dagger, sneaky; informal shifty.
> ANTONYMS open.

□ **furtively** adverb.

fury ▶ noun (plural **furies**) 1 extreme anger. 2 extreme strength or violence. 3 (**the Furies**) Greek Mythology three goddesses who punished people for their crimes.

> SYNONYMS 1 *she exploded with fury* rage, anger, wrath, outrage. 2 *the fury of the storm* ferocity, violence, turbulence, tempestuousness, savagery, severity, intensity, vehemence, force.
> ANTONYMS pleasure.

furze = GORSE.

fuse[1] ▶ verb (**fuses, fusing, fused**) 1 join or combine to form a whole. 2 melt something so it joins with something else. 3 Brit. (of an electrical appliance) stop working when a fuse melts. 4 fit a circuit or electrical appliance with a fuse.
▶ noun 1 a safety device consisting of a strip of wire that melts and breaks an electric circuit if the current goes beyond a safe level. 2 a length of material which is lit to explode a bomb or firework. 3 a device in a bomb that controls the timing of the explosion.

fuselage /**fyoo**-zuh-lah*zh*/ ▶ noun the main body of an aircraft.

fusible ▶ adjective able to be melted easily.

Fusilier /fyoo-zi-**leer**/ ▶ noun a member of a British regiment formerly armed with muskets called **fusils.**

fusillade /fyoo-zi-**layd**, fyoo-zi-**lahd**/ ▶ noun a series of shots fired at the same time or quickly one after the other.

fusion ▶ noun 1 the joining of two or more things together to form a whole. 2 a reaction in which the nuclei of atoms fuse to form a heavier nucleus, releasing a great deal of energy.

fuss ▶ noun 1 unnecessary excitement or activity. 2 a protest or complaint.

> SYNONYMS 1 *what's all the fuss about?* **commotion,** excitement, stir, confusion,

disturbance, brouhaha, uproar, furore, storm in a teacup; informal hoo-ha, to-do, song and dance, performance. **2** *he didn't put up too much of a fuss* **protest,** complaint, objection, argument, row. **3** *they settled in with very little fuss* **trouble,** bother, inconvenience, effort, exertion, labour; informal hassle.

▶ verb (usu. **fuss over**) show unnecessary concern about something.

SYNONYMS *he was still fussing about his clothes* **worry,** fret, be agitated, be worked up, make a big thing out of, make a mountain out of a molehill; informal flap, be in a tizzy.

fussy ▶ adjective (**fussier, fussiest**) **1** hard to please. **2** full of unnecessary detail.

SYNONYMS **1** *he's very fussy about what he eats* **particular,** finicky, fastidious, hard to please, faddish; informal pernickety, choosy, picky; Brit. informal faddy; N. Amer. informal persnickety. **2** *a fussy bridal gown* **over-elaborate,** ornate, fancy, busy, cluttered.

☐ **fussily** adverb **fussiness** noun.

fusty ▶ adjective **1** smelling stale or damp. **2** old-fashioned.

futile ▶ adjective pointless.

SYNONYMS **fruitless,** vain, pointless, useless, ineffectual, forlorn, hopeless. ANTONYMS useful.

☐ **futilely** adverb **futility** noun.

futon /foo-ton/ ▶ noun a padded mattress that can be rolled up.

future ▶ noun **1** (**the future**) time that is still to come. **2** a prospect of success or happiness.

SYNONYMS **1** *plans for the future* **time to come,** what lies ahead. **2** *her future lay in acting* **destiny,** fate, fortune, prospects, chances. ANTONYMS past.

▶ adjective **1** existing or happening in the future. **2** Grammar (of a verb) expressing an event yet to happen.

SYNONYMS **1** *a future date* **later,** to come, following, ensuing, succeeding, subsequent, coming. **2** *his future wife* **to be,** destined, intended, planned, prospective. ANTONYMS previous, past.

futuristic ▶ adjective **1** having very modern technology or design. **2** (of a film or book) set in the future.

futurity ▶ noun the future time.

fuzz ▶ noun **1** a frizzy mass of hair or fibre. **2** (**the fuzz**) informal the police.

fuzzy ▶ adjective (**fuzzier, fuzziest**) **1** having a frizzy texture or appearance. **2** blurred; not clear.

SYNONYMS **1** *her fuzzy hair* **frizzy,** fluffy, woolly, downy. **2** *a fuzzy picture* **blurred,** indistinct, unclear, out of focus, misty. **3** *a fuzzy concept* **unclear,** imprecise, unfocused, nebulous, vague, hazy, loose, woolly. ANTONYMS straight, smooth, sharp, clear.

Gg

G (or **g**) ▶ noun (plural **Gs** or **G's**) the seventh letter of the alphabet.
▶ abbreviation **1** grams. **2** gravity.
■ **G-string** a skimpy pair of knickers consisting of a narrow strip of cloth attached to a waistband.

gab ▶ verb (**gabs, gabbing, gabbed**) informal talk at length.
■ **the gift of the gab** the ability to speak in a fluent and persuasive way.

gabble ▶ verb (**gabbles, gabbling, gabbled**) talk very quickly and in a way that is difficult to understand.
▶ noun talk that is fast and difficult to understand.

gaberdine (or **gabardine**) /ga-ber-**deen**/ ▶ noun a smooth, hard-wearing cloth used for making raincoats.

gable ▶ noun the triangular upper part of a wall at the end of a roof.

Gabonese /gab-uh-**neez**/ ▶ noun (plural **Gabonese**) a person from Gabon, a country in West Africa.
▶ adjective relating to Gabon.

gad ▶ verb (**gads, gadding, gadded**) (**gad about**) informal enjoy yourself by visiting many different places.

gadfly ▶ noun (plural **gadflies**) **1** a fly that bites cattle. **2** an annoying person.

gadget ▶ noun a small mechanical device.

> SYNONYMS **device**, appliance, apparatus, instrument, implement, tool, utensil, contrivance, contraption, machine, mechanism, invention; informal gizmo.

□ **gadgetry** noun.

gadolinium ▶ noun a soft silvery-white metallic element.

Gaelic /**gay**-lik, **ga**-lik/ ▶ noun a language spoken in parts of Ireland and western Scotland.

gaff[1] ▶ noun a stick with a hook for landing large fish.

gaff[2] ▶ noun (**blow the gaff**) Brit. informal reveal a secret.

gaffe ▶ noun an embarrassing mistake made in a social situation.

gaffer ▶ noun informal **1** Brit. a person's boss. **2** an old man.

gag[1] ▶ noun a piece of cloth put over a person's mouth to stop them speaking.
▶ verb (**gags, gagging, gagged**) **1** put a gag on. **2** choke or retch.

> SYNONYMS **1** *the government tried to gag its critics* **silence**, muzzle, suppress, stifle, censor, curb, restrain. **2** *the stench made her gag* **retch**, heave.

gag[2] ▶ noun a joke or funny story.

> SYNONYMS *he told a few gags* **joke**, quip, jest, witticism; informal crack, wisecrack, one-liner.

gaga /**gah**-gah/ ▶ adjective informal rambling in speech or thought, especially as a result of old age.

gage US spelling of GAUGE.

gaggle ▶ noun **1** a flock of geese. **2** informal a noisy group of people.

gaiety (US spelling **gayety**) ▶ noun (plural **gaieties**) light-hearted and cheerful mood or behaviour.

gaily ▶ adverb **1** in a light-hearted and cheerful way. **2** without thinking of the effect of your actions. **3** with a bright appearance.

gain ▶ verb **1** obtain or secure something. **2** reach a place. **3** (**gain on**) get closer to a person or thing that you are chasing. **4** increase in weight or speed. **5** (**gain in**) improve or progress in some respect. **6** (of a clock or watch) become fast.

> SYNONYMS **1** *he gained a scholarship* **obtain**, get, secure, acquire, come by, procure, attain, achieve, earn, win, capture; informal land. **2** *they stood to gain from the deal* **profit**, make money, benefit, do well out of. **3** *she gained weight* **put on**, increase in, build up. **4** *they were gaining on us* **catch up (with)**, catch, reduce someone's lead, narrow the gap.
> ANTONYMS lose, fall behind.

▶ noun **1** a thing that is gained. **2** an increase in wealth or resources.

> SYNONYMS **1** *his gain from the deal* **profit**, earnings, income, yield, return, reward, advantage, benefit; informal take. **2** *weight*

gain **increase**, addition, rise, increment, advance.
ANTONYMS loss.

gainful ▸ adjective (of employment) paid; profitable.
▫ **gainfully** adverb.

gainsay ▸ verb (**gainsays, gainsaying, gainsaid**) formal deny or contradict.

gait ▸ noun a way of walking.

gaiter ▸ noun a covering of cloth or leather for the ankle and lower leg.

gala /gah-luh/ ▸ noun **1** a social occasion with special entertainments. **2** Brit. a special sports event, especially a swimming competition.

SYNONYMS **festival**, fair, fête, carnival, pageant, jubilee, jamboree, celebration.

galactic ▸ adjective relating to a galaxy.

galaxy ▸ noun (plural **galaxies**) **1** a large system of stars. **2** (**the Galaxy**) the system of stars that includes the sun and the earth; the Milky Way.

gale ▸ noun **1** a very strong wind. **2** an outburst of laughter.

SYNONYMS **1** *a howling gale* **high wind**, blast, squall, storm, tempest, hurricane, tornado, cyclone, whirlwind, typhoon. **2** *gales of laughter* **peal**, howl, hoot, shriek, scream, roar, fit, paroxysm.

gall[1] ▸ noun disrespectful or rude behaviour.
■ **gall bladder** a small organ beneath the liver, in which bile is stored.

gall[2] ▸ noun **1** annoyance; irritation. **2** a sore on the skin made by rubbing.
▸ verb annoy; irritate.
▫ **galling** adjective.

gallant ▸ adjective **1** /gal-luhnt/ brave or heroic. **2** /guh-lant/ (of a man) polite and charming to women.
▸ noun /guh-lant/ a man who is polite and charming to women.
▫ **gallantly** adverb.

gallantry ▸ noun (plural **gallantries**) **1** courageous behaviour. **2** polite attention given by men to women.

galleon ▸ noun historical a large sailing ship with three or more decks and masts.

gallery ▸ noun (plural **galleries**) **1** a room or building in which works of art are displayed or sold. **2** a balcony at the back of a large hall. **3** the highest part of a theatre.

galley ▸ noun (plural **galleys**) **1** historical a low, flat ship with one or more sails and up to three banks of oars. **2** a narrow kitchen in a ship or aircraft.

Gallic /gal-lik/ ▸ adjective having to do with France or the French.

gallivant ▸ verb informal go from place to place enjoying yourself.

gallon ▸ noun **1** a unit of volume for measuring liquids, equal to eight pints (4.55 litres). **2** (**gallons**) informal large quantities.

gallop ▸ noun **1** the fastest speed a horse can run. **2** a ride on a horse at its fastest speed.
▸ verb (**gallops, galloping, galloped**) **1** go at the speed of a gallop. **2** proceed very quickly.

gallows ▸ plural noun **1** a structure used for hanging a person. **2** (**the gallows**) execution by hanging.

gallstone ▸ noun a hard painful mass which can form in the gall bladder or bile ducts.

galore ▸ adjective in large numbers or amounts.

galoshes ▸ plural noun rubber shoes worn over normal shoes in wet weather.

galumph ▸ verb informal move in a clumsy or noisy way.

galvanic /gal-van-ik/ ▸ adjective relating to electric currents produced by chemical action.

galvanize (or **galvanise**) /gal-vuh-nyz/ ▸ verb (**galvanizes, galvanizing, galvanized**) **1** shock or excite someone into doing something. **2** (**galvanized**) (of iron or steel) coated with a protective layer of zinc.

galvanometer /gal-vuh-**nom**-i-ter/ ▸ noun an instrument for measuring small electric currents.

Gambian ▸ noun a person from Gambia.
▸ adjective relating to Gambia.

gambit ▸ noun something that somebody says or does that is meant to give them an advantage.

gamble ▸ verb (**gambles, gambling, gambled**) **1** play games of chance for money. **2** bet a sum of money. **3** risk losing something in the hope that you will be successful.

SYNONYMS **1** *he started to gamble* **bet**, place a bet, wager, hazard; Brit. informal punt, have a flutter. **2** *investors are gambling that the pound will fall* **take a chance**, take a risk; N. Amer. take a flyer; informal stick your neck out; Brit. informal chance your arm.

▸ noun a risky action.

SYNONYMS *I took a gamble* **risk**, chance, leap in the dark, speculation, lottery, pot luck.

▫ **gambler** noun.

gambol ▸ verb (**gambols, gambolling, gambolled**; US spelling **gambols, gamboling, gamboled**) run or jump about playfully.

game[1] ▸ noun **1** an activity that you take part in for amusement. **2** a competitive activity or sport played according to rules. **3** a period of play, ending in a final result. **4** a section of a tennis match, forming a unit in scoring. **5** (**games**) a meeting for sporting competitions. **6** informal a type of activity or business regarded as a game. **7** wild animals or birds that people hunt for food or as a sport.

> SYNONYMS **1** *the children invented a new game* **pastime**, diversion, entertainment, amusement, distraction, recreation, sport, activity. **2** *we lost the game* **match**, contest, fixture, meeting, tie, clash.

▸ **adjective** eager and willing to do something that is new or challenging.

> SYNONYMS *are you game?* **willing**, prepared, ready, disposed, interested, eager, keen, enthusiastic.

▸ **verb** (**games**, **gaming**, **gamed**) play at games of chance for money.
> ☐ **gamely** adverb.

game² ▸ **adjective** dated (of a person's leg) lame.

gamekeeper ▸ **noun** a person employed to breed and protect game for a large country estate.

gamesmanship ▸ **noun** the ability to win games by making your opponent feel less confident.

gamete /gam-eet/ ▸ **noun** Biology a cell which is able to unite with another of the opposite sex in sexual reproduction to form a zygote.

gamine /ga-**meen**/ ▸ **adjective** (of a girl) having a mischievous, boyish charm.

gamma /gam-muh/ ▸ **noun** the third letter of the Greek alphabet (Γ, γ).
> ■ **gamma rays** (or **gamma radiation**) electromagnetic radiation of shorter wavelength than X-rays.

gammon ▸ **noun** Brit. **1** ham which has been cured like bacon. **2** the part of a side of bacon that includes the hind leg.

gammy ▸ **adjective** Brit. informal (of a person's leg) injured or painful.

gamut /gam-**uht**/ ▸ **noun** the complete range or scope of something.
> ■ **run the gamut** experience or perform the complete range of something.

gander ▸ **noun** **1** a male goose. **2** informal a look.

gang ▸ **noun** **1** an organized group of criminals or rowdy young people. **2** informal a group of people who regularly meet and do things together. **3** an organized group of people doing manual work.

> SYNONYMS **1** *a gang of teenagers* **band**, group, crowd, pack, horde, throng, mob, herd, swarm, troop; informal bunch, gaggle, load. **2** *a gang of workmen* **crew**, team, group, squad, shift, detachment, unit.

▸ **verb** **1** (**gang together**) form a group or gang. **2** (**gang up**) join together to oppose or intimidate someone.

gangling (or **gangly**) ▸ **adjective** (of a person) tall, thin, and awkward.

ganglion ▸ **noun** (plural **ganglia** or **ganglions**) **1** a mass of nerve cells. **2** a swelling in a tendon.

gangmaster ▸ **noun** Brit. a person who organizes and supervises the work of manual labourers employed on a casual basis.

gangplank ▸ **noun** a movable plank used as a bridge between a boat and the shore.

gangrene ▸ **noun** the decay of tissue in a part of the body, caused by an obstructed blood supply or by infection.
> ☐ **gangrenous** adjective.

gangster ▸ **noun** a member of an organized gang of violent criminals.

> SYNONYMS **hoodlum**, racketeer, thug, villain, criminal, Mafioso; informal mobster, crook, tough; N. Amer. informal hood.

gangway ▸ **noun** **1** Brit. a passage between rows of seats. **2** a bridge placed between a ship and the shore.

gannet ▸ **noun** **1** a large seabird. **2** Brit. informal a greedy person.

gantry ▸ **noun** (plural **gantries**) a bridge-like structure used as a support.

gaol ➡ JAIL.

gap ▸ **noun** **1** a hole in an object or between two objects. **2** an empty space or period of time; a break in something.

> SYNONYMS **1** *a gap in the shutters* **opening**, aperture, space, breach, chink, slit, crack, crevice, cleft, cavity, hole. **2** *a gap between meetings* **pause**, intermission, interval, interlude, break, breathing space, breather, respite; N. Amer. recess. **3** *a gap in our records* **omission**, blank. **4** *the gap between rich and poor* **chasm**, gulf, separation, contrast, difference, disparity, divergence, imbalance.

> ☐ **gappy** adjective.

gape ▸ **verb** (**gapes**, **gaping**, **gaped**) **1** stare with your mouth open wide in amazement. **2** be or become wide open.

> SYNONYMS **1** *she gaped at him in astonishment* **stare**, stare open-mouthed, goggle, gaze, ogle; informal rubberneck; Brit. informal gawp. **2** *a jacket which gaped at every seam* **open**, yawn, part, split. **3** (**gaping**) **wide**, broad, vast, wide open, yawning, cavernous.

garage /ga-rahj, ga-rij/ ▸ **noun** **1** a building in which a car or other vehicle is kept. **2** a business which sells fuel or which repairs and sells motor vehicles. **3** a type of music with elements of drum and bass, house, and soul.

g

▶ verb (**garages, garaging, garaged**) keep a vehicle in a garage.

garb ▶ noun unusual or distinctive clothes.
▶ verb (**be garbed in**) be dressed in distinctive clothes.

garbage ▶ noun chiefly N. Amer. **1** domestic rubbish or waste. **2** something worthless or meaningless.

garble ▶ verb (**garbles, garbling, garbled**) confuse or distort a message or transmission.

garden ▶ noun **1** a piece of ground next to or around a house. **2** (**gardens**) a public park.
▶ verb work in a garden.
□ **gardener** noun.

gardenia ▶ noun a tree or shrub with large white or yellow sweet-smelling flowers.

gargantuan ▶ adjective enormous.

gargle ▶ verb (**gargles, gargling, gargled**) hold liquid in your mouth and throat while slowly breathing out through it.
▶ noun **1** an act of gargling. **2** a liquid used for gargling.

gargoyle ▶ noun a spout in the form of an ugly person or animal that carries water away from the roof of a building.

garish /gair-ish/ ▶ adjective unpleasantly bright and showy.

SYNONYMS gaudy, lurid, loud, harsh, showy, glittering, brash, tasteless, vulgar; informal flashy.
ANTONYMS drab, subdued, tasteful.

□ **garishly** adverb.

garland ▶ noun a wreath of flowers and leaves.
▶ verb crown or decorate with a garland.

garlic ▶ noun a plant of the onion family with a strong taste and smell.

garment ▶ noun a piece of clothing.

SYNONYMS item/article of clothing; (garments) clothes, clothing, dress, garb, wardrobe, costume; informal gear, togs, get-up; Brit. informal clobber; N. Amer. informal threads; formal attire.

garner ▶ verb (**garners, garnering, garnered**) gather or collect.

garnet ▶ noun a red semi-precious stone.

garnish ▶ verb decorate food.

SYNONYMS decorate, adorn, ornament, trim, dress, embellish.

▶ noun a decoration for food.

SYNONYMS decoration, adornment, ornament, embellishment, enhancement, finishing touch.

garret ▶ noun a room in the roof of a house.

garrison ▶ noun a group of troops stationed in a fortress or town to defend it.

SYNONYMS **1** the English garrison had left troops, forces, militia, soldiers, force, detachment, unit. **2** forces from three garrisons base, camp, station, barracks, fort, command post.

▶ verb provide a place with a garrison.

SYNONYMS troops were garrisoned in York station, post, deploy, base, site, place, billet.

garrotte /guh-rot/ (US spelling garrote) ▶ verb (**garrottes, garrotting, garrotted**) strangle someone with a wire or cord.
▶ noun a wire or cord used for garrotting.

garrulous ▶ adjective very talkative.
□ **garrulity** noun.

garter ▶ noun a band worn around the leg to keep up a stocking or sock.

gas ▶ noun (plural **gases** or chiefly US **gasses**) **1** an air-like substance which expands to fill any available space. **2** a type of gas used as a fuel. **3** a type of gas that stops you feeling pain, used during a medical operation. **4** N. Amer. gasoline.
▶ verb (**gases, gassing, gassed**) **1** attack with, expose to, or kill with gas. **2** informal talk or chat at length.
■ **gas chamber** an airtight room that can be filled with poisonous gas to kill people or animals. **gas mask** a mask used as protection against poisonous gas.

✔ In British English, the spelling of the plural is **gases**: no double **s**.

gaseous /gass-i-uhss/ ▶ adjective relating to or like a gas.

gash ▶ noun a long deep cut or wound.

SYNONYMS cut, laceration, slash, slit, split, wound, injury.

▶ verb make a gash in.

SYNONYMS cut, lacerate, slash, slit, split, wound, injure.

gasket /gass-kit/ ▶ noun a rubber seal at the junction between two surfaces in an engine.

gaslight ▶ noun light from a gas lamp.
□ **gaslit** adjective.

gasoline ▶ noun N. Amer. petrol.

gasometer /ga-som-i-ter/ ▶ noun a large tank for the storage of gas.

gasp ▶ verb **1** take a quick breath with your mouth open, because you are surprised or in pain. **2** (**gasp for**) struggle for air.

SYNONYMS **1** I gasped in surprise catch/draw in your breath, gulp. **2** he fell on the ground, gasping pant, puff, puff and blow, wheeze, breathe hard/heavily, choke, fight for breath.

▶ noun a sudden quick breath.

SYNONYMS *he could speak only between gasps* **gulp,** pant, puff.

gassy ▶ adjective (**gassier, gassiest**) full of gas.

gastric ▶ adjective having to do with the stomach.

gastritis /gas-**try**-tiss/ ▶ noun inflammation of the lining of the stomach.

gastro-enteritis ▶ noun inflammation of the stomach and intestines.

gastronomy ▶ noun the practice or art of cooking and eating good food.
□ **gastronomic** adjective.

gastropod ▶ noun a mollusc such as a snail or slug.

gasworks ▶ plural noun a place where gas is processed.

gate ▶ noun **1** a hinged barrier used to close an opening in a wall, fence, or hedge. **2** an exit from an airport building to an aircraft. **3** a barrier that controls the flow of water on a river or canal. **4** the number of people who pay to attend a sports event.

SYNONYMS **barrier,** turnstile, gateway, doorway, entrance, exit, door, portal; N. Amer. entryway.

gateau /**gat**-oh/ ▶ noun (plural **gateaus** or **gateaux** /**gat**-ohz/) Brit. a cake.

gatecrash ▶ verb go to a party without an invitation or ticket.
□ **gatecrasher** noun.

gatefold ▶ noun an oversized page in a book or magazine, intended to be opened out for reading.

gatehouse ▶ noun a house standing by the gateway to a country estate.

gatekeeper ▶ noun an attendant at a gate.

gatepost ▶ noun a post on which a gate is hinged or against which it shuts.

gateway ▶ noun **1** an opening that can be closed by a gate. **2** (**gateway to**) a means of entering somewhere or achieving something.

gather ▶ verb (**gathers, gathering, gathered**) **1** come or bring together. **2** increase in force, speed, etc. **3** understand something to be the case. **4** collect plants or fruits for food. **5** harvest a crop. **6** draw together or towards yourself. **7** pull fabric into folds by drawing thread through it.

SYNONYMS **1** *we gathered in the hotel lobby* **congregate,** assemble, meet, collect, get together, convene, muster, rally, converge. **2** *he gathered his family* **summon,** call together, bring together, assemble, convene, rally, round up, muster, marshal. **3** *they gathered the crops* **harvest,** reap, crop, pluck, collect. **4** *I gather he's a footballer* **understand,** believe, be led to believe, conclude, infer, assume, take it, surmise, hear, learn, discover. **5** *her dress was gathered at the waist* **pleat,** pucker, tuck, fold, ruffle.
ANTONYMS disperse.

▶ noun (**gathers**) a part of a piece of clothing that is gathered.

gathering ▶ noun a group of people who have come together for a purpose.

SYNONYMS **assembly,** meeting, convention, rally, council, congress, congregation, audience, crowd, group, throng, mass; informal get-together.

gauche /gohsh/ ▶ adjective awkward in social situations.

gaucho /**gow**-choh/ ▶ noun (plural **gauchos**) a cowboy from the South American plains.

gaudy /**gaw**-di/ ▶ adjective (**gaudier, gaudiest**) tastelessly bright and showy.

SYNONYMS **garish,** lurid, loud, glaring, harsh, showy, glittering, ostentatious, tasteless; informal flashy, tacky.
ANTONYMS drab, tasteful.

□ **gaudily** adverb.

gauge /gayj/ (US spelling **gage**) ▶ noun **1** an instrument for measuring the amount or level of something. **2** the thickness or size of a wire, tube, bullet, etc. **3** the distance between the rails of a railway track.

SYNONYMS *the temperature gauge* **meter,** measure, indicator, dial, scale, display.

▶ verb (**gauges, gauging, gauged**) **1** judge a situation or mood. **2** estimate or measure something.

SYNONYMS **1** *it is hard to gauge how effective the ban was* **assess,** evaluate, determine, estimate, form an opinion of, appraise, weigh up, judge, guess; informal size up. **2** *astronomers can gauge the star's brightness* **measure,** calculate, compute, work out, determine, ascertain, count, weigh, quantify, put a figure on.

✔ Spell **gauge** with **-au-** in the middle (the spelling **gage** is American).

gaunt ▶ adjective (of a person) looking thin and exhausted.

SYNONYMS **haggard,** drawn, thin, spare, bony, angular, pinched, scrawny, raw-boned, cadaverous, skeletal, emaciated.

gauntlet ▶ noun **1** a strong glove with a long loose wrist. **2** a glove worn as part of medieval armour.
■ **run the gauntlet** have to face criticism or hostility from a large number of people. **throw down the gauntlet** set a challenge.

gauze ▶ noun **1** a thin transparent fabric. **2** a fine wire mesh.
□ **gauzy** adjective.

gave past of GIVE.

gavel ▸ noun a small hammer with which a judge or auctioneer hits a surface in order to get people's attention.

gavotte /guh-**vot**/ ▸ noun a French dance, popular in the 18th century.

gawk ▸ verb stare in a stupid or rude way.

gawky ▸ adjective awkward and clumsy.

gawp ▸ verb Brit. informal gawk.

gay ▸ adjective (**gayer**, **gayest**) **1** (especially of a man) homosexual. **2** relating to homosexuals. **3** dated light-hearted and carefree. **4** dated brightly coloured.

> SYNONYMS **homosexual**, lesbian; informal queer, pink.
> ANTONYMS heterosexual.

▸ noun a homosexual person, especially a man.

gayety US spelling of GAIETY.

gaze ▸ verb (**gazes**, **gazing**, **gazed**) look steadily.

> SYNONYMS **stare**, gape, look fixedly, goggle, eye, scrutinize, ogle; informal rubberneck; Brit. informal gawp; N. Amer. informal eyeball.

▸ noun a steady look.

> SYNONYMS **stare**, gape, fixed look, regard, scrutiny.

gazebo /guh-**zee**-boh/ ▸ noun (plural **gazebos**) a summer house with a pleasant view.

gazelle ▸ noun a small antelope.

gazette ▸ noun a journal or newspaper.

gazetteer /ga-zuh-**teer**/ ▸ noun a list of place names.

gazump /guh-**zump**/ ▸ verb Brit. informal offer or accept a higher price for a house after a lower offer has already been accepted.

GB ▸ abbreviation **1** Great Britain. **2** (also **Gb**) Computing gigabytes.

GBH ▸ abbreviation Brit. grievous bodily harm.

GC ▸ abbreviation George Cross.

GCE ▸ abbreviation General Certificate of Education.

GCSE ▸ abbreviation (in the UK except Scotland) General Certificate of Secondary Education (the lower of the two main levels of the GCE exam).

gear ▸ noun **1** (**gears**) a set of machinery that connects the engine to the wheels of a vehicle and controls its speed. **2** a particular position of gears in a vehicle: *fifth gear.* **3** informal equipment or clothing.

> SYNONYMS **1** *fishing gear* **equipment**, apparatus, paraphernalia, tools, utensils, implements, instruments, rig, tackle; Brit. informal clobber. **2** *I'll pick up my gear from my hotel* **belongings**, possessions,

effects, paraphernalia, bits and pieces; informal things, stuff, kit; Brit. informal clobber, gubbins. **3** *the best designer gear* **clothes**, clothing, garments, outfits, attire, garb, wardrobe; informal togs; Brit. informal clobber, kit; N. Amer. informal threads.

▸ verb **1** adapt something for a particular purpose. **2** adjust the gears in a vehicle to a particular level. **3** (**gear up**) get prepared for something.

■ **gear lever** Brit. a lever used to change gear in a vehicle.

gearbox ▸ noun a set of gears with its casing.

gecko ▸ noun (plural **geckos** or **geckoes**) a lizard with adhesive pads on the feet, active at night.

gee ▸ exclamation **1** (**gee up**) a command to a horse to go faster. **2** (also **gee whiz**) N. Amer. informal a mild expression of surprise, enthusiasm, or sympathy.

geek ▸ noun informal **1** an awkward or unfashionable person. **2** a person who is obsessed with something: *a computer geek.* □ **geeky** adjective.

geese plural of GOOSE.

geezer ▸ noun informal a man.

Geiger counter ▸ noun a device for measuring radioactivity.

geisha /**gay**-shuh/ ▸ noun (plural **geisha** or **geishas**) a Japanese woman who is paid to accompany and entertain men.

gel¹ ▸ noun a jelly-like substance used on the hair or skin.

▸ verb (**gels**, **gelling**, **gelled**) smooth your hair with gel.

gel² ▸ verb (**gels**, **gelling**, **gelled**) **1** (of jelly or a similar substance) set or become firmer. **2** take definite form or begin to work well.

gelatin /**jel**-uh-tin/ (or **gelatine** /**jel**-uh-teen/) ▸ noun a clear substance made from animal bones and used to make jelly, glue, and photographic film.

□ **gelatinous** /ji-**lat**-i-nuhss/ adjective.

geld ▸ verb castrate a male animal.

gelding ▸ noun a castrated male horse.

gelignite /**jel**-ig-nyt/ ▸ noun a powerful explosive made from nitroglycerine.

gem ▸ noun **1** a precious stone. **2** an outstanding person or thing.

> SYNONYMS **1** *rubies and other gems* **jewel**, precious stone, semi-precious stone; informal rock. **2** *a musical gem* **masterpiece**, classic, treasure, prize, find; informal one in a million, the bee's knees.

Gemini ▸ noun a sign of the zodiac (the Twins), 21 May–20 June.

gemstone ▸ noun a gem used in a piece of jewellery.

g

gen Brit. informal ▸ noun information.
▸ verb (**gens, genning, genned**) (**gen up on**) obtain information about something.

gendarme /zhon-darm/ ▸ noun a member of the French police force.

gender ▸ noun **1** Grammar each of the classes into which nouns and pronouns are divided in some languages, usually referred to as masculine, feminine, and neuter. **2** the state of being male or female (in terms of social or cultural differences rather than biological ones). **3** the members of one or other sex.

gene ▸ noun Biology a distinct sequence of DNA forming part of a chromosome, by which offspring inherit characteristics from a parent.

genealogy /jee-ni-al-uh-ji/ ▸ noun (plural **genealogies**) **1** a line of descent traced from an ancestor. **2** the study of lines of descent.
□ **genealogical** adjective **genealogist** noun.

genera plural of GENUS.

general ▸ adjective **1** affecting or concerning all or most people or things. **2** involving only the main features of something; not detailed. **3** chief or principal: *the general manager.*

> SYNONYMS **1** *suitable for general use* **widespread,** common, extensive, universal, wide, popular, public, mainstream. **2** *a general pay increase* **comprehensive,** overall, across the board, blanket, global, universal, mass, wholesale. **3** *the general practice* **usual,** customary, habitual, traditional, normal, conventional, typical, standard, regular, accepted, prevailing, routine, established, everyday. **4** *a general description* **broad,** rough, loose, approximate, unspecific, vague, imprecise, inexact.
> ANTONYMS restricted, localized, exceptional, detailed.

▸ noun a commander of an army, or an army officer ranking above lieutenant general.
■ **general anaesthetic** an anaesthetic that affects the whole body and causes a loss of consciousness. **general election** the election of representatives to a parliament by all the people of a country. **general practitioner** a doctor who treats patients in a local community rather than at a hospital.

generality ▸ noun (plural **generalities**) **1** a general statement rather than one that is specific or detailed. **2** the quality or state of being general.

generalize (or **generalise**) ▸ verb (**generalizes, generalizing, generalized**) **1** make a general or broad statement. **2** make something more common or more widely applicable.
□ **generalization** noun.

generally ▸ adverb **1** in most cases. **2** without discussing the details of something. **3** widely.

> SYNONYMS **1** *summers were generally hot* **normally,** in general, as a rule, by and large, mainly, mostly, for the most part, predominantly, on the whole, usually. **2** *the idea was generally accepted* **widely,** commonly, extensively, universally, popularly.

generate ▸ verb (**generates, generating, generated**) create or produce something.

> SYNONYMS **create,** make, produce, engender, spawn, precipitate, prompt, provoke, trigger, spark off, stir up, induce.

□ **generative** adjective.

generation ▸ noun **1** all the people born and living at about the same time. **2** the average period in which a person grows up and has children of their own. **3** a single stage in the history of a family. **4** a stage in the development of a product. **5** the producing or creating of something.

> SYNONYMS **1** *people of the same generation* **age,** age group, peer group. **2** *the next generation of computers* **crop,** batch, wave, range.

generator ▸ noun a machine for producing electricity.

generic ▸ adjective **1** referring to a class or group of things. **2** (of goods) having no brand name.
□ **generically** adverb.

generosity ▸ noun the quality of being generous.

> SYNONYMS **liberality,** lavishness, magnanimity, bounty, munificence, open-handedness, largesse, unselfishness, altruism, charity.
> ANTONYMS meanness, selfishness.

generous ▸ adjective **1** freely giving more than is necessary or expected. **2** kind towards other people. **3** larger or more plentiful than is usual.

> SYNONYMS **1** *she is generous with money* **liberal,** lavish, magnanimous, giving, open-handed, bountiful, unselfish, ungrudging, free. **2** *a generous amount of fabric* **plentiful,** copious, ample, liberal, large, abundant.
> ANTONYMS mean, selfish, meagre.

genesis /jen-i-siss/ ▸ noun the origin or development of something.

> SYNONYMS **origin,** source, root, beginning, start.

genetic ▸ adjective **1** relating to genes. **2** relating to genetics.
□ **genetically** adverb.

g

■ **genetically modified** (of an animal or plant) containing genetic material that has been altered in order to produce a desired characteristic. **genetic engineering** the changing of the characteristics of an animal or plant by altering its genetic material. **genetic fingerprinting** the analysis of genetic material in order to identify individual people.

genetics ▶ plural noun the study of the way characteristics are passed from one generation to another.
□ **geneticist** noun.

genial /jee-ni-uhl/ ▶ adjective friendly and cheerful.
□ **geniality** noun **genially** adverb.

genie /jee-ni/ ▶ noun (in Arabian folklore) a spirit.

genital ▶ adjective referring to the external reproductive organs of a person or animal.
▶ noun (**genitals**) the external reproductive organs.

genitalia /jen-i-tay-li-uh/ ▶ plural noun formal or technical the genitals.

genitive /jen-i-tiv/ ▶ noun Grammar the form of a noun, pronoun, or adjective used to show possession.

genius ▶ noun (plural **geniuses**) **1** exceptional natural ability. **2** an exceptionally intelligent or able person.

SYNONYMS **1** *the world knew of his genius* **brilliance**, intelligence, intellect, ability, cleverness, brains. **2** *he has a genius for organization* **talent**, gift, flair, aptitude, facility, knack, ability, expertise, capacity, faculty. **3** *he is a genius* **brilliant person**, gifted person, mastermind, Einstein, intellectual, brain, prodigy; informal egghead, bright spark; Brit. informal brainbox, clever clogs; N. Amer. informal brainiac.
ANTONYMS stupidity, dunce.

genocide /jen-uh-syd/ ▶ noun the deliberate killing of a very large number of people from a particular ethnic group or nation.
□ **genocidal** adjective.

genre /zhon-ruh/ ▶ noun a type or style of art or literature.

SYNONYMS **category**, class, classification, group, set, type, sort, kind, variety.

gent ▶ noun informal a gentleman.

genteel ▶ adjective polite and refined in an affected or exaggerated way.
□ **gentility** noun.

gentian /jen-sh'n/ ▶ noun a small plant with violet or blue flowers.

Gentile /jen-tyl/ ▶ adjective not Jewish.
▶ noun a person who is not Jewish.

gentle ▶ adjective (**gentler, gentlest**) **1** (of a person) mild and kind. **2** moderate; not harsh or severe.

SYNONYMS **1** *his manner was gentle* **kind**, tender, sympathetic, considerate, understanding, compassionate, humane, mild, placid, serene. **2** *a gentle breeze | gentle music* **light**, soft, quiet, low, slow. **3** *a gentle slope* **gradual**, slight, easy, slow, imperceptible.
ANTONYMS brutal, strong, loud, steep.

□ **gentleness** noun **gently** adverb.

gentleman ▶ noun (plural **gentlemen**) **1** a polite or honourable man. **2** a man of good social position. **3** (in polite or formal use) a man.

gentrify ▶ verb (**gentrifies, gentrifying, gentrified**) renovate a house or district so that it appeals to the tastes of middle-class people.
□ **gentrification** noun.

gentry ▶ noun (**the gentry**) people of good social position.

genuflect /jen-yuu-flekt/ ▶ verb lower your body as a sign of respect by bending one knee.
□ **genuflection** noun.

genuine ▶ adjective **1** truly what it is said to be. **2** honest.

SYNONYMS **1** *a genuine Picasso* **authentic**, real, actual, original, bona fide, true; informal pukka, the real McCoy, the real thing, kosher; Austral./NZ informal dinkum. **2** *a very genuine person* **sincere**, honest, truthful, straightforward, direct, frank, candid, open, natural; informal straight, upfront.
ANTONYMS bogus, insincere.

□ **genuinely** adverb.

genus /jee-nuhss/ ▶ noun (plural **genera** /jen-uh-ruh/) a category in the classification of animals and plants.

geodesic /jee-oh-**dess**-ik, jee-oh-**dee**-sik/ ▶ adjective relating to a method of construction based on straight lines between points on a curved surface.

geographical (or **geographic**) ▶ adjective relating to geography.
□ **geographically** adverb.

geography ▶ noun **1** the study of the physical features of the earth and how people relate to them. **2** the way in which places and physical features are arranged.
□ **geographer** noun.

geology ▶ noun **1** the scientific study of the physical structure and substance of the earth. **2** the geological features of a particular area.
□ **geological** adjective **geologist** noun.

geometric ▶ adjective **1** relating to geometry. **2** (of a design) featuring regular lines and shapes.
□ **geometrical** adjective **geometrically** adverb.

g

geometry ▸ noun (plural **geometries**) **1** the branch of mathematics that deals with the properties and relationships of lines, angles, surfaces, and solids. **2** the shape and relationship of the parts of something.

geopolitical ▸ adjective relating to political relations between the countries of the world.

Geordie ▸ noun Brit. informal a person from Tyneside in NE England.

Georgian ▸ adjective relating to the reigns of the British kings George I–IV (1714–1830).

geranium ▸ noun a plant with red, pink, or white flowers.

gerbil ▸ noun a small rodent, often kept as a pet.

geriatric ▸ adjective relating to old people.
▸ noun an old person, especially one receiving special care.

germ ▸ noun **1** a microorganism, especially one which causes disease. **2** a part of an organism that is able to develop into a new one. **3** an initial stage from which something may develop.

> SYNONYMS **1** *this detergent kills germs* **microbe,** micro-organism, bacillus, bacterium, virus; informal bug. **2** *the germ of an idea* **start,** beginnings, seed, embryo, bud, root, origin, source.

German ▸ noun **1** a person from Germany. **2** the language of Germany, Austria, and parts of Switzerland.
▸ adjective relating to Germany or German.
■ **German measles** = RUBELLA. **German shepherd** a large breed of dog often used as guard dogs; an Alsatian.

germane ▸ adjective (**germane to**) relevant or appropriate to.

Germanic ▸ adjective **1** of the language family that includes English, German, Dutch, and the Scandinavian languages. **2** characteristic of Germans or Germany.

germicide ▸ noun a substance which destroys germs.
□ **germicidal** adjective.

germinal ▸ adjective **1** relating to a gamete or embryo. **2** in the earliest stage of development.

germinate ▸ verb (**germinates, germinating, germinated**) (of a seed) begin to grow.
□ **germination** noun.

gerontology ▸ noun the scientific study of old age and old people.

gerrymander ▸ verb (**gerrymanders, gerrymandering, gerrymandered**) change the boundaries of a constituency so as to give an unfair advantage to one party in an election.

gerund /je-ruhnd/ ▸ noun Grammar a verb form which functions as a noun (e.g. *asking* in *do you mind my asking?*).

Gestapo /ge-**stah**-poh/ ▸ noun the German secret police under Nazi rule.

gestation ▸ noun **1** the growth of a baby inside its mother's body. **2** the development of a plan or idea over a period of time.

gesticulate ▸ verb (**gesticulates, gesticulating, gesticulated**) make gestures instead of speaking or in order to emphasize what you are saying.
□ **gesticulation** noun.

gesture ▸ noun **1** a movement of part of the body to express an idea or meaning. **2** an action performed to convey your feelings or intentions.

> SYNONYMS **1** *a gesture of surrender* **signal,** sign, motion, indication, gesticulation. **2** *a symbolic gesture* **action,** act, deed, move.

▸ verb (**gestures, gesturing, gestured**) make a gesture.

> SYNONYMS *he gestured to her* **signal,** motion, gesticulate, wave, indicate, give a sign.

get ▸ verb (**gets, getting, got**; past participle **got,** N. Amer. or old use or **gotten**) **1** come to have or hold; receive. **2** succeed in achieving or experiencing. **3** experience or suffer. **4** fetch. **5** reach a particular state or condition: *it's getting late.* **6** move to or from a particular place. **7** travel by or catch a form of transport. **8** begin to be or do something.

> SYNONYMS **1** *where did you get that hat?* **obtain,** acquire, come by, receive, gain, earn, win, be given; informal get hold of, score. **2** *your tea's getting cold* **become,** grow, turn, go. **3** *get the children from school* **fetch,** collect, go/come for, call for, pick up, bring, deliver, convey. **4** *did the police get him?* **capture,** catch, arrest, apprehend, seize; informal collar, grab, pick up; Brit. informal nick. **5** *she got flu* **contract,** develop, go down with, catch, fall ill with. **6** *I didn't get what he said* **hear,** catch, make out, follow, take in. **7** *I don't get the joke* **understand,** comprehend, grasp, see, fathom, follow. **8** *we got there early* **arrive,** reach, make it, turn up, appear, present yourself, come along; informal show up. **9** *we got her to agree* **persuade,** induce, prevail on, influence, talk into. **10** *I'll get supper* **prepare,** get ready, cook, make; informal fix, rustle up; Brit. informal knock up.
> ANTONYMS give, shake off.

■ **get away with** escape blame or punishment for. **get by** manage to live or do something with the things that you have. **get off** informal escape a punishment.

g

get on 1 make progress with a task. **2** have a friendly relationship. **3** (**be getting on**) informal be old. **get over** recover from an illness or an unpleasant experience. **get something over** manage to communicate an idea. **get your own back** informal have your revenge. **get-together** an informal social gathering. **get-up** informal an unusual style of clothes.

getaway ▶ noun an escape.

geyser /gee-zer/ ▶ noun a hot spring that sometimes sprays water and steam into the air.

Ghanaian /gah-nay-uhn/ ▶ noun a person from Ghana.
▶ adjective relating to Ghana.

ghastly ▶ adjective (**ghastlier, ghastliest**) **1** causing great horror or fear. **2** informal very unpleasant. **3** looking very pale and ill.

> SYNONYMS **1** *a ghastly murder* **terrible,** frightful, horrible, grim, awful, horrifying, shocking, appalling, horrendous, monstrous. **2** *a ghastly building* **unpleasant,** objectionable, disagreeable, distasteful, awful, terrible, dreadful, frightful, detestable, vile; informal horrible, horrid.
> ANTONYMS pleasant.

□ **ghastliness** noun.

ghee /gee/ ▶ noun a kind of butter used in Indian cooking.

gherkin /ger-kin/ ▶ noun a small pickled cucumber.

ghetto /get-toh/ ▶ noun (plural **ghettos** or **ghettoes**) a part of a city lived in by people of a particular race, nationality, or ethnic group.
■ **ghetto blaster** informal a large portable radio and cassette or CD player.

ghost ▶ noun **1** a spirit of a dead person which is believed to appear to the living. **2** (**a** or **the ghost of**) a faint trace of.

> SYNONYMS **spectre,** phantom, wraith, spirit, presence, apparition; informal spook.

■ **ghost town** a town in which no one lives any more. **ghost writer** a person who writes something for someone else who is named as the author.

ghostly ▶ adjective like a ghost; eerie.

> SYNONYMS **supernatural,** unearthly, spectral, phantom, unnatural, eerie, weird, uncanny; informal spooky.

ghoul /gool/ ▶ noun **1** an evil spirit or phantom. **2** a person who is too interested in death or disaster.
□ **ghoulish** adjective.

GI ▶ noun (plural **GIs**) a private soldier in the US army.

giant ▶ noun **1** (in stories) a person of superhuman size and strength. **2** an

unusually large person, animal, or plant.

> SYNONYMS **colossus,** mammoth, monster, leviathan, ogre.
> ANTONYMS dwarf.

▶ adjective unusually large.

> SYNONYMS **huge,** colossal, massive, enormous, gigantic, mammoth, vast, immense, monumental, mountainous, titanic, towering, gargantuan; informal mega, monster, whopping; Brit. informal ginormous.
> ANTONYMS miniature.

gibber /jib-ber/ ▶ verb speak quickly in a way that is difficult to understand.
□ **gibbering** adjective.

gibberish /jib-ber-ish/ ▶ noun speech or writing that is impossible to understand; nonsense.

gibbet /jib-bit/ ▶ noun (in the past) a post and beam used for hanging people, or for displaying the bodies of those who had been executed.

gibbon ▶ noun a small ape with long, powerful arms, native to SE Asia.

gibe → JIBE.

giblets /jib-lits/ ▶ plural noun the liver, heart, gizzard, and neck of a chicken or other bird.

giddy ▶ adjective (**giddier, giddiest**) **1** having the feeling that everything is moving and that you are going to fall. **2** excitable and silly.

> SYNONYMS **1** *she felt giddy* **dizzy,** light-headed, faint, unsteady, wobbly, reeling; informal woozy. **2** *she was young and giddy* **flighty,** silly, frivolous, skittish, irresponsible, scatty; informal dizzy.
> ANTONYMS steady, sensible.

□ **giddily** adverb **giddiness** noun.

gift ▶ noun **1** a thing that you give to someone; a present. **2** a natural ability or talent.

> SYNONYMS **1** *he gave the staff a gift* **present,** handout, donation, offering, bonus, award, endowment; informal prezzie. **2** *a gift for music* **talent,** flair, aptitude, facility, knack, bent, ability, skill, capacity, faculty.

▶ verb **1** give something as a gift. **2** (**gifted**) having exceptional talent or ability.

> SYNONYMS (**gifted**) **talented,** skilled, accomplished, expert, able, proficient, intelligent, clever, bright, brilliant, precocious; informal crack, ace.
> ANTONYMS inept.

gig[1] ▶ noun (in the past) a light two-wheeled carriage pulled by one horse.

gig[2] ▶ noun informal a live performance by a musician.

gigabyte /gig-uh-byt, jig-uh-byt/ ▶ noun Computing a unit of information equal to one thousand million (10^9) bytes.

gigantic ▶ adjective of very great size or extent.

> SYNONYMS **huge**, enormous, vast, giant, massive, colossal, mammoth, immense, monumental, mountainous, gargantuan; informal mega, monster, whopping, humongous; Brit. informal ginormous.
> ANTONYMS tiny.

giggle ▶ verb (**giggles, giggling, giggled**) laugh lightly in a nervous or silly way.

> SYNONYMS **titter**, snigger, chuckle, chortle, laugh.

▶ noun **1** a laugh of this kind. **2** Brit. informal an amusing person or thing.

> SYNONYMS **titter**, snigger, chuckle, chortle, laugh.

□ **giggly** adjective.

gigolo /jig-uh-loh/ ▶ noun (plural **gigolos**) a young man paid to be the companion or lover of an older woman.

gild ▶ verb **1** cover thinly with gold. **2** (**gilded**) wealthy and privileged.
□ **gilding** noun.

gilet /zhi-lay/ ▶ noun a light sleeveless padded jacket.

gill[1] /gil/ ▶ noun **1** the breathing organ in fish and some amphibians. **2** the plates on the underside of mushrooms and many toadstools.

gill[2] /jil/ ▶ noun a unit for measuring liquids, equal to a quarter of a pint.

gillie /gil-li/ ▶ noun (in Scotland) a man or boy who helps someone who is on a shooting or fishing trip.

gilt ▶ adjective covered thinly with gold.
▶ noun a thin layer of gold on a surface.
■ **gilt-edged** (of investments) safe and reliable.

gimlet /gim-lit/ ▶ noun a T-shaped tool with a screw-tip for boring holes.

gimmick ▶ noun a trick or device intended to attract attention rather than fulfil a useful purpose.
□ **gimmicky** adjective.

gin[1] ▶ noun a strong, clear alcoholic drink flavoured with juniper berries.

gin[2] ▶ noun **1** a machine for separating cotton from its seeds. **2** a trap for catching small wild animals or birds.

ginger ▶ noun **1** a hot spice made from the stem of an Asian plant. **2** a light reddish-yellow colour.
■ **ginger ale** (or **ginger beer**) a fizzy drink flavoured with ginger.

gingerbread ▶ noun cake made with treacle and flavoured with ginger.

gingerly ▶ adverb in a careful or cautious way.

gingham /ging-uhm/ ▶ noun lightweight cotton cloth, typically checked.

gingivitis /jin-ji-vy-tiss/ ▶ noun inflammation of the gums.

ginormous ▶ adjective Brit. informal very large.

ginseng /jin-seng/ ▶ noun the root of an east Asian and North American plant, used in some medicines.

Gipsy → GYPSY.

giraffe ▶ noun (plural **giraffe** or **giraffes**) a large African animal with a very long neck and legs.

gird ▶ verb (**girds, girding, girded**; past participle **girded** or **girt**) literary encircle with a belt or band.
■ **gird your loins** get ready to do something.

girder ▶ noun a large metal beam.

girdle ▶ noun **1** a belt or cord worn round the waist. **2** a corset encircling the body from waist to thigh.
▶ verb (**girdles, girdling, girdled**) encircle with a girdle or belt.

girl ▶ noun **1** a female child. **2** a young woman.

> SYNONYMS **young woman**, young lady, miss; Scottish & N. English lass, lassie; Irish colleen; informal chick; Brit. informal bird; N. Amer. informal gal, broad, dame, babe; Austral./NZ informal sheila.

□ **girlish** adjective.

girlfriend ▶ noun **1** a person's regular female romantic or sexual partner. **2** a woman's female friend.

> SYNONYMS **sweetheart**, lover, partner, significant other, girl, woman; informal steady; Brit. informal bird; N. Amer. informal squeeze.

giro ▶ noun (plural **giros**) **1** a system in which money is transferred electronically from one bank or post office account to another. **2** a cheque or payment by giro.

girt past participle of GIRD.

girth ▶ noun **1** the measurement around the middle of something. **2** a strap attached to a saddle and fastened round a horse's belly.

gist /jist/ ▶ noun the main or general meaning of a speech or piece of writing.

give ▶ verb (**gives, giving, gave**; past participle **given**) **1** make someone have, get, or experience something. **2** carry out an action or make a sound. **3** show: *he gave no sign of life.* **4** state information. **5** (**give something off** or **out**) send out a smell, heat, etc. **6** bend under pressure.

> SYNONYMS **1** *he gave them £2,000* **donate**, contribute, present with, award, grant, bestow, hand (over). **2** *can I give him a message?* **convey**, pass on, impart,

communicate, transmit, send, deliver, relay. **3** *he gave his life for them* **sacrifice**, give up, relinquish, devote, dedicate. **4** *he gave a party* **organize**, arrange, lay on, throw, host, hold, have. **5** *Dominic gave a bow* **perform**, execute, make, do. **6** *she gave a shout* **utter**, let out, emit, produce, make.
ANTONYMS receive, take.

▶ **noun** the ability of something to bend under pressure.

■ **give something away** reveal something secret. **give in** stop opposing something. **give out** stop operating. **give rise to** make happen. **give up** stop making an effort and accept that you have failed. **give something up** stop doing, eating, or drinking something regularly.

given past participle of GIVE.
▶ **adjective 1** already named or stated. **2** (**given to**) inclined to.
▶ **preposition** taking into account.

■ **given name** a person's first name.

gizmo ▶ **noun** (plural **gizmos**) informal a gadget.

gizzard ▶ **noun** a muscular part of a bird's stomach for grinding food.

glacé /gla-say/ ▶ **adjective** (of fruit) preserved in sugar.

glacial /glay-sh'l, glay-si-uhl/ ▶ **adjective 1** relating to ice and glaciers. **2** very cold.

glaciation ▶ **noun** the formation of glaciers.

glacier /glass-i-er, glay-si-er/ ▶ **noun** a slowly moving mass of ice formed by the accumulation of snow on mountains.

glad ▶ **adjective** (**gladder**, **gladdest**) **1** pleased; delighted. **2** (often **glad of**) grateful. **3** giving pleasure.

SYNONYMS **1** *I'm really glad you're coming* **pleased**, happy, delighted, thrilled; informal over the moon; Brit. informal chuffed; N. English informal made up. **2** *I'd be glad to help* **willing**, eager, happy, pleased, delighted, ready, prepared.
ANTONYMS dismayed, reluctant.

■ **glad rags** informal clothes for a party or special occasion.

gladden ▶ **verb** make glad.

glade ▶ **noun** an open space in a forest.

gladiator ▶ **noun** (in ancient Rome) a man trained to fight other men or animals in a public arena.
□ **gladiatorial** adjective.

gladiolus ▶ **noun** (plural **gladioli** /glad-i-oh-ly/) a plant with tall stems and brightly coloured flowers.

gladly ▶ **adverb** with joy or pleasure.

SYNONYMS **with pleasure**, happily, cheerfully, willingly, readily, eagerly, freely, ungrudgingly.

glamorize (or **glamorise**) ▶ **verb**

(**glamorizes**, **glamorizing**, **glamorized**) often disapproving make something seem attractive or desirable.

glamorous ▶ **adjective** excitingly attractive.

SYNONYMS **1** *a glamorous woman* **beautiful**, elegant, chic, stylish, fashionable. **2** *a glamorous lifestyle* **exciting**, glittering, glossy, colourful, exotic; informal glitzy, jet-setting.
ANTONYMS dowdy, dull.

□ **glamorously** adverb.

✔ **Glamorous** drops the **u** of **glamour**: glam**or**ous.

glamour (US spelling **glamor**) ▶ **noun** an attractive and exciting quality.

SYNONYMS **1** *she had undeniable glamour* **beauty**, allure, elegance, chic, style, charisma, charm, magnetism. **2** *the glamour of TV* **allure**, attraction, fascination, charm, magic, romance, excitement, thrill; informal glitz, glam.

glance ▶ **verb** (**glances**, **glancing**, **glanced**) **1** look briefly. **2** (**glance off**) hit something at an angle and bounce off.

SYNONYMS **1** *Rachel glanced at him* **look briefly**, look quickly, peek, peep. **2** *I glanced through the report* **read quickly**, scan, skim, leaf, flick, flip, thumb, browse.
ANTONYMS study.

▶ **noun** a brief or hurried look.

SYNONYMS *a glance at his watch* **peek**, peep, brief look, quick look.

□ **glancing** adjective.

gland ▶ **noun** an organ of the body which produces a particular chemical substance.

glandular ▶ **adjective** relating to a gland or glands.

■ **glandular fever** Brit. an infectious disease which causes swelling of the lymph glands and a persistent lack of energy.

glare ▶ **verb** (**glares**, **glaring**, **glared**) **1** stare in an angry way. **2** shine with a dazzling light. **3** (**glaring**) very obvious.

SYNONYMS **1** *she glared at him* **scowl**, glower, look daggers, frown, lour; informal give someone a dirty look. **2** (**glaring**) *glaring lights* **dazzling**, blinding, blazing, strong, harsh. **3** (**glaring**) *a glaring omission* **obvious**, conspicuous, unmistakable, inescapable, unmissable, striking, flagrant, blatant.

▶ **noun 1** a fierce or angry stare. **2** strong and dazzling light.

SYNONYMS **1** *a cold glare* **scowl**, glower, angry stare, frown, black look; informal dirty look. **2** *the glare of the lights* **blaze**, dazzle, shine, beam, brilliance.

glasnost /glaz-nosst/ ▸ noun (in the former Soviet Union) the policy of more open government.

glass ▸ noun **1** a hard transparent substance made by fusing sand with soda and lime. **2** a drinking container made of glass. **3** a mirror.
■ **glass-blowing** the craft of making glass objects by blowing semi-liquid glass through a long tube.
□ **glassy** adjective.

glasses ▸ plural noun a pair of lenses set in a frame that rests on the nose and ears, used to correct eyesight.

glasshouse ▸ noun Brit. a greenhouse.

glaucoma /glaw-koh-muh/ ▸ noun a condition of increased pressure within the eyeball, causing gradual loss of sight.

glaze ▸ verb (**glazes, glazing, glazed**) **1** fit panes of glass into a window frame or similar structure. **2** enclose or cover with glass. **3** cover with a glaze. **4** (**glaze over**) (of a person's eyes) lose brightness and liveliness.

SYNONYMS *pastry glazed with caramel* **cover,** coat, varnish, lacquer, polish.

▸ noun **1** a glass-like substance fused on to the surface of pottery to form a hard coating. **2** a liquid such as milk or beaten egg, used to form a shiny coating on food.

SYNONYMS *a cake with an apricot glaze* **coating,** topping, varnish, lacquer, polish.

glazier /glay-zi-er/ ▸ noun a person who fits glass into windows and doors.

gleam ▸ verb shine brightly, especially with reflected light.

SYNONYMS *a light gleamed* **shine,** glint, glitter, shimmer, glimmer, sparkle, twinkle, flicker, wink, glisten, flash.

▸ noun **1** a faint or brief light. **2** a brief or faint show of a quality or emotion: *a gleam of hope.*

SYNONYMS *a gleam of light* **flash,** glimmer, glint, shimmer, twinkle, sparkle, flicker, beam, ray, shaft.

glean ▸ verb **1** collect information from various sources. **2** gather leftover grain after a harvest.

glee ▸ noun great delight.

gleeful ▸ adjective very happy, usually in a smug or gloating way.
□ **gleefully** adverb.

glen ▸ noun Scottish Irish a narrow valley.

glib ▸ adjective using words easily but without much thought or sincerity.
□ **glibly** adverb.

glide ▸ verb (**glides, gliding, glided**) **1** move with a smooth, quiet, continuous motion.

2 fly without power or in a glider.

SYNONYMS **1** *a gondola glided past* **slide,** slip, sail, float, drift, flow. **2** *seagulls gliding over the waves* **soar,** wheel, plane, fly.

▸ noun an instance of gliding.

glider ▸ noun a light aircraft that flies without an engine.

glimmer ▸ verb (**glimmers, glimmering, glimmered**) shine faintly with a wavering light.
▸ noun **1** a faint or wavering light. **2** a faint sign of a feeling or quality.

glimpse ▸ noun a brief look at something.

SYNONYMS *a glimpse of her face* **brief/quick look,** glance, sight, sighting, peek, peep.

▸ verb (**glimpses, glimpsing, glimpsed**) see something briefly or partially.

SYNONYMS *he glimpsed a figure* **catch sight of,** sight, spot, notice, discern, spy, pick out, make out.

glint ▸ verb give off small flashes of light.
▸ noun a sudden flash of light.

glisten ▸ verb (of something wet) shine or sparkle.

glitch ▸ noun informal a sudden problem or fault.

glitter ▸ verb **1** shine with a shimmering reflected light. **2** (**glittering**) impressively successful or glamorous.

SYNONYMS *crystal glittered in the candlelight* **sparkle,** twinkle, glint, shimmer, glimmer, wink, flash, shine.

▸ noun **1** shimmering reflected light. **2** tiny pieces of sparkling material used for decoration. **3** an attractive but superficial quality.

SYNONYMS *the glitter of light on the water* **sparkle,** twinkle, glint, shimmer, glimmer, flicker, flash.

□ **glittery** adjective.

glitz ▸ noun superficial glamour.
□ **glitzy** adjective.

gloaming ▸ noun (**the gloaming**) literary twilight; dusk.

gloat ▸ verb be smug or pleased about your own success or another person's failure.

global ▸ adjective **1** relating to the whole world; worldwide. **2** relating to all the parts of something.

SYNONYMS **1** *the global economy* **worldwide,** international, world, intercontinental, universal. **2** *a global view of the problem* **comprehensive,** overall, general, all-inclusive, all-encompassing, universal, broad.

■ **global warming** a gradual increase in the temperature of the earth's atmosphere

g

due to the increase of gases such as carbon dioxide.
□ **globally** adverb.

globalization (or **globalisation**) ▶ noun the process by which businesses start to operate on a global scale.
□ **globalize** verb.

globe ▶ noun 1 a spherical or rounded object. 2 (**the globe**) the earth. 3 a model of the earth with a map on its surface.

globetrotter ▶ noun informal a person who travels widely.
□ **globetrotting** noun & adjective.

globular ▶ adjective 1 shaped like a globe; spherical. 2 consisting of globules.

g

globule ▶ noun a small drop or ball of a substance.

globulin ▶ noun any of a group of simple proteins found in blood.

glockenspiel /glok-uhn-speel, glok-uhn-shpeel/ ▶ noun a musical instrument made of metal bars that you hit with small hammers.

gloom ▶ noun 1 darkness. 2 a feeling of sadness and hopelessness.

SYNONYMS 1 *she peered into the gloom* **darkness,** dark, murk, shadows, shade. 2 *his gloom deepened* **despondency,** depression, dejection, melancholy, unhappiness, sadness, misery, woe, despair.
ANTONYMS light, happiness.

gloomy ▶ adjective (**gloomier, gloomiest**) 1 dark or badly lit. 2 sad or depressed.

SYNONYMS 1 *a gloomy room* **dark,** shadowy, murky, sunless, dim, dingy. 2 *Joanna looked gloomy* **despondent,** depressed, downcast, downhearted, dejected, dispirited, disheartened, demoralized, crestfallen, glum, melancholy; informal down in the mouth, down in the dumps. 3 *gloomy forecasts about the economy* **pessimistic,** depressing, downbeat, disheartening, disappointing, unfavourable, bleak, black.
ANTONYMS bright, cheerful, optimistic.

□ **gloomily** adverb **gloominess** noun.

glorify ▶ verb (**glorifies, glorifying, glorified**) 1 represent something as admirable. 2 (**glorified**) made to appear more important than in reality. 3 praise and worship God.

glorious ▶ adjective 1 having or bringing glory. 2 very beautiful or impressive.

SYNONYMS **wonderful,** marvellous, magnificent, superb, sublime, spectacular, lovely, fine, delightful; informal stunning, fantastic, terrific, tremendous, sensational, heavenly,

divine, gorgeous, fabulous, awesome.
ANTONYMS undistinguished, horrid.

□ **gloriously** adverb.

glory ▶ noun (plural **glories**) 1 fame and honour. 2 magnificence; great beauty. 3 a very beautiful or impressive thing. 4 worship and praise of God.

SYNONYMS 1 *a sport that won him glory* **honour,** distinction, prestige, fame, renown, kudos, eminence, acclaim, praise, celebrity, recognition. 2 *a house restored to its former glory* **magnificence,** splendour, grandeur, majesty, greatness, nobility, opulence, beauty, elegance.
ANTONYMS shame, obscurity, modesty.

▶ verb (**glories, glorying, gloried**) (**glory in**) take great pride or pleasure in.

SYNONYMS *we gloried in our independence* **delight,** triumph, revel, rejoice, exult, relish, savour, be proud of; informal get a kick out of.

gloss[1] ▶ noun 1 the shine on a smooth surface. 2 a type of paint which dries to a bright shiny surface. 3 an attractive appearance that hides something ordinary or less attractive.

SYNONYMS *the gloss of her hair* **shine,** sheen, lustre, gleam, patina, polish, brilliance, shimmer.

▶ verb 1 give a glossy appearance to. 2 (**gloss over**) give only brief or misleading details about something.

gloss[2] ▶ noun a translation or explanation of a word, phrase, or passage.
▶ verb provide a gloss for.

glossary ▶ noun (plural **glossaries**) a list of words and their meanings.

glossy ▶ adjective (**glossier, glossiest**) 1 shiny and smooth. 2 appearing attractive and stylish.

SYNONYMS **shiny,** gleaming, lustrous, brilliant, glistening, glassy, polished, lacquered, glazed.
ANTONYMS dull.

glottal ▶ adjective having to do with the glottis.
■ **glottal stop** a speech sound made by opening and closing the glottis, sometimes used instead of a properly sounded *t*.

glottis ▶ noun the part of the larynx made up of the vocal cords and the narrow opening between them.

glove ▶ noun 1 a covering for the hand having separate parts for each finger. 2 a padded covering for the hand used in boxing and other sports.
■ **glove compartment** a small storage compartment in the dashboard of a car.

glow ▶ verb 1 give out a steady light. 2 have flushed skin, especially after exercising.

3 look very happy.

SYNONYMS **1** *lights glowed in the windows* **shine**, gleam, glimmer, flicker, flare. **2** *a fire glowed in the hearth* **smoulder**, burn.

▶ **noun** a steady light or heat.

SYNONYMS *the glow of the fire* **radiance**, light, gleam, glimmer.

■ **glow-worm** a kind of beetle which gives out light.

glower /glow-er/ ▶ **verb** have an angry or sullen expression.

▶ **noun** an angry or sullen look.

glowing ▶ **adjective** expressing great praise: *a glowing report.*

SYNONYMS **1** *glowing coals* **bright**, radiant, incandescent, luminous, smouldering. **2** *his glowing cheeks* **rosy**, pink, red, ruddy, flushed, blushing, burning. **3** *glowing colours* **vivid**, vibrant, bright, brilliant, rich, intense, radiant. **4** *a glowing report* **complimentary**, favourable, enthusiastic, admiring, rapturous, fulsome; informal rave. ANTONYMS dead, pale, drab, damning.

glucose /gloo-kohz/ ▶ **noun** a type of sugar that is easily changed into energy by the body.

glue ▶ **noun** a sticky substance used for joining things together.

SYNONYMS *a tube of glue* **adhesive**, gum, paste, cement; N. Amer. mucilage; N. Amer. informal stickum.

▶ **verb** (**glues**, **gluing** or **glueing**, **glued**) **1** join something with glue. **2** (**be glued to**) informal be paying very close attention to.

SYNONYMS *the planks were glued together* **stick**, gum, paste, fix, seal, cement.

glum ▶ **adjective** sad or miserable.

SYNONYMS **gloomy**, downcast, dejected, despondent, crestfallen, disheartened, depressed, doleful, miserable; informal fed up, down in the dumps. ANTONYMS cheerful.

□ **glumly** adverb.

glut ▶ **noun** more of something than is needed.

▶ **verb** (**gluts**, **glutting**, **glutted**) supply or provide with too much of something.

gluten ▶ **noun** a substance containing protein, found in wheat and other cereal plants.

glutinous ▶ **adjective** like glue in texture; sticky.

glutton ▶ **noun 1** a very greedy eater. **2** a person who is very eager for something difficult or challenging: *a glutton for punishment.*

gluttony ▶ **noun** the habit of eating too much.

glycerine (US spelling **glycerin**) ▶ **noun** a liquid made from fats and oils, used in medicines and cosmetics.

GM ▶ **abbreviation** genetically modified.

gm ▶ **abbreviation** grams.

GMO ▶ **abbreviation** genetically modified organism.

GMT ▶ **abbreviation** Greenwich Mean Time.

gnarled /narld/ ▶ **adjective** knobbly or twisted.

gnash /nash/ ▶ **verb** grind your teeth together, especially as a sign of anger.

gnat /nat/ ▶ **noun** a small two-winged fly.

gnaw /naw/ ▶ **verb 1** bite at or nibble something persistently. **2** cause persistent anxiety or pain.

gnome /nohm/ ▶ **noun** (in stories) a creature like a tiny man, who lives underground and guards treasure.

gnomic /**noh**-mik/ ▶ **adjective** clever but hard to understand.

Gnosticism /**noss**-ti-si-z'm/ ▶ **noun** a former religious movement teaching that the soul is saved through mystical knowledge. □ **Gnostic** adjective.

GNP ▶ **abbreviation** gross national product.

gnu /noo/ ▶ **noun** a large African antelope with a long head and a mane.

GNVQ ▶ **abbreviation** General National Vocational Qualification.

go ▶ **verb** (**goes**, **going**, **went**; past participle **gone**) **1** move to or from a place. **2** pass into or be in a particular state. **3** lie or extend in a certain direction. **4** come to an end. **5** disappear or be used up. **6** (of time) pass. **7** take part in a particular activity. **8** have a particular outcome. **9** (**be going to be** or **do**) used to express a future tense. **10** function or operate. **11** be harmonious or matching. **12** be acceptable or allowed. **13** fit into or be regularly kept in a particular place. **14** make a particular sound.

SYNONYMS **1** *he's gone into town* **travel**, move, proceed, make your way, journey, advance, progress, pass. **2** *the road goes to London* **lead**, stretch, reach, extend. **3** *it's time to go* **leave**, depart, take yourself off, go away, withdraw, absent yourself, exit, set off, start out, get under way, be on your way; Brit. make a move; informal make tracks. **4** *all our money had gone* **be used up**, be spent, be exhausted, be consumed. **5** *his hair had gone grey* **become**, get, turn, grow. **6** *everything went well* **turn out**, work out, develop, progress, result, end (up); informal pan out. **7** *those colours don't go* **match**, harmonize, blend, be complementary, coordinate, be compatible. **8** *my car won't go* **function**, work, run, operate.

g

ANTONYMS arrive, come, return, clash, malfunction.

▸ noun (plural **goes**) informal **1** an attempt. **2** a turn to do or use something. **3** spirit or energy.

SYNONYMS **1** *here, have a go* **try,** attempt, effort, bid; informal shot, stab, crack. **2** *whose go is it?* **turn,** opportunity, chance, stint, spell, time.

■ **the go-ahead** informal permission to proceed. **go along with** agree to. **go back on** fail to keep a promise. **go-between** a person who acts as a messenger or negotiator. **go-cart** (or **go-kart**) a small racing car with a lightweight body. **go for 1** decide on. **2** try to gain. **3** attack. **go in for 1** enter a contest. **2** like or habitually take part in. **go into 1** investigate or enquire into. **2** (of a whole number) be capable of dividing another. **go off 1** (of a gun or bomb) explode or fire. **2** Brit. (of food) begin to decompose. **3** Brit. informal begin to dislike. **go on** continue. **go out 1** stop shining or burning. **2** have a regular romantic relationship with someone. **go over** examine or check the details of. **go through 1** undergo a difficult experience. **2** examine carefully. **go without** suffer lack or hardship. **have a go at** attack or criticize.
□ **goer** noun.

goad ▸ verb keep annoying or criticizing someone until they react.
▸ noun **1** a thing that makes someone do something. **2** a spiked stick used for driving cattle.

goal ▸ noun **1** (in soccer, rugby, etc.) a wooden frame into or over which the ball has to be sent to score. **2** an instance of sending the ball into or over a goal. **3** an aim or desired result.

SYNONYMS **objective,** aim, end, target, intention, plan, purpose, ambition, aspiration.

□ **goalless** adjective.

goalkeeper ▸ noun (in soccer, hockey, etc.) a player whose role is to stop the ball from entering the goal.

goalpost ▸ noun either of the two upright posts of a goal.

goat ▸ noun an animal with horns and a hairy coat, often kept for milk.

goatee ▸ noun a small pointed beard like that of a goat.

goatherd ▸ noun a person who looks after goats.

gob ▸ noun Brit. informal a person's mouth.

gobbet ▸ noun a piece of flesh, food, or other matter.

gobble ▸ verb (**gobbles, gobbling, gobbled**) **1** eat hurriedly and noisily. **2** (of a turkey) make a swallowing sound in the throat.

SYNONYMS **guzzle,** bolt, gulp, devour, wolf; informal tuck into, put away, demolish; Brit. informal scoff; N. Amer. informal scarf (down/up).

gobbledegook (or **gobbledygook**)
▸ noun informal complicated language that is difficult to understand.

goblet ▸ noun a drinking glass with a foot and a stem.

goblin ▸ noun (in stories) a small, ugly, mischievous creature.

gobsmacked ▸ adjective Brit. informal utterly astonished.

gobstopper ▸ noun a hard round sweet.

goby /goh-bi/ ▸ noun (plural **gobies**) a small sea fish.

God ▸ noun **1** (in Christianity and some other religions) the creator and supreme ruler of the universe. **2** (**god**) a superhuman being or spirit.

SYNONYMS (**god**) **deity,** goddess, divine being, divinity, immortal.

■ **God-fearing** earnestly religious.

godchild ▸ noun (plural **godchildren**) a person in relation to a godparent.

god-daughter ▸ noun a female godchild.

goddess ▸ noun a female deity.

godfather ▸ noun **1** a male godparent. **2** the male leader of an illegal organization.

godforsaken ▸ adjective (of a place) remote, unattractive, or depressing.

godhead ▸ noun **1** (**the Godhead**) God. **2** divine nature.

godless ▸ adjective **1** not believing in God or a god. **2** wicked.

godly ▸ adjective very religious.

godmother ▸ noun a female godparent.

godparent ▸ noun a person who promises to be responsible for a child's religious education.

godsend ▸ noun something that is very helpful or welcome.

godson ▸ noun a male godchild.

goes 3rd person singular present of **go**.

goggle ▸ verb (**goggles, goggling, goggled**) **1** look with wide open eyes. **2** (of the eyes) stick out or open wide.
▸ noun (**goggles**) close-fitting protective glasses.

going ▸ noun **1** the condition of the ground in terms of its suitability for horse racing or walking. **2** conditions for an activity: *the going gets tough.*
▸ adjective **1** existing or available. **2** (of a price) normal or current.
■ **going concern** a thriving business. **goings-on** informal activities that are strange or dishonest.

goitre /goy-ter/ ▸ noun a swelling of the neck which is caused by enlargement of the thyroid gland.

gold ▸ noun **1** a yellow precious metal. **2** a deep yellow or yellow-brown colour. **3** things made of gold.
■ **gold leaf** gold beaten into a very thin sheet. **gold medal** a medal awarded for first place in a race or competition. **gold rush** a rapid movement of people to a place where gold has been discovered.

goldcrest ▸ noun a very small bird with a yellow or orange crest.

golden ▸ adjective **1** made of or resembling gold. **2** (of a period) very happy and prosperous. **3** excellent.

SYNONYMS **blonde,** yellow, fair, flaxen. ANTONYMS dark.

■ **golden age** the period when something is very successful. **golden eagle** a large eagle with yellow-tipped head feathers. **golden handshake** informal a payment given to someone who is made redundant or retires early. **golden jubilee** the fiftieth anniversary of an important event. **golden rule** a principle which should always be followed. **golden wedding** Brit. the fiftieth anniversary of a wedding.

goldfinch ▸ noun a brightly coloured finch with a yellow patch on each wing.

goldfish ▸ noun (plural **goldfish** or **goldfishes**) a small orange carp, often kept in ponds.

goldsmith ▸ noun a person who makes things out of gold.

golf ▸ noun a game played on an outdoor course, the aim of which is to hit a small ball into a series of small holes using a set of special clubs.
□ **golfer** noun.

golliwog ▸ noun a soft doll with a black face and fuzzy hair.

gonad /goh-nad/ ▸ noun an organ in the body that produces gametes; a testis or ovary.

gondola /gon-duh-luh/ ▸ noun a light flat-bottomed boat used on canals in Venice, worked by one oar at the stern.

gondolier /gon-duh-leer/ ▸ noun a person who propels a gondola.

gone past participle of GO.
▸ adjective no longer present or in existence.

SYNONYMS **1** *I wasn't gone long* **away,** absent, off, out, missing. **2** *those days are gone* **past,** over (and done with), no more, done, finished, ended, forgotten. **3** *the milk's all gone* **used up,** consumed, finished, spent, depleted. ANTONYMS present, here.

▸ preposition Brit. **1** (of time) past. **2** (of age) older than.

goner /gon-er/ ▸ noun informal a person or

thing that cannot be saved.

gong ▸ noun **1** a metal disc that makes a deep ringing sound when struck. **2** Brit. informal a medal or other award.

gonorrhoea /gon-uh-ree-uh/ (US spelling **gonorrhea**) ▸ noun a disease caused by bacteria that are passed on during sex.

goo ▸ noun informal a soft, sticky substance.

good ▸ adjective **1** having the right qualities; of a high standard. **2** behaving in a way that is right, polite, or obedient. **3** enjoyable or satisfying. **4** suitable or appropriate. **5** (**good for**) having a useful or helpful effect on. **6** thorough.

SYNONYMS **1** *a good product* **fine,** superior, excellent, superb, outstanding, magnificent, exceptional, marvellous, wonderful, first-rate, first-class, quality; informal great, ace, terrific, fantastic, fabulous, class, awesome, wicked; Brit. informal brilliant. **2** *a good person* **virtuous,** righteous, upright, upstanding, moral, ethical, principled, law-abiding, blameless, honourable, decent, respectable, trustworthy; informal squeaky clean. **3** *the children are good at school* **well behaved,** obedient, dutiful, polite, courteous, respectful. **4** *a good driver* **capable,** able, proficient, adept, adroit, accomplished, skilful, talented, masterly, expert; informal mean, wicked, nifty; N. Amer. informal crackerjack. **5** *a good friend* **close,** intimate, dear, bosom, special, best, firm, loyal. **6** *we had a good time* **enjoyable,** pleasant, agreeable, pleasurable, delightful, lovely, amusing. **7** *it was good of you to come* **kind,** generous, charitable, gracious, noble, altruistic, unselfish. **8** *a good time to call* **convenient,** suitable, appropriate, fitting, fit, opportune, timely, favourable. **9** *milk is good for you* **wholesome,** healthy, nourishing, nutritious, beneficial. **10** *good food* **tasty,** appetizing, flavoursome, palatable, succulent; informal scrumptious, scrummy, yummy; Brit. informal moreish; N. Amer. informal nummy. **11** *a good reason* **valid,** genuine, authentic, legitimate, sound, bona fide, convincing, compelling. **12** *good weather* **fine,** fair, dry, bright, clear, sunny, cloudless, calm, warm, mild.
ANTONYMS bad, wicked, naughty, unenjoyable, mean, inconvenient, disgusting.

▸ noun **1** behaviour that is right or acceptable. **2** something beneficial. **3** (**goods**) products or possessions. **4** Brit. (**goods**) freight.

SYNONYMS **1** *issues of good and evil* **virtue,** righteousness, goodness, morality, integrity, honesty, truth, honour. **2** *it's for your own good* **benefit,** advantage,

profit, gain, interest, welfare, well-being.
3 (**goods**) **merchandise,** wares, stock,
commodities, produce, products, articles.
ANTONYMS wickedness, disadvantage.

■ **as good as** very nearly. **for good** forever.
good faith honest or sincere intentions.
good-for-nothing worthless. **Good Friday**
the Friday before Easter Sunday, on which
Christians commemorate the Crucifixion
of Jesus. **good-looking** attractive.
good-natured kind and unselfish. **make
something good 1** compensate for loss or
damage. **2** fulfil a promise or claim.

goodbye ▶ **exclamation** used to express
good wishes when parting or ending a
conversation.

SYNONYMS **farewell,** adieu, au revoir,
ciao, adios; Austral./NZ hooray; informal bye,
bye-bye, so long, see you (later); Brit.
informal cheerio, cheers, ta-ta.

▶ **noun** (plural **goodbyes**) a parting.

goodly ▶ **adjective** (**goodlier, goodliest**)
quite large in size or quantity.

goodness ▶ **noun** the quality of being good.

SYNONYMS **1** *he had some goodness in him*
virtue, good, righteousness, morality,
integrity, rectitude, honesty, honour,
decency, respectability, nobility,
worth, merit. **2** *his goodness towards
us* **kindness,** humanity, benevolence,
tenderness, warmth, affection, love,
goodwill, sympathy, compassion, care,
concern, understanding, generosity,
charity.

goodnight ▶ **exclamation** used to express
good wishes when parting at night or
before going to bed.

goodwill ▶ **noun** friendly or helpful
feelings towards other people.

SYNONYMS **kindness,** compassion,
goodness, benevolence, consideration,
charity, decency, neighbourliness.
ANTONYMS hostility.

goody (or **goodie**) ▶ **noun** (plural **goodies**)
informal **1** Brit. a good person, especially a hero
in a story or film. **2** (**goodies**) tasty things
to eat.
■ **goody-goody** informal a person who
behaves well in order to impress other
people.

gooey ▶ **adjective** informal soft and sticky.

goof informal, chiefly N. Amer. ▶ **verb 1** make a
mistake. **2** fool around.
▶ **noun** a mistake.

goofy ▶ **adjective** informal **1** chiefly N. Amer. silly.
2 having front teeth that stick out.

goon ▶ **noun** informal **1** a silly person. **2** N. Amer.
a thug.

goose ▶ **noun** (plural **geese**) **1** a large
waterbird with a long neck and webbed
feet. **2** a female goose. **3** informal a silly
person.
■ **goose pimples** little raised bumps
on your skin, caused by feeling cold or
frightened. **goose step** a way of marching
in which the legs are kept straight.

gooseberry ▶ **noun** (plural **gooseberries**)
1 an edible yellowish-green berry with a
hairy skin. **2** Brit. informal a third person in
the company of two lovers.

gopher /goh-fer/ ▶ **noun** a burrowing
rodent found in North America.

gore¹ ▶ **noun** blood that has been shed.

gore² ▶ **verb** (**gores, goring, gored**) (of an
animal such as a bull) pierce with a horn
or tusk.

gore³ ▶ **noun** a triangular piece of material
used in making a garment, sail, or
umbrella.

gorge ▶ **noun** a narrow valley or ravine.

SYNONYMS **ravine,** canyon, gully, defile,
couloir, chasm, gulf; S. English chine;
N. English gill; N. Amer. gulch, coulee.

▶ **verb** (**gorges, gorging, gorged**) eat a large
amount greedily.

gorgeous ▶ **adjective 1** beautiful. **2** informal
very pleasant.

SYNONYMS **1** *a gorgeous girl* **good-looking,**
attractive, beautiful, pretty, handsome,
lovely, stunning; Scottish & N. English
bonny; informal fanciable, tasty, hot; Brit.
informal fit; N. Amer. informal cute, foxy. **2** *a
gorgeous view* **spectacular,** splendid,
superb, wonderful, grand, impressive,
awe-inspiring, awesome, stunning,
breathtaking; informal sensational,
fabulous, fantastic. **3** *gorgeous uniforms*
resplendent, magnificent, sumptuous,
luxurious, elegant, dazzling, brilliant.
ANTONYMS ugly, dreary, drab.

gorgon /gor-guhn/ ▶ **noun** Greek Mythology
each of three sisters with snakes for hair,
who had the power to turn anyone who
looked at them to stone.

gorilla ▶ **noun** a powerfully built ape of
central Africa.

gormless ▶ **adjective** Brit. informal stupid.

gorse ▶ **noun** a yellow-flowered shrub with
spiny leaves.

gory ▶ **adjective 1** involving violence and
bloodshed. **2** covered in blood.

goshawk /goss-hawk/ ▶ **noun** a large hawk
with short wings.

gosling ▶ **noun** a young goose.

gospel ▶ **noun 1** the teachings of Jesus.
2 (the **Gospel**) the record of Jesus's life and
teaching in the first four books of the New
Testament. **3** (**Gospel**) each of these books.
4 (also **gospel truth**) something absolutely

true. **5** (also **gospel music**) a style of black American religious singing.

gossamer ► noun a fine substance consisting of cobwebs spun by small spiders.

► adjective very fine and flimsy.

gossip ► noun **1** casual conversation about other people. **2** disapproving a person who likes talking about other people.

> SYNONYMS **1** *tell me all the gossip* **news,** rumours, scandal, hearsay; informal dirt, buzz; Brit. informal goss; N. Amer. informal scuttlebutt. **2** *they went for a gossip* **chat,** talk, conversation, chatter, heart-to-heart, tête-à-tête; informal jaw, gas; Brit. informal natter, chinwag; N. Amer. informal gabfest; Austral./NZ informal yarn. **3** *she's such a gossip* **gossip-monger,** busybody, scandalmonger, rumour-monger, muckraker.

► verb (**gossips, gossiping, gossiped**) talk about other people.

> SYNONYMS **1** *she gossiped about his wife* **talk,** whisper, tell tales; informal dish the dirt. **2** *people sat around gossiping* **chat,** talk, converse, discuss things; informal gas, chew the fat, jaw; Brit. informal natter, chinwag; N. Amer. informal shoot the breeze.

got past and past participle of **GET**.

Gothic ► adjective **1** of the style of architecture common in western Europe in the 12th to 16th centuries. **2** very gloomy or horrifying.

gotten N. Amer. or old use past participle of **GET**.

gouache /goo-**ash**/ ► noun **1** a method of painting using watercolours thickened with glue. **2** paint used in this method.

gouge /gowj, gooj/ ► verb (**gouges, gouging, gouged**) **1** make a rough hole in a surface. **2** (**gouge something out**) cut something out roughly.

► noun **1** a chisel with a concave blade. **2** a hole or groove made by gouging.

goulash /**goo**-lash/ ► noun a rich Hungarian stew of meat and vegetables.

gourd /goord/ ► noun a fruit with a hard skin, usually used as a container rather than as food.

gourmand /**goor**-muhnd/ ► noun a person who enjoys eating.

gourmet /**goor**-may/ ► noun a person who knows a lot about good food.

> SYNONYMS **gastronome,** epicure, epicurean, connoisseur; informal foodie.

► adjective suitable for a gourmet.

gout ► noun a disease causing the joints to swell and become painful.

govern ► verb **1** control the laws and affairs of a state, organization, or community. **2** control or influence.

> SYNONYMS **1** *he governs the province* **rule,** preside over, control, be in charge of, command, run, head, manage, oversee, supervise. **2** *the rules governing social behaviour* **determine,** decide, control, constrain, regulate, direct, rule, dictate, shape, affect.

governance ► noun the action or style of governing.

governess ► noun a woman employed to teach the children of a family in their home.

government ► noun **1** the group of people who govern a state. **2** the system by which a state, organization, or community is governed.

> SYNONYMS **administration,** executive, regime, authority, council, powers that be, cabinet, ministry.

□ **governmental** adjective.

> ✔ Remember that **government** is spelled with an **n** before the **m**.

governor ► noun **1** an official appointed to govern a town or region. **2** the head of a public institution. **3** a member of a governing body.

> SYNONYMS **leader,** ruler, chief, head, administrator, principal, director, chairman, chairwoman, chair, superintendent, commissioner, controller; informal boss.

gown ► noun **1** a long dress worn on formal occasions. **2** a protective garment worn in hospital by surgeons or patients. **3** a loose cloak showing your profession or status, worn by a lawyer, academic, or university student.

> SYNONYMS **dress,** frock, robe, habit, costume.

GP ► abbreviation general practitioner.

gr. ► abbreviation **1** grains. **2** grams. **3** gross.

grab ► verb (**grabs, grabbing, grabbed**) **1** seize someone or something suddenly and roughly. **2** informal take the opportunity to get something.

> SYNONYMS **seize,** grasp, snatch, take hold of, grip, clasp, clutch, catch.

► noun a sudden attempt to seize someone or something.

grace ► noun **1** attractive smoothness of movement. **2** polite respect. **3** (**graces**) attractive qualities or behaviour. **4** (in Christian belief) the unearned favour of God. **5** the condition of being trusted and respected by someone. **6** a period officially allowed to do something: *three days' grace*. **7** a short prayer of thanks said at a meal. **8** (**His, Her,** or **Your Grace**) used as a way of addressing a duke, duchess, or archbishop.

SYNONYMS **1** *the grace of a ballerina* **elegance**, poise, finesse, polish, fluency, suppleness. **2** *he had the grace to apologize* **courtesy**, decency, (good) manners, politeness, respect, tact. **3** *he fell from grace* **favour**, approval, approbation, acceptance, esteem, regard, respect.
ANTONYMS awkwardness, effrontery, disfavour.

▶ verb (**graces**, **gracing**, **graced**) **1** bring honour to someone or something by your presence. **2** make something more attractive.

SYNONYMS *a mosaic graced the floor* **adorn**, embellish, decorate, ornament, enhance.

■ **grace note** Music an extra note which is not needed for the harmony or melody.

graceful ▶ adjective having or showing grace or elegance.

SYNONYMS **elegant**, fluid, fluent, easy, polished, supple.

□ **gracefully** adverb.

graceless ▶ adjective without grace or charm.

gracious ▶ adjective **1** kind, pleasant, and polite. **2** showing the elegance associated with high social status or wealth. **3** (in Christian belief) showing divine grace.

SYNONYMS **courteous**, polite, civil, well-mannered, tactful, diplomatic, kind, considerate, thoughtful, obliging, accommodating, hospitable.
ANTONYMS ungracious.

□ **graciously** adverb.

gradation ▶ noun **1** a scale of gradual change from one thing to another. **2** a stage in such a scale.

grade ▶ noun **1** a level of rank or ability. **2** a mark indicating the quality of a student's work. **3** N. Amer. a class of school students grouped according to age or ability.

SYNONYMS **1** *hotels within the same grade* **category**, class, classification, ranking, quality, grouping, group, bracket. **2** *his job is of the lowest grade* **rank**, level, standing, position, class, status, order, echelon. **3** N. Amer. *the best grades in the school* **mark**, score, assessment, evaluation, appraisal. **4** *the fifth grade* **year**, form, class.

▶ verb (**grades**, **grading**, **graded**) **1** arrange people or things in groups according to quality, ability, etc. **2** N. Amer. give a grade to a student or their work.

SYNONYMS *eggs are graded by size* **classify**, class, categorize, bracket, sort, group, arrange, pigeonhole, rank, evaluate, rate, value.

■ **make the grade** informal succeed.

gradient /gray-di-uhnt/ ▶ noun **1** a sloping part of a road or railway. **2** the degree to which something slopes.

SYNONYMS **slope**, incline, hill, rise, ramp, bank; N. Amer. grade.

gradual ▶ adjective **1** taking place in stages over a long period of time. **2** (of a slope) not steep.

SYNONYMS **1** *a gradual transition* **slow**, steady, measured, unhurried, cautious, piecemeal, step-by-step, bit-by-bit, progressive, continuous. **2** *a gradual slope* **gentle**, moderate, slight, easy.
ANTONYMS abrupt, steep.

gradually ▶ adverb in a gradual way.

SYNONYMS **slowly**, steadily, slowly but surely, cautiously, gently, gingerly, piecemeal, bit by bit, by degrees, progressively, systematically.
ANTONYMS abruptly.

graduate ▶ noun /grad-yuu-uht/ a person who has been awarded a university degree.
▶ verb /grad-yoo-ayt/ (**graduates**, **graduating**, **graduated**) **1** successfully complete a degree or course. **2** (**graduate to**) move up to something more advanced. **3** change something gradually.
□ **graduation** noun.

graffiti /gruh-**fee**-ti/ ▶ noun writing or drawings on a wall in a public place.

✔ double **f**, single **t**: gra**ffit**i.

graft[1] ▶ noun **1** a shoot from one plant inserted into another to form a new growth. **2** a piece of body tissue that is transplanted from one part of the body to another part that has been damaged.

SYNONYMS *a skin graft* **transplant**, implant.

▶ verb **1** insert or transplant as a graft. **2** add something to something else, especially in a way that seems inappropriate.

SYNONYMS **1** *graft a bud onto the stem* **splice**, join, insert, fix. **2** *tissue is grafted on to the cornea* **transplant**, implant.

graft[2] Brit. informal ▶ noun hard work.
▶ verb work hard.

graft[3] informal ▶ noun bribery and other illegal methods used to gain advantage in politics or business.

Grail ▶ noun (in medieval legend) the cup or dish used by Jesus at the Last Supper.

grain ▶ noun **1** wheat or another cereal plant grown for food. **2** a single seed or fruit of a cereal plant. **3** a small, hard particle of a substance such as sand. **4** the smallest unit of weight in the troy and avoirdupois systems. **5** the smallest possible amount.

g

6 the arrangement of fibres in wood, fabric, etc.

SYNONYMS **1** *fields of grain* **cereal**. **2** *a grain of corn* **kernel**, seed. **3** *grains of sand* **granule**, particle, speck, bit, scrap, crumb, fragment, morsel. **4** *a grain of truth* **trace**, hint, tinge, suggestion, shadow, soupçon, ounce, iota, jot, scrap, shred; informal smidgen. **5** *the grain in paper* **texture**, weave, pattern.

■ **against the grain** conflicting with your nature or instinct.
□ **grainy** adjective.

gram (or Brit. **gramme**) ▸ noun a metric unit of mass equal to one thousandth of a kilogram.

grammar ▸ noun **1** the whole system and structure of a language. **2** knowledge and use of the rules of grammar. **3** a book on grammar.
■ **grammar school** (in the UK, especially formerly) a state secondary school to which pupils are admitted on the basis of their ability.

✔ **-ar**, not **-er**: gramm**ar**.

grammatical ▸ adjective **1** having to do with grammar. **2** conforming to the rules of grammar.
□ **grammatically** adverb.

gramophone ▸ noun dated a record player.

grampus ▸ noun (plural **grampuses**) a killer whale or other animal of the dolphin family.

gran ▸ noun Brit. informal your grandmother.

granary ▸ noun (plural **granaries**) a storehouse for grain.

grand ▸ adjective **1** magnificent and impressive. **2** large or ambitious in scale. **3** of the highest importance or rank. **4** dignified, noble, or proud. **5** informal excellent.

SYNONYMS **1** *a grand hotel* **magnificent**, imposing, impressive, awe-inspiring, splendid, resplendent, majestic, monumental, palatial, stately; Brit. upmarket; N. Amer. upscale; informal fancy, posh; Brit. informal swish. **2** *a grand scheme* **ambitious**, bold, epic, big, extravagant. **3** *a grand old lady* **august**, distinguished, illustrious, eminent, venerable, dignified, proud. **4** *you're doing a grand job* **excellent**, marvellous, splendid, first-class, first-rate, wonderful, outstanding; informal superb, terrific, great, super; Brit. informal brilliant.
ANTONYMS humble, small-scale, poor.

▸ noun (plural **grand**) informal a thousand dollars or pounds.
■ **grand piano** a large piano which has the strings arranged horizontally. **grand slam** the winning of each of a group of major sports championships or matches in the same year. **grand total** the final amount after everything is added up.
□ **grandly** adverb.

grandad (or **granddad**) ▸ noun informal your grandfather.

grandchild ▸ noun (plural **grandchildren**) the child of a person's son or daughter.

granddaughter ▸ noun the daughter of a person's son or daughter.

grandee ▸ noun a person of high status and social rank.

grandeur /gran-dyer/ ▸ noun **1** the quality of being grand and impressive. **2** high status and social rank.

SYNONYMS **splendour**, magnificence, glory, resplendence, majesty, greatness, stateliness, pomp, ceremony.

grandfather ▸ noun the father of a person's father or mother.
■ **grandfather clock** a large clock in a tall wooden case.

grandiloquent ▸ adjective pompous in style and using long and fancy words.

grandiose ▸ adjective (of a plan or building) very large and ambitious and intended to impress.

grandma ▸ noun informal your grandmother.

grandmother ▸ noun the mother of a person's father or mother.

grandpa ▸ noun informal your grandfather.

grandparent ▸ noun a grandmother or grandfather.

Grand Prix /gron pree/ ▸ noun (plural **Grands Prix** /gron pree/) a race forming part of a motor-racing or motorcycling world championship.

grandson ▸ noun the son of a person's son or daughter.

grandstand ▸ noun the main stand at a racecourse or sports ground.

grange ▸ noun Brit. a country house with farm buildings attached.

granite ▸ noun a hard grey rock.

granny (or **grannie**) ▸ noun (plural **grannies**) informal your grandmother.
■ **granny flat** a small flat that is part of or attached to a house, in which an elderly relative can live. **granny knot** a reef knot with the ends crossed the wrong way and therefore liable to slip.

grant ▸ verb **1** agree to give something to someone or to allow them to do something. **2** give something formally or legally. **3** admit to someone that something is true.

SYNONYMS **1** *he granted them leave of absence* **allow**, permit, accord, afford. **2** *he granted them £20,000* **give**, award, bestow on, confer on, present with, endow with. **3** *I grant that the difference*

is slight **admit,** accept, concede, allow, appreciate, recognize, acknowledge, confess.
ANTONYMS refuse, deny.

▶ **noun** a sum of money given by a government or public body for a particular purpose.

SYNONYMS *a grant from the council* **award,** bursary, endowment, scholarship, allowance, subsidy, contribution, handout, donation, gift.

granted ▶ **adverb** admittedly; it is true.

granulated ▶ **adjective** in the form of granules.
□ **granulation** noun.

granule ▶ **noun** a small compact particle of a substance.
□ **granular** adjective.

grape ▶ **noun** a green or purple-black berry growing in clusters on a vine, eaten as fruit and used in making wine.

grapefruit ▶ **noun** (plural **grapefruit**) a large yellow citrus fruit with a slightly bitter taste.

grapeshot ▶ **noun** (in the past) ammunition consisting of a number of small iron balls fired together from a cannon.

grapevine ▶ **noun 1** a vine which produces grapes. **2** (**the grapevine**) the spreading of information through talk or rumour.

graph ▶ **noun** a diagram showing how two or more sets of numbers relate to each other.
■ **graph paper** paper printed with small squares, used for graphs and diagrams.

graphic ▶ **adjective 1** relating to visual art, especially involving drawing and the design of printed material. **2** giving vivid details.

SYNONYMS **1** *a graphic representation* **visual,** pictorial, illustrative, diagrammatic. **2** *a graphic account* **vivid,** explicit, detailed, realistic, descriptive, powerful, colourful, lurid, shocking.
ANTONYMS vague.

▶ **noun 1** a pictorial image or symbol on a computer screen. **2** (**graphics**) the use of designs or pictures to illustrate books, magazines, etc.
■ **graphic design** the design of books, posters, and other printed material.
□ **graphically** adverb.

graphite ▶ **noun** a grey form of carbon used as pencil lead and as a lubricant in machinery.

graphology ▶ **noun** the study of handwriting as a guide to personality.
□ **graphologist** noun.

grapnel /grap-nuhl/ (or **grappling hook**)
▶ **noun** a device with iron claws, used for dragging or grasping things.

grapple ▶ **verb** (**grapples, grappling,**

grappled) **1** struggle or fight physically with someone. **2** (**grapple with**) struggle to deal with or understand.

SYNONYMS **1** *the police grappled with him* **wrestle,** struggle, tussle, scuffle, battle. **2** *grappling with addiction* **deal with,** cope with, get to grips with, tackle, confront, face.

grasp ▶ **verb 1** seize and hold something firmly. **2** understand something.

SYNONYMS **1** *she grasped his hand* **grip,** clutch, clasp, clench, squeeze, catch, seize, grab, snatch. **2** *he grasped the important points* **understand,** comprehend, take in, see, apprehend, assimilate, absorb; informal get, take on board; Brit. informal twig.
ANTONYMS release, overlook.

▶ **noun 1** a firm grip. **2** a person's ability to achieve or understand something.

SYNONYMS **1** *his grasp on her hand* **grip,** hold, squeeze. **2** *a prize lay within their grasp* **reach,** scope, power, range, sights. **3** *a grasp of history* **understanding,** comprehension, awareness, grip, knowledge, mastery, command.

grasping ▶ **adjective** greedy.

SYNONYMS **greedy,** acquisitive, avaricious, rapacious, mercenary, materialistic; informal tight-fisted, tight, money-grubbing; N. Amer. informal grabby.

grass ▶ **noun 1** plants with long narrow leaves and stalks. **2** ground covered with grass. **3** informal cannabis. **4** Brit. informal a police informer.

▶ **verb 1** cover an area with grass. **2** Brit. informal inform the police about someone's criminal activity.
■ **grass roots** the ordinary people in an organization or society, rather than the leaders.
□ **grassy** adjective.

grasshopper ▶ **noun** an insect with long hind legs which it uses for jumping and for producing a chirping sound.

grate¹ ▶ **verb** (**grates, grating, grated**)
1 shred food by rubbing it on a grater.
2 make an unpleasant rasping sound.
3 have an irritating effect.

SYNONYMS **1** *grate the cheese* **shred,** pulverize, mince, grind, crush, crumble.
2 *her bones grated together* **grind,** rub, rasp, scrape, jar, creak.

grate² ▶ **noun** a metal frame or basket in a fireplace in which the coals or wood are placed.

grateful ▶ **adjective** feeling thankful and appreciative.

synonyms **thankful,** appreciative, indebted, obliged, in someone's debt, beholden.

□ **gratefully** adverb.

✔ **grate**ful, not **great**ful.

grater ▶ noun a device having a surface covered with sharp-edged holes, used for grating food.

gratify ▶ verb (**gratifies, gratifying, gratified**) **1** give someone pleasure or satisfaction. **2** indulge or satisfy a desire.
□ **gratification** noun.

grating¹ ▶ adjective **1** sounding harsh and unpleasant. **2** irritating.

grating² ▶ noun a grid of metal bars used as a barrier.

gratis /grat-iss, grah-tiss/ ▶ adverb & adjective free of charge.

gratitude ▶ noun the feeling of being grateful.

synonyms **thanks,** gratefulness, thankfulness, appreciation, indebtedness, recognition, acknowledgement.

gratuitous /gruh-**tyoo**-i-tuhss/ ▶ adjective having no justifiable reason or purpose.
□ **gratuitously** adverb.

gratuity ▶ noun (plural **gratuities**) formal a sum of money given to someone who has provided a service; a tip.

grave¹ ▶ noun a hole dug in the ground for a coffin or dead body.

synonyms *an unmarked grave* **tomb,** burial place, last resting place, vault, mausoleum, sepulchre.

grave² ▶ adjective **1** giving cause for alarm or concern. **2** solemn.

synonyms **1** *a grave matter* **serious,** important, weighty, profound, significant, momentous, critical, urgent, pressing, dire, terrible, dreadful. **2** *Jackie looked grave* **solemn,** serious, sober, unsmiling, grim, sombre, dour.
antonyms trivial, light-hearted.

□ **gravely** adverb.

grave accent /grahv/ ▶ noun a mark (`) placed over a vowel in some languages to indicate a change in its sound quality.

gravel ▶ noun a loose mixture of small stones used for paths and roads.

gravelly ▶ adjective **1** resembling or containing gravel. **2** (of a voice) deep and rough.

graven image ▶ noun a carved figure.

gravestone ▶ noun a stone slab marking a grave.

graveyard ▶ noun a burial ground.

synonyms **cemetery,** churchyard, burial ground, necropolis, garden of remembrance; Scottish kirkyard.

gravitas /gra-vi-tahss/ ▶ noun a serious and dignified manner.

gravitate ▶ verb (**gravitates, gravitating, gravitated**) (**gravitate to/towards**) be drawn towards.

gravitation ▶ noun movement towards a centre of gravity.
□ **gravitational** adjective.

gravity ▶ noun **1** the force that attracts a body towards the centre of the earth, or towards any other physical body having mass. **2** extreme importance or seriousness. **3** a solemn manner.

synonyms **1** *the gravity of the situation* **seriousness,** importance, significance, weight, consequence, magnitude, acuteness, urgency, dreadfulness. **2** *the gravity of his demeanour* **solemnity,** seriousness, sobriety, severity, grimness, sombreness, dourness.
antonyms triviality, light-heartedness.

gravy ▶ noun (plural **gravies**) a sauce made from the fat and juices that come out of meat during cooking.
■ **gravy boat** a long, narrow jug used for serving gravy.

gray US spelling of GREY.

graze¹ ▶ verb (**grazes, grazing, grazed**) (of cattle, sheep, etc.) eat grass.

synonyms *the deer grazed* **feed,** eat, crop, nibble, browse.

graze² ▶ verb (**grazes, grazing, grazed**) **1** scrape the skin on a part of your body. **2** touch something lightly in passing.

synonyms **1** *he grazed his arm* **scrape,** skin, scratch, chafe, scuff, rasp. **2** *his shot grazed the bar* **touch,** brush, shave, skim, kiss, scrape, clip, glance off.

▶ noun an area where the skin has been scraped.

synonyms *grazes on the skin* **scratch,** scrape, abrasion.

grazing ▶ noun grassland suitable for use as pasture.

grease ▶ noun **1** a thick oily substance used as a lubricant. **2** animal fat used or produced in cooking.

synonyms **oil,** fat, lubricant.

▶ verb (**greases, greasing, greased**) smear or lubricate something with grease.

greasepaint ▶ noun a waxy substance used as make-up by actors.

greaseproof ▶ adjective not allowing grease to pass through it.

g

greasy ▸ adjective covered with or resembling grease.

> SYNONYMS **oily,** fatty, buttery, slippery, slick, slimy, slithery; informal slippy.
> ANTONYMS fat-free, clean, dry.

great ▸ adjective **1** considerably above average in extent, amount, or strength. **2** considerably above average in ability or quality. **3** informal excellent. **4** used to emphasize something: *he's a great cricket fan.*

> SYNONYMS **1** *they showed great interest* **considerable,** substantial, significant, serious, exceptional, extraordinary. **2** *a great expanse of water* **large,** big, extensive, expansive, broad, wide, vast, immense, huge, enormous, massive; informal humongous, whopping; Brit. informal ginormous. **3** *great writers* **prominent,** eminent, distinguished, illustrious, celebrated, acclaimed, admired, esteemed, renowned, notable, famous, well known, leading, top, major. **4** *a great castle* **magnificent,** imposing, impressive, awe-inspiring, grand, splendid, majestic. **5** *a great sportsman* **expert,** skilful, skilled, adept, accomplished, talented, fine, masterly, master, brilliant, virtuoso, marvellous, outstanding, first-class, superb; informal crack, class. **6** *a great fan of rugby* **keen,** eager, enthusiastic, devoted, ardent, fanatical, passionate, dedicated, committed. **7** *we had a great time* **enjoyable,** delightful, lovely, excellent, marvellous, wonderful, fine, splendid; informal terrific, fantastic, fabulous, super, cool; Brit. informal brilliant.
> ANTONYMS little, small, minor, modest, poor, apathetic, half-hearted, miserable.

■ **great-aunt** (or **great-uncle**) an aunt (or uncle) of your mother or father.

greatcoat ▸ noun a long heavy overcoat.

greatly ▸ adverb very much.

> SYNONYMS **very much,** extremely, considerably, substantially, significantly, markedly, seriously, materially, enormously, vastly, immensely, tremendously, mightily; informal majorly.
> ANTONYMS slightly.

greatness ▸ noun the quality of being great.

> SYNONYMS **1** *a woman destined for greatness* **eminence,** distinction, celebrity, fame, prominence, renown, importance. **2** *his greatness as a writer* **brilliance,** genius, prowess, talent, expertise, mastery, artistry, skill, proficiency, flair.

grebe ▸ noun a diving bird with a long neck.

Grecian /gree-sh'n/ ▸ adjective relating to ancient Greece.

greed ▸ noun **1** a strong and selfish desire for possessions, wealth, or power. **2** a desire to eat more food than you need.

> SYNONYMS **1** *human greed* **avarice,** acquisitiveness, covetousness, materialism, mercenariness; informal money-grubbing. **2** *her mouth watered with greed* **gluttony,** hunger, voracity, self-indulgence; informal piggishness. **3** *their greed for power* **desire,** appetite, hunger, thirst, craving, longing, yearning, hankering; informal itch.
> ANTONYMS generosity, temperance, indifference.

greedy ▸ adjective (**greedier, greediest**) having or showing greed.

> SYNONYMS **1** *a greedy eater* **gluttonous,** ravenous, voracious; informal piggish, piggy. **2** *his greedy manager* **avaricious,** acquisitive, covetous, grasping, materialistic, mercenary; informal money-grubbing; N. Amer. informal grabby.

□ **greedily** adverb.

Greek ▸ noun **1** a person from Greece. **2** the ancient or modern language of Greece. ▸ adjective relating to Greece.

green ▸ adjective **1** of a colour between blue and yellow, like that of grass. **2** covered with grass or other plants. **3** (also **Green**) concerned with or supporting protection of the environment. **4** inexperienced or naive.

> SYNONYMS **1** olive green, pea green, emerald green, lime green, avocado, pistachio, bottle green, Lincoln green, jade, sea green. **2** *a green island* **verdant,** grassy, leafy. **3** *Green issues* **environmental,** ecological, conservation, eco-. **4** *a green alternative to diesel* **environmentally friendly,** eco-friendly. **5** *the new supervisor was very green* **inexperienced,** callow, raw, unseasoned, untried, naive, innocent, unworldly; informal wet behind the ears.
> ANTONYMS barren, experienced.

▸ noun **1** a green colour. **2** a piece of grassy land for public use. **3** an area of smooth grass used for cricket or bowls, or surrounding a hole on a golf course. **4** (**greens**) cabbage or other green vegetables. **5** (**Green**) a supporter of a Green political party.

■ **green belt** an area of open land around a city, on which building is restricted. **green card** (in the US) a permit allowing a foreigner to live and work permanently in the US. **green fingers** Brit. natural ability in growing plants. **green light** permission to go ahead with a project. **green pepper** an unripe sweet pepper.

□ **greenness** noun.

greenery ▸ noun green leaves or plants.

greenfield ▸ adjective (of a site) previously undeveloped.

greenfinch ▸ noun a large finch with green and yellow feathers.

greenfly ▸ noun (plural **greenfly** or **greenflies**) a green aphid.

greengage ▸ noun a sweet greenish fruit like a small plum.

greengrocer ▸ noun Brit. a person who has a shop selling fruit and vegetables.

greenhouse ▸ noun a glass structure in which plants are kept to protect them from cold weather.
■ **greenhouse effect** the tendency of atmospheric temperature to rise because certain gases absorb infrared radiation from the earth. **greenhouse gas** a gas that contributes to the greenhouse effect by absorbing infrared radiation.

greet ▸ verb 1 give a word or sign of welcome when meeting someone. 2 acknowledge or react to someone or something in a particular way.

> SYNONYMS 1 *she greeted Hank cheerily* say **hello to,** address, salute, hail, welcome, meet, receive. 2 *the decision was greeted with outrage* **receive,** respond to, react to, take.

greeting ▸ noun 1 a word or sign of welcome when meeting someone. 2 (**greetings**) a formal expression of good wishes.

> SYNONYMS 1 *he shouted a greeting* **hello,** salutation, welcome, reception. 2 *birthday greetings* **best wishes,** good wishes, congratulations, compliments, regards, respects.
> ANTONYMS farewell.

gregarious ▸ adjective 1 enjoying being with people; sociable. 2 (of animals) living in flocks or colonies.

Gregorian chant ▸ noun medieval church music for voices.

gremlin ▸ noun an imaginary mischievous creature regarded as responsible for unexplained mechanical or electrical faults.

grenade ▸ noun a small bomb that is thrown by hand.

grenadier /gre-nuh-**deer**/ ▸ noun 1 historical a soldier armed with grenades. 2 (**Grenadiers** or **Grenadier Guards**) a regiment of the royal household infantry.

grew past of GROW.

grey (US spelling **gray**) ▸ adjective 1 of a colour between black and white, like that of ashes or lead. 2 (of hair) turning grey or white with age. 3 (of the weather) cloudy and dull.

> SYNONYMS 1 silvery, gunmetal, slate, charcoal, smoky. 2 *a grey day* **cloudy,**

overcast, dull, sunless, murky. 3 *her face looked grey* **pale,** wan, ashen, pasty, pallid, colourless. 4 *his grey existence* **characterless,** colourless, nondescript, flat, bland, dull, boring, tedious, monotonous. 5 *a grey area* **ambiguous,** doubtful, unclear, uncertain, indefinite, debatable.
> ANTONYMS sunny, ruddy, exciting, certain.

▸ noun a grey colour.
▸ verb (of hair) become grey with age.
■ **grey area** a subject or area of activity that does not easily fit into existing categories. **grey matter** informal the brain.

greyhound ▸ noun a swift, slender breed of dog used in racing.

grid ▸ noun 1 a set of bars lying parallel to or crossing each other. 2 a network of lines that cross each other to form a series of squares or rectangles. 3 a network of cables or pipes for distributing power.

griddle ▸ noun a heavy iron plate that is heated and used for cooking food.

gridiron /grid-I-uhn/ ▸ noun a frame of metal bars used for grilling food over an open fire.

gridlock ▸ noun a traffic jam affecting a whole network of intersecting streets.
□ **gridlocked** adjective.

grief ▸ noun 1 great sorrow and sadness, especially caused by someone's death. 2 informal trouble or annoyance.

> SYNONYMS **sorrow,** misery, sadness, anguish, pain, distress, heartache, heartbreak, agony, woe, desolation.
> ANTONYMS joy.

grievance ▸ noun a cause for complaint.

> SYNONYMS **complaint,** objection, grumble, grouse, ill feeling, bad feeling, resentment; informal gripe.

grieve ▸ verb (**grieves, grieving, grieved**) 1 feel great sorrow and sadness. 2 cause someone distress.

> SYNONYMS 1 *she grieved for her father* **mourn,** sorrow, cry, sob, weep. 2 *it grieved me to leave her* **sadden,** upset, distress, pain, hurt, wound, break someone's heart.
> ANTONYMS rejoice, please.

grievous ▸ adjective formal (of something bad) very severe or serious.
■ **grievous bodily harm** Law, Brit. serious physical injury deliberately inflicted on someone.
□ **grievously** adverb.

griffin (or **gryphon**) ▸ noun a mythical creature with the head and wings of an eagle and the body of a lion.

griffon ▸ noun a small breed of dog.

g

grill ▶ noun Brit. **1** a device on a cooker that radiates heat downwards for cooking food. **2** a frame of metal bars used for cooking food on an open fire. **3** a dish of food cooked using a grill. **4** ➡ GRILLE.
▶ verb **1** cook food with a grill. **2** informal question someone in a relentless or aggressive way.

grille (or **grill**) ▶ noun a framework of metal bars or wires.

grim ▶ adjective (**grimmer**, **grimmest**) **1** very serious and stern or forbidding. **2** horrifying or depressing.

SYNONYMS **1** *his grim expression* **stern,** forbidding, uninviting, unsmiling, dour, formidable. **2** *grim secrets* **dreadful,** ghastly, horrible, terrible, awful, appalling, frightful, shocking, grisly, gruesome, depressing, distressing, upsetting. **3** *a grim hovel* **bleak,** dismal, dingy, wretched, miserable, depressing, cheerless, joyless, gloomy, uninviting.
ANTONYMS amiable, pleasant, cheerful.

□ **grimly** adverb.

grimace ▶ noun a twisted expression on a person's face, showing disgust, pain, or wry amusement.
▶ verb (**grimaces**, **grimacing**, **grimaced**) make a grimace.

grime ▶ noun dirt ingrained on a surface.
□ **grimy** adjective.

grin ▶ verb (**grins**, **grinning**, **grinned**) smile broadly.

SYNONYMS **smile,** beam, smirk.
ANTONYMS frown, scowl.

▶ noun a broad smile.

SYNONYMS **smile,** beam, smirk.
ANTONYMS frown, scowl.

grind ▶ verb (**grinds**, **grinding**, **ground**) **1** reduce something to small particles or powder by crushing it. **2** make something sharp or smooth by rubbing it against a hard or abrasive tool or surface. **3** rub together or move gratingly. **4** (**grind someone down**) wear someone down with continuous harsh treatment. **5** (**grind something out**) produce something slowly and with effort. **6** (**grinding**) (of an unpleasant situation) seemingly endless.

SYNONYMS **1** *the ore is ground into powder* **crush,** pound, pulverize, mill, crumble. **2** *one stone grinds against another* **rub,** grate, scrape. **3** *the edge of the knife is then ground* **sharpen,** whet, hone, put an edge on, mill, machine, polish, smooth.

▶ noun **1** an act or process of grinding. **2** hard dull work.

SYNONYMS *the daily grind* **drudgery,** toil, labour, donkey work, exertion, chores, slog.

grindstone ▶ noun **1** a revolving disc of abrasive material used for sharpening or polishing metal objects. **2** a millstone.
■ **keep your nose to the grindstone** keep working hard.

grip ▶ verb (**grips**, **gripping**, **gripped**) **1** hold something tightly. **2** deeply affect someone. **3** hold someone's attention.

SYNONYMS **1** *she gripped the edge of the table* **grasp,** clutch, clasp, take hold of, clench, cling to, grab, seize, squeeze. **2** *we were gripped by the drama* **engross,** enthral, absorb, rivet, spellbind, fascinate, mesmerize.
ANTONYMS release.

▶ noun **1** a firm hold on something. **2** understanding of something. **3** a part or attachment by which something is held in the hand. **4** a travelling bag.

SYNONYMS **1** *a tight grip* **grasp,** hold. **2** *the wheels lost their grip on the road* **traction,** purchase, friction, adhesion. **3** *in the grip of an obsession* **control,** power, hold, stranglehold, clutches, influence.

■ **come** (or **get**) **to grips with** begin to deal with or understand.

gripe ▶ verb (**gripes**, **griping**, **griped**) **1** informal grumble. **2** (**griping**) (of pain in the stomach or intestines) sudden and sharp.
▶ noun **1** informal a trivial complaint. **2** pain in the stomach or intestines.

gripping ▶ adjective very interesting or exciting.

SYNONYMS **engrossing,** enthralling, absorbing, riveting, captivating, spellbinding, fascinating, compelling, thrilling, exciting, action-packed, dramatic.
ANTONYMS boring.

grisly /griz-li/ ▶ adjective (**grislier**, **grisliest**) causing horror or disgust.

❗ Don't confuse **grisly** with **grizzly**, as in *grizzly bear*.

grist ▶ noun corn that is ground to make flour.
■ **grist to the mill** useful experience or knowledge.

gristle ▶ noun tough inedible cartilage in meat.
□ **gristly** adjective.

grit ▶ noun **1** small loose particles of stone or sand. **2** (also **gritstone**) a coarse sandstone. **3** courage and determination.
▶ verb (**grits**, **gritting**, **gritted**) spread grit on an icy road.
■ **grit your teeth** resolve to do something difficult.

gritty ▶ adjective (**grittier**, **grittiest**) **1** containing or covered with grit. **2** brave

and determined. **3** showing something unpleasant as it really is.
□ **grittily** adverb.

grizzle ▶ verb (grizzles, grizzling, grizzled) Brit. informal cry fretfully.

grizzled ▶ adjective having grey or grey-streaked hair.

grizzly bear ▶ noun a large brown bear, often with white-tipped fur.

groan ▶ verb make a deep sound of pain or despair.

> SYNONYMS **1** *she groaned and rubbed her stomach* **moan,** cry. **2** *they groan about everything* **complain,** grumble, moan, mutter; informal grouse, bellyache, bitch, whinge. **3** *the tree groaned* **creak,** grate, rasp.

▶ noun a groaning sound.

> SYNONYMS **1** *a groan of anguish* **moan,** cry. **2** *she listens to all their moans and groans* **complaint,** grumble, grievance, moan, muttering; informal grouse, gripe, whinge. **3** *the groan of the timbers* **creaking,** creak, grating, grinding.

groat ▶ noun historical an English silver coin worth four old pence.

grocer ▶ noun a person who sells food and small household goods.

grocery ▶ noun (plural **groceries**) **1** a grocer's shop or business. **2** (**groceries**) items of food sold in a grocer's shop or supermarket.

grog ▶ noun spirits mixed with water.

groggy ▶ adjective (**groggier, groggiest**) dazed and unsteady.
□ **groggily** adverb.

groin ▶ noun **1** the area between the stomach and the thigh. **2** US spelling of GROYNE.

grommet ▶ noun **1** a protective metal ring or eyelet. **2** Brit. a tube fitted in the eardrum to drain fluid from the middle ear.

groom ▶ verb **1** brush and clean the coat of a horse or dog. **2** keep yourself neat and tidy in appearance. **3** train someone for a particular activity.

> SYNONYMS **1** *she groomed her pony* **curry,** brush, clean, rub down. **2** *his hair was carefully groomed* **brush,** comb, arrange, do; informal fix. **3** *groomed for stardom* **prepare,** prime, condition, coach, train, drill, teach, school.

▶ noun **1** a person employed to take care of horses. **2** a bridegroom.

> SYNONYMS *the bride and groom* **bridegroom.**

groove ▶ noun **1** a long, narrow cut in a hard surface. **2** a spiral track cut in a music record. **3** a routine or habit.

> SYNONYMS **furrow,** channel, trench, trough, rut, gutter, canal, hollow, indentation.

▶ verb (**grooves, grooving, grooved**) **1** make a groove or grooves in. **2** informal listen or dance to jazz or pop music.

groovy ▶ adjective (**groovier, grooviest**) informal, dated fashionable and exciting.

grope ▶ verb (**gropes, groping, groped**) **1** feel about with your hands. **2** ease your way forward using your hands to guide you. **3** informal feel someone's body for sexual pleasure.

> SYNONYMS **fumble,** scrabble, fish, ferret, rummage, feel, search, hunt.

gross ▶ adjective **1** unattractively large. **2** very obvious and unacceptable. **3** informal very unpleasant. **4** rude or vulgar. **5** (of income, profit, or interest) before tax has been deducted. **6** (of weight) including contents or other variable items.

> SYNONYMS **1** *the place smelled gross* **disgusting,** repulsive, revolting, foul, nasty, obnoxious, sickening, nauseating, stomach-churning. **2** *a gross distortion of the truth* **thorough,** complete, utter, out and out, shameful, serious, unacceptable, flagrant, blatant, obvious, barefaced, shameless, brazen. **3** *gross income* **total,** full, overall, combined, before deductions, before tax.
> ANTONYMS pleasant, slight, acceptable, net.

▶ adverb in total.

▶ verb earn a particular amount of money as gross profit or income.

> SYNONYMS *he grosses over a million a year* **earn,** make, bring in, take, get, receive; informal rake in.

▶ noun **1** (plural **gross**) twelve dozen; 144. **2** (plural **grosses**) a gross profit or income.
□ **grossly** adverb.

grotesque /groh-tesk/ ▶ adjective **1** ugly or distorted in a way that is funny or frightening. **2** shocking.

> SYNONYMS **1** *a grotesque creature* **misshapen,** deformed, distorted, twisted, monstrous, hideous, freakish, unnatural, abnormal, strange; informal weird. **2** *a grotesque exaggeration* **outrageous,** monstrous, shocking, appalling, preposterous, ridiculous, ludicrous, unbelievable, incredible.
> ANTONYMS normal, sensible.

▶ noun a grotesque figure or image.
□ **grotesquely** adverb.

grotto ▶ noun (plural **grottoes** or **grottos**) a small cave, especially an artificial one.

grotty ▶ adjective (**grottier, grottiest**) Brit. informal **1** unpleasant and of bad quality. **2** unwell.

grouch ▸ noun informal **1** a grumpy person. **2** a complaint.
□ **grouchy** adjective.

ground¹ ▸ noun **1** the solid surface of the earth. **2** land or soil of a particular kind. **3** an area of land or sea with a particular use. **4** (**grounds**) an area of enclosed land surrounding a large house. **5** (**grounds**) good reasons for doing or believing something. **6** (**grounds**) small pieces of solid matter in a liquid which settle at the bottom.

> SYNONYMS **1** *she collapsed on the ground* **floor**, earth, terra firma; informal deck. **2** *soggy ground* **earth**, soil, turf, land, terrain. **3** *the team's home ground* **stadium**, pitch, field, arena, track; Brit. informal park. **4** *the mansion's grounds* **estate**, gardens, park, land, property, surroundings, territory. **5** *grounds for dismissal* **reason**, cause, basis, foundation, justification, rationale, argument, occasion, excuse, pretext.

▸ verb **1** ban or prevent a pilot or aircraft from flying. **2** run a ship aground. **3** (**be grounded in** or **on**) have as a foundation or basis.

> SYNONYMS **1** *the religious life must be grounded on the law* **base**, found, establish, root, build, form. **2** *she was well grounded in the classics* **teach**, instruct, coach, tutor, educate, school, train, drill.

■ **ground control** the people who direct the flight and landing of aircraft or spacecraft. **ground floor** the floor of a building at ground level. **ground rent** Brit. rent paid by the owner of a building to the owner of the land on which it is built. **ground rules** basic rules controlling the way in which something is done.

ground² past and past participle of GRIND.

groundbreaking ▸ adjective involving completely new methods or discoveries.

grounding ▸ noun basic training or instruction in a subject.

groundless ▸ adjective not based on any good reason.

groundnut = PEANUT.

groundsel ▸ noun a plant with small yellow flowers.

groundsheet ▸ noun a waterproof sheet spread on the ground inside a tent.

groundsman ▸ noun (plural **groundsmen**) Brit. a person who maintains a sports ground or the grounds of a large building.

groundswell ▸ noun **1** a large swell in the sea. **2** a build-up of public opinion.

groundwork ▸ noun preliminary or basic work.

group ▸ noun **1** a number of people or things placed or classed together. **2** a band of pop musicians.

> SYNONYMS **1** *the exhibits are in three groups* **category**, class, classification, grouping, cluster, set, batch, type, sort, kind, variety, family. **2** *a group of tourists* **crowd**, party, body, band, company, gathering, congregation, assembly, collection, cluster, clump, knot, flock, pack, troop, gang; informal bunch. **3** *a folk group* **band**, ensemble, act; informal line-up, combo, outfit.

▸ verb put into a group.

> SYNONYMS **1** *patients were grouped according to age* **categorize**, classify, class, catalogue, sort, bracket, pigeonhole. **2** *chairs were grouped in fours* **assemble**, collect, organize, place, arrange, range, line up, lay out.

groupie ▸ noun informal a fan who follows a pop group or celebrity around.

grouse¹ ▸ noun (plural **grouse**) a game bird with a plump body.

grouse² ▸ verb (**grouses**, **grousing**, **groused**) complain; grumble.
▸ noun a grumble or complaint.

grout ▸ noun a substance used for filling the gaps between tiles.
▸ verb fill between tiles with grout.

grove ▸ noun a small wood, orchard, or group of trees.

grovel ▸ verb (**grovels**, **grovelling**, **grovelled**; US spelling **grovels**, **groveling**, **groveled**) **1** crouch or crawl on the ground. **2** act very humbly towards someone to make them forgive you or treat you favourably.

grow ▸ verb (**grows**, **growing**, **grew**; past participle **grown**) **1** (of a living thing) develop and get bigger. **2** (**grow up**) become an adult. **3** become larger or greater over a period of time. **4** become gradually or increasingly: *we grew braver.* **5** (**grow on**) become gradually more appealing to.

> SYNONYMS **1** **enlarge**, get bigger, get larger, get taller, expand, increase in size, extend, spread, swell, multiply, snowball, mushroom, balloon, build up, mount up, pile up. **2** *flowers grew among the rocks* **sprout**, germinate, spring up, develop, bud, bloom, flourish, thrive, run riot. **3** *he grew vegetables* **cultivate**, produce, propagate, raise, rear, farm. **4** *Leonora grew bored* **become**, get, turn, begin to be.
> ANTONYMS shrink, decline.

□ **grower** noun.

growl ▸ verb **1** (of a dog) make a low hostile sound in the throat. **2** say something in a low grating voice. **3** make a low or harsh rumbling sound.
▸ noun a growling sound.

grown-up ▸ adjective adult.

SYNONYMS *she has two grown-up daughters* **adult,** mature, of age, fully grown, independent.
ANTONYMS under age.

▸ noun informal an adult.

SYNONYMS *she wanted to be treated like a grown-up* **adult,** woman, man, grown man/woman.
ANTONYMS child.

growth ▸ noun 1 the process of growing. 2 something that has grown or is growing. 3 a tumour.

SYNONYMS 1 *population growth* **enlargement,** increase in size, expansion, extension, swelling, multiplication, mushrooming, snowballing, rise, escalation, build-up, development. 2 *a growth on his jaw* **tumour,** malignancy, cancer, lump, swelling.
ANTONYMS shrinkage, decline.

groyne (US spelling **groin**) ▸ noun a low wall built out into the sea from a beach to prevent the beach from shifting or being eroded.

grub ▸ noun 1 the larva of an insect. 2 informal food.
▸ verb (**grubs, grubbing, grubbed**) 1 dig or poke about in soil. 2 (**grub something up**) dig something up.

grubby ▸ adjective (**grubbier, grubbiest**) 1 rather dirty. 2 dishonest or immoral.

SYNONYMS **dirty,** grimy, filthy, mucky, unwashed, stained, soiled; informal cruddy, yucky; Brit. informal manky; Austral./NZ informal scungy.
ANTONYMS clean.

grudge ▸ noun a persistent feeling of anger or dislike.

SYNONYMS **grievance,** resentment, bitterness, rancour, ill will, animosity, antipathy, antagonism; informal a chip on your shoulder.

▸ verb (**grudges, grudging, grudged**) 1 be unwilling to give or allow something. 2 feel resentful that someone has achieved something.

grudging ▸ adjective reluctantly given or allowed.
□ **grudgingly** adverb.

gruel ▸ noun a thin liquid food of oatmeal boiled in milk or water.

gruelling (US spelling **grueling**) ▸ adjective very tiring and demanding.

SYNONYMS **exhausting,** tiring, taxing, draining, demanding, exacting, difficult, arduous, strenuous, back-breaking,

punishing, crippling; informal murderous; Brit. informal knackering.

gruesome ▸ adjective causing disgust or horror.

SYNONYMS **grisly,** ghastly, frightful, horrid, horrifying, hideous, horrible, grim, awful, dreadful, terrible, horrific; informal sick, sick-making, gross.
ANTONYMS pleasant.

gruff ▸ adjective 1 (of a voice) rough and low. 2 abrupt in manner.
□ **gruffly** adverb.

grumble ▸ verb (**grumbles, grumbling, grumbled**) 1 complain in a quiet but bad-tempered way. 2 make a low rumbling sound.

SYNONYMS **complain,** grouse, whine, mutter, carp, make a fuss; informal moan, bellyache, bitch, whinge; N. English informal mither.

▸ noun a complaint.

SYNONYMS **complaint,** grouse, grievance, protest; informal grouch, moan, whinge, beef, gripe.

grumpy ▸ adjective (**grumpier, grumpiest**) bad-tempered and sulky.

SYNONYMS **bad-tempered,** crabby, tetchy, touchy, irascible, cantankerous, curmudgeonly, surly, fractious; informal grouchy; Brit. informal ratty; N. Amer. informal cranky, ornery.
ANTONYMS good-humoured.

□ **grumpily** adverb.

grunge ▸ noun a style of rock music with a raucous guitar sound.
□ **grungy** adjective.

grunt ▸ verb 1 (of an animal) make a short, low sound. 2 (of a person) make a low sound because of physical effort or to show agreement.
▸ noun a grunting sound.

gryphon ➡ GRIFFIN.

guano /gwah-noh/ ▸ noun the excrement of seabirds, used as fertilizer.

guarantee ▸ noun 1 a promise that certain things will be done. 2 a promise that a product will remain in working order for a particular length of time. 3 something that makes a particular outcome certain. 4 an undertaking to pay or do something on behalf of someone if they fail to do it.

SYNONYMS 1 *a guarantee that the hospital will stay open* **promise,** assurance, word (of honour), pledge, vow, oath, commitment. 2 *a one-year guarantee* **warranty.** 3 *a guarantee for loans* **collateral,** security, surety, bond.

▸ verb (**guarantees, guaranteeing, guaranteed**) 1 provide a guarantee for

g

something. **2** promise something with certainty. **3** provide financial security for.

> SYNONYMS **1** *I guarantee he will accept* **promise**, swear, pledge, vow, give your word, give an assurance, give an undertaking. **2** *he agreed to guarantee the loan* **underwrite**, stand surety.

> ✔ **gua-**, not **gau-**: **gua**rantee.

guarantor /ga-ruhn-**tor**/ ▸ noun a person or organization that gives a guarantee.

guard ▸ verb **1** watch over in order to protect or control. **2** (**guard against**) take precautions against.

> SYNONYMS *troops guarded the bridge* **protect**, defend, shield, secure, cover, mind, stand guard over, watch, keep an eye on.

▸ noun **1** a person who guards or keeps watch. **2** a group of soldiers guarding a place or person. **3** a state of looking out for possible danger: *she was on guard.* **4** a device worn or fitted to prevent injury or damage. **5** Brit. an official in charge of a train. **6** N. Amer. a prison warder.

> SYNONYMS **1** *border guards* **sentry**, sentinel, nightwatchman, protector, defender, guardian, lookout, watch. **2** *a prison guard* **warder**, warden, keeper, jailer; informal screw. **3** *a metal guard* **cover**, shield, screen, fender, bumper, buffer.

> ✔ **gua-**, not **gau-**: **gua**rd.

guarded ▸ adjective cautious.

> SYNONYMS **cautious**, careful, circumspect, wary, chary, reluctant, non-committal; informal cagey.

guardian ▸ noun **1** a person who defends and protects something. **2** a person who is legally responsible for someone who cannot take care of their own affairs.

> SYNONYMS **protector**, defender, preserver, custodian, warden, guard, keeper, curator, caretaker, steward, trustee.

■ **guardian angel** a spirit who is believed to watch over and protect you.
□ **guardianship** noun.

Guatemalan /gwah-tuh-**mah**-luhn/ ▸ noun a person from Guatemala.
▸ adjective relating to Guatemala.

guava /**gwah**-vuh/ ▸ noun a tropical fruit with pink juicy flesh.

gudgeon ▸ noun a small freshwater fish.

guerrilla (or **guerilla**) /guh-**ril**-luh/ ▸ noun a member of a small independent group fighting against the government or regular forces.

> SYNONYMS **rebel**, irregular, partisan, freedom fighter, revolutionary, terrorist.

guess ▸ verb **1** estimate or suppose something without having the information you need to be sure. **2** correctly estimate or suppose.

> SYNONYMS **1** *he guessed that she was about 40* **estimate**, reckon, judge, speculate, conjecture, hypothesize, surmise. **2** *I guess I owe you an apology* **suppose**, think, imagine, expect, suspect, dare say; informal reckon.

▸ noun an attempt to guess something.

> SYNONYMS *my guess was right* **hypothesis**, theory, conjecture, surmise, estimate, belief, opinion, supposition, speculation, suspicion, impression, feeling.

guesswork ▸ noun the process or results of guessing.

guest ▸ noun **1** a person who is invited to someone's house or to a social occasion. **2** a person invited to take part in a broadcast or entertainment. **3** a person staying at a hotel.

> SYNONYMS **1** *we have guests* **visitor**, caller, company. **2** *hotel guests* **client**, customer, resident, boarder, lodger, patron, diner, holidaymaker, tourist. ANTONYMS host, staff.

■ **guest house** a kind of small hotel.

guffaw ▸ noun a loud, deep laugh.
▸ verb give a loud, deep laugh.

guidance ▸ noun advice and information given by an experienced or skilled person.

> SYNONYMS **1** *she looked to him for guidance* **advice**, counsel, instruction, suggestions, tips, hints, pointers, guidelines. **2** *under the guidance of an expert* **direction**, control, leadership, management, supervision.

guide ▸ noun **1** a person who advises or shows the way to other people. **2** a thing that helps you to form an opinion or make a decision. **3** a book providing information on a subject. **4** a structure or marking which directs the movement or positioning of something. **5** (**Guide**) a member of the Guides Association, a girls' organization corresponding to the Scouts.

> SYNONYMS **1** *our guide took us back to the hotel* **escort**, attendant, courier, leader, usher. **2** *the techniques given serve as a guide* **outline**, template, example, exemplar, model, pattern, guideline, yardstick, precedent. **3** *a guide to Paris* **guidebook**, travel guide, companion, handbook, manual, directory, A to Z, instructions, directions; informal bible.

▸ verb (**guides**, **guiding**, **guided**) **1** show someone the way. **2** direct the movement

g

or positioning of something. **3** (**guided**) directed by remote control or internal equipment.

> SYNONYMS **1** *he guided her to her seat* **lead,** conduct, show, usher, shepherd, direct, steer, pilot, escort. **2** *the chairman guides the meeting* **direct,** steer, manage, conduct, run, be in charge of, govern, preside over, supervise, oversee. **3** *he was always there to guide me* **advise,** counsel, direct.

■ **guide dog** a dog trained to lead a blind person.

guidebook ▸ noun a book containing information about a place for visitors.

guideline ▸ noun a general rule, principle, or piece of advice.

guild ▸ noun **1** a medieval association of craftsmen or merchants. **2** an association of people who do the same work or have the same interests.

> SYNONYMS **association,** society, union, league, organization, company, fellowship, club, order, lodge.

guilder /gil-der/ ▸ noun (plural **guilder** or **guilders**) the former basic unit of money in the Netherlands.

guildhall ▸ noun **1** the meeting place of a guild or corporation. **2** Brit. a town hall.

guile ▸ noun clever but dishonest or deceitful behaviour.

guileless ▸ adjective innocent and honest.

guillemot /gil-li-mot/ ▸ noun a seabird with a narrow pointed bill.

guillotine /gil-luh-teen/ ▸ noun **1** a machine with a heavy blade, used for beheading people. **2** a piece of equipment with a descending or sliding blade used for cutting paper or sheet metal.
▸ verb (**guillotines, guillotining, guillotined**) behead someone with a guillotine.

guilt ▸ noun **1** the fact of having committed an offence or crime. **2** a feeling of having done something wrong.

> SYNONYMS **1** *the proof of his guilt* **culpability,** blameworthiness, responsibility. **2** *a terrible feeling of guilt* **remorse,** shame, regret, contrition, self-reproach, a guilty conscience.
> ANTONYMS innocence, shamelessness.

□ **guiltless** adjective.

guilty ▸ adjective (**guiltier, guiltiest**) **1** responsible for doing something wrong. **2** having or showing a feeling of guilt.

> SYNONYMS **1** *the guilty party* **culpable,** to blame, at fault, in the wrong. **2** *I still feel guilty about it* **ashamed,** guilt-ridden, conscience-stricken, remorseful, sorry, contrite, repentant, penitent, regretful,

rueful, shamefaced.
> ANTONYMS innocent, unrepentant.

□ **guiltily** adverb.

guinea /gi-ni/ ▸ noun a former British gold coin worth 21 shillings (£1.05).

guineafowl ▸ noun (plural **guineafowl**) a large African bird with grey, white-spotted feathers.

Guinean /gin-i-uhn/ ▸ noun a person from Guinea, a country in West Africa.
▸ adjective relating to Guinea.

guinea pig ▸ noun **1** a South American rodent without a tail. **2** a person or thing used as a subject for experiment.

guise /gyz/ ▸ noun an outward form, appearance, or manner.

guitar ▸ noun a stringed musical instrument which you play by plucking or strumming.
□ **guitarist** noun.

Gujarati /goo-juh-**rah**-ti/ ▸ noun (plural **Gujaratis**) **1** a person from the Indian state of Gujarat. **2** the language of the Gujaratis.

gulch ▸ noun N. Amer. a narrow ravine.

gulf ▸ noun **1** a deep inlet of the sea with a narrow mouth. **2** a deep ravine. **3** a large difference in opinion between two people or groups.

> SYNONYMS **1** *our ship sailed into the gulf* **bay,** inlet, cove, bight, fjord, estuary, sound; Scottish firth. **2** *a gulf between rich and poor* **gap,** divide, separation, difference, contrast.

gull¹ ▸ noun a white seabird with long wings and a grey or black back.

gull² ▸ verb fool or deceive.

gullet ▸ noun the passage by which food passes from the mouth to the stomach.

gullible ▸ adjective easily believing what people tell you.
□ **gullibility** noun.

gully (or **gulley**) ▸ noun (plural **gullies** or **gulleys**) a ravine or channel formed by running water.

gulp ▸ verb **1** swallow food or drink quickly or in large mouthfuls. **2** swallow with difficulty because you are upset or nervous.

> SYNONYMS **1** *she gulped her juice* **swallow,** quaff, swill down; informal swig, down, knock back. **2** *he gulped down the rest of his meal* **gobble,** guzzle, devour, bolt, wolf; informal shovel down; Brit. informal scoff. **3** *Jenny gulped back her tears* **choke back,** fight/hold back, suppress, stifle, smother.
> ANTONYMS sip, nibble, let out.

▸ noun **1** an act of gulping. **2** a large mouthful of liquid hastily drunk.

> SYNONYMS *a gulp of cold beer* **mouthful,** swallow, draught; informal swig.

gum[1] ▸ noun 1 a sticky substance produced by some trees. 2 glue used for sticking paper or other light materials together. 3 chewing gum.

> SYNONYMS *stuck down with gum* **glue**, adhesive, paste, cement; N. Amer. mucilage; N. Amer. informal stickum.

▸ verb fasten or cover something with gum or glue.

> SYNONYMS *the receipts were gummed in* **stick**, glue, paste, cement, attach.

gum[2] ▸ noun the firm area of flesh around the roots of the teeth.

gumboot ▸ noun Brit. dated a tall rubber boot; a wellington.

gumdrop ▸ noun a firm, jelly-like sweet.

gummy[1] ▸ adjective sticky.

gummy[2] ▸ adjective toothless.

gumption ▸ noun informal initiative and resourcefulness.

gun ▸ noun 1 a weapon with a metal tube from which bullets or shells are fired by means of a small explosion. 2 a device using pressure to send out a substance or object.

> SYNONYMS **firearm**, side arm, handgun, weapon; informal shooter; N. Amer. informal piece, shooting iron.

▸ verb (**guns, gunning, gunned**) (**gun someone down**) shoot someone with a gun. ■ **jump the gun** act before the proper or right time. **stick to your guns** refuse to compromise.

gunboat ▸ noun a small ship armed with guns.

gunfire ▸ noun the repeated firing of a gun or guns.

gunge (N. Amer. also **gunk**) ▸ noun informal an unpleasantly sticky or messy substance.

gung-ho ▸ adjective too eager to take part in fighting or warfare.

gunman ▸ noun (plural **gunmen**) a man who uses a gun to commit a crime.

> SYNONYMS **armed criminal**, assassin, sniper, terrorist, gunfighter; informal hit man, gunslinger; N. Amer. informal shootist.

gunmetal ▸ noun 1 a grey form of bronze containing zinc. 2 a dull bluish-grey colour.

gunnel → **GUNWALE**.

gunner ▸ noun 1 a person who operates a gun. 2 a British artillery soldier.

gunnery ▸ noun the design, manufacture, or firing of heavy guns.

gunpoint ▸ noun (**at gunpoint**) while threatening someone or being threatened with a gun.

gunpowder ▸ noun an explosive consisting of a powdered mixture of saltpetre, sulphur, and charcoal.

gunrunner ▸ noun a person involved in the illegal sale or importing of firearms. □ **gunrunning** noun.

gunship ▸ noun a heavily armed helicopter.

gunwale (or **gunnel**) /**gun**-uhl/ ▸ noun the upper edge or planking of the side of a boat.

guppy ▸ noun (plural **guppies**) a small colourful fish.

gurdwara /goor-**dwah**-ruh/ ▸ noun a Sikh place of worship.

gurgle ▸ verb (**gurgles, gurgling, gurgled**) make a hollow bubbling sound. ▸ noun a hollow bubbling sound.

Gurkha /**ger**-kuh/ ▸ noun a member of a Nepalese regiment in the British army.

gurn (or **girn**) ▸ verb Brit. pull a grotesque face.

gurnard /**ger**-nerd/ ▸ noun a small sea fish.

guru ▸ noun 1 a Hindu spiritual teacher. 2 a person who is an expert on a subject and has a lot of followers.

> SYNONYMS **1** *a Hindu guru and mystic* **spiritual teacher**, tutor, sage, mentor, spiritual leader, master. **2** *a management guru* **expert**, authority, pundit, leading light, master, specialist.
> ANTONYMS disciple.

gush ▸ verb 1 flow in a strong, fast stream. 2 express approval very enthusiastically.

> SYNONYMS **1 surge**, stream, spout, spurt, jet, rush, pour, spill, cascade, flood; Brit. informal sloosh. **2** (**gushing**) **effusive**, overenthusiastic, extravagant, fulsome, lavish; informal over the top.

▸ noun a strong, fast stream.

> SYNONYMS **surge**, stream, spout, spurt, jet, rush, outpouring, spill, outflow, cascade, flood, torrent.

gusset ▸ noun a piece of material sewn into a garment to strengthen or enlarge a part of it.

gust ▸ noun 1 a brief, strong rush of wind. 2 a burst of sound or emotion.

> SYNONYMS **flurry**, blast, puff, blow, rush, squall.

▸ verb blow in gusts. □ **gusty** adjective.

gusto ▸ noun enthusiasm and energy.

gut ▸ noun 1 the stomach or intestine. 2 (**guts**) internal organs that have been removed or exposed. 3 (**guts**) the inner or most important part of something. 4 (**guts**) informal courage and determination.

> SYNONYMS **1** *an ache in his gut* **stomach**, belly, abdomen, paunch, intestines; informal tummy, insides, innards. **2** *Nicola has a lot of guts* **courage**, bravery,

backbone, nerve, pluck, spirit, daring, grit, fearlessness, determination; Brit. informal bottle; N. Amer. informal moxie.

▸ verb (guts, gutting, gutted) 1 take out the internal organs of a fish before cooking. 2 remove or destroy the internal parts of something.

> SYNONYMS 1 *gut the sardines* clean (out), disembowel, draw. 2 *builders had gutted the old place* strip, empty, devastate, lay waste, ravage, ruin, wreck.

▸ adjective informal instinctive.

> SYNONYMS *a gut feeling* instinctive, intuitive, deep-seated, involuntary, spontaneous, unthinking.

gutless ▸ adjective informal not showing courage or determination.

gutsy ▸ adjective (gutsier, gutsiest) informal brave and determined.

gutted ▸ adjective Brit. informal bitterly disappointed or upset.

gutter ▸ noun 1 a shallow trough beneath the edge of a roof, or a channel at the side of a street, for carrying off rainwater. 2 (the gutter) a very poor or unpleasant environment.

> SYNONYMS drain, trough, trench, ditch, sluice, sewer, channel, conduit, pipe.

▸ verb (gutters, guttering, guttered) (of a flame) flicker and burn unsteadily.

guttering ▸ noun the gutters of a building.

guttersnipe ▸ noun disapproving a scruffy, badly behaved child.

guttural ▸ adjective (of a speech sound) produced in the throat.

guy¹ ▸ noun 1 informal a man. 2 (guys) informal, chiefly N. Amer. people of either sex. 3 Brit. a stuffed figure that is traditionally burnt on a bonfire on 5 November.

> SYNONYMS man, fellow; informal lad; Brit. informal chap, bloke; N. Amer. informal dude, hombre.

▸ verb make fun of someone.

guy² ▸ noun a rope or line fixed to the ground to secure a tent.

Guyanese /gy-uh-neez/ ▸ noun (plural Guyanese) a person from Guyana, a country in South America.

▸ adjective relating to Guyana.

guzzle ▸ verb (guzzles, guzzling, guzzled) eat or drink greedily.

> SYNONYMS 1 *he guzzled his burger* gobble, bolt, wolf, devour; informal tuck into, shovel down; Brit. informal scoff; N. Amer. informal scarf. 2 *she guzzled down the orange juice* gulp down, quaff, swill; informal knock back, swig, down.

gybe /jyb/ ▸ verb (gybes, gybing, gybed) Sailing change course by swinging the sail across a following wind.

gym ▸ noun 1 a gymnasium. 2 a private club with equipment for improving physical fitness. 3 gymnastics.

gymkhana /jim-kah-nuh/ ▸ noun a horse-riding event consisting of a series of competitions.

gymnasium ▸ noun (plural gymnasiums or gymnasia) a hall or building equipped for gymnastics and other sports.

gymnast ▸ noun a person trained in gymnastics.

gymnastics ▸ plural noun exercises involving physical agility and coordination.
□ gymnastic adjective.

gymslip ▸ noun Brit. a pinafore dress reaching from the shoulder to the knee, formerly worn by schoolgirls.

gynaecology /gy-ni-kol-uh-ji/ (US spelling gynecology) ▸ noun the branch of medicine concerned with conditions and diseases experienced by women.
□ gynaecological adjective gynaecologist noun.

gypsophila /jip-sof-fi-luh/ ▸ noun a garden plant with small pink or white flowers.

gypsum /jip-suhm/ ▸ noun a soft white or grey mineral used to make plaster of Paris and in the building industry.

Gypsy (or Gipsy) ▸ noun (plural Gypsies) a member of a travelling people.

gyrate /jy-rayt/ ▸ verb (gyrates, gyrating, gyrated) move in a circle or spiral.

> SYNONYMS rotate, revolve, wheel, turn, whirl, circle, pirouette, twirl, swirl, spin, swivel.

□ gyration noun.

gyroscope ▸ noun a device, used to provide stability or maintain a fixed direction, consisting of a wheel or disc spinning rapidly about an axis which is itself free to alter in direction.

g

Hh

H (or **h**) ▶ noun (plural **Hs** or **H's**) the eighth letter of the alphabet.
▶ abbreviation (**h**) hours.
■ **H-bomb** a hydrogen bomb.

ha ▶ abbreviation hectares.

habeas corpus /hay-bi-uhss **kor**-puhss/ ▶ noun Law a written order saying that a person must come before a judge or court.

haberdashery ▶ noun Brit. materials used in dressmaking and sewing.

habit ▶ noun **1** a thing you do regularly and repeatedly. **2** informal an addiction to a drug. **3** a long, loose garment worn by a monk or nun.

SYNONYMS **1 custom**, practice, routine, way. **2** his cocaine habit **addiction**, dependence, craving, fixation.

habitable ▶ adjective suitable to live in.

habitat ▶ noun the natural home or environment of a plant or animal.

habitation ▶ noun **1** the fact of living somewhere. **2** formal a house or home.

habitual /huh-**bit**-yuu-uhl/ ▶ adjective **1** done constantly or as a habit. **2** regular; usual.
□ **habitually** adverb.

habituate ▶ verb (**habituates, habituating, habituated**) make or become accustomed to something.

habitué /huh-**bit**-yuu-ay/ ▶ noun a frequent visitor to a place.

hacienda /ha-si-**en**-duh/ ▶ noun (in Spanish-speaking countries) a large estate with a house.

hack¹ ▶ verb **1** cut or hit at something with rough or heavy blows. **2** use a computer to read or alter information in another computer system without permission.

SYNONYMS **cut**, chop, hew, lop, saw, slash.
□ **hacker** noun.

hack² ▶ noun **1** a journalist producing dull, unoriginal work. **2** a horse for ordinary riding.

hackles ▶ plural noun hairs along an animal's back which rise when it is angry or alarmed.

hackney ▶ noun (plural **hackneys**) (in the past) a horse-drawn vehicle kept for hire.
■ **hackney carriage** a taxi.

hackneyed ▶ adjective (especially of a phrase) not original or interesting.

hacksaw ▶ noun a saw with a narrow blade set in a frame.

had past and past participle of HAVE.

haddock ▶ noun (plural **haddock**) a silvery-grey sea fish used for food.

hadn't ▶ short form had not.

haematology /hee-muh-**tol**-uh-ji/ (US spelling **hematology**) ▶ noun the branch of medicine concerned with the blood.

haemoglobin /hee-muh-**gloh**-bin/ (US spelling **hemoglobin**) ▶ noun a red protein in the blood that carries oxygen.

haemophilia /hee-muh-**fi**-li-uh/ (US spelling **hemophilia**) ▶ noun a condition in which the ability of the blood to clot is reduced, causing severe bleeding from even a slight injury.
□ **haemophiliac** noun.

haemorrhage /**hem**-uh-rij/ (US spelling **hemorrhage**) ▶ noun an escape of blood from a burst blood vessel.
▶ verb (**haemorrhages, haemorrhaging, haemorrhaged**) have a haemorrhage.

haemorrhoid /**hem**-uh-royd/ (US spelling **hemorrhoid**) ▶ noun a swollen vein in the region of the anus.

hafnium ▶ noun a hard silver-grey metal.

haft ▶ noun the handle of a knife, axe, or spear.

hag ▶ noun an ugly old woman.

haggard ▶ adjective looking exhausted and ill.

haggis ▶ noun (plural **haggis**) a Scottish dish consisting of the internal organs of a sheep or calf mixed with suet and oatmeal.

haggle ▶ verb (**haggles, haggling, haggled**) argue or negotiate with someone about the price of something.

SYNONYMS **barter**, bargain, negotiate, wrangle.

▶ noun a period of haggling.

hagiography /ha-gi-**og**-ruh-fi/ ▶ noun **1** writing which is about the lives of saints.

2 a biography that presents its subject as better than in reality.

ha-ha ▶ noun a trench which forms a boundary to a park or garden without interrupting the view.

haiku /**hy**-koo/ ▶ noun (plural **haiku** or **haikus**) a Japanese poem of three lines and seventeen syllables.

hail¹ ▶ noun **1** pellets of frozen rain falling in showers. **2** a large number of things hurled forcefully through the air.

SYNONYMS *a hail of bullets* **barrage,** volley, shower, stream, salvo.

▶ verb (**it hails, it is hailing, it hailed**) hail falls.

hail² ▶ verb **1** call out to someone to attract their attention. **2** (**hail someone/thing as**) enthusiastically describe someone or something as. **3** (**hail from**) have your home or origins in.

SYNONYMS **1** *a friend hailed him* **call out to,** shout to, address, greet, say hello to, salute. **2** *he hailed a cab* **flag down,** wave down. **3** *critics hailed the film as a masterpiece* **acclaim,** praise, applaud. **4** *Rick hails from Australia* **come,** be, be a native of.

hailstone ▶ noun a pellet of hail.

hair ▶ noun **1** each of the thread-like strands growing from the skin of animals, or from plants. **2** strands of hair.

SYNONYMS **1** **head of hair,** shock of hair, mane, mop, locks, tresses, curls. **2** **hairstyle,** haircut; informal hairdo. **3** **fur,** wool, coat, fleece, mane.

■ **hair-raising** very alarming or frightening. **hair shirt** (in the past) a shirt made of very rough cloth worn as a way of punishing yourself. **hair trigger** a firearm trigger set for release at the slightest pressure. **let your hair down** informal behave wildly or in a very relaxed way. **split hairs** make small and unnecessary distinctions.

hairband ▶ noun a band worn on the head to keep the hair off the face.

haircut ▶ noun **1** the style in which someone's hair is cut. **2** an act of cutting someone's hair.

hairdo ▶ noun (plural **hairdos**) informal the style of a person's hair.

hairdresser ▶ noun a person who cuts and styles hair.

SYNONYMS **hairstylist,** coiffeur, coiffeuse, barber.

□ **hairdressing** noun.

hairdryer (or **hairdrier**) ▶ noun an electrical device for drying the hair with warm air.

hairgrip ▶ noun Brit. a hairpin.

hairline ▶ noun the edge of a person's hair.
▶ adjective very thin or fine.

hairnet ▶ noun a fine net for holding the hair in place.

hairpiece ▶ noun a piece of false hair worn with your own hair to make it look thicker.

hairpin ▶ noun a U-shaped pin for fastening the hair.
■ **hairpin bend** a sharp U-shaped bend in a road.

hairspray ▶ noun a solution sprayed on to hair to keep it in place.

hairstyle ▶ noun a way in which a person's hair is cut or arranged.
□ **hairstylist** noun.

hairy ▶ adjective (**hairier, hairiest**) **1** covered with or like hair. **2** informal dangerous or frightening.

SYNONYMS **1** *animals with hairy coats* **shaggy,** bushy, long-haired, woolly, furry, fleecy. **2** *his hairy face* **bearded,** unshaven, stubbly, bristly; formal hirsute. **3** *a hairy situation* **risky,** dangerous, perilous, hazardous, tricky; informal dicey; Brit. informal dodgy.
ANTONYMS short-haired, smooth-haired, shaven, safe.

Haitian /**hay**-shi-uhn, **hay**-shuhn/ ▶ noun a person from Haiti.
▶ adjective relating to Haiti.

hajj (or **haj**) /haj/ ▶ noun the pilgrimage to Mecca which all Muslims are expected to make at least once if they can afford to.

hake ▶ noun a long-bodied sea fish used for food.

halal /huh-**lahl**/ ▶ adjective (of meat) prepared according to Muslim law.

halberd /**hal**-berd/ ▶ noun historical a combined spear and battleaxe.

halcyon /**hal**-si-uhn/ ▶ adjective (of a past time) very happy and peaceful.

hale ▶ adjective (of an old person) strong and healthy.

half ▶ noun (plural **halves**) **1** either of two equal parts into which something is or can be divided. **2** Brit. informal half a pint of beer.
▶ pronoun an amount equal to a half.
▶ adverb **1** to the extent of half. **2** partly.
■ **at half mast** (of a flag) flown halfway down its mast, as a mark of respect for a person who has died. **half-and-half** in equal parts. **half-baked** informal not well planned or considered. **half board** Brit. a type of accommodation at a hotel or guest house which includes breakfast and one main meal. **half-brother** (or **half-sister**) a brother (or sister) with whom you have one parent in common. **half-caste** offensive a person whose parents are of different races. **half-crown** (or **half a crown**) a former British coin equal to two shillings and sixpence (12½p). **half-dozen** (or **half a dozen**) a group of six. **half-hearted** without

enthusiasm or energy. **half-hour** (or **half an hour**) a period of thirty minutes. **half-life** the time taken for the radioactivity of a substance to fall to half its original value. **half measures** actions or policies that are not forceful or decisive enough. **half nelson** a hold in wrestling in which you pass one arm under your opponent's arm from behind while applying your other hand to their neck. **half-term** Brit. a short holiday halfway through a school term. **half-timbered** having walls with a timber frame and a brick or plaster filling. **half-time** (in sport) a short gap between two halves of a match. **not half 1** not nearly. **2** Brit. informal to an extreme degree.

halfback ▶ noun a player in a ball game whose position is between the forwards and fullbacks.

halfpenny (or **ha'penny**) /hayp-ni/ ▶ noun (plural **halfpennies** or **halfpence** /hay-p'nss/) a former British coin equal to half an old penny.

halfway ▶ adverb & adjective **1** at or to a point equal in distance between two others. **2** to some extent.

> SYNONYMS **1** *halfway down the passage* **midway,** in the middle, in the centre, part of the way. **2** *the halfway point* **mid,** middle, midway, central, centre, intermediate.

halfwit ▶ noun informal a stupid person. □ **half-witted** adjective.

halibut ▶ noun (plural **halibut**) a large flat sea fish used for food.

halitosis /hali-**toh**-sis/ ▶ noun bad-smelling breath.

hall ▶ noun **1** (also **hallway**) a room or space inside a front door, or between a number of rooms. **2** a large room for meetings, concerts, etc. **3** (also **hall of residence**) Brit. a university building in which students live. **4** Brit. a large country house.

> SYNONYMS **1** **entrance hall,** hallway, entry, entrance, lobby, foyer, vestibule. **2** *the village hall* **assembly room,** meeting room, chamber, auditorium, theatre, house.

hallelujah /hal-li-**loo**-yuh/ (or **alleluia** /al-li-**loo**-yuh/) ▶ exclamation God be praised.

hallmark ▶ noun **1** an official mark stamped on objects made of pure gold, silver, or platinum. **2** a distinctive feature.
▶ verb stamp an object with a hallmark.

hallo → HELLO.

hallowed /hal-lohd/ ▶ adjective **1** made holy. **2** very honoured and respected.

Halloween (or **Hallowe'en**) ▶ noun the night of 31 October, the evening before All Saints' Day.

hallucinate ▶ verb (**hallucinates, hallucinating, hallucinated**) see something which is not actually there.
□ **hallucination** noun **hallucinatory** adjective.

hallucinogen /huh-**loo**-si-nuh-juhn/ ▶ noun a drug causing hallucinations.
□ **hallucinogenic** adjective.

halo /**hay**-loh/ ▶ noun (plural **haloes** or **halos**) **1** (in a painting) a circle of light surrounding the head of a holy person. **2** a circle of light round the sun or moon.

> SYNONYMS **aura,** nimbus, corona, aureole.

halogen /**hal**-uh-juhn/ ▶ noun any of a group of elements including fluorine, chlorine, bromine, and iodine.

halt¹ ▶ verb come or bring to a sudden stop.

> SYNONYMS **1** *halt at the barrier* **stop,** come to a halt, come to a stop, come to a standstill, pull up, draw up. **2** *a strike has halted production* **stop,** bring to a stop, put a stop to, suspend, arrest, check, curb, stem, staunch, block, stall.
> ANTONYMS start, continue, restart.

▶ noun **1** a stopping of movement or activity. **2** Brit. a minor stopping place on a railway line.

> SYNONYMS **1** *a bus screeched to a halt* **stop,** standstill. **2** *a halt in production* **stoppage,** break, pause, interval, interruption.
> ANTONYMS start, resumption.

halt² ▶ adjective old use lame.

halter ▶ noun a rope or strap placed around the head of an animal and used to lead it.
■ **halter neck** a style of woman's top that is fastened behind the neck, leaving the shoulders, upper back, and arms bare.

halting ▶ adjective slow and hesitant.

> SYNONYMS **hesitant,** faltering, hesitating, stumbling, stammering, stuttering, broken, imperfect.
> ANTONYMS fluent.

halve ▶ verb (**halves, halving, halved**) **1** divide into two halves. **2** reduce or be reduced by half.

halves plural of HALF.

halyard /**hal**-yerd/ ▶ noun a rope used for raising and lowering a sail, yard, or flag on a ship.

ham¹ ▶ noun **1** meat from the upper part of a pig's leg which is salted and dried or smoked. **2** (**hams**) the back of the thighs.
■ **ham-fisted** clumsy.

ham² ▶ noun **1** an actor who overacts. **2** (also **radio ham**) informal an amateur radio operator.
▶ verb (**hams, hamming, hammed**) informal overact.
□ **hammy** adjective.

hamburger ▶ noun a small cake of minced beef, fried or grilled and typically served in a bread roll.

hamlet ▶ noun a small village.

hammer ▶ noun **1** a tool with a heavy metal head and a wooden handle, for driving in nails. **2** an auctioneer's mallet, tapped to indicate a sale. **3** a part of a mechanism that hits another. **4** a heavy metal ball attached to a wire for throwing in an athletic contest.
▶ verb (hammers, hammering, hammered) **1** hit repeatedly with a hammer. **2** (hammer away) work hard and persistently. **3** (hammer something in or into) make something stick in someone's mind by constantly repeating it. **4** (hammer something out) work out the details of a plan or agreement.

SYNONYMS **1** *hammered metal* **beat**, forge, shape, form, mould, fashion. **2** *he hammered the nail in* **batter**, bang, pummel, pound, knock, thump.

hammerhead ▶ noun a shark with flattened extensions on either side of the head.

hammock ▶ noun a wide strip of canvas or rope mesh suspended at both ends, used as a bed.

hamper¹ ▶ noun a basket used for food and other items needed for a picnic.

hamper² ▶ verb (hampers, hampering, hampered) slow down or prevent the movement or progress of.

SYNONYMS **hinder**, obstruct, impede, inhibit, delay, slow down, hold up, interfere with, handicap, hamstring. ANTONYMS help.

hamster ▶ noun a burrowing rodent with a short tail and large cheek pouches.

✔ no **p**: ham**ster**, not **hamp-**.

hamstring ▶ noun any of five tendons at the back of a person's knee.
▶ verb (hamstrings, hamstringing, past and past participle hamstrung) **1** cripple by cutting the hamstrings. **2** severely restrict.

hand ▶ noun **1** the end part of the arm beyond the wrist, with four fingers and a thumb. **2** a pointer on a clock or watch indicating the passing of time. **3** (hands) a person's power or control. **4** an active role. **5** help in doing something. **6** a person's handwriting. **7** a person who does physical work. **8** the set of cards dealt to a player in a card game. **9** a unit of measurement of a horse's height, equal to 4 inches (10.16 cm).

SYNONYMS **1** **fist**, palm; informal paw, mitt. **2** *written in his own hand* **handwriting**, writing, script. **3** *a factory hand* **worker**, employee, workman, labourer, operative, craftsman, roustabout.

▶ verb give or pass something to.

SYNONYMS *hand me a spanner* **pass**, give, present, let someone have.

■ **at hand** (or **on** or **to hand**) near; easy to reach. **from hand to mouth** meeting only your immediate needs. **hand grenade** a grenade that is thrown by hand. **hand in glove** working very closely together. **hand-me-down** a piece of clothing that has been passed on from another person. **hand-pick** choose carefully. **hands-on** involving direct participation in something. **hand-to-hand** (of fighting) involving physical contact. **in hand** in progress. **out of hand** **1** not under control. **2** without taking time to think.

handbag ▶ noun Brit. a small bag used by a woman to carry everyday personal items.

handball ▶ noun **1** a game in which the ball is hit with the hand in a walled court. **2** Soccer unlawful touching of the ball with the hand or arm.

handbill ▶ noun a small printed advertisement handed out in the street.

handbook ▶ noun a book giving basic information or instructions.

SYNONYMS **manual**, instructions, ABC, A to Z, companion, guide, guidebook.

handbrake ▶ noun a brake operated by hand, used to hold an already stationary vehicle.

handcuff ▶ noun (handcuffs) a pair of lockable linked metal rings for securing a prisoner's wrists.

SYNONYMS (handcuffs) **manacles**, shackles, irons; informal cuffs, bracelets.

▶ verb put handcuffs on.

SYNONYMS *he was handcuffed* **manacle**, shackle, clap/put someone in irons; informal cuff.

handful ▶ noun **1** a quantity that fills the hand. **2** a small number or amount. **3** informal a person who is difficult to deal with or control.

SYNONYMS **few**, small number, small amount, small quantity, sprinkling, smattering, one or two, some, not many. ANTONYMS lot.

handgun ▶ noun a gun designed for use with one hand.

handhold ▶ noun something for a hand to grip on.

handicap ▶ noun **1** a condition that limits a person's ability to function physically, mentally, or socially. **2** something that makes progress or success difficult. **3** a disadvantage given to a leading competitor in a sport in order to make the chances of winning more equal, such as the extra weight given to certain racehorses. **4** the number of strokes by which a golfer normally exceeds par for a course.

h

SYNONYMS **1 disability**, infirmity, defect, impairment, affliction. **2** *a handicap to industrial competitiveness* **impediment**, hindrance, obstacle, barrier, constraint, disadvantage, stumbling block.
ANTONYMS benefit, advantage.

▸ verb (**handicaps, handicapping, handicapped**) make it difficult for someone to do something.

SYNONYMS *handicapped by lack of funding* **hamper**, impede, hinder, impair, hamstring, restrict, constrain.
ANTONYMS help.

handicapped ▸ adjective having a handicap or disability.

❗ When used to refer to people with physical and mental disabilities, the word **handicapped** sounds old-fashioned and may cause offence; it is better to use **disabled**, or, when referring to mental disability, **having learning difficulties**.

handicraft ▸ noun **1** the skilled making of decorative objects by hand. **2** an object made in this way.

handiwork ▸ noun **1** (**your handiwork**) something that you have made or done. **2** the making of things by hand.

handkerchief ▸ noun (plural **handkerchiefs** or **handkerchieves**) a square of material for wiping or blowing the nose on.

handle ▸ verb (**handles, handling, handled**) **1** feel or move something with the hands. **2** control an animal, vehicle, or tool. **3** deal with a situation. **4** control, manage, or deal in something commercially. **5** (**handle yourself**) behave.

SYNONYMS **1** *handle the vase carefully* **hold**, pick up, grasp, grip, lift, finger. **2** *a car which is easy to handle* **control**, drive, steer, operate, manoeuvre. **3** *she handled the job well* **deal with**, manage, tackle, take care of, look after, take charge of, attend to, see to, sort out. **4** *the traders handled imported goods* **trade in**, deal in, buy, sell, supply, peddle, traffic in.

▸ noun **1** the part by which a thing is held, carried, or controlled. **2** a means of understanding or approaching a person or situation.

SYNONYMS *a knife handle* **grip**, haft, hilt, stock, shaft.

□ **handler** noun.

handlebar (or **handlebars**) ▸ noun the steering bar of a bicycle or motorbike.

handmade ▸ adjective made by hand rather than machine.

handmaid (or **handmaiden**) ▸ noun old use a female servant.

handout ▸ noun **1** a parcel of food, clothes, or money given to a person in need. **2** a

piece of printed information provided free of charge.

handset ▸ noun **1** the part of a telephone that you speak into and listen to. **2** a hand-held control device for a piece of electronic equipment.

handshake ▸ noun an act of shaking a person's hand.

handsome ▸ adjective (**handsomer, handsomest**) **1** (of a man) good-looking. **2** (of a woman) striking and impressive rather than pretty. **3** (of a thing) impressive and of good quality. **4** (of an amount) large.

SYNONYMS **1** *a handsome man* **good-looking**, attractive, striking; informal hunky, dishy, tasty, fanciable; Brit. informal fit; N. Amer. informal cute. **2** *a handsome woman* **striking**, imposing, prepossessing, good-looking, attractive. **3** *a handsome profit* **substantial**, considerable, sizeable, princely, generous, lavish, ample, bumper; informal tidy, whopping; Brit. informal ginormous.
ANTONYMS ugly, meagre.

□ **handsomely** adverb.

handspring ▸ noun a jump through the air on to your hands followed by another on to your feet.

handstand ▸ noun an act of balancing on your hands with your legs in the air.

handwriting ▸ noun **1** writing with a pen or pencil rather than by typing or printing. **2** a person's particular style of writing.
□ **handwritten** adjective.

handy ▸ adjective (**handier, handiest**) **1** convenient to handle or use. **2** close by and ready for use. **3** skilful.

SYNONYMS **1** *a handy gadget* **useful**, convenient, practical, neat, easy to use, user-friendly, helpful. **2** *keep your credit card handy* **ready**, to hand, within reach, accessible, readily available, nearby, at the ready. **3** *he's handy with a needle* **skilful**, skilled, dexterous, deft, adept, proficient.
ANTONYMS useless, unwieldy, inconvenient, inept.

□ **handily** adverb.

handyman ▸ noun (plural **handymen**) a person employed to do general building repairs.

hang ▸ verb (**hangs, hanging**, past and past participle **hung** except in sense 2) **1** suspend or be suspended from above with the lower part dangling freely. **2** (past and past participle **hanged**) kill someone by suspending them from a rope tied around the neck. **3** (of a piece of clothing) fall or drape in a particular way.

SYNONYMS **1** *lights hung from the trees* **be suspended,** dangle, swing, sway, hover, float. **2** *he was hanged for murder* **send to the gallows,** execute, lynch; informal string up. **3** *the room was hung with streamers* **decorate,** adorn, drape, festoon, deck out. **4** *hang the picture at eye level* **suspend,** put up, pin up, display.

■ **get the hang of** informal learn how to do something. **hang-glider** a simple aircraft consisting of a framework from which a person is suspended while they glide through the air. **hang out** informal spend time relaxing or enjoying yourself. **hang-up** informal an emotional problem.

❗ **Hang** has two past tense and past participle forms, **hanged** and **hung**: use **hung** in general situations, as in *they hung out the washing*, and **hanged** when talking about execution by hanging, as in *the prisoner was hanged*.

hangar /hang-er/ ▸ noun a large building in which aircraft are kept.

✔ **-ar**, not **-er**: hang**ar**.

hangdog ▸ adjective having a sad or guilty appearance.

hanger ▸ noun **1** a person who hangs something. **2** (also **coat hanger**) a curved frame with a hook at the top, for hanging clothes from a rail.
■ **hanger-on** (plural **hangers-on**) a person who tries to be friendly with someone of higher status.

hanging ▸ noun a decorative piece of fabric hung on the wall of a room or around a bed.

hangman ▸ noun (plural **hangmen**) an executioner who hangs condemned people.

hangnail ▸ noun a piece of torn skin at the root of a fingernail.

hangover ▸ noun **1** a headache or other after-effects caused by drinking too much alcohol. **2** a thing that has survived from the past.

hank ▸ noun a coil or length of wool, hair, or other material.

hanker ▸ verb (**hanker after** or **for** or **to do**) feel a desire for or to do.

SYNONYMS **yearn,** long, wish, hunger, thirst, lust, ache; informal itch.

hanky (or **hankie**) ▸ noun (plural **hankies**) informal a handkerchief.

hanky-panky ▸ noun informal naughty behaviour.

hansom /han-suhm/ (or **hansom cab**) ▸ noun (in the past) a horse-drawn carriage with two wheels and a hood, for two passengers.

Hanukkah (or **Chanukkah**) /han-uu-kuh/ ▸ noun a Jewish festival of lights held in December.

haphazard ▸ adjective having no particular order or plan.
□ **haphazardly** adverb.

hapless ▸ adjective unlucky.

happen ▸ verb **1** take place without being planned or as the result of something. **2** (**happen to do**) do by chance. **3** (**happen on**) come across by chance. **4** (**happen to**) be experienced by. **5** (**happen to**) become of.

SYNONYMS **1** *remember what happened last time* **occur,** take place, come about, develop, result, transpire; N. Amer. informal go down. **2** *they happened to be in London* **chance,** have the good/bad luck.

happening ▸ noun an event or occurrence.

SYNONYMS **occurrence,** event, incident, episode, affair.

▸ adjective informal fashionable.

happily ▸ adverb **1** in a happy way. **2** fortunately.

SYNONYMS **1 cheerfully,** contentedly, cheerily, merrily, joyfully. **2** *I will happily do as you ask* **gladly,** willingly, readily, freely. **3** *happily, we arrived just in time* **fortunately,** luckily, thankfully, mercifully, as luck would have it. ANTONYMS unhappily.

happiness ▸ noun the condition of being happy.

SYNONYMS **pleasure,** contentment, satisfaction, cheerfulness, merriment, joy, well-being. ANTONYMS unhappiness.

happy ▸ adjective (**happier, happiest**) **1** feeling or showing pleasure. **2** willing to do something. **3** fortunate and convenient.

SYNONYMS **1 cheerful,** cheery, merry, joyful, jovial, jolly, carefree, in good spirits, in a good mood, pleased, contented, content, satisfied, gratified, delighted, sunny, radiant, elated, jubilant. **2** *we will be happy to advise you* **glad,** pleased, delighted, more than willing. **3** *a happy coincidence* **fortunate,** lucky, timely, convenient. ANTONYMS sad, unwilling, unfortunate.

■ **happy-go-lucky** cheerfully unconcerned about the future. **happy hour** a period of the day when drinks are sold at reduced prices in a bar.

hara-kiri /ha-ruh-ki-ri/ ▸ noun a Japanese method of ritual suicide in which a person cuts open their stomach with a sword.

harangue /huh-rang/ ▸ verb (**harangues, haranguing, harangued**) use loud and aggressive language in criticizing someone or trying to persuade them to do something.
▸ noun an act of haranguing.

harass /ha-ruhss, huh-**rass**/ ▶ verb
1 torment someone by putting constant pressure on them or by being unpleasant. **2** (**harassed**) tired or tense as a result of having too many demands made on you. **3** make repeated small-scale attacks on an enemy in order to wear down resistance.

> SYNONYMS **1** **persecute**, intimidate, hound, pester, bother; informal hassle, bug; N. Amer. informal ride. **2** (**harassed**) **stressed**, hard-pressed, careworn, worried, troubled; informal hassled.

> ✔ only one **r**: harass.

harassment ▶ noun the action of harassing.

> SYNONYMS **persecution**, intimidation, victimization, trouble, bother; informal hassle.

harbinger /**har**-bin-jer/ ▶ noun a person or thing that announces or signals the approach of something.

harbour (US spelling **harbor**) ▶ noun a sheltered area of coast, where ships can be moored.

> SYNONYMS **port**, dock, haven, marina, mooring, wharf, anchorage, waterfront.

▶ verb **1** keep a thought or feeling secretly in your mind. **2** give a refuge or shelter to. **3** carry the germs of a disease.

> SYNONYMS **1** *he is harbouring a dangerous criminal* **shelter**, conceal, hide, shield, protect, give asylum to. **2** *Rose harboured a grudge against him* **bear**, hold, nurse, foster.

hard ▶ adjective **1** solid, firm, and rigid. **2** needing a lot of endurance or effort; difficult. **3** (of a person) not showing any signs of weakness. **4** (of information) precise and definitely true: *hard science*. **5** harsh or unpleasant to the senses. **6** done with a lot of force or strength: *a hard whack*. **7** (of drink) strongly alcoholic. **8** (of a drug) very addictive.

> SYNONYMS **1** *hard ground* **firm**, solid, rigid, stiff, unbreakable, unyielding, compacted, tough, strong. **2** *hard physical work* **arduous**, strenuous, tiring, exhausting, back-breaking, gruelling, heavy, laborious, demanding; Brit. informal knackering. **3** *hard workers* **industrious**, diligent, assiduous, conscientious, energetic, keen, enthusiastic, indefatigable. **4** *a hard problem* **difficult**, puzzling, complicated, intricate, thorny, problematic. **5** *times are hard* **harsh**, grim, austere, difficult, bad, bleak, tough. **6** *a hard blow* **forceful**, heavy, strong, sharp, violent, powerful.
> ANTONYMS soft, easy, lazy, gentle.

▶ adverb **1** with a lot of effort or force. **2** so as to be solid or firm.

> SYNONYMS **1** *George pushed her hard* **forcefully**, roughly, heavily, sharply, violently. **2** *they worked hard* **diligently**, industriously, assiduously, conscientiously, energetically, doggedly; informal like mad, like crazy. **3** *she looked hard at me* **closely**, intently, critically, carefully, searchingly.
> ANTONYMS gently, lazily, casually.

■ **hard and fast** (of a rule) fixed and not able to be changed. **hard-boiled 1** (of an egg) boiled until the yolk is firm. **2** (of a person) tough and cynical. **hard cash** coins and banknotes as opposed to other forms of payment. **hard copy** a printed version of data held in a computer. **hard core 1** the most committed or uncompromising members of a group. **2** very explicit pornography. **3** pop music that is loud and aggressive in style. **hard disk** (or **hard drive**) (in a computer) a rigid magnetic disk on which a large amount of data can be stored. **hard done by** Brit. harshly or unfairly treated. **hard feelings** feelings of resentment. **hard-headed** tough and realistic. **hard-hearted** unsympathetic or uncaring. **hard line** a strict policy or attitude. **hard-nosed** realistic and tough-minded. **hard shoulder** Brit. a strip of road alongside a motorway for use in an emergency. **hard up** informal short of money. □ **hardness** noun.

hardback ▶ noun a book bound in stiff covers.

hardbitten ▶ adjective tough and cynical.

hardboard ▶ noun stiff board made of compressed wood pulp.

harden ▶ verb make or become hard or harder.

> SYNONYMS **1** *this glue hardens in four hours* **solidify**, set, stiffen, thicken. **2** *their suffering had hardened them* **toughen**, desensitize, inure, season, train, numb.
> ANTONYMS soften.

hardened ▶ adjective fixed in a bad habit or way of life: *a hardened criminal*.

> SYNONYMS **inveterate**, seasoned, habitual, chronic, compulsive, confirmed, incorrigible.

hardly ▶ adverb **1** scarcely; barely. **2** only with great difficulty.

> SYNONYMS **scarcely**, barely, only just, just.
> ANTONYMS fully, easily.

> ! Don't use **hardly** in a negative sentence, such as *I can't hardly wait*; say *I can hardly wait* instead.

hardship ▶ noun severe suffering.

SYNONYMS **difficulty,** privation, destitution, poverty, austerity, need, distress, suffering, adversity.
ANTONYMS prosperity, ease.

hardware ▸ noun **1** tools and other items used in the home and in activities such as gardening. **2** the machines, wiring, and other parts of a computer. **3** heavy military equipment such as tanks and missiles.

SYNONYMS **equipment,** apparatus, gear, paraphernalia, tackle, kit, machinery.

hardwood ▸ noun the wood from a broadleaved tree as distinguished from that of conifers.

hardy ▸ adjective (**hardier, hardiest**) capable of surviving difficult conditions.

SYNONYMS **robust,** healthy, fit, strong, sturdy, tough, rugged.
ANTONYMS delicate.

□ **hardiness** noun.

hare ▸ noun a fast-running animal like a large rabbit, with long hind legs.
▸ verb (**hares, haring, hared**) run very fast.
■ **hare-brained** foolish and unlikely to succeed.

harebell ▸ noun a plant with pale blue bell-shaped flowers.

harelip ▸ noun offensive a cleft lip.

harem /**hah**-reem, hah-**reem**/ ▸ noun **1** the separate part of a Muslim household reserved for women. **2** the women living in a harem.

haricot /**ha**-ri-koh/ ▸ noun a round white bean.

hark ▸ verb **1** literary listen. **2** (**hark back to**) recall or remind you of something in the past.

harken ➡ HEARKEN.

harlequin ▸ noun (**Harlequin**) (in traditional pantomime) a character who wears a mask and a diamond-patterned costume.
▸ adjective in varied colours.

harlot ▸ noun old use a prostitute.

harm ▸ noun **1** hurt or injury to a person. **2** damage done to a thing. **3** a bad effect on something.

SYNONYMS *it won't do you any harm* **injury,** damage, mischief.
ANTONYMS good.

▸ verb **1** hurt or injure someone. **2** damage or have a bad effect on something.

SYNONYMS **1** *he's never harmed anybody* **hurt,** injure, lay a finger on, mistreat, ill-treat. **2** *this could harm his prospects* **damage,** spoil, affect, undermine, ruin.
ANTONYMS heal, help.

harmful ▸ adjective causing or likely to cause harm.

SYNONYMS **damaging,** injurious, detrimental, dangerous, unhealthy, unwholesome, hurtful, destructive, hazardous.
ANTONYMS beneficial.

□ **harmfully** adverb.

harmless ▸ adjective not able or likely to cause harm.

SYNONYMS **1** *a harmless substance* **safe,** innocuous, gentle, mild, non-toxic. **2** *he seems harmless enough* **inoffensive,** innocuous, gentle.
ANTONYMS harmful, objectionable.

□ **harmlessly** adverb.

harmonic ▸ adjective relating to harmony.

harmonica ▸ noun a small rectangular wind instrument with a row of metal reeds that produce different notes.

harmonious ▸ adjective **1** tuneful. **2** arranged in a pleasing way so that each part goes well with the others. **3** free from conflict.
□ **harmoniously** adverb.

harmonium ▸ noun a keyboard instrument in which the notes are produced by air driven through metal reeds by foot-operated bellows.

harmonize (or **harmonise**) ▸ verb (**harmonizes, harmonizing, harmonized**) **1** add notes to a melody to produce harmony. **2** make or be harmonious.

harmony ▸ noun (plural **harmonies**) **1** the combination of musical notes sounded at the same time to produce chords with a pleasing effect. **2** a pleasing quality when things are arranged together well. **3** agreement.

SYNONYMS **1** *musical harmony* **tunefulness,** euphony, melodiousness, unison. **2** *the villagers live together in harmony* **accord,** agreement, peace, friendship, fellowship, cooperation, understanding, rapport, unity.
ANTONYMS dissonance, disagreement.

harness ▸ noun **1** a set of straps by which a horse or other animal is fastened to a cart, plough, etc. **2** an arrangement of straps used for attaching a person's body to something.
▸ verb **1** fit a person or animal with a harness. **2** control and make use of resources.

harp ▸ noun a musical instrument consisting of a frame supporting a series of strings of different lengths, played by plucking with the fingers.
▸ verb (**harp on**) keep talking about something in a boring way.
□ **harpist** noun.

harpoon ▸ noun a barbed spear-like missile used for catching whales and other large sea creatures.

▶ verb spear with a harpoon.

harpsichord ▶ noun a keyboard instrument with horizontal strings plucked by points operated by pressing the keys.

harpy ▶ noun (plural **harpies**) **1** Greek Roman Mythology a cruel creature with a woman's head and body and a bird's wings and claws. **2** an unpleasant woman.

harridan ▶ noun a bossy or aggressive old woman.

harrier ▶ noun **1** a hound used for hunting hares. **2** a bird of prey.

harrow ▶ noun a piece of equipment consisting of a heavy frame set with teeth which is dragged over ploughed land to break up or spread the soil.

▶ verb draw a harrow over.

harrowing ▶ adjective very distressing.

> SYNONYMS **distressing**, traumatic, upsetting, shocking, disturbing, painful, agonizing.

harry ▶ verb (**harries**, **harrying**, **harried**) **1** carry out repeated attacks on an enemy. **2** pester continuously.

> SYNONYMS **harass**, hound, torment, pester, worry, badger, nag, plague; informal hassle, bug.

harsh ▶ adjective **1** unpleasantly rough or jarring to the senses. **2** cruel or severe. **3** (of climate or conditions) difficult to survive in; hostile.

> SYNONYMS **1** *a harsh voice* **grating**, rasping, strident, raucous, discordant. **2** *harsh colours* **glaring**, loud, garish, gaudy, lurid. **3** *his harsh treatment of captives* **cruel**, savage, barbarous, merciless, inhumane, ruthless.
> **4** *they took harsh measures to end the crisis* **severe**, stringent, firm, stiff, stern, rigorous. **5** *harsh words* **rude**, discourteous, unfriendly, sharp, bitter, unkind, critical, disparaging. **6** *harsh conditions* **austere**, grim, spartan, hard, inhospitable. **7** *a harsh winter* **cold**, freezing, icy, bitter, hard, severe, bleak.
> ANTONYMS soft, subdued, kind, mild, friendly, comfortable.

□ **harshly** adverb **harshness** noun.

hart ▶ noun an adult male deer.

harum-scarum ▶ adjective reckless.

harvest ▶ noun **1** the process or period of gathering in crops. **2** the season's yield or crop.

> SYNONYMS *a poor harvest* **crop**, yield, vintage, produce.

▶ verb gather in a crop.

> SYNONYMS *he harvested the wheat* **gather**, bring in, reap, pick, collect.

□ **harvester** noun.

has 3rd person singular present of **HAVE**.

■ **has-been** informal a person who is no longer important.

hash¹ ▶ noun a dish of chopped cooked meat reheated with potatoes.

■ **make a hash of** informal make a mess of.

hash² = **HASHISH**.

hash³ ▶ noun Brit. the symbol #.

hashish /ha-sheesh/ ▶ noun cannabis.

hasn't ▶ short form has not.

hasp ▶ noun a hinged metal plate that is fitted over a metal loop and secured by a pin or padlock to fasten something.

hassle informal ▶ noun **1** annoying inconvenience. **2** a situation involving argument or disagreement.

> SYNONYMS *parking is such a hassle* **inconvenience,** bother, nuisance, trouble, annoyance, irritation, fuss; informal aggravation, headache, pain in the neck.

▶ verb (**hassles**, **hassling**, **hassled**) harass or pester someone.

> SYNONYMS *don't hassle me!* **harass,** pester, be on at, badger, hound, bother, nag, torment; informal bug; N. English informal mither.

hassock ▶ noun a cushion for kneeling on in church.

haste ▶ noun speed or urgency of action.

hasten ▶ verb **1** move or act quickly. **2** make something happen sooner than expected.

> SYNONYMS **1** *we hastened back* **hurry**, rush, dash, race, fly, speed; informal zip; N. Amer. informal hightail. **2** *chemicals can hasten ageing* **speed up**, bring on, precipitate, advance.
> ANTONYMS dawdle, delay.

hasty ▶ adjective (**hastier**, **hastiest**) hurried; rushed.

> SYNONYMS **hurried**, rash, impetuous, impulsive, reckless, precipitate, spur-of-the-moment.
> ANTONYMS considered.

□ **hastily** adverb.

hat ▶ noun a covering for the head.

■ **hat-trick** three successes of the same kind.

hatch¹ ▶ noun **1** a small opening in a floor, wall, or roof allowing access to an area. **2** a door in an aircraft, spacecraft, or submarine.

hatch² ▶ verb **1** (of a young bird, fish, or reptile) come out of its egg. **2** (of an egg) open and produce a young animal. **3** form a plot or plan.

hatch³ ▶ verb (in drawing) shade an area with closely drawn parallel lines.

hatchback ▶ noun a car with a door that opens upwards across the full width at the back end.

hatchet ▶ noun a small axe with a short handle.
■ **bury the hatchet** end a quarrel.

hatchling ▶ noun a newly hatched young animal.

hatchway ▶ noun an opening or hatch, especially in a ship's deck.

hate ▶ verb (**hates, hating, hated**) feel very strong dislike for.

> SYNONYMS **1** *they hate each other* **loathe**, detest, despise, dislike, abhor, shrink from, be unable to bear/stand. **2** *I hate to bother you* **be sorry**, be reluctant, be loath.
> ANTONYMS love.

▶ noun **1** very strong dislike. **2** informal a disliked person or thing.

> SYNONYMS *feelings of hate* **hatred**, loathing, abhorrence, abomination, aversion, disgust.
> ANTONYMS love.

hateful ▶ adjective very unkind or unpleasant.

hatred ▶ noun very strong dislike; hate.
> SYNONYMS See **HATE** (noun).

haughty ▶ adjective (**haughtier, haughtiest**) arrogant and superior towards other people.
□ **haughtily** adverb.

haul ▶ verb **1** pull or drag something with a lot of effort. **2** transport something in a lorry or cart.

> SYNONYMS *she hauled the basket upstairs* **drag**, pull, heave, lug, hump.

▶ noun **1** a quantity of something obtained, especially illegally. **2** a number of fish caught at one time.

> SYNONYMS *the thieves' haul* **booty**, loot, plunder, spoils, stolen goods; informal swag.

haulage ▶ noun Brit. the commercial transport of goods.

haulier ▶ noun Brit. a person or company employed in the commercial transport of goods by road.

haulm /hawm/ ▶ noun a plant stalk.

haunch ▶ noun **1** a person's or animal's buttock and thigh. **2** the leg and loin of an animal, as food.

haunt ▶ verb **1** (of a ghost) appear regularly in a place. **2** (of a person) visit a place frequently. **3** keep coming into someone's mind in a disturbing way.

> SYNONYMS *the sight haunted me* **torment**, disturb, trouble, worry, plague, prey on.

▶ noun a place where a particular type of person frequently goes.

> SYNONYMS *a favourite haunt of artists* **meeting place**, stamping ground, spot, venue; informal hang-out; N. Amer. stomping ground.

haunted ▶ adjective **1** visited by a ghost. **2** showing signs of mental suffering.

> SYNONYMS **1** *the church is haunted* **possessed**, cursed, jinxed, eerie. **2** *his haunted eyes* **tormented**, anguished, tortured, obsessed, troubled, worried.

haunting ▶ adjective making someone feel sad or thoughtful.

> SYNONYMS **evocative**, affecting, stirring, powerful, poignant, memorable.

□ **hauntingly** adverb.

haute couture /oht kuu-**tyoor**/ ▶ noun the designing and making of high-quality clothes by leading fashion houses.

haute cuisine /oht kwi-**zeen**/ ▶ noun high-quality cooking in the traditional French style.

have ▶ verb (**has, having, had**) **1** possess or own. **2** experience. **3** be able to make use of. **4** (**have to**) be obliged to; must. **5** perform an action. **6** show a personal characteristic. **7** suffer from an illness or disability. **8** cause something to be or be done. **9** place, hold, or keep something in a particular position. **10** eat or drink something.

> SYNONYMS **1** *he had a new car* **own**, be in possession of, be blessed with, boast, enjoy. **2** *the flat has five rooms* **comprise**, consist of, contain, include, incorporate, be composed of, be made up of. **3** *they had tea* **eat**, drink, take. **4** *let's have a party* **organize**, hold, give, throw, put on, lay on. **5** *I have to get up at six* **must**, be obliged to, be required to, be compelled to, be forced to, be bound to.

▶ auxiliary verb used with a past participle to form the perfect, pluperfect, and future perfect tenses, and the conditional mood.

> ❗ Be careful not to write **of** when you mean **have** or **'ve**: *I could've told you that* not *I could of told you that.*

haven ▶ noun **1** a place of safety. **2** a harbour or small port.

> SYNONYMS **refuge**, retreat, shelter, sanctuary, oasis.

haven't ▶ short form have not.

haver /**hay**-ver/ ▶ verb (**havers, havering, havered**) **1** Scottish talk foolishly. **2** Brit. be indecisive.

haversack ▶ noun a small, sturdy bag carried on the back or over the shoulder.

havoc ▶ noun great destruction, confusion, or disorder.

h

synonyms **chaos**, mayhem, bedlam, pandemonium, a shambles.

■ **play havoc with** completely disrupt.

Hawaiian /huh-wy-uhn/ ▸ noun a person from Hawaii.
▸ adjective relating to Hawaii.

hawk¹ ▸ noun **1** a fast-flying bird of prey with a long tail. **2** a person in favour of aggressive policies in foreign affairs.
▸ verb hunt with a trained hawk.
□ **hawkish** adjective.

hawk² ▸ verb offer goods for sale in the street.
□ **hawker** noun.

hawk³ ▸ verb clear the throat noisily.

hawser /haw-zer/ ▸ noun a thick rope for mooring or towing a ship.

hawthorn ▸ noun a thorny shrub or tree with small dark red fruits called **haws**.

hay ▸ noun grass that has been mown and dried for use as animal feed.
■ **hay fever** an allergy to pollen or dust, causing sneezing and watery eyes.

haystack (or **hayrick**) ▸ noun a large packed pile of hay.

haywire ▸ adjective informal out of control.

hazard ▸ noun **1** a danger. **2** an obstacle, such as a bunker, on a golf course.

synonyms **danger**, risk, peril, menace, jeopardy, threat.

▸ verb **1** dare to say. **2** put at risk.

hazardous ▸ adjective dangerous.

synonyms **risky**, dangerous, unsafe, perilous, fraught with danger, high-risk; informal dicey; Brit. informal dodgy.
antonyms safe, certain.

haze ▸ noun **1** a thin mist caused by fine particles of dust, water, etc. **2** a state of mental confusion.

synonyms **mist**, fog, cloud, vapour.

hazel ▸ noun **1** a shrub or small tree which produces round nuts called **hazelnuts**. **2** a rich reddish-brown colour.

hazy ▸ adjective (**hazier**, **haziest**) **1** covered by a haze. **2** vague or unclear.
□ **hazily** adverb.

he ▸ pronoun **1** used to refer to a man, boy, or male animal previously mentioned or easily identified. **2** used to refer to a person or animal whose sex is not specified.

❗ Until recently, **he** was used to refer to any person, male or female (as in *every child needs to know that he is loved*), but many people now think that this is old-fashioned and sexist. One solution is to use **he or she**; another is to use **they**, as in *everyone needs to feel that they matter*.

head ▸ noun **1** the upper part of the body, containing the brain, mouth, and sense organs. **2** a person in charge. **3** the front, forward, or upper part of something. **4** a person considered as a unit: *fifty pounds per head*. **5** a particular number of cattle or sheep. **6** a compact mass of leaves or flowers at the top of a stem. **7** a part of a computer or a tape or video recorder which transfers information to and from a tape or disk. **8** the source of a river or stream. **9** the foam on top of a glass of beer. **10** (**heads**) the side of a coin showing the image of a head. **11** pressure of water or steam in an enclosed space.

synonyms **1** *her head hit the wall* **skull**, cranium; informal nut. **2** *he had to use his head* **brain(s)**, brainpower, intellect, intelligence, grey matter; Brit. informal loaf; N. Amer. informal smarts. **3** *she had a head for business* **aptitude**, talent, gift, capacity. **4** *the head of the church* **leader**, chief, controller, governor, superintendent, commander, captain, director, manager, principal, president; informal boss; Brit. informal gaffer, guv'nor. **5** *the head of the queue* **front**, beginning, start, top.
antonyms back.

▸ adjective chief.

synonyms *the head waiter* **chief**, principal, leading, main, first, top, highest.

▸ verb **1** be the head of. **2** move in a particular direction. **3** (**head someone/thing off**) intercept someone or something and force them to change direction. **4** give a heading to. **5** Soccer hit the ball with the head.

synonyms *a team headed by a manager* **command**, control, lead, manage, direct, supervise, superintend, oversee, preside over.

■ **come to a head** reach a crisis. **head-on 1** with the front of a vehicle. **2** involving direct confrontation. **head start** an advantage gained at the beginning of something.
□ **headless** adjective **headship** noun.

headache ▸ noun **1** a continuous pain in the head. **2** informal something that causes worry.

synonyms **1** *I've got a headache* **sore head**, migraine, hangover. **2** *it was a real headache* **problem**, worry, hassle, pain in the neck, bind.

headband ▸ noun a band of fabric worn around the head.

headboard ▸ noun an upright panel at the head of a bed.

headbutt ▸ verb attack someone by hitting them with the head.

headdress ▸ noun a decorative covering for the head.

header ▸ noun **1** Soccer a shot or pass made with the head. **2** a line of writing at the top of each page of a book or document.

headhunt ▸ verb approach someone already employed elsewhere to fill a vacant post.

heading ▸ noun **1** a title at the head of a page or section of a book. **2** a direction or bearing.

> SYNONYMS **title**, caption, legend, rubric, headline.

headland ▸ noun a narrow piece of land that sticks out into the sea.

headlight (or **headlamp**) ▸ noun a powerful light at the front of a motor vehicle.

headline ▸ noun **1** a heading at the top of a newspaper or magazine article. **2** (**the headlines**) a summary of the most important items of news.
▸ verb (**headlines, headlining, headlined**) **1** give an article a headline. **2** appear as the star performer at a concert.

headlong ▸ adverb & adjective **1** with the head first. **2** in a rush.

headmaster (or **headmistress**) ▸ noun a teacher in charge of a school.

headphones ▸ plural noun a pair of earphones joined by a band placed over the head.

headquarters ▸ noun the place from which an organization or military operation is directed.

headset ▸ noun a set of headphones with a microphone attached.

headstone ▸ noun a stone slab set up at the head of a grave.

headstrong ▸ adjective very independent and determined to have your own way.

headway ▸ noun (**make headway**) make progress.

headwind ▸ noun a wind blowing from directly in front, towards someone or something.

headword ▸ noun a word which begins a separate entry in a dictionary or encyclopedia.

heady ▸ adjective (**headier, headiest**) **1** having a strong or exciting effect. **2** (of alcohol) strong.

> SYNONYMS **1** *the heady days of my youth* **exhilarating**, exciting, stimulating, thrilling, intoxicating. **2** *heady wine* **potent**, intoxicating, strong.
> ANTONYMS boring, weak.

heal ▸ verb **1** make or become healthy again. **2** put right.

> SYNONYMS **1** *he heals the sick* **cure**, make better, restore to health, treat. **2** *his*

knee had healed **get better,** be cured, recover, mend. **3** *we tried to heal the rift* **put right,** repair, resolve, settle; informal patch up.
ANTONYMS worsen, aggravate.

□ **healer** noun.

health ▸ noun **1** the state of being free from illness or injury. **2** a person's mental or physical condition.

> SYNONYMS **1** *he was restored to health* **well-being**, fitness, good condition, strength, robustness, vigour. **2** *poor health* **condition**, physical shape, constitution.
> ANTONYMS illness.

■ **health club** a private club where exercise facilities and health and beauty treatments are available. **health farm** a place where people stay in order to try to become healthier through dieting, exercise, and special treatments. **health food** natural food that is believed to be good for your health.

healthful ▸ adjective good for the health.

healthy ▸ adjective (**healthier, healthiest**) **1** in good health, or helping towards good health. **2** normal, sensible, or desirable. **3** of a very satisfactory size or amount.

> SYNONYMS **1** *a healthy baby* **well,** fit, in good shape, in fine fettle, in tip-top condition, strong, fighting fit. **2** *a healthy diet* **wholesome,** good for you, health-giving, nutritious, nourishing, invigorating, sanitary, hygienic.
> ANTONYMS unhealthy.

□ **healthily** adverb.

heap ▸ noun **1** a pile of a substance or of a number of objects. **2** informal a large amount or number. **3** informal an old vehicle in bad condition.

> SYNONYMS *a heap of boxes* **pile**, stack, mound, mountain.

▸ verb **1** put in or form a heap. **2** (**heap something with**) load something heavily with. **3** (**heap something on**) give a lot of praise, criticism, etc. to.

> SYNONYMS *she heaped logs on the fire* **pile (up),** stack (up), make a mound of.

hear ▸ verb (**hears, hearing, heard**) **1** be aware of a sound with the ears. **2** be told of. **3** (**have heard of**) be aware of the existence of. **4** (**hear from**) receive a letter, phone call, or email from. **5** listen to. **6** listen to and judge a case in a law court.

> SYNONYMS **1** *she could hear voices* **make out,** catch, get, perceive, overhear. **2** *they heard that I had moved* **learn,** find out, discover, gather, glean. **3** *a jury heard the case* **try,** judge, adjudicate on.

□ **hearer** noun.

hearing ▸ noun **1** the ability to hear sounds. **2** the range within which sounds can be heard. **3** an opportunity to state your case. **4** an act of listening to evidence.

SYNONYMS **1** *she moved out of hearing* **earshot**, hearing distance. **2** *I had a fair hearing* **chance to speak**, opportunity to be heard. **3** *he gave evidence at the hearing* **trial**, court case, enquiry, inquest, tribunal.

■ **hearing aid** a small device worn by a partially deaf person to make them hear better.

hearken (or **harken**) /har-k'n/ ▸ verb (usu. **hearken to**) old use listen.

hearsay ▸ noun information received from other people which is possibly unreliable.

hearse /herss/ ▸ noun a vehicle for carrying the coffin to a funeral.

heart ▸ noun **1** the organ in the chest that pumps the blood around the body. **2** the central or innermost part of something. **3** a person's ability to feel love or compassion. **4** mood or feeling. **5** courage or enthusiasm.

SYNONYMS **1** *he poured out his heart* **emotions**, feelings, sentiments, soul, mind. **2** *he has no heart* **compassion**, sympathy, humanity, feeling(s), empathy, understanding, soul, goodwill. **3** *they lost heart* **enthusiasm**, spirit, determination, resolve, nerve; Brit. informal bottle. **4** *the heart of the city* **centre**, middle, hub, core. **5** *the heart of the matter* **essence**, crux, core, nub, root, meat, substance, kernel; informal nitty-gritty. ANTONYMS edge.

■ **heart attack** a sudden failure of the heart to work properly. **heart-rending** very sad or upsetting. **heart-searching** thorough examination of your feelings and motives. **heart-throb** a very good-looking famous man. **heart-to-heart** (of a conversation) very intimate and personal. **heart-warming** arousing feelings of happiness or pleasure. **wear your heart on your sleeve** show your feelings openly.

heartache ▸ noun emotional suffering or grief.

heartbeat ▸ noun a pulsation of the heart.

heartbreak ▸ noun extreme distress.
□ **heartbreaking** adjective **heartbroken** adjective.

heartburn ▸ noun a form of indigestion felt as a burning sensation in the chest.

hearten ▸ verb make more cheerful or confident.
□ **heartening** adjective.

heartfelt ▸ adjective deeply and strongly felt.

hearth /harth/ ▸ noun the floor or surround of a fireplace.

hearthrug ▸ noun a rug laid in front of a fireplace.

heartily ▸ adverb **1** in a hearty way. **2** very.

SYNONYMS **1** *we heartily welcome the changes* **wholeheartedly**, warmly, profoundly, eagerly, enthusiastically. **2** *they were heartily sick of her* **thoroughly**, completely, absolutely, exceedingly, downright; N. Amer. quite; informal seriously; Brit. informal jolly; N. Amer. informal real, mighty.

heartless ▸ adjective feeling no pity for other people.

hearty ▸ adjective (**heartier**, **heartiest**) **1** enthusiastic and friendly. **2** strong and healthy. **3** heartfelt. **4** (of a meal) large and filling.

SYNONYMS **1** *a hearty character* **exuberant**, jovial, ebullient, cheerful, lively, loud, animated, vivacious, energetic, spirited. **2** *hearty congratulations* **wholehearted**, heartfelt, sincere, genuine, real. **3** *a hearty woman of sixty-five* **robust**, healthy, hardy, fit, vigorous, sturdy, strong. **4** *a hearty meal* **substantial**, large, ample, satisfying, filling, generous. ANTONYMS introverted, half-hearted, frail, light.

heat ▸ noun **1** the quality of being hot. **2** hot weather or high temperature. **3** strength of feeling. **4** (**the heat**) informal great pressure to do or achieve something. **5** one of a series of races or contests held to decide who will take part in the next stage of a competition.

SYNONYMS **1** *a plant sensitive to heat* **warmth**, hotness, high temperature. **2** *he took the heat out of the dispute* **passion**, intensity, vehemence, fervour, excitement, agitation, anger. ANTONYMS cold, apathy.

▸ verb **1** make or become hot or warm. **2** (**heat up**) become more intense and exciting. **3** (**heated**) passionate.

SYNONYMS **1** *the food was heated* **warm (up)**, reheat, cook, keep warm. **2** *the pipes expand as they heat up* **get hot**, get warm, warm up; Brit. informal hot up. **3** (**heated**) *a heated argument* **vehement**, passionate, impassioned, animated, lively, acrimonious, angry, bitter, furious, fierce. **4** (**heated**) *Robert grew heated as he spoke* **excited**, animated, worked up, wound up, keyed up; informal het up. ANTONYMS cool.

■ **on heat** (of a female mammal) ready for mating.
□ **heatedly** adverb.

heater ▸ noun a device for heating something.

heath ▸ noun an area of open uncultivated land covered with heather, gorse, etc.

heathen /hee-*th*uhn/ ▸ noun old use a person who does not belong to a widely held religion.

heather ▸ noun a shrub with small purple flowers, found on moors and heaths.

heating ▸ noun equipment used to provide heat.

heatstroke ▸ noun a feverish condition caused by being exposed to very high temperatures.

heatwave ▸ noun a period of abnormally hot weather.

heave ▸ verb (**heaves, heaving, heaved** or chiefly Nautical **hove**) **1** lift or move with great effort. **2** produce a sigh noisily. **3** rise and fall. **4** try to vomit. **5** (**heave to**) Nautical come to a stop. **6** (**heaving**) Brit. informal very crowded.
  ■ **heave in sight** (or **into view**) Nautical come into view.

heaven ▸ noun **1** (in Christianity and some other religions) the place where God or the gods live and where good people go when they die. **2** (**the heavens**) literary the sky. **3** a place or state of great happiness.

SYNONYMS **1** *the good will have a place in heaven* **paradise,** the hereafter, the next world, the afterworld, nirvana, Zion, Elysium. **2** *a good book is my idea of heaven* **bliss,** ecstasy, rapture, contentment, happiness, delight, joy, paradise.
ANTONYMS hell, misery.

  ■ **in seventh heaven** very happy.

heavenly ▸ adjective **1** having to do with heaven. **2** having to do with the sky. **3** informal wonderful.

SYNONYMS **1** *heavenly choirs* **divine,** holy, celestial, angelic. **2** *a heavenly body* **celestial,** cosmic, stellar, sidereal. **3** *a heavenly morning* **delightful,** wonderful, glorious, sublime, exquisite, beautiful, lovely, gorgeous, enchanting; informal divine, super, fantastic, fabulous.
ANTONYMS mortal, infernal, terrestrial, dreadful.

  ■ **heavenly body** a planet, star, etc.

heavily ▸ adverb **1** with heavy or laborious movement. **2** extensively; severely.

SYNONYMS **1** *Dad walked heavily* **laboriously,** slowly, ponderously, awkwardly, clumsily. **2** *we were heavily defeated* **decisively,** conclusively, roundly, soundly, utterly, completely, thoroughly. **3** *he drank heavily* **excessively,** immoderately, copiously, intemperately. **4** *the area is heavily planted with trees* **densely,** closely, thickly. **5** *I became heavily involved*

deeply, extremely, greatly, exceedingly, tremendously, profoundly.
ANTONYMS easily, narrowly, moderately, thinly, slightly.

heavy ▸ adjective (**heavier, heaviest**) **1** of great weight. **2** thick or dense. **3** of more than the usual size, amount, or force. **4** hard or forceful. **5** needing a lot of physical effort. **6** informal very important or serious.

SYNONYMS **1** *a heavy box* **weighty,** hefty, substantial, ponderous, solid, dense. **2** *a heavy blow to the head* **forceful,** hard, strong, violent, powerful, mighty, sharp, severe. **3** *heavy work* **strenuous,** hard, physical, difficult, arduous, demanding, back-breaking, gruelling. **4** *heavy fighting* **intense,** fierce, relentless, severe, serious. **5** *a heavy meal* **substantial,** filling, stodgy, rich, big.
ANTONYMS light.

▸ noun (plural **heavies**) informal **1** a large, strong man. **2** an important person.
  ■ **heavy-duty** designed to withstand a lot of use or wear. **heavy-handed** clumsy, insensitive, or too forceful. **heavy industry** large-scale production of large, heavy articles and materials. **heavy metal** very loud, forceful rock music.
  □ **heaviness** noun.

heavyweight ▸ noun **1** the heaviest weight in boxing. **2** informal an influential person.

Hebrew /hee-broo/ ▸ noun an ancient language still spoken in Israel.

heckle ▸ verb (**heckles, heckling, heckled**) interrupt a public speaker with comments or abuse.
  □ **heckler** noun.

hectare /hek-tair/ ▸ noun a unit of area equal to 10,000 square metres (2.471 acres).

hectic ▸ adjective full of frantic activity.

SYNONYMS **frantic,** frenetic, frenzied, feverish, manic, busy, active, fast and furious.
ANTONYMS leisurely.

  □ **hectically** adverb.

hector ▸ verb talk to someone in a bullying way.

he'd ▸ short form **1** he had. **2** he would.

hedge ▸ noun a fence formed by bushes growing closely together.
▸ verb (**hedges, hedging, hedged**) **1** surround with a hedge. **2** avoid making a definite statement or decision.
  ■ **hedge your bets** avoid committing yourself.

hedgehog ▸ noun a small animal with a spiny coat, which can roll itself into a ball for defence.

hedgerow ▸ noun a hedge of wild shrubs and trees bordering a field.

h

hedonism ▸ noun behaviour based on the belief that pleasure is the most important thing in life.
□ **hedonist** noun **hedonistic** adjective.

heebie-jeebies ▸ plural noun (**the heebie-jeebies**) informal a state of nervous fear or anxiety.

heed ▸ verb pay attention to.

> SYNONYMS *heed the warnings* **pay attention to,** take notice of, take note of, listen to, consider, take to heart, take into account, obey, adhere to, abide by, observe.
> ANTONYMS disregard.

▸ noun attention.

> SYNONYMS *he jumped with no heed for his safety* **attention,** notice, note, regard, thought.

■ **pay** (or **take**) **heed** pay careful attention.

heedless ▸ adjective showing a reckless lack of care or attention.

heel¹ ▸ noun **1** the back part of the foot below the ankle. **2** the part of a shoe or boot supporting the heel.
▸ verb renew the heel on a shoe.
■ **take to your heels** run away.

heel² ▸ verb (of a ship) lean over to one side.

heft ▸ verb lift or carry something heavy.

hefty ▸ adjective (**heftier, heftiest**) **1** large, heavy, and powerful. **2** (of a number or amount) considerable.

> SYNONYMS **1** *a hefty young man* **burly,** sturdy, strapping, bulky, strong, muscular, big, solid, well built; informal hulking, beefy. **2** *a hefty kick* **powerful,** violent, hard, forceful. **3** *a hefty fine* **substantial,** sizeable, considerable, stiff, large, heavy; informal whopping.
> ANTONYMS slight, feeble, light, small.

hegemony /hi-**jem**-uh-ni, hi-**gem**-uh-ni/ ▸ noun formal leadership or dominance.

Hegira (or **Hejira**) /**hej**-i-ruh/ ▸ noun Muhammad's departure from Mecca to Medina in AD 622.

heifer /**hef**-er/ ▸ noun a young cow.

height ▸ noun **1** measurement from head to foot or from base to top. **2** distance above sea level or the ground. **3** the quality of being tall or high. **4** a high place. **5** the most intense or extreme part.

> SYNONYMS **1** *the height of the wall* **tallness,** stature, elevation, altitude. **2** *mountain heights* **summit,** top, peak, crest, crown, tip, cap, pinnacle. **3** *the height of their fame* **highest point,** peak, zenith, pinnacle, climax.
> ANTONYMS width, depth, nadir.

heighten ▸ verb **1** make or become more intense. **2** make higher.

> SYNONYMS **intensify,** increase, enhance, add to, augment, boost, strengthen, deepen, magnify, reinforce.
> ANTONYMS reduce.

heinous /**hay**-nuhss, **hee**-nuhss/ ▸ adjective very wicked.

heir /air/ ▸ noun **1** a person who will inherit the property or rank of another when that person dies. **2** a person who continues someone else's work.

> SYNONYMS **successor,** next in line, inheritor, beneficiary, legatee.

■ **heir apparent** (plural **heirs apparent**) **1** an heir whose rights cannot be taken away by the birth of another heir. **2** someone who is most likely to take the job or role of another person.

heiress ▸ noun a female heir.

heirloom ▸ noun a valuable object that has belonged to a family for several generations.

heist /hyst/ ▸ noun informal a robbery.

held past and past participle of HOLD.

helical /**he**-li-k'l, **hee**-li-k'l/ ▸ adjective in the shape of a helix.

helicopter ▸ noun a type of aircraft which is powered and lifted by horizontally revolving blades.

heliotrope /**heel**-i-uh-trohp/ ▸ noun a plant with sweet-smelling purple or blue flowers.

heliport ▸ noun an airport or landing place for helicopters.

helium /**hee**-li-uhm/ ▸ noun a light colourless gas that does not burn.

helix /**hee**-liks/ ▸ noun (plural **helices** /**hee**-li-seez/) an object in the shape of a spiral.

hell ▸ noun **1** (in Christianity and some other religions) a place of evil and suffering where wicked people are sent after death. **2** a state or place of great suffering.

> SYNONYMS **1 the underworld,** the netherworld, eternal damnation, perdition, hellfire, fire and brimstone, the Inferno, Hades. **2** *he made her life hell* **misery,** torture, agony, purgatory, torment, a nightmare.
> ANTONYMS heaven, bliss.

■ **hell-bent** determined to achieve something.

he'll ▸ short form **1** he shall. **2** he will.

hellebore /**hel**-i-bor/ ▸ noun a poisonous plant with large white, green, or purplish flowers.

Hellenic /he-**len**-ik/ ▸ adjective Greek.

hellhole ▸ noun a very unpleasant place.

hellish ▸ adjective informal very difficult or unpleasant.
□ **hellishly** adverb.

h

hello (or **hallo** or **hullo**) ▸ exclamation **1** used as a greeting. **2** Brit. used to express surprise or to attract someone's attention.

hellraiser ▸ noun a person who causes trouble by drunken or outrageous behaviour.

helm ▸ noun **1** a wheel or tiller for steering a ship or boat. **2** (**the helm**) the position of leader.

helmet ▸ noun a hard or padded protective hat.

helmsman ▸ noun (plural **helmsmen**) a person who steers a boat.

help ▸ verb **1** make it easier for someone to do something. **2** improve a situation or problem. **3** (**help yourself**) take something without asking for it first. **4** (**cannot help**) be unable to stop yourself doing.

SYNONYMS **1 assist,** aid, abet, lend a hand (to), give assistance to, come to the aid of, be of service to, do someone a favour, do someone a service, do someone a good turn, rally round, pitch in. **2** *this credit card helps cancer research* **support,** contribute to, give money to, donate to, promote, boost, back. **3** *sore throats are helped by lozenges* **relieve,** soothe, ease, alleviate, improve, lessen. **4** *he could not help laughing* **resist,** avoid, refrain from, keep from, stop.
ANTONYMS hinder, impede, worsen.

▸ noun a person or thing that helps someone.

SYNONYMS **1** *this could be of help* **assistance,** aid, support, succour, benefit, use, advantage, service. **2** *help for his eczema* **relief,** alleviation, improvement, healing.
ANTONYMS hindrance, aggravation.

helper ▸ noun a person who helps.

SYNONYMS **assistant,** aide, deputy, auxiliary, supporter, second, mate, right-hand man/woman, attendant.

helpful ▸ adjective **1** ready to give help. **2** useful.

SYNONYMS **1** *the staff are very helpful* **obliging,** of assistance, supportive, accommodating, cooperative, eager to please. **2** *we found your comments helpful* **useful,** beneficial, valuable, constructive, informative, instructive. **3** *a helpful new tool* **handy,** useful, convenient, practical, easy-to-use, serviceable; informal neat, nifty.
ANTONYMS unhelpful, useless.

□ **helpfully** adverb.

helping ▸ noun a portion of food served to one person at one time.

SYNONYMS **portion,** serving, piece, slice, share, plateful; informal dollop.

helpless ▸ adjective **1** unable to defend yourself or to act without help. **2** uncontrollable.

SYNONYMS **dependent,** incapable, powerless, paralysed, defenceless, vulnerable, exposed, unprotected.
ANTONYMS independent.

□ **helplessly** adverb.

helpline ▸ noun a telephone service providing help with problems.

helpmate (or **helpmeet**) ▸ noun a helpful companion.

helter-skelter ▸ adjective & adverb in a hasty and confused or disorganized way.
▸ noun Brit. a tall slide winding around a tower at a fair.

hem ▸ noun the edge of a piece of cloth or clothing which has been turned under and sewn.
▸ verb (**hems, hemming, hemmed**) **1** give something a hem. **2** (**hem someone/thing in**) surround someone or something and restrict their movement.

hematology etc. US spelling of HAEMATOLOGY etc.

hemisphere ▸ noun **1** a half of a sphere. **2** a half of the earth.
□ **hemispherical** adjective.

hemline ▸ noun the level of the lower edge of a skirt or coat.

hemlock ▸ noun a poison made from a plant with small white flowers.

hemp ▸ noun **1** the cannabis plant, the fibre of which is used to make rope, fabrics, etc. **2** the drug cannabis.

hen ▸ noun a female bird, especially of a domestic fowl.
■ **hen night** Brit. informal an all-female celebration for a woman who is about to get married.

hence ▸ adverb **1** for this reason. **2** from now.

SYNONYMS **consequently,** as a consequence, for this reason, therefore, so, accordingly, as a result, that being so.

henceforth (or **henceforward**) ▸ adverb from this time on.

henchman ▸ noun (plural **henchmen**) chiefly disapproving a faithful follower or assistant.

henna ▸ noun a reddish-brown dye made from the powdered leaves of a tropical shrub.
□ **hennaed** adjective.

henpecked ▸ adjective (of a man) continually nagged or criticized by his wife.

henry ▸ noun (plural **henries** or **henrys**) the basic unit for measuring inductance.

hepatitis /he-puh-**ty**-tiss/ ▸ noun a serious disease of the liver, mainly transmitted by viruses.

h

heptagon /hep-tuh-guhn/ ▸ noun a figure with seven straight sides and angles.
□ **heptagonal** adjective.

heptathlon ▸ noun an athletic contest for women that consists of seven separate events.
□ **heptathlete** noun.

her ▸ pronoun used as the object of a verb or preposition to refer to a female person or animal previously mentioned.
▸ possessive determiner belonging to or associated with a female person or animal previously mentioned.

herald ▸ noun 1 (in the past) a person who carried official messages and supervised tournaments. 2 a sign that something is about to happen or arrive.
▸ verb 1 be a sign that something is about to happen or arrive. 2 describe in enthusiastic terms.

heraldic /he-ral-dik/ ▸ adjective having to do with heraldry.

heraldry ▸ noun the system by which coats of arms are organized and controlled.

herb ▸ noun 1 a plant used for flavouring food or in medicine. 2 Botany a plant which dies down to the ground after flowering.
□ **herbal** adjective.

herbaceous /her-bay-shuhss/ ▸ adjective relating to herbs (in the botanical sense).
■ **herbaceous border** a garden border containing plants which flower every year.

herbalism ▸ noun the use of plants in medicine and cookery.
□ **herbalist** noun.

herbicide /her-bi-syd/ ▸ noun a substance used to kill unwanted plants.

herbivore /her-bi-vor/ ▸ noun an animal that feeds on plants.
□ **herbivorous** /her-biv-uh-ruhss/ adjective.

Herculean /her-kyuu-lee-uhn/ ▸ adjective needing great strength or effort: a Herculean task.

herd ▸ noun 1 a large group of animals that live or are kept together. 2 disapproving a large group of people.

SYNONYMS **drove**, flock, pack, fold, swarm, mass, crowd, horde.

▸ verb make animals or people move in a large group.

here ▸ adverb in, at, or to this place or position.

hereabouts (or hereabout) ▸ adverb near this place.

hereafter ▸ adverb formal from now on or at some time in the future.
▸ noun (the hereafter) life after death.

hereby ▸ adverb formal as a result of this.

hereditary ▸ adjective 1 passed on by parents to their children or young.

2 having to do with inheritance.

SYNONYMS 1 a hereditary right **inherited**, bequeathed, handed down, passed down, family, ancestral. 2 a hereditary disease **genetic**, inborn, inherited, inbred, innate, in the family, in the blood, in the genes.
ANTONYMS acquired, infectious.

heredity /hi-red-i-ti/ ▸ noun 1 the passing on of characteristics from one generation to another. 2 the inheriting of a title, office, etc.

herein ▸ adverb formal in this document, book, or matter.

heresy ▸ noun (plural heresies) 1 belief which goes against traditional religious teachings. 2 opinion which is very different from what is generally accepted.

heretic ▸ noun a person who is guilty of heresy.
□ **heretical** adjective.

hereto ▸ adverb formal to this matter or document.

heretofore ▸ adverb formal before now.

herewith ▸ adverb formal with this.

heritable ▸ adjective able to be inherited.

heritage ▸ noun valued things such as historic buildings that have been passed down from previous generations.

SYNONYMS 1 Europe's cultural heritage **tradition**, history, past, background, culture, customs. 2 his Greek heritage **ancestry**, lineage, descent, extraction, parentage, roots, heredity.

hermaphrodite /her-maf-ruh-dyt/ ▸ noun a person, animal, or plant with both male and female sex organs or characteristics.

hermetic /her-met-ik/ ▸ adjective (of a seal or closure) complete and airtight.
□ **hermetically** adverb.

hermit ▸ noun a person who lives completely alone, especially for religious reasons.

SYNONYMS **recluse**, loner; historical anchorite, anchoress; old use eremite.

hernia ▸ noun a condition in which part of an organ pushes through the wall of the cavity containing it.

hero ▸ noun (plural heroes) 1 a person who is admired for their courage or outstanding achievements. 2 the chief male character in a book, play, or film.

SYNONYMS 1 a sporting hero **star**, superstar, megastar, idol, celebrity, favourite, darling; informal celeb. 2 the hero of the film **main character**, starring role, male protagonist, (male) lead, leading man; informal good guy.
ANTONYMS loser, supporting role, villain.

■ **hero worship** extreme admiration for someone.

heroic ▶ adjective **1** very brave. **2** very grand or ambitious in scale.

> SYNONYMS **brave,** courageous, valiant, intrepid, bold, fearless, daring; informal gutsy, spunky.
> ANTONYMS cowardly.

▶ noun (**heroics**) brave or dramatic behaviour or talk.
□ **heroically** adverb.

heroin ▶ noun a very addictive painkilling drug.

heroine ▶ noun **1** a woman admired for her courage or outstanding achievements. **2** the chief female character in a book, play, or film.

> SYNONYMS **1** *a sporting heroine* **star,** superstar, megastar, idol, celebrity, favourite, darling; informal celeb. **2** *the film's heroine* **main character,** female protagonist, lead, leading lady, prima donna, diva.
> ANTONYMS loser, supporting role.

heroism ▶ noun great bravery.

> SYNONYMS **bravery,** courage, valour, daring, fearlessness, pluck; informal guts, spunk; Brit. informal bottle; N. Amer. informal moxie.
> ANTONYMS cowardice.

heron ▶ noun a large fish-eating bird with long legs, a long neck, and a long pointed bill.

herpes /her-peez/ ▶ noun an infectious disease that causes blisters on the skin.

herring ▶ noun a silvery fish which is found in shoals and is used for food.

herringbone ▶ noun a zigzag pattern consisting of columns of short slanting parallel lines.

hers ▶ possessive pronoun used to refer to something belonging to or associated with a female person or animal previously mentioned.

> ✔ no apostrophe: **hers**.

herself ▶ pronoun **1** used as the object of a verb or preposition to refer to a female person or animal previously mentioned as the subject of the clause. **2** she or her personally.

hertz ▶ noun (plural **hertz**) the basic unit of frequency, equal to one cycle per second.

he's ▶ short form **1** he is. **2** he has.

hesitant ▶ adjective slow to act or speak through indecision or reluctance.

> SYNONYMS **1** *she is hesitant about buying* **uncertain,** undecided, unsure, doubtful, dubious, nervous, ambivalent, in two minds; Brit. havering, humming and hawing; informal iffy. **2** *a hesitant child* **timid,** diffident, shy, bashful, insecure.
> ANTONYMS certain, decisive, confident.

□ **hesitancy** noun **hesitantly** adverb.

hesitate ▶ verb (**hesitates, hesitating, hesitated**) **1** pause indecisively. **2** be reluctant to do something.

> SYNONYMS **1** *she hesitated, unsure of what to say* **pause,** delay, wait, stall, be uncertain, be unsure, be doubtful, be indecisive, vacillate, waver; Brit. haver; informal dilly-dally. **2** *don't hesitate to ask* **be reluctant,** be unwilling, be disinclined, scruple, have misgivings about, have qualms about, think twice about.
> ANTONYMS plunge in.

□ **hesitation** noun.

hessian ▶ noun a strong, coarse fabric.

heterodox ▶ adjective not following traditional standards or beliefs.
□ **heterodoxy** noun.

heterogeneous /het-uh-ruh-**jee**-ni-uhss/ ▶ adjective varied.
□ **heterogeneity** /het-uh-ruh-juh-**nee**-i-ti/ noun.

heterosexual ▶ adjective sexually attracted to people of the opposite sex.
▶ noun a heterosexual person.
□ **heterosexuality** noun.

het up ▶ adjective informal angry and agitated.

hew ▶ verb (**hews, hewing, hewed**; past participle **hewn** or **hewed**) chop wood, coal, etc. with an axe or other tool.

hex N. Amer. ▶ verb cast a spell on.
▶ noun a magic spell.

hexagon /**hek**-suh-guhn/ ▶ noun a figure with six straight sides and angles.
□ **hexagonal** adjective.

hexagram ▶ noun a six-pointed star formed by two intersecting triangles.

hexameter /hek-**sam**-i-ter/ ▶ noun a line of verse made up of six groups of syllables.

hey ▶ exclamation used to attract someone's attention or to express surprise, interest, etc.

heyday ▶ noun (**your heyday**) the period when you are most successful or active.

HGV ▶ abbreviation Brit. heavy goods vehicle.

hiatus /hy-**ay**-tuhss/ ▶ noun (plural **hiatuses**) a pause or gap in a series or sequence.

hibernate ▶ verb (**hibernates, hibernating, hibernated**) (of an animal) spend the winter in a state like deep sleep.
□ **hibernation** noun.

hibiscus /hi-**biss**-kuhss/ ▶ noun a plant with large brightly coloured flowers.

hiccup (or **hiccough**) /**hik**-up/ ▶ noun **1** a sudden gulping sound caused by an involuntary spasm of the diaphragm. **2** a minor setback.

▸ verb (**hiccups, hiccuping, hiccuped**) make the sound of a hiccup.

hick ▸ noun informal, chiefly N. Amer. an unsophisticated country person.

hickory ▸ noun a tree with edible nuts.

hide¹ ▸ verb (**hides, hiding, hid**; past participle **hidden**) 1 put or keep something out of sight. 2 get into a place where you cannot be seen. 3 keep secret.

SYNONYMS 1 *he hid the money* conceal, secrete, put out of sight, cache; informal stash. 2 (**hidden**) *a hidden camera* concealed, secret, invisible, unseen, camouflaged. 3 *they hid in an air vent* conceal yourself, secrete yourself, take cover, lie low, go to ground; informal hole up. 4 *clouds hid the moon* obscure, block out, blot out, obstruct, cloud, shroud, veil, eclipse. 5 *he could not hide his dislike* conceal, keep secret, cover up, keep quiet about, bottle up, suppress, disguise, mask; informal keep a/the lid on. 6 (**hidden**) *a hidden meaning* obscure, unclear, concealed, cryptic, mysterious, secret, covert, abstruse, deep.
ANTONYMS flaunt, reveal, emerge, betray.

▸ noun Brit. a concealed shelter used to watch wild animals or birds.
■ **hide-and-seek** a game in which one player hides and the others have to look for them.

hide² ▸ noun the skin of an animal.

hideaway ▸ noun a hiding place.

SYNONYMS retreat, refuge, hiding place, hideout, safe house, den, bolt-hole; informal hidey-hole.

hidebound ▸ adjective unwilling to give up old-fashioned ideas in favour of new ways of thinking.

hideous ▸ adjective 1 very ugly. 2 very unpleasant.

SYNONYMS 1 *a hideous face* ugly, repulsive, repellent, unsightly, revolting, grotesque. 2 *hideous cases of torture* horrific, terrible, appalling, awful, dreadful, frightful, horrible, horrendous, horrifying, shocking, sickening, gruesome, ghastly.
ANTONYMS beautiful, pleasant.

□ **hideously** adverb.

hideout ▸ noun a hiding place.

hiding ▸ noun a physical beating.

SYNONYMS beating, thrashing, whipping, drubbing; informal licking, belting, pasting, walloping.

hierarchy /hy-uh-rah-ki/ ▸ noun (plural **hierarchies**) 1 a system in which people are ranked one above the other according to status or authority. 2 a classification of things according to their relative importance.

SYNONYMS ranking, order, pecking order, grading, ladder, scale.

□ **hierarchical** adjective.

✔ **Hierarchy** is spelt **-ie-**, not **-ei-**, and remember the second **r**.

hieroglyphics ▸ plural noun writing in which a picture represents a word, syllable, or sound, as used in ancient Egypt.

hi-fi ▸ noun (plural **hi-fis**) a set of equipment for reproducing high-fidelity sound.
▸ adjective having to do with high-fidelity sound.

higgledy-piggledy ▸ adverb & adjective in confusion or disorder.

high ▸ adjective 1 extending far upwards. 2 of a particular height. 3 far above ground or sea level. 4 large in amount, size, or intensity. 5 (of a period or movement) at its peak. 6 great in status; important. 7 (of a sound or note) not deep or low. 8 informal under the influence of drugs or alcohol. 9 (of food) beginning to go bad.

SYNONYMS 1 *a high mountain* tall, lofty, towering, giant, big, multi-storey, high-rise, elevated. 2 *a high position in the government* high-ranking, leading, top, prominent, senior, influential, powerful, important, exalted; N. Amer. ranking. 3 *high prices* inflated, excessive, unreasonable, expensive, exorbitant, extortionate; informal steep, stiff. 4 *a high voice* high-pitched, shrill, piercing, squeaky, penetrating, soprano, treble, falsetto. 5 *high on drugs* intoxicated, befuddled, delirious, hallucinating; informal high as a kite, stoned, wrecked, off your head.
ANTONYMS low, short, lowly, deep.

▸ noun 1 a high point, level, or figure. 2 an area of high atmospheric pressure. 3 informal a state of high spirits.
▸ adverb (of a sound) at a high pitch.

SYNONYMS *a jet flew high overhead* at a great height, high up, way up, at altitude, in the sky, aloft, overhead, to a great height.
ANTONYMS low.

■ **High Church** the section of the Church of England which gives an important place to ritual and the authority of bishops and priests. **high commission** an embassy of one Commonwealth country in another. **higher education** education to degree level or its equivalent, provided at universities and colleges. **high explosive** powerful chemical explosive used in shells and bombs. **high fidelity** the reproduction of sound with little distortion. **high-flown** grand-sounding. **high-flyer** (or **high-flier**) a very successful person. **high-handed** using authority without considering the feelings of other people. **high jinks** high-spirited fun. **high jump** an athletic event in which competitors try to jump over a bar. **high-rise** (of a building) having many storeys. **high school** a secondary school. **the high seas** the areas of the sea that are not under the control of any one country. **high-spirited** lively and cheerful. **high tea** Brit. a meal eaten in the late afternoon or early evening. **high-tech** (also **hi-tech**) using advanced technology. **high technology** advanced technology. **high tide** the time when the sea is closest to the land.

highbrow ▸ adjective very intellectual or refined in taste.

highfalutin /hy-fuh-**loo**-tin/ ▸ adjective informal grand or self-important in a pretentious way.

highland (or **highlands**) ▸ noun **1** an area of high or mountainous land. **2** (**the Highlands**) the mountainous northern part of Scotland.
□ **highlander** noun.

highlight ▸ noun **1** an outstanding part of an event or period of time. **2** a bright area in a picture. **3** (**highlights**) bright tints in hair, created by bleaching or dyeing.

> SYNONYMS *the highlight of his career* **high point,** climax, peak, pinnacle, height, zenith, summit, focus, feature.
> ANTONYMS low point.

▸ verb **1** draw attention to. **2** create highlights in hair.

> SYNONYMS *he has highlighted shortcomings in the plan* **spotlight,** call attention to, focus on, underline, show up, bring out, accentuate, accent, stress, emphasize.
> ANTONYMS play down.

□ **highlighter** noun.

highly ▸ adverb **1** to a high degree or level. **2** favourably.

> SYNONYMS **very,** extremely, immensely, thoroughly, decidedly, exceptionally, extraordinarily; N. English right; informal awfully, terribly, seriously; Brit. informal dead, jolly; N. Amer. informal real, mighty, awful.
> ANTONYMS slightly.

■ **highly strung** Brit. very nervous and easily upset.

Highness ▸ noun (**His, Her, Your Highness**) a title given to a person of royal rank.

highway ▸ noun **1** chiefly N. Amer. a main road. **2** a public road.

highwayman ▸ noun (plural **highwaymen**) (in the past) a man who held up and robbed travellers.

hijack ▸ verb **1** illegally seize control of an aircraft while it is travelling somewhere.

2 take over something and use it for a different purpose.

> SYNONYMS **commandeer,** seize, take over, appropriate, expropriate.

▸ noun an act of hijacking.
□ **hijacker** noun.

hike ▸ noun **1** a long walk or walking tour. **2** a sharp increase.

> SYNONYMS **1** *a hike across country* **walk,** trek, tramp, trudge, slog, march, ramble. **2** *a price hike* **increase,** advance, boom.
> ANTONYMS reduction.

▸ verb (**hikes, hiking, hiked**) **1** go on a hike. **2** pull or lift up clothing. **3** increase a price sharply.

> SYNONYMS **1** *they hiked across Europe* **walk,** trek, tramp, trudge, slog, march, ramble, backpack. **2** *they hiked the price* **increase,** raise, up, put up, push up; informal jack up, bump up.
> ANTONYMS reduce.

□ **hiker** noun.

hilarious ▸ adjective very amusing.

> SYNONYMS **very funny,** hysterical, uproarious, rib-tickling; informal side-splitting, priceless, a scream, a hoot.
> ANTONYMS unfunny, serious.

□ **hilariously** adverb **hilarity** noun.

hill ▸ noun a naturally raised area of land, not as high as a mountain.

> SYNONYMS **high ground,** hillock, hillside, rise, mound, knoll, hummock, fell, mountain; Scottish brae.

■ **over the hill** informal old and past your best.

hillbilly ▸ noun (plural **hillbillies**) N. Amer. informal an unsophisticated country person.

hillock ▸ noun a small hill or mound.

hilly ▸ adjective (**hillier, hilliest**) having many hills.

hilt ▸ noun the handle of a sword, dagger, or knife.
■ **to the hilt** completely.

him ▸ pronoun used as the object of a verb or preposition to refer to a male person or animal previously mentioned.

himself ▸ pronoun **1** used as the object of a verb or preposition to refer to a male person or animal previously mentioned as the subject of the clause. **2** he or him personally.

hind¹ ▸ adjective situated at the back.

hind² ▸ noun a female deer.

hinder ▸ verb (**hinders, hindering, hindered**) delay or obstruct.

> SYNONYMS **hamper,** impede, inhibit, thwart, foil, delay, interfere with, slow down, hold back, hold up, restrict,

h

handicap, hamstring.
ANTONYMS ease.

Hindi ▸ noun a language of northern India.

hindmost ▸ adjective furthest back.

hindquarters ▸ plural noun the rear part and hind legs of a four-legged animal.

hindrance ▸ noun a thing that hinders someone or something.

> ✔ no **e**: hind**r**ance, not hind**er**ance.

hindsight ▸ noun understanding of a situation or event after it has happened.

Hindu ▸ noun (plural **Hindus**) a follower of Hinduism.

Hinduism ▸ noun a religion of the Indian subcontinent, with a large number of gods and goddesses.

hinge ▸ noun a movable joint or mechanism by which a door, gate, or lid opens and closes.
▸ verb (**hinges, hingeing** or **hinging, hinged**) **1** attach or join with a hinge. **2** (**hinge on**) depend entirely on.

hint ▸ noun **1** a slight or indirect suggestion. **2** a very small trace of something. **3** a small piece of practical information.

> SYNONYMS **1** *a hint that he would leave* **clue**, inkling, suggestion, indication, sign, signal, intimation. **2** *a hint of garlic* **trace**, touch, suspicion, suggestion, dash, soupçon; informal smidgen, tad. **3** *handy hints about painting* **tip**, suggestion, pointer, guideline, recommendation.

▸ verb suggest indirectly.

> SYNONYMS *what are you hinting?* **imply**, insinuate, intimate, suggest, refer to, drive at, mean; informal get at.

hinterland ▸ noun **1** the areas of a country away from the coast. **2** the area around or beyond a major town.

hip¹ ▸ noun a projection formed by the pelvis and upper thigh bone on each side of the body.

hip² ▸ noun the fruit of a rose.

hip³ ▸ adjective (**hipper, hippest**) informal fashionable.
□ **hipness** noun.

hip hop ▸ noun a style of pop music featuring rap with an electronic backing.

hippo = HIPPOPOTAMUS.

hippopotamus ▸ noun (plural **hippopotamuses** or **hippopotami** /hip-puh-pot-uh-my/) a large African animal with massive jaws, living partly on land and partly in water.

hippy (or **hippie**) ▸ noun (plural **hippies**) a young person who rejects traditional social values and dresses in an unconventional way.

hipsters ▸ plural noun Brit. trousers cut to fit and fasten at the hips.

hire ▸ verb (**hires, hiring, hired**) **1** pay to be allowed to use something temporarily. **2** (**hire something out**) allow something to be used temporarily in return for payment. **3** pay someone to work for you.

> SYNONYMS **1** *we hired a car* **rent**, lease, charter. **2** *they hire workers locally* **employ**, engage, recruit, appoint, take on, sign up.
> ANTONYMS dismiss.

▸ noun the action of hiring.
■ **hire purchase** Brit. a system by which you pay for a thing in regular instalments while having the use of it.

hireling ▸ noun a person who is willing to do any kind of work as long as they are paid.

hirsute /her-syoot/ ▸ adjective hairy.

his ▸ possessive determiner & pronoun belonging to or associated with a male person or animal previously mentioned.

Hispanic ▸ adjective having to do with Spain or other Spanish-speaking countries.

hiss ▸ verb **1** make a sharp sound like that made when pronouncing the letter *s*. **2** whisper something in an urgent or angry way.

> SYNONYMS **1** *the escaping gas hissed* **fizz**, whistle, wheeze. **2** *the audience hissed* **jeer**, catcall, whistle, hoot.
> ANTONYMS cheer.

▸ noun a hissing sound.

> SYNONYMS **1** *the hiss of steam* **fizz**, whistle, wheeze. **2** *the speaker received hisses* **jeer**, catcall, whistle, abuse, derision.
> ANTONYMS cheer.

histamine /hiss-tuh-meen/ ▸ noun a substance which is released by cells in response to an injury or allergy.

histology ▸ noun the scientific study of the structure of living tissues.
□ **histologist** noun.

historian ▸ noun an expert in history.

historic ▸ adjective famous or important in history, or likely to be seen as such in the future.

> SYNONYMS **significant**, notable, important, momentous, memorable, groundbreaking; informal earth-shattering.
> ANTONYMS insignificant.

historical ▸ adjective **1** having to do with history. **2** belonging to or set in the past.

> SYNONYMS **1** *historical evidence* **documented**, recorded, chronicled, authentic, factual, actual. **2** *historical figures* **past**, bygone, ancient, old,

former.
ANTONYMS anecdotal, contemporary.
□ **historically** adverb.

history ▸ noun (plural **histories**) **1** the study of past events. **2** the past considered as a whole. **3** the past events connected with someone or something. **4** a continuous record of past events or trends.

SYNONYMS **1** *my interest in history* **the past,** former times, the olden days, yesterday, antiquity. **2** *a history of the Civil War* **chronicle,** archive, record, report, narrative, account, study. **3** *she gave details of her history* **background,** past, life story, experiences, record.

histrionic ▸ adjective too theatrical or dramatic.
▸ noun (**histrionics**) exaggerated behaviour intended to attract attention.

hit ▸ verb (**hits, hitting, hit**) **1** bring your hand or a tool, weapon, bat, etc. against someone or something quickly and with force. **2** (of something moving) come into contact with someone or something quickly and forcefully. **3** reach a target. **4** cause harm or distress to. **5** be suddenly realized by. **6** (**hit out**) criticize or attack strongly. **7** informal reach. **8** (**hit on**) suddenly discover or think of.

SYNONYMS **1** **strike,** beat, punch, thump, thrash; informal whack, wallop, bash, clout, belt; Brit. informal stick one on; N. Amer. informal slug; Austral./NZ informal dong, quilt. **2** *a car hit the barrier* **crash into,** run into, smash into, knock into, bump into, plough into, collide with, meet head-on. **3** *the tragedy hit her hard* **devastate,** affect badly, upset, shatter, crush, traumatize; informal knock sideways; Brit. informal knock for six.

▸ noun **1** an instance of hitting or being hit. **2** a successful film, pop record, etc. **3** an instance of a website being accessed or a word being found in an Internet search. **4** informal, chiefly N. Amer. a murder carried out by a criminal organization. **5** informal a dose of an addictive drug.

SYNONYMS **1** **blow,** thump, punch, knock, bang; informal whack, wallop, bash, clout, belt; N. Amer. informal slug; Austral./NZ king-hit. **2** *he directed many big hits* **success,** sell-out, winner, triumph, sensation, best-seller; informal smash hit, chart-topper, crowd-puller.
ANTONYMS failure.

■ **hit-and-miss** not done in a careful, planned way. **hit-and-run** (of a road accident) in which the driver responsible leaves rapidly without helping the other people involved. **hit it off** informal get on well with someone.

hitch ▸ verb **1** move into a different position with a jerk. **2** fasten with a rope. **3** travel by hitchhiking.

SYNONYMS **1** *she hitched the blanket around her* **pull,** lift, raise; informal yank. **2** *Tom hitched the pony to his cart* **harness,** yoke, couple, fasten, connect, attach.

▸ noun a temporary difficulty.

SYNONYMS *it went without a hitch* **problem,** difficulty, snag, setback, obstacle, complication; informal glitch, hiccup.

□ **hitcher** noun.

hitchhike ▸ verb travel by getting free lifts in passing vehicles.
□ **hitchhiker** noun.

hither ▸ adverb old use to or towards this place.

hitherto ▸ adverb until this time.

HIV ▸ abbreviation human immunodeficiency virus (the virus causing Aids).

hive ▸ noun **1** a beehive. **2** a place full of people working hard.
■ **hive something off** transfer part of a business to new ownership.

hives ▸ plural noun a rash of red, itchy marks on the skin, caused by an allergy.

HM ▸ abbreviation Her (or His) Majesty or Majesty's.

HMS ▸ abbreviation Her or His Majesty's Ship.

HND ▸ abbreviation Higher National Diploma.

hoard ▸ noun a store of money, valued objects, or useful information.

SYNONYMS *a secret hoard* **cache,** stockpile, store, collection, supply, reserve; informal stash.

▸ verb build up a store of something.

SYNONYMS *they hoarded their rations* **stockpile,** store up, put aside, put by, lay by, set aside, cache, save, squirrel away; informal salt away.
ANTONYMS squander.

□ **hoarder** noun.

❗ Don't confuse **hoard** with **horde**: a **hoard** is a store of something valuable; a **horde** is a large group of people.

hoarding ▸ noun Brit. a large board used to display advertisements.

hoar frost ▸ noun a feathery greyish-white deposit of frost.

hoarse ▸ adjective (of a voice) rough and harsh.
□ **hoarsely** adverb.

hoary ▸ adjective (**hoarier, hoariest**) **1** greyish-white. **2** having grey hair. **3** old and unoriginal.

hoax ▸ noun a humorous or cruel trick.

SYNONYMS **practical joke**, prank, trick, deception, fraud; informal con, spoof, wind-up, scam.

▶ verb deceive with a hoax.
□ **hoaxer** noun.

hob ▶ noun Brit. the flat top part of a cooker, with hotplates or burners.

hobble ▶ verb (**hobbles, hobbling, hobbled**) **1** walk awkwardly. **2** strap together the legs of a horse to stop it wandering away.

hobby ▶ noun (plural **hobbies**) an activity that you do regularly in your leisure time for pleasure.

SYNONYMS **pastime**, leisure activity, sideline, diversion, relaxation, recreation, amusement.

■ **hobby horse 1** a child's toy consisting of a stick with a model of a horse's head at one end. **2** something that a person talks about very often.

hobgoblin ▶ noun a mischievous imp.

hobnail ▶ noun a short nail used to strengthen the soles of boots.
□ **hobnailed** adjective.

hobnob ▶ verb (**hobnobs, hobnobbing, hobnobbed**) informal spend time with rich or important people.

hobo ▶ noun (plural **hoboes** or **hobos**) N. Amer. a homeless person.

Hobson's choice ▶ noun a choice of taking what is offered or nothing at all.

hock¹ ▶ noun the middle joint in an animal's back leg.

hock² ▶ noun Brit. a dry white wine from Germany.

hock³ ▶ verb informal pawn an object.
■ **in hock** in debt.

hockey ▶ noun a team game played using hooked sticks to drive a small, hard ball towards a goal.

hocus-pocus ▶ noun **1** meaningless talk used to deceive people. **2** a form of words used by a magician.

hod ▶ noun **1** a builder's V-shaped open trough attached to a short pole, used for carrying bricks. **2** a metal container for storing coal.

hoe ▶ noun a long-handled gardening tool with a thin metal blade.
▶ verb (**hoes, hoeing, hoed**) break up soil or dig up weeds with a hoe.

hoedown ▶ noun N. Amer. a lively folk dance.

hog ▶ noun a castrated male pig reared for its meat.
▶ verb (**hogs, hogging, hogged**) informal take or hoard selfishly.
■ **go the whole hog** informal do something fully.

Hogmanay /hog-muh-nay/ ▶ noun (in Scotland) New Year's Eve.

hogshead ▶ noun a large cask.

hogwash ▶ noun informal nonsense.

hoick ▶ verb Brit. informal lift or pull with a jerk.

hoi polloi /hoy puh-loy/ ▶ plural noun disapproving the common people.

hoist ▶ verb **1** raise with ropes and pulleys. **2** haul or lift up.

SYNONYMS *we hoisted the mainsail* **raise**, lift, haul up, heave up, winch up, pull up, elevate.
ANTONYMS lower.

▶ noun a piece of equipment for hoisting something.

SYNONYMS *a mechanical hoist* **crane**, winch, pulley, windlass.

hoity-toity ▶ adjective informal snobbish.

hokey-cokey ▶ noun a group song and dance performed in a circle, involving the shaking of each limb in turn.

hokum /hoh-kuhm/ ▶ noun informal **1** nonsense. **2** unoriginal or sentimental material in a film, book, etc.

hold ▶ verb (**holds, holding, held**) **1** grasp, carry, or support. **2** contain or be able to contain. **3** have, own, or occupy. **4** keep or detain someone. **5** stay or keep at a certain level. **6** (**hold someone to**) make someone keep a promise. **7** (**hold someone/thing in**) have a particular attitude to someone or something.

SYNONYMS **1** *she held a suitcase* **clasp**, clutch, grasp, grip, clench, cling to, hold on to, embrace, hug, squeeze. **2** *he was being held by police* **detain**, imprison, lock up, keep behind bars, confine, intern. **3** *the tank held 250 gallons* **take**, contain, accommodate, fit, have room for. **4** *the court held that there was no evidence* **maintain**, consider, take the view, believe, think, feel, deem, be of the opinion, rule, decide; informal reckon. **5** *they held a meeting* **convene**, call, summon, conduct, organize, run.
ANTONYMS release.

▶ noun **1** a grip. **2** a place to grip while climbing. **3** a degree of control. **4** a storage space in the lower part of a ship or aircraft.

SYNONYMS **1** *she kept a hold on my hand* **grip**, grasp, clasp, clutch. **2** *Tom had a hold over his father* **influence**, power, control, dominance, authority, sway. **3** *the military tightened their hold on the capital* **control**, grip, power, stranglehold.

■ **hold back** hesitate. **hold fast 1** remain tightly secured. **2** stick to a principle. **hold forth** talk at length. **hold someone/thing off** resist an attacker. **hold on 1** wait. **2** keep going in difficult circumstances. **hold out 1** resist difficult circumstances. **2** continue to be enough; last. **hold something over** postpone something. **hold someone/thing up 1** delay someone or something. **2** rob someone using the threat of violence. **no holds barred** without restrictions. **on hold** waiting to be dealt with or connected by telephone.

holdall ▶ noun Brit. a large bag with handles and a shoulder strap.

holder ▶ noun **1** a person who holds something. **2** a device for holding something.

> SYNONYMS **1** *the licence holder* **bearer,** owner, possessor, keeper. **2** *a knife holder* **container,** receptacle, case, cover, housing, sheath.

holding ▶ noun **1** an area of land held by lease. **2** (**holdings**) stocks and property owned by a person or organization.

hold-up ▶ noun **1** a cause of delay. **2** a robbery carried out with the threat of violence.

> SYNONYMS **1** *a hold-up in production* **delay,** setback, hitch, snag, difficulty, problem, glitch, hiccup, traffic jam, tailback; informal snarl-up. **2** *a bank hold-up* **robbery,** raid, armed robbery, mugging; informal stick-up; N. Amer. informal heist.

hole ▶ noun **1** a hollow space or opening in a solid object or surface. **2** (in golf) a hollow in the ground which you try to hit the ball into. **3** informal an awkward or unpleasant place or situation.

> SYNONYMS **1** *a hole in the roof* **opening,** aperture, gap, space, vent, chink, breach, crack, rupture, puncture. **2** *a hole in the ground* **pit,** crater, depression, hollow, cavern, cave, chamber. **3** *the badger's hole* **burrow,** lair, den, earth, sett.

▶ verb (**holes, holing, holed**) **1** make a hole or holes in. **2** (in golf) hit the ball into a hole. **3** (**hole up**) informal hide yourself.
□ **holey** adjective.

Holi /hoh-li/ ▶ noun a Hindu spring festival.

holiday ▶ noun **1** Brit. a time spent away from home for rest or enjoyment. **2** a day when most people do not have to work.

> SYNONYMS **vacation,** break, rest, recess, time off, leave, day off, festival, feast day.

▶ verb spend a holiday.

holidaymaker ▶ noun Brit. a tourist.

holiness ▶ noun **1** the state of being holy. **2** (**His** or **Your Holiness**) the title of the Pope and some other religious leaders.

holistic ▶ adjective treating the whole person rather than just the symptoms of a disease.
□ **holism** noun.

hollandaise sauce /hol-uhn-**dayz**/ ▶ noun a creamy sauce made of butter, egg yolks, and vinegar.

holler informal ▶ verb (**hollers, hollering, hollered**) give a loud shout.
▶ noun a loud shout.

hollow ▶ adjective **1** having empty space inside. **2** curving inwards. **3** (of a sound) echoing. **4** worthless or not sincere.

> SYNONYMS **1** *a hollow tube* **empty,** hollowed out, void. **2** *hollow cheeks* **sunken,** deep-set, concave, depressed, recessed. **3** *a hollow promise* **insincere,** hypocritical, feigned.
> ANTONYMS solid, chubby, convex, sincere.

▶ noun **1** a hole. **2** a small valley.

> SYNONYMS **1** *a hollow under the tree* **hole,** pit, cavity, crater, trough, depression, indentation, dip. **2** *the village lay in a hollow* **valley,** vale, dale, dell.
> ANTONYMS rise.

▶ verb (usu. **hollow something out**) form by making a hole.

> SYNONYMS *hollowed out of rock* **gouge,** scoop, dig, cut, excavate, channel.

holly ▶ noun an evergreen shrub with prickly dark green leaves and red berries.

hollyhock ▶ noun a tall plant with large showy flowers.

holocaust /hol-uh-kawst/ ▶ noun **1** destruction or killing on a very large scale. **2** (**the Holocaust**) the mass murder of Jews under the German Nazi regime in World War II.

hologram ▶ noun a picture that looks three-dimensional when it is lit up.
□ **holographic** adjective.

holster ▶ noun a holder for carrying a handgun.

holy ▶ adjective (**holier, holiest**) **1** dedicated to God or a religious purpose. **2** morally and spiritually good.

> SYNONYMS **1** *holy men* **saintly,** godly, pious, religious, devout, God-fearing, spiritual. **2** *a holy place* **sacred,** consecrated, hallowed, sanctified, venerated, revered.
> ANTONYMS sinful, irreligious, cursed.

■ **the holy of holies** a very sacred place. **Holy Spirit** (or **Holy Ghost**) (in Christianity) God as a spirit that is active in the world. **Holy Week** the week before Easter.

homage ▶ noun honour shown to someone in public.

> SYNONYMS **respect,** honour, reverence, worship, admiration, esteem, adulation, tribute.
> ANTONYMS contempt.

homburg ▶ noun a man's felt hat with a narrow curled brim.

h

home ▸ noun **1** the place where you live. **2** a place where people who need special care live. **3** a place where something flourishes or where it started.

> SYNONYMS **1** *they fled their homes* **residence,** house, accommodation, property, quarters, lodgings, address, place; informal **pad;** formal abode, dwelling. **2** *I am far from my home* **homeland,** native land, home town, birthplace, roots, fatherland, mother country, motherland. **3** *a home for the elderly* **institution,** hospice, shelter, refuge, retreat, asylum, hostel.

▸ adjective **1** relating to your home. **2** relating to your own country. **3** (of a sports match) played at a team's own ground.

> SYNONYMS *the UK home market* **domestic,** internal, local, national.
> ANTONYMS foreign, international.

▸ adverb **1** to or at your home. **2** to the intended position.

▸ verb (**homes, homing, homed**) **1** (of an animal) return by instinct to its territory. **2** (**home in on**) move or be aimed towards.

■ **home economics** the study of cookery and household management. **home page** the main page of an individual's or organization's Internet site. **home rule** the government of a place by its own citizens. **home run** Baseball a hit that allows the batter to make a run around all the bases. **home truth** an unpleasant fact about yourself that someone else tells you.

□ **homeward** adjective & adverb **homewards** adverb.

homeland ▸ noun a person's native land.

homeless ▸ adjective not having anywhere to live.

> SYNONYMS **of no fixed abode,** without a roof over your head, on the streets, vagrant, sleeping rough, destitute.

homely ▸ adjective (**homelier, homeliest**) **1** Brit. simple but comfortable. **2** Brit. unsophisticated. **3** N. Amer. (of a person) unattractive.

> SYNONYMS **1** *a homely atmosphere* **cosy,** comfortable, snug, welcoming, friendly; informal **comfy. 2** *she's rather homely* **unattractive,** plain, unprepossessing, ugly; Brit. informal no oil painting.
> ANTONYMS uncomfortable, attractive.

homeopathy (or **homoeopathy**) /hoh-mi-**op**-uh-thi/ ▸ noun a system of treating diseases by tiny doses of substances that would normally produce symptoms of the disease.

□ **homeopath** noun **homeopathic** adjective.

homesick ▸ adjective feeling upset because you are missing your home.

homespun ▸ adjective simple and unsophisticated.

homestead ▸ noun a farmhouse with surrounding land and outbuildings.

homework ▸ noun **1** school work that you are expected to do at home. **2** preparation for an event.

homicide /**hom**-i-syd/ ▸ noun chiefly N. Amer. the killing of another person.

> SYNONYMS **murder,** manslaughter, killing, slaughter, butchery, assassination.

□ **homicidal** adjective.

homily /**hom**-i-li/ ▸ noun (plural **homilies**) **1** a talk on a religious subject. **2** a dull talk on a moral issue.

hominid ▸ noun a member of a family of primates which includes humans and the prehistoric creatures from which they developed.

homoeopathy → HOMEOPATHY.

homogeneous /hom-uh-**jee**-ni-uhss/ ▸ adjective **1** alike. **2** made up of parts which are all of the same kind.

□ **homogeneity** /hom-uh-ji-**nee**-i-ti/ noun.

> ✔ The ending is **-eous,** with an **e,** not **-ous:** homogen**eous.**

homogenize (or **homogenise**) ▸ verb (**homogenizes, homogenizing, homogenized**) **1** treat milk so that the cream is mixed in. **2** make different things more alike.

homograph ▸ noun a word that is spelled the same as another but has a different meaning (e.g. *bat* 'a flying animal' and *bat* 'a piece of wood for hitting a ball').

homonym /**hom**-uh-nim/ ▸ noun a word that is spelled or pronounced the same as another but has a different meaning.

homophobia ▸ noun extreme hatred or fear of homosexuality and homosexuals. □ **homophobic** adjective.

homophone ▸ noun a word that is pronounced the same as another but has a different meaning or spelling (e.g. *new* and *knew*).

Homo sapiens /hoh-moh **sap**-i-enz/ ▸ noun the species to which modern humans belong.

homosexual ▸ adjective sexually attracted to people of your own sex.
▸ noun a homosexual person.
□ **homosexuality** noun.

Hon. ▸ abbreviation Honorary or Honourable.

Honduran /hon-**dyoo**-ruhn/ ▸ noun a person from Honduras, a country in Central America.
▸ adjective relating to Honduras.

hone ▸ verb (**hones, honing, honed**) **1** make better or more efficient. **2** sharpen a tool with a stone.

h

honest ▸ adjective **1** truthful and sincere. **2** fairly earned. **3** simple and straightforward.

> SYNONYMS **1** *an honest man* **upright**, honourable, principled, virtuous, decent, law-abiding, trustworthy, scrupulous. **2** *I haven't been honest with you* **truthful**, sincere, candid, frank, open, forthright, straight; informal upfront. ANTONYMS dishonest.

honestly ▸ adverb in an honest way.

> SYNONYMS **1** *he earned the money honestly* **fairly**, lawfully, legally, legitimately, honourably, decently, ethically; informal on the level. **2** *we honestly believe this* **sincerely**, genuinely, truthfully, truly, wholeheartedly, to be honest, to be frank, in all honesty, in all sincerity. ANTONYMS dishonestly.

honesty ▸ noun the quality of being honest.

> SYNONYMS **1** *I can attest to his honesty* **integrity**, uprightness, honour, righteousness, virtue, goodness, probity, trustworthiness. **2** *they spoke with honesty about their fears* **sincerity**, candour, frankness, directness, truthfulness, truth, openness, straightforwardness. ANTONYMS dishonesty, insincerity.

honey ▸ noun (plural **honeys**) a sweet, sticky yellowish-brown fluid made by bees from flower nectar.

honeybee ▸ noun the common bee.

honeycomb ▸ noun a structure of six-sided wax compartments made by bees to store honey and eggs.

honeydew ▸ noun a sweet, sticky substance produced by small insects feeding on the sap of plants.
■ **honeydew melon** a variety of melon with sweet green flesh.

honeyed ▸ adjective **1** containing or coated with honey. **2** (of words) soothing and soft.

honeymoon ▸ noun **1** a holiday taken by a newly married couple. **2** an initial period of enthusiasm or goodwill.
▸ verb spend a honeymoon somewhere.

honeypot ▸ noun a place that many people are attracted to.

honeysuckle ▸ noun a climbing shrub with sweet-smelling flowers.

honk ▸ noun **1** the cry of a goose. **2** the sound of a car horn.
▸ verb make a honk.

honky-tonk ▸ noun informal **1** N. Amer. a bar. **2** ragtime piano music.

honorary ▸ adjective **1** (of a title or position) given as an honour. **2** Brit. unpaid.

> SYNONYMS **1** *an honorary doctorate* **titular**, nominal, in name only,

unofficial, token. **2** *an honorary treasurer* **unpaid**, unsalaried, voluntary, volunteer. ANTONYMS paid.

> ✔ **honor-**, not **honour-**: honorary.

honorific ▸ adjective given as a mark of respect.

honour (US spelling **honor**) ▸ noun **1** great respect. **2** a privilege. **3** a clear sense of what is right. **4** a person or thing that brings credit. **5** an award or title given as a reward for achievement. **6** (**honours**) a university course of a higher level than an ordinary one. **7** (**His**, **Your**, etc. **Honour**) a title for a judge.

> SYNONYMS **1** *a man of honour* **integrity**, honesty, uprightness, morality, principles, high-mindedness, decency, probity, scrupulousness, fairness, justness. **2** *a mark of honour* **distinction**, privilege, glory, kudos, cachet, prestige. **3** *our honour is at stake* **reputation**, good name, character, repute, image, standing, status. **4** *the honour of meeting the Queen* **privilege**, pleasure, compliment. ANTONYMS unscrupulousness, shame.

▸ verb **1** regard or treat with great respect. **2** fulfil an obligation or keep an agreement.

> SYNONYMS **1** *we should honour our parents* **respect**, esteem, admire, look up to, value, cherish, revere, venerate. **2** *they were honoured at a special ceremony* **applaud**, acclaim, praise, salute, recognize, celebrate, pay tribute to. **3** *he honoured the contract* **fulfil**, observe, keep, obey, heed, follow, carry out, keep to, abide by, adhere to, comply with, conform to, be true to. ANTONYMS scorn, disgrace, disobey, break.

honourable (US spelling **honorable**) ▸ adjective **1** deserving honour. **2** having high moral standards. **3** (**Honourable**) a title given to MPs, nobles, etc.

> SYNONYMS **1** *an honourable man* **honest**, moral, principled, righteous, decent, respectable, virtuous, good, upstanding, upright, noble, fair, trustworthy, law-abiding. **2** *an honourable career* **illustrious**, distinguished, eminent, great, glorious, prestigious. ANTONYMS crooked, deplorable.

□ **honourably** adverb.

hooch ▸ noun informal alcoholic drink.

hood[1] ▸ noun **1** a covering for the head and neck with an opening for the face. **2** Brit. a folding waterproof cover of a vehicle. **3** N. Amer. the bonnet of a vehicle. **4** a protective canopy.
□ **hooded** adjective.

hood² ▸ noun N. Amer. informal a gangster or violent criminal.

hoodlum ▸ noun a gangster or violent criminal.

hoodoo ▸ noun **1** a run or cause of bad luck. **2** voodoo.

hoodwink ▸ verb deceive or trick.

hoody (or **hoodie**) ▸ noun (plural **hoodies**) a hooded sweatshirt or other top.

hoof ▸ noun (plural **hoofs** or **hooves**) the horny part of the foot of a horse, cow, etc.
▸ verb informal **1** kick a ball powerfully. **2** (**hoof it**) go on foot.
□ **hoofed** adjective.

hook ▸ noun **1** a curved object for catching hold of things or hanging things on. **2** a punch made with the elbow bent and rigid. **3** a catchy passage in a song.

> SYNONYMS **1** *she hung her jacket on the hook* **peg**, nail. **2** *the dress has six hooks* **fastener**, clasp, hasp, clip.

▸ verb **1** catch or fasten with a hook. **2** (**hook someone/thing up**) link someone or something to electronic equipment. **3** (**be hooked**) informal be very interested or addicted. **4** (in sport) hit the ball in a curving path.

> SYNONYMS **1** *they hooked baskets onto the ladder* **attach**, hitch, fasten, fix, secure, hang, clasp. **2** *he hooked a large pike* **catch**, land, net, take, bag. **3** (**hooked**) *a hooked nose* **curved**, hook-shaped, aquiline, angular, bent. **4** informal (**hooked**) *hooked on cocaine* **addicted to**, dependent on. **5** informal (**hooked**) *he is hooked on crosswords* **keen on**, enthusiastic about, addicted to, obsessed with, fanatical about; informal mad about.

> ■ **by hook or by crook** by any possible means. **hook, line, and sinker** completely.

hookah ▸ noun a kind of tobacco pipe in which the smoke is drawn through water to cool it.

hooker ▸ noun **1** informal a prostitute. **2** Rugby the player in the middle of the front row of the scrum.

hookworm ▸ noun a worm which can infest the intestines.

hooligan ▸ noun a violent young troublemaker.

> SYNONYMS **lout**, thug, tearaway, vandal, ruffian, troublemaker; Austral. larrikin; informal **tough**, bruiser; Brit. informal yob, yobbo, lager lout; Scottish informal ned.

□ **hooliganism** noun.

hoop ▸ noun **1** a rigid circular band. **2** a large ring used as a toy or for circus performers to jump through. **3** a metal arch through which you hit the balls in croquet. **4** a contrasting horizontal band on a sports shirt.

> SYNONYMS **ring**, band, circle, wheel, circlet, loop.

□ **hooped** adjective.

hoopla ▸ noun Brit. a game in which you try to throw rings over a prize.

hooray ▸ exclamation hurrah.

hoot ▸ noun **1** a low sound made by owls, or a similar sound made by a horn, siren, etc. **2** a shout of scorn or disapproval. **3** an outburst of laughter. **4** (**a hoot**) informal an amusing person or thing.
▸ verb make a hoot.
□ **hooter** noun.

Hoover Brit. ▸ noun trademark a vacuum cleaner.
▸ verb (**hoover**) (**hoovers, hoovering, hoovered**) clean with a vacuum cleaner.

hooves plural of HOOF.

hop ▸ verb (**hops, hopping, hopped**) **1** move by jumping on one foot. **2** (of a bird or animal) move by jumping. **3** (**hop it**) Brit. informal go away.

> SYNONYMS **jump**, bound, spring, bounce, skip, leap, prance, caper.

▸ noun **1** a hopping movement. **2** an informal dance.

> SYNONYMS **jump**, bound, spring, bounce, skip, leap, prance, caper.

> ■ **on the hop** Brit. informal unprepared.

hope ▸ noun **1** a feeling that something you want may happen. **2** a cause for hope. **3** something that you wish for.

> SYNONYMS **1** *I had high hopes* **aspiration**, desire, wish, expectation, ambition, aim, plan, dream. **2** *a life filled with hope* **optimism**, expectation, confidence, faith, belief.
> ANTONYMS pessimism.

▸ verb (**hopes, hoping, hoped**) **1** expect and want something to happen. **2** intend if possible to do something.

> SYNONYMS **1** *he's hoping for a medal* **expect**, anticipate, look for, be hopeful of, dream of. **2** *we're hoping to address this issue* **aim**, intend, be looking, have the intention, have in mind, plan.

hopeful ▸ adjective feeling or inspiring hope.

> SYNONYMS **1** *he remained hopeful* **optimistic**, full of hope, confident, positive, buoyant, bullish. **2** *hopeful signs* **promising**, encouraging, heartening, reassuring, favourable, optimistic.
> ANTONYMS pessimistic, discouraging.

▸ noun a person likely or hoping to succeed.

hopefully ▸ adverb **1** in a hopeful way. **2** it is to be hoped that.

> SYNONYMS **1** *he rode on hopefully* **optimistically**, full of hope, confidently,

buoyantly, expectantly. **2** *hopefully it should finish soon* **all being well,** if all goes well, God willing, with luck, touch wood, fingers crossed.

❗ Although the meaning 'it is to be hoped that' (as in *hopefully we'll see you tomorrow*) is now the more common one, some people feel that it is wrong and so it is best avoided in formal writing.

hopeless ▸ adjective **1** feeling or causing despair. **2** not at all skilful.

SYNONYMS **1** *a hopeless case* **forlorn,** beyond hope, lost, irreparable, irreversible, incurable, impossible, futile. **2** *hopeless at maths* **bad,** poor, awful, terrible, dreadful, appalling, atrocious, incompetent; informal pathetic, useless, lousy, rotten; Brit. informal rubbish. ANTONYMS competent.

hopelessly ▸ adverb utterly: *they're hopelessly in love.*

SYNONYMS **utterly,** completely, irretrievably, impossibly, extremely, totally.

hopper ▸ noun a container that tapers downwards and empties its contents at the bottom.

hops ▸ plural noun the dried flowers of a climbing plant, used to give beer a bitter flavour.

hopscotch ▸ noun a children's game in which you hop over squares marked on the ground.

horde ▸ noun chiefly disapproving a large group of people.

SYNONYMS **crowd,** mob, pack, gang, troop, army, swarm, mass, throng.

❗ Don't confuse **horde** with **hoard**: a **horde** is a large group of people; a **hoard** is a store of something valuable.

horizon ▸ noun **1** the line at which the earth's surface and the sky appear to meet. **2** (**horizons**) the limits of a person's understanding, experience, or interest.

horizontal ▸ adjective parallel to the horizon.

SYNONYMS **level,** flat, parallel. ANTONYMS vertical.

▸ noun a horizontal line or surface.
□ **horizontally** adverb.

hormone ▸ noun a substance produced in the body that controls the action of particular cells or tissues.
□ **hormonal** adjective.

horn ▸ noun **1** a hard bony growth on the heads of cattle, sheep, and other animals. **2** the substance that horns are made of. **3** a wind instrument shaped like a cone

or wound into a spiral. **4** an instrument sounding a signal.
□ **horned** adjective.

hornbill ▸ noun a tropical bird with a very large curved beak.

hornblende /**horn**-blend/ ▸ noun a dark brown, black, or green mineral.

hornet ▸ noun a kind of large wasp.

hornpipe ▸ noun a lively solo dance traditionally performed by sailors.

horny ▸ adjective (**hornier, horniest**) **1** made of or resembling horn. **2** hard and rough.

horology /ho-**rol**-uh-ji/ ▸ noun **1** the study and measurement of time. **2** the art of making clocks and watches.

horoscope ▸ noun a forecast of a person's future based on the positions of the stars and planets at the time of their birth.

horrendous ▸ adjective very unpleasant or horrifying.
□ **horrendously** adverb.

horrible ▸ adjective **1** causing horror. **2** very unpleasant.

SYNONYMS **1** *a horrible murder* **dreadful,** awful, terrible, shocking, appalling, horrifying, horrific, horrendous, grisly, ghastly, gruesome, harrowing, unspeakable. **2** *a horrible little man* **nasty,** horrid, disagreeable, obnoxious, hateful, odious, objectionable, insufferable. ANTONYMS pleasant, agreeable.

□ **horribly** adverb.

horrid ▸ adjective horrible.

horrific ▸ adjective causing horror.

SYNONYMS **dreadful,** horrendous, horrible, terrible, atrocious, horrifying, shocking, appalling, harrowing, hideous, grisly, ghastly, sickening.

□ **horrifically** adverb.

horrify ▸ verb (**horrifies, horrifying, horrified**) fill with horror.

SYNONYMS **shock,** appal, outrage, scandalize, offend, disgust, revolt, nauseate, sicken.

horror ▸ noun **1** a strong feeling of fear, shock, disgust, or dismay. **2** a thing causing such a feeling.

SYNONYMS **1** *children screamed in horror* **terror,** fear, fright, alarm, panic. **2** *to her horror she found herself alone* **dismay,** consternation, alarm, distress, disgust, shock. ANTONYMS delight, satisfaction.

hors d'oeuvre /or **derv**/ ▸ noun (plural **hors d'oeuvre** or **hors d'oeuvres** /or **derv,** or **dervz**/) a small savoury first course of a meal.

h

horse | hot

horse ▸ noun 1 a large four-legged animal used for riding and for pulling loads. 2 cavalry.

> SYNONYMS **mount**, charger, cob, nag, hack, colt, stallion, mare, filly; N. Amer. bronco; Austral./NZ moke, yarraman; informal gee-gee.

▸ verb (**horses**, **horsing**, **horsed**) (**horse around**) informal fool about.
■ **horse chestnut 1** a large tree that produces nuts (conkers) in a spiny case. **2** a conker. **horse sense** common sense.
□ **horsey** (or **horsy**) adjective.

horseback ▸ noun (**on horseback**) mounted on a horse.

horsebox ▸ noun Brit. a vehicle or trailer for transporting horses.

horsefly ▸ noun (plural **horseflies**) a large fly that bites horses and other large animals.

horseman (or **horsewoman**) ▸ noun (plural **horsemen** or **horsewomen**) a rider on horseback.

horseplay ▸ noun rough, high-spirited play.

horsepower ▸ noun (plural **horsepower**) a unit measuring the power of an engine.

horseradish ▸ noun a plant with strong-tasting roots which are made into a sauce.

horseshoe ▸ noun a U-shaped iron band attached to the base of a horse's hoof.

horticulture ▸ noun the cultivation of gardens.
□ **horticultural** adjective.

hosanna ▸ noun an exclamation of praise or joy used in the Bible.

hose ▸ noun 1 (Brit. also **hosepipe**) a flexible tube that conveys water. 2 historical men's breeches.
▸ verb (**hoses**, **hosing**, **hosed**) spray with a hose.

hosiery /hoh-zi-uh-ri/ ▸ noun socks, tights, and stockings.

hospice ▸ noun a home for people who are very ill or dying.

hospitable ▸ adjective 1 friendly and welcoming to strangers or guests. 2 (of an environment) pleasant and favourable for living in.

> SYNONYMS **welcoming**, friendly, sociable, cordial, gracious, accommodating, warm. ANTONYMS inhospitable.

□ **hospitably** adverb.

hospital ▸ noun a place where sick or injured people are looked after.

hospitality ▸ noun the friendly and generous treatment of guests or strangers.

> SYNONYMS **friendliness**, neighbourliness, sociability, welcome, warmth, kindness, cordiality, generosity.

hospitalize (or **hospitalise**) ▸ verb (**hospitalizes**, **hospitalizing**, **hospitalized**)
admit someone to hospital.
□ **hospitalization** noun.

Host ▸ noun (**the Host**) the bread used in the Christian ceremony of Holy Communion.

host¹ ▸ noun 1 a person who receives or entertains guests. 2 the presenter of a television or radio programme. 3 the place that holds an event to which others are invited. 4 Biology an animal or plant on or in which a parasite lives.

> SYNONYMS *the host of a TV series* **presenter**, compère, anchor, anchorman, anchorwoman, announcer. ANTONYMS guest.

▸ verb act as host at.

> SYNONYMS *the show is hosted by a different presenter each week* **present**, introduce, compère, front, anchor.

host² ▸ noun (**a host** or **hosts of**) a large number of.

hostage ▸ noun a person held prisoner in an attempt to make other people give in to a demand.

> SYNONYMS **captive**, prisoner, detainee, internee.

hostel ▸ noun a place which provides cheap food and accommodation for a particular group of people.

hostelry ▸ noun (plural **hostelries**) old use or humorous a pub.

hostess ▸ noun 1 a female host. 2 a woman employed to welcome customers at a nightclub or bar.

hostile ▸ adjective 1 aggressively unfriendly. 2 having to do with a military enemy.

> SYNONYMS **1** *a hostile attitude* **unfriendly**, unkind, unsympathetic, antagonistic, aggressive, confrontational, belligerent. **2** *hostile conditions* **unfavourable**, adverse, bad, harsh, grim, inhospitable, forbidding. **3** *they are hostile to the idea* **opposed**, averse, antagonistic, ill-disposed, unsympathetic, antipathetic, against; informal anti. ANTONYMS friendly, favourable, in favour.

hostility ▸ noun (plural **hostilities**) 1 hostile behaviour. 2 (**hostilities**) acts of warfare.

> SYNONYMS **1** *he glared at her with hostility* **antagonism**, unfriendliness, malevolence, venom, hatred, aggression, belligerence. **2** *their hostility to the present regime* **opposition**, antagonism, animosity, antipathy. **3** *a cessation of hostilities* **fighting**, armed conflict, combat, warfare, war, bloodshed, violence.

hot ▸ adjective (**hotter**, **hottest**) 1 having a high temperature. 2 feeling or producing an uncomfortable sensation of heat. 3 informal currently popular or interesting.

4 informal (of goods) stolen. **5** (**hot on**) informal knowing a lot about. **6** (**hot on**) informal strict about.

> SYNONYMS **1** *hot food* **heated,** piping, sizzling, roasting, boiling, scorching, scalding, red-hot. **2** *a hot day* **very warm,** balmy, summery, tropical, scorching, searing, blistering, sweltering; informal boiling, baking, roasting. **3** *a hot chilli* **spicy,** peppery, fiery, strong, piquant, powerful. **4** *the competition was hot* **fierce,** intense, keen, competitive, cut-throat, ruthless, aggressive, strong. **5** *she is hot on local history* **knowledgeable about,** well informed about, au fait with, up on, well versed in; informal clued up about.
> ANTONYMS cold, mild, weak.

▶ verb (**hots, hotting, hotted**) (**hot up**) Brit. informal become more exciting.

■ **hot air** informal empty or boastful talk. **hot-blooded** passionate. **hot cross bun** a bun marked with a cross, eaten on Good Friday. **hot dog** a hot sausage served in a long, soft roll. **hot rod** a car specially adapted to be fast. **hot-water bottle** a container filled with hot water and used for warming a bed. **hot-wire** informal start a vehicle without using the ignition switch.

hotbed ▶ noun a place where a lot of a particular activity is happening.

hotchpotch ▶ noun a confused mixture.

hotel ▶ noun a place providing accommodation and meals for travellers.

> SYNONYMS **inn,** motel, boarding house, guest house, bed and breakfast, B & B, hostel.

hotelier ▶ noun a person who owns or manages a hotel.

hotfoot ▶ adverb quickly and eagerly.
■ **hotfoot it** hurry eagerly.

hothead ▶ noun an impetuous or quick-tempered person.

hothouse ▶ noun a heated greenhouse.

hotline ▶ noun a direct telephone line set up for a particular purpose.

hotly ▶ adverb in a passionate, intense, or angry way.

> SYNONYMS **vehemently,** passionately, vigorously, strenuously, fiercely, heatedly, angrily.
> ANTONYMS calmly.

hotplate ▶ noun a flat heated surface on an electric cooker.

hotpot ▶ noun Brit. a casserole of meat and vegetables with a covering layer of sliced potato.

hotshot ▶ noun informal an important or very skilled person.

houmous → HUMMUS.

hound ▶ noun a hunting dog.
▶ verb harass someone.

> SYNONYMS **pursue,** chase, stalk, harry, harass, pester, badger, torment.

houndstooth ▶ noun a kind of large check pattern.

hour ▶ noun **1** a twenty-fourth part of a day and night; 60 minutes. **2** (**hours**) a period set aside for a particular purpose. **3** a particular point in time. **4** (**hours**) informal a very long time.

hourglass ▶ noun an object consisting of two connected glass bulbs containing sand that takes an hour to fall from the upper to the lower bulb.

houri /hoo-ri/ ▶ noun (plural **houris**) (in Islam) one of the virgin companions of the faithful in paradise.

hourly ▶ adverb & adjective **1** every hour. **2** by the hour.

house ▶ noun /howss/ **1** a building for people to live in. **2** a firm or institution. **3** a group of pupils living in the same building at a boarding school. **4** a long-established and powerful family. **5** (also **house music**) a style of popular dance music.

> SYNONYMS **1** **residence,** home; formal dwelling. **2** *the house of Stewart* **family,** clan, tribe, dynasty, line, bloodline, lineage. **3** *a printing house* **firm,** business, company, corporation, enterprise, establishment, institution, concern, organization, operation; informal outfit. **4** *the country's upper house* **assembly,** legislative body, chamber, council, parliament, congress, senate.

▶ verb /howz/ (**houses, housing, housed**) **1** provide with accommodation. **2** provide space for. **3** enclose something.

> SYNONYMS **1** *we can house twelve adults* **accommodate,** give someone a roof over their head, lodge, quarter, board, billet, take in, sleep, put up. **2** *this panel houses the main switch* **contain,** hold, store, cover, protect, enclose.

■ **house arrest** the state of being kept as a prisoner in your own house. **House of Commons** the chamber of the UK Parliament whose members are elected. **House of Lords** the chamber of the UK Parliament whose members are peers and bishops. **house-proud** very concerned with the appearance of your home. **house-train** train a pet to urinate and defecate outside the house. **house-warming** a party held to celebrate moving into a new home. **on the house** at the management's expense.

houseboat ▶ noun a boat that people can live in.

housebound ▶ adjective unable to leave your house.

housebreaking ▸ noun the action of breaking into a building to commit a crime.

household ▸ noun a house and all the people living in it.

SYNONYMS *the household was asleep* **family,** house, occupants, clan, tribe; informal **brood.**

▸ adjective typical of or used by a household.

SYNONYMS *household expenses* **domestic,** family, everyday, workaday.

◻ **householder** noun.

housekeeper ▸ noun a person employed to shop, cook, and clean the house.
◻ **housekeeping** noun.

housemaid ▸ noun a female servant in a house.

housemaster (or **housemistress**) ▸ noun a teacher in charge of a house at a boarding school.

housemate ▸ noun a person with whom you share a house.

housewife ▸ noun (plural **housewives**) a woman whose main occupation is looking after her family and the home.

housework ▸ noun cleaning, cooking, etc. done in running a home.

housing ▸ noun 1 houses and flats as a whole. 2 a hard cover for a piece of equipment.

SYNONYMS 1 *a housing development* **houses,** homes, residences, accommodation, living quarters; formal **dwellings.** 2 *the housing for the equipment* **casing,** covering, case, cover, holder, fairing, sleeve.

hove chiefly Nautical past tense of HEAVE.

hovel ▸ noun a small house that is dirty and run-down.

SYNONYMS **shack,** slum, shanty, hut; informal **dump,** hole.

hover ▸ verb (**hovers, hovering, hovered**) 1 remain in one place in the air. 2 wait about uncertainly. 3 remain near a particular level or between two states.

SYNONYMS 1 *helicopters hovered overhead* **hang,** be poised, be suspended, float, fly, drift. 2 *a servant hovered nearby* **wait,** linger, loiter.

hovercraft ▸ noun (plural **hovercraft**) a vehicle that travels over land or water on a cushion of air.

how ▸ adverb 1 in what way or by what means. 2 in what condition. 3 to what extent or degree. 4 the way in which.

howdah /how-duh/ ▸ noun a seat for riding on the back of an elephant.

however ▸ adverb 1 used to begin a statement that contrasts with something that has just been said. 2 in whatever way or to whatever extent.

SYNONYMS **nevertheless,** nonetheless, even so, but, for all that, despite that, in spite of that.

howitzer /how-it-ser/ ▸ noun a short gun for firing shells at a high angle.

howl ▸ noun 1 a long wailing cry made by an animal. 2 a loud cry of pain, amusement, etc.

SYNONYMS 1 *the howl of a wolf* **baying,** cry, bark, yelp. 2 *a howl of anguish* **wail,** cry, yell, yelp, bellow, roar, shout, shriek, scream, screech.

▸ verb make a howl.

SYNONYMS 1 *dogs howled in the distance* **bay,** cry, bark, yelp. 2 *a baby started to howl* **wail,** cry, yell, bawl, bellow, shriek, scream, screech, caterwaul; informal **holler.**

howler ▸ noun informal a stupid mistake.

h.p. (or **HP**) ▸ abbreviation 1 Brit. hire purchase. 2 horsepower.

HQ ▸ abbreviation headquarters.

HRH ▸ abbreviation Brit. Her (or His) Royal Highness.

HTML ▸ abbreviation Computing Hypertext Markup Language.

hub ▸ noun 1 the central part of a wheel. 2 the centre of an activity or region.

SYNONYMS **centre,** core, heart, focus, focal point, nucleus, kernel, nerve centre. ANTONYMS periphery.

hubbub ▸ noun a loud confused noise caused by a crowd.

hubcap ▸ noun a cover for the hub of a motor vehicle's wheel.

hubris /hyoo-briss/ ▸ noun excessive pride or self-confidence.

huckster ▸ noun 1 a person who sells things forcefully. 2 a person who sells small items in the street.

huddle ▸ verb (**huddles, huddling, huddled**) 1 crowd together. 2 curl your body into a small space.

SYNONYMS 1 *they huddled together* **crowd,** cluster, gather, bunch, throng, flock, collect, group, congregate. 2 *he huddled beneath the sheets* **curl up,** snuggle, nestle, hunch up. ANTONYMS disperse.

▸ noun a number of people or things crowded together.

SYNONYMS *a huddle of passengers* **group,** cluster, bunch, collection; informal **gaggle.**

hue ▸ noun 1 a colour or shade. 2 a particular aspect of something.

SYNONYMS **colour,** shade, tone, tint, tinge.

hue and cry ▶ noun a strong public outcry.

huff ▶ verb (often **huff and puff**) breathe out noisily.
▶ noun a bad mood.
□ **huffy** adjective.

hug ▶ verb (**hugs**, **hugging**, **hugged**) **1** hold tightly in your arms. **2** keep close to.

SYNONYMS *they hugged each other* **embrace,** cuddle, squeeze, clasp, clutch, hold tight.

▶ noun an act of hugging.

SYNONYMS *there were hugs as we left* **embrace,** cuddle, squeeze, bear hug.

huge ▶ adjective (**huger**, **hugest**) very large.

SYNONYMS **enormous,** vast, immense, massive, colossal, prodigious, gigantic, gargantuan, mammoth, monumental, giant, towering, mountainous; informal mega, monster, astronomical; Brit. informal ginormous.
ANTONYMS tiny.

□ **hugeness** noun.

hugely ▶ adverb very; very much.

SYNONYMS **extremely,** very, tremendously, exceptionally, immensely, extraordinarily, vastly; informal terrifically, awfully, terribly, seriously; Brit. informal dead, jolly; N. Amer. informal real, mighty, awful.

hugger-mugger ▶ adjective confused or disorderly.

hula ▶ noun a dance performed by Hawaiian women, in which the dancers sway their hips.
■ **hula hoop** (also **Hula-Hoop** US trademark) a large hoop that you spin around your body by moving your hips.

hulk ▶ noun **1** an old ship stripped of fittings and no longer used. **2** a large or clumsy person or thing.

hulking ▶ adjective informal very large or clumsy.

hull[1] ▶ noun the main body of a ship.

SYNONYMS *the ship's hull* **framework,** body, shell, frame, skeleton, structure.

hull[2] ▶ noun **1** the outer covering of a fruit or seed. **2** the cluster of leaves and stalk on a strawberry or raspberry.
▶ verb remove the hulls from.

hullabaloo ▶ noun informal an uproar.

hullo → HELLO.

hum ▶ verb (**hums**, **humming**, **hummed**) **1** make a low continuous sound like that of a bee. **2** sing a tune with closed lips. **3** informal be in a state of great activity.

SYNONYMS **1** *the engine was humming* **purr,** drone, murmur, buzz, whirr, throb. **2** *the workshops are humming* **be busy,** be active, be lively, buzz, bustle, be a hive of activity, throb.

▶ noun a low continuous sound.

SYNONYMS *a low hum of conversation* **murmur,** drone, purr, buzz.

human ▶ adjective **1** having to do with men, women, or children. **2** showing the better qualities of people.

SYNONYMS **1** *they're only human* **mortal,** flesh and blood, fallible, weak, frail, imperfect, vulnerable, physical, bodily, fleshly. **2** *his human side* **compassionate,** humane, kind, considerate, understanding, sympathetic.
ANTONYMS infallible, inhuman.

▶ noun (also **human being**) a man, woman, or child.

SYNONYMS *the link between humans and animals* **person,** human being, Homo sapiens, man, woman, individual, mortal, (living) soul, earthling; (**humans**) the human race, humanity, humankind, mankind, man, people.

■ **human rights** basic rights which belong to all people, such as freedom.
□ **humanly** adverb.

humane /hyuu-**mayn**/ ▶ adjective showing concern and kindness towards other people.

SYNONYMS **compassionate,** kind, considerate, understanding, sympathetic, tolerant, forbearing, forgiving, merciful, humanitarian, charitable.
ANTONYMS cruel.

□ **humanely** adverb.

humanism ▶ noun a system of thought that sees people as able to live their lives without the need for religious beliefs.
□ **humanist** noun & adjective **humanistic** adjective.

humanitarian ▶ adjective concerned with the welfare of people.

SYNONYMS **1** *a humanitarian act* **compassionate,** humane, unselfish, altruistic, generous. **2** *a humanitarian organization* **charitable,** philanthropic, public-spirited, socially concerned, welfare, aid.
ANTONYMS selfish, commercial.

▶ noun a humanitarian person.

SYNONYMS **philanthropist,** altruist, benefactor, social reformer, good Samaritan, do-gooder.

humanity ▶ noun **1** people as a whole. **2** the condition of being human. **3** sympathy and kindness towards other people. **4** (**humanities**) studies concerned with human culture, such as literature or history.

SYNONYMS **1** *humanity evolved from the apes* **humankind,** mankind, man, people, the human race, Homo sapiens. **2** *he praised them for their humanity* **compassion,** brotherly love, fellow feeling, humaneness, kindness, consideration, understanding, sympathy, tolerance.

humanize (or humanise) ▶ verb (humanizes, humanizing, humanized) make more pleasant or suitable for people.

humankind ▶ noun people as a whole.

humanoid ▶ adjective like a human in appearance.
▶ noun a humanoid being.

humble ▶ adjective (humbler, humblest) **1** having a modest or low opinion of your own importance. **2** of low rank. **3** not large or important.

SYNONYMS **1** *she was very humble* **meek,** deferential, respectful, submissive, self-effacing, unassertive, modest, unassuming, self-deprecating; Scottish mim. **2** *a humble background* **lowly,** poor, undistinguished, mean, common, ordinary, simple. **3** *my humble abode* **modest,** plain, simple, ordinary, little.
ANTONYMS proud, illustrious, grand.

▶ verb (humbles, humbling, humbled) make someone seem less important.

SYNONYMS *it humbled him to ask for help* **humiliate,** demean, lower, degrade, debase, mortify, shame.

■ **eat humble pie** make a humble apology.
□ **humbly** adverb.

humbug ▶ noun **1** false or misleading talk or behaviour. **2** a person who is not sincere or honest. **3** Brit. a boiled peppermint sweet.

humdrum ▶ adjective ordinary; dull.

humerus /hyoo-muh-ruhss/ ▶ noun (plural humeri /hyoo-muh-ry/) the bone of the upper arm, between the shoulder and the elbow.

humid ▶ adjective (of the air or weather) damp and warm.

SYNONYMS **muggy,** close, sultry, sticky, steamy, clammy, heavy.
ANTONYMS dry, fresh.

□ **humidity** noun.

humiliate ▶ verb (humiliates, humiliating, humiliated) make someone feel ashamed or stupid.

SYNONYMS **1 embarrass,** mortify, humble, shame, disgrace, chasten, deflate, crush, squash, demean, take down a peg or two; informal show up, put down, cut down to size; N. Amer. informal make someone eat crow. **2** (humiliating) **embarrassing,** mortifying, humbling, ignominious, inglorious, shaming, undignified, chastening, demeaning, degrading, deflating.
ANTONYMS dignify.

humiliation ▶ noun the act of humiliating or state of being humiliated.

SYNONYMS **embarrassment,** mortification, shame, indignity, ignominy, disgrace, dishonour, degradation, discredit, loss of face, blow to your pride.
ANTONYMS honour.

humility ▶ noun the quality of being humble.

SYNONYMS **modesty,** humbleness, meekness, respect, deference, diffidence, unassertiveness.
ANTONYMS pride.

hummingbird ▶ noun a small bird able to hover by beating its wings very fast.

hummock ▶ noun a small hill or mound.

hummus (or houmous) /huu-muhss/ ▶ noun a Middle Eastern dip made from chickpeas, sesame seeds, etc.

humorist ▶ noun a writer or speaker who is known for being amusing.

humorous ▶ adjective **1** causing amusement. **2** showing a sense of humour.

SYNONYMS **amusing,** funny, comic, comical, entertaining, diverting, witty, jocular, light-hearted, hilarious, uproarious, riotous, farcical.
ANTONYMS serious.

□ **humorously** adverb.

✔ **-or-** not **-our-**: hum**or**ous.

humour (US spelling humor) ▶ noun **1** the quality of being amusing. **2** a state of mind.

SYNONYMS **1** *the humour of the situation* **comedy,** funny side, hilarity, ludicrousness, satire, irony. **2** *the stories are spiced up with humour* **jokes,** jests, quips, witticisms, funny remarks, wit, comedy; informal gags, wisecracks. **3** *his good humour was infectious* **mood,** temper, disposition, spirits.
ANTONYMS seriousness.

▶ verb do as someone wishes in order to keep them happy.

SYNONYMS *she was always humouring him* **indulge,** accommodate, pander to, cater to, give in to, go along with, flatter, mollify, placate.
ANTONYMS stand up to.

□ **humourless** adjective.

hump ▶ noun **1** a rounded mass of earth or land. **2** a round part projecting from the back of a camel or other animal, or as an abnormal feature on a person's back.
▶ verb informal lift or carry with difficulty.
□ **humped** adjective.

humus /hyoo-muhss/ ▸ noun a substance found in soil, made from dead leaves and plants.

hunch ▸ verb raise your shoulders and bend the top part of your body forward.
▸ noun an idea based on a feeling rather than evidence.

> SYNONYMS **feeling**, guess, suspicion, impression, inkling, idea, notion, fancy, intuition; informal gut feeling.

hunchback ▸ noun offensive a person with an abnormal hump on their back.

hundred ▸ cardinal number **1** ten more than ninety; 100. (Roman numeral: **c** or **C**.) **2** (**hundreds**) informal a large number.
□ **hundredth** ordinal number.

hundredweight ▸ noun (plural **hundredweight** or **hundredweights**) **1** Brit. a unit of weight equal to 112 lb (about 50.8 kg). **2** US a unit of weight equal to 100 lb (about 45.4 kg).

hung past and past participle of HANG.
▸ adjective **1** having no political party with an overall majority. **2** (of a jury) unable to agree on a verdict. **3** (**hung up**) informal emotionally confused or disturbed.

Hungarian ▸ noun **1** a person from Hungary. **2** the language of Hungary.
▸ adjective relating to Hungary.

hunger ▸ noun **1** a feeling of discomfort caused by a lack of food. **2** a strong desire.

> SYNONYMS **1** *she was faint with hunger* **lack of food,** starvation, malnutrition, undernourishment. **2** *a hunger for news* **desire,** craving, longing, yearning, hankering, appetite, thirst; informal itch.

▸ verb (**hungers, hungering, hungered**) (**hunger after** or **for**) have a strong desire for.
■ **hunger strike** a refusal to eat for a long period, carried out as a protest about something.

hungover ▸ adjective suffering from a hangover.

hungry ▸ adjective (**hungrier, hungriest**) **1** feeling that you want to eat something. **2** having a strong desire for something.

> SYNONYMS **1** *I was really hungry* **ravenous,** starving, starved, famished, malnourished, undernourished, underfed; informal peckish. **2** *they are hungry for success* **eager,** keen, avid, longing, yearning, aching, greedy, craving, desirous of, hankering after; informal itching, dying, gagging.
> ANTONYMS full.

□ **hungrily** adverb.

hunk ▸ noun **1** a large piece cut or broken from something larger. **2** informal a good-looking man.

> SYNONYMS **chunk**, wedge, block, slab, lump, square, gobbet; Brit. informal wodge.

□ **hunky** adjective.

hunky-dory ▸ adjective informal fine; satisfactory.

hunt ▸ verb **1** chase and kill a wild animal for food or as a sport. **2** search for something. **3** (**hunt someone down**) chase and capture someone. **4** (**hunted**) looking worried and as if you are being chased.

> SYNONYMS **1** *they hunted deer* **chase,** stalk, pursue, course, track, trail. **2** *police are hunting for her* **search,** seek, look high and low, scour the area.

▸ noun **1** an act of hunting. **2** a group of people who meet regularly to hunt animals as a sport.

> SYNONYMS **1** *the thrill of the hunt* **chase,** pursuit. **2** *a police hunt* **search,** quest.

□ **hunter** noun.

huntsman ▸ noun (plural **huntsmen**) a person who hunts.

hurdle ▸ noun **1** each of a series of upright frames that an athlete jumps over in a race. **2** a frame used as a temporary fence. **3** an obstacle or difficulty.

> SYNONYMS **obstacle**, difficulty, problem, barrier, bar, snag, stumbling block, impediment, obstruction, complication, hindrance.

▸ verb (**hurdles, hurdling, hurdled**) jump over an obstacle while running.
□ **hurdler** noun.

hurdy-gurdy ▸ noun (plural **hurdy-gurdies**) a musical instrument played by turning a handle.

hurl ▸ verb **1** throw something with great force. **2** shout insults.

> SYNONYMS **throw**, toss, fling, launch, pitch, cast, lob; informal chuck, sling, bung.

hurling (or **hurley**) ▸ noun an Irish game resembling hockey.

hurly-burly ▸ noun busy and noisy activity.

hurrah (or **hooray** or **hurray**) ▸ exclamation used to express joy or approval.

hurricane ▸ noun a severe storm with a violent wind.

> SYNONYMS **cyclone**, typhoon, tornado, storm, windstorm, whirlwind, gale, tempest; Austral. willy-willy; N. Amer. informal twister.

hurried ▸ adjective done quickly or too quickly.

> SYNONYMS **1** *hurried glances* **quick,** fast, swift, rapid, speedy, brisk, cursory, perfunctory, brief, short, fleeting. **2** *a hurried decision* **hasty,** rushed,

precipitate, spur-of-the-moment.
ANTONYMS slow, considered.

□ **hurriedly** adverb.

hurry ▶ verb (hurries, hurrying, hurried)
1 move or act quickly. **2** do something
quickly or too quickly.

> SYNONYMS **1** *hurry or you'll be late* **be
> quick,** hurry up, hasten, speed up,
> run, dash, rush, race, scurry, scramble,
> scuttle, sprint; informal get a move on; Brit.
> informal get your skates on; N. Amer. informal
> get a wiggle on. **2** *she hurried him out*
> **hustle,** hasten, push, urge, usher.
> ANTONYMS dawdle, delay.

▶ noun great haste.

> SYNONYMS *in all the hurry, we forgot* **rush,**
> haste, speed, urgency, hustle and bustle.
> ANTONYMS ease.

hurt ▶ verb (hurts, hurting, hurt) **1** make
someone feel physical pain. **2** feel pain.
3 upset someone.

> SYNONYMS **1** *my back hurts* **be painful,**
> ache, be sore, be tender, smart, sting,
> burn, throb; informal be agony. **2** *Dad hurt
> his leg* **injure,** wound, damage, disable,
> bruise, cut, gash, graze, scrape, scratch.
> **3** *his words hurt her* **distress,** pain,
> wound, sting, upset, sadden, devastate,
> grieve, mortify.
> ANTONYMS comfort.

▶ noun injury, pain, or unhappiness.

> SYNONYMS *all the hurt he had caused*
> **distress,** pain, suffering, grief, misery,
> anguish, upset, sadness, sorrow.
> ANTONYMS joy.

▶ adjective injured or causing someone pain.

> SYNONYMS **1** *my hurt hand* **injured,**
> wounded, bruised, grazed, cut, gashed,
> sore, painful, aching. **2** *Anne's hurt
> expression* **pained,** aggrieved, offended,
> distressed, upset, sad, mortified; informal
> miffed.
> ANTONYMS unhurt, pleased.

hurtful ▶ adjective upsetting; unkind.

> SYNONYMS **upsetting,** distressing,
> wounding, unkind, cruel, nasty, mean,
> malicious, spiteful.

□ **hurtfully** adverb.

hurtle ▶ verb (hurtles, hurtling, hurtled)
move very fast.

husband ▶ noun the man that a woman is
married to.
▶ verb use something carefully without
wasting it.

husbandry ▶ noun **1** farming. **2** careful
management of resources.

hush ▶ verb **1** make or become quiet. **2** (**hush
something up**) stop something from
becoming known.

> SYNONYMS *he tried to hush her* **silence,**
> quieten (down), shush, gag, muzzle;
> informal shut up.

▶ noun a silence.

> SYNONYMS *a hush descended* **silence,**
> quiet, stillness, peace, calm, tranquillity.
> ANTONYMS noise.

husk ▶ noun the dry outer covering of some
fruits or seeds.
▶ verb remove the husk from.

husky[1] ▶ adjective (huskier, huskiest) **1** (of a
voice) deep and rough. **2** big and strong.
□ **huskily** adverb.

husky[2] ▶ noun (plural huskies) a powerful dog
used for pulling sledges.

hussar /huu-**zar**/ ▶ noun historical a soldier in
a light cavalry regiment.

hussy ▶ noun (plural hussies) a girl or woman
who behaves in an immoral or cheeky way.

hustings ▶ noun the political meetings and
speeches that take place before an election.

hustle ▶ verb (hustles, hustling, hustled)
1 push or move roughly. **2** informal, chiefly
N. Amer. obtain something dishonestly.
▶ noun busy movement and activity.
□ **hustler** noun.

hut ▶ noun a small, simple house or shelter.

> SYNONYMS **shack,** shanty, cabin, shelter,
> shed, lean-to, hovel; Scottish bothy; N. Amer.
> cabana.

hutch ▶ noun a box with a front made of
wire, used for keeping rabbits.

hyacinth /**hy**-uh-sinth/ ▶ noun a plant with
bell-shaped flowers.

hyaena → HYENA.

hybrid ▶ noun **1** the offspring of two plants
or animals of different species or varieties.
2 something made by combining two
different things.

> SYNONYMS *a hybrid of a goose and a
> swan* **cross,** cross-breed, mixture, blend,
> combination, composite, fusion, amalgam.

▶ adjective composed of different elements.

> SYNONYMS *hybrid roses* **composite,**
> cross-bred, interbred, mixed, blended,
> compound.

hydra ▶ noun a minute freshwater creature
with a tube-shaped body and tentacles
around the mouth.

hydrangea /hy-**drayn**-juh/ ▶ noun a shrub
with white, blue, or pink clusters of
flowers.

hydrant ▶ noun a water pipe with a nozzle
for attaching a fire hose.

hydrate ▶ verb (hydrates, hydrating,
hydrated) make something absorb or
combine with water.
□ **hydration** noun.

hydraulic ▸ adjective operated by a liquid moving through pipes under pressure.
▸ noun (**hydraulics**) the branch of science concerned with the use of liquids moving under pressure to provide mechanical force.
□ **hydraulically** adverb.

hydrocarbon ▸ noun any of the compounds of hydrogen and carbon.

hydrocephalus /hy-druh-**sef**-uh-luhss/ ▸ noun a condition in which fluid collects in the brain.

hydrochloric acid ▸ noun an acid containing hydrogen and chlorine.

hydroelectric ▸ adjective having to do with the use of flowing water to generate electricity.

hydrofoil ▸ noun a boat designed to rise above the water when it is travelling fast.

hydrogen ▸ noun a highly flammable gas which is the lightest of the chemical elements.
■ **hydrogen bomb** a very powerful nuclear bomb. **hydrogen sulphide** a poisonous gas with a smell of bad eggs.

hydrology ▸ noun the scientific study of the water on the earth's surface.

hydrophobia ▸ noun **1** extreme fear of water, especially as a symptom of rabies. **2** rabies.
□ **hydrophobic** adjective.

hydroplane ▸ noun a light, fast motorboat designed to skim over the surface of water.

hydrous ▸ adjective containing water.

hydroxide ▸ noun a compound containing oxygen and hydrogen together with a metallic element.

hyena (or **hyaena**) ▸ noun a doglike African animal.

hygiene ▸ noun the practice of keeping yourself and your surroundings clean in order to prevent illness and disease.

> SYNONYMS **cleanliness,** sanitation, sterility, purity, disinfection.

hygienic ▸ adjective clean and not likely to spread disease.

> SYNONYMS **sanitary,** clean, germ-free, disinfected, sterilized, sterile, antiseptic, aseptic.
> ANTONYMS insanitary.

□ **hygienically** adverb.

> ✔ Remember, **i** before **e** except after **c**: hyg**ie**nic.

hygienist ▸ noun a dental worker who specializes in oral hygiene.

hymen /hy-muhn/ ▸ noun a membrane which partially closes the opening of the vagina and is usually broken when a woman or girl first has sex.

hymn ▸ noun a religious song of praise, especially a Christian one.
▸ verb praise or celebrate.

hymnal ▸ noun a book of hymns.

hype informal ▸ noun extravagant publicity given to a product.
▸ verb (**hypes, hyping, hyped**) **1** publicize a product in an extravagant way. **2** (**be hyped up**) be very excited or tense.

hyper ▸ adjective informal having a lot of nervous energy.

hyperactive ▸ adjective very active; unable to keep still.

hyperbola /hy-**per**-buh-luh/ ▸ noun (plural **hyperbolas**) a symmetrical curve formed when a cone is cut by a plane nearly parallel to the cone's axis.

hyperbole /hy-**per**-buh-li/ ▸ noun a way of speaking or writing that exaggerates things and is not meant to be understood literally.

hyperbolic ▸ adjective **1** deliberately exaggerated. **2** relating to a hyperbola.

hyperlink ▸ noun Computing a link from a hypertext document to another location.

hypermarket ▸ noun Brit. a very large supermarket.

hypersensitive ▸ adjective too sensitive.

hypersonic ▸ adjective **1** relating to speeds of more than five times the speed of sound. **2** relating to sound frequencies above about a thousand million hertz.

hypertension ▸ noun abnormally high blood pressure.

hypertext ▸ noun Computing a system that lets you move quickly between documents or sections of data.

hyperventilate ▸ verb (**hyperventilates, hyperventilating, hyperventilated**) breathe at an abnormally rapid rate.
□ **hyperventilation** noun.

hyphen ▸ noun the sign (-) used to join words together or to divide a word into parts between one line and the next.

hyphenate ▸ verb (**hyphenates, hyphenating, hyphenated**) join or divide words with a hyphen.
□ **hyphenation** noun.

hypnosis ▸ noun the practice of causing a person to enter a state in which they respond very readily to suggestions or commands.

hypnotherapy ▸ noun the use of hypnosis to treat physical or mental problems.

hypnotic ▸ adjective **1** having to do with hypnosis. **2** making you feel very relaxed or sleepy.
□ **hypnotically** adverb.

hypnotism ▸ noun the study or practice of hypnosis.
□ **hypnotist** noun.

hypnotize (or **hypnotise**) ▸ verb
(**hypnotizes, hypnotizing, hypnotized**) put
someone into a state of hypnosis.

hypoallergenic ▸ adjective unlikely to
cause an allergic reaction.

hypochondria /hy-puh-**kon**-dri-uh/ ▸ noun
extreme anxiety about your health.

hypochondriac ▸ noun a person who is too
anxious about their health.

hypocrisy /hi-**pok**-ruh-si/ ▸ noun behaviour
in which a person pretends to have higher
standards than they really have.

hypocrite ▸ noun a person who pretends
to have higher standards than they really
have.

hypocritical ▸ adjective showing hypocrisy.

SYNONYMS **sanctimonious**, pious, self-
righteous, holier-than-thou, superior,
insincere, two-faced.

hypodermic ▸ adjective (of a needle or
syringe) used to inject a drug or other
substance beneath the skin.
▸ noun a hypodermic syringe or injection.

hypotension ▸ noun abnormally low blood
pressure.

hypotenuse /hy-**pot**-uh-nyooz/ ▸ noun
the longest side of a right-angled triangle,
opposite the right angle.

hypothermia ▸ noun the condition
of having an abnormally low body
temperature.

hypothesis /hy-po-thi-siss/ ▸ noun (plural
hypotheses /hy-po-thi-seez/) an idea that
has not yet been proved to be true or
correct.

hypothesize (or **hypothesise**)
▸ verb (**hypothesizes, hypothesizing,
hypothesized**) put forward as a hypothesis.

hypothetical ▸ adjective based on a
situation which is imagined rather than
true.
□ **hypothetically** adverb.

hysterectomy ▸ noun (plural
hysterectomies) a surgical operation to
remove all or part of the womb.

hysteria ▸ noun 1 wild or uncontrollable
emotion. 2 dated a medical condition in
which a person loses control of their
emotions.

SYNONYMS **frenzy**, feverishness,
hysterics, agitation, mania, panic, alarm,
distress.
ANTONYMS calm.

hysterical ▸ adjective 1 affected by wild or
uncontrolled emotion. 2 informal very funny.

SYNONYMS 1 *Janet became hysterical*
overwrought, overemotional, out of
control, frenzied, frantic, wild, beside
yourself, manic, delirious; informal in
a state. 2 *the film was hysterical* **very
funny,** hilarious, uproarious, rib-
tickling; informal side-splitting, priceless, a
scream, a hoot.
ANTONYMS calm, unfunny, serious.

□ **hysterically** adverb.

hysterics ▸ plural noun 1 wildly emotional
behaviour. 2 informal uncontrollable
laughter.

Hz ▸ abbreviation hertz.

h

Ii

I¹ (or **i**) ▶ noun (plural **Is** or **I's**) **1** the ninth letter of the alphabet. **2** the Roman numeral for one.

I² ▶ pronoun used by a speaker to refer to himself or herself.

iambic /I-**am**-bik/ ▶ adjective (of rhythm in poetry) having one unstressed syllable followed by one stressed syllable.

Iberian /I-**beer**-i-uhn/ ▶ adjective relating to Iberia (the peninsula that consists of modern Spain and Portugal).

ibex /**I**-beks/ ▶ noun (plural **ibexes**) a wild mountain goat with long horns.

ibid. ▶ adverb in the same book as the one that has just been mentioned.
ORIGIN short for Latin *ibidem*, meaning 'in the same place'.

ibis /**I**-biss/ ▶ noun (plural **ibises**) a large wading bird with a long curved bill.

ice ▶ noun **1** water that has frozen and become solid. **2** Brit. an ice cream.
▶ verb (**ices**, **icing**, **iced**) **1** decorate a cake with icing. **2** (**ice up** or **over**) become covered with ice.
■ **ice age** a period of time when ice covered much of the earth's surface. **ice cap** a large area that is permanently covered with ice, especially at the North and South Poles. **ice cream** a frozen dessert made with sweetened milk fat. **ice hockey** a form of hockey played on an ice rink. **ice pack** a bag filled with ice and held against part of the body to reduce swelling or lower temperature. **ice skate** a boot with a blade attached to the sole, used for skating on ice. **on thin ice** in a risky situation.

iceberg ▶ noun a large mass of ice floating in the sea.

icebox ▶ noun **1** a chilled container for keeping food cold. **2** Brit. a compartment in a fridge for making and storing ice.

iced ▶ adjective **1** cooled or mixed with ice. **2** decorated with icing.

Icelandic ▶ noun the language of Iceland.
▶ adjective relating to Iceland.
□ **Icelander** noun.

ichthyology /ik-thi-**ol**-uh-ji/ ▶ noun the branch of zoology concerned with fish.
□ **ichthyologist** noun.

icicle ▶ noun a hanging piece of ice formed when dripping water freezes.

icing ▶ noun Brit. a mixture of sugar and water or fat, used to cover cakes.
■ **icing sugar** finely powdered sugar used to make icing.

icon /**I**-kon/ ▶ noun **1** (also **ikon**) (in the Orthodox Church) a painting of a holy person that is also regarded as holy. **2** a person or thing that is seen as a symbol of something. **3** Computing a symbol on a computer screen that represents a program.
□ **iconic** adjective.

iconify /I-**kon**-i-fy/ ▶ verb (**iconifies**, **iconifying**, **iconified**) Computing reduce a window to an icon.

iconoclast /I-**kon**-uh-klast/ ▶ noun a person who attacks established customs and values.
□ **iconoclasm** noun **iconoclastic** adjective.

iconography /I-kuh-**nog**-ruh-fi/ ▶ noun **1** the use or study of pictures or symbols in visual arts. **2** the pictures or symbols associated with a person or movement.
□ **iconographic** adjective.

ICT ▶ abbreviation information and computing technology.

icy ▶ adjective (**icier**, **iciest**) **1** covered with ice. **2** very cold. **3** very unfriendly; hostile.

SYNONYMS **1** *icy roads* **iced (over)**, frozen, frosty, slippery, treacherous; literary rimy. **2** *an icy wind* **freezing**, chill, biting, bitter, raw, arctic. **3** *an icy voice* **unfriendly**, hostile, forbidding, cold, chilly, frosty, stern.

□ **icily** adverb.

ID ▶ abbreviation identification or identity.

Id → EID.

id ▶ noun the part of the mind that consists of a person's unconscious instincts and feelings.

I'd ▶ short form **1** I had. **2** I should or I would.

idea ▶ noun **1** a thought or suggestion about a possible course of action. **2** a mental picture or impression. **3** a belief. **4** (**the idea**) the aim or purpose.

SYNONYMS **1** *the idea of death* **concept**, notion, conception, thought. **2** *our idea is* *to open a new shop* **plan,** scheme, design, proposal, proposition, suggestion, aim, intention, objective, goal. **3** *Liz had various ideas on the subject* **thought,** theory, view, opinion, feeling, belief. **4** *I had an idea this might happen* **sense,** feeling, suspicion, fancy, inkling, hunch, notion. **5** *an idea of the cost* **estimate,** approximation, guess, conjecture; informal guesstimate.

ideal ▸ adjective **1** most suitable; perfect. **2** existing only in the imagination.

> SYNONYMS *ideal flying weather* **perfect,** faultless, exemplary, classic, model, ultimate, theoretical, utopian. ANTONYMS bad, real.

▸ noun **1** a person or thing regarded as perfect. **2** a principle or standard that is worth trying to achieve.

> SYNONYMS **1** *an ideal to aim at* **model,** pattern, exemplar, example, perfection, epitome, last word. **2** *liberal ideals* **principle,** standard, value, belief, conviction.

□ **ideally** adverb.

idealism ▸ noun **1** the belief that ideals can be achieved. **2** the representation of things as better than they really are.
□ **idealist** noun **idealistic** adjective.

idealize (or **idealise**) ▸ verb (**idealizes, idealizing, idealized**) represent someone or something as better than they really are.
□ **idealization** noun.

identical ▸ adjective **1** exactly alike. **2** the same. **3** (of twins) very similar in appearance.

> SYNONYMS (exactly) **the same,** indistinguishable, twin, duplicate, interchangeable, alike, matching. ANTONYMS different.

□ **identically** adverb.

identification ▸ noun **1** the action of identifying. **2** an official document or other proof of your identity.

> SYNONYMS **1** *the identification of the suspect* **recognition,** singling out, pinpointing, naming. **2** *early identification of problems* **determination,** establishment, ascertainment, discovery, diagnosis. **3** *may I see your identification?* **ID,** papers, documents, credentials, card, pass, badge.

identify ▸ verb (**identifies, identifying, identified**) **1** prove or recognize that someone or something is a specified person or thing. **2** recognize as being worthy of attention. **3** (**identify with**) feel that you understand or share the feelings of. **4** (**identify someone/thing with**) associate someone or something closely with.

> SYNONYMS **1** *Gail identified her attacker* **recognize,** pick out, spot, point out, pinpoint, put your finger on, name. **2** *I identified four problem areas* **determine,** establish, ascertain, make out, discern, distinguish. **3** *we identify sport with glamour* **associate,** link, connect, relate. **4** *Peter identifies with the team captain* **empathize,** sympathize, understand, relate to, feel for.

□ **identifiable** adjective.

identity ▸ noun (plural **identities**) **1** the fact of being who or what a person or thing is. **2** a close similarity or feeling of understanding.

> SYNONYMS **individuality,** self, personality, character, originality, distinctiveness, uniqueness.

■ **identity parade** Brit. a group of people assembled so that an eyewitness may identify someone suspected of a crime from among them.

ideology /I-di-ol-uh-ji/ ▸ noun (plural **ideologies**) **1** a system of ideas that an economic or political theory is based on. **2** the set of beliefs held by a particular group.
□ **ideological** adjective **ideologically** adverb.

idiocy ▸ noun (plural **idiocies**) very stupid behaviour.

idiom ▸ noun **1** a group of words whose overall meaning is different from the meanings of the individual words (e.g. *over the moon*). **2** a form of language used by a particular group of people. **3** a style of music or art.

idiomatic ▸ adjective using expressions that are natural to a native speaker of a language.

idiosyncrasy /id-i-oh-**sing**-kruh-si/ ▸ noun (plural **idiosyncrasies**) a person's particular way of behaving or thinking.
□ **idiosyncratic** adjective.

> ✔ The ending is **-asy**, not **-acy**: idiosyncr**asy**.

idiot ▸ noun a stupid person.

> SYNONYMS **fool,** ass, halfwit, blockhead, dunce, simpleton; informal nincompoop, clod, dimwit, dummy, fathead, numbskull; Brit. informal nitwit, twit, clot, berk, prat, pillock, wally, dork, twerp, charlie; Scottish informal nyaff, balloon; N. Amer. informal schmuck, turkey; Austral./NZ informal drongo, nong, galah, boofhead. ANTONYMS genius.

□ **idiotic** adjective **idiotically** adverb.

idle ▸ adjective (**idler, idlest**) **1** avoiding work; lazy. **2** not working or in use. **3** having no purpose or effect.

> SYNONYMS **1** *an idle fellow* **lazy,** indolent, slothful, work-shy. **2** *I was bored with*

being idle **unemployed,** jobless, out of work, redundant, unoccupied; Brit. informal on the dole. **3** *their idle hours* **unoccupied,** spare, empty, unfilled. **4** *idle remarks* **frivolous,** trivial, trifling, minor, insignificant, unimportant, empty, meaningless, vain.
ANTONYMS industrious, employed, busy, serious.

▸ verb (**idles, idling, idled**) **1** spend time doing nothing. **2** (of an engine) run slowly while out of gear.
□ **idleness** noun **idler** noun **idly** adverb.

idol ▸ noun **1** a statue or picture of a god that is worshipped. **2** a person who is very much admired.

SYNONYMS **1** *an idol in a shrine* **icon,** effigy, statue, figurine, totem. **2** *the pop world's latest idol* **hero,** heroine, star, superstar, icon, celebrity, darling; informal pin-up, heart throb.

idolatry /I-**dol**-uh-tri/ ▸ noun worship of idols.

idolize (or **idolise**) ▸ verb (**idolizes, idolizing, idolized**) admire or love someone very much.

idyll /**i**-dil/ ▸ noun **1** a very happy or peaceful time or situation. **2** a short piece of writing describing a peaceful scene of country life.

idyllic ▸ adjective very happy, peaceful, or beautiful.
□ **idyllically** adverb.

i.e. ▸ abbreviation that is to say.
ORIGIN short for Latin *id est*, meaning 'that is'.

if ▸ conjunction **1** on the condition or in the event that. **2** despite the possibility that. **3** whether. **4** whenever.

SYNONYMS **1** *if the weather is fine, we can walk* **provided,** providing, on condition that, presuming, supposing, assuming, as long as, in the event that. **2** *if I go out she gets nasty* **whenever,** every time. **3** *I wonder if he noticed* **whether,** whether or not.
ANTONYMS unless.

igloo ▸ noun a dome-shaped Eskimo house built from blocks of solid snow.

igneous /**ig**-ni-uhss/ ▸ adjective (of rock) formed when molten rock has solidified.

ignite ▸ verb (**ignites, igniting, ignited**) **1** catch fire, or set on fire. **2** provoke or stir up.

SYNONYMS **1** *moments before the petrol ignited* **catch fire,** burst into flames, explode. **2** *a cigarette ignited the fumes* **light,** set fire to, set alight, kindle.
ANTONYMS go out, extinguish.

ignition ▸ noun **1** the action of igniting. **2** the mechanism in a vehicle that ignites

the fuel to start the engine.

ignoble ▸ adjective not good or honest; dishonourable.

ignominious /ig-nuh-**min**-i-uhss/ ▸ adjective deserving or causing disgrace or shame.
□ **ignominiously** adverb.

ignominy /**ig**-nuh-mi-ni/ ▸ noun public shame or disgrace.

ignoramus /ig-nuh-**ray**-muhss/ ▸ noun (plural **ignoramuses**) an ignorant or stupid person.

ignorance ▸ noun lack of knowledge or information.

SYNONYMS **1** *their attitudes are based on ignorance* **lack of knowledge,** lack of education, unenlightenment. **2** *his ignorance of economics* **unfamiliarity with,** incomprehension, inexperience, innocence.
ANTONYMS education, knowledge.

ignorant ▸ adjective **1** lacking knowledge or information. **2** informal not polite; rude.

SYNONYMS **1** *an ignorant country girl* **uneducated,** unschooled, illiterate, uninformed, unenlightened, inexperienced, unsophisticated. **2** *ignorant of working-class life* **unaware,** unconscious, unfamiliar, unacquainted, uninformed.
ANTONYMS educated, knowledgeable.

ignore ▸ verb (**ignores, ignoring, ignored**) **1** deliberately take no notice of. **2** fail to consider something important.

SYNONYMS **1** *he ignored her* **take no notice of,** pay no attention to, snub, look right through, cold-shoulder. **2** *doctors ignored her instructions* **disregard,** take no account of, fail to observe, disobey, defy, overlook, brush aside.
ANTONYMS acknowledge, obey.

iguana /i-**gwah**-nuh/ ▸ noun a large tropical American lizard with a spiny crest along the back.

ikon → ICON.

ileum /**il**-i-uhm/ ▸ noun (plural **ilea** /**il**-i-uh/) the third part of the small intestine.

ilk ▸ noun a type.

ill ▸ adjective **1** not in good health; unwell. **2** bad or harmful.

SYNONYMS **1** *she was feeling rather ill* **unwell,** sick, poorly; informal under the weather, rough; Brit. informal grotty; Austral./NZ informal crook. **2** *the ill effects of smoking* **harmful,** damaging, detrimental, deleterious, adverse, injurious, destructive, dangerous.
ANTONYMS well, beneficial.

▸ adverb **1** badly or wrongly. **2** only with difficulty.

SYNONYMS **1** *we are ill prepared* **inadequately,** insufficiently, poorly, badly. **2** *he can ill afford the loss* **barely,** scarcely, hardly, only just.
ANTONYMS well, easily.

▶ noun **1** a problem or misfortune. **2** evil or harm.

SYNONYMS *the ills of society* **problem,** trouble, difficulty, misfortune, trial, tribulation; informal headache, hassle.

■ **ill-advised** not sensible or well thought out. **ill at ease** uncomfortable or embarrassed. **ill-fated** destined to fail or be unlucky. **ill-favoured** unattractive. **ill-gotten** obtained by illegal or unfair means. **ill-starred** unlucky. **ill-treat** treat in a cruel or unkind way. **ill will** hostility.

I'll ▶ short form **1** I shall. **2** I will.

illegal ▶ adjective against the law.

SYNONYMS **unlawful,** illicit, illegitimate, criminal, fraudulent, corrupt, dishonest, outlawed, banned, forbidden, prohibited, proscribed, unlicensed, unauthorized; informal crooked, shady; Brit. informal bent, dodgy.
ANTONYMS legal.

□ **illegality** noun **illegally** adverb.

illegible ▶ adjective not clear enough to be read.

SYNONYMS **unreadable,** indecipherable, unintelligible.

□ **illegibility** noun.

illegitimate ▶ adjective **1** not allowed by law or rules. **2** (of a child) born to parents who are not married to each other.
□ **illegitimacy** noun.

illiberal ▶ adjective not allowing freedom of thought or behaviour.

illicit ▶ adjective forbidden by law, rules, or standards.

SYNONYMS **illegal,** unlawful, criminal, outlawed, banned, forbidden, prohibited, proscribed, unlicensed, unauthorized, improper, disapproved of.
ANTONYMS legal, approved.

□ **illicitly** adverb.

illiterate ▶ adjective **1** unable to read or write. **2** not knowing very much about a particular subject.
□ **illiteracy** noun.

illness ▶ noun a disease, or a period of being ill.

SYNONYMS **sickness,** poor health, disease, ailment, disorder, complaint, malady, affliction, infection; informal bug, virus.
ANTONYMS health.

illogical ▶ adjective not sensible or based on sound reasoning.
□ **illogicality** noun **illogically** adverb.

illuminate ▶ verb (illuminates, illuminating, illuminated) **1** light something up. **2** help to explain something. **3** decorate a manuscript with coloured designs.

SYNONYMS (illuminating) **informative,** enlightening, revealing, explanatory, instructive, helpful, educational.
ANTONYMS confusing.

illumination ▶ noun **1** lighting or light. **2** (illuminations) lights used in decorating a building for a special occasion. **3** understanding.

SYNONYMS **light,** lighting, radiance, gleam, glow, glare.

illumine ▶ verb literary light up; illuminate.

illusion ▶ noun **1** a false idea or belief. **2** a thing that seems to be something that it is not.

SYNONYMS **1** *I had no illusions* **delusion,** misapprehension, misconception, false impression, mistaken impression, fantasy, dream, fancy. **2** *the illusion of depth* **appearance,** impression, semblance. **3** *it's just an illusion* **mirage,** hallucination, apparition, figment of the imagination, trick of the light.

illusionist ▶ noun a magician or conjuror.

illusory (or **illusive**) ▶ adjective not real, although seeming to be.

illustrate ▶ verb (illustrates, illustrating, illustrated) **1** provide a book or magazine with pictures. **2** make something clear by using examples, charts, etc. **3** act as an example of.

SYNONYMS **1** *the photographs that illustrate the text* **decorate,** ornament, accompany, support, explain, elucidate, clarify; informal get across/over. **2** *this can be illustrated through a brief example* **demonstrate,** show, exemplify, bring home.

□ **illustrative** adjective **illustrator** noun.

illustration ▶ noun **1** a picture illustrating a book or magazine. **2** the action of illustrating. **3** an example that helps to explain something.

SYNONYMS **1** *the illustrations in children's books* **picture,** drawing, sketch, figure, plate, image, print. **2** *an illustration of such a dilemma* **example,** sample, case, instance, exemplification, demonstration.

illustrious ▶ adjective famous and admired for what you have achieved.

I'm ▶ short form I am.

image ▶ noun **1** a picture or statue of someone or something. **2** a picture seen on a television or computer screen, through a lens, or reflected in a mirror. **3** a picture in the mind. **4** the impression that a person or group gives to the public. **5** (**the image of**) a person or thing that looks very similar to another. **6** a word or phrase describing something in an imaginative way; a simile or metaphor.

SYNONYMS **1** *images of the Queen* **likeness**, depiction, portrayal, representation, painting, picture, portrait, drawing, photograph. **2** *the image of this country as a democracy* **conception**, impression, idea, perception, notion. **3** *his public image* **persona**, profile, face.

▶ verb (**images**, **imaging**, **imaged**) make or form an image of.

imagery ▶ noun **1** language that produces images in the mind. **2** pictures as a whole.

imaginary ▶ adjective existing only in the imagination.

SYNONYMS **unreal**, non-existent, fictional, pretend, make-believe, invented, made-up, illusory.
ANTONYMS real.

✔ The ending is **-ary** not **-ery**: imagin**ary**.

imagination ▶ noun **1** the part of the mind that imagines things. **2** the ability to be creative or solve problems.

SYNONYMS **1** *in your imagination* **mind's eye**, fancy. **2** *she lacked imagination* **creativity**, vision, inventiveness, resourcefulness, ingenuity, originality.

imaginative ▶ adjective using the imagination in a creative or inventive way.

SYNONYMS **creative**, visionary, inventive, resourceful, ingenious, original, innovative.

□ **imaginatively** adverb.

imagine ▶ verb (**imagines**, **imagining**, **imagined**) **1** form a mental picture of. **2** think that something is probable. **3** believe that something unreal exists.

SYNONYMS **1** *you can imagine the scene* **visualize**, envisage, picture, see in the mind's eye, dream up, think up/of, conceive. **2** *I imagine he was at home* **assume**, presume, expect, take it (as read), suppose.

□ **imaginable** adjective.

imago /i-**may**-goh/ ▶ noun (plural **imagos** or **imagines** /i-**may**-ji-neez/) the final and fully developed adult stage of an insect.

imam /i-**mahm**/ ▶ noun the person who leads prayers in a mosque.

imbalance ▶ noun a lack of proportion or balance.

imbecile /**im**-bi-seel/ ▶ noun informal a stupid person.
□ **imbecilic** adjective **imbecility** noun.

imbed → EMBED.

imbibe ▶ verb (**imbibes**, **imbibing**, **imbibed**) **1** formal drink alcohol. **2** absorb ideas or knowledge.

imbroglio /im-**broh**-li-oh/ ▶ noun (plural **imbroglios**) a very confused or complicated situation.

imbue ▶ verb (**imbues**, **imbuing**, **imbued**) fill with a feeling or quality.

imitate ▶ verb (**imitates**, **imitating**, **imitated**) **1** follow as a model; copy. **2** copy the way that a person speaks or behaves in order to amuse people.

SYNONYMS **1** *other artists have imitated his style* **copy**, emulate, follow, echo, ape, parrot; informal rip off. **2** *he could imitate Winston Churchill* **mimic**, do an impression of, impersonate; informal take someone off.

□ **imitator** noun.

imitation ▶ noun **1** a copy. **2** the action of imitating.

SYNONYMS **1** *an imitation of a sailor's hat* **copy**, simulation, reproduction, replica, forgery. **2** *learning by imitation* **emulation**, copying. **3** *a perfect imitation of Francis* **impersonation**, impression, caricature; informal take-off, spoof.

▶ adjective copied or artificial.

SYNONYMS *imitation ivory* **artificial**, synthetic, mock, fake, simulated, man-made, manufactured, ersatz, substitute.
ANTONYMS real.

imitative /**im**-i-tuh-tiv/ ▶ adjective imitating or copying something.

immaculate ▶ adjective **1** completely clean or tidy. **2** free from mistakes; perfect.

SYNONYMS **1** *an immaculate white shirt* **clean**, spotless, shining, shiny, gleaming. **2** *immaculate condition* **perfect**, pristine, mint, flawless, faultless, unblemished; informal tip-top, A1. **3** *his immaculate record* **unblemished**, spotless, impeccable, unsullied, untarnished; informal squeaky clean.
ANTONYMS dirty, damaged, sullied.

□ **immaculately** adverb.

immanent ▶ adjective present within or throughout something.
□ **immanence** noun.

immaterial ▶ adjective **1** unimportant under the circumstances. **2** spiritual rather than physical.

immature ▶ adjective **1** not fully developed. **2** behaving in a way that is typical of someone younger.
□ **immaturity** noun.

immeasurable ▶ adjective too large or extreme to measure.
□ **immeasurably** adverb.

immediate ▸ adjective **1** happening or done at once. **2** nearest in time, space, or relationship. **3** most urgent; current. **4** without anything coming between; direct.

> SYNONYMS **1** *the UN called for immediate action* **instant,** instantaneous, prompt, swift, speedy, rapid, quick. **2** *their immediate concerns* **current,** present, urgent, pressing. **3** *our immediate neighbours* **nearest,** close, next-door, adjacent, adjoining.
> ANTONYMS delayed.

□ **immediacy** noun.

immediately ▸ adverb **1** at once. **2** very close in time, space, or relationship.

> SYNONYMS **1** *you must decide immediately* **straight away,** at once, right away, instantly, now, directly, forthwith, there and then. **2** *I sat immediately behind him* **directly,** right, exactly, precisely, squarely, just, dead; informal slap bang; N. Amer. informal smack dab.
> ANTONYMS sometime, later, somewhere.

▸ conjunction chiefly Brit. as soon as.

> ✔ **-tely**, not **-tly**: immedia**tely**.

immemorial ▸ adjective existing for longer than people can remember.

immense ▸ adjective very large or great.

> SYNONYMS **huge,** vast, massive, enormous, gigantic, colossal, monumental, towering, giant, mammoth; informal monster, whopping (great); Brit. informal ginormous.
> ANTONYMS tiny.

□ **immensely** adverb **immensity** noun.

immerse ▸ verb (**immerses, immersing, immersed**) **1** dip or cover completely in a liquid. **2** (**immerse yourself in**) involve yourself deeply in an activity.

> SYNONYMS **1** *the metal was immersed in acid* **dip,** submerge, dunk, duck, sink. **2** *Elliot was immersed in his work* **absorb,** engross, occupy, engage, involve, bury, preoccupy; informal lose.

immersion ▸ noun **1** the action of immersing. **2** deep involvement in an activity.
■ **immersion heater** an electric device in a water tank which heats water for a house.

immigrant ▸ noun a person who comes to live permanently in a foreign country.

> SYNONYMS **newcomer,** settler, incomer, migrant, non-native, foreigner, alien.
> ANTONYMS native.

immigration ▸ noun the action of coming to live permanently in a foreign country.
□ **immigrate** verb.

imminent ▸ adjective about to happen.

> SYNONYMS **near,** close (at hand), impending, approaching, coming, forthcoming, on the way, expected, looming.
> ANTONYMS distant.

□ **imminence** noun **imminently** adverb.

immiscible /i-miss-i-b'l/ ▸ adjective (of liquids) not able to be mixed together.

immobile ▸ adjective not moving or able to move.
□ **immobility** noun.

immobilize (or **immobilise**) ▸ verb (**immobilizes, immobilizing, immobilized**) prevent from moving or operating normally.
□ **immobilization** noun.

immoderate ▸ adjective not sensible or controlled; excessive.

immodest ▸ adjective **1** conceited or boastful. **2** showing too much of the body.

immolate ▸ verb kill or sacrifice by burning.
□ **immolation** noun.

immoral ▸ adjective not following accepted standards of morality.

> SYNONYMS **wicked,** bad, wrong, unethical, unprincipled, unscrupulous, dishonest, corrupt, sinful, impure.
> ANTONYMS ethical, pure.

□ **immorality** noun.

immortal ▸ adjective **1** living forever. **2** deserving to be remembered forever.

> SYNONYMS **1** *our immortal souls* **undying,** deathless, eternal, everlasting, imperishable, indestructible. **2** *an immortal children's story* **timeless,** perennial, classic, time-honoured, enduring, evergreen.
> ANTONYMS mortal, ephemeral.

▸ noun **1** an immortal god. **2** a person who will be famous for a very long time.
□ **immortality** noun.

immortalize (or **immortalise**) ▸ verb (**immortalizes, immortalizing, immortalized**) prevent someone or something from being forgotten for a very long time.

immovable ▸ adjective **1** not able to be moved. **2** unable to be changed or persuaded.

immune ▸ adjective **1** having a natural ability to resist a particular infection. **2** not affected by something. **3** exempt or protected from something.

> SYNONYMS **resistant,** not subject, not liable, not vulnerable, protected from, safe from, secure against.
> ANTONYMS susceptible, liable.

immunity ▸ noun (plural **immunities**) **1** the body's ability to resist a particular infection. **2** freedom from a duty or punishment.

SYNONYMS **1** *immunity to malaria* **resistance,** protection, defence. **2** *immunity from prosecution* **exemption,** exception, freedom. **3** *diplomatic immunity* **indemnity,** privilege, prerogative, licence, exemption, impunity, protection.
ANTONYMS susceptibility, liability.

immunize (or **immunise**) ▶ verb (**immunizes, immunizing, immunized**) make immune to infection.
□ **immunization** noun.

immunology ▶ noun the branch of medicine and biology concerned with immunity to infection.
□ **immunological** adjective **immunologist** noun.

immure ▶ verb (**immures, immuring, immured**) literary shut someone up in a place.

immutable /im-**myoo**-tuh-b'l/ ▶ adjective not changing or able to be changed.

imp ▶ noun **1** (in stories) a small, mischievous devil. **2** a mischievous child.

impact ▶ noun /im-pakt/ **1** an instance of one object hitting another. **2** a noticeable effect or influence.

SYNONYMS **1** *the force of the impact* **collision,** crash, smash, bump, knock. **2** *the job losses will have a major impact* **effect,** influence, consequences, repercussions, ramifications.

▶ verb /im-**pakt**/ **1** hit another object with force. **2** (**impact on**) have a strong effect on. **3** (**impacted**) (of a tooth) wedged between another tooth and the jaw.

SYNONYMS **1** *an asteroid impacted the earth* **crash into,** smash into, collide with, hit, strike, smack into, bang into. **2** *interest rates have impacted on spending* **affect,** influence, hit, have an effect, make an impression.

impair ▶ verb weaken or damage.

SYNONYMS **weaken,** damage, harm, have a negative effect on, undermine, diminish, reduce, lessen, decrease.
ANTONYMS improve, enhance.

□ **impairment** noun.

impala /im-**pah**-luh/ ▶ noun (plural **impala**) an African antelope with curved horns.

impale ▶ verb (**impales, impaling, impaled**) pierce with a sharp instrument.

impalpable ▶ adjective **1** unable to be felt by touch. **2** not easily understood.

impart ▶ verb **1** communicate information. **2** give a particular quality to.

SYNONYMS **communicate,** pass on, convey, transmit, relay, relate, tell, make known, report, announce.

impartial ▶ adjective not favouring one person or thing more than another.

SYNONYMS **unbiased,** unprejudiced, neutral, non-partisan, disinterested, detached, dispassionate, objective.
ANTONYMS biased, partisan.

□ **impartiality** noun **impartially** adverb.

impassable ▶ adjective impossible to travel along or over.

impasse /am-**pahss**/ ▶ noun a situation in which no progress is possible.

SYNONYMS **deadlock,** dead end, stalemate, stand-off, standstill.

impassioned ▶ adjective filled with or showing great emotion.

impassive ▶ adjective not feeling or showing emotion.
□ **impassively** adverb.

impasto /im-**pass**-toh/ ▶ noun the technique of laying on paint thickly so that it stands out from the surface of a painting.

impatient ▶ adjective **1** not having much patience or tolerance. **2** restlessly eager.

SYNONYMS **1** *Melissa grew impatient* **restless,** agitated, nervous, anxious. **2** *they are impatient to get back home* **anxious,** eager, keen; informal itching, dying. **3** *an impatient gesture* **irritated,** annoyed, angry, tetchy, snappy, cross, curt, brusque.
ANTONYMS patient, reluctant, calm.

□ **impatience** noun **impatiently** adverb.

impeach ▶ verb chiefly US charge a person who holds an important public office with a serious crime.
□ **impeachment** noun.

impeccable ▶ adjective without faults or mistakes.

SYNONYMS **flawless,** faultless, unblemished, spotless, stainless, perfect, exemplary, irreproachable; informal squeaky clean.
ANTONYMS imperfect.

□ **impeccably** adverb.

impecunious /im-pi-**kyoo**-ni-uhss/ ▶ adjective having little or no money.

impedance ▶ noun the total resistance of an electric circuit to the flow of alternating current.

impede ▶ verb (**impedes, impeding, impeded**) delay or block the progress of.

SYNONYMS **hinder,** obstruct, hamper, hold back/up, delay, interfere with, disrupt, retard, slow (down).
ANTONYMS facilitate.

impediment ▶ noun **1** something that delays or blocks progress. **2** (also **speech impediment**) a defect in a person's speech, such as a stammer.

impel ▶ verb (**impels, impelling, impelled**) force to do something.

impending ▸ adjective be about to happen.

impenetrable ▸ adjective **1** impossible to get through or into. **2** impossible to understand.

impenitent ▸ adjective not feeling shame or regret.

imperative ▸ adjective **1** of vital importance. **2** giving a command. **3** Grammar (of a verb) expressing a command, as in *come here!*

> SYNONYMS **vital**, crucial, critical, essential, pressing, urgent.
> ANTONYMS unimportant.

▸ noun an essential or urgent thing.

imperceptible ▸ adjective too slight or gradual to be seen or felt.
□ **imperceptibly** adverb.

imperfect ▸ adjective **1** faulty or incomplete. **2** Grammar (of a verb) referring to a past action that is not yet completed.

> SYNONYMS **faulty**, flawed, defective, inferior, second-rate, substandard, damaged, blemished, torn, broken, cracked, scratched; Brit. informal duff.
> ANTONYMS perfect.

□ **imperfection** noun **imperfectly** adverb.

imperial ▸ adjective **1** relating to an empire or an emperor. **2** (of weights and measures) in a non-metric system formerly used in the UK.

imperialism ▸ noun a system in which one country extends its power and influence by defeating other countries in war, forming colonies, etc.
□ **imperialist** noun & adjective.

imperil ▸ verb (imperils, imperilling, imperilled; US spelling imperils, imperiling, imperiled) put into danger.

imperious /im-peer-i-uhss/ ▸ adjective expecting to be obeyed.
□ **imperiously** adverb.

impermanent ▸ adjective not permanent.
□ **impermanence** noun.

impermeable ▸ adjective not allowing a liquid or gas to pass through.

impersonal ▸ adjective **1** not influenced by or involving personal feelings. **2** lacking human feelings or atmosphere. **3** Grammar (of a verb) used only with *it* as a subject (as in *it is snowing*).
□ **impersonality** noun **impersonally** adverb.

impersonate ▸ verb (impersonates, impersonating, impersonated) pretend to be another person in order to entertain or deceive people.
□ **impersonation** noun **impersonator** noun.

impertinent ▸ adjective not showing proper respect.

> SYNONYMS **rude**, insolent, impolite, ill-mannered, disrespectful, impudent,

cheeky, presumptuous, forward.
ANTONYMS polite, respectful.

□ **impertinence** noun.

imperturbable ▸ adjective not easily upset or excited.

impervious ▸ adjective **1** not allowing a liquid or a gas to pass through. **2** (**impervious to**) unable to be affected by.

impetuous ▸ adjective acting quickly and without thinking or being careful.

> SYNONYMS **impulsive**, rash, hasty, reckless, foolhardy, imprudent, ill-considered, spontaneous, impromptu, spur-of-the-moment.
> ANTONYMS considered, cautions.

□ **impetuously** adverb.

impetus ▸ noun **1** the force or energy with which something moves. **2** the force that makes something happen.

impinge ▸ verb (impinges, impinging, impinged) (**impinge on**) have an effect or impact on.

impious /im-pi-uhss/ ▸ adjective not showing respect or reverence.

implacable ▸ adjective **1** unwilling to stop being hostile towards someone or something. **2** (of strong negative feelings) unable to be changed.
□ **implacably** adverb.

implant ▸ verb /im-plahnt/ **1** put tissue or an artificial object into someone's body, by means of a surgical operation. **2** fix an idea firmly in someone's mind.

> SYNONYMS **1** *the collagen is implanted under the skin* **insert**, embed, bury, inject, transplant, graft. **2** *he implanted the idea in my mind* **instil**, inculcate, introduce, plant, sow.
> ANTONYMS excise, banish.

▸ noun /im-plahnt/ a thing that is implanted.
□ **implantation** noun.

implausible ▸ adjective not seeming reasonable or probable.
□ **implausibility** noun **implausibly** adverb.

implement ▸ noun /im-pli-muhnt/ a tool that is used for a particular purpose.

> SYNONYMS *garden implements* **tool**, utensil, instrument, device, apparatus, gadget, contraption, appliance; informal gizmo.

▸ verb /im-pli-ment/ put something into effect.

> SYNONYMS *the cost of implementing the new law* **execute**, apply, put into effect/action, put into practice, carry out/through, perform, enact, fulfil.
> ANTONYMS abolish, cancel.

□ **implementation** noun.

implicate ▸ verb (implicates, implicating, implicated) **1** show that someone is involved in a crime. **2** (**be implicated in**) be partly responsible for.

> SYNONYMS **1** *he had been implicated in a financial scandal* **incriminate,** involve, connect, embroil, enmesh. **2** *viruses are implicated in the development of cancer* **involve in,** concern with, associate with, connect with.

implication ▶ noun **1** a conclusion that can be drawn from something. **2** a possible effect. **3** involvement in something.

> SYNONYMS **1** *he was smarting at their implication* **suggestion,** inference, insinuation, innuendo, intimation, imputation. **2** *important political implications* **consequence,** result, ramification, repercussion, reverberation, effect. **3** *his implication in the murder* **incrimination,** involvement, connection, entanglement, association. ANTONYMS exoneration.

implicit ▶ adjective **1** suggested without being directly expressed. **2** (**implicit in**) forming part of something. **3** not doubted or questioned.
> □ **implicitly** adverb.

implode ▶ verb (**implodes, imploding, imploded**) collapse violently inwards.
> □ **implosion** noun.

implore ▶ verb (**implores, imploring, implored**) beg earnestly or desperately.

> SYNONYMS **plead with,** beg, entreat, appeal to, ask, request, call on, exhort, urge.

imply ▶ verb (**implies, implying, implied**) **1** suggest rather than state directly. **2** suggest as a possible effect.

> SYNONYMS **1** *are you implying he is mad?* **insinuate,** suggest, infer, hint, intimate, give someone to understand, make out. **2** *the forecast traffic increase implies more roads* **involve,** entail, mean, point to, signify, indicate, presuppose.

> **!** Don't confuse the words **imply** and **infer.** They can describe the same situation, but from different points of view. If you **imply** something, it means that you are suggesting something though not saying it directly. If you **infer** something from what has been said, you come to the conclusion that this is what the speaker really means, although they are not saying it directly.

impolite ▶ adjective not having good manners.

> SYNONYMS **rude,** bad-mannered, ill-mannered, discourteous, uncivil, disrespectful, insolent, impudent, impertinent, cheeky; informal lippy. ANTONYMS polite.

impolitic ▶ adjective unwise.

imponderable ▶ noun something that is difficult or impossible to assess.
▶ adjective difficult or impossible to assess.

import ▶ verb /im-**port**/ **1** bring goods into a country from abroad. **2** transfer computer data into a file.

> SYNONYMS *the UK imports iron ore* **bring in,** buy in, ship in.
> ANTONYMS export.

▶ noun /**im**-port/ **1** an imported article. **2** the action of importing. **3** the implied meaning of something. **4** importance.

> SYNONYMS **1** *a matter of great import* **importance,** significance, consequence, momentousness, magnitude, substance, weight, note, gravity, seriousness. **2** *the full import of her words* **meaning,** sense, essence, gist, drift, message, thrust, substance, implication.
> ANTONYMS insignificance.

> □ **importation** noun **importer** noun.

importance ▶ noun the state or fact of being important.

> SYNONYMS **1** *an event of immense importance* **significance,** momentousness, moment, import, consequence, note, weight, seriousness, gravity. **2** *she had an exaggerated sense of her own importance* **status,** eminence, prestige, worth, influence, power, authority.
> ANTONYMS insignificance.

important ▶ adjective **1** having a great effect or value. **2** (of a person) having great authority or influence.

> SYNONYMS **1** *an important meeting* **significant,** consequential, momentous, of great import, major, valuable, necessary, crucial, vital, essential, pivotal, decisive, far-reaching, historic. **2** *he was an important man* **powerful,** influential, well-connected, high-ranking, prominent, eminent, notable, distinguished, esteemed, respected, prestigious.
> ANTONYMS unimportant, insignificant.

> □ **importantly** adverb.

importunate /im-**por**-tyuu-nuht/ ▶ adjective very persistent.

importune ▶ verb (**importunes, importuning, importuned**) ask someone persistently for something.

impose ▶ verb (**imposes, imposing, imposed**) **1** force something to be accepted. **2** (often **impose on**) take unfair advantage of someone.

> SYNONYMS **1** *he imposed his ideas on everyone* **foist,** force, inflict, press, saddle someone with. **2** *new taxes will be imposed* **levy,** charge, apply, enforce, set, establish, institute, introduce, bring

into effect.
ANTONYMS abolish.

imposing ▸ adjective grand and impressive.

SYNONYMS **impressive**, striking, dramatic, spectacular, commanding, arresting, awesome, formidable, splendid, grand, majestic.
ANTONYMS modest.

imposition ▸ noun 1 the action of imposing something. 2 an unreasonable thing that you are asked or expected to do or accept.

SYNONYMS 1 *the imposition of an alien culture* **imposing**, foisting, forcing, inflicting. 2 *the imposition of VAT* **levying**, charging, application, enforcement, enforcing, setting, establishment, introduction. 3 *it would be no imposition* **burden**, encumbrance, liberty, bother, worry; informal hassle.
ANTONYMS abolition.

impossible ▸ adjective 1 not able to exist or be done. 2 very difficult to deal with.

SYNONYMS 1 *the winds made fishing impossible* **out of the question**, impracticable, non-viable, unworkable. 2 *an impossible dream* **unattainable**, unachievable, unobtainable, hopeless, impracticable, unworkable. 3 *food shortages made life impossible* **unbearable**, intolerable, unendurable. 4 *an impossible woman* **unreasonable**, difficult, awkward, intolerable, unbearable, exasperating, maddening, infuriating.
ANTONYMS possible, attainable, bearable, reasonable.

☐ **impossibility** noun **impossibly** adverb.

impostor (or **imposter**) ▸ noun a person who pretends to be someone else in order to deceive other people.

imposture ▸ noun an act of pretending to be someone else in order to deceive.

impotent /**im**-puh-tuhnt/ ▸ adjective 1 helpless or powerless. 2 (of a man) unable to achieve an erection.
☐ **impotence** noun.

impound ▸ verb 1 officially seize something. 2 shut up domestic animals in an enclosure.

SYNONYMS **confiscate**, appropriate, take possession of, seize, commandeer, expropriate, requisition, take over.
ANTONYMS release.

impoverish ▸ verb 1 make someone poor. 2 make something worse in quality.
☐ **impoverishment** noun.

impracticable ▸ adjective not able to be done.

impractical ▸ adjective not sensible or realistic.

imprecation ▸ noun formal a spoken curse.

imprecise ▸ adjective not exact.
☐ **imprecision** noun.

impregnable ▸ adjective 1 (of a building) unable to be captured or broken into. 2 unable to be defeated.

impregnate ▸ verb (**impregnates**, **impregnating**, **impregnated**) 1 soak with a substance. 2 fill with a feeling or quality. 3 make pregnant.
☐ **impregnation** noun.

impresario /im-pri-**sah**-ri-oh/ ▸ noun (plural **impresarios**) a person who organizes plays, concerts, or operas.

impress ▸ verb 1 make someone feel admiration and respect. 2 (**impress something on**) make someone aware of something important. 3 make a mark or design using a stamp or seal.

SYNONYMS *Hazel had impressed him mightily* **make an impression on**, have an impact on, influence, affect, move, stir, rouse, excite, inspire, dazzle, awe.
ANTONYMS disappoint.

impression ▸ noun 1 an idea, feeling, or opinion. 2 the effect that something has on someone. 3 an imitation of the way that a person speaks or behaves done in order to entertain people. 4 a mark made by pressing on a surface.

SYNONYMS 1 *he got the impression she was hiding something* **feeling**, sense, fancy, (sneaking) suspicion, inkling, intuition, hunch, notion, idea. 2 *a favourable impression* **opinion**, view, image, picture, perception, reaction, judgement, verdict, estimation. 3 *school made a profound impression on me* **impact**, effect, influence. 4 *the lid had left a circular impression* **indentation**, dent, mark, outline, imprint. 5 *he did a good impression of their science teacher* **impersonation**, imitation, caricature; informal take-off.

impressionable ▸ adjective easily influenced.

Impressionism ▸ noun a style of painting concerned with showing the visual impression of a particular moment.
☐ **Impressionist** noun & adjective.

impressionist ▸ noun an entertainer who impersonates famous people.

impressionistic ▸ adjective based on personal ideas or feelings.

impressive ▸ adjective arousing admiration through size, quality, or skill.

SYNONYMS **magnificent**, majestic, imposing, splendid, spectacular, grand, awe-inspiring, stunning, breathtaking.
ANTONYMS unimpressive.

☐ **impressively** adverb.

imprimatur /im-pri-**mah**-ter/ ▸ noun the authority or approval of someone.

imprint ▸ verb /im-**print**/ make a mark on an object by pressing something on to it.

> SYNONYMS *patterns can be imprinted in the clay* **stamp**, print, impress, mark, emboss.

▸ noun /**im**-print/ 1 a mark made by pressing something on to an object. 2 a publisher's name and other details printed in a book.

> SYNONYMS *her feet left imprints on the floor* **impression**, print, mark, stamp, indentation.

imprison ▸ verb put or keep in prison.

> SYNONYMS **incarcerate**, send to prison, jail, lock up, put away, intern, detain, hold prisoner, hold captive; informal send down; Brit. informal bang up.
> ANTONYMS release.

☐ **imprisonment** noun.

improbable ▸ adjective not likely to be true or to happen.

> SYNONYMS 1 *it seemed improbable that the hot weather would continue* **unlikely**, doubtful, dubious, debatable, questionable, uncertain. 2 *an improbable exaggeration* **unconvincing**, unbelievable, implausible, unlikely.
> ANTONYMS probable, believable.

☐ **improbability** noun **improbably** adverb.

impromptu /im-**promp**-tyoo/ ▸ adjective & adverb done without being planned or rehearsed.

improper ▸ adjective 1 not fitting in with accepted standards of behaviour. 2 not modest or decent.

> SYNONYMS 1 *it is improper for police to accept gifts* **unacceptable**, unprofessional, irregular, unethical, dishonest. 2 *it was improper for young ladies to drive a young man home* **unseemly**, unfitting, unbecoming, unladylike, ungentlemanly, inappropriate, indelicate, indecent, immodest, indecorous, immoral. 3 *an extremely improper poem* **indecent**, risqué, suggestive, naughty, dirty, filthy, vulgar, crude, rude, obscene, lewd; informal blue, raunchy, steamy.
> ANTONYMS acceptable, decent, clean.

impropriety /im-pruh-**pry**-uh-ti/ ▸ noun (plural **improprieties**) improper behaviour.

improve ▸ verb (**improves**, **improving**, **improved**) 1 make or become better. 2 (**improve on**) produce something better than.

> SYNONYMS 1 *ways to improve the service* **make better**, ameliorate, upgrade, refine, enhance, boost, build on, raise. 2 *communications improved* **get better**, advance, progress, develop, make headway, make progress, pick

up, look up, move forward. 3 *the patient is improving* **recover**, get better, recuperate, rally, revive, be on the mend.
> ANTONYMS worsen, deteriorate.

improvement ▸ noun 1 the action of making or becoming better. 2 something that improves something or is better than something else.

> SYNONYMS **advance**, development, upgrade, refinement, enhancement, betterment, amelioration, boost, augmentation, rally, recovery, upswing.

improvident ▸ adjective not thinking about or preparing for the future.

improvise ▸ verb (**improvises**, **improvising**, **improvised**) 1 invent and perform music or drama without planning it in advance. 2 make something from whatever is available.

> SYNONYMS 1 *she was improvising in front of the cameras* **extemporize**, ad-lib; informal speak off the cuff, play it by ear, busk it, wing it. 2 *she improvised a sandpit* **contrive**, devise, throw together, cobble together, rig up; informal whip up, rustle up; Brit. informal knock up.

☐ **improvisation** noun.

imprudent ▸ adjective not sensible or careful.

impudent ▸ adjective not showing respect for another person.

☐ **impudence** noun **impudently** adverb.

impugn /im-**pyoon**/ ▸ verb formal express doubts about whether something is true or honest.

impulse ▸ noun 1 a sudden urge to do something. 2 a force that makes something happen.

> SYNONYMS 1 *she had an impulse to hide* **urge**, instinct, drive, compulsion, itch, whim, desire, fancy, notion. 2 *a man of impulse* **spontaneity**, impetuosity, recklessness, rashness.
> ANTONYMS forethought.

impulsive ▸ adjective acting without thinking ahead.

> SYNONYMS 1 *he had an impulsive nature* **impetuous**, spontaneous, hasty, passionate, emotional. 2 *an impulsive decision* **impromptu**, snap, spontaneous, unpremeditated, spur-of-the-moment.
> ANTONYMS cautious, premeditated.

☐ **impulsively** adverb.

impunity /im-**pyoo**-ni-ti/ ▸ noun freedom from being punished or hurt.

impure ▸ adjective 1 mixed with unwanted substances. 2 morally wrong.

impurity ▸ noun (plural **impurities**) 1 the state of being impure. 2 a thing which makes something less pure.

i

impute /im-pyoot/ ▶ verb (imputes,
imputing, imputed) (impute something to)
believe that something has been done or
caused by.
□ imputation noun.

in ▶ preposition 1 expressing the position of
something that is enclosed or surrounded.
2 expressing movement which results in
something being enclosed or surrounded.
3 expressing a period of time before
or during which something happens.
4 expressing a state or quality. 5 indicating
that something is included or involved.
6 indicating the language or material used
by someone. 7 used to express a value as a
proportion of a whole.
▶ adverb 1 expressing the state of being
enclosed or surrounded. 2 expressing
movement which results in being enclosed
or surrounded. 3 present at your home or
office. 4 having arrived at a destination.
5 (of the tide) rising or at its highest level.
▶ adjective informal fashionable.
■ in-depth thorough and detailed. in-house
within an organization. in-joke a joke
shared only by a small group. the ins and
outs informal all the details.

in. ▶ abbreviation inches.

inability ▶ noun the state of being unable to
do something.

in absentia /in ab-sen-ti-uh/ ▶ adverb while
not present.

inaccessible ▶ adjective 1 unable to be
reached or used. 2 difficult to understand.

inaccurate ▶ adjective not accurate.

SYNONYMS **inexact,** imprecise, incorrect,
wrong, erroneous, faulty, imperfect,
defective, unreliable, false, mistaken,
untrue; Brit. informal adrift.
ANTONYMS accurate.

□ inaccuracy noun (plural inaccuracies)
inaccurately adverb.

inactive ▶ adjective not active or working.
□ inaction noun.

inactivity ▶ noun lack of activity.

SYNONYMS **inaction,** inertia, idleness,
non-intervention, negligence, apathy,
indolence, laziness, slothfulness.
ANTONYMS action.

inadequate ▶ adjective 1 not enough or
not good enough. 2 unable to deal with a
situation.

SYNONYMS **1** inadequate water supplies
insufficient, deficient, poor, scant,
scarce, sparse, in short supply, paltry,
meagre. **2** he's a bit inadequate
incapable, incompetent, immature;
informal not up to scratch.
ANTONYMS adequate.

□ inadequacy noun (plural inadequacies)
inadequately adverb.

inadmissible ▶ adjective (of evidence in
court) not accepted as valid.

inadvertent ▶ adjective not deliberate or
intentional.

✔ -ent, not -ant: inadvertent.

inadvertently ▶ adverb in an inadvertent
way.

SYNONYMS **accidentally,** by accident,
unintentionally, by mistake, mistakenly,
unwittingly.
ANTONYMS intentionally.

inadvisable ▶ adjective likely to have
unfortunate results.

inalienable ▶ adjective unable to be taken
away or given away.

inane ▶ adjective silly or stupid.
□ inanely adverb inanity noun.

inanimate ▶ adjective not alive.

inapplicable ▶ adjective not relevant or
appropriate.

inappropriate ▶ adjective not suitable or
appropriate.

SYNONYMS **unsuitable,** unfitting,
unseemly, unbecoming, improper, out
of place/keeping, inapposite; informal out
of order.
ANTONYMS appropriate.

□ inappropriately adverb.

inarticulate ▶ adjective 1 unable to express
your ideas clearly. 2 not expressed in
words.

inasmuch ▶ adverb (inasmuch as) 1 to the
extent that. 2 considering that; since.

inattentive ▶ adjective not paying
attention.
□ inattention noun.

inaudible ▶ adjective unable to be heard.

SYNONYMS **unclear,** indistinct, faint,
muted, soft, low, muffled, whispered,
muttered, murmured, mumbled.

□ inaudibly adverb.

inaugural ▶ adjective marking the start of
something important.

inaugurate ▶ verb (inaugurates,
inaugurating, inaugurated) 1 begin or
introduce a system or project. 2 mark
the beginning of an organization or the
opening of a building with a ceremony.
3 establish someone in office.

SYNONYMS **1** he inaugurated a new policy
initiate, begin, start, institute, launch,
get going, get under way, establish,
bring in, usher in; informal kick off. **2** the
museum was inaugurated on September
19 **open,** open officially, declare open;
dedicate, consecrate; unveil, take the
wraps off. close. **3** the new President will
be inaugurated **install,** instate, swear in,

invest, ordain, crown.
ANTONYMS terminate, abolish, dismiss.
□ **inauguration** noun.

inauspicious ▶ adjective not likely to lead to success.

inauthentic ▶ noun not genuine or sincere.

inborn ▶ adjective existing from birth.

inbred ▶ adjective 1 produced by breeding from closely related people or animals.
2 existing from birth; inborn.

inbreeding ▶ noun breeding from closely related people or animals.

inbuilt ▶ adjective existing as an original or important part.

Inc. ▶ abbreviation N. Amer. Incorporated.

Inca ▶ noun a member of a South American Indian people living in the Andes before the Spanish conquest.

incalculable ▶ adjective too great to be calculated or estimated.

incandescent ▶ adjective glowing as a result of being heated.
□ **incandescence** noun.

incantation ▶ noun a magic spell or charm.
□ **incantatory** adjective.

incapable ▶ adjective 1 (**incapable of**) not able to do something. 2 not able to look after yourself.

SYNONYMS **incompetent**, inept, inadequate, ineffective, ineffectual, unfit, unqualified, unequal to the task; informal not up to it.
ANTONYMS competent.

incapacitate ▶ verb (**incapacitates, incapacitating, incapacitated**) prevent from working in a normal way.
□ **incapacitation** noun.

incapacity ▶ noun (plural **incapacities**) inability to do something.

incarcerate ▶ verb (**incarcerates, incarcerating, incarcerated**) imprison.
□ **incarceration** noun.

incarnate ▶ adjective in human form.

incarnation ▶ noun 1 a god, spirit, or quality in human form. 2 (**the Incarnation**) (in Christian belief) God taking human form as Jesus.

incautious ▶ adjective not concerned about possible problems.

incendiary ▶ adjective 1 (of a bomb) designed to cause fires. 2 tending to cause strong feelings.
▶ noun (plural **incendiaries**) an incendiary bomb.

incense¹ /in-senss/ ▶ noun a substance that produces a sweet smell when you burn it.

incense² /in-senss/ ▶ verb (**incenses, incensing, incensed**) make very angry.

SYNONYMS 1 **enrage**, infuriate, anger, madden, outrage, exasperate, antagonize, provoke; informal make someone see red; N. Amer. informal burn someone up. 2 (**incensed**) **enraged**, furious, infuriated, irate, raging, incandescent, fuming, seething, beside oneself, outraged; informal mad, hopping mad, wild, livid.
ANTONYMS placate, please.

incentive ▶ noun something that influences or encourages you to do something.

SYNONYMS **inducement**, motivation, motive, reason, stimulus, spur, impetus, encouragement, carrot; informal sweetener.
ANTONYMS deterrent.

inception ▶ noun the beginning of an organization or activity.

incessant ▶ adjective never stopping.
□ **incessantly** adverb.

incest ▶ noun sex between people who are very closely related in a family.

incestuous ▶ adjective 1 involving incest.
2 involving a group of people who are very close and do not want to include others.

inch ▶ noun 1 a unit of length equal to one twelfth of a foot (2.54 cm). 2 a very small amount or distance.
▶ verb move along slowly and carefully.

inchoate /in-koh-uht/ ▶ adjective just beginning and so not fully formed or developed.

incidence ▶ noun 1 the extent to which something happens. 2 Physics the meeting of a line or ray with a surface.

incident ▶ noun 1 something that happens.
2 a violent event.

SYNONYMS 1 *incidents in his youth* **event**, occurrence, episode, happening, affair, business, adventure, exploit, escapade.
2 *police are investigating another incident* **disturbance**, commotion, clash, confrontation, accident, shooting, explosion, scene, situation. 3 *the journey was not without incident* **excitement**, adventure, drama, crisis, danger.

incidental ▶ adjective 1 occurring in connection with something else. 2 relatively unimportant.

SYNONYMS 1 *incidental details* **secondary**, subsidiary, minor, peripheral, background, by-the-by, unimportant, insignificant, tangential. 2 *an incidental discovery* **chance**, accidental, random, fluky, fortuitous, serendipitous, coincidental, unlooked-for.
ANTONYMS essential.

■ **incidental music** background music in a film or play.

incidentally ▸ adverb 1 by the way. 2 in an incidental way.

SYNONYMS 1 *incidentally, I haven't had a reply yet* by the way, by the by, in passing, speaking of which; informal as it happens. 2 *the infection was discovered incidentally* by chance, by accident, accidentally, fortuitously, by a fluke, by happenstance.

incinerate ▸ verb (incinerates, incinerating, incinerated) destroy by burning.
□ **incineration** noun.

incinerator ▸ noun a device for burning rubbish.

incipient ▸ adjective beginning to happen or develop.

incise ▸ verb (incises, incising, incised) mark a surface by cutting into it.

incision ▸ noun 1 a cut made as part of a surgical operation. 2 the action of cutting into something.

incisive ▸ adjective 1 showing clear thought and good understanding. 2 quick and direct.

incisor ▸ noun a narrow-edged tooth at the front of the mouth.

incite ▸ verb (incites, inciting, incited) encourage someone to do something violent or unlawful.

SYNONYMS 1 *he was arrested for inciting racial hatred* stir up, whip up, encourage, stoke up, fuel, kindle, inflame, instigate, provoke, excite, trigger, spark off. 2 *she incited him to commit murder* provoke, encourage, urge, goad, spur on, egg on, drive, prod, prompt; informal put up to.
ANTONYMS discourage, deter.

□ **incitement** noun.

incivility ▸ noun rude speech or behaviour.

inclement /in-klem-uhnt/ ▸ adjective (of the weather) unpleasantly cold or wet.
□ **inclemency** noun.

inclination ▸ noun 1 a tendency to do things in a particular way. 2 (**inclination for** or **to do**) an interest in or liking for. 3 a slope or slant.

SYNONYMS **tendency,** propensity, leaning, predisposition, predilection, impulse, bent, liking, taste, penchant, preference.
ANTONYMS aversion.

incline ▸ verb /in-klyn/ (inclines, inclining, inclined) 1 (**incline to** or **be inclined to**) tend to do or think in a particular way. 2 lean or bend.

SYNONYMS 1 *his prejudice inclines him to overlook obvious facts* predispose, lead, make, dispose, prejudice, prompt, induce. 2 (**inclined**) *I'm inclined to believe her* disposed, minded, of a mind. 3 (**inclined**) *she's inclined to gossip* prone, given, in the habit of, liable, apt. 4 *I incline to the opposite view* tend, lean, swing, veer, gravitate, be drawn, prefer, favour, go for. 5 *he inclined his head* bend, bow, nod, bob, lower, dip.

▸ noun /in-klyn/ a slope.

SYNONYMS *a steep incline* slope, gradient, pitch, ramp, bank, ascent, rise, hill, dip, descent; N. Amer. grade.

include ▸ verb (includes, including, included) 1 have something as part of a whole. 2 make part of a whole.

SYNONYMS 1 *activities include drama and music* incorporate, comprise, encompass, cover, embrace, take in, number, contain. 2 *include the cost of repairs* allow for, count, take into account, take into consideration. 3 *include your address* add, insert, put in, append, enter.
ANTONYMS exclude, leave out.

including ▸ preposition having as part of a whole.

inclusion ▸ noun 1 the act of including. 2 a person or thing that is included.

inclusive ▸ adjective 1 including everything expected or required. 2 between the limits stated.

SYNONYMS **all-in,** comprehensive, overall, full, all-round, umbrella, catch-all, all-encompassing.
ANTONYMS exclusive, limited.

incognito /in-kog-nee-toh/ ▸ adjective & adverb having your true identity concealed.

incoherent ▸ adjective 1 hard to understand; not clear. 2 not logical or well organized.
□ **incoherence** noun **incoherently** adverb.

incombustible ▸ adjective (of a material) that does not burn.

income ▸ noun money received for work or from investments.

SYNONYMS **earnings,** salary, wages, pay, remuneration, revenue, receipts, takings, profits, proceeds, yield, dividend; N. Amer. take.
ANTONYMS expenditure, outgoings.

■ **income tax** tax that must be paid on personal income.

incomer ▸ noun Brit. a person who has come to live in an area in which they have not grown up.

incoming ▸ adjective 1 coming in or arriving. 2 (of a public official) having just been chosen to replace someone.

SYNONYMS 1 *incoming flights* arriving, approaching, inbound, inward, returning, homeward. 2 *the incoming president* new, next, future, ... elect, ... designate.
ANTONYMS outward, outgoing.

incommensurable /in-kuh-**men**-shuh-ruh-b'l/ ▸ adjective not able to be compared.

incommode ▸ verb (**incommodes, incommoding, incommoded**) formal cause someone difficulties or problems.

incommunicado /in-kuh-myoo-ni-kah-doh/ ▸ adjective & adverb not able to communicate with other people.

incomparable /in-**kom**-puh-ruh-b'l/ ▸ adjective so good that nothing can be compared to it.
□ **incomparably** adverb.

incompatible ▸ adjective 1 (of two things) not able to exist or be used together. 2 (of two people) unable to live or work together without disagreeing.

> SYNONYMS **mismatched,** unsuited, poles apart, irreconcilable, inconsistent, conflicting, opposed, opposite, contradictory, at odds, at variance. ANTONYMS well matched, harmonious, consistent.

□ **incompatibility** noun.

incompetent ▸ adjective not having the skill to do something well.

> SYNONYMS **inept,** unskilled, inexpert, amateurish, unprofessional, bungling, blundering, clumsy; informal useless, not up to it.
> ANTONYMS competent.

□ **incompetence** noun **incompetently** adverb.

incomplete ▸ adjective not complete.

> SYNONYMS 1 *the manuscript is still incomplete* **unfinished,** uncompleted, partial, half-finished. 2 *incomplete information* **deficient,** insufficient, partial, sketchy, fragmentary, scrappy, bitty.
> ANTONYMS completed, full.

□ **incompletely** adverb.

incomprehensible ▸ adjective not able to be understood.

> SYNONYMS **unintelligible,** impenetrable, unclear, indecipherable, unfathomable, abstruse, difficult, involved; Brit. informal double Dutch.
> ANTONYMS intelligible, clear.

□ **incomprehension** noun.

inconceivable ▸ adjective not able to be imagined or believed.
□ **inconceivably** adverb.

inconclusive ▸ adjective not leading to a firm conclusion.
□ **inconclusively** adverb.

incongruous /in-**kong**-groo-uhss/ ▸ adjective out of place.
□ **incongruity** noun **incongruously** adverb.

inconsequential ▸ adjective not important.
□ **inconsequentially** adverb.

inconsiderable ▸ adjective small in size or amount.

inconsiderate ▸ adjective not thinking about other people's feelings.

inconsistent ▸ adjective 1 having parts that contradict each other. 2 (**inconsistent with**) not in keeping with.

> SYNONYMS 1 *inconsistent behaviour* **erratic,** changeable, unpredictable, variable, unstable, fickle, unreliable, volatile; informal up and down. 2 *he had done nothing inconsistent with his morality* **incompatible,** conflicting, at odds, at variance, irreconcilable, out of keeping, contrary to.
> ANTONYMS consistent.

□ **inconsistency** noun (plural **inconsistencies**).

inconsolable ▸ adjective not able to be comforted.

inconspicuous ▸ adjective not noticeable.
□ **inconspicuously** adverb.

inconstant ▸ adjective 1 formal not faithful or dependable. 2 frequently changing.

incontestable ▸ adjective not able to be disputed.

incontinent ▸ adjective 1 unable to control your bladder or bowels. 2 lacking self-control.
□ **incontinence** noun.

incontrovertible ▸ adjective not able to be denied or disputed.
□ **incontrovertibly** adverb.

inconvenience ▸ noun slight trouble or difficulty.

> SYNONYMS 1 *we apologize for any inconvenience caused* **trouble,** bother, problems, disruption, difficulty, disturbance; informal aggravation, hassle. 2 *his early arrival was clearly an inconvenience* **nuisance,** trouble, bother, problem; informal headache, pain, pain in the neck, hassle.

▸ verb (**inconveniences, inconveniencing, inconvenienced**) cause someone inconvenience.

> SYNONYMS *I don't want to inconvenience you* **trouble,** bother, put out, put to any trouble, disturb, impose on.

inconvenient ▸ adjective causing trouble or difficulty.

> SYNONYMS **awkward,** difficult, inopportune, badly timed, unsuitable, inappropriate, unfortunate.
> ANTONYMS convenient.

□ **inconveniently** adverb.

incorporate ▸ verb (**incorporates, incorporating, incorporated**) include something as part of a whole.

> SYNONYMS 1 *the region was incorporated into Moldavian territory* **absorb,** include, subsume, assimilate, integrate, swallow up. 2 *the model incorporates advanced*

i

features **include,** contain, embrace, build in, offer, boast. **3** *incorporate the salt and the butter* **blend,** mix, combine, fold in, stir in.
ANTONYMS partition, separate.

□ **incorporation** noun.

incorporated ▸ adjective (of a company) formed into a legal corporation.

incorporeal /in-kor-**por**-i-uhl/ ▸ adjective without a body or form.

incorrect ▸ adjective not true or accurate.

SYNONYMS **1** *an incorrect answer* **wrong,** erroneous, mistaken, untrue, false. **2** *incorrect behaviour* **inappropriate,** unsuitable, unacceptable, improper, unseemly; informal out of order.
ANTONYMS correct.

□ **incorrectly** adverb.

incorrigible ▸ adjective having bad habits that cannot be changed.

incorruptible ▸ adjective too honest to be corrupted by taking bribes.

increase ▸ verb /in-**kreess**/ (increases, increasing, increased) make or become greater in size, amount, or strength.

SYNONYMS **1** *demand is likely to increase* **grow,** get bigger, get larger, enlarge, expand, swell, rise, climb, mount, intensify, strengthen, extend, spread, widen. **2** *higher expectations will increase user demand* **add to,** make larger, make bigger, augment, supplement, top up, build up, extend, raise, swell, inflate, intensify, heighten; informal up, bump up.
ANTONYMS decrease, reduce.

▸ noun /**in**-kreess/ a rise in amount, size, or strength.

SYNONYMS *the increase in size* | *an increase in demand* **growth,** rise, enlargement, expansion, extension, increment, gain, addition, augmentation, surge; informal hike.
ANTONYMS decrease.

increasingly ▸ adverb more and more.

incredible ▸ adjective **1** impossible or hard to believe. **2** informal very good.

SYNONYMS **1** *I find his story incredible* **unbelievable,** unconvincing, far-fetched, implausible, improbable, inconceivable, unimaginable. **2** *an incredible feat of engineering* **wonderful,** marvellous, spectacular, remarkable, phenomenal, prodigious, breathtaking; informal fantastic, terrific.
ANTONYMS believable, unremarkable.

□ **incredibly** adverb.

incredulity /in-kre-**dyoo**-li-ti/ ▸ noun unwillingness or inability to believe something.

incredulous ▸ adjective unwilling or unable to believe something.
□ **incredulously** adverb.

increment /**ing**-kri-muhnt/ ▸ noun an increase in a number or amount.
□ **incremental** adjective.

incriminate ▸ verb (incriminates, incriminating, incriminated) make it look as though someone has done something wrong or illegal.
□ **incrimination** noun.

incubate ▸ verb (incubates, incubating, incubated) **1** (of a bird) sit on eggs to keep them warm so that they hatch. **2** keep bacteria and cells at a suitable temperature so that they develop. **3** (of an infectious disease) develop slowly without obvious signs.
□ **incubation** noun **incubator** noun.

incubus /**ing**-kyuu-buhss/ ▸ noun (plural incubi /**ing**-kyuu-by/) (in folkore) a male demon believed to have sex with sleeping women.

inculcate /in-kul-kayt/ ▸ verb (inculcates, inculcating, inculcated) fix ideas in someone's mind by repeating them.
□ **inculcation** noun.

incumbency ▸ noun (plural incumbencies) the period during which an official position is held.

incumbent ▸ adjective **1** (incumbent on) necessary for someone as a duty. **2** currently holding an official position.
▸ noun the holder of an official position.

incur ▸ verb (incurs, incurring, incurred) make something unwelcome happen.

SYNONYMS **bring upon yourself,** expose yourself to, lay yourself open to, run up, earn, sustain, experience.

incurable ▸ adjective not able to be cured.
□ **incurably** adverb.

incurious ▸ adjective not curious.

incursion ▸ noun a sudden invasion or attack.

indebted ▸ adjective **1** feeling grateful to someone. **2** owing money.

indecent ▸ adjective **1** causing offence by showing too much of the body or involving sex. **2** not appropriate.

SYNONYMS **1** *indecent photographs* **obscene,** dirty, filthy, rude, naughty, vulgar, smutty, pornographic; informal blue; euphemistic adult. **2** *indecent haste* **unseemly,** improper, unbecoming, inappropriate.

□ **indecency** noun **indecently** adverb.

indecipherable ▸ adjective not able to be read or understood.

indecisive ▸ adjective **1** not able to make decisions quickly. **2** not settling an issue.
□ **indecision** noun **indecisively** adverb **indecisiveness** noun.

indeed ▸ adverb **1** used to emphasize a statement. **2** used to introduce a further and stronger point.

indefatigable ▸ adjective never tiring.

indefensible ▸ adjective not able to be justified or defended.

indefinable ▸ adjective not able to be defined or described exactly.

indefinite ▸ adjective **1** not clearly stated, seen, or heard; vague. **2** lasting for an unknown length of time.
■ **indefinite article** Grammar the word *a* or *an*.
□ **indefinitely** adverb.

indelible ▸ adjective **1** (of ink or a mark) unable to be removed. **2** unable to be forgotten.
□ **indelibly** adverb.

indelicate ▸ adjective likely to be thought rude or embarrassing.

indemnify ▸ verb (**indemnifies**, **indemnifying**, **indemnified**) **1** pay money to someone to compensate for harm or loss. **2** insure someone against legal responsibility for their actions.

indemnity ▸ noun (plural **indemnities**) **1** insurance against legal responsibility for your actions. **2** a sum of money paid to compensate for damage or loss.

indent ▸ verb /in-**dent**/ **1** form hollows or notches in. **2** begin a line of writing further from the margin than the other lines.
▸ noun /in-**dent**/ Brit. an official order for goods.
□ **indentation** noun.

indenture ▸ noun a formal agreement or contract.

independence ▸ noun the fact or state of being independent.

> SYNONYMS **1** *the struggle for American independence* **self-government**, self-rule, home rule, self-determination, sovereignty, autonomy. **2** *the adviser's independence* **impartiality**, neutrality, disinterestedness, detachment, objectivity.
> ANTONYMS dependence, partiality.

independent ▸ adjective **1** free from the control or influence of others. **2** (of a country) self-governing. **3** having or earning enough money to support yourself. **4** not connected with another; separate.

> SYNONYMS **1** *an independent country* **self-governing**, self-ruling, self-determining, sovereign, autonomous, non-aligned. **2** *two independent groups verified the results* **separate**, different, unconnected, unrelated, discrete. **3** *an independent school* **private**, non-state-run, private-sector, fee-paying, privatized, deregulated, denationalized. **4** *independent advice* **impartial**,

unbiased, unprejudiced, neutral, disinterested, uninvolved, detached, dispassionate, objective, non-partisan, with no axe to grind.
> ANTONYMS dependent, related, state, public, biased.

▸ noun an independent person or body.

> ✔ **-ent**, not **-ant**: independ**ent**.

independently ▸ adverb in an independent way.

> SYNONYMS **alone**, on your own, separately, individually, unaccompanied, solo, unaided, unassisted, without help, by your own efforts, under your own steam, single-handedly.

indescribable ▸ adjective too extreme or unusual to be described.
□ **indescribably** adverb.

indestructible ▸ adjective not able to be destroyed.

indeterminate ▸ adjective not certain; vague.

index ▸ noun (plural **indexes** or **indices** /**in**-di-seez/) **1** a list of names or subjects referred to in a book, arranged in alphabetical order. **2** an alphabetical list or catalogue of books or documents. **3** a sign or measure of something.

> SYNONYMS **list**, listing, inventory, catalogue, register, directory, database.

▸ verb record in or provide with an index.
■ **index finger** the forefinger.

Indian ▸ noun **1** a person from India. **2** an American Indian.
▸ adjective **1** relating to India. **2** relating to American Indians.
■ **Indian ink** deep black ink used in drawing. **Indian summer** a period of dry, warm weather in late autumn.

indicate ▸ verb (**indicates**, **indicating**, **indicated**) **1** point something out. **2** be a sign of. **3** mention briefly. **4** (**be indicated**) formal be necessary or recommended.

> SYNONYMS **1** *sales indicate a growing market* **point to**, be a sign of, be evidence of, demonstrate, show, testify to, be symptomatic of, denote, mark, signal, reflect, signify, suggest, imply. **2** *the president indicated his willingness to use force* **state**, declare, make known, communicate, announce, put on record. **3** *please indicate your choice of prize on the form* **specify**, designate, stipulate, show.

indication ▸ noun a sign or piece of information that indicates something.

> SYNONYMS **sign**, signal, indicator, symptom, mark, demonstration, pointer, guide, hint, clue, omen, warning.

indicative /in-**dik**-uh-tiv/ ► adjective
1 acting as a sign. **2** Grammar (of a verb)
expressing a simple statement of fact (e.g.
she left).

indicator ► noun **1** a thing that shows the
state or level of something. **2** a light on a
vehicle that flashes to show that it is about
to turn left or right.

> SYNONYMS **measure,** gauge, meter,
> barometer, guide, index, mark, sign,
> signal.

indict /in-**dyt**/ ► verb formally accuse
someone of a serious crime.
□ **indictable** adjective.

indictment /in-**dyt**-muhnt/ ► noun **1** a
formal accusation that someone has
committed a serious crime. **2** an indication
that something is bad and deserves to be
condemned.

> SYNONYMS **charge,** accusation,
> arraignment, prosecution, citation,
> summons; N. Amer. impeachment.

indifference ► noun lack of interest or
concern.

> SYNONYMS **detachment,** lack of concern,
> disinterest, lack of interest, nonchalance,
> boredom, unresponsiveness, impassivity,
> coolness.
> ANTONYMS concern.

indifferent ► adjective **1** not interested
in or caring about something. **2** not very
good; mediocre.

> SYNONYMS **1** *an indifferent shrug*
> **detached,** unconcerned, uninterested,
> uncaring, casual, nonchalant, offhand,
> unenthusiastic, unimpressed, unmoved,
> impassive, cool. **2** *an indifferent
> performance* **mediocre,** ordinary,
> average, middle-of-the-road, uninspired,
> undistinguished, unexceptional,
> pedestrian, forgettable, amateurish;
> informal no great shakes, not up to much.
> ANTONYMS enthusiastic, brilliant.

□ **indifferently** adverb.

indigenous /in-**dij**-i-nuhss/ ► adjective
belonging to a place; native.

indigent /**in**-di-juhnt/ ► adjective poor;
needy.

indigestible ► adjective difficult or
impossible to digest.

indigestion ► noun pain or discomfort
caused by difficulty in digesting food.

indignant ► adjective feeling or showing
indignation.

> SYNONYMS **aggrieved,** affronted,
> displeased, resentful, angry, annoyed,
> offended, exasperated; informal peeved,
> irked, put out; Brit. informal narked; N. Amer.
> informal sore.
> ANTONYMS content.

□ **indignantly** adverb.

indignation ► noun anger caused by
something that you consider to be unfair.

indignity ► noun (plural **indignities**) a
thing that causes you to feel ashamed or
embarrassed.

indigo /**in**-di-goh/ ► noun a dark blue colour
or dye.

indirect ► adjective **1** not going in a
straight line. **2** not saying something in
a straightforward way. **3** happening as a
secondary effect or consequence.

> SYNONYMS **1** *an indirect route*
> **roundabout,** circuitous, meandering,
> winding, tortuous. **2** *an indirect
> attack* **oblique,** implicit, implied. **3** *an
> indirect effect* **incidental,** secondary,
> subordinate, ancillary, collateral,
> concomitant, contingent.
> ANTONYMS direct.

■ **indirect speech** reported speech.
□ **indirectly** adverb.

indiscipline ► noun lack of discipline.

indiscreet ► adjective too ready to reveal
things that should remain secret or private.
□ **indiscreetly** adverb.

indiscretion ► noun **1** indiscreet behaviour.
2 an indiscreet act or remark.

indiscriminate ► adjective done or acting
without careful judgement.
□ **indiscriminately** adverb.

indispensable ► adjective absolutely
necessary.

> ✔ **-able,** not **-ible:** indispens**able.**

indisposed ► adjective **1** slightly unwell.
2 unwilling.

indisposition ► noun a slight illness.

indisputable ► adjective unable to be
challenged or denied.
□ **indisputably** adverb.

indissoluble ► adjective unable to be
destroyed; lasting.

indistinct ► adjective not clear or sharply
defined.
□ **indistinctly** adverb.

indistinguishable ► adjective not able to
be distinguished.
□ **indistinguishably** adverb.

indium ► noun a soft silvery-white metallic
element.

individual ► adjective **1** considered
separately; single. **2** having to do with one
particular person. **3** striking or unusual;
original.

> SYNONYMS **1** *exhibitions devoted to
> individual artists* **single,** separate,
> discrete, independent, lone. **2** *he had
> his own individual style of music* **unique,**
> characteristic, distinctive, distinct,
> particular, idiosyncratic, peculiar,

personal, special. **3** *a highly individual apartment* **original,** exclusive, different, unusual, novel, unorthodox, out of the ordinary.
ANTONYMS multiple, shared, ordinary.

▸ noun **1** a single person or item as distinct from a group. **2** a distinctive or original person.

SYNONYMS *a rather stuffy individual* **person,** human being, soul, creature, character; informal type, sort, customer.

individualism ▸ noun **1** the quality of doing things in your own way; independence. **2** the belief that individual people should have freedom of action.
☐ **individualist** noun & adjective **individualistic** adjective.

individuality ▸ noun the quality or character of a person or thing that makes them different from other people or things.

individualize (or **individualise**)
▸ verb (**individualizes, individualizing, individualized**) give something an individual character.

individually ▸ adverb one by one; separately.

SYNONYMS **separately,** singly, one by one, one at a time, independently.
ANTONYMS together.

indivisible ▸ adjective unable to be divided or separated.

indoctrinate ▸ verb (**indoctrinates, indoctrinating, indoctrinated**) force someone to accept a set of beliefs.
☐ **indoctrination** noun.

Indo-European ▸ noun the family of languages spoken over most of Europe and Asia as far as northern India.
▸ adjective relating to Indo-European.

indolent /in-duh-luhnt/ ▸ adjective lazy.
☐ **indolence** noun.

indomitable /in-dom-i-tuh-b'l/ ▸ adjective impossible to defeat or subdue.

Indonesian ▸ noun **1** a person from Indonesia. **2** the group of languages spoken in Indonesia.
▸ adjective relating to Indonesia.

indoor ▸ adjective situated, done, or used inside a building.
▸ adverb (**indoors**) into or inside a building.

indubitable /in-dyoo-bi-tuh-b'l/ ▸ adjective impossible to doubt; certain.
☐ **indubitably** adverb.

induce ▸ verb (**induces, inducing, induced**) **1** persuade or influence someone to do something. **2** bring about or cause. **3** make a woman begin to give birth to her baby by means of special drugs.

SYNONYMS **1** *the pickets induced many workers to stay away* **persuade,** convince, prevail upon, get, make, prompt, encourage, cajole into, talk into. **2** *these activities induce a feeling of togetherness* **bring about,** cause, produce, create, give rise to, generate, engender.
ANTONYMS dissuade, prevent.

inducement ▸ noun a thing that persuades someone to do something.

induct ▸ verb formally admit someone to an organization or establish them in a position of authority.

inductance ▸ noun a process by which a change in the current of an electric circuit produces an electromotive force.

induction ▸ noun **1** introduction to a post or organization. **2** the action of inducing. **3** a method of reasoning in which a general rule or conclusion is drawn from particular facts or examples. **4** the passing of electricity or magnetism from one object to another without them touching.
☐ **inductive** adjective.

indulge ▸ verb (**indulges, indulging, indulged**) **1** (**indulge in**) allow yourself to do something that you enjoy. **2** satisfy a desire or interest. **3** allow someone to do or have whatever they wish.

SYNONYMS **1** *Sally indulged her passion for chocolate* **satisfy,** gratify, fulfil, feed, yield to, give in to. **2** *she did not like her children to be indulged* **pamper,** spoil, overindulge, coddle, mollycoddle, cosset, pander to, wait on hand and foot.

indulgence ▸ noun **1** the action of indulging in something. **2** a thing that is indulged in; a luxury. **3** willingness to tolerate someone's faults.

SYNONYMS **1** *the indulgence of all his desires* **satisfaction,** gratification, fulfilment. **2** *indulgence contributed to his ill-health* **self-gratification,** self-indulgence, overindulgence, intemperance, excess, lack of restraint, extravagance, hedonism. **3** *they viewed holidays as an indulgence* **extravagance,** luxury, treat, non-essential, extra, frill. **4** *her indulgence left him spoilt* **pampering,** coddling, mollycoddling, cosseting. **5** *his parents view his lapses with indulgence* **tolerance,** forbearance, understanding, compassion, sympathy, leniency.
ANTONYMS asceticism, intolerance.

indulgent ▸ adjective allowing someone to do or have whatever they want or overlooking their faults.

SYNONYMS **generous,** permissive, easy-going, liberal, tolerant, forgiving, forbearing, lenient, kind, kindly, soft-hearted.
ANTONYMS strict.

☐ **indulgently** adverb.

industrial ▸ adjective having to do with industry.
 ■ **industrial action** Brit. a strike or other action taken by workers as a protest.
 industrial estate Brit. an area of land developed as a site for factories.
 □ **industrially** adverb.

industrialist ▸ noun a person who owns or controls a large factory or manufacturing business.

SYNONYMS **manufacturer,** factory owner, captain of industry, magnate, tycoon.

industrialize (or **industrialise**)
 ▸ verb (**industrializes, industrializing, industrialized**) develop industries in a country or region on a wide scale.
 □ **industrialization** noun.

industrious ▸ adjective hard-working.
 □ **industriously** adverb.

industry ▸ noun (plural **industries**) **1** the manufacture of goods in factories. **2** a branch of economic or commercial activity. **3** hard work.

SYNONYMS **1** *British industry* **manufacturing,** production, construction, trade, commerce. **2** *the publishing industry* **business,** trade, field, line of business, profession. **3** *the kitchen was a hive of industry* **activity,** energy, effort, endeavour, hard work, industriousness, diligence, application.

inebriated /i-nee-bri-ay-tid/ ▸ adjective drunk.
 □ **inebriation** noun.

inedible ▸ adjective not fit for eating.

ineffable ▸ adjective too great or extreme to be expressed in words.

ineffective ▸ adjective not having any effect or achieving what you want.

SYNONYMS **1** *an ineffective scheme* **unsuccessful,** unproductive, unprofitable, ineffectual. **2** *an ineffective president* **ineffectual,** inefficient, inadequate, incompetent, incapable, unfit, inept; informal useless, hopeless.
ANTONYMS effective.

 □ **ineffectively** adverb.

ineffectual ▸ adjective **1** ineffective. **2** not forceful enough to do something well.
 □ **ineffectually** adverb.

inefficient ▸ adjective failing to make the best use of time or resources.

SYNONYMS **1** *an inefficient worker* **ineffective,** ineffectual, incompetent, inept, disorganized, unprepared.
2 *inefficient processes* **uneconomical,** wasteful, unproductive, time-wasting, slow, unsystematic.
ANTONYMS efficient.

 □ **inefficiency** noun **inefficiently** adverb.

inelegant ▸ adjective not elegant or graceful.

ineligible ▸ adjective not qualified to have or do something.

ineluctable ▸ adjective rare unable to be resisted or avoided.

inept ▸ adjective lacking skill.
 □ **ineptitude** noun **ineptly** adverb.

inequality ▸ noun (plural **inequalities**) lack of equality.

SYNONYMS **imbalance,** inequity, inconsistency, disparity, discrepancy, dissimilarity, difference, bias, prejudice, discrimination, unfairness.
ANTONYMS equality.

inequitable ▸ adjective unfair; unjust.

inequity ▸ noun (plural **inequities**) lack of fairness or justice.

ineradicable ▸ adjective unable to be rooted out or destroyed.

inert ▸ adjective **1** lacking the ability or strength to move or act. **2** without active chemical properties.

inertia /i-ner-shuh/ ▸ noun **1** a tendency to do nothing or to remain unchanged. **2** Physics a property by which matter remains still or continues moving unless acted on by an external force.

inescapable ▸ adjective unable to be avoided or denied.

inessential ▸ adjective not absolutely necessary.

inestimable ▸ adjective too great to be measured.

inevitable ▸ adjective certain to happen; unavoidable.

SYNONYMS **unavoidable,** inescapable, inexorable, assured, certain, sure.
ANTONYMS avoidable.

 □ **inevitability** noun.

inevitably ▸ adverb unavoidably.

SYNONYMS **unavoidably,** necessarily, automatically, naturally, as a matter of course, of necessity, inescapably, certainly, surely; informal like it or not.

inexact ▸ adjective not quite accurate.

inexcusable ▸ adjective too bad to be justified or tolerated.

inexhaustible ▸ adjective (of a supply) never ending because available in unlimited quantities.

inexorable /in-ek-suh-ruh-b'l/ ▸ adjective **1** impossible to stop or prevent. **2** unable to be persuaded.
 □ **inexorably** adverb.

inexpensive ▸ adjective not costing a lot of money.

SYNONYMS **cheap,** affordable, low-cost, economical, competitive, reasonable,

budget, economy, bargain, cut-price, reduced.
ANTONYMS expensive.

inexperience ▶ noun lack of experience.

inexperienced ▶ adjective not experienced.

SYNONYMS **inexpert,** untrained, unqualified, unskilled, unseasoned, naive, new, callow, immature; informal wet behind the ears, wide-eyed.
ANTONYMS experienced.

inexpert ▶ adjective lacking skill or knowledge in a particular field.

inexplicable ▶ adjective unable to be explained.
□ **inexplicably** adverb.

inexpressive ▶ adjective showing no feelings.

in extremis /in ek-**stree**-miss/ ▶ adverb **1** in a very difficult situation. **2** at the point of death.

inextricable ▶ adjective impossible to untangle or separate.
□ **inextricably** adverb.

infallible ▶ adjective incapable of making mistakes or being wrong.
□ **infallibility** noun **infallibly** adverb.

infamous /in-fuh-muhss/ ▶ adjective well known for some bad quality or act.

SYNONYMS **notorious,** disreputable, scandalous.
ANTONYMS reputable.

□ **infamously** adverb **infamy** noun.

infancy ▶ noun **1** the state or period of early childhood or babyhood. **2** an early stage of development.

SYNONYMS **beginnings,** early days, early stages, emergence, dawn, outset, birth, inception.
ANTONYMS end.

infant ▶ noun **1** a very young child or baby. **2** Brit. a schoolchild between the ages of about four and seven.

SYNONYMS **baby,** newborn, young child, tiny tot, little one; Medicine neonate; Scottish & N. English bairn, wean; informal tiny, sprog.

infanticide /in-**fan**-ti-syd/ ▶ noun the killing of a child.

infantile ▶ adjective **1** relating to infants. **2** disapproving childish.

infantry ▶ noun soldiers who fight on foot.

infatuate ▶ verb (be infatuated with) have a strong but short-lived feeling of love for.
□ **infatuation** noun.

infect ▶ verb **1** pass a germ that causes disease to a person, animal, or plant. **2** contaminate with something harmful.

SYNONYMS **1** *they can infect their children* **pass infection to,** contaminate. **2** *nitrates*

were infecting rivers **contaminate,** pollute, taint, foul, poison.

infection ▶ noun **1** the process of infecting. **2** an infectious disease.

SYNONYMS **1** *a kidney infection* **disease,** virus, illness, ailment, disorder, sickness; informal bug. **2** *the infection in his wounds* **contamination,** poison, inflammation, germs; Medicine sepsis.

infectious ▶ adjective **1** (of a disease or germ) able to be passed on through the environment. **2** liable to spread infection. **3** likely to spread to or influence other people.

SYNONYMS **1** *infectious diseases* **communicable,** contagious, transmittable, transmissible, transferable; informal catching. **2** *her laughter is infectious* **irresistible,** compelling, contagious; informal catching.

□ **infectiously** adverb.

infer ▶ verb (**infers, inferring, inferred**) work something out from the information you have available.

❗ On the difference between the words **imply** and **infer**, see the note at **IMPLY**.

inference ▶ noun **1** a conclusion drawn from the information available to you. **2** the process of inferring.

inferior ▶ adjective lower in quality or status.

SYNONYMS **1** *she regards him as inferior* **second-class,** lower-ranking, subordinate, junior, minor, lowly, humble, menial, beneath you.
2 *inferior accommodation* **second-rate,** substandard, low-grade, unsatisfactory, shoddy, poor; informal crummy, lousy.
ANTONYMS superior, luxury.

▶ noun a person who is lower in status or less good at doing something.

SYNONYMS *how dare she treat him as an inferior?* **subordinate,** junior, underling, minion.
ANTONYMS superior.

□ **inferiority** noun.

infernal ▶ adjective **1** having to do with hell or the underworld. **2** informal very annoying.

inferno ▶ noun (plural **infernos**) a large uncontrollable fire.

infertile ▶ adjective **1** unable to have babies or other young. **2** (of land) unable to produce crops or plants.

SYNONYMS **1** **sterile,** barren, childless. **2** **barren,** unproductive, impoverished, arid.
ANTONYMS fertile.

□ **infertility** noun.

infest ▶ verb (especially of insects or rats) be present in large numbers so as to cause damage or disease.

SYNONYMS (**infested**) **overrun**, swarming, teeming, crawling, alive, plagued.

☐ **infestation** noun.

infidel /in-fi-duhl/ ▶ noun old use a person who has no religion or whose religion is not that of the majority.

infidelity ▶ noun (plural **infidelities**) the action or state of not being faithful to your sexual partner.

infighting ▶ noun conflict within a group or organization.

infiltrate ▶ verb enter or gain access to an organization or place secretly and gradually.

SYNONYMS **penetrate**, insinuate yourself into, worm your way into, sneak into, slip into, creep into, invade.

☐ **infiltration** noun.

infiltrator ▶ noun a person who infiltrates.

SYNONYMS **spy**, secret agent, plant, intruder, interloper, subversive, informer, mole, fifth columnist; N. Amer. informal **spook**.

infinite ▶ adjective 1 having no limits and impossible to measure. 2 very great in amount or degree.

SYNONYMS 1 *the universe is infinite* **boundless**, unbounded, unlimited, limitless, never-ending, incalculable, untold. 2 *in infinite combinations* **countless**, uncountable, innumerable, numberless, immeasurable.
ANTONYMS finite, limited.

☐ **infinitely** adverb.

infinitesimal /in-fi-ni-tess-i-muhl/ ▶ adjective very small.
☐ **infinitesimally** adverb.

infinitive /in-fin-i-tiv/ ▶ noun the basic form of a verb, normally occurring in English with the word *to* (as in *to see, to ask*).

infinity ▶ noun (plural **infinities**) 1 the state or quality of being infinite. 2 a very great number or amount.

infirm ▶ adjective physically weak.

infirmary ▶ noun (plural **infirmaries**) a place where sick people are cared for.

infirmity ▶ noun (plural **infirmities**) physical or mental weakness.

inflame ▶ verb (**inflames, inflaming, inflamed**) 1 make someone feel something passionately. 2 make a difficult situation worse. 3 (**inflamed**) (of a part of the body) red, swollen, and hot as a result of infection or injury.

SYNONYMS 1 *his opinions inflamed his rival* **enrage**, incense, anger, madden, infuriate, exasperate, provoke, antagonize; informal make someone see red. 2 *he inflamed a sensitive situation* **aggravate**, exacerbate, intensify, worsen, compound. 3 (**inflamed**) **swollen**, red, hot, burning, itchy, sore, painful, tender, infected.
ANTONYMS placate, calm.

inflammable ▶ adjective easily set on fire.

❗ **Inflammable** and **flammable** both mean 'easily set on fire'. It's safer to use **flammable**, however, because **inflammable** is sometimes taken to mean 'non-flammable'.

inflammation ▶ noun a condition in which an area of the skin is red, swollen, and hot.

inflammatory ▶ adjective 1 making people feel angry. 2 relating to or causing inflammation.

inflatable ▶ adjective capable of being inflated.
▶ noun an inflatable plastic or rubber boat.

inflate ▶ verb (**inflates, inflating, inflated**) 1 expand something by filling it with air or gas. 2 increase the cost or price of something by a large amount. 3 (**inflated**) exaggerated.

SYNONYMS 1 *inflate the balloon* **blow up**, pump up, fill, puff up/out, dilate, distend, swell, bloat. 2 *the demand inflated prices* **increase**, raise, boost, escalate, put up; informal hike up, jack up. 3 (**inflated**) *inflated prices* **high**, sky-high, excessive, unreasonable, outrageous, exorbitant, extortionate; Brit. over the odds; informal steep. 4 (**inflated**) *an inflated opinion of himself* **exaggerated**, immoderate, overblown, overstated.
ANTONYMS deflate, lower.

inflation ▶ noun 1 the action of inflating. 2 a general increase in prices and fall in the value of money.
☐ **inflationary** adjective.

inflect ▶ verb 1 Grammar (of a word) be changed by inflection. 2 vary the tone or pitch of your voice.

inflection ▶ noun 1 Grammar a change in the form of a word to show its grammatical function, number, or gender. 2 a variation in the tone or pitch of a voice.

inflexible ▶ adjective 1 not able to be altered or adapted. 2 unwilling to change or compromise. 3 not able to be bent.
☐ **inflexibility** noun.

inflict ▶ verb (**inflict something on**) make someone experience something unpleasant or painful.

SYNONYMS 1 *he inflicted an injury on Frank* **give**, administer, deal out, mete out,

cause someone something, exact, wreak. **2** *I won't inflict my views on my children* **impose,** force, thrust, foist.
ANTONYMS spare.

□ **infliction** noun.

inflorescence /in-fluh-**ress**-uhnss/ ▸ noun
Botany a cluster of flowers on a single stem.

influence ▸ noun **1** the power or ability to affect someone's beliefs or actions. **2** a person or thing with such ability or power. **3** the power arising out of status, contacts, or wealth.

SYNONYMS **1** *the influence of parents on their children* **effect,** impact, control, spell, hold, magic. **2** *a bad influence on young girls* **example to,** role model for, inspiration to. **3** *political influence* **power,** authority, sway, leverage, weight, pull; informal clout.

▸ verb (**influences, influencing, influenced**) have an influence on.

SYNONYMS **1** *bosses can influence our careers* **affect,** have an impact on, determine, guide, control, shape, govern, decide, change, alter. **2** *an attempt to influence the jury* **sway,** bias, prejudice, suborn, pressurize, coerce, intimidate; informal lean on; Brit. informal nobble.

influential ▸ adjective having great influence.

SYNONYMS **powerful,** controlling, important, authoritative, leading, significant, instrumental, guiding.

influenza ▸ noun a disease spread by a virus and causing fever, aching, and catarrh.

influx ▸ noun the arrival or entry of large numbers of people or things.

inform ▸ verb **1** give facts or information to. **2** (**inform on**) give information about someone's involvement in a crime to the police.

SYNONYMS **1** *she informed him that she was ill* **tell,** notify, apprise, advise, impart to, communicate to, let someone know, brief, enlighten, send word to. **2** *he informed on two colleagues* **betray,** give away, denounce, incriminate, report; informal rat, squeal, split, tell, blow the whistle, snitch; Brit. informal grass, shop; N. Amer. informal finger; Austral./NZ informal dob in.

informal ▸ adjective **1** relaxed and friendly, and not following strict rules of behaviour. **2** (of clothes) suitable for wearing when relaxing. **3** (of language) used in everyday speech and writing, rather than official contexts.

SYNONYMS **1** *an informal discussion* **unofficial,** casual, relaxed, easy-going, low-key. **2** *informal clothes* **casual,**

relaxed, comfortable, everyday, sloppy, leisure; informal comfy. **3** *informal language* **colloquial,** vernacular, idiomatic, popular, familiar, everyday; informal slangy, chatty.
ANTONYMS formal, official, smart, literary.

□ **informality** noun **informally** adverb.

informant ▸ noun a person who gives information to another.

information ▸ noun facts or details supplied to or learned by someone.

SYNONYMS **facts,** particulars, details, figures, statistics, data, knowledge, intelligence; informal info, gen.

■ **information technology** the use of computers and telecommunications for storing, retrieving, and sending information.

informative ▸ adjective providing useful information.

SYNONYMS **instructive,** illuminating, enlightening, revealing, explanatory, factual, educational, edifying.

informed ▸ adjective **1** having or showing knowledge. **2** (of a judgement) based on a sound understanding of the facts.

SYNONYMS **knowledgeable,** enlightened, educated, briefed, up to date, up to speed, in the picture, in the know, au fait; informal clued up.
ANTONYMS ignorant.

informer ▸ noun a person who informs on another person to the police.

infraction ▸ noun a breaking of a law or agreement.

infra dig /in-fruh **dig**/ ▸ adjective informal beneath your dignity.

infrared ▸ adjective (of electromagnetic radiation) having a wavelength just greater than that of red light.

infrastructure ▸ noun the basic things (e.g. buildings, roads, power supplies) needed for the operation of a society or enterprise.

infrequent ▸ adjective not happening often.
□ **infrequency** noun **infrequently** adverb.

infringe ▸ verb **1** break a law or agreement. **2** restrict a right or privilege.
□ **infringement** noun.

infuriate ▸ verb (**infuriates, infuriating, infuriated**) make someone angry.

SYNONYMS **enrage,** incense, provoke, anger, madden, exasperate; informal make someone see red; Brit. informal wind up.
ANTONYMS please.

□ **infuriating** adjective.

infuse ▸ verb (**infuses, infusing, infused**) **1** spread throughout something. **2** soak tea or herbs to extract the flavour or healing properties.

infusion ▸ noun 1 a drink prepared by soaking tea or herbs. 2 the action of infusing.

ingenious ▸ adjective clever, original, and inventive.

SYNONYMS **inventive,** creative, imaginative, original, innovative, pioneering, resourceful, enterprising, inspired, clever.
ANTONYMS unimaginative.

□ **ingeniously** adverb.

ingénue /an-zhuh-nyoo/ ▸ noun a naive young woman.

ingenuity ▸ noun the quality of being ingenious.

ingenuous /in-jen-yoo-uhss/ ▸ adjective innocent and unsuspecting.

ingest ▸ verb take food or drink into the body by swallowing it.
□ **ingestion** noun.

inglenook ▸ noun a space on either side of a large fireplace.

inglorious ▸ adjective not making you feel proud; rather shameful.

ingoing ▸ adjective going towards or into.

ingot ▸ noun a rectangular block of steel, gold, or other metal.

ingrained (or engrained) ▸ adjective 1 (of a habit or belief) firmly established. 2 (of dirt) deeply embedded.

ingratiate /in-gray-shi-ayt/ ▸ verb (ingratiates, ingratiating, ingratiated) (ingratiate yourself) do things in order to make someone like you.

ingratitude ▸ noun a lack of appropriate gratitude.

ingredient ▸ noun 1 any of the substances that are combined to make a particular dish. 2 a component part or element.

SYNONYMS **constituent,** component, element, item, part, strand, unit, feature, aspect, attribute.

ingress ▸ noun 1 the action of entering or coming in. 2 a place or means of access.

ingrown (or ingrowing) ▸ adjective (of a toenail) having grown into the flesh.

inhabit ▸ verb (inhabits, inhabiting, inhabited) live in or occupy.

SYNONYMS **live in,** occupy, settle, people, populate, colonize.

□ **inhabitable** adjective.

inhabitant ▸ noun a person or animal that lives in or occupies a place.

SYNONYMS **resident,** occupant, occupier, settler, local, native; (**inhabitants**) population, populace, people, public, community, citizenry, townsfolk, townspeople.

inhale ▸ verb (inhales, inhaling, inhaled) breathe in air, smoke, etc.

SYNONYMS **breathe in,** draw in, suck in, sniff in, drink in, gasp.
ANTONYMS exhale.

□ **inhalation** noun.

inhaler ▸ noun a portable device used for inhaling a drug.

inherent ▸ adjective existing in something as a permanent or essential quality.
□ **inherently** adverb.

inherit ▸ verb (inherits, inheriting, inherited) 1 receive money or property from someone when they die. 2 have a quality or characteristic passed on to you from your parents or ancestors. 3 be left with something previously belonging to someone else.

SYNONYMS 1 *she inherited the farm* **be left,** be bequeathed, be willed, come into. 2 *Richard inherited the title* **succeed to,** assume, take over.
ANTONYMS leave.

inheritance ▸ noun 1 a thing that is inherited. 2 the action of inheriting.

SYNONYMS **legacy,** bequest, endowment, birthright, heritage, patrimony.

inhibit ▸ verb (inhibits, inhibiting, inhibited) 1 prevent or slow down a process. 2 make someone unable to act in a relaxed and natural way.

SYNONYMS 1 **impede,** hinder, hamper, hold back, discourage, interfere with, obstruct, slow down, retard. 2 (inhibited) **reserved,** reticent, guarded, self-conscious, insecure, withdrawn, repressed, undemonstrative, shy, diffident, bashful; informal uptight.
ANTONYMS assist, allow.

inhibition ▸ noun a feeling that makes you unable to act in a relaxed and natural way.

inhospitable ▸ adjective (of an environment) harsh and difficult to live in.

inhuman ▸ adjective 1 lacking positive human qualities; cruel and barbaric. 2 not human in nature or character.

inhumane ▸ adjective without pity; cruel.

inhumanity ▸ noun (plural inhumanities) cruel and brutal behaviour.

inimical ▸ adjective having a harmful effect on something; not helpful.

inimitable ▸ adjective impossible to imitate; unique.
□ **inimitably** adverb.

iniquity ▸ noun (plural iniquities) great injustice or unfairness.
□ **iniquitous** adjective.

initial ▸ adjective existing or occurring at the beginning.

SYNONYMS **beginning,** opening, commencing, starting, first, earliest, primary, preliminary, preparatory, introductory, inaugural.
ANTONYMS final.

▶ **noun** the first letter of a name or word.
▶ **verb** (**initials, initialling, initialled**; US spelling **initials, initialing, initialed**) mark something with your initials as a sign of approval or agreement.

initially ▶ **adverb** at first.

SYNONYMS **at first,** at the start, at the outset, in/at the beginning, to begin with, to start with, originally.

initiate ▶ **verb** (**initiates, initiating, initiated**) **1** make a process or action start. **2** admit someone into a society or group with a formal ceremony. **3** introduce someone to a new activity.

SYNONYMS **1** *the government initiated the scheme* **begin,** start (off), commence, institute, inaugurate, launch, instigate, establish, set up. **2** *he was initiated into a religious cult* **introduce,** admit, induct, install, swear in, ordain, invest.
ANTONYMS finish, expel.

□ **initiation** noun.

initiative ▶ **noun** **1** the ability to act independently and with a fresh approach. **2** the power or opportunity to act before other people do. **3** a new development or approach to a problem.

SYNONYMS **1** *employers are looking for initiative* **enterprise,** resourcefulness, inventiveness, imagination, ingenuity, originality, creativity. **2** *he has lost the initiative* **advantage,** upper hand, edge, lead, start. **3** *a recent initiative on recycling* **scheme,** plan, strategy, measure, proposal, step, action.
ANTONYMS apathy.

inject ▶ **verb** **1** put a drug or other substance into the body with a syringe. **2** add a new or different quality.

SYNONYMS **1** *he injected the codeine* **administer,** take; informal shoot (up), mainline, fix. **2** *troops were injected with the vaccine* **inoculate,** vaccinate. **3** *a pump injects air into the valve* **insert,** introduce, feed, push, force, shoot. **4** *he injected new life into the team* **introduce,** instil, infuse, imbue, breathe.

injection ▶ **noun** **1** an act of giving a drug or vaccine using a syringe. **2** an additional sum of money used to help a business etc.

SYNONYMS *injections against diphtheria* **inoculation,** vaccination, immunization, booster, dose, infusion, IV, drip; informal jab, shot.

injudicious ▶ **adjective** unwise.

injunction ▶ **noun** **1** Law an order saying that someone must or must not carry out a certain action. **2** a strong warning.

SYNONYMS **order,** ruling, direction, directive, command, instruction, mandate.

injure ▶ **verb** (**injures, injuring, injured**) **1** do physical harm to; wound. **2** have a bad effect on; damage.

SYNONYMS **1** *he injured his foot* **hurt,** wound, damage, harm, disable, break; Medicine traumatize; Brit. informal knacker. **2** *a libel injured her reputation* **damage,** mar, spoil, ruin, blight, blemish, tarnish, blacken.
ANTONYMS boost.

injured ▶ **adjective** **1** physically harmed. **2** offended or upset.

SYNONYMS **1** *his injured arm* **hurt,** wounded, damaged, sore, bruised, broken, fractured; Medicine traumatized; Brit. informal gammy. **2** *an injured tone* **upset,** hurt, wounded, offended, reproachful, pained, aggrieved.
ANTONYMS healthy.

injurious /in-**joor**-i-uhss/ ▶ **adjective** causing or likely to cause injury.

injury ▶ **noun** (plural **injuries**) **1** harm done to the body. **2** hurt feelings.

SYNONYMS **1** *minor injuries* **wound,** bruise, cut, gash, scratch, graze; Medicine trauma, lesion. **2** *they escaped without injury* **harm,** hurt, damage, pain, suffering. **3** *injury to his feelings* **offence,** abuse, injustice, disservice, affront, insult.

injustice ▶ **noun** **1** lack of justice. **2** an unjust act.

SYNONYMS **1** *the injustice of the world* **unfairness,** one-sidedness, inequity, bias, prejudice, discrimination, intolerance, exploitation, corruption. **2** *his sacking was an injustice* **wrong,** offence, crime, sin, outrage, scandal, disgrace, affront.
ANTONYMS justice, just deserts.

ink ▶ **noun** **1** a coloured fluid used for writing, drawing, or printing. **2** a black liquid produced by a cuttlefish, octopus, or squid.
□ **inky** adjective.

inkling ▶ **noun** a slight suspicion; a hint.

inland ▶ **adjective & adverb** in or into the interior of a country.

SYNONYMS **interior,** inshore, internal, upcountry.
ANTONYMS coastal.

■ **inland revenue** Brit. the government department responsible for collecting income tax.

in-law ▸ noun a relative by marriage.

inlay ▸ verb (**inlays**, **inlaying**, **inlaid**) fix pieces of a different material into a surface as a form of decoration.
▸ noun decoration of this type.

inlet ▸ noun **1** a small arm of the sea, a lake, or a river. **2** a place or means of entry.

SYNONYMS **1** *a rocky inlet* **cove**, bay, bight, creek, estuary, fjord, sound; Scottish firth. **2** *an air inlet* **vent**, flue, shaft, duct, channel, pipe.

in loco parentis /in loh-koh puh-**ren**-tiss/ ▸ adverb having the same responsibility for a child or young person as a parent has.

inmate ▸ noun a person living in an institution such as a prison or hospital.

SYNONYMS **1** *the inmates of the hospital* **patient**, inpatient, resident, occupant. **2** *prison inmates* **prisoner**, convict, captive, detainee, internee.

inn ▸ noun a pub, especially in the country.
□ **innkeeper** noun (old use).

innards ▸ plural noun informal **1** internal organs. **2** the internal workings of a machine.

innate ▸ adjective natural or inborn.
□ **innately** adverb.

inner ▸ adjective **1** situated inside or close to the centre. **2** private; not expressed. **3** mental or spiritual.

SYNONYMS **1** *inner London* **central**, downtown, innermost. **2** *the inner gates* **internal**, interior, inside, innermost. **3** *the inner meaning* **hidden**, secret, deep, underlying, veiled, esoteric.
ANTONYMS outer, apparent.

■ **inner city** an area in or near the centre of a large city. **inner tube** a separate inflatable tube inside a tyre.

innermost ▸ adjective **1** furthest in; closest to the centre. **2** (of thoughts) most private.

innings ▸ noun (plural **innings**) Cricket each of the divisions of a game during which one side has a turn at batting.

innocence ▸ noun the fact or quality of being innocent.

SYNONYMS **1** *he protested his innocence* **guiltlessness**, blamelessness. **2** *she took advantage of his innocence* **naivety**, credulity, inexperience, gullibility, ingenuousness.
ANTONYMS guilt, experience.

innocent ▸ adjective **1** not guilty of a crime or offence. **2** having little experience of life. **3** not intended to cause offence.

SYNONYMS **1** *he was entirely innocent* **guiltless**, blameless, clean, irreproachable, honest, upright, law-abiding. **2** *innocent foreign*

students **naive**, ingenuous, trusting, credulous, impressionable, easily led, inexperienced, unsophisticated, artless. **3** *innocent fun* **harmless**, innocuous, safe, inoffensive.
ANTONYMS guilty, worldly, dangerous.

▸ noun an innocent person.
□ **innocently** adverb.

innocuous /in-**nok**-yoo-uhss/ ▸ adjective not harmful or offensive.

innovate ▸ verb (**innovates**, **innovating**, **innovated**) introduce new ideas or products.
□ **innovator** noun.

innovation ▸ noun **1** the introduction of new ideas or products. **2** a new idea or product.

SYNONYMS **change**, alteration, upheaval, reorganization, restructuring, novelty, departure.

innovative ▸ adjective featuring or introducing new ideas or products.

SYNONYMS **original**, new, novel, fresh, unusual, experimental, inventive, ingenious, pioneering, groundbreaking, advanced, revolutionary, radical.

innuendo /in-yuu-**en**-doh/ ▸ noun (plural **innuendoes** or **innuendos**) a remark which makes a vague and indirect reference to something.

innumerable ▸ adjective too many to be counted.

innumerate ▸ adjective without a basic knowledge of mathematics and arithmetic.

inoculate ▸ verb treat someone with a vaccine to stop them getting a disease.
□ **inoculation** noun.

✔ one **n**, one **c**: in**oc**ulate.

inoffensive ▸ adjective causing no offence or harm.

inoperable ▸ adjective **1** (of an illness) not able to be cured by an operation. **2** not able to be used or operated.

inoperative ▸ adjective not working or taking effect.

inopportune ▸ adjective happening at an inconvenient time.

inordinate ▸ adjective much greater than is usual or expected; excessive.
□ **inordinately** adverb.

inorganic ▸ adjective **1** not consisting of or coming from living matter. **2** (of a chemical compound) not containing carbon.

inpatient ▸ noun a patient who is staying day and night in a hospital.

input ▸ noun **1** what is put or taken into a system or process. **2** the putting or feeding in of something. **3** a person's contribution.
▸ verb (**inputs**, **inputting**, **input** or **inputted**) put data into a computer.

inquest ▸ noun **1** a legal enquiry to gather the facts relating to an incident. **2** Brit. an enquiry by a coroner's court into the cause of a death.

SYNONYMS enquiry, investigation, probe, examination, review, hearing.

inquire = ENQUIRE.

inquiry = ENQUIRY.

inquisition ▸ noun a long period of questioning or investigation.

inquisitive ▸ adjective **1** eager to find things out. **2** prying.
□ **inquisitively** adverb.

inquisitor ▸ noun a person conducting an inquisition.

inroad ▸ noun a gradual entry into or effect on a place or situation.

inrush ▸ noun a sudden inward rush or flow.

insalubrious /in-suh-**loo**-bri-uhss/ ▸ adjective unpleasant because not clean or well kept.

insane ▸ adjective **1** seriously mentally ill. **2** very foolish.

SYNONYMS **1** *she was declared insane* mad, of unsound mind, certifiable, psychotic, schizophrenic, unhinged; informal crazy, (stark) raving mad, bonkers, loony, round the bend; Brit. informal crackers, off your trolley; N. Amer. informal nutso, out of your tree; Austral./NZ informal bushed. **2** *an insane suggestion* stupid, idiotic, nonsensical, absurd, ridiculous, ludicrous, preposterous; informal crazy, mad; Brit. informal daft, barmy.
ANTONYMS sane, sensible.

□ **insanely** adverb **insanity** noun.

insanitary ▸ adjective so dirty as to be a danger to health.

insatiable /in-**say**-shuh-b'l/ ▸ adjective always wanting more and not able to be satisfied.
□ **insatiably** adverb.

inscribe ▸ verb (**inscribes**, **inscribing**, **inscribed**) **1** write or carve something on a surface. **2** write a dedication to someone in a book.

inscription ▸ noun words or symbols written or carved on a surface or in a book.

inscrutable ▸ adjective impossible to understand or interpret.
□ **inscrutably** adverb.

insect ▸ noun a small animal with six legs and no backbone.

SYNONYMS **bug**; informal creepy-crawly; Brit. informal minibeast.

insecticide ▸ noun a substance used for killing insects.

insectivore ▸ noun an animal that eats insects.

□ **insectivorous** adjective.

insecure ▸ adjective **1** not confident or assured. **2** not firm or firmly fixed.

SYNONYMS **1** *an insecure young man* **unconfident,** uncertain, unsure, doubtful, diffident, hesitant, self-conscious, anxious, fearful. **2** *insecure windows* **unprotected,** unguarded, vulnerable, unsecured. **3** *an insecure footbridge* **unstable,** rickety, wobbly, shaky, unsteady, precarious.
ANTONYMS confident, secure, stable.

insecurity ▸ noun the quality or state of being insecure.

SYNONYMS **lack of confidence,** uncertainty, self-doubt, diffidence, hesitancy, nervousness, self-consciousness, anxiety, worry, unease.

inseminate ▸ verb (**inseminates**, **inseminating**, **inseminated**) introduce semen into a woman or a female animal.
□ **insemination** noun.

insensate ▸ adjective lacking physical sensation.

insensible ▸ adjective **1** unconscious. **2** numb; without feeling.

insensitive ▸ adjective **1** showing or feeling no concern for the feelings of other people. **2** not sensitive to physical sensation. **3** not aware of or able to respond to something.
□ **insensitively** adverb **insensitivity** noun.

inseparable ▸ adjective unable to be separated or treated separately.
□ **inseparably** adverb.

insert ▸ verb /in-**sert**/ place, fit, or incorporate something into something else.

SYNONYMS **put,** place, push, thrust, slide, slip, load, fit, slot, install; informal pop, stick, bung.
ANTONYMS extract, remove.

▸ noun /**in**-sert/ a loose page or section in a magazine.
□ **insertion** noun.

inset ▸ noun /**in**-set/ a thing inserted.
▸ verb /in-**set**/ (**insets**, **insetting**, **inset** or **insetted**) insert.

inshore ▸ adjective & adverb **1** at sea but close to the shore. **2** towards the shore.

inside ▸ noun **1** the inner side or surface of a thing. **2** the inner part; the interior. **3** (**insides**) informal a person's stomach and bowels.

SYNONYMS **1** *the inside of the volcano* **interior,** centre, core, middle, heart, bowels. **2** *my insides are out of order* **stomach,** gut, bowels, intestines; informal tummy, belly, guts.
ANTONYMS outside.

▸ adjective situated on or in the inside.

SYNONYMS **1** *his inside pocket* **inner**, interior, internal, innermost. **2** *inside information* **confidential**, classified, restricted, privileged, private, secret, exclusive; informal hush-hush.
ANTONYMS outside, public.

▶ preposition & adverb **1** situated or moving within. **2** informal in prison. **3** within a particular time.

SYNONYMS *she ushered me inside* **indoors**, within, in.
ANTONYMS outside.

■ **inside out** with the inner surface turned outwards.

insider ▶ noun a person working within an organization.

insidious ▶ adjective proceeding in a gradual and harmful way.
□ **insidiously** adverb.

insight ▶ noun **1** the ability to understand the truth about people and situations. **2** understanding of this kind.

SYNONYMS **1** *your insight has been invaluable* **intuition**, perception, understanding, comprehension, appreciation, judgement, vision, imagination; informal nous, savvy. **2** *an insight into the government* **understanding of**, appreciation of, introduction to; informal eye-opener.
ANTONYMS stupidity.

□ **insightful** adjective.

insignia /in-sig-ni-uh/ ▶ noun (plural **insignia**) a badge or symbol showing someone's rank, position, or membership of an organization.

insignificant ▶ adjective having very little importance or value.

SYNONYMS **unimportant**, trivial, trifling, negligible, inconsequential, of no account, paltry, petty, insubstantial; informal piddling.
ANTONYMS significant.

□ **insignificance** noun **insignificantly** adverb.

insincere ▶ adjective saying or doing things that you do not mean.

SYNONYMS **false**, fake, hollow, artificial, feigned, pretended, put-on, disingenuous, hypocritical, cynical; informal phoney, pretend.
ANTONYMS sincere.

□ **insincerely** adverb **insincerity** noun.

insinuate ▶ verb (**insinuates, insinuating, insinuated**) **1** suggest or hint at something bad in an indirect way. **2** (**insinuate yourself into**) move yourself gradually into a favourable position.

insinuation ▶ noun an unpleasant hint or suggestion.

insipid ▶ adjective **1** having almost no flavour. **2** not interesting or lively.

insist ▶ verb **1** demand forcefully that something is done. **2** firmly state that something is the case, without letting anyone disagree. **3** (**insist on**) persist in doing something.

SYNONYMS **1** *be prepared to insist* **stand firm**, stand your ground, be resolute, be determined, hold out, persist, be emphatic, lay down the law, not take no for an answer; informal stick to your guns, put your foot down. **2** *she insisted that they pay up* **demand**, command, order, require. **3** *he insisted that he knew nothing* **maintain**, assert, protest, swear, declare, repeat.

insistent ▶ adjective **1** insisting that someone does something or that something is the case. **2** continuing for a long time and demanding attention.

SYNONYMS **1** *Tony's insistent questioning* **persistent**, determined, tenacious, unyielding, dogged, unrelenting, inexorable. **2** *an insistent buzzing* **incessant**, constant, unremitting.

□ **insistence** noun **insistently** adverb.

✔ **-ent**, not **-ant**: insist**ent**.

in situ /in sit-yoo/ ▶ adverb & adjective in the natural or original place.

insole ▶ noun the inner sole of a boot or shoe.

insolent ▶ adjective rude and disrespectful.
□ **insolence** noun **insolently** adverb.

insoluble ▶ adjective **1** impossible to solve. **2** (of a substance) incapable of being dissolved.

insolvent ▶ adjective not having enough money to pay your debts.
□ **insolvency** noun.

insomnia ▶ noun inability to sleep.
□ **insomniac** noun & adjective.

insouciant /in-soo-si-uhnt/ ▶ adjective carefree and unconcerned.
□ **insouciance** noun.

inspect ▶ verb **1** look at something closely. **2** make an official visit to a school, factory, etc. to check on standards.

SYNONYMS **examine**, check, scrutinize, investigate, vet, test, monitor, survey, study, look over; informal check out, give something a/the once-over.

inspection ▶ noun the action of inspecting something.

SYNONYMS **examination**, check-up, survey, scrutiny, exploration, investigation; informal once-over, going-over.

inspector ▶ noun **1** an official who makes sure that regulations are obeyed. **2** a police officer ranking below a chief inspector.

SYNONYMS **examiner**, scrutineer, investigator, surveyor, assessor, supervisor, monitor, watchdog, ombudsman, auditor.

inspiration ▶ noun **1** the process of being inspired. **2** a person or thing that inspires. **3** a sudden clever idea.

SYNONYMS **1** *she's an inspiration to others* **stimulus**, motivation, encouragement, influence, spur. **2** *his work lacks inspiration* **creativity**, invention, innovation, ingenuity, imagination, originality, insight, vision. **3** *she had a sudden inspiration* **bright idea**, revelation; informal **brainwave**; N. Amer. informal **brainstorm**.

□ **inspirational** adjective.

inspire ▶ verb (**inspires**, **inspiring**, **inspired**) **1** fill someone with the urge or ability to do something. **2** create a feeling in a person. **3** give rise to.

SYNONYMS **1** *the landscape inspired him to write* **stimulate**, motivate, encourage, influence, move, spur, energize, galvanize. **2** (**inspiring**) **inspirational**, encouraging, heartening, uplifting, stirring, rousing, electrifying, moving. **3** *the film inspired a musical* **give rise to**, lead to, bring about, prompt, spawn, engender. **4** *Charles inspired awe in her* **arouse**, awaken, prompt, induce, ignite, trigger, kindle, produce, bring out.

inspired ▶ adjective showing great creativity or imagination.

SYNONYMS **outstanding**, wonderful, marvellous, excellent, magnificent, exceptional, first-class, virtuoso, superlative; informal **tremendous**, superb, awesome, out of this world; Brit. informal **brilliant**.
ANTONYMS uninspired.

instability ▶ noun (plural **instabilities**) lack of stability.

SYNONYMS **1** *the instability of political life* **unreliability**, uncertainty, unpredictability, insecurity, volatility, capriciousness, changeability, mutability. **2** *emotional instability* **volatility**, unpredictability, variability, inconsistency.
ANTONYMS steadiness.

install ▶ verb (**installs**, **installing**, **installed**) **1** place or fix equipment in position ready for use. **2** establish someone in a new place or role.

SYNONYMS **1** *a photocopier was installed in the office* **put**, place, station, site, insert. **2** *they installed a new president* **swear in**, induct, inaugurate, invest, appoint, ordain, consecrate, anoint, enthrone,

crown. **3** *she installed herself behind the table* **ensconce**, position, settle, seat, plant, sit (down); informal **plonk**, park.
ANTONYMS remove.

installation ▶ noun **1** the installing of something. **2** a large piece of equipment installed for use. **3** a military or industrial establishment. **4** a large piece of art constructed within a gallery.

instalment (US spelling **installment**) ▶ noun **1** each of several payments made over a period of time. **2** each of several parts of something published or broadcast at intervals.

SYNONYMS **1** *they paid by monthly instalments* **payment**, tranche, repayment, part payment, planned payment, regular payment. **2** *the book was published in instalments* **part**, episode, chapter, issue, programme, section, volume.

✔ **Instalment** is spelled with only one **l** in British English, while **install** is spelled with two.

instance ▶ noun a particular example or occurrence of something.

SYNONYMS **example**, occasion, occurrence, case, illustration, sample.

▶ verb (**instances**, **instancing**, **instanced**) mention something as an example.
■ **for instance** as an example.

instant ▶ adjective **1** happening immediately. **2** (of food) processed so that it can be prepared very quickly.

SYNONYMS **1** *instant access to your money* **immediate**, instantaneous, on-the-spot, prompt, swift, speedy, rapid, quick; informal **snappy**. **2** *instant meals* **prepared**, pre-cooked, microwaveable, convenience.
ANTONYMS delayed.

▶ noun **1** a precise moment of time. **2** a very short time.

SYNONYMS **1** *come here this instant!* **moment**, minute, second. **2** *it all happened in an instant* **flash**, trice, moment, minute, (split) second, twinkling of an eye, no time (at all); informal **jiffy**.

instantaneous ▶ adjective happening or done immediately or at the same time.
□ **instantaneously** adverb.

instantly ▶ adverb at once; immediately.

SYNONYMS **immediately**, at once, straight away, right away, instantaneously, forthwith, there and then, here and now, this/that minute, this/that second.

instead ▶ adverb **1** as an alternative. **2** (**instead of**) in place of.

SYNONYMS **as an alternative,** in lieu, alternatively, rather, on second thoughts; N. Amer. alternately.
ANTONYMS as well.

instep ▸ noun the part of a person's foot between the ball and the ankle.

instigate ▸ verb (**instigates, instigating, instigated**) make something happen or come about.
□ **instigation** noun **instigator** noun.

instil (or **instill**) ▸ verb (**instils, instilling, instilled**) gradually but firmly establish an idea or attitude in someone's mind.

instinct ▸ noun 1 an inborn tendency to behave in a certain way. 2 a natural ability or skill.

SYNONYMS 1 *some instinct told me to be careful* **inclination,** urge, drive, compulsion, intuition, feeling, sixth sense, nose. 2 *a good instinct for acting* **talent,** gift, ability, aptitude, skill, flair, feel, knack.
□ **instinctual** adjective.

instinctive ▸ adjective based on instinct rather than thought or training.

SYNONYMS **intuitive,** natural, instinctual, innate, inborn, inherent, unconscious, subconscious, automatic, reflex, knee-jerk; informal gut.
ANTONYMS learned.
□ **instinctively** adverb.

institute ▸ noun an organization for the promotion of science, education, or a profession.

SYNONYMS **organization,** establishment, institution, foundation, centre, academy, school, college, university, society, association, federation, body.

▸ verb (**institutes, instituting, instituted**) set up or establish.

SYNONYMS **set up,** inaugurate, found, establish, organize, initiate, set in motion, get under way, get off the ground, start, launch.
ANTONYMS abolish, end.

institution ▸ noun 1 an important organization or public body. 2 an organization providing residential care for people who have special needs. 3 an established law or custom.

SYNONYMS 1 *an academic institution* **establishment,** organization, institute, foundation, centre, academy, school, college, university, society, association, body. 2 *they spent their lives in institutions* (**residential**) **home,** hospital, asylum, prison. 3 *the institution of marriage* **practice,** custom, convention, tradition.

institutional ▸ adjective relating to an institution.

SYNONYMS **organized,** established, bureaucratic, conventional, procedural, formal, formalized, systematic, systematized, structured, regulated.
ANTONYMS free and easy.

institutionalize (or **institutionalise**) ▸ verb (**institutionalizes, institutionalizing, institutionalized**) 1 establish something as a feature of an organization or culture. 2 place someone in a residential institution. 3 (**become institutionalized**) lose your individuality as a result of staying for a long time in a residential institution.

instruct ▸ verb 1 tell or order someone to do something. 2 teach. 3 inform someone of a fact or situation.

SYNONYMS 1 *the union instructed them to strike* **order,** direct, command, tell, mandate. 2 *nobody instructed him in how to operate it* **teach,** coach, train, educate, tutor, guide, school, show.

instruction ▸ noun 1 an order. 2 a piece of information about how something should be done. 3 teaching or education.

SYNONYMS 1 *obey my instructions* **order,** command, directive, direction, decree, injunction, mandate, commandment. 2 *read the instructions* **directions,** handbook, manual, guide, advice, guidance. 3 *he gave instruction in self defence* **tuition,** teaching, coaching, schooling, lessons, classes, lectures, training, drill, guidance.

□ **instructional** adjective.

instructive ▸ adjective useful and informative.

instructor ▸ noun a teacher.

SYNONYMS **trainer,** coach, teacher, tutor, adviser, counsellor, guide.

instrument ▸ noun 1 a tool or piece of equipment used for delicate or scientific work. 2 a measuring device. 3 (also **musical instrument**) a device for producing musical sounds.

SYNONYMS 1 *a wound made with a sharp instrument* **implement,** tool, utensil, device, apparatus, gadget. 2 *cockpit instruments* **gauge,** meter, indicator, dial, display. 3 *an instrument of learning* **agent,** agency, cause, channel, medium, means, vehicle.

instrumental ▸ adjective 1 important in making something happen. 2 (of music) performed on instruments.
▸ noun a piece of music performed by instruments, with no vocals.

instrumentalist ▸ noun a player of a musical instrument.

instrumentation ▸ noun **1** the instruments used in a piece of music. **2** the arrangement of a piece of music for particular instruments.

insubordinate ▸ adjective disobedient.
□ **insubordination** noun.

insubstantial ▸ adjective not strong or solid.

insufferable ▸ adjective unbearable.
□ **insufferably** adverb.

insufficient ▸ adjective not enough.

SYNONYMS **inadequate**, deficient, poor, scant, scanty, not enough, too little, too few.

□ **insufficiency** noun **insufficiently** adverb.

insular ▸ adjective **1** narrow-minded through being isolated from outside influences. **2** relating to an island.
□ **insularity** noun.

insulate ▸ verb (**insulates, insulating, insulated**) **1** place material between one thing and another to prevent loss of heat or intrusion of sound. **2** cover something with non-conducting material to prevent the passage of electricity. **3** protect from something unpleasant.

SYNONYMS **1** *pipes must be insulated* **wrap**, sheathe, cover, encase, enclose, lag, soundproof. **2** *they were insulated from the impact of the war* **protect**, save, shield, shelter, screen, cushion, cocoon.

□ **insulation** noun **insulator** noun.

insulin ▸ noun a hormone which regulates glucose levels in the blood.

insult ▸ verb /in-**sult**/ say or do hurtful or disrespectful things to someone.

SYNONYMS **1 abuse**, be rude to, call someone names, slight, disparage, discredit, malign, defame, denigrate, offend, hurt, humiliate; informal bad-mouth; Brit. informal slag off. **2** (**insulting**) **abusive**, rude, offensive, disparaging, belittling, derogatory, deprecating, disrespectful, uncomplimentary; informal bitchy, catty.
ANTONYMS compliment.

▸ noun /**in**-sult/ an insulting remark or action.

SYNONYMS **jibe**, affront, slight, slur, barb, indignity, abuse, aspersions; informal dig, put-down.

insuperable ▸ adjective impossible to overcome.

insupportable ▸ adjective **1** unable to be justified. **2** unbearable.

insurance ▸ noun **1** an arrangement by which you make regular payments to a company who pay an agreed amount if something is lost or damaged or someone is hurt or killed. **2** money paid by or to an insurance company. **3** a thing that provides protection in case anything bad happens.

SYNONYMS **indemnity**, assurance, protection, security, cover, safeguard, warranty.

insure ▸ verb (**insures, insuring, insured**) **1** pay money in order to receive financial compensation if something is lost or damaged or someone is hurt or killed. **2** (**insure against**) provide protection in case anything bad happens. **3** = ENSURE.

SYNONYMS **provide insurance for**, indemnify, cover, assure, protect, underwrite, warrant.

insurgent ▸ noun a rebel or revolutionary.
▸ adjective fighting against a system or authority.
□ **insurgency** noun.

insurmountable ▸ adjective too great to be overcome.

insurrection ▸ noun a violent uprising against authority.

intact ▸ adjective not damaged.

SYNONYMS **whole**, entire, complete, unbroken, undamaged, unscathed, unblemished, unmarked, in one piece.
ANTONYMS damaged.

intaglio /in-**ta**-li-oh/ ▸ noun (plural **intaglios**) an engraved design.

intake ▸ noun **1** an amount or quantity of something that is taken in. **2** a set of people entering a school or college at a particular time.

intangible ▸ adjective **1** not solid or real. **2** vague and abstract.
▸ noun an intangible thing.
□ **intangibly** adverb.

integer /**in**-ti-jer/ ▸ noun a whole number.

integral /**in**-ti-gruhl, in-**teg**-ruhl/ ▸ adjective **1** necessary to make a whole complete; fundamental. **2** included as part of a whole.

SYNONYMS **1** *an integral part of human behaviour* **essential**, fundamental, component, basic, intrinsic, inherent, vital, necessary. **2** *the dryer has an integral heat sensor* **built-in**, inbuilt, integrated, inboard, fitted. **3** *an integral approach to learning* **unified**, integrated, comprehensive, holistic, joined-up, all-embracing.
ANTONYMS peripheral, supplementary, fragmented.

integrate ▸ verb (**integrates, integrating, integrated**) **1** combine with something to form a whole. **2** make someone accepted within a social group.

SYNONYMS **combine**, amalgamate, merge, unite, fuse, blend, consolidate, meld, mix, incorporate, assimilate,

homogenize, desegregate.
ANTONYMS separate.

□ **integration** noun.

integrity ▸ noun **1** the quality of being honest, fair, and good. **2** the state of being whole or unified.

SYNONYMS **1** *I never doubted his integrity* **honesty,** probity, rectitude, honour, sincerity, truthfulness, trustworthiness. **2** *the integrity of the federation* **unity,** coherence, cohesion, solidity. **3** *the structural integrity of the aircraft* **soundness,** strength, sturdiness, solidity, durability, stability, rigidity. ANTONYMS dishonesty, division, fragility.

intellect ▸ noun the power of using your mind to think logically and understand things.

SYNONYMS **mind,** brain(s), intelligence, reason, judgement, grey matter, brain cells.

intellectual ▸ adjective **1** relating or appealing to the intellect. **2** having a highly developed intellect.

SYNONYMS **1** *his intellectual capacity* **mental,** rational, conceptual, theoretical, analytical, logical. **2** *an intellectual man* **learned,** cerebral, academic, erudite, bookish, highbrow, scholarly. ANTONYMS physical, stupid.

▸ noun a person with a highly developed intellect.
□ **intellectually** adverb.

intellectualize (or **intellectualise**) ▸ verb (**intellectualizes, intellectualizing, intellectualized**) talk or write in an intellectual way.

intelligence ▸ noun **1** the ability to gain and apply knowledge and skills. **2** the secret gathering of information about an enemy or opponent. **3** information of this sort.

SYNONYMS **1** *a man of great intelligence* **cleverness,** intellect, brainpower, judgement, reasoning, acumen, wit, insight, perception. **2** *intelligence from our agents* **information,** facts, details, particulars, data, knowledge; informal info.

intelligent ▸ adjective good at learning, understanding, and thinking.

SYNONYMS **1** *an intelligent woman* **clever,** bright, quick-witted, smart, astute, insightful, perceptive; informal brainy. **2** *intelligent machines* **self-regulating,** capable of learning, smart. ANTONYMS unintelligent, dumb.

□ **intelligently** adverb.

intelligentsia /in-tel-li-**jent**-si-uh/ ▸ noun intellectuals or highly educated people.

intelligible ▸ adjective able to be understood.

SYNONYMS **comprehensible,** understandable, accessible, digestible, user-friendly, clear, coherent, plain, unambiguous.

□ **intelligibly** adverb.

intemperate ▸ adjective lacking self-control.
□ **intemperance** noun.

intend ▸ verb **1** have something as your aim or plan. **2** plan that something should be, do, or mean something. **3** (**intend something for** or **to do**) design or plan something for a particular purpose.

SYNONYMS **plan,** mean, have in mind, aim, propose, hope, expect, envisage.

intense ▸ adjective (**intenser, intensest**) **1** of great force or strength. **2** very earnest or serious.

SYNONYMS **1** *intense heat* **extreme,** great, acute, fierce, severe, high, exceptional, extraordinary, harsh, strong, powerful; informal serious. **2** *a very intense young man* **passionate,** impassioned, zealous, vehement, earnest, eager, committed. ANTONYMS mild, apathetic.

□ **intensely** adverb.

intensify ▸ verb (**intensifies, intensifying, intensified**) make or become more intense.

SYNONYMS **escalate,** increase, step up, raise, strengthen, reinforce, pick up, build up, heighten, deepen, extend, expand, amplify, magnify, aggravate, exacerbate, worsen, inflame, compound. ANTONYMS abate.

intensity ▸ noun (plural **intensities**) the quality of having great force or strength.

SYNONYMS **1** *the intensity of the sun* **strength,** power, force, severity, ferocity, fierceness, harshness. **2** *his eyes had a glowing intensity* **passion,** ardour, fervour, vehemence, fire, emotion, eagerness.

intensive ▸ adjective **1** involving a lot of effort over a short time. **2** (of agriculture) aiming to produce the highest possible yields.

SYNONYMS **thorough,** thoroughgoing, in-depth, rigorous, exhaustive, vigorous, detailed, minute, meticulous, painstaking, methodical, extensive. ANTONYMS cursory.

■ **intensive care** special medical treatment given to a dangerously ill patient.
□ **intensively** adverb.

intent ▸ noun intention or purpose.

SYNONYMS *he tried to divine his father's intent* **aim,** intention, purpose, objective, goal.

▶ adjective **1** (**intent on**) determined to do. **2** (**intent on**) giving all your attention to. **3** showing great interest and attention.

SYNONYMS **1** *he was intent on proving his point* **bent,** set, determined, insistent, resolved, hell-bent, keen, committed to, determined to. **2** *an intent expression* **attentive,** absorbed, engrossed, fascinated, enthralled, rapt, focused, preoccupied.
ANTONYMS distracted.

■ **to all intents and purposes** in all important respects.
□ **intently** adverb.

intention ▶ noun **1** an aim or plan. **2** the fact of intending something. **3** (**intentions**) a man's plans about getting married.

SYNONYMS **aim,** purpose, intent, objective, goal.

intentional ▶ adjective deliberate.

SYNONYMS **deliberate,** done on purpose, wilful, calculated, conscious, intended, planned, meant, knowing.

□ **intentionally** adverb.

inter /in-ter/ ▶ verb (**inters, interring, interred**) place a dead body in a grave or tomb.

SYNONYMS **bury,** lay to rest, consign to the grave, entomb.
ANTONYMS exhume.

interact ▶ verb (of two people or things) do things which have an effect on each other.
□ **interaction** noun.

interactive ▶ adjective **1** influencing each other. **2** (of a computer or other electronic device) allowing a two-way flow of information between it and a user.

interbreed ▶ verb (**interbreeds, interbreeding, interbred**) breed with an animal of a different species.

intercede ▶ verb intervene on behalf of someone else.

intercept ▶ verb stop someone or something and prevent them from continuing to a destination.

SYNONYMS **stop,** head off, cut off, catch, seize, block, interrupt.

□ **interceptor** noun **interception** noun.

intercession ▶ noun **1** the action of interceding. **2** the saying of a prayer on behalf of another person.

interchange ▶ verb /in-ter-**chaynj**/ (**interchanges, interchanging, interchanged**) **1** (of two people) exchange things with each other. **2** put each of two things in the place of the other.
▶ noun /**in**-ter-chaynj/ **1** the action of interchanging things. **2** an exchange of words. **3** a road junction built on several levels.

□ **interchangeable** adjective **interchangeably** adverb.

intercity ▶ adjective existing or travelling between cities.

intercom ▶ noun a system of communication by telephone or radio inside a building or group of buildings.

interconnect ▶ verb (of two things) connect with each other.

intercontinental ▶ adjective relating to or travelling between continents.

intercourse ▶ noun **1** communication or dealings between people. **2** sexual intercourse.

SYNONYMS **1** *social intercourse* **dealings,** relations, relationships, contact, interchange, communication. **2** *she did not consent to intercourse* **sexual intercourse,** sex, sexual relations, mating, coupling, copulation.

intercut ▶ verb (**intercuts, intercutting, intercut**) alternate scenes with contrasting scenes in a film.

interdependent ▶ adjective (of two or more people or things) dependent on each other.

interdisciplinary ▶ adjective relating to more than one branch of knowledge.

interest ▶ noun **1** the state of wanting to know about something or someone. **2** the quality of making someone curious or holding their attention. **3** a subject about which you are concerned or enthusiastic. **4** money that is paid for the use of money lent. **5** a person's advantage or benefit. **6** a share, right, or stake in property or a financial undertaking.

SYNONYMS **1** *we listened with interest* **attentiveness,** attention, regard, notice, curiosity, enjoyment, delight. **2** *this will be of interest* **concern,** consequence, importance, import, significance, note, relevance, value. **3** *her interests include reading* **hobby,** pastime, leisure pursuit, amusement, recreation, diversion, passion. **4** *a financial interest in the firm* **stake,** share, claim, investment, involvement, concern.
ANTONYMS boredom.

▶ verb **1** make someone curious or attentive. **2** (**interested**) involved in something and so not impartial.

SYNONYMS **1** *a topic that interests you* **appeal to,** be of interest to, attract, intrigue, amuse, divert, entertain, arouse someone's curiosity, whet someone's appetite; informal tickle someone's fancy. **2** (**interested**) *an interested crowd* **attentive,** fascinated, riveted, gripped, captivated, agog, intrigued, curious, keen, eager. **3** (**interested**) *the*

government consulted with interested bodies **concerned**, involved, affected.
ANTONYMS bore, put off.

interesting ▸ adjective arousing curiosity or attention.

SYNONYMS **absorbing**, engrossing, fascinating, riveting, gripping, compelling, captivating, engaging, enthralling, appealing, amusing, entertaining, stimulating, diverting, intriguing.

□ **interestingly** adverb.

interface ▸ noun 1 a point where two things meet and interact. 2 a device or program enabling a user to communicate with a computer, or for connecting two items of hardware or software.
▸ verb (**interfaces, interfacing, interfaced**) (**interface with**) connect with another computer by an interface.

interfere ▸ verb (**interferes, interfering, interfered**) 1 (**interfere with**) prevent something from continuing or being carried out properly. 2 (**interfere with**) handle or adjust something without permission. 3 become involved in something without being asked.
4 (**interfere with**) Brit. sexually molest someone.

SYNONYMS *she tried not to interfere* **butt in**, barge in, intrude, meddle, tamper, encroach; informal poke your nose in, stick your oar in.

interference ▸ noun 1 the action of interfering. 2 disturbance to radio signals caused by unwanted signals from other sources.

SYNONYMS 1 *they resent state interference* **intrusion**, intervention, involvement, meddling, prying. 2 *radio interference* **disruption**, disturbance, static, noise.

interferon /in-ter-**feer**-on/ ▸ noun a protein released by animal cells which prevents a virus from reproducing itself.

intergalactic ▸ adjective relating to or situated between galaxies.

interim ▸ noun (**the interim**) the time between two events.
▸ adjective lasting for a short time, until a replacement is found.

interior ▸ adjective 1 situated within or inside; inner. 2 remote from the coast or frontier; inland.

SYNONYMS 1 *the house has interior panelling* **inside**, inner, internal.
2 *the interior deserts of the US* **inland**, upcountry, inner, central. 3 *the country's interior affairs* **internal**, home, domestic, national, state, civil, local. 4 *an interior monologue* **inner**, mental, spiritual, psychological, private, personal, secret.

ANTONYMS exterior, border, coastal, foreign.

▸ noun 1 the interior part. 2 the internal affairs of a country.

SYNONYMS 1 *the interior of the castle* **inside**, depths, recesses, bowels, belly, heart. 2 *the country's interior* **centre**, heartland.
ANTONYMS exterior, borders, coast.

interject ▸ verb say something suddenly as an interruption.

interjection ▸ noun an exclamation (e.g. *ah!*).

interlace ▸ verb (**interlaces, interlacing, interlaced**) weave together.

interleave ▸ verb 1 insert between the pages of a book. 2 place between the layers of something else.

interlock ▸ verb (of two parts, fibres, etc.) engage with each other by overlapping or fitting together.

interlocutor /in-ter-**lok**-yuu-ter/ ▸ noun formal a person who takes part in a conversation.

interloper ▸ noun a person who is in a place or situation where they are not wanted or do not belong.

interlude ▸ noun 1 a period of time that contrasts with what goes before and after. 2 a pause between the acts of a play. 3 a piece of music played between other pieces.

intermarry ▸ verb (**intermarries, intermarrying, intermarried**) (of people of different races or religions) marry each other.
□ **intermarriage** noun.

intermediary ▸ noun (plural **intermediaries**) a person who tries to settle a dispute between other people.

SYNONYMS **mediator**, go-between, negotiator, arbitrator, peacemaker, middleman, broker.

intermediate ▸ adjective 1 coming between two things in time, place, character, etc. 2 having more than basic knowledge or skills but not yet advanced.

SYNONYMS **halfway**, in-between, middle, mid, midway, intervening, transitional.

▸ noun an intermediate person or thing.

interment /in-ter-**muhnt**/ ▸ noun the burial of a dead body.

intermezzo /in-ter-**met**-soh/ ▸ noun (plural **intermezzi** /in-ter-**met**-si/ or **intermezzos**) a short piece of music connecting parts of an opera or other work.

interminable ▸ adjective lasting a very long time and therefore boring.
□ **interminably** adverb.

intermingle ▸ verb (**intermingles, intermingling, intermingled**) mix or mingle together.

intermission ▸ noun **1** a pause or break. **2** an interval between parts of a play or film.

intermittent ▸ adjective stopping and starting at irregular intervals.

SYNONYMS **sporadic,** irregular, fitful, spasmodic, discontinuous, isolated, random, patchy, scattered, occasional, periodic.
ANTONYMS continuous.

□ **intermittently** adverb.

intern ▸ verb /in-**tern**/ confine someone as a prisoner.
▸ noun /**in**-tern/ N. Amer. **1** a recent medical graduate receiving supervised training in a hospital. **2** a student or trainee doing a job to gain work experience.
□ **internment** noun.

internal ▸ adjective **1** relating to or situated on the inside. **2** inside the body. **3** relating to affairs and activities within a country. **4** existing or used within an organization. **5** within the mind.

SYNONYMS **1** an internal courtyard **inner,** interior, inside, central. **2** the state's internal affairs **domestic,** home, interior, civil, local, national, state.
ANTONYMS external, foreign.

■ **internal-combustion engine** an engine in which power is generated by the expansion of hot gases from the burning of fuel with air inside the engine.
□ **internally** adverb.

internalize (or **internalise**) ▸ verb (**internalizes, internalizing, internalized**) make a feeling or belief part of the way you think.

international ▸ adjective **1** existing or happening between nations. **2** agreed on or used by all or many nations.

SYNONYMS **global,** worldwide, world, intercontinental, universal, cosmopolitan, multiracial, multinational.
ANTONYMS national, local.

▸ noun Brit. a game or contest between teams representing different countries.
□ **internationally** adverb.

internationalism ▸ noun belief in the value of cooperation between nations.

internationalize (or **internationalise**) ▸ verb (**internationalizes, internationalizing, internationalized**) make something international.

internecine /in-ter-**nee**-syn/ ▸ adjective (of fighting) taking place between members of the same country or group.

Internet ▸ noun a very large international computer network.

interpersonal ▸ adjective having to do with relationships or communication between people.

interplanetary ▸ adjective situated or travelling between planets.

interplay ▸ noun the way in which things interact.

interpolate /in-ter-puh-layt/ ▸ verb (**interpolates, interpolating, interpolated**) **1** add a remark to a conversation. **2** add something to a piece of writing.
□ **interpolation** noun.

interpose ▸ verb (**interposes, interposing, interposed**) **1** place something between two other things. **2** say something as an interruption.

interpret ▸ verb (**interprets, interpreting, interpreted**) **1** explain the meaning of. **2** translate aloud the words of a person speaking a different language. **3** understand something as having a particular meaning.

SYNONYMS **1** the rabbis interpret the Jewish law **explain,** elucidate, expound, clarify. **2** the remark was interpreted as an invitation **understand,** construe, take (to mean), see, regard. **3** the symbols are difficult to interpret **decipher,** decode, translate, understand.

□ **interpreter** noun.

interpretation ▸ noun **1** the action of explaining the meaning of something. **2** an explanation. **3** the way in which a performer expresses a creative work.

SYNONYMS **1** the interpretation of the Bible's teachings **explanation,** elucidation, exposition, clarification, analysis. **2** she did not care what interpretation he put on her haste **meaning,** understanding, explanation, inference. **3** his interpretation of Mozart **rendition,** execution, presentation, performance, reading, playing, singing.

interracial ▸ adjective existing between or involving different races.

interregnum /in-ter-**reg**-nuhm/ ▸ noun (plural **interregnums**) a period between regimes when normal government is suspended.

interrelate ▸ verb (**interrelates, interrelating, interrelated**) (of two people or things) relate or connect to one other.
□ **interrelation** noun.

interrogate ▸ verb (**interrogates, interrogating, interrogated**) ask someone a lot of questions, often in an aggressive way.
□ **interrogation** noun **interrogator** noun.

interrogative /in-ter-**rog**-uh-tiv/ ▸ adjective in the form of or used in a question.
▸ noun a word used in questions, e.g. how or what.

interrupt ▸ verb **1** stop the continuous progress of. **2** stop a person who is speaking by saying or doing something. **3** break the continuity of a line, surface, or view.

SYNONYMS **1** *she opened her mouth to interrupt* **cut in (on)**, break in (on), barge in (on), intrude, intervene; informal butt in (on), chime in (on); Brit. informal chip in (on). **2** *the band had to interrupt their tour* **suspend**, adjourn, break off, stop, halt; informal put on ice.

✔ double **r** in the middle: inte**rr**upt.

interruption ▸ noun **1** an act or event that stops the progress of something. **2** the action of interrupting something.

SYNONYMS **1** *he was not pleased at her interruption* **cutting in**, barging in, interference, intervention, intrusion; informal butting in. **2** *an interruption of the power supply* **suspension**, breaking off, cutting.

intersect ▸ verb **1** divide something by passing or lying across it. **2** (of lines, roads, etc.) cross or cut each other.

intersection ▸ noun **1** a point or line where lines or surfaces intersect. **2** a point where roads intersect.

intersperse ▸ verb (**intersperses, interspersing, interspersed**) place or scatter among or between other things.

interstate ▸ adjective existing or carried on between states.

interstellar ▸ adjective occurring or situated between stars.

interstice /in-ter-stiss/ ▸ noun a small crack or space in something.

intertwine ▸ verb (**intertwines, intertwining, intertwined**) twist or twine together.

interval ▸ noun **1** a period of time between two events. **2** a pause or break. **3** Brit. a pause between parts of a play, concert, etc. **4** the difference in pitch between two sounds.

SYNONYMS **intermission**, interlude, break, recess, time out.

intervene ▸ verb (**intervenes, intervening, intervened**) **1** become involved in a situation in order to improve or control it. **2** happen in the time or space between other things.

SYNONYMS **intercede**, involve yourself, get involved, step in, interfere, intrude.

□ **intervention** noun.

interview ▸ noun **1** a meeting at which a journalist asks someone questions about their work or their opinions. **2** a formal meeting at which someone is asked questions to judge whether they are suitable for a job, college place, etc.

SYNONYMS *all applicants will be called for an interview* **meeting**, discussion, interrogation, cross-examination, debriefing, audience, talk, chat; informal grilling.

▸ verb ask someone questions in an interview.

SYNONYMS *we interviewed seventy subjects for the survey* **talk to**, question, quiz, interrogate, cross-examine, debrief, poll, canvass, sound out; informal grill, pump.

□ **interviewee** noun.

interviewer ▸ noun a person who interviews.

SYNONYMS **questioner**, interrogator, examiner, assessor, journalist, reporter, inquisitor.

interweave ▸ verb (**interweaves, interweaving, interwove;** past participle **interwoven**) weave two or more fibres or strands together.

intestate /in-tess-tayt/ ▸ adjective (of someone who has died) not having made a will.

intestine (or **intestines**) ▸ noun the long tube leading from the stomach to the anus. □ **intestinal** adjective.

intimacy ▸ noun (plural **intimacies**) **1** close familiarity or friendship. **2** an intimate act or remark.

SYNONYMS **closeness**, togetherness, rapport, attachment, familiarity, friendliness, affection, warmth.
ANTONYMS formality.

intimate[1] /in-ti-muht/ ▸ adjective **1** familiar. **2** private and personal. **3** (of two people) having a sexual relationship. **4** involving very close connection. **5** (of knowledge) detailed. **6** having a friendly, informal atmosphere.

SYNONYMS **1** *an intimate friend* **close**, bosom, dear, cherished, fast, firm. **2** *an intimate atmosphere* **friendly**, warm, welcoming, hospitable, relaxed, informal, cosy, comfortable. **3** *intimate thoughts* **personal**, private, confidential, secret, inward. **4** *an intimate knowledge* **detailed**, thorough, exhaustive, deep, in-depth, profound.
ANTONYMS distant, formal, cold, public, sketchy.

▸ noun a very close friend.
□ **intimately** adverb.

intimate[2] /in-ti-mayt/ ▸ verb (**intimates, intimating, intimated**) say or suggest that something is the case.

SYNONYMS **1** *he intimated his decision* **announce**, state, proclaim, make known, make public, disclose, reveal, divulge.

2 *her feelings were subtly intimated*
imply, suggest, hint at, indicate.
▢ **intimation** noun.

intimidate ▸ verb (**intimidates,
intimidating, intimidated**) frighten or
threaten someone, especially to force them
to do something.

SYNONYMS **frighten,** menace, scare,
terrorize, threaten, browbeat, bully,
harass, hound; informal lean on.

▢ **intimidation** noun.

into ▸ preposition **1** expressing motion
or direction to a point on or within.
2 expressing a change of state or the
result of an action. **3** indicating the
direction towards which something is
turned. **4** indicating an object of interest.
5 expressing division.

intolerable ▸ adjective unable to be
endured.
▢ **intolerably** adverb.

intolerant ▸ adjective not willing to
accept ideas or ways of behaving that are
different from your own.
▢ **intolerance** noun.

intonation ▸ noun the rise and fall of the
voice in speaking.

intone ▸ verb (**intones, intoning, intoned**)
say or recite something with your voice
hardly rising or falling.

intoxicate ▸ verb (**intoxicates, intoxicating,
intoxicated**) **1** (of alcoholic drink or a drug)
make someone lose control of themselves.
2 (**be intoxicated**) be excited or exhilarated
by something.
▢ **intoxication** noun.

intractable ▸ adjective **1** hard to solve or
deal with. **2** stubborn.

intranet ▸ noun a computer network for use
within an organization.

intransigent /in-**tran**-si-juhnt/ ▸ adjective
refusing to change your views or
behaviour.
▢ **intransigence** noun.

intransitive ▸ adjective (of a verb) not
taking a direct object, e.g. *look* in *look at
the sky.*

intrauterine /in-truh-**yoo**-tuh-ryn/
▸ adjective within the womb.

intravenous /in-truh-**vee**-nuhss/
▸ adjective within or into a vein.

intrepid ▸ adjective not afraid of danger or
difficulties.
▢ **intrepidly** adverb.

intricacy ▸ noun (plural **intricacies**) **1** the
quality of being intricate. **2** (**intricacies**)
details.

intricate ▸ adjective very complicated or
detailed.

SYNONYMS **complex,** complicated,
convoluted, tangled, elaborate, ornate,
detailed.
ANTONYMS simple.

▢ **intricately** adverb.

intrigue ▸ verb /in-**treeg**/ (**intrigues,
intriguing, intrigued**) **1** arouse great
curiosity in someone. **2** plot something
illegal or harmful.

SYNONYMS *her answer intrigued him*
interest, fascinate, arouse someone's
curiosity, attract, engage.

▸ noun /**in**-treeg/ **1** the plotting of something
illegal or harmful. **2** a secret plan or
relationship.

SYNONYMS **1** *the cabinet was a nest
of intrigue* **plotting,** conniving,
scheming, machination, double-dealing,
subterfuge. **2** (**intriguing**) **interesting,**
fascinating, absorbing, engaging.

▢ **intriguingly** adverb.

intrinsic ▸ adjective forming part of the
fundamental nature of something.
▢ **intrinsically** adverb.

introduce ▸ verb (**introduces, introducing,
introduced**) **1** bring something into use
or operation for the first time. **2** present
someone by name. **3** (**introduce something
to**) bring a subject to someone's attention
for the first time. **4** insert or bring
something into. **5** happen at the start of.
6 provide an opening announcement for.

SYNONYMS **1** *he has introduced a new
system* **institute,** initiate, launch,
inaugurate, establish, found, bring in,
set in motion, start, begin, get going.
2 *she introduced Lindsey to the young
man* **present,** make known, acquaint
with. **3** *introducing nitrogen into
canned beer* **insert,** inject, put, force,
shoot, feed. **4** *she introduced a note of
seriousness* **instil,** infuse, inject, add.
ANTONYMS end, remove.

introduction ▸ noun **1** the action of
introducing or being introduced. **2** a thing
which introduces another, such as a section
at the beginning of a book. **3** a thing newly
brought in. **4** a book or course intended to
introduce a newcomer to a subject of study.
5 a person's first experience of a subject or
activity.

SYNONYMS **1** *the introduction of
democratic reforms* **institution,**
establishment, initiation, launch,
inauguration, foundation. **2** *an
introduction to the king* **presentation,**
meeting, audience. **3** *the introduction to
the book* **foreword,** preface, preamble,
prologue, prelude; informal intro.
ANTONYMS ending, epilogue.

introductory ▸ adjective forming an introduction; basic.

> synonyms **1** *the introductory chapter* **opening**, initial, starting, initiatory, first, preliminary. **2** *an introductory course* **elementary**, basic, rudimentary, entry-level.
> antonyms final, advanced.

introspection ▸ noun concentration on your own thoughts or feelings.
□ **introspective** adjective.

introvert ▸ noun a shy, quiet person who is focused on their own thoughts and feelings.
▸ adjective (also **introverted**) characteristic of an introvert.

intrude ▸ verb (**intrudes, intruding, intruded**) come into a place or situation where you are unwelcome or uninvited.

> synonyms **encroach,** impinge, trespass, infringe, invade, violate, disturb, disrupt.

intruder ▸ noun **1** a person who intrudes. **2** a person who goes into a building or an area illegally.

> synonyms **trespasser,** interloper, invader, infiltrator, burglar, housebreaker; informal gatecrasher.

intrusion ▸ noun **1** the action of intruding. **2** a thing that has intruded.

intrusive ▸ adjective having a disturbing and unwelcome effect.

intuit /in-**tyoo**-it/ ▸ verb understand or work something out by intuition.

intuition ▸ noun the ability to understand or know something without conscious reasoning.

> synonyms **1** *he works by intuition* **instinct,** feeling, insight, sixth sense. **2** *this confirms an intuition I had* **hunch,** feeling in your bones, inkling, sneaking suspicion, premonition; informal gut feeling.

intuitive ▸ adjective able to understand or know something without conscious reasoning.

> synonyms **instinctive,** innate, inborn, inherent, natural, unconscious, subconscious; informal gut.

□ **intuitively** adverb.

Inuit /in-**yuu**-it, in-**uu**-it/ ▸ noun (plural **Inuit** or **Inuits**) a member of a people of northern Canada and parts of Greenland and Alaska; an Eskimo.

> ❗ **Inuit** is the official term in Canada, and many of the peoples traditionally called **Eskimos** prefer it.

inundate ▸ verb (**inundates, inundating, inundated**) **1** give or send someone so many things that they cannot deal with them all. **2** flood a place.
□ **inundation** noun.

inure /i-**nyoor**/ ▸ verb (**be inured to**) make someone used to something unpleasant.

invade ▸ verb (**invades, invading, invaded**) **1** enter a country so as to conquer or occupy it. **2** enter a place in large numbers. **3** intrude on. **4** (of a parasite or disease) spread into.

> synonyms **1** *the island was invaded* **occupy,** conquer, capture, seize, take (over), annex, overrun, storm. **2** *someone had invaded our privacy* **intrude on,** violate, encroach on, infringe on, trespass on, disturb, disrupt.
> antonyms leave, liberate.

invader ▸ noun a person who invades.

> synonyms **attacker,** raider, marauder, occupier, conqueror, intruder, trespasser.

invalid¹ /**in**-vuh-lid/ ▸ noun a person suffering from an illness or injury.
▸ verb (**be invalided**) be removed from active military service because of injury or illness.

> synonyms *an officer invalided by a chest wound* **disable,** incapacitate, hospitalize, put out of action, lay up.

invalid² /in-**val**-id/ ▸ adjective **1** not legally or officially recognized. **2** not correct because based on a mistake.

> synonyms **1** *the law was invalid* **void,** null and void, not binding, illegitimate, inapplicable. **2** *the whole theory is invalid* **false,** fallacious, spurious, unsound, wrong, untenable.
> antonyms binding, in force, true.

invalidate ▸ verb (**invalidates, invalidating, invalidated**) make something invalid.

invalidity ▸ noun **1** Brit. the condition of being an invalid. **2** the fact of not being valid.

invaluable ▸ adjective very useful.

> synonyms **indispensable,** irreplaceable, all-important, crucial, vital, worth its weight in gold.
> antonyms dispensable.

invariable ▸ adjective **1** never changing. **2** Maths (of a quantity) constant.

invariably ▸ adverb always.

> synonyms **always,** at all times, without fail, without exception, consistently, habitually, unfailingly.
> antonyms sometimes, never.

invasion ▸ noun **1** an act of invading a country. **2** the arrival of a large number of unwelcome people or things.

SYNONYMS **1** *the invasion of the islands* **occupation,** conquering, capture, seizure, annexation, takeover. **2** *an invasion of my privacy* **violation,** infringement, interruption, encroachment, disturbance, disruption, breach.
ANTONYMS withdrawal, liberation.

invasive ▶ adjective **1** tending to invade or intrude. **2** (of medical procedures) involving the introduction of instruments or other objects into the body.

invective ▶ noun strongly abusive or critical language.

inveigh /in-vay/ ▶ verb (**inveigh against**) speak or write about someone or something with great hostility.

inveigle /in-vay-g'l, in-vee-g'l/ ▶ verb (**inveigles, inveigling, inveigled**) (**inveigle someone into**) cleverly persuade someone to do something.

invent ▶ verb **1** create or design a new device or process. **2** make up a false story, name, etc.

SYNONYMS **1** *he invented television* **originate,** create, design, devise, contrive, develop. **2** *they invented the story* **make up,** fabricate, concoct, hatch, dream up; informal cook up.

invention ▶ noun **1** the action of inventing. **2** a thing that has been invented. **3** a false story. **4** creative ability.

SYNONYMS **1** *the invention of the telescope* **origination,** creation, development, design, discovery. **2** *medieval inventions* **innovation,** creation, contraption, contrivance, device, gadget. **3** *a journalistic invention* **fabrication,** concoction, (piece of) fiction, story, tale, lie, untruth, falsehood, fib.

inventive ▶ adjective having or showing creativity or original thought.

SYNONYMS **1** *the most inventive composer of his time* **creative,** original, innovative, imaginative, resourceful. **2** *a fresh, inventive comedy* **original,** innovative, unusual, fresh, novel, new, groundbreaking, unorthodox, unconventional.
ANTONYMS unimaginative, hackneyed.

□ **inventively** adverb.

inventor ▶ noun a person who invents.

SYNONYMS **originator,** creator, designer, deviser, developer, author, architect, father.

inventory /in-vuhn-tuh-ri/ ▶ noun (plural **inventories**) **1** a complete list of items. **2** a quantity of goods in stock.

SYNONYMS **list,** listing, catalogue, record, register, checklist, log, archive.

inverse ▶ adjective opposite in position, direction, order, or effect.
▶ noun **1** a thing that is the opposite or reverse of another. **2** Maths a reciprocal quantity.
□ **inversion** noun.

invert ▶ verb put something upside down or in the opposite position, order, or arrangement.
■ **inverted comma** a quotation mark.

invertebrate /in-ver-ti-bruht/ ▶ noun an animal that has no backbone.

invest ▶ verb **1** put money into financial schemes, shares, or property in the hope of making a profit. **2** put time or energy into something in the hope of worthwhile results. **3** (**invest in**) buy something expensive. **4** (**invest something with**) give something a particular quality. **5** give someone a rank, honour, official title, etc. in a special ceremony.

SYNONYMS *they invested £18 million* **put in,** plough in, put up, advance, expend, spend; informal lay out.

□ **investor** noun.

investigate ▶ verb **1** carry out a systematic enquiry so as to establish the truth of something. **2** carry out research into a subject.

SYNONYMS **enquire into,** look into, go into, probe, explore, scrutinize, analyse, study, examine; informal check out, suss out.

□ **investigative** adjective.

investigation ▶ noun **1** the act of investigating someone or something. **2** a formal enquiry or systematic study.

SYNONYMS **examination,** enquiry, study, inspection, exploration, analysis, research, scrutiny, probe, review.

investigator ▶ noun a person who investigates.

SYNONYMS **researcher,** examiner, analyst, inspector, scrutineer, detective.

investiture ▶ noun **1** the action of formally giving a person a rank, honour, or special title. **2** a ceremony at which this takes place.

investment ▶ noun **1** the process of investing in something. **2** a thing worth buying because it may be profitable or useful in the future.

SYNONYMS **1** *investment in industry* **investing,** speculation, outlay, funding, backing, financing, underwriting, buying shares. **2** *an investment of £305,000* **stake,** payment, outlay, venture, proposition.

inveterate ▸ adjective **1** having done a particular thing so often that you are now unlikely to stop doing it. **2** (of a feeling or habit) firmly established.

invidious ▸ adjective unfair and likely to arouse resentment or anger in other people.

invigilate ▸ verb (invigilates, invigilating, invigilated) Brit. supervise candidates during an exam.
□ **invigilation** noun **invigilator** noun.

invigorate ▸ verb (invigorates, invigorating, invigorated) give strength or energy to.

invincible ▸ adjective too powerful to be defeated or overcome.

inviolable ▸ adjective that must be respected; never to be broken or attacked.

inviolate ▸ adjective free from injury or violation.

invisible ▸ adjective not able to be seen.

> SYNONYMS **unseen,** imperceptible, undetectable, inconspicuous, unnoticed, unobserved, hidden, out of sight. ANTONYMS visible.

□ **invisibility** noun **invisibly** adverb.

invitation ▸ noun **1** a request that someone should join you in going somewhere or doing something. **2** the action of inviting. **3** a situation or action that is likely to provoke a particular outcome or response.

> SYNONYMS **request,** call, summons; informal invite.

invite ▸ verb (invites, inviting, invited) **1** ask someone to join you in going somewhere or doing something. **2** ask formally or politely for a response to something. **3** tend to provoke a particular outcome or response.

> SYNONYMS **1** *they invited us to lunch* **ask,** summon, have someone over/round. **2** *applications are invited for the post* **ask for,** request, call for, appeal for, solicit, seek. **3** *airing such views invites trouble* **cause,** induce, provoke, ask for, encourage, lead to, bring on yourself, arouse.

▸ noun informal an invitation.

inviting ▸ adjective tempting or attractive.

> SYNONYMS **tempting,** enticing, alluring, attractive, appealing, appetizing, mouth-watering, intriguing, seductive. ANTONYMS repellent.

□ **invitingly** adverb.

in vitro /in vee-troh/ ▸ adjective & adverb taking place in a test tube, culture dish, or elsewhere outside a living animal or plant.

invocation ▸ noun **1** the action of invoking. **2** an appeal to a god or supernatural being.

invoice ▸ noun a list of goods or services provided, with a statement of the payment that is due.
▸ verb (invoices, invoicing, invoiced) send an invoice to someone.

invoke ▸ verb (invokes, invoking, invoked) **1** appeal to someone or something as an authority or in support of an argument. **2** call on a god or supernatural being. **3** call earnestly for.

involuntary ▸ adjective **1** done without conscious control. **2** (especially of muscles or nerves) unable to be consciously controlled. **3** done against someone's will.
□ **involuntarily** adverb.

involve ▸ verb (involves, involving, involved) **1** (of a situation or event) include something as a necessary part or result. **2** make someone experience or take part in something.

> SYNONYMS **1** *the inspection involved a lot of work* **entail,** require, necessitate, demand, call for. **2** *I try to involve everyone in key decisions* **include,** bring in, consult. ANTONYMS preclude, exclude.

involved ▸ adjective **1** connected with someone or something on an emotional or personal level. **2** complicated.

> SYNONYMS **1** *social workers involved in the case* **associated,** connected, concerned. **2** *he had been involved in burglaries* **implicated,** caught up, mixed up. **3** *a long and involved story* **complicated,** intricate, complex, convoluted. **4** *they were totally involved in their work* **engrossed,** absorbed, immersed, caught up, preoccupied, intent. ANTONYMS unconnected, straightforward.

involvement ▸ noun the fact of condition of being involved.

> SYNONYMS **1** *his involvement in the plot* **participation,** collaboration, collusion, complicity, association, connection, entanglement. **2** *emotional involvement* **attachment,** friendship, intimacy, commitment.

invulnerable ▸ adjective impossible to harm or damage.

inwards (or **inward**) ▸ adverb **1** towards the inside. **2** towards the mind, spirit, or soul.

> SYNONYMS **inside,** towards the inside, into the interior, inward, within.

□ **inwardly** adverb.

iodine /I-uh-deen, I-uh-dyn/ ▸ noun **1** a black, non-metallic chemical element. **2** a solution of iodine in alcohol used as an antiseptic.

ion ▸ noun an atom or molecule with a net electric charge through loss or gain of electrons.
□ **ionic** adjective.

ionize (or **ionise**) ▶ verb convert an atom, molecule, or substance into an ion or ions. ▫ **ionization** noun.

ionizer ▶ noun a device which produces ions, used to improve the air quality in a room.

ionosphere /I-on-uh-sfeer/ ▶ noun the layer of the atmosphere above the mesosphere.

iota /I-oh-tuh/ ▶ noun a very small amount.

IOU ▶ noun a signed document acknowledging a debt.

ipso facto /ip-soh **fak**-toh/ ▶ adverb by that very fact or act.

IQ ▶ abbreviation intelligence quotient, a number representing a person's ability to reason, calculated from the results of special tests.

IRA ▶ abbreviation Irish Republican Army.

Iranian ▶ noun a person from Iran. ▶ adjective relating to Iran.

Iraqi ▶ noun (plural **Iraqis**) a person from Iraq. ▶ adjective relating to Iraq.

irascible /i-rass-i-b'l/ ▶ adjective irritable; hot-tempered.

irate ▶ adjective very angry.

ire (*rhymes with* fire) ▶ noun literary anger.

iridescent ▶ adjective showing bright colours that seem to change when seen from different angles. ▫ **iridescence** noun.

✔ just one r: iridescent.

iridium ▶ noun a hard silvery-white metallic element.

iris ▶ noun **1** the round coloured part of the eye, with the pupil in the centre. **2** a plant with sword-shaped leaves and purple, yellow, or white flowers.

Irish ▶ noun (also **Irish Gaelic**) the language of Ireland. ▶ adjective relating to Ireland or Irish. ■ **Irish coffee** coffee mixed with a dash of Irish whisky.

irk ▶ verb irritate; annoy.

irksome ▶ adjective irritating; annoying.

iron ▶ noun **1** a strong magnetic silvery-grey metal. **2** a tool made of iron. **3** a hand-held piece of equipment with a heated steel base, used to smooth clothes. **4** a golf club used for hitting the ball at a high angle. **5** (**irons**) handcuffs or chains used as a restraint. ▶ verb **1** smooth clothes with an iron. **2** (**iron something out**) settle a difficulty or problem. ▶ adjective **1** made of iron. **2** firm, strong, or resistant.

SYNONYMS **1** *an iron bar* **ferric,** ferrous. **2** *an iron will* **uncompromising,** unrelenting, unyielding, unbending, rigid, steely. ANTONYMS flexible.

■ **Iron Age** an ancient period when weapons and tools were made of iron. **Iron Curtain** an imaginary barrier separating the communist countries of the former Soviet bloc and western Europe.

ironic /I-ron-ik/ ▶ adjective **1** using irony. **2** happening in the opposite way to what is expected.

SYNONYMS **1** *Edward's tone was ironic* **sarcastic,** sardonic, dry, caustic, scathing, acerbic, bitter, trenchant, mocking, derisive, scornful; Brit. informal sarky. **2** *it's ironic that I've ended up writing* **paradoxical,** funny, strange; informal typical. ANTONYMS sincere.

▫ **ironically** adverb.

ironmonger ▶ noun Brit. a person who sells tools and other hardware. ▫ **ironmongery** noun.

ironworks ▶ noun a place where iron is smelted or iron goods are made.

irony ▶ noun (plural **ironies**) **1** the use of words that say the opposite of what you really mean in order to be funny or to make a point. **2** aspects of a situation that are opposite to what are expected.

SYNONYMS **1** *that note of irony in her voice* **sarcasm,** bitterness, mockery, ridicule, derision, scorn; Brit. informal sarkiness. **2** *the irony of the situation* **paradox.** ANTONYMS sincerity.

irradiate ▶ verb (**irradiates, irradiating, irradiated**) **1** expose to radiation. **2** shine light on. ▫ **irradiation** noun.

irrational ▶ adjective not logical or reasonable.

SYNONYMS **unreasonable,** illogical, groundless, baseless, unfounded, unjustifiable. ANTONYMS logical.

▫ **irrationality** noun **irrationally** adverb.

irreconcilable ▶ adjective **1** incompatible. **2** (of differences) not able to be settled.

irrecoverable ▶ adjective not able to be recovered.

irredeemable ▶ adjective not able to be saved, improved, or corrected.

irreducible ▶ adjective not able to be reduced or simplified.

irrefutable ▶ adjective impossible to deny or disprove.

irregular ▶ adjective **1** not regular in shape, arrangement, or occurrence. **2** against a rule, standard, or convention. **3** not belonging to regular army units. **4** Grammar (of a word) having inflections that do not conform to the usual rules.

i

SYNONYMS **1** *an irregular coastline* **uneven,** crooked, misshapen, lopsided, asymmetrical, twisted. **2** *irregular surfaces* **rough,** bumpy, uneven, pitted, rutted, lumpy, knobbly, gnarled. **3** *an irregular heartbeat* **inconsistent,** unsteady, uneven, fitful, patchy, variable, varying, changeable, inconstant, erratic, unstable, spasmodic, intermittent. **4** *irregular financial dealings* **improper,** illegitimate, unethical, unprofessional; informal shady, dodgy. **5** *an irregular army* **guerrilla,** underground, paramilitary, partisan, mercenary, terrorist.
ANTONYMS regular, above board.

□ **irregularity** noun (plural **irregularities**).

irrelevant ▸ adjective not relevant.

SYNONYMS **beside the point,** immaterial, unconnected, unrelated, peripheral, extraneous.

□ **irrelevance** noun **irrelevantly** adverb.

✔ **-ant,** not **-ent:** irrelev**ant**.

irreligious ▸ adjective indifferent or hostile to religion.

irremediable /ir-ri-**mee**-di-uh-b'l/ ▸ adjective impossible to cure or put right.

irreparable /ir-**rep**-uh-ruh-b'l/ ▸ adjective impossible to put right or repair.
□ **irreparably** adverb.

irreplaceable ▸ adjective impossible to replace if lost or damaged.

irrepressible ▸ adjective not able to be restrained.

irreproachable ▸ adjective very good and unable to be criticized.

irresistible ▸ adjective too tempting or powerful to be resisted.

SYNONYMS **1** *her irresistible smile* **captivating,** enticing, alluring, enchanting. **2** *an irresistible impulse* **uncontrollable,** overwhelming, overpowering, ungovernable.

□ **irresistibly** adverb.

✔ **-ible,** not **-able:** irresist**ible**.

irresolute ▸ adjective uncertain.

irrespective ▸ adjective (**irrespective of**) regardless of.

irresponsible ▸ adjective not showing a proper sense of responsibility.

SYNONYMS **reckless,** rash, careless, unwise, imprudent, ill-advised, injudicious, hasty, impetuous, foolhardy, foolish, unreliable, undependable, untrustworthy.
ANTONYMS responsible.

□ **irresponsibility** noun **irresponsibly** adverb.

irretrievable ▸ adjective not able to be

brought back or made right.
□ **irretrievably** adverb.

irreverent ▸ adjective disrespectful.
□ **irreverence** noun **irreverently** adverb.

irreversible ▸ adjective impossible to be reversed or altered.
□ **irreversibly** adverb.

irrevocable /ir-**rev**-uh-kuh-b'l/ ▸ adjective not able to be changed or reversed.
□ **irrevocably** adverb.

irrigate ▸ verb (**irrigates, irrigating, irrigated**) supply water to land or crops through channels.
□ **irrigation** noun.

irritable ▸ adjective **1** easily annoyed or angered. **2** Medicine unusually sensitive.

SYNONYMS **bad-tempered,** short-tempered, irascible, tetchy, testy, grumpy, grouchy.
ANTONYMS good-humoured.

□ **irritability** noun **irritably** adverb.

irritant ▸ noun **1** a substance that irritates the skin or a part of the body. **2** a source of continual annoyance.

irritate ▸ verb (**irritates, irritating, irritated**) **1** make someone annoyed or angry. **2** cause soreness, itching, or inflammation.

SYNONYMS **1** *his tone irritated her* **annoy,** bother, vex, make cross, exasperate, infuriate, anger, madden; Brit. rub up the wrong way; informal aggravate, peeve, rile, needle, get (to), bug, hack off; Brit. informal nark, get on someone's wick; N. Amer. informal tee off, tick off, burn up. **2** *some sand irritated my eyes* **inflame,** hurt, chafe, scratch, scrape, rub.
ANTONYMS delight, soothe.

irritation ▸ noun the state of being annoyed or angry.

SYNONYMS **annoyance,** exasperation, vexation, indignation, anger, displeasure, chagrin.
ANTONYMS delight.

is 3rd person singular present of BE.

ISA ▸ abbreviation individual savings account.

Islam ▸ noun **1** the religion of the Muslims, revealed through Muhammad as the Prophet of Allah. **2** the Muslim world.
□ **Islamic** adjective.

island ▸ noun **1** a piece of land surrounded by water. **2** a thing that is isolated, detached, or surrounded.

SYNONYMS **isle,** islet, atoll; Brit. holm; (**islands**) archipelago.

□ **islander** noun.

isle ▸ noun literary an island.

islet /**I**-lit/ ▸ noun a small island.

isn't ▸ short form is not.

i

isobar /I-soh-bar/ ▸ noun a line on a map connecting points having the same atmospheric pressure.

isolate ▸ verb (**isolates, isolating, isolated**) **1** place something or someone apart from others and on their own. **2** extract a substance in a pure form.

> SYNONYMS **separate,** segregate, detach, cut off, shut away, alienate, distance, cloister, seclude, cordon off, seal off, close off, fence off.
> ANTONYMS integrate.

isolated ▸ adjective **1** (of a place) remote. **2** (of a person) cut off from other people; lonely. **3** single; exceptional.

> SYNONYMS **1** *isolated communities* **remote,** out of the way, outlying, off the beaten track, in the back of beyond, godforsaken, inaccessible, cut-off; informal in the middle of nowhere, in the sticks; N. Amer. informal jerkwater, in the tall timbers; Austral./NZ informal beyond the black stump. **2** *he lived a very isolated existence* **solitary,** lonely, secluded, reclusive, hermit-like; N. Amer. lonesome. **3** *an isolated incident* **unique,** lone, solitary, unusual, exceptional, untypical, freak; informal one-off.
> ANTONYMS accessible, sociable, common.

isolation ▸ noun the fact of being isolated.

> SYNONYMS **1** *their feeling of isolation* **solitariness,** loneliness, friendlessness. **2** *the isolation of some mental hospitals* **remoteness,** inaccessibility.
> ANTONYMS contact.

isolationism ▸ noun a policy of remaining apart from the political affairs of other countries.

isomer /I-suh-mer/ ▸ noun Chemistry each of two or more compounds with the same formula but a different arrangement of atoms.

isometric ▸ adjective having equal dimensions.

isosceles /I-soss-i-leez/ ▸ adjective (of a triangle) having two sides of equal length.

isotherm /I-soh-therm/ ▸ noun a line on a map or diagram connecting points having the same temperature.

isotope /I-suh-tohp/ ▸ noun each of two or more forms of the same element that contain equal numbers of protons but different numbers of neutrons in their nuclei.

ISP ▸ abbreviation Internet service provider.

Israeli /iz-ray-li/ ▸ noun (plural **Israelis**) a person from Israel.
▸ adjective relating to the modern country of Israel.

Israelite /iz-ruh-lyt/ ▸ noun a member of the people of ancient Israel.

issue ▸ noun **1** an important topic to be discussed or settled. **2** a problem or difficulty. **3** each of a regular series of publications. **4** the action of supplying something.

> SYNONYMS **1** *the committee discussed the issue* **matter,** question, point at issue, affair, case, subject, topic, problem, situation. **2** *the latest issue of our magazine* **edition,** number, instalment, copy. **3** *the issue of a special stamp* **issuing,** release, publication.

▸ verb (**issues, issuing, issued**) **1** supply or give out. **2** formally send out or make known. **3** (**issue from**) come, go, or flow out from.

> SYNONYMS **1** *the minister issued a statement* **release,** put out, deliver, publish, broadcast, circulate, distribute. **2** *the captain issued the crew with guns* **supply,** provide, furnish, arm, equip, fit out, rig out, kit out; informal fix up.
> ANTONYMS withdraw, collect in.

■ **take issue with** challenge someone.

isthmus /isth-muhss, iss-muhss/ ▸ noun (plural **isthmuses**) a narrow strip of land with sea on either side, linking two larger areas of land.

IT ▸ abbreviation information technology.

it ▸ pronoun **1** used to refer to a thing previously mentioned or easily identified. **2** referring to an animal or child whose sex is not specified. **3** used in the normal subject position in statements about time, distance, or weather. **4** the situation or circumstances.

Italian ▸ noun **1** a person from Italy. **2** the language of Italy.
▸ adjective relating to Italy or Italian.

italic ▸ adjective (of a typeface) sloping to the right, used especially for emphasis and for foreign words.
▸ noun (also **italics**) an italic typeface or letter. □ **italicize** (or **italicise**) verb.

itch ▸ noun **1** an uncomfortable sensation that makes you want to scratch your skin. **2** informal an impatient desire.

> SYNONYMS **1** *I have an itch on my back* **tingling,** irritation, itchiness, prickle. **2** *the itch to travel* **longing,** yearning, craving, ache, hunger, thirst, urge, hankering.

▸ verb **1** experience an itch. **2** informal feel an impatient desire to do something.

> SYNONYMS **1** *my chilblains really itch* **tingle,** be irritated, be itchy, sting, hurt, be sore. **2** *he itched to do something to help* **long,** yearn, ache, burn, crave, hanker for/after, hunger, thirst, be

eager, be desperate; informal be dying, be gagging.

□ **itchy** adjective.

it'd ▶ short form **1** it had. **2** it would.

item ▶ noun an individual article or unit.

SYNONYMS **1** *an item of farm equipment* **thing**, article, object, piece, element, constituent, component, ingredient. **2** *the meeting discussed the item* **issue**, matter, affair, case, subject, topic, question, point. **3** *a news item* **report**, story, article, piece, write-up, bulletin, feature, review.

itemize (or **itemise**) ▶ verb (**itemizes**, **itemizing**, **itemized**) present a quantity as a list of individual items or parts.

itinerant /I-**tin**-uh-ruhnt/ ▶ adjective travelling from place to place.
▶ noun an itinerant person.

itinerary /I-**tin**-uh-ruh-ri/ ▶ noun (plural **itineraries**) a planned route or journey.

SYNONYMS **route**, plan, schedule, timetable, programme.

✔ itin**erary**, not -**ery**.

it'll ▶ short form **1** it shall. **2** it will.

its ▶ possessive determiner **1** belonging to or associated with a thing previously mentioned or easily identified. **2** belonging to or associated with a child or animal whose sex is not specified.

❗ Don't confuse the possessive **its** (as in *turn the camera on its side*) with the form **it's** (short for either **it is** or **it has**, as in *it's my fault* or *it's been a hot day*).

it's ▶ short form **1** it is. **2** it has.

itself ▶ pronoun **1** used to refer to something previously mentioned as the subject of the clause. **2** used to emphasize a particular thing mentioned.

ITV ▶ abbreviation Independent Television.

IUD ▶ abbreviation intrauterine device.

I've ▶ short form I have.

IVF ▶ abbreviation in vitro fertilization.

Ivorian /I-**vor**-i-uhn/ ▶ noun a person from the Ivory Coast, a country in West Africa.
▶ adjective relating to the Ivory Coast.

ivory ▶ noun (plural **ivories**) **1** the hard creamy-white substance which elephants' tusks are made of. **2** the creamy-white colour of ivory.
■ **ivory tower** a situation in which someone leads a privileged life and does not have to face normal difficulties.

ivy ▶ noun an evergreen climbing plant.

Jj

J (or **j**) ▸ noun (plural **Js** or **J's**) the tenth letter of the alphabet.
▸ abbreviation joules.

jab ▸ verb (**jabs**, **jabbing**, **jabbed**) poke someone with something sharp or pointed.

> SYNONYMS poke, prod, dig, nudge, thrust, stab, push.

▸ noun **1** a quick, sharp poke or blow. **2** Brit. informal a vaccination.

> SYNONYMS poke, prod, dig, nudge, thrust, stab, push.

jabber ▸ verb (**jabbers**, **jabbering**, **jabbered**) talk quickly and excitedly but without making much sense.

jack ▸ noun **1** a device for lifting a vehicle off the ground so that a wheel can be changed or the underside examined. **2** a playing card ranking next below a queen. **3** a connection between two pieces of electrical equipment. **4** (in bowls) a small white ball at which players aim the bowls.
▸ verb (**jack something up**) **1** raise something with a jack. **2** informal increase something by a large amount.
■ **jack-in-the-box** a toy consisting of a box containing a figure on a spring, which pops up when the lid is opened.

jackal ▸ noun a wild dog that often hunts or scavenges in packs.

jackass ▸ noun **1** a stupid person. **2** a male ass or donkey.

jackdaw ▸ noun a small crow with a grey head.

jacket ▸ noun **1** an outer garment reaching to the waist or hips, with sleeves. **2** a covering placed around something for protection or insulation. **3** Brit. the skin of a potato.

> SYNONYMS wrapping, wrapper, sleeve, coat, cover, covering, sheath.

■ **jacket potato** Brit. a potato that is baked and served with the skin on.

jackknife ▸ noun (plural **jackknives**) a large knife with a folding blade.
▸ verb (**jackknifes**, **jackknifing**, **jackknifed**) (of an articulated lorry or truck) bend into a V-shape in an uncontrolled skidding movement.

jackpot ▸ noun a large cash prize in a game or lottery.
■ **hit the jackpot** have great or unexpected success.

Jack Russell ▸ noun a small breed of terrier with short legs.

Jacobean /jak-uh-bee-uhn/ ▸ adjective having to do with the reign of James I of England (1603–1625).
▸ noun a person who lived in the Jacobean period.

Jacobite /jak-uh-byt/ ▸ noun a supporter of the deposed James II and his descendants in their claim to the British throne.

jacquard /ja-kard/ ▸ noun a fabric with a woven pattern.

jacuzzi /juh-koo-zi/ ▸ noun (plural **jacuzzis**) trademark a large, wide bath with jets of water to massage the body.

jade ▸ noun a hard bluish-green precious stone.

jaded ▸ adjective tired out or lacking enthusiasm after having had too much of something.

jagged /jag-gid/ ▸ adjective with rough, sharp points or edges sticking out.

> SYNONYMS spiky, barbed, ragged, rough, uneven, irregular, serrated.
> ANTONYMS smooth.

jaguar /jag-yuu-er/ ▸ noun a large cat with a spotted coat, found in Central and South America.

jail (or Brit. **gaol**) ▸ noun a place for holding people who are accused or convicted of a crime.

> SYNONYMS *he was thrown into jail* prison, lock-up, detention centre; N. Amer. penitentiary, jailhouse, correctional facility; informal clink, cooler, the slammer, inside; Brit. informal nick; N. Amer. informal can, pen, slam, pokey.

▸ verb put someone in jail.

> SYNONYMS *she was jailed for killing her husband* send to prison/jail, put in prison/jail, imprison, incarcerate, lock up, put away, detain; informal send down, put behind bars, put inside; Brit. informal

j

bang up.
ANTONYMS acquit, release.

□ **jailer** (or Brit. **gaoler**) noun.

jalopy /juh-**lop**-i/ ▸ noun (plural **jalopies**) informal an old car.

jam¹ ▸ verb (**jams**, **jamming**, **jammed**)
1 squeeze or pack tightly into a space.
2 push something roughly and forcibly into a position. **3** block something through crowding. **4** make or become unable to function because a part is stuck. **5** (**jam something on**) apply a brake suddenly and with force. **6** interrupt a radio transmission by causing interference. **7** informal improvise with other musicians.

SYNONYMS **1** *he jammed a finger in each ear* **stuff**, shove, force, ram, thrust, press, push, stick, cram. **2** *hundreds of people jammed into the hall* **crowd**, pack, pile, press, squeeze, cram, throng, mob, fill, block, clog, congest. **3** *the rudder had jammed* **stick**, become stuck, catch, seize (up). **4** *dust can jam the mechanism* **immobilize**, paralyse, disable, clog, block; informal bung up.

▸ noun **1** an instance of something being jammed. **2** informal a difficult situation. **3** informal an improvised performance by a group of musicians.

SYNONYMS *a traffic jam* **tailback**, hold-up, queue, congestion, bottleneck; N. Amer. gridlock; informal snarl-up.

jam² ▸ noun chiefly Brit. a spread made from fruit and sugar.

Jamaican ▸ noun a person from Jamaica.
▸ adjective relating to Jamaica.

jamb /jam/ ▸ noun a side post of a doorway, window, or fireplace.

jamboree ▸ noun a large celebration or party.

jammy ▸ adjective (**jammier**, **jammiest**)
1 covered or filled with jam. **2** Brit. informal lucky.

jangle ▸ verb (**jangles**, **jangling**, **jangled**)
1 make a ringing metallic sound. **2** (of your nerves) be set on edge.
▸ noun a ringing metallic sound.
□ **jangly** adjective.

janitor ▸ noun a caretaker of a building.

January ▸ noun (plural **Januaries**) the first month of the year.

Japanese ▸ noun (plural **Japanese**) **1** a person from Japan. **2** the language of Japan.
▸ adjective relating to Japan.

jape ▸ noun a practical joke.

jar¹ ▸ noun a cylindrical container made of glass or pottery.

SYNONYMS *a jar of honey* **pot**, container, crock.

jar² ▸ verb (**jars**, **jarring**, **jarred**) **1** send a

painful shock through a part of the body.
2 hit something with an unpleasant vibration or jolt. **3** have an unpleasant or strange effect.

SYNONYMS **1** *each step jarred my whole body* **jolt**, jerk, shake, vibrate. **2** *her shrill voice jarred on him* **grate**, set someone's teeth on edge, irritate, annoy, get on someone's nerves. **3** *the verse jars with the words that follow* **clash**, conflict, contrast, be incompatible, be at variance, be at odds, be inconsistent.

▸ noun an instance of jarring.

jardinière /zhar-din-**yair**/ ▸ noun an ornamental pot or stand for displaying plants.

jargon ▸ noun words or phrases used by a particular group that are difficult for other people to understand.

SYNONYMS **slang**, idiom, cant, argot, patter, gobbledegook; informal lingo, -speak, -ese.

jasmine ▸ noun a shrub or climbing plant with sweet-smelling flowers.

jasper ▸ noun a reddish-brown variety of quartz.

jaundice /**jawn**-diss/ ▸ noun **1** a condition in which the skin takes on a yellow colour.
2 bitterness or resentment.
□ **jaundiced** adjective.

jaunt ▸ noun a short trip or journey taken for pleasure.

jaunty ▸ adjective (**jauntier**, **jauntiest**) lively and self-confident.
□ **jauntily** adverb.

javelin ▸ noun a long spear thrown in a competitive sport or as a weapon.

jaw ▸ noun each of the upper and lower bony structures forming the framework of the mouth and containing the teeth.

SYNONYMS (**jaws**) **mouth**, maw, muzzle; informal chops.

▸ verb informal talk at length.

jawbone ▸ noun the lower jaw, or the lower part of the face.

jay ▸ noun a noisy bird of the crow family with brightly coloured feathers.

jaywalk ▸ verb chiefly N. Amer. walk in or across a road without paying proper attention to the traffic.
□ **jaywalker** noun.

jazz ▸ noun a type of music that is mainly instrumental, in which the players often improvise.
▸ verb (**jazz something up**) make something more lively.

jazzy ▸ adjective (**jazzier**, **jazziest**) **1** in the style of jazz. **2** bright, colourful, and showy.

jealous ▸ adjective **1** envious of someone else's achievements or advantages.

2 resentful of someone who you think is a sexual rival. **3** very protective of your rights or possessions.

SYNONYMS **1** *jealous of his brother* **envious,** covetous, resentful, grudging, green with envy. **2** *a jealous lover* **suspicious,** distrustful, possessive, proprietorial, overprotective. **3** *jealous of their rights* **protective,** vigilant, watchful, mindful, careful.
ANTONYMS proud, trusting, careless.

□ **jealously** adverb.

jealousy ▶ noun the state or feeling of being jealous.

SYNONYMS **envy,** resentment, bitterness, grudge.

jeans ▶ noun casual trousers made of denim.

jeep ▶ noun trademark a sturdy motor vehicle with four-wheel drive.

jeer ▶ verb (jeers, jeering, jeered) shout rude and mocking remarks at someone.

SYNONYMS *the demonstrators jeered the police* **taunt,** mock, scoff at, ridicule, sneer at, deride, insult, abuse, heckle, catcall (at), boo (at), whistle at; Brit. barrack.
ANTONYMS applaud, cheer.

▶ noun a rude and mocking remark.

SYNONYMS *the jeers of the crowd* **taunt,** sneer, insult, shout, jibe, boo, catcall, derision, teasing, scoffing, abuse, scorn, heckling, catcalling; Brit. barracking.
ANTONYMS applause, cheer.

Jehovah /ji-hoh-vuh/ ▶ noun a form of the Hebrew name of God used in some translations of the Bible.

jejune /ji-joon/ ▶ adjective **1** naive and simplistic. **2** not interesting.

jejunum /ji-joo-nuhm/ ▶ noun the part of the small intestine between the duodenum and ileum.

jell ▶ verb ➡ GEL².

jelly ▶ noun (plural **jellies**) **1** Brit. a dessert consisting of a fruit-flavoured liquid set with gelatin to form a semi-solid mass. **2** a substance with a similar semi-solid consistency.
□ **jellied** adjective.

jellyfish ▶ noun (plural **jellyfish** or **jellyfishes**) a sea creature with a soft jelly-like body that has stinging tentacles around the edge.

jemmy ▶ noun (plural **jemmies**) a short crowbar.

je ne sais quoi /zhuh nuh say kwah/ ▶ noun a quality that cannot be easily identified.

jenny ▶ noun (plural **jennies**) a female donkey or ass.

jeopardize (or **jeopardise**) ▶ verb (**jeopardizes, jeopardizing, jeopardized**) risk harming or destroying something.

SYNONYMS **threaten,** endanger, imperil, risk, put in danger/jeopardy, compromise, prejudice.
ANTONYMS safeguard.

jeopardy ▶ noun danger of loss, harm, or failure.

SYNONYMS **danger,** peril, risk.

jerboa /jer-boh-uh/ ▶ noun a desert rodent with very long hind legs.

jerk ▶ noun **1** a quick, sharp, sudden movement. **2** informal a stupid person.

SYNONYMS **1** *she gave the reins a jerk* **yank,** tug, pull, wrench. **2** *he let the clutch in with a jerk* **jolt,** lurch, bump, judder, jump, bounce, shake.

▶ verb move or raise with a jerk.

SYNONYMS **1** *she jerked her arm free* **yank,** tug, pull, wrench, wrest, drag, snatch. **2** *the car jerked along* **jolt,** lurch, bump, judder, bounce.

jerkin ▶ noun a sleeveless jacket.

jerky ▶ adjective (**jerkier, jerkiest**) moving in sudden stops and starts.
□ **jerkily** adverb.

jerry-built ▶ adjective badly or quickly built, using cheap materials.

jerrycan (or **jerrican**) ▶ noun a large flat-sided metal container for liquids.

jersey ▶ noun (plural **jerseys**) **1** a knitted garment with long sleeves. **2** a distinctive shirt worn by people who play certain sports. **3** a soft knitted fabric. **4** (**Jersey**) a breed of light brown dairy cattle.

Jerusalem artichoke ▶ noun a knobbly root vegetable with white flesh.

jest ▶ noun a joke.
▶ verb speak or behave in a joking way.

jester ▶ noun a man who entertained people in a medieval court.

Jesuit /jez-yuu-it/ ▶ noun a member of the Society of Jesus, a Roman Catholic order.

Jesus (or **Jesus Christ**) ▶ noun the central figure of the Christian religion, considered by Christians to be the son of God.

jet¹ ▶ noun **1** a rapid stream of liquid or gas forced out of a small opening. **2** an aircraft powered by jet engines.

SYNONYMS **1** *a jet of water* **stream,** spurt, spray, spout, gush, surge, burst. **2** *carburettor jets* **nozzle,** head, spout.

▶ verb (**jets, jetting, jetted**) **1** spurt out in a jet. **2** travel by jet aircraft.
■ **jet engine** an aircraft engine which gives propulsion by sending out a high-speed jet of gas obtained by burning fuel. **jet lag** extreme tiredness felt after a long flight

j

across different time zones. **the jet set** informal wealthy people who frequently travel abroad for pleasure. **jet ski** trademark a small vehicle which skims across the surface of water.

jet² ▸ noun **1** a hard black semi-precious mineral. **2** (also **jet black**) a glossy black colour.

jetsam ▸ noun unwanted material thrown overboard from a ship and washed ashore.

jettison ▸ verb **1** throw or drop something from an aircraft or ship. **2** abandon or get rid of something.

> SYNONYMS **dump,** drop, ditch, throw out, get rid of, discard, dispose of, scrap. ANTONYMS retain.

jetty ▸ noun (plural **jetties**) a landing stage or small pier where boats can be moored.

Jew ▸ noun a member of the people whose religion is Judaism and who trace their origins to the Hebrew people of ancient Israel.
∎ **Jew's harp** a small musical instrument like a U-shaped harp, held between the teeth and struck with a finger.

jewel ▸ noun **1** a precious stone. **2** (**jewels**) pieces of jewellery. **3** a highly valued person or thing.

> SYNONYMS **1** *priceless jewels* **gem,** gemstone, (precious) stone; informal sparkler, rock. **2** *the jewel of his collection* **showpiece,** pride (and joy), cream, crème de la crème, jewel in the crown, prize, pick.

□ **jewelled** (US spelling **jeweled**) adjective.

jeweller (US spelling **jeweler**) ▸ noun a person who makes or sells jewellery.

jewellery (US spelling **jewelry**) ▸ noun objects such as necklaces, rings, or bracelets worn on the body for decoration.

> SYNONYMS **jewels,** gems, gemstones, precious stones, regalia, finery, ornaments, trinkets.

Jewish ▸ adjective having to do with Jews or Judaism.
□ **Jewishness** noun.

Jewry ▸ noun Jews as a group.

Jezebel ▸ noun an immoral woman.

jib¹ ▸ noun **1** Sailing a triangular sail in front of the mast. **2** the projecting arm of a crane.

jib² ▸ verb (**jibs, jibbing, jibbed**) **1** (**jib at**) be unwilling to do or accept something. **2** (of a horse) stop and refuse to go on.

jibe (or **gibe**) ▸ noun an insulting remark.

> SYNONYMS *cruel jibes* **snide remark,** taunt, sneer, jeer, insult, barb; informal dig, put-down.

▸ verb (**jibes, jibing, jibed**) make insulting remarks.

jiffy (or **jiff**) ▸ noun informal a moment.

jig ▸ noun **1** a lively dance. **2** a device that holds something in position and guides the tools working on it.
▸ verb (**jigs, jigging, jigged**) move up and down with a quick, jerky motion.

jiggery-pokery ▸ noun informal suspicious behaviour.

jiggle ▸ verb (**jiggles, jiggling, jiggled**) move lightly and quickly from side to side or up and down.
▸ noun a quick, light shake.
□ **jiggly** adjective.

jigsaw ▸ noun **1** a picture printed on cardboard or wood and cut into many interlocking shapes that have to be fitted together. **2** a machine saw with a fine blade allowing it to cut curved lines in a sheet of wood, metal, etc.

jihad /ji-**hahd**/ ▸ noun Islam **1** a war or struggle against unbelievers. **2** the spiritual struggle within oneself against sin.

jilt ▸ verb abruptly break off a relationship with a lover.

> SYNONYMS **leave,** walk out on, throw over, finish with, break up with, stand up, leave standing at the altar; informal chuck, ditch, dump, drop, run out on, give someone the push/elbow, give someone the big E.

jingle ▸ noun **1** a light ringing sound. **2** a short easily remembered slogan, verse, or tune.

> SYNONYMS **clink,** chink, tinkle, jangle, ring.

▸ verb (**jingles, jingling, jingled**) make a jingle.
□ **jingly** adjective.

jingoism ▸ noun too much pride in your country.
□ **jingoistic** adjective.

jinx ▸ noun a person or thing that brings bad luck.

> SYNONYMS *the jinx struck six days later* **curse,** spell, the evil eye, black magic, voodoo, bad luck; N. Amer. hex.

▸ verb bring bad luck to.

> SYNONYMS *the family is jinxed* **curse,** cast a spell on, put the evil eye on; Austral. point the bone at; N. Amer. hex.

jitterbug ▸ noun a fast dance performed to swing music, popular in the 1940s.

jitters ▸ noun informal a feeling of being very nervous.
□ **jittery** adjective.

jive ▸ noun a style of lively dance popular in the 1940s and 1950s, performed to swing music or rock and roll.
▸ verb (**jives, jiving, jived**) dance the jive.

job ▸ noun **1** a paid position of regular employment. **2** a task. **3** informal a crime.

4 informal a procedure to improve the appearance of something.

> SYNONYMS **1** *my job involves a lot of travelling* **position,** post, situation, appointment, occupation, profession, trade, career, work, vocation, calling. **2** *this job will take three months* **task,** piece of work, assignment, project, chore, undertaking, venture, operation. **3** *it's your job to protect her* **responsibility,** duty, charge, task, role, function, mission; informal department.

▶ verb (**jobs, jobbing, jobbed**) do casual or occasional work.

■ **job lot** a batch of articles sold or bought at one time. **job-share** (of two part-time employees) share a single full-time job.

jobcentre ▶ noun (in the UK) a government office which gives out information about available jobs to unemployed people.

jobless ▶ adjective without a paid job.

> SYNONYMS **unemployed,** out of work, out of a job, unwaged, redundant, laid off; Brit. informal on the dole, resting; Austral./NZ informal on the wallaby track.
> ANTONYMS employed.

jockey ▶ noun (plural **jockeys**) a professional rider in horse races.

▶ verb (**jockeys, jockeying, jockeyed**) struggle to gain or achieve something.

jockstrap ▶ noun a support or protection for the male genitals.

jocose /juh-**kohss**/ ▶ adjective formal playful or humorous.

jocular /**jok**-yuu-ler/ ▶ adjective humorous. □ **jocularity** noun **jocularly** adverb.

jocund /**jok**-uhnd/ ▶ adjective formal cheerful and light-hearted.

jodhpurs /**jod**-perz/ ▶ plural noun trousers worn for horse riding that are close-fitting below the knee.

jog ▶ verb (**jogs, jogging, jogged**) **1** run at a steady, gentle pace. **2** (**jog along** or **on**) continue in a steady, uneventful way. **3** knock or nudge slightly.

> SYNONYMS **1** *he jogged along the road* **run,** trot, lope. **2** *a hand jogged his elbow* **nudge,** prod, poke, push, bump, jar.

▶ noun **1** a period of jogging. **2** a gentle running pace. **3** a slight knock or nudge.

> SYNONYMS *he set off at a jog* **run,** trot, lope.

■ **jog someone's memory** make someone remember something. □ **jogger** noun.

joggle ▶ verb (**joggles, joggling, joggled**) move with repeated small jerks.

joie de vivre /zʰwah duh **vee**-vruh/ ▶ noun lively and cheerful enjoyment of life.

join ▶ verb **1** connect things together, or become connected. **2** come together to form a whole. **3** become a member or employee of. **4** (also **join in**) take part in an activity. **5** (**join up**) become a member of the armed forces. **6** do something or go somewhere with someone else.

> SYNONYMS **1** *the two parts of the mould are joined with clay* **connect,** unite, couple, fix, affix, attach, fasten, stick, glue, fuse, weld, amalgamate, bond, link, merge, secure, make fast, tie, bind. **2** *here the path joins a major road* **meet,** touch, reach. **3** *I'm off to join the search party* **help in,** participate in, get involved in, contribute to, enlist in, join up, sign up, band together, get together, team up.
> ANTONYMS separate, leave.

▶ noun a place where two or more things are joined.

joiner ▶ noun a person who puts together the wooden parts of a building.

joinery ▶ noun **1** the wooden parts of a building. **2** the work of a joiner.

joint ▶ noun **1** a point at which parts are joined. **2** a structure in a body which joins two bones. **3** the part of a plant stem from which a leaf or branch grows. **4** Brit. a large piece of meat. **5** informal a particular kind of place: *a burger joint.* **6** informal a cannabis cigarette.

> SYNONYMS *a leaky joint* **join,** junction, intersection, link, connection, weld, seam.

▶ adjective **1** shared, held, or made by two or more people. **2** sharing in an achievement or activity.

> SYNONYMS *a joint effort* **common,** shared, communal, collective, mutual, cooperative, collaborative, concerted, combined, united.
> ANTONYMS separate.

▶ verb cut the body of an animal into joints. □ **jointed** adjective.

jointly ▶ adverb in a joint manner.

> SYNONYMS **together,** in partnership, in cooperation, cooperatively, in conjunction, in combination, mutually.
> ANTONYMS separately.

joist ▶ noun a length of timber or steel supporting the floor or ceiling of a building.

jojoba /huh-**hoh**-buh/ ▶ noun an oil extracted from the seeds of a North American shrub.

joke ▶ noun **1** a thing that someone says to cause amusement or laughter. **2** a trick played for fun. **3** informal a person or thing that is ridiculously inadequate.

> SYNONYMS **1** *telling jokes* **funny story,** jest, witticism, quip, pun; informal gag,

j

wisecrack, crack, funny, one-liner; N. Amer. informal boffola. **2** *playing stupid jokes* **trick,** prank, stunt, hoax, jape; informal leg-pull, spoof, wind-up. **3** *he soon became a joke* **laughing stock,** figure of fun, object of ridicule. **4** *the present system is a joke* **farce,** travesty, waste of time; informal shambles; N. Amer. informal shuck.

▶ verb (**jokes, joking, joked**) make jokes.

SYNONYMS *she joked with the guests* **tell jokes,** jest, banter, quip; informal wisecrack, josh.

□ **jokey** (or **joky**) adjective.

joker ▶ noun **1** a person who likes making or playing jokes. **2** a playing card with the figure of a jester, used as a wild card.

SYNONYMS **comedian,** comedienne, comic, humorist, wit, jester, prankster, practical joker, clown.

jollification ▶ noun time spent having fun.

jollity ▶ noun **1** lively and cheerful activity. **2** the quality of being cheerful.

jolly ▶ adjective (**jollier, jolliest**) **1** happy and cheerful. **2** lively and entertaining.

SYNONYMS **cheerful,** happy, cheery, good-humoured, jovial, merry, sunny, joyful, light-hearted, in high spirits, bubbly, genial; informal chipper, chirpy, perky, bright-eyed and bushy-tailed. ANTONYMS miserable.

▶ verb (**jollies, jollying, jollied**) (**jolly someone along**) informal encourage someone in a friendly way.
▶ adverb Brit. informal very.

jolt ▶ verb **1** push or shake abruptly and roughly. **2** shock someone into taking action.

SYNONYMS **1** *the train jolted the passengers to one side* **push,** thrust, jar, bump, knock, bang, shake, jog. **2** *the car jolted along* **bump,** bounce, jerk, rattle, lurch, shudder, judder. **3** *she was jolted out of her reverie* **startle,** surprise, shock, stun, shake; informal rock, knock sideways.

▶ noun **1** an act of jolting. **2** a shock.

SYNONYMS **1** *a series of sickening jolts* **bump,** bounce, shake, jerk, lurch. **2** *he woke up with a jolt* **start,** jerk, jump. **3** *the sight of the dagger gave him a jolt* **fright,** shock, scare, surprise; informal turn.

Jordanian ▶ noun a person from Jordan.
▶ adjective relating to Jordan.

josh ▶ verb informal tease playfully.

joss stick ▶ noun a thin stick covered with a substance that produces a sweet smell when you burn it.

jostle ▶ verb (**jostles, jostling, jostled**) **1** push or bump against someone roughly. **2** (**jostle for**) struggle for.

SYNONYMS **1** *she was jostled by noisy students* **push,** shove, elbow, barge. **2** *people jostled for the best position* **struggle,** vie, jockey, scramble, fight.

jot ▶ verb (**jots, jotting, jotted**) write something quickly.
▶ noun a very small amount.

jotter ▶ noun Brit. a small notebook.

joule /jool/ ▶ noun a unit of work or energy.

journal ▶ noun **1** a newspaper or magazine dealing with a particular subject. **2** a diary or daily record.

SYNONYMS **1** *a medical journal* **periodical,** magazine, gazette, review, newsletter, news-sheet, bulletin, newspaper, paper, daily, weekly, monthly, quarterly. **2** *he keeps a journal* **diary,** log, logbook, chronicle, history, yearbook; N. Amer. daybook.

journalese ▶ noun informal a bad writing style thought to be typical of that used in newspapers.

journalism ▶ noun the activity or profession of being a journalist.

journalist ▶ noun a person who writes for newspapers or magazines or prepares news to be broadcast.

SYNONYMS **reporter,** correspondent, newspaperman, newspaperwoman, newsman, newswoman, columnist; informal news hound, hack, hackette, stringer, journo; N. Amer. informal newsie.

□ **journalistic** adjective.

journey ▶ noun (plural **journeys**) an act of travelling from one place to another.

SYNONYMS *his journey round the world* **trip,** expedition, tour, trek, voyage, cruise, ride, drive, crossing, passage, flight, odyssey, pilgrimage.

▶ verb (**journeys, journeying, journeyed**) travel.

SYNONYMS *they journeyed south* **travel,** go, voyage, sail, cruise, fly, hike, trek, ride, drive, make your way.

journeyman ▶ noun (plural **journeymen**) a worker who is reliable but not outstanding.

joust ▶ verb (of medieval knights) fight each other with lances while on horseback.
▶ noun a jousting contest.

jovial ▶ adjective cheerful and friendly.

SYNONYMS **cheerful,** jolly, happy, cheery, good-humoured, convivial, genial, good-natured, affable, outgoing, smiling, merry, sunny. ANTONYMS miserable.

□ **joviality** noun **jovially** adverb.

jowl ▶ noun the lower part of a person's or animal's cheek.
□ **jowly** adjective.

joy ▸ noun **1** great pleasure and happiness. **2** something that brings joy. **3** Brit. informal success or satisfaction.

SYNONYMS **delight,** pleasure, jubilation, triumph, exultation, rejoicing, happiness, gladness, elation, euphoria, bliss, ecstasy, rapture.
ANTONYMS misery.

☐ **joyless** adjective.

joyful ▸ adjective feeling or causing joy.

SYNONYMS **1** *his joyful mood* **cheerful,** happy, jolly, merry, sunny, joyous, cheery, smiling, mirthful, jubilant, gleeful, jovial. **2** *joyful news* **pleasing,** happy, good, cheering, gladdening, welcome, heart-warming.
ANTONYMS sad.

☐ **joyfully** adverb.

joyous ▸ adjective full of happiness and joy.
☐ **joyously** adverb.

joyriding ▸ noun informal the crime of stealing a vehicle and driving it in a fast and dangerous way.
☐ **joyride** noun **joyrider** noun.

joystick ▸ noun informal **1** the rod used for controlling an aircraft. **2** a lever for controlling the movement of an image on a computer screen.

JP ▸ abbreviation Justice of the Peace.

JPEG ▸ noun Computing a format for reducing the size of images.

jubilant ▸ adjective happy and triumphant.

SYNONYMS **overjoyed,** exultant, triumphant, joyful, cock-a-hoop, elated, thrilled, gleeful, euphoric, ecstatic; informal over the moon.
ANTONYMS despondent.

☐ **jubilantly** adverb.

jubilation ▸ noun a feeling of great happiness and triumph.

jubilee ▸ noun a special anniversary.

SYNONYMS **anniversary,** commemoration, celebration, festival.

Judaism /joo-day-i-z'm/ ▸ noun the religion of the Jews, based on the Old Testament and the Talmud.
☐ **Judaic** adjective.

Judas ▸ noun a person who betrays a friend.

judder ▸ verb (**judders, juddering, juddered**) shake rapidly and violently.
☐ **juddery** adjective.

judge ▸ noun **1** a public official who has the authority to decide cases in a law court. **2** a person who decides the results of a competition. **3** a person who is qualified to give an opinion.

SYNONYMS **1** *the judge sentenced him to five years* **justice,** magistrate, recorder, sheriff, His/Her/Your Honour; N. Amer.

jurist; Brit. informal beak. **2** *a panel of judges will select the winner* **adjudicator,** referee, umpire, arbiter, assessor, examiner, moderator, scrutineer.

▸ verb (**judges, judging, judged**) **1** form an opinion about something. **2** give a verdict on a case or person in a law court. **3** decide the results of a competition.

SYNONYMS **1** *I judged that she was exhausted* **conclude,** decide, consider, believe, think, deduce, infer, gauge, estimate, guess, surmise, conjecture, regard as, rate as, class as; informal reckon, figure. **2** *she was judged innocent* **pronounce,** decree, rule, find. **3** *the competition will be judged by Alan Amey* **adjudicate,** arbitrate, moderate, referee, umpire. **4** *entries were judged by a panel of experts* **assess,** appraise, evaluate, examine, review.

judgement (or **judgment**) ▸ noun **1** the ability to make good decisions or form sensible opinions. **2** an opinion or conclusion. **3** a decision of a law court or judge.

SYNONYMS **1** *an error of judgement* **sense,** discernment, perception, discrimination, understanding, powers of reasoning, reason, logic. **2** *his beliefs affect his judgement of Milton* **opinion,** view, estimate, appraisal, conclusion, diagnosis, assessment, impression, conviction, perception, thinking. **3** *a court judgement* **verdict,** decision, adjudication, ruling, pronouncement, decree, finding, sentence.

■ **Judgement Day** the time of the Last Judgement.

judgemental (or **judgmental**) ▸ adjective **1** having to do with the use of judgement. **2** too critical of other people.

judicature ▸ noun the organization and putting into practice of justice.

judicial ▸ adjective having to do with a law court or judge.
☐ **judicially** adverb.

judiciary ▸ noun (**the judiciary**) judges as a group.

judicious /joo-di-shuhss/ ▸ adjective having or done with good judgement.

SYNONYMS **wise,** sensible, prudent, shrewd, astute, canny, discerning.
ANTONYMS ill-advised.

☐ **judiciously** adverb.

judo ▸ noun a kind of unarmed combat performed as a sport.

jug ▸ noun a cylindrical container with a handle and a lip, for holding and pouring liquids.

SYNONYMS **pitcher,** ewer, crock, jar, urn, carafe, flask, flagon, decanter; N. Amer. creamer.

■ **jugged hare** a dish made with hare that has been cooked slowly in a covered container.

juggernaut ▸ noun Brit. a large, heavy lorry.

juggle ▸ verb (**juggles, juggling, juggled**) **1** continuously toss and catch a number of objects so as to keep at least one in the air at any time. **2** do several things at the same time. **3** present facts or figures in a way that makes them seem good.
□ **juggler** noun.

jugular (or **jugular vein**) ▸ noun any of several large veins in the neck, carrying blood from the head.

juice ▸ noun **1** the liquid present in fruit and vegetables. **2** a drink made from this liquid. **3** (**juices**) fluid produced by the stomach. **4** (**juices**) liquid coming from food during cooking.

SYNONYMS **liquid,** fluid, sap, milk, gum, extract, concentrate, essence.

▸ verb (**juices, juicing, juiced**) extract the juice from.

juicy ▸ adjective (**juicier, juiciest**) **1** full of juice. **2** informal (of gossip) very interesting.

SYNONYMS **succulent,** tender, moist, ripe. ANTONYMS dry.

ju-jitsu /joo jit-soo/ ▸ noun a Japanese system of unarmed combat.

jukebox ▸ noun a machine that plays a selected musical recording when a coin is inserted.

julep /joo-lep/ ▸ noun a sweet drink made from sugar syrup.

July ▸ noun (plural **Julys**) the seventh month of the year.

jumble ▸ noun **1** an untidy collection of things. **2** Brit. articles collected for a jumble sale.

SYNONYMS *the books were in a jumble* **heap,** muddle, mess, tangle, confusion, disarray, chaos, hotchpotch; N. Amer. hodgepodge; informal shambles.

▸ verb (**jumbles, jumbling, jumbled**) mix things up in a confused way.

SYNONYMS *the photographs are all jumbled up* **mix up,** muddle up, disorganize, disorder, tangle.

■ **jumble sale** Brit. a sale of second-hand items.

jumbo informal ▸ noun (plural **jumbos**) **1** a very large person or thing. **2** (also **jumbo jet**) a very large airliner.
▸ adjective very large.

jump ▸ verb **1** push yourself off the ground using the muscles in your legs and feet.

2 move over something by jumping. **3** make a sudden involuntary movement in surprise. **4** (**jump at** or **on**) accept something eagerly. **5** (often **jump on**) informal attack someone suddenly. **6** pass abruptly from one subject or state to another.

SYNONYMS **1** *the cat jumped off his lap* **leap,** spring, bound, hop, skip, caper, dance, prance, frolic, cavort. **2** *he jumped the fence* **vault (over),** leap over, clear, sail over, hop over. **3** *pre-tax profits jumped* **rise,** go up, shoot up, soar, surge, climb, increase; informal skyrocket. **4** *the noise made her jump* **start,** jolt, flinch, recoil, shudder.

▸ noun **1** an act of jumping. **2** a large or sudden increase. **3** an obstacle to be jumped by a horse.

SYNONYMS **1** *the short jump across the gully* **leap,** spring, bound, hop, skip. **2** *a jump in profits* **rise,** leap, increase, upsurge, upswing; informal hike. **3** *I woke up with a jump* **start,** jerk, spasm, shudder.

■ **jumped-up** informal considering yourself to be more important than you really are. **jump jet** a jet aircraft that can take off and land without a runway. **jump leads** Brit. a pair of cables used to recharge a battery in a vehicle by connecting it to the battery of a vehicle whose engine is running. **jump the queue** move ahead of your proper place in a queue. **jump ship** (of a sailor) leave a ship without permission. **jump-start** start a car with jump leads or by a sudden release of the clutch while it is being pushed.

jumper ▸ noun **1** Brit. a pullover or sweater. **2** N. Amer. a pinafore dress. **3** a person or animal that jumps.

SYNONYMS **sweater,** pullover, jersey; informal woolly.

jumpsuit ▸ noun a one-piece garment incorporating trousers and a sleeved top.

jumpy ▸ adjective (**jumpier, jumpiest**) informal anxious and uneasy.

junction ▸ noun **1** a point where things meet or are joined. **2** a place where roads or railway lines meet.

SYNONYMS **crossroads,** intersection, interchange, T-junction, turn, turn-off, exit; Brit. roundabout; N. Amer. turnout, cloverleaf.

juncture ▸ noun **1** a particular point in time. **2** a place where things join.

June ▸ noun the sixth month of the year.

jungle ▸ noun **1** an area of land with thick forest and tangled vegetation. **2** a very bewildering or competitive situation.

junior ▸ adjective **1** having to do with young or younger people. **2** Brit. having to do with schoolchildren aged 7–11. **3** (after a name) referring to the younger of two with the same name in a family. **4** low or lower in status.

> SYNONYMS **1** *the junior members of the family* **younger,** youngest. **2** *a junior minister* **minor,** subordinate, lower, lesser, low-ranking, secondary.
> ANTONYMS senior, older.

▶ noun **1** a person who is a stated number of years younger than someone else: *he's five years her junior.* **2** Brit. a child at a junior school. **3** a person with low status.

juniper ▶ noun an evergreen shrub with sweet-smelling berries.

junk¹ ▶ noun informal useless or worthless articles.

> SYNONYMS **rubbish,** clutter, odds and ends, bits and pieces, bric-a-brac, refuse, litter, scrap, waste, debris; N. Amer. trash; Austral./NZ mullock.

■ **junk food** unhealthy food. **junk mail** unwanted advertising material sent to you in the post.

junk² ▶ noun a flat-bottomed sailing boat used in China and the East Indies.

junket ▶ noun **1** informal a trip or excursion made by government officials and paid for using public funds. **2** a dish of sweetened curds of milk.

junkie (or **junky**) ▶ noun informal a drug addict.

junta ▶ noun a group ruling a country after taking power by force.

Jupiter ▶ noun the largest planet in the solar system.

jurisdiction ▶ noun **1** the official power to make legal decisions. **2** the area over which the legal authority of a court or other institution extends.

jurisprudence ▶ noun the study of law.

jurist ▶ noun an expert in law.

juror ▶ noun a member of a jury.

jury ▶ noun (plural **juries**) **1** a group of people who are required to attend a legal case and come to a verdict based on the evidence given in court. **2** a group of people judging a competition.

just ▶ adjective **1** right and fair. **2** deserved. **3** (of an opinion) based on good evidence or reasons.

> SYNONYMS **1** *a just society* **fair,** fair-minded, equitable, even-handed, impartial, unbiased, objective, neutral, disinterested, unprejudiced, honourable, upright, decent, principled. **2** *a just reward* **deserved,** well deserved, well earned, merited, rightful, due, proper, fitting, appropriate.
> ANTONYMS unfair, undeserved.

▶ adverb **1** exactly. **2** exactly or nearly at that moment. **3** very recently. **4** barely. **5** only.

> SYNONYMS **1** *I just saw him* **a moment ago,** a short time ago, very recently, not long ago. **2** *she's just right for him* **exactly,** precisely, absolutely, completely, totally, entirely, perfectly, utterly, thoroughly; informal dead. **3** *we just made it* **narrowly,** only just, by a hair's breadth, by the skin of your teeth, barely, scarcely, hardly; informal by a whisker. **4** *she's just a child* **only,** merely, simply, (nothing) but, no more than.
> ANTONYMS hardly, easily.

□ **justly** adverb.

justice ▶ noun **1** just behaviour or treatment. **2** the quality of being fair and reasonable. **3** a judge or magistrate.

> SYNONYMS **1** *I appealed to his sense of justice* **fairness,** justness, fair play, fair-mindedness, equity, right, even-handedness, honesty, morality. **2** *the justice of his case* **validity,** justification, soundness, well-foundedness, legitimacy. **3** **judge,** magistrate, recorder, sheriff; N. Amer. jurist.

■ **Justice of the Peace** (in the UK) a non-professional magistrate appointed to hear minor cases.

justifiable ▶ adjective able to be shown to be right or reasonable.

> SYNONYMS **valid,** legitimate, warranted, well founded, justified, just, reasonable, defensible.
> ANTONYMS unjustifiable.

□ **justifiably** adverb.

justification ▶ noun **1** the action of justifying something. **2** good reason for something that exists or has been done.

> SYNONYMS *there is no justification for a price increase* **grounds,** reason, basis, rationale, premise, vindication, explanation, defence, argument, case.

justify ▶ verb (justifies, justifying, justified) **1** prove something to be right or reasonable. **2** be a good reason for. **3** adjust lines of type so that they form straight edges at both sides.

> SYNONYMS **1** *directors must justify the expenditure* **give grounds for,** give reasons for, explain, account for, defend, vindicate, excuse, exonerate. **2** *the situation justified further investigation* **warrant,** be good reason for, be a justification for.

jut ▶ verb (juts, jutting, jutted) extend out beyond the main body or line of something.

jute ▶ noun rough fibre made from the stems of a tropical plant, used for making rope or woven into sacking.

j

juvenile ▸ adjective **1** having to do with young people, birds, or animals. **2** childish.

> SYNONYMS **1** *juvenile offenders* **young,** teenage, adolescent, junior, pubescent. **2** *juvenile behaviour* **childish,** immature, puerile, infantile, babyish.
> ANTONYMS adult, mature.

▸ noun **1** a young person, bird, or animal. **2** Law a person below the age at which they have adult status in law (18 in most countries).

> SYNONYMS *many victims are juveniles* **young person,** youngster, child, teenager, adolescent, minor, junior; informal **kid.**
> ANTONYMS adult.

■ **juvenile delinquent** a young person who regularly commits crimes.

juxtapose ▸ verb (**juxtaposes, juxtaposing, juxtaposed**) place two things close together.
□ **juxtaposition** noun.

j

Kk

K (or **k**) ▸ noun (plural **Ks** or **K's**) the eleventh letter of the alphabet.
▸ abbreviation informal a thousand.

kaftan (or **caftan**) ▸ noun **1** a woman's long, loose dress or top. **2** a man's long tunic, worn in the East.

kaiser /ky-zer/ ▸ noun historical the German or Austrian Emperor.

kale ▸ noun a type of cabbage with large curly leaves.

kaleidoscope /kuh-ly-duh-skohp/ ▸ noun **1** a tube containing mirrors and pieces of coloured glass or paper, whose reflections produce changing patterns when the tube is turned. **2** a constantly changing pattern. □ **kaleidoscopic** adjective.

kameez /kuh-meez/ ▸ noun (plural **kameez** or **kameezes**) a long tunic worn by people from the Indian subcontinent.

kamikaze /ka-mi-kah-zi/ ▸ noun (in the Second World War) a Japanese aircraft loaded with explosives and deliberately crashed on to an enemy target in a suicide mission.
▸ adjective potentially causing death or harm to yourself.

kangaroo ▸ noun a large Australian animal with a long powerful tail and strong hind legs that enable it to travel by leaping.
■ **kangaroo court** a court set up unofficially with the aim of finding someone guilty.

kaolin /kay-uh-lin/ ▸ noun a fine soft white clay, used for making china and in medicine.

kapok /kay-pok/ ▸ noun a substance resembling cotton wool which grows around the seeds of a tropical tree, used as padding.

kaput /kuh-puut/ ▸ adjective informal broken and useless.

karaoke /ka-ri-oh-ki/ ▸ noun a form of entertainment in which people sing popular songs over pre-recorded backing tracks.

karate /kuh-rah-ti/ ▸ noun a Japanese system of fighting using the hands and feet rather than weapons.

karma ▸ noun (in Hinduism and Buddhism) a person's actions in this and previous lives, seen as affecting their future fate.

karst ▸ noun a limestone region with underground streams and many cavities in the rock.

kart ▸ noun a small racing car with no suspension and having the engine at the back.

kasbah (or **casbah**) ▸ noun a fortress in the old part of a North African city, and the narrow streets that surround it.

kayak /ky-ak/ ▸ noun a canoe made of a light frame with a watertight covering.
▸ verb (**kayaks, kayaking, kayaked**) travel in a kayak.

kazoo ▸ noun a simple musical instrument consisting of a pipe that produces a buzzing sound when you hum into it.

kebab ▸ noun a dish of pieces of meat, fish, or vegetables roasted or grilled on a skewer or spit.

kedgeree /kej-uh-ree/ ▸ noun a dish of smoked fish, rice, and hard-boiled eggs.

keel ▸ noun a structure running along the length of the base of a ship.
▸ verb (**keel over**) **1** (of a boat or ship) turn over on its side. **2** fall over.

keelhaul ▸ verb (in the past) punish someone by dragging them through the water from one side of a boat to the other.

keen[1] ▸ adjective **1** eager and enthusiastic. **2** (of a blade) sharp. **3** quick to understand. **4** (of a sense) highly developed. **5** Brit. (of prices) very low.

> SYNONYMS **1** *his publishers were keen to capitalize on his success* **eager,** anxious, intent, impatient, determined; informal raring, itching, dying. **2** *a keen birdwatcher* **enthusiastic,** avid, eager, ardent, fervent, conscientious, committed, dedicated. **3** *a girl he was keen on* **attracted to,** passionate about, interested in, fond of, taken with, smitten with, enamoured of, infatuated with; informal struck on, gone on, mad about. **4** *a keen cutting edge* **sharp,** well-honed, razor-sharp. **5** *a keen mind* **acute,** penetrating, astute, incisive, sharp, perceptive, piercing, razor-sharp, shrewd, discerning, clever, intelligent,

brilliant, bright, smart, wise, insightful.
6 *a keen sense of duty* **intense,** acute,
fierce, passionate, burning, fervent,
ardent, strong, powerful.
ANTONYMS reluctant, unenthusiastic,
dull.

□ **keenly** adverb **keenness** noun.

keen² ▸ verb **1** wail in grief for a person who
has died. **2** make an eerie wailing sound.

keep ▸ verb (**keeps, keeping, kept**)
1 continue to have something. **2** save
something for use in the future. **3** store
something in a regular place. **4** continue
in a particular condition, position, or
activity: *she kept quiet.* **5** do something
that you have promised or agreed to do.
6 (of food) remain in good condition.
7 make a note about something, or write
a diary. **8** provide accommodation and
food for someone. **9** (**kept**) dated supported
financially in return for sex.

SYNONYMS **1** *you should keep all the old
forms* **retain (possession of),** hold on to,
not part with, save, store, put by/aside,
set aside; N. Amer. set by; informal hang on
to. **2** *I tried to keep calm* **remain,** stay,
carry on being. **3** *he keeps going on
about the murder* **persist in,** keep on,
carry on, continue, insist on. **4** *I shan't
keep you long* **detain,** keep waiting,
delay, hold up, slow down. **5** *most
people kept the rules* **comply with,** obey,
observe, conform to, abide by, adhere
to, stick to, heed, follow, carry out, act
on, make good, honour, keep to, stand
by. **6** *keeping the old traditions* **preserve,**
keep alive/up, keep going, carry on,
perpetuate, maintain, uphold. **7** *where
is her umbrella kept?* **store,** house, stow,
put (away), place, deposit. **8** *he stole
to keep his family* **provide for,** support,
feed, maintain, sustain, take care of, look
after. **9** *she keeps rabbits* **breed,** rear,
raise, farm, own. **10** *his parents kept a
shop* **manage,** run, own, operate.
ANTONYMS throw away, break, abandon.

▸ noun **1** food, clothes, and other essentials
for living. **2** the strongest or central tower
of a castle.

SYNONYMS *money to pay for his keep*
maintenance, upkeep, sustenance, board
(and lodging), food, livelihood.

■ **keep-fit** regular exercises done to
improve fitness. **keep up** move at the same
rate as someone or something else. **keep
something up** continue a course of action.

keeper ▸ noun **1** a person who manages
or looks after something or someone. **2** a
goalkeeper or wicketkeeper.

SYNONYMS **curator,** custodian, guardian,
administrator, overseer, steward,
caretaker, attendant.

keeping ▸ noun (**in** (or **out of**) **keeping
with**) in (or not in) harmony or agreement
with.

SYNONYMS **care,** custody, charge,
guardianship, possession, trust,
protection.

keepsake ▸ noun a small item kept in
memory of the person who gave it or
originally owned it.

keg ▸ noun a small barrel.

kelim → KILIM.

kelp ▸ noun a very large brown seaweed.

kelvin ▸ noun a unit of temperature, equal
to one degree Celsius.

ken ▸ noun (**your ken**) the range of your
knowledge and experience.
▸ verb (**kens, kenning, kenned** or **kent**) Scottish
N. English know or recognize.

kendo ▸ noun a Japanese form of fencing
with two-handed bamboo swords.

kennel ▸ noun **1** a small shelter for a dog.
2 (**kennels**) a place where dogs are looked
after or bred.

Kenyan /ken-yuhn/ ▸ noun a person from
Kenya.
▸ adjective relating to Kenya.

kept past and past participle of KEEP.

keratin /ke-ruh-tin/ ▸ noun a protein
forming the basis of hair, feathers, hoofs,
claws, and horns.

kerb (US spelling **curb**) ▸ noun a stone
edging to a pavement.
■ **kerb-crawling** Brit. driving slowly
along the edge of the road in search of a
prostitute.

kerbstone ▸ noun a long, narrow stone or
concrete block, laid end to end with others
to form a kerb.

kerchief /ker-chif/ ▸ noun **1** a piece of
fabric used to cover the head. **2** dated a
handkerchief.

kerfuffle ▸ noun Brit. informal a fuss or
commotion.

kernel ▸ noun **1** the softer part inside the
shell of a nut, seed, or fruit stone. **2** the
seed and hard husk of a cereal. **3** the
central part of something.

✔ **-el,** not **-al:** kernel.

kerosene ▸ noun N. Amer. paraffin.

kestrel ▸ noun a small falcon that hovers in
the air with rapidly beating wings.

ketch ▸ noun a small sailing boat with two
masts.

ketchup ▸ noun a spicy sauce made from
tomatoes and vinegar.

kettle ▸ noun a container with a spout and
handle, used for boiling water.

kettledrum ▸ noun a large drum shaped
like a bowl.

k

key ▸ noun (plural **keys**) **1** a small piece of shaped metal which is inserted into a lock and turned to open or close it. **2** a lever pressed down by the finger in playing an instrument such as the organ, piano, or flute. **3** each of several buttons on a panel for operating a computer or typewriter. **4** a list explaining the symbols used in a map or table. **5** a word or system for solving a code. **6** Music a group of notes making up a scale.

> SYNONYMS **1** *the key to the mystery* **answer,** clue, solution, explanation, basis, foundation. **2** *the key to success* **means,** way, route, path, passport, secret, formula.

▸ adjective of great importance.

> SYNONYMS *a key figure* **crucial,** central, essential, indispensable, pivotal, critical, dominant, vital, principal, prime, major, leading, main, important. ANTONYMS peripheral.

▸ verb (**keys, keying, keyed**) **1** enter data using a computer keyboard. **2** (**be keyed up**) be nervous, tense, or excited.

keyboard ▸ noun **1** a panel of keys for use with a computer or typewriter. **2** a set of keys on a musical instrument. **3** an electronic musical instrument with keys arranged as on a piano.

▸ verb enter data by means of a keyboard. ▢ **keyboarder** noun.

keyhole ▸ noun a hole in a lock into which the key is inserted.

■ **keyhole surgery** surgery carried out through a very small cut in the patient's body.

keynote ▸ noun **1** a central theme of a book, speech, etc. **2** Music the note on which a key is based.

▸ adjective (of a speech) setting out the theme of a conference.

keypad ▸ noun a small keyboard or set of buttons for operating a portable electronic device or telephone.

keystone ▸ noun **1** the most important part of a policy or system. **2** a central stone at the top of an arch.

keystroke ▸ noun a single act of pressing a key on a keyboard.

keyword ▸ noun **1** a significant word mentioned in an index. **2** a word used in a computer system to indicate the content of a document.

kg ▸ abbreviation kilograms.

khaki /kah-ki/ ▸ noun (plural **khakis**) **1** a dull greenish- or yellowish-brown colour. **2** a cotton or wool fabric of this colour.

khan ▸ noun a title given to rulers and officials in central Asia, Afghanistan, and certain other Muslim countries.

kHz ▸ abbreviation kilohertz.

kibbutz /kib-buuts/ ▸ noun a farming settlement in Israel in which work is shared between all of its members.

kibosh /ky-bosh/ ▸ noun (**put the kibosh on**) informal firmly put an end to.

kick ▸ verb **1** hit or propel something forcibly with the foot. **2** hit out with the foot or feet. **3** informal succeed in giving up a habit. **4** (**kick off**) (of a football match) start or restart with a kick of the ball from the centre. **5** (**kick someone out**) informal force someone to leave. **6** (of a gun) spring back when fired.

> SYNONYMS *kick the ball* **boot,** punt.

▸ noun **1** an instance of kicking. **2** informal a thrill of excitement. **3** informal the strong effect of alcohol or a drug.

> SYNONYMS *I get a kick out of driving* **thrill,** excitement, stimulation, tingle, frisson; informal buzz, high; N. Amer. informal charge.

■ **kick-boxing** a form of martial art which combines boxing with kicking with bare feet. **kick-off** the start of a football match. **kick-start 1** start a motorcycle engine with a downward thrust of a lever. **2** take action to make something start or develop more quickly. **kick the bucket** informal die. ▢ **kicker** noun.

kickback ▸ noun **1** informal an underhand payment to someone who has helped in a business deal. **2** an instance of a gun springing back when fired.

kid¹ ▸ noun **1** informal a child or young person. **2** a young goat.

> SYNONYMS **child,** youngster, little one, baby, toddler, tot, infant, boy, girl, young person, minor, juvenile, adolescent, teenager, youth, stripling; Scottish bairn; informal kiddie, nipper, kiddiewink; Brit. informal sprog; N. Amer. informal rug rat; Austral./NZ ankle-biter; derogatory brat.

kid² ▸ verb (**kids, kidding, kidded**) informal fool someone into believing something.

kidnap ▸ verb (**kidnaps, kidnapping, kidnapped**; US spelling **kidnaps, kidnaping, kidnaped**) take someone by force and hold them captive.

> SYNONYMS **abduct,** carry off, capture, seize, snatch, take hostage.

▸ noun an instance of kidnapping someone. ▢ **kidnapper** noun.

kidney ▸ noun (plural **kidneys**) **1** each of a pair of organs that remove waste products from the blood and produce urine. **2** the kidney of a sheep, ox, or pig as food.

■ **kidney bean** an edible dark red bean shaped like a kidney. **kidney machine** a device that performs the functions of a kidney, used if a person has a damaged kidney. **kidney stone** a hard mass formed in the kidneys.

k

kilim (or **kelim**) /ki-**leem**/ ▶ noun a carpet or rug of a kind made in Turkey and neighbouring areas.

kill ▶ verb **1** cause the death of. **2** put an end to. **3** informal cause someone pain. **4** pass time.

> SYNONYMS **1 murder**, take the life of, assassinate, eliminate, terminate, dispatch, finish off, put to death, execute, slaughter, exterminate; informal bump off, do away with, do in, top, take out, blow away; N. Amer. informal rub out, waste; literary slay. **2** Congress killed the bill veto, defeat, vote down, rule against, reject, throw out, overturn, put a stop to.

▶ noun **1** an act of killing. **2** an animal or animals killed by a hunter or another animal.

killer ▶ noun **1** a person or thing that kills. **2** informal something that is very difficult or very impressive.

> SYNONYMS **murderer**, assassin, butcher, serial killer, gunman, terminator, executioner; informal hit man.

■ **killer whale** = ORCA.

killing ▶ noun an act of causing death.

> SYNONYMS **murder**, assassination, homicide, manslaughter, execution, slaughter, massacre, butchery, bloodshed, extermination.

▶ adjective informal exhausting.
■ **make a killing** make a lot of money out of something.

killjoy ▶ noun a person who spoils the enjoyment of other people.

kiln ▶ noun a furnace for baking or drying things.

kilo ▶ noun (plural **kilos**) a kilogram.

kilobyte ▶ noun Computing a unit of memory or data equal to 1,024 bytes.

kilocalorie ▶ noun a unit of energy of one thousand calories.

kilogram (or **kilogramme**) ▶ noun a unit of mass, equal to 1,000 grams (approximately 2.205 lb).

kilohertz ▶ noun a measure of frequency equal to 1,000 hertz.

kilometre /**kil**-uh-mee-ter, ki-**lom**-i-ter/ (US spelling **kilometer**) ▶ noun a metric unit of measurement equal to 1,000 metres (0.62 miles).

kiloton (or **kilotonne**) ▶ noun a unit of explosive power equivalent to 1,000 tons of TNT.

kilovolt ▶ noun 1,000 volts.

kilowatt ▶ noun 1,000 watts.
■ **kilowatt-hour** a measure of electrical energy equivalent to one kilowatt operating for one hour.

kilt ▶ noun a skirt of pleated tartan cloth, traditionally worn by men as part of Scottish Highland dress.

kilter ▶ noun (**out of kilter**) out of balance.

kimono /ki-**moh**-noh/ ▶ noun (plural **kimonos**) a long, loose Japanese robe with wide sleeves, tied with a sash.

kin ▶ plural noun your family and relations.

kind¹ ▶ noun a class or type of similar people or things.

> SYNONYMS all kinds of gifts **sort**, type, variety, style, form, class, category, genre.

■ **in kind 1** in the same way. **2** (of payment) in goods or services instead of money.

> ❗ Use **this kind of** to refer to a singular noun (e.g. this kind of behaviour is not acceptable), and **these kinds of** to refer to a plural noun (e.g. these kinds of questions are not relevant).

kind² ▶ adjective considerate and generous.

> SYNONYMS a kind and caring person **kindly**, good-natured, kind-hearted, warm-hearted, caring, affectionate, loving, warm, considerate, obliging, compassionate, sympathetic, understanding, benevolent, benign; Brit. informal decent.
> ANTONYMS unkind.

kindergarten ▶ noun a nursery school.

kindle ▶ verb (**kindles**, **kindling**, **kindled**) **1** light a flame; make a fire start burning. **2** arouse an emotion.

kindling ▶ noun small sticks used for lighting fires.

kindly ▶ adverb **1** in a kind way. **2** please (used in a polite request).

> SYNONYMS he looked at her kindly **nicely**, warmly, affectionately, tenderly, lovingly, compassionately, considerately, obligingly, generously.
> ANTONYMS unkindly, harshly.

▶ adjective (**kindlier**, **kindliest**) kind.

> SYNONYMS a kindly old lady **benevolent**, kind, kind-hearted, warm-hearted, generous, good-natured, gentle, warm, compassionate, caring, loving, benign, well meaning, considerate.
> ANTONYMS unkind, cruel.

■ **not take kindly to** not be pleased by.
□ **kindliness** noun.

kindness ▶ noun **1** the quality of being kind. **2** a kind act.

> SYNONYMS **kindliness**, affection, warmth, gentleness, concern, care, consideration, altruism, compassion, sympathy, benevolence, generosity.
> ANTONYMS unkindness.

kindred ▶ plural noun your family and relations.

k

▶ adjective having similar qualities.
■ **kindred spirit** a person whose interests or attitudes are similar to your own.

kinetic ▶ adjective relating to or resulting from motion.
□ **kinetically** adverb.

kinfolk → **KINSFOLK**.

king ▶ noun **1** the male ruler of an independent state. **2** the best or most important person or thing of their kind. **3** a playing card ranking next below an ace. **4** the most important chess piece, which the opponent has to checkmate in order to win.

SYNONYMS **ruler**, sovereign, monarch, Crown, His Majesty, emperor, prince, potentate.

■ **king-sized** (or **king-size**) of a larger than normal size.
□ **kingly** adjective **kingship** noun.

kingdom ▶ noun **1** a country, state, or territory ruled by a king or queen. **2** each of the three divisions (animal, vegetable, and mineral) in which natural objects are classified.

SYNONYMS **realm**, domain, dominion, country, empire, land, territory, nation, (sovereign) state, province.

kingfisher ▶ noun a colourful bird with a long sharp beak which dives to catch fish in streams and ponds.

kingpin ▶ noun **1** a person or thing that is essential to the success of an organization or operation. **2** a large bolt in a central position.

kink ▶ noun **1** a sharp twist in something long and narrow. **2** a flaw or difficulty. **3** a peculiar habit or characteristic.
▶ verb form a kink.

kinky ▶ adjective (**kinkier**, **kinkiest**) **1** informal having to do with unusual sexual behaviour. **2** having kinks or twists.

kinsfolk (or **kinfolk**) ▶ plural noun your family and relations.

kinship ▶ noun **1** the relationship between members of the same family. **2** a state of having similar characteristics or origins.

kinsman (or **kinswoman**) ▶ noun (plural **kinsmen** or **kinswomen**) one of your relations.

kiosk ▶ noun **1** a small open-fronted hut from which newspapers, refreshments, or tickets are sold. **2** Brit. a public telephone booth.

kip Brit. informal ▶ noun a sleep.
▶ verb (**kips**, **kipping**, **kipped**) sleep.

kipper ▶ noun a herring that has been split open, salted, and dried or smoked.
■ **kipper tie** a very wide tie.

kirk ▶ noun Scottish N. English a church.

kismet /kiz-mit/ ▶ noun fate.

kiss ▶ verb touch someone or something with the lips as a sign of love, affection, or greeting.

SYNONYMS **1** *he kissed her* informal **peck**, smooch, canoodle, neck, pet; Brit. informal snog; N. Amer. informal buss. **2** *the ball just kissed the crossbar* brush (against), caress, touch, stroke, skim.

▶ noun an act of kissing.

SYNONYMS informal peck, smack, smacker, smooch; Brit. informal snog; N. Amer. informal buss.

■ **kiss curl** a small curl of hair on the forehead or in front of the ear. **the kiss of life** mouth-to-mouth resuscitation.

kit ▶ noun **1** a set of equipment or clothes for a specific purpose. **2** a set of drums, cymbals, and other percussion instruments.

SYNONYMS **1** *the dental kit for the hospital* **equipment**, tools, implements, instruments, gadgets, utensils, appliances, gear, tackle, hardware, paraphernalia; informal things, stuff; Military accoutrements. **2** *their football kit* **clothes**, clothing, garments, outfit, dress, costume, attire, garb; informal gear, get-up, rig-out. **3** *a tool kit* **set**, selection, collection, pack.

▶ verb (**kits**, **kitting**, **kitted**) (**kit someone out**) provide someone with the clothes or equipment needed for a particular activity.

kitbag ▶ noun a long canvas bag for carrying a soldier's possessions.

kitchen ▶ noun **1** a room where food is prepared and cooked. **2** a set of fittings and units installed in a kitchen.
■ **kitchen garden** a part of a garden where vegetables, fruit, and herbs are grown.

kitchenette ▶ noun a small kitchen or cooking area.

kite ▶ noun **1** a toy consisting of a light frame with thin material stretched over it, flown in the wind at the end of a long string. **2** a long-winged bird of prey with a forked tail. **3** Geometry a four-sided figure having two pairs of equal sides next to each other.

kith ▶ noun (**kith and kin**) your family and relations.

kitsch /kich/ ▶ noun art, objects, or design that are thought to be unpleasantly bright and showy or too sentimental.
□ **kitschy** adjective.

kitten ▶ noun a young cat.

kittenish ▶ adjective playful, lively, or flirtatious.

kittiwake ▶ noun a small gull that nests on sea cliffs.

kitty[1] ▶ noun (plural **kitties**) **1** a fund of money for use by a number of people. **2** a pool of money in some card games.

k

kitty² ▸ noun (plural **kitties**) informal a cat.

kiwi ▸ noun (plural **kiwis**) **1** a bird from New Zealand that cannot fly. **2** (**Kiwi**) informal a person from New Zealand.
  ■ **kiwi fruit** the fruit of an Asian plant, with green flesh and black seeds.

klaxon /klak-suhn/ ▸ noun trademark a vehicle horn or warning hooter.

kleptomania ▸ noun a compulsive urge to steal.
  □ **kleptomaniac** noun & adjective.

km ▸ abbreviation kilometres.

knack ▸ noun **1** a skill at performing a task. **2** a habit of doing something.

> SYNONYMS **1** *a knack for making money* **gift,** talent, flair, genius, instinct, ability, capability, capacity, aptitude, bent, facility, trick; informal the hang of something. **2** *he has a knack of getting injured* **tendency,** habit, liability, propensity.

knacker ▸ verb (**knackers, knackering, knackered**) Brit. informal **1** damage or injure something. **2** (**knackered**) very tired.

knacker's yard ▸ noun Brit. informal a place where old or injured animals are taken to be killed.

knapsack ▸ noun a bag with shoulder straps, carried on the back.

knave ▸ noun **1** old use a dishonest man. **2** (in cards) a jack.
  □ **knavish** adjective.

knead ▸ verb **1** work dough or clay with the hands. **2** massage something as if kneading it.

knee ▸ noun **1** the joint between the thigh and the lower leg. **2** the upper surface of your thigh when you are in a sitting position.
▸ verb (**knees, kneeing, kneed**) hit someone with your knee.
  ■ **knee-jerk** done automatically and without thinking. **knees-up** Brit. informal a lively party.

kneecap ▸ noun the bone in front of the knee joint.
▸ verb (**kneecaps, kneecapping, kneecapped**) shoot someone in the knee.

kneel ▸ verb (**kneels, kneeling, knelt** or **kneeled**) be in a position in which you rest your weight on your knees.

knell ▸ noun literary the sound of a bell ringing to mark a person's death.

knew past of KNOW.

knickerbockers ▸ plural noun loose-fitting trousers or knickers gathered at the knee or calf.

knickers ▸ plural noun Brit. women's or girls' underpants.

> SYNONYMS **underpants,** briefs; Brit. pants; informal **panties,** undies; Brit. informal knicks, smalls; dated drawers; historical bloomers.

knick-knack ▸ noun a small worthless object.

knife ▸ noun (plural **knives**) a cutting tool consisting of a blade fixed into a handle.

> SYNONYMS **blade,** cutter.

▸ verb (**knifes, knifing, knifed**) **1** stab someone with a knife. **2** cut through or into something like a knife.

> SYNONYMS *he was knifed in the back* **stab,** hack, gash, slash, lacerate, cut, bayonet.

  ■ **at knifepoint** under threat of injury from a knife. **knife-edge** a very tense or dangerous situation.

knight ▸ noun **1** (in the Middle Ages) a man of noble rank with a duty to fight for his king. **2** (in the UK) a man awarded a title by the king or queen and entitled to use 'Sir' in front of his name. **3** a chess piece that moves by jumping to the opposite corner of a rectangle two squares by three.
▸ verb give a man the title of knight.
  □ **knighthood** noun.

knit ▸ verb (**knits, knitting, knitted** or **knit**) **1** make a garment by looping yarn together with knitting needles or on a machine. **2** make a plain stitch in knitting. **3** join together. **4** tighten your eyebrows in a frown.

> SYNONYMS **1** *disparate regions began to knit together* **unite,** unify, come together, bond, fuse, coalesce, merge, meld, blend. **2** *we expect broken bones to knit* **heal,** mend, join, fuse. **3** *Marcus knitted his brows* **furrow,** contract, gather, wrinkle.

knitwear ▸ noun knitted clothes.

knob ▸ noun **1** a rounded lump at the end or on the surface of something. **2** a ball-shaped handle. **3** a round button on a machine. **4** a small lump of something.

> SYNONYMS **lump,** bump, protrusion, bulge, swelling, knot, boss.

knobble ▸ noun Brit. a small lump on something.
  □ **knobbly** adjective.

knock ▸ verb **1** hit a surface noisily to attract attention. **2** collide with. **3** hit someone or something so that they move or fall. **4** make a hole, dent, etc. in something by hitting it. **5** informal criticize. **6** (of a motor) make a thumping or rattling noise.

> SYNONYMS **1** *he knocked on the door* **bang,** tap, rap, thump, pound, hammer, beat, strike, hit. **2** *she knocked her knee on the table* **bump,** bang, hit, strike, crack, injure, hurt, bruise; informal bash, whack. **3** *he knocked into an elderly man*

k

collide with, bump into, bang into, run into, crash into, smash into, plough into; N. Amer. **impact;** informal **bash into.**

▶ noun **1** a sound of knocking. **2** a blow or collision. **3** a setback.

SYNONYMS **1** *a knock at the door* **tap,** rap, rat-tat, knocking, bang, banging, pounding, hammering, thump, thud. **2** *the casing can withstand knocks* **bump,** blow, bang, jolt, jar, shock, collision, crash, smash, impact.

■ **knock-kneed** having legs that curve inward at the knee. **knock off** informal stop work. **knock something off** informal produce a piece of work quickly and easily. **knock-on effect** an effect or result that causes a series of other things to happen. **knock someone out 1** make someone unconscious. **2** eliminate a person or team from a knockout competition.

knockabout ▶ adjective (of comedy) lively and involving deliberately clumsy or rough actions.

knocker ▶ noun a hinged object fixed to a door and rapped by visitors to attract attention.

knockout ▶ noun **1** an act of knocking someone out. **2** Brit. a competition in which the loser in each round is eliminated. **3** informal a very impressive person or thing.

knoll ▶ noun a small hill or mound.

knot ▶ noun **1** a fastening made by looping a piece of string or rope and tightening it. **2** a tangled mass in hair, wool, etc. **3** a hard mass in wood at the point where the trunk and a branch join. **4** a hard lump of muscle tissue. **5** a small group of people. **6** a unit of speed of a ship, aircraft, or the wind, equivalent to one nautical mile per hour.

SYNONYMS *a knot of people* **cluster,** group, band, huddle, bunch, circle, ring.

▶ verb (**knots, knotting, knotted**) **1** fasten with a knot. **2** tangle. **3** make a muscle tense and hard.

SYNONYMS **1** *a scarf knotted round her throat* **tie,** fasten, secure, bind, do up. **2** (**knotted**) **tangled,** matted, snarled, unkempt, tousled; informal **mussed up.**

■ **tie the knot** informal get married.

knotty ▶ adjective (**knottier, knottiest**) **1** full of knots. **2** very complex.

know ▶ verb (**knows, knowing, knew;** past participle **known**) **1** be aware of something as a result of observing, asking, or being told. **2** be absolutely sure of something. **3** be familiar with. **4** have a good grasp of a subject or language. **5** have personal experience of. **6** (**be known as**) be thought of as having a particular quality or title.

SYNONYMS **1** *she doesn't know I'm here* **be aware,** realize, be conscious. **2** *do*

you know the rules? **be familiar with,** be conversant with, be acquainted with, be versed in, have mastered, have a grasp of, understand, comprehend; informal be clued up on. **3** *I don't know many people here* **be acquainted with,** have met, be familiar with; Scottish ken.

■ **be in the know** informal be aware of something known only to a few people. **know-all** informal a person who behaves as if they know everything. **know the ropes** have experience of the right way of doing something.
□ **knowable** adjective.

know-how ▶ noun practical knowledge or skill.

SYNONYMS **expertise,** skill, proficiency, knowledge, understanding, mastery, technique; informal **savvy.**

knowing ▶ adjective suggesting that you know something that is meant to be secret.

SYNONYMS **significant,** meaningful, expressive, suggestive, superior.
□ **knowingly** adverb.

knowledge ▶ noun **1** information and awareness gained through experience or education. **2** the state of knowing about something.

SYNONYMS **1** *his knowledge of history* **understanding,** comprehension, grasp, command, mastery; informal know-how. **2** *people anxious to display their knowledge* **learning,** erudition, education, scholarship, schooling, wisdom. **3** *he slipped away without my knowledge* **awareness,** consciousness, realization, cognition, apprehension, perception, appreciation. **4** *a knowledge of the countryside* **familiarity,** acquaintance, conversance, intimacy.
ANTONYMS ignorance.

✔ Remember the **d**: knowle**d**ge.

knowledgeable (or **knowledgable**) ▶ adjective intelligent and well informed.

SYNONYMS **1** *a knowledgeable old man* **well informed,** learned, well read, (well) educated, erudite, scholarly, cultured, cultivated, enlightened. **2** *he is knowledgeable about modern art* **conversant with,** familiar with, well acquainted with, au fait with, up on, up to date with, abreast of; informal clued up on.
ANTONYMS ignorant.
□ **knowledgeably** adverb.

known past participle of **KNOW.**
▶ adjective **1** identified as being: *a known criminal.* **2** Maths (of a quantity or variable) having a value that can be stated.

knuckle ▶ noun **1** each of the joints of a finger. **2** a knee joint of a four-legged animal, or the part joining the leg to the foot.
▶ verb (**knuckles, knuckling, knuckled**) **1** (**knuckle down**) apply yourself seriously to a task. **2** (**knuckle under**) accept someone's authority.

knuckleduster ▶ noun a metal fitting worn over the knuckles in fighting to increase the effect of blows.

koala /koh-**ah**-luh/ ▶ noun a bear-like Australian animal that lives in trees.

kohl ▶ noun a black powder used as eye make-up.

kohlrabi ▶ noun a variety of cabbage with an edible thick, round stem.

kookaburra /**kuu**-kuh-bur-ruh/ ▶ noun a very large, noisy kingfisher found in Australia and New Zealand.

Koran /ko-**rahn**/ ▶ noun the sacred book of Islam, believed to be the word of God as told to Muhammad and written down in Arabic.

Korean ▶ noun **1** a person from Korea. **2** the language of Korea.
▶ adjective relating to Korea.

kosher /**koh**-sher/ ▶ adjective **1** (of food) prepared according to the requirements of Jewish law. **2** informal genuine and legitimate.

kowtow /kow-**tow**/ ▶ verb **1** be too meek and obedient towards someone. **2** (in the past, as part of Chinese custom) kneel and touch the ground with the forehead, in worship or as a sign of respect.

kraal /krahl/ ▶ noun S. African **1** a traditional African village of huts. **2** an enclosure for sheep and cattle.

krill ▶ plural noun small shrimp-like crustaceans which are the main food of baleen whales.

krona ▶ noun **1** (plural **kronor**) the basic unit of money of Sweden. **2** (plural **kronur**) the unit of money of Iceland.

krone /**kroh**-nuh/ ▶ noun (plural **kroner**) the basic unit of money of Denmark and Norway.

krypton /**krip**-ton/ ▶ noun a gaseous chemical element used in some kinds of electric light.

kudos ▶ noun praise and honour.

❗ **Kudos** is a singular word and it is wrong to use it as if it were a plural; for example, you should say *he received much kudos for his work*, not *he received many kudos for his work*.

kumquat /**kum**-kwot/ ▶ noun a very small orange-like fruit.

kung fu /kung **foo**/ ▶ noun a Chinese martial art resembling karate.

Kurd ▶ noun a member of a mainly Islamic people living in Kurdistan, a region in the Middle East.

Kuwaiti /kuu-**way**-ti/ ▶ noun a person from Kuwait.
▶ adjective relating to Kuwait.

kV ▶ abbreviation kilovolts.

kW ▶ abbreviation kilowatts.

Ll

L (or **l**) ► noun (plural **Ls** or **L's**) **1** the twelfth letter of the alphabet. **2** the Roman numeral for 50.

► abbreviation **1** Brit. learner driver: *L-plates*. **2** (**l**) litres. **3** (**l.**) old use pounds.

lab ► noun informal a laboratory.

label ► noun **1** a small piece of paper, fabric, etc. attached to an object and giving information about it. **2** the name or trademark of a fashion company. **3** a company that produces recorded music. **4** a classifying name given to a person or thing.

> SYNONYMS **1** *the price is clearly stated on the label* **tag**, ticket, tab, sticker, marker, docket. **2** *a designer label* **brand (name)**, (trade) name, trademark, make, logo. **3** *the label the media came up with for me* **designation**, description, tag, name, epithet, nickname, title.

► verb (**labels**, **labelling**, **labelled**; US spelling **labels**, **labeling**, **labeled**) **1** attach a label to. **2** put someone or something in a category.

> SYNONYMS **1** *label each jar with the date* **tag**, ticket, mark, stamp. **2** *tests labelled him an underachiever* **categorize**, classify, class, describe, designate, identify, mark, stamp, brand, call, name, term, dub.

> ✔ **-el**, not **-le**: label.

labia /lay-bi-uh/ ► plural noun (singular **labium**) the inner and outer folds of a woman's genitals.
□ **labial** adjective.

labor etc. US spelling of **LABOUR** etc.

laboratory ► noun (plural **laboratories**) a room or building for scientific research or teaching, or for the making of drugs or chemicals.

laborious ► adjective **1** needing a lot of time and effort. **2** showing obvious signs of effort.

> SYNONYMS **1** *a laborious job* **arduous**, hard, heavy, difficult, strenuous, gruelling, punishing, exacting, tough, onerous, burdensome, back-breaking, trying, challenging. **2** *Doug's laborious style* **laboured**, strained, forced, stiff, stilted, unnatural, artificial,

overwrought, heavy, ponderous.
ANTONYMS easy, effortless.

□ **laboriously** adverb.

labour (US spelling **labor**) ► noun **1** work. **2** workers as a group. **3** (**Labour** or **the Labour Party**) a left-wing political party formed to represent ordinary working people. **4** the process of giving birth.

> SYNONYMS **1** *manual labour* **work**, toil, exertion, industry, drudgery, effort; informal slog, grind. **2** *the conflict between capital and labour* **workers**, employees, working people, labourers, workforce, staff, labour force. **3** *a difficult labour* **childbirth**, birth, delivery.
> ANTONYMS rest, management.

► verb **1** do hard physical work. **2** have difficulty doing something in spite of working hard. **3** move with difficulty and effort. **4** (**labour under**) believe something that is not true.

> SYNONYMS **1** *a project on which he had laboured for many years* **work (hard)**, toil, slave (away), grind away, struggle, strive, exert yourself; informal slog away, plug away. **2** *Newcastle laboured to break down their defence* **strive**, struggle, endeavour, work, try hard, make every effort, do your best, do your utmost, do all one can, give your all, go all out, fight, exert yourself; informal bend/lean over backwards, pull out all the stops.

■ **labour camp** a prison camp where prisoners have to do hard physical work. **labour force** the members of a population who are able to work. **labour-intensive** needing a lot of work. **labour the point** repeat something that has already been said and understood.

laboured (US spelling **labored**) ► adjective **1** done with great difficulty. **2** not spontaneous or natural.

> SYNONYMS **1** *laboured breathing* **strained**, difficult, forced, laborious. **2** *a rather laboured joke* **contrived**, strained, forced, unconvincing, unnatural, artificial, overdone, ponderous, over-elaborate.
> ANTONYMS natural, easy.

labourer (US spelling **laborer**) ▸ noun a person who does hard physical work that does not need any special skill or training.

SYNONYMS **workman,** worker, working man, manual worker, unskilled worker, blue-collar worker, (hired) hand, roustabout, drudge, menial; Austral./NZ rouseabout.

Labrador ▸ noun a breed of dog with a black or yellow coat, used as a retriever and as a guide dog.

laburnum ▸ noun a small tree with hanging clusters of yellow flowers.

labyrinth ▸ noun a complicated network of passages.
□ **labyrinthine** /lab-uh-**rin**-thyn/ adjective.

lace ▸ noun **1** a delicate open fabric made by looping, twisting, or knitting thread in patterns. **2** a cord used to fasten a shoe or garment.
▸ verb (**laces, lacing, laced**) **1** fasten something with a lace or laces. **2** add an ingredient to a drink or dish to make it stronger or improve the flavour.

SYNONYMS **1** *he laced up his running shoes* **fasten,** do up, tie up, secure, knot. **2** *tea laced with rum* **flavour,** mix, blend, fortify, strengthen, season, spice (up), liven up, doctor, adulterate; informal spike.
ANTONYMS untie.

lacerate ▸ verb (**lacerates, lacerating, lacerated**) tear or deeply cut the flesh or skin.
□ **laceration** noun.

lachrymal (or **lacrimal**) /**lak**-ri-muhl/ ▸ adjective connected with weeping or tears.

lachrymose /**lak**-ri-mohss/ ▸ adjective literary tearful.

lack ▸ noun the state of being without or not having enough of something.

SYNONYMS *a lack of cash* **absence,** want, need, deficiency, dearth, shortage, shortfall, scarcity, paucity, scarceness.
ANTONYMS abundance.

▸ verb (also **lack for**) be without or without enough of.

SYNONYMS *she lacks judgement* **be without,** be in need of, be short of, be deficient in, be low on, be pressed for; informal be strapped for.
ANTONYMS have, possess.

lackadaisical ▸ adjective not showing enthusiasm or thoroughness.

lackey ▸ noun (plural **lackeys**) **1** a servant. **2** a person who is too willing to serve or obey other people.

lacklustre (US spelling **lackluster**)
▸ adjective **1** not exciting or interesting. **2** (of the hair or eyes) not shining.

laconic /luh-**kon**-ik/ ▸ adjective using very few words.

□ **laconically** adverb.

lacquer /**lak**-ker/ ▸ noun **1** a liquid applied to wood or metal to give it a hard, glossy surface. **2** decorative wooden goods coated with lacquer. **3** hairspray.
□ **lacquered** adjective.

lacrimal ➔ LACHRYMAL.

lacrosse /luh-**kross**/ ▸ noun a team game in which a ball is thrown, caught, and carried with a long-handled stick which has a net at one end.

lactate /lak-**tayt**/ ▸ verb (**lactates, lactating, lactated**) (of a woman or female animal) produce milk in the breasts or mammary glands, for feeding babies or young.
□ **lactation** noun.

lactic ▸ adjective relating to or obtained from milk.
■ **lactic acid** an acid present in sour milk, and produced in the muscles during strenuous exercise.

lactose ▸ noun a sugar present in milk.

lacuna /luh-**kyoo**-nuh/ ▸ noun (plural **lacunae** /luh-**kyoo**-nee/ or **lacunas**) a gap or missing part.

lacy ▸ adjective (**lacier, laciest**) made of, resembling, or trimmed with lace.

lad ▸ noun informal a boy or young man.

SYNONYMS **1** *a young lad* **boy,** schoolboy, youth, youngster, juvenile, stripling; informal kid, nipper; Scottish informal laddie; derogatory brat. **2** *a hard-working lad* **(young) man;** informal guy, fellow, geezer; Brit. informal chap, bloke; N. Amer. informal dude, hombre.

ladder ▸ noun **1** a structure consisting of a series of bars or steps between two uprights, used for climbing up or down. **2** a series of stages by which progress can be made: *the career ladder*. **3** Brit. a hole in tights or stockings where the threads have come undone.
▸ verb (**ladders, laddering, laddered**) Brit. cause a ladder to develop in a pair of tights or a stocking.

laddish ▸ adjective behaving in a way thought to be typical of young men, especially in being rowdy or drinking too much.

laden ▸ adjective heavily loaded or weighed down.

SYNONYMS **loaded,** burdened, weighed down, overloaded, piled high, full, packed, stuffed, crammed; informal chock-full, chock-a-block.

la-di-da (or **lah-di-dah**) ▸ adjective informal affected or snobbish.

ladle ▸ noun a large spoon with a cup-shaped bowl and a long handle, for serving soup, stew, etc.

▶ **verb** (**ladles, ladling, ladled**) serve or transfer soup, stew, etc. with a ladle.

lady ▶ **noun** (plural **ladies**) **1** (in polite or formal use) a woman. **2** a well-mannered woman, or a woman of high social position. **3** (**Lady**) a title used by peeresses, female relatives of peers, and the wives and widows of knights.

> SYNONYMS **1** *several ladies were present* **woman**, female, girl; Scottish & N. English lass, lassie; N. Amer. informal dame. **2** *lords and ladies* **noblewoman**, duchess, countess, peeress, viscountess, baroness.

■ **lady-in-waiting** (plural **ladies-in-waiting**) a woman who accompanies and looks after a queen or princess.

ladybird ▶ **noun** a small beetle that has a red back with black spots.

ladykiller ▶ **noun** informal a man who is successful in seducing women.

ladylike ▶ **adjective** typical of a well-mannered woman or girl.

Ladyship ▶ **noun** (**Her/Your Ladyship**) a respectful way of referring to or addressing a Lady.

lag[1] ▶ **verb** (**lags, lagging, lagged**) fall behind.
▶ **noun** (also **time lag**) a period of time between two events.

lag[2] ▶ **verb** (**lags, lagging, lagged**) cover a water tank or pipes with material designed to prevent heat loss.

lager ▶ **noun** a light fizzy beer.

laggard ▶ **noun** a person who falls behind other people.

lagging ▶ **noun** material wrapped round a water tank and pipes to prevent heat loss.

lagoon ▶ **noun** a stretch of salt water separated from the sea by a low sandbank or coral reef.

lah-di-dah ➡ LA-DI-DA.

laid past and past participle of LAY[1].

laid-back ▶ **adjective** relaxed and easy-going.

> SYNONYMS **relaxed**, easy-going, free and easy, casual, nonchalant, unexcitable, blasé, cool, calm, unconcerned, leisurely, unhurried; informal unflappable.
> ANTONYMS uptight.

lain past participle of LIE[1].

lair ▶ **noun** **1** a wild animal's resting place. **2** a person's secret den.

laird ▶ **noun** (in Scotland) a person who owns a large estate.

laissez-faire /less-ay-**fair**/ ▶ **noun** a policy of leaving things to take their own course, without interfering.

laity /**lay**-i-ti/ ▶ **noun** (**the laity**) people who are not priests or ministers of the Church; ordinary people.

lake ▶ **noun** a large area of water surrounded by land.

> SYNONYMS **pool**, pond, tarn, reservoir, lagoon, waterhole, inland sea; Scottish loch; Anglo-Irish lough; N. Amer. bayou.

lama /**lah**-muh/ ▶ **noun** **1** a title given to a spiritual leader in Tibetan Buddhism. **2** a Tibetan or Mongolian Buddhist monk.

lamb ▶ **noun** **1** a young sheep. **2** a gentle or innocent person.
▶ **verb** (of a female sheep) give birth to lambs. □ **lambing** noun.

lambada /lam-**bah**-duh/ ▶ **noun** a fast Brazilian dance.

lambaste /lam-**bayst**/ (or **lambast** /lam-**bast**/) ▶ **verb** (**lambastes** or **lambasts, lambasting, lambasted**) criticize someone harshly.

lambent /**lam**-buhnt/ ▶ **adjective** literary lit up or flickering with a soft glow.

lame ▶ **adjective** **1** walking with difficulty because of an injury or illness affecting the leg or foot. **2** (of an explanation or excuse) unconvincing and feeble. **3** (of something meant to be entertaining) dull.

> SYNONYMS **1** *the mare was lame* **limping**, hobbling, crippled, disabled, incapacitated; informal gammy. **2** *a lame excuse* **feeble**, weak, thin, flimsy, poor, unconvincing, implausible, unlikely.
> ANTONYMS sound, convincing.

▶ **verb** (**lames, laming, lamed**) make a person or animal lame.
■ **lame duck** an unsuccessful person or thing. □ **lamely** adverb **lameness** noun.

lamé /**lah**-may/ ▶ **noun** fabric with interwoven gold or silver threads.

lament /luh-**ment**/ ▶ **noun** **1** a passionate expression of grief. **2** a song or poem expressing grief or regret.
▶ **verb** **1** mourn a person's death. **2** express regret or disappointment about.

> SYNONYMS **1** *he was lamenting the death of his daughter* **mourn**, grieve, sorrow, weep, cry. **2** *entrepreneurs lamented the red tape* **complain about**, bewail, bemoan, deplore, be disappointed at.
> ANTONYMS celebrate, welcome.

□ **lamentation** noun.

lamentable /**la**-muhn-tuh-b'l/ ▶ **adjective** very bad or disappointing.
□ **lamentably** adverb.

laminate ▶ **verb** /**lam**-i-nayt/ (**laminates, laminating, laminated**) **1** cover a flat surface with a layer of protective material. **2** make something by sticking layers of material together. **3** split into layers or leaves. **4** beat or roll metal into thin plates.
▶ **noun** /**lam**-i-nuht/ a laminated product or material.
□ **lamination** noun.

lamp ▸ noun a device using electricity, oil, or gas to give light.

lampoon ▸ verb mock or ridicule.
▸ noun a mocking attack.

lamprey /lam-pri/ ▸ noun (plural **lampreys**) a fish like an eel, having a round sucking mouth with horny teeth.

lance ▸ noun (in the past) a weapon with a long shaft and a pointed steel head, used by people on horseback.
▸ verb (**lances**, **lancing**, **lanced**) Medicine prick or cut open a boil or wound with a sharp instrument.
   ■ **lance corporal** a rank of non-commissioned officer in the army, below corporal.

lancer ▸ noun (in the past) a soldier armed with a lance.

lancet /lahn-sit/ ▸ noun a small two-edged knife with a sharp point, used in surgery.

land ▸ noun 1 the part of the earth's surface that is not covered by water. 2 an area of ground. 3 (**the land**) ground or soil used for farming. 4 a country or state.

> SYNONYMS 1 *the lookout sighted land* **dry land**, terra firma, coast, coastline, shore. 2 *Lyme Park has 1323 acres of land* **grounds**, fields, open space, property, territory, acres, acreage, estate, lands, real estate. 3 *many people are leaving the land* **the countryside**, the country, rural areas. 4 *Tunisia is a land of variety* **country**, nation, state, realm, kingdom, province, region, area, domain.

▸ verb 1 put or go ashore. 2 come or bring something down to the ground. 3 bring a fish out of the water with a net or rod. 4 informal succeed in obtaining or achieving something. 5 (**land up**) reach a particular place or destination. 6 (**land someone in**) informal put someone in a difficult situation. 7 (**land someone with**) inflict something unwelcome on someone. 8 informal inflict a blow on someone.

> SYNONYMS 1 *Allied troops landed in France* **disembark**, go ashore, debark, alight, get off. 2 *the ship landed at Le Havre* **berth**, dock, moor, (drop) anchor, tie up, put in. 3 *their plane landed at Chicago* **touch down**, make a landing, come in to land, come down. 4 *Nick landed the job of editor* **get**, obtain, acquire, secure, gain, net, win, achieve, attain, bag, carry off; informal swing.
> ANTONYMS embark, take off.

landau /lan-dor/ ▸ noun an enclosed horse-drawn carriage.

landed ▸ adjective owning a lot of land.

landfall ▸ noun arrival on land after a sea journey.

landfill ▸ noun 1 the disposal of rubbish by burying it. 2 buried rubbish.

landing ▸ noun 1 a level area at the top of a staircase. 2 a place where people and goods can be landed from a boat.
   ■ **landing gear** the undercarriage of an aircraft.

landless ▸ adjective owning no land.

landlocked ▸ adjective (of a place) surrounded by land.

landlord (or **landlady**) ▸ noun 1 a person who rents out property or land. 2 Brit. a person who runs a pub.

> SYNONYMS 1 *the landlady had objected to the noise* **owner**, proprietor, lessor, householder, landowner. 2 *the landlord of the pub* **licensee**, innkeeper, owner, hotelier, restaurateur; Brit. publican.
> ANTONYMS tenant.

landlubber ▸ noun informal a person who is not familiar with the sea or sailing.

landmark ▸ noun 1 an object or feature that is easily seen from a distance. 2 an important stage or turning point.

> SYNONYMS 1 *one of London's most famous landmarks* **feature**, sight, monument, building. 2 *the ruling was hailed as a landmark* **turning point**, milestone, watershed, critical point.

landmine ▸ noun an explosive mine laid on or just under the surface of the ground.

landscape ▸ noun 1 all the visible features of an area of land. 2 a picture of an area of countryside.

> SYNONYMS **scenery**, country, countryside, topography, terrain, view, panorama.

▸ verb (**landscapes**, **landscaping**, **landscaped**) improve the appearance of land by changing its contours, planting trees and shrubs, etc.

landslide ▸ noun 1 (Brit. also **landslip**) a mass of earth or rock that slides down a mountain or cliff. 2 an overwhelming majority of votes for one party in an election.

> SYNONYMS 1 *floods and landslides* **landslip**, rockfall, mudslide, avalanche. 2 *the Labour landslide* **decisive victory**, runaway triumph, overwhelming majority; informal whitewash.

lane ▸ noun 1 a narrow road. 2 a division of a road for a single line of traffic. 3 a strip of track or water for each of the competitors in a race. 4 a course followed by ships or aircraft.

> SYNONYMS **country road**, track, course, trail, street, alley, alleyway, passage.

language ▸ noun 1 human communication through the use of spoken or written words. 2 a particular system or style of spoken or written communication. 3 a system of symbols and rules for writing computer programs.

> SYNONYMS **1** *the structure of language* **speech,** speaking, conversation, talking, talk, discourse, communication, words, writing, vocabulary, text. **2** *the English language* **tongue,** mother tongue, native tongue, dialect; informal lingo. **3** *the booklet is written in simple, everyday language* **wording,** phrasing, phraseology, style, vocabulary, terminology, expressions, turn of phrase, parlance; informal lingo.

> ✔ **-guage**, not **-gauge**: lan**guage**.

languid /**lang**-gwid/ ▸ adjective relaxed and not inclined to be physically active.
□ **languidly** adverb.

languish ▸ verb **1** become weak or faint. **2** be kept in an unpleasant place or situation.

> SYNONYMS **1** *the plants languished and died* **weaken,** deteriorate, decline, go downhill, wither, droop, wilt, fade, waste away. **2** *the general is languishing in prison* **waste away,** rot, be abandoned, be neglected, be forgotten, suffer, lie. ANTONYMS thrive.

languor /**lang**-ger/ ▸ noun a pleasant feeling of being tired or without energy.
□ **languorous** adjective.

lank ▸ adjective (of hair) long, limp, and straight.

lanky ▸ adjective (**lankier**, **lankiest**) tall, thin, and moving in an awkward or ungraceful way.

lanolin ▸ noun a fatty substance from sheep's wool, used in skin cream.

lantern ▸ noun a lamp enclosed in a metal frame with glass panels.

lanthanum /**lan**-thuh-nuhm/ ▸ noun a silvery-white metallic element.

lanyard /**lan**-yerd/ ▸ noun **1** a rope used on a ship. **2** a cord around the neck or shoulder for holding a whistle or similar object.

lap¹ ▸ noun the flat area between the waist and knees of a seated person.

lap² ▸ noun **1** one circuit of a track or racetrack. **2** an overlapping part.

> SYNONYMS *a race of eight laps* **circuit,** leg, circle, revolution, round.

▸ verb (**laps**, **lapping**, **lapped**) overtake a competitor in a race to become a lap ahead.

> SYNONYMS *she lapped the other runners* **overtake,** outstrip, leave behind, pass, go past, catch up with.

lap³ ▸ verb (**laps**, **lapping**, **lapped**) **1** (of an animal) take up liquid with the tongue. **2** (**lap something up**) accept something

with obvious pleasure. **3** (of water) wash against something with a gentle rippling sound.

> SYNONYMS **1** *the dog lapped water out of a puddle* **drink,** lick up, sup, swallow, slurp, gulp. **2** *waves lapped against the sea wall* **splash,** wash, swish, slosh, break.

lapdog ▸ noun **1** a small pampered pet dog. **2** a person who is completely under the influence of someone else.

lapel ▸ noun the part which is folded back at the front opening of a jacket or coat.

lapidary /la-pi-duh-ri/ ▸ adjective **1** relating to the engraving, cutting, or polishing of stone or gems. **2** (of language) elegant and concise.

lapis lazuli /lap-iss **laz**-yuu-ly/ ▸ noun a bright blue stone used in jewellery.

Lapp ▸ noun a member of a people of the extreme north of Scandinavia.

> ❗ The people themselves prefer to be called **Sami**.

lapse ▸ noun **1** a brief failure of concentration, memory, or judgement. **2** a decline from previously high standards. **3** an interval of time.

> SYNONYMS **1** *a lapse of concentration* **failure,** slip, error, mistake, blunder, fault, omission; informal slip-up. **2** *his lapse into petty crime* **decline,** fall, falling, slipping, deterioration, degeneration, backsliding, regression. **3** *a lapse of time* **interval,** gap, pause, interlude, lull, hiatus, break.

▸ verb (**lapses**, **lapsing**, **lapsed**) **1** (of a right, agreement, etc.) become invalid because it is not used or renewed. **2** stop following a religion or doctrine. **3** (**lapse into**) pass gradually into a different state.

> SYNONYMS **1** *the planning permission has lapsed* **expire,** become void, become invalid, run out. **2** (**lapsed**) *a lapsed season ticket* **expired,** void, invalid, out of date. **3** *do not let friendships lapse* **(come to an) end,** cease, stop, terminate, pass, fade, wither, die. **4** (**lapsed**) *a lapsed Catholic* **non-practising,** backsliding, apostate. **5** *she lapsed into silence* **revert,** relapse, drift, slide, slip, sink.

laptop ▸ noun a portable computer.

lapwing ▸ noun a black and white bird with a crest on the head.

larboard = PORT³.

larceny /**lar**-suh-ni/ ▸ noun (plural **larcenies**) theft of personal property.

larch ▸ noun a coniferous tree with needles that fall in winter.

lard ▶ noun fat from a pig, used in cooking.
▶ verb **1** insert strips of fat or bacon in meat before cooking. **2** add technical or obscure expressions to talk or writing.

larder ▶ noun a room or large cupboard for storing food.

large ▶ adjective **1** of relatively great size, extent, or capacity. **2** of wide range or scope.

> SYNONYMS **big**, great, sizeable, substantial, considerable, extensive, voluminous, vast, huge, immense, enormous, colossal, massive, heavy, mammoth, gigantic, giant, fat, stout, bulky.
> ANTONYMS small.

■ **at large 1** escaped or not yet captured. **2** as a whole.

largely ▶ adverb on the whole; mostly.

> SYNONYMS **mostly**, mainly, to a large/ great extent, chiefly, predominantly, primarily, principally, for the most part, in the main, typically, commonly.

largesse /lar-zhess/ ▶ noun **1** generosity. **2** money or gifts given generously.

largo /lar-goh/ ▶ adverb & adjective Music in a slow tempo and dignified style.

lariat /la-ri-uht/ ▶ noun a rope used as a lasso or for tying an animal to a post.

lark¹ ▶ noun a brown bird that sings while flying.

lark² informal ▶ noun **1** something done for fun or as a joke. **2** Brit. an activity viewed as foolish or a waste of time.
▶ verb (**lark about** or **around**) behave in a playful and mischievous way.

larkspur ▶ noun a plant resembling a delphinium, with tall spikes of blue, pink, or white flowers.

larva ▶ noun (plural **larvae** /lar-vee/) an immature form of an insect that looks very different from the adult creature, e.g. a caterpillar.

laryngitis /la-rin-jy-tiss/ ▶ noun inflammation of the larynx.

larynx /la-rinks/ ▶ noun (plural **larynxes** or **larynges** /luh-rin-jeez/) the area at the top of the throat forming an air passage to the lungs and containing the vocal cords.

lasagne /luh-zan-yuh/ ▶ noun pasta in the form of sheets, baked in layers with meat or vegetables and a cheese sauce.

lascivious /luh-siv-i-uhss/ ▶ adjective showing strong or inappropriate sexual desire.
□ **lasciviously** adverb **lasciviousness** noun.

laser ▶ noun a device that produces an intense narrow beam of light.

laserdisc ▶ noun a disc resembling a large compact disc, used for high-quality video and multimedia.

lash ▶ verb **1** beat with a whip or stick. **2** beat strongly against. **3** (**lash out**) attack someone verbally or physically. **4** (of an animal) move its tail quickly and violently. **5** fasten securely with a cord or rope.

> SYNONYMS **1** *rain lashed the window panes* **beat against,** dash against, pound, batter, strike, drum. **2** *the tiger lashed his tail* **swish,** flick, twitch, whip. **3** *two boats were lashed together* **fasten,** bind, tie (up), tether, hitch, knot, rope.

▶ noun **1** an eyelash. **2** a sharp blow with a whip or stick. **3** the flexible part of a whip.

> SYNONYMS *he brought the lash down upon the prisoner's back* **whip,** scourge, flail, birch, cane; historical cat-o'-nine-tails, cat.

lashings ▶ plural noun Brit. informal a large amount of something.

lass (or **lassie**) ▶ noun Scottish N. English a girl or young woman.

lassitude ▶ noun lack of energy.

lasso /luh-soo/ ▶ noun (plural **lassos** or **lassoes**) a rope with a noose at one end, used for catching cattle.
▶ verb (**lassoes, lassoing, lassoed**) catch with a lasso.

last¹ ▶ adjective **1** coming after all others in time or order. **2** most recent in time. **3** lowest in importance or rank. **4** (**the last**) the least likely or suitable. **5** only remaining.

> SYNONYMS **1** *Rembrandt's last years* **final,** closing, concluding, end, terminal, later, latter. **2** *the last woman in the queue* **rearmost,** hindmost, endmost, furthest (back), ultimate. **3** *the candidate coming last is eliminated* **at the end,** at/in the rear, bringing up the rear, at the back. **4** *last year* **previous,** preceding, prior, former. **5** *the last edition* **latest,** most recent.
> ANTONYMS first, next.

▶ adverb on the last occasion before the present.
▶ noun (plural **last**) **1** the last person or thing. **2** (**the last of**) the only remaining part of.
■ **Last Judgement** (in some religions) the judgement of humankind expected to take place at the end of the world. **last rites** a Christian religious ceremony performed for a person who is about to die.
□ **lastly** adverb.

last² ▶ verb **1** continue for a particular period of time. **2** remain operating for a considerable or particular length of time. **3** be enough for someone to use for a particular length of time.

> SYNONYMS **1** *the hearing lasted for six days* **continue,** go on, carry on, keep on/going, take. **2** *how long will he last as manager?*

survive, endure, hold on/out, keep going, persevere, persist, stay, remain; informal stick it out, hang on, go the distance. **3** *the car is built to last* **endure,** wear well, stand up, bear up; informal go the distance.
ANTONYMS end, wear out.

last³ ▸ noun a block used by a shoemaker for shaping or repairing shoes.

lasting ▸ adjective enduring or able to endure for a long time.

SYNONYMS **enduring,** long-lasting, long-lived, abiding, continuing, long-term, permanent, durable, stable, secure, long-standing, eternal, undying, everlasting, unending, never-ending.
ANTONYMS ephemeral.

latch ▸ noun **1** a bar with a catch and lever used for fastening a door or gate. **2** a type of door lock which can be opened from the outside only with a key.
▸ verb **1** fasten a door or gate with a latch. **2** (**latch on to**) associate yourself enthusiastically with.

latchkey ▸ noun (plural **latchkeys**) a key to an outer door of a house.

late ▸ adjective **1** acting, arriving, or happening after the proper or usual time. **2** far on in a period. **3** far on in the day or night. **4** (**the late**) (of a person) recently dead. **5** (**latest**) of most recent date or origin.

SYNONYMS **1** *the train was late* **behind schedule,** tardy, overdue, delayed. **2** *some late news* **recent,** fresh, new, up to date, latter-day, current. **3** (**later**) *a later chapter* **subsequent,** following, succeeding, future, upcoming, to come, ensuing, next. **4** *her late husband* **dead,** departed, lamented, passed on/away; formal deceased. **5** (**latest**) **most recent,** newest, just out, up to the minute, state-of-the-art, current; informal in, with it, trendy, hip, hot, happening, cool.
ANTONYMS punctual, early, living, old.

▸ adverb **1** after the proper or usual time. **2** towards the end of a period. **3** far on in the day or night. **4** (**later**) afterwards or in the near future.

SYNONYMS **1** *she had arrived late* **behind schedule,** belatedly, tardily, at the last minute. **2** (**later**) *later, the film rights were sold* **subsequently,** eventually, then, next, later on, after this/that, afterwards, at a later date, in the future, in due course, by and by, in a while, in time; formal thereafter.

■ **of late** recently.
□ **lateness** noun.

lately ▸ adverb recently; not long ago.

SYNONYMS **recently,** not long ago, of late, latterly, in recent times.

latent ▸ adjective existing but not yet developed, showing, or active.
□ **latency** noun.

lateral ▸ adjective of, at, towards, or from the side or sides.
■ **lateral thinking** chiefly Brit. the solving of a problem by thinking of new ways to approach it.
□ **laterally** adverb.

latex ▸ noun **1** a milky fluid in some plants which thickens when exposed to the air. **2** a synthetic product resembling this, used to make paints, coatings, etc.

lath /lahth, lath/ ▸ noun (plural **laths**) a thin, flat strip of wood.

lathe ▸ noun a machine that shapes pieces of wood or metal by turning them against a cutting tool.

lather ▸ noun **1** a frothy mass of bubbles produced by soap when mixed with water. **2** heavy sweat visible on a horse's coat as a white foam.
▸ verb (**lathers, lathering, lathered**) **1** cover with or form a lather. **2** cover or spread generously with a substance.

Latin ▸ noun the language of ancient Rome and its empire.
▸ adjective relating to the Latin language.
■ **Latin America** the parts of the American continent where Spanish or Portuguese is spoken.

Latino /luh-tee-noh/ ▸ noun (plural **Latinos**) N. Amer. a Latin American inhabitant of the United States.

latitude ▸ noun **1** the distance of a place north or south of the equator. **2** (**latitudes**) regions at a particular distance from the equator. **3** scope for freedom of action or thought.

SYNONYMS **freedom,** scope, leeway, (breathing) space, flexibility, liberty, independence, free rein, licence, slack.
ANTONYMS restriction.

latrine ▸ noun a communal toilet, especially a temporary one in a camp.

latter ▸ adjective **1** nearer to the end than to the beginning. **2** recent. **3** (**the latter**) referring to the second-mentioned of two people or things.

SYNONYMS **1** *the latter half of the season* **later,** closing, end, concluding, final. **2** *the latter option* **last-mentioned,** second, last, final.
ANTONYMS earlier, former.

■ **latter-day** modern or contemporary.
□ **latterly** adverb.

lattice ▸ noun a structure or pattern of strips crossing each other with square or diamond-shaped spaces left between.

Latvian ▸ noun a person from Latvia.
▸ adjective relating to Latvia.

laud /lawd/ ▸ verb formal praise highly.

laudable ▸ adjective deserving praise.

laudanum /**law**-duh-nuhm/ ▸ noun a liquid containing opium, formerly used as a sedative.

laudatory /**law**-duh-tuh-ri/ ▸ adjective formal expressing praise.

laugh ▸ verb 1 make sounds and movements that express amusement. 2 (**laugh at**) make fun of. 3 (**laugh something off**) dismiss something by treating it light-heartedly.

> SYNONYMS *he started to laugh* **chuckle**, chortle, guffaw, giggle, titter, snigger, roar, hoot with laughter, split your sides; informal be in stitches, be rolling in the aisles, crease up, fall about, crack up; Brit. informal kill yourself.

▸ noun 1 an act of laughing. 2 (**a laugh**) informal someone or something that makes people laugh.

> SYNONYMS 1 *he gave a short laugh* **chuckle**, chortle, guffaw, giggle, titter, snigger, roar, hoot, shriek. 2 *I entered the contest for a laugh* **joke**, prank, bit of fun, jest; informal lark, hoot, scream.

■ **laughing gas** nitrous oxide, used as an anaesthetic. **laughing stock** a person who is made fun of.

laughable ▸ adjective ridiculous or absurd; deserving to be laughed at.
□ **laughably** adverb.

laughter ▸ noun the action or sound of laughing.

> SYNONYMS 1 *the laughter subsided* **laughing**, chuckling, chortling, guffawing, giggling, tittering, sniggering. 2 *a source of laughter* **amusement**, entertainment, humour, mirth, merriment, gaiety, hilarity, jollity, fun.

launch¹ ▸ verb 1 move a boat or ship from land into the water. 2 send a rocket or missile on its course. 3 begin an enterprise or introduce a new product. 4 (**launch into**) begin something energetically and enthusiastically.

> SYNONYMS 1 *a chair was launched at him* **propel**, throw, hurl, fling, pitch, lob, let fly, fire, shoot; informal chuck, heave, sling. 2 *the government launched a new campaign* **start**, begin, initiate, put in place, set up, inaugurate, introduce; informal kick off.

▸ noun an act of launching something.
□ **launcher** noun.

launch² ▸ noun a large motorboat.

launder ▸ verb (**launders, laundering, laundered**) 1 wash and iron clothes, sheets, etc. 2 informal pass illegally obtained money through a bank or business to conceal its origins.

launderette (or **laundrette**) ▸ noun Brit. a place with coin-operated washing machines and dryers for public use.

laundry ▸ noun (plural **laundries**) 1 clothes, sheets, etc. that need to be washed or that have been newly washed. 2 a room or building where clothes, sheets, etc. are washed.

laurel ▸ noun 1 an evergreen shrub or small tree with dark green glossy leaves. 2 (**laurels**) a crown of bay leaves awarded as a mark of honour in classical times. 3 (**laurels**) honour or praise.
■ **rest on your laurels** be so satisfied with what you have achieved that you make no more effort.

lava ▸ noun hot molten rock that erupts from a volcano, or solid rock formed when this cools.

lavatorial ▸ adjective (of humour) referring to bodily functions in a rude way.

lavatory ▸ noun (plural **lavatories**) a toilet.

> SYNONYMS **toilet**, WC, convenience, privy, latrine; Brit. cloakroom; N. Amer. washroom, bathroom, rest room, men's/ladies' room, comfort station; informal little girls'/boys' room, smallest room; Brit. informal loo, bog, the Ladies, the Gents, khazi; N. Amer. informal can, john; Austral./NZ informal dunny.

lavender ▸ noun 1 a strong-smelling shrub with bluish-purple flowers. 2 a pale bluish-purple colour.

lavish ▸ adjective 1 very rich, elaborate, or luxurious. 2 giving or given in large amounts.

> SYNONYMS 1 *a lavish apartment* **sumptuous**, luxurious, gorgeous, costly, expensive, opulent, grand, splendid, rich, fancy; informal posh. 2 *he was lavish with his hospitality* **generous**, liberal, bountiful, unstinting, unsparing, free, munificent, extravagant, prodigal. 3 *lavish praise* **extravagant**, excessive, wasteful, prodigal, fulsome, effusive. 4 *lavish amounts of champagne* **abundant**, copious, plentiful, liberal, prolific, generous; literary plenteous.
> ANTONYMS meagre, mean, frugal.

▸ verb give something in large or generous quantities.

> SYNONYMS *she lavished money on her children* **shower**, heap, pour, deluge, throw at, squander, dissipate.
> ANTONYMS begrudge, stint.

□ **lavishly** adverb.

law ▸ noun 1 a rule or system of rules that regulates the actions of the people in a country or community. **2** a rule laying down the correct procedure or behaviour in a sport. **3** a statement of fact to the effect that a particular phenomenon always occurs if certain conditions are present.

> SYNONYMS **1** *the law* **legislation,** constitution, rules, regulations, legal code. **2** *a new law* **regulation,** statute, act, bill, decree, edict, rule, ruling, dictum, command, order, directive, dictate, diktat, fiat, by-law; N. Amer. formal ordinance. **3** *the laws of the game* **rule,** regulation, principle, convention, instruction, guideline. **4** *a moral law* **principle,** rule, precept, commandment, belief, creed, credo, maxim, tenet, doctrine, canon.

lawful ▶ adjective allowed by or obeying law or rules.
  □ **lawfully** adverb.

lawless ▶ adjective not governed by or obeying laws.
  □ **lawlessness** noun.

lawn ▶ noun **1** an area of mown grass in a garden or park. **2** a fine linen or cotton fabric.

lawnmower ▶ noun a machine for cutting the grass on a lawn.

lawrencium ▶ noun a radioactive metallic element that is produced artificially.

lawsuit ▶ noun a claim brought to a law court to be decided.

lawyer ▶ noun a person who practises or studies law.

> SYNONYMS **legal adviser,** legal representative, solicitor, barrister, advocate, counsel, Queen's Counsel, QC; N. Amer. attorney, counselor(-at-law); informal brief, legal eagle.

lax ▶ adjective **1** not strict, severe, or careful enough. **2** (of limbs or muscles) relaxed.
  □ **laxity** noun.

laxative ▶ adjective tending to make someone empty their bowels.
▶ noun a laxative drug or medicine.

lay[1] ▶ verb (**lays, laying,** past and past participle **laid**) **1** put something down gently or carefully. **2** put something down in position for use. **3** assign or place. **4** (of a female bird, reptile, etc.) produce an egg from inside the body. **5** stake an amount of money in a bet.

> SYNONYMS **1** *Curtis laid the newspaper on the table* **put (down),** place, set (down), deposit, rest, position, shove; informal stick, dump, park, plonk; Brit. informal bung. **2** *I'd lay money on it* **bet,** wager, gamble, stake. **3** *we laid plans for the next voyage* **devise,** arrange, prepare, work out, hatch, design, plan, scheme, plot, conceive, put together, draw up, produce, develop, formulate; informal cook up.

■ **lay-by** (plural **lay-bys**) Brit. an area at the side of a road where vehicles may stop. **lay off** informal stop doing something. **lay someone off** dismiss a worker because of a shortage of work. **lay something on** Brit. provide food or entertainment. **lay something out** construct or arrange something according to a plan.

> ! Don't confuse **lay** and **lie**. You *lay* something, as in *they are going to lay the carpet,* but you *lie* down on a bed or other flat surface. The past tense and past participle of **lay** is **laid,** as in *they laid the groundwork;* the past tense of **lie** is **lay** (*he lay on the floor*) and the past participle is **lain** (*she had lain on the bed for hours*).

lay[2] ▶ adjective **1** not having an official position in the Church. **2** not having professional qualifications or expert knowledge.

> SYNONYMS **1** *a lay preacher* **non-ordained,** non-clerical. **2** *a lay audience* **non-expert,** non-professional, non-specialist, non-technical, amateur, unqualified, untrained.

lay[3] ▶ noun a short poem intended to be sung.

lay[4] past of LIE[1].

layabout ▶ noun disapproving a person who does little or no work.

layer ▶ noun a sheet or thickness of material covering a surface.

> SYNONYMS **sheet,** stratum, level, tier, seam, coat, coating, film, covering, blanket, skin.

▶ verb arrange or cut in a layer or layers.

layette ▶ noun a set of clothing and bedclothes for a newborn baby.

layman (or **laywoman**) ▶ noun (plural **laymen** or **laywomen**) **1** a member of a Church who is not a priest or minister. **2** a person without professional or specialized knowledge.

layout ▶ noun the way in which something is laid out.

> SYNONYMS **arrangement,** design, plan, formation, format, configuration, composition, organization, geography, structure.

laze ▶ verb (**lazes, lazing, lazed**) spend time relaxing or doing very little.

> SYNONYMS **idle,** relax, unwind, do nothing, loaf (around/about), lounge (around/about), loll (around/about), lie (around/about), take it easy; informal hang around/round, veg (out).

lazy ▸ adjective (**lazier**, **laziest**) **1** unwilling to work or use energy. **2** showing a lack of effort or care.

> SYNONYMS **1** *a lazy worker* **idle**, indolent, slothful, bone idle, work-shy, shiftless. **2** *a lazy stream* **slow**, slow-moving, languid, leisurely, lethargic, sluggish. ANTONYMS industrious, fast.

□ **lazily** adverb **laziness** noun.

lazybones ▸ noun informal a lazy person.

lb ▸ abbreviation pounds (in weight).
ORIGIN short for Latin *libra* 'pound, balance'.

lbw ▸ abbreviation Cricket leg before wicket.

lea ▸ noun literary an area of grassy land.

leach ▸ verb (of chemicals or minerals) be removed from soil by water passing through it.

lead¹ ▸ verb (**leads**, **leading**, **led**) **1** cause a person or animal to go with you. **2** be a route or means of access. **3** (**lead to**) result in. **4** cause someone to do or believe something. **5** be in charge of. **6** have the advantage in a race or game. **7** have a particular way of life. **8** (**lead up to**) come before or result in. **9** (**lead someone on**) deceive someone into believing that you are attracted to them.

> SYNONYMS **1** *Michelle led them into the house* **guide**, conduct, show (the way), usher, escort, steer, shepherd, accompany, see, take. **2** *he led us to believe they were lying* **cause**, induce, prompt, move, persuade, drive, make. **3** *she led a coalition of radicals* **control**, preside over, head, command, govern, run, manage, rule, be in charge of; informal head up. **4** *Rangers were leading at half-time* **be ahead**, be winning, be (out) in front, be in the lead, be first. **5** *the champion was leading the field* **be ahead of**, head, outrun, outstrip, outpace, leave behind, outdo, outclass, beat. **6** *I just want to lead a normal life* **live**, have, spend, follow, pass, enjoy. ANTONYMS follow.

▸ noun **1** an example for other people to copy. **2** a position of advantage in a contest. **3** the chief part in a play or film. **4** a clue to follow when trying to solve a problem. **5** Brit. a strap or cord for controlling and guiding a dog. **6** a wire conveying electric current.

> SYNONYMS **1** *sixth-formers should give a lead to younger pupils* **example**, model, pattern, standard, guidance, direction, role model. **2** *I was in the lead early on* **first place**, winning position, vanguard. **3** *Newcastle built up a 3–0 lead* **margin**, advantage, gap, edge, interval. **4** *playing the lead* **leading role**, star/starring role, title role, principal role. **5** *detectives were*

following up a new lead **clue**, pointer, hint, tip, tip-off, suggestion, indication, sign. **6** *a dog on a lead* **leash**, tether, rope, chain.

▸ adjective first or most prominent.

> SYNONYMS *the lead position* **leading**, first, top, foremost, front, pole, head, chief, principal, premier.

lead² ▸ noun **1** a heavy bluish-grey metal. **2** the part of a pencil that makes a mark.

leaded ▸ adjective **1** framed or covered with lead. **2** (of petrol) containing lead.

leaden ▸ adjective **1** dull, heavy, or slow. **2** dull grey in colour.

leader ▸ noun **1** a person or thing that leads. **2** the most successful or advanced person or thing in a particular area. **3** the main player in a music group. **4** a newspaper article giving the editor's opinion.

> SYNONYMS **chief**, head, principal, commander, captain, controller, superior, chairman, chair, director, manager, superintendent, supervisor, overseer, master, mistress, prime minister, president, premier, governor, ruler, monarch, sovereign; informal boss, skipper, gaffer, guv'nor, number one. ANTONYMS follower, supporter.

leadership ▸ noun **1** the state or position of being a leader. **2** the action of leading.

> SYNONYMS **1** *the leadership of the Party* **control**, rule, command, dominion, headship, directorship, premiership, chairmanship, governorship, captaincy. **2** *firm leadership* **guidance**, direction, authority, management, supervision, government.

leading ▸ adjective most important, or in first place.

> SYNONYMS **main**, chief, top, front, major, prime, principal, foremost, key, central, dominant, most powerful, most important, greatest, pre-eminent, star. ANTONYMS subordinate, minor.

■ **leading light** a prominent or influential person. **leading question** a question that encourages someone to give the answer that you want.

leaf ▸ noun (plural **leaves**) **1** a flat green part of a plant that is attached to a stem. **2** a single sheet of paper in a book. **3** gold or silver in the form of a very thin sheet. **4** a hinged or detachable part of a table.

> SYNONYMS *a folder of loose leaves* **page**, sheet, folio.

▸ verb (**leaf through**) turn over pages or papers, reading them quickly or casually.

> SYNONYMS *he leafed through the documents* **flick**, flip, thumb, skim,

browse, glance, riffle, scan, run your eye over, peruse.

■ **turn over a new leaf** start to behave in a better way.
□ **leafy** adjective.

leaflet ▸ noun **1** a printed sheet of paper containing information or advertising. **2** a small leaf.

synonyms **pamphlet,** booklet, brochure, handbill, circular, flyer, handout; N. Amer. folder, dodger.

▸ verb (**leaflets, leafleting, leafleted**) distribute leaflets to.

league¹ ▸ noun **1** a collection of people, countries, or groups that combine to help or protect each other. **2** a group of sports clubs that play each other over a period for a championship. **3** a class of quality or excellence.

synonyms **1** *a league of nations* **alliance,** confederation, confederacy, federation, union, association, coalition, consortium, affiliation, cooperative, partnership, fellowship, syndicate. **2** *the store is not in the same league* **class,** group, category, level, standard.

■ **in league** (of two or more people) making secret plans.

league² ▸ noun a former measure of distance, of about three miles.

leak ▸ verb **1** accidentally allow contents to escape or enter through a hole or crack. **2** (of liquid, gas, etc.) escape or enter accidentally through a hole or crack. **3** deliberately give out secret information.

synonyms **1** *oil was leaking from the tanker* **seep,** escape, ooze, drip, dribble, drain, run. **2** *civil servants leaking information* **disclose,** divulge, reveal, make public, tell, expose, release, bring into the open.

▸ noun **1** a hole or crack through which contents leak. **2** an instance of leaking.

synonyms **1** *check that there are no leaks in the bag* **hole,** opening, puncture, perforation, gash, slit, break, crack, fissure, rupture, tear. **2** *a gas leak* **escape,** leakage, discharge, seepage. **3** *leaks to the media* **disclosure,** revelation, exposé.

□ **leakage** noun **leaky** adjective.

lean¹ ▸ verb (**leans, leaning,** past and past participle **leaned** or Brit. **leant**) **1** be in a sloping position. **2** (**lean against** or **on**) rest against. **3** (**lean on**) rely on for support. **4** (**lean to** or **towards**) favour a particular point of view.

synonyms **1** *trees leaning in the wind* **slant,** incline, bend, tilt, slope, tip, list. **2** *Polly leaned against the door* **rest,** recline. **3** *someone to lean on* **depend,**

rely, count, bank, trust in. **4** *he leans towards existentialist philosophy* **tend,** incline, gravitate, have a preference for, have an affinity with.

■ **lean-to** (plural **lean-tos**) a small building sharing a wall with a larger building.

lean² ▸ adjective **1** (of a person) having little fat; thin. **2** (of meat) containing little fat. **3** (of a period of time) unproductive.

synonyms **1** *a tall, lean man* **slim,** thin, slender, spare, spindly, wiry, lanky. **2** *a lean harvest* **meagre,** sparse, poor, mean, inadequate, insufficient, paltry.
antonyms fat, abundant.

leaning ▸ noun a tendency or preference.

synonyms **inclination,** tendency, bent, propensity, penchant, preference, predisposition, predilection.

leap ▸ verb (**leaps, leaping,** past and past participle **leaped** or **leapt**) **1** jump high or a long way. **2** move quickly and suddenly. **3** (**leap at**) accept something eagerly. **4** increase dramatically.

synonyms **1** *he leapt over the gate* **jump,** vault, spring, bound, hop, clear. **2** *profits leapt by 55%* **rise,** jump, soar, rocket, skyrocket, shoot up.

▸ noun an act of leaping.

synonyms *a leap of 33%* **rise,** surge, upsurge, upswing, upturn.

■ **leap year** a year with 366 days, occurring every four years.

leapfrog ▸ noun a game in which players in turn jump over others who are bending down.
▸ verb (**leapfrogs, leapfrogging, leapfrogged**) **1** jump over someone in leapfrog. **2** overtake others to move into a leading position.

learn ▸ verb (**learns, learning,** past and past participle **learned** or **learnt**) **1** gain knowledge or skill through study or experience. **2** become aware of something through observing or hearing about it. **3** memorize.

synonyms **1** *learn a foreign language* **acquire,** grasp, master, take in, absorb, assimilate, digest, familiarize yourself with, be taught; informal get the hang of. **2** *she learnt the poem* **memorize,** learn by heart, commit to memory, learn parrot-fashion, get off/down pat. **3** *he learned that the school would be closing* **discover,** find out, become aware, be informed, hear, understand, gather; informal get wind of the fact.

learned /ler-nid/ ▸ adjective having gained a lot of knowledge by studying.

synonyms **scholarly,** erudite, knowledgeable, widely read, cultured, intellectual, academic, literary, bookish,

highbrow; informal **brainy**.
ANTONYMS ignorant.

learner ▸ noun a person who is learning a subject of skill.

SYNONYMS **beginner**, novice, starter, trainee, apprentice, pupil, student, fledgling.
ANTONYMS expert, veteran.

learning ▸ noun knowledge or skills gained by studying.

SYNONYMS **study**, knowledge, education, schooling, tuition, teaching, scholarship, erudition, research, understanding, wisdom.
ANTONYMS ignorance.

lease ▸ noun an agreement by which one person uses land, property, etc. which belongs to another person for a stated time in return for payment.
▸ verb (leases, leasing, leased) let out or rent land, property, etc. by a lease.

SYNONYMS **1** *the film crew leased a large hangar* **rent**, hire, charter. **2** *they leased the mill to a reputable family* **rent (out)**, let (out), hire (out), charter (out), loan (out).

leasehold ▸ noun the holding of property by a lease.

leash ▸ noun a dog's lead.

least ▸ determiner & pronoun (usu. the least) smallest in amount, extent, or significance.
▸ adverb to the smallest extent or degree.
■ at least **1** not less than. **2** if nothing else. **3** anyway.

leather ▸ noun a material made from the skin of an animal by tanning or a similar process.

leathery ▸ adjective tough and hard like leather.

leave¹ ▸ verb (leaves, leaving, left) **1** go away from. **2** stop attending or working for. **3** go away without taking someone or something. **4** (be left) remain to be used or dealt with. **5** let someone do something without interfering. **6** put something somewhere to be collected or dealt with. **7** give something to someone in a will. **8** (leave someone/thing out) fail to include someone or something.

SYNONYMS **1** *I left the hotel* **go away from**, depart from, withdraw from, retire from, take yourself off from, take your leave of, pull out of, quit, escape from, flee, abandon, desert, vacate; informal push off, shove off, clear out/off, split, make tracks. **2** *the next morning we left for Leicester* **set off**, head, make, set sail, get going. **3** *he's left his wife* **abandon**, desert, jilt, leave in the lurch, leave high and dry, throw over; informal dump, ditch, walk/run out on. **4** *he left his job*

in November **resign from**, retire from, step down from, withdraw from, pull out of, give up; informal quit, jack in. **5** *she left her handbag on a bus* **leave behind**, forget, lose, mislay. **6** *I thought I'd leave it to the experts* **entrust**, hand over, pass on, refer, delegate. **7** *he left her £100,000* **bequeath**, will, endow, hand down.
ANTONYMS arrive.

□ **leaver** noun.

leave² ▸ noun **1** (also **leave of absence**) time when you have permission to be absent from work or duty. **2** formal permission.

SYNONYMS **1** *the judge granted leave to appeal* **permission**, consent, authorization, sanction, dispensation, approval, clearance, blessing, agreement, assent; informal the go-ahead, the green light. **2** *he was on leave* **holiday**, vacation, break, furlough, sabbatical, leave of absence; informal vac.

■ take your leave formal say goodbye.

leaven /lev-uhn/ ▸ noun a substance added to dough to make it ferment and rise.
▸ verb make something less serious or dull by adding something.

leaves plural of LEAF.

Lebanese /le-buh-neez/ ▸ noun (plural **Lebanese**) a person from Lebanon.
▸ adjective relating to Lebanon.

lecher ▸ noun a lecherous man.
□ **lechery** noun.

lecherous ▸ adjective (of a man) showing sexual desire in an offensive way.

lectern ▸ noun a tall stand with a sloping top from which a speaker can read while standing up.

lecture ▸ noun **1** an educational talk to an audience. **2** a long telling-off or critical talk.

SYNONYMS **1** *a lecture on children's literature* **speech**, talk, address, discourse, presentation, oration. **2** *Dave got a severe lecture* **reprimand**, scolding, rebuke, reproach; informal dressing-down, telling-off, talking-to, tongue-lashing.

▸ verb (lectures, lecturing, lectured) **1** give a lecture, or a series of lectures. **2** give someone a long telling-off.

SYNONYMS **1** *he lectures on drugs* **talk**, speak, discourse, hold forth, teach; informal spout, sound off. **2** *he was lectured by the headmaster* **reprimand**, scold, rebuke, reproach, take to task; informal tell off, bawl out; Brit. informal tick off, carpet.
ANTONYMS praise.

□ **lecturer** noun.

led past and past participle of LEAD¹.

ledge ▸ noun a narrow horizontal surface sticking out from a wall, cliff, etc.

ledger ▸ noun a book in which financial accounts are kept.

lee ▸ noun the side of something that provides shelter from wind or weather.

leech ▸ noun 1 a worm that sucks the blood of animals or people. 2 a person who lives off other people.

leek ▸ noun a plant with a long cylindrical bulb which is eaten as a vegetable.

leer ▸ verb look or smile at someone in a lustful or unpleasant way.
▸ noun a lustful or unpleasant look or smile.

leery ▸ adjective informal wary.

lees /leez/ ▸ plural noun the sediment left in the bottom of a bottle or barrel of wine.

leeward ▸ adjective & adverb on or towards the side that is sheltered from the wind.

leeway ▸ noun the amount of freedom to move or act that is available.

> SYNONYMS **freedom,** scope, latitude, space, room, liberty, flexibility, licence, free hand, free rein.

left¹ ▸ adjective 1 on or towards the side of a person or thing which is to the west when the person or thing is facing north. 2 left-wing.

> SYNONYMS **left-hand,** sinistral; Nautical port.
> ANTONYMS right, starboard.

▸ adverb on or to the left side.
▸ noun 1 (the left) the left-hand part, side, or direction. 2 a left turn. 3 (often the Left) a left-wing group or party.
■ **left-field** unconventional or experimental.

left² past and past participle of LEAVE¹.

leftovers ▸ plural noun food remaining after the rest has been eaten.
▸ adjective (**leftover**) remaining after the rest of something has been eaten.

left-wing ▸ adjective socialist, or supporting political or social change.

> SYNONYMS **socialist,** communist, leftist, Labour; informal Commie, lefty, red, pinko.
> ANTONYMS right-wing, conservative.

leg ▸ noun 1 each of the limbs on which a person or animal moves and stands. 2 each of the parts of a table, chair, etc. that rest on the floor and support its weight. 3 a section of a journey, race, etc. 4 (in sport) each of two or more games making up a round of a competition.

> SYNONYMS the first leg of a European tour **part,** stage, section, phase, stretch, lap.

▸ verb (**legs, legging, legged**) (**leg it**) informal run away.

legacy ▸ noun (plural **legacies**) 1 an amount of money or property left to someone in a will. 2 something handed down by a predecessor.

> SYNONYMS 1 a legacy from a great aunt **bequest,** inheritance, endowment, gift, birthright, estate, heirloom. 2 the legacy of the war **consequence,** effect, repercussion, aftermath, by-product, result.

legal ▸ adjective 1 having to do with the law. 2 permitted by law.

> SYNONYMS 1 a legal tax-avoidance scheme **lawful,** legitimate, within the law, legalized, valid, permissible, permitted, allowable, allowed, above board, acceptable, constitutional; informal legit. 2 the legal profession **judicial,** juridical, forensic.
> ANTONYMS illegal.

■ **legal aid** money given to people who cannot afford to pay for a lawyer. **legal tender** accepted methods of payment such as coins or banknotes.
□ **legality** noun **legally** adverb.

legalize (or **legalise**) ▸ verb (**legalizes, legalizing, legalized**) make something legal.
□ **legalization** noun.

legate /le-guht/ ▸ noun a representative of the Pope.

legation /li-gay-sh'n/ ▸ noun 1 a diplomat below the rank of ambassador, and their staff. 2 the official residence of a diplomat.

legato /li-gah-toh/ ▸ adverb & adjective Music in a smooth, flowing way.

legend ▸ noun 1 a traditional story from long ago which is not definitely true. 2 a very famous person. 3 an inscription, caption, or list explaining the symbols used in a map or table.

> SYNONYMS 1 the Arthurian legends **myth,** saga, epic, folk tale, folk story, fable, lore, folklore, mythology, folk tradition. 2 pop legends **celebrity,** star, superstar, icon, phenomenon, luminary, giant, hero; informal celeb, megastar. 3 the wording of the legend **caption,** inscription, dedication, slogan, heading, title.

legendary ▸ adjective 1 described in legends. 2 remarkable enough to be famous.

> SYNONYMS 1 legendary kings **fabled,** heroic, traditional, fairy-tale, storybook, mythical, mythological. 2 a legendary figure in the trade-union movement **famous,** celebrated, famed, renowned, acclaimed, illustrious, esteemed, honoured, exalted, venerable, distinguished, great, eminent.
> ANTONYMS historical, insignificant.

legerdemain /lej-er-di-mayn/ ▸ noun 1 skilful use of your hands when performing magic tricks. 2 trickery.

leggings ▶ plural noun **1** women's tight-fitting stretchy trousers. **2** strong protective coverings for the legs, worn over trousers.

leggy ▶ adjective (**leggier, leggiest**) long-legged.

legible ▶ adjective (of handwriting or print) clear enough to read.
□ **legibility** noun **legibly** adverb.

legion ▶ noun **1** a division of 3,000 to 6,000 men in the army of ancient Rome. **2** (a legion or legions of) a vast number of.

SYNONYMS **horde,** throng, multitude, crowd, mass, mob, gang, swarm, flock, herd, army.

▶ adjective literary great in number.

legionary ▶ noun (plural **legionaries**) a soldier in an ancient Roman legion.

legionnaire /lee-juh-**nair**/ ▶ noun a member of a legion.
■ **legionnaires' disease** a form of pneumonia.

legislate ▶ verb (**legislates, legislating, legislated**) **1** make laws. **2** (legislate for or against) prepare for or try to prevent a situation.
□ **legislator** noun.

legislation ▶ noun laws.

SYNONYMS **law,** rules, rulings, regulations, acts, bills, statutes; N. Amer. formal ordinances.

legislative ▶ adjective **1** having the power to make laws. **2** relating to laws.

legislature ▶ noun the group of people who make a country's laws.

legitimate ▶ adjective /li-**jit**-i-muht/ **1** allowed by the law or rules. **2** able to be defended; reasonable. **3** (of a child) born to parents who are married to each other.

SYNONYMS **1** *legitimate gambling* **legal,** lawful, authorized, permitted, sanctioned, approved, licensed; informal legit. **2** *the legitimate heir* **rightful,** lawful, genuine, authentic, real, true, proper. **3** *legitimate grounds for unease* **valid,** sound, admissible, acceptable, well founded, justifiable, reasonable, sensible, just, fair, bona fide.
ANTONYMS illegal, invalid.

▶ verb /li-**jit**-i-mayt/ (**legitimates, legitimating, legitimated**) make something legitimate.
□ **legitimacy** noun **legitimately** adverb.

✔ **leg-,** not **lig-:** le**git**imate.

legitimize (or **legitimise**) ▶ verb (**legitimizes, legitimizing, legitimized**) make something legitimate.

legume /**leg**-yoom/ ▶ noun a plant with seeds in pods, such as the pea.
□ **leguminous** adjective.

leisure ▶ noun time for relaxation or enjoyment.

SYNONYMS **free time,** spare time, time off, rest, recreation, relaxation.
ANTONYMS work.

■ **at leisure 1** not occupied; free. **2** in an unhurried way.

leisurely ▶ adjective relaxed and unhurried.

SYNONYMS **unhurried,** relaxed, easy, gentle, sedate, comfortable, restful, undemanding, slow.
ANTONYMS hurried.

▶ adverb without hurry.

lemming ▶ noun a small Arctic rodent, some kinds of which periodically migrate in large numbers (they are popularly believed to run headlong into the sea and drown).

lemon ▶ noun **1** a pale yellow citrus fruit with thick skin and acidic juice. **2** a pale yellow colour.
■ **lemon curd** a sweet spread made with lemons.

lemonade ▶ noun a sweet drink made with lemon juice or flavouring.

lemur /**lee**-mer/ ▶ noun an animal resembling a monkey, found only in Madagascar.

lend ▶ verb (**lends, lending, lent**) **1** allow someone to use something on the understanding that they will return it. **2** give someone money on condition that they will pay it back later. **3** add or contribute a particular quality. **4** (lend itself to) be suitable for.

SYNONYMS **1** *I'll lend you my towel* **loan,** let someone use, advance; Brit. informal sub. **2** *these examples lend weight to his assertions* **add,** impart, give, bestow, confer, provide, supply, furnish, contribute.
ANTONYMS borrow.

□ **lender** noun.

length ▶ noun **1** the measurement or extent of something from end to end. **2** the amount of time that something lasts. **3** the quality of being long. **4** a stretch or piece of something. **5** the extent to which someone does something: *going to great lengths.*

SYNONYMS **1** *the whole length of the valley* **extent,** distance, span, reach, area, expanse, stretch, range, scope. **2** *a considerable length of time* **period,** duration, stretch, span. **3** *a length of blue silk* **piece,** strip.

lengthen ▶ verb make or become longer.

SYNONYMS **1** *he lengthened his stride* **elongate,** make longer, extend, expand, widen, broaden, enlarge. **2** *you'll need to lengthen the cooking time* **prolong,**

make longer, increase, extend, expand, protract, stretch out.
ANTONYMS shorten.

lengthways (or lengthwise) ▶ adverb in a direction parallel with a thing's length.

lengthy ▶ adjective (lengthier, lengthiest) lasting a long time.

SYNONYMS **(very) long**, long-lasting, protracted, extended, long-drawn-out, prolonged, interminable, time-consuming, long-winded.
ANTONYMS short.

□ **lengthily** adverb.

lenient /lee-ni-uhnt/ ▶ adjective not strict; merciful or tolerant.

SYNONYMS **merciful**, forgiving, forbearing, tolerant, charitable, humane, indulgent, magnanimous.
ANTONYMS severe.

□ **leniency** noun **leniently** adverb.

lens ▶ noun **1** a piece of transparent curved material that concentrates or spreads out light rays, used in cameras, glasses, etc. **2** the transparent part of the eye that focuses light on to the retina.

Lent ▶ noun (in the Christian Church) the period immediately before Easter.

lent past and past participle of LEND.

lentil ▶ noun an edible seed with one flat and one curved side.

lento ▶ adverb & adjective Music slow or slowly.

Leo ▶ noun a sign of the zodiac (the Lion), 23 July–22 August.

leonine /lee-uh-nyn/ ▶ adjective relating to or like a lion or lions.

leopard ▶ noun (feminine **leopardess**) a large cat with a spotted coat, found in Africa and southern Asia.

leotard /lee-uh-tard/ ▶ noun a close-fitting, stretchy one-piece garment covering the body to the top of the thighs, worn for dance, exercise, etc.

leper ▶ noun **1** a person who has leprosy. **2** someone who is rejected or avoided by other people.

lepidopterist ▶ noun a person who studies or collects butterflies or moths.

leprechaun /lep-ruh-kawn/ ▶ noun (in Irish folklore) a mischievous elf.

leprosy ▶ noun a contagious disease that affects the skin and can cause deformities.
□ **leprous** adjective.

lesbian ▶ noun a woman who is sexually attracted to other women.
▶ adjective relating to lesbians.
□ **lesbianism** noun.

lesion /lee-zhuhn/ ▶ noun an area of skin or part of the body which has been damaged.

less ▶ determiner & pronoun **1** a smaller amount of; not as much. **2** fewer in number.
▶ adverb to a smaller extent; not so much.
▶ preposition minus.

❗ Make sure you distinguish between **less** and **fewer**. Use **fewer** with plural nouns, as in *there are fewer tourists this year*; use **less** with nouns referring to things that cannot be counted, as in *there is less blossom on this tree*. Using **less** with a plural noun (*less tourists*) is wrong.

lessee ▶ noun a person who holds the lease of a property.

lessen ▶ verb make or become less.

SYNONYMS **1** *exercise lessens the risk of heart disease* **reduce**, make less/smaller, minimize, decrease, attenuate, narrow, moderate. **2** *the pain began to lessen* **grow less**, grow smaller, decrease, diminish, decline, subside, slacken, abate, fade, die down, let up, ease off, tail off, drop (off/away), dwindle, ebb, wane, recede.
ANTONYMS increase.

lesser ▶ adjective not so great, large, or important as the other or the rest.

SYNONYMS **1** *a lesser offence* **less important**, minor, secondary, subsidiary, peripheral. **2** *you look down at us lesser mortals* **subordinate**, minor, inferior, second-class, subservient, lowly, humble.
ANTONYMS greater, superior.

lesson ▶ noun **1** a period of learning or teaching. **2** a thing that has been learned. **3** a thing that acts as a warning or encouragement. **4** a passage from the Bible read aloud during a church service.

SYNONYMS **1** *a maths lesson* **class**, session, seminar, tutorial, lecture, period. **2** *Stuart's accident should be a lesson to all parents* **warning**, deterrent, caution, example, message, moral.

lessor ▶ noun a person who lets a property to someone else.

lest ▶ conjunction formal **1** with the intention of preventing; to avoid the risk of. **2** because of the possibility of.

let ▶ verb (lets, letting, let) **1** allow. **2** used to express an intention, suggestion, or order: *let's have a drink.* **3** allow someone to use a room or property in return for payment.

SYNONYMS **1** *let him sleep for now* **allow**, permit, give permission to, give leave to, authorize, license, empower, enable, entitle. **2** *they've let their flat* **rent (out)**, let out, lease, hire (out).
ANTONYMS prevent, prohibit.

▶ noun **1** Brit. a period during which a room or property is rented. **2** (in racket sports) a situation in which a point is not counted and is played for again.

■ **let alone** not to mention. **let someone down** fail to support or help someone. **let someone go** allow someone to go free. **let yourself go 1** act in a relaxed way. **2** become careless in your habits or appearance. **let someone off 1** choose not to punish someone. **2** excuse someone from a task. **let something off** cause a gun, firework, etc. to fire or explode. **let up** informal become less strong or severe.

lethal ▸ adjective **1** able to cause death. **2** very harmful or destructive.

> SYNONYMS **fatal,** deadly, mortal, terminal, life-threatening, murderous, poisonous, toxic, noxious, venomous, dangerous. ANTONYMS harmless, safe.

□ **lethally** adverb.

lethargic ▸ adjective lacking energy or enthusiasm.
□ **lethargically** adverb.

lethargy /leth-er-ji/ ▸ noun a lack of energy and enthusiasm.

let's ▸ short form let us.

letter ▸ noun **1** any of the symbols of an alphabet. **2** a written communication, usually sent by post. **3** (**letters**) old use knowledge of literature.

> SYNONYMS **1** *capital letters* **character,** sign, symbol, figure. **2** *she received a letter* **message,** note, line, missive, dispatch, communication, correspondence, post, mail.

▸ verb (**letters, lettering, lettered**) **1** write something with letters. **2** (**lettered**) old use able to read and write.
■ **letter bomb** an explosive device hidden in a small package, which explodes when the package is opened. **letter box** a slot in a door through which letters are delivered. **the letter of the law** the precise terms of a law or rule.

letterhead ▸ noun a printed heading on stationery.

lettuce ▸ noun a plant whose leaves are eaten in salads.

leucocyte (or **leukocyte**) /loo-koh-syt/ ▸ noun technical a white blood cell.

leukaemia /loo-kee-mi-uh/ (US spelling **leukemia**) ▸ noun a serious disease in which too many white blood cells are produced.

levee /lev-i/ ▸ noun an embankment built to stop a river overflowing.

level ▸ noun **1** a position on a scale. **2** the amount of something that is present. **3** a horizontal line or surface. **4** height in relation to the ground. **5** a particular floor in a building.

> SYNONYMS **1** *the post is at a senior level* **rank,** position, degree, grade, stage, standard, class, group, set, classification. **2** *a high level of employment* **quantity,** amount, extent, measure, degree, volume.

▸ adjective **1** having a flat horizontal surface. **2** having the same relative height or position as someone or something else.

> SYNONYMS **1** *a smooth and level surface* **flat,** smooth, even, uniform, plane, flush, horizontal. **2** *he kept his voice level* **steady,** even, uniform, regular, constant. **3** *the scores were level* **equal,** even, drawn, tied, all square, neck and neck, level pegging, on a par, evenly matched; informal even-stevens. **4** *his eyes were level with hers* **at the same height,** on a level, in line. ANTONYMS uneven, unsteady, unequal.

▸ verb (**levels, levelling, levelled;** US spelling **levels, leveling, leveled**) **1** make or become level. **2** aim or direct a weapon, criticism, or accusation. **3** (**level with**) informal be honest with.

> SYNONYMS **1** *tilt the tin to level the mixture* **even off/out,** flatten, smooth (out). **2** *bulldozers levelled the building* **raze (to the ground),** demolish, flatten, bulldoze, destroy. **3** *Carl levelled the score* **equalize,** equal, even (up), make level. **4** *he levelled his pistol at me* **aim,** point, direct, train, focus, turn.

■ **level crossing** Brit. a place where a road crosses a railway at the same level. **level-headed** calm and sensible.
□ **levelly** adverb.

lever ▸ noun **1** a bar used to move a load with one end when pressure is applied to the other. **2** an arm or handle that is moved to operate a mechanism.

> SYNONYMS *the lid can be removed with a lever* **handle,** arm, switch, crowbar, bar, jemmy.

▸ verb (**levers, levering, levered**) lift or move with a lever.

> SYNONYMS *he levered the door open* **prise,** force, wrench; N. Amer. pry; informal jemmy.

leverage ▸ noun **1** the application of force with a lever. **2** the power to influence other people.

> SYNONYMS **1** *the long handles provide increased leverage* **force,** purchase, grip, hold, anchorage. **2** *they have significant leverage in negotiations* **influence,** power, authority, weight, sway, pull, control, say, advantage, pressure; informal clout, muscle, teeth.

leveret ▸ noun a young hare.

leviathan /li-vy-uh-thuhn/ ▸ noun **1** (in the Bible) a sea monster. **2** a very large or powerful thing.

levitate ▸ verb (**levitates, levitating, levitated**) rise and hover in the air.
□ **levitation** noun.

levity ▸ noun the treatment of a serious matter with humour or lack of respect.

levy ▸ verb (**levies, levying, levied**) make a person, organization, etc. pay a tax or fine.

> SYNONYMS **impose**, charge, exact, raise, collect.

▸ noun (plural **levies**) **1** a sum of money paid as a tax. **2** old use a group of enlisted troops.

> SYNONYMS **tax**, tariff, toll, excise, duty.

lewd ▸ adjective referring to sex in a crude and offensive way.

lexical ▸ adjective relating to the words of a language.

lexicography ▸ noun the writing of dictionaries.
□ **lexicographer** noun.

lexicon ▸ noun **1** the vocabulary of a person, language, or branch of knowledge. **2** a dictionary.

ley line ▸ noun a line of energy believed by some people to connect some ancient sites.

liability ▸ noun (plural **liabilities**) **1** the state of being liable. **2** an amount of money that a person or company owes. **3** a person or thing likely to cause you embarrassment or trouble.

> SYNONYMS **1** they have big liabilities **obligations**, debts, arrears, dues, commitments. **2** he's become a bit of a liability **hindrance**, encumbrance, burden, handicap, nuisance, inconvenience, embarrassment, impediment, disadvantage, millstone. ANTONYMS asset.

liable ▸ adjective **1** responsible by law. **2** (**liable to**) able to be punished by law for something. **3** (**liable to do**) likely to do or to be affected by.

> SYNONYMS **1** they are liable for negligence **responsible**, accountable, answerable, chargeable, blameworthy, at fault, culpable, guilty. **2** my income is liable to fluctuate wildly **likely**, inclined, tending, apt, prone, given. **3** areas liable to flooding **exposed**, prone, subject, susceptible, vulnerable, in danger of, at risk of.

liaise /li-**ayz**/ ▸ verb (**liaises, liaising, liaised**) **1** (of two or more people or groups) cooperate with each other and share information. **2** (**liaise between**) act as a link between two or more people or groups.

> SYNONYMS **cooperate**, collaborate, communicate, network, interface, link up.

> ✔ Remember the second **i** in **liaise** and **liaison**.

liaison ▸ noun **1** communication or cooperation between people or organizations. **2** a sexual relationship.

> SYNONYMS **1** the branches work in close liaison **cooperation**, contact, association, connection, collaboration, communication, alliance, partnership. **2** Dave was my White House liaison **intermediary**, mediator, middleman, contact, link, go-between. **3** a secret liaison **love affair**, relationship, romance, attachment, fling.

liana ▸ noun a tropical climbing plant that hangs from trees.

liar ▸ noun a person who tells lies.

> SYNONYMS **fibber**, deceiver, perjurer, dissembler, faker, hoaxer, impostor.

libation ▸ noun (in the past) a drink poured as an offering to a god.

libel ▸ noun the crime of publishing something false that is damaging to a person's reputation.

> SYNONYMS she sued two newspapers for libel **defamation (of character)**, character assassination, calumny, misrepresentation, scandalmongering, aspersions, malicious gossip, slur, smear; informal mud-slinging.

▸ verb (**libels, libelling, libelled;** US spelling **libels, libeling, libeled**) publish something false about.

> SYNONYMS she claimed the magazine had libelled her **defame**, malign, blacken someone's name, sully someone's reputation, smear, cast aspersions on, drag someone's name through the mud/mire, denigrate; N. Amer. slur.

□ **libellous** (US spelling **libelous**) adjective.

liberal ▸ adjective **1** willing to respect and accept behaviour or opinions different from your own. **2** (in politics) supporting the freedom of individuals and in favour of moderate political reform. **3** (**Liberal**) relating to the Liberal or Liberal Democrat Party. **4** generous in applying or adding something.

> SYNONYMS **1** the values of a liberal society **tolerant**, unprejudiced, broad-minded, open-minded, enlightened, permissive, free (and easy), easy-going, libertarian, indulgent, lenient. **2** a liberal social agenda **progressive**, advanced, modern, forward-looking, forward-thinking, enlightened, reformist, radical; informal go-ahead. **3** a liberal interpretation of divorce laws **flexible**, broad, loose, rough, free, non-literal. **4** liberal coatings of paint **abundant**, copious, ample, plentiful, generous, lavish. **5** they were liberal with their cash **generous**, open-handed, unsparing, unstinting, lavish,

free, munificent.
ANTONYMS reactionary, strict, miserly.

▶ noun 1 a person with liberal views.
2 (Liberal) a supporter of the Liberal or
Liberal Democrat Party.
□ liberalism noun liberality noun liberally
adverb.

liberalize (or liberalise) ▶ verb (liberalizes,
liberalizing, liberalized) remove or loosen
restrictions on.
□ liberalization noun.

liberate ▶ verb (liberates, liberating,
liberated) 1 set free. 2 (liberated) free from
traditional ideas about social behaviour.

SYNONYMS (set) free, release, let out, let
go, set loose, save, rescue, emancipate,
enfranchise.
ANTONYMS imprison, enslave.

□ liberation noun liberator noun.

libertarian ▶ noun a person who believes
that people should have the freedom to act
and think as they wish.

libertine ▶ noun a man who is immoral and
indulges too much in sexual pleasure.

liberty ▶ noun (plural liberties) 1 the state
of being free. 2 a right or privilege. 3 the
ability to act as you please. 4 informal a rude
remark or disrespectful act.

SYNONYMS freedom, independence,
immunity, self-determination,
autonomy, emancipation, sovereignty,
self-government, self-rule, self
determination, civil liberties, human
rights.
ANTONYMS constraint, slavery.

■ take liberties behave in a disrespectful or
overfamiliar way.

libidinous /li-bid-i-nuhss/ ▶ adjective
having a strong sexual drive.

libido /li-bee-doh/ ▶ noun (plural libidos)
sexual desire.

Libra /lee-bruh/ ▶ noun a sign of the zodiac
(the Scales or Balance), 23 September–
22 October.

librarian ▶ noun a person who works in a
library.

library ▶ noun (plural libraries) 1 a building
or room containing a collection of books
which people can read or borrow. 2 a
private collection of books.

libretto ▶ noun (plural libretti /li-bret-ti/ or
librettos) the words of an opera or musical.
□ librettist noun.

Libyan ▶ noun a person from Libya.
▶ adjective relating to Libya.

lice plural of LOUSE.

licence (US spelling license) ▶ noun
1 an official permit to own, use, or do
something. 2 the freedom to say or do what
you want.

SYNONYMS 1 a driving licence permit,
certificate, document, documentation,
authorization, warrant, credentials, pass,
papers. 2 they manufacture footwear
under licence franchise, consent,
sanction, warrant, charter, concession.
3 the army have too much licence
freedom, liberty, free rein, latitude,
independence, scope, carte blanche;
informal a blank cheque. 4 poetic licence
disregard, inventiveness, invention,
creativity, imagination, fancy, freedom.

■ license plate N. Amer. a number plate.

✔ Licence is the spelling for the noun, and
license for the verb; in American English the
-ense spelling is used for both.

license ▶ verb (licenses, licensing, licensed)
1 grant a licence to. 2 authorize or permit.

SYNONYMS permit, allow, authorize,
grant/give authority to, grant/give
permission to, certify, empower, entitle,
enable, sanction.
ANTONYMS ban.

licensee ▶ noun a person who holds a
licence to sell alcoholic drinks.

licentious /ly-sen-shuhss/ ▶ adjective
behaving in a sexually immoral way.

lichen /ly-kuhn, li-chuhn/ ▶ noun a plant
resembling moss which grows on rocks,
walls, and trees.

lick ▶ verb 1 pass the tongue over something.
2 move lightly and quickly.
▶ noun 1 an act of licking. 2 informal a small
amount or quick application of something.

licorice US spelling of LIQUORICE.

lid ▶ noun 1 a removable or hinged cover for
the top of a container. 2 an eyelid.

SYNONYMS cover, top, cap, covering.

lido /lee-doh/ ▶ noun (plural lidos) a public
open-air swimming pool.

lie[1] ▶ verb (lies, lying, lay; past participle
lain) 1 be in a horizontal position on a
supporting surface. 2 be in a particular
state. 3 be situated or found.

SYNONYMS 1 he was lying on the bed
recline, lie down/back, be recumbent,
be prostrate, be supine, be prone, be
stretched out, sprawl, rest, repose,
lounge, loll. 2 her handbag lay on the
chair be, be situated, be positioned, be
located, be placed, be found, be sited, be
arranged, rest.
ANTONYMS stand.

■ the lie of the land 1 the features or
characteristics of an area. 2 the current
situation.

! Don't confuse lay and lie: see the note at
LAY[1].

lie[2] ▸ noun a false statement made deliberately by someone who knows it is not true.

SYNONYMS *it was a lie* **untruth,** falsehood, fib, fabrication, deception, invention, (piece of) fiction, falsification, white lie; informal tall story, whopper; humorous terminological inexactitude.
ANTONYMS truth.

▸ verb (**lies, lying, lied**) tell a lie or lies.

SYNONYMS *he had lied to the police* **tell a lie,** tell an untruth, fib, dissemble, tell a white lie, perjure yourself.

liege /leej/ ▸ noun historical **1** (also **liege lord**) a lord under the feudal system. **2** a person who served a feudal lord.

lieu /lyoo/ ▸ noun (**in lieu of**) instead of.

lieutenant /lef-ten-uhnt/ ▸ noun **1** a deputy or substitute acting for a superior. **2** a rank of officer in the army and navy.

life ▸ noun (plural **lives**) **1** the condition of being alive. **2** the existence of an individual human being or animal. **3** a particular type or aspect of existence: *college life.* **4** living things and their activity. **5** vitality or energy. **6** informal a sentence of imprisonment for life.

SYNONYMS **1** *the joy of giving life to a child* **existence,** being, living, animation, sentience, creation, viability. **2** *life on Earth* **living beings/creatures,** human/animal/plant life, fauna, flora, the ecosystem, the biosphere, the ecosphere. **3** *an easy life* **way of life,** lifestyle, situation, fate, lot. **4** *the last nine months of his life* **lifetime,** lifespan, days, time (on earth), existence. **5** *the life of a Parliament* **duration,** lifetime, existence. **6** *he is full of life* **vitality,** animation, liveliness, vivacity, verve, high spirits, exuberance, zest, enthusiasm, energy, vigour, dynamism, elan, gusto, bounce, spirit, fire. **7** *a life of Chopin* **biography,** autobiography, life story/history, chronicle, account, memoirs, diary.
ANTONYMS death.

■ **life insurance** (or **life assurance**) insurance that pays out money either when the insured person dies or after a set period. **life jacket** a jacket for keeping a person afloat in water. **life peer** (in the UK) a peer whose title cannot be inherited. **life raft** an inflatable raft used in an emergency at sea.

lifebelt ▸ noun a ring used to help a person who has fallen into water to stay afloat.

lifeblood ▸ noun a vital factor or force.

lifeboat ▸ noun a boat which is launched from land to rescue people at sea, or which is kept on a ship for use in an emergency.

lifeguard ▸ noun a person employed to rescue people who get into difficulty at a beach or swimming pool.

lifeless ▸ adjective **1** dead or apparently dead. **2** not containing living things. **3** lacking energy or excitement.

lifelike ▸ adjective accurate in its representation of a living person or thing.

lifeline ▸ noun **1** a thing on which someone or something depends. **2** a rope thrown to rescue someone in difficulties in water.

lifelong ▸ adjective lasting or remaining throughout a person's life.

lifespan ▸ noun the length of time that a person or animal is likely to live.

lifestyle ▸ noun the way in which a person lives.

SYNONYMS **way of life,** life, situation, conduct, behaviour, ways, habits, mores.

lifetime ▸ noun the length of time that a person lives or a thing functions.

SYNONYMS **lifespan,** life, days, time (on earth), existence, career.

lift ▸ verb **1** raise to a higher position. **2** pick up and move to a different position. **3** formally end a restriction. **4** (**lift off**) (of an aircraft, spacecraft, etc.) take off.

SYNONYMS **1** *lift the pack on to your back* **raise,** hoist, heave, haul up, heft, raise up/aloft, elevate, hold high, pick up, grab, take up, winch up, jack up; informal hump. **2** *the fog had lifted* **clear,** rise, disperse, dissipate, disappear, vanish, dissolve. **3** *the ban has been lifted* **cancel,** remove, withdraw, revoke, rescind, end, stop, terminate.
ANTONYMS drop, put down.

▸ noun **1** Brit. a device for moving people or things between different levels of a building. **2** a free ride in another person's vehicle. **3** a device for carrying people up or down a mountain. **4** a feeling of increased cheerfulness. **5** upward force exerted by the air on an aircraft wing or similar structure.

SYNONYMS **1** *give me a lift up* **push,** hand, heave, thrust, shove. **2** *he gave me a lift to the airport* **ride,** run, drive. **3** *that goal will give his confidence a real lift* **boost,** fillip, impetus, encouragement, spur, push; informal shot in the arm.

ligament /lig-uh-muhnt/ ▸ noun a band of tissue which connects two bones or holds together a joint.

ligature /lig-uh-cher/ ▸ noun a thing used for tying something tightly, especially a cord used to stop the flow of blood from a bleeding artery.

light[1] ▸ noun **1** the natural energy that makes things visible. **2** a device that uses electricity, oil, or gas to give light. **3** a match or cigarette lighter. **4** understanding or enlightenment.

> SYNONYMS **1** *the light of the candles* **illumination,** brightness, shining, gleam, brilliance, radiance, glow, blaze, glare. **2** *there was a light on in the hall* **lamp,** lantern, torch, beacon, candle, bulb. **3** *we'll be driving in the light* **daylight,** daytime, day, natural light, sunlight.
> ANTONYMS darkness.

▶ verb (**lights, lighting, lit**; past participle **lit** or **lighted**) **1** provide an area or object with light. **2** make something start burning. **3** (**light up**) become lively or happy. **4** (**light on**) discover by chance.
▶ adjective **1** having a lot of light. **2** pale in colour.

> SYNONYMS **1** *a light bedroom* **bright,** well lit, sunny. **2** *light blue* **pale,** pastel, delicate, subtle, insipid, faint.
> ANTONYMS dark.

■ **in the light of** taking something into consideration. **light-fingered** informal tending to steal things. **light-headed** dizzy and slightly faint. **light-hearted 1** amusing and entertaining. **2** cheerful and carefree. **light year** the distance that light travels in one year, nearly 6 million million miles.

light² ▶ adjective **1** of little weight; not heavy. **2** not heavy enough. **3** not strongly or heavily built. **4** relatively low in density, amount, or strength. **5** gentle or delicate. **6** not profound or serious.

> SYNONYMS **1** *it's light and compact* **lightweight,** portable, underweight. **2** *a light cotton dress* **flimsy,** lightweight, thin, floaty, gauzy, diaphanous. **3** *she is light on her feet* **nimble,** agile, lithe, graceful, quick, sprightly. **4** *a light dinner* **small,** modest, simple, insubstantial, quick. **5** *light duties* **easy,** simple, undemanding, untaxing; informal cushy. **6** *light reading* **entertaining,** lightweight, diverting, undemanding, middle-of-the-road, mainstream, frivolous, superficial, trivial. **7** *a light touch* **gentle,** delicate, dainty, soft, faint, careful, sensitive, subtle.
> ANTONYMS heavy.

□ **lightness** noun.

lighten¹ ▶ verb make or become brighter.

> SYNONYMS **1** *the sky was beginning to lighten* **become/grow/get lighter,** brighten. **2** *the first touch of dawn lightened the sky* **brighten,** make brighter, light up, illuminate. **3** *he used lemon juice to lighten his hair* **make lighter,** whiten, bleach, blanch.
> ANTONYMS darken.

lighten² ▶ verb make or become lighter in weight.

> SYNONYMS **1** *lightening the burden of taxation* **reduce,** lessen, decrease, diminish, ease, alleviate, relieve. **2** *an attempt to lighten her mood* **cheer (up),** brighten, gladden, lift, boost, buoy (up), revive, restore, revitalize.
> ANTONYMS increase, depress.

lighter¹ ▶ noun a device producing a small flame, used to light cigarettes.

lighter² ▶ noun a barge used to transfer goods to and from ships in harbour.

lighthouse ▶ noun a tower containing a powerful light to guide ships at sea.

lighting ▶ noun **1** equipment for producing light. **2** the arrangement or effect of lights.

lightly ▶ adverb in a light way.

> SYNONYMS **1** *Maisie kissed him lightly on the cheek* **softly,** gently, faintly, delicately. **2** *season very lightly* **sparingly,** sparsely, moderately, delicately, subtly. **3** *her views are not to be dismissed lightly* **carelessly,** airily, readily, heedlessly, uncaringly, unthinkingly, thoughtlessly, flippantly.
> ANTONYMS hard, heavily, seriously.

lightning ▶ noun a flow of high-voltage electricity between a cloud and the ground or within a cloud, accompanied by a bright flash.
▶ adjective very quick.
■ **lightning conductor** (or N. Amer. **lightning rod**) a rod or wire fixed to a high place to divert lightning into the ground.

> ✔ The spelling is **lightning**, not **-tening**.

lights ▶ plural noun the lungs of sheep, pigs, or bullocks as food.

lightweight ▶ noun **1** a weight in boxing between featherweight and welterweight. **2** informal a person who is not very important: *a political lightweight.*
▶ adjective **1** of thin material or build. **2** lacking seriousness or importance.

> SYNONYMS **1** *a lightweight jacket* **thin,** light, flimsy, insubstantial, summery. **2** *lightweight entertainment* **trivial,** insubstantial, superficial, shallow, undemanding, frivolous.
> ANTONYMS heavy, serious.

ligneous /lig-ni-uhss/ ▶ adjective consisting of, or resembling, wood.

lignite ▶ noun soft brownish coal.

like¹ ▶ preposition **1** similar to. **2** in a similar way to. **3** in a way appropriate to. **4** such as.

> SYNONYMS **1** *you're just like a teacher* **similar to,** the same as, identical to, akin to, resembling. **2** *the figure landed like a cat* **in the manner of,** in the same way/manner as, in a similar way to.

3 *big cities, like Birmingham* **such as,** for example, for instance, in particular, namely, viz. **4** *Richard sounded mean, which isn't like him* **characteristic of,** typical of, in character with.
ANTONYMS unlike.

▸ **conjunction** informal **1** in the same way that. **2** as though.
▸ **noun** (**the like**) things of the same kind.
▸ **adjective** having similar characteristics to someone or something else.

> ❗ Don't use **like** to mean 'as if', as in *he's behaving like he owns the place.* Use **as if** or **as though** instead.

like² ▸ **verb** (**likes, liking, liked**) **1** find pleasant or satisfactory. **2** wish for; want.

> SYNONYMS **1** *I like him* **be fond of,** have a soft spot for, think well/highly of, admire, respect, be attracted to, fancy, find attractive, be keen on, be taken with; informal rate. **2** *she likes gardening* **enjoy,** have a taste for, have a liking for, be partial to, find/take pleasure in, be keen on, appreciate, love, adore, relish; informal have a thing about, be into, be mad about/for, be hooked on. **3** *feel free to say what you like* **choose,** please, wish, want, see/think fit, care to, will.
> ANTONYMS hate.

▸ **noun** (**likes**) the things that you like.
likeable (or **likable**) ▸ **adjective** pleasant; easy to like.
likelihood ▸ **noun** the state of being likely; probability.

> SYNONYMS **probability,** chance, prospect, possibility, odds, risk, threat, danger, hope, promise.

likely ▸ **adjective** (**likelier, likeliest**) **1** probable. **2** promising.

> SYNONYMS **1** *it seemed likely that a scandal would break* **probable,** (distinctly) possible, odds-on, plausible, imaginable; informal on the cards. **2** *a likely explanation* **plausible,** reasonable, feasible, acceptable, believable, credible, tenable.
> ANTONYMS improbable, unbelievable.

▸ **adverb** probably.
liken ▸ **verb** (**liken someone/thing to**) point out the resemblance of someone or something to.

> SYNONYMS **compare,** equate, set beside.
> ANTONYMS contrast.

likeness ▸ **noun 1** resemblance. **2** outward appearance. **3** a portrait or representation.

> SYNONYMS **1** *her likeness to Anne is quite uncanny* **resemblance,** similarity, correspondence. **2** *a likeness of the president* **representation,** image, depiction, portrayal, picture, drawing,

sketch, painting, portrait, photograph, study.
ANTONYMS dissimilarity.

likewise ▸ **adverb 1** also; moreover. **2** similarly.

> SYNONYMS **1** *an ambush was out of the question, likewise poison* **also,** equally, in addition, too, as well, to boot, besides, moreover, furthermore. **2** *encourage your family and friends to do likewise* **the same,** similarly, correspondingly.
> ANTONYMS differently.

liking ▸ **noun 1** a fondness for someone or something. **2** (**your liking**) your taste: *the coffee was just to her liking.*

> SYNONYMS **fondness,** love, affection, penchant, attachment, taste, passion, preference, partiality, predilection.
> ANTONYMS dislike.

lilac ▸ **noun 1** a shrub or small tree with sweet-smelling violet, pink, or white blossom. **2** a pale pinkish-violet colour.
lilo ▸ **noun** (plural **lilos**) an inflatable mattress used for floating on water.
lilt ▸ **noun 1** a rising and falling of the voice when speaking. **2** a gentle rhythm in a tune.
◻ **lilting** adjective.
lily ▸ **noun** (plural **lilies**) a plant with large trumpet-shaped flowers on a tall, slender stem.
■ **lily-livered** cowardly. **lily of the valley** a plant with broad leaves and white bell-shaped flowers.
limb ▸ **noun 1** an arm, leg, or wing. **2** a large branch of a tree.

> SYNONYMS **arm, leg,** wing, appendage; archaic member.

■ **out on a limb** not supported by other people.
limber ▸ **verb** (**limbers, limbering, limbered**) (**limber up**) warm up in preparation for exercise or activity.
▸ **adjective** supple; flexible.
limbo¹ ▸ **noun** an uncertain period of waiting.
limbo² ▸ **noun** (plural **limbos**) a West Indian dance in which you bend backwards to pass under a horizontal bar.
lime¹ ▸ **noun** a white alkaline substance used as a building material or fertilizer.
lime² ▸ **noun 1** a green citrus fruit similar to a lemon. **2** a bright light green colour.
lime³ ▸ **noun** a deciduous tree with heart-shaped leaves and yellowish blossom.
limelight ▸ **noun** (**the limelight**) the focus of public attention.

> SYNONYMS **attention,** interest, scrutiny, the public eye/gaze, the glare of

publicity, prominence, the spotlight, fame, celebrity.
ANTONYMS obscurity.

limerick ▸ noun a humorous five-line poem with a rhyme scheme *aabba*.

limestone ▸ noun a hard rock composed mainly of calcium carbonate.

limit ▸ noun **1** a point beyond which something does not or may not pass. **2** a restriction on the size or amount of something.

SYNONYMS **1** *the city limits* **boundary (line)**, border, frontier, edge, perimeter, margin. **2** *a limit of 4,500 supporters* **maximum**, ceiling, upper limit.

▸ verb (**limits, limiting, limited**) put a limit on.

SYNONYMS *the pressure to limit costs* **restrict**, curb, cap, (hold in) check, restrain, regulate, control, govern.

■ **off limits** out of bounds.
□ **limitless** adjective.

limitation ▸ noun **1** a restriction. **2** a fault or failing.

SYNONYMS **1** *a limitation on the number of newcomers* **restriction**, curb, restraint, control, check. **2** *he is aware of his own limitations* **imperfection**, flaw, defect, failing, shortcoming, weak point, deficiency, frailty, weakness.
ANTONYMS strength.

limited ▸ adjective restricted in size, amount, extent, or ability.

SYNONYMS **restricted**, finite, small, tight, slight, in short supply, short, meagre, scanty, sparse, inadequate, insufficient, paltry, poor, minimal.
ANTONYMS limitless, ample.

■ **limited company** Brit. a company whose owners have only a limited responsibility for its debts.

limo ▸ noun (plural **limos**) informal a limousine.

limousine ▸ noun a large, luxurious car.

limp¹ ▸ verb **1** walk with difficulty because of an injured leg or foot. **2** (of a damaged ship or aircraft) proceed with difficulty.

SYNONYMS *she limped out of the house* **hobble**, hop, lurch, stagger, shuffle, shamble.

▸ noun a limping walk.

limp² ▸ adjective **1** not stiff or firm. **2** without energy or strength.

SYNONYMS *a limp handshake* **soft**, flaccid, loose, slack, lax, floppy, drooping, droopy, sagging.
ANTONYMS firm.

□ **limply** adverb.

limpet ▸ noun a shellfish with a muscular foot for clinging tightly to rocks.

limpid ▸ adjective (of a liquid or the eyes) clear.

linchpin (or **lynchpin**) ▸ noun **1** a very important person or thing. **2** a pin through the end of an axle keeping a wheel in position.

linctus ▸ noun Brit. thick liquid medicine, especially cough mixture.

line¹ ▸ noun **1** a long, narrow mark or band. **2** a length of cord, wire, etc. **3** a row or series of people or things. **4** a row of written or printed words. **5** a direction, course, or channel. **6** a telephone connection. **7** a railway track or route. **8** a series of military defences facing an enemy force. **9** a wrinkle in the skin. **10** a range of commercial products. **11** an area of activity: *their line of work*. **12** (**lines**) a way of doing or thinking about something. **13** (**lines**) the words of an actor's part. **14** (**lines**) Brit. a school punishment in which you have to write out the same sentence a stated number of times.

SYNONYMS **1** *he drew a line through the name* **stroke**, dash, score, underline, underscore, slash, stripe, strip, band, belt; Brit. oblique. **2** *there were lines round her eyes* **wrinkle**, furrow, crease, crinkle, crow's foot. **3** *the classic lines of the Bentley* **contour**, outline, configuration, shape, design, profile. **4** *the county line* **boundary**, limit, border, frontier, touchline, margin, perimeter. **5** *the clothes line* **cord**, rope, cable, wire, thread, string. **6** *a line of soldiers* **file**, rank, column, string, train, procession, row, queue; Brit. informal crocodile. **7** *their line of flight* **course**, route, track, path, trajectory.

▸ verb (**lines, lining, lined**) **1** be positioned at intervals along a route. **2** (**line someone/thing up**) arrange people or things in a row. **3** (**line something up**) have something prepared. **4** (**lined**) marked or covered with lines.

SYNONYMS **1** *the driveway was lined by poplars* **border**, edge, fringe, bound. **2** *her face was lined with age* **furrow**, wrinkle, crease. **3** (**lined**) *his lined face* **wrinkled**, wrinkly, furrowed, wizened. **4** (**lined**) *lined paper* **ruled**, feint, striped, banded.

■ **in line** under control. **in line for** likely to receive. **line dancing** country and western dancing in which a line of dancers follow a set pattern of steps. **on the line** at serious risk. **out of line** informal behaving badly or wrongly.

line² ▸ verb (**lines, lining, lined**) cover the inner surface of something with different material.

SYNONYMS **back**, pad, cover, insulate, seal.

lineage /lin-i-ij/ ▸ noun ancestry or pedigree.

lineal /lin-i-uhl/ ▸ adjective in a direct line of descent or ancestry.

lineament /lin-i-uh-muhnt/ ▸ noun literary a distinctive feature, especially of the face.

linear /lin-i-er/ ▸ adjective **1** arranged in or extending along a straight line. **2** consisting of lines or outlines. **3** involving one dimension only. **4** progressing from one stage to another in a series of steps.
□ **linearity** noun.

linen ▸ noun **1** cloth woven from flax. **2** articles such as sheets, pillowcases, and duvet covers.

liner¹ ▸ noun **1** a large passenger ship. **2** a cosmetic for outlining or emphasizing a facial feature.

liner² ▸ noun a lining of a garment, container, etc.

linesman ▸ noun (plural **linesmen**) (in sport) an official who helps the referee or umpire to decide whether the ball is out of play.

line-up ▸ noun a group of people or things assembled for a particular purpose.

> SYNONYMS **1** *a star-studded line-up* **cast,** bill, programme. **2** *United's line-up* **team,** squad, side, configuration.

ling¹ ▸ noun a long-bodied sea fish.

ling² ▸ noun heather.

linger ▸ verb **1** be slow or reluctant to leave. **2** (**linger over**) spend a long time over. **3** be slow to fade, disappear, or die.

> SYNONYMS **1** *the crowd lingered* **wait (around),** stand (around), remain, loiter; informal stick around, hang around/round. **2** *the infection can linger for years* **persist,** continue, remain, stay, endure, carry on, last.
> ANTONYMS vanish.

lingerie /lan-zhuh-ri/ ▸ noun women's underwear and nightclothes.

lingo ▸ noun (plural **lingos** or **lingoes**) informal **1** a foreign language. **2** the jargon of a particular subject or group.

lingua franca /ling-gwuh frang-kuh/ ▸ noun (plural **lingua francas**) a language used as a common language between speakers whose native languages are different.

linguine /ling-gwee-ni/ ▸ plural noun small ribbons of pasta.

linguist ▸ noun **1** a person who is good at foreign languages. **2** a person who studies linguistics.

linguistic ▸ adjective relating to language or linguistics.

linguistics ▸ noun the scientific study of language.

liniment ▸ noun an ointment rubbed on the body to relieve pain or bruising.

lining ▸ noun a layer of material covering or attached to the inside of something.

> SYNONYMS **backing,** facing, padding, insulation.

link ▸ noun **1** a relationship or connection between people or things. **2** something that lets people communicate. **3** a means of contact or transport between two places. **4** a code or instruction that connects one part of a computer program, website, etc. to another. **5** a loop in a chain.

> SYNONYMS **1** *the links between transport and the environment* **connection,** relationship, association, linkage, tie-up. **2** *their links with the labour movement* **bond,** tie, attachment, connection, association, affiliation.

▸ verb connect or join.

> SYNONYMS **1** *four boxes were linked together* **join,** connect, fasten, attach, bind, secure, fix, tie, couple, yoke. **2** *the evidence linking him with the body* **associate,** connect, relate, bracket.
> ANTONYMS separate.

linkage ▸ noun **1** the action of linking or the state of being linked. **2** a system of links.

links ▸ plural noun a golf course, especially one near the sea.

linnet ▸ noun a type of finch (songbird).

lino ▸ noun Brit. informal linoleum.

linoleum /li-noh-li-uhm/ ▸ noun a floor covering made from a mixture of linseed oil and powdered cork.

linseed ▸ noun the seeds of the flax plant, which are crushed to make an oil used in paint, varnish, etc.

lint ▸ noun **1** short, fine fibres which separate from cloth when it is being made. **2** a fabric used for dressing wounds.

lintel ▸ noun a horizontal support across the top of a door or window.

lion ▸ noun (feminine **lioness**) a large cat of Africa and NW India, the male of which has a shaggy mane.
■ **the lion's share** the largest part of something.

lionize (or **lionise**) ▸ verb (**lionizes, lionizing, lionized**) treat as a celebrity.

lip ▸ noun **1** either of the two fleshy parts forming the edges of the mouth opening. **2** the edge of a hollow container or an opening. **3** informal cheeky talk.

> SYNONYMS *the lip of the crater* **edge,** rim, brim, border, verge, brink.

■ **lip-read** understand speech from watching a speaker's lip movements.

liposuction ▸ noun a technique in cosmetic surgery for sucking out excess fat from under the skin.

lippy ▸ adjective informal cheeky.

lipstick ▸ noun coloured cosmetic applied to the lips from a small solid stick.

liquefy /lik-wi-fy/ ▸ verb (liquefies, liquefying, liquefied) make or become liquid.
□ liquefaction noun.

> ✔ lique**fy**, not **-ify**.

liqueur /li-kyoor/ ▸ noun a strong, sweet alcoholic drink.

liquid ▸ noun a substance such as water or oil that flows freely.

> SYNONYMS *a vat of liquid* **fluid**, moisture, liquor, solution, juice, sap.
> ANTONYMS solid.

▸ adjective 1 in the form of a liquid. 2 clear, like water. 3 (of assets) held in cash, or easily converted into cash.

> SYNONYMS *liquid fuels* **fluid**, liquefied, melted, molten, thawed, dissolved.
> ANTONYMS solid.

liquidate ▸ verb (liquidates, liquidating, liquidated) 1 close a business and sell what it owns so as to pay its debts. 2 convert assets into cash. 3 pay off a debt. 4 informal kill.
□ liquidation noun.

liquidity /li-kwid-i-ti/ ▸ noun the state of owning assets that are held in or easily converted to cash.

liquidize (or liquidise) ▸ verb (liquidizes, liquidizing, liquidized) Brit. convert solid food into a liquid or purée.
□ liquidizer noun.

liquor /lik-er/ ▸ noun 1 alcoholic drink, especially spirits. 2 liquid that has been produced in cooking.

> SYNONYMS 1 *alcoholic liquor* **alcohol**, spirits, (alcoholic) drink; informal booze, the hard stuff, hooch, moonshine.
> 2 *strain the liquor into the sauce* **stock**, broth, bouillon, juice, liquid.

liquorice /lik-uh-riss, lik-uh-rish/ (US spelling licorice) ▸ noun a black substance made from the juice of a root and used as a sweet and in medicine.

lira /leer-uh/ ▸ noun (plural lire /leer-uh/) the basic unit of money of Turkey and formerly also of Italy.

lisp ▸ noun a speech defect in which the sound s is pronounced like th.
▸ verb speak with a lisp.

lissom (or lissome) ▸ adjective slim, supple, and graceful.

list[1] ▸ noun a number of connected items or names written one after the other.

> SYNONYMS *a list of the world's wealthiest people* **catalogue**, inventory, record,
register, roll, file, index, directory, checklist.

▸ verb 1 make a list of. 2 include in a list.

> SYNONYMS *the accounts are listed below* **record**, register, enter, itemize, enumerate, catalogue, file, log, minute, categorize, inventory, classify, group, sort, rank, index.

list[2] ▸ verb (of a ship) lean over to one side.

> SYNONYMS *the boat listed to one side* **lean (over)**, tilt, tip, heel (over), pitch, incline, slant, slope, bank.

listed ▸ adjective (of a building in the UK) officially protected because of its historical importance.

listen ▸ verb 1 give your attention to a sound. 2 make an effort to hear something. 3 pay attention to advice or a request.

> SYNONYMS 1 *are you listening?* **pay attention**, be attentive, attend, concentrate, keep your ears open, prick up your ears; informal be all ears. 2 *policymakers should listen to popular opinion* **heed**, take heed of, take notice/note of, bear in mind, take into consideration/account.

▸ noun an act of listening.
□ listener noun.

listeria ▸ noun a type of bacterium which infects humans and animals through contaminated food.

listing ▸ noun 1 a list or catalogue. 2 an entry in a list.

listless ▸ adjective lacking energy or enthusiasm.
□ listlessly adverb.

lit past and past participle of LIGHT[1].

litany ▸ noun (plural litanies) 1 a series of prayers to God used in church services. 2 a long, boring list of complaints, reasons, etc.

liter US spelling of LITRE.

literacy ▸ noun the ability to read and write.

literal ▸ adjective 1 using or interpreting words in their usual or most basic sense. 2 (of a translation) representing the exact words of the original piece of writing. 3 not exaggerated or distorted.

> SYNONYMS **strict**, technical, concrete, original, true.
> ANTONYMS figurative.

literally ▸ adverb 1 in a literal way. 2 informal used to emphasize what you are saying: *we were literally killing ourselves laughing*.

literary ▸ adjective 1 having to do with literature. 2 (of language) characteristic of literature or formal writing.

SYNONYMS **1** *literary works* **artistic,** poetic, dramatic. **2** *her literary friends* **scholarly,** intellectual, academic, bookish, erudite.

literate ▸ adjective **1** able to read and write. **2** knowledgeable in a particular field: *computer-literate.*

SYNONYMS **(well) educated,** well read, widely read, scholarly, learned, knowledgeable, cultured, cultivated, well informed.
ANTONYMS ignorant.

literati /li-tuh-**rah**-ti/ ▸ plural noun educated people who are interested in literature.

literature ▸ noun **1** written works that are regarded as having artistic merit. **2** books and printed information on a particular subject.

SYNONYMS **1** *English literature* **writing,** poetry, drama, prose. **2** *the literature on prototype theory* **publications,** reports, studies, material. **3** *election literature* **documentation,** material, publicity, blurb, propaganda, advertising; informal bumf.

lithe /lyth/ ▸ adjective slim, supple, and graceful.

lithium /**li**-thi-uhm/ ▸ noun a silver-white metallic element.

lithograph /**li**-thuh-grahf/ ▸ noun a print made by lithography.

lithography /li-**thog**-ruh-fi/ ▸ noun printing from a flat metal surface which has been prepared so that ink sticks only where it is required.

Lithuanian ▸ noun a person from Lithuania. ▸ adjective relating to Lithuania.

litigant ▸ noun a person who is involved in a dispute or claim being heard in a law court.

litigation ▸ noun the process of taking a dispute to a law court.

SYNONYMS **legal/judicial proceedings,** legal action, lawsuit, legal dispute, legal case, prosecution, indictment.

litigious /li-**ti**-juhss/ ▸ adjective frequently choosing to go to a law court to settle a dispute.

litmus ▸ noun a dye that is red under acid conditions and blue under alkaline conditions.
■ **litmus paper** paper stained with litmus, used as a test for acids or alkalis. **litmus test** a reliable test of the quality or truth of something.

litre (US spelling **liter**) ▸ noun a metric unit of capacity equal to 1,000 cubic centimetres (about 1.75 pints).

litter ▸ noun **1** rubbish left in an open or public place. **2** an untidy collection of things. **3** a number of young born to an animal at one time. **4** (also **cat litter**) absorbent material that is put into a tray for a cat to use as a toilet indoors. **5** straw or other material used as bedding for animals. **6** (also **leaf litter**) decomposing leaves forming a layer on top of soil. **7** (in the past) an enclosed chair or bed carried by men or animals.

SYNONYMS **1** *never drop litter* **rubbish,** refuse, junk, waste, debris; N. Amer. trash, garbage. **2** *the litter of glasses around her* **clutter,** jumble, muddle, mess, heap; informal shambles.

▸ verb (**litters, littering, littered**) make a place untidy by dropping litter.

SYNONYMS *clothes littered the floor* **cover,** clutter up, pepper.

little ▸ adjective **1** small in size, amount, or degree. **2** (of a person) young or younger. **3** (of distance or time) short.

SYNONYMS **1** *a little writing desk* **small,** compact, miniature, tiny, toy, baby, undersized, dwarf, midget; Scottish wee; informal teeny-weeny; Brit. informal titchy, dinky; N. Amer. informal vest-pocket. **2** *a little man* **short,** small, slight, petite, diminutive, tiny; Scottish wee; informal teeny-weeny, pint-sized. **3** *my little sister* **young,** younger, baby. **4** *a little while* **brief,** short, quick, hasty, cursory. **5** *a few little problems* **minor,** unimportant, insignificant, trivial, trifling, petty, paltry, inconsequential.
ANTONYMS big, large, elder, major.

▸ determiner & pronoun not much.

SYNONYMS *they have little political influence* **hardly any,** not much, scant, limited, restricted, modest, little or no, minimal, negligible.
ANTONYMS considerable.

▸ adverb hardly, or not at all.

SYNONYMS **1** *he is little known as a teacher* **hardly,** barely, scarcely, not much, only slightly. **2** *this disease is little seen nowadays* **rarely,** seldom, infrequently, hardly (ever), scarcely ever, not much.
ANTONYMS well, often.

■ **a little 1** a small amount of. **2** a short time or distance. **3** to a limited extent.

littoral ▸ adjective relating to the shore of the sea or a lake.

liturgy /**li**-ter-ji/ ▸ noun (plural **liturgies**) a set form of public worship used in the Christian Church.
□ **liturgical** adjective.

live¹ /liv/ ▸ verb (**lives, living, lived**) **1** remain alive. **2** be alive at a particular time. **3** spend your life in a particular way. **4** have your home in a particular place. **5** obtain the things necessary for staying alive.

SYNONYMS **1** *the greatest mathematician who ever lived* **exist,** be alive, be, have life, breathe, draw breath, walk the earth. **2** *I live in London* **reside,** have your home, lodge, inhabit, occupy, populate; Scottish stay. **3** *she had lived a difficult life* **experience,** spend, pass, lead, have, go through, undergo. **4** *Freddy lived by scavenging* **survive,** make a living, eke out a living, subsist, support yourself, sustain yourself, make ends meet, keep body and soul together.
ANTONYMS die, be dead.

■ **live something down** manage to make other people forget something embarrassing. **live rough** live outdoors with no home.
□ **liveable** (or **livable**) adjective.

live² /lyv/ ▶ adjective **1** living. **2** (of music) played in front of an audience; not recorded. **3** (of a broadcast) transmitted at the time it happens, rather than recorded. **4** (of a wire or device) connected to a source of electric current. **5** containing explosive that can be detonated.

SYNONYMS **1** *live bait* **living,** alive, conscious. **2** *a live rail* **electrified,** charged, powered up, active, switched on. **3** *a live grenade* **unexploded,** explosive, active, primed. **4** *a live issue* **topical,** current, controversial, burning, pressing, important, relevant.
ANTONYMS dead, inanimate.

▶ adverb as a live performance.
■ **live wire** informal an energetic and lively person.

livelihood ▶ noun a way of earning enough money to live on.

SYNONYMS **(source of) income,** means of support, living, subsistence, bread and butter, job, work, employment, occupation.

lively ▶ adjective (**livelier, liveliest**) **1** full of life and energy. **2** (of a place) full of activity.

SYNONYMS **1** *a lively young woman* **energetic,** active, animated, dynamic, full of life, outgoing, spirited, high-spirited, vivacious, enthusiastic, vibrant, buoyant, exuberant, effervescent, cheerful; informal full of beans. **2** *a lively bar* **busy,** crowded, bustling, buzzing, vibrant, boisterous, jolly. **3** *a lively debate* **heated,** vigorous, animated, spirited, enthusiastic, forceful. **4** *a lively portrait of the local community* **vivid,** colourful, striking, graphic. **5** *he bowled at a lively pace* **brisk,** quick, fast, rapid, swift, speedy, smart.
ANTONYMS quiet, dull, slow.

□ **liveliness** noun.

liven ▶ verb (**liven someone/thing up** or **liven up**) make or become more lively or interesting.

liver ▶ noun **1** a large organ in the abdomen that produces bile. **2** the liver of some animals used as food.

livery ▶ noun (plural **liveries**) **1** a special uniform worn by a servant or official. **2** a distinctive design and colour scheme used on the vehicles or products of a company.
■ **livery stable** a stable where people can pay to keep their horses, or hire a horse to ride.
□ **liveried** adjective.

lives plural of LIFE.

livestock ▶ noun farm animals.

livid ▶ adjective **1** furiously angry. **2** dark bluish grey in colour.

SYNONYMS **very angry,** enraged, furious, infuriated, irate, incensed, fuming, ranting, raving, seething, beside yourself, outraged; informal hopping mad, wild.

living ▶ noun **1** being alive. **2** an income which is enough to live on.

SYNONYMS **1** *she cleaned floors for a living* **livelihood,** (source of) income, means of support, subsistence, keep, daily bread, bread and butter, job, work, employment, occupation. **2** *healthy living* **way of life,** lifestyle, life, conduct, behaviour, activities, habits.

▶ adjective alive.

SYNONYMS **1** *living organisms* **alive,** live, animate, sentient, breathing, existing. **2** *a living language* **current,** contemporary, active.
ANTONYMS dead, extinct.

■ **living room** a room in a house used for relaxing in.

lizard ▶ noun a small four-legged reptile with a long body and tail.

llama /lah-muh/ ▶ noun a South American animal related to the camel.

lo ▶ exclamation old use used to draw attention to something.

loach ▶ noun a small freshwater fish.

load ▶ noun **1** a heavy or bulky thing that is being carried. **2** a weight or source of pressure. **3** the total number or amount carried in a vehicle or container. **4** (**a load** or **loads of**) informal a lot of.

SYNONYMS **1** *MacDowell's got a load to deliver* **cargo,** freight, consignment, delivery, shipment, goods, pack, bundle, parcel. **2** *a heavy teaching load* **commitment,** responsibility, duty, obligation, burden.

▶ verb **1** put a load on or in. **2** put ammunition into a gun. **3** put something into a device so that it will operate.

SYNONYMS 1 *we quickly loaded the van*
fill (up), pack, lade, charge, stock, stack.
2 *Larry loaded boxes into the jeep* **pack,**
stow, store, stack, bundle, place, deposit,
put away. **3** *loading the committee with*
responsibilities **burden,** weigh down,
saddle, charge, overburden, overwhelm,
encumber, tax, strain, trouble, worry.
4 *he loaded a gun* **prime,** charge, set
up, prepare. **5** *load the cassette into the*
camcorder **insert,** put, place, slot, slide.

loaded ▸ adjective **1** carrying or supporting
a load. **2** biased towards a particular
outcome. **3** having an underlying meaning:
a loaded question. **4** informal wealthy.

SYNONYMS 1 *a loaded freight train* **full,**
filled, laden, packed, stuffed, crammed,
brimming, stacked; informal chock-full,
chock-a-block. **2** *a politically loaded word*
charged, emotive, sensitive, delicate.

loaf[1] ▸ noun (plural **loaves**) a quantity of bread
that is shaped and baked in one piece.

loaf[2] ▸ verb spend your time in a lazy or
aimless way.

SYNONYMS laze, lounge, loll, idle; informal
hang around/round; Brit. informal **hang**
about, mooch about/around; N. Amer.
informal bum around.

loafer ▸ noun **1** a person who spends their
time in a lazy or aimless way. **2** a casual
leather shoe with a flat heel.

loam ▸ noun a fertile soil of clay and sand
containing humus.

loan ▸ noun **1** a sum of money that is lent
to someone. **2** the action of lending
something.

SYNONYMS credit, advance, mortgage,
overdraft; Brit. informal sub.

▸ verb give something as a loan.
■ **loan shark** informal a moneylender who
charges very high rates of interest.

loath (or **loth**) ▸ adjective (**loath to do**)
reluctant or unwilling to do.

SYNONYMS reluctant, unwilling,
disinclined, averse, opposed, resistant.
ANTONYMS willing.

❗ Don't confuse **loath** with **loathe**, which
means 'feel hatred for'.

loathe ▸ verb (**loathes, loathing, loathed**)
feel hatred or disgust for.

SYNONYMS 1 hate, detest, abhor, not be
able to bear/stand. **2** (**loathing**) **hatred,**
hate, abhorrence, antipathy, dislike,
hostility, animosity, malice, enmity,
repugnance.
ANTONYMS love.

loathsome ▸ adjective causing hatred or
disgust.

SYNONYMS hateful, detestable, abhorrent,
repulsive, odious, repugnant, repellent,
disgusting, revolting, sickening,
abominable, despicable, contemptible,
reprehensible, vile, horrible, nasty,
obnoxious, gross, foul; informal horrid;
literary noisome.

loaves plural of **LOAF**[1].

lob ▸ verb (**lobs, lobbing, lobbed**) throw or
hit something in a high arc.
▸ noun (in soccer or tennis) a ball lobbed over
an opponent.

lobby ▸ noun (plural **lobbies**) **1** an open area
inside the entrance of a public building.
2 any of several large halls in the Houses
of Parliament in which MPs meet members
of the public. **3** each of two corridors in
the Houses of Parliament where MPs vote.
4 a group of people who try to influence
politicians on a particular issue.

SYNONYMS 1 *the hotel lobby* **entrance**
(**hall**), hallway, hall, vestibule, foyer,
reception area. **2** *the anti-hunt lobby*
pressure group, interest group,
movement, campaign, crusade, faction,
camp.

▸ verb (**lobbies, lobbying, lobbied**) try to
influence a politician on an issue.

SYNONYMS 1 *readers are urged to lobby*
their MPs **approach,** contact, importune,
sway, petition, solicit, appeal to,
pressurize. **2** *a group lobbying for*
better rail services **campaign,** crusade,
press, push, ask, call, demand, promote,
advocate, champion.

◻ **lobbyist** noun.

lobe ▸ noun **1** a roundish and flattish part
that projects from or divides something.
2 the rounded fleshy part at the lower edge
of the ear. **3** each of the sections of the
main part of the brain.

lobelia /luh-**bee**-li-uh/ ▸ noun a garden
plant with blue or red flowers.

lobotomy /luh-**bot**-uh-mi/ ▸ noun (plural
lobotomies) an operation that involves
cutting into part of the brain, formerly
used to treat mental illness.

lobster ▸ noun a large edible shellfish with
large pincers.
■ **lobster pot** a basket-like trap in which
lobsters are caught.

local ▸ adjective having to do with a
particular area, or with the place where
you live.

SYNONYMS 1 *the local council* **community,**
district, neighbourhood, regional, town,
municipal, provincial, village, parish.
2 *a local restaurant* **neighbourhood,**
nearby, near, at hand, close by, handy,
convenient. **3** *a local infection* **confined,**

I

restricted, contained, localized.
ANTONYMS national, widespread.

▸ noun 1 a person who lives in a particular place. 2 Brit. informal a pub near where you live.

SYNONYMS *complaints from the locals* **local person,** native, inhabitant, resident, parishioner.
ANTONYMS outsider.

■ **local anaesthetic** an anaesthetic that causes a loss of feeling in a particular part of the body.
□ **locally** adverb.

locale /loh-**kahl**/ ▸ noun a place where something happens.

locality ▸ noun (plural **localities**) 1 an area or neighbourhood. 2 the position or site of something.

localize (or **localise**) ▸ verb (**localizes, localizing, localized**) restrict to a particular place.
□ **localization** noun.

locate ▸ verb (**locates, locating, located**) 1 discover the exact place or position of. 2 (**be located**) be situated in a particular place.

SYNONYMS 1 *spotter planes located the submarines* **find,** pinpoint, track down, unearth, sniff out, smoke out, search out, uncover. 2 *a company located near Pittsburgh* **situate,** site, position, place, base, put, build, establish, station.

location ▸ noun 1 a place where something is located. 2 the action of locating someone or something. 3 an actual place in which a film or broadcast is made, as distinct from a studio.

SYNONYMS **position,** place, situation, site, locality, locale, spot, whereabouts, scene, setting, area, environment, venue, address.

loch /lok, lokh/ ▸ noun Scottish a lake, or a narrow strip of sea that is almost surrounded by land.

loci plural of **locus**.

lock[1] ▸ noun 1 a mechanism for keeping a door or container fastened, operated by a key. 2 a similar device used to prevent a vehicle or other machine from operating. 3 a short section of a canal or river with gates at each end which can be opened or closed to change the water level, used for raising and lowering boats. 4 a hold in wrestling that prevents an opponent from moving a limb. 5 the maximum extent that the front wheels of a vehicle can be turned.

SYNONYMS *the lock on the door* **bolt,** catch, fastener, clasp, hasp, latch.

▸ verb 1 fasten with a lock. 2 shut in or imprison by locking a door. 3 become fixed in one position.

SYNONYMS 1 *he locked the door* **bolt,** fasten, secure, padlock, latch, chain. 2 *the police locked arms* **join,** interlock, link, engage, combine, connect, couple. 3 *the wheels locked* **become stuck,** stick, jam, seize. 4 *he locked her in an embrace* **clasp,** clench, grasp, embrace, hug, squeeze.
ANTONYMS unlock, open, separate, divide.

■ **lock, stock, and barrel** including everything. **lock-up** 1 a place used as a temporary jail. 2 Brit. a small shop or rented garage that is separate from other premises.
□ **lockable** adjective.

lock[2] ▸ noun 1 a coil or hanging piece of a person's hair. 2 (**locks**) literary a person's hair.

SYNONYMS *a lock of hair* **tuft,** tress, curl, ringlet, hank, strand, wisp, coil.

locker ▸ noun a small cupboard or compartment that can be locked.

SYNONYMS **cupboard,** cabinet, chest, safe, box, case, coffer, storeroom.

locket ▸ noun a piece of jewellery in the form of a small case on a chain, worn round a person's neck and used to hold a tiny photograph, a lock of hair, etc.

lockjaw ▸ noun a form of the disease tetanus in which the jaws become stiff and tightly closed.

lockout ▸ noun a situation in which an employer refuses to allow employees to enter their place of work until they agree to certain conditions.

locksmith ▸ noun a person who makes and repairs locks.

locomotion ▸ noun movement from one place to another.

locomotive ▸ noun a powered railway vehicle used for pulling trains.
▸ adjective relating to locomotion.

locum /**loh**-kuhm/ ▸ noun a doctor or priest standing in for another who is temporarily away.

locus /**loh**-kuhss/ ▸ noun (plural **loci** /**loh**-sy/) technical a particular position, point, or place.

locust ▸ noun a large tropical grasshopper which migrates in vast swarms.

locution ▸ noun 1 a word or phrase. 2 a person's particular way of speaking.

lode ▸ noun a vein of metal ore in the earth.

lodestone ▸ noun a piece of magnetic iron ore used as a magnet.

lodge ▸ noun 1 a small house at the gates of a large house with grounds. 2 a room for a porter at the entrance of a large building. 3 a small country house where people stay while hunting and shooting. 4 a branch of

an organization such as the Freemasons.
5 a beaver's den.

> SYNONYMS **1** *the porter's lodge* **gatehouse,** cottage. **2** *a hunting lodge* **house,** cottage, cabin, chalet. **3** *a Masonic lodge* **section,** branch, wing, hall, clubhouse, meeting room; N. Amer. chapter.

▸ verb (**lodges, lodging, lodged**) **1** formally present a complaint, appeal, etc. **2** firmly fix something in a place. **3** rent accommodation in another person's house. **4** leave something valuable in a safe place or with someone reliable.

> SYNONYMS **1** *the government lodged a protest* **submit,** register, enter, put forward, advance, lay, present, tender, proffer, put on record, record, table, file. **2** *the bullet lodged in his back* **become embedded,** get/become stuck, stick, catch, become caught, wedge. **3** *William lodged at our house* **reside,** board, stay, live, stop; N. Amer. room. **4** *the money was lodged in a bank* **deposit,** put, bank, stash, store, stow, put away.

lodger ▸ noun a person who pays rent to live in a house or flat with the owner.

lodging ▸ noun **1** temporary accommodation. **2** (usu. **lodgings**) a rented room or rooms, usually in the same house as the owner.

> SYNONYMS **accommodation,** rooms, chambers, living quarters, a roof over your head, housing, shelter; informal digs; formal residence, dwelling.

loft ▸ noun **1** a room or storage space directly under the roof of a house. **2** a large, open flat in a converted warehouse or factory. **3** a gallery in a church or hall.
▸ verb kick, hit, or throw a ball high into the air.

lofty ▸ adjective (**loftier, loftiest**) **1** tall and impressive. **2** morally good; noble. **3** proud and superior.

> SYNONYMS **1** *a lofty tower* **tall,** high. **2** *lofty ideals* **noble,** exalted, high, high-minded, worthy, grand, fine, elevated. **3** *lofty disdain* **haughty,** arrogant, disdainful, supercilious, condescending, scornful, contemptuous, self-important, conceited, snobbish; informal stuck-up, snooty; Brit. informal toffee-nosed. ANTONYMS low, short, base, lowly, modest.

□ **loftily** adverb.

log¹ ▸ noun **1** a part of the trunk or a large branch of a tree that has fallen or been cut off. **2** an official record of the voyage of a ship or aircraft.
▸ verb (**logs, logging, logged**) **1** record facts in a log. **2** achieve a certain distance, speed, or time. **3** (**log in/on** or **out/off**) begin

or finish using a computer system. **4** cut down an area of forest to use the wood commercially.

> SYNONYMS **1** *all complaints are logged* **register,** record, note, write down, put in writing, enter, file. **2** *the pilot had logged 95 hours* **attain,** achieve, chalk up, make, do, go, cover, clock up.

□ **logger** noun.

log² ▸ noun a logarithm.

loganberry ▸ noun (plural **loganberries**) an edible red soft fruit, similar to a raspberry.

logarithm ▸ noun each of a series of numbers which allow you to do calculations by adding and subtracting rather than multiplying and dividing.
□ **logarithmic** adjective.

logbook ▸ noun **1** a log of a ship or aircraft. **2** Brit. a document recording details about a vehicle and its owner.

loggerheads ▸ plural noun (**at loggerheads**) in strong disagreement.

loggia /**loh**-juh/ ▸ noun a long room with one or more open sides.

logic ▸ noun **1** the science of reasoning. **2** clear, sound reasoning. **3** a set of principles used in preparing a computer or electronic device to perform a task.

> SYNONYMS **1** *this case appears to defy all logic* **reason,** judgement, rationality, wisdom, sense, good sense, common sense, sanity. **2** *the logic of their argument* **reasoning,** line, rationale, argument.

□ **logician** noun.

logical ▸ adjective **1** following the rules of logic. **2** using clear, sound reasoning. **3** expected or reasonable under the circumstances.

> SYNONYMS **1** *information displayed in a logical fashion* **reasoned,** rational, sound, cogent, valid, coherent, clear, systematic, orderly, methodical, analytical, consistent. **2** *the logical outcome* **natural,** reasonable, sensible, understandable, predictable, unsurprising, likely. ANTONYMS illogical, unlikely.

□ **logically** adverb.

logistics ▸ noun the detailed organization of a large and complex project or event.
▸ adjective (**logistic**) relating to logistics.
□ **logistic** adjective **logistical** adjective.

logjam ▸ noun a situation in which progress is difficult or impossible.

logo /**loh**-goh/ ▸ noun (plural **logos**) a design or symbol used by an organization to identify its products.

loin ▸ noun **1** the part of the body between the ribs and the hip bones. **2** a joint of meat from this part of an animal. **3** (**loins**) literary a person's sexual organs.

loincloth ▸ noun a piece of cloth wrapped round the hips, worn by men in some hot countries.

loiter ▸ verb (loiters, loitering, loitered) stand around without any obvious purpose.

loll ▸ verb 1 sit, lie, or stand in a lazy, relaxed way. 2 hang loosely.

lollipop ▸ noun a large, flat, rounded boiled sweet on the end of a stick.

lollop ▸ verb (lollops, lolloping, lolloped) move in a series of clumsy bounding steps.

lolly ▸ noun (plural lollies) Brit. informal 1 a lollipop. 2 (also ice lolly) a piece of flavoured ice or ice cream on a stick. 3 money.

lone ▸ adjective 1 having no companions. 2 not having the support of other people.

> SYNONYMS 1 *a lone police officer* **solitary,** single, solo, unaccompanied, sole, isolated. 2 *a lone parent* **single,** unmarried, separated, divorced, widowed.

■ **lone wolf** a person who prefers to be alone.

loneliness ▸ noun the condition of being lonely.

> SYNONYMS 1 *his loneliness was unbearable* **isolation,** friendlessness, abandonment, rejection; N. Amer. lonesomeness. 2 *the enforced loneliness of a prison cell* **solitariness,** solitude, separation, seclusion.
> ANTONYMS popularity, company.

lonely ▸ adjective (lonelier, loneliest) 1 sad because of having no friends or company. 2 (of time) spent alone. 3 (of a place) remote.

> SYNONYMS 1 *I felt very lonely* **isolated,** alone, friendless, with no one to turn to, abandoned, rejected, unloved, unwanted; N. Amer. lonesome. 2 *a lonely road* **deserted,** uninhabited, desolate, solitary, isolated, remote, out of the way, secluded, in the back of beyond, godforsaken; informal in the middle of nowhere.
> ANTONYMS popular, crowded.

loner ▸ noun a person who prefers to be alone.

lonesome ▸ adjective N. Amer. lonely.

long[1] ▸ adjective (longer, longest) 1 of great length in space or time. 2 having or lasting a particular length, distance, or time. 3 (of odds in betting) reflecting a low level of probability.

> SYNONYMS *a long silence* **lengthy,** extended, prolonged, protracted, long-lasting, drawn-out, endless, lingering, interminable.
> ANTONYMS short, brief.

▸ adverb (longer, longest) 1 for a long time. 2 at a distant time. 3 throughout a stated period of time.

■ **long-haul** involving transport over a long distance. **long in the tooth** rather old. **long johns** informal underpants with close-fitting legs extending to the ankles. **long jump** an athletic event in which competitors jump as far as possible. **long-lived** living or lasting a long time. **long shot** a scheme or guess that has only the slightest chance of succeeding. **long-sighted** unable to see things clearly if they are close to the eyes. **long-suffering** patiently putting up with problems or annoying behaviour. **long-winded** long and boring.

long[2] ▸ verb (long for or to do) have a strong wish to do or have something.

> SYNONYMS *I longed for the holidays* **yearn,** pine, ache, hanker for/after, hunger, thirst, itch, be eager, be desperate, crave, dream of; informal be dying.

longboat ▸ noun 1 historical the largest boat carried by a sailing ship. 2 = LONGSHIP.

longbow ▸ noun a large bow formerly used for shooting arrows.

longevity /lon-jev-i-ti/ ▸ noun long life.

longhand ▸ noun ordinary handwriting (as opposed to shorthand, typing, or printing).

longing ▸ noun a strong wish to do or have something.

> SYNONYMS **yearning,** craving, ache, burning, hunger, thirst, hankering; informal yen, itch.

▸ adjective strongly wishing for something. □ **longingly** adverb.

longitude /long-i-tyood/ ▸ noun the distance of a place east or west of the Greenwich meridian, measured in degrees.

longitudinal /long-i-tyoo-di-n'l/ ▸ adjective 1 extending lengthwise. 2 relating to longitude. □ **longitudinally** adverb.

longship ▸ noun a long, narrow warship with oars and a sail, used by the Vikings.

long-standing ▸ adjective having existed for a long time.

> SYNONYMS **well established,** long-established, time-honoured, traditional, abiding, enduring.
> ANTONYMS new, recent.

longways ▸ adverb lengthways.

loo ▸ noun Brit. informal a toilet.

loofah /loo-fuh/ ▸ noun a long, rough object used to wash yourself with in the bath, consisting of the dried inner parts of a tropical fruit.

look ▸ verb 1 direct your eyes in a particular direction. 2 have the appearance of being; seem. 3 face in a particular direction.

SYNONYMS 1 *Mrs Wright looked at him* **glance,** gaze, stare, gape, peer, peep, peek, watch, observe, view, regard, examine, inspect, eye, scan, scrutinize, survey, study, contemplate, take in, ogle; informal take a gander, rubberneck, get a load of; Brit. informal gawp; N. Amer. informal eyeball. **2** *they looked shocked* **seem (to be),** appear (to be), come across/over as. **ANTONYMS** ignore.

▶ **noun 1** an act of looking. **2** appearance. **3** (**looks**) a person's facial appearance. **4** a style or fashion.

SYNONYMS 1 *have a look at this report* **glance,** examination, study, inspection, scrutiny, peep, peek, glimpse; informal eyeful, once-over, squint. **2** *the look on her face* **expression,** mien. **3** *that rustic look* **appearance,** air, aspect, manner, mien, demeanour, impression, effect, ambience, style; informal thing. **4** *this season's look* **fashion,** style; informal thing.

■ **look after** take care of. **look down on** think that you are better than. **look for** try to find. **looking glass** a mirror. **look into** investigate. **look on** watch without getting involved. **look out** be alert for possible trouble. **look up** improve. **look someone/ thing up 1** search for information in a reference book. **2** informal visit or contact a friend. **look up to** have a lot of respect for.

lookalike ▶ **noun** a person who looks very similar to another.

lookout ▶ **noun 1** a place from which you can keep watch or view landscape. **2** a person who keeps watch for danger or trouble.

SYNONYMS 1 *the lookout sighted sails* **watchman,** watch, guard, sentry, sentinel, observer. **2** *that's your lookout* **problem,** concern, business, affair, responsibility, worry; informal pigeon.

loom¹ ▶ **noun** a machine for weaving cloth.

loom² ▶ **verb 1** appear as a vague and threatening shape. **2** (of something bad) seem about to happen.

SYNONYMS 1 *ghostly shapes loomed out of the fog* **emerge,** appear, materialize, reveal itself. **2** *the church loomed above him* **soar,** tower, rise, rear up, hang, overshadow. **3** *without reforms, disaster looms* **be imminent,** be on the horizon, impend, threaten, brew, be just around the corner.

loony informal ▶ **noun** (plural **loonies**) a mad or silly person.
▶ **adjective** mad or silly.

loop ▶ **noun 1** a shape produced by a curve that bends round and crosses itself. **2** a strip of tape or film with the ends joined, which allows sounds or images to be continuously repeated. **3** a complete circuit for an electric current.

SYNONYMS *a loop of rope* **coil,** ring, circle, noose, spiral, curl, bend, curve, arc, twirl, whorl, twist, helix.

▶ **verb** form into or have the shape of a loop.

SYNONYMS 1 *Dave looped rope around their hands* **coil,** wind, twist, snake, spiral, curve, bend, turn. **2** *he looped the cables together* **fasten,** tie, join, connect, knot, bind.

■ **loop the loop** (of an aircraft) fly in a vertical circle.

loophole ▶ **noun** a mistake or piece of vague wording that lets someone avoid obeying a law or keeping to a contract.

SYNONYMS **flaw,** discrepancy, inconsistency, ambiguity, omission, excuse; Brit. get-out.

loopy ▶ **adjective** informal mad or silly.

loose ▶ **adjective 1** not firmly or tightly fixed in place. **2** not fastened or packaged together. **3** not tied up or shut in. **4** (of a garment) not fitting tightly. **5** not exact: *a loose translation.* **6** careless and indiscreet. **7** dated immoral.

SYNONYMS 1 *a loose floorboard* **not secure,** unsecured, unattached, detached, wobbly, unsteady, dangling, free. **2** *she wore her hair loose* **untied,** free, down. **3** *there's a wolf loose* **free,** at large, at liberty, on the loose. **4** *a loose interpretation* **vague,** imprecise, approximate, broad, general, rough, liberal. **5** *a loose jacket* **baggy,** generously cut, slack, roomy, oversized, shapeless, sloppy.
ANTONYMS secure, literal, narrow, tight.

▶ **verb** (**looses, loosing, loosed**) **1** unfasten or set free. **2** (**loose something off**) fire a shot, bullet, etc.

SYNONYMS 1 *the hounds have been loosed* **free,** let loose, release, untie, unchain, unfasten, unleash. **2** *the fingers loosed their hold* **relax,** slacken, loosen.
ANTONYMS confine, tighten.

■ **be at a loose end** have nothing definite to do. **loose cannon** a person who behaves in an unpredictable and potentially harmful way. **loose-leaf** (of a folder) having sheets of paper that can be added or removed.
□ **loosely** adverb **looseness** noun.

❗ Don't confuse **loose** with **lose**, which means 'no longer have' or 'become unable to find'.

loosen ▶ **verb 1** make or become loose. **2** (**loosen up**) warm up in preparation for an activity.

SYNONYMS 1 *you simply loosen two screws* **undo,** slacken, unfasten, detach, release, disconnect. **2** *her fingers loosened* **slacken,** become loose, let go, ease. **3** *Philip loosened his grip* **weaken,** relax, slacken, loose.
ANTONYMS tighten.

loot ▸ verb steal goods from empty buildings during a war, riot, etc.

SYNONYMS *troops looted the cathedral* **plunder,** pillage, ransack, sack, rifle, rob, strip, gut.

▸ noun **1** goods stolen from empty buildings during a war, riot, etc. **2** goods stolen by a thief. **3** informal money.

SYNONYMS *a bag full of loot* **booty,** spoils, plunder, stolen goods, contraband; informal **swag.**

□ **looter** noun.

lop ▸ verb (**lops, lopping, lopped**) cut off a branch or limb from a tree or body.
■ **lop-eared** (of an animal) having drooping ears.

lope ▸ verb (**lopes, loping, loped**) run with long, relaxed strides.

lopsided ▸ adjective with one side lower or smaller than the other.

loquacious /luh-**kway**-shuhss/ ▸ adjective formal talkative.
□ **loquacity** noun.

lord ▸ noun **1** a nobleman. **2** (**Lord**) a title given to certain British peers or high officials. **3** (**the Lords**) the House of Lords. **4** a master or ruler. **5** (**Lord**) a name for God or Jesus.

SYNONYMS 1 *lords and ladies* **noble,** nobleman, peer, aristocrat. **2** *it is my duty to obey my lord's wishes* **master,** ruler, leader, chief, superior, monarch, sovereign, king, emperor, prince, governor, commander.
ANTONYMS commoner, servant, inferior.

■ **lord it over** act in an arrogant and bullying way towards someone. **Lord Mayor** the title of the mayor in London and some other large cities.

lordly ▸ adjective proud or superior.

Lordship ▸ noun (**His/Your Lordship**) a form of address to a judge, bishop, or nobleman.

lore ▸ noun all the traditions and knowledge relating to a particular subject.

lorgnette (or **lorgnettes**) /lor-**nyet**/ ▸ noun a pair of glasses held by a long handle at one side.

lorry ▸ noun (plural **lorries**) Brit. a large motor vehicle for transporting goods.

lose ▸ verb (**loses, losing, lost**) **1** have something or someone taken away from you; no longer have. **2** become unable to find. **3** fail to win a game or contest. **4** earn less money than you are spending. **5** waste an opportunity. **6** (**be lost**) be destroyed or killed. **7** escape from. **8** (**lose yourself in** or **be lost in**) be or become deeply involved in. **9** (of a clock or watch) become slow.

SYNONYMS 1 *I've lost my watch* **mislay,** misplace, be unable to find, lose track of. **2** *he lost his pursuers* **escape from,** evade, elude, dodge, avoid, give someone the slip, shake off, throw off, leave behind, outdistance, outrun. **3** *you've lost your opportunity* **waste,** squander, let pass, miss; informal pass up, blow. **4** *they always lose at football* **be defeated,** be/get beaten; informal come a cropper, go down.
ANTONYMS find, seize, win.

■ **lose out** not get a fair chance or share.

❗ Don't confuse **lose** with **loose,** which means 'not fixed in place or tied up'.

loser ▸ noun **1** the person who loses a contest. **2** informal a person who is generally unsuccessful in life.

SYNONYMS **failure,** underachiever, dead loss, write-off, has-been; informal also-ran, non-starter, no-hoper.
ANTONYMS success.

loss ▸ noun **1** the losing of something or someone. **2** a person or thing that is lost. **3** the feeling of sadness after losing a valued person or thing.

SYNONYMS 1 *the loss of the papers* **mislaying,** misplacement, destruction, theft. **2** *loss of earnings* **forfeiture,** diminution, erosion, reduction, depletion. **3** *the loss of her husband* **death,** demise, passing away, end. **4** *British losses in the war* **casualty,** fatality, victim, dead. **5** *a loss of £15,000* **deficit,** debit, debt.
ANTONYMS recovery, profit.

■ **at a loss 1** uncertain or puzzled. **2** losing more money than is being made. **loss-leader** a product sold at a very low price to attract customers.

lost past and past participle of **LOSE.**

SYNONYMS 1 *her lost keys* **missing,** mislaid, misplaced, stolen. **2** *I think we're lost* **off course,** going round in circles, adrift, at sea. **3** *a lost opportunity* **missed,** wasted, squandered, gone by the board; informal down the drain. **4** *lost traditions* **bygone,** past, former, old, vanished, forgotten, dead. **5** *lost species and habitats* **extinct,** died out, defunct, vanished, gone, destroyed, wiped out, exterminated. **6** *lost in thought* **engrossed,** absorbed, rapt, immersed, deep, intent, engaged, wrapped up.
ANTONYMS current, living, saved.

■ **be lost for words** be so surprised or upset that you cannot think what to say. **be lost**

on not be noticed or understood by. **lost cause** something that has no chance of success.

lot ▸ pronoun & adverb (**a lot** or informal **lots**) a large number or amount.

SYNONYMS **1** *a lot of money* | *lots of friends* **a large amount,** a good/great deal, an abundance, a wealth, a profusion, plenty, many, a great many, a large number, a considerable number; informal hundreds, loads, masses, heaps, piles, stacks, tons; Brit. informal a shedload, lashings. **2** *I work in pastels a lot* **a great deal,** a good deal, much, often, frequently, regularly.
ANTONYMS a little, a few.

▸ noun **1** an item or set of items for sale at an auction. **2** informal a particular group of people. **3** (**the lot**) informal the whole number or quantity. **4** a method of deciding something by chance in which one piece is chosen from a number of marked pieces of paper. **5** a person's luck or situation in life. **6** chiefly N. Amer. a plot of land.

SYNONYMS **1** *an auction lot* **item,** article, batch, group, bundle, parcel. **2** *what do your lot think?* **group,** crowd, circle, crew; informal bunch, gang, mob. **3** *his lot in life* **fate,** destiny, fortune, situation, circumstances, plight, predicament.

✔ **a lot** is a two-word phrase; don't spell it as one word.

loth ➙ LOATH.

Lothario /luh-**thah**-ri-oh/ ▸ noun (plural **Lotharios**) a man who has many casual sexual relationships with women.

lotion ▸ noun a creamy liquid put on the skin as a medicine or cosmetic.

SYNONYMS **ointment,** cream, balm, rub, moisturizer, lubricant, embrocation.

lottery ▸ noun (plural **lotteries**) **1** a way of raising money by selling numbered tickets and giving prizes to the holders of numbers drawn at random. **2** something whose success is controlled by luck.

SYNONYMS **raffle,** (prize) draw, sweepstake, sweep, tombola, lotto, pools.

lotus ▸ noun a kind of large water lily.
■ **lotus position** a cross-legged position with the feet resting on the thighs, used in meditation.

louche /loosh/ ▸ adjective having a bad reputation but still attractive.

loud ▸ adjective **1** producing a lot of noise. **2** expressed forcefully. **3** very brightly coloured and in bad taste.

SYNONYMS **1** *loud music* **noisy,** blaring, booming, deafening, roaring, thunderous, ear-splitting, powerful, stentorian; Music forte, fortissimo. **2** *loud*

complaints **vociferous,** clamorous, insistent, vehement, emphatic. **3** *a loud T-shirt* **garish,** gaudy, lurid, showy, ostentatious, vulgar, tasteless; informal flashy.
ANTONYMS quiet, gentle, sober, tasteful.

□ **loudness** noun.

loudhailer ▸ noun an electronic device for making the voice louder.

loudly ▸ adverb in a loud way.

SYNONYMS **at high volume,** at the top of your voice, noisily, stridently, vociferously, shrilly.
ANTONYMS quietly.

loudspeaker ▸ noun a device that converts electrical impulses into sound.

lough /lok, lokh/ ▸ noun Irish a loch.

lounge ▸ verb (**lounges, lounging, lounged**) lie, sit, or stand in a relaxed way.

SYNONYMS *lounging around* **laze,** lie, loll, recline, relax, rest, take it easy, sprawl, slump, slouch, loaf, idle, do nothing.

▸ noun **1** Brit. a sitting room. **2** a room in a hotel, airport, etc. in which people can relax or wait.

SYNONYMS *sitting in the lounge* **living room,** sitting room, front room, drawing room.

■ **lounge bar** Brit. a bar in a pub or hotel that is more comfortable than the public bar. **lounge suit** Brit. a man's ordinary suit.

lounger ▸ noun an outdoor chair that you can lie back in.

lour (or **lower**) (*rhymes with* flour) ▸ verb **1** (of the sky) look dark and threatening. **2** scowl.

louse ▸ noun **1** (plural **lice**) a small insect which lives as a parasite on animals or plants. **2** (plural **louses**) informal an unpleasant person.

lousy ▸ adjective (**lousier, lousiest**) informal very bad.

lout ▸ noun a rude or aggressive man or boy.

SYNONYMS **hooligan,** ruffian, thug, boor, oaf, rowdy; informal tough, bruiser; Brit. informal yob, yobbo.
ANTONYMS gentleman.

□ **loutish** adjective.

louvre /**loo**-ver/ (US spelling **louver**) ▸ noun each of a set of slanting slats fixed at intervals in a door, shutter, etc. to allow air or light through.

lovable (or **loveable**) ▸ adjective easy to love or feel affection for.

lovage ▸ noun a herb used in cookery.

love ▸ noun **1** a very strong feeling of affection. **2** a strong feeling of affection linked with sexual attraction. **3** a great interest and pleasure in something. **4** a person or thing that you love. **5** (in tennis, squash, etc.) a score of zero.

> SYNONYMS **1** *a friendship that blossomed into love* **infatuation,** adoration, attachment, devotion, fondness, tenderness, warmth, intimacy, passion, desire, lust, yearning, besottedness. **2** *her love of fashion* **liking,** taste, passion, zeal, zest, enthusiasm, keenness, fondness, weakness, partiality, predilection, penchant. **3** *their love for their fellow human beings* **compassion,** care, regard, concern, altruism, unselfishness, philanthropy, benevolence, humanity. **4** *he was her one true love* **beloved,** loved one, dearest, darling, sweetheart, sweet, angel, honey.
> ANTONYMS hatred.

▸ **verb** (**loves, loving, loved**) **1** feel love for. **2** like very much.

> SYNONYMS **1** *she loves him dearly* **be in love with,** be infatuated with, be smitten with, be besotted with, adore, idolize, worship, think the world of, be devoted to, dote on, care for, hold dear; informal be mad/crazy/nuts/wild/potty about, carry a torch for. **2** *Laura loved painting* **like,** delight in, enjoy, have a passion for, take pleasure in, have a weakness for, be partial to, be taken with; informal have a thing about, be mad/crazy/nuts/wild/potty about, be hooked on.
> ANTONYMS hate.

■ **love affair** a romantic or sexual relationship between two people who are not married to each other. **love child** a child born to parents who are not married to each other. **make love** have sex.
□ **loveless** adjective.

lovelorn ▸ **adjective** unhappy because you love someone who does not feel the same way about you.

lovely ▸ **adjective** (**lovelier, loveliest**) **1** very beautiful. **2** very pleasant.

> SYNONYMS **1** *a lovely young woman* **beautiful,** pretty, attractive, good-looking, handsome, adorable, enchanting, gorgeous, alluring, ravishing, glamorous; Scottish & N. English bonny; informal tasty, stunning, drop-dead gorgeous; Brit. informal fit; N. Amer. informal cute, foxy. **2** *a lovely view* **scenic,** picturesque, pleasing, magnificent, stunning, splendid. **3** *we had a lovely day* **delightful,** very pleasant, very nice, marvellous, wonderful, sublime, superb; informal terrific, fabulous, heavenly, amazing, glorious.
> ANTONYMS ugly, horrible.

□ **loveliness** noun.

lovemaking ▸ **noun** sex and other sexual activity.

lover ▸ **noun** **1** a person having a sexual or romantic relationship with someone. **2** a person who enjoys a particular thing.

> SYNONYMS **1** *she had a secret lover* **boyfriend, girlfriend,** beloved, sweetheart, mistress, partner; informal bit on the side, fancy man, fancy woman. **2** *a dog lover* **devotee,** admirer, fan, enthusiast, aficionado; informal buff, nut, ...head.

lovesick ▸ **adjective** unable to think clearly or act normally as a result of being in love.

loving ▸ **adjective** showing love or great care.

> SYNONYMS **affectionate,** fond, devoted, adoring, doting, caring, tender, warm, close, amorous, passionate.
> ANTONYMS cold, cruel.

low¹ ▸ **adjective** **1** not high or tall or far above the ground. **2** below average in amount, extent, or strength. **3** not good or important. **4** (of a sound) deep or quiet. **5** depressed or without energy. **6** not honest or moral.

> SYNONYMS **1** *a low fence* **short,** small, little, squat, stubby, stunted. **2** *low prices* **cheap,** economical, moderate, reasonable, affordable, modest, bargain, bargain-basement, rock-bottom. **3** *supplies were low* **scarce,** scant, meagre, sparse, few, little, reduced, depleted, diminished. **4** *low quality* **inferior,** substandard, poor, low-grade, unsatisfactory. **5** *a low voice* **quiet,** soft, faint, gentle, muted, subdued, muffled, hushed. **6** *a low note* **bass,** low-pitched, deep, rumbling, booming, sonorous. **7** *she was feeling low* **depressed,** dejected, despondent, downhearted, downcast, down, miserable, dispirited, flat; informal fed up, down in the dumps, blue.
> ANTONYMS high, expensive, plentiful, superior, loud, cheerful, lively.

▸ **noun** **1** a low point or level. **2** an area of low atmospheric pressure.
▸ **adverb** (of a sound) at a low pitch.
■ **Low Church** the section of the Church of England that places little emphasis on ritual and the authority of bishops and priests. **the low-down** informal the important facts about something. **lowest common denominator** the lowest number that the bottom number of a group of fractions can be divided into exactly. **low-key** not elaborate or showy. **low life** dishonest or immoral people or activities. **low tide** the time when the sea is furthest out.

low² ▸ **verb** (of a cow) moo.

lowbrow ▸ **adjective** not intellectual or interested in culture.

lower¹ ▸ **adjective** **1** less high. **2** (in place names) situated to the south.

SYNONYMS **1** *the lower house of parliament* **subordinate,** inferior, lesser, junior, minor, secondary, subsidiary, subservient. **2** *her lower lip* **bottom,** bottommost, nether, under. **3** *a lower price* **cheaper,** reduced, cut.
ANTONYMS upper, higher, increased.

▶ verb (lowers, lowering, lowered) **1** make or become lower. **2** move downwards. **3** (lower yourself) behave in a way that makes other people lose respect for you.

SYNONYMS **1** *she lowered the mask* **let down,** take down, drop, let fall. **2** *lower your voice* **soften,** modulate, quieten, hush, tone down, muffle, turn down. **3** *they are lowering their prices* **reduce,** decrease, lessen, bring down, cut, slash.
ANTONYMS raise, increase.

■ lower case small letters as opposed to capitals.

lower² ➡ LOUR.

lowland (or lowlands) ▶ noun **1** low-lying country. **2** (the Lowlands) the part of Scotland lying south and east of the Highlands.
□ lowlander noun.

lowly ▶ adjective (lowlier, lowliest) low in status or importance.

SYNONYMS **humble,** low, low-ranking, common, ordinary, plain, modest, simple, obscure.
ANTONYMS aristocratic, exalted.

□ lowliness noun.

loyal ▶ adjective firm and faithful in your support for a person, organization, etc.

SYNONYMS **faithful,** true, devoted, constant, steadfast, staunch, dependable, reliable, trustworthy, trusty, patriotic.
ANTONYMS disloyal.

□ loyally adverb.

loyalist ▶ noun **1** a person who remains loyal to the established ruler or government. **2** (Loyalist) a person who believes that Northern Ireland should remain part of Great Britain.
□ loyalism noun.

loyalty ▶ noun (plural loyalties) **1** the state of being loyal. **2** a strong feeling of support.

SYNONYMS **allegiance,** faithfulness, obedience, adherence, devotion, steadfastness, staunchness, dedication, commitment, patriotism.
ANTONYMS disloyalty.

lozenge ▶ noun **1** a tablet of medicine that is sucked to soothe a sore throat. **2** a diamond-shaped figure.

LP ▶ abbreviation long-playing (record).

LSD ▶ noun lysergic acid diethylamide, a drug that causes hallucinations.

Ltd ▶ abbreviation Brit. Limited.

lubricant ▶ noun a substance, e.g. oil, for lubricating part of a machine.

lubricate /loo-bri-kayt/ ▶ verb (lubricates, lubricating, lubricated) apply oil or grease to machinery so that it moves easily.
□ lubrication noun.

lubricious /loo-bri-shuhss/ ▶ adjective formal referring to sexual matters in a rude or offensive way.

lucid /loo-sid/ ▶ adjective **1** easy to understand; clear. **2** able to think clearly.

SYNONYMS **rational,** sane, in possession of your faculties, compos mentis, clear-headed, sober; informal all there.
ANTONYMS confused.

□ lucidity noun lucidly adverb.

Lucifer /loo-si-fer/ ▶ noun the Devil.

luck ▶ noun **1** good things that happen by chance. **2** chance considered as a force that causes good or bad things to happen.

SYNONYMS **1** *with luck you'll make it* **good fortune,** good luck, stroke of luck; informal lucky break. **2** *I wish you luck* **success,** prosperity, good fortune, good luck. **3** *it is a matter of luck whether it hits or misses* **fortune,** fate, serendipity, chance, accident, a twist of fate.
ANTONYMS bad luck, misfortune.

luckily ▶ adverb it is fortunate that.

SYNONYMS **fortunately,** happily, providentially, by good fortune, as luck would have it, mercifully, thankfully.
ANTONYMS unluckily.

luckless ▶ adjective unlucky.

lucky ▶ adjective (luckier, luckiest) having, bringing, or resulting from good luck.

SYNONYMS **1** *the lucky winner* **fortunate,** in luck, favoured, charmed, successful; Brit. informal jammy. **2** *a lucky escape* **providential,** fortunate, timely, opportune, serendipitous, chance, fortuitous, accidental.
ANTONYMS unlucky.

■ lucky dip Brit. a game in which prizes are hidden in a container for people to pick out at random.

lucrative ▶ adjective making a large profit.

SYNONYMS **profitable,** gainful, remunerative, moneymaking, well paid, rewarding, worthwhile.
ANTONYMS unprofitable.

lucre /loo-ker/ ▶ noun money.

Luddite /lud-dyt/ ▶ noun a person who is opposed to new technology.

ludicrous /loo-di-kruhss/ ▶ adjective absurd; ridiculous.

SYNONYMS **absurd,** ridiculous, farcical, laughable, risible, preposterous, mad, insane, idiotic, stupid, asinine,

nonsensical; informal crazy.
ANTONYMS sensible.

□ **ludicrously** adverb.

ludo ▶ noun Brit. a board game in which players move counters according to throws of a dice.

lug¹ ▶ verb (**lugs, lugging, lugged**) carry or drag with great effort.

lug² ▶ noun 1 informal an ear. 2 a projection on an object for carrying it or fixing it in place.

luggage ▶ noun suitcases or other bags for a traveller's belongings.

SYNONYMS **baggage**, bags, suitcases, cases.

lugubrious /luu-**goo**-bri-uhss/ ▶ adjective sad and gloomy.

lukewarm ▶ adjective 1 only slightly warm. 2 unenthusiastic.

SYNONYMS 1 *lukewarm coffee* **tepid**, warmish, at room temperature. 2 *a lukewarm response* **indifferent**, cool, half-hearted, apathetic, unenthusiastic, tepid, offhand.
ANTONYMS hot, cold, warm.

lull ▶ verb 1 make someone relaxed or calm. 2 make someone feel safe or confident, even if they are at risk of something bad.

SYNONYMS *the sound of the bells lulled us to sleep* **soothe**, calm, hush, rock to sleep.
ANTONYMS waken, arouse.

▶ noun a quiet period between times of activity.

SYNONYMS 1 *a lull in the fighting* **pause**, respite, interval, break, suspension, breathing space; informal let-up, breather. 2 *the lull before the storm* **calm**, stillness, quiet, tranquillity, peace, silence, hush.
ANTONYMS agitation, activity.

lullaby ▶ noun (plural **lullabies**) a soothing song sung to send a child to sleep.

lumbago /lum-**bay**-goh/ ▶ noun pain in the lower back.

lumbar ▶ adjective relating to the lower back.

lumber ▶ noun 1 Brit. disused furniture. 2 chiefly N. Amer. timber sawn into rough planks.
▶ verb (**lumbers, lumbering, lumbered**) 1 Brit. informal give someone an unwanted responsibility. 2 move in a heavy, awkward way.

SYNONYMS 1 *elephants lumbered past* **trundle**, stumble, lurch, shamble, shuffle, trudge, clump. 2 (**lumbering**) **clumsy**, awkward, slow, blundering, bumbling, ponderous; informal clodhopping.

lumberjack ▶ noun a person who cuts down trees and saws them into logs.

luminary /**loo**-mi-nuh-ri/ ▶ noun (plural

luminaries) an important or influential person.

luminescence ▶ noun light given off by a substance that has not been heated, e.g. fluorescent light.
□ **luminescent** adjective.

luminous ▶ adjective bright or shining, especially in the dark.
□ **luminosity** noun **luminously** adverb.

lump ▶ noun 1 an irregularly shaped piece of something hard or solid. 2 a swelling under the skin.

SYNONYMS 1 *a lump of coal* **chunk**, hunk, piece, block, wedge, slab, ball, knob, clod. 2 *a lump on his head* **swelling**, bump, bulge, protuberance, protrusion, growth, tumour.

▶ verb (**lump together**) casually group different people or things together.

SYNONYMS *it is convenient to lump them together* **combine**, put, group, bunch, throw.

■ **lump it** informal put up with something whether you like it or not. **lump sum** a single payment as opposed to a number of smaller payments.
□ **lumpy** adjective.

lumpen ▶ adjective 1 lumpy and misshapen. 2 stupid or loutish.

lunacy ▶ noun 1 insanity; mental illness. 2 great stupidity.

lunar ▶ adjective having to do with the moon.
■ **lunar eclipse** an eclipse in which the moon is hidden by the earth's shadow.

lunatic ▶ noun 1 a person who is mentally ill. 2 a very foolish person.

SYNONYMS *he drives like a lunatic* **maniac**, madman, madwoman, fool, idiot; informal loony, nutcase; Brit. informal nutter; N. Amer. informal screwball.

▶ adjective extremely foolish or eccentric.

SYNONYMS *a lunatic idea* **stupid**, foolish, idiotic, absurd, ridiculous, ludicrous, preposterous; informal crazy, mad; Brit. informal barmy, daft.
ANTONYMS sensible.

lunch ▶ noun a meal eaten in the middle of the day.
▶ verb eat lunch.

luncheon ▶ noun formal lunch.

lung ▶ noun each of a pair of organs in the chest into which humans and animals draw air when breathing.

lunge ▶ noun a sudden forward movement of the body.

SYNONYMS *Darren made a lunge at his attacker* **thrust**, dive, rush, charge, grab.

▶ verb (**lunges, lunging** or **lungeing, lunged**) make a sudden forward movement.

SYNONYMS *he lunged at Finn with a knife* **thrust,** dive, spring, launch yourself, rush.

lupin ▸ noun a plant with spikes of tall flowers.

lupine /**loo**-pyn/ ▸ adjective resembling a wolf.

lurch ▸ verb make a sudden, unsteady movement.

SYNONYMS **1** *he lurched into the kitchen* **stagger,** stumble, sway, reel, roll, totter. **2** *the car lurched to the left* **swing,** list, roll, pitch, veer, swerve.

▸ noun a sudden, unsteady movement.
■ **leave someone in the lurch** leave someone in a difficult situation without help or support.

lurcher ▸ noun Brit. a dog that is a cross between a greyhound and a retriever, collie, or sheepdog.

lure ▸ verb (**lures, luring, lured**) tempt someone to do something by offering a reward.

SYNONYMS *consumers are frequently lured into debt* **tempt,** entice, attract, induce, coax, persuade, inveigle, seduce. ANTONYMS deter, put off.

▸ noun **1** the attractive and tempting qualities of something. **2** a type of bait used in fishing or hunting.

SYNONYMS *the lure of the stage* **temptation,** attraction, pull, draw, appeal, inducement, allure, fascination, interest, glamour.

lurex ▸ noun trademark yarn or fabric containing a glittering metallic thread.

lurid ▸ adjective **1** unpleasantly bright in colour. **2** (of a description) deliberately containing many shocking details.
□ **luridly** adverb.

lurk ▸ verb wait in hiding to attack someone.

SYNONYMS **skulk,** loiter, lie in wait, hide.

luscious ▸ adjective **1** having a pleasantly rich, sweet taste. **2** (of a woman) very attractive.

lush ▸ adjective **1** (of plants) growing thickly and strongly. **2** rich or luxurious.

SYNONYMS **1** *lush vegetation* **profuse,** rich, abundant, luxuriant, riotous, vigorous, dense, thick, rampant. **2** *a lush apartment* **luxurious,** sumptuous, palatial, opulent, lavish, elaborate, extravagant, fancy; informal plush, posh, swanky; Brit. informal swish; N. Amer. informal swank. ANTONYMS sparse, shrivelled, austere.

▸ noun N. Amer. informal a drunkard.
□ **lushly** adverb **lushness** noun.

lust ▸ noun **1** strong sexual desire. **2** a passionate desire for something.

SYNONYMS **1** *his lust for her* **desire,** longing, passion, libido, sex drive, sexuality, lechery, lasciviousness; informal horniness; Brit. informal randiness. **2** *a lust for power* **greed,** desire, craving, eagerness, longing, yearning, hunger, thirst, appetite, hankering. ANTONYMS dread, aversion.

▸ verb feel lust.
□ **lustful** adjective.

lustre (US spelling **luster**) ▸ noun **1** a soft glow or shine. **2** prestige or honour.
□ **lustrous** adjective.

lusty ▸ adjective (**lustier, lustiest**) healthy and strong.
□ **lustily** adverb.

lute ▸ noun a stringed instrument with a long neck and a rounded body, which you play by plucking.

lutetium /loo-**tee**-shi-uhm/ ▸ noun a rare silvery-white metallic element.

luxuriant /lug-z**hoor**-i-uhnt/ ▸ adjective growing thickly and strongly.
□ **luxuriance** noun **luxuriantly** adverb.

luxuriate /lug-z**hoor**-i-ayt/ ▸ verb (**luxuriates, luxuriating, luxuriated**) (**luxuriate in**) relax and enjoy something very pleasant.

luxurious ▸ adjective very comfortable or elegant and expensive.

SYNONYMS **opulent,** sumptuous, grand, palatial, magnificent, extravagant, fancy; Brit. upmarket; informal plush, posh, classy, swanky; Brit. informal swish; N. Amer. informal swank. ANTONYMS plain, basic.

□ **luxuriously** adverb.

luxury ▸ noun (plural **luxuries**) **1** comfortable and expensive living or surroundings. **2** something that is expensive and enjoyable but not essential.

SYNONYMS **1** *we'll live in luxury* **opulence,** sumptuousness, grandeur, magnificence, splendour, affluence. **2** *a TV is his only luxury* **indulgence,** extravagance, treat, extra, frill. ANTONYMS simplicity, necessity.

lychee /**ly**-chee/ ▸ noun a small, sweet fruit with thin, rough skin.

lychgate ▸ noun a roofed gateway to a churchyard.

Lycra ▸ noun trademark an elastic fabric used for close-fitting clothing.

lye ▸ noun an alkaline solution used for washing or cleaning.

lying present participle of LIE[1], LIE[2].

SYNONYMS **1** *she was no good at lying* **dishonesty,** fabrication, fibbing, perjury, untruthfulness, mendacity, misrepresentation, deceit, duplicity.

2 *he was a lying womanizer* **dishonest,** false, untruthful, mendacious, deceitful, duplicitous, double-dealing, two-faced. ANTONYMS honesty, honest.

lymph ▸ noun a colourless fluid in the body that contains white blood cells.
■ **lymph node** (or **lymph gland**) each of a number of small swellings where lymph is filtered.
□ **lymphatic** adjective.

lymphocyte /lim-fuh-syt/ ▸ noun a type of white blood cell.

lynch ▸ verb (of a group) kill someone believed to be guilty of a crime without a legal trial.

lynchpin ➝ LINCHPIN.

lynx ▸ noun a wild cat with a short tail and tufted ears.

lyre ▸ noun a stringed instrument like a small harp, used in ancient Greece.

lyric ▸ noun **1** (also **lyrics**) the words of a song. **2** a poem that expresses the writer's thoughts and emotions.
▸ adjective (of poetry) expressing the writer's thoughts and emotions.

lyrical ▸ adjective **1** (of writing or music) expressing the writer's emotions in an imaginative and beautiful way. **2** relating to the words of a popular song.

SYNONYMS **1** *a subtle, lyrical film* **expressive,** emotional, deeply felt, personal, passionate. **2** *she was lyrical about her success* **enthusiastic,** effusive, rapturous, ecstatic, euphoric.
ANTONYMS unenthusiastic.

■ **wax lyrical** talk about something in a very enthusiastic way.
□ **lyrically** adverb.

lyricism ▸ noun expression of emotion in writing or music in an imaginative and beautiful way.

lyricist ▸ noun a person who writes the words to popular songs.

Mm

M (or **m**) ▶ noun (plural **Ms** or **M's**) **1** the thirteenth letter of the alphabet. **2** the Roman numeral for 1,000.
▶ abbreviation **1** Monsieur. **2** motorway. **3** (m) metres. **4** (m) miles. **5** (m) millions.

MA ▶ abbreviation Master of Arts.

ma'am ▶ noun madam.

mac ▶ noun Brit. informal a mackintosh.

macabre /muh-**kah**-bruh/ ▶ adjective disturbing and horrifying because concerned with death and injury.

macadam ▶ noun broken stone used for surfacing roads and paths.

macadamia ▶ noun the round edible nut of an Australian tree.

macaque /muh-**kak**/ ▶ noun a monkey with a long face and cheek pouches for holding food.

macaroni ▶ noun pasta in the form of narrow tubes.

macaroon ▶ noun a light biscuit made with ground almonds or coconut.

macaw /muh-**kaw**/ ▶ noun a brightly coloured parrot found in Central and South America.

mace¹ ▶ noun **1** a decorated stick carried by an official such as a mayor. **2** (in the past) a heavy club with a spiked metal head.

mace² ▶ noun a spice made from the dried outer covering of nutmeg.

Macedonian /mass-i-**doh**-ni-uhn/ ▶ noun a person from the republic of Macedonia (formerly part of Yugoslavia), ancient Macedonia, or the modern Greek region of Macedonia.
▶ adjective relating to Macedonia.

macerate /**mass**-uh-rayt/ ▶ verb (**macerates, macerating, macerated**) soften food by soaking it in a liquid.
◻ **maceration** noun.

Mach /mak/ ▶ noun (**Mach 1, Mach 2**, etc.) the speed of sound, twice the speed of sound, etc.

machete /muh-**shet**-i/ ▶ noun a broad, heavy knife used as a tool or weapon.

Machiavellian /ma-ki-uh-**vel**-li-uhn/ ▶ adjective using cunning and underhand methods to get what you want.

machinations /ma-shi-**nay**-shuhnz/ ▶ plural noun plots and scheming.

machine ▶ noun **1** a mechanical device for performing a particular task. **2** an efficient group of influential people.

> SYNONYMS **1** device, appliance, apparatus, engine, gadget, mechanism. **2** *an efficient publicity machine* **organization,** system, structure, machinery; informal set-up.

▶ verb (**machines, machining, machined**) make or work on something with a machine.
■ **machine gun** a gun that fires many bullets in rapid succession. **machine-readable** in a form that a computer can process.

machinery ▶ noun **1** machines as a whole, or the parts of a machine. **2** an organized system or structure.

> SYNONYMS **1** equipment, apparatus, plant, hardware, gear, gadgetry, technology. **2** *the machinery of local government* **workings,** organization, system, structure, institution; informal set-up.

machinist ▶ noun a person who operates a machine or makes machinery.

machismo /muh-**kiz**-moh/ ▶ noun strong or aggressive male pride.

macho /**mach**-oh/ ▶ adjective showing aggressive pride in being male.

> SYNONYMS **manly**, male, masculine, virile, red-blooded; informal butch, laddish.
> ANTONYMS wimpish.

mackerel ▶ noun an edible sea fish.

mackintosh (or **macintosh**) ▶ noun Brit. a full-length waterproof coat.

macramé /muh-**krah**-mi/ ▶ noun the craft of knotting cord to make decorative articles.

macrobiotic ▶ adjective (of diet) consisting of foods grown or produced without the use of chemicals.

macrocosm ▶ noun the whole of a complex structure, contrasted with a small or representative part of it (a microcosm).

mad ▶ adjective (**madder, maddest**) **1** seriously mentally ill. **2** very foolish.

m

3 done without thought or control. **4** informal very enthusiastic about something. **5** informal very angry.

SYNONYMS **1** *he was killed by his mad brother* **insane,** out of your mind, deranged, demented, crazed, lunatic, unbalanced, unhinged; informal crazy, mental, off your head, round the bend; Brit. informal barmy, crackers, barking (mad), potty, round the twist. **2** *I'm still mad at him* **angry,** furious, infuriated, enraged, fuming, incensed, beside yourself; informal livid, spare; N. Amer. informal sore. **3** *some mad scheme* **foolish,** insane, stupid, lunatic, idiotic, absurd, silly, asinine, wild; informal crazy, crackpot; Brit. informal daft. **4** *he's mad about jazz* **passionate,** fanatical, ardent, fervent, devoted to, infatuated with, in love with; informal crazy, dotty, nuts, wild, hooked on; Brit. informal potty; N. Amer. informal nutso. **5** *it was a mad dash to get ready* **frenzied,** frantic, frenetic, feverish, hysterical, wild, hectic, manic. ANTONYMS sane, pleased, sensible, indifferent, calm.

■ **mad cow disease** BSE.

Madagascan ▶ noun a person from Madagascar.
▶ adjective relating to Madagascar.

madam ▶ noun **1** a polite form of address for a woman. **2** Brit. informal a bossy or cheeky girl. **3** a woman who runs a brothel.

Madame /muh-**dam**/ ▶ noun (plural **Mesdames** /may-**dam**/) a form of address for a French woman.

madcap ▶ adjective acting without thought; reckless.

madden ▶ verb make someone mad or very annoyed.

SYNONYMS **infuriate,** exasperate, irritate, incense, anger, enrage, provoke, make someone see red; informal aggravate, make someone's blood boil; Brit. informal nark; N. Amer. informal tee off, tick off. ANTONYMS calm.

madder ▶ noun a red dye obtained from the roots of a plant.

made past and past participle of MAKE.

Madeira ▶ noun a strong sweet white wine from the island of Madeira.
■ **Madeira cake** Brit. a rich kind of sponge cake.

Mademoiselle /ma-duh-mwah-**zel**/ ▶ noun (plural **Mesdemoiselles** /may-duh-mwa-**zel**/) a form of address for an unmarried French woman.

madly ▶ adverb **1** in a mad way. **2** with extreme intensity. **3** very.

SYNONYMS **1** *she was smiling madly* **insanely,** wildly; informal crazily. **2** *it was*

fun, hurtling madly downhill **furiously,** hurriedly, speedily, energetically; informal like mad, like crazy. **3** *he loved her madly* **intensely,** fervently, wildly, to distraction. **4** *his job isn't madly exciting* **very,** tremendously, wildly, all that, hugely; informal awfully, terribly. ANTONYMS sanely, slowly, slightly.

madman (**madwoman**) ▶ noun **1** a person who is mentally ill. **2** a foolish or reckless person.

SYNONYMS **lunatic,** maniac, psychotic, psychopath; informal loony, nut, nutcase, head case; Brit. informal nutter; N. Amer. informal screwball.

madness ▶ noun **1** the state of being mad. **2** extremely foolish behaviour. **3** wild or chaotic activity.

SYNONYMS **1** *today madness is called mental illness* **insanity,** mental illness, dementia, derangement, lunacy, mania, psychosis. **2** *it would be madness to do otherwise* **folly,** foolishness, idiocy, stupidity, insanity, lunacy. **3** *it's absolute madness in here* **bedlam,** mayhem, chaos, pandemonium, uproar, turmoil, all hell broken loose; N. Amer. three-ring circus. ANTONYMS sanity, sense.

Madonna ▶ noun (**the Madonna**) the Virgin Mary.

madrigal ▶ noun a 16th- or 17th-century song for several voices without instrumental accompaniment.

maelstrom /**mayl**-struhm/ ▶ noun **1** a situation of confusion or upheaval. **2** a powerful whirlpool.

maestro /**my**-stroh/ ▶ noun (plural **maestros**) a famous and talented man, especially a classical musician.

Mafia ▶ noun **1** (**the Mafia**) an international criminal organization originating in Sicily. **2** (**mafia**) a powerful group who secretly influence matters.

Mafioso /ma-fi-**oh**-soh/ ▶ noun (plural **Mafiosi** /ma-fi-**oh**-si/) a member of the Mafia.

magazine ▶ noun **1** a weekly or monthly publication that contains articles and pictures. **2** the part of a gun that holds bullets before they are fired. **3** a store for weapons, ammunition, and explosives.

SYNONYMS **journal,** periodical, supplement, colour supplement; informal glossy, mag, 'zine.

magenta ▶ noun a light crimson.

maggot ▶ noun the soft-bodied larva of a fly or other insect.

Magi /**may**-jy/ ▶ plural noun the three wise men from the East who brought gifts to the infant Jesus.

magic ▸ noun **1** the use of mysterious or supernatural forces to influence events. **2** conjuring tricks performed to entertain people. **3** a mysterious or wonderful quality.

> SYNONYMS **1** *do you believe in magic?* **sorcery,** witchcraft, wizardry, necromancy, enchantment, the supernatural, occultism, the occult, black magic, the black arts, voodoo. **2** *he does magic at children's parties* **conjuring (tricks),** illusion, sleight of hand; formal prestidigitation. **3** *the magic of the stage* **allure,** excitement, fascination, charm, glamour. **4** *the old Liverpool magic* **brilliance,** skill, accomplishment, expertise, art, finesse, talent.

▸ adjective **1** having supernatural powers. **2** informal wonderful.
▸ verb (**magics, magicking, magicked**) use magic to make something happen.

magical ▸ adjective **1** relating to or using magic. **2** wonderful; very enjoyable.

> SYNONYMS **1** *magical powers* **supernatural,** magic, mystical, otherworldly. **2** *the news had a magical effect* **extraordinary,** remarkable, incredible, amazing, astonishing, astounding, staggering, miraculous. **3** *this magical island* **enchanting,** entrancing, spellbinding, bewitching, fascinating, captivating, alluring, enthralling, charming, lovely, delightful, beautiful; informal heavenly, gorgeous.
> ANTONYMS predictable, boring.

□ **magically** adverb.

magician ▸ noun **1** a person with magic powers. **2** a conjuror.

> SYNONYMS **1** **sorcerer,** sorceress, witch, wizard, warlock, enchanter, enchantress, necromancer. **2** **conjuror,** illusionist; formal prestidigitator.

magisterial /ma-ji-**steer**-i-uhl/ ▸ adjective **1** having or showing great authority. **2** relating to a magistrate.

magistrate ▸ noun an official who judges minor cases and holds preliminary hearings.
□ **magistracy** noun (plural **magistracies**).

magma /**mag**-muh/ ▸ noun very hot fluid or semi-fluid rock under the earth's crust.

magnanimous ▸ adjective generous or forgiving towards a rival or enemy.
□ **magnanimity** noun.

magnate ▸ noun a wealthy and influential person, especially in business.

magnesium /mag-**nee**-zi-uhm/ ▸ noun a silvery-white substance which burns with a brilliant white flame.

magnet ▸ noun **1** a piece of iron that attracts objects containing iron and that points north and south when suspended. **2** a person, place, etc. that someone or something is strongly attracted to.

magnetic ▸ adjective **1** having the property of magnetism. **2** very attractive.

> SYNONYMS **attractive,** irresistible, seductive, charismatic, hypnotic, alluring, fascinating, captivating.
> ANTONYMS repellent.

■ **magnetic pole** each of the points near the geographical North and South Poles, which the needle of a compass points to. **magnetic tape** tape used in recording sound, pictures, or computer data.
□ **magnetically** adverb.

magnetism ▸ noun **1** the property displayed by magnets of attracting or pushing away metal objects. **2** the ability to attract and charm people.

magnetize (or **magnetise**) ▸ verb (**magnetizes, magnetizing, magnetized**) make magnetic.

magneto /mag-**nee**-toh/ ▸ noun (plural **magnetos**) a small generator that uses a magnet to produce pulses of electricity.

magnification ▸ noun **1** the action of magnifying something. **2** the degree to which something is magnified.

magnificent ▸ adjective **1** very attractive and impressive; splendid. **2** very good.

> SYNONYMS **1** *a magnificent view* **splendid,** spectacular, impressive, striking, glorious, superb, majestic, awe-inspiring, breathtaking. **2** *a magnificent apartment* **sumptuous,** grand, impressive, imposing, monumental, palatial, opulent, luxurious, lavish, rich, dazzling, beautiful; informal posh, classy; Brit. informal swish.
> ANTONYMS uninspiring, modest, tawdry.

□ **magnificence** noun **magnificently** adverb.

magnify ▸ verb (**magnifies, magnifying, magnified**) **1** make something appear larger than it is with a lens or microscope. **2** make larger or stronger. **3** old use praise.

> SYNONYMS **enlarge,** increase, augment, extend, expand, boost, enhance, maximize, amplify, intensify; informal blow up.
> ANTONYMS reduce, minimize, understate.

■ **magnifying glass** a lens used to help you see something very small by magnifying it.

magnitude ▸ noun **1** great size or importance. **2** size.

magnolia ▸ noun a tree or shrub with large white or pale pink flowers.

magnum ▸ noun (plural **magnums**) a wine bottle of twice the standard size, normally 1½ litres.

magnum opus ▸ noun a work of art, music, or literature which is the most important that a person has produced.

m

magpie ▶ noun **1** a black and white bird with a long tail. **2** a person who collects things of little use or value.

Magyar /mag-yar/ ▶ noun **1** a member of the predominant people in Hungary. **2** the Hungarian language.

maharaja (or **maharajah**) ▶ noun (in the past) an Indian prince.

mah-jong (or **mah-jongg**) /mah-**jong**/ ▶ noun a Chinese game played with small rectangular tiles.

mahogany ▶ noun **1** hard reddish-brown wood from a tropical tree. **2** a rich reddish-brown colour.

mahout /muh-**howt**/ ▶ noun (in the Indian subcontinent and SE Asia) a person who works with elephants.

maid ▶ noun **1** a female servant. **2** old use a girl or young unmarried woman.

maiden ▶ noun **1** old use a girl or young unmarried woman. **2** (also **maiden over**) Cricket an over in which no runs are scored. ▶ adjective first of its kind: *a maiden voyage.* ■ **maiden name** the surname of a married woman before her marriage.

maidenhair fern ▶ noun a fern with long, thin stems and delicate leaves.

maidenhead ▶ noun old use a girl's or woman's virginity.

mail[1] ▶ noun **1** letters and parcels sent by post. **2** the postal system. **3** email.

SYNONYMS **1** *the mail arrived* **post,** letters, correspondence, email. **2** *we sent it by mail* **post,** postal system, postal service, post office; informal snail mail; N. Amer. the mails.

▶ verb **1** send by post. **2** send post or email to.

SYNONYMS *we mailed the parcels* **send,** post, dispatch, forward, ship, email.

■ **mail order** the buying or selling of goods by post.

mail[2] ▶ noun (in the past) armour made of metal rings or plates.

mailshot ▶ noun Brit. a piece of advertising material posted to a large number of people.

maim ▶ verb inflict a permanent injury on.

SYNONYMS **injure,** wound, cripple, disable, incapacitate, mutilate, disfigure, mangle.

main ▶ adjective greatest or most important.

SYNONYMS **principal,** chief, leading, foremost, most important, major, dominant, central, focal, key, prime, primary, first, fundamental, predominant, pre-eminent. ANTONYMS subsidiary, minor.

▶ noun **1** a chief water or gas pipe or electricity cable. **2** (**the mains**) Brit. the network of pipes and cables supplying water, gas, and electricity. ■ **in the main** on the whole.

mainframe ▶ noun a large high-speed computer supporting a network of workstations.

mainland ▶ noun the main area of land of a country, not including islands and separate territories.

mainly ▶ adverb for the most part; chiefly.

SYNONYMS **mostly,** for the most part, in the main, on the whole, largely, by and large, to a large extent, predominantly, chiefly, principally, primarily.

mainspring ▶ noun the most important or influential part of something.

mainstay ▶ noun a thing on which something depends or is based.

mainstream ▶ noun the ideas, attitudes, or activities that are shared by most people.

maintain ▶ verb **1** keep something in the same state or at the same level. **2** regularly check and repair a building, machine, etc. **3** provide someone with financial support. **4** strongly state that something is the case.

SYNONYMS **1** *they wanted to maintain peace* **preserve,** conserve, keep, retain, keep going, prolong, perpetuate, sustain, carry on, continue. **2** *the council maintains the roads* **look after,** service, care for, take care of. **3** *the costs of maintaining a family* **support,** provide for, keep, sustain. **4** *he maintains that he is innocent* **insist,** declare, assert, protest, affirm, profess, claim, contend, argue. ANTONYMS break, discontinue, neglect, deny.

maintenance ▶ noun **1** the action of maintaining something. **2** Brit. financial support that someone gives to their former husband or wife after divorce.

SYNONYMS **1** *the maintenance of peace* **preservation,** conservation, keeping, carrying on, prolongation, continuation. **2** *car maintenance* **servicing,** service, repair(s), running repairs, care. **3** *the maintenance of his children* **support,** keeping, upkeep, sustenance, nurture. **4** *absent fathers are forced to pay maintenance* **financial support,** child support, alimony, upkeep. ANTONYMS breakdown, discontinuation, neglect.

✔ **-ten-,** not **-tain-:** main**ten**ance.

maisonette ▶ noun a flat on two storeys of a larger building.

maize ▶ noun Brit. a cereal plant whose large yellow grains are eaten as a vegetable.

majestic ▶ adjective impressively grand or beautiful.

SYNONYMS **stately,** dignified, distinguished, solemn, magnificent, grand, splendid, glorious, impressive, noble, awe-inspiring, monumental, palatial, imposing.
ANTONYMS modest, wretched.

□ **majestically** adverb.

majesty ▸ noun (plural **majesties**)
1 impressive beauty or grandeur. **2** (**His, Your,** etc. **Majesty**) a title given to a king or queen or their wife or widow.

SYNONYMS **stateliness,** dignity, solemnity, magnificence, pomp, grandeur, grandness, splendour, glory, impressiveness, nobility.
ANTONYMS modesty, wretchedness.

major ▸ adjective **1** important or serious. **2** greater or more important; main. **3** Music (of a scale) having intervals of a semitone between the third and fourth, and seventh and eighth notes.

SYNONYMS **1** *a major factor* **crucial,** vital, important, big, significant, considerable, weighty, serious, key, utmost, great, paramount, prime. **2** *the major English poets* **greatest,** best, finest, most important, chief, main, prime, principal, leading, foremost, outstanding, pre-eminent.
ANTONYMS trivial, minor.

▸ noun **1** the rank of army officer above captain. **2** N. Amer. a student specializing in a particular subject.
▸ verb (**major in**) N. Amer. or Austral./NZ specialize in a particular subject at college or university.
■ **major general** the rank of army officer above brigadier.

major-domo ▸ noun (plural **major-domos**) a person employed to manage a large household.

majority ▸ noun (plural **majorities**) **1** the greater number. **2** Brit. the number of votes by which one party or candidate in an election defeats the opposition. **3** the age when a person is legally an adult, usually 18 or 21.

SYNONYMS **1** *the majority of cases* **most,** bulk, mass, larger part/number, best/better part, more than half, lion's share, (main) body, preponderance, predominance. **2** *a majority in the election* (**winning**) **margin,** landslide, whitewash.
ANTONYMS minority.

make ▸ verb (**makes, making, made**) **1** form something by putting parts together or mixing substances. **2** cause something to happen or come into existence. **3** force someone to do something. **4** add up to. **5** be suitable as. **6** estimate as or decide on. **7** earn money or profit. **8** arrive at or achieve. **9** prepare to go in a particular direction or to do something.

SYNONYMS **1** *he makes models* **construct,** build, assemble, put together, manufacture, produce, fabricate, create, form, fashion, model, improvise. **2** *she made me drink it* **force,** compel, coerce, press, drive, pressurize, oblige, require; informal railroad, steamroller. **3** *don't make such a noise* **cause,** create, produce, generate, effect. **4** *she made a little bow* **perform,** execute, give, do, accomplish, achieve, bring off, carry out. **5** *they made him chairman* **appoint,** designate, name, nominate, select, elect, vote in. **6** *he's made a lot of money* **acquire,** obtain, gain, get, secure, win, earn. **7** *he made tea* **prepare,** get ready, put together, concoct, cook, dish up, throw together, whip up, brew; informal fix.
ANTONYMS destroy, lose.

▸ noun the manufacturer or trade name of a product.

SYNONYMS **brand,** marque, label.

■ **make-believe** fantasy or pretence. **make do** manage with something that is not satisfactory. **make for** move towards. **make it** become successful. **make off** leave hurriedly. **make off with** steal. **make out** claim or pretend to be. **make something out** manage with difficulty to see, hear, or understand something. **make up** be friendly again after a quarrel. **make someone up** apply cosmetics to someone. **make something up 1** put something together from parts or ingredients. **2** invent a story. **make up for** compensate for. **make up your mind** make a decision. **on the make** informal trying to make money or gain an advantage.

makeover ▸ noun a transformation of someone's appearance with cosmetics, hairstyling, and clothes.

maker ▸ noun a person or thing that creates something.

SYNONYMS **creator,** manufacturer, constructor, builder, producer.

makeshift ▸ adjective temporary and improvised.

SYNONYMS **temporary,** provisional, stopgap, standby, rough and ready, improvised, ad hoc.
ANTONYMS permanent.

make-up ▸ noun **1** cosmetics applied to the face. **2** the way in which something is formed.

SYNONYMS **1** *she used too much make-up* **cosmetics;** informal warpaint, slap. **2** *the cellular make-up of plants* **composition,** constitution, structure, configuration, arrangement. **3** *jealousy isn't part of his*

m

make-up **character,** nature, temperament, personality, mentality, persona.

makeweight ▸ noun an unimportant person or thing that is only added or included to make up the correct number, amount, etc.

makings ▸ plural noun necessary qualities: *she had the makings of a great teacher.*

> SYNONYMS **qualities,** characteristics, ingredients, potential, capacity, capability, stuff.

malachite /ma-luh-kyt/ ▸ noun a bright green mineral.

maladjusted ▸ adjective not able to cope well with normal life.

maladroit /mal-uh-**droyt**/ ▸ adjective clumsy.

malady ▸ noun (plural **maladies**) literary a disease or illness.

malaise /ma-**layz**/ ▸ noun **1** a general feeling of illness or low spirits. **2** a long-standing problem that is difficult to identify.

malapropism /mal-uh-prop-i-z'm/ ▸ noun the mistaken use of a word in place of a similar-sounding one.

malaria ▸ noun a disease that causes fever and is transmitted by the bite of some mosquitoes.
□ **malarial** adjective.

malarkey ▸ noun informal nonsense.

Malawian /muh-**lah**-wi-uhn/ ▸ noun a person from Malawi, a country in Africa.
▸ adjective relating to Malawi.

Malay ▸ noun **1** a member of a people inhabiting Malaysia and Indonesia. **2** the language of the Malays.

Malayan ▸ noun = **MALAY.**
▸ adjective relating to Malays or Malaya (which is now part of Malaysia).

Malaysian ▸ noun a person from Malaysia.
▸ adjective relating to Malaysia.

malcontent ▸ noun a person who is dissatisfied and rebellious.

Maldivian /mawl-**div**-i-uhn/ ▸ noun a person from the Maldives.
▸ adjective relating to the Maldives.

male ▸ adjective **1** of the sex that can fertilize or inseminate the female. **2** having to do with men. **3** (of a plant or flower) having stamens but not a pistil. **4** (of a fitting) made to fit inside a corresponding part.

> SYNONYMS **masculine,** manly, virile, macho.
> ANTONYMS female.

▸ noun a male person, animal, or plant.

malediction /mal-i-**dik**-sh'n/ ▸ noun formal a curse.

malefactor /**mal**-i-fak-ter/ ▸ noun formal a criminal or wrongdoer.

malevolent /muh-**lev**-uh-luhnt/ ▸ adjective wishing to harm other people.
□ **malevolence** noun.

malformation ▸ noun the state of being abnormally shaped or formed.
□ **malformed** adjective.

malfunction ▸ verb (of equipment or machinery) fail to function normally.

> SYNONYMS *the computer has malfunctioned* **crash,** go wrong, break down, fail, stop working; informal conk out, go kaput; Brit. informal play up, pack up.

▸ noun a failure to function normally.

Malian /**mah**-li-uhn/ ▸ noun a person from Mali, a country in West Africa.
▸ adjective relating to Mali.

malice ▸ noun the desire to harm someone.

malicious ▸ adjective meaning to harm other people.

> SYNONYMS **spiteful,** malevolent, vindictive, vengeful, resentful, malign, nasty, hurtful, cruel.
> ANTONYMS benevolent.

□ **maliciously** adverb.

malign /muh-**lyn**/ ▸ adjective harmful or evil.
▸ verb say unpleasant things about.
□ **malignity** /muh-**lig**-ni-ti/ noun.

malignancy ▸ noun (plural **malignancies**) **1** a cancerous growth. **2** the quality of being harmful or evil.

malignant ▸ adjective **1** (of a tumour) cancerous. **2** having or showing a desire to harm other people.

malinger ▸ verb (**malingers, malingering, malingered**) pretend to be ill in order to avoid work.
□ **malingerer** noun.

mall /mawl/ ▸ noun **1** a large enclosed shopping area. **2** a sheltered walk.

mallard ▸ noun a kind of duck, the male of which has a dark green head.

malleable /**mal**-li-uh-b'l/ ▸ adjective **1** able to be hammered or pressed into shape. **2** easily influenced.

mallet ▸ noun **1** a hammer with a large wooden head. **2** a wooden stick with a head like a hammer, for hitting a croquet or polo ball.

mallow ▸ noun a plant with pink or purple flowers.

malnourished ▸ adjective suffering from malnutrition.

malnutrition ▸ noun bad health caused by not having enough food, or not enough of the right food.

malodorous ▸ adjective smelling very unpleasant.

m

malpractice ▸ noun illegal, corrupt, or careless behaviour by a professional person.

malt ▸ noun barley or other grain that has been soaked in water and then dried.
□ **malted** adjective.

maltreat ▸ verb treat badly or cruelly.

> SYNONYMS **ill-treat,** mistreat, abuse, ill-use, mishandle, persecute, molest.

□ **maltreatment** noun.

mama (or **mamma**) ▸ noun dated or N. Amer. your mother.

mamba ▸ noun a large, highly poisonous African snake.

mammal ▸ noun a warm-blooded animal that has hair or fur, produces milk, and gives birth to live young.
□ **mammalian** adjective.

mammary ▸ adjective relating to the breasts or the milk-producing organs of other mammals.

Mammon ▸ noun money thought of as being worshipped like a god.

mammoth ▸ noun a large extinct form of elephant with a hairy coat and long curved tusks.
▸ adjective huge.

man ▸ noun (plural **men**) **1** an adult human male. **2** a person. **3** human beings in general. **4** a figure or token used in a board game.

> SYNONYMS **1** *a handsome man* **male,** adult male, gentleman, youth; informal guy, fellow, gent; Brit. informal bloke, chap, lad; N. Amer. informal dude, hombre. **2** *all men are mortal* **human being,** human, person, mortal, individual, soul. **3** *the evolution of man* **the human race,** the human species, Homo sapiens, humankind, humanity, human beings, humans, people, mankind.

▸ verb (**mans, manning, manned**) provide a place or machine with people to operate or defend it.

> SYNONYMS **1** *the office is manned from 9 to 5* **staff,** crew, occupy, people. **2** *firemen manned the pumps* **operate,** work, use.

■ **man-of-war** historical an armed sailing ship.
□ **manhood** noun.

manacle ▸ noun a metal band fastened round a person's hands or ankles to restrict their movement.
▸ verb (**manacles, manacling, manacled**) restrict someone with manacles.

manage ▸ verb (**manages, managing, managed**) **1** be in charge of people or an organization. **2** succeed in doing. **3** be able to cope despite difficulties. **4** control the use of money or other resources.

> SYNONYMS **1** *she manages a staff of 80* **be in charge of,** run, head, direct, control, preside over, lead, govern, rule, command, supervise, oversee, administer; informal head up. **2** *how much work can you manage this week?* **accomplish,** achieve, carry out, perform, undertake, deal with, cope with, get through. **3** *will you be able to manage without him?* **cope,** get along/on, make do, do all right, carry on, survive, get by, muddle through/along, make ends meet; informal make out, hack it.

□ **manageable** adjective.

management ▸ noun **1** the action of managing. **2** the managers of an organization.

> SYNONYMS **1** *he's responsible for the management of the firm* **administration,** running, managing, organization, direction, leadership, control, governance, rule, command, supervision, guidance, operation. **2** *workers are in dispute with the management* **managers,** employers, directors, board, directorate, executive, administration; informal bosses.
> ANTONYMS employees, workforce.

manager ▸ noun **1** a person who manages staff, an organization, or a sports team. **2** a person in charge of the business affairs of a performer, group of musicians, etc.

> SYNONYMS **executive,** head, supervisor, principal, director, superintendent, foreman, forewoman, overseer, organizer, administrator; informal boss, chief, governor; Brit. informal gaffer, guv'nor.

□ **managerial** adjective.

manageress ▸ noun a woman who manages a business.

manatee /man-uh-tee/ ▸ noun a large plant-eating animal that lives in tropical seas.

mandarin ▸ noun **1** (**Mandarin**) the official form of the Chinese language. **2** (in the past) a high-ranking Chinese official. **3** a powerful official. **4** a small citrus fruit with a loose yellow-orange skin.

mandate ▸ noun /**man**-dayt/ **1** an official order or permission to do something. **2** the authority to carry out a policy that is given by voters to the winner of an election.

> SYNONYMS **1** *a mandate from the UN* **instruction,** directive, decree, command, order, injunction. **2** *he sought a mandate for his policies* **authority,** approval, ratification, endorsement, sanction, authorization.

▸ verb /man-**dayt**/ (**mandates, mandating, mandated**) give someone authority to do something.

mandatory /man-**duh-tuh-ri**/ ▸ adjective required by law or rules; compulsory.

m

SYNONYMS **obligatory,** compulsory, binding, required, requisite, necessary.
ANTONYMS optional.

mandible ► noun **1** the lower jawbone in mammals or fish. **2** either of the upper and lower parts of a bird's beak. **3** either of the parts of an insect's mouth that crush its food.

mandolin ► noun a musical instrument with a rounded back and metal strings.

mandrake ► noun a plant whose root is used in herbal medicine and magic.

mandrill ► noun a large baboon with a red and blue face.

mane ► noun **1** a growth of long hair on the neck of a horse, lion, etc. **2** a person's long hair.

maneuver US spelling of MANOEUVRE.

manful ► adjective brave and determined.
□ **manfully** adverb.

manganese ► noun a hard grey metallic element.

mange ► noun a skin disease of some animals that causes itching and hair loss.

mangel-wurzel ► noun a variety of beet grown as feed for farm animals.

manger ► noun a long trough from which horses or cattle eat.

mangetout /monzh-too/ ► noun (plural **mangetout** or **mangetouts** /monzh-too/) chiefly Brit. a variety of pea with an edible pod.

mangle ► verb (**mangles, mangling, mangled**) destroy or severely damage by crushing or twisting.
► noun a machine with rollers for squeezing wet laundry to remove the water.

mango ► noun (plural **mangoes** or **mangos**) a tropical fruit with yellow flesh.

mangrove ► noun a tropical tree or shrub found in coastal swamps.

mangy /mayn-ji/ ► adjective **1** (of an animal) having mange. **2** in bad condition; shabby.

manhandle ► verb (**manhandles, manhandling, manhandled**) **1** move a heavy object with effort. **2** push or drag someone roughly.

manhole ► noun a covered opening giving access to a sewer or other underground structure.

mania /may-ni-uh/ ► noun **1** mental illness in which a person imagines things and has periods of wild excitement. **2** an extreme enthusiasm.

SYNONYMS **obsession,** compulsion, fixation, fetish, fascination, preoccupation, passion, enthusiasm, desire, urge, craving, craze, fad, rage; informal thing.

maniac /may-ni-ak/ ► noun **1** a person who behaves in a very wild or violent way. **2** informal a person who is very enthusiastic about something.

SYNONYMS **lunatic,** madman, madwoman, psychopath; informal loony, nutcase, nut, head case, headbanger, sicko; Brit. informal nutter; N. Amer. informal screwball.

□ **maniacal** /muh-ny-uh-k'l/ adjective.

manic ► adjective **1** having to do with mania. **2** showing wild excitement and energy.
■ **manic depression** a mental disorder with alternating periods of excitement and depression.
□ **manically** adverb.

manicure ► noun treatment to improve the appearance of the hands and nails.
□ **manicured** adjective **manicurist** noun.

manifest ► adjective clear and obvious.

SYNONYMS **obvious,** clear, plain, apparent, evident, patent, distinct, definite, blatant, overt, transparent, conspicuous, undisguised.
ANTONYMS secret.

► verb **1** show or display. **2** appear; become apparent.

SYNONYMS **display,** show, exhibit, demonstrate, betray, present, reveal.
ANTONYMS hide.

► noun a document listing the cargo, crew, and passengers of a ship or aircraft.
□ **manifestly** adverb.

manifestation ► noun **1** a sign or evidence of something. **2** an appearance of a ghost or spirit.

SYNONYMS **1** *the manifestation of anxiety* display, demonstration, show, exhibition, presentation. **2** *manifestations of global warming* sign, indication, evidence, symptom, testimony, proof, mark, reflection, example, instance.

manifesto ► noun (plural **manifestos**) a public declaration of the policy and aims of a political party.

manifold ► adjective of many kinds.
► noun a pipe with several openings, especially in a car engine.

manikin ► noun a very small person.

Manila (or **Manilla**) ► noun strong brown paper, used especially for envelopes.

manioc /man-i-ok/ = CASSAVA.

manipulate ► verb (**manipulates, manipulating, manipulated**) **1** handle skilfully. **2** control or influence in a clever or underhand way.

SYNONYMS **1** *he manipulated some levers* operate, work, turn, pull, push, twist, slide. **2** *the government tried to manipulate the situation* control,

influence, use to your advantage, exploit, twist.
□ **manipulation** noun **manipulator** noun.

manipulative ▸ adjective manipulating other people in a clever or underhand way.

mankind ▸ noun human beings as a whole.

SYNONYMS **the human race,** humankind, humanity, human beings, humans, Homo sapiens, people, man, men and women.

manky ▸ adjective Brit. informal dirty or of bad quality.

manly ▸ adjective (**manlier, manliest**) **1** having good qualities associated with men, such as courage and strength. **2** suitable for a man.

SYNONYMS **virile,** masculine, strong, all-male, red-blooded, muscular, muscly, strapping, well built, rugged, tough, powerful, brawny; informal hunky. ANTONYMS effeminate.

□ **manliness** noun.

man-made ▸ adjective made or caused by human beings.

SYNONYMS **artificial,** synthetic, manufactured, imitation, ersatz, simulated, mock, fake. ANTONYMS natural, real.

manna ▸ noun **1** (in the Bible) the substance supplied by God as food to the Israelites in the wilderness. **2** something unexpected and beneficial.

mannequin /man-ni-kin/ ▸ noun a dummy used to display clothes in a shop window.

manner ▸ noun **1** a way in which something is done or happens. **2** a person's outward behaviour. **3** (**manners**) polite social behaviour. **4** literary a kind or sort.

SYNONYMS **1** *it was dealt with in a very efficient manner* **way,** fashion, mode, means, method, system, style, approach, technique, procedure, process. **2** *her rather unfriendly manner* **behaviour,** attitude, demeanour, air, aspect, bearing, conduct. **3** *the life and manners of Victorian society* **customs,** habits, ways, practices, conventions, usages. **4** *you ought to teach him some manners* **etiquette,** social graces, protocol, politeness, decorum, propriety, civility, Ps and Qs.

mannered ▸ adjective **1** behaving in a particular way: *a well-mannered girl.* **2** artificial and exaggerated.

mannerism ▸ noun a distinctive gesture or way of speaking.

SYNONYMS **idiosyncrasy,** quirk, oddity, foible, trait, peculiarity, habit, characteristic.

mannerly ▸ adjective well mannered; polite.

mannish ▸ adjective (of a woman) like a man in appearance or behaviour.

manoeuvre /muh-**noo**-ver/ (US spelling **maneuver**) ▸ noun **1** a movement or series of moves needing skill and care. **2** a carefully planned scheme. **3** (**manoeuvres**) a large-scale military exercise.

SYNONYMS **1** *a tricky parking manoeuvre* **operation,** exercise, move, movement, action. **2** *diplomatic manoeuvres* **stratagem,** tactic, gambit, ploy, trick, dodge, ruse, scheme, device, plot, machination, artifice, subterfuge, intrigue.

▸ verb (**manoeuvres, manoeuvring, manoeuvred**) **1** make a movement or series of moves skilfully and carefully. **2** cleverly influence someone or something in order to achieve an aim.

SYNONYMS **1** *I manoeuvred the car into the space* **steer,** guide, drive, negotiate, navigate, pilot, direct, manipulate, move, work. **2** *he manoeuvred things to suit himself* **manipulate,** contrive, manage, engineer, fix, organize, arrange, orchestrate, choreograph, stage-manage; informal wangle.

□ **manoeuvrable** adjective.

✔ The British spelling has **-oeu-** in the middle and **-re** at the end: man**oeu**v**re**.

manometer ▸ noun an instrument for measuring the pressure of fluids.

manor ▸ noun a large country house with lands.
□ **manorial** adjective.

manpower ▸ noun the number of people working or available for work.

manse ▸ noun the house provided for a minister of certain Christian Churches.

mansion ▸ noun a large, impressive house.

SYNONYMS **country house,** stately home, hall, manor house; informal palace, pile. ANTONYMS hovel.

manslaughter ▸ noun the crime of killing a person without meaning to do so.

mantel ▸ noun a mantelpiece or mantelshelf.

mantelpiece ▸ noun **1** a structure surrounding a fireplace. **2** (also **mantelshelf**) a shelf forming the top of a mantelpiece.

mantilla /man-til-luh/ ▸ noun a lace or silk scarf worn by Spanish women over the hair and shoulders.

mantis (or **praying mantis**) ▸ noun (plural **mantis** or **mantises**) a large insect that waits for its prey with its forelegs folded like hands in prayer.

mantle ▸ noun **1** a woman's loose sleeveless cloak. **2** a close covering, e.g. of snow. **3** a cover around a gas jet that produces a glowing light when heated. **4** a role or responsibility that passes from one person to another. **5** the region of very hot, dense rock between the earth's crust and its core.

mantra ▸ noun a word or sound repeated to aid concentration when meditating.

manual ▸ adjective **1** having to do with the hands. **2** operated by or using the hands.

> SYNONYMS **1** *manual work* **physical**, labouring, blue-collar. **2** *a manual typewriter* **hand-operated**, hand.

▸ noun a book giving instructions or information.

> SYNONYMS *a training manual* **handbook**, instructions, guide, companion, ABC, guidebook; informal bible.

□ **manually** adverb.

manufacture ▸ verb (manufactures, manufacturing, manufactured) **1** make something on a large scale using machinery. **2** invent evidence or a story.

> SYNONYMS **1** *the company manufactures laser printers* **make**, produce, mass-produce, build, construct, assemble, put together, turn out. **2** *a story manufactured by the press* **make up**, invent, fabricate, concoct, hatch, dream up, think up, contrive; informal cook up.

▸ noun the manufacturing of things.

> SYNONYMS *the manufacture of aircraft engines* **production**, making, manufacturing, mass production, construction, building, assembly.

manufacturer ▸ noun a person or organization that manufactures.

> SYNONYMS **maker**, producer, builder, constructor, industrialist.

manure ▸ noun animal dung used for fertilizing land.

manuscript ▸ noun **1** a handwritten book, document, etc. **2** an author's handwritten or typed work, before printing and publication.

Manx ▸ adjective relating to the Isle of Man. ■ **Manx cat** a breed of cat that has no tail.

many ▸ determiner, pronoun, & adjective a large number of.

> SYNONYMS **numerous**, a lot of, plenty of, countless, innumerable, scores of, untold, copious, abundant; informal lots of, umpteen, loads of, masses of, stacks of, heaps of, a slew of; Brit. informal a shedload of; Austral./NZ informal a swag of; literary myriad.
> ANTONYMS few.

▸ noun (**the many**) the majority of people.

Maori /mow-ri/ ▸ noun (plural **Maori** or **Maoris**) a member of the aboriginal people of New Zealand.

map ▸ noun a flat diagram of an area showing physical features, cities, roads, etc.

> SYNONYMS **plan**, chart, A to Z, atlas.

▸ verb (maps, mapping, mapped) **1** show something on a map. **2** (**map something out**) plan something in detail.

> SYNONYMS *the region was mapped from the air* **chart**, plot, draw, record.

maple ▸ noun a tree with five-pointed leaves.

mar ▸ verb (mars, marring, marred) spoil the appearance or quality of.

> SYNONYMS **1** *an ugly bruise marred his features* **spoil**, impair, disfigure, blemish, scar. **2** *the celebrations were marred by violence* **spoil**, ruin, damage, wreck, taint, tarnish.
> ANTONYMS enhance.

maraca /muh-rak-uh/ ▸ noun a container filled with small beans or stones, shaken as a musical instrument.

marathon ▸ noun **1** a long-distance running race, strictly one of 26 miles 385 yards (42.195 km). **2** a long-lasting and difficult task.

maraud ▸ verb go about a place in search of things to steal or people to attack. □ **marauder** noun.

marble ▸ noun **1** a hard stone, usually white with coloured streaks, which can be polished and used in sculpture and building. **2** a small ball of coloured glass used as a toy.

marbled ▸ adjective patterned with coloured streaks.

marcasite /mar-kuh-syt, mar-kuh-zeet/ ▸ noun a semi-precious stone used in jewellery.

March ▸ noun the third month of the year.

march ▸ verb **1** walk in time and with regular paces, like a soldier. **2** walk quickly and with determination. **3** force someone to walk quickly. **4** take part in an organized procession to make a protest.

> SYNONYMS **1** *the men marched past* **stride**, walk, troop, step, pace, tread, slog, tramp, hike, trudge, parade, file. **2** *she marched in without even knocking* **stride**, stalk, strut, flounce, storm, stomp, sweep.

▸ noun **1** an act of marching. **2** a procession organized as a protest. **3** (**Marches**) land on the border between two territories.

> SYNONYMS **1** *a 20-mile march* **walk**, trek, slog, route march, hike. **2** *police sought to ban the march* **parade**, procession,

m

cortège, demonstration; informal demo.
3 *the march of technology* **progress,**
advance, development, evolution,
passage.
□ **marcher** noun.

marchioness /mar-shuh-**ness**/ ▶ noun **1** the
wife or widow of a marquess. **2** a woman
who holds the rank of marquess.

Mardi Gras /mar-di **grah**/ ▶ noun a carnival
held in some countries on Shrove Tuesday.

mare ▶ noun the female of a horse or related
animal.

margarine ▶ noun a butter substitute made
from vegetable oils or animal fats.

margin ▶ noun **1** an edge or border. **2** the
blank border on each side of the print on
a page. **3** an amount by which something
is won.

> SYNONYMS **1** *the margin of the lake* **edge,**
> side, verge, border, perimeter, brink,
> brim, rim, fringe, boundary, periphery,
> extremity. **2** *there's no margin for error*
> **leeway,** latitude, scope, room, space,
> allowance. **3** *they won by a narrow*
> *margin* **gap,** majority, amount.

■ **margin of** (or **for**) **error** a small amount
allowed for or included so as to be sure of
success or safety.

marginal ▶ adjective **1** in a margin. **2** slight,
or of minor importance. **3** Brit. (of a
parliamentary seat) held by only a small
majority.

> SYNONYMS **1** *the difference is marginal*
> **slight,** small, tiny, minute, insignificant,
> minimal, negligible. **2** *a very*
> *marginal case* **borderline,** disputable,
> questionable, doubtful.
> ANTONYMS considerable, clear-cut.

□ **marginality** noun **marginally** adverb.

marginalize (or **marginalise**) ▶ verb
(**marginalizes, marginalizing, marginalized**)
reduce the power or importance of.
□ **marginalization** noun.

marigold ▶ noun a plant of the daisy family
with yellow or orange flowers.

marijuana /ma-ri-yoo-**ah**-nuh/ ▶ noun
cannabis.

marina ▶ noun a purpose-built harbour with
moorings for yachts and small boats.

marinade ▶ noun /ma-ri-**nayd**/ a mixture of
ingredients in which food is soaked before
cooking to flavour or soften it.
▶ verb /**ma**-ri-nayd/ (**marinades, marinading,**
marinaded) = MARINATE.

marinate ▶ verb (**marinates, marinating,**
marinated) soak food in a marinade.

marine ▶ adjective **1** relating to the
sea. **2** relating to shipping or matters
concerning a navy.

> SYNONYMS **1** *marine plants* **seawater,** sea,
> saltwater, aquatic. **2** *a marine insurance*
> *company* **maritime,** nautical, naval,
> seafaring, seagoing, ocean-going.

▶ noun a soldier trained to serve on land or
sea.

mariner ▶ noun literary a sailor.

> SYNONYMS **sailor,** seaman, seafarer.

marionette ▶ noun a puppet worked by
strings.

marital ▶ adjective having to do with
marriage.

> SYNONYMS **matrimonial,** married,
> wedded, conjugal, nuptial, marriage,
> wedding.

maritime ▶ adjective **1** relating to shipping
or other activity taking place at sea.
2 living or found in or near the sea.
3 (of a climate) moist and having a mild
temperature due to the influence of the
sea.

> SYNONYMS **naval,** marine, nautical,
> seafaring, seagoing, sea, ocean-going.

marjoram ▶ noun **1** a sweet-smelling
plant of the mint family, used as a herb in
cooking. **2** = OREGANO.

mark[1] ▶ noun **1** a small area on a surface
having a different colour from its
surroundings. **2** something that indicates
position or acts as a pointer. **3** a line, figure,
or symbol made to identify or record
something. **4** a sign of a quality or feeling.
5 a characteristic feature of something. **6** a
point awarded for a correct answer or for
a piece of work. **7** a particular model of a
vehicle or machine.

> SYNONYMS **1** *a dirty mark* **blemish,** streak,
> spot, fleck, blot, stain, smear, speck,
> smudge; informal splodge. **2** *a punctuation*
> *mark* **symbol,** sign, character, accent,
> diacritic. **3** *the mark of a well-known*
> *bookseller* **logo,** seal, stamp, symbol,
> emblem, device, insignia, badge, brand,
> trademark, monogram, hallmark. **4** *a*
> *mark of respect* **sign,** token, symbol,
> indication, symptom, proof. **5** *the mark*
> *of a civilized society* **characteristic,**
> feature, trait, attribute, quality,
> hallmark, indicator. **6** *he got a good*
> *mark for maths* **grade,** grading, rating,
> score, percentage.

▶ verb **1** make a mark on. **2** write a word or
symbol on an object in order to identify
it. **3** indicate the position of. **4** (**mark**
someone/thing out) show someone or
something to be different or special. **5** do
something to celebrate or remember a
significant event. **6** (**mark something up** or
down) increase or reduce the price of an
item. **7** assess and give a mark to a piece of

m

work. **8** pay careful attention to. **9** Brit. (in team games) stay close to an opponent in order to prevent them getting or passing the ball.

> SYNONYMS **1** *be careful not to mark the paintwork* **discolour,** stain, smear, smudge, streak, dirty; informal splodge. **2** *her possessions were clearly marked* **label,** identify, flag, initial, name. **3** *I've marked the relevant passages* **indicate,** label, tick, identify, highlight. **4** *a festival to mark the town's 200th anniversary* **celebrate,** observe, recognize, acknowledge, keep, honour, commemorate, remember. **5** *these incidents marked a new phase* **represent,** signify, indicate, herald. **6** *his style is marked by simplicity* **characterize,** distinguish, identify, typify. **7** *I have a pile of essays to mark* **assess,** evaluate, appraise, correct; N. Amer. grade.

■ **mark time 1** fill in time with routine activities. **2** (of troops) march on the spot without moving forward. **on your marks** be ready to start (used to instruct competitors in a race). **up to the mark** up to the required standard.

mark² ▸ noun the former basic unit of money in Germany.

marked ▸ adjective **1** having an identifying mark. **2** clearly noticeable. **3** singled out as a target for attack.

> SYNONYMS **noticeable,** pronounced, decided, distinct, striking, clear, unmistakable, obvious, conspicuous, notable.
> ANTONYMS imperceptible.

□ **markedly** adverb.

marker ▸ noun **1** an object used to indicate a position, place, or route. **2** a felt-tip pen with a broad tip. **3** (in team games) a player who marks an opponent.

market ▸ noun **1** a regular gathering for the buying and selling of food, livestock, or other goods. **2** an outdoor space or large hall where traders offer their goods for sale. **3** a particular area of trade or competitive activity. **4** demand for a particular product or service.

> SYNONYMS **shopping centre,** marketplace, mart, bazaar, souk, fair.

▸ verb (**markets, marketing, marketed**) advertise or promote a product.

> SYNONYMS *the product was marketed worldwide* **sell,** retail, merchandise, trade, advertise, promote.

■ **market garden** a place where vegetables and fruit are grown to be sold. **market research** the gathering of information about what people choose to buy. **market town** a medium-sized town where a regular

market is held. **market value** the amount for which something can be sold. **on the market** available for sale.
□ **marketable** adjective.

marketing ▸ noun the promoting and selling of products or services.

marketplace ▸ noun **1** an open space where a market is held. **2** the world of trade and commerce.

marking ▸ noun **1** an identification mark. **2** (also **markings**) a pattern of marks on an animal's fur, feathers, or skin.

marksman ▸ noun (plural **marksmen**) a person skilled in shooting.
□ **marksmanship** noun.

markup ▸ noun the difference between the basic cost of producing something and the amount it is sold for.

marl¹ ▸ noun a rock or soil consisting of clay and lime.

marl² ▸ noun a type of yarn or fabric with differently coloured threads.

marlin ▸ noun a large edible fish with a pointed snout.

marmalade ▸ noun a thick spread made from oranges.

marmoreal /mar-mor-i-uhl/ ▸ adjective literary made of or resembling marble.

marmoset ▸ noun a small tropical American monkey with a long tail.

marmot ▸ noun a heavily built burrowing rodent.

maroon¹ ▸ noun a dark brownish-red colour.

maroon² ▸ verb (**be marooned**) be abandoned or isolated in a place which cannot be reached.

marque ▸ noun a make of car, as distinct from a specific model.

marquee ▸ noun **1** chiefly Brit. a large tent used for special events. **2** N. Amer. a roof-like canopy over the entrance to a building.

marquess ▸ noun a British nobleman ranking above an earl and below a duke.

marquetry /mar-ki-tri/ ▸ noun patterns or pictures made from small pieces of coloured wood inlaid into a surface, used to decorate furniture.

marquis /mar-kwiss/ ▸ noun (in some European countries) a nobleman ranking above a count and below a duke.

marquise /mar-keez/ ▸ noun the wife or widow of a marquis, or a woman holding the rank of marquis in her own right.

marriage ▸ noun **1** the formal union of a man and woman, by which they become husband and wife. **2** the relationship between a husband and wife.

> SYNONYMS **1** *a proposal of marriage* **matrimony,** wedlock. **2** *the marriage*

took place at St Margaret's **wedding**, wedding ceremony, nuptials, union, match. **3** *a marriage of jazz, pop, and gospel* **union,** fusion, mixture, mix, blend, amalgamation, combination, hybrid.
ANTONYMS divorce, separation.

☐ **marriageable** adjective.

marrow ▶ noun **1** Brit. a long vegetable with a green skin and white flesh. **2** (also **bone marrow**) a soft fatty substance inside bones, in which blood cells are produced.

marrowbone ▶ noun a bone containing edible bone marrow.

marry ▶ verb (**marries, marrying, married**) **1** become the husband or wife of. **2** join two people in marriage. **3** join two things together.

SYNONYMS **1** *the couple married last year* **get/be married,** wed, be wed, become man and wife; informal tie the knot, walk down the aisle, get spliced, get hitched, say 'I do'. **2** *John wanted to marry her* **wed**; informal make an honest woman of. **3** *the show marries poetry with art* **join,** unite, combine, fuse, mix, blend, merge, amalgamate.
ANTONYMS divorce, separate.

Mars ▶ noun the fourth planet from the sun in the solar system and the nearest to the earth.

marsh ▶ noun an area of low-lying land which usually remains waterlogged.

SYNONYMS **swamp,** marshland, bog, swampland, morass, mire, quagmire, slough, fen.

☐ **marshy** adjective.

marshal ▶ noun **1** an officer of the highest rank in the armed forces of some countries. **2** (in the US) a type of law enforcement officer. **3** an official responsible for supervising public events.
▶ verb (**marshals, marshalling, marshalled**; US spelling **marshals, marshaling, marshaled**) **1** assemble a group of people in order. **2** bring facts together in an organized way.

SYNONYMS **assemble,** gather (together), collect, muster, call together, draw up, line up, array, organize, group, arrange, deploy, position, summon, round up.

marshmallow ▶ noun a spongy sweet made from sugar, egg white, and gelatin.

marsupial /mar-soo-pi-uhl/ ▶ noun a mammal whose young are carried and suckled in a pouch on the mother's belly.

mart ▶ noun **1** N. Amer. a shop. **2** a trade centre or market.

marten ▶ noun a forest animal resembling a weasel.

martial ▶ adjective having to do with war.

SYNONYMS **military,** soldierly, army, warlike, fighting, militaristic; informal gung-ho.

■ **martial arts** sports which started as forms of self-defence or attack, such as judo and karate. **martial law** government by the military forces of a country.

Martian ▶ noun a supposed inhabitant of the planet Mars.
▶ adjective relating to Mars.

martin ▶ noun a small short-tailed swallow.

martinet ▶ noun a person who is very strict and insists on being obeyed.

martingale ▶ noun a strap running from the noseband or reins to the girth of a horse's saddle, which prevents the horse from raising its head too high.

martyr ▶ noun **1** a person who is killed because of their beliefs. **2** a person who exaggerates their difficulties in order to obtain sympathy or admiration.
▶ verb make a martyr of.
☐ **martyrdom** noun.

marvel ▶ verb (**marvels, marvelling, marvelled**; US spelling **marvels, marveling, marveled**) be filled with wonder.

SYNONYMS *she marvelled at their courage* **be amazed,** be astonished, be in awe, wonder; informal be gobsmacked.

▶ noun a person or thing that causes a feeling of wonder.

SYNONYMS *a marvel of technology* **wonder,** miracle, sensation, spectacle, phenomenon.

marvellous (US spelling **marvelous**) ▶ adjective wonderful; very good.

SYNONYMS **excellent,** splendid, wonderful, magnificent, superb, glorious, sublime, lovely, delightful; informal super, great, amazing, fantastic, terrific, tremendous; Brit. informal smashing, brilliant.
ANTONYMS commonplace, awful.

☐ **marvellously** adverb.

Marxism ▶ noun the political and economic theories of Karl Marx and Friedrich Engels, which formed the basis for communism.
☐ **Marxist** noun & adjective.

marzipan ▶ noun a sweet paste of ground almonds, sugar, and egg whites.

mascara ▶ noun a cosmetic for darkening the eyelashes.

mascot ▶ noun a person, animal, or object that is supposed to bring good luck.

masculine ▶ adjective **1** relating to men. **2** having the qualities or appearance traditionally associated with men. **3** Grammar referring to a gender of nouns and adjectives seen as male.

m

SYNONYMS 1 *a masculine trait* **male,** man's, men's, male-oriented. **2** *a powerfully masculine man* **virile,** macho, manly, all-male, muscular, muscly, strong, strapping, well built, rugged, robust, brawny, powerful, red-blooded, vigorous; informal hunky. **3** *a rather masculine woman* **mannish,** unfeminine, unladylike; informal butch.
ANTONYMS feminine, effeminate.

□ **masculinity** noun.

mash ▶ verb crush or beat something into a soft mass.
▶ noun **1** a soft mass made by crushing a substance. **2** Brit. informal boiled and mashed potatoes.

mask ▶ noun **1** a covering for all or part of the face, worn for protection, as a disguise, or for theatrical effect. **2** a likeness of a person's face moulded in clay or wax.

SYNONYMS *a mask of respectability* **pretence,** semblance, veil, screen, front, facade, veneer, disguise, cover, cloak, camouflage.

▶ verb **1** (**masked**) wearing a mask. **2** conceal or disguise.

SYNONYMS *poplar trees masked the factory* **hide,** conceal, disguise, cover up, obscure, screen, cloak, camouflage.

masochism /mass-uh-ki-z'm/ ▶ noun enjoyment felt in being hurt or humiliated by someone.
□ **masochist** noun **masochistic** adjective.

mason ▶ noun **1** a person who works with stone. **2** (**Mason**) a Freemason.

Masonic ▶ adjective relating to Freemasons.

masonry ▶ noun the parts of a building that are made of stone.

masque /mahsk/ ▶ noun (in the past) a form of entertainment consisting of dancing and acting performed by masked players.

masquerade /mass-kuh-**rayd**/ ▶ noun **1** a pretence. **2** a ball at which people wear masks.
▶ verb (**masquerades, masquerading, masqueraded**) pretend to be someone or something else.

Mass ▶ noun **1** the Christian service of the Eucharist or Holy Communion. **2** a musical setting of parts of this service.

mass ▶ noun **1** an amount of matter with no definite shape. **2** a large number of people or objects gathered together. **3** (**the masses**) the ordinary people. **4** (**a mass of**) a large amount of. **5** Physics the quantity of matter which something contains.

SYNONYMS **1** *a soggy mass of fallen leaves* **pile,** heap, accumulation, mess, mat, tangle. **2** *a mass of cyclists* **crowd,** horde, throng, host, troop, army, herd, flock, swarm, mob, pack, flood, multitude.

3 *the mass of the population* **majority,** greater part/number, best/better part, major part, bulk, main body.

▶ adjective done by or affecting large numbers of people or things.

SYNONYMS *mass hysteria* **widespread,** general, extensive, large-scale, wholesale, universal, indiscriminate.

▶ verb gather together in a mass.

SYNONYMS *they began massing troops in the region* **assemble,** gather together, collect, rally.

■ **mass-market** (of goods) produced in large quantities and appealing to a large number of people. **mass-produce** produce goods in large quantities in a factory.

massacre ▶ noun a brutal killing of a large number of people.

SYNONYMS *a cold-blooded massacre* **slaughter,** mass killing, mass murder, mass execution, ethnic cleansing, genocide, holocaust, annihilation, liquidation, extermination, carnage, butchery, bloodbath, bloodletting.

▶ verb (**massacres, massacring, massacred**) brutally kill a large number of people.

SYNONYMS *thousands were massacred* **slaughter,** butcher, murder, kill, annihilate, exterminate, execute, liquidate, eliminate, mow down, cut to pieces.

massage ▶ noun the rubbing and kneading of parts of the body with the hands to relieve tension or pain.

SYNONYMS **rub,** rub-down, kneading.

▶ verb (**massages, massaging, massaged**) **1** give a massage to. **2** alter facts or figures to make them seem better than they really are.

SYNONYMS **1** *he massaged her tired muscles* **rub,** knead, manipulate, pummel, work. **2** *the statistics have been massaged* **alter,** tamper with, manipulate, doctor, falsify, juggle, fiddle with, tinker with, distort, rig; informal cook, fiddle.

■ **massage parlour 1** a place where massage is provided. **2** a brothel.

masseur /ma-ser/ ▶ noun (feminine **masseuse** /ma-**serz**/) a person who gives massages professionally.

massif /ma-**seef**/ ▶ noun a compact group of mountains.

massive ▶ adjective **1** large and heavy or solid. **2** very large, powerful, or severe.

SYNONYMS **huge,** enormous, vast, immense, mighty, great, colossal, tremendous, gigantic, mammoth, monumental, giant, mountainous; informal monster, whopping, astronomical; Brit.

m

informal **whacking**, **ginormous**.
ANTONYMS tiny.

□ **massively** adverb.

mast¹ ▶ noun **1** a tall upright post on a boat carrying a sail or sails. **2** any tall upright post or structure.

mast² ▶ noun nuts and other fruit that has fallen from trees.

mastectomy ▶ noun (plural **mastectomies**) an operation to remove a breast.

master ▶ noun **1** a man in a position of authority, control, or ownership. **2** a person skilled in a particular art or activity. **3** the head of a college or school. **4** chiefly Brit. a male schoolteacher. **5** a person who holds a second or further degree. **6** an original film, recording, or document from which copies can be made.

SYNONYMS **1** *he acceded to his master's wishes* **lord**, ruler, sovereign, monarch. **2** *a chess master* **expert**, genius, maestro, virtuoso, authority; informal ace, wizard, whizz, hotshot; Brit. informal dab hand; N. Amer. informal maven, crackerjack. **3** *the geography master* **teacher**, schoolteacher, schoolmaster, tutor, instructor. **4** *their spiritual master* **guru**, teacher, leader, guide, mentor. ANTONYMS servant, amateur, pupil.

▶ adjective having great skill or expertise.

SYNONYMS *a master craftsman* **expert**, adept, proficient, skilled, skilful, deft, dexterous, adroit, practised, experienced, masterly, accomplished; informal crack, ace; N. Amer. informal crackerjack. ANTONYMS amateur.

▶ verb (**masters**, **mastering**, **mastered**) **1** gain great knowledge of or skill in. **2** gain control of.

SYNONYMS **1** *it took ages to master the technique* **learn**, become proficient in, pick up, grasp, understand; informal get the hang of. **2** *I managed to master my fears* **overcome**, conquer, beat, quell, suppress, control, triumph over, subdue, vanquish, subjugate, curb, check, defeat, get the better of; informal lick. ANTONYMS succumb to.

■ **master key** a key that opens several locks, each of which has its own key. **master of ceremonies** a person in charge of proceedings at a special event.

masterclass ▶ noun a class given to students by a leading musician.

masterful ▶ adjective **1** powerful and able to control other people. **2** performed or performing very skilfully.

SYNONYMS **commanding**, powerful, imposing, authoritative. ANTONYMS weak.

□ **masterfully** adverb.

masterly ▶ adjective performed or performing very skilfully.

SYNONYMS **expert**, adept, skilful, skilled, adroit, proficient, deft, dexterous, accomplished, polished, consummate. ANTONYMS inept.

mastermind ▶ noun a person who plans and directs a complex scheme or project.

SYNONYMS *the mastermind behind the project* **genius**, intellect; informal brain, brains.

▶ verb plan and direct a complex scheme or project.

SYNONYMS *he masterminded the whole campaign* **plan**, control, direct, be in charge of, run, conduct, organize, arrange, preside over, orchestrate, stage-manage, engineer, manage, coordinate.

masterpiece ▶ noun a work of outstanding skill.

SYNONYMS **magnum opus**, chef-d'œuvre, masterwork, pièce de résistance, tour de force, classic.

mastery ▶ noun **1** complete knowledge or command of a subject or skill. **2** control or superiority.

SYNONYMS **1** *her mastery of the language* **proficiency**, ability, capability, knowledge, understanding, comprehension, command, grasp. **2** *man's mastery over nature* **control**, domination, command, supremacy, superiority, power, authority, jurisdiction, dominion, sovereignty.

masthead ▶ noun **1** the highest part of a ship's mast. **2** the name of a newspaper or magazine printed at the top of the first page.

mastic ▶ noun **1** a gum from the bark of a Mediterranean tree, used in making varnish and chewing gum. **2** a waterproof substance like putty, used in building.

masticate ▶ verb (**masticates**, **masticating**, **masticated**) chew food.
□ **mastication** noun.

mastiff ▶ noun a dog of a large, strong breed with drooping ears and lips.

mastitis /ma-sty-tiss/ ▶ noun painful inflammation of glands in the breast or udder.

mastodon ▶ noun a large extinct elephant-like mammal.

mastoid ▶ noun a part of the bone behind the ear, which has air spaces linked to the middle ear.

masturbate ▶ verb (**masturbates**, **masturbating**, **masturbated**) stimulate your genitals with your hand for sexual pleasure.
□ **masturbation** noun.

m

mat ▸ noun **1** a thick piece of material placed on the floor, used for decoration or to protect the floor. **2** a piece of springy material for landing on in gymnastics or similar sports. **3** a small piece of material placed on a surface to protect it. **4** a thick layer of hairy or woolly material.

SYNONYMS **1** *the hall mat* **rug,** carpet, doormat. **2** *a thick mat of hair* **mass,** tangle, mop, thatch, shock, mane.

matador ▸ noun a bullfighter.

match¹ ▸ noun **1** an event at which two people or teams compete against each other. **2** a person or thing that can compete with another as an equal in quality or strength. **3** an exact equivalent. **4** a pair of things which correspond or are very similar.

SYNONYMS **1** *a football match* **contest,** competition, game, tournament, tie, fixture, meet, friendly, (local) derby, bout, fight. **2** *the vase was an exact match of hers* **lookalike,** double, twin, duplicate, mate, companion, counterpart, pair, replica, copy; informal spitting image, dead ringer.

▸ verb **1** correspond or fit with something. **2** be equal to. **3** place a person or team in competition with another.

SYNONYMS **1** *the curtains matched the duvet cover* **go with,** coordinate with, complement, suit, set off. **2** *did their statements match?* **correspond,** tally, agree, match up, coincide, square. **3** (matching) **corresponding,** equivalent, parallel, complementary, paired, twin, identical, alike. **4** *no one can match him at chess* **equal,** compare with, be in the same league as, touch, rival, compete with; informal hold a candle to.

■ **match point** (in sports) a point which if won by one of the players will also win them the match.

match² ▸ noun a short, thin stick tipped with a substance that ignites when rubbed against a rough surface.

matchbox ▸ noun a small box in which matches are sold.

matchless ▸ adjective so good that nothing is an equal.

matchmaker ▸ noun a person who tries to bring about marriages or relationships between other people.

matchstick ▸ noun the stem of a match.

mate ▸ noun **1** Brit. informal a friend. **2** the sexual partner of an animal. **3** an assistant to a skilled worker.

SYNONYMS **1** *he's gone out with his mates* **friend,** companion, schoolmate, classmate, workmate; informal pal, chum; N. Amer. informal buddy, amigo, compadre. **2** *she's finally found her ideal mate*

partner, husband, wife, spouse, consort, lover; informal better half; Brit. informal other half. **3** *a plumber's mate* **assistant,** helper, apprentice.

▸ verb (**mates, mating, mated**) (of animals or birds) come together for breeding.

SYNONYMS *pandas rarely mate in captivity* **breed,** couple, pair.

matelot /mat-uh-loh/ ▸ noun Brit. informal a sailor.

material ▸ noun **1** the matter from which something is or can be made. **2** items needed for doing or creating something. **3** cloth.

SYNONYMS **1** *organic material* **matter,** substance, stuff. **2** *the materials for a new building* **constituent,** raw material, component, supplies. **3** *cleaning materials* **things,** items, articles, stuff, supplies; Brit. informal gubbins. **4** *curtain material* **fabric,** cloth, textiles. **5** *material for a magazine article* **information,** data, facts, facts and figures, statistics, evidence, details, particulars, background, notes; informal info.

▸ adjective **1** having to do with physical things rather than the mind or spirit. **2** essential or relevant.

SYNONYMS **1** *the material world* **physical,** corporeal, tangible, mundane, worldly, earthly, secular, temporal, concrete, real. **2** *she was too fond of material pleasures* **sensual,** physical, carnal, corporal, fleshly, bodily. **3** *information that could be material to the enquiry* **relevant,** pertinent, applicable, germane, vital, essential, key.
ANTONYMS spiritual, aesthetic, irrelevant.

□ **materially** adverb.

materialism ▸ noun a strong interest in possessions and physical comfort rather than spiritual values.
□ **materialist** adjective & noun **materialistic** adjective.

materialize (or **materialise**) ▸ verb (**materialize, materializing, materialized**) **1** happen. **2** appear suddenly.

maternal ▸ adjective **1** having to do with a mother. **2** related through the mother's side of the family.

SYNONYMS **motherly,** protective, caring, nurturing, maternalistic.

□ **maternally** adverb.

maternity ▸ noun motherhood.

matey ▸ adjective (**matier, matiest**) Brit. informal very friendly.

mathematics ▸ noun the branch of science concerned with numbers, quantities, and space.
□ **mathematical** adjective **mathematically** adverb **mathematician** noun.

maths (or N. Amer. **math**) ▸ noun mathematics.

matinee /**ma**-ti-nay/ ▸ noun an afternoon performance in a theatre or cinema.

matins ▸ noun a Christian service of morning prayer.

matriarch /**may**-tri-ark/ ▸ noun a woman who is the head of a family or tribe.

matriarchy ▸ noun a society led or controlled by women.
□ **matriarchal** adjective.

matricide /**ma**-tri-syd/ ▸ noun **1** the killing by someone of their own mother. **2** a person who kills their mother.

matriculate ▸ verb (**matriculates**, **matriculating**, **matriculated**) enrol or be enrolled at a college or university.
□ **matriculation** noun.

matrimony ▸ noun the state of being married.
□ **matrimonial** adjective.

matrix /**may**-triks/ ▸ noun (plural **matrices** /**may**-tri-seez/ or **matrixes**) **1** an environment or material in which something develops. **2** a mould in which something is cast or shaped. **3** a grid-like arrangement of elements.

matron ▸ noun **1** a woman in charge of medical and living arrangements at a boarding school. **2** Brit. dated a woman in charge of nursing in a hospital. **3** an older married woman.
■ **matron of honour** a married woman attending the bride at a wedding.
□ **matronly** adjective.

matt (or **matte**) ▸ adjective not shiny.

matted ▸ adjective (of hair or fur) tangled into a thick mass.

SYNONYMS **tangled,** knotted, tousled, dishevelled, uncombed, unkempt, ratty.

matter ▸ noun **1** physical substance or material. **2** a subject or situation to be considered or dealt with. **3** (**the matter**) the reason for a problem.

SYNONYMS **1** *vegetable matter* **material,** stuff, substance. **2** *a serious matter* **affair,** business, situation, concern, incident, episode, subject, topic, issue, question, point at issue, case.

▸ verb (**matters**, **mattering**, **mattered**) be important.

SYNONYMS *it doesn't matter what you wear* **be important,** make any difference, be of consequence, be relevant, count.

matter-of-fact ▸ adjective unemotional and practical.

SYNONYMS **unemotional,** practical, down-to-earth, sensible, realistic, unsentimental, pragmatic, businesslike, commonsensical, level-headed, hardheaded, no-nonsense, straightforward.

mattock ▸ noun a farming tool similar to a pickaxe.

mattress ▸ noun a fabric case filled with soft or firm material and sometimes incorporating springs, used for sleeping on.

mature ▸ adjective **1** fully grown. **2** like a sensible adult. **3** (of certain foods or drinks) developed over a long period in order to achieve a full flavour.

SYNONYMS **1** *a mature woman* **adult,** grown, fully grown, in your prime. **2** *he's very mature for his age* **grown-up,** sensible, responsible, adult, levelheaded. **3** *mature cheese* **ripe,** mellow, rich, strong, flavoursome, full-bodied. ANTONYMS immature.

▸ verb (**matures**, **maturing**, **matured**) **1** become mature. **2** (of an insurance policy) reach the end of its term and so become payable.

SYNONYMS **1** *kittens mature when they are about a year old* **become fully grown,** come of age, reach adulthood, reach maturity. **2** *he's matured since he left home* **grow up,** blossom. **3** *leave the cheese to mature* **ripen,** mellow, age. **4** *their friendship didn't have time to mature* **develop,** grow, evolve, bloom, blossom, flourish, thrive.

□ **maturation** noun **maturely** adverb.

maturity ▸ noun **1** the state or period of being mature. **2** the time when an insurance policy matures.

SYNONYMS **1** *her progress from childhood to maturity* **adulthood,** coming of age, manhood, womanhood. **2** *he displayed a maturity beyond his years* **responsibility,** sense, level-headedness.

maudlin /**mawd**-lin/ ▸ adjective sentimental in a self-pitying way.

maul ▸ verb **1** wound by scratching and tearing. **2** treat roughly.

SYNONYMS **savage,** attack, claw, scratch, lacerate, mangle, tear.

maunder ▸ verb (**maunders**, **maundering**, **maundered**) move, talk, or act in a rambling way.

Mauritanian ▸ noun a person from Mauritania, a country in West Africa.
▸ adjective relating to Mauritania.

mausoleum /maw-suh-**lee**-uhm/ ▸ noun (plural **mausolea** /maw-suh-**lee**-uh/ or **mausoleums**) a building containing a tomb or tombs.

mauve ▸ noun a pale or reddish-purple colour.

maverick ▸ noun an unconventional and independent-minded person.

m

synonyms **individualist**, nonconformist, free spirit, original, eccentric, rebel, dissenter, dissident.
antonyms conformist.

maw ▸ noun the jaws or throat.

mawkish ▸ adjective foolishly sentimental.

max ▸ abbreviation maximum.

maxim ▸ noun a short statement expressing a general truth or rule of behaviour.

maximize (or maximise) ▸ verb (maximizes, maximizing, maximized) **1** make something as large or great as possible. **2** make the best use of.

maximum ▸ noun (plural maxima or maximums) the greatest amount, size, or strength that is possible or that has been gained.

synonyms *production levels are near their maximum* **upper limit,** limit, utmost, greatest, most, peak, height, ceiling, top.
antonyms minimum.

▸ adjective greatest in amount, size, or strength.

synonyms *the maximum amount* **greatest,** highest, biggest, largest, top, most, utmost.
antonyms minimum.

☐ **maximal** adjective.

May ▸ noun **1** the fifth month of the year. **2** (may) the hawthorn or its blossom.

may ▸ modal verb (3rd singular present may; past might) **1** expressing possibility. **2** expressing permission. **3** expressing a wish or hope.

maybe ▸ adverb perhaps.

synonyms **perhaps,** possibly, for all one knows; N. English happen; literary perchance.

Mayday ▸ noun an international distress signal used by ships and aircraft.

mayfly ▸ noun (plural mayflies) an insect which lives as an adult for only a very short time.

mayhem ▸ noun violent disorder.

synonyms **chaos,** havoc, bedlam, pandemonium, uproar, turmoil, a riot, anarchy; informal a madhouse.

mayn't ▸ short form may not.

mayonnaise /may-uh-**nayz**/ ▸ noun a creamy dressing made from egg yolks, oil, and vinegar.

mayor ▸ noun the elected head of a city or borough council.
☐ **mayoral** adjective.

mayoralty /**mair**-uhl-ti/ ▸ noun (plural mayoralties) the period of office of a mayor.

mayoress ▸ noun **1** the wife of a mayor. **2** a woman elected as mayor.

maypole ▸ noun a decorated pole with long ribbons attached to the top, traditionally used for dancing round on the first day of May.

maze ▸ noun a complicated network of paths and walls or hedges designed as a challenge to find a way through.

synonyms **labyrinth,** network, warren, web, tangle, confusion, jungle.

mazurka ▸ noun a lively Polish dance.

MBA ▸ abbreviation Master of Business Administration.

MBE ▸ abbreviation Member of the Order of the British Empire.

MC ▸ abbreviation **1** master of ceremonies. **2** Military Cross.

MD ▸ abbreviation **1** Doctor of Medicine. **2** Brit. Managing Director.

ME ▸ abbreviation myalgic encephalomyelitis, a medical condition causing aching and prolonged tiredness.

me ▸ pronoun used as the object of a verb or preposition or after 'than', 'as', or the verb 'to be', to refer to the speaker himself or herself.

❗ It is wrong to use *me* as the subject of a verb, as in *John and me went to the shops*; in this case use *I* instead.

mead ▸ noun an alcoholic drink made from fermented honey and water.

meadow ▸ noun an area of grassland.

synonyms **field,** paddock, pasture; literary lea.

meadowsweet ▸ noun a tall plant with creamy-white sweet-smelling flowers.

meagre (US spelling meager) ▸ adjective small in quantity and of bad quality.
☐ **meagreness** noun.

meal¹ ▸ noun **1** any of the regular daily occasions when food is eaten. **2** the food eaten on such an occasion.

meal² ▸ noun the edible part of any grain or pulse ground to powder.
☐ **mealy** adjective.

mealy-mouthed ▸ adjective not wanting to speak honestly or frankly.

mean¹ ▸ verb (means, meaning, meant) **1** intend to say or show something. **2** (of a word) have as its explanation in the same language or its equivalent in another language. **3** intend something to happen or be the case. **4** have something as a result. **5** intend something for a particular purpose. **6** have a particular level of importance: *animals mean more to him than people.*

synonyms **1** *flashing lights mean the road is blocked* **signify,** denote, indicate, show, express, spell out, stand for, represent, symbolize, imply, suggest, intimate. **2** *she didn't mean to break it* **intend,** aim, plan, have in mind, set out, want. **3** *this will mean war* **entail,** involve, necessitate, lead to, result in, give rise to, bring about, cause, engender, produce.

mean[2] ▸ adjective **1** unwilling to give or share things. **2** unkind or unfair. **3** N. Amer. vicious or aggressive. **4** (of a place) poor and dirty in appearance.

> SYNONYMS **1** *he's too mean to leave a tip* **miserly,** niggardly, parsimonious, penny-pinching, cheese-paring; informal tight-fisted, stingy, tight; N. Amer. informal cheap. **2** *a mean trick* **unkind,** nasty, unpleasant, spiteful, malicious, unfair, shabby, despicable, contemptible, obnoxious, vile, loathsome, base, low; informal horrible, rotten.
> ANTONYMS generous, kind.

▢ **meanly** adverb **meanness** noun.

mean[3] ▸ noun **1** the average value of a set of quantities. **2** something in the middle of two extremes.
▸ adjective **1** calculated as a mean. **2** equally far from two extremes.

meander /mi-an-der/ ▸ verb (**meanders, meandering, meandered**) **1** follow a winding course. **2** wander in a leisurely way.
▸ noun a winding bend of a river or road.

meaning ▸ noun **1** the thing or idea that a word, signal, or action represents. **2** a sense of purpose.

> SYNONYMS **1** *the meaning of his remark* **significance,** sense, signification, import, gist, thrust, drift, implication, message. **2** *the word has several different meanings* **definition,** sense, explanation, interpretation.

meaningful ▸ adjective **1** having meaning. **2** worthwhile. **3** expressive.

> SYNONYMS **1** *a meaningful remark* **significant,** relevant, important, telling. **2** *a meaningful relationship* **sincere,** deep, serious, earnest, significant, important. **3** *a meaningful glance* **expressive,** eloquent, pointed, pregnant, revealing, suggestive.
> ANTONYMS inconsequential, insincere.

▢ **meaningfully** adverb.

meaningless ▸ adjective having no meaning or significance.

> SYNONYMS **unintelligible,** incomprehensible, incoherent.

▢ **meaninglessly** adverb.

means ▸ plural noun **1** a thing or method used to achieve a result. **2** money or wealth.

> SYNONYMS **1** *the best means to achieve your goal* **method,** way, manner, course, procedure. **2** *she doesn't have the means to support herself* **money,** resources, capital, income, finance, funds, cash, the wherewithal, assets, wealth, riches, affluence, fortune.

■ **by all means** of course. **by no means** certainly not. **means test** an official investigation into how much money or income a person has, to find out whether they qualify for welfare benefits.

meant past and past participle of MEAN[1].

meantime ▸ adverb (**in the meantime**) meanwhile.

meanwhile ▸ adverb **1** in the period of time between two events. **2** at the same time.

> SYNONYMS **1** *meanwhile, I'll stay here* **for now,** for the moment, for the present, for the time being, in the meanwhile, in the meantime, in the interim. **2** *cook for a further half hour; meanwhile, make the stuffing* **at the same time,** simultaneously, concurrently.

measles ▸ noun an infectious disease causing fever and a red rash.

measly ▸ adjective informal ridiculously small or few.

measure ▸ verb (**measures, measuring, measured**) **1** find out what the size, amount, or degree of something is in standard units. **2** be of a particular size, amount, or degree. **3** (**measure something out**) take an exact quantity of. **4** (**measure up**) reach the required standard.

> SYNONYMS **quantify,** gauge, size, count, weigh, evaluate, assess, determine, calculate, compute.

▸ noun **1** a course of action taken to achieve a purpose. **2** a proposal for a new law. **3** a standard unit used to express size, amount, or degree. **4** a measuring device marked with such units. **5** (**a measure of**) an indication of the extent or quality of.

> SYNONYMS **1** *cost-cutting measures* **action,** act, course of action, deed, procedure, step, expedient, initiative, programme. **2** *the Senate passed the measure* **statute,** act, bill, law. **3** *use a measure to check the size* **ruler,** tape measure, gauge, meter, scale, level. **4** *sales are the measure of the company's success* **yardstick,** test, standard, barometer, touchstone, benchmark.

■ **for good measure** as an amount or item that is additional to what is strictly necessary. **have the measure of** understand the character of.

▢ **measurable** adjective **measurably** adverb.

measured ▸ adjective **1** slow and regular in rhythm. **2** carefully considered.

m

SYNONYMS **1** *his measured tread* **regular,** steady, even, rhythmic, unfaltering, slow, dignified, stately, sedate, leisurely, unhurried. **2** *his measured tones* **thoughtful,** careful, considered, deliberate, restrained.

measurement ▶ noun **1** the action of measuring. **2** an amount, size, or extent found by measuring.

SYNONYMS **1** *measurement of the effect is difficult* **quantification,** evaluation, assessment, calculation, computation. **2** *all measurements are in metric units* **size,** dimension, proportions, value, amount, quantity.

meat ▶ noun the flesh of an animal used as food.

meatball ▶ noun a ball of minced or chopped meat.

meaty ▶ adjective (**meatier, meatiest**) **1** full of meat. **2** fleshy or muscular. **3** substantial or challenging.

Mecca ▶ noun **1** the holiest city for Muslims, in Saudi Arabia. **2** a place which attracts many people.

mechanic ▶ noun a skilled worker who repairs and maintains machinery.

mechanical ▶ adjective **1** relating to or operated by a machine or machinery. **2** done without thought. **3** relating to physical forces or movement.

SYNONYMS **1** *a mechanical device* **mechanized,** machine-driven, automated, automatic. **2** *a mechanical response* **automatic,** knee-jerk, unthinking, instinctive, habitual, routine, unemotional, unfeeling. ANTONYMS manual, thoughtful.

□ **mechanically** adverb.

mechanics ▶ noun **1** the branch of study concerned with the forces producing movement. **2** machinery or working parts. **3** the practical aspects of something.

mechanism ▶ noun **1** a piece of machinery. **2** the way in which something works or is made to happen.

SYNONYMS **1** *an electrical mechanism* **apparatus,** machine, appliance, device, instrument, contraption, gadget; informal gizmo. **2** *the train's safety mechanism* **machinery,** gear, system, equipment. **3** *a complaints mechanism* **procedure,** process, system, method, means, medium, channel.

mechanize (or **mechanise**) ▶ verb (**mechanizes, mechanizing, mechanized**) equip with machines or automatic devices. □ **mechanization** noun.

medal ▶ noun a metal disc with an inscription or design on it, awarded to someone for a special achievement.

medallion ▶ noun **1** a piece of jewellery in the shape of a medal, worn as a pendant. **2** a decorative oval or circular painting, panel, or design.

medallist (US spelling **medalist**) ▶ noun a person who has been awarded a medal.

meddle ▶ verb (**meddles, meddling, meddled**) interfere in something that is not your concern. □ **meddler** noun.

meddlesome ▶ adjective fond of interfering in other people's affairs.

media ▶ noun **1** television, radio, and newspapers as providers of information. **2** plural of MEDIUM.

❗ The word **media** comes from the Latin plural of **medium**. In its normal sense, 'television, radio, and newspapers', it can be used with either a singular or a plural verb.

mediaeval ➞ MEDIEVAL.

medial /mee-di-uhl/ ▶ adjective situated in the middle.

median ▶ adjective technical situated in the middle.
▶ noun **1** a median value. **2** Geometry a straight line drawn from one of the angles of a triangle to the middle of the opposite side.

mediate ▶ verb (**mediates, mediating, mediated**) try to settle a dispute between other people or groups.

SYNONYMS **1** *Austria tried to mediate between the two sides* **arbitrate,** conciliate, moderate, make peace, intervene, intercede, act as an intermediary, liaise. **2** *a tribunal was set up to mediate disputes* **resolve,** settle, arbitrate in, umpire, reconcile, referee, mend, clear up; informal patch up.

mediation ▶ noun the action of mediating.

SYNONYMS **arbitration,** conciliation, reconciliation, intervention, intercession, negotiation, shuttle diplomacy.

mediator ▶ noun a person who mediates.

SYNONYMS **arbitrator,** arbiter, negotiator, conciliator, peacemaker, go-between, middleman, intermediary, moderator, honest broker, liaison officer, umpire, referee, adjudicator, judge.

medic ▶ noun informal a doctor or medical student.

medical ▶ adjective relating to the science or practice of medicine.
▶ noun an examination to see how healthy someone is. □ **medically** adverb.

medicament ▶ noun a medicine.

medicate ▶ verb (**medicates, medicating, medicated**) **1** give medicine or a drug to.

m

2 (medicated) containing a substance that has healing properties.

medication ▸ noun **1** a medicine or drug. **2** treatment with medicines.

medicinal ▸ adjective **1** having healing properties. **2** relating to medicines.
□ **medicinally** adverb.

medicine ▸ noun **1** the science or practice of the treatment and prevention of disease. **2** a substance taken by mouth in order to treat or prevent disease.

> SYNONYMS **medication**, drug, prescription, treatment, remedy, cure, nostrum, panacea, cure-all.

■ **medicine man** a person believed to have supernatural healing powers.

medieval (or **mediaeval**) /me-di-ee-v'l/ ▸ adjective relating to the Middle Ages, the period between about 1000 and 1450.

medievalist (or **mediaevalist**) ▸ noun a person who studies medieval history or literature.

mediocre /mee-di-oh-ker/ ▸ adjective of only average or fairly low quality.

> SYNONYMS **average**, ordinary, undistinguished, uninspired, indifferent, unexceptional, unexciting, unremarkable, run-of-the-mill, pedestrian, prosaic, lacklustre, forgettable, amateurish; informal so-so.
> ANTONYMS excellent.

□ **mediocrity** noun.

meditate ▸ verb (meditates, meditating, meditated) **1** focus your mind and free it of uncontrolled thoughts, as a spiritual exercise or for relaxation. **2** (meditate on or about) think carefully about.

> SYNONYMS **contemplate**, think, consider, ponder, muse, reflect, deliberate, ruminate, brood, mull over.

□ **meditation** noun **meditative** adjective **meditatively** adverb.

Mediterranean ▸ adjective relating to the Mediterranean Sea or the countries around it.

> ✔ one **d**, one **t**, double **r**: Mediterranean.

medium ▸ noun (plural **media** or **mediums**) **1** a means by which something is communicated or achieved. **2** a substance that something lives or exists in, or through which it travels. **3** the type of material used by an artist. **4** (plural **mediums**) a person who claims to be able to communicate with the spirits of dead people. **5** the middle state between two extremes.

> SYNONYMS a medium of expression **means**, method, avenue, channel, vehicle, organ, instrument, mechanism.

▸ adjective between two extremes.

> SYNONYMS he is of medium build **average**, middling, medium-sized, middle-sized, moderate, normal, standard.

medlar ▸ noun a fruit resembling a small brown apple.

medley ▸ noun (plural **medleys**) a varied mixture.

meek ▸ adjective quiet, gentle, and obedient.
□ **meekly** adverb.

meerkat ▸ noun a small southern African mongoose.

meet ▸ verb (meets, meeting, met) **1** come together with someone at the same place and time. **2** be introduced to or come across someone for the first time. **3** touch or join. **4** come across a situation. **5** (meet with) receive a particular reaction. **6** fulfil or satisfy a requirement.

> SYNONYMS **1** I met an old friend on the train **encounter**, come face to face with, run into, run across, come across/upon, chance on, happen on, stumble across; informal bump into. **2** she first met Paul at a party **get to know**, be introduced to, make the acquaintance of. **3** the committee met on Saturday **assemble**, gather, come together, get together, congregate, convene. **4** the place where three roads meet **converge**, connect, touch, link up, intersect, cross, join.

▸ noun a gathering or meeting.

meeting ▸ noun **1** an occasion when people meet to discuss or decide something. **2** a situation in which people come together.

> SYNONYMS **1** he stood up to address the meeting **gathering**, assembly, conference, congregation, convention, summit, rally; informal get-together. **2** she demanded a meeting with the minister **consultation**, audience, interview. **3** he intrigued her on their first meeting **encounter**, contact, appointment, assignation, rendezvous. **4** the meeting of land and sea **convergence**, coming together, confluence, conjunction, union, intersection, crossing. **5** an athletics meeting **event**, tournament, meet, rally, competition, match, game, contest.

mega ▸ adjective informal **1** very large. **2** excellent.

megabyte ▸ noun Computing a unit of information equal to one million bytes.

megalith ▸ noun a large stone that forms a prehistoric monument or part of one.
□ **megalithic** adjective.

megalomania ▸ noun **1** the false belief that you are very powerful and important. **2** a strong desire for power.
□ **megalomaniac** noun & adjective.

megaphone ▸ noun a cone-shaped device for making the voice sound louder.

megapixel ▸ noun a unit for measuring the resolution of a digital image, equal to one million pixels.

megaton ▸ noun a unit for measuring the power of an explosive, equivalent to one million tons of TNT.

megawatt ▸ noun a unit of power equal to one million watts.

melamine /mel-uh-meen/ ▸ noun a hard plastic used to coat the surfaces of tables or worktops.

melancholia /me-luhn-**koh**-li-uh/ ▸ noun great sadness or depression.

melancholy ▸ noun deep and long-lasting sadness.

> SYNONYMS *a feeling of melancholy* **sadness**, sorrow, unhappiness, depression, despondency, gloom, misery; informal **the blues**.
> ANTONYMS happiness.

▸ adjective sad or depressed.

> SYNONYMS *a melancholy mood* **sad**, sorrowful, unhappy, gloomy, despondent, glum, miserable, morose; informal **down in the dumps**, blue.
> ANTONYMS cheerful.

□ **melancholic** adjective.

melanin ▸ noun a dark pigment in the hair and skin, responsible for the tanning of skin exposed to sunlight.

melanoma ▸ noun a form of skin cancer.

meld ▸ verb blend.

melee /mel-ay/ ▸ noun **1** a confused fight or scuffle. **2** a disorderly crowd of people.

mellifluous ▸ adjective pleasingly smooth and musical to hear.

mellow ▸ adjective **1** pleasantly smooth or soft in sound, taste, or colour. **2** relaxed and good-humoured.

> SYNONYMS **1** *she loved the mellow tone of his voice* **sweet-sounding**, dulcet, soft, smooth, warm, full, rich. **2** *a mellow wine* **full-bodied**, mature, full-flavoured, rich, smooth. **3** *a mellow mood* **genial**, affable, amiable, good-humoured, good-natured, pleasant, relaxed, easy-going.
> ANTONYMS harsh, rough, irritable.

▸ verb make or become mellow.

melodic ▸ adjective **1** relating to melody. **2** sounding pleasant.
□ **melodically** adverb.

melodious ▸ adjective tuneful.

melodrama ▸ noun **1** a play full of exciting events, in which the characters seem too exaggerated to be realistic. **2** behaviour or events that are very dramatic.

melodramatic ▸ adjective too dramatic and exaggerated.

□ **melodramatically** adverb.

melody ▸ noun (plural **melodies**) **1** a piece of music with a clear or simple tune. **2** the main tune in a piece of music.

> SYNONYMS **tune**, air, strain, theme, song, refrain.

melon ▸ noun a large round fruit with sweet pulpy flesh.

melt ▸ verb **1** make or become liquid by heating. **2** (**melt away**) gradually disappear. **3** become more tender or loving.

> SYNONYMS **1** *the snow was beginning to melt* **liquefy**, thaw, defrost, soften, dissolve. **2** *his anger melted away* **vanish**, disappear, fade, dissolve, evaporate.
> ANTONYMS freeze, grow.

■ **melting pot** a place where different peoples, ideas, or styles are mixed together.

meltdown ▸ noun an accident in a nuclear reactor in which the fuel overheats and melts the reactor core.

member ▸ noun **1** a person or organization belonging to a group or society. **2** old use a part of the body.

> SYNONYMS **subscriber**, associate, supporter, fellow, representative.

□ **membership** noun.

membrane ▸ noun **1** a skin-like tissue that connects, covers, or lines cells or parts of the body. **2** a layer of thin, skin-like material.
□ **membranous** adjective.

memento ▸ noun (plural **mementos** or **mementoes**) an object kept as a reminder.

memo ▸ noun (plural **memos**) a written note sent from one person to another within an organization.

memoir /mem-war/ ▸ noun **1** a historical account or biography written from personal knowledge. **2** (**memoirs**) an account written by a public figure of their life and experiences.

> SYNONYMS **1** *a touching memoir of her childhood* **account**, history, record, chronicle, narrative, story, portrayal, depiction, portrait, profile. **2** *he published his memoirs in 1955* **autobiography**, life story, journal, diary.

memorabilia ▸ plural noun objects kept or collected because of their associations with people or events.

memorable ▸ adjective worth remembering or easily remembered.

> SYNONYMS **unforgettable**, indelible, catchy, haunting, momentous, significant, historic, notable, noteworthy, outstanding, arresting.

□ **memorably** adverb.

memorandum ▸ noun (plural **memoranda** or **memorandums**) **1** formal a memo. **2** a note recording something for future use.

memorial ▸ noun a column or other structure made or built in memory of a person or event.

> SYNONYMS **1** *the war memorial* **monument,** cenotaph, mausoleum, statue, plaque, cairn, shrine. **2** *the festival is a memorial to his life's work* **tribute,** testimonial, remembrance, memento.

▸ adjective created or done in memory of someone.

> SYNONYMS *a memorial service* **commemorative,** remembrance.

memorize (or memorise) ▸ verb (**memorizes, memorizing, memorized**) learn and remember exactly.

> SYNONYMS **commit to memory,** remember, learn (by heart), become word-perfect in.

memory ▸ noun (plural **memories**) **1** the power that the mind has to store and remember information. **2** a thing remembered. **3** the length of time over which you can remember things. **4** a computer's equipment or capacity for storing data.

> SYNONYMS **1** *happy memories of her childhood* **recollection,** remembrance, reminiscence. **2** *the town built a statue in memory of him* **commemoration,** remembrance, honour, tribute, recognition, respect.

men plural of MAN.

menace ▸ noun **1** a dangerous or troublesome person or thing. **2** a threatening quality.

> SYNONYMS **1** *an atmosphere full of menace* **threat,** intimidation, malevolence, oppression. **2** *a menace to society* **danger,** peril, risk, hazard, threat. **3** *that child is a menace* **nuisance,** pest, troublemaker, mischief-maker; informal bad news.

▸ verb (**menaces, menacing, menaced**) threaten.

> SYNONYMS **1** *the elephants are still menaced by poaching* **threaten,** endanger, put at risk, jeopardize, imperil. **2** *a gang of skinheads menaced local residents* **intimidate,** threaten, terrorize, frighten, scare, terrify. **3** (**menacing**) **threatening,** ominous, intimidating, frightening, forbidding, hostile, sinister, baleful.

ménage à trois /may-nahzh ah trwah/ ▸ noun an arrangement in which a married couple and the lover of one of them live together.

menagerie /muh-**naj**-uh-ri/ ▸ noun a small zoo.

mend ▸ verb **1** restore something so that it is no longer broken, torn, or out of action. **2** improve an unpleasant situation.

> SYNONYMS **repair,** fix, restore, sew (up), stitch, darn, patch, renew, renovate, fill in; informal patch up.
> ANTONYMS break.

▸ noun a repair.

mendacious /men-**day**-shuss/ ▸ adjective untruthful; lying.
□ **mendacity** noun.

mendicant /**men**-di-kuhnt/ ▸ adjective **1** living by begging. **2** (of a religious order) originally dependent on charitable donations.
▸ noun **1** a beggar. **2** a member of a mendicant religious order.

menhir /**men**-heer/ ▸ noun a tall upright prehistoric stone erected as a monument.

menial /**mee**-ni-uhl/ ▸ adjective (of work) needing little skill and lacking status.
▸ noun a person with a menial job.

meningitis /men-in-**jy**-tiss/ ▸ noun an infectious disease in which the membranes enclosing the brain and spinal cord become inflamed.

meniscus /mi-**niss**-kuhss/ ▸ noun (plural **menisci** /mi-**niss**-I/) **1** the curved upper surface of a liquid in a tube. **2** a thin lens curving outwards on one side and inwards on the other.

menopause ▸ noun the time when a woman gradually stops having menstrual periods, on average around the age of 50.
□ **menopausal** adjective.

menorah /mi-**nor**-uh/ ▸ noun a large candlestick with several branches, used in Jewish worship.

menstrual ▸ adjective having to do with menstruation.

menstruate ▸ verb (**menstruates, menstruating, menstruated**) (of a woman) have a flow of blood from the lining of the womb each month.
□ **menstruation** noun.

mental ▸ adjective **1** having to do with the mind. **2** relating to disorders of the mind. **3** informal mad.

> SYNONYMS **1** *mental faculties* **intellectual,** cerebral, rational, cognitive. **2** *a mental disorder* **psychiatric,** psychological, behavioural.
> ANTONYMS physical.

mentality ▸ noun (plural **mentalities**) a characteristic way of thinking.

> SYNONYMS **way of thinking,** mindset, mind, psychology, attitude, outlook, make-up.

m

mentally ▸ adverb in the mind.

> SYNONYMS **psychologically,** intellectually, in your mind, in your head, inwardly, internally.

menthol ▸ noun a substance found in peppermint oil, used in medicines and as a flavouring.
□ **mentholated** adjective.

mention ▸ verb refer to something or someone briefly.

> SYNONYMS **1** *don't mention the war* **allude to,** refer to, touch on/upon, bring up, raise, broach. **2** *Jim mentioned that he'd met them before* **state,** say, indicate, let someone know, disclose, divulge, reveal.

▸ noun **1** a brief reference to someone or something. **2** a formal acknowledgement that someone has done something well.

> SYNONYMS **reference,** allusion, comment, citation; informal namecheck, plug.

mentor ▸ noun an experienced person who advises you over a period of time.

> SYNONYMS **adviser,** counsellor, guide, guru, consultant, confidant(e), trainer, teacher, tutor, instructor.

menu ▸ noun **1** a list of dishes available in a restaurant. **2** the food to be served in a restaurant or at a meal. **3** Computing a list of commands or facilities displayed on screen.

> SYNONYMS **bill of fare,** tariff, carte du jour, set menu, table d'hôte.

meow → MIAOW.

MEP ▸ abbreviation Member of the European Parliament.

mercantile /mer-kuhn-tyl/ ▸ adjective relating to trade or commerce.

mercenary ▸ adjective wanting to do only things that make you money.
▸ noun (plural **mercenaries**) a professional soldier who is hired to serve in a foreign army.

merchandise ▸ noun goods for sale.

> SYNONYMS **goods,** wares, stock, commodities, produce, products.

merchant ▸ noun a trader who sells goods in large quantities.

> SYNONYMS **trader,** tradesman, dealer, wholesaler, broker, agent, seller, retailer, supplier, buyer, vendor, distributor.

▸ adjective (of ships, sailors, or shipping activity) involved with commerce.
■ **merchant bank** a bank whose customers are large businesses. **merchant navy** a country's commercial shipping.

merchantable ▸ adjective suitable for sale.

merciful ▸ adjective **1** showing mercy.
2 giving relief from suffering.
□ **mercifully** adverb.

merciless ▸ adjective showing no mercy.
□ **mercilessly** adverb.

mercurial /mer-**kyoor**-i-uhl/ ▸ adjective
1 tending to change mood suddenly.
2 having to do with the element mercury.

mercury ▸ noun **1** a heavy silvery-white liquid metallic element used in some thermometers and barometers. **2** (**Mercury**) the planet closest to the sun in the solar system.

mercy ▸ noun (plural **mercies**) **1** kindness or forgiveness shown towards someone who is in your power. **2** something to be grateful for.

> SYNONYMS **pity,** compassion, leniency, clemency, charity, forgiveness, forbearance, kindness, sympathy, indulgence, tolerance, generosity, magnanimity.
> ANTONYMS ruthlessness, cruelty.

■ **at the mercy of** in the power of.

mere ▸ adjective **1** being no more than what is stated or described. **2** (**the merest**) the smallest or slightest.

merely ▸ adverb only.

> SYNONYMS **only,** purely, solely, simply, just, but.

meretricious /me-ri-**tri**-shuhss/ ▸ adjective superficially attractive but having no real value.

merge ▸ verb (**merges, merging, merged**)
1 combine or be combined into a whole.
2 blend gradually into something else.

> SYNONYMS **1** *the company merged with a European firm* **join (together),** join forces, amalgamate, unite, affiliate, team up. **2** *the two organizations were merged* **amalgamate,** bring together, join, consolidate, conflate, unite, unify, combine, incorporate, integrate. **3** *the two colours merged* **mingle,** blend, fuse, mix, intermix, intermingle, coalesce.
> ANTONYMS separate.

merger ▸ noun a merging of two organizations into one.

> SYNONYMS **amalgamation,** combination, union, fusion, coalition, affiliation, unification, incorporation, consolidation, link-up, alliance.
> ANTONYMS split.

meridian ▸ noun a circle passing at the same longitude through a given place on the earth's surface and the two poles.

meringue /muh-**rang**/ ▸ noun beaten egg whites and sugar baked until crisp.

merino ▸ noun (plural **merinos**) a soft wool obtained from a breed of sheep with a long fleece.

merit ▸ noun **1** the quality of being good and deserving praise. **2** a good point or feature.

SYNONYMS 1 *composers of outstanding merit* **excellence,** quality, calibre, worth, value, distinction, eminence. **2** *the merits of the scheme* **good point,** strong point, advantage, benefit, value, asset, plus. **ANTONYMS** inferiority, fault, disadvantage.

▶ verb (**merits, meriting, merited**) deserve.

SYNONYMS *the accusation did not merit a response* **deserve,** warrant, justify, earn, rate, be worthy of, be entitled to, have a right to, have a claim to/on.

meritocracy ▶ noun (plural **meritocracies**) a society in which power is held by those people who have the greatest ability.
□ **meritocratic** adjective.

meritorious ▶ adjective deserving reward or praise.

merlin ▶ noun a small falcon.

Merlot /mer-loh/ ▶ noun a type of red wine.

mermaid ▶ noun a mythical sea creature with a woman's head and body and a fish's tail instead of legs.

merriment ▶ noun fun.

merry ▶ adjective (**merrier, merriest**) **1** cheerful and lively. **2** informal slightly drunk.

SYNONYMS **cheerful,** cheery, in high spirits, sunny, smiling, light-hearted, lively, carefree, joyful, joyous, jolly, convivial, festive, gleeful, happy, laughing; informal **chirpy**. **ANTONYMS** miserable.

■ **merry-go-round** a revolving platform fitted with model horses or cars, on which people ride for fun.
□ **merrily** adverb.

merrymaking ▶ noun lively celebration and fun.

Mesdames plural of **MADAME**.

Mesdemoiselles plural of **MADEMOISELLE**.

mesh ▶ noun **1** material made of a network of wire or thread. **2** the spacing of the strands of a net.

SYNONYMS *wire mesh* **netting,** net, grille, screen, lattice, gauze.

▶ verb **1** fit together or be in harmony. **2** (of a gearwheel) lock together with another.

SYNONYMS 1 *our ideas just do not mesh* **harmonize,** fit together, match, dovetail, connect, interconnect. **2** *one gear meshes with the input gear* **engage,** connect, lock, interlock.

mesmeric ▶ adjective hypnotic.

mesmerism ▶ noun hypnotism.

mesmerize (or **mesmerise**) ▶ verb (**mesmerizes, mesmerizing, mesmerized**) capture someone's attention so that they are completely enthralled.

Mesolithic ▶ adjective relating to the middle part of the Stone Age.

mess ▶ noun **1** a dirty or untidy state. **2** a state of confusion or difficulty. **3** a portion of semi-solid food. **4** a dog or cat's excrement. **5** a place where members of the armed forces eat and relax.

SYNONYMS 1 *please clear up the mess* **untidiness,** disorder, disarray, clutter, muddle, chaos; informal **shambles**; Brit. informal **tip**. **2** *I've got to get out of this mess* **plight,** predicament, tight spot, tight corner, difficulty, trouble, quandary, dilemma, problem, muddle, mix-up; informal **jam, fix, pickle, hole**.

▶ verb **1** make something untidy or dirty. **2** (**mess about** or **around**) behave in a silly or playful way. **3** (**mess with**) informal meddle with.

message ▶ noun **1** a spoken, written, or electronic communication. **2** a significant point or central theme.

SYNONYMS 1 *are there any messages for me?* **communication,** news, note, memo, email, letter, missive, report, bulletin, communiqué, dispatch. **2** *the message of his teaching* **meaning,** sense, import, idea, point, thrust, moral, gist, essence, implication.

▶ verb (**messages, messaging, messaged**) send a message to.

messenger ▶ noun a person who carries a message.

SYNONYMS **courier,** postman, runner, dispatch rider, envoy, emissary, agent, go-between.

messiah ▶ noun **1** (the Messiah) (in Judaism) the person who will be sent by God as the saviour of the Jewish people. **2** (the Messiah) (in Christianity) Jesus, regarded as this saviour. **3** a great leader seen as the saviour of a country, group, etc.

messianic /mess-i-an-ik/ ▶ adjective relating to a messiah.

Messieurs plural of **MONSIEUR**.

Messrs plural of **MR**.

messy ▶ adjective (**messier, messiest**) **1** untidy or dirty. **2** confused and difficult to deal with.

SYNONYMS 1 *messy clothes* **dirty,** filthy, grubby, soiled, grimy, mucky, muddy, stained, smeared, smudged, dishevelled, scruffy, unkempt, rumpled, matted, tousled; informal **yucky**. **2** *a messy kitchen* **untidy,** disordered, in a muddle, chaotic, confused, disorganized, in disarray, cluttered, in a jumble; informal **like a bomb's hit it**; Brit. informal **shambolic**. **3** *a messy legal battle* **complex,** tangled, confused, convoluted, unpleasant, nasty,

m

bitter, acrimonious.
ANTONYMS clean, tidy.
□ **messily** adverb **messiness** noun.

met past and past participle of MEET.

metabolism /mi-**tab**-uh-li-z'm/ ▸ noun the process by which food is used for the growth of tissue or the production of energy.
□ **metabolic** adjective.

metabolize (or metabolise) ▸ verb (metabolizes, metabolizing, metabolized) process by metabolism.

metal ▸ noun **1** a hard, solid, shiny material which conducts electricity and heat. **2** (also **road metal**) broken stone used in making road surfaces.

metalled ▸ adjective Brit. (of a road) having a hard surface.

metallic ▸ adjective **1** having to do with metal. **2** (of sound) sharp and ringing.

metallurgy /mi-**tal**-ler-ji, **met**-uh-ler-ji/ ▸ noun the scientific study of metals.
□ **metallurgical** adjective **metallurgist** noun.

metamorphic ▸ adjective (of rock) having been changed by heat and pressure.

metamorphosis /met-uh-**mor**-fuh-siss/ ▸ noun (plural **metamorphoses** /met-uh-**mor**-fuh-seez/) **1** the transformation of an insect or amphibian from an immature form or larva to an adult form. **2** a change in form or nature.
□ **metamorphose** verb.

metaphor /**met**-uh-fer/ ▸ noun a word or phrase used in an imaginative way to represent or stand for something else (e.g. *the long arm of the law*).

SYNONYMS **figure of speech,** image, trope, analogy, comparison, symbol.

metaphorical /met-uh-**fo**-ri-k'l/ (or metaphoric) ▸ adjective having to do with metaphor.
□ **metaphorically** adverb.

metaphysical ▸ adjective **1** relating to metaphysics. **2** beyond physical matter.
□ **metaphysically** adverb.

metaphysics ▸ noun the branch of philosophy dealing with the nature of existence, truth, and knowledge.

mete ▸ verb (metes, meting, meted) (**mete something out**) give someone a punishment, or subject them to harsh treatment.

meteor ▸ noun a small body of matter from space that glows as a result of friction with the earth's atmosphere, and appears as a shooting star.

meteoric ▸ adjective **1** relating to meteors or meteorites. **2** rapid in achieving success or promotion.

meteorite ▸ noun a piece of rock or metal that has fallen to the earth from space.

meteorology ▸ noun the study of conditions in the atmosphere, especially for weather forecasting.
□ **meteorological** adjective **meteorologist** noun.

meter[1] ▸ noun a device that measures and records the quantity, degree, or rate of something.
▸ verb (meters, metering, metered) measure something with a meter.

meter[2] US spelling of METRE[1], METRE[2].

methadone ▸ noun a powerful painkiller, used as a substitute for morphine and heroin in treating people addicted to these drugs.

methane ▸ noun a flammable gas which is the main constituent of natural gas.

methanol ▸ noun a poisonous flammable alcohol, used to make methylated spirit.

methinks ▸ verb (past **methought**) old use it seems to me.

method ▸ noun **1** a way of doing something. **2** the quality of being well planned and organized.

SYNONYMS **1** *they use very old-fashioned methods* **procedure,** technique, system, practice, routine, modus operandi, process, strategy, tactic, approach. **2** *there's no method in his approach* **order,** organization, structure, form, system, logic, planning, design, consistency.
ANTONYMS disorder.

methodical (or methodic) ▸ adjective done or doing something in a well-organized and systematic way.

SYNONYMS **orderly,** well ordered, well organized, (well) planned, efficient, businesslike, systematic, structured, logical, disciplined, consistent, scientific.

□ **methodically** adverb.

Methodist ▸ noun a member of a Christian Protestant group which separated from the Church of England in the 18th century.
▸ adjective relating to Methodists or their beliefs.
□ **Methodism** noun.

methodology ▸ noun (plural **methodologies**) a particular system of methods.
□ **methodological** adjective.

meths ▸ noun Brit. informal methylated spirit.

methylated spirit (or methylated spirits) ▸ noun alcohol for use as a solvent or fuel, made unfit for drinking by the addition of methanol and a violet dye.

meticulous ▸ adjective very careful and precise.

SYNONYMS **careful,** conscientious, diligent, scrupulous, punctilious,

painstaking, thorough, studious, rigorous, detailed, perfectionist, fastidious.
ANTONYMS careless.

□ **meticulously** adverb.

métier /**may**-ti-ay/ ▶ noun a person's trade, profession, or special ability.

metre[1] (US spelling **meter**) ▶ noun the basic unit of length in the metric system, equal to 100 centimetres (approximately 39.37 inches).

metre[2] (US spelling **meter**) ▶ noun the rhythm of a piece of poetry.

metric ▶ adjective relating to or using the metric system.
■ **metric system** the decimal measuring system based on the metre, litre, and gram. **metric ton** (or **metric tonne**) a unit of weight equal to 1,000 kilograms (2,205 lb).

metrical ▶ adjective having to do with poetic metre.
□ **metrically** adverb.

metricate ▶ verb (**metricates, metricating, metricated**) convert a system of measurement to the metric system.
□ **metrication** noun.

metro ▶ noun (plural **metros**) an underground railway system in a city.

metronome ▶ noun a device that marks time at a selected rate by giving a regular tick, used by musicians.
□ **metronomic** adjective.

metropolis ▶ noun the main city of a country or region.

metropolitan ▶ adjective relating to the main city of a country or region.

mettle ▶ noun spirit and strength of character.

mew ▶ verb (of a cat or gull) make a soft, high-pitched sound like a cry.

mewl ▶ verb **1** cry feebly. **2** mew.

mews ▶ noun (plural **mews**) Brit. a row of houses or flats converted from stables in a small street or square.

Mexican ▶ noun a person from Mexico.
▶ adjective relating to Mexico.

mezzanine /**mets**-uh-neen/ ▶ noun a floor extending over only part of the full area of a building, built between two full floors.

mezzo /**met**-soh/ (or **mezzo-soprano**) ▶ noun (plural **mezzos**) a female singer with a voice pitched between soprano and contralto.

mg ▶ abbreviation milligrams.

MHz ▶ abbreviation megahertz.

miaow (or **meow**) ▶ noun the cry of a cat.
▶ verb make a miaow.

miasma /mi-**az**-muh/ ▶ noun an unpleasant or unhealthy atmosphere.

mica /**my**-kuh/ ▶ noun a mineral found as tiny shiny scales in rocks.

mice plural of MOUSE.

mickey ▶ noun **(take the mickey)** Brit. informal tease or mock someone.

microbe ▶ noun a bacterium; a germ.

SYNONYMS **microorganism**, bacterium, bacillus, germ; informal bug.

□ **microbial** adjective.

microbiology ▶ noun the scientific study of living creatures that are so tiny that they can only be seen using a microscope.

microchip ▶ noun a miniature electronic circuit made from a tiny wafer of silicon.

microclimate ▶ noun the climate of a very small or restricted area.

microcosm ▶ noun a thing that has the features and qualities of something much larger.

microfiche /**my**-kroh-feesh/ (or **microfilm**) ▶ noun a piece of film containing very small-sized photographs of the pages of a newspaper, book, etc.

microlight ▶ noun Brit. a very small, light one- or two-seater aircraft.

micrometer /my-**krom**-i-ter/ ▶ noun an instrument which measures small distances or thicknesses.

microorganism ▶ noun an organism that is so small that it can only be seen using a microscope.

microphone ▶ noun an instrument for changing sound waves into electrical energy which is then amplified and transmitted or recorded.

microprocessor ▶ noun an integrated circuit which can function as the main part of a computer.

microscope ▶ noun an instrument for magnifying very small objects.

microscopic ▶ adjective so small as to be visible only with a microscope.
□ **microscopically** adverb.

microscopy /my-**kross**-kuh-pi/ ▶ noun the use of a microscope.

microsurgery ▶ noun surgery performed using very small instruments and a microscope.

microwave ▶ noun **1** an electromagnetic wave with a wavelength in the range $0.001–0.3$ m. **2** (also **microwave oven**) an oven that uses microwaves to cook or heat food.
▶ verb (**microwaves, microwaving, microwaved**) cook food in a microwave oven.

mid ▶ adjective having to do with the middle position of a range.
▶ preposition literary amid; in the middle of.

Midas touch ▶ noun the ability to make a lot of money out of anything you do.

midday ▶ noun twelve o'clock in the day; noon.

m

SYNONYMS **noon,** twelve noon, high noon, noonday.
ANTONYMS midnight.

midden ▸ noun a heap of dung or refuse.

middle ▸ adjective **1** positioned at an equal distance from the edges or ends of something. **2** medium in rank, quality, or ability.

SYNONYMS *the middle point* **central,** mid, mean, medium, median, midway, halfway.

▸ noun **1** a middle point or position. **2** informal a person's waist and stomach.

SYNONYMS **1 centre,** midpoint, halfway point, dead centre, hub, eye, heart, core, kernel. **2** *he had a towel round his middle* **midriff,** waist, belly, stomach; informal tummy.
ANTONYMS edge.

■ **middle age** the period when a person is between about 45 and 60 in age. **Middle Ages** the period of European history between about 1000 and 1450. **middle class** the social group between the aristocracy and the working class. **middle ear** the air-filled central cavity of the ear, behind the eardrum. **Middle East** an area of SW Asia and northern Africa, stretching from the Mediterranean to Pakistan. **middle-of-the-road 1** (of views) not extreme. **2** (of music) generally popular but rather unadventurous.

middleman ▸ noun (plural **middlemen**) **1** a person who buys goods from the company who makes them and sells them on to shops or consumers. **2** a person who arranges business or political deals between other people.

middling ▸ adjective average in size, amount, or rank.

midfield ▸ noun the central part of a sports field.
□ **midfielder** noun.

midge ▸ noun a small fly that breeds near water.

midget ▸ noun a very small person.
▸ adjective very small.

midland ▸ noun **1** the middle part of a country. **2** (**the Midlands**) the inland counties of central England.

midnight ▸ noun twelve o'clock at night.

midriff ▸ noun the front of the body between the chest and the waist.

midship ▸ noun the middle part of a ship or boat.

midshipman ▸ noun (plural **midshipmen**) a low-ranking officer in the Royal Navy.

midships = AMIDSHIPS.

midst old use ▸ preposition in the middle of.
▸ noun the middle point or part.

midstream ▸ noun the middle of a stream or river.

midsummer ▸ noun **1** the middle part of summer. **2** the summer solstice.
■ **Midsummer Day** (or **Midsummer's Day**) 24 June.

midterm ▸ noun the middle of a period of office, an academic term, or a pregnancy.

midway ▸ adverb & adjective in or towards the middle.

midweek ▸ noun the middle of the week.
▸ adjective & adverb in the middle of the week.

midwife ▸ noun (plural **midwives**) a nurse trained to help women during childbirth.
□ **midwifery** /mid-**wif**-uh-ri/ noun.

midwinter ▸ noun **1** the middle part of winter. **2** the winter solstice.

mien /meen/ ▸ noun a person's look or manner.

miffed ▸ adjective informal slightly angry or upset.

might[1] ▸ modal verb (3rd singular present **might**) past of MAY. **1** used to express possibility or make a suggestion. **2** used politely in questions and requests.

might[2] ▸ noun great power or strength.

SYNONYMS **strength,** force, power, vigour, energy, brawn.

mightn't ▸ short form might not.

mighty ▸ adjective (**mightier, mightiest**) very strong or powerful.

SYNONYMS **powerful,** forceful, hard, heavy, violent, vigorous, hefty.
ANTONYMS feeble.

▸ adverb informal very.
□ **mightily** adverb.

migraine /**mee**-grayn, **my**-grayn/ ▸ noun a severe headache which is accompanied by symptoms such as nausea and disturbed vision.

migrant ▸ noun **1** a worker who moves from one place to another to find work. **2** an animal that migrates.

SYNONYMS *economic migrants* **immigrant, emigrant,** nomad, itinerant, traveller, transient, wanderer, drifter.

▸ adjective tending to migrate or having migrated.

SYNONYMS *migrant workers* **travelling,** mobile, wandering, drifting, nomadic, itinerant, transient.

migrate ▸ verb (**migrates, migrating, migrated**) **1** (of an animal) move to warmer regions in the winter and back to colder regions in the summer. **2** move to settle in a new area in order to find work.

SYNONYMS **1** *wildebeest migrate across the Serengeti* **roam,** wander, drift, rove, travel. **2** *rural populations migrated to* *towns* **relocate,** resettle, move (house), emigrate, go abroad.

◻ **migration** noun **migratory** adjective.

mike ► noun informal a microphone.

milch ► adjective (of an animal) giving or kept for milk.

mild ► adjective **1** not severe or harsh. **2** (of weather) fairly warm. **3** not sharp or strong in flavour. **4** (of a person or their behaviour) calm and gentle.

> SYNONYMS **1** *a mild tone of voice* **gentle,** tender, soft, sympathetic, peaceable, quiet, reasonable. **2** *a mild punishment* **lenient,** light. **3** *he was eyeing her with mild interest* **slight,** faint, vague. **4** *mild weather* **warm,** balmy, temperate, clement. **5** *a mild curry* **bland,** light, insipid.
> ANTONYMS harsh, strong, cold, severe, hot.

► noun Brit. a kind of dark beer not strongly flavoured with hops.

◻ **mildly** adverb **mildness** noun.

mildew ► noun a coating of tiny fungi on plants or damp material such as paper or leather.

◻ **mildewed** adjective.

mile ► noun **1** a unit of length equal to 1,760 yards (approximately 1.609 kilometres). **2** (**miles**) informal a very long way.

mileage ► noun **1** a number of miles covered. **2** informal advantage.

mileometer ➡ MILOMETER.

milestone ► noun **1** a stone set up beside a road, marking the distance in miles to a place further along the road. **2** an event marking a significant new development or stage.

milieu /**mee**-lyer/ ► noun (plural **milieux** /**mee**-lyer/ or **milieus** /**mee**-lyerz/) the social environment that you live or work in.

militant ► adjective supporting a cause in a forceful and aggressive way.

> SYNONYMS *militant workers* **hard-line,** extreme, active, extremist, committed, zealous, fanatical, radical.

► noun a militant person.

> SYNONYMS *a confrontation with militants* **activist,** extremist, radical, zealot.

◻ **militancy** noun **militantly** adverb.

militarism ► noun a belief in the value of military strength.

◻ **militarist** noun & adjective **militaristic** adjective.

militarized (or **militarised**) ► adjective supplied with soldiers and military equipment.

military ► adjective having to do with soldiers or armed forces.

> SYNONYMS **fighting,** service, army, armed, defence, martial.
> ANTONYMS civilian.

► noun (**the military**) the armed forces of a country.

> SYNONYMS *the military took power* (**armed**) **forces,** services, militia, army, navy, air force, marines.

◻ **militarily** adverb.

militate ► verb (**militates, militating, militated**) (**militate against**) make it very difficult for something to happen or exist.

> ❗ Don't confuse **militate** with **mitigate,** which means 'make something bad less severe'.

militia /mi-li-shuh/ ► noun **1** a group of people who are not professional soldiers but who act as an army. **2** a rebel force opposing a regular army.

milk ► noun **1** a white fluid produced by female mammals to feed their young. **2** the milk of cows as a food and drink for humans. **3** the milk-like juice of certain plants.

► verb **1** draw milk from an animal. **2** take money from someone dishonestly and over a period of time. **3** take full advantage of a situation.

> SYNONYMS *milking rich clients* **exploit,** take advantage of, suck dry; informal bleed, squeeze, fleece.

■ **milk chocolate** solid chocolate made with milk. **milk float** Brit. an electrically powered van with open sides, used for delivering milk to houses. **milk tooth** a temporary tooth in a child or young mammal.

milkmaid ► noun old use a girl or woman who worked in a dairy.

milkman ► noun (plural **milkmen**) a man who delivers milk to houses.

milkshake ► noun a cold drink made from milk whisked with ice cream or a flavouring.

milksop ► noun a timid person.

milky ► adjective **1** containing milk. **2** having a soft white colour or clouded appearance.

■ **Milky Way** the galaxy of which our solar system is a part, visible at night as a faint band of light crossing the sky.

◻ **milkily** adverb **milkiness** noun.

mill ► noun **1** a building equipped with machinery for grinding grain into flour. **2** a device for grinding coffee beans, peppercorns, etc. **3** a building fitted with machinery for a manufacturing process.

> SYNONYMS *a steel mill* **factory,** plant, works, workshop, shop, foundry.

► verb **1** grind something in a mill. **2** cut or shape metal with a rotating tool. **3** (**milled**) (of a coin) having ribbed markings on the edge. **4** (**mill about** or **around**) move around in a confused mass.

SYNONYMS *the wheat is milled into flour* **grind,** pulverize, powder, granulate, pound, crush, press.

■ **mill wheel** a wheel used to drive a watermill.

millennium /mi-**len**-i-uhm/ ▶ noun (plural **millennia** or **millenniums**) **1** a period of a thousand years. **2** (**the millennium**) the point at which one period of a thousand years ends and another begins. **3** an anniversary of a thousand years.
□ **millennial** adjective.

✔ double **l**, double **n**: mille**nn**ium.

miller ▶ noun a person who owns or works in a grain mill.

millet ▶ noun a cereal plant used to make flour or alcoholic drinks.

millibar ▶ noun a unit for measuring the pressure of the atmosphere.

milligram (or **milligramme**) ▶ noun one thousandth of a gram.

millilitre (US spelling **milliliter**) ▶ noun one thousandth of a litre.

millimetre (US spelling **millimeter**) ▶ noun one thousandth of a metre.

milliner ▶ noun a person who makes or sells women's hats.
□ **millinery** noun.

million ▶ cardinal number (plural **millions** or (with another word or number) **million**) **1** a thousand times a thousand; 1,000,000. **2** (also **millions**) informal a very large number or amount.
□ **millionth** ordinal number.

millionaire ▶ noun a person whose money and property are worth one million pounds or dollars or more.

✔ just one **n**: millio**n**aire.

millipede ▶ noun an insect-like creature with a long body and a lot of legs.

millisecond ▶ noun one thousandth of a second.

millpond ▶ noun **1** a pool created to provide the water that turns the wheel of a watermill. **2** a very still and calm stretch of water.

millstone ▶ noun **1** each of a pair of circular stones used for grinding grain. **2** a heavy responsibility that you cannot escape from.

milometer (or **mileometer**) /my-**lom**-i-ter/ ▶ noun Brit. an instrument on a vehicle for recording the number of miles travelled.

mime ▶ noun the use of silent gestures and facial expressions to tell a story or show feelings.
▶ verb (**mimes, miming, mimed**) **1** use mime to tell a story or show feelings. **2** pretend to sing or play an instrument as a recording is being played.

mimic ▶ verb (**mimics, mimicking, mimicked**) **1** imitate the voice or actions of someone else. **2** (of an animal or plant) take on the appearance of another in order to hide or for protection.

SYNONYMS **imitate,** copy, impersonate, do an impression of, ape, caricature, parody; informal send up, take off.

▶ noun a person skilled in mimicking others.

SYNONYMS **impersonator,** impressionist; informal copycat.

□ **mimicry** noun.

mimosa ▶ noun an acacia tree with delicate leaves and yellow flowers.

minaret /min-uh-**ret**/ ▶ noun a slender tower of a mosque, with a balcony from which Muslims are called to prayer.

minatory /**min**-uh-tuh-ri/ ▶ adjective formal threatening.

mince ▶ verb **1** cut or grind meat into very small pieces. **2** walk with short, quick steps and swinging hips.

SYNONYMS **grind,** chop up, cut up, dice, crumble; N. Amer. hash.

▶ noun Brit. minced meat.
■ **mince pie** a small tart containing mincemeat, eaten at Christmas. **not mince your words** speak plainly.

mincemeat ▶ noun a mixture of dried fruit, candied peel, sugar, spices, and suet.

mind ▶ noun **1** the faculty of consciousness and thought. **2** a person's intellect or memory. **3** a person's attention or will.

SYNONYMS **1** *a good teacher must stretch pupils' minds* **brain,** intelligence, intellect, brains, brainpower, wits, understanding, reasoning, judgement, sense, head; informal grey matter; N. Amer. informal smarts. **2** *he kept his mind on the job* **attention,** thoughts, concentration. **3** *the tragedy affected her mind* **sanity,** mental faculties, senses, wits, reason, reasoning, judgement. **4** *a great mind* **intellect,** thinker, brain, scholar.

▶ verb **1** be upset or annoyed by. **2** remember or take care to do. **3** watch out for. **4** temporarily take care of. **5** (**be minded**) be inclined to do.

SYNONYMS **1** *do you mind if I smoke?* **object,** care, be bothered, be annoyed, be upset, take offence, disapprove, look askance; informal give/care a damn. **2** *mind the step!* **be careful of,** watch out for, look out for, beware of. **3** *mind you wipe your feet* **make sure,** see, remember to, don't forget to. **4** *her husband was minding the baby* **look after,** take care of, keep an eye on, attend to, care for.

■ **out of your mind** not thinking sensibly; crazy.

minded ▶ adjective inclined to think in a particular way.

minder ▶ noun a person whose job is to take care of or protect someone or something.

mindful ▶ adjective (**mindful of** or **that**) aware of or recognizing that.

mindless ▶ adjective **1** acting or done without good reason and with no concern for the consequences. **2** (of an activity) simple and repetitive.
　□ **mindlessly** adverb.

mindset ▶ noun a person's particular way of thinking and set of beliefs.

mine¹ ▶ possessive pronoun referring to a thing or things belonging to or associated with the person speaking.
▶ possessive determiner old use my.

mine² ▶ noun **1** a hole or channel dug in the earth for extracting coal or other minerals. **2** an abundant source. **3** a type of bomb placed on or in the ground or water, which explodes on contact.

> SYNONYMS **1** *a coal mine* **pit,** colliery, excavation, quarry. **2** *a mine of information* **store,** storehouse, reservoir, repository, gold mine, treasure house, treasury.

▶ verb (**mines, mining, mined**) **1** obtain coal or other minerals from a mine. **2** lay explosive mines on or in.

> SYNONYMS *the iron ore was mined from shallow pits* **quarry,** excavate, dig, extract.

minefield ▶ noun **1** an area planted with explosive mines. **2** a subject or situation presenting unseen dangers.

miner ▶ noun a person who works in a mine.

mineral ▶ noun **1** a solid substance occurring naturally, such as copper and silicon. **2** an inorganic substance needed by the human body for good health, such as calcium and iron.
　■ **mineral water** water from a natural spring, containing dissolved mineral salts.

mineralogy ▶ noun the scientific study of minerals.
　□ **mineralogical** adjective **mineralogist** noun.

mineshaft ▶ noun a deep, narrow shaft that gives access to a mine.

minestrone /mi-ni-stroh-ni/ ▶ noun an Italian soup containing vegetables and pasta.

minesweeper ▶ noun a warship equipped for detecting and removing or destroying explosive mines.

mingle ▶ verb (**mingles, mingling, mingled**) mix together.

> SYNONYMS **1** *fact and fiction are mingled* **mix,** blend, intermingle, intermix, interweave, interlace, combine, merge, fuse, unite, join, amalgamate. **2** *guests mingled in the marquee* **socialize,** circulate, associate, fraternize, get together; informal hobnob.
> ANTONYMS separate.

mingy /min-ji/ ▶ adjective informal not generous.

mini ▶ adjective very small of its kind.
▶ noun (plural **minis**) a very short skirt.

miniature ▶ adjective of a much smaller size than normal.

> SYNONYMS **small,** mini, little, small-scale, baby, toy, pocket, diminutive; Scottish wee; N. Amer. vest-pocket.
> ANTONYMS giant.

▶ noun **1** a thing that is much smaller than normal. **2** a tiny, detailed portrait or picture.

> ✔ **-ia-** in the middle: min**ia**ture.

miniaturist ▶ noun an artist who paints miniatures.

miniaturize (or **miniaturise**) ▶ verb (**miniaturizes, miniaturizing, miniaturized**) make a smaller version of.

minibar ▶ noun a small fridge in a hotel room containing a selection of drinks.

minibus ▶ noun a small bus for about ten to fifteen passengers.

minicab ▶ noun Brit. a taxi that you order by telephone but cannot hail in the street.

minidisc ▶ noun a disc similar to a small CD but able to record sound or data as well as play it back.

minim ▶ noun a musical note that lasts as long as two crotchets.

minimal ▶ adjective of a minimum amount, quantity, or degree.

> SYNONYMS **very little/small,** minimum, the least (possible), nominal, token, negligible.
> ANTONYMS maximum.

　□ **minimally** adverb.

minimalist ▶ adjective **1** (of art) using simple forms and structures. **2** deliberately simple or basic in design.
▶ noun an artist who uses simple forms and structures.
　□ **minimalism** noun.

minimize (or **minimise**) ▶ verb (**minimizes, minimizing, minimized**) **1** make something as small as possible. **2** represent something as less important or significant than it really is.

> SYNONYMS **1** *the aim is to minimize costs* **keep down,** keep to a minimum, reduce, decrease, cut (down), lessen,

curtail, prune; informal slash. **2** *we should not minimize his contribution* belittle, make light of, play down, underrate, downplay, undervalue.
ANTONYMS maximize, exaggerate.

minimum ▸ noun (plural **minima** or **minimums**) the smallest amount, extent, or strength possible.

SYNONYMS *costs will be kept to the minimum* **lowest level,** lower limit, rock bottom, least, lowest, slightest.
ANTONYMS maximum.

▸ adjective smallest in amount, extent, or strength.

SYNONYMS *with the minimum effort* **minimal,** least, smallest, least possible, slightest, lowest, minutest.
ANTONYMS maximum.

minion ▸ noun a worker or assistant who has a low or unimportant status.

miniskirt ▸ noun a very short skirt.

minister ▸ noun **1** a head of a government department. **2** a person who represents their government in a foreign country. **3** a person who carries out religious duties in the Christian Church.

SYNONYMS **1** *a government minister* **member of the government,** member of the cabinet, secretary of state.
2 *a minister of religion* **clergyman,** clergywoman, cleric, pastor, vicar, rector, priest, parson, curate; informal reverend, padre.

▸ verb (**ministers, ministering, ministered**) (**minister to**) attend to the needs of.

SYNONYMS *doctors were ministering to the injured* **tend,** care for, take care of, look after, nurse, treat, attend to, see to, help.

□ **ministerial** adjective.

ministrations ▸ plural noun the providing of help or care.

ministry ▸ noun (plural **ministries**) **1** a government department headed by a minister. **2** a period of government under one Prime Minister. **3** the work of a minister in the Christian Church.

SYNONYMS **1** *the ministry for foreign affairs* **department,** bureau, agency, office. **2** *he's training for the ministry* **the priesthood,** holy orders, the cloth, the church.

mink ▸ noun a small stoat-like animal that is farmed for its fur.

minnow ▸ noun a small freshwater fish.

minor ▸ adjective **1** not important or serious. **2** Music (of a scale) having intervals of a semitone between the second and third, fifth and sixth, and, in the harmonic minor, seventh and eighth notes.

SYNONYMS **1** *a minor problem* **slight,** small, unimportant, insignificant, inconsequential, negligible, trivial, trifling, paltry, petty; N. Amer. nickel-and-dime; informal piffling. **2** *a minor poet* **little known,** unknown, lesser, unimportant, insignificant, obscure; N. Amer. minor-league; informal small-time; N. Amer. informal two-bit.
ANTONYMS major, important.

▸ noun a person under the age of full legal responsibility.

SYNONYMS *the accused was a minor* **child,** infant, youth, adolescent, teenager, boy, girl; informal kid.
ANTONYMS adult.

minority ▸ noun (plural **minorities**) **1** the smaller number or part. **2** a relatively small group of people differing from the majority in race, religion, etc.

minster ▸ noun Brit. a large or important church.

minstrel ▸ noun a medieval singer or musician.

mint¹ ▸ noun **1** a sweet-smelling plant, used as a herb in cookery. **2** the flavour of mint. **3** a peppermint sweet.
□ **minty** adjective.

mint² ▸ noun **1** a place where money is made. **2** (**a mint**) informal a large sum of money.

▸ verb make a coin by stamping metal.

SYNONYMS **coin,** stamp, strike, cast, manufacture.

■ **in mint condition** new, or as good as new.

minuet ▸ noun a ballroom dance popular in the 18th century.

minus ▸ preposition **1** with the subtraction of. **2** (of temperature) falling below zero by. **3** informal lacking.

▸ adjective **1** (before a number) below zero. **2** (after a grade) slightly below. **3** having a negative electric charge.

▸ noun **1** (also **minus sign**) the symbol −, indicating subtraction or a negative value. **2** informal a disadvantage.

minuscule /**min**-uhss-kyool/ ▸ adjective very tiny.

✔ **-u-**, not **-i-**, in the middle: min**u**scule.

minute¹ /**mi**-nit/ ▸ noun **1** a period of time equal to sixty seconds or a sixtieth of an hour. **2** (**a minute**) informal a very short time. **3** a measurement of an angle equal to one sixtieth of a degree.

SYNONYMS **1** *it'll only take a minute* **moment,** short time, little while, second, instant; informal sec, jiffy; Brit. informal tick, mo, two ticks. **2** *at that minute, Tony walked in* **point (in time),** moment, instant, second, juncture.

minute[2] /my-**nyoot**/ ▸ adjective (**minutest**)
1 very small. **2** precise and careful.

> SYNONYMS **1** *minute particles* **tiny**,
> minuscule, microscopic, miniature; Scottish
> wee; informal teeny, teeny-weeny; Brit. informal
> titchy, tiddly. **2** *a minute chance of success*
> **negligible,** slight, infinitesimal, minimal.
> **3** *in minute detail* **exhaustive,** painstaking,
> meticulous, rigorous, thorough.
> ANTONYMS huge.

□ **minutely** adverb.

minute[3] /**mi**-nit/ ▸ noun **1** (**minutes**) a
written summary of the points discussed at
a meeting. **2** an official written message.

> SYNONYMS (**minutes**) *their objection
> was noted in the minutes* **record(s)**,
> proceedings, log, notes, transcript,
> summary.

▸ verb (**minutes, minuting, minuted**) record
the points discussed at a meeting.

minutiae /mi-**nyoo**-shi-ee/ ▸ plural noun
small or precise details.

minx ▸ noun a cheeky, cunning, or flirtatious
girl or young woman.

miracle ▸ noun **1** a welcome event that is so
extraordinary that it is thought to be the
work of God or a saint. **2** an outstanding
example or achievement.

> SYNONYMS **wonder,** marvel, sensation,
> phenomenon.

■ **miracle play** a medieval play based on
stories from the Bible.

miraculous ▸ adjective like a miracle; very
surprising and welcome.

> SYNONYMS **amazing,** astounding,
> remarkable, extraordinary, incredible,
> unbelievable, sensational, phenomenal.

□ **miraculously** adverb.

mirage /mi-**rah**zh/ ▸ noun **1** an effect
caused by hot air, in which a sheet of
water seems to appear in a desert or on a
hot road. **2** something that appears real or
possible but is not in fact so.

mire ▸ noun **1** a stretch of swampy or boggy
ground. **2** a difficult situation from which
it is hard to escape.

▸ verb (**be mired**) **1** become stuck in mud.
2 be in a difficult situation.

mirror ▸ noun **1** a surface which reflects a
clear image. **2** something that accurately
represents something else.

> SYNONYMS **1** *a quick look in the
> mirror* **looking glass**; Brit. glass. **2** *the
> Frenchman's life was a mirror of his own
> reflection*, replica, copy, match, parallel.

▸ verb reflect.

> SYNONYMS *pop music mirrored the mood
> of desperation* **reflect**, match, reproduce,
> imitate, copy, mimic, echo, parallel.

■ **mirror image** an image which is identical
in form to another but is reversed, as if
seen in a mirror.

mirth ▸ noun laughter.
□ **mirthful** adjective.

misadventure ▸ noun **1** (also **death
by misadventure**) Law death caused
accidentally and not involving crime. **2** a
mishap.

misalliance ▸ noun an unsuitable or
unhappy relationship or marriage.

misanthrope /**mi**-zuhn-throhp/ ▸ noun
a person who dislikes and avoids other
people.
□ **misanthropic** adjective **misanthropy** noun.

misapprehension ▸ noun a mistaken
belief.

misappropriate ▸ verb (**misappropriates,
misappropriating, misappropriated**)
dishonestly take something for your own
use.
□ **misappropriation** noun.

misbegotten ▸ adjective badly thought out
or planned.

misbehave ▸ verb (**misbehaves,
misbehaving, misbehaved**) behave badly.

> SYNONYMS **behave badly,** be naughty, be
> disobedient, get up to mischief, get up to
> no good, be rude; informal carry on, act up.

□ **misbehaviour** noun.

miscalculate ▸ verb (**miscalculates,
miscalculating, miscalculated**) calculate or
assess wrongly.
□ **miscalculation** noun.

miscarriage ▸ noun the birth of a baby or
fetus before it is able to survive outside the
mother's womb.
■ **miscarriage of justice** a situation in which
a court of law fails to achieve justice.

miscarry ▸ verb (**miscarries, miscarrying,
miscarried**) **1** (of a pregnant woman) have a
miscarriage. **2** (of a plan) fail.

miscast ▸ verb (**be miscast**) (of an actor) be
given an unsuitable role.

miscellaneous /mi-suh-**lay**-ni-uhss/
▸ adjective consisting of many different
kinds.

> SYNONYMS **various,** varied, different,
> assorted, mixed, sundry, diverse,
> disparate.

miscellany /mi-**sel**-luh-ni/ ▸ noun (plural
miscellanies) a collection of different
things.

mischance ▸ noun bad luck.

mischief ▸ noun **1** playful bad behaviour
that does not cause serious damage or
harm. **2** harm caused by someone or
something.

> SYNONYMS **1** *the boys are always getting
> up to mischief* **naughtiness**, bad

behaviour, misbehaviour, misconduct, disobedience. **2** *the mischief in her eyes* **impishness**, roguishness, glint, twinkle.

mischievous /miss-chi-vuhss/ ▶ adjective **1** causing mischief. **2** intended to cause trouble.
□ **mischievously** adverb.

✔ The ending is **-ous**, not **-ious**: mischiev**ous**.

miscible /miss-i-b'l/ ▶ adjective (of liquids) able to be mixed together.

misconceived ▶ adjective badly judged or planned.

misconception ▶ noun a failure to understand something correctly.

misconduct ▶ noun /miss-kon-dukt/ bad behaviour.

misconstruction ▶ noun a failure to interpret something correctly.

misconstrue ▶ verb (misconstrues, misconstruing, misconstrued) interpret something wrongly.

miscreant /miss-kri-uhnt/ ▶ noun a person who behaves badly or unlawfully.

misdeed ▶ noun a bad or evil act.

misdemeanour (US spelling **misdemeanor**) ▶ noun an action that is bad or unacceptable, but does not amount to a serious crime.

misdiagnose ▶ verb (misdiagnoses, misdiagnosing, misdiagnosed) diagnose something incorrectly.
□ **misdiagnosis** noun (plural **misdiagnoses**).

misdirect ▶ verb direct or instruct wrongly.
□ **misdirection** noun.

miser ▶ noun a person who hoards wealth and spends as little as possible.

SYNONYMS **penny-pincher**, Scrooge; informal skinflint, cheapskate; N. Amer. informal tightwad.
ANTONYMS spendthrift.

miserable ▶ adjective **1** very unhappy or depressed. **2** causing unhappiness or discomfort. **3** (of a person) gloomy and humourless. **4** very small or inadequate.

SYNONYMS **1** *I'm too miserable to eat* **unhappy**, sad, sorrowful, dejected, depressed, down, despondent, disconsolate, wretched, glum, forlorn; informal blue, down in the dumps. **2** *their miserable surroundings* **dreary**, dismal, gloomy, drab, wretched, depressing, grim, cheerless, bleak, desolate.
ANTONYMS cheerful, lovely.

□ **miserably** adverb.

misericord /mi-zerr-i-kord/ ▶ noun a ledge projecting from the underside of a hinged seat in the choir of a church, giving support to someone standing when the seat is folded up.

miserly ▶ adjective **1** not willing to spend money. **2** (of a quantity) too small.
□ **miserliness** noun.

misery ▶ noun (plural **miseries**) **1** great unhappiness. **2** a cause of this. **3** Brit. informal a person who is constantly miserable.

SYNONYMS **unhappiness**, distress, wretchedness, suffering, anguish, anxiety, angst, torment, pain, grief, heartache, heartbreak, despair, despondency, dejection, depression, gloom, sorrow; informal the blues.
ANTONYMS contentment, pleasure.

misfire ▶ verb (misfires, misfiring, misfired) **1** (of a gun) fail to fire properly. **2** (of an internal-combustion engine) fail to ignite the fuel correctly. **3** fail to produce the intended result.

misfit ▶ noun a person whose attitudes and actions set them apart from other people.

misfortune ▶ noun **1** bad luck. **2** an unfortunate event.

SYNONYMS **problem**, difficulty, setback, trouble, adversity, (stroke of) bad luck, misadventure, mishap, blow, failure, accident, disaster.

misgivings ▶ plural noun feelings of doubt or worry.

misguided ▶ adjective badly judged.

SYNONYMS **unwise**, ill-advised, ill-judged, ill-considered, injudicious, imprudent, unsound, mistaken, misplaced.
ANTONYMS wise.

mishandle ▶ verb (mishandles, mishandling, mishandled) handle a situation badly or wrongly.

mishap ▶ noun an unlucky accident.

mishear ▶ verb (mishears, mishearing, misheard) hear incorrectly.

mishit ▶ verb (mishits, mishitting, mishit) hit or kick a ball badly.

mishmash ▶ noun a confused mixture.

misinform ▶ verb give someone false or inaccurate information.
□ **misinformation** noun.

misinterpret ▶ verb (misinterprets, misinterpreting, misinterpreted) interpret something wrongly.
□ **misinterpretation** noun.

misjudge ▶ verb (misjudges, misjudging, misjudged) **1** form a wrong opinion about. **2** estimate wrongly.
□ **misjudgement** (or **misjudgment**) noun.

mislay ▶ verb (mislays, mislaying, mislaid) lose something because you have forgotten where you put it.

SYNONYMS **lose**, misplace, be unable to find.
ANTONYMS find.

mislead ▸ verb (misleads, misleading, misled) give someone a wrong impression or wrong information.

> SYNONYMS **1 deceive**, delude, take in, lie to, fool, hoodwink, misinform; informal lead up the garden path; N. Amer. informal give someone a bum steer. **2** (**misleading**) **deceptive**, confusing, deceiving, equivocal, false.

mismanage ▸ verb (mismanages, mismanaging, mismanaged) manage something badly or wrongly.
  □ **mismanagement** noun.

mismatch ▸ noun a combination of things or people that do not go together well.
▸ verb match people or things unsuitably or incorrectly.

misnomer /miss-noh-mer/ ▸ noun **1** a name or term that is wrong or inaccurate. **2** the wrong use of a name or term.

misogynist /mi-soj-uh-nist/ ▸ noun a man who hates women.
  □ **misogynistic** adjective **misogyny** noun.

misplace ▸ verb (misplaces, misplacing, misplaced) put in the wrong place.

misplaced ▸ adjective **1** wrongly placed. **2** unwise or inappropriate.

misprint ▸ noun a mistake in printed material.

mispronounce ▸ verb (mispronounces, mispronouncing, mispronounced) pronounce wrongly.
  □ **mispronunciation** noun.

misquote ▸ verb (misquotes, misquoting, misquoted) quote inaccurately.

misread ▸ verb (misreads, misreading, misread) read or interpret wrongly.

misrepresent ▸ verb give a false or misleading account of.
  □ **misrepresentation** noun.

misrule ▸ noun **1** bad government. **2** disorder.

miss[1] ▸ verb **1** fail to hit, reach, or come into contact with. **2** be too late for. **3** fail to notice, hear, or understand. **4** fail to be present at. **5** avoid something unpleasant. **6** (**miss someone/thing out**) fail to include someone or something. **7** feel sad because of the absence of.

> SYNONYMS **1** the shot missed her by inches **go wide of**, fall short of, pass, overshoot. **2** I left early to miss the traffic **avoid**, beat, evade, escape, dodge, sidestep, elude, circumvent, bypass. **3** she missed him when he was away **pine for**, yearn for, ache for, long for. **4** she never missed a meeting **fail to attend**, be absent from, play truant from, cut, skip, omit; Brit. informal skive off.
> ANTONYMS hit, catch, attend.

▸ noun a failure to hit, catch, or reach something.

> SYNONYMS one hit and three misses **failure**, omission, slip, error, mistake.

miss[2] ▸ noun **1** (**Miss**) a title coming before the name of an unmarried woman or girl. **2** (**Miss**) used as a form of address to a teacher. **3** a girl or young woman.

missal ▸ noun a book containing the prayers and responses used in the Catholic Mass.

misshapen ▸ adjective not having the normal or natural shape.

missile ▸ noun an object or weapon that is thrown or fired at a target.

missing ▸ adjective **1** absent and unable to be found. **2** not present when expected to be.

> SYNONYMS **1** his wallet is missing **lost**, mislaid, misplaced, absent, gone (astray), unaccounted for. **2** passion was missing from her life **absent**, lacking, gone, wanting.
> ANTONYMS present.

mission ▸ noun **1** an important assignment, typically involving travel abroad. **2** an organization involved in a long-term assignment abroad. **3** a military or scientific expedition. **4** the work of teaching people about Christianity. **5** a strongly felt aim or calling.

> SYNONYMS **1** a mercy mission to Romania **assignment**, commission, expedition, journey, trip, undertaking, operation, project. **2** her mission in life **vocation**, calling, goal, aim, quest, purpose, function, task, job, labour, work, duty.

missionary ▸ noun (plural **missionaries**) a person sent on a religious mission.

> SYNONYMS **evangelist**, apostle, proselytizer, preacher.

▸ adjective having to do with a religious mission.

missive ▸ noun formal a letter.

misspell ▸ verb (misspells, misspelling, past and past participle **misspelled** or chiefly Brit. **misspelt**) spell wrongly.

misspend ▸ verb (misspends, misspending, misspent) spend time or money foolishly.

mist ▸ noun a thin cloud of tiny water droplets that makes it difficult to see.

> SYNONYMS **haze**, fog, smog, murk, cloud, vapour, steam, spray, condensation.

▸ verb cover or become covered with mist.

mistake ▸ noun **1** a thing that is incorrect. **2** an error of judgement.

> SYNONYMS it was all a mistake **error**, fault, inaccuracy, omission, slip, blunder, miscalculation, misunderstanding, oversight, misinterpretation, gaffe, faux pas; informal slip-up, boo-boo, howler; Brit. informal **boob**, clanger; N. Amer. informal goof.

▸ verb (**mistakes, mistaking, mistook**; past participle **mistaken**) **1** be wrong about. **2** (**mistake someone/thing for**) confuse someone or something with.

> synonyms **1** *men are apt to mistake their own feelings* **misunderstand**, misinterpret, get wrong, misconstrue, misread. **2** *children often mistake pills for sweets* **confuse with**, mix up with, take for.

mistaken ▸ adjective **1** wrong in your opinion or judgement. **2** based on or resulting from a misunderstanding.

> synonyms **1** *such a mistaken view* **inaccurate**, wrong, erroneous, incorrect, off beam, false, fallacious, unfounded, misguided. **2** *you are mistaken there* **misinformed**, wrong, in error, under a misapprehension, barking up the wrong tree.
> antonyms correct.

□ **mistakenly** adverb.

mister ▸ noun **1** (Mister) = **Mr. 2** informal a form of address to a man.

mistime ▸ verb (**mistimes, mistiming, mistimed**) choose an inappropriate moment to do or say something.

> synonyms (**mistimed**) **ill-timed**, badly timed, inopportune, inappropriate, untimely.
> antonyms opportune.

mistletoe ▸ noun a plant which grows as a parasite on trees, producing white berries in winter.

mistral /**miss**-truhl, mis-**trahl**/ ▸ noun a strong north-westerly wind that blows through southern France.

mistreat ▸ verb treat badly or unfairly.
□ **mistreatment** noun.

mistress ▸ noun **1** a woman in a position of authority. **2** a woman who is very skilled in something. **3** a woman having a sexual relationship with a man who is married to someone else. **4** Brit. a female schoolteacher. **5** (Mistress) old use Mrs.

mistrial ▸ noun a trial that is not considered valid because of a mistake in proceedings.

mistrust ▸ verb have no trust in.

> synonyms **be suspicious of**, be sceptical of, be wary of, be chary of, distrust, have doubts about, have misgivings about, have reservations about, suspect.

▸ noun lack of trust.

misty ▸ adjective (**mistier, mistiest**) **1** covered with mist. **2** having an outline that is not clear.

misunderstand ▸ verb (**misunderstands, misunderstanding, misunderstood**) fail to understand correctly.

> synonyms **misapprehend**, misinterpret, misconstrue, misconceive, mistake, misread, be mistaken, get the wrong idea; informal get (hold of) the wrong end of the stick.

misunderstanding ▸ noun **1** a failure to understand something correctly. **2** a disagreement with someone.

> synonyms **1** *a misunderstanding of juvenile crime* **misinterpretation**, misreading, misapprehension, misconception, false impression. **2** *we have had some misunderstandings* **disagreement**, difference (of opinion), dispute, falling-out, quarrel, argument, clash.

misuse ▸ verb (**misuses, misusing, misused**) **1** use wrongly. **2** treat badly or unfairly.

> synonyms *misusing public funds* **embezzle**, misappropriate, abuse, waste, squander.

▸ noun the action of misusing.

> synonyms *a misuse of company assets* **embezzlement**, fraud, squandering, waste.

mite ▸ noun **1** a tiny insect-like creature. **2** a small child or animal. **3** a very small amount.

mitigate ▸ verb (**mitigates, mitigating, mitigated**) make something bad less severe or serious.
□ **mitigation** noun.

> ❗ Don't confuse **mitigate** with **militate**: **militate against** means 'make it very difficult for something to happen or exist'.

mitre (US spelling **miter**) ▸ noun **1** a tall headdress that tapers to a point at the front and back, worn by bishops. **2** a joint made between two pieces of wood cut at an angle in order to form a corner of 90°.

mitt ▸ noun **1** a mitten. **2** informal a person's hand.

mitten ▸ noun a glove having a single section for all four fingers, with a separate section for the thumb.

mix ▸ verb **1** combine or be combined to form a whole. **2** make by mixing ingredients. **3** combine different recordings to form one piece of music. **4** (**mix something up**) spoil the arrangement of something. **5** (**mix someone/thing up**) confuse one person or thing with another. **6** meet different people socially.

> synonyms **1** *mix all the ingredients together* **blend**, mingle, combine, jumble, fuse, unite, join, amalgamate, incorporate, meld, homogenize; technical admix; literary commingle. **2** *she mixes*

with all sorts **associate,** socialize, keep company, consort, mingle, circulate; Brit. rub shoulders; N. Amer. rub elbows; informal hang out/around, hobnob.
ANTONYMS separate.

▶ noun **1** a mixture. **2** the proportion of different people or things making up a mixture. **3** a version of a piece of music mixed in a different way from the original.

SYNONYMS *a mix of ancient and modern* **mixture,** blend, combination, compound, fusion, union, amalgamation, medley, selection, assortment, variety.

mixed ▶ adjective **1** made up of different qualities or things. **2** having to do with males and females.

SYNONYMS **1** *a mixed collection* **assorted,** varied, variegated, miscellaneous, disparate, diverse, diversified, motley, sundry, jumbled, heterogeneous. **2** *mixed reactions* **ambivalent,** equivocal, contradictory, conflicting, confused, muddled.
ANTONYMS homogeneous.

■ **mixed bag** an assortment of people or things of very different types.

mixer ▶ noun **1** a machine or device for mixing things. **2** a soft drink that can be mixed with alcohol.

mixture ▶ noun **1** a substance made by mixing other substances together. **2** (a **mixture of**) a combination of different things in which each thing is distinct.

SYNONYMS **1** *the pudding mixture* **blend,** mix, brew, combination, concoction, composition, compound, alloy, amalgam. **2** *a strange mixture of people* **assortment,** miscellany, medley, blend, variety, mixed bag, mix, diversity, collection, selection, hotchpotch, ragbag; N. Amer. hodgepodge.

mix-up ▶ noun a misunderstanding or mistake.

SYNONYMS **misunderstanding,** mistake, muddle, error, confusion.

mizzen (or **mizzenmast**) ▶ noun the mast behind a ship's mainmast.

ml ▶ abbreviation **1** miles. **2** millilitres.

mm ▶ abbreviation millimetres.

MMR ▶ abbreviation measles, mumps, and rubella (a vaccination given to children).

mnemonic /ni-**mon**-ik/ ▶ noun a pattern of letters or words used to help remember something.
▶ adjective designed to help remember something.

moan ▶ noun **1** a low mournful sound, usually expressing suffering. **2** informal a complaint.
▶ verb **1** make a moan. **2** complain; grumble.

SYNONYMS **1** *he moaned in agony* **groan,** wail, whimper, sob, cry. **2** *you're always moaning about the weather* **complain,** grouse, grumble, whine, carp; informal gripe, grouch, bellyache, bitch, beef, whinge.

moat ▶ noun a wide defensive ditch surrounding a castle or town.

mob ▶ noun **1** a disorderly crowd of people. **2** Brit. informal a group of people. **3** (**the Mob**) N. Amer. the Mafia. **4** (**the mob**) disapproving the ordinary people.

SYNONYMS *troops dispersed the mob* **crowd,** horde, multitude, rabble, mass, throng, gathering, assembly.

▶ verb (**mobs, mobbing, mobbed**) (of a large group of people) crowd round someone.

SYNONYMS *the Chancellor was mobbed* **surround,** crowd round, besiege, jostle.

mobile ▶ adjective **1** able to move or be moved freely or easily. **2** (of a shop, library, etc.) set up inside a vehicle and able to travel around. **3** able to change your occupation, social class, or where you live. **4** (of a person's face) easily changing expression.

SYNONYMS **1** *both patients are mobile* **able to move (around),** able to walk, walking; informal up and about. **2** *a mobile library* **travelling,** transportable, portable, movable, itinerant, peripatetic.
ANTONYMS immobilized, fixed.

▶ noun **1** a decoration that is hung so as to turn freely in the air. **2** (also **mobile phone**) a portable telephone.

mobility ▶ noun the quality of being mobile.

mobilize (or **mobilise**) ▶ verb (**mobilizes, mobilizing, mobilized**) **1** organize troops for active service. **2** organize people or resources for a particular task.

SYNONYMS **1** *the government mobilized the troops* **marshal,** deploy, muster, rally, call up, assemble, mass, organize, prepare. **2** *mobilizing support for the party* **generate,** arouse, awaken, excite, stimulate, stir up, encourage, inspire, whip up.

▫ **mobilization** noun.

mobster ▶ noun informal a gangster.

moccasin ▶ noun a soft leather shoe with the sole turned up and sewn to the upper, originally worn by North American Indians.

mocha /**mok**-uh/ ▶ noun **1** a type of fine-quality coffee. **2** a drink made with coffee and chocolate.

mock ▶ verb tease or imitate someone in an unkind way.

m

SYNONYMS **1** *the local children mocked the old people* **ridicule,** jeer at, sneer at, deride, make fun of, laugh at, scoff at, tease, taunt; informal take the mickey out of; N. Amer. informal goof on, rag on; Austral./NZ informal chiack, sling off at. **2** (**mocking**) **sneering,** derisive, contemptuous, scornful, sardonic, ironic, sarcastic.

▶ adjective **1** not genuine or real. **2** (of an exam, battle, etc.) arranged for training or practice.

SYNONYMS *mock leather* **imitation,** artificial, man-made, simulated, synthetic, ersatz, fake, reproduction, false, counterfeit; informal pretend. ANTONYMS genuine.

▶ noun (**mocks**) Brit. informal exams taken in school as a practice for public exams.
■ **mock-up** a model of a machine or structure that is used for teaching or testing.

mockery ▶ noun (plural **mockeries**) **1** unkind teasing; ridicule. **2** (**a mockery of**) an absurd or worthless version of something.
■ **make a mockery of** make something seem ridiculous or useless.

mockingbird ▶ noun a long-tailed American songbird, noted for copying the calls of other birds.

modal verb ▶ noun Grammar an auxiliary verb expressing necessity or possibility, e.g. *must, shall, will.*

mode ▶ noun **1** a way in which something occurs or is done. **2** a style in clothes, art, etc.

SYNONYMS **1** *an informal mode of policing* **manner,** way, means, method, system, style, approach. **2** *the camera is in manual mode* **function,** position, operation, setting, option.

model ▶ noun **1** a three-dimensional representation of something. **2** something used as an example. **3** a person or thing seen as an excellent example of a quality: *he was a model of self-control.* **4** a person whose job is to display clothes by wearing them. **5** a person who poses for an artist or photographer. **6** a particular design or version of a product. **7** a simplified mathematical description of a system or process.

SYNONYMS **1** *a working model* **replica,** copy, representation, mock-up, dummy, imitation, duplicate, reproduction, facsimile. **2** *the American model of airline deregulation* **prototype,** archetype, type, version, mould, template, framework, pattern, design, blueprint. **3** *a top model* **fashion model,** supermodel, mannequin; informal clothes horse.

▶ adjective **1** representing or copied from something, and typically smaller. **2** regarded as an excellent example.

SYNONYMS **1** *model trains* **replica,** toy, miniature, dummy, imitation, duplicate, reproduction, facsimile. **2** *a model teacher* **ideal,** perfect, exemplary, classic, flawless, faultless.

▶ verb (**models, modelling, modelled;** US spelling **models, modeling, modeled**) **1** make a figure in clay, wax, etc. **2** (**model something on**) design or plan something using another thing as an example. **3** work as a fashion model. **4** devise a mathematical model of.

modem /moh-dem/ ▶ noun a device that connects a computer to a telephone line.

moderate ▶ adjective **1** average in amount, strength, or degree. **2** (of a political position) not extreme.

SYNONYMS **1** *moderate success* **average,** modest, medium, middling, tolerable, passable, adequate, fair; informal OK, so-so, bog-standard, fair-to-middling. **2** *moderate prices* **reasonable,** acceptable, affordable, inexpensive, fair, modest. **3** *moderate views* **middle-of-the-road,** non-extremist, liberal, pragmatic. ANTONYMS great, unreasonable, extreme.

▶ noun a person with moderate views.
▶ verb (**moderates, moderating, moderated**) **1** make or become less extreme or strong. **2** check exam papers to ensure that they have been marked consistently.

SYNONYMS **1** *the wind has moderated* **die down,** abate, let up, calm down, lessen, decrease, diminish, recede, weaken, subside. **2** *you can help her moderate her temper* **curb,** control, check, temper, restrain, subdue, tame, lessen, decrease, lower, reduce, diminish, alleviate, allay, appease, ease, soothe, calm, tone down. ANTONYMS increase.

moderately ▶ adverb to a certain extent.

SYNONYMS **somewhat,** quite, fairly, reasonably, comparatively, relatively, to some extent, tolerably, adequately; informal pretty.

moderation ▶ noun **1** the avoidance of extremes in your actions or opinions. **2** the process of moderating.

moderator ▶ noun **1** a person who helps others to solve a dispute. **2** a chairman of a debate. **3** a person who moderates exam papers.

modern ▶ adjective **1** relating to the present or to recent times. **2** using the most up-to-date techniques or equipment. **3** (of art, architecture, music, etc.) new and intended to be different from traditional styles.

SYNONYMS **1** *modern times* **present-day,** contemporary, present, current, twenty-

first-century, latter-day, recent. **2** *her clothes are very modern* **fashionable,** up to date, trendsetting, stylish, chic, à la mode, the latest, new, newest, newfangled, advanced; informal trendy, cool, in.
ANTONYMS past, old-fashioned.

□ **modernity** noun.

modernism ▸ noun **1** modern ideas, methods, or styles. **2** a movement in the arts or religion that aims to break with traditional forms or ideas.
□ **modernist** noun & adjective.

modernize (or modernise) ▸ verb (**modernizes, modernizing, modernized**) bring up to date with modern equipment, techniques, etc.
□ **modernization** noun.

modest ▸ adjective **1** not boasting about your abilities or achievements. **2** relatively moderate, limited, or small. **3** not showing off the body; decent.

SYNONYMS **1** *she was modest about her poetry* **humble,** self-deprecating, self-effacing, unassuming, shy, diffident, reserved, coy. **2** *modest success* **moderate,** fair, limited, tolerable, passable, adequate, satisfactory, acceptable, unexceptional. **3** *a modest house* **small,** ordinary, simple, plain, humble, inexpensive, unostentatious, unpretentious. **4** *her modest dress* **demure,** decent, seemly, decorous, proper.
ANTONYMS conceited, great, grand, indecent.

□ **modestly** adverb.

modesty ▸ noun the quality or state of being humble, decent, or moderate.

SYNONYMS **humility,** self-effacement, shyness, bashfulness, self-consciousness, reserve.

modicum /**mod**-i-kuhm/ ▸ noun a small quantity of something.

modification ▸ noun **1** the action of modifying something. **2** a change made.

SYNONYMS **change,** adjustment, alteration, adaptation, refinement, revision, amendment; informal tweak.

modifier ▸ noun **1** a person or thing that modifies. **2** Grammar a word that qualifies the sense of a noun (e.g. *family* in *a family house*).

modify ▸ verb (**modifies, modifying, modified**) make partial changes to.

SYNONYMS **1** *their economic policy has been modified* **change,** alter, adjust, adapt, amend, revise, refine; informal tweak. **2** *he modified his more extreme views* **moderate,** temper, soften, tone down, qualify.

modish ▸ adjective fashionable.

modular ▸ adjective made up of separate units.

modulate ▸ verb (**modulates, modulating, modulated**) **1** adjust, change, or control something. **2** vary the strength, tone, or pitch of your voice. **3** Music change from one key to another.
□ **modulation** noun.

module ▸ noun **1** each of a set of parts or units that can be used to create a more complex structure. **2** a unit forming part of a course. **3** an independent unit of a spacecraft.

moggie (or moggy) ▸ noun (plural **moggies**) Brit. informal a cat.

mogul /**moh**-guhl/ ▸ noun informal an important or powerful person.

mohair ▸ noun a yarn or fabric made from the hair of the angora goat.

Mohican /moh-**hee**-kuhn/ ▸ noun a hair style in which the sides of the head are shaved and a central strip of hair is made to stand up.

moiety /**moy**-i-ti/ ▸ noun (plural **moieties**) formal a half.

moist ▸ adjective slightly wet; damp.

SYNONYMS **1** *the air was moist* **damp,** steamy, humid, muggy, clammy, dank, wet, soggy, sweaty, sticky. **2** *a moist fruitcake* **succulent,** juicy, soft, tender.
ANTONYMS dry.

moisten ▸ verb make or become slightly wet.

SYNONYMS **dampen,** wet, damp, water, humidify.

moisture ▸ noun tiny droplets of water making something damp.

SYNONYMS **wetness,** wet, water, liquid, condensation, steam, vapour, dampness, damp, humidity.

moisturize (or moisturise) ▸ verb (**moisturizes, moisturizing, moisturized**) make something, especially the skin, less dry.
□ **moisturizer** noun.

molar ▸ noun a grinding tooth at the back of the mouth.

molasses /muh-**lass**-iz/ ▸ noun a thick brown liquid obtained from raw sugar.

mold US spelling of MOULD¹, MOULD².

Moldovan /mol-**doh**-vuhn/ ▸ noun a person from Moldova, a country in SE Europe. ▸ adjective relating to Moldova.

mole¹ ▸ noun **1** a small burrowing mammal with dark fur, a long muzzle, and very small eyes. **2** someone within an organization who secretly passes confidential information to another organization or country.

mole² ▸ noun a dark brown mark on the skin.

mole³ ▸ noun **1** a pier, breakwater, or causeway. **2** a harbour formed by a mole.

mole⁴ ▸ noun Chemistry the amount of a particular substance which contains as many atoms or molecules as there are atoms in a standard amount of carbon.

molecule /mol-i-kyool/ ▸ noun a group of atoms forming the smallest unit into which a substance can be divided.
□ **molecular** adjective.

molehill ▸ noun a small mound of earth thrown up by a burrowing mole.

moleskin ▸ noun **1** the skin of a mole used as fur. **2** a thick cotton fabric with a soft surface.

molest ▸ verb **1** sexually assault someone. **2** dated pester someone in a hostile way.
□ **molestation** noun **molester** noun.

moll ▸ noun informal a gangster's girlfriend.

mollify ▸ verb (**mollifies, mollifying, mollified**) make someone feel less angry.

mollusc (US spelling **mollusk**) ▸ noun an animal of a group with a soft unsegmented body and often an external shell, such as slugs and snails.

mollycoddle ▸ verb (**mollycoddles, mollycoddling, mollycoddled**) treat someone too indulgently or protectively.

molt US spelling of **MOULT**.

molten ▸ adjective (especially of metal and glass) made liquid by heat.

molto /mol-toh/ ▸ adverb Music very.

molybdenum /muh-**lib**-duh-nuhm/ ▸ noun a brittle silver-grey metallic element.

mom N. Amer. = **MUM¹**.

moment ▸ noun **1** a brief period of time. **2** an exact point in time. **3** formal importance.

> SYNONYMS **1** *he thought for a moment* **little while,** short time, bit, minute, instant, (split) second; informal sec, jiffy; Brit. informal tick, mo, two ticks. **2** *just at that moment* **point (in time),** stage, juncture, instant, time, hour, second, minute, day.

momentarily ▸ adverb **1** for a very short time. **2** N. Amer. very soon.

momentary ▸ adjective very brief or short-lived.

> SYNONYMS **brief,** short, short-lived, fleeting, passing.
> ANTONYMS lengthy.

momentous ▸ adjective of great importance or significance.

> SYNONYMS **important,** significant, historic, critical, crucial, decisive, pivotal, consequential, far-reaching;

informal earth-shattering.
> ANTONYMS insignificant.

momentum ▸ noun (plural **momenta**)
1 the force gained by a moving object.
2 the force caused by the development of something.

> SYNONYMS **impetus,** energy, force, power, strength, thrust, speed, velocity.

mommy N. Amer. = **MUMMY¹**.

monarch ▸ noun a king, queen, or emperor.

> SYNONYMS **sovereign,** ruler, Crown, crowned head, potentate, king, queen, emperor, empress, prince, princess.

□ **monarchical** adjective.

monarchist ▸ noun someone who believes a country should be ruled by a king or queen.
□ **monarchism** noun.

monarchy ▸ noun (plural **monarchies**)
1 government by a monarch. **2** a state with a monarch.

monastery ▸ noun (plural **monasteries**) a community of monks living under religious vows.

> SYNONYMS **monastic community,** friary, abbey, priory, cloister.

monastic ▸ adjective **1** relating to monks or nuns. **2** resembling monks or their way of life.

Monday ▸ noun the day of the week before Tuesday and following Sunday.

monetarism ▸ noun the theory that inflation is best controlled by limiting the supply of money.
□ **monetarist** noun & adjective.

monetary ▸ adjective having to do with money.

> SYNONYMS **financial,** fiscal, pecuniary, money, cash, capital, economic, budgetary.

money ▸ noun **1** a means of paying for things in the form of coins and banknotes.
2 wealth. **3** payment or financial gain.
4 (**moneys** or **monies**) formal sums of money.

> SYNONYMS **cash,** hard cash, means, wherewithal, funds, capital, finances, notes, coins, change, currency; informal dough, bread, loot; Brit. informal dosh, brass, lolly; N. Amer. informal dinero, mazuma.

■ **money order** a postal order. **money spider** a very small black spider.

moneyed (or **monied**) ▸ adjective having a lot of money.

Mongol ▸ noun **1** a person from Mongolia.
2 (**mongol**) offensive a person with Down's syndrome.
□ **Mongolian** noun & adjective.

mongoose ▸ noun (plural **mongooses**) a small meat-eating animal with a long body and tail, native to Africa and Asia.

mongrel ▸ noun a dog of no definite breed.

moniker ▸ noun informal a name.

monitor ▸ noun 1 a person or device that monitors something. 2 a television used to view a picture from a particular camera or a display from a computer. 3 a school pupil with special duties. 4 (also **monitor lizard**) a large tropical lizard.

> SYNONYMS 1 *monitors covered all entrances* detector, scanner, recorder, sensor, security camera, CCTV. 2 *UN monitors* observer, watchdog, overseer, supervisor, scrutineer. 3 *a computer monitor* screen, display, VDU.

▸ verb keep under observation.

> SYNONYMS *his movements were closely monitored* observe, watch, track, keep an eye on, keep under surveillance, record, note, oversee; informal keep tabs on.

monk ▸ noun a man belonging to a religious community typically living under vows of poverty, chastity, and obedience.

monkey ▸ noun (plural **monkeys**) a primate typically having a long tail and living in trees in tropical countries.
▸ verb (**monkeys, monkeying, monkeyed**) 1 (**monkey about** or **around**) behave in a silly or playful way. 2 (**monkey with**) tamper with.
■ **monkey nut** Brit. a peanut. **monkey puzzle** a coniferous tree with branches covered in spirals of tough spiny leaves. **monkey wrench** a spanner with large adjustable jaws.

mono ▸ noun sound reproduction which uses only one transmission channel.

monochrome ▸ adjective (of a photograph or picture) produced in black and white or in varying tones of one colour.
□ **monochromatic** adjective.

monocle ▸ noun a single lens worn at one eye.

monogamy /muh-**nog**-uh-mi/ ▸ noun the practice of having only one wife or husband at any one time.
□ **monogamous** adjective.

monogram ▸ noun a motif of two or more interwoven letters, typically a person's initials.
□ **monogrammed** adjective.

monograph ▸ noun a book or academic paper written on a single subject.

monolingual ▸ adjective speaking or expressed in only one language.

monolith ▸ noun a large single upright block of stone.

monolithic ▸ adjective 1 formed of a single large block of stone. 2 very large and impersonal.

monologue ▸ noun 1 a long speech by one actor in a play or film. 2 a long, boring speech by one person.

monomania ▸ noun an obsession with one thing.
□ **monomaniac** noun.

monomer /**mon**-uh-mer/ ▸ noun Chemistry a molecule that can be linked to other identical molecules to form a polymer.

monophonic ▸ adjective (of sound reproduction) using only one channel.

monoplane ▸ noun an aircraft with one pair of wings.

monopolize (or **monopolise**) ▸ verb (**monopolizes, monopolizing, monopolized**) dominate or take control of.

monopoly ▸ noun (plural **monopolies**) the complete control of the supply of a product or service by one person or organization.

monorail ▸ noun a railway in which the track consists of a single rail.

monosodium glutamate ▸ noun a compound used to add flavour to food.

monosyllabic ▸ adjective 1 (of a word) having one syllable. 2 (of a person) saying very little.

monosyllable ▸ noun a word of one syllable.

monotheism /**mon**-oh-thee-i-z'm/ ▸ noun the belief that there is only one god.
□ **monotheistic** adjective.

monotone ▸ noun a continuing sound that does not change pitch.

monotonous ▸ adjective boring and unchanging.
□ **monotonously** adverb **monotony** noun.

monoxide ▸ noun Chemistry an oxide containing one atom of oxygen.

Monsieur /muh-**syer**/ ▸ noun (plural **Messieurs** /mess-**yer**/) a title for a French man, corresponding to *Mr* or *sir*.

Monsignor /mon-**seen**-yer/ ▸ noun (plural **Monsignori** /mon-seen-**yor**-i/) the title of a senior Roman Catholic priest.

monsoon ▸ noun 1 a seasonal wind in the Indian subcontinent and SE Asia. 2 the rainy season accompanying the monsoon.

monster ▸ noun 1 a frightening imaginary creature. 2 a cruel or wicked person. 3 something that is very large: *a monster of a book.*

> SYNONYMS 1 *legendary sea monsters* giant, mammoth, demon, dragon, colossus, leviathan, creature. 2 *her husband is a monster* fiend, animal, beast, devil, demon, barbarian, savage, brute; informal swine.

monstrosity ▸ noun (plural **monstrosities**) something that is very large and ugly.

m

monstrous ▸ adjective **1** very large, ugly, or frightening. **2** shocking and morally wrong.

> SYNONYMS **1** *a monstrous creature* **grotesque,** hideous, ugly, ghastly, gruesome, horrible, horrific, horrifying, grisly, disgusting, repulsive, dreadful, frightening, terrible, terrifying. **2** *monstrous acts of violence* **appalling,** wicked, abominable, terrible, horrible, dreadful, vile, outrageous, unspeakable, despicable, vicious, savage, barbaric, inhuman.
> ANTONYMS lovely, kind.

□ **monstrously** adverb.

montage /mon-**tah**zh/ ▸ noun a picture or film made by putting together pieces from other pictures or films.

month ▸ noun **1** each of the twelve periods of time into which a year is divided. **2** a period of time between a date in one month and the same date in the next month. **3** a period of 28 days or four weeks.

monthly ▸ adjective & adverb happening or produced once a month.

monty ▸ noun (**the full monty**) Brit. informal the full amount or extent.

monument ▸ noun **1** a statue or structure built in memory of a person or event. **2** a site of historical importance. **3** a lasting example of something: *a monument to good taste*.

> SYNONYMS **memorial,** statue, pillar, cairn, column, obelisk, cross, cenotaph, tomb, mausoleum, shrine.

monumental ▸ adjective **1** very large or impressive. **2** forming a monument.

> SYNONYMS **1** *a monumental task* **huge,** enormous, gigantic, massive, colossal, mammoth, immense, tremendous, mighty, stupendous. **2** *his monumental career* **significant,** important, majestic, memorable, noteworthy, momentous, defining, grand, awe-inspiring, heroic, epic.
> ANTONYMS tiny, insignificant.

□ **monumentally** adverb.

moo ▸ verb (**moos, mooing, mooed**) (of a cow) make a long, deep sound.

mooch ▸ verb Brit. informal stand or walk around in a bored way.

mood ▸ noun **1** the way you feel at a particular time. **2** a period of being bad-tempered. **3** the atmosphere of a work of art. **4** Grammar a form of a verb expressing fact, command, question, wish, or a condition.

> SYNONYMS **1** *she's in a good mood* **frame of mind,** state of mind, humour, temper. **2** *he's obviously in a mood* **bad mood,** temper, bad temper, sulk, low spirits, the doldrums, the blues; Brit. informal paddy.

3 *the mood of the film* **atmosphere,** feeling, spirit, ambience, aura, character, flavour, feel, tone.

moody ▸ adjective (**moodier, moodiest**) **1** having moods that change quickly. **2** gloomy or bad-tempered.

> SYNONYMS **temperamental,** emotional, volatile, capricious, sullen, sulky, morose, glum, depressed, dejected, despondent, doleful.
> ANTONYMS cheerful.

moon ▸ noun **1** (also **Moon**) the natural satellite of the earth. **2** a natural satellite of any planet. **3** literary a month.

> SYNONYMS **satellite.**

▸ verb **1** (**moon about** or **around**) behave or walk about in a dreamy way. **2** informal expose your buttocks to someone as an insult or joke.

> SYNONYMS **1** *stop mooning about* **waste time,** loaf, idle, mope; Brit. informal mooch; N. Amer. informal lollygag. **2** *he's mooning over her photograph* **mope,** pine, brood, daydream.

■ **over the moon** informal delighted.

moonlight ▸ noun the light of the moon. ▸ verb (**moonlights, moonlighting, moonlighted**) informal do a second job without declaring it for tax purposes.
□ **moonlit** adjective.

moonscape ▸ noun a landscape that is rocky and barren like the moon.

moonshine ▸ noun informal **1** foolish talk or ideas. **2** N. Amer. alcohol that is made and sold illegally.

moonstone ▸ noun a white semi-precious mineral.

moony ▸ adjective dreamy as a result of being in love.

Moor ▸ noun a member of a NW African Muslim people.
□ **Moorish** adjective.

moor¹ ▸ noun a high open area of land that is not cultivated.

> SYNONYMS *a walk on the moor* **upland,** heath, moorland; Brit. fell, wold.

moor² ▸ verb fasten a boat to the shore or to an anchor.

> SYNONYMS *a boat was moored to the quay* **tie (up),** secure, make fast, berth, dock.

moorhen ▸ noun a waterbird with black feathers.

mooring (or **moorings**) ▸ noun a place where a boat is moored, or the ropes used to moor it.

moose = ELK.

moot ▸ adjective uncertain or undecided: *a moot point*.

▶ **verb** put forward a topic for discussion.

mop ▶ **noun 1** a bundle of thick strings or a sponge attached to a handle, used for wiping floors. **2** a thick mass of hair.

> SYNONYMS *her tousled mop of hair* **shock,** mane, tangle, mass.

▶ **verb** (**mops, mopping, mopped**) **1** clean or soak up by wiping. **2** (**mop something up**) complete something by dealing with the things that remain.

> SYNONYMS *a man was mopping the floor* **wash,** clean, wipe, sponge.

mope ▶ **verb** (**mopes, moping, moped**) be listless and gloomy.

moped /**moh**-ped/ ▶ **noun** a motorcycle with a small engine.

moraine ▶ **noun** rocks and stones deposited by a glacier.

moral ▶ **adjective 1** concerned with the principles of right and wrong behaviour. **2** conforming to accepted standards of behaviour.

> SYNONYMS **1** *moral issues* **ethical. 2** *a very moral man* **good,** virtuous, righteous, upright, upstanding, high-minded, principled, honourable, honest, just, noble. **3** *moral support* **psychological,** emotional, mental.
> ANTONYMS dishonourable, practical.

▶ **noun 1** a lesson about right or wrong that you learn from a story or experience. **2** (**morals**) standards of good behaviour.

> SYNONYMS **1** *the moral of the story* **lesson,** message, meaning, significance, import, point, teaching. **2** (**morals**) **moral code,** code of ethics, values, principles, standards, (sense of) morality, scruples.

□ **morally** adverb.

morale ▶ **noun** a feeling of confidence and satisfaction.

> SYNONYMS **confidence,** self-confidence, self-esteem, spirit(s), team spirit, motivation.

moralist ▶ **noun** a person with strict views about morals.

□ **moralistic** adjective.

morality ▶ **noun** (plural **moralities**) **1** principles concerning the difference between right and wrong or good and bad behaviour. **2** moral behaviour. **3** the extent to which an action is right or wrong.

> SYNONYMS **1** *the morality of nuclear weapons* **ethics,** rights and wrongs, whys and wherefores. **2** *a sharp decline in morality* **virtue,** good behaviour, righteousness, uprightness, morals, principles, honesty, integrity, propriety, honour, decency. **3** *Christian morality* **morals,** standards, ethics, principles, mores.

moralize (or **moralise**) ▶ **verb** (**moralizes, moralizing, moralized**) comment on moral issues, usually in a disapproving way.

morass /muh-**rass**/ ▶ **noun 1** an area of muddy or boggy ground. **2** a complicated or confused situation.

moratorium ▶ **noun** (plural **moratoriums** or **moratoria**) a temporary ban on an activity.

moray (or **moray eel**) ▶ **noun** an eel-like fish.

morbid ▶ **adjective 1** having a strong interest in unpleasant subjects, especially death and disease. **2** Medicine having to do with disease.

> SYNONYMS **ghoulish,** macabre, unhealthy, gruesome, unwholesome; informal sick.
> ANTONYMS wholesome.

□ **morbidity** noun **morbidly** adverb.

mordant ▶ **adjective** (of humour) sharply sarcastic.

more ▶ **determiner & pronoun** a greater or additional amount or degree.

> SYNONYMS *some more clothes* **extra,** further, added, additional, supplementary, increased, new.
> ANTONYMS less, fewer.

▶ **adverb 1** forming the comparative of adjectives and adverbs. **2** to a greater extent. **3** again. **4** (**more than**) very.

morel /muh-**rel**/ ▶ **noun** an edible fungus with a brown cap.

morello ▶ **noun** (plural **morellos**) a kind of sour dark cherry.

moreover ▶ **adverb** in addition to what has been said already.

> SYNONYMS **besides,** furthermore, what's more, in addition, also, as well, too, to boot, additionally, on top of that, into the bargain.

mores /**mor**-ayz/ ▶ **plural noun** the customs of a community.

morgue ▶ **noun** a mortuary.

moribund ▶ **adjective 1** at the point of death. **2** about to come to an end.

Mormon ▶ **noun** a member of the Church of Jesus Christ of Latter-Day Saints.
□ **Mormonism** noun.

morn ▶ **noun** literary morning.

morning ▶ **noun 1** the period of time between midnight and noon, especially from sunrise to noon. **2** sunrise.

> SYNONYMS **1** *I've got a meeting this morning* **before lunch(time),** a.m.; literary morn; Nautical N. Amer. forenoon. **2** *morning is on its way* **dawn,** daybreak, sunrise, first light; N. Amer. sunup.

■ **morning sickness** nausea felt by a woman when she is pregnant.

Moroccan ▶ **noun** a person from Morocco.
▶ **adjective** relating to Morocco.

m

moron ▶ noun informal a stupid person.
□ **moronic** adjective.

morose ▶ adjective unhappy and bad-tempered.
□ **morosely** adverb.

morph ▶ verb (in computer animation) change smoothly and gradually from one image to another.

morphine ▶ noun a drug made from opium and used to relieve pain.

morphology ▶ noun the scientific study of the form and structure of animals and plants, or of the forms of words.
□ **morphological** adjective.

morris dancing ▶ noun traditional English folk dancing.

morrow ▶ noun (the morrow) old use the next day.

Morse (or Morse code) ▶ noun a code in which letters are represented by combinations of long and short sounds or flashes of light.

morsel ▶ noun a small piece of food.

mortal ▶ adjective 1 having to die at some time. 2 causing death. 3 (of a battle or enemy) lasting until death.

> SYNONYMS **1** *all men are mortal* **perishable**, physical, bodily, corporeal, human, fleshly, earthly, impermanent, transient, ephemeral. **2** *a mortal blow* **deadly**, fatal, lethal, death-dealing, murderous, terminal.
> ANTONYMS eternal.

▶ noun a human being.

> SYNONYMS *we are mere mortals* **human (being)**, person, man, woman, earthling.

■ **mortal sin** (in Christian belief) a sin so serious as to result in damnation.
□ **mortally** adverb.

mortality ▶ noun 1 the state of being mortal. 2 death. 3 (also **mortality rate**) the number of deaths in a particular area or period of time.

mortar ▶ noun 1 a mixture of lime with cement, sand, and water, used to stick bricks or stones together. 2 a cup-shaped container in which substances are crushed with a pestle. 3 a short cannon for firing shells at high angles.
■ **mortar board** an academic cap with a flat square top and a tassel.

mortgage ▶ noun 1 a legal agreement by which a bank or building society lends you money, using your house as security. 2 an amount of money borrowed or lent under such an agreement.
▶ verb (mortgages, mortgaging, mortgaged) give a bank or building society the right to hold your house as security for the money they agree to lend you.

mortician ▶ noun N. Amer. an undertaker.

mortify ▶ verb (mortifies, mortifying, mortified) make someone feel embarrassed or ashamed.
□ **mortification** noun.

mortise (or **mortice**) ▶ noun a slot cut in a piece of wood in order to hold the end of another piece of wood.
■ **mortise lock** a lock fitted into a hole in a door.

mortuary ▶ noun (plural mortuaries) a room or building in which dead bodies are kept until they are buried or cremated.

> SYNONYMS **morgue**, funeral parlour; Brit. chapel of rest.

mosaic ▶ noun a picture or pattern made by fitting together small coloured pieces of stone, tile, or glass.

mosey ▶ verb (moseys, moseying, moseyed) informal walk in a leisurely way.

Moslem → **MUSLIM**.

mosque ▶ noun a Muslim place of worship.

mosquito ▶ noun (plural mosquitoes) a small long-legged fly, some kinds of which transmit diseases through their bite.

moss ▶ noun a very small green spreading plant which grows in damp places.
□ **mossy** adjective.

most ▶ determiner & pronoun 1 greatest in amount or degree. 2 the majority of.
▶ adverb 1 to the greatest extent. 2 forming the superlative of adjectives and adverbs. 3 very.

mostly ▶ adverb 1 on the whole; mainly. 2 usually.

> SYNONYMS **1** *the other passengers were mostly businessmen* **mainly**, for the most part, on the whole, in the main, largely, chiefly, predominantly, principally, primarily. **2** *I mostly wear jeans* **usually**, generally, in general, as a rule, ordinarily, normally, customarily, typically, most of the time, almost always.

mote ▶ noun a speck.

motel ▶ noun a roadside hotel designed for motorists.

motet /moh-tet/ ▶ noun a short piece of choral music.

moth ▶ noun an insect like a butterfly, which is active at night.
■ **moth-eaten 1** eaten by the larvae of moths. **2** shabby and worn.

mothball ▶ noun a small ball of camphor, placed among stored clothes to deter moths.

mother ▶ noun 1 a female parent. 2 (Mother) (especially as a title or form of address) the head of a convent.

m

SYNONYMS informal **ma**; Brit. informal **mum**, **mummy**; N. Amer. informal **mom**, **mommy**; Brit. informal, dated **mater**.

▶ verb look after somebody protectively.

SYNONYMS *her colleagues mothered her* **look after,** care for, take care of, nurse, protect, tend, raise, rear, pamper, coddle, cosset, fuss over.
ANTONYMS neglect.

■ **mother-in-law** (plural **mothers-in-law**) the mother of a person's husband or wife. **mother-of-pearl** a smooth pearly substance lining the shells of oysters. **mother tongue** a person's native language.
□ **motherhood** noun.

motherland ▶ noun your native country.

motherly ▶ adjective relating to or like a mother, especially in being caring, protective, and kind.

SYNONYMS **maternal,** maternalistic, protective, caring, loving, affectionate, nurturing.

motif /moh-**teef**/ ▶ noun **1** a pattern or design. **2** a theme that is repeated in a work of literature or piece of music.

SYNONYMS **1** *a colourful tulip motif* **design,** pattern, decoration, figure, shape, device, emblem. **2** *a recurring motif in Pinter's work* **theme,** idea, concept, subject, topic, leitmotif.

motion ▶ noun **1** the action of moving. **2** a movement or gesture. **3** a formal proposal that is discussed at a meeting. **4** Brit. an emptying of the bowels.

SYNONYMS **1** *a planet's motion around the sun* **movement,** locomotion, progress, passage, transit, course, travel, orbit. **2** *a motion of the hand* **gesture,** movement, signal, sign, indication, wave, nod, gesticulation. **3** *the motion was passed* **proposal,** proposition, recommendation.

▶ verb direct someone with a gesture.

SYNONYMS *he motioned her to sit down* **gesture,** signal, direct, indicate, wave, beckon, nod.

■ **motion picture** N. Amer. a cinema film.
□ **motionless** adjective.

motivate ▶ verb (**motivates, motivating, motivated**) **1** provide someone with a motive for doing something. **2** make someone want to do something.

SYNONYMS **1** *motivated by greed* **prompt,** drive, move, inspire, stimulate, influence, activate, impel, propel, spur (on). **2** *the teacher must motivate the child* **inspire,** stimulate, encourage, spur (on), excite, incentivize, fire (with enthusiasm).

□ **motivator** noun.

motivation ▶ noun **1** the reason for your actions or behaviour. **2** enthusiasm.

SYNONYMS **motive,** motivating force, incentive, stimulus, stimulation, inspiration, inducement, incitement, spur.

□ **motivational** adjective.

motive ▶ noun something that makes someone act in a particular way.

SYNONYMS **reason,** motivation, motivating force, rationale, grounds, cause, basis.

▶ adjective causing motion.

motley ▶ adjective made up of a variety of different things.

motocross ▶ noun cross-country racing on motorcycles.

motor ▶ noun **1** a device that produces power and movement for a vehicle or machine. **2** Brit. informal a car.

▶ adjective giving or producing motion.
▶ verb travel in a car.
■ **motor vehicle** a road vehicle powered by an engine.
□ **motorized** adjective.

motorbike ▶ noun a motorcycle.

motorboat ▶ noun a boat powered by a motor.

motorcade ▶ noun a procession of motor vehicles.

motorcycle ▶ noun a two-wheeled vehicle powered by a motor.
□ **motorcycling** noun **motorcyclist** noun.

motorist ▶ noun the driver of a car.

motorway ▶ noun Brit. a road designed for fast traffic, typically with three lanes in each direction.

mottled ▶ adjective marked with patches of a different colour.

motto ▶ noun (plural **mottoes** or **mottos**) a short sentence or phrase that expresses a belief or aim.

SYNONYMS **slogan,** maxim, saying, proverb, aphorism, adage, saw, axiom, formula, catchphrase.

mould[1] (US spelling **mold**) ▶ noun **1** a container into which you pour hot liquid in order to produce a solid object of a desired shape when it cools. **2** a distinctive style or character.

SYNONYMS **1** *a clay mould* **cast,** die, form, matrix, shape, template, pattern, frame. **2** *an actress in the traditional Hollywood mould* **pattern,** form, type, style, tradition, school.

▶ verb **1** form an object of a particular shape out of a soft substance. **2** influence the development of something.

m

SYNONYMS **1** *a figure moulded from clay* **shape,** form, fashion, model, work, construct, make, create, sculpt, cast. **2** *the ideas that mould US policy* **determine,** direct, control, guide, influence, shape, form, fashion, make.

mould² (US spelling **mold**) ▸ noun a furry growth of tiny fungi that occurs in moist warm conditions.
□ **mouldy** adjective.

moulder (US spelling **molder**) ▸ verb (**moulders, mouldering, mouldered**) slowly decay.

moulding (US spelling **molding**) ▸ noun a carved or moulded strip of wood, stone, or plaster as a decorative feature on a building.

moult (US spelling **molt**) ▸ verb shed old feathers, hair, or skin.
▸ noun a period of moulting.

mound ▸ noun **1** a raised mass of earth or other material. **2** a small hill. **3** a heap or pile.

SYNONYMS **1** *high on the mound* **hillock,** hill, knoll, rise, hummock, hump; Scottish brae. **2** *a mound of books* **heap,** pile, stack, mountain.

▸ verb heap up into a mound.

m **mount¹** ▸ verb **1** climb up or on to. **2** get up on an animal or bicycle to ride it. **3** increase in size, number, or strength. **4** organize a campaign, bid, etc. **5** put or fix something in place or on a support.

SYNONYMS **1** *he mounted the stairs* **go up,** ascend, climb (up), scale. **2** *they mounted their horses* **get on to,** bestride, climb on to, leap on to, hop on to. **3** *the museum is mounting an exhibition* **put on,** present, install, organize, stage, set up, prepare, launch, set in motion. **4** *their losses mounted rapidly* **increase,** grow, rise, escalate, soar, spiral, shoot up, rocket, climb, accumulate, build up, multiply. ANTONYMS descend, dismount, fall.

▸ noun **1** (also **mounting**) something on which an object is mounted for support or display. **2** a horse used for riding.

SYNONYMS *a picture mount* **setting,** backing, support, mounting, frame, stand.

mount² ▸ noun old use a mountain or hill.

mountain ▸ noun **1** a very high and steep hill. **2** a large pile or quantity.

SYNONYMS **1** *climb a mountain* **peak,** summit; (**mountains**) range, massif, sierra; Scottish ben. **2** *a mountain of work* **lot;** informal heap, pile, stack, slew, lots, loads, tons, masses.

mountaineering ▸ noun the sport or activity of climbing mountains.

□ **mountaineer** noun.

mountainous ▸ adjective **1** having many mountains. **2** huge.

mountebank ▸ noun a person who tricks people in order to get money from them.

mourn ▸ verb feel deep sorrow following the death or loss of.

SYNONYMS **1** *Isobel mourned her husband* **grieve for,** sorrow over, lament for, weep for. **2** *he mourned the loss of the beautiful buildings* **deplore,** bewail, bemoan, rue, regret.

mourner ▸ noun a person who attends a funeral.

mournful ▸ adjective very sad or depressing.
□ **mournfully** adverb.

mourning ▸ noun **1** the expression of deep sorrow for someone who has died. **2** black clothes worn in a period of mourning.

SYNONYMS **grief,** grieving, sorrowing, lamentation.

mouse ▸ noun (plural **mice**) **1** a small rodent with a pointed snout and a long thin tail. **2** a timid and quiet person. **3** (plural also **mouses**) Computing a small hand-held device which controls the cursor on a computer screen.

moussaka /moo-**sah**-kuh/ ▸ noun a Greek dish of minced lamb layered with aubergines and tomatoes and topped with a cheese sauce.

mousse ▸ noun **1** a dish made from whipped cream and egg whites. **2** a light substance used to style hair.

moustache (US spelling **mustache**) ▸ noun a strip of hair above a man's upper lip.

mousy (or **mousey**) ▸ adjective **1** (of hair) of a light brown colour. **2** timid and shy.

mouth ▸ noun **1** the opening in the body through which food is taken and sounds are made. **2** an opening or entrance to something. **3** the place where a river enters the sea.

SYNONYMS **1** **lips,** jaws, muzzle; informal trap, chops, kisser; Brit. informal gob; N. Amer. informal puss, bazoo. **2** *the mouth of the cave* **entrance,** opening. **3** *the mouth of the river* **estuary,** delta, firth, outlet, outfall.

▸ verb **1** move your lips as if you were saying something. **2** say something in a pompous way.
■ **mouth organ** a harmonica. **mouth-watering** smelling or looking delicious.

mouthful ▸ noun **1** an amount of food or drink that fills your mouth. **2** a long or complicated word or phrase.

mouthpiece ▸ noun a part of a musical instrument, telephone, etc. that is put in or against the mouth.

mouthwash ▸ noun an antiseptic liquid for rinsing the mouth or gargling.

mouthy ▸ adjective informal inclined to talk a lot.

move ▸ verb (**moves, moving, moved**) **1** go or make something go in a particular direction or way. **2** change or make something change position. **3** change the place where you live. **4** change from one state or activity to another. **5** take action. **6** make progress. **7** provoke a strong feeling in someone.

SYNONYMS **1** *she moved to the door | don't move!* **go,** walk, step, proceed, progress, advance, budge, stir, shift, change position. **2** *he moved the chair closer to the fire* **carry,** transfer, shift, push, pull, lift, slide. **3** *things were moving too fast* **go,** progress, advance, develop, evolve, change, happen. **4** *he urged the council to move quickly* **act,** take steps, do something, take measures; informal get moving. **5** *she's moved to Cambridge* **relocate,** move house, move away/out, change address, go (away), decamp. **6** *I was deeply moved by the story* **affect,** touch, impress, shake, upset, disturb. **7** *she was moved to find out more about it* **inspire,** prompt, stimulate, motivate, provoke, influence, rouse, induce, incite. **8** *I move that we adjourn* **propose,** submit, suggest, advocate, recommend, urge.

▸ noun **1** an instance of moving. **2** an action taken towards achieving a purpose. **3** a player's turn during a board game.

SYNONYMS **1** *his eyes followed her every move* **movement,** motion, action, gesture. **2** *his recent move to London* **relocation,** change of house/address, transfer, posting. **3** *the latest move in the war against drugs* **initiative,** step, action, measure, manoeuvre, tactic, stratagem. **4** *it's your move* **turn,** go; Scottish shot.

□ **movable** (or **moveable**) adjective.

movement ▸ noun **1** an act of moving. **2** the process of moving. **3** a group of people who share the same aims. **4** a trend or development. **5** (**movements**) a person's activities during a particular period of time. **6** a main division of a piece of music.

SYNONYMS **1** *Rachel made a sudden movement* **motion,** move, gesture, sign, signal, action. **2** *the movement of supplies* **transportation,** shifting, conveyance, moving, transfer. **3** *a political movement* **group,** party, faction, wing, lobby, camp. **4** *a movement to declare war on poverty* **campaign,** crusade, drive, push, initiative.

movie ▸ noun N. Amer. a cinema film.

SYNONYMS **film,** picture, feature film; informal flick.

moving ▸ adjective **1** in motion. **2** arousing strong emotion.

SYNONYMS **1 in motion,** operating, operational, working, on the move, active, movable, mobile. **2** *a moving book* **affecting,** touching, poignant, heart-warming, heart-rending, emotional, inspiring, inspirational, stimulating, stirring.
ANTONYMS stationary, fixed.

□ **movingly** adverb.

mow ▸ verb (**mows, mowing, mowed**; past participle **mowed** or **mown**) **1** cut down or trim grass, hay, etc. **2** (**mow someone down**) kill someone with a gun or by knocking them down with a vehicle.

SYNONYMS **cut,** trim, crop, clip, shear.

□ **mower** noun.

Mozambican ▸ noun a person from Mozambique, a country in southern Africa.
▸ adjective relating to Mozambique.

mozzarella /mot-suh-**rel**-luh/ ▸ noun a firm white Italian cheese made from buffalo's or cow's milk.

MP ▸ abbreviation Member of Parliament.

MP3 ▸ noun a method of compressing a sound sequence into a very small file, used as a way of downloading sound files from the Internet.

Mr ▸ noun a title used before a man's surname or full name.

Mrs ▸ noun a title used before a married woman's surname or full name.

MS ▸ abbreviation **1** manuscript. **2** multiple sclerosis.

Ms ▸ noun a title used before a married or unmarried woman's surname or full name.

MSc ▸ abbreviation Master of Science.

Mt ▸ abbreviation Mount.

much ▸ determiner & pronoun a large amount.

SYNONYMS **1** *is there much food?* **a lot of,** a great/good deal of, a great/large amount of, plenty of, ample, abundant, plentiful; informal lots of, loads of, heaps of, masses of, tons of, stacks of. **2** *he did much for our team* **a lot,** a great/good deal, plenty; informal lots, loads, heaps, masses, tons.
ANTONYMS little.

▸ adverb **1** to a great extent. **2** often.

SYNONYMS **1** *it didn't hurt much* **greatly,** a great deal, a lot, considerably, appreciably. **2** *does he come here much?* **often,** frequently, many times, regularly, habitually, routinely, usually, normally, commonly; informal a lot.

muck ▸ noun **1** dirt or rubbish. **2** manure.

SYNONYMS **1** *I'll just clean off the muck* **dirt,** grime, filth, mud, mess; Brit. informal gunge; N. Amer. informal guck. **2** *spreading*

m

muck on the fields **dung,** manure, excrement, droppings.

▶ verb chiefly Brit. **1** (**muck something up**) informal spoil something. **2** (**muck about** or **around**) informal behave in a silly way. **3** (**muck about with** or **around with**) informal interfere with. **4** (**muck in**) informal share a task. **5** (**muck something out**) remove manure and dirt from a stable.
□ **mucky** adjective.

mucous /**myoo**-kuhss/ ▶ adjective having to do with mucus.
■ **mucous membrane** a tissue that produces mucus, lining the nose, mouth, and other organs.

mucus /**myoo**-kuhss/ ▶ noun a slimy substance produced by the mucous membranes.

mud ▶ noun soft, wet, sticky earth.

> SYNONYMS **dirt,** sludge, ooze, silt, clay, mire, soil.

muddle ▶ verb (**muddles, muddling, muddled**) **1** put things in the wrong order or mix them up. **2** confuse someone. **3** (**muddle something up**) confuse two or more things with each other. **4** (**muddle along** or **through**) manage to cope in spite of a lack of skill, knowledge, etc.

> SYNONYMS **1** *the papers have got muddled up* **confuse,** mix up, jumble (up), disarrange, disorganize, disorder, mess up. **2** *it would only muddle you* **bewilder,** confuse, bemuse, perplex, puzzle, baffle, nonplus, mystify.

▶ noun a muddled state.

> SYNONYMS **mess,** confusion, jumble, tangle, chaos, disorder, disarray, disorganization.

muddy ▶ adjective (**muddier, muddiest**) **1** covered in mud. **2** not bright or clear.

> SYNONYMS **1** *muddy ground* **marshy,** boggy, swampy, waterlogged, squelchy, squishy, mucky, slimy, wet, soft. **2** *muddy boots* **dirty,** filthy, mucky, grimy, soiled. **3** *muddy water* **murky,** cloudy, turbid.
> ANTONYMS clean, clear.

▶ verb (**muddies, muddying, muddied**) make something muddy.

mudflap ▶ noun a flap hung behind the wheel of a vehicle to protect against mud and stones thrown up from the road.

mudflat ▶ noun a stretch of muddy land left uncovered at low tide.

mudguard ▶ noun a curved strip fitted over a wheel of a bicycle or motorcycle to protect against water and dirt thrown up from the road.

muesli /**myooz**-li/ ▶ noun (plural **mueslis**) a mixture of oats, dried fruit, and nuts, eaten

with milk.

muezzin /moo-**ez**-zin/ ▶ noun a man who calls Muslims to prayer.

muff¹ ▶ noun a short tube made of fur or other warm material into which you place your hands for warmth.

muff² ▶ verb informal handle something clumsily or badly.

muffin ▶ noun **1** a type of flat bread roll, usually eaten toasted with butter. **2** a type of small cake.

muffle ▶ verb (**muffles, muffling, muffled**) **1** wrap or cover for warmth. **2** make a sound quieter.

> SYNONYMS **1** *everyone was muffled up in coats* **wrap (up),** swathe, enfold, envelop, cloak. **2** *the sound of their footsteps was muffled* **deaden,** dull, dampen, mute, soften, quieten, mask, stifle, smother.

muffler ▶ noun a scarf.

mufti /**muf**-ti/ ▶ noun (plural **muftis**) **1** a Muslim legal expert allowed to give rulings on religious matters. **2** civilian clothes when worn by military or police staff.

mug¹ ▶ noun **1** a large cylindrical cup with a handle. **2** informal a person's face. **3** Brit. informal a stupid or gullible person.

> SYNONYMS *a china mug* **beaker,** cup, tankard, glass, stein.

▶ verb (**mugs, mugging, mugged**) attack and rob someone in a public place.

> SYNONYMS *he was mugged by youths* **assault,** attack, set upon, beat up, rob; informal **jump.**

mug² ▶ verb (**mugs, mugging, mugged**) (**mug something up**) Brit. informal learn as much as you can about a subject in a short time.

mugger ▶ noun a person who attacks and robs someone in a public place.

muggins ▶ noun (plural **muggins** or **mugginses**) Brit. informal a foolish person.

muggy ▶ adjective (of the weather) unpleasantly warm and humid.

> SYNONYMS **humid,** close, sultry, sticky, oppressive, airless, stifling, suffocating, stuffy, heavy.
> ANTONYMS fresh.

mugshot ▶ noun informal a photograph of a person's face made for an official purpose.

mulatto ▶ noun (plural **mulattoes** or **mulattos**) offensive a person with one white and one black parent.

mulberry ▶ noun (plural **mulberries**) **1** a dark red or white fruit resembling the loganberry. **2** a dark red or purple colour.

mulch ▶ noun a mass of leaves or compost, used to protect the base of a plant or to

enrich the soil.
▶ verb cover with mulch.

mule ▶ noun the offspring of a male donkey and a female horse.

mulish ▶ adjective stubborn.

mull¹ ▶ verb (mull something over) think about something at length.

> SYNONYMS she began to mull over the possibilities **ponder,** consider, think over/about, reflect on, contemplate, chew over; formal cogitate on.

mull² ▶ verb warm wine or beer and add sugar and spices to it.

mullah /muul-luh/ ▶ noun a Muslim who is an expert in Islamic theology and sacred law.

mullet ▶ noun a sea fish that is caught for food.

mulligatawny ▶ noun a spicy meat soup originally made in India.

mullion ▶ noun a vertical bar between the panes of glass in a window.
□ mullioned adjective.

multicoloured (or multicolour) (US spelling multicolored or multicolor)
▶ adjective having many colours.

> SYNONYMS **kaleidoscopic,** psychedelic, colourful, rainbow, jazzy, variegated.
> ANTONYMS monochrome.

multicultural ▶ adjective relating to or made up of several cultural or ethnic groups.
□ multiculturalism noun.

multifaceted ▶ adjective having many sides or aspects.

multifarious ▶ adjective having great variety.

multilateral ▶ adjective involving three or more participants.

multilingual ▶ adjective in or using several languages.

multimedia ▶ noun the use of sound and pictures as well as text on a computer screen.

multinational ▶ adjective involving several countries.
▶ noun a company operating in several countries.

multiple ▶ adjective **1** having or involving several parts or elements. **2** (of a disease or injury) affecting several parts of the body.

> SYNONYMS **numerous,** many, various, different, diverse, several, manifold.
> ANTONYMS single.

▶ noun a number that may be divided by another number without a remainder.
■ multiple-choice (of a question in an exam) giving several possible answers, from which you must choose one. multiple

sclerosis ➡ SCLEROSIS.

multiplex ▶ noun a cinema with several separate screens.

multiplication ▶ noun the process of multiplying.
■ multiplication sign the symbol ×, indicating that one number is to be multiplied by another.

multiplicity ▶ noun (plural multiplicities) a large number or variety of something.

multiply ▶ verb (multiplies, multiplying, multiplied) **1** add a number to itself a stated number of times. **2** increase in number or quantity. **3** increase in number by reproducing.

> SYNONYMS **increase,** grow, accumulate, proliferate, mount up, mushroom, snowball.
> ANTONYMS decrease.

□ multiplier noun.

multiracial ▶ adjective having to do with people of many races.

multi-storey ▶ adjective (of a building) having several storeys.
▶ noun Brit. a multi-storey car park.

multitask ▶ verb **1** Computing operate more than one program at the same time. **2** do several things at the same time.

multitude ▶ noun **1** a large number of people or things. **2** (the multitude) the mass of ordinary people.

multitudinous ▶ adjective very numerous.

mum¹ ▶ noun Brit. informal your mother.

mum² ▶ adjective (keep mum) informal stay silent so as not to reveal a secret.
■ mum's the word it's a secret.

mumble ▶ verb (mumbles, mumbling, mumbled) say something in a quiet voice that is difficult to hear or understand.

> SYNONYMS **mutter,** murmur, talk under your breath.

▶ noun quiet speech that is difficult to hear or understand.

mumbo-jumbo ▶ noun informal language that sounds mysterious but has no real meaning.

mummify ▶ verb (mummifies, mummifying, mummified) preserve a body as a mummy.
□ mummification noun.

mummy¹ ▶ noun (plural mummies) Brit. informal your mother.

mummy² ▶ noun (plural mummies) (especially in ancient Egypt) a body that has been embalmed and wrapped in bandages in order to preserve it.

mumps ▶ noun a disease causing swelling of the glands at the sides of the face.

munch ▶ verb eat something steadily and often noisily.

m

mundane ▸ adjective lacking interest or excitement.

synonyms **humdrum,** dull, boring, tedious, monotonous, tiresome, unexciting, uninteresting, uneventful, unremarkable, routine, ordinary. antonyms extraordinary.

municipal ▸ adjective relating to a municipality.

synonyms **civic,** civil, metropolitan, urban, city, town, borough, council. antonyms private, rural.

municipality ▸ noun (plural **municipalities**) a town or district with its own local government.

munificent ▸ adjective very generous. □ munificence noun.

munitions ▸ plural noun military weapons, ammunition, and equipment.

mural ▸ noun a painting done directly on a wall.

murder ▸ noun the unlawful planned killing of one person by another.

synonyms *a brutal murder* **killing,** homicide, assassination, extermination, execution, slaughter, butchery, massacre, manslaughter; literary slaying.

▸ verb (**murders, murdering, murdered**) kill someone unlawfully, having planned to in advance.

synonyms *someone tried to murder him* **kill,** put/do to death, assassinate, execute, butcher, slaughter, massacre, wipe out; informal bump off; N. Amer. informal ice, waste; literary slay.

murderer (or **murderess**) ▸ noun a person who commits murder.

synonyms **killer,** assassin, serial killer, butcher; informal hit man, hired gun.

murderous ▸ adjective capable of murdering someone or being very violent.

synonyms **homicidal,** brutal, violent, savage, ferocious, fierce, vicious, bloodthirsty, barbarous, barbaric, fatal, lethal, deadly.

murk ▸ noun darkness or fog.

murky ▸ adjective (**murkier, murkiest**) 1 dark and gloomy. 2 (of water) dirty or cloudy. 3 suspicious and kept hidden.

synonyms 1 *a murky winter afternoon* **dark,** gloomy, grey, leaden, dull, dim, overcast, cloudy, clouded, sunless, dismal, dreary, bleak. 2 *murky water* **dirty,** muddy, cloudy, turbid. antonyms bright, clear.

murmur ▸ verb 1 say something quietly. 2 make a low continuous sound.

synonyms *he heard them murmuring in the hall* **mutter,** mumble, whisper, talk under your breath.

▸ noun 1 the sound made by a person speaking quietly. 2 a low continuous background noise.

synonyms 1 *his voice was a murmur* **whisper,** mutter, mumble. 2 *the murmur of bees* **hum,** buzz, drone.

muscle ▸ noun 1 a band of body tissue that can be tightened or relaxed to move a part of the body. 2 power or strength.

synonyms 1 *he had muscle but no brains* **strength,** power, brawn; informal beef, beefiness. 2 *financial muscle* **influence,** power, strength, might, force, forcefulness, weight; informal clout.

▸ verb (**muscles, muscling, muscled**) (**muscle in**) informal involve yourself in something that does not concern you. □ muscly adjective.

muscular ▸ adjective 1 having to do with the muscles. 2 having well-developed muscles.

synonyms **strong,** brawny, muscly, well built, burly, strapping, sturdy, powerful, athletic; informal hunky, beefy.

■ muscular dystrophy an inherited condition in which the muscles gradually become weaker.

musculature ▸ noun the arrangement of muscles in a body.

muse[1] ▸ noun 1 (**Muse**) (in Greek and Roman mythology) each of nine goddesses representing or associated with a particular art or science. 2 a woman who is the inspiration for a creative artist.

muse[2] ▸ verb (**muses, musing, mused**) 1 be absorbed in thought. 2 say something to yourself in a thoughtful way.

synonyms **ponder,** consider, think over/about, mull over, reflect on, contemplate, turn over in your mind, chew over.

museum ▸ noun a building in which objects of interest are kept and shown to the public.

mush ▸ noun 1 a soft, wet, pulpy mass. 2 something that is too sentimental. □ mushy adjective.

mushroom ▸ noun a fungus in the form of a domed cap on a short stalk, many kinds of which are edible.

▸ verb increase or develop quickly. ■ mushroom cloud a mushroom-shaped cloud of dust formed after a nuclear explosion.

music ▸ noun 1 the sounds of voices or instruments arranged in a pleasing way. 2 the art of writing or playing music. 3 the written or printed signs representing a piece of music.

■ **music hall 1** (in the past) a popular form of entertainment involving singing, dancing, and comedy. **2** a theatre where such entertainment took place.

musical ▸ adjective **1** relating to or accompanied by music. **2** fond of or skilled in music. **3** having a pleasant sound.

> SYNONYMS **tuneful**, melodic, melodious, harmonious, sweet-sounding.
> ANTONYMS discordant.

▸ noun a play or film which involves singing or dancing.
□ **musically** adverb.

musician ▸ noun a person who plays a musical instrument or writes music.
□ **musicianship** noun.

musicology ▸ noun the study of the history and theory of music.

musk ▸ noun a strong-smelling substance produced by the male of a small breed of deer, used as an ingredient in perfume.
□ **musky** adjective.

musket ▸ noun (in the past) a light gun with a long barrel.

musketeer ▸ noun (in the past) a soldier armed with a musket.

muskrat ▸ noun a large North American rodent with a musky smell.

Muslim (or Moslem) ▸ noun a follower of Islam.
▸ adjective relating to Muslims or Islam.

muslin ▸ noun lightweight cotton cloth in a plain weave.

musquash ▸ noun Brit. the fur of the muskrat.

mussel ▸ noun a small shellfish with a dark brown or purplish-black shell.

must[1] ▸ modal verb (past **had to** or in reported speech **must**) **1** be obliged to; should. **2** used to insist on something. **3** used to say that something is very likely: *you must be tired.*

> SYNONYMS **ought to**, should, have (got) to, need to, be obliged to, be required to, be compelled to.

▸ noun informal something that should not be missed.

must[2] ▸ noun grape juice before it is fermented.

mustache US spelling of MOUSTACHE.

mustang ▸ noun a small wild horse of the south-western US.

mustard ▸ noun **1** a hot-tasting yellow or brown paste made from the crushed seeds of a plant. **2** a brownish-yellow colour.
■ **mustard gas** a liquid whose vapour causes severe irritation and blistering of the skin, used in chemical weapons.

muster ▸ verb (musters, mustering, mustered) **1** summon up a feeling or attitude. **2** bring troops together in preparation for battle. **3** (of people) gather together.

> SYNONYMS **1** *she mustered her courage* **summon (up)**, screw up, call up, rally. **2** *they mustered 50,000 troops* **assemble**, mobilize, rally, raise, summon, gather, mass, call up, call to arms, recruit, conscript; US draft. **3** *reporters mustered outside her house* **congregate**, assemble, gather (together), come together, collect, convene, mass, rally.

▸ noun an instance of mustering troops.
■ **pass muster** be accepted as satisfactory.

mustn't ▸ short form must not.

musty ▸ adjective having a stale or mouldy smell.
□ **mustiness** noun.

mutable ▸ adjective able or tending to change.
□ **mutability** noun.

mutant ▸ adjective resulting from or showing the effect of mutation.
▸ noun a mutant form.

mutate ▸ verb (mutates, mutating, mutated) undergo mutation.

mutation ▸ noun **1** the process of changing. **2** a change in genetic structure which may be passed on to subsequent generations. **3** a distinct form resulting from such a change.

> SYNONYMS **1** **alteration**, change, transformation, metamorphosis, transmutation. **2** *a genetic mutation* **mutant**, freak (of nature), deviant, monstrosity, monster.

mute ▸ adjective **1** not speaking. **2** unable to speak. **3** (of a letter) not pronounced.

> SYNONYMS **1** *Yasmin remained mute* **silent**, speechless, dumb, unspeaking, tight-lipped, taciturn; informal mum. **2** *a mute appeal* **wordless**, silent, dumb, unspoken.
> ANTONYMS voluble, spoken.

▸ noun **1** dated a person who is unable to speak. **2** a device used to make the sound of a musical instrument quieter or softer.
▸ verb (mutes, muting, muted) **1** make the sound of something quieter or softer. **2** reduce the strength or intensity of.

> SYNONYMS **1** *the noise was muted by the heavy curtains* **deaden**, muffle, dampen, soften, stifle, smother, suppress. **2** (muted) *the muted hum of traffic* **muffled**, faint, indistinct, quiet, soft, low, distant, faraway. **3** (muted) *muted tones* **subdued**, pastel, delicate, subtle, understated, restrained.

□ **mutely** adverb.

mutilate ▸ verb (mutilates, mutilating, mutilated) severely injure or damage.

> SYNONYMS **1** *the bodies had been mutilated* **mangle**, maim, disfigure, dismember, slash, hack. **2** *the carved screen had been mutilated* **vandalize**, damage, slash, hack, deface, violate, desecrate.

□ **mutilation** noun.

mutineer ▶ noun a person who takes part in a mutiny.

mutinous ▶ adjective rebellious.

mutiny ▶ noun (plural **mutinies**) an open rebellion against authority, especially by soldiers or sailors against their officers.

> SYNONYMS *a naval mutiny* **insurrection**, rebellion, revolt, riot, uprising, insurgence, insubordination.

▶ verb (**mutinies, mutinying, mutinied**) take part in a mutiny; rebel.

> SYNONYMS *the crew mutinied* **rise up**, rebel, revolt, riot, strike.

mutt ▶ noun informal a mongrel dog.

mutter ▶ verb (**mutters, muttering, muttered**) **1** say something in a voice which can barely be heard. **2** talk or grumble in private.

> SYNONYMS **1** *a group of men stood muttering* **talk under your breath**, murmur, mumble, whisper. **2** *residents muttered about the charge* **grumble**, complain, grouse, carp, whine; informal moan, whinge.

▶ noun speech that can barely be heard.

mutton ▶ noun the flesh of a fully grown sheep used as food.

mutual ▶ adjective **1** experienced by two or more people equally. **2** shared by two or more people: *a mutual friend*.

> SYNONYMS **reciprocal**, reciprocated, requited, returned, common, joint, shared.

□ **mutuality** noun **mutually** adverb.

muzzle ▶ noun **1** the nose and mouth of an animal. **2** a guard fitted over an animal's muzzle to stop it biting. **3** the open end of the barrel of a gun.

▶ verb (**muzzles, muzzling, muzzled**) **1** put a muzzle on an animal. **2** prevent someone speaking freely.

muzzy ▶ adjective **1** dazed or confused. **2** blurred or indistinct.

my ▶ possessive determiner belonging to or associated with the speaker.

myalgia /my-**al**-juh/ ▶ noun pain in a muscle.

mycology ▶ noun the scientific study of fungi.

mynah bird ▶ noun an Asian or Australasian bird, some kinds of which can mimic human speech.

myopia /my-**oh**-pi-uh/ ▶ noun short-sightedness.
□ **myopic** adjective.

myriad /**mi**-ri-uhd/ ▶ noun (also **myriads**) a countless or very great number.
▶ adjective countless.

myrrh /mer/ ▶ noun a sweet-smelling substance obtained from certain trees, used in perfumes and incense.

myrtle ▶ noun an evergreen shrub with white flowers and purple-black berries.

myself ▶ pronoun **1** used by a speaker to refer to himself or herself as the object of a verb or preposition when he or she is the subject of the clause. **2** I or me personally.

mysterious ▶ adjective difficult or impossible to understand or explain.

> SYNONYMS **1** *mysterious circumstances* **puzzling**, strange, peculiar, curious, funny, odd, weird, bizarre, mystifying, inexplicable, baffling, perplexing. **2** *he was being very mysterious* **secretive**, inscrutable, enigmatic, reticent, evasive, furtive, surreptitious.
> ANTONYMS straightforward.

□ **mysteriously** adverb.

mystery ▶ noun (plural **mysteries**) **1** something that is difficult or impossible to understand or explain. **2** secrecy. **3** a novel, film, etc. dealing with a puzzling crime.

> SYNONYMS **1** *his death remains a mystery* **puzzle**, enigma, conundrum, riddle, secret, paradox. **2** *her past is shrouded in mystery* **secrecy**, obscurity, uncertainty, mystique.

■ **mystery play** a medieval play based on biblical stories or the lives of the saints.

mystic ▶ noun a person who seeks to know God through prayer and contemplation.
▶ adjective mystical.

> SYNONYMS **spiritual**, religious, transcendental, paranormal, other-worldly, supernatural, occult, metaphysical.

mystical ▶ adjective **1** relating to mystics or mysticism. **2** having a spiritual significance that goes beyond human understanding. **3** inspiring a sense of spiritual mystery and awe.

mysticism ▶ noun **1** the belief that knowledge of God can be found through prayer and contemplation. **2** vague or ill-defined religious or spiritual belief.

mystify ▶ verb (**mystifies, mystifying, mystified**) **1** completely bewilder someone. **2** make something uncertain or mysterious.

> SYNONYMS **bewilder**, puzzle, perplex, baffle, confuse, confound, bemuse, throw; informal flummox, stump, bamboozle.

□ **mystification** noun.

m

mystique ▸ noun a quality of mystery, glamour, or power that makes someone or something seem impressive or attractive.

myth ▸ noun 1 a traditional story that describes the early history of a people or explains a natural event. 2 a widely held but false belief. 3 an imaginary person or thing.

> SYNONYMS 1 *ancient Greek myths* **folk tale,** folk story, legend, fable, saga, lore, folklore. 2 *the myths surrounding childbirth* **misconception,** fallacy, old wives' tale, fairy story, fiction; informal cock and bull story.

mythical ▸ adjective 1 found in or characteristic of myths or folk tales. 2 imaginary or not real.

mythology ▸ noun (plural **mythologies**) 1 a collection of myths. 2 a set of widely held but exaggerated or false beliefs. ▫ **mythological** adjective.

myxomatosis /mik-suh-muh-**toh**-siss/ ▸ noun a highly infectious and usually fatal disease of rabbits.

m

Nn

N (or n) ▶ noun (plural **Ns** or **N's**) the fourteenth letter of the alphabet.
▶ abbreviation North or Northern.

n/a ▶ abbreviation not applicable.

naan → NAN².

nab ▶ verb (**nabs, nabbing, nabbed**) informal catch a wrongdoer.

nacho /**na**-choh/ ▶ noun (plural **nachos**) a small piece of tortilla topped with melted cheese, peppers, etc.

nadir /**nay**-deer/ ▶ noun **1** the lowest or most unsuccessful point. **2** the point in space directly opposite the zenith and below an observer.

naevus /**nee**-vuhss/ (US spelling **nevus**)
▶ noun (plural **naevi** /**nee**-vy/) a birthmark or a mole on the skin.

naff ▶ adjective Brit. informal lacking taste or style.

nag¹ ▶ verb (**nags, nagging, nagged**)
1 constantly tell someone they should be doing something. **2** be constantly worrying or painful.

> SYNONYMS **1** *she's constantly nagging me* **harass,** keep on at, go on at, badger, chivvy, hound, criticize, find fault with, moan at, grumble at, henpeck; informal hassle; N. Amer. informal ride. **2** *this has been nagging me for weeks* **trouble,** worry, bother, plague, torment, niggle, prey on your mind; informal bug.

▶ noun **1** a person who nags. **2** a persistent feeling of anxiety.

nag² ▶ noun informal an old horse.

naiad /**ny**-ad/ ▶ noun (in classical mythology) a water nymph.

nail ▶ noun **1** a small metal spike with a flat head, used for joining pieces of wood together. **2** a thin hard layer covering the upper part of the tip of the finger and toe.

> SYNONYMS *fastened with nails* **tack,** pin, brad, clout, spike, staple.

▶ verb **1** fasten with a nail or nails. **2** informal catch a criminal.

> SYNONYMS *a board was nailed to the wall* **fasten,** attach, fix, affix, secure, tack, hammer, pin.

■ **nail-biting** making you feel great anxiety or tension.

naive (or **naïve**) /ny-**eev**/ ▶ adjective lacking experience or judgement.

> SYNONYMS **innocent,** unsophisticated, artless, inexperienced, unworldly, trusting, gullible, credulous, immature, callow, raw, green; informal wet behind the ears.
> ANTONYMS worldly.

□ **naively** adverb.

naivety /ny-**eev**-ti/ (or **naiveté** /ny-**eev**-tay/) ▶ noun lack of experience, wisdom, or judgement.

naked ▶ adjective **1** without clothes. **2** (of an object) without the usual covering or protection. **3** (of feelings) not hidden; open. **4** vulnerable.

> SYNONYMS **nude,** bare, in the nude, stark naked, having nothing on, stripped, unclothed, undressed; informal without a stitch on, in your birthday suit, in the raw/buff, in the altogether; Brit. informal starkers; N. Amer. informal buck naked.
> ANTONYMS clothed.

■ **the naked eye** the normal power of the eyes, without using a telescope, microscope, etc.
□ **nakedly** adverb **nakedness** noun.

namby-pamby ▶ adjective lacking strength or courage; feeble.

name ▶ noun **1** a word or words by which someone or something is known. **2** a famous person. **3** a reputation: *he made a name for himself.*

> SYNONYMS *her name's Gemma* **title,** honorific, designation, tag, epithet, label; informal moniker, handle.

▶ verb (**names, naming, named**) **1** give a name to. **2** identify or mention by name. **3** specify a sum of money, time, or place.

> SYNONYMS **1** *they named the child Pamela* **call,** dub, label, style, term, title, baptize, christen. **2** *he has named his successor* **nominate,** designate, select, pick, decide on, choose.

■ **name-dropping** mentioning the names of famous people as if you know them, in order to impress other people.

nameless ▸ adjective **1** having no name.
2 having a name that is kept secret.

namely ▸ adverb that is to say.

> SYNONYMS **that is (to say),** to be specific,
> specifically, viz., to wit, in other words.

namesake ▸ noun a person or thing with
the same name as another.

Namibian /nuh-**mib**-i-uhn/ ▸ noun a person
from Namibia, a country in southern
Africa.
▸ adjective relating to Namibia.

nan¹ ▸ noun Brit. informal your grandmother.

nan² (or **naan**) /nahn/ ▸ noun a type of soft
flat Indian bread.

nanny ▸ noun (plural **nannies**) **1** a woman
employed to look after a child in its own
home. **2** (also **nanny goat**) a female goat.

nanosecond ▸ noun one thousand
millionth of a second.

nap¹ ▸ noun a short sleep.

> SYNONYMS **sleep,** catnap, siesta, doze, lie-
> down, rest; informal snooze, forty winks,
> shut-eye; Brit. informal kip.

▸ verb (**naps, napping, napped**) have a nap.

nap² ▸ noun short raised fibres on the
surface of certain fabrics.

napalm /**nay**-pahm/ ▸ noun a highly
flammable form of petrol, used in
firebombs.

nape ▸ noun the back of the neck.

naphtha /**naf**-thuh/ ▸ noun a flammable oil
extracted from coal and petroleum.

napkin ▸ noun a piece of cloth or paper used
at a meal to wipe the fingers or lips and to
protect clothes.

nappy ▸ noun (plural **nappies**) Brit. a piece of
material wrapped round a baby's bottom
and between its legs to absorb urine and
faeces.

narcissism /**nar**-si-si-z'm/ ▸ noun too much
interest in yourself and your appearance.
□ **narcissist** noun **narcissistic** adjective.

narcissus /nar-**si**-suhss/ ▸ noun (plural
narcissi /nar-**si**-sy/ or **narcissuses**) a daffodil
with a flower that has pale outer petals and
an orange or yellow centre.

narcotic ▸ noun **1** an addictive drug which
affects mood or behaviour. **2** a drug which
causes drowsiness or unconsciousness, or
relieves pain.

> SYNONYMS *illegal narcotics* **drug,** sedative,
> opiate, painkiller, analgesic, palliative.

▸ adjective relating to narcotics.

> SYNONYMS *a narcotic effect* **soporific,**
> sedative, calming, sleep-inducing, opiate,
> painkilling, pain-relieving, analgesic,
> anodyne.

nark Brit. informal ▸ noun a police informer.
▸ verb annoy.

narrate ▸ verb (**narrates, narrating,
narrated**) **1** give an account of something.
2 provide a commentary for a film,
television programme, etc.

> SYNONYMS **tell,** relate, recount, describe,
> chronicle, report, present.

□ **narration** noun.

narrative ▸ noun an account of connected
events; a story.

> SYNONYMS **account,** chronicle, history,
> description, record, report, story, tale.

▸ adjective having to do with stories or the
telling of stories.

narrator ▸ noun a person who narrates.

> SYNONYMS **storyteller,** relater, chronicler,
> commentator, presenter, author.
> ANTONYMS listener, audience.

narrow ▸ adjective (**narrower, narrowest**)
1 of small width in comparison to length.
2 limited in extent, amount, or scope.
3 only just achieved: *a narrow escape.*

> SYNONYMS **1** *her narrow waist* **slender,**
> slim, small, slight, spare, attenuated,
> tapering, thin, tiny. **2** *a narrow space*
> **confined,** cramped, tight, restricted,
> limited, constricted, small, tiny. **3** *a
> narrow range of products* **limited,**
> restricted, small, inadequate,
> insufficient, deficient.
> ANTONYMS wide, broad.

▸ verb **1** become or make narrower. **2** (**narrow
something down**) reduce the number of
possibilities of something.

> SYNONYMS *narrowing the gap between
> rich and poor* **become/make narrower,**
> become/make smaller, taper, diminish,
> decrease, reduce, contract, shrink,
> constrict.
> ANTONYMS widen.

▸ noun (**narrows**) a narrow channel
connecting two larger areas of water.
□ **narrowness** noun.

narrowboat ▸ noun Brit. a canal boat less
than 7 ft (2.1 metres) wide.

narrowly ▸ adverb by only a small margin.

> SYNONYMS **(only) just,** barely, scarcely,
> hardly, by a hair's breadth; informal by a
> whisker.

narrow-minded ▸ adjective unwilling
to listen to or accept the views of other
people.

> SYNONYMS **intolerant,** illiberal,
> reactionary, conservative, parochial,
> provincial, insular, small-minded, petty,
> blinkered, inward-looking, narrow,
> hidebound, prejudiced, bigoted.
> ANTONYMS tolerant.

n

NASA ▶ abbreviation (in the US) National Aeronautics and Space Administration.

nasal ▶ adjective relating to the nose.
□ **nasally** adverb.

nascent /**na**-suhnt, **nay**-suhnt/ ▶ adjective just coming into existence and beginning to develop.

nasturtium /nuh-**ster**-shuhm/ ▶ noun a garden plant with bright orange, yellow, or red flowers.

nasty ▶ adjective (**nastier, nastiest**)
1 unpleasant or disgusting. **2** spiteful, violent, or bad-tempered. **3** painful or harmful: *a nasty bang on the head.*

> SYNONYMS **1** *a nasty smell* **unpleasant,** disagreeable, disgusting, vile, foul, abominable, revolting, repulsive, repellent, obnoxious, unsavoury, noxious, foul-smelling, smelly, stinking, rank; informal ghastly, horrid, yucky; N. Amer. informal lousy. **2** *she can be really nasty* **unkind,** unpleasant, unfriendly, disagreeable, rude, spiteful, malicious, mean, vicious, malevolent, hurtful. **3** *a nasty accident* **serious,** dangerous, bad, awful, dreadful, terrible, severe, painful, ugly.
> ANTONYMS nice, slight.

□ **nastily** adverb **nastiness** noun.

natal /**nay**-t'l/ ▶ adjective relating to the place or time of your birth.

nation ▶ noun a large group of people sharing the same language, culture, or history and inhabiting a particular territory.

> SYNONYMS **country,** state, land, realm, people, race, tribe, clan.

national ▶ adjective **1** having to do with a nation. **2** owned, controlled, or financially supported by the state.

> SYNONYMS **1** *national politics* **state,** public, federal, governmental. **2** *a national strike* **nationwide,** countrywide, state, general, widespread.
> ANTONYMS local, international.

▶ noun a citizen of a particular country.

> SYNONYMS *a French national* **citizen,** subject, native, resident, inhabitant, voter, passport holder.

■ **national curriculum** a programme of study that must be taught in state schools. **national debt** the total amount of money which a country's government has borrowed. **national grid** Brit. **1** the network of power lines between major power stations. **2** the system of geographical coordinates used in maps of the British Isles. **National Insurance** (in the UK) a system of payments made by employees and employers to provide help for people who are ill, unemployed, or retired.

national park an area of countryside that is protected by the state. **national service** a period of compulsory service in the armed forces during peacetime.
□ **nationally** adverb.

nationalism ▶ noun **1** very strong feelings of support for and pride in your own country. **2** belief in independence for a particular country.

> SYNONYMS **patriotism,** allegiance, xenophobia, chauvinism, jingoism.

□ **nationalist** noun & adjective **nationalistic** adjective.

nationality ▶ noun (plural **nationalities**)
1 the status of belonging to a particular nation. **2** an ethnic group.

nationalize (or **nationalise**) ▶ verb (**nationalizes, nationalizing, nationalized**) put an industry or business under the control of the government.
□ **nationalization** noun.

nationwide ▶ adjective & adverb throughout the whole nation.

> SYNONYMS **national,** countrywide, state, general, widespread, extensive.
> ANTONYMS local.

native ▶ noun **1** a person born in a particular place. **2** a local inhabitant. **3** an animal or plant that lives or grows naturally in a particular area. **4** dated, offensive a non-white person living in a country before the arrival of white colonists or settlers.

> SYNONYMS *a native of Sweden* **inhabitant,** resident, local, citizen, national, countryman.
> ANTONYMS foreigner.

▶ adjective **1** associated with the place where you were born. **2** (of a plant or animal) living or growing naturally in a place. **3** having to do with the original inhabitants of a place. **4** in a person's character: *his native wit.*

> SYNONYMS **1** *the native population* **indigenous,** original. **2** *native produce* **domestic,** home-grown, home-made, local, indigenous. **3** *her native tongue* **mother,** home, local, vernacular.
> ANTONYMS immigrant, imported.

■ **native speaker** a person who has spoken a particular language from earliest childhood. **Native American** a member of any of the original peoples of North and South America.

nativity ▶ noun (plural **nativities**) **1** (the Nativity) the birth of Jesus. **2** formal a person's birth.

NATO (or **Nato**) ▶ abbreviation North Atlantic Treaty Organization.

natter informal ▶ verb (**natters, nattering, nattered**) chat for a long time.
▶ noun a long chat.

natty ▸ adjective (**nattier, nattiest**) informal smart and fashionable.
□ **nattily** adverb.

natural ▸ adjective **1** existing in or obtained from nature; not made or caused by people. **2** as you would expect; normal. **3** born with a particular skill or quality: *a natural leader.* **4** having a relaxed, easy manner. **5** (of a parent or child) related by blood. **6** Music (of a note) not sharp or flat.

> SYNONYMS **1** *a natural occurrence* **normal,** ordinary, everyday, usual, regular, common, commonplace, typical, routine, standard. **2** *natural products* **unprocessed,** organic, pure, unrefined, additive-free, green, GM-free. **3** *Alex is a natural leader* **born,** instinctive, congenital, pathological. **4** *his natural instincts* **innate,** inborn, inherent, native, hereditary, inherited, inbred. **5** *she seemed very natural* **unaffected,** spontaneous, uninhibited, relaxed, unselfconscious, genuine, open, artless, guileless, unpretentious. **6** *it was quite natural to think she admired him* **reasonable,** logical, understandable, (only) to be expected, predictable. ANTONYMS abnormal, artificial, affected.

▸ noun **1** a person with a particular gift or talent. **2** Music a natural note or a sign (♮) denoting one.
■ **natural gas** gas found underground and used as fuel. **natural history** the scientific study of animals or plants. **natural selection** the evolutionary process by which creatures better adapted to their environment tend to survive and produce more offspring.

naturalism ▸ noun a style in art or literature that shows things how they are in everyday life.

naturalist ▸ noun a person who studies animals or plants.

naturalistic ▸ adjective **1** having to do with real life or nature. **2** based on the theory of naturalism.

naturalize (or **naturalise**) ▸ verb (**naturalizes, naturalizing, naturalized**) **1** make a foreigner a citizen of a country. **2** introduce a plant or animal into a region where it is not native.

naturally ▸ adverb **1** in a natural way. **2** of course.

> SYNONYMS **1** *try to act naturally* **normally,** in a natural manner, spontaneously, genuinely, unpretentiously; informal natural. **2** *he's naturally shy* **by nature,** by character, inherently, innately, congenitally, pathologically. **3** *naturally, they wanted everything kept quiet* **of course,** as might be expected, needless to say, obviously, clearly, it goes without

saying.
ANTONYMS self-consciously.

nature ▸ noun **1** the physical world, including plants, animals, and all things that are not made by people. **2** the typical qualities or character of a person, animal, or thing. **3** a type or kind of something.

> SYNONYMS **1** *the beauty of nature* **the natural world,** the environment, the universe, the cosmos, wildlife, the countryside, the land, the landscape. **2** *the very nature of such crimes* **essence,** inherent features, character, complexion. **3** *nastiness was not in her nature* **character,** personality, disposition, temperament, make-up, psyche. **4** *experiments of a similar nature* **kind,** sort, type, variety, category, genre, order; N. Amer. stripe.

naturism ▸ noun nudism.
□ **naturist** noun & adjective.

naught ▸ pronoun old use nothing.

naughty ▸ adjective (**naughtier, naughtiest**) **1** (of a child) disobedient; badly behaved. **2** informal mildly rude or indecent.

> SYNONYMS **1** *a naughty boy* **badly behaved,** disobedient, bad, wayward, defiant, unruly, insubordinate, wilful, delinquent, undisciplined, disruptive, mischievous, impish. **2** *naughty jokes* **indecent,** risqué, rude, racy, vulgar, dirty, filthy, smutty, crude, coarse. ANTONYMS well behaved, clean.

□ **naughtily** adverb **naughtiness** noun.

nausea /naw-zi-uh/ ▸ noun a feeling of sickness and wanting to vomit.

> SYNONYMS **sickness,** biliousness, queasiness, vomiting, retching.

nauseate ▸ verb (**nauseates, nauseating, nauseated**) make someone feel sick or disgusted.

nauseous ▸ adjective **1** suffering from nausea. **2** causing nausea.

nautical ▸ adjective having to do with sailors or navigation.

> SYNONYMS **maritime,** marine, naval, seafaring, boating, sailing.

■ **nautical mile** a unit used to measure distances at sea, equal to 1,852 metres (approximately 2,025 yards).

nautilus ▸ noun (plural **nautiluses**) a swimming mollusc with a spiral shell and short tentacles round the mouth.

naval ▸ adjective having to do with a navy or navies.

nave ▸ noun the central part of a church.

navel ▸ noun the small hollow in the centre of a person's belly where the umbilical cord was cut at birth.

navigable ▸ adjective able to be used by boats and ships.

navigate ▸ verb (**navigates, navigating, navigated**) **1** plan and direct the route of a ship, aircraft, etc. **2** guide a boat or vehicle over a particular route.

SYNONYMS **1** *he navigated the yacht across the Atlantic* **steer,** pilot, guide, direct, captain; informal skipper. **2** *I'll drive—you can navigate* **map-read,** give directions.

□ **navigator** noun.

navigation ▸ noun **1** the activity of navigating. **2** the movement of ships.
□ **navigational** adjective.

navvy ▸ noun (plural **navvies**) Brit. dated a labourer employed in building a road, railway, or canal.

navy ▸ noun (plural **navies**) **1** the branch of a country's armed forces which fights at sea. **2** (also **navy blue**) a dark blue colour.

SYNONYMS **fleet,** flotilla, armada, squadron, task force.

nay ▸ adverb old use or dialect no.

Nazi /naht-si/ ▸ noun (plural **Nazis**) historical a member of the far-right National Socialist German Workers' Party.
□ **Nazism** noun.

NB ▸ abbreviation note well.
ORIGIN short for Latin *nota bene.*

NE ▸ abbreviation north-east or north-eastern.

Neanderthal /ni-an-der-tahl/ ▸ noun an extinct human living in Europe between about 120,000 and 35,000 years ago.

neap tide ▸ noun the tide when there is least difference between high and low water.

near ▸ adverb **1** at or to a short distance in space or time. **2** almost.
▸ preposition (also **near to**) **1** at or to a short distance in space or time from. **2** close to.
▸ adjective **1** at a short distance away. **2** close to being.

SYNONYMS **1** *the house is quite near* **close,** nearby, (close/near) at hand, a stone's throw away, within reach, accessible, handy, convenient; informal within spitting distance. **2** *the final judgement is near* **imminent,** in the offing, (close/near) at hand, (just) around the corner, on its way, coming, impending, looming.
ANTONYMS far, distant.

▸ verb approach.
■ **Near East** the countries of SW Asia between the Mediterranean and India (including the Middle East).
□ **nearness** noun.

nearby ▸ adjective & adverb not far away.

SYNONYMS **not far away/off,** close at hand, close by, near, within reach, neighbouring, local, accessible, handy, convenient.
ANTONYMS faraway.

nearly ▸ adverb very close to; almost.

SYNONYMS **almost,** just about, more or less, practically, virtually, all but, as good as, not far off, to all intents and purposes, not quite; informal pretty well.

nearside ▸ noun the side of a vehicle nearest the kerb.

nearsighted ▸ adjective chiefly N. Amer. short-sighted.

neat ▸ adjective **1** tidy or carefully arranged. **2** clever but simple. **3** (of a drink of spirits) not diluted. **4** N. Amer. informal excellent.

SYNONYMS **1** *the bedroom was neat and clean* **tidy,** orderly, well ordered, in (good) order, spick and span, uncluttered, straight, trim. **2** *he's very neat* **smart,** spruce, dapper, trim, well groomed, well turned out; informal natty. **3** *her neat handwriting* **clear,** regular, precise, elegant; informal easy to read. **4** *this neat little gadget* **compact,** well designed, handy; Brit. informal dinky, nifty. **5** *his neat footwork* **skilful,** deft, dexterous, adroit, adept, expert; informal nifty. **6** *a neat solution* **clever,** ingenious, inventive, imaginative. **7** *neat gin* **undiluted,** straight, unmixed; N. Amer. informal straight up.
ANTONYMS untidy.

□ **neatly** adverb.

neaten ▸ verb make something neat.

nebula /neb-yuu-luh/ ▸ noun (plural **nebulae** /neb-yuu-lee/ or **nebulas**) a cloud of gas or dust in outer space.

nebulous ▸ adjective not clearly defined; vague.

necessarily ▸ adverb as a necessary result; unable to be avoided.

SYNONYMS **as a consequence,** as a result, automatically, as a matter of course, certainly, incontrovertibly, inevitably, unavoidably, inescapably, of necessity.

necessary ▸ adjective **1** needing to be present, or to be done or achieved. **2** unavoidable.

SYNONYMS **1** *planning permission is necessary* **obligatory,** requisite, required, compulsory, mandatory, imperative, needed. **2** *a necessary consequence* **inevitable,** unavoidable, inescapable, inexorable.

✔ one **c**, double **s**: ne**cess**ary.

necessitate ▸ verb (**necessitates, necessitating, necessitated**) make something necessary.

necessity ▸ noun (plural **necessities**) **1** the fact of being necessary. **2** a thing that it is essential to have.

SYNONYMS **1** *the VCR is now regarded as a necessity* **essential**, requisite, prerequisite, necessary, basic; informal must-have. **2** *political necessity forced him to resign* **force of circumstance**, obligation, need, call, exigency.

neck ▸ noun **1** the part connecting the head to the rest of the body. **2** the part of a bottle near the mouth. **3** the part of a violin, guitar, etc. to which the fingerboard is fixed.
▸ verb informal kiss and caress.
■ **neck and neck** level in a race or other competition.

neckerchief ▸ noun a square of cloth worn round the neck.

necklace ▸ noun a piece of jewellery consisting of a chain, string of beads, etc., worn round the neck.

necklet ▸ noun a close-fitting ornament worn round the neck.

neckline ▸ noun the edge of a dress or top at or below the neck.

necromancy /nek-ruh-man-si/ ▸ noun **1** attempted communication with dead people in order to predict the future. **2** witchcraft or black magic.
□ **necromancer** noun.

necrophilia /nek-ruh-fil-i-uh/ ▸ noun sexual activity with or interest in dead bodies.
□ **necrophiliac** noun.

necropolis /ne-**krop**-uh-liss/ ▸ noun a cemetery.

necrosis /ne-**kroh**-siss/ ▸ noun the death of cells in an organ or tissue.

nectar ▸ noun **1** a fluid produced by flowers and made into honey by bees. **2** (in Greek and Roman mythology) the drink of the gods.

nectarine ▸ noun a variety of peach with smooth skin.

née /nay/ ▸ adjective born (used in giving a married woman's maiden name).

need ▸ verb **1** require something because it is essential or very important. **2** used to express what should or must be done.

SYNONYMS **1** *do you need money?* **require**, be in/have need of, want, be crying out for, be desperate for, demand, call for, necessitate, entail, involve, lack, be without, be short of. **2** (**needed**) **necessary**, required, called for, wanted, desired, lacking. **3** *do I need to come?* **have to,** be meant to, be supposed to, be expected to.

▸ noun **1** a situation in which something is necessary or must be done. **2** a thing that is needed. **3** the state of being very poor.

SYNONYMS **1** *there's no need to apologize* **necessity**, requirement, call, demand. **2** *basic human needs* **requirement**, necessity, want, requisite, prerequisite. **3** *my hour of need* **difficulty**, trouble, distress, crisis, emergency, urgency, extremity.

needful ▸ adjective formal necessary.

needle ▸ noun **1** a very thin pointed piece of metal with a hole or eye for thread at the blunter end, used in sewing. **2** a long, thin rod used in knitting. **3** the pointed hollow end of a hypodermic syringe. **4** a stylus used to play records. **5** a thin pointer on a dial, compass, etc. **6** the thin, stiff leaf of a fir or pine tree.
▸ verb (**needles, needling, needled**) informal deliberately annoy someone.

needlecord ▸ noun Brit. a lightweight corduroy fabric with narrow ridges.

needlepoint ▸ noun closely stitched embroidery done on canvas.

needless ▸ adjective unnecessary; avoidable.

SYNONYMS **unnecessary**, unneeded, uncalled for, gratuitous, pointless, superfluous, redundant, excessive. ANTONYMS necessary.

□ **needlessly** adverb.

needlework ▸ noun sewing or embroidery.

needn't ▸ short form need not.

needy ▸ adjective (**needier, neediest**) very poor.

SYNONYMS **poor**, deprived, disadvantaged, underprivileged, in need, needful, hard up, poverty-stricken, impoverished, destitute, penniless; informal broke, strapped (for cash); Brit. informal skint. ANTONYMS wealthy.

ne'er /nair/ ▸ short form old use or dialect never.
■ **ne'er-do-well** a useless or lazy person.

nefarious /ni-**fair**-i-uhss/ ▸ adjective bad or illegal.

negate ▸ verb (**negates, negating, negated**) **1** stop or undo the effect of. **2** say that something does not exist.
□ **negation** noun.

negative ▸ adjective **1** showing the absence rather than the presence of something. **2** expressing denial, disagreement, or refusal. **3** not hopeful or favourable. **4** (of a quantity) less than zero. **5** having to do with the kind of electric charge carried by electrons. **6** (of a photograph) showing light and shade or colours reversed from those of the original.

SYNONYMS **1** *a negative reply* **opposing**, opposed, contrary, anti-, dissenting, in the negative. **2** *stop being so negative* **pessimistic**, defeatist, gloomy, cynical, fatalistic, dismissive, unenthusiastic,

apathetic, unresponsive. **3** *a negative effect on the economy* **harmful,** bad, adverse, damaging, detrimental, unfavourable, disadvantageous.
ANTONYMS positive, optimistic, favourable.

▶ noun **1** a negative word or statement. **2** a negative photograph, from which positive prints may be made.
□ **negatively** adverb **negativity** noun.

neglect ▶ verb **1** fail to give enough care or attention to. **2** fail to do.

> SYNONYMS **1** *she neglected the children* **fail to look after,** leave alone, abandon. **2** *(neglected) neglected animals* **uncared for,** abandoned, mistreated, maltreated. **3** *(neglected) a neglected cottage* **derelict,** dilapidated, tumbledown, ramshackle, untended. **4** *he's neglecting his work* **pay no attention to,** let slide, not attend to, be remiss about, be lax about, leave undone. **5** *(neglected) a neglected masterpiece* **disregarded,** forgotten, overlooked, ignored, unrecognized, unnoticed, unsung, underrated. **6** *I neglected to inform her* **fail,** omit, forget.
> ANTONYMS cherish, heed, remember.

▶ noun the action of neglecting.

> SYNONYMS **1** *the place had an air of neglect* **disrepair,** dilapidation, shabbiness, disuse, abandonment. **2** *her doctor was guilty of neglect* **negligence,** dereliction (of duty), carelessness, laxity, slackness, irresponsibility.
> ANTONYMS care.

neglectful ▶ adjective failing to give enough care or attention.

negligee /neg-li-zhay/ ▶ noun a woman's dressing gown made of a very light, thin fabric.

negligence ▶ noun a failure to give someone or something enough care or attention.

negligent ▶ adjective failing to take proper care.

> SYNONYMS **neglectful,** remiss, careless, lax, irresponsible, inattentive, thoughtless, unmindful, forgetful, slack, sloppy; N. Amer. derelict.
> ANTONYMS dutiful.

negligible ▶ adjective so small or unimportant as to be not worth considering.

> SYNONYMS **trivial,** trifling, insignificant, unimportant, minor, inconsequential, minimal, small, slight, infinitesimal; informal minuscule.
> ANTONYMS significant.

negotiate ▶ verb (negotiates, negotiating, negotiated) **1** reach an agreement by discussion. **2** bring something about by

discussion. **3** find a way through a difficult path or route.

> SYNONYMS **1** *she refused to negotiate* **discuss (terms),** talk, consult, confer, debate, compromise, bargain, haggle. **2** *he negotiated a new contract* **arrange,** broker, work out, thrash out, agree on. **3** *I negotiated the obstacles* **get round,** get past, get over, clear, cross, surmount, deal with, cope with.

□ **negotiable** adjective.

> ✔ **-tiate**, not **-ciate**: nego**tiate**.

negotiation ▶ noun **1** (also negotiations) discussion aimed at reaching an agreement or compromise. **2** the act of bringing something about by discussion.

> SYNONYMS **1** *the negotiations resume next week* **discussion(s),** talks, conference, debate, dialogue, consultation. **2** *the negotiation of a deal* **arrangement,** brokering, settlement, conclusion, completion.

negotiator ▶ noun a person who negotiates.

> SYNONYMS **mediator,** arbitrator, go-between, middleman, intermediary, representative, spokesperson, broker.

Negro ▶ noun (plural **Negroes**) a black person.

> ❗ The term **Negro** is now regarded as old-fashioned or even offensive.

neigh ▶ noun a high-pitched cry made by a horse.
▶ verb make this cry.

neighbour (US spelling **neighbor**) ▶ noun a person who lives next door to you, or very close by.

neighbourhood (US spelling **neighborhood**) ▶ noun **1** a district within a town or city. **2** the area surrounding a place, person, or object.

> SYNONYMS **1** *a quiet neighbourhood* **district,** area, locality, locale, quarter, community; N. Amer. informal hood, nabe. **2** *in the neighbourhood of Canterbury* **vicinity,** environs.

neighbouring ▶ adjective situated next to or very near something.

> SYNONYMS **adjacent,** adjoining, bordering, connecting, next-door, nearby.
> ANTONYMS remote.

neighbourly ▶ adjective characteristic of a good neighbour.

> SYNONYMS **obliging,** helpful, friendly, kind, considerate, amicable, sociable, hospitable, companionable, civil, cordial.
> ANTONYMS unfriendly.

neither ▶ determiner & pronoun not either.
▶ adverb used to show that a negative

statement is true of two things, or also true of something else.

> ✔ Remember that **neither** is spelled with the **e** before the **i**.

nematode /**nem**-uh-tohd/ ▸ noun a type of worm with a thin tube-shaped body.

nemesis ▸ noun (plural **nemeses** /**nem**-i-seez/) something that brings about someone's deserved and unavoidable downfall.

neoclassical ▸ adjective relating to the revival of a classical style in the arts. ◻ **neoclassicism** noun.

neodymium ▸ noun a silvery-white metallic element.

Neolithic ▸ adjective relating to the later part of the Stone Age.

neologism /ni-**ol**-uh-ji-z'm/ ▸ noun a new word or expression.

neon ▸ noun a gas that glows when electricity is passed through it, used in fluorescent lighting.

neonatal ▸ adjective relating to birth and newborn children.

neophyte /**nee**-oh-fyt/ ▸ noun **1** a person who is new to a subject, skill, or belief. **2** a novice in a religious order, or a newly ordained priest.

Nepali /ni-**paw**-li/ ▸ noun (plural **Nepali** or **Nepalis**) a person from Nepal. ◻ **Nepalese** noun & adjective.

nephew ▸ noun a son of your brother or sister.

nephritis /ni-**fry**-tiss/ ▸ noun inflammation of the kidneys.

nepotism /**nep**-uh-ti-z'm/ ▸ noun favouritism shown to relatives or friends.

Neptune ▸ noun the eighth planet from the sun in the solar system.

neptunium ▸ noun a rare radioactive metallic element.

nerd ▸ noun informal an unfashionable person who is obsessed with a particular subject or interest.

nerve ▸ noun **1** a fibre or bundle of fibres in the body along which impulses of sensation pass. **2** steadiness and courage in a difficult or demanding situation. **3** (**nerves**) nervousness. **4** informal cheekily disrespectful or inappropriate behaviour.

> SYNONYMS **1** *the match will be a test of nerve* **confidence,** assurance, courage, bravery, determination, will power, spirit, grit; informal **guts**; Brit. informal **bottle**; N. Amer. informal **moxie. 2** *he had the nerve to chat her up* **audacity,** cheek, effrontery, gall, temerity, presumption, impudence, impertinence, arrogance; informal **face, front, brass neck, chutzpah. 3** (**nerves**) **anxiety,** tension,

nervousness, stress, worry, cold feet, apprehension; informal **butterflies (in your stomach), collywobbles, jitters.**

▸ verb (**nerves, nerving, nerved**) (**nerve yourself**) brace yourself for a difficult situation.

■ **get on someone's nerves** informal irritate someone. **nerve cell** a neuron. **nerve gas** a poisonous gas which affects the nervous system. **nerve-racking** (or **nerve-wracking**) causing nervousness or fear.

nerveless ▸ adjective **1** lacking strength or feeling. **2** confident.

nervous ▸ adjective **1** easily frightened or worried. **2** anxious. **3** having to do with the nerves.

> SYNONYMS **1** *a nervous woman* **highly strung,** anxious, edgy, nervy, tense, excitable, jumpy, neurotic. **2** *he was so nervous he couldn't eat* **anxious,** worried, apprehensive, on edge, edgy, tense, stressed, agitated, uneasy, restless, worked up, keyed up, overwrought; informal **jittery, twitchy, in a state, uptight, wired, in a flap;** Brit. informal **having kittens;** N. Amer. informal **squirrelly.**
> ANTONYMS relaxed, calm.

■ **nervous breakdown** a period of mental illness resulting from severe depression or stress. **nervous system** the network of nerves which transmits nerve impulses between parts of the body. ◻ **nervously** adverb **nervousness** noun.

nervy ▸ adjective (**nervier, nerviest**) Brit. nervous or tense.

nest ▸ noun **1** a structure made by a bird in which it lays eggs and shelters its young. **2** a place where an animal or insect breeds or shelters. **3** a set of similar objects that are designed to fit inside each other.
▸ verb **1** use or build a nest. **2** fit an object inside a larger one.
■ **nest egg** a sum of money saved for the future.

nestle ▸ verb (**nestles, nestling, nestled**) **1** settle comfortably within or against something. **2** (of a place) lie in a sheltered position.

> SYNONYMS **snuggle,** cuddle, huddle, nuzzle, settle, burrow.

nestling ▸ noun a bird that is too young to leave the nest.

net[1] ▸ noun **1** a material made of strands of cord or string that are knotted together to form small open squares. **2** a piece or structure of net for catching fish or insects, surrounding a goal, etc. **3** a thin fabric with a very open weave. **4** (**the Net**) the Internet.

> SYNONYMS *a dress of green net* **netting,** mesh, tulle, fishnet, lace.

▸ verb (**nets, netting, netted**) **1** catch

n

something in a net. **2** earn or obtain something.

> SYNONYMS *they netted some big criminals* **catch,** capture, trap, snare; informal nab, bag, collar, bust; Brit. informal nick.

net² (or Brit. **nett**) ▶ adjective **1** (of a sum of money) remaining after tax or expenses have been deducted. **2** (of a weight) not including the packaging. **3** (of an effect or result) overall.

> SYNONYMS **1** *net earnings* **after tax,** after deductions, take-home, clear, final; informal bottom line. **2** *the net result* **final,** end, ultimate, closing, overall, actual, effective.
> ANTONYMS gross.

▶ verb (**nets, netting, netted**) gain a sum of money as clear profit.

> SYNONYMS *she netted £50,000* **earn,** make, clear, take home, bring in, pocket, realize, be paid.

netball ▶ noun a team game in which goals are scored by throwing a ball through a net hanging from a hoop.

nether ▶ adjective lower in position.

nettle ▶ noun a plant with leaves that are covered with stinging hairs.
▶ verb (**nettles, nettling, nettled**) annoy.

network ▶ noun **1** an arrangement of intersecting horizontal and vertical lines. **2** a complex system of railways, roads, etc. that cross or connect with each other. **3** a group of radio or television stations that connect to broadcast a programme at the same time. **4** a number of interconnected computers, operations, etc. **5** a group of people who keep in contact with each other to exchange information.

> SYNONYMS **1** *a network of arteries* **web,** lattice, net, matrix, mesh, criss-cross, grid. **2** *a network of lanes* **maze,** labyrinth, warren, tangle.

▶ verb keep in contact with other people to exchange information.
□ **networker** noun.

neural /**nyoor**-uhl/ ▶ adjective relating to a nerve or the nervous system.

neuralgia /nyoo-**ral**-juh/ ▶ noun severe pain along a nerve in the head or face.
□ **neuralgic** adjective.

neurology ▶ noun the branch of medicine concerned with the nervous system.
□ **neurological** adjective **neurologist** noun.

neuron (or **neurone**) ▶ noun a cell that transmits nerve impulses.

neurosis /nyoo-**roh**-siss/ ▶ noun (plural **neuroses** /nyoo-**roh**-seez/) a mild mental illness in which a person feels depressed or anxious, or behaves in an obsessive way.

neurosurgery ▶ noun surgery performed on the nervous system.
□ **neurosurgeon** noun.

neurotic ▶ adjective **1** having to do with neurosis. **2** informal obsessive, or too sensitive or anxious.

> SYNONYMS **overanxious,** oversensitive, nervous, tense, highly strung, paranoid, obsessive, fixated, hysterical, overwrought, irrational.
> ANTONYMS stable, calm.

neuter ▶ adjective **1** (of a noun) neither masculine nor feminine. **2** having no sexual or reproductive organs.
▶ verb (**neuters, neutering, neutered**) operate on an animal so that it cannot produce young.

neutral ▶ adjective **1** not supporting either side in a dispute or war. **2** lacking noticeable or strong qualities. **3** Chemistry neither acid nor alkaline; having a pH of about 7.

> SYNONYMS **1** *she's neutral on this issue* **impartial,** unbiased, unprejudiced, objective, open-minded, non-partisan, even-handed, disinterested, dispassionate, detached. **2** *Switzerland remained neutral* **unaligned,** non-aligned, unaffiliated, uninvolved. **3** *a neutral topic of conversation* **inoffensive,** bland, unobjectionable, unexceptionable, anodyne, uncontroversial, safe, harmless, innocuous. **4** *a neutral background* **pale,** light, colourless, indeterminate, drab, insipid, nondescript, dull.
> ANTONYMS biased, partisan, provocative, colourful.

▶ noun a position of a gear mechanism in which the engine is disconnected from the driven parts.
□ **neutrality** noun **neutrally** adverb.

neutralize (or **neutralise**) ▶ verb (**neutralizes, neutralizing, neutralized**) **1** stop something from having an effect. **2** make neutral.
□ **neutralization** noun.

neutrino /nyoo-**tree**-noh/ ▶ noun (plural **neutrinos**) a subatomic particle with a mass close to zero and no electric charge.

neutron ▶ noun a subatomic particle of about the same mass as a proton but without an electric charge.

never ▶ adverb **1** not ever. **2** not at all.
■ **the never-never** Brit. informal hire purchase.

nevermore ▶ adverb never again.

nevertheless ▶ adverb in spite of that.

nevus US spelling of **NAEVUS**.

new ▶ adjective **1** made, introduced, discovered, or experienced recently. **2** not previously used or owned. **3** (**new to**) not experienced in. **4** different from a recent previous one. **5** better than before; renewed or reformed.

SYNONYMS **1** *new technology* **recent,** up to date, the latest, current, state-of-the-art, contemporary, advanced, cutting-edge, modern. **2** *is your boat new?* **unused,** brand new, pristine, fresh. **3** *new neighbours moved in* **different,** another, alternative, unfamiliar, unknown, strange. **4** *they had a new classroom built* **additional,** extra, supplementary, further, another, fresh. **5** *I came back a new woman* **reinvigorated,** restored, revived, improved, refreshed, regenerated. ANTONYMS old, hackneyed, second-hand, present.

▶ adverb newly.
■ **New Age** an alternative movement concerned with spirituality, care for the environment, etc. **new moon** the phase of the moon when it first appears as a thin crescent. **New Testament** the second part of the Christian Bible, recording the life and teachings of Jesus. **New World** North and South America. **new year** the calendar year that has just begun or is about to begin, following 31 December.

newborn ▶ adjective recently born.

newcomer ▶ noun **1** a person who has recently arrived. **2** a person who is new to an activity or situation.

SYNONYMS **1** *a newcomer to the village* **new arrival,** immigrant, incomer, settler, stranger, outsider, foreigner, alien; informal new kid on the block; Austral. informal blow-in. **2** *photography tips for the newcomer* **beginner,** novice, learner, trainee, apprentice, probationer; N. Amer. tenderfoot; informal rookie, newbie.

newel /**nyoo**-uhl/ ▶ noun the post at the top or bottom of a stair rail.

newfangled ▶ adjective disapproving newly developed and unfamiliar.

newly ▶ adverb recently.

SYNONYMS **recently,** only just, lately, freshly, not long ago, a short time ago.

■ **newly-wed** a person who has recently married.

news ▶ noun **1** new information about recent events. **2** (**the news**) a broadcast or published news report.

SYNONYMS **report,** story, account, announcement, press release, communication, communiqué, bulletin, intelligence, disclosure, revelation, gossip; informal scoop.

newsagent ▶ noun Brit. a shopkeeper who sells newspapers and magazines.

newscast ▶ noun N. Amer. a broadcast news report.
□ **newscaster** noun.

newsflash ▶ noun a brief item of important news, interrupting other radio or television programmes.

newsgroup ▶ noun a group of Internet users who exchange information about a particular subject online.

newsletter ▶ noun a bulletin issued on a regular basis to the members of a society or organization.

newspaper ▶ noun a daily or weekly publication containing news and articles on current affairs.

newsprint ▶ noun cheap, low-quality paper used for newspapers.

newsreader ▶ noun Brit. a person who reads the news on radio or television.

newsreel ▶ noun a short cinema film showing news and current affairs.

newsroom ▶ noun the area in a newspaper or broadcasting office where news is processed.

newsworthy ▶ adjective important enough to be mentioned as news.

newt ▶ noun a small animal with a slender body and a long tail, that can live in water or on land.

newton ▶ noun Physics a unit of force.

next ▶ adjective **1** coming immediately after the present one in time, space, or order. **2** (of a day of the week) nearest (or the nearest but one) after the present.

SYNONYMS **1** *the next chapter* **following,** succeeding, upcoming, to come. **2** *the next house in the street* **neighbouring,** adjacent, adjoining, next-door, bordering, connected, closest, nearest. ANTONYMS previous.

▶ adverb immediately afterwards.

SYNONYMS *where shall we go next?* **then,** after, afterwards, after this/that, later, subsequently; formal thereafter. ANTONYMS before.

■ **next door** in or to the next house or room. **next of kin** a person's closest living relative or relatives.

nexus ▶ noun (plural **nexus** or **nexuses**) a connection or series of connections.

NHS ▶ abbreviation National Health Service.

nib ▶ noun the pointed end part of a pen.

nibble ▶ verb (**nibbles, nibbling, nibbled**) **1** take small bites out of. **2** bite gently.
▶ noun **1** a small piece of food bitten off. **2** (**nibbles**) informal small savoury snacks.

Nicaraguan /ni-kuh-**rag**-yuu-uhn/ ▶ noun a person from Nicaragua.
▶ adjective relating to Nicaragua.

nice ▶ adjective **1** enjoyable or attractive; pleasant. **2** good-natured; kind. **3** involving a very small detail or difference.

SYNONYMS **1** *have a nice time* **enjoyable**, pleasant, agreeable, good, satisfying, entertaining, amusing; informal **lovely**, great; N. Amer. informal **neat**. **2** *nice people* **pleasant**, likeable, agreeable, personable, congenial, amiable, affable, genial, friendly, charming, delightful, engaging, sympathetic. **3** *nice manners* **polite**, courteous, civil, refined, polished, genteel, elegant. **4** *that's a rather nice distinction* **subtle**, fine, delicate, precise, strict, close, careful, meticulous, scrupulous. **5** *it's a nice day* **fine**, pleasant, agreeable, dry, sunny, warm, mild.
ANTONYMS unpleasant, nasty, rough.

◻ **nicely** adverb **niceness** noun.

nicety ▸ noun (plural **niceties**) **1** a very small detail or difference. **2** accuracy.

niche /neesh, nich/ ▸ noun **1** a small hollow in a wall. **2** (**your niche**) a role or job that suits you.

SYNONYMS **1** *a niche in the wall* **recess**, alcove, nook, cranny, hollow, bay, cavity, cubbyhole, pigeonhole. **2** *he found his niche in life* (**ideal**) **position**, slot, place, function, vocation, calling, métier, station, job, level.

nick ▸ noun **1** a small cut. **2** (**the nick**) Brit. informal **prison or a police station**. **3** Brit. informal **condition**.

SYNONYMS *a slight nick in the blade* **cut**, scratch, incision, notch, chip, dent, indentation.

▸ verb **1** make a nick or nicks in. **2** Brit. informal steal. **3** Brit. informal arrest.

SYNONYMS *I nicked the edge of the table* **cut**, scratch, graze, chip, dent.

▪ **in the nick of time** only just in time.

nickel ▸ noun **1** a silvery-white metallic element. **2** N. Amer. a five-cent coin.

nickname ▸ noun another name by which someone is known.

SYNONYMS **pet name**, diminutive, endearment, tag, label, sobriquet, epithet; informal **moniker**.

▸ verb (**nicknames, nicknaming, nicknamed**) give a nickname to.

nicotine ▸ noun a poisonous oily liquid found in tobacco.

niece ▸ noun a daughter of your brother or sister.

✔ **i** before **e** except after **c**: ni**e**ce.

nifty ▸ adjective (**niftier, niftiest**) informal very skilful, effective, or useful.

Nigerian ▸ noun a person from Nigeria.
▸ adjective relating to Nigeria.

niggardly ▸ adjective not generous; mean.

nigger ▸ noun offensive a black person.

niggle ▸ verb (**niggles, niggling, niggled**) slightly worry or annoy.
▸ noun a minor worry or criticism.

nigh ▸ adverb, preposition, & adjective old use near.

night ▸ noun **1** the time from sunset to sunrise. **2** an evening.

SYNONYMS **night-time**, (hours of) darkness, dark.
ANTONYMS day.

nightcap ▸ noun **1** a hot or alcoholic drink taken at bedtime. **2** (in the past) a soft hat worn in bed.

nightclub ▸ noun a club that is open at night, with a bar and music.

nightdress (or **nightgown**) ▸ noun a light, loose garment worn by a woman or girl in bed.

nightfall ▸ noun dusk.

nightie ▸ noun informal a nightdress.

nightingale ▸ noun a small bird with a tuneful song, often heard at night.

nightjar ▸ noun a bird with grey-brown feathers and a distinctive call, active at night.

nightlife ▸ noun social activities or entertainment available at night.

nightly ▸ adjective **1** happening or done every night. **2** happening or done during the night.

SYNONYMS **1** *nightly raids* **every night**, night after night. **2** *his nightly wanderings* **nocturnal**, night-time.

▸ adverb every night.

SYNONYMS *a band plays there nightly* **every night**, each night, night after night.

nightmare ▸ noun **1** a frightening or unpleasant dream. **2** a very unpleasant experience.

SYNONYMS **ordeal**, trial, hell, misery, agony, torture, murder, purgatory, disaster; informal **the pits**.

◻ **nightmarish** adjective.

nightshirt ▸ noun a long shirt worn in bed.

nightspot ▸ noun informal a nightclub.

nihilism /ny-hi-li-z'm/ ▸ noun the belief that nothing has any value.
◻ **nihilist** noun **nihilistic** adjective.

nil ▸ noun nothing; zero.

SYNONYMS **nothing**, none, nought, zero; Tennis **love**; Cricket **a duck**.

nimble ▸ adjective (**nimbler, nimblest**) **1** quick and light in movement. **2** able to think and understand quickly.

SYNONYMS **1** *he was nimble on his feet* **agile,** sprightly, light, spry, quick, lithe, skilful, deft, dexterous, adroit; informal nippy. **2** *a nimble mind* **quick,** alert, lively, astute, perceptive, penetrating, discerning, shrewd, sharp, intelligent, bright, smart, clever, brilliant; informal quick on the uptake.
ANTONYMS clumsy, dull.

□ **nimbly** adverb.

nimbus ▸ noun (plural **nimbi** /**nim**-by/ or **nimbuses**) a large grey rain cloud.

nincompoop ▸ noun a stupid person.

nine ▸ cardinal number one less than ten; 9. (Roman numeral: **ix** or **IX**.)

nineteen ▸ cardinal number one more than eighteen; 19. (Roman numeral: **xix** or **XIX**.)
□ **nineteenth** ordinal number.

ninety ▸ cardinal number (plural **nineties**) ten less than one hundred; 90. (Roman numeral: **xc** or **XC**.)
□ **ninetieth** ordinal number.

ninny ▸ noun (plural **ninnies**) informal a silly person.

ninth ▸ ordinal number **1** at number nine in a sequence; 9th. **2** (**a ninth** or **one ninth**) each of nine equal parts into which something is divided.

niobium ▸ noun a silver-grey metallic element.

nip[1] ▸ verb (**nips, nipping, nipped**) **1** pinch, squeeze, or bite sharply. **2** Brit. informal go quickly.

SYNONYMS **bite,** nibble, peck, pinch, tweak.

▸ noun **1** a sharp bite or pinch. **2** a sharp feeling of coldness.

SYNONYMS **bite,** nibble, peck, pinch, tweak.

nip[2] ▸ noun a small quantity or sip of spirits.

nipper ▸ noun informal a child.

nipple ▸ noun a small projection in the centre of each breast, from which (in a woman who has recently had a baby) a baby is able to suck milk.

nippy ▸ adjective (**nippier, nippiest**) informal **1** able to move quickly. **2** chilly.

nirvana /neer-**vah**-nuh/ ▸ noun (in Buddhism) a state of perfect happiness.

nit ▸ noun informal **1** the egg of a human head louse. **2** Brit. a stupid person.
■ **nit-picking** criticism of small or unimportant details.

nitrate ▸ noun a salt or ester of nitric acid.

nitric acid ▸ noun a very corrosive acid.

nitrite ▸ noun a salt or ester of nitrous acid.

nitrogen ▸ noun a gas forming about 78 per cent of the earth's atmosphere.

nitroglycerine (US spelling **nitroglycerin**) ▸ noun an explosive liquid used in dynamite.

nitrous oxide ▸ noun a colourless gas used as an anaesthetic.

nitty-gritty ▸ noun informal the most important details.

nitwit ▸ noun informal a stupid person.

no ▸ determiner not any.
▸ exclamation used to refuse or disagree with something.
▸ adverb not at all.

SYNONYMS **absolutely not,** definitely not, of course not, under no circumstances, not at all, negative, never; informal nope, no way, not a chance; Brit. informal no fear; archaic nay.
ANTONYMS yes.

▸ noun (plural **noes**) a decision or vote against something.
■ **no-claims bonus** Brit. a reduction in an insurance premium when no claim has been made over an agreed period. **no-ball** a ball in cricket that is unlawfully bowled, counting as an extra run to the batting side.

no. ▸ abbreviation number.

nob ▸ noun Brit. informal an upper-class person.

nobble ▸ verb (**nobbles, nobbling, nobbled**) Brit. informal **1** try to influence someone using unfair or illegal methods. **2** stop someone and talk to them.

nobelium ▸ noun a radioactive chemical element that is produced artificially.

nobility ▸ noun **1** the quality of being noble. **2** the aristocracy.

noble ▸ adjective (**nobler, noblest**) **1** belonging to the aristocracy. **2** having personal qualities that people admire, such as courage and honesty. **3** magnificent; impressive.

SYNONYMS **1** *a noble family* **aristocratic,** blue-blooded, high-born, titled. **2** *a noble cause* **worthy,** righteous, virtuous, good, honourable, worthwhile. **3** *a noble pine forest* **magnificent,** splendid, grand, stately, imposing, dignified, proud, striking, majestic.
ANTONYMS humble, base, unimpressive.

▸ noun a nobleman or noblewoman.

SYNONYMS *Scottish nobles* **aristocrat,** nobleman, noblewoman, lord, lady, peer (of the realm), peeress; informal aristo.
ANTONYMS commoner.

□ **nobly** adverb.

nobleman (or **noblewoman**) ▸ noun (plural **noblemen** or **noblewomen**) a member of the aristocracy.

nobody ▸ pronoun no person.
▸ noun (plural **nobodies**) a person who is not considered important.

nocturnal ▸ adjective done or active at night.
□ **nocturnally** adverb.

n

nocturne ▶ noun a short piece of music in a dreamy, romantic style.

nod ▶ verb (**nods, nodding, nodded**) **1** lower and raise your head briefly to show agreement or as a greeting or signal. **2** let your head fall forward when you are drowsy or asleep. **3** (**nod off**) informal fall asleep.

SYNONYMS **1** *she nodded her head* **incline,** bob, bow, dip. **2** *he nodded to me to start* **signal,** gesture, gesticulate, motion, sign, indicate.

▶ noun an act of nodding.

SYNONYMS **1** *a nod of his head* **inclination,** bob, bow, dip. **2** *she gave a nod to the manager* **signal,** indication, sign, cue, gesture.

node ▶ noun technical **1** a point in a network at which lines cross or branch. **2** the part of a plant stem from which one or more leaves grow. **3** a small mass of tissue in the body.

nodule ▶ noun a small swelling or lump.
□ **nodular** adjective.

Noel ▶ noun Christmas.

noggin ▶ noun a small quantity of alcoholic drink.

Noh ▶ noun a type of traditional Japanese theatre with dance and song.

noise ▶ noun **1** a sound or series of sounds, especially an unpleasant one. **2** disturbances that accompany and interfere with an electrical signal.

SYNONYMS **sound,** din, hubbub, clamour, racket, uproar, tumult, commotion; informal hullabaloo; Brit. informal row.
ANTONYMS silence.

□ **noiseless** adjective.

noisome /**noy**-suhm/ ▶ adjective literary having a very unpleasant smell.

noisy ▶ adjective (**noisier, noisiest**) full of or making a lot of noise.

SYNONYMS **1** *a noisy crowd* **rowdy,** raucous, clamorous, boisterous, chattering, talkative, vociferous, shouting, screaming. **2** *noisy music* **loud,** blaring, booming, deafening, thunderous, ear-splitting, piercing, strident, cacophonous.
ANTONYMS quiet, soft.

□ **noisily** adverb.

nomad ▶ noun a member of a people that travels from place to place to find fresh pasture for its animals.

nomadic ▶ adjective having the life of a nomad; wandering.

nom de plume /nom duh **ploom**/ ▶ noun (plural **noms de plume** /nom duh **ploom**/) a name used by a writer instead of their real name; a pen name.

nomenclature /noh-**men**-kluh-cher/ ▶ noun a system of names used in a particular subject.

nominal ▶ adjective **1** in name but not in reality. **2** (of a sum of money) very small.

SYNONYMS **1** *the nominal head of the campaign* **in name only,** titular, formal, official, theoretical, supposed, ostensible, so-called. **2** *a nominal rent* **token,** symbolic, minimal; Brit. peppercorn.
ANTONYMS real, considerable.

□ **nominally** adverb.

nominate ▶ verb (**nominates, nominating, nominated**) **1** put someone forward as a candidate for a job or award. **2** arrange a time, date, or place.

SYNONYMS **1** *any member may nominate a candidate* **propose,** put forward, put up, submit, present, recommend, suggest. **2** *the President nominated her to the Supreme Court* **appoint,** designate, assign, select, choose, decide on, promote.

□ **nomination** noun **nominee** noun.

nominative ▶ noun Grammar the case used for the subject of a verb.

non- ▶ prefix not: *non-existent*.

nonagenarian /noh-nuh-juh-**nair**-i-uhn/ ▶ noun a person between 90 and 99 years old.

nonchalant /**non**-shuh-luhnt/ ▶ adjective relaxed and unconcerned.
□ **nonchalance** noun **nonchalantly** adverb.

non-commissioned ▶ adjective (of a military officer) appointed from the lower ranks.

non-committal ▶ adjective not showing what you think or which side you are on.
□ **non-committally** adverb.

non compos mentis /non kom-poss **men**-tiss/ ▶ adjective not in your right mind; distracted or mad.

nonconformist ▶ noun **1** a person who does not follow accepted ideas or behaviour. **2** (**Nonconformist**) a member of a Protestant Church which does not follow the beliefs of the established Church of England.
□ **nonconformity** noun.

nondescript ▶ adjective having no interesting or special features.

none ▶ pronoun **1** not any. **2** no one.
▶ adverb (**none the**) not at all.

nonentity ▶ noun (plural **nonentities**) an unimportant person or thing.

nonetheless (or **none the less**) ▶ adverb in spite of that; nevertheless.

non-event ▶ noun a very disappointing or uninteresting event.

n

non-existent ▸ adjective not real or present.

SYNONYMS **imaginary,** imagined, unreal, fictional, fictitious, made up, invented, fanciful, mythical, illusory.
ANTONYMS real.

no-nonsense ▸ adjective simple and straightforward; sensible.

nonpareil /non-puh-**rayl**/ ▸ noun a person or thing that is better than all others of the same kind.

nonplussed ▸ adjective surprised and confused.

non-proliferation ▸ noun the prevention of an increase in the number of nuclear weapons that are produced.

nonsense ▸ noun **1** words or statements that make no sense. **2** silly behaviour.

SYNONYMS **1** *he was talking nonsense* **rubbish,** gibberish, claptrap, garbage; informal baloney, tripe, drivel, gobbledegook, twaddle; Brit. informal cobblers, codswallop, double Dutch; Scottish & N. English informal havers; N. Amer. informal flapdoodle, bushwa, applesauce. **2** *she stands no nonsense* **mischief,** messing about, misbehaviour, funny business; informal tomfoolery, monkey business, shenanigans; Brit. informal monkey tricks, jiggery-pokery. **3** *the whole thing is a nonsense* **joke,** farce, travesty, insanity, madness.
ANTONYMS sense, wisdom.

nonsensical ▸ adjective making no sense; ridiculous.

non sequitur /non **sek**-wi-ter/ ▸ noun a statement that does not follow on logically from what has just been said.

non-starter ▸ noun informal something that has no chance of succeeding.

non-stick ▸ adjective (of a pan) covered with a substance that prevents food sticking to it during cooking.

non-stop ▸ adjective **1** continuing without stopping. **2** having no stops on the way to a destination.

SYNONYMS *non-stop entertainment* **continuous,** constant, continual, incessant, ceaseless, uninterrupted, perpetual, round-the-clock, unremitting, relentless, persistent.
ANTONYMS intermittent, occasional.

▸ adverb without stopping.

SYNONYMS *we worked non-stop* **continuously,** continually, incessantly, ceaselessly, all the time, constantly, perpetually, round the clock, steadily, relentlessly, persistently; informal 24-7.
ANTONYMS intermittently, occasionally.

noodles ▸ plural noun thin, long strips of pasta.

nook ▸ noun a place that is sheltered or hidden.

noon ▸ noun twelve o'clock in the day; midday.

SYNONYMS **midday,** twelve o'clock, twelve hundred hours, twelve noon, high noon, noonday.

noonday ▸ adjective taking place or appearing in the middle of the day.

no one ▸ pronoun no person.

noose ▸ noun a loop with a knot which tightens as the rope or wire is pulled, used to hang people or trap animals.

nor ▸ conjunction & adverb and not; and not either.

Nordic ▸ adjective relating to Scandinavia, Finland, and Iceland.

norm ▸ noun **1** (the norm) the usual or standard thing. **2** a standard that is required or acceptable.

SYNONYMS **1** *such teams are now the norm* **normal,** usual, the rule, standard, typical, average, par for the course, expected. **2** *norms of behaviour* **standard,** convention, criterion, yardstick, benchmark, touchstone, rule, formula, pattern.

normal ▸ adjective usual and typical; what you would expect.

SYNONYMS **1** *they issue books in the normal way* **usual,** standard, ordinary, customary, conventional, habitual, accustomed, typical, common, regular, routine, traditional. **2** *a normal couple* **ordinary,** average, typical, run-of-the-mill, middle-of-the-road, common, conventional, mainstream; N. Amer. garden-variety; Brit. informal common or garden, bog-standard. **3** *the man was not normal* **sane,** in your right mind, right in the head, of sound mind, compos mentis; informal all there.
ANTONYMS unusual, insane.

▸ noun the normal state or condition.
□ **normality** noun.

normalize (or **normalise**) ▸ verb (**normalizes, normalizing, normalized**) make or become normal.
□ **normalization** noun.

normally ▸ adverb **1** in a normal way. **2** under normal conditions.

SYNONYMS **1** *she wanted to be able to walk normally* **naturally,** conventionally, properly, like everyone else. **2** *normally we'd keep quiet about this* **usually,** ordinarily, as a rule, generally, in general, mostly, for the most part, by and large, mainly, most of the time, on the whole, typically, traditionally.

Norman ▸ noun a member of a people from Normandy in northern France who conquered England in 1066.

▸ **adjective** relating to the Normans or Normandy.

normative ▸ **adjective** relating to or setting a standard or norm.

Norse ▸ **noun** ancient or medieval Norwegian or another Scandinavian language.

▸ **adjective** relating to ancient or medieval Norway or Scandinavia.

north ▸ **noun** **1** the direction which is on your left-hand side when you are facing east. **2** the northern part of a place.

▸ **adjective** **1** lying towards or facing the north. **2** (of a wind) blowing from the north.

▸ **adverb** to or towards the north.
  □ **northward** adjective & adverb **northwards** adverb.

north-east ▸ **noun** the direction or region halfway between north and east.

▸ **adjective & adverb** **1** towards or facing the north-east. **2** (of a wind) blowing from the north-east.
  □ **north-eastern** adjective.

north-easterly ▸ **adjective & adverb 1** facing or moving towards the north-east. **2** (of a wind) blowing from the north-east.

northerly ▸ **adjective & adverb 1** facing or moving towards the north. **2** (of a wind) blowing from the north.

northern ▸ **adjective 1** situated in or facing the north. **2** coming from or characteristic of the north.
  ■ **Northern Lights** the aurora borealis.

northerner ▸ **noun** a person from the north of a region.

north-west ▸ **noun** the direction or region halfway between north and west.

▸ **adjective & adverb 1** towards or facing the north-west. **2** (of a wind) blowing from the north-west.
  □ **north-western** adjective.

north-westerly ▸ **adjective & adverb 1** facing or moving towards the north-west. **2** (of a wind) blowing from the north-west.

Norwegian ▸ **noun 1** a person from Norway. **2** the language spoken in Norway.

▸ **adjective** relating to Norway.

nose ▸ **noun 1** the part of the face containing the nostrils and used in breathing and smelling. **2** the front end of an aircraft, car, or other vehicle. **3** a talent for finding something. **4** the characteristic smell of a wine.

SYNONYMS **1 snout**, muzzle, proboscis, trunk; informal beak, conk, schnozz, schnozzle, hooter. **2** *a nose for scandal* **instinct**, feeling, sixth sense, intuition, insight, feel.

▸ **verb** (**noses, nosing, nosed**) **1** make your way slowly forward. **2** look around or pry into something. **3** (of an animal) push its nose against or into.

SYNONYMS **1** *he nosed the car into the traffic* **ease**, inch, edge, move, manoeuvre, steer, guide. **2** *she's nosing into my business* **pry**, enquire, poke about/around, interfere (in), meddle (in), be a busybody, stick/poke your nose in; informal be nosy (about), snoop; Austral./NZ informal stickybeak.

nosebag ▸ **noun** a bag containing fodder, hung from a horse's head.

nosebleed ▸ **noun** an instance of bleeding from the nose.

nosedive ▸ **noun 1** a sudden dramatic decline. **2** a steep downward plunge by an aircraft.

▸ **verb** (**nosedives, nosediving, nosedived**) **1** fall or decline suddenly. **2** (of an aircraft) make a nosedive.

nosegay ▸ **noun** a small bunch of flowers.

nosh informal ▸ **noun** food.

▸ **verb** eat enthusiastically.

nostalgia ▸ **noun** longing for a happier or better time in the past.

SYNONYMS **reminiscence**, remembrance, recollection, wistfulness, regret, sentimentality.

nostalgic ▸ **adjective** characterized by nostalgia.

SYNONYMS **wistful**, romantic, sentimental, emotional, homesick, regretful, dewy-eyed, maudlin.

□ **nostalgically** adverb.

nostril ▸ **noun** either of the two openings of the nose through which air passes to the lungs.

nostrum ▸ **noun 1** a favourite method for improving something. **2** an ineffective medicine.

nosy (or **nosey**) ▸ **adjective** (**nosier, nosiest**) informal too inquisitive about other people's affairs.

not ▸ **adverb 1** used to express a negative. **2** less than.

notable ▸ **adjective** deserving to be noticed or given attention.

SYNONYMS **1** *notable examples of workmanship* **noteworthy**, remarkable, outstanding, important, significant, memorable, marked, striking, impressive. **2** *a notable author* **prominent**, important, well known, famous, famed, noted.
ANTONYMS unremarkable, unknown.

▸ **noun** a famous or important person.

SYNONYMS *movie stars and other notables* **celebrity**, public figure, VIP, dignitary, luminary, star, superstar, big name;

informal **celeb**, bigwig, megastar.
ANTONYMS nonentity.

notably ▸ adverb **1** in particular. **2** in a way
that is noticeable or remarkable.

> SYNONYMS **1** *other countries, notably
> the USA* **in particular,** particularly,
> especially, primarily, principally. **2** *these
> are notably short-lived birds* **remarkably,**
> especially, exceptionally, singularly,
> particularly, peculiarly, distinctly,
> significantly, unusually, uncommonly,
> conspicuously.

notary ▸ noun (plural **notaries**) a lawyer who
is authorized to be a witness when people
sign documents.

notation ▸ noun a system of symbols used
in music, mathematics, etc.

notch ▸ noun **1** a V-shaped cut on an edge or
surface. **2** a point or level on a scale.

> SYNONYMS **nick,** cut, incision, score,
> scratch, slit, snick, slot, groove.

▸ verb **1** make notches in. **2** (**notch something
up**) score or achieve something.

note ▸ noun **1** a brief written record of
something. **2** a short written message.
3 Brit. a banknote. **4** a single sound of a
particular pitch and length made by a
musical instrument or voice, or a symbol
representing this.

> SYNONYMS **1** *a note in her diary* **record,**
> entry, reminder; informal memo. **2** *notes
> of the meeting* **minutes,** record, details,
> report, account, transcript, summary.
> **3** *notes in the margins* **annotation,**
> footnote, comment. **4** *he wrote me
> a note* **message,** letter, line. **5** *a £20
> note* **banknote;** N. Amer. bill; US informal
> greenback. **6** *a note of hopelessness in
> her voice* **tone,** hint, indication, sign,
> element, suggestion, sense.

▸ verb (**notes, noting, noted**) **1** pay attention
to. **2** record something in writing.

> SYNONYMS **1** *we will note your suggestion*
> **bear in mind,** be mindful of, consider,
> take notice of, register, record, enter.
> **2** *the letter noted the ministers' concern*
> **mention,** refer to, touch on, indicate,
> point out, make known, state. **3** *note
> the date in your diary* **write down,** put
> down, jot down, take down, enter, mark,
> record, register, pencil.

■ **of note** important. **take note** pay
attention.

notebook ▸ noun **1** a small book for writing
notes in. **2** a portable computer smaller
than a laptop.

> SYNONYMS **notepad,** exercise book,
> register, logbook, log, diary, journal,
> record; Brit. jotter, pocketbook.

noted ▸ adjective well known.

> SYNONYMS **famous,** famed, well known,
> renowned, prominent, notable,
> important, eminent, acclaimed,
> celebrated.
> ANTONYMS unknown.

notepaper ▸ noun paper for writing letters
on.

noteworthy ▸ adjective interesting or
important.

nothing ▸ pronoun **1** not anything.
2 something that is not important or
interesting. **3** nought.

> SYNONYMS **1** *there's nothing I can do* **not
> a thing,** zero; N. English nowt; informal zilch,
> sweet FA, not a dicky bird; Brit. informal
> damn all, not a sausage; N. Amer. informal
> zip, nada, diddly-squat. **2** *the price fell to
> nothing* **zero,** nought, nil, o; Tennis love;
> Cricket a duck.
> ANTONYMS something.

▸ adverb not at all.

nothingness ▸ noun a state of not existing,
or in which nothing exists.

notice ▸ noun **1** the fact of being aware of or
paying attention to something. **2** warning
that something is going to happen. **3** a
formal statement that you are going to
leave a job or end an agreement. **4** a sheet
of paper displaying information. **5** a small
published announcement or advertisement
in a newspaper. **6** a short published review
of a new film, play, or book.

> SYNONYMS **1** *nothing escaped his notice*
> **attention,** observation, awareness,
> consciousness, perception, regard,
> consideration, scrutiny. **2** *a notice on the
> wall* **sign,** announcement, advertisement,
> poster, bill, bulletin. **3** *we will give
> you notice of any changes* **notification,**
> (advance) warning, news, word.

▸ verb (**notices, noticing, noticed**) become
aware of.

> SYNONYMS *I noticed that the door was
> open* **observe,** note, see, discern, detect,
> spot; Brit. informal clock.
> ANTONYMS overlook.

noticeable ▸ adjective easily seen or
noticed.

> SYNONYMS **obvious,** evident, apparent,
> manifest, plain, clear, conspicuous,
> perceptible, discernible, detectable,
> observable, visible, appreciable.

□ **noticeably** adverb.

> ✔ Remember the **e** in the middle: notic**e**able.

notifiable ▸ adjective (of an infectious
disease) that must be reported to the
health authorities.

notify ▸ verb (**notifies, notifying, notified**)
formally tell someone about something.

n

SYNONYMS **inform,** tell, advise, give (advance) warning, let someone know, alert, warn.

□ **notification** noun.

notion ▸ noun **1** an idea or belief. **2** an understanding.

SYNONYMS **1** *he had a notion that something was wrong* **idea,** impression, (funny) feeling, (sneaking) suspicion, intuition, hunch, belief, opinion. **2** *Claire had no notion of what he meant* **understanding,** idea, clue, inkling.

notional ▸ adjective based on an idea rather than reality.

□ **notionally** adverb.

notoriety /noh-tuh-**ry**-i-ti/ ▸ noun the state of being notorious.

notorious ▸ adjective famous for something bad.

SYNONYMS **infamous,** scandalous, disreputable.

□ **notoriously** adverb.

notwithstanding ▸ preposition in spite of. ▸ adverb nevertheless.

nougat /**noo**-gah, **nug**-uht/ ▸ noun a sweet made from sugar or honey, nuts, and egg white.

nought ▸ noun the figure 0.

SYNONYMS **nil,** zero, nothing; Tennis **love;** Cricket a **duck;** informal **zilch;** Brit. informal **not a sausage;** N. Amer. informal **zip, nada.**

▸ pronoun nothing.

noun ▸ noun a word (other than a pronoun) that refers to a person, place, or thing.

nourish ▸ verb **1** give a person, animal, or plant the food and other substances they need in order to grow and be healthy. **2** keep a feeling or belief in your mind for a long time.

SYNONYMS **1** *patients must be well nourished* **feed,** sustain, provide for, maintain. **2** (**nourishing**) **nutritious,** wholesome, good for you, full of goodness, healthy, health-giving, beneficial. **3** *we nourish the talents of children* **encourage,** promote, foster, nurture, cultivate, boost, strengthen, enrich.

nourishment ▸ noun the food and other substances necessary for life, growth, and good health.

nous /nowss/ ▸ noun Brit. informal common sense.

nouveau riche /noo-voh **reesh**/ ▸ noun people who have recently become rich and who display their wealth in an obvious or tasteless way.

nova ▸ noun (plural **novae** /**noh**-vee/ or **novas**) a star that suddenly becomes very bright

for a short period.

novel[1] ▸ noun a story of book length about imaginary people and events.

SYNONYMS *a good novel* **story,** tale, narrative, romance.

novel[2] ▸ adjective new in an interesting or unusual way.

SYNONYMS *a novel way of making money* **new,** original, unusual, unconventional, unorthodox, different, fresh, imaginative, innovative. ANTONYMS traditional.

novelist ▸ noun a person who writes novels.

novella /nuh-**vel**-luh/ ▸ noun a short novel or long short story.

novelty ▸ noun (plural **novelties**) **1** the quality of being new and unusual. **2** a new or unfamiliar thing. **3** a small toy or ornament.

SYNONYMS **1** *the novelty of our approach* **originality,** newness, freshness, unconventionality, creativity, innovation, unfamiliarity, strangeness. **2** *we sell seasonal novelties* **knick-knack,** trinket, bauble, toy, trifle, ornament; N. Amer. **kickshaw.**

November ▸ noun the eleventh month of the year.

novice ▸ noun **1** a person who is new to and lacks experience in a job or situation. **2** a person who has entered a religious community but has not yet taken their vows.

SYNONYMS **beginner,** learner, newcomer, fledgling, trainee, probationer, student, pupil, apprentice; informal **rookie, newie;** N. Amer. informal **greenhorn.** ANTONYMS expert, veteran.

novitiate (or **noviciate**) ▸ noun a period of being a novice in a religious community.

now ▸ adverb **1** at the present time. **2** immediately.

SYNONYMS **1** *I'm busy now* **at the moment,** at present, at this moment in time, at this time, currently; N. Amer. **presently. 2** *television is now the main source of news* **nowadays,** these days, today, in this day and age. **3** *you must leave now* **at once,** straight away, right away, this minute, this instant, immediately, instantly, directly; informal **pronto, asap.**

▸ conjunction as a result of the fact.

nowadays ▸ adverb at the present time, in contrast with the past.

nowhere ▸ adverb not anywhere. ▸ pronoun no place.

noxious ▸ adjective harmful or very unpleasant.

nozzle ▸ noun a spout used to control a stream of liquid or gas.

nuance /**nyoo**-ahnss/ ▸ noun a very slight difference in meaning, expression, sound, etc.

nub ▸ noun **1** (the nub) the central point of a matter. **2** a small lump.

nubile ▸ adjective (of a girl or young woman) sexually attractive.

nubuck /**nyoo**-buk/ ▸ noun a type of leather which has been rubbed on one side to make it feel like suede.

nuclear ▸ adjective **1** relating to the nucleus of an atom or cell. **2** using energy released in the fission (splitting) or fusion of atomic nuclei. **3** possessing or involving nuclear weapons.
■ **nuclear family** a couple and their children. **nuclear physics** the science of atomic nuclei and the way they interact.

nucleic acid /nyoo-**klay**-ik/ ▸ noun either of two substances, DNA and RNA, that are present in all living cells.

nucleus /**nyoo**-kli-uhss/ ▸ noun (plural **nuclei** /**nyoo**-kli-I/) **1** the central and most important part of an object or group. **2** Physics the positively charged central core of an atom. **3** Biology a structure present in most cells, containing the genetic material.

SYNONYMS **core**, centre, heart, hub, middle, focal point, pivot, crux.

nude ▸ adjective wearing no clothes.

SYNONYMS **naked**, stark naked, bare, unclothed, undressed, stripped, with nothing on; informal without a stitch on, in your birthday suit, in the raw/buff, in the altogether; Brit. informal **starkers**; N. Amer. informal **buck naked**.
ANTONYMS clothed.

▸ noun a painting or sculpture of a naked human figure.
□ **nudity** noun.

nudge ▸ verb (**nudges**, **nudging**, **nudged**) **1** prod someone with your elbow to attract their attention. **2** touch or push something gently.

SYNONYMS **1** *he nudged Ben* **prod**, elbow, dig, poke, jab. **2** *the canoe nudged the bank* **touch**, bump (against), push (against), run into. **3** *we nudged them towards a decision* **prompt**, encourage, persuade, prod.

▸ noun a light prod or push.

SYNONYMS *Maggie gave him a nudge* **prod**, dig (in the ribs), poke, jab, push.

nudist ▸ noun a person who prefers to wear no clothes.
□ **nudism** noun.

nugatory /**noo**-guh-tuh-ri/ ▸ adjective formal having no purpose or value.

nugget ▸ noun a small lump of precious metal found in the earth.

nuisance ▸ noun a person or thing that causes annoyance or difficulty.

SYNONYMS **annoyance**, inconvenience, bore, bother, irritation, trial, burden, pest; informal **pain (in the neck)**, hassle, bind, drag, headache.
ANTONYMS blessing.

nuke informal ▸ noun a nuclear weapon.
▸ verb (**nukes**, **nuking**, **nuked**) attack with nuclear weapons.

null ▸ adjective (**null and void**) having no legal force; invalid.

nullify ▸ verb (**nullifies**, **nullifying**, **nullified**) **1** make something legally invalid. **2** cancel out the effect of.
□ **nullification** noun.

nullity ▸ noun the state of being legally invalid.

numb ▸ adjective **1** (of a part of the body) having no sensation. **2** lacking the power to feel, think, or react.

SYNONYMS **1** *my fingers are numb* **dead**, without sensation, without feeling, numbed, desensitized, frozen, anaesthetized. **2** *the news left me numb* **dazed**, stunned, unfeeling, stupefied, paralysed, immobilized.
ANTONYMS sensitive.

▸ verb make something numb.

SYNONYMS **1** *the cold weather numbed his fingers* **deaden**, desensitize, anaesthetize, immobilize, freeze. **2** *the news updates numb us* **daze**, stun, dull, stupefy, paralyse, immobilize.
ANTONYMS sensitize.

□ **numbly** adverb **numbness** noun.

number ▸ noun **1** a quantity or value expressed by a word or symbol. **2** a quantity or amount: *huge numbers of visitors*. **3** (a number of) several. **4** a single issue of a magazine. **5** a song, dance, or piece of music. **6** a grammatical classification of words depending on whether one or more people or things are being referred to.

SYNONYMS **1** *a whole number* **numeral**, integer, figure, digit, character. **2** *a large number of complaints* **quantity**, total, aggregate, tally, quota. **3** *the wedding of one of their number* **group**, crowd, circle, party, band, crew, set, company; informal **gang**. **4** *the band performed another number* **song**, piece, tune, track, dance.

▸ verb (**numbers**, **numbering**, **numbered**) **1** amount to. **2** give a number to each thing in a series. **3** count. **4** include as a member of a group.

n

SYNONYMS **1** *visitors numbered more than two million* **add up to,** amount to, total, come to. **2** *he numbers her among his friends* **include,** count, reckon, deem.

■ **number plate** Brit. a sign on the front and rear of a vehicle showing its registration number.

numberless ▸ adjective too many to be counted.

numbskull (or **numskull**) ▸ noun informal a stupid person.

numeral ▸ noun a symbol or word representing a number.

numerate /nyoo-muh-ruht/ ▸ adjective having a good basic knowledge of arithmetic. □ **numeracy** noun.

numeration ▸ noun the action of numbering or calculating.

numerator ▸ noun Maths the number above the line in a fraction.

numerical ▸ adjective having to do with numbers. □ **numerically** adverb.

numerology ▸ noun the study of the supposed magical power of numbers. □ **numerologist** noun.

numerous ▸ adjective **1** many. **2** consisting of many members.

SYNONYMS **many,** a number of, a lot of, several, plenty of, copious, an abundance of, frequent; informal umpteen. ANTONYMS few.

numinous ▸ adjective having a strong religious or spiritual quality.

numismatic ▸ adjective having to do with coins or medals.
▸ noun (**numismatics**) the study or collection of coins, banknotes, and medals. □ **numismatist** noun.

numskull ➞ NUMBSKULL.

nun ▸ noun a member of a female religious community who has taken vows of chastity and obedience.

nuncio /nun-si-oh/ ▸ noun (plural **nuncios**) a person who represents the Pope in a foreign country.

nunnery ▸ noun (plural **nunneries**) a convent.

nuptial /nup-sh'l/ ▸ adjective having to do with marriage or weddings.
▸ noun (**nuptials**) a wedding.

nurse ▸ noun **1** a person who is trained to care for sick or injured people. **2** dated a person employed to look after young children.
▸ verb (**nurses, nursing, nursed**) **1** look after a sick person. **2** treat or hold carefully or protectively. **3** feed a baby from the breast. **4** hold on to a belief or feeling for a long time.

SYNONYMS **1** *they nursed smallpox patients* **care for,** take care of, look after, tend, minister to. **2** *they nursed old grievances* **harbour,** foster, bear, have, hold (on to), retain.

■ **nursing home** a place providing accommodation and health care for old people.

nursemaid ▸ noun dated a woman or girl employed to look after a young child.

nursery ▸ noun (plural **nurseries**) **1** a room in a house where young children sleep or play. **2** a nursery school. **3** a place where young plants and trees are grown for sale or for planting elsewhere.
■ **nursery rhyme** a simple traditional song or poem for children. **nursery school** a school for young children between the ages of three and five.

nurture ▸ verb (**nurtures, nurturing, nurtured**) **1** care for and protect a child or young plant while they are growing and developing. **2** have a feeling or belief for a long time.

SYNONYMS **1** *she nurtured her children into adulthood* **bring up,** care for, take care of, look after, tend, rear, support. **2** *we nurtured these plants* **cultivate,** grow, keep, tend, raise. **3** *he nurtured my love of art* **encourage,** promote, stimulate, develop, foster, cultivate, boost, strengthen, fuel. ANTONYMS neglect, hinder.

▸ noun the state of being nurtured.

nut ▸ noun **1** a fruit consisting of a hard shell around an edible kernel. **2** the kernel of such a fruit. **3** a small flat piece of metal with a hole through the centre, for screwing on to a bolt. **4** (also **nutcase**) informal a crazy person. **5** (**nuts**) informal mad. **6** informal a person's head.

SYNONYMS **1** informal *some nut arrived at the office* **maniac,** lunatic, madman, madwoman; informal loony, nutcase, head case; Brit. informal nutter; N. Amer. informal screwball. **2** *a movie nut* **enthusiast,** fan, devotee, aficionado; informal freak, fanatic, addict, buff.

■ **in a nutshell** in the fewest possible words. **nuts and bolts** informal basic facts or practical details. □ **nutty** adjective.

nutcrackers ▸ plural noun a device for cracking nuts.

nutmeg ▸ noun a spice made from the seed of a tropical tree.

nutrient ▸ noun a substance that provides nourishment.

nutriment ▸ noun nourishment.

nutrition ▸ noun the process of eating or taking nourishment.

□ **nutritional** adjective **nutritionist** noun.

nutritious ▸ adjective full of nourishing things; good for you.

> SYNONYMS **nourishing**, wholesome, good for you, full of goodness, healthy, health-giving, beneficial.

nutritive ▸ adjective **1** having to do with nutrition. **2** nutritious.

nutter ▸ noun Brit. informal a mad person.

nuzzle ▸ verb (nuzzles, nuzzling, nuzzled) gently rub or push against someone or something with the nose.

NVQ ▸ abbreviation (in the UK) National Vocational Qualification.

NW ▸ abbreviation north-west or north-western.

nylon ▸ noun **1** a strong, lightweight synthetic material. **2** (nylons) nylon stockings or tights.

nymph ▸ noun **1** (in Greek and Roman mythology) a spirit in the form of a beautiful young woman. **2** an immature form of an insect such as a dragonfly.

nymphet ▸ noun an attractive and sexually mature young girl.

nymphomania ▸ noun uncontrollable or abnormally strong sexual desire in a woman. □ **nymphomaniac** noun.

n

Oo

O (or o) ▶ noun (plural **Os** or **O's**) **1** the fifteenth letter of the alphabet. **2** zero.
■ **O level** (in the past in the UK) the lower of the two main levels of the GCE exam.

oaf ▶ noun a stupid, rude, or clumsy man.
□ **oafish** adjective.

oak ▶ noun a large tree which produces acorns and a hard wood used in building and for furniture.

oaken ▶ adjective literary made of oak.

OAP ▶ abbreviation Brit. old-age pensioner.

oar ▶ noun a pole with a flat blade, used for rowing a boat.

oarsman (or **oarswoman**) ▶ noun (plural **oarsmen** or **oarswomen**) a rower.

oasis ▶ noun (plural **oases**) a fertile place in a desert where water rises to ground level.

oast house ▶ noun a building containing a kiln for drying hops.

oat ▶ noun **1** a cereal plant grown in cool climates. **2** (**oats**) the grain of this plant.

oatcake ▶ noun an oatmeal biscuit.

oath ▶ noun (plural **oaths**) **1** a solemn promise to do something or that something is true. **2** a swear word.

> SYNONYMS **1** *an oath of allegiance* **vow,** pledge, promise, affirmation, word (of honour), guarantee. **2** *a stream of oaths* **swear word,** profanity, expletive, four-letter word, dirty word, obscenity, curse.

oatmeal ▶ noun ground oats, used in making porridge and oatcakes.

obdurate /ob-dyuu-ruht/ ▶ adjective refusing to change your mind; stubborn.
□ **obduracy** noun.

OBE ▶ abbreviation Officer of the Order of the British Empire.

obedient ▶ adjective willingly doing what you are told.

> SYNONYMS **compliant,** biddable, acquiescent, good, law-abiding, deferential, governable, docile, submissive.
> ANTONYMS rebellious.

□ **obedience** noun **obediently** adverb.

obeisance /oh-bay-suhnss/ ▶ noun **1** respect for someone and willingness to

obey them. **2** a gesture expressing this, such as a bow.

obelisk ▶ noun a stone pillar that tapers to a point, set up as a monument.

obese ▶ adjective very fat.
□ **obesity** noun.

obey ▶ verb do what a person or a rule tells you to do.

> SYNONYMS **1** *I obeyed him* **do what someone says,** submit to, defer to, do as one is told. **2** *he refused to obey the order* **carry out,** perform, act on, execute, discharge, implement. **3** *the rules have to be obeyed* **comply with,** adhere to, observe, abide by, act in accordance with, conform to, respect, follow, keep to, stick to.
> ANTONYMS defy, ignore.

obfuscate /ob-fuss-kayt/ ▶ verb (**obfuscates, obfuscating, obfuscated**) make something unclear or hard to understand.
□ **obfuscation** noun.

obituary /oh-bi-tyuu-ri/ ▶ noun (plural **obituaries**) a short piece of writing about a person and their life which is published in a newspaper when they die.

object ▶ noun /ob-jikt/ **1** a thing that you can see and touch. **2** a person or thing to which an action or feeling is directed. **3** a purpose. **4** Grammar a noun acted on by a transitive verb or by a preposition.

> SYNONYMS **1** *wooden objects* **thing,** article, item, entity. **2** *the object of criticism* **target,** butt, focus, recipient, victim. **3** *his object was to resolve the crisis* **objective,** aim, goal, target, purpose, end, plan, point, ambition, intention, idea.

▶ verb /uhb-**jekt**/ say that you disagree with or disapprove of something.

> SYNONYMS *teachers objected to the scheme* **protest about,** oppose, take exception to, take issue with, take a stand against, argue against, quarrel with, condemn, draw the line at, demur at, mind, complain about; informal kick up a fuss/stink about.
> ANTONYMS approve of, accept.

□ **objector** noun.

objectify ▸ verb (objectifies, objectifying, objectified) **1** refer to something abstract as if it has a physical form. **2** treat someone as an object rather than a person.
□ **objectification** noun.

objection ▸ noun a statement expressing disagreement or disapproval.

SYNONYMS **protest,** protestation, complaint, opposition, demurral, counter-argument, disagreement, disapproval, dissent.

objectionable ▸ adjective unpleasant or offensive.

objective ▸ adjective **1** considering the facts about something without being influenced by personal feelings or opinions. **2** having actual existence outside the mind.

SYNONYMS **1** *try to be objective* **impartial,** unbiased, unprejudiced, non-partisan, disinterested, neutral, uninvolved, even-handed, fair, dispassionate, detached. **2** *objective knowledge* **factual,** actual, real, empirical, verifiable.
ANTONYMS subjective, emotional.

▸ noun a goal or aim.

SYNONYMS *our objective is to make a profit* **aim,** intention, purpose, target, goal, object, idea, plan.

□ **objectivity** noun.

objectively ▸ adverb in an objective way.

SYNONYMS **impartially,** without bias/prejudice, even-handedly, fairly, dispassionately, with an open mind, without fear or favour.

objet d'art /ob-zhay dar/ ▸ noun (plural objets d'art /ob-zhay dar/) a small decorative object or piece of art.

oblation ▸ noun a thing presented or offered to a god.

obligate ▸ verb (be obligated) having a moral or legal duty to do something.

obligation ▸ noun **1** something you must do in order to keep to an agreement or fulfil a duty. **2** the state of having to do something of this kind.

SYNONYMS **1** *his professional obligations* **commitment,** duty, responsibility, function, task, job, charge, onus, liability, requirement, debt. **2** *a sense of obligation* **duty,** compulsion, indebtedness, necessity, pressure, constraint.

obligatory ▸ adjective required by a law, rule, or custom; compulsory.

SYNONYMS **compulsory,** mandatory, prescribed, required, statutory, enforced, binding, requisite, necessary, imperative.
ANTONYMS optional.

oblige ▸ verb (obliges, obliging, obliged)

1 make someone do something because it is a law, a necessity, or their duty. **2** do something to help someone. **3** (be obliged) be grateful.

SYNONYMS **1** *we are obliged to accept the decision* **compel,** force, require, bind, constrain. **2** *I'll be happy to oblige you* **do someone a favour,** accommodate, help, assist, indulge, humour. **3** (obliged) **thankful,** grateful, appreciative, beholden, indebted, in someone's debt.

obliging ▸ adjective willing to help.

SYNONYMS **helpful,** accommodating, cooperative, agreeable, amenable, generous, kind; Brit. informal decent.
ANTONYMS unhelpful.

□ **obligingly** adverb.

oblique /uh-**bleek**/ ▸ adjective **1** at an angle; slanting. **2** not done in a direct way.
□ **obliquely** adverb.

obliterate /uh-**bli**-tuh-rayt/ ▸ verb (obliterates, obliterating, obliterated) destroy or remove all signs of something.
□ **obliteration** noun.

oblivion ▸ noun **1** the state of being unaware of what is happening around you. **2** the state of being forgotten or destroyed.

oblivious ▸ adjective not aware of what is happening around you.

oblong ▸ adjective rectangular in shape.
▸ noun an oblong shape.

obloquy /**ob**-luh-kwi/ ▸ noun **1** strong public criticism. **2** disgrace.

obnoxious /uhb-**nok**-shuhss/ ▸ adjective very unpleasant and offensive.

oboe ▸ noun a woodwind instrument of treble pitch, that you play by blowing through a reed.
□ **oboist** noun.

obscene ▸ adjective **1** dealing with sex in an offensive way. **2** (of a payment, pay rise, etc.) unacceptably large.

SYNONYMS **1** *obscene literature* **pornographic,** indecent, smutty, dirty, filthy, X-rated, explicit, lewd, rude, vulgar, coarse, scatological; informal blue, porn; euphemistic adult. **2** *an obscene amount* **scandalous,** shocking, outrageous, immoral.
ANTONYMS clean, family.

□ **obscenely** adverb.

obscenity ▸ noun (plural obscenities) obscene language or behaviour, or an obscene action or word.

obscure ▸ adjective **1** not discovered or known about. **2** hard to understand or see.

SYNONYMS **1** *his origins remain obscure* **unclear,** uncertain, unknown, mysterious, hazy, vague, indeterminate. **2** *obscure references to Proust* **abstruse,**

o

oblique, opaque, cryptic, enigmatic, puzzling, perplexing, baffling, elliptical. **3** *an obscure Peruvian painter* **little known,** unknown, unheard of, unsung, unrecognized, forgotten.
ANTONYMS clear, plain, famous.

▶ verb (**obscures, obscuring, obscured**) make something difficult to see, hear, or understand.

SYNONYMS **1** *clouds obscured the sun* **hide,** conceal, cover, veil, shroud, screen, mask, cloak, block, obliterate, eclipse. **2** *recent events have obscured the issue* **confuse,** complicate, obfuscate, cloud, blur, muddy.
ANTONYMS reveal, clarify.

□ **obscurely** adverb.

obscurity ▶ noun (plural **obscurities**) **1** the state of being unknown or forgotten. **2** the quality of being hard to understand.

obsequies /ob-si-kwiz/ ▶ plural noun funeral ceremonies.

obsequious /uhb-**see**-kwi-uhss/ ▶ adjective too attentive and respectful towards someone.
□ **obsequiously** adverb **obsequiousness** noun.

observance ▶ noun **1** the obeying of a rule or following of a custom. **2** (**observances**) acts performed for religious or ceremonial reasons.

observant ▶ adjective quick to notice things.

observation ▶ noun **1** the close watching of someone or something. **2** the ability to notice important details. **3** a comment.

SYNONYMS **1** *detailed observation of their behaviour* **monitoring,** watching, scrutiny, survey, surveillance, attention, study. **2** *his observations were correct* **remark,** comment, opinion, impression, thought, reflection.

□ **observational** adjective.

observatory ▶ noun (plural **observatories**) a building containing a telescope for looking at the stars and planets.

observe ▶ verb (**observes, observing, observed**) **1** notice. **2** watch something carefully. **3** make a remark. **4** obey a rule. **5** celebrate or take part in a particular festival.

SYNONYMS **1** *she observed that he was drunk* **notice,** see, note, perceive, discern, spot. **2** *he had been observing her* **watch,** look at, contemplate, view, survey, regard, keep an eye on, scrutinize, keep under surveillance, keep watch on, monitor; informal keep tabs on, keep a beady eye on. **3** *'You look tired,' she observed* **remark,** comment, say, mention, declare, announce, state. **4** *they agreed to observe the ceasefire* **comply**

with, abide by, keep, obey, adhere to, heed, honour, fulfil, respect, follow, consent to, accept.

□ **observable** adjective.

observer ▶ noun a person who observes.

SYNONYMS **1** *the casual observer* **spectator,** onlooker, watcher, fly on the wall, viewer, witness. **2** *industry observers are worried* **commentator,** reporter, monitor.

obsess ▶ verb preoccupy someone to a disturbing extent.

SYNONYMS **1** *it obsessed him for years* **preoccupy,** prey on (someone's mind), possess, take over, haunt, consume, plague, torment. **2** (**obsessed**) *you're obsessed by this music* **fixated,** possessed, consumed, infatuated, besotted; informal smitten, hung up; N. Amer. informal hipped.

obsession ▶ noun **1** the state of being obsessed. **2** something that you cannot stop thinking about.

SYNONYMS **fixation,** passion, mania, compulsion, preoccupation, infatuation, hobby horse, phobia, complex, neurosis; informal bee in your bonnet, hang-up, thing.

□ **obsessional** adjective.

obsessive ▶ adjective unable to stop thinking about someone or something.

SYNONYMS **consuming,** all-consuming, compulsive, controlling, fanatical, neurotic, excessive; informal pathological.

□ **obsessively** adverb **obsessiveness** noun.

obsidian /uhb-**sid**-i-uhn/ ▶ noun a dark glass-like volcanic rock.

obsolescent /ob-suh-**less**-uhnt/ ▶ adjective becoming obsolete.
□ **obsolescence** noun.

obsolete ▶ adjective no longer produced or used; out of date.

SYNONYMS **out of date,** outdated, outmoded, old-fashioned, passé, antiquated, antediluvian, anachronistic, archaic, ancient, fossilized, extinct, defunct; informal out of the ark; Brit. informal past its sell-by date.
ANTONYMS current, modern.

obstacle ▶ noun a thing that blocks the way or makes it difficult to do something.

SYNONYMS **barrier,** hurdle, stumbling block, obstruction, bar, block, impediment, hindrance, snag, catch, drawback, hitch, fly in the ointment, handicap, difficulty, problem, disadvantage; Brit. spanner in the works.
ANTONYMS advantage, aid.

obstetrician /ob-stuh-**tri**-sh'n/ ▶ noun a doctor who is trained in obstetrics.

obstetrics ▸ noun the branch of medicine concerned with childbirth.
 □ **obstetric** adjective.

obstinate ▸ adjective 1 refusing to change your mind or stop what you are doing. 2 hard to deal with.

SYNONYMS **stubborn,** pig-headed, unyielding, inflexible, unbending, intransigent, intractable, self-willed. ANTONYMS compliant.

 □ **obstinacy** noun **obstinately** adverb.

obstreperous ▸ adjective noisy and difficult to control.

obstruct ▸ verb be in the way or stop the progress of.

SYNONYMS **1** *ensure that vents are not obstructed* **block (up),** clog (up), occlude, cut off, bung up, choke, dam up. **2** *he was obstructing the traffic* **hold up,** bring to a standstill, stop, halt, block. **3** *they may obstruct aid distribution* **impede,** hinder, interfere with, hamper, block, interrupt, hold up, stand in the way of, frustrate, slow down, delay. ANTONYMS clear, facilitate.

obstruction ▸ noun 1 a thing that is in the way; an obstacle or blockage. 2 the obstructing of someone or something.

SYNONYMS **obstacle,** barrier, stumbling block, impediment, hindrance, difficulty, check, restriction, blockage, stoppage, congestion, bottleneck, hold-up.

obstructive ▸ adjective deliberately causing a delay or difficulty.

obtain ▸ verb 1 get possession of. 2 formal be established or usual.

SYNONYMS **get,** acquire, come by, secure, procure, pick up, be given, gain, earn, achieve, attain; informal get hold of, lay your hands on, land. ANTONYMS lose.

obtainable ▸ adjective able to be obtained.

SYNONYMS **available,** to be had, in circulation, on the market, on offer, in season, at your disposal, accessible; informal up for grabs, on tap.

obtrude ▸ verb (**obtrudes, obtruding, obtruded**) become noticeable in an unpleasant or unwelcome way.

obtrusive ▸ adjective noticeable in an unwelcome way.

obtuse /uhb-**tyooss**/ ▸ adjective 1 annoyingly slow to understand. 2 (of an angle) more than 90° and less than 180°. 3 not sharp or pointed; blunt.

obverse ▸ noun 1 the side of a coin or medal showing the head or main design. 2 the opposite of something.

obviate /**ob**-vi-ayt/ ▸ verb (**obviates, obviating, obviated**) remove or prevent a need or difficulty.

obvious ▸ adjective easily seen or understood; clear.

SYNONYMS **clear,** plain, evident, apparent, manifest, conspicuous, pronounced, prominent, distinct, noticeable, perceptible, visible; informal sticking out a mile. ANTONYMS imperceptible.

obviously ▸ adverb in an obvious way.

SYNONYMS **clearly,** plainly, evidently, patently, visibly, discernibly, manifestly, noticeably, of course, naturally, needless to say, it goes without saying. ANTONYMS perhaps.

ocarina /o-kuh-**ree**-nuh/ ▸ noun a small egg-shaped wind instrument with holes for the fingers.

occasion ▸ noun 1 a particular event, or the time at which it happens. 2 a special event or celebration. 3 a suitable time for something. 4 formal reason or cause.

SYNONYMS **1** *a previous occasion* **time,** instance, juncture, point, moment, experience, case. **2** *a special occasion* **event,** affair, function, celebration, party, get-together, gathering; informal do, bash.

▸ verb formal cause.

✔ two **c**s and one **s**: oc**ca**sion.

occasional ▸ adjective happening or done from time to time.

SYNONYMS **infrequent,** intermittent, irregular, periodic, sporadic, odd; N. Amer. sometime. ANTONYMS regular, frequent.

occasionally ▸ adverb sometimes; irregularly and infrequently.

SYNONYMS **sometimes,** from time to time, (every) now and then, (every) now and again, at times, every so often, (every) once in a while, on occasion, periodically. ANTONYMS often.

occidental /ok-si-**den**-tuhl/ ▸ adjective relating to the countries of the West.

occlude ▸ verb (**occludes, occluding, occluded**) technical close up; block.

occult /o-**kult**, o-kult/ ▸ noun (**the occult**) the world of magic and supernatural beliefs and practices.

▸ adjective relating to the occult.

SYNONYMS **supernatural,** magic, magical, satanic, mystical, unearthly, esoteric, psychic.

 □ **occultism** noun **occultist** noun.

occupancy ▸ noun 1 the action of occupying a place. 2 the proportion of accommodation that is occupied.

occupant ▸ noun a person who occupies a place.

SYNONYMS **resident**, inhabitant, owner, householder, tenant, leaseholder, lessee; Brit. occupier, owner-occupier.

occupation ▸ noun 1 a job or profession. 2 a way of spending time. 3 the occupying of a place.

SYNONYMS 1 *his father's occupation* **job**, profession, work, line of work, trade, employment, business, career, métier, calling. 2 *among her leisure occupations is birdwatching* **pastime**, activity, leisure activity, hobby, pursuit, interest, entertainment, recreation. 3 *the Roman occupation of Britain* **conquest**, capture, invasion, seizure, annexation, colonization, subjugation.

occupational ▸ adjective having to do with a job or profession.
■ **occupational therapy** the use of certain activities and crafts to help someone recover from an illness.

occupy ▸ verb (occupies, occupying, occupied) 1 live or work in a building. 2 fill or take up a space, time, or position. 3 keep someone busy. 4 enter and take control of a place.

SYNONYMS 1 *Carol occupied the basement flat* **live in**, inhabit, lodge in, move into, people, populate, settle. 2 (occupied) *only two flats are occupied* **inhabited**, lived in. 3 (occupied) *the table was occupied* **in use**, full, engaged, taken. 4 *he occupies a post at the Treasury* **hold**, fill, have; informal hold down. 5 *something to occupy my mind* **engage**, busy, distract, absorb, engross, hold, interest, involve, entertain. 6 (occupied) *tasks which kept her occupied* **busy**, working, at work, active; informal tied up, hard at it, on the go. 7 *the region was occupied by Japan* **capture**, seize, conquer, invade, colonize, annex, subjugate.

□ occupier noun.

occur ▸ verb (occurs, occurring, occurred) 1 happen. 2 be found or present. 3 (occur to) come into someone's mind.

SYNONYMS 1 *an accident occurred at 3.30* **happen**, take place, come about; N. Amer. informal go down. 2 *the disease occurs in the tropics* **be found**, be present, exist, appear, develop. 3 *enter someone's head/mind*, cross someone's mind, come/spring to mind, strike someone, come to someone, dawn on someone, suggest itself.

✔ double **c** and double **r** in **occurred**, **occurring**, and **occurrence**.

occurrence /uh-**kur**-ruhnss/ ▸ noun 1 a thing that happens or exists. 2 the fact of

something happening or existing.

SYNONYMS 1 *a rare occurrence* **event**, incident, happening, phenomenon, circumstance. 2 *the occurrence of cancer* **existence**, instance, appearance, frequency, incidence, rate, prevalence; Statistics distribution.

ocean ▸ noun a very large area of sea.

oceanic /oh-si-**an**-ik/ ▸ adjective relating to the ocean.

oceanography ▸ noun the study of the sea.
□ oceanographer noun.

ocelot /**oss**-i-lot/ ▸ noun a medium-sized striped and spotted wild cat, found in South and Central America.

ochre /**oh**-ker/ (US spelling ocher) ▸ noun a type of light yellow or reddish earth, used as a pigment.

o'clock ▸ adverb used to say which hour it is when telling the time.

octagon ▸ noun a figure with eight straight sides and eight angles.
□ octagonal adjective.

octahedron /ok-tuh-**hee**-druhn/ ▸ noun (plural **octahedra** or **octahedrons**) a three-dimensional shape with eight flat faces.

octane ▸ noun a liquid hydrocarbon present in petroleum.

octave ▸ noun 1 a series of eight musical notes occupying the interval between (and including) two notes. 2 the interval between two such notes.

octavo /ok-**tah**-voh/ ▸ noun (plural **octavos**) a size of book page that results from folding each printed sheet into eight leaves (sixteen pages).

octet ▸ noun 1 a group of eight musicians. 2 a piece of music for an octet.

October ▸ noun the tenth month of the year.

octogenarian /ok-tuh-ji-**nair**-i-uhn/ ▸ noun a person who is between 80 and 89 years old.

octopus ▸ noun (plural **octopuses**) a sea creature with a soft body and eight long tentacles.

ocular ▸ adjective having to do with the eyes.

OD ▸ verb (OD's, OD'ing, OD'd) informal take an overdose of a drug.

odd ▸ adjective 1 unusual or unexpected; strange. 2 (of whole numbers such as 3 and 5) having one left over as a remainder when divided by two. 3 occasional. 4 spare; available. 5 separated from a pair or set. 6 in the region of.

SYNONYMS 1 *an odd man* **strange**, peculiar, queer, funny, bizarre, eccentric, unusual, weird, quirky, zany; informal wacky, off the wall. 2 *some odd things had happened* **unusual**, strange, peculiar, funny, curious, weird, bizarre, queer,

abnormal, puzzling, mystifying, baffling, unaccountable. **3** *he does odd jobs* **occasional,** casual, irregular, isolated, sporadic, periodic, miscellaneous, various, varied, sundry. **4** *an odd shoe* **mismatched,** unmatched, unpaired, single, lone, solitary, extra, leftover, spare.
ANTONYMS normal, ordinary, regular.

☐ **oddly** adverb **oddness** noun.

oddball ▶ noun informal a strange or eccentric person.

oddity ▶ noun (plural **oddities**) **1** the quality of being strange. **2** a strange person or thing.

oddment ▶ noun an item or piece left over from a larger piece or set.

odds ▶ plural noun **1** the ratio between the amount placed as a bet and the money which would be received if the bet was won. **2** (**the odds**) the chances of something happening. **3** (**the odds**) the advantage thought to be possessed by one person or side compared to another.

SYNONYMS **likelihood,** probability, chances.

■ **at odds** in conflict or disagreement. **odds-on 1** (of a horse) with betting odds in favour of winning. **2** very likely to happen or succeed.

ode ▶ noun a poem addressed to a person or thing or celebrating an event.

odious ▶ adjective very unpleasant.

odium ▶ noun widespread hatred or disgust.

odoriferous ▶ adjective smelly.

odour (US spelling **odor**) ▶ noun a smell.

SYNONYMS **smell,** stench, stink, reek, aroma, bouquet, scent, perfume, fragrance; Brit. informal pong, whiff; N. Amer. informal funk.

☐ **odorous** adjective **odourless** adjective.

odyssey /od-i-si/ ▶ noun (plural **odysseys**) a long, eventful journey.

SYNONYMS **journey,** voyage, trip, trek, travels, quest, crusade, pilgrimage.

oedema /i-**dee**-muh/ (US spelling **edema**) ▶ noun a build-up of watery fluid in the tissues of the body.

oesophagus /i-so-fuh-guhss/ (US spelling **esophagus**) ▶ noun (plural **oesophagi** /i-so-fuh-jy/) the muscular tube which connects the throat to the stomach.

oestrogen /ee-struh-juhn/ (US spelling **estrogen**) ▶ noun a hormone which produces female physical and sexual characteristics.

oeuvre /er-vruh/ ▶ noun all the works of a particular artist, composer, or author.

of ▶ preposition **1** expressing the relationship between a part and a whole. **2** belonging to; coming from. **3** used in expressions of measurement, value, or age. **4** made from. **5** used to show position. **6** used to show that something belongs to a category.

❗ It is wrong to write **of** instead of **have** in sentences such as *I could have told you* (don't write *I could of told you*).

off ▶ adverb **1** away from a place. **2** so as to be removed or separated. **3** starting a journey or race. **4** so as to finish or be discontinued. **5** (of an electrical appliance or power supply) not working or connected. **6** having a particular level of wealth.
▶ preposition **1** away from. **2** situated or leading in a direction away from. **3** so as to be removed or separated from. **4** having a temporary dislike of.
▶ adjective (of food) no longer fresh.

SYNONYMS **1** *Kate's off today* **away,** absent, not at work, off duty, on holiday, on leave, free; N. Amer. on vacation. **2** *the game's off* **cancelled,** postponed, called off. **3** *the fish was off* **rotten,** bad, stale, mouldy, sour, rancid, turned, spoiled.
ANTONYMS in, on, good.

▶ noun Brit. informal the start of a race or journey.
■ **off-colour** Brit. slightly unwell. **off-licence** Brit. a shop selling alcoholic drink to be drunk elsewhere. **off-peak** at a time when demand is less. **off-putting** unpleasant or unsettling. **off white** a white colour with a grey or yellowish tinge.

❗ Use **off,** not **off of,** in a sentence like *the cup fell off the table.*

offal ▶ noun the internal organs of an animal used as food.

offbeat ▶ adjective unconventional; unusual.

offcut ▶ noun a piece of wood, fabric, etc. left behind after a larger piece has been cut off.

offence (US spelling **offense**) ▶ noun **1** an act that breaks a law or rule. **2** a feeling of hurt or annoyance.

SYNONYMS **1** *he has committed an offence* **crime,** illegal act, misdemeanour, breach of the law, felony, infringement, violation, wrongdoing, sin. **2** *I do not want to cause offence* **annoyance,** resentment, indignation, displeasure, bad feeling, animosity.

offend ▶ verb **1** make someone feel upset, insulted, or annoyed. **2** seem unpleasant to. **3** do something illegal.

SYNONYMS **1** *I'm sorry if I offended him* **upset,** give offence to, affront, hurt someone's feelings, insult, hurt, wound, slight. **2** *criminals who offend repeatedly* **break the law,** commit a crime, do wrong.

offender ▶ noun a person who offends.

> SYNONYMS **wrongdoer,** criminal, lawbreaker, crook, villain, miscreant, felon, delinquent, culprit, guilty party.

offensive ▶ adjective **1** causing someone to feel upset, insulted, or annoyed. **2** used in attack.

> SYNONYMS **1** *offensive remarks* **insulting,** rude, derogatory, disrespectful, personal, hurtful, upsetting, wounding, abusive. **2** *an offensive smell* **unpleasant,** disagreeable, nasty, distasteful, objectionable, off-putting, dreadful, frightful, obnoxious, abominable, disgusting, repulsive, repellent, vile, foul, sickening, nauseating; informal ghastly, horrible, horrid, gross; Brit. informal beastly. **3** *offensive operations* **hostile,** attacking, aggressive, invading, incursive, combative, threatening, martial, warlike, belligerent, bellicose. ANTONYMS complimentary, pleasant, defensive.

▶ noun a campaign to attack or achieve something.

> SYNONYMS *a military offensive* **attack,** assault, onslaught, invasion, push, thrust, charge, raid, incursion, blitz, campaign.

□ **offensively** adverb.

offer ▶ verb (offers, offering, offered) **1** present something for a person to accept or reject as they wish. **2** say you are willing to do something for someone. **3** provide.

> SYNONYMS **1** *Frank offered a suggestion* **put forward,** proffer, give, present, come up with, suggest, propose, advance, submit, tender. **2** *she offered to help* **volunteer,** step/come forward, show willing. **3** *he offered $200* **bid,** tender, put in a bid/offer of. ANTONYMS withdraw, refuse.

▶ noun **1** an expression of readiness to do or give something. **2** an amount of money that someone is willing to pay for something. **3** a specially reduced price.

> SYNONYMS **1** *an offer of help* **proposal,** proposition, suggestion, submission, approach, overture. **2** *the highest offer* **bid,** tender, bidding price.

■ **on offer 1** available. **2** for sale at a reduced price.

offering ▶ noun something that is offered; a gift or contribution.

> SYNONYMS **contribution,** donation, gift, present, sacrifice, tribute.

offertory /off-er-tuh-ri/ ▶ noun (plural **offertories**) **1** the offering of the bread

and wine at the Christian service of Holy Communion. **2** a collection of money made at a Christian church service.

offhand ▶ adjective rudely casual or cool in manner.
▶ adverb without previous thought.

office ▶ noun **1** a room, set of rooms, or building where people work at desks. **2** a position of authority. **3** (**offices**) formal things done for other people.

> SYNONYMS **1** *we met at her office* **place of work,** place of business, workplace, workroom. **2** *the company's Paris office* **branch,** division, section, bureau, department. **3** *the office of President* **post,** position, appointment, job, occupation, role, situation, function.

officer ▶ noun **1** a person holding a position of authority, especially in the armed forces. **2** a policeman or policewoman.

> SYNONYMS **official,** office-holder, committee member, board member, functionary, executive.

official ▶ adjective **1** relating to an authority or public organization. **2** agreed or done by a person or group in a position of authority.

> SYNONYMS **1** *an official enquiry* **authorized,** approved, validated, authenticated, certified, accredited, endorsed, sanctioned, licensed, recognized, legitimate, legal, lawful, valid, bona fide, proper; informal kosher. **2** *an official function* **ceremonial,** formal, solemn, bureaucratic. ANTONYMS unauthorized, informal.

▶ noun a person holding public office or having official duties.

> SYNONYMS *a union official* **officer,** office-holder, executive, functionary, administrator, bureaucrat, mandarin, representative, agent; derogatory apparatchik.

□ **officialdom** noun **officially** adverb.

officiate /uh-fi-shi-ayt/ ▶ verb (officiates, officiating, officiated) **1** act as an official in charge of something. **2** perform a religious service or ceremony.

officious ▶ adjective using your authority or interfering in a bossy way.

offing ▶ noun (in the offing) likely to happen or appear soon.

offline ▶ adjective not connected to a computer.

offload ▶ verb **1** unload a cargo. **2** get rid of.

offset ▶ verb (offsets, offsetting, offset) cancel out something with an equal and opposite force or effect.

> SYNONYMS **counteract,** balance (out), even out/up, counterbalance,

compensate for, make up for, neutralize, cancel (out).

offshoot ▶ noun a thing that develops from something else.

offshore ▶ adjective & adverb **1** at sea some distance from the shore. **2** (of the wind) blowing towards the sea from the land. **3** situated or registered abroad.

offside ▶ adjective & adverb (in games such as football) occupying a position on the field where playing the ball is not allowed.

offspring ▶ noun (plural **offspring**) a person's child or children.

> SYNONYMS **children,** sons and daughters, progeny, youngsters, babies, infants, brood, descendants, heirs, successors; informal kids; Brit. informal sprogs, brats.

offstage ▶ adjective & adverb (in a theatre) not on the stage.

often ▶ adverb **1** frequently. **2** in many instances.

> SYNONYMS **frequently,** many times, on many/numerous occasions, a lot, repeatedly, again and again, regularly, commonly, generally, ordinarily; N. Amer. oftentimes.
> ANTONYMS seldom.

ogle ▶ verb (**ogles, ogling, ogled**) stare at someone in a lecherous way.

ogre /oh-guh/ ▶ noun **1** (in stories) a man-eating giant. **2** a cruel or terrifying person.

ohm ▶ noun the basic unit of electrical resistance.

oik ▶ noun informal a rude person.

oil ▶ noun **1** a thick, sticky liquid obtained from petroleum. **2** a thick liquid which cannot be dissolved in water and is obtained from plants. **3** (also **oils**) oil paint.
▶ verb treat or coat with oil.
   ■ **oil paint** artist's paint made from powder mixed with linseed or other oil.

oilcloth ▶ noun cotton fabric treated with oil to make it waterproof.

oilfield ▶ noun an area where oil is found beneath the ground or seabed.

oilskin ▶ noun **1** heavy cotton cloth waterproofed with oil. **2** (**oilskins**) a set of clothes made of oilskin.

oily ▶ adjective (**oilier, oiliest**) **1** containing, covered with, or like oil. **2** (of a person) insincerely polite and flattering.

> SYNONYMS **greasy,** fatty, buttery, rich.

   □ **oiliness** noun.

oink ▶ noun the grunting sound made by a pig.
▶ verb make such a sound.

ointment ▶ noun a smooth substance that is rubbed on the skin to heal a wound or sore place.

> SYNONYMS **lotion,** cream, salve, liniment, embrocation, rub, gel, balm, emollient, unguent.

OK (or **okay**) informal ▶ exclamation said to express agreement or acceptance.
▶ adjective **1** satisfactory, but not especially good. **2** allowed.
▶ adverb in a satisfactory way.
▶ noun permission to do something.
▶ verb (**OK's, OK'ing, OK'd**) approve or authorize.

okapi /oh-kah-pi/ ▶ noun (plural **okapi** or **okapis**) a large plant-eating African animal with stripes on the hindquarters and upper legs.

okra /ok-ruh/ ▶ noun the long seed pods of a tropical plant, eaten as a vegetable.

old ▶ adjective (**older, oldest**) **1** having lived for a long time. **2** made, built, or originating long ago. **3** owned or used for a long time. **4** former. **5** of a stated age.

> SYNONYMS **1** old people **elderly,** aged, older, senior, venerable, in your dotage, long in the tooth, ancient, decrepit, doddery, senescent, senile; informal getting on, past it, over the hill. **2** old clothes **worn,** worn out, shabby, threadbare, frayed, patched, tattered, moth-eaten, ragged; informal tatty. **3** old cars **antique,** veteran, vintage, classic. **4** an old girlfriend **former,** previous, earlier, past, ex-, one-time, sometime, erstwhile.
> ANTONYMS young, new, modern, current.

■ **old age** the later part of normal life. **Old English** the language spoken in England until about 1150. **the old guard** the long-standing members of a group, who are often unwilling to accept change. **old hand** a very experienced person. **old hat** informal boringly familiar or out of date. **old maid** disapproving a single woman thought of as too old for marriage. **old master** a great painter of former times. **Old Nick** the Devil. **Old Testament** the first part of the Christian Bible. **old wives' tale** a widely held traditional belief that is incorrect. **Old World** Europe, Asia, and Africa.

olden ▶ adjective of a former age.

old-fashioned ▶ adjective no longer current or modern.

> SYNONYMS **out of date,** outdated, dated, out of fashion, outmoded, unfashionable, passé, outworn, behind the times, archaic, obsolescent, obsolete; informal out of the ark; N. Amer. informal horse-and-buggy.
> ANTONYMS modern.

oleaginous /oh-li-aj-i-nuhss/ ▶ adjective **1** oily. **2** insincerely flattering.

oleander /oh-li-an-der/ ▶ noun an evergreen shrub with white, pink, or red flowers.

olfactory /ol-**fak**-tuh-ri/ ▶ adjective relating to the sense of smell.

oligarch /**ol**-i-gark/ ▶ noun a ruler in an oligarchy.

oligarchy ▶ noun (plural **oligarchies**) **1** a small group of people having control of a state. **2** a state governed by a small group of people.
□ oligarchic adjective.

olive ▶ noun **1** a small oval fruit with a hard stone and bitter flesh. **2** (also **olive green**) a greyish-green colour like that of an unripe olive.
▶ adjective (of a person's complexion) yellowish brown.
■ **olive branch** an offer to restore friendly relations. **olive oil** oil obtained from olives, used in cookery and salad dressing.

Olympiad ▶ noun a staging of the Olympic Games.

Olympian ▶ adjective **1** relating to the Olympic Games. **2** having to do with Mount Olympus, traditional home of the Greek gods.
▶ noun **1** a competitor in the Olympic Games. **2** any of the twelve main Greek gods.

Olympic ▶ adjective relating to the Olympic Games.
▶ noun (**the Olympics** or **the Olympic Games**) a sports competition held every four years, or the ancient Greek festival of sport and arts that it was based on.

ombudsman /om-**buudz**-muhn/ ▶ noun (plural **ombudsmen**) an official who investigates people's complaints against companies and the government.

omega /**oh**-mi-guh/ ▶ noun the last letter of the Greek alphabet (Ω, ω).

omelette (US spelling **omelet**) ▶ noun a dish of beaten eggs cooked in a frying pan, usually with a savoury filling.

omen ▶ noun an event seen as a sign of future good or bad luck.

ominous ▶ adjective giving the impression that something bad is going to happen.

SYNONYMS **threatening**, menacing, baleful, forbidding, foreboding, fateful, sinister, black, dark, gloomy.
ANTONYMS promising.

□ ominously adverb.

omission ▶ noun **1** the action of leaving something out. **2** a failure to do something. **3** something that has been left out or not done.

SYNONYMS **1** *the omission of certain news items* **exclusion**, leaving out, deletion, elimination. **2** *I regret any omission on my part* **negligence**, neglect, dereliction, oversight, lapse, failure.

omit ▶ verb (**omits**, **omitting**, **omitted**) **1** leave out or exclude. **2** fail to do.

SYNONYMS **1** *they omitted his name from the list* **leave out**, exclude, leave off, miss out, miss, cut, drop, skip. **2** *I omitted to mention this* **forget**, neglect, fail.
ANTONYMS add, include, remember.

✔ just one **m**: o**m**it.

omni- ▶ combining form **1** of all things: *omniscient*. **2** in all ways or places: *omnipresent*.

omnibus ▶ noun **1** a volume containing several works previously published separately. **2** a single edition of two or more programmes previously broadcast separately. **3** dated a bus.

omnipotent /om-**ni**-puh-tuhnt/ ▶ adjective having unlimited or very great power.
□ omnipotence noun.

omnipresent ▶ adjective **1** (of God) present everywhere at the same time. **2** widespread.
□ omnipresence noun.

omniscient /om-**ni**-si-uhnt/ ▶ adjective knowing everything.
□ omniscience noun.

omnivore /**om**-ni-vor/ ▶ noun an animal that eats both plants and meat.

omnivorous /om-**ni**-vuh-ruhss/ ▶ adjective eating both plants and meat.

on ▶ preposition & adverb in contact with and supported by a surface.
▶ preposition **1** (also **on to**) into contact with a surface, or aboard a vehicle. **2** about; concerning. **3** as a member of. **4** stored in or broadcast by. **5** in the course of. **6** indicating a day or date when something takes place. **7** engaged in. **8** regularly taking a drug or medicine. **9** informal paid for by.
▶ adverb **1** with continued movement or action. **2** (of clothing) being worn. **3** taking place or being presented. **4** (of an electrical appliance or power supply) functioning.

once ▶ adverb **1** on one occasion or for one time only. **2** formerly. **3** multiplied by one.

SYNONYMS **1** *I only met him once* **on one occasion**, one time. **2** *he didn't help once* **ever**, at any time, on any occasion, at all. **3** *they were friends once* **formerly**, previously, in the past, at one time, at one point, once upon a time, in days/times gone by, in the (good) old days, long ago.
ANTONYMS often, now.

▶ conjunction as soon as.

SYNONYMS *once she's gone* **as soon as**, the moment, when, after.

■ **at once 1** immediately. **2** at the same time. **once-over** informal a quick inspection, or act of cleaning something.

oncology /ong-**kol**-uh-ji/ ▶ noun the study and treatment of tumours.
□ oncologist noun.

oncoming ▸ adjective moving towards you.

one ▸ cardinal number **1** the lowest cardinal number; 1. (Roman numeral: i or I.) **2** single, or a single person or thing. **3** (before a person's name) a certain. **4** the same.
▸ pronoun **1** used to refer to a person or thing previously mentioned or easily identified. **2** used to refer to the speaker, or to represent people in general.
■ **one-armed bandit** informal a fruit machine operated by pulling a long handle at the side. **one-liner** informal a short joke or witty remark. **one-off** Brit. informal done, made, or happening only once. **one-upmanship** informal the technique of gaining an advantage over someone else.

oneness ▸ noun the state of being whole or in agreement.

onerous /oh-nuh-ruhss/ ▸ adjective involving a lot of effort and difficulty.

oneself ▸ pronoun **1** used as the object of a verb or preposition when this is the same as the subject of the clause and the subject is 'one'. **2** used to emphasize that you are doing something individually or without help. **3** in your normal state of body or mind.

one-sided ▸ adjective **1** giving only one point of view; biased. **2** involving poorly matched opponents.

> SYNONYMS **1** *a one-sided account* **biased,** prejudiced, partisan, partial, slanted, distorted, unfair. **2** *a one-sided game* **unequal,** uneven, unbalanced. ANTONYMS impartial, equal.

ongoing ▸ adjective still in progress.

> SYNONYMS **in progress,** under way, going on, continuing, proceeding.

onion ▸ noun a vegetable consisting of a round bulb with a strong taste and smell.

online ▸ adjective & adverb **1** controlled by or connected to a computer. **2** available on or carried out via the Internet.

onlooker ▸ noun a spectator.

> SYNONYMS **eyewitness,** witness, observer, spectator, bystander; informal rubberneck.

only ▸ adverb **1** and no one or nothing more besides. **2** no longer ago than. **3** not until. **4** with the negative result that.

> SYNONYMS **1** *only enough for two* **at most,** at best, just, no more than, hardly, barely, scarcely. **2** *for your eyes only* **exclusively,** solely, purely. **3** *you're only saying that* **merely,** simply, just.

▸ adjective **1** single or solitary. **2** alone deserving consideration.

> SYNONYMS *their only son* **sole,** single, one (and only), solitary, lone, unique, exclusive.

▸ conjunction informal except that.

onomatopoeia /on-uh-mat-uh-**pee**-uh/
▸ noun the use of words that sound like the thing they refer to (e.g. *sizzle*).
□ **onomatopoeic** adjective.

onrush ▸ noun a surging rush forward.
□ **onrushing** adjective.

onset ▸ noun the beginning of something.

> SYNONYMS **start,** beginning, commencement, arrival, appearance, inception, day one, outbreak. ANTONYMS end.

onshore ▸ adjective & adverb **1** situated on land. **2** (of the wind) blowing from the sea towards the land.

onside ▸ adjective & adverb (in sport) not offside.

onslaught ▸ noun **1** a fierce or destructive attack. **2** an overwhelmingly large quantity of people or things.

> SYNONYMS **attack,** assault, offensive, advance, charge, blitz, bombardment, barrage.

onstage ▸ adjective & adverb (in a theatre) on the stage.

onto ▸ on to at on.

ontology ▸ noun philosophy concerned with the nature of being.
□ **ontological** adjective.

onus ▸ noun a duty or responsibility.

onward ▸ adjective & adverb in a forward direction.
□ **onwards** adverb.

onyx /on-iks/ ▸ noun a semi-precious stone with layers of different colours.

oodles ▸ plural noun informal a very great number or amount.

oomph ▸ noun informal excitement or energy.

ooze ▸ verb (oozes, oozing, oozed) slowly seep out.

> SYNONYMS **1** *blood oozed from the wound* **seep,** discharge, flow, exude, trickle, drip, dribble, drain, leak. **2** *positively oozing charm* **exude,** gush, drip, emanate, radiate.

▸ noun the very slow flow of a liquid.
□ **oozy** adjective.

opacity /oh-**pa**-si-ti/ ▸ noun the condition of being opaque.

opal ▸ noun a semi-transparent gemstone in which small points of shifting colour can be seen.

opalescent ▸ adjective having small points of shifting colour.

opaque /oh-**payk**/ ▸ adjective **1** not able to be seen through. **2** difficult or impossible to understand.

op. cit. ▸ adverb in the work already cited. ORIGIN short for Latin *opere citato*.

open ▸ adjective **1** not closed, fastened, or restricted. **2** not covered or protected. **3** (**open to**) likely to suffer from or be affected by. **4** spread out, expanded, or unfolded. **5** accessible or available. **6** not hiding thoughts and feelings. **7** not disguised or hidden. **8** not finally settled.

> SYNONYMS **1** *the door's open* **unlatched,** unlocked, off the latch, ajar, gaping, yawning. **2** *a silk shirt, open at the neck* **unfastened,** undone, unbuttoned, unzipped. **3** *an open packet* **opened,** undone, unsealed, uncorked, unstoppered. **4** *open countryside | open spaces* **unenclosed,** rolling, sweeping, wide open, exposed, spacious, uncluttered. **5** *a map was open beside him* **spread out,** unfolded, unfurled, unrolled, stretched out. **6** *the bank wasn't open* **open for business,** open to the public, working, accessible. **7** *the position is still open* **available,** vacant, free, unfilled; informal up for grabs. **8** *open to abuse* **vulnerable,** subject, susceptible, liable, exposed. **9** *she was very open* **frank,** candid, honest, forthcoming, communicative, forthright, direct, unreserved, plain-spoken, outspoken; informal upfront. **10** *open hostility* **overt,** manifest, conspicuous, plain, undisguised, unconcealed, clear, naked, blatant, flagrant, barefaced, brazen. **11** *I'm open to suggestions* **receptive,** amenable, willing to listen, responsive. **12** *what other options are open to us?* **available,** accessible, on hand, on offer. **13** *an open meeting* **public,** general, unrestricted.
> ANTONYMS shut, fastened, enclosed, closed, filled, protected, reticent, suppressed, private.

▸ verb **1** make or become open. **2** formally begin or establish. **3** (**open on to** or **into**) give access to. **4** (**open out** or **up**) begin to talk freely.

> SYNONYMS **1** *she opened the front door* **unfasten,** unlock, throw wide. **2** *Katherine opened the parcel* **unwrap,** undo, untie. **3** *shall I open another bottle?* **uncork,** crack open. **4** *Adam opened the map* **spread out,** unfold, unfurl, unroll, straighten out. **5** *we'll be opening next week* **start trading,** set up shop. **6** *Bryan opened the meeting* **begin,** start, commence, initiate, set in motion, get going, get under way, get off the ground; informal kick off. **7** *the lounge opens on to a patio* **give access,** lead.
> ANTONYMS close, shut, end.

▸ noun (**the open**) fresh air or open countryside.
■ **open-and-shut** straightforward. **open-heart surgery** surgery in which the heart is exposed. **open house** a place or situation in which all visitors are welcome. **open letter** a letter addressed to a particular person but intended to be published. **open market** a situation in which companies can trade without restrictions. **open-plan** having large rooms with few or no dividing walls. **open verdict** Law a verdict that a person's death is suspicious but that the cause is not known.
□ **opener** noun **openness** noun.

open air ▸ noun (**the open air**) an unenclosed space outdoors.
▸ adjective (**open-air**) located or taking place outdoors.

> SYNONYMS **outdoor,** out-of-doors, outside, alfresco.
> ANTONYMS indoor.

opencast ▸ adjective Brit. (of mining) in which coal or ore is extracted from a level near the earth's surface, rather than from shafts.

opening ▸ noun **1** a gap. **2** the beginning of something. **3** a ceremony at which a building, show, etc. is declared to be open. **4** an opportunity to achieve something. **5** an available job or position.

> SYNONYMS **1** *an opening in the roof* **hole,** gap, aperture, orifice, vent, crack, slit, chink. **2** *the opening of the session* **beginning,** start, commencement, outset; informal kick-off. **3** *a gallery opening* **launch,** inauguration, opening/first night, premiere.

▸ adjective coming at the beginning.

> SYNONYMS *her opening remarks* **first,** initial, introductory, preliminary, maiden, inaugural.
> ANTONYMS final, closing.

openly ▸ adverb in a frank, honest, or public way.

> SYNONYMS **1** *drugs were openly on sale* **publicly,** blatantly, flagrantly, overtly. **2** *he spoke openly of his problems* **frankly,** candidly, explicitly, honestly, sincerely, forthrightly, freely.
> ANTONYMS secretly, privately.

open-minded ▸ adjective willing to consider new ideas.

> SYNONYMS **unbiased,** unprejudiced, neutral, objective, disinterested, tolerant, liberal, permissive, broad-minded.
> ANTONYMS prejudiced, narrow-minded.

opera[1] ▸ noun a dramatic work that is set to music for singers and musicians.
■ **opera glasses** small binoculars used at the opera or theatre.

opera[2] plural of OPUS.

operable ▸ adjective **1** able to be used. **2** able to be treated by a surgical operation.

operate ▸ verb (operates, operating, operated) 1 function or work. 2 use or control a machine. 3 (of an organization or armed force) carry out activities. 4 be in effect. 5 carry out a surgical operation.

SYNONYMS 1 *he can operate the crane* work, run, use, handle, control, manage, drive, steer, manoeuvre. 2 *the machine ceased to operate* function, work, go, run. 3 *the way the law operates* take effect, act, apply, work, function. 4 *we operated the mines until 1979* direct, control, manage, run, be in control/charge of.

operatic ▸ adjective having to do with opera.

operation ▸ noun 1 the action of operating. 2 an act of cutting into a patient's body to remove or repair a damaged part. 3 an organized action involving a number of people. 4 a business organization.

SYNONYMS 1 *the sliders ensure smooth operation* functioning, working, running, performance, action. 2 *the operation of the factory* management, running, administration, supervision. 3 *a military operation* action, exercise, undertaking, enterprise, manoeuvre, campaign. 4 *their mining operation* business, enterprise, company, firm.

operational ▸ adjective 1 ready for use, or being used. 2 relating to the functioning of an organization.

SYNONYMS running, up and running, working, functioning, operative, in operation, in use, in action, ready for use, in working order, serviceable, functional.

□ **operationally** adverb.

operative ▸ adjective 1 working or functioning. 2 (of a word) having the most significance in a phrase. 3 relating to surgery.

SYNONYMS 1 *the steam railway is operative* running, up and running, working, functioning, operational, in operation, in use, in action, in effect. 2 *the operative word* key, significant, relevant, crucial, critical.
ANTONYMS inoperative, invalid.

▸ noun a worker.

SYNONYMS 1 *the operatives clean the machines* machinist, operator, mechanic, engineer, worker, workman, (factory) hand. 2 *a CIA operative* agent, secret/undercover agent, spy, mole, plant; N. Amer. informal spook.

operator ▸ noun 1 a person who operates equipment or a machine. 2 a person who works at the switchboard of a telephone exchange. 3 a person or company that runs a business or enterprise. 4 informal a person who acts in a particular way: *a smooth operator*.

SYNONYMS 1 *a machine operator* operative, mechanic, handler, driver, worker, engineer, machinist. 2 *a tour operator* contractor, entrepreneur, promoter.

operetta ▸ noun a short opera on a light or humorous theme.

ophthalmic ▸ adjective relating to the eye and its diseases.

ophthalmology /off-thal-**mol**-uh-ji, op-thal-**mol**-uh-ji/ ▸ noun the study and treatment of disorders and diseases of the eye.
□ **ophthalmologist** noun.

opiate /**oh**-pi-uht/ ▸ noun a drug containing opium.

opine ▸ verb (opines, opining, opined) formal say something as your opinion.

opinion ▸ noun 1 a personal view not necessarily based on fact or knowledge. 2 the views of people in general. 3 a formal statement of advice by an expert.

SYNONYMS belief, thought(s), idea, way of thinking, feeling, mind, view, point of view, assessment, estimation, judgement.

■ **opinion poll** the questioning of a small number of people in order to assess the views of people in general.

opinionated ▸ adjective having strong opinions that you are not willing to change.

opium ▸ noun an addictive drug made from the juice of a poppy.

opossum /uh-**poss**-uhm/ ▸ noun 1 an American animal with a tail which it can use for grasping. 2 Austral./NZ a possum.

opponent ▸ noun 1 a person who competes with another in a contest or argument. 2 a person who disagrees with a proposal or practice.

SYNONYMS 1 *his Republican opponent* rival, adversary, competitor, enemy, antagonist, combatant, contender, challenger. 2 *an opponent of the reforms* critic, objector, dissenter.
ANTONYMS ally, supporter.

opportune /**op**-per-tyoon/ ▸ adjective happening at a good or convenient time.

opportunist ▸ noun a person who takes advantage of opportunities without worrying about whether or not they are right to do so.
▸ adjective (also **opportunistic**) taking advantage of opportunities when they come up.
□ **opportunism** noun.

opportunity ▸ noun (plural **opportunities**) 1 a good time or set of circumstances for doing something. 2 a chance for employment or promotion.

SYNONYMS **chance**, time, occasion, moment, opening, option, window, possibility, scope, freedom; informal **shot**, break, look-in.

✔ two **p**s: op**p**ortunity.

oppose ▸ verb (opposes, opposing, opposed) **1** (also **be opposed to**) disapprove of and try to prevent or resist. **2** compete with or fight. **3** (**opposed**) (of two or more things) contrasting or conflicting. **4** (**opposing**) opposite.

SYNONYMS **1** be against, object to, be hostile to, be dead set against, disagree with, disapprove of, resist, take a stand against, put up a fight against, fight, counter, challenge; informal be anti. **2** (**opposing**) *opposing points of view* **conflicting**, contrasting, opposite, incompatible, irreconcilable, contradictory, clashing, at variance, at odds, opposed. **3** (**opposing**) *opposing sides* **rival**, opposite, enemy, competing.
ANTONYMS support.

opposite ▸ adjective **1** facing. **2** completely different. **3** being the other of a contrasted pair: *the opposite sex.*

SYNONYMS **1** *they sat opposite each other* **facing**, face to face with, across from. **2** *the opposite page* **facing**, opposing. **3** *opposite views* **conflicting**, contrasting, incompatible, irreconcilable, contradictory, at variance, at odds, differing. **4** *opposite sides* **rival**, opposing, competing, enemy.
ANTONYMS same, similar, allied.

▸ noun an opposite person or thing.

SYNONYMS *the opposite was true* **reverse**, converse, antithesis, contrary.
ANTONYMS same.

▸ adverb in an opposite position.
▸ preposition in a position opposite to.

opposition ▸ noun **1** resistance or disagreement. **2** a group of opponents. **3** (**the Opposition**) Brit. the main party in parliament that is opposed to the one in government. **4** a contrast or direct opposite.

SYNONYMS **1** *the proposal met with opposition* **resistance**, hostility, antipathy, antagonism, objection, dissent, disapproval. **2** *they beat the opposition* **opponent(s)**, opposing side, other side/team, competition, rival(s), adversary, adversaries.
ANTONYMS agreement, goodwill.

◻ **oppositional** adjective.

oppress ▸ verb **1** treat in a harsh and unfair way. **2** make someone feel distressed or anxious.

SYNONYMS **persecute**, tyrannize, crush, repress, subjugate, subdue, keep down.

◻ **oppressor** noun.

✔ double **p**, double **s**: o**pp**re**ss**.

oppression ▸ noun the act of oppressing or state of being oppressed.

SYNONYMS **persecution**, abuse, ill-treatment, tyranny, repression, suppression, subjection, subjugation, cruelty, brutality, injustice.
ANTONYMS freedom.

oppressive ▸ adjective **1** harsh and unfair. **2** causing depression or anxiety. **3** (of weather) hot and airless.

SYNONYMS **1** *an oppressive dictatorship* **harsh**, cruel, brutal, repressive, tyrannical, despotic, ruthless, merciless, pitiless. **2** *it was overcast and oppressive* **muggy**, close, heavy, hot, humid, sticky, airless, stuffy, stifling, sultry.
ANTONYMS kindly, fresh.

◻ **oppressively** adverb.

opprobrious /uh-**proh**-bri-uhss/ ▸ adjective formal very critical or scornful.

opprobrium /uh-**proh**-bri-uhm/ ▸ noun formal **1** harsh criticism or scorn. **2** public disgrace as a result of bad behaviour.

opt ▸ verb make a choice.

SYNONYMS **choose**, select, pick, decide, elect.

■ **opt out** choose not to take part.

optic ▸ adjective relating to the eye or vision.
▸ noun Brit. trademark a device fastened to the neck of an upside-down bottle for measuring out spirits.

optical ▸ adjective relating to vision, light, or optics.
■ **optical fibre** a thin glass fibre through which light can be transmitted. **optical illusion** something that deceives the eye by appearing to be different from what it really is.
◻ **optically** adverb.

optician ▸ noun a person qualified to examine people's eyes and to prescribe glasses and contact lenses.

optics ▸ noun the study of vision and the behaviour of light.

optimal ▸ adjective best or most favourable.
◻ **optimally** adverb.

optimism ▸ noun hopefulness and confidence about the future or success of something.
◻ **optimist** noun.

optimistic ▸ adjective hopeful and confident about the future.

SYNONYMS **1** *she felt optimistic about the future* **positive**, confident, hopeful,

sanguine, bullish, buoyant; informal upbeat. **2** *the forecast is optimistic* **encouraging,** promising, hopeful, reassuring, favourable.
ANTONYMS pessimistic, depressing.

□ **optimistically** adverb.

optimize (or **optimise**) ▸ verb (**optimizes, optimizing, optimized**) make the best use of.

optimum ▸ adjective most likely to lead to a favourable outcome.

SYNONYMS **best,** most favourable, most advantageous, ideal, perfect, prime, optimal.

▸ noun (plural **optima** or **optimums**) the most favourable conditions for growth or success.

option ▸ noun **1** a thing that you may choose. **2** the freedom or right to choose. **3** a right to buy or sell something at a stated price within a set time.

SYNONYMS **choice,** preference, alternative, selection, possibility.
ANTONYMS impossibility.

optional ▸ adjective available to be chosen, but not compulsory.

SYNONYMS **voluntary,** non-compulsory, elective, discretionary.
ANTONYMS compulsory.

□ **optionally** adverb.

optometry ▸ noun the occupation of measuring people's eyesight, prescribing lenses, and detecting eye disease.
□ **optometrist** noun.

opulent ▸ adjective expensive and luxurious.

SYNONYMS **luxurious,** sumptuous, palatial, lavishly appointed, rich, splendid, magnificent, grand, fancy; informal plush; Brit. informal swish; N. Amer. informal swank.
ANTONYMS spartan.

□ **opulence** noun **opulently** adverb.

opus /**oh**-puhss/ ▸ noun (plural **opuses** or **opera**) **1** a musical work or set of works. **2** a literary work.

or ▸ conjunction **1** used to link alternatives. **2** introducing a word that means the same as a preceding word or phrase, or that explains it. **3** otherwise.

oracle ▸ noun (in ancient Greece or Rome) a priest or priestess through whom the gods were believed to give prophecies about the future.

oracular /o-**rak**-yuu-ler/ ▸ adjective having to do with an oracle.

oral ▸ adjective **1** spoken rather than written. **2** relating to the mouth. **3** done or taken by the mouth.

SYNONYMS **spoken,** verbal, unwritten, vocal, uttered.
ANTONYMS written.

▸ noun a spoken exam.
□ **orally** adverb.

orange ▸ noun **1** a large round citrus fruit with a tough reddish-yellow rind. **2** a bright reddish-yellow colour.

orangeade ▸ noun Brit. a fizzy soft drink flavoured with orange.

orangery ▸ noun (plural **orangeries**) a type of large conservatory where orange trees are grown.

orang-utan (or **orang-utang**) ▸ noun a large ape with long reddish hair.

oration ▸ noun a formal speech.

orator /o-**ruh**-ter/ ▸ noun a person who is good at public speaking.

oratorio ▸ noun (plural **oratorios**) a large-scale musical work on a religious theme for orchestra and voices.

oratory[1] ▸ noun (plural **oratories**) a small chapel.

oratory[2] ▸ noun **1** formal public speaking. **2** exciting and inspiring speech.
□ **oratorical** adjective.

orb ▸ noun **1** an object shaped like a ball. **2** a golden globe with a cross on top, carried by a king or queen.

orbit ▸ noun **1** the regularly repeated course of a moon, spacecraft, etc. around a star or planet. **2** a particular area of activity or influence.

SYNONYMS **circuit,** course, path, track, trajectory, rotation, revolution.

▸ verb (**orbits, orbiting, orbited**) move in orbit round a star or planet.

SYNONYMS **circle,** go round, revolve round, travel round, circumnavigate.

orbital ▸ adjective **1** relating to an orbit or orbits. **2** Brit. (of a road) passing round the outside of a town.

orca ▸ noun a large whale with teeth and black and white markings.

orchard ▸ noun a piece of enclosed land planted with fruit trees.

orchestra ▸ noun **1** a large group of musicians with string, woodwind, brass, and percussion sections. **2** (also **orchestra pit**) the part of a theatre where the orchestra plays.

SYNONYMS **ensemble,** group; informal band, combo.

□ **orchestral** adjective.

orchestrate ▸ verb (**orchestrates, orchestrating, orchestrated**) **1** arrange music to be performed by an orchestra. **2** organize a situation to produce a particular effect.

SYNONYMS **1** *the piece was orchestrated by Mozart* **arrange,** adapt, score, set. **2** *orchestrating a protest campaign* **organize,** arrange, plan, set up, mobilize, mount, stage, mastermind, coordinate, direct.

□ **orchestration** noun.

orchid ▸ noun a plant with bright, unusually shaped flowers.

ordain ▸ verb **1** make someone a priest or minister. **2** order officially.

SYNONYMS **1** *the decision to ordain women* **confer holy orders on,** admit to the priesthood, priest, appoint, anoint, consecrate. **2** *the path ordained by God* **determine,** predestine, preordain, predetermine, prescribe, designate.

ordeal ▸ noun a prolonged painful or horrific experience.

SYNONYMS **unpleasant experience,** trial, hardship, suffering, nightmare, trauma, hell, torture, torment, agony.

order ▸ noun **1** the arrangement of people or things according to a particular sequence or method. **2** a situation in which everything is in its correct or appropriate place. **3** a situation in which the law is being obeyed and no one is behaving badly. **4** a statement telling someone to do something. **5** a request for something to be made, supplied, or served. **6** the procedure followed in a meeting, court, or religious service. **7** quality or class. **8** a social class or system. **9** a classifying category of plants and animals. **10** (**orders** or **holy orders**) the rank of an ordained Christian minister. **11** a group of people living in a religious community. **12** an institution founded by a ruler to honour people: *the Order of the Garter.*

SYNONYMS **1** *alphabetical order* **sequence,** arrangement, organization, system, series, succession. **2** *some semblance of order* **tidiness,** neatness, orderliness. **3** *the police managed to keep order* **peace,** control, law and order, calm. **4** *his sense of order* **orderliness,** organization, method, symmetry, uniformity, regularity, routine. **5** *in good order* **condition,** state, repair, shape; Brit. informal nick. **6** *I had to obey his orders* **command,** instruction, directive, direction, decree, edict, injunction. **7** *the company has won the order* **commission,** request, requisition. **8** *the lower orders of society* **class,** level, rank, grade, caste. **9** *a religious order* **community,** brotherhood, sisterhood. **10** *the Orange Order* **organization,** association, society, fellowship, fraternity, lodge, guild, league, union, club.
ANTONYMS chaos.

▸ verb (**orders, ordering, ordered**) **1** tell someone to do something. **2** request that something be made, supplied, or served. **3** organize or arrange.

SYNONYMS **1** *he ordered me to return* **instruct,** tell, command, direct, charge, require, enjoin. **2** *he ordered that their assets be confiscated* **rule,** ordain, decree, direct. **3** *order your tickets by phone* **request,** apply for, book, reserve. **4** *the messages are ordered chronologically* **organize,** arrange, sort out, lay out, group, classify, categorize, catalogue.
ANTONYMS forbid.

■ **of** (or **in**) **the order of** approximately. **out of order 1** not functioning. **2** Brit. informal unacceptable.

orderly ▸ adjective **1** arranged in a neat, organized way. **2** well behaved.

SYNONYMS **1** *an orderly desk* **neat,** tidy, well ordered, in order, trim, in apple-pie order. **2** *the orderly presentation of information* **organized,** efficient, methodical, systematic, coherent, structured, logical. **3** *the crowd was orderly* **well behaved,** law-abiding, disciplined, peaceful, peaceable, non-violent.
ANTONYMS untidy, disorganized, unruly.

▸ noun (plural **orderlies**) **1** a hospital attendant who is responsible for various non-medical tasks. **2** a soldier who carries orders or performs minor tasks.
□ **orderliness** noun.

ordinal ▸ adjective relating to order in a series.

■ **ordinal number** a number defining a thing's position in a series, such as 'first' or 'second'.

ordinance ▸ noun formal **1** an official order. **2** a religious rite.

ordinary ▸ adjective **1** normal or usual. **2** not interesting or exceptional.

SYNONYMS **1** *the ordinary course of events* **usual,** normal, standard, typical, common, customary, habitual, everyday, regular, routine, day-to-day. **2** *my life seemed very ordinary* **average,** normal, run-of-the-mill, standard, typical, middle-of-the-road, conventional, unremarkable, unexceptional; informal bog-standard; Brit. informal common or garden; N. Amer. informal ornery.
ANTONYMS unusual.

■ **out of the ordinary** unusual.
□ **ordinarily** adverb **ordinariness** noun.

ordination ▸ noun the ordaining of someone as a priest or minister.

ordnance ▸ noun **1** mounted guns. **2** US military equipment and stores.

ordure ▸ noun formal dung; excrement.

ore ▸ noun a naturally occurring material from which a metal or mineral can be extracted.

oregano /o-ri-**gah**-noh/ ▸ noun a sweet-smelling plant used in cooking.

organ ▸ noun **1** a part of the body that has a particular function, e.g. the heart or kidneys. **2** a musical keyboard instrument with rows of pipes supplied with air from bellows, or one that produces similar sounds electronically. **3** a newspaper which puts forward particular views.

SYNONYMS **newspaper**, paper, journal, periodical, magazine, voice, mouthpiece.

□ **organist** noun.

organdie ▸ noun a thin, slightly stiff cotton fabric.

organic ▸ adjective **1** having to do with living matter. **2** produced without the aid of artificial chemicals such as fertilizers. **3** (of chemical compounds) containing carbon. **4** having to do with an organ of the body. **5** (of development or change) continuous or natural.

SYNONYMS **1** *organic matter* **living**, live, animate, biological. **2** *organic vegetables* **additive-free**, chemical-free, pesticide-free, bio-, natural. **3** *a society is an organic whole* **structured**, organized, coherent, integrated, coordinated, ordered, harmonious.

□ **organically** adverb.

organism ▸ noun **1** an individual animal, plant, or life form. **2** a whole made up of parts which are dependent on each other.

SYNONYMS **1** *fish and other organisms* **living thing**, being, creature, animal, plant, life form. **2** *a complex political organism* **structure**, system, organization, entity.

organization (or **organisation**) ▸ noun **1** an organized group of people, e.g. a business. **2** the action of organizing. **3** a systematic arrangement or approach.

SYNONYMS **1** *a large organization* **institution**, body, group, company, firm, business, corporation, agency, association, society; informal outfit. **2** *the organization of conferences* **planning**, arrangement, coordination, organizing, running, management. **3** *the overall organization of the book* **structure**, arrangement, plan, pattern, order, form, format, framework, composition. **4** *his lack of organization* **efficiency**, order, orderliness, planning.

□ **organizational** adjective.

organize (or **organise**) ▸ verb (**organizes**, **organizing**, **organized**) **1** arrange in a particular order or structure. **2** make arrangements for an event or activity.

SYNONYMS **1** *organize the information* **order**, arrange, sort, assemble, marshal, put straight, group, classify, collate, categorize, catalogue. **2** *they organized a search party* **arrange**, coordinate, sort out, put together, fix up, set up, lay on, orchestrate, see to, mobilize. ANTONYMS muddle.

□ **organizer** noun.

orgasm ▸ noun an intensely pleasurable sensation that is felt as the climax of sexual activity.
▸ verb have an orgasm.
□ **orgasmic** adjective.

orgiastic /or-ji-**ass**-tik/ ▸ adjective like an orgy.

orgy ▸ noun (plural **orgies**) **1** a wild party with a lot of drinking and sexual activity. **2** an excessive amount of a particular activity.

oriel ▸ noun a projecting part of an upper storey with a window.

orient ▸ noun (**the Orient**) literary the countries of the East.
▸ verb (also **orientate**) **1** position something in relation to the points of a compass or other points. **2** (**orient yourself**) find your position in relation to your surroundings. **3** adapt something to meet particular needs.

SYNONYMS **1** *the stones are oriented from north to south* **align**, place, position, arrange. **2** *she found it hard to orient herself* **acclimatize**, familiarize, adjust, accustom, find your feet, get/find your bearings. **3** *oriented to the business community* **aim**, direct, pitch, design, intend.

oriental ▸ adjective having to do with the Far East.
▸ noun dated or offensive a person of Far Eastern descent.

orientation ▸ noun **1** the action of orienting. **2** a position in relation to something else. **3** a person's attitude or natural tendency.

SYNONYMS **1** *the orientation of the radar station* **positioning**, location, position, situation, placement, alignment. **2** *broadly Marxist in orientation* **attitude**, inclination. **3** *orientation courses* **induction**, training, initiation, briefing.

orienteering ▸ noun the sport of finding your way across country using a map and compass.

orifice ▸ noun an opening.

origami /o-ri-**gah**-mi/ ▸ noun the Japanese art of folding paper into decorative shapes.

origin ▸ noun **1** the point where something begins. **2** a person's background or ancestry.

SYNONYMS **1** *the origins of life* **beginning,** start, genesis, birth, dawning, dawn, emergence, creation, source, basis, cause, root(s). **2** *the origin of the word* **source,** derivation, root(s), provenance, etymology; N. Amer. provenience. **3** *his Scottish origins* **descent,** ancestry, parentage, pedigree, lineage, line (of descent), heritage, birth, extraction, family, roots.

original ▸ adjective **1** existing from the beginning. **2** not a copy. **3** new in an interesting or unusual way.

SYNONYMS **1** *the original inhabitants* **indigenous,** native, first, earliest, early. **2** *an original Rembrandt* **authentic,** genuine, actual, true, bona fide. **3** *a highly original film* **innovative,** creative, imaginative, inventive, new, novel, fresh, unusual, unconventional, unorthodox, groundbreaking, pioneering, unique, distinctive.

▸ noun the earliest form of something, from which copies can be made.

SYNONYMS *a copy of the original* **prototype,** source, master.

■ **original sin** (in Christian belief) the tendency to be sinful that is thought to be present in all people.
□ **originality** noun.

originally ▸ adverb from or in the beginning.

SYNONYMS **at first,** in the beginning, to begin with, initially, in the first place, at the outset.

originate ▸ verb (**originates, originating, originated**) **1** begin in a particular place or situation. **2** create.

SYNONYMS **1** *the disease originates from Africa* **arise,** have its origin, begin, start, stem, spring, emerge, emanate. **2** *Bill originated the idea* **invent,** create, devise, think up, dream up, conceive, formulate, form, develop, produce, mastermind, pioneer.

□ **origination** noun **originator** noun.

oriole /or-i-ohl/ ▸ noun a brightly coloured songbird.

ormolu /or-muh-loo/ ▸ noun a gold-coloured alloy of copper, zinc, and tin.

ornament ▸ noun **1** an object used as a decoration. **2** decorative items considered together.

SYNONYMS **1** *cheap ornaments* **knick-knack,** trinket, bauble; N. Amer. informal tchotchke, kickshaw. **2** *a dress with no ornament at all* **decoration,** adornment, embellishment, ornamentation, trimming, accessories, frills.

□ **ornamentation** noun.

ornamental ▸ adjective acting or intended as an ornament.

SYNONYMS **decorative,** fancy, ornate, ornamented, for show.

ornate ▸ adjective elaborately decorated.

SYNONYMS **elaborate,** decorated, embellished, adorned, ornamented, fancy, fussy, ostentatious, showy; informal flashy.
ANTONYMS plain.

□ **ornately** adverb.

ornithology ▸ noun the scientific study of birds.
□ **ornithological** adjective **ornithologist** noun.

orphan ▸ noun a child whose parents are dead.
▸ verb (**be orphaned**) (of a child) be made an orphan.

orphanage ▸ noun a place where orphans are looked after.

orthodontist /or-thuh-**don**-tist/ ▸ noun a dentist who treats irregularities in the position of the teeth and jaws.
□ **orthodontic** adjective **orthodontics** noun.

orthodox ▸ adjective **1** in keeping with generally accepted beliefs. **2** normal. **3** (**Orthodox**) relating to the Orthodox Church.

SYNONYMS **1** *orthodox views* **conventional,** mainstream, conformist, established, traditional, traditionalist, prevalent, popular, conservative, received. **2** *an orthodox Hindu* **conservative,** traditional, observant, devout, strict.
ANTONYMS unconventional, liberal.

■ **Orthodox Church** a branch of the Christian Church in Greece and eastern Europe.

orthodoxy ▸ noun (plural **orthodoxies**) **1** the traditional beliefs or practices of a religion. **2** a generally accepted idea.

orthography ▸ noun (plural **orthographies**) the spelling system of a language.
□ **orthographic** adjective.

orthopaedics /or-thuh-**pee**-diks/ (US spelling **orthopedics**) ▸ noun the branch of medicine concerned with bones and muscles.
□ **orthopaedic** adjective.

Oscar ▸ noun a gold statuette given annually for achievement in various categories of film-making; an Academy award.

oscillate /oss-i-layt/ ▸ verb (**oscillates, oscillating, oscillated**) **1** move back and forth in a regular rhythm. **2** waver in your opinions or emotions.
□ **oscillation** noun **oscillator** noun.

osier /**oh**-zi-er/ ▸ noun a type of willow tree with long, flexible shoots that are used for making baskets.

osmium ▸ noun a hard, dense silvery-white metallic element.

osmosis /oz-**moh**-siss/ ▸ noun **1** a process by which molecules pass through a membrane from a less concentrated solution into a more concentrated one. **2** the gradual absorbing of ideas.
□ osmotic adjective.

osprey ▸ noun (plural ospreys) a large fish-eating bird of prey.

osseous /oss-i-uhss/ ▸ adjective consisting of bone.

ossify /oss-i-fy/ ▸ verb (ossifies, ossifying, ossified) **1** turn into bone or bony tissue. **2** stop developing or progressing.
□ ossification noun.

ostensible ▸ adjective apparently true, but not necessarily so.
□ ostensibly adverb.

ostentation ▸ noun a showy display of wealth, knowledge, etc. which is intended to impress.

ostentatious ▸ adjective expensive or showy in a way that is designed to impress.
□ ostentatiously adverb.

osteoarthritis ▸ noun a disease that causes pain and stiffness in the joints of the body.

osteopathy /oss-ti-**op**-uh-thi/ ▸ noun a system of complementary medicine involving manipulation of the bones and muscles.
□ osteopath noun.

osteoporosis /oss-ti-oh-puh-**roh**-siss/ ▸ noun a medical condition in which the bones become brittle.

ostinato /oss-ti-**nah**-toh/ ▸ noun (plural ostinatos or ostinati /oss-ti-**nah**-ti/) a continually repeated musical phrase or rhythm.

ostler /oss-ler/ ▸ noun (in the past) a man employed at an inn to look after customers' horses.

ostracize (or ostracise) ▸ verb (ostracizes, ostracizing, ostracized) exclude someone from a society or group.
□ ostracism noun.

ostrich ▸ noun a large African bird with a long neck and long legs which is unable to fly.

other ▸ adjective & pronoun **1** used to refer to a person or thing that is different from one already mentioned or known. **2** additional. **3** the alternative of two. **4** those not already mentioned.

SYNONYMS **1** these homes use other fuels **alternative**, different, distinct, separate, various. **2** are there any other questions? **more**, further, additional, extra, fresh, new, added, supplementary.

■ other-worldly **1** relating to an imaginary or spiritual world. **2** not aware of the realities of life.

otherness ▸ noun the quality of being different or unusual.

otherwise ▸ adverb **1** in different circumstances. **2** in other respects. **3** in a different way. **4** alternatively.

SYNONYMS **1** hurry up, otherwise we'll be late **or (else)**, if not. **2** she's exhausted, but otherwise she's fine **in other respects,** apart from that. **3** he could not have acted otherwise **in any other way,** differently.

otiose /oh-ti-ohss/ ▸ adjective serving no practical purpose.

otter ▸ noun a fish-eating animal with a long body, living partly in water and partly on land.

ottoman ▸ noun (plural ottomans) a low padded seat without a back or arms.

oubliette /oo-bli-et/ ▸ noun a secret dungeon with access only through a trapdoor in its ceiling.

ought ▸ modal verb (3rd singular present and past ought) **1** used to indicate duty or correctness. **2** used to indicate something that is probable. **3** used to indicate a desirable or expected state. **4** used to give or ask advice.

❗ When using **ought** in a negative sentence, say, for example, he ought not to have gone rather than he didn't/hadn't ought to have gone.

oughtn't ▸ short form ought not.

Ouija board /wee-juh/ ▸ noun trademark a board marked with letters, used at a seance supposedly to receive messages from dead people.

ounce ▸ noun **1** a unit of weight of one sixteenth of a pound (approximately 28 grams). **2** a very small amount.

our ▸ possessive determiner **1** belonging to or associated with the speaker and one or more other people. **2** belonging to or associated with people in general.

ours ▸ possessive pronoun used to refer to something belonging to or associated with the speaker and one or more other people.

✔ no apostrophe: **ours**.

ourselves ▸ pronoun **1** used as the object of a verb or preposition when this is the same as the subject of the clause and the subject is the speaker and one or more other people. **2** we or us personally.

oust ▸ verb force someone out from a job or position.

SYNONYMS **expel**, drive out, force out, remove from office/power, eject, get rid of, depose, topple, unseat, overthrow, bring down, overturn, dismiss, dislodge.

out ▸ adverb **1** away from a place. **2** away from your home or office. **3** outdoors. **4** so as to be revealed, heard, or known. **5** to an end. **6** not possible or worth considering. **7** (of the tide) falling or at its lowest level. **8** (of the ball in tennis, squash, etc.) not in the playing area. **9** (in cricket, baseball, etc.) no longer batting.

> SYNONYMS **1** *she's out at the moment* **not here,** not at home, not in, away, gone away, elsewhere. **2** *the secret was out* **revealed,** (out) in the open, common/public knowledge. **3** *the roses are out* **in flower,** flowering, in (full) bloom, blooming, in blossom, blossoming. **4** *the book should be out soon* **available,** obtainable, to be had, in the shops, published, in print. **5** *grunge is out* **unfashionable,** out of fashion, dated, outdated, passé; informal old hat. **6** *smoking is out* **forbidden,** not permitted, not allowed, unacceptable; informal not on. **7** *he was slightly out in his calculations* **mistaken,** inaccurate, incorrect, wrong, in error.
> ANTONYMS in.

▶ verb informal reveal that someone is homosexual.

> SYNONYMS *it was not our intention to out him* **expose,** unmask.

■ **out of 1** from. **2** not having a supply of something. **out of date 1** old-fashioned. **2** no longer valid.

❗ You should say **out of** rather than just **out** in sentences such as *he threw it out of the window.*

outback ▶ noun (**the outback**) the part of Australia that is remote and has few inhabitants.

outbid ▶ verb (**outbids, outbidding, outbid**) bid more than.

outboard ▶ adjective & adverb on, towards, or near the outside of a ship or aircraft.
■ **outboard motor** a motor attached to the outside of a boat.

outbreak ▶ noun a sudden occurrence of war, disease, etc.

> SYNONYMS **1** *outbreaks of violence* **eruption,** flare-up, upsurge, rash, wave, spate, burst, flurry. **2** *the outbreak of war* **start,** beginning, commencement, onset.

outbuilding ▶ noun a smaller building in the grounds of a main building.

outburst ▶ noun **1** a sudden release of strong emotion. **2** a sudden or violent occurrence of something.

> SYNONYMS **eruption,** explosion, flare-up, storm, outpouring, surge, fit.

outcast ▶ noun a person who is rejected by their social group.

outclass ▶ verb be far better than.

outcome ▶ noun a result or effect.

> SYNONYMS **result,** end result, net result, consequence, upshot, conclusion, end product; informal pay-off.

outcrop ▶ noun a part of a rock formation that is visible on the surface.

outcry ▶ noun (plural **outcries**) a strong expression of public disapproval.

> SYNONYMS **protest,** protestation, complaints, objections, furore, fuss, uproar, opposition, dissent; informal hullabaloo, ructions, stink.

outdated ▶ adjective no longer used or fashionable.

> SYNONYMS **old-fashioned,** out of date, outmoded, out of fashion, unfashionable, dated, passé, old, behind the times; informal out, old hat, square; N. Amer. informal horse-and-buggy.
> ANTONYMS modern.

outdistance ▶ verb (**outdistances, outdistancing, outdistanced**) leave a competitor or pursuer far behind.

outdo ▶ verb (**outdoes, outdoing, outdid;** past participle **outdone**) do better than someone else.

outdoor ▶ adjective done, situated, or used outdoors.

> SYNONYMS **open-air,** out-of-doors, outside, al fresco.
> ANTONYMS indoor.

outdoors ▶ adverb in or into the open air.
▶ noun any area outside buildings or shelter.

outer ▶ adjective **1** outside. **2** further from the centre or the inside.

> SYNONYMS **1** *the outer layer* **outside,** outermost, outward, exterior, external, surface. **2** *the outer islands* **outlying,** distant, remote, faraway, far-flung, furthest.
> ANTONYMS inner.

■ **outer space** the universe beyond the earth's atmosphere.

outermost ▶ adjective furthest from the centre.

outface ▶ verb (**outfaces, outfacing, outfaced**) unsettle or defeat someone by confronting them in a brave or confident way.

outfall ▶ noun the place where a river or drain empties into the sea, a river, or a lake.

outfit ▶ noun **1** a set of clothes worn together. **2** informal a group of people working together as a business, team, etc.

> SYNONYMS **1** *a new outfit* **costume,** suit, uniform, ensemble, clothes, clothing, dress, garb; informal get-up; Brit. informal kit. **2** *a local manufacturing outfit* **organization,** enterprise, company,

firm, business, group, body, team; informal set-up.

▶ verb (**outfits, outfitting, outfitted**) provide someone with an outfit of clothes.
□ **outfitter** noun.

outflank ▶ verb **1** surround in order to attack. **2** defeat.

outgoing ▶ adjective **1** friendly and confident. **2** leaving an office or position. **3** going out or away from a place.

SYNONYMS **1** *he's very outgoing* **extrovert**, uninhibited, unreserved, demonstrative, affectionate, warm, sociable, convivial, lively, gregarious. **2** *the outgoing president* **departing**, retiring, leaving.
ANTONYMS introverted, incoming.

▶ plural noun (**outgoings**) Brit. money that you spend regularly.

SYNONYMS **expenses**, expenditure, spending, outlay, payments, costs, overheads.

outgrow ▶ verb (**outgrows, outgrowing, outgrew**; past participle **outgrown**) **1** grow too big for. **2** stop doing something as you grow older.

outhouse ▶ noun a smaller building attached or close to a house.

outing ▶ noun a short trip made for pleasure.

SYNONYMS **trip**, excursion, jaunt, expedition, day out, tour, drive, ride, run; informal spin.

outlandish ▶ adjective bizarre or unfamiliar.

outlast ▶ verb last longer than.

outlaw ▶ noun a person who has broken the law and remains at large.

SYNONYMS *a band of outlaws* **fugitive**, wanted criminal, bandit, robber.

▶ verb make something illegal.

SYNONYMS *fox-hunting has been outlawed* **ban**, bar, prohibit, forbid, make illegal, proscribe.
ANTONYMS permit.

outlay ▶ noun an amount of money spent.

outlet ▶ noun **1** a pipe or hole through which water or gas may escape. **2** a point from which goods are sold or distributed. **3** a way of expressing your talents, energy, or emotions.

SYNONYMS **1** *a central-heating outlet* **vent**, way out, outfall, opening, channel, conduit, duct. **2** *an outlet for farm produce* **market**, retail outlet, shop, store. **3** *an outlet for their energies* **means of expression**, means of release, vent, avenue, channel.

outline ▶ noun **1** a sketch or diagram showing the shape of an object. **2** the outer edges of an object. **3** a general description of something, with no detail.

SYNONYMS **1** *the outline of the building* **silhouette**, profile, shape, contours, form, lines. **2** *an outline of our proposal* **rough idea**, thumbnail sketch, rundown, summary, synopsis, résumé, precis, main points, gist, bare bones.

▶ verb (**outlines, outlining, outlined**) **1** draw the outer edge or shape of. **2** give a summary of.

SYNONYMS *she outlined the plan briefly* **rough out**, sketch out, draft, give a rough idea of, summarize, precis.

outlive ▶ verb live or last longer than.

outlook ▶ noun **1** a person's attitude to life. **2** a view. **3** what is likely to happen in the future.

SYNONYMS **1** *a positive outlook* **point of view**, viewpoint, way of thinking, perspective, attitude, standpoint, stance, frame of mind. **2** *a lovely open outlook* **view**, vista, prospect, panorama. **3** *the outlook for the economy* **prospects**, future, expectations, prognosis.

outlying ▶ adjective situated far from a centre.

outmanoeuvre ▶ verb (**outmanoeuvres, outmanoeuvring, outmanoeuvred**) gain an advantage over an opponent by using skill and cunning.

outmoded ▶ adjective old-fashioned.

outnumber ▶ verb (**outnumbers, outnumbering, outnumbered**) be more numerous than.

outpace ▶ verb (**outpaces, outpacing, outpaced**) go faster than.

outpatient ▶ noun a patient attending a hospital for treatment without staying overnight.

outperform ▶ verb perform better than.

outplay ▶ verb play better than.

outpost ▶ noun **1** a small military camp at a distance from the main army. **2** a remote part of a country or empire.

outpouring ▶ noun **1** something that streams out rapidly. **2** an outburst of strong emotion.

output ▶ noun **1** the amount of something produced. **2** the process of producing something. **3** the power, energy, etc. supplied by a device or system. **4** a place where power, information, etc. leaves a system.

SYNONYMS **production**, yield, product, productivity, work, result, processed data.

outrage ▶ noun **1** a very strong reaction of anger or annoyance. **2** a very immoral or shocking act.

SYNONYMS **1** *public outrage* **indignation,** fury, anger, rage, wrath. **2** *it is an outrage* **scandal,** offence, insult, affront, disgrace, atrocity.

▶ verb (**outrages, outraging, outraged**) make someone feel outrage.

SYNONYMS *his remarks outraged everyone* **enrage,** infuriate, incense, anger, scandalize, offend, affront, shock.

outrageous ▶ adjective **1** shockingly bad or unacceptable. **2** very unusual and slightly shocking.

SYNONYMS **1** *outrageous behaviour* **shocking,** disgraceful, scandalous, atrocious, appalling, dreadful. **2** *an outrageous claim* **exaggerated,** improbable, preposterous, ridiculous, unwarranted. **3** *outrageous clothes* **eye-catching,** flamboyant, showy, gaudy, ostentatious; informal **flashy.**

□ **outrageously** adverb.

outran past of **OUTRUN.**

outrank ▶ verb have a higher rank than.

outré /oo-tray/ ▶ adjective unusual and rather shocking.

outreach ▶ noun an organization's involvement with the community.

outrider ▶ noun a person in a vehicle or on horseback who escorts another vehicle.

outrigger ▶ noun a structure fixed to a boat's side to help keep it stable.

outright ▶ adverb **1** altogether. **2** openly. **3** immediately.

SYNONYMS **1** *he rejected the proposal outright* **completely,** entirely, wholly, totally, categorically, absolutely, utterly, flatly, unreservedly, out of hand. **2** *I told her outright* **explicitly,** directly, frankly, candidly, bluntly, plainly, to someone's face; Brit. informal **straight up. 3** *they were killed outright* **instantly,** instantaneously, immediately, at once, straight away, then and there, on the spot.

▶ adjective **1** open and direct. **2** complete.

SYNONYMS **1** *an outright lie* **complete,** absolute, out-and-out, downright, utter, sheer, categorical. **2** *the outright winner* **definite,** unequivocal, clear, unmistakable, overall.

outrun ▶ verb (**outruns, outrunning, outran;** past participle **outrun**) run or travel faster or further than.

outsell ▶ verb (**outsells, outselling, outsold**) be sold in greater quantities than.

outset ▶ noun the beginning.

SYNONYMS **start,** starting point, beginning; informal **the word go.** ANTONYMS end.

outshine ▶ verb (**outshines, outshining, outshone**) **1** shine more brightly than. **2** be much better than.

outside ▶ noun **1** the external side or surface of something. **2** the external appearance of someone or something. **3** the side of a curve where the edge is longer.

SYNONYMS *the outside of the building* **exterior,** outer/external surface, case, skin, shell, covering, facade.

▶ adjective **1** situated on or near the outside. **2** not belonging to a particular group.

SYNONYMS **1** *outside lights* **exterior,** external, outer, outdoor, out-of-doors. **2** *outside contractors* **independent,** freelance, consultant, external.

▶ preposition & adverb **1** situated or moving beyond the boundaries of. **2** beyond the limits of. **3** not being a member of.

SYNONYMS *shall we eat outside?* **outdoors,** out of doors, alfresco. ANTONYMS inside.

outsider ▶ noun **1** a person who does not belong to a particular group. **2** a competitor thought to have little chance of success.

SYNONYMS **stranger,** visitor, non-member, foreigner, alien, interloper, immigrant, incomer, newcomer.

outsize (or **outsized**) ▶ adjective very large.

outskirts ▶ plural noun the outer parts of a town or city.

SYNONYMS **edges,** fringes, suburbs, suburbia, periphery.

outsmart ▶ verb defeat someone by being cleverer than them.

outsold past and past participle of **OUTSELL.**

outspoken ▶ adjective stating your opinions in an open and direct way.

SYNONYMS **forthright,** direct, candid, frank, straightforward, open, straight from the shoulder, plain-spoken, blunt.

outstanding ▶ adjective **1** exceptionally good. **2** clearly noticeable. **3** not yet dealt with or paid.

SYNONYMS **1** *an outstanding painter* **excellent,** marvellous, magnificent, superb, fine, wonderful, superlative, exceptional; informal **great, terrific, tremendous, super;** Brit. informal **brilliant;** N. Amer. informal **neat. 2** *how much work is still outstanding?* **to be done,** undone, unfinished, incomplete, remaining, pending. **3** *outstanding debts* **unpaid,** unsettled, owing, owed, to be paid, payable, due, overdue; N. Amer. **delinquent.**

□ **outstandingly** adverb.

outstay ▶ verb stay for longer than the expected or allowed time.

outstrip ▸ verb (outstrips, outstripping, outstripped) 1 move faster than. 2 surpass.

outvote ▸ verb (outvotes, outvoting, outvoted) defeat by gaining more votes.

outward ▸ adjective & adverb 1 on or from the outside. 2 out or away from a place.

> SYNONYMS **external,** surface, superficial, seeming, apparent, ostensible.
> ANTONYMS inward.

□ **outwardly** adverb **outwards** adverb.

outweigh ▸ verb be more significant than.

> SYNONYMS **be greater than,** exceed, be superior to, prevail over, override, supersede, offset, cancel out, more than make up for, outbalance, compensate for.

outwit ▸ verb (outwits, outwitting, outwitted) deceive someone through being cleverer than them.

ouzo /oo-zoh/ ▸ noun an aniseed-flavoured Greek spirit.

ova plural of **ovum**.

oval ▸ adjective having a rounded and slightly elongated outline.
▸ noun an oval object or design.

ovary ▸ noun (plural **ovaries**) 1 a female reproductive organ in which eggs are produced. 2 the base of the reproductive organ of a flower.
□ **ovarian** adjective.

ovation ▸ noun a long, enthusiastic round of applause.

> SYNONYMS **applause,** round of applause, cheers, bravos, acclaim, standing ovation; informal (big) hand.

oven ▸ noun 1 an enclosed compartment in which food is cooked or heated. 2 a small furnace or kiln.

ovenproof ▸ adjective suitable for use in an oven.

over ▸ preposition 1 extending upwards from or above. 2 above so as to cover or protect. 3 expressing movement across. 4 expressing length of time. 5 beyond and falling or hanging from. 6 higher or more than. 7 expressing authority or control. 8 on the subject of.

> SYNONYMS **1** there was cloud over the hills **above,** on top of, higher (up) than, atop, covering. **2** he walked over the grass **across,** on. **3** over 2,000 people **more than,** above, in excess of, upwards of. **4** he has three people over him **superior to,** above, higher up than, in charge of, responsible for. **5** an argument over money **about,** on the subject of, concerning, with reference to, regarding, relating to, in connection with.
> ANTONYMS under.

▸ adverb 1 expressing movement across an area. 2 beyond and falling or hanging

from a point. 3 in or to the place indicated. 4 expressing action and result. 5 finished. 6 expressing repetition of a process.

> SYNONYMS **1** a plane flew over **overhead,** past, by. **2** the relationship is over **at an end,** finished, ended, no more, a thing of the past.

▸ noun Cricket a sequence of six balls bowled by a bowler from one end of the pitch.

overact ▸ verb act a role in an exaggerated way.

overactive ▸ adjective more active than is normal or desirable.

overall ▸ adjective including everything.

> SYNONYMS the overall cost **total,** all-inclusive, gross, final, inclusive, complete, entire.

▸ adverb taken as a whole.

> SYNONYMS overall, things are better **generally (speaking),** in general, altogether, all in all, on balance, on average, for the most part, in the main, on the whole, by and large.

▸ noun (also **overalls**) Brit. a loose-fitting garment worn over ordinary clothes to protect them.

overarching ▸ adjective covering or dealing with everything.

overarm ▸ adjective & adverb done with the hand brought forward and down from above shoulder level.

overawe ▸ verb (overawes, overawing, overawed) impress someone so much that they are nervous or silent.

overbalance ▸ verb (overbalances, overbalancing, overbalanced) fall due to loss of balance.

overbearing ▸ adjective trying to control other people; domineering.

overblown ▸ adjective made to seem more important or impressive than it really is.

overboard ▸ adverb from a ship into the water.
■ **go overboard** be very enthusiastic.

overcast ▸ adjective cloudy.

overcharge ▸ verb (overcharges, overcharging, overcharged) charge too high a price.

overcoat ▸ noun 1 a long, warm coat. 2 a top layer of paint or varnish.

overcome ▸ verb (overcomes, overcoming, overcome; past participle **overcome**) 1 succeed in dealing with a problem. 2 defeat; overpower.

> SYNONYMS **1** he overcame his pain **conquer,** defeat, beat, prevail over, control, get/bring under control, master, get the better of; informal lick, best. **2** she was overcome with excitement

overwhelm, move, affect, render speechless.

overcompensate ▸ verb (**overcompensates, overcompensating, overcompensated**) do too much when trying to correct a problem.

overcrowded ▸ adjective filled beyond what is usual or comfortable.

overdo ▸ verb (**overdoes, overdoing, overdid;** past participle **overdone**) **1** do something excessively or in an exaggerated way. **2** (**overdone**) cooked too much.

overdose ▸ noun an excessive and dangerous dose of a drug.
▸ verb (**overdoses, overdosing, overdosed**) take an overdose.

overdraft ▸ noun an arrangement with a bank that lets you take out more money than your account holds.

overdrawn ▸ adjective having taken out more money than there is in your bank account.

overdressed ▸ adjective dressed too elaborately or formally.

overdrive ▸ noun **1** a mechanism in a motor vehicle providing an extra gear above the usual top gear. **2** a state of high activity.

overdue ▸ adjective not having arrived, happened, or been done at the expected or required time.

SYNONYMS **1** *the ship is overdue* **late,** behind schedule, behind time, delayed. **2** *overdue payments* **unpaid,** unsettled, owing, owed, payable, due, outstanding, undischarged; N. Amer. delinquent. ANTONYMS early, punctual.

overestimate ▸ verb (**overestimates, overestimating, overestimated**) estimate that something is larger or better than it really is.
▸ noun an estimate which is too high.

overexpose ▸ verb (**overexposes, overexposing, overexposed**) **1** subject photographic film to too much light. **2** (**overexposed**) seen too much on television, in the newspapers, etc.

overflow ▸ verb **1** flow over the edge of a container. **2** be too full or crowded. **3** (**overflow with**) be very full of an emotion.

SYNONYMS *chemicals overflowed from the tank* **spill over,** flow over, brim over, well over, flood.

▸ noun **1** the number of people or things that do not fit into a particular space. **2** an outlet for excess water.

SYNONYMS *offices to accommodate the overflow* **surplus,** excess, additional people/things, extra, remainder, overspill.

overground ▸ adverb & adjective on or above the ground.

overgrown ▸ adjective **1** covered with plants that have grown wild. **2** having grown too large.

overhang ▸ verb (**overhangs, overhanging, overhung**) project outwards over.
▸ noun an overhanging part.

overhaul ▸ verb **1** examine and repair or improve something. **2** Brit. overtake.

SYNONYMS **service,** maintain, repair, mend, fix up, rebuild, renovate, recondition, refit, refurbish.

▸ noun an act of overhauling something.

overhead ▸ adverb & adjective above your head.

SYNONYMS **1** *the sky overhead* **above,** high up, in the sky, on high, above your head. **2** *overhead lines* **aerial,** elevated, raised, suspended, overhanging. ANTONYMS below, surface, underground.

▸ plural noun (**overheads**) regular expenses involved in running a business or organization.

SYNONYMS **running costs,** operating costs, fixed costs, expenses.

overhear ▸ verb (**overhears, overhearing, overheard**) hear something accidentally.

overheat ▸ verb make or become too hot.

overindulge ▸ verb (**overindulges, overindulging, overindulged**) **1** have too much of something enjoyable. **2** give in to the wishes of someone too easily.
□ **overindulgence** noun.

overjoyed ▸ adjective very happy.

overkill ▸ noun too much of something.

overland ▸ adjective & adverb by land.

overlap ▸ verb (**overlaps, overlapping, overlapped**) **1** extend over something so as to cover it partially. **2** (of two events) happen at the same time for part of their duration.
▸ noun an overlapping part or amount.

overlay ▸ verb (**overlays, overlaying, overlaid**) **1** coat the surface of. **2** add a quality, feeling, etc. to.
▸ noun a covering.

overleaf ▸ adverb on the other side of the page.

overload ▸ verb **1** load too heavily. **2** put too great a demand on.
▸ noun too much of something.

overlook ▸ verb **1** fail to notice. **2** ignore or disregard. **3** have a view of something from above.

SYNONYMS **1** *he overlooked the mistake* **fail to notice,** fail to spot, miss. **2** *his work has been overlooked* **disregard,** neglect, ignore, pass over, forget. **3** *she* *was willing to overlook his faults* **ignore,** disregard, take no notice of, make allowances for, turn a blind eye to, excuse, pardon, forgive. **4** *the lounge overlooks the garden* **have a view of,** look over/across, look on to, look out on/over.

overlord ▶ noun a ruler.

overly ▶ adverb excessively.

overmuch ▶ adverb & pronoun too much.

overnight ▶ adverb & adjective **1** during or for a night. **2** happening suddenly or very quickly.

overpass ▶ noun a bridge by which a road or railway line passes over another.

overplay ▶ verb give too much importance to.

overpower ▶ verb (**overpowers, overpowering, overpowered**) **1** defeat through having greater strength. **2** overwhelm.

> SYNONYMS **1 overwhelm,** get the better of, overthrow, subdue, suppress, subjugate, repress, bring someone to their knees. **2** (**overpowering**) *overpowering grief* **overwhelming,** oppressive, unbearable, unendurable, intolerable, shattering. **3** (**overpowering**) *an overpowering smell* **stifling,** suffocating, strong, pungent, powerful, nauseating, offensive, acrid, fetid.

overpriced ▶ adjective too expensive.

overqualified ▶ adjective too highly qualified.

overrate ▶ verb (often **overrated**) have too high an opinion of someone or something.

> SYNONYMS **overestimate,** overvalue, think too much of.
> ANTONYMS underestimate.

overreach ▶ verb (**overreach yourself**) fail through being too ambitious or trying too hard.

overreact ▶ verb react more strongly than is justified.
□ **overreaction** noun.

override ▶ verb (**overrides, overriding, override;** past participle **overridden**) **1** use your authority to reject someone else's decision or order. **2** be more important than. **3** interrupt the action of an automatic device.

> SYNONYMS **1** *the court overrode the decision* **disallow,** overrule, countermand, veto, quash, overturn, overthrow, cancel, reverse, rescind, revoke, repeal. **2** *our interests should override all others* **outweigh,** supersede, take precedence over, take priority over, be more important than, cancel out, outbalance.

▶ noun a device on a machine for overriding

an automatic process.

overrule ▶ verb (**overrules, overruling, overruled**) use your authority to reject someone else's decision or order.

> SYNONYMS **countermand,** cancel, reverse, rescind, repeal, revoke, disallow, override, veto, quash, overturn, overthrow.

overrun ▶ verb (**overruns, overrunning, overran;** past participle **overrun**) **1** occupy a place in large numbers. **2** use more time or money than expected.

> SYNONYMS **invade,** storm, occupy, swarm into, surge into, inundate, overwhelm.

overseas ▶ adverb & adjective in or to a foreign country.

oversee ▶ verb (**oversees, overseeing, oversaw;** past participle **overseen**) supervise.
□ **overseer** noun.

oversexed ▶ adjective having unusually strong sexual desires.

overshadow ▶ verb **1** appear more important or successful than. **2** make something sad or less enjoyable. **3** tower above and cast a shadow over.

> SYNONYMS **outshine,** eclipse, surpass, exceed, outclass, outstrip, outdo, upstage; informal be head and shoulders above.

overshoot ▶ verb (**overshoots, overshooting, overshot**) go past the place you intended to stop at.

oversight ▶ noun an unintentional failure to notice or do something.

oversimplify ▶ verb (**oversimplifies, oversimplifying, oversimplified**) simplify something so much that an inaccurate impression of it is given.

oversized (or **oversize**) ▶ adjective bigger than the usual size.

oversleep ▶ verb (**oversleeps, oversleeping, overslept**) sleep later than you intended to.

overspend ▶ verb (**overspends, overspending, overspent**) spend too much.

overspill ▶ noun Brit. people who move from an overcrowded area to live elsewhere.

overstate ▶ verb (**overstates, overstating, overstated**) state too strongly; exaggerate.
□ **overstatement** noun.

overstay ▶ verb stay longer than is allowed by.

overstep ▶ verb (**oversteps, overstepping, overstepped**) go beyond a limit.

overstretch ▶ verb make too many demands on a resource.

oversubscribed ▶ adjective offering too few places to satisfy demand.

overt ▶ adjective done or shown openly.

> SYNONYMS **undisguised,** unconcealed, plain (to see), clear, conspicuous,

obvious, noticeable, manifest, patent, open, blatant.
ANTONYMS covert.

□ **overtly** adverb.

overtake ▸ verb (**overtakes, overtaking, overtook**; past participle **overtaken**) **1** pass while travelling in the same direction. **2** suddenly affect.

SYNONYMS **1** *a green car overtook us* **pass**, go past, pull ahead of. **2** *Goa overtook Ibiza as the favourite destination* **outstrip**, surpass, overshadow, eclipse, outshine, outclass, exceed, top, cap. **3** *the calamity which overtook us* **befall**, happen to, come upon, hit, strike, overwhelm, overcome.

overthrow ▸ verb (**overthrows, overthrowing, overthrew**; past participle **overthrown**) remove from power by force.

SYNONYMS *the regime was overthrown* **oust**, remove, bring down, topple, depose, displace, unseat, defeat, conquer.

▸ noun a removal from power.

SYNONYMS *the overthrow of capitalism* **ousting**, removal, downfall, toppling, supplanting, displacement, unseating, defeat, fall, collapse, demise.

overtime ▸ noun time worked in addition to normal working hours.

overtone ▸ noun a subtle or secondary quality or implication.

overture ▸ noun **1** an orchestral piece at the beginning of a musical work. **2** an orchestral composition in one movement. **3** (**overtures**) approaches made with the aim of opening negotiations or establishing a relationship.

SYNONYMS **1** *the overture to a long debate* **preliminary**, prelude, introduction, lead-in, precursor, start, beginning. **2** *peace overtures* **opening move**, approach, advances, feeler, signal.

overturn ▸ verb **1** turn over and come to rest upside down. **2** abolish or reverse a decision, system, etc.

SYNONYMS **1** *the boat overturned* **capsize**, turn turtle, keel over, tip over, topple over. **2** *I overturned the stool* **upset**, tip over, topple over, turn over, knock over, upend. **3** *the Senate may overturn this ruling* **cancel**, reverse, rescind, repeal, revoke, countermand, disallow, override, overrule, veto, quash, overthrow.

overuse ▸ verb (**overuses, overusing, overused**) use too much.
▸ noun excessive use.

overview ▸ noun a general review or summary.

overweening ▸ adjective showing too much confidence or pride.

overweight ▸ adjective heavier or fatter than is usual or desirable.

SYNONYMS **fat**, obese, stout, plump, portly, chubby, pot-bellied, flabby; informal tubby; Brit. informal podgy.
ANTONYMS underweight.

overwhelm ▸ verb **1** have a strong emotional effect on. **2** overpower. **3** bury or drown beneath a huge mass.

SYNONYMS **1** *she was overwhelmed by a sense of tragedy* **overcome**, move, stir, affect, touch, strike, dumbfound, shake, leave speechless; informal bowl over, knock sideways, floor; Brit. informal knock/hit for six. **2** *Spain overwhelmed Russia in the hockey* **defeat heavily**, trounce, rout, beat hollow, conquer, be victorious over, crush; informal thrash, lick, wipe the floor with.

overwhelming ▸ adjective **1** very great in amount. **2** (especially of an emotion) very strong.

SYNONYMS **1** *an overwhelming number of people* **very large**, enormous, immense, inordinate, massive, huge. **2** *an overwhelming desire to laugh* **very strong**, powerful, uncontrollable, irrepressible, irresistible, overpowering, compelling.

overwork ▸ verb **1** work too hard. **2** use a word or idea too much.
▸ noun too much work.

overwrite ▸ verb (**overwrites, overwriting, overwrote**; past participle **overwritten**) destroy computer data by entering new data in its place.

overwrought ▸ adjective **1** in a state of nervous excitement or anxiety. **2** too elaborate or complicated.

ovoid /**oh**-voyd/ ▸ adjective **1** egg-shaped. **2** oval.

ovulate /ov-yuu-layt/ ▸ verb (**ovulates, ovulating, ovulated**) (of a woman or female animal) release ova (reproductive cells) from the ovary.
□ **ovulation** noun.

ovule /ov-yool/ ▸ noun the part of the ovary of plants that after fertilization becomes the seed.

ovum /**oh**-vuhm/ ▸ noun (plural **ova**) a female reproductive cell, which can develop into an embryo if fertilized by a male cell.

owe ▸ verb (**owes, owing, owed**) **1** be required to give money or goods to someone in return for something received. **2** be obliged to show someone gratitude, respect, etc. **3** (**owe something to**) have something because of.

SYNONYMS **be in debt (to),** be indebted (to), be in arrears (to), be under an obligation (to).

owing ▸ adjective yet to be paid or supplied.

SYNONYMS *the rent was owing* **unpaid,** to be paid, payable, due, overdue, undischarged, owed, outstanding, in arrears; N. Amer. delinquent.
ANTONYMS paid.

■ **owing to** because of.

owl ▸ noun a bird of prey with large eyes, which is active at night.

owlish ▸ adjective resembling an owl.

own ▸ adjective & pronoun belonging to or done by the person specified.

SYNONYMS *he has his own reasons* **personal,** individual, particular, private, personalized, unique.

▸ verb **1** have something as your property. **2** formal admit that something is the case. **3** (**own up**) admit that you have done something wrong or embarrassing.

SYNONYMS *I own this house* **possess,** keep, hold, be the owner of, have to your name.

■ **come into your own** become fully effective. **hold your own** remain in a strong position.

owner ▸ noun a person who owns something.

SYNONYMS **possessor,** holder, proprietor, homeowner, freeholder, landlord, landlady.

ownership ▸ noun the state of possessing or the right to possess something.

SYNONYMS **possession,** freehold, proprietorship, proprietary rights, title.

ox ▸ noun (plural **oxen**) **1** a cow or bull. **2** a castrated bull.

Oxbridge ▸ noun Oxford and Cambridge universities classed together.

oxidation ▸ noun the process of oxidizing, or the result of being oxidized.

oxide ▸ noun a compound of oxygen with another substance.

oxidize (or **oxidise**) ▸ verb (**oxidizes, oxidizing, oxidized**) cause to combine with oxygen.
□ **oxidization** noun.

oxtail ▸ noun the tail of an ox, used in making soup.

oxygen ▸ noun a colourless, odourless gas that forms about 20 per cent of the earth's atmosphere.

oxygenate ▸ verb (**oxygenates, oxygenating, oxygenated**) supply or treat with oxygen.

oxymoron /ok-si-**mor**-on/ ▸ noun a figure of speech in which apparently contradictory terms appear together (e.g. *bittersweet*).

oyster ▸ noun **1** a shellfish with two hinged shells, some kinds of which are edible. **2** a shade of greyish white.

oystercatcher ▸ noun a wading bird with black or black-and-white feathers.

oz ▸ abbreviation ounces.

ozone ▸ noun **1** a strong-smelling, poisonous form of oxygen. **2** informal fresh air blowing from the sea.
■ **ozone layer** a layer in the stratosphere containing a lot of ozone, which protects the earth from the sun's ultraviolet radiation.

o

Pp

P (or **p**) ▸ noun (plural **Ps** or **P's**) the sixteenth letter of the alphabet.
▸ abbreviation **1** page. **2** Brit. penny or pence.

PA ▸ abbreviation **1** Brit. personal assistant.
2 public address.

p.a. ▸ abbreviation per year.
ORIGIN short for Latin *per annum*.

pace ▸ noun **1** a single step taken when walking or running. **2** the rate at which something happens or develops.

> SYNONYMS **1** *ten paces* **step. 2** *a slow, steady pace* **gait,** stride, walk, march. **3** *a furious pace* **speed,** rate, velocity, tempo.

▸ verb (**paces, pacing, paced**) **1** walk to and fro in a small area. **2** measure a distance by counting the number of steps taken to cover it. **3** (**pace yourself**) do something at a controlled and steady rate.

> SYNONYMS *she paced up and down* **walk,** stride, march, pound.

■ **keep pace with** progress at the same speed as. **put someone through their paces** make someone demonstrate their abilities.

pacemaker ▸ noun a device for stimulating and regulating the heart muscle.

pachyderm /pak-i-derm/ ▸ noun an elephant or other very large mammal with thick skin.

pacific ▸ adjective **1** formal peaceful.
2 (**Pacific**) having to do with the Pacific Ocean.

pacifism ▸ noun the belief that disputes should be settled by peaceful means and that violence should never be used.
□ **pacifist** noun & adjective.

pacify ▸ verb (**pacifies, pacifying, pacified**)
1 make someone less angry or upset.
2 make a country peaceful.
□ **pacification** noun.

pack ▸ noun **1** a cardboard or paper container and the items inside it. **2** Brit. a set of playing cards. **3** a group of animals that live and hunt together. **4** chiefly disapproving a group of similar things or people. **5** (**the pack**) the main group of competitors following the leader in a race. **6** Rugby a team's forwards. **7** (**Pack**) an organized group of Cub Scouts or Brownies. **8** a

rucksack. **9** an absorbent pad used for treating an injury.

> SYNONYMS **1** *a pack of cigarettes* **packet,** container, package, box, carton, parcel.
> **2** *a pack of wolves* **group,** herd, troop.
> **3** *a pack of hooligans* **crowd,** mob, group, band, party, set, gang, rabble, horde, throng, huddle, mass, assembly, gathering, host; informal crew, bunch.

▸ verb **1** fill a bag with items needed for travel. **2** put something in a container for transport or storage. **3** cram a large number of things into. **4** (**packed**) crowded.
5 cover, surround, or fill.

> SYNONYMS **1** *she helped pack the car* **fill (up),** put things in, load. **2** *they packed their belongings* **stow,** put away, store, box up. **3** *the glasses were packed in straw* **wrap (up),** package, parcel, swathe, swaddle, encase, envelop, bundle.
> **4** *shoppers packed the store* **throng,** crowd, fill, cram, jam, squash into, squeeze into.

■ **pack ice** a mass of ice floating in the sea. **pack something in** informal give up an activity or job. **pack someone off** informal send someone somewhere without much notice. **pack up** Brit. informal (of a machine) break down. **send someone packing** informal dismiss someone abruptly.

package ▸ noun **1** an object or group of objects wrapped in paper or packed in a box. **2** N. Amer. a packet. **3** a set of proposals or terms as a whole.

> SYNONYMS **1** *the delivery of a package* **parcel,** packet, box. **2** *a package of services* **collection,** bundle, combination, range, complement, raft, platform.

▸ verb (**packages, packaging, packaged**) **1** put into a box or wrapping. **2** present in an attractive way.

> SYNONYMS *goods packaged in recyclable materials* **wrap,** gift-wrap, pack, box, seal.

packet ▸ noun **1** a paper or cardboard container or parcel. **2** (**a packet**) informal a lot of money.

> SYNONYMS **pack,** carton, container, case, package.

packhorse ▸ noun a horse that is used to carry loads.

pact ▸ noun a formal agreement between two or more people, groups, or countries.

SYNONYMS **agreement,** treaty, entente, protocol, deal, settlement, armistice, truce.

pacy ▸ adjective fast-moving.

pad ▸ noun **1** a thick piece of soft or absorbent material. **2** a number of sheets of blank paper fastened together at one edge. **3** the fleshy underpart of an animal's foot or of a human finger. **4** a protective guard worn by a sports player. **5** a structure or area used for helicopter take-off and landing or for launching rockets. **6** informal a person's home.

SYNONYMS **1** a pad over the eye **dressing,** pack, wad. **2** making notes on a pad **notebook,** notepad, writing pad, jotter; N. Amer. scratch pad.

▸ verb (pads, padding, padded) **1** fill or cover with padding. **2** (pad something out) add unnecessary material to a speech, article, or book to make it longer. **3** walk with quiet, steady steps.

SYNONYMS **1** you'll need to pad the vase inside its box **cushion,** insulate, line, quilt, stuff, lag. **2** he padded along the landing **creep,** sneak, steal, tiptoe, pussyfoot.

padding ▸ noun **1** soft material used to pad or stuff something. **2** unnecessary material added to make a speech, article, or book longer.

SYNONYMS **1** padding around the ankle **wadding,** cushioning, stuffing, packing, filling, lining. **2** a concise style with no padding **verbiage,** wordiness; Brit. informal waffle.

paddle ▸ noun **1** a short pole with a broad end, used to propel a small boat. **2** a paddle-shaped tool for stirring or mixing. **3** a short-handled bat used e.g. in table tennis.

SYNONYMS use the paddles to row ashore **oar,** scull.

▸ verb (paddles, paddling, paddled) **1** walk with bare feet in shallow water. **2** propel a boat with a paddle or paddles.

SYNONYMS children were paddling in the water **splash (about),** dabble, wade.

■ **paddle steamer** a boat powered by steam and propelled by large wheels which move the water as they turn.

paddock ▸ noun **1** a small field or enclosure for horses. **2** an enclosure where horses or cars are displayed before a race.

paddy[1] ▸ noun (plural **paddies**) a field where rice is grown.

paddy[2] ▸ noun Brit. informal a fit of temper.

padlock ▸ noun a detachable lock which is attached by a hinged hook.
▸ verb secure with a padlock.

padre /pah-dray/ ▸ noun informal a chaplain in the armed services.

paean /pee-uhn/ ▸ noun formal a song of praise or triumph.

paediatrics /pee-di-at-riks/ (US spelling **pediatrics**) ▸ noun the branch of medicine concerned with children and their diseases.
□ **paediatric** adjective **paediatrician** noun.

paedophile /pee-duh-fyl/ (US spelling **pedophile**) ▸ noun a person who is sexually attracted to children.
□ **paedophilia** noun.

paella /py-el-luh/ ▸ noun a Spanish dish of rice, chicken, seafood, etc.

pagan ▸ noun a person who holds religious beliefs other than those of the main world religions.

SYNONYMS **heathen,** infidel, non-Christian.

▸ adjective relating to pagans or their beliefs.

SYNONYMS **heathen,** infidel, non-Christian.

□ **paganism** noun.

page[1] ▸ noun **1** one side of a sheet of paper in a book, magazine, etc. **2** both sides of such a sheet of paper considered as a single unit. **3** a section of data displayed on a computer screen.

SYNONYMS **folio,** sheet, side, leaf.

▸ verb (pages, paging, paged) (page through) turn the pages of a book, magazine, etc.

page[2] ▸ noun **1** a boy or young man employed in a hotel to run errands, open doors, etc. **2** a young boy who attends a bride at a wedding. **3** historical a boy in training for knighthood.

SYNONYMS **1** a page in a hotel **errand boy,** messenger boy; N. Amer. bellboy, bellhop. **2** a page at a wedding **attendant,** pageboy, train-bearer.

▸ verb (pages, paging, paged) summon someone over a public address system or with a pager.

SYNONYMS could you please page Mr Johnson? **call (for),** summon, send for.

pageant /pa-juhnt/ ▸ noun an entertainment performed by people in elaborate or historical costumes.

SYNONYMS **parade,** procession, cavalcade, tableau, spectacle, extravaganza, show.

pageantry ▸ noun elaborate display or ceremonial events.

SYNONYMS **spectacle,** display, ceremony, magnificence, pomp, splendour,

p

grandeur, show; informal razzle-dazzle, razzmatazz.

pageboy ▸ noun a page in a hotel or attending a bride at a wedding.

pager ▸ noun a small device which bleeps or vibrates to inform you that it has received a message.

paginate ▸ verb (paginates, paginating, paginated) give numbers to the pages of a book, magazine, etc.
□ pagination noun.

pagoda ▸ noun a Hindu or Buddhist temple or other sacred building.

paid past and past participle of PAY.
■ put paid to informal stop something abruptly.

pail ▸ noun a bucket.

pain ▸ noun 1 a strongly unpleasant physical sensation caused by illness or injury. 2 mental suffering. 3 (pains) great care or trouble. 4 informal an annoying or boring person or thing.

SYNONYMS 1 *she endured great pain* **suffering,** agony, torture, torment, discomfort. 2 *a pain in the stomach* **ache,** aching, soreness, throbbing, sting, twinge, stab, pang, discomfort, irritation. 3 *the pain of losing a loved one* **sorrow,** grief, heartache, heartbreak, sadness, unhappiness, distress, misery, despair, agony, torment, torture. 4 *he took great pains to hide his feelings* **care,** effort, bother, trouble.

▸ verb 1 cause pain to. 2 (pained) showing that you are annoyed or upset.

SYNONYMS *it pained him to watch* **sadden,** grieve, distress, trouble, perturb, oppress, cause anguish to.

■ on (or under) pain of with the threat of being punished by.

painful ▸ adjective suffering or causing pain.

SYNONYMS 1 *a painful arm* **sore,** hurting, tender, aching, throbbing. 2 *a painful experience* **disagreeable,** unpleasant, nasty, distressing, upsetting, traumatic, miserable, sad, heartbreaking, agonizing, harrowing.

painfully ▸ adverb 1 in a painful way. 2 exceedingly.

SYNONYMS *this much was painfully obvious* **distressingly,** disturbingly, uncomfortably, unpleasantly, dreadfully.

painkiller ▸ noun a medicine for relieving pain.

painless ▸ adjective 1 not causing pain. 2 involving little effort or stress.
□ painlessly adverb.

painstaking ▸ adjective very careful and thorough.

SYNONYMS **careful,** meticulous, thorough, assiduous, attentive, conscientious, punctilious, scrupulous, rigorous. ANTONYMS slapdash.
□ painstakingly adverb.

paint ▸ noun a coloured substance which is spread over a surface to give a thin decorative or protective coating.

SYNONYMS **colouring,** colour, tint, dye, stain, pigment.

▸ verb 1 put paint on something. 2 produce a picture with paint. 3 give a description of.

SYNONYMS 1 *I painted the ceiling* **colour,** decorate, whitewash, emulsion, gloss, spray-paint, airbrush. 2 *painting slogans on a wall* **daub,** smear, spray-paint, airbrush. 3 *Rembrandt painted his mother* **portray,** picture, paint a picture/portrait of, depict, represent.

painter¹ ▸ noun 1 an artist who paints pictures. 2 a person who paints buildings.

painter² ▸ noun a rope attached to the bow of a boat for tying it to a quay.

painting ▸ noun 1 the action of painting. 2 a painted picture.

SYNONYMS **picture,** illustration, portrayal, depiction, representation, image, artwork, canvas, oil, watercolour.

paintwork ▸ noun painted surfaces in a building or on a vehicle.

pair ▸ noun 1 a set of two things used together or seen as a unit. 2 an article consisting of two joined or corresponding parts. 3 two people or animals related in some way or considered together.

SYNONYMS *a matching pair* **set,** brace, couple, duo, two.

▸ verb 1 join or connect to form a pair. 2 (pair off or up) form a couple.

SYNONYMS *a cardigan paired with a matching skirt* **match,** put together, couple, combine.

paisley ▸ noun an intricate pattern of curved feather-shaped figures.

pajamas US spelling of PYJAMAS.

Pakistani ▸ noun a person from Pakistan. ▸ adjective relating to Pakistan.

pal informal ▸ noun a friend.
▸ verb (pals, palling, palled) (pal up) form a friendship.

palace ▸ noun a large building where a king, queen, president, etc. lives.

SYNONYMS **castle,** château, mansion, stately home, residence.

palaeography /pa-li-**og**-ruh-fi/ (US spelling paleography) ▸ noun the study of ancient writing systems and manuscripts.

Palaeolithic /pa-li-uh-**li**-thik/ (US spelling

Paleolithic) ▸ adjective relating to the early part of the Stone Age.

palaeontology /pa-li-on-**tol**-uh-ji/ (US spelling paleontology) ▸ noun the study of fossil animals and plants.
□ palaeontologist noun.

palatable ▸ adjective **1** pleasant to taste. **2** acceptable.

palate ▸ noun **1** the roof of the mouth. **2** a person's ability to distinguish between different flavours.

palatial /puh-**lay**-sh'l/ ▸ adjective large and impressive, like a palace.

palaver /puh-**lah**-ver/ ▸ noun informal a lot of fuss about something.

pale¹ ▸ adjective **1** of a light shade or colour. **2** (of a person's face) having little colour, especially as a result of illness or shock.

> SYNONYMS **1** *pale colours* light, pastel, muted, subtle, soft, faded, bleached, washed out. **2** *she looked pale* white, pallid, pasty, wan, colourless, anaemic, washed out, peaky, ashen, sickly; informal like death warmed up. **3** *the pale light of morning* dim, faint, weak, feeble. ANTONYMS dark, rosy-cheeked.

▸ verb (pales, paling, paled) **1** become pale in your face. **2** seem or become less important.

> SYNONYMS *he paled at the news* go/turn white, grow/turn pale, blanch, lose colour.

pale² ▸ noun **1** a wooden stake used with others to form a fence. **2** a boundary.
■ beyond the pale (of behaviour) considered by most people to be unacceptable.

Palestinian ▸ adjective relating to Palestine. ▸ noun a member of the native Arab population of Palestine.

palette /pa-lit/ ▸ noun **1** a thin board on which an artist lays and mixes paints. **2** the range of colours used by an artist.
■ palette knife a blunt knife with a flexible blade, for applying or removing paint.

palimpsest ▸ noun an ancient sheet of parchment from which the original writing has been removed to make room for new writing.

palindrome ▸ noun a word or phrase that reads the same backwards as forwards, e.g. *madam*.

paling ▸ noun **1** a fence made from stakes. **2** a stake used in such a fence.

palisade ▸ noun a fence of stakes or iron railings.

pall¹ /pawl/ ▸ noun **1** a cloth spread over a coffin, hearse, or tomb. **2** a dark cloud of smoke or dust. **3** a general atmosphere of gloom or fear.
■ pall-bearer a person helping to carry a coffin at a funeral.

pall² /pawl/ ▸ verb become less appealing through being too familiar.

palladium ▸ noun a rare silvery-white metallic element.

pallet ▸ noun **1** a portable platform on which goods can be moved, stacked, and stored. **2** a straw mattress.

palliate ▸ verb (palliates, palliating, palliated) **1** reduce the pain or bad effects of a disease, though not curing it. **2** make something bad easier to cope with.
□ palliative adjective.

pallid ▸ adjective **1** pale, especially because of bad health. **2** (of colours or light) not strong or bright.

pallor ▸ noun an unhealthy pale appearance.

pally ▸ adjective informal having a close, friendly relationship.

palm¹ ▸ noun an evergreen tree of warm regions, with a crown of large feathered or fan-shaped leaves.

palm² ▸ noun the inner surface of the hand between the wrist and fingers.
▸ verb informal **1** (palm something off) sell or dispose of something in a way that is dishonest or unfair. **2** (palm someone off with) persuade someone to accept something that is unwanted or has no value.

palmistry ▸ noun the activity of interpreting a person's character or predicting their future by examining the palm of their hand.
□ palmist noun.

palmtop ▸ noun a computer small and light enough to be held in one hand.

palmy ▸ adjective comfortable and prosperous.

palomino /pa-luh-**mee**-noh/ ▸ noun (plural palominos) a tan-coloured horse with a white mane and tail.

palpable ▸ adjective **1** able to be touched or felt. **2** (of a feeling or quality) very strong or obvious.
□ palpably adverb.

palpate ▸ verb (palpates, palpating, palpated) (of a doctor or nurse) examine a part of the body by touching it.

palpitate ▸ verb (palpitates, palpitating, palpitated) **1** (of the heart) beat fast or irregularly. **2** shake; tremble.

palpitations ▸ plural noun a noticeably fast, strong, or irregular heartbeat.

palsy /**pawl**-zi/ ▸ noun (plural palsies) dated paralysis.
□ palsied adjective.

paltry ▸ adjective (paltrier, paltriest) (of an amount) very small.

pampas ▸ noun large treeless plains in South America.

p

pamper ▸ verb (pampers, pampering, pampered) give someone a great deal of care and attention.

SYNONYMS **spoil,** indulge, overindulge, cosset, mollycoddle, coddle, baby, wait on someone hand and foot.

pamphlet ▸ noun a small booklet or leaflet.

SYNONYMS **brochure,** leaflet, booklet, circular; N. Amer. mailer, folder.

pan¹ ▸ noun 1 a metal container for cooking food in. 2 a bowl fitted at either end of a pair of scales. 3 Brit. the bowl of a toilet. 4 a hollow in the ground in which water collects.

SYNONYMS *a pan of water* **saucepan,** pot, bowl, frying pan, skillet.

▸ verb (pans, panning, panned) 1 informal criticize harshly. 2 (pan out) informal end up or conclude. 3 wash gravel in a pan to separate out gold.

pan² ▸ verb (pans, panning, panned) swing a video or film camera to give a wide view or follow a subject.

SYNONYMS *the camera panned to the building* **swing (round),** sweep, move, turn.

pan- ▸ combining form including everything or everyone: *pan-African.*

panacea /pan-uh-**see**-uh/ ▸ noun something that will cure all diseases or solve all difficulties.

panache /puh-**nash**/ ▸ noun impressive skill and confidence.

panama ▸ noun a man's wide-brimmed hat made of straw-like material.

Panamanian /pan-uh-**may**-ni-uhn/ ▸ noun a person from Panama.
▸ adjective relating to Panama.

panatella ▸ noun a long, thin cigar.

pancake ▸ noun a thin, flat cake of batter, cooked in a frying pan.

pancreas /**pang**-kri-uhss/ ▸ noun (plural pancreases) a large gland behind the stomach which produces insulin and a liquid used in digestion.
□ **pancreatic** adjective.

panda ▸ noun 1 (also giant panda) a large black and white bear-like animal native to bamboo forests in China. 2 (also red panda) a Himalayan animal like a raccoon, with thick reddish-brown fur and a bushy tail.

pandemic /pan-**dem**-ik/ ▸ adjective (of a disease) widespread over a whole country or large part of the world.
▸ noun an outbreak of such a disease.

pandemonium ▸ noun a state of uproar and confusion.

pander ▸ verb (panders, pandering, pandered) (pander to) indulge someone in an unreasonable desire or bad habit.

pane ▸ noun a single sheet of glass in a window or door.

panegyric /pa-ni-**ji**-rik/ ▸ noun a speech or piece of writing praising someone or something.

panel ▸ noun 1 a section in a door, vehicle, garment, etc. 2 a flat board on which instruments or controls are fixed. 3 a small group of people brought together to investigate a matter, or to take part in a broadcast quiz or game.

SYNONYMS 1 *a control panel* **console,** instrument panel, dashboard, instruments, controls, dials, array. 2 *a panel of judges* **group,** team, body, committee, board.

□ **panelled** (US spelling **paneled**) adjective **panellist** (US spelling **panelist**) noun.

pang ▸ noun a sudden sharp pain or painful emotion.

panic ▸ noun 1 sudden uncontrollable fear or anxiety. 2 frenzied hurry to do something.

SYNONYMS *a wave of panic* **alarm,** anxiety, fear, fright, trepidation, dread, terror, hysteria, apprehension; informal flap, fluster, cold sweat; N. Amer. informal swivet. ANTONYMS calm.

▸ verb (panics, panicking, panicked) feel sudden uncontrollable fear or anxiety, or make someone feel it.

SYNONYMS 1 *there's no need to panic* **be alarmed,** be scared, be afraid, take fright, be hysterical, lose your nerve, get overwrought, get worked up; informal get in a flap, run around like a headless chicken; Brit. informal get the wind up, go into a flat spin, have kittens. 2 *talk of love panicked her* **frighten,** alarm, scare, unnerve; Brit. informal put the wind up. ANTONYMS stay calm, calm down.

□ **panicky** adjective.

pannier ▸ noun each of a pair of containers fitted on either side of a bicycle or motorcycle, or carried by a horse or donkey.

panoply /**pan**-uh-pli/ ▸ noun a large and impressive collection or number of things.

panorama ▸ noun 1 a broad view of a surrounding region. 2 a complete survey of a subject or sequence of events.

SYNONYMS **view,** vista, prospect, scenery, landscape, seascape, cityscape, skyline.

□ **panoramic** adjective.

pan pipes ▸ plural noun a musical instrument made from a row of short pipes fixed together.

pansy ▸ noun (plural pansies) 1 a garden plant with brightly coloured flowers. 2 informal a homosexual man.

pant ▶ verb breathe with short, quick breaths.

> SYNONYMS **breathe heavily,** breathe hard, puff and blow, huff and puff, gasp, heave, wheeze.

▶ noun a short, quick breath.

pantaloons ▶ plural noun **1** women's baggy trousers gathered at the ankles. **2** (in the past) men's close-fitting trousers fastened below the calf or at the foot.

pantechnicon ▶ noun Brit. dated a large van for transporting furniture.

pantheism /**pan**-thee-i-z'm/ ▶ noun the belief that God is all around us and is present in all things.
□ **pantheist** noun **pantheistic** adjective.

pantheon /**pan**-thi-uhn/ ▶ noun **1** all the gods of a people or religion. **2** an ancient temple dedicated to all the gods. **3** a group of particularly famous or important people.

panther ▶ noun **1** a black leopard. **2** N. Amer. a puma or a jaguar.

panties ▶ plural noun knickers.

pantile /**pan**-tyl/ ▶ noun a curved roof tile, fitted to overlap its neighbour.

panto ▶ noun (plural **pantos**) Brit. informal a pantomime.

pantomime ▶ noun Brit. an entertainment in the theatre involving music and slapstick comedy.

pantry ▶ noun (plural **pantries**) a small room or cupboard for storing food.

pants ▶ plural noun **1** Brit. underpants or knickers. **2** chiefly N. Amer. trousers.

> SYNONYMS **1 underpants,** briefs, boxer shorts, boxers, knickers; N. Amer. shorts, undershorts; informal panties; N. Amer. dated step-ins. **2 trousers,** slacks; Brit. informal trews, strides, kecks; Austral. informal daks.

pantyhose ▶ plural noun N. Amer. women's thin nylon tights.

pap ▶ noun **1** bland soft or semi-liquid food suitable for babies or invalids. **2** trivial books, television programmes, etc.

papa ▶ noun N. Amer. or dated your father.

papacy ▶ noun (plural **papacies**) the position or role of the Pope.

papal ▶ adjective relating to the Pope or the papacy.

paparazzo /pa-puh-**rat**-soh/ ▶ noun (plural **paparazzi** /pa-puh-**rat**-si/) a photographer who follows celebrities to get photographs of them.

papaya /puh-**py**-uh/ ▶ noun a tropical fruit like a long melon, with orange flesh and small black seeds.

paper ▶ noun **1** material manufactured in thin sheets from the pulp of wood, used for writing or printing on or as wrapping material. **2** (**papers**) sheets of paper covered with writing or printing. **3** a newspaper. **4** a government report or policy document. **5** an academic article read at a conference or published in a journal. **6** a set of exam questions.

> SYNONYMS **1 newspaper,** journal, gazette, periodical, tabloid, broadsheet, daily, weekly; informal rag; N. Amer. informal tab. **2** *a three-hour paper* **exam,** examination, test. **3** *he has written a paper on global warming* **essay,** article, monograph, thesis, work, dissertation, treatise, study, report, analysis; N. Amer. theme. **4** *personal papers* **document,** certificate, letter, file, deed, record, archive; (**papers**) paperwork, documentation. **5** *they asked us for our papers* **identification,** identity card, ID, credentials.

▶ verb (**papers, papering, papered**) **1** cover a wall with wallpaper. **2** (**paper something over**) conceal or disguise an awkward problem instead of resolving it.
■ **on paper 1** in writing. **2** in theory rather than in reality. **paper clip** a piece of bent wire or plastic used for holding sheets of paper together. **paper tiger** a person or thing that appears threatening but is actually weak.
□ **papery** adjective.

paperback ▶ noun a book bound in stiff paper or thin cardboard.

paperknife ▶ noun a blunt knife used for opening envelopes.

paperweight ▶ noun a small, heavy object for keeping loose papers in place.

paperwork ▶ noun routine work involving written documents.

papier mâché /pa-pi-ay **mash**-ay/ ▶ noun a mixture of paper and glue that becomes hard when dry.

papist /**pay**-pist/ ▶ noun disapproving a Roman Catholic.

paprika /**pap**-ri-kuh, puh-**pree**-kuh/ ▶ noun a powdered spice made from sweet red peppers.

papyrus /puh-**py**-ruhss/ ▶ noun (plural **papyri** /puh-**py**-ry/ or **papyruses**) a material made in ancient Egypt from the stem of a water plant, used for writing or painting on.

par ▶ noun Golf the number of strokes a first-class player normally requires for a particular hole or course.
■ **above** (or **below** or **under**) **par** above (or below) the usual or expected level or amount. **on a par with** equal to.

parable ▶ noun a simple story that teaches a moral or spiritual lesson.

> SYNONYMS **allegory,** moral tale, fable.

parabola /puh-**rab**-uh-luh/ ▶ noun (plural **parabolas** or **parabolae** /puh-**rab**-uh-

lee/) a curve of the kind formed by the intersection of a cone with a plane parallel to its side.
□ **parabolic** adjective.

paracetamol ▸ noun (plural **paracetamol** or **paracetamols**) Brit. a drug used to relieve pain and reduce fever.

parachute ▸ noun a cloth canopy which allows a person or heavy object attached to it to descend slowly when dropped from a high position.
▸ verb (**parachutes, parachuting, parachuted**) drop by parachute.
□ **parachutist** noun.

parade ▸ noun 1 a public procession. 2 a formal occasion when soldiers march or stand in line in order to be inspected or for display. 3 a series or succession. 4 Brit. a row of shops.

SYNONYMS 1 *a victory parade* **procession,** march, cavalcade, motorcade, spectacle, display, pageant, review, tattoo; Brit. march past. 2 *she walked along the parade* **promenade,** walkway, esplanade, mall; N. Amer. boardwalk; Brit. informal prom.

▸ verb (**parades, parading, paraded**) 1 walk, march, or display in a parade. 2 display something publicly in order to impress people or attract attention.

SYNONYMS 1 *the teams paraded through the city* **march,** process, file, troop. 2 *she paraded up and down* **strut,** swagger, stride. 3 *he was keen to parade his knowledge* **display,** exhibit, make a show of, flaunt, show (off), demonstrate.

paradigm /pa-ruh-dym/ ▸ noun a typical example, pattern, or model of something.
□ **paradigmatic** adjective.

paradise ▸ noun 1 (in some religions) heaven. 2 the Garden of Eden. 3 an ideal place or state.

SYNONYMS 1 **heaven,** the promised land, the Elysian Fields. 2 *a tropical paradise* **Utopia,** Shangri-La, Eden, heaven, idyll. 3 *this is sheer paradise!* **bliss,** heaven, ecstasy, delight, joy, happiness, heaven on earth.
ANTONYMS hell.

paradox ▸ noun 1 a statement that sounds absurd or seems to contradict itself, but is in fact true. 2 a person or thing that combines two contradictory features or qualities.

SYNONYMS **contradiction,** self-contradiction, inconsistency, incongruity, conflict, enigma, puzzle, conundrum.

□ **paradoxical** adjective **paradoxically** adverb.

paraffin ▸ noun 1 Brit. an oily liquid obtained from petroleum, used as a fuel. 2 a waxy substance obtained from petroleum, used

for sealing and waterproofing and in candles.

paragliding ▸ noun a sport in which a person glides through the air attached to a wide parachute after jumping from a high place.

paragon ▸ noun a model of excellence or of a particular quality.

paragraph ▸ noun a distinct section of a piece of writing, beginning on a new line.

SYNONYMS **section,** division, part, portion, segment, passage, clause.

Paraguayan /pa-ruh-gwy-uhn/ ▸ noun a person from Paraguay.
▸ adjective relating to Paraguay.

parakeet (or **parrakeet**) ▸ noun a small parrot with green feathers and a long tail.

parallax ▸ noun the apparent difference in the position of an object when viewed from different positions.

parallel ▸ adjective 1 (of lines or surfaces) side by side and having the same distance continuously between them. 2 happening or existing at the same time or in a similar way; corresponding.

SYNONYMS 1 *parallel lines* **aligned,** side by side, equidistant. 2 *parallel careers* **similar,** analogous, comparable, corresponding, like, equivalent, matching.
ANTONYMS divergent, different.

▸ noun 1 a person or thing that is similar to or can be compared to another. 2 a similarity or comparison. 3 each of the imaginary parallel circles of latitude on the earth's surface.

SYNONYMS 1 *an exact parallel* **counterpart,** analogue, equivalent, match, twin, duplicate, mirror. 2 *there is an interesting parallel between these figures* **similarity,** likeness, resemblance, analogy, correspondence, comparison, equivalence, symmetry.
ANTONYMS divergence, difference.

▸ verb (**parallels, paralleling, paralleled**) correspond to or happen at the same time as.

✔ double l in the middle: parallel.

parallelogram ▸ noun a figure with four straight sides and opposite sides parallel.

paralyse (US spelling **paralyze**) ▸ verb (**paralyses, paralysing, paralysed**) 1 make someone unable to move a part of their body. 2 prevent something from functioning normally.

SYNONYMS 1 *both of his legs were paralysed* **disable,** cripple, immobilize, incapacitate; (**paralysed**) Medicine paraplegic, quadriplegic. 2 *the capital was paralysed by a strike* **bring to a**

standstill, immobilize, bring to a halt, freeze, cripple, disable.

paralysis /puh-**ral**-i-siss/ ▶ noun (plural **paralyses** /puh-**ral**-i-seez/) **1** the loss of the ability to move part of the body. **2** inability to do things or function normally.

SYNONYMS **1** *the disease can cause paralysis* **immobility,** powerlessness, incapacity; Medicine paraplegia, quadriplegia. **2** *complete paralysis of the ports* **shutdown,** immobilization, stoppage, gridlock, standstill, blockage.

paralytic ▶ adjective **1** relating to paralysis. **2** informal very drunk.

paramedic ▶ noun a person who is trained to do medical work but is not a fully qualified doctor.

parameter /puh-**ram**-i-ter/ ▶ noun a thing which decides or limits the way in which something can be done.

paramilitary ▶ adjective organized on similar lines to a military force.
▶ noun (plural **paramilitaries**) a member of a paramilitary organization.

paramount ▶ adjective **1** more important than anything else. **2** having the highest position or the greatest power.

SYNONYMS **most important,** supreme, chief, overriding, predominant, foremost, prime, primary, principal, main, key, central; informal number-one.

paramour ▶ noun old use a person's lover.

paranoia ▶ noun a mental condition in which someone wrongly believes that other people want to harm them, or that they are very important.

paranoid ▶ adjective **1** wrongly believing that other people want to harm you. **2** having to do with paranoia.

SYNONYMS **suspicious,** mistrustful, anxious, fearful, insecure, obsessive.

paranormal ▶ adjective beyond the scope of scientific knowledge.

parapet ▶ noun a low wall along the edge of a roof, bridge, or balcony.

paraphernalia ▶ noun the objects needed for a particular activity.

paraphrase ▶ verb (**paraphrases, paraphrasing, paraphrased**) express the meaning of something using different words.

SYNONYMS **reword,** rephrase, express differently, rewrite, gloss.

▶ noun a rewording of something written or spoken.

paraplegia /pa-ruh-**plee**-juh/ ▶ noun paralysis of the legs and lower body.
□ **paraplegic** adjective & noun.

paraquat ▶ noun a powerful weedkiller.

parasite ▶ noun **1** an animal or plant which lives on or inside another, and gets its food from it. **2** a person who relies on or benefits from someone else but gives nothing in return.

SYNONYMS **hanger-on,** cadger, leech, passenger; informal sponger, scrounger, freeloader; N. Amer. informal mooch; Austral./NZ informal bludger.

□ **parasitic** adjective **parasitism** noun.

parasol ▶ noun a light umbrella used to give shade from the sun.

paratroops ▶ plural noun troops trained to be dropped by parachute from aircraft.
□ **paratrooper** noun.

parboil ▶ verb boil something until it is partly cooked.

parcel ▶ noun an object or collection of objects wrapped in paper in order to be carried or sent by post.

SYNONYMS *a parcel of clothes* **package,** packet, pack, bundle, box, case, bale.

▶ verb (**parcels, parcelling, parcelled;** US spelling **parcels, parceling, parceled**) **1** (**parcel something up**) make something into a parcel. **2** (**parcel something out**) divide something between several people.

SYNONYMS *she parcelled up the papers* **pack (up),** package, wrap (up), gift-wrap, tie up, bundle up.

parch ▶ verb **1** make something dry through strong heat. **2** (**parched**) informal very thirsty.

parchment ▶ noun **1** (in the past) a stiff material made from the skin of a sheep or goat and used for writing on. **2** thick paper resembling parchment.

pardon ▶ noun **1** forgiveness for a mistake, sin, or crime. **2** a cancellation of the punishment for a crime.

SYNONYMS **1** *pardon for your sins* **forgiveness,** absolution. **2** *he offered them a full pardon* **reprieve,** amnesty, exoneration, release, acquittal, discharge.

▶ verb **1** forgive or excuse a person, mistake, sin, or crime. **2** give an offender a pardon.

SYNONYMS **1** *I know she will pardon me* **forgive,** absolve. **2** *they were subsequently pardoned* **exonerate,** acquit, reprieve; informal let off.
ANTONYMS blame, punish.

▶ exclamation used to ask a speaker to repeat something because you did not hear or understand it.
□ **pardonable** adjective.

pare ▶ verb (**pares, paring, pared**) **1** trim something by cutting away the outer edges. **2** (**pare something away** or **down**) gradually reduce the amount of something.

parent ▸ noun **1** a father or mother. **2** an animal or plant from which young or new ones are produced. **3** an organization or company which owns or controls a number of smaller organizations or companies.
▸ verb be or act as a parent to.
□ **parental** adjective **parenthood** noun.

parentage ▸ noun the identity and origins of your parents.

parenthesis /puh-**ren**-thi-siss/ ▸ noun (plural **parentheses** /puh-**ren**-thi-seez/) **1** a word or phrase added as an explanation or afterthought, indicated in writing by a pair of brackets, dashes, or commas. **2** (**parentheses**) a pair of round brackets () surrounding a word or phrase.
□ **parenthetic** (or **parenthetical**) adjective.

par excellence /par ek-suh-**lonss**/ ▸ adjective better or more than all others of the same kind: *a designer par excellence.*

pariah /puh-**ry**-uh/ ▸ noun a person who is rejected by other people; an outcast.

parings ▸ plural noun thin strips pared off from something.

parish ▸ noun **1** (in the Christian Church) a district with its own church and church ministers. **2** Brit. the smallest unit of local government in country areas.

> SYNONYMS **1** *the parish of Upton* **district**, community. **2** *the vicar scandalized the parish* **parishioners**, churchgoers, congregation, fold, flock, community.

parishioner ▸ noun a person who lives in a particular Church parish.

parity ▸ noun the quality of being equal with or equivalent to something.

park ▸ noun **1** a large public garden in a town. **2** a large area of land attached to a country house. **3** an area used for a particular purpose.

> SYNONYMS **1** **public garden**, recreation ground, playground, play area. **2** **parkland**, grassland, woodland, garden(s), lawns, grounds, estate.

▸ verb leave a vehicle somewhere for a time.

> SYNONYMS **1** *he parked his car* **leave**, position, stop, pull up. **2** *park your bag by the door* **put (down)**, place, deposit, leave, stick, shove, dump; informal **plonk**; Brit. informal **bung**.

parka ▸ noun a windproof hooded jacket.

Parkinson's disease ▸ noun a disease of the brain and nervous system marked by trembling, stiffness in the muscles, and slowness of movement.

parky ▸ adjective Brit. informal chilly.

parlance ▸ noun a way of speaking.

parley ▸ noun (plural **parleys**) a meeting between enemies to discuss terms for a truce.

▸ verb (**parleys**, **parleying**, **parleyed**) hold a parley.

parliament ▸ noun **1** (**Parliament**) (in the UK) the assembly that makes laws, consisting of the king or queen, the House of Lords, and the House of Commons. **2** a similar assembly in other countries.

> SYNONYMS **legislature**, assembly, chamber, house, congress, senate, diet.

> ✔ **-lia-** in the middle, not **-la-**: par**lia**ment.

parliamentarian ▸ noun a member of a parliament.

parliamentary ▸ adjective relating to a parliament.

> SYNONYMS **legislative**, law-making, governmental, congressional, democratic, elected.

parlour (US spelling **parlor**) ▸ noun **1** dated a sitting room. **2** a shop providing particular goods or services.

parlous /**par**-luhss/ ▸ adjective old use dangerously uncertain; precarious.

Parmesan /**par**-mi-zan/ ▸ noun a hard, dry Italian cheese.

parochial /puh-**roh**-ki-uhl/ ▸ adjective **1** relating to a parish. **2** having a narrow outlook.

> SYNONYMS **narrow-minded**, small-minded, provincial, small-town, conservative; N. Amer. informal **jerkwater**. ANTONYMS broad-minded.

□ **parochialism** noun.

parody ▸ noun (plural **parodies**) a piece of writing, art, or music that deliberately copies the style of someone or something, in order to be funny.

> SYNONYMS **1** *a parody of the news* **satire**, burlesque, lampoon, pastiche, caricature, imitation; informal **spoof**, take-off, send-up. **2** *a parody of the truth* **distortion**, travesty, caricature, misrepresentation, perversion, corruption.

▸ verb (**parodies**, **parodying**, **parodied**) produce a parody of.

parole ▸ noun the temporary or permanent release of a prisoner before the end of their sentence, on the condition that they behave well.
▸ verb (**paroles**, **paroling**, **paroled**) release a prisoner on parole.

paroxysm /**pa**-ruhk-si-z'm/ ▸ noun a sudden attack of pain, coughing, etc., or a sudden feeling of overwhelming emotion.

parquet /**par**-kay/ ▸ noun flooring consisting of wooden blocks arranged in a geometric pattern.

parrakeet ➡ PARAKEET.

parricide ▸ noun the killing by someone of their own parent or other close relative.

parrot ▸ noun a tropical bird with brightly coloured feathers and a hooked bill, some kinds of which can copy human speech.
▸ verb (**parrots, parroting, parroted**) repeat something mechanically, without thought or understanding.
■ **parrot-fashion** repeated without thought or understanding.

parry ▸ verb (**parries, parrying, parried**)
1 ward off a weapon or attack. **2** say something in order to avoid answering a question directly.

> SYNONYMS **1** *Sharpe parried the blow* **ward off,** fend off, deflect, block. **2** *I parried her questions* **evade,** sidestep, avoid, dodge, field.

parse /parz/ ▸ verb analyse a sentence in terms of grammar.

parsimony /**par**-si-muh-ni/ ▸ noun the fact of being very unwilling to spend money.
□ **parsimonious** adjective.

parsley ▸ noun a herb with crinkly or flat leaves, used in cooking.

parsnip ▸ noun a long tapering cream-coloured root vegetable.

parson ▸ noun (in the Church of England) a parish priest.

> SYNONYMS **priest,** minister, clergyman, vicar, rector, cleric, chaplain, pastor, curate; informal reverend, padre; Austral. informal josser.

parsonage ▸ noun a house provided by the Church for a parson.

part ▸ noun **1** a piece or section which is combined with others to make up a whole. **2** some but not all of something. **3** a role played by an actor or actress. **4** a person's contribution to an action or situation. **5** (**parts**) informal a region.

> SYNONYMS **1** *a large part of their life* **piece,** amount, portion, proportion, percentage, fraction; informal slice, chunk. **2** *car parts* **component,** bit, constituent, element, module. **3** *body parts* **organ,** limb, member. **4** *the third part of the book* **section,** division, volume, chapter, act, scene, instalment. **5** *another part of the country* **district,** neighbourhood, quarter, section, area, region. **6** *the part of Juliet* **role,** character. **7** *he was jailed for his part in the affair* **involvement,** role, function, hand, responsibility, capacity, participation, contribution; informal bit. ANTONYMS whole.

▸ verb **1** move apart or divide to leave a central space. **2** (of two or more people) leave each other. **3** (**part with**) give up possession of; hand over.

> SYNONYMS **1** *the curtains parted* **separate,** divide, split, move apart. **2** *we parted on bad terms* **leave each other,** part

company, say goodbye/farewell, say your goodbyes/farewells, go your separate ways, take your leave.
ANTONYMS join, meet.

▸ adverb partly.
■ **part company** go in different directions. **part of speech** a category in which a word is placed according to its function in grammar, e.g. noun, adjective, and verb. **part song** a song with three or more voice parts and no musical accompaniment. **part-time** for only part of the usual working day or week. **take part** join in or be involved in an activity. **take someone's part** support someone in an argument.

partake ▸ verb (**partakes, partaking, partook;** past participle **partaken**) formal **1** (**partake of**) eat or drink. **2** (**partake in**) participate in.

partial ▸ adjective **1** not complete or whole. **2** favouring one side in a dispute. **3** (**partial to**) liking something.

> SYNONYMS **1** *a partial recovery* **incomplete,** limited, qualified, imperfect, fragmentary, unfinished. **2** *a very partial view of the situation* **biased,** prejudiced, partisan, one-sided, slanted, skewed, coloured, unbalanced. ANTONYMS complete, unbiased.

□ **partiality** noun.

partially ▸ adverb to some extent; in part.

> SYNONYMS **somewhat,** to a limited extent, to a certain extent, partly, in part, up to a point, slightly. ANTONYMS wholly.

participant ▸ noun a person who takes part in something.

> SYNONYMS **participator,** contributor, party, member, entrant, competitor, player, contestant, candidate.

participate ▸ verb (**participates, participating, participated**) join in something; take part.

> SYNONYMS **take part,** join, engage, get involved, share, play a part, play a role, contribute, partake, have a hand in.

□ **participation** noun **participatory** adjective.

participle ▸ noun Grammar a word such as *going* or *burnt* that is formed from a verb and used as an adjective or noun (as in *burnt toast* or *the going was good*), or to make compound verb forms (as in *was going*).

particle ▸ noun **1** a tiny portion of matter. **2** a minute piece of matter smaller than an atom, e.g. an electron.

> SYNONYMS **(tiny) bit,** (tiny) piece, speck, spot, fragment, sliver, splinter.

particular ▸ adjective **1** relating to an individual member of a group or class.

2 more than is usual. **3** very careful or concerned about something.

> SYNONYMS **1** *a particular group of companies* **specific,** certain, distinct, separate, definite, precise. **2** *an issue of particular importance* **special,** exceptional, unusual, uncommon, notable, noteworthy, remarkable, unique. **3** *he was particular about what he ate* **fussy,** fastidious, finicky, discriminating, selective; informal pernickety, choosy, picky; Brit. informal faddy.
> ANTONYMS general, indiscriminate.

▶ **noun** a detail.

> SYNONYMS *the same in every particular* **detail,** item, point, element, fact, circumstance, feature.

■ **in particular** especially.

particularly ▶ adverb **1** more than is usual. **2** in particular; especially.

> SYNONYMS **1** *the acoustics are particularly good* **especially,** specially, exceptionally, unusually, remarkably, outstandingly, uncommonly, uniquely. **2** *he particularly asked that I should help you* **specifically,** explicitly, expressly, in particular, especially, specially.

> ✔ particula**rly**, not **-culy**.

parting ▶ noun **1** an act of leaving someone and going away. **2** Brit. a line of scalp which is visible when the hair is combed in different directions.

> SYNONYMS *an emotional parting* **farewell,** leave-taking, goodbye, adieu, departure.

partisan /par-ti-zan/ ▶ noun **1** a committed supporter of a cause, group, or person. **2** a member of an armed group fighting secretly against an occupying force.

> SYNONYMS **guerrilla,** freedom fighter, resistance fighter, underground fighter, irregular.

▶ **adjective** prejudiced.

> SYNONYMS **biased,** prejudiced, one-sided, discriminatory, partial, sectarian, factional.
> ANTONYMS unbiased.

partition ▶ noun **1** a structure that divides a space into separate areas. **2** division into parts.

> SYNONYMS **1** *room partitions* **screen,** room divider, dividing wall, barrier, panel. **2** *the partition of the country* **division,** partitioning, separation, dividing up, splitting up, breaking up, break-up.

▶ **verb 1** divide into parts. **2** divide a room with a partition.

> SYNONYMS **1** *moves to partition Poland* **divide,** separate, split up, break up. **2** *the hall was partitioned* **subdivide,** divide (up), separate, section off, screen off.

partly ▶ adverb not completely but to some extent.

> SYNONYMS **in part,** partially, somewhat, a little, up to a point, in some measure, slightly, to some extent.
> ANTONYMS wholly.

partner ▶ noun **1** each of two people doing something as a pair. **2** the person you are having a sexual relationship with. **3** each of two or more people who are involved in a project or undertaking or who own a business.

> SYNONYMS **1** *his partner in crime* **accomplice,** confederate, accessory, collaborator, fellow conspirator, helper; informal sidekick. **2** *your relationship with your partner* **spouse,** husband, wife, lover, girlfriend, boyfriend, fiancé, fiancée, significant other, live-in lover, mate; Brit. informal other half. **3** *business partners* **colleague,** associate, co-worker, fellow worker, collaborator, comrade, teammate; Austral./NZ informal offsider.

▶ **verb** (**partners, partnering, partnered**) be the partner of.

partnership ▶ noun **1** the state of being a partner or partners. **2** an association of two or more people as partners.

> SYNONYMS **1** *in close partnership* **cooperation,** association, collaboration, coalition, alliance, union, affiliation, connection. **2** *thriving partnerships* **company,** association, consortium, syndicate, firm, business, organization.

partook past of **PARTAKE.**

partridge ▶ noun (plural **partridge** or **partridges**) a game bird with brown feathers and a short tail.

parturition ▶ noun formal or technical the action of giving birth.

party ▶ noun (plural **parties**) **1** a social event with food and drink and sometimes dancing. **2** an organized political group that puts forward candidates for election to government. **3** a group of people taking part in an activity or trip. **4** a person or group forming one side in an agreement or dispute.

> SYNONYMS **1** *150 people attended the party* **social gathering,** function, get-together, celebration, reunion, festivity, reception, soirée, social; informal bash, do; Austral./NZ informal shivoo. **2** *a party of visitors* **group,** company, body, gang, band, crowd, pack, contingent; informal bunch, crew, load. **3** *a left-wing party*

faction, group, bloc, camp, caucus, alliance.

▶ verb (**parties, partying, partied**) informal enjoy yourself at a party.
■ **be party to** be involved in. **party line** a policy officially adopted by a political party. **party wall** a wall between two adjoining houses or rooms.

parvenu /par-vuh-nyoo/ ▶ noun disapproving a person from a poor background who has recently joined a group of wealthy or famous people.

pascal ▶ noun a unit of pressure.

pass[1] ▶ verb 1 move or go onward, past, through, or across. 2 change from one state or condition to another. 3 transfer something to someone. 4 kick, hit, or throw the ball to a teammate. 5 (of time) go by. 6 spend time. 7 be done or said. 8 come to an end. 9 be successful in an exam or test. 10 declare something to be satisfactory. 11 approve a proposal or law by voting. 12 express an opinion or judgement.

SYNONYMS 1 *the traffic passing through the village* **go,** proceed, move, progress, make your way, travel. 2 *a car passed him* **overtake,** go past/by, pull ahead of, leave behind. 3 *time passed* **elapse,** go by/past, advance, wear on, roll by, tick by. 4 *he passed the time reading* **occupy,** spend, fill, use (up), employ, while away. 5 *pass the salt* **hand,** let someone have, give, reach. 6 *her estate passed to her grandson* **be transferred,** go, be left, be bequeathed, be handed down/on, be passed on; Law devolve. 7 *his death passed unnoticed* **happen,** occur, take place. 8 *the storm passed* **come to an end,** fade (away), blow over, run its course, die out/down, finish, end, cease. 9 *he passed the exam* **be successful in,** succeed in, gain a pass in, get through; informal sail through, scrape through. 10 *the Senate passed the bill* **approve,** vote for, accept, ratify, adopt, agree to, authorize, endorse, legalize, enact; informal OK.
ANTONYMS start, fail, reject.

▶ noun 1 an act of passing. 2 a success in an exam. 3 an official document which allows you to go somewhere or use something. 4 informal a sexual advance. 5 a particular situation.

SYNONYMS *you must show your pass* **permit,** warrant, authorization, licence.

■ **pass away** die. **pass off** happen in a particular way. **pass something off as** pretend that something is something else. **pass out** become unconscious. **pass something up** choose not to take up an opportunity.

pass[2] ▶ noun a route over or through mountains.

passable ▶ adjective 1 acceptable, but not outstanding. 2 able to be travelled along or on.
□ **passably** adverb.

passage ▶ noun 1 the passing of someone or something. 2 a way through or across something. 3 a journey by sea or air. 4 the right to pass through a place. 5 a short section from a book, document, or musical work.

SYNONYMS 1 *their passage through the country* **progress,** transit, advance, journey, trip, voyage. 2 *the passage of time* **passing,** advance, course, march. 3 *clearing a passage to the front door* **way,** route, path. 4 *the passage to the kitchen* **corridor,** hall, hallway. 5 *a passage between the buildings* **alley,** alleyway, passageway, lane, path, footpath, track, thoroughfare; N. Amer. areaway. 6 *a passage from 'Macbeth'* **extract,** excerpt, quotation, quote.

passageway ▶ noun a corridor or other narrow passage between buildings or rooms.

passé /pass-ay/ ▶ adjective no longer fashionable.

passenger ▶ noun a person travelling in a car, bus, train, ship, or aircraft, other than the driver, pilot, or crew.

SYNONYMS **traveller,** commuter, fare-payer, rider, fare.

passer-by ▶ noun (plural **passers-by**) a person who happens to be walking past something or someone.

passerine /pass-uh-ryn, pass-uh-reen/ ▶ adjective referring to birds whose feet are adapted for perching (including all songbirds).

passim ▶ adverb used to show that a reference appears at various places throughout a document.

passing ▶ adjective 1 done quickly and casually. 2 (of a similarity) slight.

SYNONYMS 1 *of passing interest* **fleeting,** transient, transitory, ephemeral, brief, short-lived, temporary, momentary. 2 *a passing glance* **hasty,** rapid, hurried, brief, quick, cursory, superficial, casual, perfunctory.

▶ noun 1 the ending of something. 2 a person's death.

SYNONYMS 1 *the passing of time* **passage,** course, progress, advance. 2 *Jack's passing* **death,** demise, passing away, end, loss.

passion ▶ noun 1 very strong emotion. 2 strong sexual love. 3 a strong enthusiasm for something. 4 (**the Passion**) Jesus's suffering and death on the Cross.

p

SYNONYMS **1** *the passion of activists* **enthusiasm**, ardour, fervour, eagerness, zeal, vigour, fire, energy, spirit, fanaticism. **2** *he worked himself up into a passion* **rage**, fit of anger, temper, tantrum, fury, frenzy; Brit. informal paddy. **3** *hot with passion* **love**, desire, lust, ardour, lasciviousness, lustfulness. **4** *his passion for football* **enthusiasm**, love, mania, fascination, obsession, preoccupation, fanaticism, fixation, compulsion, appetite, addiction; informal thing.
ANTONYMS apathy, calm.

■ **passion flower** a climbing plant with distinctive flowers. **passion fruit** the edible fruit of some species of passion flower. **passion play** a play about Jesus's crucifixion.

passionate ▶ adjective showing or caused by passion.

SYNONYMS **1** *a passionate entreaty* **intense**, impassioned, ardent, fervent, vehement, fiery, heated, emotional, heartfelt, excited. **2** *McGregor is passionate about sport* **very keen**, very enthusiastic, addicted; informal mad, crazy, hooked; Austral./NZ informal shook. **3** *a passionate kiss* **amorous**, ardent, hot-blooded, loving, sexy, sensual, erotic, lustful; informal steamy, hot, turned on.
ANTONYMS apathetic, cool.

□ **passionately** adverb.

passive ▶ adjective **1** accepting what happens without resisting or trying to change anything. **2** Grammar (of a verb) having the form used when the subject is affected by the action of the verb (e.g. *they were killed* as opposed to the active form *he killed them*).

SYNONYMS **1** *a passive role* **inactive**, non-active, non-participative, uninvolved. **2** *passive victims* **submissive**, acquiescent, unresisting, compliant, docile.
ANTONYMS active, resistant.

■ **passive smoking** the inhaling of smoke from other people's cigarettes.
□ **passively** adverb **passivity** noun.

Passover ▶ noun the major Jewish spring festival, commemorating the liberation of the Israelites from slavery in Egypt.

passport ▶ noun an official document that identifies you as a citizen of a particular country and is required in order to enter and leave other countries.

password ▶ noun a secret word or phrase used to enter a place or use a computer.

past ▶ adjective **1** gone by in time and no longer existing. **2** (of time) that has gone by. **3** Grammar (of a tense of a verb) expressing a past action or state.

SYNONYMS **1** *times past* **gone by**, bygone, former, previous, old, of old, olden, long-ago. **2** *the past few months* **last**, recent, preceding. **3** *a past chairman* **previous**, former, foregoing, erstwhile, one-time, sometime, ex-.
ANTONYMS present, future.

▶ noun **1** a past period or the events in it. **2** a person's or thing's history or earlier life.

SYNONYMS *details of her past* **history**, background, past life, life story.

▶ preposition **1** beyond in time or space. **2** in front of or from one side to the other of. **3** beyond the scope or power of.

SYNONYMS **1** *I drove past the cafe* **in front of**, by. **2** *it's past 9 o'clock* **beyond**, after, later than.

▶ adverb **1** so as to pass from one side to the other. **2** used to indicate the passage of time.

SYNONYMS *they hurried past* **along**, by, on.

■ **past master** a person who is an expert in a particular activity. **past participle** Grammar the form of a verb which is used in perfect tenses (e.g. *have you looked*?), to form passive sentences (e.g. *it was broken*), and sometimes as an adjective (e.g. *lost property*).

pasta ▶ noun a type of food made from flour and water, formed into various shapes and cooked in boiling water.

paste ▶ noun **1** a soft, moist substance. **2** a glue made from water and starch. **3** a hard substance used in making imitation gems.

SYNONYMS **1** *blend the ingredients to a paste* **purée**, pulp, mush, spread, pâté. **2** *wallpaper paste* **adhesive**, glue, gum; N. Amer. mucilage.

▶ verb (**pastes**, **pasting**, **pasted**) **1** coat or stick with paste. **2** (in computing) insert a section of text into a document.

SYNONYMS *a notice was pasted on the door* **stick**, glue, gum, fix, affix.

pasteboard ▶ noun thin board made by pasting together sheets of paper.

pastel ▶ noun **1** a soft coloured chalk or crayon used for drawing. **2** a pale shade of a colour.
▶ adjective (of a colour) pale.

SYNONYMS **pale**, soft, light, delicate, muted.
ANTONYMS dark, bright.

pasteurize (or **pasteurise**) ▶ verb (**pasteurizes**, **pasteurizing**, **pasteurized**) destroy the germs in milk by a process of heating and cooling.
□ **pasteurization** noun.

pastiche /pa-steesh/ ▶ noun a piece of writing or work of art produced in a style which imitates that of another work, artist, or period.

pastille /**pass**-tuhl/ ▶ noun a small sweet or throat lozenge.

pastime ▶ noun an activity done regularly for enjoyment.

> synonyms **hobby,** leisure activity, leisure pursuit, recreation, game, amusement, diversion, entertainment, interest.

pastor ▶ noun a minister in charge of a Christian church or group.

> synonyms **priest,** minister, parson, clergyman, cleric, chaplain, vicar, rector, curate; informal reverend, padre; Austral. informal josser.

pastoral ▶ adjective **1** relating to or portraying country life. **2** relating to the farming or grazing of sheep or cattle. **3** relating to the work of a Christian minister in giving personal and spiritual guidance. **4** relating to a teacher's responsibility for the well-being of students.

> synonyms **1** *a pastoral scene* **rural,** country, rustic, agricultural, bucolic. **2** *his pastoral duties* **priestly,** clerical, ecclesiastical, ministerial.
> antonyms urban, lay.

▶ noun a pastoral poem, picture, or piece of music.

pastrami /pass-**trah**-mi/ ▶ noun highly seasoned smoked beef.

pastry ▶ noun (plural **pastries**) **1** dough made from flour, fat, and water, used in baked dishes such as pies. **2** a cake consisting of sweet pastry with a filling.

pasture ▶ noun land covered with grass, suitable for grazing cattle or sheep.

> synonyms **grassland,** grass, grazing, meadow, field; Austral./NZ run.

▶ verb (**pastures, pasturing, pastured**) put animals to graze in a pasture.
> □ **pasturage** noun.

pasty[1] (or **pastie**) /**pass**-ti/ ▶ noun (plural **pasties**) Brit. a folded pastry case filled with seasoned meat and vegetables.

pasty[2] /**pay**-sti/ ▶ adjective (**pastier, pastiest**) (of a person's skin) unhealthily pale.

pat[1] ▶ verb (**pats, patting, patted**) tap quickly and gently with the flat of your hand.

> synonyms **tap,** clap, touch, stroke.

▶ noun **1** an act of patting. **2** a compact mass of a soft substance.

> synonyms **tap,** clap, touch, stroke.

pat[2] ▶ adjective (of something said) too quick or easy; not convincing.
> ■ **have something off pat** know facts or words perfectly so that you can repeat them without hesitation.

patch ▶ noun **1** a small area differing in colour or texture from its surroundings. **2** a piece of material used to mend a hole or strengthen a weak point. **3** a cover worn over an injured eye. **4** a small plot of land. **5** Brit. informal a period of time. **6** Brit. informal an area for which someone is responsible or in which they operate.

> synonyms **1** *a reddish patch on her wrist* **blotch,** mark, spot, smudge, smear, stain, streak, blemish; informal splodge. **2** *a patch of ground* **plot,** area, piece, strip, tract, parcel, bed; Brit. allotment; N. Amer. lot. **3** *going through a difficult patch* **period,** time, spell, phase, stretch.

▶ verb **1** mend, strengthen, or protect with a patch. **2** (**patch something up**) treat injuries or repair damage quickly or temporarily.

> synonyms *her jeans were neatly patched* **mend,** repair, sew up, stitch up, cover, reinforce.

■ **not a patch on** Brit. informal much less good than.

patchwork ▶ noun needlework in which small pieces of cloth of different colours are sewn edge to edge.

patchy ▶ adjective (**patchier, patchiest**) **1** existing or happening in small, isolated areas. **2** uneven in quality; inconsistent.

pate (*rhymes with* gate) ▶ noun old use a person's head.

pâté /**pa**-tay/ ▶ noun a rich savoury paste made from meat, fish, etc.

patella /puh-**tel**-luh/ ▶ noun (plural **patellae** /puh-**tel**-lee/) the kneecap.

patent /**pay**-t'nt, **pa**-t'nt/ ▶ noun a government licence giving someone the sole right to make, use, or sell their invention for a set period.

▶ verb obtain a patent for.

▶ adjective **1** /**pay**-t'nt/ easily recognizable; obvious. **2** made and marketed under a patent.

> synonyms **1** *patent nonsense* **obvious,** clear, plain, evident, manifest, conspicuous, blatant, barefaced, flagrant. **2** *patent medicines* **proprietary,** patented, licensed, branded.

■ **patent leather** shiny varnished leather.
> □ **patently** adverb.

paterfamilias /pay-ter-fuh-**mi**-li-ass/ ▶ noun the man who is the head of a family or household.

paternal ▶ adjective **1** having to do with or like a father. **2** related through the father.
> □ **paternally** adverb.

paternalism ▶ noun the policy of protecting the people you have control over but also of restricting their freedom.
> □ **paternalist** noun & adjective **paternalistic** adjective.

p

paternity ▸ noun 1 the state of being a father. 2 descent from a father.

paternoster ▸ noun (in the Roman Catholic Church) the Lord's Prayer.

path ▸ noun 1 a way or track laid down for walking or made by repeated treading. 2 the direction in which a person or thing moves. 3 a course of action.

> SYNONYMS 1 *the path to the beach* footpath, pathway, track, trail, bridle path, lane, cycle track; N. Amer. bikeway. 2 *journalists blocked his path* route, way, course. 3 *the best path to follow* course of action, route, road, avenue, line, approach, tack.

pathetic ▸ adjective 1 arousing pity or sadness. 2 informal weak or inadequate.

> SYNONYMS 1 *a pathetic sight* pitiful, moving, touching, poignant, plaintive, wretched. 2 *a pathetic excuse* feeble, woeful, sorry, poor, pitiful, lamentable, deplorable, contemptible.
> ANTONYMS funny, plausible, commendable.

□ **pathetically** adverb.

pathogen /pa-thuh-juhn/ ▸ noun a microscopic organism that can cause disease.
□ **pathogenic** adjective.

pathological ▸ adjective 1 relating to or caused by a disease. 2 informal unable to stop yourself doing something; compulsive.
□ **pathologically** adverb.

pathology ▸ noun 1 the study of the causes and effects of diseases. 2 the typical behaviour of a disease.
□ **pathologist** noun.

pathos /pay-thoss/ ▸ noun a quality that arouses pity or sadness.

pathway ▸ noun a path or route.

patience ▸ noun 1 the ability to accept delay, trouble, or suffering without becoming angry or upset. 2 Brit. a card game for one player.

> SYNONYMS 1 *she tried everyone's patience* forbearance, tolerance, restraint, equanimity, understanding, indulgence. 2 *a task requiring patience* perseverance, persistence, endurance, tenacity, application, staying power, doggedness.

patient ▸ adjective having or showing patience.

> SYNONYMS 1 *I must ask you to be patient* forbearing, uncomplaining, tolerant, long-suffering, accommodating, understanding, indulgent. 2 *patient research* persevering, persistent, tenacious, dogged, determined.

▸ noun a person receiving or registered to receive medical treatment.

> SYNONYMS *a doctor's patient* sick person, case, sufferer.

□ **patiently** adverb.

patina /pa-ti-nuh/ ▸ noun 1 a green or brown film on the surface of old bronze. 2 a soft glow on wooden furniture produced by age and polishing.

patio ▸ noun (plural patios) a paved area outside a house.

patisserie /puh-tiss-uh-ri/ ▸ noun a shop where pastries and cakes are sold.

patois /pat-wah/ ▸ noun (plural patois /pat-wahz/) the dialect of a region.

patriarch /pay-tri-ark/ ▸ noun 1 a man who is the head of a family or tribe. 2 a biblical figure regarded as a father of the human race. 3 a respected older man.

patriarchy ▸ noun (plural patriarchies) a society led or controlled by men.
□ **patriarchal** adjective.

patrician /puh-tri-sh'n/ ▸ noun an aristocrat.
▸ adjective relating to or characteristic of aristocrats.

patricide ▸ noun 1 the killing by someone of their own father. 2 a person who kills their father.

patrimony /pa-tri-muh-ni/ ▸ noun (plural patrimonies) property inherited from your father or male ancestor.

patriot ▸ noun a person who strongly supports their country and is prepared to defend it.
□ **patriotism** noun.

patriotic ▸ adjective devoted to and vigorously supporting your country.

> SYNONYMS nationalistic, loyalist, loyal, chauvinistic, jingoistic, flag-waving.
> ANTONYMS traitorous.

patrol ▸ noun 1 a person or group sent to keep watch over an area. 2 the action of patrolling an area.

> SYNONYMS 1 *ships on patrol in the straits* guard, watch, vigil. 2 *the patrol stopped a woman* squad, detachment, party, force.

▸ verb (patrols, patrolling, patrolled) keep watch over an area by regularly walking or travelling around it.

> SYNONYMS *a guard was patrolling the estate* guard, keep watch on, police, make the rounds of, stand guard (over), defend, safeguard.

patron ▸ noun 1 a person who gives financial support to a person or organization. 2 a regular customer of a restaurant, hotel, etc.

> SYNONYMS 1 *a patron of the arts* sponsor, backer, benefactor, contributor,

p

subscriber, donor, philanthropist, promoter, friend, supporter. **2** *club patrons* **customer,** client, consumer, user, visitor, guest; informal regular.

■ **patron saint** a saint who is believed to protect a particular place or group of people.

patronage ▸ noun **1** support given by a patron. **2** custom attracted by a restaurant, hotel, etc.

SYNONYMS **1** *arts patronage* **sponsorship,** backing, funding, financing, assistance, support. **2** *thank you for your patronage* **custom,** trade, business.

patronize (or **patronise**) ▸ verb (**patronizes, patronizing, patronized**) **1** treat someone as if they lack experience or are not very intelligent. **2** go regularly to a restaurant, hotel, etc.

SYNONYMS **1** *don't patronize me!* **talk down to,** treat like a child. **2** (**patronizing**) **condescending,** supercilious, superior, imperious, scornful; informal uppity, high and mighty. **3** *they patronized local tradesmen* **use,** buy from, shop at, be a customer/client of, deal with, frequent, support.

patter[1] ▸ verb (**patters, pattering, pattered**) make a repeated light tapping sound.
▸ noun a repeated light tapping sound.

patter[2] ▸ noun fast continuous talk.

pattern ▸ noun **1** a repeated decorative design. **2** a regular form or order in which a series of things happen. **3** a model, design, or set of instructions for making something. **4** an example for other people to follow.

SYNONYMS **1** *the pattern on the wallpaper* **design,** decoration, motif, device, marking. **2** *working patterns* **system,** order, arrangement, form, method, structure, scheme, plan, format. **3** *this set the pattern for a generation* **model,** example, criterion, standard, norm, yardstick, touchstone, benchmark, blueprint.

patterned ▸ adjective decorated with a pattern.

patty ▸ noun (plural **patties**) a small pie or pasty.

paucity /paw-si-ti/ ▸ noun a very small or inadequate amount of something.

paunch ▸ noun an abdomen or stomach that is large and sticks out.
□ **paunchy** adjective.

pauper ▸ noun a very poor person.

pause ▸ verb (**pauses, pausing, paused**) stop talking or doing something for a short time before continuing again.

SYNONYMS *let's pause here* **stop,** break off, take a break, adjourn, rest, wait, hesitate; informal take a breather.

▸ noun a temporary stop.

SYNONYMS *five minutes' pause* **break,** interruption, lull, respite, breathing space, gap, interlude, adjournment, rest, wait, hesitation; informal let-up, breather.

pave ▸ verb (**paves, paving, paved**) cover a piece of ground with flat stones.

SYNONYMS **surface,** floor, cover, tile, flag.

□ **paving** noun.

pavement ▸ noun Brit. a raised path for pedestrians at the side of a road.

SYNONYMS **footpath,** walkway; N. Amer. sidewalk.

pavilion ▸ noun **1** Brit. a building at a sports ground used for changing and taking refreshments. **2** a summer house in a park or large garden. **3** a temporary display stand at a trade exhibition.

pavlova ▸ noun a dessert consisting of a meringue base covered with whipped cream and fruit.

paw ▸ noun an animal's foot that has claws and pads.
▸ verb **1** feel or scrape something with a paw or hoof. **2** informal touch someone in a way that is clumsy or unwanted.

pawn[1] ▸ noun **1** a chess piece of the smallest size and value. **2** a person used by more powerful people for their own purposes.

pawn[2] ▸ verb leave an object with a pawnbroker in exchange for money.

pawnbroker ▸ noun a person who is licensed to lend money in exchange for an object that is left with them, and which they can sell if the borrower fails to pay the money back.

pawnshop ▸ noun a pawnbroker's shop.

pawpaw ▸ noun Brit. a papaya.

pay ▸ verb (**pays, paying, paid**) **1** give someone money for work or goods. **2** give a sum of money that is owed. **3** be profitable, or result in an advantage. **4** suffer something as a result of an action. **5** give someone attention, respect, or a compliment. **6** make a visit or a call to.

SYNONYMS **1** *I must pay him for his work* **reward,** reimburse, recompense, remunerate. **2** *I paid £7 for a ticket* **spend,** pay out; informal lay out, shell out, fork out, cough up; N. Amer. informal ante up, pony up. **3** *he paid his debts* **discharge,** settle, pay off, clear. **4** *he made the buses pay* **be profitable,** make money, make a profit. **5** *it may pay you to be early* **be advantageous to,** benefit, be of advantage to, be beneficial to. **6** *he will pay for his mistakes* **suffer (the**

p

consequences), be punished, atone, pay the penalty/price.

▶ noun money that you get for work that you have done.

SYNONYMS *equal pay* **salary**, wages, payment, earnings, remuneration, fee, reimbursement, income, revenue.

■ **pay someone back** take revenge on someone. **pay-off** informal a payment made to someone as a bribe or so that they will not cause trouble.

payable ▶ adjective **1** that must be paid. **2** able to be paid.

SYNONYMS **due**, owed, owing, outstanding, unpaid, overdue; N. Amer. delinquent.

PAYE ▶ abbreviation pay as you earn, a system by which employers pay their employees' income tax directly to the government.

payee ▶ noun a person to whom money is paid.

payload ▶ noun **1** passengers and cargo as the part of a vehicle's load for which money is paid. **2** an explosive warhead carried by an aircraft or missile.

paymaster ▶ noun an official who pays troops or workers.

payment ▶ noun **1** the process of paying someone or of being paid. **2** an amount that is paid.

SYNONYMS **1** *discounts for early payment* **remittance**, settlement, discharge, clearance. **2** *monthly payments* **instalment**, premium. **3** *extra payment for good performance* **salary**, wages, pay, earnings, fees, remuneration, reimbursement, income.

payola /pay-**oh**-luh/ ▶ noun N. Amer. the illegal payment of money to someone in return for their promoting a product in the media.

payroll ▶ noun a list of a company's employees and the amount of money they are to be paid.

PC ▶ abbreviation **1** personal computer. **2** police constable. **3** politically correct, or political correctness.

PDF ▶ noun Computing a kind of electronic file which can be sent by any system and displayed on any computer.

PE ▶ abbreviation physical education.

pea ▶ noun an edible round green seed growing in pods on a climbing plant.

peace ▶ noun **1** freedom from disturbance, noise, or anxiety. **2** freedom from war, or the ending of war.

SYNONYMS **1** *peace at last!* **quiet**, silence, peace and quiet, hush, stillness, still. **2** *peace of mind* **serenity**, peacefulness,

tranquillity, calm, calmness, composure, ease, contentment. **3** *we pray for peace* **order**, harmony, agreement. **4** *a lasting peace* **treaty**, truce, ceasefire, armistice. ANTONYMS noise, agitation, war.

peaceable ▶ adjective **1** wanting to avoid war. **2** free from conflict; peaceful. □ **peaceably** adverb.

peaceful ▶ adjective **1** free from disturbance or noise. **2** not involving war or violence. **3** wanting to avoid conflict.

SYNONYMS **1** *peaceful surroundings* **tranquil**, calm, restful, quiet, still, relaxing. **2** *his peaceful mood* **serene**, calm, tranquil, composed, placid, at ease, untroubled, unworried, content. **3** *peaceful relations* **harmonious**, on good terms, amicable, friendly, cordial, non-violent. ANTONYMS noisy, agitated, hostile.

□ **peacefully** adverb.

peach ▶ noun **1** a round fruit with yellow and red skin and juicy yellow flesh, with a rough stone inside. **2** a pinkish-orange colour.

peacock ▶ noun a large, colourful bird with very long tail feathers that can be fanned out in display.

peahen ▶ noun the female of the peacock.

peak ▶ noun **1** the pointed top of a mountain, or a mountain with a pointed top. **2** a stiff brim at the front of a cap. **3** the point of highest strength, activity, or achievement.

SYNONYMS **1** *the peaks of the mountains* **summit**, top, crest, pinnacle, cap. **2** *the highest peak* **mountain**, hill, height. **3** *the peak of his career* **height**, high point, pinnacle, summit, top, climax, culmination, apex, zenith, acme.

▶ verb reach a maximum or the highest point.

SYNONYMS *Labour support has peaked* **reach its height**, climax, culminate.

▶ adjective **1** greatest; maximum. **2** involving the greatest number of people; busiest.

SYNONYMS *at peak times* **maximum**, greatest, busiest, highest.

peaked¹ ▶ adjective (of a cap) having a peak.

peaked² (or **peaky**) ▶ adjective pale from illness or tiredness.

peal ▶ noun **1** the loud ringing sound of a bell or bells. **2** a loud sound of thunder or laughter. **3** a set of bells.
▶ verb ring or sound loudly.

peanut ▶ noun **1** an oval edible seed that develops in a pod underground. **2** (**peanuts**) informal a very small sum of money.
■ **peanut butter** a spread made from ground roasted peanuts.

p

pear ▸ noun a green edible fruit which has a narrow top and rounded base.

pearl ▸ noun 1 a small hard, shiny white ball that sometimes forms inside the shell of an oyster and has great value as a gem. 2 a thing that is highly valued.
■ **pearl barley** barley that is reduced to small round grains by grinding.
□ **pearly** adjective.

pearlescent ▸ adjective seeming to shine with many soft colours, like mother-of-pearl.

peasant ▸ noun (in the past, or in poor countries) an agricultural worker.
□ **peasantry** noun.

peat ▸ noun a soft brown or black substance formed in damp areas from decayed plants.
□ **peaty** adjective.

pebble ▸ noun a small, smooth round stone.
■ **pebble-dash** mortar mixed with small pebbles, used to coat the outside of houses.
□ **pebbly** adjective.

pecan /pee-k'n/ ▸ noun the smooth edible nut of a hickory tree of the southern US.

peccadillo /pek-kuh-**dil**-loh/ ▸ noun (plural **peccadilloes** or **peccadillos**) a small sin or fault.

peck¹ ▸ verb 1 (of a bird) hit or bite something with its beak. 2 kiss someone lightly or casually.
▸ noun 1 an act of pecking. 2 a light or casual kiss.
■ **pecking order** the order of importance that people or animals give each other within a group.

peck² ▸ noun a measure of dry goods, equal to a quarter of a bushel.

pecker ▸ noun (**keep your pecker up**) Brit. informal remain cheerful.

peckish ▸ adjective informal hungry.

pectin ▸ noun a substance present in ripe fruits, used as a setting agent in jams and jellies.

pectoral ▸ adjective relating to the breast or chest.
▸ noun each of four large paired muscles which cover the front of the ribcage.

peculiar ▸ adjective 1 strange or odd. 2 (**peculiar to**) belonging only to.

> SYNONYMS 1 *something peculiar happened* **strange,** unusual, odd, funny, curious, bizarre, weird, eccentric, abnormal, unconventional, outlandish; informal wacky. 2 *customs peculiar to this area* **distinctive,** exclusive, unique, characteristic, distinct, individual, typical, special, personal. ANTONYMS ordinary.

□ **peculiarly** adverb.

> ✔ **-ar,** not **-er:** peculi**ar**.

peculiarity ▸ noun (plural **peculiarities**) 1 a feature or habit that is strange or unusual, or that belongs only to a particular person, thing, or place. 2 the state of being peculiar.

pecuniary /pi-**kyoo**-ni-uh-ri/ ▸ adjective formal relating to money.

pedagogue /**ped**-uh-gog/ ▸ noun formal a teacher.
□ **pedagogy** noun.

pedal ▸ noun 1 each of a pair of levers that you press with your foot to make a bicycle move along. 2 a lever that you press with your foot to operate an accelerator, brake, or clutch in a motor vehicle. 3 a similar lever on a piano or organ used to sustain or soften the tone.
▸ verb (**pedals, pedalling, pedalled;** US spelling **pedals, pedaling, pedaled**) work the pedals of a bicycle to move along.

> ❗ Don't confuse **pedal** with **peddle,** which means 'sell goods'.

pedalo /**ped**-uh-loh/ ▸ noun (plural **pedalos** or **pedaloes**) Brit. a small pedal-operated pleasure boat.

pedant ▸ noun a person who cares too much about small details or rules.
□ **pedantry** noun.

pedantic ▸ adjective relating to or like a pedant.

> SYNONYMS **finicky,** fussy, fastidious, dogmatic, purist, hair-splitting, quibbling; informal nit-picking, pernickety.

peddle ▸ verb (**peddles, peddling, peddled**) 1 sell goods by going from house to house. 2 sell an illegal drug or stolen item. 3 disapproving spread an idea or view widely or persistently.

> SYNONYMS **sell,** hawk, tout, trade, deal in, traffic in.

> ❗ Don't confuse **peddle** with **pedal.**

peddler ➡ PEDLAR.

pederast /**ped**-uh-rasst/ ▸ noun a man who has sexual intercourse with a boy.
□ **pederasty** noun.

pedestal ▸ noun 1 the base or support on which a statue or column is mounted. 2 the supporting column of a washbasin or toilet.

pedestrian ▸ noun a person who is walking rather than travelling in a vehicle.

> SYNONYMS **walker,** person on foot. ANTONYMS driver.

▸ adjective dull.

> SYNONYMS **dull,** boring, tedious, monotonous, unremarkable, uninspired, unimaginative, unexciting, routine, commonplace, ordinary, everyday, run-

p

of-the-mill, mundane, humdrum; informal bog-standard.
ANTONYMS exciting.

pediatrics US spelling of PAEDIATRICS.

pedicure ▶ noun treatment to improve the appearance of the feet and toenails.

pedigree ▶ noun 1 the record of an animal's origins, showing that all the animals from which it is descended are of the same breed. 2 a person's family history and background.

> SYNONYMS *a fine pedigree* ancestry, lineage, line, descent, genealogy, extraction, parentage, bloodline.

▶ adjective Brit. pure-bred.

> SYNONYMS *a pedigree cat* pure-bred, full-blooded, thoroughbred.

pediment ▶ noun the triangular upper part of the front of a classical building, above the columns.

pedlar (or **peddler**) ▶ noun 1 a trader who sells goods by going from house to house. 2 a person who sells illegal drugs or stolen goods.

pedometer /pi-**dom**-i-ter/ ▶ noun an instrument for estimating how far you are walking by recording the number of steps you take.

peek ▶ verb 1 look quickly or secretly. 2 be just visible.
▶ noun a quick look.

peel ▶ verb 1 remove the skin or rind from a fruit or vegetable. 2 remove a thin covering or layer from. 3 (of a surface) come off in small pieces.

> SYNONYMS 1 *peel and core the fruit* pare, skin, hull, shell. 2 *the wallpaper was peeling* flake (off), come off, fall off.

▶ noun the outer covering or rind of a fruit or vegetable.

> SYNONYMS *orange peel* rind, skin, covering, zest.

peep¹ ▶ verb 1 look quickly and secretly. 2 (**peep out**) be just visible.

> SYNONYMS *I peeped through the keyhole* peek, look, sneak a look, glance; informal squint.

▶ noun 1 a quick or secret look. 2 a momentary or partial view of something.

> SYNONYMS *I'll just take a peep* peek, look, glance; informal squint.

■ **peeping Tom** a person who likes to spy on people undressing or having sex. **peep show** a series of pictures in a box which you look at through a small opening.

peep² ▶ noun a short, high-pitched sound.
▶ verb make a short, high-pitched sound.

peephole ▶ noun a small hole in a door or wall which you can look through.

peer¹ ▶ verb (**peers, peering, peered**) 1 look at something with difficulty or concentration. 2 be just visible.

> SYNONYMS *he peered at the manuscript* look closely, squint, gaze.

peer² ▶ noun 1 a member of the nobility in Britain or Ireland. 2 a person of the same age or social status as you.

> SYNONYMS 1 *hereditary peers* aristocrat, lord, lady, noble, nobleman, noblewoman. 2 *his academic peers* equal, fellow, contemporary.

■ **peer group** a group of people of approximately the same age, status, and interests.

peerage ▶ noun 1 the title and rank of peer or peeress. 2 (**the peerage**) all the peers in Britain or Ireland.

peeress ▶ noun 1 a woman holding the rank of a peer in her own right. 2 the wife or widow of a peer.

peerless ▶ adjective better than all others.

peeved ▶ adjective informal annoyed; irritated.

peevish ▶ adjective irritable.

peewit ▶ noun Brit. a lapwing.

peg ▶ noun 1 a pin or bolt used for hanging things on, securing something in place, or marking a position. 2 a clip for holding things together or hanging up clothes.

> SYNONYMS *a tent peg* pin, nail, dowel.

▶ verb (**pegs, pegging, pegged**) 1 fix, attach, or mark something with a peg or pegs. 2 fix a price, rate, etc. at a particular level.

> SYNONYMS 1 *the flysheet is pegged to the ground* fix, pin, attach, fasten, secure. 2 *we decided to peg our prices* set, hold, fix, freeze, keep down, hold down.

■ **off the peg** (of clothes) not made to order; ready-made.

peignoir /**pay**-nwar/ ▶ noun a woman's light dressing gown or negligee.

pejorative /pi-**jorr**-uh-tiv/ ▶ adjective expressing contempt or disapproval.
□ **pejoratively** adverb.

Pekinese ▶ noun (plural **Pekinese**) a small dog with long hair and a snub nose.

pelican ▶ noun a large waterbird with a bag of skin hanging from a long bill.
■ **pelican crossing** (in the UK) a pedestrian crossing with traffic lights that are operated by the pedestrians.

pellagra /pel-**lag**-ruh/ ▶ noun a disease caused by an inadequate diet, whose symptoms include inflamed skin and diarrhoea.

pellet ▶ noun 1 a small compressed mass of a substance. 2 a lightweight bullet or piece of small shot.

pell-mell ▸ adjective & adverb in a confused or rushed way.

pellucid /pel-**loo**-sid/ ▸ adjective translucent or transparent; clear.

pelmet ▸ noun a structure or strip of fabric fitted across the top of a window to conceal the curtain fittings.

pelt¹ ▸ verb 1 hurl missiles at. 2 (**pelt down**) fall very heavily.
■ (**at**) **full pelt** as fast as possible.

pelt² ▸ noun the skin of an animal with the fur, wool, or hair still on it.

pelvis ▸ noun the large bony frame at the base of the spine to which the legs are attached.
□ **pelvic** adjective.

pen¹ ▸ noun an instrument for writing or drawing with ink.
▸ verb (**pens, penning, penned**) write or compose.

SYNONYMS *he penned a number of articles* **write,** compose, draft, dash off, scribble.

■ **pen name** a name used by a writer that is not their real name.

pen² ▸ noun a small enclosure for farm animals.

SYNONYMS *a sheep pen* **enclosure,** fold, pound, compound, stockade, sty, coop; N. Amer. corral.

▸ verb (**pens, penning, penned**) 1 put or keep animals in a pen. 2 (**pen someone/thing up** or **in**) shut a person or animal up in a small space.

SYNONYMS *the hostages were penned up in a basement* **confine,** coop, cage, shut, box, lock, trap, imprison, incarcerate.

penal ▸ adjective 1 relating to the use of punishment as part of the legal system. 2 very severe.

penalize (or **penalise**) ▸ verb (**penalizes, penalizing, penalized**) 1 give someone a penalty or punishment. 2 put in an unfavourable position.

SYNONYMS 1 *if you break the rules you will be penalized* **punish,** discipline. 2 *a new tax would penalize the poor* **handicap,** disadvantage, discriminate against. ANTONYMS reward, benefit.

penalty ▸ noun (plural **penalties**) 1 a punishment given to someone for breaking a law, rule, or contract. 2 something unpleasant suffered as a result of an action or circumstance. 3 (also **penalty kick**) Soccer a free shot at the goal awarded to the attacking team after a foul within the area around the goal (the **penalty area**).

SYNONYMS **punishment,** sanction, fine, forfeit, sentence. ANTONYMS reward.

penance ▸ noun 1 something that you yourself do or that a priest gives you to do as punishment for having done wrong. 2 a religious act in which someone confesses their sins to a priest and is given penance or formal forgiveness.

pence plural of PENNY.

❗ It is wrong to use **pence** in the singular to mean 'penny'; say *one penny* not *one pence*.

penchant /**pon**-shon/ ▸ noun a strong liking for something.

pencil ▸ noun an instrument for writing or drawing, consisting of a thin stick of graphite enclosed in a wooden case.
▸ verb (**pencils, pencilling, pencilled;** US spelling **pencils, penciling, penciled**) 1 write or draw something with a pencil. 2 (**pencil something in**) enter a time or date in your diary on the understanding that it might have to be changed later.

pendant ▸ noun 1 a piece of jewellery worn hanging from a chain around the neck. 2 a light designed to hang from the ceiling.
▸ adjective (also **pendent**) hanging downwards.

pending ▸ adjective 1 waiting to be decided or settled. 2 about to happen.

SYNONYMS 1 *nine cases were still pending* **unresolved,** undecided, unsettled, up in the air, ongoing, outstanding; informal on the back burner. 2 *with a general election pending* **imminent,** impending, about to happen, forthcoming, on the way, coming, approaching, looming, near, on the horizon, in the offing.

▸ preposition awaiting the outcome of.

SYNONYMS *they were released on bail pending an appeal* **awaiting,** until.

pendulous ▸ adjective hanging down; drooping.

pendulum ▸ noun a weight hung from a fixed point so that it can swing freely, used in regulating the mechanism of a clock.

penetrate ▸ verb (**penetrates, penetrating, penetrated**) 1 force a way into or through. 2 gain access to an enemy organization or a competitor's market.

SYNONYMS 1 *the knife penetrated his lungs* **pierce,** puncture, enter, perforate, stab, gore. 2 *they penetrated enemy lines* **infiltrate,** slip through, enter. 3 *his words finally penetrated* **register,** sink in, become clear, fall into place; informal click.

□ **penetration** noun **penetrative** adjective.

penetrating ▸ adjective 1 clearly heard through or above other sounds. 2 (of someone's look) intent. 3 having or showing clear insight.

SYNONYMS 1 *a penetrating voice* **shrill,** strident, piercing, ear-splitting. 2 *her*

p

penetrating gaze **intent,** searching, piercing, probing, sharp, keen. **3** *a penetrating analysis* **perceptive,** insightful, keen, sharp, intelligent, clever, smart, incisive, trenchant, astute. ANTONYMS soft, stupid.

penfriend ▸ noun a person with whom you form a friendship through exchanging letters.

penguin ▸ noun a black and white seabird living in the Antarctic and unable to fly.

penicillin ▸ noun a type of antibiotic.

peninsula ▸ noun a long, narrow piece of land projecting into the sea.
□ **peninsular** adjective.

penis ▸ noun the male organ used for urinating and having sex.

penitent ▸ adjective feeling sorrow and regret for having done wrong.
▸ noun a person who is doing penance.
□ **penitence** noun **penitential** adjective.

penitentiary /pen-i-ten-shuh-ri/ ▸ noun (plural **penitentiaries**) N. Amer. a prison for people convicted of serious crimes.

penknife ▸ noun a small knife with a blade which folds into the handle.

pennant ▸ noun a long, narrow pointed flag.

penne /pen-nay/ ▸ plural noun pasta in the form of short wide tubes.

penniless ▸ adjective having no money.

pennon = PENNANT.

penny ▸ noun (plural **pennies** (for separate coins); **pence** (for a sum of money)) **1** a British bronze coin worth one hundredth of a pound. **2** (in the past) a British coin worth one twelfth of a shilling and 240th of a pound.
■ **penny-farthing** an early type of bicycle with a very large front wheel and a small rear wheel. **penny-pinching** unwilling to spend money.

pension¹ /pen-sh'n/ ▸ noun a regular payment made to retired people, widows, etc., either by the state or from an investment fund.

SYNONYMS **old-age pension,** retirement pension, superannuation, allowance, benefit, support, welfare.

▸ verb (**pension someone off**) dismiss someone from employment and pay them a pension.
□ **pensionable** adjective.

pension² /pon-syon/ ▸ noun a small hotel in France and other European countries.

pensioner ▸ noun a person who receives a pension.

SYNONYMS **retired person,** old-age pensioner, OAP, senior citizen; N. Amer. senior, retiree.

pensive ▸ adjective thinking deeply about something.

□ **pensively** adverb.

pentacle ▸ noun a pentagram.

pentagon ▸ noun **1** a figure with five straight sides and five angles. **2** (**the Pentagon**) the headquarters of the US Department of Defense.

pentagram ▸ noun a five-pointed star used as a magical symbol.

pentameter /pen-tam-i-ter/ ▸ noun a line of poetry with five stressed syllables.

Pentateuch /pen-tuh-tyook/ ▸ noun the first five books of the Old Testament and Hebrew Scriptures.

pentathlon ▸ noun an athletic event consisting of five different activities.
□ **pentathlete** noun.

Pentecost ▸ noun **1** the Christian festival celebrating the coming of the Holy Spirit to the disciples of Jesus after his Ascension. **2** a Jewish festival that takes place fifty days after the second day of Passover.

Pentecostal ▸ adjective having to do with a Christian movement which emphasizes the gifts of the Holy Spirit, e.g. the healing of the sick.

penthouse ▸ noun a flat on the top floor of a tall building.

pent-up ▸ adjective not expressed or released.

penultimate ▸ adjective last but one.

penumbra /pi-num-bruh/ ▸ noun the partially shaded outer part of a shadow.

penurious /pi-nyoor-i-uhss/ ▸ adjective formal very poor.

penury /pen-yuu-ri/ ▸ noun extreme poverty.

peony /pee-uh-ni/ ▸ noun a plant with large red, pink, or white flowers.

people ▸ plural noun **1** human beings in general. **2** (**the people**) all those living in a country or society. **3** (plural **peoples**) the members of a particular nation, community, or ethnic group.

SYNONYMS **1** *crowds of people* **human beings,** persons, individuals, humans, mortals, living souls, personages, (men, women, and children); informal folk. **2** *the British people* **citizens,** subjects, electors, voters, taxpayers, residents, inhabitants, public, citizenry, nation, population, populace. **3** *a man of the people* **the common people,** the proletariat, the masses, the populace, the rank and file; derogatory the hoi polloi; informal, derogatory the proles, the plebs. **4** *her people don't live far away* **family,** parents, relatives, relations, folk, kinsfolk, flesh and blood, nearest and dearest; informal folks. **5** *a proud people* **race,** ethnic group, tribe, clan, nation.

p

▶ verb (**peoples, peopling, peopled**) live in a place or fill it with people.

> SYNONYMS *those who once peopled Newfoundland* **populate**, settle (in), colonize, inhabit, live in, occupy.

pep informal ▶ verb (**peps, pepping, pepped**) (**pep someone/thing up**) make someone or something more lively.
▶ noun liveliness.
■ **pep talk** a talk given to someone to make them feel braver or more enthusiastic.

pepper ▶ noun **1** a hot-tasting powder made from peppercorns, used to flavour food. **2** the fruit of a tropical American plant, of which sweet peppers and chilli peppers are varieties.
▶ verb (**peppers, peppering, peppered**) **1** season food with pepper. **2** (**pepper something with**) scatter large amounts of something over an area. **3** hit a place repeatedly with small missiles or gunshot.

> SYNONYMS **1** *stars peppered the desert skies* **sprinkle**, fleck, dot, spot, stipple. **2** *gunfire peppered the area* **bombard**, pelt, shower, rain down on, strafe, rake, blitz.

□ **pepperiness** noun **peppery** adjective.

peppercorn ▶ noun the dried berry of a climbing vine, used whole as a spice or crushed to make pepper.
■ **peppercorn rent** a very low rent.

peppermint ▶ noun **1** a plant of the mint family whose leaves and oil are used as a flavouring in food. **2** a sweet flavoured with peppermint oil.

pepperoni /pep-puh-**roh**-ni/ ▶ noun a dried sausage made from beef and pork and seasoned with pepper.

peptic ▶ adjective relating to digestion.
■ **peptic ulcer** an ulcer in the lining of the stomach or small intestine.

per ▶ preposition **1** for each. **2** by means of. **3** (**as per**) according to.

perambulate ▶ verb (**perambulates, perambulating, perambulated**) formal walk or travel from place to place.
□ **perambulation** noun.

perambulator ▶ noun dated a pram.

per annum ▶ adverb for each year.

per capita ▶ adverb & adjective for each person.

perceive ▶ verb (**perceives, perceiving, perceived**) **1** become aware of something through starting to see, smell, or hear it. **2** (**perceive something as**) understand or interpret something in a particular way.

> SYNONYMS **1** *he perceived a tear in her eye* **see**, discern, detect, catch sight of, spot, observe, notice. **2** *he was perceived as too negative* **regard**, look on, view, consider, think of, judge, deem.

□ **perceivable** adjective.

> ✔ Remember, **i** before **e** except after **c**: perc**ei**ve.

per cent (also US **percent**) ▶ adverb by a stated amount in or for every hundred.
▶ noun one part in every hundred.

percentage ▶ noun **1** a rate, number, or amount in each hundred. **2** a proportion or share of a whole.

percentile /per-**sen**-tyl/ ▶ noun Statistics each of 100 equal groups into which a population can be divided.

perceptible ▶ adjective able to be noticed or felt.
□ **perceptibly** adverb.

perception ▶ noun **1** the ability to see, hear, or become aware of something. **2** a particular understanding of something. **3** the process of perceiving.

> SYNONYMS **1** *popular perceptions about old age* **impression**, idea, conception, notion, thought, belief. **2** *he talks with great perception* **insight**, perceptiveness, understanding, intelligence, intuition, incisiveness.

perceptive ▶ adjective having a good understanding of people and situations.

> SYNONYMS **insightful**, discerning, sensitive, intuitive, observant, penetrating, intelligent, clever, canny, keen, sharp, astute, shrewd, quick, smart, acute; informal on the ball; N. Amer. informal heads-up.
> ANTONYMS obtuse.

□ **perceptively** adverb.

perceptual ▶ adjective relating to the ability to perceive.

perch¹ ▶ noun **1** a branch, bar, or ledge on which a bird rests or roosts. **2** a high or narrow seat or resting place.
▶ verb **1** sit or rest somewhere. **2** place or balance something somewhere.

> SYNONYMS **1** *a swallow perched on the telegraph wire* **sit**, rest, alight, settle, land, roost. **2** *she perched her glasses on her nose* **put**, place, set, rest, balance.

perch² ▶ noun (plural **perch** or **perches**) a freshwater fish with a spiny fin on its back.

perchance ▶ adverb old use perhaps.

percipient ▶ adjective having good insight or understanding.

percolate ▶ verb (**percolates, percolating, percolated**) **1** filter through a porous surface or substance. **2** (of information or ideas) spread gradually through a group of people. **3** prepare coffee in a percolator.
□ **percolation** noun.

percolator ▶ noun a machine for making coffee, consisting of a pot in which

p

boiling water is circulated through a small chamber that holds the ground beans.

percussion ▸ noun musical instruments that you play by hitting or shaking them.
□ **percussionist** noun.

perdition ▸ noun (in Christian thinking) a state of eternal damnation into which people who have sinned and not repented pass when they die.

peregrinations ▸ plural noun old use journeys or wanderings from place to place.

peregrine ▸ noun a powerful falcon with a bluish-grey back and wings.

peremptory ▸ adjective insisting on immediate attention or obedience.
□ **peremptorily** adverb.

perennial ▸ adjective 1 lasting or doing something for a very long time. 2 (of a plant) living for several years.

> SYNONYMS **lasting,** enduring, abiding, long-lasting, long-lived, perpetual, continuing, continual, recurring.
> ANTONYMS ephemeral.

▸ noun a perennial plant.
□ **perennially** adverb.

perestroika /pe-ri-**stroy**-kuh/ ▸ noun (in the former Soviet Union) the economic and political reforms introduced during the 1980s.

perfect ▸ adjective /**per**-fikt/ 1 having all the parts and qualities that are needed or wanted, and no flaws or weaknesses. 2 total; complete: *it made perfect sense.* 3 Grammar (of a verb) referring to a completed action or to a state in the past.

> SYNONYMS 1 *a perfect wife* **ideal,** model, faultless, flawless, consummate, exemplary, best, ultimate, copybook. 2 *in perfect condition* **flawless,** mint, as good as new, pristine, immaculate, optimum, prime, peak; informal tip-top, A1. 3 *a perfect copy* **exact,** precise, accurate, faithful, true; Brit. informal spot on; N. Amer. informal on the money. 4 *the perfect Christmas present* **ideal,** just right, appropriate, fitting, suitable, tailor-made, very; Brit. informal spot on, just the job. 5 *she felt a perfect idiot* **absolute,** complete, total, real, out-and-out, thorough, downright, utter; Brit. informal right; Austral./NZ informal fair.

▸ verb /per-**fekt**/ make something perfect.

> SYNONYMS *he's perfecting his style* **improve,** polish (up), hone, refine, brush up, fine-tune.

perfection ▸ noun the process of perfecting, or the state of being perfect.

> SYNONYMS **the ideal,** a paragon, the last word, the ultimate; informal the tops, the bee's knees.

perfectionism ▸ noun the refusal to be satisfied with something unless it is done perfectly.
□ **perfectionist** noun & adjective.

perfectly ▸ adverb 1 in a perfect way. 2 completely (used for emphasis).

> SYNONYMS 1 *a perfectly cooked meal* **superbly,** superlatively, excellently, flawlessly, faultlessly, to perfection, immaculately, exquisitely, consummately; N. Amer. to a fare-thee-well; informal like a dream, to a T. 2 *we understand each other perfectly* **absolutely,** completely, altogether, entirely, wholly, totally, fully, in every respect.
> ANTONYMS badly, partly.

perfidious /per-**fid**-i-uhss/ ▸ adjective deceitful and disloyal.

perfidy /**per**-fi-di/ ▸ noun literary deceit; disloyalty.

perforate ▸ verb (perforates, perforating, perforated) pierce and make a hole or holes in.
□ **perforation** noun.

perforce ▸ adverb formal necessarily; inevitably.

perform ▸ verb 1 carry out an action, task, or function. 2 work, function, or do something to a particular standard. 3 entertain an audience by playing a piece of music, acting in a play, etc.

> SYNONYMS 1 *duties to perform* **carry out,** do, execute, discharge, conduct, implement; informal pull off. 2 *the car performs well* **function,** work, operate, run, go, respond, behave, act. 3 *the play was performed in Britain* **stage,** put on, present, mount, act, produce. 4 *the band performed live* **play,** sing, appear.
> ANTONYMS neglect.

performance ▸ noun 1 an act of performing a play, piece of music, etc. 2 the process of performing. 3 informal a fuss. 4 the capabilities of a machine or product.

> SYNONYMS 1 *the evening performance* **show,** production, showing, presentation, staging, concert, recital; informal gig. 2 *their performance was excellent* **rendition,** interpretation, playing, acting. 3 *the performance of his duty* **carrying out,** execution, discharge, completion, fulfilment. 4 *the performance of the processor* **functioning,** working, operation, running, behaviour, response, economy.

■ **performance art** an art form that combines visual art with drama.

performer ▸ noun a person who performs.

SYNONYMS **actor, actress,** artiste, artist, entertainer, trouper, player, musician, singer, dancer, comic, comedian, comedienne.

perfume /**per**-fyoom/ ▶ noun **1** a sweet-smelling liquid put on the body. **2** a pleasant smell.

SYNONYMS **1** *a bottle of perfume* **scent,** fragrance, eau de toilette, toilet water. **2** *the heady perfume of lilacs* **smell,** scent, fragrance, aroma, bouquet.

▶ verb /per-**fyoom**/ (**perfumes, perfuming, perfumed**) **1** give a pleasant smell to. **2** put perfume on or in.
☐ **perfumery** noun.

perfunctory ▶ adjective carried out without much care or effort.
☐ **perfunctorily** adverb.

pergola /**per**-guh-luh/ ▶ noun an arched structure forming a framework for climbing plants.

perhaps ▶ adverb possibly; maybe.

SYNONYMS **maybe,** for all one knows, it could be, it may be, it's possible, possibly, conceivably; N. English happen.

peril ▶ noun a situation of serious and immediate danger.

SYNONYMS **danger,** jeopardy, risk, hazard, menace, threat.
ANTONYMS safety.

perilous ▶ adjective full of danger or risk.
☐ **perilously** adverb.

perimeter ▶ noun the boundary or outside edge of something.

SYNONYMS **boundary,** border, limits, bounds, edge, margin, fringe(s), periphery.
ANTONYMS centre.

perinatal /per-i-**nay**-t'l/ ▶ adjective at the time immediately before and after a birth.

perineum /pe-ri-**nee**-uhm/ ▶ noun (plural **perinea**) the area between the anus and the genitals.

period ▶ noun **1** a length or portion of time. **2** a lesson in a school. **3** (also **menstrual period**) a flow of blood each month from the lining of a woman's womb. **4** N. Amer. a full stop.

SYNONYMS **1** *a six-week period* **time,** spell, interval, stretch, term, span, phase, bout; Brit. informal patch. **2** *the post-war period* **era,** age, epoch, time, days, years.

▶ adjective belonging to or characteristic of a past historical time.
■ **period piece** an object made or a book or play set in an earlier period.

periodic ▶ adjective appearing or happening at intervals.

SYNONYMS **regular,** at fixed intervals, recurrent, recurring, repeated, cyclical, seasonal, occasional, intermittent, sporadic, odd.

■ **periodic table** a table of all the chemical elements.

periodical ▶ adjective **1** happening or appearing at intervals. **2** (of a magazine or newspaper) published at regular intervals.
▶ noun a periodical magazine or newspaper.

SYNONYMS **journal,** magazine, newspaper, paper, review, digest, gazette, newsletter, organ; informal mag, glossy.

☐ **periodically** adverb.

peripatetic /pe-ri-puh-**tet**-ik/ ▶ adjective travelling from place to place.

peripheral /puh-**rif**-uh-ruhl/ ▶ adjective **1** relating to or situated on an edge or boundary. **2** outside the most important part of something; marginal.

SYNONYMS **secondary,** subsidiary, incidental, tangential, marginal, minor, unimportant, ancillary.
ANTONYMS central.

☐ **peripherally** adverb.

periphery /puh-**rif**-uh-ri/ ▶ noun (plural **peripheries**) **1** the outside edge or boundary of something. **2** an area of activity that is outside the most important part of something.

periscope ▶ noun a device consisting of a tube attached to a set of mirrors, through which you can see things that are above or behind something else.

perish ▶ verb **1** die. **2** be completely ruined or destroyed. **3** (of rubber or a similar material) rot or decay. **4** (**be perished**) Brit. informal feel very cold. **5** (**perishing**) Brit. informal very cold.

SYNONYMS **1** *millions of soldiers perished* **die,** lose your life, be killed, fall, be lost; informal buy it. **2** *the rubber had perished* **go bad,** spoil, rot, decay, decompose.

perishable ▶ adjective (of food) not able to be kept beyond a certain time because it will rot or decay.

peristalsis ▶ noun the contraction and relaxation of muscles in the digestive system and intestines, creating wave-like movements which push food through the body.

peritoneum /pe-ri-tuh-**nee**-uhm/ ▶ noun (plural **peritoneums** or **peritonea** /pe-ri-tuh-**nee**-uh/) a membrane lining the inside of the abdomen.
☐ **peritoneal** adjective.

peritonitis ▶ noun inflammation of the peritoneum.

periwinkle ▶ noun **1** a plant with purple flowers and glossy leaves. **2** = WINKLE.

p

perjure ▸ verb (perjures, perjuring, perjured) (perjure yourself) tell a lie in court after swearing to tell the truth.

perjury /per-juh-ri/ ▸ noun the offence of deliberately telling a lie in court after swearing to tell the truth.

perk[1] ▸ verb (perk up) become more cheerful or lively.

perk[2] ▸ noun informal an extra benefit given to an employee in addition to their wages.

> SYNONYMS **fringe benefit,** advantage, bonus, extra, plus; informal freebie.

perky ▸ adjective (perkier, perkiest) cheerful and lively.

perm ▸ noun (also permanent wave) a method of setting the hair in waves or curls and treating it with chemicals so that the style lasts for several months.
▸ verb treat hair in such a way.

permafrost ▸ noun a layer of soil beneath the surface that remains below freezing point throughout the year.

permanent ▸ adjective lasting for a long time or forever.

> SYNONYMS **1** *permanent brain damage* **lasting,** enduring, indefinite, continuing, constant, irreparable, irreversible, lifelong, indelible, standing. **2** *a permanent job* **long-term,** stable, secure.
> ANTONYMS temporary.

☐ **permanence** noun.

✔ perm**anent**, not **-enant** or **-anant**.

permanently ▸ adverb in a permanent way.

> SYNONYMS **1** *the attack left her permanently disabled* **forever,** for all time, for good, irreversibly, incurably, irreparably, indelibly; informal for keeps. **2** *I was permanently hungry* **continually,** constantly, perpetually, always.

permeable ▸ adjective allowing liquids or gases to pass through.

permeate ▸ verb (permeates, permeating, permeated) spread throughout.

permissible ▸ adjective permitted.

permission ▸ noun the act of allowing someone to do something.

> SYNONYMS **authorization,** consent, leave, authority, sanction, licence, dispensation, assent, agreement, approval, blessing, clearance; informal the go-ahead, the green light, say-so.
> ANTONYMS ban.

permissive ▸ adjective allowing someone a lot of freedom of behaviour.
☐ **permissiveness** noun.

permit ▸ verb /per-mit/ (permits, permitting, permitted) **1** say that someone is allowed to do something. **2** make something possible.

> SYNONYMS *other synthetic drugs would be permitted* **allow,** let, authorize, sanction, grant, license, consent to, assent to; informal give the go-ahead to, give the green light to.
> ANTONYMS ban.

▸ noun /per-mit/ an official document saying that someone is allowed to do something or go somewhere.

> SYNONYMS *a work permit* **authorization,** licence, pass, ticket, warrant, passport, visa.

permutation ▸ noun each of several possible ways in which a number of things can be ordered or arranged.

pernicious ▸ adjective having a harmful effect.

pernickety ▸ adjective fussy.

peroration ▸ noun the concluding part of a speech.

peroxide ▸ noun (also hydrogen peroxide) a chemical that is used as a bleach or disinfectant.

perpendicular ▸ adjective at an angle of 90° to the ground, or to another line or surface.
▸ noun a perpendicular line.

perpetrate ▸ verb (perpetrates, perpetrating, perpetrated) carry out a bad or illegal action.
☐ **perpetration** noun **perpetrator** noun.

perpetual ▸ adjective **1** never ending or changing. **2** so frequent as to seem continual.

> SYNONYMS **1** *a perpetual state of fear* **constant,** permanent, uninterrupted, continuous, unremitting, unending, everlasting, eternal, unceasing, without end, persistent, lasting, abiding. **2** *perpetual nagging* **interminable,** incessant, ceaseless, endless, relentless, unrelenting, persistent, continual, continuous, non-stop, never-ending, repeated, unremitting, round-the-clock, unabating; informal eternal.
> ANTONYMS temporary, intermittent.

☐ **perpetually** adverb.

perpetuate ▸ verb (perpetuates, perpetuating, perpetuated) cause something to continue indefinitely.
☐ **perpetuation** noun.

perpetuity ▸ noun (plural perpetuities) the state of lasting forever.

perplex ▸ verb puzzle someone very much.

> SYNONYMS **puzzle,** baffle, mystify, bewilder, confuse, disconcert, worry.

☐ **perplexing** adjective.

perplexity ▸ noun (plural perplexities) **1** the state of being puzzled. **2** a puzzling situation or thing.

p

perquisite /per-kwi-zit/ ▸ noun formal a special right or privilege.

perry ▸ noun (plural **perries**) an alcoholic drink made from pear juice.

per se /per say/ ▸ adverb in itself.

persecute ▸ verb (**persecutes, persecuting, persecuted**) **1** treat badly over a long period. **2** harass.

SYNONYMS **1** *they were persecuted for their beliefs* **oppress,** abuse, victimize, ill-treat, mistreat, maltreat, torment, torture. **2** *she was persecuted by the press* **harass,** hound, plague, badger, harry, intimidate, pick on, pester; informal hassle.

□ **persecution** noun **persecutor** noun.

persevere ▸ verb continue doing something in spite of difficulty or lack of success.
□ **perseverance** noun.

Persian ▸ noun **1** a person from Persia (now Iran). **2** the language of ancient Persia or modern Iran. **3** a breed of cat with long hair.
▸ adjective relating to Persia or Iran.

persiflage /per-si-flahzh/ ▸ noun formal light teasing or joking.

persimmon /per-sim-muhn/ ▸ noun a fruit that looks like a large tomato but is very sweet.

persist ▸ verb **1** continue doing something in spite of difficulty or opposition. **2** continue to exist.

SYNONYMS **1** *Corbett persisted with his questioning* **persevere,** continue, carry on, go on, keep on, keep going, hammer away, keep at it; informal soldier on, plug away. **2** *if dry weather persists, water the lawn thoroughly* **continue,** hold, carry on, last, keep on, remain, linger, stay, endure.
ANTONYMS give up, stop.

persistence ▸ noun the quality of being persistent.

SYNONYMS **perseverance,** tenacity, determination, staying power, endurance, doggedness, stamina; informal stickability; N. Amer. informal stick-to-it-iveness.

persistent ▸ adjective **1** continuing to do something in spite of difficulty or opposition. **2** continuing or recurring over a long period.

SYNONYMS **1** *a very persistent man* **tenacious,** determined, resolute, dogged, tireless, indefatigable, insistent, unrelenting. **2** *persistent rain* **constant,** continuous, continuing, continual, non-stop, never-ending, steady, uninterrupted, unbroken, interminable, incessant, endless, unending, unrelenting. **3** *a persistent cough*

chronic, nagging, frequent, repeated, habitual.
ANTONYMS irresolute, intermittent.

□ **persistently** adverb.

✔ persist**ent**, not **-ant**.

person ▸ noun (plural **people** or **persons**) **1** an individual human being. **2** a person's body. **3** Grammar a category used in classifying pronouns and verb forms according to whether they indicate the speaker (**first person**), the person spoken to (**second person**), or a third party (**third person**).

SYNONYMS **human being,** individual, man, woman, human, being, living soul, mortal, creature; informal type, sort, beggar, cookie.

■ **in person** physically present.

persona /per-soh-nuh/ ▸ noun (plural **personas** or **personae** /per-soh-nee/) the part of a person's character that is revealed to other people.

personable ▸ adjective having a pleasant appearance and manner.

personage ▸ noun a person of importance or high status.

personal ▸ adjective **1** having to do with or belonging to a particular person. **2** done by a particular person themselves, rather than someone acting for them. **3** concerning a person's private rather than professional or public life. **4** referring to someone's character or appearance in a way that is offensive. **5** relating to a person's body.

SYNONYMS **1** *a highly personal style* **distinctive,** characteristic, unique, individual, idiosyncratic. **2** *a personal appearance* **in person,** in the flesh, actual, live, physical. **3** *his personal life* **private,** intimate. **4** *personal remarks* **derogatory,** disparaging, belittling, insulting, rude, disrespectful, offensive, pejorative.
ANTONYMS common, public, complimentary.

■ **personal pronoun** Grammar each of the pronouns that show person, gender, number, and case (such as *I, you, he, she,* etc.). **personal stereo** a small portable cassette or compact disc player, used with headphones.

personality ▸ noun (plural **personalities**) **1** the qualities that form a person's character. **2** qualities that make someone interesting or popular. **3** a celebrity.

SYNONYMS **1** *her cheerful personality* **character,** nature, disposition, temperament, make-up, psyche. **2** *she had loads of personality* **charisma,** magnetism, character, charm, presence. **3** *a famous personality* **celebrity,** VIP, star, superstar, big name, somebody,

p

leading light, luminary, notable; informal celeb.
ANTONYMS nobody.

personalize (or personalise) ▸ verb (personalizes, personalizing, personalized) **1** design or produce something to meet someone's individual requirements. **2** cause an issue or argument to become concerned with personalities or feelings.

personally ▸ adverb **1** in person. **2** from your own viewpoint.

> SYNONYMS **1** *I'd like to thank him personally* **in person**, yourself. **2** *personally, I like it* **for my part**, for myself, as far as I am concerned, subjectively.

persona non grata /per-soh-nuh nohn grah-tuh/ ▸ noun a person who is not welcome in a place.

personify ▸ verb (personifies, personifying, personified) **1** give human characteristics to something that is not human. **2** be an example of a quality or characteristic.
□ **personification** noun.

personnel ▸ plural noun people employed in an organization.

> SYNONYMS **staff**, employees, workforce, workers, labour force, manpower, human resources.

perspective ▸ noun **1** the art of representing things in a picture so that they seem to have height, width, depth, and relative distance. **2** a way of seeing something. **3** understanding of how important things are in relation to others.

> SYNONYMS **outlook**, view, viewpoint, point of view, standpoint, position, stand, stance, angle, slant, attitude.

perspex ▸ noun trademark a tough transparent plastic.

perspicacious ▸ adjective quickly gaining insight into things.
□ **perspicacity** noun.

perspicuous ▸ adjective **1** clearly expressed and easily understood. **2** (of a person) expressing things clearly.

perspiration ▸ noun **1** sweat. **2** the process of sweating.

perspire ▸ verb (perspires, perspiring, perspired) produce sweat through the pores of your skin.

persuade ▸ verb (persuades, persuading, persuaded) use reasoning or argument to make someone do or believe something.

> SYNONYMS **1** *he persuaded her to go with him* **prevail on**, talk into, coax, convince, get, induce, win over, bring round, influence, sway; informal sweet-talk. **2** *lack of money persuaded them to abandon*

the scheme **cause**, lead, move, dispose, incline.
ANTONYMS dissuade, deter.

persuasion ▸ noun **1** the process of persuading or of being persuaded. **2** a belief or set of beliefs.

> SYNONYMS **1** *Monica needed a lot of persuasion* **coaxing**, urging, inducement, convincing, encouragement, enticement; informal sweet-talking. **2** *various religious persuasions* **group**, grouping, sect, denomination, party, camp, side, faction, school of thought, belief, creed, faith.

persuasive ▸ adjective **1** good at persuading someone to do or believe something. **2** providing evidence or reasoning that makes you believe something.

> SYNONYMS **convincing**, compelling, effective, telling, forceful, powerful, eloquent, impressive, sound, cogent, valid, strong, plausible, credible.
> ANTONYMS unconvincing.

□ **persuasively** adverb.

pert ▸ adjective **1** attractively lively or cheeky. **2** (of a bodily feature) attractively small and firm.

pertain ▸ verb (pertain to) be appropriate, related, or relevant to.

pertinacious ▸ adjective formal persistent.
□ **pertinacity** noun.

pertinent ▸ adjective relevant or appropriate.

> SYNONYMS **relevant**, to the point, apposite, appropriate, suitable, applicable, material, germane.
> ANTONYMS irrelevant.

□ **pertinence** noun **pertinently** adverb.

perturb ▸ verb make someone worried or anxious.
□ **perturbation** noun.

peruse ▸ verb (peruses, perusing, perused) formal read or examine thoroughly or carefully.
□ **perusal** noun.

Peruvian /puh-roo-vi-uhn/ ▸ noun a person from Peru.
▸ adjective relating to Peru.

pervade ▸ verb (pervades, pervading, pervaded) spread or be present throughout.

pervasive ▸ adjective spreading widely through something.
□ **pervasively** adverb **pervasiveness** noun.

perverse ▸ adjective **1** deliberately choosing to behave in a way that other people find unacceptable. **2** contrary to what is accepted or expected.

> SYNONYMS **1** *he is being deliberately perverse* **awkward**, contrary, difficult, unreasonable, uncooperative, unhelpful,

obstructive, stubborn, obstinate; Brit. informal bloody-minded. **2** *a verdict that is manifestly perverse* **illogical,** irrational, wrong-headed.
ANTONYMS accommodating, reasonable.

□ **perversely** adverb **perversity** noun.

perversion ▶ noun **1** the action of perverting. **2** abnormal or unacceptable sexual behaviour.

pervert ▶ verb **1** change the form or meaning of something in a way that distorts it. **2** make someone perverted.

SYNONYMS *perverting the course of justice* **distort,** warp, corrupt, subvert, twist, bend, abuse, divert.

▶ noun a person whose sexual behaviour is abnormal and unacceptable.

SYNONYMS *a nasty pervert* **deviant,** degenerate; informal perv, dirty old man, sicko.

perverted ▶ adjective sexually abnormal or unacceptable.

SYNONYMS **unnatural,** deviant, warped, twisted, abnormal, unhealthy, depraved, perverse, aberrant, debased, degenerate; informal sick, kinky.

pervious /**per**-vi-uhss/ ▶ adjective allowing water to pass through.

peseta /puh-**say**-tuh/ ▶ noun the former basic unit of money in Spain.

pesky ▶ adjective informal annoying.

peso /**pay**-soh/ ▶ noun (plural **pesos**) the basic unit of money of several Latin American countries.

pessary ▶ noun (plural **pessaries**) a solid medical preparation designed to dissolve after being inserted into the vagina, used to treat infection or as a contraceptive.

pessimism ▶ noun a tendency to expect the worst to happen.
□ **pessimist** noun.

pessimistic ▶ adjective tending to expect the worst to happen.

SYNONYMS **gloomy,** negative, defeatist, downbeat, cynical, bleak, fatalistic, depressed.
ANTONYMS optimistic.

□ **pessimistically** adverb.

pest ▶ noun **1** a destructive insect or other animal that attacks plants, crops, or livestock. **2** informal an annoying person or thing.

SYNONYMS **nuisance,** annoyance, irritant, thorn in your flesh/side, trial, menace, trouble, problem, worry, bother; informal pain in the neck, headache.

pester ▶ verb (**pesters, pestering, pestered**) annoy someone with repeated questions or requests.

SYNONYMS **badger,** hound, harass, plague, annoy, bother, harry, worry; informal hassle, bug.

pesticide ▶ noun a substance for destroying insects or other pests.

pestilence ▶ noun old use a disease that spreads widely and causes many deaths.
□ **pestilent** adjective.

pestilential ▶ adjective **1** old use relating to or causing a pestilence. **2** informal annoying.

pestle /**pess**-uhl/ ▶ noun a small, heavy tool with a rounded end, used for grinding substances in a mortar.

pesto ▶ noun a sauce of crushed basil leaves, pine nuts, garlic, Parmesan cheese, and olive oil, served with pasta.

pet ▶ noun **1** an animal or bird that you keep for pleasure. **2** a person treated with special favour.
▶ adjective favourite.

SYNONYMS **1** *a pet lamb* **tame,** domesticated, companion; Brit. house-trained; N. Amer. housebroken. **2** *his pet theory* **favourite,** favoured, cherished, particular, special, personal.

▶ verb (**pets, petting, petted**) **1** stroke or pat an animal. **2** caress someone sexually.

SYNONYMS **1** *the cats came to be petted* **stroke,** caress, fondle, pat, tickle. **2** *couples petting in their cars* **cuddle,** embrace, caress, kiss; informal canoodle, neck, smooch; Brit. informal snog; N. Amer. informal make out.

■ **pet name** a name used to express fondness or familiarity.

petal ▶ noun each of the segments forming the outer part of a flower.

petard /pi-**tard**/ ▶ noun (**be hoist with your own petard**) have problems when your schemes against other people backfire on you.

peter ▶ verb (**peters, petering, petered**) (**peter out**) gradually come to an end.

petite ▶ adjective (of a woman) small and dainty.

petit four /puh-ti **for**/ ▶ noun (plural **petits fours** /puh-ti **forz**/) a very small fancy cake, biscuit, or sweet.

petition ▶ noun **1** an appeal or request, especially a written one signed by a large number of people and presented formally to someone in authority. **2** Law an application to a court for a writ, legal action, etc.

SYNONYMS *2,500 people have signed a petition* **appeal,** round robin, letter, request, entreaty, application, plea.

▶ verb make or present a petition to.

p

p

SYNONYMS *the islanders petitioned the government to help them* **appeal to,** request, ask, call on, entreat, beg, implore, plead with, apply to, press, urge.

petrel ▸ noun a seabird that flies far from land.

Petri dish ▸ noun a shallow transparent dish with a flat lid, used in laboratories.

petrify ▸ verb (petrifies, petrifying, petrified) **1** make someone so frightened that they cannot move. **2** change organic matter into stone.

petrochemical ▸ adjective relating to petroleum and natural gas.
▸ noun a chemical obtained from petroleum and natural gas.

petrol ▸ noun Brit. a liquid obtained by refining petroleum, used as fuel in motor vehicles.
■ petrol bomb a simple firebomb consisting of a bottle containing petrol and a cloth wick.

petroleum ▸ noun an oil that is refined to produce fuels including petrol, paraffin, and diesel oil.

petticoat ▸ noun a woman's light undergarment in the form of a skirt or dress.

pettifogging ▸ adjective petty; trivial.

pettish ▸ adjective childishly sulky.
□ pettishly adverb.

petty ▸ adjective (pettier, pettiest) **1** of little importance. **2** too concerned with unimportant things. **3** minor.

SYNONYMS **1** *petty regulations* **trivial,** trifling, minor, insignificant, inconsequential, footling; informal piffling. **2** *a petty form of revenge* **small-minded,** mean, shabby, spiteful.
ANTONYMS important, magnanimous.

■ petty cash a store of money that is available for spending on small items. petty officer a rank of naval officer.
□ pettiness noun.

petulant ▸ adjective childishly sulky or bad-tempered.
□ petulance noun **petulantly** adverb.

petunia ▸ noun a plant with white, purple, or red funnel-shaped flowers.

pew ▸ noun **1** a long wooden bench with a back, arranged with others in rows to provide seating in a church. **2** Brit. informal a seat.

pewter ▸ noun a metal made by mixing tin with copper and antimony.

pfennig /pfen-nig/ ▸ noun a former unit of money in Germany, equal to one hundredth of a mark.

PG ▸ abbreviation Brit. (in film classification) parental guidance.

pH ▸ noun a figure expressing how acid or alkaline a substance is.

phalanx ▸ noun (plural phalanxes) a group of people standing or moving forward closely together.

phallic ▸ adjective relating to or resembling a penis.

phallus ▸ noun (plural phalli /fal-lee/ or phalluses) a penis.

phantasm ▸ noun literary a thing that exists only in the imagination.

phantasmagoria ▸ noun a sequence of real or imaginary images like that seen in a dream.

phantom ▸ noun **1** a ghost. **2** a thing that exists only in the imagination.

SYNONYMS **ghost,** apparition, spirit, spectre, wraith; informal spook.

▸ adjective not really existing.

pharaoh /fair-oh/ ▸ noun a ruler in ancient Egypt.

✔ Remember, -aoh, not -oah: pharaoh.

Pharisee ▸ noun a member of an ancient Jewish sect who followed religious laws very strictly.

pharmaceutical ▸ adjective relating to medicinal drugs.
▸ noun a medicinal drug.

pharmacist ▸ noun a person who is qualified to prepare and dispense medicinal drugs.

pharmacology ▸ noun the branch of medicine concerned with drugs.
□ pharmacological adjective **pharmacologist** noun.

pharmacy ▸ noun (plural pharmacies) **1** a place where medicinal drugs are prepared or sold. **2** the science or practice of preparing and dispensing medicinal drugs.

pharynx ▸ noun (plural pharynges /fa-rin-jeez/) the cavity connecting the nose and mouth to the throat.

phase ▸ noun a distinct period or stage in a process of change or development.

SYNONYMS **1** *the final phase of the campaign* **stage,** period, chapter, episode, part, step. **2** *he's going through a difficult phase* **period,** stage, time, spell; Brit. informal patch.

▸ verb (phases, phasing, phased) **1** carry something out in gradual stages. **2** (phase something in or out) gradually introduce or withdraw something.

PhD ▸ abbreviation Doctor of Philosophy.

pheasant ▸ noun a large long-tailed game bird.

phenomenal ▸ adjective remarkable or outstanding.

SYNONYMS **remarkable**, exceptional, extraordinary, marvellous, miraculous, wonderful, outstanding, unprecedented; informal fantastic, terrific, tremendous, stupendous.
ANTONYMS ordinary.

□ **phenomenally** adverb.

phenomenon ▸ noun (plural **phenomena**)
1 a fact or situation that is known to exist or happen. 2 a remarkable person or thing.

SYNONYMS 1 *a rare phenomenon* **occurrence**, event, happening, fact, situation, circumstance, experience, case, incident, episode. 2 *a pop phenomenon* **marvel**, sensation, wonder, prodigy.

! The word **phenomenon** comes from Greek, and its plural form is **phenomena**. Don't use **phenomena** as a singular form: say *this is a strange phenomenon*, not *this is a strange phenomena*.

pheromone /**ferr**-uh-mohn/ ▸ noun a chemical substance released by an animal and causing a response in others of its species.

phial /**fy**-uhl/ ▸ noun a small cylindrical glass bottle.

philander ▸ verb (**philanders, philandering, philandered**) (of a man) have many casual sexual relationships with women.
□ **philanderer** noun.

philanthropy ▸ noun the practice of helping people in need.
□ **philanthropic** adjective **philanthropist** noun.

philately /fi-**lat**-uh-li/ ▸ noun the hobby of collecting postage stamps.
□ **philatelist** noun.

philharmonic ▸ adjective devoted to music (used in the names of orchestras).

philippic ▸ noun a verbal attack.

Philistine ▸ noun 1 a member of a people of ancient Palestine who fought with the Israelites. 2 (**philistine**) a person who is not interested in culture and the arts.
□ **philistinism** noun.

philology ▸ noun the study of the structure and development of language and the relationships between languages.
□ **philological** adjective **philologist** noun.

philosopher ▸ noun 1 a person who is engaged in philosophy. 2 a person who thinks deeply about things.

SYNONYMS **thinker**, theorist, theoretician, scholar, intellectual, sage.

philosophical ▸ adjective 1 relating to the study of philosophy. 2 having a calm attitude when things are difficult.

SYNONYMS 1 *a philosophical question* **theoretical**, metaphysical. 2 *a philosophical mood* **thoughtful**,

reflective, pensive, meditative, contemplative, introspective. 3 *he was very philosophical about it* **stoical**, self-possessed, serene, dispassionate, phlegmatic, long-suffering, resigned.

□ **philosophically** adverb.

philosophize (or **philosophise**) ▸ verb (**philosophizes, philosophizing, philosophized**) talk about serious issues, especially in a boring way.

philosophy ▸ noun (plural **philosophies**)
1 the study of the fundamental nature of knowledge, reality, and existence. 2 a set or system of beliefs.

SYNONYMS 1 *the philosophy of Aristotle* **thinking**, thought, reasoning, logic. 2 *her political philosophy* **beliefs**, credo, ideology, ideas, thinking, theories, doctrine, principles, views, outlook.

phlegm /flem/ ▸ noun mucus in the nose and throat.

phlegmatic /fleg-**mat**-ik/ ▸ adjective calm and reasonable, and tending not to get upset.

phlox /floks/ ▸ noun a garden plant with colourful sweet-scented flowers.

phobia ▸ noun a strong irrational fear of something.

SYNONYMS **fear**, dread, horror, terror, aversion, antipathy, revulsion; informal hang-up.

□ **phobic** adjective.

phoenix /**fee**-niks/ ▸ noun (in classical mythology) a bird that lived for hundreds of years before burning itself to death and being born again from its ashes.

✔ **-oe-**, not **-eo-**: pho**e**nix.

phone ▸ noun a telephone.

SYNONYMS *she spent hours on the phone* **telephone**; Brit. informal blower.

▸ verb (**phones, phoning, phoned**) make a telephone call to someone.

SYNONYMS *I'll phone you later* **call**, telephone; Brit. ring, ring up, give someone a ring; informal call up, give someone a buzz; Brit. informal give someone a bell, give someone a tinkle, get on the blower to; N. Amer. informal get someone on the horn.

■ **phone-in** a radio or television programme in which listeners or viewers participate over the telephone.

phonecard ▸ noun a card which you can use instead of cash to make calls on a public telephone.

phonetic ▸ adjective 1 having to do with speech sounds. 2 (of a system of writing) using symbols that represent sounds.
▸ noun (**phonetics**) the study of speech sounds.
□ **phonetically** adverb.

p

phoney (or **phony**) informal ▸ adjective (**phonier, phoniest**) not genuine.

SYNONYMS *a phoney address* **bogus,** false, fake, fraudulent, counterfeit, forged, imitation, affected, insincere; informal pretend; Brit. informal cod.
ANTONYMS authentic.

▸ noun (plural **phoneys** or **phonies**) a person or thing that is not genuine.

SYNONYMS **1** *he's a phoney* **impostor,** sham, fake, fraud, charlatan; informal con artist. **2** *the diamond's a phoney* **fake,** imitation, counterfeit, forgery.

phonic ▸ adjective relating to speech sounds.
▸ noun (**phonics**) a way of teaching people to read based on the sounds that letters represent.

phonograph ▸ noun **1** Brit. an early form of record player that could record as well as reproduce sound. **2** N. Amer. a record player.

phonology ▸ noun the relationships between the speech sounds of a language.

phosphate ▸ noun a salt or ester of phosphoric acid.

phosphorescence ▸ noun a faint light that is given out by a substance with little or no heat.
□ **phosphorescent** adjective.

phosphorus ▸ noun a yellowish waxy solid which can ignite spontaneously and which glows in the dark.
□ **phosphorous** adjective.

photo ▸ noun (plural **photos**) a photograph.
■ **photo finish** a close finish of a race in which the winner can be identified only from a photograph of competitors crossing the line.

photocall ▸ noun Brit. a prearranged occasion on which famous people pose for photographers.

photocopy ▸ noun (plural **photocopies**) a photographic copy of something produced by a process involving the action of light on a specially prepared surface.

SYNONYMS *a photocopy of the letter* **copy,** duplicate, reproduction, facsimile; trademark Xerox, photostat.

▸ verb (**photocopies, photocopying, photocopied**) make a photocopy of.

SYNONYMS *I photocopied the form* **copy,** duplicate, xerox, photostat, reproduce.

□ **photocopier** noun.

photoelectric ▸ adjective involving the production of electrons as a result of the action of light on a surface.

photofit ▸ noun Brit. a picture of a person made up from photographs of parts of other people's faces.

photogenic ▸ adjective looking attractive in photographs.

photograph ▸ noun a picture made with a camera.

SYNONYMS *a colour photograph* **picture,** photo, snap, snapshot, shot, print, still.

▸ verb take a photograph of.

SYNONYMS *he was photographed in Paris* **take a picture/photo of,** take someone's picture, snap, shoot, film.

□ **photographer** noun.

photographic ▸ adjective **1** relating to photography. **2** as accurate as photographs.

SYNONYMS **1** *a photographic record* **pictorial,** graphic, in photographs. **2** *a photographic memory* **detailed,** exact, precise, accurate, vivid.

photography ▸ noun the taking and processing of photographs.

photometer /foh-**tom**-i-ter/ ▸ noun an instrument measuring the strength of light.

photon /**foh**-ton/ ▸ noun a particle representing a quantum of light or other electromagnetic radiation.

photosensitive ▸ adjective responding to light.

photostat ▸ noun trademark **1** a type of machine for making photocopies on special paper. **2** a copy made by a photostat.
▸ verb (**photostats, photostatting, photostatted**) copy something with a photostat.

photosynthesis ▸ noun the process by which green plants use sunlight to form nutrients from carbon dioxide and water.

phrase ▸ noun **1** a group of words forming a unit within a sentence. **2** Music a group of notes forming a unit within a longer passage.

SYNONYMS *an elegant phrase* **expression,** construction, term, turn of phrase, idiom, saying.

▸ verb (**phrases, phrasing, phrased**) put an idea into a particular form of words.

SYNONYMS *how did you phrase the question?* **express,** put into words, put, word, formulate, couch, frame.

■ **phrase book** a book listing and translating useful phrases in a foreign language.
□ **phrasal** adjective.

phraseology /fray-zi-**ol**-uh-ji/ ▸ noun (plural **phraseologies**) a form of words used to express an idea.

phrenology ▸ noun (mainly in the past) the study of the shape and size of the skull in the belief that this can indicate someone's character.

phylum /**fy**-luhm/ ▸ noun (plural **phyla** /**fy**-luh/) a category used in the classification of animals.

p

physical ▶ adjective **1** relating to the body rather than the mind. **2** relating to things that you can see, hear, or feel. **3** involving bodily contact or activity. **4** relating to physics and natural forces such as heat, light, sound, etc.

> SYNONYMS **1** *physical pleasure* **bodily,** corporeal, corporal, carnal, fleshly, non-spiritual. **2** *physical work* **manual,** labouring, blue-collar. **3** *the physical universe* **material,** concrete, tangible, palpable, solid, substantial, real, actual, visible. ANTONYMS mental, spiritual.

▶ noun a medical examination to find out the state of someone's health.
   ■ **physical education** instruction in physical exercise, sports, and games.
   □ **physicality** noun **physically** adverb.

physician ▶ noun a person qualified to practise medicine.

> SYNONYMS **doctor,** medical practitioner, general practitioner, GP, clinician, specialist, consultant; informal doc, medic.

physics ▶ noun the branch of science concerned with the nature and properties of matter and energy.
   □ **physicist** noun.

physiognomy /fi-zi-on-uh-mi/ ▶ noun (plural **physiognomies**) a person's face or facial expression.

physiology ▶ noun the scientific study of the way in which living things function.
   □ **physiological** adjective **physiologist** noun.

physiotherapy ▶ noun Brit. the treatment of disease and injury by massage and exercise.
   □ **physiotherapist** noun.

physique ▶ noun the shape and size of a person's body.

pi /py/ ▶ noun the numerical value of the ratio of the circumference of a circle to its diameter (approximately 3.14159).

pianissimo /pi-uh-**niss**-i-moh/ ▶ adverb & adjective Music very soft or softly.

piano[1] /pi-**an**-oh/ ▶ noun (plural **pianos**) a musical instrument which you play by pressing black or white keys on a large keyboard, the sound being produced by small hammers hitting metal strings.
   □ **pianist** noun.

piano[2] /pi-**ah**-noh/ ▶ adverb & adjective Music soft or softly.

pianoforte /pi-an-oh-**for**-tay/ ▶ noun formal a piano.

piazza /pi-**at**-suh/ ▶ noun a public square or marketplace.

picador ▶ noun (in bullfighting) a person on horseback who goads the bull with a lance.

picaresque ▶ adjective (of fiction) dealing with the adventures of a dishonest but appealing hero.

piccalilli ▶ noun a pickle of chopped vegetables, mustard, and hot spices.

piccaninny ▶ noun (plural **piccaninnies**) offensive a small black child.

piccolo ▶ noun (plural **piccolos**) a small flute sounding an octave higher than the ordinary flute.

pick[1] ▶ verb **1** choose from a number of alternatives. **2** (often **pick something up**) take hold of something and lift or move it. **3** remove a flower or fruit from where it is growing.

> SYNONYMS **1** *pick a time that suits you* **choose,** select, single out, opt for, plump for, elect, decide on, settle on, fix on, name, nominate, identify. **2** *they were picking apples* **harvest,** gather (in), collect, pluck. **3** *he tried to pick a fight* **provoke,** start, cause, incite, instigate, prompt. ANTONYMS reject, avoid.

▶ noun **1** an act of choosing something. **2** (**the pick of**) the best person or thing in a particular group.

> SYNONYMS *the pick of the crop* **best,** finest, choice, choicest, cream, flower, crème de la crème, elite.

   ■ **pick at 1** repeatedly pull at something with your fingers. **2** eat food in small amounts. **pick holes in** criticize. **pick a lock** open a lock with something other than the proper key. **pick on** single someone out for unfair treatment. **pick someone's pockets** steal something from a person's pocket. **pick up** improve or increase. **pick someone/ thing up 1** go to collect someone. **2** informal flirtatiously start talking to a stranger with the aim of having a sexual relationship with them. **3** detect or receive a signal or sound. **4** obtain or learn something.
   □ **picker** noun.

pick[2] ▶ noun **1** (also **pickaxe**) a tool consisting of a curved iron bar with pointed ends and a wooden handle, used for breaking up hard ground or rock. **2** a plectrum.

picket ▶ noun **1** a group of people standing outside a workplace and trying to persuade others not to work during a strike. **2** a pointed wooden stake driven into the ground.

> SYNONYMS **1** *forty pickets were arrested* **demonstrator,** striker, protester. **2** *they decided to organize a picket* **demonstration,** picket line, blockade, boycott, strike.

▶ verb (**pickets, picketing, picketed**) act as a picket outside a workplace.

> SYNONYMS *workers picketed the factory* **demonstrate at,** blockade, boycott.

pickings ▶ plural noun **1** profits or gains. **2** scraps or leftovers.

p

pickle ▶ noun 1 Brit. a thick, spicy, cold sauce made from chopped vegetables and fruit. 2 a preserve of vegetables or fruit in vinegar or salt water. 3 (a pickle) informal a difficult situation.
▶ verb (pickles, pickling, pickled) preserve food in vinegar or salt water.

pickpocket ▶ noun a person who steals from people's pockets.

pickup ▶ noun 1 a small truck with low sides. 2 the part of a record player that holds the stylus. 3 a device on an electric guitar which converts sound vibration into electrical signals for amplification. 4 an improvement after poor performance.

SYNONYMS **improvement**, recovery, revival, upturn, upswing, rally, resurgence, renewal, turnaround.
ANTONYMS slump.

picky ▶ adjective informal fussy.

picnic ▶ noun a meal that is eaten outdoors and away from home.
▶ verb (picnics, picnicking, picnicked) have a picnic.
□ picnicker noun.

Pict ▶ noun a member of an ancient people inhabiting northern Scotland in Roman times.

pictograph (or pictogram) ▶ noun a small image or picture representing a word or phrase.

pictorial ▶ adjective having to do with or expressed in pictures.

picture ▶ noun 1 a painting, drawing, or photograph. 2 an image on a television screen. 3 a cinema film. 4 (the pictures) the cinema. 5 an image formed in the mind.

SYNONYMS 1 *pictures in an art gallery* **painting**, **drawing**, sketch, watercolour, print, canvas, portrait, illustration, depiction, likeness, representation, image. 2 *we were told not to take pictures* **photograph**, photo, snap, snapshot, shot, frame, exposure, still, print. 3 *my picture of the ideal woman* **concept**, idea, impression, (mental) image, vision, visualization, notion. 4 *the picture of health* **personification**, embodiment, epitome, essence, quintessence, soul.

▶ verb (pictures, picturing, pictured) 1 represent in a picture. 2 form an image of something in your mind.

SYNONYMS 1 *they were pictured playing in the snow* **depict**, portray, show, represent, **draw**, sketch, photograph, paint. 2 *Anne still pictured Richard as he had been* **visualize**, see (in your mind's eye), imagine, remember.

■ picture window a large window consisting of a single pane of glass.

picturesque ▶ adjective (of a place) very pleasant to look at.

SYNONYMS **attractive**, pretty, beautiful, lovely, scenic, charming, quaint, pleasing, delightful.
ANTONYMS ugly.

pidgin ▶ noun a simple form of a language with elements taken from local languages.

pie ▶ noun a baked dish of meat, vegetables, fruit, etc. inside a pastry case.
■ pie chart a diagram in which a circle is divided into segments to show the size of particular amounts in relation to the whole.

piebald ▶ adjective (of a horse) having irregular patches of two colours.

piece ▶ noun 1 a portion that is separated or seen separately from the whole. 2 an item used in building something or forming part of a set. 3 a musical or written work. 4 a token used to make moves in a board game. 5 a coin of a particular value.

SYNONYMS 1 *a piece of cheese* **bit**, slice, chunk, segment, section, lump, hunk, wedge, slab, block, cake, bar, stick, length. 2 *the pieces of a clock* **component**, part, bit, constituent, element, section, unit, module. 3 *a piece of furniture* **item**, article, specimen. 4 *a piece of the profit* **share**, portion, slice, quota, part, percentage, amount, quantity, ration, fraction; Brit. informal whack. 5 *pieces from his collection* **work (of art)**, artwork, artefact, composition, opus. 6 *the reporter who wrote the piece* **article**, item, story, report, essay, feature, review, column.

▶ verb (pieces, piecing, pieced) (piece something together) assemble something from individual parts.

pièce de résistance /pyess duh ray-ziss-tonss/ ▶ noun the most important or impressive part of something.

piecemeal ▶ adjective & adverb done in stages over a period of time.

piecework ▶ noun work that is paid for by the amount done and not the hours worked.

pied (*rhymes with* ride) ▶ adjective having two or more different colours.

pied-à-terre /pyay-dah-tair/ ▶ noun (plural pieds-à-terre /pyay-dah-tair/) a small flat or house kept for occasional use.

pier ▶ noun 1 a structure leading out to sea or into a lake, used as a landing stage for boats. 2 a pillar supporting an arch or bridge.

SYNONYMS **jetty**, quay, wharf, dock, landing stage.

pierce ▶ verb (pierces, piercing, pierced) 1 make a hole in something with a sharp object. 2 force or cut a way through. 3 (piercing) very sharp, cold, or high-pitched.

p

SYNONYMS **1 penetrate,** puncture, perforate, prick, spike, stab, drill, bore. **2 (piercing)** *a piercing shriek* **shrill,** ear-splitting, high-pitched, penetrating, strident. **3 (piercing)** *his piercing gaze* **searching,** probing, penetrating, sharp, keen.

piety /py-uh-ti/ ▸ noun (plural **pieties**) the quality of being religious in a respectful and serious way.

piffle ▸ noun informal nonsense.

pig ▸ noun **1** an animal with a short, curly tail and a flat snout. **2** informal a greedy, dirty, or unpleasant person.
▸ verb (**pigs, pigging, pigged**) informal eat too much food.
■ **pig-headed** stupidly stubborn. **pig iron** iron when it is first taken out of a smelting furnace.
□ **piggish** adjective **piglet** noun.

pigeon ▸ noun a plump grey and white bird with a cooing voice.
■ **pigeon-toed** having the toes and feet turned inwards.

✔ Note that there is no **d**: pigeon.

pigeonhole ▸ noun **1** a small hole in a wall leading into a place where pigeons nest. **2** each of a set of small compartments in a workplace, college, etc. where letters or messages may be left for individuals. **3** a category in which someone or something is put.
▸ verb (**pigeonholes, pigeonholing, pigeonholed**) put into a particular category.

piggery ▸ noun (plural **piggeries**) a place where pigs are kept.

piggy ▸ noun (plural **piggies**) a child's word for a pig or piglet.
▸ adjective like a pig.
■ **piggy bank** a money box shaped like a pig.

piggyback ▸ noun a ride on someone's back and shoulders.
▸ adverb on the back and shoulders of another person.

pigment ▸ noun **1** the substance that gives natural colouring to animal or plant tissue. **2** a coloured powder mixed with a liquid to make paints, crayons, etc.

SYNONYMS **colouring,** colour, tint, dye, stain.

□ **pigmentation** noun **pigmented** adjective.

pigmy → PYGMY.

pigskin ▸ noun leather made from the hide of a pig.

pigsty ▸ noun (plural **pigsties**) **1** an enclosure for a pig or pigs. **2** a very dirty or untidy place.

pigswill ▸ noun kitchen refuse and scraps fed to pigs.

pigtail ▸ noun a length of hair worn in a plait at the back or on each side of the head.

pike¹ ▸ noun (plural **pike**) a freshwater fish with a long body and sharp teeth.

pike² ▸ noun (in the past) a weapon with a pointed metal head on a long wooden shaft.

pikestaff ▸ noun (as plain as a pikestaff) very obvious.

pilaster /pi-**lass**-ter/ ▸ noun a column that projects from a wall.

pilchard ▸ noun a small fish of the herring family.

pile¹ ▸ noun **1** a heap of things lying one on top of another. **2** informal a large amount. **3** a large and impressive building.

SYNONYMS **1** *a pile of stones* **heap,** stack, mound, pyramid, mass, collection, accumulation, assemblage, stockpile, hoard. **2** *I've a pile of work to do* **lot,** mountain, reams, abundance; informal load, heap, mass, slew, stack, ton; Brit. informal **shedload;** Austral./NZ informal **swag.**

▸ verb (**piles, piling, piled**) **1** place things one on top of the other. **2** (**pile up**) form a pile or very large quantity. **3** (**pile into** or **out of**) get into or out of a vehicle in a disorganized way.

SYNONYMS **1** *he piled up the plates* **heap,** stack. **2** *he piled his plate with salad* **load,** heap, fill (up), stack, charge. **3** *we piled into the car* **crowd,** clamber, pack, squeeze, scramble, struggle.

pile² ▸ noun the soft surface of a carpet or a fabric, consisting of the cut ends of many small threads.

SYNONYMS *a carpet with a short pile* **nap,** fibres, threads.

pile³ ▸ noun a heavy post driven into the ground to support foundations.

piledriver ▸ noun a machine for driving piles into the ground.

piles ▸ plural noun haemorrhoids.

pile-up ▸ noun a crash involving a lot of vehicles.

SYNONYMS **crash,** collision, smash, accident; Brit. RTA; N. Amer. **wreck;** Brit. informal **shunt.**

pilfer ▸ verb (**pilfers, pilfering, pilfered**) steal small items of little value.

pilgrim ▸ noun a person who travels to a sacred place for religious reasons.

SYNONYMS **traveller,** wayfarer, worshipper, devotee, believer; Islam haji, alhaji.

pilgrimage ▸ noun a pilgrim's journey.

SYNONYMS **journey,** expedition, mission, hajj, visit, trek, trip, odyssey.

p

pill ▸ noun **1** a small round mass of solid medicine for swallowing whole. **2** (**the Pill**) a contraceptive pill.

> SYNONYMS **tablet**, capsule, pellet, lozenge, pastille.

pillage ▸ verb (**pillages, pillaging, pillaged**) steal from a place in a rough and violent way.
▸ noun the action of pillaging.

pillar ▸ noun **1** a tall upright structure used as a support for a building. **2** a source of help and support.

> SYNONYMS **1** *stone pillars* **column**, post, support, upright, pier, pile, prop, stanchion, obelisk. **2** *a pillar of the community* **stalwart**, mainstay, bastion, leading light, worthy, backbone, supporter, upholder, champion.

■ **from pillar to post** from one place to another without achieving anything. **pillar box** (in the UK) a red cylindrical public postbox.

pillbox ▸ noun **1** a small round hat with a flat top and no brim. **2** a small concrete fort.

pillion ▸ noun a seat for a passenger behind a motorcyclist.

pillory ▸ noun (plural **pillories**) (in the past) a wooden framework with holes for the head and hands, in which people were locked and left on display as a punishment.
▸ verb (**pillories, pillorying, pilloried**) criticize or ridicule someone publicly.

pillow ▸ noun a soft pad used to support the head when you lie down in bed.
■ **pillow talk** intimate conversation between a couple in bed.

pillowcase ▸ noun a removable cloth cover for a pillow.

pilot ▸ noun **1** a person who flies an aircraft. **2** a person qualified to take charge of a ship entering or leaving a harbour. **3** something done or produced as a test before being introduced more widely.

> SYNONYMS **1** *a fighter pilot* **airman**, **airwoman**, flyer, captain; informal **skipper**; N. Amer. informal **jock**; dated **aviator**. **2** *a harbour pilot* **navigator**, helmsman, steersman, coxswain. **3** *a pilot for a TV series* **trial**, sample, experiment.

▸ adjective done as an experiment or test before being introduced more widely.

> SYNONYMS *a pilot project* **experimental**, exploratory, trial, test, sample, preliminary.

▸ verb (**pilots, piloting, piloted**) **1** act as a pilot of an aircraft or ship. **2** test a scheme, project, etc. before introducing it more widely.

> SYNONYMS *he piloted the jet to safety* **navigate**, guide, manoeuvre, steer, control, direct, captain, fly, drive, sail; informal **skipper**.

■ **pilot light** a small gas burner that is kept alight permanently, used to fire a boiler.

pimento (or **pimiento**) ▸ noun (plural **pimentos**) a sweet red pepper.

pimp ▸ noun a man who controls prostitutes and takes part of their earnings.
▸ verb act as a pimp.

pimple ▸ noun a small inflamed lump on the skin.
□ **pimply** adjective.

PIN (or **PIN number**) ▸ abbreviation personal identification number.

pin ▸ noun **1** a very thin pointed piece of metal with a round head, used to hold pieces of fabric together or as a fastener. **2** a metal projection from an electric plug. **3** a small brooch. **4** a steel rod used to join the ends of broken bones while they heal. **5** a metal peg in a hand grenade that prevents it exploding. **6** a skittle in bowling. **7** (**pins**) informal legs.

> SYNONYMS **1** *fasten the hem with a pin* **tack**, safety pin, nail, staple, fastener. **2** *a broken pin in the machine* **bolt**, peg, rod, rivet, dowel. **3** *they wore name pins* **badge**, brooch.

▸ verb (**pins, pinning, pinned**) **1** attach or fasten with a pin or pins. **2** hold someone firmly so they are unable to move. **3** (**pin someone down**) force someone to be specific about their plans. **4** (**pin someone down**) trap an enemy by firing at them. **5** (**pin something on**) fix blame or responsibility on.

> SYNONYMS **1** *she pinned the brooch to her dress* **attach**, fasten, affix, fix, join, secure, clip, nail. **2** *they pinned him to the ground* **hold**, press, pinion.

■ **pin money** a small sum of money for spending on everyday items. **pins and needles** a tingling sensation in a part of the body that is recovering from numbness. **pin-up** a poster of an attractive person.

pinafore ▸ noun a collarless, sleeveless dress worn over a blouse or jumper.

pinball ▸ noun a game in which balls are shot across a sloping board and score points by hitting targets.

pince-nez /panss-nay/ ▸ noun a pair of glasses kept in place with a nose clip instead of parts that rest on the ears.

pincer ▸ noun **1** (**pincers**) a metal tool with blunt inward-curving jaws for gripping and pulling things. **2** a front claw of a lobster or similar shellfish.

pinch ▸ verb **1** grip flesh tightly between your finger and thumb. **2** (of a shoe) hurt a foot by being too tight. **3** informal steal.

> SYNONYMS **1** *he pinched my arm* **nip,** tweak, squeeze, grasp. **2** *my new shoes pinch my toes* **hurt,** squeeze, crush, cramp.

▶ noun **1** an act of pinching. **2** an amount of an ingredient that can be held between your fingers and thumb.

> SYNONYMS **1** *he gave her arm a pinch* **nip,** tweak, squeeze. **2** *a pinch of salt* **bit,** touch, dash, spot, trace, soupçon, speck, taste; informal smidgen, tad.

■ **feel the pinch** experience financial hardship.

pinched ▶ adjective (of a person's face) tight with cold or suffering.

pincushion ▶ noun a small pad into which you stick pins to store them.

pine¹ ▶ noun an evergreen tree that produces cones and has clusters of long needle-shaped leaves.
■ **pine nut** the edible seed of various pines. **pine marten** an animal resembling a weasel that lives in trees.

pine² ▶ verb (**pines, pining, pined**) **1** become very sad or weak because you miss someone so much. **2** (**pine for**) miss or long for.

> SYNONYMS *she thinks I am pining away from love* **fade,** waste away, weaken, decline, languish, wilt, sicken.

pineapple ▶ noun a large juicy tropical fruit consisting of yellow flesh surrounded by a tough skin.

ping ▶ noun a short high-pitched ringing sound.
▶ verb make such a sound.
■ **ping-pong** (also **Ping-Pong** US trademark) informal table tennis.

pinion¹ ▶ verb tie or hold someone's arms or legs so that they cannot move.
▶ noun the outer part of a bird's wing.

pinion² ▶ noun a small cogwheel or spindle that engages with a large cogwheel.

pink¹ ▶ adjective of a colour midway between red and white.

> SYNONYMS **rose,** rosy, rosé, pale red, salmon, coral, flushed, blushing.

▶ noun a pink colour.
■ **in the pink** informal in the best condition.

pink² ▶ noun a plant with sweet-smelling pink or white flowers.

pinking shears ▶ plural noun scissors with a thick serrated blade, used for cutting a zigzag edge on fabric to prevent it fraying.

pinky (or **pinkie**) ▶ noun informal the little finger.

pinnace /pin-nis/ ▶ noun a small boat forming part of the equipment of a larger one.

pinnacle ▶ noun **1** the most successful point. **2** a high pointed piece of rock. **3** a small pointed turret on a roof.

> SYNONYMS **1** *the pinnacle of his career* **height,** peak, high point, top, apex, zenith, acme. **2** *pinnacles of rock* **peak,** needle, crag, tor.
> ANTONYMS low point.

pinpoint ▶ verb locate or identify something precisely.

> SYNONYMS *the technology can pinpoint a cellphone's position* **identify,** determine, distinguish, discover, find, locate, detect, track down, spot, diagnose, recognize, pin down, home in on.

▶ adjective absolutely precise.

> SYNONYMS *pinpoint accuracy* **precise,** exact, strict, absolute, complete, scientific.

▶ noun a tiny dot.

pinprick ▶ noun a very small dot or amount.

pinstripe ▶ noun a very narrow white stripe woven into dark material.
□ **pinstriped** adjective.

pint ▶ noun **1** a unit of liquid or dry capacity equal to one eighth of a gallon, in Britain equal to 0.568 litre. **2** Brit. a pint of beer.
■ **pint-sized** informal very small.

pinwheel ▶ noun chiefly N. Amer. a Catherine wheel firework.

pioneer ▶ noun **1** a person who explores or settles in a new region. **2** a developer of new ideas or techniques.

> SYNONYMS **1** *the pioneers of the Wild West* **settler,** colonist, colonizer, frontiersman, explorer. **2** *a pioneer of motoring* **developer,** innovator, trailblazer, groundbreaker, founding father, architect, creator.

▶ verb (**pioneers, pioneering, pioneered**) be a pioneer of a new idea or technique.

> SYNONYMS *he pioneered the sale of insurance* **introduce,** develop, launch, instigate, initiate, spearhead, institute, establish, found.

pious ▶ adjective **1** religious in a very respectful and serious way. **2** pretending to be moral and good in order to impress other people. **3** (of a hope) very much wanted, but unlikely to be achieved.

> SYNONYMS **religious,** devout, God-fearing, churchgoing, holy, godly, saintly, reverent, righteous.
> ANTONYMS irreligious.

□ **piously** adverb.

pip ▶ noun **1** a small hard seed in a fruit. **2** Brit. a short, high-pitched sound used as a signal on the radio or in a telephone.
■ **pip someone at** (or **to**) **the post** Brit. informal

p

defeat someone by a small margin or at the last moment.

pipe ▸ noun **1** a tube through which water, gas, oil, etc. can flow. **2** a device for smoking tobacco, consisting of a narrow tube that opens into a small bowl in which the tobacco is burned. **3** a wind instrument consisting of a single tube with holes along its length that you cover with your fingers to produce different notes. **4** each of the tubes by which notes are produced in an organ. **5** (**pipes**) bagpipes.

SYNONYMS *a central-heating pipe* **tube**, conduit, hose, main, duct, line, channel, pipeline, drain.

▸ verb (**pipes, piping, piped**) **1** send a liquid through a pipe. **2** transmit music, a programme, a signal, etc. by wire or cable. **3** play a tune on a pipe. **4** sing or say something in a high voice. **5** decorate something with piping.

SYNONYMS **1** *the beer is piped into barrels* **feed**, siphon, channel, run, convey. **2** *programmes piped in from London* **relay**, feed, patch, transmit.

■ **piped music** pre-recorded background music played through loudspeakers. **pipe dream** a hope or plan that is impossible to achieve. **pipe down** informal be less noisy. **pipe up** informal say something suddenly.

pipeline ▸ noun a long pipe for carrying oil, gas, etc. over a distance.
■ **in the pipeline** in the process of being developed.

piper ▸ noun a person who plays a pipe or bagpipes.

pipette ▸ noun a thin tube used in a laboratory for transferring small quantities of liquid.

piping ▸ noun **1** lengths of pipe. **2** lines of icing or cream used to decorate cakes and desserts. **3** thin cord covered in fabric and used for decorating a garment or piece of furniture.
■ **piping hot** (of food or water) very hot.

pipistrelle ▸ noun a small insect-eating bat.

pipit ▸ noun a bird that lives on the ground in open country.

pippin ▸ noun a sweet red and yellow apple.

pipsqueak ▸ noun informal an unimportant person.

piquant /**pee**-kuhnt/ ▸ adjective having a pleasantly strong and sharp taste.
□ **piquancy** noun **piquantly** adverb.

pique /peek/ ▸ noun a feeling of irritation mixed with hurt pride.
▸ verb (**piques, piquing, piqued**) **1** (**be piqued**) feel both irritated and hurt. **2** stimulate someone's interest.

piracy ▸ noun **1** the attacking and robbing of ships at sea. **2** the reproduction of a film or

recording without permission and so as to make a profit.

piranha /pi-**rah**-nuh/ ▸ noun a freshwater fish with very sharp teeth.

pirate ▸ noun a person who attacks and robs ships at sea.

SYNONYMS *pirates boarded the ship* **raider**, hijacker, marauder, freebooter; historical privateer, buccaneer.

▸ adjective **1** (of a film or recording) having been reproduced and used for profit without permission. **2** (of an organization) broadcasting without permission.
▸ verb (**pirates, pirating, pirated**) reproduce a film or recording for profit without permission.

SYNONYMS *designers may pirate good ideas* **steal**, copy, plagiarize, poach, appropriate, bootleg; informal crib, lift, rip off.

pirouette ▸ noun a movement in ballet involving spinning on one foot.
▸ verb (**pirouettes, pirouetting, pirouetted**) perform a pirouette.

piscatorial /piss-kuh-**tor**-i-uhl/ ▸ adjective having to do with fish.

Pisces /**py**-seez/ ▸ noun a sign of the zodiac (the Fish or Fishes), 21 February–19 March.

pistachio /pi-**stah**-shi-oh/ ▸ noun (plural **pistachios**) a small pale green nut.

piste /peest/ ▸ noun a course or run for skiing.

pistil ▸ noun Botany the female organs of a flower (the stigma, style, and ovary).

pistol ▸ noun a small gun designed to be held in one hand.

piston ▸ noun a sliding disc or cylinder fitting closely inside a tube in which it moves up and down as part of an engine or pump.

pit[1] ▸ noun **1** a large hole in the ground. **2** a mine for coal, chalk, etc. **3** a hollow in a surface. **4** a sunken area in a workshop floor where people can work on the underside of vehicles. **5** an area at the side of a track where racing cars are serviced and refuelled. **6** a part of a theatre where the orchestra plays. **7** (**the pits**) informal a very bad place or situation.

SYNONYMS **1** *we dug a pit* **hole**, trough, hollow, excavation, cavity, crater, pothole. **2** *pit closures* **coal mine**, colliery, quarry, shaft.

▸ verb (**pits, pitting, pitted**) **1** (**pit someone/ thing against**) test someone or something in a contest with. **2** make a hollow in the surface of something.

SYNONYMS *his skin had been pitted by acne* **mark**, pockmark, pock, scar, dent, indent.

■ **pit bull terrier** a fierce breed of bull terrier. **the pit of the stomach** an area low down in the stomach.

pit² ▶ noun chiefly N. Amer. the stone of a fruit.

> SYNONYMS **stone**, pip, seed.

▶ verb (**pits**, **pitting**, **pitted**) remove the stone from a fruit.

pitch¹ ▶ noun **1** Brit. an area of ground used for outdoor team games. **2** the degree of highness or lowness in a sound or tone. **3** a particular level of intensity. **4** a form of words used when trying to sell something: *a sales pitch*. **5** Brit. a place on a street where someone performing or selling something has settled. **6** the steepness of a roof.

> SYNONYMS **1** *a football pitch* **playing field**, ground, sports field, stadium; Brit. park. **2** *her voice rose in pitch* **tone**, key, modulation, frequency. **3** *the pitch of the roof* **gradient**, slope, slant, angle, tilt, incline. **4** *at fever pitch* **level**, intensity, point, degree, height, extent. **5** *his sales pitch* **patter**, talk; informal spiel, line.

▶ verb **1** throw heavily or roughly. **2** set your voice, a sound, or a piece of music at a particular pitch. **3** aim something at a particular level, target, or audience. **4** set up a tent or camp. **5** (**pitch in**) informal join in enthusiastically with an activity. **6** (**pitch up**) informal arrive. **7** (of a moving ship, aircraft, or vehicle) rock up and down. **8** (**pitched**) (of a roof) sloping.

> SYNONYMS **1** *a kid pitched a snowball* **throw**, toss, fling, hurl, cast, lob, flip; informal chuck, sling, heave, bung. **2** *he pitched overboard* **fall**, tumble, topple, plunge, plummet. **3** *they pitched their tents* **put up**, set up, erect, raise. **4** *the boat pitched* **lurch**, toss, plunge, roll, reel, sway, rock, list.

■ **pitched battle** a battle in which the time and place are decided beforehand.

pitch² ▶ noun a sticky black substance made from tar or turpentine and used for waterproofing.

■ **pitch-black** (or **pitch-dark**) completely dark.

pitcher ▶ noun a large jug.

pitchfork ▶ noun a farm tool with a long handle and two sharp metal prongs, used for lifting hay.

piteous ▶ adjective deserving or arousing pity.
□ **piteously** adverb.

pitfall ▶ noun a hidden danger or difficulty.

> SYNONYMS **hazard**, danger, risk, peril, difficulty, catch, snag, stumbling block, drawback.

pith ▶ noun **1** spongy white tissue lining the rind of citrus fruits. **2** spongy tissue in the stems and branches of many plants. **3** the most important part of something.

■ **pith helmet** a lightweight hat made from the dried pith of a plant, used for protection from the sun.

pithead ▶ noun the top of a mineshaft and the area around it.

pithy ▶ adjective (**pithier**, **pithiest**) (of language) concise and clear.

pitiable ▶ adjective **1** deserving or arousing pity. **2** deserving contempt.

pitiful ▶ adjective **1** deserving or arousing pity. **2** very small or inadequate.
□ **pitifully** adverb.

pitiless ▶ adjective showing no pity.

piton ▶ noun (in rock climbing) a peg or spike driven into a crack to support a climber or hold a rope.

pitta ▶ noun a type of flat bread which can be split open to hold a filling.

pittance ▶ noun a very small or inadequate amount of money.

pitter-patter ▶ noun the sound of quick light steps or taps.

pituitary gland /pi-tyoo-i-tuh-ri/ ▶ noun a gland at the base of the brain which controls growth and development.

pity ▶ noun (plural **pities**) **1** a feeling of sympathy and sadness caused by the suffering of other people. **2** a cause for regret or disappointment.

> SYNONYMS **1** *a voice full of pity* **compassion**, commiseration, condolence, sympathy, fellow feeling, understanding. **2** *it's a pity he never had children* **shame**, misfortune, too bad; informal bummer.
> ANTONYMS indifference, cruelty.

▶ verb (**pities**, **pitying**, **pitied**) feel pity for.

> SYNONYMS *they pitied me* **feel sorry for**, feel for, sympathize with, empathize with, commiserate with, take pity on, be moved by, bleed for.

pivot ▶ noun the central point, pin, or shaft on which a mechanism turns or is balanced.
▶ verb (**pivots**, **pivoting**, **pivoted**) **1** turn on or as if on a pivot. **2** (**pivot on**) depend on.

pivotal ▶ adjective of central importance.

pixel ▶ noun any of the tiny areas of light on a computer screen which make up an image.

pixie (or **pixy**) ▶ noun (plural **pixies**) an imaginary being portrayed as a tiny man with pointed ears.

pizza ▶ noun a flat, round base of dough baked with a topping of tomatoes, cheese, and other ingredients.

pizzeria /peet-suh-**ree**-uh/ ▶ noun a pizza restaurant.

pizzicato /pit-si-**kah**-toh/ ▶ adverb & adjective plucking the strings of a stringed instrument such as a violin with your finger.

placard ▶ noun a large written sign fixed to a wall or carried during a demonstration.

placate ▶ verb (**placates**, **placating**, **placated**) make someone less angry or upset.
□ **placatory** adjective.

place ▶ noun **1** a particular position or location. **2** an opportunity to study on a course or be a member of a team. **3** a position in a sequence. **4** (in place names) a square or short street.

> synonyms **1** *an ideal place for dinner* **location**, site, spot, setting, position, situation, area, region, locale, venue. **2** *foreign places* **country**, state, area, region, town, city. **3** *a place of her own* **home**, house, flat, apartment, accommodation, property, rooms, quarters; informal pad; Brit. informal gaff; formal residence, abode, dwelling. **4** *in your place, I'd agree* **situation**, position, circumstances; informal shoes. **5** *a place was reserved for her* **seat**, chair, space. **6** *I offered him a place in the company* **job**, position, post, appointment, situation, employment. **7** *I know my place* **status**, position, standing, rank, niche. **8** *it was not her place to sort it out* **responsibility**, duty, job, task, role, function, concern, affair, charge.

▶ verb (**places**, **placing**, **placed**) **1** put something in a particular position or situation. **2** find an appropriate place or role for. **3** remember where you have seen someone before. **4** make a reservation or order.

> synonyms **1** *books were placed on the table* **put (down)**, set (down), lay, deposit, position, plant, rest, stand, station, situate, leave; informal stick, dump, bung, park, plonk, pop; N. Amer. informal plunk. **2** *the trust you placed in me* **put**, lay, set, invest. **3** *a survey placed the company sixth* **rank**, order, grade, class, classify, put. **4** *Joe couldn't quite place her* **identify**, recognize, remember, put a name to, pin down, locate, pinpoint. **5** *we were placed with foster parents* **accommodate**, house, home, allocate, assign.

■ **take place** happen.

placebo /pluh-see-boh/ ▶ noun (plural **placebos**) a medicine given to a patient to make them feel happier or more confident rather than for any physical effect.

placement ▶ noun **1** the action of placing. **2** a temporary job undertaken to gain work experience.

placenta /pluh-sen-tuh/ ▶ noun (plural **placentae** /pluh-sen-tee/ or **placentas**) an organ that is formed in the womb during pregnancy and which supplies blood and nourishment to the fetus through the umbilical cord.

placid ▶ adjective not easily upset or excited.
□ **placidity** noun **placidly** adverb.

placket ▶ noun an opening in a garment, covering fastenings or giving access to a pocket.

plagiarize (or **plagiarise**) /play-juh-ryz/ ▶ verb (**plagiarizes**, **plagiarizing**, **plagiarized**) copy another person's words or ideas and pretend that they are your own.
□ **plagiarism** noun **plagiarist** noun.

plague ▶ noun **1** an infectious disease causing fever and delirium. **2** an unusually and unpleasantly large number of insects or animals.

> synonyms **1** *they died in a plague* **pandemic**, epidemic, disease, sickness; dated contagion; archaic pestilence. **2** *a plague of fleas* **infestation**, invasion, swarm, epidemic.

▶ verb (**plagues**, **plaguing**, **plagued**) **1** cause continual trouble to. **2** pester someone.

> synonyms **1** *he was plagued by poor health* **afflict**, trouble, torment, beset, dog, curse, bedevil. **2** *he plagued her with questions* **pester**, harass, badger, bother, torment, harry, hound, trouble, nag, molest; informal hassle, bug; N. English informal mither; N. Amer. informal devil.

plaice ▶ noun (plural **plaice**) a flat brown fish with orange spots, used for food.

plaid /plad/ ▶ noun fabric woven in a chequered or tartan design.

plain ▶ adjective **1** simple or ordinary. **2** without a pattern. **3** unmarked. **4** easy to understand; clear. **5** (of a woman or girl) not attractive.

> synonyms **1** *it was plain that something was wrong* **obvious**, clear, evident, apparent, manifest, unmistakable. **2** *plain English* **intelligible**, comprehensible, understandable, clear, lucid, simple, straightforward, user-friendly. **3** *plain speaking* **candid**, frank, outspoken, forthright, direct, honest, truthful, blunt, bald, unequivocal; informal upfront. **4** *a plain dress* **simple**, ordinary, unadorned, homely, basic, modest, unsophisticated, restrained. **5** *a plain girl* **unattractive**, unprepossessing, ugly, ordinary; N. Amer. homely; Brit. informal no oil painting. **6** *it was plain bad luck* **sheer**, pure, downright, out-and-out.
> antonyms obscure, fancy, attractive, pretentious.

▶ noun a large area of flat land with few trees.

> synonyms *the plains of North America* **grassland**, flatland, prairie, savannah, steppe, tundra, pampas, veld, plateau.

■ **plain chocolate** Brit. dark, slightly bitter chocolate made without added milk. **plain clothes** ordinary clothes rather than uniform. **plain sailing** smooth and easy progress.
▫ **plainly** adverb **plainness** noun.

plainsong (or **plainchant**) ▸ noun a kind of medieval church music that was sung by a number of voices without any accompanying instruments.

plaintiff ▸ noun a person who brings a case against someone in a court of law.

plaintive ▸ adjective sounding sad and mournful.
▫ **plaintively** adverb.

plait ▸ noun Brit. a length of hair or rope made up of strands woven together.
▸ verb form into a plait or plaits.

plan ▸ noun **1** a detailed proposal for doing or achieving something. **2** an intention. **3** a map or diagram. **4** a scheme for making regular payments towards a pension, insurance policy, etc.

SYNONYMS **1** *a plan for raising money* **scheme,** idea, proposal, proposition, project, programme, system, method, strategy, stratagem, formula, recipe. **2** *her plan was to break even* **intention,** aim, idea, objective, object, goal, target, ambition. **3** *a plan of the new office* **map,** diagram, chart, blueprint, drawing, sketch, impression; N. Amer. plat.

▸ verb (**plans, planning, planned**) **1** decide on and arrange something in advance. **2** intend to do something. **3** (**plan for**) make preparations for. **4** make a plan of a building, town, garden, etc.

SYNONYMS **1** *plan your route in advance* **organize,** arrange, work out, outline, map out, prepare, formulate, frame, develop, devise. **2** *he plans to buy a house* **intend,** aim, propose, mean, hope. **3** *I'm planning a new garden* **design,** draw up a plan for, sketch out, map out; N. Amer. plat.

▫ **planner** noun.

plane¹ ▸ noun **1** a completely flat surface. **2** a level of existence or thought.

SYNONYMS *a higher plane of achievement* **level,** degree, standard, stratum, dimension.

▸ adjective **1** completely flat. **2** relating to two-dimensional surfaces or sizes.
▸ verb (**planes, planing, planed**) **1** (of a bird) soar without moving its wings. **2** skim over the surface of water.

SYNONYMS *boats planed across the water* **skim,** glide.

plane² ▸ noun an aeroplane.

SYNONYMS *the plane took off* **aircraft,** airliner, jet, flying machine; Brit. aeroplane; N. Amer. airplane, ship.

plane³ (or **planer**) ▸ noun a tool used to smooth a wooden surface by cutting thin shavings from it.
▸ verb (**planes, planing, planed**) smooth a surface with a plane.

plane⁴ ▸ noun a tall tree with broad leaves and peeling bark.

planet ▸ noun a large round mass in space that orbits a star.
▫ **planetary** adjective.

planetarium ▸ noun (plural **planetariums** or **planetaria** /plan-i-**tair**-i-uh/) a building in which images of stars, planets, and constellations are projected on to a domed ceiling.

plangent /**plan**-juhnt/ ▸ adjective (of a sound) loud and melancholy.

plank ▸ noun a long, flat piece of timber.

plankton ▸ noun tiny creatures living in the sea or fresh water.

plant ▸ noun **1** a living thing that absorbs substances through its roots and makes nutrients in its leaves by photosynthesis. **2** a place where a manufacturing process takes place. **3** machinery used in a manufacturing process. **4** a person placed in a group as a spy.

SYNONYMS **1** *garden plants* **flower,** vegetable, herb, shrub, bush, weed; (**plants**) vegetation, greenery, flora. **2** *a chemical plant* **factory,** works, facility, refinery, mill. **3** *investment in new plant* **machinery,** machines, equipment, apparatus, appliances, gear. **4** *a CIA plant* **spy,** informant, informer, secret agent, mole, infiltrator, operative; N. Amer. informal spook.

▸ verb **1** place a seed, bulb, or plant in the ground so that it can grow. **2** place in a particular position. **3** secretly place a bomb. **4** hide something among someone's belongings to make them appear guilty of something. **5** send someone to join a group to act as a spy. **6** fix an idea in someone's mind.

SYNONYMS **1** *plant the seeds* **sow,** scatter. **2** *he planted his feet on the ground* **place,** put, set, position, situate, settle; informal plonk. **3** *she planted the idea in his mind* **instil,** implant, put, place, introduce, fix, establish, lodge.

▫ **planter** noun.

Plantagenet /plan-**taj**-uh-nuht/ ▸ noun a member of the English royal house which ruled 1154–1485.

plantain ▸ noun **1** a type of banana eaten as a vegetable. **2** a wild plant with small green flowers and broad leaves that spread out near the ground.

p

plantation ▸ noun 1 a large estate on which crops such as coffee, sugar, and tobacco are grown. 2 an area in which trees have been planted.

plaque ▸ noun 1 an ornamental tablet fixed to a wall in memory of a person or event. 2 a sticky deposit that forms on teeth and in which bacteria grow quickly.

plasma /plaz-muh/ ▸ noun 1 the clear fluid part of blood in which blood cells are suspended. 2 a gas of positive ions and free electrons with little or no overall electric charge.

plaster ▸ noun 1 a soft mixture of lime with sand or cement and water for spreading on walls and ceilings to form a smooth, hard surface when dried. 2 (also **plaster of Paris**) a hard white substance made by adding water to powdered gypsum, used for setting broken bones and making sculptures and casts. 3 a sticky strip of material for covering cuts and wounds.

> SYNONYMS 1 *the plaster covering the bricks* **plasterwork**, stucco. 2 *a statuette made of plaster* **plaster of Paris**, gypsum. 3 *waterproof plasters* **sticking plaster**, adhesive dressing; trademark Elastoplast, Band-Aid.

▸ verb (**plasters, plastering, plastered**) 1 apply plaster to. 2 coat something thickly. 3 make hair lie flat by applying liquid to it. 4 (**plastered**) informal drunk.

> SYNONYMS 1 *bread plastered with butter* **spread**, smother, smear, cake, coat. 2 *his hair was plastered down with sweat* **flatten (down)**, smooth down, slick down.

□ plasterer noun.

plasterboard ▸ noun board made of plaster set between two sheets of paper, used to line interior walls and ceilings.

plastic ▸ noun a chemically produced material that can be moulded into shape while soft and then set into a hard or slightly flexible form.
▸ adjective 1 made of plastic. 2 easily shaped.

> SYNONYMS 1 *at high temperatures the rocks become plastic* **soft**, pliable, pliant, flexible, malleable, workable, mouldable; informal bendy. 2 *a plastic smile* **artificial**, false, fake, bogus, insincere; informal phoney, pretend.
> ANTONYMS rigid, genuine.

■ plastic surgery surgery performed to repair or reconstruct parts of the body.
□ plasticity noun plasticky adjective.

plasticine ▸ noun trademark a soft modelling material.

plate ▸ noun 1 a flat dish for holding food. 2 bowls, cups, and other utensils made of gold or silver. 3 a thin, flat piece of metal, plastic, etc. 4 a small, flat piece of metal with writing on it, fixed to a wall or door. 5 a printed photograph or illustration in a book. 6 each of the several rigid pieces which together make up the earth's surface.

> SYNONYMS 1 *a dinner plate* **dish**, platter, salver; historical trencher; archaic charger. 2 *a plate of spaghetti* **plateful**, helping, portion, serving. 3 *steel plates* **panel**, sheet, slab. 4 *a brass plate on the door* **plaque**, sign, tablet. 5 *the book has colour plates* **picture**, print, illustration, photograph, photo.

▸ verb (**plates, plating, plated**) cover a metal object with a thin coating of a different metal.

> SYNONYMS *the roof was plated with steel* **cover**, coat, overlay, laminate, veneer, armour, gild, chrome.

■ plate glass thick glass used for shop windows and doors.

plateau /plat-oh/ ▸ noun (plural plateaux /plat-ohz/ or plateaus) 1 an area of fairly level high ground. 2 a state of little or no change after a period of activity or progress.

> SYNONYMS **upland**, mesa, highland, tableland.

▸ verb (**plateaus, plateauing, plateaued**) reach a plateau.

platelet ▸ noun a disc-shaped cell fragment found in large numbers in blood and involved in clotting.

platen /plat-uhn/ ▸ noun a cylindrical roller in a typewriter against which the paper is held.

platform ▸ noun 1 a raised level surface on which people or things can stand. 2 a raised structure along the side of a railway track where passengers get on and off trains. 3 a raised structure standing in the sea from which oil or gas wells can be drilled. 4 the stated policy of a political party or group. 5 an opportunity for the expression or exchange of views. 6 a very thick sole on a shoe.

> SYNONYMS 1 *he made a speech from the platform* **stage**, dais, rostrum, podium, stand. 2 *the Democratic Party's platform* **programme**, manifesto, policies, principles, party line.

platinum ▸ noun a precious silvery-white metallic element.

platitude ▸ noun a remark that has been used too often to be interesting.
□ platitudinous adjective.

platonic /pluh-ton-ik/ ▸ adjective 1 (of love or friendship) intimate and affectionate but not sexual. 2 (**Platonic**) having to do with the ideas of Plato, a philosopher of ancient Greece.

p

platoon ▶ noun a subdivision of a company of soldiers.

platter ▶ noun a large flat serving dish.

platypus (or **duck-billed platypus**) ▶ noun (plural **platypuses**) an animal with a duck-like bill and webbed feet, which lays eggs.

plaudits ▶ plural noun praise.

plausible ▶ adjective 1 seeming reasonable or probable. 2 skilled at making people believe something.

> SYNONYMS **credible**, believable, reasonable, likely, possible, conceivable, imaginable, convincing, persuasive. ANTONYMS unlikely.

□ **plausibility** noun **plausibly** adverb.

play ▶ verb 1 take part in games for enjoyment. 2 take part in a sport or contest. 3 compete against another player or team. 4 act the role of a character in a play or film. 5 perform on a musical instrument. 6 perform a piece of music. 7 make a CD, tape, or record produce sounds. 8 move a piece or display a playing card when it is your turn in a game. 9 move or flicker over a surface.

> SYNONYMS **1** *the children played with toys* **amuse yourself**, entertain yourself, enjoy yourself, have fun, relax, occupy yourself, frolic, romp; informal mess about/around. **2** *I used to play football* **take part in**, participate in, be involved in, compete in, do. **3** *Liverpool play Oxford on Sunday* **compete against**, take on, meet. **4** *he was to play Macbeth* **act the part of**, take the role of, appear as, portray, perform.

▶ noun 1 a piece of writing performed by actors. 2 games that people take part in for enjoyment. 3 the performing of a sports match. 4 a move in a sport or game. 5 freedom of movement. 6 constantly changing movement.

> SYNONYMS **1** *a Shakespeare play* **drama**, theatrical work, piece, comedy, tragedy, production, performance. **2** *work and play* **amusement**, relaxation, recreation, diversion, leisure, enjoyment, pleasure, fun. **3** *there was no play in the rope* **movement**, slack, give.

■ **make a play for** informal attempt to attract or gain. **play along** pretend to cooperate with someone. **play something by ear** 1 perform music without having seen a score. 2 (**play it by ear**) informal proceed without having formed a plan. **play something down** disguise the importance of something. **playing card** each of a set of rectangular pieces of card with numbers and symbols on one side, used in various games. **play-off** an extra match played to decide the outcome of a contest. **play on** take advantage of someone's weak point.

play up Brit. informal cause problems.

playboy ▶ noun a wealthy man who spends his time enjoying himself.

player ▶ noun 1 a person taking part in a sport or game. 2 a person who plays a musical instrument. 3 a device for playing CDs, cassettes, etc. 4 a person who has influence in a particular area. 5 an actor.

> SYNONYMS **1** *a tournament for young players* **participant**, contestant, competitor, contender, sportsman, sportswoman. **2** *the players in the orchestra* **musician**, performer, artist, virtuoso, instrumentalist. **3** *the players of the Royal Shakespeare Company* **actor**, **actress**, performer, thespian, entertainer, artiste, trouper.

playful ▶ adjective 1 fond of games and amusement. 2 light-hearted.

> SYNONYMS **1** *a playful mood* **frisky**, lively, full of fun, frolicsome, high-spirited, exuberant, mischievous, impish; informal full of beans. **2** *a playful remark* **light-hearted**, jokey, teasing, humorous, jocular, facetious, frivolous, flippant. ANTONYMS serious.

□ **playfully** adverb.

playground ▶ noun an outdoor area provided for children to play in.

playgroup (or **playschool**) ▶ noun Brit. a regular supervised play session for preschool children.

playhouse ▶ noun 1 a theatre. 2 a toy house for children to play in.

playmate ▶ noun a friend with whom a child plays.

playpen ▶ noun a small portable enclosure in which a baby or small child can play safely.

plaything ▶ noun 1 a person who is treated as amusing but unimportant. 2 a toy.

playwright ▶ noun a person who writes plays.

plaza ▶ noun 1 an open public space in a built-up area. 2 N. Amer. a shopping centre.

plc (or **PLC**) ▶ abbreviation Brit. public limited company.

plea ▶ noun 1 a request made in an urgent and emotional way. 2 a formal statement made by or on behalf of a person charged with an offence in a law court.

> SYNONYMS **appeal**, entreaty, supplication, petition, request, call.

plead ▶ verb (**pleads**, **pleading**, **pleaded** or US or dialect **pled**) 1 make an emotional appeal. 2 argue in support of something. 3 state formally in court whether you are guilty or not guilty of the offence with which you are charged. 4 present something as an excuse for doing or not doing something.

SYNONYMS *she pleaded ignorance* **claim,** use as an excuse, assert, allege, argue.

□ **pleadingly** adverb.

pleasant ▶ adjective **1** satisfactory and enjoyable. **2** friendly and likeable.

SYNONYMS **1** *a pleasant evening* **enjoyable,** pleasurable, nice, agreeable, entertaining, amusing, delightful, charming; informal lovely, great. **2** *the staff are pleasant* **friendly,** charming, agreeable, amiable, nice, delightful, sweet, genial, cordial, good-natured, personable, hospitable, polite.
ANTONYMS unpleasant.

□ **pleasantly** adverb.

pleasantry ▶ noun (plural **pleasantries**) **1** an unimportant remark made as part of a polite conversation. **2** a mildly amusing joke.

please ▶ verb (**pleases, pleasing, pleased**) **1** make someone feel happy and satisfied. **2** wish or choose to do something. **3** (**please yourself**) consider only your own wishes.

SYNONYMS **1** *he'd do anything to please her* **make happy,** give pleasure to, make someone feel good, delight, charm, amuse, satisfy, gratify, humour, oblige. **2** *do as you please* **like,** want, wish, desire, see fit, think fit, choose, will, prefer.
ANTONYMS annoy.

▶ adverb used in polite requests or questions, or to accept an offer.

pleased ▶ adjective feeling or showing pleasure and satisfaction.

SYNONYMS **happy,** glad, delighted, gratified, grateful, thankful, content, contented, satisfied, thrilled; informal over the moon, on cloud nine; Brit. informal chuffed; N. English informal made up; Austral. informal wrapped.
ANTONYMS unhappy.

pleasing ▶ adjective pleasant, satisfying, or attractive.

SYNONYMS **1** *a pleasing result* **good,** agreeable, pleasant, pleasurable, satisfying, gratifying, great. **2** *her pleasing manner* **friendly,** amiable, pleasant, agreeable, affable, nice, genial, likeable, charming, engaging, delightful; informal lovely.
ANTONYMS poor, unfriendly.

pleasurable ▶ adjective enjoyable.
□ **pleasurably** adverb.

pleasure ▶ noun **1** a feeling of happy satisfaction and enjoyment. **2** an event or activity which you enjoy.

SYNONYMS **1** *she smiled with pleasure* **happiness,** delight, joy, gladness, glee,

satisfaction, gratification, contentment, enjoyment, amusement. **2** *his greatest pleasure in life* **joy,** amusement, diversion, recreation, pastime, treat, thrill. **3** *don't mix business and pleasure* **enjoyment,** fun, entertainment, recreation, leisure, relaxation.
ANTONYMS unhappiness, trial, duty, work.

▶ verb (**pleasures, pleasuring, pleasured**) give pleasure to.

pleat ▶ noun a fold in fabric, held by stitching at the top or side.
▶ verb fold or form into pleats.

pleb ▶ noun informal, disapproving a member of the lower social classes.

plebeian /pli-**bee**-uhn/ ▶ adjective ordinary or unsophisticated.
▶ noun a member of the ordinary people or the lower classes.

plebiscite /**pleb**-i-syt/ ▶ noun a vote made by everyone entitled to do so on an important public question.

plectrum ▶ noun (plural **plectrums** or **plectra**) a thin flat piece of plastic used to pluck the strings of a guitar.

pled US or dialect past and past participle of PLEAD.

pledge ▶ noun **1** a solemn promise or undertaking. **2** something valuable promised as a guarantee that a debt will be paid or a promise kept. **3** a thing given as a token of love or loyalty.

SYNONYMS *his election pledge* **promise,** vow, undertaking, word, commitment, assurance, oath, guarantee.

▶ verb (**pledges, pledging, pledged**) **1** solemnly undertake to do or give something. **2** promise something as a pledge.

SYNONYMS *he pledged to root out corruption* **promise,** vow, undertake, swear, commit yourself, declare, affirm.

plenary /**plee**-nuh-ri/ ▶ adjective **1** (of a meeting at a conference or assembly) to be attended by all participants. **2** full; complete.

plenipotentiary /plen-i-puh-**ten**-shuh-ri/ ▶ noun (plural **plenipotentiaries**) a person given full power by a government to act on its behalf.
▶ adjective having full power to take independent action.

plenitude ▶ noun formal a large amount of something.

plenteous ▶ adjective literary plentiful.

plentiful ▶ adjective existing in or producing great quantities.

SYNONYMS **abundant,** copious, ample, profuse, rich, lavish, generous, bountiful, bumper, prolific; informal galore.
ANTONYMS scarce.

p

◻ **plentifully** adverb.

plenty ▸ pronoun as much as is wanted or needed; quite enough.

SYNONYMS *there are plenty of books* **a lot of,** many, a great deal of, a plethora of, enough and to spare, no lack of, a wealth of; informal loads of, heaps of, stacks of, masses of.

▸ noun a situation in which food and other necessities are available in large enough quantities.

SYNONYMS *times of plenty* **prosperity,** affluence, wealth, opulence, comfort, luxury, abundance.

plenum /plee-nuhm/ ▸ noun an assembly of all the members of a group or committee.

plethora /pleth-uh-ruh/ ▸ noun an excessive amount or number of something.

pleurisy /ploor-i-si/ ▸ noun inflammation of the membranes around the lungs, causing pain during breathing.

plexus ▸ noun (plural **plexus** or **plexuses**) a complex network or web-like structure.

pliable /ply-uh-b'l/ ▸ adjective **1** easily bent. **2** easily influenced or persuaded.
◻ **pliability** noun.

pliant ▸ adjective pliable.

pliers ▸ plural noun pincers having jaws with flat surfaces, used for gripping small objects and bending or cutting wire.

plight[1] ▸ noun a dangerous or difficult situation.

SYNONYMS **predicament,** difficult situation, dire straits, trouble, difficulty, bind; informal tight corner, tight spot, hole, pickle, jam, fix.

plight[2] ▸ verb (**plight your troth**) old use promise to marry.

plimsoll ▸ noun Brit. a light rubber-soled canvas sports shoe.

plinth ▸ noun a heavy block or slab supporting a statue or forming the base of a column.

PLO ▸ abbreviation Palestine Liberation Organization.

plod ▸ verb (**plods, plodding, plodded**) **1** walk slowly with heavy steps. **2** work slowly and steadily at a dull task.

SYNONYMS **trudge,** walk heavily, clump, stomp, tramp, lumber, slog.
ANTONYMS stride, skip.

▸ noun a slow, heavy walk.

plonk[1] ▸ verb informal put something down heavily or carelessly.

plonk[2] ▸ noun Brit. informal cheap wine.

plop ▸ noun a sound like that of a small, solid object dropping into water without a splash.
▸ verb (**plops, plopping, plopped**) fall or drop with a plop.

plot ▸ noun **1** a secret plan to do something illegal or harmful. **2** the main sequence of events in a play, novel, or film. **3** a small piece of ground marked out for building, gardening, etc.

SYNONYMS **1** *a plot to overthrow him* **conspiracy,** intrigue, stratagem, plan. **2** *the plot of her novel* **storyline,** story, scenario, action, thread, narrative. **3** *a three-acre plot* **piece of ground,** patch, area, tract, acreage; Brit. allotment; N. Amer. lot, plat; N. Amer. & Austral./NZ homesite.

▸ verb (**plots, plotting, plotted**) **1** secretly make plans to carry out something illegal or harmful. **2** mark a route or position on a chart or graph.

SYNONYMS **1** *he plotted their downfall* **plan,** scheme, arrange, organize, contrive. **2** *his brother was plotting against him* **conspire,** scheme, intrigue, connive. **3** *the points were plotted on a graph* **mark,** chart, map.

◻ **plotter** noun.

plough (US spelling **plow**) ▸ noun **1** a piece of farming equipment with one or more blades fixed in a frame, used to turn over soil. **2** (**the Plough**) a formation of seven stars shaped like a simple plough, in the constellation Ursa Major (the Great Bear).
▸ verb **1** turn earth with a plough. **2** move forward with difficulty or force. **3** (of a ship or boat) travel through an area of water. **4** (**plough something in**) invest money in a business.

SYNONYMS **1** *the fields were ploughed* **till,** furrow, harrow, cultivate, work. **2** *the car ploughed into a wall* **crash,** smash, career, plunge, bulldoze, hurtle, cannon.

ploughman's lunch ▸ noun Brit. a meal of bread, cheese, and pickle.

ploughshare ▸ noun the main cutting blade of a plough.

plover (*rhymes with* lover) ▸ noun a wading bird with a short bill.

ploy ▸ noun a cunning act performed to gain an advantage.

SYNONYMS **ruse,** tactic, move, device, stratagem, scheme, trick, gambit, plan, manoeuvre, dodge, subterfuge; Brit. informal wheeze.

pluck ▸ verb **1** take hold of something and quickly remove it from its place. **2** pull out a hair or feather. **3** pull the feathers from a bird's carcass to prepare it for cooking. **4** pull at. **5** sound a stringed instrument with your fingers or a plectrum.

SYNONYMS **1** *he plucked a thread from his lapel* **remove,** pick, pull, extract. **2** *she plucked at his T-shirt* **pull,** tug, clutch, snatch, grab, catch, tweak, jerk; informal

p

yank. **3** *she plucked the guitar strings*
strum, pick, thrum, twang.

▶ noun courage.

> SYNONYMS *it took a lot of pluck* **courage,**
> bravery, nerve, daring, spirit, grit; informal
> guts; Brit. informal **bottle;** N. Amer. informal
> moxie.

■ **pluck up courage** summon up enough
courage to do something frightening.

plucky ▶ adjective (**pluckier, pluckiest**)
having a lot of courage and determination.
□ **pluckily** adverb.

plug ▶ noun **1** a piece of solid material that
tightly blocks a hole. **2** a device with metal
pins that fit into holes in a socket to make
an electrical connection. **3** an electrical
socket. **4** informal a piece of publicity
promoting a product or event.

> SYNONYMS **1** *she pulled out the plug*
> **stopper,** bung, cork, connector; N. Amer.
> stopple. **2** *a plug for his new book*
> **advertisement,** promotion, commercial,
> recommendation, mention, good word;
> informal **hype,** push, puff.

▶ verb (**plugs, plugging, plugged**) **1** block a
hole. **2** (**plug something in**) connect an
appliance to an electric circuit. **3** informal
promote a product or event by mentioning
it publicly. **4** (**plug away**) informal proceed
steadily with a task.

> SYNONYMS **1** *plug the holes* **stop,** seal,
> close, block, fill. **2** *she plugged her new
> film* **publicize,** promote, advertise,
> mention, bang the drum for, draw
> attention to; informal **hype,** push.

plughole ▶ noun Brit. a hole at the bottom or
end of a sink or bath, through which the
water drains away.

plum ▶ noun **1** an oval fruit which is purple,
reddish, or yellow when ripe. **2** a reddish-
purple colour.

▶ adjective informal highly desirable: *a plum job.*

plumage ▶ noun a bird's feathers.

plumb¹ ▶ verb **1** explore or experience
something fully. **2** measure the depth of
water. **3** test an upright surface to find out
if it is vertical.

> SYNONYMS *an attempt to plumb her
> psyche* **explore,** probe, delve into, search,
> examine, investigate, fathom, penetrate,
> understand.

▶ noun a heavy object attached to a plumb
line.
▶ adverb informal exactly.

> SYNONYMS *it went plumb through the
> screen* **right,** exactly, precisely, directly,
> dead, straight; informal (**slap**) bang.

▶ adjective vertical.
■ **plumb line** a line with a heavy object
attached to it, used for measuring the

depth of water or checking that a wall,
post, etc. is vertical.

plumb² ▶ verb (**plumb something in**) install
a bath, washing machine, etc. and connect
it to water and drainage pipes.

plumber ▶ noun a person who fits and
repairs the pipes and fittings used in the
supply of water and heating in a building.

plumbing ▶ noun the system of pipes and
fittings required for the water supply and
heating in a building.

plume ▶ noun **1** a long, soft feather or group
of feathers. **2** a long spreading cloud of
smoke or vapour.
□ **plumed** adjective.

plummet ▶ verb (**plummets, plummeting,
plummeted**) **1** fall straight down very
quickly. **2** decrease rapidly in value or
amount.

> SYNONYMS **1** *the plane plummeted to the
> ground* **plunge,** dive, drop, fall, hurtle.
> **2** *share prices plummeted* **fall steeply,**
> plunge, tumble, drop rapidly, slump;
> informal **crash,** nosedive.
> ANTONYMS soar.

▶ noun a steep and rapid fall or drop.

plummy ▶ adjective (**plummier, plummiest**)
Brit. informal (of a person's voice) typical of
the English upper classes.

plump¹ ▶ adjective **1** rather fat. **2** full and
rounded in shape.

> SYNONYMS **fat,** chubby, rotund, ample,
> round, stout, portly, overweight; informal
> **tubby,** roly-poly, pudgy; Brit. informal
> **podgy;** N. Amer. informal **zaftig,** corn-fed.
> ANTONYMS thin.

▶ verb (**plump something up**) make
something more full and rounded.

plump² ▶ verb **1** set or sit down heavily.
2 (**plump for**) decide in favour of one of
two or more possibilities.

plunder ▶ verb (**plunders, plundering,
plundered**) force your way into a place and
steal everything of value.

> SYNONYMS **1** *they plundered the
> countryside* **pillage,** loot, rob, raid,
> ransack, rifle, strip, sack. **2** *money
> plundered from pension funds* **steal,** seize,
> thieve, pilfer, embezzle.

▶ noun **1** goods obtained by plundering. **2** the
action of plundering.

> SYNONYMS *huge quantities of plunder*
> **booty,** loot, stolen goods, spoils, ill-
> gotten gains; informal **swag.**

plunge ▶ verb (**plunges, plunging,
plunged**) **1** fall or move suddenly and
uncontrollably. **2** jump or dive quickly.
3 push or thrust something quickly.
4 (**plunge in**) begin a course of action
without thought or care. **5** (**be plunged**

into) be suddenly brought into a particular state.

> SYNONYMS **1** *Joy plunged into the sea* **dive,** jump, throw yourself. **2** *the aircraft plunged to the ground* **plummet,** nosedive, drop, fall, tumble, descend. **3** *the car plunged down an alley* **charge,** hurtle, career, plough, tear; N. Amer. informal barrel. **4** *oil prices plunged* **fall sharply,** plummet, drop, tumble, slump; informal crash, nosedive. **5** *he plunged the dagger into her back* **thrust,** stab, sink, stick, ram, drive, push, shove, force. **6** *plunge the pears into water* **immerse,** submerge, dip, dunk. **7** *the room was plunged into darkness* **throw,** cast.
> ANTONYMS soar.

▶ noun an act of plunging.

> SYNONYMS **1** *a plunge in the pool* **dive,** jump, dip. **2** *a plunge in profits* **fall,** drop, slump; informal nosedive, crash.
> ANTONYMS rise.

■ **take the plunge** informal finally decide to do something difficult or challenging.

plunger ▶ noun **1** a part of a device that works with a plunging or thrusting movement. **2** a rubber cup on a long handle, used to clear blocked pipes by means of suction.

pluperfect ▶ adjective Grammar (of a tense) referring to an action completed earlier than some past point of time, formed by *had* and the past participle (as in *he had gone by then*).

plural ▶ adjective **1** more than one in number. **2** Grammar (of a word or form) referring to more than one.
▶ noun Grammar a plural word or form.

pluralism ▶ noun **1** a system in which power is shared among a number of political parties. **2** the acceptance within a society of a number of groups with different beliefs or ethnic backgrounds.
□ **pluralist** noun & adjective.

plurality ▶ noun (plural **pluralities**) **1** the fact or state of being plural. **2** a large number of people or things.

plus ▶ preposition **1** with the addition of. **2** together with; as well as.

> SYNONYMS *four novels plus various poems* **as well as,** together with, along with, in addition to, and, added to, not to mention.
> ANTONYMS minus.

▶ adjective **1** (after a number or amount) at least. **2** (after a grade) rather better than. **3** (before a number) above zero. **4** having a positive electric charge.
▶ noun **1** (also **plus sign**) the symbol +, indicating addition or a positive value. **2** informal an advantage.

> SYNONYMS *one of the pluses of the job* **advantage,** good point, asset, pro, benefit, bonus, attraction; informal perk.
> ANTONYMS disadvantage.

▶ conjunction informal also.
■ **plus fours** men's trousers that are cut wide over the thigh and are gathered in at mid-calf length.

plush ▶ noun a fabric with a thick, velvety surface.
▶ adjective informal luxurious.

> SYNONYMS **luxurious,** luxury, de luxe, sumptuous, opulent, magnificent, rich, expensive, fancy; Brit. upmarket; informal posh, classy; Brit. informal swish; N. Amer. informal swank.
> ANTONYMS austere.

Pluto ▶ noun the furthest planet from the sun in the solar system.

plutocracy /ploo-**tok**-ruh-si/ ▶ noun (plural **plutocracies**) **1** government by the richest people in a country. **2** a society governed by the richest people in it.

plutocrat ▶ noun a person who is powerful because of their wealth.

plutonium /ploo-**toh**-ni-uhm/ ▶ noun a radioactive metallic element used as a fuel in nuclear reactors and as an explosive in atomic weapons.

ply¹ ▶ noun (plural **plies**) a thickness or layer of a material.

ply² ▶ verb (**plies, plying, plied**) **1** (**ply someone with**) keep presenting someone with food or drink, or asking them questions. **2** (of a ship or vehicle) travel regularly over a route. **3** work steadily with a tool.

> SYNONYMS **1** *she plied me with scones* **provide,** supply, shower. **2** *he plied her with questions* **bombard,** assail, pester, plague, harass; informal hassle. **3** *he plied a profitable trade* **engage in,** carry on, pursue, conduct, practise. **4** *ferries ply between all lake resorts* **travel,** shuttle, go back and forth.

■ **ply your trade** do your job or business.

plywood ▶ noun board consisting of layers of wood glued together.

PM ▶ abbreviation Prime Minister.

p.m. ▶ abbreviation after noon.
ORIGIN short for Latin *post meridiem*.

pneumatic /nyoo-**mat**-ik/ ▶ adjective containing or operated by air or gas under pressure.

pneumonia /nyoo-**moh**-ni-uh/ ▶ noun an infection causing inflammation in the lungs.

poach¹ ▶ verb cook something by simmering it in a small amount of liquid.

poach² ▶ verb **1** hunt game or catch fish illegally from private or protected areas.

2 unfairly entice customers, workers, etc. away from someone else.

SYNONYMS **1** *he's been poaching salmon* **hunt illegally,** catch illegally, steal. **2** *workers were poached by other firms* **steal,** appropriate, headhunt; informal nab, swipe; Brit. informal nick, pinch.

□ **poacher** noun.

pocked ▸ adjective having pockmarks.

pocket ▸ noun **1** a small bag sewn into or on clothing, used for carrying small articles. **2** a small area or group that is different from its surroundings. **3** informal the money that you have available: *gifts to suit every pocket.* **4** an opening at the corner or on the side of a billiard table into which balls are struck.

SYNONYMS **1** *a bag with two pockets* **pouch,** compartment. **2** *pockets of resistance* **area,** patch, region, cluster.

▸ adjective of a suitable size for carrying in a pocket.

SYNONYMS *a pocket dictionary* **small,** little, miniature, mini, compact, concise, abridged, portable, travel; N. Amer. vest-pocket.

▸ verb (**pockets, pocketing, pocketed**) **1** put something into your pocket. **2** take something that is not yours.

SYNONYMS **1** *he pocketed $4m for a few months' work* **acquire,** obtain, gain, get, secure, win, make, earn. **2** *they were pocketing money supposed to be used for repairs* **steal,** appropriate, purloin, misappropriate, embezzle.

■ **pocket money 1** a small amount of money given to children regularly by their parents. **2** a small amount of money for minor expenses.

pockmark ▸ noun **1** a hollow scar or mark on the skin left by a spot. **2** a mark or hollow area on a surface.
□ **pockmarked** adjective.

pod¹ ▸ noun a long seed case of a pea, bean, etc.

SYNONYMS **shell,** husk, hull, case; N. Amer. shuck.

▸ verb (**pods, podding, podded**) remove peas or beans from their pods before cooking.

pod² ▸ noun a small herd of whales or similar sea mammals.

podcast ▸ noun a digital recording of a radio broadcast which is made available on the Internet for downloading to a personal computer or MP3 player.
□ **podcasting** noun.

podgy ▸ adjective (**podgier, podgiest**) Brit. informal rather fat.

podium ▸ noun (plural **podiums** or **podia**) a small platform on which a person stands to

conduct an orchestra or give a speech.

SYNONYMS **platform,** stage, dais, rostrum, stand.

poem ▸ noun a piece of imaginative writing in verse.

SYNONYMS **verse,** rhyme, lyric, piece of poetry.

poesy /poh-i-zi/ ▸ noun old use poetry.

poet ▸ noun a person who writes poems.
■ **Poet Laureate** (plural **Poets Laureate**) a poet appointed by the British king or queen, formerly responsible for writing poems for important occasions.

poetic (or **poetical**) ▸ adjective **1** having to do with poetry. **2** expressed in a sensitive and imaginative way.

SYNONYMS **expressive,** figurative, symbolic, flowery, artistic, imaginative, creative.

■ **poetic justice** a situation in which something bad happens to someone who has done something wrong. **poetic licence** freedom to change facts or the normal rules of language to achieve a special effect in writing.
□ **poetically** adverb.

poetry ▸ noun **1** poems as a whole or as a form of literature. **2** a quality of beauty and sensitivity.

SYNONYMS **poems,** verse, versification, rhyme.

po-faced ▸ adjective Brit. informal serious and disapproving.

pogo stick ▸ noun a toy for bouncing around on, consisting of a pole on a spring, with a bar to stand on and a handle at the top.

pogrom ▸ noun an organized massacre of an ethnic group, originally that of Jews in Russia or eastern Europe.

poignant /**poy**-nyuhnt/ ▸ adjective making you feel sadness or regret.

SYNONYMS **touching,** moving, sad, affecting, pitiful, pathetic, plaintive.

□ **poignancy** noun **poignantly** adverb.

poinsettia ▸ noun a shrub with large red leaves which resemble petals.

point ▸ noun **1** the tapered, sharp end of a tool, weapon, or other object. **2** a particular place or moment. **3** an item, detail, or idea. **4** (**the point**) the most important part of what is being discussed. **5** the advantage or purpose of something: *what's the point of it all?* **6** a unit of scoring, value, or measurement. **7** a small dot used as punctuation or in decimal numbers. **8** each of thirty-two directions marked at equal distances round a compass. **9** a narrow piece of land jutting out into the sea. **10** (**points**) Brit. a junction of two railway lines. **11** (also **power point**) Brit. an electrical socket. **12** (**points**) a set of electrical contacts in the distributor of a motor vehicle.

> SYNONYMS **1** *the point of a needle* **tip,** (sharp) end, extremity, prong, spike, tine, nib, barb. **2** *points of light* **pinpoint,** dot, spot, speck. **3** *a meeting point* **place,** position, location, site, spot. **4** *this point in her life* **time,** stage, juncture, period, phase. **5** *the tension had reached such a high point* **level,** degree, stage, pitch, extent. **6** *an important point* **detail,** item, fact, thing, argument, consideration, factor, element, subject, issue, topic, question, matter. **7** *get to the point* **heart of the matter,** essence, nub, core, crux; informal nitty-gritty. **8** *what's the point of this?* **purpose,** aim, object, objective, goal, intention, use, sense, value, advantage. **9** *he had his good points* **attribute,** characteristic, feature, trait, quality, property, aspect, side.

▶ verb **1** direct someone's attention by extending your finger. **2** aim, indicate, or face in a particular direction: *a sign pointing left.* **3** (**point something out**) make someone aware of something. **4** (**point to**) indicate that something is likely to happen. **5** fill in the joints of brickwork or tiling with mortar or cement.

> SYNONYMS *she pointed the gun at him* **aim,** direct, level, train.

■ **point-blank 1** (of a shot or missile) fired from very close to its target. **2** in a blunt and very direct way. **point of view** a particular attitude or opinion. **point-to-point** (plural **point-to-points**) Brit. a cross-country race for horses used in hunting.

pointed ▶ adjective **1** having a sharpened or tapered tip or end. **2** (of a remark or look) directed towards a particular person and expressing a clear message.

> SYNONYMS **1** *a pointed stick* **sharp,** spiky, spiked, tapering, barbed; informal pointy. **2** *a pointed remark* **cutting,** biting, incisive, acerbic, caustic, scathing, venomous, sarcastic; informal sarky; N. Amer. informal snarky.

pointer ▶ noun **1** a long, thin piece of metal on a scale or dial which moves to give a reading. **2** a hint or tip. **3** a breed of dog that, when it scents game, stands rigid and looks towards it.

> SYNONYMS **1** *the pointer moved to 100rpm* **indicator,** needle, arrow, hand. **2** *a pointer to the outcome of the election* **indication,** indicator, clue, hint, sign, signal, evidence. **3** *I can give you a few pointers* **tip,** hint, suggestion, guideline, recommendation.

pointless ▶ adjective having little or no sense or purpose.

> SYNONYMS **senseless,** futile, hopeless, unavailing, aimless, idle, worthless, valueless.
> ANTONYMS valuable.

□ **pointlessly** adverb.

poise ▶ noun **1** a graceful way of holding your body. **2** a calm and confident manner.

> SYNONYMS **1** *poise and good deportment* **grace,** gracefulness, elegance, balance, control. **2** *in spite of the setback she retained her poise* **composure,** equanimity, self-possession, aplomb, self-assurance, self-control, sangfroid, dignity; informal cool.

▶ verb **1** cause something to be balanced or suspended. **2** (**poised**) calm and confident. **3** (**be poised to do**) be ready to do.

> SYNONYMS **1** (**poised**) *she was poised on one foot* **balanced,** suspended, motionless, hanging, hovering. **2** (**poised**) *he was poised for action* **prepared,** ready, braced, geared up, all set, standing by.

poison ▶ noun **1** a substance that causes death or injury to a person or animal that swallows or absorbs it. **2** a harmful influence.

> SYNONYMS **toxin,** venom.

▶ verb **1** harm or kill a person or animal with poison. **2** put poison on or in. **3** have a harmful effect on.

> SYNONYMS **1** *her mother poisoned her* **give poison to,** murder. **2** *the Amazon is being poisoned* **pollute,** contaminate, taint, spoil. **3** *they poisoned his mind* **twist,** warp, corrupt.

□ **poisoner** noun.

poisonous ▶ adjective **1** (of an animal) producing poison. **2** (of a plant or substance) capable of causing death or illness if taken into the body. **3** very unpleasant or spiteful.

> SYNONYMS **1** *a poisonous snake* **venomous,** deadly. **2** *a poisonous chemical* **toxic,** noxious, deadly, fatal, lethal, mortal. **3** *a poisonous glance* **malicious,** malevolent, hostile, spiteful, bitter, venomous, malign.
> ANTONYMS harmless, non-toxic, benevolent.

poke ▶ verb (**pokes, poking, poked**) **1** prod with a finger or a sharp object. **2** (**poke about** or **around**) look or search around. **3** push or stick out in a particular direction.

> SYNONYMS **1** *she poked him in the ribs* **prod,** jab, dig, elbow, nudge, shove, jolt, stab, stick. **2** *leave the cable poking out*

p

stick out, jut out, protrude, project, extend.

▶ **noun** an act of poking.

SYNONYMS *Carrie gave him a poke* **prod,** jab, dig, elbow, nudge.

poker¹ ▶ **noun** a metal rod used for prodding an open fire.

poker² ▶ **noun** a card game in which the players bet on the value of the hands dealt to them.
■ **poker face** a blank expression that hides your true feelings.

poky (or **pokey**) ▶ **adjective** (**pokier, pokiest**) (of a room or building) uncomfortably small and cramped.

SYNONYMS **small,** little, tiny, cramped, confined, restricted, boxy.
ANTONYMS spacious.

polar ▶ **adjective 1** relating to the North or South Poles or the regions around them. **2** having an electrical or magnetic field. **3** completely opposite.
■ **polar bear** a large white bear from the Arctic.

polarity ▶ **noun** (plural **polarities**) **1** the state of having poles or opposites. **2** the direction of a magnetic or electric field.

polarize (or **polarise**) ▶ **verb** (**polarizes, polarizing, polarized**) **1** divide people into two sharply contrasting groups with different opinions. **2** Physics restrict the vibrations of a wave of light to one direction. **3** give magnetic or electric polarity to.
◻ **polarization** noun.

p

Polaroid ▶ **noun** trademark **1** a material that polarizes the light passing through it, used in sunglasses. **2** a camera that produces a finished print rapidly after each exposure.

polder ▶ **noun** (in the Netherlands) a piece of land reclaimed from the sea or a river.

Pole ▶ **noun** a person from Poland.

pole¹ ▶ **noun** a long, thin rounded piece of wood or metal, used as a support.

SYNONYMS **post,** pillar, stanchion, stake, support, prop, stick, paling, staff.

■ **pole position** the most favourable position at the start of a motor race. **pole vault** an athletic event in which competitors vault over a high bar with the aid of a long pole.

pole² ▶ **noun 1** either of the two points (**North Pole** or **South Pole**) at opposite ends of the earth's axis. **2** each of the two opposite points of a magnet at which magnetic forces are strongest. **3** the positive or negative terminal of an electric cell or battery.
■ **be poles apart** have nothing in common.

poleaxe (US spelling **poleax**) ▶ **verb**

(**poleaxes, poleaxing, poleaxed**) **1** kill or knock down with a heavy blow. **2** shock someone very much.

polecat ▶ **noun 1** a dark brown weasel-like animal with an unpleasant smell. **2** N. Amer. a skunk.

polemic /puh-**lem**-ik/ ▶ **noun 1** a speech or piece of writing that argues strongly for or against something. **2** (also **polemics**) the practice of using fierce argument or discussion.
▶ **adjective** (also **polemical**) having to do with fierce argument or discussion.
◻ **polemicist** noun.

police ▶ **noun** an official body of people employed by a state to prevent and solve crime and keep public order.

SYNONYMS **police force, police service,** police officers, policemen, policewomen; Brit. **constabulary;** informal the cops, the fuzz, the law, the boys in blue; Brit. informal the (Old) Bill; N. Amer. informal the heat.

▶ **verb** (**polices, policing, policed**) **1** keep law and order in an area. **2** make sure that a particular set of rules is obeyed.

SYNONYMS **1** *we must police the area* **guard,** watch over, protect, defend, patrol. **2** *the regulations will be policed by the ministry* **enforce,** regulate, oversee, supervise, monitor, observe, check.

■ **police state** a state in which the government requires the police to watch people secretly and control their activities.

policeman (or **policewoman**) ▶ **noun** (plural **policemen** or **policewomen**) a member of a police force.

police officer ▶ **noun** a member of a police force.

SYNONYMS **policeman, policewoman;** Brit. **constable;** N. Amer. **patrolman, trooper, roundsman;** informal cop; Brit. informal rozzer; N. Amer. informal uniform.

policy ▶ **noun** (plural **policies**) **1** a plan of action adopted by an organization or person. **2** a contract of insurance.

SYNONYMS **plans,** approach, code, system, guidelines, theory, line, position, stance.

polio (or **poliomyelitis**) /poh-li-oh-my-uh-**ly**-tiss/ ▶ **noun** a disease that can cause temporary or permanent paralysis.

Polish ▶ **noun** the language of Poland.
▶ **adjective** relating to Poland.

polish ▶ **verb 1** make something smooth and shiny by rubbing. **2** (**polish something up**) improve a skill. **3** (**polish something off**) finish eating or doing something quickly.

SYNONYMS **1** *I polished his shoes* **shine,** wax, buff, rub up/down, gloss, burnish. **2** (**polished**) *a polished table* **shiny,** glossy, gleaming, lustrous, glassy, waxed, buffed, burnished. **3** *polish up your essay* **perfect,** refine, improve, hone, enhance, brush up, revise, edit, correct, rewrite, go over, touch up. **4** (**polished**) *a polished performance* **expert,** accomplished, masterly, skilful, adept, adroit, dexterous, consummate, superb, superlative.

▸ noun **1** a substance used to polish something. **2** an act of polishing. **3** a shiny appearance produced by polishing. **4** refinement or elegance.

SYNONYMS *his poetry has clarity and polish* **sophistication,** refinement, urbanity, suaveness, elegance, style, grace, finesse; informal class.

□ **polisher** noun.

polite ▸ adjective (**politer, politest**) **1** respectful and considerate towards other people; courteous. **2** civilized or refined.

SYNONYMS **1** *a very polite girl* **well mannered,** civil, courteous, respectful, well behaved, well bred, gentlemanly, ladylike, genteel, gracious, tactful, diplomatic. **2** *polite society* **civilized,** refined, cultured, sophisticated. ANTONYMS rude, uncivilized.

□ **politely** adverb **politeness** noun.

politic ▸ adjective (of an action) sensible and wise in the circumstances.

SYNONYMS **wise,** prudent, sensible, judicious, expedient, advantageous, beneficial, profitable. ANTONYMS unwise.

political ▸ adjective **1** relating to the government or public affairs of a country. **2** related to or interested in politics.

SYNONYMS **governmental,** government, constitutional, ministerial, parliamentary, diplomatic, legislative, administrative.

■ **political correctness** the avoidance of language or behaviour that could offend certain groups of people. **political prisoner** a person who is imprisoned for their beliefs rather than because they have committed a crime.
□ **politically** adverb.

politician ▸ noun a person who holds an elected position within the government.

SYNONYMS **legislator,** Member of Parliament, MP, representative, minister, statesman, stateswoman, senator, congressman, congresswoman; informal politico.

politicize (or **politicise**) ▸ verb (**politicizes, politicizing, politicized**) **1** make someone interested in politics. **2** make something a political issue.

□ **politicization** noun.

politics ▸ noun **1** the activities concerned with governing a country or area. **2** a particular set of political beliefs. **3** activities concerned with gaining or using power within an organization or group: *office politics.*

SYNONYMS **1** *a career in politics* **government,** affairs of state, public affairs, diplomacy. **2** *he studies politics* **political science,** civics. **3** *what are his politics?* **political views,** political leanings. **4** *office politics* **power struggles,** machinations, manoeuvring, realpolitik.

polity ▸ noun (plural **polities**) **1** a form of government. **2** a society as a politically organized state.

polka ▸ noun a lively dance for couples.
■ **polka dot** each of a number of dots that are evenly spaced to form a pattern.

poll (*rhymes with* pole *or* doll) ▸ noun **1** the process of voting in an election. **2** a record of the number of votes cast.

SYNONYMS **1** *the poll to elect a new leader* **vote,** ballot, show of hands, referendum, plebiscite, election. **2** *a poll to investigate holiday choices* **survey,** opinion poll, market research, census.

▸ verb **1** record the opinion or vote of. **2** (of a candidate in an election) receive a particular number of votes.

SYNONYMS **1** *most of those polled supported him* **canvass,** survey, ask, question, interview, ballot. **2** *she polled 119 votes* **get,** gain, register, record, return.

■ **poll tax** a tax paid at the same rate by every adult.

pollard ▸ verb cut off the top and side branches of a tree to encourage new growth.

pollen ▸ noun a powder produced by the male part of a flower, which is carried by bees, the wind, etc. and can fertilize other flowers.
■ **pollen count** a measure of the amount of pollen in the air.

pollinate ▸ verb (**pollinates, pollinating, pollinated**) carry pollen to and fertilize a flower or plant.
□ **pollination** noun.

pollster ▸ noun a person who carries out opinion polls.

pollutant ▸ noun a substance that causes pollution.

pollute ▸ verb (**pollutes, polluting, polluted**) make something dirty or poisonous with unwanted or harmful substances.

p

SYNONYMS **contaminate**, taint, poison, foul, dirty, soil, infect.
ANTONYMS purify.

□ **polluter** noun.

pollution ▶ noun the presence in the air, soil, or water of a substance with unpleasant or harmful effects.

SYNONYMS **contamination**, impurity, dirt, filth, infection.

polo ▶ noun a game similar to hockey, played on horseback with a long-handled mallet.
■ **polo neck** Brit. a high, tight, turned-over collar on a sweater. **polo shirt** a casual short-sleeved shirt with a collar and two or three buttons at the neck.

polonium ▶ noun a rare radioactive metallic element.

poltergeist /pol-ter-gyst/ ▶ noun a kind of ghost that is said to make loud noises and throw objects around.

polychrome ▶ adjective consisting of several colours.
□ **polychromatic** adjective.

polyester ▶ noun a synthetic fibre used to make fabric for clothes.

polygamy /puh-**lig**-uh-mi/ ▶ noun the practice of having more than one wife or husband at the same time.
□ **polygamist** noun **polygamous** adjective.

polyglot ▶ adjective knowing or using several languages.

polygon ▶ noun a figure with three or more straight sides and angles.

polygraph ▶ noun a lie detector.

polyhedron /po-li-**hee**-druhn/ ▶ noun (plural **polyhedra** or **polyhedrons**) a solid figure with many sides.

polymath ▶ noun a person with a wide knowledge of many subjects.

polymer ▶ noun a substance with a molecular structure formed from many identical small molecules bonded together.

polymorphic (or **polymorphous**)
▶ adjective having several different forms.

Polynesian ▶ noun a person from Polynesia, a large group of Pacific islands including New Zealand and Hawaii.
▶ adjective relating to Polynesia.

polyp ▶ noun **1** a simple sea creature which remains fixed in the same place, such as coral. **2** Medicine a small lump sticking out from a mucous membrane.

polyphony /puh-**li**-fuh-ni/ ▶ noun the combination of a number of musical parts, each forming an individual melody and harmonizing with each other.
□ **polyphonic** adjective.

polystyrene ▶ noun a light synthetic material.

polysyllabic ▶ adjective having more than one syllable.

polytechnic ▶ noun (in the past in the UK) a college offering courses at degree level (now called a university).

polytheism /po-li-thee-i-z'm/ ▶ noun the worship of more than one god.
□ **polytheistic** adjective.

polythene ▶ noun Brit. a tough, light, flexible plastic.

polyunsaturated ▶ adjective (of a fat) having a chemical structure that is thought not to lead to the formation of cholesterol in the blood.

polyurethane ▶ noun a synthetic material used in paints and varnishes.

Pom ▶ noun Austral./NZ informal a British person.
□ **Pommy** adjective & noun.

pomade ▶ noun a scented oil or cream for making the hair glossy and smooth.

pomander ▶ noun a ball or container of sweet-smelling substances used to perfume a room or cupboard.

pomegranate ▶ noun a round tropical fruit with a tough orange outer skin and red flesh containing many seeds.

pommel ▶ noun **1** the curving or projecting front part of a saddle. **2** a rounded knob on the handle of a sword.

pomp ▶ noun the special clothes, music, and customs that are part of a grand public ceremony.

pompom ▶ noun a small woollen ball attached to a garment for decoration.

pompous ▶ adjective showing in a rather solemn or arrogant way that you have a high opinion of yourself and your own views.

SYNONYMS **self-important**, overbearing, sententious, grandiose, affected, pretentious, puffed up, haughty, proud, conceited, supercilious, condescending, patronizing.
ANTONYMS modest.

□ **pomposity** noun **pompously** adverb.

ponce Brit. informal ▶ noun **1** a man who lives off a prostitute's earnings. **2** disapproving an effeminate man.
▶ verb (**ponces**, **poncing**, **ponced**) (**ponce about** or **around**) behave in a way that wastes time or looks silly.
□ **poncey** (or **poncy**) adjective.

poncho ▶ noun (plural **ponchos**) a garment made of a thick piece of cloth with a slit in the middle for the head.

pond ▶ noun a small area of still water.

ponder ▶ verb (**ponders**, **pondering**, **pondered**) consider something carefully.

SYNONYMS **think about**, contemplate, consider, review, reflect on, mull over, meditate on, muse on, dwell on.

p

ponderous ▸ adjective **1** moving slowly and heavily. **2** boringly solemn or long-winded.
□ **ponderously** adverb.

pondweed ▸ noun a plant that grows in still or running water.

pong Brit. informal ▸ noun a strong, unpleasant smell.
▸ verb smell strongly and unpleasantly.
□ **pongy** adjective.

pontiff ▸ noun the Pope.

pontifical ▸ adjective having to do with a pope; papal.

pontificate ▸ verb /pon-ti-fi-kayt/ (**pontificates, pontificating, pontificated**) express your opinions in a pompous and overbearing way.
▸ noun (**the Pontificate**) /pon-ti-fi-kuht/ the official position of a pope or bishop.

pontoon¹ ▸ noun Brit. a card game in which players try to obtain cards with a value totalling twenty-one.

pontoon² ▸ noun **1** a flat-bottomed boat or hollow cylinder used with others to support a temporary bridge or floating landing stage. **2** a bridge or landing stage supported by pontoons.

pony ▸ noun (plural **ponies**) a small breed of horse, especially one below 15 hands.
■ **pony-trekking** Brit. the riding of ponies across country as a leisure activity.

ponytail ▸ noun a hairstyle in which the hair is drawn back and tied at the back of the head.

pooch ▸ noun informal a dog.

poodle ▸ noun a breed of dog with a curly coat that is usually clipped.

poof (or **pouf**) ▸ noun Brit. informal a homosexual man.

pooh-pooh ▸ verb informal dismiss an idea as being silly or impractical.

pool¹ ▸ noun **1** a small area of still water. **2** (also **swimming pool**) an artificial pool for swimming in. **3** a small, shallow patch of liquid on a surface.

> SYNONYMS **1** *pools of water* **puddle,** pond, lake. **2** *the hotel has a pool* **swimming pool,** baths; Brit. swimming baths; N. Amer. natatorium.

pool² ▸ noun **1** a supply of vehicles, goods, money, etc. that is shared between a number of people and available for use when needed. **2** (**the pools** or **football pools**) a form of gambling on the results of football matches. **3** a game played on a billiard table using sixteen balls.

> SYNONYMS **1** *a pool of skilled labour* **supply,** reserve(s), reservoir, fund, store, bank, stock, cache. **2** *a pool of money for emergencies* **fund,** reserve, kitty, pot, bank, purse.

▸ verb put something into a common fund to be used by a number of people.

> SYNONYMS *they pooled their skills* **combine,** group, join, unite, merge, share.

poop (or **poop deck**) ▸ noun a raised deck at the back of a ship.

poor ▸ adjective **1** having very little money. **2** of a low standard or quality. **3** (**poor in**) not having enough of something. **4** deserving pity or sympathy.

> SYNONYMS **1** *a poor family* **poverty-stricken,** penniless, impoverished, impecunious, needy, destitute; Brit. on the breadline; informal hard up, strapped, on your uppers. **2** *poor workmanship* **substandard,** bad, deficient, defective, faulty, imperfect, inferior, unsatisfactory, shoddy, crude, inadequate, unacceptable; informal crummy, rubbishy, rotten; Brit. informal ropy, duff, rubbish, dodgy. **3** *a poor crop* **meagre,** scanty, scant, paltry, reduced, modest, sparse, spare, deficient, insubstantial, skimpy, lean; informal measly, stingy. **4** *the poor thing* **unfortunate,** unlucky, unhappy, hapless, wretched.
> ANTONYMS rich, superior, abundant, lucky.

poorhouse ▸ noun Brit. a workhouse.

poorly ▸ adverb badly.

> SYNONYMS *the text is poorly written* **badly,** imperfectly, incompetently, crudely, shoddily, inadequately.

▸ adjective chiefly Brit. unwell.

> SYNONYMS *she felt poorly* **ill,** unwell, not very well, ailing, indisposed, out of sorts, under par, peaky; Brit. off colour; informal under the weather, rough; Brit. informal ropy, grotty; Scottish informal wabbit; Austral./NZ informal crook.

pootle ▸ verb (**pootles, pootling, pootled**) Brit. informal move or travel in a leisurely way.

pop¹ ▸ verb (**pops, popping, popped**) **1** make a sudden short explosive sound. **2** go or come quickly or unexpectedly. **3** put something somewhere quickly or for a short time. **4** (of a person's eyes) open wide and appear to bulge.

> SYNONYMS **1** *champagne corks popped* **go bang,** go off, crack, snap, burst, explode. **2** *I'm just popping home* **go**; informal tootle, whip; Brit. informal nip. **3** *pop a bag over the pot* **put,** place, slip, throw, slide, stick, set, lay, position.

▸ noun **1** a sudden short explosive sound. **2** informal, dated a sweet fizzy drink.

pop² ▸ noun (also **pop music**) modern popular music, usually with a strong melody and beat.

▶ **adjective 1** relating to pop music. **2** often disapproving made easy for the general public to understand; popularized: *pop psychology*.
■ **pop art** a style of art that uses images taken from popular culture, such as advertisements or films.

pop³ ▶ noun informal, chiefly US father.

popcorn ▶ noun a snack consisting of maize kernels which are heated until they burst open.

pope ▶ noun the Bishop of Rome as head of the Roman Catholic Church.

popery ▶ noun disapproving Roman Catholicism.
□ **popish** adjective.

popinjay ▶ noun old use a person who is vain and dresses in a showy way.

poplar ▶ noun a tall, slender tree with soft wood.

poplin ▶ noun a cotton fabric with a finely ribbed surface.

poppadom ▶ noun (in Indian cookery) a thin circular piece of spiced bread that is fried until crisp.

popper ▶ noun Brit. informal a press stud.

poppet ▶ noun Brit. informal a pretty or charming child.

poppy ▶ noun a plant with bright flowers and small black seeds.

poppycock ▶ noun informal nonsense.

populace ▶ noun the general public.

popular ▶ adjective **1** liked or admired by many people. **2** suited to the tastes of the general public. **3** connected with or carried out by ordinary people.

> SYNONYMS **1** *the restaurant is very popular* **well liked,** sought-after, in demand, commercial, marketable, fashionable, in vogue, all the rage, hot; informal in, cool, big. **2** *popular science books* **non-specialist,** non-technical, amateur, lay person's, general, middle-of-the-road, accessible, simplified, understandable, mass-market. **3** *popular opinion* **widespread,** general, common, current, prevailing, standard, ordinary, conventional.
> ANTONYMS unpopular, specialist, restricted.

□ **popularly** adverb.

popularity ▶ noun the state of being liked or supported by many people.

popularize (or **popularise**) ▶ verb (**popularizes, popularizing, popularized**) **1** make something popular. **2** make something understandable or interesting to the general public.
□ **popularization** noun.

populate ▶ verb (**populates, populating, populated**) **1** live in an area and form its population. **2** cause people to settle in an area.

population ▶ noun **1** all the people living in an area. **2** the number of people living in an area.

> SYNONYMS **inhabitants,** residents, people, citizens, public, community, populace, society, natives, occupants.

populist ▶ adjective aiming to appeal to ordinary people, especially in politics.
▶ noun a populist politician.
□ **populism** noun.

populous ▶ adjective having a large population.

porcelain /por-suh-lin/ ▶ noun a type of delicate china.

porch ▶ noun a covered shelter at the entrance to a building.

porcine /por-syn/ ▶ adjective relating to pigs, or like a pig.

porcupine ▶ noun an animal with long protective spines on the body and tail.

pore¹ ▶ noun each of many tiny openings in the skin or another surface.

pore² ▶ verb (**pores, poring, pored**) (**pore over** or **through**) study or read something with close attention.

> ! Don't confuse **pore** and **pour**: you **pore over** a book, not **pour over** it.

pork ▶ noun the flesh of a pig used as food.

porker ▶ noun a young pig raised and fattened for food.

porn ▶ noun informal pornography.

pornographic ▶ adjective relating to or constituting pornography.

> SYNONYMS **obscene,** indecent, dirty, smutty, filthy, erotic, titillating, sexy, risqué, X-rated, adult.

pornography ▶ noun pictures, writing, or films that are intended to arouse sexual excitement.

porous ▶ adjective having tiny spaces through which liquid or air can pass.
□ **porosity** noun.

porpoise ▶ noun a type of small whale with a rounded snout.

porridge ▶ noun a dish consisting of oats or oatmeal boiled with water or milk.

port¹ ▶ noun **1** a town or city with a harbour. **2** a harbour.

> SYNONYMS **harbour,** docks, marina, haven, seaport.

■ **port of call** a place where a ship or person stops on a journey.

port² ▶ noun a strong, sweet dark red wine from Portugal.

port³ ▶ noun the side of a ship or aircraft that is on the left when you are facing forward.

port⁴ ▶ noun **1** an opening in the side of a

ship for boarding or loading. **2** an opening in an aircraft or vehicle through which a gun can be fired. **3** a socket in a computer network into which a device can be plugged.

portable ▸ adjective able to be carried or moved easily.

> SYNONYMS **transportable**, movable, mobile, battery, wireless, lightweight, compact, handy, convenient.

□ **portability** noun.

portal ▸ noun a large and impressive doorway or gate.

portcullis ▸ noun a strong, heavy grating that can be lowered to block a gateway to a castle.

portend ▸ verb be a sign or warning that something important or unpleasant is likely to happen.

portent ▸ noun a sign or warning that something important or unpleasant is likely to happen.

portentous ▸ adjective **1** warning or showing that something important is likely to happen. **2** very serious or solemn.
□ **portentously** adverb.

porter ▸ noun **1** a person employed to carry luggage and other loads. **2** a hospital employee who moves equipment or patients. **3** Brit. an employee in charge of the entrance of a large building. **4** dark brown bitter beer.

> SYNONYMS *a porter helped with the bags* **carrier**, bearer; N. Amer. redcap, skycap.

portfolio ▸ noun (plural **portfolios**) **1** a thin, flat case for carrying drawings, maps, etc. **2** a set of pieces of creative work collected together to show someone's ability. **3** a range of investments held by a person or organization. **4** the position and duties of a government minister.

porthole ▸ noun a small window in the side of a ship or aircraft.

portico ▸ noun (plural **porticoes** or **porticos**) a roof supported by columns, built over the entrance to a building.

portion ▸ noun **1** a part or share of something. **2** an amount of food for one person.

> SYNONYMS **1** *the upper portion of the chimney* **part**, piece, bit, section, segment. **2** *her portion of the allowance* **share**, slice, quota, ration, allocation, tranche; Brit. informal whack. **3** *a portion of cake* **helping**, serving, plateful, slice, piece.

▸ verb share something out in portions.

portly ▸ adjective rather fat.

portmanteau /port-man-toh/ ▸ noun (plural **portmanteaus** or **portmanteaux** /port-man-

tohz/) a large travelling bag that opens into two parts.

portrait ▸ noun **1** a painting, drawing, or photograph of a particular person. **2** a piece of writing or film about a particular person.

> SYNONYMS **1** *a portrait of the King* **picture**, likeness, painting, drawing, photograph, image. **2** *a vivid portrait of Italy* **description**, portrayal, representation, depiction, impression, account, profile.

portraiture ▸ noun the art of making portraits.

portray ▸ verb **1** show or describe in a work of art or literature. **2** describe in a particular way.

> SYNONYMS **1** *he always portrays Windermere in sunny weather* **paint**, draw, sketch, picture, depict, represent, illustrate, render, show. **2** *the man portrayed by Waugh* **describe**, depict, characterize, represent. **3** *he portrays her as a doormat* **represent**, depict, characterize, describe, present. **4** *the actor portrays a spy* **play**, act the part of, take the role of, represent, appear as.

portrayal ▸ noun the action or an act of portraying.

> SYNONYMS **1** *her portrayal of adolescence* **description**, representation, characterization, depiction, evocation. **2** *Brando's portrayal of Corleone* **performance as**, representation, interpretation, rendering.

Portuguese ▸ noun (plural **Portuguese**) **1** a person from Portugal. **2** the language of Portugal and Brazil.
▸ adjective relating to Portugal.

> ✔ -**guese**, not -**gese**: Portu**guese**.

pose ▸ verb (**poses, posing, posed**) **1** present a problem, question, etc. **2** sit or stand in a particular position in order to be photographed, painted, or drawn. **3** (**pose as**) pretend to be. **4** behave in a way that is intended to impress people.

> SYNONYMS **1** *pollution poses a threat to health* **constitute**, present, offer. **2** *the question posed earlier* **raise**, ask, put, submit, advance, propose. **3** *the guys posing at the bar* **posture**, attitudinize, put on airs; informal show off, ponce about.

▸ noun **1** a position adopted in order to be painted, drawn, or photographed. **2** a way of behaving that is intended to impress people.

> SYNONYMS **1** *a formal pose* **posture**, position, stance, attitude. **2** *her pose of aggrieved innocence* **act**, affectation, show, display, posture, expression.

poser ▸ noun **1** a person who behaves in a way intended to impress other people. **2** a puzzling question or problem.

p

poseur /poh-zer/ ▶ noun a person who poses in order to impress; a poser.

posh ▶ adjective informal **1** very elegant or luxurious. **2** chiefly Brit. upper-class.

> SYNONYMS **1** *a posh hotel* **smart**, stylish, fancy, high-class, fashionable, chic, luxurious, luxury, exclusive; Brit. upmarket; informal classy, plush, flash; Brit. informal swish; N. Amer. informal swank, tony. **2** *a posh accent* **upper-class**, aristocratic.

posit ▶ verb (**posits, positing, posited**) present something as a fact or as a basis for argument.

position ▶ noun **1** a place where something is situated. **2** a way in which someone or something is placed or arranged. **3** a situation or set of circumstances. **4** a job. **5** a person's place or importance in relation to others. **6** a point of view.

> SYNONYMS **1** *the aircraft's position* **location**, place, situation, spot, site, locality, setting, area, whereabouts, bearings. **2** *a standing position* **posture**, stance, attitude, pose. **3** *our financial position* **situation**, state, condition, circumstances, predicament, plight. **4** *a secretarial position* **job**, post, situation, appointment, opening, vacancy, placement. **5** *their position in society* **status**, place, level, rank, standing, stature, prestige, reputation. **6** *the government's position on the matter* **viewpoint**, opinion, outlook, attitude, stand, standpoint, stance, perspective, thinking, policy, feelings.

▶ verb put or arrange in a particular position.

> SYNONYMS *he positioned a chair between them* **put**, place, locate, situate, set, site, stand, station, plant, stick; informal plonk, park.

☐ **positional** adjective.

positive ▶ adjective **1** indicating agreement with or support for something. **2** hopeful, favourable, or confident. **3** with no possibility of doubt; certain. **4** (of the rèsults of a test or experiment) showing the presence of something. **5** (of a quantity) greater than zero. **6** having to do with the kind of electric charge opposite to that carried by electrons. **7** (of an adjective or adverb) expressing the basic degree of a quality (e.g. *brave*).

> SYNONYMS **1** *a positive response* **affirmative**, favourable, good, enthusiastic, supportive, encouraging. **2** *say something positive* **constructive**, useful, productive, helpful, worthwhile, beneficial. **3** *she seems a lot more positive* **optimistic**, hopeful, confident, cheerful, sanguine, buoyant; informal upbeat. **4** *positive economic signs* **favourable**, good, promising, encouraging,

heartening, propitious, auspicious. **5** *positive proof* **definite**, certain, reliable, concrete, tangible, clear-cut, explicit, firm, decisive, real, actual. **6** *I'm positive he's coming back* **certain**, sure, convinced, confident, satisfied. ANTONYMS negative, pessimistic, doubtful, unsure.

▶ noun a positive quality.

■ **positive discrimination** Brit. the policy of giving jobs or other opportunities to people who belong to groups which suffer discrimination.

☐ **positivity** noun.

positively ▶ adverb **1** with certainty. **2** absolutely.

> SYNONYMS **1** *I could not positively identify the voice* **confidently**, definitely, firmly, categorically, with certainty, conclusively. **2** *he was positively livid* **absolutely**, utterly, downright, simply, virtually; informal plain.

positivism ▶ noun a system of philosophy that recognizes only things that can be scientifically or logically proved.

☐ **positivist** noun & adjective.

positron ▶ noun a subatomic particle with the same mass as an electron and an equal but positive charge.

posse /poss-i/ ▶ noun **1** N. Amer. (in the past) a group of men summoned by a sheriff to enforce the law. **2** informal a group of people.

possess ▶ verb **1** have or own something. **2** (also **be possessed of**) have a particular ability or quality. **3** dominate or have complete power over someone.

> SYNONYMS **1** *the only hat she possessed* **own**, have (to your name), be in possession of. **2** *he did not possess a sense of humour* **have**, be blessed with, be endowed with, enjoy, boast. **3** *an evil force possessed him* **take control of**, take over, bewitch, enchant, enslave.

☐ **possessor** noun.

> ✔ double s in the middle as well as at the end: po**ss**e**ss**.

possession ▶ noun **1** the state of having or owning something. **2** a thing owned.

> SYNONYMS **1** *the estate came into their possession* **ownership**, control, hands, keeping, care, custody, charge. **2** *she packed her possessions* **belongings**, things, property, worldly goods, personal effects, stuff, bits and pieces; informal gear, junk; Brit. informal clobber.

possessive ▶ adjective **1** demanding someone's total attention and love. **2** unwilling to share your possessions. **3** Grammar (of a pronoun or determiner) showing that someone owns something.

p

□ **possessively** adverb.

possibility ▸ noun (plural **possibilities**)
1 a thing that is possible. **2** the state of being possible. **3** (**possibilities**) qualities suggesting that something might be good or could be improved.

> SYNONYMS **1** *a possibility that he might be alive* **chance**, likelihood, probability, potentiality, hope, risk, hazard, danger, fear. **2** *buying a smaller house is one possibility* **option**, alternative, choice, course of action, solution.
> **3** (**possibilities**) *the idea has distinct possibilities* **potential**, promise, prospects.

possible ▸ adjective **1** capable of existing, happening, or being done. **2** that may be so.

> SYNONYMS **1** *it's not possible to check the figures* **feasible**, practicable, viable, attainable, achievable, workable; informal **on**, doable. **2** *a possible reason for his disappearance* **likely**, plausible, imaginable, believable, potential, probable, credible. **3** *a possible future leader* **potential**, prospective, likely, probable.
> ANTONYMS unlikely.

▸ noun a person or thing that may be chosen.

possibly ▸ adverb **1** perhaps. **2** in accordance with what is possible.

> SYNONYMS **1** *possibly he took her with him* **perhaps**, maybe, it is possible.
> **2** *you can't possibly refuse* **conceivably**, under any circumstances, by any means.
> **3** *could you possibly help me?* **please**, kindly, be so good as to.

possum ▸ noun **1** a marsupial that lives in trees. **2** N. Amer. informal an opossum.

post¹ ▸ noun **1** a strong, upright piece of timber or metal used as a support or a marker. **2** (**the post**) a post marking the start or finish of a race.

> SYNONYMS *wooden posts* **pole**, stake, upright, shaft, prop, support, picket, strut, pillar.

▸ verb **1** display a notice in a public place. **2** send a message to an Internet bulletin board or newsgroup.

> SYNONYMS **1** *the notice posted on the wall* **affix**, attach, fasten, display, pin up, put up, stick up. **2** *the group posted a net profit* **announce**, report, make known, publish.

post² chiefly Brit. ▸ noun **1** the official service or system that delivers letters and parcels. **2** letters and parcels delivered. **3** a single collection or delivery of post.

> SYNONYMS **1** *the winners will be notified by post* **mail**; informal snail mail. **2** *did we get any post?* **letters**, correspondence, mail.

▸ verb send something via the postal system.

> SYNONYMS *post the order form today* **send (off)**, mail, put in the post/mail, get off.

■ **keep someone posted** keep someone up to date with the latest news about something. **post office 1** the organization responsible for postal services. **2** a building where postal business is carried out.

post³ ▸ noun **1** a place where someone is on duty or where an activity is carried out. **2** a job.

> SYNONYMS **1** *back to your posts* **assigned position**, station, place, base. **2** *there were seventy candidates for the post* **job**, position, appointment, situation, place, vacancy, opening.

▸ verb **1** put a soldier, police officer, etc. in a particular place. **2** send someone to a place to take up a job.

> SYNONYMS *armed guards were posted* **put on duty**, mount, station.

post- ▸ prefix after: *postgraduate*.

postage ▸ noun **1** the sending of letters and parcels by post. **2** the charge for sending something by post.

postal ▸ adjective relating to or carried out by post.
■ **postal order** Brit. a document that can be bought from a post office and sent to someone who exchanges it for money.

postbox ▸ noun a large public box into which letters are posted for collection by the post office.

postcard ▸ noun a card for sending a message by post without an envelope.

postcode ▸ noun Brit. a group of letters and numbers added to a postal address to help in the sorting of mail.

post-date ▸ verb **1** put a date later than the actual one on a cheque or document. **2** happen, exist, or be found later than.

poster ▸ noun a large picture or notice used for decoration or advertisement.

> SYNONYMS **notice**, placard, bill, sign, advertisement, playbill.

poste restante /pohst ress-tuhnt/ ▸ noun Brit. a department in a post office that keeps people's letters until they are collected.

posterior ▸ adjective at or near the rear.
▸ noun humorous a person's bottom.

posterity ▸ noun all future generations of people.

postgraduate ▸ adjective relating to study done after completing a first degree.
▸ noun a person taking a course of postgraduate study.

post-haste ▸ adverb very fast.

posthumous /poss-tyuu-muhss/ ▸ adjective happening or appearing after the person involved has died.
□ **posthumously** adverb.

posting[1] ▶ noun chiefly Brit. an appointment to a job abroad.

posting[2] ▶ noun a message sent to an Internet bulletin board or newsgroup.

postman ▶ noun (plural **postmen**) Brit. a man employed to deliver or collect post.

postmark ▶ noun an official mark stamped on a letter or parcel, giving the date of posting and cancelling the postage stamp.
▶ verb stamp a letter or parcel with a postmark.

postmaster (or **postmistress**) ▶ noun a person in charge of a post office.

postmodernism ▶ noun a movement in the arts that features a deliberate mixing of different styles.
◻ **postmodern** adjective **postmodernist** noun & adjective.

post-mortem ▶ noun an examination of a dead body to find out the cause of death.

post-natal ▶ adjective having to do with the period after childbirth.

postpone ▶ verb (**postpones, postponing, postponed**) arrange for something to take place at a time later than that first planned.

> SYNONYMS **put off**, put back, delay, defer, hold over, reschedule, adjourn, shelve; informal put on ice, put on the back burner. ANTONYMS bring forward.

◻ **postponement** noun.

postscript ▶ noun a remark added at the end of a letter.

postulant ▶ noun a person who has recently entered a religious order.

postulate ▶ verb (**postulates, postulating, postulated**) assume that something is true, as a basis for a theory or discussion.
◻ **postulation** noun.

posture ▶ noun 1 a particular position of the body. 2 the usual way in which a person holds their body. 3 an approach or attitude towards something.

> SYNONYMS 1 *a kneeling posture* **position**, pose, attitude, stance. 2 *good posture* **bearing**, carriage, stance, comportment; Brit. deportment. 3 *trade unions adopted a militant posture* **attitude**, stance, standpoint, point of view, opinion, position.

▶ verb (**postures, posturing, postured**) behave in a way that is meant to impress or mislead other people.

> SYNONYMS *Keith postured, flexing his biceps* **pose**, strike an attitude, strut.

◻ **postural** adjective.

posy ▶ noun (plural **posies**) a small bunch of flowers.

pot[1] ▶ noun a rounded container used for storage or cooking.

> SYNONYMS 1 *a pot of soup* **pan**, saucepan, casserole. 2 *Neolithic pots* **vessel**, bowl, earthenware, pottery.

▶ verb (**pots, potting, potted**) 1 plant a young plant in a flowerpot. 2 preserve food in a sealed pot or jar. 3 Billiards Snooker hit a ball into a pocket. 4 informal hit or kill by shooting.
■ **go to pot** informal be ruined through neglect. **pot belly** a large stomach that sticks out. **pot luck** a situation in which you take a chance that whatever is available will be acceptable. **potting shed** a shed used for potting plants and storing garden tools.

pot[2] ▶ noun informal cannabis.

potable /poh-tuh-b'l/ ▶ adjective formal (of water) safe to drink.

potash ▶ noun a substance obtained from potassium, used in making soap and fertilizers.

potassium ▶ noun a soft silvery-white metallic element.

potato ▶ noun (plural **potatoes**) an oval vegetable with starchy white or yellow flesh and a brown skin, that grows underground as a tuber.

> ✔ The singular has no **e** on the end: potat**o**.

potent ▶ adjective 1 very powerful. 2 (of a man) able to achieve an erection.

> SYNONYMS 1 *a potent political force* **powerful**, strong, mighty, formidable, influential, dominant. 2 *a potent argument* **forceful**, convincing, cogent, compelling, persuasive, powerful, strong. 3 *a potent drug* **strong**, powerful, effective; formal efficacious. ANTONYMS weak.

◻ **potency** noun.

potentate ▶ noun a monarch or ruler.

potential ▶ adjective capable of becoming or developing into something.

> SYNONYMS *a potential source of conflict* **possible**, likely, prospective, future, probable.

▶ noun 1 qualities or abilities that may be developed and lead to future success. 2 the possibility of something happening.

> SYNONYMS *he has great potential* **possibilities**, potentiality, prospects, promise, capability, capacity.

◻ **potentiality** noun **potentially** adverb.

pothole ▶ noun 1 a deep underground cave. 2 a hole in the surface of a road.
◻ **potholed** adjective.

potholing ▶ noun exploring potholes as a pastime.

potion ▶ noun a drink with healing, magical, or poisonous powers.

potpourri /poh-puh-ree/ ▶ noun (plural

potpourris) a mixture of dried petals and spices used to perfume a room.

potshot ▸ noun a shot aimed unexpectedly or at random.

pottage ▸ noun old use soup or stew.

potted ▸ adjective **1** preserved in a sealed pot. **2** put into a short, easily understandable form.

potter[1] ▸ verb (**potters, pottering, pottered**) **1** spend your time doing small tasks in a relaxed way. **2** move in an unhurried way.

SYNONYMS **amble,** wander, meander, stroll, saunter; informal mosey, tootle, toddle; N. Amer. informal putter.

potter[2] ▸ noun a person who makes pottery.

pottery ▸ noun (plural **potteries**) **1** articles made of fired clay. **2** the craft of making such articles. **3** a place where pottery is made.

SYNONYMS **ceramics,** crockery, earthenware, terracotta, stoneware, china, porcelain.

potty[1] ▸ adjective (**pottier, pottiest**) Brit. informal **1** mad; crazy. **2** very enthusiastic about someone or something.

potty[2] ▸ noun (plural **potties**) a bowl for a child to sit on and use as a toilet.

pouch ▸ noun **1** a small flexible bag. **2** a pocket of skin in an animal's body, especially that in which animals such as kangaroos carry their young.

pouf ➡ POOF or POUFFE.

pouffe (or **pouf**) /poof/ ▸ noun a large, firm cushion used as a seat or for resting your feet on.

poulterer ▸ noun Brit. a person who sells poultry.

poultice /**pohl**-tiss/ ▸ noun a soft, moist mass of flour or plant material that is put on the skin to reduce inflammation.

poultry ▸ noun chickens, turkeys, ducks, and geese.

pounce ▸ verb (**pounces, pouncing, pounced**) **1** suddenly spring to seize or attack something. **2** (**pounce on**) quickly notice and criticize something that someone has said or done.

SYNONYMS **jump,** spring, leap, dive, lunge, swoop, attack.

▸ noun an act of pouncing.

pound[1] ▸ noun **1** a unit of weight equal to 16 oz avoirdupois (0.4536 kg), or 12 oz troy (0.3732 kg). **2** (also **pound sterling**) the basic unit of money of the UK, equal to 100 pence.

pound[2] ▸ verb **1** hit something heavily again and again. **2** walk or run with heavy steps. **3** beat or throb with a strong regular rhythm. **4** crush or grind something into a

powder or paste.

SYNONYMS **1** *the two men pounded him with their fists* **beat,** strike, hit, batter, thump, pummel, punch, rain blows on, belabour, hammer; informal bash, clobber, wallop. **2** *waves pounded the seafront* **beat against,** crash against, batter, dash against, lash, buffet. **3** *gunships pounded the capital* **bombard,** bomb, shell. **4** *pound the garlic to a paste* **crush,** grind, pulverize, mash, pulp. **5** *I heard him pounding along the gangway* **stomp,** stamp, clomp, clump, tramp, lumber. **6** *her heart was pounding* **throb,** thump, thud, hammer, pulse, race.

pound[3] ▸ noun a place where stray dogs or illegally parked vehicles are officially taken and kept until claimed.

SYNONYMS *a dog pound* **enclosure,** compound, pen, yard, corral.

pour ▸ verb **1** flow or cause to flow in a steady stream. **2** (of rain) fall heavily. **3** prepare and serve a drink. **4** come or go in large numbers. **5** (**pour something out**) express your feelings freely.

SYNONYMS **1** *blood was pouring from his nose* **stream,** flow, run, gush, course, jet, spurt, surge, spill. **2** *it was pouring* **rain heavily/hard,** teem down, pelt down, tip down, rain cats and dogs; informal be chucking it down; Brit. informal bucket down; N. Amer. informal rain pitchforks. **3** *Amy poured wine into his glass* **tip,** splash, spill, decant; informal slosh, slop. **4** *people poured off the train* **crowd,** throng, swarm, stream, flood.

❗ Don't confuse **pour** and **pore**: you **pore over** a book, not **pour over** it.

pout ▸ verb push your lips forward as a sign of sulking or to make yourself look sexually attractive.

▸ noun a pouting expression.
  ◻ **pouty** adjective.

poverty ▸ noun **1** the state of being very poor. **2** the state of lacking in a particular quality.

SYNONYMS **1** *abject poverty* **pennilessness,** destitution, penury, impoverishment, neediness, hardship, impecuniousness. **2** *the poverty of choice* **scarcity,** deficiency, dearth, shortage, paucity, absence, lack. **3** *the poverty of her imagination* **inferiority,** mediocrity, sterility.

ANTONYMS wealth, abundance, fertility.

powder ▸ noun **1** a mass of fine dry particles. **2** a cosmetic in this form applied to a person's face.

▸ verb (**powders, powdering, powdered**) **1** sprinkle powder over. **2** make something into a powder.

■ **powder room** a women's toilet in a public building.

powdery ▸ adjective like or constituting powder.

SYNONYMS **fine**, dry, fine-grained, powder-like, dusty, chalky, floury, sandy, crumbly, friable.

power ▸ noun **1** the ability to do something. **2** the ability to influence people or events. **3** the right or authority to do something. **4** political authority or control. **5** a country seen as having international influence and military strength. **6** strength, force, or energy. **7** capacity or performance of an engine or other device. **8** energy that is produced by mechanical, electrical, or other means. **9** Physics the rate of doing work, measured in watts or horse power. **10** Maths the product obtained when a number is multiplied by itself a certain number of times.

SYNONYMS **1** *the power of speech* **ability**, capacity, capability, potential, faculty. **2** *the union has enormous power* **control**, authority, influence, dominance, sway, leverage; informal clout, teeth; N. Amer. informal drag. **3** *the power to stop and search* **authority**, right, authorization. **4** *a major European power* **state**, country, nation. **5** *he hit the ball with as much power as he could* **strength**, might, force, vigour, energy; Brit. informal welly. **6** *the power of his arguments* **forcefulness**, powerfulness, strength, force, cogency, persuasiveness. **7** *the new engine has more power* **driving force**, horsepower, acceleration, torque; informal oomph, poke. **8** *generating power from waste* **energy**, electricity.
ANTONYMS inability, weakness.

▸ verb (**powers, powering, powered**) **1** supply with power. **2** move with speed or force.
■ **power cut** a temporary interruption in an electricity supply. **power station** a building where electrical power is generated. **power steering** steering aided by power from a vehicle's engine.

powerboat ▸ noun a fast motorboat.

powerful ▸ adjective having power.

SYNONYMS **1** *powerful shoulders* **strong**, muscular, muscly, sturdy, strapping, robust, brawny, burly, athletic, manly, well built, solid; informal beefy. **2** *a powerful drink* **intoxicating**, hard, strong, stiff. **3** *a powerful blow* **violent**, forceful, hard, mighty. **4** *he felt a powerful urge to kiss her* **intense**, keen, fierce, strong, irresistible, overpowering, overwhelming. **5** *a powerful nation* **influential**, strong, important, dominant, commanding, formidable. **6** *a powerful critique* **cogent**, compelling,

convincing, persuasive, forceful.
ANTONYMS weak, gentle.

□ **powerfully** adverb.

powerhouse ▸ noun a person or thing having great energy or power.

powerless ▸ adjective without the power to take action.

SYNONYMS **impotent**, helpless, ineffectual, ineffective, useless, defenceless, vulnerable.

powwow ▸ noun **1** informal a meeting for discussion. **2** a North American Indian ceremony involving feasting and dancing.

pox ▸ noun **1** any disease that produces a rash of pus-filled pimples that leave pockmarks on healing. **2** (**the pox**) informal syphilis.

poxy ▸ adjective Brit. informal of bad quality.

pp (or **p.p.**) ▸ abbreviation used when signing a letter on someone else's behalf.
ORIGIN short for Latin *per procurationem*, literally 'through the agency of'.

PR ▸ abbreviation **1** proportional representation. **2** public relations.

practicable ▸ adjective able to be done successfully.

SYNONYMS **realistic**, feasible, possible, viable, reasonable, sensible, workable, achievable; informal doable.

□ **practicability** noun.

practical ▸ adjective **1** relating to the actual doing or use of something rather than theory. **2** likely to be successful or useful. **3** skilled at making or doing things.

SYNONYMS **1** *practical experience* **empirical**, hands-on, actual. **2** *there are no practical alternatives* **feasible**, practicable, realistic, viable, workable, possible, reasonable, sensible; informal doable. **3** *practical clothes* **functional**, sensible, utilitarian. **4** *try to be more practical* **realistic**, sensible, down-to-earth, businesslike, commonsensical, hard-headed, no-nonsense; informal hard-nosed. **5** *a practical certainty* **virtual**, effective, near.
ANTONYMS theoretical, impractical.

▸ noun Brit. an exam or lesson in which students have to do or make things.
■ **practical joke** a trick played on someone to make them look silly.

practicality ▸ noun (plural **practicalities**) **1** the state of being practical. **2** (**practicalities**) the real facts or aspects of a situation.

practically ▸ adverb **1** almost; virtually. **2** in a practical way.

SYNONYMS **1** *the cinema was practically empty* **almost**, very nearly, virtually, just about, all but, more or less, as good as, to all intents and purposes; informal pretty nearly, pretty well. **2** *'You can't afford it,' he pointed out practically* **realistically,** sensibly, reasonably, rationally, matter-of-factly.

practice ▸ noun **1** the actual doing of something rather than the theories about it. **2** the usual way of doing something. **3** the work, business, or place of work of a doctor, dentist, or lawyer. **4** the doing of something repeatedly to improve your skill.

> SYNONYMS **1** *the practice of radiotherapy* **application,** exercise, use, operation, implementation, execution. **2** *it is common practice* **custom,** procedure, policy, convention, tradition. **3** *the team's final practice* **training,** rehearsal, repetition, preparation, dummy run, run-through; informal dry run. **4** *the practice of medicine* **profession,** career, business, work. **5** *a small legal practice* **business,** firm, office, company; informal outfit.

▸ verb US spelling of **PRACTISE**.

> ❗ Do you mean **practice** or **practise**?
> **Practice** is the spelling for the noun, and in America for the verb as well; **practise** is the British spelling of the verb.

practise (US spelling practice) ▸ verb (**practises, practising, practised**) **1** do something repeatedly to improve your skill. **2** (**practised**) skilful as a result of experience. **3** do something regularly as part of your normal behaviour. **4** be working in a particular profession. **5** follow the teaching and rules of a religion.

> SYNONYMS **1** *he practised the songs every day* **rehearse,** run through, go over/through, work on/at, polish, perfect. **2** (**practised**) **expert,** experienced, seasoned, skilled, skilful, accomplished, proficient, talented, able, adept. **3** *the performers were practising* **train,** rehearse, prepare, go through your paces. **4** *she practises medicine* **work at/in,** pursue a career in. **5** *we still practise these rituals today* **carry out,** perform, observe.

practitioner ▸ noun a person who practises a profession or activity.

pragmatic ▸ adjective dealing with things in a sensible and realistic way.

> SYNONYMS **practical,** matter of fact, sensible, down-to-earth, commonsensical, businesslike, hard-headed, no-nonsense; informal hard-nosed.
> ANTONYMS impractical.

☐ **pragmatically** adverb.

pragmatism ▸ noun a realistic and sensible attitude or approach to something.
☐ **pragmatist** noun.

prairie ▸ noun (in North America) a large open area of grassland.

praise ▸ verb (**praises, praising, praised**) **1** show approval of or admiration for. **2** express thanks to or respect for God.

> SYNONYMS **commend,** applaud, pay tribute to, speak highly of, compliment, congratulate, sing the praises of, rave about.
> ANTONYMS criticize.

▸ noun words that show approval or admiration.

> SYNONYMS **approval,** acclaim, admiration, approbation, plaudits, congratulations, commendation, accolade, compliment, a pat on the back, eulogy.
> ANTONYMS criticism.

praiseworthy ▸ adjective deserving praise.

praline /prah-leen, pray-leen/ ▸ noun a sweet substance made from nuts boiled in sugar.

pram ▸ noun Brit. a four-wheeled vehicle for a baby, pushed by a person on foot.

prance ▸ verb (**prances, prancing, pranced**) walk with exaggerated steps.

prang ▸ verb Brit. informal crash a motor vehicle or aircraft.

prank ▸ noun a practical joke or mischievous act.

prankster ▸ noun a person who is fond of playing pranks.

prat ▸ noun Brit. informal a stupid person.

prate ▸ verb (**prates, prating, prated**) talk too much in a silly or boring way.

prattle ▸ verb (**prattles, prattling, prattled**) talk too much in a silly or trivial way.
▸ noun foolish or silly talk.

prawn ▸ noun an edible shellfish like a large shrimp.

pray ▸ verb **1** say a prayer. **2** hope strongly for something.
▸ adverb formal or old use please.
■ **praying mantis** ➡ MANTIS.

prayer ▸ noun **1** a request for help or expression of thanks made to God or a god. **2** (**prayers**) a religious service at which people gather to pray together. **3** an earnest hope or wish.

pre- ▸ prefix before: *prearrange*.

preach ▸ verb **1** give a religious talk to a group of people. **2** recommend a particular way of thinking or behaving. **3** (**preach at**) tell someone how they should think or behave in a way that is boring or annoying.

> SYNONYMS **1** *he preached to a large congregation* **give a sermon,** sermonize, address, speak. **2** *preaching the gospel* **proclaim,** teach, spread, propagate, expound. **3** *they preach toleration*

p

advocate, recommend, advise, urge, teach, counsel.

□ **preacher** noun.

preamble /pree-**am**-b'l/ ▸ noun an opening statement; an introduction.

prearrange ▸ verb (**prearranges**, **prearranging**, **prearranged**) arrange something in advance.

prebendary ▸ noun (plural **prebendaries**) (in the Church of England) a person holding an administrative or honorary position at certain cathedrals.

precarious ▸ adjective 1 likely to tip over or fall. 2 (of a situation) not safe or certain.

SYNONYMS **insecure**, uncertain, unpredictable, risky, parlous, hazardous, dangerous, unsafe, unstable, unsteady, shaky; informal dicey, iffy; Brit. informal dodgy.
ANTONYMS safe.

□ **precariously** adverb.

precaution ▸ noun something done to avoid problems or danger.

SYNONYMS **safeguard**, preventive measure, safety measure, insurance; informal backstop.

□ **precautionary** adjective.

precede ▸ verb (**precedes**, **preceding**, **preceded**) 1 happen before something in time or order. 2 go somewhere in front of someone.

SYNONYMS 1 *adverts preceded the film* go/**come before**, lead up to, pave the way for, herald, introduce, usher in. 2 *Catherine preceded him into the studio* go **ahead of**, go in front of, lead the way.
ANTONYMS follow.

precedence ▸ noun the state of coming before others in order or importance.

precedent ▸ noun an earlier event, action, or legal case that is taken as an example to be followed in similar situations.

SYNONYMS **model**, exemplar, example, pattern, paradigm, criterion, yardstick, standard.

precept ▸ noun a general rule about how to behave.

precinct ▸ noun 1 Brit. an area in a town that is closed to traffic. 2 an enclosed area around a place or building. 3 N. Amer. each of the districts into which a city or town is divided for elections or policing.

SYNONYMS **district**, zone, sector, quarter, area.

precious ▸ adjective 1 rare and worth a lot of money. 2 greatly loved or valued. 3 sophisticated in a way that is artificial and exaggerated.

SYNONYMS 1 *precious works of art* **valuable**, costly, expensive, invaluable, priceless. 2 *her most precious possession* **valued**, cherished, treasured, prized, favourite, dear, beloved, special. 3 *his precious manners* **affected**, pretentious; informal la-di-da; Brit. informal poncey.

■ **precious little** (or **few**) informal very little (or few). **precious metal** a valuable metal such as gold, silver, or platinum. **precious stone** an attractive and valuable piece of mineral, used in jewellery.

precipice ▸ noun a tall and very steep rock face or cliff.

precipitate ▸ verb /pri-**sip**-i-tayt/ (**precipitates**, **precipitating**, **precipitated**) 1 make something bad happen suddenly or sooner than it should. 2 make something move or happen suddenly and with force. 3 Chemistry cause a substance to be deposited in solid form from a solution. 4 cause moisture in the air to condense and fall as rain, snow, etc.

SYNONYMS 1 *the incident precipitated a crisis* **bring about**/**on**, cause, lead to, give rise to, instigate, trigger, spark off, touch off, provoke. 2 *they were precipitated down the mountain* **hurl**, catapult, throw, plunge, launch, fling, propel.

▸ adjective /pri-**sip**-i-tuht/ done or happening suddenly or without careful thought.

SYNONYMS *their actions were precipitate* **hasty**, overhasty, rash, hurried, rushed, impetuous, impulsive, precipitous, incautious, imprudent, injudicious, ill-advised, reckless.

▸ noun /pri-**sip**-i-tayt/ Chemistry a substance precipitated from a solution.

precipitation ▸ noun 1 rain, snow, sleet, or hail. 2 Chemistry the action of precipitating a substance from a solution.

precipitous ▸ adjective dangerously high or steep.

SYNONYMS 1 *a precipitous drop* **steep**, sheer, perpendicular, abrupt, sharp, vertical. 2 *his precipitous fall from power* **sudden**, rapid, swift, abrupt, headlong, speedy, quick, fast.

precis /**pray**-si/ (also **précis**) ▸ noun (plural **precis** /**pray**-si, **pray**-seez/) a short summary.

▸ verb (**precises** /**pray**-seez/, **precising** /**pray**-see-ing/, **precised** /**pray**-seed/) make a precis of.

precise ▸ adjective 1 presented in a detailed and accurate way. 2 taking care to be exact and accurate. 3 particular.

SYNONYMS 1 *precise measurements* **exact**, accurate, correct, specific, detailed, explicit, careful, meticulous, strict, rigorous. 2 *at that precise moment* **exact**,

p

particular, very, specific.
ANTONYMS inaccurate.

precisely ▸ adverb **1** exactly. **2** in exact terms; without vagueness. **3** used as a reply to confirm or agree with a previous statement.

SYNONYMS **1** *at 2 o'clock precisely* **exactly,** sharp, on the dot, promptly, on the stroke of ...; informal bang (on); Brit. informal spot on; N. Amer. informal on the button. **2** *precisely the man I am looking for* **exactly,** just, in all respects; informal to a T. **3** *fertilization can be timed precisely* **accurately,** exactly. **4** *'So you knew?' 'Precisely.'* **yes,** exactly, absolutely, (that's) right, quite so.

precision ▸ noun the quality of being exact, accurate, and careful.

SYNONYMS **exactness,** accuracy, exactitude, correctness, care, meticulousness, scrupulousness, punctiliousness, rigour.

preclude ▸ verb (**precludes, precluding, precluded**) prevent something from happening.

precocious ▸ adjective having developed certain abilities or tendencies at an earlier age than usual.
□ **precocity** noun.

precognition ▸ noun knowledge of an event before it happens.

preconceived ▸ adjective (of an idea or opinion) formed before full knowledge or evidence is available.

preconception ▸ noun a preconceived idea or opinion.

precondition ▸ noun something that must exist or happen before other things can happen or be done.

precursor ▸ noun a person or thing that comes before another of the same kind.

pre-date ▸ verb happen, exist, or be found earlier than.

predation /pri-**day**-sh'n/ ▸ noun the preying of one animal on others.

predator ▸ noun an animal that hunts and kills others for food.

predatory ▸ adjective **1** (of an animal) killing other animals for food. **2** taking advantage of weaker people.

predecease ▸ verb (**predeceases, predeceasing, predeceased**) formal die before another person.

predecessor ▸ noun **1** a person who held a job or office before the current holder. **2** a thing that has been followed or replaced by another.

SYNONYMS **1** *the Prime Minister's predecessor* **forerunner,** precursor, antecedent. **2** *our Victorian predecessors*

ancestor, forefather, forebear, antecedent.
ANTONYMS successor, descendant.

predestination ▸ noun the belief that everything that happens has been decided in advance by God or fate.

predestined ▸ adjective already decided by God or fate.

predetermine ▸ verb (**predetermines, predetermining, predetermined**) establish or decide in advance.

predicament ▸ noun a difficult situation.

SYNONYMS **difficulty,** mess, plight, quandary, muddle, dilemma; informal hole, fix, jam, pickle.

predicate ▸ noun /**pred**-i-kuht/ Grammar the part of a sentence or clause containing a verb and stating something about the subject (e.g. *went home* in *she went home*).
▸ verb /**pred**-i-kayt/ (**predicates, predicating, predicated**) (**predicate something on**) base something on.

predicative /pri-**dik**-uh-tiv/ ▸ adjective Grammar (of an adjective) coming after a verb, as *old* in *the dog is old*.

predict ▸ verb state that an event will happen in the future.

SYNONYMS **forecast,** foretell, prophesy.

□ **predictive** adjective **predictor** noun.

predictable ▸ adjective **1** able to be predicted. **2** always behaving or happening in the way that you would expect.

SYNONYMS **foreseeable,** to be expected, anticipated, likely, foreseen, unsurprising, reliable; informal inevitable.
ANTONYMS unpredictable.

□ **predictability** noun **predictably** adverb.

prediction ▸ noun **1** a statement saying that something will happen; a forecast. **2** the action of predicting.

SYNONYMS **forecast,** prophecy, prognosis, prognostication.

predilection /pree-di-**lek**-sh'n/ ▸ noun a preference or special liking for something.

predispose ▸ verb (**predisposes, predisposing, predisposed**) make someone likely to be, do, or think something.
□ **predisposition** noun.

predominant ▸ adjective **1** present as the main part of something. **2** having the greatest power.
□ **predominance** noun.

predominantly ▸ adverb mainly; for the most part.

SYNONYMS **mainly,** mostly, for the most part, chiefly, principally, primarily, in the main, on the whole, largely, by and large, typically, generally, usually.

p

predominate ▸ verb (predominates, predominating, predominated) **1** be the main part of something. **2** have control or power.

pre-eminent ▸ adjective better than all others.
□ **pre-eminence** noun.

pre-empt ▸ verb **1** take action so as to prevent something happening. **2** stop someone from saying something by speaking first.
□ **pre-emption** noun **pre-emptive** adjective.

preen ▸ verb **1** (of a bird) tidy and clean its feathers with its beak. **2** attend to and admire your appearance. **3** (**preen yourself**) feel very pleased with yourself.

pre-existing ▸ adjective existing from an earlier time.

prefab ▸ noun informal a prefabricated building.

prefabricated ▸ adjective (of a building) made in previously constructed sections that can be easily put together on site.

preface /pref-uhss/ ▸ noun an introduction to a book.
▸ verb (prefaces, prefacing, prefaced) (preface something with or by) say or do something to introduce a book, speech, or event.

prefect ▸ noun **1** Brit. a senior pupil in a school who has some authority over younger pupils. **2** a chief officer or regional governor in certain countries.

prefecture ▸ noun (in certain countries) a district administered by a prefect.

prefer ▸ verb (prefers, preferring, preferred) like one person or thing better than another.

SYNONYMS **like better,** would rather (have), would sooner (have), favour, be more partial to, choose, select, pick, opt for, go for, plump for.

✔ double the **r** when forming the past tense: preferred.

preferable ▸ adjective more desirable or suitable.

SYNONYMS **better,** best, more desirable, more suitable, advantageous, superior, preferred, recommended.

preferably ▸ adverb ideally; if possible.

SYNONYMS **ideally,** if possible, for preference, from choice.

preference ▸ noun **1** a greater liking for one person or thing than another. **2** a thing preferred. **3** favour shown to one person over another.

SYNONYMS **1** *her preference for gin* **liking,** partiality, fondness, taste, inclination, leaning, bent, penchant, predisposition. **2** *preference was given to female*

applicants **priority,** favour, precedence, preferential treatment.

preferential ▸ adjective favouring a particular person or group.
□ **preferentially** adverb.

preferment ▸ noun formal promotion to a job or position.

prefigure ▸ verb (prefigures, prefiguring, prefigured) be an early sign or version of.

prefix ▸ noun **1** a letter or group of letters placed at the beginning of a word to alter its meaning (e.g. *non-*). **2** a word, letter, or number placed before another.
▸ verb add a prefix to.

pregnancy ▸ noun (plural pregnancies) the state or period of being pregnant.

pregnant ▸ adjective **1** (of a woman) having a baby developing inside her womb. **2** full of meaning.

SYNONYMS **1** *she is pregnant* **expecting,** expectant, carrying a child; informal in the family way, preggers. **2** *a pregnant pause* **meaningful,** significant, suggestive, expressive, charged.

prehensile /pri-hen-syl/ ▸ adjective (of an animal's limb or tail) capable of grasping things.

prehistoric ▸ adjective relating to the period before written records of events were made.

prehistory ▸ noun **1** the period of time before written records were made. **2** the early stages in the development of something.

pre-industrial ▸ adjective before the development of industries.

prejudge ▸ verb (prejudges, prejudging, prejudged) make a judgement before you have all the necessary information.

prejudice ▸ noun **1** an opinion that is not based on reason or experience. **2** unfair reactions or behaviour based on such opinions.

SYNONYMS **1** *male prejudices about women* **preconceived idea,** preconception. **2** *they are motivated by prejudice* **bigotry,** bias, partiality, intolerance, discrimination, unfairness, inequality.

▸ verb (prejudices, prejudicing, prejudiced) **1** influence someone so that they form an opinion that is not based on reason or experience. **2** cause harm to.

SYNONYMS **1** *the article could prejudice the jury* **bias,** influence, sway, predispose, make partial, colour. **2** *this could prejudice his chances* **damage,** be detrimental to, be prejudicial to, injure, harm, hurt, spoil, impair, undermine, compromise.

prejudiced ▸ adjective having or showing

a dislike or distrust that is derived from prejudice.

SYNONYMS **biased,** bigoted, discriminatory, partisan, intolerant, narrow-minded, unfair, unjust, inequitable, coloured.
ANTONYMS impartial.

prejudicial ▸ adjective harmful to someone or something.

prelate /prel-uht/ ▸ noun a bishop or other high-ranking minister in the Christian Church.

preliminary ▸ adjective taking place before a main action or event.

SYNONYMS *at a preliminary stage* **preparatory,** introductory, initial, opening, early, exploratory.
ANTONYMS final.

▸ noun (plural **preliminaries**) a preliminary action or event.

SYNONYMS *he began without any preliminaries* **introduction,** preamble, preface, opening remarks, formalities.

prelude ▸ noun 1 an action or event acting as an introduction to something more important. 2 a piece of music introducing a longer piece.

SYNONYMS **preliminary,** overture, opening, preparation, introduction, lead-in, precursor.

premarital ▸ adjective happening before marriage.

premature ▸ adjective 1 happening or done before the proper time. 2 (of a baby) born before the normal length of pregnancy is completed.

SYNONYMS 1 *his premature death* **untimely,** too early, before time, unseasonable. 2 *such a step would be premature* **rash,** overhasty, hasty, precipitate, impulsive, impetuous; informal previous.
ANTONYMS overdue.

□ **prematurely** adverb.

premeditated ▸ adjective (of a crime or other bad action) planned in advance.
□ **premeditation** noun.

premenstrual ▸ adjective happening or experienced in the days of the month before menstruation.

premier ▸ adjective first in importance, order, or position.

SYNONYMS *Germany's premier rock band* **leading,** foremost, chief, principal, head, top-ranking, top, prime, primary, first, highest, pre-eminent, senior, outstanding; N. Amer. ranking.

▸ noun a Prime Minister or other head of government.

SYNONYMS *the British premier* **head of government,** prime minister, PM, president, chancellor.

□ **premiership** noun.

premiere /prem-i-air/ ▸ noun the first performance or showing of a play, film, ballet, etc.

SYNONYMS **first performance,** first night, opening night, debut.

premise (or Brit. **premiss**) /prem-iss/ ▸ noun a statement or idea that forms the basis for a theory or argument.

SYNONYMS **proposition,** assumption, hypothesis, thesis, presupposition, supposition, presumption, assertion.

premises ▸ plural noun the building and land occupied by a business.

SYNONYMS **building(s),** property, site, office, establishment.

premium ▸ noun (plural **premiums**) 1 an amount paid for an insurance policy. 2 an extra sum added to a basic price.

SYNONYMS 1 *monthly premiums of £30* **(regular) payment,** instalment. 2 *you must pay a premium for organic fruit* **surcharge,** additional payment, extra.

▸ adjective of high quality and more expensive.
■ **at a premium 1** scarce and in demand. **2** above the usual price.

premonition ▸ noun a strong feeling that something is going to happen.
□ **premonitory** adjective.

prenatal ▸ adjective N. Amer. before birth.

preoccupation ▸ noun 1 the state of being preoccupied. 2 a matter that preoccupies someone.

SYNONYMS **obsession,** fixation, concern, passion, enthusiasm, hobby horse; informal bee in your bonnet.

preoccupy ▸ verb (**preoccupies, preoccupying, preoccupied**) completely fill someone's mind.

SYNONYMS 1 (**preoccupied**) *he's preoccupied with work* **obsessed,** fixated, concerned, absorbed, engrossed, involved, wrapped up. 2 (**preoccupied**) *she looked preoccupied* **lost in thought,** deep in thought, oblivious, pensive, distracted.

preordained ▸ adjective decided or determined beforehand.

prep ▸ noun Brit. informal school work done outside lessons.
■ **prep school** a preparatory school.

prepaid ▸ adjective paid for in advance.

preparation ▸ noun 1 the process of getting ready for something. 2 something

p

that is done to get ready for something. **3** a substance prepared for use as a medicine, cosmetic, etc.

SYNONYMS **1** *the preparation of a plan* **devising**, putting together, drawing up, construction, composition, production, getting ready, development. **2** *preparations for the party* **arrangements**, planning, plans, groundwork, provisions. **3** *a preparation to kill mites* **mixture**, compound, concoction, solution, medicine, potion.

preparatory ▸ adjective done in order to prepare for something.
■ **preparatory school** Brit. a private school for pupils aged seven to thirteen.

prepare ▸ verb (prepares, preparing, prepared) **1** make something ready for use. **2** get ready to do or deal with something. **3** (**be prepared to do**) be willing to do.

SYNONYMS **1** *I will prepare a report* **make/get ready**, put together, draw up, produce, arrange, assemble, construct, compose, formulate. **2** *the meal is easy to prepare* **cook**, make, get, put together, concoct; informal fix, rustle up; Brit. informal knock up. **3** *preparing for war* **get ready**, make preparations, arrange things, make provision. **4** (**prepared**) *prepared for action* **ready**, (all) set, equipped, primed, waiting, poised. **5** *athletes preparing for the Olympics* **train**, get into shape, practise, get ready, warm up, limber up. **6** *prepare yourself for a shock* **brace**, ready, tense, steel, steady. **7** (**prepared**) *I'm prepared to negotiate* **willing**, ready, disposed, (favourably) inclined, of a mind, minded.

preparedness ▸ noun readiness.

preponderance ▸ noun a greater number or incidence of something.

preponderant ▸ adjective greater in number or happening more often.

preposition /prep-uh-**zi**-sh'n/ ▸ noun Grammar a word used with a noun or pronoun to show place, time, or method.
□ **prepositional** adjective.

prepossessing ▸ adjective attractive or appealing in appearance.

preposterous ▸ adjective completely ridiculous or outrageous.
□ **preposterously** adverb.

prepubescent ▸ adjective having to do with the period before puberty.

prerequisite /pree-**rek**-wi-zit/ ▸ noun a thing that must exist or happen before something else can exist or happen.

prerogative /pri-**rog**-uh-tiv/ ▸ noun a right or privilege belonging to a particular person or group.

presage /**press**-ij/ ▸ verb also /pri-**sayj**/

(presages, presaging, presaged) be a sign or warning of.
▸ noun an omen.

Presbyterian /prez-bi-**teer**-i-uhn/
▸ adjective relating to a Protestant Church governed by elders who are all of equal rank.
▸ noun a member of a Presbyterian Church.
□ **Presbyterianism** noun.

presbytery /**prez**-bi-tuh-ri/ ▸ noun (plural **presbyteries**) **1** an administrative body in a Presbyterian Church. **2** the house of a Roman Catholic parish priest. **3** the eastern part of a church near the altar.

prescient /**press**-i-uhnt/ ▸ adjective knowing about things before they happen.
□ **prescience** noun.

prescribe ▸ verb (prescribes, prescribing, prescribed) **1** (of a doctor) state officially that someone should take a particular medicine or have a particular treatment. **2** state officially that something should be done.

SYNONYMS **1** *a doctor may prescribe antibiotics* **advise**, recommend, advocate, suggest. **2** *rules prescribing your duty* **stipulate**, lay down, dictate, order, direct, specify, determine.

prescription ▸ noun **1** a piece of paper on which a doctor states that a patient may be supplied with a medicine or treatment. **2** the action of prescribing a medicine or treatment.

prescriptive ▸ adjective stating what should be done.

presence ▸ noun **1** the state of being in a particular place. **2** a person's impressive manner or appearance. **3** a person or thing that seems to be present but is not seen.

SYNONYMS **1** *the presence of an intruder* **existence**. **2** *I requested the presence of a lawyer* **attendance**, appearance. **3** *a woman of great presence* **aura**, charisma, personality.
ANTONYMS absence.

■ **presence of mind** the ability to remain calm and act sensibly in a difficult situation.

present¹ /**pre**-z'nt/ ▸ adjective **1** being or existing in a particular place. **2** existing or happening now. **3** Grammar (of a tense of a verb) expressing an action or state happening or existing now.

SYNONYMS **1** *a doctor must be present* **in attendance**, here, there, near, nearby, at hand, available. **2** *organic compounds are present* **in existence**, detectable, occurring, here, there. **3** *the present economic climate* **current**, present-day, existing, extant.
ANTONYMS absent.

p

▸ **noun** the period of time happening now.

SYNONYMS *think about the present* **now,** today, the present time, the here and now, modern times.
ANTONYMS past, future.

■ **present participle** Grammar the form of a verb, ending in *-ing*, which is used in forming tenses describing continuous action (e.g. *I'm thinking*), as a noun (e.g. *good thinking*), and as an adjective (e.g. *running water*).

present² ▸ verb /pri-**zent**/ **1** formally give someone something. **2** offer something for consideration or payment. **3** formally introduce someone to someone else. **4** produce a show, broadcast, etc. for the public. **5** introduce and take part in a television or radio show. **6** be the cause of a problem. **7** give a particular impression to other people: *we must present a united front.* **8** (**present yourself**) appear at or attend a formal or official occasion.

SYNONYMS **1** *Eddy presented a cheque to the winner* **hand over,** give (out), confer, bestow, award, grant, accord. **2** *the committee presented its report* **submit,** set forth, put forward, offer, tender, table. **3** *may I present my wife?* **introduce,** make known, acquaint someone with. **4** *she presents a TV show* **host,** introduce, compère; N. Amer. informal emcee. **5** *they present him as a criminal* **represent,** describe, portray, depict.

▸ **noun** /**pre**-z'nt/ a thing given to someone as a gift.

SYNONYMS *a birthday present* **gift,** donation, offering, contribution, gratuity, tip, hand-out; informal prezzie.

□ **presenter** noun.

presentable ▸ adjective looking smart enough to be seen in public.

presentation ▸ noun the action of presenting something, or the way in which it is presented.

SYNONYMS **1** *the presentation of his certificate* **awarding,** presenting, giving, handing over, bestowal, granting. **2** *the presentation of food* **appearance,** arrangement, packaging, layout. **3** *a sales presentation* **demonstration,** talk, lecture, address, speech, show, exhibition, display, introduction, launch, launching, unveiling.

□ **presentational** adjective.

presentiment /pri-**zen**-ti-muhnt/ ▸ noun a feeling that something unpleasant is going to happen.

presently ▸ adverb **1** soon. **2** now.

SYNONYMS **1** *I shall see you presently* **soon,** shortly, quite soon, in a short time, in a little while, at any moment/

minute/second, before long; N. Amer. momentarily; Brit. informal in a mo. **2** *he is presently abroad* **at present,** currently, at the/this moment.

preservation ▸ noun the action of preserving something.

SYNONYMS **1** *wood preservation* **conservation,** protection, care. **2** *the preservation of the status quo* **continuation,** conservation, maintenance, upholding, sustaining, perpetuation.

preservative ▸ noun a substance used to prevent food or wood from decaying.

preserve ▸ verb (preserves, preserving, preserved) **1** keep something in its original state or in good condition. **2** keep someone safe from harm. **3** treat food to prevent it from decaying.

SYNONYMS **1** *oil preserves the wood* **conserve,** protect, maintain, care for, look after. **2** *the wish to preserve the status quo* **continue (with),** conserve, keep going, maintain, uphold, sustain, perpetuate, prolong. **3** *preserving him from harm* **guard,** protect, keep, defend, safeguard, shelter, shield.
ANTONYMS attack, abandon.

▸ **noun 1** a food preserved in sugar, salt, vinegar, or alcohol, such as jam or pickle. **2** something reserved for a particular person or group. **3** a place where game is protected and kept for private hunting.

SYNONYMS **1** *the preserve of the rich* **domain,** area, field, sphere, orbit, realm, province, territory; informal turf, bailiwick. **2** *a game preserve* **sanctuary,** (game) reserve, reservation.

□ **preserver** noun.

preset ▸ verb (presets, presetting, preset) set the controls of an electrical device before it is used.

preside ▸ verb (presides, presiding, presided) lead or be in charge of a meeting or event.

SYNONYMS *the President continued to preside over cabinet meetings* **be in charge of,** be responsible for, head, manage, administer, control, direct, chair, conduct, officiate at, lead, govern, rule, command, supervise, oversee; informal **head up**.

presidency ▸ noun (plural **presidencies**) the job of president, or the period of time it is held.

president ▸ noun **1** the elected head of a republic. **2** the head of an organization.
□ **presidential** adjective.

presidium /pri-**si**-di-uhm/ ▸ noun a permanent decision-making committee

p

within a political organization, especially a communist one.

press¹ ▸ verb **1** (**press against** or **to**) move into contact with something by using steady force. **2** push something that operates a device. **3** apply pressure to something to flatten or shape it. **4** move by pushing. **5** (**press on** or **ahead**) continue in what you are doing. **6** express or repeat an opinion or claim in a forceful way. **7** make strong efforts to persuade someone to do something. **8** (**be pressed for**) have too little of. **9** (**be pressed to do**) have difficulty doing.

SYNONYMS **1** *press the paper down firmly* **push (down)**, press down, depress, hold down, force, thrust, squeeze, compress. **2** *his shirt was pressed* **iron**. **3** *she pressed the child to her bosom* **clasp**, hold close, hug, cuddle, squeeze, clutch, grasp, embrace. **4** *the crowd pressed round* **cluster**, gather, converge, congregate, flock, swarm, crowd. **5** *the government pressed its claim* **plead**, urge, advance, present, submit, put forward. **6** *they pressed him to agree* **urge**, put pressure on, pressurize, force, push, coerce, dragoon, steamroller, browbeat; informal lean on, put the screws on, twist someone's arm, railroad, bulldoze. **7** *they pressed for a ban* **call**, ask, clamour, push, campaign, demand.

▸ noun **1** a device for crushing, flattening, or shaping something. **2** a printing press. **3** (**the press**) newspapers or journalists as a whole.

SYNONYMS **1** *the freedom of the press* **the media**, the newspapers, journalism, reporters; Brit. dated Fleet Street. **2** *the company had some bad press* (**press**) **reports**, press coverage, press articles, press reviews.

■ **press conference** a meeting with journalists in order to make an announcement or answer questions. **press release** a statement or piece of publicity issued to journalists. **press stud** Brit. a small fastener with two parts that fit together when pressed. **press-up** Brit. an exercise in which you lie face down on the floor and push your body up by pressing down with your hands and arms.

press² ▸ verb (in the past) force someone to serve in the army or navy.

■ **press gang** (in the past) a group of men employed to force men to serve in the army or navy. **press-gang** force someone into doing something. **press someone/thing into service** use someone or something for a particular purpose as a temporary or emergency measure.

pressing ▸ adjective **1** needing urgent action. **2** strongly expressed and difficult to refuse or ignore.

SYNONYMS **1** *a pressing problem* **urgent**, critical, crucial, acute, desperate, serious, grave, life-and-death. **2** *a pressing engagement* **important**, high-priority, critical, crucial, unavoidable.

▸ noun an object made by pressing.

pressure ▸ noun **1** steady force applied to an object by something that is in contact with it. **2** the use of persuasion or threats to make someone do something. **3** a feeling of stress caused by the need to do something. **4** the force per unit area applied by a fluid against a surface.

SYNONYMS **1** *atmospheric pressure* **force**, load, stress, thrust, compression, weight. **2** *there was pressure to conform* **persuasion**, intimidation, coercion, compulsion, duress, harassment, nagging, badgering. **3** *she had a lot of pressure at work* **strain**, stress, tension, trouble, difficulty, burden; informal hassle.

▸ verb (**pressures**, **pressuring**, **pressured**) persuade or force someone into doing something.

SYNONYMS *they pressured him into resigning* **coerce**, push, persuade, force, bulldoze, hound, nag, badger, browbeat, bully, intimidate, dragoon, twist someone's arm; informal railroad, lean on; N. Amer. informal hustle.

■ **pressure cooker** a large airtight saucepan in which food is cooked quickly in steam held under pressure. **pressure group** a group that tries to influence the government or public opinion in order to help a cause.

pressurize (or **pressurise**) ▸ verb (**pressurizes**, **pressurizing**, **pressurized**) **1** persuade or force someone into doing something. **2** keep the air pressure in an aircraft cabin the same as it is at ground level.

SYNONYMS *he pressurized us into selling* **coerce**, pressure, push, persuade, force, bulldoze, hound, nag, badger, browbeat, bully, bludgeon, intimidate, dragoon, twist someone's arm; informal railroad, lean on; N. Amer. informal hustle.

prestige ▸ noun respect and admiration resulting from achievements or high quality.

SYNONYMS **status**, standing, kudos, cachet, stature, reputation, repute, renown, honour, esteem, importance, prominence.

prestigious /press-ti-juhss/ ▸ adjective having or bringing prestige.

SYNONYMS **reputable**, distinguished, respected, high-status, esteemed,

eminent, highly regarded, renowned, influential.
ANTONYMS disreputable, obscure.

presto ▸ adverb & adjective Music in a quick tempo.

prestressed ▸ adjective (of concrete) strengthened by means of rods inserted under tension before setting.

presumably ▸ adverb as may be supposed.

SYNONYMS I **presume**, I expect, I assume, I take it, I imagine, I dare say, doubtless, no doubt, apparently, probably.

presume ▸ verb (presumes, presuming, presumed) **1** suppose that something is probably true. **2** show a lack of respect by doing something that you do not have authority or permission to do. **3** (**presume on**) take advantage of someone's kindness, friendship, etc.

SYNONYMS **1** *I presume it was once an attic* **assume**, suppose, surmise, imagine, take it, expect. **2** *I wouldn't presume to advise you* **dare**, venture, have the effrontery, be so bold as, go so far as, take the liberty of.

presumption ▸ noun **1** something that is thought to be true or probable. **2** an act of presuming. **3** behaviour that is too confident.

presumptuous ▸ adjective behaving too confidently.
☐ **presumptuously** adverb.

✔ **-uous**, not **-ious**: presumpt**uous**.

presuppose ▸ verb (presupposes, presupposing, presupposed) **1** need something to have happened in order to exist or be true. **2** assume, without knowing for sure, that something exists or is true and act on that basis.
☐ **presupposition** noun.

pretence (US spelling **pretense**) ▸ noun **1** an act of pretending. **2** a claim to have or be something.

SYNONYMS **1** *cease this pretence* **make-believe**, acting, faking, play-acting, posturing, deception, trickery. **2** *he made a pretence of being concerned* (**false**) **show**, semblance, affectation, (false) appearance, outward appearance, impression, guise, facade.
ANTONYMS honesty.

pretend ▸ verb **1** make it seem that something is the case when in fact it is not. **2** give the appearance of feeling or having an emotion or quality. **3** (**pretend to**) claim to have a skill, quality, or title.

SYNONYMS **1** *they pretend to listen* **make as if**, act like, affect, go through the motions, fake it. **2** *I'll pretend to be*

the dragon **make believe**, play at, act, impersonate.

▸ adjective informal artificial; imaginary.

SYNONYMS **mock**, fake, sham, simulated, artificial, false, pseudo; informal **phoney**.

pretender ▸ noun a person who claims a right to a title or position.

pretension ▸ noun **1** the act of trying to appear more important or better than you actually are. **2** (also **pretensions**) a claim to have or be something.

pretentious ▸ adjective trying to appear more important or better than you actually are so as to impress other people.
☐ **pretentiousness** noun.

preternatural ▸ adjective beyond what is normal or natural.
☐ **preternaturally** adverb.

pretext ▸ noun a false reason used to justify an action.

prettify ▸ verb (prettifies, prettifying, prettified) try to make something look pretty.

pretty ▸ adjective (prettier, prettiest) **1** (of a woman or girl) having an attractive face. **2** pleasant to look at.

SYNONYMS *a pretty girl* **attractive**, good-looking, nice-looking, personable, fetching, prepossessing, appealing, charming, delightful, cute; Scottish & N. English **bonny**.
ANTONYMS plain, ugly.

▸ adverb informal to a certain extent; fairly.

SYNONYMS *it's pretty cold* **quite**, rather, somewhat, fairly.

☐ **prettily** adverb **prettiness** noun.

pretzel ▸ noun a crisp salty biscuit in the shape of a knot or stick.

prevail ▸ verb **1** be widespread or current. **2** (**prevail against** or **over**) be more powerful than. **3** (**prevail on**) persuade someone to do something.

SYNONYMS **1** *common sense will prevail* **win** (**out/through**), triumph, be victorious, carry the day, come out on top, succeed, rule, reign. **2** *the conditions that prevailed in the 1950s* **exist**, be present, be the case, occur, be prevalent, be in force. **3** (**prevailing**) **current**, existing, prevalent, usual, common, general, widespread.

prevalent ▸ adjective widespread; common.

SYNONYMS **widespread**, frequent, usual, common, current, popular, general.
ANTONYMS rare.

☐ **prevalence** noun.

prevaricate ▸ verb (prevaricates, prevaricating, prevaricated) avoid giving a direct answer to a question.

p

❑ **prevarication** noun.

prevent ▶ verb **1** keep something from happening. **2** stop someone from doing something.

> SYNONYMS **stop,** avert, nip in the bud, foil, inhibit, thwart, prohibit, forbid. ANTONYMS allow.

❑ **preventable** adjective **prevention** noun.

preventive (or **preventative**) ▶ adjective designed to prevent something from happening.

preview ▶ noun **1** a viewing or showing of something before it becomes generally available. **2** a review of a forthcoming film, book, or performance.

previous ▶ adjective **1** coming before something else in time or order. **2** (**previous to**) before.

> SYNONYMS **1** *the previous five years* **preceding,** foregoing, prior, past, last. **2** *her previous boyfriend* **former,** preceding, old, earlier, ex-, past, last, sometime, one-time, erstwhile. **3** *I was a bit previous* **overhasty,** hasty, premature; informal ahead of yourself. ANTONYMS next.

previously ▶ adverb at a previous or earlier time.

> SYNONYMS **formerly,** earlier (on), before, hitherto, at one time, in the past.

prey ▶ noun **1** an animal that is hunted and killed by another for food. **2** a person who is harmed or deceived by someone or something.

> SYNONYMS **1** *the lions' prey* **quarry,** kill. **2** *con men choose their prey carefully* **victim,** target, dupe; informal sucker; Brit. informal mug. ANTONYMS predator.

▶ verb (**prey on**) **1** hunt and kill another animal for food. **2** take advantage of or cause distress to someone.

price ▶ noun **1** the amount of money for which something is bought or sold. **2** something unwelcome that must be done in order to achieve something. **3** the odds in betting.

> SYNONYMS **1** *the purchase price* **cost,** charge, fee, fare, amount, sum; informal damage. **2** *the price of success* **consequence,** result, cost, penalty, toll, sacrifice, downside, drawback, disadvantage, minus.

▶ verb (**prices, pricing, priced**) decide the price of.

priceless ▶ adjective **1** very valuable. **2** informal very amusing.

> SYNONYMS **invaluable,** beyond price, irreplaceable, expensive, costly. ANTONYMS worthless, cheap.

pricey ▶ adjective (**pricier, priciest**) informal expensive.

prick ▶ verb **1** make a small hole in something with a sharp point. **2** cause someone to feel a small, sharp pain.

> SYNONYMS *prick the potatoes* **pierce,** puncture, stab, perforate, spike, penetrate, jab.

▶ noun a mark, hole, or pain caused by pricking.

> SYNONYMS *a prick in the leg* **jab,** sting, pinprick, stab, pinhole, wound.

■ **prick up your ears 1** (of a horse or dog) raise the ears when alert. **2** suddenly begin to pay attention.

prickle ▶ noun **1** a small thorn on a plant or a pointed spine on an animal. **2** a tingling feeling on the skin.
▶ verb (**prickles, prickling, prickled**) have a tingling feeling on the skin.

prickly ▶ adjective **1** having prickles. **2** causing a prickling feeling. **3** easily offended or annoyed.

> SYNONYMS **spiky,** spiked, thorny, barbed, spiny, bristly.

■ **prickly pear** a cactus which produces prickly, pear-shaped fruits.

pride ▶ noun **1** deep pleasure or satisfaction felt if you or people close to you have done something well. **2** a source of pride: *the team is the pride of the town.* **3** self-respect. **4** the feeling that you are better than other people. **5** a group of lions.

> SYNONYMS **1** *a source of pride* **self-esteem,** dignity, honour, self-respect. **2** *pride in a job well done* **pleasure,** joy, delight, gratification, fulfilment, satisfaction, sense of achievement. **3** *he refused out of pride* **arrogance,** vanity, self-importance, hubris, conceitedness, egotism, snobbery. ANTONYMS shame, humility.

▶ verb (**prides, priding, prided**) (**pride yourself on**) be especially proud of a quality or skill.
■ **pride of place** the most noticeable or important position.

priest ▶ noun **1** a person who is qualified to perform religious ceremonies in the Christian Church. **2** (also **priestess**) a person who performs ceremonies in a non-Christian religion.

> SYNONYMS **clergyman,** clergywoman, minister, cleric, pastor, vicar, rector, parson, churchman, churchwoman, father, curate; Scottish kirkman; N. Amer. dominie; informal reverend, padre.

❑ **priesthood** noun **priestly** adjective.

prig ▶ noun a person who behaves as if they are morally superior to other people.
❑ **priggish** adjective.

p

prim ▸ adjective very formal and correct and disapproving of anything rude.
□ **primly** adverb.

prima ballerina /pree-muh bal-luh-**ree**-nuh/ ▸ noun the chief female dancer in a ballet company.

primacy ▸ noun the fact of being most important.

prima donna /pree-muh **don**-uh/ ▸ noun **1** the chief female singer in an opera. **2** a very temperamental and self-important person.

primaeval ➡ PRIMEVAL.

prima facie /pry-muh **fay**-shi-ee/ ▸ adjective & adverb Law accepted as correct until proved otherwise.

primal ▸ adjective having to do with early human life; primeval.

primarily ▸ adverb for the most part; mainly.

SYNONYMS **1** *he was primarily a singer* **first and foremost,** firstly, essentially, in essence, fundamentally, principally, predominantly. **2** *work is done primarily for large institutions* **mostly,** for the most part, chiefly, mainly, in the main, on the whole, largely, principally, predominantly.

primary ▸ adjective **1** of chief importance. **2** earliest in time or order. **3** (of education) for children between the ages of about five and eleven.

SYNONYMS **main,** chief, key, prime, central, principal, foremost, first, most important, predominant, paramount; informal **number-one.**
ANTONYMS secondary.

▸ noun (plural **primaries**) (in the US) a preliminary election to appoint delegates to a party conference or to choose candidates for an election.
■ **primary colour** each of the colours blue, red, and yellow, from which all other colours can be obtained by mixing.

primate ▸ noun **1** an animal belonging to the group that includes monkeys, apes, and humans. **2** (in the Christian Church) an archbishop.

prime¹ ▸ adjective **1** of chief importance. **2** of the highest quality; excellent. **3** (of a number) that can be divided only by itself and one (e.g. 2, 3, 5).

SYNONYMS **1** *his prime reason for leaving* **main,** chief, key, primary, central, principal, foremost, first, most important, paramount, major; informal **number-one.** **2** *prime agricultural land* **top-quality,** top, best, first-class, superior, choice, select, finest; informal tip-top, A1.
ANTONYMS secondary, inferior.

▸ noun the time in a person's life when they are the strongest and most successful.

SYNONYMS *he is in his prime* **heyday,** peak, pinnacle, high point/spot, zenith, flower, bloom, flush.

■ **prime minister** the head of a government. **prime time** the time at which a radio or television audience is greatest.

prime² ▸ verb (primes, priming, primed) **1** prepare someone for a situation by giving them information. **2** make something ready for use or action. **3** cover a surface with primer.

SYNONYMS *Lucy had primed him carefully* **brief,** fill in, prepare, advise, instruct, coach, drill, train.

primer ▸ noun **1** a substance painted on a surface as a base coat. **2** a book for teaching children to read or giving a basic introduction to a subject.

primeval (or **primaeval**) /pry-**mee**-v'l/ ▸ adjective relating to the earliest times in history.

primitive ▸ adjective **1** relating to the earliest times in history or stages in development. **2** offering a very basic level of comfort. **3** (of behaviour or emotion) not based on reason; instinctive.

SYNONYMS **1** *primitive times* **ancient,** earliest, first, prehistoric, primordial, primeval. **2** *primitive tools* **crude,** simple, rough (and ready), basic, rudimentary, makeshift.
ANTONYMS modern, sophisticated.

□ **primitively** adverb.

primogeniture ▸ noun **1** the state of being the first child born in a family. **2** the system by which the eldest son inherits all his parents' property.

primordial /pry-**mor**-di-uhl/ ▸ adjective existing at the beginning of time.

primp ▸ verb make small adjustments to your appearance.

primrose ▸ noun a plant of woods and hedges with pale yellow flowers.

primula ▸ noun a plant of a group that includes primroses and cowslips.

prince ▸ noun a son or other close male relative of a king or queen.

SYNONYMS **ruler,** sovereign, monarch, crowned head.

■ **prince consort** the husband of a reigning queen who is himself a prince. **Prince of Wales** the title given to the eldest son of a British king or queen.

princeling ▸ noun **1** the ruler of a small country. **2** a young prince.

princely ▸ adjective **1** relating to or suitable for a prince. **2** (of a sum of money) generous.

p

princess ▸ noun **1** a daughter or other close female relative of a king or queen. **2** the wife or widow of a prince.
■ **Princess Royal** a title given to the eldest daughter of a British king or queen.

principal ▸ adjective most important; main.

> SYNONYMS **main,** chief, primary, leading, foremost, first, most important, predominant, dominant, pre-eminent, highest, top; informal number-one.
> ANTONYMS minor.

▸ noun **1** the most important person in an organization or group. **2** the head of a school or college. **3** a sum of money lent or invested, on which interest is paid.

> SYNONYMS **head teacher,** headmaster, headmistress, head, dean, rector, master, mistress, chancellor, vice-chancellor, president, provost, warden; N. Amer. informal prexy.

■ **principal boy** Brit. a woman who takes the leading male role in a pantomime.

❗ Don't confuse the words **principal** and **principle**. Principal is usually an adjective meaning 'main or most important', whereas **principle** is a noun meaning 'a law, rule, or theory on which something is based'.

principality ▸ noun (plural **principalities**) **1** a state ruled by a prince. **2** (**the Principality**) Brit. Wales.

principally ▸ adverb mainly.

> SYNONYMS **mainly,** mostly, chiefly, for the most part, in the main, on the whole, largely, predominantly, primarily.

principle ▸ noun **1** a law, rule, or theory on which something is based. **2** (**principles**) rules or beliefs that govern the way you behave. **3** a scientific theorem or natural law that explains why something happens or how it works.

> SYNONYMS **1** *a basic principle of science* **truth,** concept, idea, theory, fundamental, essential, precept, rule, law. **2** *the principle of laissez-faire* **doctrine,** belief, creed, credo, code, ethic. **3** *a woman of principle* **morals,** morality, ethics, ideals, standards, integrity, virtue, probity, honour, decency, conscience, scruples.

■ **in principle** in theory. **on principle** because of your moral principles.

principled ▸ adjective acting according to strong moral principles.

print ▸ verb **1** produce a book, newspaper, etc. by a process involving the transfer of words or pictures to paper. **2** produce a photographic print from a negative. **3** write words clearly without joining the letters. **4** mark fabric with a coloured design.

> SYNONYMS **1** *when was the book printed?* **publish,** issue, release, circulate, run off, copy, reproduce. **2** *patterns were printed on the cloth* **imprint,** impress, stamp, mark.

▸ noun **1** printed words in a book, newspaper, etc. **2** a mark where something has pressed or touched a surface. **3** a printed picture or design.

> SYNONYMS **1** *large print* **type,** printing, letters, lettering, characters, typeface, font. **2** *a print of his left hand* **impression,** handprint, fingerprint, footprint. **3** *sporting prints* **picture,** engraving, etching, lithograph, woodcut. **4** *prints and negatives* **photograph,** photo, snap, snapshot, picture, still, enlargement, copy, reproduction.

■ **in** (or **out of**) **print** (of a book) available (or no longer available) from the publisher. □ **printer** noun.

printing ▸ noun **1** the transfer of words or pictures to paper in the production of books, newspapers, etc. **2** handwriting in which the letters are written separately.
■ **printing press** a machine for printing books, newspapers, etc. by pressing an ink-covered surface on to paper.

printout ▸ noun a page of printed material from a computer's printer.

prion /pree-on/ ▸ noun a protein particle believed to be the cause of brain diseases such as BSE and CJD.

prior¹ ▸ adjective **1** coming before in time, order, or importance. **2** (**prior to**) before.

> SYNONYMS **earlier,** previous, preceding, advance, pre-existing.
> ANTONYMS subsequent.

prior² ▸ noun (feminine **prioress**) **1** (in an abbey) the person next in rank below an abbot or abbess. **2** the head of a house of friars or nuns.

prioritize (or **prioritise**) ▸ verb (**prioritizes, prioritizing, prioritized**) **1** decide the order of importance of a number of tasks. **2** treat something as being more important than other things.

priority ▸ noun (plural **priorities**) **1** the condition of being more important than other things. **2** a thing seen as more important than others. **3** Brit. the right to go before other traffic.

> SYNONYMS **1** *safety is our priority* **prime concern,** main consideration. **2** *giving priority to education* **precedence,** preference, pre-eminence, predominance, primacy. **3** *oncoming traffic has priority* **right of way,** precedence, supremacy, seniority.

priory ▸ noun (plural **priories**) a monastery or nunnery governed by a prior or prioress.

prise (US spelling **prize**) ▸ verb (**prises, prising, prised**) force something open or apart.

prism ▸ noun **1** a piece of glass or other transparent material with facets, used to separate white light into a spectrum of colours. **2** a solid geometric figure whose two ends are parallel and of the same size and shape, and whose sides are parallelograms.
□ **prismatic** adjective.

prison ▸ noun a building where criminals are kept as a punishment.

> SYNONYMS **jail**, penal institution; N. Amer. jailhouse, penitentiary, correctional facility; informal clink, slammer; Brit. informal nick; N. Amer. informal can, pen.

prisoner ▸ noun **1** a person who has been found guilty of a crime and sent to prison. **2** a person who has been captured by someone and kept confined.

> SYNONYMS **1** *a prisoner serving a life sentence* **convict**, detainee, inmate; informal jailbird, con; Brit. informal lag; N. Amer. informal yardbird. **2** *the army took many prisoners* **prisoner of war**, POW, internee, captive, hostage.

■ **prisoner of war** a person captured and imprisoned by the enemy in war.

prissy ▸ adjective too concerned with behaving in a correct and respectable way.

pristine ▸ adjective **1** in its original condition. **2** clean and fresh as if new.

> SYNONYMS **immaculate**, perfect, in mint condition, as new, spotless, unspoilt.
> ANTONYMS dirty, spoilt.

privacy ▸ noun a state in which you are not watched or disturbed by other people.

> SYNONYMS **seclusion**, solitude, isolation.

private ▸ adjective **1** intended for or involving a particular person or group. **2** (of thoughts, feelings, etc.) that you do not tell other people about. **3** not sharing thoughts and feelings with other people. **4** where you will not be disturbed; secluded. **5** (of a service or industry) provided by an individual or commercial company rather than the state. **6** not connected with a person's work or official role.

> SYNONYMS **1** *his private plane* **personal**, own, special, exclusive. **2** *private talks* **confidential**, secret, classified. **3** *private thoughts* **intimate**, personal, secret, innermost, undisclosed, unspoken, unvoiced. **4** *a very private man* **reserved**, introverted, self-contained, reticent, retiring, unsociable, withdrawn, solitary, reclusive. **5** *somewhere private to talk* **secluded**, undisturbed, remote,

isolated. **6** *private industry* **independent**, non-state, privatized, commercial, private-enterprise. **7** *in a private capacity* **unofficial**, personal.
> ANTONYMS public, open, extrovert, busy, crowded, nationalized, official, state.

▸ noun (also **private soldier**) a soldier of the lowest rank in the army.

> SYNONYMS *a private in the army* **private soldier**, trooper; Brit. sapper, gunner; US GI; Brit. informal Tommy, squaddie.

■ **private company** Brit. a company whose shares may not be offered to the public for sale. **private detective** a detective who is not a police officer and who carries out investigations for clients. **private enterprise** business or industry managed by independent companies rather than the state. **private eye** informal a private detective. **private member** a member of parliament who does not hold a government office. **private parts** a person's genitals. **private practice** the work of a doctor, lawyer, etc. who is self-employed. **private school** Brit. an independent school financed mainly by the fees paid by pupils. **private secretary 1** a secretary who deals with the personal matters of their employer. **2** a civil servant acting as an assistant to a senior government official. **private sector** the part of the national economy not under direct state control.
□ **privately** adverb.

privateer ▸ noun (in the past) an armed but privately owned ship, authorized by a government for use in war.

privation ▸ noun a state in which you do not have the basic things you need, such as food and warmth.

privatize (or **privatise**) ▸ verb (**privatizes, privatizing, privatized**) transfer a business or industry from ownership by the state to private ownership.
□ **privatization** noun.

privet ▸ noun a shrub with small white flowers.

privilege ▸ noun **1** a special right or advantage for a particular person or group. **2** an opportunity to do something regarded as a special honour. **3** the advantages available to people who are rich and powerful.

> SYNONYMS **1** *senior pupils have certain privileges* **advantage**, benefit, prerogative, entitlement, right, concession, freedom, liberty. **2** *it was a privilege to meet her* **honour**, pleasure.

> ✔ **-il-**, not **-el-**, and no **d**: privi**leg**e.

privileged ▸ adjective **1** having a privilege or privileges. **2** (of information) protected from being made public.

SYNONYMS **1** *a privileged background* **wealthy,** rich, affluent, prosperous. **2** *I feel very privileged* **honoured,** advantaged, favoured, valued, appreciated. **3** *privileged information* **confidential,** private, secret, restricted, classified, not for publication, off the record, inside; informal hush-hush. ANTONYMS underprivileged, disadvantaged, snubbed, public.

privy ▸ adjective (**privy to**) sharing in the knowledge of something secret.
▸ noun (plural **privies**) a toilet in a small shed outside a house.
■ **Privy Council** a group of politicians appointed to advise a king or queen.

prize¹ ▸ noun **1** a thing given to someone who wins a competition or race or to mark an outstanding achievement. **2** something that is worth struggling to achieve.

SYNONYMS *an art prize* **award,** reward, trophy, medal, cup, winnings, purse, honour.

▸ adjective **1** having been awarded a prize. **2** outstanding or complete.

SYNONYMS **1** *a prize bull* **champion,** award-winning, top, best. **2** *a prize idiot* **utter,** complete, total, absolute, real, perfect; Brit. informal right.
ANTONYMS second-rate.

▸ verb (**prizes, prizing, prized**) value highly.
prize² US spelling of PRISE.
pro¹ informal ▸ noun (plural **pros**) a professional, especially in sport.
▸ adjective professional.
pro² ▸ noun (plural **pros**) (usu. in **pros and cons**) an advantage of or argument in favour of something.

proactive ▸ adjective creating or controlling a situation rather than just responding to it.
□ **proactively** adverb.

probability ▸ noun (plural **probabilities**) **1** the extent to which something is probable. **2** an event that is likely to happen.

SYNONYMS **1** *the probability of winning* **likelihood,** prospect, expectation, chance(s), odds. **2** *relegation is a distinct probability* **prospect,** possibility.

probable ▸ adjective likely to happen or be the case.

SYNONYMS **likely,** odds-on, expected, anticipated, predictable; informal on the cards, a safe bet.
ANTONYMS improbable, unlikely.

probably ▸ adverb almost certainly.

SYNONYMS **in all likelihood,** in all probability, as likely as not, ten to one, the chances are, doubtless.

probate ▸ noun the official process of proving that a will is valid.

probation ▸ noun **1** a system in which a person who has committed a crime does not have to go to prison if they behave well and report regularly to an official. **2** a period of training and testing when you start a new job.

SYNONYMS **trial,** trial period, test period, apprenticeship, training.

□ **probationary** adjective **probationer** noun.

probe ▸ noun **1** an investigation. **2** a surgical instrument used to examine the body. **3** a small device for measuring or testing something. **4** (also **space probe**) an unmanned spacecraft used for exploration.

SYNONYMS *a probe into city hall corruption* **investigation,** enquiry, examination, inquest, study.

▸ verb (**probes, probing, probed**) **1** physically explore or examine something. **2** investigate something closely.

SYNONYMS **1** *their long beaks are suited to probing the ground* **prod,** poke, dig into, delve into, explore, feel around in, examine. **2** *an enquiry probed the cause of the disaster* **investigate,** enquire into, look into, go into, study, examine, explore.

□ **probing** adjective.

probiotic ▸ noun a substance which stimulates the growth of beneficial microorganisms in the body.

probity ▸ noun formal the quality of being honest and having high moral standards.

problem ▸ noun a thing that is difficult to deal with or understand.

SYNONYMS **1** *there's a problem* **difficulty,** worry, complication, snag, hitch, drawback, stumbling block, obstacle, hiccup, setback, catch; informal dilemma, headache. **2** *I don't want to be a problem* **nuisance,** bother; informal drag, pain. **3** *arithmetical problems* **puzzle,** question, poser, riddle, conundrum; informal brain-teaser.

problematic (or **problematical**) ▸ adjective difficult to deal with or understand.

SYNONYMS **difficult,** troublesome, tricky, awkward, controversial, ticklish, complicated, complex, knotty.
ANTONYMS easy, straightforward.

proboscis /pruh-**boss**-iss/ ▸ noun (plural **probosces** /pruh-**boss**-eez/ or **proboscises**) **1** a mammal's long, flexible snout, e.g. an elephant's trunk. **2** the long, thin mouth of some insects.

procedure ▸ noun **1** an established or official way of doing something. **2** a series of actions done in a certain way.

SYNONYMS **course of action,** method, system, strategy, way, approach, formula, mechanism, technique, routine, drill, practice.

□ **procedural** adjective.

proceed ▸ verb **1** begin a course of action. **2** go on to do something. **3** carry on or continue.

SYNONYMS **1** *she was uncertain how to proceed* **begin,** make a start, get going, move. **2** *he proceeded down the road* **go,** make your way, advance, move, progress, carry on, press on, push on. **3** *we should proceed with the talks* **go ahead,** carry on, go on, continue, keep on, get on.
ANTONYMS stop.

proceedings ▸ plural noun **1** an event or a series of actions. **2** action taken in a law court to settle a dispute.

SYNONYMS **1** *the evening's proceedings* **events,** activities, happenings, goings-on. **2** *the proceedings of the meeting* **report,** transactions, minutes, account, story, record(s). **3** *legal proceedings* **legal action,** litigation, lawsuit, case, prosecution.

proceeds ▸ plural noun money obtained from an event or activity.

SYNONYMS **profits,** earnings, receipts, returns, takings, income, revenue, profit, yield; Sport gate (money); N. Amer. take.

process¹ /proh-sess/ ▸ noun **1** a series of actions that are done to achieve a particular end. **2** a natural series of changes: *the ageing process.*

SYNONYMS **1** *investigation is a long process* **procedure,** operation, action, activity, exercise, affair, business, job, task, undertaking. **2** *a new canning process* **method,** system, technique, means, practice, way, approach.

▸ verb **1** perform a series of actions on something to change or preserve it. **2** deal with someone or something using an established procedure.

SYNONYMS *applications are processed rapidly* **deal with,** attend to, see to, sort out, handle, take care of.

□ **processor** noun.

process² /pruh-sess/ ▸ verb walk in procession.

procession ▸ noun **1** a number of people or vehicles moving forward in an orderly way. **2** a large number of people or things that come one after another.

SYNONYMS **parade,** march, march past, cavalcade, motorcade, cortège, column, file; Brit. informal crocodile.

proclaim ▸ verb **1** announce officially or publicly. **2** show something clearly.

SYNONYMS **declare,** announce, pronounce, state, make known, give out, advertise, publish, broadcast, trumpet.

□ **proclamation** noun.

proclivity ▸ noun (plural **proclivities**) a tendency to do something regularly.

procrastinate ▸ verb (**procrastinates, procrastinating, procrastinated**) delay or postpone action.

□ **procrastination** noun.

procreate ▸ verb (**procreates, procreating, procreated**) produce a baby or young animal.

□ **procreation** noun.

proctor ▸ noun Brit. an officer in charge of discipline at some universities.

procurator fiscal ▸ noun (plural **procurators fiscal** or **procurator fiscals**) (in Scotland) a local coroner and public prosecutor.

procure ▸ verb (**procures, procuring, procured**) obtain.

□ **procurement** noun.

prod ▸ verb (**prods, prodding, prodded**) **1** push someone or something with a finger or pointed object. **2** prompt or remind someone to do something.

SYNONYMS **1** *Cassie prodded him in the chest* **poke,** jab, stab, dig, nudge, elbow. **2** *the Department was prodded into action* **spur,** stimulate, prompt, push, galvanize, persuade, urge, chivvy, remind.

▸ noun **1** an act of prodding. **2** a prompt or reminder. **3** a pointed object like a stick.

SYNONYMS **1** *a sharp prod in the ribs* **poke,** jab, stab, dig, nudge, elbow. **2** *he might need a prod to get him to come* **urging,** stimulus, push, prompt, reminder, chivvying.

prodigal ▸ adjective **1** using time, money, etc. in a wasteful way. **2** lavish.

SYNONYMS **wasteful,** extravagant, spendthrift.
ANTONYMS thrifty.

▸ noun (also **prodigal son**) a person who leaves home and leads a wasteful life but is later sorry for their actions and returns.

□ **prodigality** noun.

prodigious ▸ adjective impressively large.

□ **prodigiously** adverb.

prodigy ▸ noun (plural **prodigies**) a young person with exceptional abilities.

SYNONYMS **genius,** mastermind, virtuoso, wunderkind; informal whizz-kid, whizz.
ANTONYMS dunce, amateur.

produce ▸ verb /pruh-**dyooss**/ (**produces, producing, produced**) **1** make, manufacture, or create. **2** make something happen or exist. **3** show or provide

p

something for consideration. **4** be in charge of the financial aspects of a film or the staging of a play. **5** supervise the making of a musical recording.

> SYNONYMS **1** *the company produces furniture* **manufacture**, make, construct, build, fabricate, put together, assemble, turn out, create, mass-produce. **2** *the vineyards produce excellent wines* **yield**, grow, give, supply, provide, furnish, bear. **3** *she produced ten puppies* **give birth to**, bear, deliver, bring forth, bring into the world. **4** *he produced five novels* **create**, fashion, turn out, compose, write, pen, paint. **5** *she produced an ID card* **pull out**, extract, fish out, present, offer, proffer, show. **6** *that will produce a reaction* **cause**, bring about, give rise to, occasion, generate, lead to, result in, provoke, precipitate, spark off, trigger. **7** *James produced the play* **stage**, put on, mount, present, exhibit.

▸ noun /prod-yooss/ things that have been produced or grown.

> SYNONYMS *local produce* **food**, foodstuff(s), products, crops, fruit and vegetables.

producer ▸ noun a person, company, or country that produces something.

> SYNONYMS **1** *a car producer* **manufacturer**, maker, builder, constructor. **2** *coffee producers* **grower**, farmer. **3** *the producer of the show* **impresario**, manager, administrator, promoter, director.

product ▸ noun **1** an article or substance manufactured for sale. **2** a result of an action or process. **3** a substance produced during a natural, chemical, or manufacturing process. **4** Maths a quantity obtained by multiplying one number by another.

> SYNONYMS **1** *household products* **artefact**, commodity; (**products**) goods, ware(s), merchandise, produce. **2** *a product of experience* **result**, consequence, outcome, effect, upshot.

production ▸ noun **1** the action of producing something. **2** the amount of something produced.

> SYNONYMS **1** *the production of cars* **manufacture**, making, construction, building, fabrication, assembly, creation, mass production. **2** *the production of literary works* **creation**, origination, fashioning, composition, writing. **3** *agricultural production* **output**, yield, productivity. **4** *a theatre production* **performance**, staging, presentation, show, piece, play.

■ **production line** an assembly line.

productive ▸ adjective **1** producing large amounts of goods or crops. **2** doing or achieving a lot.

> SYNONYMS **1** *productive land* **fertile**, fruitful, rich, fecund. **2** *a productive artist* **prolific**, inventive, creative. **3** *productive talks* **useful**, constructive, profitable, fruitful, valuable, effective, worthwhile, helpful.
> ANTONYMS unproductive.

□ **productively** adverb.

productivity ▸ noun **1** the quality of being productive. **2** the efficiency with which things are produced.

> SYNONYMS **efficiency**, work rate, output, yield, production.

profane ▸ adjective **1** not religious; secular. **2** not having respect for God or holy things.
▸ verb (**profanes**, **profaning**, **profaned**) treat something holy with a lack of respect.

profanity ▸ noun (plural **profanities**) **1** language or behaviour that shows a lack of respect for God or holy things. **2** a swear word.

profess ▸ verb **1** claim that something is true. **2** declare your faith in a religion.

> SYNONYMS **1** *he professed his love* **declare**, announce, proclaim, assert, state, affirm, maintain, protest. **2** (**professed**) *a professed Christian* **declared**, self-acknowledged, self-confessed, confessed, sworn, confirmed. **3** (**professed**) *their professed independence* **claimed**, supposed, ostensible, self-styled, apparent, pretended, purported. **4** *she professed to loathe publicity* **claim**, pretend, purport, affect, make out.

profession ▸ noun **1** a job that needs special training and a formal qualification. **2** all the people working in a particular profession. **3** a claim. **4** a declaration of belief in a religion.

> SYNONYMS **career**, occupation, calling, vocation, métier, line of work, job, business, trade, craft.

professional ▸ adjective **1** relating to or belonging to a profession. **2** doing something as a job rather than as a hobby. **3** having the skills or qualities of a professional person.

> SYNONYMS **1** *professional occupations* **white-collar**, non-manual, graduate, qualified, chartered. **2** *a professional cricketer* **paid**, salaried. **3** *a very professional job* **expert**, accomplished, skilful, masterly, fine, polished, skilled, proficient, competent, able, businesslike, deft. **4** *not a professional way to behave* **appropriate**, fitting, proper, honourable, ethical.

ANTONYMS manual, amateur, amateurish, inappropriate, unethical.

▸ noun **1** a professional person. **2** a person who is very skilled in a particular activity.

SYNONYMS *she was a real professional* **expert**, virtuoso, old hand, master, maestro, past master; informal pro, ace. ANTONYMS amateur.

☐ **professionally** adverb.

✔ only one **f**: professional.

professionalism ▸ noun the ability or skill that you expect from a professional person.

professor ▸ noun **1** a university teacher or scholar of the highest rank. **2** N. Amer. a university teacher.
☐ **professorial** adjective **professorship** noun.

proffer ▸ verb (proffers, proffering, proffered) offer something for someone to accept.

proficient ▸ adjective competent; skilled.
☐ **proficiency** noun.

profile ▸ noun **1** an outline of someone's face, seen from the side. **2** a short article that describes someone or something. **3** the extent to which someone attracts attention: *her high profile.*

SYNONYMS **1** *his handsome profile* **outline**, silhouette, side view, contour, shape, form, lines. **2** *a profile of the organization* **description**, account, study, portrait, rundown, sketch, outline.

▸ verb (profiles, profiling, profiled) describe in a short article.
■ **keep a low profile** try not to attract attention.

profit ▸ noun **1** a financial gain. **2** advantage or benefit.

SYNONYMS **1** *the firm made a profit* **financial gain**, return(s), yield, proceeds, earnings, winnings, surplus; informal pay dirt, bottom line. **2** *there was little profit in going on* **advantage**, benefit, value, use, good; informal mileage. ANTONYMS loss, disadvantage.

▸ verb (profits, profiting, profited) benefit someone.

SYNONYMS **1** *we will not profit from the deal* **make money**, earn; informal rake it in, clean up, make a killing; N. Amer. informal make a fast buck. **2** *how will that profit us?* **benefit**, be advantageous to, be of use to, do someone good, help, be of service to, serve. ANTONYMS lose, disadvantage.

■ **profit margin** the difference between the cost of producing something and the price at which it is sold.

✔ Note that the forms **profited** and **profiting** have a single rather than a double **t**.

profitable ▸ adjective **1** (of a business or activity) making a profit. **2** useful.

SYNONYMS **1** *a profitable company* **moneymaking**, profit-making, paying, lucrative, commercial, successful, money-spinning, gainful. **2** *profitable study* **beneficial**, useful, advantageous, valuable, productive, worthwhile, rewarding, fruitful, illuminating, informative, well spent. ANTONYMS unprofitable, loss-making, fruitless, useless.

☐ **profitability** noun **profitably** adverb.

profiteering ▸ noun the making of a large profit in an unfair way.
☐ **profiteer** noun.

profiterole ▸ noun a small ball of choux pastry filled with cream and covered with chocolate.

profligate ▸ adjective **1** using time, money, in a wasteful or extravagant way. **2** indulging too much in physical pleasures.
▸ noun a profligate person.
☐ **profligacy** noun.

profound ▸ adjective (profounder, profoundest) **1** very great. **2** showing great knowledge or understanding. **3** needing a lot of study or thought.

SYNONYMS **1** *profound relief* **heartfelt**, intense, keen, extreme, acute, severe, sincere, earnest, deep, deep-seated, overpowering, overwhelming. **2** *a profound change* **far-reaching**, radical, extensive, sweeping, exhaustive, thoroughgoing. **3** *a profound analysis* **wise**, learned, intelligent, scholarly, discerning, penetrating, perceptive, astute, thoughtful, insightful. ANTONYMS superficial, mild, slight.

☐ **profoundly** adverb **profundity** noun.

profuse ▸ adjective produced or appearing in large quantities.
☐ **profusely** adverb.

profusion ▸ noun a very large quantity of something.

progenitor /proh-**jen**-i-ter/ ▸ noun **1** an ancestor or parent. **2** the person who started an artistic, political, or intellectual movement.

progeny /**proj**-uh-ni/ ▸ noun offspring.

progesterone /pruh-**jess**-tuh-rohn/ ▸ noun a hormone that stimulates the uterus to prepare for pregnancy.

prognosis /prog-**noh**-siss/ ▸ noun (plural prognoses /prog-**noh**-seez/) **1** an opinion about how an illness is likely to develop. **2** the likely course of a situation.
☐ **prognostic** adjective.

programmatic ▸ adjective having to do with or following a programme.

p

programme (US spelling **program**) ▶ noun
1 a plan of future events or things to be
done. **2** a radio or television broadcast.
3 a sheet or booklet giving details about
a play, concert, etc. **4** (**program**) a series
of software instructions to control the
operation of a computer.

> SYNONYMS **1** *our programme for the day*
> **schedule,** agenda, calendar, timetable,
> order, line-up. **2** *the government's*
> *reform programme* **scheme,** plan,
> package, strategy, initiative, proposal.
> **3** *a television programme* **broadcast,**
> production, show, presentation,
> transmission, performance; informal prog.
> **4** *a programme of study* **course,** syllabus,
> curriculum.

▶ verb (**programmes, programming,**
programmed) **1** (**program**) provide
a computer with a program. **2** make
something behave in a particular way.
3 arrange something according to a plan.

> SYNONYMS *they programmed the day well*
> **arrange,** organize, schedule, plan, map
> out, timetable, line up; N. Amer. slate.

□ **programmable** adjective **programmer** noun.

progress ▶ noun **1** forward movement
towards a place. **2** the process of improving
or developing.

> SYNONYMS **1** *snow made progress difficult*
> **(forward) movement,** advance, going,
> headway, passage. **2** *scientific progress*
> **development,** advance, advancement,
> headway, step forward, improvement,
> growth.
> ANTONYMS regression.

▶ verb **1** move forwards. **2** improve or
develop.

> SYNONYMS **1** *they progressed slowly down*
> *the road* **go,** make your way, move,
> proceed, advance, go on, continue, make
> headway, work your way. **2** *the school*
> *has progressed rapidly* **develop,** make
> progress, advance, make headway, take
> steps forward, move on, get on, gain
> ground, improve, get better, come on,
> come along, make strides; informal be
> getting there.
> ANTONYMS regress, lapse.

progression ▶ noun **1** a gradual movement
from one place or state to another. **2** a
number of things coming one after
another.

> SYNONYMS **1** *progression to the next stage*
> **progress,** advancement, movement,
> passage, development, evolution,
> growth. **2** *a progression of peaks on the*
> *graph* **succession,** series, sequence,
> string, stream, chain, train, row, cycle.

progressive ▶ adjective **1** proceeding
gradually or in stages. **2** favouring new

ideas or social reform.

> SYNONYMS **1** *progressive deterioration*
> **continuing,** continuous, ongoing,
> gradual, step-by-step, cumulative.
> **2** *progressive views* **modern,** liberal,
> advanced, forward-thinking,
> enlightened, pioneering, reforming,
> reformist, radical; informal go-ahead.
> ANTONYMS sporadic, conservative,
> reactionary.

▶ noun a person who is in favour of social
reform.
□ **progressively** adverb.

prohibit ▶ verb (**prohibits, prohibiting,**
prohibited) **1** formally forbid something by
law. **2** prevent something from happening.

> SYNONYMS **1** *state law prohibits gambling*
> **forbid,** ban, bar, proscribe, make illegal,
> outlaw, disallow. **2** *a cash shortage*
> *prohibited the visit* **prevent,** stop, rule
> out, preclude, make impossible.
> ANTONYMS allow.

prohibition ▶ noun **1** the action of
prohibiting. **2** an order that forbids
something.

> SYNONYMS **ban,** bar, veto, embargo,
> boycott, injunction, moratorium.

prohibitive ▶ adjective **1** forbidding or
restricting something. **2** (of a price) too
high.
□ **prohibitively** adverb.

project ▶ noun /**pro**-jekt/ **1** a piece of
work that is carefully planned to achieve
a particular aim. **2** a piece of work by a
school or college student in which they
carry out their own research.

> SYNONYMS **1** *an engineering project*
> **scheme,** plan, programme, enterprise,
> undertaking, venture, proposal, idea,
> concept. **2** *a history project* **assignment,**
> piece of work, piece of research, task.

▶ verb /pruh-**jekt**/ **1** estimate or predict
something based on what is happening
now. **2** (**be projected**) be planned. **3** stick
out beyond something else. **4** make light
or an image fall on a surface or screen.
5 present yourself to other people in a
particular way.

> SYNONYMS **1** *profits are projected to rise*
> **forecast,** predict, expect, estimate,
> calculate, reckon. **2** *his projected book*
> **intend,** plan, propose. **3** *balconies*
> *projected over the lake* **stick out,** jut
> (out), protrude, extend, stand out, bulge
> out. **4** *the sun projected his shadow on the*
> *wall* **cast,** throw, send, shed, shine.

projectile ▶ noun an object that is fired or
thrown at a target.

projection ▶ noun **1** a prediction about
something based on what is happening

now. **2** the projecting of an image, sound, etc. **3** a thing that sticks out from something else.

SYNONYMS **1** *a sales projection* **forecast,** prediction, prognosis, expectation, estimate. **2** *tiny projections on the cliff face* **outcrop,** outgrowth, overhang, ledge, shelf, prominence, protrusion, protuberance; informal sticky-out bit.

◻ **projectionist** noun.

projector ▸ noun a device for projecting slides or film on to a screen.

prolapse ▸ noun a condition in which an organ of the body has slipped forward or down from its normal position.

proletarian /proh-li-**tair**-i-uhn/ ▸ adjective relating to the proletariat.
▸ noun a member of the proletariat.

proletariat ▸ noun workers or working-class people.

proliferate ▸ verb (**proliferates, proliferating, proliferated**) reproduce rapidly; increase rapidly in number.

SYNONYMS **increase,** grow, multiply, rocket, mushroom, snowball, burgeon, spread, expand, run riot.
ANTONYMS decrease, dwindle.

◻ **proliferation** noun.

prolific ▸ adjective **1** (of a plant or animal) producing a lot of fruit, leaves, or young. **2** (of an artist, author, etc.) producing many works.

SYNONYMS **1** *a prolific crop of tomatoes* **plentiful,** abundant, bountiful, profuse, copious, luxuriant, rich, lush, fruitful. **2** *a prolific composer* **productive,** fertile, creative, inventive.
ANTONYMS meagre, unproductive.

◻ **prolifically** adverb.

prolix /**proh**-liks/ ▸ adjective (of speech or writing) long and boring.
◻ **prolixity** noun.

prologue ▸ noun **1** a separate introductory part of a play, book, or piece of music. **2** an event that leads to another.

prolong ▸ verb make something last longer.

SYNONYMS **lengthen,** extend, drag out, draw out, protract, spin out, carry on, continue, keep up, perpetuate.
ANTONYMS shorten.

◻ **prolongation** noun.

prolonged ▸ adjective continuing for a long time.

prom ▸ noun informal **1** Brit. a promenade by the sea. **2** Brit. a promenade concert. **3** N. Amer. a formal dance at a high school or college.

promenade ▸ noun **1** a paved walkway along a seafront. **2** a leisurely walk.
▸ verb (**promenades, promenading,**

promenaded**) go for a leisurely walk.
■ **promenade concert** Brit. a concert of classical music at which part of the audience stands.

promethium ▸ noun a radioactive metallic element.

prominence ▸ noun the state of being prominent.

SYNONYMS **1** *his rise to prominence* **fame,** celebrity, eminence, importance, distinction, greatness, prestige, stature, standing. **2** *the press gave prominence to the reports* **wide coverage,** importance, precedence, weight, a high profile, top billing.

prominent ▸ adjective **1** important; famous. **2** sticking out. **3** particularly noticeable.

SYNONYMS **1** *a prominent surgeon* **important,** well known, leading, eminent, distinguished, notable, noteworthy, noted, illustrious, celebrated, famous, renowned; N. Amer. major-league. **2** *prominent cheekbones* **jutting (out),** protruding, projecting, protuberant, standing out, sticking out, proud, bulging. **3** *a prominent feature of the landscape* **conspicuous,** noticeable, obvious, unmistakable, eye-catching, pronounced, salient, striking, dominant, obtrusive.
ANTONYMS unimportant, unknown, flat, inconspicuous.

◻ **prominently** adverb.

promiscuous /pruh-**miss**-kyuu-uhss/ ▸ adjective having a lot of sexual relationships.
◻ **promiscuity** noun.

promise ▸ noun **1** an assurance that you will do something or that something will happen. **2** qualities or abilities that may lead to future success.

SYNONYMS **1** *you broke your promise* **word (of honour),** assurance, pledge, vow, guarantee, oath, bond, undertaking, agreement, commitment, contract. **2** *he shows promise* **potential,** ability, talent, aptitude, possibility.

▸ verb (**promises, promising, promised**) **1** make a promise. **2** give good grounds for expecting something.

SYNONYMS **1** *she promised to go* **give your word,** swear, pledge, vow, undertake, guarantee, warrant, contract, give an assurance, commit yourself. **2** *the skies promised sunshine* **indicate,** lead one to expect, point to, be a sign of, give hope of, augur, herald, portend.

promising ▸ adjective showing signs of future success.

SYNONYMS **1** *a promising start* **good,** encouraging, favourable, hopeful,

auspicious, propitious, bright, rosy, heartening. **2** *a promising actor* **with potential,** gifted, talented, budding, up-and-coming, rising, coming, in the making.
ANTONYMS unfavourable, hopeless.

□ **promisingly** adverb.

promissory note ▸ noun a signed document containing a written promise to pay a stated amount of money.

promo ▸ noun (plural **promos**) informal a promotional film, video, etc.

promontory /prom-uhn-tuh-ri/ ▸ noun (plural **promontories**) a point of high land jutting out into the sea.

promote ▸ verb (**promotes, promoting, promoted**) **1** help something to happen. **2** give publicity to a product, event, etc. in order to increase sales or make people aware of it. **3** raise someone to a higher position or rank.

SYNONYMS **1** *she's been promoted* **upgrade,** give promotion to, elevate, advance, move up. **2** *an organization promoting justice* **encourage,** further, advance, foster, develop, boost, stimulate, work for. **3** *she is promoting her new film* **advertise,** publicize, give publicity to, beat/bang the drum for, market, merchandise; informal push, plug, hype; N. Amer. informal flack.
ANTONYMS demote, obstruct, play down.

□ **promoter** noun.

promotion ▸ noun **1** movement to a higher position or rank. **2** activity that supports or encourages a cause or aim. **3** the action of promoting a product, event, etc.

SYNONYMS **1** *her promotion at work* **upgrading,** preferment, elevation, advancement, step up (the ladder). **2** *the promotion of justice* **encouragement,** furtherance, furthering, advancement, contribution to, fostering, boosting, stimulation; N. Amer. boosterism. **3** *the promotion for her new film* **advertising,** marketing, publicity, campaign, propaganda; informal hard sell, plug, hype, puff.

□ **promotional** adjective.

prompt ▸ verb **1** make something happen. **2** (**prompt someone to**) make someone take a course of action. **3** encourage someone to speak. **4** tell an actor a word that they have forgotten.

SYNONYMS **1** *curiosity prompted him to look* **induce,** make, move, motivate, lead, dispose, persuade, incline, encourage, stimulate, prod, impel, spur on, inspire. **2** *the statement prompted a hostile reaction* **give rise to,** bring about, cause, occasion, result in, lead to, elicit, produce, precipitate, trigger,

spark off, provoke. **3** *the actors needed prompting* **remind,** cue, feed, help out, jog someone's memory.
ANTONYMS deter, avoid.

▸ noun **1** a word or phrase used to prompt an actor. **2** a symbol on a computer screen to show that more input is needed.
▸ adjective done without delay.

SYNONYMS *a prompt reply* **quick,** swift, rapid, speedy, fast, direct, immediate, instant, early, punctual, in good time, on time.
ANTONYMS slow, late.

▸ adverb Brit. exactly or punctually.

SYNONYMS *at 3.30 prompt* **exactly,** precisely, sharp, on the dot, dead, punctually; informal bang on; N. Amer. informal on the button, on the nose.

□ **prompter** noun.

promptly ▸ adverb in a prompt way.

SYNONYMS **1** *William arrived promptly at 7.30* **punctually,** on time; informal on the dot, bang on; Brit. informal spot on; N. Amer. informal on the button, on the nose. **2** *I expect the matter to be dealt with promptly* **without delay,** straight/right away, at once, immediately, now, as soon as possible, quickly, swiftly, rapidly, speedily, fast; informal pronto, asap.
ANTONYMS late, slowly.

promulgate ▸ verb (**promulgates, promulgating, promulgated**) **1** make an idea widely known. **2** announce the official beginning of a new law.
□ **promulgation** noun.

prone ▸ adjective **1** (**prone to** or **to do**) likely to suffer from, do, or experience something unfortunate. **2** lying flat, especially face downwards.

SYNONYMS **1** *softwood is prone to rotting* **susceptible,** vulnerable, subject, open, liable, given, predisposed, likely, disposed, inclined, apt. **2** *his prone body* **lying face down,** on your stomach/front, lying flat, lying down, horizontal, prostrate.
ANTONYMS resistant, immune, upright.

prong ▸ noun **1** each of two or more long pointed parts on a fork. **2** each of the separate parts of an attack.
□ **pronged** adjective.

pronoun ▸ noun a word used instead of a noun to indicate someone or something already mentioned or known, e.g. *I, this.*

pronounce ▸ verb (**pronounces, pronouncing, pronounced**) **1** make the sound of a word or part of a word. **2** declare or announce. **3** (**pronounce on**) pass judgement or make a decision on.

p

SYNONYMS **1** *his name is difficult to pronounce* say, enunciate, utter, voice, sound, vocalize, get your tongue round. **2** *the doctor pronounced her fit for work* declare, proclaim, judge, rule, decree.
□ **pronouncement** noun.

pronounced ▸ adjective very noticeable.

SYNONYMS **noticeable,** marked, strong, conspicuous, striking, distinct, prominent, unmistakable, obvious. ANTONYMS slight.

pronto ▸ adverb informal promptly.

pronunciation ▸ noun the way in which a word is pronounced.

✔ **Pronunciation** has no **o** in the middle.

proof ▸ noun **1** evidence that shows that something is true. **2** the process of finding out whether something is true. **3** a series of stages in the solving of a mathematical problem. **4** a copy of printed material used for making corrections before final printing. **5** a standard used to measure the strength of alcohol.

SYNONYMS **evidence,** verification, corroboration, demonstration, authentication, confirmation, certification, documentation.

▸ adjective resistant to: *damp-proof.*

SYNONYMS **resistant,** immune, unaffected, impervious.

proofread ▸ verb read written or printed material and mark any mistakes.
□ **proofreader** noun.

prop¹ ▸ noun **1** a pole or beam used as a temporary support. **2** a source of support or assistance. **3** (also **prop forward**) Rugby a forward at either end of the front row of a scrum.

SYNONYMS **1** *the roof is held up by props* pole, post, support, upright, brace, buttress, stay, strut. **2** *a prop for the economy* mainstay, pillar, anchor, support, cornerstone.

▸ verb (**props, propping, propped**) **1** support with a prop. **2** lean something against something else. **3** (**prop something up**) help something that is in difficulty.

SYNONYMS *he propped his bike against the wall* lean, rest, stand, balance.

prop² ▸ noun a portable object used by actors during a play or film.

propaganda ▸ noun false or exaggerated information, used to win support for a political cause or point of view.

SYNONYMS **information,** promotion, advertising, publicity, disinformation; informal hype.

□ **propagandist** noun.

✔ **propa-**, not **propo-**: propaganda.

propagate ▸ verb (**propagates, propagating, propagated**) **1** grow a new plant from a parent plant. **2** spread an idea or information widely.
□ **propagation** noun.

propane ▸ noun a flammable gas present in natural gas and used as fuel.

propel ▸ verb (**propels, propelling, propelled**) drive or push forwards.

SYNONYMS **1** *a boat propelled by oars* move, power, push, drive. **2** *the impact propelled him into the street* throw, thrust, toss, fling, hurl, pitch, send, shoot.

propellant ▸ noun a gas which forces out the contents of an aerosol.

propeller (or **propellor**) ▸ noun a device which uses two or more angled blades to propel a ship or aircraft.

propensity ▸ noun (plural **propensities**) a tendency to behave in a particular way.

proper ▸ adjective **1** truly what it is said to be; real. **2** in its true form: *the World Cup proper.* **3** appropriate or correct. **4** (**proper to**) belonging exclusively to.

SYNONYMS **1** *he's not a proper scientist* real, genuine, actual, true, bona fide; informal kosher. **2** *the proper channels* right, correct, accepted, conventional, established, official, regular, acceptable, appropriate. **3** *they were terribly proper* formal, conventional, correct, orthodox, polite, punctilious, respectable. ANTONYMS fake, inappropriate, wrong, unconventional.

■ **proper fraction** a fraction that is less than one. **proper noun** (or **proper name**) a name of a person, place, or organization, written with a capital letter.
□ **properly** adverb.

property ▸ noun (plural **properties**) **1** a thing or things belonging to someone. **2** a building and the land belonging to it. **3** a characteristic or quality.

SYNONYMS **1** *lost property* possessions, belongings, things, effects, stuff, goods; informal gear. **2** *private property* building(s), premises, house(s), land; N. Amer. real estate. **3** *healing properties* quality, attribute, characteristic, feature, power, trait, hallmark.

prophecy /prof-i-si/ ▸ noun (plural **prophecies**) **1** a prediction about what will happen in the future. **2** the ability to predict the future.

SYNONYMS **prediction,** forecast, prognostication, prognosis, divination.

prophesy /prof-i-sy/ ▸ verb (**prophesies, prophesying, prophesied**) predict that a particular thing will happen in the future.

p

SYNONYMS **predict,** foretell, forecast, foresee, prognosticate.

prophet ▸ noun **1** a person regarded as being sent by God to teach people. **2** a person who predicts the future.

SYNONYMS **forecaster,** seer, soothsayer, fortune teller, clairvoyant, oracle.

prophetic ▸ adjective **1** accurately predicting the future. **2** having to do with a prophet or prophecy.

prophylactic /prof-i-lak-tik/ ▸ adjective intended to prevent disease.
▸ noun a medicine intended to prevent disease.

propinquity /pruh-ping-kwi-ti/ ▸ noun nearness in time or space.

propitiate ▸ verb (propitiates, propitiating, propitiated) win or regain the favour of.
▢ **propitiation** noun **propitiatory** adjective.

propitious ▸ adjective indicating a good chance of success; favourable.

proponent ▸ noun a person who proposes a theory or plan.

proportion ▸ noun **1** a part or share of a whole. **2** the relationship of one thing to another in terms of quantity or size. **3** the correct relationship between one thing and another. **4** (**proportions**) the size and shape of something.

SYNONYMS **1** *a proportion of the land* **part,** portion, amount, quantity, bit, piece, percentage, fraction, section, segment, share. **2** *the proportion of water to alcohol* **ratio,** distribution, relative amount/number, relationship. **3** *a sense of proportion* **balance,** symmetry, harmony, correspondence, correlation, agreement. **4** (**proportions**) *men of huge proportions* **size,** dimensions, magnitude, measurements, mass, volume, bulk, expanse, extent.

proportional (or **proportionate**) ▸ adjective corresponding in size or amount to something else.

SYNONYMS **corresponding,** comparable, in proportion, pro rata, commensurate, equivalent, consistent.
ANTONYMS disproportionate.

■ **proportional representation** an electoral system in which parties gain seats in proportion to the number of votes cast for them.
▢ **proportionally** adverb.

proposal ▸ noun **1** a plan or suggestion. **2** the action of proposing something. **3** an offer of marriage.

SYNONYMS **scheme,** plan, idea, project, programme, motion, proposition, suggestion, submission.

propose ▸ verb (proposes, proposing, proposed) **1** put forward an idea or plan for consideration by other people. **2** nominate someone for an official position. **3** plan or intend to do something. **4** make an offer of marriage to someone.

SYNONYMS **1** *he proposed a solution* **put forward,** suggest, submit, advance, offer, present, move, come up with. **2** *do you propose to go?* **intend,** mean, plan, have in mind, aim. **3** *he proposed to her!* **ask someone to marry you,** ask for someone's hand in marriage; informal pop the question.
ANTONYMS withdraw.

proposition ▸ noun **1** a statement that expresses an opinion. **2** a plan of action. **3** a problem to be dealt with.

SYNONYMS **1** *a business proposition* **proposal,** scheme, plan, project, idea, programme. **2** *doing it for real is a very different proposition* **task,** job, undertaking, venture, activity, affair.

▸ verb informal offer to have sex with someone.

propound ▸ verb put forward an idea or theory for consideration.

proprietary ▸ adjective **1** having to do with an owner or ownership. **2** (of a product) marketed under a registered trademark.
■ **proprietary name** a name of a product or service registered as a trademark.

proprietor ▸ noun the owner of a business.

SYNONYMS **owner,** possessor, holder, householder, master, mistress, landowner, landlord, landlady, shopkeeper.

proprietorial ▸ adjective behaving as if you owned something; possessive.

propriety ▸ noun (plural **proprieties**) **1** correctness of behaviour or morals. **2** the condition of being right or appropriate.

propulsion ▸ noun the action of propelling or driving something forward.
▢ **propulsive** adjective.

pro rata /proh rah-tuh/ ▸ adjective proportional.
▸ adverb proportionally.

prosaic /proh-zay-ik/ ▸ adjective ordinary or unimaginative; dull.
▢ **prosaically** adverb.

proscenium /pruh-see-ni-uhm/ ▸ noun (plural **prosceniums** or **proscenia** /pruh-see-ni-uh/) **1** the part of a stage in front of the curtain. **2** (also **proscenium arch**) an arch framing the opening between the stage and the part of the theatre in which the audience sits.

proscribe ▸ verb (proscribes, proscribing, proscribed) **1** forbid. **2** criticize or condemn.

prose ▸ noun ordinary written or spoken language.

p

prosecute ▸ verb (prosecutes, prosecuting, prosecuted) **1** take legal proceedings against someone. **2** continue doing or taking part in something.

> synonyms **charge,** take to court, take legal action against, sue, try, bring to trial, put on trial, put in the dock, indict; N. Amer. impeach.
> antonyms defend, let off.

☐ **prosecutor** noun.

prosecution ▸ noun **1** the action of prosecuting. **2** (**the prosecution**) the party prosecuting someone in a lawsuit.

proselyte /pross-i-lyt/ ▸ noun a person who has converted from one religion or belief to another.

proselytize (or proselytise) /pross-i-li-tyz/ ▸ verb (proselytizes, proselytizing, proselytized) convert someone from one religion or belief to another.

prosody /pross-uh-di/ ▸ noun **1** the patterns of rhythm and sound used in poetry. **2** the study of these patterns.

prospect ▸ noun **1** a possibility of something happening. **2** an idea about what will happen in the future. **3** (**prospects**) chances of being successful. **4** a person who is likely to be successful.

> synonyms **1** *there is little prospect of success* **likelihood,** hope, expectation, chance, odds, probability, possibility, promise, lookout, fear, danger. **2** *her job prospects* **possibilities,** potential, expectations, outlook. **3** *a daunting prospect* **vision,** thought, idea, task, undertaking.

▸ verb search for mineral deposits.

> synonyms *prospecting for oil* **search,** look, explore, survey, scout, hunt, dowse.

☐ **prospector** noun.

prospective ▸ adjective expected or likely to happen or be something in the future.

> synonyms **potential,** possible, probable, likely, future, eventual, -to-be, soon-to-be, in the making, intending, aspiring, would-be.

☐ **prospectively** adverb.

prospectus ▸ noun (plural **prospectuses**) a printed booklet advertising a school, university, or business.

> synonyms **brochure,** syllabus, curriculum, catalogue, programme, list, schedule.

prosper ▸ verb (prospers, prospering, prospered) be successful, especially in making money.

> synonyms **flourish,** thrive, do well, bloom, blossom, burgeon, progress, do all right for yourself, get ahead, get on

(in the world), be successful; informal go places.
> antonyms fail, flounder.

prosperity ▸ noun the state of being prosperous.

> synonyms **success,** affluence, wealth, ease, plenty.
> antonyms hardship, failure.

prosperous ▸ adjective rich and successful.

> synonyms **thriving,** flourishing, successful, strong, vigorous, profitable, lucrative, expanding, booming, burgeoning, **affluent,** wealthy, rich, moneyed, well off, well-to-do; informal in the money.
> antonyms ailing, poor.

prostate ▸ noun a gland in men and male mammals that produces the fluid part of semen.

prostitute ▸ noun a person who has sex for money.

> synonyms **whore,** sex worker, call girl, rent boy; informal working girl; Brit. informal tom; N. Amer. informal hooker, hustler.

▸ verb (prostitutes, prostituting, prostituted) (**prostitute yourself**) **1** work as a prostitute. **2** put your talents to an unworthy use in order to earn money.

> synonyms *they prostituted their art* **betray,** sacrifice, sell, sell out, debase, degrade, demean, devalue, cheapen, lower, shame, misuse.

☐ **prostitution** noun.

prostrate ▸ adjective /pross-trayt/ **1** lying stretched out on the ground with the face downwards. **2** completely overcome or helpless.
▸ verb /pross-**trayt**/ (prostrates, prostrating, prostrated) **1** (**prostrate yourself**) throw yourself flat on the ground. **2** (**be prostrated**) be completely overcome with stress or exhaustion.
☐ **prostration** noun.

protactinium ▸ noun a rare radioactive metallic element.

protagonist ▸ noun **1** the leading character in a drama, film, or novel. **2** an important person in a real event.

protean /proh-tee-uhn/ ▸ adjective tending or able to change or adapt.

protect ▸ verb keep someone or something safe from harm or injury.

> synonyms **keep safe,** keep from harm, guard, defend, shield, save, safeguard, preserve, cushion, insulate, shelter, screen, keep, look after.
> antonyms expose, neglect, attack, harm.

protection ▸ noun **1** the action of protecting. **2** a person or thing that

p

protects. **3** the payment of money to criminals so that they will not attack your property.

> SYNONYMS **1** *protection against frost* **defence,** security, safeguard, safety, sanctuary, shelter, refuge, immunity, indemnity. **2** *the protection of the Church* **safe keeping,** care, charge, umbrella, guardianship, support, aegis, patronage. **3** *a good protection against noise* **barrier,** buffer, shield, screen, cushion, bulwark, armour, insulation.

protectionism ▸ noun the practice of protecting a country's industries from foreign competition by taxing imported goods.
□ **protectionist** noun & adjective.

protective ▸ adjective **1** protecting someone or something. **2** having a strong wish to protect someone.

> SYNONYMS **1** *protective clothing* **special,** safety, thick, heavy, insulated, ...-proof, ...-resistant. **2** *he felt protective towards her* **solicitous,** caring, defensive, paternal, maternal, overprotective, possessive, jealous.

□ **protectively** adverb.

protector ▸ noun a person or thing that protects someone or something.

> SYNONYMS **1** *a protector of the environment* **defender,** preserver, guardian, champion, patron, custodian. **2** *ear protectors* **guard,** shield, buffer, cushion, pad, screen.

protectorate ▸ noun a state that is controlled and protected by another.

protégé /prot-i-zhay/ ▸ noun (feminine **protégée**) a person who is guided and supported by an older and more experienced person.

protein ▸ noun a substance which forms part of body tissues and is an important part of the human diet.

> ✔ **Protein** is an exception to the usual rule of **i** before **e** except after **c**.

protest ▸ noun /proh-test/ a statement or action expressing disapproval or objection to something.

> SYNONYMS **1** *a storm of protest* **objection,** complaint, challenge, dissent, demurral, remonstration, fuss, outcry. **2** *the women staged a protest* **demonstration,** rally, vigil, sit-in, occupation, work-to-rule, stoppage, strike, walkout, mutiny, picket, boycott; informal demo.
> ANTONYMS support, approval.

▸ verb /pruh-test/ **1** express an objection to what someone has said or done. **2** take part in a public protest. **3** state something strongly in response to an accusation: *she protested her innocence.*

> SYNONYMS **1** *residents protested at the plans* **object,** express opposition, dissent, take issue, take a stand, put up a fight, take exception, complain, express disapproval, disagree, make a fuss, speak out; informal kick up a fuss. **2** *he protested his innocence* **insist on,** maintain, assert, affirm, announce, proclaim, declare, profess.
> ANTONYMS acquiesce, support, deny.

□ **protester** (or **protestor**) noun.

Protestant /pro-tiss-tuhnt/ ▸ noun a member or follower of any of the Western Christian Churches that are separate from the Roman Catholic Church.
▸ adjective relating to or belonging to any of the Protestant Churches.
□ **Protestantism** noun.

protestation ▸ noun **1** a firm declaration that something is or is not the case. **2** an objection or protest.

proto- ▸ combining form original, primitive, or first: *prototype* | *protozoan.*

protocol ▸ noun **1** the system of rules governing formal occasions. **2** the accepted way to behave in a particular situation.

> SYNONYMS **etiquette,** convention, formalities, custom, the rules, procedure, ritual, decorum, the done thing.

proton ▸ noun a subatomic particle with a positive electric charge.

prototype ▸ noun a first form of something from which other forms are copied or developed.

> SYNONYMS **original,** master, template, pattern, sample.

protozoan /proh-tuh-zoh-uhn/ ▸ noun a microscopic animal that is made up of a single cell.

protracted ▸ adjective lasting for a long time.

> SYNONYMS **prolonged,** extended, long-drawn-out, lengthy, long.
> ANTONYMS short.

protractor ▸ noun an instrument for measuring angles, in the form of a flat semicircle marked with degrees.

protrude ▸ verb (protrudes, protruding, protruded) stick out from a surface.
□ **protrusion** noun.

protuberance ▸ noun a thing that sticks out from a surface.
□ **protuberant** adjective.

> ✔ There is no **r** immediately after the **t**: pro**tub**erance.

proud ▸ adjective **1** feeling pleased or satisfied by your own or another's achievements. **2** having too high an opinion of yourself. **3** having respect for yourself. **4** slightly sticking out from a surface.

> SYNONYMS **1** *the proud parents* **pleased,** glad, happy, delighted, thrilled, satisfied, gratified. **2** *a proud day* **pleasing,** gratifying, satisfying, cheering, heart-warming, happy, glorious. **3** *he is too proud to admit to being in the wrong* **arrogant,** conceited, vain, self-important, full of yourself, overbearing, bumptious, presumptuous, overweening, haughty, high and mighty; informal big-headed, too big for your boots, stuck-up.
> ANTONYMS ashamed, shameful, humble, modest.

□ **proudly** adverb.

prove ▸ verb (**proves, proving, proved;** past participle **proved** or **proven** /**proo**-v'n, **proh**-v'n/) **1** use evidence to show that something is true or exists. **2** be found to be. **3** (**prove yourself**) show your abilities or courage. **4** (**proven**) found through experience to be effective or true.

> SYNONYMS **1** *that proves I'm right* **show (to be true),** demonstrate (the truth of), provide proof, substantiate, verify, validate, authenticate. **2** *the rumour proved to be correct* **turn out,** be found.
> ANTONYMS disprove.

□ **provable** adjective.

provenance ▸ noun the place where something originally comes from.

provender ▸ noun old use food or animal fodder.

proverb ▸ noun a short saying that gives advice or states something that is generally true.

> SYNONYMS **saying,** adage, saw, maxim, axiom, motto, aphorism, epigram.

proverbial ▸ adjective **1** referred to in a proverb. **2** well known.
□ **proverbially** adverb.

provide ▸ verb (**provides, providing, provided**) **1** make something available for someone to use. **2** (**provide for**) make enough preparation for a possible event.

> SYNONYMS **1** *we will provide funds* **supply,** give, furnish, come up with, dispense, produce, yield, deliver, donate, contribute; informal fork out, lay out. **2** *he was provided with tools* **equip,** furnish, issue, supply, fit out, rig out, kit out, arm, provision; informal fix up. **3** *the test may provide the answer* **offer,** present, afford, give, add, bring, yield, impart, reveal.
> ANTONYMS refuse, withhold, deprive, neglect.

provided (or **providing**) ▸ conjunction on the condition that.

> SYNONYMS **if,** on condition that, provided that, presuming (that), assuming (that), as long as, with/on the understanding that.

providence ▸ noun **1** the protective care of God or of nature. **2** careful preparation for the future.

provident ▸ adjective careful in preparing for the future.

providential ▸ adjective happening at a favourable time.

provider ▸ noun a person who provides.

> SYNONYMS **supplier,** donor, giver, contributor, source.

province ▸ noun **1** a main administrative division of a country or empire. **2** (**the provinces**) the whole of a country outside the capital city.

> SYNONYMS **1** *a province of the Roman Empire* **territory,** region, state, department, canton, area, district, sector, zone, division. **2** (**the provinces**) **the regions,** the rest of the country, rural areas/districts, the countryside; informal the sticks, the middle of nowhere; N. Amer. informal the boondocks. **3** *that's outside my province, I'm afraid* **domain,** area, department, responsibility, sphere, world, realm, field, discipline, territory; informal bailiwick.

provincial ▸ adjective **1** relating to a province or the provinces. **2** unsophisticated or narrow-minded.

> SYNONYMS **1** *the provincial government* **regional,** state, territorial, district, local, county. **2** *provincial areas* **rural,** country, rustic, small-town, outlying, backwoods, backwater; informal one-horse. **3** *they're so dull and provincial* **unsophisticated,** narrow-minded, parochial, small-town, suburban, insular, inward-looking; N. Amer. informal corn-fed.
> ANTONYMS national, metropolitan, cosmopolitan, sophisticated, broad-minded.

▸ noun a person who lives in a province.
□ **provincialism** noun.

provision ▸ noun **1** the action of providing. **2** something supplied or provided. **3** (**provision for** or **against**) arrangements for possible future events or needs. **4** (**provisions**) supplies of food, drink, or equipment. **5** a condition or requirement in a legal document.

> SYNONYMS **1** *the provision of weapons to guerrillas* **supply,** giving, donation, equipping, furnishing, distribution. **2** *limited provision for young children* **facilities,** services, amenities,

p

resource(s), arrangements, means, funds, assistance. **3** (**provisions**) *provisions for the trip* **supplies,** food and drink, stores, groceries, foodstuff(s), rations. **4** *the provisions of the Act* **term,** requirement, specification, stipulation.

▶ verb supply with provisions.

provisional ▶ adjective arranged for the present time only, possibly to be changed later.

SYNONYMS **interim,** temporary, transitional, changeover, stopgap, short-term, fill-in, acting, working.
ANTONYMS permanent, definite.

◻ **provisionally** adverb.

proviso /pruh-vy-zoh/ ▶ noun (plural **provisos**) a condition attached to an agreement.

provocation ▶ noun action or speech that makes someone angry or causes a strong reaction.

SYNONYMS **goading,** prodding, incitement, pressure, harassment, teasing, taunting, torment; informal hassle, aggravation.

provocative ▶ adjective **1** intended to make someone annoyed or angry. **2** intended to make someone sexually interested.

SYNONYMS **annoying,** irritating, maddening, galling, insulting, offensive, inflammatory, incendiary; informal aggravating.
ANTONYMS soothing, calming.

◻ **provocatively** adverb.

provoke ▶ verb (**provokes, provoking, provoked**) **1** cause a strong reaction. **2** deliberately make someone feel angry. **3** stir someone up to do something.

SYNONYMS **1** *the plan has provoked outrage* **arouse,** produce, evoke, cause, give rise to, excite, spark off, touch off, kindle, generate, engender, instigate, result in, lead to, bring on, precipitate, prompt, trigger. **2** *he was provoked into replying* **goad,** spur, prick, sting, prod, incite, rouse, stimulate. **3** *he's dangerous if provoked* **annoy,** anger, enrage, irritate, madden, nettle; Brit. rub up the wrong way; informal aggravate, rile, needle, get/put someone's back up; Brit. informal wind up.
ANTONYMS allay, deter, pacify, appease.

provost ▶ noun **1** Brit. the head of certain university colleges and public schools. **2** N. Amer. a senior administrative officer in certain universities. **3** Scottish a mayor.

prow ▶ noun the pointed front part of a ship.

prowess ▶ noun skill or expertise.

SYNONYMS **skill,** expertise, mastery, ability, capability, capacity, talent,

aptitude, dexterity, proficiency, finesse; informal know-how.
ANTONYMS inability, ineptitude.

prowl ▶ verb move about stealthily or restlessly.

SYNONYMS **steal,** slink, skulk, sneak, stalk, creep; informal snoop.

■ **on the prowl** moving about in a stealthy way.
◻ **prowler** noun.

proximity ▶ noun nearness or closeness.
◻ **proximate** adjective.

proxy ▶ noun (plural **proxies**) **1** the authority to represent someone else. **2** a person authorized to act on behalf of another.

SYNONYMS **deputy,** representative, substitute, delegate, agent, surrogate, stand-in, go-between.

prude ▶ noun a person who is easily shocked by matters relating to sex.
◻ **prudish** adjective.

prudent ▶ adjective acting in a cautious and sensible way.

SYNONYMS **1** *it is prudent to obtain consent* **wise,** sensible, politic, judicious, shrewd, advisable. **2** *a prudent approach to borrowing* **cautious,** careful, provident, far-sighted, judicious, shrewd, circumspect, thrifty, economical.
ANTONYMS unwise, reckless, extravagant.

◻ **prudence** noun **prudently** adverb.

prudential ▶ adjective prudent.

prune¹ ▶ noun a dried plum.

prune² ▶ verb (**prunes, pruning, pruned**) **1** trim a tree or bush by cutting away dead or overgrown branches. **2** remove unwanted parts from.

SYNONYMS **1** *I pruned the roses* **cut back,** trim, clip, shear, shorten, thin, shape. **2** *staff numbers have been pruned* **reduce,** cut (back/down), pare (down), slim down, trim, downsize, axe, shrink; informal slash.
ANTONYMS increase.

▶ noun an instance of pruning.

prurient ▶ adjective having too much interest in sexual matters.
◻ **prurience** noun.

pry¹ ▶ verb (**pries, prying, pried**) ask someone unwelcome questions about their private life.

pry² = PRISE.

PS ▶ abbreviation postscript.

psalm /sahm/ ▶ noun a song or poem that praises God.

psalter /sawl-ter/ ▶ noun a copy of the Book of Psalms in the Bible.

pseudo ▶ adjective informal not genuine; false.

pseudonym ▶ noun a false name, especially one used by an author.

p

PSHE ► abbreviation personal, social, and health education (as a school subject).

psoriasis /suh-**ry**-uh-siss/ ► noun a condition in which patches of skin become red and itchy.

psych /syk/ ► verb **1** (**psych yourself up**) informal prepare yourself mentally for a difficult task. **2** (**psych someone out**) intimidate an opponent by appearing very confident or aggressive.

psyche /**sy**-ki/ ► noun the human soul, mind, or spirit.

psychedelia /sy-kuh-**dee**-li-uh/ ► noun music or art based on the experiences produced by taking psychedelic drugs.

psychedelic /sy-kuh-**del**-ik/ ► adjective **1** (of drugs) producing hallucinations. **2** having a strong, vivid colour or a swirling abstract pattern.

psychiatrist ► noun a doctor specializing in mental illness.

SYNONYMS **psychotherapist**, psychoanalyst, analyst; informal **shrink**.

psychiatry ► noun the branch of medicine concerned with mental illness.
□ **psychiatric** adjective.

psychic ► adjective **1** relating to or possessing abilities that cannot be explained by science, e.g. telepathy or clairvoyance. **2** relating to the mind.

SYNONYMS **1** *psychic powers* **supernatural**, paranormal, other-worldly, metaphysical, extrasensory, magic(al), mystic(al), occult. **2** *I'm not psychic* **clairvoyant**, telepathic.
ANTONYMS normal.

► noun a person considered or claiming to have psychic powers.

SYNONYMS *she is a psychic* **clairvoyant**, fortune teller, medium, spiritualist, telepath, mind-reader.

□ **psychically** adverb.

psycho ► noun (plural **psychos**) informal a psychopath.

psychoanalyse (US spelling **psychoanalyze**) ► verb (**psychoanalyses**, **psychoanalysing**, **psychoanalysed**) treat someone using psychoanalysis.

psychoanalysis ► noun a method of treating mental disorders by investigating the unconscious elements of the mind.
□ **psychoanalyst** noun **psychoanalytic** adjective.

psychological ► adjective **1** having to do with the mind. **2** relating to psychology.

SYNONYMS **1** *his psychological state* **mental**, emotional, inner, cognitive. **2** *her pain was psychological* (**all) in the mind**, psychosomatic, emotional,

subjective, subconscious, imaginary, irrational.
ANTONYMS physical.

□ **psychologically** adverb.

psychology ► noun **1** the scientific study of the human mind. **2** the way in which someone thinks or behaves.

SYNONYMS *the psychology of the road user* **mind**, thought processes, way of thinking, mentality, psyche, attitude(s), make-up, character, temperament; informal what makes someone tick.

□ **psychologist** noun.

psychopath ► noun a person suffering from a serious mental illness which makes them behave violently.
□ **psychopathic** adjective.

psychosis /sy-**koh**-siss/ ► noun (plural **psychoses** /sy-**koh**-seez/) a serious mental illness in which a person loses contact with external reality.

psychosomatic ► adjective (of a physical illness) caused or made worse by a mental factor such as stress.

psychotherapy ► noun the treatment of mental disorders by psychological rather than medical means.
□ **psychotherapist** noun.

psychotic /sy-**kot**-ik/ ► adjective relating to or suffering from a psychosis.

PT ► abbreviation physical training.

Pt ► abbreviation **1** Part. **2** (**pt**) pint. **3** (in scoring) point.

PTA ► abbreviation parent–teacher association.

ptarmigan /**tar**-mi-guhn/ ► noun a grouse with grey and black feathers which change to white in winter.

Pte ► abbreviation Private (in the army).

pterodactyl /te-ruh-**dak**-til/ ► noun a fossil flying reptile with a long, slender head and neck.

PTO ► abbreviation please turn over.

pub ► noun Brit. a building in which beer and other drinks are served.

SYNONYMS **bar**, inn, tavern, hostelry; Brit. public house; Austral./NZ hotel; informal watering hole; Brit. informal local, boozer; N. Amer. historical saloon.

puberty ► noun the period during which adolescents reach sexual maturity.

pubes /**pyoo**-beez/ ► noun the lower front part of the abdomen.

pubescence ► noun the time when puberty begins.
□ **pubescent** adjective & noun.

pubic ► adjective relating to the pubes or pubis.

pubis /**pyoo**-biss/ ► noun (plural **pubes** /**pyoo**-beez/) either of a pair of bones forming the two sides of the pelvis.

p

public ▸ adjective **1** having to do with the people as a whole. **2** involved in the affairs of the community: *a public figure.* **3** intended to be seen or heard by people in general. **4** provided by the government rather than an independent company.

SYNONYMS **1** *public affairs* **state,** national, government, constitutional, civic, civil, official, social, municipal, community, nationalized. **2** *by public demand* **popular,** general, common, communal, collective, shared, joint, universal, widespread. **3** *a public figure* **prominent,** well known, important, leading, eminent, distinguished, celebrated, household, famous; N. Amer. major-league. **4** *public places* **open (to the public),** communal, available, free, unrestricted, community. **5** *the news became public* **known,** published, publicized, open, obvious.

ANTONYMS private, obscure, unknown, restricted, secret.

▸ noun **1** (**the public**) ordinary people in general. **2** a group of people with a particular interest: *the reading public.*

SYNONYMS **1** *the British public* **people,** citizens, subjects, electors, electorate, voters, taxpayers, residents, inhabitants, citizenry, population, populace, community, society, country, nation, everyone. **2** *his adoring public* **audience,** spectators, followers, following, fans, devotees, admirers.

■ **in public** when other people are present. **public address system** a system of microphones and loudspeakers used to amplify speech or music. **public company** (or **public limited company**) a company whose shares are traded freely on a stock exchange. **public house** a pub. **public relations** the business of creating a good public image for an organization or famous person. **public school** (in the UK) a private fee-paying secondary school. **public sector** the part of an economy that is controlled by the state. **public transport** buses, trains, and other forms of transport that are available to the public and run on fixed routes. ▢ **publicly** adverb.

publican ▸ noun Brit. a person who owns or manages a pub.

publication ▸ noun **1** the action of publishing something. **2** a book or journal that is published.

SYNONYMS **1** *the author of this publication* **book,** volume, title, opus, tome, newspaper, paper, magazine, periodical, newsletter, bulletin, journal, report. **2** *the publication of her new book* **issuing,** publishing, printing, distribution, spreading, appearance.

publicist ▸ noun a person responsible for publicizing a product or celebrity.

publicity ▸ noun **1** attention given to someone or something by television, newspapers, etc. **2** information used for advertising or promoting a product, person, event, etc.

SYNONYMS **1** *the blaze of publicity* **public attention/interest,** media attention/interest, exposure, glare, limelight. **2** *publicity should boost sales* **promotion,** advertising, propaganda, boost, push; informal hype, ballyhoo, puff, build-up, plug.

publicize (or **publicise**) ▸ verb (**publicizes, publicizing, publicized**) **1** make something widely known. **2** give out information about a product, person, event, etc. in order to advertise or promote them.

publish ▸ verb **1** produce a book, newspaper, etc., for public sale. **2** print something in a book or newspaper.

SYNONYMS **1** *we publish novels* **issue,** bring out, produce, print. **2** *he ought to publish his views* **make known,** make public, publicize, announce, broadcast, issue, put out, distribute, spread, promulgate, disseminate, circulate, air.

▢ **publisher** noun.

puce /pyooss/ ▸ noun a dark red or purple-brown colour.

puck ▸ noun a black disc made of hard rubber, used in ice hockey.

pucker ▸ verb (**puckers, puckering, puckered**) tightly gather into wrinkles or small folds.
▸ noun a wrinkle or small fold.

pudding ▸ noun chiefly Brit. **1** a cooked sweet dish eaten at the end of a meal. **2** the dessert course of a meal. **3** a savoury dish made with suet and flour.

SYNONYMS **dessert,** sweet, last course; Brit. informal afters, pud.

puddle ▸ noun a small pool of liquid, especially of rain on the ground.

pudgy ▸ adjective (**pudgier, pudgiest**) informal rather fat.

puerile /pyoor-yl/ ▸ adjective childishly silly.

Puerto Rican /pwair-toh ree-kuhn/ ▸ noun a person from Puerto Rico.
▸ adjective relating to Puerto Rico.

puff ▸ noun **1** a small amount of air or smoke that is blown out from somewhere. **2** an act of breathing in smoke from a pipe, cigarette, or cigar. **3** a hollow piece of light pastry that is filled with cream or jam. **4** informal breath: *out of puff.*

SYNONYMS **1** *a puff of wind* **gust,** blast, flurry, rush, draught, waft, breeze, breath. **2** *he took a puff at his cigar* **pull**; informal drag, toke.

▶ verb **1** breathe in repeated short gasps. **2** move with short, noisy puffs of air or steam. **3** smoke a pipe, cigarette, or cigar. **4** (**be puffed** or **puffed out**) informal be out of breath. **5** (**puff out** or **up**) swell.

SYNONYMS **1** *he walked fast, puffing a little* **breathe heavily,** pant, blow, gasp. **2** *she puffed at her cigarette* **smoke,** draw on, drag on, suck at/on, inhale; informal toke on.

■ **puff pastry** light flaky pastry.

puffball ▶ noun a fungus with a round head that bursts to release its seeds.

puffin ▶ noun a seabird with a large brightly coloured triangular bill.

puffy ▶ adjective (**puffier, puffiest**) **1** (of a part of the body) swollen and soft. **2** softly rounded: *puffy clouds.*

pug ▶ noun a very small breed of dog with a broad flat nose and a wrinkled face.

pugilist /**pyoo**-ji-list/ ▶ noun chiefly humorous a boxer.
  □ **pugilistic** adjective.

pugnacious ▶ adjective eager or quick to argue or fight.
  □ **pugnaciously** adverb **pugnacity** noun.

puke informal ▶ verb (**pukes, puking, puked**) vomit.
▶ noun vomit.

pukka informal ▶ adjective **1** genuine. **2** socially acceptable. **3** excellent.

pulchritude /**pul**-kri-tyood/ ▶ noun literary beauty.

pull ▶ verb **1** apply force to something so as to move it towards yourself. **2** remove from a place by pulling. **3** move steadily: *the bus pulled away.* **4** strain a muscle. **5** attract someone as a customer. **6** Brit. informal attract a potential sexual partner. **7** informal bring out a weapon for use.

SYNONYMS **1** *he pulled the box towards him* **tug,** haul, drag, draw, tow, heave, jerk, wrench; informal yank. **2** *she pulled a muscle* **strain,** sprain, wrench, tear. **3** *race day pulled big crowds* **attract,** draw, bring in, pull in, lure, seduce, entice, tempt.
ANTONYMS push, repel.

▶ noun **1** an act of pulling. **2** a force, influence, or attraction. **3** a deep drink of something or a deep breath of smoke from a cigarette, pipe, etc.

SYNONYMS **1** *give the chain a pull* **tug,** jerk, heave; informal yank. **2** *the pull of the theatre* **attraction,** draw, lure, magnetism, fascination, appeal, allure. **3** *she took a pull at her beer* **gulp,** draught, drink, swallow, mouthful, slug; informal swig. **4** *a pull on a cigarette* **puff;** informal drag, toke.

■ **pull back** retreat. **pull someone's leg** deceive someone for a joke. **pull something off** informal succeed in doing something difficult. **pull out** withdraw. **pull strings** use your influence to gain an advantage. **pull yourself together** regain your self-control. **pull your weight** do your fair share of work.

pullet ▶ noun a young hen.

pulley ▶ noun (plural **pulleys**) a wheel around which a rope or chain passes, used to raise heavy objects.

pullover ▶ noun a knitted garment for the upper body.

pulmonary /**pul**-muh-nuh-ri/ ▶ adjective relating to the lungs.

pulp ▶ noun **1** a soft, wet mass of crushed material. **2** the soft fleshy part of a fruit.

SYNONYMS **1** *he ground it into a pulp* **mush,** mash, paste, purée, slop, slush, mulch. **2** *the sweet pulp on cocoa seeds* **flesh,** marrow, meat.

▶ verb crush into a pulp.

SYNONYMS *pulp the gooseberries* **mash,** purée, cream, crush, press, liquidize.

▶ adjective (of writing) popular and badly written: *pulp fiction.*
  □ **pulpy** adjective.

pulpit ▶ noun a raised platform in a church from which the preacher gives a sermon.

pulsar ▶ noun a star that gives off regular rapid pulses of radio waves.

pulsate ▶ verb (**pulsates, pulsating, pulsated**) **1** expand and contract with strong regular movements. **2** produce a regular throbbing sensation or sound.
  □ **pulsation** noun.

pulse[1] ▶ noun **1** the regular beat of the blood as it is pumped around the body. **2** a single vibration or short burst of sound, electric current, light, etc. **3** a regular musical rhythm.

SYNONYMS **1** *the pulse in her neck* **heartbeat,** heart rate. **2** *the pulse of the engine* **rhythm,** beat, tempo, pounding, throbbing, thudding, drumming. **3** *pulses of ultrasound* **burst,** blast, surge.

▶ verb (**pulses, pulsing, pulsed**) pulsate.

SYNONYMS *music pulsed through the building* **throb,** pulsate, vibrate, beat, pound, thud, thump, drum, reverberate, echo.

pulse[2] ▶ noun the edible seeds of various plants, such as lentils or beans.

pulverize (or **pulverise**) ▶ verb (**pulverizes, pulverizing, pulverized**) **1** crush into fine particles. **2** informal completely defeat.

puma ▶ noun a large American wild cat with a yellowish-brown or grey coat.

pumice /**pum**-iss/ ▶ noun a very light rock formed from lava.

p

pummel ▸ verb (pummels, pummelling, pummelled; US spelling pummels, pummeling, pummeled) hit repeatedly with the fists.

pump¹ ▸ noun a device used to move liquids and gases or to force air into inflatable objects.
▸ verb 1 move with a pump, or with something that works like a pump. 2 fill something with liquid, gas, etc. 3 move something up and down energetically. 4 informal try to get information from someone.

> SYNONYMS 1 *they pumped air down the tube* **force,** drive, push, inject, suck, draw. 2 *she pumped up the tyre* **inflate,** blow up, fill up, swell, enlarge, distend, expand, dilate, puff up. 3 *blood was pumping from his leg* **spurt,** spout, squirt, jet, surge, spew, gush, stream, flow, pour, spill, well, cascade.

■ **pump iron** informal exercise with weights.

pump² ▸ noun 1 chiefly N. English a plimsoll. 2 a light shoe for dancing.

pumpkin ▸ noun 1 a large round fruit with a thick orange skin and edible flesh. 2 Brit. = SQUASH².

pun ▸ noun a joke that uses a word or words with more than one meaning.
▸ verb (puns, punning, punned) make a pun.

punch¹ ▸ verb 1 hit with the fist. 2 press a button or key on a machine.

> SYNONYMS *Jim punched him in the face* **hit,** strike, thump, jab, smash; informal sock, slug, biff, bop; Brit. informal stick one on, slosh; N. Amer. informal boff, bust; Austral./NZ informal quilt.

▸ noun 1 a blow with the fist. 2 informal the power to impress someone.

> SYNONYMS *a punch on the nose* **blow,** hit, knock, thump, box, jab, clip; informal sock, slug, biff, bop; N. Amer. informal boff, bust.

■ **punch-drunk** 1 dazed by a series of punches. 2 very confused or shocked. **punch-up** informal a fight.

punch² ▸ noun a device for cutting holes in paper, metal, leather, etc.
▸ verb pierce a hole in something.

> SYNONYMS *he punched her ticket* **perforate,** puncture, pierce, prick, hole, spike, skewer.

punch³ ▸ noun a drink made from wine or spirits mixed with water, fruit juices, and spices.

punchbag ▸ noun Brit. a heavy bag hung on a rope, used for punching as exercise or training.

punchline ▸ noun the final part of a joke that makes it funny.

punchy ▸ adjective (punchier, punchiest) effective; forceful.

punctilious ▸ adjective showing great attention to detail or correct behaviour.

punctual ▸ adjective happening or doing something at the agreed or proper time.

> SYNONYMS **on time,** prompt, on schedule, in (good) time; informal on the dot. ANTONYMS late.

□ **punctuality** noun **punctually** adverb.

punctuate ▸ verb (punctuates, punctuating, punctuated) 1 interrupt something at intervals. 2 add punctuation marks to a piece of writing.

> SYNONYMS **break up,** interrupt, intersperse, pepper, sprinkle, scatter.

punctuation ▸ noun the marks, such as full stop, comma, and brackets, used in writing to separate sentences and make meaning clear.

puncture ▸ noun a small hole caused by a sharp object.

> SYNONYMS 1 *the tyre developed a puncture* **hole,** perforation, rupture, cut, gash, slit, leak. 2 *my car has a puncture* **flat tyre;** informal flat.

▸ verb (punctures, puncturing, punctured) make a puncture in.

> SYNONYMS *he punctured the balloon* **prick,** pierce, stab, rupture, perforate, cut, slit, deflate.

pundit ▸ noun a person who frequently gives opinions about a subject in public.

pungent ▸ adjective 1 having a sharply strong taste or smell. 2 (of remarks or humour) having a strong effect.
□ **pungency** noun.

punish ▸ verb 1 make someone experience something unpleasant because they have done something criminal or wrong. 2 treat harshly or unfairly.

> SYNONYMS 1 *they punished their children* **discipline,** penalize, correct, sentence, teach someone a lesson; informal come down on (like a ton of bricks), have someone's guts for garters; dated chastise. 2 *higher charges would punish the poor* **disadvantage,** handicap, hurt, penalize. 3 (**punishing**) *a punishing trek in tropical heat* **arduous,** demanding, taxing, strenuous, rigorous, stressful, trying, heavy, difficult, tough, exhausting, tiring, gruelling.

□ **punishable** adjective.

punishment ▸ noun 1 an unpleasant experience imposed on someone because they have done something criminal or wrong. 2 the action of punishing. 3 harsh or rough treatment.

> SYNONYMS **penalty,** sanction, penance, discipline, forfeit, sentence.

p

punitive /pyoo-ni-tiv/ ▶ adjective intended as punishment.

SYNONYMS **penal,** disciplinary, corrective, retributive, retaliatory.

Punjabi ▶ noun (plural **Punjabis**) **1** a person from Punjab, a region of NW India and Pakistan. **2** the language of Punjab.

punk ▶ noun **1** (also **punk rock**) a loud and aggressive form of rock music. **2** (also **punk rocker**) a person who likes or plays punk music. **3** N. Amer. informal a worthless person.

punnet ▶ noun Brit. a small container for fruit or vegetables.

punt¹ ▶ noun a long, narrow boat with a flat bottom, moved forward with a long pole.
▶ verb travel in a punt.

punt² ▶ verb kick a ball after it has dropped from the hands and before it reaches the ground.
▶ noun a kick of this kind.

punt³ ▶ noun Brit. informal a bet.

punt⁴ /puunt/ ▶ noun the former basic unit of money in the Republic of Ireland.

punter ▶ noun Brit. informal **1** a person who gambles. **2** a customer or client.

puny ▶ adjective (**punier, puniest**) **1** small and weak. **2** not very impressive.

SYNONYMS **1** *a puny boy* **small,** weak, feeble, slight, undersized, stunted; informal weedy. **2** *their puny efforts* **pitiful,** pitiable, miserable, sorry, meagre, paltry; informal pathetic, measly.
ANTONYMS sturdy, substantial.

pup ▶ noun **1** a young dog. **2** a young wolf, seal, rat, or other animal.

pupa /pyoo-puh/ ▶ noun (plural **pupae** /pyoo-pee/) an insect in the form between larva and adult.
□ **pupal** adjective.

pupate ▶ verb (**pupates, pupating, pupated**) become a pupa.

pupil¹ ▶ noun a person who is being taught.

SYNONYMS **1** *former pupils of the school* **student,** scholar, schoolchild, schoolboy, schoolgirl. **2** *the guru's pupils* **disciple,** follower, student, protégé, apprentice, trainee, novice.
ANTONYMS teacher.

pupil² ▶ noun the dark circular opening in the centre of the iris of the eye.

puppet ▶ noun **1** a model of a person or animal which can be moved either by strings or by a hand inside it. **2** a person under the control of someone else.

SYNONYMS **1** *a show with puppets* **marionette,** glove puppet, finger puppet. **2** *a puppet of the government* **pawn,** tool, instrument, cat's paw, poodle, mouthpiece, stooge.

□ **puppeteer** noun **puppetry** noun.

puppy ▶ noun (plural **puppies**) a young dog.
■ **puppy fat** fat on a child's body that disappears as they grow up. **puppy love** strong but short-lived love.

purblind ▶ adjective literary **1** partially sighted. **2** lacking awareness or understanding.

purchase ▶ verb (**purchases, purchasing, purchased**) buy.

SYNONYMS *we purchased new software* **buy,** acquire, obtain, pick up, procure, pay for, invest in; informal get hold of, score.
ANTONYMS sell.

▶ noun **1** the action of buying. **2** a thing bought. **3** firm contact or grip.

SYNONYMS **1** *he's happy with his purchase* **acquisition,** buy, investment, order, bargain, shopping, goods. **2** *he could get no purchase on the wall* **grip,** grasp, hold, foothold, toehold, anchorage, support, traction, leverage.
ANTONYMS sale.

□ **purchaser** noun.

purdah ▶ noun the practice in certain Muslim and Hindu societies of screening women from men or strangers.

pure ▶ adjective **1** not mixed with any other substance or material: *pure wool.* **2** not containing any harmful or polluting substances. **3** innocent or morally good. **4** sheer; nothing but: *a shout of pure anger.* **5** theoretical rather than practical: *pure mathematics.* **6** (of a sound) perfectly in tune and with a clear tone.

SYNONYMS **1** *pure gold* **unadulterated,** undiluted, sterling, solid, 100%. **2** *the air is so pure* **clean,** clear, fresh, sparkling, unpolluted, uncontaminated, untainted. **3** *pure in body and mind* **virtuous,** moral, good, righteous, honourable, reputable, wholesome, clean, honest, upright, upstanding, exemplary, chaste, decent, worthy, noble; informal squeaky clean. **4** *three hours of pure magic* **sheer,** utter, absolute, out-and-out, complete, total, perfect.
ANTONYMS adulterated, polluted, immoral, practical.

purée /pyoor-ay/ ▶ noun a mass of crushed fruit or vegetables.
▶ verb (**purées, puréeing, puréed**) make a purée of.

purely ▶ adverb entirely; exclusively.

SYNONYMS **entirely,** wholly, exclusively, solely, only, just, merely.

purgative ▶ adjective having a strong laxative effect.
▶ noun a laxative.

purgatory ▸ noun (plural **purgatories**) (in Roman Catholic belief) a place inhabited by the souls of sinners who are making up for their sins before going to heaven. □ **purgatorial** adjective.

purge ▸ verb (**purges**, **purging**, **purged**) rid someone or something of undesirable or harmful people or things.

> SYNONYMS **1** *this purges the system of impurities* **cleanse**, clear, purify, rid, empty, strip, scour. **2** *the founders were purged from the firm* **remove**, get rid of, eliminate, clear out, sweep out, expel, eject, evict, dismiss, sack, oust, axe, depose, root out, weed out.

▸ noun an act of purging.

> SYNONYMS **removal**, elimination, expulsion, ejection, exclusion, eviction, dismissal, sacking, ousting.

purify ▸ verb (**purifies**, **purifying**, **purified**) make something pure.

> SYNONYMS **clean**, cleanse, refine, decontaminate, filter, clear, freshen, deodorize, sanitize, disinfect, sterilize.

□ **purification** noun.

> ✔ i not e: purify.

purist ▸ noun a person who insists on following traditional rules, especially in language or style.
□ **purism** noun.

puritan ▸ noun **1** (**Puritan**) a member of a group of English Protestants in the 16th and 17th centuries who tried to simplify forms of worship. **2** a person with strong moral beliefs who is critical of the behaviour of other people.
□ **puritanical** adjective.

purity ▸ noun the state of being pure.

> SYNONYMS **1** *the purity of our tap water* **cleanness**, freshness, cleanliness, wholesomeness. **2** *they sought purity in a foul world* **virtue**, morality, goodness, righteousness, piety, honour, honesty, integrity, decency, innocence.

purl ▸ adjective (of a knitting stitch) made by putting the needle through the front of the stitch from right to left.
▸ verb knit with a purl stitch.

purlieus /per-lyooz/ ▸ plural noun literary the area around or near a place.

purloin ▸ verb formal steal.

purple ▸ adjective of a colour between red and blue.
▸ noun a purple colour.
■ **purple patch** informal a run of success or good luck. **purple prose** prose that is too elaborate.

purport ▸ verb /per-**port**/ appear or claim to be or do.

▸ noun /**per**-port/ the meaning or purpose of something.

purpose ▸ noun **1** the reason for which something is done or for which something exists. **2** strong determination.

> SYNONYMS **1** *the purpose of his visit* **motive**, motivation, grounds, occasion, reason, point, basis, justification. **2** *their purpose was to subvert the economy* **intention**, aim, object, objective, goal, plan, ambition, aspiration. **3** *the original purpose of the porch* **function**, role, use. **4** *they started with some purpose* **determination**, resolution, resolve, enthusiasm, ambition, motivation, commitment, conviction, dedication; informal get-up-and-go.

■ **on purpose** intentionally.

purposeful ▸ adjective **1** having or showing determination. **2** having a purpose.

> SYNONYMS **determined**, resolute, steadfast, single-minded, committed. ANTONYMS aimless.

□ **purposefully** adverb.

purposely ▸ adverb on purpose.

> SYNONYMS **deliberately**, intentionally, on purpose, wilfully, knowingly, consciously.

purposive ▸ adjective having or done with a purpose.

purr ▸ verb **1** (of a cat) make a low continuous sound expressing contentment. **2** (of an engine) run smoothly while making a similar sound.
▸ noun a purring sound.

purse ▸ noun **1** chiefly Brit. a small pouch for carrying money. **2** N. Amer. a handbag. **3** money for spending. **4** a sum of money given as a prize.

> SYNONYMS **1** *the money fell out of her purse* **wallet**, money bag; N. Amer. change purse, billfold. **2** *a woman's purse* **handbag**, shoulder bag, clutch bag; N. Amer. pocketbook. **3** *the fight will net him a $75,000 purse* **prize**, reward, winnings, stake(s).

▸ verb (**purses**, **pursing**, **pursed**) form the lips into a tight round shape.

> SYNONYMS *he pursed his lips* **press together**, compress, tighten, pucker, pout.

purser ▸ noun a ship's officer who keeps the accounts.

pursuance ▸ noun formal the carrying out of a plan or action.

pursuant ▸ adverb (**pursuant to**) formal in accordance with.

pursue ▸ verb (**pursues**, **pursuing**, **pursued**) **1** follow someone or something in order to catch or attack them. **2** try to achieve

p

a goal. **3** follow a course of action.
4 continue to investigate or discuss a topic.

SYNONYMS **1** *I pursued him down the garden* **follow,** run after, chase, hunt, stalk, track, trail, hound. **2** *pursue the goal of political union* **strive for,** work towards, seek, search for, aim at/for, aspire to. **3** *she pursued a political career* **engage in,** be occupied in, practise, follow, conduct, ply, take up, undertake, carry on, continue, take further, stick with/at.
ANTONYMS avoid, shun.

□ **pursuer** noun.

✔ **pur-**, not **per-**: **pur**sue.

pursuit ▸ noun **1** the action of pursuing someone or something. **2** a leisure or sporting activity.

SYNONYMS **1** *the pursuit of profit* **striving for,** quest after/for, search for. **2** *a worthwhile pursuit* **activity,** hobby, pastime, diversion, recreation, amusement, occupation.

purulent /pyoor-uh-luhnt/ ▸ adjective made up of or giving out pus.

purvey ▸ verb formal provide or supply food or drink as a business.
□ **purveyor** noun.

purview ▸ noun formal the range of something's influence or concerns.

pus ▸ noun a thick yellowish or greenish liquid produced in infected body tissue.

push ▸ verb **1** apply force to something so as to move it away from yourself. **2** move part of your body into a particular position. **3** move by using force. **4** encourage someone to work hard. **5** (**push for**) repeatedly demand something. **6** informal promote the use, sale, or acceptance of. **7** informal sell an illegal drug.

SYNONYMS **1** *she tried to push him away* **shove,** thrust, propel, send, drive, force, prod, poke, nudge, elbow, shoulder, sweep, ram. **2** *she pushed her way into the flat* **force,** shove, thrust, squeeze, jostle, elbow, shoulder, bundle, hustle, work, inch. **3** *he pushed the panic button* **press,** depress, hold down, squeeze, operate, activate. **4** *don't push her to join in* **urge,** press, pressure, pressurize, force, coerce, nag; informal lean on, twist someone's arm.
ANTONYMS pull.

▸ noun **1** an act of pushing. **2** a great effort: *one last push.*

SYNONYMS **1** *I felt a push in the back* **shove,** thrust, nudge, bump, jolt, prod, poke. **2** *the army's eastward push* **advance,** drive, thrust, charge, attack, assault, onslaught, onrush, offensive.

□ **pusher** noun.

pushbike ▸ noun Brit. informal a bicycle.

pushchair ▸ noun Brit. a folding chair on wheels, in which a young child can be pushed along.

pushover ▸ noun informal **1** a person who is easy to influence or defeat. **2** a thing that is easily done.

pushy ▸ adjective (**pushier, pushiest**) too assertive or ambitious.

pusillanimous ▸ adjective weak or cowardly.
□ **pusillanimity** noun.

pussy (or **puss**) ▸ noun (plural **pussies** or **pusses**) (also **pussycat**) informal a cat.
■ **pussy willow** a willow with soft, fluffy catkins that appear before the leaves.

pussyfoot ▸ verb (**pussyfoots, pussyfooting, pussyfooted**) act very cautiously.

pustule ▸ noun a small blister on the skin containing pus.
□ **pustular** adjective.

put ▸ verb (**puts, putting, put**) **1** move something into a particular position. **2** bring into a particular state or condition: *she tried to put me at ease.* **3** (**put something on** or **on to**) make a person or thing subject to something. **4** give a value, figure, or limit to. **5** express something in a particular way. **6** (of a ship) go in a particular direction: *the boat put out to sea.* **7** throw a shot or weight as a sport.

SYNONYMS **1** *she put the parcel on a chair* **place,** set, lay, deposit, position, leave, plant; informal stick, dump, park, plonk, pop; N. Amer. informal plunk. **2** *she put it bluntly* **express,** word, phrase, frame, formulate, render, convey, state.

■ **put someone/thing down 1** end a riot by using force. **2** kill a sick, old, or injured animal. **3** pay a sum as a deposit. **4** informal criticize someone in public. **put someone/thing off 1** postpone something. **2** make someone feel dislike or lose enthusiasm. **3** distract someone. **put something on 1** organize an event. **2** gain weight. **3** adopt an expression, accent, etc. **put someone out** cause someone trouble or inconvenience. **put someone/thing up 1** present, provide, or offer something. **2** give someone a place to stay. **put someone up to** informal encourage someone to do something wrong. **put up with** tolerate.

putative /pyoo-tuh-tiv/ ▸ adjective formal generally considered to be.

putrefy ▸ verb (**putrefies, putrefying, putrefied**) decay or rot and produce a very unpleasant smell.
□ **putrefaction** noun.

putrid ▸ adjective **1** decaying or rotting and producing a very unpleasant smell. **2** informal very unpleasant.

p

putsch /puuch/ ▶ noun a violent attempt to overthrow a government.

putt ▶ verb (**putts, putting, putted**) hit a golf ball gently so that it rolls into or near a hole.
▶ noun a stroke of this kind.
■ **putting green** a smooth area of short grass surrounding a hole on a golf course.

putter[1] ▶ noun a golf club designed for putting.

putter[2] ▶ noun the rapid irregular sound of a small petrol engine.
▶ verb (**putters, puttering, puttered**) move with this sound.

putty ▶ noun a soft paste that hardens as it dries, used for sealing glass in window frames.

puzzle ▶ verb (**puzzles, puzzling, puzzled**) **1** make someone feel confused because they cannot understand something. **2** think hard about something difficult to understand.

> SYNONYMS **1** *her decision puzzled me* **baffle,** perplex, bewilder, confuse, bemuse, mystify, nonplus; informal stump, beat. **2** (**puzzling**) *a puzzling remark* **baffling,** perplexing, bewildering, confusing, complicated, unclear, mysterious, enigmatic.

▶ noun **1** a game, toy, or problem designed to test mental skills or knowledge. **2** a person or thing that is difficult to understand.

> SYNONYMS *the poem has always been a puzzle* **enigma,** mystery, paradox, conundrum, poser, riddle, problem.

□ **puzzlement** noun **puzzler** noun.

PVC ▶ abbreviation polyvinyl chloride, a sort of plastic.

pygmy (or **pigmy**) ▶ noun (plural **pygmies**) **1** (**Pygmy**) a member of a race of very short people living in parts of Africa. **2** a very small person or thing.
▶ adjective very small.

pyjamas (US spelling **pajamas**) ▶ plural noun a loose jacket and trousers for sleeping in.

pylon ▶ noun a tall tower-like structure for carrying electricity cables.

pyramid ▶ noun a very large stone structure with a square or triangular base and sloping sides that meet in a point at the top.
□ **pyramidal** adjective.

pyre ▶ noun a large pile of wood for the ritual burning of a dead body.

pyrites /py-ry-teez/ (or **pyrite**) ▶ noun a shiny yellow mineral that is a compound of iron and sulphur.

pyromania ▶ noun a strong urge to set fire to things.
□ **pyromaniac** noun.

pyrotechnics ▶ plural noun **1** a firework display. **2** the art of making fireworks or staging firework displays.
□ **pyrotechnic** adjective.

pyrrhic /pir-rik/ ▶ adjective (of a victory) won at too great a cost to have been worthwhile.

python ▶ noun a large snake which crushes its prey.

p

Qq

Q (or **q**) ▸ noun (plural **Qs** or **Q's**) the seventeenth letter of the alphabet.
▸ abbreviation question.

Qatari /ka-**tah**-ri/ ▸ noun a person from Qatar, a country in the Persian Gulf.
▸ adjective relating to Qatar.

QC ▸ abbreviation Law Queen's Counsel.

QED ▸ abbreviation used to say that something proves the truth of your claim. ORIGIN short for Latin *quod erat demonstrandum* 'which was to be demonstrated'.

qt ▸ abbreviation quarts.

qua /kway, kwah/ ▸ conjunction formal in the role or capacity of.

quack¹ ▸ noun the harsh sound made by a duck.
▸ verb make this sound.

quack² ▸ noun 1 an unqualified person who claims to have medical knowledge. 2 Brit. informal a doctor.

quad ▸ noun 1 a quadrangle. 2 a quadruplet.
■ **quad bike** a motorcycle with four large tyres, for off-road use.

quadrangle ▸ noun 1 a square or rectangular courtyard enclosed by buildings. 2 a four-sided geometrical figure.
▫ **quadrangular** adjective.

quadrant ▸ noun 1 a quarter of a circle or of a circle's circumference. 2 historical an instrument for measuring angles in astronomy and navigation.

quadraphonic (or **quadrophonic**) /kwod-ruh-**fon**-ik/ ▸ adjective (of sound reproduction) using four channels.

quadratic /kwod-**rat**-ik/ ▸ adjective Maths involving the second and no higher power of an unknown quantity.

quadriceps /**kwod**-ri-seps/ ▸ noun (plural **quadriceps**) a large muscle at the front of the thigh.

quadrilateral ▸ noun a four-sided figure.
▸ adjective having four straight sides.

quadrille /kwod-**ril**/ ▸ noun a square dance performed by four couples.

quadriplegia /kwod-ri-**plee**-juh/ ▸ noun paralysis of all four limbs.

▫ **quadriplegic** adjective & noun.

quadruped /**kwod**-ruu-ped/ ▸ noun an animal which has four feet.

quadruple ▸ adjective 1 consisting of four parts. 2 four times as much or as many.
▸ verb (**quadruples**, **quadrupling**, **quadrupled**) multiply by four.

quadruplet ▸ noun each of four children born at one birth.

quaff /kwoff/ ▸ verb drink a large amount of something quickly.

quagmire /**kwog**-my-er/ ▸ noun a soft, wet area of land.

quail¹ ▸ noun (plural **quail** or **quails**) a small short-tailed game bird.

quail² ▸ verb feel or show fear.

quaint ▸ adjective attractively unusual or old-fashioned.

> SYNONYMS 1 *a quaint town* **picturesque**, charming, sweet, attractive, old-fashioned, old-world; Brit. twee; N. Amer. cunning. 2 *quaint customs* **unusual**, curious, eccentric, quirky, bizarre, whimsical, unconventional; informal offbeat.
> ANTONYMS ugly, ordinary.

▫ **quaintly** adverb.

quake ▸ verb (**quakes**, **quaking**, **quaked**) 1 (especially of the earth) shake or tremble. 2 shudder with fear.

> SYNONYMS **shake**, tremble, quiver, shudder, sway, rock, wobble, move, heave, convulse.

▸ noun informal an earthquake.

Quaker ▸ noun a member of the Religious Society of Friends, a Christian movement devoted to peaceful principles and rejecting set forms of worship.
▫ **Quakerism** noun.

qualification ▸ noun 1 the action of qualifying. 2 a pass of an exam or an official completion of a course. 3 a quality that makes someone suitable for a job or activity. 4 a statement that limits the meaning of another statement.

> SYNONYMS 1 *a teaching qualification* **certificate**, diploma, degree, licence,

q

document, warrant. **2** *I can't accept it without qualification* **modification**, limitation, reservation, stipulation, alteration, amendment, revision, moderation, mitigation, condition, proviso, caveat.

qualify ▸ verb (**qualifies, qualifying, qualified**) **1** meet the necessary standard or conditions to be able to do or receive something. **2** become officially recognized as able to do a particular job. **3** add something to a statement to limit its meaning. **4** Grammar (of a word or phrase) give a quality to another word.

> SYNONYMS **1** *I qualify for free travel* **be eligible,** meet the requirements, be entitled to, be permitted. **2** *they qualify as refugees* **count,** be considered, be designated, be eligible. **3** *she qualified as a solicitor* **be certified,** be licensed, pass, graduate, succeed. **4** *the course qualified them to teach* **authorize,** empower, allow, permit, license. **5** (**qualified**) *a qualified engineer* **certified,** certificated, chartered, licensed, professional. **6** *they qualified their findings* **modify,** limit, restrict, make conditional, moderate, temper, modulate, mitigate. **7** (**qualified**) *qualified approval* **limited,** conditional, restricted, contingent, circumscribed, guarded, equivocal, modified, adapted, amended, adjusted, moderated, reduced.

□ **qualifier** noun.

qualitative /kwol-i-tuh-tiv/ ▸ adjective relating to or measured by quality.
□ **qualitatively** adverb.

quality ▸ noun (plural **qualities**) **1** the standard of something as measured against other similar things; how good or bad something is. **2** general excellence. **3** a distinctive characteristic.

> SYNONYMS **1** *a poor quality of signal* **standard,** grade, class, calibre, condition, character, nature, form, rank, value, level. **2** *work of such quality* **excellence,** superiority, merit, worth, value, virtue, calibre, distinction. **3** *her good qualities* **feature,** trait, attribute, characteristic, point, aspect, facet, side, property.

qualm /kwahm/ ▸ noun a feeling of doubt about what you are doing.

quandary /kwon-duh-ri/ ▸ noun (plural **quandaries**) a state of uncertainty.

quango /kwang-goh/ ▸ noun (plural **quangos**) disapproving an organization that works independently but with support from the government.

quantify ▸ verb (**quantifies, quantifying, quantified**) express or measure the quantity of.
□ **quantifiable** adjective.

quantitative /kwon-ti-tuh-tiv/ ▸ adjective relating to or measured by quantity.
□ **quantitatively** adverb.

quantity ▸ noun (plural **quantities**) **1** a certain amount or number. **2** the property of something that can be measured in number, amount, size, or weight. **3** a large number or amount.

> SYNONYMS **amount,** total, aggregate, sum, quota, mass, weight, volume, bulk.

■ **quantity surveyor** Brit. a person who calculates the amount and cost of materials needed for building work.

quantum /kwon-tuhm/ ▸ noun (plural **quanta**) Physics a distinct quantity of energy corresponding to that involved in the absorption or emission of energy by an atom.

■ **quantum leap** a sudden large increase or advance. **quantum mechanics** the branch of physics concerned with describing the behaviour of subatomic particles in terms of quanta.

quarantine ▸ noun a period of time when an animal or person that may have a disease is kept in isolation.
▸ verb (**quarantines, quarantining, quarantined**) put in quarantine.

quark /kwark/ ▸ noun any of a group of subatomic particles which carry a very small electric charge and are believed to form protons, neutrons, and other particles.

quarrel ▸ noun **1** an angry argument or disagreement. **2** a reason for disagreement.

> SYNONYMS *they had a quarrel* **argument,** disagreement, squabble, fight, dispute, wrangle, clash, altercation, feud; informal tiff, slanging match, run-in; Brit. informal row, bust-up.
> ANTONYMS agreement, harmony.

▸ verb (**quarrels, quarrelling, quarrelled**; US spelling **quarrels, quarreling, quarreled**) **1** have a quarrel. **2** (**quarrel with**) disagree with.

> SYNONYMS *don't quarrel over it* **argue,** fight, disagree, fall out, differ, be at odds, bicker, squabble, cross swords; Brit. informal row.
> ANTONYMS agree, get on.

quarrelsome ▸ adjective tending to quarrel with people.

quarry[1] ▸ noun (plural **quarries**) a place where stone or other materials are dug out of the earth.
▸ verb (**quarries, quarrying, quarried**) dig out stone or other materials from a quarry.

quarry[2] ▸ noun (plural **quarries**) an animal or person that is being hunted or chased.

> SYNONYMS **prey,** victim, object, goal, target, kill, game, prize.

quart ▸ noun a unit of liquid capacity equal to a quarter of a gallon or two pints, in Britain equal to 1.13 litres and in the US to 0.94 litre.

quarter ▸ noun **1** each of four equal parts of something. **2** a period of three months. **3** a quarter of an hour; fifteen minutes. **4** one fourth of a pound weight, equal to 4 oz avoirdupois. **5** a part of a town. **6** a US or Canadian coin worth 25 cents. **7** one fourth of a hundredweight, in Britain equal to 28 lb and in the US equal to 25 lb. **8** (**quarters**) rooms to live in. **9** a person or area seen as the source of something: *help from an unexpected quarter*. **10** mercy shown to an opponent.
▸ verb (**quarters, quartering, quartered**) **1** divide into quarters. **2** (**be quartered**) be provided with rooms to live in. **3** historical cut the body of an executed person into four parts.
■ **quarter-final** a match of a competition coming before the semi-final.

quarterdeck ▸ noun the part of a ship's upper deck near the stern.

quarterly ▸ adjective & adverb produced or happening once every quarter of a year.
▸ noun (plural **quarterlies**) a publication produced four times a year.

quartermaster ▸ noun an army officer in charge of accommodation and supplies.

quartet ▸ noun **1** a group of four people playing music or singing together. **2** a piece of music for a quartet. **3** a set of four.

quarto /kwor-toh/ ▸ noun (plural **quartos**) a size of page for a book, resulting from folding a sheet into four leaves.

quartz ▸ noun a hard mineral consisting of silica.

quasar /kway-zar/ ▸ noun (in astronomy) a kind of galaxy which gives off enormous amounts of energy.

quash ▸ verb **1** officially declare that a legal decision is no longer valid. **2** put an end to.

> SYNONYMS **1** *he may quash the sentence* **cancel**, reverse, rescind, repeal, revoke, retract, countermand, withdraw, overturn, overrule. **2** *we want to quash these rumours* **stop**, put an end to, stamp out, crush, put down, check, curb, nip in the bud, squash, suppress, stifle. ANTONYMS validate, encourage, perpetuate.

quasi- /kway-zy/ ▸ combining form seemingly; as if: *quasi-scientific*.

quatrain /kwot-rayn/ ▸ noun a poem or verse of four lines.

quaver ▸ verb (**quavers, quavering, quavered**) (of a voice) tremble.
▸ noun **1** a tremble in a voice. **2** chiefly Brit. a musical note that lasts as long as half a crotchet.

□ **quavery** adjective.

quay /kee/ ▸ noun a platform in a harbour for loading and unloading ships.

quayside ▸ noun a quay and the area around it.

queasy ▸ adjective (**queasier, queasiest**) feeling sick.
□ **queasiness** noun.

queen ▸ noun **1** the female ruler of an independent state. **2** (also **queen consort**) a king's wife. **3** the best or most important woman or thing in a particular group. **4** a playing card ranking next below a king. **5** the most powerful chess piece, able to move in any direction. **6** a female that lays eggs for a colony of ants, bees, wasps, or termites. **7** informal a homosexual man who behaves like a woman.

> SYNONYMS **monarch**, sovereign, ruler, head of state, Crown, Her Majesty.

■ **queen mother** the widow of a king who is also mother of the current king or queen.
□ **queenly** adjective.

Queensberry Rules ▸ plural noun the standard rules of boxing.

queer ▸ adjective **1** strange; odd. **2** disapproving (of a man) homosexual.

> SYNONYMS **odd**, strange, unusual, funny, peculiar, curious, bizarre, weird, uncanny, freakish, eerie, unnatural, abnormal, anomalous; informal spooky. ANTONYMS normal.

▸ noun disapproving a homosexual man.

quell ▸ verb **1** put an end to a rebellion by force. **2** suppress a feeling.

quench ▸ verb **1** satisfy thirst by drinking. **2** put out a fire.

querulous /kwe-ruu-luhss/ ▸ adjective complaining in an irritable way.
□ **querulously** adverb.

query ▸ noun (plural **queries**) a question, especially one expressing a doubt about something.

> SYNONYMS **1** *we can answer any queries* **question**, enquiry. **2** *there was a query as to who owned the hotel* **doubt**, uncertainty, question (mark), reservation.

▸ verb (**queries, querying, queried**) ask a question expressing doubt about something.

> SYNONYMS **1** *'Why do that?' queried Isobel* **ask**, enquire, question; Brit. informal quiz. **2** *folk may query his credentials* **challenge**, question, dispute, doubt, have suspicions about, distrust. ANTONYMS accept, trust.

quest ▸ noun a long or difficult search.

> SYNONYMS **1** *their quest for her killer* **search**, hunt, pursuance of. **2** *Sir*

q

Galahad's quest **expedition,** journey, voyage, trek, travels, odyssey, adventure, exploration, search, crusade, mission, pilgrimage.
▶ **verb** search for something.

question ▶ **noun 1** a sentence worded so as to obtain information. **2** doubt, or the raising of a doubt about something. **3** a problem needing to be solved. **4** a matter depending on stated conditions: *it's only a question of time.*

SYNONYMS **1** *please answer my question* **enquiry,** query, interrogation. **2** *there is no question that he is ill* **doubt,** dispute, argument, debate, uncertainty, reservation. **3** *the political questions of the day* **issue,** matter, topic, business, problem, concern, debate, argument, dispute, controversy.
ANTONYMS answer, certainty.

▶ **verb 1** ask someone questions. **2** express doubt about something.

SYNONYMS **1** *the magistrate questions the suspect* **interrogate,** cross-examine, cross-question, quiz, interview, debrief, examine; informal grill, pump. **2** *she questioned his motives* **query,** challenge, dispute, cast aspersions on, doubt, suspect.

■ **out of the question** not possible. **question mark** a punctuation mark (?) indicating a question.
□ **questioner** noun.

questionable ▶ **adjective** likely to be wrong.

SYNONYMS **suspicious,** suspect, dubious, irregular, odd, strange, murky, dark, unsavoury, disreputable; informal funny, fishy, shady, iffy; Brit. informal dodgy.
ANTONYMS honest.

questionnaire ▶ **noun** a set of questions written for a survey.

SYNONYMS **question sheet,** survey form, opinion poll, test, quiz.

✔ There are two **n**s: questio**nn**aire.

queue ▶ **noun** a line of people or vehicles waiting their turn for something.

SYNONYMS **row,** column, file, chain, string, procession, waiting list; N. Amer. line, wait list.

▶ **verb** (**queues, queuing** or **queueing, queued**) wait in a queue.
■ **queue-jump** Brit. move forward out of turn in a queue.

quibble ▶ **noun** a minor objection.
▶ **verb** (**quibbles, quibbling, quibbled**) raise a minor objection.

quiche /keesh/ ▶ **noun** a baked flan with a savoury filling thickened with eggs.

quick ▶ **adjective 1** moving fast. **2** lasting or taking a short time. **3** with little or no delay. **4** intelligent. **5** (of temper) easily roused.

SYNONYMS **1** *a quick worker* **fast,** swift, rapid, speedy, brisk, smart, lightning, whirlwind, whistle-stop, breakneck; informal nippy, zippy. **2** *a quick look* **hasty,** hurried, cursory, perfunctory, desultory, superficial, brief. **3** *a quick end to the recession* **sudden,** instantaneous, instant, immediate, abrupt, precipitate. **4** *she isn't as quick as the others* **intelligent,** bright, clever, gifted, able, astute, sharp-witted, smart, alert, sharp, perceptive; informal brainy, on the ball.
ANTONYMS slow, long.

▶ **noun** (**the quick**) the tender flesh below the growing part of a fingernail or toenail.
■ **cut someone to the quick** upset someone very much. **quick-tempered** easily angered. **quick-witted** able to think or respond quickly.

quicken ▶ **verb 1** make or become quicker. **2** make or become active or alive.

SYNONYMS **1** *she quickened her pace* **speed up,** accelerate, step up, hasten, hurry (up). **2** *the film quickened his interest in nature* **stimulate,** excite, arouse, rouse, stir up, activate, whet, inspire, kindle.

quicklime ▶ **noun** a white alkaline substance consisting of calcium oxide, obtained by heating limestone.

quickly ▶ **adverb** with speed or haste.

SYNONYMS **1** *he walked quickly* **fast,** swiftly, briskly, rapidly, speedily, at full tilt, at a gallop, at the double, post-haste, hotfoot; informal like (greased) lightning, hell for leather, like blazes, like the wind; Brit. informal like the clappers, like billy-o; N. Amer. informal lickety-split. **2** *you'd better leave quickly* **immediately,** directly, at once, straight away, right away, instantly, forthwith; N. Amer. momentarily; informal like a shot, asap, p.d.q., pronto. **3** *he quickly inspected it* **briefly,** fleetingly, briskly, hastily, hurriedly, cursorily, perfunctorily, superficially, desultorily.

quicksand (or **quicksands**) ▶ **noun** loose wet sand that sucks in anything resting on it.

quicksilver ▶ **noun** mercury.
▶ **adjective** moving or changing rapidly.

quickstep ▶ **noun** a fast foxtrot.

quid ▶ **noun** (plural **quid**) Brit. informal one pound sterling.

quid pro quo /kwid proh kwoh/ ▶ **noun** (plural **quid pro quos**) a favour given in return for something.

quiescent /kwi-ess-uhnt/ ▶ **adjective** not active.
□ **quiescence** noun.

quiet ▸ adjective (quieter, quietest) **1** making little or no noise. **2** free from activity or excitement. **3** without being disturbed: *a quiet drink*. **4** discreet: *a quiet word*. **5** (of a person) shy and not tending to talk very much.

SYNONYMS **1** *the whole pub went quiet* **silent**, still, hushed, noiseless, soundless, mute, dumb, speechless. **2** *a quiet voice* **soft**, low, muted, muffled, faint, hushed, whispered, suppressed. **3** *a quiet village* **peaceful**, sleepy, tranquil, calm, still, restful.
ANTONYMS loud, busy.

▸ noun absence of noise or disturbance.

SYNONYMS *the quiet of the countryside* **silence**, still, hush, restfulness, calm, tranquillity, serenity, peace.

▸ verb N. Amer. make or become quiet.

quieten ▸ verb Brit. make or become quiet and calm.

quietly ▸ adverb in a quiet way.

SYNONYMS **1** *she read quietly* **silently**, noiselessly, soundlessly, inaudibly. **2** *he spoke quietly* **softly**, faintly, in a low voice, in a whisper, in a murmur, under your breath, in an undertone.
ANTONYMS out loud, loudly.

quietude ▸ noun a state of calmness and quiet.

quiff ▸ noun Brit. a piece of hair brushed upwards and backwards from the forehead.

quill ▸ noun **1** a main wing or tail feather of a bird. **2** the hollow shaft of a feather. **3** a pen made from a quill. **4** a spine of a porcupine or hedgehog.

quilt ▸ noun a warm bed covering made of padding enclosed between layers of fabric.

SYNONYMS **duvet**, cover(s); Brit. eiderdown; N. Amer. comforter, puff; Austral. trademark Doona.
□ **quilting** noun.

quilted ▸ adjective made of two layers of cloth filled with padding.

quin ▸ noun Brit. informal a quintuplet.

quince ▸ noun a hard yellow pear-shaped fruit.

quinine /kwi-**neen**/ ▸ noun a bitter drug made from the bark of a South American tree.

quintessence ▸ noun **1** a perfect example of something. **2** the central and most important part or quality of something.

quintessential ▸ adjective representing the most perfect example.
□ **quintessentially** adverb.

quintet ▸ noun **1** a group of five people playing music or singing together. **2** a piece of music for a quintet. **3** a set of five.

quintuple ▸ adjective **1** consisting of five parts or elements. **2** five times as much or as many.

quintuplet ▸ noun each of five children born at one birth.

quip ▸ noun a witty remark.
▸ verb (quips, quipping, quipped) make a witty remark.

quire ▸ noun **1** four sheets of paper folded to form eight leaves. **2** 25 sheets of paper.

quirk ▸ noun **1** a peculiar habit. **2** a strange thing that happens by chance.

SYNONYMS **1** *they all know his quirks* **idiosyncrasy**, peculiarity, oddity, eccentricity, foible, whim, vagary, habit, characteristic, trait, fad. **2** *a quirk of fate* **chance**, fluke, freak, anomaly, twist.

quirky ▸ adjective (quirkier, quirkiest) having peculiar or unexpected habits or qualities.

SYNONYMS **eccentric**, idiosyncratic, unconventional, unorthodox, unusual, strange, bizarre, peculiar, zany; informal wacky, way-out, offbeat.
ANTONYMS conventional.

quisling ▸ noun a traitor who collaborates with an enemy force that has occupied their country.

quit ▸ verb (quits, quitting, quitted or quit) **1** leave a place. **2** resign from a job. **3** informal, chiefly N. Amer. stop doing something.

SYNONYMS **1** *he quit the office at 12.30* **leave**, vacate, exit, depart from. **2** informal *he quit his job* **resign from**, leave, give up, hand in your notice; informal chuck, pack in. **3** informal *quit living in the past* **give up**, stop, discontinue, drop, abandon, abstain from; informal pack in, leave off.
ANTONYMS arrive at, continue, start.
□ **quitter** noun.

quite ▸ adverb **1** to a certain extent; fairly. **2** to the greatest degree; completely.

SYNONYMS **1** *two quite different types* **completely**, entirely, totally, wholly, absolutely, utterly, thoroughly, altogether. **2** *red hair was quite common* **fairly**, rather, somewhat, relatively, comparatively, moderately, reasonably; informal pretty.
ANTONYMS slightly, not at all.

▸ exclamation expressing agreement.

quits ▸ adjective on equal terms because a debt or score has been settled.

quiver¹ ▸ verb (quivers, quivering, quivered) shake or vibrate slightly.
▸ noun a quivering movement.

quiver² ▸ noun a case for carrying arrows.

quixotic /kwik-**sot**-ik/ ▸ adjective idealistic but impractical.

q

quiz ▸ noun (plural **quizzes**) a competition in which people answer questions that test their knowledge.

> SYNONYMS **competition**, test of knowledge.

▸ verb (**quizzes**, **quizzing**, **quizzed**) question someone.

> SYNONYMS *a man was quizzed by police* **question**, interrogate, cross-examine, cross-question, interview; informal grill, pump.

quizzical ▸ adjective showing mild or amused puzzlement.
> □ **quizzically** adverb.

quoin /koyn, kwoyn/ ▸ noun **1** an external angle of a wall or building. **2** a cornerstone.

quoit /koyt, kwoyt/ ▸ noun a ring that you throw over an upright peg in the game of **quoits**.

quorate /kwor-uht/ ▸ adjective Brit. (of a meeting) having a quorum.

quorum ▸ noun (plural **quorums**) the minimum number of people that must be present at a meeting to make its business valid.

quota ▸ noun **1** a limited quantity of people or things that is officially allowed. **2** a share of something that you have to contribute.

> SYNONYMS **share**, allocation, allowance, ration, portion, slice; Brit. informal whack.

quotation ▸ noun **1** a passage or remark repeated by someone other than the person who originally said or wrote it. **2** a formal statement of the estimated cost of a job or service.

> SYNONYMS **1** *a quotation from Dryden* **extract**, quote, citation, excerpt, passage; N. Amer. cite. **2** *a quotation for the work* **estimate**, quote, price, tender, bid, costing.

■ **quotation marks** a pair of punctuation marks, (' ') or (" "), used to mark the beginning and end of a quotation or passage of speech.

quote ▸ verb (**quotes**, **quoting**, **quoted**) **1** repeat a passage or remark by another person. **2** (**quote something as**) mention something as an example to support a point. **3** give someone an estimated price. **4** give a company a listing on a stock exchange.

> SYNONYMS **1** *he quoted from the book* **recite**, repeat, reproduce, retell, echo. **2** *she quoted one case in which a girl died* **mention**, cite, refer to, name, instance, allude to, point out.

▸ noun **1** a quotation. **2** (**quotes**) quotation marks.

> SYNONYMS See **QUOTATION**.

> □ **quotable** adjective.

quoth (*rhymes with* oath) ▸ verb old use said.

quotidian /kwuh-**tid**-i-uhn/ ▸ adjective formal **1** daily. **2** ordinary or everyday.

quotient /**kwoh**-shuhnt/ ▸ noun Maths a result obtained by dividing one quantity by another.

q.v. ▸ abbreviation used to direct a reader to another part of a book for further information.
> ORIGIN short for Latin *quod vide*, literally 'which see'.

q

Rr

R (or **r**) ▶ noun (plural **Rs** or **R's**) the eighteenth letter of the alphabet.
▶ abbreviation **1** Regina or Rex. **2** (**R.**) River.

R & B ▶ abbreviation **1** rhythm and blues. **2** a kind of pop music with soulful vocals.

rabbi /rab-by/ ▶ noun (plural **rabbis**) a Jewish religious leader or teacher of Jewish law.
□ **rabbinic** (or **rabbinical**) adjective.

rabbit ▶ noun a burrowing animal with long ears and a short tail.
▶ verb (**rabbits, rabbiting, rabbited**) Brit. informal chatter.

rabble ▶ noun **1** a disorderly crowd of people. **2** (**the rabble**) disapproving ordinary people.
■ **rabble-rouser** a person who makes speeches intended to make people angry or excited, usually for political reasons.

rabid /rab-id, ray-bid/ ▶ adjective **1** having extreme opinions; fanatical. **2** having rabies.
□ **rabidly** adverb.

rabies /ray-beez/ ▶ noun a dangerous disease of dogs and other animals, that can be transmitted through saliva to humans.

raccoon (or **racoon**) ▶ noun a greyish-brown American animal with a black face and striped tail.

race¹ ▶ noun **1** a competition to see who or which is fastest over a set course. **2** a strong current flowing through a narrow channel.

SYNONYMS **1** *Dave won the race* **contest,** competition, event, fixture, heat, trial(s). **2** *the race for naval domination* **competition,** rivalry, contention, quest.

▶ verb (**races, racing, raced**) **1** compete against someone or something in a race. **2** move or progress rapidly. **3** (of an engine) operate at too high a speed.

SYNONYMS **1** *he will race in the final* **compete,** contend, run. **2** *Claire raced after him* **hurry,** dash, rush, run, sprint, bolt, charge, shoot, hurtle, hare, fly, speed; informal tear, belt.

□ **racer** noun.

race² ▶ noun **1** each of the major divisions of humankind. **2** a group of people or things with a common feature. **3** a subdivision of a species.

SYNONYMS **1** *pupils of different races* **ethnic group,** racial type, origin, stock, blood, tribe. **2** *a bloodthirsty race* **people,** nation.

■ **race relations** relations between members of different races within a country.

racecourse ▶ noun a ground or track for horse or dog racing.

racehorse ▶ noun a horse bred and trained for racing.

raceme /ra-seem/ ▶ noun a flower cluster with separate flowers along a central stem.

racetrack ▶ noun **1** a racecourse. **2** a track for motor racing.

racial ▶ adjective **1** having to do with race. **2** relating to relations or differences between races.

SYNONYMS **ethnic,** ethnological, race-related, cultural, national, tribal, genetic.

□ **racially** adverb.

racialism ▶ noun racism.
□ **racialist** noun & adjective.

racism ▶ noun **1** the belief that certain races are better than others. **2** discrimination against, or hostility towards, other races.
□ **racist** noun & adjective.

rack ▶ noun **1** a framework for holding or storing things. **2** (**the rack**) (in the past) a frame on which people were tortured by being stretched. **3** a joint of meat that includes the front ribs.

SYNONYMS *the boots live on that rack* **frame,** framework, stand, holder, trestle, support, shelf.

▶ verb **1** (also **wrack**) cause great pain to. **2** (**rack something up**) achieve a score or amount.

SYNONYMS *he was racked with guilt* **torment,** afflict, torture, agonize, harrow, plague, persecute, trouble, worry.

■ **go to rack and ruin** fall into a bad condition. **rack** (or **wrack**) **your brains** think very hard.

r

racket¹ (or **racquet**) ► noun **1** a bat with a round or oval frame, used in tennis, badminton, and squash. **2** (**rackets**) a ball game played with rackets in a four-walled court.

racket² ► noun **1** a loud, unpleasant noise. **2** informal a dishonest scheme for making money.

> SYNONYMS **1** noise, din, hubbub, clamour, uproar, tumult, commotion, rumpus; informal hullabaloo; Brit. informal row. **2** *a gold-smuggling racket* fraud, swindle, sharp practice; informal game, scam, rip-off.

□ **rackety** adjective.

racketeer ► noun a person who makes money through dishonest activities. □ **racketeering** noun.

raconteur /ra-kon-**ter**/ ► noun a person who tells stories in an interesting and amusing way.

racoon → RACCOON.

racy ► adjective lively and exciting.

radar ► noun a system for detecting aircraft, ships, etc., by sending out radio waves which are reflected back off the object.

raddled ► adjective showing signs of age and tiredness.

radial ► adjective **1** arranged in lines coming out from a central point to the edge of a circle. **2** (of a tyre) in which the layers of fabric run at right angles to the circumference of the tyre. □ **radially** adverb.

radian /**ray**-di-uhn/ ► noun an angle of 57.3 degrees, equal to the angle at the centre of a circle formed by an arc equal in length to the radius.

radiant ► adjective **1** shining or glowing brightly. **2** glowing with joy, love, or health. **3** transmitted by radiation. □ **radiance** noun **radiantly** adverb.

radiate ► verb (**radiates**, **radiating**, **radiated**) **1** (of light, heat, or other energy) be sent out in rays or waves. **2** show a strong feeling or quality. **3** spread out from a central point.

> SYNONYMS **1** *stars radiate energy* emit, give off, discharge, diffuse, scatter, shed, cast. **2** *light radiated from the hall* shine, beam, emanate, pour. **3** *four spokes radiate from the hub* fan out, spread out, branch out/off, extend, issue.

radiation ► noun energy sent out as electromagnetic waves or subatomic particles.

radiator ► noun **1** a metal device for heating a room, usually filled with hot water pumped in through pipes. **2** a cooling device in a vehicle or aircraft engine.

radical ► adjective **1** having to do with the basic nature of something; fundamental. **2** supporting complete political or social reform. **3** departing from tradition; new. **4** Maths relating to the root of a number or quantity.

> SYNONYMS **1** *radical reform* thorough, complete, total, comprehensive, exhaustive, sweeping, far-reaching, wide-ranging, extensive, profound, major. **2** *radical differences between the two theories* fundamental, basic, essential, quintessential, structural, deep-seated. **3** *a radical political movement* revolutionary, progressive, reformist, revisionist, progressivist, extreme, fanatical, militant.
> ANTONYMS superficial, minor, conservative.

► noun **1** a supporter of radical reform. **2** Chemistry a group of atoms behaving as a unit in a compound. □ **radicalism** noun **radically** adverb.

radii plural of RADIUS.

radio ► noun (plural **radios**) **1** the sending and receiving of electromagnetic waves carrying sound messages. **2** the activity or medium of broadcasting in sound. **3** a device for receiving radio programmes, or for sending and receiving radio messages. ► verb (**radioes**, **radioing**, **radioed**) send a message to someone by radio.

radioactive ► adjective giving out harmful radiation or particles.

radioactivity ► noun harmful radiation or particles sent out when atomic nuclei break up.

radiocarbon ► noun a radioactive isotope of carbon used in carbon dating.

radiogram ► noun Brit. dated a combined radio and record player.

radiography ► noun the production of images by X-rays or other radiation. □ **radiographer** noun.

radioisotope ► noun a radioactive isotope.

radiology ► noun the science of X-rays and similar radiation, especially as used in medicine. □ **radiologist** noun.

radiotherapy ► noun the treatment of disease using X-rays or similar radiation.

radish ► noun a crisp, hot-tasting root vegetable, eaten raw in salads.

radium ► noun a radioactive metallic element.

radius ► noun (plural **radii** /**ray**-di-I/ or **radiuses**) **1** a straight line from the centre to the edge of a circle or sphere. **2** a stated distance from a centre in all directions. **3** the thicker and shorter of the two bones in the human forearm.

radon ► noun a rare radioactive gas.

RAF ▸ abbreviation Royal Air Force.

raffia ▸ noun fibre from the leaves of a tropical palm tree.

raffish ▸ adjective slightly disreputable, but in an attractive way.

raffle ▸ noun a lottery with goods as prizes.
▸ verb (**raffles, raffling, raffled**) offer something as a prize in a raffle.

raft ▸ noun 1 a flat structure used as a boat or floating platform. 2 a small inflatable boat. 3 a large amount.

rafter ▸ noun a beam forming part of the internal framework of a roof.

rag ▸ noun 1 a piece of old cloth. 2 (**rags**) old or tattered clothes. 3 informal a low-quality newspaper. 4 Brit. a programme of entertainments organized by students to raise money for charity. 5 a piece of ragtime music.
  ■ **the rag trade** informal the clothing or fashion industry.

ragamuffin ▸ noun a person in ragged, dirty clothes.

ragbag ▸ noun a collection of widely different things.

rage ▸ noun violent, uncontrollable anger.

> SYNONYMS 1 *his rage is due to frustration* **fury,** anger, wrath, outrage, indignation, temper, spleen, resentment, pique, annoyance, vexation, displeasure; informal grump, strop. 2 *the current rage for DIY* **craze,** passion, fashion, taste, trend, vogue, fad, mania; informal thing.

▸ verb (**rages, raging, raged**) 1 feel or express rage. 2 continue with great force.

> SYNONYMS *she raged silently* **be angry,** be furious, be enraged, be incensed, seethe, be beside yourself, rave, storm, fume, spit; informal be livid, be wild, be steamed up.

  ■ **all the rage** temporarily very popular or fashionable.

ragged ▸ adjective 1 (of cloth or clothes) old and torn. 2 rough or irregular. 3 not smooth or steady.

> SYNONYMS 1 *ragged jeans* **tattered,** torn, ripped, frayed, worn (out), threadbare, scruffy, shabby; informal tatty. 2 *a ragged coastline* **jagged,** craggy, rugged, uneven, rough, irregular, indented. ANTONYMS new, smart, sound, smooth.

  □ **raggedly** adverb.

ragout /ra-**goo**/ ▸ noun a spicy stew of meat and vegetables.

ragtag ▸ adjective disorganized and made up of a mixture of different types of people.

ragtime ▸ noun an early form of jazz played especially on the piano.

ragwort ▸ noun a plant with yellow flowers and ragged leaves.

raid ▸ noun 1 a sudden attack on an enemy, or on a building to commit a crime. 2 a surprise visit by police to arrest suspects or seize illegal goods.

> SYNONYMS 1 *the raid on Dieppe* **attack,** assault, descent, blitz, incursion, sortie, onslaught, storming. 2 *a raid on a shop* **robbery,** burglary, hold-up, break-in, ram raid; informal smash-and-grab, stick-up; N. Amer. informal heist. 3 *a police raid* **swoop,** search; N. Amer. informal bust, takedown.

▸ verb make a raid on.

> SYNONYMS 1 *they raided shipping in the harbour* **attack,** assault, set upon, descend on, swoop on, storm. 2 *armed men raided the store* **rob,** hold up, break into, plunder, steal from, pillage, loot, ransack; informal stick up. 3 *homes were raided by police* **search,** swoop on; N. Amer. informal bust.

raider ▸ noun a person who raids.

> SYNONYMS **robber,** burglar, thief, housebreaker, plunderer, pillager, looter, marauder, attacker, assailant, invader.

rail¹ ▸ noun 1 a fixed bar forming part of a fence or barrier or used to hang things on. 2 each of the two metal bars laid on the ground to form a railway track. 3 railways as a means of transport.
▸ verb 1 enclose with a rail or rails. 2 (**rail against** or **at**) complain strongly about.
  ■ **go off the rails** informal behave in an uncontrolled way.

rail² ▸ noun a waterside bird with grey and brown feathers.

railing ▸ noun a fence or barrier made of rails.

> SYNONYMS **fence,** fencing, rail(s), palisade, balustrade, banister.

raillery ▸ noun good-humoured teasing.

railroad ▸ noun N. Amer. a railway.
▸ verb informal rush or force someone into doing something.

railway ▸ noun Brit. 1 a track made of rails along which trains run. 2 a system of tracks and trains.

raiment /**ray**-muhnt/ ▸ noun old use or literary clothing.

rain ▸ noun 1 condensed moisture from the atmosphere falling in separate drops. 2 (**rains**) falls of rain. 3 a large quantity of things falling together.
▸ verb 1 (**it rains, it is raining, it rained**) rain falls. 2 (**be rained off**) (of an event) be prevented by rain from continuing or taking place. 3 fall in large quantities.

rainbow ▸ noun an arch of colours in the sky, caused by the sun shining through water droplets in the atmosphere.

r

raincoat ▸ noun a coat made from water-resistant fabric.

rainfall ▸ noun the amount of rain falling.

rainforest ▸ noun a dense forest found in tropical areas with consistently heavy rainfall.

rainy ▸ adjective (rainier, rainiest) having a lot of rain.

> SYNONYMS **wet,** showery, drizzly, damp, inclement.
> ANTONYMS dry, fine.

■ **a rainy day** a time in the future when money may be needed.

raise ▸ verb (raises, raising, raised) **1** lift or move upwards or into an upright position. **2** increase the amount, level, or strength of. **3** express doubts, objections, etc. **4** collect money. **5** bring up a child. **6** breed or grow animals or plants. **7** (**raise something to**) Maths multiply a quantity to a particular power.

> SYNONYMS **1** *he raised a hand* **lift (up),** hold aloft, elevate, uplift, hoist, haul up, hitch up; Brit. informal hoick up. **2** *they raised prices* **increase,** put up, push up, up, mark up, inflate; informal hike (up), jack up, bump up. **3** *he raised his voice* **amplify,** louden, magnify, intensify, boost, lift, increase. **4** *how will you raise the money?* **get,** obtain, acquire, accumulate, amass, collect, fetch, net, make. **5** *he raised several objections* **bring up,** air, present, table, propose, submit, advance, suggest, put forward. **6** *the disaster raised doubts about safety* **give rise to,** occasion, cause, produce, engender, elicit, create, result in, lead to, prompt. **7** *most parents raise their children well* **bring up,** rear, nurture. **8** *he raised cattle* **breed,** rear, nurture, keep, tend, farm, produce.
> ANTONYMS lower, reduce, demolish.

▸ noun N. Amer. an increase in salary.
■ **raise the roof** cheer very loudly.

raisin ▸ noun a partially dried grape.

raison d'être /ray-zon det-ruh/ ▸ noun (plural **raisons d'être** /ray-zon det-ruh/) the most important reason for someone or something's existence.

Raj /rahj/ ▸ noun (**the Raj**) the period of British rule in India.

raja (or **rajah**) /rah-juh/ ▸ noun historical an Indian king or prince.

rake¹ ▸ noun a pole with metal prongs at the end, used for drawing together leaves, smoothing soil, etc.
▸ verb (rakes, raking, raked) **1** draw together or smooth with a rake. **2** scratch or sweep with a long broad movement. **3** search through.

> SYNONYMS **1** *he raked the leaves into a pile* **scrape,** collect, gather. **2** *she raked the gravel smooth* **smooth (out),** level, even out, flatten, comb. **3** *I raked through my pockets* **rummage,** search, hunt, sift, rifle.

■ **rake it in** informal make a lot of money.
rake something up bring up something that is best forgotten.

rake² ▸ noun a fashionable, rich, but immoral man.

rake³ ▸ verb (rakes, raking, raked) set something at a sloping angle.
▸ noun the angle at which something slopes.

rakish ▸ adjective having a dashing, jaunty, or slightly disreputable appearance.

rally ▸ noun (plural **rallies**) **1** a mass meeting held as a protest or in support of a cause. **2** a long-distance competition for motor vehicles over roads or rough ground. **3** a quick or strong recovery. **4** (in tennis and similar games) a long exchange of strokes between players.

> SYNONYMS **1** *a rally in support of the strike* (**mass**) **meeting,** gathering, assembly, demonstration, (protest) march; informal demo. **2** *a rally in oil prices* **recovery,** upturn, improvement, comeback, resurgence.
> ANTONYMS slump.

▸ verb (rallies, rallying, rallied) **1** (of troops) come together again to continue fighting. **2** come together to support a person or cause. **3** recover health or strength. **4** (of shares or currency) increase in value after a fall. **5** (**rallying**) the sport of taking part in a motor rally.

> SYNONYMS **1** *the troops rallied and held their ground* **regroup,** reassemble, re-form, reunite. **2** *share prices rallied* **recover,** improve, get better, pick up, revive, bounce back, perk up, look up, turn a corner.
> ANTONYMS disperse, slump.

ram ▸ noun **1** an adult male sheep. **2** a long, heavy object swung against a door to break it down. **3** a striking or plunging device in a machine.
▸ verb (rams, ramming, rammed) **1** hit with force. **2** roughly force into place.

> SYNONYMS **1** *a van rammed the car* **hit,** strike, crash into, collide with, impact, smash into, butt. **2** *he rammed his sword into its sheath* **force,** thrust, plunge, stab, push, sink, dig, stick, cram, jam, stuff.

■ **ram raid** a robbery in which people ram a shop window with a vehicle to steal goods.

Ramadan /ram-uh-dan/ ▸ noun the ninth month of the Muslim year, during which Muslims do not eat from dawn to sunset.

ramble ▸ verb (rambles, rambling, rambled)

1 walk for pleasure in the countryside. **2** talk or write in a confused way.

> SYNONYMS **1** *we rambled around the lanes* **walk,** hike, tramp, trek, backpack. **2** *she does ramble on* **chatter,** babble, prattle, blather, gabble, jabber, twitter, rattle; Brit. informal witter, chunter, rabbit.

▶ noun a country walk taken for pleasure.
□ **rambler** noun.

ramekin /ra-mi-kin/ ▶ noun a small dish for baking and serving an individual portion of food.

ramifications ▶ plural noun complex results of an action or event.

ramp ▶ noun **1** a sloping surface joining two different levels. **2** a set of steps for entering or leaving an aircraft.

> SYNONYMS **slope,** bank, incline, gradient, rise, drop.

rampage ▶ verb /ram-**payj**/ (rampages, rampaging, rampaged) rush around in a wild and violent way.

> SYNONYMS **riot,** run amok, go berserk, storm, charge, tear.

▶ noun /**ram**-payj/ a period of wild and violent behaviour.

rampant ▶ adjective **1** flourishing or spreading in an uncontrolled way. **2** Heraldry (of an animal) shown standing on its left hind foot with its forefeet in the air.

> SYNONYMS **uncontrolled,** unrestrained, unchecked, unbridled, out of control, out of hand, widespread, rife, spreading.
> ANTONYMS controlled.

rampart ▶ noun a wall defending a castle or town, having a broad top with a walkway.

ramrod ▶ noun a rod formerly used to ram down the charge of a firearm.

ramshackle ▶ adjective in a very bad condition.

ran past of RUN.

ranch ▶ noun a large farm in America where cattle or other animals are bred.
□ **rancher** noun.

rancid ▶ adjective (of fatty or oily food) stale and smelling or tasting unpleasant.

rancour (US spelling rancor) ▶ noun bitter feeling or resentment.
□ **rancorous** adjective.

rand ▶ noun the basic unit of money of South Africa.

random ▶ adjective done or happening without any plan, purpose, or regular pattern.

> SYNONYMS **unsystematic,** unmethodical, arbitrary, unplanned, chance, casual, indiscriminate, non-specific, haphazard, stray, erratic.
> ANTONYMS systematic, deliberate.

■ **at random** without thinking or planning in advance.
□ **randomly** adverb **randomness** noun.

randy ▶ adjective (randier, randiest) Brit. informal sexually excited.

rang past of RING².

range ▶ noun **1** the limits between which something varies. **2** a set of different things of the same general type. **3** the distance over which a sound, missile, etc. can travel. **4** a line of mountains or hills. **5** a large area of open land for grazing or hunting. **6** an area for testing military equipment or practising shooting. **7** a large stove with several burners or hotplates.

> SYNONYMS **1** *his range of vision* **extent,** limit, reach, span, scope, compass, sweep, area, field, orbit, ambit, horizon, latitude. **2** *a range of foods* **assortment,** variety, diversity, mixture, collection, array, selection, choice. **3** *a range of mountains* **row,** chain, sierra, ridge, massif.

▶ verb (ranges, ranging, ranged) **1** vary between particular limits. **2** arrange things in a particular way. **3** (be ranged against) be in opposition to. **4** travel over a wide area.

> SYNONYMS **1** *charges range from 1% to 5%* **vary,** fluctuate, differ, extend, stretch, reach, go, run, cover. **2** *they ranged over the steppes* **roam,** wander, travel, journey, rove, traverse, walk, hike, trek.

ranger ▶ noun a keeper of a park, forest, or area of countryside.

rangy /**rayn**-ji/ ▶ adjective (of a person) tall and slim with long limbs.

rank¹ ▶ noun **1** a position within the armed forces or an organization. **2** a row of people or things. **3** high social position. **4** (the ranks) (in the armed forces) those who are not commissioned officers.

> SYNONYMS **1** *he was elevated to ministerial rank* **position,** level, grade, echelon, class, status, standing. **2** *a family of rank* **high standing,** blue blood, high birth, nobility, aristocracy. **3** *a rank of riflemen* **row,** line, file, column, string, train, procession.

▶ verb **1** give a rank to. **2** hold a particular rank. **3** arrange in a row or rows.

> SYNONYMS **1** *the plant is ranked as endangered* **classify,** class, categorize, rate, grade, bracket, group, designate, list. **2** *tulips were ranked like guardsmen* **line up,** align, order, arrange, dispose, set out, array, range.

■ **close ranks** unite to defend shared interests. **pull rank** use your higher rank to take advantage of someone. **rank and file** the ordinary members of an organization.

r

rank² ▸ adjective **1** having a very unpleasant smell. **2** complete: *a rank amateur*. **3** (of plants) growing too thickly.

> SYNONYMS **1** *a rank smell* **offensive,** nasty, revolting, sickening, obnoxious, foul, fetid, high, rancid, putrid; Brit. informal **pongy, humming. 2** *rank stupidity* **downright,** utter, out-and-out, absolute, complete, sheer, blatant, arrant, thorough, unqualified. **3** *rank vegetation* **abundant,** lush, luxuriant, dense, profuse, vigorous, overgrown; informal **jungly.**
> ANTONYMS pleasant, sparse.

rankle ▸ verb (**rankles, rankling, rankled**) cause continuing annoyance or resentment.

ransack ▸ verb go hurriedly through a place stealing or searching for things.

ransom ▸ noun a sum of money demanded for the release of someone who is held captive.

> SYNONYMS **pay-off,** payment, sum, price.

▸ verb cause someone to be released by paying a ransom.
■ **hold someone to ransom 1** hold someone captive and demand payment for their release. **2** force someone to do something by threatening them.

rant ▸ verb speak in a loud, angry, and forceful way.

> SYNONYMS **shout,** sound off, hold forth, go on, fulminate, spout, bluster; informal **mouth off.**

rap ▸ verb (**raps, rapping, rapped**) **1** hit a hard surface several times. **2** hit sharply. **3** informal criticize sharply. **4** say sharply or suddenly.

> SYNONYMS **hit,** knock, strike, smack, bang; informal **whack, thwack, bash, wallop.**

▸ noun **1** a quick, sharp knock or blow. **2** a type of popular music in which words are spoken rhythmically over an instrumental backing.
■ **take the rap** informal be punished or blamed for something.
□ **rapper** noun.

rapacious ▸ adjective very greedy.

rapacity /ruh-**pa**-si-ti/ ▸ noun greed.

rape¹ ▸ verb (**rapes, raping, raped**) **1** (of a man) force someone to have sex with him against their will. **2** spoil or destroy a place.
▸ noun an act of raping.

rape² ▸ noun a plant with bright yellow flowers, grown for its oil-rich seed.

rapid ▸ adjective very fast.

> SYNONYMS **quick,** fast, swift, speedy, express, brisk, lightning, meteoric, whirlwind, sudden, instantaneous, instant, immediate.
> ANTONYMS slow.

▸ noun (**rapids**) a part of a river where the water flows very fast.
□ **rapidity** noun **rapidly** adverb.

rapier ▸ noun a thin, light sword.

rapist ▸ noun a man who commits rape.

rapport /rap-**por**/ ▸ noun a close relationship in which people understand each other and communicate well.

rapprochement /ra-**prosh**-mon/ ▸ noun a renewal of friendly relations between two countries or groups.

rapscallion ▸ noun old use a rascal.

rapt ▸ adjective completely fascinated or absorbed.

raptor ▸ noun a bird of prey.

rapture ▸ noun **1** great pleasure or joy. **2** (**raptures**) the expression of great pleasure or enthusiasm.

rapturous ▸ adjective very pleased or enthusiastic.
□ **rapturously** adverb.

rare ▸ adjective (**rarer, rarest**) **1** not happening or found very often. **2** unusually good. **3** (of red meat) lightly cooked, so that the inside is still red.

> SYNONYMS **1** *rare moments of privacy* **infrequent,** scarce, sparse, few and far between, occasional, limited, odd, isolated, unaccustomed. **2** *rare stamps* **unusual,** recherché, uncommon, thin on the ground, like gold dust, unfamiliar, atypical. **3** *a man of rare talent* **exceptional,** outstanding, unparalleled, peerless, matchless, unique, unrivalled.
> ANTONYMS common, commonplace.

rarebit = WELSH RAREBIT at WELSH.

rarefied ▸ adjective **1** (of air) of lower pressure than usual; thin. **2** understood by only a limited group of people.

> ✔ **-ref-,** not **-rif-:** ra**ref**ied.

rarely ▸ adverb not often.

> SYNONYMS **seldom,** infrequently, hardly (ever), scarcely.
> ANTONYMS often.

raring ▸ adjective (**raring to do**) informal very eager to do something.

> SYNONYMS **eager,** keen, enthusiastic, impatient, longing, desperate; informal **dying, itching, gagging.**

rarity ▸ noun (plural **rarities**) **1** the state of being rare. **2** a rare thing.

> SYNONYMS **1** *the rarity of earthquakes in the UK* **infrequency,** scarcity. **2** *this book is a rarity* **curiosity,** oddity, collector's item, rare bird, wonder, nonpareil, one of a kind; Brit. informal **one-off.**

rascal ▸ noun **1** a mischievous or cheeky person. **2** a dishonest man.

r

□ **rascally** adjective.

rash¹ ▸ adjective acting or done without careful consideration of the possible results.

> SYNONYMS **reckless**, impulsive, impetuous, hasty, foolhardy, incautious, precipitate, careless, heedless, thoughtless, imprudent, foolish.
> ANTONYMS prudent.

□ **rashly** adverb.

rash² ▸ noun **1** an area of red spots or patches on a person's skin. **2** a series of unpleasant things happening within a short time.

> SYNONYMS **1** *he broke out in a rash* **spots**, eruption, nettlerash, hives. **2** *a rash of articles in the press* **series**, succession, spate, wave, flood, deluge, torrent, outbreak, epidemic, flurry.

rasher ▸ noun a thin slice of bacon.

rasp ▸ noun **1** a harsh, grating noise. **2** a tool with a rough edge, used for smoothing surfaces.
▸ verb **1** make a harsh, grating noise. **2** scrape roughly. **3** file with a rasp.

raspberry ▸ noun (plural **raspberries**) **1** a reddish-pink soft fruit. **2** informal a rude sound made with the tongue and lips.

Rasta ▸ noun informal a Rastafarian.

Rastafarian /rass-tuh-**fair**-i-uhn/ ▸ noun a member of a Jamaican religious movement which worships Haile Selassie, the former Emperor of Ethiopia.
□ **Rastafarianism** noun.

rat ▸ noun **1** a rodent resembling a large mouse. **2** informal an unpleasant person.
▸ verb (**rats, ratting, ratted**) (**rat on**) informal **1** inform on someone. **2** break an agreement or promise.
■ **the rat race** informal a way of life which is a fiercely competitive struggle for money or power.

ratatouille /ra-tuh-**too**-i/ ▸ noun a vegetable dish of stewed onions, courgettes, tomatoes, etc.

ratchet ▸ noun a device with a set of angled teeth in which a cog, tooth, or bar fits, allowing movement in one direction only.

rate¹ ▸ noun **1** a measure, quantity, or frequency measured against another. **2** the speed of something. **3** a fixed price paid or charged for something. **4** (**rates**) (in the UK) a tax on land and buildings paid to a local authority by a business.

> SYNONYMS **1** *a fixed rate of interest* **percentage**, ratio, proportion, scale, standard. **2** *the rate of change* **speed**, pace, tempo, velocity. **3** *an hourly rate of £30* **charge**, price, cost, tariff, fare, fee, remuneration, payment.

▸ verb (**rates, rating, rated**) **1** give something

a standard or value according to a particular scale. **2** consider to be of a certain quality or standard. **3** be worthy of; deserve. **4** informal have a high opinion of.

> SYNONYMS **1** *they rated their ability at driving* **assess**, evaluate, appraise, judge, weigh up, estimate, gauge. **2** *he rated only a brief mention* **merit**, deserve, warrant, be worthy of.

□ **rateable** (or **ratable**) adjective.

rate² ▸ verb old use scold angrily.

rather ▸ adverb **1** (**would rather**) would prefer. **2** to some extent; fairly. **3** used to correct something you have said or to be more precise. **4** instead of.

> SYNONYMS **1** *I'd rather you went* **sooner**, by preference, by choice. **2** *it's rather complicated* **quite**, a bit, a little, fairly, slightly, somewhat, relatively, comparatively; informal pretty. **3** *she seemed sad rather than angry* **more**, as opposed to, instead of.

ratify ▸ verb (**ratifies, ratifying, ratified**) make a treaty, contract, etc. valid by signing or agreeing to it.

> SYNONYMS **confirm**, approve, sanction, endorse, agree to, accept, uphold, authorize, formalize, sign.
> ANTONYMS reject.

□ **ratification** noun.

rating ▸ noun **1** a classification based on quality, standard, or performance. **2** (**ratings**) the estimated audience size of a television or radio programme. **3** Brit. a sailor in the navy who does not hold a commission.

> SYNONYMS **grade**, classification, ranking, position, category, assessment, evaluation, mark, score.

ratio ▸ noun (plural **ratios**) an indication of the relationship between two amounts, showing the number of times one contains the other.

> SYNONYMS **proportion**, relationship, rate, percentage, fraction, correlation.

ratiocination /ra-ti-oss-i-**nay**-sh'n/ ▸ noun formal the process of thinking in a logical way; reasoning.

ration ▸ noun **1** a fixed amount of food, fuel, etc., officially allowed to each person. **2** (**rations**) a regular allowance of food supplied to members of the armed forces.

> SYNONYMS **1** *a daily ration of chocolate* **allowance**, allocation, quota, share, portion, helping. **2** (**rations**) *the garrison ran out of rations* **supplies**, provisions, food, stores.

▸ verb limit the supply of food, fuel, etc.

> SYNONYMS *fuel supplies were rationed* **control**, limit, restrict, conserve.

r

rational ▸ adjective **1** based on reason or logic. **2** able to think sensibly or logically.

> SYNONYMS **logical,** reasoned, sensible, reasonable, realistic, cogent, intelligent, shrewd, common-sense, sane, sound.
> ANTONYMS irrational.

□ **rationality** noun **rationally** adverb.

rationale /ra-shuh-**nahl**/ ▸ noun the reasons for doing or believing something.

> SYNONYMS **reason(s),** thinking, logic, grounds, sense.

rationalism ▸ noun the belief that opinions and actions should be based on reason rather than on religious belief or emotions.
□ **rationalist** noun.

rationalize (or **rationalise**) ▸ verb (**rationalizes, rationalizing, rationalized**) **1** try to find a logical reason for an action or attitude. **2** reorganize a business, system, etc. to make it more efficient.
□ **rationalization** noun.

rattan /ruh-**tan**/ ▸ noun the thin stems of a tropical palm, used to make furniture.

rattle ▸ verb (**rattles, rattling, rattled**) **1** make a rapid series of short, sharp sounds. **2** informal make someone nervous or irritated. **3** (**rattle something off**) say or do something quickly and easily.

> SYNONYMS **1** *hailstones rattled against the window* **clatter,** patter, clink, clunk. **2** *he rattled some coins* **jingle,** jangle, clink, tinkle. **3** *the government was rattled by the strike* **unnerve,** disconcert, disturb, fluster, shake, perturb, throw; informal faze.

▸ noun **1** a rattling sound. **2** a toy that makes a rattling sound.

rattlesnake ▸ noun an American viper with horny rings on the tail that produce a rattling sound.

ratty ▸ adjective Brit. informal irritable.

raucous ▸ adjective sounding loud and harsh.
□ **raucously** adverb.

raunchy ▸ adjective (**raunchier, raunchiest**) informal sexually exciting or explicit.

ravage ▸ verb (**ravages, ravaging, ravaged**) cause great damage to.

> SYNONYMS **lay waste,** devastate, ruin, destroy, wreak havoc on.

▸ noun (**ravages**) the destruction caused by something.

rave ▸ verb (**raves, raving, raved**) **1** talk angrily or without making sense. **2** speak or write about someone or something with great enthusiasm.

> SYNONYMS **1** *I raved and swore at them* **rant,** rage, lose your temper, storm, fume, shout; informal fly off the handle,

hit the roof; Brit. informal go spare; N. Amer. informal flip your wig. **2** *he raved about her talent* **enthuse,** go into raptures, wax lyrical, rhapsodize, sing the praises of, acclaim, eulogize, extol; N. Amer. informal ballyhoo.
> ANTONYMS criticize.

▸ noun a large event with dancing to loud, fast electronic music.

raven ▸ noun a large black crow.
▸ adjective (of hair) of a glossy black colour.

ravening ▸ adjective literary very fierce and hungry.

ravenous ▸ adjective very hungry.
□ **ravenously** adverb.

raver ▸ noun informal a person who has an exciting or wild social life.

ravine ▸ noun a deep, narrow gorge.

raving ▸ noun (**ravings**) wild talk that makes no sense.
▸ adjective & adverb informal used for emphasis: *raving mad.*

ravioli /rav-i-**oh**-li/ ▸ plural noun small pasta cases containing minced meat, cheese, or vegetables.

ravish ▸ verb **1** dated rape. **2** (**ravishing**) very beautiful.

raw ▸ adjective **1** (of food) not cooked. **2** (of a material) in its natural state. **3** (of the skin) red and painful from being rubbed or scraped. **4** (of an emotion or quality) strong and undisguised. **5** (of the weather) cold and damp. **6** new to an activity and lacking experience.

> SYNONYMS **1** *raw carrot* **uncooked,** fresh, natural. **2** *raw materials* **unprocessed,** untreated, unrefined, crude, natural. **3** *raw recruits* **inexperienced,** new, untrained, untried, untested, callow, green. **4** *his skin is raw* **sore,** red, painful, tender, chafed.
> ANTONYMS cooked, processed, experienced, sound.

■ **a raw deal** unfair treatment.
□ **rawness** noun.

ray¹ ▸ noun **1** a narrow line or beam of light or radiation. **2** a trace of something good: *a ray of hope.*

> SYNONYMS **beam,** shaft, stream, streak, flash, glimmer, flicker, spark.

ray² ▸ noun a broad flat fish with a long, thin tail.

rayon ▸ noun a synthetic fabric made from viscose.

raze ▸ verb (**razes, razing, razed**) completely destroy a building, town, etc.

razor ▸ noun an instrument used to shave hair.

razzle ▸ noun (**on the razzle**) Brit. informal out celebrating or enjoying yourself.

razzmatazz (or **razzamatazz**) ▸ noun informal noisy and exciting activity designed to attract attention.

RC ▸ abbreviation Roman Catholic.

re /ree, ray/ ▸ preposition with reference to.

reach ▸ verb **1** stretch out an arm to touch or grasp something. **2** be able to touch something with an outstretched arm or leg. **3** arrive at; get as far as. **4** come to a particular level or point. **5** make contact with.

> SYNONYMS **1** *Travis reached out a hand* **extend,** stretch, outstretch, thrust, stick, hold. **2** *she reached Helen's house* **arrive at,** get to, come to, end up at. **3** *the temperature reached 94 degrees* **attain,** get to, rise to, fall to, sink to, drop to; informal hit. **4** *the leaders reached an agreement* **achieve,** work out, draw up, put together, negotiate, thrash out, hammer out. **5** *I have been trying to reach you all day* **contact,** get in touch with, get through to, get, speak to; informal get hold of.

▸ noun **1** the distance to which someone can stretch out their arm or arms to touch something. **2** a continuous stretch of river between two bends.

> SYNONYMS **1** *Bobby moved out of her reach* **grasp,** range, stretch. **2** *small goals within your reach* **capabilities,** capacity. **3** *beyond the reach of the law* **jurisdiction,** authority, influence, power, scope, range, compass, ambit.

react ▸ verb **1** respond to something in a particular way. **2** interact and undergo a chemical or physical change.

> SYNONYMS **respond,** act in response, reply, answer, behave.

□ **reactive** adjective.

reaction ▸ noun **1** something done or experienced as a result of an event. **2** (**reactions**) a person's ability to respond to an event. **3** a bad response by the body to a drug or substance. **4** a process in which substances interact causing chemical or physical change. **5** a force exerted in opposition to an applied force.

> SYNONYMS **1** *his reaction bewildered her* **response,** answer, reply, rejoinder, retort, riposte; informal comeback. **2** *a reaction against modernism* **backlash,** counteraction.

reactionary ▸ adjective opposing political or social progress or reform.

> SYNONYMS *a reactionary policy* **right-wing,** conservative, traditionalist, conventional. ANTONYMS radical, progressive.

▸ noun (plural **reactionaries**) a person holding reactionary views.

> SYNONYMS *an extreme reactionary* **right-winger,** conservative, traditionalist. ANTONYMS radical.

reactivate ▸ verb (**reactivates, reactivating, reactivated**) bring something back into action.
□ **reactivation** noun.

reactor ▸ noun an apparatus in which material is made to undergo a controlled nuclear reaction that releases energy.

read ▸ verb (**reads, reading, read**) **1** understand the meaning of written or printed words or symbols. **2** speak written or printed words aloud. **3** have a particular wording. **4** understand the nature or meaning of. **5** (**read something into**) think that something has a meaning that it may not possess. **6** Brit. study a subject at a university. **7** (of an instrument) show a measurement or figure.

> SYNONYMS **1** *he was reading the newspaper* **peruse,** study, scrutinize, look through, pore over, run your eye over, cast an eye over, leaf through, scan. **2** *he read the letter to me* **read out/aloud,** recite, declaim. **3** *I can't read my writing* **understand,** make out, make sense of, interpret, decipher.

▸ noun informal a book that is interesting to read.
■ **take something as read** assume something.
□ **readable** adjective **reader** noun.

readership ▸ noun the readers of a publication regarded as a group.

readily ▸ adverb **1** willingly. **2** easily.

> SYNONYMS **1** *Durkin readily offered to drive* **willingly,** unhesitatingly, ungrudgingly, gladly, happily, eagerly. **2** *the island is readily accessible* **easily,** without difficulty. ANTONYMS reluctantly, with difficulty.

readiness ▸ noun the state or quality of being ready.

> SYNONYMS **1** *their readiness to accept change* **willingness,** eagerness, keenness, enthusiasm. **2** *a state of readiness* **preparedness.**

reading ▸ noun **1** the action of reading. **2** something that is read. **3** a figure recorded on a measuring instrument.

> SYNONYMS **1** *a cursory reading of the page* **perusal,** study, scanning, browse, look, glance, leaf. **2** *a man of wide reading* **learning,** scholarship, education, erudition. **3** *a poetry reading* **recital,** recitation, performance. **4** *a Bible reading* **lesson,** passage, excerpt. **5** *my reading of the situation* **interpretation,**

r

understanding, explanation, analysis, construction.

readjust ▸ verb **1** adjust again. **2** adapt to a changed situation.
□ **readjustment** noun.

ready ▸ adjective (**readier, readiest**)
1 prepared for an activity or situation. **2** made available for immediate use. **3** easily available or obtained. **4** (**ready to do**) willing or eager to do. **5** immediate or quick.

> SYNONYMS **1** *are you ready?* **prepared,** all set, organized, primed; informal fit, psyched up, geared up. **2** *everything is ready* **completed,** finished, prepared, organized, done, arranged, fixed. **3** *he's always ready to help* **willing,** prepared, pleased, inclined, disposed, eager, keen, happy, glad; informal game. **4** *a ready supply of food* (**easily**) **available,** accessible, handy, close/near at hand, to/on hand, convenient, within reach, near, at your fingertips. **5** *a ready answer* **prompt,** quick, swift, speedy, fast, immediate, unhesitating, clever, sharp, astute, shrewd, keen, perceptive, discerning.

▸ noun (**readies** or **the ready**) Brit. informal available money.
▸ verb (**readies, readying, readied**) prepare.

> SYNONYMS **prepare,** organize, gear up; informal psych up.

reagent /ri-ay-juhnt/ ▸ noun a substance that produces a chemical reaction, used to detect the presence of another substance.

real ▸ adjective **1** actually existing or happening. **2** not artificial; genuine. **3** worthy of the description; proper.

> SYNONYMS **1** *based on real events* **actual,** true, non-fictional, factual, historical, material, physical, tangible, concrete. **2** *real gold* **genuine,** authentic, bona fide; informal pukka, kosher. **3** *tears of real grief* **sincere,** genuine, true, unfeigned, heartfelt. **4** *a real man* **proper,** true; informal regular. **5** *you're a real idiot* **complete,** utter, thorough, absolute, total, prize, perfect; Brit. informal right, proper.
> ANTONYMS imaginary, imitation.

▸ adverb N. Amer. informal really; very.
■ **real estate** N. Amer. land or housing. **real tennis** the original form of tennis, played with a solid ball on an enclosed court.

realign ▸ verb change something to a different position or state.
□ **realignment** noun.

realism ▸ noun **1** the acceptance of a situation as it is. **2** the presentation of things in a way that is accurate and true to life.

> SYNONYMS **1** *optimism tinged with realism* **pragmatism,** practicality, common sense, level-headedness. **2** *a degree of realism* **authenticity,** accuracy, fidelity, verisimilitude, truthfulness.
> ANTONYMS fancy, inauthenticity.

□ **realist** noun.

realistic ▸ adjective **1** having a sensible and practical idea of what can be achieved. **2** showing things in a way that is accurate and true to life.

> SYNONYMS **1** *you've got to be realistic* **practical,** pragmatic, matter-of-fact, down-to-earth, sensible, commonsensical, rational, level-headed; informal no-nonsense. **2** *a realistic aim* **achievable,** attainable, feasible, practicable, reasonable, sensible, workable; informal doable. **3** *a realistic portrayal of war* **authentic,** accurate, true to life, lifelike, truthful, faithful, natural, naturalistic.
> ANTONYMS idealistic, impracticable, inauthentic.

□ **realistically** adverb.

reality ▸ noun (plural **realities**) **1** the state of things as they actually exist. **2** a thing that is real. **3** the state of being real.

> SYNONYMS **1** *distinguishing fantasy from reality* **the real world,** real life, actuality, truth. **2** *the harsh realities of life* **fact,** actuality, truth. **3** *the reality of the detail* **authenticity,** verisimilitude, fidelity, truthfulness, accuracy.
> ANTONYMS fantasy, inaccuracy.

■ **reality TV** television programmes based on real people or situations, presented as entertainment.

realization ▸ noun the action or an act of realizing.

> SYNONYMS **1** *a growing realization of the danger* **awareness,** understanding, comprehension, consciousness, appreciation, recognition, discernment. **2** *the realization of our dreams* **fulfilment,** achievement, accomplishment, attainment.

realize (or **realise**) ▸ verb (**realizes, realizing, realized**) **1** become fully aware of a fact. **2** achieve or fulfil a wish or plan. **3** be sold for a particular amount. **4** convert property, shares, etc. into money by selling them.

> SYNONYMS **1** *he suddenly realized what she meant* **register,** perceive, understand, grasp, comprehend, see, recognize; informal tumble to; Brit. informal twig. **2** *they realized their dream* **fulfil,** achieve, accomplish, make happen, bring to fruition, bring about/off. **3** *the company realized significant profits* **make,** clear,

gain, earn, return, produce. **4** *the goods realized £30* **be sold for,** fetch, go for, make, net.

really ▸ adverb **1** in actual fact. **2** very; thoroughly.

> SYNONYMS **1** *he is really very wealthy* **in (actual) fact,** actually, in reality, in truth. **2** *he really likes her* **genuinely,** truly, certainly, honestly, undoubtedly, unquestionably.

▸ exclamation expressing interest, surprise, doubt, etc.

realm ▸ noun **1** chiefly literary a kingdom. **2** an area of activity or interest.

> SYNONYMS **1** *peace in the realm* **kingdom,** country, land, dominion, nation. **2** *the realm of academia* **domain,** sphere, area, field, world, province, territory.

ream ▸ noun **1** 500 sheets of paper. **2** (**reams**) a large quantity.

reap ▸ verb **1** gather in a crop or harvest. **2** receive a reward or benefit as a result of your actions.

> SYNONYMS **1** *the corn was reaped* **harvest,** cut, pick, gather, garner. **2** *reaping the benefits* **receive,** obtain, get, derive, acquire, secure, realize.

reaper ▸ noun a person or machine that harvests a crop.
▪ **the Grim Reaper** death, shown as a cloaked skeleton holding a scythe.

rear¹ ▸ noun the back part of something.

> SYNONYMS **1** *the rear of the building* **back (part),** hind part; Nautical stern. **2** *the rear of the queue* **end,** tail (end), back (end). ANTONYMS front, bow, head.

▸ adjective at the back.

> SYNONYMS *the rear bumper* **back,** end, rearmost, hind, last. ANTONYMS front.

▪ **rear admiral** the naval rank above commodore.
□ **rearmost** adjective **rearward** adjective & adverb **rearwards** adverb.

rear² ▸ verb **1** bring up offspring. **2** breed animals. **3** (of an animal) raise itself upright on its hind legs. **4** extend to a great height.

> SYNONYMS **1** *I was reared in Newcastle* **bring up,** care for, look after, nurture; N. Amer. raise. **2** *he reared cattle* **breed,** raise, keep. **3** *laboratory-reared plants* **grow,** cultivate. **4** *houses reared up on either side* **rise,** tower, soar, loom.

rearguard ▸ noun a group of soldiers protecting the rear of the main force.

rearm ▸ verb provide with or obtain a new supply of weapons.
□ **rearmament** noun.

rearrange ▸ verb (**rearranges, rearranging, rearranged**) arrange again in a different way.
□ **rearrangement** noun.

reason ▸ noun **1** a cause or explanation. **2** good or obvious cause to do something. **3** the power to think and draw conclusions logically. **4** (**your reason**) your sanity. **5** what is right, practical, or possible.

> SYNONYMS **1** *the main reason for his decision* **cause,** ground(s), basis, rationale, motive, explanation, justification, defence, vindication, excuse. **2** *postmodern voices railing against reason* **rationality,** logic, cognition. **3** *he was losing his reason* **sanity,** mind, mental faculties, senses, wits; informal marbles.

▸ verb **1** think and draw conclusions logically. **2** (**reason with**) persuade someone by using logical arguments.

> SYNONYMS *Scott reasoned that Annabel might be ill* **calculate,** conclude, reckon, think, judge, deduce, infer, surmise; informal figure.

▪ **stand to reason** be logical.

reasonable ▸ adjective **1** fair and sensible. **2** appropriate in a particular situation. **3** fairly good. **4** not too expensive.

> SYNONYMS **1** *a reasonable explanation* **sensible,** rational, logical, fair, just, equitable, intelligent, wise, level-headed, practical, realistic, sound, valid, commonsensical, tenable, plausible, credible, believable. **2** *take all reasonable precautions* **practicable,** sensible, appropriate, suitable. **3** *cars in reasonable condition* **fairly good,** acceptable, satisfactory, average, adequate, fair, tolerable, passable; informal OK. **4** *reasonable prices* **inexpensive,** affordable, moderate, low, cheap, budget, bargain.

□ **reasonably** adverb.

reassure ▸ verb (**reassures, reassuring, reassured**) make someone feel less worried or afraid.

> SYNONYMS **put someone's mind at rest,** encourage, hearten, buoy up, cheer up, comfort, soothe. ANTONYMS alarm.

□ **reassurance** noun.

rebarbative ▸ adjective unpleasant.

rebate /ree-bayt/ ▸ noun **1** a partial refund to someone who has paid too much for tax, rent, etc. **2** a discount on a sum that is due.

> SYNONYMS **partial refund,** partial repayment, discount, deduction, reduction.

rebel ▸ verb /ri-**bel**/ (**rebels, rebelling, rebelled**) **1** refuse to obey the government or ruler. **2** oppose authority, or refuse to behave conventionally.

> SYNONYMS *the citizens rebelled* **revolt**, mutiny, riot, rise up, take up arms.
> ANTONYMS comply.

▶ noun /**reb**-uhl/ a person who rebels.

> SYNONYMS **1** *the rebels took control of the capital* **revolutionary**, insurgent, insurrectionist, mutineer, guerrilla, terrorist, freedom fighter. **2** *the concept of the artist as a rebel* **nonconformist**, dissenter, dissident, maverick.
> ANTONYMS loyalist, conformist.

▶ adjective refusing to obey authority.

> SYNONYMS **1** *rebel troops* **rebellious**, insurgent, revolutionary, mutinous. **2** *rebel MPs* **defiant**, disobedient, insubordinate, subversive, rebellious, nonconformist, maverick.
> ANTONYMS loyal, compliant.

rebellion ▶ noun **1** an act of rebelling. **2** opposition to authority or control.

> SYNONYMS **1** *troops suppressed the rebellion* **revolt**, uprising, insurrection, mutiny, revolution, insurgence. **2** *an act of rebellion* **defiance**, disobedience, insubordination, subversion, resistance.
> ANTONYMS compliance.

rebellious ▶ adjective choosing to rebel.

> SYNONYMS **1** *rebellious troops* **rebel**, insurgent, mutinous, revolutionary. **2** *a rebellious adolescent* **defiant**, disobedient, insubordinate, unruly, mutinous, obstreperous, recalcitrant, intractable; Brit. informal bolshie.
> ANTONYMS loyal, compliant.

□ **rebelliously** adverb.

rebirth ▶ noun a return to life or activity.

reborn ▶ adjective brought back to life or activity.

rebound ▶ verb /ri-**bownd**/ **1** bounce back after hitting a hard surface. **2** increase again. **3** (**rebound on**) have an unexpected and unpleasant effect on.

> SYNONYMS **1** *the ball rebounded* **bounce (back)**, spring back, ricochet, boomerang. **2** *Thomas's tactics rebounded on him* **backfire**, boomerang.

▶ noun /**ree**-bownd/ a ball or shot that rebounds.

■ **on the rebound** while still upset after the ending of a romantic relationship.

rebuff ▶ verb reject in an abrupt or unkind way.

> SYNONYMS *his offer was rebuffed* **reject**, turn down, spurn, refuse, decline, snub, slight, dismiss, brush off.
> ANTONYMS accept.

▶ noun an abrupt or unkind rejection.

> SYNONYMS *for fear of a rebuff* **rejection**, snub, slight, refusal, spurning; informal brush-off, kick in the teeth, slap in the face.
> ANTONYMS acceptance.

rebuke ▶ verb (rebukes, rebuking, rebuked) sharply criticize or tell off.

> SYNONYMS *she never rebuked him* **reprimand**, reproach, scold, admonish; informal tell off; Brit. informal tick off; N. Amer. informal chew out.
> ANTONYMS praise.

▶ noun a sharp criticism.

> SYNONYMS *a severe rebuke* **reprimand**, reproach, scolding, admonition; informal telling-off; Brit. informal ticking-off.
> ANTONYMS praise.

rebus ▶ noun (plural rebuses) a puzzle in which words are represented by combinations of pictures and letters.

rebut ▶ verb (rebuts, rebutting, rebutted) claim or prove that something is false.
□ **rebuttal** noun.

recalcitrant /ri-**kal**-si-truhnt/ ▶ adjective unwilling to cooperate; disobedient.
□ **recalcitrance** noun.

recall ▶ verb **1** remember. **2** make someone think of; bring to mind. **3** officially order someone to return. **4** (of a manufacturer) ask for faulty products to be returned.

> SYNONYMS **1** *he recalled his student days* **remember**, recollect, call to mind, think back on/to, reminisce about. **2** *their exploits recall the days of chivalry* **remind someone of**, bring to mind, call up, conjure up, evoke. **3** *the ambassador was recalled* **call back**, order home, withdraw.
> ANTONYMS forget, post.

▶ noun **1** the action of remembering. **2** an official order for someone to return.

> SYNONYMS **1** *their recall of dreams* **recollection**, remembrance, memory. **2** *the recall of the ambassador* **calling back**, ordering home, withdrawal.

recant ▶ verb withdraw a former opinion or belief.

recap ▶ verb (recaps, recapping, recapped) recapitulate.

recapitulate ▶ verb (recapitulates, recapitulating, recapitulated) give a summary of.
□ **recapitulation** noun.

recapture ▶ verb (recaptures, recapturing, recaptured) **1** capture a person or animal that has escaped. **2** recover something taken or lost. **3** bring back or experience again a past time or feeling.
▶ noun an act of recapturing.

recast ▶ verb (recasts, recasting, recast) present something in a different form.

recce /**rek**-ki/ ▶ noun Brit. informal a reconnaissance.

recede ▶ verb (recedes, receding, receded) **1** move back or further away. **2** gradually become weaker or smaller. **3** (**receding**) (of part of the face) sloping backwards.

> SYNONYMS **1** *the waters receded* **retreat,** go back/down/away, withdraw, ebb, subside, abate, return, retire. **2** *fears of violence have receded* **diminish,** lessen, dwindle, fade, abate, subside.
> ANTONYMS advance, grow.

receipt ▶ noun **1** a written statement confirming that something has been paid for or received. **2** the action of receiving something. **3** (**receipts**) the amount of money received over a period by a business.

> SYNONYMS **1** *the receipt of a letter* **receiving,** getting, obtaining, gaining. **2** *make sure you get a receipt* **proof of purchase,** sales ticket, till receipt, acknowledgement.

receive ▶ verb (receives, receiving, received) **1** be given or paid. **2** accept something sent or offered. **3** experience or meet with. **4** form an idea or impression from an experience. **5** entertain someone as a guest. **6** detect or pick up broadcast signals. **7** (**received**) widely accepted as true.

> SYNONYMS **1** *Tony received an award* **be given,** be presented with, be awarded, be sent, be told, hear, collect, get, obtain, gain, acquire, be paid. **2** *he received her suggestion with a lack of interest* **hear,** listen to, respond to, react to. **3** *she received an injury* **experience,** sustain, undergo, meet with, suffer, bear.
> ANTONYMS give, send, inflict.

■ **received pronunciation** the standard form of British English pronunciation, based on educated speech in southern England.

> ✔ Remember, the rule is **i** before **e** except after **c**: rec**ei**ve.

receiver ▶ noun **1** a radio or television apparatus that converts broadcast signals into sound or images. **2** the part of a telephone that converts electrical signals into sounds. **3** (also **official receiver**) a person appointed to manage the financial affairs of a bankrupt business.
□ **receivership** noun.

recent ▶ adjective having happened or been done shortly before the present.

> SYNONYMS **new,** the latest, current, fresh, modern, late, contemporary, up to date, up to the minute.
> ANTONYMS old.

recently ▶ adverb at a recent date.

> SYNONYMS **not long ago,** a little while back, just now, newly, freshly, of late, lately, latterly.

receptacle ▶ noun an object used to contain something.

reception ▶ noun **1** the action of receiving. **2** the way in which people react to something. **3** a formal social occasion held to welcome someone or celebrate an event. **4** the area in a hotel, office, etc. where visitors are greeted. **5** the quality with which broadcast signals are received.

> SYNONYMS **1** *a chilly reception* **response,** reaction, treatment, welcome. **2** *a wedding reception* **party,** function, social occasion, celebration, get-together, gathering, soirée; N. Amer. levee; informal do.

receptionist ▶ noun a person who greets and deals with visitors to an office, hotel, etc.

receptive ▶ adjective **1** able or willing to receive something. **2** willing to consider new ideas.
□ **receptivity** noun.

receptor ▶ noun a nerve ending in the body that responds to a stimulus such as light.

recess ▶ noun **1** a small space set back in a wall or in a surface. **2** a break between sessions of a parliament, law court, etc. **3** (**recesses**) remote or hidden places.

> SYNONYMS **1** *two recesses fitted with bookshelves* **alcove,** bay, niche, nook, corner. **2** *the Christmas recess* **break,** adjournment, interlude, interval, rest, holiday, vacation.

▶ verb fit something so that it is set back into a surface.

recession ▶ noun a period during which trade and industrial activity in a country are reduced.

> SYNONYMS **downturn,** depression, slump, slowdown.
> ANTONYMS boom.

recessive ▶ adjective (of a gene) appearing in offspring only if a contrary gene is not also inherited.

recharge ▶ verb (recharges, recharging, recharged) charge a battery or device again.
□ **rechargeable** adjective **recharger** noun.

recherché /ruh-**shair**-shay/ ▶ adjective unusual and not easily understood.

recidivist /ri-**sid**-i-vist/ ▶ noun a person who constantly commits crimes.
□ **recidivism** noun.

recipe ▶ noun **1** a list of ingredients and instructions for preparing a dish. **2** something likely to lead to a particular outcome: *a recipe for disaster.*

r

SYNONYMS *a recipe for success* **formula,** prescription, blueprint.

recipient ▸ noun a person who receives something.

reciprocal /ri-**sip**-ruh-k'l/ ▸ adjective
1 given or done in return. **2** affecting two parties equally.
□ **reciprocally** adverb.

reciprocate ▸ verb (**reciprocates, reciprocating, reciprocated**) respond to an action or emotion with a similar one.

reciprocity /re-si-**pross**-i-ti/ ▸ noun a situation in which two parties provide the same help to each other.

recital ▸ noun **1** the performance of a programme of music by a soloist or small group. **2** a long account of a series of facts or events.

SYNONYMS **1** *a piano recital* **performance,** concert, rendering, recitation, reading. **2** *her recital of Adam's failures* **report,** account, listing, catalogue, litany.

recite ▸ verb (**recites, reciting, recited**) **1** repeat a passage aloud from memory. **2** state facts, events, etc. in order.

SYNONYMS **1** *he began to recite the Koran* **quote,** say, speak, read aloud, declaim, deliver, render. **2** *Sir John recited the facts* **recount,** list, detail, reel off, relate, enumerate.

□ **recitation** noun.

reckless ▸ adjective without thought or care for the results of an action.

SYNONYMS **rash,** careless, thoughtless, heedless, precipitate, impetuous, impulsive, irresponsible, foolhardy.
ANTONYMS cautious.

□ **recklessly** adverb **recklessness** noun.

reckon ▸ verb **1** have an opinion about something; think. **2** (**reckon on**) rely on or expect. **3** calculate. **4** (**reckon with** or **without**) take (or fail to take) something into account.

SYNONYMS **1** *the cost was reckoned at £60* **calculate,** compute, work out, figure, count (up), add up, total; Brit. tot up. **2** *Anselm reckoned Hugh among his friends* **include,** count, regard as, look on as. **3** *it was reckoned a failure* **regard as,** consider, judge, think of as, deem, rate, gauge, count.

■ **to be reckoned with** to be treated as important.

reckoning ▸ noun **1** the action of calculating or estimating something. **2** punishment for past actions.

SYNONYMS **calculation,** estimation, computation, working out, addition, count.

reclaim ▸ verb **1** get possession of something again. **2** make land usable.

SYNONYMS **1** *expenses can be reclaimed* **get back,** claim back, recover, retrieve, recoup. **2** *Henrietta had reclaimed him from a life of vice* **save,** rescue, redeem, salvage.

□ **reclamation** noun.

recline ▸ verb (**reclines, reclining, reclined**) lie back in a relaxed position.

SYNONYMS **lie (down/back),** lean back, relax, loll, lounge, sprawl, stretch out.

recluse /ri-**klooss**/ ▸ noun a person who avoids other people and lives alone.
□ **reclusive** adjective.

recognition ▸ noun **1** the action of recognizing. **2** appreciation or acknowledgement.

SYNONYMS **1** *there was no sign of recognition on his face* **identification,** recollection, remembrance. **2** *his recognition of his lack of experience* **acknowledgement,** acceptance, admission, confession. **3** *you deserve recognition for your work* **appreciation,** gratitude, thanks, congratulations, credit, commendation, acclaim, acknowledgement.

recognize (or **recognise**) ▸ verb (**recognizes, recognizing, recognized**) **1** know someone or something from having come across them before. **2** accept something as genuine, legal, or valid. **3** show official appreciation of.

SYNONYMS **1** *Hannah recognized him at once* **identify,** place, know, put a name to, remember, recall, recollect; Scottish & N. English ken. **2** *they recognized Alan's ability* **acknowledge,** accept, admit, concede, confess, realize. **3** *the Trust recognized their hard work* **pay tribute to,** appreciate, be grateful for, acclaim, commend.

□ **recognizable** adjective.

recoil ▸ verb **1** suddenly move back in fear, horror, or disgust. **2** (of a gun) suddenly move backwards as a reaction to being fired. **3** (**recoil on**) have an unpleasant effect on.
▸ noun the action of recoiling.

recollect ▸ verb remember.

SYNONYMS **remember,** recall, call to mind, think of, think back to, reminisce about.
ANTONYMS forget.

recollection ▸ noun the action of remembering, or something remembered.

SYNONYMS **memory,** recall, remembrance, impression, reminiscence.

recommend ▸ verb **1** say that someone or something is suitable for a particular purpose or role. **2** make something seem appealing or desirable.

SYNONYMS **1** *his former employer recommended him* **advocate**, endorse, commend, suggest, put forward, propose, nominate, put up, speak favourably of, put in a good word for, vouch for; informal plug. **2** *the committee recommended a cautious approach* **advise**, counsel, urge, exhort, enjoin, prescribe, argue for, back, support.
ANTONYMS advise against.

✔ one **c** and two **m**s: re**c**o**mm**end.

recommendation ▸ noun **1** a suggestion or proposal as to the best course of action. **2** the action or recommending.

SYNONYMS **1** *the adviser's recommendations* **advice**, counsel, guidance, suggestion, proposal. **2** *a personal recommendation* **commendation**, endorsement, good word, testimonial, tip; informal plug.

recompense /**rek**-uhm-penss/ ▸ verb (**recompenses**, **recompensing**, **recompensed**) **1** compensate someone for loss or harm suffered. **2** pay or reward someone for effort or work.
▸ noun compensation or reward.

reconcile ▸ verb (**reconciles**, **reconciling**, **reconciled**) **1** make two people or groups friendly again. **2** find a satisfactory way of dealing with opposing facts, ideas, etc. **3** (**reconcile someone to**) make someone accept something unwelcome.

reconciliation ▸ noun **1** the end of a disagreement and the return to friendly relations. **2** the action of reconciling opposing ideas, facts, etc.

recondite /**rek**-uhn-dyt/ ▸ adjective not known about or understood by many people.

recondition ▸ verb Brit. bring back to a good condition; renovate.

reconnaissance /ri-**kon**-ni-suhnss/ ▸ noun military observation of an area to gain information.

reconnoitre /rek-uh-**noy**-ter/ (US spelling **reconnoiter**) ▸ verb (**reconnoitres**, **reconnoitring**, **reconnoitred**) make a military observation of an area.

reconsider ▸ verb (**reconsiders**, **reconsidering**, **reconsidered**) consider again, with the possibility of changing a decision.

SYNONYMS **rethink**, review, revise, re-evaluate, reassess, have second thoughts, change your mind.

◻ **reconsideration** noun.

reconstitute ▸ verb (**reconstitutes**, **reconstituting**, **reconstituted**) **1** change the form of an organization. **2** restore dried food to its original state by adding water.
◻ **reconstitution** noun.

reconstruct ▸ verb **1** construct again. **2** show how a past event happened by using the evidence that has been gathered.

SYNONYMS **1** *the building had to be reconstructed* **rebuild**, recreate, remake, restore, reassemble. **2** *reconstructing events* **recreate**, piece together, re-enact.

◻ **reconstruction** noun.

record ▸ noun /**rek**-ord/ **1** a permanent account of something, kept for evidence or information. **2** the previous behaviour or performance of a person or thing. **3** (also **criminal record**) a list of a person's previous criminal convictions. **4** the best performance of its kind that has been officially recognized. **5** a thin plastic disc carrying recorded sound in grooves on each surface.

SYNONYMS **1** *written records* **account**, document, data, file, dossier, evidence, report, annals, archive, chronicle, minutes, transactions, proceedings, transcript, certificate, deed, register, log. **2** *listening to records* **album**, vinyl; dated LP, single. **3** *a good attendance record* **previous conduct**, previous performance, history, reputation. **4** *a new British record* **best performance**, highest achievement, best time, fastest time.

▸ verb /ri-**kord**/ **1** make a record of. **2** convert sound or vision into a permanent form so that it can be reproduced later.

SYNONYMS **1** *the doctor recorded her blood pressure* **write down**, take down, note, jot down, put down on paper, document, enter, minute, register, log. **2** *the thermometer recorded a high temperature* **indicate**, register, show, display. **3** *the recital was recorded live* **capture on film/tape/disk**, film, photograph, tape, tape-record, video-record, videotape.

■ **off the record** not made as an official statement. **record player** a device for playing records.
◻ **recording** noun.

recorder ▸ noun **1** a device for recording sound, pictures, etc. **2** a person who keeps records. **3** a musical instrument which you play by blowing through a mouthpiece and putting your fingers over holes.

recount[1] ▸ verb describe something to someone.

SYNONYMS **tell**, relate, narrate, describe, report, relay, convey, communicate, impart.

r

recount² ▸ verb count again.
▸ noun an act of counting something again.

recoup ▸ verb recover an amount of money that has been lost or spent.

recourse ▸ noun 1 a source of help in a difficult situation. 2 (**recourse to**) the use of a particular source of help.

recover ▸ verb (**recovers, recovering, recovered**) 1 return to a normal state of health or strength. 2 regain possession or control of. 3 regain an amount of money that has been spent or lent.

> SYNONYMS 1 *he's recovering from a heart attack* **get better,** improve, recuperate, convalesce, be on the mend, respond to treatment, heal, bounce back. 2 *later, shares recovered* **rally,** improve, pick up, rebound, bounce back. 3 *the stolen material has been recovered* **retrieve,** regain, get back, recoup, reclaim, repossess. 4 *gold coins recovered from a wreck* **salvage,** save, rescue, retrieve. ANTONYMS deteriorate, lose.

□ **recoverable** adjective.

recovery ▸ noun (plural **recoveries**) the action or an act of recovering.

> SYNONYMS 1 *her recovery may be slow* **improvement,** recuperation, convalescence, rally, mend. 2 *the recovery of stolen goods* **retrieval,** repossession, reclamation. ANTONYMS relapse, loss.

recreate ▸ verb (**recreates, recreating, recreated**) make or do again.

recreation¹ /rek-ri-**ay**-sh'n/ ▸ noun enjoyable leisure activity.

> SYNONYMS 1 *she cycles for recreation* **pleasure,** leisure, relaxation, fun, enjoyment, entertainment, amusement. 2 *his favourite recreations* **pastime,** hobby, leisure activity. ANTONYMS work.

□ **recreational** adjective.

recreation² /ree-kri-**ay**-sh'n/ ▸ noun the action of recreating something.

recrimination ▸ noun an accusation made in response to one from someone else.

recrudescence /ree-kroo-**dess**-'nss/ ▸ noun formal a recurrence.

recruit ▸ verb take on someone to serve in the armed forces or work for an organization.

> SYNONYMS 1 *more soldiers were recruited* **enlist,** call up, conscript; US draft. 2 *the king recruited an army* **muster,** form, raise, mobilize. 3 *the company is recruiting staff* **hire,** employ, take on, enrol, sign up, engage. ANTONYMS demobilize, disband, dismiss.

▸ noun a newly recruited person.

> SYNONYMS 1 *new recruits were enlisted* **conscript;** US draftee; N. Amer. informal yardbird. 2 *top-quality recruits* **new member,** newcomer, initiate, joiner, beginner, novice.

□ **recruitment** noun.

rectal ▸ adjective relating to or affecting the rectum.

rectangle ▸ noun a flat shape with four right angles and four straight sides, two of which are longer than the others.
□ **rectangular** adjective.

rectify ▸ verb (**rectifies, rectifying, rectified**) 1 put right; correct. 2 convert alternating current to direct current.
□ **rectification** noun **rectifier** noun.

rectilinear ▸ adjective having or moving in a straight line or lines.

rectitude ▸ noun morally correct behaviour.

recto ▸ noun (plural **rectos**) a right-hand page of an open book, or the front of a loose document.

rector ▸ noun 1 a Christian priest in charge of a parish. 2 the head of certain universities, colleges, and schools.

rectory ▸ noun (plural **rectories**) the house of a rector.

rectum ▸ noun the final section of the large intestine, ending at the anus.

recumbent ▸ adjective lying down.

recuperate ▸ verb (**recuperates, recuperating, recuperated**) 1 recover from illness or tiredness. 2 get back something that has been lost or spent.
□ **recuperation** noun.

recur ▸ verb (**recurs, recurring, recurred**) happen again or repeatedly.

> SYNONYMS **happen again,** reoccur, repeat (itself), come back, return, reappear.

□ **recurrence** noun.

recurrent ▸ adjective happening often or repeatedly.

recycle ▸ verb (**recycles, recycling, recycled**) 1 convert waste into a form in which it can be reused. 2 use something again.

> SYNONYMS **reuse,** reprocess, reclaim, recover, salvage.

□ **recyclable** adjective.

red ▸ adjective (**redder, reddest**) 1 of the colour of blood or fire. 2 (of hair or fur) of a reddish-brown colour.

> SYNONYMS 1 *a red dress* **scarlet,** vermilion, ruby, cherry, cerise, cardinal, carmine, wine. 2 *he was red in the face* **flushed,** blushing, pink, rosy, florid, ruddy. 3 *red hair* auburn, Titian, chestnut, carroty, ginger.

▸ noun 1 red colour. 2 informal, chiefly disapproving a communist or socialist.

■ **in the red** having spent more than is in your bank account. **red blood cell** a blood cell which contains haemoglobin and carries oxygen to the tissues. **red-blooded** (of a man) energetic and healthy. **red-brick** (of a British university) founded in the late 19th or early 20th century. **red card** (in soccer) a red card shown by the referee to a player being sent off the field. **red-handed** in the act of doing something wrong. **red herring** a thing that takes people's attention away from something important. **red-hot 1** so hot that it glows red. **2** very exciting. **Red Indian** dated, often offensive an American Indian. **red-letter day** an important or memorable day. **red-light district** an area with many brothels, strip clubs, etc. **red pepper** a ripe sweet pepper. **red tape** complicated official rules which cause irritation because they take up your time. **see red** informal suddenly become very angry.
□ **reddish** adjective.

redcurrant ▸ noun a small edible red berry.

redden ▸ verb make or become red.

redeem ▸ verb **1** make up for the faults of. **2** save someone from sin or evil. **3** fulfil a promise. **4** pay a debt. **5** exchange a coupon for goods or money. **6** regain possession of something in exchange for payment.

> SYNONYMS **1** *redeeming sinners* **save,** deliver from sin, absolve. **2** *Billy redeemed his drums from the pawnbrokers* **retrieve,** regain, recover, get back, reclaim, repossess, buy back. **3** *this voucher can be redeemed at any branch* **exchange,** convert, trade in, cash in.
> ANTONYMS damn, pawn, buy.

Redeemer ▸ noun (the Redeemer) Jesus.

redemption ▸ noun the action of redeeming.

> SYNONYMS **1** *God's redemption of his people* **saving,** freeing from sin, absolution. **2** *the redemption of their possessions* **retrieval,** recovery, reclamation, repossession, return. **3** *the redemption of vouchers* **exchange,** conversion, trade-in, cashing in.
> ANTONYMS condemnation, pawning, purchase.

redeploy ▸ verb move troops, resources, etc. to a new place or task.
□ **redeployment** noun.

redhead ▸ noun a person with red hair.

redneck ▸ noun US informal a conservative working-class white person.

redolent /red-uh-luhnt/ ▸ adjective (**redolent of** or **with**) **1** making you think of a particular thing. **2** literary smelling of.
□ **redolence** noun.

redouble ▸ verb (redoubles, redoubling, redoubled) make or become greater or stronger.

redoubt ▸ noun a small or temporary structure from which soldiers can defend a place under attack.

redoubtable ▸ adjective worthy of respect or fear; formidable.

redound ▸ verb (**redound to**) formal be to someone's credit.

redress /ri-**dress**/ ▸ verb put right something that is unfair or wrong.

> SYNONYMS **1** *we redressed the problem* **rectify,** correct, right, compensate for, amend, remedy, make good. **2** *we aim to redress the balance* **even up,** regulate, equalize.

▸ noun payment or action to make amends for a wrong.

> SYNONYMS *your best hope of redress* **compensation,** reparation, restitution, recompense, repayment, amends.

redskin ▸ noun dated or offensive an American Indian.

reduce ▸ verb (reduces, reducing, reduced) **1** make or become less. **2** (**reduce something to**) change something to a simpler form. **3** (**reduce someone to**) bring someone to a particular state or condition. **4** boil a liquid so that it becomes thicker.

> SYNONYMS **1** *the aim to reduce pollution* **lessen,** make smaller, lower, bring down, decrease, diminish, minimize, shrink, narrow, contract, shorten; informal chop. **2** *he reduced her to tears* **bring to,** drive to.
> ANTONYMS increase.

■ **reduced circumstances** a state in which you have become poorer than you were before.
□ **reducible** adjective.

reduction ▸ noun **1** the action of reducing. **2** the amount by which something is reduced.

> SYNONYMS **1** *a reduction in pollution* **lessening,** lowering, decrease, diminution. **2** *a reduction in staff* **cut,** cutback, axing, downsizing.

reductive ▸ adjective presenting something in an oversimplified form.

redundancy ▸ noun (plural **redundancies**) **1** the state of being redundant. **2** dismissal from a job that has become redundant.

> SYNONYMS **dismissal,** sacking, lay-off, discharge, unemployment.

redundant ▸ adjective **1** Brit. unemployed because your job is no longer needed. **2** no longer needed or useful.

> SYNONYMS *redundant churches* **unnecessary,** not required, unneeded,

r

redwood | reflect

surplus (to requirements), superfluous. ANTONYMS necessary.

redwood ▸ noun a giant coniferous tree with reddish wood.

reed ▸ noun 1 a tall, slender plant that grows in water or on marshy ground. 2 a piece of thin cane or metal in musical instruments such as the clarinet, which vibrates when air is blown over it and produces sound.

reedy ▸ adjective 1 (of a sound or voice) high and thin in tone. 2 full of reeds.

reef ▸ noun 1 a ridge of jagged rock or coral just above or below the surface of the sea. 2 each of several strips across a sail that can be taken in when the wind is strong.
▸ verb make a sail smaller by taking in a reef.
■ reef knot a type of secure knot.

reefer ▸ noun informal a cannabis cigarette.

reefer jacket ▸ noun a thick close-fitting double-breasted jacket.

reek ▸ verb have a very unpleasant smell.
▸ noun a very unpleasant smell.

reel ▸ noun 1 a cylinder on which film, thread, etc. can be wound. 2 a lively Scottish or Irish folk dance.
▸ verb 1 (reel something in) bring something towards you by turning a reel. 2 (reel something off) recite something quickly and with ease. 3 stagger. 4 feel giddy, shocked, or bewildered.

SYNONYMS 1 *he reeled as the ship began to roll* stagger, lurch, sway, rock, stumble, totter, wobble. 2 *the room reeled* go round (and round), whirl, spin, revolve, swirl, twirl, turn, swim.

re-entry ▸ noun (plural re-entries) 1 the action of entering again. 2 the return of a spacecraft or missile into the earth's atmosphere.

refectory ▸ noun (plural refectories) a room used for meals in an educational or religious institution.

refer ▸ verb (refers, referring, referred) (refer to) 1 write or say something about; mention. 2 (of a word or phrase) describe. 3 turn to a person, book, etc. for information. 4 (refer someone/thing to) pass a person or matter on to someone else for help or a decision.

SYNONYMS *the matter has been referred to my insurers* pass, direct, hand on/over, send on, transfer, entrust, assign.

referee ▸ noun 1 an official who supervises a game to ensure that players keep to the rules. 2 Brit. a person who is willing to provide a reference for a person applying for a job. 3 a person who reads academic work before it is published.

SYNONYMS 1 *the referee blew his whistle* umpire, judge, adjudicator; informal ref.

2 *include the names of two referees* supporter, character witness, advocate.
▸ verb (referees, refereeing, refereed) be a referee of.

SYNONYMS *he refereed the game* umpire, judge, adjudicate; informal ref.

reference ▸ noun 1 the action of referring to something. 2 a mention of a source of information in a book or article. 3 a letter giving information about how suitable someone is for a new job.

SYNONYMS 1 *a reference to his book* mention, allusion, quotation, comment, remark. 2 *references are given in the bibliography* source, citation, authority, credit. 3 *a glowing reference* testimonial, recommendation, character reference, credentials.

✔ one **r** in the middle, not two: refe**r**ence.

referendum ▸ noun (plural referendums or referenda) a vote by the people of a country on a single political issue.

SYNONYMS (popular) vote, ballot, poll, plebiscite.

referral ▸ noun the action of referring someone or something to a specialist or higher authority.

refine ▸ verb (refines, refining, refined) 1 make something pure by removing unwanted substances. 2 improve something by making minor changes. 3 (refined) well educated, elegant, and having good taste.

SYNONYMS 1 *refining our cereal foods* purify, filter, distil, process, treat. 2 (refined) *refined sugar* purified, processed, treated. 3 *helping students to refine their skills* improve, perfect, polish (up), hone, fine-tune. 4 (refined) *a refined lady* cultivated, cultured, polished, elegant, sophisticated, urbane, polite, gracious, well bred. 5 (refined) *a person of refined taste* discriminating, discerning, fastidious, exquisite, impeccable, fine.

refinement ▸ noun 1 the process of refining. 2 an improvement. 3 the quality of being well educated, elegant, and having good taste.

refinery ▸ noun (plural refineries) a factory where a substance such as oil is refined.

refit ▸ verb (refits, refitting, refitted) replace or repair equipment and fittings in a ship, building, etc.
▸ noun an act of refitting.

reflect ▸ verb 1 throw back heat, light, or sound from a surface. 2 (of a mirror) show an image of. 3 show in a realistic or appropriate way. 4 (reflect well or badly

on) give a good or bad impression of.
5 (**reflect on**) think seriously about.

> SYNONYMS **1** *the snow reflects light*
> **mirror,** send back, throw back, echo.
> **2** *their expressions reflected their feelings*
> **indicate,** show, display, demonstrate, be
> evidence of, reveal, betray. **3** *he reflected*
> *on his task* **think,** consider, review, mull,
> contemplate, cogitate, meditate, muse,
> brood.

reflection ▶ noun **1** the process of
reflecting. **2** a reflected image. **3** a sign of
something's true nature. **4** something that
brings discredit. **5** serious thought.

> SYNONYMS **1** *her reflection in the mirror*
> **image,** likeness. **2** *your hands are a*
> *reflection of your well-being* **indication,**
> display, demonstration, manifestation,
> expression, evidence. **3** *after some*
> *reflection, he turned it down* **thought,**
> consideration, contemplation,
> deliberation, pondering, meditation,
> musing.

reflective ▶ adjective **1** providing a
reflection. **2** thoughtful.
□ **reflectively** adverb.

reflector ▶ noun a piece of glass or plastic
on the back of a vehicle for reflecting light.

reflex ▶ noun an action done without
conscious thought as a response to
something.
▶ adjective **1** done as a reflex. **2** (of an angle)
more than 180°.

reflexive ▶ adjective Grammar referring back
to the subject of a clause or verb, e.g.
myself in *I hurt myself.*

reflexology ▶ noun a system of massage
used to relieve tension and treat illness.
□ **reflexologist** noun.

refocus ▶ verb (**refocuses, refocusing** or
refocussing, refocused or **refocussed**)
1 adjust the focus of a lens or your eyes.
2 focus attention on something new or
different.

reform ▶ verb **1** change something to
improve it. **2** make someone improve their
behaviour.

> SYNONYMS **1** *a plan to reform the*
> *system* **improve,** better, ameliorate,
> correct, rectify, restore, revise, refine,
> adapt, revamp, redesign, reconstruct,
> reorganize. **2** *after his marriage he*
> *reformed* **mend your ways,** change for
> the better, turn over a new leaf.

▶ noun an act of reforming.

> SYNONYMS *the reform of the prison*
> *system* **improvement,** amelioration,
> refinement, rectification, restoration,
> adaptation, revision, redesign, revamp,
> reconstruction, reorganization.

□ **reformer** noun.

reformation ▶ noun **1** the action of
reforming. **2** (**the Reformation**) a 16th-
century movement for reforming the
Roman Catholic Church, leading to the
establishment of the Protestant Churches.

reformist ▶ adjective supporting political or
social reform.
▶ noun a supporter of such reform.
□ **reformism** noun.

refract ▶ verb (of water, air, or glass) make a
ray of light change direction when it enters
at an angle.
□ **refraction** noun **refractive** adjective.

refractory ▶ adjective **1** stubborn or
difficult to control. **2** (of an illness) not
responding to treatment.

refrain[1] ▶ verb (**refrain from**) stop yourself
from doing something.

> SYNONYMS **abstain,** desist, hold back, stop
> yourself, forbear, avoid; informal swear off.

refrain[2] ▶ noun a part of a song that is
repeated at the end of each verse.

refresh ▶ verb make someone feel less tired
or hot.

> SYNONYMS **1** *the cool air will refresh me*
> **reinvigorate,** revitalize, revive, restore,
> perk up, brace, freshen, wake up; informal
> buck up. **2** *let me refresh your memory*
> **jog,** stimulate, prompt, prod.
> ANTONYMS weary.

refresher ▶ noun a course intended
to improve or update your skills or
knowledge.

refreshing ▶ adjective **1** making you feel
less tired or hot. **2** pleasingly new or
different.

> SYNONYMS **1** *a refreshing drink*
> **invigorating,** revitalizing, reviving,
> bracing, fortifying, enlivening,
> stimulating. **2** *a refreshing change of*
> *direction* **welcome,** stimulating, fresh,
> new, imaginative, innovative.
> ANTONYMS wearying.

□ **refreshingly** adverb.

refreshment ▶ noun **1** a snack or drink.
2 the giving of fresh energy.

> SYNONYMS **food and drink,** snacks, titbits;
> informal nibbles.

refrigerate ▶ verb (**refrigerates,**
refrigerating, refrigerated) make food or
drink cold to keep it fresh.
□ **refrigeration** noun.

refrigerator ▶ noun a fridge.

> ✔ no **d** in the middle: ref**rig**erator, not **-ridg-**.

refuel ▶ verb (**refuels, refuelling, refuelled;**
US spelling **refuels, refueling, refueled**)
supply with more fuel.

refuge ▶ noun **1** shelter from danger or
trouble. **2** a safe place.

r

SYNONYMS **1** *homeless people seeking refuge* **shelter,** protection, safety, security, asylum, sanctuary. **2** *a refuge for mountain gorillas* **sanctuary,** shelter, haven, sanctum, retreat, bolt-hole, hiding place.

refugee ▸ noun a person who has been forced to leave their country because of a war or because they are being persecuted.

SYNONYMS **asylum seeker,** fugitive, displaced person, exile, émigré.

refulgent /ri-**ful**-juhnt/ ▸ adjective literary shining very brightly.

refund ▸ verb pay back money to.

SYNONYMS **1** *we will refund your money* **repay,** give back, return, pay back. **2** *they refunded the subscribers* **reimburse,** compensate, recompense.

▸ noun a repayment of a sum of money.

SYNONYMS *a full refund* **repayment,** reimbursement, compensation, rebate.

refurbish ▸ verb redecorate and improve a building or room.

SYNONYMS **renovate,** recondition, rehabilitate, revamp, overhaul, restore, redecorate, upgrade, refit; informal do up.

□ **refurbishment** noun.

refusal ▸ noun **1** an act of refusing to do something. **2** an expression of unwillingness to accept an offer or grant a request.

SYNONYMS **1** *we had one refusal to our invitation* **non-acceptance,** no, rejection, rebuff, turndown; informal knock-back. **2** *the refusal of planning permission* **withholding,** denial.
ANTONYMS acceptance, granting.

refuse[1] /ri-**fyooz**/ ▸ verb (**refuses, refusing, refused**) say that you are unwilling to do or accept something.

SYNONYMS **1** *he refused the invitation* **decline,** turn down, say no to, reject, spurn, rebuff; informal pass up. **2** *the Council refused planning permission* **withhold,** deny.
ANTONYMS accept, grant.

refuse[2] /**ref**-yooss/ ▸ noun things thrown away; rubbish.

SYNONYMS *piles of refuse* **rubbish,** waste, litter; N. Amer. garbage, trash; informal dreck, junk.

refute ▸ verb (**refutes, refuting, refuted**) prove a statement or person to be wrong.
□ **refutation** noun.

regain ▸ verb **1** get something back after losing possession of it. **2** get back to a place.

SYNONYMS **1** *government troops regained the capital* **recover,** get back, win back, recoup, retrieve, repossess, take back, retake, recapture, reconquer. **2** *they regained dry land* **return to,** get back to, reach again, rejoin.

regal ▸ adjective having to do with a king or queen, especially in being magnificent or dignified.

SYNONYMS **1** *his regal forebears* **royal,** kingly, queenly, princely, majestic. **2** *a regal feast.* See **SPLENDID** (sense 1).

□ **regally** adverb.

regale ▸ verb (**regales, regaling, regaled**) **1** entertain someone with anecdotes or stories. **2** supply someone generously with food or drink.

regalia /ri-**gay**-li-uh/ ▸ noun **1** objects such as the crown and sceptre used at coronations or other state occasions. **2** the distinctive clothes and items worn or carried on official occasions by important people.

regard ▸ verb **1** think of in a particular way. **2** look steadily at.

SYNONYMS **1** *we regard the results as encouraging* **consider,** look on, view, see, think of, judge, deem, estimate, assess, reckon, rate. **2** *he regarded her coldly* **look at,** contemplate, eye, gaze at, stare at, observe, view, study, scrutinize.

▸ noun **1** concern or care. **2** high opinion; respect. **3** a look. **4** (**regards**) best wishes.

SYNONYMS **1** *he has no regard for life* **consideration,** care, concern, thought, notice, heed, attention. **2** *doctors are held in high regard* **esteem,** respect, admiration, approval, honour, estimation. **3** *his steady regard* (**fixed**) **look,** gaze, stare, observation, contemplation, study, scrutiny. **4** (**regards**) **best wishes,** greetings, respects, compliments, best, love.

■ **as regards** (or **with regard to**) concerning.

regarding ▸ preposition about; concerning.

SYNONYMS **concerning,** as regards, with/in regard to, with respect to, with reference to, relating to, respecting, re, about, apropos, on the subject of, in connection with, vis-à-vis.

regardless ▸ adverb **1** (**regardless of**) without concern for. **2** despite what is happening.

SYNONYMS **anyway,** anyhow, in any case, nevertheless, nonetheless, despite everything, even so, all the same, in any event, come what may.

regatta ▸ noun a sports event consisting of a series of boat or yacht races.

regency /**ree**-juhn-si/ ▸ noun (plural regencies) 1 a period of government by a regent. 2 (the Regency) the period when George, Prince of Wales, acted as regent in Britain (1811–20).

regenerate ▸ verb (regenerates, regenerating, regenerated) 1 bring new life or strength to. 2 grow new tissue.
□ regeneration noun.

regent ▸ noun a person appointed to rule a state because the king or queen is too young or ill to rule, or is absent.

reggae /**reg**-gay/ ▸ noun a style of popular music originating in Jamaica.

regicide ▸ noun 1 the killing of a king. 2 a person who kills a king.

regime /ray-z**h**eem/ ▸ noun 1 a government, especially one that strictly controls a state. 2 an ordered way of doing something; a system.

synonyms **1** *regime change* **government,** administration, leadership, authority, control, rule, command. **2** *a health regime* **system,** arrangement, scheme, policy, method, course, plan, programme.

regimen /**rej**-i-muhn/ ▸ noun a course of medical treatment, diet, or exercise.

regiment ▸ noun 1 a permanent unit of an army. 2 a large number of people.
□ regimental adjective.

regimented ▸ adjective organized according to a strict system.

Regina ▸ noun the reigning queen (used in referring to lawsuits).

region ▸ noun 1 an area of a country or the world. 2 an administrative district of a city or country. 3 (the regions) the parts of a country outside the capital. 4 a part of the body.

synonyms **district,** province, territory, division, area, section, sector, zone, belt, quarter.

■ in the region of approximately.

regional ▸ adjective relating to or typical of a region.

synonyms **1** *regional variation* **geographical,** territorial. **2** *a regional parliament* **local,** provincial, district, parochial, zonal.
antonyms national.

□ regionally adverb.

register ▸ noun 1 an official list or record. 2 a particular part of the range of a musical instrument or voice. 3 the level and style of a piece of writing or speech (e.g. informal, formal).

synonyms **1** *the register of electors* **list,** roll, roster, index, directory, catalogue, inventory. **2** *the parish register* **record,**

chronicle, log, ledger, archive, annals, files.

▸ verb (registers, registering, registered) 1 enter in a register. 2 put your name on a register. 3 express an opinion or emotion. 4 become aware of. 5 (of a measuring instrument) show a reading.

synonyms **1** *I wish to register a complaint* **record,** enter, file, lodge, write down, submit, report, note, minute, log. **2** *I'd like to register for the course* **enrol,** put your name down, enlist, sign on/up, apply. **3** *her face registered anger* **display,** show, express, exhibit, betray, reveal. **4** *the dial registered 100mph* **indicate,** read, record, show.

■ register office (in the UK) a government building where marriages are performed and births, marriages, and deaths are recorded.

registrar ▸ noun 1 an official responsible for keeping official records. 2 Brit. a hospital doctor who is training to be a specialist.

registration ▸ noun 1 the action of registering. 2 (also registration number) Brit. the series of letters and figures shown on a vehicle's number plate.

registry ▸ noun (plural registries) a place where registers are kept.
■ registry office a register office.

regress /ri-**gress**/ ▸ verb return to an earlier or less advanced state.
□ regression noun.

regressive ▸ adjective 1 returning to a less advanced state. 2 (of a tax) taking a proportionally greater amount from those on lower incomes.

regret ▸ verb (regrets, regretting, regretted) feel sorry or disappointed about something you have done or should have done.

synonyms **1** *they came to regret their decision* **be sorry about,** feel contrite about, feel remorse for, rue. **2** *regretting the passing of youth* **mourn,** grieve for/over, weep over, sigh over, lament, sorrow for.
antonyms welcome.

▸ noun a feeling of regretting something.

synonyms **1** *both players expressed regret* **remorse,** contrition, repentance, compunction. **2** *they left with genuine regret* **sadness,** sorrow, disappointment, unhappiness, grief.
antonyms satisfaction.

regretful ▸ adjective feeling or showing regret.
□ regretfully adverb.

regrettable ▸ adjective causing regret.
□ regrettably adverb.

regular ▸ adjective 1 following or arranged in an evenly spaced pattern or sequence.

r

2 done or happening frequently. **3** doing the same thing often. **4** following an accepted standard. **5** usual. **6** Grammar (of a word) following the normal pattern of inflection. **7** belonging to the permanent professional armed forces of a country. **8** (of a geometrical figure) having all sides and angles equal.

SYNONYMS **1** *plant them at regular intervals* **uniform**, even, consistent, constant, unchanging, unvarying, fixed. **2** *the subject of regular protests* **frequent**, repeated, continual, recurrent, periodic, constant, perpetual, numerous. **3** *his regular route to work* **usual**, normal, customary, habitual, routine, typical, accustomed, established. ANTONYMS erratic, occasional, unusual.

▶ noun a regular customer, member of a team, etc.

□ **regularity** noun **regularly** adverb.

regularize (or **regularise**) ▶ verb (**regularizes, regularizing, regularized**) **1** make regular. **2** make a temporary situation legal or official.

regulate ▶ verb (**regulates, regulating, regulated**) **1** control the rate or speed of a machine or process. **2** control or supervise by means of rules.

SYNONYMS **1** *the flow has been regulated* **control**, adjust, manage, govern. **2** *a new act regulating businesses* **police**, supervise, monitor, check (up on), be responsible for, control, manage, direct, govern.

□ **regulator** noun **regulatory** adjective.

regulation ▶ noun **1** a rule made by an authority. **2** the action of regulating.

SYNONYMS **1** *EC regulations* **rule**, order, directive, act, law, by-law, statute, dictate, decree. **2** *the regulation of blood sugar* **adjustment**, control, management, balancing. **3** *the regulation of financial services* **policing**, supervision, superintendence, monitoring, control, governance, management, responsibility for.

regurgitate /ri-ger-ji-tayt/ ▶ verb (**regurgitates, regurgitating, regurgitated**) **1** bring swallowed food up again to the mouth. **2** repeat information without understanding it.

□ **regurgitation** noun.

rehabilitate ▶ verb (**rehabilitates, rehabilitating, rehabilitated**) **1** help someone who has been ill or in prison to return to normal life. **2** restore the reputation of someone previously out of favour.

□ **rehabilitation** noun.

rehash ▶ verb reuse old ideas or material.
▶ noun a reuse of old ideas or material.

rehearsal ▶ noun a trial performance of a play or other work for later public performance.

SYNONYMS **practice**, trial performance, read-through, run-through, drill, training, coaching; informal dry run.

rehearse ▶ verb (**rehearses, rehearsing, rehearsed**) **1** practise a play, piece of music, etc. for later public performance. **2** state points that have been made many times before.

SYNONYMS **1** *I rehearsed the role* **prepare**, practise, read through, run through/over, go over. **2** *he rehearsed the Vienna Philharmonic* **train**, drill, prepare, coach. **3** *the document rehearsed all the arguments* **list**, enumerate, itemize, detail, spell out, catalogue, recite, repeat, go over, run through; informal recap.

rehydrate ▶ verb (**rehydrates, rehydrating, rehydrated**) add moisture to something dehydrated.

□ **rehydration** noun.

Reich /ryk, rykh/ ▶ noun the former German state, in particular the **Third Reich** (the Nazi regime, 1933–45).

reign ▶ verb **1** rule as king or queen. **2** be the main quality or aspect: *confusion reigned.* **3** (**reigning**) currently holding a particular title in sport.

SYNONYMS **1** *Robert II reigned for nineteen years* **be king/queen**, sit on the throne, wear the crown, be supreme, rule. **2** *chaos reigned* **prevail**, exist, be present, be the case, occur, be rife, be rampant, be the order of the day.

▶ noun the period of rule of a king or queen.

SYNONYMS *Henry's reign* **rule**, sovereignty, monarchy, dominion.

reimburse ▶ verb (**reimburses, reimbursing, reimbursed**) repay money to.
□ **reimbursement** noun.

rein ▶ noun (**reins**) **1** long, narrow straps attached to a horse's bit, used to control the horse. **2** the power to direct and control something.
▶ verb **1** control a horse by pulling on its reins. **2** (**rein someone/thing in** or **back**) restrain someone or something.

SYNONYMS *they reined back costs* **restrain**, check, curb, constrain, hold back/in, keep under control, regulate, restrict, control, curtail, limit.

■ **free rein** freedom of action.

reincarnate ▶ verb (**be reincarnated**) be born again in another body.
□ **reincarnation** noun.

reindeer ▶ noun (plural **reindeer** or **reindeers**) a deer with large antlers, found in cold northern regions.

reinforce ▸ verb (reinforces, reinforcing, reinforced) **1** make something stronger. **2** strengthen a military force with additional personnel.

> SYNONYMS **1** *contractors reinforced the dam* **strengthen**, fortify, bolster up, shore up, buttress, prop up, underpin, brace, support. **2** *reinforcing links between colleges and companies* **strengthen**, fortify, cement, boost, deepen, enrich, enhance, intensify, improve. **3** *the need to reinforce NATO troops* **augment**, increase, add to, supplement, boost, top up.

reinforcement ▸ noun **1** the action of reinforcing. **2** (**reinforcements**) extra personnel sent to strengthen a military force.

> SYNONYMS **1** *the reinforcement of our defences* **strengthening**, fortification, bolstering, shoring up, buttressing, bracing. **2** (**reinforcements**) **additional troops**, auxiliaries, reserves, support, backup, help.

reinstate ▸ verb (reinstates, reinstating, reinstated) restore to a former position.

> SYNONYMS **restore**, put back, bring back, reinstitute, reinstall, re-establish.

▫ **reinstatement** noun.

reiterate ▸ verb (reiterates, reiterating, reiterated) say something again or repeatedly.

▫ **reiteration** noun.

reject ▸ verb /ri-jekt/ **1** refuse to accept or agree to. **2** fail to show proper affection or concern for. **3** (of the body) react against a transplanted organ or tissue.

> SYNONYMS **1** *the miners rejected the offer* **turn down**, refuse, decline, say no to, spurn. **2** *Jamie rejected her* **rebuff**, spurn, shun, snub, cast off/aside, discard, abandon, desert, turn your back on.
> ANTONYMS accept, welcome.

▸ noun /**ree**-jekt/ a rejected person or thing.

> SYNONYMS **1** *what a reject!* **failure**, loser, incompetent. **2** *it is only a reject* **second**, discard, misshape, faulty item, cast-off.

rejection ▸ noun an act or the action of rejecting.

> SYNONYMS **1** *a rejection of the offer* **refusal**, declining, turning down, dismissal, spurning. **2** *Madeleine's rejection of him* **repudiation**, rebuff, spurning, abandonment, desertion; informal brush-off.
> ANTONYMS agreement, acceptance, welcome.

rejig ▸ verb (rejigs, rejigging, rejigged) Brit. rearrange.

rejoice ▸ verb (rejoices, rejoicing, rejoiced) feel or show great joy.

> SYNONYMS **be happy**, be glad, be delighted, celebrate, make merry; informal be over the moon.
> ANTONYMS mourn.

rejoin[1] ▸ verb join again.

> SYNONYMS **return to**, be reunited with, join again, reach again, regain.

rejoin[2] ▸ verb formal say in reply; retort.

rejoinder ▸ noun a quick reply.

rejuvenate ▸ verb (rejuvenates, rejuvenating, rejuvenated) make more lively or youthful.

▫ **rejuvenation** noun.

rekindle ▸ verb (rekindles, rekindling, rekindled) **1** revive a past feeling, relationship, etc. **2** relight a fire.

relapse /ri-**laps**/ ▸ verb (relapses, relapsing, relapsed) **1** become ill again after a period of improvement. **2** (**relapse into**) return to a worse state.
▸ noun /**ree**-laps/ a return to bad health after a temporary improvement.

relate ▸ verb (relates, relating, related) **1** make or show a connection between. **2** (**be related**) be connected by blood or marriage. **3** (**relate to**) have to do with; concern. **4** (**relate to**) feel sympathy with. **5** give a spoken or written account of.

> SYNONYMS **1** *he related stories* **tell**, recount, narrate, report, recite. **2** (**related**) *a related incident* **connected**, interconnected, associated, linked, allied, corresponding, analogous, parallel, comparable, equivalent.

relation ▸ noun **1** the way in which people or things are connected or related. **2** (**relations**) the way in which people or groups behave towards each other. **3** a relative.

> SYNONYMS **1** *the relation between church and state* **connection**, relationship, association, link, correlation, correspondence, parallel. **2** (**relations**) *improving relations with India* **dealings**, communication, relationship, connections, contact, interaction. **3** *are you a relation of his?* **relative**, member of the family, kinsman, kinswoman; (**relations**) family, kin, kith and kin, kindred.

relationship ▸ noun **1** the way in which people or things are connected or related. **2** the way in which people or groups behave towards each other. **3** an emotional and sexual association between two people.

> SYNONYMS **1** *the relationship between diet and diabetes* **connection**, relation, association, link, correlation,

r

correspondence, parallel. **2** *their relationship to a common ancestor* **family ties/connections,** blood relationship, kinship, affinity, common ancestry/ lineage. **3** *the end of their relationship* **romance,** affair, love affair, liaison, amour, fling.

relative ▸ adjective **1** considered in relation or in proportion to something else. **2** existing or possessing a quality only in comparison to something else. **3** Grammar referring to an earlier noun, sentence, or clause.

> SYNONYMS **1** *the relative importance of each factor* **comparative,** respective, comparable. **2** *food required is relative to body weight* **proportionate,** in proportion, commensurate, corresponding.
> ANTONYMS disproportionate.

▸ noun a person connected to another by blood or marriage.

> SYNONYMS *he's a relative of mine* **relation,** member of the family, kinsman, kinswoman; (**relatives**) family, kin, kith and kin, kindred.

relatively ▸ adverb **1** in comparison or proportion to something else. **2** quite.

relativism ▸ noun the idea that truth, morality, etc. exist only in relation to other things and are not absolute.
□ relativist noun.

relativity ▸ noun **1** the state of being relative; ability to be judged only in comparison with something else. **2** Physics a description of matter, energy, space, and time according to Albert Einstein's theories.

relax ▸ verb **1** become less tense, anxious, or rigid. **2** rest from work; do something recreational. **3** make a rule or restriction less strict.

> SYNONYMS **1** *relax after work* **rest,** loosen up, ease up/off, slow down, de-stress, unbend, unwind, put your feet up, take it easy; informal chill out; N. Amer. informal hang loose. **2** *a walk will relax you* **calm,** unwind, rest, loosen up, make less tense, make less uptight, soothe. **3** *he relaxed his grip* **loosen,** slacken, unclench, weaken, lessen. **4** *they relaxed the restrictions* **moderate,** temper, ease, loosen, lighten, dilute, weaken, reduce, decrease; informal let up on.
> ANTONYMS tense, tighten.

relaxation ▸ noun **1** the state of being free from tension and worry. **2** the action of making something less strict.

> SYNONYMS **recreation,** enjoyment, amusement, entertainment, fun,

pleasure, leisure.
> ANTONYMS activity, work.

relay ▸ noun **1** a group of people or animals carrying out a task for a time and then replaced by a similar group. **2** a race between teams of runners, each team member in turn covering part of the total distance. **3** an electrical device which opens or closes a circuit in response to a current in another circuit. **4** a device which receives, strengthens, and transmits a signal again.

> SYNONYMS *a live relay of the performance* **broadcast,** transmission, showing, feed, patch.

▸ verb **1** receive and pass on information. **2** broadcast something by means of a relay.

> SYNONYMS *I'd relayed the messages* **pass on,** hand on, transfer, repeat, communicate, send, transmit, circulate.

release ▸ verb (**releases, releasing, released**) **1** set someone free from a place where they have been kept or trapped. **2** free someone from a duty, responsibility, etc. **3** allow to move freely. **4** allow information to be made available. **5** make a film or recording available to the public.

> SYNONYMS **1** *all prisoners were released* **free,** set free, let go/out, liberate, discharge. **2** *Burke released the animal* **untie,** undo, loose, let go, unleash. **3** *police released the news yesterday* **make public,** make known, issue, put out, publish, broadcast, circulate, launch.
> ANTONYMS imprison, tie up, embargo.

▸ noun **1** the action of releasing. **2** a film or recording made available to the public.

> SYNONYMS **1** *the release of political prisoners* **freeing,** liberation, deliverance, freedom, liberty. **2** *the release of the news* **issuing,** announcement, publication, broadcasting, circulation, launch.
> ANTONYMS imprisonment, embargo.

relegate ▸ verb (**relegates, relegating, relegated**) **1** place in a lower rank or position. **2** Brit. transfer a sports team to a lower division of a league.

> SYNONYMS **downgrade,** demote, lower, put down, move down.
> ANTONYMS upgrade, promote.

□ relegation noun.

relent ▸ verb **1** finally agree to something after first refusing it. **2** become less severe or intense.

relentless ▸ adjective **1** never stopping or ending. **2** harsh or inflexible.

> SYNONYMS **1** *their relentless pursuit of quality* **persistent,** unfaltering, unremitting, unflagging, untiring,

unwavering, dogged, single-minded, tireless, indefatigable. **2** *a relentless taskmaster* **harsh,** cruel, remorseless, merciless, pitiless, implacable, ruthless.

☐ **relentlessly** adverb.

relevant ▸ adjective closely connected or appropriate to the current subject.

> **SYNONYMS pertinent,** applicable, apposite, material, apropos, to the point, germane.
> **ANTONYMS** irrelevant.

☐ **relevance** noun.

> ✔ **-ant,** not **-ent:** relev**ant**.

reliable ▸ adjective able to be depended on or trusted.

> **SYNONYMS dependable,** trustworthy, good, safe, authentic, faithful, genuine, sound, true, loyal, unfailing.
> **ANTONYMS** unreliable.

☐ **reliability** noun **reliably** adverb.

reliance ▸ noun dependence on or trust in someone or something.

> **SYNONYMS 1** *reliance on the state* **dependence. 2** *reliance on his judgement* **trust,** confidence, faith, belief, conviction.

☐ **reliant** adjective.

relic ▸ noun **1** an object or custom that survives from an earlier time. **2** a part of a holy person's body or belongings kept after their death.

> **SYNONYMS artefact,** historical object, antiquity, remnant, vestige, remains.

relief ▸ noun **1** a feeling of reassurance and relaxation after anxiety or stress. **2** a cause of relief. **3** the action of relieving. **4** (also **light relief**) a temporary break in a tense or boring situation. **5** help given to people in need or difficulty. **6** a person or group replacing others who have been on duty. **7** a way of carving in which the design stands out from the surface.

> **SYNONYMS 1** *a bit of relief from work* **freedom,** release, liberation, deliverance, comfort, respite, diversion. **2** *pain relief* **alleviation,** relieving, palliation, soothing, easing, lessening. **3** *a little light relief* **respite,** amusement, diversion, entertainment, jollity, recreation. **4** *bringing relief to the starving* **help,** aid, assistance, charity. **5** *his relief arrived to take over* **replacement,** substitute, deputy, reserve, cover, stand-in, supply, locum, understudy.
> **ANTONYMS** intensification.

■ **relief map** a map that indicates hills and valleys by shading.

relieve ▸ verb (**relieves, relieving, relieved**)

1 lessen or remove pain, difficulty, etc. **2** (**be relieved**) stop feeling anxious or stressed. **3** replace someone who is on duty. **4** (**relieve someone of**) take a responsibility from someone. **5** bring military support for a place which is surrounded by the enemy. **6** make something less boring. **7** (**relieve yourself**) go to the toilet.

> **SYNONYMS 1** *this helps relieve pain* **alleviate,** mitigate, ease, counteract, dull, reduce. **2** *the helpers relieved us* **replace,** take over from, stand in for, fill in for, substitute for, deputize for, cover for. **3** *this relieves the teacher of a heavy load* **free,** release, exempt, excuse, absolve, let off.
> **ANTONYMS** aggravate, inflict.

> ✔ **i** before **e** except after **c:** rel**ie**ve.

religion ▸ noun **1** belief in and worship of a God or gods. **2** a particular system of faith and worship.

> **SYNONYMS faith,** belief, worship, creed, church, sect, denomination, cult.

religious ▸ adjective **1** concerned with or believing in a religion. **2** very careful and regular.

> **SYNONYMS 1** *a religious person* **devout,** pious, reverent, godly, God-fearing, churchgoing. **2** *religious beliefs* **spiritual,** theological, scriptural, doctrinal, ecclesiastical, church, holy, divine, sacred. **3** *religious attention to detail* **scrupulous,** conscientious, meticulous, punctilious, strict, rigorous.
> **ANTONYMS** atheistic, secular, casual.

☐ **religiously** adverb.

> ✔ reli**gious,** not **-gous**.

relinquish ▸ verb give up something, especially unwillingly.

> **SYNONYMS 1** *he relinquished control of the company* **renounce,** give up/away, hand over, let go of. **2** *he relinquished his post* **leave,** resign from, stand down from, bow out of, give up; informal quit, chuck.
> **ANTONYMS** retain, continue.

reliquary /rel-i-kwuh-ri/ ▸ noun (plural **reliquaries**) a container for holy relics.

relish ▸ noun **1** great enjoyment or anticipation. **2** a strongly flavoured sauce or pickle.

> **SYNONYMS 1** *he dug into his food with relish* **enjoyment,** gusto, delight, pleasure, glee, appreciation, enthusiasm. **2** *a hot relish* **condiment,** sauce, dressing.
> **ANTONYMS** distaste.

▸ verb enjoy or look forward to.

> **SYNONYMS 1** *he was relishing his moment of glory* **enjoy,** delight in, love, adore,

r

take pleasure in, rejoice in, appreciate, savour, revel in, luxuriate in, glory in. **2** *I don't relish the drive* **look forward to,** fancy.
ANTONYMS dislike.

relive ▸ verb (**relives, reliving, relived**) live through an experience or feeling again in your mind.

reload ▸ verb load something, especially a gun, again.

relocate ▸ verb (**relocates, relocating, relocated**) move your home or business to a new place.
□ **relocation** noun.

reluctance ▸ noun unwillingness to do something.

SYNONYMS **unwillingness,** disinclination, hesitation, wavering, vacillation, doubts, second thoughts, misgivings.

reluctant ▸ adjective unwilling and hesitant.

SYNONYMS **unwilling,** disinclined, unenthusiastic, resistant, opposed, hesitant, loath.
ANTONYMS willing, eager.

□ **reluctantly** adverb.

rely ▸ verb (**relies, relying, relied**) (**rely on**) **1** need or be dependent on. **2** have faith in; trust.

SYNONYMS *I knew I could rely on him* **depend on,** count on, bank on, be confident of, be sure of, have faith in, trust in. informal swear by. N. Amer. informal figure on.

remain ▸ verb **1** still be in the same place or condition. **2** continue to be: *he remained alert.* **3** be left over.

SYNONYMS **1** *the problem will remain* **continue,** endure, last, abide, carry on, persist, stay around, survive, live on. **2** *he remained in hospital* **stay,** stay behind, stay put, wait behind, be left, hang on; informal hang around/round. **3** *union leaders remain sceptical* **continue to be,** stay, keep.

remainder ▸ noun **1** a part, number, or amount that is left over. **2** a part that is still to come. **3** the number left over when one quantity does not exactly divide another.

SYNONYMS **rest,** balance, residue, others, remnant(s), leftovers, surplus, extra, excess.

remains ▸ plural noun **1** things that remain or are left. **2** historical or archaeological relics. **3** a person's body after death.

SYNONYMS **1** *the remains of her drink* **remainder,** residue, rest, remnant(s), leftovers. **2** *Roman remains* **antiquities,** relics, artefacts. **3** *the saint's remains* **corpse,** body, carcass, bones.

remand ▸ verb send a defendant to wait for their trial, either on bail or in jail.
■ **on remand** in jail before being tried.

remark ▸ verb **1** say as a comment. **2** notice.

SYNONYMS *'You're quiet,' he remarked* **comment,** say, observe, mention, reflect.

▸ noun a comment.

SYNONYMS *he made a few remarks* **comment,** statement, utterance, observation, reflection.

remarkable ▸ adjective extraordinary or striking.

SYNONYMS **extraordinary,** exceptional, outstanding, notable, striking, memorable, unusual, conspicuous, momentous.
ANTONYMS ordinary.

□ **remarkably** adverb.

rematch ▸ noun a second match between two teams or players.

remedial ▸ adjective **1** intended as a remedy. **2** provided for children with learning difficulties.

remedy ▸ noun (plural **remedies**) **1** a medicine or treatment for a disease or injury. **2** a means of dealing with something undesirable.

SYNONYMS **1** *herbal remedies* **treatment,** cure, medicine, medication, medicament, drug. **2** *a remedy for all kinds of problems* **solution,** answer, cure, fix, antidote, resolution.

▸ verb (**remedies, remedying, remedied**) put right an undesirable situation.

SYNONYMS *remedying the situation* **put right,** set right, rectify, solve, sort out, straighten out, resolve, correct, repair, mend, fix.

remember ▸ verb (**remembers, remembering, remembered**) **1** have in your mind someone or something from the past. **2** not forget to do something necessary or important. **3** (**remember someone to**) pass on greetings from one person to another.

SYNONYMS **1** *remembering happy times* **recall,** call to mind, recollect, think of, reminisce about, look back on. **2** *can you remember all that?* **memorize,** retain, learn off by heart. **3** *you must remember she's only five* **bear in mind,** be mindful of, take into account. **4** *remember to feed the cat* **be sure,** be certain, mind that you, make sure that you. **5** *the nation remembered those who gave their lives* **commemorate,** pay tribute to, honour, salute, pay homage to.
ANTONYMS forget.

remembrance ▸ noun **1** the action of remembering. **2** a memory. **3** a thing acting as a reminder of someone.

> SYNONYMS **1** *an expression of remembrance* **recollection,** reminiscence, recall. **2** *we sold poppies in remembrance* **commemoration,** memory, recognition.

remind ▶ verb **1** help someone to remember something. **2** (**remind someone of**) make someone think of someone or something because of a resemblance.

> SYNONYMS **jog someone's memory,** prompt.

reminder ▶ noun a thing that makes someone remember something.

reminisce /re-mi-**niss**/ ▶ verb (**reminisces, reminiscing, reminisced**) think or talk about the past.

reminiscence ▶ noun **1** an account of something that you remember. **2** the enjoyable remembering of past events.

reminiscent ▶ adjective **1** (**reminiscent of**) tending to remind you of something. **2** absorbed in memories.

> SYNONYMS **similar to,** comparable with, evocative of, suggestive of, redolent of, that reminds one of.

remiss /ri-**miss**/ ▶ adjective not giving something proper attention or care.

remission ▶ noun **1** a temporary period during which a serious illness becomes less severe. **2** Brit. the reduction of a prison sentence as a reward for good behaviour. **3** the cancellation of a debt, penalty, etc.

remit ▶ noun /**ree**-mit/ the task or area of activity officially given to a person or organization.
▶ verb /ri-**mit**/ (**remits, remitting, remitted**) **1** send money in payment. **2** cancel a debt or punishment. **3** refer a matter to an authority for a decision.

remittance ▶ noun **1** a sum of money sent as payment. **2** the action of remitting money.

remix ▶ verb produce a different version of a musical recording by altering the balance of the separate parts.
▶ noun a remixed recording.

remnant ▶ noun a small remaining quantity of something.

> SYNONYMS **remains,** remainder, leftovers, offcut, residue, rest.

remonstrate /**rem**-uhn-strayt/
▶ verb (**remonstrates, remonstrating, remonstrated**) complain or protest strongly.
□ **remonstrance** noun **remonstration** noun.

remorse ▶ noun deep regret or guilt for something wrong that you have done.

> SYNONYMS **regret,** guilt, contrition, repentance, shame.

□ **remorseful** adjective.

remorseless ▶ adjective **1** (of something unpleasant) never ending or improving. **2** without remorse.
□ **remorselessly** adverb.

remote ▶ adjective (**remoter, remotest**) **1** far away in space or time. **2** situated far from the main centres of population. **3** having very little connection. **4** (of a chance or possibility) unlikely to happen. **5** unfriendly and distant in manner. **6** operating or operated by means of radio or infrared signals.

> SYNONYMS **1** *a remote village* **isolated,** faraway, distant, out of the way, off the beaten track, secluded, lonely; N. Amer. in the backwoods; informal in the middle of nowhere. **2** *a remote possibility* **unlikely,** improbable, doubtful, dubious, faint, slight, slim, small, slender. **3** *she seems very remote* **aloof,** distant, detached, withdrawn, unforthcoming, unapproachable, unresponsive, unfriendly, unsociable, introspective, introverted; informal stand-offish.
> ANTONYMS close, distinct, friendly.

■ **remote control 1** control of a machine from a distance by means of signals transmitted from a radio or electronic device. **2** a device that controls a machine in this way.
□ **remotely** adverb **remoteness** noun.

removal ▶ noun **1** the action of removing. **2** Brit. the transfer of furniture and other items when moving house.

> SYNONYMS **1** *the removal of church treasures* **taking away,** moving, carrying away, transporting. **2** *his removal from office* **dismissal,** ejection, expulsion, ousting; N. Amer. ouster; informal sacking, firing. **3** *the removal of customs barriers* **withdrawal,** elimination, abolition, taking away. **4** *her removal to France* **move,** transfer, relocation.
> ANTONYMS installation, appointment, imposition.

remove ▶ verb (**removes, removing, removed**) **1** take something away from the position it occupies. **2** abolish or get rid of. **3** dismiss from a post. **4** (**be removed**) be very different from. **5** (**removed**) separated by a particular number of steps of descent: *a second cousin once removed.*

> SYNONYMS **1** *she removed the lid* **take off,** take away, take out, pull out, withdraw, detach, undo, unfasten, disconnect. **2** *he was removed from his post* **dismiss,** discharge, get rid of, expel, oust, depose; informal sack, fire, kick out. **3** *tax relief was removed* **abolish,** withdraw, eliminate, get rid of, do away with, stop, cut, axe.

r

ANTONYMS attach, insert, replace, appoint, impose.

▶ noun the amount by which things are separated.
□ **removable** adjective.

remunerate /ri-**myoo**-nuh-rayt/ ▶ verb (remunerates, remunerating, remunerated) formal pay someone for work they have done.
□ **remuneration** noun.

remunerative ▶ adjective formal paying a lot of money.

Renaissance /ri-**nay**-sonss/ ▶ noun 1 the revival of classical styles in art and literature in the 14th–16th centuries. 2 (**renaissance**) a period of renewed interest in something.

SYNONYMS (**renaissance**) **revival**, renewal, resurrection, reawakening, re-emergence, rebirth, reappearance, resurgence.

renal /**ree**-n'l/ ▶ adjective technical having to do with the kidneys.

rename ▶ verb (renames, renaming, renamed) give a new name to.

renascence /ri-**nass**-uhnss/ ▶ noun formal a revival or rebirth.
□ **renascent** adjective.

rend ▶ verb (rends, rending, rent) literary tear something to pieces.

render ▶ verb (renders, rendering, rendered) 1 provide or give a service, help, etc. 2 hand over for inspection, consideration, or payment. 3 cause to be or become: *he was rendered speechless.* 4 perform a piece of music or drama. 5 melt down fat to separate out its impurities. 6 cover a wall with a coat of plaster.

SYNONYMS 1 *her fury rendered her speechless* **make,** cause to be/become, leave, turn. 2 *rendering assistance* **give,** provide, supply, furnish, contribute. 3 *the characters are vividly rendered* **act,** perform, play, depict, portray, interpret, represent, draw, paint, execute.

rendezvous /**ron**-day-voo/ ▶ noun (plural **rendezvous** /**ron**-day-voo/ or /**ron**-day-vooz/) 1 a meeting at an agreed time and place. 2 a meeting place.
▶ verb (**rendezvouses** /**ron**-day-vooz/, **rendezvousing** /**ron**-day-voo-ing/, **rendezvoused** /**ron**-day-vood/) meet at an agreed time and place.

rendition ▶ noun a performance or version of a piece of music or drama.

renegade /**ren**-i-gayd/ ▶ noun a person who deserts and betrays an organization, country, or set of principles.

renege /ri-**nayg**, ri-**neeg**/ ▶ verb (reneges, reneging, reneged) go back on an agreement or promise.

renew ▶ verb 1 start doing something again after an interruption. 2 give fresh life or strength to. 3 make a licence, subscription, etc. valid for a further period. 4 replace something broken or worn out.

SYNONYMS 1 *I renewed my search* **resume,** return to, take up again, come back to, begin again, restart, recommence, continue (with), carry on (with). 2 *they renewed their vows* **reaffirm,** repeat, reiterate, restate. 3 *something to renew her interest in life* **revive,** regenerate, revitalize, reinvigorate, restore, resuscitate. 4 *the hotel was completely renewed* **renovate,** restore, refurbish, revamp, remodel, modernize; informal do up; N. Amer. informal rehab.

□ **renewable** adjective **renewal** noun.

rennet ▶ noun a substance used to curdle milk in order to make cheese.

renounce ▶ verb (renounces, renouncing, renounced) 1 formally give up a title or possession. 2 state that you no longer have a particular belief or allegiance. 3 abandon a cause, habit, etc.

SYNONYMS 1 *Edward renounced his claim to the throne* **give up,** relinquish, abandon, surrender, waive, forego, desist from, keep off; informal say goodbye to. 2 *she renounced her family* **reject,** repudiate, deny, abandon, wash your hands of, turn your back on, disown, spurn, shun.
ANTONYMS assert, continue, keep, accept.

renovate ▶ verb (renovates, renovating, renovated) restore something old to a good state; repair.

SYNONYMS **modernize,** restore, refurbish, revamp, recondition, rehabilitate, update, upgrade, refit; informal do up; N. Amer. informal rehab.

□ **renovation** noun.

renown ▶ noun the state of being famous.

SYNONYMS (**renowned**) *a renowned scientist* **famous,** well known, celebrated, famed, eminent, distinguished, acclaimed, illustrious, prominent, great, esteemed.
ANTONYMS unknown.

rent¹ ▶ noun a regular payment made for the use of property or land.

SYNONYMS *I can't afford to pay the rent* **hire charge,** rental.

▶ verb 1 regularly pay money to someone for the use of property or land. 2 let someone use property or land in return for payment.

SYNONYMS 1 *she rented a car* **hire,** lease, charter. 2 *why don't you rent it out?* **let (out),** lease (out), hire (out), charter (out).

r

rent² past and past participle of **REND**.
▸ **noun** a large tear in a piece of fabric.

rental ▸ **noun** 1 an amount paid as rent.
2 the action of renting.

renunciation ▸ **noun** the action of renouncing or giving up something.

reorganize (or **reorganise**) ▸ **verb** (reorganizes, reorganizing, reorganized) change the organization of.
□ **reorganization** noun.

rep ▸ **noun** informal 1 a representative.
2 repertory.

repaid past and past participle of **REPAY**.

repair¹ ▸ **verb** restore something damaged or worn to a good condition.

> SYNONYMS 1 *the car was repaired* **mend,** fix (up), put/set right, restore (to working order), darn; informal patch up. 2 *repairing relations with other countries* **put/set right,** mend, fix, straighten out, improve; informal patch up. 3 *she sought to repair the wrong she had done* **rectify,** make good, (put) right, correct, make up for, make amends for.

▸ **noun** 1 an act of repairing something. 2 the condition of an object: *in good repair.*

> SYNONYMS 1 *in need of repair* **restoration,** fixing (up), mending, renovation. 2 *an invisible repair* **mend,** darn, patch. 3 *in good repair* **condition,** working order, state, shape, fettle; Brit. informal nick.

□ **repairer** noun.

repair² ▸ **verb** (repair to) go to a place.

reparable ▸ **adjective** able to be repaired.

reparation ▸ **noun** 1 something done to make up for a wrong. 2 (reparations) compensation for war damage paid by a defeated country.

repartee /rep-ar-**tee**/ ▸ **noun** quick, witty comments or conversation.

repast /ri-**pahst**/ ▸ **noun** formal a meal.

repatriate /ree-**pat**-ri-ayt/ ▸ **verb** (repatriates, repatriating, repatriated) send someone back to their own country.
□ **repatriation** noun.

repay ▸ **verb** (repays, repaying, repaid) 1 pay back money owed to someone. 2 do something as a reward for a favour or kindness. 3 be worthy of investigation, attention, etc.

> SYNONYMS 1 *repaying customers who have been cheated* **reimburse,** refund, pay back, recompense, compensate. 2 *the grants have to be repaid* **pay back,** return, refund, reimburse. 3 *I'd like to repay her generosity* **reciprocate,** return, requite, reward.

□ **repayment** noun.

repeal ▸ **verb** make a law no longer valid.

> SYNONYMS *the Act was repealed* **cancel,** abolish, reverse, rescind, revoke, annul, quash.
> ANTONYMS enact.

▸ **noun** the action of repealing.

> SYNONYMS *the repeal of the law* **cancellation,** abolition, reversal, rescinding, annulment.

repeat ▸ **verb** 1 say or do again. 2 (repeat yourself) say the same thing again. 3 (repeat itself) happen again in the same way or form.

> SYNONYMS 1 *she repeated her story* **say again,** restate, reiterate, go/run through again, recapitulate; informal recap. 2 *children can repeat chunks of text* **recite,** quote, parrot, regurgitate, echo; informal trot out. 3 *Steele was invited to repeat his work* **do again,** redo, replicate, duplicate. 4 *the episodes were repeated* **rebroadcast,** rerun, reshow.

▸ **noun** 1 something that happens or is done again. 2 a repeated broadcast of a television or radio programme.

> SYNONYMS 1 *a repeat of the previous year's final* **repetition,** replication, duplicate. 2 *repeats of his TV show* **rerun,** rebroadcast, reshowing, replay.

repeatedly ▸ **adverb** frequently.

> SYNONYMS **frequently,** often, again and again, over and over (again), time and (time) again, many times, persistently, recurrently, constantly, continually, regularly; N. Amer. oftentimes.

repel ▸ **verb** (repels, repelling, repelled) 1 drive back or away. 2 make someone feel disgust. 3 force away something with a similar magnetic charge.

> SYNONYMS 1 *the US repelled an Iraqi attack* **fight off,** repulse, drive back, force back, beat back, hold off; Brit. see off. 2 *the sight of the food repelled me* **revolt,** disgust, repulse, sicken, nauseate, turn someone's stomach; informal turn off; N. Amer. informal gross out.
> ANTONYMS attract, delight.

repellent ▸ **adjective** 1 causing disgust or distaste. 2 able to keep a particular substance out: *water-repellent nylon.*
▸ **noun** 1 a substance that keeps insects away. 2 a substance used to treat something so that water cannot pass through it.

repent ▸ **verb** feel sorry for something bad that you have done.
□ **repentance** noun **repentant** adjective.

repercussions ▸ **plural noun** the consequences of an event or action.

repertoire /**rep**-er-twar/ ▸ **noun** the material known or regularly performed by a performer or company.

r

SYNONYMS **collection,** range, repertory, list, store, stock, repository, supply.

repertory /rep-er-tuh-ri/ ▸ noun (plural **repertories**) **1** the performance by a company of various plays, operas, etc. at regular intervals. **2** a repertoire.

repetition ▸ noun **1** the action of repeating. **2** a repeat of something.

SYNONYMS **1** *the statistics bear repetition* **reiteration,** restatement, retelling. **2** *a repetition of the scene in the kitchen* **recurrence,** rerun, repeat. **3** *there is some repetition* **repetitiousness,** repetitiveness, redundancy, tautology.

repetitious ▸ adjective having too much repetition; repetitive.

repetitive ▸ adjective involving repetition; repeated many or too many times.

SYNONYMS **recurring,** recurrent, repeated, unvaried, unchanging, routine, mechanical, automatic, monotonous, boring.
ANTONYMS unique, varied.

□ **repetitively** adverb.

rephrase ▸ verb (**rephrases, rephrasing, rephrased**) express something in an alternative way.

repine ▸ verb (**repines, repining, repined**) literary be unhappy or anxious.

replace ▸ verb (**replaces, replacing, replaced**) **1** take the place of. **2** provide a substitute for. **3** put something back in its previous position.

SYNONYMS **1** *a new chairman came in to replace him* **take the place of,** succeed, take over from, supersede, stand in for, substitute for, deputize for; informal step into someone's shoes/boots. **2** *she replaced the spoon with a fork* **substitute,** exchange, change, swap. **3** *Adam replaced the receiver* **put back,** return, restore.
ANTONYMS remove.

□ **replaceable** adjective.

replacement ▸ noun **1** the action of replacing. **2** a person or thing that takes the place of another.

SYNONYMS **1** *we have to find a replacement* **substitute,** stand-in, locum, understudy, relief, cover, successor. **2** *the wiring was in need of replacement* **renewal.**

replay ▸ noun **1** a match that is played again because the previous game was a draw. **2** an act of playing a recording again.
▸ verb **1** play back a recording. **2** play a match again.

replenish ▸ verb fill up a supply again after using some of it.
□ **replenishment** noun.

replete ▸ adjective **1** (**replete with**) filled or well supplied with. **2** very full with food.
□ **repletion** noun.

replica ▸ noun an exact copy or model of something.

SYNONYMS **1** *is it real or a replica?* **copy,** model, duplicate, reproduction, dummy, imitation, facsimile. **2** *a replica of her mother* **perfect likeness,** double, lookalike, living image, twin, clone; informal spitting image, dead ringer.

replicate ▸ verb (**replicates, replicating, replicated**) make an exact copy of.
□ **replication** noun.

reply ▸ verb (**replies, replying, replied**) **1** say or write a response to something said or written. **2** respond with a similar action.

SYNONYMS *Rachel didn't reply* **respond,** answer, write back, rejoin, retort, riposte, counter, come back.

▸ noun (plural **replies**) a spoken or written response.

SYNONYMS *he waited for a reply* **answer,** response, rejoinder, retort, riposte; informal comeback.

report ▸ verb **1** give a spoken or written account of something. **2** (**be reported**) be said or rumoured. **3** make a formal complaint about. **4** tell someone in authority that you have arrived or are ready to do something. **5** (**report to**) be responsible to a manager.

SYNONYMS **1** *the press reported the story* **communicate,** announce, divulge, disclose, reveal, make public, publish, broadcast, proclaim, publicize. **2** *I reported him to the police* **inform on**; informal shop, tell on, squeal on, rat on; Brit. informal grass on. **3** *Juliet reported for duty* **present yourself,** arrive, turn up; informal show up.

▸ noun **1** a spoken or written account of something. **2** Brit. a teacher's written assessment of a pupil's progress. **3** the sound of an explosion or a gun being fired.

SYNONYMS **1** *a full report on the meeting* **account,** record, minutes, proceedings, transcript. **2** *reports of drug dealing* **news,** information, word, intelligence. **3** *newspaper reports* **story,** account, article, piece, item, column, feature, bulletin, dispatch. **4** *a school report* **assessment,** evaluation, appraisal. **5** *reports of his imminent resignation* **rumour,** whisper; informal buzz. **6** *the report of a gun* **bang,** crack, explosion, boom.

reportage /rep-or-tah*zh*/ ▸ noun the reporting of news by the press and the broadcasting media.

reporter ▸ noun a person who reports news for a newspaper or broadcasting company.

> SYNONYMS **journalist,** correspondent, newsman, newswoman, columnist; Brit. pressman; informal hack, stringer, journo; N. Amer. informal newsie.

repose ▸ noun a state of restfulness, peace, or calm.
▸ verb (**reposes, reposing, reposed**) lie or be kept in a particular place.

repository ▸ noun (plural **repositories**) **1** a place or container for storage. **2** a place where a lot of something is found.

repossess ▸ verb take possession of something when a buyer fails to make the required payments.
□ **repossession** noun.

reprehensible ▸ adjective deserving condemnation; bad.

represent ▸ verb **1** act and speak on behalf of. **2** amount to. **3** be a specimen or example of. **4** show or describe in a particular way. **5** depict in a work of art. **6** signify or symbolize.

> SYNONYMS **1** *a character representing a single quality* **stand for,** symbolize, personify, epitomize, typify, embody, illustrate. **2** *Hathor is represented as a woman with cow's horns* **depict,** portray, render, picture, delineate, show, illustrate. **3** *his solicitor represented him in court* **appear for,** act for, speak on behalf of. **4** *the Queen was represented by Lord Lewin* **deputize for,** substitute for, stand in for.

representation ▸ noun **1** the action of representing. **2** an image, model, etc. of something. **3** (**representations**) statements made to an authority.

> SYNONYMS **1** *Rossetti's representation of women* **portrayal,** depiction, presentation, rendition. **2** *representations of the human form* **likeness,** painting, drawing, picture, illustration, sketch, image, model, figure, statue.

representational ▸ adjective **1** relating to representation. **2** (of art) not abstract.

representative ▸ adjective **1** typical of a class or group. **2** consisting of people chosen to act and speak on behalf of a wider group. **3** portraying or symbolizing something.

> SYNONYMS **1** *a representative sample* **typical,** characteristic, illustrative. **2** *a female figure representative of Britain* **symbolic,** emblematic.
> ANTONYMS atypical.

▸ noun **1** a person chosen to act and speak for another or others. **2** a person who travels around trying to sell their company's products. **3** an example of a class or group.

> SYNONYMS **1** *a representative of the Royal Society* **spokesperson,** spokesman, spokeswoman, agent, official, mouthpiece. **2** *he acted as his father's representative* **deputy,** substitute, stand-in, proxy, delegate, ambassador, emissary. **3** *a sales representative* **salesman,** saleswoman, commercial traveller, agent, negotiator; informal rep; N. Amer. informal drummer.

repress ▸ verb **1** bring under control by force. **2** try not to have or show a thought or feeling. **3** (**repressed**) tending to keep your feelings or desires hidden.

> SYNONYMS **1** *the rebellion was repressed* **suppress,** quell, quash, subdue, put down, crush, extinguish, stamp out, defeat, contain. **2** *the peasants were repressed* **oppress,** subjugate, keep down, tyrannize. **3** *these emotions may well be repressed* **restrain,** hold back/in, suppress, keep in check, control, curb, stifle, bottle up; informal button up, keep the lid on.
> ANTONYMS express.

repression ▸ noun the act of repressing.

> SYNONYMS **1** *the repression of the protests* **suppression,** quashing, subduing, crushing, stamping out. **2** *political repression* **oppression,** subjugation, suppression, tyranny, authoritarianism. **3** *the repression of sexual urges* **restraint,** suppression, control, curbing, stifling, bottling up.

repressive ▸ adjective restricting personal freedom.

reprieve ▸ noun **1** the cancellation or postponement of a punishment, especially the death penalty. **2** a brief delay before something undesirable happens.

> SYNONYMS *she was given a reprieve* **pardon,** stay of execution, amnesty.

▸ verb (**reprieves, reprieving, reprieved**) give someone a reprieve.

> SYNONYMS *she was reprieved* **pardon,** spare, amnesty; informal let off (the hook).

reprimand ▸ verb speak severely to someone because they have done something wrong.

> SYNONYMS *he was publicly reprimanded* **rebuke,** reproach, scold, admonish; informal tell off; Brit. informal tick off; N. Amer. informal chew out.
> ANTONYMS praise, pardon.

▸ noun an act of reprimanding someone.

> SYNONYMS *a severe reprimand* **rebuke,** reproach, scolding, admonition; informal telling-off; Brit. informal ticking-off.
> ANTONYMS praise, pardon.

r

reprint ▸ verb print again.
▸ noun **1** an act of reprinting. **2** a copy of a book that has been reprinted.

reprisal ▸ noun an act of retaliation.

reprise /ri-**preez**/ ▸ noun **1** a repeated passage in music. **2** a further performance of something.
▸ verb (**reprises**, **reprising**, **reprised**) repeat a piece of music or a performance.

reproach ▸ verb express disapproval of or disappointment with.
▸ noun an expression of disapproval or disappointment.
□ **reproachful** adjective **reproachfully** adverb.

reprobate /**rep**-ruh-bayt/ ▸ noun a person who behaves in an immoral way.

reproduce ▸ verb (**reproduces**, **reproducing**, **reproduced**) **1** produce a copy or representation of. **2** recreate in a different medium or context. **3** produce young or offspring.

SYNONYMS **1** *each artwork is reproduced in colour* **copy,** duplicate, replicate, photocopy, xerox, photostat, print. **2** *this work has not been reproduced in other laboratories* **repeat,** replicate, recreate, redo, simulate, imitate, emulate, mimic. **3** *some animals reproduce prolifically* **breed,** procreate, propagate, multiply.

reproduction ▸ noun **1** the process of reproducing. **2** a copy of a work of art.

SYNONYMS **1** *a reproduction of the original* **print,** copy, reprint, duplicate, facsimile, photocopy; trademark Xerox. **2** *the process of reproduction* **breeding,** procreation, multiplying, propagation.

□ **reproductive** adjective.

reproof ▸ noun a reprimand.

reprove ▸ verb (**reproves**, **reproving**, **reproved**) reprimand; tell off.

reptile ▸ noun a cold-blooded animal of a class that includes snakes, lizards, crocodiles, and tortoises.
□ **reptilian** adjective.

republic ▸ noun a state in which power is held by the people and their elected representatives, and which has a president rather than a king or queen.

republican ▸ adjective **1** belonging to or characteristic of a republic. **2** in favour of republican government. **3** (**Republican**) (in the US) relating to or supporting the Republican Party.
▸ noun **1** a person in favour of republican government. **2** (**Republican**) (in the US) a member or supporter of the Republican Party. **3** (**Republican**) a person who wants Ireland to be one country.
□ **republicanism** noun.

repudiate ▸ verb (**repudiates**, **repudiating**, **repudiated**) **1** refuse to accept or support.

2 deny that something is true or valid.
□ **repudiation** noun.

repugnance ▸ noun great disgust.

repugnant ▸ adjective very unpleasant.

repulse ▸ verb (**repulses**, **repulsing**, **repulsed**) **1** drive back by force. **2** reject or refuse to accept. **3** give someone a feeling of strong disgust.
▸ noun the action of repulsing.

repulsion ▸ noun **1** a feeling of strong disgust. **2** a force by which objects tend to push each other away.

repulsive ▸ adjective arousing a feeling of strong disgust.

SYNONYMS **disgusting,** revolting, foul, nasty, obnoxious, sickening, nauseating, stomach-churning.
ANTONYMS attractive.

reputable /**rep**-yuu-tuh-b'l/ ▸ adjective having a good reputation.

reputation ▸ noun the beliefs or opinions that people generally hold about someone or something.

SYNONYMS **name,** good name, character, repute, standing, stature, position, renown, esteem, prestige.

repute ▸ noun **1** the opinion that people have of someone or something. **2** good reputation.
▸ verb **1** (**be reputed**) have a particular reputation. **2** (**reputed**) believed to exist.
□ **reputedly** adverb.

request ▸ noun **1** an act of asking politely or formally for something. **2** something that is asked for in this way.

SYNONYMS **1** *requests for assistance* **appeal,** entreaty, plea, petition, application, demand, call. **2** *Charlotte spoke, at Ursula's request* **bidding,** entreaty, demand, insistence. **3** *indicate your requests on the form* **requirement,** wish, desire, choice.

▸ verb politely or formally ask for something, or ask someone to do something.

SYNONYMS **1** *the government requested aid* **ask for,** appeal for, call for, seek, solicit, plead for, apply for, demand. **2** *I requested him to help* **ask,** call on, beg, entreat, implore; literary beseech.

requiem /**rek**-wi-em/ ▸ noun **1** a Christian Mass for the souls of dead people. **2** a musical work based on such a Mass.

require ▸ verb (**requires**, **requiring**, **required**) **1** need or want something for a purpose. **2** instruct or expect someone to do something. **3** regard a particular thing as necessary or compulsory.

SYNONYMS **1** *the child required hospital treatment* **need. 2** *a situation requiring patience* **necessitate,** demand, call for, involve, entail. **3** *unquestioning obedience is required* **demand,** insist on, call for, ask for, expect. **4** *she was required to pay costs* **order,** instruct, command, enjoin, oblige, compel, force. **5** *do you require anything else?* **want,** desire, lack, be short of.

requirement ▸ noun **1** something that you need or want. **2** something that is compulsory.

> SYNONYMS **need,** necessity, prerequisite, stipulation, demand, want, essential.

requisite /rek-wi-zit/ ▸ adjective necessary because of circumstances or regulations.
▸ noun a thing that is needed for a particular purpose.

requisition ▸ noun **1** an official order allowing property or materials to be taken or used. **2** the taking of goods for military or public use.
▸ verb officially take possession of something, especially during a war.

reredos /reer-doss/ ▸ noun (plural **reredos**) an ornamental screen at the back of an altar in a church.

rerun ▸ verb (**reruns, rerunning, reran;** past participle **rerun**) show, stage, or perform again.
▸ noun a rerun event, competition, or programme.

resat past and past participle of RESIT.

reschedule ▸ verb (**reschedules, rescheduling, rescheduled**) change the timing of.

rescind /ri-sind/ ▸ verb cancel or repeal a law, order, etc.

rescue ▸ verb (**rescues, rescuing, rescued**) save from danger or distress.

> SYNONYMS **1** *an attempt to rescue the hostages* **save,** free, set free, release, liberate, deliver. **2** *Boyd rescued his papers* **retrieve,** recover, salvage.

▸ noun an act of rescuing or being rescued.

> SYNONYMS *the rescue of ten crewmen* **saving,** rescuing, release, freeing, liberation, deliverance.

□ **rescuer** noun.

research ▸ noun the study of materials and sources in order to establish facts and reach new conclusions.

> SYNONYMS *medical research* **investigation,** experimentation, testing, analysis, fact-finding, examination, scrutiny.

▸ verb carry out research into a subject, or for a book, programme, etc.

> SYNONYMS *the phenomenon has been widely researched* **investigate,** study, enquire into, look into, probe, explore, analyse, examine, scrutinize.

□ **researcher** noun.

resemblance ▸ noun **1** the state of resembling. **2** a way in which things resemble each other.

> SYNONYMS **similarity,** likeness, similitude, correspondence, congruence, conformity, comparability, parallelism.
> ANTONYMS dissimilarity.

resemble ▸ verb (**resembles, resembling, resembled**) look or be like.

> SYNONYMS **look like,** be similar to, remind one of, take after, approximate to, smack of, correspond to, echo, mirror, parallel.
> ANTONYMS differ from.

resent ▸ verb feel bitter towards.

> SYNONYMS **begrudge,** feel aggrieved at/about, feel bitter about, grudge, be resentful of, take exception to, object to, take amiss, take offence at.
> ANTONYMS welcome.

resentful ▸ adjective bitter about something you think is unfair.
□ **resentfully** adverb.

resentment ▸ noun a feeling of bitterness about something unfair.

> SYNONYMS **bitterness,** indignation, irritation, pique, dissatisfaction, disgruntlement, discontentment, acrimony, rancour.

reservation ▸ noun **1** the action of reserving. **2** an arrangement for something to be reserved. **3** an expression of doubt about a statement. **4** an area of land set aside for a native people.

> SYNONYMS **1** *grave reservations* **doubt,** qualm, scruple; (**reservations**) misgivings, scepticism, unease, hesitation, objection. **2** *an Indian reservation* **reserve,** enclave, sanctuary, territory, homeland.

reserve ▸ verb (**reserves, reserving, reserved**) **1** keep something to be used in the future. **2** arrange for a seat, ticket, etc. to be kept for a particular person. **3** have or keep a right or power.

> SYNONYMS **1** *ask your newsagent to reserve you a copy* **put aside,** set aside, keep (back), save, hold back, keep in reserve, earmark. **2** *he reserved a table* **book,** order, arrange for, secure. **3** *all rights reserved* **retain,** keep, hold. **4** *reserve your judgement until you know him better* **defer,** postpone, put off, delay, withhold.

▸ noun **1** a supply of something available for use if required. **2** money kept available by a bank, company, etc. **3** a military force kept to reinforce others or for use in an emergency. **4** an extra player in a team, who can be called on to play if necessary. **5** (**the reserves**) the second-choice team. **6** an area of land set aside for wildlife or for a native people. **7** a lack of warmth or openness.

SYNONYMS **1** *reserves of petrol* **stock,** store, supply, stockpile, pool, hoard, cache. **2** *the army are calling up reserves* **reinforcements,** extras, auxiliaries. **3** *a nature reserve* **national park,** sanctuary, preserve, conservation area. **4** *his natural reserve* **shyness,** diffidence, timidity, taciturnity, inhibition, reticence, detachment, distance, remoteness. **5** *she trusted him without reserve* **reservation,** qualification, condition, limitation, hesitation, doubt.

▸ **adjective** available for use if required.

SYNONYMS *a reserve goalkeeper* **substitute,** stand-in, relief, replacement, fallback, spare, extra.

reserved ▸ **adjective** slow to reveal emotion or opinions.

SYNONYMS **1** *Sewell is rather reserved* **uncommunicative,** reticent, unforthcoming, quiet, silent, taciturn, withdrawn, secretive, shy, retiring, diffident, timid, introverted; informal stand-offish. **2** *that table is reserved* **booked,** taken, spoken for, prearranged. ANTONYMS outgoing.

reservist ▸ **noun** a member of a military reserve force.

reservoir ▸ **noun 1** a large lake used as a source of water supply. **2** a place where fluid collects. **3** a supply or source of something.

SYNONYMS **1** *sailing on the reservoir* **lake,** pool, pond, basin. **2** *an ink reservoir* **receptacle,** container, holder, tank. **3** *the reservoir of managerial talent* **stock,** store, stockpile, reserve(s), supply, bank, pool.

reshuffle ▸ **verb** (**reshuffles, reshuffling, reshuffled**) **1** change the roles or positions of government ministers. **2** rearrange.
▸ **noun** an act of reshuffling.

reside ▸ **verb** (**resides, residing, resided**) formal **1** live in a particular place. **2** (**reside in or with**) (of a right or power) belong to a person or group. **3** (**reside in**) (of a quality) be naturally present in.

residence ▸ **noun 1** the fact of living somewhere. **2** the place where a person lives.

SYNONYMS **home,** house, address, quarters, lodgings; informal pad; formal dwelling.

residency ▸ **noun** (plural **residencies**) the fact of living in a place.

resident ▸ **noun 1** a person who lives somewhere on a long-term basis. **2** Brit. a guest in a hotel.

SYNONYMS *the residents of New York City* **inhabitant,** local, citizen, native, householder, homeowner, occupier, tenant.

▸ **adjective** living somewhere on a long-term basis.

SYNONYMS **1** *resident in the UK* **living,** residing; formal dwelling. **2** *a resident nanny* **live-in.**

residential ▸ **adjective 1** involving residence. **2** providing accommodation. **3** occupied by private houses.

residual ▸ **adjective** remaining after the greater part has gone or been taken away.

residue ▸ **noun** a small amount of something that remains after the main part has gone or been taken.

SYNONYMS **remainder,** rest, remnant(s), surplus, extra, excess, remains, leftovers.

resign ▸ **verb 1** voluntarily leave a job or position of office. **2** (**be resigned**) accept that something bad cannot be avoided.

SYNONYMS **1** *the manager resigned* **leave,** give notice, stand down, step down; informal quit. **2** *19 MPs resigned their seats* **give up,** leave, vacate, stand down from; informal quit, pack in. **3** (**resigned**) **patient,** long-suffering, uncomplaining, forbearing, stoical, philosophical, fatalistic.

resignation ▸ **noun 1** an act of resigning. **2** a document stating that you intend to resign. **3** acceptance of something bad but inevitable.

SYNONYMS **1** *his resignation from his post* **departure,** leaving, standing down, stepping down; informal quitting. **2** *he accepted his fate with resignation* **patience,** forbearance, stoicism, fortitude, fatalism, acceptance.

resilient ▸ **adjective 1** able to spring back into shape after bending, stretching, or being compressed. **2** able to withstand or recover quickly from difficult conditions. □ **resilience** noun.

resin ▸ **noun 1** a sticky substance produced by some trees. **2** a synthetic substance used as the basis of plastics, adhesives, etc.

resist ▸ **verb 1** withstand the action or effect of. **2** try to prevent or fight against. **3** stop yourself having or doing something tempting.

SYNONYMS **1** *built to resist cold winters* **withstand,** be proof against, combat, weather, endure, be resistant to, keep out. **2** *they resisted his attempts to change*

things **oppose,** fight against, object to, defy, kick against; informal be anti. **3** *I resisted the urge to retort* **refrain from,** abstain from, forbear from, desist from, not give in to, restrain yourself from.
ANTONYMS welcome, submit to.

resistance ▸ noun **1** the action of resisting. **2** a secret organization that fights against an occupying enemy. **3** the ability not to be affected by something. **4** the degree to which a material or device resists the passage of an electric current.

SYNONYMS **1** *resistance to change* **opposition,** hostility. **2** *a spirited resistance* **struggle,** fight, battle, stand, opposition, defiance. **3** *the body's resistance to disease* **immunity,** defences. **4** *the French resistance* **freedom fighters,** underground, partisans.

resistant ▸ adjective offering resistance.

SYNONYMS **1** *resistant to water* **impervious,** immune, invulnerable, proof, unaffected. **2** *resistant to change* **opposed,** averse, hostile, inimical, against; informal anti.
ANTONYMS vulnerable, favourable.

resistor ▸ noun a device that resists the passage of an electric current.

resit ▸ verb (**resits, resitting, resat**) Brit. take an exam again after failing.

resolute /rez-uh-loot/ ▸ adjective determined.
▢ **resolutely** adverb.

resolution ▸ noun **1** a firm decision. **2** a formal statement of opinion by a parliament. **3** determination. **4** the resolving of a problem or dispute. **5** the degree to which detail is visible in a photograph or an image on a computer or television screen.

SYNONYMS **1** *her resolution not to smoke* **intention,** resolve, decision, intent, aim, plan, commitment, pledge, promise. **2** *the committee passed the resolution* **motion,** proposal, proposition; N. Amer. resolve. **3** *she handled the work with resolution* **determination,** purpose, resolve, single-mindedness; informal guts. **4** *a satisfactory resolution of the problem* **solution,** answer, end, settlement, conclusion.

resolve ▸ verb (**resolves, resolving, resolved**) **1** find a solution to. **2** decide firmly on a course of action. **3** take a decision by a formal vote. **4** (**resolve into**) separate into different parts.

SYNONYMS **1** *this matter cannot be resolved overnight* **settle,** sort out, solve, fix, straighten out, deal with, put right, rectify; informal hammer out, thrash out.

2 *David resolved to wait* **determine,** decide, make up your mind. **3** *the committee resolved to back the project* **vote,** rule, decide formally, agree.

▸ noun determination.

SYNONYMS *he reaffirmed his resolve* **determination,** purpose, resolution, single-mindedness; informal guts.

resonant ▸ adjective **1** (of sound) deep, clear, and ringing. **2** having the power to bring images, memories, or feelings into your mind.
▢ **resonance** noun.

resonate ▸ verb (**resonates, resonating, resonated**) make a deep, clear, ringing sound.

resort ▸ noun **1** a place visited for holidays. **2** a strategy or course of action.

SYNONYMS *strike action is our last resort* **option,** alternative, choice, possibility, hope, measure, step, recourse, expedient.

▸ verb (**resort to**) turn to a strategy or course of action so as to resolve a difficult situation.

resound ▸ verb **1** make a ringing, booming, or echoing sound. **2** (**resounding**) definite; unmistakable.

SYNONYMS **1** **echo,** reverberate, ring, boom, thunder, rumble, resonate. **2** (**resounding**) *a resounding voice* **reverberating,** resonating, echoing, ringing, sonorous, deep, rich. **3** (**resounding**) *a resounding success* **enormous,** huge, very great, tremendous, terrific, colossal, emphatic, outstanding, remarkable, phenomenal.

resource ▸ noun **1** (**resources**) a stock or supply of materials or assets. **2** something that can be used to help achieve an aim. **3** (**resources**) personal qualities that help you to cope with difficult circumstances.

SYNONYMS **1** *your tutor is there as a resource* **facility,** amenity, aid, help, support. **2** *a person of resource* **initiative,** resourcefulness, enterprise, ingenuity, inventiveness. **3** (**resources**) *use your resources efficiently* **assets,** funds, wealth, money, capital, supplies, materials, stores, stocks, reserves.

▸ verb (**be resourced**) be provided with resources.

resourceful ▸ adjective able to find quick and clever ways to overcome difficulties.

SYNONYMS **ingenious,** enterprising, inventive, creative, clever, talented, able, capable.

▢ **resourcefully** adverb **resourcefulness** noun.

respect ▸ noun **1** a feeling of admiration for someone because of their qualities

r

or achievements. **2** consideration for the feelings or rights of other people. **3** (**respects**) polite greetings. **4** a particular aspect, point, or detail.

> SYNONYMS **1** *the respect due to a great artist* **esteem,** regard, high opinion, admiration, reverence, deference, honour. **2** *he spoke to her with respect* **due regard,** politeness, courtesy, civility, deference. **3** (**respects**) *paying your respects* **regards,** compliments, greetings, best/good wishes. **4** *the report was accurate in every respect* **aspect,** regard, feature, way, sense, particular, point, detail.
> ANTONYMS contempt.

▶ verb **1** have respect for. **2** avoid harming or interfering with. **3** agree to observe a law, principle, etc.

> SYNONYMS **1** *he is highly respected for his industry* **esteem,** admire, think highly of, have a high opinion of, look up to, revere, honour. **2** *they respected our privacy* **show consideration for,** have regard for, observe, be mindful of, be heedful of. **3** *father respected her wishes* **abide by,** comply with, follow, adhere to, conform to, act in accordance with, obey, observe, keep (to).
> ANTONYMS despise, disregard, disobey.

respectable ▶ adjective **1** regarded by society as being correct or proper. **2** adequate or acceptable.

> SYNONYMS **1** *a respectable middle-class background* **reputable,** upright, honest, honourable, trustworthy, decent, good, well bred, clean-living. **2** *a respectable salary* **fairly good,** decent, fair-sized, reasonable, moderately good, large, sizeable, considerable.
> ANTONYMS disreputable, paltry.

□ **respectability** noun **respectably** adverb.

respectful ▶ adjective feeling or showing respect.

> SYNONYMS **deferential,** reverent, dutiful, polite, well mannered, civil, courteous, gracious.
> ANTONYMS rude.

□ **respectfully** adverb.

respecting ▶ preposition with reference to.

respective ▶ adjective belonging or relating separately to each of two or more people or things.

> SYNONYMS **separate,** personal, own, particular, individual, specific, special.

respectively ▶ adverb individually and in the order already mentioned.

respiration ▶ noun the action of breathing.

respirator ▶ noun **1** a device worn over the face to prevent you breathing in

dust, smoke, etc. **2** a device that enables someone to breathe when they cannot do so naturally.

respiratory /ri-spi-ruh-tuh-ri/ ▶ adjective relating to breathing.

respire ▶ verb (**respires, respiring, respired**) technical breathe.

respite /ress-pyt/ ▶ noun a short period of rest or relief from something difficult or unpleasant.

> SYNONYMS **rest,** break, breathing space, interval, lull, pause, time out, relief; informal breather, let-up.

resplendent ▶ adjective attractive and impressive.

respond ▶ verb say or do something in reply or as a reaction.

> SYNONYMS **1** *they do not respond to questions* **answer,** reply, write back, come back, rejoin, retort, riposte, counter. **2** *they were slow to respond* **react,** reciprocate, retaliate.

respondent ▶ noun **1** Law a person against whom a petition is filed, especially one in a divorce case. **2** a person who responds to a questionnaire or advertisement.

response ▶ noun an answer or reaction.

> SYNONYMS **1** *his response to the question* **answer,** reply, rejoinder, retort, riposte; informal comeback. **2** *an angry response* **reaction,** reply, retaliation; informal comeback.
> ANTONYMS question.

responsibility ▶ noun (plural **responsibilities**) **1** the state of being responsible. **2** the opportunity to act independently. **3** a thing which you are required to do as part of a job, role, or obligation.

> SYNONYMS **1** *it was his responsibility to find witnesses* **duty,** task, function, job, role, business; Brit. informal pigeon. **2** *they denied responsibility for the attack* **blame,** fault, guilt, culpability, liability. **3** *a sense of responsibility* **trustworthiness,** (common) sense, maturity, reliability, dependability. **4** *managerial responsibility* **authority,** control, power, leadership.
> ANTONYMS irresponsibility.

responsible ▶ adjective **1** obliged to do something or look after someone. **2** being the cause of something and so able to be blamed or credited for it. **3** able to be trusted. **4** (of a job) involving important duties or decisions. **5** (**responsible to**) having to report to a senior person.

> SYNONYMS **1** *who is responsible for prisons?* **in charge of,** in control of, at the helm of, accountable for, liable for. **2** *I am responsible for the mistake*

accountable, answerable, to blame, guilty, culpable, blameworthy, at fault, in the wrong. **3** *a responsible job* **important,** powerful, executive. **4** *a responsible tenant* **trustworthy,** sensible, mature, reliable, dependable.
ANTONYMS irresponsible.

□ **responsibly** adverb.

✔ responsi**ble**, not **-able**.

responsive ▸ adjective responding readily and positively.

SYNONYMS **reactive,** receptive, open to suggestions, amenable, flexible, forthcoming.
ANTONYMS unresponsive.

rest[1] ▸ verb **1** stop working or moving in order to relax or recover your strength. **2** place something so that it stays in a particular position. **3** remain or be left in a particular condition: *rest assured.* **4** (**rest on**) depend or be based on. **5** (**rest with**) (of power, responsibility, etc.) belong to.

SYNONYMS **1** *he needed to rest* **relax,** ease up/off, let up, slow down, have/take a break, unbend, unwind, take it easy, put your feet up; informal take five, have/take a breather, chill out. **2** *his hands rested on the rail* **lie,** be laid, repose, be placed, be positioned, be supported by. **3** *she rested her basket on the ground* **support,** prop (up), lean, lay, set, stand, position, place, put.

▸ noun **1** a period of resting. **2** a motionless state. **3** an object that is used to hold or support something. **4** a brief interval of silence in a piece of music.

SYNONYMS **1** *get some rest* **relaxation,** repose, leisure, respite, time off, breathing space; informal lie-down. **2** *a short rest from work* **holiday,** vacation, break, breathing space, interval, interlude, intermission, time off/out; informal breather. **3** *she took the poker from its rest* **stand,** base, holder, support, rack, frame, shelf. **4** *we came to rest 100 metres lower* **a standstill,** a halt, a stop.

rest[2] ▸ noun the remaining part, people, or things.

SYNONYMS *the rest of the board are appointees* **remainder,** residue, balance, others, those left, remnant(s), surplus, excess.

restaurant /ress-tuh-ront/ ▸ noun a place where people pay to sit and eat meals that are cooked on the premises.

restaurateur /ress-tuh-ruh-**ter**/ ▸ noun a person who owns and manages a restaurant.

✔ Note that there is no **n**: restau**rat**eur.

restful ▸ adjective having a quiet and soothing quality.

SYNONYMS **relaxing,** quiet, calm, tranquil, soothing, peaceful, leisurely, undisturbed, untroubled.
ANTONYMS exciting.

restitution ▸ noun **1** the restoration of something lost or stolen to its proper owner. **2** payment for injury or loss that has been suffered.

restive ▸ adjective unable to keep still or silent; restless.

restless ▸ adjective unable to rest or relax.

SYNONYMS **1** *Maria was restless* **uneasy,** ill at ease, fidgety, edgy, tense, worked up, nervous, nervy, agitated, anxious; informal jumpy, jittery, twitchy, uptight. **2** *a restless night* **sleepless,** wakeful, fitful, broken, disturbed, troubled, unsettled.

□ **restlessly** adverb.

restoration ▸ noun the action of restoring something or someone.

SYNONYMS **1** *the restoration of democracy* **reinstatement,** reinstitution, re-establishment, reimposition, return. **2** *the restoration of derelict housing* **repair,** fixing, mending, refurbishment, reconditioning, rehabilitation, rebuilding, reconstruction, renovation; N. Amer. informal rehab.

restorative ▸ adjective able to restore health or strength.

restore ▸ verb (**restores, restoring, restored**) **1** bring back a previous practice, situation, etc. **2** return someone or something to a previous condition, place, position, etc. **3** repair or renovate a building, work of art, etc.

SYNONYMS **1** *the aim to restore democracy* **reinstate,** bring back, reinstitute, reimpose, reinstall, re-establish. **2** *he restored it to its rightful owner* **return,** give back, hand back. **3** *the building has been restored* **repair,** fix, mend, refurbish, recondition, rehabilitate, renovate; informal do up; N. Amer. informal rehab. **4** *a good sleep can restore you* **reinvigorate,** revitalize, revive, refresh, energize, freshen.
ANTONYMS abolish, tire.

□ **restorer** noun.

restrain ▸ verb **1** keep under control or within limits. **2** stop someone moving or acting freely.

SYNONYMS **1** *Charles restrained his anger* **control,** check, curb, suppress, contain, rein back/in; informal keep the lid on. **2** *she could barely restrain herself from swearing* **prevent,** stop, keep, hold back.
ANTONYMS vent, allow.

r

restrained ▸ adjective **1** reserved or unemotional. **2** not richly decorated or brightly coloured; subtle.

SYNONYMS **1** *Julie was quite restrained* **self-controlled,** not given to excesses, sober, steady, unemotional, undemonstrative. **2** *restrained elegance* **muted,** soft, discreet, subtle, quiet, unobtrusive, unostentatious, understated, tasteful.
ANTONYMS impetuous, ostentatious.

restraint ▸ noun **1** the action of keeping someone or something under control. **2** a device which limits or prevents freedom of movement. **3** self-controlled behaviour.

SYNONYMS **1** *a restraint on their impulsiveness* **constraint,** check, control, restriction, limitation, curtailment, rein, brake. **2** *the customary restraint of the police* **self-control,** self-discipline, control, moderation, judiciousness. **3** *the room has been decorated with restraint* **subtlety,** understatedness, taste, discretion, discrimination.
ANTONYMS impetuousness, ostentation.

restrict ▸ verb **1** put a limit on. **2** stop someone moving or acting freely.

SYNONYMS **1** *a busy job restricted his leisure activities* **limit,** keep within bounds, regulate, control, moderate, cut down. **2** *the belt rather restricts movement* **hinder,** interfere with, impede, hamper, obstruct, block, check, curb.

restricted ▸ adjective **1** limited in extent, number, or scope. **2** not open to the public; secret.

SYNONYMS **1** *restricted space* **cramped,** confined, constricted, small, narrow, tight. **2** *a restricted calorie intake* **limited,** controlled, regulated, reduced. **3** *a restricted zone* **out of bounds,** off limits, private, exclusive. **4** *restricted information* **secret,** classified; informal hush-hush.
ANTONYMS generous, unlimited, public, open.

restriction ▸ noun **1** a rule, law, etc. that prevents free movement or action. **2** the action of restricting.

SYNONYMS **1** *there is no restriction on the number of places* **limitation,** constraint, control, check, curb. **2** *the restriction of personal freedom* **reduction,** limitation, diminution, curtailment. **3** *restriction of movement* **hindrance,** impediment, slowing, reduction, limitation.

restrictive ▸ adjective preventing freedom of action or movement.

restroom ▸ noun N. Amer. a toilet in a public building.

restructure ▸ verb (restructures, restructuring, restructured) **1** organize differently. **2** convert a debt into another debt that can be repaid at a later time.

result ▸ noun **1** a thing that is caused or produced by something else. **2** a piece of information obtained by experiment or calculation. **3** a final score or mark in an exam or sports event. **4** a satisfactory or favourable outcome.

SYNONYMS *stress is the result of overwork* **consequence,** outcome, upshot, sequel, effect, reaction, repercussion.
ANTONYMS cause.

▸ verb **1** happen because of something else. **2** (**result from**) be caused by something.

SYNONYMS *anger may result from an argument* **follow,** ensue, develop, stem, spring, arise, derive, proceed; (**result from**) be caused by, be brought about by, be produced by, originate in.

resultant ▸ adjective happening or produced as a result.

resume ▸ verb (resumes, resuming, resumed) begin again or continue after a pause.

SYNONYMS **restart,** recommence, begin again, start again, reopen, renew, return to, continue with, carry on with.
ANTONYMS suspend, abandon.

résumé /rez-yuu-may/ ▸ noun **1** a summary. **2** N. Amer. a curriculum vitae.

SYNONYMS **summary,** precis, synopsis, abstract, outline, abridgement, overview.

resumption ▸ noun the action of beginning again after a pause.

SYNONYMS **restart,** recommencement, reopening, continuation, renewal, return, revival.

resurgence ▸ noun an increase in strength or popularity after a period of weakness or unpopularity.

SYNONYMS **renewal,** revival, renaissance, recovery, comeback, reawakening, resurrection, reappearance, re-emergence, resumption, continuation.

resurgent ▸ adjective becoming stronger or more popular again.

resurrect ▸ verb **1** restore to life. **2** start using or doing again.

SYNONYMS **revive,** restore, regenerate, revitalize, breathe new life into, reinvigorate, resuscitate, rejuvenate, re-establish, relaunch.

resurrection ▸ noun **1** the action of resurrecting. **2** (**the Resurrection**) (in Christian belief) the time when Jesus rose from the dead.

r

resuscitate /ri-**suss**-i-tayt/ ▶ verb
(**resuscitates, resuscitating, resuscitated**)
make someone conscious again.
□ **resuscitation** noun.

> ✔ Note that it is -**susc**-, not -**suss**-:
> re**susc**itate.

retail ▶ noun the sale of goods to the public.
▶ verb **1** sell goods to the public. **2** (**retail at** or
for) be sold for a particular price.
□ **retailer** noun.

retain ▶ verb **1** continue to have; keep
possession of. **2** absorb and continue to
hold a substance. **3** (**retaining**) keeping
something in place.

> synonyms **1** *the government retained a*
> *share in the industries* **keep (possession**
> **of),** keep hold of, hang on to. **2** *existing*
> *footpaths are to be retained* **maintain,**
> keep, preserve, conserve.
> antonyms give up, abolish.

retainer ▶ noun **1** a fee paid in advance to
a barrister to secure their services. **2** a
servant who has worked for a family for a
long time.

retake ▶ verb (**retakes, retaking, retook**; past
participle **retaken**) **1** take a test or exam again.
2 regain possession of.
▶ noun a test or exam that is retaken.

retaliate ▶ verb (**retaliates, retaliating,**
retaliated) make an attack in return for a
similar attack.

> synonyms **fight back,** hit back, respond,
> react, reply, reciprocate, counter-attack,
> get back at someone, pay someone back;
> informal get your own back.

□ **retaliatory** adjective.

retaliation ▶ noun the action or an act of
retaliating.

> synonyms **revenge,** vengeance, reprisal,
> retribution, repayment, response,
> reaction, reply, counter-attack.

retard ▶ verb stop from developing or
progressing.

> synonyms **delay,** slow down/up, hold
> back/up, postpone, detain, decelerate,
> hinder, impede, check.
> antonyms accelerate, bring forward.

□ **retardation** noun.

retarded ▶ adjective offensive less developed
mentally than is usual at a particular age.

retch ▶ verb make the sound and movements
of vomiting.

retention ▶ noun the action of retaining, or
the state of being retained.

retentive ▶ adjective (of a person's
memory) effective in retaining facts and
impressions.

rethink ▶ verb (**rethinks, rethinking,**
rethought) consider a policy or course of

action again.
▶ noun an instance of rethinking.

reticent /**ret**-i-suhnt/ ▶ adjective not
revealing your thoughts or feelings readily.

> synonyms **uncommunicative,**
> unforthcoming, unresponsive, tight-
> lipped, quiet, taciturn, silent, reserved.
> antonyms expansive.

□ **reticence** noun.

retina ▶ noun (plural **retinas** or **retinae** /**ret**-i-
nee/) a layer at the back of the eyeball that
is sensitive to light and sends impulses to
the brain.

retinue ▶ noun a group of assistants
accompanying an important person.

retire ▶ verb (**retires, retiring, retired**)
1 leave your job and stop working,
especially because you have reached a
particular age. **2** withdraw from a race
or match because of accident or injury.
3 formal leave a place. **4** (of a jury) leave the
courtroom to decide the verdict of a trial.
5 go to bed.

> synonyms **1** *he has retired* **give up work,**
> stop work. **2** *Gillian retired to her office*
> **withdraw,** go away, take yourself off,
> shut yourself away. **3** *everyone retired*
> *early* **go to bed,** call it a day; informal turn
> in, hit the hay/sack.
> antonyms emerge, get up.

retired ▶ adjective having left your job and
stopped working.

> synonyms *a retired teacher* **former,** ex-,
> pensioned-off, past, elderly.

▶ noun retired people as a class.

> synonyms (**the retired**) (**old-age**)
> **pensioners,** OAPs, senior citizens, the
> elderly; N. Amer. seniors.

retirement ▶ noun **1** the action of retiring.
2 the period of life after retiring from
work.

retiring ▶ adjective tending to avoid
company; shy.

> synonyms **shy,** diffident, self-effacing,
> unassuming, reserved, reticent, quite,
> timid.

retook past of RETAKE.

retort[1] ▶ verb say something sharp or witty
in answer to a remark or accusation.

> synonyms *'Oh, sure,' she retorted* **answer,**
> reply, respond, return, counter, riposte,
> retaliate.

▶ noun a sharp or witty reply.

> synonyms *a sarcastic retort* **answer,** reply,
> response, counter, rejoinder, riposte;
> informal comeback.

retort[2] ▶ noun a glass container with a long
neck, used for distilling liquids and heating
chemicals.

r

retouch ▸ verb make slight improvements to a painting, photograph, etc.

retrace ▸ verb (**retraces, retracing, retraced**) **1** go back over the route that you have just taken. **2** follow a route taken by someone else. **3** trace something back to its source.

retract ▸ verb **1** draw something back. **2** withdraw a statement or accusation. **3** go back on an undertaking.

> synonyms **take back,** withdraw, recant, disavow, go back on, backtrack on.

□ **retractable** adjective **retraction** noun.

retreat ▸ verb **1** (of an army) withdraw from confrontation with enemy forces. **2** move back from a difficult situation. **3** withdraw to a quiet or secluded place.

> synonyms *the army retreated* **withdraw,** retire, draw back, pull back/out, fall back, give way, give ground.
> antonyms advance.

▸ noun **1** an act of retreating. **2** a quiet or secluded place. **3** a quiet place where people go for a time to pray and meditate.

> synonyms **1** *the retreat of the army* **withdrawal,** retirement, pullback, flight. **2** *her rural retreat* **refuge,** haven, sanctuary, hideaway, hideout, hiding place; informal hidey-hole.

retrench ▸ verb reduce costs or spending in times of economic difficulty.
□ **retrenchment** noun.

retrial ▸ noun a second or further trial.

retribution ▸ noun severe punishment inflicted as revenge.

retrieve ▸ verb (**retrieves, retrieving, retrieved**) **1** get or bring back. **2** find or extract information stored in a computer. **3** improve a bad situation.

> synonyms **1** *I retrieved our ball from their garden* **get back,** bring back, recover, recapture, regain, recoup. **2** *they tried to retrieve the situation* **put/set right,** rectify, remedy, restore, sort out, straighten out, resolve.

□ **retrieval** noun.

retriever ▸ noun a breed of dog used for finding and bringing back game that has been shot.

retrograde ▸ adjective directed or moving backwards or to a worse state.

retrogressive ▸ adjective going back to an earlier and inferior state.
□ **retrogression** noun.

retrorocket ▸ noun a small rocket on a spacecraft or missile, fired in the direction of travel to slow it down.

retrospect ▸ noun (**in retrospect**) when looking back on a past event.

retrospective ▸ adjective **1** looking back on or dealing with past events or situations. **2** taking effect from a date in the past.

▸ noun an exhibition showing the development of an artist's work over a period of time.
□ **retrospectively** adverb.

retroussé /ruh-**troo**-say/ ▸ adjective (of a person's nose) turned up at the tip.

retsina /ret-**see**-nuh/ ▸ noun a Greek white wine flavoured with resin.

return ▸ verb **1** come or go back to a place. **2** (**return to**) go back to a particular state or activity. **3** give, send, or put back. **4** feel, say, or do the same thing in response. **5** (in tennis) hit the ball back to an opponent. **6** (of a judge or jury) give a verdict. **7** produce a profit. **8** elect someone to a political office.

> synonyms **1** *he returned to London* **go back,** come back, arrive back, come home. **2** *the symptoms returned* **recur,** reoccur, repeat (itself), reappear. **3** *he returned the money* **give back,** hand back, pay back, repay. **4** *Peter returned the book to the shelf* **restore,** put back, replace, reinstall. **5** *the jury returned a verdict* **deliver,** bring in, hand down.
> antonyms keep.

▸ noun **1** an act of returning. **2** a profit from an investment. **3** Brit. a ticket that lets you travel to a place and back again.

> synonyms **1** *the return of hard times* **recurrence,** reoccurrence, repeat, repetition, reappearance. **2** *I requested the return of my books* **giving back,** handing back, replacement, restoration, reinstatement, restitution. **3** *a quick return on investments* **yield,** profit, gain, revenue, interest, dividend.

reunify ▸ verb (**reunifies, reunifying, reunified**) make a place a united country again.
□ **reunification** noun.

reunion ▸ noun **1** the process of reuniting. **2** a gathering of people who have not seen each other for some time.

reunite ▸ verb (**reunites, reuniting, reunited**) bring two or more people or things together again.

reuse ▸ verb (**reuses, reusing, reused**) use something again.
□ **reusable** adjective.

rev informal ▸ noun (**revs**) the number of revolutions of an engine per minute.
▸ verb (**revs, revving, revved**) make an engine run quickly by pressing the accelerator.

Rev. (or **Revd**) ▸ abbreviation Reverend.

revamp ▸ verb alter something so as to improve it.

> synonyms **renovate,** redecorate, refurbish, remodel, refashion, redesign,

restyle; informal do up, give something a facelift, give something a makeover, vamp up; Brit. informal tart up.

▶ noun a new and improved version of something.

reveal ▶ verb **1** make previously unknown or secret information known. **2** allow something hidden to be seen.

> SYNONYMS **1** *the police can't reveal his whereabouts* **disclose,** make known, make public, broadcast, publicize, circulate, divulge, tell, let slip/drop, give away/out, blurt out, release, leak; informal let on. **2** *he revealed his new car* **show,** display, exhibit, unveil, uncover.
> ANTONYMS keep secret, hide.

revealing ▶ adjective **1** giving out interesting or significant information. **2** (of a piece of clothing) allowing a lot of your body to be seen.

reveille /ri-**val**-li/ ▶ noun a signal sounded on a bugle, drum, etc. to wake up soldiers in the morning.

revel ▶ verb (**revels, revelling, revelled**; US spelling **revels, reveling, reveled**) **1** spend time enjoying yourself in a lively, noisy way. **2** (**revel in**) get great pleasure from.

> SYNONYMS *they revelled all night* **celebrate,** make merry; informal party, live it up, whoop it up, paint the town red.

▶ noun (**revels**) lively, noisy celebrations.

> SYNONYMS *late-night revels* **celebration,** festivity, jollification, merrymaking, party; informal rave, shindig, bash; Brit. informal rave-up; N. Amer. informal wingding, blast.

> □ **reveller** noun **revelry** noun (plural **revelries**).

revelation ▶ noun **1** the revealing of something previously unknown. **2** a surprising or remarkable thing.

> SYNONYMS **1** *revelations about his personal life* **disclosure,** announcement, report, admission, confession. **2** *the revelation of a secret* **disclosure,** divulging, letting slip/drop, giving away/out, leak, betrayal, publicizing.

revelatory ▶ adjective revealing something previously unknown.

revenge ▶ noun something harmful done to someone in return for something bad that they did to you.

> SYNONYMS *she is seeking revenge* **retaliation,** retribution, vengeance, reprisal, recrimination, an eye for an eye (and a tooth for a tooth), redress.
> ANTONYMS forgiveness.

▶ verb (**revenges, revenging, revenged**) (**revenge yourself** or **be revenged**) harm someone in return for something bad that they did to you.

> SYNONYMS *he revenged his brother's murder* **avenge,** exact retribution for, take reprisals for, get redress for, make someone pay for; informal get your own back for.
> ANTONYMS forgive.

revenue ▶ noun the income received by an organization, or by a government from taxes.

> SYNONYMS **income,** takings, receipts, proceeds, earnings, profit(s), gain, yield.
> ANTONYMS expenditure.

reverberate ▶ verb (**reverberates, reverberating, reverberated**) **1** (of a loud noise) be repeated as an echo. **2** have continuing serious effects.
□ **reverberation** noun.

revere ▶ verb (**reveres, revering, revered**) respect or admire deeply.

> SYNONYMS **respect,** admire, think highly of, esteem, venerate, look up to, be in awe of.
> ANTONYMS despise.

reverence ▶ noun deep respect.

reverend ▶ adjective a title given to Christian ministers.

reverent ▶ adjective showing reverence; deeply respectful.
□ **reverential** adjective **reverently** adverb.

reverie /**rev**-uh-ri/ ▶ noun a daydream.

reversal ▶ noun **1** a change to an opposite direction, position, or course of action. **2** a harmful change of fortune.

reverse ▶ verb (**reverses, reversing, reversed**) **1** move backwards. **2** make something the opposite of what it was. **3** turn something the other way round. **4** cancel a judgement by a lower court.

> SYNONYMS **1** *the car reversed* **back,** move back/backwards. **2** *reverse the bottle in the ice bucket* **turn upside down,** turn over, upend, invert, turn back to front. **3** *reverse your roles* **swap (round),** change (round), exchange, switch (round), transpose. **4** *the umpire reversed the decision* **alter,** change, overturn, overthrow, disallow, override, overrule, veto, revoke.

▶ adjective **1** going in or turned towards the opposite direction. **2** opposite to the usual way.

> SYNONYMS *in reverse order* **backward(s),** inverted, transposed, opposite.

▶ noun **1** a complete change of direction or action. **2** (**the reverse**) the opposite or contrary. **3** a setback or defeat. **4** the opposite side of something to the observer.

> SYNONYMS **1** *the reverse is the case* **opposite,** contrary, converse, inverse,

r

antithesis. **2** *successes and reverses* **setback,** reversal, upset, failure, misfortune, mishap, disaster, blow, disappointment, adversity, hardship, affliction, vicissitude, defeat. **3** *the reverse of the page* **other side,** back, underside, wrong side.
ANTONYMS success, front.

▢ **reversible** adjective.

reversion ▸ noun a return to a previous state, practice, etc.

revert ▸ verb (**revert to**) return to a previous state, practice, etc.

SYNONYMS **return,** go back, change back, default, relapse.

review ▸ noun **1** an examination of something to decide whether changes are necessary. **2** a critical assessment of a book, play, etc. **3** a report of an event that has already happened. **4** a ceremonial display of military forces.

SYNONYMS **1** *the Council undertook a review* **analysis,** evaluation, assessment, appraisal, examination, investigation, enquiry, probe, inspection, study. **2** *the rent is due for review* **reconsideration,** reassessment, re-evaluation, reappraisal. **3** *book reviews* **criticism,** critique, assessment, evaluation, commentary.

▸ verb **1** examine or consider something again. **2** write a review of.

SYNONYMS **1** *I reviewed the evidence* **survey,** study, research, consider, analyse, examine, scrutinize, explore, look into, probe, investigate, inspect, assess, appraise; informal size up. **2** *the referee reviewed his decision* **reconsider,** re-examine, reassess, re-evaluate, reappraise, rethink. **3** *she reviewed the play* **comment on,** evaluate, assess, appraise, judge, criticize.

reviewer ▸ noun a person who reviews.

SYNONYMS **critic,** commentator, judge.

revile ▸ verb (**reviles, reviling, reviled**) criticize in a rude or scornful way.

revise ▸ verb (**revises, revising, revised**) **1** examine and alter a piece of writing. **2** reconsider and change an opinion. **3** Brit. reread work in order to prepare for an exam.

SYNONYMS **1** *she revised her opinion* **reconsider,** review, re-examine, reassess, re-evaluate, reappraise, rethink, change, alter, modify. **2** *the editor revised the text* **amend,** correct, alter, change, edit, rewrite, redraft, rephrase, rework. **3** *revise your lecture notes* **go over,** reread, memorize, cram; informal bone up on; Brit. informal swot up (on), mug up (on).

revision ▸ noun **1** the action of revising

something. **2** a revised edition or form of something.

SYNONYMS **1** *a revision of the Prayer Book* **alteration,** adaptation, editing, rewriting, redrafting, correction, updating. **2** *a major revision of the system* **reconsideration,** review, re-examination, reassessment, re-evaluation, reappraisal, rethink, change, alteration, modification. **3** *he was doing some revision* **rereading,** memorizing, cramming; Brit. informal swotting.

revisionism ▸ noun disapproving the changing of accepted theories or principles.
▢ **revisionist** noun & adjective.

revitalize (or revitalise) ▸ verb (**revitalizes, revitalizing, revitalized**) give new life and vitality to.
▢ **revitalization** noun.

revival ▸ noun **1** an improvement in the condition, strength, or popularity of something. **2** a new production of an old play.

SYNONYMS **1** *a revival in the economy* **improvement,** rallying, picking up, turn for the better, upturn, upswing, resurgence. **2** *the revival of traditional crafts* **comeback,** re-establishment, reintroduction, restoration, reappearance, resurrection.
ANTONYMS downturn, disappearance.

revivalism ▸ noun **1** the process of trying to reawaken interest in a particular religious faith. **2** the practice of returning to former customs, fashions, etc.
▢ **revivalist** noun & adjective.

revive ▸ verb (**revives, reviving, revived**) **1** make conscious, healthy, or strong again. **2** start doing, using, or performing something again.

SYNONYMS **1** *attempts to revive her failed* **resuscitate,** bring round, bring back to consciousness. **2** *the man soon revived* **regain consciousness,** come round, wake up. **3** *a cup of tea revived her* **reinvigorate,** revitalize, refresh, energize, reanimate. **4** *reviving old traditions* **reintroduce,** re-establish, restore, resurrect, bring back.

revivify /ri-**viv**-i-fy/ ▸ verb (**revivifies, revivifying, revivified**) formal revive.

revoke ▸ verb (**revokes, revoking, revoked**) make a decree, law, etc. no longer valid.
▢ **revocation** noun.

revolt ▸ noun an act of rebellion or defiance.

SYNONYMS *an armed revolt* **rebellion,** revolution, insurrection, mutiny, uprising, riot, insurgence, coup (d'état).

▸ verb **1** rebel against an authority. **2** make someone feel disgust.

SYNONYMS **1** *the people revolted* **rebel,** rise up, take to the streets, riot, mutiny. **2** *the smell revolted him* **disgust,** sicken, nauseate, turn someone's stomach, put off, offend; informal turn off; N. Amer. informal gross out.

revolting ▶ adjective very unpleasant; disgusting.

SYNONYMS **disgusting,** sickening, nauseating, stomach-turning, repulsive, repugnant, hideous, nasty, foul, offensive; N. Amer. vomitous; informal ghastly, horrid, gross.
ANTONYMS attractive, pleasant.

revolution ▶ noun **1** the overthrow of a government by force, in favour of a new system. **2** a dramatic and far-reaching change. **3** a single circular movement around a central point.

SYNONYMS **1** *the French Revolution* **rebellion,** revolt, insurrection, mutiny, rising, uprising, riot, insurgence, coup (d'état). **2** *a revolution in printing techniques* **dramatic change,** sea change, metamorphosis, transformation, innovation, reorganization, restructuring; informal shake-up; N. Amer. informal shakedown. **3** *one revolution of a wheel* (**single**) **turn,** rotation, circle, spin, orbit, circuit, lap.

revolutionary ▶ adjective **1** involving or causing dramatic change. **2** taking part in, or relating to, political revolution.

SYNONYMS **1** *revolutionary troops* **rebellious,** rebel, insurgent, rioting, mutinous, renegade. **2** *a revolutionary kind of wheelchair* **new,** novel, original, unusual, unconventional, unorthodox, newfangled, innovatory, modern, state-of-the-art, futuristic, pioneering.

▶ noun (plural **revolutionaries**) a person who starts or supports a political revolution.

SYNONYMS *political revolutionaries* **rebel,** insurgent, mutineer, insurrectionist, agitator.

revolutionize (or **revolutionise**) ▶ verb (**revolutionizes, revolutionizing, revolutionized**) change something completely or fundamentally.

revolve ▶ verb (**revolves, revolving, revolved**) **1** move in a circle around a central point. **2** (**revolve around**) treat as the most important element.

SYNONYMS **1** *a fan revolved slowly* **go round,** turn round, rotate, spin. **2** *the moon revolves around the earth* **circle,** travel, orbit.

revolver ▶ noun a pistol with revolving chambers that allow several shots to be fired without reloading.

revue ▶ noun a theatrical show with short sketches, songs, and dances.

revulsion ▶ noun a sense of disgust and loathing.

reward ▶ noun something given in recognition of service, effort, or achievement.

SYNONYMS *a reward for long service* **award,** honour, decoration, bonus, premium, bounty, present, gift, payment, recompense, prize; informal pay-off.

▶ verb **1** give a reward to. **2** show appreciation of an action or quality by giving a reward.

SYNONYMS *they were well rewarded* **recompense,** pay, remunerate.
ANTONYMS punish.

rewarding ▶ adjective providing satisfaction.

SYNONYMS **satisfying,** gratifying, pleasing, fulfilling, enriching, illuminating, worthwhile, productive, fruitful.

rewind ▶ verb (**rewinds, rewinding, rewound**) wind a film or tape back to the beginning.

rewire ▶ verb (**rewires, rewiring, rewired**) provide with new wiring.

rework ▶ verb alter something in order to improve or update it.

rhapsodize (or **rhapsodise**) ▶ verb (**rhapsodizes, rhapsodizing, rhapsodized**) express great enthusiasm about someone or something.

rhapsody ▶ noun (plural **rhapsodies**) **1** an expression of great enthusiasm. **2** a piece of music in one extended movement.
□ **rhapsodic** adjective.

rhenium /ree-ni-uhm/ ▶ noun a rare silvery-white metallic element.

rheostat /ree-uh-stat/ ▶ noun a device for varying the amount of resistance in an electrical circuit.

rhesus factor /ree-suhss/ ▶ noun a substance found in the red blood cells of many humans.

rhesus monkey ▶ noun a small monkey found in southern Asia.

rhetoric /ret-uh-rik/ ▶ noun **1** effective or persuasive public speaking. **2** persuasive but insincere language.

SYNONYMS **1** *a form of rhetoric* **oratory,** eloquence, command of language, way with words. **2** *empty rhetoric* **wordiness,** verbosity, grandiloquence, bombast, pomposity, extravagant language, purple prose, turgidity; informal hot air.

rhetorical /ri-torr-i-k'l/ ▶ adjective **1** relating to rhetoric. **2** intended to

r

persuade or impress. **3** (of a question) asked for effect or to make a statement rather than to obtain an answer.

> SYNONYMS **1** *rhetorical devices* **stylistic,** oratorical, linguistic, verbal. **2** *rhetorical exchanges in parliament* **extravagant,** grandiloquent, high-flown, bombastic, grandiose, pompous, pretentious, overblown, oratorical, turgid, flowery; informal highfalutin.

□ **rhetorically** adverb.

rheumatic ▸ adjective relating to, or suffering from, rheumatism.

rheumatism /roo-muh-ti-z'm/ ▸ noun a disease with inflammation and pain in the joints and muscles.

rheumy /roo-mi/ ▸ adjective (of a person's eyes) watery.

rhinestone ▸ noun an imitation diamond.

rhino ▸ noun (plural **rhino** or **rhinos**) informal a rhinoceros.

rhinoceros /ry-noss-uh-ruhss/ ▸ noun (plural **rhinoceros** or **rhinoceroses**) a large plant-eating animal with one or two horns on the nose and thick skin, found in Africa and Asia.

rhizome /ry-zohm/ ▸ noun a horizontal underground plant stem producing both roots and shoots.

rhodium /roh-di-uhm/ ▸ noun a hard silvery-white metallic element.

rhododendron ▸ noun a shrub with large clusters of bright flowers.

rhombus ▸ noun (plural **rhombuses** or **rhombi** /rom-by/) a flat shape with four straight sides of equal length.

rhubarb ▸ noun the thick leaf stalks of a plant, cooked and eaten as fruit.

rhumba → RUMBA.

rhyme ▸ noun **1** a word that has the same sound or ends with the same sound as another. **2** similarity of sound between words or the endings of words. **3** a short poem with rhyming lines.

> SYNONYMS **poem,** verse, ode; (**rhymes**) poetry, doggerel.

▸ verb (**rhymes, rhyming, rhymed**) have or end with the same sound as another word or line.
■ **rhyming slang** slang in which you use words that rhyme with the word you mean (e.g. *butcher's,* short for *butcher's hook,* meaning 'look').

> ✔ Remember the first **h**, following the **r**, in r**h**yme and r**h**ythm.

rhythm ▸ noun **1** a strong, regular repeated pattern of sound or movement. **2** a regularly recurring sequence of events or actions.

> SYNONYMS **1** *the rhythm of the music* **beat,** cadence, tempo, time, pulse, throb, swing. **2** *poetic features such as rhythm* **metre,** measure, stress, accent, cadence. **3** *the rhythm of daily life* **pattern,** flow, tempo.

■ **rhythm and blues** a type of music that is a combination of blues and jazz.

rhythmic ▸ adjective **1** having or relating to rhythm. **2** happening regularly.
□ **rhythmically** adverb.

rib ▸ noun **1** each of a series of bones that are attached to the spine and curve around the chest. **2** a curved structure supporting an arched roof or forming part of a boat's framework.
▸ verb (**ribs, ribbing, ribbed**) informal tease someone good-naturedly.

ribald ▸ adjective referring to sex in a rude but humorous way.
□ **ribaldry** noun.

riband ▸ noun old use a ribbon.

ribbed ▸ adjective having a pattern of raised bands.

ribbon ▸ noun **1** a long, narrow strip of fabric, used for tying something or for decoration. **2** a long, narrow strip. **3** a narrow band of inked material used to produce the characters in some typewriters.

ribcage ▸ noun the bony frame formed by the ribs.

riboflavin /ry-boh-**flay**-vin/ ▸ noun vitamin B₂.

rice ▸ noun grains of a cereal plant which is grown for food on wet land in warm countries.

ricepaper ▸ noun thin edible paper made from a type of plant, used in oriental painting and in baking biscuits and cakes.

rich ▸ adjective **1** having a lot of money, assets, or resources. **2** made of expensive materials. **3** plentiful. **4** having or producing something in large amounts. **5** (of food) containing a lot of fat, sugar, etc. **6** (of a colour, sound, or smell) pleasantly deep and strong. **7** (of soil or land) fertile.

> SYNONYMS **1** *rich people* **wealthy,** affluent, moneyed, well off, well-to-do, prosperous; informal loaded, well heeled, made of money. **2** *rich furnishings* **sumptuous,** opulent, luxurious, lavish, gorgeous, splendid, magnificent, costly, expensive, fancy; informal plush; Brit. informal swish; N. Amer. informal swank. **3** *a garden rich in flowers* **well stocked,** well provided, abounding, crammed, packed, teeming, bursting. **4** *a rich supply of restaurants* **plentiful,** abundant, copious, ample, profuse, lavish, liberal, generous.

5 *rich soil* **fertile,** productive, fruitful.
6 *a rich sauce* **creamy,** fatty, heavy, full-flavoured. **7** *rich colours* **strong,** deep, full, intense, vivid, brilliant.
ANTONYMS poor, cheap, light.

□ **richness** noun.

riches ▸ plural noun **1** large amounts of money or valuable possessions. **2** valuable natural resources.

SYNONYMS **money,** wealth, funds, cash, means, assets, capital, resources; informal bread, loot; Brit. informal dosh, brass, lolly, spondulicks; N. Amer. informal bucks; US informal greenbacks.

richly ▸ adverb **1** in a rich way. **2** fully; thoroughly.

SYNONYMS **1** *richly furnished* **sumptuously,** opulently, luxuriously, lavishly, gorgeously, splendidly, magnificently. **2** *the joy she richly deserves* **fully,** amply, well, thoroughly, completely, wholly, totally, entirely, absolutely, utterly.
ANTONYMS meanly.

Richter scale /rik-ter/ ▸ noun a scale for measuring the severity of an earthquake.

rick¹ ▸ noun a stack of hay, corn, or straw.

rick² Brit. ▸ verb strain part of your body slightly.
▸ noun a slight sprain or strain.

rickets /ri-kits/ ▸ noun a disease of children in which the bones are softened and distorted.

rickety ▸ adjective badly made and likely to collapse.

rickshaw ▸ noun a light two-wheeled vehicle pulled by a person walking or riding a bicycle.

ricochet /ri-kuh-shay/ ▸ verb (**ricochets, ricocheting, ricocheted**) (of a bullet or other fast-moving object) rebound off a surface.
▸ noun a shot or hit that ricochets.

rictus ▸ noun a fixed grimace or grin.

rid ▸ verb (**rids, ridding, rid**) **1** (**rid someone/thing of**) free a person or place of something unwanted. **2** (**be** or **get rid of**) be or make yourself free of.

SYNONYMS *the aim was to rid the town of malaria* **clear,** free, purge, empty, strip.

riddance ▸ noun (**good riddance**) said when expressing relief at getting rid of someone or something.

ridden past participle of RIDE.
▸ adjective full of a particular unpleasant thing: *disease-ridden*.

riddle¹ ▸ noun **1** a cleverly worded question that is asked as a game. **2** a puzzling person or thing.

SYNONYMS **puzzle,** conundrum, brain-teaser, problem, question, poser, enigma, mystery.

riddle² ▸ verb (usu. **be riddled with**) **1** make a lot of holes in. **2** fill with something bad or unpleasant.
▸ noun a type of large sieve.

ride ▸ verb (**rides, riding, rode**; past participle **ridden**) **1** sit on and control the movement of a horse, bicycle, or motorcycle. **2** travel in a vehicle. **3** be carried or supported by. **4** (**ride up**) (of clothing) gradually move upwards out of its proper position. **5** (**ride on**) depend on.

SYNONYMS **1** *she can ride a horse* **sit on,** mount, control, manage, handle. **2** *riding round the town* **travel,** move, proceed, drive, cycle, trot, canter, gallop.

▸ noun **1** an act of riding. **2** a roller coaster, roundabout, etc. ridden at a fair or amusement park. **3** a path for horse riding.

SYNONYMS *he took us for a ride* **trip,** journey, drive, run, excursion, outing, jaunt, lift; informal spin.

■ **take someone for a ride** informal deceive someone.

rider ▸ noun **1** a person who rides a horse, bicycle, etc. **2** an added condition on an official document.

ridge ▸ noun **1** a long, narrow hilltop or mountain range. **2** a narrow raised band on a surface. **3** the edge formed where the two sloping sides of a roof meet at the top.
□ **ridged** adjective.

ridicule ▸ noun making fun of someone in an unkind way; mockery.

SYNONYMS *he was subjected to ridicule* **mockery,** derision, laughter, scorn, scoffing, jeering.
ANTONYMS respect.

▸ verb (**ridicules, ridiculing, ridiculed**) make fun of.

SYNONYMS *his theory was ridiculed* **mock,** deride, laugh at, heap scorn on, jeer at, make fun of, scoff at, satirize, caricature, parody.
ANTONYMS respect.

ridiculous ▸ adjective very silly or unreasonable; absurd.

SYNONYMS **1** *that looks ridiculous* **laughable,** absurd, comical, funny, hilarious, risible, droll, amusing, farcical. **2** *a ridiculous suggestion* **foolish,** silly, senseless, foolhardy, stupid, idiotic. **3** *a ridiculous exaggeration* **absurd,** preposterous, ludicrous, laughable, risible, nonsensical, outrageous.
ANTONYMS sensible.

□ **ridiculously** adverb.

riding ▸ noun each of three former administrative divisions of Yorkshire.

Riesling /reez-ling/ ▸ noun a type of dry white wine.

rife ▸ adjective 1 (of something bad or unpleasant) widespread. 2 (**rife with**) full of something bad or unpleasant.

> SYNONYMS **widespread**, general, common, universal, extensive, ubiquitous, endemic, inescapable.
> ANTONYMS unknown.

riff ▸ noun a short repeated phrase in pop music or jazz.

riffle ▸ verb (**riffles, riffling, riffled**) (**riffle through**) turn over the pages of a book quickly and casually.

riff-raff ▸ noun people who are considered socially undesirable.

rifle ▸ noun a gun with a long barrel.
▸ verb (**rifles, rifling, rifled**) 1 search through something hurriedly to find or steal something. 2 hit or kick a ball hard and straight.

> SYNONYMS 1 *she rifled through her wardrobe* **rummage**, search, hunt, forage. 2 *a thief rifled her home* **burgle**, rob, steal from, loot, raid, plunder, ransack.

rift ▸ noun 1 a crack, split, or break. 2 a serious break in friendly relations.

> SYNONYMS 1 *a deep rift in the ice* **crack**, split, breach, fissure, fracture, cleft, crevice, opening. 2 *the rift between them* **breach**, division, split, quarrel, disagreement, falling-out, row, conflict, feud; Brit. informal bust-up.

rig ▸ verb (**rigs, rigging, rigged**) 1 secretly arrange something in order to gain an advantage. 2 fit sails and rigging on a boat. 3 (often **rig something up**) set up a device or structure. 4 (**rig someone out**) provide with clothes of a particular type.

> SYNONYMS 1 *they rigged the election* **manipulate**, engineer, distort, misrepresent, pervert, tamper with, falsify, fake; informal fix; Brit. informal fiddle. 2 *the boats were rigged with a single sail* **equip**, kit out, fit out, supply, furnish, provide, arm. 3 *he will rig up a shelter* **set up**, erect, assemble, put together, whip up, improvise, contrive; Brit. informal knock up. 4 *I rigged myself out in black* **dress**, clothe, attire, robe, garb, get up; informal doll up.

▸ noun 1 a piece of equipment for a particular purpose: *a lighting rig*. 2 a large piece of equipment for extracting oil or gas from the ground.

rigging ▸ noun the system of ropes or chains supporting a ship's masts.

right ▸ adjective 1 on or towards the side of a person or thing which is to the east when the person or thing is facing north. 2 justified or morally good. 3 factually correct. 4 most appropriate. 5 satisfactory, sound, or normal. 6 right-wing.

> SYNONYMS 1 *on my right side* **right-hand**; Nautical starboard. 2 *it wouldn't be right to do that* **just**, fair, proper, good, upright, righteous, virtuous, moral, ethical, honourable, honest, lawful, legal. 3 *the right answer* **correct**, accurate, exact, precise, proper, valid, conventional, established, official, formal; Brit. informal spot on. 4 *the right person for the job* **suitable**, appropriate, fitting, correct, proper, desirable, preferable, ideal. 5 *you've come at the right time* **opportune**, advantageous, favourable, good, lucky, fortunate.
> ANTONYMS left, port, wrong, bad.

▸ adverb 1 on or to the right side. 2 completely; totally. 3 exactly; directly. 4 correctly or satisfactorily.

> SYNONYMS 1 *she was right at the limit of her patience* **completely**, fully, totally, absolutely, utterly, thoroughly, quite. 2 *right in the middle of the village* **exactly**, precisely, directly, immediately, just, squarely, dead; informal (slap) bang, smack, plumb. 3 *I think I heard right* **correctly**, accurately, properly, precisely, perfectly. 4 *make sure you're treated right* **well**, properly, justly, fairly, equitably, impartially, honourably, lawfully, legally. 5 *things will turn out right* **well**, for the best, favourably, happily, advantageously, profitably, luckily, conveniently.
> ANTONYMS wrong, badly.

▸ noun 1 what is morally right. 2 an entitlement to have or do something. 3 (**rights**) the authority to perform, publish, or film a work or event. 4 (**the right**) the right-hand part, side, or direction. 5 a right turn. 6 (often **the Right**) a right-wing group or party.

> SYNONYMS 1 *the difference between right and wrong* **goodness**, righteousness, virtue, integrity, propriety, morality, truth, honesty, honour, justice, fairness, equity. 2 *you have the right to say no* **entitlement**, prerogative, privilege, liberty, authority, power, licence, permission, dispensation, leave, due.
> ANTONYMS wrong.

▸ verb 1 put something back in a normal or upright position. 2 correct or make up for a wrong.

> SYNONYMS *we must right the situation* **remedy**, rectify, retrieve, fix, resolve,

sort out, settle, square, straighten out, correct, repair, mend, redress.

■ **by rights** if things were fair or correct. **in your own right** as a result of your own qualifications or efforts. **right angle** an angle of 90°, as in a corner of a square. **right of way 1** the legal right to go through someone's property along a specific route. **2** a public path through someone's property. **3** the right to proceed before another vehicle.
□ **rightly** adverb.

righteous /**ry**-chuhss/ ▶ adjective morally right.

SYNONYMS **good,** virtuous, upright, upstanding, decent, ethical, principled, moral, honest, honourable, blameless. ANTONYMS wicked.

□ **righteously** adverb.

rightful ▶ adjective **1** having a clear right to something. **2** proper; fitting.
□ **rightfully** adverb.

right-wing ▶ adjective conservative or opposed to political or social change.

SYNONYMS **conservative,** rightist, reactionary, traditionalist, conventional. ANTONYMS left-wing.

rigid ▶ adjective **1** unable to bend or be put out of shape. **2** (of a person) stiff and unmoving. **3** not able to be changed or adapted.

SYNONYMS **1** *a rigid container* **stiff,** hard, firm, inflexible, unbending, unyielding. **2** *a rigid routine* **fixed,** set, firm, inflexible, invariable, hard and fast, cast-iron. **3** *a rigid approach to funding* **strict,** stringent, rigorous, inflexible, uncompromising, intransigent. ANTONYMS flexible, lenient.

□ **rigidity** noun **rigidly** adverb.

rigmarole /**rig**-muh-rohl/ ▶ noun a lengthy and complicated procedure.

rigor mortis /ri-ger **mor**-tiss/ ▶ noun stiffening of the joints and muscles that happens a few hours after death.

rigorous ▶ adjective **1** very thorough or accurate. **2** (of a rule, system, etc.) strictly applied or followed. **3** harsh or severe.

SYNONYMS **1** *rigorous attention to detail* **meticulous,** conscientious, punctilious, careful, scrupulous, painstaking, exact, precise, accurate, particular, strict. **2** *the rigorous enforcement of rules* **strict,** stringent, rigid, inflexible, draconian, intransigent, uncompromising. **3** *rigorous conditions* **harsh,** severe, bleak, extreme, demanding. ANTONYMS slapdash, lax, mild.

□ **rigorously** adverb.

rigour (US spelling **rigor**) ▶ noun **1** the quality of being rigorous. **2** (**rigours**) difficult or extreme conditions.

rile ▶ verb (**riles, riling, riled**) informal annoy or irritate.

rill ▶ noun literary a small stream.

rim ▶ noun **1** the upper or outer edge of something circular. **2** a limit or boundary.

SYNONYMS **edge,** brim, lip, border, side, margin, brink, boundary, perimeter, circumference, limits, periphery.

▶ verb (**rims, rimming, rimmed**) provide with a rim.

rime ▶ noun literary hoar frost.

rind ▶ noun a tough outer layer or covering of fruit, cheese, bacon, etc.

ring¹ ▶ noun **1** a small circular metal band worn on a finger. **2** a circular band, object, or mark. **3** an enclosed space in which a sport, performance, or show takes place. **4** each of the flat plates on a cooker that are used for cooking on. **5** a group of people with a shared interest or goal.

SYNONYMS **1** *a ring round the moon* **circle,** band, halo, disc. **2** *the horses entered the ring* **arena,** enclosure, circus, amphitheatre, bowl. **3** *a spy ring* **gang,** syndicate, cartel, mob, band, circle, organization, association, society, alliance, league.

▶ verb **1** surround. **2** draw a circle round.

SYNONYMS *police ringed the building* **surround,** circle, encircle, enclose, hem in, confine, seal off.

■ **ring binder** a binder with ring-shaped clasps. **ring pull** Brit. a ring on a can that you pull to open it. **ring road** Brit. a road encircling a town.

ring² ▶ verb (**rings, ringing, rang;** past participle **rung**) **1** make a clear and repeated or long-lasting sound. **2** (**ring with**) echo with such a sound. **3** Brit. telephone someone. **4** (**ring off**) Brit. end a telephone call by replacing the receiver. **5** call for attention by sounding a bell. **6** (of the ears) be filled with a buzzing or humming sound. **7** (**ring something up**) record an amount on a cash register.

SYNONYMS **1** *church bells rang* **chime,** sound, peal, toll, clang, bong; literary knell. **2** *the room rang with laughter* **resound,** reverberate, resonate, echo. **3** *I'll ring you tomorrow* **telephone,** phone (up), call (up); informal give someone a buzz; Brit. informal give someone a bell, give someone a tinkle, get on the blower to.

▶ noun **1** an act of ringing. **2** a loud, clear sound or tone. **3** a quality or feeling conveyed by words: *a ring of truth.*
■ **give someone a ring** Brit. informal telephone someone.
□ **ringer** noun.

r

ringing ▸ adjective **1** having a clear, resonant sound. **2** forceful and clear.

ringleader ▸ noun a person who leads others in committing a crime or causing trouble.

ringlet ▸ noun a corkscrew-shaped curl of hair.

ringmaster ▸ noun the person who directs a circus performance.

ringside ▸ noun the area beside a boxing ring or circus ring.

ringtone ▸ noun a sound made by a mobile phone when an incoming call is received.

ringworm ▸ noun a skin disease that causes small, itchy circular patches.

rink ▸ noun **1** (also **ice rink**) an enclosed area of ice for skating, ice hockey, or curling. **2** the strip of a bowling green used for a match.

rinse ▸ verb (**rinses, rinsing, rinsed**) **1** wash with clean water to remove soap or dirt. **2** remove soap or dirt by rinsing.

> SYNONYMS **wash (out)**, clean, cleanse, bathe, dip, drench, splash, swill, sluice.

▸ noun **1** an act of rinsing. **2** an antiseptic solution for cleaning the mouth. **3** a liquid for conditioning or colouring the hair.

Rioja /ri-o-kuh/ ▸ noun a red or white Spanish wine.

riot ▸ noun **1** a violent disturbance caused by an angry crowd. **2** a confused combination or display. **3** (**a riot**) informal a very entertaining person or thing.

> SYNONYMS **1** *a riot in the capital* **disorder**, disturbance, lawlessness, upheaval, uproar, commotion. **2** *a riot of colour* **mass**, sea, splash, show, profusion.

▸ verb take part in a riot.

> SYNONYMS *the miners rioted* **(go on the) rampage**, run wild, run amok, run riot, go berserk; informal **raise hell**.

■ **run riot** behave in an uncontrolled way.
□ **rioter** noun.

riotous ▸ adjective **1** wild and uncontrolled. **2** involving public disorder.

RIP ▸ abbreviation rest in peace.

rip ▸ verb (**rips, ripping, ripped**) **1** suddenly tear or become torn. **2** pull forcibly away.

> SYNONYMS **1** *he ripped the posters down* **tug**, wrench, pull, snatch, tear, heave, drag, peel, pluck; informal **yank**. **2** *she ripped Leo's note into pieces* **tear**, claw, hack, slit.

▸ noun a long tear.
■ **let rip** informal move or act without restraint. **rip someone/thing off** informal **1** cheat someone. **2** steal something. **rip-roaring** very energetic and exciting. **rip tide** a stretch of fast-flowing rough water

caused by currents meeting.

riparian /ri-**pair**-i-uhn/ ▸ adjective technical relating to or on the banks of a river.

ripcord ▸ noun a cord that you pull to open a parachute.

ripe ▸ adjective **1** ready for harvesting and eating. **2** (of a cheese or wine) fully matured. **3** (**ripe for**) having reached the right time for. **4** (of a person's age) advanced.

> SYNONYMS **1** *a ripe tomato* **mature**, full grown. **2** *ripe for development* **ready**, fit, suitable, right. **3** *the time is ripe for his return* **opportune**, advantageous, favourable, auspicious, good, right.
> ANTONYMS young, unsuitable, unfavourable.

□ **ripely** adverb **ripeness** noun.

ripen ▸ verb become or make ripe.

riposte /ri-**posst**/ ▸ noun a quick reply.

ripple ▸ noun **1** a small wave or series of waves. **2** a feeling, effect, or sound that spreads through someone or something. **3** ice cream with wavy lines of syrup running through it.

▸ verb (**ripples, rippling, rippled**) **1** form ripples. **2** (of a sound, feeling, etc.) spread through a person or place.

rise ▸ verb (**rises, rising, rose**; past participle **risen**) **1** come or go up. **2** get up after lying, sitting, or kneeling. **3** increase in number, size, strength, etc. **4** (of land) slope upwards. **5** (of the sun, moon, or stars) appear above the horizon. **6** (**rise above**) manage not to be restricted by. **7** (**rise to**) respond well to a difficult situation. **8** (**rise up**) rebel. **9** (of a river) have its source.

> SYNONYMS **1** *the sun rose* **climb**, come up, arise, ascend, mount, soar. **2** *the mountains rising above us* **loom**, tower, soar. **3** *prices rose* **go up**, increase, soar, shoot up, surge, leap, jump, rocket, escalate, spiral. **4** *living standards have risen* **improve**, get better, advance. **5** *his voice rose* **get higher**, grow, increase, become louder, swell, intensify. **6** *he rose from his chair* **stand up**, get to your feet, get up, jump up, leap up. **7** *he rises at dawn* **get up**, stir, bestir yourself, be up and about; informal **surface**.
> ANTONYMS fall, sit down, go to bed.

▸ noun **1** an act of rising. **2** an upward slope or hill. **3** Brit. a pay increase.

> SYNONYMS **1** *a price rise* **increase**, hike, leap, upsurge, upswing, climb. **2** *he got a rise of 4%* **raise**, increase, hike, increment. **3** *a rise in standards* **improvement**, advance. **4** *his rise to power* **progress**, climb, promotion, elevation. **5** *we walked up the rise* **slope**, incline, hill.

riser ▸ noun **1** a person who gets up at a particular time. **2** a vertical section between the treads of a staircase.

risible /ri-zi-b'l/ ▸ adjective causing laughter. □ **risibly** adverb.

rising ▸ noun a rebellion or revolt.
▸ adjective approaching a particular age.
■ **rising damp** Brit. moisture absorbed from the ground into a wall.

risk ▸ noun **1** a situation that involves being exposed to danger. **2** the possibility that something bad will happen. **3** a person or thing that causes a risk.

> SYNONYMS **1** *there is a certain amount of risk* **chance,** uncertainty, unpredictability, instability, insecurity. **2** *the risk of fire* **possibility,** chance, probability, likelihood, danger, peril, threat, menace, prospect. ANTONYMS certainty, safety, impossibility.

▸ verb **1** expose to danger or loss. **2** act in such a way that there is a chance of something bad happening.

> SYNONYMS *he risked his life to save them* **endanger,** imperil, jeopardize, hazard, gamble (with), chance, put on the line.

risky ▸ adjective (**riskier, riskiest**) involving the possibility of danger or a bad outcome.

> SYNONYMS **dangerous,** hazardous, perilous, unsafe, insecure, precarious, touch-and-go, treacherous, uncertain, unpredictable; informal dicey; N. Amer. informal gnarly.

□ **riskily** adverb **riskiness** noun.

risotto ▸ noun (plural **risottos**) a dish of rice with meat, seafood, etc.

> ✔ only one **s**: risotto.

risqué /riss-kay/ ▸ adjective slightly indecent or rude.

rissole ▸ noun Brit. a small flat mass of chopped meat that is coated in breadcrumbs and fried.

rite ▸ noun a religious ceremony, or other solemn procedure.

> SYNONYMS **ceremony,** ritual, ceremonial, custom, service, observance, liturgy, worship, office.

■ **rite of passage** a ceremony or event that marks an important stage in someone's life.

ritual ▸ noun **1** a ceremony that involves a series of actions performed in a set order. **2** something that is habitually done in the same way.

> SYNONYMS *an elaborate civic ritual* **ceremony,** rite, act, practice, custom, tradition, convention, formality, protocol.

▸ adjective done as a ritual.

> SYNONYMS *a ritual burial* **ceremonial,** prescribed, set, formal, traditional, conventional.

□ **ritually** adverb.

ritzy ▸ adjective (**ritzier, ritziest**) informal expensively stylish.

rival ▸ noun **1** a person or thing competing with another for the same thing. **2** a person or thing equal to another in quality.

> SYNONYMS **1** *his rival for the nomination* **opponent,** challenger, competitor, contender, adversary, antagonist, enemy. **2** *the tool has no rival* **equal,** match, peer, equivalent. ANTONYMS ally.

▸ adjective competing.

> SYNONYMS *rival candidates* **competing,** opposing.

▸ verb (**rivals, rivalling, rivalled;** US spelling **rivals, rivaling, rivaled**) be comparable to.

> SYNONYMS *few countries can rival it for scenery* **match,** compare with, compete with, vie with, equal, measure up to, touch; informal hold a candle to.

rivalry ▸ noun (plural **rivalries**) a situation in which two people or groups are competing for the same thing.

> SYNONYMS **competition,** contention, opposition, conflict, feuding; informal keeping up with the Joneses.

riven /ri-vuhn/ ▸ adjective literary torn apart; split.

river ▸ noun **1** a large natural flow of water moving in a channel to the sea or another river. **2** a large quantity of a flowing substance.

> SYNONYMS **1** **stream,** brook, watercourse, rivulet, tributary; Scottish & N. English **burn;** N. English **beck;** S. English **bourn;** N. Amer. & Austral./NZ **creek. 2** *a river of molten lava* **stream,** torrent, flood, deluge, cascade.

rivet ▸ noun a short metal pin or bolt for holding together two metal plates.
▸ verb (**rivets, riveting, riveted**) **1** fasten with a rivet or rivets. **2** (**be riveted**) be completely fascinated by something.

> SYNONYMS (**riveting**) **fascinating,** gripping, engrossing, intriguing, absorbing, captivating, enthralling, compelling, spellbinding, mesmerizing; informal unputdownable. ANTONYMS boring.

riviera /ri-vi-air-uh/ ▸ noun a coastal area of a warm country, especially in southern France and northern Italy.

rivulet ▸ noun a small stream.

RN ▸ abbreviation Royal Navy.

r

RNA ▸ noun a substance in living cells which carries instructions from DNA.
ORIGIN short for *ribonucleic acid.*

roach[1] ▸ noun (plural **roach**) a common freshwater fish of the carp family.

roach[2] ▸ noun N. Amer. informal a cockroach.

road ▸ noun **1** a wide track with a hard surface for vehicles to travel on. **2** a way to achieving a particular outcome.

SYNONYMS **1** **street,** thoroughfare, roadway, highway, lane; Brit. motorway. **2** *on the road to recovery* **way,** path, route, course.

■ **road rage** informal violent anger caused by conflict with the driver of another vehicle. **road test** a test of the performance of a vehicle or of other equipment.

roadblock ▸ noun a barrier put across a road by the police or army to stop and examine traffic.

roadholding ▸ noun the ability of a moving vehicle to remain stable.

roadie ▸ noun informal a person who sets up equipment for a rock group.

roadshow ▸ noun **1** a show broadcast from a different place each day. **2** a touring political or promotional campaign.

roadster ▸ noun an open-top sports car.

roadway ▸ noun **1** a road. **2** the part of a road intended for vehicles.

roadworks ▸ plural noun Brit. repairs to roads or to pipes under roads.

roadworthy ▸ adjective (of a vehicle) fit to be used on the road.

roam ▸ verb travel aimlessly over a wide area.

SYNONYMS **wander,** rove, ramble, drift, walk, traipse, range, travel, tramp, trek; Scottish & Irish stravaig; informal cruise, mosey.

roaming ▸ noun the use of a mobile phone on another operator's network, typically while abroad.

roan ▸ adjective (of a horse) having a bay, chestnut, or black coat mixed with hairs of another colour.

roar ▸ noun a loud, deep sound made by a lion, engine, etc., or by a person who is angry, amused, or in pain.

SYNONYMS **1** *the roars of the crowd* **shout,** bellow, yell, cry, howl, clamour; informal holler. **2** *the roar of the sea* **boom,** crash, rumble, roll, thunder.

▸ verb **1** make a roar. **2** laugh loudly. **3** move very fast.

SYNONYMS **1** *'Get out!' roared Angus* **bellow,** yell, shout, bawl, howl; informal holler. **2** *thunder roared* **boom,** rumble, crash, roll, thunder.

roaring ▸ adjective very active or successful: *a roaring trade.*

roast ▸ verb **1** cook food in an oven or over a fire. **2** make or become very warm.
▸ adjective (of food) having been roasted.
▸ noun a joint of meat that has been roasted.

roasting informal ▸ adjective very hot and dry.
▸ noun a severe telling-off.

rob ▸ verb (**robs, robbing, robbed**) **1** steal property from a person or place by using force or threatening violence. **2** deprive someone of something.

SYNONYMS **1** *the gang robbed a bank* **burgle,** steal from, hold up, break into, raid, loot, plunder, pillage; N. Amer. burglarize. **2** *he robbed an old woman* **steal from,** hold up; informal mug. **3** *he was robbed of his savings* **cheat,** swindle, defraud; informal do out of, con out of. **4** *defeat robbed him of his title* **deprive,** strip, deny.

robber ▸ noun a person who commits robbery.

SYNONYMS **burglar,** thief, housebreaker, mugger, shoplifter, raider, looter.

robbery ▸ noun (plural **robberies**) the action of robbing a person or place.

SYNONYMS *they were arrested for the robbery* **burglary,** theft, stealing, housebreaking, shoplifting, embezzlement, fraud, hold-up, raid; informal mugging, smash-and-grab, stick-up; N. Amer. informal heist.

robe ▸ noun **1** a loose garment reaching to the ankles, worn on formal or ceremonial occasions. **2** a dressing gown.

SYNONYMS **1** *the women wore black robes* **cloak,** kaftan, djellaba, wrap, mantle, cape; N. Amer. wrapper. **2** *ceremonial robes* **garb,** regalia, costume, finery, vestments.

▸ verb (**robes, robing, robed**) clothe someone in a robe.

robin ▸ noun a small bird with a red breast and brown back and wings.

robot ▸ noun a machine capable of carrying out a complex series of actions automatically.

SYNONYMS **machine,** automaton, android, golem; informal bot, droid.

robotic ▸ adjective **1** relating to robots. **2** mechanical, stiff, or unemotional.

robotics ▸ plural noun the science of constructing and using robots.

robust ▸ adjective **1** sturdy or able to withstand difficult conditions. **2** strong and healthy. **3** determined and forceful.

SYNONYMS **1** *a robust man* **strong,** vigorous, sturdy, tough, powerful,

r

solid, rugged, hardy, strapping, healthy, (fighting) fit, hale and hearty. **2** *these knives are robust* **durable,** resilient, tough, hard-wearing, long-lasting, sturdy, strong.
ANTONYMS frail, fragile.

□ **robustly** adverb.

rock[1] ▶ noun **1** the hard material that makes up the earth's crust. **2** a projecting mass of rock. **3** a boulder. **4** Brit. a hard sweet in the form of a cylindrical stick. **5** informal a diamond or other precious stone.

SYNONYMS **boulder,** stone, pebble.

■ **on the rocks** informal **1** in difficulties and likely to fail. **2** (of a drink) served undiluted and with ice cubes. **rock bottom** the lowest possible level. **rock salt** salt occurring naturally as a mineral.

rock[2] ▶ verb **1** move gently to and fro or from side to side. **2** shake violently. **3** shock or distress very much.

SYNONYMS **1** *the ship rocked on the water* **move to and fro,** sway, see-saw, roll, pitch, plunge, toss, lurch. **2** *Wall Street was rocked by the news* **stun,** shock, stagger, astonish, startle, surprise, shake, take aback, throw, unnerve, disconcert.

▶ noun **1** (also **rock music**) a type of loud popular music with a heavy beat. **2** a rocking movement.
■ **rock and roll** a type of popular music with simple melodies, originating in the 1950s. **rocking chair** a chair mounted on curved bars. **rocking horse** a model horse mounted on curved bars for a child to ride on.

rockabilly ▶ noun music that combines rock and roll and country music.

rocker ▶ noun **1** a curved piece of wood on the bottom of a rocking chair. **2** a person who performs or likes rock music.
■ **off your rocker** informal mad.

rockery ▶ noun (plural **rockeries**) an arrangement of rocks in a garden with plants growing between them.

rocket ▶ noun **1** a tube-shaped missile or spacecraft propelled by a stream of burning gases. **2** a firework that shoots high in the air and explodes. **3** Brit. informal a severe telling-off. **4** a plant similar to lettuce, eaten in salads.
▶ verb (**rockets, rocketing, rocketed**) move or increase very quickly and suddenly.

rocky[1] ▶ adjective (**rockier, rockiest**) **1** consisting or formed of rock. **2** full of rocks.

SYNONYMS *a rocky path* **stony,** pebbly, shingly, rough, bumpy, craggy, mountainous.

rocky[2] ▶ adjective (**rockier, rockiest**) unsteady or unstable.

SYNONYMS **unsteady,** shaky, unstable, wobbly, tottery, rickety.
ANTONYMS steady, stable.

rococo /ruh-**koh**-koh/ ▶ adjective (of furniture or architecture) in a highly decorated style popular in the 18th century.

rod ▶ noun **1** a thin straight bar of wood, metal, etc. **2** (also **fishing rod**) a long stick with a line and hook attached, for catching fish.

SYNONYMS **bar,** stick, pole, baton, staff, shaft, strut, rail, spoke.

rode past of RIDE.

rodent ▶ noun a mammal of a large group including rats, mice, and squirrels, with large front teeth.

rodeo /**roh**-di-oh/ ▶ noun (plural **rodeos**) a contest or entertainment in which cowboys show their horse-riding and lassoing skills.

roe ▶ noun the eggs or sperm of a fish, used as food.

roebuck ▶ noun a male roe deer.

roe deer ▶ noun a small deer with a coat that is reddish in summer.

roentgen /**runt**-yuhn/ ▶ noun a unit of radiation.

rogue ▶ noun **1** a dishonest or immoral man. **2** a mischievous but likeable person. **3** an elephant that is living apart from the herd.

SYNONYMS **1** *a rogue without ethics* **scoundrel,** rascal, good-for-nothing, wretch, villain, criminal, lawbreaker; informal crook. **2** *your boy's a little rogue* **rascal,** imp, devil, monkey; informal scamp, scallywag.

roguish ▶ adjective mischievous.

roister ▶ verb (**roisters, roistering, roistered**) old use enjoy yourself in a lively, noisy way.

role ▶ noun **1** an actor's part in a play, film, etc. **2** a person's or thing's function in a particular situation.

SYNONYMS **1** *a small role in the film* **part,** character. **2** *his role as President* **capacity,** position, function, job, post, office, duty, responsibility.

■ **role model** a person that others look up to as an example to be imitated. **role play** the acting out of a role or situation.

❗ Don't confuse **role** with **roll**, which mainly means 'move by turning over and over' or 'a rolling movement'.

roll ▶ verb **1** move by turning over and over. **2** move forward on wheels or with a smooth motion. **3** (of a moving ship, aircraft, etc.) sway from side to side. **4** (of a machine or device) begin operating. **5** (often **roll something up**) turn something flexible over and over on itself. **6** (**roll**

r

up) curl up tightly. **7** (**roll something out**) officially launch a new product. **8** flatten with a roller. **9** (of a loud, deep sound) reverberate. **10** (**roll up**) informal arrive.

> SYNONYMS **1** *the bottle rolled down the table* **bowl,** turn over and over, spin, rotate, wheel, trundle. **2** *tears rolled down her cheeks* **flow,** run, course, stream, pour, trickle. **3** *he rolled his handkerchief into a ball* **wind,** coil, fold, curl, twist. **4** *the ship began to roll* **rock,** sway, reel, list, pitch, plunge, lurch, toss.

▶ noun **1** a cylinder formed by rolling flexible material. **2** a rolling movement. **3** a long, deep, reverberating sound. **4** a very small loaf of bread. **5** an official list or register of names.

> SYNONYMS **1** *a roll of paper* **cylinder,** tube, scroll, reel, spool. **2** *a roll of the dice* **throw,** toss, turn, spin. **3** *the electoral roll* **list,** register, directory, record, file, index, catalogue, inventory. **4** *a roll of thunder* **rumble,** reverberation, echo, boom, clap, crack, roar.

■ **roll call** an occasion when a list of names is read out to discover who is present. **rolling pin** a cylinder for rolling out dough. **rolling stock** locomotives, carriages, and other vehicles used on a railway. **roll neck** a high turned-over collar. **roll-on** applied by means of a rotating ball.

> ❗ Don't confuse **roll** with **role**, which means 'an actor's part in a play or film'.

roller ▶ noun **1** a rotating cylinder used to move, flatten, or spread something. **2** a small cylinder on which you roll your hair to make it curly. **3** a long wave moving towards the shore.

■ **roller coaster** a fairground attraction in which you ride in an open carriage on a steep, twisting track. **roller skate** a boot with wheels on which you can glide across a hard surface.

Rollerblade ▶ noun trademark a roller skate with wheels in a single line along the sole. ☐ **rollerblading** noun.

rollicking ▶ adjective cheerfully lively and amusing.
▶ noun Brit. informal a severe telling-off.

rollmop ▶ noun a rolled pickled herring fillet.

roly-poly ▶ adjective informal round and plump.
▶ noun Brit. a hot pudding made of suet pastry covered with jam and rolled up.

Roman ▶ adjective **1** relating to Rome or its ancient empire. **2** referring to the alphabet used for writing Latin, English, and most European languages. **3** (**roman**) (of a typeface) plain and upright, used in ordinary print.

▶ noun **1** an inhabitant of Rome. **2** (**roman**) roman type.

■ **Roman Catholic 1** of the Christian Church which has the Pope as its head. **2** a member of the Roman Catholic Church. **Roman numeral** each of the letters, I, V, X, L, C, D, and M, used in ancient Rome to represent numbers.

romance /roh-**manss**/ ▶ noun **1** a pleasurable feeling of excitement associated with love. **2** a love affair. **3** a book or film that deals with love in a sentimental or idealized way. **4** a feeling of mystery, excitement, and remoteness from everyday life. **5** (**Romance**) French, Spanish, Italian, and other languages descended from Latin.

> SYNONYMS **1** *he's had many romances* **love affair,** relationship, liaison, courtship, attachment, amour. **2** *an author of romances* **story,** tale, legend, fairy tale. **3** *the romance of the Far East* **mystery,** glamour, excitement, exoticism, mystique, appeal, allure, charm.

▶ verb (**romances, romancing, romanced**) try to win the love of someone.

Romanesque /roh-muh-**nesk**/ ▶ adjective relating to a style of architecture common in Europe *c*.900–1200.

Romanian (or **Rumanian**) ▶ noun **1** a person from Romania. **2** the language of Romania.
▶ adjective relating to Romania.

romantic ▶ adjective **1** having to do with love or romance. **2** thinking about or showing life in an idealized rather than realistic way. **3** (**Romantic**) relating to the artistic and literary movement of Romanticism.

> SYNONYMS **1** *he's so romantic* **loving,** amorous, passionate, tender, affectionate; informal lovey-dovey. **2** *romantic songs* **sentimental,** hearts-and-flowers, mawkish, sickly, saccharine, syrupy; informal slushy, mushy, sloppy, schmaltzy; Brit. informal soppy. **3** *a romantic setting* **idyllic,** picturesque, fairy-tale, beautiful, lovely, charming, pretty. **4** *romantic notions of rural communities* **idealistic,** unrealistic, fanciful, impractical, head-in-the-clouds, starry-eyed, utopian, fairy-tale.
> ANTONYMS unsentimental, realistic.

▶ noun **1** a person with romantic beliefs or attitudes. **2** (**Romantic**) an artist or writer of the Romantic movement.

> SYNONYMS *an incurable romantic* **idealist,** sentimentalist, dreamer, fantasist.
> ANTONYMS realist.

☐ **romantically** adverb.

Romanticism ▶ noun a literary and artistic movement which emphasized creative inspiration and individual feeling.

romanticize (or **romanticise**) ▸ verb (**romanticizes**, **romanticizing**, **romanticized**) make something seem more attractive and inspiring than it really is.

Romany /roh-muh-ni/ ▸ noun (plural **Romanies**) 1 the language of the Gypsies. 2 a Gypsy.

Romeo ▸ noun (plural **Romeos**) an attractive, passionate male lover.

romp ▸ verb 1 play about roughly and energetically. 2 (**romp ahead** or **home**) easily lead or win a race. 3 (**romp through**) informal do or achieve something easily.

SYNONYMS **play,** frolic, frisk, gambol, skip, prance, caper, cavort.

rompers (or **romper suit**) ▸ plural noun a young child's one-piece garment.

rondo ▸ noun (plural **rondos**) a piece of music with a recurring leading theme.

röntgen = ROENTGEN.

rood screen ▸ noun a screen of wood or stone separating the nave from the chancel of a church.

roof ▸ noun (plural **roofs**) 1 the upper covering of a building or vehicle. 2 the top inner surface of a covered space.
▸ verb put a roof over.
■ **roof rack** a framework for carrying luggage on the roof of a vehicle.

roofer ▸ noun a person who builds or repairs roofs.

rook[1] ▸ noun a crow that nests in colonies in treetops.

rook[2] ▸ noun a chess piece that can move in any direction except diagonally.

rookery ▸ noun (plural **rookeries**) 1 a collection of rooks' nests high in a clump of trees. 2 a breeding place of seabirds.

rookie ▸ noun informal a new recruit.

room ▸ noun 1 a part of a building enclosed by walls, a floor, and a ceiling. 2 (**rooms**) a set of rooms rented out to a lodger. 3 empty space in which you can do or put things.

SYNONYMS 1 *there isn't much room* **space,** headroom, legroom, area, expanse, extent. 2 *room for improvement* **scope,** capacity, leeway, latitude, freedom.

▸ verb N. Amer. share a rented room or flat.

roomy ▸ adjective (**roomier, roomiest**) having plenty of space.

roost ▸ noun a place where birds regularly settle to rest.
▸ verb (of a bird or birds) settle or gather for rest.

rooster ▸ noun N. Amer. a male chicken.

root[1] ▸ noun 1 the part of a plant that is normally below ground, which acts as a support and collects water and nourishment. 2 the part of a hair, tooth, nail, etc. that is fixed in the body tissue.

3 the basic cause or origin of something. 4 (**roots**) your family or origins. 5 Maths a number that when multiplied by itself one or more times gives a particular number.

SYNONYMS 1 *the root of the problem* **source,** origin, cause, reason, basis, foundation, bottom, seat. 2 (**roots**) **origins,** beginnings, family, birth, heritage.

▸ verb 1 (of a plant or cutting) grow roots. 2 (**be rooted**) be firmly established. 3 (**root something out**) find and get rid of something.
■ **root vegetable** a vegetable which grows as the root of a plant.

root[2] ▸ verb 1 (of an animal) turn up the ground with its snout in search of food. 2 rummage. 3 (**root for**) informal support someone enthusiastically.

SYNONYMS *he rooted around in the cupboard* **rummage,** hunt, search, rifle, delve, forage, dig, nose, poke.

rootless ▸ adjective having nowhere where you feel settled and at home.

rootstock ▸ noun 1 a rhizome. 2 a plant on to which another variety is grafted.

rope ▸ noun 1 a length of thick cord made by twisting together thinner strands of fibre. 2 a number of objects strung together. 3 (**the ropes**) the ropes enclosing a boxing or wrestling ring. 4 (**the ropes**) informal the established way of doing something.

SYNONYMS **cord,** cable, line, hawser, string.

▸ verb (**ropes, roping, roped**) 1 secure something with rope. 2 (**rope someone in** or **into**) informal persuade someone to take part in something.

ropy (or **ropey**) ▸ adjective Brit. informal of bad quality, or in bad health.

rosary ▸ noun (plural **rosaries**) a string of beads used by some Roman Catholics for keeping count of how many prayers they have said.

rose[1] ▸ noun 1 a sweet-smelling flower that grows on a prickly bush. 2 a cap with holes in it attached to a spout, hose, shower, etc. to produce a spray. 3 a soft pink colour.
■ **rose hip** the fruit of a rose.

rose[2] past of RISE.

rosé /roh-zay/ ▸ noun light pink wine made from red grapes, coloured by only brief contact with the skins.

rosemary ▸ noun an evergreen shrub with sweet-smelling leaves which are used as a herb in cooking.

rosette ▸ noun 1 a rose-shaped decoration made of ribbon, worn by supporters of a sports team or political party or awarded as a prize. 2 a piece of decoration in the shape of a rose.

r

rosewood ▶ noun the wood of a tropical tree, used for making furniture and musical instruments.

Rosh Hashana (or Rosh Hashanah) /rosh huh-**shah**-nuh/ ▶ noun the Jewish New Year festival.

rosin /ro-zin/ ▶ noun a kind of resin that is rubbed on the bows of stringed instruments.

roster ▶ noun 1 a list of people's names and the jobs they have to do at a particular time. 2 a list of sports players available for team selection.
▶ verb (rosters, rostering, rostered) put a person's name on a roster.

rostrum ▶ noun (plural rostra or rostrums) a platform on which a person stands to make a speech, receive a prize, or conduct an orchestra.

rosy ▶ adjective (rosier, rosiest) 1 of a soft pink colour. 2 promising: *a rosy future*.

> SYNONYMS 1 *a rosy complexion* pink, roseate, reddish, glowing, healthy, fresh, radiant, blooming, blushing, flushed, ruddy. 2 *his future looks rosy* promising, optimistic, auspicious, hopeful, encouraging, favourable, bright, golden.
> ANTONYMS pale, bleak.

rot ▶ verb (rots, rotting, rotted) gradually decay.

> SYNONYMS 1 *the floorboards rotted* decay, decompose, disintegrate, crumble, perish. 2 *the meat began to rot* go bad, go off, spoil, moulder, putrefy, fester. 3 *poor neighbourhoods have been left to rot* deteriorate, degenerate, decline, decay, go to seed, go downhill; informal go to pot, go to the dogs.
> ANTONYMS improve.

▶ noun 1 the process of decaying. 2 informal rubbish.

> SYNONYMS *the leaves turned black with rot* decay, decomposition, mould, mildew, blight, canker.

rota ▶ noun Brit. a list showing when each of a number of people has to do a particular job.

rotary ▶ adjective 1 revolving around a centre or axis. 2 having a rotating part or parts.

rotate ▶ verb (rotates, rotating, rotated) 1 move in a circle round an axis. 2 (of a job) pass on a regular basis to each member of a group in turn. 3 grow different crops one after the other on a piece of land.

> SYNONYMS 1 *the wheels rotate continually* revolve, go round, turn (round), spin, gyrate, whirl, twirl, swivel, circle, pivot. 2 *many nurses rotate jobs* alternate, take turns, change, switch, interchange, exchange, swap.

□ **rotator** noun **rotatory** adjective.

rotation ▶ noun the action or an act of rotating.

> SYNONYMS 1 *the rotation of the wheels* revolving, turning, spinning, gyration, circling. 2 *a rotation of the Earth* turn, revolution, orbit, spin. 3 *each member is chair for six months in rotation* sequence, succession, alternation, cycle.

rote ▶ noun regular repetition of something to be learned.

rotisserie /roh-**tiss**-uh-ri/ ▶ noun a rotating spit for roasting meat.

rotor ▶ noun 1 the rotating part of a turbine, electric motor, or other device. 2 a hub with a number of blades spreading out from it that is rotated to provide the lift for a helicopter.

rotten ▶ adjective 1 decayed. 2 corrupt. 3 informal very bad.

> SYNONYMS 1 *rotten meat* decaying, bad, off, decomposing, putrid, perished, rancid, festering, fetid. 2 *he's rotten to the core* corrupt, unprincipled, dishonest, dishonourable, unscrupulous, untrustworthy, immoral; informal crooked; Brit. informal bent.
> ANTONYMS fresh, honourable.

rotter ▶ noun informal, dated an unkind or unpleasant person.

Rottweiler /rot-vy-ler/ ▶ noun a large, powerful breed of dog.

rotund ▶ adjective rounded and plump.

rotunda ▶ noun a round building or room.

rouble (or ruble) /roo-b'l/ ▶ noun the basic unit of money in Russia.

roué /roo-ay/ ▶ noun a man who leads an immoral life.

rouge /roozh/ ▶ noun a red powder or cream used for colouring the cheeks.

rough ▶ adjective 1 not smooth or level. 2 not gentle. 3 (of weather or the sea) wild and stormy. 4 plain and basic. 5 not worked out in every detail. 6 harsh in sound or taste. 7 unsophisticated. 8 informal difficult and unpleasant.

> SYNONYMS 1 *rough ground* uneven, irregular, bumpy, stony, rocky, rugged, rutted, pitted. 2 *the terrier's rough coat* coarse, bristly, scratchy, prickly, shaggy, hairy, bushy. 3 *rough skin* dry, leathery, weather-beaten, chapped, calloused, scaly. 4 *his voice was rough* gruff, hoarse, harsh, rasping, husky, throaty, gravelly. 5 *he gets rough when he's drunk* violent, brutal, vicious, aggressive, belligerent, pugnacious, boisterous, rowdy, disorderly, unruly, riotous. 6 *a machine that can take rough handling* careless, clumsy, inept,

r

unskilful. **7** *rough manners* **boorish,** loutish, oafish, brutish, coarse, crude, uncouth, vulgar, unrefined, unladylike, ungentlemanly, uncultured. **8** *rough seas* **turbulent,** stormy, tempestuous, violent, heavy, choppy. **9** *a rough draft* **preliminary,** hasty, quick, sketchy, cursory, basic, crude, rudimentary, raw, unpolished, incomplete, unfinished. **10** *a rough estimate* **approximate,** inexact, imprecise, vague, estimated; N. Amer. informal ballpark.
ANTONYMS smooth, sleek, soft, dulcet, sweet, gentle, careful, refined, calm, exact.

▶ noun **1** a basic draft of a design, piece of writing, etc. **2** (on a golf course) the area of longer grass around the fairway and the green.

SYNONYMS *the artist's initial roughs* **sketch,** draft, outline, mock-up.

▶ verb **1** (**rough something out**) make a draft or first version of something. **2** (**rough it**) informal live with only very basic necessities. **3** (**rough someone up**) informal beat someone up.
■ **rough diamond** Brit. a person who lacks good manners and education but has a good character. **rough justice** treatment that is not fair or in accordance with the law. **sleep rough** Brit. sleep outside or without a bed.
□ **roughness** noun.

roughage ▶ noun material in cereals, fruit, and vegetables that cannot be digested.

roughen ▶ verb make or become rough.

roughly ▶ adverb **1** in a rough way. **2** approximately.

roughneck ▶ noun informal **1** a rough, rude person. **2** a person who works on an oil rig.

roughshod ▶ adjective (**ride roughshod over**) fail to consider someone's needs or wishes.

roulette ▶ noun a gambling game in which a ball is dropped on to a revolving wheel.

round ▶ adjective **1** shaped like a circle, sphere, or cylinder. **2** having a curved surface with no sharp projections. **3** (of a person's shoulders) bent forward. **4** (of a sound) rich and smooth. **5** (of a number) expressed in convenient units rather than exactly.

SYNONYMS *a round window* **circular,** spherical, globular, cylindrical.

▶ noun **1** a circular shape or piece. **2** a route by which you visit a number of people or places in turn. **3** a sequence of things that you do regularly. **4** each of a sequence of stages in a process. **5** a single division of a boxing or wrestling match. **6** a song for three or more voices or parts, each singing the same theme but starting one after

another. **7** the amount of ammunition needed to fire one shot. **8** a set of drinks bought for all the members of a group. **9** Brit. the quantity of sandwiches made from two slices of bread.

SYNONYMS **1** *mould the dough into rounds* **ball,** sphere, globe, orb, circle, disc, ring, hoop. **2** *a policeman on his rounds* **circuit,** beat, route, tour. **3** *the first round of the contest* **stage,** level, heat, game, bout, contest. **4** *an endless round of parties* **succession,** sequence, series, cycle.

▶ adverb Brit. **1** so as to rotate or cause rotation. **2** so as to cover the whole area surrounding a particular centre. **3** so as to turn and face in the opposite direction. **4** used in describing the position of something: *the wrong way round.* **5** so as to surround someone or something. **6** so as to reach a new place or position.

▶ preposition chiefly Brit. **1** on every side of. **2** so as to encircle. **3** from or on the other side of. **4** so as to cover the whole area of.

SYNONYMS **1** *the alleys round the station* **around,** about, encircling, near, orbiting. **2** *casinos dotted round France* **throughout,** all over.

▶ verb **1** pass and go round. **2** (**round something up** or **down**) make a figure less exact but easier to use in calculations. **3** make or become round in shape.

SYNONYMS *the ship rounded the point* **go round,** travel round, skirt, circumnavigate, orbit.

■ **round something off** complete in a suitable or satisfying way. **round on** make a sudden attack on. **round robin 1** a tournament in which every player or team plays against every other player or team. **2** a petition. **round trip** a journey to a place and back again. **round someone/thing up** collect a number of people or animals together.

roundabout ▶ noun Brit. **1** a road junction at which traffic moves in one direction round a central island to reach one of the roads leading off it. **2** a large revolving device in a playground, for children to ride on. **3** a merry-go-round.

▶ adjective not following a direct route.

SYNONYMS **1** *a roundabout route* **circuitous,** indirect, meandering, serpentine, tortuous. **2** *I asked in a roundabout sort of way* **indirect,** oblique, circuitous, circumlocutory.
ANTONYMS direct.

rounded ▶ adjective **1** round or curved. **2** complete and balanced.

roundel ▶ noun a small disc or circular design.

r

rounders ▸ noun a ball game in which players run round a circuit after hitting the ball with a cylindrical wooden bat.

Roundhead ▸ noun a supporter of the Parliamentary party in the English Civil War.

roundly ▸ adverb in a firm or thorough way.

roundworm ▸ noun a parasitic worm found in the intestines of animals.

rouse ▸ verb (rouses, rousing, roused) **1** wake someone up. **2** make someone move or take an interest in something.

> SYNONYMS **1** *he roused Ralph at dawn* **wake (up)**, awaken, arouse; Brit. informal knock up. **2** *she roused and looked around* **wake up**, awake, come to, get up, rise, bestir yourself. **3** *he roused the crowd* **stir up**, excite, galvanize, electrify, stimulate, inspire, inspirit, move, inflame, agitate, goad, provoke, prompt. **4** *he's got a temper when he's roused* **provoke**, annoy, anger, infuriate, madden, incense, vex, irk; informal aggravate.
> ANTONYMS calm, pacify, allay.

rousing ▸ adjective stirring.

> SYNONYMS **stirring**, inspiring, exciting, stimulating, moving, electrifying, invigorating, energizing, exhilarating.

rout /rowt/ ▸ noun **1** a disorderly retreat of defeated troops. **2** a decisive defeat.

> SYNONYMS *the army's ignominious rout* **defeat**, beating, retreat, flight; informal licking, hammering, thrashing, pasting, drubbing.
> ANTONYMS victory.

▸ verb defeat troops decisively and force them to retreat.

> SYNONYMS *his army was routed* **defeat**, beat, conquer, vanquish, crush, put to flight, drive off, scatter; informal lick, hammer, clobber, thrash; Brit. informal stuff.

route /root/ ▸ noun a way taken in getting from a starting point to a destination.

> SYNONYMS **way**, course, road, path, direction.

▸ verb (routes, routeing or routing, routed) send along a particular route.

routine ▸ noun **1** the order and way in which you regularly do things. **2** a set sequence in a stage performance.

> SYNONYMS **1** *his morning routine* **procedure**, practice, pattern, drill, regime, programme, schedule, plan. **2** *a stand-up routine* **act**, performance, number, turn, piece; informal spiel, patter.

▸ adjective **1** performed as part of a regular procedure. **2** without variety.

> SYNONYMS **1** *a routine health check* **standard**, regular, customary, normal, usual, ordinary, typical, everyday. **2** *a routine action movie* **boring**, tedious, monotonous, humdrum, run-of-the-mill, pedestrian, predictable, hackneyed, unimaginative, unoriginal, banal, trite.
> ANTONYMS unusual.

□ **routinely** adverb.

roux /roo/ ▸ noun (plural **roux**) a mixture of butter and flour used in making sauces.

rove ▸ verb (roves, roving, roved) **1** travel from place to place without a fixed destination. **2** (of eyes) look around in all directions.
□ **rover** noun.

row[1] /roh/ ▸ noun a number of people or things in a more or less straight line.

> SYNONYMS **1** *rows of children* **line**, column, file, queue, procession, chain, string, succession; informal crocodile. **2** *the middle row of seats* **tier**, line, rank, bank.

row[2] /roh/ ▸ verb move a boat through water with oars.

row[3] /row/ Brit. ▸ noun **1** an angry quarrel. **2** a loud noise.

> SYNONYMS **1** *have you two had a row?* **argument**, quarrel, squabble, fight, dispute; informal tiff, run-in, slanging match, spat; Brit. informal bust-up. **2** *I couldn't hear for the row* **din**, noise, racket, uproar, hubbub, rumpus; informal hullabaloo.

▸ verb have an angry quarrel.

> SYNONYMS *they rowed about money* **argue**, quarrel, squabble, bicker, fight, fall out, disagree, have words; informal scrap.

rowan /roh-uhn/ ▸ noun a small tree with white flowers and red berries.

rowdy ▸ adjective (rowdier, rowdiest) noisy and disorderly.
▸ noun (plural **rowdies**) a rowdy person.
□ **rowdily** adverb **rowdiness** noun.

rowlock /rol-luhk/ ▸ noun a fitting on the side of a boat for holding an oar.

royal ▸ adjective **1** having the status of a king or queen or a member of their family. **2** having to do with a king or queen. **3** of a quality or size suitable for a king or queen.

> SYNONYMS **regal**, kingly, queenly, princely, sovereign.

▸ noun informal a member of a royal family.
■ **royal blue** a deep, vivid blue. **royal jelly** a substance produced by worker bees and fed by them to larvae raised to be queen bees.
□ **royally** adverb.

royalist ▸ noun a person who supports the principle of having a king or queen.

royalty ▸ noun (plural **royalties**) **1** the members of a royal family. **2** the status or power of a king or queen. **3** a sum of money paid for the use of a patent, to an author for each copy of a book sold, or to a composer for each performance of a work.

RSPCA ▸ abbreviation Royal Society for the Prevention of Cruelty to Animals.

RSVP ▸ abbreviation please reply.
ORIGIN short for French *répondez s'il vous plaît*.

Rt Hon. ▸ abbreviation Brit. Right Honourable.

rub ▸ verb (**rubs, rubbing, rubbed**) **1** move your hand, a cloth, etc. over the surface while pressing down firmly. **2** apply a substance with a rubbing action. **3** (**rub off**) come off a surface through being rubbed. **4** (**rub something out**) erase pencil marks with a rubber. **5** (**rub something down**) dry, smooth, or clean something by rubbing. **6** (**rub it in**) informal keep reminding someone of an embarrassing fact they would rather forget.

SYNONYMS **1** *Polly rubbed her arm* **massage**, knead, stroke, pat. **2** *he rubbed sun lotion on her back* **apply**, smear, spread, work in. **3** *my shoes rub painfully* **chafe**, scrape, pinch.

▸ noun **1** an act of rubbing. **2** a substance for rubbing on the skin.

SYNONYMS **1** *she gave his back a rub* **massage**, rub-down. **2** *I gave my shoes a rub* **polish**, wipe, clean.

rubber¹ ▸ noun **1** a tough stretchy waterproof substance obtained from a tropical plant or from chemicals. **2** Brit. a piece of this or a similar substance used for erasing pencil marks. **3** N. Amer. informal a condom.
■ **rubber band** a stretchy loop of rubber for holding things together. **rubber plant** an evergreen plant with large shiny leaves. **rubber-stamp** approve something automatically without proper consideration.
□ **rubbery** adjective.

rubber² ▸ noun a unit of play in the card game bridge.

rubberneck ▸ verb informal turn to look at something as you pass it.

rubbing ▸ noun **1** the action of rubbing. **2** an impression of a design on brass or stone, made by placing paper over it and rubbing it with chalk or pencil.

rubbish Brit. ▸ noun **1** waste material and discarded items. **2** something that has no value or makes no sense.

SYNONYMS **1** *throw away that rubbish* **refuse**, waste, litter, scrap, dross; N. Amer. garbage, trash; informal dreck, junk. **2** *she's talking rubbish* **nonsense**, gibberish, claptrap, garbage; informal baloney, tripe, drivel, bilge, bunk, piffle, poppycock, twaddle, gobbledegook; Brit. informal codswallop, cobblers, tosh.

▸ verb informal say that something is bad.
□ **rubbishy** adjective.

rubble ▸ noun rough fragments of stone, brick, or concrete.

rubella /roo-**bel**-luh/ ▸ noun a disease with symptoms like mild measles.

rubicund /**roo**-bi-kuhnd/ ▸ adjective having a red complexion.

ruble ➡ ROUBLE.

rubric /**roo**-brik/ ▸ noun **1** a heading on a document. **2** a set of instructions.

ruby ▸ noun (plural **rubies**) **1** a deep red precious stone. **2** a deep red colour.
■ **ruby wedding** Brit. the fortieth anniversary of a wedding.

ruche /roosh/ ▸ noun a frill or pleat of fabric.
□ **ruched** adjective.

ruck¹ ▸ noun **1** Rugby a loose scrum formed around a player with the ball on the ground. **2** a crowd of people.

ruck² ▸ verb (often **ruck up**) form creases or folds.
▸ noun a crease.

rucksack ▸ noun a bag with two shoulder straps, that you carry on your back.

ruckus ▸ noun a row or commotion.

ructions ▸ plural noun Brit. informal angry reactions or protests.

rudder ▸ noun a flat piece hinged in an upright position at the back of a boat, used for steering.

ruddy ▸ adjective (**ruddier, ruddiest**) **1** (of a person's face) having a healthy red colour. **2** reddish.

rude ▸ adjective **1** saying impolite things that offend and hurt someone. **2** referring to sex or the body in a way that people find offensive or embarrassing. **3** very abrupt. **4** Brit. hearty: *rude health*.

SYNONYMS **1** *a rude man* **ill-mannered**, bad-mannered, impolite, discourteous, uncivil, impertinent, insolent, impudent, disparaging, abusive. **2** *rude jokes* **vulgar**, coarse, smutty, dirty, filthy, crude, lewd, obscene, risqué; informal blue; Brit. informal near the knuckle. **3** *a rude awakening* **abrupt**, sudden, sharp. ANTONYMS polite, clean, gentle.

□ **rudely** adverb **rudeness** noun.

rudimentary /roo-di-**men**-tuh-ri/ ▸ adjective **1** involving only basic matters or facts. **2** undeveloped.

rudiments /**roo**-di-muhnts/ ▸ plural noun **1** the essential matters or facts relating to a subject. **2** a basic form of something.

rue ▸ verb (**rues, rueing** or **ruing, rued**) bitterly regret a past event or action.

r

rueful ▸ adjective expressing regret.
  ◻ **ruefully** adverb.

ruff ▸ noun **1** a frill worn round the neck. **2** a ring of feathers or hair round the neck of a bird or mammal.

ruffian ▸ noun a rough person.

ruffle ▸ verb (**ruffles, ruffling, ruffled**) **1** disturb the smooth surface of. **2** upset or worry. **3** (**ruffled**) gathered into a frill.

> SYNONYMS **1** *he ruffled her hair* **disarrange,** tousle, dishevel, rumple, mess up; N. Amer. informal muss up. **2** *don't let him ruffle you* **disconcert,** unnerve, fluster, agitate, upset, disturb, discomfit, put off, perturb, unsettle; informal faze, throw, get to.
> ANTONYMS smooth, calm.

▸ noun a gathered frill on a garment.

rug ▸ noun **1** a small carpet. **2** Brit. a thick woollen blanket.

rugby (or **rugby football**) ▸ noun a team game played with an oval ball that may be kicked, carried, and passed by hand.

rugged /**rug**-gid/ ▸ adjective **1** having a rocky surface. **2** tough and determined. **3** (of a man) having attractively masculine features.

> SYNONYMS **1** *the rugged path* **rough,** uneven, bumpy, rocky, stony, pitted. **2** *a rugged vehicle* **robust,** durable, sturdy, strong, tough, resilient. **3** *rugged manly types* **well built,** burly, strong, muscular, muscly, brawny, strapping, tough, hardy, robust, sturdy, solid; informal hunky. **4** *his rugged features* **strong,** craggy, rough-hewn, manly, masculine.
> ANTONYMS smooth, flimsy, weedy, delicate.

> ◻ **ruggedly** adverb **ruggedness** noun.

rugger ▸ noun Brit. informal rugby.

ruin ▸ verb **1** completely spoil or destroy something. **2** make someone bankrupt or very poor.

> SYNONYMS **1** *don't ruin my plans* **spoil,** wreck, blight, shatter, dash, torpedo, scotch, mess up, sabotage; informal screw up; Brit. informal scupper. **2** *the bank's collapse ruined them* **bankrupt,** make insolvent, impoverish, pauperize, wipe out, break, cripple, bring someone to their knees. **3** *a country ruined by civil war* **destroy,** devastate, lay waste, ravage, raze, demolish, wreck, wipe out, flatten.
> ANTONYMS save, rebuild.

▸ noun **1** the destruction or collapse of something. **2** (also **ruins**) a building that has been badly damaged. **3** the complete loss of a person's money and property.

> SYNONYMS **1** *the buildings were saved from ruin* **disintegration,** decay, disrepair,

dilapidation, destruction, demolition. **2** *the ruins of a church* **remains,** remnants, fragments, rubble, debris, wreckage. **3** *electoral ruin for Labour* **downfall,** collapse, defeat, undoing, failure. **4** *shopkeepers are facing ruin* **bankruptcy,** insolvency, penury, poverty, destitution.
> ANTONYMS preservation, triumph, wealth.

ruination ▸ noun the process of ruining something.

ruinous ▸ adjective **1** disastrous or destructive. **2** in ruins.

rule ▸ noun **1** a statement saying what you must or must not do. **2** authority and control over a people or country. **3** (**the rule**) the normal state of things. **4** a ruler (for measuring or drawing).

> SYNONYMS **1** *health and safety rules* **regulation,** directive, order, law, statute. **2** *church attendance on Sunday was the general rule* **procedure,** practice, protocol, convention, norm, routine, custom, habit. **3** *moderation is the golden rule* **principle,** precept, standard, axiom, truth, maxim. **4** *under British rule* **government,** jurisdiction, command, power, dominion, control, administration, sovereignty, leadership.

▸ verb (**rules, ruling, ruled**) **1** have authority and control over a people or country. **2** control or influence. **3** state with legal authority that something is the case. **4** (**rule something out**) say that something is not possible. **5** (**ruled**) (of paper) marked with thin horizontal lines.

> SYNONYMS **1** *El Salvador was ruled by Spain* **govern,** preside over, control, lead, dominate, run, head, administer. **2** *Mary ruled for six years* **reign,** be on the throne, be in power, govern. **3** *the judge ruled that they be set free* **decree,** order, pronounce, judge, adjudge, ordain, decide, find. **4** *subversion ruled* **prevail,** predominate, be the order of the day, reign supreme.

■ **rule of thumb** a rough guide.

ruler ▸ noun **1** a person who has authority and control over a people or country. **2** a strip of rigid material marked with centimetres or inches, used to measure short distances or draw straight lines.

> SYNONYMS **leader,** sovereign, monarch, potentate, king, queen, emperor, empress, prince, princess, crowned head, head of state, president, premier, governor.
> ANTONYMS subject.

ruling ▸ noun a decision or statement made by an authority.

SYNONYMS *the judge's ruling* **judgement,** decision, adjudication, finding, verdict, pronouncement, resolution, decree, injunction.

▶ **adjective** in control; governing.

SYNONYMS **1** *Japan's ruling party* **governing,** controlling, commanding, supreme. **2** *football was their ruling passion* **main,** chief, principal, major, dominating, consuming; informal number-one.

rum¹ ▶ **noun** a strong alcoholic drink made from sugar cane.

rum² ▶ **adjective** (**rummer, rummest**) Brit. informal, dated peculiar.

Rumanian → ROMANIAN.

rumba (or **rhumba**) ▶ **noun** a rhythmic dance with Spanish and African elements.

rumble ▶ **verb** (**rumbles, rumbling, rumbled**) **1** make a continuous deep sound, like distant thunder. **2** (**rumble on**) (of a dispute) continue in a low-key way. **3** Brit. informal discover that someone is doing something wrong.
▶ **noun** a continuous deep sound like that of distant thunder.

rumbustious /rum-**buss**-chuhss/ ▶ **adjective** Brit. informal high-spirited or difficult to control.

ruminant ▶ **noun** an animal that chews the cud, such as a cow or sheep.

ruminate ▶ **verb** (**ruminates, ruminating, ruminated**) **1** think deeply about something. **2** (of an animal) chew the cud.

rummage ▶ **verb** (**rummages, rummaging, rummaged**) search for something by turning things over or moving them about in an untidy way.
▶ **noun** an act of rummaging.

rummy ▶ **noun** a card game in which the players try to form sets and sequences of cards.

rumour (US spelling **rumor**) ▶ **noun** a piece of information spread among a number of people which is not confirmed and may be false.

SYNONYMS **gossip,** hearsay, talk, tittle-tattle, speculation, word, report, story, whisper; informal the grapevine, the word on the street, the buzz.

▶ **verb** (**be rumoured**) be spread as a rumour.

rump ▶ **noun** **1** the hind part of the body of a mammal. **2** a piece left over from something larger.

rumple ▶ **verb** (**rumples, rumpling, rumpled**) make something less smooth and neat.

rumpus ▶ **noun** (plural **rumpuses**) a noisy disturbance.

run ▶ **verb** (**runs, running, ran**; past participle **run**) **1** move at a speed faster than a walk, never having both feet on the ground at the same time. **2** be in charge of people or an organization. **3** continue, operate, or proceed. **4** function or cause to function. **5** pass into or reach a particular state or level. **6** (of a liquid) flow. **7** (**run in**) (of a quality) be common or lasting in. **8** (of dye or colour) dissolve and spread when wet. **9** stand as a candidate in an election. **10** compete in a race. **11** (of a bus or train) make a regular journey on a particular route. **12** take someone somewhere in a car. **13** publish a story in a newspaper. **14** smuggle goods.

SYNONYMS **1** *she ran across the road* **sprint,** race, dart, rush, dash, hasten, hurry, scurry, scamper, gallop, jog, trot; informal leg it. **2** *the robbers turned and ran* **flee,** take flight, make off, take off, take to your heels, bolt, make your getaway, escape; informal beat it, clear off/out, scram; Brit. informal scarper. **3** *the road runs the length of the valley* **extend,** stretch, reach, continue. **4** *water ran from the eaves* **flow,** pour, stream, gush, flood, cascade, roll, course, spill, trickle, drip, dribble, leak. **5** *a bus runs to Sorrento* **travel,** shuttle, go. **6** *he runs a transport company* **be in charge of,** manage, direct, control, head, govern, supervise, superintend, oversee. **7** *it's expensive to run a car* **maintain,** keep, own, possess, have, use, operate. **8** *he left the engine running* **operate,** function, work, go. **9** *the lease runs for twenty years* **last,** continue, survive.

▶ **noun** **1** an act or period of running. **2** a journey or route. **3** a course that is regularly used: *a ski run.* **4** a continuous period or sequence. **5** an enclosed area in which chickens or animals can run around. **6** (**the run of**) unrestricted use of or access to a place. **7** a point scored in cricket or baseball. **8** a ladder in stockings or tights.

SYNONYMS **1** *his morning run* **jog,** sprint, dash, gallop, trot. **2** *she did the school run* **route,** journey, circuit, round, beat. **3** *a run in the car* **drive,** ride, turn, trip, excursion, outing, jaunt; informal spin, tootle. **4** *an unbeaten run of victories* **series,** succession, sequence, string, streak, spate. **5** *a chicken run* **enclosure,** pen, coop. **6** *a ski run* **slope,** track, piste; N. Amer. trail.

■ **run across** meet or find by chance. **run down** gradually lose power. **run someone down 1** knock someone down with a vehicle. **2** criticize someone unfairly or unkindly. **run-of-the-mill** ordinary. **run into 1** collide with. **2** meet someone by chance. **run out 1** be used up. **2** be no longer valid. **run someone out** Cricket dismiss a batsman by hitting the bails with the ball while the batsman is still running. **run someone over** knock someone down with a vehicle. **run through** (or **over**) go over something as a quick rehearsal or reminder. **run something up 1** allow a bill to build up. **2** make something quickly. **run-up** the period before an important event.

runaway ▸ noun a person who has run away from their home or an institution.
▸ adjective **1** (of an animal or vehicle) running out of control. **2** happening or done quickly or uncontrollably.

rundown ▸ noun a brief summary.

> SYNONYMS **summary,** synopsis, precis, run-through, review, overview, briefing, sketch, outline; informal low-down, recap.

▸ adjective (**run-down**) **1** in a bad or neglected state. **2** tired and rather unwell.

> SYNONYMS **1** *a run-down area of London* **dilapidated,** tumbledown, ramshackle, derelict, crumbling, neglected, uncared-for, slummy. **2** *she was feeling rather run down* **unwell,** ill, poorly, unhealthy, peaky, tired, drained, exhausted, worn out, below par, washed out; Brit. off colour; informal under the weather; Brit. informal **off**; Austral./NZ informal crook.

rune ▸ noun **1** a letter of an ancient Germanic alphabet. **2** a symbol with mysterious or magical significance.
□ **runic** adjective.

rung[1] ▸ noun **1** a horizontal support on a ladder for the foot. **2** a level or rank.

rung[2] past participle of RING[2].

runnel ▸ noun **1** a gutter. **2** a stream.

runner ▸ noun **1** a person who runs in a race or for exercise. **2** a messenger. **3** a rod, groove, or blade on which something slides. **4** a shoot which grows along the ground and can take root at points along its length. **5** a long, narrow rug.

> SYNONYMS **1 athlete,** sprinter, hurdler, racer, jogger. **2** *the bookmaker employed runners* **messenger,** courier, errand boy; informal gofer.

■ **runner bean** a climbing bean plant with long edible pods. **runner-up** (plural **runners-up**) a competitor who comes second.

running ▸ noun **1** the activity or movement of a runner. **2** the action of managing or operating something.

> SYNONYMS **1** *the running of the school* **administration,** management, organization, coordination, orchestration, handling, direction, control, supervision. **2** *the smooth running of her department* **operation,** working, function, performance.

▸ adjective **1** (of water) flowing naturally or supplied through pipes and taps. **2** producing liquid or pus. **3** continuous or recurring. **4** done while running. **5** in

succession: *the third week running.*

> SYNONYMS **1** *running water* **flowing,** gushing, rushing, moving. **2** *a running argument* **ongoing,** continuous, incessant, ceaseless, constant, perpetual. **3** *she was late two days running* **in succession,** in a row, in sequence, consecutively, straight, together; informal on the trot.

■ **in** (or **out of**) **the running** in (or no longer in) with a chance of success. **running board** a board acting as a step which extends along the side of a vehicle. **running commentary** a description of events given as they happen.

runny ▸ adjective (**runnier, runniest**) **1** more liquid than is usual. **2** (of a person's nose) producing mucus.

> SYNONYMS **liquid,** liquefied, fluid, melted, molten, watery, thin.
> ANTONYMS solid, thick.

runt ▸ noun the smallest animal in a litter.

runway ▸ noun a strip of hard ground where aircraft take off and land.

rupee /roo-pee/ ▸ noun the basic unit of money of India and Pakistan.

rupture ▸ verb (**ruptures, rupturing, ruptured**) **1** break or burst suddenly. **2** (**be ruptured** or **rupture yourself**) develop a hernia in the abdomen.

> SYNONYMS **break,** fracture, crack, burst, split, fissure, breach.

▸ noun **1** an instance of rupturing. **2** a hernia in the abdomen.

> SYNONYMS **break,** fracture, crack, burst, split, fissure, breach.

rural ▸ adjective having to do with the countryside.

> SYNONYMS **country,** rustic, bucolic, pastoral, agricultural, agrarian.
> ANTONYMS urban.

□ **rurally** adverb.

ruse ▸ noun something done to deceive or trick someone.

> SYNONYMS **ploy,** stratagem, tactic, scheme, trick, gambit, dodge, subterfuge, machination, wile; Brit. informal wheeze.

rush[1] ▸ verb **1** move or act very quickly, often too quickly. **2** produce, deal with, or transport very quickly. **3** (of air or a liquid) flow strongly. **4** dash towards a person or place as a form of attack.

> SYNONYMS **1** *she rushed home* **hurry,** dash, run, race, sprint, bolt, dart, gallop, career, charge, shoot, hurtle, hare, fly, speed, zoom, scurry, scuttle, scamper, hasten; informal tear, belt, pelt, scoot, zip, whip; Brit. informal bomb. **2** *water rushed*

along gutters **gush**, pour, surge, stream, course, cascade. **3** *the tax was rushed through parliament* **push**, hurry, hasten, speed, hustle, press, force. **4** *they rushed the cordon of troops* **attack**, charge, storm.

▸ **noun 1** a sudden quick movement towards something. **2** a sudden period of hasty activity. **3** a sudden strong demand for a product. **4** a sudden strong feeling. **5** informal a sudden thrill experienced after taking certain drugs. **6** (**rushes**) the first prints made of a film after a period of shooting.

> SYNONYMS **1** *Tim made a rush for the exit* **dash**, run, sprint, dart, bolt, charge, scramble. **2** *the lunchtime rush* **hustle and bustle**, commotion, hubbub, hurly-burly, stir. **3** *a rush for tickets* **demand**, clamour, call, request, run on. **4** *he was in no rush to leave* **hurry**, haste, urgency. **5** *I made a sudden rush at him* **charge**, onslaught, attack, assault.

▸ **adjective** done in a hurry.

> SYNONYMS *a rush job* **urgent**, high-priority, emergency, hurried, hasty, fast, quick, swift.

■ **rush hour** a time at the start and end of the working day when traffic is at its heaviest.

rush² ▸ **noun** a water plant used in making mats, baskets, etc.

rusk ▸ **noun** a dry biscuit or piece of baked bread.

russet ▸ **adjective** reddish brown.
▸ **noun** a kind of apple with a greenish-brown skin.

Russian ▸ **noun 1** a person from Russia. **2** the language of Russia.
▸ **adjective** relating to Russia.
■ **Russian roulette** a dangerous game of chance in which a person loads one bullet into a revolver, spins the cylinder, and then pulls the trigger while pointing the gun at their own head.

rust ▸ **noun** a brown flaky coating which forms on iron or steel when it is wet.
▸ **verb** be affected by rust.

> SYNONYMS **corrode**, oxidize, tarnish.

rustic ▸ **adjective 1** having to do with life in the country. **2** simple and charming in a way seen as typical of the countryside.

> SYNONYMS **1** *a rustic setting* **rural**, country, pastoral, bucolic, agricultural, agrarian. **2** *rustic wooden tables* **plain**, simple, homely, unsophisticated, rough, crude.
> ANTONYMS urban, ornate, sophisticated.

▸ **noun** an unsophisticated country person.

> SYNONYMS **peasant**, countryman, countrywoman, bumpkin, yokel, country cousin; N. Amer. informal hillbilly, hayseed, hick; Austral./NZ informal bushy.

□ **rusticity** noun.

rustle ▸ **verb 1** make a soft crackling sound. **2** round up and steal cattle, horses, or sheep. **3** (**rustle something up**) informal produce food or a drink quickly.
▸ **noun** a rustling sound.
□ **rustler** noun.

rusty ▸ **adjective 1** affected by rust. **2** of the colour of rust; reddish-brown. **3** (of knowledge or a skill) less good than it used to be because of a lack of recent practice.

rut¹ ▸ **noun 1** a long deep track made by the wheels of vehicles. **2** a way of living or working that has become routine and dull but is hard to change.

rut² ▸ **noun** an annual period of sexual activity in deer and some other animals, during which the males fight each other for access to the females.
▸ **verb** (**ruts, rutting, rutted**) be in such a period of activity.

ruthenium ▸ **noun** a hard silvery-white metallic element.

ruthless ▸ **adjective** hard, determined, and showing no sympathy.

> SYNONYMS **merciless**, pitiless, cruel, heartless, hard-hearted, cold-hearted, cold-blooded, harsh, callous.
> ANTONYMS merciful.

□ **ruthlessly** adverb **ruthlessness** noun.

Rwandan /ruu-**an**-duhn/ ▸ **noun** a person from Rwanda, a country in central Africa.
▸ **adjective** relating to Rwanda.

rye ▸ **noun 1** a type of cereal plant. **2** whisky made from rye.

ryegrass ▸ **noun** a grass used for lawns and as food for farm animals.

Ss

S (or s) ▸ noun (plural **Ss** or **S's**) the nineteenth letter of the alphabet.
▸ abbreviation South or Southern.

sabbath ▸ noun (often **the Sabbath**) a day for rest and religious worship.

sabbatical ▸ noun a period of paid leave for study or travel.

sable ▸ noun a marten native to Japan and Siberia, hunted for its dark brown fur.

sabotage /sab-uh-tah*z*h/ ▸ verb (**sabotages, sabotaging, sabotaged**) deliberately damage or destroy.

> SYNONYMS **vandalize,** wreck, damage, destroy, incapacitate, obstruct, disrupt, spoil, ruin, undermine.

▸ noun the action of sabotaging.

> SYNONYMS **vandalism,** wrecking, destruction, damage, obstruction, disruption; Brit. informal a spanner in the works.

saboteur /sab-uh-**ter**/ ▸ noun a person who sabotages something.

sabre /**say**-ber/ (US spelling **saber**) ▸ noun **1** a heavy sword with a curved blade. **2** a light fencing sword with a thin blade.

sabretooth tiger (or **sabre-toothed tiger**) ▸ noun a large extinct member of the cat family with massive curved upper canine teeth.

sac ▸ noun a hollow, flexible structure resembling a bag or pouch.

saccharin /sak-kuh-rin/ ▸ noun a sweet-tasting substance used as a low-calorie substitute for sugar.

saccharine /sak-kuh-rin/ ▸ adjective too sweet or sentimental.

sacerdotal /sak-er-**doh**-t'l/ ▸ adjective relating to priests.

sachet /sa-shay/ ▸ noun Brit. a small sealed bag or packet.

sack¹ ▸ noun **1** a large bag made of rough material or thick paper, used for storing and carrying goods. **2** (**the sack**) informal dismissal from employment. **3** (**the sack**) informal bed.

> SYNONYMS **bag,** pouch, pocket, pack.

▸ verb informal dismiss someone from employment.

> SYNONYMS **dismiss,** discharge, lay off, make redundant, let go, throw out; informal fire, give someone the sack; Brit. informal give someone their cards.

□ **sackable** adjective.

sack² ▸ verb violently attack, steal from, and destroy a town or city (used when talking about the past).
▸ noun the sacking of a town or city.

sackcloth ▸ noun a rough fabric woven from flax or hemp.

sacra plural of SACRUM.

sacrament /sak-ruh-muhnt/ ▸ noun **1** (in the Christian Church) an important religious ceremony in which the people taking part are believed to receive the grace of God. **2** (also **the Blessed Sacrament** or **the Holy Sacrament**) (in Catholic use) the bread and wine used in the Mass.
□ **sacramental** adjective.

sacred /say-krid/ ▸ adjective **1** connected with God or a god or goddess, and treated as holy. **2** (of a piece of writing) containing the teachings of a religion. **3** religious.

> SYNONYMS **1** *a sacred place* **holy,** hallowed, blessed, consecrated, sanctified. **2** *sacred music* **religious,** spiritual, devotional, church, ecclesiastical.
> ANTONYMS secular, profane.

■ **sacred cow** a thing that people believe must not be criticized.

sacrifice ▸ noun **1** the killing of an animal or person or giving up of a possession as an offering to a god or goddess. **2** an animal, person, or object offered in this way. **3** an act of giving up something you value for the sake of something that is more important.

> SYNONYMS **1** *the sacrifice of animals* **(ritual) slaughter,** (votive) offering. **2** *the sacrifice of privileges* **surrender,** giving up, abandonment, renunciation.

▸ verb (**sacrifices, sacrificing, sacrificed**) offer as a sacrifice.

> SYNONYMS **1** *two goats were sacrificed* **offer up,** slaughter. **2** *he sacrificed his*

principles **give up,** abandon, renounce, relinquish, betray. **3** *he sacrificed his life* **give (up),** lay down, surrender, forfeit.
□ **sacrificial** adjective.

sacrilege /sak-ri-lij/ ▶ noun an act of treating a sacred or highly valued thing without respect.
□ **sacrilegious** adjective.

✔ sac**rilege**, not **-religo** or **-rilige**.

sacristan ▶ noun a person in charge of a sacristy.

sacristy ▶ noun (plural **sacristies**) a room in a church where a priest prepares for a service.

sacrosanct ▶ adjective too important or valuable to be changed.

sacrum /say-kruhm/ ▶ noun (plural **sacra** or **sacrums**) a triangular bone in the lower back between the two hip bones.

sad ▶ adjective (**sadder, saddest**) **1** unhappy. **2** causing sorrow. **3** informal very inadequate or unfashionable.

SYNONYMS **1** *we felt sad* **unhappy,** sorrowful, depressed, downcast, miserable, down, despondent, wretched, glum, gloomy, doleful, melancholy, mournful, forlorn, heartbroken; informal blue, down in the mouth, down in the dumps. **2** *a sad story* **tragic,** unhappy, miserable, wretched, sorry, pitiful, pathetic, heartbreaking, heart-rending. **3** *a sad state of affairs* **unfortunate,** regrettable, sorry, deplorable, lamentable, pitiful, shameful, disgraceful.
ANTONYMS happy, cheerful, fortunate.

□ **sadly** adverb.

sadden ▶ verb make someone unhappy.

SYNONYMS **depress,** dispirit, deject, dishearten, grieve, discourage, upset, get down.

saddle ▶ noun **1** a seat with a raised ridge at the front and back, fastened on the back of a horse for riding. **2** a seat on a bicycle or motorcycle. **3** a piece of meat from the back of an animal.
▶ verb (**saddles, saddling, saddled**) **1** put a saddle on a horse. **2** (**saddle someone with**) give someone an unpleasant responsibility or task.

SYNONYMS **burden,** encumber, lumber, land, impose something on.

saddlebag ▶ noun a bag attached to a saddle.

saddler ▶ noun a person who makes, sells, and repairs saddles and other equipment for horses.
□ **saddlery** (plural **saddleries**).

sadism /say-di-z'm/ ▶ noun enjoyment felt

in hurting or humiliating other people.
□ **sadist** noun **sadistic** adjective.

sadness ▶ noun the quality or condition of being sad.

SYNONYMS **unhappiness,** sorrow, dejection, depression, misery, despondency, wretchedness, gloom, gloominess, melancholy.

sadomasochism /say-doh-**mass**-uh-ki-z'm/ ▶ noun enjoyment felt in hurting or being hurt by someone else, especially during sex.
□ **sadomasochist** noun **sadomasochistic** adjective.

safari ▶ noun (plural **safaris**) an expedition to observe or hunt animals in their natural environment.
■ **safari park** an area of parkland where wild animals are kept in the open and may be observed by visitors.

safe ▶ adjective **1** protected from danger or risk. **2** not leading to harm or injury; not risky. **3** (of a place) giving security or protection. **4** based on good reasons and not likely to be proved wrong.

SYNONYMS **1** *the jewels are safe in the bank* **secure,** protected, out of harm's way. **2** *the children are all safe* **unharmed,** unhurt, uninjured, unscathed, all right, fine, well, in one piece, out of danger. **3** *a safe place* **secure,** sound, impregnable, invulnerable, secret. **4** *a safe driver* **cautious,** circumspect, prudent, careful, unadventurous, conservative. **5** *the drug is safe* **harmless,** innocuous, benign, non-toxic, non-poisonous.
ANTONYMS insecure, dangerous, reckless, harmful.

▶ noun a strong fireproof cabinet with a complex lock, used for storing valuable items.
■ **safe house** a house in a secret location, used by people in hiding.
□ **safely** adverb.

safeguard ▶ noun a thing done in order to protect or prevent something.

SYNONYMS **protection,** defence, buffer, provision, security, cover, insurance.

▶ verb protect with a safeguard.

SYNONYMS **protect,** preserve, conserve, save, secure, shield, guard, keep safe.
ANTONYMS jeopardize.

safekeeping ▶ noun the keeping of something in a safe place.

safety ▶ noun (plural **safeties**) the condition of being safe.

SYNONYMS **1** *the safety of the residents* **welfare,** well-being, protection, security. **2** *the safety of ferries* **security,** soundness, dependability, reliability.

S

3 *the safety of the shore* **shelter,** sanctuary, refuge.

■ **safety belt** a belt that secures a person to their seat in a vehicle or aircraft. **safety net 1** a net placed to catch an acrobat should they fall. **2** something arranged as a safeguard. **safety pin** a pin with a point that is bent back to the head and held in a guard when closed.

saffron ▶ noun a yellow spice made from the dried stigmas of a crocus.

sag ▶ verb (**sags, sagging, sagged**) **1** sink downwards gradually under weight or pressure or through weakness. **2** hang down loosely or unevenly.

SYNONYMS **1** *he sagged back in his chair* **sink,** slump, loll, flop, crumple. **2** *the floors all sag* **dip,** droop, bulge, bag.

▶ noun an instance of sagging.
□ **saggy** adjective.

saga ▶ noun **1** a long traditional story describing brave acts. **2** a story which covers a long period of time. **3** a long and complicated series of incidents.

SYNONYMS **1** *Icelandic sagas* **epic,** legend, (folk) tale, romance, narrative, myth. **2** *the saga of how they met* **story,** tale, yarn.

sagacious ▶ adjective having good judgement; wise.
□ **sagacity** noun.

sage¹ ▶ noun a sweet-smelling Mediterranean plant with greyish-green leaves, used as a herb in cookery.

sage² ▶ noun a very wise man.

SYNONYMS **wise man/woman,** philosopher, scholar, guru, prophet, mystic.

▶ adjective wise.
□ **sagely** adverb.

Sagittarius /saj-i-**tair**-i-uhss/ ▶ noun a sign of the zodiac (the Archer), 22 November–20 December.

sago ▶ noun a pudding made with starchy granules obtained from a palm tree, cooked with milk.

sahib /sahb/ ▶ noun Indian a polite form of address for a man.

said past and past participle of **SAY.**
▶ adjective referring to someone or something already mentioned.

sail ▶ noun **1** a piece of material spread on a mast to catch the wind and propel a boat or ship. **2** a trip in a sailing boat or ship. **3** a flat board attached to the arm of a windmill.

▶ verb **1** travel in a sailing boat as a sport or pastime. **2** travel in a ship or boat using sails or engine power. **3** begin a voyage. **4** direct or control a boat or ship. **5** move smoothly or confidently. **6** (**sail through**) informal succeed easily at.

SYNONYMS **1** *we sailed across the Atlantic* **voyage,** travel, navigate, cruise. **2** *we sail tonight* **set sail,** put to sea, leave, weigh anchor. **3** *who is sailing the ship?* **steer,** pilot, captain; informal skipper. **4** *clouds were sailing past* **glide,** drift, float, flow, sweep, skim, coast, flit, scud.

■ **sail close to the wind** take risks. **sailing boat** (N. Amer. **sailboat**) a boat propelled by sails.

sailboard ▶ noun a board with a mast and a sail, used in windsurfing.

sailcloth ▶ noun strong fabric used for making sails.

sailor ▶ noun **1** a member of the crew of a ship or boat. **2** a person who sails as a sport or pastime. **3** (**a good** or **bad sailor**) a person who rarely (or often) becomes seasick.

SYNONYMS **seaman,** seafarer, mariner, yachtsman, yachtswoman, hand, merchant seaman.

saint ▶ noun **1** a good person who Christians believe will go to heaven when they die. **2** a person of great goodness who after their death is formally declared by the Church to be a saint, and to whom people offer prayers. **3** informal a very good or kind person.

■ **saint's day** (in the Christian Church) a day each year when a particular saint is honoured.
□ **sainthood** noun.

sainted ▶ adjective dated very good or kind, like a saint.

St George's cross ▶ noun a red cross on a white background.

saintly ▶ adjective very holy or good.
□ **saintliness** noun.

sake¹ ▶ noun **1** (**for the sake of**) in the interest of. **2** (**for the sake of**) out of consideration for. **3** (**for old times' sake**) in memory of former times.

SYNONYMS **1** *for the sake of clarity* **purpose(s),** reason(s). **2** *for her son's sake* **benefit,** advantage, good, well-being, welfare.

sake² /**sah**-ki/ ▶ noun a Japanese alcoholic drink made from rice.

salaam /suh-**lahm**/ ▶ noun a low bow with the hand touching the forehead, used by Muslims as a gesture of respect.
▶ verb make a salaam.

salacious /suh-**lay**-shuhss/ ▶ adjective containing too much sexual detail.

salad ▶ noun a cold dish of raw vegetables.
■ **your salad days** the time when you are young and inexperienced.

salamander ▸ noun **1** an animal like a newt that can live in water or on land. **2** a mythical creature resembling a lizard, said to be able to stay alive in fire.

salami ▸ noun (plural **salami** or **salamis**) a type of spicy preserved sausage.

salary ▸ noun (plural **salaries**) a fixed payment made every month to an employee.

> SYNONYMS **pay**, wages, earnings, payment, remuneration, fee(s), stipend, income.

□ **salaried** adjective.

sale ▸ noun **1** the exchange of something for money. **2** (**sales**) the activity or profession of selling. **3** a period in which goods in a shop are sold at reduced prices. **4** a public event at which goods are sold or auctioned.

> SYNONYMS **1** *the sale of firearms* **selling**, dealing, trading. **2** *they make a sale every minute* **deal**, transaction, bargain. ANTONYMS purchase.

□ **saleable** (or **salable**) adjective.

saleroom (or **salesroom**) ▸ noun a room in which auctions are held or cars are sold.

salesman (or **saleswoman**) ▸ noun (plural **salesmen** or **saleswomen**) a person whose job involves selling goods.
□ **salesmanship** noun.

salient /say-li-uhnt/ ▸ adjective most noticeable or important.
□ **salience** noun.

saline /say-lyn/ ▸ adjective containing salt.
□ **salinity** noun.

saliva ▸ noun a watery liquid in the mouth produced by glands, that helps chewing, swallowing, and digestion.
□ **salivary** adjective.

salivate ▸ verb (**salivates**, **salivating**, **salivated**) have a lot of saliva in the mouth.
□ **salivation** noun.

sallow ▸ adjective (of a person's skin) yellowish or pale brown in colour.

sally ▸ noun (plural **sallies**) **1** a sudden charge out of a place surrounded by an enemy. **2** a witty or lively reply.
▸ verb (**sallies**, **sallying**, **sallied**) (**sally forth**) set out.

salmon (*rhymes with* gammon) ▸ noun (plural **salmon** or **salmons**) a large fish with pink flesh, that matures in the sea and moves to freshwater streams to release eggs.

salmonella /sal-muh-nel-luh/ ▸ noun a germ that can cause food poisoning.

salon ▸ noun **1** a place where a hairdresser, beautician, or clothes designer works. **2** a reception room in a large house. **3** (in the past) a regular gathering of writers and artists held in someone's house.

saloon ▸ noun **1** Brit. a car with a separate boot. **2** Brit. a lounge bar in a pub. **3** a large

room for use as a public lounge on a ship. **4** N. Amer. old use a bar.

salopettes /sal-uh-**pets**/ ▸ plural noun padded trousers with a high waist and shoulder straps, worn for skiing.

salsa ▸ noun **1** a Latin American dance performed to music that combines jazz and rock. **2** a spicy sauce.

salt ▸ noun **1** sodium chloride, a white substance in the form of crystals, used for flavouring or preserving food. **2** Chemistry any compound formed by the reaction of an acid with a base.
▸ verb **1** season or preserve food with salt. **2** sprinkle a road or path with salt in order to melt snow or ice.
■ **salt cellar** a container for salt. **the salt of the earth** a person who is very kind, reliable, or honest. **take something with a pinch** (or **grain**) **of salt** recognize that something may be exaggerated or untrue.

saltings ▸ noun Brit. an area of coastal land regularly covered by the tide.

saltpetre /sawlt-**pee**-ter/ (US spelling **saltpeter**) ▸ noun a white powder (potassium nitrate) used to make gunpowder and preserve meat.

salty ▸ adjective (**saltier**, **saltiest**) **1** containing or tasting of salt. **2** (of language or humour) rather rude.

> SYNONYMS **salt**, salted, saline, briny, brackish.

□ **saltiness** noun.

salubrious ▸ adjective **1** good for your health. **2** (of a place) well maintained and pleasant to be in.

salutary /sal-yuu-tuh-ri/ ▸ adjective (with reference to something unpleasant) producing a good effect because it teaches you something.

salutation ▸ noun a greeting.

salute ▸ noun **1** a raising of a hand to the head, made as a formal gesture of respect by a member of a military force. **2** a gesture of admiration or respect. **3** the shooting of a gun or guns as a formal sign of respect or celebration.

> SYNONYMS **tribute**, testimonial, homage, honour, celebration (of), acknowledgement (of).

▸ verb (**salutes**, **saluting**, **saluted**) **1** make a formal salute to. **2** greet. **3** express admiration and respect for.

> SYNONYMS **pay tribute to**, pay homage to, honour, celebrate, acknowledge, take your hat off to.

Salvadorean /sal-vuh-**dor**-i-uhn/ ▸ noun a person from El Salvador, a country in Central America.
▸ adjective relating to El Salvador.

S

salvage ▸ verb (salvages, salvaging, salvaged) **1** rescue something that is in danger of being lost or destroyed. **2** rescue a ship or its contents from being lost at sea.

SYNONYMS **rescue**, save, recover, retrieve, reclaim.

▸ noun **1** the action of salvaging. **2** contents rescued from a wrecked ship.
■ **salvage yard** a place where disused machinery and vehicles are broken up so that the metal or parts can be used again.

salvation ▸ noun **1** the saving of a person from sin and its consequences, believed by Christians to be brought about by faith in Jesus. **2** the protecting or saving of someone or something from harm or loss.

SYNONYMS **1** *praying for salvation* **redemption**, deliverance. **2** *that man was her salvation* **lifeline**, means of escape, saviour.
ANTONYMS damnation, ruin.

salve ▸ noun **1** an ointment that soothes the skin. **2** something that makes you feel less guilty.
▸ verb (salves, salving, salved) reduce feelings of guilt.

salver ▸ noun a tray.

salvia ▸ noun a plant with bright red flowers.

salvo ▸ noun (plural salvos or salvoes) **1** a shooting of a number of guns at the same time. **2** a sudden series of aggressive statements or acts.

salwar /sul-**wah**/ (also shalwar) ▸ noun light, loose trousers that fit tightly around the ankles, worn by women from the Indian subcontinent.

Samaritan ▸ noun **1** (good Samaritan) a helpful person. **2** a member of a people living in Samaria, an ancient city and region of Palestine.

samba /sam-buh/ ▸ noun a Brazilian dance of African origin.

same ▸ adjective **1** (the same) exactly alike. **2** (this or that same) referring to a person or thing just mentioned.

SYNONYMS **1** *we stayed at the same hotel* **identical**, selfsame, very same. **2** *they had the same symptoms* **matching**, identical, alike, carbon-copy, twin, indistinguishable, interchangeable, corresponding, equivalent, parallel, like, comparable, similar.
ANTONYMS another, different, dissimilar, varying.

▸ pronoun **1** (the same) the same thing as previously mentioned. **2** (the same) identical people or things.
▸ adverb in the same way.
□ **sameness** noun.

samey ▸ adjective Brit. informal lacking in variety.

Samoan ▸ noun a person from Samoa.
▸ adjective relating to Samoa.

samovar /sam-uh-var/ ▸ noun a highly decorated Russian tea urn.

sampan ▸ noun (in SE Asia) a small flat-bottomed boat propelled with an oar.

samphire ▸ noun a plant which grows on rocks near the sea.

sample ▸ noun **1** a small part or quantity of something intended to show what the whole is or will be like. **2** a specimen taken for scientific testing.

SYNONYMS **1** *a sample of the fabric* **specimen**, example, snippet, swatch, taste, taster. **2** *a representative sample* **cross section**, selection.

▸ adjective produced to show what a larger version is or will be like.

SYNONYMS *a sample copy* **specimen**, test, trial, pilot, dummy.

▸ verb (samples, sampling, sampled) **1** take a sample of. **2** try out. **3** take a short extract from one musical recording and reuse it as part of another recording.

SYNONYMS *we sampled the food* **try (out)**, taste, test, put to the test, appraise, evaluate; informal check out.

sampler ▸ noun **1** a piece of fabric decorated with a number of different embroidery stitches. **2** a device for sampling music.

samurai /sam-yuu-ry/ ▸ noun (plural samurai) (in the past) a member of a powerful Japanese military class.

sanatorium ▸ noun (plural sanatoriums or sanatoria) **1** a place like a hospital where people who have a long-term illness or who are recovering from an illness are treated. **2** Brit. a place in a boarding school for children who are ill.

sanctify ▸ verb (sanctifies, sanctifying, sanctified) **1** make something holy. **2** make something legal or right.
□ **sanctification** noun.

sanctimonious ▸ adjective disapproving making a show of being morally superior to other people.

sanction ▸ noun **1** (sanctions) measures taken by a state to try to force another state to behave well. **2** a penalty for disobeying a law or rule. **3** official permission or approval.

SYNONYMS **1** *trade sanctions* **penalty**, punishment, deterrent, restriction, embargo, ban, prohibition, boycott. **2** *the scheme has the sanction of the court* **authorization**, consent, leave, permission, authority, dispensation, assent, acquiescence, agreement, approval, endorsement, blessing; informal

s

the thumbs up, the OK.
ANTONYMS reward, prohibition.

▶ verb give official permission for.

SYNONYMS *the rally was sanctioned by the government* **authorize**, permit, allow, endorse, approve, accept, back, support; informal OK.
ANTONYMS prohibit.

sanctity ▶ noun (plural **sanctities**) **1** the state of being holy. **2** the state of being very important.

sanctuary ▶ noun (plural **sanctuaries**) **1** a place of safety. **2** a nature reserve. **3** a place where injured or unwanted animals are cared for. **4** a holy place. **5** the part of the chancel of a church containing the high altar.

SYNONYMS **1** *the garden is our sanctuary* **refuge**, haven, oasis, shelter, retreat, bolt-hole, hideaway. **2** *he was given sanctuary in the embassy* **safety**, protection, shelter, immunity, asylum. **3** *a bird sanctuary* **reserve**, park.

sanctum ▶ noun **1** a sacred place. **2** a private place.

sand ▶ noun **1** a substance consisting of very fine particles resulting from the wearing down of rocks, found in beaches and deserts and on the seabed. **2** (**sands**) a wide area of sand.

▶ verb smooth a surface with sandpaper or a sander.

sandal ▶ noun a shoe with a partly open upper part or straps attaching the sole to the foot.

sandalwood ▶ noun the sweet-smelling wood of an Asian tree.

sandbag ▶ noun a bag of sand, used to protect or strengthen a structure or as a weight.

sandbank ▶ noun a deposit of sand forming a shallow area in the sea or a river.

sandbar ▶ noun a long, narrow sandbank.

sandblast ▶ verb roughen or clean a surface with a jet of sand.

sandcastle ▶ noun a model of a castle built out of sand.

sander ▶ noun a power tool used for smoothing a surface.

sandpaper ▶ noun paper coated with sand or another rough substance, used for smoothing surfaces.

▶ verb smooth with sandpaper.

sandpiper ▶ noun a wading bird with a long bill and long legs.

sandpit ▶ noun Brit. a shallow box or hollow containing sand, for children to play in.

sandstone ▶ noun rock formed from compressed sand.

sandstorm ▶ noun a strong wind in a desert carrying clouds of sand.

sandwich ▶ noun two pieces of bread with a filling between them.

▶ verb (**sandwich someone/thing between**) squeeze someone or something between two people or things.
■ **sandwich board** a pair of boards hung in front of and behind a person's body as they walk around, used especially to advertise something. **sandwich course** Brit. a course of study which includes periods working in business or industry.

sandy ▶ adjective (**sandier, sandiest**) **1** covered in or consisting of sand. **2** light yellowish brown.

sane ▶ adjective **1** not mad. **2** sensible.

SYNONYMS **1** *he is presumed to be sane* **of sound mind**, in your right mind, compos mentis, lucid, rational, balanced, normal; informal all there. **2** *a sane suggestion* **sensible**, practical, realistic, prudent, reasonable, rational, level-headed.
ANTONYMS mad, foolish.

sang past of SING.

sangfroid /song-frwah/ ▶ noun the ability to stay calm in difficult circumstances.

sangria ▶ noun a Spanish drink of red wine and lemonade with fruit and spices.

sanguinary /sang-gwi-nuh-ri/ ▶ adjective old use involving a lot of bloodshed.

sanguine /sang-gwin/ ▶ adjective cheerful and confident about things that are going to happen.

sanitarium US = SANATORIUM.

sanitary ▶ adjective **1** relating to sanitation. **2** hygienic.
■ **sanitary towel** a pad worn by women to absorb blood during a menstrual period.

sanitation ▶ noun arrangements to protect public health, such as the provision of clean drinking water and the disposal of sewage.

sanitize (or **sanitise**) ▶ verb (**sanitizes, sanitizing, sanitized**) **1** make something hygienic. **2** make something unpleasant seem more acceptable.

sanity ▶ noun **1** the condition of being sane. **2** reasonable behaviour.

sank past of SINK.

Sanskrit /san-skrit/ ▶ noun an ancient language of India.

Santa Claus ▶ noun Father Christmas.

sap ▶ noun the liquid that circulates in plants, carrying food to all parts.

SYNONYMS *tree sap* **juice**, secretion, fluid, liquid.

▶ verb (**saps, sapping, sapped**) gradually weaken a person's strength.

S

SYNONYMS *illness sapped his energy* **erode,** wear away/down, deplete, reduce, lessen, undermine, drain, bleed.

sapient /**say**-pi-uhnt/ ▶ adjective formal wise or intelligent.

sapling ▶ noun a young tree.

sapper ▶ noun a military engineer who lays or finds and defuses mines or (Brit.) a soldier in the Royal Engineers.

sapphic /**saf**-fik/ ▶ adjective literary relating to lesbians.

sapphire /**saf**-fy-er/ ▶ noun 1 a transparent blue precious stone. 2 a bright blue colour.

saprophyte /**sap**-ruh-fyt/ ▶ noun a plant or fungus that lives on decaying matter.
□ **saprophytic** adjective.

Saracen ▶ noun an Arab or Muslim at the time of the Crusades.

sarcasm ▶ noun the use of words which say the opposite of what you mean, as a way of hurting or mocking someone.

sarcastic ▶ adjective using sarcasm.
□ **sarcastically** adverb.

sarcoma /sar-**koh**-muh/ ▶ noun (plural **sarcomas**) a cancer that grows in parts of the body such as muscle or bone.

sarcophagus /sar-**kof**-fuh-guhss/ ▶ noun (plural **sarcophagi** /sar-**kof**-fuh-gy/) a stone coffin.

sardine ▶ noun a small edible sea fish.

sardonic ▶ adjective mocking.
□ **sardonically** adverb.

sari (or **saree**) ▶ noun (plural **saris** or **sarees**) a length of fabric draped around the body, worn by women from the Indian subcontinent.

sarky ▶ adjective Brit. informal sarcastic.
□ **sarkily** adverb.

sarnie ▶ noun Brit. informal a sandwich.

sarong ▶ noun a long piece of cloth wrapped round the body and tucked at the waist or under the armpits.

sartorial ▶ adjective having to do with the way a person dresses.
□ **sartorially** adverb.

sash[1] ▶ noun a strip of fabric worn over one shoulder or round the waist.

sash[2] ▶ noun a frame holding the glass in a window.
■ **sash window** a window with two sashes which can be slid up and down to open it.

sashay ▶ verb informal swing the hips from side to side when walking.

Sassenach /**sass**-uh-nak/ Scottish Irish disapproving ▶ noun an English person.
▶ adjective English.

sassy ▶ adjective (**sassier, sassiest**) informal confident, spirited, and cheeky.

SAT ▶ abbreviation standard assessment task.

sat past and past participle of SIT.

Satan ▶ noun the Devil.

satanic ▶ adjective having to do with Satan or the worship of Satan.

SYNONYMS **diabolical,** fiendish, devilish, demonic, ungodly, hellish, infernal, wicked, evil, sinful.
ANTONYMS godly.

satanism ▶ noun the worship of Satan.
□ **satanist** noun & adjective.

satay (or **saté**) /**sat**-ay/ ▶ noun an Indonesian and Malaysian dish consisting of small pieces of meat grilled on a skewer, usually served with a peanut sauce.

satchel ▶ noun a bag with a long strap worn over one shoulder.

sated ▶ adjective having had as much as or more of something than you want.

satellite ▶ noun 1 a man-made device placed in orbit round the earth or another planet in order to collect information or for communication. 2 a celestial body that moves in orbit round a planet. 3 a thing that is separate from but controlled by something else.
■ **satellite television** television in which the signals are broadcast via satellite.

satiate /**say**-shi-ayt/ ▶ verb give someone as much or more of something than they want.
□ **satiation** noun.

satiety /suh-**ty**-i-ti/ ▶ noun the state of being fully satisfied or of having had too much of something.

satin ▶ noun a smooth, glossy fabric.
□ **satiny** adjective.

satire /**sa**-ty-er/ ▶ noun 1 the use of humour, irony, exaggeration, or ridicule to reveal and criticize people's bad points. 2 a play or other piece of writing that uses satire.

SYNONYMS **parody,** burlesque, caricature, irony, lampoon, skit; informal spoof, take-off, send-up.
□ **satirist** noun.

satirical (or **satiric**) ▶ adjective using satire.

SYNONYMS **mocking,** ironic, sardonic, critical, irreverent, disparaging, disrespectful.
□ **satirically** adverb.

satirize (or **satirise**) /**sat**-i-ryz/ ▶ verb (**satirizes, satirizing, satirized**) mock or criticize using satire.

satisfaction ▶ noun the feeling of pleasure that arises when you have the things you need or want or when the things you want to happen have happened.

SYNONYMS **contentment,** content, pleasure, gratification, fulfilment, enjoyment, happiness, pride.

S

satisfactory ▸ adjective acceptable.

> SYNONYMS **adequate**, all right, acceptable,
> good enough, sufficient, reasonable,
> competent, fair, decent, average,
> passable, fine, in order, up to scratch, up
> to the mark.
> ANTONYMS unsatisfactory.

□ **satisfactorily** adverb.

satisfy ▸ verb (**satisfies, satisfying, satisfied**)
1 give someone the things they need or
want or bring about the things they want
to happen. **2** meet a particular demand,
desire, or need.

> SYNONYMS **1** *a chance to satisfy his lust*
> **fulfil**, gratify, meet, fill, indulge,
> appease, assuage, quench, slake, satiate.
> **2** *she satisfied herself that it was an
> accident* **convince**, assure, reassure.
> **3** *products which satisfy EC law* **comply
> with**, meet, fulfil, answer, conform to,
> measure up to, come up to.
> ANTONYMS frustrate.

satsuma /sat-**soo**-muh/ ▸ noun a kind of
tangerine with a loose skin.

saturate ▸ verb (**saturates, saturating,
saturated**) **1** soak thoroughly with a liquid.
2 make a substance combine with, dissolve,
or hold the greatest possible quantity of
another substance. **3** put more than is
needed of a particular product into the
market.

> SYNONYMS **1** *rain had saturated the ground*
> **soak**, drench, waterlog. **2** *the company
> has saturated the market* **flood**, glut,
> oversupply, overfill, overload.

□ **saturation** noun.

saturated ▸ adjective Chemistry (of fats)
having only single bonds between carbon
atoms in their molecules and therefore
being less easily processed by the body.

> SYNONYMS **1** *his trousers were saturated*
> **soaked**, soaking (wet), wet through,
> sopping (wet), sodden, dripping,
> wringing wet, drenched, soaked to the
> skin. **2** *the saturated pitch* **waterlogged**,
> flooded, boggy, awash.
> ANTONYMS dry.

Saturday ▸ noun the day of the week before
Sunday and following Friday.

Saturn ▸ noun the sixth planet from the sun
in the solar system, circled by broad flat
rings.

saturnine /sat-er-nyn/ ▸ adjective **1** (of
a person or their manner) gloomy. **2** (of
looks) dark and brooding.

satyr /sat-er/ ▸ noun (in Greek mythology) a
lecherous woodland god, with a man's face
and body and a horse's or goat's ears, tail,
and legs.

sauce ▸ noun **1** a thick liquid served with

food to add moistness and flavour. **2** informal
cheeky talk or behaviour.

> SYNONYMS **relish**, condiment, ketchup,
> dip, dressing, jus, coulis, gravy.

■ **sauce boat** a boat-shaped jug for serving
sauce.

saucepan ▸ noun a deep cooking pan, with
one long handle and a lid.

saucer ▸ noun a small shallow dish on which
a cup stands.

saucy ▸ adjective (**saucier, sauciest**) informal
1 sexually suggestive in a light-hearted
way. **2** cheeky.
□ **saucily** adverb.

Saudi /**sow**-di/ ▸ noun (plural **Saudis**) a person
from Saudi Arabia.
▸ adjective relating to Saudi Arabia.

sauerkraut /**sow**-er-krowt/ ▸ noun a
German dish of pickled cabbage.

sauna /**saw**-nuh/ ▸ noun **1** a small room
used as a hot-air or steam bath for cleaning
and refreshing the body. **2** a session in a
sauna.

saunter ▸ verb (**saunters, sauntering,
sauntering**) walk in a slow, relaxed way.
▸ noun a leisurely stroll.

sausage ▸ noun **1** a short tube of raw
minced meat encased in a skin and grilled
or fried before eating. **2** a tube of seasoned
minced meat that is cooked or preserved
and eaten cold in slices.
■ **sausage dog** Brit. informal a dachshund.
sausage meat minced meat used in
sausages or as a stuffing. **sausage roll** a
portion of sausage meat baked in a roll of
pastry.

sauté /**soh**-tay/ ▸ adjective fried quickly in
shallow fat or oil.
▸ verb (**sautés, sautéing, sautéed** or **sautéd**)
cook in such a way.

Sauvignon /**soh**-vin-yon/ ▸ noun a type of
white wine.

savage ▸ adjective **1** fierce and violent.
2 cruel and vicious. **3** primitive and
uncivilized.

> SYNONYMS **1** *savage dogs* **ferocious**,
> fierce, vicious, wild, feral. **2** *a savage
> assault* **vicious**, brutal, cruel, sadistic,
> ferocious, fierce, violent. **3** *a savage
> attack on free trade* **fierce**, blistering,
> scathing, searing, stinging, devastating,
> withering, virulent, vitriolic.
> ANTONYMS tame, mild.

▸ noun **1** a member of a people seen as
primitive and uncivilized. **2** a brutal
person.

> SYNONYMS *she described her assailants as
> savages* **brute**, beast, monster, barbarian,
> sadist, animal.

▸ verb (**savages, savaging, savaged**) **1** attack
ferociously; maul. **2** criticize severely.

S

SYNONYMS **1** *savaged by a dog* **maul,** attack, lacerate, claw, bite. **2** *critics savaged the film* **criticize,** attack, lambaste, condemn, denounce, pillory, revile; informal **pan;** Brit. informal **slate;** N. Amer. informal **trash.**

□ **savagely** adverb **savagery** noun.

savannah (or **savanna**) ▶ noun a grassy plain in hot regions.

savant (or **savante**) /sav-uhnt/ ▶ noun a wise and knowledgeable person.

save¹ ▶ verb (**saves, saving, saved**) **1** rescue or protect someone or something from harm or danger. **2** prevent someone from dying. **3** store or keep for future use. **4** (in computing) store data. **5** avoid, lessen, or guard against. **6** prevent an opponent from scoring a goal. **7** (in Christian use) prevent a soul from being damned.

SYNONYMS **1** *the captain was saved by his crew* **rescue,** set free, free, liberate, deliver. **2** *the house was saved from demolition* **preserve,** keep, protect, safeguard, salvage, retrieve, reclaim, rescue. **3** *start saving old newspapers* **put/set aside,** put by/to one side, keep, retain, store, hoard; informal **squirrel away. 4** *asking her saved a lot of trouble* **prevent,** avoid, forestall, spare, stop, obviate, avert.

▶ noun an act of preventing an opponent's goal.

□ **saver** noun.

save² ▶ preposition & conjunction formal except.

saveloy /sav-uh-loy/ ▶ noun Brit. a smoked pork sausage.

saving ▶ noun **1** a reduction in money, time, or some other resource. **2** (**savings**) money saved.

SYNONYMS **1** *a considerable saving in cost* **reduction,** cut, decrease, economy. **2** (**savings**) **nest egg,** capital, assets, funds, resources, reserves.

▶ preposition except.

■ **saving grace** a good quality that makes up for someone or something's faults.

saviour (US spelling **savior**) ▶ noun **1** a person who saves someone or something from danger or harm. **2** (**Saviour**) (in Christianity) God or Jesus.

SYNONYMS **rescuer,** liberator, deliverer, champion, protector, redeemer.

savoir faire /sav-war fair/ ▶ noun the ability to act appropriately in social situations.

savory ▶ noun a plant used as a herb in cookery.

savour (US spelling **savor**) ▶ verb **1** eat or drink something slowly while enjoying its full flavour. **2** enjoy a feeling or experience thoroughly.

SYNONYMS *she savoured every moment* **relish,** enjoy, appreciate, delight in, revel in, luxuriate in.

▶ noun a characteristic flavour or smell.

SYNONYMS *the subtle savour of wood smoke* **smell,** aroma, fragrance, scent, perfume, bouquet, taste, flavour, tang, smack.

savoury (US spelling **savory**) ▶ adjective **1** (of food) salty or spicy rather than sweet. **2** morally acceptable or respectable.

▶ noun (plural **savouries**) Brit. a savoury snack.

savoy ▶ noun a type of cabbage.

savvy informal ▶ noun intelligence and good judgement.

▶ adjective having intelligence and good judgement.

saw¹ ▶ noun a tool with a long, thin jagged blade, used with a backwards and forwards movement to cut wood and other hard materials.

▶ verb (**saws, sawing, sawed**; past participle Brit. **sawn** or N. Amer. **sawed**) cut through or cut off with a saw.

saw² past of SEE¹.

saw³ ▶ noun a proverb or wise saying.

sawdust ▶ noun powdery particles of wood produced by sawing.

sawmill ▶ noun a place where logs are sawn by machine.

sawtooth (or **sawtoothed**) ▶ adjective shaped like the jagged teeth of a saw.

sawyer ▶ noun a person who saws timber.

sax ▶ noun informal a saxophone.

saxifrage /saks-i-frayj/ ▶ noun a plant which grows on rocky or stony ground, with small red, white, or yellow flowers.

Saxon ▶ noun a member of a people from Germany that settled in southern England in the 5th and 6th centuries.

saxophone ▶ noun a metal wind instrument with a reed in the mouthpiece.

□ **saxophonist** noun.

say ▶ verb (**says, saying, said**) **1** speak words to communicate something. **2** (of a piece of writing or a symbol) convey information or instructions. **3** (of a clock or watch) indicate a time. **4** (**be said**) be reported. **5** assume something in order to work out what its consequences would be.

SYNONYMS **1** *he said her name* **speak,** utter, voice, pronounce. **2** *'I must go,'* she *said* **declare,** state, announce, remark, observe, mention, comment, note, add. **3** *they said a prayer* **recite,** repeat, utter, deliver, perform. **4** *her watch said one twenty* **indicate,** show, read.

▶ noun an opportunity to state your opinion.

saying ▶ noun a well-known statement expressing a general truth.

scab ▶ noun **1** a crust that forms over a wound as it heals. **2** informal, disapproving a person who refuses to take part in a strike. □ **scabby** adjective.

scabbard ▶ noun a cover for the blade of a sword or dagger.

scabies ▶ noun a skin disease that causes itching and small red spots.

scabrous ▶ adjective **1** rough and covered with scabs. **2** indecent or sordid.

scaffold ▶ noun **1** (in the past) a raised wooden platform on which people stood when they were to be executed. **2** a structure made using scaffolding.

scaffolding ▶ noun **1** a structure made of wooden planks and metal poles, for people to stand on when building or repairing a building. **2** the planks and poles used in such a structure.

scald ▶ verb **1** burn with very hot liquid or steam. **2** heat a liquid to near boiling point. **3** dip something briefly in boiling water.
▶ noun an injury caused by hot liquid or steam.

scale¹ ▶ noun **1** each of the small overlapping plates protecting the skin of fish and reptiles. **2** a dry flake of skin. **3** a white deposit which is left in a kettle, water pipe, etc. when water containing lime is heated. **4** a hard deposit that forms on teeth.
▶ verb (**scales, scaling, scaled**) **1** remove the scales from. **2** form or flake off in scales.

scale² ▶ noun **1** (usu. **scales**) an instrument for weighing. **2** either of the dishes on a simple set of scales.

scale³ ▶ noun **1** a range of values forming a system for measuring or grading something. **2** a measuring instrument based on such a system. **3** relative size or extent. **4** a ratio of size in a map, model, drawing, or plan. **5** Music an arrangement of notes in order of pitch.

▶ verb (**scales, scaling, scaled**) **1** climb up or over something high and steep. **2** (**scale something down** or **up**) reduce (or increase) something in size, number, or extent. **3** represent something in a size that is larger or smaller than the original but exactly in proportion to it.

■ **to scale** reduced or enlarged in proportion to something.

scallion ▶ noun N. Amer. a spring onion.

scallop /skol-luhp, skal-luhp/ ▶ noun **1** an edible shellfish with two hinged fan-shaped shells. **2** each of a series of small curves like the edge of a scallop shell, forming a decorative edging.

scalloped ▶ adjective (of the edge of something) decorated with a series of small curves.

scallywag ▶ noun informal a mischievous person.

scalp ▶ noun **1** the skin covering the top and back of the head. **2** (in the past, among American Indians) the scalp and hair cut away from an enemy's head as a battle trophy.
▶ verb historical take the scalp of an enemy.

scalpel ▶ noun a knife with a small sharp blade, used by a surgeon.

scaly ▶ adjective (**scalier, scaliest**) **1** covered in scales. **2** (of skin) dry and flaking.

scam ▶ noun informal a dishonest scheme for making money.

scamp ▶ noun informal a mischievous person.

scamper ▶ verb (**scampers, scampering, scampered**) run with quick light steps.

scampi ▶ plural noun the tails of large prawns, covered in breadcrumbs or batter and fried.

scan ▶ verb (**scans, scanning, scanned**) **1** look at something quickly in order to find the parts that are most relevant or important. **2** move a detector or beam across. **3** convert a document or picture into digital form for storing or processing on a computer. **4** analyse the metre of a line of verse. **5** (of poetry) follow metrical rules.

▶ noun **1** an act of scanning. **2** a medical examination using a scanner. **3** an image obtained by scanning.

scandal ▶ noun **1** an action or event that causes public outrage. **2** outrage or gossip arising from such an action or event. **3** an action or situation that you find shocking and unacceptable.

> SYNONYMS **1** *a scandal that led him to resign* **affair,** issue, incident, outrage, skeleton in the cupboard; informal ...-gate. **2** *it's a scandal* **disgrace,** outrage, (crying) shame, sin. **3** *a name tarnished by scandal* **gossip,** rumour(s), slander, libel, aspersions, muckraking; informal **dirt.**

scandalize (or **scandalise**) ▶ verb (**scandalizes, scandalizing, scandalized**) shock other people by acting in way that is considered shameful or immoral.

scandalous ▶ adjective **1** causing public outrage. **2** shocking and unacceptable.
□ **scandalously** adverb.

Scandinavian ▶ adjective relating to the countries of Scandinavia, especially Norway, Sweden, and Denmark.
▶ noun a person from Scandinavia.

scandium ▶ noun a soft silvery-white metallic element.

scanner ▶ noun **1** a machine that uses X-rays or ultrasound to record images, used by doctors to examine the inside of someone's body. **2** a device that scans documents or pictures and converts them into digital data.

scansion ▶ noun **1** the action of scanning a line of verse to find out its rhythm. **2** the rhythm of a line of verse.

scant ▶ adjective barely reaching the amount specified or needed.

> SYNONYMS **little,** little or no, minimal, limited, negligible, meagre, insufficient, inadequate.
> ANTONYMS abundant, ample.

scanty ▶ adjective (**scantier, scantiest**) too little in size or amount for what is needed.
□ **scantily** adverb.

scapegoat ▶ noun a person who is blamed for the things other people do wrong.

> SYNONYMS **whipping boy,** Aunt Sally; informal **fall guy;** N. Amer. informal **patsy.**

▶ verb make a scapegoat of.

scapula ▶ noun the shoulder blade.

scar¹ ▶ noun **1** a mark left on the skin or in body tissue after the healing of a wound. **2** a lasting effect left after an unpleasant experience. **3** a mark left at the point where a leaf or other part separates from a plant.

> SYNONYMS **1** *the scar on his arm* **mark,** blemish, disfigurement, discoloration, pockmark, pit, lesion, stitches. **2** *psychological scars* **trauma,** damage, injury.

▶ verb (**scars, scarring, scarred**) mark or be marked with a scar.

> SYNONYMS *scarred for life* **disfigure,** mark, blemish.

scar² ▶ noun a steep high cliff or outcrop of rock.

scarab /ska-ruhb/ ▶ noun **1** a kind of large beetle, seen as sacred in ancient Egypt. **2** an ancient Egyptian gem in the form of a scarab beetle.

scarce ▶ adjective **1** (of a resource) only available in small quantities that do not meet a demand. **2** rarely found.

> SYNONYMS **1** *food was scarce* **in short supply,** scant, meagre, sparse, hard to come by. **2** *wading birds are now scarce* **rare,** few and far between, thin on the ground.
> ANTONYMS plentiful.

□ **scarcity** noun.

scarcely ▶ adverb **1** only just. **2** just moments before. **3** definitely or very probably not.

> SYNONYMS **1** *she could scarcely hear him* **hardly,** barely, only just. **2** *I scarcely see her* **rarely,** seldom, infrequently, not often, hardly ever; informal once in a blue moon. **3** *this could scarcely be an accident* **surely not,** not, hardly.
> ANTONYMS often.

scare ▶ verb (**scares, scaring, scared**) **1** frighten or become frightened. **2** (**scare someone away** or **off**) drive or keep someone away by frightening them.

> SYNONYMS **1** *stop it, you're scaring me* **frighten,** startle, alarm, terrify, unnerve, worry, intimidate, terrorize, cow; informal freak out; Brit. informal put the wind up; N. Amer. informal spook. **2** (**scared**) **frightened,** afraid, fearful, nervous, panicky, terrified; informal in a cold sweat; N. Amer. informal **spooked.**

▶ noun **1** a sudden attack of fright. **2** a period of general alarm.

> SYNONYMS *you gave me a scare* **fright,** shock, start, turn, jump.

scarecrow ▶ noun an object made to look like a person, set up to scare birds away from crops.

scarf ▶ noun (plural **scarves** or **scarfs**) a length or square of fabric worn around the neck or head.

scarify ▶ verb (**scarifies, scarifying, scarified**) **1** rake out unwanted material from a lawn. **2** break up the surface of soil. **3** make shallow cuts in the skin.

scarlatina (or **scarletina**) ▶ noun scarlet fever.

scarlet ▶ noun a bright red colour.
■ **scarlet fever** an infectious disease that affects children, causing fever and a scarlet rash.

s

scarp ▸ noun a very steep slope.

scarper ▸ verb (**scarpers, scarpering, scarpered**) Brit. informal run away.

scarves plural of **SCARF**.

scary ▸ adjective (**scarier, scariest**) informal frightening.

> SYNONYMS **frightening,** terrifying, hair-raising, spine-chilling, blood-curdling, eerie, sinister; informal creepy, spine-tingling, spooky.

□ **scarily** adverb.

scathing ▸ adjective severely critical.
□ **scathingly** adverb.

scatological ▸ adjective obsessed with excrement and excretion.
□ **scatology** noun.

scatter ▸ verb (**scatters, scattering, scattered**) **1** throw in various random directions. **2** separate and move off in different directions. **3** (**be scattered**) be found at various places.

> SYNONYMS **1** *scatter the seeds evenly* **spread,** sprinkle, distribute, strew, disseminate, sow. **2** *the crowd scattered* **disperse,** break up, disband, separate, dissolve. **3** *the floor was scattered with books* **cover,** dot, sprinkle, spot, pepper, litter.
> ANTONYMS gather, assemble.

scatty (or **scatterbrained**) ▸ adjective informal disorganized and rather silly.

scavenge ▸ verb (**scavenges, scavenging, scavenged**) **1** search through waste for anything that can be used again. **2** (of an animal) search for and eat dead animals.
□ **scavenger** noun.

scenario ▸ noun (plural **scenarios**) **1** a possible sequence of events in the future. **2** a written outline of a film, play, or novel.

> SYNONYMS **1** *Walt wrote scenarios for various studios* **plot,** outline, storyline, framework, screenplay, script. **2** *consider every possible scenario* **situation,** chain of events, course of events.

scene ▸ noun **1** the place where an incident happens. **2** a view or landscape as seen by a spectator. **3** an incident: *scenes of violence.* **4** a sequence of continuous action in a play, film, etc. **5** an area of activity or interest: *the literary scene.* **6** a public display of emotion or anger.

> SYNONYMS **1** *the scene of the accident* **location,** site, place, position. **2** *the scene is London in the 1890s* **background,** setting, context, milieu, backdrop. **3** *scenes of violence* **incident,** event, episode, happening. **4** *an impressive mountain scene* **view,** vista, outlook, panorama, landscape, scenery. **5** *she made a scene* **fuss,** exhibition of yourself,

performance, tantrum, commotion, disturbance, row; informal carry-on. **6** *the political scene* **arena,** stage, sphere, world, milieu, realm. **7** *a scene from a movie* **clip,** section, segment, part, sequence, extract.

■ **behind the scenes** out of public view.

scenery ▸ noun **1** a landscape considered in terms of its appearance. **2** the background used to represent a place on a stage or film set.

> SYNONYMS **1** *beautiful scenery* **landscape,** countryside, country, terrain, setting, surroundings, environment. **2** *scenery and costumes* **set,** setting, backdrop.

scenic ▸ adjective having beautiful natural scenery.

> SYNONYMS **picturesque,** pretty, attractive, beautiful, charming, impressive, striking, spectacular, breathtaking, panoramic.

□ **scenically** adverb.

scent ▸ noun **1** a distinctive smell, especially a pleasant one. **2** pleasant-smelling liquid worn on the skin; perfume. **3** a trail left by an animal, indicated by its smell.

> SYNONYMS **1** *the scent of freshly cut hay* **smell,** fragrance, aroma, perfume, savour, odour. **2** *a bottle of scent* **perfume,** fragrance, eau de toilette, eau de cologne. **3** *the hounds picked up the scent* **spoor,** trail, track.

▸ verb **1** give a pleasant scent to. **2** find or recognize something by using the sense of smell. **3** sense that something is about to happen.

> SYNONYMS **1** (**scented**) **perfumed,** fragranced, fragrant, sweet-smelling, aromatic. **2** *sharks soon scent the blood* **smell,** nose out, detect, pick up, sense.

sceptic /skep-tik/ (US spelling **skeptic**) ▸ noun a person who questions accepted opinions.

> SYNONYMS **cynic,** doubter, unbeliever, doubting Thomas.

sceptical (US spelling **skeptical**) ▸ adjective not easily convinced; having doubts.

> SYNONYMS **dubious,** doubtful, doubting, cynical, distrustful, suspicious, disbelieving, unconvinced.
> ANTONYMS certain, convinced.

□ **sceptically** adverb.

scepticism ▸ noun a sceptical attitude.

> SYNONYMS **doubt,** a pinch of salt, disbelief, cynicism, distrust, suspicion, incredulity.

sceptre /sep-ter/ (US spelling **scepter**) ▸ noun a decorated rod carried by a king or queen on ceremonial occasions.

S

schedule /shed-yool, sked-yool/ ▸ noun 1 a plan for doing something, with a list of intended events and times. 2 a timetable.

SYNONYMS 1 *our production schedule* **plan**, programme, timetable, scheme. 2 *I have a busy schedule* **timetable**, agenda, diary, calendar, itinerary.

▸ verb (**schedules, scheduling, scheduled**) 1 plan for something to happen at a particular time. 2 (**scheduled**) (of a flight) forming part of a regular service rather than specially chartered.

SYNONYMS *a meeting has been scheduled* **arrange**, organize, plan, programme, timetable, set up, line up; N. Amer. slate.

schema /skee-muh/ ▸ noun (plural **schemata** /skee-muh-tuh/ or **schemas**) technical an outline of a plan or theory.

schematic ▸ adjective 1 (of a diagram) simplified and using symbols. 2 presented according to a plan.
□ **schematically** adverb.

scheme ▸ noun 1 a careful plan for achieving something. 2 a secret or devious plan; a plot. 3 a system or pattern.

SYNONYMS 1 *fund-raising schemes* **plan**, project, programme, strategy, stratagem, tactic; Brit. informal wheeze. 2 *his schemes and plots* **plot**, intrigue, conspiracy, ruse, ploy, stratagem, manoeuvre, subterfuge, machinations; informal racket, scam.

▸ verb (**schemes, scheming, schemed**) make secret plans; plot.

SYNONYMS 1 *he schemed endlessly* **plot**, conspire, intrigue, connive, manoeuvre, plan. 2 (**scheming**) **cunning**, crafty, calculating, devious, conniving, wily, sly, tricky, artful.

scherzo /skair-tsoh/ ▸ noun (plural **scherzos** or **scherzi** /skair-tsi/) a short, lively piece of music.

schism /si-z'm, ski-z'm/ ▸ noun a disagreement or division between two groups or within an organization.
□ **schismatic** adjective.

schist /shist/ ▸ noun a metamorphic rock which consists of layers of different minerals.

schizoid /skit-soyd/ ▸ adjective having a mental condition similar to schizophrenia.

schizophrenia ▸ noun a mental disorder whose symptoms include a withdrawal from reality into fantasy.

schizophrenic ▸ adjective 1 suffering from schizophrenia. 2 having contradictory elements.
▸ noun a schizophrenic person.

schmaltz ▸ noun informal the quality of being too sentimental.
□ **schmaltzy** adjective.

schnapps ▸ noun a strong alcoholic drink.

scholar ▸ noun 1 a person who is studying at an advanced level. 2 a student who has a scholarship.

SYNONYMS **academic**, intellectual, learned person, man/woman of letters, authority, expert; informal egghead; N. Amer. informal pointy-head.

scholarly ▸ adjective 1 relating to serious academic study. 2 very knowledgeable and keen on studying.

SYNONYMS **learned**, educated, erudite, academic, well read, intellectual, literary, highbrow.
ANTONYMS uneducated, illiterate.

scholarship ▸ noun 1 academic work. 2 an amount of money given to a student to help pay for their education.

SYNONYMS 1 *a centre of scholarship* **learning**, knowledge, erudition, education, academic study. 2 *a scholarship of £2,000* **grant**, award, endowment; Brit. bursary.

scholastic ▸ adjective having to do with schools and education.

school ▸ noun 1 a place where children are educated. 2 a place where instruction is given in a particular subject. 3 a group of artists, philosophers, etc. sharing similar ideas. 4 a large group of fish or sea mammals.

SYNONYMS 1 *the village school* **college**, academy, alma mater. 2 *the university's School of English* **department**, faculty, division. 3 *the Columbia school of history* **tradition**, approach, style, way of thinking, persuasion, creed, credo, doctrine, belief, opinion, point of view.

▸ verb 1 formal or N. Amer. educate. 2 train in a particular skill or activity.

SYNONYMS *he schooled her in horsemanship* **train**, teach, tutor, coach, instruct, drill.

■ **school of thought** a particular way of thinking.

schooling ▸ noun education received at school.

schooner /skoo-ner/ ▸ noun 1 a sailing ship with two or more masts. 2 Brit. a large glass for sherry.

sciatic /sy-at-ik/ ▸ adjective having to do with the hip or with the nerve which goes down the back of the thigh (the **sciatic nerve**).

sciatica ▸ noun pain affecting the back, hip, and leg, caused by pressure on the sciatic nerve.

science ▸ noun 1 study or knowledge of the physical and natural world, based on observation and experiment. **2** a particular branch of science. **3** a body of knowledge on any subject.

> SYNONYMS *the science of criminology* **subject,** discipline, field, branch of knowledge, body of knowledge, area of study.

■ **science fiction** fiction set in the future and dealing with imagined scientific advances. **science park** an area where a number of science-based companies are located.

scientific ▶ adjective **1** relating to or based on science. **2** systematic; methodical.

> SYNONYMS **1** *scientific research* **technological,** technical, evidence-based, empirical. **2** *a more scientific approach* **systematic,** methodical, organized, ordered, rigorous, exact, precise, accurate, mathematical.

□ **scientifically** adverb.

scientist ▶ noun a person who studies or is an expert in science.

sci-fi ▶ noun science fiction.

scimitar /sim-i-ter/ ▶ noun a short sword with a curved blade.

scintillating ▶ adjective very skilful and exciting.

scion /sy-uhn/ ▶ noun **1** a young shoot or twig of a plant. **2** literary a descendant of a notable family.

scissors ▶ plural noun a device for cutting cloth and paper, consisting of two crossing blades pivoted in the middle.

sclerosis ▶ noun **1** abnormal hardening of body tissue. **2** (also **multiple sclerosis**) a serious disease of the nervous system that can cause partial paralysis.

scoff¹ ▶ verb speak about something in a scornful way.

> SYNONYMS **sneer,** jeer, laugh; (**scoff at**) mock, deride, ridicule, dismiss, belittle; informal pooh-pooh.

scoff² ▶ verb informal eat something quickly and greedily.

scold ▶ verb angrily criticize or tell off.

sconce ▶ noun a candle holder attached to a wall.

scone /skon, skohn/ ▶ noun a small plain cake, usually eaten with butter.

scoop ▶ noun **1** an implement like a spoon, with a short handle and a deep bowl. **2** the bowl-shaped part of a digging machine. **3** informal a piece of news printed by one newspaper before its rivals.

> SYNONYMS *a measuring scoop* **spoon,** ladle, dipper.

▶ verb **1** pick something up with a scoop. **2** create a hollow or hole in something.

3 pick someone or something up in a quick, smooth movement. **4** informal be quicker than other newspapers to print a piece of news.

scoot ▶ verb informal move or go quickly.

scooter ▶ noun **1** (also **motor scooter**) a light motorcycle. **2** a child's vehicle with two wheels and a long steering handle, which you move by pushing one foot against the ground.

scope ▶ noun **1** the opportunity or possibility for doing something. **2** the extent of the area or subject matter that something deals with.

> SYNONYMS **1** *the scope of the investigation* **extent,** range, breadth, reach, sweep, span, area, sphere, realm, compass, orbit, ambit, terms of reference, remit. **2** *the scope for change is limited* **opportunity,** freedom, latitude, leeway, capacity, room (to manoeuvre).

scorch ▶ verb **1** burn something on the surface or edges. **2** (**scorched**) dried out and withered as a result of extreme heat.

> SYNONYMS **1** *trees were scorched by the fire* **burn,** sear, singe, char, blacken, discolour. **2** *grass scorched by the sun* **dry up,** parch, wither, shrivel. **3** (**scorching**) **hot,** red-hot, blazing, flaming, fiery, burning, blistering, searing; informal boiling, baking, sizzling.

scorcher ▶ noun informal a very hot day.

score ▶ noun **1** the number of points, goals, etc. achieved by a person or team in a game. **2** (plural **score**) a group or set of twenty. **3** (**scores of**) a lot of. **4** the written music for a composition.

> SYNONYMS **1** *the final score was 4–3* **result,** outcome, total, tally, count. **2** *an IQ score of 161* **rating,** grade, mark, percentage.

▶ verb (**scores, scoring, scored**) **1** win a point, goal, etc. in a game. **2** record the score during a game. **3** cut or scratch a mark on a surface. **4** (**score something out**) cross out a word or words. **5** arrange a piece of music.

> SYNONYMS **1** *he's scored 13 goals this season* **get,** gain, chalk up, achieve, make, record, rack up, notch up; informal bag, knock up. **2** *the piece was scored for horn and strings* **arrange,** set, adapt, orchestrate, write, compose. **3** *score the wood in criss-cross patterns* **scratch,** cut, notch, incise, scrape, nick, gouge.

scoreline ▶ noun Brit. the final score in a game.

scorn ▶ noun a strong feeling that someone or something is worthless; contempt.

> SYNONYMS *the scorn in his voice* **contempt,** derision, disdain, mockery, sneering. ANTONYMS admiration, respect.

S

▸ **verb 1** express scorn for. **2** reject in a contemptuous way.

> SYNONYMS **1** *critics scorned the talks* **deride**, treat with contempt, mock, scoff at, sneer at, jeer at, laugh at. **2** *they scorned my offers of help* **spurn**, rebuff, reject, ignore, shun, snub.
> ANTONYMS admire, respect.

scornful ▸ adjective showing or feeling scorn.
□ **scornfully** adverb.

Scorpio ▸ noun a sign of the zodiac (the Scorpion), 23 October–21 November.

scorpion ▸ noun a small creature with six legs, pincers, and a poisonous sting at the end of its tail.

Scot ▸ noun a person from Scotland.

Scotch ▸ noun (also **Scotch whisky**) whisky distilled in Scotland.
▸ adjective dated Scottish.
■ **Scotch egg** Brit. a hard-boiled egg enclosed in sausage meat.

> ! Use **Scots** or **Scottish** rather than **Scotch** to refer to people or things from Scotland.

scotch ▸ verb decisively put an end to.

scot-free ▸ adverb without suffering any punishment or injury.

Scots ▸ adjective Scottish.
▸ noun the form of English used in Scotland.

Scottie (or **Scottie dog**) ▸ noun informal a Scottish terrier.

Scottish ▸ adjective relating to Scotland or its people.
■ **Scottish terrier** a small breed of terrier with a rough coat.

scoundrel ▸ noun old use a dishonest or immoral person.

scour¹ ▸ verb clean by rubbing with rough material.

> SYNONYMS *the saucepan needs scouring* **scrub**, rub, clean, polish, buff, shine, burnish, grind, abrade.

scour² ▸ verb search a place thoroughly.

> SYNONYMS *Christine scoured the shops* **search**, comb, hunt through, rummage through, look high and low in, ransack, turn upside-down.

scourge /skerj/ ▸ noun **1** a cause of great suffering. **2** old use a whip.
▸ verb (**scourges, scourging, scourged**) **1** cause great suffering to. **2** old use whip someone.

Scouse Brit. informal ▸ noun **1** the dialect or accent of people from Liverpool. **2** (also **Scouser**) a person from Liverpool.

scout ▸ noun **1** a person who is sent ahead to gather information about the enemy. **2** a member of the Scout Association, an organization for young people. **3** (also **talent scout**) a person whose job is

searching for talented performers.

> SYNONYMS **1** *scouts reported that the Romans were advancing* **lookout**, outrider, spy. **2** *a lengthy scout round the area* **reconnaissance**, reconnoitre, survey, exploration, search; informal recce; Brit. informal shufti.

▸ **verb 1** search a place to find something or gather information. **2** act as a scout.

> SYNONYMS **1** *I scouted around for some logs* **search**, look, hunt, ferret around, root around. **2** *a patrol was sent to scout out the area* **reconnoitre**, explore, inspect, investigate, spy out, survey, scan, study; informal check out, case.

scowl ▸ noun a bad-tempered expression.
▸ verb frown in an angry or bad-tempered way.

scrabble ▸ verb (**scrabbles, scrabbling, scrabbled**) **1** grope around with your fingers to find or hold on to something. **2** move quickly and awkwardly; scramble.

scraggy ▸ adjective thin and bony.

scram ▸ verb (**scrams, scramming, scrammed**) informal leave quickly.

scramble ▸ verb (**scrambles, scrambling, scrambled**) **1** move quickly and awkwardly, using hands as well as feet. **2** muddle. **3** put a transmission into a form that can only be understood by using a decoding device. **4** cook beaten eggs in a pan. **5** (of fighter aircraft) take off immediately in an emergency.

> SYNONYMS **1** *we scrambled over the boulders* **clamber**, climb, crawl, claw your way, scrabble, struggle; N. Amer. shinny. **2** *the speaker can scramble the words* **muddle**, confuse, mix up, jumble (up), disarrange, disorganize, disorder, disturb, mess up.

▸ noun **1** an act of scrambling. **2** Brit. a motorcycle race over rough and hilly ground.

> SYNONYMS **1** *a short scramble over the rocks* **clamber**, climb. **2** *the scramble for a seat* **struggle**, jostle, scrimmage, scuffle, tussle, free-for-all, jockeying, competition, race.

scrap¹ ▸ noun **1** a small piece or amount of something. **2** (**scraps**) bits of uneaten food left after a meal. **3** unwanted metal that can be used again.

> SYNONYMS **1** *a scrap of paper* **fragment**, piece, bit, snippet, shred, oddment, remnant. **2** *there wasn't a scrap of evidence* **bit**, shred, speck, iota, particle, ounce, jot. **3** *the foxes ate all our scraps* **leftovers**, crumbs, remains, remnants, residue. **4** *a sculpture made from scrap* **waste**, rubbish, refuse, debris; N. Amer. garbage, trash; informal junk.

S

▶ verb (scraps, scrapping, scrapped) 1 abolish or cancel a plan, policy, etc. 2 remove from use.

SYNONYMS 1 *the scheme is to be scrapped* **abandon**, drop, abolish, withdraw, do away with, put an end to, cancel, axe; informal ditch, dump, junk. 2 *old computers are scrapped* **throw away**, throw out, dispose of, get rid of, discard, dispense with, bin, decommission, break up, demolish; informal chuck (away/out), ditch, dump, junk; Brit. informal get shot of; N. Amer. informal trash.
ANTONYMS keep, preserve.

scrap² ▶ noun a short fight or quarrel.
▶ verb (scraps, scrapping, scrapped) be involved in a scrap.

scrapbook ▶ noun a book for sticking cuttings or pictures in.

scrape ▶ verb (scrapes, scraping, scraped) 1 drag something hard or sharp across a surface to remove dirt or waste matter. 2 rub against a rough or hard surface. 3 just manage to achieve, succeed, or pass.

SYNONYMS 1 *we scraped all the paint off the windows* **rub**, scratch, scour, grind, sand, sandpaper, abrade, file. 2 *their boots scraped along the floor* **grate**, creak, rasp, scratch. 3 *Ellen scraped her shins on the wall* **graze**, scratch, scuff, rasp, skin, cut, lacerate, bark, chafe.

▶ noun 1 an act or sound of scraping. 2 an injury or mark caused by scraping. 3 informal an awkward or difficult situation.

SYNONYMS 1 *the scrape of her key in the lock* **grating**, creaking, rasp, scratch. 2 *a long scrape on his shin* **graze**, scratch, abrasion, cut, laceration, wound.

scrappy ▶ adjective disorganized, untidy, or incomplete.

scrapyard ▶ noun a place where scrap metal is collected.

scratch ▶ verb 1 make a long mark or wound on a surface with something sharp or pointed. 2 rub part of the body with your fingernails to relieve itching. 3 (scratch something out) cross out a word or words. 4 withdraw from a competition. 5 cancel or abandon a plan, project, etc.

SYNONYMS 1 *the paintwork was scratched* **score**, abrade, scrape, scuff. 2 *thorns scratched her skin* **graze**, scrape, skin, cut, lacerate, bark, chafe.

▶ noun 1 a mark or wound made by scratching. 2 informal a slight injury.

SYNONYMS 1 *a scratch on the paintwork* **score**, mark, line, scrape. 2 *he had scratches on his cheek* **graze**, scrape, abrasion, cut, laceration.

▶ adjective put together from whatever is available: *a scratch squad.*

■ **from scratch** from the very beginning. **up to scratch** up to the required standard. **scratch card** a card with a section which you scratch to reveal whether a prize has been won.
□ **scratchy** adjective.

scrawl ▶ verb write in a hurried, careless way.
▶ noun scrawled handwriting.

scrawny ▶ adjective (scrawnier, scrawniest) thin and bony.

scream ▶ verb make a loud, piercing cry or sound.

SYNONYMS **shriek**, screech, yell, howl, bawl, yelp, squeal, wail, squawk.

▶ noun 1 a loud, piercing cry or sound. 2 (a scream) informal a very funny person or thing.

scree ▶ noun a mass of small loose stones on a mountain slope.

screech ▶ noun a loud, harsh cry or sound.
▶ verb make a screech.

screed ▶ noun 1 a long speech or piece of writing. 2 a layer of material applied to make a floor level.

screen ▶ noun 1 an upright partition used to divide a room or conceal something. 2 the front part of a television or computer monitor, on which images and data are displayed. 3 a blank surface on which films are projected. 4 (the screen) films or television.

SYNONYMS 1 *he dressed behind the screen* **partition**, divider, windbreak. 2 *a computer with a 15-inch screen* **display**, monitor, visual display unit. 3 *a screen to keep out mosquitoes* **mesh**, net, netting. 4 *the hedge acts as a screen against the wind* **buffer**, protection, shield, shelter, guard.

▶ verb 1 conceal or protect with a screen. 2 test a group of people for the presence of a disease. 3 show or broadcast a film or television programme.

SYNONYMS 1 *the end of the hall had been screened off* **partition**, divide, separate, curtain. 2 *the cottage was screened by the trees* **conceal**, hide, veil, shield, shelter, shade, protect. 3 *all blood is screened for the virus* **check**, test, examine, investigate, vet; informal check out. 4 *the programme is screened on Thursday* **show**, broadcast, transmit, televise, put out, air.

■ **screen printing** a process in which ink is forced through a screen of fine material to create a picture or pattern. **screen saver** a moving image displayed by a computer screen when the computer is switched on but has not been used for a particular length of time. **screen test** a filmed audition for a film part.

screenplay ▸ noun the script of a film, including acting instructions.

screenwriter ▸ noun a person who writes a screenplay.

screw ▸ noun 1 a metal pin with a spiral thread running around it, which is turned and pressed into a surface to join things together. 2 a ship's or aircraft's propeller. 3 informal a prison warder.

SYNONYMS 1 *four steel screws* **bolt**, fastener. 2 *the ship's twin screws* **propeller**, rotor.

▸ verb 1 fasten or tighten with a screw or screws. 2 rotate something to attach or remove it. 3 informal cheat or swindle.

SYNONYMS 1 *he screwed the lid back on the jar* **tighten**, turn, twist, wind. 2 *the bracket was screwed in place* **fasten**, secure, fix, attach. 3 *she intended to screw more money out of them* **extort**, force, extract, wrest, wring, squeeze; informal bleed.

■ screw someone/thing up 1 crush something into a tight mass. 2 informal make something fail or go wrong. 3 informal make someone emotionally disturbed.

screwdriver ▸ noun a tool with a tip that fits into the head of a screw to turn it.

screwy ▸ adjective informal rather odd or eccentric.

scribble ▸ verb (scribbles, scribbling, scribbled) write or draw carelessly or hurriedly.

SYNONYMS *he scribbled a note* **scrawl**, scratch, dash off, jot (down), doodle, sketch.

▸ noun a scribbled picture or piece of writing.

SYNONYMS *I can't read this scribble* **scrawl**, squiggle(s), jottings, doodle, doodlings.

scribe ▸ noun (in the past) a person who copied out documents.

scrimmage ▸ noun a confused struggle or fight.

scrimp ▸ verb be very careful with money; economize.

script ▸ noun 1 the written text of a play, film, or broadcast. 2 handwriting as distinct from print.

SYNONYMS 1 *her neat, tidy script* **handwriting**, writing, hand. 2 *the script of the play* **text**, screenplay, libretto, score, lines, dialogue, words.

▸ verb write a script for.

scripture (or scriptures) ▸ noun 1 the sacred writings of Christianity contained in the Bible. 2 the sacred writings of another religion.

□ scriptural adjective.

scrofula ▸ noun the name in the past for a form of tuberculosis.

□ scrofulous adjective.

scroll ▸ noun a roll of parchment or paper for writing or painting on.

▸ verb move data on a computer screen in order to view different parts of it.

Scrooge ▸ noun a person who is mean with money.

scrotum ▸ noun (plural scrota or scrotums) the pouch of skin containing the testicles.

scrounge ▸ verb (scrounges, scrounging, scrounged) informal try to get something from someone without having to pay or work for it.

□ scrounger noun.

scrub¹ ▸ verb (scrubs, scrubbing, scrubbed) rub something hard to clean it.

SYNONYMS 1 *he scrubbed the kitchen floor* **brush**, scour, rub, clean, cleanse, wash. 2 *the plans were scrubbed* **abandon**, scrap, drop, cancel, call off, axe; informal ditch, dump, junk.

▸ noun an act of scrubbing.

scrub² ▸ noun 1 vegetation consisting mainly of bushes and small trees. 2 land covered with such vegetation.

□ scrubby adjective.

scruff¹ ▸ noun the back of a person's or animal's neck.

scruff² ▸ noun Brit. informal a scruffy person.

scruffy ▸ adjective (scruffier, scruffiest) shabby and untidy or dirty.

□ scruffiness noun.

scrum ▸ noun 1 (also scrummage) Rugby a formation in which players push against each other with heads down and try to gain possession of the ball when it is thrown in between them. 2 Brit. informal a disorderly crowd.

scrummy ▸ adjective informal delicious.

scrump ▸ verb Brit. informal steal fruit from an orchard or garden.

scrumptious ▸ adjective informal delicious.

scrumpy ▸ noun strong cider made in the west of England.

scrunch ▸ verb crush or squeeze into a tight mass.

scruple ▸ noun a feeling of doubt as to whether an action is morally right.

▸ verb (not scruple to do) formal not hesitate to do something, even if it may be wrong.

scrupulous ▸ adjective 1 very careful and thorough. 2 very concerned to avoid doing wrong.

□ scrupulously adverb.

scrutinize (or scrutinise) ▸ verb (scrutinizes, scrutinizing, scrutinized) examine thoroughly.

SYNONYMS **examine**, inspect, survey, study, look at, peruse, investigate,

S

explore, probe, enquire into, go into, check.

scrutiny ▸ noun (plural **scrutinies**) close and critical examination.

scuba diving ▸ noun swimming underwater using an aqualung.

scud ▸ verb (**scuds, scudding, scudded**) move quickly, driven by the wind.

scuff ▸ verb **1** make a mark on the surface of something by scraping it against something rough. **2** drag your feet when walking.
▸ noun a mark made by scuffing.

scuffle ▸ noun a short, confused fight or struggle.
▸ verb (**scuffles, scuffling, scuffled**) take part in a scuffle.

scull ▸ noun **1** each of a pair of small oars used by a single rower. **2** a light, narrow boat propelled by a single rower.
▸ verb propel a boat with sculls.

scullery ▸ noun (plural **sculleries**) a small room in an old house, used for washing dishes and laundry.

sculpt ▸ verb carve or shape.

sculptor ▸ noun (feminine **sculptress**) an artist who makes sculptures.

sculpture ▸ noun **1** the art of making three-dimensional figures and shapes by carving or shaping wood, stone, metal, etc. **2** a work of such a kind.

SYNONYMS **carving,** statue, statuette, figure, figurine, effigy, bust, head, model.

▸ verb (**sculptures, sculpturing, sculptured**) **1** make or represent by sculpture. **2** (**sculptured**) pleasingly shaped, with strong, smooth lines.
□ **sculptural** adjective.

scum ▸ noun **1** a layer of dirt or froth on the surface of a liquid. **2** informal a worthless person or group of people.
□ **scummy** adjective.

scupper ▸ verb (**scuppers, scuppering, scuppered**) Brit. **1** informal stop something working or succeeding. **2** sink your own ship deliberately.

scurf ▸ noun flakes of skin.

scurrilous ▸ adjective rude and insulting; slanderous.

scurry ▸ verb (**scurries, scurrying, scurried**) move hurriedly with short, quick steps.

scurvy ▸ noun a disease caused by a lack of vitamin C.

scut ▸ noun the short tail of a hare, rabbit, or deer.

scuttle[1] ▸ noun a metal container used to store coal for a domestic fire.

scuttle[2] ▸ verb (**scuttles, scuttling, scuttled**) run hurriedly or secretively with short, quick steps.

scuttle[3] ▸ verb (**scuttles, scuttling, scuttled**) **1** cause a scheme to fail. **2** sink your own ship deliberately.

scythe ▸ noun a tool with a long curved blade for cutting grass or corn.
▸ verb (**scythes, scything, scythed**) cut with a scythe.

SE ▸ abbreviation south-east or south-eastern.

sea ▸ noun **1** the salt water that surrounds the land masses of the earth. **2** a particular area of sea. **3** a vast expanse or quantity.

SYNONYMS **1 ocean,** waves; informal the drink; Brit. informal the briny; literary the deep. **2** *a sea of roofs* **expanse,** stretch, area, tract, sweep, carpet, mass. ANTONYMS land.

▸ adjective connected with the sea.

SYNONYMS *a sea story* **marine,** ocean, oceanic, maritime, naval, nautical.

■ **at sea** very confused and uncertain. **sea anemone** a sea creature with stinging tentacles that make it resemble a flower. **sea change** a great or remarkable change in a situation. **sea cow** a manatee or other large plant-eating sea animal. **sea horse** a small sea fish that swims upright and has a head rather like a horse's. **sea level** the average level of the sea's surface, used in calculating the height of land. **sea lion** a large seal with a mane on the neck and shoulders. **sea urchin** a small sea creature with a shell covered in spines.

seabird ▸ noun a bird that lives near the sea.

seaboard ▸ noun a region bordering the sea; the coastline.

seafaring ▸ adjective & noun travelling by sea.
□ **seafarer** noun.

seafood ▸ noun shellfish and sea fish as food.

seafront ▸ noun the part of a coastal town facing the sea.

seagoing ▸ adjective travelling on the sea.

seagull ▸ noun a gull.

seal[1] ▸ noun **1** a device or substance used to join two things together or to stop fluid getting in. **2** a piece of wax with a design stamped into it, attached to letters and documents to guarantee they are genuine. **3** a confirmation or guarantee: *a seal of approval.*

SYNONYMS *the seal round the bath* **sealant,** adhesive, mastic, joint.

▸ verb **1** fasten or close securely. **2** (**seal something off**) stop people entering and leaving an area. **3** coat a surface to stop fluid passing through it. **4** conclude; make definite.

SYNONYMS **1** *seal each bottle while hot* **stop up,** seal up, cork, stopper, plug.

S

2 *they sealed the bargain* **clinch,** secure, settle, conclude, complete, finalize, confirm.

□ **sealer** noun.

seal² ▸ noun a sea mammal with flippers and a streamlined body.

sealant ▸ noun material used to make something airtight or watertight.

seam ▸ noun **1** a line where two pieces of fabric are sewn together. **2** an underground layer of a mineral.

> SYNONYMS **1** *the seam was coming undone* **join,** stitching, joint. **2** *a seam of coal* **layer,** stratum, vein, lode.

□ **seamed** adjective.

seaman ▸ noun (plural **seamen**) a sailor, especially one below the rank of officer.

> SYNONYMS **sailor,** seafarer, mariner, boatman, hand, merchant seaman. ANTONYMS landlubber.

seamless ▸ adjective smooth and without seams or obvious joins.
□ **seamlessly** adverb.

seamstress ▸ noun a woman who sews, especially as a job.

seamy ▸ adjective (**seamier, seamiest**) immoral and unpleasant.

seance /say-onss/ ▸ noun a meeting at which people attempt to make contact with the dead.

seaplane ▸ noun an aircraft designed to land on and take off from water.

sear ▸ verb **1** scorch with a sudden intense heat. **2** (of pain) be experienced as a burning sensation.

> SYNONYMS **1** *the heat of the blast seared his face* **scorch,** burn, singe, char. **2** *sear the meat* **flash-fry,** seal, brown.

search ▸ verb **1** try to find something by looking carefully and thoroughly. **2** examine something thoroughly in order to find something or someone. **3** look for information on the Internet by using a search engine. **4** (**searching**) investigating very deeply.

> SYNONYMS **1** *I searched for the key* **hunt,** look, seek, forage, fish, look high and low, ferret, root, rummage. **2** *he searched the house* **look through,** scour, go through, sift through, comb, turn upside down; Austral./NZ informal fossick through. **3** *the guards searched him* **examine,** inspect, check, frisk. **4** (**searching**) **penetrating,** piercing, probing, keen, shrewd, sharp, intent.

▸ noun an act of searching.

> SYNONYMS *we continued our search* **hunt,** look, quest, examination, exploration.

■ **search engine** a computer program

that searches the Internet for web pages containing a specified word or words. **search warrant** a document authorizing a police officer to enter and search a place.
□ **searcher** noun **searchingly** adverb.

searchlight ▸ noun a powerful electric light with a concentrated beam that can be turned in any direction.

seascape ▸ noun a view or picture of the sea.

seashell ▸ noun the shell of a marine shellfish.

seashore ▸ noun an area of sandy, stony, or rocky land next to the sea.

seasick ▸ adjective suffering from nausea caused by the motion of a ship at sea.
□ **seasickness** noun.

seaside ▸ noun a place by the sea, especially a beach-area or holiday resort.

> SYNONYMS **coast,** shore, seashore, beach, sand, sands.

season ▸ noun **1** each of the four divisions of the year (spring, summer, autumn, and winter). **2** a part of the year with particular weather, or when a particular sport is played.

> SYNONYMS *the seasons of the year* **period,** time, time of year, spell, term.

▸ verb **1** add salt, herbs, or spices to food. **2** dry wood for use as timber. **3** (**seasoned**) experienced.

> SYNONYMS **1** *a well seasoned dish* **flavour,** add salt/pepper to, spice. **2** (**seasoned**) **experienced,** practised, well versed, knowledgeable, established, veteran, hardened.

■ **in season 1** (of food) available and ready to eat. **2** (of a female mammal) ready to mate. **season ticket** a ticket that lets you travel within a particular period or gain admission to a series of events.

seasonable ▸ adjective usual or appropriate for a particular season of the year.

seasonal ▸ adjective **1** relating to or characteristic of a particular season of the year. **2** changing according to the season.
□ **seasonally** adverb.

seasoning ▸ noun salt or spices added to food to improve the flavour.

> SYNONYMS **flavouring,** salt and pepper, herbs, spices, condiments.

seat ▸ noun **1** a thing made or used for sitting on. **2** the part of a chair designed for sitting on. **3** a place for a person to sit in a vehicle, theatre, etc. **4** a person's bottom. **5** a place in an elected parliament or council. **6** Brit. a parliamentary constituency. **7** a site or location. **8** Brit. a large country house belonging to an aristocratic family.

S

SYNONYMS **1** *a wooden seat* **chair,** bench, stool; (seats) seating. **2** *the seat of government* **headquarters,** base, centre, nerve centre, hub, heart, location, site. **3** *the family's country seat* **residence,** ancestral home, mansion.

▶ verb **1** arrange for someone to sit somewhere. **2** (**seat yourself** or **be seated**) formal sit down. **3** (of a place) have enough seats for.

SYNONYMS **1** *they seated themselves round the table* **position,** put, place, ensconce, install, settle. **2** *the hall seats 500* **have room for,** contain, take, sit, hold, accommodate.

■ **seat belt** a belt used to secure someone in the seat of a motor vehicle or aircraft.

seaweed ▶ noun plants growing in the sea or on rocks by the sea.

seaworthy ▶ adjective (of a boat) in a good enough condition to sail on the sea.

sebaceous /si-**bay**-shuhss/ ▶ adjective technical producing oil or fat.

secateurs /sek-uh-**terz**/ ▶ plural noun Brit. a cutting tool like a pair of strong scissors, used for pruning plants, bushes, etc.

secede ▶ verb (secedes, seceding, seceded) withdraw formally from an alliance or federation of states.

secession ▶ noun the action of seceding.

secluded ▶ adjective (of a place) sheltered and private.

seclusion ▶ noun the state of being private and away from other people.

second[1] ▶ ordinal number **1** that is number two in a sequence; 2nd. **2** lower in position, rank, or importance. **3** (**seconds**) goods that are not of perfect quality. **4** a person who helps someone fighting in a duel or boxing match. **5** Brit. a place in the second highest grade in an exam for a degree.

SYNONYMS **1** *the second day of the trial* **next,** following, subsequent. **2** *a second pair of glasses* **additional,** extra, alternative, another, spare, backup; N. Amer. alternate. **3** *second prize* **secondary,** subordinate, subsidiary, lesser, inferior. ANTONYMS first.

▶ verb **1** formally support a nomination or resolution before voting or discussion. **2** express agreement with.

SYNONYMS *George seconded the motion* **support,** vote for, back, approve, endorse.

■ **second best** not quite as good as the best. **second class 1** the second-best accommodation in a train, ship, etc. **2** of a lower standard or quality than the best. **second-degree** (of burns) causing blistering but not permanent scars.

second-guess predict someone's actions or thoughts by guesswork. **second nature** a habit that has become instinctive. **second-rate** of bad quality. **second sight** the supposed ability to know what will happen in the future. **second thoughts** a change of opinion after reconsidering something. **second wind** fresh energy gained during exercise after having been out of breath.

second[2] ▶ noun **1** a unit of time equal to one sixtieth of a minute. **2** (**a second**) informal a very short time. **3** a measurement of an angle equal to one sixtieth of a minute.

SYNONYMS *I'll be gone for a second* **moment,** bit, little while, instant, flash; informal sec, jiffy; Brit. informal mo, tick.

second[3] /si-**kond**/ ▶ verb Brit. temporarily move a worker to another position or role.
□ **secondment** noun.

secondary ▶ adjective **1** coming after, or less important than, something else. **2** (of education) for children from the age of eleven to sixteen or eighteen.

SYNONYMS **1** *a secondary issue* **less important,** subordinate, lesser, minor, peripheral, incidental, subsidiary. **2** *secondary infections* **accompanying,** attendant, concomitant, consequential, resulting, resultant. ANTONYMS primary, main.

□ **secondarily** adverb.

second-hand ▶ adjective & adverb **1** having had a previous owner. **2** heard from another person.

SYNONYMS **1** *second-hand clothes* **used,** old, worn, pre-owned, nearly new, handed-down, hand-me-down, cast-off. **2** *second-hand information* **indirect.** **3** *I heard this second-hand* **indirectly;** informal on the grapevine. ANTONYMS new, direct, directly.

secondly ▶ adverb in the second place.

SYNONYMS **furthermore,** also, moreover, additionally, second, in the second place, next.

secrecy ▶ noun the action of keeping something secret.

SYNONYMS **confidentiality,** privacy, mystery, concealment, stealth.

secret ▶ adjective **1** hidden from, or not known by, other people. **2** secretive.

SYNONYMS **1** *a secret plan* **confidential,** top secret, classified, undisclosed, unknown, private, under wraps; informal hush-hush. **2** *a secret drawer in the table* **hidden,** concealed, disguised. **3** *a secret campaign* **clandestine,** covert, undercover, underground, surreptitious, cloak-and-dagger; informal hush-hush. **4** *a secret code* **cryptic,** mysterious, abstruse,

S

recondite, arcane, esoteric.
ANTONYMS public, open.

▶ noun **1** something that other people do not know about. **2** a method of achieving something that is not generally known.

SYNONYMS **1** *it's a secret* **confidential matter,** confidence, skeleton in the cupboard. **2** *the secrets of the universe* **mystery,** enigma. **3** *the secret of their success* **recipe,** magic formula, blueprint, key, answer, solution.

■ **secret agent** a spy acting for a country. **secret police** a police force working in secret against a government's political opponents. **secret service** a government department concerned with spying.

secretariat /sek-ri-**tair**-i-uht/ ▶ noun a government office or department.

secretary ▶ noun (plural **secretaries**) **1** a person employed to type letters, keep records, etc. **2** an official of a society or other organization.
■ **Secretary of State 1** (in the UK) the head of a major government department. **2** (in the US) the government official responsible for foreign affairs.
☐ **secretarial** adjective.

✔ **-ary**, not **-ery**: secret**ary**.

secrete ▶ verb (**secretes, secreting, secreted**) **1** (of a cell, gland, or organ) produce a liquid substance. **2** hide an object.
☐ **secretion** noun.

secretive ▶ adjective inclined to hide your feelings or not to give out information.

SYNONYMS **uncommunicative,** secret, unforthcoming, playing your cards close to your chest, reticent, tight-lipped.
ANTONYMS open, communicative.

☐ **secretively** adverb.

secretly ▶ adverb in a secret way.

SYNONYMS **in secret,** in private, privately, behind closed doors, under cover, furtively, stealthily, on the quiet, covertly.

sect ▶ noun a small religious or political group with different beliefs from those of the larger group that they belong to.

SYNONYMS **group,** cult, denomination, order, splinter group, faction, camp.

sectarian ▶ adjective having to do with a sect or group.
☐ **sectarianism** noun.

section ▶ noun **1** any of the parts into which something is divided. **2** a distinct group within a larger body of people or things. **3** the shape that results from cutting through something.

SYNONYMS **1** *the separate sections of the box* **part,** bit, portion, segment,

compartment, module. **2** *the last section of the questionnaire* **passage,** subsection, chapter, subdivision, clause. **3** *the reference section of the library* **department,** area, division.

▶ verb divide into sections.

sector ▶ noun **1** a distinct area or part. **2** a part of a circle between two lines drawn from its centre to its circumference.

SYNONYMS **1** *every sector of the industry* **part,** branch, arm, division, area, department, field, sphere. **2** *the north-eastern sector of the town* **district,** quarter, section, zone, region, area, belt.

secular ▶ adjective not religious or spiritual.

SYNONYMS **non-religious,** lay, temporal, civil, worldly, earthly, profane.
ANTONYMS sacred, religious.

☐ **secularism** noun.

secure ▶ adjective **1** certain to remain safe. **2** fixed or fastened so as to not give way or become loose. **3** free from fear or anxiety.

SYNONYMS **1** *a secure future* **certain,** assured, reliable, dependable, settled, fixed. **2** *check that all bolts are secure* **fastened,** fixed, secured, done up, closed, shut, locked. **3** *a place where children feel secure* **safe,** protected, safe and sound, out of harm's way, in safe hands, invulnerable, at ease, unworried, relaxed, happy, confident.
ANTONYMS uncertain, loose, vulnerable.

▶ verb (**secures, securing, secured**) **1** protect against danger or threat. **2** firmly fix or fasten. **3** succeed in obtaining.

SYNONYMS **1** *secure the handle to the main body* **fix,** attach, fasten, affix, connect, couple. **2** *the doors had been secured* **fasten,** close, shut, lock, bolt, chain, seal. **3** *the division secured a major contract* **obtain,** acquire, gain, get; informal land.

☐ **securely** adverb.

security ▶ noun (plural **securities**) **1** the state of being or feeling secure. **2** the safety of a state or organization. **3** a valuable item offered as a guarantee that you will repay a loan.

SYNONYMS **1** *the security of our citizens* **safety,** protection. **2** *he could give her security* **peace of mind,** stability, certainty. **3** *security at the court was tight* **safety measures,** safeguards, surveillance, defence, protection, policing. **4** *additional security for your loan* **guarantee,** collateral, surety, pledge, bond.
ANTONYMS insecurity.

sedan ▶ noun **1** an enclosed chair carried between two horizontal poles. **2** N. Amer. a car for four or more people.

S

sedate ▸ adjective **1** calm and unhurried. **2** respectable and rather dull.
▸ verb (**sedates, sedating, sedated**) give someone a sedative drug.
□ **sedately** adverb.

sedation ▸ noun the action of sedating someone.

sedative ▸ adjective having the effect of making someone calm or sleepy.
▸ noun a sedative drug.

sedentary /sed-uhn-tri/ ▸ adjective **1** involving a lot of sitting and not much exercise. **2** sitting down a lot; taking little exercise.

sedge ▸ noun a grass-like plant that grows in wet ground.

sediment ▸ noun **1** matter that settles to the bottom of a liquid. **2** material carried by water or wind and deposited on land.

SYNONYMS **dregs,** grounds, lees, residue, deposit, silt.

□ **sedimentary** adjective.

sedition ▸ noun things done or said to stir up rebellion against a ruler or government.
□ **seditious** adjective.

seduce ▸ verb (**seduces, seducing, seduced**) **1** persuade someone to do something unwise. **2** persuade someone to have sex with you.

SYNONYMS **1** *customers are seduced by the advertising* **attract,** allure, lure, tempt, entice, beguile, inveigle, manipulate. **2** *he tried to seduce her* **have your (wicked) way with,** take advantage of.

□ **seduction** noun.

seductive ▸ adjective tempting and attractive.

SYNONYMS **tempting,** inviting, enticing, alluring, beguiling, attractive.

□ **seductively** adverb.

sedulous ▸ adjective showing great care or effort; diligent.

sedum /see-duhm/ ▸ noun a plant with fleshy leaves.

see¹ ▸ verb (**sees, seeing, saw;** past participle **seen**) **1** become aware of with the eyes. **2** experience or witness. **3** realize something after thinking or getting information. **4** think of in a particular way. **5** meet someone socially or by chance. **6** meet someone regularly as a boyfriend or girlfriend. **7** consult a specialist or professional. **8** guide or lead someone somewhere.

SYNONYMS **1** *he saw her in the street* **discern,** spot, notice, catch sight of, glimpse, make out, pick out, spy; informal clap eyes on, clock; literary behold. **2** *I saw a programme about it* **watch,** look at, view, catch. **3** *would you like to see the house?* **inspect,** view, look round, tour, survey, examine, scrutinize. **4** *I finally saw what she meant* **understand,** grasp, comprehend, follow, realize, appreciate, recognize, work out, fathom; informal get, latch on to, tumble to, figure out; Brit. informal twig, suss (out). **5** *I must see what Victor is up to* **find out,** discover, learn, ascertain, determine, establish. **6** *see that no harm comes to him* **ensure,** make sure/certain, see to it, take care, mind. **7** *I see trouble ahead* **foresee,** predict, forecast, prophesy, anticipate. **8** *later, I saw him in town* **encounter,** meet, run into, come across, stumble across, happen on, chance on; informal bump into. **9** *you'd better see a doctor* **consult,** confer with, talk to, have recourse to, call in, turn to. **10** *he's seeing someone else now* **go out with,** date, take out, be involved with; informal go steady with; dated court.

■ **see someone off** go with a person who is leaving to their point of departure. **see something through** carry on with a project until it is completed. **see-through** transparent or semi-transparent. **see to** deal with.

see² ▸ noun the district or position of a bishop or archbishop.

seed ▸ noun **1** a small, hard object produced by a plant, from which a new plant may grow. **2** the beginning of a feeling, process, etc. **3** any of the stronger competitors in a sports tournament who are kept from playing each other in the early rounds. **4** old use a man's semen.

SYNONYMS **pip,** stone, kernel.

▸ verb **1** sow land with seeds. **2** remove the seeds from. **3** (**be seeded**) be made a seed in a sports tournament.

seedling ▸ noun a young plant raised from seed.

seedy ▸ adjective (**seedier, seediest**) unpleasant because dirty or immoral.
□ **seediness** noun.

seeing ▸ conjunction because; since.

seek ▸ verb (**seeks, seeking, sought**) **1** try to find or get. **2** ask for. **3** (**seek to do**) try or want to do. **4** (**seek someone/thing out**) search for and find someone or something.

SYNONYMS **1** *he is seeking work* **search for,** try to find, look for, be after, hunt for. **2** *he sought help from a motorist* **ask for,** request, solicit, call for, appeal for, apply for. **3** *we constantly seek to improve the service* **try,** attempt, endeavour, strive, work, do your best.

□ **seeker** noun.

seem ▸ verb **1** give the impression of being. **2** (**cannot seem to do**) be unable to do, despite having tried.

SYNONYMS **appear (to be)**, have the appearance/air of being, give the impression of being, look, sound, come across as, strike someone as.

seeming ▶ adjective appearing to be real or true.
□ **seemingly** adverb.

seemly ▶ adjective respectable or in good taste.

seen past participle of SEE[1].

seep ▶ verb (of a liquid) flow or leak slowly through a substance.

SYNONYMS **ooze**, trickle, exude, drip, dribble, flow, leak, drain, bleed, filter, percolate, soak.

□ **seepage** noun.

seer ▶ noun a person supposedly able to see visions of the future.

seersucker ▶ noun a fabric with a crinkled surface.

see-saw ▶ noun a long plank supported in the middle, on each end of which children sit and move up and down by pushing the ground with their feet.
▶ verb repeatedly change between two states or positions.

seethe ▶ verb (seethes, seething, seethed) **1** be very angry but try not to show it. **2** be filled with a crowd that is moving about. **3** (of a liquid) boil or churn.

SYNONYMS **1** *the water seethed with fish* **teem**, swarm, boil, swirl, churn, surge, bubble, heave. **2** *I seethed at the injustice of it all* **be angry**, be furious, be enraged, be incensed, be beside yourself, boil, rage, rant, fume; informal be livid, foam at the mouth.

segment ▶ noun /seg-muhnt/ each of the parts into which something is divided.

SYNONYMS **piece**, bit, section, part, portion, division, slice, wedge.

▶ verb /seg-**ment**/ divide into segments.

segregate ▶ verb (segregates, segregating, segregated) **1** keep separate from the rest or from each other. **2** keep people of different races, sexes, or religions separate.

SYNONYMS **separate**, set apart, keep apart, isolate, quarantine, partition, divide, discriminate against.
ANTONYMS integrate.

□ **segregation** noun.

segue /seg-way/ ▶ verb (segues, segueing or seguing, segued) move without interruption from one song or film scene to another.

seine (*rhymes with* rain) ▶ noun a fishing net which hangs vertically in the water, with floats at the top.

seismic /syz-mik/ ▶ adjective **1** having to do

with earthquakes. **2** enormous in size or effect.

seismology ▶ noun the study of earthquakes.
□ **seismologist** noun.

seize ▶ verb (seized, seizing, seized) **1** take hold of suddenly and forcibly. **2** (of the police) officially take possession of. **3** take an opportunity eagerly and decisively. **4** (seize on) take advantage of eagerly. **5** (often seize up) (of a machine) become jammed.

SYNONYMS **1** *she seized the microphone* **grab**, grasp, snatch, take hold of. **2** *rebels seized the air base* **capture**, take, overrun, occupy, conquer, take over. **3** *the drugs were seized by customs* **confiscate**, impound, commandeer, requisition, appropriate, expropriate. **4** *terrorists seized his wife* **kidnap**, abduct, take captive, take prisoner, take hostage; informal snatch.
ANTONYMS liberate, relinquish, release.

✔ **Seize** is an exception to the usual rule of **i** before **e** except after **c**.

seizure ▶ noun **1** the action of seizing. **2** a sudden attack of illness, especially a stroke or an epileptic fit.

SYNONYMS **1** *Napoleon's seizure of Spain* **capture**, takeover, annexation, invasion, occupation. **2** *the seizure of banned goods* **confiscation**, appropriation, expropriation. **3** *the seizure of UN staff* **kidnap**, abduction. **4** *the baby suffered a seizure* **convulsion**, fit, spasm, paroxysm.
ANTONYMS liberation, release.

seldom ▶ adverb not often.

SYNONYMS **rarely**, infrequently, hardly (ever), scarcely (ever); informal once in a blue moon.
ANTONYMS often.

select ▶ verb carefully choose from a group.

SYNONYMS *select the correct tool for the job* **choose**, pick (out), single out, sort out, take, adopt.

▶ adjective **1** carefully chosen as being among the best. **2** used by, or made up of, wealthy people.

SYNONYMS **1** *a small, select group* **choice**, hand-picked, elite; informal top-flight. **2** *a very select area* **exclusive**, privileged, wealthy; informal posh.
ANTONYMS inferior.

■ **select committee** a small parliamentary committee appointed for a special purpose.
□ **selector** noun.

selection ▶ noun **1** the action of selecting. **2** a number of selected things. **3** a range of things from which you can choose.

S

SYNONYMS **1** *Jim made his selection* **choice,** pick, option, preference. **2** *a wide selection of dishes* **range,** array, diversity, variety, assortment, mixture. **3** *a selection of his poems* **anthology,** assortment, collection, assemblage, miscellany, medley.

selective ▸ adjective **1** involving selection. **2** choosing carefully. **3** affecting some things and not others.

SYNONYMS **discerning,** discriminating, exacting, demanding, particular; informal choosy, picky.
ANTONYMS indiscriminate.

□ **selectively** adverb **selectivity** noun.

selenium /si-lee-ni-uhm/ ▸ noun a grey crystalline chemical element.

self ▸ noun (plural **selves**) **1** a person's essential being that distinguishes them from other people. **2** a person's particular nature or personality.

self-absorbed ▸ adjective obsessed with your own emotions or interests.

self-addressed ▸ adjective (of an envelope) addressed to yourself.

self-adhesive ▸ adjective sticking without needing to be moistened.

self-appointed ▸ adjective having taken up a position or role without the approval of other people.

self-assessment ▸ noun **1** assessment of your own performance. **2** a system in which you calculate yourself how much tax you owe.

self-assurance ▸ noun confidence in your own abilities or character.
□ **self-assured** adjective.

self-aware ▸ adjective knowledgeable about your own character, feelings, motives, etc.
□ **self-awareness** noun.

self-catering ▸ adjective Brit. (of a holiday or accommodation) offering facilities for you to cook your own meals.

self-centred ▸ adjective obsessed with yourself and your affairs.

self-confessed ▸ adjective admitting to having certain characteristics.

self-confidence ▸ noun a feeling of trust in your abilities and judgement.
□ **self-confident** adjective.

self-conscious ▸ adjective nervous or awkward through being worried about what other people think of you.

self-contained ▸ adjective **1** complete in itself. **2** not depending on or influenced by other people.

self-control ▸ noun the ability to control your emotions or behaviour.
□ **self-controlled** adjective.

self-defeating ▸ adjective making things worse rather than achieving the desired aim.

self-defence ▸ noun defence of yourself.

self-denial ▸ noun not allowing yourself to have things that you want.

self-deprecating ▸ adjective modest about yourself.
□ **self-deprecation** noun.

self-destruct ▸ verb explode or disintegrate automatically.

self-destructive ▸ adjective causing harm to yourself.

self-determination ▸ noun the right or ability of a country or person to manage their own affairs.

self-discipline ▸ noun the ability to control your feelings and actions.
□ **self-disciplined** adjective.

self-doubt ▸ noun lack of confidence in yourself and your abilities.

self-effacing ▸ adjective not wanting to attract attention.

self-employed ▸ adjective working for yourself rather than for an employer.
□ **self-employment** noun.

self-esteem ▸ noun confidence in your own worth or abilities.

self-evident ▸ adjective obvious.

self-explanatory ▸ adjective not needing explanation; clearly understood.

self-expression ▸ noun the expression of your feelings or thoughts.

self-fulfilling ▸ adjective (of a prediction) bound to come true because people behave in a way that makes it happen.

self-help ▸ noun reliance on your own efforts and resources to achieve things.

self-importance ▸ noun an exaggerated sense of your own value or importance.
□ **self-important** adjective.

self-indulgent ▸ adjective allowing yourself to have or do things that you like, especially to an excessive extent.
□ **self-indulgence** noun.

self-interest ▸ noun your personal interest or advantage.

selfish ▸ adjective concerned mainly with your own needs and wishes.

SYNONYMS **egocentric,** egotistic, self-centred, self-absorbed, self-obsessed, wrapped up in yourself, mean, greedy; informal looking after number one.
ANTONYMS altruistic.

□ **selfishly** adverb **selfishness** noun.

selfless ▸ adjective concerned more with the needs and wishes of other people than with your own.

self-made ▸ adjective having become successful by your own efforts.

S

self-pity ▸ noun too much sorrow and concern for yourself and your own problems.
□ **self-pitying** adjective.

self-portrait ▸ noun a portrait by an artist of himself or herself.

self-possessed ▸ adjective calm, confident, and in control of your feelings.
□ **self-possession** noun.

self-raising flour ▸ noun Brit. flour that has baking powder already added.

self-reliance ▸ noun reliance on your own powers and resources.
□ **self-reliant** adjective.

self-respect ▸ noun pride and confidence in yourself.

self-righteous ▸ adjective certain that you are right or morally superior.

self-sacrifice ▸ noun the giving up of your own needs or wishes to help other people.
□ **self-sacrificing** adjective.

selfsame ▸ adjective (the selfsame) the very same.

self-satisfied ▸ adjective smugly pleased with yourself.
□ **self-satisfaction** noun.

self-seeking (or self-serving) ▸ adjective concerned only with your own welfare and interests.

self-service ▸ adjective (of a shop or restaurant) where customers choose goods for themselves and pay at a checkout.

self-styled ▸ adjective using a description or title that you have given yourself: *self-styled experts*.

self-sufficient ▸ adjective able to satisfy your basic needs without outside help.
□ **self-sufficiency** noun.

self-worth ▸ noun self-esteem.

sell ▸ verb (sells, selling, sold) **1** hand over something in exchange for money. **2** (of goods) be bought. **3** (sell up) sell all your property or assets. **4** persuade someone that something is good.

SYNONYMS **1** *they are selling their house* **put up for sale**, put on the market, auction (off), trade in. **2** *he sells cakes* **trade in**, deal in, traffic in, peddle, retail, market. ANTONYMS buy.

■ **sell out 1** sell all your stock of something. **2** (of tickets for an event) be all sold. **3** abandon your principles for reasons of convenience.

seller ▸ noun a person who sells something.

SYNONYMS **vendor**, dealer, retailer, trader, merchant, agent, hawker, pedlar, purveyor, supplier, stockist. ANTONYMS buyer.

Sellotape ▸ noun Brit. trademark transparent adhesive tape.

selvedge /sel-vij/ ▸ noun an edge on woven fabric that prevents it from fraying or unravelling.

selves plural of SELF.

semantic ▸ adjective having to do with meaning.
□ **semantically** adverb.

semantics ▸ plural noun **1** the study of the meaning of words and phrases. **2** the meaning of words, phrases, etc.

semaphore ▸ noun a system of sending messages by holding the arms or two flags in positions that represent letters of the alphabet.

semblance ▸ noun the way that something looks or seems.

semen /see-muhn/ ▸ noun a fluid containing sperm that is produced by men and male animals.

semester ▸ noun a half-year term in a school or university.

semi ▸ noun (plural semis) informal **1** Brit. a semi-detached house. **2** a semi-final.

semi-automatic ▸ adjective (of a gun) able to load bullets automatically but not fire continuously.

semibreve ▸ noun Brit. a musical note that lasts as long as two minims or four crotchets.

semicircle ▸ noun a half of a circle.
□ **semicircular** adjective.

semicolon ▸ noun a punctuation mark (;) indicating a bigger pause than that indicated by a comma.

semiconductor ▸ noun a solid which conducts electricity, but to a smaller extent than a metal.

semi-detached ▸ adjective Brit. (of a house) joined to another house on one side by a common wall.

semi-final ▸ noun (in sport) a match or round coming immediately before the final.
□ **semi-finalist** noun.

seminal ▸ adjective **1** strongly influencing later developments. **2** referring to semen.

seminar ▸ noun **1** a meeting for discussion or training. **2** a university class for discussion of topics with a teacher.

seminary ▸ noun (plural seminaries) a training college for priests or rabbis.

semiotics ▸ plural noun the study of signs and symbols.
□ **semiotic** adjective.

semi-precious ▸ adjective (of minerals) used as gems but less valuable than precious stones.

semiquaver ▸ noun Brit. a musical note lasting half as long as a quaver.

S

semi-skimmed ▶ adjective Brit. (of milk) having had some of the cream removed.

Semite /see-myt/ ▶ noun a member of a people speaking a Semitic language, especially the Jews and Arabs.

Semitic /si-mit-ik/ ▶ noun a group of languages that includes Hebrew and Arabic.
▶ adjective relating to Semitic or Semites, especially the Jews and Arabs.

semitone ▶ noun Brit. a musical interval equal to half a tone.

semolina ▶ noun the hard grains left after flour has been milled, used to make puddings and pasta.

Semtex ▶ noun a powerful explosive.

senate ▶ noun 1 the smaller but higher law-making assembly in the US, France, etc. 2 the governing body of a university or college. 3 the state council of ancient Rome.

senator ▶ noun a member of a senate.

send ▶ verb (sends, sending, sent) 1 cause to go or be taken to a destination. 2 cause to move sharply or quickly. 3 put someone into a particular state.

> SYNONYMS 1 *they sent a message to HQ* **dispatch,** post, mail, consign, forward, transmit, convey, communicate, broadcast. 2 *the pump sent out a jet of petrol* **propel,** project, eject, deliver, discharge, spout, fire, shoot, release, fling, cast. 3 *it's enough to send one mad* **make,** drive, turn.
> ANTONYMS receive.

■ **send someone down** Brit. 1 expel a student from a university. 2 informal sentence someone to imprisonment. **send someone up** informal make fun of someone by imitating them.

send-off ▶ noun a gathering to say goodbye to someone who is leaving.

> SYNONYMS **farewell,** goodbye, adieu, leave-taking, funeral.
> ANTONYMS welcome.

Senegalese /sen-i-guh-**leez**/ ▶ noun (plural Senegalese) a person from Senegal, a country in West Africa.
▶ adjective relating to Senegal.

senescence /si-**ness**-uhnss/ ▶ noun the process of growing old and gradually deteriorating.
□ senescent adjective.

senile ▶ adjective suffering a loss of mental faculties because of old age.
□ senility noun.

senior ▶ adjective 1 having to do with older people. 2 Brit. having to do with schoolchildren above the age of about eleven. 3 US of the final year at a university or high school. 4 (after a name) referring

to the elder of two with the same name in a family. 5 high or higher in status.

> SYNONYMS 1 *senior school pupils* **older,** elder. 2 *a senior officer* **superior,** higher-ranking, more important; N. Amer. ranking.
> ANTONYMS junior, subordinate.

▶ noun 1 a person who is a stated number of years older than someone else: *she was two years his senior.* 2 a student at a senior school. 3 (in sport) a competitor of above a certain age or of the highest status.
■ **senior citizen** an old-age pensioner.
□ seniority noun.

senna ▶ noun a laxative prepared from the dried pods of a tree.

sensation ▶ noun 1 a feeling resulting from something that happens to or comes into contact with the body. 2 the ability to have such feelings. 3 a vague awareness or impression. 4 a widespread reaction of interest and excitement, or a person or thing that causes it.

> SYNONYMS 1 *a sensation of heaviness* **feeling,** sense, perception, impression. 2 *she caused a sensation* **commotion,** stir, uproar, furore, scandal, impact; informal splash, to-do.

sensational ▶ adjective 1 causing or trying to cause great public interest and excitement. 2 informal very impressive or attractive.

> SYNONYMS 1 *a sensational murder trial* **shocking,** scandalous, appalling, fascinating, thrilling, interesting, dramatic, momentous, historic, newsworthy. 2 *sensational stories* **overdramatized,** melodramatic, exaggerated, sensationalist, graphic, explicit, lurid; informal shock-horror, juicy. 3 *she looked sensational* **gorgeous,** stunning, wonderful, superb, excellent, first-class; informal great, terrific, tremendous, fantastic, fabulous, out of this world; Brit. informal smashing.
> ANTONYMS dull, understated, unremarkable.

□ sensationalism noun sensationalist noun & adjective sensationally adverb.

sensationalize (or sensationalise)
▶ verb (sensationalizes, sensationalizing, sensationalized) present information in an exaggerated way to make it seem more interesting.

sense ▶ noun 1 any of the powers of sight, smell, hearing, taste, and touch, which allow the body to perceive things. 2 a feeling that something is the case. 3 (sense of) awareness of or sensitivity to. 4 a sensible and practical attitude or way of behaving. 5 a meaning of a word or expression.

S

SYNONYMS **1** *the sense of touch* **feeling,** faculty, awareness, sensation, recognition, perception. **2** *a sense of humour* **appreciation,** awareness, understanding, comprehension. **3** *she had the sense to leave* **wisdom,** common sense, wit, intelligence, judgement, reason, brain(s); informal gumption, nous, horse sense, savvy; Brit. informal loaf, common; N. Amer. informal smarts. **4** *I can't see the sense in this* **purpose,** point, use, value, advantage, benefit. **5** *different senses of the word* **meaning,** definition, nuance, drift, gist, thrust, tenor, message.
ANTONYMS stupidity.

▶ **verb** (**senses, sensing, sensed**) **1** perceive by a sense or senses. **2** be vaguely aware of.

SYNONYMS *she sensed their hostility* **detect,** feel, observe, notice, recognize, pick up, be aware of, distinguish, make out; informal catch on to.

■ **make sense** be understandable or sensible.

senseless ▶ **adjective 1** lacking meaning, purpose, or common sense. **2** unconscious.

SYNONYMS **pointless,** futile, useless, needless, meaningless, absurd, foolish, insane, stupid, idiotic, mindless, illogical.
ANTONYMS wise.

sensibility ▶ **noun** (plural **sensibilities**) **1** the ability to experience and understand emotion or art; sensitivity. **2** (**sensibilities**) the degree to which a person can be offended or shocked.

sensible ▶ **adjective 1** having or showing common sense. **2** practical rather than decorative.

SYNONYMS **practical,** realistic, responsible, reasonable, commonsensical, rational, logical, sound, no-nonsense, level-headed, down-to-earth, wise.
ANTONYMS foolish.

□ **sensibly** adverb.

sensitive ▶ **adjective 1** quick to detect or be affected by slight changes. **2** appreciating the feelings of other people. **3** easily offended or upset. **4** secret or controversial.

SYNONYMS **1** *she's sensitive to changes in temperature* **responsive to,** reactive to, sensitized to, aware of, conscious of, susceptible to, affected by, vulnerable to. **2** *sensitive skin* **delicate,** fragile, tender, raw, sore. **3** *the matter needs sensitive handling* **tactful,** careful, thoughtful, diplomatic, delicate, subtle, kid-glove. **4** *he's sensitive about his bald patch* **touchy,** oversensitive, hypersensitive,

easily offended, thin-skinned, defensive, paranoid, neurotic. **5** *a sensitive issue* **difficult,** delicate, tricky, awkward, problematic, ticklish, controversial, emotive.
ANTONYMS impervious, resilient, clumsy, thick-skinned, uncontroversial.

□ **sensitively** adverb.

sensitivity ▶ **noun** (plural **sensitivities**) **1** the quality of being sensitive. **2** (**sensitivities**) a person's feelings which might be offended or hurt.

SYNONYMS **1** *the sensitivity of the skin* **responsiveness,** sensitiveness, reactivity, susceptibility. **2** *the job calls for sensitivity* **tact,** diplomacy, delicacy, subtlety, understanding. **3** *her sensitivity on the subject* **touchiness,** oversensitivity, hypersensitivity, defensiveness. **4** *the sensitivity of the issue* **delicacy,** trickiness, awkwardness, ticklishness.

sensitize (or **sensitise**) ▶ **verb** (**sensitizes, sensitizing, sensitized**) make sensitive or aware.

sensor ▶ **noun** a device which detects or measures a light, heat, pressure, etc.

sensory ▶ **adjective** relating to sensation or the senses.

sensual ▶ **adjective** relating to the physical senses as a source of pleasure.

SYNONYMS **1** *sensual pleasure* **physical,** carnal, bodily, fleshly, animal. **2** *a very sensual woman* **passionate,** sexual, physical, tactile, hedonistic.
ANTONYMS spiritual, passionless.

□ **sensuality** noun **sensually** adverb.

sensuous ▶ **adjective 1** relating to or affecting the senses rather than the intellect. **2** attractive or pleasing physically.

SYNONYMS **1** *big sensuous canvases* **rich,** sumptuous, luxurious. **2** *sensuous lips* **voluptuous,** sexy, seductive, luscious, lush, ripe.

□ **sensuously** adverb.

sent past and past participle of SEND.

sentence ▶ **noun 1** a set of words that is complete in itself, conveying a statement, question, exclamation, or command. **2** the punishment given to someone found guilty by a court.

SYNONYMS **1** *the judge delivered his sentence* **judgement,** ruling, decision, verdict. **2** *a long sentence* **punishment,** prison term; informal time, stretch.

▶ **verb** (**sentences, sentencing, sentenced**) say officially in a law court that an offender is to receive a particular punishment.

S

SYNONYMS *they were sentenced to death* **condemn,** doom, punish, convict.

sententious /sen-**ten**-shuhss/ ▸ adjective given to making pompous comments on moral issues.

sentient ▸ adjective able to perceive or feel things.

sentiment ▸ noun **1** an opinion or feeling. **2** exaggerated feelings of tenderness, sadness, or nostalgia.

SYNONYMS **1** *the comments echo my own sentiments* **view,** feeling, attitude, thought, opinion, belief. **2** *there's no room for sentiment* **sentimentality,** emotion, softness; informal schmaltz, slush; Brit. informal soppiness; N. Amer. informal sappiness.

sentimental ▸ adjective having or causing exaggerated feelings of tenderness, sadness, or nostalgia.

SYNONYMS **1** *she kept the vase for sentimental reasons* **nostalgic,** emotional. **2** *the film is too sentimental* **mawkish,** overemotional, cloying, sickly, romantic; Brit. twee; informal slushy, schmaltzy, corny; Brit. informal soppy; N. Amer. informal sappy. ANTONYMS practical, gritty.

□ **sentimentality** noun **sentimentally** adverb.

sentinel ▸ noun a guard whose job is to stand and keep watch.

sentry ▸ noun (plural **sentries**) a soldier whose job is to guard or control access to a place.

sepal /sep-uhl/ ▸ noun each of the leaf-like parts of a flower that surround the petals.

separable ▸ adjective able to be separated or treated separately.

separate ▸ adjective /sep-uh-ruht/ **1** forming a unit by itself. **2** different; distinct.

SYNONYMS **1** *his personal life was separate from his job* **unconnected,** unrelated, different, distinct, discrete, detached, divorced, disconnected, independent. **2** *the infirmary was separate from the school* **set apart,** detached, cut off, segregated, isolated, free-standing, self-contained. ANTONYMS linked, attached.

▸ verb /sep-uh-rayt/ (**separates, separating, separated**) **1** move or come apart. **2** stop living together as a couple. **3** divide into distinct parts. **4** form a distinction or boundary between.

SYNONYMS **1** *they separated the two youths* **split (up),** break up, part, pull apart. **2** *the connectors can be separated* **disconnect,** detach, disengage, uncouple, split. **3** *the wall that separated the two estates* **partition,** divide, keep apart. **4** *the south aisle was separated off* **isolate,** partition off, section off, close

off, shut off, cordon off. **5** *they separated at the airport* **part (company),** go their separate ways, split up, disperse, scatter. **6** *the road separated* **fork,** divide, branch, diverge. **7** *her parents separated* **split up,** break up, part, divorce. ANTONYMS unite, join, link, meet, merge, marry.

✔ The middle is **-par-,** not **-per-:** se**par**ate.

separately ▸ adverb in a separate way.

SYNONYMS **individually,** one by one, one at a time, singly, severally, apart, independently, alone, by yourself, on your own.

separation ▸ noun **1** the action of separating. **2** the state in which a husband and wife remain married but live apart.

SYNONYMS **1** *the separation of the two companies* **disconnection,** splitting, division, breaking up. **2** *her parents' separation* **break-up,** split, estrangement, divorce; Brit. informal bust-up.

separatism ▸ noun separation of a group of people from a larger group. □ **separatist** noun & adjective.

sepia /see-pi-uh/ ▸ noun a reddish-brown colour.

sepoy /see-poy/ ▸ noun historical an Indian soldier who served the British.

sepsis ▸ noun the infection of body tissues with harmful bacteria.

September ▸ noun the ninth month of the year.

septet ▸ noun a group of seven people playing music or singing together.

septic ▸ adjective (of a wound or a part of the body) infected with bacteria. ■ **septic tank** an underground tank in which sewage is allowed to decompose before draining slowly into the soil.

septicaemia /sep-ti-see-mi-uh/ (US spelling **septicemia**) ▸ noun blood poisoning caused by bacteria.

septuagenarian ▸ noun a person who is between 70 and 79 years old.

septum ▸ noun (plural **septa**) a partition separating two hollow areas in the body, such as that between the nostrils.

sepulchral ▸ adjective **1** having to do with a tomb or burial. **2** gloomy.

sepulchre /sep-uhl-ker/ (US spelling **sepulcher**) ▸ noun a stone tomb.

sequel ▸ noun **1** a book, film, or programme that continues the story of an earlier one. **2** something that takes place after or as a result of an earlier event.

SYNONYMS **continuation,** further episode, follow-up.

S

sequence ▸ noun **1** a particular order in which things follow each other. **2** a set of things that follow each other in a particular order.

SYNONYMS **1** *the sequence of events* **succession**, order, course, series, chain, train, progression, chronology, pattern, flow. **2** *a sequence from his film* **excerpt**, clip, extract, section.

▸ verb (**sequences, sequencing, sequenced**) arrange in a sequence.

sequential ▸ adjective following in a logical order or sequence.
□ **sequentially** adverb.

sequester ▸ verb (**sequesters, sequestering, sequestered**) **1** isolate or hide away. **2** sequestrate.

sequestrate ▸ verb (**sequestrates, sequestrating, sequestrated**) take legal possession of assets until a debt has been paid.
□ **sequestration** noun.

sequin ▸ noun a small, shiny disc sewn on to clothing for decoration.
□ **sequinned** (or **sequined**) adjective.

sequoia ▸ noun a redwood tree.

seraglio /si-**rah**-li-oh/ ▸ noun (plural **seraglios**) **1** the women's apartments in a Muslim palace. **2** a harem.

seraph ▸ noun (plural **seraphim** or **seraphs**) an angelic being associated with light and purity.
□ **seraphic** adjective.

Serbian ▸ noun **1** the language of the Serbs. **2** (also **Serb**) a person from Serbia.
▸ adjective relating to Serbia.

serenade ▸ noun a piece of music sung or played by a man for a woman he loves, outdoors and at night.
▸ verb (**serenades, serenading, serenaded**) perform a serenade for.

serendipity ▸ noun the occurrence of something by chance in a fortunate way.
□ **serendipitous** adjective.

serene ▸ adjective calm and peaceful.
□ **serenely** adverb **serenity** noun.

serf ▸ noun (in the feudal system) an agricultural labourer who had to work on a particular estate and was not allowed to leave.
□ **serfdom** noun.

serge ▸ noun a hard-wearing woollen fabric.

sergeant ▸ noun **1** the rank of officer in the army or air force above corporal. **2** Brit. a police officer just below the rank of inspector.
■ **sergeant major** an officer in the British army who helps with administrative duties.

serial ▸ adjective **1** arranged in a series. **2** repeatedly committing the same offence or doing the same thing: *a serial killer*.

▸ noun a story published or broadcast in regular instalments.
■ **serial number** an identification number given to a manufactured item.

serialize (or **serialise**) ▸ verb (**serializes, serializing, serialized**) **1** publish or broadcast a story in regular instalments. **2** arrange in a series.
□ **serialization** noun.

series ▸ noun (plural **series**) **1** a number of related things coming one after another. **2** a sequence of related television or radio programmes.

SYNONYMS **succession**, sequence, string, chain, run, round, spate, wave, rash, course, cycle, row.

serious ▸ adjective **1** dangerous or very bad: *a serious injury*. **2** needing careful consideration or action. **3** solemn or thoughtful. **4** sincere and in earnest.

SYNONYMS **1** *serious injuries* **severe**, grave, bad, critical, acute, terrible, dire, dangerous. **2** *serious decisions* **important**, significant, momentous, weighty, far-reaching. **3** *serious consideration* **careful**, detailed, in-depth. **4** *a serious play* **intellectual**, highbrow, heavyweight, deep, profound, literary, learned, scholarly; informal heavy. **5** *a serious expression* **solemn**, earnest, grave, sombre, unsmiling, stern, grim, humourless, stony. **6** *we're serious about equality* **sincere**, earnest, genuine, wholehearted, committed, resolute, determined.
ANTONYMS minor, trivial, superficial, lowbrow, light-hearted, half-hearted.

□ **seriousness** noun.

seriously ▸ adverb **1** in a serious way. **2** extremely.

SYNONYMS **1** *Faye nodded seriously* **solemnly**, earnestly, gravely, sombrely, sternly, grimly, humourlessly. **2** *seriously injured* **severely**, gravely, badly, critically, dangerously. **3** *seriously, I'm very pleased* **really**, honestly, truthfully, truly, actually; Brit. informal straight up. **4** *she's seriously rich* **extremely**, very, exceptionally, especially, extraordinarily, tremendously, immensely, hugely, supremely, highly, mightily; informal awfully, terribly; Brit. informal jolly; N. Amer. informal mighty.

sermon ▸ noun a talk on a religious or moral subject, especially one given during a church service.

SYNONYMS **address**, homily, talk, speech, lecture.

serpent ▸ noun literary a large snake.

serpentine ▸ adjective winding or twisting like a snake.

serrated ▸ adjective having a jagged edge like the teeth of a saw.

serration ▸ noun a tooth or point of a serrated edge.

serried ▸ adjective (of rows of people or things) standing close together.

serum ▸ noun (plural **sera** or **serums**) a thin liquid which separates out when blood solidifies.

servant ▸ noun a person employed to perform domestic duties in a household or for a person.

> SYNONYMS **attendant**, domestic, maid, housemaid, retainer, flunkey, minion, slave.

serve ▸ verb (**serves**, **serving**, **served**) **1** perform duties or services for. **2** be employed as a member of the armed forces. **3** spend a period in a job or in prison. **4** present food or drink to. **5** (of food or drink) be enough for. **6** attend to a customer in a shop. **7** fulfil a purpose. **8** treat in a particular way. **9** (in tennis, badminton, etc.) hit the ball or shuttlecock to begin play for each point of a game.

> SYNONYMS **1** *they served their masters faithfully* **work for,** obey, do the bidding of. **2** *this job serves the community* **benefit,** help, assist, aid, make a contribution to, do your bit for. **3** *he served his apprenticeship in Scotland* **carry out,** perform, do, fulfil, complete, discharge, spend. **4** *serve the soup hot* **present,** offer, give out, distribute, dish up, provide, supply. **5** *she served another customer* **attend to,** deal with, see to, assist, help, look after. **6** *a saucer serving as an ashtray* **act,** function, work, perform. **7** *official forms will serve in most cases* **suffice,** do, be good enough, be adequate, fit/fill the bill, suit.

▸ noun an act of serving in tennis, badminton, etc.

■ **serve someone right** be someone's deserved punishment.

server ▸ noun **1** a person or thing that serves. **2** a computer or program that controls or supplies information to a network of computers.

service ▸ noun **1** the action of serving. **2** a period of employment with an organization. **3** an act of assistance. **4** a ceremony of religious worship. **5** a system supplying a public need such as water or electricity. **6** a department or organization run by the state. **7** (**the services**) the armed forces. **8** a set of matching crockery. **9** (in tennis, badminton, etc.) a serve. **10** a routine inspection and maintenance of a vehicle or machine. **11** (**services** or **service area**) a roadside area with a petrol station, cafe, toilets, etc. for motorists.

> SYNONYMS **1** *conditions of service* **work,** employment, labour. **2** *he has done us a service* **favour,** kindness, good turn, helping hand. **3** *the service was excellent* **waiting,** serving, attendance, attention. **4** *products which give reliable service* **use,** usage, functioning, operation. **5** *he took his car in for a service* **overhaul,** check, maintenance. **6** *a marriage service* **ceremony,** ritual, rite, liturgy. **7** *a range of local services* **amenity,** facility, resource, utility. **8** *soldiers leaving the services* **(armed) forces,** military, army, navy, air force.

▸ verb (**services**, **servicing**, **serviced**) **1** perform routine maintenance or repair work on. **2** provide a service or services for someone. **3** pay interest on a debt.

> SYNONYMS *the appliances are serviced regularly* **overhaul,** check, go over, maintain.

■ **in service** dated employed as a servant. **service industry** a business that provides a service rather than manufacturing things. **service station** a garage selling petrol, oil, etc.

serviceable ▸ adjective **1** in working order. **2** useful and hard-wearing.

serviceman (or **servicewoman**) ▸ noun (plural **servicemen** or **servicewomen**) a member of the armed forces.

serviette ▸ noun Brit. a table napkin.

servile ▸ adjective **1** too willing to serve or please other people. **2** of a slave or slaves. □ **servility** noun.

serving ▸ noun a quantity of food for one person.

servitude ▸ noun the state of being a slave, or of being under the complete control of someone more powerful.

servo ▸ noun a device in a vehicle which converts a force into a larger force.

sesame /sess-uh-mi/ ▸ noun a tropical plant grown for its oil-rich seeds.

session ▸ noun **1** a period devoted to a particular activity. **2** a meeting of a council, court, etc., or the period when such meetings are held.

> SYNONYMS **1** *a session of the committee* **meeting,** sitting, assembly, conclave; N. Amer. & NZ caucus. **2** *this parliamentary session* **period,** time, term, year.

set ▸ verb (**sets**, **setting**, **set**) **1** put in a particular place or position. **2** bring into a particular state. **3** give someone a task. **4** decide on or fix a time or limit. **5** establish as an example or record. **6** adjust a device as required. **7** prepare a table for a meal. **8** harden into a solid, semi-solid, or fixed state. **9** arrange damp hair into the required style. **10** put a

S

broken or dislocated bone into the right position for healing. **11** (of the sun, moon, etc.) appear to move towards and below the earth's horizon.

> SYNONYMS **1** *Beth set the bag on the table* **put (down),** place, lay, deposit, position, settle, leave, stand, plant; informal stick, dump, park, plonk, pop. **2** *the fence is set in concrete* **fix,** embed, insert, mount. **3** *a ring set with precious stones* **adorn,** ornament, decorate, embellish. **4** *I'll set the table* **lay,** prepare, arrange, fix. **5** *we set them some work* **assign,** allocate, give, allot. **6** *they set a date for the election* **arrange,** schedule, fix (on), settle on, determine, designate, name, specify. **7** *he set his watch* **adjust,** regulate, synchronize, calibrate, put right, correct. **8** *the adhesive will set in an hour* **solidify,** harden, stiffen, thicken, gel, cake, congeal, coagulate, clot.
> ANTONYMS melt.

▶ noun **1** a number of things or people grouped together. **2** the way in which something is set. **3** a radio or television receiver. **4** (in tennis and similar games) a group of games counting as a unit towards a match. **5** a collection of scenery, furniture, etc., used for a scene in a play or film.

> SYNONYMS **1** *a set of postcards* **series,** collection, group, batch, arrangement, array, assortment, selection. **2** *the literary set* **group,** circle, crowd, crew, band, fraternity, company, ring, camp, school, clique, faction; informal gang, bunch.

▶ adjective **1** fixed or arranged in advance. **2** firmly fixed and unchanging. **3** having a conventional or fixed wording. **4** ready, prepared, or likely to do something.

> SYNONYMS **1** *a set routine* **fixed,** established, predetermined, hard and fast, unvarying, unchanging, invariable, rigid, inflexible, strict, settled. **2** *she had very set ideas* **inflexible,** rigid, fixed, entrenched. **3** *I was all set for the evening* **ready,** prepared, organized, equipped, primed; informal geared up, psyched up.
> ANTONYMS variable, flexible, unprepared.

■ **set about** start doing. **set something aside 1** temporarily stop using land for growing crops. **2** declare that a legal decision is no longer valid. **set off** begin a journey. **set something off** make a bomb or alarm go off. **set on** attack violently. **set out 1** begin a journey. **2** aim or intend to do something. **set piece 1** a formal or elaborate arrangement in a novel, film, etc. **2** Brit. a carefully organized move in a team game. **set square** a flat triangular piece of plastic or metal with a right angle, for drawing lines and angles. **set-top box** a

device which converts a digital television signal into a form which can be viewed on an ordinary television. **set something up** establish a business or other organization.

setback ▶ noun a difficulty or problem that holds back progress.

> SYNONYMS **problem,** difficulty, hitch, complication, upset, blow; informal glitch, hiccup.
> ANTONYMS breakthrough.

sett ▶ noun a badger's burrow.

settee ▶ noun Brit. a long padded seat for more than one person.

setter ▶ noun a breed of dog trained to stand rigid when it scents game.

setting ▶ noun **1** the way or place in which something is set. **2** the metal in which a precious stone or gem is fixed to form a piece of jewellery. **3** a piece of music composed for particular words. **4** (also **place setting**) a complete set of crockery and cutlery for one person at a meal.

> SYNONYMS **surroundings,** position, situation, environment, background, backdrop, spot, place, location, locale, site, scene.

settle¹ ▶ verb (settles, settling, settled) **1** resolve a dispute or difficulty. **2** decide or arrange something finally. **3** make your home in a new place. **4** (often **settle down**) start to live in a more steady or secure way. **5** make or become calmer. **6** sit or rest comfortably or securely. **7** (often **settle in**) begin to feel comfortable in a new situation. **8** pay a debt. **9** (**settle for**) accept after negotiation.

> SYNONYMS **1** *they settled the dispute* **resolve,** sort out, clear up, end, fix, work out, iron out, set right, reconcile; informal patch up. **2** *she settled her affairs* **put in order,** sort out, tidy up, arrange, organize, order, clear up. **3** *they settled on a date for the wedding* **decide on,** set, fix, agree on, name, establish, arrange, choose, pick. **4** *she went to settle her bill* **pay,** square, clear. **5** *he settled in London* **make your home,** set up home, take up residence, put down roots, establish yourself, live, move to. **6** *immigrants settled much of Australia* **colonize,** occupy, populate. **7** *a brandy will settle your nerves* **calm,** quieten, quiet, soothe, pacify, quell. **8** *a butterfly settled on the flower* **land,** come to rest, alight, perch.
> ANTONYMS stir up, take off.

settle² ▶ noun a wooden bench with a high back and arms.

settlement ▶ noun **1** the process of settling. **2** an agreement that is intended to settle a dispute. **3** a place where people establish a community.

S

SYNONYMS **1** *a pay settlement* **agreement,** deal, arrangement, resolution, understanding, pact. **2** *the settlement of the dispute* **resolution,** settling, solution, reconciliation. **3** *a frontier settlement* **community,** colony, outpost, encampment, post, village.

settler ▶ noun a person who establishes a community in a new area.

SYNONYMS **colonist,** frontiersman, pioneer, immigrant, newcomer, incomer. ANTONYMS native.

seven ▶ cardinal number one more than six; 7. (Roman numeral: **vii** or **VII**.)

seventeen ▶ cardinal number one more than sixteen; 17. (Roman numeral: **xvii** or **XVII**.)
□ **seventeenth** ordinal number.

seventh ▶ ordinal number **1** at number seven in a sequence; 7th. **2** (**a seventh** or **one seventh**) each of seven equal parts of something.

seventy ▶ cardinal number (plural **seventies**) ten less than eighty; 70. (Roman numeral: **lxx** or **LXX**.)
□ **seventieth** ordinal number.

sever ▶ verb (**severs, severing, severed**) **1** cut off, or cut into two pieces. **2** put an end to a connection or relationship.

SYNONYMS **1** *the head was severed from the body* **cut off,** chop off, detach, separate, amputate. **2** *a knife had severed the artery* **cut (through),** rupture, split, pierce. **3** *they severed diplomatic relations* **break off,** discontinue, suspend, end, cease, dissolve.
ANTONYMS join, maintain.

several ▶ determiner & pronoun more than two but not many.
▶ adjective separate or respective.

SYNONYMS **some,** a number of, a few, various, assorted.

□ **severally** adverb.

severance ▶ noun **1** the ending of a connection, relationship, or period of employment. **2** the state of being separated or cut off.

severe ▶ adjective **1** (of something bad or difficult) very great. **2** strict or harsh. **3** very plain in style or appearance.

SYNONYMS **1** *severe injuries* **acute,** very bad, serious, grave, critical, dangerous, life-threatening. **2** *severe storms* **fierce,** violent, strong, powerful. **3** *a severe winter* **harsh,** bitter, cold, freezing, icy, arctic. **4** *severe criticism* **harsh,** scathing, sharp, strong, fierce, savage, devastating, withering. **5** *his severe expression* **stern,** dour, grim, forbidding, disapproving, unsmiling, unfriendly, sombre, stony, cold, frosty. **6** *a severe style of*

architecture **plain,** simple, austere, unadorned, stark, clinical, uncluttered.
ANTONYMS minor, gentle, mild, friendly, ornate.

□ **severity** noun.

severely ▶ adverb in a severe way.

SYNONYMS **1** *he was severely injured* **badly,** seriously, critically. **2** *murderers should be treated more severely* **harshly,** strictly, sternly, rigorously. **3** *she looked severely at Harriet* **sternly,** grimly, dourly, disapprovingly.

sew ▶ verb (**sews, sewing, sewed;** past participle **sewn** or **sewed**) join or repair by making stitches with a needle and thread or a machine.

SYNONYMS **stitch,** tack, seam, hem, embroider.

sewage /soo-ij/ ▶ noun human waste and water carried away from drains in sewers.

sewer /soo-er/ ▶ noun an underground channel for carrying away human waste and water from drains.
□ **sewerage** noun.

sex ▶ noun **1** either of the two main categories (male and female) into which humans and most other living things are divided. **2** the fact of being male or female. **3** the group of all members of either sex. **4** sexual intercourse.

SYNONYMS **1** *they talked about sex* **sexual intercourse,** lovemaking, making love, the sex act, sexual relations, mating, copulation. **2** *adults of both sexes* **gender.**

■ **sex symbol** a celebrity famous for being sexually attractive. **sex something up** informal present something in a more interesting way.

sexagenarian ▶ noun a person between 60 and 69 years old.

sexism ▶ noun prejudice or discrimination on the basis of a person's sex.
□ **sexist** adjective & noun.

sexless ▶ adjective **1** not sexually attractive or active. **2** neither male nor female.

sextant ▶ noun an instrument for measuring angles and distances, used in navigation and surveying.

sextet ▶ noun **1** a group of six musicians. **2** a piece of music for a sextet.

sexton ▶ noun a person who looks after a church and churchyard.

sextuple ▶ adjective **1** made up of six parts or elements. **2** six times as much or as many.

sextuplet ▶ noun each of six children born at one birth.

sexual ▶ adjective **1** relating to sex, or to physical attraction or contact between individuals. **2** connected with the state of

S

being male or female. **3** (of reproduction) involving the fusion of male and female cells.

> SYNONYMS **1** *the sexual organs* **reproductive,** genital, sex. **2** *sexual activity* **carnal,** erotic.

■ **sexual harassment** the making of unwanted sexual advances or remarks to someone, especially at work. **sexual intercourse** sexual contact in which the man inserts his erect penis into the woman's vagina.
□ **sexually** adverb.

sexuality ▸ noun (plural **sexualities**) **1** capacity for sexual feelings. **2** a person's sexual preference.

> SYNONYMS **1** *she had a powerful sexuality* **sensuality,** sexiness, seductiveness, eroticism, physicality, sexual appetite, passion, desire, lust. **2** *I'm open about my sexuality* **sexual orientation,** sexual preference, leaning, persuasion.

sexy ▸ adjective (**sexier, sexiest**) **1** sexually attractive or exciting. **2** sexually aroused. **3** informal exciting and interesting.

> SYNONYMS **1** *she's so sexy* **sexually attractive,** seductive, desirable, alluring; informal **fanciable;** Brit. informal **fit;** N. Amer. informal **foxy. 2** *sexy videos* **erotic,** sexually explicit, titillating, naughty, X-rated, rude, pornographic, crude; informal raunchy, steamy; euphemistic adult. **3** *they weren't feeling sexy* **sexually aroused,** sexually excited, amorous, lustful, passionate; informal **turned on;** Brit. informal randy.

□ **sexily** adverb **sexiness** noun.

shabby ▸ adjective (**shabbier, shabbiest**) **1** worn out or scruffy. **2** mean and unfair.

> SYNONYMS **1** *a shabby little bar* **run down,** scruffy, dilapidated, squalid, sordid; informal **crummy;** Brit. informal **grotty;** N. Amer. informal **shacky. 2** *a shabby grey coat* **scruffy,** old, worn out, threadbare, ragged, frayed, tattered, battered, faded, moth-eaten; informal **tatty;** N. Amer. informal **raggedy. 3** *her shabby treatment of Ben* **mean,** unkind, unfair, shameful, shoddy, unworthy, contemptible, despicable, discreditable; informal **rotten.** ANTONYMS smart, decent.

□ **shabbily** adverb **shabbiness** noun.

shack ▸ noun a roughly built hut or cabin.

> SYNONYMS **hut,** cabin, shanty, lean-to, shed, hovel; Scottish **bothy.**

▸ verb (**shack up with**) informal live with someone as a lover.

shackle ▸ noun (**shackles**) **1** rings connected by a chain, used to fasten a prisoner's wrists or ankles together. **2** restraints or restrictions.

▸ verb (**shackles, shackling, shackled**) **1** chain with shackles. **2** restrain; limit.

shade ▸ noun **1** relative darkness and coolness caused by shelter from direct sunlight. **2** a colour, especially in terms of how light or dark it is. **3** a variety. **4** a slight amount. **5** (**shades**) informal sunglasses. **6** literary a ghost.

> SYNONYMS **1** *they sat in the shade* **shadow,** shelter, cover, cool. **2** *shades of blue* **colour,** hue, tone, tint, tinge. **3** *shades of meaning* **nuance,** gradation, degree, difference, variation, variety, nicety, subtlety, undertone, overtone. **4** *her skirt was a shade too short* **little,** bit, trace, touch, modicum, tinge; informal **tad, smidgen;** (**a shade**) slightly, rather, somewhat. **5** *the window shade* **blind,** curtain, screen, cover, covering, awning, canopy.
> ANTONYMS light.

▸ verb (**shades, shading, shaded**) **1** screen from direct light. **2** cover or lessen the light of. **3** represent a darker area with pencil or a block of colour. **4** change gradually into something else.

> SYNONYMS *vines shaded the garden* **cast a shadow over,** shadow, shelter, cover, screen.

shadow ▸ noun **1** a dark area or shape produced by an object coming between light rays and a surface. **2** partial or complete darkness. **3** sadness or gloom. **4** the slightest trace. **5** a weak or less good version. **6** a person who constantly accompanies or secretly follows another.

> SYNONYMS **1** *he saw her shadow in the doorway* **silhouette,** outline, shape, contour, profile. **2** *he emerged from the shadows* **shade,** darkness, twilight, gloom.

▸ verb **1** cast a shadow over. **2** follow and observe secretly.

> SYNONYMS *he is shadowing a suspect* **follow,** trail, track, stalk, pursue; informal tail, keep tabs on.

■ **shadow-boxing** boxing against an imaginary opponent as a form of training. **Shadow Cabinet** Brit. those members of the main opposition party who would become government ministers if their party won the next election.
□ **shadowy** adjective.

shady ▸ adjective (**shadier, shadiest**) **1** giving, or situated in, shade. **2** informal seeming to be dishonest or illegal.

> SYNONYMS **1** *a shady garden* **shaded,** shadowy, dim, dark, sheltered, leafy. **2** *shady deals* **suspicious,** suspect, questionable, dubious, irregular, underhand; N. Amer. **snide;** informal **fishy,**

S

murky; Brit. informal **dodgy**; Austral./NZ informal **shonky**.
ANTONYMS bright, honest.

shaft ▶ noun **1** the long, narrow handle of a tool or club, body of a spear or arrow, etc. **2** a ray of light or bolt of lightning. **3** a narrow vertical passage giving access to a mine, accommodating a lift, etc. **4** each of the pair of poles between which a horse is harnessed to a vehicle. **5** a rotating rod for transmitting mechanical power in a machine.

SYNONYMS **1** *the shaft of a golf club* **pole**, shank, stick, rod, staff, handle, stem. **2** *shafts of sunlight* **ray**, beam, gleam, streak. **3** *a ventilation shaft* **tunnel**, passage, hole, bore, duct, well, flue, vent.

shag¹ ▶ noun coarse tobacco.
▶ adjective (of pile on a carpet) long and rough.

shag² ▶ noun a cormorant (seabird) with greenish-black feathers.

shaggy ▶ adjective (**shaggier, shaggiest**) **1** (of hair or fur) long, thick, and untidy. **2** having shaggy hair or fur.

shah ▶ noun (in the past) the title of the king of Iran.

shake ▶ verb (**shakes, shaking, shook**; past participle **shaken**) **1** move quickly and jerkily up and down or to and fro. **2** tremble. **3** shock or upset. **4** get rid of or put an end to.

SYNONYMS **1** *the building shook* **vibrate**, tremble, quiver, quake, shiver, shudder, judder, wobble, rock, sway, convulse. **2** *she shook the bottle* **jiggle**, agitate; informal wiggle, waggle. **3** *he shook his stick* **brandish**, wave, flourish, swing, wield. **4** *what she saw shook her* **upset**, distress, disturb, unsettle, disconcert, discompose, unnerve, throw off balance, agitate, fluster, shock, alarm, scare, worry; informal rattle.
ANTONYMS soothe.

▶ noun **1** an act of shaking. **2** informal a milkshake.

SYNONYMS **1** *camera shake* **judder**, trembling, quivering, quake, tremor, shiver, shudder, wobble. **2** *he gave his coat a shake* **jiggle**, joggle; informal waggle. **3** *a shake of his fist* **flourish**, wave.

■ **shake hands (with someone)** clasp someone's right hand in your own when meeting or leaving them, to congratulate them, or as a sign of agreement. **shake someone/thing up 1** stir someone into action. **2** make major changes to an institution or system.
□ **shaker** noun.

Shakespearean (or **Shakespearian**) ▶ adjective having to do with the English dramatist William Shakespeare or his works.

shaky ▶ adjective (**shakier, shakiest**) **1** shaking; unsteady. **2** not safe or certain.

SYNONYMS **1** *shaky legs* **unsteady**, unstable, rickety, wobbly; Brit. informal wonky. **2** *I feel a bit shaky* **faint**, dizzy, light-headed, giddy, weak, wobbly, in shock. **3** *the evidence is shaky* **unreliable**, untrustworthy, questionable, dubious, doubtful, tenuous, suspect, flimsy, weak; informal iffy; Brit. informal dodgy.
ANTONYMS steady, stable, sound.

□ **shakily** adverb.

shale ▶ noun soft rock formed from compressed mud or clay.

shall ▶ modal verb (3rd singular present **shall**) **1** used with *I* and *we* to express the future tense. **2** expressing a strong statement, intention, or order. **3** Brit. used in questions to make offers or suggestions: *shall we go?*

❗ The traditional rule is that you should use **shall** when forming the future tense with **I** and **we** (*I shall be late*) and **will** with **you**, **he**, **she**, **it**, and **they** (*he will not be there*).

shallot /shuh-**lot**/ ▶ noun a vegetable like a small onion.

shallow ▶ adjective **1** having a short distance between the top and the bottom; not deep. **2** not thinking or thought out seriously.

SYNONYMS **superficial**, trivial, facile, insubstantial, lightweight, empty, trifling, surface, skin-deep, frivolous, foolish, silly.
ANTONYMS profound.

▶ noun (**shallows**) a shallow area of water.
□ **shallowly** adverb.

shalwar = SALWAR.

sham ▶ noun **1** a thing that is not what it appears to be or is not as good as it seems. **2** a person who pretends to be something they are not.

SYNONYMS *it's all a sham* **pretence**, fake, act, simulation, fraud, lie, counterfeit, humbug.

▶ adjective not genuine; false.

SYNONYMS *a sham marriage* **fake**, pretended, feigned, simulated, false, artificial, bogus, insincere, affected, make-believe; informal pretend, put-on, phoney.
ANTONYMS genuine.

▶ verb (**shams, shamming, shammed**) pretend.

SYNONYMS *he's shamming* **pretend**, fake, malinger; informal put it on; Brit. informal swing the lead.

shaman /**shay**-muhn/ ▶ noun (plural **shamans**) (in some societies) a person believed to be able to contact good and evil spirits.
□ **shamanic** adjective **shamanism** noun.

S

shamble ▸ verb (shambles, shambling, shambled) walk in a slow, shuffling, awkward way.

shambles ▸ noun informal a state of complete disorder.

SYNONYMS **1** *we have to sort out this shambles* **chaos,** muddle, jumble, confusion, disorder, havoc. **2** *the room was a shambles* **mess,** pigsty; informal disaster area; Brit. informal tip.

shambolic ▸ adjective Brit. informal very disorganized.

shame ▸ noun **1** the feeling you have of embarrassment or distress when you know you have done something wrong or foolish. **2** loss of respect; dishonour. **3** a cause of shame. **4** a cause for regret or disappointment.

SYNONYMS **1** *a sense of shame* **guilt,** remorse, contrition. **2** *he brought shame on the family* **humiliation,** embarrassment, indignity, mortification, disgrace, dishonour, discredit, ignominy, disrepute, infamy, scandal. **3** *it's a shame she never married* **pity,** sad thing, bad luck; informal crime, sin.
ANTONYMS pride, honour.

▸ verb (shames, shaming, shamed) make someone feel shame.

SYNONYMS **1** *you shamed your family* **disgrace,** dishonour, discredit, blacken, drag through the mud. **2** *he was shamed in public* **humiliate,** embarrass, humble, take down a peg or two, cut down to size; informal show up; N. Amer. informal make someone eat crow.
ANTONYMS honour.

■ **put someone/thing to shame** be much better than someone or something.

shamefaced ▸ adjective showing shame.

shameful ▸ adjective causing a feeling of shame.

SYNONYMS **1** *shameful behaviour* **disgraceful,** deplorable, despicable, contemptible, discreditable, reprehensible, unworthy, shabby, shocking, scandalous, outrageous, abominable, atrocious, appalling, inexcusable, unforgivable. **2** *a shameful secret* **embarrassing,** mortifying, humiliating, ignominious.
ANTONYMS admirable.

□ **shamefully** adverb.

shameless ▸ adjective showing no shame.
□ **shamelessly** adverb.

shammy ▸ noun (plural shammies) informal chamois leather.

shampoo ▸ noun **1** a liquid soap for washing the hair. **2** a similar substance for cleaning a carpet, car, etc. **3** an act of washing with shampoo.

▸ verb (shampoos, shampooing, shampooed) wash or clean with shampoo.

shamrock ▸ noun a clover-like plant with three leaves on each stem, the national emblem of Ireland.

shandy ▸ noun (plural shandies) beer mixed with lemonade or ginger beer.

shanghai /shang-**hy**/ ▸ verb (shanghais, shanghaiing, shanghaied) informal force or trick into doing something.

shank ▸ noun **1** the lower part of the leg. **2** the shaft of a tool.
■ **Shanks's pony** your own legs as a means of transport.

shan't ▸ short form shall not.

shantung ▸ noun a type of silk fabric with a rough surface.

shanty¹ ▸ noun (plural shanties) a small roughly built hut.
■ **shanty town** a settlement in or near a town where poor people live in shanties.

shanty² ▸ noun (plural shanties) a song with alternating solo and chorus, sung by sailors when working.

shape ▸ noun **1** the form of something produced by its outline. **2** a piece of material, paper, etc. cut in a particular form. **3** a particular condition or state. **4** well-defined structure or arrangement.

SYNONYMS **1** *the shape of the dining table* **form,** appearance, configuration, structure, contours, lines, outline, silhouette, profile. **2** *a spirit in the shape of a fox* **guise,** likeness, semblance, form, appearance, image. **3** *in good shape* **condition,** health, trim, fettle, order; Brit. informal nick.

▸ verb (shapes, shaping, shaped) **1** give a shape to. **2** have a big influence on.

SYNONYMS **1** *the metal is shaped into tools* **form,** fashion, make, mould, model. **2** *attitudes shaped by his report* **determine,** form, fashion, mould, develop, influence, affect.

■ **shape up 1** develop in a particular way. **2** improve your fitness, behaviour, etc.

shapeless ▸ adjective lacking a definite or attractive shape.

shapely ▸ adjective having an attractive shape.

shard ▸ noun a sharp piece of broken pottery, glass, etc.

share ▸ noun **1** a part of a larger amount which is divided among or contributed to by a number of people. **2** any of the equal parts into which a company's wealth is divided, which can be bought by people in return for a proportion of the profits. **3** an amount thought to be normal or acceptable.

S

SYNONYMS *her share of the profits* **portion,** part, division, quota, allowance, ration, allocation; informal cut, slice; Brit. informal whack.

▶ verb (**shares, sharing, shared**) **1** have or give a share of. **2** have, use, or experience jointly with others.

SYNONYMS **1** *we share the bills* **split,** divide, go halves on; informal go fifty-fifty on. **2** *they shared out the peanuts* **apportion,** divide up, allocate, portion out, measure out, carve up; Brit. informal divvy up. **3** *we all share in the learning process* **participate,** take part, play a part, be involved, have a hand.

□ **sharer** noun.

shareholder ▶ noun an owner of shares in a company.

shark¹ ▶ noun a large and sometimes aggressive sea fish with a triangular fin on its back.

shark² ▶ noun informal a person who dishonestly obtains money from other people.

sharp ▶ adjective **1** having a cutting or piercing edge or point. **2** tapering to a point or edge. **3** sudden and noticeable. **4** clear and definite. **5** producing a sudden, piercing feeling. **6** quick to understand, notice, or respond. **7** (of a taste or smell) strong and slightly bitter. **8** (of a note or key) higher by a semitone than a stated note or key. **9** (of musical sound) above true or normal pitch.

SYNONYMS **1** *a sharp knife* **keen,** razor-edged, sharpened, well-honed. **2** *a sharp pain* **intense,** acute, severe, agonizing, excruciating, stabbing, shooting, searing. **3** *a sharp taste* **tangy,** piquant, acidic, acid, sour, tart, pungent. **4** *a sharp wind* **cold,** chilly, icy, bitter, biting, brisk, keen, penetrating. **5** *sharp words* **harsh,** bitter, cutting, spiteful, hurtful, cruel. **6** *a sharp photo* **clear,** distinct, crisp, focused. **7** *a sharp increase* **sudden,** abrupt, rapid, steep. **8** *she was sharp and witty* **astute,** intelligent, bright, incisive, keen, quick-witted, shrewd, canny, perceptive, smart, quick; informal on the ball, quick on the uptake; N. Amer. informal heads-up. ANTONYMS blunt, mild, sweet, soft, kind, indistinct, gradual, slow, stupid.

▶ adverb **1** precisely. **2** suddenly or abruptly.

SYNONYMS **precisely,** exactly, promptly, prompt, punctually; informal on the dot; N. Amer. informal on the button. ANTONYMS roughly.

▶ noun a musical note raised a semitone above natural pitch, shown by the sign ♯.

■ **sharp practice** dishonest business

dealings.
□ **sharply** adverb **sharpness** noun.

sharpen ▶ verb make or become sharp.

SYNONYMS **hone,** whet, strop, grind, file.

□ **sharpener** noun.

sharpshooter ▶ noun a person skilled in shooting.

shatter ▶ verb (**shatters, shattering, shattered**) **1** break suddenly and violently into pieces. **2** damage or destroy. **3** upset someone greatly. **4** (**shattered**) Brit. informal completely exhausted.

SYNONYMS **1** *the glasses shattered* **smash,** break, splinter, crack, fracture, fragment, disintegrate. **2** *the announcement shattered their hopes* **destroy,** wreck, ruin, dash, crush, devastate, demolish, torpedo, scotch; informal do for, put paid to; Brit. informal scupper. **3** (**shattered**) *he was shattered by the reviews* **devastated,** shocked, stunned, dazed, traumatized. **4** (**shattered**) *I feel too shattered to move* **exhausted,** tired, worn out, weary, fatigued, ready to drop; informal done in, all in, dead beat; Brit. informal knackered, whacked, zonked; N. Amer. informal pooped, tuckered out.

shave ▶ verb (**shaves, shaving, shaved**) **1** remove hair by cutting it off close to the skin with a razor. **2** cut a thin slice or slices from something. **3** reduce something by a small amount.

SYNONYMS **1** *he shaved his beard* **cut off,** crop, trim, barber. **2** *shave off excess wood* **plane,** pare, whittle, scrape.

▶ noun an act of shaving.

shaven ▶ adjective shaved.

shaver ▶ noun an electric razor.

shaving ▶ noun a thin strip cut off a surface.

shawl ▶ noun a large piece of fabric worn by women over the shoulders or head or wrapped round a baby.

she ▶ pronoun **1** used to refer to a female person or animal previously mentioned or easily identified. **2** used to refer to a ship, country, or other thing thought of as female.

sheaf ▶ noun (plural **sheaves**) **1** a bundle of papers. **2** a bundle of grain stalks tied together after reaping.

shear ▶ verb (**shears, shearing, sheared**; past participle **shorn** or **sheared**) **1** cut the wool off a sheep. **2** cut off something such as wool or grass with shears. **3** (**be shorn of**) have something taken away from you. **4** (**shear off**) tear or break off under pressure.
□ **shearer** noun.

❗ Don't confuse **shear** with **sheer**, which is a verb meaning 'change course quickly' and also an adjective meaning 'nothing but; absolute'.

shears ▸ plural noun a cutting tool like very large scissors.

sheath ▸ noun (plural **sheaths**) **1** a cover for the blade of a knife or sword. **2** a condom. **3** a close-fitting covering.

> SYNONYMS **covering**, cover, case, casing, sleeve, scabbard.

sheathe ▸ verb (**sheathes, sheathing, sheathed**) **1** put a knife or sword into a sheath. **2** encase something in a close-fitting or protective covering.

shebang /shi-**bang**/ ▸ noun (**the whole shebang**) informal the whole thing.

shed¹ ▸ noun a simple building used for storage.

> SYNONYMS *a shed in the garden* **hut**, lean-to, outhouse, outbuilding, cabin, shack.

shed² ▸ verb (**sheds, shedding, shed**) **1** allow leaves, hair, skin, etc. to fall off naturally. **2** get rid of. **3** take off clothes. **4** give off light. **5** (of a vehicle) accidentally drop what it is carrying.

> SYNONYMS **1** *the trees shed their leaves* **drop**, scatter, spill. **2** *the caterpillar shed its skin* **throw off**, cast off, discard, slough off, moult. **3** *we shed our clothes* **take off**, remove, discard, climb out of, slip out of; Brit. informal peel off. **4** *the moon shed a watery light* **cast**, radiate, emit, give out.
> ANTONYMS keep, put on.

■ **shed tears** cry.

she'd ▸ short form **1** she had. **2** she would.

sheen ▸ noun a soft shine on a surface.

> SYNONYMS **shine**, lustre, gloss, patina, burnish, polish, shimmer.

sheep ▸ noun (plural **sheep**) an animal with a thick woolly coat, kept in flocks for its wool or meat.

■ **sheep dip** a liquid in which sheep are dipped to clean and disinfect their wool.

sheepdog ▸ noun a breed of dog trained to guard and herd sheep.

sheepish ▸ adjective feeling embarrassed from shame or shyness.
□ **sheepishly** adverb.

sheepskin ▸ noun a sheep's skin with the wool on.

sheer¹ ▸ adjective **1** nothing but; absolute. **2** (of a cliff or wall) vertical or almost vertical. **3** (of fabric) very thin.

> SYNONYMS **1** *the sheer audacity of the plan* **utter**, complete, absolute, total, pure, downright, out-and-out. **2** *a sheer drop* **steep**, abrupt, sharp, precipitous, vertical. **3** *a sheer dress* **thin**, fine, gauzy, diaphanous, transparent, see-through, flimsy.
> ANTONYMS gradual, thick.

❗ Don't confuse **sheer** with **shear**: see the note at SHEAR.

sheer² ▸ verb (**sheers, sheering, sheered**) **1** (especially of a boat) change course quickly. **2** move away from an unpleasant topic.

sheet¹ ▸ noun **1** a large rectangular piece of cotton or other fabric, used on a bed to lie on or under. **2** a broad flat piece of metal or glass. **3** a rectangular piece of paper. **4** a wide expanse or moving mass of water, flames, etc.

> SYNONYMS **1** *a sheet of ice* **layer**, covering, blanket, coat, film, veneer, crust, skin, surface, stratum. **2** *a sheet of glass* **pane**, panel, slab, plate, piece. **3** *a fresh sheet of paper* **page**, leaf, piece. **4** *a sheet of water* **expanse**, area, stretch, sweep.

■ **sheet music** music printed on loose sheets of paper.

sheet² ▸ noun a rope attached to the lower corner of a sail.

sheikh (or **sheik**) /shayk/ ▸ noun a Muslim or Arab leader.

sheila ▸ noun Austral./NZ informal a girl or woman.

shekel ▸ noun the basic unit of money of modern Israel.

shelf ▸ noun (plural **shelves**) **1** a flat length of wood or other rigid material, fixed horizontally and used to display or store things. **2** a ledge of rock.
■ **off the shelf** taken from existing supplies, not made to order. **on the shelf** (of a woman) past an age when she might expect to be married. **shelf life** the length of time for which an item to be sold can be stored.

shell ▸ noun **1** the hard protective outer case of an animal such as a shellfish or turtle. **2** the outer covering of an egg, nut kernel, or seed. **3** a metal case filled with explosive, to be fired from a large gun. **4** a hollow case. **5** an outer structure or framework.

> SYNONYMS **1** *peanut shells* **pod**, hull, husk; N. Amer. shuck. **2** *the metal shell of the car* **body**, case, casing, framework, hull, fuselage, hulk.

▸ verb **1** fire explosive shells at. **2** remove the shell or pod from. **3** (**shell something out**) informal pay an amount of money.

> SYNONYMS **1** *they were shelling peas* **pod**, hull, husk; N. Amer. shuck. **2** *rebel artillery shelled the city* **bombard**, fire on, attack, bomb, blitz.

■ **shell shock** a mental condition which resembles a state of shock and can affect soldiers who have been in battle for a long time. **shell suit** Brit. an outfit consisting of a top and trousers with a soft lining and shiny outer layer.

S

she'll ▸ short form **1** she shall. **2** she will.

shellfish ▸ noun a water animal that has a shell and that can be eaten, such as a crab or oyster.

shelter ▸ noun **1** a place giving protection from bad weather or danger. **2** a place providing food and accommodation for the homeless. **3** protection from danger or bad weather.

> SYNONYMS **1** *the trees provide shelter for animals* **protection,** cover, shade, safety, security, refuge. **2** *a shelter for abandoned cats* **sanctuary,** refuge, home, haven, safe house.
> ANTONYMS exposure, danger.

▸ verb (**shelters, sheltering, sheltered**)
1 provide with shelter. **2** find protection or take cover. **3** (**sheltered**) protected from the more unpleasant aspects of life. **4** (**sheltered**) Brit. (of accommodation) designed for elderly or disabled people, and staffed by a warden.

> SYNONYMS **1** *the hut sheltered him from the sun* **protect,** shield, screen, cover, shade, defend, cushion, guard, insulate. **2** *the convoy sheltered in a bay* **take shelter,** take refuge, take cover; informal hole up. **3** (**sheltered**) *a sheltered stretch of water* **protected,** tranquil, still, shady. **4** (**sheltered**) *a sheltered life* **protected,** cloistered, insulated, privileged, secure, safe, quiet.
> ANTONYMS expose.

shelve ▸ verb (**shelves, shelving, shelved**)
1 decide not to continue with a plan for the time being. **2** place something on a shelf. **3** (of ground) slope downwards.

> SYNONYMS **postpone,** put off, delay, defer, put back, reschedule, hold over/off, put to one side, suspend, stay, mothball; N. Amer. put over, table; informal put on ice, put on the back burner.
> ANTONYMS execute, bring forward, revive.

shelves plural of SHELF.

shenanigans ▸ plural noun informal mischievous behaviour.

shepherd ▸ noun a person who looks after sheep.
▸ verb guide or direct someone.

> SYNONYMS **usher,** steer, herd, lead, take, escort, guide, conduct, marshal, walk.

■ **shepherd's pie** Brit. a dish of minced meat under a layer of mashed potato. □ **shepherdess** noun.

sherbet ▸ noun **1** Brit. a sweet fizzing powder eaten alone or made into a drink. **2** (in Arab countries) a drink of sweet diluted fruit juices.

sheriff ▸ noun **1** (also **high sheriff**) (in England and Wales) the chief executive officer in a county, working on behalf of a king or queen. **2** (in Scotland) a judge. **3** (in the US) an elected officer in a county, responsible for keeping the peace.

Sherpa ▸ noun (plural **Sherpa** or **Sherpas**) a member of a Himalayan people living on the borders of Nepal and Tibet.

sherry ▸ noun (plural **sherries**) a strong wine from southern Spain.

she's ▸ short form **1** she is. **2** she has.

Shetland pony ▸ noun a small breed of pony with a rough coat.

Shia /shi-uh/ ▸ noun (plural **Shia** or **Shias**) **1** one of the two main branches of Islam. The other is SUNNI. **2** a Muslim who follows the Shia branch of Islam.

shiatsu /shi-at-soo/ ▸ noun a medical treatment from Japan in which pressure is applied with the hands to points on the body.

shibboleth /shib-buh-leth/ ▸ noun a long-standing belief or principle held by a group of people.

shied past and past participle of SHY².

shield ▸ noun **1** a broad piece of armour held for protection against blows or missiles. **2** a person or thing that acts as a protective barrier or screen. **3** a sports trophy consisting of an engraved metal plate mounted on a piece of wood. **4** a drawing or model of a shield used for displaying a coat of arms.

> SYNONYMS *a shield against radiation* **protection,** guard, defence, cover, screen, shelter.

▸ verb protect or hide.

> SYNONYMS *he shielded his eyes* **protect,** guard, defend, cover, screen, shade, shelter.
> ANTONYMS expose.

shift ▸ verb **1** move or change from one position to another. **2** transfer blame or responsibility to someone else. **3** Brit. informal move quickly.

> SYNONYMS **1** *he shifted some chairs* **move,** transfer, transport, switch, relocate, reposition, rearrange. **2** *the cargo has shifted* **move,** slide, slip, be displaced. **3** *the wind shifted* **veer,** alter, change, turn. **4** *this brush really shifts the dirt* **get rid of,** remove, get off, budge, lift.
> ANTONYMS leave.

▸ noun **1** a slight change in position or direction. **2** a period of time worked by someone who starts work as another finishes. **3** a straight dress without a fitted waist. **4** a key used to switch between two sets of characters or functions on a keyboard.

> SYNONYMS **1** *a shift in public opinion* **change,** alteration, adjustment, variation, modification, revision,

S

reversal, U-turn. **2** *they worked three shifts* **stint**, stretch, spell.

shiftless ▸ adjective lazy and lacking ambition.

shifty ▸ adjective informal seeming dishonest or untrustworthy.

Shiite /shee-It/ ▸ noun a follower of the Shia branch of Islam.

shilling ▸ noun **1** a former British coin worth one twentieth of a pound or twelve old pence (five p). **2** the basic unit of money of Kenya, Tanzania, and Uganda.

shilly-shally ▸ verb (shilly-shallies, shilly-shallying, shilly-shallied) be unable to make up your mind.

shimmer ▸ verb (shimmers, shimmering, shimmered) shine with a soft wavering light.

SYNONYMS *the sea shimmered in the sunset* **glint**, glisten, twinkle, sparkle, flash, gleam, glow, glimmer, wink.

▸ noun a soft wavering light or shine.

SYNONYMS *a shimmer of moonlight* **glint**, twinkle, sparkle, flash, gleam, glow, glimmer, lustre, glitter.

□ **shimmery** adjective.

shimmy ▸ verb (shimmies, shimmying, shimmied) move quickly and smoothly.

shin ▸ noun the front of the leg below the knee.

▸ verb (shins, shinning, shinned) (shin up or down) climb quickly up or down by gripping with your arms and legs.

shindig ▸ noun informal a lively party.

shine ▸ verb (shines, shining, past and past participle **shone** or **shined**) **1** give out or reflect light. **2** direct a torch or other light somewhere. **3** (of a person's eyes) be bright with an emotion. **4** be very good at something. **5** (past and past participle **shined**) polish.

SYNONYMS **1** *the sun shone* **beam**, gleam, radiate, glow, glint, glimmer, sparkle, twinkle, glitter, glisten, shimmer, flash. **2** *she shone her shoes* **polish**, burnish, buff, rub up, brush, clean. **3** *they shone at university* **excel**, stand out.

▸ noun a quality of brightness.

SYNONYMS *linseed oil restores the shine* **polish**, gleam, gloss, lustre, sheen, patina.

■ **take a shine to** informal develop a liking for.

shiner ▸ noun informal a black eye.

shingle¹ ▸ noun a mass of small rounded pebbles on a seashore.

shingle² ▸ noun a wooden tile used on walls or roofs.
□ **shingled** adjective.

shingles ▸ noun a disease in which painful blisters form along the path of a nerve.

Shinto Japan ▸ noun a Japanese religion involving the worship of ancestors and nature spirits.

shiny ▸ adjective (shinier, shiniest) reflecting light.

SYNONYMS **glossy**, bright, glassy, polished, gleaming, satiny, lustrous. ANTONYMS matt.

ship ▸ noun a large boat for transporting people or goods by sea.

SYNONYMS **boat**, vessel, craft.

▸ verb (ships, shipping, shipped) **1** transport goods on a ship or by other means. **2** (of a boat) take in water over the side.

SYNONYMS *goods are shipped within 24 hours* **deliver**, send, dispatch, transport, carry, distribute.

shipbuilder ▸ noun a person or company that designs and builds ships.
□ **shipbuilding** noun.

shipment ▸ noun **1** the action of transporting goods. **2** an amount of goods shipped.

shipping ▸ noun **1** ships as a whole. **2** the transport of goods.

shipshape ▸ adjective orderly and neat.

shipwreck ▸ noun **1** the sinking or breaking up of a ship at sea. **2** a ship that has been lost or destroyed at sea.

▸ verb (be shipwrecked) suffer a shipwreck.

shipyard ▸ noun a place where ships are built and repaired.

shire ▸ noun **1** Brit. a county in England. **2** (the Shires) country areas of England regarded as strongholds of traditional country life.

■ **shire horse** a heavy, powerful breed of horse.

shirk ▸ verb avoid work or a duty.
□ **shirker** noun.

shirred ▸ adjective (of fabric) gathered by means of threads in parallel rows.

shirt ▸ noun a garment for the upper body, with a collar and sleeves and buttons down the front.

shirtsleeves ▸ plural noun (in your shirtsleeves) wearing a shirt without a jacket.

shirty ▸ adjective Brit. informal irritated or annoyed.

shish kebab ▸ noun a dish of pieces of meat and vegetables cooked and served on skewers.

shiver ▸ verb (shivers, shivering, shivered) shake slightly from fear, cold, or excitement.

S

SYNONYMS *she was shivering with fear* **tremble,** quiver, shake, shudder, quake.

▶ noun a trembling movement.

SYNONYMS *she gave a shiver* **shudder,** twitch, start.

□ **shivery** adjective.

shoal¹ ▶ noun a large number of fish swimming together.

shoal² ▶ noun 1 an area of shallow water. 2 a submerged sandbank that can be seen at low tide.

shock¹ ▶ noun 1 a sudden upsetting or surprising event or experience. 2 an unpleasant feeling of sudden surprise and distress. 3 a serious medical condition associated with a fall in blood pressure, caused by loss of blood, severe burns, etc. 4 a violent shaking movement caused by an impact, explosion, or earthquake. 5 an electric shock.

SYNONYMS 1 *the news came as a shock* **blow,** upset, surprise, revelation, bolt from the blue, rude awakening, eye-opener. 2 *you gave me a shock* **fright,** scare, start; informal turn. 3 *suffering from shock* **trauma,** collapse, breakdown, post-traumatic stress disorder. 4 *the first shock of the earthquake* **vibration,** reverberation, shake, jolt, impact, blow.

▶ verb 1 greatly surprise and upset someone. 2 make someone feel outraged or disgusted.

SYNONYMS *the murder shocked the nation* **appal,** horrify, outrage, scandalize, disgust, traumatize, distress, upset, disturb, stun, rock, shake. ANTONYMS delight.

■ **shock absorber** a device for absorbing jolts and vibrations on a vehicle. **shocking pink** a very bright shade of pink. **shock troops** troops trained to carry out sudden attacks. **shock wave** a moving wave of very high pressure caused by an explosion or by something travelling faster than sound.

shock² ▶ noun an untidy or thick mass of hair.

SYNONYMS *a shock of red hair* **mass,** mane, mop, thatch, head, bush, tangle, cascade, halo.

shocking ▶ adjective 1 causing shock or disgust. 2 Brit. informal very bad.

SYNONYMS **appalling,** horrifying, horrific, dreadful, awful, terrible, scandalous, outrageous, disgraceful, abominable, atrocious, disgusting, distressing, upsetting, disturbing, startling.

□ **shocker** noun **shockingly** adverb.

shoddy ▶ adjective (shoddier, shoddiest) 1 badly made or done. 2 dishonest or unfair.

□ **shoddily** adverb.

shoe ▶ noun 1 a covering for the foot with a stiff sole. 2 a horseshoe.

▶ verb (shoes, shoeing, shod) 1 fit a horse with a shoe or shoes. 2 (be shod) be wearing shoes of a particular kind.

■ **shoe tree** a shaped block put into a shoe when it is not being worn, to keep it in shape.

shoehorn ▶ noun a curved piece of metal or plastic, used for easing your heel into a shoe.

▶ verb force into a tight space.

shoelace ▶ noun a cord passed through holes or hooks on opposite sides of the opening in a shoe to fasten it.

shoestring ▶ noun (on a shoestring) informal with only a very small amount of money.

shogun ▶ noun (in the past, in Japan) a hereditary leader of the army.

shone past and past participle of SHINE.

shook past of SHAKE.

shoot ▶ verb (shoots, shooting, shot) 1 kill or wound someone with a bullet, arrow, etc. 2 fire a gun. 3 move suddenly and rapidly. 4 direct a glance, question, or remark at someone. 5 (in sport) kick, hit, or throw the ball in an attempt to score a goal. 6 photograph or film a scene or film. 7 (shooting) (of a pain) sudden and piercing. 8 (of a boat) travel quickly down rapids. 9 move a bolt to fasten a door. 10 send out buds or shoots. 11 (shoot up) informal inject yourself with an illegal drug.

SYNONYMS 1 *they shot him in the street* **gun down,** mow down, hit, wound, injure, shoot someone dead, kill. 2 *they shot at the police* **fire,** open fire, snipe, let fly, bombard, shell. 3 *it can shoot bullets or grenades* **discharge,** fire, launch, propel, release. 4 *a car shot past* **race,** speed, flash, dash, rush, hurtle, streak, whizz, zoom, career, fly; informal belt, tear, zip, whip; Brit. informal bomb; N. Amer. informal hightail it, barrel. 5 *the film was shot in Tunisia* **film,** photograph, take, make, record.

▶ noun 1 a new part growing from a plant. 2 an occasion of taking photographs or making a film. 3 an occasion when a group of people hunt and shoot animals or birds as a sport.

SYNONYMS *new shoots* **sprout,** bud, runner, tendril.

■ **shooting star** a small rapidly moving meteor that burns up on entering the earth's atmosphere. **shooting stick** a walking stick with a handle that unfolds to form a seat.

shooter ▶ noun 1 a person who uses a gun. 2 informal a gun.

shop ▸ noun **1** a building or part of a building where goods are sold. **2** a place where things are manufactured or repaired; a workshop.

SYNONYMS **store,** retail outlet, boutique, emporium, department store, supermarket, hypermarket, superstore, chain store; N. Amer. minimart.

▸ verb (**shops, shopping, shopped**) **1** go to a shop or shops to buy goods. **2** (**shop around**) look for the best available price or rate for something. **3** Brit. informal inform on.
■ **shop floor** Brit. the area in a factory where things are made or put together by the workers. **shop-soiled** Brit. (of an article) dirty or damaged from being displayed or handled in a shop. **shop steward** Brit. a person elected by workers in a factory to represent them in dealings with the management. **talk shop** discuss work matters with a colleague when you are not at work.
□ **shopper** noun **shopping** noun.

shopkeeper ▸ noun the owner and manager of a shop.

shoplifting ▸ noun the stealing of goods from a shop.
□ **shoplifter** noun.

shore¹ ▸ noun **1** the land along the edge of a sea or other stretch of water. **2** (**shores**) literary a foreign country or region.

SYNONYMS **seashore,** beach, sand(s), shoreline, coast.

■ **on shore** on land.

shore² ▸ verb (**shores, shoring, shored**) (**shore something up**) **1** support or strengthen something. **2** hold something up with a prop or beam.

shoreline ▸ noun the line along which a sea or other stretch of water meets the land.

shorn past participle of SHEAR.

short ▸ adjective **1** of a small length in space or time. **2** small in height. **3** smaller than is usual or expected. **4** (**short of** or **on**) not having enough of. **5** not available in large enough quantities; scarce. **6** rude and abrupt. **7** (of odds in betting) reflecting a high level of probability. **8** (of pastry) containing a high proportion of fat to flour and therefore crumbly.

SYNONYMS **1** short people **small,** little, petite, tiny, diminutive, elfin; Scottish wee. **2** a short report **concise,** brief, succinct, compact, pithy, abridged, abbreviated, condensed. **3** a short visit **brief,** fleeting, lightning, quick, cursory. **4** money is a bit short **scarce,** scant, meagre, sparse, insufficient, deficient, inadequate, lacking. **5** he was rather short with her **curt,** sharp, abrupt, blunt, brusque, terse, offhand.
ANTONYMS tall, long, plentiful, courteous.

▸ adverb not as far as expected or required.

SYNONYMS she stopped short **abruptly,** suddenly, sharply, all of a sudden, unexpectedly, without warning.

▸ noun Brit. a small drink of spirits.
▸ verb have a short circuit.
■ **short-change** cheat someone by giving them less than the correct change. **short circuit** a faulty connection in an electrical circuit in which the current flows along a shorter route than it should do. **short-circuit** cause a short circuit in. **short cut** a way of going somewhere or doing something that is quicker than usual. **short-handed** (or **short-staffed**) having fewer staff than you need or than is usual. **short-lived** lasting only a short time. **short shrift** abrupt and unsympathetic treatment. **short-sighted** Brit. **1** unable to see things clearly unless they are close to your eyes. **2** not thinking carefully about the consequences of something. **short-tempered** losing your temper quickly. **stop short** suddenly stop.
□ **shortness** noun.

shortage ▸ noun a lack of something needed.

SYNONYMS **scarcity,** dearth, poverty, insufficiency, deficiency, inadequacy, famine, lack, deficit, shortfall.
ANTONYMS abundance.

shortbread (or **shortcake**) ▸ noun a rich, crumbly type of biscuit made with butter, flour, and sugar.

shortcoming ▸ noun a fault in someone's character or in a system.

SYNONYMS **fault,** defect, flaw, imperfection, deficiency, limitation, failing, drawback, weakness, weak point.
ANTONYMS strength.

shortcrust pastry ▸ noun Brit. crumbly pastry made with flour, fat, and a little water.

shorten ▸ verb make or become shorter.

SYNONYMS **abbreviate,** abridge, condense, contract, compress, reduce, shrink, diminish, cut (down), trim, pare (down), prune, curtail, truncate.
ANTONYMS lengthen.

shortening ▸ noun fat used for making pastry.

shortfall ▸ noun a situation in which something amounts to less than is required.

shorthand ▸ noun a way of writing very quickly when recording what someone is saying, by using abbreviations and symbols.

shortlist ▸ noun a list of selected candidates from which a final choice is made.
▸ verb put on a shortlist.

S

shortly ▶ adverb **1** in a short time; soon. **2** abruptly or sharply.

> SYNONYMS **soon,** presently, in a little while, at any moment, in a minute, in next to no time, before long, by and by; N. Amer. momentarily; informal anon, any time now, in a jiffy; Brit. informal in a mo.

shorts ▶ plural noun short trousers that reach to the thighs or knees.

shot[1] ▶ noun **1** the firing of a gun, arrow, etc. **2** (in sport) a hit, stroke, or kick of the ball as an attempt to score. **3** informal an attempt. **4** a photograph. **5** a film sequence photographed continuously by one camera. **6** a person with a particular level of ability in shooting. **7** (also **lead shot**) tiny lead pellets used in a shotgun. **8** a heavy ball thrown in the sport of shot put. **9** the launch of a rocket. **10** informal a small drink of spirits. **11** informal an injection of a drug or vaccine.

> SYNONYMS **1** *a shot rang out* **report,** crack, bang, blast; (**shots**) gunfire, firing. **2** *a winning shot* **stroke,** hit, strike, kick, throw. **3** *Mike was an excellent shot* **marksman,** markswoman, shooter. **4** *a shot of us on holiday* **photograph,** photo, snap, snapshot, picture, print, slide, still.

■ **like a shot** informal without hesitation. **shot put** an athletic contest in which a very heavy round ball is thrown as far as possible.

shot[2] past and past participle of **SHOOT**.
> ▶ adjective woven with a warp and weft of different colours, giving a contrasting effect.

■ **shot through with** filled with a quality.

shotgun ▶ noun a gun for firing small bullets at short range.

■ **shotgun wedding** informal a wedding arranged quickly because the bride is pregnant.

should ▶ modal verb (3rd singular **should**) **1** used to indicate what is right or ought to be done. **2** used to indicate what is probable. **3** formal used to state what would happen if something else was the case: *if you should change your mind, I'll be at the hotel.* **4** used with *I* and *we* to express a polite request, opinion, or hope.

shoulder ▶ noun the joint between the upper arm and the main part of the body.
> ▶ verb (**shoulders, shouldering, shouldered**) **1** take on a responsibility. **2** push aside with your shoulder. **3** carry on your shoulder.

> SYNONYMS **1** *I shouldered the responsibility* **take on (yourself),** undertake, accept, assume, bear, carry. **2** *another lad shouldered him aside* **push,** shove, thrust, jostle, force, bulldoze, bundle.

■ **shoulder blade** either of the triangular bones at the top of the back.

shouldn't ▶ short form should not.

shout ▶ verb **1** speak or call out very loudly. **2** (**shout someone down**) prevent someone from being heard by shouting.

> SYNONYMS *he shouted a warning* **yell,** cry, call, roar, howl, bellow, bawl; informal holler.

▶ noun **1** a loud cry or call. **2** (**your shout**) Brit. informal your turn to buy a round of drinks.

> SYNONYMS *I heard a shout* **yell,** cry (out), call (out), roar, howl, bellow, bawl, raise your voice; informal holler.
> ANTONYMS whisper.

shove ▶ verb (**shoves, shoving, shoved**) **1** push roughly. **2** place carelessly or roughly. **3** (**shove off**) informal go away.

> SYNONYMS **1** *she shoved him back* **push,** thrust, propel, drive, force, ram, knock, elbow, shoulder. **2** *she shoved past him* **push (your way),** force your way, barge (your way), elbow (your way), shoulder your way.

▶ noun a strong push.

> SYNONYMS *a hefty shove* **push,** thrust, bump, jolt, barge.

shovel ▶ noun a tool resembling a spade with a broad blade and upturned sides, used for moving earth, snow, etc.
> ▶ verb (**shovels, shovelling, shovelled;** US spelling **shovels, shoveling, shoveled**) move earth, snow, etc. with a shovel.

show ▶ verb (**shows, showing, showed;** past participle **shown** or **showed**) **1** be or make visible. **2** offer for inspection or viewing. **3** present an image of. **4** lead or guide. **5** behave in a particular way towards someone. **6** be evidence of; prove. **7** make someone understand something by explaining it or doing it yourself. **8** (also **show up**) informal arrive for an appointment.

> SYNONYMS **1** *the stitches do not show* **be visible,** be seen, be in view, be obvious. **2** *he wouldn't show the picture* **display,** exhibit, put on show, put on display, put on view. **3** *Frank showed his frustration* **manifest,** exhibit, reveal, convey, communicate, make known, express, make plain, make obvious, disclose, betray. **4** *I'll show you how to cook* **demonstrate,** explain, describe, illustrate, teach, instruct. **5** *events show this to be true* **prove,** demonstrate, confirm, substantiate, corroborate, verify, bear out. **6** *she showed them to their seats* **escort,** accompany, take, conduct, lead, usher, guide, direct.
> ANTONYMS conceal.

▶ noun **1** a stage performance involving singing and dancing. **2** an entertainment programme on television or radio. **3** an

S

event or competition in which animals, plants, or products are displayed. **4** an impressive or pleasing sight. **5** a display of a quality or feeling. **6** a display intended to give a false impression.

> SYNONYMS **1** *a spectacular show of bluebells* **display,** array, sight, spectacle. **2** *the motor show* **exhibition,** display, fair, festival, parade; N. Amer. exhibit. **3** *a TV show* **programme,** broadcast, presentation, production, episode. **4** *she's only doing it for show* **appearance,** display, image. **5** *Drew made a show of looking busy* **pretence,** outward appearance, (false) front, guise, pose.

■ **show business** the world of theatre, films, television, and pop music as a profession or industry. **show off** try to impress other people by talking about your abilities or possessions. **show something off** display something that you are proud of. **show trial** a public trial held to influence or please people, rather than to ensure that justice is done. **show someone/thing up 1** reveal someone or something to be bad or at fault. **2** informal humiliate someone.

showbiz ▸ noun informal show business.

showcase ▸ noun **1** an occasion for presenting someone or something to their best advantage. **2** a glass case used for displaying articles.

showdown ▸ noun a final argument, fight, or test, to settle a dispute.

> SYNONYMS **confrontation,** clash, face-off.

shower ▸ noun **1** a short period of rain or snow. **2** a large number of things that fall or arrive together. **3** a device that creates a spray of water under which you stand to wash yourself. **4** an act of washing yourself in a shower.

> SYNONYMS **1** *a shower of rain* **fall,** drizzle, sprinkling. **2** *a shower of missiles* **volley,** hail, salvo, barrage.

▸ verb (**showers, showering, showered**) **1** fall or make things fall in a shower. **2** (**shower someone with**) give large quantities of something to someone. **3** wash yourself in a shower.

> SYNONYMS **1** *confetti showered down on us* **rain,** fall, hail. **2** *she showered them with gifts* **deluge,** flood, inundate, swamp, overwhelm, snow under.

□ **showery** adjective.

showgirl ▸ noun an actress who sings and dances in a musical or variety show.

showjumping ▸ noun the competitive sport of riding horses over a course of obstacles in an arena.

showman ▸ noun (plural **showmen**) **1** a person who is very good at entertaining

people or getting their attention. **2** the manager or presenter of a circus, fair, etc. □ **showmanship** noun.

shown past participle of **show**.

show-off ▸ noun a person who tries to impress other people by showing off.

> SYNONYMS **exhibitionist,** extrovert, poser, poseur, swaggerer, self-publicist.

showpiece ▸ noun an outstanding example of something.

showroom ▸ noun a room used to display cars, furniture, or other goods for sale.

showy ▸ adjective very bright or colourful and attracting a lot of attention.

> SYNONYMS **ostentatious,** flamboyant, gaudy, garish, brash, vulgar, loud, fancy, ornate; informal flash, flashy. ANTONYMS restrained.

shrank past of **shrink**.

shrapnel ▸ noun small metal fragments from an exploding shell or bomb.

shred ▸ noun **1** a strip of material that has been torn, cut, or scraped from something. **2** a very small amount.

> SYNONYMS **1** *her dress was torn to shreds* **tatter,** ribbon, rag, fragment, sliver. **2** *not a shred of evidence* **scrap,** bit, speck, particle, ounce, jot, crumb, fragment, grain, drop, trace.

▸ verb (**shreds, shredding, shredded**) tear or cut into shreds.

> SYNONYMS *shredding vegetables* **grate,** mince, grind.

□ **shredder** noun.

shrew ▸ noun **1** a small mouse-like animal with a long pointed snout. **2** a bad-tempered woman.

shrewd ▸ adjective having or showing good judgement.

> SYNONYMS **astute,** sharp, smart, intelligent, clever, canny, perceptive; informal on the ball. ANTONYMS stupid.

□ **shrewdly** adverb **shrewdness** noun.

shrewish ▸ adjective (of a woman) bad-tempered or nagging.

shriek ▸ verb make a piercing cry.

> SYNONYMS **scream,** screech, squeal, squawk, roar, howl, shout, yelp.

▸ noun a piercing cry.

> SYNONYMS **scream,** screech, squeal, squawk, roar, howl, shout, yelp.

shrike ▸ noun a songbird with a strong hooked bill.

shrill ▸ adjective high-pitched and piercing. ▸ verb make a shrill noise. □ **shrilly** adverb.

S

shrimp ▸ noun (plural **shrimp** or **shrimps**) a small edible shellfish.

shrine ▸ noun **1** a place connected with a holy person or event, where people go to pray. **2** a place containing a religious statue or object.

shrink ▸ verb (**shrinks**, **shrinking**, **shrank**; past participle **shrunk** or (especially as adjective) **shrunken**) **1** become or make smaller. **2** move back or away in fear or disgust. **3** (**shrink from**) be unwilling to do.

> SYNONYMS **1** *the number of competitors shrank* **get smaller**, contract, diminish, lessen, reduce, decrease, dwindle, decline, fall off. **2** *he doesn't shrink from naming names* **recoil**, shy away, flinch, be averse, be afraid, hesitate.
> ANTONYMS expand, increase.

▸ noun informal a psychiatrist.
  ■ **shrinking violet** informal a very shy person.
  shrink-wrap wrap in clinging plastic film.
  □ **shrinkage** noun.

shrivel ▸ verb (**shrivels**, **shrivelling**, **shrivelled**; US spelling **shrivels**, **shriveling**, **shriveled**) wrinkle and shrink through loss of moisture.

> SYNONYMS **wither**, shrink, wilt, dry up, dehydrate, parch, frazzle.

shroud ▸ noun **1** a length of cloth in which a dead person is wrapped for burial. **2** a thing that closely surrounds or hides something. **3** (**shrouds**) a set of ropes supporting the mast of a sailing boat.

> SYNONYMS *a shroud of mist* **covering**, cover, cloak, mantle, blanket, layer, cloud, veil, winding sheet.

▸ verb **1** wrap in a shroud. **2** cover or hide.

> SYNONYMS *shrouded by cloud* **cover**, envelop, veil, cloak, blanket, screen, conceal, hide, mask, obscure.

shrub ▸ noun a woody plant which is smaller than a tree and divided into separate stems from near the ground.
  □ **shrubby** adjective.

shrubbery ▸ noun (plural **shrubberies**) an area planted with shrubs.

shrug ▸ verb (**shrugs**, **shrugging**, **shrugged**) **1** raise your shoulders slightly and briefly as a sign that you do not know or care about something. **2** (**shrug something off**) treat something as unimportant.

▸ noun an act of shrugging your shoulders.

shudder ▸ verb (**shudders**, **shuddering**, **shuddered**) tremble or shake violently.

> SYNONYMS *the ground shuddered* **shake**, shiver, tremble, quiver, judder.

▸ noun an act of shuddering.

> SYNONYMS *the truck's shudders and jolts* **shake**, shiver, tremor, trembling, quivering, vibration, judder.

shuffle ▸ verb (**shuffles**, **shuffling**, **shuffled**) **1** walk without lifting your feet completely from the ground. **2** move about restlessly while sitting or standing. **3** rearrange a pack of cards by sliding them over and under each other quickly. **4** rearrange people or things.

> SYNONYMS **1** *they shuffled along the passage* **shamble**, dodder, drag your feet. **2** *she shuffled her feet* **scrape**, drag, scuffle. **3** *he shuffled the cards* **mix (up)**, rearrange, jumble (up).

▸ noun an act of shuffling.

shun ▸ verb (**shuns**, **shunning**, **shunned**) avoid or reject.

> SYNONYMS **avoid**, steer clear of, give a wide berth to, have nothing to do with; informal freeze out; Brit. informal send to Coventry.
> ANTONYMS welcome.

shunt ▸ verb **1** push or pull a railway vehicle from one set of tracks to another. **2** move something around or along. **3** move someone to a less important position.
  □ **shunter** noun.

shut ▸ verb (**shuts**, **shutting**, **shut**) **1** move something into position to block an opening. **2** (**shut someone/thing in** or **out**) keep a person or animal in or out by closing a door, gate, etc. **3** prevent access to a place or along a route. **4** (with reference to a shop or other business) stop operating for business. **5** close a book, curtains, etc.

> SYNONYMS *please shut the door* **close**, pull to, push to, slam, fasten, put the lid on, lock, secure.
> ANTONYMS open, unlock.

  ■ **shut down** stop opening for business, or stop operating. **shut up** informal stop talking.

shutter ▸ noun **1** each of a pair of hinged panels inside or outside a window that can be closed for security or to keep out the light. **2** a device that opens and closes to expose the film in a camera.

▸ verb (**shutters**, **shuttering**, **shuttered**) close the shutters of a window or building.

shuttle ▸ noun **1** a form of transport that travels regularly between two places. **2** (in weaving) a bobbin for carrying the weft thread across the warp.

▸ verb (**shuttles**, **shuttling**, **shuttled**) **1** travel regularly between places. **2** transport in a shuttle.

> SYNONYMS **commute**, run, ply, go/travel back and forth, ferry.

shuttlecock ▸ noun a light cone-shaped object that is struck with rackets in the game of badminton.

S

shy[1] ▸ adjective (**shyer**, **shyest**) nervous about meeting or talking to other people.

> SYNONYMS **bashful**, diffident, timid, reserved, introverted, retiring, self-effacing, withdrawn.
> ANTONYMS confident.

▸ verb (**shies**, **shying**, **shied**) **1** (of a horse) turn aside in fright. **2** (**shy away from**) avoid doing something through lack of confidence.
  □ **shyly** adverb.

shy[2] ▸ verb (**shies**, **shying**, **shied**) throw something at a target.

shyster ▸ noun informal a dishonest person, especially a lawyer.

SI ▸ abbreviation Système International, the international system of units of measurement.

Siamese ▸ adjective relating to Siam (the old name for Thailand).
  ■ **Siamese cat** a breed of cat that has short pale fur with darker face, ears, feet, and tail. **Siamese twins** twins whose bodies are joined at birth.

sibilant ▸ adjective making a hissing sound.
  □ **sibilance** noun.

sibling ▸ noun a brother or sister.

sibyl ▸ noun (in ancient Greece and Rome) a woman supposedly able to pass on messages from a god.
  □ **sibylline** adjective.

sic ▸ adverb (after a copied word that seems odd or wrong) written exactly as it stands in the original.

sick ▸ adjective **1** physically or mentally ill. **2** wanting to vomit. **3** (**sick of**) bored by or annoyed about. **4** informal behaving in an abnormal or cruel way. **5** informal (of humour) dealing with unpleasant subjects in a way that is offensive.

> SYNONYMS **1** the children are sick **ill**, unwell, poorly, ailing, indisposed; informal laid up, under the weather; Austral./NZ informal crook. **2** he was feeling sick **nauseous**, queasy, bilious, green about the gills. **3** I'm sick of this music **fed up**, bored, tired, weary. **4** a sick joke **macabre**, tasteless, ghoulish, morbid, black, gruesome, gallows, cruel.
> ANTONYMS well.

▸ noun Brit. informal vomit.
  ■ **be sick 1** be ill. **2** Brit. vomit.

sickbay ▸ noun a room set aside for sick people.

sickbed ▸ noun the bed of a person who is ill.

sicken ▸ verb **1** disgust or shock. **2** (**be sickening for**) start to develop an illness.

> SYNONYMS **1** the stench sickened him **nauseate**, make sick, turn someone's stomach, disgust; N. Amer. informal gross

out. **2** (sickening) **nauseating**, stomach-turning, repulsive, revolting, disgusting, offensive, off-putting, distasteful, obscene, gruesome, grisly; N. Amer. vomitous; informal gross. **3** she sickened and died **fall ill**, catch something.
> ANTONYMS please, recover.

sickle ▸ noun a tool for cutting corn, with a semicircular blade and a short handle.

sickly ▸ adjective (**sicklier**, **sickliest**) **1** often ill. **2** looking or seeming unhealthy. **3** (of flavour, colour, etc.) so bright or sweet as to cause sickness.

sickness ▸ noun **1** the state of being ill. **2** a particular type of illness or disease. **3** nausea or vomiting.

> SYNONYMS **1** she was absent through sickness **illness**, disease, ailment, infection, malady, infirmity; informal bug, virus; Brit. informal lurgy; Austral. informal wog. **2** a wave of sickness **nausea**, biliousness, queasiness. **3** sickness and diarrhoea **nausea**, vomiting, retching; informal throwing up, puking.

side ▸ noun **1** a position to the left or right of an object, place, or central point. **2** either of the two halves into which something can be divided. **3** an upright or sloping surface of something that is not the top, bottom, front, or back. **4** each of the flat surfaces of a solid object, or either of the two surfaces of something flat and thin, e.g. paper. **5** either of the two surfaces of a record or the corresponding parts of a cassette tape. **6** a part near the edge of something. **7** a person or group opposing another in a dispute or contest. **8** a sports team. **9** a particular aspect. **10** Geometry each of the lines forming the boundary of a plane figure.

> SYNONYMS **1** the side of the road **edge**, border, verge, boundary, margin, fringe(s), flank, bank, perimeter, extremity, periphery, limit(s). **2** the wrong side of the road **half**, part, carriageway, lane. **3** the east side of the city **district**, quarter, area, region, part, neighbourhood, sector, zone. **4** one side of the paper **surface**, face. **5** his side of the argument **point of view**, viewpoint, perspective, opinion, standpoint, position, outlook, slant, angle. **6** the losing side **faction**, camp, bloc, party. **7** the players in their side **team**, squad, line-up.
> ANTONYMS centre, end.

▸ adjective additional or less important.

> SYNONYMS **1** elaborate side pieces **lateral**, wing, flanking. **2** a side issue **subordinate**, secondary, minor, peripheral, incidental, subsidiary.
> ANTONYMS front, central.

S

▸ verb (**sides, siding, sided**) (**side with** or **against**) support or oppose in a conflict or dispute.
■ **side effect** a secondary effect of a drug. **side road** (or **street**) a minor road. **side-saddle** (of a rider) sitting with both feet on the same side of the horse. **take sides** support one person or cause against another.

sideboard ▸ noun **1** a piece of furniture with cupboards and drawers, used for storing crockery, glasses, etc. **2** (**sideboards**) Brit. sideburns.

sideburns ▸ plural noun a strip of hair growing down each side of a man's face in front of his ears.

sidecar ▸ noun a small, low vehicle attached to the side of a motorcycle for carrying passengers.

sidekick ▸ noun informal a person's assistant.

sidelight ▸ noun Brit. a small additional light on either side of a motor vehicle's headlights.

sideline ▸ noun **1** something you do in addition to your main job. **2** either of the two lines along the longer sides of a sports field or court. **3** (**the sidelines**) a position of watching a situation rather than being directly involved in it.
▸ verb (**sidelines, sidelining, sidelined**) remove from a team, game, or influential position.

sidelong ▸ adjective & adverb to or from one side; sideways.

sidereal /sy-**deer**-i-uhl/ ▸ adjective relating to the distant stars or their apparent positions in the sky.

sideshow ▸ noun a small show or stall at an exhibition, fair, or circus.

sidestep ▸ verb (**sidesteps, sidestepping, sidestepped**) **1** avoid dealing with a difficult issue. **2** avoid someone or something by stepping sideways.

sideswipe ▸ noun a critical or harsh remark made while discussing another matter.

sidetrack ▸ verb distract someone from the main issues of what they are discussing or doing.

sidewalk ▸ noun N. Amer. a pavement.

sideways ▸ adverb & adjective to, towards, or from the side.

SYNONYMS **1** *she slid sideways* **to the side,** laterally. **2** *the expansion slots are mounted sideways* **edgewise,** edgeways, side first, end on. **3** *sideways force* **lateral,** sideward, on the side, side to side. **4** *a sideways look* **indirect,** oblique, sidelong, surreptitious, furtive, covert, sly.

siding ▸ noun a short track beside a main railway line, where trains are left.

sidle ▸ verb (**sidles, sidling, sidled**) walk in a secretive or timid way.

siege ▸ noun **1** a military operation in which forces surround a town and cut off its supplies. **2** a similar operation by a police team to force an armed person to surrender.

✔ Remember, **i** before **e** in **siege** and **sieve**.

sienna ▸ noun a kind of earth used as a brown colouring in painting.

sierra /si-**air**-uh/ ▸ noun (in Spain and the US) a long chain of mountains with jagged peaks.

siesta ▸ noun an afternoon rest or nap.

sieve /siv/ ▸ noun a piece of mesh held in a frame, used for straining solids from liquids or separating coarser from finer particles.
▸ verb (**sieves, sieving, sieved**) put a substance through a sieve.

sift ▸ verb **1** put a substance through a sieve. **2** examine something thoroughly to sort out what is important or useful.

SYNONYMS **1** *sift the flour into a large bowl* **sieve,** strain, screen, filter. **2** *we sift out unsuitable applications* **separate out,** filter out, sort out, weed out, get rid of, remove. **3** *sifting through the wreckage* **search,** look, examine, inspect, scrutinize, pore over.

sigh ▸ verb let out a long, deep breath expressing sadness, relief, etc.
▸ noun such a breath.

sight ▸ noun **1** the ability to see. **2** the act of seeing something. **3** the area or distance within which you can see something. **4** a thing that you see. **5** (**sights**) places of interest to tourists. **6** (**a sight**) informal a person or thing that looks ridiculous or unattractive. **7** (also **sights**) a device that you look through to aim a gun or see with a telescope.

SYNONYMS **1** *she has excellent sight* **eyesight,** vision, eyes. **2** *her first sight of it* **view,** glimpse, glance, look. **3** *historic sights* **landmark,** place of interest, monument, spectacle, marvel, wonder.

▸ verb see or glimpse.

SYNONYMS *one of the helicopters sighted wreckage* **glimpse,** catch sight of, see, spot, spy, make out, pick out, notice, observe.

■ **raise** (or **lower**) **your sights** increase (or lower) your expectations. **set your sights on** have something as an ambition. **sight-read** read a musical score and play it without preparation.

❗ Don't confuse **sight** with **site**, which means 'a place where something is located or happens'.

S

sighted ▸ adjective **1** having the ability to see; not blind. **2** having a particular kind of sight.

sightless ▸ adjective blind.

sightseeing ▸ noun the activity of visiting places of interest.
□ **sightseer** noun.

sign ▸ noun **1** an indication that something exists, is happening, or may happen. **2** a signal, gesture, or notice giving information or an instruction. **3** a symbol used to represent something in algebra, music, or other subjects. **4** each of the twelve divisions of the zodiac.

> SYNONYMS **1** *a sign of affection* **indication,** signal, symptom, pointer, suggestion, intimation, mark, manifestation, demonstration, token. **2** *a sign of things to come* **warning,** omen, portent, threat, promise. **3** *signs saying 'danger'* **notice,** board, placard, signpost. **4** *the dancers were daubed with signs* **symbol,** figure, emblem, device, logo, character.

▸ verb **1** write your name on something to show that you have written it, or to authorize it. **2** recruit a sports player, musician, etc. by signing a contract. **3** use gestures to give information or instructions.

> SYNONYMS **1** *he signed the letter* **write your name on,** autograph, initial, countersign. **2** *the government signed the treaty* **endorse,** validate, agree to, approve, ratify, adopt. **3** *he signed his name* **write,** inscribe, pen.

■ **sign language** a system of hand movements and facial expressions used to communicate with people who are deaf. **sign off** end a letter, broadcast, or other message. **sign on 1** commit yourself to a job. **2** Brit. register as unemployed. **sign someone on** employ someone. **sign up** commit yourself to a course, job, etc.
□ **signer** noun.

signal ▸ noun **1** a gesture, action, or sound giving information or an instruction. **2** a sign indicating a particular situation. **3** a device that uses lights or a movable arm to tell drivers to stop or beware on a road or railway. **4** an electrical impulse or radio wave that is sent or received.

> SYNONYMS **1** *a signal to stop* **gesture,** sign, wave, cue, indication, warning, prompt, reminder. **2** *a clear signal that we're in trouble* **indication,** sign, symptom, hint, pointer, clue, demonstration, evidence, proof.

▸ verb (**signals, signalling, signalled;** US spelling **signals, signaling, signaled**) give a signal.

> SYNONYMS **1** *the driver signalled to her* **gesture,** sign, indicate, motion, wave,

beckon, nod. **2** *they signalled their displeasure* **indicate,** show, express, communicate. **3** *his death signals the end of an era* **mark,** signify, mean, be a sign of, be evidence of.

▸ adjective noteworthy.

■ **signal box** Brit. a building beside a railway track from which signals and points are controlled.

signatory ▸ noun (plural **signatories**) a person who has signed an agreement.

signature ▸ noun **1** a person's name written in a distinctive way, used in signing something. **2** a distinctive product or quality by which someone or something can be recognized.

■ **signature tune** a tune announcing a particular television or radio programme.

signet ▸ noun (in the past) a small seal used to authorize an official document.

■ **signet ring** a ring with letters or a design set into it.

significance ▸ noun **1** importance. **2** the meaning of something.

> SYNONYMS **importance,** import, consequence, seriousness, gravity, weight, magnitude.
> ANTONYMS insignificance.

significant ▸ adjective **1** important or large enough to have an effect or be noticed. **2** having a particular or secret meaning.

> SYNONYMS **1** *a significant fact* **notable,** noteworthy, remarkable, important, of consequence. **2** *a significant increase* **large,** considerable, sizeable, appreciable, conspicuous, obvious, sudden. **3** *a significant look* **meaningful,** expressive, eloquent, suggestive, knowing, telling.
> ANTONYMS insignificant.

□ **significantly** adverb.

signify ▸ verb (**signifies, signifying, signified**) **1** be a sign of; mean. **2** make a feeling or intention known.

> SYNONYMS **mean,** denote, designate, represent, symbolize, stand for.

□ **signification** noun.

signing ▸ noun **1** Brit. a person who has recently been recruited to a sports team, record company, etc. **2** an event at which an author signs copies of their book. **3** the use of sign language.

signpost ▸ noun a sign on a post, giving information such as the direction and distance to a nearby place.

Sikh /seek/ ▸ noun a follower of a religion that developed from Hinduism.
□ **Sikhism** noun.

silage /sy-lij/ ▸ noun grass or other green crops that are stored in a silo without being dried, used as animal feed in the winter.

silence ▸ noun **1** complete lack of sound. **2** a situation in which someone is unwilling to speak or discuss something.

> SYNONYMS **1** *the silence of the night* **quietness**, quiet, still, stillness, hush, tranquillity, peace. **2** *her silence was answer enough* **failure to speak**, dumbness, reticence, taciturnity.
> ANTONYMS sound, loquacity.

▸ verb (**silences, silencing, silenced**) **1** stop someone from speaking. **2** make something silent.

> SYNONYMS **1** *he silenced her with a kiss* **quieten**, quiet, hush. **2** *dissidents have been silenced* **gag**, muzzle, censor.

silencer ▸ noun a device for reducing the noise made by a gun or exhaust system.

silent ▸ adjective **1** without any sound. **2** not speaking or not spoken aloud.

> SYNONYMS **1** *the forest was silent* **quiet**, still, hushed, noiseless, soundless, inaudible. **2** *the right to remain silent* **speechless**, quiet, unspeaking, dumb, mute, taciturn, uncommunicative, tight-lipped. **3** *silent thanks* **unspoken**, wordless.
> ANTONYMS audible, noisy, spoken.

□ **silently** adverb.

silhouette ▸ noun a dark shape and outline seen against a lighter background.

> SYNONYMS *silhouettes of aircraft* **outline**, contour(s), profile, form, shape.

▸ verb (**silhouettes, silhouetting, silhouetted**) show as a silhouette.

> SYNONYMS *silhouetted against the window* **outline**, define.

silica ▸ noun a hard substance formed from silicon and oxygen that occurs as quartz and is found in sandstone and other rocks.

silicon ▸ noun a chemical element that is a semiconductor and is used to make electronic circuits.
■ **silicon chip** a microchip.

silicone ▸ noun a synthetic substance made from silicon.

silk ▸ noun a fine, soft shiny fibre produced by silkworms, made into thread or fabric.

silken ▸ adjective **1** smooth and shiny like silk. **2** made of silk.

silkworm ▸ noun a caterpillar that spins a silk cocoon from which silk fibre is obtained.

silky ▸ adjective (**silkier, silkiest**) smooth and shiny like silk.

sill ▸ noun a shelf or slab at the foot of a window or doorway.

silly ▸ adjective (**sillier, silliest**) showing a lack of good judgement or common sense.

> SYNONYMS **1** *don't be so silly* **foolish**, stupid, scatterbrained, frivolous, inane, immature, childish, empty-headed; informal dotty, scatty. **2** *that was a silly thing to do* **unwise**, imprudent, thoughtless, foolish, stupid, unintelligent, idiotic, rash, reckless, foolhardy, irresponsible; informal crazy, mad; Brit. informal daft. **3** *he would worry about silly things* **trivial**, trifling, frivolous, petty, small, insignificant, unimportant; informal piffling.
> ANTONYMS sensible, serious.

□ **silliness** noun.

silo ▸ noun (plural **silos**) **1** a tower used to store grain. **2** a pit or airtight structure for storing silage. **3** an underground chamber in which a guided missile is kept ready for firing.

silt ▸ noun fine sand or clay carried by running water and deposited as a sediment.
▸ verb (**silt up**) fill or block with silt.
□ **silty** adjective.

silver ▸ noun **1** a shiny greyish-white precious metal. **2** a shiny grey-white colour. **3** coins made from silver or from a metal that looks like silver. **4** silver dishes, containers, or cutlery.
▸ verb (**silvers, silvering, silvered**) cover or plate with silver.
■ **silver birch** a birch tree with silver-grey bark. **silver jubilee** the twenty-fifth anniversary of an important event. **silver medal** a medal awarded for second place in a race or competition. **silver plate 1** a thin layer of silver applied as a coating to another metal. **2** plates, dishes, etc. made of or plated with silver. **silver wedding** Brit. the twenty-fifth anniversary of a wedding.
□ **silvery** adjective.

silverfish ▸ noun (plural **silverfish**) a small silvery wingless insect that lives in buildings.

silverside ▸ noun the upper side of a cut of beef from the outside of the leg.

silversmith ▸ noun a person who makes silver articles.

SIM card ▸ noun a small card inside a mobile phone that stores information such as details of calls made and received.

simian ▸ adjective relating to or like apes or monkeys.
▸ noun an ape or monkey.

similar ▸ adjective like something but not exactly the same.

> SYNONYMS **1** *you two are very similar* **alike**, the same; informal much of a muchness. **2** *northern India and similar areas* **comparable**, like, corresponding, equivalent.
> ANTONYMS different, unlike.

□ **similarly** adverb.

similarity ▸ noun (plural **similarities**) the state or fact of being similar.

SYNONYMS **resemblance**, likeness, comparability, correspondence, parallel, equivalence, uniformity.

simile /sim-i-li/ ▸ noun a word or phrase that compares one thing to another of a different kind (e.g. *the family was as solid as a rock*).

simmer ▸ verb (**simmers**, **simmering**, **simmered**) 1 stay or cause to stay just below boiling point. 2 be in a state of anger or excitement which you only just keep under control. 3 (**simmer down**) become calmer and quieter.

SYNONYMS 1 *the soup was simmering on the stove* **boil gently**, cook gently, bubble. 2 *she was simmering with resentment* **seethe**, fume, smoulder.

simper ▸ verb (**simpers**, **simpering**, **simpered**) smile in a coy and silly way. ▸ noun a coy and silly smile.

simple ▸ adjective (**simpler**, **simplest**) 1 easily understood or done. 2 plain and basic. 3 composed of a single element; not compound. 4 of very low intelligence.

SYNONYMS 1 *it's really pretty simple* **straightforward**, easy, uncomplicated, uninvolved, undemanding, elementary. 2 *simple language* **clear**, plain, straightforward, unambiguous, understandable, comprehensible, accessible; informal user-friendly. 3 *a simple white blouse* **plain**, unadorned, basic, unsophisticated, no-frills, classic, understated, uncluttered, restrained. 4 *simple country people* **unpretentious**, unsophisticated, ordinary, unaffected, unassuming, natural, straightforward; N. Amer. cracker-barrel. ANTONYMS difficult, complex, fancy, sophisticated.

■ **simple fracture** a fracture of a bone without any breaking of the skin.

simpleton ▸ noun a foolish or unintelligent person.

simplicity ▸ noun the quality of being simple.

SYNONYMS 1 *the simplicity of the recipes is an advantage* **straightforwardness**, ease. 2 *the simplicity of the language* **clarity**, plainness, intelligibility, comprehensibility, accessibility. 3 *the building's simplicity* **austerity**, plainness, spareness, clean lines. 4 *the simplicity of their lifestyle* **plainness**, modesty, naturalness. ANTONYMS difficulty, complexity, adornment, sophistication.

simplify ▸ verb (**simplifies**, **simplifying**, **simplified**) make something easier to do or understand.

SYNONYMS **make simpler**, clarify, put into words of one syllable, streamline; informal dumb down. ANTONYMS complicate.

□ **simplification** noun.

simplistic ▸ adjective treating complex issues as more simple than they really are. □ **simplistically** adverb.

simply ▸ adverb 1 in a simple way. 2 just; merely. 3 absolutely.

SYNONYMS 1 *he always spoke simply and forcefully* **straightforwardly**, directly, clearly, plainly, lucidly, unambiguously. 2 *she was dressed simply* **plainly**, soberly, unfussily, classically. 3 *they lived simply* **modestly**, plainly, quietly. 4 *they are welcomed simply because they are rich* **merely**, just, purely, solely, only. 5 *she was simply delighted* **utterly**, absolutely, completely, positively, just; informal plain. ANTONYMS confusingly, elaborately.

simulacrum /sim-yuu-lay-kruhm/ ▸ noun (plural **simulacra** or **simulacrums**) something that is similar to something else.

simulate ▸ verb (**simulates**, **simulating**, **simulated**) 1 imitate the appearance or nature of. 2 use a computer to create a model of something or conditions that are like those in real life. 3 pretend to have or feel a particular emotion.

SYNONYMS 1 *they simulated pleasure* **feign**, pretend, fake, affect, put on. 2 *simulating conditions in space* **imitate**, reproduce, replicate, duplicate, mimic.

□ **simulation** noun **simulator** noun.

simultaneous ▸ adjective happening or done at the same time.

SYNONYMS **concurrent**, happening at the same time, contemporaneous, coinciding, coincident, synchronized. ANTONYMS separate.

□ **simultaneity** noun.

✔ The ending is **-eous**, not **-ious**: simultan**eous**.

simultaneously ▸ adverb at the same time.

SYNONYMS **at the same time**, at one and the same time, at once, concurrently, (all) together, in unison, in concert, in chorus.

sin ▸ noun 1 an act that breaks a religious or moral law. 2 an act that causes strong disapproval.

SYNONYMS 1 *a sin in the eyes of God* **wrong**, act of wickedness, transgression, crime, offence, misdeed. 2 *the human capacity for sin* **wickedness**, wrongdoing, evil, immorality, iniquity, vice, crime. ANTONYMS virtue.

▶ verb (**sins**, **sinning**, **sinned**) commit a sin.

SYNONYMS *I have sinned* **transgress**, do wrong, misbehave, err, go astray.

since ▶ preposition in the period between a time in the past and the present.
▶ conjunction **1** during or in the time after. **2** because.
▶ adverb **1** from the time mentioned until the present. **2** ago.

sincere ▶ adjective (**sincerer**, **sincerest**) not pretending anything or deceiving anyone; genuine and honest.

SYNONYMS **1** *our sincere gratitude* **heartfelt**, wholehearted, profound, deep, true, honest. **2** *a sincere person* **honest**, genuine, truthful, direct, frank, candid; informal straight, on the level; N. Amer. informal on the up and up.

sincerely ▶ adverb in a sincere or genuine way.

SYNONYMS **genuinely**, honestly, really, truly, truthfully, wholeheartedly, earnestly.

sincerity ▶ noun the quality of being sincere.

SYNONYMS **genuineness**, honesty, truthfulness, integrity, directness, openness, candour.

sine (*rhymes with* line) ▶ noun Maths (in a right-angled triangle) the ratio of the side opposite a particular acute angle to the hypotenuse.

sinecure /sin-i-kyoor/ ▶ noun a job for which you are paid but which requires little or no work.

sine qua non /see-nay kwah nohn/ ▶ noun a thing that is absolutely necessary.

sinew /sin-yoo/ ▶ noun a band of strong tissue that joins a muscle to a bone.
□ **sinewy** adjective.

sinful ▶ adjective **1** wicked. **2** disgraceful.
□ **sinfully** adverb **sinfulness** noun.

sing ▶ verb (**sings**, **singing**, **sang**; past participle **sung**) **1** make musical sounds with your voice; perform a song. **2** make a whistling sound.

SYNONYMS **1** *he began to sing* **chant**, trill, intone, croon, chorus. **2** *the birds were singing* **trill**, warble, chirp, chirrup, cheep.

■ **sing-song 1** a rising and falling sound in someone's voice. **2** informal an informal gathering for singing.

singalong ▶ noun an informal occasion when people sing together.

Singaporean ▶ noun a person from Singapore.
▶ adjective relating to Singapore.

singe ▶ verb (**singes**, **singeing**, **singed**) burn the surface of something slightly.

SYNONYMS **scorch**, burn, sear, char.

▶ noun a slight burn.

singer ▶ noun a person who sings.

SYNONYMS **vocalist**, songster, songstress, soloist, chorister, cantor.

single ▶ adjective **1** one only. **2** designed for one person. **3** consisting of one part. **4** taken separately from others. **5** not involved in a romantic or sexual relationship. **6** Brit. (of a ticket) for an outward journey only.

SYNONYMS **1** *a single red rose* **sole**, one, lone, solitary, unaccompanied, alone. **2** *every single word* **individual**, separate, distinct. **3** *is she single?* **unmarried**, unwed, unattached, free, a bachelor, a spinster.
ANTONYMS double, multiple, married.

▶ noun **1** a single person or thing. **2** a short record or CD. **3** (**singles**) a game or competition for individual players.
▶ verb (**singles**, **singling**, **singled**) (**single someone/thing out**) choose someone or something from a group for special treatment.
■ **single-breasted** (of a jacket or coat) fastened by one row of buttons at the centre of the front. **single file** a line of people moving one behind another. **single-handed** done without help from other people. **single-minded** determined to concentrate on one particular aim. **single parent** a person bringing up a child or children without a partner.

singlet ▶ noun Brit. a vest or similar sleeveless garment.

singleton ▶ noun a single person or thing.

singly ▶ adverb as a single person or thing.

SYNONYMS **one by one**, one at a time, one after the other, individually, separately.
ANTONYMS together.

singular ▶ adjective **1** Grammar (of a word or form) referring to just one person or thing. **2** very good or interesting; remarkable.
▶ noun Grammar the singular form of a word.
□ **singularity** noun **singularly** adverb.

Sinhalese /sin-huh-**leez**, sin-uh-**leez**/ ▶ noun (plural **Sinhalese**) **1** a member of an Indian people living in Sri Lanka. **2** the language of the Sinhalese.
▶ adjective relating to the Sinhalese.

sinister ▶ adjective seeming evil or dangerous.

SYNONYMS **1** *there was a sinister undertone in his words* **menacing**, threatening, ominous, forbidding, frightening, alarming, disturbing, dark. **2** *a sinister motive* **evil**, wicked, criminal, nefarious, villainous, base, malicious; informal shady.
ANTONYMS unthreatening, innocent.

S

sink ▸ verb (sinks, sinking, sank; past participle sunk) **1** go down below the surface of liquid. **2** go or cause to go to the bottom of the sea. **3** move slowly downwards. **4** gradually decrease in amount or strength. **5** (sink something into) force something sharp through a surface. **6** (sink in) become fully understood. **7** pass into a particular state. **8** (sink something into) put money or resources into.

> SYNONYMS **1** *the coffin sank below the waves* **submerge**, founder, go down, be engulfed, drop, fall, descend. **2** *they sank their ships* **scuttle**; Brit. scupper. **3** *the sun was sinking* **set**, go down. **4** *Loretta sank into an armchair* **lower yourself**, flop, collapse, drop, slump; informal plonk yourself. **5** *sink the pots into the ground* **embed**, insert, drive, plant.
> ANTONYMS float, rise.

▸ noun a fixed basin with a water supply and a drainage pipe.

sinker ▸ noun a weight used to keep a fishing line beneath the water.

sinner ▸ noun a person who sins.

Sino- /sy-noh/ ▸ combining form Chinese; Chinese and ...: *Sino-American*.

sinuous ▸ adjective **1** having many curves and turns. **2** moving in a graceful, swaying way. □ **sinuously** adverb.

sinus /sy-nuhss/ ▸ noun a hollow space within the bones of the face that connects with the nostrils.

sinusitis ▸ noun inflammation of a sinus.

Sioux /soo/ ▸ noun (plural **Sioux**) a member of an American Indian people, many of whom live in South Dakota.

sip ▸ verb (sips, sipping, sipped) drink something in small mouthfuls.

> SYNONYMS *she sipped her martini* **drink**, taste, sample, nip.

▸ noun a small mouthful of liquid.

> SYNONYMS *have a sip* **mouthful**, swallow, drink, drop, dram, nip; informal swig.

siphon (or **syphon**) ▸ noun a tube used to move liquid from one container to another, using air pressure to maintain the flow.
▸ verb **1** draw off or move liquid by means of a siphon. **2** (siphon something off) take small amounts of money over a period of time.

sir ▸ noun **1** a polite form of address to a man. **2** used as a title for a knight or baronet.

sire ▸ noun **1** the male parent of an animal. **2** literary a father. **3** old use a respectful form of address to a king.
▸ verb (sires, siring, sired) be the male parent of.

siren ▸ noun **1** a device that makes a loud prolonged warning sound. **2** Greek Mythology

each of a group of creatures who were part woman, part bird, whose singing lured sailors on to rocks. **3** a woman whose attractiveness is regarded as dangerous to men.

sirloin ▸ noun the best part of a loin of beef.

sirocco /si-rok-koh/ ▸ noun (plural **siroccos**) a hot wind that blows from Africa to southern Europe.

sirup US spelling of SYRUP.

sisal /sy-z'l/ ▸ noun fibre made from the leaves of a tropical Mexican plant, used for ropes or matting.

sissy ▸ noun (plural **sissies**) informal a weak or cowardly person.

sister ▸ noun **1** a woman or girl in relation to other children of her parents. **2** a female friend or colleague. **3** a member of a religious order of women. **4** Brit. a senior female nurse.
■ **sister-in-law** (plural **sisters-in-law**) **1** the sister of a person's wife or husband. **2** the wife of a person's brother or brother-in-law.
□ **sisterly** adjective.

sisterhood ▸ noun **1** the relationship between sisters. **2** a bond of friendship and understanding between women. **3** a group of women linked by a shared interest.

sit ▸ verb (sits, sitting, sat) **1** rest your weight on your bottom with your back upright. **2** be in a particular position or state. **3** serve as a member of a council, jury, or other official body. **4** (of a parliament, committee, or court of law) be carrying on its business. **5** Brit. take an exam. **6** (sit for) pose for an artist or photographer.

> SYNONYMS **1** *you'd better sit down* **take a seat**, be seated, perch, ensconce yourself, flop; informal take the load off your feet; Brit. informal take a pew. **2** *she sat the package on the table* **put**, place, set, lay, deposit, rest, stand; informal stick, park. **3** *the committee sits on Saturday* **be in session**, meet, be convened. **4** *she sits on the tribunal* **serve on**, have a seat on, be a member of.
> ANTONYMS stand.

■ **sit-in** the occupation of a college or workplace as a form of protest.

> ❗ Use **sitting** rather than **sat** with the verb 'to be': say *we were sitting there for hours* rather than *we were sat there for hours*.

sitar ▸ noun an Indian lute with a long neck.

sitcom ▸ noun a situation comedy.

site ▸ noun **1** a place where something is located or happens. **2** a website.

> SYNONYMS *the site of the battle* **location**, place, position, situation, locality, whereabouts.

S

▶ verb (sites, siting, sited) build or establish something in a particular place.

SYNONYMS *sited in an industrial area* place, put, position, situate, locate.

❗ Don't confuse site with sight, which means 'the ability to see'.

sitter ▶ noun 1 a person who sits for a portrait. 2 a person who looks after children, pets, or a house while the parents or owners are away.

sitting ▶ noun 1 a period of time during which a court of law, committee, or parliament is carrying on its business. 2 a period of time when a group of people are served a meal. 3 a period of posing for a portrait.
■ sitting duck informal a person or thing that is easy to attack. sitting room a room for sitting and relaxing in. sitting tenant Brit. a tenant who has the legal right to remain living in a property.

situate ▶ verb (situates, situating, situated) 1 put in a particular place. 2 (be situated) be in a particular set of circumstances.

situation ▶ noun 1 a set of circumstances. 2 the location and surroundings of a place. 3 a job.

SYNONYMS 1 *their financial situation* circumstances, state of affairs, state, condition. 2 *I'll fill you in on the situation* the facts, how things stand, the lie of the land, what's going on; Brit. the state of play; N. Amer. the lay of the land; informal the score. 3 *the hotel's pleasant situation* location, position, spot, site, setting, environment.

■ situation comedy a comedy series in which the same characters are involved in various amusing situations.
❑ situational adjective.

six ▶ cardinal number 1 one more than five; 6. (Roman numeral: vi or VI.) 2 Cricket a hit that reaches the boundary without first hitting the ground, scoring six runs.
■ at sixes and sevens in a state of confusion. knock someone for six Brit. informal take someone completely by surprise.

sixpence ▶ noun Brit. (in the past) a coin worth six old pence (2½p).

sixteen ▶ cardinal number one more than fifteen; 16. (Roman numeral: xvi or XVI.)
❑ sixteenth ordinal number.

sixth ▶ ordinal number 1 being number six in a sequence; 6th. 2 (a sixth or one sixth) each of six equal parts of something.
■ sixth-form college Brit. a college for students aged 16 to 18. sixth sense a supposed ability to know things by intuition rather than using your sight, hearing, etc.

sixty ▶ cardinal number (plural sixties) ten more than fifty; 60. (Roman numeral: lx or LX.)
❑ sixtieth ordinal number.

size¹ ▶ noun 1 the overall measurements or extent of something. 2 each of the series of standard measurements in which clothes, shoes, and other goods are made.

SYNONYMS dimensions, measurements, proportions, magnitude, largeness, area, expanse, breadth, width, length, height, depth.

▶ verb (sizes, sizing, sized) 1 group things according to size. 2 (size someone/thing up) informal form a judgement of a person or thing.

size² ▶ noun a sticky solution used to glaze paper, stiffen textiles, and prepare plastered walls for decoration.

▶ verb (sizes, sizing, sized) treat with size.

sizeable (or sizable) ▶ adjective fairly large.

SYNONYMS large, substantial, considerable, respectable, significant, goodly.
ANTONYMS small.

sizzle ▶ verb (sizzles, sizzling, sizzled) 1 (of food) make a hissing sound when being fried. 2 (sizzling) informal very hot or exciting.

SYNONYMS crackle, frizzle, sputter, hiss, spit.

skate¹ ▶ noun an ice skate or roller skate.
▶ verb (skates, skating, skated) 1 move on skates. 2 (skate over or round) pass over or refer only briefly to.
❑ skater noun.

skate² ▶ noun (plural skate or skates) an edible sea fish with a diamond-shaped body.

skateboard ▶ noun a short narrow board fitted with two small wheels at either end, on which a person can ride.
❑ skateboarder noun skateboarding noun.

skedaddle ▶ verb (skedaddles, skedaddling, skedaddled) informal leave quickly.

skein ▶ noun a length of yarn held in a loose coil or knot.

skeletal ▶ adjective 1 having to do with a skeleton. 2 very thin.

skeleton ▶ noun 1 a framework of bone or cartilage supporting or containing the body of an animal. 2 a supporting framework or structure.
▶ adjective referring to an essential or minimum number of people: *a skeleton staff*.
■ skeleton in the cupboard a shocking or embarrassing fact that someone wishes to keep secret. skeleton key a key designed to fit a number of locks.

skeptic US spelling of SCEPTIC.

S

skeptical US spelling of SCEPTICAL.

sketch ▸ noun **1** a rough drawing or painting. **2** a short humorous scene in a comedy show. **3** a brief written or spoken account.

SYNONYMS *a sketch of the proposed design* **drawing,** outline, draft, diagram, design, plan; informal **rough.**

▸ verb **1** make a sketch of. **2** give a brief account of.

SYNONYMS *he sketched the garden* **draw,** make a drawing of, pencil, rough out, outline.

sketchbook ▸ noun a pad of drawing paper for sketching on.

sketchy ▸ adjective (**sketchier, sketchiest**) not thorough or detailed; rough.
□ **sketchily** adverb.

skew ▸ verb **1** suddenly change direction or move at an angle. **2** make something biased or distorted.
▸ noun a bias towards one particular group or subject.
■ **skew-whiff** Brit. informal not straight; askew.

skewbald ▸ adjective (of a horse) having patches of white and brown.

skewer ▸ noun a long piece of metal or wood used for holding pieces of food together during cooking.
▸ verb (**skewers, skewering, skewered**) hold or pierce with a pin or skewer.

ski ▸ noun (plural **skis**) each of a pair of long, narrow pieces of wood, metal, or plastic, attached to boots for travelling over snow.
▸ verb (**skis, skiing, skied**) travel on skis.
■ **ski jump** a steep slope levelling off before a sharp drop to allow a skier to leap through the air. **ski lift** a system of moving seats attached to an overhead cable, used for taking skiers to the top of a run.
□ **skier** noun.

✔ The plural of the noun is **skis**, without an **e**.

skid ▸ verb (**skids, skidding, skidded**) **1** (of a vehicle) slide sideways in an uncontrolled way. **2** slip; slide.
▸ noun **1** an act of skidding. **2** a runner attached to the underside of a helicopter and some other aircraft.
■ **skid row** N. Amer. informal a run-down part of a town or city where homeless people and alcoholics live.

skiff ▸ noun a light rowing boat.

skilful (US spelling **skillful**) ▸ adjective having or showing skill.

SYNONYMS **expert,** accomplished, skilled, masterly, talented, deft, dexterous, handy; informal **mean, crack, ace;** N. Amer. informal **crackerjack.**
ANTONYMS incompetent.

□ **skilfully** adverb.

✔ There is only one **l** in the middle: skil**f**ul. The spelling with two **l**s is American.

skill ▸ noun **1** the ability to do something well. **2** a particular ability.

SYNONYMS **expertise,** accomplishment, skilfulness, mastery, talent, deftness, dexterity, prowess, competence, artistry.
ANTONYMS incompetence.

skilled ▸ adjective **1** having or showing skill. **2** (of work) needing special abilities or training.

skillet ▸ noun N. Amer. a frying pan.

skim ▸ verb (**skims, skimming, skimmed**) **1** remove a substance from the surface of a liquid. **2** move quickly and lightly over a surface or through the air. **3** read through quickly. **4** (**skim over**) deal with briefly.

SYNONYMS **1** *skim off the fat* **remove,** scoop off, separate. **2** *the boat skimmed over the water* **glide,** move lightly, slide, sail, skate. **3** *she skimmed through the newspaper* **glance,** flick, flip, leaf, thumb, scan, run your eye over.

■ **skimmed milk** milk from which the cream has been removed.

skimp ▸ verb spend less money or use less of something than is really needed in an attempt to economize.

skimpy ▸ adjective (**skimpier, skimpiest**) **1** not large enough in amount or size. **2** (of clothes) short and revealing.

skin ▸ noun **1** the thin layer of tissue forming the outer covering of the body. **2** the skin of a dead animal used for clothing or other items. **3** the peel or outer layer of a fruit or vegetable.

SYNONYMS **1** *leopard skins* **hide,** pelt, fell, fleece. **2** *a banana skin* **peel,** rind. **3** *milk with a skin on it* **film,** layer, membrane, crust, covering, coating.

▸ verb (**skins, skinning, skinned**) **1** remove the skin from. **2** graze a part of your body.

SYNONYMS **1** *skin the tomatoes* **peel,** pare. **2** *he skinned his knee* **graze,** scrape, abrade, bark, rub raw, chafe.

■ **by the skin of your teeth** only just. **have a thick skin** be unaffected by criticism or insults. **skin-deep** not deep or lasting; superficial. **skin-diving** swimming underwater without a diving suit, using an aqualung and flippers.

skinflint ▸ noun informal a very mean person.

skinhead ▸ noun a young person of a group with very short shaved hair.

skinny ▸ adjective (**skinnier, skinniest**) **1** (of a person) very thin. **2** (of a garment) tight-fitting.

SYNONYMS **thin,** underweight, scrawny, bony, gaunt, emaciated, skeletal, wasted, pinched, spindly, gangly; informal anorexic.

skint ▸ adjective Brit. informal having little or no money.

skintight ▸ adjective (of a garment) very tight-fitting.

skip¹ ▸ verb (**skips, skipping, skipped**) **1** move along lightly, stepping from one foot to the other with a little jump. **2** Brit. jump repeatedly with a rope turned over the head and under the feet. **3** leave out or move quickly over. **4** fail to attend or deal with.

SYNONYMS **1** *skipping down the path* **caper,** prance, trip, dance, bound, bounce, gambol. **2** *we skipped the boring stuff* **omit,** leave out, miss out, dispense with, pass over, skim over, disregard; informal give something a miss.

▸ noun a skipping movement.

skip² ▸ noun Brit. a large open-topped container for holding and carrying away large unwanted items, builders' rubbish, etc.

skipper informal ▸ noun **1** the captain of a ship, boat, or aircraft. **2** the captain of a sports team.
▸ verb (**skippers, skippering, skippered**) be captain of.

skirl ▸ noun a shrill sound made by bagpipes.
▸ verb make such a sound.

skirmish ▸ noun a short period of fighting.
▸ verb take part in a skirmish.

skirt ▸ noun a woman's garment that hangs from the waist and surrounds the lower body and legs.
▸ verb **1** go round or past the edge of. **2** (also **skirt round**) avoid dealing with.

SYNONYMS **1** *he skirted the city* **go round,** walk round, circle. **2** *the fields that skirt the park* **border,** edge, flank, line. **3** *he carefully skirted round the subject* **avoid,** evade, sidestep, dodge, pass over, gloss over; informal duck; Austral./NZ informal duck-shove.

skirting (or **skirting board**) ▸ noun Brit. a wooden board running along the base of the walls of a room.

skit ▸ noun a short comedy sketch that makes fun of something by imitating it.

skitter ▸ verb (**skitters, skittering, skittered**) move lightly and quickly.

skittish ▸ adjective **1** (of a horse) nervous and tending to shy. **2** lively or changeable.
□ **skittishly** adverb.

skittle ▸ noun **1** (**skittles**) a game played with wooden pins set up to be bowled down with a ball. **2** a pin used in the game of skittles.

skive ▸ verb (**skives, skiving, skived**) Brit. informal avoid work or a duty by staying away or leaving early.
□ **skiver** noun.

skivvy ▸ noun (plural **skivvies**) Brit. informal a female domestic servant.

skua ▸ noun a large seabird like a gull.

skulduggery (or **skullduggery**) ▸ noun underhand behaviour.

skulk ▸ verb hide or move around in a secretive way.

skull ▸ noun the bony framework that surrounds and protects the brain.
■ **skull and crossbones** a picture of a skull with two thigh bones crossed below it, used in the past by pirates and now as a sign of danger.

skullcap ▸ noun a small close-fitting cap without a peak.

skunk ▸ noun an animal with black and white stripes that can spray foul-smelling liquid at attackers.

sky ▸ noun (plural **skies**) the region of the upper atmosphere seen from the earth.

skydiving ▸ noun the sport of jumping from an aircraft and performing movements in the air before landing by parachute.
□ **skydiver** noun.

skylark ▸ noun a lark that sings while flying.
▸ verb behave in a playful and mischievous way.

skylight ▸ noun a window set in a roof.

skyline ▸ noun an outline of land and buildings seen against the sky.

skyrocket ▸ verb (**skyrockets, skyrocketing, skyrocketed**) informal (of a price or amount) increase rapidly.

skyscraper ▸ noun a very tall building.

slab ▸ noun **1** a large, thick, flat piece of stone or concrete. **2** a thick slice of cake, bread, etc.

SYNONYMS **piece,** block, hunk, chunk, lump, cake, tablet, brick, panel, plate, sheet.

slack ▸ adjective **1** not taut or held tightly. **2** (of business or trade) quiet. **3** careless or lazy. **4** (of a tide) between the ebb and the flow.

SYNONYMS **1** *the rope went slack* **limp,** loose. **2** *slack skin* **sagging,** flabby, flaccid, loose, saggy. **3** *business is slack* **sluggish,** slow, quiet, slow-moving, flat, depressed, stagnant. **4** *slack procedure* **lax,** negligent, careless, slapdash, slipshod; informal sloppy.
ANTONYMS taut, firm, busy, strict.

▸ noun **1** the part of a rope or line which is not held taut. **2** (**slacks**) casual trousers.
▸ verb **1** (**slack off** or **up**) become slower or less intense. **2** Brit. informal work slowly or lazily.

SYNONYMS *no slacking!* **idle**, shirk, be lazy, be indolent, waste time, lounge about; Brit. informal skive; N. Amer. informal goof off.

□ **slacker** noun **slackly** adverb **slackness** noun.

slacken ▶ verb **1** make or become less active or intense. **2** make or become less tight.

slag ▶ noun **1** stony waste matter left when metal has been separated from ore by smelting or refining. **2** Brit. informal, disapproving a woman who has many sexual partners.

▶ verb (**slags**, **slagging**, **slagged**) (**slag someone/thing off**) Brit. informal criticize someone or something rudely.

■ **slag heap** a mound of waste material from a mine.

slain past participle of SLAY.

slake ▶ verb (**slakes**, **slaking**, **slaked**) satisfy a desire, thirst, etc.

slalom /slah-luhm/ ▶ noun a skiing or canoeing race following a winding course marked out by poles.

slam ▶ verb (**slams**, **slamming**, **slammed**) **1** shut forcefully and loudly. **2** put down with great force. **3** hit a ball with great force. **4** informal criticize severely.

SYNONYMS **1** *he slammed the door* **bang**, shut with a bang. **2** *the car slammed into a lamp post* **crash**, smash, plough, run, bump, collide with, hit, strike, ram; N. Amer. impact.

▶ noun a loud bang caused when a door is slammed.

slander ▶ noun the crime of saying something untrue that harms a person's reputation.

▶ verb (**slanders**, **slandering**, **slandered**) say something untrue and damaging about. □ **slanderous** adjective.

slang ▶ noun very informal words and phrases that are more common in speech than in writing and are used by a particular group of people.

■ **slanging match** Brit. an angry argument in which people insult each other. □ **slangy** adjective.

slant ▶ verb **1** slope or lean. **2** present information from a particular point of view.

SYNONYMS **1** *the floor slanted* **slope**, tilt, incline, be at an angle, tip, lean, dip, pitch, shelve, list, bank. **2** *their findings were slanted in our favour* **bias**, distort, twist, skew, weight.

▶ noun **1** a sloping position. **2** a point of view.

SYNONYMS **1** *the slant of the roof* **slope**, incline, tilt, gradient, pitch, angle, camber. **2** *a feminist slant* **point of view**, viewpoint, standpoint, stance, angle, perspective, approach, view, attitude, position, bias.

slap ▶ verb (**slaps**, **slapping**, **slapped**) **1** hit with the palm of your hand or a flat object. **2** hit against a surface with a slapping sound. **3** (**slap something on**) put something on a surface quickly or carelessly.

SYNONYMS *he slapped her hard* **smack**, strike, hit, cuff, clip, spank; informal whack.

▶ noun an act or sound of slapping.

SYNONYMS *a slap across the face* **smack**, blow, cuff, clip, spank; informal whack.

▶ adverb (also **slap bang**) informal suddenly and with great force.

■ **slap-up** Brit. informal (of a meal) large and extravagant.

slapdash ▶ adjective done too hurriedly and carelessly.

slapstick ▶ noun comedy consisting of deliberately clumsy actions and embarrassing situations.

slash ▶ verb **1** cut with a violent sweeping movement. **2** informal greatly reduce a price or quantity.

SYNONYMS **1** *her tyres had been slashed* **cut**, gash, slit, lacerate, knife. **2** *the company slashed prices* **reduce**, cut, lower, bring down, mark down.

▶ noun **1** a cut made with a wide sweeping stroke. **2** a slanting stroke (/) used between alternatives and in fractions and ratios.

SYNONYMS *a slash across his temple* **cut**, gash, slit, laceration, incision, wound.

slat ▶ noun each of a series of thin, narrow pieces of wood or other material, arranged so as to overlap or fit into each other. □ **slatted** adjective.

slate ▶ noun a dark grey rock that is easily split into smooth, flat plates, used in building and in the past for writing on.

▶ verb (**slates**, **slating**, **slated**) Brit. informal severely criticize.

slather ▶ verb (**slathers**, **slathering**, **slathered**) informal spread or smear thickly over.

slattern ▶ noun old use a dirty, untidy woman. □ **slatternly** adjective.

slaughter ▶ noun **1** the killing of farm animals for food. **2** the killing of a large number of people in a cruel or violent way.

SYNONYMS *a scene of slaughter* **massacre**, (mass) murder, (mass) killing, (mass) execution, extermination, carnage, bloodshed, bloodletting, bloodbath; literary slaying.

▶ verb (**slaughters**, **slaughtering**, **slaughtered**) **1** kill animals for food. **2** kill a number of people in a cruel or violent way.

S

SYNONYMS 1 *the cattle were slaughtered* **kill,** butcher, cull, put down. **2** *civilians are being slaughtered* **massacre,** murder, butcher, kill, exterminate, wipe out, put to death, execute; literary slay.

slaughterhouse ▸ noun a place where animals are killed for food.

Slav /slahv/ ▸ noun a member of a group of peoples in central and eastern Europe.
□ **Slavic** adjective.

slave ▸ noun **1** (in the past) a person who was the legal property of another and was forced to obey them. **2** a person who is strongly influenced or controlled by something.

SYNONYMS *the work was done by slaves* **servant,** lackey; Brit. informal skivvy, dogsbody; historical serf, vassal.
ANTONYMS freeman, master.

▸ verb (**slaves, slaving, slaved**) work very hard.

SYNONYMS *we slaved away* **toil,** labour, sweat, work like a Trojan/dog; informal kill yourself, sweat blood, slog away; Brit. informal graft; Austral./NZ informal bullock.

■ **slave-driver** informal a person who makes other people work very hard. **slave labour** very demanding work that is very badly paid.

slaver /sla-ver, slay-ver/ ▸ verb (**slavers, slavering, slavered**) let saliva run from the mouth.
▸ noun saliva running from the mouth.

slavery ▸ noun **1** the state of being a slave. **2** the practice or system of owning slaves.

SYNONYMS **enslavement,** servitude, serfdom, bondage, captivity.
ANTONYMS freedom.

slavish ▸ adjective showing no attempt to be original.
□ **slavishly** adverb.

slay ▸ verb (**slays, slaying, slew**; past participle **slain**) old use or N. Amer. violently kill.

sleaze ▸ noun informal immoral or dishonest behaviour.

sleazy ▸ adjective (**sleazier, sleaziest**) **1** immoral or dishonest. **2** (of a place) dirty and seedy.

SYNONYMS 1 *sleazy politicians* **corrupt,** immoral. **2** *a sleazy bar* **squalid,** seedy, seamy, sordid, insalubrious.
ANTONYMS honest, reputable, upmarket.

sled ▸ noun & verb (**sleds, sledding, sledded**) N. Amer. = SLEDGE.

sledge ▸ noun **1** a vehicle on runners for travelling over snow or ice, sometimes pulled by dogs. **2** Brit. a toboggan.
▸ verb (**sledges, sledging, sledged**) ride or carry on a sledge.

sledgehammer ▸ noun a large, heavy hammer.

sleek ▸ adjective **1** smooth and glossy. **2** having a wealthy and smart appearance. **3** elegant and streamlined.

SYNONYMS 1 *his sleek dark hair* **smooth,** glossy, shiny, shining, lustrous, silken, silky. **2** *the car's sleek lines* **streamlined,** elegant, graceful.
ANTONYMS scruffy, crude.

□ **sleekly** adverb.

sleep ▸ noun a condition of rest in which the eyes are closed, the muscles are relaxed, and the mind is unconscious.

SYNONYMS **nap,** doze, siesta, catnap; informal snooze, forty winks, shut-eye; Brit. informal kip; literary slumber.
ANTONYMS wakefulness.

▸ verb (**sleeps, sleeping, slept**) **1** be asleep. **2** (**sleep in**) remain asleep or in bed later than usual in the morning. **3** provide a particular number of people with beds. **4** (**sleep with**) have sex or be involved in a sexual relationship with. **5** (**sleep around**) have many sexual partners.

SYNONYMS **be asleep,** doze, take a siesta, take a nap, catnap; informal snooze, snatch forty winks, get some shut-eye; Brit. informal kip; N. Amer. informal catch some Zs; literary slumber.
ANTONYMS wake up.

■ **put something to sleep** kill an animal painlessly. **sleeping bag** a warm padded bag for sleeping in when camping or travelling. **sleeping car** a railway carriage fitted with beds or berths. **sleeping partner** Brit. a partner who puts money into a business but is not involved in running it. **sleeping policeman** Brit. a hump in the road for slowing down traffic.
□ **sleepless** adjective.

sleeper ▸ noun **1** Brit. each of the wooden supports on which a railway track rests. **2** Brit. a ring or bar worn in a pierced ear to keep the hole from closing. **3** a train carrying sleeping cars.

sleepover ▸ noun a night spent by children at another person's house.

sleepwalk ▸ verb walk around while asleep.
□ **sleepwalker** noun.

sleepy ▸ adjective (**sleepier, sleepiest**) **1** ready for, or needing, sleep. **2** (of a place) without much activity.

SYNONYMS 1 *she felt very sleepy* **drowsy,** tired, somnolent, heavy-eyed; informal dopey. **2** *a sleepy little village* **quiet,** peaceful, tranquil, placid, slow-moving, dull, boring.
ANTONYMS awake, alert.

□ **sleepily** adverb **sleepiness** noun.

S

sleet ▸ noun rain containing some ice, or snow melting as it falls.
▸ verb (**it sleets, it is sleeting, it sleeted**) sleet falls.

sleeve ▸ noun **1** the part of a garment covering a person's arm. **2** a protective cover for a record. **3** a tube fitting over a rod or smaller tube.
■ **up your sleeve** kept secret and ready for use when needed.
□ **sleeveless** adjective.

sleigh ▸ noun a sledge pulled by horses or reindeer.

sleight (*rhymes with* slight) ▸ noun (**sleight of hand**) **1** skilful use of the hands when performing magic tricks. **2** skilful deception.

slender ▸ adjective (**slenderer, slenderest**) **1** gracefully thin. **2** barely enough.

> SYNONYMS **1** *her tall, slender figure* **slim,** lean, willowy, svelte, lissom, graceful, slight, thin, skinny. **2** *slender evidence* **meagre,** limited, slight, scanty, scant, sparse, flimsy, insubstantial. **3** *the chances seemed slender* **faint,** remote, tenuous, fragile, slim.
> ANTONYMS plump, strong.

slept past and past participle of SLEEP.

sleuth (*rhymes with* truth) ▸ noun informal a detective.
□ **sleuthing** noun.

slew¹ ▸ verb turn or slide violently or uncontrollably.

slew² past of SLAY.

slice ▸ noun **1** a thin, broad piece of food cut from a larger portion. **2** a portion or share. **3** a kitchen implement with a broad, flat blade for lifting cake, fish, etc. **4** (in sports) a sliced stroke or shot.

> SYNONYMS **1** *a slice of cake* **piece,** portion, slab, wedge, rasher, sliver, wafer. **2** *a huge slice of public spending* **share,** part, portion, tranche, percentage, proportion, allocation.

▸ verb (**slices, slicing, sliced**) **1** cut into slices. **2** cut with something sharp. **3** (in sport) hit the ball so that it spins or curves away to the side.

> SYNONYMS *slice the cheese thinly* **cut,** carve, divide.

slick ▸ adjective **1** impressively smooth and efficient. **2** self-confident but insincere. **3** (of a surface) smooth, glossy, or slippery.

> SYNONYMS **1** *a slick advertising campaign* **efficient,** smooth, smooth-running, polished, well organized, well run, streamlined. **2** *a slick salesman* **glib,** polished, assured, self-assured, smooth-talking, plausible; informal smarmy.
> ANTONYMS incompetent, hesitant.

▸ noun a smooth patch of oil.
▸ verb make hair smooth and glossy with water, oil, or cream.

> SYNONYMS *his hair was slicked down* **smooth,** plaster, sleek, grease, oil, gel.

□ **slickly** adverb.

slide ▸ verb (**slides, sliding, slid**) **1** move along a smooth surface while remaining in contact with it. **2** move smoothly, quickly, or without being noticed. **3** become gradually lower or worse.

> SYNONYMS **glide,** slip, slither, skim, skate, skid, slew.

▸ noun **1** a structure with a smooth sloping surface for children to slide down. **2** an act of sliding. **3** a rectangular piece of glass which you place an object on to look at it through a microscope. **4** a small piece of photographic film which you view using a projector.
■ **slide rule** a ruler with a sliding central strip, used for making calculations quickly. **sliding scale** a scale of fees, wages, etc. that varies according to some other factor.

slight ▸ adjective **1** small in degree. **2** not sturdy or strongly built. **3** lacking depth; trivial.

> SYNONYMS **1** *the chance of success is slight* **small,** tiny, minute, negligible, insignificant, minimal, remote, slim, faint. **2** *Elizabeth's slight figure* **slim,** slender, delicate, dainty, fragile.
> ANTONYMS good, plump.

▸ verb insult someone by treating them without proper respect or attention.

> SYNONYMS *he had been slighted* **insult,** snub, rebuff, spurn, give someone the cold shoulder, cut (dead), scorn.
> ANTONYMS respect.

▸ noun an insult.

> SYNONYMS *an unintended slight* **insult,** affront, snub, rebuff; informal put-down.
> ANTONYMS compliment.

slightly ▸ adverb to a small degree.

> SYNONYMS **a little,** a bit, somewhat, faintly, vaguely, a shade.
> ANTONYMS very.

slim ▸ adjective (**slimmer, slimmest**) **1** gracefully thin. **2** small in width and long and narrow in shape. **3** very small: *a slim chance*.

> SYNONYMS **1** *tall and slim* **slender,** lean, thin, willowy, sylphlike, svelte, lissom, trim. **2** *a slim silver bracelet* **narrow,** slender. **3** *a slim chance* **slight,** small, slender, faint, poor, remote.
> ANTONYMS plump, wide, good.

▸ verb (**slims, slimming, slimmed**) Brit. make or become thinner.

S

SYNONYMS *I'm trying to slim* **lose weight,** get into shape; N. Amer. slenderize.
ANTONYMS put on weight.

□ **slimmer** noun.

slime ▸ noun an unpleasantly moist, soft, and slippery substance.

slimy ▸ adjective (**slimier, slimiest**) **1** like or covered by slime. **2** informal polite and flattering in a way that is not sincere.

SYNONYMS **slippery,** slithery, greasy; informal slippy, gloopy.
ANTONYMS firm, grippy.

sling ▸ noun **1** a loop of fabric used to support or raise a hanging weight. **2** a strap or loop used to hurl small missiles.
▸ verb (**slings, slinging, slung**) **1** hang or carry with a sling or strap. **2** informal throw.

SYNONYMS **1** *a hammock was slung between two trees* **hang,** suspend, string, swing. **2** *she slung her jacket on the sofa* **throw,** toss, fling, hurl, cast, pitch, lob, flip; informal chuck, heave, bung.

slingback ▸ noun a shoe held in place by a strap around the ankle.

slingshot ▸ noun a hand-held catapult.

slink ▸ verb (**slinks, slinking, slunk**) move quietly in a secretive way.

SYNONYMS **creep,** sneak, steal, slip, slide, sidle, tiptoe.

slinky ▸ adjective (**slinkier, slinkiest**) informal (of a woman's garment) close-fitting and sexy.

slip¹ ▸ verb (**slips, slipping, slipped**) **1** lose your balance and slide for a short distance. **2** accidentally slide out of position or from someone's grasp. **3** fail to grip a surface. **4** get gradually worse. **5** (usu. **slip up**) make a careless mistake. **6** move or place quietly, quickly, or secretly. **7** get free from.

SYNONYMS **1** *she slipped on the ice* **slide,** skid, slither, fall (over), lose your balance, tumble. **2** *the envelope slipped through Luke's fingers* **fall,** drop, slide. **3** *we slipped out by a back door* **creep,** steal, sneak, slide, sidle, slope, slink, tiptoe. **4** *she slipped the map into her pocket* **put,** tuck, shove; informal pop, stick, stuff.

▸ noun **1** an act of slipping. **2** a minor or careless mistake. **3** a loose-fitting short petticoat. **4** Cricket a fielding position close behind the batsman to one side.

SYNONYMS **1** *a single slip could send them plummeting down* **false step,** slide, skid, fall, tumble. **2** *a careless slip* **mistake,** error, blunder, gaffe, oversight, omission, lapse; informal slip-up, boo-boo, howler; Brit. informal boob, clanger, bloomer; N. Amer. informal goof, blooper.

■ **slip knot** a knot that can be undone by a pull, or that can slide along the rope on which it is tied. **slip-on** (of shoes or clothes) having no fastenings. **slipped disc** a displaced disc in the spine that presses on nearby nerves and causes pain. **slip road** Brit. a road entering or leaving a motorway or dual carriageway.

□ **slippage** noun.

slip² ▸ noun **1** a small piece of paper. **2** a cutting from a plant.

slipper ▸ noun a comfortable slip-on shoe worn indoors.

slippery ▸ adjective **1** difficult to hold firmly or stand on through being smooth, wet, or slimy. **2** (of a person) difficult to pin down.

SYNONYMS **1** *the roads are slippery* **slithery,** greasy, oily, icy, glassy, smooth, slimy, wet; informal slippy. **2** *a slippery customer* **sneaky,** sly, devious, crafty, cunning, tricky, evasive, scheming, unreliable, untrustworthy; N. Amer. snide; informal shady, shifty; Brit. informal dodgy; Austral./NZ informal shonky.

□ **slipperiness** noun.

slippy ▸ adjective (**slippier, slippiest**) informal slippery.

slipshod ▸ adjective careless, thoughtless, or disorganized.

slipstream ▸ noun **1** a current of air or water driven back by a propeller or jet engine. **2** the partial vacuum created in the wake of a moving vehicle.

slipway ▸ noun a slope leading into water, used for launching and landing boats and ships.

slit ▸ noun a long, narrow cut or opening.

SYNONYMS **1** *three diagonal slits* **cut,** incision, split, slash, gash. **2** *a slit in the curtains* **opening,** gap, chink, crack, aperture, slot.

▸ verb (**slits, slitting, slit**) make a slit in.

SYNONYMS *he threatened to slit her throat* **cut,** slash, split open, slice open.

slither ▸ verb (**slithers, slithering, slithered**) **1** move smoothly over a surface with a twisting motion. **2** slide unsteadily on a loose or slippery surface.
▸ noun a slithering movement.
□ **slithery** adjective.

sliver ▸ noun a small, narrow, sharp piece cut or split off a larger piece.

slob Brit. informal ▸ noun a lazy, untidy person.
▸ verb (**slobs, slobbing, slobbed**) behave in a lazy, untidy way.

slobber ▸ verb (**slobbers, slobbering, slobbered**) have saliva dripping from the mouth.
▸ noun saliva dripping from the mouth.
□ **slobbery** adjective.

S

sloe ▸ noun the small bluish-black fruit of the blackthorn.

slog ▸ verb (**slogs, slogging, slogged**) **1** work hard over a period of time. **2** move with difficulty or effort. **3** hit forcefully. **4** (**slog it out**) fight or compete fiercely.
▸ noun a period of difficult, tiring work or travelling.

slogan ▸ noun a short, memorable phrase used in advertising or associated with a political group.

> SYNONYMS **catchphrase**, catchline, motto, jingle; N. Amer. informal **tag line**.

sloop ▸ noun a type of sailing boat with one mast.

slop ▸ verb (**slops, slopping, slopped**) **1** (of a liquid) spill over the edge of a container. **2** (**slop about** or **around**) Brit. informal spend time relaxing in casual or scruffy clothes.
▸ noun (**slops**) **1** waste liquid that has to be emptied by hand. **2** unappetizing semi-liquid food.

slope ▸ noun **1** a surface with one end at a higher level than another. **2** a part of the side of a hill or mountain.

> SYNONYMS the slope of the roof **tilt**, pitch, slant, angle, gradient, incline, inclination, fall, camber; N. Amer. **grade**.

▸ verb (**slopes, sloping, sloped**) **1** slant up or down. **2** (**slope off**) informal leave without attracting attention.

> SYNONYMS **1** the garden sloped down to a stream **tilt**, slant, incline, lean, drop/fall away, descend, shelve, camber, rise, ascend, climb. **2** (**sloping**) **slanting**, leaning, inclined, angled, cambered, tilted.

sloppy ▸ adjective (**sloppier, sloppiest**) **1** careless and disorganized. **2** containing too much liquid. **3** too sentimental.

> SYNONYMS **1** their defending was sloppy **careless**, slapdash, slipshod, untidy, slack, slovenly; informal slap-happy. **2** sloppy chicken curry **runny**, watery, liquid, mushy; informal gloopy. **3** sloppy letters **sentimental**, mawkish, romantic; informal slushy, schmaltzy; Brit. informal soppy; N. Amer. informal cornball, sappy, hokey.

□ **sloppily** adverb **sloppiness** noun.

slosh ▸ verb **1** (of liquid in a container) move around with a splashing sound. **2** move through liquid with a splashing sound. **3** pour liquid clumsily.

sloshed ▸ adjective informal drunk.

slot ▸ noun **1** a long, narrow opening into which something may be inserted. **2** a place in an arrangement or scheme.

> SYNONYMS **1** he slid a coin into the slot **aperture**, slit, crack, hole, opening. **2** a

mid-morning slot **time**, spot, period, niche, space; informal **window**.

▸ verb (**slots, slotting, slotted**) **1** place into a slot. **2** (**slot in** or **into**) fit easily into a new role or situation.

> SYNONYMS he slotted a cassette into the machine **insert**, slide, fit, put, place.

■ **slot machine** a fruit machine or (Brit.) vending machine.

sloth /slohth/ ▸ noun **1** laziness. **2** a slow-moving animal that hangs upside down.
□ **slothful** adjective.

slouch ▸ verb stand, move, or sit in a lazy, drooping way.
▸ noun a lazy, drooping posture.
■ **be no slouch** informal be fast or good at something.

slough[1] (rhymes with plough) ▸ noun **1** a swamp. **2** a situation without progress or activity.

slough[2] (rhymes with rough) ▸ verb (of an animal) cast off an old skin.

Slovakian (also **Slovak**) ▸ noun a person from Slovakia.
▸ adjective relating to Slovakia.

Slovene /sloh-veen/ ▸ noun **1** a person from Slovenia. **2** the language of Slovenia.
□ **Slovenian** noun & adjective.

slovenly ▸ adjective **1** untidy and dirty. **2** careless.
□ **slovenliness** noun.

slow ▸ adjective **1** moving or capable of moving only at a low speed. **2** taking a long time. **3** (of a clock or watch) showing a time earlier than the correct time. **4** not quick to understand, think, or learn.

> SYNONYMS **1** their slow walk home **unhurried**, leisurely, steady, sedate, sluggish, plodding. **2** a slow process **lengthy**, time-consuming, long-drawn-out, protracted, prolonged, gradual. **3** he's a bit slow **stupid**, unintelligent, obtuse; informal dense, dim, thick, slow on the uptake, dumb, dopey; Brit. informal dozy.
> ANTONYMS quick.

▸ verb (often **slow down** or **up**) **1** reduce speed. **2** be less busy or active.

> SYNONYMS **1** the traffic forced him to slow down **reduce speed**, go slower, decelerate, brake. **2** this would slow down economic growth **hold back/up**, delay, retard, set back, check, curb.
> ANTONYMS accelerate.

■ **slow motion** the showing of film or video more slowly than it was made or recorded. **slow-worm** a small snake-like lizard.
□ **slowness** noun.

slowcoach ▸ noun Brit. informal a person who acts or moves slowly.

S

slowly ▸ adverb at low speed.

> SYNONYMS **1** *Rose walked off slowly* **unhurriedly,** without hurrying, steadily, at a leisurely pace, at a snail's pace. **2** *her health is improving slowly* **gradually,** bit by bit, little by little, slowly but surely, step by step.
> ANTONYMS quickly.

sludge ▸ noun thick, soft, wet mud or a similar mixture.
> □ **sludgy** adjective.

slug[1] ▸ noun **1** a small creature like a snail without a shell. **2** informal a small amount of an alcoholic drink. **3** informal a bullet.
▸ verb (**slugs, slugging, slugged**) informal gulp a drink.

slug[2] informal ▸ verb (**slugs, slugging, slugged**) **1** hit with a hard blow. **2** (**slug it out**) settle a dispute by fighting or competing fiercely.

sluggard ▸ noun a lazy, inactive person.

sluggish ▸ adjective **1** slow-moving or inactive. **2** not energetic or alert.

> SYNONYMS **lethargic,** listless, lacking in energy, lifeless, inactive, slow; N. Amer. logy.
> ANTONYMS vigorous.

> □ **sluggishly** adverb.

sluice /slooss/ ▸ noun **1** (also **sluice gate**) a sliding device for controlling the flow of water. **2** a channel for carrying off surplus water.
▸ verb (**sluices, sluicing, sluiced**) wash or rinse with water.

slum ▸ noun **1** a rundown area of a city or town inhabited by very poor people. **2** a house or building which is unfit to be lived in.

> SYNONYMS **hovel;** (**slums**) ghetto, shanty town.

▸ verb (**slums, slumming, slummed**) (**slum it**) informal choose to spend time in uncomfortable conditions or at a low social level.

slumber ▸ verb (**slumbers, slumbering, slumbered**) sleep.
▸ noun a sleep.

slump ▸ verb **1** sit, lean, or fall heavily and limply. **2** fall in price, value, number, etc. suddenly and by a large amount.

> SYNONYMS **1** *he slumped into a chair* **sit heavily,** flop, collapse, sink; informal plonk yourself. **2** *house prices slumped* **fall,** plummet, tumble, collapse, drop; informal crash, nosedive.
> ANTONYMS rise, boom.

▸ noun an instance of slumping.

> SYNONYMS **1** *a slump in profits* **fall,** drop, tumble, downturn, downswing, slide, decline, decrease; informal nosedive. **2** *an economic slump* **recession,** decline,

depression, slowdown.
> ANTONYMS rise, boom.

slung past and past participle of SLING.

slunk past and past participle of SLINK.

slur ▸ verb (**slurs, slurring, slurred**) **1** speak in a way that is difficult to understand. **2** perform a group of musical notes in a smooth, flowing way.
▸ noun **1** an insult or accusation intended to damage someone's reputation. **2** a curved line indicating that notes are to be slurred.

slurp ▸ verb eat or drink with a loud sucking sound.
▸ noun a slurping sound.

slurry ▸ noun (plural **slurries**) a semi-liquid mixture of water and manure, cement, or coal.

slush ▸ noun **1** partially melted snow or ice. **2** informal very sentimental talk or writing.
■ **slush fund** a reserve of money used for something illegal.
> □ **slushy** adjective.

slut ▸ noun disapproving a woman who has many sexual partners, or who is untidy and lazy.
> □ **sluttish** adjective.

sly ▸ adjective (**slyer, slyest**) **1** cunning and deceitful. **2** (of a remark, glance, or expression) suggesting secret knowledge.

> SYNONYMS **1** *she's very sly* **cunning,** crafty, clever, wily, artful, tricky, scheming, devious, underhand, sneaky. **2** *a sly grin* **roguish,** mischievous, impish, playful, wicked, arch, knowing. **3** *she took a sly sip of water* **surreptitious,** furtive, stealthy, covert.
> ANTONYMS open, straightforward.

> □ **slyly** adverb.

smack[1] ▸ noun **1** a sharp blow with the palm of the hand. **2** a loud, sharp sound. **3** a loud kiss.

> SYNONYMS *she gave him a smack* **slap,** blow, cuff, clip, spank; informal whack.

▸ verb **1** give someone a smack. **2** smash or drive into. **3** part your lips noisily.
▸ adverb informal exactly or directly.

> SYNONYMS *smack in the middle* **exactly,** precisely, straight, right, directly, squarely, dead, plumb; informal slap, bang; N. Amer. informal smack dab.

smack[2] ▸ verb (**smack of**) **1** seem to contain or involve something wrong or unpleasant. **2** smell or taste of.

smack[3] ▸ noun Brit. a sailing boat with one mast.

smack[4] ▸ noun informal heroin.

smacker ▸ noun informal **1** a loud kiss. **2** Brit. one pound sterling.

small ▸ adjective **1** of less than normal size. **2** not great in amount, number, strength, or power. **3** young.

SYNONYMS **1** *a small flat* **little**, compact, tiny, miniature, mini, minute, toy, baby, poky, cramped; Scottish **wee**; informal **tiddly**; Brit. informal **titchy**; N. Amer. informal **little-bitty**. **2** *a very small man* **short**, little, petite, diminutive, elfin, tiny; Scottish **wee**; informal **teeny**, pint-sized. **3** *a few small changes* **slight**, minor, unimportant, trifling, trivial, insignificant, inconsequential, negligible; informal **minuscule**, piffling.
ANTONYMS big, tall, major.

■ **small arms** guns that can be carried in the hands. **small beer** Brit. something unimportant. **small fry** young or unimportant people or things. **the small hours** the early hours of the morning after midnight. **the small of the back** the lower part of a person's back where the spine curves in. **small print** details printed so small that they are not easily noticed in an agreement or contract. **small talk** polite conversation about unimportant things.
□ **smallness** noun.

smallholding ▶ noun Brit. a piece of agricultural land that is smaller than a farm.
□ **smallholder** noun.

smallpox ▶ noun a serious disease which causes blisters that usually leave permanent scars.

smarmy ▶ adjective Brit. informal friendly or flattering in an unpleasant and insincere way.

smart ▶ adjective **1** clean, tidy, and stylish. **2** bright and fresh in appearance. **3** (of a place) fashionable and upmarket. **4** informal quick-witted. **5** chiefly N. Amer. cheekily clever. **6** quick.

SYNONYMS **1** *you look very smart* **well dressed**, stylish, chic, fashionable, modish, elegant, dapper; N. Amer. **trig**; informal **natty**, snappy; N. Amer. informal **fly**. **2** *a smart restaurant* **fashionable**, stylish, high-class, exclusive, chic, fancy; Brit. **upmarket**; N. Amer. **high-toned**; informal **trendy**, classy, swanky; Brit. informal **swish**; N. Amer. informal **swank**. **3** *he's very smart* **clever**, bright, intelligent, quick-witted, shrewd, astute, perceptive; informal **brainy**, quick on the uptake. **4** *a smart pace* **brisk**, quick, fast, rapid, lively, energetic, vigorous; informal **cracking**.
ANTONYMS untidy, downmarket, stupid, slow, gentle.

▶ verb **1** give a sharp, stinging pain. **2** feel upset and annoyed.

SYNONYMS **1** *her eyes were smarting* **sting**, burn, tingle, prickle, hurt. **2** *she smarted at the accusations* **feel hurt**, feel upset, take offence, feel aggrieved, feel indignant, be put out.

■ **smart card** a plastic card on which information is stored in electronic form.
□ **smartish** adjective **smartly** adverb **smartness** noun.

smarten ▶ verb (**smarten up**) make or become smarter.

smash ▶ verb **1** break violently into pieces. **2** hit or collide forcefully. **3** (in sport) hit the ball hard. **4** completely defeat or destroy.

SYNONYMS **1** *he smashed a window* **break**, shatter, splinter, crack; informal **bust**. **2** *she's smashed the car* **crash**, wreck; Brit. **write off**; N. Amer. informal **total**. **3** *they smashed into a wall* **crash**, smack, slam, plough, run, bump, hit, strike, ram, collide with; N. Amer. **impact**.

▶ noun **1** an act or sound of smashing. **2** (also **smash hit**) informal a very successful song, film, or show.

SYNONYMS *a motorway smash* **crash**, collision, accident; N. Amer. **wreck**; informal **pile-up**; Brit. informal **shunt**.

smashing ▶ adjective Brit. informal excellent.
□ **smasher** noun.

smattering ▶ noun **1** a small amount. **2** a slight knowledge of a language.

smear ▶ verb **1** coat or mark with a greasy or sticky substance. **2** blur or smudge. **3** make false accusations about someone so as to damage their reputation.

SYNONYMS **1** *the table was smeared with grease* **streak**, smudge, mark. **2** *smear the meat with olive oil* **cover**, coat, grease. **3** *she smeared sunblock on her skin* **spread**, rub, daub, slap, smother, plaster. **4** *they are trying to smear our reputation* **sully**, tarnish, blacken, drag through the mud, damage, defame, malign, slander, libel; N. Amer. **slur**.

▶ noun **1** a greasy or sticky mark. **2** a false accusation.

SYNONYMS **1** *smears of blood* **streak**, smudge, daub, dab, spot, patch, blotch, mark; informal **splodge**. **2** *press smears about his closest aides* **accusation**, lie, untruth, slur, slander, libel, defamation.

■ **smear test** Brit. a test to detect signs of cervical cancer.

smell ▶ noun **1** the ability to sense different things by means of the organs in the nose. **2** something sensed by the organs in the nose; an odour. **3** an act of smelling.

SYNONYMS *the smell of the kitchen* **odour**, aroma, fragrance, scent, perfume, bouquet, nose, stench, stink; Brit. informal **pong**.

▶ verb (**smells**, **smelling**, **smelt** or **smelled**) **1** sense by means of the organs in the nose. **2** sniff at something to find out its smell.

S

3 send out a smell. **4** have a strong or unpleasant smell. **5** sense or detect.

> SYNONYMS **1** *he smelled her perfume* **scent**, get a sniff of, detect. **2** *the dogs smelled each other* **sniff**, nose. **3** *the cellar smells* **stink**, reek; Brit. informal pong.

■ **smell a rat** informal suspect a trick. **smelling salts** a strong-smelling liquid formerly sniffed by people who felt faint.

smelly ▸ adjective (**smellier, smelliest**) having a strong or unpleasant smell.

> SYNONYMS **foul-smelling**, stinking, reeking, rank; informal stinky; Brit. informal pongy.

smelt¹ ▸ verb extract metal from its ore by heating and melting it.

smelt² past and past participle of SMELL.

smidgen (or **smidgeon**) ▸ noun informal a tiny amount.

smile ▸ verb (**smiles, smiling, smiled**) form your features into a pleased, friendly, or amused expression, with the corners of the mouth turned up.

> SYNONYMS *he smiled at her* **beam**, grin (from ear to ear), smirk, simper, leer. ANTONYMS frown.

▸ noun an act of smiling.

> SYNONYMS *the smile on her face* **beam**, grin, smirk, simper, leer.

smirk ▸ verb smile in a smug or silly way. ▸ noun a smug or silly smile.

smite ▸ verb (**smites, smiting, smote**; past participle **smitten**) **1** old use hit with a hard blow. **2** (**be smitten**) be strongly attracted to someone. **3** (**be smitten**) be severely affected by a disease.

smith ▸ noun **1** a person who works in metal. **2** a blacksmith.

smithereens ▸ plural noun informal small pieces.

smithy ▸ noun (plural **smithies**) a blacksmith's workshop.

smock ▸ noun **1** a loose dress or blouse with the upper part gathered into decorative stitched pleats. **2** a loose overall worn to protect your clothes.

smog ▸ noun fog or haze made worse by pollution in the atmosphere.

smoke ▸ noun **1** a visible vapour in the air produced by a burning substance. **2** an act of smoking tobacco. **3** informal a cigarette or cigar. **4** (**the Smoke** or **the Big Smoke**) Brit. a big city.

▸ verb (**smokes, smoking, smoked**) **1** give out smoke. **2** breathe smoke from a cigarette, pipe, etc. in and out again. **3** preserve meat or fish by exposing it to smoke. **4** (**smoke someone/thing out**) drive someone or something out of a place by using smoke. **5** (**smoked**) (of glass) darkened.

□ **smokeless** adjective **smoker** noun.

smokescreen ▸ noun **1** something designed to disguise your real intentions or activities. **2** a cloud of smoke created to conceal military operations.

smokestack ▸ noun a chimney or funnel which takes away smoke produced by a locomotive, ship, factory, etc.

smoky ▸ adjective (**smokier, smokiest**) producing, filled with, or like smoke.

smolder US spelling of SMOULDER.

smooch ▸ verb informal kiss and cuddle.

smooth ▸ adjective **1** having an even and regular surface. **2** (of a liquid) without lumps. **3** (of movement) without jerks. **4** without difficulties. **5** charming in a very confident or flattering way. **6** (of a flavour) not harsh or bitter.

> SYNONYMS **1** *the smooth flat rocks* **even**, level, flat, glassy, glossy, silky, polished. **2** *a smooth sauce* **creamy**, fine, velvety. **3** *a smooth sea* **calm**, still, tranquil, undisturbed, unruffled, even, flat, like a millpond. **4** *smooth operation* **steady**, regular, uninterrupted, unbroken, straightforward, easy, effortless, trouble-free. **5** *a smooth, confident man* **suave**, urbane, sophisticated, polished, debonair, courteous, gracious, glib, slick; informal smarmy. ANTONYMS uneven, rough, lumpy, irregular, gauche.

▸ verb (also **smoothe**) (**smooths** or **smoothes, smoothing, smoothed**) **1** make something smooth. **2** (**smooth something over**) deal successfully with a problem.

> SYNONYMS **1** *she smoothed the soil* **flatten**, level (out/off), even out/off, press, roll, iron, plane. **2** *brokers smooth the passage of goods* **ease**, facilitate, expedite, assist, aid. ANTONYMS roughen, hinder.

■ **smooth-talking** informal using very persuasive or flattering language. □ **smoothly** adverb **smoothness** noun.

smoothie ▸ noun **1** a thick, smooth drink of fresh fruit with milk, yogurt, or ice cream. **2** informal a man with a charming, confident manner.

smorgasbord ▸ noun a meal at which you choose from a range of open sandwiches and savoury items.

smote past of SMITE.

smother ▸ verb (**smothers, smothering, smothered**) **1** suffocate someone by covering their nose and mouth. **2** (**smother someone/thing in** or **with**) cover someone or something thickly with. **3** be oppressively protective or loving towards someone.

S

SYNONYMS **1** *she tried to smother her baby* **suffocate**, asphyxiate, stifle, choke. **2** *we smothered the flames* **extinguish**, put out, snuff out, douse, stamp out. **3** *we smothered ourselves with suncream* **smear**, daub, spread, cover. **4** *she smothered a sigh* **stifle**, muffle, strangle, suppress, hold back, fight back, swallow, conceal.

smoulder (US spelling **smolder**) ▶ verb (**smoulders, smouldering, smouldered**) **1** burn slowly with smoke but no flame. **2** feel strong and barely hidden anger, hatred, lust, etc.

SMS ▶ abbreviation Short Message (or Messaging) Service, a system for sending and receiving text messages.
▶ noun a message sent by SMS.

smudge ▶ verb (**smudges, smudging, smudged**) make or become blurred or smeared.
▶ noun a smudged mark or image.
□ **smudgy** adjective.

smug ▶ adjective (**smugger, smuggest**) irritatingly pleased with yourself.

SYNONYMS **self-satisfied**, conceited, complacent, superior, pleased with yourself.

□ **smugly** adverb **smugness** noun.

smuggle ▶ verb (**smuggles, smuggling, smuggled**) **1** move goods illegally into or out of a country. **2** secretly convey.
□ **smuggler** noun.

smut ▶ noun **1** a small flake of soot or dirt. **2** indecent talk, writing, or pictures.
□ **smutty** adjective.

snack ▶ noun a small quantity of food eaten between meals or in place of a meal.

SYNONYMS **light meal**, sandwich, refreshments, nibbles, titbit(s); informal bite (to eat).

▶ verb eat a snack.

snaffle ▶ noun a bit on a horse's bridle.
▶ verb (**snaffles, snaffling, snaffled**) Brit. informal quickly take for yourself.

snag ▶ noun **1** an unexpected difficulty. **2** a sharp or jagged projection. **3** a small tear.

SYNONYMS *we've met a snag* **complication**, difficulty, catch, hitch, obstacle, pitfall, problem, setback, disadvantage, drawback.

▶ verb (**snags, snagging, snagged**) catch or tear on a snag.

SYNONYMS *thorns snagged his sweater* **catch**, hook, tear.

snail ▶ noun a small, slow-moving creature with a spiral shell into which it can withdraw its whole body.

snake ▶ noun a reptile with no legs and a long slender body.

▶ verb (**snakes, snaking, snaked**) move with the twisting motion of a snake.
■ **snake in the grass** a person who pretends to be someone's friend but is secretly working against them.
□ **snaky** adjective.

snap ▶ verb (**snaps, snapping, snapped**) **1** break with a sharp cracking sound. **2** open or close with a brisk movement or sharp sound. **3** (of an animal) make a sudden bite. **4** say something quickly and irritably. **5** suddenly lose self-control. **6** take a snapshot of.

SYNONYMS **1** *the ruler snapped* **break**, fracture, splinter, split, crack; informal bust. **2** *'Shut up!' Anna snapped* **bark**, snarl, growl, retort. **3** *photographers snapped the royals* **photograph**, picture, take, shoot, film, capture.

▶ noun **1** an act or sound of snapping. **2** a snapshot. **3** Brit. a card game in which players compete to call 'snap' as soon as two cards of the same type are exposed.

SYNONYMS **1** *she closed her purse with a snap* **click**, crack, pop. **2** *holiday snaps* **photograph**, picture, photo, shot, snapshot, print, slide.

▶ adjective done on the spur of the moment: *a snap decision*.
■ **snap something up** quickly buy something that is in short supply. **snap out of** informal get out of a bad mood by a sudden effort.

snapdragon ▶ noun a plant with brightly coloured flowers which have a mouth-like opening.

snapper ▶ noun a sea fish noted for snapping its jaws.

snappy ▶ adjective (**snappier, snappiest**) informal **1** short and clever or amusing: *snappy slogans*. **2** neat and stylish. **3** irritable; speaking sharply.
■ **make it snappy** do it quickly.

snapshot ▶ noun an informal photograph, taken quickly.

snare ▶ noun **1** a trap for catching animals, consisting of a loop of wire that pulls tight. **2** a thing likely to lure someone into trouble. **3** (also **snare drum**) a drum with a length of wire stretched across the head to produce a rattling sound.

SYNONYMS *a fox caught in a snare* **trap**, gin, wire, net, noose.

▶ verb (**snares, snaring, snared**) catch in a snare or trap.

SYNONYMS *game birds were snared* **trap**, catch, net, bag, ensnare, hook.

snarl ▶ verb **1** growl with bared teeth. **2** say something aggressively. **3** (**snarl something up**) make something tangled.
▶ noun an act of snarling.

■ **snarl-up** Brit. informal a traffic jam.

snatch ▸ verb **1** seize quickly in a rude or eager way. **2** informal steal or kidnap. **3** quickly take the chance to have.

SYNONYMS **1** *she snatched the microphone* **grab**, seize, take hold of, take, pluck, grasp at, clutch at. **2** *someone snatched my bag* **steal**, take, thieve; informal swipe, nab, lift; Brit. informal nick, pinch, whip.

▸ noun **1** an act of snatching. **2** a short spell of doing something. **3** a fragment of music or talk.

SYNONYMS **1** *brief snatches of sleep* **period**, spell, time, fit, bout, interval, stretch. **2** *a snatch of conversation* **fragment**, snippet, bit, scrap, extract, excerpt, portion.

snazzy ▸ adjective (**snazzier**, **snazziest**) informal smart and stylish.

sneak ▸ verb (**sneaks**, **sneaking**, **sneaked** or N. Amer. informal **snuck**) **1** move or take in a secretive way. **2** Brit. informal tell someone in authority of a person's wrongdoings. **3** (**sneaking**) (of a feeling) persistent but reluctant or unrecognized.

SYNONYMS **1** *I sneaked out* **creep**, slink, steal, slip, slide, sidle, tiptoe, pad. **2** *she sneaked a camera in* **smuggle**, spirit, slip. **3** (**sneaking**) *a sneaking admiration for him* **secret**, private, hidden, concealed, unvoiced. **4** (**sneaking**) *a sneaking feeling* **niggling**, nagging, lurking, insidious, lingering, persistent.

▸ noun Brit. informal a telltale.
▸ adjective secret or unofficial: *a sneak preview*.

SYNONYMS *a sneak preview* **furtive**, secret, stealthy, sly, surreptitious, clandestine, covert, private, quick, exclusive.

sneaker ▸ noun chiefly N. Amer. a soft shoe worn for sports or casual occasions.

sneaky ▸ adjective (**sneakier**, **sneakiest**) secretive in a sly or dishonest way.

SYNONYMS **sly**, crafty, cunning, wily, scheming, devious, deceitful, underhand. ANTONYMS honest.

□ **sneakily** adverb.

sneer ▸ noun a scornful or mocking smile or remark.

SYNONYMS **1** *a sneer on her face* **smirk**, curled lip. **2** *the sneers of others* **jibe**, jeer, taunt, insult; informal dig.

▸ verb (**sneers**, **sneering**, **sneered**) smile or speak in a scornful or mocking way.

SYNONYMS **1** *he looked at me and sneered* **smirk**, curl your lip. **2** *it is easy to sneer at them* **scoff**, laugh, scorn, disdain, mock, ridicule, deride; N. Amer. slur.

sneeze ▸ verb (**sneezes**, **sneezing**, **sneezed**) suddenly expel air from the nose and mouth due to irritation of the nostrils.

▸ noun an act of sneezing.
■ **not to be sneezed at** informal worth having or considering.

snick ▸ verb cut a small notch in.
▸ noun a small notch or cut.

snicker ▸ verb (**snickers**, **snickering**, **snickered**) **1** snigger. **2** (of a horse) make a gentle high-pitched neigh.
▸ noun a sound of snickering.

snide ▸ adjective disrespectful or mocking in an indirect way.

sniff ▸ verb **1** draw in air audibly through the nose. **2** (**sniff around** or **round**) informal investigate secretly. **3** (**sniff something out**) informal discover something by investigation.

SYNONYMS **1** *she sniffed and blew her nose* **inhale**, snuffle. **2** *Tom sniffed the fruit* **smell**, scent, get a whiff of.

▸ noun an act of sniffing.

SYNONYMS **1** *she gave a loud sniff* **snuffle**, snort. **2** *a sniff of fresh air* **smell**, scent, whiff, lungful.

■ **not to be sniffed at** informal worth having or considering. **sniffer dog** a dog trained to find drugs or explosives by smell.
□ **sniffer** noun **sniffy** adjective.

sniffle ▸ verb (**sniffles**, **sniffling**, **sniffled**) sniff slightly or repeatedly.
▸ noun **1** an act of sniffling. **2** a slight cold.
□ **sniffly** adjective.

snifter ▸ noun Brit. informal a small quantity of an alcoholic drink.

snigger ▸ verb (**sniggers**, **sniggering**, **sniggered**) give a half-suppressed laugh.

SYNONYMS **giggle**, titter, snicker, chortle, laugh, sneer, smirk.

▸ noun a half-suppressed laugh.

SYNONYMS **giggle**, titter, snicker, chortle, laugh, sneer, smirk.

snip ▸ verb (**snips**, **snipping**, **snipped**) cut with small, quick strokes.
▸ noun **1** an act of snipping. **2** Brit. informal a bargain.

snipe ▸ verb (**snipes**, **sniping**, **sniped**) **1** shoot at someone from a hiding place at long range. **2** criticize someone in an unpleasant or petty way.
▸ noun (plural **snipe** or **snipes**) a wading bird with brown feathers and a long straight bill.
□ **sniper** noun.

snippet ▸ noun a small piece or brief extract.

snitch informal ▸ verb **1** steal. **2** inform on someone.
▸ noun an informer.

snivel ▸ verb (**snivels**, **snivelling**, **snivelled**; US spelling **snivels**, **sniveling**, **sniveled**) cry or complain in a whining way.

S

snob ▸ noun **1** a person who has great respect for people with social status or wealth and looks down on lower-class people. **2** a person who believes that they have superior taste in a particular area: *a wine snob*.
□ **snobbery** noun.

snobbish (or **snobby**) ▸ adjective relating to or typical of a snob.

SYNONYMS **elitist**, superior, supercilious, arrogant, condescending, pretentious, affected; informal snooty, high and mighty, la-di-da, stuck-up; Brit. informal toffee-nosed.

snog Brit. informal ▸ verb (**snogs, snogging, snogged**) kiss.
▸ noun an act or period of kissing.

snood ▸ noun a hairnet worn at the back of a woman's head.

snook ▸ noun (**cock a snook at**) Brit. informal openly show contempt or disrespect for.

snooker ▸ noun **1** a game played with cues on a billiard table. **2** a position in a game of snooker or pool in which a player cannot make a direct shot at any permitted ball.
▸ verb (**snookers, snookering, snookered**) **1** (in snooker or pool) put your opponent in a snooker. **2** (**be snookered**) Brit. informal be placed in an impossible position.

snoop informal ▸ verb look around or investigate secretly in order to find out something.
▸ noun an act of snooping.
□ **snooper** noun.

snooty ▸ adjective (**snootier, snootiest**) informal behaving as if you are better or more important than other people.
□ **snootily** adverb.

snooze informal ▸ noun a short, light sleep.
▸ verb (**snoozes, snoozing, snoozed**) have a snooze.

snore ▸ noun a snorting sound in a person's breathing while they are asleep.
▸ verb (**snores, snoring, snored**) make a snorting sound while asleep.

snorkel ▸ noun a tube for a swimmer to breathe through while underwater.
□ **snorkelling** (US spelling **snorkeling**) noun.

snort ▸ verb **1** make a loud explosive sound by forcing breath out through the nose. **2** informal inhale cocaine.
▸ noun a snorting sound.

snot ▸ noun informal mucus in the nose.

snotty ▸ adjective informal **1** full of, or covered with, mucus from the nose. **2** superior or arrogant.

snout ▸ noun **1** the projecting nose and mouth of an animal. **2** the projecting front or end of something such as a pistol.

snow ▸ noun **1** frozen water vapour in the atmosphere that falls in light white flakes.

2 (**snows**) falls of snow.
▸ verb **1** (**it snows, it is snowing, it snowed**) snow falls. **2** (**be snowed in** or **up**) be unable to leave a place because of heavy snow. **3** (**be snowed under**) be overwhelmed with a large quantity of something, especially work.

snowball ▸ noun a ball of packed snow.
▸ verb increase rapidly in size, strength, or importance.

snowboard ▸ noun a board that resembles a short, broad ski, used for sliding downhill on snow.
□ **snowboarder** noun **snowboarding** noun.

snowbound ▸ adjective **1** unable to travel or go out because of snow. **2** (of a place) cut off by snow.

snowdrift ▸ noun a bank of deep snow heaped up by the wind.

snowdrop ▸ noun a plant with drooping white flowers that appear during late winter.

snowfall ▸ noun **1** a fall of snow. **2** the quantity of snow falling within a certain area in a given time.

snowflake ▸ noun each of the many ice crystals that fall as snow.

snowline ▸ noun the altitude above which some snow remains on the ground throughout the year.

snowman ▸ noun (plural **snowmen**) a model of a human figure made with compressed snow.

snowplough (US spelling **snowplow**) ▸ noun a device or vehicle for clearing roads of snow.

snowshoe ▸ noun a flat device attached to the sole of a boot and used for walking on snow.

snowy ▸ adjective (**snowier, snowiest**) **1** having a lot of snow. **2** pure white.

snub ▸ verb (**snubs, snubbing, snubbed**) **1** insult someone by ignoring them when you meet. **2** refuse to attend or accept something.

SYNONYMS *sponsors find themselves snubbed by politicians* rebuff, spurn, cold-shoulder, cut (dead), ignore, insult, slight; informal freeze out; N. Amer. informal stiff.

▸ noun an act of snubbing.

SYNONYMS *a very public snub* rebuff, slap in the face; informal brush-off, put-down.

■ **snub nose** a nose that is short and turned up at the end.

snuck N. Amer. informal past and past participle of SNEAK.

snuff[1] ▸ verb **1** put out a candle. **2** (**snuff something out**) abruptly put an end to something. **3** (**snuff it**) Brit. informal die.

snuff² ▸ noun powdered tobacco that is sniffed up the nostril.
▸ verb sniff at.

snuffle ▸ verb (**snuffles, snuffling, snuffled**)
1 breathe noisily through a partially blocked nose. **2** (of an animal) make repeated sniffing sounds.
▸ noun a snuffling sound.

snug ▸ adjective (**snugger, snuggest**) **1** warm and cosy. **2** close-fitting.

> SYNONYMS **1** *our tents were snug* **cosy,** comfortable, warm, sheltered, secure; informal comfy. **2** *a snug dress* **tight,** skintight, close-fitting, figure-hugging. ANTONYMS bleak, loose.

▸ noun Brit. a small, cosy bar in a pub or hotel.
□ **snugly** adverb.

snuggle ▸ verb (**snuggles, snuggling, snuggled**) settle into a warm, comfortable position.

so ▸ adverb **1** to such a great extent. **2** extremely; very much. **3** to the same extent; as. **4** that is the case. **5** similarly. **6** thus.
▸ conjunction **1** therefore. **2** (**so that**) with the result or aim that. **3** and then. **4** in the same way.
■ **or so** approximately. **so-and-so** (plural **so-and-sos**) informal **1** a person whose name you do not know. **2** a person that you do not like: *a nosy so-and-so.* **so long!** informal goodbye. **so-so** neither very good nor very bad.

soak ▸ verb **1** make something thoroughly wet by leaving it in liquid. **2** (of a liquid) spread completely throughout. **3** (**soak something up**) absorb a liquid. **4** (**soak something up**) expose yourself to something enjoyable.

> SYNONYMS **1** *soak the beans in water* **dip,** immerse, steep, submerge, douse, marinate, souse. **2** *we got soaked outside* **drench,** wet through, saturate, waterlog. **3** *the sweat soaked through his clothes* **permeate,** penetrate, impregnate, percolate, seep, spread. **4** *use towels to soak up the water* **absorb,** suck up, blot, mop up.

▸ noun **1** a period of soaking. **2** informal a heavy drinker.

soaking (also **soaking wet**) ▸ adjective very wet.

> SYNONYMS **drenched,** wet (through), soaked (through), sodden, soggy, waterlogged, saturated, sopping, dripping, wringing. ANTONYMS parched.

soap ▸ noun **1** a substance used with water for washing and cleaning. **2** informal a soap opera.
▸ verb wash with soap.

■ **soap opera** a television or radio serial that deals with the daily lives of a group of characters.
□ **soapy** adjective.

soapbox ▸ noun a box that someone stands on to speak in public.

soapstone ▸ noun a soft rock used for making ornaments.

soar ▸ verb **1** fly or rise high into the air. **2** increase rapidly.

> SYNONYMS **1** *the bird soared into the air* **rise,** ascend, climb. **2** *the gulls soared on the winds* **glide,** plane, float, hover. **3** *the cost of living soared* **increase,** escalate, shoot up, spiral; informal go through the roof, skyrocket. ANTONYMS plummet.

sob ▸ verb (**sobs, sobbing, sobbed**) **1** cry with loud gasps. **2** say while sobbing.

> SYNONYMS **weep,** cry, snivel, whimper; Scottish greet; informal blubber; Brit. informal grizzle.

▸ noun a sound of sobbing.

sober ▸ adjective (**soberer, soberest**) **1** not drunk. **2** serious. **3** (of a colour) not bright or likely to attract attention.

> SYNONYMS **1** *the driver was clearly sober* **clear-headed,** teetotal, abstinent, dry; informal on the wagon. **2** *a sober view of life* **serious,** solemn, sensible, grave, sombre, level-headed, businesslike, down-to-earth. **3** *a sober suit* **sombre,** subdued, severe, quiet, drab, plain. ANTONYMS drunk, frivolous, sensational, flamboyant.

▸ verb (**sobers, sobering, sobered**) **1** (**sober up**) make or become sober after being drunk. **2** make or become serious.
□ **soberly** adverb.

sobriety /suh-bry-uh-ti/ ▸ noun the state of being sober.

sobriquet /soh-bri-kay/ (or **soubriquet** /soo-bri-kay/) ▸ noun a person's nickname.

so-called ▸ adjective wrongly or inappropriately called a particular thing.

> SYNONYMS **supposed,** alleged, presumed, inappropriately named, ostensible, reputed, self-styled.

soccer ▸ noun a form of football played with a round ball which may not be handled during play except by the goalkeepers.

sociable ▸ adjective **1** liking to talk to and do things with other people. **2** friendly and welcoming.

> SYNONYMS **friendly,** amicable, affable, companionable, gregarious, cordial, warm, genial. ANTONYMS unfriendly.

□ **sociability** noun **sociably** adverb.

S

social ▸ adjective **1** having to do with society and its organization. **2** needing the company of other people. **3** (of an activity) in which people meet each other for pleasure. **4** (of animals) breeding or living in organized communities.

SYNONYMS **1** *a social problem* communal, community, collective, group, general, popular, civil, public. **2** *a social club* recreational, leisure, entertainment. ANTONYMS individual, professional.

▸ noun an informal social gathering.

SYNONYMS *the club has a social once a month* party, gathering, function, get-together, celebration; informal do.

■ **social science 1** the study of human society and social relationships. **2** a subject within this field, such as economics. **social security** (in the UK) money provided by the state for poor or unemployed people. **social services** services provided by the state such as education and medical care. **social worker** a person whose job is to help improve the conditions of the poor, the old, etc.
□ **socially** adverb.

socialism ▸ noun the theory that a country's land, transport, industries, etc. should be owned or controlled by the community as a whole.
□ **socialist** noun & adjective.

socialite ▸ noun a person who mixes in fashionable society.

socialize (or **socialise**) ▸ verb (socializes, socializing, socialized) **1** mix socially with other people. **2** make someone behave in a socially acceptable way.

society ▸ noun (plural **societies**) **1** people living together in an ordered community. **2** a community of people. **3** (also **high society**) people who are fashionable, wealthy, and influential. **4** an organization formed for a particular purpose. **5** the situation of being in the company of other people.

SYNONYMS **1** *a danger to society* the community, the (general) public, the people, the population, civilization, humankind, mankind. **2** *an industrial society* culture, community, civilization, nation, population. **3** *Lady Angela will help you enter society* high society, polite society, the upper classes, the gentry, the elite, the smart set; informal the upper crust. **4** *a local history society* club, association, group, circle, institute, guild, lodge, league, union, alliance. **5** *the society of others* company, companionship, fellowship, friendship.

□ **societal** adjective.

sociology ▸ noun the study of human society.

□ **sociological** adjective **sociologist** noun.

sock ▸ noun **1** a knitted garment for the foot and lower part of the leg. **2** informal a hard blow.
▸ verb informal hit forcefully.
■ **pull your socks up** informal make an effort to improve.

socket ▸ noun **1** a hollow in which something fits or revolves. **2** an electrical device which a plug or light bulb fits into.

sod ▸ noun **1** grass-covered ground. **2** a piece of turf.

soda ▸ noun **1** (also **soda water**) carbonated water. **2** N. Amer. a sweet fizzy drink. **3** a compound of sodium.

sodden ▸ adjective **1** soaked through. **2** having drunk too much alcohol: *whisky-sodden.*

sodium ▸ noun a soft silver-white metallic element.
■ **sodium bicarbonate** a white powder used in fizzy drinks and as a raising agent in baking. **sodium chloride** the chemical name for salt. **sodium hydroxide** a strongly alkaline white compound; caustic soda.

sodomite ▸ noun a person who engages in sodomy.

sodomy ▸ noun anal intercourse.

sofa ▸ noun a long padded seat with a back and arms.

SYNONYMS settee, couch, divan, chaise longue, chesterfield.

soft ▸ adjective **1** easy to mould, cut, compress, or fold. **2** not rough in texture. **3** quiet and gentle. **4** (of light or colour) not harsh. **5** not strict enough. **6** informal not needing much effort. **7** informal foolish. **8** (**soft on**) informal having romantic feelings for. **9** (of a drink) not alcoholic. **10** (of a drug) not likely to cause addiction. **11** (of water) free from mineral salts.

SYNONYMS **1** *soft fruit* mushy, squashy, pulpy, slushy, squelchy, squishy, doughy; informal gooey; Brit. informal squidgy. **2** *soft ground* swampy, marshy, boggy, muddy, squelchy. **3** *a soft cushion* squashy, spongy, supple, springy, elastic, resilient. **4** *soft fabric* smooth, velvety, fleecy, downy, furry, silky. **5** *soft light* dim, low, faint, subdued, muted. **6** *soft colours* pale, pastel, muted, restrained, subdued, subtle. **7** *soft voices* quiet, low, gentle, faint, muted, subdued, muffled, hushed, whispered. **8** *soft outlines* blurred, vague, hazy, misty, foggy, nebulous, fuzzy, indistinct. **9** *soft words* kind, gentle, sympathetic, soothing, tender, sensitive, affectionate, loving, warm, sweet, sentimental. **10** *she's too soft with her pupils* lenient, easy-going, tolerant, forgiving, forbearing, indulgent, liberal, lax.

S

ANTONYMS hard, firm, rough, harsh, lurid, strident, sharp, strict.

■ **have a soft spot for** be fond of. **soft focus** deliberate slight blurring in a photograph or film. **soft-hearted** kind and sympathetic. **softly-softly** Brit. cautious and patient. **soft-pedal** play down the unpleasant aspects of. **soft sell** the selling of something in a gently persuasive way. **soft-soap** informal use flattery to persuade someone. **soft top** a car with a roof that can be folded back. **soft touch** informal a person who is easily persuaded. □ **softly** adverb **softness** noun.

softball ▶ noun a form of baseball played with a larger, softer ball.

soften ▶ verb **1** make or become soft or softer. **2** (**soften someone up**) make someone more likely to agree or agree to something.

SYNONYMS *the compensation should soften the blow* **ease,** alleviate, relieve, soothe, take the edge off, cushion, lessen, diminish, blunt, deaden.

software ▶ noun programs and other operating information used by a computer.

softwood ▶ noun the wood from a conifer as opposed to that from a broadleaved tree.

soggy ▶ adjective (**soggier, soggiest**) very wet and soft.

soil ▶ noun **1** the upper layer of earth, in which plants grow. **2** the territory of a particular nation.

SYNONYMS **1** *acid soil* **earth,** dirt, clay, ground, loam. **2** *British soil* **territory,** land, region, country, domain, dominion.

▶ verb **1** make dirty. **2** bring discredit to.

SYNONYMS *he soiled his tie* **dirty,** stain, smear, smudge, spoil, foul.

soirée /swah-ray/ ▶ noun an evening social gathering.

sojourn /so-juhn/ literary ▶ noun a temporary stay.
▶ verb stay temporarily.

solace /sol-iss/ ▶ noun comfort in a difficult time.
▶ verb (**solaces, solacing, solaced**) give comfort to.

solar ▶ adjective having to do with the sun or its rays.
■ **solar eclipse** an eclipse in which the sun is hidden by the moon. **solar plexus** a network of nerves at the pit of the stomach. **solar system** the sun together with the planets, asteroids, comets, etc. in orbit around it.

solarium ▶ noun a room equipped with sunlamps or sunbeds.

sold past and past participle of SELL.

solder ▶ noun a soft alloy used for joining metals.

▶ verb (**solders, soldering, soldered**) join with solder.
■ **soldering iron** an electrical tool for melting and applying solder.

soldier ▶ noun **1** a person who serves in an army. **2** a private in an army. **3** Brit. informal a strip of bread or toast for dipping into a boiled egg.

SYNONYMS **fighter,** trooper, serviceman, servicewoman, warrior; US GI; Brit. informal squaddie.

▶ verb (**soldiers, soldiering, soldiered**) **1** serve as a soldier. **2** (**soldier on**) informal keep trying or working.
■ **soldier of fortune** a mercenary.
□ **soldierly** adjective.

soldiery ▶ noun soldiers as a group.

sole¹ ▶ noun **1** the underside of the foot. **2** the underside of a piece of footwear.
▶ verb (**soles, soling, soled**) put a new sole on a shoe.

sole² ▶ noun (plural **sole**) a kind of edible flatfish.

sole³ ▶ adjective **1** one and only. **2** belonging or restricted to one person or group.

SYNONYMS **only,** one, single, solitary, lone, unique, exclusive.

solecism /sol-i-si-z'm/ ▶ noun **1** a grammatical mistake. **2** an example of bad manners or incorrect behaviour.

solely ▶ adverb not involving anyone or anything else.

SYNONYMS **only,** simply, purely, just, merely, uniquely, exclusively, entirely, wholly, alone.

solemn ▶ adjective **1** formal and dignified. **2** serious. **3** deeply sincere.

SYNONYMS **1** *a solemn occasion* **dignified,** ceremonial, stately, formal, majestic, imposing, splendid, magnificent, grand. **2** *he looked very solemn* **serious,** grave, sober, sombre, unsmiling, stern, grim, dour, humourless. **3** *a solemn promise* **sincere,** earnest, honest, genuine, firm, heartfelt, wholehearted, sworn. ANTONYMS frivolous, light-hearted, insincere.

□ **solemnly** adverb.

solemnity ▶ noun (plural **solemnities**) **1** the quality of being solemn. **2** (**solemnities**) solemn rites or ceremonies.

solemnize (or **solemnise**) ▶ verb (**solemnizes, solemnizing, solemnized**) **1** perform a ceremony. **2** mark an occasion with a ceremony.

solenoid ▶ noun a coil of wire which becomes magnetic when an electric current is passed through it.

solicit ▶ verb (**solicits, soliciting, solicited**) **1** try to obtain something from someone.

S

2 (of a prostitute) approach someone and offer sex for money.
□ **solicitation** noun.

solicitor ▸ noun Brit. a lawyer qualified to advise on property, wills, etc., instruct barristers, and represent clients in lower courts.

solicitous ▸ adjective showing interest or concern about a person's well-being.
□ **solicitously** adverb.

solicitude ▸ noun care or concern.

solid ▸ adjective (**solider**, **solidest**) **1** firm and stable in shape. **2** strongly built or made. **3** not hollow or having spaces or gaps. **4** consisting of the same substance throughout. **5** (of time) uninterrupted. **6** three-dimensional.

SYNONYMS **1** *the plaster was solid* **hard**, rock-hard, rigid, firm, solidified, set, frozen. **2** *solid gold* **pure**, unadulterated, genuine. **3** *solid houses* **well built**, sound, substantial, strong, sturdy, durable. **4** *a solid argument* **well founded**, valid, sound, logical, authoritative, convincing. **5** *solid support from their colleagues* **unanimous**, united, consistent, undivided.
ANTONYMS liquid, alloyed, flimsy, untenable, half-hearted.

▸ noun **1** a solid substance or object. **2** (**solids**) food that is not liquid.
■ **solid-state** (of an electronic device) using solid semiconductors, e.g. transistors, as opposed to valves.
□ **solidity** noun **solidly** adverb.

solidarity ▸ noun agreement and support resulting from shared interests, feelings, or opinions.

SYNONYMS **unanimity**, unity, agreement, team spirit, accord, harmony, consensus; formal concord.

solidify ▸ verb (**solidifies**, **solidifying**, **solidified**) make or become hard or solid.
□ **solidification** noun.

soliloquy /suh-lil-uh-kwi/ ▸ noun (plural **soliloquies**) a speech in which a character speaks their thoughts aloud when alone on stage.

solipsism ▸ noun the view that the self is all that can be known to exist.
□ **solipsist** noun **solipsistic** adjective.

solitaire ▸ noun **1** Brit. a game for one player played by removing pegs from a board by jumping others over them. **2** N. Amer. the card game patience. **3** a single gem in a piece of jewellery.

solitary ▸ adjective **1** done or existing alone. **2** (of a place) secluded or isolated. **3** single.

SYNONYMS **1** *a solitary man* **lonely**, unaccompanied, by yourself, on your own, alone, friendless, unsociable,

withdrawn, reclusive; N. Amer. lonesome. **2** *solitary farmsteads* **isolated**, remote, lonely, out of the way, in the back of beyond, outlying, off the beaten track, secluded; N. Amer. in the backwoods. **3** *a solitary piece of evidence* **single**, lone, sole, only, one, individual.
ANTONYMS sociable, accessible.

■ **solitary confinement** the isolating of a prisoner in a separate cell as a punishment.

solitude ▸ noun the state of being alone.

solo ▸ noun (plural **solos**) **1** a piece of music or dance for one performer. **2** a flight undertaken by a single pilot.
▸ adjective & adverb for or done by one person.
▸ verb (**soloes**, **soloing**, **soloed**) perform a solo.
□ **soloist** noun.

solstice ▸ noun each of the two times in the year when the sun reaches its highest or lowest point in the sky at noon, marked by the longest and shortest days.

soluble ▸ adjective **1** (of a substance) able to be dissolved. **2** (of a problem) able to be solved.
□ **solubility** noun.

solution ▸ noun **1** a way of solving a problem. **2** the correct answer to a puzzle. **3** a mixture formed when a substance is dissolved in a liquid. **4** the process of dissolving.

SYNONYMS **1** *a solution to the problem* **answer**, result, resolution, key, explanation. **2** *a solution of salt and water* **mixture**, blend, compound.

solve ▸ verb (**solves**, **solving**, **solved**) find an answer to, or way of dealing with, a problem or mystery.

SYNONYMS **answer**, resolve, work out, puzzle out, fathom, decipher, decode, clear up, straighten out, get to the bottom of, unravel, explain; informal figure out, crack; Brit. informal suss out.

solvency ▸ noun the state of having more money than you owe.

solvent ▸ adjective **1** having more money than you owe. **2** able to dissolve other substances.
▸ noun the liquid in which another substance is dissolved to form a solution.

Somali /suh-mah-li/ ▸ noun (plural **Somali** or **Somalis**) **1** a person from Somalia. **2** the language of the Somali.
▸ adjective relating to Somalia.

somatic ▸ adjective having to do with the body rather than the mind.

sombre (US spelling **somber**) ▸ adjective **1** dark or dull. **2** very solemn or serious.

SYNONYMS **1** *sombre clothes* **dark**, drab, dull, dingy, restrained, subdued, sober,

S

funereal. **2** *a sombre expression* **solemn,** earnest, serious, grave, sober, unsmiling, stern, grim, dour, gloomy, sad, mournful, lugubrious.
ANTONYMS bright, cheerful.

□ **sombrely** adverb.

sombrero ▸ noun (plural **sombreros**) a broad-brimmed felt or straw hat.

some ▸ determiner **1** an unspecified amount or number of. **2** unknown or unspecified. **3** approximately. **4** a considerable amount or number of. **5** used to express admiration.
▸ pronoun a certain amount or number of people or things.

somebody ▸ pronoun someone.

some day (or **someday**) ▸ adverb at some time in the future.

somehow ▸ adverb **1** by one means or another. **2** for an unknown or unspecified reason.

SYNONYMS **one way or another,** no matter how, by fair means or foul, by hook or by crook, come what may.

someone ▸ pronoun **1** an unknown or unspecified person. **2** an important or famous person.

someplace ▸ adverb & pronoun N. Amer. informal somewhere.

somersault ▸ noun a movement in which a person turns head over heels and finishes on their feet.
▸ verb perform a somersault.

something ▸ pronoun an unspecified or unknown thing or amount.

sometime ▸ adverb at some unspecified or unknown time.
▸ adjective former.

sometimes ▸ adverb occasionally.

SYNONYMS **occasionally,** from time to time, now and then, every so often, once in a while, on occasion, at times, off and on.

somewhat ▸ adverb to some extent.

somewhere ▸ adverb in or to an unspecified or unknown place.
▸ pronoun some unspecified place.

somnambulism ▸ noun formal sleepwalking.
□ **somnambulist** noun.

somnolent ▸ adjective sleepy or drowsy.
□ **somnolence** noun.

son ▸ noun **1** a boy or man in relation to his parents. **2** a male descendant. **3** (**the Son**) Jesus.
■ **son-in-law** (plural **sons-in-law**) the husband of a person's daughter.

sonar ▸ noun a system for detecting objects underwater by giving out sound pulses.

sonata /suh-**nah**-tuh/ ▸ noun a piece of music for a solo instrument, sometimes

with piano accompaniment.

song ▸ noun **1** a set of words set to music. **2** singing. **3** the musical phrases uttered by some birds, whales, and insects. **4** literary a poem.

SYNONYMS **air,** strain, ditty, chant, number, track, melody, tune.

■ **for a song** informal very cheaply. **on song** Brit. informal performing well.

songbird ▸ noun a bird with a musical song.

songster ▸ noun (feminine **songstress**) a person who sings.

sonic ▸ adjective relating to or using sound waves.
■ **sonic boom** an explosive noise caused by the shock wave from an object travelling faster than the speed of sound.
□ **sonically** adverb.

sonnet ▸ noun a poem of fourteen lines using a fixed rhyme scheme.

sonorous ▸ adjective **1** (of a sound) deep and full. **2** (of speech) using powerful language.
□ **sonority** noun **sonorously** adverb.

soon ▸ adverb **1** after a short time. **2** early. **3** (**sooner**) rather: *I would sooner walk.*

SYNONYMS **1 shortly,** presently, in the near future, before long, in a little while, in a minute, in a moment; Brit. informal in a tick. **2** (**sooner**) *he should have done it sooner* **earlier,** before now. **3** (**sooner**) *I would sooner stay* **rather,** preferably, given the choice.

soot ▸ noun a black powdery substance produced when wood, coal, etc. is burned.
□ **sooty** adjective.

soothe ▸ verb (**soothes, soothing, soothed**) **1** gently calm. **2** relieve pain or discomfort.

SYNONYMS **1** *Rachel tried to soothe him* **calm (down),** pacify, comfort, hush, quiet, settle (down), appease, mollify; Brit. quieten (down). **2** (**soothing**) *soothing music* **relaxing,** restful, calm, calming, tranquil, peaceful. **3** *an anaesthetic to soothe the pain* **ease,** alleviate, relieve, take the edge off, allay, lessen, reduce.
ANTONYMS agitate, aggravate.

soothsayer ▸ noun a person supposed to be able to foresee the future.

sop ▸ noun a thing given or done to calm or please someone who is angry or disappointed.
▸ verb (**sops, sopping, sopped**) (**sop something up**) soak up liquid.

sophism ▸ noun a false argument.

sophist ▸ noun a person who uses clever but false arguments.
□ **sophistry** noun.

sophisticate ▸ noun a sophisticated person.

S

sophisticated ▸ adjective **1** having experience and taste in matters of culture or fashion. **2** highly developed and complex.

> SYNONYMS **1** *a sophisticated woman* **worldly,** worldly-wise, experienced, cosmopolitan, urbane, cultured, cultivated, polished, refined.
> **2** *sophisticated technology* **advanced,** state-of-the-art, the latest, up-to-the-minute, cutting-edge, trailblazing, complex.
> ANTONYMS naive, crude.

sophistication ▸ noun the quality or fact of being sophisticated.

> SYNONYMS **worldliness,** experience, urbanity, culture, polish, refinement, elegance, style, poise, finesse, savoir faire.

sophomore ▸ noun N. Amer. a second-year university or high-school student.

soporific ▸ adjective causing drowsiness or sleep.

sopping ▸ adjective wet through.

soppy ▸ adjective (**soppier, soppiest**) Brit. informal **1** too sentimental. **2** feeble.
□ **soppily** adverb.

soprano ▸ noun (plural **sopranos**) the highest singing voice.

sorbet /sor-bay/ ▸ noun a water ice.

sorcerer ▸ noun (feminine **sorceress**) a person who practises magic.
□ **sorcery** noun.

sordid ▸ adjective **1** dishonest or immoral. **2** very dirty and unpleasant.
□ **sordidly** adverb.

sore ▸ adjective **1** painful or aching. **2** urgent: *in sore need.* **3** N. Amer. informal upset and angry.

> SYNONYMS **1** *a sore leg* **painful,** hurting, hurt, aching, throbbing, smarting, stinging, inflamed, sensitive, tender, raw. **2** *they were sore at us* **upset,** angry, annoyed, cross, disgruntled, dissatisfied, irritated; informal aggravated, miffed, peeved; Brit. informal narked; N. Amer. informal ticked off.

▸ noun a raw or painful place on the body.
▸ adverb old use very: *sore afraid.*
■ **sore point** an issue about which someone feels distressed or annoyed.
□ **soreness** noun.

sorely ▸ adverb extremely; badly.

sorghum /sor-guhm/ ▸ noun a cereal plant found in warm regions, grown for grain and animal feed.

sorority ▸ noun (plural **sororities**) N. Amer. a society for female students in a university or college.

sorrel ▸ noun **1** an edible plant with a bitter flavour. **2** a light reddish-brown colour.

sorrow ▸ noun **1** deep distress caused by loss or disappointment. **2** a cause of sorrow.

> SYNONYMS **1** *he felt sorrow at her death* **sadness,** unhappiness, misery, despondency, regret, despair, desolation, heartache, grief. **2** *the sorrows of life* **trouble,** difficulty, problem, woe, affliction, trial, tribulation, misfortune.
> ANTONYMS joy.

sorrowful ▸ adjective feeling or showing sorrow.
□ **sorrowfully** adverb.

sorry ▸ adjective (**sorrier, sorriest**) **1** feeling sympathy for someone else's misfortune. **2** feeling or expressing regret. **3** in a bad or pitiful state. **4** unpleasant and regrettable.

> SYNONYMS **1** *I was sorry to hear about his accident* **sad,** moved, sorrowful, distressed. **2** *he felt sorry for her* **full of pity,** sympathetic, compassionate, moved, concerned. **3** *I'm sorry I was rude* **regretful,** apologetic, remorseful, contrite, repentant, rueful, penitent, guilty, shamefaced, ashamed.
> ANTONYMS glad, unsympathetic, unrepentant.

sort ▸ noun **1** a category of people or things with a common feature or features. **2** informal a person: *a friendly sort.*

> SYNONYMS *what sort of book is it?* **type,** kind, variety, class, category, style, form, genre, species, make, model.

▸ verb **1** arrange systematically in groups. **2** (often **sort someone/thing out**) separate someone or something from a mixed group. **3** (**sort something out**) deal with a problem or difficulty.

> SYNONYMS **1** *they sorted the books alphabetically* **classify,** class, group, organize, arrange, order. **2** *the problem was soon sorted out* **resolve,** settle, solve, fix, work out, straighten out, deal with, put right, set right, rectify, iron out.

■ **out of sorts** slightly unwell or unhappy.

❗ Use **this sort of** to refer to a singular noun (e.g. *this sort of job*), and **these sorts of** to refer to a plural noun (e.g. *these sorts of questions*).

sorted ▸ adjective Brit. informal **1** organized; arranged. **2** emotionally stable.

sortie ▸ noun **1** an attack made by troops from a position of defence. **2** a flight by an aircraft on a military operation. **3** a short trip.

SOS ▸ noun **1** an international signal sent when in great trouble. **2** an urgent appeal for help.
ORIGIN letters chosen to be easily transmitted and recognized in Morse code,

S

but often thought to be short for *save our souls*.

sot ▸ noun old use a person who is regularly drunk.
◻ **sottish** adjective.

sotto voce /sot-toh **voh**-chay/ ▸ adverb & adjective in a quiet voice.

soubriquet ➡ SOBRIQUET.

soufflé /soo-flay/ ▸ noun a light, spongy dish made by mixing egg yolks with beaten egg whites.

sough (*rhymes with* cow *or* cuff) ▸ verb literary (of the wind or sea) make a moaning, whistling, or rushing sound.

sought past and past participle of SEEK.
■ **sought after** in great demand.

souk /sook/ ▸ noun an Arab market.

soul ▸ noun 1 the spiritual element of a person, believed by some to be immortal. 2 a person's inner nature. 3 emotional energy or power. 4 (**the soul of**) a perfect example of a particular quality. 5 an individual: *poor soul!* 6 a kind of music that expresses strong emotions, made popular by black Americans.

> SYNONYMS 1 *his soul cried out* **spirit,** psyche, (inner) self. 2 *their music lacked soul* **feeling,** emotion, passion, animation, intensity, warmth, energy, vitality, spirit.

■ **soul-destroying** unbearably dull and repetitive. **soul-searching** close examination of your emotions and motives.

soulful ▸ adjective expressing deep feeling.
◻ **soulfully** adverb.

soulless ▸ adjective 1 lacking character or interest. 2 lacking human feelings.

soulmate ▸ noun a person ideally suited to another.

sound[1] ▸ noun 1 vibrations which travel through the air and are sensed by the ear. 2 a thing that can be heard. 3 an impression given by words.

> SYNONYMS 1 *the sound of a car* **noise,** din, racket, row, resonance, reverberation. 2 *she did not make a sound* **utterance,** cry, word, noise, peep. 3 *the sound of the flute* **tone,** timbre, call, song, voice. ANTONYMS silence.

▸ verb 1 make sound. 2 make a sound to show or warn of something. 3 give a particular impression. 4 (**sound off**) express your opinions loudly or forcefully.

> SYNONYMS 1 *the buzzer sounded* **make a noise,** resonate, resound, reverberate, go off, ring, chime, ping. 2 *drivers must sound their horns* **blow,** blast, toot, ring, use, operate, activate, set off. 3 *it sounds a crazy idea* **appear,** look (like), seem, give every indication of being.

■ **sound barrier** the point at which an aircraft approaches the speed of sound. **sound bite** a short, memorable extract from a speech or interview. **sound effect** a sound other than speech or music that is used in a play, film, etc. **sound wave** a wave by which sound travels through water, air, etc.
◻ **soundless** adjective.

sound[2] ▸ adjective 1 in good condition. 2 based on solid judgement. 3 financially secure. 4 competent or reliable. 5 (of sleep) deep and unbroken. 6 severe or thorough.

> SYNONYMS 1 *your heart is sound* **healthy,** in good condition/shape, fit, hale and hearty, in fine fettle, undamaged, unimpaired. 2 *a sound building* **well built,** solid, substantial, strong, sturdy, durable, stable, intact. 3 *sound advice* **well founded,** valid, reasonable, logical, weighty, authoritative, reliable. 4 *a sound judge of character* **reliable,** dependable, trustworthy, fair, good. 5 *financially sound* **solvent,** debt-free, in the black, in credit, creditworthy, secure. 6 *a sound sleep* **deep,** undisturbed, uninterrupted, untroubled, peaceful. ANTONYMS unhealthy, unsound, unsafe, unreliable, insolvent.

◻ **soundly** adverb.

sound[3] ▸ verb 1 find out the depth of water using a line, pole, or sound echoes. 2 (**sound someone out**) question someone about their opinions or feelings.

sound[4] ▸ noun a narrow stretch of water connecting two larger areas of water.

sounding ▸ noun 1 a measurement of the depth of water. 2 (**soundings**) information found out before taking action.
■ **sounding board** a person or group that you talk to in order to test out new ideas.

soundproof ▸ adjective preventing sound getting in or out.
▸ verb make soundproof.

soundtrack ▸ noun the sound accompaniment to a film.

soup ▸ noun a savoury liquid dish made by boiling meat, fish, or vegetables.
▸ verb (**soup something up**) informal make a car more powerful.
■ **soup kitchen** a place where free food is served to homeless or very poor people.

soupçon /soop-son/ ▸ noun a very small quantity of something.

sour ▸ adjective 1 having a sharp taste like lemon or vinegar. 2 (especially of milk) stale and unpleasant. 3 resentful or angry.

> SYNONYMS 1 *sour wine* **acid,** acidic, tart, bitter, sharp, vinegary, pungent. 2 *sour milk* **bad,** off, turned, curdled, rancid, high, fetid. 3 *a sour old man* **embittered,** resentful, jaundiced, bitter, cross,

S

crabby, crotchety, cantankerous; informal grouchy.
ANTONYMS sweet, fresh, amiable.

▶ verb make or become sour.

> SYNONYMS *the dispute soured relations* **spoil**, mar, damage, harm, impair, wreck, upset, poison, blight.
> ANTONYMS improve.

■ **sour cream** cream that has been made sour by adding bacteria. **sour grapes** an attitude of pretending that something is worthless or undesirable because you cannot have it yourself.
□ **sourly** adverb **sourness** noun.

source ▶ noun **1** a place, person, or thing from which something originates. **2** a place where a river or stream starts. **3** a person, book, or document that provides information.

> SYNONYMS **1** *the source of the river* **spring**, origin. **2** *the source of the rumour* **origin**, starting point, root, author, originator. **3** *historical sources* **reference**, authority, informant, document.

▶ verb (**sources, sourcing, sourced**) obtain from a particular source.

sourpuss ▶ noun informal a bad-tempered or sulky person.

souse /sowss/ ▶ verb (**souses, sousing, soused**) **1** soak in liquid. **2** (**soused**) pickled or marinated.

south ▶ noun **1** the direction which is on your right-hand side when you are facing east. **2** the southern part of a place.
▶ adjective **1** lying towards or facing the south. **2** (of a wind) blowing from the south.
▶ adverb to or towards the south.
□ **southward** adjective & adverb **southwards** adverb.

south-east ▶ noun the direction or region halfway between south and east.
▶ adjective & adverb **1** towards or facing the south-east. **2** (of a wind) blowing from the south-east.
□ **south-eastern** adjective.

south-easterly ▶ adjective & adverb **1** in or towards the south-east. **2** (of a wind) blowing from the south-east.

southerly ▶ adjective & adverb **1** facing or moving towards the south. **2** (of a wind) blowing from the south.

southern ▶ adjective **1** situated in or facing the south. **2** coming from or characteristic of the south.

southerner ▶ noun a person from the south of a region.

south-west ▶ noun the direction or region halfway between south and west.
▶ adjective & adverb **1** towards or facing the south-west. **2** (of a wind) blowing from the

south-west.
□ **south-western** adjective.

south-westerly ▶ adjective & adverb **1** in or towards the south-west. **2** (of a wind) blowing from the south-west.

souvenir ▶ noun a thing that is kept as a reminder of a person, place, or event.

> SYNONYMS **memento**, keepsake, reminder, memorial, trophy.

sou'wester /sow-wess-ter/ ▶ noun a waterproof hat with a brim that covers the back of the neck.

sovereign ▶ noun **1** a king or queen who is the supreme ruler of a country. **2** a former British gold coin worth one pound sterling.

> SYNONYMS *the sovereign's prerogative* **ruler**, monarch, potentate, overlord, king, queen, emperor, empress, prince, princess.

▶ adjective **1** possessing supreme power. **2** (of a country) independent.

> SYNONYMS *a sovereign state* **autonomous**, independent, self-governing, self-determining, non-aligned, free.

sovereignty ▶ noun (plural **sovereignties**) **1** supreme power or authority. **2** a self-governing state.

> SYNONYMS **1** *their sovereignty over the islands* **power**, rule, supremacy, dominion, jurisdiction, ascendancy, domination, authority, control. **2** *full sovereignty was achieved in 1955* **autonomy**, independence, self-government, self-rule, home rule, self-determination, freedom.

Soviet ▶ noun **1** a citizen of the former Soviet Union. **2** (**soviet**) an elected council in the former Soviet Union.
▶ adjective having to do with the former Soviet Union.

sow[1] /soh/ ▶ verb (past **sowed**; past participle **sown** or **sowed**) **1** plant seed by scattering it on or in the earth. **2** spread or introduce something unwelcome.

> SYNONYMS **plant**, scatter, disperse, strew, broadcast, seed.

sow[2] /sow/ ▶ noun an adult female pig.

soya bean ▶ noun an edible bean that is high in protein.

soy sauce ▶ noun a sauce made with fermented soya beans, used in Chinese and Japanese cooking.

sozzled ▶ adjective informal very drunk.

spa ▶ noun **1** a mineral spring considered to have health-giving properties. **2** a place with a mineral spring.

space ▶ noun **1** unoccupied ground or area. **2** a blank between typed or written words or characters. **3** the dimensions of height,

s

depth, and width within which all things exist and move. **4** (also **outer space**) the universe beyond the earth's atmosphere. **5** an interval of time. **6** freedom to live and develop as you wish.

> SYNONYMS **1** *there was not enough space* **room,** capacity, latitude, margin, leeway, play, elbow room, clearance. **2** *green spaces in London* **area,** expanse, stretch, sweep, tract. **3** *a space between the timbers* **gap,** interval, opening, aperture, cavity, niche. **4** *write your name in the appropriate space* **blank,** gap, box, field. **5** *a space of seven years* **period,** span, time, duration, stretch, course, interval, gap. **6** *the first woman in space* **outer space,** deep space, the universe.

▶ verb (**spaces, spacing, spaced**) **1** position items at a distance from one another. **2** (**be spaced out**) informal be confused or not completely conscious.

> SYNONYMS *the chairs were spaced widely* **position,** arrange, range, array, spread, lay out, set.

■ **space shuttle** a spacecraft used for journeys between earth and craft which are orbiting the earth. **space station** a large spacecraft used as a base for manned operations in space.

spacecraft ▶ noun (plural **spacecraft** or **spacecrafts**) a vehicle used for travelling in space.

spaceman ▶ noun (plural **spacemen**) a male astronaut.

spaceship ▶ noun a manned spacecraft.

spacesuit ▶ noun a pressurized suit covering the whole body that allows an astronaut to survive in space.

spacious ▶ adjective (of a room or building) having plenty of space.

> SYNONYMS **roomy,** capacious, commodious, voluminous, sizeable, generous.
> ANTONYMS cramped.

spade ▶ noun a tool with a rectangular metal blade and a long handle, used for digging.
■ **call a spade a spade** speak plainly and frankly.

spades ▶ noun one of the four suits in a pack of playing cards, represented by a black heart-shaped figure with a small stalk.
■ **in spades** informal in large amounts or to a high degree.

spadework ▶ noun hard or routine work done to prepare for something.

spaghetti /spuh-get-ti/ ▶ plural noun pasta made in long, thin strands.

spake old-fashioned past of SPEAK.

spam ▶ noun **1** (**Spam**) trademark a canned meat product made mainly from ham.

2 unwanted email sent to many Internet users.

span ▶ noun **1** the length of time for which something lasts. **2** width or extent from side to side. **3** a part of a bridge between the uprights supporting it. **4** the maximum distance between the tips of the thumb and little finger.

> SYNONYMS **1** *the span of one week* **period,** space, time, duration, course, interval. **2** *a six-foot wing span* **extent,** length, width, reach, stretch, spread, distance, range.

▶ verb (**spans, spanning, spanned**) extend across or over.

> SYNONYMS **1** *an arch spanned the stream* **bridge,** cross, traverse, pass over. **2** *his career spanned twenty years* **last,** cover, extend, spread over.

spangle ▶ noun **1** a small piece of decorative glittering material. **2** a spot of bright colour or light.
□ **spangled** adjective **spangly** adjective.

Spaniard ▶ noun a person from Spain.

spaniel ▶ noun a breed of dog with a long silky coat and drooping ears.

Spanish ▶ noun the main language of Spain and of much of Central and South America.
▶ adjective relating to Spain or Spanish.

spank ▶ verb slap someone on the buttocks with your hand or a flat object.
▶ noun a slap on the buttocks.

spanking ▶ adjective **1** brisk. **2** informal impressive or pleasing.
▶ noun a series of spanks.

spanner ▶ noun Brit. a tool for gripping and turning a nut or bolt.
■ **spanner in the works** something that prevents a plan being carried out successfully.

spar[1] ▶ noun **1** a thick, strong pole used to support the sails on a ship. **2** the main supporting structure of an aircraft's wing.

spar[2] ▶ verb (**spars, sparring, sparred**) **1** make the motions of boxing without landing heavy blows, as a form of training. **2** argue in a friendly way.

spare ▶ adjective **1** additional to what is required for ordinary use. **2** not being used or occupied. **3** thin.

> SYNONYMS **1** *a spare set of keys* **extra,** supplementary, additional, second, other, alternative, emergency, reserve, backup, relief, substitute; N. Amer. alternate. **2** *they sold off the spare land* **surplus,** superfluous, excess, leftover, redundant, unnecessary, unwanted; informal going begging. **3** *your spare time* **free,** leisure, own. **4** *her spare, elegant form* **slender,** lean, willowy, svelte,

S

lissom, thin, skinny, gaunt, lanky, spindly.

▶ noun an item kept in case another is lost, broken, or worn out.

▶ verb (**spares, sparing, spared**) **1** let someone have something that you have enough of. **2** refrain from killing or harming. **3** protect from something unpleasant.

SYNONYMS **1** *he couldn't spare any money* **afford,** manage, part with, give, provide. **2** *they were spared by their captors* **pardon,** let off, forgive, have mercy on, reprieve, release, free.

■ **go spare** Brit. informal become very angry. **spare no expense** be prepared to pay any amount. **spare ribs** trimmed ribs of pork. **spare tyre** informal a roll of fat around a person's waist.

sparing ▶ adjective not wasteful; economical.

SYNONYMS **thrifty,** economical, frugal, careful, prudent, cautious. ANTONYMS lavish, extravagant.

□ **sparingly** adverb.

spark ▶ noun **1** a small fiery particle produced by burning or caused by friction. **2** a flash of light produced by an electrical discharge. **3** a small amount of a quality or feeling. **4** a sense of liveliness and excitement.

SYNONYMS *a spark of light* **flash,** glint, twinkle, flicker, flare.

▶ verb **1** give out or produce sparks. **2** ignite a fire. **3** (usu. **spark something off**) cause something.

SYNONYMS *the arrest sparked off riots* **cause,** give rise to, occasion, bring about, start, precipitate, prompt, trigger (off), provoke, stimulate, stir up.

■ **spark plug** a device that produces a spark to ignite the fuel in a vehicle engine. □ **sparky** adjective.

sparkle ▶ verb (**sparkles, sparkling, sparkled**) **1** shine brightly with flashes of light. **2** be attractively lively and witty. **3** (**sparkling**) (of a drink) fizzy.

SYNONYMS **glitter,** glint, glisten, twinkle, flicker, flash, shimmer.

▶ noun **1** a glittering flash of light. **2** attractive liveliness and wit.

SYNONYMS **1** **glitter,** glint, glisten, twinkle, flicker, flash, shimmer. **2** (**sparkling**) *a sparkling performance* **brilliant,** dazzling, scintillating, exciting, exhilarating, stimulating, invigorating, vivacious, lively, vibrant. **3** (**sparkling**) *sparkling wine* **effervescent,** fizzy, carbonated, aerated.

□ **sparkly** adjective.

sparkler ▶ noun a hand-held firework that gives out sparks.

sparrow ▶ noun a small bird with brown and grey feathers.

sparrowhawk ▶ noun a small hawk that preys on small birds.

sparse ▶ adjective thinly scattered. □ **sparsely** adverb **sparsity** noun.

spartan ▶ adjective not comfortable or luxurious.

spasm ▶ noun **1** a sudden involuntary contraction of a muscle. **2** a sudden period of an activity or sensation.

spasmodic ▶ adjective happening or done in brief, irregular bursts. □ **spasmodically** adverb.

spastic ▶ adjective **1** relating to or affected by muscle spasm. **2** offensive having to do with cerebral palsy.

▶ noun offensive a person with cerebral palsy. □ **spasticity** noun.

❗ Say *person with cerebral palsy* rather than **spastic**, which many people find offensive.

spat¹ past and past participle of **SPIT¹**.

spat² ▶ noun informal a quarrel about something unimportant.

spat³ ▶ noun a cloth covering formerly worn by men over their ankles and shoes.

spate ▶ noun **1** a large number of similar things coming quickly one after another. **2** a sudden flood in a river.

SYNONYMS **series,** succession, run, cluster, string, rash, epidemic, outbreak, wave, flurry.

spathe /spay*th*/ ▶ noun a large sheath enclosing the flower cluster of certain plants.

spatial ▶ adjective having to do with space. □ **spatially** adverb.

spatter ▶ verb (**spatters, spattering, spattered**) cover something with drops or spots of a liquid.

▶ noun a spray or splash.

spatula ▶ noun an object with a broad, flat, blunt blade, used for mixing or spreading.

spawn ▶ verb **1** (of a fish, frog, etc.) release or deposit eggs. **2** give rise to.

▶ noun the eggs of fish, frogs, etc.

spay ▶ verb sterilize a female animal by removing the ovaries.

speak ▶ verb (**speaks, speaking, spoke;** past participle **spoken**) **1** say something. **2** communicate, or be able to communicate, in a particular language. **3** (**speak up**) speak more loudly. **4** (**speak out** or **up**) express your opinions frankly and publicly.

SYNONYMS **1** *she refused to speak about it* **talk,** converse, communicate, chat, have a word, gossip, commune, say anything/something. **2** *she spoke her words carefully* **say,** utter, state, declare, voice, express, pronounce, articulate, enunciate, verbalize. **3** *the Minister spoke for two hours* **give a speech,** talk, lecture, hold forth; informal spout, sound off.

■ **speak in tongues** speak in an unknown language during religious worship. **speak volumes** convey a great deal without using words.

speakeasy ▶ noun (plural **speakeasies**) (in the US during Prohibition) a secret illegal drinking club.

speaker ▶ noun **1** a person who speaks. **2** (**Speaker**) the person who is in charge of proceedings in a parliament. **3** a loudspeaker.

SYNONYMS **speech-maker,** lecturer, talker, orator, spokesperson, spokesman/woman, reader, commentator, broadcaster, narrator.

spear ▶ noun **1** a weapon with a pointed metal tip and a long shaft. **2** a pointed stem of asparagus or broccoli.
▶ verb pierce with a spear or other pointed object.

spearhead ▶ verb lead a campaign or attack.
▶ noun a person or group that leads a campaign or attack.

spearmint ▶ noun a type of garden mint, used in cooking.

spec ▶ noun informal **1** (**on spec**) without any specific preparation or plan. **2** a detailed working description.

special ▶ adjective **1** better or different from what is usual. **2** designed for or belonging to a particular person, place, or event.

SYNONYMS **1** *a very special person* **exceptional,** unusual, remarkable, outstanding, unique. **2** *our town's special character* **distinctive,** distinct, individual, particular, specific, peculiar. **3** *a special occasion* **momentous,** significant, memorable, important, historic. **4** *a special tool for cutting tiles* **specific,** particular, purpose-built, tailor-made, custom-built.
ANTONYMS ordinary, general.

▶ noun **1** something designed or organized for a particular occasion or purpose. **2** a dish not on the regular menu but served on a particular day.

■ **special constable** a person trained to act as a police officer on particular occasions. **special effects** illusions created for films and television by camerawork, computer graphics, etc.

specialist ▶ noun an expert in a particular subject, area of activity, etc.

SYNONYMS **expert,** authority, pundit, professional, connoisseur, master,

maestro; informal buff.
ANTONYMS amateur.

▶ adjective involving detailed knowledge within a subject, area of activity, etc.
□ **specialism** noun.

speciality (US spelling **specialty**) ▶ noun (plural **specialities**) **1** a skill or area of study in which someone is an expert. **2** a product for which a person or region is famous. **3** (usu. **specialty**) a branch of medicine or surgery.

SYNONYMS **1** *his speciality was watercolours* **strength,** strong point, forte, métier, strong suit, party piece, pièce de résistance; informal bag, thing. **2** *a speciality of the region* **delicacy.**

specialize (or **specialise**) ▶ verb (**specializes, specializing, specialized**) **1** concentrate on and become expert in a particular skill or area. **2** (**specialized**) adapted or designed for a particular purpose or area of activity.
□ **specialization** noun.

specially ▶ adverb **1** for a special purpose. **2** particularly.

specie /spee-shee/ ▶ noun money in the form of coins rather than notes.

species ▶ noun (plural **species**) **1** a group of animals or plants that are capable of breeding with each other. **2** a kind.

SYNONYMS **type,** kind, sort, breed, strain, variety, class, classification, category.

specific ▶ adjective **1** clearly defined or identified. **2** precise and clear. **3** (**specific to**) belonging or relating only to.

SYNONYMS **1** *a specific purpose* **particular,** specified, fixed, set, determined, distinct, definite. **2** *I gave specific instructions* **detailed,** explicit, express, clear-cut, unequivocal, precise, exact.
ANTONYMS general, vague.

▶ noun (**specifics**) precise details.
□ **specifically** adverb.

specification ▶ noun **1** the action of specifying. **2** (usu. **specifications**) a detailed description of the design and materials used to make something. **3** the standard of workmanship and materials in a piece of work.

SYNONYMS **1** *clear specification of objectives* **statement,** identification, definition, description, setting out. **2** *a shelter built to their specifications* **instruction,** guideline, parameter, stipulation, requirement, condition, order, detail.

specify ▶ verb (**specifies, specifying, specified**) state, identify, or require clearly and definitely.

SYNONYMS **state,** name, identify, define, set out, itemize, detail, list, spell out, stipulate, lay down.

specimen ▸ noun **1** an example of an animal, plant, object, etc. used for study or display. **2** a sample for medical testing. **3** a typical example of something. **4** informal a person of a specific type: *a sorry specimen.*

SYNONYMS **sample,** example, model, instance, illustration, demonstration.

specious /spee-shuhss/ ▸ adjective seeming right or reasonable, but actually wrong.

speck ▸ noun a tiny spot or particle.
▸ verb mark with small spots.

speckle ▸ noun a small spot or patch of colour.
▸ verb (**speckles, speckling, speckled**) mark with speckles.

specs ▸ plural noun informal spectacles.

spectacle ▸ noun a visually striking performance or display.

SYNONYMS **1** *his love of spectacle* **display,** show, pageantry, performance, exhibition, pomp and circumstance, extravaganza, spectacular. **2** *they were rather an odd spectacle* **sight,** vision, scene, prospect, picture.

spectacles ▸ plural noun Brit. a pair of glasses.

spectacular ▸ adjective very impressive, striking, or dramatic.

SYNONYMS **1** *a spectacular view* **striking,** picturesque, eye-catching, breathtaking, arresting, glorious; informal out of this world. **2** *a spectacular victory* **impressive,** magnificent, splendid, dazzling, sensational, dramatic, outstanding, memorable, unforgettable.
ANTONYMS dull, unimpressive.

▸ noun a spectacular performance or event.
□ **spectacularly** adverb.

spectate ▸ verb (**spectates, spectating, spectated**) be a spectator.

spectator ▸ noun a person who is watching a show, game, etc.

SYNONYMS **watcher,** viewer, observer, onlooker, bystander, witness.
ANTONYMS participant.

spectral ▸ adjective **1** like a spectre. **2** having to do with the spectrum.

spectre (US spelling **specter**) ▸ noun **1** a ghost. **2** a possible unpleasant or dangerous occurrence.

SYNONYMS **ghost,** phantom, apparition, spirit, wraith, presence; informal spook.

spectrum ▸ noun (plural **spectra**) **1** a band of colours produced by separating light into elements with different wavelengths, e.g. in a rainbow. **2** the entire range of

wavelengths of light. **3** a range of sound waves or different types of wave. **4** an entire range of beliefs, ideas, etc.: *the political spectrum.*

speculate ▸ verb (**speculates, speculating, speculated**) **1** form a theory without firm evidence. **2** invest in stocks, property, etc. in the hope of gain but with the risk of loss.

SYNONYMS **1** *they speculated about my private life* **conjecture,** theorize, hypothesize, guess, surmise, wonder, muse. **2** *investors speculate on the stock market* **gamble,** venture, wager, invest, play the market; Brit. informal punt.

□ **speculation** noun **speculator** noun.

speculative ▸ adjective **1** based on theory or guesswork rather than knowledge. **2** (of an investment) risky.

SYNONYMS **1** *any discussion is largely speculative* **conjectural,** suppositional, theoretical, hypothetical, tentative, unproven, unfounded, groundless, unsubstantiated. **2** *a speculative investment* **risky,** hazardous, unsafe, uncertain, unpredictable; informal chancy.

□ **speculatively** adverb.

speculum ▸ noun (plural **specula**) a metal instrument that is used to make an opening or canal in the body wider so that it can be examined.

speech ▸ noun **1** the expression of thoughts and feelings using spoken language. **2** a formal talk given to an audience. **3** a sequence of lines written for one character in a play.

SYNONYMS **1** *the power of speech* **speaking,** talking, verbal expression, verbal communication. **2** *her speech was slurred* **diction,** elocution, articulation, enunciation, pronunciation, delivery, words. **3** *an after-dinner speech* **talk,** address, lecture, discourse, oration, presentation, sermon. **4** *in popular speech* **language,** parlance, tongue, idiom, dialect, vernacular; informal lingo.

■ **speech marks** inverted commas. **speech therapy** treatment to help people with speech problems.

speechify ▸ verb (**speechifies, speechifying, speechified**) deliver a speech in a boring or pompous way.

speechless ▸ adjective unable to speak due to shock or strong emotion.

speed ▸ noun **1** the rate at which someone or something moves or operates. **2** a fast rate of movement or action. **3** each of the possible gear ratios of a vehicle or bicycle. **4** the sensitivity of photographic film to light. **5** informal an amphetamine drug.

SYNONYMS **1** *the speed of their progress* **rate,** pace, tempo, momentum, velocity;

informal **lick. 2** *the speed with which they responded* **rapidity,** swiftness, promptness, briskness, haste, hurry.
ANTONYMS slowness.

▶ verb (**speeds, speeding, speeded** or **sped**)
1 move quickly. **2** (**speed up**) move or work more quickly. **3** (of a motorist) travel at a speed greater than the legal limit. **4** old use make prosperous or successful.

SYNONYMS **1** *I sped home* **hurry,** rush, dash, race, sprint, career, shoot, hurtle, hare, fly, zoom, hasten; informal tear, belt, pelt; Brit. informal bomb. **2** *a holiday will speed his recovery* **hasten,** speed up, accelerate, advance, further, promote, boost, stimulate, aid, assist, facilitate.
ANTONYMS dawdle, slow, hinder.

speedboat ▶ noun a motorboat designed for high speed.

speedometer ▶ noun an instrument that indicates a vehicle's speed.

speedway ▶ noun Brit. a form of motorcycle racing in which the riders race around an oval dirt track.

speedwell ▶ noun a small plant with blue or pink flowers.

speedy ▶ adjective (**speedier, speediest**) done, happening, or moving quickly.

SYNONYMS **fast,** swift, quick, rapid, prompt, immediate, brisk, hasty, hurried, precipitate, rushed.
ANTONYMS slow.

□ **speedily** adverb.

speleology /spee-li-**ol**-uh-ji/ ▶ noun the study or exploration of caves.
□ **speleologist** noun.

spell[1] ▶ verb (**spells, spelling, spelled** or chiefly Brit. **spelt**) **1** write or name the letters that form a word in correct sequence. **2** (of letters) form a word. **3** be a sign of. **4** (**spell something out**) explain something clearly and in detail.

SYNONYMS *the drought spelled disaster* **signal,** signify, mean, amount to, add up to, constitute.

spell[2] ▶ noun **1** a form of words with magical power. **2** a state of enchantment caused by a spell. **3** an ability to control or influence other people.

SYNONYMS **1** *the witch muttered a spell* **charm,** incantation, formula, curse; N. Amer. hex; (**spells**) magic, sorcery, witchcraft. **2** *she surrendered to his spell* **influence,** charm, magnetism, charisma, magic.

spell[3] ▶ noun a short period of time.

SYNONYMS **1** *a spell of dry weather* **period,** time, interval, season, stretch, run; Brit. informal patch. **2** *a spell of dizziness* **bout,** fit, attack.

spellbound ▶ adjective with your attention completely held by something.
□ **spellbinding** adjective.

spellchecker ▶ noun a computer program which checks the spelling of words in an electronic document.

spelling ▶ noun **1** the process of spelling a word. **2** the way in which a word is spelled.

spend ▶ verb (**spends, spending, spent**)
1 pay out money to buy or hire goods or services. **2** pass time in a particular way. **3** use up energy or resources.

SYNONYMS **1** *she spent £185 on shoes* **pay out,** expend; informal blow, splurge. **2** *the morning was spent gardening* **pass,** occupy, fill, take up, while away. **3** *I've spent hours on this essay* **put in,** devote, waste, squander.

□ **spender** noun.

spendthrift ▶ noun a person who spends too much money or wastes money.

sperm ▶ noun (plural **sperm** or **sperms**)
1 semen. **2** a spermatozoon.
■ **sperm whale** a toothed whale that feeds largely on squid.

spermatozoon /sper-muh-tuh-**zoh**-on/ ▶ noun (plural **spermatozoa** /sper-muh-tuh-**zoh**-uh/) the male sex cell of an animal, that fertilizes the egg.

spermicide ▶ noun a contraceptive substance that kills spermatozoa.

spew ▶ verb **1** pour out in large quantities. **2** informal vomit.

sphagnum /**sfag**-nuhm/ ▶ noun a kind of moss that grows in boggy areas.

sphere ▶ noun **1** a round solid figure in which every point on the surface is at an equal distance from the centre. **2** an area of activity or interest.

SYNONYMS **1** *a glass sphere* **globe,** ball, orb, bubble. **2** *sphere of influence* **area,** field, compass, orbit, range, scope, extent. **3** *the sphere of foreign affairs* **domain,** realm, province, field, area, territory, arena, department.

spherical ▶ adjective shaped like a sphere.
□ **spherically** adverb.

sphincter ▶ noun a ring of muscle surrounding an opening such as the anus.

sphinx ▶ noun an ancient Egyptian stone figure having a lion's body and a human or animal head.

spice ▶ noun **1** a strong-tasting substance used to flavour food. **2** an element that provides interest and excitement.

SYNONYMS **1** *the spices in curry powder* **seasoning,** flavouring, condiment. **2** *the risk added spice to their affair* **excitement,** interest, colour, piquancy, zest, an edge.

S

▸ verb (**spices, spicing, spiced**) **1** flavour with spice. **2** (**spice something up**) make something more exciting or interesting.

spick and span ▸ adjective neat, clean, and well looked after.

spicy ▸ adjective (**spicier, spiciest**) **1** strongly flavoured with spice. **2** mildly indecent.

> SYNONYMS **hot,** tangy, peppery, piquant, spiced, highly seasoned, pungent. ANTONYMS bland.

□ **spiciness** noun.

spider ▸ noun a small insect-like creature (an arachnid) with eight legs.
□ **spidery** adjective.

spiel /shpeel, speel/ ▸ noun informal an elaborate and insincere speech made in an attempt to persuade someone.

spigot ▸ noun **1** a small peg or plug. **2** the end of a section of a pipe that fits into the socket of the next one.

spike ▸ noun **1** a thin, pointed piece of metal or wood. **2** each of several metal points set into the sole of a sports shoe to prevent slipping. **3** a cluster of flower heads attached directly to a long stem.

> SYNONYMS **prong,** pin, barb, point, skewer, stake, spit.

▸ verb (**spikes, spiking, spiked**) **1** impale on or pierce with a spike. **2** cover with sharp points. **3** informal secretly add alcohol or a drug to drink or food.
□ **spiky** adjective.

spill¹ ▸ verb (**spills, spilling, spilt** or **spilled**) **1** flow, or allow to flow, over the edge of a container. **2** move or empty out from a place.

> SYNONYMS **1** *Kevin spilled his drink* **knock over,** tip over, upset, overturn. **2** *the bath water spilled on to the floor* **overflow,** slop, slosh, splash, leak. **3** *students spilled out of the building* **stream,** pour, surge, swarm, flood, throng, crowd.

▸ noun **1** a quantity of liquid spilt. **2** informal a fall from a horse or bicycle.
■ **spill the beans** informal reveal confidential information. **spill blood** kill or wound people.
□ **spillage** noun.

spill² ▸ noun a thin strip of wood or paper used for lighting a fire.

spin ▸ verb (**spins, spinning, spun**) **1** turn round quickly. **2** (of a person's head) have a dizzy sensation. **3** (of a ball) move through the air with a revolving motion. **4** draw out and twist the fibres of wool, cotton, etc. to convert them into yarn. **5** (of a spider, silkworm, etc.) produce silk or a web by forcing out a fine thread from a special gland. **6** (**spin something out**) make something last as long as possible.

> SYNONYMS **1** *the wheels are spinning* **revolve,** rotate, turn, go round, whirl. **2** *she spun round to face him* **whirl,** wheel, twirl, turn, swing, twist, swivel, pivot.

▸ noun **1** a spinning motion. **2** informal a brief trip in a vehicle for pleasure. **3** a favourable slant given to a news story.

> SYNONYMS **1** *a spin of the wheel* **rotation,** revolution, turn, whirl, twirl. **2** *a spin in the car* **trip,** jaunt, outing, excursion, journey, drive, ride, run, turn; informal tootle. **3** *a positive spin* **slant,** angle, twist, bias.

■ **spin doctor** informal a person employed by a political party to give a favourable interpretation of events to the media. **spin dryer** a machine that removes water from washed clothes by spinning them in a drum. **spinning wheel** a piece of equipment for spinning yarn or thread with a spindle driven by a wheel operated by hand or foot. **spin-off** something unexpected but useful resulting from an activity.
□ **spinner** noun.

spina bifida /spy-nuh bi-fi-duh/ ▸ noun a condition in which part of the spinal cord is exposed, sometimes causing paralysis.

spinach ▸ noun a plant with large dark green leaves which are eaten as a vegetable.

spinal ▸ adjective relating to the spine.
■ **spinal column** the spine. **spinal cord** the nerve fibres enclosed in the spine and connected to the brain.

spindle ▸ noun **1** a slender rod with tapered ends used for spinning wool, flax, etc. by hand. **2** a rod around which something revolves.

spindly ▸ adjective long or tall and thin.

spindrift ▸ noun spray blown from the sea by the wind.

spine ▸ noun **1** a series of bones extending from the skull to the small of the back, enclosing the spinal cord; the backbone. **2** the part of a book that encloses the inner edges of the pages. **3** a hard pointed projection found on certain plants and animals.

> SYNONYMS **1** *he injured his spine* **backbone,** spinal column, back. **2** *cactus spines* **needle,** quill, bristle, barb, spike, prickle, thorn.

■ **spine-chiller** a story or film that causes terror and excitement.
□ **spiny** adjective.

spineless ▸ adjective **1** lacking courage and determination. **2** having no backbone; invertebrate. **3** having no spines.

spinet ▸ noun a kind of small harpsichord.

spinnaker ▸ noun a large three-cornered sail used on a racing yacht when the wind is coming from behind.

S

spinney ▸ noun (plural **spinneys**) Brit. a small area of trees and bushes.

spinster ▸ noun disapproving a single woman beyond the usual age for marriage.
□ **spinsterhood** noun.

spiral ▸ adjective winding in a continuous curve around a central point or axis.

SYNONYMS *a spiral column* **coiled,** helical, curling, winding, twisting.

▸ noun 1 a spiral curve, shape, or pattern. 2 a continuous rise or fall of prices, wages, etc.

SYNONYMS *a spiral of smoke* **coil,** curl, twist, whorl, scroll, helix, corkscrew.

▸ verb (**spirals, spiralling, spiralled;** US spelling **spirals, spiraling, spiraled**) 1 follow a spiral course. 2 show a continuous increase or decrease.

SYNONYMS *smoke spiralled up* **coil,** wind, swirl, twist, snake.

□ **spirally** adverb.

spire ▸ noun a pointed structure on the top of a church tower.

spirit ▸ noun 1 the part of a person that consists of their character and feelings rather than their body. 2 a supernatural being. 3 typical character, quality, or mood. 4 (**spirits**) a person's mood or state of mind. 5 courage, energy, and determination. 6 the real meaning of something as opposed to its strict interpretation. 7 (also **spirits**) chiefly Brit. strong alcoholic drink, e.g. rum. 8 purified distilled alcohol, e.g. methylated spirit.

SYNONYMS 1 *body and spirit* **soul,** psyche, inner self, inner man/woman, mind. 2 *a spirit haunts the island* **ghost,** phantom, spectre, apparition, presence. 3 *in good spirits* **mood,** frame/state of mind, humour, temper. 4 *team spirit* **morale,** esprit de corps. 5 *the spirit of the age* **ethos,** essence, atmosphere, mood, feeling, climate. 6 *they played with spirit* **enthusiasm,** energy, verve, vigour, dynamism, dash, sparkle, exuberance, gusto, fervour, zeal, fire, passion; informal get-up-and-go. 7 *the spirit of the law* **real meaning,** true meaning, essence, substance, idea.
ANTONYMS body, flesh.

▸ verb (**spirits, spiriting, spirited**) (**spirit someone/thing away**) take someone or something away quickly and secretly.
■ **spirit level** a glass tube partially filled with a liquid, containing an air bubble whose position reveals whether a surface is perfectly level.

spirited ▸ adjective energetic and determined.

SYNONYMS **lively,** energetic, enthusiastic, vigorous, dynamic, passionate; informal

feisty, gutsy; N. Amer. informal peppy.
ANTONYMS apathetic, lifeless.

□ **spiritedly** adverb.

spiritual ▸ adjective 1 having to do with the human spirit as opposed to material or physical things. 2 having to do with religion or religious belief.

SYNONYMS 1 *your spiritual self* **inner,** mental, psychological, incorporeal, non-material. 2 *spiritual writings* **religious,** sacred, divine, holy, devotional.
ANTONYMS physical, secular.

▸ noun a religious song of a kind associated with black Christians of the southern US.
□ **spirituality** noun **spiritually** adverb.

spiritualism ▸ noun the belief that the spirits of the dead can communicate with the living.
□ **spiritualist** noun.

spirogyra /spy-ruh-jy-ruh/ ▸ noun a type of algae consisting of long green threads.

spit¹ ▸ verb (**spits, spitting, spat** or **spit**) 1 forcibly eject saliva, or food, liquid, etc., from the mouth. 2 say in a hostile way. 3 give out small bursts of sparks or hot fat. 4 (**it spits, it is spitting**) Brit. light rain falls.

SYNONYMS 1 *Cranston coughed and spat* **expectorate,** hawk; Brit. informal gob. 2 *the fat began to spit* **sizzle,** hiss, crackle, sputter.

▸ noun 1 saliva. 2 an act of spitting.

SYNONYMS *spit dribbled from his mouth* **spittle,** saliva, sputum, slobber, dribble; Brit. informal gob.

■ **be the spitting image of** informal look exactly like.

spit² ▸ noun 1 a metal rod pushed through meat in order to hold and turn it while it is roasted. 2 a narrow point of land sticking out into the sea.

spite ▸ noun a desire to hurt, annoy, or offend someone.

SYNONYMS *he said it out of spite* **malice,** malevolence, ill will, vindictiveness, meanness, nastiness; informal bitchiness, cattiness.
ANTONYMS kindness.

▸ verb (**spites, spiting, spited**) deliberately hurt, annoy, or offend someone.

SYNONYMS *he did it to spite me* **upset,** hurt, wound.
ANTONYMS please.

■ **in spite of** without being affected by.

spiteful ▸ adjective deliberately hurtful; malicious.
□ **spitefully** adverb.

spitfire ▸ noun a person with a fierce temper.

spittle ▸ noun saliva.

spittoon ▸ noun a container for spitting into.

spiv ▸ noun Brit. informal a flashily dressed man who makes a living by dishonest business dealings.

splash ▸ verb **1** (of a liquid) fall in scattered drops. **2** make wet with scattered drops. **3** move around in water, causing it to fly about. **4** (**splash down**) (of a spacecraft) land on water. **5** prominently display a story or photograph in a newspaper or magazine. **6** (**splash out**) Brit. informal spend money freely.

> SYNONYMS **1** *splash your face with water* **sprinkle**, spray, shower, wash, squirt, daub, wet. **2** *his boots were splashed with rain* **spatter**, splatter, speck, smear, stain, mark. **3** *waves splashing on the beach* **wash**, break, lap, pound. **4** *children splashed in the water* **paddle**, wade, wallow.

▸ noun **1** an instance of splashing. **2** a small quantity of liquid splashed on to a surface. **3** a small quantity of liquid added to a drink. **4** a bright patch of colour. **5** informal a prominent news story.

> SYNONYMS **1** *a splash of rain* **spot**, blob, smear, speck. **2** *a splash of lemonade* **drop**, dash, bit, spot, soupçon, dribble; Scottish informal scoosh. **3** *a splash of colour* **patch**, burst, streak.

■ **make a splash** informal attract a lot of attention.

splatter ▸ verb (**splatters, splattering, splattered**) splash with a sticky or thick liquid.

▸ noun a splash of a sticky or thick liquid.

splay ▸ verb spread out wide apart.

spleen ▸ noun **1** an organ involved in producing and removing blood cells. **2** bad temper.

splendid ▸ adjective **1** magnificent; very impressive. **2** informal excellent.

> SYNONYMS **1** *splendid costumes* **magnificent**, sumptuous, grand, imposing, superb, spectacular, resplendent, rich, lavish, ornate, gorgeous, glorious, dazzling, handsome, beautiful; informal plush; Brit. informal swish. **2** *a splendid holiday* **excellent**, wonderful, marvellous, superb, glorious, lovely, delightful, first-class; informal super, great, amazing, fantastic, terrific, tremendous; Brit. informal smashing, brilliant.
> ANTONYMS simple, modest, awful.

□ **splendidly** adverb.

splendour (US spelling **splendor**) ▸ noun magnificent and impressive appearance.

> SYNONYMS **magnificence**, sumptuousness, grandeur, resplendence,

richness, glory, majesty.
> ANTONYMS simplicity, modesty.

splenetic ▸ adjective bad-tempered or spiteful.

splice ▸ verb (**splices, splicing, spliced**) **1** join ropes by weaving together the strands at the ends. **2** join pieces of film, tape, etc. at the ends.

▸ noun a spliced join.

spliff ▸ noun informal a cannabis cigarette.

splint ▸ noun a rigid support for a broken bone.

splinter ▸ noun a small, thin, sharp piece of wood, glass, etc. broken off from a larger piece.

> SYNONYMS *a splinter of wood* **sliver**, chip, shard, fragment, shred; Scottish skelf.

▸ verb (**splinters, splintering, splintered**) break into splinters.

> SYNONYMS *the glass splintered* **shatter**, smash, break into smithereens, fracture, split, crack, disintegrate.

■ **splinter group** a small breakaway group.

split ▸ verb (**splits, splitting, split**) **1** break into parts by force. **2** divide into parts or groups. **3** (often **split up**) end a marriage or other relationship. **4** (**be splitting**) informal (of a person's head) be suffering from a bad headache.

> SYNONYMS **1** *the force split the wood* **break**, cut, burst, snap, crack. **2** *the ice split under him* **break**, fracture, rupture, burst, snap, crack, come apart, splinter. **3** *her dress was split* **tear**, rip, slash, slit. **4** *they split the profit* **share**, divide up, distribute, dole out, parcel out, carve up, slice up. **5** *the path split* **fork**, divide, branch, diverge. **6** *the band split up last year* **break up**, separate, part, part company, go their separate ways.
> ANTONYMS mend, join, unite, pool, converge, get together.

▸ noun **1** a tear or crack. **2** an instance of splitting. **3** (**the splits**) a leap or seated position with the legs straight and at right angles to the body.

> SYNONYMS **1** *a split in the rock face* **crack**, fissure, cleft, crevice, break, fracture, breach. **2** *a split in the curtain* **rip**, tear, cut, rent, slash, slit. **3** *a split in the Party* **division**, rift, breach, schism, rupture, partition. **4** *the acrimonious split with his wife* **break-up**, split-up, separation, parting, estrangement, rift.
> ANTONYMS join, merger, marriage.

■ **split infinitive** Grammar an infinitive construction in which an adverb or other word is placed between *to* and the verb (e.g. *she used to secretly admire him*), traditionally regarded as bad English. **split-level** (of a room or building) having the floor divided into two levels. **split second** a very brief moment of time.

splodge (or **splotch**) ▶ noun Brit. a spot, splash, or smear.

splosh informal ▶ verb make a soft splashing sound.
▶ noun a splashing sound.

splurge informal ▶ verb (**splurges**, **splurging**, **splurged**) spend extravagantly.
▶ noun a sudden burst of extravagance.

splutter ▶ verb (**splutters**, **spluttering**, **spluttered**) **1** make a series of short explosive spitting or choking sounds. **2** say in a rapid, unclear way.
▶ noun a spluttering sound.

spoil ▶ verb (**spoils**, **spoiling**, past and past participle **spoilt** (chiefly Brit.) or **spoiled**) **1** make something less good or enjoyable. **2** (of food) become unfit for eating. **3** harm the character of a child by not being strict enough. **4** treat with great or excessive kindness. **5** (**be spoiling for**) be very eager for.

> SYNONYMS **1** *smoking spoils your complexion* **damage**, ruin, impair, blemish, disfigure, blight, deface, harm, destroy, wreck. **2** *rain spoiled my plans* **ruin**, wreck, upset, undo, mess up, sabotage, scotch, torpedo; informal muck up, screw up, do for; Brit. informal cock up, scupper. **3** *his sisters spoil him* **overindulge**, pamper, indulge, mollycoddle, cosset, wait on someone hand and foot. **4** *stockpiled food may spoil* **go bad**, go off, go rancid, turn, go sour, rot, perish.
> ANTONYMS improve, enhance, further, neglect, be strict with, keep.

▶ noun (**spoils**) stolen goods.

spoiler ▶ noun **1** a flap on an aircraft wing which can be raised to create drag and slow it down. **2** a similar device on a car intended to improve roadholding at high speeds.

spoilsport ▶ noun a person who spoils the pleasure of other people.

spoke¹ ▶ noun each of the rods connecting the centre of a wheel to its rim.

spoke² past of SPEAK.

spoken past participle of SPEAK.
▶ adjective speaking in a particular way: *a soft-spoken man*.

> SYNONYMS **verbal**, oral, vocal, unwritten, word-of-mouth.
> ANTONYMS non-verbal, written.

■ **be spoken for** be already claimed.

spokesman (or **spokeswoman**) ▶ noun (plural **spokesmen** or **spokeswomen**) a person who makes statements on behalf of a group.

> SYNONYMS See SPOKESPERSON.

spokesperson ▶ noun (plural **spokespersons** or **spokespeople**) a spokesman or spokeswoman.

> SYNONYMS **spokesman**, **spokeswoman**, representative, voice, mouthpiece, agent, official; informal spin doctor.

spoliation /spoh-li-ay-shuhn/ ▶ noun **1** the action of destroying or ruining something. **2** the action of plundering.

sponge ▶ noun **1** a simple sea creature with no backbone and a soft porous body. **2** a piece of a light, absorbent substance used for washing, as padding, etc. **3** Brit. a cake made with little or no fat.
▶ verb (**sponges**, **sponging** or **spongeing**, **sponged**) **1** wipe or clean with a wet sponge or cloth. **2** informal obtain money or food from other people without giving anything in return.
■ **sponge bag** Brit. a toilet bag.
□ **sponger** noun **spongy** adjective.

sponsor ▶ noun **1** a person or organization that helps pays for an event in return for advertising. **2** a person who promises to give money to a charity if another person completes a task or activity. **3** a person who proposes a new law.

> SYNONYMS **backer**, patron, promoter, benefactor, supporter, contributor.

▶ verb be a sponsor for.

> SYNONYMS **finance**, fund, subsidize, back, promote, support, contribute to; N. Amer. informal bankroll.

□ **sponsorship** noun.

> ✔ **-or**, not **-er**: spons**or**.

spontaneous ▶ adjective **1** done or happening as a result of an impulse. **2** open, natural, and relaxed. **3** happening without apparent external cause.

> SYNONYMS **1** *a spontaneous display of affection* **unplanned**, unpremeditated, impulsive, impromptu, spur-of-the-moment, unprompted; informal off-the-cuff. **2** *a spontaneous kind of person* **natural**, uninhibited, relaxed, unselfconscious, unaffected.
> ANTONYMS planned, inhibited.

□ **spontaneity** noun **spontaneously** adverb.

spoof ▶ noun informal a humorous imitation of something.

spook informal ▶ noun **1** a ghost. **2** N. Amer. a spy.
▶ verb frighten.

spooky ▶ adjective (**spookier**, **spookiest**) informal sinister or ghostly.
□ **spookily** adverb.

spool ▶ noun a cylindrical device on which thread, film, etc. can be wound.
▶ verb wind on to a spool.

spoon ▸ noun an implement consisting of a small, shallow bowl on a long handle, used for eating and serving food.
▸ verb transfer food with a spoon.
■ **spoon-feed 1** feed someone with a spoon. **2** provide someone with so much help that they do not need to think for themselves.
□ **spoonful** noun.

spoonbill ▸ noun a tall wading bird that has a long bill with a very broad flat tip.

spoonerism ▸ noun a mistake in speech in which the initial sounds or letters of two or more words are accidentally swapped around, as in *you have hissed the mystery lectures*.

spoor ▸ noun the track or scent of an animal.

sporadic ▸ adjective happening at irregular intervals or only in a few places.
□ **sporadically** adverb.

spore ▸ noun a tiny reproductive cell produced by fungi and plants such as mosses and algae.

sporran ▸ noun a small pouch worn around the waist as part of men's Scottish Highland dress.

sport ▸ noun **1** a competitive activity which involves physical effort and skill. **2** informal a person who behaves well when teased or defeated.

SYNONYMS **game**, physical recreation.

▸ verb **1** wear a distinctive item. **2** literary amuse yourself or play in a lively way.

SYNONYMS *he was sporting a new tie* **wear**, have on, dress in, show off, parade, flaunt.

■ **sports car** a small, fast car. **sports jacket** a man's informal jacket resembling a suit jacket.

sporting ▸ adjective **1** connected with or interested in sport. **2** fair and generous.

SYNONYMS **sportsmanlike**, generous, considerate, fair; Brit. informal decent.
ANTONYMS dirty, unfair.

■ **sporting chance** a reasonable chance of winning or succeeding.
□ **sportingly** adverb.

sportive ▸ adjective playful; light-hearted.

sportsman (or **sportswoman**) ▸ noun (plural **sportsmen** or **sportswomen**) **1** a person who takes part in a sport. **2** a person who behaves in a fair and generous way.
□ **sportsmanship** noun.

sporty ▸ adjective (**sportier**, **sportiest**) informal **1** fond of or good at sport. **2** (of clothing) suitable for sport or casual wear. **3** (of a car) compact and fast.

SYNONYMS **athletic**, fit, active, energetic.
ANTONYMS unfit, lazy.

spot ▸ noun **1** a small round mark on a surface. **2** a pimple. **3** a particular place,

point, or position. **4** a small amount of something.

SYNONYMS **1** *a grease spot* **mark**, patch, dot, fleck, smudge, smear, stain, blotch, splash; informal splodge. **2** *a spot on his nose* **pimple**, pustule, blackhead, boil; informal zit; Scottish informal plook; (**spots**) acne. **3** *a secluded spot* **place**, site, position, situation, setting, location, venue.

▸ verb (**spots**, **spotting**, **spotted**) **1** notice or recognize, especially with difficulty or effort. **2** mark with spots.

SYNONYMS *she spotted him* **see**, notice, observe, detect, make out, recognize, identify, locate; Brit. informal clock.

■ **on the spot 1** immediately. **2** at the scene of an action or event. **spot check** a test made without warning on a person or thing selected at random. **spot on** completely accurate.
□ **spotter** noun.

spotless ▸ adjective absolutely clean or pure.
□ **spotlessly** adverb.

spotlight ▸ noun **1** a lamp projecting a narrow, strong beam of light directly on to a place or person. **2** (**the spotlight**) intense public attention.

SYNONYMS **attention**, glare of publicity, limelight, public eye.

▸ verb (**spotlights**, **spotlighting**, past and past participle **spotlighted** or **spotlit**) light up with a spotlight.

spotted ▸ adjective decorated or covered with spots.

SYNONYMS **spotty**, dotted, polka-dot, freckled, mottled.
ANTONYMS plain.

spotty ▸ adjective marked with or having spots.

SYNONYMS **1** *a spotty dress* **polka-dot**, spotted, dotted. **2** *his spotty face* **pimply**, pimpled, acned; Scottish informal plooky.

spouse ▸ noun formal a husband or wife.

SYNONYMS **partner**, husband, wife, mate, consort; informal better half; Brit. informal other half.

spout ▸ noun **1** a projecting tube or lip through or over which liquid can be poured from a container. **2** a stream of liquid flowing out.
▸ verb **1** send out or flow in a stream. **2** express your views in a lengthy and forceful way.
■ **up the spout** Brit. informal useless or ruined.

sprain ▸ verb wrench a joint violently so as to cause pain and swelling.
▸ noun an instance of wrenching a joint.

sprang past of SPRING.

sprat ▶ noun a small sea fish of the herring family.

sprawl ▶ verb 1 sit, lie, or fall with your arms and legs spread out awkwardly. 2 spread out irregularly over a large area.

> SYNONYMS **stretch out**, lounge, loll, slump, flop, slouch.

▶ noun 1 a sprawling position or movement. 2 the disorganized expansion of a town or city.

spray ▶ noun 1 liquid sent through the air in tiny drops. 2 a liquid which can be forced out of an aerosol or other container in a spray. 3 a stem or small branch with flowers and leaves. 4 a small bunch of cut flowers worn on clothing.

> SYNONYMS 1 *a spray of water* **shower**, sprinkle, jet, squirt, mist, spume, foam, froth. 2 *a perfume spray* **aerosol**, vaporizer, atomizer, sprinkler.

▶ verb 1 apply a spray of liquid to something. 2 scatter something over an area with great force.

> SYNONYMS 1 *we sprayed water on the soil* **sprinkle**, dribble, drizzle. 2 *spray the plants with weedkiller* **water**, mist, soak, douse, drench. 3 *water sprayed into the air* **spout**, jet, gush, spurt, shoot, squirt.

spread ▶ verb (spreads, spreading, spread) 1 open out fully. 2 stretch out hands, fingers, wings, etc. 3 extend over a wide area or a specified period of time. 4 apply a substance in an even layer.

> SYNONYMS 1 *he spread the map out* **lay out**, open out, unfurl, unroll, roll out, straighten out, fan out, stretch out, extend. 2 *the landscape spread out below* **extend**, stretch, sprawl. 3 *papers were spread all over his desk* **scatter**, strew, disperse, distribute. 4 *he's spreading rumours* **circulate**, broadcast, put about, publicize, propagate, repeat. 5 *the disease spread rapidly* **travel**, move, be borne, sweep, diffuse, reproduce, be passed on, be transmitted. 6 *she spread sun cream on her arms* **smear**, daub, plaster, apply, rub.
> ANTONYMS fold up, suppress.

▶ noun 1 the process of spreading. 2 the extent, width, or area covered by something. 3 the range of something. 4 a soft paste that can be spread on bread. 5 an article covering several pages of a newspaper or magazine. 6 informal a large and elaborate meal.

> SYNONYMS 1 *the spread of learning* **expansion**, proliferation, dissemination, diffusion, transmission, propagation. 2 *a spread of six feet* **span**, width, extent, stretch, reach.

□ **spreader** noun.

spreadeagle ▶ verb (be spreadeagled) be stretched out with the arms and legs extended.

spreadsheet ▶ noun a computer program in which figures are arranged in a grid and used in calculations.

spree ▶ noun a short period of time spent doing a lot of a particular thing: *a shopping spree*.

> SYNONYMS **bout**, orgy; informal binge, splurge.

sprig ▶ noun a small stem with leaves or flowers, taken from a bush or plant.

sprightly ▶ adjective (sprightlier, sprightliest) (of an old person) lively, energetic.
□ **sprightliness** noun.

spring ▶ verb (springs, springing, sprang or sprung; past participle sprung) 1 move suddenly upwards or forwards. 2 (spring from) come or appear from. 3 (spring up) suddenly develop or appear. 4 (sprung) having springs.

> SYNONYMS 1 *the cat sprang off her lap* **leap**, jump, bound, vault. 2 *the branch sprang back* **fly**, whip, flick, whisk, kick, bounce. 3 *all art springs from feelings* **originate**, derive, arise, stem, emanate, evolve.

▶ noun 1 the season after winter and before summer. 2 a spiral metal coil that returns to its former shape after being pressed or pulled. 3 a sudden jump upwards or forwards. 4 a place where water wells up from an underground source. 5 the quality of being elastic.

> SYNONYMS *the mattress has lost its spring* **springiness**, bounce, resilience, elasticity, flexibility, stretch, stretchiness, give.

■ **spring-clean** clean a house or building thoroughly. **spring-loaded** containing a spring that presses one part against another. **spring onion** Brit. an onion taken from the ground before the bulb has formed.
□ **springy** adjective.

springboard ▶ noun 1 a flexible board from which a diver or gymnast jumps in order to push off more powerfully. 2 something that starts off an activity or enterprise.

springbok ▶ noun a southern African gazelle which leaps when disturbed.

sprinkle ▶ verb (sprinkles, sprinkling, sprinkled) 1 scatter or pour small drops or particles over an object or surface. 2 distribute something randomly throughout.

> SYNONYMS 1 *he sprinkled water on the cloth* **splash**, trickle, drizzle, spray, shower, drip. 2 *sprinkle sesame seeds over*

S

the top **scatter**, strew. **3** *sprinkle the cake with icing sugar* **dredge**, dust.

▶ **noun** a small amount that is sprinkled.

sprinkler ▶ **noun 1** a device for watering lawns. **2** an automatic fire extinguisher installed in a ceiling.

sprint ▶ **verb** run at full speed over a short distance.

> SYNONYMS **run**, race, rush, dash, bolt, fly, charge, shoot, speed; informal hotfoot it, leg it.
> ANTONYMS walk.

▶ **noun 1** a period of sprinting. **2** a short, fast race.
> □ **sprinter** noun.

sprite ▶ **noun** an elf or fairy.

spritzer ▶ **noun** a mixture of wine and soda water.

sprocket ▶ **noun** each of several projections on the rim of a wheel that engage with the links of a chain or with holes in film, paper, etc.

sprout ▶ **verb** produce shoots; begin to grow.

> SYNONYMS **1** *the seeds begin to sprout* **germinate**, put/send out shoots, bud. **2** *parsley sprouted from the pot* **spring**, come up, grow, develop, appear.

▶ **noun 1** a shoot of a plant. **2** a Brussels sprout.

spruce¹ ▶ **adjective** neat and smart.
▶ **verb** (**spruces, sprucing, spruced**) (**spruce someone/thing up**) make someone or something smarter.

spruce² ▶ **noun** an evergreen tree with hanging cones.

sprung past and past participle of **SPRING**.

spry ▶ **adjective** (of an old person) lively.

spud ▶ **noun** informal a potato.

spume ▶ **noun** literary froth or foam.

spun past and past participle of **SPIN**.

spunk ▶ **noun** informal courage and determination.
> □ **spunky** adjective.

spur ▶ **noun 1** a spiked device worn on a rider's heel for urging a horse forward. **2** an encouragement. **3** an area of high ground that sticks out from a mountain. **4** a short branch road or railway line.

> SYNONYMS *the spur of competition* **stimulus**, incentive, encouragement, inducement, impetus, motivation.
> ANTONYMS disincentive.

▶ **verb** (**spurs, spurring, spurred**) **1** encourage someone to do something, or make something happen faster or sooner. **2** urge a horse forward with spurs.

> SYNONYMS *the thought spurred him into action* **stimulate**, encourage, prompt,

prod, impel, motivate, move, galvanize, inspire, drive.
> ANTONYMS discourage.

■ **on the spur of the moment** on a sudden impulse; without planning in advance.

spurious (*rhymes with* curious) ▶ **adjective 1** false or fake. **2** (of reasoning) apparently but not actually correct.
> □ **spuriously** adverb.

spurn ▶ **verb** reject in a contemptuous way.

> SYNONYMS **reject**, rebuff, scorn, turn down, treat with contempt, disdain, look down your nose at; informal turn your nose up at.
> ANTONYMS welcome, accept.

spurt ▶ **verb 1** gush out in a stream. **2** move with a sudden burst of speed.
▶ **noun 1** a gushing stream. **2** a sudden burst of activity or speed.

sputter ▶ **verb** (**sputters, sputtering, sputtered**) make a series of soft explosive sounds.
▶ **noun** a sputtering sound.

sputum ▶ **noun** saliva and mucus that is coughed up.

spy ▶ **noun** (plural **spies**) a person who secretly collects information about an enemy or competitor.

> SYNONYMS *a foreign spy* **agent**, mole, plant; N. Amer. informal spook.

▶ **verb** (**spies, spying, spied**) **1** see or notice. **2** (**spy on**) watch secretly. **3** be a spy.

> SYNONYMS **1** *she spied a coffee shop* **notice**, observe, see, spot, sight, catch sight of, glimpse, make out, discern, detect. **2** (**spying**) **espionage**, intelligence gathering, surveillance, infiltration.

spyglass ▶ **noun** a small telescope.

spyhole ▶ **noun** Brit. a peephole.

sq. ▶ **abbreviation** square.

squab ▶ **noun** a young pigeon that has not yet left the nest.

squabble ▶ **noun** a noisy quarrel about something unimportant.

> SYNONYMS *there was a brief squabble* **quarrel**, disagreement, row, argument, dispute, wrangle, clash, altercation; informal tiff, set-to, run-in, scrap, dust-up; Brit. informal barney, ding-dong; N. Amer. informal rhubarb.

▶ **verb** (**squabbles, squabbling, squabbled**) have a squabble.

> SYNONYMS *they squabbled over money* **quarrel**, row, argue, bicker, disagree; informal scrap.

squad ▶ **noun 1** a division of a police force. **2** a group of sports players from which a team is chosen. **3** a small group of soldiers.

S

SYNONYMS **1** *a maintenance squad* **team,** crew, gang, force. **2** *a squad of marines* **detachment,** detail, unit, platoon, battery, troop, patrol, squadron, commando.

squaddie ▸ noun (plural **squaddies**) Brit. informal a private soldier.

squadron ▸ noun **1** a unit of an air force. **2** a group of warships.

squalid ▸ adjective **1** very dirty and unpleasant. **2** immoral or dishonest.

squall ▸ noun **1** a sudden violent gust of wind. **2** a loud cry.
▸ verb (of a baby) cry noisily and continuously.

squalor ▸ noun the state of being squalid.

squander ▸ verb (**squanders, squandering, squandered**) waste time, money, etc. in a reckless or foolish way.

SYNONYMS **waste,** throw away, misuse, fritter away, spend like water; informal blow, go through, splurge, pour down the drain.
ANTONYMS manage, make good use of, save.

square ▸ noun **1** a flat shape with four equal straight sides and four right angles. **2** an open area surrounded by buildings. **3** the product of a number multiplied by itself. **4** an L-shaped or T-shaped instrument used for obtaining or testing right angles. **5** informal an old-fashioned or boring person.
▸ adjective **1** having the shape of a square. **2** having or forming a right angle. **3** (of a unit of measurement) equal to the area of a square whose side is of the unit specified: *2,000 square feet.* **4** referring to the length of each side of a square shape or object: *ten metres square.* **5** level or parallel. **6** broad and solid in shape. **7** fair or honest. **8** informal old-fashioned or boringly conventional.

SYNONYMS *the sides were square at half-time* **level,** even, drawn, equal, tied, level pegging; informal even-steven(s).
ANTONYMS uneven.

▸ verb (**squares, squaring, squared**) **1** make something square or rectangular. **2** (**squared**) marked out in squares. **3** multiply a number by itself. **4** (**square with**) make or be consistent with. **5** settle a bill or debt. **6** make the score of a game even. **7** (**square up**) take up the position of a person about to fight.

SYNONYMS **1** *this does not square with the data* **agree,** tally, be in agreement, be consistent, match up, correspond, fit. **2** *Tom squared things with his boss* **resolve,** sort out, settle, clear up, work out, iron out, straighten out, set right, rectify, remedy; informal patch up.

■ **square dance** a country dance that starts with four couples facing one another in a square. **square meal** a large and balanced meal. **square root** the number which produces a given number when multiplied by itself.
□ **squarely** adverb.

squash¹ ▸ verb **1** crush or squeeze something so that it becomes flat or distorted. **2** force into a restricted space. **3** stop something from continuing or developing.

SYNONYMS **1** *the fruit got squashed* **crush,** squeeze, mash, pulp, flatten, compress, distort, pound, trample. **2** *she squashed her clothes inside the bag* **force,** ram, thrust, push, cram, jam, stuff, pack, squeeze, wedge.

▸ noun **1** a state of being squashed. **2** Brit. a concentrated liquid mixed with water to make a fruit-flavoured drink. **3** (also **squash rackets**) a game in which two players use rackets to hit a small rubber ball against the walls of a closed court.
□ **squashy** adjective.

squash² ▸ noun a type of vegetable like a marrow.

squat ▸ verb (**squats, squatting, squatted**) **1** crouch or sit with the knees bent and the heels close to the thighs. **2** unlawfully occupy an uninhabited building or area of land.
▸ adjective short or low and wide.
▸ noun **1** a squatting position. **2** a building occupied by squatters.
□ **squatter** noun.

squaw ▸ noun offensive an American Indian woman or wife.

squawk ▸ verb **1** (of a bird) make a loud, harsh noise. **2** say something in a loud, ugly tone.
▸ noun a squawking sound.

squeak ▸ noun a short, high-pitched sound or cry.
▸ verb **1** make a squeak. **2** say something in a high-pitched tone.
□ **squeaky** adjective.

squeal ▸ noun a long, high-pitched cry or noise.
▸ verb **1** make a squeal. **2** say something in a high-pitched tone. **3** (**squeal on**) informal inform on.

squeamish ▸ adjective **1** easily disgusted or made to feel sick. **2** having very strong moral views.

squeegee ▸ noun a scraping tool with a rubber-edged blade, used for cleaning windows.

squeeze ▸ verb (**squeezes, squeezing, squeezed**) **1** firmly press from opposite sides. **2** extract liquid from something by

S

squeezing. **3** manage to get into or through a restricted space.

SYNONYMS **1** *I squeezed the bottle* **compress,** press, crush, squash, pinch, nip, grasp, grip, clutch. **2** *squeeze the juice from both oranges* **extract,** press, force, express. **3** *Sally squeezed her feet into the sandals* **force,** thrust, cram, ram, jam, stuff, pack, wedge, press, squash. **4** *we all squeezed into Steve's van* **crowd,** crush, cram, pack, jam, squash, shove, push, force your way.

▶ **noun 1** an act of squeezing. **2** a hug. **3** a small amount of liquid extracted by squeezing. **4** a strong financial demand or pressure.

SYNONYMS **1** *he gave her hand a squeeze* **press,** pinch, nip, grasp, grip, clutch, hug. **2** *it was quite a squeeze* **crush,** jam, squash, congestion.

□ **squeezy** adjective.

squelch ▶ **verb** make a soft sucking sound, e.g. by treading in thick mud.
▶ **noun** a squelching sound.
□ **squelchy** adjective.

squib ▶ **noun** a small firework.

squid ▶ **noun** (plural **squid** or **squids**) a sea creature with a long body, eight arms, and two long tentacles.

squiffy ▶ **adjective** Brit. informal slightly drunk.

squiggle ▶ **noun** a short line that curls and loops irregularly.
□ **squiggly** adjective.

squint ▶ **verb 1** look at someone or something with your eyes partly closed. **2** have a squint affecting one eye.
▶ **noun 1** a condition in which one eye looks in a different direction from the other. **2** informal a quick or casual look.

squire ▶ **noun 1** a country gentleman. **2** (in the past) a young nobleman who acted as an attendant to a knight.

squirm ▶ **verb 1** wriggle or twist the body from side to side. **2** be embarrassed or ashamed.
▶ **noun** a wriggling movement.

squirrel ▶ **noun** a bushy-tailed rodent which lives in trees.
▶ **verb** (**squirrels, squirrelling, squirrelled;** US spelling **squirrels, squirreling, squirreled**) (**squirrel something away**) hide money or valuables in a safe place.

squirt ▶ **verb 1** force liquid out in a thin jet from a small opening. **2** wet with a jet of liquid.
▶ **noun 1** a thin jet of liquid. **2** informal a weak or insignificant person.

squish ▶ **verb 1** make a soft squelching sound. **2** informal squash.
▶ **noun** a soft squelching sound.
□ **squishy** adjective.

Sri Lankan ▶ **noun** a person from Sri Lanka.
▶ **adjective** relating to Sri Lanka.

SS ▶ **abbreviation 1** Saints. **2** steamship.
▶ **noun** the Nazi special police force.

St ▶ **abbreviation 1** Saint. **2** Street. **3** (**st**) stone (in weight).

stab ▶ **verb** (**stabs, stabbing, stabbed**) **1** thrust a knife or other pointed weapon into. **2** thrust a pointed object at. **3** (of a pain) cause a sudden sharp feeling.

SYNONYMS *he stabbed him in the stomach* **knife,** run through, skewer, spear, gore, spike, impale.

▶ **noun 1** an act of stabbing. **2** a sudden sharp feeling or pain. **3** (**a stab at**) informal an attempt to do.

SYNONYMS **1** *a stab of pain* **twinge,** pang, throb, spasm, cramp, prick, flash, thrill. **2** *a stab at writing* **attempt,** try; informal go, shot, crack, bash.

stability ▶ **noun** the state of being stable.

SYNONYMS **1** *the stability of the equipment* **firmness,** solidity, steadiness. **2** *his mental stability* **balance (of mind),** (mental) health, sanity, reason. **3** *the stability of their relationship* **strength,** durability, lasting nature, permanence.

stabilize (or **stabilise**) ▶ **verb** (**stabilizes, stabilizing, stabilized**) make or become stable.
□ **stabilization** noun **stabilizer** noun.

stable[1] ▶ **adjective 1** not likely to give way or overturn; firmly fixed. **2** not worsening in health after an injury or operation. **3** emotionally well balanced. **4** not likely to change or fail.

SYNONYMS **1** *a stable vehicle* **firm,** solid, steady, secure. **2** *a stable person* **well balanced,** of sound mind, compos mentis, sane, normal, rational. **3** *a stable relationship* **secure,** solid, strong, steady, firm, sure, steadfast, established, enduring, lasting.
ANTONYMS wobbly, unbalanced, rocky, changeable.

□ **stably** adverb.

stable[2] ▶ **noun 1** a building in which horses are kept. **2** an establishment where racehorses are kept and trained.
▶ **verb** (**stables, stabling, stabled**) put or keep a horse in a stable.

stablemate ▶ **noun** a horse from the same stable as another.

staccato /stuh-kah-toh/ ▶ **adjective** Music with each sound or note sharply separated from the others.

stack ▶ **noun 1** a neat pile of objects. **2** a rectangular or cylindrical pile of hay, straw, etc. **3** informal a large quantity. **4** a chimney.

S

SYNONYMS *a stack of boxes* **heap**, pile, mound, mountain, pyramid, tower.

▶ verb **1** arrange in a stack. **2** fill or cover with stacks of things. **3** cause aircraft to fly at different altitudes while waiting to land. **4** arrange a pack of cards dishonestly.

SYNONYMS **1** *Leo was stacking plates* **heap (up)**, pile (up), assemble, put together, collect. **2** *they stacked the shelves* **load,** fill (up), pack, charge, stuff, cram, stock.
ANTONYMS clear.

stadium ▶ noun (plural **stadiums** or **stadia**) a sports ground with rows of seats for spectators.

staff ▶ noun **1** the employees of an organization. **2** a group of military officers assisting an officer in command. **3** a long stick used as a support or weapon. **4** a rod or sceptre held as a symbol of office or authority. **5** Music a stave.

SYNONYMS **1** *we'll take on new staff* **employees,** workers, workforce, personnel, human resources, manpower, labour. **2** *a wooden staff* **stick,** stave, pole, rod.

▶ verb provide an organization with staff.

SYNONYMS *the centre is staffed by teachers* **man,** people, crew, work, operate.

■ **staff nurse** Brit. an experienced nurse less senior than a sister.

stag ▶ noun a fully adult male deer.
■ **stag night** an all-male celebration held for a man who is about to get married.

stage ▶ noun **1** a point or step in a process or development. **2** a raised platform on which actors, entertainers, or speakers perform. **3** (**the stage**) the acting profession. **4** a platform on to which passengers or cargo can be landed from a boat.

SYNONYMS **1** *this stage of the development* **phase,** period, juncture, step, point, level. **2** *the last stage of the race* **part,** section, portion, stretch, leg, lap, circuit. **3** *a raised stage* **platform,** dais, stand, rostrum, podium.

▶ verb (**stages, staging, staged**) **1** present a performance of a play. **2** organize an event.
■ **stage fright** nervousness before or during a performance. **stage-manage** arrange something carefully to create a certain effect. **stage manager** the person responsible for lighting and other technical arrangements for a play. **stage-struck** having a strong desire to become an actor. **stage whisper** a loud whisper by an actor on stage, intended to be heard by the audience. **staging post** a regular stop on a journey.

stagecoach ▶ noun a horse-drawn vehicle formerly used to carry passengers along a regular route.

stagehand ▶ noun a person who deals with the scenery or props for a play.

stagger ▶ verb (**staggers, staggering, staggered**) **1** walk or move unsteadily. **2** astonish. **3** spread over a period of time.

SYNONYMS **1** *he staggered to the door* **lurch,** reel, sway, teeter, totter, stumble. **2** *I was absolutely staggered* **amaze,** astound, astonish, surprise, stun, confound, daze, take aback; informal flabbergast; Brit. informal gobsmack.

▶ noun an unsteady walk.

stagnant ▶ adjective **1** (of water or air) not moving and having an unpleasant smell. **2** showing little activity.

stagnate ▶ verb (**stagnates, stagnating, stagnated**) become stagnant.
□ **stagnation** noun.

stagy (or **stagey**) ▶ adjective very theatrical or exaggerated.

staid ▶ adjective respectable and unadventurous.

stain ▶ verb **1** mark or discolour with something that is not easily removed. **2** damage someone's reputation. **3** colour with a dye or chemical.

SYNONYMS **1** *her clothing was stained with blood* **discolour,** soil, mark, spot, spatter, splatter, smear, splash, smudge. **2** *the wood was stained* **colour,** tint, dye, pigment.

▶ noun **1** a discoloured patch or mark. **2** a thing that damages someone's reputation. **3** a dye or chemical used to colour materials.

SYNONYMS **1** *a mud stain* **mark,** spot, blotch, smudge, smear. **2** *a stain on his character* **blemish,** taint, blot, smear, dishonour.

■ **stained glass** coloured glass used to form pictures or designs. **stainless steel** a form of steel containing chromium, resistant to tarnishing and rust.
□ **stainless** adjective.

stair ▶ noun **1** each of a set of fixed steps. **2** (**stairs**) a set of steps leading from one floor of a building to another.

staircase (or **stairway**) ▶ noun a set of stairs and its surrounding structure.

stairwell ▶ noun a shaft in which a staircase is built.

stake¹ ▶ noun a strong post driven into the ground to support a tree, form part of a fence, etc.

SYNONYMS *a stake in the ground* **post,** pole, stick, spike, upright, support, cane.

▶ verb (**stakes, staking, staked**) **1** support with a stake. **2** (**stake something out**) mark an area with stakes to claim ownership.

S

3 (stake someone/thing out) informal keep a place or person under observation.

stake² ▸ noun **1** a sum of money gambled. **2** a share or interest in a business or situation. **3** (stakes) prize money, especially in horse racing. **4** (stakes) a competitive situation.

SYNONYMS **1** *high stakes* **bet**, wager, ante. **2** *a 40% stake in the business* **share**, interest, ownership, involvement.

▸ verb (stakes, staking, staked) gamble money or valuables.

SYNONYMS *he staked his week's pay* **bet**, wager, lay, put on, gamble.

■ at stake **1** at risk. **2** in question.

stakeholder ▸ noun a person who has an interest in a business, project, etc., especially because they have invested money in it.

stalactite ▸ noun a tapering structure hanging from the roof of a cave, formed of calcium salts deposited by dripping water.

stalagmite ▸ noun a tapering column rising from the floor of a cave, formed of calcium salts deposited by dripping water.

stale ▸ adjective **1** (of food) no longer fresh. **2** no longer new and interesting. **3** no longer interested or motivated.

SYNONYMS **1** *stale food* **old**, past its best, off, dry, hard, musty, rancid. **2** *stale air* **stuffy**, musty, fusty, stagnant. **3** *stale beer* **flat**, spoiled, off, insipid, tasteless. **4** *stale jokes* **overused**, hackneyed, tired, worn out, overworked, threadbare, banal, clichéd; N. Amer. played out. ANTONYMS fresh, original.

□ staleness noun.

stalemate ▸ noun **1** a situation in which further progress by opposing sides seems impossible. **2** Chess a position in which a player is not in check but can only move into check.

stalk¹ ▸ noun **1** the stem of a plant or support of a leaf, flower, or fruit. **2** a slender support or stem.

stalk² ▸ verb **1** follow or approach stealthily. **2** obsessively follow, watch, or try to communicate with a particular person. **3** walk in a proud, stiff, or angry way.

SYNONYMS **1** *he was stalking a deer* **trail**, follow, shadow, track, go after, hunt; informal tail. **2** *she stalked out* **strut**, stride, march, flounce, storm, stomp, sweep.

□ stalker noun.

stall ▸ noun **1** a stand or booth where goods are sold in a market. **2** a compartment for an animal in a stable or cowshed. **3** a compartment in which a horse is held before the start of a race. **4** a compartment in a set of toilets. **5** (stalls) Brit. the ground-floor seats in a theatre. **6** a seat in the choir or chancel of a church.

SYNONYMS **1** *a market stall* **stand**, table, counter, booth, kiosk. **2** *stalls for larger animals* **pen**, coop, sty, corral, enclosure, compartment.

▸ verb **1** (of a vehicle's engine) suddenly stop running. **2** stop making progress. **3** be vague or indecisive so as to gain more time to deal with something. **4** (of an aircraft) be moving too slowly to be controlled effectively.

SYNONYMS **1** *quit stalling* **delay**, play for time, procrastinate, hedge, drag your feet, filibuster, stonewall. **2** *stall him for a bit* **delay**, divert, distract, hold off.

stallion ▸ noun an adult male horse that has not been castrated.

stalwart ▸ adjective loyal, reliable, and hard-working.

SYNONYMS **staunch**, loyal, faithful, committed, devoted, dedicated, dependable, reliable. ANTONYMS disloyal, unfaithful, unreliable.

▸ noun a stalwart supporter or member of an organization.

stamen /stay-muhn/ ▸ noun a male fertilizing organ of a flower.

stamina ▸ noun the ability to keep up effort over a long period.

SYNONYMS **endurance**, staying power, energy, toughness, determination, tenacity, perseverance, grit.

stammer ▸ verb (stammers, stammering, stammered) speak or say with difficulty, making sudden pauses and repeating the first letters of words.

SYNONYMS **stutter**, stumble over your words, hesitate, falter, pause, splutter.

▸ noun a tendency to stammer.

stamp ▸ verb **1** bring down your foot heavily. **2** walk with heavy, forceful steps. **3** (stamp something out) decisively put an end to something. **4** press with a device that leaves a mark or pattern.

SYNONYMS **1** *he stamped on my toe* **trample**, step, tread, tramp, crush, squash, flatten. **2** *John stamped off, muttering* **stomp**, stump, clump. **3** *the name is stamped on the cover* **imprint**, print, impress, punch, inscribe, emboss.

▸ noun **1** a small piece of paper stuck to a letter or parcel to record payment of postage. **2** an instrument for stamping a pattern or mark. **3** a mark or pattern made by a stamp. **4** a characteristic impression or quality. **5** an act of stamping the foot.

SYNONYMS *the stamp of authority* **mark,** hallmark, sign, seal, sure sign, smack, savour, air.

■ **stamp duty** a tax on some legal documents. **stamping ground** a place you regularly visit or spend time in.

stampede ▸ noun **1** a sudden panicked rush of a number of horses, cattle, etc. **2** a sudden mass movement or reaction due to interest or panic.
▸ verb (**stampedes, stampeding, stampeded**) take part in a stampede.

stance ▸ noun **1** the way in which someone stands. **2** an attitude or standpoint.

SYNONYMS **1** *a natural golfer's stance* **posture,** body position, pose, attitude. **2** *a liberal stance* **attitude,** opinion, standpoint, position, approach, policy, line.

stanch US spelling of STAUNCH².

stanchion ▸ noun an upright bar, post, or frame forming a support or barrier.

stand ▸ verb (**stands, standing, stood**) **1** be or become upright, supported by the feet. **2** place or be situated in a particular position. **3** remain stationary, undisturbed, or unchanged. **4** be in a particular state or condition. **5** tolerate or like. **6** Brit. be a candidate in an election.

SYNONYMS **1** *the men stood up* **rise,** get to your feet, get up, pick yourself up. **2** *today a house stands on the site* **be situated,** be located, be positioned, be sited, have been built. **3** *he stood the vase on the shelf* **put,** set, erect, place, position, prop, install, arrange; informal park. **4** *my decision stands* **remain in force,** remain in operation, hold, hold good, apply, be the case, exist. **5** *his heart could not stand the strain* **withstand,** endure, bear, put up with, take, cope with, handle, sustain, resist, stand up to. **6** *I won't stand cheek* **put up with,** endure, tolerate, accept, take, abide, stand for, support, countenance; formal brook.
ANTONYMS sit, lie down.

▸ noun **1** an attitude towards an issue. **2** a determined effort to hold your ground or resist something. **3** a structure for holding or displaying something. **4** a large structure for spectators to sit or stand in. **5** a raised platform for a band, orchestra, or speaker. **6** a stall from which goods are sold or displayed. **7** (**the stand**) the witness box in a law court. **8** a stopping of motion or progress.

SYNONYMS **1** *the party's stand on immigration* **attitude,** stance, opinion, standpoint, position, approach, policy, line. **2** *a stand against tyranny*

opposition, resistance. **3** *a mirror on a stand* **base,** support, platform, rest, plinth, tripod, rack, trivet. **4** *a newspaper stand* **stall,** counter, booth, kiosk.

■ **stand by 1** look on without becoming involved. **2** support or remain loyal to. **3** be ready to take action if needed. **stand down** (or **aside**) resign from a position or office. **stand for 1** be an abbreviation of or symbol for. **2** put up with. **stand in** deputize for someone. **stand-off** a deadlock between two opponents. **stand-offish** informal distant and cold in manner. **stand out 1** stick out or be easily noticeable. **2** be clearly better. **stand someone up** informal fail to keep a date with someone. **stand up for** speak or act in support of.

❗ Use **standing** rather than **stood** with the verb 'to be': say *we were standing in a line for hours* rather than *we were stood in a line for hours.*

standard ▸ noun **1** a level of quality or achievement. **2** a measure or model used to make comparisons. **3** (**standards**) principles of good behaviour. **4** a military or ceremonial flag.

SYNONYMS **1** *the standard of her work* **quality,** level, calibre, merit, excellence. **2** *a safety standard* **guideline,** norm, yardstick, benchmark, measure, criterion, guide. **3** *a standard to live by* **principle,** ideal; (**standards**) code of behaviour, morals, ethics. **4** *the regiment's standard* **flag,** banner, ensign, colour(s).

▸ adjective used or accepted as normal or average.

SYNONYMS **1** *the standard way of doing it* **normal,** usual, typical, stock, common, ordinary, customary, conventional, established. **2** *the standard work on the subject* **definitive,** classic, recognized, accepted.
ANTONYMS unusual, special.

■ **standard-bearer 1** a leading figure in a cause or movement. **2** a soldier who carries a military or ceremonial flag. **standard English** the dialect of English used by most educated English speakers. **standard lamp** a tall lamp that is placed on the floor. **standard of living** the degree of comfort that a person or community has.

standardize (or **standardise**) ▸ verb (**standardizes, standardizing, standardized**) make something fit in with a standard. ▢ **standardization** noun.

standby ▸ noun (plural **standbys**) **1** readiness for duty or action. **2** a person or thing ready to be used in an emergency.
▸ adjective (of tickets) sold only at the last minute.

S

standing ▶ noun **1** position, status, or reputation. **2** duration or length.

SYNONYMS **1** *his standing in the community* **status**, ranking, position, reputation, stature. **2** *a person of some standing* **prestige**, rank, eminence, seniority, repute, stature, esteem, importance, account.

▶ adjective remaining in force or use: *a standing invitation.*
■ **standing joke** something that regularly causes amusement. **standing order** Brit. an instruction to a bank to make regular fixed payments to someone. **standing ovation** a long period of applause during which the audience rise to their feet.

standpoint ▶ noun an attitude towards a particular issue.

standstill ▶ noun a situation or condition without movement or activity.

stank past of STINK.

stanza ▶ noun a group of lines forming the basic unit in a poem.

staple¹ ▶ noun **1** a small piece of wire used to fasten papers together. **2** a small U-shaped metal bar driven into wood to hold things in place.
▶ verb (**staples, stapling, stapled**) secure with a staple or staples.
□ **stapler** noun.

staple² ▶ noun **1** a main item of trade or production. **2** a main or important element.
▶ adjective main or important.

SYNONYMS **main**, principal, chief, major, primary, leading, foremost, first, most important, predominant, dominant, basic, prime; informal number-one.

star ▶ noun **1** a large ball of burning gas which appears as a glowing point in the night sky. **2** a simplified representation of a star with five or six points. **3** a famous entertainer or sports player.

SYNONYMS **1** *the sky was full of stars* **celestial/heavenly body**, sun. **2** *the stars of the film* **principal**, leading lady/man, lead, hero, heroine. **3** *a star of the world of chess* **celebrity**, superstar, famous name, household name, leading light, VIP, personality, luminary; informal celeb, big shot, megastar.
ANTONYMS nobody.

▶ adjective **1** outstandingly successful. **2** very famous.

SYNONYMS **1** *a star pupil* **outstanding**, exceptional. **2** *the star attraction* **top**, leading, greatest, foremost, major, pre-eminent.
ANTONYMS poor, minor.

▶ verb (**stars, starring, starred**) **1** have someone as a leading performer. **2** have a leading role in a film, play, etc.

■ **Stars and Stripes** the national flag of the US. **star sign** a sign of the zodiac.
□ **stardom** noun.

starboard ▶ noun the side of a ship or aircraft that is on the right when you are facing forward.

starch ▶ noun **1** a carbohydrate which is obtained from potatoes, flour, rice, etc. and is an important part of the human diet. **2** powder or spray used to stiffen fabric.
▶ verb stiffen with starch.

starchy ▶ adjective (**starchier, starchiest**) **1** containing a lot of starch. **2** informal stiff and formal in manner.

stare ▶ verb (**stares, staring, stared**) look with concentration and the eyes wide open.

SYNONYMS **gaze**, gape, goggle, glare, ogle, peer; informal gawk; Brit. informal gawp.

▶ noun an act of staring.

starfish ▶ noun (plural **starfish** or **starfishes**) a sea creature having five or more arms extending from a central point.

stark ▶ adjective **1** severe or bare in appearance. **2** unpleasantly or sharply clear. **3** complete; sheer: *stark terror.*

SYNONYMS **1** *a stark silhouette* **sharp**, crisp, distinct, clear, clear-cut. **2** *a stark landscape* **desolate**, bare, barren, empty, bleak. **3** *a stark room* **austere**, severe, plain, simple, bare, unadorned. **4** *stark terror* **sheer**, utter, absolute, total, pure, downright, out-and-out, outright. **5** *the stark facts* **blunt**, bald, bare, simple, plain, unvarnished, harsh, grim.
ANTONYMS fuzzy, indistinct, lush, ornate, disguised.

■ **stark naked** completely naked.
□ **starkly** adverb.

starkers ▶ adjective Brit. informal completely naked.

starlet ▶ noun informal a promising young actress or performer.

starling ▶ noun a bird with shiny dark speckled feathers.

starry ▶ adjective (**starrier, starriest**) full of or lit by stars.
■ **starry-eyed** full of unrealistic hopes or dreams.

starship ▶ noun (in science fiction) a spaceship for travel between stars.

start ▶ verb **1** begin to do or happen. **2** begin to operate or start working. **3** make something happen or start working. **4** begin to move or travel. **5** (**start out** or **up**) begin a project or undertaking. **6** jump or jerk from surprise.

SYNONYMS **1** *the meeting starts at 7.45* **begin**, commence, get under way, get going, go ahead; informal kick off. **2** *this was how her illness started* **come into being/existence**, begin, commence, be

born, arise, originate, develop. **3** *she started her own charity* **establish**, set up, found, create, bring into being, institute, initiate, inaugurate, introduce, open, launch. **4** *you can start the machine* **activate**, switch/turn on, start up, fire up, boot up. **5** *the machine started* **begin working**, start up, get going, spring into life. **6** *'Oh my!' she said, starting* **flinch**, jerk, jump, twitch, wince.
ANTONYMS finish, stop, wind up, close down.

▶ noun **1** an act of beginning. **2** the point at which something begins. **3** an advantage given to a competitor at the beginning of a race. **4** a sudden movement of surprise.

SYNONYMS **1** *the start of the event* **beginning**, commencement, inception. **2** *the start of her illness* **onset**, emergence. **3** *a quarter of an hour's start* **lead**, head start, advantage. **4** *she awoke with a start* **jerk**, twitch, spasm, jump.
ANTONYMS end, finish.

starter ▶ noun **1** a person or thing that starts. **2** the first course of a meal.

startle ▶ verb (**startles, startling, startled**) make someone feel sudden shock or alarm.

SYNONYMS **surprise**, frighten, scare, alarm, shock, give someone a fright, make someone jump.
ANTONYMS put at ease.

☐ **startled** adjective.

startling ▶ adjective very surprising.
☐ **startlingly** adverb.

starve ▶ verb (**starves, starving, starved**) **1** suffer or die from hunger. **2** make someone starve. **3** (**be starving** or **starved**) informal feel very hungry. **4** (**be starved of**) be deprived of.

SYNONYMS (**starving**) **hungry**, undernourished, malnourished, starved, ravenous, famished.
ANTONYMS full.

☐ **starvation** noun.

stash informal ▶ verb store safely in a secret place.
▶ noun a secret store.

stasis /stay-sis/ ▶ noun formal a period or state when there is no activity or change.

state ▶ noun **1** the condition of someone or something at a particular time. **2** a country considered as an organized political community. **3** an area forming part of a federal republic. **4** (**the States**) the United States of America. **5** the government of a country. **6** the ceremonial procedures associated with monarchy or government. **7** (**a state**) informal an agitated, untidy, or dirty condition.

SYNONYMS **1** *the state of the economy* **condition**, shape, position, predicament,

plight. **2** *an autonomous state* **country**, nation, land, kingdom, realm, power, republic. **3** *the country is divided into thirty-two states* **province**, region, territory, canton, department, county, district; Brit. shire. **4** *the power of the state* **government**, parliament, administration, regime, authorities.

▶ verb (**states, stating, stated**) express definitely in speech or writing.

SYNONYMS **express**, voice, utter, put into words, declare, announce, make known, put across/over, communicate, air.

■ **state-of-the-art** very up to date.
☐ **stateless** adjective.

stately ▶ adjective (**statelier, stateliest**) dignified, imposing, or grand.

SYNONYMS **dignified**, majestic, ceremonious, courtly, imposing, solemn, regal, grand.
ANTONYMS undignified.

■ **stately home** Brit. a large and fine house occupied or formerly occupied by an aristocratic family.

statement ▶ noun **1** a clear expression of something in speech or writing. **2** an account of events given to the police or in court. **3** a list of amounts paid into and out of a bank account.

SYNONYMS **declaration**, expression, affirmation, assertion, announcement, utterance, communication, bulletin, communiqué.

stateroom ▶ noun **1** a private room on a ship. **2** a large room in a palace or public building, for use on formal occasions.

stateside ▶ adjective & adverb informal relating to or towards the US.

statesman (or **stateswoman**) ▶ noun (plural **statesmen** or **stateswomen**) an experienced and respected political leader.

static ▶ adjective not moving, acting, or changing.
▶ noun **1** (also **static electricity**) an electric charge acquired by an object that is not a conductor of electricity. **2** crackling or hissing on a telephone, radio, etc.
☐ **statically** adverb.

station ▶ noun **1** a place where passenger trains stop on a railway line. **2** a place where an activity or service is based. **3** a broadcasting company. **4** the place where someone or something stands or is placed. **5** dated a person's social rank or position.

SYNONYMS **1** *a research station* **establishment**, base, camp, post, depot, mission, site, facility, installation. **2** *a police station* **office**, depot, base, headquarters; N. Amer. precinct, station house. **3** *a radio station* **channel**, wavelength.

S

▶ **verb** put someone in a particular place or position.

> SYNONYMS *the regiment was stationed at Woolwich* **base,** post, establish, deploy, garrison.

■ **station wagon** N. Amer. Austral./NZ an estate car.

stationary ▶ **adjective** not moving or changing.

> SYNONYMS **static,** parked, motionless, immobile, still, stock-still, at a standstill, at rest.
> ANTONYMS moving, shifting.

> ❗ Don't confuse **stationary** and **stationery**: **stationary** means 'not moving or changing', whereas **stationery** means 'paper and other writing materials'.

stationer ▶ **noun** a person who sells stationery.

stationery ▶ **noun** paper and other materials needed for writing.

stationmaster ▶ **noun** a person in charge of a railway station.

statistic ▶ **noun 1** (**statistics**) the collection and analysis of large amounts of information shown in numbers. **2** a fact or piece of data obtained from a study of statistics.
□ **statistician** noun.

statistical ▶ **adjective** relating to statistics.
□ **statistically** adverb.

statuary ▶ **noun** statues.

statue ▶ **noun** a model of a person or animal made of stone, metal, etc.

statuesque ▶ **adjective** (of a woman) attractively tall and dignified.

statuette ▶ **noun** a small statue.

stature ▶ **noun 1** a person's height when they are standing. **2** importance or reputation.

> SYNONYMS **1** *small in stature* **height,** size, build. **2** *an architect of international stature* **reputation,** repute, standing, status, position, prestige, distinction, eminence, prominence, importance.

status ▶ **noun 1** a person's social or professional position. **2** high rank or social standing. **3** the situation at a particular time.

> SYNONYMS **1** *the status of women* **standing,** rank, position, level, place. **2** *wealth and status* **prestige,** kudos, cachet, standing, stature, esteem, image, importance, authority, fame.

■ **status symbol** a possession intended to show a person's wealth or high status.

status quo /stay-tuhss kwoh/ ▶ **noun** the existing situation.

statute ▶ **noun 1** a written law. **2** a rule of an organization or institution.

statutory ▶ **adjective 1** required or permitted by law. **2** done or happening regularly and therefore expected.

staunch[1] ▶ **adjective** very loyal and committed.

> SYNONYMS *a staunch supporter* **stalwart,** loyal, faithful, committed, devoted, dedicated, reliable.
> ANTONYMS disloyal, unfaithful, unreliable.

□ **staunchly** adverb.

staunch[2] (US spelling **stanch**) ▶ **verb** stop or slow down a flow of blood.

> SYNONYMS *try to staunch the flow* **stem,** stop, halt, check, curb; N. Amer. stanch.

stave ▶ **noun 1** any of the lengths of wood fixed side by side to make a barrel, bucket, etc. **2** a strong stick, post, or pole. **3** (also **staff**) Music a set of five parallel lines which notes are written on or between.
▶ **verb** (**staves, staving,** past and past participle **staved** or **stove**) **1** (**stave something in**) break something by forcing it inwards. **2** (past and past participle **staved**) (**stave something off**) stop or delay something bad or dangerous.

stay ▶ **verb 1** remain in the same place. **2** remain in a particular state or position. **3** live somewhere temporarily as a visitor or guest. **4** stop, delay, or prevent.

> SYNONYMS **1** *he stayed where he was* **remain (behind),** wait, linger, stick, be left, hold on, hang on; informal hang around; Brit. informal hang about. **2** *they won't stay hidden* **continue (to be),** remain, keep, carry on being, go on being. **3** *our aunt is staying with us* **visit,** stop (off/over), holiday, lodge; N. Amer. vacation.
> ANTONYMS leave, stop being.

▶ **noun 1** a period of staying somewhere. **2** a brace or support. **3** (**stays**) historical a corset stiffened by strips of whalebone.

> SYNONYMS *a stay at a hotel* **visit,** stop, stopover, break, holiday; N. Amer. vacation.

■ **staying power** informal endurance or stamina. **stay of execution** a delay in carrying out the orders of a law court.

stead ▶ **noun** (**in someone's or something's stead**) instead of someone or something.
■ **stand someone in good stead** be useful to someone over time.

steadfast ▶ **adjective** not changing in your attitudes or aims.
□ **steadfastly** adverb.

steady ▶ **adjective** (**steadier, steadiest**) **1** firmly fixed, supported, or balanced. **2** not faltering or wavering. **3** sensible and

S

reliable. **4** regular, even, and continuous.

SYNONYMS **1** *the ladder must be steady* **stable,** firm, fixed, secure. **2** *keep the camera steady* **still,** motionless, static, stationary. **3** *a steady gaze* **fixed,** intent, unwavering, unfaltering. **4** *a steady income* **constant,** regular, consistent, reliable. **5** *steady rain* **continuous,** continual, unceasing, ceaseless, perpetual, unremitting, endless. **6** *a steady boyfriend* **regular,** settled, firm, committed, long-term.
ANTONYMS unstable, loose, shaky, darting, fluctuating, sporadic, occasional.

▸ verb (**steadies, steadying, steadied**) make steady.

SYNONYMS **1** *he steadied the rifle* **stabilize,** hold steady, brace, support, balance, rest. **2** *she needed to steady her nerves* **calm,** soothe, quieten, compose, settle, subdue, quell.

□ **steadily** adverb **steadiness** noun.

steak ▸ noun **1** high-quality beef cut into thick slices for grilling or frying. **2** a thick slice of other meat or fish. **3** poorer-quality beef for stewing.

steal ▸ verb (**steals, stealing, stole**; past participle **stolen**) **1** take something without permission and without intending to return it. **2** move quietly or secretively.

SYNONYMS **1** *burglars stole the TV* **take,** thieve, help yourself to, pilfer, embezzle; informal swipe, lift, filch; Brit. informal nick, pinch, knock off; N. Amer. informal heist. **2** *his work was stolen by his tutor* **plagiarize,** copy, pirate; informal rip off, lift, pinch, crib; Brit. informal nick. **3** *he stole out of the room* **creep,** sneak, slink, slip, glide, tiptoe, slope.

▸ noun informal a bargain.
■ **steal the show** attract the most attention and praise.

stealth ▸ noun cautious and secretive action or movement.

SYNONYMS **furtiveness,** secretiveness, secrecy, surreptitiousness.
ANTONYMS openness.

stealthy ▸ adjective (**stealthier, stealthiest**) cautious and secretive.

SYNONYMS **furtive,** secretive, secret, surreptitious, sneaky, sly.
ANTONYMS open.

□ **stealthily** adverb.

steam ▸ noun **1** the hot vapour into which water is converted when heated. **2** power produced by steam under pressure. **3** momentum.
▸ verb **1** give off or produce steam. **2** (**steam up**) mist over with steam. **3** cook food by heating it in steam from boiling water.

4 (of a ship or train) travel under steam power. **5** informal move quickly or forcefully.
□ **steamer** noun.

steamroller ▸ noun a heavy, slow vehicle with a roller, used to flatten the surfaces of roads.
▸ verb (**steamrollers, steamrollering, steamrollered**) **1** force someone into doing or accepting something. **2** forcibly pass a law.

steamship ▸ noun a ship that is propelled by a steam engine.

steamy ▸ adjective (**steamier, steamiest**) **1** producing or filled with steam. **2** informal involving passionate sexual activity.

steed ▸ noun literary a horse.

steel ▸ noun **1** a hard, strong metal that is a mixture of iron and carbon. **2** strength and determination.
▸ verb mentally prepare yourself for something difficult.
■ **steel band** a band that plays music on drums made from empty oil containers.

steelworks ▸ plural noun a factory where steel is produced.

steely ▸ adjective (**steelier, steeliest**) **1** like steel. **2** coldly determined.

steep[1] ▸ adjective **1** rising or falling sharply. **2** (of a rise or fall in an amount) very large or rapid. **3** informal (of a price or demand) too great.

SYNONYMS **1** *steep cliffs* **sheer,** precipitous, abrupt, sharp, perpendicular, vertical. **2** *a steep increase* **sharp,** sudden, dramatic.
ANTONYMS gentle, gradual, reasonable.

□ **steepen** verb **steeply** adverb.

steep[2] ▸ verb **1** soak in water or other liquid. **2** (**be steeped in**) have a lot of a particular quality or atmosphere.

SYNONYMS (**steeped in**) *a city steeped in history* **imbued with,** filled with, permeated with, suffused with, soaked in, pervaded by.

steeple ▸ noun a church tower and spire.

steeplechase ▸ noun **1** a horse race with ditches and hedges as jumps. **2** a race in which runners must clear hurdles and water jumps.
□ **steeplechaser** noun.

steeplejack ▸ noun a person who climbs tall structures such as chimneys and steeples to repair them.

steer[1] ▸ verb **1** guide or control the movement of a vehicle, ship, etc. **2** direct or guide.

SYNONYMS **guide,** direct, manoeuvre, drive, pilot, navigate.

■ **steer clear of** take care to avoid. **steering**

S

wheel a wheel that a driver turns in order to steer a vehicle.

steer² ▸ noun a bullock.

steerage ▸ noun (in the past) the cheapest accommodation in a ship.

steersman ▸ noun (plural **steersmen**) a person who steers a boat or ship.

stegosaurus ▸ noun a plant-eating dinosaur with large bony plates along the back.

stein /styn/ ▸ noun a large earthenware beer mug.

stellar ▸ adjective having to do with a star or stars.

stem¹ ▸ noun 1 the long, thin main part of a plant or shrub, or support of a fruit, flower, or leaf. 2 a long, thin supporting part of a wine glass, tobacco pipe, etc. 3 a vertical stroke in a letter or musical note. 4 the root or main part of a word.

SYNONYMS *a plant stem* **stalk**, shoot, trunk.

▸ verb (**stems, stemming, stemmed**) (**stem from**) come from or be caused by.

stem² ▸ verb (**stems, stemming, stemmed**) stop or slow down the flow or progress of something.

SYNONYMS *they stemmed the flow of blood* **stop**, staunch, halt, check, curb; N. Amer. stanch.

stench ▸ noun a strong and very unpleasant smell.

stencil ▸ noun a thin sheet with a pattern or letters cut out of it, used to produce a design by applying ink or paint through the holes.

▸ verb (**stencils, stencilling, stencilled;** US spelling **stencils, stenciling, stenciled**) decorate or form something with a stencil.

stenographer /sti-**nog**-ruh-fer/ ▸ noun N. Amer. a shorthand typist.

stentorian ▸ adjective (of a person's voice) loud and powerful.

step ▸ noun 1 an act of lifting and putting down the foot or feet in walking. 2 the distance covered by a step. 3 a flat surface on which to place the feet when moving from one level to another. 4 a position or grade in a scale or ranking. 5 a measure or action taken to deal with something.

SYNONYMS 1 *Frank took a step forward* **pace**, stride. 2 *she heard a step on the stairs* **footstep**, footfall, tread. 3 *the top step* **stair**, tread; (**steps**) stairs, staircase, flight of stairs. 4 *resigning is a very serious step* **action**, act, course of action, measure, move, operation. 5 *a significant step towards a ceasefire* **advance**, development, move, movement, breakthrough. 6 *the first step on the*

managerial ladder **stage**, level, grade, rank, degree, phase.

▸ verb (**steps, stepping, stepped**) lift and put down your foot or feet.

SYNONYMS *she stepped forward* **walk**, move, tread, pace, stride.

■ **step down** resign from a job or post. **step in** become involved in a difficult situation. **stepping stone 1** a raised stone which you can step on when crossing a stream. **2** something that helps you make progress towards a goal. **step something up** increase the amount, speed, or strength of.

stepbrother ▸ noun a son of a person's stepfather or stepmother.

stepchild ▸ noun (plural **stepchildren**) a child of a person's husband or wife from a previous marriage.

stepdaughter ▸ noun a daughter of a person's husband or wife from a previous marriage.

stepfather ▸ noun a man who is married to a person's mother but is not his or her father.

stepladder ▸ noun a short free-standing folding ladder.

stepmother ▸ noun a woman who is married to a person's father but is not his or her mother.

steppe ▸ noun a large area of flat unforested grassland in SE Europe and Siberia.

stepsister ▸ noun a daughter of a person's stepfather or stepmother.

stepson ▸ noun a son of a person's husband or wife from a previous marriage.

stereo ▸ noun (plural **stereos**) 1 music or sound that come from two or more speakers and seems to surround you. 2 a CD player, record player, etc. that has two or more speakers.

▸ adjective (also **stereophonic**) relating to this kind of sound.

stereotype ▸ noun an oversimplified idea of the typical characteristics of a person or thing.

SYNONYMS *the stereotype of the woman as carer* **conventional idea**, standard image, cliché, formula.

▸ verb (**stereotypes, stereotyping, stereotyped**) represent as a stereotype.

SYNONYMS *bodybuilders are stereotyped as 'muscleheads'* **typecast**, pigeonhole, conventionalize, categorize, label, tag.

□ **stereotypical** adjective.

sterile ▸ adjective 1 not able to produce children, young, crops, or fruit. 2 not imaginative, creative, or exciting. 3 free from bacteria.

SYNONYMS 1 *sterile desert* **unproductive**, infertile, unfruitful, barren. 2 *sterile*

S

conditions **hygienic,** clean, pure, uncontaminated, sterilized, disinfected, germ-free, antiseptic. **ANTONYMS** fertile, productive, septic.

□ **sterility** noun.

sterilize (or **sterilise**) ▶ verb (**sterilizes, sterilizing, sterilized**) make sterile.
□ **sterilization** noun.

sterling ▶ noun British money.
▶ adjective **1** excellent. **2** (of silver) of at least 92¼ per cent purity.

stern¹ ▶ adjective **1** grimly serious or strict. **2** severe.

SYNONYMS 1 *a stern expression* unsmiling, frowning, serious, severe, forbidding, grim, unfriendly, austere, dour. **2** *stern measures* strict, severe, stringent, harsh, drastic, hard, tough, extreme, draconian. **ANTONYMS** genial, friendly, lenient, lax.

□ **sternly** adverb.

stern² ▶ noun the rear end of a ship or boat.

sternum ▶ noun the breastbone.

steroid /ste-royd, steer-oyd/ ▶ noun **1** any of a class of substances that includes certain hormones and vitamins. **2** an anabolic steroid.

stertorous /ster-tuh-ruhss/ ▶ adjective (of breathing) noisy and laboured.

stethoscope ▶ noun a device used by doctors for listening to the sound of a person's heart or breathing.

Stetson ▶ noun (trademark) a hat with a high crown and a very wide brim, worn by cowboys and ranchers in the US.

stevedore ▶ noun a person employed at a dock to load and unload ships.

stew ▶ noun **1** a dish of meat and vegetables cooked slowly in a closed dish. **2** informal a state of anxiety or agitation.
▶ verb **1** cook slowly in a closed dish. **2** Brit. (of tea) become strong and bitter with prolonged brewing. **3** informal be anxious or agitated.

steward ▶ noun **1** a person who looks after the passengers on a ship or aircraft. **2** an official who supervises arrangements at a large public event. **3** a person employed to manage a large house or estate. **4** a person responsible for supplies of food to a college, club, etc.
□ **stewardship** noun.

stewardess ▶ noun a woman who looks after the passengers on a ship or aircraft.

stick¹ ▶ noun **1** a thin piece of wood that has fallen or been cut from a tree. **2** a piece of wood used for support in walking or as a weapon. **3** a long, thin implement used in hockey, polo, etc. to hit the ball or puck. **4** a long, thin object or piece. **5** Brit. informal severe criticism or treatment. **6** (**the sticks**) informal remote country areas.

SYNONYMS 1 *a fire made of sticks* branch, twig. **2** *he walks with a stick* walking stick, cane, staff, crutch. **3** *the plants need supporting on sticks* post, pole, cane, stake. **4** *he beat me with a stick* club, cudgel, truncheon, baton, cane, switch, rod; Brit. informal cosh.

■ **stick insect** a long, slender insect that resembles a twig.

stick² ▶ verb (**sticks, sticking, stuck**) **1** push something pointed into or through something. **2** be fixed with its point embedded in something. **3** protrude or extend. **4** informal put something somewhere quickly or carelessly. **5** cling firmly to a surface; adhere. **6** (**be stuck**) be fixed or unable to move. **7** (**be stuck**) be unable to complete a task. **8** (**be stuck with**) informal be unable to get rid of or escape from. **9** (**stick around**) informal remain in or near a place. **10** (**stick to**) continue doing or using. **11** (**stick up for**) informal support.

SYNONYMS 1 *he stuck his fork into the sausage* thrust, push, insert, jab, poke, dig, plunge. **2** *the bristles stuck into his skin* pierce, penetrate, puncture, prick, stab. **3** *the mug stuck to the mat* adhere, cling. **4** *stick the stamp there* attach, fasten, affix, fix, paste, glue, gum, tape. **5** *the wheels stuck fast* jam, get jammed, catch, get caught, get trapped. **6** *that sticks in his mind* remain, stay, linger, persist, continue, endure. **7** *I can't stick it* tolerate, put up with, take, stand, stomach, endure, bear; informal abide.

sticker ▶ noun a sticky label or notice.

stickleback ▶ noun a small fish with sharp spines along its back.

stickler ▶ noun a person who insists on people behaving in a particular way.

sticky ▶ adjective (**stickier, stickiest**) **1** tending or designed to stick. **2** like glue in texture. **3** (of the weather) hot and humid. **4** awkward or difficult.

SYNONYMS 1 *sticky tape* adhesive, self-adhesive, gummed. **2** *sticky clay* tacky, gluey, gummy, treacly, glutinous; informal gooey. **3** *sticky weather* humid, muggy, close, sultry, steamy, sweaty. **4** *a sticky situation* awkward, difficult, tricky, ticklish, delicate, embarrassing, sensitive; informal hairy. **ANTONYMS** dry, fresh, cool, easy.

stiff ▶ adjective **1** not easily bent. **2** difficult to turn or operate. **3** unable to move easily and without pain. **4** not relaxed or friendly. **5** severe or strong.

SYNONYMS 1 *stiff cardboard* rigid, hard, firm. **2** *a stiff paste* thick, firm, viscous, semi-solid. **3** *I'm stiff all over* aching, achy, painful, arthritic. **4** *a rather stiff*

manner **formal,** reserved, wooden, forced, strained, stilted; *informal* starchy, uptight. **5** *a stiff fine* **harsh,** severe, heavy, stringent, drastic, draconian; Brit. swingeing. **6** *stiff resistance* **vigorous,** determined, strong, spirited, resolute, tenacious, dogged, stubborn. **7** *a stiff climb* **difficult,** hard, arduous, tough, strenuous, laborious, exacting, tiring, demanding. **8** *a stiff breeze* **strong,** fresh, brisk. **9** *a stiff drink* **strong,** potent, alcoholic.
ANTONYMS flexible, limp, runny, supple, relaxed, informal, lenient, mild, half-hearted, easy, gentle, weak.

▶ **noun** informal a dead body.
■ **stiff upper lip** the tendency to hide your feelings and not complain.
□ **stiffly** adverb **stiffness** noun.

stiffen ▶ verb **1** make or become stiff. **2** make or become stronger.

stifle ▶ verb (**stifles, stifling, stifled**) **1** prevent from breathing freely; suffocate. **2** restrain or suppress.

> SYNONYMS **suppress,** smother, restrain, check, curb, silence, hinder, hamper, impede, prevent, inhibit.
> ANTONYMS encourage, let out.

stifling ▶ adjective unpleasantly hot and stuffy.

stigma ▶ noun (plural **stigmas** or **stigmata**) **1** a mark or sign of disgrace. **2** (**stigmata**) marks on a person's body believed by some Christians to correspond to those left on Jesus's body by the Crucifixion. **3** the part of a plant that receives the pollen during pollination.

stigmatize (or **stigmatise**) ▶ verb (**stigmatizes, stigmatizing, stigmatized**) regard or treat as shameful.

stile ▶ noun an arrangement of steps in a fence or wall that allows people to climb over.

stiletto ▶ noun (plural **stilettos**) **1** a thin, high heel on a woman's shoe. **2** a short dagger with a tapering blade.

still ▶ adjective **1** not moving. **2** Brit. (of a drink) not fizzy.

> SYNONYMS **1** *Polly lay still* **motionless,** unmoving, stock-still, immobile, rooted to the spot, transfixed, static, stationary. **2** *a still night* **quiet,** silent, calm, peaceful, serene, windless. **3** *the lake was still* **calm,** flat, smooth, like a millpond.
> ANTONYMS moving, active, noisy, rough.

▶ **noun 1** deep, quiet calm. **2** a photograph or a single shot from a cinema film. **3** a piece of equipment for distilling alcoholic drinks such as whisky.
▶ **adverb 1** even now or at a particular time. **2** nevertheless. **3** even.

> SYNONYMS **1** *he's still here* **even now,** yet. **2** *He's crazy. Still, he's harmless* **nevertheless,** nonetheless, all the same, even so, but, however, despite that, in spite of that, for all that.

▶ **verb** make or become still.

> SYNONYMS *he stilled the crowd* **quieten,** quiet, silence, hush, calm, settle, pacify, subdue.
> ANTONYMS stir up.

■ **still life** (plural **still lifes**) a painting or drawing of an arrangement of objects such as flowers or fruit.
□ **stillness** noun.

stillborn ▶ adjective (of a baby) born dead.
□ **stillbirth** noun.

stilt ▶ noun **1** either of a pair of upright poles that are used to walk raised above the ground. **2** each of a set of posts supporting a building.

stilted ▶ adjective (of speech or writing) stiff and unnatural.

Stilton ▶ noun trademark a kind of strong, rich blue cheese.

stimulant ▶ noun something that stimulates.

stimulate ▶ verb (**stimulates, stimulating, stimulated**) **1** cause a reaction in the body. **2** make more active or interested.

> SYNONYMS **1** **encourage,** prompt, motivate, trigger, spark, spur on, galvanize, fire, inspire, excite; N. Amer. light a fire under. **2** (**stimulating**) **thought-provoking,** interesting, inspiring, inspirational, lively, exciting, provocative.
> ANTONYMS discourage.

□ **stimulation** noun.

stimulus ▶ noun (plural **stimuli**) something that stimulates.

> SYNONYMS **motivation,** encouragement, impetus, prompt, spur, incentive, inspiration.
> ANTONYMS deterrent, discouragement.

sting ▶ noun **1** a sharp-pointed part of an insect, capable of inflicting a wound by injecting poison. **2** a wound from a sting. **3** a sharp tingling sensation.

> SYNONYMS **1** *a bee sting* **prick,** wound, injury. **2** *this cream will take the sting away* **pain,** pricking, smart, soreness, hurt, irritation.

▶ **verb** (**stings, stinging, stung**) **1** wound with a sting. **2** produce a stinging sensation. **3** upset someone.

> SYNONYMS **1** *she was stung by a scorpion* **prick,** wound. **2** *the smoke made her eyes sting* **smart,** burn, hurt, be irritated,

S

be sore. **3** *the criticism stung her* **upset,** wound, hurt, pain, mortify.

stingray ▸ noun a ray (fish) with a poisonous spine at the base of the tail.

stingy /stin-ji/ ▸ adjective (**stingier, stingiest**) informal mean.

stink ▸ verb (**stinks, stinking, stank** or **stunk**; past participle **stunk**) **1** have a strong, unpleasant smell. **2** informal be very bad or unpleasant.

> SYNONYMS *his clothes stank of sweat* **reek,** smell.

▸ noun **1** a strong, unpleasant smell. **2** informal a row or fuss.

> SYNONYMS *the stink of sweat* **stench,** reek; Brit. informal pong; N. Amer. informal funk.

□ **stinker** noun.

stinking ▸ adjective **1** foul-smelling. **2** informal very unpleasant or bad.
▸ adverb informal very: *stinking rich.*

stint ▸ verb (**stint on**) be very economical or mean about spending or providing something.
▸ noun a period of work.

> SYNONYMS **spell,** stretch, turn, session, term, time, shift, tour of duty.

stipend /sty-pend/ ▸ noun a fixed regular sum paid as a salary to a priest, teacher, or official.

stipendiary ▸ adjective receiving a stipend; working for pay.

stipple ▸ verb (**stipples, stippling, stippled**) mark a surface with many small dots or specks.

stipulate ▸ verb (**stipulates, stipulating, stipulated**) demand or specify as part of an agreement.

> SYNONYMS **specify,** set out, lay down, demand, require, insist on.

□ **stipulation** noun.

stir ▸ verb (**stirs, stirring, stirred**) **1** move an implement round and round in a liquid or soft substance to mix it. **2** move slightly. **3** wake or get up. **4** (often **stir something up**) arouse a strong feeling in someone. **5** Brit. informal deliberately cause trouble by spreading rumours or gossip.

> SYNONYMS **1** *stir the mixture well* **mix,** blend, beat, whip, whisk, fold in; N. Amer. muddle. **2** *James stirred in his sleep* **move,** change your position, shift. **3** *a breeze stirred the leaves* **disturb,** rustle, shake, move, agitate. **4** *the war stirred him to action* **spur,** drive, rouse, prompt, propel, motivate, encourage, urge, impel, provoke.

▸ noun **1** an act of stirring. **2** a disturbance or commotion.

> SYNONYMS *the news caused a stir* **commotion,** disturbance, fuss, excitement, sensation; informal to-do, hoo-ha.

■ **stir-fry** fry quickly over a high heat while stirring.
□ **stirrer** noun.

stirring ▸ adjective causing great excitement or strong emotion.

stirrup ▸ noun each of a pair of loops attached to a horse's saddle to support the rider's foot.

stitch ▸ noun **1** a loop of thread made by a single pass of the needle in sewing or knitting. **2** a method of sewing or knitting that produces a particular pattern. **3** a sudden sharp pain in the side of the body, caused by strenuous exercise.
▸ verb make or mend with stitches.
■ **in stitches** informal laughing uncontrollably. **stitch someone up** Brit. informal make someone appear to be guilty of something that they did not do.

stoat ▸ noun a small meat-eating animal of the weasel family.

stock ▸ noun **1** a supply of goods or materials available for sale or use. **2** farm animals; livestock. **3** money raised by selling shares in a company. **4** (**stocks**) shares in a company. **5** water in which bones, meat, fish, or vegetables have been simmered. **6** a person's ancestry. **7** a breed, variety, or population of an animal or plant. **8** the trunk or stem of a tree or shrub. **9** a plant with sweet-smelling lilac, pink, or white flowers. **10** (**the stocks**) (in the past) a wooden structure in which criminals were locked as a public punishment.

> SYNONYMS **1** *the shop doesn't carry much stock* **merchandise,** goods, wares. **2** *a stock of fuel* **store,** supply, stockpile, reserve, hoard, cache, bank. **3** *farm stock* **animals,** livestock, beasts, flocks, herds. **4** *his mother was of French stock* **descent,** ancestry, origin(s), lineage, birth, extraction, family, blood, pedigree.

▸ adjective common or conventional: *stock characters.*

> SYNONYMS *the stock response* **usual,** routine, predictable, set, standard, staple, customary, familiar, conventional, traditional, stereotyped, clichéd, hackneyed, unoriginal, formulaic.
> ANTONYMS non-standard, original.

▸ verb **1** have or keep a stock of. **2** provide or fill with a stock of something. **3** (**stock up**) collect stocks of something.

> SYNONYMS *we do not stock GM food* **sell,** carry, keep (in stock), offer, supply, provide, furnish.

S

■ **stock car** a car used in a type of racing in which cars collide with each other. **stock exchange** (or **stock market**) a place where stocks and shares are bought and sold. **stock-in-trade** the typical thing a person or company uses or deals in. **stock-still** completely still. **take stock** assess your situation.

stockade ▸ noun a barrier or enclosure formed from wooden posts.

stockbroker ▸ noun a person who buys and sells stocks and shares on behalf of clients.

stocking ▸ noun 1 either of a pair of women's close-fitting nylon garments covering the foot and leg. 2 US or old use a long sock.
□ **stockinged** adjective.

stockist ▸ noun Brit. a retailer that sells goods of a particular type.

stockpile ▸ noun a large stock of goods or materials.
▸ verb (**stockpiles, stockpiling, stockpiled**) gather together a large stock of.

stocktaking ▸ noun the process of listing all the stock held by a business.

stocky ▸ adjective (**stockier, stockiest**) (of a person) short and sturdy.

stodge ▸ noun Brit. informal food that is heavy and filling.
□ **stodgy** adjective.

stoic /stoh-ik/ ▸ noun a stoical person.
▸ adjective stoical.

stoical ▸ adjective enduring pain and hardship without complaining.
□ **stoically** adverb **stoicism** noun.

stoke ▸ verb (**stokes, stoking, stoked**) 1 add coal to a fire, furnace, etc. 2 encourage a strong emotion.
□ **stoker** noun.

stole[1] ▸ noun a woman's long scarf or shawl.

stole[2] past of STEAL.

stolen past participle of STEAL.

stolid ▸ adjective calm, dependable, and unemotional.
□ **stolidly** adverb.

stomach ▸ noun 1 the internal organ in which the first part of digestion occurs. 2 the front part of the body below the chest; the belly. 3 inclination or desire.

SYNONYMS 1 *a pain in my stomach* **abdomen,** belly, gut, middle; informal tummy, insides. 2 *his fat stomach* **paunch,** belly, beer belly, girth; informal pot, tummy, spare tyre, middle-aged spread; N. Amer. informal bay window. 3 *no stomach for a fight* **appetite,** taste, inclination, desire, wish.

▸ verb 1 consume food or drink without feeling ill. 2 accept or approve of something.

SYNONYMS *they couldn't stomach it* **tolerate,** put up with, take, stand, endure, bear; informal hack, abide; Brit. informal stick.

stomp ▸ verb 1 tread heavily and noisily. 2 dance with stamping steps.

stone ▸ noun 1 the hard material that rock is made of. 2 a small piece of stone found on the ground. 3 a piece of stone shaped as a memorial, a boundary marker, etc. 4 a gem. 5 the hard seed of certain fruits. 6 (plural **stone**) Brit. a unit of weight equal to 14 lb (6.35 kg).

SYNONYMS 1 *someone threw a stone* **rock,** pebble, boulder. 2 *a precious stone* **gem,** gemstone, jewel; informal rock, sparkler. 3 *a peach stone* **kernel,** seed, pip, pit.

▸ verb (**stones, stoning, stoned**) 1 throw stones at. 2 remove the stone from a fruit.
▸ adverb extremely or totally: *stone cold*.
■ **Stone Age** the prehistoric period when tools were made of stone. **a stone's throw** a short distance.

stoned ▸ adjective informal strongly affected by drugs or alcohol.

stonewall ▸ verb 1 refuse to answer questions, or give evasive replies. 2 Cricket bat very defensively.

stony ▸ adjective (**stonier, stoniest**) 1 full of stones. 2 made of or like stone. 3 cold and unfeeling.
□ **stonily** adverb.

stood past and past participle of STAND.

stooge ▸ noun 1 disapproving a less important person used by someone to do routine or unpleasant work. 2 a performer whose act involves being the butt of a comedian's jokes.

stool ▸ noun 1 a seat without a back or arms. 2 Medicine a piece of faeces.
■ **stool pigeon** informal a police informer.

stoop ▸ verb 1 bend the head or body forwards and downwards. 2 lower your standards to do something wrong.

SYNONYMS *she stooped to pick up the pen* **bend,** lean, crouch, bow, duck.

▸ noun a stooping posture.

SYNONYMS *a man with a stoop* **hunch,** round shoulders.

stop ▸ verb (**stops, stopping, stopped**) 1 come or bring to an end. 2 prevent from happening or from doing something. 3 no longer move or operate. 4 (of a bus or train) call at a place to pick up or let off passengers. 5 block up a hole or leak.

SYNONYMS 1 *we can't stop the decline* **end,** halt, finish, terminate, wind up, discontinue, cut short, interrupt, nip in the bud, shut down. 2 *he stopped running* **cease,** discontinue, desist from,

break off, give up, abandon, cut out; informal quit, pack in; Brit. informal jack in. **3** *the car stopped* **pull up,** draw up, come to a stop/halt, come to rest, pull in/over. **4** *the music stopped* **cease,** end, come to an and, halt, finish, draw to a close, be over, conclude. **5** *the police stopped her leaving* **prevent,** obstruct, impede, block, bar, preclude, dissuade from.
ANTONYMS start, begin, continue, allow, encourage.

▶ noun **1** an act of stopping. **2** a place for a bus or train to stop at. **3** an object or part of a mechanism which prevents movement. **4** a set of organ pipes.

SYNONYMS **1** *all business came to a stop* **halt,** end, finish, close, standstill. **2** *a brief stop in the town* **break,** stopover, stop-off, stay, visit. **3** *the next stop is Oxford Street* **stopping place,** station, halt.
ANTONYMS start, beginning, continuation.

■ **pull out all the stops** make a very great effort to achieve something. **stop press** Brit. news added to a newspaper at the last minute.

stopcock ▶ noun a valve which controls the flow of a liquid or gas through a pipe.

stopgap ▶ noun a temporary solution or substitute.

stoppage ▶ noun **1** an instance of being stopped. **2** an instance of industrial action. **3** a blockage. **4** (**stoppages**) Brit. deductions from wages for tax, National Insurance, etc.

stopper ▶ noun a plug for sealing a hole.
▶ verb (**stoppers, stoppering, stoppered**) seal with a stopper.

stopwatch ▶ noun a watch with buttons that start and stop the display, used to time races.

storage ▶ noun **1** the action of storing. **2** space available for storing.
■ **storage heater** Brit. an electric heater that stores up heat during the night and releases it during the day.

store ▶ noun **1** an amount or supply kept to be used when needed. **2** (**stores**) equipment and food kept for use by an army, navy, etc. **3** a place where things are kept for future use or sale. **4** Brit. a large shop selling different types of goods. **5** N. Amer. a shop.

SYNONYMS **1** *a store of food* **stock,** supply, stockpile, hoard, cache, reserve, bank, pool. **2** *a grain store* **storeroom,** storehouse, repository, depository, stockroom, depot, warehouse. **3** *ship's stores* **supplies,** provisions, stocks, food, rations, materials, equipment, hardware. **4** *a DIY store* **shop,** (retail) outlet, boutique, department store,

supermarket, hypermarket, superstore, megastore.

▶ verb (**stores, storing, stored**) **1** keep for future use. **2** enter information in the memory of a computer.

SYNONYMS *rabbits don't store food* **keep,** stockpile, lay in, set aside, put aside, put away/by, save, collect, accumulate, hoard; informal squirrel away.
ANTONYMS use, discard.

■ **in store** about to happen. **set store by** consider to be important.

storey (US spelling **story**) ▶ noun (plural **storeys** or **stories**) a particular level of a building.

❗ Don't confuse **storey** with **story**, which means 'an account of events told for entertainment'. In American English, the spelling **story** is used for both senses.

stork ▶ noun a tall long-legged bird with a long, heavy bill.

storm ▶ noun **1** a violent disturbance of the atmosphere with strong winds and rain, thunder, etc. **2** an uproar or controversy.

SYNONYMS **1** *battered by a storm* **tempest,** squall, gale, hurricane, tornado, cyclone, typhoon, thunderstorm, rainstorm, monsoon, hailstorm, snowstorm, blizzard. **2** *there was a storm over his remarks* **uproar,** outcry, fuss, furore, rumpus, trouble; informal to-do, hoo-ha, ructions, stink; Brit. informal row.

▶ verb **1** move angrily or forcefully. **2** (of troops) suddenly attack and capture a place. **3** shout angrily.

SYNONYMS **1** *she stormed out* **stride,** march, stomp, stamp, stalk, flounce, fling. **2** *police stormed the building* **attack,** charge, rush, swoop on.

■ **a storm in a teacup** Brit. great anger or excitement about something that is not very important.

stormy ▶ adjective (**stormier, stormiest**) **1** affected by a storm. **2** full of angry or violent outbursts of feeling.

SYNONYMS **1** *stormy weather* **blustery,** squally, windy, gusty, blowy, thundery, wild, violent, rough, foul. **2** *a stormy debate* **angry,** heated, fierce, furious, passionate, acrimonious.
ANTONYMS calm, fine, peaceful.

story[1] ▶ noun (plural **stories**) **1** an account of imaginary or real events told for entertainment. **2** an item of news. **3** (also **storyline**) the plot of a novel, film, etc. **4** informal a lie.

SYNONYMS **1** *an adventure story* **tale,** narrative, account, history, anecdote, saga; informal yarn. **2** *the novel has a good story* **plot,** storyline, scenario. **3** *the story* appeared in the papers **news,** report, item, feature, piece. **4** *there have been a lot of stories going round* **rumour,** whisper, allegation, speculation, gossip; Austral./NZ informal furphy.

❗ Don't confuse **story** with **storey:** see the note at **STOREY**.

story² US spelling of **STOREY**.

stoup /stoop/ ▶ noun a basin for holy water in a church.

stout ▶ adjective **1** rather fat or heavily built. **2** sturdy and thick. **3** brave and determined.

SYNONYMS **1** *a short stout man* **fat,** plump, portly, rotund, dumpy, corpulent; informal tubby; Brit. informal podgy; N. Amer. informal zaftig, corn-fed. **2** *stout leather shoes* **strong,** sturdy, solid, robust, tough, durable, hard-wearing. **3** *stout resistance* **determined,** vigorous, forceful, spirited, committed, brave; informal gutsy.
ANTONYMS thin, flimsy, feeble.

▶ noun a kind of strong, dark beer.
□ **stoutly** adverb.

stove¹ ▶ noun a device for cooking or heating.

stove² past and past participle of **STAVE**.

stow ▶ verb **1** pack or store an object tidily. **2** (**stow away**) hide on a ship, aircraft, etc. to travel secretly and without paying.

stowaway ▶ noun a person who stows away.

straddle ▶ verb (**straddles, straddling, straddled**) **1** sit or stand with one leg on either side of. **2** extend across both sides of.

strafe /strahf, strayf/ ▶ verb (**strafes, strafing, strafed**) attack with gunfire or bombs from a low-flying aircraft.

straggle ▶ verb (**straggles, straggling, straggled**) **1** trail slowly behind the person or people in front. **2** grow or spread out in an untidy way.
□ **straggler** noun **straggly** adjective.

straight ▶ adjective **1** extending in one direction only; without a curve or bend. **2** level, upright, or symmetrical. **3** in proper order or condition. **4** honest and direct. **5** in continuous succession. **6** (of an alcoholic drink) undiluted. **7** informal conventional or respectable. **8** informal heterosexual.

SYNONYMS **1** *a long, straight road* **direct,** linear, unswerving, undeviating. **2** *that picture isn't straight* **level,** even, in line, aligned, square, vertical, upright, perpendicular, horizontal. **3** *we must get the place straight* **in order,** tidy, neat, shipshape, orderly, organized, arranged, sorted out, straightened out.

4 *a straight answer* **honest,** direct, frank, candid, truthful, sincere, forthright, straightforward, plain-spoken, blunt, unambiguous; informal upfront. **5** *straight brandy* **neat,** undiluted, pure; N. Amer. informal straight up.
ANTONYMS winding, crooked, untidy, evasive.

▶ adverb **1** in a straight line or in a straight way. **2** without delay. **3** clearly and logically.

SYNONYMS **1** *he looked me straight in the eyes* **right,** directly, squarely, full; informal smack, (slap) bang; N. Amer. informal spang, smack dab. **2** *she drove straight home* **directly,** right. **3** *I told her straight* **frankly,** directly, candidly, honestly, forthrightly, plainly, point-blank, bluntly, flatly; Brit. informal straight up. **4** *he can't think straight* **logically,** rationally, clearly, lucidly, coherently, cogently.

■ **straight away** immediately. **straight-faced** having a serious expression. **straight-laced** ➔ **STRAIT-LACED**.

straighten ▶ verb make or become straight.

SYNONYMS **1** *Rory straightened his tie* **put straight,** adjust, arrange, rearrange, tidy. **2** *we must straighten things out with Viola* **put right,** sort out, clear up, settle, resolve, rectify, remedy; informal patch up.

straightforward ▶ adjective **1** easy to do or understand. **2** honest and open.

SYNONYMS **1** *the process was remarkably straightforward* **uncomplicated,** simple, plain sailing. **2** *a straightforward man* **honest,** frank, candid, open, truthful, sincere, on the level, forthright, plain-speaking, direct; informal upfront; N. Amer. informal on the up and up.
ANTONYMS complicated, devious.

□ **straightforwardly** adverb.

straightjacket ➔ **STRAITJACKET**.

strain¹ ▶ verb **1** make an unusually great effort. **2** injure a muscle, limb, etc. by making it work too hard. **3** make great or excessive demands on. **4** pour a mainly liquid substance through a sieve to separate out solid matter.

SYNONYMS **1** *take care that you don't strain yourself* **overtax,** overwork, overextend, overreach, overdo it, exhaust, wear out; informal knacker, knock yourself out. **2** *you have strained a muscle* **injure,** damage, pull, wrench, twist, sprain. **3** *strain the mixture* **sieve,** sift, filter, screen.

▶ noun **1** a force tending to strain something to an extreme degree. **2** an injury caused by straining a muscle, limb, etc. **3** a severe demand on strength or resources. **4** a state

S

of tension or exhaustion. **5** the sound of a piece of music.

> SYNONYMS **1** *the rope snapped under the strain* **tension,** tightness, tautness. **2** *muscle strain* **injury,** sprain, wrench, twist. **3** *the strain of her job* **pressure,** demands, burdens, stress; informal hassle. **4** *Melissa was showing signs of strain* **stress,** (nervous) tension, exhaustion, fatigue, pressure, overwork.

□ **strainer** noun.

strain² ▸ noun **1** a breed or variety of an animal or plant. **2** a tendency in a person's character.

> SYNONYMS *a different strain of flu* **variety,** kind, type, sort, breed, genus.

strained ▸ adjective **1** not relaxed or comfortable; showing signs of strain. **2** produced by deliberate effort; not graceful or spontaneous.

> SYNONYMS **1** *relations were strained* **awkward,** tense, uneasy, uncomfortable, edgy, difficult, troubled. **2** *a strained smile* **forced,** unnatural, artificial, insincere, false, affected, put-on. ANTONYMS friendly, genuine.

strait ▸ noun **1** (also **straits**) a narrow passage of water connecting two other large areas of water. **2** (**straits**) trouble or difficulty: *in dire straits.*

> SYNONYMS **1** **channel,** sound, narrows, stretch of water. **2** (**straits**) **difficulty,** trouble, crisis, mess, predicament, plight; informal hot water, jam, hole, fix, scrape.

straitened ▸ adjective without enough money; poor.

straitjacket (or **straightjacket**) ▸ noun a strong garment with long sleeves which can be tied together to confine the arms of a violent person.

strait-laced (or **straight-laced**) ▸ adjective very strictly moral and conventional.

strand¹ ▸ verb **1** drive or leave a ship, whale, etc. aground on a shore. **2** leave someone or something without the means to move from a place.

> SYNONYMS **1** (**stranded**) *stranded on a desert island* **shipwrecked,** wrecked, marooned, high and dry, grounded, aground, beached. **2** (**stranded**) *stranded in a strange city* **helpless,** abandoned, lost, adrift.

▸ noun literary a beach or shore.

strand² ▸ noun **1** a single thin length of thread, wire, etc. **2** an element that forms part of a complex whole.

> SYNONYMS **thread,** filament, fibre, length.

strange ▸ adjective **1** unusual or surprising. **2** not previously visited or encountered.

> SYNONYMS **1** *strange things have been happening* **unusual,** odd, curious, peculiar, funny, bizarre, weird, uncanny, anomalous; informal fishy. **2** *visiting a strange house* **unfamiliar,** unknown, new, novel. ANTONYMS ordinary, familiar.

□ **strangely** adverb.

stranger ▸ noun **1** a person that you do not know. **2** a person who does not know a particular place.

> SYNONYMS **newcomer,** new arrival, visitor, guest, outsider, foreigner.

strangle ▸ verb (**strangles, strangling, strangled**) **1** kill or injure someone by squeezing their neck. **2** prevent from growing or developing.

> SYNONYMS **throttle,** choke, garrotte, asphyxiate.

□ **strangler** noun.

stranglehold ▸ noun **1** a firm grip around a person's neck that deprives them of oxygen. **2** complete or overwhelming control.

strangulation ▸ noun the action of strangling.

strap ▸ noun a strip of flexible material used for fastening, carrying, or holding on to.

> SYNONYMS *thick leather straps* **belt,** tie, band, thong.

▸ verb (**straps, strapping, strapped**) fasten or secure with a strap.

> SYNONYMS *a bag was strapped to the bicycle* **tie,** lash, secure, fasten, bind, make fast, truss.

□ **strapless** adjective **strappy** adjective.

strapping ▸ adjective (of a person) big and strong.

> SYNONYMS **big,** strong, well-built, brawny, burly, muscular; informal beefy. ANTONYMS weedy.

stratagem ▸ noun a plan or scheme intended to outwit an opponent.

strategic ▸ adjective **1** forming part of a long-term plan to achieve something. **2** relating to the gaining of long-term military advantage. **3** (of weapons) for use against enemy territory rather than in battle.

> SYNONYMS **planned,** calculated, deliberate, tactical, judicious, prudent, shrewd.

□ **strategically** adverb.

strategy ▸ noun (plural **strategies**) **1** a plan designed to achieve a long-term aim. **2** the planning and directing of military activity in a war or battle.

SYNONYMS **plan**, grand design, game plan, policy, programme, scheme.

□ **strategist** noun.

stratify ▶ verb (**stratifies, stratifying, stratified**) form or arrange into strata.
□ **stratification** noun.

stratosphere ▶ noun **1** the layer of the earth's atmosphere above the lowest layer, at a height of about 10–50 km. **2** informal the very highest levels of something.
□ **stratospheric** adjective.

stratum ▶ noun (plural **strata**) **1** a layer or series of layers of rock. **2** a level or class of society.

straw ▶ noun **1** dried stalks of grain. **2** a single dried stalk of grain. **3** a thin hollow tube used for sucking drink from a container. **4** a pale yellow colour.
■ **clutch at straws** turn to something in desperation. **draw the short straw** be chosen to do something unpleasant. **the last** (or **final**) **straw** the final difficulty that makes a situation unbearable. **straw poll** an unofficial test of opinion.

strawberry ▶ noun (plural **strawberries**) a sweet red fruit with seeds on the surface.
■ **strawberry blonde** (of hair) light reddish-blonde.

stray ▶ verb move away aimlessly from a group or from the right course or place.

SYNONYMS **1** *the gazelle had strayed from the herd* **wander off**, get separated, get lost, drift away. **2** *we strayed from our original topic* **digress**, deviate, wander, get sidetracked, go off at a tangent, get off the subject.

▶ adjective **1** not in the right place; separated from a group. **2** (of a domestic animal) having no home or having wandered away from home.

SYNONYMS **1** *a stray dog* **homeless**, lost, abandoned, feral. **2** *a stray bullet* **random**, chance, freak, unexpected.

▶ noun a stray person or thing.

streak ▶ noun **1** a long, thin mark. **2** an element in someone's character: *a ruthless streak*. **3** a period of success or luck of a certain kind: *a winning streak*.

SYNONYMS **1** *a streak of light* **band**, line, strip, stripe, vein, slash, ray, smear. **2** *a streak of self-destructiveness* **element**, vein, strain, touch. **3** *a winning streak* **period**, spell, stretch, run; Brit. informal patch.

▶ verb **1** mark with streaks. **2** move very fast. **3** informal run naked in a public place to shock or amuse people.

SYNONYMS **1** *the sky was streaked with red* **stripe**, band, fleck, smear, mark. **2** *Miranda streaked across the road* **race**,

speed, flash, shoot, dash, rush, hurtle, whizz, zoom, career, fly; informal belt, tear, zip, whip; Brit. informal **bomb**; N. Amer. informal barrel.

□ **streaker** noun **streaky** adjective.

stream ▶ noun **1** a small, narrow river. **2** a continuous flow of liquid, air, people, etc. **3** Brit. a group in which schoolchildren of the same age and ability are taught.

SYNONYMS **1** *a mountain stream* **brook**, rivulet, tributary; Scottish & N. English burn; N. English beck; S. English bourn; N. Amer. & Austral./NZ creek. **2** *a stream of boiling water* **jet**, flow, rush, gush, surge, torrent, flood, cascade. **3** *a steady stream of visitors* **succession**, series, string.

▶ verb **1** move in a continuous flow. **2** run with tears, sweat, etc. **3** float out in the wind. **4** Brit. put schoolchildren in streams.

SYNONYMS **1** *tears were streaming down her face* **flow**, pour, course, run, gush, surge, flood, cascade, spill. **2** *children streamed out of the classrooms* **pour**, surge, flood, swarm, pile, crowd.

■ **on stream** in operation or existence.

streamer ▶ noun a long, narrow flag or strip of decorative material.

streamline ▶ verb (**streamlines, streamlining, streamlined**) **1** (be **streamlined**) have a shape that allows quick, easy movement through air or water. **2** make an organization or system more efficient.

SYNONYMS **1** (**streamlined**) *streamlined cars* **aerodynamic**, smooth, sleek. **2** (**streamlined**) *a streamlined organization* **efficient**, smooth-running, well run, slick.

street ▶ noun a public road in a city, town, or village.

SYNONYMS **road**, thoroughfare, avenue, drive, boulevard, lane; N. Amer. highway.

■ **street value** the price something, especially drugs, would fetch if sold illegally.

streetcar ▶ noun N. Amer. a tram.

streetwalker ▶ noun a prostitute who seeks clients in the street.

streetwise ▶ adjective informal able to deal with the difficulties and dangers of life in a big city.

strength ▶ noun **1** the quality or state of being strong. **2** a good or useful quality or attribute. **3** the number of people making up a group.

SYNONYMS **1** *enormous physical strength* **power**, muscle, might, brawn, force. **2** *Oliver began to regain his strength* **health**, fitness, vigour, stamina. **3** *her great inner strength* **fortitude**, resilience,

S

spirit, backbone, courage, bravery, pluck, grit; informal **guts**. **4** *the strength of the retaining wall* **robustness**, sturdiness, firmness, toughness, soundness, solidity, durability. **5** *political strength* **power**, influence; informal **clout**. **6** *strength of feeling* **intensity**, vehemence, force, depth. **7** *the strength of their argument* **force**, weight, power, persuasiveness, soundness, cogency, validity. **8** *what are your strengths?* **strong point**, advantage, asset, forte, aptitude, talent, skill, speciality. **9** *the strength of the army* **size**, extent, magnitude.
ANTONYMS weakness.

■ **on the strength of** on the basis of.

✔ Remember the **g** before the **-th**: stren**g**th.

strengthen ▸ verb make or become stronger.

SYNONYMS **1** *calcium strengthens growing bones* **make strong/stronger**, build up, harden, toughen, fortify, stiffen, reinforce. **2** *the wind had strengthened* **become strong/stronger**, gain strength, intensify, pick up.
ANTONYMS weaken.

strenuous ▸ adjective needing or using a lot of effort or exertion.

SYNONYMS **1** *a strenuous climb* **difficult**, arduous, hard, tough, taxing, demanding, exacting, exhausting, tiring, gruelling, back-breaking; Brit. informal knackering. **2** *strenuous efforts* **vigorous**, energetic, forceful, strong, spirited, intense, determined, resolute, dogged.
ANTONYMS easy, half-hearted.

▢ **strenuously** adverb.

streptococcus /strep-tuh-kok-kuhss/ ▸ noun (plural **streptococci** /strep-tuh-kok-ky/) a type of bacterium which can cause various serious infections.
▢ **streptococcal** adjective.

stress ▸ noun **1** pressure or tension exerted on an object. **2** mental or emotional strain or tension. **3** particular emphasis. **4** emphasis given to a syllable or word in speech.

SYNONYMS **1** *he's under a lot of stress* **strain**, pressure, (nervous) tension, worry, anxiety, trouble, difficulty; informal hassle. **2** *laying greater stress on education* **emphasis**, importance, weight.

▸ verb **1** emphasize. **2** subject to pressure, tension, or strain.

SYNONYMS **1** *they stress the need for reform* **emphasize**, draw attention to, underline, underscore, point up, highlight. **2** *all the staff were stressed* **overstretch**, overtax, pressurize,

pressure, worry, harass; informal hassle.
ANTONYMS play down.

stressful ▸ adjective causing mental or emotional stress.
▢ **stressfully** adverb.

stretch ▸ verb **1** be able to be made longer or wider without tearing or breaking. **2** extend something without tearing or breaking it. **3** extend part of the body to its full length. **4** extend over an area or period of time. **5** make demands on.

SYNONYMS **1** *this material stretches* **expand**, give, be elastic, be stretchy. **2** *he stretched the elastic* **pull (out)**, draw out, extend, lengthen, elongate, expand. **3** *stretching the truth* **bend**, strain, distort, exaggerate, embellish. **4** *she stretched out her arm* **reach out**, hold out, extend, straighten (out). **5** *she stretched out on the sofa* **lie down**, recline, lean back, sprawl, lounge, loll. **6** *the desert stretches for miles* **extend**, spread, continue, go on.
ANTONYMS shorten, contract, fold up.

▸ noun **1** an act of stretching. **2** the capacity to stretch or be stretched; elasticity. **3** a continuous expanse or period.

SYNONYMS **1** *magnificent stretches of forest* **expanse**, area, tract, belt, sweep, extent. **2** *a four-hour stretch* **period**, time, spell, run, stint, session, shift.

▢ **stretchy** adjective.

stretcher ▸ noun a long framework covered with canvas, used for carrying sick, injured, or dead people.
▸ verb (**stretchers**, **stretchering**, **stretchered**) carry on a stretcher.

strew ▸ verb (**strews**, **strewing**, past participle **strewn** or **strewed**) **1** scatter untidily over a surface or area. **2** (**be strewn with**) be covered with untidily scattered things.

striated ▸ adjective marked with ridges or furrows.
▢ **striation** noun.

stricken North American or old-fashioned past participle of STRIKE.
▸ adjective **1** seriously affected by something unpleasant. **2** showing great distress.

strict ▸ adjective **1** demanding that rules are obeyed. **2** following rules or beliefs exactly.

SYNONYMS **1** *a strict interpretation of the law* **precise**, exact, literal, faithful, accurate, careful, meticulous, rigorous. **2** *strict controls on spending* **stringent**, rigorous, severe, harsh, hard, rigid, tough. **3** *strict parents* **stern**, severe, harsh, uncompromising, authoritarian, firm. **4** *in strict confidence* **absolute**, utter, complete, total.
ANTONYMS loose, liberal.

▢ **strictly** adverb **strictness** noun.

S

stricture ▶ noun **1** a rule restricting behaviour or action. **2** a sternly critical remark.

stride ▶ verb (**strides, striding, strode**; past participle **stridden**) walk with long, decisive steps.

> SYNONYMS **step,** pace, march.

▶ noun **1** a long, decisive step. **2** a step made towards an aim.

> SYNONYMS **step,** pace, march.

■ **take something in your stride** deal calmly with something difficult.

strident ▶ adjective **1** loud and harsh. **2** presenting a point of view in a way that is too forceful.

□ **stridency** noun **stridently** adverb.

strife ▶ noun angry or bitter disagreement.

> SYNONYMS **conflict,** friction, discord, disagreement, dissension, dispute, argument, quarrelling.
> ANTONYMS peace.

strike ▶ verb (**strikes, striking, struck**) **1** hit someone or something with force. **2** attack suddenly. **3** (of a disaster) happen suddenly and have harmful effects on. **4** refuse to work as a form of organized protest. **5** discover gold, oil, etc. by digging or drilling. **6** light a match by rubbing it against a rough surface. **7** (of a clock) show the time by sounding a chime or stroke. **8** reach an agreement.

> SYNONYMS **1** *the teacher struck Mary* **hit,** slap, smack, thump, punch, beat, bang; informal clout, wallop, belt, whack, thwack, bash, clobber, bop, biff; Austral./NZ informal quilt. **2** *the car struck a tree* **crash into,** collide with, hit, run into, bump into, smash into; N. Amer. impact. **3** *a thought struck her* **occur to,** come to (mind), dawn on you, hit, spring to mind, enter your head. **4** *you strike me as intelligent* **seem to,** appear to, give someone the impression of being. **5** *train drivers are to strike* **take industrial action,** go on strike, down tools, walk out.

▶ noun **1** an act of striking by employees. **2** a sudden attack. **3** an act of hitting a ball.

> SYNONYMS **1** *a 48-hour strike* **industrial action,** walkout. **2** *a military strike* **attack,** assault, bombing.

■ **strike someone off** officially expel someone from a professional group. **strike out** start out on a new course. **strike up** begin to play a piece of music. **strike something up** begin a friendship or conversation with someone.

striker ▶ noun **1** an employee who is on strike. **2** (in soccer) a forward.

striking ▶ adjective **1** very noticeable. **2** dramatically good-looking.

> SYNONYMS **1** *a striking resemblance* **noticeable,** obvious, conspicuous, marked, unmistakable, strong, remarkable. **2** *Kenya's striking landscape* **impressive,** imposing, magnificent, spectacular, breathtaking, marvellous, wonderful, stunning, sensational, dramatic.
> ANTONYMS unremarkable.

□ **strikingly** adverb.

string ▶ noun **1** material consisting of threads twisted together to form a thin length. **2** a length of catgut or wire on a musical instrument, producing a note when it is made to vibrate. **3** (**strings**) the stringed instruments in an orchestra. **4** a sequence of similar items or events.

> SYNONYMS **1** *a ball of string* **twine,** cord, yarn, thread. **2** *a string of brewers* **chain,** group, consortium. **3** *a string of convictions* **series,** succession, chain, sequence, run, streak. **4** *a string of wagons* **queue,** procession, line, file, column, convoy, train, cavalcade. **5** (**strings**) *a guaranteed loan with no strings* **conditions,** qualifications, provisions, provisos, caveats, stipulations, riders, limitations, restrictions; informal catches.

▶ verb (**strings, stringing, strung**) **1** thread things together on a string. **2** (**be strung** or **be strung out**) be arranged in a long line. **3** fit strings to a musical instrument, bow, etc.

> SYNONYMS *lights were strung across the promenade* **hang,** suspend, sling, stretch, run, thread, loop, festoon.

■ **with no strings attached** informal with no special conditions or restrictions. **string someone along** informal deliberately mislead someone. **string bean** any of various beans eaten in their pods. **string quartet** a chamber music group consisting of two violinists and a viola and cello player. □ **stringed** adjective.

stringent ▶ adjective (of regulations or requirements) strict and precise.

> SYNONYMS **strict,** firm, rigid, rigorous, severe, harsh, tough, tight, exacting, demanding.
> ANTONYMS lax.

□ **stringency** noun **stringently** adverb.

stringy ▶ adjective **1** like string. **2** (of meat) containing tough fibres that are difficult to chew.

strip¹ ▶ verb (**strips, stripping, stripped**) **1** remove all coverings or clothes from. **2** take off your clothes. **3** remove all the contents or fittings of a room, vehicle, etc. **4** remove paint from a surface. **5** (**strip someone of**) deprive someone of rank, power, or property.

SYNONYMS **1** *he stripped and got into bed* **undress,** strip off, take your clothes off, disrobe. **2** *stripping the paint off the door* **peel,** remove, scrape, clean. **3** *I stripped down the engine* **dismantle,** disassemble, take to bits/pieces, take apart. **4** *the house had been stripped* **empty,** clear, clean out, plunder, rob, burgle, loot, pillage, ransack, sack.
ANTONYMS dress, reassemble.

▶ noun **1** an act of undressing. **2** Brit. the identifying outfit worn by a sports team.

strip² ▶ noun **1** a long, narrow piece of cloth, paper, etc. **2** a long, narrow area of land.

SYNONYMS *a strip of paper* (**narrow**) **piece,** band, belt, ribbon, slip, shred, stretch.

■ **strip light** Brit. a fluorescent lamp in the shape of a tube.

stripe ▶ noun a long, narrow band or strip of a different colour or texture from the areas next to it.
▶ verb (**stripes, striping, striped**) mark with stripes.
□ **stripy** (or **stripey**) adjective.

stripling ▶ noun old use a young man.

stripper ▶ noun **1** a striptease performer. **2** a device or substance for stripping paint, varnish, etc. off a surface.

striptease ▶ noun a form of entertainment in which a performer gradually undresses to music in an erotic way.

strive ▶ verb (**strives, striving, strove** or **strived; past participle striven** or **strived**) try very hard to do or achieve something.

strobe ▶ noun a bright light which shines at rapid intervals.

strode past of STRIDE.

stroke ▶ noun **1** an act of hitting. **2** a sound made by a striking clock. **3** an act of stroking with the hand. **4** a mark made by drawing a pen, pencil, etc. across paper or canvas. **5** a short diagonal line separating characters or figures. **6** each of a series of repeated movements, e.g. in rowing or swimming. **7** a style of moving the arms and legs in swimming. **8** a sudden disabling attack caused by an interruption in the flow of blood to the brain.

SYNONYMS **1** *five hammer strokes* **blow,** hit. **2** *light upward strokes* **movement,** action, motion. **3** *broad brush strokes* **mark,** line. **4** *he suffered a stroke* **thrombosis,** seizure, apoplexy.

▶ verb (**strokes, stroking, stroked**) gently move your hand over.

SYNONYMS *she stroked the cat* **caress,** fondle, pat, pet, touch, rub, massage, soothe.

stroll ▶ verb walk in a leisurely way.

SYNONYMS **walk,** amble, wander, meander, ramble, promenade, saunter; informal **mosey.**

▶ noun a short leisurely walk.

SYNONYMS **walk,** amble, wander, meander, ramble, promenade, saunter; informal **mosey.**

strong ▶ adjective (**stronger, strongest**) **1** physically powerful. **2** done with or supplying great force. **3** able to withstand great force or pressure. **4** secure or stable. **5** great in power, influence, or ability. **6** great in intensity or degree. **7** having a lot of flavour. **8** (of a solution or drink) containing a large proportion of a substance. **9** used after a number to indicate the size of a group.

SYNONYMS **1** *a strong lad* **powerful,** sturdy, robust, athletic, tough, rugged, lusty. **2** *she isn't very strong* **well,** healthy, fit. **3** *a strong character* **forceful,** determined, spirited, self-assertive, tough, formidable, strong-minded; informal gutsy, feisty. **4** *a strong fortress* **secure,** well built, well fortified, well protected, solid. **5** *strong cotton bags* **durable,** hard-wearing, heavy-duty, tough, sturdy, well made, long-lasting. **6** *a strong interest in literature* **keen,** passionate, fervent. **7** *strong feelings* **intense,** forceful, passionate, ardent, fervent, deep-seated. **8** *strong arguments* **forceful,** compelling, powerful, convincing, persuasive, sound, valid, cogent, well founded. **9** *a strong voice* **loud,** powerful, forceful, resonant, sonorous, rich, deep, booming. **10** *strong language* **bad,** foul, obscene, profane. **11** *a strong blue colour* **intense,** deep, rich, bright, brilliant, vivid, vibrant. **12** *strong lights* **bright,** brilliant, dazzling, glaring. **13** *strong coffee* **concentrated,** undiluted. **14** *strong cheese* **highly flavoured,** mature, ripe, piquant, tangy, spicy. **15** *strong drink* **alcoholic,** intoxicating, hard, stiff.
ANTONYMS weak, gentle, mild.

■ **going strong** informal continuing to be healthy, active, or successful.
□ **strongly** adverb.

strongbox ▶ noun a small metal box in which valuables are kept.

stronghold ▶ noun **1** a place of strong support for a cause or political party. **2** a place that has been strengthened against attack.

SYNONYMS **1** *the enemy stronghold* **fortress,** fort, castle, citadel, garrison. **2** *a Tory stronghold* **bastion,** centre, hotbed.

strongroom ▶ noun a room designed to protect valuable items against fire and theft.

S

strontium ▸ noun a soft silver-white metallic element.

stroppy ▸ adjective Brit. informal bad-tempered or argumentative.

strove past of STRIVE.

struck past and past participle of STRIKE.

structural ▸ adjective relating to or forming part of a structure.
□ **structurally** adverb.

structure ▸ noun 1 the putting together of different parts to form a whole. 2 a building or other object constructed from several parts. 3 good organization.

SYNONYMS 1 *a vast Gothic structure* **building**, edifice, construction, erection. 2 *the structure of local government* **construction**, organization, system, arrangement, framework, form, formation, shape, composition, anatomy, make-up.

▸ verb (**structures, structuring, structured**) put parts together to form a whole.

SYNONYMS *the programme is structured around periods of study* **arrange**, organize, design, shape, construct, build.

strudel /stroo-duhl/ ▸ noun a dessert of thin pastry rolled up round a fruit filling and baked.

struggle ▸ verb (**struggles, struggling, struggled**) 1 make great efforts to get free. 2 try hard to do something. 3 make your way with difficulty.

SYNONYMS 1 *they struggled to do better* **strive**, try hard, endeavour, make every effort. 2 *James struggled with the raiders* **fight**, battle, grapple, wrestle, scuffle. 3 *she struggled over the dunes* **scramble**, flounder, stumble, fight/battle your way, labour.

▸ noun 1 an act of struggling. 2 a very difficult task.

SYNONYMS 1 *the struggle for justice* **striving**, endeavour, campaign, battle, crusade, drive, push. 2 *no signs of a struggle* **fight**, scuffle, brawl, tussle, fracas; informal bust-up, ding-dong. 3 *many perished in the struggle* **conflict**, fight, battle, confrontation, clash, hostilities, fighting, war, warfare, campaign. 4 *a struggle within the leadership* **contest**, competition, fight, clash, rivalry, friction, feuding, conflict.

□ **struggler** noun.

strum ▸ verb (**strums, strumming, strummed**) play a guitar or similar instrument by sweeping the thumb or a plectrum up or down the strings.
▸ noun an instance of strumming.

strumpet ▸ noun old use a woman who has a lot of sexual partners.

strung past and past participle of STRING.

strut ▸ noun 1 a bar used to support or strengthen a structure. 2 a proud, confident walk.
▸ verb (**struts, strutting, strutted**) walk in a proud and confident way.

SYNONYMS **swagger**, prance, parade, stride, sweep; N. Amer. informal sashay.
ANTONYMS slink.

strychnine /strik-neen/ ▸ noun a bitter and highly poisonous substance obtained from an Asian tree.

Stuart (or **Stewart**) ▸ adjective relating to the royal family ruling Scotland 1371–1714 and Britain 1603–1714.

stub ▸ noun 1 the remaining part of a pencil, cigarette, etc. after use. 2 the counterfoil of a cheque, ticket, etc.
▸ verb (**stubs, stubbing, stubbed**) 1 accidentally bump your toe against something. 2 (often **stub something out**) put out a cigarette by pressing the lighted end against something.
□ **stubby** adjective.

stubble ▸ noun 1 short, stiff hairs growing on a man's face when he has not shaved for a while. 2 the cut stalks of cereal plants left in the ground after harvesting.
□ **stubbly** adjective.

stubborn ▸ adjective 1 determined not to change your attitude or position. 2 difficult to move or remove.

SYNONYMS 1 *you're too stubborn to admit it* **obstinate**, headstrong, wilful, strong-willed, pig-headed, inflexible, uncompromising, unbending; informal stiff-necked. 2 *stubborn stains* **indelible**, permanent, persistent, tenacious, resistant.
ANTONYMS compliant, removable.

□ **stubbornly** adverb **stubbornness** noun.

stucco ▸ noun plaster used for coating wall surfaces or moulding into decoration.
□ **stuccoed** adjective.

stuck past participle of STICK².

SYNONYMS 1 *a message was stuck to his screen* **fixed**, fastened, attached, glued, pinned. 2 *the gate was stuck* **jammed**, immovable. 3 *if you get stuck, leave a blank* **baffled**, beaten, at a loss; informal stumped, bogged down, flummoxed, bamboozled.

■ **stuck-up** informal having snobbish views and thinking that you are better than other people.

stud¹ ▸ noun 1 a piece of metal with a large head that projects from a surface. 2 Brit. a small projection fixed to the base of a shoe or boot to provide better grip. 3 a small piece of jewellery which is pushed through a pierced ear or nostril. 4 a fastener

S

consisting of two buttons joined with a bar.
▸ verb (**studs**, **studding**, **studded**) decorate with studs or similar small objects.

stud² ▸ noun **1** an establishment where horses are kept for breeding. **2** a stallion. **3** informal a man who has many sexual partners.

student ▸ noun **1** a person studying at a university or college. **2** a school pupil.

> SYNONYMS **1** *a university student* **undergraduate**, postgraduate. **2** *a former student* **pupil**, schoolchild, schoolboy, schoolgirl, scholar. **3** *a nursing student* **trainee**, apprentice, probationer, novice, learner.

studio ▸ noun (plural **studios**) **1** a room from which television or radio programmes are broadcast. **2** a place where film or sound recordings are made. **3** a room where an artist works or where dancers practise.

> SYNONYMS **workshop**, workroom, atelier.

■ **studio flat** Brit. a flat containing one main room.

studious ▸ adjective **1** spending a lot of time studying or reading. **2** done with careful effort.

> SYNONYMS **scholarly**, academic, bookish, intellectual, erudite, learned, donnish; informal brainy.

□ **studiously** adverb.

study ▸ noun (plural **studies**) **1** the reading of books or examination of other materials to gain knowledge. **2** a detailed investigation into a subject or situation. **3** a room used for reading and writing. **4** a piece of work done for practice or as an experiment.

> SYNONYMS **1** *two years of study* **learning**, education, schooling, scholarship, tuition, research. **2** *a study of global warming* **investigation**, enquiry, research, examination, analysis, review, survey. **3** *Bob was in the study* **office**, workroom, studio.

▸ verb (**studies**, **studying**, **studied**) **1** learn about something. **2** investigate a subject or situation in detail. **3** look at something closely in order to observe or read it. **4** (**studied**) done with careful effort.

> SYNONYMS **1** *Anne studied hard* **work**, revise; informal swot, cram. **2** *he studied maths* **learn**, read, be taught. **3** *Thomas studied ants* **investigate**, research, look at, examine, analyse. **4** *she studied him thoughtfully* **scrutinize**, examine, inspect, consider, regard, look at, observe, watch, survey; informal check out.

stuff ▸ noun **1** material, articles, or activities of a particular kind, or of a mixed or unspecified kind. **2** basic characteristics. **3** (**your stuff**) informal the things that you are

good at or responsible for.

> SYNONYMS **1** *suede is tough stuff* **material**, substance, fabric, cloth. **2** *first-aid stuff* **items**, articles, objects, goods; informal things, bits and pieces, odds and ends. **3** *all my stuff is in the suitcase* **belongings**, possessions, effects, paraphernalia; informal gear, things, kit; Brit. informal clobber.

▸ verb **1** fill a container or space tightly with something. **2** fill out the skin of a dead animal or bird with material to restore its original appearance.

> SYNONYMS **1** *stuffing pillows* **fill**, pack, pad, upholster. **2** *Robyn stuffed her clothes into a bag* **shove**, thrust, push, ram, cram, squeeze, force, jam, pack, pile.

stuffing ▸ noun **1** a mixture used to stuff poultry or meat before cooking. **2** padding used to stuff cushions, furniture, or soft toys.

> SYNONYMS **padding**, wadding, filling, packing.

stuffy ▸ adjective (**stuffier**, **stuffiest**) **1** lacking fresh air or ventilation. **2** conventional and narrow-minded. **3** (of a person's nose) blocked up.

> SYNONYMS **1** *a stuffy atmosphere* **airless**, close, musty, stale. **2** *a stuffy young man* **staid**, sedate, sober, priggish, strait-laced, conformist, conservative, old-fashioned; informal straight, starchy, fuddy-duddy.
> ANTONYMS airy, clear, informal, modern.

stultify ▸ verb (**stultifies**, **stultifying**, **stultified**) make someone feel bored or drained of energy.

stumble ▸ verb (**stumbles**, **stumbling**, **stumbled**) **1** trip and momentarily lose your balance. **2** walk unsteadily. **3** make a mistake in speaking. **4** (**stumble across** or **on**) find by chance.

> SYNONYMS **1** *he stumbled and fell* **trip**, lose your balance, lose your footing, slip. **2** *he stumbled back home* **stagger**, totter, blunder, hobble.

▸ noun an act of stumbling.
■ **stumbling block** an obstacle.

stump ▸ noun **1** the part of a tree trunk left sticking out of the ground after the rest has fallen or been cut down. **2** a remaining piece. **3** Cricket each of the three upright pieces of wood which form a wicket.
▸ verb informal baffle.

> SYNONYMS **baffle**, perplex, puzzle, confound, defeat, put at a loss; informal flummox, fox, throw, floor.

stumpy ▸ adjective (**stumpier**, **stumpiest**) short and thick; squat.

S

stun ▸ verb (stuns, stunning, stunned) **1** knock someone into a dazed or unconscious state. **2** greatly astonish or shock someone.

> SYNONYMS **1** *the force of the blow stunned him* **daze,** stupefy, knock out, lay out. **2** *she was stunned by the news* **astound,** amaze, astonish, dumbfound, stupefy, stagger, shock, take aback; informal flabbergast, knock sideways.

stung past and past participle of STING.

stunk past and past participle of STINK.

stunner ▸ noun informal a strikingly attractive or impressive person or thing.

stunning ▸ adjective very impressive or attractive.

> SYNONYMS **beautiful,** lovely, glorious, wonderful, marvellous, magnificent, superb, sublime, spectacular, fine, delightful; informal fantastic, terrific, tremendous, sensational, heavenly, divine, gorgeous, fabulous, awesome. ANTONYMS ordinary.

□ **stunningly** adverb.

stunt¹ ▸ verb slow down the growth or development of.

> SYNONYMS (**stunted**) **small,** undersized, underdeveloped, diminutive.

stunt² ▸ noun **1** an action displaying spectacular skill and daring. **2** something unusual done to attract attention.

> SYNONYMS **feat,** exploit, trick.

stuntman ▸ noun (plural **stuntmen**) a person taking an actor's place in performing dangerous stunts.

stupefy ▸ verb (stupefies, stupefying, stupefied) make someone unable to think properly.
□ **stupefaction** noun.

stupendous ▸ adjective very impressive.
□ **stupendously** adverb.

stupid ▸ adjective **1** lacking intelligence or common sense. **2** dazed and unable to think clearly.

> SYNONYMS **1** *he's really stupid* **unintelligent,** dense, foolish, slow, idiotic, simple-minded; informal thick, dim, dumb, dopey, dozy; Brit. informal daft. **2** *a stupid idea* **foolish,** silly, senseless, idiotic, ill-advised, ill-considered, unwise; informal crazy, half-baked, cockeyed, hare-brained; Brit. informal potty. ANTONYMS intelligent, sensible.

□ **stupidity** noun **stupidly** adverb.

stupor ▸ noun a state of being very dazed or nearly unconscious.

sturdy ▸ adjective (sturdier, sturdiest) **1** strong and solidly built or made. **2** confident and determined.

> SYNONYMS **1** *a sturdy lad* **strapping,** well built, muscular, strong, hefty, brawny, powerful, solid, burly; informal beefy. **2** *sturdy boots* **robust,** strong, well built, solid, stout, tough, durable, long-lasting, hard-wearing. ANTONYMS feeble, flimsy.

□ **sturdily** adverb **sturdiness** noun.

sturgeon /ster-juhn/ ▸ noun a very large fish with bony plates on the body, from whose roe (eggs) caviar is made.

stutter ▸ verb (stutters, stuttering, stuttered) **1** have difficulty talking because you are sometimes unable to stop repeating the first sounds of a word. **2** (of a machine or gun) produce a series of short, sharp sounds.
▸ noun a tendency to stutter while speaking.
□ **stutterer** noun.

sty¹ ▸ noun (plural **sties**) a pigsty.

sty² (or **stye**) ▸ noun (plural **sties** or **styes**) an inflamed swelling on the edge of an eyelid.

Stygian /sti-ji-uhn/ ▸ adjective literary very dark.

style ▸ noun **1** a way of doing something. **2** a particular appearance, design, or arrangement. **3** a way of painting, writing, etc. characteristic of a particular period or person. **4** elegance and sophistication. **5** Botany a narrow extension of the ovary, carrying the stigma.

> SYNONYMS **1** *differing styles of management* **manner,** way, technique, method, approach, system, form. **2** *dressing with style* **flair,** elegance, taste, grace, poise, polish, sophistication, dash; informal class. **3** *Laura travelled in style* **comfort,** luxury. **4** *modern styles* **fashion,** trend, vogue.

▸ verb (styles, styling, styled) **1** design, make, or arrange in a particular form. **2** give a particular name, description, or title to.

> SYNONYMS *sportswear styled by Karl* **design,** fashion, tailor, cut.

stylish ▸ adjective having a good sense of style; fashionably elegant.

> SYNONYMS **fashionable,** modern, up to date, modish, smart, sophisticated, elegant, chic, dapper, dashing; informal trendy, natty; N. Amer. informal kicky, tony. ANTONYMS unfashionable.

□ **stylishly** adverb.

stylist ▸ noun a person who designs fashionable clothes or cuts hair.

stylistic ▸ adjective relating to style.
□ **stylistically** adverb.

stylized (or **stylised**) ▸ adjective represented in an artificial style.

stylus ▸ noun (plural **styli** /sty-ly/) **1** a hard point that follows a groove in a gramophone record and transmits the recorded sound for reproduction. **2** a pointed implement used for scratching or tracing letters or engraving.

stymie ▸ verb (**stymies, stymying** or **stymieing, stymied**) informal prevent or slow down the progress of.

styptic /stip-tik/ ▸ adjective able to make bleeding stop.

suave /swahv/ ▸ adjective (of a man) charming, confident, and elegant.
□ **suavely** adverb **suavity** noun.

sub informal ▸ noun **1** a submarine. **2** a subscription. **3** a substitute in a sports team.
▸ verb (**subs, subbing, subbed**) act as a substitute.

subaltern /sub-uhl-tern/ ▸ noun an officer in the British army below the rank of captain.

subatomic ▸ adjective smaller than or occurring within an atom.

subconscious ▸ adjective concerning the part of the mind which you are not aware of but which influences your actions and feelings.
▸ noun this part of the mind.
□ **subconsciously** adverb.

subcontinent ▸ noun a large part of a continent considered as a particular area, such as North America or southern Africa.

subcontract ▸ verb employ a firm or person outside your company to do work.
□ **subcontractor** noun.

subculture ▸ noun a distinct group within a society or class, having beliefs or interests that are different from those of the larger group.

subcutaneous ▸ adjective situated or applied under the skin.

subdivide ▸ verb (**subdivides, subdividing, subdivided**) divide a part into smaller parts.
□ **subdivision** noun.

subdue ▸ verb (**subdues, subduing, subdued**) **1** overcome, quieten, or control. **2** bring a group or country under control by force.

SYNONYMS **conquer,** defeat, vanquish, overcome, overwhelm, crush, beat, subjugate, suppress.

subdued ▸ adjective **1** quiet and thoughtful or depressed. **2** (of colour or lighting) soft; muted.

SYNONYMS **1** *Lewis's subdued air* **sombre,** downcast, sad, dejected, depressed, gloomy, despondent. **2** *subdued voices* **hushed,** muted, quiet, low, soft, faint, muffled, indistinct. **3** *subdued lighting* **dim,** muted, soft, low, mood.
ANTONYMS cheerful, loud, bright.

subedit ▸ verb (**subedits, subediting, subedited**) check and correct newspaper or magazine text before printing.
□ **subeditor** noun.

subhuman ▸ adjective not behaving like a human being.

subject ▸ noun /sub-jekt/ **1** a person or thing that is being discussed, studied, or dealt with. **2** a branch of knowledge that is studied or taught. **3** Grammar the word or words in a sentence that come before the verb and which the verb says something about, e.g. *Joe* in *Joe ran home.* **4** each of the people in a population ruled by a king or queen.

SYNONYMS **1** *the subject of this chapter* **theme,** subject matter, topic, issue, question, concern. **2** *popular university subjects* **branch of study,** discipline, field. **3** *British subjects* **citizen,** national, resident, taxpayer, voter.

▸ adjective /sub-jekt/ (**subject to**) **1** able to be affected by. **2** dependent or conditional on. **3** under the control or authority of.
▸ adverb /sub-jekt/ (**subject to**) if certain conditions are fulfilled.
▸ verb /suhb-jekt/ (**subject someone/thing to**) make someone or something undergo an unpleasant experience.

SYNONYMS *subjected to violence* **expose to,** treat with, put through.

□ **subjection** noun.

subjective ▸ adjective based on or influenced by personal opinions.

SYNONYMS **personal,** individual, emotional, biased, intuitive.
ANTONYMS objective.

□ **subjectively** adverb **subjectivity** noun.

sub judice /sub joo-di-si/ ▸ adjective being considered by a court of law and therefore not to be publicly discussed elsewhere.

subjugate ▸ verb (**subjugates, subjugating, subjugated**) bring someone under your control by force.
□ **subjugation** noun.

subjunctive ▸ adjective Grammar (of a verb) expressing what is imagined or wished or possible.

sublet ▸ verb (**sublets, subletting, sublet**) let a property or part of a property that you are already renting to someone else.

sublimate ▸ verb **1** direct energy, especially sexual energy, into socially acceptable activities such as exercise, work, or art. **2** Chemistry = SUBLIME.
□ **sublimation** noun.

sublime ▸ adjective **1** of great beauty or excellence. **2** extreme: *sublime confidence.*
▸ verb (**sublimes, subliming, sublimed**) Chemistry (of a solid substance) change directly into vapour when heated.
□ **sublimely** adverb.

S

subliminal ▶ adjective affecting your mind without your being aware of it.
□ **subliminally** adverb.

sub-machine gun ▶ noun a hand-held lightweight machine gun.

submarine ▶ noun a streamlined warship designed to operate completely submerged in the sea.
▶ adjective existing, occurring, or used under the surface of the sea.
□ **submariner** noun.

submerge ▶ verb (**submerges, submerging, submerged**) **1** push or hold something underwater. **2** go down below the surface of water. **3** completely cover or hide.

> SYNONYMS **1** *submerge the bowl in water* **immerse,** plunge, sink. **2** *the farmland was submerged* **flood,** deluge, swamp, overwhelm, inundate. **3** *the U-boat submerged* **go under (water),** dive, sink, plunge, blow its tanks.
> ANTONYMS drain, surface.

submerse ▶ verb submerge.
□ **submersion** noun.

submersible ▶ adjective designed to operate while submerged.

submicroscopic ▶ adjective too small to be seen by a microscope.

submission ▶ noun **1** the action of submitting. **2** a proposal or application submitted for consideration.

> SYNONYMS **1** *submission to authority* **yielding,** capitulation, surrender, resignation, acceptance, consent, compliance, acquiescence, obedience, subjection, subservience, servility.
> **2** *a report for submission to the Board* **presentation,** proffering, tendering, proposing. **3** *his original submission* **proposal,** suggestion, proposition, entry, recommendation. **4** *the judge rejected his submission* **argument,** assertion, contention, statement, claim, allegation.
> ANTONYMS defiance, resistance.

submissive ▶ adjective very obedient or passive.
□ **submissively** adverb.

submit ▶ verb (**submits, submitting, submitted**) **1** give in to the authority, control, or greater strength of someone or something. **2** present a proposal or application for consideration. **3** subject to a particular process or treatment.

> SYNONYMS **1** *she was forced to submit* **yield,** give in/way, back down, cave in, capitulate, surrender. **2** *he refused to submit to their authority* **be governed by,** abide by, comply with, accept, be subject to, agree to, consent to, conform to. **3** *we submitted an application* **put forward,** present, offer, tender, propose, suggest,

enter, put in, send in. **4** *they submitted that the judgement was incorrect* **contend,** assert, argue, state, claim.
ANTONYMS resist, withdraw.

subordinate ▶ adjective /suh-**bor**-di-nuht/ **1** lower in rank or position. **2** of less importance.

> SYNONYMS **inferior,** junior, lower-ranking, lower, supporting.
> ANTONYMS superior, senior.

▶ noun /suh-**bor**-di-nuht/ a person who is under the authority of someone else.

> SYNONYMS **junior,** assistant, second (in command), number two, deputy, aide, underling, minion.
> ANTONYMS superior, senior.

▶ verb /suh-**bor**-di-nayt/ (**subordinates, subordinating, subordinated**) treat someone or something as less important than another.
□ **subordination** noun.

suborn ▶ verb pay or persuade someone to commit an unlawful act, especially perjury.

subplot ▶ noun a secondary plot in a play, novel, etc.

subpoena /suhb-**pee**-nuh/ Law ▶ noun a written order instructing someone to attend a court.
▶ verb (**subpoenas, subpoenaing, subpoenaed**) summon someone with a subpoena.

subscribe ▶ verb (**subscribes, subscribing, subscribed**) **1** (often **subscribe to**) arrange to receive something regularly by paying in advance. **2** (**subscribe to**) contribute a sum of money to a project or cause. **3** (**subscribe to**) say you agree with an idea or proposal.

> SYNONYMS *we subscribe to charity* **contribute,** donate, give, pay.

□ **subscriber** noun.

subscript ▶ adjective (of a letter, figure, or symbol) printed below the line.

subscription ▶ noun **1** money paid to subscribe to something. **2** the action of subscribing.

> SYNONYMS **membership fee,** dues, annual payment, charge.

subsection ▶ noun a division of a section.

subsequent ▶ adjective coming after something.

> SYNONYMS **following,** ensuing, succeeding, later, future, coming, to come, next.
> ANTONYMS previous.

subsequently ▶ adverb after a particular event.

SYNONYMS **later (on)**, at a later date, afterwards, in due course, following this/that, eventually; formal thereafter.

subservient ▸ adjective too ready to obey other people.
□ **subservience** noun.

subside ▸ verb (**subsides, subsiding, subsided**) 1 become less strong, violent, or severe. 2 (of water) go down to a lower level. 3 (of a building) sink lower into the ground. 4 (of the ground) cave in; sink. 5 (**subside into**) give way to a strong feeling.

SYNONYMS 1 *wait until the storm subsides* **abate,** let up, quieten down, calm, slacken (off), ease (up), relent, die down, diminish, decline. 2 *the flood has subsided* **recede,** ebb, fall, go down, get lower. 3 *the house is gradually subsiding* **sink,** settle, cave in, collapse, give way. ANTONYMS intensify, rise.

subsidence ▸ noun the gradual caving in or sinking of an area of land.

subsidiary ▸ adjective 1 related but less important. 2 (of a company) controlled by another company.

SYNONYMS *a subsidiary company* **subordinate,** secondary, subservient, supplementary, peripheral, auxiliary. ANTONYMS principal.

▸ noun (plural **subsidiaries**) a subsidiary company.

SYNONYMS *the firm's Spanish subsidiary* **branch,** division, subdivision, derivative, offshoot. ANTONYMS headquarters, holding company.

subsidize (or **subsidise**) ▸ verb (**subsidizes, subsidizing, subsidized**) 1 support an organization or activity financially. 2 pay part of the cost of producing something to reduce its price.

SYNONYMS **finance,** fund, support, contribute to, give money to, underwrite, sponsor; informal shell out for; N. Amer. informal **bankroll.**

subsidy ▸ noun (plural **subsidies**) a sum of money given to help keep the price of a product or service low.

SYNONYMS **finance,** funding, backing, support, grant, sponsorship, allowance, contribution, handout.

subsist ▸ verb maintain or support yourself at a basic level.

subsistence ▸ noun the action or fact of subsisting.
▸ adjective (of production) at a level which is enough only for your own use, without any surplus for trade.

subsoil ▸ noun soil lying under the surface soil.

subsonic ▸ adjective relating to or flying at a speed less than that of sound.

substance ▸ noun 1 a type of solid, liquid, or gas that has particular qualities. 2 the real physical matter of which a person or thing consists. 3 solid basis in reality or fact. 4 the quality of being important, valid, or significant. 5 the most important or essential part or meaning.

SYNONYMS 1 *organic substances* **material,** compound, matter, stuff. 2 *none of the objections has any substance* **significance,** importance, import, validity, foundation. 3 *the substance of the tale is very thin* **content,** subject matter, theme, message, essence. 4 *men of substance* **wealth,** fortune, riches, affluence, prosperity, money, means.

substandard ▸ adjective below the usual or required standard.

substantial ▸ adjective 1 of considerable importance, size, or value. 2 strongly built or made. 3 concerning the essential points of something.

SYNONYMS 1 *substantial progress had been made* **considerable,** real, significant, important, major, valuable, useful. 2 *substantial damages* **sizeable,** considerable, significant, large, ample, appreciable. 3 *substantial Victorian villas* **sturdy,** solid, stout, strong, well built, durable, long-lasting, hard-wearing. ANTONYMS little, meagre, flimsy.

substantially ▸ adverb 1 to a great extent. 2 for the most part; mainly.

substantiate ▸ verb (**substantiates, substantiating, substantiated**) provide evidence to support or prove the truth of something.

substantive ▸ adjective real and meaningful.
□ **substantively** adverb.

substitute ▸ noun a person or thing that does something or is used in place of someone or something else.

SYNONYMS *substitutes for permanent employees* **replacement,** deputy, relief, proxy, reserve, surrogate, cover, stand-in, understudy; informal **sub.**

▸ adjective acting in place of another.

SYNONYMS *a substitute teacher* **acting,** replacement, deputy, relief, reserve, surrogate, stand-in. ANTONYMS permanent.

▸ verb (**substitutes, substituting, substituted**) make someone or something act as a substitute for.

S

SYNONYMS **1** *curd cheese can be substituted for yogurt* **exchange,** swap, use instead of, use as an alternative to, use in place of, replace with. **2** *the Senate was empowered to substitute for the President* **deputize,** stand in, cover.

□ **substitution** noun.

subsume ▸ verb (**subsumes, subsuming, subsumed**) include or absorb something in something else.

subterfuge ▸ noun secretive or dishonest actions.

subterranean ▸ adjective existing or happening under the earth's surface.

subtext ▸ noun an underlying theme in a piece of writing or speech.

subtitle ▸ noun **1** (**subtitles**) words displayed at the bottom of a cinema or television screen that translate what is being said. **2** a secondary title of a published work.
▸ verb (**subtitles, subtitling, subtitled**) provide something with a subtitle or subtitles.

subtle ▸ adjective (**subtler, subtlest**) **1** so delicate or precise as to be difficult to analyse or describe. **2** capable of making fine distinctions. **3** making use of clever and indirect methods to achieve something.

SYNONYMS **1** *subtle colours* **understated,** muted, subdued, delicate, soft. **2** *subtle distinctions* **fine,** nice. **3** *a subtle change* **gentle,** slight, gradual.
ANTONYMS gaudy, crude, dramatic.

□ **subtly** adverb.

subtlety ▸ noun (plural **subtleties**) **1** the quality or state of being subtle. **2** a subtle distinction or feature.

SYNONYMS **delicacy,** understatedness, refinement, mutedness, softness.

subtotal ▸ noun the total of one set within a larger set of figures.

subtract ▸ verb take away a number or amount from another to calculate the difference.
□ **subtraction** noun.

subtropical ▸ adjective having to do with regions near or next to the tropics.

suburb ▸ noun a residential district that is outside the central part of a city.
□ **suburban** adjective.

suburbia ▸ noun suburbs, and the way of life of the people who live in them.

subversive ▸ adjective trying to damage or weaken the power of an established system or institution.

SYNONYMS *subversive literature* **disruptive,** troublemaking, insurrectionary, seditious, dissident.

▸ noun a subversive person.

SYNONYMS *suspected of being a subversive* **troublemaker,** dissident, agitator, renegade.

□ **subversively** adverb.

subvert ▸ verb damage or weaken the power of an established system or institution.
□ **subversion** noun.

subway ▸ noun **1** Brit. a passage under a road for use by pedestrians. **2** N. Amer. an underground railway.

sub-zero ▸ adjective (of temperature) lower than zero; below freezing.

succeed ▸ verb **1** achieve an aim or purpose. **2** gain wealth or status. **3** take over a job, role, or title from someone else. **4** come after and take the place of.

SYNONYMS **1** *Darwin finally succeeded* **triumph,** achieve success, be successful, do well, flourish, thrive; informal make it, make the grade. **2** *the plan succeeded* **be successful,** turn out well, work (out), be effective; informal come off, pay off. **3** *he succeeded Gladstone as Prime Minister* **replace,** take over from, follow, supersede.
ANTONYMS fail, precede.

success ▸ noun **1** the achievement of an aim or purpose. **2** the gaining of wealth or status. **3** a person or thing that achieves success.

SYNONYMS **1** *the success of the scheme* **favourable outcome,** triumph. **2** *the trappings of success* **prosperity,** affluence, wealth, riches, opulence. **3** *a box-office success* **triumph,** best-seller, sell-out; informal hit, smash, winner.
ANTONYMS failure.

✔ double **c** and double **s** in **success, successful, succession,** and **successive.**

successful ▸ adjective **1** having achieved an aim or purpose. **2** having gained wealth or status.

SYNONYMS **1** *a successful designer* **prosperous,** affluent, wealthy, rich, famous, eminent, top, respected. **2** *successful companies* **flourishing,** thriving, booming, buoyant, doing well, profitable, moneymaking, lucrative.

□ **successfully** adverb.

succession ▸ noun **1** a number of people or things following one after the other. **2** the action, process, or right of inheriting a position or title.

SYNONYMS **sequence,** series, progression, chain, string, train, line, run.

successive ▸ adjective following one another or following others.

SYNONYMS **consecutive,** in a row, sequential, in succession, running; informal on the trot.

□ **successively** adverb.

successor ▸ noun a person or thing that succeeds another.

succinct /suhk-**singkt**/ ▸ adjective briefly and clearly expressed.
□ **succinctly** adverb.

succour /**suk**-ker/ (US spelling **succor)**
▸ noun help and support in difficult times.
▸ verb give help and support to.

succulent ▸ adjective **1** (of food) tender, juicy, and tasty. **2** (of a plant) having thick fleshy leaves or stems that store water.
▸ noun a succulent plant.
□ **succulence** noun.

succumb ▸ verb **1** give in to pressure or temptation. **2** die from the effect of a disease or injury.

SYNONYMS **1** *she finally succumbed to temptation* **yield,** give in/way, submit, surrender, capitulate, cave in. **2** *he succumbed to the disease* **die from/of.**
ANTONYMS resist.

such ▸ determiner & pronoun **1** of the type previously mentioned or about to be mentioned. **2** to so high a degree; so great.
■ **such as 1** for example. **2** of a kind that; like.

suchlike ▸ pronoun things of the type mentioned.

suck ▸ verb **1** draw something into your mouth by tightening your lip muscles to make a partial vacuum. **2** hold something in your mouth and draw at it by tightening your lip and cheek muscles. **3** draw something in a particular direction by creating a vacuum. **4** (**suck someone in** or **into)** involve someone in a situation or activity without them being able to choose or resist it. **5** (**suck up to)** informal do things to please someone in authority in order to gain advantage for yourself. **6** N. Amer. informal be very bad or unpleasant.

SYNONYMS **1** *they sucked orange juice through straws* **sip,** sup, siphon, slurp, drink. **2** *Fran sucked in a deep breath* **draw,** pull, breathe, gasp.

▸ noun an act of sucking.

sucker ▸ noun **1** a rubber cup that sticks to a surface by suction. **2** an organ that allows an animal to cling to a surface by suction. **3** informal a person who is easily fooled. **4** (**a sucker for)** informal a person who is very fond of a particular thing. **5** a shoot springing from the base of a tree or other plant.

suckle ▸ verb (**suckles, suckling, suckled)** feed at the breast or a teat.

suckling ▸ noun a young child or animal that is still feeding on its mother's milk.

sucrose /**soo**-krohz/ ▸ noun the main substance in cane or beet sugar.

suction ▸ noun the force produced when a partial vacuum is created by the removal of air.

Sudanese ▸ noun a person from Sudan.
▸ adjective relating to Sudan.

sudden ▸ adjective happening or done quickly and unexpectedly.

SYNONYMS **unexpected,** unforeseen, immediate, instantaneous, instant, precipitous, abrupt, rapid, swift, quick.

□ **suddenness** noun.

suddenly ▸ adverb happening or done quickly or unexpectedly.

SYNONYMS **all of a sudden,** all at once, abruptly, swiftly, unexpectedly, without warning, out of the blue.
ANTONYMS gradually.

sudoku /soo-**dok**-koo, soo-**doh**-koo/ ▸ noun a type of number puzzle.

suds ▸ plural noun froth made from soap and water.

sue ▸ verb (**sues, suing, sued) 1** start legal proceedings against someone that you claim has harmed you. **2** (**sue for)** formal appeal formally to a person for.

SYNONYMS **take legal action (against),** go to court, take to court.

suede ▸ noun leather with the flesh side rubbed to give it a velvety surface.

suet ▸ noun hard white fat obtained from cattle, sheep, and other animals, used in cooking.

suffer ▸ verb (**suffers, suffering, suffered) 1** experience something bad. **2** (**suffer from)** be affected by an illness or condition. **3** become worse in quality. **4** old use tolerate.

SYNONYMS **1** *I hate to see him suffer* **hurt,** ache, be in pain, be in distress, be upset, be miserable. **2** (**suffering)** **hardship,** distress, misery, adversity, pain, agony, anguish, trauma, torment, torture, hurt, affliction. **3** *he suffers from asthma* **be afflicted by,** be affected by, be troubled with, have. **4** *England suffered a humiliating defeat* **undergo,** experience, be subjected to, receive, endure, face. **5** *our reputation has suffered* **be impaired,** be damaged, decline.

□ **sufferer** noun.

sufferance ▸ noun toleration, rather than genuine approval.

suffice ▸ verb (**suffices, sufficing, sufficed)** be enough or adequate.

sufficiency ▸ noun (plural **sufficiencies) 1** the quality of being enough or adequate. **2** an adequate amount.

S

sufficient ▸ adjective enough; adequate.

> SYNONYMS **enough,** adequate, plenty of, ample.
> ANTONYMS inadequate.

□ **sufficiently** adverb.

suffix ▸ noun a part added on to the end of a word (e.g. *-ly*, *-ation*).

suffocate ▸ verb (**suffocates, suffocating, suffocated**) die or cause to die from lack of air or being unable to breathe.
□ **suffocation** noun.

suffrage /suf-frij/ ▸ noun the right to vote in political elections.

suffragette /suf-fruh-**jet**/ ▸ noun (in the past, when only men could vote) a woman who campaigned for the right to vote in an election.

suffuse ▸ verb (**suffuses, suffusing, suffused**) gradually spread through or over.
□ **suffusion** noun.

sugar ▸ noun 1 a sweet substance obtained from sugar cane or sugar beet. 2 a type of sweet soluble carbohydrate found in plant and animal tissue.
▸ verb sweeten, sprinkle, or coat with sugar. ■ **sugar beet** a type of beet from which sugar is extracted. **sugar cane** a tropical grass with tall thick stems from which sugar is extracted. **sugar daddy** informal a rich older man who gives presents and money to a much younger woman.
□ **sugary** adjective.

suggest ▸ verb 1 put forward an idea or plan for people to consider. 2 make you think that something exists or is the case. 3 say or indicate something indirectly. 4 (**suggest itself**) (of an idea) come into your mind.

> SYNONYMS 1 *Ruth suggested a holiday* **propose,** put forward, recommend, advocate, advise. 2 *evidence suggests that voters are unhappy* **indicate,** lead to the belief, demonstrate, show. 3 *what exactly are you suggesting?* **hint,** insinuate, imply, intimate.

suggestible ▸ adjective quick to accept other people's ideas or suggestions.

suggestion ▸ noun 1 an idea or plan put forward for people to consider. 2 a thing that suggests that something is the case. 3 a slight trace or indication.

> SYNONYMS 1 *some suggestions for tackling this problem* **proposal,** proposition, recommendation, advice, counsel, hint, tip, clue, idea. 2 *the suggestion of a smirk* **hint,** trace, touch, suspicion, ghost, semblance, shadow, glimmer. 3 *a suggestion that he knew about the plot* **insinuation,** hint, implication.

suggestive ▸ adjective 1 making you think of a particular thing. 2 hinting at sexual matters.

> SYNONYMS 1 *an odour suggestive of a brewery* **redolent,** evocative, reminiscent, characteristic, indicative, typical. 2 *suggestive remarks* **indecent,** indelicate, improper, unseemly, sexual, sexy, smutty, dirty.

□ **suggestively** adverb.

suicide ▸ noun 1 the action of killing yourself intentionally. 2 a person who commits suicide.
□ **suicidal** adjective **suicidally** adverb.

suit ▸ noun 1 a set of clothes made of the same fabric, consisting of a jacket and trousers or a skirt. 2 a set of clothes for a particular activity. 3 any of the sets into which a pack of playing cards is divided (spades, hearts, diamonds, and clubs). 4 a lawsuit.

> SYNONYMS 1 *a pinstriped suit* **outfit,** ensemble. 2 *a medical malpractice suit* **legal action,** lawsuit, (court) case, action, (legal/judicial) proceedings, litigation.

▸ verb 1 be right or good for. 2 (of clothes, colours, etc.) be right for someone's features or figure. 3 (**suit yourself**) do as you wish.

> SYNONYMS 1 *savings schemes to suit all pockets* **be convenient for,** be acceptable to, be suitable for, meet the requirements of; informal fit. 2 *recipes suited to students* **be appropriate,** tailor, fashion, adjust, adapt, modify, fit, gear, design. 3 *blue really suits you* **look attractive on,** look good on, become, flatter.

suitable ▸ adjective right or good for a particular person or situation.

> SYNONYMS 1 *suitable employment* **acceptable,** satisfactory, fitting; informal right up someone's street. 2 *a drama suitable for all ages* **appropriate,** fitting, fit, acceptable, right. 3 *music suitable for a dinner party* **appropriate,** suited, befitting, in keeping with. 4 *they treated him with suitable respect* **proper,** seemly, decent, appropriate, fitting, correct, due.
> ANTONYMS inappropriate.

□ **suitability** noun **suitably** adverb.

suitcase ▸ noun a case with a handle and a hinged lid, used for carrying clothes and other possessions.

suite ▸ noun 1 a set of rooms. 2 a set of furniture. 3 (in music) a set of instrumental compositions to be played one after the other.

> SYNONYMS **apartment,** flat, rooms.

suitor ▸ noun dated a man who pays attention to a woman because he wants to marry her.

sulfur US spelling of **sulphur**.

sulk ▸ verb be quietly bad-tempered and resentful because you are annoyed.
▸ noun a period of sulking.

sulky ▸ adjective quietly bad-tempered and resentful.
□ **sulkily** adverb.

sullen ▸ adjective silent and bad-tempered.
□ **sullenly** adverb.

sully ▸ verb (**sullies, sullying, sullied**) literary spoil the purity or cleanness of something.

sulphate (US spelling **sulfate**) ▸ noun a salt or ester of sulphuric acid.

sulphide (US spelling **sulfide**) ▸ noun a compound of sulphur with another substance.

sulphur (US spelling **sulfur**) ▸ noun a chemical element in the form of yellow crystals, which easily catches fire.
■ **sulphur dioxide** a poisonous gas formed by burning sulphur.

sulphuric (US spelling **sulfuric**) ▸ adjective containing sulphur.
■ **sulphuric acid** a strong corrosive acid.

sulphurous (US spelling **sulfurous**)
▸ adjective containing or obtained from sulphur.

sultan ▸ noun a Muslim king or ruler.

sultana ▸ noun 1 Brit. a light brown seedless raisin. 2 the wife of a sultan.

sultry ▸ adjective 1 (of the weather) hot and humid. 2 suggesting sexual passion.

sum ▸ noun 1 a particular amount of money. 2 (also **sum total**) the total amount resulting from the addition of two or more numbers or amounts. 3 a calculation in arithmetic.

> SYNONYMS 1 *a large sum of money* **amount,** quantity, price, charge, fee, cost. 2 *the sum of two numbers* **total,** sum total, grand total, tally. 3 *the sum of his wisdom* **entirety,** totality, total, whole, beginning and end. 4 *we did sums at school* **calculation,** problem; (**sums**) arithmetic, mathematics; Brit. informal maths; N. Amer. informal math.
> ANTONYMS difference.

▸ verb (**sums, summing, summed**) (**sum someone/thing up**) 1 describe the nature or character of someone or something concisely. 2 summarize something briefly.

summarize (or **summarise**) ▸ verb (**summarizes, summarizing, summarized**) give a summary of.

> SYNONYMS **sum up,** abridge, condense, outline, put in a nutshell, precis.

summary ▸ noun (plural **summaries**) a brief statement of the main points of something.

> SYNONYMS *a summary of the findings* **synopsis,** precis, résumé, abstract, outline, rundown, summing-up, overview.

▸ adjective 1 not including many details; brief. 2 (of a legal process or judgement) done or made immediately and without following the normal procedures.
□ **summarily** adverb.

summation ▸ noun 1 the process of adding things together. 2 the action of summing up. 3 a summary.

summer ▸ noun the season after spring and before autumn.
■ **summer house** a small building in a garden, used for relaxing in during hot weather.
□ **summery** adjective.

summit ▸ noun 1 the highest point of a hill or mountain. 2 the highest possible level of achievement. 3 a meeting between heads of government.

> SYNONYMS 1 *the summit of Mont Blanc* (mountain) **top,** peak, crest, crown, apex, tip, cap, hilltop. 2 *the next superpower summit* **meeting,** conference, talk(s).
> ANTONYMS base.

summon ▸ verb 1 order someone to be present. 2 urgently ask for help. 3 call people to attend a meeting. 4 make an effort to produce a quality or reaction from within yourself.

> SYNONYMS 1 *he was summoned to the Embassy* **send for,** call for, request the presence of, ask, invite. 2 *they were summoned as witnesses* **summons,** subpoena. 3 *he summoned the courage to move closer* **muster,** gather, collect, rally, screw up.

summons ▸ noun (plural **summonses**) 1 an order to appear in a law court. 2 an act of summoning.

sumo /soo-moh/ ▸ noun a Japanese form of wrestling.

sump ▸ noun the base of an internal-combustion engine, in which a reserve of oil is stored.

sumptuous ▸ adjective splendid and expensive-looking.

> SYNONYMS **lavish,** luxurious, opulent, magnificent, resplendent, gorgeous, splendid; informal plush; Brit. informal swish.
> ANTONYMS plain.

□ **sumptuously** adverb.

sun ▸ noun 1 (also **Sun**) the star round which the earth orbits. 2 any similar star. 3 the light or warmth received from the sun.
▸ verb (**suns, sunning, sunned**) (**sun yourself**) sit or lie outside in the heat of the sun.

sunbathe ▸ verb (**sunbathes, sunbathing, sunbathed**) sit or lie outside in the sun to get a suntan.

S

sunbeam ▸ noun a ray of sunlight.

sunbed ▸ noun Brit. **1** a long chair that you lie on when sunbathing. **2** a bed between two banks of sunlamps, which you lie on to get an artificial suntan.

sunblock ▸ noun a cream or lotion used on the skin for complete protection from sunburn.

sunburn ▸ noun inflammation of the skin caused by too much exposure to the ultraviolet rays of the sun.
□ **sunburned** (or **sunburnt**) adjective.

sundae ▸ noun a dish of ice cream with added fruit and syrup.

> ✔ **-ae**, not **-ay**: sund**ae**.

Sunday ▸ noun the day of the week before Monday and following Saturday, observed by Christians as a day of worship.
■ **Sunday school** a class held on Sundays to teach children about Christianity or Judaism.

sunder ▸ verb (**sunders, sundering, sundered**) literary split apart.

sundial ▸ noun an instrument showing the time by the shadow cast by a pointer.

sundry ▸ adjective of various kinds.
▸ noun (**sundries**) various items not important enough to be mentioned individually.

sunflower ▸ noun a tall plant with very large yellow flowers.

sung past participle of SING.

sunglasses ▸ plural noun glasses tinted to protect the eyes from sunlight.

sunk past participle of SINK.

sunken ▸ adjective **1** having sunk. **2** at a lower level than the surrounding area.

sunlamp ▸ noun a lamp giving off ultraviolet rays, under which you lie to get an artificial suntan.

sunlight ▸ noun light from the sun.
□ **sunlit** adjective.

Sunni ▸ noun (plural **Sunni** or **Sunnis**) **1** one of the two main branches of Islam. The other is SHIA. **2** a Muslim who follows the Sunni branch of Islam.

sunny ▸ adjective (**sunnier, sunniest**) **1** bright with or receiving a lot of sunlight. **2** cheerful.

> SYNONYMS **1** *a sunny day* **bright,** sunlit, clear, fine, cloudless. **2** *a sunny disposition* **cheerful,** cheery, happy, bright, merry, joyful, bubbly, jolly.
> ANTONYMS dull, miserable.

sunrise ▸ noun **1** the time when the sun rises. **2** the colours and light visible in the sky at sunrise.

> SYNONYMS **dawn,** crack of dawn, daybreak, break of day, first light, early morning; N. Amer. sunup.

sunroof ▸ noun a panel in the roof of a car that can be opened to let air in.

sunscreen ▸ noun a cream or lotion rubbed on to the skin to protect it from the sun.

sunset ▸ noun **1** the time when the sun sets. **2** the colours and light visible in the sky at sunset.

> SYNONYMS **nightfall,** twilight, dusk, evening; N. Amer. sundown.

sunshade ▸ noun a light umbrella or awning giving protection from the sun.

sunshine ▸ noun sunlight unbroken by cloud.

sunspot ▸ noun a temporary darker and cooler patch on the sun's surface.

sunstroke ▸ noun heatstroke brought about by staying in the sun for too long.

suntan ▸ noun a golden-brown colouring of the skin caused by spending time in the sun.
□ **suntanned** adjective.

sup¹ ▸ verb (**sups, supping, supped**) dated or N. English take drink or liquid food by sips or spoonfuls.
▸ noun a sip.

sup² ▸ verb (**sups, supping, supped**) old use eat supper.

super ▸ adjective informal excellent.

superannuate ▸ verb (**superannuates, superannuating, superannuated**) **1** arrange for someone to retire with a pension. **2** (**superannuated**) humorous too old to be effective or useful.

superannuation ▸ noun regular payment made by an employee into a fund from which a future pension will be paid.

superb ▸ adjective **1** very good; excellent. **2** magnificent or splendid.

> SYNONYMS **1** *a superb goal* **excellent,** first-class, outstanding, marvellous, wonderful, splendid, admirable, fine, exceptional, glorious; informal great, fantastic, fabulous, terrific, super, awesome, ace; Brit. informal brilliant, smashing. **2** *a superb house* **magnificent,** splendid, grand, impressive, imposing, awe-inspiring, breathtaking, gorgeous, beautiful.
> ANTONYMS poor, unimpressive.

□ **superbly** adverb.

supercharger ▸ noun a device that makes an engine more efficient by forcing extra air or fuel into it.
□ **supercharged** adjective.

supercilious ▸ adjective having a manner that shows you think you are better than other people.

superficial ▸ adjective **1** existing or happening at or on the surface. **2** apparent rather than real. **3** not thorough. **4** lacking the ability to think deeply about things.

> SYNONYMS **1** *superficial burns* **surface,** exterior, external, outer, slight. **2** *a superficial investigation* **cursory,** perfunctory, casual, sketchy, desultory, token, slapdash, offhand, rushed, hasty, hurried. **3** *a superficial resemblance* **apparent,** seeming, outward, ostensible, cosmetic, slight. **4** *a superficial person* **facile,** shallow, flippant, empty-headed, trivial, frivolous, silly, inane.
> ANTONYMS deep, thorough, strong, intelligent.

□ **superficiality** noun **superficially** adverb.

superfluous /soo-per-floo-uhss/ ▸ adjective more than what is needed.

> SYNONYMS **surplus (to requirements),** redundant, unneeded, unnecessary, excess, extra, (to) spare, remaining, unused, left over, waste.
> ANTONYMS necessary.

□ **superfluity** noun.

superglue ▸ noun a very strong quick-setting glue.

supergrass ▸ noun Brit. informal a person who secretly gives the police information about the criminal activities of a large number of people.

superhuman ▸ adjective having exceptional ability or powers.

superimpose ▸ verb (superimposes, superimposing, superimposed) lay one thing over another.
□ **superimposition** noun.

superintend ▸ verb manage or oversee.

superintendent ▸ noun **1** a person who supervises and controls a group or activity. **2** a senior police officer.

superior ▸ adjective **1** higher in status, quality, or power. **2** of high quality. **3** arrogant and conceited.

> SYNONYMS **1** *a superior officer* **senior,** higher-level, higher-ranking, higher. **2** *the superior candidate* **better,** worthier, finer, preferred. **3** *superior chocolate* **top-quality,** choice, select, exclusive, prime, fine, excellent, best, choicest, finest. **4** *a superior smile* **condescending,** supercilious, patronizing, haughty, disdainful; informal high and mighty.
> ANTONYMS junior, inferior, modest.

▸ noun a person of higher rank or status.

> SYNONYMS *my immediate superior* **manager,** chief, supervisor, senior, controller, foreman; informal boss.
> ANTONYMS subordinate.

superiority ▸ noun the state of being superior.

> SYNONYMS **supremacy,** advantage, lead, dominance, primacy, ascendancy, eminence.

superlative ▸ adjective **1** of the highest quality or degree. **2** (of an adjective or adverb) expressing the highest degree of a quality (e.g. *bravest*).
▸ noun an exaggerated expression of praise.

superman ▸ noun (plural **supermen**) informal a man who is unusually strong or intelligent.

supermarket ▸ noun a large self-service shop selling foods and household goods.

supermodel ▸ noun a very successful and famous fashion model.

supernatural ▸ adjective not able to be explained by the laws of nature.

> SYNONYMS **1** *supernatural powers* **paranormal,** psychic, magic, magical, occult, mystic, mystical. **2** *a supernatural being* **ghostly,** phantom, spectral, other-worldly, unearthly.

▸ noun (the supernatural) supernatural events.
□ **supernaturally** adverb.

supernova ▸ noun (plural **supernovae** /soo-per-noh-vee/ or **supernovas**) a star that undergoes an explosion, becoming suddenly very much brighter.

supernumerary ▸ adjective **1** present in more than the required number. **2** not belonging to a regular staff but employed for extra work.

superpower ▸ noun a very powerful and influential country.

superscript ▸ adjective (of a letter, figure, or symbol) printed above the line.

supersede ▸ verb (supersedes, superseding, superseded) take the place of.

> SYNONYMS **replace,** take the place of, take over from, succeed, supplant.

✔ **-sede**, not **-cede**: super**sede**.

supersonic ▸ adjective involving or flying at a speed greater than that of sound.

superstar ▸ noun a very famous and successful performer or sports player.

superstition ▸ noun a belief in the supernatural, especially that particular things bring good or bad luck.

superstitious ▸ adjective believing in the supernatural and in the power of particular things to bring good or bad luck.
□ **superstitiously** adverb.

superstore ▸ noun a very large out-of-town supermarket.

superstructure ▸ noun **1** a structure built on top of something else. **2** the part of a structure that is built above a supporting base or foundation.

S

supertanker ▶ noun a very large oil tanker.

supervene ▶ verb happen so as to interrupt or change an existing situation.

supervise ▶ verb be in charge of the carrying out of a task or the work done by a person, ensuring that everything is done correctly.

> SYNONYMS **oversee**, be in charge of, superintend, preside over, direct, manage, run, look after, be responsible for, govern, keep an eye on, observe, monitor, mind.

□ **supervision** noun.

supervisor ▶ noun a person who supervises.

> SYNONYMS **manager**, director, overseer, controller, superintendent, governor, chief, head, foreman; informal **boss**; Brit. informal **gaffer**.

□ **supervisory** adjective.

supine ▶ adjective **1** lying face upwards. **2** failing to act as a result of laziness or weakness.

supper ▶ noun a light or informal evening meal.

supplant ▶ verb take the place of.

supple ▶ adjective (**suppler**, **supplest**) able to bend and move parts of your body easily; flexible.

> SYNONYMS **1** *her supple body* **lithe**, lissom, willowy, flexible, agile, acrobatic, nimble. **2** *supple leather* **pliable**, flexible, soft, bendy, workable, stretchy, springy. ANTONYMS stiff, rigid.

supplement ▶ noun **1** a thing added to something else to improve or complete it. **2** a separate section added to a newspaper or magazine. **3** an additional charge payable for an extra service or facility.

> SYNONYMS **1** *a dietary supplement* **extra**, add-on, accessory, adjunct. **2** *a special supplement with today's paper* **pull-out**, insert. **3** *a supplement to the essay* **appendix**, addendum, postscript, addition, coda. **4** *a single room supplement* **surcharge**, addition, increase.

▶ verb add an extra thing or amount to.

> SYNONYMS *he supplemented his income by teaching* **add to**, augment, increase, boost, swell, amplify, enlarge, top up.

□ **supplemental** adjective.

supplementary ▶ adjective completing or improving something.

suppliant /sup-pli-uhnt/ ▶ noun a person who makes a humble request.

▶ adjective making a humble request.

supplicate ▶ verb (**supplicates**, **supplicating**, **supplicated**) humbly ask for something.

□ **supplicant** noun **supplication** noun.

supply ▶ verb (**supplies**, **supplying**, **supplied**) provide someone with something that is needed or wanted.

> SYNONYMS **1** *they supplied money to the rebels* **give**, contribute, provide, furnish, donate, confer, dispense. **2** *the lake supplies the city with water* **provide**, furnish, serve, endow, equip, arm. **3** *windmills supply their power needs* **satisfy**, meet, fulfil, cater for.

▶ noun (plural **supplies**) **1** a stock or amount of something supplied or available. **2** the action of supplying. **3** (**supplies**) provisions and equipment necessary for a large group of people or for an expedition.

> SYNONYMS **1** *a limited supply of food* **stock**, store, reserve, reservoir, stockpile, hoard, cache, fund, bank. **2** *the supply of alcoholic liquor* **provision**, distribution, serving. **3** (**supplies**) **provisions**, stores, rations, food, necessities.

□ **supplier** noun.

support ▶ verb **1** carry all or part of the weight of. **2** give help, encouragement, or approval to. **3** confirm or back up. **4** provide someone with a home and the things they need in order to live. **5** like a particular sports team and watch or go to their matches.

> SYNONYMS **1** *a roof supported by pillars* **hold up**, bear, carry, prop up, keep up, brace, shore up, underpin, buttress, reinforce. **2** *he struggled to support his family* **provide for**, maintain, sustain, keep, take care of, look after. **3** *she supported him to the end* **stand by**, defend, back, stand/stick up for. **4** *evidence to support the argument* **back up**, substantiate, bear out, corroborate, confirm. **5** *the money supports charitable projects* **help**, aid, assist, contribute to, back, subsidize, fund, finance; N. Amer. informal **bankroll**. **6** *a candidate supported by local people* **back**, champion, favour, be in favour of, advocate, encourage, promote, endorse, espouse.
> ANTONYMS neglect, contradict, oppose.

▶ noun **1** encouragement, help, or approval. **2** a person or thing that supports. **3** the action of supporting.

> SYNONYMS **1** *I was lucky to have their support* **encouragement**, friendship, backing, endorsement, help, assistance, comfort. **2** *bridge supports* **pillar**, post, prop, upright, brace, buttress, foundation. **3** *thank you for your support* **contributions**, backing, donations, money, subsidy, funding, funds, finance, capital.
> ANTONYMS opposition.

supporter ▶ noun a person who supports a sports team, political party, etc.

SYNONYMS **1** *the team's supporters* **fan,** follower, enthusiast, devotee, admirer. **2** *the charity relies on its supporters* **contributor,** donor, benefactor, sponsor, backer, patron, subscriber, well-wisher.

supportive ▶ adjective providing encouragement or emotional help.

SYNONYMS **encouraging,** caring, sympathetic, reassuring, understanding, concerned, helpful.

suppose ▶ verb (**supposes, supposing, supposed**) **1** think that something is true or likely, but lack proof. **2** consider something as a possibility. **3** (**be supposed to do**) be required or expected to do.

SYNONYMS **1** *I suppose he's used to it* **assume,** presume, expect, dare say, take it, guess. **2** *suppose you had a spacecraft* **imagine,** assume, (let's) say, hypothesize, theorize, speculate. **3** (**supposed**) *the supposed phenomena* **alleged,** reputed, rumoured, claimed, purported. **4** (**supposed**) *I'm supposed to meet him at 8.30* **meant,** intended, expected, required, obliged.

supposedly ▶ adverb according to what is generally believed.

supposition ▶ noun a belief that something is likely to be true.

suppository ▶ noun (plural **suppositories**) a solid medical preparation designed to dissolve after being inserted into the rectum or vagina.

suppress ▶ verb **1** forcibly put an end to. **2** prevent from acting or developing. **3** stop something from being stated or published.

SYNONYMS **1** *they will suppress any criticism* **subdue,** repress, crush, quell, quash, squash, stamp out, put down, crack down on. **2** *she suppressed her irritation* **conceal,** restrain, stifle, smother, check, curb, contain. **3** *the report was suppressed* **censor,** keep secret, conceal, hide, hush up, gag, withhold, cover up, stifle. ANTONYMS allow, encourage, reveal.

□ **suppressant** noun **suppression** noun.

✔ two **p**s: su**pp**ress.

suppurate ▶ verb (**suppurates, suppurating, suppurated**) form pus.
□ **suppuration** noun.

supremacist ▶ noun a person who believes that a particular group is superior to all others.

supremacy ▶ noun the state of being superior to all others.

SYNONYMS **control,** power, rule, sovereignty, dominance, superiority, predominance, primacy, dominion, authority, mastery, ascendancy.

supreme ▶ adjective **1** highest in authority or rank. **2** very great or greatest; most important.

SYNONYMS **1** *the supreme commander* **highest,** chief, head, top, foremost, principal, superior, premier, first, prime. **2** *a supreme achievement* **extraordinary,** remarkable, phenomenal, exceptional, outstanding, incomparable, unparalleled. **3** *the supreme sacrifice* **ultimate,** greatest, highest, extreme, final, last. ANTONYMS subordinate, insignificant.

■ **supreme court** the highest law court in a country or state.
□ **supremely** adverb.

supremo ▶ noun (plural **supremos**) Brit. informal a person in overall charge.

surcharge ▶ noun an extra charge or payment.

surd ▶ noun Maths a number which cannot be expressed as a ratio of two whole numbers.

sure ▶ adjective **1** completely confident that you are right. **2** (**sure of** or **to do**) certain to receive, get, or do. **3** undoubtedly true. **4** steady and confident.

SYNONYMS **1** *I'm sure they knew* **certain,** positive, convinced, confident, definite, satisfied, persuaded. **2** *someone was sure to find out* **bound,** likely, destined, fated. **3** *a sure winner* **guaranteed,** unfailing, infallible, unerring, certain, inevitable; informal sure-fire. **4** *a sure sign that he's worried* **reliable,** dependable, trustworthy, certain, unambiguous. ANTONYMS uncertain, unlikely.

▶ adverb informal certainly.
□ **sureness** noun.

surely ▶ adverb **1** it must be true that. **2** certainly.

surety ▶ noun (plural **sureties**) **1** a person who guarantees that somebody else will do something or pay a debt. **2** money given as a guarantee that someone will do something.

surf ▶ noun the breaking of large waves on a seashore or reef.
▶ verb **1** stand or lie on a surfboard and ride on the crest of a wave towards the shore. **2** move from site to site on the Internet.
□ **surfer** noun **surfing** noun.

surface ▶ noun **1** the outside or top layer of something. **2** outward appearance.

SYNONYMS **1** *the surface of the wall* **outside,** exterior, top, side, finish. **2** *the surface of polite society* **outward appearance,** facade, veneer. ANTONYMS inside, interior.

▶ verb (**surfaces, surfacing, surfaced**) **1** rise to the surface. **2** become apparent. **3** provide a road, floor, etc. with a top layer.

S

SYNONYMS **1** *a submarine surfaced* **come to the surface**, come up, rise. **2** *the idea first surfaced in the sixties* **emerge**, arise, appear, come to light, crop up, materialize, spring up.
ANTONYMS dive.

surfboard ▸ noun a long, narrow board used in surfing.

surfeit ▸ noun an amount that is more than is needed or wanted.

surge ▸ noun **1** a sudden powerful movement forwards or upwards. **2** a sudden increase. **3** a powerful rush of an emotion or feeling.

SYNONYMS **1** *a surge of water* **gush**, rush, outpouring, stream, flow. **2** *a surge in demand* **increase**, rise, growth, upswing, upsurge, escalation, leap. **3** *a sudden surge of anger* **rush**, storm, torrent, blaze, outburst, eruption.

▸ verb (**surges, surging, surged**) **1** move in a surge. **2** increase suddenly and powerfully.

SYNONYMS **1** *the water surged into people's homes* **gush**, rush, stream, flow, burst, pour, cascade, spill, sweep, roll. **2** *the Dow Jones index surged 47.63 points* **increase**, rise, grow, leap.

surgeon ▸ noun a doctor who is qualified to practise surgery.

surgery ▸ noun (plural **surgeries**) **1** medical treatment that involves cutting open the body and repairing or removing parts. **2** Brit. a place where a doctor or nurse sees patients.

surgical ▸ adjective relating to or used in surgery.
■ **surgical spirit** Brit. methylated spirit used for cleaning the skin before injections or surgery.
□ **surgically** adverb.

surly ▸ adjective (**surlier, surliest**) bad-tempered and unfriendly.

surmise ▸ verb (**surmises, surmising, surmised**) suppose something without having evidence.
▸ noun a guess.

surmount ▸ verb **1** overcome a difficulty or obstacle. **2** stand or be placed on top of.

surname ▸ noun an inherited name used by all the members of a family.

surpass ▸ verb be greater or better than.

SYNONYMS **excel**, exceed, transcend, outdo, outshine, outstrip, outclass, eclipse, improve on, top, trump, cap, beat, better, outperform.

surplice ▸ noun a white robe worn over a cassock by Christian ministers and people singing in church choirs.

surplus ▸ noun an amount left over.

SYNONYMS *food surpluses* **excess**, surfeit, superfluity, oversupply, glut, remainder, residue, remains, leftovers.
ANTONYMS dearth.

▸ adjective more than what is needed or used.

SYNONYMS *surplus cash* **excess**, leftover, unused, remaining, extra, additional, spare, superfluous, redundant, unwanted, unneeded, dispensable.
ANTONYMS insufficient.

surprise ▸ noun **1** a feeling of mild astonishment or shock caused by something unexpected. **2** an unexpected or astonishing thing.

SYNONYMS **1** *Kate looked at me in surprise* **astonishment**, amazement, wonder, bewilderment, disbelief. **2** *the test came as a big surprise* **shock**, bolt from the blue, bombshell, revelation, rude awakening, eye-opener.

▸ verb (**surprises, surprising, surprised**) **1** make someone feel surprise. **2** attack or discover suddenly and unexpectedly.

SYNONYMS **1** *I was so surprised that I dropped it* **astonish**, amaze, startle, astound, stun, stagger, shock; informal bowl over, floor, flabbergast; Brit. informal knock for six. **2** (**surprising**) **unexpected**, unforeseen, astonishing, amazing, startling, astounding, staggering, incredible, extraordinary. **3** *she surprised a burglar* **take by surprise**, catch unawares, catch off guard, catch red-handed.

✔ Don't forget the first **r**, and note also that **surprise** can't be spelled with an **-ize** ending: surprise.

surreal ▸ adjective strange and having the qualities of a dream.
□ **surreally** adverb.

surrealism ▸ noun an artistic movement which combined normally unrelated images in a bizarre way.
□ **surrealist** noun & adjective.

surrender ▸ verb (**surrenders, surrendering, surrendered**) **1** give in to an opponent. **2** give up a right or possession. **3** (**surrender yourself to**) abandon yourself to a powerful emotion or influence.

SYNONYMS **1** *the gunmen surrendered* **give up**, give yourself up, give in, cave in, capitulate, concede (defeat), submit, lay down your arms/weapons. **2** *they surrendered power to the government* **give up**, relinquish, renounce, cede, abdicate, forfeit, sacrifice, hand over, turn over, yield.
ANTONYMS resist, seize.

▸ noun an act of surrendering.

SYNONYMS **1** *the surrender of the hijackers* **capitulation,** submission, yielding. **2** *a surrender of power* **relinquishment,** renunciation, abdication, resignation.

surreptitious ▸ adjective done secretly.
□ **surreptitiously** adverb.

surrogate ▸ noun a person who stands in for someone else.
■ **surrogate mother** a woman who gives birth to a child on behalf of another woman.
□ **surrogacy** noun.

surround ▸ verb **1** be all round someone or something. **2** be associated with.

SYNONYMS **1 encircle,** enclose, encompass, ring, hem in, confine, cut off, besiege, trap. **2** (**surrounding**) **neighbouring,** enclosing, nearby, near, local, adjoining, adjacent.

▸ noun **1** a border or edging. **2** (**surrounds**) the area around something.

surroundings ▸ plural noun the conditions or area around a person or thing.

SYNONYMS **environment,** setting, background, backdrop, vicinity, locality, habitat.

surtax ▸ noun an extra tax on something already taxed.

surtitle ▸ noun a caption projected on a screen above the stage in an opera, translating the words that are being sung.

surveillance /ser-**vay**-luhnss/ ▸ noun close observation, especially of a suspected spy or criminal.

survey ▸ verb (**surveys, surveying, surveyed**) **1** look carefully and thoroughly at. **2** examine and record the features of an area of land in order to produce a map or description. **3** Brit. examine and report on the condition of a building. **4** question a group of people to find out their opinions.

SYNONYMS **1** *he surveyed his work* **look at,** look over, view, contemplate, regard, gaze at, stare at, eye, scrutinize, examine, inspect, scan, study; informal size up. **2** *they surveyed 4,000 drug users* **interview,** question, canvass, poll, investigate, research, study. **3** *he was asked to survey the house* **inspect,** assess, appraise, prospect.

▸ noun **1** an investigation into the opinions or experience of a group of people, based on a series of questions. **2** a general view, examination, or description. **3** an act of surveying. **4** a map or report obtained by surveying.

SYNONYMS **1** *a survey of the current literature* **study,** review, overview, examination. **2** *a survey of sexual behaviour* **poll,** investigation, enquiry,

study, probe, questionnaire, census, research. **3** *a thorough survey of the property* **inspection,** assessment, appraisal.
□ **surveyor** noun.

survival ▸ noun **1** the state or fact of surviving. **2** an object or practice that has survived from an earlier time.

survive ▸ verb (**survives, surviving, survived**) **1** continue to live or exist. **2** remain alive after an accident or ordeal. **3** remain alive after someone has died.

SYNONYMS **1** *he survived by escaping through a hole* **remain alive,** live, sustain yourself, pull through, hold out, make it. **2** *the theatre must survive* **continue,** remain, persist, endure, live on, persevere, abide, go on, carry on. **3** *he was survived by his sons* **outlive,** outlast.

□ **survivor** noun.

susceptibility ▸ noun (plural **susceptibilities**) the quality of being easily influenced or hurt.

susceptible ▸ adjective **1** (**susceptible to**) likely to be influenced or harmed by. **2** easily influenced by feelings or emotions.

sushi /soo-shi/ ▸ noun a Japanese dish consisting of balls of cold rice with raw seafood, vegetables, etc.

suspect ▸ verb **1** believe something to be likely or possible. **2** believe that someone is guilty of a crime or offence, without having definite proof. **3** feel that something may not be genuine or true.

SYNONYMS **1** *I suspected she'd made a mistake* **have a suspicion,** have a feeling, feel, be inclined to think, fancy, reckon, guess, surmise, have a hunch, fear. **2** *he had no reason to suspect me* **doubt,** distrust, mistrust, have misgivings about, have qualms about, be suspicious of.

▸ noun a person suspected of a crime or offence.
▸ adjective possibly dangerous or false.

SYNONYMS *a suspect package* **suspicious,** dubious, doubtful, untrustworthy; informal fishy, funny; Brit. informal dodgy.

suspend ▸ verb **1** temporarily bring a stop to something. **2** temporarily stop someone from doing their job or attending school, as a punishment or during an investigation. **3** postpone or delay an action, event, or judgement. **4** (**suspended**) (of a sentence given by a court) not enforced as long as no further offence is committed. **5** hang something in the air.

SYNONYMS **1** *the court case was suspended* **adjourn,** interrupt, break off, cut short, discontinue; N. Amer. table. **2** *he was suspended from college* **exclude,** debar,

S

remove, expel, eject, rusticate. **3** *lights were suspended from the ceiling* **hang**, sling, string, swing, dangle.

suspender ▸ noun **1** Brit. an elastic strap attached to a belt and fastened to the top of a stocking to hold it up. **2** (**suspenders**) N. Amer. braces for holding up trousers.

suspense ▸ noun a state or feeling of excited or anxious uncertainty about what may happen.

> SYNONYMS **tension**, uncertainty, doubt, anticipation, excitement, anxiety, strain.

suspension ▸ noun **1** the action of suspending something or the state of being suspended. **2** a system of springs and shock absorbers which supports a vehicle on its wheels and makes it more comfortable to ride in. **3** a mixture in which particles are spread throughout a fluid.
■ **suspension bridge** a bridge which is suspended from cables running between towers.

suspicion ▸ noun **1** an idea that something is possible or likely or that someone has done something wrong. **2** a feeling of distrust. **3** a very slight trace.

> SYNONYMS **1** *she had a suspicion that he didn't like her* **intuition**, feeling, impression, inkling, hunch, fancy, notion, idea, theory, premonition; informal gut feeling. **2** *I confronted him with my suspicions* **misgiving**, doubt, qualm, reservation, hesitation, question. ANTONYMS trust.

suspicious ▸ adjective **1** having a feeling that someone has done something wrong. **2** making you feel that something is wrong. **3** not able to trust other people.

> SYNONYMS **1** *she gave him a suspicious look* **doubtful**, unsure, dubious, wary, sceptical, mistrustful. **2** *a suspicious character* **suspect**, dubious, unsavoury, disreputable; informal shifty, shady; Brit. informal dodgy. **3** *in suspicious circumstances* **strange**, odd, questionable, irregular, funny, doubtful, mysterious, murky; informal fishy; Brit. informal dodgy. ANTONYMS trusting, honest, innocent.

□ **suspiciously** adverb.

suss ▸ verb (**susses, sussing, sussed**) (often **suss someone/thing out**) Brit. informal realize or understand the true character or nature of.

sustain ▸ verb **1** strengthen or support someone physically or mentally. **2** keep something going over time or continuously. **3** experience something unpleasant. **4** carry the weight of an object.

> SYNONYMS **1** *she had bread and cheese to sustain her* **nourish**, feed, nurture, keep alive, keep going. **2** *her memories*

sustained her **comfort**, help, assist, encourage, support, give strength to, buoy up. **3** *they were unable to sustain a coalition* **continue**, carry on, keep up, keep alive, maintain, preserve. **4** (**sustained**) **continuous**, ongoing, steady, continual, constant, prolonged, persistent, non-stop, perpetual, relentless. **5** *she sustained slight injuries* **suffer**, experience, undergo, receive. **6** *the allegation was not sustained* **confirm**, corroborate, substantiate, bear out, prove, authenticate, back up, uphold.

sustainable ▸ adjective **1** able to be sustained. **2** (of industry, development, or agriculture) avoiding using up natural resources.
□ **sustainability** noun **sustainably** adverb.

sustenance ▸ noun **1** the food needed to keep someone alive. **2** the process of keeping something going.

suture ▸ noun a stitch holding together the edges of a wound or surgical cut.
▸ verb (**sutures, suturing, sutured**) stitch up a wound or cut.

suzerainty /soo-zuh-rayn-ti/ ▸ noun the right of one country to rule over another country which has its own ruler but is not fully independent.

svelte ▸ adjective slender and elegant.

SW ▸ abbreviation south-west or south-western.

swab ▸ noun **1** a pad used for cleaning a wound or taking liquid from the body for testing. **2** a sample of liquid taken with a swab.
▸ verb (**swabs, swabbing, swabbed**) **1** clean or take liquid from a wound or part of the body with a swab. **2** wash down a surface with water and a cloth or mop.

swaddle ▸ verb (**swaddles, swaddling, swaddled**) wrap in clothes or a cloth.
■ **swaddling clothes** (in the past) strips of cloth wrapped round a baby to calm it.

swag ▸ noun **1** a curtain hanging in a drooping curve. **2** informal property stolen by a burglar.

swagger ▸ verb (**swaggers, swaggering, swaggered**) walk or behave in a very confident or arrogant way.
▸ noun a swaggering walk or way of behaving.

swain ▸ noun old use **1** a young male lover. **2** a country youth.

swallow[1] ▸ verb **1** contract the muscles of the mouth and throat so that food, drink, or saliva pass down the throat. **2** (**swallow someone/thing up**) surround or cover someone or something so that they disappear. **3** believe an untrue statement without question.

S

SYNONYMS **eat,** drink, gulp down, consume, devour, put away, quaff, slug; informal swig, swill, down; Brit. informal scoff.

▶ noun an act of swallowing.

swallow² ▶ noun a fast-flying bird with a forked tail.

swam past of SWIM.

swamp ▶ noun an area of boggy or marshy land.

SYNONYMS *he got stuck in the swamp* **marsh,** bog, fen, quagmire.

▶ verb **1** flood an area with water. **2** overwhelm with too much of something.

SYNONYMS **1** *the rain was swamping the boat* **flood,** inundate, deluge, fill. **2** *he was swamped by media attention* **overwhelm,** inundate, flood, deluge, engulf, snow under.

□ **swampy** adjective.

swan ▶ noun a large white waterbird with a long flexible neck.

▶ verb (**swans, swanning, swanned**) Brit. informal go around enjoying yourself in a way that makes other people jealous or annoyed.

swank informal ▶ verb show off your achievements, knowledge, or wealth.
▶ noun the act of showing off.

swanky ▶ adjective (**swankier, swankiest**) informal stylishly luxurious and expensive.

swansong ▶ noun the final performance or activity of a person's career.

swap (or **swop**) ▶ verb (**swaps, swapping, swapped**) exchange or substitute something for something else.

SYNONYMS **exchange,** trade, barter, switch, change, replace.

▶ noun an act of swapping.

sward ▶ noun literary an area of grass.

swarm ▶ noun **1** a large group of insects flying closely together. **2** a large number of honeybees that leave a hive with a queen in order to form a new colony. **3** a large group of people or things.

SYNONYMS **1** *a swarm of bees* **hive,** flock. **2** *a swarm of reporters* **crowd,** horde, mob, throng, mass, army, herd, pack.

▶ verb **1** move in or form a swarm. **2** (**swarm with**) be crowded or overrun with. **3** (**swarm up**) climb something rapidly by gripping with your hands and feet.

SYNONYMS *reporters were swarming all over the place* **flock,** crowd, throng, surge, stream.

swarthy ▶ adjective (**swarthier, swarthiest**) having a dark skin.

swashbuckling ▶ adjective having many daring and romantic adventures.
□ **swashbuckler** noun.

swastika /swoss-ti-kuh/ ▶ noun an ancient symbol in the form of a cross with its arms bent at a right angle, used in the 20th century as the emblem of the Nazi party.

swat ▶ verb (**swats, swatting, swatted**) hit or crush something with a sharp blow from a flat object.

swatch ▶ noun a piece of fabric used as a sample.

swathe¹ /swayth/ (US spelling **swath** /swawth/) ▶ noun (plural **swathes** or **swaths**) **1** a broad strip or area. **2** a row or line of grass, corn, etc. as it falls when cut down.

swathe² /swayth/ ▶ verb (**swathes, swathing, swathed**) wrap in several layers of fabric.

SYNONYMS **wrap,** envelop, bandage, cover, shroud, drape, wind, enfold.

sway ▶ verb **1** move slowly and rhythmically backwards and forwards or from side to side. **2** make someone change their opinion.

SYNONYMS **1** *the curtains swayed in the breeze* **swing,** shake, undulate, move to and fro. **2** *she swayed on her feet* **stagger,** wobble, rock, lurch, reel, roll. **3** *we are swayed by the media* **influence,** affect, manipulate, bend, mould.

▶ noun **1** a swaying movement. **2** influence or control over people.

SYNONYMS **1** *the sway of her hips* **swing,** roll, shake, undulation. **2** *a province under the sway of the Franks* **power,** rule, government, sovereignty, dominion, control, jurisdiction, authority.

■ **hold sway** have power or influence.

swear ▶ verb (**swears, swearing, swore;** past participle **sworn**) **1** promise something solemnly or on oath. **2** use offensive or obscene language.

SYNONYMS **1** *they swore to protect each other* **promise,** vow, pledge, give your word, undertake, guarantee. **2** *she swore she would never go back* **insist,** declare, proclaim, assert, maintain, emphasize, stress. **3** *Kate spilled her wine and swore* **curse,** blaspheme, use bad language; informal cuss, eff and blind. **4** (**swearing**) **bad language,** strong language, cursing, blaspheming, obscenities, expletives, swear words; informal effing and blinding, four-letter words.

■ **swear by** informal have or express great confidence in. **swear someone in** admit someone to a new post by making them take a formal oath. **swear word** an offensive or obscene word.

sweat ▶ noun moisture that comes out through the pores of the skin when you are hot, making a physical effort, or anxious.

S

synonyms *drenched with sweat* **perspiration**.

▶ verb (**sweats, sweating,** past and past participle **sweated** or N. Amer. **sweat**) **1** give off sweat. **2** (**sweat over**) make a lot of effort in doing something. **3** be very anxious.

synonyms **1** *she was sweating heavily* **perspire. 2** *I've sweated over this book* **work,** labour, toil, slog, slave, work your fingers to the bone.

□ **sweaty** adjective.

sweatband ▶ noun a band of absorbent material worn round the head or wrists to soak up sweat.

sweater ▶ noun a pullover with long sleeves.

sweatshirt ▶ noun a loose, warm cotton sweater.

sweatshop ▶ noun a factory or workshop employing workers for long hours in bad conditions.

swede ▶ noun **1** (**Swede**) a person from Sweden. **2** Brit. a round yellow root vegetable.

Swedish ▶ noun the language of Sweden. ▶ adjective relating to Sweden.

sweep ▶ verb (**sweeps, sweeping, swept**) **1** clean an area by brushing away dirt or litter. **2** move quickly or forcefully. **3** (**sweep something away** or **aside**) remove or abolish something quickly and suddenly. **4** search an area.

synonyms **1** *she swept the floor* **brush,** clean, scrub, mop, scour. **2** *he was swept out to sea* **carry,** pull, drag, tow. **3** *riots swept the country* **engulf,** overwhelm, flood, spread across. **4** *she swept down the stairs* **glide,** sail, breeze, drift, race, speed, stride.

▶ noun **1** an act of sweeping. **2** a long, swift, curving movement. **3** a long curved stretch of road, river, etc. **4** the range or scope of something. **5** (also **chimney sweep**) a person who cleans out the soot from chimneys.

synonyms **1** *a sweep of his hand* **gesture,** stroke, wave, movement. **2** *a long sweep of golden sand* **expanse,** tract, stretch, extent. **3** *the broad sweep of our interests* **range,** scope, compass, reach, spread, extent.

□ **sweeper** noun.

sweeping ▶ adjective **1** extending or performed in a long, continuous curve. **2** wide in range or effect. **3** (of a statement) too general.

synonyms **1** *sweeping changes* **extensive,** wide-ranging, broad, comprehensive, far-reaching, thorough, radical. **2** *sweeping statements* **wholesale,** blanket, general, unqualified, indiscriminate, oversimplified.
antonyms limited, focused.

sweepstake (or **sweepstakes**) ▶ noun a form of gambling in which the winner receives all the money bet by the other players.

sweet ▶ adjective **1** having the pleasant taste characteristic of sugar. **2** having a pleasant smell. **3** pleasing or satisfying. **4** charming and endearing. **5** kind and thoughtful.

synonyms **1** *sweet biscuits* **sugary,** sweetened, sugared, honeyed, sickly, cloying. **2** *the sweet scent of roses* **fragrant,** aromatic, perfumed. **3** *her sweet voice* **musical,** melodious, dulcet, tuneful, soft, harmonious, silvery. **4** *life was still sweet* **pleasant,** agreeable, delightful, nice, satisfying, gratifying, good. **5** *she has a sweet nature* **likeable,** appealing, engaging, amiable, pleasant, agreeable, kind, thoughtful, considerate, delightful, lovely. **6** *she looks sweet* **cute,** lovable, adorable, endearing, charming.
antonyms sour, savoury, harsh, disagreeable.

▶ noun Brit. **1** a small item of sweet food made with sugar, chocolate, etc. **2** a sweet dish forming a course of a meal.

synonyms **1** *sweets for the children* **confectionery,** bonbon; N. Amer. candy; informal sweetie. **2** *a delicious sweet for the guests* **dessert,** pudding; Brit. informal afters, pud.

■ **sweet-and-sour** cooked with both sugar and vinegar. **sweet pea** a climbing plant of the pea family with colourful, sweet-smelling flowers. **sweet pepper** a large pepper with a mild or sweet flavour. **sweet potato** the pinkish-orange tuber of a tropical climbing plant, eaten as a vegetable. **sweet-talk** informal use charming or flattering words to persuade someone to do something. **sweet tooth** a great liking for sweet-tasting foods.
□ **sweetly** adverb **sweetness** noun.

sweetbread ▶ noun an animal's pancreas, eaten as food.

sweetcorn ▶ noun a kind of maize with sweet-tasting yellow kernels which are eaten as a vegetable.

sweeten ▶ verb **1** make or become sweet or sweeter. **2** make more pleasant or acceptable.

sweetener ▶ noun **1** a substance used to sweeten food or drink. **2** informal a bribe.

sweetheart ▶ noun a person you are in love with.

synonyms **1** *you look lovely, sweetheart* **darling,** dear, dearest, love, beloved, sweet; informal honey, sweetie, sugar, baby, poppet. **2** *my high-school sweetheart* **lover,** love, girlfriend, boyfriend, beloved; informal steady, flame.

sweetmeat ▶ noun old use a sweet or other item of sweet food.

swell ▶ verb (swells, swelling, swelled; past participle **swollen** or **swelled**) **1** become larger or more rounded. **2** increase in strength, amount, or loudness.

> SYNONYMS **1** *her lip swelled up* **expand,** bulge, distend, inflate, dilate, bloat, puff up, balloon, fatten, fill out. **2** *the population swelled* **grow,** enlarge, increase, expand, rise, escalate, multiply, proliferate, snowball, mushroom. ANTONYMS shrink, decrease.

▶ noun **1** a slow, regular, rolling movement of the sea. **2** a full or gently rounded form. **3** a gradual increase in strength, amount, or loudness.

> SYNONYMS *a heavy swell on the sea* **surge,** wave, roll.

▶ adjective N. Amer. informal, dated excellent.

swelling ▶ noun a place on the body that has swollen as a result of illness or an injury.

> SYNONYMS **bump,** lump, bulge, protuberance, protrusion, distension.

swelter ▶ verb (swelters, sweltering, sweltered) be uncomfortably hot.

swept past and past participle of SWEEP.

swerve ▶ verb (swerves, swerving, swerved) abruptly go off from a straight course.
▶ noun an abrupt change of course.

swift ▶ adjective **1** happening quickly or promptly. **2** moving or able to move very fast.

> SYNONYMS **1** *a swift decision* **prompt,** rapid, quick, sudden, immediate, instant, abrupt, hasty, hurried. **2** *swift runners* **fast,** rapid, quick, speedy, brisk, lively. ANTONYMS slow, leisurely.

▶ noun a fast-flying bird with long, slender wings.
□ **swiftly** adverb **swiftness** noun.

swig ▶ verb (swigs, swigging, swigged) drink deeply and quickly.
▶ noun a quick, deep drink.

swill ▶ verb Brit. **1** rinse something out with large amounts of water. **2** (of liquid) swirl round in a container or cavity.
▶ noun waste food mixed with water for feeding to pigs.

swim ▶ verb (swims, swimming, swam; past participle **swum**) **1** move through water using your arms and legs. **2** be covered with liquid. **3** experience a dizzy, confusing feeling.
▶ noun a period of swimming.
□ **swimmer** noun.

swimmingly ▶ adverb informal smoothly and satisfactorily.

swimsuit ▶ noun a woman's one-piece garment for swimming.

swindle ▶ verb (swindles, swindling, swindled) cheat someone in order to get money from them.
▶ noun a dishonest scheme to get money from someone.
□ **swindler** noun.

swine ▶ noun **1** (plural **swine**) a pig. **2** (plural **swine** or **swines**) informal an unpleasant person.
□ **swinish** adjective.

swing ▶ verb (swings, swinging, swung) **1** move backwards and forwards or from side to side while suspended. **2** move by grasping a support and leaping. **3** move in a smooth, curving line. **4** (**swing at**) attempt to hit. **5** change from one opinion, mood, or situation to another. **6** have a decisive influence on a vote or opinion. **7** informal succeed in bringing something about.

> SYNONYMS **1** *the sign swung in the wind* **sway,** move back and forth, oscillate, wave, rock, swivel, pivot, turn, rotate. **2** *Helen swung the bottle* **brandish,** wave, flourish, wield. **3** *the road swings round* **curve,** bend, veer, turn, bear, wind, twist, deviate, slew. **4** *the needle swings to the right* **rotate,** swivel, pivot, turn.

▶ noun **1** a seat suspended by ropes or chains, on which you can sit and swing backwards and forwards. **2** an act of swinging. **3** a clear change in public opinion. **4** a style of jazz or dance music with an easy flowing rhythm.

> SYNONYMS **1** *a swing of the pendulum* **oscillation,** sway, wave. **2** *the swing to the Conservatives* **change,** move, turnaround, turnabout, reversal. **3** *mood swings* **fluctuation,** change, shift, variation, oscillation.

swingeing /swin-jing/ ▶ adjective Brit. extreme or severe.

swinging ▶ adjective informal lively, exciting, and fashionable.

swipe informal ▶ verb (swipes, swiping, swiped) **1** hit or try to hit something with a swinging blow. **2** steal. **3** pass a swipe card through an electronic reader.
▶ noun a swinging blow.
■ **swipe card** a plastic card carrying coded information which is read when the card is slid through an electronic device.

swirl ▶ verb move in a twisting or spiralling pattern.

> SYNONYMS **whirl,** eddy, billow, spiral, twist, twirl, circulate, revolve, spin.

▶ noun a swirling movement or pattern.
□ **swirly** adjective.

swish ▶ verb move with a soft rushing sound.

▶ **noun** a soft rushing sound or movement.
▶ **adjective** Brit. informal impressively smart.

Swiss ▶ **adjective** relating to Switzerland.
▶ **noun** (plural **Swiss**) a person from Switzerland.
  ■ **Swiss roll** Brit. a thin sponge cake spread with jam or cream and rolled up.

switch ▶ **noun 1** a device for making and breaking an electrical connection. **2** a change or exchange. **3** a flexible shoot cut from a tree.

> SYNONYMS **1** *the switch on top of the telephone* **button,** lever, control. **2** *a switch from direct to indirect taxation* **change,** move, shift, transition, transformation, reversal, turnaround, U-turn, changeover, transfer, conversion.

▶ **verb 1** change in position, direction, or focus. **2** exchange one thing for another. **3** (**switch something off** or **on**) turn an electrical device off or on. **4** (**switch off**) informal stop paying attention.

> SYNONYMS **1** *he switched sides* **change,** shift; informal chop and change. **2** *he managed to switch the envelopes* **exchange,** swap, interchange, change round, rotate.

switchback ▶ **noun** Brit. a road that alternately slopes up and down very steeply.

switchblade ▶ **noun** N. Amer. a flick knife.

switchboard ▶ **noun** a device for putting phone calls made to an organization through to the right person.

swivel ▶ **verb** (**swivels, swivelling, swivelled;** US spelling **swivels, swiveling, swiveled**) turn around a central point.
▶ **noun** a connecting device between two parts enabling one to revolve without turning the other.

swizz ▶ **noun** Brit. informal an instance of being mildly cheated or disappointed.

swollen past participle of SWELL.

swoon literary ▶ **verb** faint, especially from strong emotion.
▶ **noun** an act of fainting.

swoop ▶ **verb 1** move rapidly downwards through the air. **2** carry out a sudden raid.

> SYNONYMS **1** *pigeons swooped down after the grain* **dive,** descend, pounce, plunge, pitch, nosedive. **2** *police swooped on the flat* **raid,** descend on, pounce on, attack; N. Amer. informal bust.

▶ **noun** an act of swooping.

swop ➡ SWAP.

sword ▶ **noun** a weapon with a long, sharp metal blade.

swordfish ▶ **noun** (plural **swordfish** or **swordfishes**) a large sea fish with a sword-like snout.

swore past of SWEAR.

sworn past participle of SWEAR.
▶ **adjective 1** made after having sworn to tell the truth. **2** determined to remain so: *sworn enemies.*

swot Brit. informal ▶ **verb** (**swots, swotting, swotted**) study hard.
▶ **noun** a person who spends a lot of time studying.

swum past participle of SWIM.

swung past and past participle of SWING.

sybarite /si-buh-ryt/ ▶ **noun** a person who is very fond of luxury.
  □ **sybaritic** adjective.

sycamore ▶ **noun 1** a tree with five-pointed leaves and seeds shaped like wings. **2** N. Amer. a plane tree.

sycophant /si-kuh-fant/ ▶ **noun** a person who tries to gain favour with someone important by saying flattering things to them.
  □ **sycophancy** noun **sycophantic** adjective.

syllable ▶ **noun** a unit of pronunciation having one vowel sound and forming all or part of a word.
  □ **syllabic** adjective.

syllabub ▶ **noun** a dessert made of whipped cream flavoured with white wine or sherry.

syllabus ▶ **noun** (plural **syllabuses** or **syllabi** /sil-luh-by/) all the things covered in a course of study or teaching.

syllogism /sil-luh-ji-z'm/ ▶ **noun** a form of reasoning in which a conclusion is drawn from two propositions.

sylph ▶ **noun 1** a slender woman or girl. **2** an imaginary spirit of the air.
  □ **sylphlike** adjective.

sylvan ▶ **adjective** literary having to do with woods and trees.

symbiosis /sim-by-oh-siss/ ▶ **noun** (plural **symbioses** /sim-by-oh-seez/) Biology a situation in which two living things are connected with and dependent on each other to the advantage of both.
  □ **symbiotic** adjective.

symbol ▶ **noun 1** an object, person, or event that represents something else. **2** a letter, mark, or character used as a representation of something.

> SYNONYMS **1** *the lotus is the symbol of purity* **representation,** token, sign, emblem, figure, image, metaphor, allegory. **2** *the chemical symbol for helium* **sign,** character, mark, letter. **3** *the Red Cross symbol* **logo,** emblem, badge, stamp, trademark, crest, insignia, coat of arms, seal, device, monogram, hallmark, motif.

symbolic ▶ **adjective 1** acting as a symbol. **2** involving the use of symbols or symbolism.
  □ **symbolically** adverb.

S

symbolism ▸ noun the use of symbols to represent ideas or qualities.
  □ **symbolist** noun & adjective.

symbolize (or **symbolise**) ▸ verb (**symbolizes, symbolizing, symbolized**) **1** be a symbol of. **2** represent something by means of symbols.

symmetrical ▸ adjective exactly the same on each side.

> SYNONYMS **regular**, uniform, consistent, even, equal, balanced, proportional.

  □ **symmetrically** adverb.

symmetry ▸ noun (plural **symmetries**) **1** the exact match in size or shape between two halves, parts, or sides of something. **2** the quality of being exactly the same or very similar.

sympathetic ▸ adjective **1** feeling or showing sympathy. **2** showing approval of an idea or action. **3** pleasing or likeable.

> SYNONYMS **1** *a sympathetic listener* **compassionate**, caring, concerned, understanding, sensitive, supportive. **2** *the most sympathetic character in the book* **likeable**, pleasant, agreeable, congenial.
> ANTONYMS unsympathetic, unfeeling, unlikeable.

  □ **sympathetically** adverb.

sympathize (or **sympathise**) ▸ verb (**sympathizes, sympathizing, sympathized**) **1** feel or express sympathy. **2** agree with an opinion.

> SYNONYMS **commiserate**, show concern, offer condolences; (**sympathize with**) pity, feel sorry for, feel for, identify with, understand, relate to.

sympathy ▸ noun (plural **sympathies**) **1** the feeling of being sorry for someone. **2** support for or approval of something. **3** understanding between people.

> SYNONYMS **compassion**, care, concern, commiseration, pity.
> ANTONYMS indifference.

  ■ **in sympathy** fitting in; in keeping.

symphonic ▸ adjective having the form of a symphony.

symphony ▸ noun (plural **symphonies**) a long, elaborate piece of music for a full orchestra.

symposium /sim-**poh**-zi-uhm/ ▸ noun (plural **symposia** /sim-**poh**-zi-uh/ or **symposiums**) a conference to discuss a particular academic subject.

symptom ▸ noun **1** a change in the body or mind which is the sign of a disease. **2** a sign of an undesirable situation.

> SYNONYMS **indication**, indicator, manifestation, sign, mark, feature, trait, clue, hint, warning, evidence, proof.

  □ **symptomatic** adjective.

synagogue /**sin**-uh-gog/ ▸ noun a building where Jews meet for worship and teaching.

synapse /**sy**-naps, si-**naps**/ ▸ noun a connection between two nerve cells.
  □ **synaptic** adjective.

sync (or **synch**) ▸ noun informal synchronization.
  ■ **in** (or **out of**) **sync** working well (or badly) together.

synchromesh ▸ noun a system of gear changing in which the gearwheels are made to revolve at the same speed during engagement.

synchronize (or **synchronise**) ▸ verb (**synchronizes, synchronizing, synchronized**) make things happen or operate at the same time or rate.
  □ **synchronization** noun.

synchronous /**sing**-kruh-nuhss/ ▸ adjective existing or happening at the same time.

syncopate ▸ verb (**syncopates, syncopating, syncopated**) alter the beats or accents of music so that strong beats become weak and vice versa.
  □ **syncopation** noun.

syndicate ▸ noun /**sin**-di-kuht/ a group of people or organizations who get together to promote a common interest.
  ▸ verb /**sin**-di-kayt/ (**syndicates, syndicating, syndicated**) **1** control or manage an operation through a syndicate. **2** publish or broadcast something in a number of different ways at the same time.
  □ **syndication** noun.

syndrome ▸ noun a set of medical symptoms which tend to occur together.

synergy ▸ noun the working together of two or more people or things to produce a combined effect that is greater than the sum of their separate effects.

synod ▸ noun an official meeting of Church ministers and members.

synonym /**sin**-uh-nim/ ▸ noun a word or phrase that means the same as another word or phrase in the same language.

synonymous /si-**non**-i-muhss/ ▸ adjective **1** (of a word or phrase) having the same meaning as another word or phrase in the same language. **2** closely associated.

synopsis ▸ noun (plural **synopses**) a brief summary or survey.

syntax ▸ noun the way in which words and phrases are put together to form sentences.
  □ **syntactic** adjective **syntactical** adjective.

synthesis /**sin**-thuh-siss/ ▸ noun (plural **syntheses** /**sin**-thuh-seez/) **1** the combination of parts to form a connected whole. **2** the production of chemical compounds from simpler materials.

S

synthesize (or **synthesise**) ▶ verb (**synthesizes, synthesizing, synthesized**) **1** combine parts into a connected whole. **2** make something by chemical synthesis. **3** produce sound with a synthesizer.

synthesizer (or **synthesiser**) ▶ noun an electronic musical instrument that produces sounds by generating and combining signals of different frequencies.

synthetic ▶ adjective **1** made by chemical synthesis, especially to imitate a natural product. **2** not genuine.

> SYNONYMS **artificial**, fake, imitation, mock, simulated, man-made, manufactured; informal pretend.
> ANTONYMS natural.

□ **synthetically** adverb.

syphilis ▶ noun a disease caused by bacteria that are passed on during sex.
□ **syphilitic** adjective.

syphon ➡ SIPHON.

Syrian ▶ noun a person from Syria.
▶ adjective relating to Syria.

syringe ▶ noun a tube with a nozzle and a piston that is fitted with a hollow needle for injecting drugs or withdrawing blood.

syrup (US spelling **sirup**) ▶ noun **1** a thick sweet liquid made by dissolving sugar in boiling water. **2** a thick sweet liquid containing medicine or diluted to make a drink.

syrupy (US spelling **sirupy**) ▶ adjective **1** like syrup. **2** too sentimental.

system ▶ noun **1** a set of things that are connected or that work together. **2** an organized scheme or method. **3** (**the system**) the laws and rules that govern society.

> SYNONYMS **1** *a system of canals* **structure**, organization, arrangement, complex, network; informal set-up. **2** *a system for regulating sales* **method**, technique, procedure, means, way, scheme, plan, policy, programme, formula, routine. **3** (**the system**) **the establishment**, the administration, the authorities, the powers that be, bureaucracy, officialdom.

systematic ▶ adjective done according to a system.

> SYNONYMS **structured**, methodical, organized, orderly, planned, regular, routine, standardized, standard, logical, coherent, consistent.
> ANTONYMS unstructured, disorganized.

□ **systematically** adverb.

systematize (or **systematise**) ▶ verb (**systematizes, systematizing, systematized**) arrange things according to an organized system.

systemic /si-steem-ik/ ▶ adjective affecting the whole of a system.

systole /siss-tuh-li/ ▶ noun the stage of the heartbeat when the heart muscle contracts and pumps blood into the arteries.
□ **systolic** /si-stol-lik/ adjective.

S

Tt

T (or **t**) ▸ noun (plural **Ts** or **T's**) the twentieth letter of the alphabet.
■ **to a T** informal to perfection. **T-bone** a large piece of steak containing a T-shaped bone. **T-shirt** a short-sleeved casual top. **T-square** a T-shaped instrument for drawing or testing right angles.

TA ▸ abbreviation Territorial Army.

ta ▸ exclamation Brit. informal thank you.

tab¹ ▸ noun **1** a small flap or strip of material attached to something. **2** informal, chiefly N. Amer. a restaurant bill.
■ **keep tabs on** informal keep a watch on.

tab² = TABULATOR.

tab³ ▸ noun informal a tablet containing an illegal drug.

tabard ▸ noun a sleeveless jacket consisting only of front and back pieces with a hole for the head.

tabby ▸ noun (plural **tabbies**) a grey or brownish cat with dark stripes.

tabernacle ▸ noun **1** a place of worship for some religions. **2** (in the Bible) a tent in which the Israelites kept the Ark of the Covenant during the Exodus.

table ▸ noun **1** a piece of furniture with a flat top and legs, for eating, writing, or working at. **2** a set of facts or figures arranged in rows and columns. **3** (**tables**) multiplication sums arranged in sets.

> SYNONYMS **chart**, diagram, figure, graphic, graph, plan, list.

▸ verb (**tables**, **tabling**, **tabled**) Brit. present something for discussion at a meeting.
■ **table tennis** a game played with small round bats and a small hollow ball which is hit across a table over a net. **turn the tables** reverse a situation.

tableau /tab-loh/ ▸ noun (plural **tableaux** /tab-lohz/) a group of models or motionless figures representing a scene.

tablecloth ▸ noun a cloth spread over a table.

table d'hôte /tah-bluh **doht**/ ▸ noun a restaurant menu or meal offered at a fixed price and with limited choices.

tableland ▸ noun a wide area of high, level ground; a plateau.

tablespoon ▸ noun a large spoon for serving food.

tablet ▸ noun **1** a pill. **2** a slab of stone or other hard material on which an inscription is written.

tabloid ▸ noun a newspaper that has small pages and is written in a popular style.

taboo ▸ noun (plural **taboos**) a social custom that prevents people from doing or talking about something.

> SYNONYMS the taboo against lying **prohibition**, proscription, veto, ban.

▸ adjective banned or restricted by social custom.

> SYNONYMS taboo language **forbidden**, prohibited, banned, proscribed, outlawed, off limits, unmentionable, unspeakable, unutterable; informal no go.
> ANTONYMS acceptable.

tabular ▸ adjective (of facts or figures) arranged in columns or tables.

tabulate ▸ verb (**tabulates**, **tabulating**, **tabulated**) arrange facts or figures in columns or tables.
☐ **tabulation** noun.

tabulator ▸ noun a facility in a word-processing program, or a device on a typewriter, used for moving to fixed positions in a document when creating tables or columns.

tachograph ▸ noun an instrument used in commercial road vehicles to provide a record of their speed and the distance travelled.

tachometer /ta-kom-i-ter/ ▸ noun an instrument which measures the working speed of an engine.

tachycardia /ta-ki-kar-di-uh/ ▸ noun an abnormally fast heart rate.

tacit /ta-sit/ ▸ adjective understood or meant without being stated.
☐ **tacitly** adverb.

taciturn /ta-si-tern/ ▸ adjective not saying very much.
☐ **taciturnity** noun.

tack¹ ▸ noun **1** a small broad-headed nail. **2** N. Amer. a drawing pin. **3** a long stitch used to fasten fabrics together temporarily. **4** a course of action. **5** Sailing a sailing boat's course relative to the direction of the wind.

> SYNONYMS *tacks held the carpet down* **pin,** nail, staple, rivet.

▸ **verb 1** fasten or fix with tacks. **2** (**tack something on**) casually add something to something else. **3** change course by turning a boat's head into and through the wind. **4** make a series of such changes of course while sailing.

> SYNONYMS *a photo tacked to the wall* **pin,** nail, staple, fix, fasten, attach, secure.

tack² ▸ noun equipment used in horse riding.

tackle ▸ verb (**tackles, tackling, tackled**) **1** start to deal with a problem or task. **2** confront someone about a difficult issue. **3** (in soccer, hockey, rugby, etc.) try to take the ball from or prevent the movement of an opponent.

> SYNONYMS **1** *we must tackle the problems* **deal with,** take care of, attend to, see to, handle, manage, get to grips with, address, take on. **2** *he tackled an intruder* **confront,** face up to, take on, challenge, attack, grab, struggle with, intercept, block, stop, bring down, floor, fell; informal have a go at.

▸ **noun 1** the equipment needed for a task or sport. **2** a mechanism consisting of ropes, pulley blocks, and hooks for lifting heavy objects. **3** (in sport) an act of tackling an opponent.

> SYNONYMS **1** *fishing tackle* **gear,** equipment, apparatus, kit, hardware; informal things, clobber. **2** *a tackle by the scrum half* **interception,** challenge, block, attack.

□ **tackler** noun.

tacky ▸ adjective (**tackier, tackiest**) **1** (of glue, paint, etc.) not fully dry. **2** informal showing bad taste and quality.

taco ▸ noun (plural **tacos**) (in Mexican cookery) a folded tortilla filled with spicy meat or beans.

tact ▸ noun sensitivity and skill in dealing with other people.

tactful ▸ adjective having or showing tact.

> SYNONYMS **diplomatic,** discreet, considerate, sensitive, understanding, thoughtful, delicate, judicious, subtle.

□ **tactfully** adverb.

tactic ▸ noun **1** the method you use to achieve something. **2** (**tactics**) the art of organizing and directing the movement of soldiers and equipment during a war.

> SYNONYMS **1** *a tax-saving tactic* **scheme,** plan, manoeuvre, method, trick, ploy. **2** (**tactics**) **strategy,** policy, campaign, game plan, planning, generalship, manoeuvres, logistics.

□ **tactician** noun.

tactical ▸ adjective **1** planned in order to achieve a particular end. **2** (of weapons) for use in direct support of military or naval operations. **3** (of voting) done to prevent the strongest candidate from winning, rather than indicating your true political choice.

> SYNONYMS **calculated,** planned, strategic, prudent, politic, diplomatic, judicious, shrewd.

□ **tactically** adverb.

tactile ▸ adjective **1** having to do with the sense of touch. **2** liking to touch other people in a friendly way.

tactless ▸ adjective thoughtless and insensitive.

> SYNONYMS **insensitive,** inconsiderate, thoughtless, indelicate, undiplomatic, indiscreet, unsubtle, inept, gauche, blunt.

□ **tactlessly** adverb.

tad ▸ adverb (**a tad**) informal to a small extent.

tadpole ▸ noun the larva of a frog or toad, which lives in water and has gills, a large head, and a tail.

taffeta ▸ noun a crisp shiny fabric.

tag ▸ noun **1** a label giving information about something. **2** an electronic device attached to someone to monitor their movements. **3** a nickname or commonly used description. **4** a nickname or identifying mark written as the signature of a graffiti artist. **5** a frequently repeated phrase. **6** a metal or plastic point at the end of a shoelace. **7** a chasing game played by children.

> SYNONYMS *a price tag* **label,** ticket, badge, mark, tab, sticker, docket.

▸ **verb** (**tags, tagging, tagged**) **1** attach a tag to. **2** (**tag something on**) add something to the end of something else as an afterthought. **3** (**tag along**) accompany someone without being invited.

> SYNONYMS *bottles tagged with stickers* **label,** mark, ticket, identify, flag, indicate.

tagliatelle /tal-yuh-**tel**-li/ ▸ plural noun pasta in narrow ribbons.

Tahitian /tah-**hee**-shuhn/ ▸ noun a person from Tahiti.

▸ adjective relating to Tahiti.

tail ▸ noun **1** the part at the rear of an animal that sticks out and can be moved. **2** the rear part of an aircraft, with the tailplane and rudder. **3** the final, more distant, or weaker part. **4** (**tails**) the side of a coin without the image of a head on it. **5** (**tails**) informal a tailcoat.

SYNONYMS *the tail of the queue* **rear**, end, back, extremity, bottom.
ANTONYMS head, front, start.

▸ verb 1 informal secretly follow someone. 2 (**tail off** or **away**) gradually become smaller or weaker.

SYNONYMS *the detectives tailed him to his hide-out* **follow**, shadow, stalk, trail, track, keep under surveillance.

tailback ▸ noun Brit. a long queue of stationary traffic.

tailcoat ▸ noun Brit. a man's formal jacket with a long skirt divided at the back into tails and cut away in front.

tailgate ▸ noun 1 a hinged flap at the back of a truck. 2 the door at the back of an estate or hatchback car.

tailor ▸ noun a person who makes men's clothing for individual customers.

SYNONYMS **outfitter**, couturier, costumier, dressmaker, fashion designer.

▸ verb 1 make clothes to fit individual customers. 2 make or adapt for a particular purpose or person.

SYNONYMS *services can be tailored to requirements* **customize**, adapt, adjust, modify, change, convert, alter, mould, gear, fit, shape, tune.

■ **tailor-made** made for a particular purpose.

tailored ▸ adjective (of clothes) smart, fitted, and well cut.

tailplane ▸ noun Brit. a small wing at the tail of an aircraft.

tailspin ▸ noun a fast spinning motion made by a rapidly descending aircraft.

tailwind ▸ noun a wind blowing from behind.

taint ▸ verb 1 contaminate or pollute. 2 affect with a bad or unpleasant quality.

SYNONYMS 1 *the wilderness is tainted by pollution* **contaminate**, pollute, adulterate, infect, blight, spoil, soil, ruin. 2 *fraudulent firms taint our reputation* **tarnish**, sully, blacken, stain, blot, damage.
ANTONYMS clean, improve.

▸ noun a trace of something bad or unpleasant.

Taiwanese ▸ noun (plural **Taiwanese**) a person from Taiwan.
▸ adjective relating to Taiwan.

take ▸ verb (**takes**, **taking**, **took**; past participle **taken**) 1 reach for and hold. 2 occupy a place or position. 3 gain possession of by force. 4 carry or bring with you. 5 remove from a place. 6 subtract. 7 consume. 8 bring into a particular state. 9 experience or be affected by. 10 use as

a route or a means of transport. 11 accept or receive. 12 require or use up. 13 act on an opportunity. 14 see or deal with in a particular way. 15 tolerate or endure. 16 study a subject. 17 do an exam or test.

SYNONYMS 1 *she took his hand* **grasp**, get hold of, grip, clasp, clutch, grab. 2 *he took an envelope from his pocket* **remove**, pull, draw, withdraw, extract, fish. 3 *a passage taken from my book* **extract**, quote, cite, excerpt, derive, abstract, copy, cull. 4 *many prisoners were taken* **capture**, seize, catch, arrest, apprehend, take into custody, carry off, abduct. 5 *someone's taken my car* **steal**, remove, appropriate, make off with, pilfer, purloin; informal filch, swipe, snaffle; Brit. informal pinch, nick. 6 *take four from the total* **subtract**, deduct, remove, discount; informal knock off, minus. 7 *all the seats had been taken* **occupy**, use, utilize, fill, hold, reserve, engage; informal bag. 8 *he took notes* **write**, note (down), jot (down), scribble, scrawl, record, register, document, minute. 9 *I took it back to London* **bring**, carry, bear, transport, convey, move, transfer, shift, ferry; informal cart, tote. 10 *the priest took her home* **escort**, accompany, help, assist, show, lead, guide, see, usher, convey. 11 *he took the train* **travel on/by**, journey on, go via, use. 12 *I can't take much more* **endure**, bear, tolerate, stand, put up with, abide, stomach, accept, allow, countenance, support, shoulder; formal brook.
ANTONYMS give, free, add.

▸ noun 1 a sequence of sound or vision photographed or recorded continuously. 2 a particular approach to something. 3 an amount gained.
■ **take after** look or behave like a parent or ancestor. **take someone/thing for granted** 1 be too familiar with someone or something to appreciate them properly. 2 assume that something is true. **take someone/thing in** 1 cheat or deceive someone. 2 make a garment tighter by altering its seams. 3 understand something. **take off** 1 become airborne. 2 leave hastily. **take someone/thing off** 1 remove clothing. 2 informal mimic someone. **take-off** an act of taking off. **take someone/thing on** 1 employ someone. 2 undertake a task. 3 begin to have a meaning or quality. **take over** begin to have control of or responsibility for something, in place of someone else. **take to** 1 get into the habit of. 2 start liking. 3 go to a place to escape danger. **take something up** 1 start to do something. 2 occupy time, space, or attention. 3 pursue a matter further.

takeaway ▸ noun Brit. 1 a restaurant or shop selling cooked food to be eaten elsewhere.

2 a meal of such food.

takeout ▸ noun N. Amer. a takeaway.

takeover ▸ noun an act of taking control of something from someone else.

> SYNONYMS **buyout**, purchase, acquisition, merger, amalgamation.

takings ▸ plural noun money received by a shop for goods sold.

talc ▸ noun **1** talcum powder. **2** a soft mineral.

talcum powder ▸ noun a powder used to make the skin feel smooth and dry.

tale ▸ noun **1** a story. **2** a lie.

> SYNONYMS **story**, narrative, anecdote, account, history, legend, fable, myth, saga; informal yarn.

talent ▸ noun **1** natural ability or skill. **2** people possessing natural ability or skill. **3** an ancient weight and unit of currency.

> SYNONYMS **flair**, aptitude, facility, gift, knack, technique, bent, ability, forte, genius, brilliance.

talented ▸ adjective having talent.

> SYNONYMS **gifted**, skilful, accomplished, brilliant, expert, consummate, able; informal ace.
> ANTONYMS untalented, inept.

talisman ▸ noun (plural **talismans**) an object thought to have magic powers and to bring good luck.
> □ **talismanic** adjective.

talk ▸ verb **1** speak in order to give information or express ideas or feelings. **2** be able to speak. **3** (**talk something over** or **through**) discuss something thoroughly. **4** (**talk back**) reply in a defiant or cheeky way. **5** (**talk down to**) speak to someone in a superior way. **6** (**talk someone round**) persuade someone to accept or agree to something. **7** (**talk someone into** or **out of**) persuade someone to do or not to do something.

> SYNONYMS **1** *I was talking to a friend* **speak**, chat, chatter, gossip, jabber; informal yak; Brit. informal natter. **2** *they were able to talk in peace* **converse**, communicate, speak, confer, consult, negotiate, parley; informal have a confab.

▸ noun **1** conversation. **2** a speech or lecture. **3** (**talks**) formal discussions.

> SYNONYMS **1** *he was bored with all this talk* **chatter**, gossip, prattle, jabbering; informal yak; Brit. informal nattering. **2** *she needed a talk with Vi* **conversation**, chat, discussion, tête-à-tête, heart-to-heart, dialogue; informal confab, gossip. **3** (**talks**) **negotiations**, discussions, conference, summit, meeting, consultation, dialogue. **4** *she gave a talk on her travels* **lecture**,

speech, address, discourse, oration, presentation, report, sermon.

> ■ **talking-to** informal a telling-off.

talkative ▸ adjective fond of talking.

> SYNONYMS **chatty**, garrulous, loquacious, voluble, communicative; informal mouthy.
> ANTONYMS taciturn.

tall ▸ adjective **1** of great or more than average height. **2** measuring a stated distance from top to bottom.

> SYNONYMS **1** *a tall man* **big**, large, huge, towering, gigantic, giant, leggy, gangling. **2** *tall buildings* **high**, big, lofty, towering, sky-high. **3** *a tall order* **demanding**, exacting, difficult, unreasonable, impossible. **4** *a tall tale* **unlikely**, improbable, exaggerated, far-fetched, implausible, dubious, unbelievable, incredible, untrue; informal cock and bull.
> ANTONYMS short, low, wide, easy, credible.

> ■ **a tall order** a difficult challenge. **tall ship** a sailing ship with high masts. **a tall story** (or **tale**) an account of something that seems unlikely to be true.

tallow ▸ noun a hard substance made from animal fat, used in making candles and soap.

tally ▸ noun (plural **tallies**) **1** a current score or amount. **2** a record of a score or amount.

> SYNONYMS *a tally of the score* **running total**, count, record, reckoning, register, account, roll.

▸ verb (**tallies, tallying, tallied**) **1** agree or correspond. **2** calculate the total number of.

> SYNONYMS *these statistics tally with government figures* **correspond**, agree, accord, concur, coincide, match, fit, be consistent, conform, equate, parallel; informal square.
> ANTONYMS disagree.

tally-ho ▸ exclamation a huntsman's cry to the hounds on sighting a fox.

Talmud /tal-muud/ ▸ noun a collection of ancient writings on Jewish law and legend.

talon ▸ noun a curved claw.

tamarind ▸ noun a fruit with sticky brown pulp used in Asian cookery.

tamarisk ▸ noun a small tree with tiny leaves on slender branches.

tambourine ▸ noun a shallow drum with metal discs around the edge, which you play by shaking or hitting with your hand.

tame ▸ adjective **1** (of an animal) not dangerous or frightened of people. **2** not exciting, adventurous, or controversial.

> SYNONYMS **1** *a tame elephant* **domesticated**, docile, broken, trained,

gentle, mild, pet. **2** *a tame affair* **unexciting**, uninteresting, uninspiring, dull, bland, flat, pedestrian, humdrum, boring.
ANTONYMS wild, exciting.

▸ verb (**tames, taming, tamed**) **1** make an animal tame. **2** make less powerful and easier to control.

> SYNONYMS **1** *wild rabbits can be tamed* **domesticate**, break, train, master, subdue. **2** *she learned to tame her emotions* **subdue**, curb, control, calm, master, moderate, discipline, suppress, temper, bridle.

▫ **tamely** adverb.

Tamil ▸ noun **1** a member of a people living in parts of South India and Sri Lanka. **2** the language of the Tamils.

tamp ▸ verb firmly ram or pack a substance into something.

tamper ▸ verb (**tampers, tampering, tampered**) (**tamper with**) interfere with something without permission.

tampon ▸ noun a plug of soft material that a woman puts into her vagina to absorb blood during a period.

tan ▸ noun **1** a golden-brown shade of skin developed by pale-skinned people after being in the sun. **2** a yellowish-brown colour.

▸ verb (**tans, tanning, tanned**) **1** become golden-brown from being in the sun. **2** convert animal skin into leather.

tandem ▸ noun a bicycle for two riders, one sitting behind the other.

▸ adverb one behind another.
■ **in tandem** together or at the same time.

tandoori /tan-**door**-i/ ▸ adjective (of Indian food) cooked in a clay oven called a **tandoor**.

tang ▸ noun **1** a strong flavour or smell. **2** the projection on the blade of a tool that holds it firmly in the handle.
▫ **tangy** adjective.

tangent ▸ noun **1** a straight line that touches a curve but does not cross it at that point. **2** Maths (in a right-angled triangle) the ratio of the sides opposite and adjacent to a particular angle. **3** a completely different line of thought or action.

tangential /tan-**jen**-sh'l/ ▸ adjective **1** only slightly relevant. **2** relating to or along a tangent.

tangerine ▸ noun a small citrus fruit with a loose skin.

tangible ▸ adjective **1** able to be perceived by touch. **2** real.

> SYNONYMS **real**, actual, physical, solid, palpable, material, substantial, concrete, visible, definite, perceptible, discernible.
> ANTONYMS abstract, theoretical.

▫ **tangibility** noun **tangibly** adverb.

tangle ▸ verb (**tangles, tangling, tangled**) **1** twist together into a knotted mass. **2** (**tangle with**) informal come into conflict with.

> SYNONYMS *the wool got tangled up* **entangle**, snarl, catch, entwine, twist, knot, mat, jumble.

▸ noun **1** a twisted, knotted mass. **2** a muddle.

> SYNONYMS **1** *a tangle of branches* **snarl**, mass, knot, mesh, mishmash. **2** *the defence got into an awful tangle* **muddle**, jumble, mix-up, confusion, shambles.

tango ▸ noun (plural **tangos**) a South American ballroom dance with abrupt pauses.

▸ verb (**tangoes, tangoing, tangoed**) dance the tango.

tank ▸ noun **1** a large container for liquid or gas. **2** the container holding the fuel supply in a vehicle. **3** a clear container for keeping pet fish. **4** a heavy armoured fighting vehicle that moves on a continuous metal track.
■ **tank engine** a steam locomotive carrying fuel and water holders in its own frame, not in a separate wagon. **tank top** a sleeveless top worn over a shirt or blouse.

tankard ▸ noun a large beer mug, sometimes with a hinged lid.

tanker ▸ noun a ship, road vehicle, or aircraft for carrying liquids in bulk.

tannin ▸ noun a bitter-tasting substance present in tea, grapes, etc.

tannoy ▸ noun Brit. trademark a type of public address system.

tantalize (or **tantalise**) ▸ verb (**tantalizes, tantalizing, tantalized**) tease someone by showing or promising them something that they cannot have.

tantalum ▸ noun a hard silver-grey metallic element.

tantamount ▸ adjective (**tantamount to**) equivalent in seriousness to.

tantrum ▸ noun an uncontrolled outburst of anger and frustration.

> SYNONYMS **fit of temper**, fit of rage, outburst, pet, paroxysm, frenzy; informal paddy, wobbly; N. Amer. informal hissy fit.

Tanzanian /tan-zuh-**nee**-uhn/ ▸ noun a person from Tanzania.

▸ adjective relating to Tanzania.

Taoiseach /**tee**-shuhkh/ ▸ noun the Prime Minister of the Irish Republic.

tap[1] ▸ noun a device for controlling the flow of liquid or gas from a pipe or container.

> SYNONYMS *she turned the tap on* **valve**, stopcock; N. Amer. faucet, spigot.

▸ verb (**taps, tapping, tapped**) **1** make use of

t

a supply or resource. **2** connect a device to a telephone so as to listen to conversations secretly. **3** draw liquid from a cask, barrel, etc. **4** draw sap from a tree by cutting into it.

> SYNONYMS **1** *the resources were to be tapped for our benefit* **draw on,** exploit, milk, mine, use, utilize, turn to account. **2** *their telephones were tapped* **bug,** wiretap, monitor, overhear, eavesdrop on.

■ **on tap 1** ready to be poured from a tap. **2** informal freely available whenever needed.

tap² ▸ verb (**taps, tapping, tapped**) hit with a quick, light blow.

> SYNONYMS *she tapped on the door* **knock,** rap, strike, beat, pat, drum.

▸ noun a quick, light blow.
■ **tap dancing** a style of dancing performed in shoes with metal pieces on the toes and heels.

tapas /tap-uhss/ ▸ plural noun small Spanish savoury dishes served with drinks at a bar.

tape ▸ noun **1** light, flexible material in a narrow strip, used to hold, fasten, or mark off something. **2** tape with magnetic properties, used for recording sound, pictures, or computer data. **3** a cassette or reel containing magnetic tape.

> SYNONYMS **1** *a package tied with tape* **binding,** ribbon, string, braid, band. **2** *they made a tape of the concert* (**audio**) **cassette,** (tape) recording, video.

▸ verb (**tapes, taping, taped**) **1** record sound or pictures on magnetic tape. **2** fasten, attach, or mark off with tape.

> SYNONYMS **1** *police taped his confession* **record,** tape-record, video. **2** *a card was taped to the box* **bind,** stick, fix, fasten, secure, attach.

■ **tape measure** a strip of tape marked for measuring the length of things. **tape recorder** a device for recording and then reproducing sounds on magnetic tape.

taper ▸ verb (**tapers, tapering, tapered**) **1** reduce in thickness towards one end. **2** (**taper off**) gradually lessen.
▸ noun a thin candle.

tapestry ▸ noun (plural **tapestries**) a piece of thick fabric with a design woven or embroidered on it.

tapeworm ▸ noun a long ribbon-like worm which lives as a parasite in the intestines of a person or animal.

tapioca ▸ noun hard white grains of cassava, used for making puddings.

tapir /tay-peer/ ▸ noun a piglike animal with a short flexible snout.

tappet ▸ noun a moving part in a machine which transmits motion between a cam and another part.

taproot ▸ noun a tapering root that grows straight downwards, from which other roots grow.

tar ▸ noun **1** a dark, thick liquid distilled from wood or coal. **2** a similar substance formed by burning tobacco.
▸ verb (**tars, tarring, tarred**) cover with tar.

taramasalata ▸ noun a dip made from the roe (eggs) of certain fish.

tarantula ▸ noun **1** a very large hairy spider found in warm parts of America. **2** a large black spider of southern Europe.

tardy ▸ adjective (**tardier, tardiest**) formal **1** late. **2** slow to act or respond.
□ **tardily** adverb **tardiness** noun.

tare ▸ noun the weight of a vehicle without its fuel or load.

target ▸ noun **1** a person, object, or place that is aimed at in an attack. **2** a board marked with a series of circles that you aim at in archery or shooting. **3** something that you aim to achieve.

> SYNONYMS **1** *their profit target* **objective,** goal, aim, mark, end, plan, intention, aspiration, ambition. **2** *she was the target for abuse* **victim,** butt, recipient, focus, object, subject.

▸ verb (**targets, targeting, targeted**) **1** select as an object of attention or attack. **2** aim or direct.

> SYNONYMS **1** *he was targeted by a gunman* **pick out,** single out, earmark, fix on, attack, aim at, fire at. **2** *the product is targeted at a specific market* **aim,** direct, level, intend, focus.

> ✔ Note that **targeted** and **targeting** have a single **t** in the middle.

tariff ▸ noun **1** a tax to be paid on a particular class of imports or exports. **2** a list of the charges made by a hotel, restaurant, etc.

> SYNONYMS **1** *import tariffs* **tax,** duty, toll, excise, levy, charge, rate, fee. **2** *the bar tariff* **price list,** menu.

> ✔ one **r**, double **f**: tari**ff**.

tarmac ▸ noun **1** (trademark) a mixture of broken stone and tar used for making road surfaces. **2** (**the tarmac**) a runway or other area with a tarmac surface.
▸ verb (**tarmacs, tarmacking, tarmacked**) give a road or runway a tarmac surface.

tarn ▸ noun a small mountain lake.

tarnish ▸ verb **1** make metal lose its shine by exposure to air or damp. **2** make something less respected.

> SYNONYMS **1** *gold does not tarnish easily* **discolour,** rust, oxidize, corrode, stain, dull, blacken. **2** *it tarnished his reputation*

sully, blacken, stain, blemish, ruin, disgrace, mar, damage, harm.
ANTONYMS polish, enhance.

▶ noun a film or stain formed on the exposed surface of metal.

SYNONYMS **1** *the tarnish on the candlesticks* **discoloration,** oxidation, rust, verdigris. **2** *the tarnish on his reputation* **smear,** stain, blemish, blot, taint, stigma.

tarot /ta-roh/ ▶ noun a set of cards used for fortune telling.

tarpaulin ▶ noun a sheet of heavy waterproof cloth.

tarragon ▶ noun a herb with narrow strong-tasting leaves.

tarry ▶ verb (**tarries, tarrying, tarried**) literary stay longer than intended.

tarsus ▶ noun (plural **tarsi** /tar-sy/) the group of small bones in the ankle and upper foot.

tart[1] ▶ noun an open pastry case containing a sweet or savoury filling.

SYNONYMS *a jam tart* **pastry,** flan, quiche, tartlet, vol-au-vent, pie.

□ **tartlet** noun.

tart[2] informal ▶ noun disapproving a woman who has many sexual partners.
▶ verb Brit. **1** (**tart yourself up**) make yourself look attractive with clothes or make-up. **2** (**tart something up**) improve the appearance of something.

SYNONYMS **1** *she tarted herself up* **dress up,** make up, smarten up; informal doll yourself up, titivate yourself. **2** *we must tart this place up a bit* **decorate,** renovate, refurbish, redecorate, smarten up; informal do up, fix up.

□ **tarty** adjective.

tart[3] ▶ adjective **1** sharp or acid in taste. **2** (of a remark or tone of voice) sharp or hurtful.

SYNONYMS **1** *a tart apple* **sour,** sharp, acidic, zesty, tangy, piquant. **2** *a tart reply* **scathing,** sharp, biting, cutting, sarcastic, acrimonious, nasty, rude, vicious, spiteful.
ANTONYMS sweet, kind.

□ **tartly** adverb.

tartan ▶ noun **1** a pattern of coloured checks and intersecting lines. **2** cloth with a tartan pattern.

tartar[1] ▶ noun a person who is fierce or difficult to deal with.

tartar[2] ▶ noun **1** a hard deposit that forms on the teeth. **2** a deposit formed during the fermentation of wine.

tartare sauce ▶ noun a sauce consisting of mayonnaise mixed with chopped onions, gherkins, and capers.

task ▶ noun a piece of work to be done.

SYNONYMS **job,** duty, chore, charge, assignment, detail, mission, engagement, occupation, undertaking, exercise.

■ **task force 1** an armed force organized for a special operation. **2** a group of people specially organized to deal with a particular problem. **take someone to task** criticize or reprimand someone.

taskmaster ▶ noun a person who gives someone a lot of difficult tasks.

tassel ▶ noun a tuft of threads that are knotted together at one end.
□ **tasselled** (US spelling **tasseled**) adjective.

taste ▶ noun **1** the sensation of flavour perceived in the mouth when it comes into contact with a particular substance. **2** the sense by which taste is perceived. **3** a small sample of food or drink. **4** a brief experience of something. **5** a liking for something. **6** the ability to pick out things that are of good quality or appropriate.

SYNONYMS **1** *a distinctive sharp taste* **flavour,** savour, relish, tang, smack. **2** *a taste of brandy* **mouthful,** drop, bit, sip, nip, touch, soupçon, dash. **3** *it's too sweet for my taste* **palate,** appetite, stomach. **4** *a taste for adventure* **liking,** love, fondness, fancy, desire, penchant, inclination. **5** *my first taste of prison* **experience,** impression, exposure to, contact with, involvement with. **6** *the house was furnished with taste* **judgement,** discrimination, discernment, refinement, elegance, grace, style. **7** *the photo was rejected on grounds of taste* **sensitivity,** decorum, propriety, etiquette, nicety, discretion.
ANTONYMS dislike.

▶ verb (**tastes, tasting, tasted**) **1** have a particular flavour. **2** perceive or recognize the flavour of. **3** test the flavour of. **4** have a brief experience of.

SYNONYMS **1** *a beer that tasted of cashews* **have the flavour,** savour, smack, be reminiscent. **2** *he could taste blood* **perceive,** discern, make out, distinguish. **3** *Adam tasted the wine* **sample,** test, try, savour.

■ **taste bud** any of the clusters of nerve endings on the tongue and in the mouth which provide the sense of taste.
□ **taster** noun.

tasteful ▶ adjective showing good judgement of quality, appearance, or appropriate behaviour.

SYNONYMS **stylish,** refined, cultured, elegant, smart, chic, exquisite.
ANTONYMS tasteless.

□ **tastefully** adverb.

tasteless ▶ adjective **1** having little or no flavour. **2** not showing good judgement

t

of quality, appearance, or appropriate behaviour.
□ **tastelessly** adverb.

tasty ▶ adjective (**tastier**, **tastiest**) **1** (of food) having a pleasant flavour. **2** Brit. informal attractive; appealing.

SYNONYMS **delicious**, palatable, luscious, mouth-watering, delectable, appetizing, tempting; informal yummy, scrumptious, moreish.
ANTONYMS bland.

tat ▶ noun Brit. informal tasteless or badly made articles.

tattered ▶ adjective old and torn.

tatters ▶ plural noun torn pieces of cloth, paper, etc.
■ **in tatters 1** torn in many places. **2** destroyed; ruined.

tattle ▶ noun gossip.
▶ verb (**tattles**, **tattling**, **tattled**) engage in gossip.

tattoo¹ ▶ noun (plural **tattoos**) a permanent design made on the skin with a needle and ink.
▶ verb (**tattoos**, **tattooing**, **tattooed**) give someone a tattoo.
□ **tattooist** noun.

tattoo² ▶ noun (plural **tattoos**) **1** Brit. a military display with music and marching. **2** a rhythmic tapping or drumming.

tatty ▶ adjective (**tattier**, **tattiest**) informal worn and shabby.

taught past and past participle of TEACH.

taunt ▶ noun a remark made in order to anger or upset someone.

SYNONYMS *the taunts of his classmates* **jeer**, gibe, sneer, insult, barb; informal dig, put-down; (**taunts**) teasing, provocation, goading, derision, mockery.

▶ verb anger or upset with taunts.

SYNONYMS *she taunted him about his job* **jeer at**, sneer at, scoff at, poke fun at, make fun of, get at, insult, tease, torment, ridicule, deride, mock; N. Amer. ride; informal rib, needle.

taupe (*rhymes with* rope) ▶ noun a brownish-grey colour.

Taurus ▶ noun a sign of the zodiac (the Bull), 21 April–20 May.

taut ▶ adjective **1** stretched or pulled tight. **2** (of muscles or nerves) tense.
□ **tauten** verb **tautly** adverb.

tautology ▶ noun (plural **tautologies**) the saying of the same thing twice in different words.
□ **tautological** adjective **tautologous** adjective.

tavern ▶ noun old use an inn or pub.

tawdry ▶ adjective **1** showy but cheap and of bad quality. **2** sleazy or unpleasant.
□ **tawdriness** noun.

tawny ▶ adjective of an orange-brown or yellowish-brown colour.

tax ▶ noun money that must be paid to the state, charged as a proportion of income and profits or added to the cost of some goods and services.

SYNONYMS *they have to pay tax* **duty**, excise, customs, dues, levy, tariff, toll, tithe, charge.

▶ verb **1** impose a tax on. **2** pay tax on a vehicle. **3** make heavy demands on. **4** accuse someone of doing something wrong.

SYNONYMS *his whining taxed her patience* **strain**, stretch, overburden, overload, overwhelm, try, wear out, exhaust, sap, drain, weary, weaken.

■ **tax-deductible** allowed to be deducted from income before the amount of tax to be paid is calculated. **tax exile** a rich person who chooses to live somewhere with low rates of taxation. **tax haven** a country or independent area where low rates of taxes are charged. **tax return** a form on which a person states their income, used to assess how much tax they should pay.
□ **taxable** adjective.

taxation ▶ noun **1** the imposing of tax. **2** money paid as tax.

taxi ▶ noun (plural **taxis**) a vehicle which takes fare-paying passengers to the place of their choice.
▶ verb (**taxies**, **taxiing** or **taxying**, **taxied**) (of an aircraft) move slowly along the ground before take-off or after landing.
■ **taxi rank** Brit. a place where taxis wait to be hired.

taxicab ▶ noun a taxi.

taxidermy ▶ noun the art of preparing and stuffing the skins of dead animals so that they look like living ones.
□ **taxidermist** noun.

taxing ▶ adjective physically or mentally demanding.

taxonomy ▶ noun **1** the branch of science concerned with classification. **2** a system of classifying things.
□ **taxonomic** adjective.

TB ▶ abbreviation tuberculosis.

tbsp (or **tbs**) ▶ abbreviation tablespoonful.

tea ▶ noun **1** a hot drink made by soaking the dried leaves of an evergreen Asian shrub in boiling water. **2** the dried leaves used to make tea. **3** Brit. a light afternoon meal of sandwiches, cakes, etc., with tea to drink. **4** Brit. a cooked evening meal.
■ **tea bag** a sachet of tea leaves on to which boiling water is poured to make tea. **tea room** a cafe serving tea, cakes, etc. **tea towel** (or **tea cloth**) Brit. a cloth for drying washed crockery, cutlery, etc. **tea tree** a

shrub of Australia and New Zealand that produces an oil with antiseptic qualities.

teacake ▸ noun Brit. a kind of bun containing currants.

teach ▸ verb (**teaches, teaching, taught**) **1** give lessons in a particular subject to a class or pupil. **2** show someone how to do something. **3** make someone realize or understand something.

SYNONYMS **educate,** instruct, school, tutor, inform, coach, train, drill.

teacher ▸ noun a person who teaches in a school.

SYNONYMS **educator,** tutor, instructor, schoolteacher, master, mistress, schoolmarm, governess, coach, trainer, lecturer, professor, don, guide, mentor, guru.

teacup ▸ noun a cup from which you drink tea.

teak ▸ noun hard wood obtained from a tree native to India and SE Asia.

teal ▸ noun (plural **teal** or **teals**) a small freshwater duck.

team ▸ noun **1** a group of players forming one side in a game or sport. **2** two or more people working together. **3** two or more horses harnessed together to pull something.

SYNONYMS *the sales team* **group,** squad, company, party, crew, troupe, band, side, line-up; informal bunch, gang.

▸ verb **1** (**team up**) work together to achieve a shared goal. **2** (**team something with**) wear an item of clothing with another.

SYNONYMS *ankle boots teamed with jeans* **match,** coordinate, complement, pair up.

■ **team spirit** trust and cooperation among the members of a team.

teammate ▸ noun a fellow member of a team.

teamwork ▸ noun organized effort as a group.

teapot ▸ noun a pot with a handle, spout, and lid, in which tea is made.

tear¹ ▸ verb (**tears, tearing, tore**; past participle **torn**) **1** rip a hole or split in. **2** (usu. **tear something up**) pull something apart or to pieces. **3** damage a muscle or ligament by overstretching it. **4** (**tear something down**) demolish or destroy something. **5** (**be torn**) be unsure about which of two options to choose. **6** informal move very quickly. **7** (**tear into**) attack verbally.

SYNONYMS **1** *your shirt's torn* **rip,** split, slit, pull apart, pull to pieces, shred, rupture, sever. **2** *his flesh was torn* **lacerate,** cut (open), gash, slash, scratch, hack, pierce, stab. **3** *Gina tore the book from his hands*

SYNONYMS **snatch,** grab, seize, rip, wrench, wrest, pull, pluck; informal yank.

▸ noun a hole or split caused by tearing.

SYNONYMS *a tear in her dress* **rip,** hole, split, slash, slit, ladder, snag.

tear² ▸ noun a drop of clear salty liquid produced in a person's eye when they are crying or when the eye is irritated.
■ **tear gas** gas that causes severe irritation to the eyes, used in warfare and riot control. **tear-jerker** informal a very sad book, film, or song.

tearaway ▸ noun Brit. a person who behaves in a wild or reckless way.

teardrop ▸ noun a single tear.

tearful ▸ adjective **1** crying or about to cry. **2** causing tears.
□ **tearfully** adverb.

tease ▸ verb (**teases, teasing, teased**) **1** playfully make fun of or attempt to provoke. **2** tempt sexually. **3** (**tease something out**) find out something by searching through a mass of information. **4** gently pull tangled wool, hair, etc. into separate strands.

SYNONYMS **make fun of,** laugh at, deride, mock, ridicule, guy, make a monkey (out) of, taunt, bait, goad, pick on; informal take the mickey out of, rag, have on, pull someone's leg; Brit. informal wind up.

▸ noun a person who teases.
□ **teaser** noun.

teasel (or **teazle**) ▸ noun a tall prickly plant with spiny flower heads.

teaspoon ▸ noun a small spoon for adding sugar to hot drinks.

teat ▸ noun **1** a nipple on an animal's udder or similar organ. **2** Brit. a plastic nipple-shaped device for sucking milk from a bottle.

technetium /tek-nee-shi-uhm/ ▸ noun a radioactive metallic element that is produced artificially.

technical ▸ adjective **1** having to do with the techniques of a particular subject, art, or craft. **2** needing specialized knowledge. **3** having to do with the practical use of machinery and methods in science and industry. **4** according to the law or rules when applied strictly.

SYNONYMS **1** *an important technical achievement* **practical,** scientific, technological, high-tech. **2** *this might seem very technical* **specialist,** specialized, scientific, complex, complicated, esoteric.

■ **technical college** a college specializing in applied sciences and other practical subjects.
□ **technically** adverb.

technicality ▸ noun (plural **technicalities**)
1 a small formal detail in a set of rules.
2 (**technicalities**) small details of how
something works or is done. **3** the use of
technical terms or methods.

technician ▸ noun **1** a person who looks
after equipment or does practical work
in a laboratory. **2** a person skilled in the
technique of an art, science, craft, or sport.

Technicolor ▸ noun trademark a process of
producing cinema films in colour.

technique ▸ noun **1** a particular way of
carrying out a task. **2** a person's level of
skill in doing something.

SYNONYMS **1** *different techniques for
solving the problem* **method**, approach,
procedure, system, way, means, strategy.
2 *I was impressed with his technique* **skill**,
ability, proficiency, expertise, artistry,
craftsmanship, adroitness, deftness,
dexterity.

techno ▸ noun a style of fast, loud electronic
dance music.

technology ▸ noun (plural **technologies**)
1 the application of scientific knowledge
for practical purposes. **2** machinery or
equipment developed from this knowledge.
3 the branch of knowledge concerned with
applied sciences.
□ **technological** adjective **technologically** adverb
technologist noun.

tectonic ▸ adjective Geology having to do with
the earth's crust.

teddy (or **teddy bear**) ▸ noun (plural **teddies**)
a soft toy bear.

Teddy boy ▸ noun (in Britain during the
1950s) a young man of a group who had
their hair slicked up in a quiff and liked
rock-and-roll music.

tedious ▸ adjective too long, slow, or dull.

SYNONYMS **boring**, dull, monotonous,
repetitive, unrelieved, unvaried,
uneventful, lifeless, uninteresting,
unexciting, uninspiring, lacklustre,
dreary, soul-destroying; informal deadly;
N. Amer. informal dullsville.
ANTONYMS exciting.

□ **tediously** adverb.

tedium ▸ noun the state of being tedious.

tee ▸ noun **1** a place on a golf course from
which the ball is struck at the beginning
of each hole. **2** a small peg placed in the
ground to support a golf ball before it is
struck from a tee. **3** a mark aimed at in
bowls.
▸ verb (**tees**, **teeing**, **teed**) Golf **1** (**tee up**) place
the ball on a tee ready to begin a round or
hole. **2** (**tee off**) begin a round or hole.

teem ▸ verb **1** (**teem with**) be swarming
with. **2** (of rain) fall heavily.

teen informal ▸ adjective having to do with
teenagers.
▸ noun a teenager.

teenage ▸ adjective having to do with
teenagers.
□ **teenaged** adjective.

teenager ▸ noun a person aged between 13
and 19 years.

SYNONYMS **adolescent**, youth, young
person, minor, juvenile; informal teen.

teens ▸ plural noun the years of a person's
age from 13 to 19.

teeny (or **teensy**) ▸ adjective (**teenier**,
teeniest) informal tiny.

teepee → TEPEE.

tee shirt ▸ noun a T-shirt.

teeter ▸ verb (**teeters**, **teetering**, **teetered**)
move or sway unsteadily.

teeth plural of TOOTH.

teethe ▸ verb (**teethes**, **teething**, **teethed**)
(of a baby) develop its first teeth.
■ **teething troubles** problems that occur in
the early stages of a new project.

teetotal ▸ adjective choosing not to drink
alcohol.
□ **teetotaller** noun.

telecommunications ▸ noun the
technology concerned with long-distance
communication by means of cable,
telephone, broadcasting, satellite, etc.

telegram ▸ noun a message sent by
telegraph and delivered in written or
printed form.

telegraph ▸ noun a system or device for
transmitting messages from a distance
along a wire.
▸ verb send a message to someone by
telegraph.
■ **telegraph pole** a tall pole used to carry
telegraph or telephone wires.
□ **telegraphic** adjective.

telekinesis /te-li-ky-**nee**-siss/ ▸ noun the
movement of objects supposedly as a result
of using mental power.
□ **telekinetic** adjective.

telepathy ▸ noun the supposed
communication of thoughts or ideas by
means other than the known senses.
□ **telepathic** adjective.

telephone ▸ noun **1** a system for
transmitting voices over a distance using
wire or radio. **2** an instrument used in a
telephone system for speaking into.

SYNONYMS *Sophie picked up the telephone*
phone, handset, receiver; informal blower;
N. Amer. informal horn.

▸ verb (**telephones**, **telephoning**, **telephoned**)
contact someone by telephone.

SYNONYMS *he telephoned me* **phone**, call,
dial; Brit. ring (up); informal call up, give
someone a buzz, get on the blower to; Brit.

informal give someone a bell, give someone a tinkle; N. Amer. informal get someone on the horn.

telephonist ▸ noun Brit. an operator of a telephone switchboard.

telephony /ti-lef-fuh-ni/ ▸ noun the working or use of telephones.

telephoto lens ▸ noun a lens that produces a magnified image of a distant object.

teleprinter ▸ noun Brit. a device for transmitting telegraph messages as they are keyed.

telesales ▸ plural noun the selling of goods or services over the telephone.

telescope ▸ noun an instrument designed to make distant objects appear nearer.
▸ verb (**telescopes, telescoping, telescoped**) **1** (of an object made up of several tubes) slide into itself so as to become smaller. **2** condense or combine to occupy less space or time.
□ **telescopic** adjective.

teletext ▸ noun an information service transmitted to televisions.

telethon ▸ noun a long television programme broadcast to raise money for a charity.

televise ▸ verb (**televises, televising, televised**) show on television.

television ▸ noun **1** a system for transmitting visual images with sound and displaying them electronically on a screen. **2** (also **television set**) a device with a screen for receiving television signals. **3** the activity or medium of broadcasting on television.

SYNONYMS TV; informal the small screen; Brit. informal telly, the box; N. Amer. informal the tube.

□ **televisual** adjective.

telex ▸ noun **1** an international system in which printed messages are transmitted and received by teleprinters. **2** a message sent by telex.
▸ verb send a message to someone by telex.

tell ▸ verb (**tells, telling, told**) **1** communicate information to. **2** say that someone must do something. **3** relate a story. **4** (**tell on**) informal inform someone about a person's wrongdoings. **5** (**tell someone off**) reprimand someone. **6** establish that something is the case. **7** have a noticeable effect on someone.

SYNONYMS **1** *why didn't you tell me?* **inform,** notify, let know, make aware, acquaint with, advise, put in the picture, brief, fill in, alert, warn; informal clue in/up. **2** *she told the story slowly* **relate,** recount, narrate, report, recite, describe, sketch. **3** *she told him to leave* **instruct,** order, command, direct, charge, enjoin,

call on, require. **4** *it was hard to tell what he said* **ascertain,** determine, work out, make out, deduce, discern, perceive, see, identify, recognize, understand, comprehend; informal figure out; Brit. informal suss out. **5** *he couldn't tell one from the other* **distinguish,** differentiate, discriminate. **6** *the strain began to tell on him* **take its toll,** leave its mark, affect.

■ **telling-off** (plural **tellings-off**) informal a reprimand.

teller ▸ noun **1** chiefly N. Amer. a person who deals with customers' transactions in a bank. **2** a person who counts votes. **3** a person who tells something.

telling ▸ adjective having a striking or revealing effect.

SYNONYMS **revealing,** significant, weighty, important, meaningful, influential, striking, potent, powerful, compelling.
ANTONYMS insignificant.

□ **tellingly** adverb.

telltale ▸ adjective revealing or betraying something: *telltale signs of stress.*
▸ noun informal a person who reports things that other people have done wrong.

telly ▸ noun informal television.

temerity ▸ noun very confident behaviour that other people are likely to consider rude or disrespectful.

temp informal ▸ noun a person who is employed on a temporary basis.
▸ verb work as a temp.

temper ▸ noun **1** a person's state of mind. **2** a tendency to become angry easily. **3** an angry state of mind. **4** the degree of hardness of a metal.

SYNONYMS **1** *he walked out in a temper* **rage,** fury, fit of pique, tantrum, bad mood, pet, sulk, huff; Brit. informal strop, paddy; N. Amer. informal hissy fit. **2** *a display of temper* **anger,** fury, rage, annoyance, irritation, pique, petulance; Brit. informal stroppiness. **3** *she struggled to keep her temper* **composure,** self-control, self-possession, calm, good humour; informal cool.

▸ verb (**tempers, tempering, tempered**) **1** make something less extreme. **2** harden metal by heating and then cooling it.

SYNONYMS *their idealism is tempered with realism* **moderate,** modify, modulate, mitigate, alleviate, reduce, weaken, lighten, soften.

tempera ▸ noun a method of painting with powdered colours mixed with egg yolk.

temperament ▸ noun a person's nature in terms of the way it affects their behaviour.

temperamental ▸ adjective **1** tending to have sudden or unreasonable changes of mood. **2** relating to or caused by temperament.

> SYNONYMS **volatile,** excitable, emotional, unpredictable, hot-headed, quick-tempered, impatient, touchy, moody, sensitive, highly strung.
> ANTONYMS placid.

□ **temperamentally** adverb.

temperance ▸ noun the practice of never drinking alcohol.

temperate ▸ adjective **1** (of a region or climate) having mild temperatures. **2** showing self-control.

temperature ▸ noun **1** the degree of heat in a place, substance, or object. **2** a body temperature above the normal.

> ✔ **-era-** in the middle: temp**era**ture.

tempest ▸ noun a violent windy storm.

tempestuous ▸ adjective **1** very stormy. **2** full of strong and changeable emotions.

template ▸ noun **1** a shaped piece of rigid material used as a pattern for cutting out, shaping, or drilling. **2** a model for others to copy.

temple¹ ▸ noun a building for the worship of a god or gods.

> SYNONYMS **house of God,** shrine, sanctuary, church, cathedral, mosque, synagogue.

temple² ▸ noun the flat part either side of the head between the forehead and the ear.

tempo ▸ noun (plural **tempos** or **tempi** /ˈtem-pi/) **1** the speed at which a passage of music is played. **2** the pace of an activity or process.

temporal ▸ adjective **1** relating to time. **2** having to do with the physical world rather than spiritual matters.
□ **temporally** adverb.

temporarily ▸ adverb **1** for the time being. **2** for a short time.

> SYNONYMS **1** *they are temporarily abroad* **for the time being,** for the moment, for now, for the present, provisionally, pro tem. **2** *he was temporarily blinded by the light* **briefly,** for a short time, momentarily, fleetingly.
> ANTONYMS permanently.

temporary ▸ adjective lasting for only a short time.

> SYNONYMS **1** *temporary accommodation* **provisional,** short-term, interim, makeshift, stopgap, acting, fill-in, stand-in, caretaker. **2** *a temporary loss of self-control* **brief,** short-lived, momentary, fleeting, passing, ephemeral.
> ANTONYMS permanent, lasting.

temporize (or **temporise**) ▸ verb (**temporizes, temporizing, temporized**) delay making a decision.

tempt ▸ verb **1** try to persuade someone to do something appealing but wrong. **2** (**be tempted to do**) have an urge or inclination to do.

> SYNONYMS **1** *the manager tried to tempt me to stay* **entice,** persuade, convince, inveigle, induce, cajole, coax, lure; informal sweet-talk. **2** *more customers are being tempted by credit* **attract,** allure, appeal to, whet the appetite of, seduce.
> ANTONYMS discourage, deter.

■ **tempt fate** do something risky or dangerous.

temptation ▸ noun **1** the action of tempting. **2** a tempting thing.

> SYNONYMS **1** *Mary resisted the temptation to answer back* **desire,** urge, itch, impulse, inclination. **2** *the temptations of London* **lure,** enticement, attraction, draw, pull. **3** *the temptation of exotic travel* **allure,** appeal, attraction, fascination.

tempting ▸ adjective appealing or attractive, even if wrong or unwise.

> SYNONYMS **enticing,** alluring, attractive, appealing, inviting, seductive, beguiling, fascinating.
> ANTONYMS off-putting, uninviting.

□ **temptingly** adverb.

temptress ▸ noun a woman who sets out to make a man desire her.

ten ▸ cardinal number one more than nine; 10. (Roman numeral: **x** or **X**.)
■ **Ten Commandments** (in the Bible) the ten rules of conduct given by God to Moses.
□ **tenfold** adjective & adverb.

tenable ▸ adjective **1** able to be defended against attack or objection. **2** (of an academic post, grant, etc.) able to be held or used for a stated period.

tenacious ▸ adjective **1** firmly holding on to something. **2** continuing to exist or do something for longer than might be expected.
□ **tenaciously** adverb **tenacity** noun.

tenancy ▸ noun (plural **tenancies**) possession of land or property as a tenant.

tenant ▸ noun a person who rents land or property from a landlord.

> SYNONYMS **occupant,** resident, inhabitant, leaseholder, lessee, lodger; Brit. occupier.
> ANTONYMS owner, freeholder.

▸ verb occupy property as a tenant.

tench ▸ noun (plural **tench**) a freshwater fish of the carp family.

tend¹ ▸ verb **1** frequently behave in a particular way or have certain characteristics. **2** go or move in a particular direction.

SYNONYMS **1** *I tend to get very involved in my work* **be inclined**, be apt, be disposed, be prone, be liable. **2** *younger voters tended towards the tabloid press* **incline**, lean, gravitate, prefer, favour; N. Amer. trend.

tend² ▸ verb care for or look after.

SYNONYMS *she tended her cattle* **look after**, take care of, minister to, attend to, see to, watch over, keep an eye on, mind, protect, guard.
ANTONYMS neglect.

tendency ▸ noun (plural **tendencies**) an inclination to act in a particular way.

SYNONYMS **inclination**, propensity, proclivity, proneness, aptness, likelihood, bent, leaning, liability.

tendentious ▸ adjective formal expressing a strong, often controversial, opinion.

tender¹ ▸ adjective (**tenderer**, **tenderest**) **1** gentle and sympathetic. **2** (of food) easy to cut or chew. **3** (of a part of the body) sensitive. **4** young and vulnerable. **5** (of a plant) easily damaged by severe weather.

SYNONYMS **1** *a gentle, tender man* **caring**, kind, kind-hearted, soft-hearted, compassionate, sympathetic, warm, gentle, mild, benevolent. **2** *a tender kiss* **affectionate**, fond, loving, romantic, emotional; informal lovey-dovey. **3** *simmer until the meat is tender* **soft**, succulent, juicy, melt-in-the-mouth. **4** *her ankle was swollen and tender* **sore**, sensitive, inflamed, raw, painful, hurting, aching, throbbing. **5** *the tender age of fifteen* **young**, youthful, impressionable, inexperienced; informal wet behind the ears.
ANTONYMS hard-hearted, callous, tough, ripe.

□ **tenderly** adverb **tenderness** noun.

tender² ▸ verb (**tenders**, **tendering**, **tendered**) **1** offer or present formally. **2** make a formal written offer to do work, supply goods, etc. for a stated fixed price. **3** offer money as payment.

SYNONYMS *she tendered her resignation* **offer**, proffer, present, put forward, propose, suggest, advance, submit, hand in.

▸ noun a tendered offer.

SYNONYMS *contractors were invited to submit tenders* **bid**, offer, quotation, quote, estimate, price.

tender³ ▸ noun **1** a vehicle used by a fire service or the armed forces for carrying supplies. **2** a wagon attached to a steam locomotive to carry fuel and water. **3** a boat used to ferry people and supplies to and from a ship.

tenderize (or **tenderise**) ▸ verb (**tenderizes**, **tenderizing**, **tenderized**) make meat more tender by beating it or cooking it slowly.

tenderloin ▸ noun the tenderest part of a loin of pork or beef.

tendon ▸ noun a strong band or cord of tissue attaching a muscle to a bone.

tendril ▸ noun **1** a thin curling stem of a climbing plant, which twines round a support. **2** a slender ringlet of hair.

tenebrous ▸ adjective literary dark; shadowy.

tenement ▸ noun a building divided into flats.

tenet ▸ noun a central principle or belief.

tenner ▸ noun Brit. informal a ten-pound note.

tennis ▸ noun a game in which players use rackets to hit a ball over a net stretched across a grass or clay court.
■ **tennis elbow** inflammation of the tendons of the elbow caused by overuse of the forearm muscles.

tenon ▸ noun a projecting piece of wood that fits into a slot in another piece of wood.

tenor¹ ▸ noun the male singing voice below alto or countertenor.

tenor² ▸ noun the general meaning or character of something.

tenpin bowling ▸ noun a game in which ten skittles are bowled down with hard balls.

tense¹ ▸ adjective **1** feeling, causing, or showing anxiety and nervousness. **2** stretched tight or rigid.

SYNONYMS **1** *Loretta was feeling tense* **anxious**, nervous, on edge, edgy, strained, stressed, under pressure, ill at ease, uneasy, restless, worked up, keyed up, overwrought, jumpy, nervy; informal a bundle of nerves, jittery, twitchy, uptight. **2** *tense muscles* **taut**, tight, rigid, stretched, strained, stiff. **3** *a tense moment* **nerve-racking**, stressful, anxious, worrying, fraught, charged, strained, nail-biting.
ANTONYMS calm, slack, relaxed.

▸ verb (**tenses**, **tensing**, **tensed**) make or become tense.

SYNONYMS *Hebden tensed his muscles* **tighten**, tauten, flex, contract, brace, stiffen.
ANTONYMS relax.

□ **tensely** adverb.

tense² ▸ noun Grammar a set of forms of a verb that indicate the time or completeness of the action referred to.

tensile ▸ adjective **1** relating to tension. **2** capable of being drawn out or stretched.

tension ▸ noun **1** a situation that is strained because of differing views or aims. **2** mental or emotional strain. **3** the state of being stretched tight. **4** voltage of a particular magnitude: *high tension*.

> SYNONYMS **1** *months of tension between the military and the government* **strained relations,** strain, ill feeling, friction, antagonism, antipathy, hostility. **2** *the tension was unbearable* **strain,** stress, anxiety, pressure, worry, nervousness, jumpiness, edginess, restlessness, suspense, uncertainty. **3** *the tension of the rope* **tightness,** tautness, rigidity, pull.

tent ▸ noun a portable shelter made of cloth and supported by poles and cords.
□ **tented** adjective.

tentacle ▸ noun a long, thin, flexible part extending from the body of certain animals, used for feeling or holding things or moving about.

tentative ▸ adjective **1** done without confidence. **2** not certain or fixed.

> SYNONYMS **1** *tentative arrangements* **provisional,** unconfirmed, preliminary, exploratory, experimental. **2** *he took a few tentative steps* **hesitant,** uncertain, cautious, timid, hesitating, faltering, shaky, unsteady, halting.
> ANTONYMS definite, confident.

□ **tentatively** adverb.

tenterhook ▸ noun (**on tenterhooks**) in a state of nervous suspense.

tenth ▸ ordinal number **1** that is number ten in a sequence; 10th. **2** (**a tenth** or **one tenth**) each of ten equal parts into which something is divided.

tenuous ▸ adjective very slight or weak.
□ **tenuously** adverb.

tenure ▸ noun **1** the conditions under which land or buildings are held or occupied. **2** the period of time when someone holds a job or position. **3** the right to stay permanently in a particular job.

tenured ▸ adjective having permanent employment in a particular job.

tepee (or **teepee**) ▸ noun a cone-shaped tent used by American Indians.

tepid ▸ adjective **1** lukewarm. **2** unenthusiastic.

tequila /ti-kee-luh/ ▸ noun a clear Mexican alcoholic spirit.

tercentenary ▸ noun (plural **tercentenaries**) a three-hundredth anniversary.

term ▸ noun **1** a word or phrase used to describe a thing or to express an idea. **2** (**terms**) requirements or conditions. **3** (**terms**) relations between people: *we're on good terms.* **4** a period for which something lasts. **5** each of the periods in the year during which teaching is given in a school or college. **6** (also **full term**) the completion of a normal length of

pregnancy. **7** Maths each of the quantities in a ratio, equation, etc.

> SYNONYMS **1** *scientific terms* **word,** expression, phrase, name, title, designation, label, description. **2** *the terms of the contract* **condition,** stipulation, specification, provision, proviso, restriction, qualification. **3** *the President is elected for a four-year term* **period,** length of time, spell, stint, duration, stretch, run, session.

▸ verb call by a particular term.

> SYNONYMS *he has been termed the father of modern theology* **call,** name, entitle, title, style, designate, describe as, dub, label, tag.

■ **come to terms with** become able to accept or deal with.
□ **termly** adjective & adverb.

termagant ▸ noun a bossy woman.

terminal ▸ adjective **1** having to do with or situated at the end. **2** (of a disease) predicted to lead to death.

> SYNONYMS **1** *a terminal illness* **incurable,** untreatable, inoperable, fatal, lethal, mortal, deadly. **2** *a terminal bonus may be payable* **final,** last, concluding, closing, end.
> ANTONYMS curable, initial.

▸ noun **1** the station at the end of a railway or bus route. **2** a departure and arrival building for passengers at an airport. **3** a point at which connection can be made in an electric circuit. **4** a keyboard and screen joined to a central computer system.

> SYNONYMS **1** *a railway terminal* **station,** last stop, end of the line, depot; Brit. terminus. **2** *a computer terminal* **workstation,** VDU, visual display unit.

□ **terminally** adverb.

terminate ▸ verb (**terminates, terminating, terminated**) **1** bring or come to an end. **2** (of a train or bus service) end its journey.

> SYNONYMS **1** *treatment was terminated* **bring to an end,** bring to a close, close, conclude, finish, stop, wind up, discontinue, cease, cut short, abort, axe; informal pull the plug on. **2** *the pregnancy was terminated* **abort,** end.
> ANTONYMS begin, start, continue.

termination ▸ noun **1** the ending of something. **2** a medical procedure to end a pregnancy at an early stage.

terminology ▸ noun (plural **terminologies**) a set of terms relating to a subject.
□ **terminological** adjective.

terminus ▸ noun (plural **termini** /ter-mi-**ny**/ or **terminuses**) **1** Brit. a railway or bus terminal. **2** a final point or end.

termite ▶ noun a small insect which eats wood and lives in colonies in large nests of earth.

tern ▶ noun a white seabird with long pointed wings and a forked tail.

ternary ▶ adjective composed of three parts.

terpsichorean /terp-si-kuh-**ree**-uhn/ ▶ adjective relating to dancing.

terrace ▶ noun **1** a paved area next to a house; a patio. **2** Brit. a row of houses built in one block. **3** each of a series of flat areas on a slope, used for growing plants and crops. **4** Brit. a flight of wide, shallow steps for standing spectators in a stadium.
▶ verb (**terraces, terracing, terraced**) make sloping land into terraces.
□ **terraced** adjective **terracing** noun.

terracotta ▶ noun brownish-red earthenware that has not been glazed.

terra firma ▶ noun dry land; the ground.

terrain ▶ noun a stretch of land seen in terms of its physical features.

SYNONYMS **land,** ground, territory, topography, landscape, countryside, country.

terrapin ▶ noun a small freshwater turtle.

terrarium /ter-**rair**-i-uhm/ ▶ noun a glass container in which plants are grown, or in which small reptiles or amphibians are kept.

terrestrial ▶ adjective **1** having to do with the earth or dry land. **2** (of an animal or plant) living on or in the ground. **3** (of television broadcasting) not using a satellite.

SYNONYMS **earthly,** worldly, mundane, earthbound.

terrible ▶ adjective **1** very bad, serious, or unpleasant. **2** troubled or guilty. **3** causing terror.

SYNONYMS **1** *the film was terrible* **very bad,** dreadful, awful, frightful, atrocious, poor; informal pathetic, pitiful, useless, lousy, appalling; Brit. informal chronic, rubbish, pants. **2** *he was in terrible pain* **severe,** extreme, intense, excruciating, agonizing, unbearable. **3** *a terrible crime* **dreadful,** awful, appalling, horrific, horrible, horrendous, atrocious, monstrous, sickening, heinous, vile.
ANTONYMS excellent, slight, minor.

terribly ▶ adverb **1** extremely. **2** very badly.

SYNONYMS **1** *I shall miss you terribly* **very much,** greatly, a great deal, a lot; informal loads. **2** *he played terribly* **very badly,** atrociously, awfully, dreadfully, appallingly, execrably; informal abysmally, pitifully.

terrier ▶ noun a small, lively breed of dog.

terrific ▶ adjective **1** of great size, amount, or strength. **2** informal excellent.

SYNONYMS **1** *a terrific bang* **tremendous,** huge, massive, gigantic, colossal, mighty, considerable; informal mega, whopping; Brit. informal ginormous. **2** *a terrific game of top-quality football* **marvellous,** wonderful, sensational, outstanding, superb, excellent, first-rate, dazzling, out of this world, breathtaking; informal great, fantastic, fabulous, super, ace, wicked, awesome; Brit. informal brilliant.
□ **terrifically** adverb.

terrify ▶ verb (**terrifies, terrifying, terrified**) make someone feel very frightened.

SYNONYMS **frighten,** horrify, petrify, scare, strike terror into, paralyse, transfix.

terrine /tuh-**reen**/ ▶ noun a mixture of chopped savoury food that is pressed into a container and served cold.

territorial ▶ adjective **1** relating to a territory or area. **2** (of an animal) having a territory which it defends.
■ **Territorial Army** (in the UK) a military reserve force of volunteers.
□ **territorially** adverb.

territory ▶ noun (plural **territories**) **1** an area controlled by a ruler or state. **2** a division of a country. **3** an area defended by an animal against others. **4** an area in which a person has special rights, responsibilities, or knowledge.

SYNONYMS **1** *British overseas territories* **region,** area, enclave, country, state, land, dependency, colony, dominion. **2** *mountainous territory* **terrain,** land, ground, countryside. **3** *the territory of biblical scholarship* **domain,** province, department, field, preserve, sphere, arena, realm, world.

terror ▶ noun **1** extreme fear. **2** a cause of terror. **3** the use of terror to intimidate people. **4** informal a person causing trouble or annoyance.

SYNONYMS **fear,** dread, horror, fright, alarm, panic, shock.

terrorism ▶ noun the unofficial or unauthorized use of violence and intimidation in the attempt to achieve political aims.
□ **terrorist** noun & adjective.

terrorize (or **terrorise**) ▶ verb (**terrorizes, terrorizing, terrorized**) threaten and frighten over a period of time.

terry ▶ noun a towelling fabric.

terse ▶ adjective (**terser, tersest**) using few words.
□ **tersely** adverb.

t

tertiary /ter-shuh-ri/ ▸ adjective **1** third in order or level. **2** Brit. relating to university education.

tessellated ▸ adjective decorated with mosaics.
□ **tessellation** noun.

test ▸ noun **1** a procedure intended to establish how reliable or good something is, or whether something is present. **2** a short examination of skill or knowledge. **3** a medical examination of part of the body. **4** a difficult situation. **5** (**Test** or **Test match**) an international cricket or rugby match.

SYNONYMS **1** *a series of scientific tests* **trial,** experiment, check, examination, assessment, evaluation, appraisal, investigation. **2** *candidates must take a test* **exam,** examination; N. Amer. quiz.

▸ verb **1** subject someone or something to a test. **2** make great demands on someone's endurance or patience.

SYNONYMS **1** *a small-scale prototype was tested* **try out,** trial, put through its paces, experiment with, check, examine, assess, evaluate, appraise, investigate, sample. **2** (**testing**) **difficult,** challenging, tough, hard, demanding, taxing, stressful.

■ **test case** Law a case that sets an example for future cases. **test tube** a thin glass tube used to hold material in laboratory tests. **test-tube baby** informal a baby conceived by in vitro fertilization.
□ **tester** noun.

testament ▸ noun **1** a person's will. **2** evidence or proof. **3** (**Testament**) each of the two divisions of the Bible.
□ **testamentary** adjective.

testate ▸ adjective having made a valid will before dying.

testicle ▸ noun either of the two oval organs that produce sperm in male mammals, enclosed in the scrotum.
□ **testicular** adjective.

testify ▸ verb (**testifies, testifying, testified**) **1** give evidence as a witness in a law court. **2** (**testify to**) be evidence or proof of.

SYNONYMS **swear,** attest, give evidence, state on oath, declare, assert, affirm.

testimonial ▸ noun **1** a formal statement of a person's good character and qualifications. **2** a public tribute to someone.

SYNONYMS **reference,** letter of recommendation, commendation.

testimony ▸ noun (plural **testimonies**) **1** a formal statement, especially one given in a court of law. **2** (**testimony to**) evidence or proof of.

SYNONYMS **evidence,** sworn statement, attestation, affidavit, statement, declaration, assertion.

testis /tess-tiss/ ▸ noun (plural **testes** /tess-teez/) a testicle.

testosterone ▸ noun a hormone that stimulates the development of male physical characteristics.

testy ▸ adjective (**testier, testiest**) easily irritated.
□ **testily** adverb.

tetanus ▸ noun a disease that causes the muscles to stiffen and go into spasms.

tetchy ▸ adjective (**tetchier, tetchiest**) bad-tempered and irritable.
□ **tetchily** adverb.

tête-à-tête /tet-ah-**tet**/ ▸ noun a private conversation between two people.
▸ adjective & adverb happening privately between two people.

tether ▸ verb (**tethers, tethering, tethered**) tie an animal to a post with a rope or chain.
▸ noun a rope or chain used to tether an animal.

tetrahedron /tet-ruh-**hee**-druhn/ ▸ noun (plural **tetrahedra** or **tetrahedrons**) a solid figure with four triangular faces.

Teutonic /tyoo-**ton**-ik/ ▸ adjective often disapproving German.

text ▸ noun **1** a book or other written or printed work. **2** the main part of a work as distinct from illustrations, notes, etc. **3** written or printed words or computer data. **4** a text message.

SYNONYMS **1** *a text which explores pain and grief* **book,** work, textbook. **2** *the pictures relate well to the text* **words,** content, body, wording, script, copy.

▸ verb send someone a text message.
■ **text message** an electronic message sent and received via mobile phone.
□ **textual** adjective.

textbook ▸ noun a book used for the study of a subject.
▸ adjective done in exactly the recommended way.

textile ▸ noun any type of cloth.

SYNONYMS **cloth,** fabric, material.

texture ▸ noun the feel, appearance, or consistency of a surface, substance, or fabric.

SYNONYMS **feel,** touch, appearance, finish, surface, grain, consistency.

▸ verb (**textures, texturing, textured**) give a rough or raised texture to.
□ **textural** adjective.

Thai /ty/ ▸ noun (plural **Thai** or **Thais**) **1** a person from Thailand. **2** the official language of Thailand.

thalidomide /thuh-lid-uh-myd/ ▸ noun a sedative drug which was found to cause abnormalities in the fetus when taken by pregnant women.

thallium ▸ noun a soft silvery-white metallic element whose compounds are very poisonous.

than ▸ conjunction & preposition **1** used to introduce the second part of a comparison. **2** used to introduce an exception or contrast. **3** used in expressions indicating one thing happening immediately after another.

thane ▸ noun an Anglo-Saxon or medieval Scottish landowner or nobleman.

thank ▸ verb **1** express gratitude to. **2** ironic blame or hold responsible.

> synonyms **express your gratitude to,** say thank you to, show your appreciation to.

■ **thank you** a polite expression of gratitude.

> ✔ **Thank you** is a two-word phrase: don't spell it as one word.

thankful ▸ adjective pleased and relieved.

> synonyms **grateful,** relieved, pleased, glad.

□ **thankfulness** noun.

thankfully ▸ adverb **1** in a thankful way. **2** fortunately.

thankless ▸ adjective **1** (of a job or task) unpleasant and unlikely to be appreciated by other people. **2** not showing or feeling gratitude.

thanks ▸ plural noun **1** an expression of gratitude. **2** = THANK YOU (see THANK).

> synonyms *they expressed their thanks and wished her well* **gratitude,** appreciation, acknowledgement, recognition, credit.

■ **thanks to** due to.

thanksgiving ▸ noun **1** the expression of gratitude to God. **2** (**Thanksgiving**) (in North America) a national holiday held in November in the US and October in Canada.

that ▸ pronoun & determiner **1** (plural **those**) used to refer to a person or thing seen or heard or already mentioned or known. **2** (plural **those**) referring to the more distant of two things.
▸ pronoun used instead of which, who, when, etc. to introduce a clause that defines or identifies something.
▸ adverb to such a degree; so.
▸ conjunction introducing a statement or suggestion.

thatch ▸ noun a roof covering of straw, reeds, etc.
▸ verb cover with thatch.
□ **thatcher** noun.

thaw ▸ verb **1** make or become liquid or soft after being frozen. **2** make or become friendlier.

> synonyms **melt,** unfreeze, defrost, soften, liquefy.
> antonyms freeze.

▸ noun **1** a period of warmer weather that thaws ice and snow. **2** an increase in friendliness.

the ▸ determiner **1** used to refer to one or more people or things already mentioned or easily understood; the definite article. **2** used to refer to someone or something that is the only one of its kind. **3** used to refer to something in a general rather than specific way.

theatre (US spelling **theater**) ▸ noun **1** a building in which plays are performed. **2** the writing and production of plays. **3** the dramatic quality of a play or event. **4** a room where specific things are done: *an operating theatre.* **5** the area in which something happens: *a theatre of war.*

theatrical ▸ adjective **1** having to do with acting or the theatre. **2** exaggerated and too dramatic.

> synonyms **1** *a theatrical career* **stage,** dramatic, thespian, show-business; informal showbiz. **2** *Henry looked over his shoulder with theatrical caution* **exaggerated,** ostentatious, stagy, showy, melodramatic, affected.

▸ noun (**theatricals**) theatrical performances or behaviour.
□ **theatricality** noun **theatrically** adverb.

theatrics ▸ noun theatricals.

thee old-fashioned or dialect form of **you**, as the singular object of a verb or preposition.

theft ▸ noun the action or crime of stealing.

> synonyms **robbery,** stealing, larceny, shoplifting, burglary, embezzlement, raid, hold-up; informal smash-and-grab; N. Amer. informal heist.

their ▸ possessive determiner **1** belonging to or associated with the people or things previously mentioned or easily identified. **2** belonging to or associated with a person whose sex is not specified.

> ❗ Don't confuse **their** with **there**, which means 'in or to that place' or **they're**, which is short for 'they are'.

theirs ▸ possessive pronoun used to refer to something belonging to or associated with two or more people or things previously mentioned.

> ✔ no apostrophe: **theirs**.

them ▸ pronoun **1** used as the object of a verb or preposition to refer to two or more people or things previously mentioned or

t

easily identified. **2** referring to a person whose sex is not specified.

thematic ▸ adjective arranged according to subject, or connected with a subject.
□ **thematically** adverb.

theme ▸ noun **1** a subject which a person speaks, writes, or thinks about. **2** a prominent or recurring melody in a piece of music. **3** an idea that is often repeated in a work of art or literature. **4** (also **theme tune** or **music**) a piece of music played at the beginning and end of a film or programme.

SYNONYMS **1** *the theme of her speech* **subject**, topic, argument, idea, thrust, thread, motif, keynote. **2** *the first violin takes up the theme* **melody**, tune, air, motif, leitmotif.

■ **theme park** a large amusement park based around a particular idea.
□ **themed** adjective.

themselves ▸ pronoun **1** used as the object of a verb or preposition to refer to a group of people or things previously mentioned as the subject of the clause. **2** they or them personally. **3** used instead of 'himself' or 'herself' to refer to a person whose sex is not specified.

❗ Note that you should use **themselves** rather than **themself** to refer to a person whose sex is not specified, e.g. *helping someone to help themselves*, not *helping someone to help themself*.

then ▸ adverb **1** at that time. **2** after that. **3** also. **4** therefore.

SYNONYMS **1** *I was living in Cairo then* **at that time**, in those days, at that point (in time), at that moment, on that occasion. **2** *she won the first and then the second game* **next**, after that, afterwards, subsequently; formal thereafter.

thence (or **from thence**) ▸ adverb formal **1** from a place or source previously mentioned. **2** as a consequence.

thenceforth (or **thenceforward**) ▸ adverb formal from that time, place, or point onward.

theocracy ▸ noun (plural **theocracies**) a system of government by priests.
□ **theocratic** adjective.

theodolite /thi-od-uh-lyt/ ▸ noun an instrument used in surveying for measuring horizontal and vertical angles.

theologian /thi-uh-loh-juhn/ ▸ noun a person who is an expert in or is studying theology.

theology ▸ noun (plural **theologies**) **1** the study of God and religious belief. **2** a system of religious beliefs and theory.
□ **theological** adjective **theologist** noun.

theorem ▸ noun a scientific or

mathematical rule or proposition that can be proved by reasoning.

theoretical ▸ adjective **1** concerned with the theory of a subject rather than its practical application. **2** based on theory rather than experience or practice.

SYNONYMS **hypothetical**, speculative, academic, conjectural, suppositional, notional, unproven.
ANTONYMS actual, real, practical.

□ **theoretically** adverb.

theoretician ▸ noun a person who develops or studies the theoretical framework of a subject.

theorist ▸ noun a theoretician.

theorize (or **theorise**) ▸ verb (**theorizes**, **theorizing**, **theorized**) form a theory or theories about something.

theory ▸ noun (plural **theories**) **1** an idea or system of ideas intended to explain something. **2** a set of principles on which an activity is based.

SYNONYMS **1** *that confirms my theory* **hypothesis**, thesis, conjecture, supposition, speculation, postulation, proposition, premise, opinion, view, belief, contention. **2** *modern economic theory* **principles**, ideas, concepts, philosophy, ideology, thinking.

therapeutic /the-ruh-**pyoo**-tik/ ▸ adjective **1** relating to the healing of disease. **2** having a good effect on the body or mind.

SYNONYMS **healing**, curative, remedial, medicinal, restorative, health-giving.
ANTONYMS harmful.

□ **therapeutically** adverb.

therapist ▸ noun a person who gives therapy.

SYNONYMS **psychologist**, psychotherapist, analyst, psychoanalyst, psychiatrist, counsellor; informal shrink.

therapy ▸ noun (plural **therapies**) **1** treatment of a physical problem or illness. **2** treatment of mental or emotional problems using psychological methods.

SYNONYMS **1** *complementary therapies* **treatment**, remedy, cure. **2** *he's currently in therapy* **psychotherapy**, psychoanalysis, counselling.

there ▸ adverb **1** in, at, or to that place or position. **2** on that issue.
■ **there is** (or **there are**) used to indicate that something exists or is true.

❗ Don't confuse **there** with **their** or **they're**: see the note at **THEIR**.

thereabouts ▸ adverb near that place, time, or amount.

thereafter ▸ adverb after that time.

thereby ▶ adverb by that means; as a result of that.

therefore ▶ adverb for that reason.

SYNONYMS **consequently,** because of that, for that reason, that being the case, so, as a result, hence, accordingly.

therein ▶ adverb formal in that place, document, or respect.

thereof ▶ adverb formal of the thing just mentioned.

there's ▶ short form **1** there is. **2** there has.

thereupon ▶ adverb formal immediately or shortly after that.

therewith ▶ adverb old use or formal **1** with or in the thing mentioned. **2** soon or immediately after that.

thermal ▶ adjective **1** relating to heat. **2** (of a garment) designed to keep the body warm by stopping heat from escaping.
▶ noun an upward current of warm air.
□ **thermally** adverb.

thermodynamics ▶ noun the study of the relationship between heat and other forms of energy.
□ **thermodynamic** adjective.

thermometer ▶ noun an instrument for measuring temperature, usually containing mercury or alcohol which expands when heated.

thermonuclear ▶ adjective relating to or using nuclear fusion reactions that occur at very high temperatures.

Thermos ▶ noun trademark a vacuum flask.

thermostat ▶ noun a device that automatically controls temperature or activates a device at a set temperature.
□ **thermostatic** adjective **thermostatically** adverb.

thesaurus /thi-**saw**-ruhss/ ▶ noun a book containing lists of words which have the same or a similar meaning.

these plural of THIS.

thesis ▶ noun (plural **theses**) **1** a statement or theory that is put forward to be supported or proved. **2** a long piece of work involving research, written as part of a university degree.

SYNONYMS **1** the central thesis of his lecture **theory,** contention, argument, proposal, proposition, premise, assumption, hypothesis. **2** a doctoral thesis **dissertation,** essay, paper, treatise, composition, study; N. Amer. theme.

thespian ▶ noun an actor or actress.
▶ adjective relating to drama and the theatre.

they ▶ pronoun **1** used to refer to two or more people or things previously mentioned or easily identified. **2** people in general. **3** used to refer to a person whose sex is not specified (in place of either 'he' or 'he or she').

they'd ▶ short form **1** they had. **2** they would.

they'll ▶ short form **1** they shall. **2** they will.

they're ▶ short form they are.

❗ Don't confuse **they're** with **their** or **there**: see the note at THEIR.

they've ▶ short form they have.

thiamine (or thiamin) ▶ noun vitamin B_1, found in grains, nuts, beans, and liver.

thick ▶ adjective **1** with opposite sides or surfaces relatively far apart. **2** (of a garment or fabric) made of heavy material. **3** made up of a large number of things or people close together. **4** (**thick with**) filled or covered with. **5** (of the air or atmosphere) difficult to see through or breathe. **6** (of something liquid or semi-liquid) relatively firm in consistency. **7** informal stupid. **8** (of a voice) hoarse or husky. **9** (of an accent) strong and difficult to understand. **10** informal having a very close, friendly relationship.

SYNONYMS **1** thick stone walls **broad,** wide, deep, stout, bulky, hefty, chunky, solid, plump. **2** the station was thick with people **crowded,** full, packed, teeming, seething, swarming, crawling, crammed, thronged, bursting at the seams, solid, overflowing; informal jam-packed, chock-a-block, stuffed; Austral./NZ informal chocker. **3** the thick vegetation **plentiful,** abundant, profuse, luxuriant, bushy, rich, riotous, exuberant, rank, rampant, dense; informal jungly. **4** a thick paste **semi-solid,** firm, stiff, heavy, viscous, gelatinous. **5** thick fog **dense,** heavy, opaque, impenetrable, soupy, murky. ANTONYMS thin, slender, sparse.

▶ noun (**the thick**) the middle or the busiest part.
■ **through thick and thin** under all circumstances.
□ **thickly** adverb.

thicken ▶ verb make or become thick or thicker.

SYNONYMS **stiffen,** condense, solidify, set, gel, congeal, clot, coagulate.

thicket ▶ noun a dense group of bushes or trees.

thickness ▶ noun **1** the distance through an object, as distinct from width or height. **2** the state or quality of being thick. **3** a layer of material.

thickset ▶ adjective heavily built.

thief ▶ noun (plural **thieves**) a person who steals another person's property.

SYNONYMS **robber,** burglar, housebreaker, shoplifter, pickpocket, mugger, kleptomaniac; informal crook.

t

✔ **i** before **e** except after **c**: th**ie**f.

thieve ▸ verb (thieves, thieving, thieved) steal things.

SYNONYMS **steal,** take, purloin, help yourself to, snatch, pilfer, embezzle, misappropriate; informal rob, swipe, nab, lift; Brit. informal nick, pinch, knock off; N. Amer. informal heist.

▫ **thievery** noun.

thigh ▸ noun the part of the leg between the hip and the knee.

thimble ▸ noun a small covering that you wear to protect the end of the finger and push the needle in sewing.

thin ▸ adjective (thinner, thinnest) **1** having opposite surfaces or sides close together. **2** (of a garment or fabric) made of light material. **3** having little flesh or fat on the body. **4** having few parts or members in relation to the area covered or filled. **5** not dense or heavy. **6** containing a lot of liquid and not much solid substance. **7** (of a sound) faint and high-pitched. **8** weak and inadequate.

SYNONYMS **1** *a thin white line* **narrow,** fine, attenuated. **2** *a thin cotton nightdress* **lightweight,** light, fine, delicate, flimsy, diaphanous, gossamer, sheer, filmy, transparent, see-through. **3** *a tall, thin woman* **slim,** lean, slender, willowy, svelte, sylphlike, spare, slight, skinny, underweight, scrawny, scraggy, bony, gaunt, emaciated, skeletal, lanky, spindly, gangly; informal anorexic. **4** *thin soup* **watery,** weak, runny, sloppy. ANTONYMS thick, broad, fat.

▸ verb (thins, thinning, thinned) (often **thin out**) make or become less thick or dense.

SYNONYMS **1** *some paint must be thinned down* **dilute,** water down, weaken. **2** *the crowds were beginning to thin out* **disperse,** dissipate, scatter. ANTONYMS thicken, gather.

▫ **thinly** adverb **thinness** noun.

t

thine ▸ pronoun & possessive determiner old use your or yours.

thing ▸ noun **1** an inanimate object. **2** an unspecified object, action, activity, etc. **3** (your things) personal belongings. **4** (the thing) informal what is needed or required. **5** (your thing) informal your special interest.

SYNONYMS **1** *the room was full of strange things* **object,** article, item, artefact, commodity; informal doodah, whatsit, whatchamacallit, thingummy, thingy; Brit. informal gubbins. **2** (things) *I'll collect my things* **belongings,** possessions, stuff, property, worldly goods, effects, paraphernalia, bits and pieces, luggage, baggage; informal gear, junk; Brit. informal

clobber. **3** (things) *his gardening things* **equipment,** apparatus, gear, kit, tackle, stuff, implements, tools, utensils, accoutrements.

think ▸ verb (thinks, thinking, thought) **1** have a particular opinion, belief, or idea. **2** use or direct your mind. **3** (think of or about) take into account or consideration. **4** intend. **5** (think something over) consider something carefully. **6** (think something up) informal invent something.

SYNONYMS **1** *I think he's gone home* **believe,** be of the opinion, be of the view, be under the impression, expect, imagine, anticipate, suppose, guess, fancy; informal reckon, figure. **2** *his family was thought to be rich* **consider,** judge, hold, reckon, deem, presume, estimate, regard as, view as. **3** *Jack thought for a moment* **ponder,** reflect, deliberate, consider, meditate, contemplate, muse, brood. **4** *she thought of all the visits she had made* **recall,** remember, recollect, call to mind. **5** *I can't think how bad it must be* **imagine,** picture, visualize, envisage.

▸ noun an act of thinking.
■ **think better of** reconsider and decide not to do. **think tank** a group of experts providing advice and ideas.

thinker ▸ noun a person who thinks deeply and seriously.

SYNONYMS **intellectual,** philosopher, scholar, sage, ideologist, theorist, intellect, mind; informal brain.

thinking ▸ noun a person's ideas or opinions.

SYNONYMS *the thinking behind the campaign* **reasoning,** idea(s), theory, thoughts, philosophy, beliefs, opinion(s), view(s).

▸ adjective using thought or rational judgement.

SYNONYMS *a thinking man* **intelligent,** sensible, reasonable, rational, logical, analytical, thoughtful. ANTONYMS stupid, irrational.

thinner ▸ noun a solvent used to thin paint or other solutions.

third ▸ ordinal number **1** that is number three in a sequence; 3rd. **2** (a third or one third) each of three equal parts into which something is divided. **3** Brit. a place in the third grade in an exam for a degree.
■ **third-degree** (of burns) of the most severe kind, affecting tissue below the skin. **the third degree** lengthy and harsh questioning. **third party 1** a person besides the two main ones involved in a situation. **2** Brit. (of insurance) covering damage or injury suffered by someone other than the

person who is insured. **Third World** the developing countries of Asia, Africa, and Latin America.
□ **thirdly** adverb.

thirst ▸ noun **1** a feeling of needing or wanting to drink. **2** the state of not having enough water to drink. **3** (**thirst for**) a strong desire for.

> SYNONYMS *his thirst for knowledge* **craving**, desire, longing, yearning, hunger, hankering, eagerness, lust, appetite; informal yen, itch.

▸ verb **1** (**thirst for** or **after**) have a strong desire for. **2** old use feel a need to drink.

thirsty ▸ adjective (**thirstier**, **thirstiest**) **1** feeling or causing thirst. **2** (**thirsty for**) having a strong desire for.

> SYNONYMS **longing for a drink**, dry, dehydrated; informal parched, gasping.

□ **thirstily** adverb.

thirteen ▸ cardinal number one more than twelve; 13. (Roman numeral: **xiii** or **XIII**.)
□ **thirteenth** ordinal number.

thirty ▸ cardinal number (plural **thirties**) ten less than forty; 30. (Roman numeral: **xxx** or **XXX**.)
□ **thirtieth** ordinal number.

this ▸ pronoun & determiner (plural **these**) **1** used to identify a specific person or thing close at hand, just mentioned, or being indicated or experienced. **2** referring to the nearer of two things close to the speaker.
▸ adverb to the degree or extent indicated.

thistle ▸ noun a plant with a prickly stem and leaves and purple flowers.

thistledown ▸ noun the light fluffy down of thistle seeds.

thither ▸ adverb old use to or towards that place.

tho' (or **tho**) informal spelling of THOUGH.

thong ▸ noun **1** a narrow strip used as a fastening or as the lash of a whip. **2** a pair of knickers like a G-string.

thorax ▸ noun (plural **thoraces** /**thor**-uh-seez/ or **thoraxes**) **1** the part of the body between the neck and the abdomen. **2** the middle section of an insect's body, to which the legs and wings are attached.
□ **thoracic** adjective.

thorium ▸ noun a white radioactive metallic element.

thorn ▸ noun **1** a stiff sharp-pointed projection on a plant. **2** a thorny bush, shrub, or tree.

> SYNONYMS **prickle**, spike, barb, spine.

■ **a thorn in someone's side** (or **flesh**) a source of continual annoyance or trouble.

thorny ▸ adjective (**thornier**, **thorniest**) **1** having many thorns. **2** causing difficulty.

thorough ▸ adjective **1** complete with regard to every detail. **2** very careful and complete. **3** absolute; utter.

> SYNONYMS **1** *a thorough investigation* **rigorous**, in-depth, exhaustive, minute, detailed, close, meticulous, methodical, careful, complete, comprehensive.
> **2** *he is slow but thorough* **meticulous**, scrupulous, assiduous, conscientious, painstaking, punctilious, methodical, careful. **3** *the child is being a thorough nuisance* **utter**, downright, absolute, complete, total, out-and-out, real, perfect, proper; Brit. informal **right**; Austral./NZ informal **fair**.
> ANTONYMS superficial, cursory, careless.

□ **thoroughly** adverb.

thoroughbred ▸ adjective descended from animals that were all of the same breed.
▸ noun a thoroughbred animal.

thoroughfare ▸ noun a road or path between two places.

thoroughgoing ▸ adjective **1** thorough. **2** complete; absolute.

those plural of THAT.

thou ▸ pronoun old use you (as the singular subject of a verb).

though ▸ conjunction **1** despite the fact that; although. **2** however; but.

> SYNONYMS *though she smiled bravely, she looked tired* **although**, even though, even if, despite the fact that, notwithstanding (the fact) that, for all that.

▸ adverb however.

> SYNONYMS *You can't always do that. You can try, though.* **nevertheless**, nonetheless, even so, however, be that as it may, for all that, despite that, having said that; informal still and all.

thought[1] ▸ noun **1** an idea or opinion produced by thinking, or occurring suddenly in the mind. **2** the process of thinking. **3** (**thought of**) intention, hope, or idea of. **4** the forming of opinions, or the opinions so formed.

> SYNONYMS **1** *what are your thoughts on the matter?* **idea**, notion, opinion, view, impression, feeling, theory. **2** *he gave up any thought of taking a degree* **hope**, aspiration, ambition, dream, intention, idea, plan, design, aim. **3** *it only took a moment's thought* **thinking**, contemplation, musing, pondering, consideration, reflection, deliberation, meditation. **4** *have you no thought for others?* **consideration**, understanding, regard, sensitivity, compassion, sympathy, care, concern.

thought[2] past and past participle of THINK.

thoughtful ▸ adjective **1** absorbed in thought. **2** showing careful consideration. **3** showing consideration for other people.

SYNONYMS **1** *a thoughtful expression* **pensive**, reflective, contemplative, musing, meditative, philosophical, preoccupied. **2** *how very thoughtful of you!* **considerate**, caring, attentive, understanding, sympathetic, solicitous, concerned, helpful, obliging, accommodating, kind, compassionate.
ANTONYMS vacant, inconsiderate.

□ **thoughtfully** adverb.

thoughtless ▸ adjective **1** not showing consideration for other people. **2** without considering the consequences.
□ **thoughtlessly** adverb.

thousand ▸ cardinal number **1** the product of a hundred and ten; 1,000. (Roman numeral: m or M.) **2** (**thousands**) informal an unspecified large number.
□ **thousandth** ordinal number.

thrall ▸ noun the state of being in another person's power.

thrash ▸ verb **1** beat repeatedly and violently with a stick or whip. **2** move in a violent or uncontrolled way. **3** informal defeat heavily. **4** (**thrash something out**) discuss an issue frankly and thoroughly.

SYNONYMS **1** *she thrashed him with a whip* **hit**, beat, strike, batter, thump, hammer, pound; informal belt. **2** *he was thrashing around in pain* **flail**, writhe, thresh, jerk, toss, twist, twitch.

thread ▸ noun **1** a thin strand of cotton or other fibres used in sewing or weaving. **2** a spiral ridge on the outside of a screw or bolt or on the inside of a hole, to allow two parts to be screwed together. **3** a theme running through a situation or piece of writing.

SYNONYMS **1** *a needle and thread* **cotton**, yarn, filament, fibre. **2** *she lost the thread of the conversation* **train of thought**, drift, direction, theme, tenor.

▸ verb **1** pass a thread through. **2** weave in and out of obstacles.

SYNONYMS **1** *he threaded the rope through a pulley* **pass**, string, work, ease, push, poke. **2** *she threaded her way through the tables* **weave**, inch, squeeze, navigate, negotiate.

threadbare ▸ adjective thin and tattered with age.

threat ▸ noun **1** a stated intention to inflict harm on someone. **2** a person or thing likely to cause harm. **3** the possibility of trouble or danger.

SYNONYMS **1** *Maggie ignored his threats* **threatening remark**, warning, ultimatum. **2** *a possible threat to aircraft* **danger**, peril, hazard, menace, risk. **3** *the company faces the threat of liquidation*

possibility, chance, probability, likelihood, risk.

threaten ▸ verb **1** make a threat to. **2** put at risk. **3** seem likely to produce an unwelcome result.

SYNONYMS **1** *how dare you threaten me?* **menace**, intimidate, browbeat, bully, terrorize. **2** *these events could threaten the stability of Europe* **endanger**, jeopardize, imperil, put at risk. **3** *the grey skies threatened snow* **herald**, bode, warn of, presage, foreshadow, indicate, point to, be a sign of, signal.

□ **threatening** adjective **threateningly** adverb.

three ▸ cardinal number one more than two; 3. (Roman numeral: iii or III.)
■ **three-dimensional** having or appearing to have length, breadth, and depth.
□ **threefold** adjective & adverb.

threepence /thrup-uhnss/ ▸ noun Brit. the sum of three old pence before decimalization (1971).
□ **threepenny** adjective.

threesome ▸ noun a group of three people.

threnody /thren-uh-di/ ▸ noun (plural **threnodies**) a song, piece of music, or poem expressing grief or regret.

thresh ▸ verb **1** separate grains of corn from the rest of the plant. **2** move in an uncontrolled way.
□ **thresher** noun.

threshold ▸ noun **1** a strip of wood or stone forming the bottom of a doorway. **2** a level or point marking the start of something.

SYNONYMS **1** *the threshold of the church* **doorstep**, entrance, entry, gate. **2** *on the threshold of a new era* **start**, beginning, commencement, brink, verge, dawn, inception, day one, opening, debut. **3** *the human threshold of pain* **limit**, minimum.

✔ There is only one **h** in the middle: thre**sh**old.

threw past of THROW.

❗ Don't confuse **threw** with **through**, which means 'in one side of an opening or place and out of the other'.

thrice ▸ adverb old use three times.

thrift ▸ noun the quality of spending money very carefully, so that none is wasted.

thrifty ▸ adjective careful with money.

SYNONYMS **frugal**, economical, sparing, careful with money, provident, prudent, abstemious, parsimonious, penny-pinching.
ANTONYMS extravagant.

thrill ▸ noun **1** a sudden feeling of excitement and pleasure. **2** an exciting or enjoyable experience. **3** a wave of emotion or sensation.

t

SYNONYMS *the thrill of jumping out of an aeroplane* **excitement,** stimulation, pleasure, tingle; informal buzz, kick; N. Amer. informal charge.
ANTONYMS boredom.

▶ verb **1** give someone a thrill. **2** (**thrill to**) experience something exciting.

SYNONYMS **1** *his words thrilled her* **excite,** stimulate, arouse, rouse, inspire, delight, exhilarate, intoxicate, stir, electrify, move; informal give someone a buzz, give someone a kick; N. Amer. informal give someone a charge. **2** *he thrilled at the sound of her voice* **feel excited,** tingle; informal get a buzz out of, get a kick out of; N. Amer. informal get a charge out of.
ANTONYMS bore.

thriller ▶ noun a novel, play, or film with an exciting plot, typically involving crime or spying.

thrilling ▶ adjective very exciting and pleasurable.

SYNONYMS **exciting,** stimulating, stirring, action-packed, rip-roaring, gripping, electrifying, riveting, fascinating, dramatic, hair-raising.
ANTONYMS boring.

thrive ▶ verb (thrives, thriving, thrived or throve; past participle thrived or thriven) **1** grow or develop well. **2** be successful; flourish.

SYNONYMS **1** **flourish,** prosper, burgeon, bloom, blossom, do well, advance, succeed, boom. **2** (**thriving**) **flourishing,** prospering, growing, developing, blooming, healthy, successful, booming, profitable; informal going strong.
ANTONYMS decline, wither.

throat ▶ noun **1** the passage which leads from the back of the mouth to the lungs and stomach. **2** the front part of the neck.

throaty ▶ adjective (throatier, throatiest) sounding deep and husky.
□ **throatily** adverb.

throb ▶ verb (throbs, throbbing, throbbed) **1** beat or sound with a strong, regular rhythm. **2** feel pain in a series of pulsations.

SYNONYMS *her arms and legs throbbed with tiredness* **pulsate,** beat, pulse, palpitate, pound, thud, thump, drum, judder, vibrate, quiver.

▶ noun a strong, regular beat or sound.

SYNONYMS *the throb of the ship's engines* **pulsation,** beat, pulse, palpitation, pounding, thudding, thumping, drumming, juddering, vibration, quivering.

throes ▶ plural noun severe or violent pain and struggle.

■ **in the throes of** in the middle of doing or dealing with something difficult.

thrombosis ▶ noun (plural thromboses) the formation of a blood clot in a blood vessel or the heart.

throne ▶ noun **1** a chair for a king or queen, used during ceremonies. **2** (**the throne**) the power or rank of a king or queen.

throng ▶ noun a large, densely packed crowd.

SYNONYMS *throngs of people blocked her way* **crowd,** horde, mass, army, herd, flock, drove, swarm, sea, troupe, pack; informal gaggle, bunch, gang.

▶ verb gather somewhere in large numbers.

SYNONYMS **1** *the pavements were thronged with tourists* **fill,** crowd, pack, cram, jam. **2** *people thronged to see the play* **flock,** stream, swarm, troop. **3** *visitors thronged round him* **crowd,** cluster, mill, swarm, congregate, gather.

throttle ▶ noun a device controlling the flow of fuel or power to an engine.

▶ verb (throttles, throttling, throttled) **1** attack or kill by choking or strangling. **2** control an engine or vehicle with a throttle.

SYNONYMS **choke,** strangle, garrotte.

through ▶ preposition & adverb **1** in one side and out of the other side of an opening or place. **2** continuing in time towards. **3** from beginning to end. **4** by means of.

SYNONYMS **1** *he worked through the night* **throughout,** for the duration of, until/to the end of, all. **2** *he got the job through an advertisement* **by means of,** by way of, by dint of, via, using, thanks to, by virtue of, as a result of, as a consequence of, on account of, owing to.

▶ adjective **1** (of public transport) continuing to the final destination. **2** (of traffic, roads, etc.) passing straight through a place. **3** having successfully reached the next stage of a competition. **4** informal having finished an activity, relationship, etc.

❗ Don't confuse **through** with **threw,** which is the past of **throw.**

throughout ▶ preposition & adverb all the way through.

SYNONYMS **1** *it had repercussions throughout Europe* **all over,** in every part of, everywhere in. **2** *Rose had been very fit throughout her life* **all through,** for the duration of, for the whole of, until the end of, all.

throughput ▶ noun the amount of material or number of items passing through a process.

throve past of THRIVE.

t

throw ▸ verb (throws, throwing, threw; past participle **thrown**) **1** send through the air with a rapid movement of the arm and hand. **2** move or place hurriedly or roughly. **3** project, direct, or cast light, an expression, etc. in a particular direction. **4** send suddenly into a particular position or condition. **5** upset or confuse.

SYNONYMS **1 hurl**, toss, fling, pitch, cast, lob, launch, bowl; informal chuck, heave, sling, bung. **2** *he threw the door open* **push**, thrust, fling, bang. **3** *a chandelier threw its light over the walls* **cast**, send, give off, emit, radiate, project. **4** *his intervention threw me* **disconcert**, unnerve, fluster, ruffle, put off, throw off balance, unsettle, confuse; informal rattle, faze.

▸ noun **1** an act of throwing. **2** a small rug or light cover for furniture.

SYNONYMS **lob**, toss, pitch, bowl.

■ **throw something away** (or **out**) get rid of something. **throw up** informal vomit.

throwaway ▸ adjective **1** intended to be thrown away after use. **2** (of a remark) said without careful thought.

throwback ▸ noun a person or thing that resembles someone or something that existed in the past.

thrum ▸ verb (thrums, thrumming, thrummed) make a continuous rhythmic humming sound.
▸ noun a thrumming sound.

thrush[1] ▸ noun a bird with a brown back and spotted breast.

thrush[2] ▸ noun an infection of the mouth and throat or the genitals.

thrust ▸ verb (thrusts, thrusting, thrust) **1** push suddenly or violently. **2** make your way forcibly.

SYNONYMS **1** *a spear was thrust into the sack* **shove**, push, force, plunge, stick, drive, ram. **2** *fame had been thrust on him* **force**, foist, impose, inflict. **3** *he thrust his way past her* **push**, shove, force, elbow, shoulder, barge.

▸ noun **1** a sudden or violent lunge or attack. **2** the main point of an argument. **3** the force produced by an engine to push forward a jet, rocket, etc.

SYNONYMS **1** *a hard thrust* **shove**, push, lunge, poke. **2** *a thrust by the Third Army* **advance**, push, drive, attack, assault, onslaught, offensive. **3** *only one engine is producing thrust* **force**, propulsion, power, impetus. **4** *the thrust of the speech* **gist**, substance, drift, message, import, tenor.

thrusting ▸ adjective aggressively ambitious.

thud ▸ noun a dull, heavy sound.

▸ verb (thuds, thudding, thudded) move, fall, or strike with a thud.

thug ▸ noun a violent man.

SYNONYMS **ruffian**, hooligan, bully boy, hoodlum, gangster, villain; informal tough, bruiser, heavy; Brit. informal rough, bovver boy; N. Amer. informal hood, goon.

□ **thuggery** noun **thuggish** adjective.

thulium ▸ noun a soft silvery-white metallic element.

thumb ▸ noun the short, thick first digit of the hand.
▸ verb **1** turn over pages with your thumb. **2** ask for a free ride in a passing vehicle by signalling with your thumb.
■ **thumb index** lettered notches cut into the side of a book to help you find the section you want. **thumbs up** (or **down**) informal an indication of approval (or disapproval). **under someone's thumb** under someone's control.

thumbnail ▸ noun the nail of the thumb.
■ **thumbnail sketch** a brief, concise description.

thumbscrew ▸ noun an instrument of torture that crushes the thumbs.

thump ▸ verb **1** hit heavily with your fist or a blunt object. **2** put down forcefully. **3** (of a person's heart) beat strongly.

SYNONYMS **1** *he thumped the policeman* **hit**, punch, strike, smack; informal whack, wallop, bash, biff, bop, clobber; Brit. informal slosh; N. Amer. informal slug. **2** *her heart thumped with fright* **throb**, pound, thud, hammer.

▸ noun a dull, heavy blow or noise.

SYNONYMS **1** *a thump in the eye* **blow**, punch, box, cuff, smack; informal whack, wallop, bash, biff; Brit. informal slosh; N. Amer. informal boff, slug. **2** *she put the box down with a thump* **thud**, clunk, clonk, crash, smack, bang.

thumping ▸ adjective informal very big.

thunder ▸ noun **1** a loud rumbling or crashing noise heard after a lightning flash due to the expansion of rapidly heated air. **2** a loud, deep noise.

SYNONYMS **rumble**, boom, roar, pounding, thud, crash, reverberation.

▸ verb **1** (it thunders, it is thundering, it thundered) thunder is sounding. **2** make a loud, deep noise. **3** speak loudly and angrily.

SYNONYMS **1** *below me the surf thundered* **rumble**, boom, roar, pound, thud, thump, bang. **2** *'Answer me!' he thundered* **shout**, roar, bellow, bark, bawl.

thunderbolt ▸ noun a flash of lightning with a crash of thunder at the same time.

thunderclap ▶ noun a sudden crash of thunder.

thundercloud ▶ noun a cloud charged with electricity and producing thunder and lightning.

thunderous ▶ adjective 1 very loud. 2 (of a person's expression) very angry or threatening.

thunderstorm ▶ noun a storm with thunder and lightning.

thunderstruck ▶ adjective very surprised or shocked.

Thursday ▶ noun the day of the week before Friday and following Wednesday.

thus ▶ adverb formal 1 as a result or consequence of this; therefore. 2 in this way. 3 to this point; so.

> SYNONYMS 1 *the studio handled production, thus cutting its costs* **consequently,** so, therefore, accordingly, hence, as a result. 2 *legislation forbids such data being held thus* **like this/that,** in this/that way, so, like so, as follows.

thwack ▶ verb hit with a sharp blow. ▶ noun a sharp blow.

thwart ▶ verb prevent someone from accomplishing something.

> SYNONYMS **foil,** frustrate, forestall, stop, check, block, prevent, defeat, impede, obstruct, derail, snooker; informal put paid to, do for, stymie; Brit. informal scupper. ANTONYMS help.

thy (or, before a vowel, **thine**) ▶ possessive determiner old use your.

thyme (*rhymes with* time) ▶ noun a low-growing, sweet-smelling plant used in cooking.

thymus /thy-muhss/ ▶ noun (plural **thymi** /thy-my/) a gland in the neck which produces white blood cells for the immune system.

thyroid ▶ noun a large gland in the neck which produces hormones regulating growth and development.

tiara ▶ noun a jewelled ornamental band worn above the forehead.

Tibetan ▶ noun a person from Tibet. ▶ adjective relating to Tibet.

tibia ▶ noun (plural **tibiae** /ti-bi-ee/ or **tibias**) the inner of the two bones between the knee and the ankle.

tic ▶ noun a recurring spasm in the muscles of the face.

tick¹ ▶ noun 1 Brit. a mark (✓) used to show that something is correct or has been chosen or checked. 2 a regular short, sharp sound. 3 Brit. informal a moment. ▶ verb 1 Brit. mark with a tick. 2 make regular ticking sounds. 3 (**tick away** or **by** or **past**) (of time) keep passing. 4 (**tick over**) (of an engine) run slowly while the vehicle is not moving. 5 (**tick someone off**) Brit. informal tell someone off.

tick² ▶ noun a tiny insect-like creature which attaches itself to the skin and sucks blood.

ticker ▶ noun 1 informal a person's heart. 2 N. Amer. a machine that prints out data on a strip of paper. ■ **ticker tape** strips of paper on which data is printed by a machine.

ticket ▶ noun 1 a piece of paper or card giving you the right to travel on public transport or letting you in to a place or an event. 2 an official notice that you have committed a parking or driving offence. 3 a label attached to a product, giving its price, size, etc.

> SYNONYMS 1 *a bus ticket* **pass,** authorization, permit, token, coupon, voucher. 2 *a price ticket* **label,** tag, sticker, tab, slip, docket.

ticking ▶ noun a hard-wearing material used to cover mattresses.

tickle ▶ verb (**tickles, tickling, tickled**) 1 lightly touch in a way that causes itching or twitching and often laughter. 2 be appealing or amusing to.

> SYNONYMS 1 **stroke,** pet, chuck. 2 *something tickled his imagination* **stimulate,** interest, appeal to, arouse, excite. 3 *the idea tickled Lewis* **amuse,** entertain, divert, please, delight.

▶ noun an act of tickling, or the sensation of being tickled.
□ **tickly** adjective.

ticklish ▶ adjective 1 sensitive to being tickled. 2 needing care and tact.

tidal ▶ adjective relating to or affected by tides. ■ **tidal wave** a huge sea wave caused by an earthquake, storm, etc. □ **tidally** adverb.

tidbit ▶ US spelling of TITBIT.

tiddler ▶ noun Brit. informal a small fish.

tiddly ▶ adjective informal 1 slightly drunk. 2 Brit. little; tiny.

tiddlywinks ▶ plural noun a game in which small plastic counters are flicked into a cup.

tide ▶ noun 1 the alternate rising and falling of the sea due to the attraction of the moon and sun. 2 a powerful surge of feeling or trend of events.

> SYNONYMS 1 **current,** flow, stream, ebb. 2 *the tide of history* **course,** movement, direction, trend, current, drift, run.

▶ verb (**tides, tiding, tided**) (**tide someone over**) help someone through a difficult period.

tidings ▶ plural noun literary news; information.

t

tidy ▶ adjective (**tidier**, **tidiest**) **1** arranged neatly and in order. **2** liking to keep yourself and your possessions neat and in order. **3** informal (of a sum of money) large.

> synonyms **1** *a tidy room* **neat**, orderly, well ordered, well kept, in apple-pie order, uncluttered, straight. **2** *a very tidy person* **organized**, neat, methodical, meticulous.
> antonyms messy, disorganized.

▶ verb (**tidies**, **tidying**, **tidied**) (often **tidy up**) make a place tidy.

> synonyms *I'd better tidy up the living room* **put in order**, clear up, sort out, straighten (up), clean up, spruce up.
> antonyms mess up.

▶ noun (plural **tidies**) **1** an act of tidying. **2** a container for holding small objects.
□ **tidily** adverb **tidiness** noun.

tie ▶ verb (**ties**, **tying**, **tied**) **1** attach or fasten with string, cord, ribbon, etc. **2** form into a knot or bow. **3** restrict to a particular situation or place. **4** connect or link. **5** achieve the same score or ranking as another competitor.

> synonyms **1** *he tied the boat to the jetty* **bind**, tie up, tether, hitch, strap, truss, fetter, rope, make fast, moor, lash. **2** *he bent to tie his shoelaces* **do up**, lace, knot. **3** *women can feel tied by childcare responsibilities* **restrict**, restrain, limit, tie down, constrain, cramp, hamper, handicap, hamstring, encumber, shackle. **4** *a pay deal tied to productivity* **link**, connect, couple, relate, join, marry. **5** *they tied for second place* **draw**, be equal, be even.

▶ noun (plural **ties**) **1** a strip of material worn beneath a collar and tied in a knot at the front. **2** a thing that ties. **3** a result in a game or match in which two or more competitors are equal. **4** Brit. a sports match in which the winners go on to the next round.

> synonyms **1** *he tightened the ties of his robe* **lace**, string, cord, fastening. **2** *family ties* **bond**, connection, link, relationship, attachment, affiliation. **3** *pets can be a tremendous tie* **restriction**, constraint, curb, limitation, restraint, hindrance, encumbrance, handicap, obligation, commitment. **4** *a tie for first place* **draw**, dead heat.

■ **tie-dye** produce patterns on fabric by tying knots in it before it is dyed. **tie in** fit or be in harmony. **tie someone/thing up 1** restrict someone's movement by tying their arms or legs. **2** bring something to a conclusion. **3** informal occupy someone so that they have no time for other activities.

tiebreaker (also **tiebreak**) ▶ noun a means of deciding a winner from competitors who are equal at the end of a game or match.

tied ▶ adjective Brit. **1** (of accommodation) rented by someone on condition that they work for the owner. **2** (of a pub) owned and controlled by a brewery.

tiepin ▶ noun an ornamental pin for holding a tie in place.

tier ▶ noun one of a series of rows or levels placed one above and behind the other.

> synonyms **1** *six tiers of seats* **row**, rank, bank, line, layer, level. **2** *a tier of management* **grade**, gradation, echelon, rung on the ladder.

□ **tiered** adjective.

tiff ▶ noun informal a quarrel about something unimportant.

tiffin ▶ noun dated or Indian a snack or light meal.

tiger ▶ noun a large cat with a yellow coat striped with black, native to the forests of Asia.

tight ▶ adjective **1** firmly fixed, closed, or fastened. **2** (of clothes) fitting very closely. **3** well sealed against water or air. **4** (of a rope, fabric, or surface) stretched so as to leave no slack. **5** (of an area or space) allowing little room for movement. **6** closely packed together. **7** (of a form of control) very strict. **8** (of money or time) limited.

> synonyms **1** *a tight grip* **firm**, secure. **2** *the rope was pulled tight* **taut**, rigid, stiff, tense, stretched, strained. **3** *tight jeans* **close-fitting**, narrow, figure-hugging, skintight; informal sprayed on. **4** *a tight mass of fibres* **compact**, compressed, dense, solid. **5** *a tight space* **small**, tiny, narrow, limited, restricted, confined, cramped, constricted. **6** *a tight joint* **sealed**, sound, impenetrable, impervious.
> antonyms slack, loose, roomy, leaky.

▶ adverb very closely or firmly.
■ **tight-fisted** informal not willing to spend your money. **tight-knit** (or **tightly knit**) (of a group of people) closely connected to each other through family or social relationships. **tight-lipped** unwilling to express emotion or give away information.
□ **tightly** adverb **tightness** noun.

tighten ▶ verb make or become tight or tighter.

> synonyms **1** *he tightened his grip* **strengthen**, harden. **2** *she tightened the rope* **stretch**, tauten, strain, stiffen, tense.
> antonyms loosen, slacken, relax.

tightrope ▶ noun a rope or wire stretched high above the ground, on which acrobats balance.

tights ▶ plural noun a close-fitting garment

made of stretchy material, covering the hips, legs, and feet.

tigress ▸ noun a female tiger.

tikka /tik-uh, **tee**-kuh/ ▸ noun an Indian dish of meat or vegetables marinated in spices.

tilde /til-duh/ ▸ noun an accent (∼) placed over the Spanish *n* or Portuguese *a* or *o* to change the way they are pronounced.

tile ▸ noun a thin square or rectangular piece of fired clay, concrete, cork, etc., used for covering roofs, floors, or walls.
▸ verb (**tiles, tiling, tiled**) cover with tiles.
□ **tiler** noun.

till¹ less formal way of saying **until**.

till² ▸ noun a cash register or drawer for money.

till³ ▸ verb prepare and cultivate land for crops.

tiller ▸ noun a horizontal bar fitted to a boat's rudder and used for steering.

tilt ▸ verb 1 slip or move into a sloping position. 2 (**tilt at**) (in the past, in jousting) thrust at someone with a lance.

SYNONYMS *the ground seemed to tilt* **slope,** tip, lean, list, bank, slant, incline, pitch, cant, angle.

▸ noun 1 a tilting position or movement. 2 a leaning or bias. 3 (in the past) a joust. 4 (**tilt at**) an attempt at winning something.

SYNONYMS *a tilt of some 45°* **slope,** list, camber, gradient, bank, slant, incline, pitch, cant, bevel, angle.

■ (**at**) **full tilt** with maximum speed or force.

tilth ▸ noun soil that has been prepared for crops.

timber ▸ noun 1 wood prepared for use in building and carpentry. 2 a wooden beam used in building.

SYNONYMS 1 *houses built of timber* **wood;** N. Amer. lumber. 2 *the timbers of wrecked ships* **beam,** spar, plank, batten, lath, board, joist, rafter.

timbre /**tam**-ber/ ▸ noun the quality of the sound in a voice or piece of music.

time ▸ noun 1 the continuing and unlimited progress of existence and events in the past, present, and future. 2 a point or period within this. 3 a point of time as measured in hours and minutes past midnight or noon. 4 the right or agreed moment to do something. 5 time as a resource to be used. 6 an instance of something happening or being done. 7 (**times**) (following a number) expressing multiplication. 8 the rhythmic pattern or tempo of a piece of music.

SYNONYMS 1 *the best time to leave* **moment,** point (in time), occasion, instant, juncture, stage. 2 *he worked*

there for a time **while,** spell, stretch, stint, interval, period, length of time, duration, phase. 3 *the time of the dinosaurs* **era,** age, epoch, period, years, days.

▸ verb (**times, timing, timed**) 1 arrange a time for. 2 do at a particular time. 3 measure the time taken by.

SYNONYMS *the meeting is timed for 4 o'clock* **schedule,** arrange, set, organize, fix, book, line up, timetable, plan; N. Amer. slate.

■ **behind the times** not using the latest ideas or techniques. **for the time being** until some other arrangement is made. **in time** 1 not late. 2 eventually. **on time** punctual, or punctually. **time-honoured** (of a custom or tradition) respected or valued because it has existed for a long time. **time off** time spent away from your usual work or studies. **time-server** a person who makes little effort at work because they are waiting to leave or retire. **time signature** a sign at the start of a piece of music showing the number of beats in a bar.

timekeeper ▸ noun 1 a person who records the amount of time taken by a process or activity. 2 a person regarded in terms of their punctuality.
□ **timekeeping** noun.

timeless ▸ adjective not affected by the passing of time.

SYNONYMS **lasting,** enduring, classic, ageless, permanent, perennial, abiding, unchanging, unvarying, never-changing, eternal, everlasting.
ANTONYMS ephemeral.

timely ▸ adjective done or happening at a good or appropriate time.

SYNONYMS **opportune,** well timed, convenient, appropriate, expedient, seasonable, propitious.
ANTONYMS ill-timed.

□ **timeliness** noun.

timepiece ▸ noun a clock or watch.

timer ▸ noun 1 a device that records how long something is taking. 2 a device that stops or starts a machine at a preset time.

timescale ▸ noun the time allowed for or taken by a process or events.

timeshare ▸ noun an arrangement in which joint owners use a property as a holiday home at different times.

timetable ▸ noun a list or plan of times at which events are scheduled to take place.

SYNONYMS **schedule,** programme, agenda, calendar, diary.

▸ verb (**timetables, timetabling, timetabled**) schedule events to take place at particular times.

SYNONYMS **schedule**, arrange, programme, organize, fix, time, line up; Brit. diarize; N. Amer. slate.

timid ▸ adjective not brave or confident.

SYNONYMS **fearful**, afraid, faint-hearted, timorous, nervous, scared, frightened, shy, diffident.
ANTONYMS bold.

◻ **timidity** noun **timidly** adverb.

timorous ▸ adjective easily frightened.

timpani (or **tympani**) /tim-puh-ni/ ▸ plural noun kettledrums.

tin ▸ noun 1 a silvery-white metal. 2 an airtight container with a lid, made of tinplate or aluminium. 3 Brit. a sealed tinplate or aluminium container for preserving food. 4 Brit. an open metal container for baking food.
▸ verb (**tins**, **tinning**, **tinned**) 1 cover another metal with a thin layer of tin. 2 (**tinned**) Brit. (of food) preserved in a tin.
■ **tin whistle** a metal musical instrument like a small flute.

tincture ▸ noun 1 a medicine made by dissolving a drug in alcohol. 2 a slight trace.

tinder ▸ noun dry material used in lighting a fire.

tinderbox ▸ noun (in the past) a box containing tinder, flint, and other items for lighting fires.

tine ▸ noun a prong or sharp point.

tinfoil ▸ noun metal foil used for covering or wrapping food.

tinge ▸ noun a slight trace of a colour, feeling, or quality.

SYNONYMS **1** *a blue tinge* **tint**, colour, shade, tone, hue. **2** *a tinge of cynicism* **trace**, note, touch, suggestion, hint, flavour, element, streak, suspicion, soupçon.

▸ verb (**tinges**, **tinging** or **tingeing**, **tinged**) give a tinge to.

SYNONYMS **1** *white blossom tinged with pink* **tint**, colour, stain, shade, wash. **2** *his optimism is tinged with realism* **influence**, affect, touch, flavour, colour.

tingle ▸ verb (**tingles**, **tingling**, **tingled**) have a slight prickling or stinging feeling.
▸ noun a slight prickling or stinging sensation.
◻ **tingly** adjective.

tinker ▸ noun (in the past) a person who travelled from place to place mending pots, kettles, etc.
▸ verb (**tinkers**, **tinkering**, **tinkered**) (**tinker with**) casually try to repair or improve.

SYNONYMS **fiddle**, play about, mess about, adjust, try to mend; Brit. informal muck about.

tinkle ▸ verb (**tinkles**, **tinkling**, **tinkled**) make or cause to make a light, clear ringing sound.
▸ noun a tinkling sound.

tinnitus /tin-ni-tuhss/ ▸ noun a ringing or buzzing in the ears.

tinny ▸ adjective 1 having a thin, metallic sound. 2 made of thin or poor-quality metal.

tinplate ▸ noun thin sheets of steel or iron coated with a layer of tin.

tinpot ▸ adjective informal not important or effective.

tinsel ▸ noun thin strips of shiny metal foil attached to a length of thread, used to decorate a Christmas tree.

tint ▸ noun 1 a shade of a colour. 2 a dye for colouring the hair.

SYNONYMS **1** *an apricot tint* **shade**, colour, tone, hue, tinge, cast, flush, blush. **2** *a hair tint* **dye**, colourant, colouring, wash.

▸ verb 1 colour something slightly. 2 dye hair with a tint.

SYNONYMS *she had her hair tinted* **dye**, colour, tinge.

tintinnabulation ▸ noun a ringing or tinkling sound.

tiny ▸ adjective (**tinier**, **tiniest**) very small.

SYNONYMS **minute**, minuscule, microscopic, very small, mini, diminutive, miniature, baby, toy, dwarf; Scottish wee; informal teeny, tiddly; Brit. informal titchy; N. Amer. informal little-bitty.
ANTONYMS huge.

tip¹ ▸ noun 1 the pointed or rounded end of something slender or tapering. 2 a small part fitted to the end of an object.

SYNONYMS **1** *the tip of the spear* **point**, end, extremity, head, spike, prong, nib. **2** *the tips of the mountains* **peak**, top, summit, apex, crown, crest, pinnacle.

■ **tip-top** of the very best quality.
◻ **tipped** adjective.

tip² ▸ verb (**tips**, **tipping**, **tipped**) 1 overbalance so as to fall or turn over. 2 be or put in a sloping position. 3 empty out the contents of a container by holding it at an angle.

SYNONYMS **1** *the boat tipped over* **overturn**, turn over, topple (over), fall (over), keel over, capsize, roll over. **2** *a whale could tip over a small boat* **upset**, overturn, topple over, turn over, push over, upend, capsize; informal roll. **3** *the car tipped to one side* **lean**, tilt, list, slope, bank, slant, incline, pitch, cant. **4** *she tipped the water into the trough* **pour**, empty, drain, dump, discharge, decant.

▸ noun 1 Brit. a place where rubbish is left.

2 informal a dirty or untidy place.

> SYNONYMS *rubbish must be taken to the tip* **dump**, rubbish dump, landfill site.

tip³ ► noun **1** a small extra amount of money that you give to someone for their good service in a restaurant, taxi, etc. **2** a piece of practical advice. **3** a prediction about the likely winner of a race or contest.

> SYNONYMS **1** *a generous tip* **gratuity**, baksheesh, present, gift, reward. **2** *useful tips* **piece of advice**, suggestion, word of advice, pointer, hint; informal wrinkle.

► verb (**tips, tipping, tipped**) **1** give a tip to. **2** Brit. predict that a particular horse, competitor, etc. is likely to win something. **3** (**tip someone off**) informal give someone secret information.

tipple informal ► noun an alcoholic drink.
► verb (**tipples, tippling, tippled**) drink alcohol regularly.
□ **tippler** noun.

tipster ► noun a person who gives tips as to the likely winner of a race or contest.

tipsy ► adjective slightly drunk.
□ **tipsily** adverb.

tiptoe ► verb (**tiptoes, tiptoeing, tiptoed**) walk quietly and carefully with your heels raised.
■ **on tiptoe** (or **tiptoes**) with your heels raised.

tirade ► noun a long angry speech.

tire¹ ► verb (**tires, tiring, tired**) **1** make or become in need of rest or sleep. **2** (**tire of**) become impatient or bored with.

> SYNONYMS **1** *he began to tire* **get tired**, weaken, flag, droop. **2** *the journey had tired him* **fatigue**, tire out, exhaust, wear out, drain, weary; informal knock out, take it out of; Brit. informal knacker. **3** (**tiring**) **exhausting**, wearying, taxing, draining, hard, arduous, strenuous, onerous, gruelling; informal killing; Brit. informal knackering. **4** *they tired of his difficult behaviour* **weary**, get tired, get fed up, get sick, get bored.

tire² US spelling of TYRE.

tired ► adjective **1** in need of sleep or rest. **2** (**tired of**) bored with. **3** (of a statement or idea) boring because it has been said or used too often.

> SYNONYMS **1** *tired from travelling* **exhausted**, worn out, weary, fatigued, ready to drop, drained; informal all in, dead beat, shattered; Brit. informal knackered, whacked; N. Amer. informal pooped, tuckered out; Austral./NZ informal stonkered. **2** *are you tired of having him here?* **fed up with**, weary of, bored with/by, sick (and tired) of; informal up to here with. **3** *tired jokes* **hackneyed**, overused, stale, clichéd, predictable, unimaginative, unoriginal,

dull, boring; informal corny.
ANTONYMS energetic, lively, fresh.
□ **tiredness** noun.

tireless ► adjective having or showing great effort or energy.
□ **tirelessly** adverb.

tiresome ► adjective making you feel impatient or bored.
□ **tiresomely** adverb.

'tis ► short form literary it is.

tissue /ti-shoo/ ► noun **1** any of the distinct types of material of which animals or plants are made. **2** a disposable paper handkerchief.
■ **a tissue of lies** a story that is full of lies.
tissue paper a very thin, soft paper.

tit¹ ► noun a small bird that searches for food among leaves and branches.

tit² ► noun (**tit for tat**) a situation in which you insult or hurt someone because they have done the same to you.

Titan ► noun **1** any of a family of giant gods in Greek mythology. **2** (**titan**) a person of very great strength, intelligence, or importance.

titanic ► adjective of exceptional strength, size, or power.

titanium ► noun a silver-grey metal used in making strong alloys.

titbit (US spelling **tidbit**) ► noun **1** a small piece of tasty food. **2** a small item of very interesting information.

titch ► noun Brit. informal a small person.
□ **titchy** adjective.

tithe ► noun (in the past) one tenth of what people produced or earned in a year, taken as a tax to support the Church.

titillate ► verb (**titillates, titillating, titillated**) make someone feel interested or mildly excited, especially sexually.
□ **titillation** noun.

> ✔ one **t**, two **l**s: titillate.

> ! Don't confuse **titillate** with **titivate**, which means 'make smarter or more attractive'.

titivate ► verb (**titivates, titivating, titivated**) informal make smarter or more attractive.
□ **titivation** noun.

title ► noun **1** the name of a book, piece of music, or other work. **2** a name that describes someone's position or job. **3** a word, such as *Dr*, *Mrs*, or *Lord*, used before or instead of someone's name to indicate their rank or profession. **4** a descriptive name that someone has earned or chosen. **5** the position of being the champion of a major sports competition. **6** a caption or credit in a film or broadcast.

SYNONYMS **1** *the title of the article* **heading,** label, inscription, caption, subheading, legend. **2** *the title of Duke of Marlborough* **name,** designation, form of address, rank, office, position; informal moniker, handle. **3** *an Olympic title* **championship,** crown, first place.

▶ verb (**titles, titling, titled**) give a title to.
■ **title deed** a legal document giving evidence of someone's right to own a property. **title role** the part in a play or film from which the title is taken.

titled ▶ adjective having a title indicating nobility, e.g. *Lord* or *Lady*.

titration ▶ noun the calculation of the amount of a substance in a solution by measuring the volume of a reagent required to react with it.

titter ▶ verb (**titters, tittering, tittered**) laugh quietly.
▶ noun a short, quiet laugh.

tittle-tattle ▶ noun gossip.

titular /tit-yuu-ler/ ▶ adjective **1** holding a formal position or title without any real authority. **2** relating to a title.

tizzy ▶ noun (plural **tizzies**) informal a state of nervous excitement or worry.

TNT ▶ abbreviation trinitrotoluene, a high explosive.

to ▶ preposition **1** expressing direction or position in relation to a particular location, point, or condition. **2** Brit. (in telling the time) before the hour mentioned. **3** identifying the person or thing affected by an action. **4** identifying a particular relationship between one person or thing and another. **5** indicating a rate of return on something: *ten miles to the gallon.* **6** indicating that two things are attached.
▶ infinitive marker used with the base form of a verb to indicate that the verb is in the infinitive.
▶ adverb so as to be closed or nearly closed.
■ **to and fro** backwards and forwards or from side to side. **to-do** informal a fuss or commotion.

❗ Don't confuse **to** with **too** or **two**. **To** mainly means 'in the direction of' (as in *the next train to London*), while **too** means 'excessively' (as in *she was driving too fast*) or 'in addition', and **two** is the number meaning 'one less than three'.

toad ▶ noun an amphibian with a short body, short legs, and no tail.

toadstool ▶ noun a fungus with a rounded cap on a stalk.

toady ▶ noun (plural **toadies**) a person who is too polite and respectful to someone in order to gain their favour.
▶ verb (**toadies, toadying, toadied**) act in a way that is too polite and respectful.

toast ▶ noun **1** sliced bread that has been held a source of heat until it is brown and crisp. **2** an act of raising glasses at a gathering and drinking together in honour of a person or thing. **3** a person who is greatly respected or admired.

SYNONYMS **1** *he raised his glass in a toast* **tribute,** salutation. **2** *he was the toast of the West End* **darling,** favourite, pet, heroine, hero, talk; Brit. informal blue-eyed boy/girl.

▶ verb **1** make bread brown and crisp by holding it against a source of heat. **2** drink a toast to.

SYNONYMS *we toasted the couple with champagne* **drink (to) the health of,** salute, honour, pay tribute to.

toaster ▶ noun an electrical device for making toast.

tobacco ▶ noun (plural **tobaccos**) a preparation of the dried nicotine-rich leaves of an American plant, used for smoking or chewing.

tobacconist ▶ noun Brit. a shopkeeper who sells cigarettes and tobacco.

toboggan ▶ noun a light, narrow vehicle on runners, used for sliding downhill over snow or ice.
□ **tobogganist** noun.

toccata /tuh-kah-tuh/ ▶ noun a piece of music for a keyboard instrument designed to show the performer's skill and technique.

tod ▶ noun (**on your tod**) Brit. informal on your own.

today ▶ adverb **1** on or in the course of this present day. **2** at the present period of time.
▶ noun **1** this present day. **2** the present period of time.

toddle ▶ verb (**toddles, toddling, toddled**) **1** (of a young child) move with short unsteady steps while learning to walk. **2** informal walk or go about in a leisurely way.

toddler ▶ noun a young child who is just beginning to walk.

toddy ▶ noun (plural **toddies**) a drink of spirits mixed with hot water.

toe ▶ noun **1** any of the five digits at the end of the foot. **2** the lower end, tip, or point of something.
■ **on your toes** ready and alert. **toe the line** be obedient.

toecap ▶ noun a piece of steel or leather fitted over the front part of a boot or shoe.

toehold ▶ noun a small foothold.

toenail ▶ noun a nail on the upper surface of the tip of each toe.

toff ▶ noun Brit. informal, disapproving a rich, upper-class person.

toffee ▸ noun a kind of firm sweet which softens when sucked or chewed, made by boiling together sugar and butter.
■ **toffee-nosed** Brit. informal snobbish.

tofu /toh-foo/ ▸ noun a soft white substance made from mashed soya beans.

tog¹ informal ▸ noun (**togs**) clothes.
▸ verb (**be togged up**) be fully dressed for a particular occasion or activity.

tog² ▸ noun Brit. a unit for measuring the warmth of duvets or quilts.

toga ▸ noun a loose outer garment made of a single piece of cloth, worn in ancient Rome.

together ▸ adverb **1** with or near to another person or people. **2** so as to touch, combine, or be united. **3** regarded as a whole. **4** (of two people) married or in a sexual relationship. **5** at the same time. **6** without interruption.

SYNONYMS **1** *friends who work together* **with each other,** in conjunction, jointly, in cooperation, in collaboration, in partnership, in combination, in league, side by side; informal in cahoots. **2** *they both spoke together* **simultaneously,** at the same time, at once, concurrently, as a group, in unison, in chorus.
ANTONYMS separately, successively.

▸ adjective informal level-headed and well organized.

SYNONYMS *she looks a very together young woman* **level-headed,** well adjusted, sensible, practical, realistic, mature, stable, full of common sense, well organized, efficient, methodical, self-confident, self-assured; informal unflappable.
ANTONYMS flighty, disorganized.

□ **togetherness** noun.

toggle ▸ noun a narrow piece of wood or plastic attached to a garment, pushed through a loop to act as a fastener.

Togolese /toh-guh-leez/ ▸ noun (plural **Togolese**) a person from Togo, a country in West Africa.
▸ adjective relating to Togo.

toil ▸ verb **1** work very hard. **2** move somewhere slowly and with difficulty.

SYNONYMS **1** *she toiled all night* **work,** labour, slave, strive; informal slog, beaver; Brit. informal graft. **2** *she began to toil up the path* **struggle,** drag yourself, trudge, slog, plod; N. Amer. informal schlep.
ANTONYMS rest, relax.

▸ noun exhausting work.

SYNONYMS *a life of toil* **hard work,** labour, exertion, slaving, drudgery, effort, (blood, sweat, and tears); informal slog, elbow grease; Brit. informal graft.

toilet ▸ noun **1** a large bowl for urinating or defecating into. **2** old use the process of washing yourself, dressing, brushing your hair, etc.

SYNONYMS **lavatory,** WC, (public) convenience, cloakroom, powder room, latrine, privy, urinal; N. Amer. bathroom, washroom, rest room, men's/ladies' room, comfort station; Brit. informal loo, the Ladies, the Gents; N. Amer. informal can, john; Austral./NZ informal dunny.

■ **toilet bag** Brit. a waterproof bag for toothpaste, soap, etc., used when travelling. **toilet-train** teach a young child to use the toilet. **toilet water** a diluted form of perfume.

toiletries ▸ plural noun articles used in washing and taking care of your body, such as soap and shampoo.

token ▸ noun **1** a thing that represents a feeling, fact, or quality. **2** a voucher that can be exchanged for goods or services. **3** a disc used to operate a machine.

SYNONYMS **1** *a token of our appreciation* **symbol,** sign, emblem, badge, representation, indication, mark, expression, demonstration. **2** *a book token* **voucher,** coupon, note.

▸ adjective involving little effort or commitment and done only for show.

SYNONYMS *token resistance* **symbolic,** nominal, perfunctory, slight, minimal, superficial, emblematic, indicative.

tokenism ▸ noun the practice of doing something in a superficial way, so as to be seen to be obeying the law or satisfying a particular group of people.
□ **tokenistic** adjective.

told past and past participle of TELL.

tolerable ▸ adjective **1** able to be tolerated. **2** fairly good.
□ **tolerably** adverb.

tolerance ▸ noun **1** the ability to accept things you do not like or agree with. **2** an allowable amount of variation in the dimensions of a machine or part.

SYNONYMS **1** *an attitude of tolerance towards people* **acceptance,** open-mindedness, broad-mindedness, forbearance, patience, charity, understanding. **2** *the plant's tolerance of pollution* **endurance,** resilience, resistance, immunity. **3** *a 1% maximum tolerance in measurement* **deviation,** variation, play, inaccuracy, imprecision.

tolerant ▸ adjective **1** able to accept things you do not like or agree with. **2** able to cope with particular conditions.

SYNONYMS **open-minded,** forbearing, broad-minded, liberal, unprejudiced,

t

unbiased, patient, long-suffering, understanding, charitable, lenient, easy-going.
ANTONYMS intolerant, strict.

tolerate ▸ verb (tolerates, tolerating, tolerated) **1** allow someone to do something you do not like or agree with. **2** patiently accept something unpleasant. **3** be able to be exposed to a drug, toxin, etc. without a bad reaction.

> SYNONYMS **1** *a regime unwilling to tolerate dissent* **allow**, permit, condone, accept, swallow, countenance. **2** *he couldn't tolerate her moods any longer* **endure**, put up with, bear, take, stand, support, stomach; informal abide; Brit. informal stick.

□ **toleration** noun.

toll¹ ▸ noun **1** a charge you have to pay for the use of certain roads or bridges. **2** the number of deaths or casualties arising from an accident, war, etc. **3** the cost or damage resulting from something.

> SYNONYMS **1** *a motorway toll* **charge**, fee, payment, levy, tariff, tax. **2** *the toll of dead and injured* **number**, count, tally, total, sum. **3** *the toll on the environment has been high* **harm**, damage, hurt, injury, detriment, adverse effect, cost, price, loss.

toll² ▸ verb (of a bell) sound with slow, even strokes, especially as a sign that someone has died.

> SYNONYMS *I heard the bell toll* **ring**, sound, clang, chime, strike, peal.

▸ noun a single ring of a bell.

tom (or **tomcat**) ▸ noun a male domestic cat.

tomahawk ▸ noun a light axe used in the past by American Indians.

tomato ▸ noun (plural **tomatoes**) a red fruit eaten as a vegetable or in salads.

> ✔ no **e** on the end: toma**to**.

tomb ▸ noun **1** a burial place consisting of a stone structure built above ground, or an underground vault. **2** a monument to a dead person, built over their burial place.

> SYNONYMS **burial chamber**, vault, crypt, catacomb, sepulchre, mausoleum, grave.

tombola ▸ noun Brit. a game in which tickets are drawn from a revolving drum to win prizes.

tomboy ▸ noun a girl who enjoys rough, noisy activities traditionally associated with boys.
□ **tomboyish** adjective.

tombstone ▸ noun a flat stone with an inscription, standing or laid over a grave.

tome ▸ noun a large, serious book.

tomfoolery ▸ noun silly behaviour.

tomography /tuh-**mog**-ruh-fi/ ▸ noun a technique for seeing a cross section through a human body or other solid object using X-rays or ultrasound.
□ **tomographic** adjective.

tomorrow ▸ adverb on the day after today. ▸ noun **1** the day after today. **2** the future.

> ✔ one **m**, two **r**s: to**m**o**rr**ow.

tom-tom ▸ noun a drum beaten with the hands.

ton /tun/ ▸ noun **1** (also **long ton**) a unit of weight equal to 2,240 lb avoirdupois (1016.05 kg). **2** (also **short ton**) N. Amer. a unit of weight equal to 2,000 lb avoirdupois (907.19 kg). **3** a metric ton. **4** a unit of measurement of a ship's weight equal to 2,240 lb or 35 cubic feet (0.99 cubic metres). **5** (also **tons**) informal a large number or amount. **6** Brit. informal a speed of one hundred miles per hour.

tonal ▸ adjective **1** relating to tone. **2** (of music) written using traditional keys and harmony.
□ **tonality** noun **tonally** adverb.

tone ▸ noun **1** the quality of a musical sound. **2** the feeling or mood expressed in a person's voice. **3** general character. **4** a particular brightness, deepness, or shade in a colour. **5** firmness in a resting muscle. **6** a basic interval in classical Western music, equal to two semitones.

> SYNONYMS **1** *the tone of the tuba* **sound**, timbre, voice, colour, tonality. **2** *the impatient tone of his letter* **mood**, air, feel, flavour, note, attitude, character. **3** *a dialling tone* **note**, signal, bleep. **4** *tones of lavender and rose* **shade**, colour, hue, tint, tinge.

▸ verb (tones, toning, toned) **1** (often **tone something up**) give greater strength or firmness to a part of your body. **2** (**tone something down**) make a statement or piece of writing less harsh, extreme, or strong.

> SYNONYMS *the shirt toned well with her cream skirt* **harmonize**, go, blend, coordinate, team, match, suit, complement.

■ **tone deaf** unable to hear differences in musical pitch.

toner ▸ noun **1** a liquid applied to the skin to reduce oiliness. **2** a type of powder or ink used in photocopiers.

tongs ▸ plural noun a tool with two arms that are joined at one end, used for picking up and holding things.

tongue ▸ noun **1** the fleshy organ in the mouth, used for tasting, licking, swallowing, and speaking. **2** a person's way of speaking: *a sharp tongue*. **3** a language. **4** a strip of leather or fabric under the laces in a shoe.

■ **tongue and groove** wooden boards which are joined by means of interlocking ridges and grooves down their sides. **tongue-tied** too shy or embarrassed to speak. **tongue-twister** a sequence of words that are difficult to pronounce. **with tongue in cheek** not seriously meaning what you are saying.

tonic ▸ noun **1** a drink taken as a kind of medicine, to make you feel energetic and healthy. **2** something that makes you feel happier or healthier. **3** (also **tonic water**) a fizzy drink with a slightly bitter flavour, often mixed with gin.

SYNONYMS **stimulant,** boost, restorative, refresher, fillip; informal shot in the arm, pick-me-up, bracer.

tonight ▸ adverb on the evening or night of the present day.
▸ noun the evening or night of the present day.

tonnage ▸ noun **1** weight in tons. **2** the size or carrying capacity of a ship measured in tons.

tonne /tun/ ▸ noun a metric ton.

tonsil ▸ noun each of two small masses of tissue in the throat.

tonsillectomy ▸ noun (plural **tonsillectomies**) an operation to remove the tonsils.

tonsillitis ▸ noun inflammation of the tonsils.

tonsure ▸ noun a circular area on a monk's or priest's head where the hair is shaved off.

too ▸ adverb **1** to a higher degree than is desirable, allowed, or possible; excessively. **2** in addition.

SYNONYMS **1** invasion would be too risky **excessively,** overly, unduly, immoderately, inordinately, unreasonably, extremely, very. **2** he was unhappy, too, you know **also,** as well, in addition, into the bargain, besides, furthermore, moreover.

! Don't confuse **too** with **to** or **two**: see the note at **TO**.

took past of TAKE.

tool ▸ noun **1** an object or device used to carry out a particular function. **2** a thing that helps you to do your job or achieve something.

SYNONYMS **implement,** utensil, instrument, device, apparatus, gadget, appliance, machine, contrivance, contraption; informal gizmo.

▸ verb **1** impress a design on leather with a heated tool. **2** equip an organization with tools for industrial production.

toot ▸ noun a short sound made by a horn, trumpet, or similar instrument.
▸ verb make a toot.

tooth ▸ noun (plural **teeth**) **1** each of the hard white projections in the mouth, used for biting and chewing. **2** a projecting part such as a cog on a gearwheel or a point on a saw or comb.
□ **toothed** adjective **toothless** adjective.

toothache ▸ noun pain in a tooth.

toothbrush ▸ noun a small long-handled brush for cleaning your teeth.

toothpaste ▸ noun a paste for cleaning the teeth.

toothpick ▸ noun a thin, pointed piece of wood or plastic for removing bits of food from between your teeth.

toothsome ▸ adjective **1** (of food) appetizing or tasty. **2** informal attractive.

toothy ▸ adjective having large or prominent teeth.

tootle ▸ verb (**tootles, tootling, tootled**) **1** make a series of sounds on a horn, trumpet, etc. **2** walk or drive somewhere without hurrying.

top¹ ▸ noun **1** the highest or uppermost point, part, or surface. **2** a thing placed on, fitted to, or covering the upper part of something. **3** (**the top**) the highest or most important level or position. **4** the utmost degree. **5** a garment covering the upper part of the body.

SYNONYMS **1** the top of the cliff **summit,** peak, pinnacle, crest, crown, brow, head, tip, apex. **2** the top of the coffee jar **lid,** cap, cover. **3** he was at the top of his profession **height,** peak, pinnacle, zenith, culmination, climax, prime. ANTONYMS bottom, base.

▸ adjective highest in position, status, or degree.

SYNONYMS **1** the top floor **highest,** topmost, uppermost. **2** top scientists **foremost,** leading, principal, pre-eminent, greatest, best, finest, elite. **3** the organization's top management **chief,** principal, main, leading, highest, ruling, commanding, most powerful, most important. **4** a top hotel **prime,** premier, excellent, superior, choice, select, five-star, grade A, best, finest. **5** at top speed **maximum,** greatest, utmost. ANTONYMS bottom, lowest, minimum.

▸ verb (**tops, topping, topped**) **1** be more, better, or taller than. **2** be at the highest place or rank in. **3** reach the top of a hill or rise. **4** provide with a top or topping.

SYNONYMS **1** sales topped £1 billion **exceed,** surpass, go beyond, better, beat, outstrip, outdo, outshine, eclipse. **2** their CD is currently topping the charts **lead,**

t

head, be at the top of. **3** *mousse topped with cream* **cover,** cap, coat, finish, garnish.

■ **on top of 1** so as to cover. **2** in command or control of. **3** in addition to. **over the top** Brit. informal excessive or exaggerated. **top hat** a man's tall formal black hat. **top-heavy** too heavy at the top and therefore likely to fall. **top something up 1** add to a number or amount to bring it up to a certain level. **2** fill up a partly full container.

top² ▶ noun a toy shaped like a cone with a point at the base, that can be made to spin.

topaz ▶ noun a colourless, yellow, or pale blue precious stone.

topcoat ▶ noun **1** an overcoat. **2** an outer coat of paint.

topiary ▶ noun (plural **topiaries**) **1** the art of clipping evergreen shrubs into interesting shapes. **2** shrubs clipped in this way.

topic ▶ noun a subject that you talk, write, or learn about.

> SYNONYMS **subject,** theme, issue, matter, point, question, concern, argument, thesis.

topical ▶ adjective **1** relating to or dealing with current affairs. **2** relating to a particular subject.

> SYNONYMS **current,** up to date, up to the minute, contemporary, recent, relevant, in the news.
> ANTONYMS out of date.

□ **topicality** noun **topically** adverb.

topknot ▶ noun a knot of hair arranged on the top of the head.

topless ▶ adjective having the breasts uncovered.

topography ▶ noun **1** the arrangement of the physical features of an area of land. **2** the representation of these features on a map.
□ **topographical** (or **topographic**) adjective.

topping ▶ noun a layer of food poured or spread over another food.

topple ▶ verb (**topples, toppling, toppled**) **1** overbalance and fall down. **2** remove a government or leader from power.

> SYNONYMS **1** *she toppled off the chair* **fall,** tumble, tip, overbalance, overturn, keel over, lose your balance. **2** *protesters toppled a statue* **knock over,** upset, push over, tip over, upend. **3** *a plot to topple the government* **overthrow,** oust, unseat, overturn, bring down, defeat, get rid of, dislodge, eject.

topsoil ▶ noun the top layer of soil.

topspin ▶ noun a fast forward spin given to a moving ball.

topsy-turvy ▶ adjective & adverb **1** upside down. **2** in a state of confusion.

tor ▶ noun a small steep hill or rocky peak.

Torah /**tor**-uh, tor-**ah**/ ▶ noun (in Judaism) the law of God as revealed to Moses and recorded in the Pentateuch.

torch ▶ noun **1** Brit. a portable lamp powered by a battery. **2** (in the past) a piece of wood or cloth soaked in fat and set on fire.
▶ verb informal set fire to.

tore past of TEAR¹.

toreador ▶ noun a bullfighter.

torment ▶ noun /**tor**-ment/ **1** great suffering. **2** a cause of suffering.

> SYNONYMS *emotional torment* **agony,** suffering, torture, pain, anguish, misery, distress, trauma.

▶ verb /tor-**ment**/ **1** make someone suffer very much. **2** annoy or tease in a cruel or unkind way.

> SYNONYMS **1** *she was tormented by shame* **torture,** afflict, rack, harrow, plague, haunt, distress, agonize. **2** *she began to torment the boys* **tease,** taunt, bait, provoke, harass, bother, persecute; informal needle.

□ **tormentor** noun.

torn past participle of TEAR¹.

> SYNONYMS **1** *a torn shirt* **ripped,** rent, cut, slit, ragged, tattered. **2** *she was torn between the two options* **wavering,** vacillating, irresolute, dithering, uncertain, unsure, undecided, in two minds.

tornado ▶ noun (plural **tornadoes** or **tornados**) a violent rotating wind storm.

> SYNONYMS **whirlwind,** cyclone, typhoon, storm, hurricane; N. Amer. informal **twister.**

torpedo ▶ noun (plural **torpedoes**) a long narrow underwater missile.
▶ verb (**torpedoes, torpedoing, torpedoed**) attack using torpedoes.

torpid ▶ adjective inactive and having no energy.
□ **torpidity** noun.

torpor ▶ noun the state of being inactive and having no energy.

torque /tork/ ▶ noun a force causing rotation.

torrent ▶ noun **1** a strong, fast-moving stream of water or other liquid. **2** a large outpouring.

> SYNONYMS **1** *a torrent of water* **flood,** deluge, spate, cascade, rush. **2** *a torrent of abuse* **outburst,** outpouring, stream, flood, volley, barrage, tide.
> ANTONYMS trickle.

torrential ▶ adjective (of rain) falling rapidly and heavily.

torrid ▶ adjective **1** very hot and dry. **2** full of sexual passion. **3** full of difficulty.

torsion ▸ noun the state of being twisted.

torso ▸ noun (plural **torsos**) the trunk of the human body.

tort ▸ noun Law a wrongful act or a violation of a right.

tortellini /tor-tuhl-lee-ni/ ▸ plural noun stuffed pasta parcels rolled into small rings.

tortilla /tor-tee-yuh/ ▸ noun 1 (in Mexican cookery) a thin, flat maize pancake. 2 (in Spanish cookery) an omelette.

tortoise /tor-tuhss/ ▸ noun a slow-moving reptile with a hard, round shell into which it can draw its head and legs.

tortoiseshell ▸ noun 1 the semi-transparent mottled yellow and brown shell of certain turtles, used to make jewellery or ornaments. 2 a domestic cat with markings resembling tortoiseshell. 3 a butterfly with mottled orange, yellow, and black markings.

tortuous ▸ adjective 1 full of twists and turns. 2 very long and complicated.
□ **tortuously** adverb.

torture ▸ noun 1 severe pain inflicted on someone, especially to make them say something. 2 great suffering or anxiety.

SYNONYMS 1 *the torture of political prisoners* **abuse,** ill-treatment, mistreatment, maltreatment, persecution, cruelty, atrocity. 2 *the torture of losing a loved one* **torment,** agony, suffering, pain, anguish, misery, distress, heartbreak, trauma.

▸ verb (**tortures, torturing, tortured**) subject someone to torture.

SYNONYMS 1 *the forces routinely tortured suspects* **abuse,** ill-treat, mistreat, maltreat, persecute. 2 *he was tortured by grief* **torment,** rack, afflict, harrow, plague, distress, trouble.

□ **torturer** noun **torturous** adjective.

Tory ▸ noun (plural **Tories**) a member or supporter of the British Conservative Party.

toss ▸ verb 1 throw lightly or casually. 2 move something from side to side or backwards and forwards. 3 jerk your head or hair backwards. 4 throw a coin into the air and see which side is facing upwards when it lands, using this to help decide something. 5 shake or turn food in a liquid to coat it lightly.

SYNONYMS 1 *he tossed his tools into the boot* **throw,** hurl, fling, sling, pitch, lob, launch; informal heave, chuck, bung. 2 *he tossed a coin* **flip,** flick, spin. 3 *the ship tossed about on the waves* **pitch,** lurch, rock, roll, plunge, reel, sway. 4 *toss the ingredients together* **mix,** combine, stir, turn, shake.

▸ noun an act of tossing.
■ **toss-up 1** a situation in which any of two or more outcomes is equally possible. 2 the tossing of a coin to make a decision.

tot¹ ▸ noun 1 a very young child. 2 Brit. a small drink of spirits.

tot² ▸ verb (**tots, totting, totted**) (**tot something up**) Brit. add up numbers or amounts.

total ▸ adjective 1 consisting of the whole number or amount. 2 complete.

SYNONYMS 1 *the total cost* **entire,** complete, whole, full, combined, aggregate, gross, overall. 2 *a total disaster* **utter,** complete, absolute, thorough, perfect, downright, out-and-out, outright, sheer, unmitigated.
ANTONYMS partial, net.

▸ noun a total number or amount.

SYNONYMS *a total of £16* **sum,** aggregate, whole, entirety, totality.

▸ verb (**totals, totalling, totalled;** US spelling **totals, totaling, totaled**) 1 amount to a total number. 2 find the total of.

SYNONYMS 1 *the prize money totalled £33,050* **add up to,** amount to, come to, run to, make. 2 *he totalled up his score* **add,** count, reckon, tot up, compute, work out.

□ **totality** noun.

totalitarian ▸ adjective (of a system of government) consisting of only one leader or party and having complete power and control over the people.
□ **totalitarianism** noun.

totalizator (or **totalisator**) ▸ noun 1 a device showing the number of bets and amount of money staked on a race. 2 the system of betting based on this; the tote.

totally ▸ adverb completely.

SYNONYMS **completely,** entirely, wholly, thoroughly, fully, utterly, absolutely, perfectly, unreservedly, unconditionally, downright, one hundred per cent.
ANTONYMS partly.

tote¹ ▸ noun (**the tote**) informal a system of betting based on the use of the totalizator, in which winnings are calculated according to the amount staked rather than odds offered.

tote² ▸ verb (**totes, toting, toted**) informal carry.

totem ▸ noun a natural object or animal believed to have spiritual meaning and adopted as an emblem by a particular society.
■ **totem pole** a pole on which totems are hung or on which images of totems are carved.
□ **totemic** adjective.

totter ▸ verb (totters, tottering, tottered)
1 move in an unsteady way. **2** shake or rock as if about to collapse.

toucan /too-kuhn/ ▸ noun a tropical bird with a massive bill and brightly coloured feathers.

touch ▸ verb **1** bring your fingers or another part of your body into contact with. **2** come into or be in physical contact with. **3** have an effect on. **4** (**be touched**) feel moved with gratitude or sympathy because of someone's actions or situation. **5** harm or interfere with. **6** use or consume. **7** (**touched**) informal mad.

> SYNONYMS **1** *his feet touched the floor* **contact,** meet, brush, graze, come up against, be in contact with, border, abut. **2** *he touched her cheek* **feel,** pat, tap, stroke, fondle, caress, pet, handle. **3** *sales touched twenty grand* **reach,** attain, come to, make, rise to, soar to, sink to, plummet to; informal hit. **4** *nobody can touch him when he's on form* **compare with,** be on a par with, equal, match, rival, measure up to, better, beat; informal hold a candle to. **5** *you're not supposed to touch the computer* **handle,** hold, pick up, move, use, meddle with, play about with, fiddle with, interfere with, tamper with, disturb. **6** *Lisa felt touched by her kindness* **affect,** move, stir.

▸ noun **1** an act or way of touching. **2** the ability to become aware of something and learn what it is like through physical contact, especially with the fingers. **3** a small amount. **4** a distinctive detail or feature. **5** a distinctive or skilful way of dealing with something.

> SYNONYMS **1** *her touch on his shoulder* **tap,** pat, contact, stroke, caress. **2** *his political touch* **skill,** expertise, dexterity, deftness, adroitness, adeptness, ability, talent, flair, facility, proficiency, knack. **3** *there was a touch of bitterness in her voice* **trace,** bit, suggestion, suspicion, hint, scintilla, tinge, dash, taste, spot, drop, dab, soupçon. **4** *the gas lights are a nice touch* **detail,** feature, point, element, addition. **5** *have you been in touch with him?* **contact,** communication, correspondence.

■ **in touch 1** in or into communication. **2** having up-to-date knowledge. **out of touch** lacking up-to-date knowledge or awareness. **touch-and-go** (of a particular outcome) possible but very uncertain. **touch down** (of an aircraft or spacecraft) land. **touch on** deal briefly with. **touch-type** type using all of your fingers and without needing to look at the keys. **touch something up** make small improvements to something.

touchdown ▸ noun **1** the moment at which an aircraft touches down. **2** (in rugby) an act of scoring by touching the ball down behind the opponents' goal line.

touché /too-shay/ ▸ exclamation used to acknowledge a good point made at your own expense.

touching ▸ adjective making you feel gratitude or sympathy; moving.

> SYNONYMS **moving,** affecting, heart-warming, emotional, emotive, poignant, sad, tear-jerking.

touchline ▸ noun (in football) the boundary line on each side of the field.

touchstone ▸ noun a standard by which something is judged.

touchy ▸ adjective **1** quick to take offence. **2** (of a situation or issue) needing careful treatment.

tough ▸ adjective **1** strong enough to withstand wear and tear. **2** able to deal with pain or difficulty. **3** strict. **4** involving problems or difficulties. **5** (of a person) rough or violent.

> SYNONYMS **1** *tough leather* **durable,** strong, resilient, sturdy, rugged, solid, stout, robust, hard-wearing, long-lasting, heavy-duty, well built, made to last. **2** *he'll survive—he's pretty tough* **robust,** resilient, strong, hardy, rugged, fit; informal hard. **3** *tough sentencing for offenders* **strict,** stern, severe, stringent, rigorous, hard, firm, hard-hitting, uncompromising. **4** *the training was pretty tough* **difficult,** hard, strenuous, onerous, gruelling, exacting, arduous, demanding, taxing, tiring, exhausting, punishing. **5** *tough questions* **difficult,** hard, knotty, thorny, tricky. ANTONYMS weak, lenient, light, easy.

▸ noun informal a rough or violent man.

> SYNONYMS *a gang of toughs* **ruffian,** thug, hoodlum, hooligan, bully boy; Brit. rough; informal heavy, bruiser; Brit. informal yob.

□ **toughness** noun.

toughen ▸ verb make or become tough.

toupee /too-pay/ ▸ noun a small wig or hairpiece worn to cover a bald spot.

tour ▸ noun **1** a journey for pleasure in which several different places are visited. **2** a short trip to view or inspect something. **3** a series of plays, matches, etc. performed in several different places.

> SYNONYMS **1** *a three-day walking tour* **trip,** excursion, journey, expedition, jaunt, outing, trek, safari. **2** *a tour of the factory* **visit,** inspection, walkabout.

▸ verb make a tour of.

> SYNONYMS **1** *this hotel is well placed for touring Devon* **travel round,** explore, holiday in; informal do. **2** *the Prince toured*

a local factory **visit**, inspect, go round, walk round.

tour de force /toor duh **forss**/ ▶ noun (plural **tours de force** /toor duh **forss**/) a performance or achievement accomplished with great skill.

tourism ▶ noun the business of organizing and operating holidays and visits to places of interest.

tourist ▶ noun 1 a person who travels for pleasure. 2 Brit. a member of a touring sports team.

SYNONYMS **holidaymaker,** traveller, sightseer, visitor, backpacker, globetrotter, tripper; N. Amer. vacationer.
ANTONYMS local.

touristy ▶ adjective informal visited by a lot of tourists.

tournament ▶ noun 1 a series of contests between a number of competitors. 2 a medieval sporting event in which knights jousted with blunted weapons.

SYNONYMS **competition,** contest, championship, meeting, event.

tourney /**toor**-ni, **ter**-ni/ ▶ noun (plural **tourneys**) a joust or tournament.

tourniquet /**toor**-ni-kay, **tor**-ni-kay/ ▶ noun a cord or tight bandage tied round a limb to stop the flow of blood through an artery.

tousle ▶ verb (**tousles, tousling, tousled**) make someone's hair untidy.

tout /towt/ ▶ verb 1 try to sell. 2 try to persuade people of something's value. 3 Brit. resell a ticket for a popular event at a higher price than you paid for it.
▶ noun a person who buys up tickets for an event to resell them at a profit.

tow ▶ verb use a vehicle or boat to pull another vehicle or boat along.

SYNONYMS **pull,** haul, drag, draw, tug, lug.

▶ noun an act of towing.
■ **in tow 1** (also **on tow**) being towed. 2 accompanying or following someone.

towards (or **toward**) ▶ preposition 1 in the direction of. 2 getting nearer to. 3 in relation to. 4 contributing to the cost of.

SYNONYMS **1** they were driving towards her flat **in the direction of,** to, on the way to, on the road to. **2** towards evening dark clouds gathered **just before,** shortly before, near, around, approaching, getting on for. **3** her attitude towards politics **with regard to,** regarding, in/with regard to, in relation to, concerning, about, apropos.

towel ▶ noun a piece of absorbent cloth used for drying.
▶ verb (**towels, towelling, towelled**; US spelling **towels, toweling, toweled**) dry someone or something with a towel.

towelling (US spelling **toweling**) ▶ noun absorbent cloth used for towels.

tower ▶ noun 1 a tall, narrow building or part of a building, especially of a church or castle. 2 a tall structure containing special equipment.
▶ verb (**towers, towering, towered**) 1 rise to or reach a great height. 2 (**towering**) very important or influential. 3 (**towering**) very great: a towering rage.

SYNONYMS snow-capped peaks towered over the valley **soar,** rise, rear, overshadow, overhang, hang over, dominate.

■ **tower block** Brit. a tall modern building containing many floors of offices or flats.

town ▶ noun 1 a settlement larger than a village and generally smaller than a city. 2 the central part of a town or city containing its shopping area.
■ **go to town** informal do something thoroughly or enthusiastically. **town crier** (in the past) a person employed to shout out public announcements in the streets. **town hall** the building where local government offices are located.

township ▶ noun (in South Africa) a suburb or city occupied chiefly by black people.

towpath ▶ noun a path beside a river or canal, originally used as a pathway for horses towing barges.

toxaemia /tok-see-mi-uh/ (US spelling **toxemia**) ▶ noun a form of blood poisoning.

toxic ▶ adjective 1 poisonous. 2 relating to or caused by poison.

SYNONYMS **poisonous,** dangerous, harmful, injurious, noxious, pernicious, deadly, lethal.
ANTONYMS harmless.

□ **toxicity** noun.

toxicology ▶ noun the branch of science concerned with how poisons work.
□ **toxicologist** noun.

toxin ▶ noun a poison caused by a germ, to which the body reacts by producing antibodies.

toy ▶ noun an object for a child to play with.

SYNONYMS playing with their toys **plaything,** game.

▶ verb (**toy with**) 1 casually consider an idea. 2 fiddle with something.
▶ adjective (of a breed of dog) very small.

SYNONYMS a toy gun **model,** imitation, replica, miniature.

■ **toy boy** Brit. informal a male lover who is much younger than his partner.

trace ▶ verb (**traces, tracing, traced**) 1 find by careful investigation. 2 find or describe the origin or development of. 3 follow the course or position of something with your eye or finger. **4** copy something by drawing over its lines on a piece of transparent paper placed on top of it. **5** draw a pattern or outline.

> SYNONYMS **1** *police hope to trace the owner* **track down**, find, discover, detect, unearth, turn up, hunt down, ferret out, run to ground. **2** *she traced a pattern in the sand* **draw**, outline, mark.

▶ noun **1** a mark or other sign of the existence or passing of something. **2** a very small amount. **3** a barely noticeable indication. **4** a line or pattern on paper or a screen showing information recorded by a machine.

> SYNONYMS **1** *no trace had been found of the missing plane* **sign**, mark, indication, evidence, clue, vestige, remains, remnant. **2** *a trace of bitterness crept into her voice* **bit**, touch, hint, suggestion, suspicion, shadow, dash, tinge; informal smidgen, tad.

■ **trace element** a chemical element that is present in tiny amounts.

tracer ▶ noun a bullet or shell whose course is made visible by a trail of flames or smoke.

tracery ▶ noun (plural **traceries**) **1** a decorative design of holes and outlines in stone. **2** a delicate branching pattern.

trachea /truh-kee-uh/ ▶ noun (plural **tracheae** /truh-kee-ee/ or **tracheas**) the tube carrying air between the larynx and the lungs; the windpipe.

tracheotomy /tra-ki-ot-uh-mi/ (or **tracheostomy** /tra-ki-oss-tuh-mi/) ▶ noun (plural **tracheotomies**) a surgical cut in the windpipe, made to enable someone to breathe when their windpipe is blocked.

track ▶ noun **1** a rough path or small road. **2** a course or circuit for racing. **3** a line of marks left on the ground by a person, animal, or vehicle as they move along. **4** a continuous line of rails on a railway. **5** a section of a CD, record, or cassette tape containing one song or piece of music. **6** a strip or rail along which something may be moved.

> SYNONYMS **1** *a gravel track* **path**, footpath, lane, trail, route. **2** *the final lap of the track* **course**, racecourse, racetrack, velodrome; Brit. circuit. **3** *he found the tracks of a fox* **traces**, marks, prints, footprints, trail, spoor. **4** *the railway tracks* **rail**, line. **5** *the album's title track* **song**, recording, number, piece.

▶ verb **1** follow the trail or movements of. **2** (**track someone/thing down**) find someone or something after a thorough search. **3** follow a particular course. **4** (of a camera) move along with the subject being filmed.

> SYNONYMS *he tracked a bear for 40 km* **follow**, trail, pursue, shadow, stalk; informal tail.

■ **keep** (or **lose**) **track of** keep (or fail to keep) fully aware of or informed about. **on the right** (or **wrong**) **track** following a course that is likely to result in success (or failure). **track events** athletic events that take place on a running track. **track record** someone's past achievements.
□ **tracker** noun.

tracksuit ▶ noun an outfit consisting of a sweatshirt and loose trousers.

tract¹ ▶ noun **1** a large area of land. **2** a system of connected organs or tissues in the body along which something passes.

tract² ▶ noun a short piece of religious writing in the form of a pamphlet.

tractable ▶ adjective **1** (of a person) easy to control or influence. **2** (of a difficulty) easy to resolve.

traction ▶ noun **1** the action of pulling a thing along a surface. **2** the power used in pulling. **3** a way of treating a broken bone by gradually pulling it back into position. **4** the grip of a tyre on a road or a wheel on a rail.

■ **traction engine** a steam- or diesel-powered road vehicle used for pulling heavy loads.

tractor ▶ noun a powerful motor vehicle with large rear wheels, used for pulling farm machinery.

trade ▶ noun **1** the buying and selling of goods and services. **2** a particular area of commercial activity: *the tourist trade*. **3** a job requiring special skills and training: *a carpenter by trade*.

> SYNONYMS **1** *the trade in stolen cattle* **dealing**, buying and selling, commerce, traffic, business. **2** *the glazier's trade* **occupation**, work, craft, job, career, profession, business, line (of work), métier.

▶ verb (**trades**, **trading**, **traded**) **1** buy and sell goods and services. **2** exchange. **3** (**trade something in**) exchange a used article as part of the payment for another. **4** (**trade on**) take advantage of. **5** (**trade something off**) exchange something of value as part of a compromise.

> SYNONYMS **1** *he made his fortune trading in diamonds* **deal**, do business, bargain, negotiate, traffic, buy and sell. **2** *the business is trading at a loss* **operate**, run, do business, deal. **3** *I traded the old machine for a newer model* **swap**, exchange, barter, part-exchange.

■ **trade union** (or Brit. **trades union**) an association formed within an industry or particular workplace to protect the rights of the workers. **trade wind** a wind blowing steadily towards the equator.

trademark ▶ noun **1** a symbol, word, or words chosen to represent a company or product. **2** a distinctive characteristic.

trader ▶ noun a person who trades goods, currency, or shares.

> SYNONYMS **dealer,** merchant, buyer, seller, vendor, purveyor, supplier, trafficker.

tradesman ▶ noun (plural **tradesmen**) **1** a person who has a small shop. **2** a person working at a skilled trade.

tradition ▶ noun **1** the passing on of customs or beliefs from generation to generation. **2** a long-established custom or belief passed on in this way. **3** a method or style established by an artist, writer, or movement, and followed by others.

> SYNONYMS **custom,** practice, convention, ritual, observance, way, usage, habit, institution, unwritten law; formal praxis.

traditional ▶ adjective having to do with or following tradition.

> SYNONYMS **customary,** long-established, time-honoured, classic, wonted, accustomed, standard, regular, normal, conventional, habitual, ritual, age-old, folk.

□ **traditionally** adverb.

traditionalism ▶ noun the upholding of tradition, especially so as to resist change.
□ **traditionalist** noun & adjective.

traduce ▶ verb (**traduces, traducing, traduced**) formal say things about someone that are unpleasant or untrue.

traffic ▶ noun **1** vehicles moving on public roads. **2** the movement of ships or aircraft. **3** the commercial transportation of goods or passengers. **4** the messages or signals sent through a communications system. **5** the action of trading in something illegal.

> SYNONYMS **1** *the increased use of railways for goods traffic* **transport,** freight, shipping. **2** *the traffic in stolen art* **trade,** dealing, commerce, business, buying and selling.

▶ verb (**traffics, trafficking, trafficked**) buy or sell something illegal.

> SYNONYMS *he confessed to trafficking in ivory* **trade,** deal, do business, buy and sell.

■ **traffic jam** a congestion in the flow of traffic so that it is at or almost at a standstill. **traffic lights** a set of automatically operated lights for controlling the flow of traffic. **traffic warden** Brit. an official who locates and reports on cars breaking parking regulations.

□ **trafficker** noun.

tragedian /truh-**jee**-di-uhn/ ▶ noun **1** a person who writes tragedies for the theatre. **2** a person who acts in tragedies.

tragedy ▶ noun (plural **tragedies**) **1** a very sad event or situation. **2** a serious play with an unhappy ending.

> SYNONYMS **disaster,** calamity, catastrophe, cataclysm, misfortune, adversity.

tragic ▶ adjective **1** very sad. **2** relating to tragedy in a literary work.

> SYNONYMS **1** *a tragic accident* **disastrous,** calamitous, catastrophic, cataclysmic, devastating, terrible, dreadful, awful, appalling, horrendous, fatal. **2** *a tragic tale* **sad,** unhappy, pathetic, moving, distressing, painful, harrowing, heart-rending, sorry.
> ANTONYMS fortunate, happy.

□ **tragically** adverb.

tragicomedy ▶ noun (plural **tragicomedies**) a play or novel containing elements of both comedy and tragedy.
□ **tragicomic** adjective.

trail ▶ noun **1** a line of marks or signs left behind by someone or something as it moves along. **2** a track or scent used in following someone or hunting an animal. **3** a path through rough country. **4** a route planned or followed for a particular purpose. **5** a long thin part stretching behind or hanging down from something.

> SYNONYMS **1** *a trail of clues* **series,** string, chain, succession, sequence. **2** *wolves on the trail of their prey* **track,** spoor, path, scent, traces, marks, signs, prints, footprints. **3** *the plane's vapour trail* **wake,** tail, stream. **4** *nature trails* **path,** way, footpath, track, route.

▶ verb **1** draw or be drawn along behind. **2** follow the trail of. **3** walk or move slowly or wearily. **4** (**trail away** or **off**) become gradually quieter and then stop. **5** be losing to an opponent in a contest. **6** (of a plant) grow along the ground or so as to hang down.

> SYNONYMS **1** *her robe trailed along the ground* **drag,** sweep, be drawn, dangle. **2** *Sharpe suspected they were trailing him* **follow,** pursue, track, shadow, stalk, hunt; informal tail. **3** *the defending champions were trailing 10–5* **lose,** be down, be behind, lag behind. **4** *the roses trailed over the banks* **hang,** droop, fall, spill, cascade.
> ANTONYMS lead.

trailblazer ▶ noun **1** a person who is the first to do something new. **2** a person who finds a new way through wild country.
□ **trailblazing** adjective.

t

trailer ▸ noun **1** an unpowered vehicle pulled by another. **2** the rear section of an articulated truck. **3** N. Amer. a caravan. **4** an extract from a film or programme used to advertise it.

train ▸ verb **1** teach a person or animal a particular skill or type of behaviour. **2** be taught a particular skill. **3** make or become physically fit through a course of exercise. **4** (**train something on**) point something at. **5** make a plant grow in a particular direction or into a required shape.

> SYNONYMS **1** *an engineer trained in remote-sensing techniques* **instruct,** teach, coach, tutor, school, educate, prime, drill, ground. **2** *she's training to be a hairdresser* **study,** learn, prepare, take instruction. **3** *with the Olympics in mind, athletes are training hard* **exercise,** work out, get into shape, practise. **4** *she trained the gun on him* **aim,** point, direct, level, focus.

▸ noun **1** a series of railway carriages or wagons moved by a locomotive. **2** a number of vehicles or animals moving in a line. **3** a series of connected events, thoughts, etc. **4** a long piece of trailing material attached to the back of a formal dress or robe.

> SYNONYMS *a bizarre train of events* **chain,** string, series, sequence, succession, set, course.

■ **in train** in progress.

trainee ▸ noun a person undergoing training for a job or profession.

trainer ▸ noun **1** a person who trains people or animals. **2** Brit. a soft shoe for sports or casual wear.

> SYNONYMS **coach,** instructor, teacher, tutor, handler.

trainspotter ▸ noun Brit. a person who collects locomotive numbers as a hobby. □ **trainspotting** noun.

traipse ▸ verb (**traipses, traipsing, traipsed**) walk or move wearily or reluctantly. ▸ noun a boring walk.

trait /trayt, tray/ ▸ noun a distinguishing quality or characteristic.

> SYNONYMS **characteristic,** attribute, feature, quality, habit, mannerism, idiosyncrasy, peculiarity.

traitor ▸ noun a person who betrays their country, an organization, or a cause.

> SYNONYMS **betrayer,** back-stabber, double-crosser, renegade, Judas, quisling, fifth columnist, turncoat, defector; informal snake in the grass.

□ **traitorous** adjective.

trajectory ▸ noun (plural **trajectories**) the path followed by a moving object.

tram (or **tramcar**) ▸ noun Brit. a passenger vehicle powered by electricity and running on rails laid in a road.

tramlines ▸ plural noun rails for a tram.

trammel ▸ noun (**trammels**) literary restrictions on someone's freedom.
▸ verb (**trammels, trammelling, trammelled**; US spelling **trammels, trammeling, trammeled**) restrict or limit.

tramp ▸ noun **1** a homeless person who travels around and lives by begging or doing casual work. **2** the sound of heavy steps. **3** a long walk. **4** N. Amer. informal a woman who has a lot of sexual partners.

> SYNONYMS **1** *a dirty old tramp* **vagrant,** vagabond, homeless person, down-and-out, traveller, drifter; N. Amer. hobo; N. Amer. informal bum. **2** *the tramp of boots* **tread,** step, footstep, footfall. **3** *a tramp round York* **trek,** walk, hike, slog, march, roam, ramble; N. Amer. informal schlep.

▸ verb **1** walk heavily or noisily. **2** walk over a long distance.

> SYNONYMS **1** *men were tramping through the shrubbery* **trudge,** plod, stamp, trample, lumber; informal traipse. **2** *he spent ten days tramping through the jungle* **trek,** walk, hike, slog, march, roam, ramble, rove; informal traipse; N. Amer. informal schlep.

trample ▸ verb (**tramples, trampling, trampled**) **1** tread on and crush. **2** (**trample on** or **over**) treat with contempt.

> SYNONYMS **tread,** stamp, walk, squash, crush, flatten.

trampoline ▸ noun a strong fabric sheet connected by springs to a frame, used as a springboard and landing area in doing acrobatic or gymnastic exercises. □ **trampolining** noun.

trance ▸ noun a half-conscious state in which someone does not respond to things happening around them.

> SYNONYMS **daze,** stupor, hypnotic state, dream, reverie.

tranche (*rhymes with* branch) ▸ noun one of the parts into which something is divided, especially an amount of money.

tranquil ▸ adjective free from disturbance; calm.

> SYNONYMS **1** *a tranquil village* **peaceful,** calm, restful, quiet, still, relaxing, undisturbed. **2** *Martha smiled, perfectly tranquil* **calm,** serene, relaxed, unruffled, unperturbed, unflustered, untroubled, composed; informal unflappable.
> ANTONYMS busy, excitable.

□ **tranquillity** (or **tranquility**) noun **tranquilly** adverb.

tranquillize (or **tranquillise**) (US spelling **tranquilize**) ▸ verb (**tranquillizes,**

tranquillizing, tranquillized) give a calming or sedative drug to.

tranquillizer (or tranquilliser) (US spelling tranquilizer) ▶ noun a drug taken to reduce tension or anxiety.

transact ▶ verb conduct or carry out business.

transaction ▶ noun 1 an act of buying or selling. 2 the process of carrying out business.

> SYNONYMS **deal**, bargain, agreement, undertaking, arrangement, negotiation, settlement.

transatlantic ▶ adjective 1 crossing the Atlantic. 2 concerning countries on either side of the Atlantic.

transceiver ▶ noun a combined radio transmitter and receiver.

transcend ▶ verb 1 be or go beyond the range or limits of. 2 be superior to.

transcendent ▶ adjective 1 going beyond normal or physical human experience. 2 (of God) existing apart from the material world.
□ transcendence noun.

transcendental ▶ adjective going beyond the limits of human knowledge in a religious or spiritual context.
□ transcendentally adverb.

transcontinental ▶ adjective crossing or extending across a continent or continents.

transcribe ▶ verb (transcribes, transcribing, transcribed) 1 put thoughts, speech, or data into written form, or into a different written form. 2 arrange a piece of music for a different instrument or voice.

transcript ▶ noun a written or printed version of material that was originally spoken or presented in another form.

transcription ▶ noun 1 a transcript. 2 the process of transcribing. 3 a transcribed piece of music.

transducer ▶ noun a device that produces an electrical signal from another form of energy such as pressure or brightness.

transept ▶ noun (in a cross-shaped church) either of the two parts extending at right angles from the nave.

transfer ▶ verb (transfers, transferring, transferred) 1 move someone or something from one place to another. 2 move to another department, job, etc. 3 change to another place, route, or means of transport during a journey. 4 pass a property, right, or responsibility to another person.

> SYNONYMS **move**, take, bring, shift, convey, remove, carry, transport, relocate.

▶ noun 1 an act of transferring. 2 Brit. a small coloured picture or design on paper, which

can be transferred to another surface by being pressed or heated.
□ transference noun.

transfigure ▶ verb (be transfigured) be transformed into something more beautiful or spiritual.
□ transfiguration noun.

transfix ▶ verb 1 make motionless with horror, wonder, or astonishment. 2 pierce with a sharp object.

transform ▶ verb 1 change or be changed in nature, form, or appearance. 2 change the voltage of an electric current.

> SYNONYMS **change**, alter, convert, revolutionize, overhaul, reconstruct, rebuild, reorganize, rearrange, rework.

□ transformation noun.

transformer ▶ noun a device for changing the voltage of an electric current.

transfusion ▶ noun a medical process in which someone is given a supply of someone else's blood.

transgress ▶ verb go beyond the limits of what is morally, socially, or legally acceptable.
□ transgression noun transgressor noun.

transient ▶ adjective 1 lasting only for a short time. 2 staying or working in a place for a short time only.
▶ noun a transient person.
□ transience noun transiently adverb.

transistor ▶ noun 1 a silicon-based device which is able to amplify or rectify electric currents. 2 (also transistor radio) a portable radio using circuits containing transistors.

transit ▶ noun 1 the carrying of people or things from one place to another. 2 an act of passing through or across a place.

transition ▶ noun 1 the process of changing from one state or condition to another. 2 a period of such change.

> SYNONYMS **change**, passage, move, transformation, conversion, metamorphosis, alteration, changeover, shift, switch.

transitional ▶ adjective relating to or characterized by transition.

> SYNONYMS 1 *a transitional period* **intermediate**, interim, changeover, changing, fluid, unsettled. 2 *the transitional government* **interim**, temporary, provisional, pro tem, acting, caretaker.

transitive ▶ adjective (of a verb) able to take a direct object, e.g. *saw* in *he saw the donkey*.
□ transitivity noun.

transitory ▶ adjective lasting for only a short time.

translate ▶ verb (translates, translating, translated) 1 express the sense of words

t

or a piece of writing in another language. **2** (**translate into**) change or be changed into another form.

> SYNONYMS **interpret,** convert, render, put, change, express, decipher, reword, decode, gloss, explain.

translation ▸ noun **1** the action of translating. **2** a piece of writing or word that is translated.

> SYNONYMS **interpretation,** rendition, conversion, change, alteration, adaptation.

translator ▸ noun a person who translates writing or speech from one language into another.

transliterate ▸ verb (**transliterates, transliterating, transliterated**) write a letter or word using the corresponding letters of a different alphabet or language.
□ **transliteration** noun.

translucent ▸ adjective allowing light to pass through partially; semi-transparent.
□ **translucence** (or **translucency**) noun.

transmission ▸ noun **1** the passing of something from one place or person to another. **2** a transmitted programme or signal. **3** the mechanism by which power is passed from an engine to the axle in a motor vehicle.

> SYNONYMS **1** *the transmission of knowledge* **transfer,** communication, passing on, conveyance, dissemination, spread, circulation, relaying. **2** *the transmission of the film* **broadcasting,** airing, televising. **3** *a live transmission* **broadcast,** programme, show.

transmit ▸ verb (**transmits, transmitting, transmitted**) **1** cause to pass from one place or person to another. **2** broadcast or send out an electrical signal or a radio or television programme. **3** allow heat, light, etc. to pass through a material.

> SYNONYMS **1** *the use of computers to transmit information* **transfer,** communicate, pass on, hand on, convey, impart, channel, carry, relay, dispatch, disseminate, spread, circulate. **2** *the programme will be transmitted on Sunday* **broadcast,** send out, air, televise.

transmitter ▸ noun a device used to produce and transmit electromagnetic waves carrying messages or signals, especially those of radio or television.

transmogrify ▸ verb (**transmogrifies, transmogrifying, transmogrified**) humorous change into something completely different.

transmute ▸ verb (**transmutes, transmuting, transmuted**) change in form, nature, or substance.

□ **transmutation** noun.

transom ▸ noun **1** the flat surface forming the stern of a boat. **2** a strengthening crossbar.

transparency ▸ noun (plural **transparencies**) **1** the condition of being transparent. **2** a positive transparent photograph printed on plastic or glass, and viewed using a slide projector.

transparent ▸ adjective **1** allowing light to pass through so that objects behind can be distinctly seen. **2** obvious or evident.

> SYNONYMS **1** *transparent blue water* **clear,** translucent, limpid. **2** *fine transparent fabrics* **see-through,** sheer, filmy, gauzy, diaphanous. **3** *a transparent attempt to buy votes* **obvious,** blatant, unambiguous, unequivocal, clear, plain, apparent, unmistakable, manifest, conspicuous, patent.
> ANTONYMS opaque, obscure.

□ **transparently** adverb.

transpire ▸ verb (**transpires, transpiring, transpired**) **1** come to be known. **2** take place; happen. **3** (of a plant or leaf) give off water vapour through pores in the surface layer.
□ **transpiration** noun.

transplant ▸ verb **1** take living tissue or an organ and implant it in another part of the body or in another body. **2** transfer to another place or situation.

> SYNONYMS **1** *kidneys are frequently transplanted* **transfer,** implant, graft. **2** *these ideas were transplanted to America* **transfer,** move, remove, shift, relocate, take, replant.

▸ noun **1** an operation in which an organ or tissue is transplanted. **2** a person or thing that has been transplanted.
□ **transplantation** noun.

transport ▸ verb **1** carry people or goods from one place to another by means of a vehicle, aircraft, or ship. **2** (**be transported**) be overwhelmed with a strong emotion. **3** (in the past) send someone to a distant place as a punishment.

> SYNONYMS *the blocks were transported by lorry* **convey,** carry, take, transfer, move, shift, send, deliver, bear, ship, ferry; informal cart.

▸ noun **1** a system or method of carrying people or goods from one place to another. **2** the action of transporting. **3** a large vehicle, ship, or aircraft for carrying troops or stores. **4** (**transports**) very strong emotions.

> SYNONYMS *the transport of crude oil* **conveyance,** carriage, delivery, shipping, freight, shipment, haulage.

□ **transportation** noun **transporter** noun.

transpose ▶ verb (transposes, transposing, transposed) **1** cause two or more things to change places with each other. **2** move something to a different place or context. **3** write or play music in a different key from the original.
□ **transposition** noun.

transsexual (or transexual) ▶ noun a person who emotionally and psychologically feels that they belong to the opposite sex.

transubstantiation ▶ noun (in Christian thinking) the doctrine that the bread and wine served in the service of Holy Communion become the actual body and blood of Jesus after they have been blessed.

transverse ▶ adjective placed or extending across something.
□ **transversely** adverb.

transvestite ▶ noun a person, especially a man, who likes to dress in clothes worn by the opposite sex.
□ **transvestism** noun.

trap ▶ noun **1** a device, pit, or enclosure designed to catch and hold animals. **2** an unpleasant situation from which you cannot escape. **3** a trick causing someone to say or do something which they do not intend. **4** a container or device used to collect a particular thing. **5** a light, two-wheeled carriage pulled by a horse or pony.

SYNONYMS **1** *an animal caught in a trap* **snare**, net, mesh, gin; N. Amer. deadfall. **2** *the question was set as a trap* **trick**, ploy, ruse, deception, subterfuge; informal set-up.

▶ verb (traps, trapping, trapped) **1** catch and hold in a trap. **2** trick into doing something.

SYNONYMS **1** *police trapped the men* **snare**, entrap, capture, catch, ambush. **2** *a rat trapped in a barn* **confine**, cut off, corner, shut in, pen in, hem in, imprison. **3** *I hoped to trap him into an admission* **trick**, dupe, deceive, fool, hoodwink.

trapdoor ▶ noun a hinged or removable panel in a floor, ceiling, or roof.

trapeze ▶ noun a horizontal bar hanging on two ropes high above the ground, used by acrobats in a circus.

trapezium ▶ noun (plural trapezia or trapeziums) (in geometry) a quadrilateral with one pair of sides parallel.

trapper ▶ noun a person who traps wild animals.

trappings ▶ plural noun **1** the signs or objects associated with a particular situation or role. **2** a horse's ornamental harness.

Trappist ▶ noun a monk belonging to an order that speaks only at certain times.

trash ▶ noun **1** N. Amer. waste material.
2 poor-quality writing, art, etc. **3** N. Amer. a person or people of very low social status.

SYNONYMS **1** *the entrance was blocked with trash* **rubbish**, refuse, waste, litter, junk; N. Amer. garbage. **2** *they read trash* **rubbish**, nonsense, trivia, pulp fiction, pap; N. Amer. garbage; informal drivel.

▶ verb informal wreck or destroy.
■ **trash can** N. Amer. a dustbin.
□ **trashy** adjective.

trauma /traw-muh/ ▶ noun (plural traumas) **1** a deeply disturbing experience. **2** emotional shock following a stressful event. **3** (in medicine) physical injury.

SYNONYMS **1** *the trauma of divorce* **shock**, upheaval, distress, stress, strain, pain, anguish, suffering, upset, ordeal. **2** *trauma to the liver* **injury**, damage, wound.

traumatic ▶ adjective deeply disturbing or distressing.

SYNONYMS **disturbing**, shocking, distressing, upsetting, painful, agonizing, hurtful, stressful, devastating, harrowing.
ANTONYMS comforting.

traumatize (or traumatise) ▶ verb (be traumatized) suffer lasting shock as a result of a disturbing experience or injury.

travail (or travails) ▶ noun old use a situation involving a lot of hard work or difficulty.

travel ▶ verb (travels, travelling, travelled; US spelling travels, traveling, traveled) **1** go from one place to another, especially over a long distance. **2** journey along a particular road or through a particular region.

SYNONYMS **journey**, tour, take a trip, voyage, go sightseeing, globetrot, backpack, trek.

▶ noun **1** the action of travelling. **2** (travels) journeys over a long distance.

SYNONYMS (travels) **travelling**, journeys, expeditions, trips, tours, excursions, voyages, treks, wanderings, jaunts.

■ **travel agent** a person or agency that makes the necessary arrangements for travellers.

traveller (US spelling traveler) ▶ noun **1** a person who is travelling or who often travels. **2** Brit. a Gypsy or other travelling person.

SYNONYMS **tourist**, tripper, holidaymaker, sightseer, globetrotter, backpacker, passenger, commuter; N. Amer. vacationer.

■ **traveller's cheque** a cheque for a fixed amount that can be exchanged for cash in foreign countries.

travelogue ▶ noun a film, book, or talk about a person's travels.

t

traverse ▶ verb (traverses, traversing, traversed) travel or extend across or through.

travesty ▶ noun (plural travesties) a ridiculous or shocking version of something.

trawl ▶ verb 1 catch fish with a trawl net. 2 search through something thoroughly.
▶ noun 1 an act of trawling. 2 a large wide-mouthed fishing net dragged by a boat along the bottom of the sea.

trawler ▶ noun a fishing boat used for trawling.

tray ▶ noun a flat container with a raised rim, used for carrying plates, cups, etc.

treacherous ▶ adjective 1 guilty of or involving betrayal. 2 having hidden or unpredictable dangers.
□ treacherously adverb treachery noun.

treacle ▶ noun Brit. 1 molasses. 2 golden syrup.
□ treacly adjective.

tread ▶ verb (treads, treading, trod; past participle **trodden** or **trod**) 1 walk in a particular way. 2 press down or crush with your feet. 3 walk on or along.

> SYNONYMS 1 *he trod purposefully down the hall* **walk,** step, stride, pace, march, tramp, plod, stomp, trudge. 2 *the snow had been trodden down by the horses* **crush,** flatten, press down, squash, trample on, stamp on.

▶ noun 1 a way or the sound of walking. 2 the top surface of a step or stair. 3 the part of a vehicle tyre that grips the road. 4 the part of the sole of a shoe that touches the ground.

> SYNONYMS *we heard his heavy tread on the stairs* **step,** footstep, footfall, tramp.

■ tread water stay in an upright position in deep water by moving the feet with a walking movement.

treadle ▶ noun a lever which you work with your foot to operate a machine.

treadmill ▶ noun 1 a job or situation that is tiring or boring and difficult to escape from. 2 a large wheel turned by the weight of people or animals treading on steps fitted into it, used in the past to drive machinery. 3 a device used for exercise consisting of a continuous moving belt on which you walk or run.

treason (or high treason) ▶ noun the crime of betraying your country.

> SYNONYMS **treachery,** disloyalty, betrayal, sedition, subversion, mutiny, rebellion. ANTONYMS allegiance, loyalty.

□ treasonable adjective.

treasure ▶ noun 1 a quantity of precious coins, gems, or other valuable objects. 2 a very valuable object. 3 informal a much loved or highly valued person.

> SYNONYMS 1 *a casket of treasure* **riches,** valuables, jewels, gems, gold, silver, precious metals, money, cash, wealth, fortune. 2 *art treasures* **masterpiece,** gem, pearl, jewel.

▶ verb (treasures, treasuring, treasured) 1 look after carefully. 2 value highly.

> SYNONYMS *I treasure the photographs* **cherish,** hold dear, prize, set great store by, value greatly.

■ treasure hunt a game in which players search for hidden objects by following a trail of clues. treasure trove a store of valuable or pleasant things.

treasurer ▶ noun a person appointed to manage the finances of a society, company, etc.

treasury ▶ noun (plural treasuries) 1 the funds or revenue of a state, institution, or society. 2 (Treasury) (in some countries) the government department responsible for the overall management of the economy.

> SYNONYMS **storehouse,** repository, treasure house, exchequer, fund, mine, bank, coffers, purse.

treat ▶ verb 1 behave towards or deal with in a certain way. 2 give medical care or attention to. 3 use a substance or process to protect or preserve something, or give it particular properties. 4 present or discuss a subject. 5 (treat someone to) provide a person with food, drink, or entertainment that you have paid for. 6 (treat yourself) do or have something very enjoyable.

> SYNONYMS 1 *Charlotte treated him badly* **behave towards,** act towards, use, deal with, handle. 2 *police are treating the fires as arson* **regard,** consider, view, look on, put down as. 3 *the book treats its subject with insight* **deal with,** tackle, handle, discuss, explore, investigate. 4 *she was treated in hospital* **tend,** nurse, attend to, give medical attention to. 5 *a cream used to treat sunburn* **cure,** heal, remedy. 6 *he treated her to lunch* **buy,** take out for, stand, give, pay for, entertain, wine and dine; informal foot the bill for. 7 *delegates were treated to dance performances* **entertain with/to,** regale with, fête with, amuse with.

▶ noun a gift or event that gives someone great pleasure.

> SYNONYMS 1 *a birthday treat* **celebration,** entertainment, amusement, surprise. 2 *I bought you some chocolate as a treat* **present,** gift, titbit, delicacy, luxury, indulgence, extravagance; informal goody.

3 *it was a real treat to see them* **pleasure,** delight, thrill, joy.

treatise /tree-tiss/ ▶ noun a formal piece of writing on a subject.

treatment ▶ noun **1** a way of behaving towards someone or dealing with something. **2** medical care for an illness or injury. **3** the use of a substance or process to preserve or give particular properties to something. **4** the presentation or discussion of a subject.

SYNONYMS **1** *the company's treatment of its workers* **behaviour towards,** conduct towards, handling of, dealings with. **2** *she's responding well to treatment* **medical care,** therapy, nursing, medication, drugs. **3** *her treatment of the topic* **discussion,** handling, investigation, exploration, consideration, study, analysis.

treaty ▶ noun (plural **treaties**) a formal agreement between states.

SYNONYMS **agreement,** settlement, pact, deal, entente, concordat, accord, protocol, compact, convention; formal concord.

treble¹ ▶ adjective **1** consisting of three parts. **2** multiplied or occurring three times.
▶ pronoun an amount which is three times as large as usual.
▶ verb (**trebles, trebling, trebled**) make or become treble.

treble² ▶ noun **1** a high-pitched voice, especially a boy's singing voice. **2** the high-frequency output of a radio or audio system.
■ **treble clef** (in music) a clef placing G above middle C on the second-lowest line of the stave.

tree ▶ noun a plant consisting of a thick wooden stem and a number of branches, that can grow to a great height and live for many years.
■ **tree diagram** a diagram with a structure of branching lines. **tree house** a structure built in the branches of a tree for children to play in.

treeline ▶ noun a height up a mountain above which trees do not grow.

trefoil ▶ noun **1** a small plant with yellow flowers and clover-like leaves. **2** a shape or design in the form of three rounded lobes like a clover leaf.

trek ▶ noun a long, difficult journey, especially one made on foot.

SYNONYMS **journey,** trip, expedition, safari, hike, march, tramp, walk.

▶ verb (**treks, trekking, trekked**) go on a trek.
□ **trekker** noun.

trellis ▶ noun a framework of bars used as a support for climbing plants.

tremble ▶ verb (**trembles, trembling, trembled**) **1** shake in a way that you cannot control, usually as a result of fear, excitement, or weakness. **2** be in a state of great worry or fear.

SYNONYMS **1** *Joe's hands were trembling* **shake,** quiver, twitch. **2** *the entire building trembled* **shudder,** shake, judder, vibrate, wobble, rock, move, sway.

▶ noun a trembling feeling, movement, or sound.

tremendous ▶ adjective **1** very great in amount, scale, or force. **2** informal very good or impressive.

SYNONYMS **1** *tremendous sums of money* **huge,** enormous, immense, colossal, massive, prodigious, stupendous; informal whopping, astronomical; Brit. informal ginormous. **2** *a tremendous result* **excellent,** first-class, outstanding, marvellous, wonderful, splendid, admirable; informal great, fantastic, fabulous, terrific, super, awesome, ace; Brit. informal brilliant, smashing. ANTONYMS tiny, poor.

□ **tremendously** adverb.

tremolo ▶ noun (plural **tremolos**) a wavering effect in singing or created in certain musical instruments.

tremor ▶ noun **1** a quivering movement that cannot be controlled. **2** (also **earth tremor**) a slight earthquake. **3** a sudden feeling of fear or excitement.

tremulous ▶ adjective **1** shaking or quivering slightly. **2** nervous.

trench ▶ noun **1** a long, narrow ditch. **2** a ditch dug by troops to provide shelter from enemy fire. **3** (also **ocean trench**) a long, deep depression in the ocean bed.

SYNONYMS **ditch,** channel, trough, excavation, furrow, rut, conduit.

■ **trench coat** a belted, double-breasted raincoat.

trenchant ▶ adjective (of something said or written) expressed strongly and clearly.
□ **trenchantly** adverb.

trencher ▶ noun (in the past) a flat piece of wood from which food was served or eaten.

trend ▶ noun **1** a general direction in which something is developing or changing. **2** a fashion.

SYNONYMS **1** *an upward trend in unemployment* **tendency,** movement, drift, swing, shift, course, current, direction, inclination, leaning. **2** *the latest trend in music* **fashion,** vogue, style, mode, craze, mania, rage; informal fad, thing.

t

trendsetter ▶ noun a person who leads the way in fashion or ideas.

trendy ▶ adjective (**trendier**, **trendiest**) informal very fashionable.

trepidation ▶ noun a feeling of fear or nervousness.

trespass ▶ verb **1** enter someone's land or property without their permission. **2** (**trespass on**) take advantage of someone's time, good nature, etc. **3** (**trespass against**) old use do wrong or harm to.

SYNONYMS **intrude**, encroach, invade, enter without permission.

▶ noun **1** Law the entering of someone's land or property without their permission. **2** old use a bad or wrongful act.
□ **trespasser** noun.

tress ▶ noun literary a long lock of hair.

trestle ▶ noun a structure consisting of a horizontal bar on sloping legs, used in pairs to support a surface such as a table top.

triad ▶ noun **1** a group of three people or things. **2** a Chinese secret society involved in criminal activity.

trial ▶ noun **1** a formal examination in a court of law to decide if someone is guilty of a crime. **2** a test of performance, qualities, or suitability. **3** (**trials**) an event in which horses or dogs compete or perform. **4** something that tests a person's endurance or patience.

SYNONYMS **1** *a county court trial* **case**, lawsuit, hearing, tribunal, litigation, proceedings. **2** *the drug is undergoing clinical trials* **test**, experiment, pilot study, examination, check, assessment, audition, evaluation, appraisal; informal dry run. **3** *trials and tribulations* **trouble**, affliction, ordeal, tribulation, difficulty, problem, misfortune, mishap, misadventure.

▶ verb (**trials**, **trialling**, **trialled**; US spelling **trials**, **trialing**, **trialed**) test something to assess its suitability or performance.
■ **on trial 1** being tried in a court of law. **2** undergoing tests. **trial and error** the process of trying out various methods until you find one that works well.

triangle ▶ noun **1** a figure with three straight sides and three angles. **2** a musical instrument consisting of a steel rod bent into a triangle, sounded with a rod. **3** an emotional relationship involving a couple and a third person.
□ **triangular** adjective.

triangulation ▶ noun the division of an area into a series of triangles in order to determine distances and relative positions.

triathlon ▶ noun an athletic contest involving three different events, typically swimming, cycling, and long-distance running.
□ **triathlete** noun.

tribalism ▶ noun behaviour and attitudes that result from a system in which people belong to tribes.

tribe ▶ noun **1** a group of people within a traditional society sharing customs and beliefs and led by a chief. **2** informal a large number of people.

SYNONYMS **ethnic group**, people, family, clan, race, dynasty, house, nation.

□ **tribal** adjective.

tribesman ▶ noun (plural **tribesmen**) a member of a tribe in a traditional society.

tribulation ▶ noun trouble, suffering, or difficulty.

tribunal ▶ noun **1** Brit. a group of people established to settle disputes. **2** a court of justice.

SYNONYMS **court**, board, panel, committee.

tribune ▶ noun (in ancient Rome) an official chosen by the ordinary people to protect their interests.

tributary ▶ noun (plural **tributaries**) a river or stream that flows into a larger river or lake.

tribute ▶ noun **1** an act, statement, or gift intended to show respect or admiration for someone. **2** historical payment made by a state to a more powerful one.

SYNONYMS **accolade**, praise, commendation, salute, testimonial, homage, congratulations, compliments, plaudits.
ANTONYMS criticism, condemnation.

trice ▶ noun (**in a trice**) in a moment.

tricentenary ▶ noun (plural **tricentenaries**) a three-hundredth anniversary.

triceps /**try**-seps/ ▶ noun (plural **triceps**) the large muscle at the back of the upper arm.

triceratops /try-se-ruh-tops/ ▶ noun a large plant-eating dinosaur with two large horns.

trichology /tri-kol-uh-ji/ ▶ noun the branch of medicine concerned with the hair and scalp.
□ **trichologist** noun.

trick ▶ noun **1** something intended to deceive or outwit someone. **2** a skilful act performed to entertain people. **3** an illusion. **4** a habit or mannerism. **5** (in card games) a single round of play.

SYNONYMS **1** *a mean trick* **stratagem**, ploy, ruse, scheme, device, manoeuvre, dodge, subterfuge, swindle, fraud; informal con, set-up, scam, sting. **2** *he's playing a trick on us* **practical joke**, prank; informal leg-pull, spoof, put-on. **3** *it was probably a trick of the light* **illusion**, figment of the imagination, mirage. **4** *the tricks of the trade* **knack,** skill, technique, secret, art.

▸ verb cunningly deceive or outwit someone.

> SYNONYMS *tricked by villains* **deceive,** delude, hoodwink, mislead, take in, dupe, fool, cheat, defraud, swindle; informal con, diddle, take for a ride, shaft, do; N. Amer. informal sucker.

□ **trickery** noun.

trickle ▸ verb (**trickles, trickling, trickled**) **1** (of a liquid) flow in a small stream. **2** come or go slowly or gradually.

> SYNONYMS *blood was trickling from two cuts* **dribble,** drip, ooze, leak, seep, spill.
> ANTONYMS pour, gush.

▸ noun **1** a small flow of liquid. **2** a small number of people or things moving slowly.

> SYNONYMS *trickles of water* **dribble,** drip, thin stream, rivulet.

trickster ▸ noun a person who cheats or deceives people.

tricksy ▸ adjective clever or mischievous.

tricky ▸ adjective (**trickier, trickiest**) **1** difficult or awkward. **2** likely to deceive you; crafty.

> SYNONYMS **1** *a tricky situation* **difficult,** awkward, problematic, delicate, ticklish, sensitive; informal sticky. **2** *a tricky politician* **cunning,** crafty, wily, devious, sly, scheming, calculating, deceitful.
> ANTONYMS straightforward, honest.

tricolour /tri-kuh-ler/ (US spelling **tricolor**) ▸ noun a flag with three bands of different colours, especially the French national flag.

tricycle ▸ noun a vehicle similar to a bicycle but having three wheels.

trident ▸ noun a three-pronged spear.

tried past and past participle of TRY.

triennial ▸ adjective lasting for or happening every three years.

trier ▸ noun a person who always tries hard.

trifle ▸ noun **1** something of little value or importance. **2** a small amount. **3** Brit. a cold dessert of sponge cake and fruit with layers of custard, jelly, and cream.

> SYNONYMS **triviality,** thing of no consequence, bagatelle, inessential, nothing, technicality; (**trifles**) trivia, minutiae.

▸ verb (**trifles, trifling, trifled**) (**trifle with**) treat without seriousness or respect.

trifling ▸ adjective unimportant; trivial.

> SYNONYMS **trivial,** unimportant, insignificant, inconsequential, petty, minor, of little/no account, footling, incidental; informal piffling.
> ANTONYMS important.

trigger ▸ noun **1** a small lever that sets off a gun or other mechanism when pulled. **2** an event that causes something to happen.

▸ verb (**triggers, triggering, triggered**) **1** cause a device to function. **2** make something happen.

> SYNONYMS **start,** set off, initiate, spark (off), activate, touch off, provoke, precipitate, prompt, stir up, cause, give rise to, lead to, set in motion, bring about.

■ **trigger-happy** tending to fire a gun on the slightest provocation.

trigonometry ▸ noun the branch of mathematics concerned with the relationships between the sides and angles of triangles.

trilby ▸ noun (plural **trilbies**) Brit. a man's soft felt hat with a narrow brim.

trill ▸ noun a high warbling sound.
▸ verb make a high warbling sound.

trillion ▸ cardinal number **1** a million million ($1,000,000,000,000$ or 10^{12}). **2** Brit. dated a million million million ($1,000,000,000,000,000,000$ or 10^{18}).
□ **trillionth** ordinal number.

trilobite /try-luh-byt/ ▸ noun a fossil sea creature with a rear part divided into segments.

trilogy ▸ noun (plural **trilogies**) a group of three related novels, plays, or films.

trim ▸ verb (**trims, trimming, trimmed**) **1** cut away unwanted parts from something. **2** reduce the size, amount, or number of. **3** decorate something along its edges. **4** adjust a sail.

> SYNONYMS **1** *his hair had been trimmed* **cut,** crop, bob, shorten, clip, snip, shear, dock, lop off, prune, shave, pare. **2** *gloves trimmed with fake fur* **decorate,** adorn, ornament, embellish, edge, border, fringe.

▸ noun **1** decoration along the edges of something. **2** the upholstery or interior lining of a car. **3** an act of trimming. **4** good condition.

> SYNONYMS **1** *white curtains with a blue trim* **decoration,** ornamentation, adornment, embellishment, border, edging, piping, fringe, frill. **2** *hair in need of a trim* **haircut,** cut, clip, snip.

▸ adjective (**trimmer, trimmest**) neat and smart.

> SYNONYMS **1** *a very trim garden* **neat,** tidy, orderly, uncluttered, well kept, well maintained, immaculate, spick and span, spruce, dapper. **2** *her trim figure* **slim,** slender, lean, sleek, willowy.
> ANTONYMS untidy, messy.

■ **in trim** slim and fit.

trimaran /try-muh-ran/ ▸ noun a yacht with three hulls side by side.

trimming ▸ noun **1** (trimmings) small pieces trimmed off. **2** decoration, or the traditional accompaniments to something.

> SYNONYMS **1** *a black dress with lace trimming* **decoration,** ornamentation, adornment, borders, edging, piping, fringes, frills. **2** (trimmings) **accompaniments,** extras, frills, accessories, accoutrements, trappings, paraphernalia, garnish.

trinity ▸ noun (plural **trinities**) **1** (the Trinity or the Holy Trinity) (in Christian belief) the three persons (Father, Son, and Holy Spirit) that make up God. **2** a group of three people or things.

trinket ▸ noun a small inexpensive ornament or item of jewellery.

trio ▸ noun (plural **trios**) **1** a set or group of three. **2** a group of three musicians.

> SYNONYMS **threesome,** three, triumvirate, triad, troika, trinity, trilogy.

trip ▸ verb (**trips, tripping, tripped**) **1** catch your foot on something and stumble or fall. **2** (**trip up**) make a mistake. **3** walk, run, or dance with quick, light steps. **4** make a mechanism start working. **5** informal experience hallucinations as a result of taking a drug such as LSD.

> SYNONYMS **1** *he tripped on the stones* **stumble,** lose your footing, catch your foot, slip, fall (down), tumble. **2** *they tripped up the steps* **skip,** dance, prance, bound, spring, scamper.

▸ noun **1** a journey to a place and back again, especially for pleasure. **2** an instance of tripping or falling. **3** informal a period of hallucinations caused by taking a drug such as LSD. **4** a device that trips a mechanism.

> SYNONYMS **1** *a trip to Paris* **excursion,** outing, jaunt, holiday, break, visit, tour, journey, expedition, voyage, drive, run; informal **spin. 2** *trips cause many accidents* **stumble,** slip, fall, misstep.

tripartite ▸ adjective **1** consisting of three parts. **2** shared by or involving three parties.

tripe ▸ noun **1** the stomach of a cow or sheep used as food. **2** informal nonsense.

triplane ▸ noun an early type of aircraft with three pairs of wings, one above the other.

triple ▸ adjective **1** consisting of three parts, things, or people. **2** having three times the usual size, quality, or strength.

> SYNONYMS **1** *a triple alliance* **threefold,** tripartite, three-way. **2** *triple the going rate* **three times,** treble.

▸ noun a thing that is three times as large as usual or is made up of three parts.

▸ verb (**triples, tripling, tripled**) make or become triple.

■ **triple jump** an athletic event in which competitors perform a hop, a step, and a jump from a running start.
□ **triply** adverb.

triplet ▸ noun **1** each of three children born at the same birth. **2** a group of three musical notes to be performed in the time of two or four.

triplicate ▸ adjective /trip-li-kuht/ existing in three copies or examples.
▸ verb /trip-li-kayt/ (**triplicates, triplicating, triplicated**) **1** make three copies of. **2** multiply by three.

tripod ▸ noun a three-legged stand for a camera or other device.

tripper ▸ noun Brit. informal a person who goes on a pleasure trip.

triptych /trip-tik/ ▸ noun a picture or carving on three panels.

tripwire ▸ noun a wire that is stretched close to the ground and sets off a trap or alarm when disturbed.

trite ▸ adjective (of a remark or idea) unoriginal and dull.

triumph ▸ noun **1** a great victory or achievement. **2** joy or satisfaction resulting from a success or victory. **3** a very successful example of something.

> SYNONYMS **1** *Napoleon's triumphs* **victory,** win, conquest, success, achievement. **2** *his eyes shone with triumph* **jubilation,** exultation, elation, delight, joy, happiness, glee, pride, satisfaction.
> ANTONYMS defeat, disappointment.

▸ verb be successful or victorious.

> SYNONYMS *he triumphed in the Grand Prix* **win,** succeed, come first, be victorious, carry the day, prevail.
> ANTONYMS lose.

□ **triumphal** adjective.

triumphant ▸ adjective **1** having won a battle or contest. **2** joyful after a victory or achievement.

> SYNONYMS **1** *the triumphant team* **victorious,** successful, winning, conquering. **2** *a triumphant expression* **jubilant,** exultant, celebratory, elated, joyful, delighted, gleeful, proud, cock-a-hoop.
> ANTONYMS unsuccessful, defeated, despondent.

□ **triumphantly** adverb.

triumvirate /try-um-vi-ruht/ ▸ noun a group of three powerful or important people or things.

trivet ▸ noun a metal stand on which hot dishes are placed.

trivia ▸ plural noun unimportant details or pieces of information.

trivial ▶ adjective of little value or importance.

> SYNONYMS **unimportant**, insignificant, inconsequential, minor, of no account, of no importance, petty, trifling, footling, negligible; informal piffling.
> ANTONYMS important, significant.

☐ **triviality** noun (plural **trivialities**) **trivially** adverb.

trivialize (or **trivialise**) ▶ verb (**trivializes**, **trivializing**, **trivialized**) make something seem less important or complex than it really is.
☐ **trivialization** noun.

trod past and past participle of TREAD.

trodden past participle of TREAD.

troglodyte ▶ noun a person who lives in a cave.

troika ▶ noun **1** a Russian vehicle pulled by a team of three horses side by side. **2** a group of three people working together.

Trojan ▶ noun an inhabitant of ancient Troy in Asia Minor (present-day Turkey).
▶ adjective relating to Troy.
■ **Trojan Horse** something intended to weaken or defeat an enemy secretly.

troll¹ ▶ noun (in stories) an ugly giant or dwarf.

troll² ▶ verb fish by trailing a baited line along behind a boat.

trolley ▶ noun (plural **trolleys**) **1** Brit. a large metal basket with wheels, for transporting heavy or bulky items. **2** a small table on wheels.

trolleybus ▶ noun Brit. a bus powered by electricity obtained from overhead wires.

trollop ▶ noun dated or humorous a woman who has a lot of sexual partners.

trombone ▶ noun a large brass wind instrument with a sliding tube which you move to produce different notes.
☐ **trombonist** noun.

troop ▶ noun **1** (**troops**) soldiers or armed forces. **2** a unit of troops. **3** a group of people or animals.

> SYNONYMS **1** a troop of musicians **group**, party, band, gang, body, company, troupe, crowd, squad, unit. **2** (**troops**) **soldiers**, armed forces, soldiery, servicemen, servicewomen.

▶ verb come or go as a group.

> SYNONYMS we trooped out of the hall **walk**, march, file, flock, crowd, throng, stream, swarm.

trooper ▶ noun **1** a soldier in a cavalry or armoured unit. **2** US a state police officer.

trophy ▶ noun (plural **trophies**) **1** a cup or other object awarded as a prize. **2** a souvenir of an achievement.

> SYNONYMS **1** a swimming trophy **cup**, medal, prize, award. **2** trophies from his travels **souvenir**, memento, keepsake, spoils, booty.

tropic ▶ noun **1** the line of latitude 23°26′ north (**tropic of Cancer**) or south (**tropic of Capricorn**) of the equator. **2** (**the tropics**) the region between the tropics of Cancer and Capricorn.

tropical ▶ adjective **1** having to do with the tropics. **2** very hot and humid.

> SYNONYMS **hot**, sweltering, humid, sultry, steamy, sticky, oppressive, stifling.
> ANTONYMS cold.

☐ **tropically** adverb.

trot ▶ verb (**trots**, **trotting**, **trotted**) **1** (of a horse) move at a pace faster than a walk. **2** run at a moderate pace with short steps. **3** (**trot something out**) informal repeat something that has been said many times before.

> SYNONYMS **run**, jog, scuttle, scurry, bustle, scamper.

▶ noun **1** a trotting pace. **2** a period of trotting.
■ **on the trot** Brit. informal one after another.

troth ▶ noun (**plight your troth**) old use promise to marry.

trotter ▶ noun a pig's foot.

troubadour /troo-buh-dor/ ▶ noun a travelling singer and poet in medieval France.

trouble ▶ noun **1** difficulty or problems. **2** effort that you make to do something. **3** a cause of worry or inconvenience. **4** a situation in which you can be punished or blamed. **5** a situation in which people are angry or violent.

> SYNONYMS **1** you've caused enough trouble **difficulty**, problems, bother, inconvenience, worry, anxiety, distress, stress, agitation, harassment, unpleasantness; informal hassle. **2** she poured out all her troubles **problem**, misfortune, difficulty, trial, tribulation, woe, grief, heartache, misery, affliction, suffering. **3** he's gone to a lot of trouble **bother**, inconvenience, fuss, effort, exertion, work, labour. **4** I wouldn't want to be a trouble to her **nuisance**, bother, inconvenience, irritation, problem, trial, pest; informal headache, pain, drag. **5** you're too gullible, that's your trouble **shortcoming**, weakness, failing, fault. **6** he had heart trouble **disease**, illness, sickness, ailment, complaint, problem, disorder, disability. **7** the crash was due to engine trouble **malfunction**, failure, breakdown. **8** a match marred by crowd trouble **disturbance**, disorder, unrest, fighting, scuffles, breach of the peace.

t

▸ verb (**troubles, troubling, troubled**) **1** cause distress or inconvenience to. **2** (**troubled**) feeling anxious or experiencing problems. **3** (**trouble to do**) make the effort required to do.

> SYNONYMS **1** *this matter had been troubling her for some time* **worry**, bother, concern, disturb, upset, agitate, distress, perturb, annoy, nag, prey on someone's mind; informal bug. **2** *he was troubled by ill health* **afflict**, burden, suffer from, be cursed with. **3** *there is nothing you need trouble about* **worry**, upset yourself, fret, be anxious, be concerned. **4** *I'm sorry to trouble you* **inconvenience**, bother, impose on, disturb, put out, disoblige; informal hassle.

troublemaker ▸ noun a person who regularly causes trouble.

troubleshooter ▸ noun a person who investigates and solves problems or faults. □ **troubleshooting** noun.

troublesome ▸ adjective causing difficulty or problems.

> SYNONYMS **1** *a troublesome problem* **annoying**, irritating, exasperating, maddening, infuriating, bothersome, tiresome, nagging, difficult, awkward; N. Amer. informal pesky. **2** *a troublesome child* **difficult**, awkward, uncooperative, rebellious, unmanageable, unruly, obstreperous, disruptive, disobedient, naughty, recalcitrant.
> ANTONYMS simple, cooperative.

trough ▸ noun **1** a long, narrow open container for animals to eat or drink out of. **2** (in weather forecasting) a long region of low atmospheric pressure. **3** a point of low activity or achievement.

trounce ▸ verb (**trounces, trouncing, trounced**) defeat heavily.

troupe ▸ noun a touring group of entertainers.

trouper ▸ noun **1** an entertainer with many years of experience. **2** a reliable and uncomplaining person.

trousers ▸ plural noun an outer garment that covers the body from the waist down and has a separate part for each leg.

trousseau /troo-soh/ ▸ noun (plural **trousseaux** or **trousseaus** /troo-sohz/) clothes and other belongings collected by a bride for her marriage.

trout ▸ noun (plural **trout** or **trouts**) an edible fish of the salmon family.

trove ▸ noun a store of valuable things.

trowel ▸ noun **1** a small tool with a curved scoop for lifting plants or earth. **2** a small tool with a flat blade for applying mortar or plaster.

troy ▸ noun a system of weights used mainly

for precious metals and gems, with a pound of 12 ounces.

truant ▸ noun a pupil who stays away from school without permission or explanation.
▸ verb (also **play truant**) stay away from school without permission or explanation. □ **truancy** noun.

truce ▸ noun an agreement between enemies to stop fighting for a certain time.

> SYNONYMS **ceasefire**, armistice, cessation, peace.

truck[1] ▸ noun **1** a large road vehicle for carrying goods. **2** Brit. an open railway vehicle for carrying goods. □ **trucker** noun.

truck[2] ▸ noun (**have no truck with**) refuse to have any dealings or association with.

truculent /truk-yuu-luhnt/ ▸ adjective quick to argue or fight. □ **truculence** noun **truculently** adverb.

trudge ▸ verb (**trudges, trudging, trudged**) walk slowly and with heavy steps.
▸ noun a difficult or long and tiring walk.

true ▸ adjective (**truer, truest**) **1** in accordance with fact or reality. **2** rightly so called: *true love*. **3** real or actual. **4** accurate and exact. **5** (**true to**) in keeping with what is usual or expected. **6** loyal or faithful. **7** upright or level.

> SYNONYMS **1** *what I say is true* **correct**, accurate, right, verifiable, the case, so. **2** *true craftsmanship* **genuine**, authentic, real, actual, bona fide, proper. **3** *true repentance* **sincere**, genuine, real, unfeigned, heartfelt. **4** *a true friend* **loyal**, faithful, constant, devoted, trustworthy, reliable, dependable. **5** *a true reflection of life* **accurate**, faithful, telling it like it is, realistic, factual, lifelike.
> ANTONYMS untrue, false, disloyal, inaccurate.

truffle ▸ noun **1** an underground fungus that is eaten as a delicacy. **2** a soft chocolate sweet.

trug ▸ noun Brit. a wooden basket for carrying flowers, fruit, and vegetables.

truism ▸ noun a statement that is obviously true and says nothing new or interesting.

truly ▸ adverb **1** in a truthful way. **2** sincerely or genuinely. **3** in actual fact; really. **4** absolutely (used for emphasis).

> SYNONYMS **1** *tell me truly what you want* **truthfully**, honestly, frankly, candidly, openly. **2** *I'm truly grateful* **sincerely**, genuinely, really, indeed, heartily, profoundly. **3** *this is truly a miracle* **without (a) doubt**, unquestionably, certainly, surely, definitely, undeniably, really, actually, in fact. **4** *a truly dreadful song* **really**, absolutely, simply,

t

utterly, totally, perfectly, thoroughly, completely.

✔ Note that there's no **e** in **truly**.

trump ▸ noun (in card games) a card of the suit chosen to rank above the others.
▸ verb **1** play a trump on a card of another suit. **2** beat by saying or doing something better. **3** (**trump something up**) invent a false accusation or excuse.
■ **come** (or **turn**) **up trumps** Brit. informal **1** unexpectedly do very well. **2** be especially generous or helpful.

trumpery ▸ adjective old use showy but worthless.

trumpet ▸ noun **1** a brass musical instrument with a flared end. **2** the loud cry of an elephant.
▸ verb (**trumpets, trumpeting, trumpeted**) **1** announce widely or enthusiastically. **2** (of an elephant) make its characteristic loud cry. **3** play a trumpet.

> SYNONYMS **proclaim,** announce, declare, noise abroad, shout from the rooftops. ANTONYMS keep quiet about.

■ **blow your own trumpet** talk boastfully about your achievements.
□ **trumpeter** noun.

truncate ▸ verb (**truncates, truncating, truncated**) shorten by cutting off the top or end.
□ **truncation** noun.

truncheon ▸ noun Brit. a short, thick stick carried as a weapon by a police officer.

trundle ▸ verb (**trundles, trundling, trundled**) move or roll slowly and heavily.

trunk ▸ noun **1** the main woody stem of a tree. **2** a person's or animal's body apart from the limbs and head. **3** the long nose of an elephant. **4** a large box for storing or transporting articles. **5** N. Amer. the boot of a car.

> SYNONYMS **1** *the trunk of a tree* **stem,** bole, stock, stalk. **2** *his powerful trunk* **torso,** body. **3** *an elephant's trunk* **proboscis,** nose, snout. **4** *an enormous tin trunk* **chest,** box, crate, coffer, case, portmanteau.

■ **trunk call** Brit. dated a long-distance telephone call. **trunk road** an important main road.

trunks ▸ plural noun men's shorts worn for swimming or boxing.

truss ▸ noun **1** a framework which supports a roof, bridge, or other structure. **2** a padded belt worn to support a hernia.
▸ verb **1** tie someone up tightly. **2** tie up the wings and legs of a bird before cooking.

trust ▸ noun **1** firm belief in the truth, reliability, or ability of someone or something. **2** responsibility for someone or something. **3** an arrangement by which someone manages property for the benefit of another person or people. **4** an organization or company managed by trustees.

> SYNONYMS *good relationships are built on trust* **confidence,** belief, faith, certainty, assurance, conviction, credence, reliance. ANTONYMS distrust, mistrust, doubt.

▸ verb **1** have trust in. **2** (**trust someone with**) allow someone to have, use, or look after. **3** (**trust someone/thing to**) give someone or something to another person for safekeeping. **4** (**trust to**) rely on luck, fate, etc. **5** expect or hope.

> SYNONYMS **1** *I should never have trusted her* **have faith in,** have (every) confidence in, believe in, pin your hopes/faith on. **2** *he can be trusted to carry out an impartial investigation* **rely on,** depend on, bank on, count on, be sure of. **3** *I trust we shall meet again* **hope,** expect, take it, assume, presume. **4** *they won't trust their money to strangers* **entrust,** consign, commit, give, hand over, turn over, assign. ANTONYMS distrust, mistrust, doubt.

■ **trust fund** a fund of money or property that is held for someone by a trust.

trustee ▸ noun a person who is given legal powers to manage property for the benefit of others.

trustful ▸ adjective having total trust in someone.
□ **trustfully** adverb.

trusting ▸ adjective tending to trust other people; not suspicious.

> SYNONYMS **trustful,** unsuspecting, unquestioning, naive, innocent, childlike, ingenuous, wide-eyed, credulous, gullible, easily taken in. ANTONYMS distrustful, suspicious.

□ **trustingly** adverb.

trustworthy ▸ adjective honest and reliable.

> SYNONYMS **reliable,** dependable, honest, as good as your word, above suspicion; informal on the level. ANTONYMS unreliable.

□ **trustworthiness** noun.

trusty ▸ adjective (**trustier, trustiest**) old use or humorous reliable or faithful.

truth ▸ noun (plural **truths**) **1** the quality or state of being true. **2** true facts. **3** a fact or belief that is accepted as true.

> SYNONYMS **1** *he doubted the truth of her statement* **accuracy,** correctness, authenticity, veracity, verity. **2** *truth is stranger than fiction* **fact(s),** reality, real life, actuality. ANTONYMS lies, fiction, falsehood.

t

truthful ▸ adjective **1** telling or expressing the truth. **2** accurate; true to life.

> SYNONYMS **true**, accurate, correct, factual, faithful, reliable.
> ANTONYMS deceitful, untrue.

□ **truthfully** adverb **truthfulness** noun.

try ▸ verb (**tries**, **trying**, **tried**) **1** make an attempt to do something. **2** (also **try something out**) test something new or different. **3** attempt to open a door. **4** (**try something on**) put on an item of clothing to see if it fits or looks good. **5** put someone on trial.

> SYNONYMS **1** *try to help him* **attempt**, endeavour, make an effort, strive, do your best, do your utmost, aim; informal have a go, go all out. **2** *try it and see what you think* **test**, sample, taste, inspect, investigate, examine, appraise, evaluate, assess; informal check out. **3** *Mary tried everyone's patience* **tax**, strain, test, stretch, sap, drain, exhaust, wear out.

▸ noun (plural **tries**) **1** an attempt. **2** an act of testing something new or different. **3** Rugby an act of touching the ball down behind the opposing goal line to score points.

> SYNONYMS *I'll have one last try* **attempt**, effort, endeavour; informal go, shot, crack, stab, bash.

■ **try someone's patience** make someone feel irritated or annoyed.

> ! When writing, it is better to use **try to** rather than **try and** (*we should try to help them* rather than *we should try and help them*).

trying ▸ adjective difficult or annoying.

> SYNONYMS **1** *a trying day* **stressful**, taxing, demanding, difficult, challenging, pressured, frustrating, fraught; informal hellish. **2** *Steve was very trying* **annoying**, irritating, exasperating, maddening, infuriating, tiresome, troublesome.
> ANTONYMS easy, accommodating.

tryst /trist/ ▸ noun literary a private, romantic meeting between lovers.

tsar (or **czar** or **tzar**) /zar/ ▸ noun an emperor of Russia before 1917.
□ **tsarist** adjective.

tsetse fly /tset-si/ ▸ noun an African bloodsucking fly which transmits diseases.

tsp ▸ abbreviation teaspoonful.

tsunami /tsoo-**nah**-mi/ ▸ noun a tidal wave caused by an underwater earthquake or other disturbance.

tub ▸ noun **1** a low, wide, open container with a flat bottom. **2** a small plastic or cardboard container for food.
■ **tub-thumping** informal loud, aggressive expression of opinions.

tuba ▸ noun a large low-pitched brass wind instrument.

tubby ▸ adjective (**tubbier**, **tubbiest**) informal (of a person) short and rather fat.

tube ▸ noun **1** a long, hollow cylinder for conveying or holding something. **2** a flexible container sealed at one end and having a cap at the other. **3** (**the Tube**) Brit. trademark the underground railway system in London.

tuber ▸ noun a thick underground part of the stem or root of some plants, from which new plants grow.

tubercular ▸ adjective relating to, or suffering from, tuberculosis.

tuberculosis /tyoo-ber-kyuu-**loh**-siss/ ▸ noun a serious infectious disease in which small swellings (**tubercles**) appear, especially in the lungs.

tubular ▸ adjective **1** long, round, and hollow like a tube. **2** made from a tube or tubes.

TUC ▸ abbreviation Trades Union Congress.

tuck ▸ verb **1** push, fold, or turn between two surfaces. **2** put neatly into a small space. **3** (**tuck someone in** or **up**) settle someone in bed by pulling the edges of the bedclothes under the mattress. **4** (**tuck in** or **into**) informal eat food heartily.

> SYNONYMS **push**, insert, slip, thrust, stuff, stick, cram; informal pop.

▸ noun **1** a flattened, stitched fold in a garment or material. **2** Brit. informal food eaten by children at school as a snack.

tucker ▸ noun Austral./NZ informal food.

Tudor ▸ adjective relating to the royal family which ruled England 1485–1603.

Tuesday ▸ noun the day of the week before Wednesday and following Monday.

tufa ▸ noun **1** rock formed as a deposit from mineral springs. **2** rock formed from volcanic ash.

tuffet ▸ noun **1** a tuft or clump. **2** a footstool or low seat.

tuft ▸ noun a bunch of threads, grass, or hair held or growing together at the base.
□ **tufted** adjective **tufty** adjective.

tug ▸ verb (**tugs**, **tugging**, **tugged**) pull hard or suddenly.

> SYNONYMS **1** *Ben tugged at her sleeve* **pull**, pluck, tweak, twitch, jerk, catch hold of; informal yank. **2** *she tugged him towards the door* **drag**, pull, lug, draw, haul, heave, tow, trail.

▸ noun **1** a hard or sudden pull. **2** (also **tugboat**) a small, powerful boat for towing larger boats and ships.
■ **tug of war** a contest in which two teams pull at opposite ends of a rope.

tuition ▸ noun teaching or instruction.

tulip ▸ noun a plant with brightly coloured cup-shaped flowers.

tulle /tyool/ ▸ noun a soft, fine net material, used for making veils and dresses.

tumble ▸ verb (**tumbles, tumbling, tumbled**) **1** fall suddenly or clumsily. **2** move in a headlong way. **3** decrease rapidly in amount or value.

SYNONYMS **1** *he tumbled over* **fall (over/down)**, topple over, lose your balance, take a spill, trip (up), stumble. **2** *oil prices tumbled* **plummet**, plunge, dive, nosedive, drop, slump, slide; informal crash.
ANTONYMS rise.

▸ noun **1** a sudden or clumsy fall. **2** an untidy or confused arrangement.
■ **tumble dryer** a machine that dries washed clothes by turning them in hot air inside a revolving drum.

tumbledown ▸ adjective (of a building) ruined or falling into ruin.

tumbler ▸ noun **1** a drinking glass with straight sides and no handle or stem. **2** an acrobat. **3** a part of a lock that holds the bolt until lifted by a key.

tumbril ▸ noun an open cart of a kind used to take prisoners to the guillotine during the French Revolution.

tumescent /tyuu-**mess**-uhnt/ ▸ adjective swollen or becoming swollen.

tumid ▸ adjective (of a part of the body) swollen.

tummy ▸ noun (plural **tummies**) informal a person's stomach or abdomen.
■ **tummy button** the navel.

tumour (US spelling **tumor**) ▸ noun an abnormal growth of tissue in the body.

SYNONYMS **cancer**, growth, lump, malignancy; Medicine carcinoma, sarcoma.

tumult ▸ noun **1** a loud, confused noise. **2** confusion or disorder.

tumultuous /tyuu-**mul**-tyuu-uhss/ ▸ adjective **1** very loud and showing strong feelings: *tumultuous applause.* **2** excited, confused, or disorderly.

tumulus /tyoo-myuu-luhss/ ▸ noun (plural **tumuli** /tyoo-myuu-ly/) an ancient burial mound.

tun ▸ noun a large beer or wine cask.

tuna ▸ noun (plural **tuna** or **tunas**) a large edible fish of warm seas.

tundra ▸ noun the vast, flat, treeless regions of Europe, Asia, and North America in which the soil under the surface is permanently frozen.

tune ▸ noun **1** a sequence of notes that form a piece of music; a melody. **2** correct musical pitch.

SYNONYMS *she hummed a tune* **melody**, air, strain, theme, song, jingle, ditty.

▸ verb (**tunes, tuning, tuned**) **1** adjust a musical instrument to the correct pitch. **2** adjust a radio or television to a particular frequency. **3** adjust an engine so that it runs smoothly and efficiently. **4** adjust or adapt to a purpose or situation.

SYNONYMS *a body clock tuned to the tides* **attune**, adapt, adjust, regulate.

■ **tuning fork** a two-pronged steel device which produces a specific note when hit against a surface.

tuneful ▸ adjective having a pleasing tune.
□ **tunefully** adverb.

tuneless ▸ adjective not having a pleasing tune.
□ **tunelessly** adverb.

tuner ▸ noun **1** a person or device that tunes musical instruments. **2** a part of a stereo system that receives radio broadcasts.

tungsten ▸ noun a hard grey metal used to make electric light filaments.

tunic ▸ noun **1** a loose sleeveless garment reaching to the thighs or knees. **2** a close-fitting short coat worn as part of a uniform.

Tunisian ▸ noun a person from Tunisia.
▸ adjective relating to Tunisia.

tunnel ▸ noun a passage built underground for a road or railway or by a burrowing animal.

SYNONYMS **underground passage**, underpass, subway, shaft, burrow, hole, warren, labyrinth.

▸ verb (**tunnels, tunnelling, tunnelled**; US spelling **tunnels, tunneling, tunneled**) dig a tunnel.

SYNONYMS **dig**, burrow, mine, bore, drill.

■ **tunnel vision 1** a condition in which things cannot be seen properly if they are not straight ahead. **2** informal the tendency to focus only on a single aspect of a situation.

tunny ▸ noun (plural **tunny** or **tunnies**) a tuna.

tuppence ➡ TWOPENCE.

turban ▸ noun a long length of material worn wound round the head by Muslim and Sikh men.
□ **turbaned** (or **turbanned**) adjective.

turbid ▸ adjective (of a liquid) cloudy or muddy; not clear.

turbine ▸ noun a machine in which a wheel or rotor is made to revolve by a fast-moving flow of water, air, etc.

turbocharger (or **turbo**) ▸ noun a supercharger driven by a turbine powered by the engine's exhaust gases.

t

□ **turbocharged** adjective.

turbofan ▸ noun a jet engine in which a turbine-driven fan provides additional thrust.

turbojet ▸ noun a jet engine in which the exhaust gases also operate a device for compressing the air drawn into the engine.

turboprop ▸ noun a jet engine in which a turbine is used to drive a propeller.

turbot ▸ noun (plural **turbot** or **turbots**) an edible flatfish.

turbulence ▸ noun 1 violent or unsteady movement of air or water. 2 conflict or confusion.

turbulent ▸ adjective 1 involving a lot of conflict, disorder, or confusion. 2 (of air or water) moving unsteadily or violently.

SYNONYMS **tempestuous**, stormy, unstable, unsettled, tumultuous, chaotic, anarchic, lawless.
ANTONYMS peaceful.

□ **turbulently** adverb.

tureen ▸ noun a deep covered dish from which soup is served.

turf ▸ noun (plural **turfs** or **turves**) 1 grass and earth held together by its roots. 2 a piece of turf cut from the ground. 3 (**the turf**) horse racing. 4 (**your turf**) informal your territory.

SYNONYMS **grass**, lawn, sod; literary sward.

▸ verb 1 (**turf someone out**) Brit. informal force someone to leave. 2 cover with turf.
■ **turf accountant** Brit. a bookmaker.

turgid ▸ adjective 1 (of language) pompous and boring. 2 swollen or full.

Turk ▸ noun a person from Turkey.

turkey ▸ noun (plural **turkeys**) a large game bird bred for food.

Turkish ▸ noun the language of Turkey.
▸ adjective relating to Turkey or its language.
■ **Turkish bath** a period of sitting in a room filled with very hot air or steam, followed by washing and massage. **Turkish delight** a sweet made from syrup and cornflour, coated in icing sugar.

turmeric /ter-muh-rik/ ▸ noun a bright yellow powder obtained from a plant, used in Asian cookery.

turmoil ▸ noun a state of great disturbance, confusion, or uncertainty.

SYNONYMS **confusion**, upheaval, turbulence, tumult, disorder, disturbance, ferment, chaos, mayhem.
ANTONYMS peace, order.

turn ▸ verb 1 move around a central point. 2 move so as to face or go in a different direction. 3 make or become: *she turned pale.* 4 shape on a lathe. 5 twist or sprain an ankle.

SYNONYMS 1 *the wheels were still turning* **go round**, revolve, rotate, spin, roll, circle, wheel, whirl, gyrate, swivel, pivot. 2 *I turned and headed back* **change direction**, change course, make a U-turn, turn about/round, wheel round. 3 *the path turned to right and left* **bend**, curve, wind, twist, meander, snake, zigzag. 4 *Emma turned red* **become**, go, grow, get. 5 *the milk had turned* **(go) sour**, go off, curdle, become rancid, go bad, spoil.

▸ noun 1 an act of turning. 2 a bend in a road, river, etc. 3 a place where a road meets or branches off another. 4 the time when a member of a group must or is allowed to do something. 5 a time when one period of time ends and another begins. 6 a short walk or ride. 7 a brief feeling of illness. 8 a short performance.

SYNONYMS 1 *a turn of the wheel* **rotation**, revolution, spin, whirl, gyration, swivel. 2 *a turn to the left* **change of direction**, veer, divergence. 3 *we're approaching the turn* **bend**, corner, junction, twist, dog-leg; Brit. hairpin bend. 4 *you'll get your turn* **opportunity**, chance, say, stint, time, try; informal go, shot, stab, crack. 5 *she did me some good turns* **service**, deed, act, favour, kindness, disservice, wrong.

■ **be turned out** be dressed in a particular way. **do someone a good turn** do something that is helpful for someone. **to a turn** to exactly the right degree. **turn someone/thing down 1** reject an offer made by someone. **2** reduce the volume or strength of sound, heat, etc. produced by a device. **turn in** informal go to bed. **turn someone in** hand someone over to the authorities. **turn something off** switch something off. **turn on** suddenly attack. **turn someone/thing on 1** switch something on. **2** informal excite someone sexually. **turn out 1** prove to be the case. **2** be present at an event. **turn something out** switch off an electric light. **turn over** (of an engine) start to run. **turn up 1** be found. **2** arrive. **turn something up** increase the volume or strength of sound, heat, etc. produced by a device. **turn-up** Brit. **1** the end of a trouser leg folded upwards on the outside. **2** informal an unusual or unexpected event.

turncoat ▸ noun a person who deserts one party or cause in order to join an opposing one.

turning ▸ noun a place where a road branches off another.

SYNONYMS **junction**, turn-off, side road, exit; N. Amer. turnout.

turning point ▸ noun a time when a decisive change happens, especially one with good results.

t

SYNONYMS **watershed**, critical moment, decisive moment, moment of truth, crossroads, crisis.

turnip ▸ noun a round root which is eaten as a vegetable.

turnkey ▸ noun (plural **turnkeys**) old use a jailer.

turnout ▸ noun the number of people attending or taking part in an event.

SYNONYMS **1** *the lecture attracted a good turnout* **attendance**, audience, house, congregation, crowd, gate, gathering. **2** *his turnout was very elegant* **outfit**, clothing, dress, garb, attire, ensemble; informal get-up.

turnover ▸ noun **1** the amount of money taken by a business in a particular period. **2** the rate at which employees leave a workforce and are replaced. **3** the rate at which goods are sold and replaced in a shop. **4** a small pie made by folding a piece of pastry over on itself to enclose a filling.

SYNONYMS **1** *a turnover of £2 million* **gross revenue**, income, yield, sales. **2** *staff turnover* **replacement**, change, movement.

turnpike ▸ noun US historical a road on which a toll is charged.

turnstile ▸ noun a gate with revolving arms allowing only one person at a time to pass through.

turntable ▸ noun a circular revolving platform or support, e.g. for the record in a record player.

turpentine ▸ noun a liquid obtained from certain trees, used to thin paint and clean brushes.

turpitude ▸ noun formal wickedness.

turps ▸ noun informal turpentine.

turquoise ▸ noun **1** a greenish-blue or sky-blue semi-precious stone. **2** a greenish-blue colour.

turret ▸ noun **1** a small tower at the corner of a building or wall. **2** an armoured tower for a gun on a ship, aircraft, or tank.
□ **turreted** adjective.

turtle ▸ noun a reptile with a bony or leathery shell, that lives in the sea.
■ **turn turtle** (of a boat) turn upside down.
turtle dove a small dove with a soft call.

turtleneck ▸ noun **1** Brit. a high, round, close-fitting neck on a garment. **2** N. Amer. a polo neck.

turves plural of TURF.

tusk ▸ noun a long, pointed tooth which protrudes from the closed mouth of an elephant, walrus, or wild boar.

tussle ▸ noun a short struggle or scuffle.
▸ verb (**tussles**, **tussling**, **tussled**) be involved in a tussle.

tussock ▸ noun a dense clump or tuft of grass.

tutelage /**tyoo**-ti-lij/ ▸ noun formal **1** protection or authority. **2** instruction.

tutelary /**tyoo**-ti-luh-ri/ ▸ adjective formal acting as a protector, guardian, or patron.

tutor ▸ noun **1** a person who teaches a single pupil or a very small group. **2** Brit. a university or college teacher with extra responsibility for students.

SYNONYMS *a history tutor* **teacher**, instructor, coach, educator, lecturer, trainer, mentor.

▸ verb act as a tutor to.

SYNONYMS *he was tutored at home* **teach**, instruct, educate, school, coach, train, drill.

tutorial ▸ noun a period of teaching by a university or college tutor.
▸ adjective relating to a tutor.

tutu ▸ noun a female ballet dancer's very short, stiff skirt that sticks out from the waist.

tuxedo /tuk-**see**-doh/ ▸ noun (plural **tuxedos** or **tuxedoes**) chiefly N. Amer. a man's dinner jacket.

TV ▸ abbreviation television.

twaddle ▸ noun informal silly talk or writing.

twain old-fashioned form of TWO.

twang ▸ noun **1** a strong ringing sound made by the plucked string of a musical instrument. **2** a distinctive nasal way of speaking.
▸ verb make a twang.
□ **twangy** adjective.

tweak ▸ verb **1** twist or pull with a small but sharp movement. **2** informal improve by making small adjustments.
▸ noun an act of tweaking.

twee ▸ adjective Brit. too sentimental or sweet.

tweed ▸ noun a rough woollen cloth flecked with mixed colours.
□ **tweedy** adjective.

tweet ▸ noun the chirp of a small or young bird.
▸ verb make a chirping noise.

tweeter ▸ noun a loudspeaker that reproduces high frequencies.

tweezers ▸ plural noun a small pair of pincers for plucking out hairs and picking up small objects.

twelfth ▸ ordinal number being number twelve in a sequence; 12th.

twelve ▸ cardinal number two more than ten; 12. (Roman numeral: **xii** or **XII**.)

twenty ▸ cardinal number (plural **twenties**) ten less than thirty; 20. (Roman numeral: **xx** or **XX**.)
■ **twenty-twenty vision** normal vision.

t

◻ **twentieth** ordinal number.

twerp ▸ noun informal a silly person.

twice ▸ adverb **1** two times. **2** double in degree or quantity.

twiddle ▸ verb (**twiddles, twiddling, twiddled**) fiddle with something in an aimless or nervous way.
 ■ **twiddle your thumbs** have nothing to do.
 ◻ **twiddly** adjective.

twig¹ ▸ noun a slender woody shoot growing from a branch or stem of a tree or shrub.

twig² ▸ verb (**twigs, twigging, twigged**) Brit. informal understand or realize something.

twilight ▸ noun **1** the soft glowing light from the sky when the sun is below the horizon. **2** a period or state of gradual decline.

> SYNONYMS **1** *we arrived at twilight* **dusk**, sunset, sundown, nightfall, evening, close of day. **2** *it was scarcely visible in the twilight* **half-light**, semi-darkness, gloom. ANTONYMS dawn.

◻ **twilit** adjective.

twill ▸ noun a fabric with a slightly ridged surface.

twin ▸ noun **1** each of two children born at the same birth. **2** a thing that is exactly like another.

> SYNONYMS *a sitting room that was the twin of her own* **duplicate**, double, carbon copy, likeness, mirror image, replica, lookalike, clone, match, pair; informal spitting image, dead ringer.

▸ adjective forming or being one of a pair of twins.

> SYNONYMS **1** *the twin towers of the stadium* **matching**, identical, paired. **2** *the twin aims of conservation and recreation* **twofold**, double, dual, related, linked, connected, parallel, complementary.

▸ verb (**twins, twinning, twinned**) link or combine as a pair.

> SYNONYMS *the company twinned its brewing with distilling* **combine**, join, link, couple, pair.

twine ▸ noun strong string consisting of strands twisted together.

▸ verb (**twines, twining, twined**) wind round something.

twinge ▸ noun **1** a sudden, sharp pain. **2** a brief, sharp pang of emotion.

twinkle ▸ verb (**twinkles, twinkling, twinkled**) **1** shine with a gleam that changes constantly from bright to faint. **2** (of a person's eyes) sparkle with amusement or liveliness.

> SYNONYMS **glitter**, sparkle, shine, glimmer, shimmer, glint, gleam, glisten, flicker, flash, wink.

▸ noun a twinkling sparkle or gleam.

> SYNONYMS **glitter**, sparkle, shine, glimmer, shimmer, glint, gleam, glisten, flicker, flash, wink.

◻ **twinkly** adjective.

twinset ▸ noun a woman's matching cardigan and jumper.

twirl ▸ verb spin quickly and lightly round.
▸ noun an act of twirling.
 ◻ **twirly** adjective.

twist ▸ verb **1** bend, curl, or distort. **2** force out of the natural position. **3** have a winding course. **4** deliberately change the meaning of. **5** (**twisted**) unpleasantly abnormal; perverted.

> SYNONYMS **1** *the impact twisted the chassis* **crumple**, crush, buckle, mangle, warp, deform, distort, contort. **2** *he twisted round in his seat* **turn**, swivel, spin, pivot, rotate, revolve, twiddle. **3** *I twisted my ankle* **sprain**, wrench, turn, rick, crick. **4** *she twisted her hair round her finger* **wind**, twirl, coil, curl, wrap. **5** *the wires were twisted together* **intertwine**, interlace, weave, plait, braid, coil, wind. **6** *the road twisted and turned* **wind**, bend, curve, turn, meander, weave, zigzag, snake.

▸ noun **1** an act of twisting. **2** a thing with a spiral shape. **3** a new or unexpected development or treatment. **4** (**the twist**) a dance with a twisting movement of the body, popular in the 1960s.

> SYNONYMS **1** *the twist of a dial* **turn**, twirl, spin. **2** *the twists of the road* **bend**, curve, turn, zigzag, dog-leg. **3** *the twists of the plot* **convolution**, complication, complexity, intricacy, surprise, revelation.

■ **twist someone's arm** informal forcefully persuade someone to do something.
 ◻ **twister** noun.

twit¹ ▸ noun Brit. informal a silly person.

twit² ▸ verb (**twits, twitting, twitted**) informal tease good-humouredly.

twitch ▸ verb make a short jerking movement.

> SYNONYMS **1** *he twitched and then lay still* **jerk**, convulse, have a spasm, quiver, tremble, shiver, shudder. **2** *he twitched the note out of my hand* **snatch**, tweak, pluck, pull, tug; informal yank.

▸ noun a twitching movement.

> SYNONYMS **1** *a twitch of her lips* **spasm**, convulsion, quiver, tremor, shiver, shudder, tic. **2** *he gave a twitch at his moustache* **pull**, tug, tweak; informal yank.

twitcher ▸ noun Brit. informal a keen birdwatcher.

twitchy ▸ adjective informal nervous.

twitter ▸ verb (twitters, twittering, twittered) **1** (of a bird) make a series of short, high sounds. **2** talk rapidly in a nervous or silly way.
▸ noun a twittering sound.

two ▸ cardinal number one less than three; 2. (Roman numeral: **ii** or **II**.)
■ **put two and two together** draw a conclusion from what is known or evident. **two-dimensional** having or appearing to have length and breadth but no depth. **two-faced** insincere and deceitful. **two-time** be unfaithful to a husband, wife, or lover.
□ **twofold** adjective & adverb.

! Don't confuse **two** with **to** or **too**: see the note at **TO**.

twopence (or **tuppence**) /**tup**-puhnss/
▸ noun Brit. the sum of two pence before decimalization (1971).
□ **twopenny** (or **tuppenny**) adjective.

twosome ▸ noun a set of two people or things.

tycoon ▸ noun a wealthy, powerful person in business or industry.

SYNONYMS **magnate,** mogul, businessman, captain of industry, industrialist, financier, entrepreneur; informal, derogatory fat cat.

tying present participle of **TIE**.

tyke (or **tike**) ▸ noun informal a mischievous child.

tympani → **TIMPANI**.

tympanum ▸ noun (plural **tympanums** or **tympana**) the eardrum.

type ▸ noun **1** a category of people or things that share particular qualities or features. **2** informal a person of a particular nature: *a sporty type.* **3** printed characters or letters.

SYNONYMS **1** *six types of coffee* **kind,** sort, variety, class, category, set, genre, species, order, breed. **2** *italic type* **print,** typeface, characters, lettering, font; Brit. fount.

▸ verb (**types, typing, typed**) write using a typewriter or computer.
□ **typist** noun.

typecast ▸ verb (**be typecast**) (of an actor) always be cast in the same type of role.

typeface ▸ noun a particular design of printed letters or numbers.

typescript ▸ noun a typed copy of a written work.

typeset ▸ verb (**typeset, typesetting, typeset**) arrange or generate the data or type for text to be printed.
□ **typesetter** noun.

typewriter ▸ noun a machine with keys that are pressed to produce characters similar to printed ones.
□ **typewriting** noun **typewritten** adjective.

typhoid ▸ noun an infectious fever that causes red spots on the chest and severe pain in the intestines.

typhoon ▸ noun a tropical storm with very high winds.

typhus ▸ noun an infectious disease that causes a purple rash, headaches, fever, and usually delirium.

typical ▸ adjective **1** having the distinctive qualities of a particular type of person or thing. **2** characteristic of a particular person or thing.

SYNONYMS **1** *a typical example of art deco* **representative,** characteristic, classic, quintessential, archetypal. **2** *a fairly typical day* **normal,** average, ordinary, standard, regular, routine, run-of-the-mill, conventional, unremarkable; informal bog-standard.
ANTONYMS unusual, exceptional.

□ **typically** adverb.

typify ▸ verb (**typifies, typifying, typified**) be typical of.

typo ▸ noun (plural **typos**) informal a small error in typed or printed writing.

typography ▸ noun **1** the setting and arrangement of printed characters. **2** the style and appearance of printed material.
□ **typographer** noun **typographical** (or **typographic**) adjective.

tyrannical ▸ adjective using power in a cruel or unfair way.
□ **tyrannically** adverb.

tyrannize (or **tyrannise**) ▸ verb (**tyrannizes, tyrannizing, tyrannized**) rule or dominate in a cruel or unfair way.

tyrannosaurus rex ▸ noun a large meat-eating dinosaur that walked on its strong hind legs.

tyranny ▸ noun (plural **tyrannies**) cruel and oppressive government or rule.

SYNONYMS **despotism,** absolute power, autocracy, dictatorship, totalitarianism, fascism, oppression, repression, subjugation, enslavement.

✔ one **r**, two **n**s : tyra**nn**y.

tyrant ▸ noun a cruel and oppressive ruler.

tyre (US spelling **tire**) ▸ noun a rubber covering, usually inflated, that fits round a wheel.

tyro ▸ noun (plural **tyros**) a beginner or novice.

tzar → **TSAR**.

tzatziki /tsat-**see**-ki/ ▸ noun a Greek side dish of yogurt with cucumber and garlic.

Uu

U (or **u**) ▸ noun (plural **Us** or **U's**) the twenty-first letter of the alphabet.
▸ abbreviation Brit. (in film classification) universal.

■ **U-boat** a German submarine of the First or Second World War. **U-turn 1** the turning of a vehicle in a U-shaped course so as to face the opposite way. **2** a complete hange in policy.

ubiquitous /yoo-bi-kwi-tuhss/ ▸ adjective appearing or found everywhere.

> SYNONYMS **everywhere,** omnipresent, all over the place, all-pervasive, universal, worldwide, global.
> ANTONYMS rare.

□ **ubiquitously** adverb **ubiquity** noun.

udder ▸ noun the bag-like milk-producing organ of female cattle, sheep, horses, etc.

UFO ▸ noun (plural **UFOs**) a mysterious object seen in the sky that some people believe is carrying beings from outer space (short for *unidentified flying object*).

Ugandan ▸ noun a person from Uganda.
▸ adjective relating to Uganda.

ugly ▸ adjective (**uglier, ugliest**) **1** unpleasant or unattractive in appearance. **2** hostile or threatening.

> SYNONYMS **1 unattractive,** unsightly, ill-favoured, hideous, plain, unprepossessing, horrible, ghastly, repellent; N. Amer. homely; Brit. informal no oil painting. **2** *things got pretty ugly* **unpleasant,** nasty, disagreeable, alarming, charged, dangerous, perilous, threatening, menacing, hostile, ominous, sinister.
> ANTONYMS beautiful, pleasant.

■ **ugly duckling** a person who unexpectedly turns out to be beautiful or talented.
□ **ugliness** noun.

UK ▸ abbreviation United Kingdom.

Ukrainian /yoo-kray-ni-uhn/ ▸ noun a person from Ukraine.
▸ adjective relating to Ukraine.

ukulele (or **ukelele**) /yoo-kuh-lay-li/ ▸ noun a small four-stringed guitar.

ulcer ▸ noun an open sore on the body or on an internal organ.

□ **ulcerated** adjective **ulceration** noun.

ulna ▸ noun (plural **ulnae** /ul-nee/ or **ulnas**) the thinner and longer of the two bones in the human forearm.

ulterior ▸ adjective other than what is obvious or admitted: *she had an ulterior motive.*

ultimate ▸ adjective **1** happening at the end of a process. **2** being the best or most extreme example of its kind. **3** basic or fundamental.

> SYNONYMS **1** *the ultimate collapse of the Empire* **eventual,** final, concluding, terminal, end. **2** *the ultimate gift for cat lovers* **best,** ideal, greatest, supreme, quintessential. **3** *ultimate truths* **fundamental,** basic, primary, elementary, absolute, central, crucial, essential, pivotal.

▸ noun (**the ultimate**) the best of its kind that is imaginable.

ultimately ▸ adverb **1** finally. **2** at the most basic level.

> SYNONYMS **1** *the cost will ultimately fall on us* **eventually,** in the end, in the long run, at length, finally, in time, one day. **2** *two ultimately contradictory reasons* **fundamentally,** basically, primarily, essentially, at heart, deep down.

ultimatum ▸ noun a final warning that action will be taken against you if you do not agree to another party's demands.

ultramarine ▸ noun a brilliant deep blue colour or pigment.

ultrasonic ▸ adjective involving sound waves with a frequency above the upper limit of human hearing.

ultrasound ▸ noun sound or other vibrations with an ultrasonic frequency, used in medical scans.

ultraviolet ▸ adjective (of electromagnetic radiation) having a wavelength just shorter than that of violet light.

ululate ▸ verb (**ululates, ululating, ululated**) howl or wail.
□ **ululation** noun.

umber ▸ noun a dark brown or yellowish-brown colour.

u

umbilical ▸ adjective relating to the navel or umbilical cord.
■ **umbilical cord** a flexible tube which connects a developing fetus with the placenta while it is in the womb.

umbilicus ▸ noun the navel.

umbra ▸ noun (plural **umbras** or **umbrae** /umbree/) the shadow cast by the earth or the moon in an eclipse.

umbrage ▸ noun (**take umbrage**) take offence; become annoyed.

umbrella ▸ noun a folding device used as protection against rain.
▸ adjective including or containing many different parts.

umlaut /uum-lowt/ ▸ noun a mark (¨) placed over a vowel in some languages to indicate how it should sound.

umpire ▸ noun (in certain sports) an official who supervises a game to make sure that players keep to the rules.

> SYNONYMS **referee**, judge, line judge, linesman, touch judge, adjudicator, arbitrator, moderator; informal ref.

▸ verb (**umpires**, **umpiring**, **umpired**) be the umpire of.

umpteen ▸ cardinal number informal very many.
□ **umpteenth** ordinal number.

UN ▸ abbreviation United Nations.

unabashed ▸ adjective not embarrassed or ashamed.

unabated ▸ adjective not reduced in intensity or strength.

unable ▸ adjective not able to do something.

> SYNONYMS **incapable**, powerless, impotent, inadequate, incompetent, unqualified, unfit.

unacceptable ▸ adjective not satisfactory or allowable.
□ **unacceptably** adverb.

unaccountable ▸ adjective **1** unable to be explained. **2** not having to explain your actions or decisions.
□ **unaccountably** adverb.

unaccustomed ▸ adjective **1** not usual. **2** (**unaccustomed to**) not familiar with or used to.

unadulterated ▸ adjective not mixed with any different or extra elements.

unaided ▸ adjective without any help.

unalloyed ▸ adjective complete; total: *unalloyed delight.*

unambiguous ▸ adjective not open to more than one interpretation.
□ **unambiguously** adverb.

unanimous ▸ adjective **1** fully in agreement. **2** (of an opinion, decision, or vote) held or carried by everyone involved.

> SYNONYMS **1** *doctors were unanimous about the effects* **in agreement**, of one mind, in accord, united, undivided. **2** *a unanimous vote* **uniform**, consistent, united.
> ANTONYMS split.

□ **unanimity** noun **unanimously** adverb.

unannounced ▸ adjective without warning or notice.

unappetizing (or unappetising) ▸ adjective not inviting or attractive.

unapproachable ▸ adjective not welcoming or friendly.

unarguable ▸ adjective not able to be disagreed with.
□ **unarguably** adverb.

unarmed ▸ adjective not equipped with or carrying weapons.

> SYNONYMS **defenceless**, unprotected, unguarded.
> ANTONYMS armed.

unassailable ▸ adjective unable to be attacked, questioned, or defeated.

unassuming ▸ adjective not drawing attention to yourself or your abilities.

unattached ▸ adjective without a husband or wife or established lover.

unattended ▸ adjective not being supervised or looked after.

unauthorized (or unauthorised) ▸ adjective not having official permission or approval.

unavailing ▸ adjective achieving little or nothing.

unavoidable ▸ adjective not able to be avoided or prevented.
□ **unavoidably** adverb.

unaware ▸ adjective having no knowledge of a situation or fact.

> SYNONYMS **ignorant**, oblivious, unconscious, unwitting, unsuspecting, uninformed, unenlightened, innocent; informal in the dark.
> ANTONYMS aware.

unawares ▸ adverb so as to surprise someone; unexpectedly.

unbalanced ▸ adjective emotionally or mentally disturbed.

unbearable ▸ adjective not able to be endured.
□ **unbearably** adverb.

unbeknown (or unbeknownst) ▸ adjective (**unbeknown to**) without the knowledge of.

unbelievable ▸ adjective **1** unlikely to be true. **2** extraordinary.

> SYNONYMS **incredible**, inconceivable, unthinkable, unimaginable, unconvincing, far-fetched, implausible, improbable; informal hard to swallow.
> ANTONYMS believable.

u

□ **unbelievably** adverb.

unbeliever ▸ noun a person without religious belief.

unbending ▸ adjective unwilling to compromise or change your mind.

unbiased (or **unbiassed**) ▸ adjective showing no prejudice.

> SYNONYMS **impartial**, unprejudiced, neutral, non-partisan, disinterested, objective, even-handed, fair.

unbidden ▸ adjective without having been invited.

unborn ▸ adjective not yet born.

> SYNONYMS **expected**, embryonic, fetal, in utero.

unbounded ▸ adjective having no limits.

unbowed ▸ adjective not having given in or been defeated.

unbridgeable ▸ adjective (of a gap or difference between people) not able to be made smaller or less significant.

unbridled ▸ adjective uncontrolled: *unbridled lust.*

unbroken ▸ adjective 1 not broken. 2 not interrupted or disturbed. 3 (of a record) not beaten.

> SYNONYMS 1 *the last unbroken window* **undamaged**, unharmed, unscathed, untouched, sound, intact, whole. 2 *an unbroken chain of victories* **uninterrupted**, continuous, endless, constant, unremitting, ongoing. 3 *his record is still unbroken* **unbeaten**, undefeated, unsurpassed, unrivalled, unmatched, supreme.

unburden ▸ verb (**unburden yourself**) confide in someone about your worries or problems.

uncalled ▸ adjective (**uncalled for**) not fair or appropriate; unnecessary.

uncanny ▸ adjective (**uncannier**, **uncanniest**) strange or mysterious.

> SYNONYMS 1 *the silence was uncanny* **eerie**, unnatural, unearthly, other-worldly, ghostly, strange, abnormal, weird; informal creepy, spooky. 2 *an uncanny resemblance* **striking**, remarkable, extraordinary, exceptional, incredible.

□ **uncannily** adverb.

unceasing ▸ adjective not ceasing; continuous.
□ **unceasingly** adverb.

unceremonious ▸ adjective rude or abrupt.
□ **unceremoniously** adverb.

uncertain ▸ adjective 1 not known, reliable, or definite. 2 not completely confident or sure.

> SYNONYMS 1 *the effects are uncertain* **unknown**, debatable, open to question, in doubt, unsure, in the balance, up in the air, unpredictable, unforeseeable; informal iffy. 2 *Ed was uncertain about the decision* **unsure**, doubtful, dubious, undecided, irresolute, hesitant, vacillating, vague, unclear, ambivalent, in two minds.
> ANTONYMS certain, predictable, sure.

■ **in no uncertain terms** clearly and forcefully.

□ **uncertainly** adverb **uncertainty** noun.

uncharitable ▸ adjective unkind or unsympathetic to other people.
□ **uncharitably** adverb.

uncharted ▸ adjective (of an area of land or sea) not mapped or surveyed.

unchristian ▸ adjective 1 not in line with the teachings of Christianity. 2 not generous or fair.

uncle ▸ noun the brother of your father or mother or the husband of your aunt.
■ **Uncle Sam** the United States.

unclean ▸ adjective 1 dirty. 2 immoral. 3 (of food) forbidden by a religion.

unclear ▸ adjective 1 difficult to see, hear, or understand. 2 confused or not certain about something.

> SYNONYMS **uncertain**, unsure, unsettled, up in the air, in doubt, ambiguous, equivocal, indefinite, vague, mysterious, obscure, hazy, nebulous.
> ANTONYMS clear, evident.

uncomfortable ▸ adjective 1 not physically comfortable. 2 uneasy or awkward.

> SYNONYMS 1 *an uncomfortable chair* **painful**, awkward, lumpy, confining, cramped. 2 *I felt uncomfortable in her presence* **uneasy**, awkward, nervous, tense, edgy, restless, embarrassed, anxious; informal rattled, twitchy.
> ANTONYMS comfortable, relaxed.

□ **uncomfortably** adverb.

uncommon ▸ adjective 1 out of the ordinary; unusual. 2 remarkably great.

> SYNONYMS **unusual**, abnormal, rare, atypical, exceptional, unconventional, unfamiliar, strange, extraordinary, peculiar, scarce, few and far between, isolated, infrequent.
> ANTONYMS common.

□ **uncommonly** adverb.

uncomprehending ▸ adjective unable to understand something.
□ **uncomprehendingly** adverb.

uncompromising ▸ adjective unwilling to compromise.
□ **uncompromisingly** adverb.

unconcern ▸ noun a lack of worry or interest.

□ **unconcerned** adjective.

unconditional ▶ adjective not subject to any conditions.

SYNONYMS **unquestioning,** unqualified, unreserved, unlimited, unrestricted, wholehearted, complete, total, entire, full, absolute, unequivocal.

□ **unconditionally** adverb.

unconfined ▶ adjective **1** not confined to a limited space. **2** (of joy or excitement) very great.

unconscionable /un-kon-shuh-nuh-b'l/ ▶ adjective formal not right or reasonable.
□ **unconscionably** adverb.

unconscious ▶ adjective **1** not awake and aware of your surroundings. **2** done or existing without you realizing. **3** (**unconscious of**) unaware of.

SYNONYMS **1** *she made sure he was unconscious* **knocked out,** senseless, comatose, inert; informal out cold, out for the count. **2** *an unconscious desire* **subconscious,** instinctive, involuntary, uncontrolled, subliminal; informal gut. **3** *blissfully unconscious of these problems* **unaware of,** oblivious to, insensible to, impervious to, unaffected by. ANTONYMS conscious, voluntary, aware.

▶ noun the part of the mind which you are not aware of but which affects behaviour and emotions.
□ **unconsciously** adverb **unconsciousness** noun.

unconstitutional ▶ adjective not allowed by the constitution of a country or the rules of an organization.
□ **unconstitutionally** adverb.

unconstrained ▶ adjective not restricted or limited.

uncontrollable ▶ adjective not able to be controlled.
□ **uncontrollably** adverb.

unconventional ▶ adjective not fitting in with what is generally done or believed.
□ **unconventionally** adverb.

unconvincing ▶ adjective failing to convince or impress.
□ **unconvincingly** adverb.

uncooperative ▶ adjective unwilling to help other people or do what they ask.

uncoordinated ▶ adjective **1** clumsy. **2** badly organized.

uncouth ▶ adjective lacking good manners.

SYNONYMS **uncivilized,** uncultured, rough, coarse, crude, loutish, boorish, rude, discourteous, disrespectful, bad-mannered, ill-bred. ANTONYMS civilized.

uncover ▶ verb (**uncovers, uncovering. uncovered**) **1** remove a cover or covering from. **2** discover something previously secret or unknown.

SYNONYMS **1** *she uncovered the sandwiches* **expose,** reveal, lay bare, unwrap, unveil, strip. **2** *they uncovered a plot* **discover,** detect, come across, stumble on, chance on, find, turn up, unearth, dig up.

unction ▶ noun **1** formal the smearing of someone with oil or ointment as part of a religious ceremony. **2** excessive politeness or flattery.

unctuous ▶ adjective excessively polite or flattering.
□ **unctuously** adverb.

undaunted ▶ adjective not discouraged by difficulty or danger.

undeceive ▶ verb tell someone that an idea or belief is mistaken.

undecided ▶ adjective **1** not having made a decision. **2** not yet settled or resolved.

undemonstrative ▶ adjective not tending to express feelings openly.

undeniable ▶ adjective unable to be denied or disputed.
□ **undeniably** adverb.

under ▶ preposition **1** extending or directly below. **2** at a lower level or grade than. **3** expressing control by another person. **4** in accordance with rules. **5** used to express grouping or classification. **6** undergoing a process.

SYNONYMS **1** *they hid under a bush* **below,** beneath, underneath. **2** *the rent is under £250* **less than,** lower than, below. **3** *branch managers are under the retail director* **subordinate to,** answerable to, responsible to, subject to, junior to, inferior to. ANTONYMS above, over.

▶ adverb extending or directly below something.
■ **under way 1** having started and making progress. **2** (of a boat) moving through the water.

underachieve ▶ verb (**underachieves, underachieving, underachieved**) do less well than is expected.

underarm ▶ adjective & adverb done with the arm or hand below shoulder level.

undercarriage ▶ noun the wheeled structure which supports an aircraft when it is on the ground.

underclass ▶ noun the lowest social class, consisting of very poor and unemployed people.

underclothes ▶ plural noun underwear.

undercoat ▶ noun a layer of paint applied before the top layer.

undercover ▶ adjective & adverb involving secret work for investigation or spying.

SYNONYMS **secret,** covert, clandestine, underground, surreptitious, furtive,

u

cloak-and-dagger, stealthy; informal hush-hush.
ANTONYMS overt.

undercurrent ▸ noun an underlying feeling or influence.

undercut ▸ verb (**undercuts**, **undercutting**, **undercut**) **1** offer products or services at a lower price than a competitor. **2** weaken or undermine.

underdog ▸ noun a competitor thought to have little chance of winning a fight or contest.

underdone ▸ adjective not cooked enough.

underdressed ▸ adjective wearing clothes that are too plain or casual.

underestimate ▸ verb (**underestimates**, **underestimating**, **underestimated**) **1** estimate something to be smaller or less important than it really is. **2** think of someone as less capable than they really are.

> SYNONYMS **underrate**, undervalue, miscalculate, misjudge, do an injustice to.
> ANTONYMS overestimate.

▸ noun an estimate that is too low.
□ **underestimation** noun.

underfoot ▸ adverb **1** on the ground. **2** constantly present and in the way.

undergarment ▸ noun a piece of underwear.

undergo ▸ verb (**undergoes**, **undergoing**, **underwent**; past participle **undergone**) experience something unpleasant or difficult.

> SYNONYMS **experience**, go through, submit to, face, be subjected to, receive, endure, brave, bear, withstand, weather.

undergraduate ▸ noun a student at a university who has not yet taken a first degree.

underground ▸ adjective & adverb **1** beneath the surface of the ground. **2** in secrecy or hiding.

> SYNONYMS **1** *an underground car park* **subterranean**, buried, sunken, basement. **2** *underground organizations* **secret**, clandestine, surreptitious, covert, undercover, closet, cloak-and-dagger, resistance, subversive.

▸ noun **1** Brit. an underground railway. **2** a secret group working against the government or an enemy.

> SYNONYMS **1** *he took the underground* **metro**; N. Amer. **subway**; Brit. informal **tube**. **2** *information from the French underground* **resistance**, partisans, guerrillas, freedom fighters.

undergrowth ▸ noun a mass of shrubs and other plants growing closely together.

underhand ▸ adjective done in a secret or dishonest way.

underlay ▸ noun material laid under a carpet.

underlie ▸ verb (**underlies**, **underlying**, **underlay**; past participle **underlain**) lie or be situated under.

underline ▸ verb (**underlines**, **underlining**, **underlined**) **1** draw a line under. **2** emphasize.

> SYNONYMS **1** *she underlined a phrase* **underscore**, mark, pick out, emphasize, highlight. **2** *the programme underlines the benefits of exercise* **emphasize**, stress, highlight, accentuate, accent, focus on, spotlight.

underling ▸ noun disapproving a person of lower status.

underlying ▸ adjective lying under or beneath the surface.

> SYNONYMS **fundamental**, basic, primary, central, essential, principal, elementary, initial.

undermine ▸ verb (**undermines**, **undermining**, **undermined**) **1** damage or weaken. **2** wear away the base or foundation of.

> SYNONYMS **weaken**, diminish, reduce, impair, mar, spoil, ruin, damage, sap, shake, threaten, subvert, compromise, sabotage.
> ANTONYMS strengthen, support.

underneath ▸ preposition & adverb **1** situated directly below. **2** so as to be concealed by.
▸ noun the part or side facing towards the ground.

underpants ▸ plural noun a piece of underwear covering the lower part of the body and having two holes for the legs.

underpart ▸ noun a lower part.

underpass ▸ noun a road or tunnel passing under another road or a railway.

underpin ▸ verb (**underpins**, **underpinning**, **underpinned**) **1** support or form the basis for an argument, claim, etc. **2** support a structure from below.

underplay ▸ verb represent something as being less important than it really is.

underprivileged ▸ adjective not having the same rights or standard of living as the majority of the population.

underrated ▸ verb rated less highly than is deserved.

underscore ▸ verb underline.

undersea ▸ adjective found or situated below the surface of the sea.

undersecretary ▸ noun (plural **undersecretaries**) (in the UK) a junior minister or senior civil servant.

undersell ▶ verb (**undersells, underselling, undersold**) sell something at a lower price than a competitor.

underside ▶ noun the bottom or lower side or surface of something.

undersigned ▶ noun formal the person or people who have signed the document in question.

undersized (or **undersize**) ▶ adjective of less than the usual size.

understaffed ▶ adjective having too few members of staff.

understand ▶ verb (**understands, understanding, understood**) **1** know or realize the real or intended meaning or cause of. **2** know how someone feels or why they behave in a particular way. **3** interpret or view in a particular way. **4** believe that something is the case because of information that you have received.

> SYNONYMS **1** *he couldn't understand anything we said* **comprehend,** grasp, take in, see, apprehend, follow, make sense of, fathom; informal work out, figure out, make head or tail of, get; Brit. informal twig, suss. **2** *she understood how hard he'd worked* **know,** realize, recognize, acknowledge, appreciate, be aware of, be conscious of. **3** *I understand that you wish to go* **believe,** gather, take it, hear (tell), notice, see, learn.

understandable ▶ adjective **1** able to be understood. **2** natural, reasonable, or forgivable.

> SYNONYMS **1** *make it understandable to the layman* **comprehensible,** intelligible, clear, plain, unambiguous, transparent, straightforward, explicit, coherent. **2** *an understandable desire* **unsurprising,** expected, predictable, inevitable, reasonable, acceptable, logical, rational, normal, natural, justifiable, excusable, pardonable, forgivable.
> ANTONYMS incomprehensible, surprising, illogical, abnormal, unforgivable.

□ **understandably** adverb.

understanding ▶ noun **1** the ability to understand something. **2** a person's intellect. **3** the way in which a person looks at a situation. **4** sympathetic awareness or tolerance. **5** an informal or unspoken agreement or arrangement.

> SYNONYMS **1** *test your understanding of the language* **comprehension,** grasp, mastery, appreciation, knowledge, awareness, skill, expertise, proficiency; informal know-how. **2** *a young man of brilliant understanding* **intellect,** intelligence, brainpower, judgement, insight, intuition, acumen, sagacity, wisdom; informal nous. **3** *it was my*

understanding that this was free **belief,** perception, view, conviction, feeling, opinion, intuition, impression. **4** *he treated me with understanding* **sympathy,** compassion, pity, feeling, concern, consideration, kindness, sensitivity, decency, goodwill. **5** *we had a tacit understanding* **agreement,** arrangement, deal, bargain, settlement, pledge, pact.
> ANTONYMS ignorance, indifference.

▶ adjective sympathetically aware of other people's feelings.

> SYNONYMS *an understanding friend* **sympathetic,** compassionate, sensitive, considerate, kind, thoughtful, tolerant, patient, forbearing, lenient, forgiving.

□ **understandingly** adverb.

understate ▶ verb (**understates, understating, understated**) represent something as being smaller or less significant than it really is.

> SYNONYMS **play down,** underrate, underplay, trivialize, minimize, diminish, downgrade, brush aside, gloss over.
> ANTONYMS exaggerate.

□ **understatement** noun.

understated ▶ adjective pleasingly subtle.

understudy ▶ noun (plural **understudies**) an actor who learns another's role in order to take their place if necessary.
▶ verb (**understudies, understudying, understudied**) be an understudy for.

undertake ▶ verb (**undertake, undertaking, undertook**; past participle **undertaken**) **1** begin an activity. **2** formally guarantee or promise.

> SYNONYMS **1** *we undertook a survey of the site* **set about,** embark on, go about, engage in, take on, be responsible for, get down to, get to grips with, tackle, attempt; informal have a go at. **2** *the Minister undertook to attend* **promise,** pledge, vow, give your word, swear, guarantee, contract, give an assurance, commit yourself.

undertaker ▶ noun a person whose job is preparing dead bodies for burial or cremation and making arrangements for funerals.

> SYNONYMS **funeral director**; N. Amer. mortician.

undertaking ▶ noun **1** a formal promise to do something. **2** a task.

> SYNONYMS **1** *a risky undertaking* **enterprise,** venture, project, campaign, scheme, plan, operation, endeavour, effort, task. **2** *sign this undertaking to comply with the rules* **promise,** pledge,

u

agreement, oath, covenant, vow, commitment, guarantee, assurance.

undertone ▸ noun **1** a subdued or muted tone. **2** an underlying quality or feeling.

undertow ▸ noun a current under the surface of water.

underused ▸ adjective not used as much as it could or should be.
□ **underuse** noun.

underwater ▸ adjective & adverb situated, happening, or used beneath the surface of the water.

> synonyms **submerged,** sunken, undersea, submarine.

underwear ▸ noun clothing worn under other clothes next to the skin.

> synonyms **underclothes,** undergarments, underthings, lingerie; informal **undies;** Brit. informal smalls.

underweight ▸ adjective below a normal or desirable weight.

underwent past of **UNDERGO.**

underwhelmed ▸ verb humorous not very impressed.

underworld ▸ noun **1** the world of criminals or of organized crime. **2** (in myths and legends) the home of the dead, imagined as being under the earth.

underwrite ▸ verb (**underwrites, underwriting, underwrote;** past participle **underwritten) 1** accept legal responsibility for an insurance policy. **2** accept financial responsibility for an undertaking.

> synonyms **sponsor,** support, back, insure, indemnify, subsidize, pay for, finance, fund; N. Amer. informal bankroll.

□ **underwriter** noun.

undesirable ▸ adjective harmful, offensive, or unpleasant.

> synonyms **unpleasant,** disagreeable, nasty, unwelcome, unwanted, unfortunate.
> antonyms pleasant.

▸ noun an unpleasant or offensive person.

undeterred ▸ adjective persevering despite setbacks.

undeviating ▸ adjective constant and steady.

undies ▸ plural noun informal pieces of underwear.

undisputed ▸ adjective not disputed or called into question.

undistinguished ▸ adjective not particularly good or successful.

undivided ▸ adjective **1** not divided or broken into parts. **2** complete; total: *my undivided attention.*

undo ▸ verb (**undoes, undoing, undid;** past

participle **undone) 1** unfasten or loosen. **2** reverse the effects of something previously done. **3** formal cause the downfall or ruin of.

> synonyms **1** *he undid his shirt* **unfasten,** unbutton, unhook, untie, unlace, unlock, unbolt, loosen, detach, free, open. **2** *they will undo a decision by the lords* **cancel,** reverse, overrule, overturn, repeal, rescind, countermand, revoke, annul, invalidate, negate. **3** *she undid much of the good work* **ruin,** undermine, overturn, scotch, sabotage, spoil, impair, mar, destroy, wreck; informal blow; Brit. informal scupper.
> antonyms fasten, ratify, enhance.

undoing ▸ noun formal a person's ruin or downfall.

undoubted ▸ adjective not questioned or doubted.

undoubtedly ▸ adverb without or beyond any doubt.

> synonyms **doubtless,** indubitably, unquestionably, indisputably, undeniably, incontrovertibly, without (a) doubt, clearly.

undreamed (or Brit. **undreamt**) ▸ adjective (**undreamed of**) not previously thought to be possible.

undress ▸ verb **1** (also **get undressed**) take off your clothes. **2** take the clothes off someone else.
▸ noun formal the state of being naked or only partially clothed.

undue ▸ adjective more than is reasonable or necessary.
□ **unduly** adverb.

undulate ▸ verb (**undulates, undulating, undulated) 1** move with a smooth wave-like motion. **2** have a wavy form or outline.
□ **undulation** noun.

undying ▸ adjective lasting forever.

unearth ▸ verb **1** find in the ground by digging. **2** discover by investigation or searching.

> synonyms **1** *workmen unearthed an artillery shell* **dig up,** excavate, exhume, disinter, root out. **2** *I unearthed an interesting fact* **discover,** uncover, find, come across, hit on, bring to light, expose, turn up.

unearthly ▸ adjective **1** unnatural or mysterious. **2** informal very early and therefore inconvenient or annoying.

unease ▸ noun anxiety or discontent.

uneasy ▸ adjective (**uneasier, uneasiest**) anxious or uncomfortable.

> synonyms **1** *the doctor made him feel uneasy* **worried,** anxious, troubled, disturbed, nervous, nervy, tense, edgy,

apprehensive, fearful, uncomfortable, unsettled; informal jittery. **2** *an uneasy peace* **tense,** awkward, strained, fraught, precarious, unstable, insecure.
ANTONYMS calm, stable.

□ **uneasily** adverb **uneasiness** noun.

unedifying ▸ adjective distasteful or unpleasant.

unemployable ▸ adjective not having enough skills or qualifications to get paid employment.

unemployed ▸ adjective without a paid job but available to work.

SYNONYMS **jobless,** out of work, unwaged, redundant, laid off, on benefit; Brit. signing on; N. Amer. on welfare; Brit. informal on the dole, resting.

unemployment ▸ noun **1** the state of being unemployed. **2** the number or proportion of unemployed people.

unencumbered ▸ adjective not burdened or held back.

unending ▸ adjective seeming to last forever.

unenviable ▸ adjective difficult, undesirable, or unpleasant.

unequal ▸ adjective **1** not equal. **2** not fair or even. **3** (**unequal to**) not having the ability to meet a challenge.
□ **unequally** adverb.

unequalled (US spelling **unequaled**) ▸ adjective better or greater than all others.

unequivocal ▸ adjective leaving no doubt; unambiguous.
□ **unequivocally** adverb.

unerring ▸ adjective always right or accurate.
□ **unerringly** adverb.

uneven ▸ adjective **1** not level or smooth. **2** not regular or equal.

SYNONYMS **1** *uneven ground* **bumpy,** rough, lumpy, stony, rocky, rutted. **2** *uneven teeth* **irregular,** crooked, lopsided, askew, asymmetrical. **3** *uneven quality* **inconsistent,** variable, fluctuating, irregular, erratic, patchy.
ANTONYMS flat, regular.

□ **unevenly** adverb **unevenness** noun.

uneventful ▸ adjective not marked by interesting or exciting events.
□ **uneventfully** adverb.

unexceptionable ▸ adjective not able to be objected to, but not particularly new or exciting.

unexceptional ▸ adjective not out of the ordinary; usual.
□ **unexceptionally** adverb.

unexpected ▸ adjective not expected or thought likely to happen.
□ **unexpectedly** adverb.

unexpurgated ▸ adjective (of a written work) complete and containing all the original material.

unfailing ▸ adjective reliable or never changing.
□ **unfailingly** adverb.

unfair ▸ adjective not fair or just.

SYNONYMS **1** *the trial was unfair* **unjust,** prejudiced, biased, discriminatory, one-sided, unequal, uneven, unbalanced, partisan. **2** *his comments were unfair* **undeserved,** unmerited, unreasonable, unjustified; Brit. informal out of order. **3** *unfair play* **unsporting,** dirty, underhand, dishonourable, dishonest.
ANTONYMS fair, just, justified.

□ **unfairly** adverb **unfairness** noun.

unfaithful ▸ adjective **1** having sex with someone who is not your husband, wife, or usual partner. **2** disloyal.

unfasten ▸ verb open the fastening of something.

SYNONYMS **undo,** open, disconnect, remove, untie, unbutton, unzip, loosen, free, unlock, unbolt.

unfathomable ▸ adjective incapable of being fully understood.

unfavourable (US spelling **unfavorable**) ▸ adjective **1** not approving. **2** not good or likely to lead to success.
□ **unfavourably** adverb.

unfazed ▸ adjective informal not worried or confused by something unexpected.

unfeasible ▸ adjective not able to be done or achieved.
□ **unfeasibly** adverb.

unfit ▸ adjective **1** unsuitable. **2** not in good physical condition.

SYNONYMS **1** *the film is unfit for children* **unsuitable,** inappropriate, not designed. **2** *unfit for duty* **incapable of,** not up to, not equal to, unequipped, inadequate; informal not cut out for. **3** *I am unfit* **unhealthy,** out of condition/shape.
ANTONYMS fit, suitable, capable, healthy.

unflagging ▸ adjective not becoming weak or tired.

unflappable ▸ adjective informal calm in a crisis.

unflinching ▸ adjective not afraid or hesitant.
□ **unflinchingly** adverb.

unfold ▸ verb **1** open or spread out from a folded position. **2** reveal or be revealed.

SYNONYMS **1** *May unfolded the map* **open out,** spread out, flatten, straighten out, unroll. **2** *I watched the events unfold* **develop,** evolve, happen, take place, occur.
ANTONYMS fold up.

u

unforeseen ▸ adjective not anticipated or predicted; unexpected.
□ **unforeseeable** adjective.

✔ Remember the **e** before the **s**: unfor**e**seen.

unforgettable ▸ adjective very memorable.
□ **unforgettably** adverb.

unforgivable ▸ adjective so bad as to be unable to be forgiven.
□ **unforgivably** adverb.

unforgiving ▸ adjective **1** not willing to forgive. **2** (of conditions) harsh.

unforthcoming ▸ adjective **1** not willing to give out information. **2** not available when needed.

unfortunate ▸ adjective **1** unlucky.
2 regrettable or inappropriate.

SYNONYMS **1** *unfortunate people* **unlucky,** hapless, wretched, forlorn, poor, pitiful; informal down on your luck. **2** *an unfortunate start to our holiday* **unwelcome,** disadvantageous, unfavourable, unlucky, adverse, unpromising, inauspicious. **3** *an unfortunate remark* **regrettable,** inappropriate, unsuitable, tactless, injudicious.
ANTONYMS fortunate, lucky, auspicious, well-chosen.

▸ noun a person who suffers bad luck.
□ **unfortunately** adverb.

unfounded ▸ adjective having no basis in fact.

unfurl ▸ verb open something that is rolled or folded.

ungainly ▸ adjective clumsy; awkward.

SYNONYMS **awkward,** clumsy, graceless, inelegant, gawky, gauche, uncoordinated.
ANTONYMS graceful.

□ **ungainliness** noun.

ungodly ▸ adjective **1** immoral or disrespectful to God. **2** informal very early or late, and therefore annoying.

ungovernable ▸ adjective impossible to control or govern.

ungrateful ▸ adjective not grateful.
□ **ungratefully** adverb.

unguarded ▸ adjective **1** without protection. **2** not well considered; careless: *an unguarded remark*.

unguent /ung-yuu-uhnt/ ▸ noun a soft greasy or thick substance used as ointment or for lubrication.

ungulate ▸ noun the name in zoology for a hoofed mammal.

unhappy ▸ adjective (unhappier, unhappiest) **1** not happy. **2** unfortunate.

SYNONYMS **1** *why are you looking so unhappy?* **sad,** miserable, sorrowful, dejected, despondent, disconsolate, morose, heartbroken, down, dispirited, downhearted, depressed, melancholy, mournful, gloomy, glum; informal down in the mouth, fed up, blue. **2** *I was unhappy with the service* **dissatisfied,** displeased, discontented, disappointed, disgruntled. **3** *an unhappy coincidence* **unfortunate,** unlucky, ill-starred, ill-fated, doomed; informal jinxed.
ANTONYMS happy, pleased, cheerful, lucky.

□ **unhappily** adverb **unhappiness** noun.

unharmed ▸ adjective not harmed.

unhealthy ▸ adjective (unhealthier, unhealthiest) **1** not having good health. **2** not good for your health.

SYNONYMS **1** *an unhealthy lifestyle* **harmful,** detrimental, destructive, injurious, damaging, noxious, poisonous. **2** *he's pretty unhealthy* **sick,** poorly, ill, unwell, unfit, ailing, weak, frail, infirm, washed out, run down. **3** *an unhealthy obsession* **abnormal,** morbid, macabre, twisted, unwholesome, warped, depraved, unnatural; informal sick.

□ **unhealthily** adverb.

unheard ▸ adjective **1** not heard or listened to. **2** (unheard of) previously unknown.

unhelpful ▸ adjective not helpful.
□ **unhelpfully** adverb.

unheralded ▸ adjective not previously announced, expected, or recognized.

unhesitating ▸ adjective without doubt or hesitation.
□ **unhesitatingly** adverb.

unhinged ▸ adjective mentally ill or unbalanced.

unholy ▸ adjective **1** sinful; wicked.
2 unnatural and likely to be harmful.
3 informal dreadful.

unhurried ▸ adjective moving or doing things in a leisurely way.
□ **unhurriedly** adverb.

unhurt ▸ adjective not hurt or harmed.

unicameral ▸ adjective (of a parliament) consisting of only one main part.

unicorn ▸ noun (in stories) a creature like a horse with a single long horn on its forehead.

unicycle ▸ noun a cycle with a single wheel.
□ **unicyclist** noun.

unidentified ▸ adjective not recognized or identified.

unification ▸ noun the process of uniting or of being united.

uniform ▸ noun the distinctive clothing worn by members of the same organization or school.

SYNONYMS *a soldier in uniform* **costume,** outfit, suit, ensemble, livery, regalia; *informal* get-up, rig, gear.

▶ **adjective** not varying; the same in all cases and at all times.

SYNONYMS **1** *a uniform temperature* **constant,** consistent, steady, invariable, unchanging, stable, static, regular, fixed, even. **2** *pieces of uniform size* **identical,** matching, similar, equal, same, like, consistent.
ANTONYMS variable.

□ **uniformed** adjective **uniformity** noun **uniformly** adverb.

unify ▶ **verb** (**unifies, unifying, unified**) make or become united.

SYNONYMS **unite,** combine, bring together, join, merge, fuse, amalgamate, coalesce, consolidate.
ANTONYMS separate.

unilateral ▶ **adjective** done by or affecting only one person or group.
□ **unilaterally** adverb.

unimaginable ▶ **adjective** impossible to imagine or understand.
□ **unimaginably** adverb.

unimaginative ▶ **adjective** not using or showing imagination or new ideas; dull.
□ **unimaginatively** adverb.

unimpeachable ▶ **adjective** not able to be doubted or criticized.

unimportant ▶ **adjective** not important.
□ **unimportance** noun.

uninhabited ▶ **adjective** having no people living there.
□ **uninhabitable** adjective.

uninhibited ▶ **adjective** saying or doing things without concern about what other people think.

uninitiated ▶ **adjective** without knowledge or experience of something.

uninspired ▶ **adjective** **1** not original or exciting; dull. **2** feeling no excitement.
□ **uninspiring** adjective.

unintelligible ▶ **adjective** impossible to understand.
□ **unintelligibility** noun **unintelligibly** adverb.

unintentional ▶ **adjective** not done on purpose.
□ **unintentionally** adverb.

uninterested ▶ **adjective** not interested or concerned.

SYNONYMS **indifferent,** unconcerned, uninvolved, apathetic.

❗ Don't confuse **uninterested** and **disinterested**. **Disinterested** means 'impartial', while **uninterested** means 'not interested'.

uninteresting ▶ **adjective** not interesting.

SYNONYMS **boring,** dull, unexciting, tiresome, tedious, dreary, lifeless, humdrum, colourless, bland, insipid, banal, dry.
ANTONYMS interesting, exciting.

uninterrupted ▶ **adjective** not interrupted; continuous.

union ▶ **noun** **1** the act of uniting two or more things. **2** a trade union. **3** a club, society, or association. **4** (also **Union**) a political unit consisting of a number of states or provinces with the same central government. **5** a state of harmony or agreement. **6** a marriage.

SYNONYMS **1** *the union of art and nature* **unification,** joining, merger, fusion, amalgamation, coalition, combination, synthesis, blend. **2** *a trade union* **association,** league, guild, confederation, federation.
ANTONYMS separation, parting.

■ **Union Jack** (or **Union Flag**) the national flag of the United Kingdom.

unionist ▶ **noun** **1** a member of a trade union. **2** (**Unionist**) a person in favour of the union of Northern Ireland with Great Britain.

unionize (or **unionise**) ▶ **verb** (**unionizes, unionizing, unionized**) make or become members of a trade union.
□ **unionization** noun.

unique ▶ **adjective** **1** being the only one of its kind. **2** (**unique to**) belonging or connected to one particular person, group, or place. **3** very special or unusual.

SYNONYMS **1** *each town has its unique quality* **distinctive,** individual, special, particular, specific, idiosyncratic, single, sole, lone, unrepeated, solitary, exclusive; *informal* one-off. **2** *a unique insight into history* **remarkable,** special, notable, unequalled, unparalleled, unmatched, unsurpassed, incomparable.
ANTONYMS common.

□ **uniquely** adverb.

unisex ▶ **adjective** designed to be suitable for both sexes.

unison ▶ **noun** (**in unison**) at the same time; together.

unit ▶ **noun** **1** a single thing or group that is complete in itself but can also form part of something larger. **2** a device, part, or item of furniture with a particular function: *a sink unit.* **3** a self-contained section of a building or group of buildings. **4** a subdivision of a larger military grouping. **5** a quantity used as a standard measure.

SYNONYMS **1** *the family is the fundamental unit of society* **component,** element, constituent, subdivision. **2** *a unit* of currency **quantity,** measure, denomination. **3** *a guerrilla unit* **group,** detachment, contingent, division, cell, faction, department, office, branch.

■ **unit trust** Brit. a company that invests money in various different businesses on behalf of individuals, who can buy small units.

Unitarian ▸ noun a member of a Christian Church that believes that God is one being and rejects the idea of the Trinity.

unitary ▸ adjective **1** forming a single unit or entity. **2** relating to a unit or units.

unite ▸ verb (**unites, uniting, united**) **1** join together with others in order to do something as a group. **2** bring people or things together to form a unit or whole.

> SYNONYMS **1** *uniting the nation* **unify,** join, link, connect, combine, amalgamate, fuse, weld, bond, bring together. **2** *environmentalists and activists united* **join together,** join forces, combine, band together, ally, cooperate, collaborate, work together, team up. **3** *he sought to unite comfort with elegance* **merge,** mix, blend, mingle, combine.
> ANTONYMS divide.

□ **united** adjective.

unity ▸ noun (plural **unities**) **1** the state of being united or forming a whole. **2** a thing forming a complex whole. **3** Maths the number one.

> SYNONYMS **1** *European unity* **union,** unification, integration, amalgamation, coalition, federation, confederation. **2** *unity between opposing factions* **harmony,** accord, cooperation, collaboration, agreement, consensus, solidarity. **3** *the organic unity of the universe* **oneness,** singleness, wholeness, uniformity, homogeneity.
> ANTONYMS division, discord.

universal ▸ adjective **1** affecting or done by all people or things in the world or in a particular group. **2** true or right in all cases.

> SYNONYMS **general,** common, widespread, ubiquitous, comprehensive, global, worldwide, international.

□ **universality** noun.

universally ▸ adverb in every case; by everyone.

> SYNONYMS **always,** without exception, by everyone, in all cases, everywhere, worldwide, globally, internationally, commonly, generally.

universe ▸ noun the whole of space and everything in it.

> SYNONYMS **cosmos,** macrocosm, space, infinity, nature, all existence.

university ▸ noun (plural **universities**) an institution where students study for a degree, and where academic research is done.

unjust ▸ adjective not just; unfair.
□ **unjustly** adverb.

unjustifiable ▸ adjective impossible to justify.
□ **unjustifiably** adverb.

unjustified ▸ adjective not justified; unfair.

unkempt ▸ adjective having an untidy appearance.

unkind ▸ adjective not caring or kind.

> SYNONYMS **1** *everyone was being unkind to him* **unpleasant,** disagreeable, nasty, mean, cruel, vicious, spiteful, malicious, callous, unsympathetic; informal bitchy. **2** *unkind weather* **inclement,** intemperate, rough, severe, filthy.

□ **unkindly** adverb **unkindness** noun.

unknowing ▸ adjective not knowing or aware.
□ **unknowingly** adverb.

unknown ▸ adjective not known or familiar.

> SYNONYMS **1** *the outcome was unknown* **undisclosed,** unrevealed, secret, undetermined, undecided. **2** *unknown country* **unexplored,** uncharted, unmapped, undiscovered. **3** *persons unknown* **unidentified,** unnamed, anonymous. **4** *firearms were unknown to the Indians* **unfamiliar,** unheard of, new, novel, strange. **5** *unknown artists* **obscure,** unheard of, unsung, minor, undistinguished.
> ANTONYMS known, familiar.

▸ noun an unknown person or thing.
■ **unknown quantity** a person or thing that is not known about and whose actions or effects are unpredictable. **Unknown Soldier** an unidentified member of a country's armed forces killed in war, buried in a national memorial to represent all those killed but unidentified.

unladylike ▸ adjective not typical of a well-mannered woman or girl.

unlawful ▸ adjective not obeying or allowed by law or rules.
□ **unlawfully** adverb.

unleaded ▸ adjective (of petrol) without added lead.

unleash ▸ verb release something from a leash or restraint; set free.

unleavened ▸ adjective (of bread) flat because made without yeast.

unless ▸ conjunction except when; if not.

unlike ▸ preposition **1** different from; not like. **2** in contrast to. **3** not characteristic of.

SYNONYMS **1** *England is totally unlike Jamaica* **different from,** dissimilar to. **2** *unlike Lyn, Chris was a bit of a radical* **in contrast to,** as opposed to.
ANTONYMS similar to.

▶ adjective different from each other.

unlikely ▶ adjective (unlikelier, unlikeliest) **1** not likely to happen. **2** not what you would expect.

SYNONYMS **improbable,** doubtful, dubious, questionable, unconvincing, implausible, far-fetched, unrealistic, incredible, unbelievable, inconceivable.
ANTONYMS probable, believable.

□ **unlikelihood** noun.

unlimited ▶ adjective not limited or restricted.

unload ▶ verb remove goods from a vehicle, ship, aircraft, or container.

SYNONYMS **1** *we unloaded the van* **unpack,** empty. **2** *they unloaded the cases from the lorry* **remove,** offload, discharge, dump.
ANTONYMS load.

unlock ▶ verb undo the lock of a door, container, etc. using a key.

unlooked ▶ adjective (unlooked for) not planned or expected.

unloose (or unloosen) ▶ verb (unlooses, unloosing, unloosed) release something.

unlucky ▶ adjective (unluckier, unluckiest) having, bringing, or resulting from bad luck.

SYNONYMS **1** *the unlucky victim* **unfortunate,** hapless, ill-fated. **2** *an unlucky number* **unfavourable,** inauspicious, unpropitious, ominous, jinxed.
ANTONYMS fortunate, favourable.

□ **unluckily** adverb.

unmade ▶ adjective Brit. (of a road) without a hard, smooth surface.

unmanageable ▶ adjective difficult or impossible to manage or control.

unmanned ▶ adjective not having or needing a crew or staff.

unmarked ▶ adjective **1** not marked. **2** not noticed.

unmarried ▶ adjective not married.

unmask ▶ verb reveal the true character of.

unmatched ▶ adjective not matched or equalled.

unmentionable ▶ adjective too embarrassing or shocking to be spoken about.

unmerciful ▶ adjective showing no mercy.
□ **unmercifully** adverb.

unmetalled ▶ adjective Brit. (of a road) not having a hard surface.

unmindful ▶ adjective (unmindful of) not

conscious or aware of.

unmissable ▶ adjective that should not or cannot be missed.

unmistakable (or unmistakeable) ▶ adjective not able to be mistaken for anything else.
□ **unmistakably** adverb.

unmitigated ▶ adjective complete: *an unmitigated disaster.*

unmoved ▶ adjective not affected by emotion or excitement.

unnameable ▶ adjective too bad or frightening to mention.

unnatural ▶ adjective **1** different from what is found in nature or what is normal in society. **2** not spontaneous.

SYNONYMS **1** *the life of a battery hen is completely unnatural* **abnormal,** unusual, uncommon, extraordinary, strange, unorthodox, exceptional, irregular, untypical. **2** *an unnatural colour* **artificial,** man-made, synthetic, manufactured. **3** *her voice sounded unnatural* **affected,** artificial, stilted, forced, false, fake, insincere; informal put on, phoney.
ANTONYMS normal, genuine.

□ **unnaturally** adverb.

unnecessary ▶ adjective not necessary, or more than is necessary.

SYNONYMS **unneeded,** inessential, not required, uncalled for, unwarranted, dispensable, optional, extraneous, expendable, redundant.
ANTONYMS necessary.

□ **unnecessarily** adverb.

unnerve ▶ verb (unnerves, unnerving, unnerved) make someone feel fearful or lacking in confidence.

unnoticeable ▶ adjective not easily seen or noticed.

unnoticed ▶ adjective not being or having been seen or noticed.

unobtainable ▶ adjective not able to be obtained.

unobtrusive ▶ adjective not conspicuous or attracting attention.
□ **unobtrusively** adverb.

unofficial ▶ adjective not officially authorized or confirmed.
□ **unofficially** adverb.

unopposed ▶ adjective not opposed or challenged.

unorthodox ▶ adjective different from what is usual, traditional, or accepted.

unpack ▶ verb take things out of a suitcase, bag, or package.

unpaid ▶ adjective **1** (of a debt) not yet paid. **2** done without payment. **3** not receiving payment for work done.

u

unpalatable ▸ adjective 1 not pleasant to taste. 2 difficult to accept.

unparalleled ▸ adjective having no equal; exceptional.

unpardonable ▸ adjective (of a fault or offence) unforgivable.
□ **unpardonably** adverb.

unperturbed ▸ adjective not concerned or worried about something.

unpick ▸ verb 1 undo the sewing of stitches or a garment. 2 carefully analyse the different elements of something.

unpleasant ▸ adjective 1 not pleasant or comfortable. 2 not friendly or kind.

SYNONYMS 1 *a very unpleasant situation* **disagreeable,** irksome, distressing, nasty, horrible, terrible, awful, dreadful, invidious, objectionable. 2 *an unpleasant man* **unlikeable,** unlovable, disagreeable, unfriendly, rude, impolite, obnoxious, nasty, spiteful, mean, insufferable, objectionable, unbearable, annoying, irritating. 3 *an unpleasant taste* **unappetizing,** unpalatable, unsavoury, unappealing, disgusting, revolting, nauseating, sickening.
ANTONYMS agreeable, likeable.

□ **unpleasantly** adverb **unpleasantness** noun.

unplug ▸ verb (unplugs, unplugging, unplugged) disconnect an electrical device from a socket.

unpopular ▸ adjective not liked or popular.

SYNONYMS **disliked,** friendless, unloved, unwelcome, avoided, ignored, rejected, shunned, out of favour.

□ **unpopularity** noun.

unprecedented ▸ adjective never done or known before.

unpredictable ▸ adjective not able to be predicted; changeable.
□ **unpredictability** noun **unpredictably** adverb.

unprejudiced ▸ adjective without prejudice; unbiased.

unpremeditated ▸ adjective not planned beforehand.

unprepared ▸ adjective not ready or able to deal with something.

unprepossessing ▸ adjective not attractive or interesting.

unprincipled ▸ adjective without moral principles.

unprintable ▸ adjective (of words or comments) too rude or offensive to be published.

unproductive ▸ adjective 1 not able to produce the required quantity of goods or crops. 2 not achieving much; not very useful.

unprofessional ▸ adjective not in accordance with professional standards or behaviour.
□ **unprofessionally** adverb.

unprofitable ▸ adjective 1 not making a profit. 2 not helpful or useful.

unprompted ▸ adjective without being prompted; spontaneous.

unpronounceable ▸ adjective too difficult to pronounce.

unproven (or unproved) ▸ adjective not proved or tested.

unprovoked ▸ adjective (of an attack or crime) not directly provoked.

unqualified ▸ adjective 1 not having the necessary qualifications or requirements. 2 complete.

unquantifiable ▸ adjective impossible to express or measure in terms of quantity.

unquestionable ▸ adjective not able to be denied or doubted.
□ **unquestionably** adverb.

unquestioned ▸ adjective not denied or doubted.

unravel ▸ verb (unravels, unravelling, unravelled; US spelling unravels, unraveling, unraveled) 1 undo twisted, knitted, or woven threads. 2 (of threads) become undone. 3 solve a mystery or puzzle.

SYNONYMS 1 *he unravelled the strands* **untangle,** disentangle, separate out, unwind, untwist. 2 *detectives are trying to unravel the mystery* **solve,** resolve, clear up, puzzle out, get to the bottom of, explain, clarify; informal figure out.
ANTONYMS entangle.

unreadable ▸ adjective 1 not clear enough to read. 2 too dull or difficult to be worth reading.

unreal ▸ adjective 1 strange and not seeming real. 2 not related to reality; unrealistic.

SYNONYMS **imaginary,** fictitious, pretend, make-believe, made-up, dreamed-up, mock, false, illusory, mythical, fanciful, hypothetical, theoretical; informal phoney.
ANTONYMS real.

□ **unreality** noun.

unrealistic ▸ adjective 1 not showing things in a way that is accurate and true to life. 2 not having a sensible understanding of what can be achieved.
□ **unrealistically** adverb.

unreasonable ▸ adjective 1 not based on good sense. 2 beyond what is achievable or acceptable.
□ **unreasonably** adverb.

unrecognizable (or unrecognisable) ▸ adjective not able to be recognized.

unrelenting ▸ adjective 1 not stopping or becoming less severe. 2 not giving in to requests.
□ **unrelentingly** adverb.

unreliable ▸ adjective not able to be relied on.
◻ **unreliability** noun **unreliably** adverb.

unrelieved ▸ adjective lacking variation or change.

unremarkable ▸ adjective not particularly interesting or surprising.

unremitting ▸ adjective never stopping or easing.

unrepeatable ▸ adjective **1** not able to be repeated. **2** too offensive or shocking to be said again.

unrepentant ▸ adjective showing no shame or regret for your actions.

unrequited ▸ adjective (of love) not given in return.

unreserved ▸ adjective **1** without any doubts or reservations. **2** not set apart or booked in advance.
◻ **unreservedly** adverb.

unrest ▸ noun **1** a situation in which people are feeling discontented and rebellious. **2** a state of uneasiness.

SYNONYMS **disturbance,** trouble, turmoil, disruption, disorder, chaos, anarchy, dissatisfaction, dissent, strife, agitation, protest, rebellion, uprising, rioting. ANTONYMS peace, contentment.

unrivalled (US spelling unrivaled)
▸ adjective greater or better than all others.

unroll ▸ verb open out something that is rolled up.

unruffled ▸ adjective calm and undisturbed.

unruly ▸ adjective (unrulier, unruliest) difficult to control; disorderly.
◻ **unruliness** noun.

unsafe ▸ adjective **1** not safe; dangerous. **2** (of a decision in a court of law) not based on good evidence.

SYNONYMS **1** the building was unsafe **dangerous,** risky, hazardous, high-risk, treacherous, insecure, unsound, harmful, injurious, toxic. **2** the verdict was unsafe **unreliable,** insecure, unsound, questionable, doubtful, dubious, suspect; informal iffy; Brit. informal dodgy. ANTONYMS safe, harmless, secure.

unsatisfactory ▸ adjective not good enough.

SYNONYMS **disappointing,** displeasing, inadequate, unacceptable, poor, bad, substandard, weak, mediocre, not up to par, defective, deficient; informal leaving a lot to be desired.

◻ **unsatisfactorily** adverb.

unsaturated ▸ adjective Chemistry (of fats) having double or triple bonds between carbon atoms in their molecules and therefore being more easily processed by the body.

unsavoury (US spelling unsavory)
▸ adjective **1** unpleasant to taste, smell, or look at. **2** not respectable.

unscathed ▸ adjective without suffering any injury, damage, or harm.

unschooled ▸ adjective lacking schooling or training.

unscientific ▸ adjective not using proper scientific methods.
◻ **unscientifically** adverb.

unscrew ▸ verb unfasten something by twisting it or undoing screws.

unscrupulous ▸ adjective without moral principles; dishonest or unfair.

SYNONYMS **dishonest,** deceitful, devious, underhand, unethical, immoral, shameless, exploitative, corrupt, unprincipled, dishonourable, disreputable; informal crooked, shady.

◻ **unscrupulously** adverb.

unseasonable ▸ adjective (of weather) unusual for the time of year.
◻ **unseasonably** adverb.

unseasonal ▸ adjective unusual or inappropriate for the time of year.

unseat ▸ verb **1** make someone fall from a saddle or seat. **2** remove someone from a position of power.

unseeing ▸ adjective having your eyes open but not noticing anything.

unseemly ▸ adjective (of behaviour or actions) not proper or appropriate.

unseen ▸ adjective **1** not seen or noticed. **2** (of a passage for translation in an exam) not previously read or prepared.

unselfconscious ▸ adjective not self-conscious; not shy or embarrassed.
◻ **unselfconsciously** adverb.

unselfish ▸ adjective putting other people's needs before your own.
◻ **unselfishly** adverb.

unserviceable ▸ adjective not in working order; unfit for use.

unsettle ▸ verb (unsettles, unsettling, unsettled) make someone anxious or uneasy.

SYNONYMS **disturb,** disconcert, unnerve, upset, disquiet, perturb, alarm, dismay, trouble, bother, agitate, fluster, ruffle, shake (up), throw; informal rattle, faze.

unsettled ▸ adjective **1** frequently changing, or likely to change. **2** anxious or uneasy. **3** not yet resolved.

unshakeable (or unshakable) ▸ adjective (of a belief or feeling) firm and unable to be changed.

unshaven ▸ adjective not having shaved.

unsightly ▸ adjective unpleasant to look at; ugly.

u

SYNONYMS **unattractive,** ugly, unprepossessing, hideous, horrible, repulsive, revolting, offensive, grotesque.
ANTONYMS attractive.

unskilled ▶ adjective not having or needing special skill or training.

unsociable ▶ adjective not enjoying the company of other people.

SYNONYMS **unfriendly,** uncongenial, unneighbourly, unapproachable, introverted, reserved, withdrawn, retiring, aloof, distant, remote, detached; informal stand-offish.
ANTONYMS sociable, friendly.

unsocial ▶ adjective (of hours of work) not falling within the normal working day.

unsolicited ▶ adjective not asked for.

unsophisticated ▶ adjective 1 not having much experience in matters of culture or fashion. 2 not complicated or highly developed; basic.

unsound ▶ adjective 1 not safe or strong; in bad condition. 2 not based on reliable evidence or reasoning.

unsparing ▶ adjective 1 very severe or harsh. 2 giving generously.

unspeakable ▶ adjective too bad or horrific to express in words.
□ **unspeakably** adverb.

unspoilt (or **unspoiled**) ▶ adjective (of a place) beautiful because it has not been changed or built on.

unstable ▶ adjective 1 likely to fall or collapse. 2 likely to change; unsettled. 3 tending to experience mental health problems or sudden changes of mood.

SYNONYMS 1 *icebergs are notoriously unstable* **unsteady,** rocky, wobbly, rickety, shaky, unsafe, insecure, precarious. 2 *unstable coffee prices* **changeable,** volatile, variable, fluctuating, irregular, unpredictable, erratic. 3 *he was mentally unstable* **unbalanced,** of unsound mind, mentally ill, deranged, demented, disturbed, unhinged.
ANTONYMS stable, steady, firm.

unsteady ▶ adjective 1 liable to fall or shake; not firm. 2 not uniform or even.
□ **unsteadily** adverb.

unstick ▶ verb (**unsticks, unsticking, unstuck**) separate things that have been stuck together.
■ **come unstick** informal fail.

unstinting ▶ adjective given or giving freely or generously.

unsuccessful ▶ adjective not successful.

SYNONYMS 1 *an unsuccessful attempt* **failed,** abortive, ineffective, fruitless, profitless, unproductive, vain, futile. 2 *an unsuccessful business* **unprofitable,** loss-making. 3 *an unsuccessful candidate* **failed,** losing, beaten, unlucky.
□ **unsuccessfully** adverb.

unsuitable ▶ adjective not right or appropriate for a particular purpose or occasion.

SYNONYMS 1 *an unsuitable product* **inappropriate,** ill-suited, inapposite, unacceptable, unfitting, incompatible, out of place, out of keeping. 2 *an unsuitable moment* **inopportune,** badly timed, unfortunate, difficult, infelicitous.
ANTONYMS appropriate, opportune.

□ **unsuitability** noun **unsuitably** adverb.

unsung ▶ adjective not celebrated or praised.

unsure ▶ adjective having doubts about something; not certain.

SYNONYMS 1 *she felt very unsure* **unconfident,** unassertive, insecure, hesitant, diffident, anxious, apprehensive. 2 *Sally was unsure what to do* **undecided,** uncertain, irresolute, dithering, in two minds, in a quandary. 3 *some teachers are unsure about the proposed strike* **dubious,** doubtful, sceptical, uncertain, unconvinced.
ANTONYMS confident.

unsurpassed ▶ adjective better or greater than any other.

unsurprising ▶ adjective expected and so not causing surprise.
□ **unsurprisingly** adverb.

unsuspecting ▶ adjective not aware of the presence of danger.

unsustainable ▶ adjective 1 not able to be maintained at the current level. 2 upsetting the ecological balance by using up natural resources.

unswerving ▶ adjective not changing or becoming weaker.

unsympathetic ▶ adjective 1 not sympathetic. 2 not showing approval of an idea or action. 3 not likeable.
□ **unsympathetically** adverb.

unsystematic ▶ adjective not done or acting according to a fixed plan.
□ **unsystematically** adverb.

untangle ▶ verb undo something that has become twisted or tangled.

SYNONYMS **disentangle,** unravel, unsnarl, straighten out, untwist, unknot, sort out.
ANTONYMS tangle.

untapped ▶ adjective (of a resource) available but not yet used.

untenable ▶ adjective (of a theory or view)

u

not able to be defended against criticism or attack.

unthinkable ▸ adjective too unlikely or unpleasant to be considered a possibility.

SYNONYMS **unimaginable,** inconceivable, unbelievable, incredible, implausible, out of the question, impossible, unconscionable, unreasonable.

unthinking ▸ adjective not thinking about the effects of what you do or say.
□ **unthinkingly** adverb.

untidy ▸ adjective (**untidier, untidiest**) **1** not arranged tidily. **2** not inclined to be neat.

SYNONYMS **1** *untidy hair* **scruffy,** tousled, dishevelled, unkempt, messy, rumpled, bedraggled, uncombed, tangled, matted. **2** *the room was untidy* **disordered,** messy, disorganized, cluttered, in chaos, haywire, in disarray; informal higgledy-piggledy.
ANTONYMS tidy, neat, orderly.

□ **untidily** adverb **untidiness** noun.

untie ▸ verb (**unties, untying, untied**) undo or unfasten something that is tied.

until ▸ preposition & conjunction up to the time or event mentioned.

> ✔ just one **l** at the end: unti**l**.

untimely ▸ adjective **1** happening or done at an unsuitable time. **2** (of a death or end) happening too soon or sooner than normal.

unto ▸ preposition old use **1** to. **2** until.

untold ▸ adjective **1** too much or too many to be counted. **2** (of a story) not told to anyone.

untouchable ▸ adjective **1** not able to be touched. **2** not able to be criticized or rivalled.
▸ noun offensive a member of the lowest Hindu caste (social class).

> ❗ The official term today for the lowest Hindu social class is **scheduled caste**.

untouched ▸ adjective **1** not handled, used, or consumed. **2** not affected, changed, or damaged.

untoward ▸ adjective unexpected and unwanted.

SYNONYMS **unexpected,** unforeseen, surprising, unusual, inappropriate, inconvenient, unwelcome, unfavourable, adverse, unfortunate, infelicitous.

untrammelled (US spelling **untrammeled**) ▸ adjective not restricted or hampered.

untrue ▸ adjective **1** false. **2** not faithful or loyal.

SYNONYMS **false,** invented, made up, fabricated, concocted, trumped up,

erroneous, wrong, incorrect, inaccurate.
ANTONYMS true, correct.

untrustworthy ▸ adjective unable to be trusted.

unused ▸ adjective **1** not used. **2** (**unused to**) not accustomed to.

unusual ▸ adjective **1** not often done or happening. **2** exceptional.

SYNONYMS **1** *an unusual sight* **uncommon,** abnormal, atypical, unexpected, surprising, unfamiliar, different, strange, odd, curious, extraordinary, unorthodox, unconventional, peculiar; informal weird, offbeat. **2** *a man of unusual talent* **remarkable,** extraordinary, exceptional, particular, outstanding, notable, noteworthy, distinctive, striking, significant, special, unique, unparalleled, prodigious.
ANTONYMS common.

□ **unusually** adverb.

unutterable ▸ adjective too great or bad to describe.
□ **unutterably** adverb.

unvarnished ▸ adjective **1** not varnished. **2** plain and straightforward.

unveil ▸ verb **1** show or announce something publicly for the first time. **2** remove a veil or covering from.

unwaged ▸ adjective Brit. unemployed or doing unpaid work.

unwanted ▸ adjective not wanted.

unwarrantable ▸ adjective not reasonable or justifiable.

unwarranted ▸ adjective not justified.

SYNONYMS **1** *the criticism is unwarranted* **unjustified,** indefensible, inexcusable, unforgivable, unpardonable, uncalled for, unnecessary, unjust, groundless. **2** *an unwarranted invasion of privacy* **unauthorized,** unsanctioned, unapproved, uncertified, unlicensed, illegal, unlawful, illicit, illegitimate, criminal, actionable.
ANTONYMS justified.

unwavering ▸ adjective not changing or becoming weaker.

unwelcome ▸ adjective not wanted.

unwell ▸ adjective ill.

unwholesome ▸ adjective **1** harmful to health. **2** unpleasant or unnatural.

unwieldy ▸ adjective hard to move or manage because of its size, shape, or weight.

SYNONYMS **awkward,** unmanageable, unmanoeuvrable, cumbersome, clumsy, massive, heavy, hefty, bulky.

unwilling ▸ adjective not willing.

u

SYNONYMS **1** *unwilling conscripts* **reluctant**, unenthusiastic, hesitant, resistant, grudging, involuntary, forced. **2** *he was unwilling to take on responsibility* **disinclined**, reluctant, averse, loath; (**be unwilling to do something**) baulk at, demur at, shy away from, flinch from, shrink from, not have the heart to, have qualms about, have misgivings about, have reservations about.
ANTONYMS willing, keen.

□ **unwillingly** adverb **unwillingness** noun.

unwind ▶ verb (unwinds, unwinding, unwound) **1** undo something that has been wound or twisted. **2** relax after a period of work or tension.

unwise ▶ adjective foolish.
□ **unwisely** adverb.

unwitting ▶ adjective **1** not aware of the full facts. **2** unintentional.
□ **unwittingly** adverb.

unwonted /un-**wohn**-tid/ ▶ adjective not usual or expected.

unworldly ▶ adjective **1** having little awareness of the realities of life. **2** not seeming to belong to this world.

unworthy ▶ adjective not deserving effort, attention, or respect.
□ **unworthiness** noun.

unwrap ▶ verb (unwraps, unwrapping, unwrapped) remove the wrapping from.

unwritten ▶ adjective (of a rule or law) generally known about and accepted, although not made official.

unyielding ▶ adjective **1** not bending or breaking; firm. **2** (of a person) not changing their mind.

unzip ▶ verb (unzips, unzipping, unzipped) **1** unfasten the zip of. **2** Computing decompress a file.

up ▶ adverb **1** towards a higher place or position. **2** to the place where someone is. **3** at or to a higher level or value. **4** into the desired condition or position. **5** out of bed. **6** (of the sun) visible in the sky.
▶ preposition **1** from a lower to a higher point of. **2** from one end of a street to another.
▶ adjective **1** directed or moving towards a higher place or position. **2** at an end.
▶ verb (ups, upping, upped) increase a level or an amount.
■ **up-and-coming** likely to be successful.

upbeat ▶ adjective positive and cheerful or enthusiastic.

SYNONYMS **cheerful**, optimistic, cheery, positive, confident, hopeful, bullish, buoyant.
ANTONYMS pessimistic, negative.

upbraid ▶ verb scold or criticize.

upbringing ▶ noun the way in which a

person is taught and looked after as a child.

SYNONYMS **childhood**, early life, formative years, teaching, instruction, rearing.

upcoming ▶ adjective forthcoming.

update ▶ verb (updates, updating, updated) **1** make something more modern. **2** give someone the latest information on something.

SYNONYMS **1** *security measures are continually updated* **modernize**, upgrade, improve, overhaul. **2** *I'll update him on developments* **brief**, bring up to date, inform, fill in, tell, notify, keep posted; informal clue in, put in the picture, bring/keep up to speed.

▶ noun an act of updating, or an updated version of something.

upend ▶ verb set something on its end or upside down.

upfront informal ▶ adjective **1** not trying to hide your thoughts or intentions; frank. **2** (of a payment) made in advance.
▶ adverb (usu. **up front**) (of a payment) in advance.

upgrade ▶ verb (upgrades, upgrading, upgraded) raise something to a higher standard or rank.

SYNONYMS **improve**, modernize, update, reform.
ANTONYMS downgrade.

▶ noun an act of upgrading, or an upgraded version of something.

upheaval ▶ noun a big change that causes a lot of upset or disruption.

SYNONYMS **disturbance**, disruption, trouble, turbulence, disorder, confusion, turmoil.

uphill ▶ adverb towards the top of a slope.
▶ adjective **1** sloping upwards. **2** difficult: *an uphill struggle*.

SYNONYMS **1** *an uphill path* **upward**, rising, ascending, climbing. **2** *an uphill job* **difficult**, hard, tough, demanding, arduous, taxing, exacting, stiff, gruelling, onerous.
ANTONYMS downhill.

uphold ▶ verb (upholds, upholding, upheld) **1** confirm or support something which has been questioned. **2** maintain a custom or practice.

SYNONYMS **1** *the court upheld his claim* **confirm**, endorse, sustain, approve, support, back (up). **2** *they've a tradition to uphold* **maintain**, sustain, continue, preserve, protect, keep, hold to, keep alive, keep going.
ANTONYMS overturn, oppose.

upholster ▶ verb (upholsters, upholstering,

upholstered) provide an armchair, sofa, etc. with a soft, padded covering.
□ **upholsterer** noun.

upholstery ▸ noun **1** the soft, padded covering on an armchair, sofa, etc. **2** the art of upholstering furniture.

upkeep ▸ noun the process or cost of keeping something in good condition or of supporting a person.

> SYNONYMS **1** *the upkeep of the road* **maintenance,** repair(s), servicing, care, preservation, conservation, running. **2** *the child's upkeep* **(financial) support,** maintenance, keep, subsistence, care.

upland (or **uplands**) ▸ noun an area of high or hilly land.

uplift ▸ verb make someone feel hope or happiness.

> SYNONYMS (uplifting) **inspiring,** stirring, inspirational, rousing, moving, touching, affecting, cheering, heartening, encouraging.

▸ noun **1** an act of lifting or raising something. **2** a feeling of hope or happiness.

upload ▸ verb transfer data to a larger computer system.

upmarket ▸ adjective chiefly Brit. expensive or of high quality.

upon more formal term for **on.**

upper ▸ adjective **1** situated above another part. **2** higher in position or status. **3** situated on higher ground.

> SYNONYMS **1** *the upper floor* **higher,** superior, top. **2** *the upper echelons of the party* **senior,** superior, higher-level, higher-ranking, top.
> ANTONYMS lower.

▸ noun the part of a boot or shoe above the sole.

■ **have the upper hand** have an advantage or control over someone. **upper case** capital letters. **the Upper House** (in the UK) the House of Lords.

upper class ▸ noun the social group with the highest status.

▸ adjective (**upper-class**) belonging or relating to the upper class.

> SYNONYMS **aristocratic,** noble, patrician, titled, blue-blooded, high-born, elite; Brit. county; informal upper-crust, top-drawer; Brit. informal posh.

uppercut ▸ noun a punch delivered with an upward motion and the arm bent.

uppermost ▸ adjective & adverb highest in place, rank, or importance.

uppity ▸ adjective informal behaving as if you are more important than you really are.

upright ▸ adjective **1** in a vertical position. **2** greater in height than breadth. **3** strictly honest and respectable. **4** (of a piano) having vertical strings.

> SYNONYMS **1** *an upright position* **vertical,** perpendicular, plumb, straight (up), erect, on end, on your feet. **2** *an upright member of the community* **honest,** honourable, upstanding, respectable, high-minded, law-abiding, worthy, righteous, decent, good, virtuous, principled.
> ANTONYMS flat, horizontal, dishonourable.

▸ adverb in or into an upright position.
▸ noun a vertical post, structure, or line.

uprising ▸ noun a rebellion.

> SYNONYMS **rebellion,** revolt, insurrection, mutiny, revolution, insurgence, rioting, coup.

upriver ➡ UPSTREAM.

uproar ▸ noun **1** a loud noise or disturbance made by people who are angry or upset about something. **2** a public expression of outrage.

> SYNONYMS **1** *the uproar in the kitchen continued* **commotion,** disturbance, rumpus, disorder, confusion, chaos, tumult, mayhem, pandemonium, bedlam, noise, din, clamour, hubbub, racket; informal hullabaloo; Brit. informal row. **2** *there was an uproar when he was dismissed* **outcry,** furore, fuss, commotion, hue and cry, rumpus; informal hullabaloo, stink, ructions; Brit. informal row.
> ANTONYMS calm.

uproarious ▸ adjective **1** very noisy and lively. **2** very funny.
□ **uproariously** adverb.

uproot ▸ verb **1** pull a tree or other plant out of the ground. **2** move someone from their home or usual surroundings.

upscale ▸ adjective N. Amer. upmarket.

upset ▸ verb (**upsets, upsetting, upset**) **1** make someone unhappy, disappointed, or worried. **2** knock something over. **3** disrupt or disturb a situation or arrangement.

> SYNONYMS **1** *the accusation upset her* **distress,** trouble, perturb, dismay, sadden, grieve, disturb, unsettle, disconcert, disquiet, worry, bother, agitate, fluster, throw, ruffle, unnerve, shake. **2** *he upset the soup* **knock over,** overturn, upend, tip over, topple, spill. **3** *the dam will upset the ecological balance* **disrupt,** interfere with, disturb, throw into confusion, mess up.
> ANTONYMS calm, reassure.

▸ noun **1** a difficult or unexpected result or situation. **2** a state of being upset.

> SYNONYMS **1** *a legal dispute will cause upset* **distress,** trouble, dismay, disquiet,

u

worry, bother, agitation, hurt, grief.
2 *a stomach upset* **disorder,** complaint, ailment, illness, sickness; informal bug; Brit. informal lurgy.
ANTONYMS reassurance.

▸ **adjective 1** unhappy, disappointed, or worried. **2** (of a person's stomach) not digesting food normally.

> SYNONYMS **1** *I was upset by the news* **distressed,** troubled, perturbed, dismayed, disturbed, unsettled, disconcerted, worried, bothered, anxious, agitated, flustered, ruffled, unnerved, shaken, saddened, grieved; informal cut up, choked; Brit. informal gutted. **2** *an upset stomach* **disturbed,** unsettled, queasy, bad, poorly; informal gippy.
> ANTONYMS unperturbed, calm.

upshot ▸ noun the eventual outcome or conclusion of something.

upside ▸ noun the positive aspect of something.

upside down ▸ adjective with the upper part where the lower part should be.

> SYNONYMS **1** *an upside-down canoe* **upturned,** upended, wrong side up, overturned, inverted, capsized. **2** *they left the flat upside down* **in disarray,** in disorder, jumbled up, in a muddle, untidy, disorganized, in chaos, in confusion; informal higgledy-piggledy.

upstage ▸ verb (upstages, upstaging, upstaged) draw attention away from someone so that people notice you instead.
▸ adverb & adjective at or towards the back of a stage.

upstairs ▸ adverb & adjective on or to an upper floor.
▸ noun an upper floor.

upstanding ▸ adjective very respectable and responsible.

upstart ▸ noun disapproving a person who thinks they are more important than they really are.

upstate ▸ adjective & adverb US in or to a part of a state remote from its large cities.

upstream (or **upriver**) ▸ adverb & adjective at or to a point nearer the source of a stream or river.

upsurge ▸ noun an increase.

uptake ▸ noun the action of taking up or making use of something.
■ **be quick (or slow) on the uptake** informal be quick (or slow) to understand something.

uptight ▸ adjective informal nervously tense or angry, and unable to express your feelings.

up to date ▸ adjective using or aware of the latest developments and trends.

> SYNONYMS **1** *up-to-date equipment* **modern,** contemporary, the latest, state-of-the-art, new, up-to-the-minute, advanced. **2** *the newsletter will keep you up to date* **informed,** up to speed, in the picture, in touch, au fait, conversant, familiar, knowledgeable, acquainted.
> ANTONYMS out of date, old-fashioned.

upturn ▸ noun an improvement or upward trend.
▸ verb (**be upturned**) be turned upwards or upside down.

upward ▸ adjective & adverb towards a higher level.
□ **upwards** adverb.

upwind ▸ adverb & adjective into the wind.

uranium /yuu-**ray**-ni-uhm/ ▸ noun a radioactive metallic element used as a fuel in nuclear reactors.

Uranus /yoo-**ray**-nuhss, **yoo**-ruh-nuhss/ ▸ noun the seventh planet from the sun in the solar system.

urban ▸ adjective having to do with a town or city.

> SYNONYMS **town,** city, municipal, metropolitan, built-up, inner-city, suburban.
> ANTONYMS rural.

urbane /er-**bayn**/ ▸ adjective (of a man) confident, polite, and sophisticated.
□ **urbanity** noun.

urchin ▸ noun a poor child dressed in ragged clothes.

Urdu /**oor**-doo, **er**-doo/ ▸ noun a language of Pakistan and India.

ureter /yuu-**ree**-ter/ ▸ noun the duct by which urine passes from the kidney to the bladder.

urethra /yuu-**ree**-thruh/ ▸ noun the duct by which urine passes out of the body, and which in males also carries semen.
□ **urethral** adjective.

urge ▸ verb (urges, urging, urged)
1 encourage or earnestly ask someone to do something. **2** strongly recommend.

> SYNONYMS **1** *she urged him to try* **encourage,** exhort, press, entreat, implore, call on, appeal to, beg, plead with. **2** *I urge caution in interpreting these results* **advise,** counsel, advocate, recommend.

▸ noun a strong desire or impulse.

> SYNONYMS *his urge to travel* **desire,** wish, need, compulsion, longing, yearning, hankering, craving, hunger, thirst; informal yen, itch.

urgent ▸ adjective needing immediate action or attention.

SYNONYMS **pressing**, acute, dire, desperate, critical, serious, grave, intense, crying, burning, compelling, extreme, high-priority, life-and-death.

□ **urgency** noun **urgently** adverb.

urinal ► noun a container into which men urinate, attached to the wall in a public toilet.

urinate ► verb (urinates, urinating, urinated) pass urine out of the body.
□ **urination** noun.

urine /**yoo**-rin, **yoo**-ryn/ ► noun a yellowish liquid that is stored in the bladder and which contains waste substances that are passed with it out of the body.
□ **urinary** adjective.

URL ► abbreviation uniform (or universal) resource locator, the address of a World Wide Web page.

urn ► noun **1** a container for storing a cremated person's ashes. **2** a metal container with a tap, in which tea or coffee is made and kept hot.

ursine ► adjective having to do with bears.

Uruguayan /yoor-uh-**gwy**-uhn/ ► noun a person from Uruguay.
► adjective relating to Uruguay.

US ► abbreviation United States.

us ► pronoun used by a speaker to refer to himself or herself and one or more other people as the object of a verb or preposition.

USA ► abbreviation United States of America.

usable (or useable) ► adjective able to be used.
□ **usability** noun.

usage ► noun the using of something.

SYNONYMS **1** *energy usage* **consumption**, use. **2** *the usage of equipment* **use**, utilization, operation, manipulation, running, handling. **3** *English usage* **language**, expression, phraseology, parlance, idiom.

use ► verb (uses, using, used) **1** do something with an object or adopt a method in order to achieve a purpose. **2** (use something up) consume all of something. **3** take unfair advantage of a person or situation. **4** (used to) did something repeatedly in the past, or existed or happened in the past. **5** (be or get used to) be or become familiar with something through experience.

SYNONYMS **1** *she used her key to open the door* **utilize**, employ, avail yourself of, work, operate, wield, ply, apply, put into service. **2** *the court will use its discretion* **exercise**, employ, bring into play, practise, apply. **3** *she was using me* **take advantage of**, exploit, manipulate, take liberties with, impose on, abuse, capitalize on, profit from, trade on, milk;

informal **cash in on**, walk all over. **4** *we have used up our funds* **consume**, get/go through, exhaust, deplete, expend, spend.

► noun **1** the using of something. **2** the ability to use a part of the body. **3** a purpose for something, or a way in which something can be used. **4** value.

SYNONYMS **1** *the use of such weapons* **utilization**, application, employment, operation, manipulation. **2** *his use of other people for his own ends* **exploitation**, manipulation, abuse. **3** *what is the use of that?* **advantage**, benefit, good, point, object, purpose, sense, reason, service, utility, help, gain, avail, profit, value, worth.

used ► adjective second-hand.

SYNONYMS *a used car* **second-hand**, preowned, nearly new, old, worn, hand-medown, cast-off.
ANTONYMS new.

useful ► adjective able to be used for a practical purpose or in several ways.

SYNONYMS **1** *a useful tool* **functional**, practical, handy, convenient, utilitarian, serviceable, of service; informal **nifty**. **2** *a useful experience* **beneficial**, advantageous, helpful, worthwhile, profitable, rewarding, productive, constructive, valuable, fruitful.
ANTONYMS useless, disadvantageous.

□ **usefully** adverb **usefulness** noun.

useless ► adjective **1** serving no purpose. **2** informal having no ability or skill.

SYNONYMS **1** *it was useless to try* **futile**, pointless, to no avail, vain, to no purpose, unavailing, hopeless, ineffectual, fruitless, unprofitable, unproductive. **2** *he was useless at his job* **incompetent**, inept, ineffective, incapable, inadequate, hopeless, bad; informal **a dead loss**.
ANTONYMS useful, beneficial, competent.

□ **uselessly** adverb.

user ► noun a person who uses or operates something.
■ **user-friendly** easy for people to use or understand.

u

usher ► noun **1** a person who shows people to their seats in a theatre or cinema or in church. **2** an official in a law court who swears in jurors and generally keeps order.

SYNONYMS *ushers showed them to their seats* **guide**, attendant, escort.

► verb (ushers, ushering, ushered) guide someone somewhere.

SYNONYMS *she ushered him to a seat* **escort**, accompany, take, show, see, lead, conduct, guide.

usherette ▸ noun a woman who shows people to their seats in a cinema or theatre.

USSR ▸ abbreviation historical Union of Soviet Socialist Republics.

usual ▸ adjective happening or done typically, regularly, or frequently.

> SYNONYMS **normal,** customary, accustomed, wonted, habitual, routine, regular, standard, typical, established, set, stock, conventional, traditional, expected, familiar.
> ANTONYMS unusual, exceptional.

usually ▸ adverb generally speaking.

> SYNONYMS **normally,** generally, habitually, customarily, routinely, typically, ordinarily, commonly, as a rule, in general, more often than not, mainly, mostly.

> ✔ Remember that **usually** is spelled with a double **l**.

usurp /yuu-**zerp**/ ▸ verb take over someone's position or power without having the right to do so.
□ **usurper** noun.

usury /**yoo**-zhuh-ri/ ▸ noun formal the practice of lending money at unreasonably high rates of interest.
□ **usurer** noun.

utensil ▸ noun a tool or container, especially for household use.

> SYNONYMS **implement,** tool, instrument, device, apparatus, gadget, appliance, contrivance, contraption; informal gizmo.

uterus /**yoo**-tuh-ruhss/ ▸ noun the womb.
□ **uterine** adjective.

utilitarian ▸ adjective useful or practical rather than attractive.

utilitarianism ▸ noun the doctrine that the right course of action is the one that will lead to the greatest happiness of the greatest number of people.

utility ▸ noun (plural utilities) **1** the state of being useful or profitable. **2** an organization supplying electricity, gas, water, or sewerage to the public.

> SYNONYMS **usefulness,** use, benefit, value, advantage, help, practicality, effectiveness, service.

▪ **utility room** a room where a washing machine and other domestic equipment are kept.

utilize (or utilise) ▸ verb (utilizes, utilizing, utilized) make practical and effective use of.

> SYNONYMS **use,** employ, avail yourself of, press into service, bring into play, deploy, draw on, exploit.

□ **utilization** noun.

utmost ▸ adjective most extreme; greatest.

> SYNONYMS **greatest,** highest, maximum, most, extreme, supreme, paramount.

▸ noun (**the utmost**) the greatest or most extreme extent or amount.

Utopia /yoo-**toh**-pi-uh/ ▸ noun an imagined world or society where everything is perfect.

> SYNONYMS **paradise,** heaven, Eden, Shangri-La, idyll, nirvana.

utopian ▸ adjective idealistic.

utter[1] ▸ adjective complete; absolute.

> SYNONYMS *that's utter nonsense* **complete,** total, absolute, thorough, perfect, downright, out-and-out, outright, sheer, arrant, positive, prize, pure, unmitigated.

□ **utterly** adverb.

utter[2] ▸ verb (utters, uttering, uttered) make a sound, or say something.

> SYNONYMS **say,** speak, voice, mouth, express, articulate, pronounce, enunciate, emit, let out, give, produce.

utterance ▸ noun **1** a word, statement, or sound uttered. **2** the action of saying or uttering something.

> SYNONYMS **remark,** comment, word, statement, observation, declaration, pronouncement.

uttermost = UTMOST.

uvula /**yoo**-vyuu-luh/ ▸ noun (plural uvulae /**yoo**-vyuu-lee/) a small piece of flesh that hangs down at the top of the throat.

uxorious /uk-**sor**-i-uhss/ ▸ adjective (of a man) very fond of his wife.

u

Vv

V (or **v**) ▸ noun (plural **Vs** or **V's**) **1** the twenty-second letter of the alphabet. **2** the Roman numeral for five.
▸ abbreviation **1** volts. **2** (**v**) versus.
■ **V-neck** a V-shaped neckline. **V-sign 1** an insulting gesture made with the first two fingers pointing up and the back of the hand facing outwards. **2** a similar sign made with the palm facing outwards, used as a symbol of victory.

vacancy ▸ noun (plural **vacancies**) **1** a job or position that is available. **2** an available room in a hotel, guest house, etc. **3** empty space.

> SYNONYMS **opening**, position, post, job, opportunity.

vacant ▸ adjective **1** empty. **2** (of a job or position) available. **3** showing no intelligence or interest.

> SYNONYMS **1** *a vacant house* **empty**, unoccupied, not in use, free, unfilled, uninhabited, untenanted. **2** *a vacant look* **blank**, expressionless, unresponsive, emotionless, impassive, vacuous, empty, glazed.
> ANTONYMS full, occupied, expressive.

□ **vacantly** adverb.

vacate ▸ verb (**vacates, vacating, vacated**) **1** go out of a place, leaving it empty. **2** give up a position.

> SYNONYMS **1** *he was forced to vacate the premises* **leave**, move out of, evacuate, quit, depart from. **2** *he will be vacating his post next year* **resign from**, leave, stand down from, give up, bow out of, relinquish, retire from; informal quit.
> ANTONYMS occupy, take up.

vacation ▸ noun **1** a period when universities, law courts, etc. are closed. **2** N. Amer. a holiday. **3** the action of vacating a place.

> SYNONYMS **holiday**, trip, tour, break, leave, time off, recess.

▸ verb N. Amer. take a holiday.

vaccinate ▸ verb (**vaccinates, vaccinating, vaccinated**) give a person or animal an injection of a vaccine to protect them against a disease.

□ **vaccination** noun.

vaccine /vak-seen/ ▸ noun a substance injected into the body that causes the production of antibodies and so provides immunity against a disease.

vacillate /va-si-layt/ ▸ verb (**vacillates, vacillating, vacillated**) keep changing your mind about something.

□ **vacillation** noun.

vacuous ▸ adjective showing a lack of thought or intelligence.

□ **vacuity** noun.

vacuum /vak-yuum/ ▸ noun (plural **vacuums** or **vacua** /vak-yuu-uh/) **1** a completely empty space in which there is no air or other matter. **2** a gap left by the loss of someone or something important.
▸ verb clean a surface using a vacuum cleaner.
■ **vacuum cleaner** an electrical machine that collects dust by means of suction. **vacuum flask** a container with a double wall enclosing a vacuum, used for keeping drinks hot or cold.

vagabond ▸ noun a person who has no settled home or job.

vagary /vay-guh-ri/ ▸ noun (plural **vagaries**) a change that is difficult to predict or control.

vagina /vuh-jy-nuh/ ▸ noun (in a woman or girl) a tube leading from the external genitals to the womb.

□ **vaginal** adjective.

vagrant /vay-gruhnt/ ▸ noun a person who has no settled home or job.

> SYNONYMS **tramp**, drifter, down-and-out, beggar, itinerant, wanderer, nomad, traveller; N. Amer. **hobo**; N. Amer. informal bum.

▸ adjective having no settled home or job.
□ **vagrancy** noun.

vague ▸ adjective **1** not certain or definite. **2** saying things or thinking in a way that is not clear.

> SYNONYMS **1** *a vague shape* **indistinct**, indefinite, indeterminate, unclear, ill-defined, hazy, fuzzy, misty, blurry, out of focus, shadowy, obscure. **2** *a vague description* **imprecise**, rough,

v

approximate, inexact, non-specific, ambiguous, hazy, uncertain. **3** *she was so vague in life* **absent-minded,** forgetful, dreamy, abstracted; informal scatty, not with it.
ANTONYMS clear, precise, certain, sharp.

□ **vaguely** adverb **vagueness** noun.

vain ▸ adjective **1** having too high an opinion of yourself. **2** useless or meaningless.

> SYNONYMS **1** *their flattery made him vain* **conceited,** proud, arrogant, boastful, cocky, immodest; informal big-headed. **2** *a vain attempt* **futile,** useless, pointless, ineffective, fruitless, unproductive, unsuccessful, failed, abortive.
> ANTONYMS modest, successful.

■ **in vain** without success.
□ **vainly** adverb.

vainglorious ▸ adjective literary boastful or vain.
□ **vainglory** noun.

valance /**va**-luhnss/ ▸ noun a length of fabric fitted over the base of the bed under the mattress.

vale ▸ noun literary a valley.

valediction /va-li-**dik**-sh'n/ ▸ noun **1** the action of saying farewell. **2** a farewell statement.

valedictory /va-li-**dik**-tuh-ri/ ▸ adjective (especially of a speech) saying farewell.

valency /**vay**-luhn-si/ (or **valence**) ▸ noun (plural **valencies**) Chemistry the combining power of an element, especially as measured by the number of hydrogen atoms it can displace or combine with.

valentine ▸ noun **1** a card that you send to a person you love on St Valentine's Day (14 February). **2** a person to whom you send such a card.

valerian /vuh-**leer**-i-uhn/ ▸ noun **1** a plant with small pink, red, or white flowers. **2** a sedative drug obtained from valerian roots.

valet /**va**-lay, **va**-lit/ ▸ noun **1** a person who looks after a man's clothes and other personal needs. **2** N. Amer. a person employed to clean or park cars.
▸ verb (**valets, valeting, valeted**) **1** clean a car as a professional service. **2** act as a valet to.

valetudinarian /va-li-tyoo-di-**nair**-i-uhn/ ▸ noun a person who is in bad health, or worries too much about their health.

valiant ▸ adjective showing courage or determination.
□ **valiantly** adverb.

valid ▸ adjective **1** (of a reason, argument, etc.) sound or logical. **2** legally binding or acceptable.

> SYNONYMS **1** *a valid criticism* **well founded,** sound, reasonable, rational, logical, justifiable, defensible, cogent, credible, forceful. **2** *a valid contract*

legally binding, lawful, official, in force, in effect.
ANTONYMS invalid.

□ **validity** noun.

validate ▸ verb (**validates, validating, validated**) make valid, or show to be valid.
□ **validation** noun.

valise /vuh-**leez**/ ▸ noun a small travelling bag or suitcase.

Valium ▸ noun trademark a tranquillizing drug used to relieve anxiety.

valley ▸ noun (plural **valleys**) a low area between hills or mountains.

> SYNONYMS **dale,** vale, hollow, gully, gorge, ravine, canyon, rift; Brit. combe; Scottish glen.

valour (US spelling **valor**) ▸ noun great courage in the face of danger.
□ **valorous** adjective.

valuable ▸ adjective **1** worth a lot of money. **2** very useful or important.

> SYNONYMS **1** *a valuable watch* **precious,** costly, high-priced, expensive, dear, priceless. **2** *a valuable contribution* **useful,** helpful, beneficial, invaluable, productive, worthwhile, worthy, important.
> ANTONYMS cheap, worthless, useless.

▸ plural noun (**valuables**) valuable items.

> SYNONYMS **precious items,** costly items, prized possessions, treasures.

valuation ▸ noun an estimation of how much something is worth.

value ▸ noun **1** the importance or usefulness of something. **2** the amount of money that something is worth. **3** (**values**) standards of behaviour. **4** Maths the amount represented by a letter or symbol. **5** the relative length of the sound represented by a musical note.

> SYNONYMS **1** *the value of adequate preparation* **worth,** usefulness, advantage, benefit, gain, profit, good, help. **2** *houses exceeding £250,000 in value* **price,** cost, worth, market price. **3** (**values**) **principles,** ethics, morals, standards, code of behaviour.

▸ verb (**values, valuing, valued**) **1** estimate how much something is worth. **2** consider something to be important or useful.

> SYNONYMS **1** *his estate was valued at £45,000* **evaluate,** assess, estimate, appraise, price. **2** *she valued his opinion* **think highly of,** have a high opinion of, rate highly, esteem, set great store by, respect.
> ANTONYMS despise.

■ **value added tax** a tax on the amount by which goods rise in value at each stage of production.

valve ▶ noun **1** a device for controlling the flow of a liquid or gas through a pipe or duct. **2** a mechanism that varies the length of the tube in a brass musical instrument. **3** a structure in the heart or a vein which allows blood to flow in one direction only.

vamp¹ ▶ verb (**vamp something up**) informal improve something by adding something more interesting to it.

vamp² ▶ noun informal a woman who uses her sexual attractiveness to control men.
□ **vampish** adjective.

vampire ▶ noun **1** (in stories) a dead person who leaves their grave at night to drink the blood of living people. **2** (also **vampire bat**) a bloodsucking bat found mainly in tropical America.
□ **vampirism** noun.

van¹ ▶ noun **1** a motor vehicle used for moving goods or a group of people. **2** Brit. a railway carriage used for large luggage, mail, etc.

van² ▶ noun (**the van**) the leading part of an advancing group of people.

vanadium ▶ noun a hard grey metallic chemical element, used to make some types of steel.

vandal ▶ noun a person who deliberately destroys or damages property.
□ **vandalism** noun.

vandalize (or **vandalise**) ▶ verb (**vandalizes, vandalizing, vandalized**) deliberately destroy or damage property.

vane ▶ noun a broad blade that is moved by wind or water, forming part of a windmill, propeller, or turbine.

vanguard ▶ noun **1** the leading part of an advancing army. **2** a group of people leading the way in new developments or ideas.

vanilla ▶ noun a substance obtained from the pods of a tropical plant, used as a flavouring or scent.

vanish ▶ verb **1** disappear suddenly and completely. **2** gradually cease to exist.

> SYNONYMS **1** *he vanished into the darkness* **disappear,** be lost to sight, become invisible, recede from view. **2** *all hope vanished* **fade (away),** evaporate, melt away, end, cease to exist, pass away, die out.
> ANTONYMS appear, materialize.

vanity ▶ noun (plural **vanities**) **1** too much pride in your own appearance or achievements. **2** the quality of being pointless or futile.

> SYNONYMS **conceit,** self-love, self-admiration, egotism, pride, arrogance, boastfulness, cockiness, swagger; informal big-headedness.
> ANTONYMS modesty.

vanquish ▶ verb literary defeat completely.

vantage (or **vantage point**) ▶ noun a place or position giving the best view.

vapid ▶ adjective offering no stimulation or challenge.
□ **vapidity** noun.

vaporize (or **vaporise**) ▶ verb (**vaporizes, vaporizing, vaporized**) convert something into vapour.
□ **vaporization** noun **vaporizer** noun.

vapour (US spelling **vapor**) ▶ noun **1** moisture suspended in the air. **2** Physics a gaseous substance that can be made into liquid by pressure alone.

variable ▶ adjective **1** not consistent or having a fixed pattern. **2** able to be changed or adapted.

> SYNONYMS **changeable,** shifting, fluctuating, irregular, inconstant, inconsistent, fluid, unstable; informal up and down.
> ANTONYMS constant.

▶ noun a variable element, feature, or quantity.
□ **variability** noun **variably** adverb.

variance ▶ noun **1** the fact or quality of being different or inconsistent. **2** the state of disagreeing or quarrelling.

variant ▶ noun a version that varies from other forms of the same thing.

> SYNONYMS *variants of the same idea* **variation,** form, alternative, version, adaptation, alteration, modification.

▶ adjective varying from other forms of the same thing.

> SYNONYMS *a variant spelling* **alternative,** other, different, divergent.

variation ▶ noun **1** a change or slight difference in condition, amount, or level. **2** a different or distinct form or version. **3** a new but still recognizable version of a musical theme.

> SYNONYMS **1** *regional variations in farming* **difference,** dissimilarity, disparity, contrast, discrepancy, imbalance. **2** *opening times are subject to variation* **change,** alteration, modification. **3** *there was very little variation from the pattern* **deviation,** variance, divergence, departure, fluctuation.

varicose ▶ adjective (of a vein) swollen, twisted, and lengthened, as a result of bad circulation.

varied ▶ adjective involving a number of different types or elements.

> SYNONYMS **diverse,** assorted, miscellaneous, mixed, sundry, wide-ranging, disparate, motley.
> ANTONYMS similar, unchanging.

v

variegated /vair-i-gay-tid/ ▶ adjective having irregular patches or streaks of a different colour or colours.
□ **variegation** noun.

✔ Remember the **e** in the middle: vari**e**gated.

variety ▶ noun (plural **varieties**) **1** the quality of being varied. **2** (**a variety of**) a number of things of the same type that are distinct in character. **3** a thing which differs in some way from others of the same general class. **4** a form of entertainment involving singing, dancing, and comedy.

SYNONYMS **1** *the lack of variety in the curriculum* **diversity,** variation, diversification, change, difference. **2** *a wide variety of flowers* **assortment,** miscellany, range, array, collection, selection, mixture, medley. **3** *fifty varieties of pasta* **sort,** kind, type, class, category, style, form, make, model, brand, strain, breed.
ANTONYMS uniformity.

various ▶ adjective of different kinds or sorts.

SYNONYMS **diverse,** different, differing, varied, assorted, mixed, sundry, miscellaneous, disparate, motley.
ANTONYMS similar.

▶ determiner & pronoun more than one; individual and separate.
□ **variously** adverb.

varnish ▶ noun a liquid applied to wood to give a hard, clear, shiny surface when dry.
▶ verb put varnish on.

vary ▶ verb (**varies, varying, varied**) **1** differ in size, degree, or nature from something else of the same general class. **2** change from one form or state to another. **3** alter something to make it less uniform.

SYNONYMS **1** *estimates of the cost vary* **differ,** be dissimilar, disagree. **2** *rates of interest vary over time* **fluctuate,** rise and fall, go up and down, change, alter, shift, swing. **3** *the diaphragm is used for varying the aperture* **modify,** change, alter, adjust, regulate, control, set.

vascular ▶ adjective referring to the system of vessels for carrying blood or (in plants) the tissues carrying sap, water, and nutrients.

vas deferens /vass def-uh-renz/ ▶ noun (plural **vasa deferentia** /vay-suh def-uh-**ren**-shuh/) the duct carrying sperm from a testicle to the urethra.

vase ▶ noun a container for displaying cut flowers.

vasectomy /vuh-**sek**-tuh-mi/ ▶ noun (plural **vasectomies**) the surgical cutting and sealing of part of each vas deferens as a means of sterilization.

Vaseline ▶ noun trademark a type of petroleum jelly used as an ointment and lubricant.

vassal ▶ noun (in the feudal system) a man who promised to support and fight for a king or lord in return for holding a piece of land.

vast ▶ adjective of very great extent or quantity; immense.

SYNONYMS **huge,** extensive, broad, wide, boundless, enormous, immense, great, massive, colossal, gigantic, mammoth, giant, mountainous; informal mega, whopping; Brit. informal ginormous.
ANTONYMS tiny.

□ **vastly** adverb **vastness** noun.

VAT ▶ abbreviation value added tax.

vat ▶ noun a large tank or tub used to hold liquid.

Vatican ▶ noun the official residence of the Pope in Rome.

vaudeville /vaw-duh-vil/ ▶ noun a type of entertainment featuring a mixture of musical and comedy acts.

vault¹ ▶ noun **1** a large room used for storage, especially in a bank. **2** a chamber beneath a church or in a graveyard, used for burials. **3** a roof in the form of an arch or a series of arches.

SYNONYMS **1** *the vault under the church* **cellar,** basement, crypt, undercroft, catacomb, burial chamber. **2** *valuables stored in the vault* **strongroom,** safe deposit.

□ **vaulted** adjective.

vault² ▶ verb leap or spring using your hands or a pole to push yourself.

SYNONYMS *he vaulted over the gate* **jump,** leap, spring, bound, clear.

▶ noun an act of vaulting.

vaunted ▶ adjective praised or boasted about.

VC ▶ abbreviation Victoria Cross.

VCR ▶ abbreviation video cassette recorder.

VDU ▶ abbreviation Brit. visual display unit.

veal ▶ noun meat from a young calf.

vector ▶ noun **1** Maths a quantity having direction as well as magnitude. **2** the carrier of a disease or infection.

Veda /vay-duh, vee-duh/ ▶ noun the most ancient Hindu scriptures.

veer ▶ verb (**veers, veering, veered**) **1** change direction suddenly. **2** (of the wind) change direction clockwise around the points of the compass.

SYNONYMS **turn,** swerve, swing, weave, wheel, change direction, change course, deviate.

vegan ▶ noun a person who does not eat or use any animal products.

V

vegetable ▸ noun **1** a plant used as food. **2** offensive a person who is incapable of normal mental or physical activity as a result of brain damage.

✔ **vege-**, not **vega-**: veg**e**table.

vegetal ▸ adjective relating to plants.

vegetarian ▸ noun a person who does not eat meat or fish.
▸ adjective eating or including no meat or fish.
□ **vegetarianism** noun.

vegetate ▸ verb (**vegetates, vegetating, vegetated**) spend your time in a dull way that involves little mental stimulation.

vegetation ▸ noun plants.

vegetative ▸ adjective **1** relating to vegetation. **2** Medicine alive but showing no sign of brain activity or responsiveness.

vehement /vee-uh-muhnt/ ▸ adjective showing strong feeling.
□ **vehemence** noun **vehemently** adverb.

vehicle ▸ noun a car, lorry, truck, etc. used for transporting people or goods on land.

SYNONYMS **1** *a stolen vehicle* **means of transport,** conveyance. **2** *a vehicle for the communication of ideas* **channel,** medium, means, agent, instrument, mechanism, organ, apparatus.

□ **vehicular** /vi-**hik**-yuu-ler/ adjective.

veil ▸ noun **1** a piece of thin material worn to protect or hide the face. **2** the part of a nun's headdress that covers the head and shoulders. **3** a thing that hides or disguises.

SYNONYMS *a thin veil of cloud* **covering,** screen, curtain, mantle, cloak, mask, blanket, shroud, canopy, cloud, pall.

▸ verb **1** cover with a veil. **2** (**veiled**) partially hidden or disguised.

SYNONYMS *the peak was veiled in mist* **cover,** surround, swathe, enfold, envelop, conceal, hide, obscure, screen, shield, cloak, blanket, shroud.

vein ▸ noun **1** any of the tubes that carry blood from all parts of the body towards the heart. **2** a blood vessel. **3** (in plants) a thin rib running through a leaf. **4** (in insects) a hollow rib forming part of the supporting framework of a wing. **5** a streak of a different colour in wood, marble, cheese, etc. **6** a fracture in rock containing a deposit of minerals or ore. **7** a source of a particular quality: *a vein of humour.*

SYNONYMS **1** *veins of quartz* **layer,** seam, lode, stratum, deposit. **2** *he closes his article in a humorous vein* **mood,** humour, attitude, tone, spirit, character, feel, flavour, quality, atmosphere, manner, way, style.

□ **veined** adjective.

Velcro ▸ noun trademark a fastener consisting of two strips of fabric covered with tiny hooks.

veld (or **veldt**) /velt/ ▸ noun open uncultivated country or grassland in southern Africa.

vellum ▸ noun fine parchment made from animal skin.

velociraptor /vi-**los**-si-rap-ter/ ▸ noun a small meat-eating dinosaur.

velocity ▸ noun (plural **velocities**) speed in a particular direction.

SYNONYMS **speed,** pace, rate, tempo, rapidity.

velodrome ▸ noun a track used for cycle racing.

velour /vuh-**loor**/ ▸ noun a thick, soft fabric resembling velvet.

velvet ▸ noun a fabric with a soft, short pile on one side.
□ **velvety** adjective.

velveteen ▸ noun a cotton fabric resembling thin velvet.

venal /vee-n'l/ ▸ adjective open to bribery.
□ **venality** noun.

vend ▸ verb sell small items.
■ **vending machine** a machine from which you can buy drinks, snacks, etc. by inserting coins.

vendetta ▸ noun **1** a feud in which the family of a murdered person seeks vengeance on the murderer or the murderer's family. **2** a long and bitter quarrel.

vendor (US spelling **vender**) ▸ noun **1** a person selling small items. **2** Law a person who is selling a property.

veneer ▸ noun **1** a thin covering of fine wood applied to a cheaper wood or other material. **2** an outward appearance that hides the true nature of a person or thing.
□ **veneered** adjective.

venerable ▸ adjective given great respect because of age, wisdom, or character.

venerate ▸ verb (**venerates, venerating, venerated**) respect someone highly.
□ **veneration** noun.

venereal disease ▸ noun a disease caught by having sex with an infected person.

Venetian ▸ adjective relating to Venice.
■ **venetian blind** a window blind consisting of horizontal slats which can be turned to control the amount of light that passes through.

Venezuelan /ve-ni-**zway**-luhn/ ▸ noun a person from Venezuela.
▸ adjective relating to Venezuela.

vengeance ▸ noun an act of harming or punishing someone in return for what they have done to you or someone close to you.

V

synonyms **revenge**, retribution, retaliation, requital, reprisal, an eye for an eye.
antonyms forgiveness.

■ **with a vengeance** with great intensity.

vengeful ▸ adjective wanting to punish or harm someone in return for something they have done.

venial /vee-ni-uhl/ ▸ adjective (of a fault or offence) slight and able to be forgiven.

venison ▸ noun meat from a deer.

Venn diagram ▸ noun a diagram representing mathematical sets as circles, with overlapping sections representing elements shared between sets.

venom ▸ noun **1** the poisonous liquid produced by some animals that bite or sting, such as snakes and scorpions. **2** a strong feeling of hatred or bitterness.

venomous ▸ adjective **1** producing venom. **2** full of hatred or bitterness.

synonyms **poisonous**, toxic, dangerous, deadly, lethal, fatal.
antonyms harmless.

□ **venomously** adverb.

venous /vee-nuhss/ ▸ adjective relating to a vein or the veins.

vent¹ ▸ noun an opening that allows air, gas, or liquid to pass out of or into a confined space.

synonyms *an air vent* **outlet**, **inlet**, opening, aperture, hole, gap, orifice, space, duct, flue, shaft, well, passage, airway.

▸ verb **1** allow yourself to express a strong emotion. **2** let air, gas, or liquid pass through a vent.

synonyms *the crowd vented their fury* **let out**, release, pour out, utter, express, air, voice.

vent² ▸ noun a slit in a garment.

ventilate ▸ verb (ventilates, ventilating, ventilated) cause air to enter and circulate freely in a room or building.
□ **ventilation** noun.

ventilator ▸ noun **1** an opening or a machine for ventilating a room or building. **2** a machine that pumps air in and out of a person's lungs to help them to breathe.

ventral ▸ adjective having to do with the underside or abdomen.

ventricle ▸ noun each of the two larger and lower cavities of the heart.

ventriloquist /ven-**tril**-uh-kwist/ ▸ noun an entertainer who can make their voice seem to come from elsewhere.
□ **ventriloquism** noun.

venture ▸ noun **1** a business enterprise involving considerable risk. **2** a risky or daring journey or undertaking.

synonyms *a business venture* **enterprise**, undertaking, project, scheme, operation, endeavour, speculation.

▸ verb (ventures, venturing, ventured) **1** dare to do something dangerous or risky. **2** dare to say something.

synonyms **1** *we ventured across the moor* **set out**, go, travel, journey. **2** *may I venture an opinion?* **put forward**, advance, proffer, offer, air, suggest, volunteer, submit, propose. **3** *I ventured to invite her* **dare**, be so bold as, presume, have the audacity, have the nerve, take the liberty of.

venturesome ▸ adjective literary willing to take on something risky or difficult.

venue ▸ noun the place where an event or meeting is held.

Venus ▸ noun the second planet from the sun in the solar system.
■ **Venus flytrap** a plant with hinged leaves that spring shut on and digest insects which land on them.

veracious ▸ adjective formal truthful.

veracity ▸ noun the quality of being truthful and accurate.

veranda (or verandah) ▸ noun a roofed structure with an open front along the outside of a house.

verb ▸ noun a word expressing an action or occurrence.

verbal ▸ adjective **1** relating to or in the form of words. **2** spoken rather than written. **3** relating to a verb.

synonyms **oral**, spoken, word-of-mouth, stated, said, unwritten.

□ **verbally** adverb.

verbalize (or verbalise) ▸ verb (verbalizes, verbalizing, verbalized) express something in words.

verbatim /ver-**bay**-tim/ ▸ adverb & adjective in exactly the same words as were used originally.

verbena ▸ noun a garden plant with brightly coloured flowers.

verbiage ▸ noun speech or writing that is too long or detailed.

verbose ▸ adjective using more words than are needed.
□ **verbosity** noun.

verdant ▸ adjective green with grass or other lush vegetation.

verdict ▸ noun **1** a decision made by a jury in a court of law about whether someone is innocent or guilty. **2** an opinion or judgement formed after trying or testing something.

SYNONYMS **judgement,** adjudication, decision, finding, ruling, sentence.

verdigris /ver-di-gree/ ▶ noun a bright bluish-green substance formed on copper or brass by oxidation.

verdure ▶ noun literary lush green vegetation.

verge ▶ noun **1** Brit. a grass edging by the side of a road or path. **2** a limit beyond which a particular thing will happen: *I was on the verge of tears.*

SYNONYMS **1** *the verge of the lake* **edge,** border, margin, side, brink, rim, lip, fringe, boundary, perimeter. **2** *I was on the verge of tears* **brink,** threshold, edge, point.

▶ verb (**verges, verging, verged**) (**verge on**) be very close or similar to.

verger ▶ noun an official in a church who acts as a caretaker and attendant.

verify ▶ verb (**verifies, verifying, verified**) make sure or show that something is true and accurate.

SYNONYMS **confirm,** prove, substantiate, corroborate, back up, bear out, justify, support, uphold, testify to, validate, authenticate.
ANTONYMS refute.

□ **verifiable** adjective **verification** noun.

verily ▶ adverb old use truly; certainly.

verisimilitude ▶ noun the appearance of being true or real.

veritable ▶ adjective genuine.
□ **veritably** adverb.

verity ▶ noun (plural **verities**) formal truthfulness, or a truth.

vermicelli /ver-mi-**chel**-li/ ▶ plural noun **1** pasta made in long thin threads. **2** Brit. shreds of chocolate used to decorate cakes.

vermilion ▶ noun a bright red colour.

vermin ▶ noun wild animals or birds which carry disease or harm crops.
□ **verminous** adjective.

vermouth /ver-**muhth**/ ▶ noun a red or white wine flavoured with herbs.

vernacular ▶ noun the language or dialect spoken by the ordinary people of a country or region.

vernal ▶ adjective relating to the season of spring.

verruca /vuh-**roo**-kuh/ ▶ noun a contagious wart on the sole of the foot.

versatile ▶ adjective able to adapt or be adapted to many different functions or activities.

SYNONYMS **1** *a versatile player* **adaptable,** flexible, all-round, multitalented, resourceful. **2** *a versatile device*

adjustable, adaptable, multi-purpose, all-purpose.

□ **versatility** noun.

verse ▶ noun **1** writing arranged with a metrical rhythm. **2** a group of lines that form a unit in a poem or song. **3** each of the short numbered divisions of a chapter in the Bible.

SYNONYMS **1** *Elizabethan verse* **poetry,** lyrics. **2** *a verse he'd composed* **poem,** lyric, rhyme, ditty, lay. **3** *a poem with sixty verses* **stanza.**
ANTONYMS prose.

versed ▶ adjective (**versed in**) experienced or skilled in.

versify ▶ verb (**versifies, versifying, versified**) write verse, or turn a piece of writing into verse.
□ **versification** noun.

version ▶ noun **1** a particular form of something which differs from other forms of the same type of thing. **2** an account of something told from a particular person's point of view.

SYNONYMS **1** *the English version will be published next year* **edition,** translation, impression. **2** *his version of events* **account,** report, statement, description, record, story, rendering, interpretation, explanation, understanding, reading, impression, side. **3** *they have replaced coal-burning fires with gas versions* **type,** sort, kind, form, equivalent, variety, variant, design, model, style.

verso /ver-soh/ ▶ noun (plural **versos**) a left-hand page of an open book, or the back of a loose document.

versus ▶ preposition **1** against. **2** as opposed to.

vertebra /ver-ti-bruh/ ▶ noun (plural **vertebrae** /**ver**-ti-bray, **ver**-ti-bree/) each of the series of small bones forming the backbone.

vertebrate ▶ noun an animal having a backbone, e.g. a mammal, bird, reptile, amphibian, or fish.

vertex ▶ noun (plural **vertices** /**ver**-ti-seez/ or **vertexes**) **1** the highest point. **2** a meeting point of two lines that form an angle.

vertical ▶ adjective going straight up or down, at a right angle to a horizontal line or surface.

SYNONYMS **upright,** erect, perpendicular, plumb, on end, standing.
ANTONYMS flat, horizontal.

▶ noun a vertical line or surface.
□ **vertically** adverb.

vertiginous /ver-**tij**-i-nuhss/ ▶ adjective very high or steep.

V

vertigo /ver-ti-goh/ ▸ noun a feeling of giddiness caused by looking down from a great height.

vervain ▸ noun a plant with small blue, white, or purple flowers, used in herbal medicine.

verve ▸ noun energy, spirit, and style.

very ▸ adverb in a high degree.

> SYNONYMS *that's very kind of you* **extremely,** exceedingly, exceptionally, extraordinarily, tremendously, immensely, acutely, abundantly, singularly, decidedly, highly, remarkably, really; informal awfully, terribly, majorly, seriously, mega, ultra; Brit. informal ever so, well, dead, jolly; N. Amer. informal real, mighty.
> ANTONYMS slightly.

▸ adjective **1** actual; precise. **2** extreme. **3** mere.

> SYNONYMS **1** *those were his very words* **exact,** actual, precise. **2** *the very thought of food made her feel ill* **mere,** simple, pure, sheer.

vespers ▸ noun a Christian service of evening prayer.

vessel ▸ noun **1** a ship or large boat. **2** a tube or duct carrying a liquid within the body, or within a plant. **3** old use a bowl, cup, or other container for liquids.

> SYNONYMS **1** *a fishing vessel* **boat,** ship, craft. **2** *a cooking vessel* **container,** receptacle, basin, bowl, pan, pot, jug.

vest ▸ noun **1** Brit. a sleeveless garment or undergarment worn on the upper part of the body. **2** N. Amer. Austral. a waistcoat or sleeveless jacket.

▸ verb (**vest something in**) give someone power or property, or the legal right to hold power or own property.

■ **vested interest** a personal reason for wanting something to happen.

vestibule ▸ noun a room or hall just inside the outer door of a building.

vestige ▸ noun **1** a last remaining trace of something. **2** the smallest amount.

> SYNONYMS **remnant,** fragment, relic, echo, trace, mark, legacy, reminder.

◻ **vestigial** adjective.

vestment ▸ noun a robe worn by ministers or members of the choir during church services.

vestry ▸ noun (plural **vestries**) a small room in a church, used as an office and for changing into ceremonial robes.

vet ▸ noun a person qualified to treat sick or injured animals.

▸ verb (**vets, vetting, vetted**) find out about someone's background and past before employing them.

> SYNONYMS **check up on,** screen, investigate, examine, scrutinize, inspect, look over, assess, evaluate, appraise; informal check out.

vetch ▸ noun a plant of the pea family grown as food for farm animals.

veteran ▸ noun **1** a person who has had many years of experience in a particular field. **2** a person who used to serve in the armed forces.

> SYNONYMS *a veteran of many political campaigns* **old hand,** past master, doyen, doyenne; informal old-timer; N. Amer. informal vet.
> ANTONYMS novice.

▸ adjective with long experience in a particular field.

> SYNONYMS *a veteran diplomat* **long-serving,** seasoned, old, hardened, practised, experienced; informal battle-scarred.

veterinarian ▸ noun N. Amer. a vet.

veterinary /vet-uhn-ri, vet-uh-ri-nuh-ri/ ▸ adjective relating to the treatment of diseases and injuries in animals.

■ **veterinary surgeon** a vet.

> ✔ Note the **-er-** before the **-in-**: vet**er**inary.

veto /vee-toh/ ▸ noun (plural **vetoes**) **1** the right or power to reject a ruling or decision made by others. **2** a refusal to allow something.

> SYNONYMS *parliament's right of veto* **rejection,** dismissal, prohibition, proscription, embargo, ban.
> ANTONYMS approval.

▸ verb (**vetoes, vetoing, vetoed**) use a veto against, or refuse to allow.

> SYNONYMS *the president vetoed the bill* **reject,** turn down, throw out, dismiss, prohibit, forbid, proscribe, disallow, embargo, ban; informal kill.
> ANTONYMS approve.

vex ▸ verb make someone annoyed or worried.

◻ **vexation** noun **vexatious** adjective.

vexed ▸ adjective **1** (of an issue) difficult to deal with and causing a lot of debate. **2** annoyed or worried.

VHF ▸ abbreviation very high frequency.

VHS ▸ abbreviation trademark video home system.

via ▸ preposition **1** travelling through a particular place on the way to a destination. **2** by way of; through. **3** by means of.

viable ▸ adjective **1** capable of working successfully. **2** (of a plant, animal, or cell) able to live.

SYNONYMS **feasible,** workable, practicable, practical, realistic, achievable, attainable; informal doable.
ANTONYMS impracticable.

□ **viability** noun.

viaduct ▸ noun a long bridge-like structure carrying a road or railway across a valley or other low ground.

vial ▸ noun a small cylindrical glass bottle for medicines etc.

viands ▸ plural noun old use food.

vibe (or **vibes**) ▸ noun informal the atmosphere of a place, or a feeling passing between people.

vibrant ▸ adjective **1** full of energy and enthusiasm. **2** (of sound) strong or resonant. **3** (of colour) bright.

SYNONYMS **1** *a vibrant performance* **spirited,** lively, energetic, vigorous, storming, dynamic, passionate, fiery; informal feisty. **2** *vibrant colours* **vivid,** bright, striking, brilliant, glowing, strong, rich.
ANTONYMS lifeless, pale.

□ **vibrancy** noun **vibrantly** adverb.

vibraphone ▸ noun an electrical percussion instrument giving a vibrato effect.

vibrate ▸ verb (**vibrates, vibrating, vibrated**) **1** move with rapid small movements to and fro. **2** (of a sound) resonate.

SYNONYMS **shake,** tremble, shiver, quiver, shudder, throb, pulsate.

□ **vibration** noun.

vibrato /vi-**brah**-toh/ ▸ noun a rapid, slight variation in pitch in singing or playing some musical instruments.

vicar ▸ noun (in the Church of England) a minister in charge of a parish.

vicarage ▸ noun a vicar's house.

vicarious /vi-**kair**-i-uhss/ ▸ adjective experienced in the imagination rather than directly: *a vicarious thrill.*
□ **vicariously** adverb.

vice¹ ▸ noun **1** immoral or wicked behaviour. **2** criminal activities that involve sex or drugs. **3** a bad personal characteristic. **4** a bad habit.

SYNONYMS **1** *youngsters may be driven to vice* **immorality,** wrongdoing, wickedness, evil, iniquity, villainy, corruption, misconduct, sin, depravity. **2** *smoking is my only vice* **fault,** failing, flaw, defect, shortcoming, weakness, deficiency, foible, frailty.
ANTONYMS virtue.

vice² (US spelling **vise**) ▸ noun a metal tool with movable jaws which are used to hold an object firmly in place while work is done on it.

vice- ▸ combining form next in rank to; deputy: *vice-president.*

viceroy ▸ noun a person sent by a king or queen to govern a colony.

vice versa ▸ adverb reversing the order of the items just mentioned.

vicinity ▸ noun (plural **vicinities**) the area near or surrounding a place.

vicious ▸ adjective **1** cruel or violent. **2** (of an animal) wild and dangerous.

SYNONYMS **1** *a vicious killer* **brutal,** ferocious, savage, violent, ruthless, merciless, heartless, callous, cruel, cold-blooded, inhuman, barbaric, bloodthirsty. **2** *a vicious hate campaign* **malicious,** spiteful, vindictive, cruel, bitter, acrimonious, hostile, nasty; informal catty.
ANTONYMS gentle, kindly.

■ **vicious circle** a situation in which one problem leads to another, which then makes the first one worse.
□ **viciously** adverb **viciousness** noun.

✔ no **s** in the middle: vi**c**ious.

vicissitudes /vi-**sis**-si-tyoodz/ ▸ plural noun the ups and downs and changes in your life.

victim ▸ noun a person who is harmed or killed as a result of a crime, injustice, or accident.

SYNONYMS **sufferer,** injured party, casualty, fatality, loss, survivor.

victimize (or **victimise**) ▸ verb (**victimizes, victimizing, victimized**) single someone out for cruel or unfair treatment.
□ **victimization** noun.

victor ▸ noun a person who defeats an opponent in a battle, game, or competition.

Victorian ▸ adjective relating to the reign of Queen Victoria (1837–1901).

victorious ▸ adjective having won a victory.

SYNONYMS **triumphant,** conquering, vanquishing, winning, champion, successful.
ANTONYMS unsuccessful, losing.

victory ▸ noun (plural **victories**) an act of defeating an opponent.

SYNONYMS **success,** triumph, conquest, win, coup; informal walkover.
ANTONYMS defeat, loss.

victuals /vi-t'lz/ ▸ plural noun old use food and provisions.

video ▸ noun (plural **videos**) **1** a system of recording and reproducing moving images using magnetic tape. **2** a film or other recording on magnetic tape. **3** Brit. a video recorder.
▸ verb (**videoes, videoing, videoed**) film or make a video recording of.

V

■ **video game** a computer game played on a television screen. **video recorder** a machine linked to a television, used for recording programmes and playing videotapes.

videotape ▸ noun **1** magnetic tape for recording and reproducing visual images and sound. **2** a cassette on which this magnetic tape is held.
▸ verb (**videotapes, videotaping, videotaped**) record on videotape.

vie ▸ verb (**vies, vying, vied**) compete eagerly with others in order to do or achieve something.

> SYNONYMS **compete,** contend, struggle, fight, battle, jockey.

Vietnamese ▸ noun (plural **Vietnamese**) **1** a person from Vietnam. **2** the language of Vietnam.
▸ adjective relating to Vietnam.

view ▸ noun **1** the ability to see something or to be seen from a particular position. **2** something seen from a particular position, especially natural scenery. **3** an attitude or opinion.

> SYNONYMS **1** *the church came into view* **sight,** perspective, vision, visibility. **2** *the view from her flat* **outlook,** prospect, panorama, vista, scene, scenery, landscape. **3** *we agree with this view* **opinion,** viewpoint, belief, judgement, thinking, notion, idea, conviction, persuasion, attitude, feeling, sentiment.

▸ verb **1** look at or inspect. **2** have a particular attitude towards.

> SYNONYMS **1** *they viewed the landscape* **look at,** observe, eye, gaze at, contemplate, regard, scan, survey, inspect, scrutinize; informal check out; N. Amer. informal eyeball. **2** *the law was viewed as a last resort* **consider,** regard, look on, see, perceive, judge, deem, reckon.

■ **in view of** because or as a result of. **with a view to** with the intention of.

viewer ▸ noun **1** a person who views something. **2** a device for looking at images.

> SYNONYMS **watcher,** spectator, onlooker, observer; (**viewers**) audience, crowd.

viewfinder ▸ noun a device on a camera that you look through to see what will appear in the picture.

viewpoint ▸ noun an opinion.

viewscreen ▸ noun the screen on a television or computer on which images and information are displayed.

vigil /vi-jil/ ▸ noun a period of staying awake through the night to keep watch or pray.

vigilant ▸ adjective keeping careful watch for possible danger or difficulties.

> SYNONYMS **watchful,** observant, attentive, alert, eagle-eyed, on the lookout, on your guard; informal beady-eyed.
> ANTONYMS inattentive.

□ **vigilance** noun **vigilantly** adverb.

vigilante /vi-ji-**lan**-ti/ ▸ noun a member of a group of people who take it on themselves to prevent crime or punish criminals without legal authority.
□ **vigilantism** noun.

vignette /vee-**nyet**/ ▸ noun **1** a brief, vivid description or episode. **2** a small illustration or photograph which fades into its background without a definite border.

vigorous ▸ adjective **1** strong, healthy, and full of energy. **2** involving physical strength, effort, or energy.

> SYNONYMS **1** *the child was vigorous* **robust,** healthy, hale and hearty, strong, sturdy, fit, hardy, tough, energetic, lively, active. **2** *a vigorous defence* **strenuous,** powerful, forceful, spirited, determined, aggressive, passionate; informal punchy, feisty.
> ANTONYMS weak, feeble.

vigorously ▸ adverb in a vigorous way.

> SYNONYMS **strenuously,** strongly, powerfully, forcefully, energetically, heartily, all out, fiercely, hard; informal like mad; Brit. informal like billy-o.

vigour (US spelling **vigor**) ▸ noun **1** physical strength and good health. **2** effort, energy, and enthusiasm.

> SYNONYMS **health,** strength, robustness, energy, life, vitality, spirit, passion, determination, dynamism, drive; informal oomph, get-up-and-go.
> ANTONYMS lethargy.

Viking ▸ noun a member of the Scandinavian people who settled in parts of Britain and elsewhere in NW Europe between the 8th and 11th centuries.

vile ▸ adjective **1** very unpleasant. **2** wicked.

> SYNONYMS **foul,** nasty, unpleasant, bad, horrid, repulsive, disgusting, hateful, nauseating; informal gross.
> ANTONYMS pleasant.

□ **vilely** adverb.

vilify ▸ verb (**vilifies, vilifying, vilified**) speak or write about someone in a very unpleasant way.
□ **vilification** noun.

villa ▸ noun **1** Brit. a rented holiday home abroad. **2** (especially in southern Europe) a large country house in its own grounds. **3** a large house in ancient Rome.

village ▸ noun a small community of streets and houses in a country area.
□ **villager** noun.

villain ▶ noun **1** a bad person. **2** a bad character in a novel or play whose actions are important to the plot.

> SYNONYMS **criminal**, lawbreaker, offender, felon, miscreant, wrongdoer, rogue, scoundrel, reprobate; informal crook, baddy.

□ **villainous** adjective **villainy** noun.

villein /**vil**-luhn, vil-**layn**/ ▶ noun (in medieval England) a poor man who had to work for a lord in return for a small piece of land on which to grow food.

vim ▶ noun informal energy; enthusiasm.

vinaigrette /vi-ni-**gret**, vi-nay-**gret**/ ▶ noun a salad dressing consisting of oil mixed with vinegar.

vindicate ▶ verb (vindicates, vindicating, vindicated) **1** clear someone of blame or suspicion. **2** show something to be right or justified.

> SYNONYMS **1** *he was vindicated by the jury* **acquit**, clear, absolve, exonerate; informal let off. **2** *our concerns were vindicated* **justify**, warrant, substantiate, confirm, corroborate, prove, defend, support, back, endorse.
> ANTONYMS incriminate.

□ **vindication** noun.

vindictive ▶ adjective having or showing a strong or inappropriate desire for revenge.
□ **vindictiveness** noun.

vine ▶ noun a climbing plant, especially one that produces grapes.

vinegar ▶ noun a sour liquid made from wine, cider, or beer, used as a seasoning or for pickling.
□ **vinegary** adjective.

vineyard /**vin**-yard/ ▶ noun a plantation of grapevines producing grapes used in winemaking.

vintage ▶ noun **1** the year or place in which wine was produced. **2** a wine of high quality made from the crop of a single identified district in a good year. **3** the harvesting of grapes for winemaking. **4** the grapes or wine of a particular season. **5** the time that something was produced.
▶ adjective **1** referring to vintage wine. **2** referring to something from the past of high quality.

> SYNONYMS **1** *vintage French wine* **high-quality**, quality, choice, select, superior. **2** *vintage motor vehicles* **classic**, ageless, timeless, old, antique, heritage, historic.

vintner ▶ noun a wine merchant.

vinyl ▶ noun a type of strong flexible plastic, used in making floor coverings, paints, and gramophone records.

viol /**vy**-uhl/ ▶ noun an early instrument like a violin, but with six strings.

viola[1] /vi-**oh**-luh/ ▶ noun an instrument of the violin family, larger than the violin and tuned to a lower pitch.

viola[2] /**vy**-uh-luh/ ▶ noun a plant of a group that includes pansies and violets.

violate ▶ verb (violates, violating, violated) **1** break a rule or formal agreement. **2** treat something with disrespect. **3** rape or sexually assault someone.

> SYNONYMS **1** *this violates human rights* **contravene**, breach, infringe, break, transgress, disobey, defy, flout, disregard, ignore. **2** *the tomb was violated* **desecrate**, profane, defile, degrade, debase, damage, vandalize, deface, destroy.
> ANTONYMS respect.

violation ▶ noun an act of the action of violating.

> SYNONYMS **1** *a traffic violation* **contravention**, breach, infringement, transgression, defiance, flouting, disregard. **2** *the violation of the relics* **desecration**, defilement, damage, vandalism, destruction.

violence ▶ noun **1** actions using physical force and intended to hurt or kill someone or to cause damage. **2** an unpleasant or destructive natural force. **3** strength of emotion.

> SYNONYMS **1** *police violence* **brutality**, savagery, cruelty, barbarity. **2** *the violence of the blow* **force**, power, strength, might. **3** *the violence of his passion* **intensity**, severity, strength, force, vehemence, power, ferocity, fury.

violent ▶ adjective **1** using or involving violence. **2** very forceful or powerful.

> SYNONYMS **1** *a violent alcoholic* **brutal**, vicious, savage, rough, aggressive, threatening, fierce, ferocious. **2** *a violent blow* **powerful**, forceful, hard, sharp, smart, strong, vigorous, mighty, hefty. **3** *violent jealousy* **intense**, extreme, strong, powerful, unbridled, uncontrollable, ungovernable, consuming, passionate.
> ANTONYMS gentle, weak, mild.

□ **violently** adverb.

violet ▶ noun **1** a small plant with purple or blue flowers. **2** a bluish-purple colour.

violin ▶ noun a musical instrument with four strings, that you play with a bow.
□ **violinist** noun.

violoncello /vy-uh-luhn-**chel**-loh/ formal term for CELLO.

VIP ▶ noun a very important person.

viper ▶ noun a poisonous snake with large fangs and a patterned body.

V

virago /vi-**rah**-goh/ ▶ **noun** (plural **viragos** or **viragoes**) a domineering, violent, or bad-tempered woman.

viral ▶ **adjective** having to do with a virus or viruses.

virgin ▶ **noun 1** a person who has never had sex. **2** (**the Virgin**) the Virgin Mary, mother of Jesus.
▶ **adjective 1** having had no sexual experience. **2** not yet used, touched, or spoiled: *virgin forest*. **3** (of olive oil) made from the first pressing of olives.

> SYNONYMS **1** *virgin girls* **chaste,** celibate, abstinent, pure, uncorrupted, undefiled, innocent, immaculate.
> **2** *virgin forest* **untouched,** unspoilt, untainted, pristine, spotless, unpolluted, undefiled, perfect, intact, unexplored, uncharted.

□ **virginal** adjective **virginity** noun.

Virgo ▶ **noun** a sign of the zodiac (the Virgin), 23 August–22 September.

virile ▶ **adjective** (of a man) having strength, energy, and a strong sex drive.
□ **virility** noun.

virology ▶ **noun** the scientific study of viruses.
□ **virologist** noun.

virtual ▶ **adjective 1** almost or nearly the thing described, but not completely. **2** not existing in reality but made by computer software to appear to do so.

> SYNONYMS **effective,** near (enough), essential, practical, to all intents and purposes, in all but name, implied, unacknowledged.

■ **virtual reality** a system in which images that look like real objects are created by computer.

virtually ▶ **adverb** nearly.

> SYNONYMS **nearly,** almost, all but, more or less, practically, close to, verging on, just about, effectively, as good as, essentially, to all intents and purposes.

virtue ▶ **noun 1** behaviour showing high moral standards. **2** a good or useful quality. **3** old use virginity or chastity.

> SYNONYMS **1** *the simple virtue of peasant life* **goodness,** righteousness, morality, integrity, dignity, rectitude, honour.
> **2** *promptness was not one of his virtues* **good point,** good quality, strong point, asset, forte, attribute, strength, talent.
> **3** *I can see no virtue in this* **merit,** advantage, benefit, usefulness, strength.
> ANTONYMS vice, failing, disadvantage.

■ **by virtue of** because or as a result of.

virtuoso /ver-tyoo-**oh**-soh/ ▶ **noun** (plural **virtuosi** /ver-tyoo-**oh**-si/ or **virtuosos**) a person highly skilled in music or another art.

□ **virtuosity** noun.

virtuous ▶ **adjective 1** having high moral standards. **2** old use chaste.
□ **virtuously** adverb.

virulent ▶ **adjective 1** (of a disease or poison) very harmful in its effects. **2** bitterly hostile or critical.
□ **virulence** noun **virulently** adverb.

virus ▶ **noun 1** a submicroscopic organism which can cause disease. **2** an infection or disease caused by a virus. **3** a piece of code introduced secretly into a computer system in order to damage or destroy data.

visa ▶ **noun** a note on your passport indicating that you are allowed to enter, leave, or stay in a country.

visage /**vi**-zij/ ▶ **noun** literary a person's facial features or expression.

vis-à-vis /veez-ah-**vee**/ ▶ **preposition** in relation to.

viscera /**vis**-suh-ruh/ ▶ **plural noun** the internal organs of the body.

visceral ▶ **adjective 1** relating to deep inward feelings rather than to the intellect. **2** relating to the viscera.
□ **viscerally** adverb.

viscid /**viss**-id/ ▶ **adjective** technical sticky.

viscose ▶ **noun** a smooth synthetic fabric made from cellulose.

viscosity ▶ **noun** the state of being viscous.

viscount /**vy**-kownt/ ▶ **noun** a British nobleman ranking above a baron and below an earl.
□ **viscountess** noun.

viscous /**viss**-kuhss/ ▶ **adjective** having a thick, sticky consistency between solid and liquid.

vise US spelling of VICE².

visibility ▶ **noun 1** the state of being able to see or be seen. **2** the distance you can see, as determined by light and weather conditions.

visible ▶ **adjective** able to be seen or noticed.

> SYNONYMS **observable,** perceptible, noticeable, detectable, discernible, in sight, in view, on display, evident, apparent, manifest, plain.
> ANTONYMS invisible.

□ **visibly** adverb.

vision ▶ **noun 1** the ability to see. **2** the ability to think about the future with imagination or wisdom. **3** an experience of seeing something in a dream, trance, etc. **4** the images seen on a television screen. **5** a person or sight of unusual beauty.

> SYNONYMS **1** *her vision was blurred* **eyesight,** sight, observation, eyes, view, perspective. **2** *visions of the ancestral pilgrims* **apparition,** spectre, phantom, ghost, wraith, manifestation,

hallucination, illusion, mirage; informal spook. **3** *visions of a better future* **dream,** reverie, plan, hope, fantasy, delusion. **4** *his speech lacked vision* **imagination,** creativity, inventiveness, innovation, inspiration, intuition, perception, insight.

visionary ▸ adjective **1** thinking about the future with imagination or wisdom. **2** relating to supernatural or dreamlike visions.
▸ noun (plural **visionaries**) a person with imaginative and original ideas about the future.

visit ▸ verb (**visits, visiting, visited**) **1** go to spend time with a person or in a place. **2** view a website or web page. **3** (**visit with**) N. Amer. chat with someone. **4** (**visit something on**) literary cause something harmful or unpleasant to affect someone.

> SYNONYMS **1** *I visited my uncle* **call on,** go to see, look in on, stay with, holiday with, stop by, drop by; informal pop in on, drop in on, look up. **2** *Alex was visiting America* **stay in,** stop over in, spend time in, holiday in, vacation in, tour, explore, see; informal do.

▸ noun an act of visiting.

> SYNONYMS **1** *she paid a visit to her mum* (**social**) **call. 2** *a visit to the museum* **trip,** tour of, look round, stopover, stay, holiday, break, vacation.

visitation ▸ noun **1** an official or formal visit. **2** the appearance of a god, goddess, etc. **3** a disaster or difficulty seen as a punishment from God.

visitor ▸ noun a person who visits.

> SYNONYMS **1** *I am expecting a visitor* **guest,** caller, company. **2** *the monument attracts many visitors* **tourist,** traveller, holidaymaker, tripper, vacationer, sightseer, pilgrim, foreigner, stranger.

visor (or **vizor**) ▸ noun **1** a movable part of a helmet that can be pulled down to cover the face. **2** a screen for protecting the eyes from light.

vista ▸ noun a pleasing view.

> SYNONYMS **view,** scene, prospect, panorama, sight, scenery, landscape.

visual ▸ adjective relating to seeing or sight.

> SYNONYMS **1** *visual defects* **optical,** ocular, eye, vision, sight. **2** *a visual indication that the alarm works* **visible,** observable, perceptible, discernible.
> ANTONYMS acoustic.

▸ noun a picture, piece of film, or display used to illustrate or accompany something.
■ **visual display unit** Brit. a device that displays information from a computer on a screen.

□ **visually** adverb.

visualize (or **visualise**) ▸ verb (**visualizes, visualizing, visualized**) form an image of something in the mind.

> SYNONYMS **envisage,** conjure up, picture, call to mind, see, imagine, dream up.

□ **visualization** noun.

vital ▸ adjective **1** absolutely necessary. **2** essential for life. **3** full of energy.

> SYNONYMS **1** *it is vital that action is taken* **essential,** critical, crucial, indispensable, all-important, imperative, mandatory, high-priority. **2** *he is young and vital* **lively,** energetic, active, sprightly, spirited, vivacious, exuberant, dynamic, vigorous; informal full of beans.
> ANTONYMS unimportant, listless.

▸ noun (**vitals**) the body's important internal organs.
■ **vital statistics** informal the measurements of a woman's bust, waist, and hips.
□ **vitally** adverb.

vitality ▸ noun the state of being strong and active.

> SYNONYMS **life,** energy, spirit, vivacity, exuberance, dynamism, vigour, passion, drive; informal get-up-and-go.

vitalize (or **vitalise**) ▸ verb (**vitalizes, vitalizing, vitalized**) give strength and energy to.

vitamin ▸ noun any of a group of natural substances which are present in many foods and are essential for normal nutrition.

vitiate /vi-shee-ayt/ ▸ verb (**vitiates, vitiating, vitiated**) formal make something less good or effective.

viticulture ▸ noun the cultivation of grapevines.

vitreous ▸ adjective containing or like glass.
■ **vitreous humour** the transparent jelly-like tissue that fills the eyeball.

vitrify ▸ verb (**vitrifies, vitrifying, vitrified**) convert into glass or a glass-like substance by exposure to heat.

vitriol ▸ noun **1** very cruel or bitter remarks. **2** old use sulphuric acid.
□ **vitriolic** adjective.

vituperation ▸ noun bitter and abusive language.
□ **vituperative** adjective.

viva[1] /vee-vuh/ ▸ exclamation long live!

viva[2] /vy-vuh/ (or **viva voce** /vy-vuh voh-chi/) ▸ noun Brit. an oral exam for an academic qualification.

vivacious ▸ adjective attractively lively.
□ **vivaciously** adverb **vivacity** noun.

vivarium ▸ noun (plural **vivaria**) a place for keeping animals in natural conditions for study or as pets.

v

vivid | void

vivid ▸ adjective **1** producing powerful feelings or strong, clear images in the mind. **2** (of a colour) very deep or bright.

SYNONYMS **1** *a vivid blue* **bright,** colourful, brilliant, radiant, vibrant, strong, bold, deep, intense, rich, warm. **2** *a vivid account* **graphic,** realistic, lifelike, faithful, authentic, striking, evocative, arresting, colourful, dramatic, memorable, powerful, stirring, moving, haunting.
ANTONYMS dull, vague.

□ **vividly** adverb **vividness** noun.

vivify ▸ verb (**vivifies, vivifying, vivified**) formal make more lively or interesting; enliven.

viviparous /vi-vi-puh-ruhss/ ▸ adjective (of an animal) giving birth to live young.

vivisection ▸ noun the performance of operations on live animals for scientific research.

vixen ▸ noun **1** a female fox. **2** a spirited or hot-tempered woman.

viz. ▸ adverb namely; in other words.
ORIGIN short for Latin *videlicet*.

vizier /vi-zeer/ ▸ noun (in the past) an important official in some Muslim countries.

vizor → VISOR.

vocabulary ▸ noun (plural **vocabularies**) **1** all the words used in a particular language or activity. **2** all the words known to a person. **3** a list of words and their meanings, provided with a piece of technical or foreign writing.

vocal ▸ adjective **1** relating to the human voice. **2** expressing opinions or feelings freely or loudly. **3** (of music) consisting of or including singing.

SYNONYMS **1** *vocal sounds* **spoken,** said, voiced, uttered, articulated, oral. **2** *a vocal critic* **vociferous,** outspoken, forthright, plain-spoken, blunt, frank, candid, passionate, vehement, vigorous.

▸ noun (also **vocals**) a part of a piece of music that is sung.
■ **vocal cords** strips of muscle in the throat that vibrate to produce the voice.
□ **vocally** adverb.

vocalist ▸ noun a singer.

vocalize (or **vocalise**) ▸ verb (**vocalizes, vocalizing, vocalized**) **1** make a sound or say a word. **2** express something with words.
□ **vocalization** noun.

vocation ▸ noun **1** a strong feeling that you ought to pursue a particular career or occupation. **2** a person's career or occupation.

SYNONYMS **calling,** life's work, mission, purpose, profession, occupation, career,

job, employment, trade, craft, line (of work).

□ **vocational** adjective.

vocative /vok-uh-tiv/ ▸ noun Grammar the case of nouns, pronouns, and adjectives used in addressing a person or thing.

vociferous /vuh-sif-uh-ruhss/ ▸ adjective expressing opinions in a loud and forceful way.
□ **vociferously** adverb.

vodka ▸ noun a clear alcoholic spirit, originally from Russia.

vogue ▸ noun the fashion or style current at a particular time.

SYNONYMS **fashion,** trend, fad, fancy, craze, rage, enthusiasm, passion.

□ **voguish** adjective.

voice ▸ noun **1** the sound produced in a person's larynx and uttered through the mouth, as speech or song. **2** the ability to speak or sing. **3** a vocal part in a piece of music. **4** Grammar a form of a verb showing the relation of the subject to the action.

SYNONYMS **1** *the voice of the people* **opinion,** view, feeling, wish, desire, vote. **2** *a powerful voice for conservation* **mouthpiece,** representative, spokesperson, agent, vehicle.

▸ verb (**voices, voicing, voiced**) express something in words.

SYNONYMS *they voiced their opposition* **express,** communicate, declare, state, vent, utter, say, speak, articulate; informal come out with.

■ **voice box** the larynx. **voice-over** a piece of speech in a film or broadcast that is spoken by a person who is not seen on the screen.
□ **voiceless** adjective.

voicemail ▸ noun an electronic system which can store messages from telephone callers.

void ▸ adjective **1** not valid or legally binding. **2** completely empty. **3** (**void of**) free from; lacking.

SYNONYMS **1** *the election was void* **invalid,** null, ineffective, worthless. **2** *vast void spaces* **empty,** vacant, blank, bare, clear, free.
ANTONYMS valid, full.

▸ noun a completely empty space.

SYNONYMS *the void of space* **vacuum,** emptiness, nothingness, blankness, (empty) space, gap, cavity, chasm, gulf.

▸ verb **1** empty waste matter from the bladder or bowels. **2** declare to be not valid or legally binding.

SYNONYMS *the contract was voided* **invalidate,** annul, nullify, negate, quash, cancel, countermand, repeal, revoke, rescind, retract, withdraw, reverse. ANTONYMS validate, fill.

voile /voyl, vwahl/ ▸ noun a thin, semi-transparent fabric.

volatile ▸ adjective **1** liable to change rapidly and unpredictably. **2** (of a substance) easily evaporated at normal temperatures.

SYNONYMS **1** *a volatile personality* **unpredictable,** temperamental, capricious, fickle, impulsive, emotional, excitable, turbulent, erratic, unstable. **2** *the atmosphere is too volatile for an election* **tense,** strained, fraught, uneasy, uncomfortable, charged, explosive, inflammatory, turbulent. ANTONYMS stable, calm.

▢ **volatility** noun.

vol-au-vent /vol-oh-von/ ▸ noun a small round case of puff pastry filled with a savoury mixture.

volcanic ▸ adjective relating to or produced by a volcano or volcanoes.

volcano ▸ noun (plural **volcanoes** or **volcanos**) a mountain with an opening through which lava, rock, and gas are forced from the earth's crust.

vole ▸ noun a small mouse-like rodent.

volition ▸ noun a person's will or power of independent action.

volley ▸ noun (plural **volleys**) **1** a number of bullets, arrows, etc. fired at one time. **2** a series of questions, insults, etc. directed rapidly at someone. **3** (in sport) an act of hitting the ball before it touches the ground.

SYNONYMS **barrage,** cannonade, battery, bombardment, salvo, burst, storm, hail, shower, deluge, torrent.

▸ verb (**volleys, volleying, volleyed**) hit the ball before it touches the ground.

volleyball ▸ noun a team game in which a ball is hit by hand over a net and must be kept from touching the ground.

volt ▸ noun the basic unit of electric potential.

voltage ▸ noun an electrical force expressed in volts.

volte-face /volt-fass/ ▸ noun an abrupt and complete change of attitude or policy.

voluble ▸ adjective talking easily and at length.
▢ **volubility** noun **volubly** adverb.

volume ▸ noun **1** the amount of space occupied by something or enclosed within a container. **2** the amount or quantity of something. **3** degree of loudness. **4** a book, especially one forming part of a larger work or series.

SYNONYMS **1** *a syringe of known volume* **capacity,** mass, bulk, extent, size, dimensions. **2** *a huge volume of water* **quantity,** amount, mass, bulk, measure. **3** *she turned the volume down* **loudness,** sound, amplification. **4** *a volume from the library* **book,** publication, tome, work, title.

voluminous ▸ adjective **1** (of clothing) loose and full. **2** (of writing) very lengthy.

voluntarily ▸ adverb in a voluntary way.

SYNONYMS **of your own free will,** of your own volition, by choice, by preference, spontaneously, willingly, readily, freely. ANTONYMS compulsorily.

voluntary ▸ adjective **1** done or acting of your own free will. **2** working or done without payment.

SYNONYMS **1** *attendance is voluntary* **optional,** discretionary, elective, non-compulsory. **2** *voluntary work* **unpaid,** unsalaried, for free, without charge, for nothing, honorary. ANTONYMS compulsory, paid.

▸ noun (plural **voluntaries**) an organ solo played before, during, or after a church service.

volunteer ▸ noun **1** a person who freely offers to do something. **2** a person who does work without being paid. **3** a person who freely joins the armed forces.
▸ verb (**volunteers, volunteering, volunteered**) **1** freely offer to do something. **2** say or suggest something without being asked.

SYNONYMS **1** *I volunteered my services* **offer,** tender, proffer, put forward, put up, venture. **2** *he volunteered as a driver* **offer your services,** present yourself, make yourself available, come forward. ANTONYMS withdraw, refuse.

voluptuary ▸ noun (plural **voluptuaries**) a person who loves luxury and pleasure.

voluptuous /vuh-**lup**-tyuu-uhss/ ▸ adjective **1** (of a woman) curvaceous and sexually attractive. **2** giving sensual pleasure.
▢ **voluptuously** adverb.

vomit ▸ verb (**vomits, vomiting, vomited**) **1** bring up food from the stomach through the mouth. **2** send out in an uncontrolled stream.

SYNONYMS **1** *he needed to vomit* **be sick,** spew, fetch up, heave, retch, gag; informal throw up, puke; N. Amer. informal barf. **2** *I vomited my breakfast* **bring up,** regurgitate, spew up; informal throw up, puke up; Brit. informal sick up.

▸ noun food vomited from the stomach.

SYNONYMS *a coat stained with vomit* **sick;** informal puke, spew; N. Amer. informal barf.

voodoo ▸ noun a religious cult practised mainly in the Caribbean and involving sorcery and possession by spirits.

V

voracious ▸ adjective **1** wanting or eating great quantities of food. **2** doing something eagerly and enthusiastically.
□ **voraciously** adverb **voracity** noun.

vortex ▸ noun (plural **vortexes** or **vortices** /**vor**-ti-seez/) a whirling mass of water or air.

votary ▸ noun (plural **votaries**) **1** a person who has dedicated themselves to God or religious service. **2** a devoted follower or supporter.

vote ▸ noun **1** a formal choice made between two or more candidates or courses of action. **2** (**the vote**) the right to take part in an election.

> SYNONYMS **1** *a rigged vote* **ballot,** poll, election, referendum, plebiscite, show of hands. **2** *in 1918 women got the vote* **suffrage,** franchise, voting rights, voice, say.

▸ verb (**votes, voting, voted**) give or register a vote.

> SYNONYMS *I vote we have one more game* **suggest,** propose, recommend, advocate, move, submit.

□ **voter** noun.

votive ▸ adjective offered to a god as a sign of thanks.

vouch ▸ verb (**vouch for**) **1** state that something is true or accurate. **2** state that someone is who they claim to be, or that they are of good character.

voucher ▸ noun a piece of paper that entitles you to a discount, or that may be exchanged for goods or services.

> SYNONYMS **coupon,** token, ticket, pass, chit, slip, stub, docket; Brit. informal chitty.

vouchsafe ▸ verb (**vouchsafes, vouchsafing, vouchsafed**) formal give or say in a gracious or superior way.

vow ▸ noun a solemn promise.

> SYNONYMS *a vow of silence* **promise,** pledge, oath, bond, covenant, commitment, word (of honour).

▸ verb solemnly promise to do something.

> SYNONYMS *I vowed to do better* **promise,** pledge, swear, undertake, make a commitment, give your word, guarantee.

vowel ▸ noun a letter of the alphabet representing a sound in which the mouth is open and the tongue is not touching the top of the mouth, the teeth, or the lips (in English *a*, *e*, *i*, *o*, and *u*).

voyage ▸ noun a long journey by sea or in space.

> SYNONYMS **journey,** trip, cruise, passage, sail, crossing, expedition.

▸ verb (**voyages, voyaging, voyaged**) go on a voyage.
□ **voyager** noun.

voyeur /vwa-**yer**, voy-**er**/ ▸ noun **1** a person who gains sexual pleasure from watching other people when they are naked or having sex. **2** a person who enjoys seeing the pain or distress of other people.
□ **voyeurism** noun **voyeuristic** adjective.

vs ▸ abbreviation versus.

vulcanized (or **vulcanised**) ▸ adjective (of rubber) hardened by being treated with sulphur at a high temperature.

vulgar ▸ adjective **1** lacking sophistication or good taste. **2** referring to sex or bodily functions in a rude or inappropriate way.

> SYNONYMS **1** *the decor was lavish but vulgar* **tasteless,** crass, tawdry, ostentatious, flamboyant, showy, gaudy, garish; informal flash, tacky. **2** *a vulgar joke* **rude,** crude, dirty, filthy, smutty, naughty, indecent, obscene, coarse, risqué; informal blue.
> **3** *it was vulgar for a woman to whistle* **impolite,** ill-mannered, boorish, uncouth, unsophisticated, unrefined.
> ANTONYMS tasteful, clean, decent.

■ **vulgar fraction** Brit. a fraction shown by numbers above and below a line, not decimally.
□ **vulgarity** noun **vulgarly** adverb.

vulgarize (or **vulgarise**) ▸ verb (**vulgarizes, vulgarizing, vulgarized**) spoil something by making it less refined or exclusive.

Vulgate ▸ noun the main Latin version of the Bible, prepared in the 4th century.

vulnerable ▸ adjective able to be attacked or harmed.

> SYNONYMS **1** *a vulnerable city* **in danger,** in peril, in jeopardy, at risk, unprotected, undefended, unguarded, open to attack, exposed. **2** *he is vulnerable to criticism* **exposed,** open, liable, prone, prey, susceptible, subject.
> ANTONYMS invulnerable, safe.

□ **vulnerability** noun **vulnerably** adverb.

vulpine ▸ adjective having to do with foxes, or like a fox.

vulture ▸ noun a large bird of prey that feeds mainly on dead animals.

vulva ▸ noun the female external genitals.

vying present participle of VIE.

Ww

W (or **w**) ▸ noun (plural **Ws** or **W's**) the twenty-third letter of the alphabet.
▸ abbreviation **1** watts. **2** West or Western.

wacky (or **whacky**) ▸ adjective (**wackier**, **wackiest**) informal funny or amusing in a slightly odd way.

wad ▸ noun **1** a lump or bundle of a soft material. **2** a bundle of paper or banknotes.
▸ verb (**wads**, **wadding**, **wadded**) **1** press a soft material into a wad. **2** line or fill with soft material.

waddle ▸ verb (**waddles**, **waddling**, **waddled**) walk with short steps and a clumsy swaying motion.

> SYNONYMS **toddle**, totter, wobble, shuffle.

▸ noun a waddling way of walking.

wade ▸ verb (**wades**, **wading**, **waded**) **1** walk through water or mud. **2** (**wade through**) read or deal with something that is boring or takes a long time. **3** (**wade in** or **into**) informal attack or intervene in a forceful way.

> SYNONYMS **1** *they waded in the water* **paddle**, wallow, splash; informal splosh. **2** *I had to wade through some hefty documents* **plough**, plod, trawl, labour, toil.

wader ▸ noun **1** a long-legged bird that feeds in shallow water. **2** (**waders**) high waterproof boots.

wafer ▸ noun **1** a very thin, light, sweet biscuit. **2** a thin disc of unleavened bread used in the Christian service of Holy Communion.

waffle¹ Brit. informal ▸ verb (**waffles**, **waffling**, **waffled**) speak or write at length without saying anything interesting or important.
▸ noun lengthy talk or writing that does not say anything interesting or important.

waffle² ▸ noun a small, crisp batter cake, eaten hot with butter or syrup.

waft ▸ verb pass easily or gently through the air.
▸ noun a gentle movement of air.

wag ▸ verb (**wags**, **wagging**, **wagged**) move rapidly to and fro.

> SYNONYMS **1** *the dog's tail wagged* **swing**, swish, switch, sway, shake; informal

waggle. **2** *he wagged his stick at them* **shake**, wave, wiggle, flourish, brandish.

▸ noun **1** a wagging movement. **2** informal a person who likes making jokes.
□ **waggish** adjective.

wage ▸ noun (also **wages**) a fixed regular payment for work.

> SYNONYMS *the workers' wages* **pay**, salary, stipend, fee, remuneration, income, earnings.

▸ verb (**wages**, **waging**, **waged**) carry on a war or campaign.

> SYNONYMS *they waged war on the guerrillas* **engage in**, carry on, conduct, execute, pursue, prosecute, proceed with.

wager more formal term for BET.

waggle ▸ verb (**waggles**, **waggling**, **waggled**) move with short, quick movements from side to side or up and down.

wagon (or Brit. **waggon**) ▸ noun **1** a vehicle, especially a horse-drawn one, for transporting goods. **2** Brit. a railway vehicle for carrying goods in bulk.
■ **on the wagon** informal not drinking alcohol.

wagtail ▸ noun a slender bird with a long tail that it frequently wags up and down.

waif ▸ noun **1** a poor, helpless person, especially a child. **2** a person who is thin and pale.

wail ▸ noun **1** a long high-pitched cry of pain, grief, or anger. **2** a sound resembling this.

> SYNONYMS **howl**, cry, bawl, moan, groan, yowl, whine, lament.

▸ verb make a wail.

> SYNONYMS **howl**, cry, bawl, moan, groan, yowl, whine, lament.

wain ▸ noun old use a wagon or cart.

wainscot /wayn-skuht/ ▸ noun an area of wooden panelling on the lower part of the walls of a room.

waist ▸ noun **1** the part of the human body below the ribs and above the hips. **2** a narrow part in the middle of something.

waistband ▸ noun a strip of cloth forming the waist of a skirt or pair of trousers.

waistcoat ▸ noun Brit. a waist-length garment with buttons down the front and no sleeves or collar.

waistline ▸ noun the measurement around a person's body at the waist.

wait ▸ verb 1 stay in a particular place or delay doing anything until a particular time or event. 2 be delayed or postponed. 3 (wait on) act as an attendant to. 4 serve people at a meal or in a restaurant.

> SYNONYMS 1 *we'll wait in the airport* **stay (put)**, remain, rest, stop, halt, pause, linger, loiter; informal stick around. 2 *she had to wait until her bags arrived* **stand by**, hold back, bide your time, mark time, kill time, waste time, kick your heels, twiddle your thumbs; informal hold on, hang around, sit tight. 3 *that job will have to wait* **be postponed**, be delayed, be put off, be deferred; informal be put on the back burner, be put on ice.

▸ noun a period of waiting.

> SYNONYMS *a long wait* **delay**, hold-up, interval, interlude, pause, break, suspension, stoppage, halt, interruption, lull, gap.

waiter (or **waitress**) ▸ noun a person whose job is to serve customers at their tables in a restaurant.

> SYNONYMS **server**, steward, stewardess, attendant, butler, servant; N. Amer. waitperson.

waive ▸ verb (**waives, waiving, waived**) choose not to insist on a claim or right.

> SYNONYMS 1 *he waived his right to a hearing* **give up**, abandon, renounce, relinquish, surrender, sacrifice, turn down. 2 *the manager waived the rules* **disregard**, ignore, overlook, set aside, forgo.

waiver ▸ noun an instance of waiving a right or claim, or a document recording this.

wake[1] ▸ verb (**wakes, waking, woke**; past participle **woken**) 1 (often **wake up**) stop sleeping. 2 bring to life, or make more alert. 3 (**wake up to**) become aware of.

> SYNONYMS 1 *at 4.30 a.m. Mark woke up* **awake**, waken, stir, come to, come round. 2 *she woke her husband* **rouse**, waken.
> ANTONYMS go to sleep, send to sleep.

▸ noun 1 a party held after a funeral. 2 a gathering held beside the body of someone who has died.

> SYNONYMS **vigil**, watch, funeral.

wake[2] ▸ noun a trail of disturbed water or air left by a ship or aircraft.

> SYNONYMS *the cruiser's wake* **backwash**, slipstream, trail, path, track.

■ **in the wake of** following as a result of.

wakeful ▸ adjective 1 not sleeping. 2 alert and aware of possible dangers.
□ **wakefulness** noun.

waken ▸ verb wake from sleep.

walk ▸ verb 1 move fairly slowly using the legs. 2 travel over a route or area on foot. 3 accompany someone on foot. 4 take a dog out for exercise.

> SYNONYMS 1 *they walked along the road* **stroll**, saunter, amble, trudge, plod, hike, tramp, trek, march, stride, troop, wander, ramble, promenade, traipse; informal mosey, hoof it. 2 *he walked her home* **accompany**, escort, guide, show, see, take.

▸ noun 1 a journey on foot. 2 a fairly slow rate of movement on foot. 3 a person's way of walking. 4 a path for walking.

> SYNONYMS 1 *country walks* **ramble**, hike, tramp, march, stroll, promenade, constitutional, turn. 2 *her elegant walk* **gait**, step, stride, tread. 3 *the riverside walk* **path**, pathway, footpath, track, walkway, promenade, footway, pavement, trail, towpath.

■ **walking stick** a stick used for support when walking. **walk of life** the position in society that someone holds.

walkabout ▸ noun 1 chiefly Brit. an informal stroll among a crowd by an important visitor. 2 Austral. a journey (originally on foot) made by an Australian Aboriginal in order to live in the traditional way.

walker ▸ noun a person who walks.

> SYNONYMS **rambler**, hiker, trekker, stroller, pedestrian.

walkie-talkie ▸ noun a portable two-way radio.

Walkman ▸ noun (plural **Walkmans** or **Walkmen**) trademark a personal stereo.

walkout ▸ noun a sudden angry departure as a protest or strike.

walkover ▸ noun an easy victory.

walkway ▸ noun a raised passageway or a wide path.

wall ▸ noun 1 a continuous upright structure forming a side of a building or room, or enclosing or dividing an area of land. 2 a barrier. 3 the outer layer or lining of an organ or cavity in the body.
▸ verb enclose or block with walls.
■ **go to the wall** informal (of a business) fail. **wall-eyed** informal having an eye that squints outwards.

wallaby ▸ noun (plural **wallabies**) an Australian animal like a small kangaroo.

wallet ▸ noun a small flat, folding holder for money and plastic cards.

w

SYNONYMS **purse,** case, pouch, holder; N. Amer. billfold, pocketbook.

wallflower ▸ noun **1** a plant with sweet-smelling flowers that bloom in early spring. **2** informal a girl who has no one to dance with at a party.

wallop informal ▸ verb (**wallops, walloping, walloped**) hit very hard.
▸ noun a heavy blow.

wallow ▸ verb **1** roll about or lie in mud or water. **2** (of a boat or aircraft) roll from side to side. **3** (**wallow in**) indulge in.
▸ noun **1** an act of wallowing. **2** an area of mud or shallow water where animals go to wallow.

wallpaper ▸ noun **1** paper pasted in strips over the walls of a room as decoration. **2** a background pattern or picture on a computer screen.

wally ▸ noun (plural **wallies**) Brit. informal a stupid person.

walnut ▸ noun an edible nut with a wrinkled shell.

walrus ▸ noun a large sea mammal with downward-pointing tusks.

waltz ▸ noun a ballroom dance in triple time performed by a couple.
▸ verb **1** dance a waltz. **2** move in a casual or inconsiderate way.

waltzer ▸ noun a fairground ride in which cars are carried round a track that moves up and down.

wan (*rhymes with* gone) ▸ adjective **1** (of a person) pale and appearing ill or exhausted. **2** (of light) pale or weak. **3** (of a smile) lacking enthusiasm; strained.
□ **wanly** adverb.

wand ▸ noun a long, thin rod, especially one used in casting magic spells or performing tricks.

wander ▸ verb (**wanders, wandering, wandered**) **1** move in a leisurely, casual, or aimless way. **2** move slowly away from the correct place.

SYNONYMS **1** *I wandered around the estate* **stroll,** amble, saunter, walk, potter, ramble, meander, roam, range, drift; Scottish & Irish stravaig; informal traipse, mosey. **2** *we are wandering from the point* **stray,** depart, diverge, deviate, digress, drift, get sidetracked.

▸ noun a period of wandering.
□ **wanderer** noun.

wanderlust ▸ noun a strong desire to travel.

wane ▸ verb (**wanes, waning, waned**) **1** (of the moon) appear to decrease in size day by day. **2** become weaker.

SYNONYMS **decline,** diminish, decrease, dwindle, shrink, tail off, ebb, fade, lessen, peter out, fall off, recede, slump, weaken, wither, evaporate, die out.
ANTONYMS wax, grow.

■ **on the wane** becoming weaker.

wangle ▸ verb (**wangles, wangling, wangled**) informal get something by using persuasion or a clever plan.

want ▸ verb **1** have a desire to possess or do. **2** (**be wanted**) (of a suspected criminal) be searched for by the police. **3** (also **want for**) lack or be short of. **4** feel sexual desire for.

SYNONYMS **desire,** wish for, hope for, fancy, care for, like, long for, yearn for, crave, hanker after, hunger for, thirst for, cry out for, covet; informal have a yen for, be dying for.

▸ noun **1** lack or shortage. **2** poverty. **3** a desire for something.

SYNONYMS **1** *his want of vigilance* **lack,** absence, non-existence, dearth, deficiency, inadequacy, insufficiency, paucity, shortage, scarcity. **2** *a time of want* **need,** austerity, privation, deprivation, poverty, destitution. **3** *her wants would be taken care of* **wish,** desire, demand, longing, fancy, craving, need, requirement; informal yen.

wanting ▸ adjective **1** not having something required or desired. **2** not good enough.

SYNONYMS **deficient,** inadequate, lacking, insufficient, imperfect, flawed, unsound, substandard, inferior, second-rate.
ANTONYMS sufficient.

wanton ▸ adjective **1** (of a cruel or violent action) deliberate and unprovoked. **2** having many sexual partners.

SYNONYMS **deliberate,** wilful, malicious, gratuitous, unprovoked, motiveless, arbitrary, unjustifiable, senseless.
ANTONYMS justifiable.

□ **wantonly** adverb.

WAP ▸ abbreviation Wireless Application Protocol, a means of enabling a mobile phone to browse the Internet.

wapiti /wop-i-ti/ ▸ noun (plural **wapitis**) a large North American red deer.

war ▸ noun **1** a state of armed conflict between different nations, states, or groups. **2** a long contest between rivals or campaign against something.

SYNONYMS **1** *the Napoleonic wars* **conflict,** warfare, combat, fighting, action, bloodshed, struggle, fight, campaign, hostilities, crusade. **2** *the war against drugs* **campaign,** crusade, battle, fight, struggle.
ANTONYMS peace.

▸ verb (**wars, warring, warred**) be involved in a war.

W

SYNONYMS *rival Emperors warred against each other* **fight,** battle, combat, wage war, take up arms, feud, quarrel, struggle, contend, wrangle, cross swords.

■ **be on the warpath** be very angry with someone. **war crime** an action that breaks accepted international rules of war.

warble ▶ verb (**warbles, warbling, warbled**) sing in a trilling or quavering voice.

warbler ▶ noun a small songbird with a warbling song.

ward ▶ noun **1** a room in a hospital for one or more patients. **2** a division of a city or borough that is represented by a councillor or councillors. **3** a young person looked after by a guardian appointed by their parents or a court. **4** a ridge or bar in a lock that engages with grooves on a key.

SYNONYMS **1** *the surgical ward* **room,** department, unit, area. **2** *the most marginal ward in Westminster* **district,** constituency, division, quarter, zone, parish. **3** *the boy is my ward* **dependant,** charge, protégé.

▶ verb (**ward someone/thing off**) prevent someone or something from harming you.

warden ▶ noun **1** a person supervising a place or procedure. **2** Brit. the head of certain schools, colleges, etc. **3** N. Amer. a prison governor.

SYNONYMS **1** *the flats have a resident warden* **superintendent,** caretaker, porter, steward, custodian, watchman, concierge, doorman, commissionaire. **2** *a game warden* **ranger,** keeper, guardian, protector. **3** *he was handcuffed to a warden* **prison officer,** guard, jailer, warder, keeper; informal **screw. 4** *the college warden* **principal,** head, governor, master, mistress, rector, provost, dean, president, director, chancellor.

warder ▶ noun (feminine **wardress**) Brit. a prison guard.

wardrobe ▶ noun **1** a large, tall cupboard for hanging clothes in. **2** a person's entire collection of clothes. **3** the costume department of a theatre or film company.

wardroom ▶ noun the room on a warship where the officers eat.

ware ▶ noun **1** pottery of a particular type. **2** manufactured articles. **3** (**wares**) articles offered for sale.

SYNONYMS (**wares**) **goods,** merchandise, products, produce, stock, commodities.

warehouse ▶ noun **1** a large building for storing raw materials or manufactured goods. **2** a large wholesale or retail store.

SYNONYMS **storeroom,** depot, depository, stockroom, magazine, granary; informal lock-up.

warfare ▶ noun the activity of fighting a war.

SYNONYMS **fighting,** war, combat, conflict, action, hostilities.

warhead ▶ noun the explosive head of a missile, torpedo, etc.

warhorse ▶ noun informal a very experienced soldier, politician, etc.

warlike ▶ adjective **1** hostile. **2** intended for war.

warlock ▶ noun a man who practises witchcraft.

warlord ▶ noun a military commander, especially one controlling a region.

warm ▶ adjective **1** at a fairly high temperature. **2** helping the body to stay warm. **3** enthusiastic, affectionate, or kind. **4** (of a colour) containing red, yellow, or orange tones. **5** (of a scent or trail) fresh and easy to follow.

SYNONYMS **1** *a warm kitchen* **hot,** cosy, snug. **2** *a warm day* **balmy,** summery, sultry, hot, mild, temperate. **3** *warm water* **tepid,** lukewarm. **4** *a warm sweater* **thick,** chunky, thermal, winter, woolly. **5** *a warm welcome* **friendly,** cordial, amiable, genial, kind, pleasant, fond, welcoming, hospitable, hearty.
ANTONYMS cold, chilly, light, hostile.

▶ verb **1** make or become warm. **2** (**warm to** or **towards**) become more interested in or enthusiastic about.

SYNONYMS *warm the soup in that pan* **heat (up),** reheat.
ANTONYMS chill.

▶ noun (**the warm**) a warm place or area.
■ **warm-blooded** (of animals) keeping a constant body temperature by their body's chemical processes. **warm up** prepare for physical exertion by doing gentle stretches and exercises. **warm something up** entertain an audience before the arrival of the main act.
□ **warmly** adverb.

warmonger ▶ noun a person who tries to bring about war.

warmth ▶ noun **1** the quality of being warm. **2** enthusiasm, affection, or kindness. **3** strength of emotion.

SYNONYMS **1** *the warmth of the fire* **heat,** cosiness, snugness. **2** *the warmth of their welcome* **friendliness,** amiability, geniality, cordiality, kindness, tenderness, fondness.

warn ▶ verb **1** tell someone of a possible danger or problem. **2** advise someone not to do something. **3** (**warn someone off**) order someone to keep away.

w

> SYNONYMS **1** *David warned her that it was too late* **inform,** notify, tell, alert, apprise, make someone aware, remind; informal tip off. **2** *police are warning galleries to be alert* **advise,** exhort, urge, counsel, caution.

warning ▶ noun **1** a statement or event that indicates a possible danger or problem. **2** advice against wrong or foolish behaviour. **3** advance notice.

> SYNONYMS **1** *the earthquake came without warning* **(advance) notice,** alert, hint, signal, sign, alarm bells; informal a tip-off. **2** *a health warning* **caution,** notification, information, exhortation, advice. **3** *a warning of things to come* **omen,** premonition, foreboding, prophecy, prediction, forecast, token, portent, signal, sign. **4** *his sentence is a warning to other drunk drivers* **example,** deterrent, lesson, caution, message, moral. **5** *a written warning* **reprimand,** caution, remonstrance, admonition, censure; informal dressing-down, talking-to, telling-off.

warp ▶ verb **1** make or become bent or twisted. **2** make abnormal or strange.

> SYNONYMS **1** *timber which is too dry will warp* **buckle,** twist, bend, distort, deform, curve, bow, contort. **2** *he warped the mind of her child* **corrupt,** twist, pervert, deprave.
> ANTONYMS straighten.

▶ noun **1** a distortion or twist in shape. **2** the lengthwise threads on a loom over and under which the weft threads are passed to make cloth.

warrant ▶ noun **1** an official authorization allowing police, soldiers, etc. to make an arrest, search premises, etc. **2** a document that entitles you to receive goods, money, or services. **3** justification or authority.

> SYNONYMS **1** *a warrant for his arrest* **authorization,** order, writ, mandate, licence, permit, summons. **2** *a travel warrant* **voucher,** chit, slip, ticket, coupon, pass.

▶ verb **1** justify or make necessary. **2** officially state or guarantee.

> SYNONYMS **1** *the charges warranted a severe sentence* **justify,** deserve, vindicate, call for, sanction, permit, authorize, excuse, account for, legitimize, support, license, merit, qualify for, rate. **2** *we warrant that the texts do not infringe copyright* **guarantee,** promise, affirm, swear, vouch, vow, pledge, undertake, declare, testify.

■ **warrant officer** a rank of military officer below the commissioned officers.

warranty ▶ noun (plural **warranties**) a written guarantee promising to repair or replace an article if necessary within a stated period.

> SYNONYMS **guarantee,** assurance, promise, commitment, undertaking, pledge, agreement, covenant.

warren ▶ noun **1** a network of interconnecting rabbit burrows. **2** a complex network of paths or passages.

warrior ▶ noun a brave or experienced soldier or fighter.

> SYNONYMS **fighter,** soldier, serviceman, combatant.

warship ▶ noun an armed ship designed to take part in warfare at sea.

wart ▶ noun a small, hard growth on the skin. □ **warty** adjective.

warthog ▶ noun an African wild pig with warty lumps on the face.

wary ▶ adjective (**warier, wariest**) cautious about possible dangers or problems.

> SYNONYMS **1** *he was trained to be wary* **cautious,** careful, circumspect, on your guard, chary, alert, on the lookout, attentive, heedful, watchful, vigilant, observant. **2** *we are wary of strangers* **suspicious,** chary, leery, careful, distrustful.
> ANTONYMS inattentive, trustful.

□ **warily** adverb **wariness** noun.

was 1st and 3rd person singular past of BE.

wash ▶ verb **1** clean with water and usually soap or detergent. **2** (of water) flow freely in a particular direction. **3** (**wash over**) happen all around someone without affecting them very much. **4** informal seem convincing or genuine.

> SYNONYMS **1** *he washed in the bath* **clean yourself,** bathe, shower. **2** *she washed her hands* **clean,** cleanse, scrub, wipe, shampoo, lather, sluice, swill, douse, swab, disinfect. **3** *she washed off the blood* **remove,** expunge, eradicate, sponge off, scrub off, wipe off, rinse off. **4** *the women were washing clothes* **launder,** clean, rinse. **5** *waves washed against the hull* **splash,** lap, dash, break, beat, surge, ripple, roll. **6** *the wreckage was washed downriver* **sweep,** carry, convey, transport, deposit.
> ANTONYMS dirty.

▶ noun **1** an act of washing. **2** a quantity of clothes needing to be washed. **3** the water or air disturbed by a moving boat or aircraft. **4** a medicinal or cleansing solution. **5** a thin coating of paint.

> SYNONYMS **1** *that shirt should go in the wash* **laundry,** washing. **2** *the wash of a motor boat* **backwash,** wake, trail, path.

w

■ **be washed out 1** be postponed or cancelled because of rain. **2** (**washed out**) pale and tired. **wash your hands of** take no further responsibility for. **wash up 1** Brit. wash crockery and cutlery after use. **2** (**washed up**) informal no longer effective or successful.

washbasin ▶ noun a basin for washing your hands and face.

washboard ▶ noun a ridged or corrugated board formerly used for scrubbing clothes when washing them.

washer ▶ noun **1** a person or device that washes. **2** a small flat ring fixed between a nut and bolt.

washing ▶ noun clothes, sheets, towels, etc. that need washing or have just been washed.

■ **washing-up** Brit. crockery, cutlery, etc. that need washing.

washout ▶ noun informal a disappointing failure.

washroom ▶ noun N. Amer. a room with washing and toilet facilities.

washstand ▶ noun a piece of furniture formerly used to hold a bowl or basin for washing the hands and face.

wasn't ▶ short form was not.

wasp ▶ noun a stinging winged insect with a black and yellow striped body.

■ **wasp waist** a very narrow waist.

waspish ▶ adjective sharply irritable.
□ **waspishly** adverb.

wassail /wos-sayl/ old use ▶ noun lively festivities involving the drinking of a lot of alcohol.
▶ verb **1** celebrate with a lot of alcohol. **2** go carol-singing at Christmas.

wastage ▶ noun **1** the process of wasting. **2** an amount wasted. **3** (also **natural wastage**) Brit. the reduction in the size of a workforce through people resigning or retiring.

waste ▶ verb (**wastes, wasting, wasted**) **1** use more of something than is necessary. **2** fail to make good use of. **3** (**be wasted on**) not be appreciated by. **4** (often **waste away**) gradually become weaker and thinner. **5** (**wasted**) informal under the influence of alcohol or illegal drugs.

SYNONYMS **1** *he doesn't like to waste money* **squander,** misspend, misuse, fritter away, throw away, lavish, dissipate; informal blow, splurge. **2** *kids are wasting away in the streets* **grow weak,** grow thin, shrink, wilt, fade, flag, deteriorate. **3** *the disease wasted his legs* **emaciate,** atrophy, wither, shrivel, shrink, weaken.
ANTONYMS conserve, thrive.

▶ adjective **1** discarded because no longer useful or required. **2** (of land) not used, cultivated, or built on.

SYNONYMS **1** *waste material* **unwanted,** excess, superfluous, left over, scrap, unusable, unprofitable. **2** *waste ground* **uncultivated,** barren, desert, arid, bare, desolate.

▶ noun **1** an instance of wasting. **2** material that is not wanted or useful. **3** a large area of barren, uninhabited land.

SYNONYMS **1** *a waste of money* **misuse,** misapplication, abuse, extravagance, lavishness. **2** *household waste* **rubbish,** refuse, litter, debris, junk, sewage, effluent; N. Amer. garbage, trash. **3** (**wastes**) **desert,** wasteland, wilderness, emptiness, wilds.

■ **lay waste to** completely destroy.
□ **waster** noun.

wasteful ▶ adjective using more of something than is necessary.

SYNONYMS **prodigal,** profligate, uneconomical, extravagant, lavish, excessive, imprudent, improvident, spendthrift.
ANTONYMS frugal.

□ **wastefully** adverb.

wasteland ▶ noun a barren or empty area of land.

wastrel ▶ noun literary a lazy person who spends their time or money wastefully.

watch ▶ verb **1** look at attentively. **2** keep under careful observation. **3** be cautious about. **4** (**watch for**) look out for. **5** (**watch out**) be careful.

SYNONYMS **1** *she watched him as he spoke* **observe,** view, look at, eye, gaze at, peer at, contemplate, inspect, scrutinize, scan; informal check out, get a load of, recce, eyeball. **2** *he was being watched by the police* **spy on,** keep in sight, keep under surveillance, track, monitor, tail; informal keep tabs on, stake out. **3** *we stayed to watch the boat* **guard,** mind, protect, look after, keep an eye on, take care of, shield, defend.
ANTONYMS ignore, neglect.

▶ noun **1** a small clock worn on a strap on your wrist. **2** an instance of watching. **3** a period of keeping watch during the night. **4** a shift worked by firefighters or police officers.

SYNONYMS **1** *Bill looked at his watch* **wristwatch,** timepiece, chronometer. **2** *we kept watch on the yacht* **guard,** vigil, lookout, an eye, observation, surveillance.

■ **keep watch** be alert for danger or trouble.
□ **watchable** adjective **watcher** noun.

watchdog ▶ noun **1** a dog kept to guard property. **2** a person or group that monitors the practices of companies providing a particular service.

synonyms **ombudsman**, monitor, scrutineer, inspector, supervisor.

watchful ▸ adjective alert to possible difficulty or danger.
□ **watchfully** adverb **watchfulness** noun.

watchman ▸ noun (plural **watchmen**) a man employed to look after an empty building.

watchtower ▸ noun a tower built as a high observation point.

watchword ▸ noun a word or phrase expressing a central aim or belief.

water ▸ noun **1** the liquid which forms the seas, lakes, rivers, and rain. **2** (**waters**) an area of sea under the authority of a particular country. **3** (**waters**) fluid that passes from a woman's body shortly before she gives birth.
▸ verb (**waters**, **watering**, **watered**) **1** pour water over a plant. **2** give a drink of water to an animal. **3** (of the eyes or mouth) produce tears or saliva. **4** dilute a drink with water. **5** (**water something down**) make something less forceful or controversial.

> synonyms **1** *water the plants* sprinkle, moisten, dampen, wet, spray, splash. **2** *my mouth watered* moisten, become wet, salivate.

■ **hold water** (of a theory) seem valid or reasonable. **water buffalo** a kind of Asian buffalo used for carrying heavy loads. **water cannon** a device that sends out a powerful jet of water, used to make a crowd disperse. **water closet** dated a flush toilet. **water ice** a frozen dessert consisting of fruit juice or purée in a sugar syrup. **watering can** a portable container with a long spout, used for watering plants. **watering hole** informal a pub or bar. **water lily** a plant that grows in water, with large round floating leaves. **water meadow** a meadow that is periodically flooded by a stream or river. **water polo** a game played by swimmers in a pool, who try to throw the ball into their opponents' net. **water table** the level below which the ground is saturated with water. **water tower** a tower that raises up a water tank to create enough pressure to distribute the water through pipes.
□ **waterless** adjective.

waterbed ▸ noun a bed with a water-filled mattress.

watercolour (US spelling **watercolor**)
▸ noun **1** artists' paint that is thinned with water. **2** a picture painted with watercolours.

watercourse ▸ noun a stream or artificial water channel.

watercress ▸ noun a kind of cress which grows in running water.

waterfall ▸ noun a place where a stream of water falls from a height.

> synonyms **falls**, cascade, cataract, rapids.

waterfowl ▸ plural noun ducks, geese, or other large birds living in water.

waterfront ▸ noun a part of a town or city alongside an area of water.

waterhole ▸ noun a water-filled hollow where animals drink.

waterline ▸ noun the level normally reached by the water on the side of a ship.

waterlogged ▸ adjective saturated with water.

watermark ▸ noun a faint design made in some paper that can be seen when held against the light.

watermelon ▸ noun a very large fruit with smooth green skin, red pulp, and watery juice.

watermill ▸ noun a mill worked by a waterwheel.

waterproof ▸ adjective unable to be penetrated by water.
▸ noun Brit. a waterproof garment.
▸ verb make waterproof.

watershed ▸ noun **1** an area of land that separates waters flowing to different rivers, seas, etc. **2** a turning point in a situation.

waterski ▸ noun (plural **waterskis**) each of a pair of skis that let you skim the surface of the water when towed by a motorboat.
▸ verb (**waterskis**, **waterskiing**, **waterskied**) travel on waterskis.
□ **waterskier** noun.

waterspout ▸ noun a column of water formed by a whirlwind over the sea.

watertight ▸ adjective **1** not allowing any water to pass through. **2** unable to be called into question.

waterway ▸ noun a river, canal, or other route for travel by water.

waterwheel ▸ noun a large wheel driven by flowing water, used to work machinery or to raise water to a higher level.

waterworks ▸ noun a place with equipment for managing a water supply.

watery ▸ adjective like water, especially thin and tasteless.

> synonyms *very watery soup* runny, thin, diluted, weak, tasteless, bland, soggy, sloppy.
> antonyms thick, tasty.

watt ▸ noun the basic unit of power.

wattage ▸ noun an amount of electrical power expressed in watts.

wattle[1] ▸ noun rods interlaced with twigs or branches, used for making fences, walls, etc.
■ **wattle and daub** wattle covered with mud or clay, formerly used in building walls.

w

wattle² ▸ noun a fleshy part hanging from the head or neck of the turkey and some other birds.

wave ▸ verb (waves, waving, waved) **1** move your hand, or something held in it, to and fro, especially when greeting someone. **2** move to and fro with a swaying motion.

SYNONYMS **1** *he waved his flag* **flap,** wag, shake, swish, swing, brandish, flourish, wield. **2** *the grass waved in the breeze* **ripple,** flutter, undulate, stir, flap, sway, shake, quiver. **3** *the waiter waved them closer* **gesture,** signal, beckon, motion.

▸ noun **1** a ridge of water moving along the surface of the sea or breaking on the shore. **2** a sudden occurrence of or increase in a phenomenon or emotion. **3** a gesture made by waving your hand. **4** a slightly curling lock of hair. **5** a regular to-and-fro motion of particles of matter involved in transmitting sound, light, heat, etc.

SYNONYMS **1** *he surfs the big waves* **breaker,** roller, comber, boomer, ripple; (**waves**) swell, surf. **2** *a wave of emigration* **rush,** flow, surge, flood, stream, tide, deluge, spate. **3** *a wave of self-pity* **surge,** rush, stab, upsurge, sudden feeling. **4** *she gave him a friendly wave* **signal,** sign, motion, gesture.

waveband ▸ noun a range of wavelengths used in radio transmission.

wavelength ▸ noun **1** the distance between successive crests of a wave of sound, light, radio, etc. **2** a person's way of thinking.

wavelet ▸ noun a small wave.

waver ▸ verb (wavers, wavering, wavered) **1** move in a quivering way; flicker. **2** begin to weaken; falter. **3** be indecisive.

SYNONYMS **1** *the candlelight wavered in the draught* **flicker,** quiver. **2** *his voice wavered* **falter,** wobble, tremble, quaver. **3** *he wavered between the choices* **hesitate,** dither, be irresolute, be undecided, vacillate, blow hot and cold; Brit. haver, hum and haw; informal shilly-shally, sit on the fence.

wavy ▸ adjective (wavier, waviest) having a series of wave-like curves.

wax¹ ▸ noun **1** a soft solid substance used for making candles or polishes. **2** a substance produced by bees to make honeycombs; beeswax.

▸ verb polish or treat with wax.
▢ **waxen** adjective **waxy** adjective.

wax² ▸ verb **1** (of the moon) gradually appear to increase in size. **2** literary become larger or stronger. **3** literary speak or write in a particular way: *they waxed lyrical.*

waxwork ▸ noun **1** a lifelike dummy made of wax. **2** (**waxworks**) an exhibition of waxworks.

way ▸ noun **1** a method, style, or manner of doing something. **2** a road, track, or path. **3** a route or means taken in order to reach, enter, or leave a place. **4** a direction. **5** the distance in space or time between two points. **6** condition or state. **7** (**ways**) parts into which something divides.

SYNONYMS **1** *a way of reducing the damage* **method,** process, procedure, technique, system, plan, strategy, scheme, means, mechanism, approach. **2** *she kissed him in her brisk way* **manner,** style, fashion, mode. **3** *I've changed my ways* **practice,** wont, habit, custom, convention, routine, trait, attribute, peculiarity, idiosyncrasy, conduct, behaviour, manner, style. **4** *which way leads home?* **route,** course, direction, track, path, access, gate, exit, entrance, door. **5** *a short way downstream* **distance,** length, stretch, journey. **6** *April is a long way away* **time,** stretch, term, span, duration. **7** *a car coming the other way* **direction,** bearing, course, orientation, line, tack. **8** *in some ways, he may be better off* **respect,** regard, aspect, facet, sense, detail, point, particular. **9** *the country is in a bad way* **state,** condition, situation, circumstances, position, predicament, plight; informal shape.

▸ adverb informal at or to a considerable distance or extent.
■ **by the way** used to introduce a comment that is not connected to the current subject of conversation. **give way 1** yield. **2** collapse or break under pressure. **3** (**give way to**) be replaced by. **in the way** obstructing someone's progress. **make way** allow room for someone or something else. **way-out** informal very unconventional.

wayfarer ▸ noun literary a person who travels on foot.

waylay ▸ verb (waylays, waylaying, waylaid) **1** intercept someone in order to attack them. **2** stop someone and talk to them.

wayside ▸ noun the edge of a road.

wayward ▸ adjective unpredictable and hard to control.

WC ▸ abbreviation Brit. water closet.

we ▸ pronoun **1** used by a speaker to refer to himself or herself and one or more other people considered together. **2** people in general.

weak ▸ adjective **1** lacking strength and energy. **2** likely to break or give way under pressure. **3** not secure or stable. **4** lacking power, influence, or ability. **5** (of a liquid or solution) heavily diluted.

SYNONYMS **1** *they are too weak to move* **feeble,** frail, delicate, fragile, infirm,

debilitated, decrepit, exhausted;
informal weedy. **2** *bats have weak eyes*
inadequate, poor, feeble, defective,
faulty, deficient, imperfect, substandard.
3 *a weak excuse* **unconvincing,** tenuous,
implausible, unsatisfactory, poor,
inadequate, feeble, flimsy, lame, hollow;
informal pathetic. **4** *a weak bridge* **fragile,**
frail, rickety, insubstantial, wobbly,
unstable, ramshackle, jerry-built,
shoddy. **5** *I was too weak to be a rebel*
spineless, craven, cowardly, timid,
irresolute, indecisive, ineffectual, meek,
tame, soft, faint-hearted; informal yellow,
gutless. **6** *a weak light* **dim,** pale, wan,
faint, feeble, muted. **7** *a weak voice*
indistinct, muffled, muted, hushed,
faint, low. **8** *weak coffee* **watery,** dilute,
watered down, thin.
ANTONYMS strong, powerful, convincing,
solid, resolute, bright, loud.

☐ **weakly** adverb.

weaken ▸ verb make or become weak.

SYNONYMS **1** *the virus weakened him*
enfeeble, debilitate, incapacitate, sap,
tire, exhaust. **2** *our morale weakened*
decrease, dwindle, diminish, wane, ebb,
subside, peter out, fizzle out, tail off,
decline, falter. **3** *the move weakened
her authority* **impair,** undermine,
compromise, lessen.
ANTONYMS strengthen, bolster.

weakling ▸ noun a weak person or animal.
weakness ▸ noun **1** the state of being weak.
2 a fault. **3** (**weakness for**) a liking for
something that you find difficult to resist.

SYNONYMS **1** *with old age came weakness*
frailty, feebleness, fragility, delicacy,
debility, incapacity, decrepitude;
informal weediness. **2** *he has worked
on his weaknesses* **fault,** flaw, defect,
deficiency, failing, shortcoming,
imperfection, Achilles heel. **3** *a
weakness for champagne* **fondness,**
liking, partiality, love, penchant,
predilection, inclination, taste. **4** *the
President was accused of weakness*
timidity, cravenness, cowardliness,
indecision, irresolution, ineffectuality,
ineffectiveness, impotence. **5** *the
weakness of this argument* **inadequacy,**
implausibility, poverty, untenability,
transparency, flimsiness, hollowness.

weal ▸ noun a red swollen mark left on flesh
by a blow or pressure.
wealth ▸ noun **1** a large amount of money,
property, or possessions. **2** the state of
being rich. **3** a large amount of something
desirable.

SYNONYMS **1** *a gentleman of wealth*
affluence, prosperity, riches, means,
fortune, money, cash, capital, treasure,

finance; informal wherewithal, dough,
bread. **2** *a wealth of information*
abundance, profusion, plethora, mine,
store; informal lot, load, mountain, stack,
ton; Brit. informal shedload.
ANTONYMS poverty, dearth.

wealthy ▸ adjective (**wealthier, wealthiest**)
rich.

SYNONYMS **rich,** affluent, moneyed, well
off, well-to-do, prosperous; informal well
heeled, rolling in it, made of money,
loaded, flush.
ANTONYMS poor.

wean ▸ verb **1** make a young mammal
used to food other than its mother's milk.
2 (**wean someone off**) make someone give
up a habit or addiction. **3** (**be weaned on**)
be strongly influenced by something from
an early age.
weapon ▸ noun **1** a thing used to cause
physical harm or damage. **2** a means of
gaining an advantage or defending yourself.
☐ **weaponry** noun.

wear ▸ verb (**wears, wearing, wore;** past
participle **worn**) **1** have something on your
body as clothing, decoration, or protection.
2 have a particular facial expression.
3 damage something by continuous
use or rubbing. **4** (**wear off**) stop being
effective or strong. **5** (**wear someone out**)
exhaust someone. **6** (**wearing**) mentally
or physically tiring. **7** (**wear on**) (of time)
pass in a slow or boring way.

SYNONYMS **1** *he wore a suit* **dress in,** be
clothed in, have on, sport. **2** *Barbara wore
a smile* **bear,** have (on your face), show,
display, exhibit, give, put on, assume.
3 *the bricks have been worn down* **erode,**
abrade, rub away, grind away, wash
away, crumble (away), eat away (at).
4 *the tyres are wearing well* **last,** endure,
hold up, bear up. **5** (**wearing**) *tours
were very wearing* **tiring,** exhausting,
wearying, fatiguing, enervating,
draining, sapping, demanding, exacting,
taxing, gruelling, punishing.

▸ noun **1** clothing of a particular type.
2 damage caused by continuous use.

SYNONYMS **1** *evening wear* **clothes,**
garments, dress, attire, garb, wardrobe;
informal get-up, gear, togs; Brit. informal kit,
clobber. **2** *the varnish will withstand wear*
damage, friction, abrasion, erosion.
3 *you won't get much wear out of that
use,* service, value; informal mileage.

☐ **wearer** noun.

wearisome ▸ adjective making you feel
tired or bored.
weary ▸ adjective (**wearier, weariest**) **1** tired.
2 causing tiredness. **3** (**weary of**) bored with.

w

synonyms **1** *he was weary after cycling* **tired,** worn out, exhausted, fatigued, sapped, spent, drained; informal done in, ready to drop, bushed, shattered; Brit. informal knackered, whacked; N. Amer. informal pooped. **2** *a weary journey* **tiring,** exhausting, fatiguing, enervating, draining, sapping, demanding, taxing, arduous, gruelling.
antonyms fresh, keen, refreshing.

▶ verb (**wearies, wearying, wearied**) **1** make someone weary. **2** (**weary of**) grow bored with.
□ **wearily** adverb **weariness** noun.

weasel ▶ noun a small, slender meat-eating animal with reddish-brown fur.

weather ▶ noun the state of the atmosphere in terms of temperature, wind, rain, etc.

synonyms *what's the weather like?* **conditions,** climate, elements, forecast, outlook.

▶ verb (**weathers, weathering, weathered**) **1** wear something away by long exposure to the weather. **2** come safely through a difficult or dangerous situation.

synonyms *we weathered the recession* **survive,** come through, ride out, pull through, withstand, endure, rise above; informal stick out.

■ **make heavy weather of** informal have unnecessary difficulty in dealing with. **under the weather** informal slightly unwell.

weathercock ▶ noun a weathervane in the form of a cockerel.

weatherman ▶ noun (plural **weathermen**) a man who gives a description and forecast of weather conditions on television or radio.

weathervane ▶ noun a revolving pointer that shows the direction of the wind.

weave¹ ▶ verb (**weaves, weaving, wove;** past participle **woven** or **wove**) **1** make fabric by interlacing long threads with others. **2** make facts, events, etc. into a story.

synonyms **1** *flowers were woven into their hair* **entwine,** lace, twist, knit, braid, plait. **2** *he weaves colourful plots* **invent,** make up, fabricate, construct, create, spin.

▶ noun a particular way in which fabric is woven.
□ **weaver** noun.

weave² ▶ verb (**weaves, weaving, weaved**) move from side to side to get around obstructions.

synonyms *he had to weave his way through the crowds* **thread,** wind, wend, dodge, zigzag.

web ▶ noun **1** a network of fine threads made by a spider to catch its prey. **2** a

complex system of interconnected elements. **3** (**the Web**) the World Wide Web. **4** the skin between the toes of a bird or animal living in water.

synonyms **1** *a spider's web* **mesh,** net, lattice, lacework, gauze, gossamer. **2** *a web of friendships* **network,** nexus, complex, tangle, chain.

■ **web page** a document that can be accessed via the Internet.

webbed ▶ adjective (of an animal's feet) having the toes connected by a web.

webbing ▶ noun strong fabric used for making straps, belts, etc.

webcam ▶ noun (trademark) a video camera connected to a computer, so that the moving image produced may be viewed on the Internet.

webcast ▶ noun a live video broadcast of an event transmitted on the Internet.

weblog ▶ noun a personal website on which someone regularly writes about their interests, experiences, etc.

website ▶ noun a location on the Internet that maintains one or more web pages.

wed ▶ verb (**weds, wedding, wedded** or **wed**) **1** formal or literary marry. **2** (**wedded**) having to do with marriage. **3** combine two desirable factors or qualities. **4** (**be wedded to**) be entirely devoted to a particular activity or belief.

synonyms **1** (**wedded**) *wedded bliss* **married,** matrimonial, marital, conjugal, nuptial. **2** (**wedded**) *he is wedded to his work* **dedicated,** devoted, attached, fixated.

we'd ▶ short form **1** we had. **2** we would.

wedding ▶ noun a marriage ceremony.

synonyms **marriage (service),** nuptials, union.

wedge ▶ noun **1** a piece of wood, metal, etc. with a thick end that tapers to a thin edge. **2** a golf club for hitting the ball as high as possible into the air. **3** a shoe with a fairly high heel forming a solid block with the sole.

synonyms **1** *the door was secured by a wedge* **chock,** stop. **2** *a wedge of cheese* **triangle,** segment, slice, section, chunk, lump, slab, hunk, block, piece.

▶ verb (**wedges, wedging, wedged**) **1** fix in position using a wedge. **2** force into a narrow space.

synonyms *she wedged her case between two bags* **squeeze,** cram, jam, ram, force, push, shove; informal stuff, bung.

■ **the thin end of the wedge** informal something unimportant in itself which is likely to lead to a more serious or unpleasant situation.

w

wedlock ▸ noun formal the state of being married.

Wednesday ▸ noun the day of the week before Thursday and following Tuesday.

✔ Remember the **d** before the **n**: We**dn**esday.

wee ▸ adjective Scottish little.

weed ▸ noun 1 a wild plant growing where it is not wanted. 2 informal cannabis. 3 (**the weed**) informal tobacco. 4 Brit. informal a weak or skinny person. 5 (**weeds**) old use black clothes worn by a widow in mourning for her husband.
▸ verb 1 remove weeds from. 2 (**weed someone/thing out**) remove unwanted members or items.

weedkiller ▸ noun a substance used to destroy weeds.

weedy ▸ adjective (**weedier, weediest**) 1 Brit. informal thin and weak. 2 containing or covered with many weeds.

week ▸ noun 1 a period of seven days. 2 the five days from Monday to Friday, when many people work. 3 Brit. a week after a stated day.

weekday ▸ noun a day of the week other than Saturday or Sunday.

weekend ▸ noun Saturday and Sunday.

weekly ▸ adjective & adverb happening or produced once a week.

weeny ▸ adjective (**weenier, weeniest**) informal tiny.

weep ▸ verb (**weeps, weeping, wept**) 1 shed tears; cry. 2 (of a wound) produce liquid.

SYNONYMS **cry**, shed tears, sob, snivel, whimper, wail, bawl, keen; Scottish greet; informal boohoo, blub.
ANTONYMS rejoice.

▸ noun a period of shedding tears.

weepy ▸ adjective (**weepier, weepiest**) informal 1 tearful. 2 sentimental.

weevil ▸ noun a small beetle which eats crops or stored food.

weft ▸ noun (in weaving) the threads that are passed over and under the warp threads to make cloth.

weigh ▸ verb 1 find out how heavy someone or something is. 2 have a particular weight. 3 (**weigh something out**) measure and take out a portion of a particular weight. 4 (**weigh someone down**) be a burden to someone. 5 (**weigh on**) be depressing or worrying to. 6 (**weigh in**) (of a boxer or jockey) be officially weighed before or after a contest. 7 (often **weigh something up**) consider something carefully. 8 (often **weigh against**) influence a decision or action. 9 (**weigh in**) informal join in something enthusiastically or forcefully.

SYNONYMS 1 *she weighs the vegetables* **put on the scales**. 2 *he weighed 118 kg*

tip the scales at. 3 *he has to weigh up the possibilities* **consider**, contemplate, think about, mull over, chew over, reflect on, ruminate about, muse on, assess, examine, review, explore, take stock of. 4 *they need to weigh benefit against risk* **balance**, evaluate, compare, juxtapose, contrast.

weighbridge ▸ noun a machine on to which vehicles are driven to be weighed.

weight ▸ noun 1 the heaviness of a person or thing. 2 the quality of being heavy. 3 a unit used for expressing how much something weighs. 4 a piece of metal known to weigh a definite amount and used on scales to find out how heavy something is. 5 a heavy object. 6 ability to influence decisions. 7 the importance attached to something.

SYNONYMS 1 *the weight of the book* **mass**, heaviness, load, burden. 2 *his recommendation will carry great weight* **influence**, force, leverage, sway, pull, power, authority; informal clout. 3 *a weight off her mind* **burden**, load, millstone, trouble, worry. 4 *the weight of the evidence is against him* **most**, bulk, majority, preponderance, body, lion's share.

▸ verb 1 make heavier or keep in place with a weight. 2 (**be weighted**) be arranged so as to give one party an advantage.
□ **weightless** adjective.

weighting ▸ noun 1 adjustment made to take account of special circumstances. 2 Brit. additional wages paid to allow for a higher cost of living in a particular area.

weightlifting ▸ noun the sport or activity of lifting heavy weights.
□ **weightlifter** noun.

weighty ▸ adjective (**weightier, weightiest**) 1 heavy. 2 very serious and important. 3 very influential.

weir (*rhymes with* here) ▸ noun a low dam built across a river to control its flow.

weird ▸ adjective 1 informal very strange. 2 mysterious or strange in a frightening way; eerie.

SYNONYMS 1 *weird apparitions* **uncanny**, eerie, unnatural, supernatural, unearthly, other-worldly, ghostly, mysterious, strange, abnormal, unusual; informal creepy, spooky, freaky. 2 *a weird sense of humour* **bizarre**, odd, curious, strange, quirky, outlandish, eccentric, unconventional, unorthodox, idiosyncratic, surreal, crazy, absurd, grotesque, peculiar; informal wacky, freaky; N. Amer. informal wacko.
ANTONYMS normal, conventional.

□ **weirdly** adverb **weirdness** noun.

W

✔ **Weird** is an exception to the usual rule of **i** before **e** except after **c**.

weirdo ▸ noun (plural **weirdos**) informal a strange or eccentric person.

welch → WELSH.

welcome ▸ noun 1 an instance or way of greeting someone. 2 a pleased or approving reaction.

> SYNONYMS *a welcome from the vicar* **greeting**, salutation, reception, hospitality, the red carpet.

▸ verb (**welcomes, welcoming, welcomed**)
1 greet someone in a polite or friendly way when they arrive somewhere. 2 be glad to receive or hear of.

> SYNONYMS 1 *welcome your guests in their own language* **greet**, salute, receive, meet, usher in. 2 *we welcomed their decision* **be pleased by**, be glad about, approve of, applaud, appreciate, embrace.
> ANTONYMS resent, object to.

▸ adjective 1 gladly received. 2 very pleasing because much needed or wanted. 3 allowed or invited to do a particular thing.

> SYNONYMS *welcome news* **pleasing**, agreeable, encouraging, gratifying, heartening, promising, favourable, pleasant.
> ANTONYMS unwelcome.

weld ▸ verb 1 join together metal parts by heating the surfaces and pressing or hammering them together. 2 make two things combine into a whole.

> SYNONYMS **fuse**, bond, stick, join, attach, seal, splice, melt, solder.

▸ noun a welded joint.
□ **welder** noun.

welfare ▸ noun 1 the general health, happiness, and safety of a person or group. 2 organized help given to people in need.

> SYNONYMS 1 *the welfare of children* **well-being**, health, comfort, security, safety, protection, success, interest, good. 2 *we cannot claim welfare* **social security**, benefit, public assistance, pension, credit, support, sick pay, unemployment benefit; Brit. informal the dole.

■ **welfare state** a system under which the state provides pensions, health care, etc.

well¹ ▸ adverb 1 in a good way. 2 thoroughly. 3 to a great extent or degree. 4 very probably. 5 without difficulty. 6 with good reason.

> SYNONYMS 1 *please behave well* **satisfactorily**, nicely, correctly, properly, fittingly, suitably, appropriately.
> 2 *they get on well together* **amicably**, agreeably, pleasantly, nicely, happily,

harmoniously, amiably, peaceably; informal **famously**. 3 *he plays the piano well* **skilfully**, ably, competently, proficiently, adeptly, deftly, expertly, excellently.
4 *treat your employees well* **decently**, fairly, kindly, generously. 5 *mix the ingredients well* **thoroughly**, completely, effectively, rigorously, carefully.
6 *I know her quite well* **intimately**, thoroughly, deeply, profoundly, personally. 7 *they studied the car market well* **carefully**, closely, attentively, rigorously, in depth, exhaustively, in detail, meticulously, scrupulously, methodically, comprehensively, fully, extensively. 8 *they speak well of him* **admiringly**, highly, approvingly, favourably, appreciatively, warmly, enthusiastically, glowingly. 9 *she lives well* **comfortably**, in luxury, prosperously. 10 *you may well be right* **quite possibly**, conceivably, probably.
11 *he is well over forty* **considerably**, very much, a great deal, substantially, easily, comfortably, significantly. 12 *she could well afford it* **easily**, comfortably, readily, effortlessly.
ANTONYMS badly, negligently, disparagingly, barely.

▸ adjective 1 in good health. 2 in a satisfactory state or position. 3 sensible; advisable.

> SYNONYMS 1 *she was completely well again* **healthy**, fine, fit, robust, strong, vigorous, blooming, thriving, in fine fettle; informal in the pink. 2 *all is not well* **satisfactory**, all right, fine, in order, as it should be, acceptable; informal OK, hunky-dory.
> ANTONYMS poorly, unsatisfactory.

▸ exclamation used to express surprise, anger, resignation, etc.

■ **as well 1** in addition. 2 with equal reason or an equally good result. **well advised** sensible; wise. **well appointed** having a high standard of equipment or furnishing. **well-being** the state of being comfortable, healthy, or happy. **well disposed** having a sympathetic or friendly attitude. **well heeled** informal wealthy. **well nigh** almost. **well off 1** wealthy. 2 in a good situation. **well read** having read widely. **well spoken** having an educated and refined voice. **well-to-do** wealthy. **well-wisher** a person who wants someone else to be happy or successful.

❗ **Well** is often used with a past participle such as *known* or *dressed* to form adjectives such as **well known**, **well dressed**, etc. Write these adjectives without a hyphen when they come after a noun or pronoun (*she is well known*) but with a hyphen when they come directly in front of a noun (*a well-known writer*).

well² ▸ noun 1 a shaft sunk into the ground to obtain water, oil, or gas. 2 a hollow made to hold liquid. **3** a space in the middle of a building for stairs, a lift, etc.

> SYNONYMS *she drew water from the well* **borehole,** spring, waterhole, shaft.

▸ **verb** (often **well up**) **1** (of a liquid) rise up to the surface. **2** (of an emotion) develop and become stronger.

> SYNONYMS *tears welled from her eyes* **flow,** spill, stream, gush, roll, cascade, flood, spout, burst, issue.

we'll ▸ **short form 1** we shall. **2** we will.

well built ▸ **adjective** (of a person) strong and sturdy.

wellington ▸ **noun** Brit. a knee-length waterproof rubber or plastic boot.

welly (or **wellie**) ▸ **noun** Brit. informal a wellington boot.

Welsh ▸ **noun** the language of Wales.
▸ **adjective** relating to Wales.
■ **Welsh rarebit** (or **Welsh rabbit**) a dish of melted cheese on toast.

welsh (or **welch**) ▸ **verb** (**welsh on**) fail to repay a debt or fulfil an obligation.

welt ▸ **noun 1** a leather rim to which the sole of a shoe is attached. **2** a red swollen mark left on the skin by a blow or pressure.

welter ▸ **noun** a large and confused or disorganized number of items.

welterweight ▸ **noun** a weight in boxing between lightweight and middleweight.

wench ▸ **noun** old use or humorous a girl or young woman.

wend ▸ **verb** (**wend your way**) go slowly or by an indirect route.

Wendy house ▸ **noun** Brit. a toy house large enough for children to play in.

went past of GO.

wept past and past participle of WEEP.

were 2nd person singular past, plural past, and past subjunctive of BE.

we're ▸ **short form** we are.

weren't ▸ **short form** were not.

werewolf /wair-wuulf/ ▸ **noun** (plural **werewolves**) (in stories) a person who periodically changes into a wolf, especially when there is a full moon.

west ▸ **noun 1** the direction in which the sun sets. **2** the western part of a place. **3** (**the West**) Europe and North America.
▸ **adjective & adverb 1** towards or facing the west. **2** (of a wind) blowing from the west.
□ **westward** adjective & adverb **westwards** adverb.

westerly ▸ **adjective & adverb 1** facing or moving towards the west. **2** (of a wind) blowing from the west.

western ▸ **adjective 1** situated in or facing the west. **2** (**Western**) having to do with the west, in particular Europe and North America.
▸ **noun** a film or novel about cowboys in western North America.

westerner ▸ **noun** a person from the west of a region.

westernize (or **westernise**) ▸ **verb** (**westernizes, westernizing, westernized**) bring under the influence of Europe and North America.

wet ▸ **adjective** (**wetter, wettest**) **1** covered or soaked with liquid. **2** (of the weather) rainy. **3** not yet having dried or hardened. **4** Brit. informal feeble.

> SYNONYMS **1** *wet clothes* **damp,** moist, soaked, drenched, saturated, sopping, dripping, soggy, waterlogged, squelchy. **2** *it was cold and wet* **rainy,** pouring, teeming, showery, drizzly. **3** *the paint is still wet* **sticky,** tacky.
> ANTONYMS dry, fine.

▸ **verb** (**wets, wetting, wet** or **wetted**) **1** cover or touch with liquid. **2** urinate in or on.

> SYNONYMS *wet the clothes before ironing them* **dampen,** moisten, sprinkle, spray, splash, soak, saturate, flood, douse, drench.
> ANTONYMS dry.

▸ **noun 1** (**the wet**) rainy weather. **2** liquid that makes something damp. **3** Brit. informal a feeble person.
■ **wet blanket** informal a person who spoils other people's enjoyment by being disapproving or unenthusiastic. **wet nurse** a woman employed to breastfeed another woman's child.
□ **wetly** adverb **wetness** noun.

wether ▸ **noun** a castrated ram.

wetland ▸ **noun** (also **wetlands**) swampy or marshy land.

wetsuit ▸ **noun** a close-fitting rubber garment covering the entire body, worn in water sports or diving.

we've ▸ **short form** we have.

whack informal ▸ **verb 1** hit forcefully. **2** (**whacked**) Brit. completely exhausted. **3** (**whacking**) Brit. very large.
▸ **noun 1** a sharp blow. **2** Brit. a share or contribution.

whacky → WACKY.

whale ▸ **noun** (plural **whales**) a very large sea mammal with a blowhole on top of the head for breathing.
■ **have a whale of a time** informal enjoy yourself very much.

whalebone ▸ **noun** a hard substance growing in plates in the upper jaw of some whales, used by them to strain plankton from the seawater.

whaler ▸ **noun 1** a ship used for hunting whales. **2** a sailor who hunts and kills whales.

w

whaling ▸ noun the practice of hunting and killing whales.

whammy ▸ noun (plural **whammies**) informal an event with a powerful and unpleasant effect.

wharf /worf/ ▸ noun (plural **wharves** or **wharfs**) a level area where ships are moored to load and unload.

> SYNONYMS **quay**, pier, dock, berth, landing, jetty, harbour, dockyard.

what ▸ pronoun & determiner **1** asking for information about something. **2** whatever. **3** used to emphasize something surprising or remarkable.
▸ pronoun **1** asking someone to repeat something. **2** the thing or things that.
▸ adverb to what extent?

whatever (or **whatsoever**) ▸ pronoun & determiner everything or anything that; no matter what.
▸ pronoun used for emphasis instead of 'what' in questions.
▸ adverb at all; of any kind.

whatnot ▸ noun informal an unspecified item or items.

wheat ▸ noun a cereal crop whose grain is ground to make flour.

wheatear ▸ noun a small songbird.

wheatgerm ▸ noun a nutritious food consisting of the centre parts of grains of wheat.

wheatmeal ▸ noun flour made from wheat from which some of the bran and germ has been removed.

wheedle ▸ verb (**wheedles, wheedling, wheedled**) try to persuade someone to do something by flattering them or saying nice things that you do not mean.

wheel ▸ noun **1** a revolving circular object that is fixed below a vehicle to enable it to move along, or that forms part of a machine. **2** (**the wheel**) a steering wheel. **3** a turn or rotation.
▸ verb **1** push or pull a vehicle with wheels. **2** carry on a vehicle with wheels. **3** fly or turn in a wide curve. **4** turn round quickly. **5** (**wheel something out**) informal resort to something that has been frequently seen or heard before.

> SYNONYMS **1** *she wheeled the trolley away* **push**, trundle, roll. **2** *the flock of doves wheeled round* **turn**, go round, circle, orbit.

■ **wheel and deal** take part in commercial or political scheming.

wheelbarrow ▸ noun a small cart with a wheel at the front and two handles at the rear.

wheelbase ▸ noun the distance between the front and rear axles of a vehicle.

wheelchair ▸ noun a chair on wheels for a person who is ill or disabled.

wheeler-dealer ▸ noun a person who wheels and deals.

wheelwright ▸ noun a person who makes or repairs wooden wheels.

wheeze ▸ verb (**wheezes, wheezing, wheezed**) **1** breathe with a whistling or rattling sound in the chest. **2** make a rattling or spluttering sound.
▸ noun **1** a sound of wheezing. **2** Brit. informal a clever or amusing scheme or trick.
□ **wheezy** adjective

whelk ▸ noun a shellfish with a pointed spiral shell.

whelp ▸ noun old use **1** a puppy. **2** disapproving a boy or young man.
▸ verb give birth to a puppy.

when ▸ adverb **1** at what time? **2** in what circumstances? **3** at which time or in which situation.
▸ conjunction **1** at or during the time that. **2** at any time that; whenever. **3** in view of the fact that. **4** although; whereas.

whence (or **from whence**) ▸ adverb formal **1** from what place or source? **2** from which or from where. **3** to the place from which. **4** as a consequence of which.

whenever (or formal **whensoever**)
▸ conjunction **1** at whatever time or on whatever occasion. **2** every time that.
▸ adverb used for emphasis instead of 'when' in questions.

where ▸ adverb **1** in or to what place or position? **2** in what direction or respect? **3** at, in, or to which. **4** in or to a place or situation in which.

whereabouts ▸ adverb where or approximately where?
▸ noun the place where someone or something is.

> SYNONYMS **location**, position, site, situation, spot, point, home, address, neighbourhood.

whereas ▸ conjunction **1** in contrast or comparison with the fact that. **2** taking into consideration the fact that.

whereby ▸ adverb by which.

wherefore old use ▸ adverb for what reason?
▸ adverb & conjunction as a result of which.

wherein ▸ adverb formal **1** in which. **2** in what place or respect?

whereof ▸ adverb formal of what or which.

whereupon ▸ conjunction immediately after which.

wherever (or formal **wheresoever**) ▸ adverb **1** in or to whatever place. **2** used for emphasis instead of 'where' in questions.
▸ conjunction in every case when.

wherewithal ▸ noun the money or other resources needed for something.

wherry (*rhymes with* sherry) ► noun (plural **wherries**) a light rowing boat or barge.

whet /wet/ ► verb (**whets, whetting, whetted**) **1** sharpen a blade. **2** stimulate someone's interest or appetite.

whether ► conjunction **1** expressing a doubt or choice between alternatives. **2** indicating that a statement applies whichever of the alternatives mentioned is the case.

whetstone ► noun a stone used for sharpening cutting tools.

whey /way/ ► noun the watery part of milk that remains after curds have formed.

which ► pronoun & determiner **1** asking for information specifying one or more people or things from a set. **2** used to refer to something previously mentioned when introducing a clause giving further information.

whichever ► determiner & pronoun **1** any which; that or those which. **2** regardless of which.

whiff ► noun **1** a smell that is smelt only briefly or faintly. **2** Brit. informal an unpleasant smell. **3** a trace or hint of something bad or exciting. **4** a puff or breath of air or smoke.

Whig ► noun historical a member of a British political party that became the Liberal Party.

while ► noun **1** (a while) a period of time. **2** (a while) for some time. **3** (the while) meanwhile.

> SYNONYMS *we chatted for a while* time, spell, stretch, stint, span, interval, period; Brit. informal patch.

► conjunction **1** at the same time as. **2** whereas. **3** although.

► adverb during which.

► verb (**whiles, whiling, whiled**) (**while something away**) pass time in a leisurely way.

> SYNONYMS *tennis helped to while away the time* pass, spend, occupy, use up, kill.

■ **worth while** (or **worth your while**) worth the time or effort spent.

whilst ► conjunction & adverb chiefly Brit. while.

whim ► noun a sudden desire or change of mind.

> SYNONYMS **impulse**, urge, notion, fancy, caprice, vagary, inclination.

whimper ► verb (**whimpers, whimpering, whimpered**) make low, feeble sounds expressing fear, pain, or discontent.

► noun a whimpering sound.

whimsical ► adjective **1** playfully unusual. **2** showing sudden changes of mood or behaviour.

□ **whimsically** adverb.

whimsy ► noun (plural **whimsies**) **1** playfully unusual behaviour or humour. **2** an odd or unusual thing. **3** a whim.

whin ► noun chiefly N. English gorse.

whine ► noun **1** a long, high-pitched complaining cry. **2** a long, high-pitched sound.

► verb (**whines, whining, whined**) give or make a whine.

> SYNONYMS **1** *a child was whining* wail, whimper, cry, mewl, moan, howl, yowl. **2** *the lift began to whine* hum, drone, beep. **3** *he's always whining about something* complain, grouse, grouch, grumble, moan, carp; informal gripe, bellyache, whinge.

□ **whiny** adjective.

whinge Brit. informal ► verb (**whinges, whingeing, whinged**) complain persistently and irritably.

► noun an act of whingeing.

whinny ► noun (plural **whinnies**) a gentle, high-pitched neigh.

► verb (**whinnies, whinnying, whinnied**) (of a horse) make a whinny.

whip ► noun **1** a length of leather or cord fastened to a handle, used for beating a person or urging on an animal. **2** an official of a political party who is appointed to keep parliamentary discipline among its members. **3** a written notice from a party whip telling members how to vote in a debate. **4** a dessert made from cream or eggs beaten into a light fluffy mass.

> SYNONYMS *he used a whip on his dogs* lash, scourge, strap, belt.

► verb (**whips, whipping, whipped**) **1** hit a person or animal with a whip. **2** beat or move violently. **3** move or take out fast or suddenly. **4** beat cream, eggs, etc. into a froth.

> SYNONYMS **1** *he whipped the boy* flog, lash, scourge, strap, belt, thrash, beat. **2** *then whip the cream* whisk, beat. **3** *he whipped his listeners into a frenzy* rouse, stir up, excite, galvanize, electrify, stimulate, inspire, fire up, inflame, provoke.

■ **the whip hand** a position of power or control over someone. **whipping boy** a person who is blamed or punished for other people's faults. **whip-round** Brit. informal a collection of money. **whip someone/thing up 1** make or prepare something very quickly. **2** deliberately excite or provoke someone.

whiplash ► noun **1** injury caused by a severe jerk to the head. **2** the flexible part of a whip.

whippersnapper ► noun informal a young and inexperienced but overconfident person.

whippet ▸ noun a small, slender breed of dog.

whippoorwill /**wip**-per-wil/ ▸ noun an American bird with a distinctive call.

whirl ▸ verb 1 move rapidly round and round. 2 (of the head or mind) seem to spin round.

> SYNONYMS 1 *leaves whirled in the wind* **rotate**, circle, wheel, turn, revolve, orbit, spin, twirl. 2 *they whirled past* **hurry**, race, dash, rush, run, sprint, bolt, career, charge, shoot, hurtle, hare, fly, speed; informal tear, belt; Brit. informal bomb. 3 *his mind was whirling* **spin**, reel, swim.

▸ noun 1 a rapid movement round and round. 2 busy or hurried activity.

> SYNONYMS 1 *a whirl of dust* **swirl**, flurry, eddy. 2 *the mad social whirl* **hurly-burly**, activity, round, bustle, rush, flurry. 3 *Laura's mind was in a whirl* **spin**, daze, muddle, jumble, confusion; informal dither.

whirligig ▸ noun 1 a toy that spins round. 2 a roundabout at a fair.

whirlpool ▸ noun a current of water that whirls in a circle.

whirlwind ▸ noun 1 a column of air moving rapidly round and round. 2 a situation in which many things happen very quickly.

▸ adjective very quick and unexpected: *a whirlwind romance.*

whirr (or **whir**) ▸ verb (**whirs** or **whirrs**, **whirring**, **whirred**) (of something rapidly rotating or moving) make a low, continuous, regular sound.

▸ noun a whirring sound.

whisk ▸ verb 1 beat eggs, cream, etc. with a light, rapid movement. 2 move or take suddenly and quickly.

> SYNONYMS 1 *whisk the egg yolks* **whip**, beat, mix. 2 *she whisked the cloth away* **pull**, snatch, pluck, tug, jerk; informal whip, yank. 3 *the cable car will whisk you to the top* **speed**, hurry, rush, sweep, hurtle, shoot.

▸ noun 1 a device for whisking eggs, cream, etc. 2 a bunch of grass, twigs, etc. for flicking away dust or flies.

> SYNONYMS *an egg whisk* **beater**, mixer, blender.

whisker ▸ noun 1 each of the long hairs or bristles growing from the face of an animal. 2 (**whiskers**) the hair growing on a man's face. 3 (**a whisker**) informal a very small amount.

whisky (Irish US & spelling **whiskey**) ▸ noun (plural **whiskies**) a strong alcoholic drink distilled from malted grain.

> ✔ Scotch whis**ky**, but Irish whis**key**.

whisper ▸ verb (**whispers**, **whispering**, **whispered**) 1 speak very softly. 2 literary rustle or murmur softly.

> SYNONYMS *Alison whispered in his ear* **murmur**, mutter, mumble, speak softly, breathe.
> ANTONYMS shout.

▸ noun 1 something whispered. 2 a very soft voice. 3 literary a soft rustling or murmuring. 4 a rumour or piece of gossip. 5 a slight trace.

> SYNONYMS 1 *she spoke in a whisper* **murmur**, mutter, mumble, low voice, undertone. 2 *I heard a whisper that he's left town* **rumour**, story, report, gossip, speculation, suggestion, hint; informal buzz.
> ANTONYMS shout.

whist ▸ noun a card game in which points are scored according to the number of tricks won.

whistle ▸ noun 1 a clear, high-pitched sound made by forcing breath between the lips or teeth. 2 any similar high-pitched sound. 3 a device used to produce a whistling sound.

▸ verb (**whistles**, **whistling**, **whistled**) 1 give out a whistle. 2 move rapidly with a whistling sound. 3 blow a whistle.

■ **whistle-stop** very fast and with only brief pauses.

Whit ▸ noun Whitsun.

■ **Whit Sunday** a Christian festival held on the seventh Sunday after Easter.

whit ▸ noun a very small part or amount.

white ▸ adjective 1 having the colour of milk or fresh snow. 2 very pale. 3 relating to people with light-coloured skin. 4 Brit. (of coffee or tea) with milk. 5 (of wine) yellowish in colour. 6 innocent and pure.

> SYNONYMS *her face went white* **pale**, pallid, wan, ashen, chalky, pasty, peaky, washed out, ghostly, deathly.

▸ noun 1 white colour. 2 the visible pale part of the eyeball around the iris. 3 the outer part which surrounds the yolk of an egg; the albumen. 4 a white person.

■ **white blood cell** a cell in the blood or lymph which acts against foreign substances and disease. **white-collar** relating to work in an office or other professional environment. **white elephant** a useless or troublesome possession. **white flag** a white flag waved as a symbol of surrender or truce. **white-hot** so hot that it glows white. **white lie** a harmless lie told to avoid hurting someone's feelings. **white magic** magic used only for good purposes. **White Paper** (in the UK) a government report giving information or proposals on an issue. **white sauce** a sauce made with flour, butter, and milk or stock. **white spirit** Brit. a colourless liquid distilled from

petroleum, used as a paint thinner and solvent.
□ **whiteness** noun.

whitebait ▸ noun the young of various sea fish used as food.

whiten ▸ verb make or become white.
□ **whitener** noun.

whitewash ▸ noun 1 a solution of lime or chalk and water, used for painting walls white. 2 a deliberate concealment of mistakes or faults.
▸ verb 1 paint with whitewash. 2 conceal mistakes or faults.

whither ▸ adverb formal or old use 1 to what place or state. 2 what is the likely future of?

whiting ▸ noun (plural **whiting**) a sea fish with white flesh eaten as food.

Whitsun (or **Whitsuntide**) ▸ noun the weekend or week including Whit Sunday.

whittle ▸ verb (**whittles**, **whittling**, **whittled**) 1 carve wood by cutting small slices from it. 2 (**whittle something away** or **down**) gradually reduce something.

whizz ▸ verb (**whizzes**, **whizzing**, **whizzed**) 1 move quickly through the air. 2 move or go fast.
▸ noun informal a person who is very clever at something.
■ **whizz-kid** informal a young person who is very successful or skilful.

who ▸ pronoun 1 what or which person or people? 2 introducing a clause giving further information about a person or people previously mentioned.

! The rule is that you should use **who** as the subject of a verb (*who decided this?*) and **whom** as the object of a verb or preposition (*whom do you think we should support?*). When speaking, however, it's acceptable to use **who** instead of **whom** (*who do you think we should support?*).

whoa /woh/ ▸ exclamation used as a command to a horse to stop or slow down.

who'd ▸ short form 1 who had. 2 who would.

whodunnit (US spelling **whodunit**) ▸ noun informal a crime story in which the identity of the murderer is not revealed until the end.

whoever (or formal **whosoever**) ▸ pronoun 1 the person or people who; any person who. 2 regardless of who. 3 used for emphasis instead of 'who' in questions.

whole ▸ adjective 1 complete; entire. 2 in one piece.

SYNONYMS 1 *the whole report* **entire,** complete, full, unabridged, uncut. 2 *the eggs emerge whole* **intact,** in one piece, unbroken, undamaged, flawless, unmarked, perfect.
ANTONYMS incomplete.

▸ noun 1 a thing that is complete in itself. 2 (**the whole**) all of something.

SYNONYMS 1 *a single whole* **entity,** unit, body, ensemble. 2 *the whole of the year* **all,** every part, the lot, the sum.

■ **on the whole** taking everything into account; in general.
□ **wholeness** noun.

wholefood ▸ noun Brit. food that has been processed as little as possible and is free from additives.

wholehearted ▸ adjective completely sincere and committed.

SYNONYMS **unqualified,** unreserved, unconditional, complete, full, total, absolute.
ANTONYMS half-hearted.

□ **wholeheartedly** adverb.

wholemeal ▸ adjective Brit. (of flour or bread) made from whole grains of wheat including the husk.

wholesale ▸ noun the selling of goods in large quantities to be sold to the public by others.
▸ adverb 1 being sold in such a way. 2 as a whole and in an indiscriminate way.

SYNONYMS *the images were removed wholesale* **extensively,** on a large scale, comprehensively, indiscriminately, without exception.
ANTONYMS selectively.

▸ adjective done on a large scale; extensive.

SYNONYMS *wholesale destruction* **extensive,** widespread, large-scale, wide-ranging, comprehensive, total, mass, indiscriminate.
ANTONYMS partial.

▸ verb (**wholesales**, **wholesaling**, **wholesaled**) sell goods wholesale.
□ **wholesaler** noun.

wholesome ▸ adjective 1 good for health or well-being. 2 morally good.

wholly ▸ adverb entirely; fully.

SYNONYMS **completely,** totally, absolutely, entirely, fully, thoroughly, utterly, downright, in every respect; informal one hundred per cent.

✔ two **l**s, no **e**: wholly, not **-ely**.

whom ▸ pronoun used instead of 'who' as the object of a verb or preposition.

whoop ▸ noun a loud cry of joy or excitement.
▸ verb give or make a whoop.
■ **whooping cough** an illness which mainly affects children, marked by coughs followed by a noisy drawing in of breath.

whoopee ▸ exclamation informal expressing excitement or joy.

whoosh ▸ verb move quickly with a rushing sound.
▸ noun a whooshing movement.

w

whopper ▶ noun informal **1** something that is very large. **2** a blatant lie.

whopping ▶ adjective informal very large.

whore (*rhymes with* door) ▶ noun **1** a prostitute. **2** disapproving a woman who has many sexual partners.

whorl /worl, werl/ ▶ noun **1** each of the turns in a spiral or coil. **2** a spiral or coil. **3** a coil of leaves, flowers, or branches encircling a stem.

who's ▶ short form **1** who is. **2** who has.

> ❗ Don't confuse **who's** with **whose**. **Who's** is short for either **who is** or **who has**, as in *he has a son who's a doctor* or *who's done the reading?*, whereas **whose** means 'belonging to which person' or 'of whom or which', as in *whose is this?* or *he's a man whose opinion I respect.*

whose ▶ possessive determiner & pronoun **1** belonging to or associated with which person. **2** of whom or which.

why ▶ adverb **1** for what reason or purpose? **2** on account of which; the reason that.
▶ exclamation expressing surprise, annoyance, etc.

wick ▶ noun a length of cord in a candle, lamp, or lighter which carries liquid fuel to the flame.

wicked ▶ adjective **1** very bad; evil. **2** playfully mischievous. **3** informal excellent; wonderful.

> SYNONYMS **1** *wicked deeds* **evil,** sinful, immoral, wrong, bad, iniquitous, corrupt, base, vile, villainous, criminal, nefarious; informal **crooked. 2** *a wicked sense of humour* **mischievous,** playful, naughty, impish, roguish, puckish, cheeky.
> ANTONYMS virtuous.

□ **wickedly** adverb **wickedness** noun.

wicker ▶ noun twigs plaited or woven to make items such as furniture and baskets.
□ **wickerwork** noun.

wicket ▶ noun **1** Cricket each of the two sets of three stumps with two bails across the top that are defended by a batsman. **2** a small door or gate.

wicketkeeper ▶ noun Cricket a fielder positioned close behind a batsman's wicket.

wide ▶ adjective (**wider, widest**) **1** of great or more than average width. **2** having a particular width. **3** open to the full extent. **4** including a great variety of people or things. **5** spread among a large number or over a large area. **6** at a distance from a point or mark. **7** (in football) at or near the side of the field.

> SYNONYMS **1** *a wide river* **broad,** extensive, spacious, vast, spread out. **2** *a wide range of opinion* **comprehensive,** ample, broad, extensive, large, exhaustive, all-inclusive. **3** *his shot was wide* **off target,**

off the mark, inaccurate.
> ANTONYMS narrow.

▶ adverb **1** to the full extent. **2** far from the target.

> SYNONYMS **1** *he opened his eyes wide* **fully,** to the fullest/furthest extent, as far/much as possible. **2** *he shot wide* **off target,** wide of the mark/target, inaccurately.

■ **wide awake** fully awake. **wide boy** Brit. informal a man involved in petty criminal activities.
□ **widely** adverb.

widen ▶ verb make or become wider.

> SYNONYMS **broaden,** open up/out, expand, extend, enlarge.

widespread ▶ adjective spread among a large number or over a large area.

> SYNONYMS **general,** extensive, universal, common, global, worldwide, omnipresent, ubiquitous, across the board, predominant, prevalent, rife, broad.
> ANTONYMS limited.

widgeon → WIGEON.

widget ▶ noun informal a small gadget or mechanical device.

widow ▶ noun a woman whose husband has died and who has not married again.
▶ verb (**be widowed**) become a widow or widower.

widower ▶ noun a man whose wife has died and who has not married again.

width ▶ noun **1** the measurement or extent of something from side to side. **2** wide range or extent.

> SYNONYMS **breadth,** thickness, span, diameter, girth.

widthways (or **widthwise**) ▶ adverb in a direction parallel with a thing's width.

wield ▶ verb **1** hold and use a weapon or tool. **2** have power or influence.

> SYNONYMS **1** *he was wielding a sword* **brandish,** flourish, wave, swing, use, employ, handle. **2** *he has wielded power since 1972* **exercise,** exert, hold, maintain, command, control.

> ✔ Remember, the usual rule is **i** before **e** except after **c**: w**ie**ld.

wife ▶ noun (plural **wives**) the woman a man is married to.

> SYNONYMS **spouse,** partner, mate, consort, bride; informal **better half, missus;** Brit. informal **other half.**

□ **wifely** adjective.

wig ▶ noun a covering for the head made of real or artificial hair.

w

wigeon (or **widgeon**) ▸ noun a duck with mainly reddish-brown and grey feathers.

wiggle ▸ verb (**wiggles, wiggling, wiggled**) move with short movements up and down or from side to side.
▸ noun a wiggling movement.
□ **wiggly** adjective.

wigwam ▸ noun a tent consisting of animal skins fixed over a framework of poles, formerly lived in by some North American Indian peoples.

wild ▸ adjective 1 (of animals or plants) living or growing in their natural environment. 2 (of scenery or a region) not lived in or changed by people. 3 lacking discipline or control. 4 not based on reason or evidence. 5 informal very enthusiastic or excited.

> SYNONYMS 1 *wild animals* **untamed,** undomesticated, feral, fierce, ferocious, savage. 2 *wild flowers* **uncultivated,** native, indigenous. 3 *wild hill country* **uninhabited,** unpopulated, uncultivated, rugged, rough, inhospitable, desolate, barren. 4 *a wild night* **stormy,** squally, tempestuous, turbulent, boisterous. 5 *wild behaviour* **uncontrolled,** unrestrained, undisciplined, unruly, rowdy, disorderly, riotous. 6 *Bill's wild schemes* **foolish,** ridiculous, ludicrous, stupid, foolhardy, idiotic, madcap, absurd, silly, impractical, impracticable, unworkable; informal crazy, crackpot. 7 *a wild guess* **random,** arbitrary, haphazard, uninformed.
> ANTONYMS tame, cultivated, calm, disciplined.

▸ noun 1 (**the wild**) a natural state. 2 (**the wilds**) a remote area.
■ **wild card 1** a playing card which can take on any value, suit, or colour that the player holding it needs. 2 Computing a character that will match any character or sequence of characters in a search. 3 an opportunity to enter a sports competition without having qualified in the usual way. **wild goose chase** a hopeless search for something that you will never find.
□ **wildly** adverb **wildness** noun.

wildcat ▸ adjective (of a strike) sudden and unofficial.

wildebeest /wil-duh-beest/ ▸ noun a gnu (a kind of antelope).

wilderness ▸ noun a wild, uninhabited, and unwelcoming region.

> SYNONYMS 1 *the Siberian wilderness* **wilds,** wastes, desert. 2 *a litter-strewn wilderness* **wasteland.**

wildfire ▸ noun (**spread like wildfire**) spread very fast.

wildfowl ▸ plural noun birds that are hunted for sport or food.

wildlife ▸ noun all the animals, birds, and insects that naturally inhabit a particular region.

wiles ▸ plural noun cunning methods used by someone to get what they want.

wilful (US spelling **willful**) ▸ adjective 1 (of a bad act) deliberate. 2 stubborn and determined.

> SYNONYMS 1 *wilful destruction* **deliberate,** intentional, premeditated, planned, conscious. 2 *a wilful child* **headstrong,** strong-willed, obstinate, stubborn, pig-headed, recalcitrant, uncooperative; Brit. informal bloody-minded, bolshie.
> ANTONYMS accidental, amenable.

□ **wilfully** adverb **wilfulness** noun.

will¹ ▸ modal verb (3rd singular present **will**; past **would**) 1 expressing the future tense. 2 expressing a request. 3 expressing desire, consent, or willingness. 4 expressing facts about ability or capacity.

> ❗ The traditional rule is that you should use **shall** when forming the future tense with **I** and **we** (*I shall be late*) and **will** with **you**, **he**, **she**, **it**, and **they** (*he will not be there*). Nowadays, people do not follow this rule so strictly and are more likely to use the shortened forms **I'll**, **she'll**, etc.

will² ▸ noun 1 the power you have to decide on something and take action. 2 (also **willpower**) the ability to control your thoughts and actions in order to achieve something. 3 a desire or intention. 4 a legal document in which someone gives instructions about what should be done with their money and property after their death.

> SYNONYMS 1 *the will to succeed* **determination,** strength of character, resolve, single-mindedness, drive, commitment, dedication, doggedness, tenacity, staying power. 2 *they stayed against their will* **desire,** wish, preference, inclination, intention. 3 *God's will* **wish,** desire, decision, choice, decree, command.

▸ verb 1 intend or desire that something should happen. 2 bring something about by using your mental powers. 3 leave money or property to someone in a will.

> SYNONYMS 1 *do what you will* **want,** wish, please, see fit, think fit/best, like, choose, prefer. 2 *God willed it* **decree,** order, ordain, command.

■ **at will** whenever or in whatever way you like.

willing ▸ adjective 1 ready, eager, or prepared to do something. 2 given or done readily.

> SYNONYMS 1 *I'm willing to give it a try* **ready,** prepared, disposed, inclined, minded, happy, glad, pleased, agreeable,

amenable; informal **game. 2** *willing help* **readily given,** ungrudging.
ANTONYMS reluctant.

willingly ▸ adverb in a willing manner.

> SYNONYMS **voluntarily,** of your own free will, of your own accord, readily, without reluctance, ungrudgingly, cheerfully, happily, gladly, with pleasure.
> ANTONYMS reluctantly.

willingness ▸ noun the quality or state of being willing.

> SYNONYMS **readiness,** inclination, will, wish, desire.
> ANTONYMS reluctance.

will-o'-the-wisp ▸ noun **1** a thing that is impossible to obtain. **2** a faint flickering light seen at night over marshy ground, thought to result from natural gases burning.

willow ▸ noun a tree which has narrow leaves and produces catkins.

willowy ▸ adjective tall and slim.

willy-nilly ▸ adverb **1** whether you like it or not. **2** without any direction or plan.

wilt ▸ verb **1** (of a plant) become limp through heat or lack of water. **2** feel tired and weak.

> SYNONYMS **1** *the roses had begun to wilt* **droop,** sag, become limp, flop. **2** *we were wilting in the heat* **languish,** flag, droop, become listless.
> ANTONYMS flourish.

wily (*rhymes with* highly) ▸ adjective clever in a cunning or crafty way.

wimp ▸ noun informal a person who is not strong, brave, or confident.
□ **wimpish** adjective **wimpy** adjective.

wimple ▸ noun a cloth headdress covering the head, neck, and sides of the face, worn in the past by women and still today by some nuns.

win ▸ verb (**wins, winning, won**) **1** be the most successful in a contest or conflict. **2** gain something as a result of success in a contest or conflict. **3** gain someone's attention, support, or love. **4** (**win someone over**) gain someone's agreement or support by persuading them that you are right.

> SYNONYMS **1** *Steve won the race* **come first in,** take first prize in, triumph in, be successful in. **2** *she was determined to win* **come first,** be victorious, carry/win the day, come out on top, succeed, triumph, prevail. **3** *he won a cash prize* **earn,** gain, secure, collect, pick up, walk away/off with, carry off; informal land, net, bag, scoop.
> ANTONYMS lose.

▸ noun a victory in a game or contest.

> SYNONYMS *a 3–0 win* **victory,** triumph, conquest.
> ANTONYMS defeat.

wince ▸ verb (**winces, wincing, winced**) flinch slightly on feeling pain or distress.

> SYNONYMS **grimace,** pull a face, flinch, blench, start.

▸ noun an act of wincing.

winceyette ▸ noun Brit. a soft brushed cotton fabric.

winch ▸ noun a hauling or lifting device consisting of a rope or chain winding around a rotating drum.
▸ verb hoist or haul something with a winch.

wind[1] ▸ noun **1** a natural movement of the air. **2** breath needed to play an instrument or do exercise. **3** wind or woodwind instruments forming a band or section of an orchestra. **4** Brit. air or gas in the stomach or intestines.

> SYNONYMS **1** *the trees were swaying in the wind* **breeze,** current of air, gale, hurricane, gust, draught; informal **blow;** literary **zephyr. 2** *Jez got his wind back* **breath;** informal **puff.**

▸ verb **1** make someone unable to breathe easily for a short time. **2** Brit. pat a baby on its back to help it bring up air swallowed while feeding.
■ **get wind of** informal hear a rumour of. **put the wind up** Brit. informal alarm or frighten. **wind instrument 1** a musical instrument which you play by blowing into it. **2** a woodwind instrument as distinct from a brass instrument. **wind tunnel** a tunnel-like structure in which a strong current of air is created, to test the effect of wind and air flow on vehicles.

wind[2] ▸ verb (**winds, winding, wound**) **1** move in or take a twisting or spiral course. **2** pass something around a thing or person so as to encircle or enfold them. **3** (with reference to something long) twist or be twisted around itself or a central thing. **4** make a clockwork device work by turning a key or handle. **5** turn a key or handle repeatedly. **6** move an audio tape, videotape, or film backwards or forwards.

> SYNONYMS **1** *the road winds up the mountain* **twist (and turn),** bend, curve, loop, zigzag, weave, snake. **2** *he wound a towel around his waist* **wrap,** furl, entwine, lace. **3** *Anne wound the wool into a ball* **coil,** roll, twist, twine.

■ **wind down 1** (of a clockwork mechanism) gradually lose power. **2** (also **wind something down**) draw or bring something gradually to an end. **3** informal relax. **wind up** informal end up in a particular situation or place. **wind someone/thing up 1** gradually bring something to an end.

W

2 Brit. informal tease or irritate someone.

windbag ▸ noun informal a person who talks a lot but without saying anything interesting or important.

windbreak ▸ noun a screen providing shelter from the wind.

windcheater ▸ noun Brit. a wind-resistant jacket with a close-fitting neck and cuffs.

windfall ▸ noun **1** a piece of unexpected good fortune. **2** an apple or other fruit blown from a tree by the wind.

SYNONYMS **bonanza,** jackpot, pennies from heaven, godsend.

windlass ▸ noun a winch used on a ship or in a harbour.

windmill ▸ noun a building with sails or vanes that turn in the wind and generate power to grind corn, generate electricity, or draw water.

window ▸ noun **1** an opening in a wall, fitted with glass to let in light and allow people to see out. **2** a framed area on a computer screen for viewing information.
■ **window dressing 1** the arrangement of an attractive display in a shop window. **2** the presentation of something in a superficially attractive way to give a good impression. **window-shop** spend time looking at the goods displayed in shop windows.

windowpane ▸ noun a pane of glass in a window.

windowsill ▸ noun a ledge or sill at the bottom of a window.

windpipe ▸ noun the tube carrying air down the throat and into the lungs; the trachea.

windscreen ▸ noun Brit. a glass screen at the front of a motor vehicle.

windshield ▸ noun N. Amer. a windscreen.

windsock ▸ noun a light, flexible cone mounted on a mast to show the direction and strength of the wind.

windsurfing ▸ noun the sport of riding on a sailboard on water.
□ **windsurf** verb **windsurfer** noun.

windswept ▸ adjective exposed to strong winds.

windward ▸ adjective & adverb facing the wind, or on the side facing the wind.

windy ▸ adjective marked by or exposed to strong winds.

SYNONYMS **breezy,** blowy, fresh, blustery, gusty, wild, stormy, squally.
ANTONYMS still.

wine ▸ noun an alcoholic drink made from fermented grape juice.

winery ▸ noun (plural **wineries**) an establishment where wine is made.

wing ▸ noun **1** a kind of limb used by a bird, bat, or insect for flying. **2** a rigid structure projecting from both sides of an aircraft and supporting it in the air. **3** a part of a large building. **4** a group or faction within an organization. **5** (**the wings**) the sides of a theatre stage out of view of the audience. **6** the part of a soccer or rugby field close to the sidelines. **7** Brit. the part of a car above and extending slightly over a wheel. **8** an air force unit of several squadrons.

SYNONYMS **1** the east wing of the house **part,** section, side, annexe, extension. **2** the radical wing of the party **faction,** camp, caucus, arm, branch, group, section, set.

▸ verb **1** fly, or move quickly as if flying. **2** shoot a bird so as to wound it in the wing. **3** (**wing it**) informal speak or act without preparation.

SYNONYMS **1** a seagull winged its way over the sea **fly,** glide, soar. **2** the eagle was shot at and winged **wound,** graze, hit.

■ **wing nut** a nut with a pair of projections for the fingers to turn it on a screw.
□ **winged** adjective.

winger ▸ noun an attacking player on the wing in soccer, hockey, etc.

wingspan ▸ noun the full extent from tip to tip of the wings of an aircraft, bird, etc.

wink ▸ verb **1** close and open one eye quickly as a private signal. **2** shine with an unsteady light; flash on and off.

SYNONYMS **1** he winked an eye at her **blink,** flutter, bat. **2** the diamond winked in the moonlight **sparkle,** twinkle, flash, glitter, gleam, shine, scintillate.

▸ noun an act of winking.

winkle ▸ noun a small edible shellfish with a spiral shell.
▸ verb (**winkles, winkling, winkled**) (**winkle something out**) Brit. **1** extract something with difficulty. **2** get information from someone who is reluctant to give it.

winner ▸ noun a person who wins.

SYNONYMS **victor,** champion, conqueror, vanquisher, medallist; informal champ, top dog.
ANTONYMS loser.

winning ▸ adjective attractive.

SYNONYMS **1** the winning team **victorious,** successful, triumphant, undefeated, conquering, first, top. **2** a winning smile **engaging,** charming, appealing, endearing, sweet, cute, winsome, attractive, prepossessing, fetching, disarming, captivating.

▸ plural noun (**winnings**) money won by gambling.

W

SYNONYMS **prize money,** gains, booty, spoils, proceeds, profits, takings, purse.
□ **winningly** adverb.

winnow ▸ verb **1** remove people or things from a group until only the best ones are left. **2** blow air through grain in order to remove the chaff.

wino ▸ noun (plural **winos**) informal a person who sits all day in the streets drinking alcohol.

winsome ▸ adjective appealing.

winter ▸ noun the coldest season of the year, after autumn and before spring.
▸ verb (**winters, wintering, wintered**) spend the winter in a particular place.

wintry ▸ adjective cold or bleak.

wipe ▸ verb (**wipes, wiping, wiped**) **1** clean or dry something by rubbing it with a cloth or your hand. **2** remove something from a surface in this way. **3** erase data from a computer, tape, etc.

SYNONYMS **1** *Beth wiped the table* **rub,** mop, sponge, swab, clean, dry, polish. **2** *he wiped the marks off the window* **rub off,** clean off, remove, erase, efface.

▸ noun **1** an act of wiping. **2** an absorbent cleaning cloth.
■ **wipe someone/thing out 1** remove or eliminate something. **2** kill a large number of people.
□ **wiper** noun.

wire ▸ noun **1** metal in the form of a thin flexible strand. **2** a length of wire used for fencing, to carry an electric current, etc. **3** a concealed listening device. **4** informal a telegram.
▸ verb (**wires, wiring, wired**) **1** install electric circuits or wires in a room or building. **2** fasten or reinforce with wire. **3** informal send a telegram to.

wireless ▸ adjective using radio, microwaves, etc. (as opposed to wires) to transmit signals.
▸ noun dated **1** a radio. **2** broadcasting using radio signals.

wiretapping ▸ noun the secret tapping of telephone lines in order to listen to other people's conversations.

wiring ▸ noun a system of wires providing electric circuits for a device or building.

wiry ▸ adjective **1** resembling wire. **2** lean, tough, and sinewy.

W

wisdom ▸ noun **1** the quality of being wise. **2** the knowledge that a particular society or culture has gained over a period of time.

SYNONYMS **1** *we questioned the wisdom of the decision* **understanding,** intelligence, sagacity, sense, common sense, shrewdness, astuteness, judgement, prudence, circumspection, advisability. **2** *the*

wisdom of the East **knowledge,** learning, erudition, scholarship, philosophy, lore.
ANTONYMS folly.

■ **wisdom tooth** each of the four molars at the back of the mouth which usually appear at about the age of twenty.

wise[1] ▸ adjective **1** having or showing experience, knowledge, and good judgement. **2** (**wise to**) informal aware of.

SYNONYMS *a wise old man* **sage,** sagacious, intelligent, clever, learned, knowledgeable, enlightened, astute, smart, shrewd, sharp-witted, canny, knowing, sensible, prudent, discerning, perceptive.
ANTONYMS foolish.

▸ verb (**wises, wising, wised**) (**wise up**) informal become aware of something.
□ **wisely** adverb.

wise[2] ▸ noun old use the manner or extent of something.

wisecrack informal ▸ noun a witty remark or joke.
▸ verb make a wisecrack.

wish ▸ verb **1** feel a strong desire for something. **2** silently express a hope that something will happen. **3** say that you hope that someone will be happy, successful, etc.

SYNONYMS **1** *they can do as they wish* **want,** desire, feel inclined, feel like, care, choose, please, think fit. **2** *I wish you to send them a message* **want,** desire, require.

▸ noun **1** a desire or hope. **2** (**wishes**) an expression of hope that someone will be happy, successful, etc. **3** a thing wished for.

SYNONYMS **1** *his wish to own a Mercedes* **desire,** longing, yearning, whim, craving, hunger, hope, aspiration, aim, ambition, dream; informal hankering, yen. **2** *her parents' wishes* **request,** requirement, bidding, instruction, direction, demand, order, command, want, desire, will.

wishbone ▸ noun a forked bone between the neck and breast of a bird.

wishful ▸ adjective wishing for something to happen.
■ **wishful thinking** expectations that are based on optimistic wishes rather than facts.

wishy-washy ▸ adjective not firm or forceful; feeble.

wisp ▸ noun a small, thin bunch or strand of something.
□ **wispy** adjective.

wisteria /wi-**steer**-i-uh/ ▸ noun a climbing plant with hanging clusters of bluish-lilac flowers.

wistful ▸ adjective having a feeling of vague or regretful longing.
□ **wistfully** adverb **wistfulness** noun.

wit ▸ noun **1** (also **wits**) the ability to think quickly and make good decisions. **2** a natural talent for using words and ideas in a quick and funny way. **3** a witty person.

SYNONYMS **1** *he needed all his wits to escape* **intelligence,** shrewdness, astuteness, cleverness, canniness, sense, judgement, acumen, insight, brains, mind; informal nous. **2** *my sparkling wit* **wittiness,** humour, drollery, repartee, badinage, banter, wordplay, jokes, witticisms, quips, puns. **3** *she's such a wit* **comedian,** humorist, comic, joker; informal wag.

■ **at your wits' end** not knowing what to do.

witch ▸ noun a woman believed to have evil magic powers.

SYNONYMS **1** *the witch cast a spell* **sorceress,** enchantress, hex, Wiccan. **2** *she's a right old witch* **hag,** crone, harpy, harridan, she-devil; informal battleaxe.

■ **witch doctor** a person believed to have magic powers that cure illness. **witch hazel** a lotion made from the bark and leaves of a shrub, used for treating injuries on the skin. **witch-hunt** a campaign against a person who holds unpopular views.

witchcraft ▸ noun the use of evil magic powers.

SYNONYMS **sorcery,** (black) magic, wizardry, spells, incantations, necromancy, Wicca.

with ▸ preposition **1** accompanied by. **2** in the same direction as. **3** possessing; having. **4** indicating the instrument used to perform an action or the material used for a purpose. **5** in opposition to or competition with. **6** indicating the way or attitude in which a person does something. **7** in relation to.
■ **with it** informal **1** up to date or fashionable. **2** alert and able to understand.

withdraw ▸ verb (**withdraws, withdrawing, withdrew**; past participle **withdrawn**) **1** remove or take away. **2** leave or cause to leave a place. **3** stop taking part in an activity. **4** take back something you have said. **5** take money out of an account. **6** go away to another place in search of quiet or privacy. **7** stop taking an addictive drug. **8** (**withdrawn**) very shy or reserved.

SYNONYMS **1** *she withdrew her hand from his* **remove,** extract, pull out, take out, take back. **2** *the ban on advertising was withdrawn* **abolish,** cancel, lift, set aside, end, stop, remove, reverse, revoke, rescind, repeal, annul. **3** *she withdrew the allegation* **retract,** take back, go back on, recant, repudiate, renounce, back down, climb down, backtrack, back-pedal, do a U-turn, eat your words. **4** *the troops withdrew from the city* **retreat,**

pull out of, evacuate, quit, leave. **5** *his partner withdrew from the project* **pull out of,** back out of, bow out of. **6** *they withdrew to their rooms* **retire,** retreat, adjourn, decamp, leave, depart, absent yourself; formal repair.
ANTONYMS insert, introduce, deposit, enter.

withdrawal ▸ noun the action of withdrawing.

SYNONYMS **1** *the withdrawal of subsidies* **removal,** abolition, cancellation, discontinuation, termination, elimination. **2** *the withdrawal of the troops* **departure,** pull-out, exit, exodus, evacuation, retreat.

wither ▸ verb (**withers, withering, withered**) **1** (of a plant) become dry and shrivelled. **2** become shrunken or wrinkled from age or disease. **3** become weaker; decline. **4** (**withering**) scornful.

SYNONYMS **1** *the flowers withered in the sun* **shrivel (up),** dry up, wilt, droop, go limp, fade, perish. **2** *the muscles in his leg withered* **waste (away),** shrivel (up), shrink, atrophy. **3** *her confidence withered* **diminish,** dwindle, shrink, lessen, fade, wane, evaporate, disappear. **4** (**withering**) **scornful,** contemptuous, scathing, stinging, devastating, humiliating, mortifying.
ANTONYMS thrive, grow.

withers ▸ plural noun the highest part of a horse's back, at the base of the neck.

withhold ▸ verb (**withholds, withholding, withheld**) **1** refuse to give. **2** hold back an emotion or reaction.

SYNONYMS **1** *he withheld the information* **hold back,** keep back, refuse to give, retain, hold on to, hide, conceal, keep secret; informal sit on. **2** *she could not withhold her tears* **suppress,** repress, hold back, fight back, choke back, control, check, restrain, contain.
ANTONYMS release.

✔ Remember to double the **h**: wit**hh**old.

within ▸ preposition **1** before a particular period of time has passed. **2** inside the range or bounds of something. **3** inside something.
▸ adverb inside.

without ▸ preposition not accompanied by, using, or having.
▸ adverb old use outside.

withstand ▸ verb (**withstands, withstanding, withstood**) remain undamaged by; resist.

SYNONYMS **resist,** weather, survive, endure, cope with, stand, tolerate, bear, defy, brave, hold out against.

W

witless ▸ adjective foolish; stupid.

witness ▸ noun **1** a person who sees an event take place. **2** a person who gives evidence in a court of law. **3** a person who is present at the signing of a document and signs it themselves to confirm this.

> SYNONYMS *witnesses claimed that he started the fight* **observer,** onlooker, eyewitness, spectator, viewer, watcher, bystander, passer-by.

▸ verb **1** be a witness to. **2** be the place, period, etc. in which an event takes place.

> SYNONYMS **1** *who witnessed the incident?* **see,** observe, watch, view, notice, spot, be present at, attend. **2** *the will is correctly witnessed* **countersign,** sign, endorse, validate.

witter ▸ verb (witters, wittering, wittered) Brit. informal talk for a long time about unimportant things.

witticism ▸ noun a witty remark.

witty ▸ adjective (wittier, wittiest) able to say clever and amusing things.

> SYNONYMS **humorous,** amusing, droll, funny, comic, jocular, sparkling, scintillating, entertaining, clever, quick-witted.

□ **wittily** adverb.

wives plural of WIFE.

wizard ▸ noun **1** a man who has magical powers. **2** a person who is very skilled in something.

> SYNONYMS **1** *the wizard cast a spell* **sorcerer,** warlock, magus, (black) magician, enchanter. **2** *a financial wizard* **genius,** expert, master, virtuoso, maestro, marvel; informal hotshot, whizz-kid; Brit. informal dab hand; N. Amer. informal maven.

□ **wizardry** noun.

wizened ▸ adjective shrivelled or wrinkled with age.

WMD ▸ abbreviation weapon (or weapons) of mass destruction.

woad ▸ noun a plant whose leaves were used in the past to make blue dye.

wobble ▸ verb (wobbles, wobbling, wobbled) **1** move unsteadily from side to side. **2** (of the voice) tremble.

> SYNONYMS **1** *the table wobbled* **rock,** teeter, jiggle, sway, see-saw, shake. **2** *he wobbled across to the door* **teeter,** totter, stagger, lurch. **3** *her voice wobbled* **tremble,** shake, quiver, quaver, waver.

▸ noun a wobbling movement or sound.

wobbly ▸ adjective **1** tending to wobble. **2** weak an unsteady from illness.

> SYNONYMS **1** *a wobbly table* **unsteady,** unstable, shaky, rocky, rickety, unsafe, precarious; informal wonky. **2** *her legs*

were a bit wobbly **shaky,** quivery, weak, unsteady; informal like jelly.
ANTONYMS stable.

woe ▸ noun literary **1** great sadness or distress. **2** (woes) troubles.

> SYNONYMS **1** *a tale of woe* **misery,** sorrow, distress, sadness, unhappiness, heartache, heartbreak, despair, adversity, misfortune, disaster, suffering, hardship. **2** *financial woes* **trouble,** difficulty, problem, trial, tribulation, misfortune, setback, reverse.
> ANTONYMS joy.

■ **woe betide someone** a person will be in trouble if they do a particular thing.

woebegone /woh-bi-gon/ ▸ adjective looking sad or miserable.

woeful ▸ adjective **1** very sad. **2** very bad. □ **woefully** adverb.

wok ▸ noun a bowl-shaped frying pan used in Chinese cookery.

woke past of WAKE¹.

woken past participle of WAKE¹.

wold ▸ noun an area of high, open land.

wolf ▸ noun (plural wolves) a wild animal of the dog family, that lives and hunts in packs.

▸ verb (wolfs, wolfing, wolfed) eat food quickly and greedily.

■ **cry wolf** keep raising false alarms, so that when you really need help you are ignored. **wolf whistle** a whistle with a rising and falling note, used by a man to show that he finds a woman sexually attractive. □ **wolfish** adjective.

wolfhound ▸ noun a large breed of dog originally used to hunt wolves.

wolfram ▸ noun tungsten or its ore.

wolverine ▸ noun a heavily built meat-eating animal found in cold northern areas.

woman ▸ noun (plural women) an adult human female.

> SYNONYMS **lady,** female; Scottish & N. English lass; Irish colleen; informal chick; N. Amer. informal sister, dame, broad; Austral./NZ informal sheila; literary damsel.

□ **womanhood** noun.

womanize (or womanise) ▸ verb (womanizes, womanizing, womanized) (of a man) have a lot of casual affairs with women.
□ **womanizer** noun.

womankind ▸ noun women as a whole.

womanly ▸ adjective characteristic of a woman or women.

> SYNONYMS **1** *womanly virtues* **feminine,** female. **2** *her womanly figure* **voluptuous,** curvaceous, shapely, ample, buxom, full-figured; informal curvy, busty.
> ANTONYMS manly, boyish.

w

womb ▸ noun the organ in a woman's body in which a baby develops before it is born.

wombat ▸ noun an Australian animal resembling a small bear with short legs.

won past and past participle of WIN.

wonder ▸ verb (wonders, wondering, wondered) 1 be interested to know about something. 2 feel doubt. 3 feel amazement and admiration.

SYNONYMS 1 *I wondered what was on her mind* ponder, think about, reflect on, muse on, speculate about, conjecture, be curious about. 2 *people wondered at such bravery* marvel, be amazed, be astonished, stand in awe, be dumbfounded; informal be flabbergasted.

▸ noun 1 a feeling of amazement and admiration. 2 a person or thing that causes such a feeling.

SYNONYMS 1 *she was speechless with wonder* awe, admiration, fascination, surprise, astonishment, amazement. 2 *the wonders of nature* marvel, miracle, phenomenon, sensation, spectacle, beauty, curiosity.

■ no wonder it is not surprising.

wonderful ▸ adjective very good, pleasant, or remarkable.

SYNONYMS marvellous, magnificent, superb, glorious, sublime, lovely, delightful; informal super, great, fantastic, terrific, tremendous, sensational, fabulous, awesome, magic, wicked; Brit. informal smashing, brilliant; N. Amer. informal peachy, dandy, neat; Austral./NZ informal beaut, bonzer.

□ wonderfully adverb.

wonderland ▸ noun a place full of wonderful things.

wondrous ▸ adjective literary inspiring wonder.

wonky ▸ adjective informal 1 not straight; crooked. 2 unsteady or faulty.

wont /wohnt/ ▸ noun (your wont) formal your normal behaviour.
▸ adjective (wont to) literary in the habit of doing something.

won't ▸ short form will not.

wonted /wohn-tid/ ▸ adjective literary usual.

woo ▸ verb (woos, wooing, wooed) 1 (of a man) try to make a woman love him. 2 try to get someone's support or custom.

SYNONYMS 1 *Richard wooed Joan* pay court to, pursue, chase (after); dated court, romance, seek the hand of. 2 *the party wooed voters with promises* seek, pursue, curry favour with, try to win, try to attract, try to cultivate. 3 *an attempt to woo him out of retirement* entice,

tempt, coax, persuade, wheedle, seduce; informal sweet-talk.

wood ▸ noun 1 the hard material forming the trunk and branches of a tree. 2 (also woods) a small forest.

SYNONYMS 1 *polished wood* timber, planks, logs; N. Amer. lumber. 2 *a walk through the woods* forest, woodland, trees, copse, coppice, grove; Brit. spinney.

□ woody adjective.

woodbine ▸ noun Brit. honeysuckle.

woodcock ▸ noun (plural woodcock) a woodland bird with a long beak and brown feathers.

woodcut ▸ noun a print made with a block of wood in which a design has been cut.

woodcutter ▸ noun a person who cuts down trees for wood.

wooded ▸ adjective (of land) covered with woods.

SYNONYMS forested, afforested, tree-covered; literary sylvan.

wooden ▸ adjective 1 made of wood. 2 acting or speaking in a stiff and awkward way.

SYNONYMS 1 *a wooden door* wood, timber. 2 *wooden acting* stilted, stiff, unnatural, awkward, flat, stodgy, lifeless, soulless. 3 *her face was wooden* expressionless, impassive, poker-faced, emotionless, blank, vacant, unresponsive.

□ woodenly adverb.

woodland (or woodlands) ▸ noun land covered with trees.

woodlouse ▸ noun (plural woodlice) a small insect-like creature with a grey segmented body.

woodpecker ▸ noun a bird with a strong bill that pecks at tree trunks to find insects.

woodturning ▸ noun the activity of shaping wood with a lathe.

woodwind ▸ noun wind instruments other than brass instruments forming a section of an orchestra.

woodwork ▸ noun 1 the wooden parts of a room, building, or other structure. 2 the activity of making things from wood.
□ woodworker noun.

woodworm ▸ noun the larva of a kind of beetle, that bores into wood.

woof¹ ▸ noun the barking sound made by a dog.
▸ verb bark.

woof² = WEFT.

woofer ▸ noun a loudspeaker that reproduces low frequencies.

wool ▸ noun the fine, soft hair forming the coat of a sheep.

w

synonyms **fleece**, hair, coat.

woollen (US spelling **woolen**) ▶ adjective
1 made of wool. **2** relating to the
production of wool.
▶ noun (**woollens**) woollen clothes.

woolly ▶ adjective **1** made of wool.
2 covered with wool or hair resembling
wool. **3** resembling wool. **4** confused or
unclear.
▶ noun (plural **woollies**) informal a woollen
jumper or cardigan.

woozy ▶ adjective informal unsteady, dizzy, or
dazed.
□ **woozily** adverb.

word ▶ noun **1** a unit of language which
has meaning and is used with others to
form sentences. **2** a remark or statement.
3 (**words**) angry talk. **4** (**the word**) a
command, slogan, or signal. **5** (**your word**)
your account of the truth of something
that happened. **6** (**your word**) a thing that
you promise. **7** news.

synonyms **1** *the Italian word for 'ham'*
term, name, expression, designation.
2 *his words were meant kindly* **remark**,
comment, observation, statement,
utterance. **3** *I've got three weeks to learn
my words* **script**, lines, lyrics, libretto.
4 *I give you my word* **promise**, assurance,
guarantee, undertaking, pledge, vow,
oath, bond. **5** *I want a word with you*
talk, conversation, chat, tête-à-tête,
heart-to-heart, one-to-one, discussion;
informal confab. **6** *there's no word
from the hospital* **news**, information,
communication, intelligence, message,
report, communiqué, dispatch, bulletin.

▶ verb express something in particular words.

synonyms *the question was carefully
worded* **phrase**, express, put, couch,
frame, formulate, style.

■ **in a word** briefly. **word class** a category
in which a word is placed according to its
function in grammar; a part of speech.
word of mouth talking as a way of passing
on information. **word processor** a computer
or program for creating and printing a
document or piece of text.

wording ▶ noun the way in which
something is worded.

synonyms **phrasing**, phraseology,
language, words, expression,
terminology.

wordy ▶ adjective using too many words.

synonyms **long-winded**, verbose,
lengthy, rambling, garrulous, voluble;
informal windy; Brit. informal waffly.
antonyms succinct.

wore past of **wear**.

work ▶ noun **1** activity involving mental or
physical effort done in order to achieve a
result. **2** the activity or job that a person
does in order to earn money. **3** a task or
tasks to be done. **4** a thing or things done
or made. **5** (**works**) a place where industrial
or manufacturing processes are carried out.
6 (**works**) activities involving the building
or repair of something. **7** (**works**) the
mechanism of a clock or other machine.

synonyms **1** *a day's work in the fields*
labour, toil, slog, drudgery, exertion,
effort; informal grind, sweat; Brit.
informal graft. **2** *I'm looking for work*
employment, job, post, position,
situation, occupation, profession, career,
vocation, calling. **3** *haven't you got any
work?* **tasks**, jobs, duties, assignments,
projects, chores. **4** *works of literature*
composition, piece, creation, opus.
5 *this is the work of a radical faction*
handiwork, doing, act, deed. **6** *a lifetime
spent doing good works* **deeds**, acts,
actions, turns. **7** *the complete works of
Shakespeare* **writings**, oeuvre, canon,
output. **8** *a car works* **factory**, plant, mill,
workshop, facility. **9** *the works of a clock*
mechanism, machinery, workings, parts,
movement, action; informal insides.
antonyms leisure, pleasure.

▶ verb **1** do work as your job. **2** make someone
do work. **3** (of a machine or system)
function properly. **4** (of a machine) be
in operation. **5** have the desired result.
6 bring a material or mixture to a desired
shape or consistency. **7** cultivate land, or
extract materials from a mine or quarry.
8 move something gradually or with
difficulty into another position.

synonyms **1** *staff worked late into the
night* **labour**, toil, exert yourself, slave
(away); informal slog (away), beaver
away; Brit. informal graft. **2** *he worked in
education for years* **be employed**, have
a job, earn your living, do business.
3 *farmers worked the land* **cultivate**,
farm, till, plough. **4** *his car was working
perfectly* **function**, go, run, operate;
informal behave. **5** *how do I work this
machine?* **operate**, use, handle, control,
manipulate, run. **6** *their ploy worked*
succeed, turn out well, go as planned,
get results, be effective; informal come
off, pay off, do the trick. **7** *blusher can
work miracles* **achieve**, accomplish, bring
about, produce, perform. **8** *he worked
the crowd into a frenzy* **stir (up)**, excite,
drive, move, rouse, fire, galvanize; whip
up, agitate. **9** *work the mixture into a
paste* **knead**, squeeze, form; mix, stir,
blend. **10** *he worked the blade into the
padlock* **manipulate**, manoeuvre, guide,
squeeze, edge. **11** *he worked his way
through the crowd* **manoeuvre**, make,

thread, wind, weave, wend, elbow.
ANTONYMS rest, fail.

■ **get worked up** become stressed or angry.
work out 1 develop in the desired way.
2 do energetic physical exercise. **work something out 1** solve something. **2** plan something in detail. **work permit** an official document giving a foreigner permission to take a job in a country. **work-to-rule** a situation in which people refuse to do overtime or extra work, as a form of protest. **work up to** proceed gradually towards something more demanding or advanced.

workaday ▸ adjective ordinary.

workbench ▸ noun a bench at which carpentry and other work is done.

worker ▸ noun **1** a person who works. **2** a neuter or undeveloped female bee, wasp, ant, etc., large numbers of which perform the basic work of a colony.

> SYNONYMS **employee**, member of staff, workman, labourer, hand, operator, operative, agent, wage-earner, breadwinner, proletarian.

workforce ▸ noun the people working or available for work in a particular area, firm, or industry.

workhouse ▸ noun (in the past in the UK) a place where poor people were given accommodation and food in return for work.

working ▸ adjective **1** having paid employment. **2** doing manual work. **3** functioning or able to function. **4** used as a basis for work or discussion and likely to be changed later.
▸ noun **1** a mine from which minerals are being extracted. **2** (**workings**) the way in which a machine, organization, or system operates.

■ **working class** the social group consisting mainly of people who do manual or industrial work. **working party** a group set up to study and report on a particular question and make recommendations.

workload ▸ noun the amount of work to be done by someone or something.

workman ▸ noun (plural **workmen**) a man employed to do manual work.

workmanlike ▸ adjective showing efficient skill.

workout ▸ noun a session of energetic physical exercise.

workshop ▸ noun **1** a room or building in which things are made or repaired. **2** a meeting for discussion and activity on a particular subject or project.

> SYNONYMS **1** *an ideal set of tools for a workshop* **workroom**, studio, factory, works, plant, industrial unit. **2** *a*

workshop on combating stress **study group**, discussion group, seminar, forum, class.

workstation ▸ noun a desktop computer that is part of a network.

worktop ▸ noun Brit. a flat surface for working on in a kitchen.

world ▸ noun **1** (**the world**) the earth with all its countries and peoples. **2** all that belongs to a particular region, period, or area of activity.

> SYNONYMS **1** *he travelled the world* **earth**, globe, planet, sphere. **2** *the academic world* **sphere**, society, circle, arena, milieu, province, domain, preserve, realm, field. **3** (**the world**) *the world would hear of her achievements* **everyone**, people, mankind, humankind, humanity, the public, all and sundry.

■ **world-weary** bored with or cynical about life. **World Wide Web** an information system on the Internet which allows documents to be connected to each other using hypertext links.

worldly ▸ adjective **1** relating to material things rather than spiritual ones. **2** experienced and sophisticated.

> SYNONYMS **1** *worldly pursuits* **earthly**, terrestrial, temporal, mundane, mortal, human, material, physical. **2** *a worldly man* **sophisticated**, experienced, worldly-wise, knowledgeable, knowing, enlightened, mature, seasoned, cosmopolitan, urbane, cultured.
> ANTONYMS spiritual, naive.

■ **worldly-wise** having a lot of experience of life.

worldwide ▸ adjective & adverb throughout the world.

> SYNONYMS **global**, international, intercontinental, universal, ubiquitous.
> ANTONYMS local.

worm ▸ noun **1** an earthworm or other creeping or burrowing creature with a long, thin body and no limbs. **2** (**worms**) long, thin creatures that live as parasites in a person's or animal's intestines.
▸ verb **1** move by crawling or wriggling. **2** (**worm your way into**) gradually move into. **3** (**worm something out of**) cleverly obtain information from someone who is reluctant to give it.

■ **worm cast** a small spiral of earth or sand thrown up at the surface by a burrowing worm.

wormwood ▸ noun a plant with a bitter flavour, used in drinks such as vermouth.

worn past participle of WEAR.
▸ adjective thin or damaged as a result of wear.

w

SYNONYMS **shabby,** worn out, threadbare, in tatters, falling to pieces, ragged, frayed, moth-eaten, scruffy, having seen better days.
ANTONYMS new, smart.

■ **worn out 1** exhausted. **2** damaged by wear, and no longer usable.

worried ▶ adjective feeling anxiety or concern.

SYNONYMS **anxious,** troubled, bothered, concerned, uneasy, fretful, agitated, nervous, edgy, tense, apprehensive, fearful, afraid, frightened; Brit. informal in a stew, in a flap.
ANTONYMS carefree.

□ **worriedly** adverb.

worrisome ▶ adjective causing anxiety or concern.

worry ▶ verb (**worries, worrying, worried**) **1** feel or cause to feel troubled over unwelcome things that have happened or may happen. **2** annoy or disturb. **3** (of a dog) repeatedly push at and bite something. **4** (of a dog) chase and attack livestock.

SYNONYMS **1** *she worries about his health* **be anxious,** be concerned, fret, agonize, brood, panic, lose sleep, get worked up; informal get in a flap, get in a state. **2** *is something worrying you?* **trouble,** bother, make anxious, disturb, distress, upset, concern, unsettle, perturb, scare, prey on someone's mind; informal bug, get to.

▶ noun (plural **worries**) **1** the state of being worried. **2** a source of anxiety.

SYNONYMS **1** *I'm beside myself with worry* **anxiety,** distress, concern, unease, disquiet, nerves, agitation, edginess, tension, apprehension, fear, misgiving; informal butterflies. **2** *the rats are a worry* **problem,** cause for concern, nuisance, pest, trial, trouble, bane, bugbear; informal pain, headache, hassle.
ANTONYMS peace of mind.

□ **worrier** noun.

worse ▶ adjective **1** less good, satisfactory, or pleasing. **2** more serious or severe. **3** more ill or unhappy.

▶ adverb **1** less well. **2** more seriously or severely.

▶ noun a worse event or circumstance.

worsen ▶ verb make or become worse.

SYNONYMS **1** *insomnia can worsen a patient's distress* **aggravate,** add to, intensify, increase, compound, magnify, heighten, inflame, exacerbate. **2** *the recession worsened* **deteriorate,** degenerate, decline; informal go downhill.
ANTONYMS improve.

worship ▶ noun **1** the practice of praising and praying to God or a god or goddess.

2 religious rites and ceremonies. **3** a strong feeling of admiration and respect for someone.

SYNONYMS **1** *the worship of saints* **reverence,** veneration, adoration, glorification, exaltation, devotion, praise, thanksgiving, homage, honour. **2** *morning worship* **service,** rite, prayer, praise, devotion, observance.

▶ verb (**worships, worshipping, worshipped**; US spelling **worships, worshiping, worshiped**) **1** offer praise and prayers to God or a god or goddess. **2** feel great admiration and respect for.

SYNONYMS **1** *they worship pagan gods* **revere,** pray to, pay homage to, honour, adore, venerate, praise, glorify, exalt. **2** *he absolutely worshipped her* **love,** cherish, treasure, hold dear, esteem, adulate, idolize, deify, hero-worship, lionize; informal put on a pedestal.
ANTONYMS mock, despise, shun.

□ **worshipper** noun.

worshipful ▶ adjective **1** feeling or showing great respect and admiration. **2** (**Worshipful**) Brit. a title given to Justices of the Peace.

worst ▶ adjective most bad, severe, or serious.

▶ adverb **1** most severely or seriously. **2** least well.

▶ noun the worst part, event, or circumstance.

worsted /wuus-tid/ ▶ noun a smooth woollen fabric of good quality.

worth ▶ adjective **1** equivalent in value to a particular sum or item. **2** deserving to be treated in a particular way.

▶ noun **1** the value of someone or something. **2** an amount of something that is equivalent to a particular sum of money.

SYNONYMS **1** *evidence of the rug's worth* **value,** price, cost, valuation, estimate. **2** *the intrinsic worth of education* **benefit,** good, advantage, use, value, virtue, desirability, sense.

worthless ▶ adjective **1** having no practical or financial value. **2** having no good qualities.

SYNONYMS **1** *the item was worthless* **valueless. 2** *a mountain of worthless information* **useless,** pointless, meaningless, senseless, inconsequential, ineffective, ineffectual, fruitless, unproductive, unavailing, valueless. **3** *his worthless son* **good-for-nothing,** ne'er-do-well, useless, despicable, contemptible, degenerate; informal no-good, lousy.
ANTONYMS valuable, useful, worthy.

worthwhile ▶ adjective worth the time, money, or effort spent.

W

SYNONYMS **valuable,** useful, of service, beneficial, rewarding, advantageous, positive, helpful, profitable, gainful, fruitful, productive, constructive, effective.

worthy ▸ adjective (**worthier, worthiest**)
1 deserving effort, attention, or respect.
2 (**worthy of**) deserving or good enough for. **3** well intended but too serious and dull.

SYNONYMS *a worthy citizen* **good,** righteous, virtuous, moral, ethical, upright, respectable, upstanding, high-minded, principled, reputable, decent.
ANTONYMS disreputable.

▸ noun (plural **worthies**) humorous an important person.

SYNONYMS *local worthies* **dignitary,** personage, grandee, VIP, notable, pillar of society, luminary, leading light; informal bigwig.
ANTONYMS nobody.

□ **worthily** adverb **worthiness** noun.

would ▸ modal verb (3rd singular present **would**)
1 past of **WILL**[1]. **2** indicating the result of an imagined event. **3** expressing a desire or inclination. **4** expressing a polite request.
5 expressing an opinion or assumption.
6 literary expressing a wish or regret.

would-be ▸ adjective wishing to be a particular type of person.

SYNONYMS **aspiring,** budding, promising, prospective, potential, hopeful, keen, eager, ambitious; informal wannabe.

wouldn't ▸ short form would not.

wound[1] ▸ noun **1** an injury to the body caused by a cut, blow, or bullet. **2** an injury to a person's feelings.

SYNONYMS **1** *a chest wound* **injury,** cut, gash, laceration, graze, scratch, abrasion, puncture, lesion; Medicine trauma. **2** *the wounds inflicted by the media* **insult,** blow, slight, offence, affront, hurt, damage, injury.

▸ verb **1** inflict a wound on. **2** injure someone's feelings.

SYNONYMS **1** *he was critically wounded* **injure,** hurt, harm, lacerate, cut, graze, gash, stab, slash, wing. **2** *her words had wounded him* **hurt,** insult, slight, offend, affront, distress, grieve, pain, sting.

wound[2] past and past participle of **WIND**[2].
wove past of **WEAVE**[1].
woven past participle of **WEAVE**[1].
wow informal ▸ exclamation expressing great surprise or admiration.
▸ verb impress someone very much.
WPC ▸ abbreviation woman police constable.
wrack[1] ➡ **RACK**.

wrack[2] ▸ noun a brown seaweed.
wraith /rayth/ ▸ noun a ghost.
wrangle ▸ noun a long dispute or argument.
▸ verb (**wrangles, wrangling, wrangled**) be involved in a wrangle.

wrap ▸ verb (**wraps, wrapping, wrapped**)
1 enclose something in paper or soft material. **2** encircle or wind round.

SYNONYMS **1** *she wrapped herself in a towel* **enclose,** enfold, envelop, encase, cover, fold, wind, swathe, bundle, swaddle. **2** *I wrapped the vase carefully* **pack,** package, parcel up, bundle (up), gift-wrap.

▸ noun **1** a loose outer garment or piece of material. **2** paper or material used for wrapping.

SYNONYMS *he put a wrap round her* **shawl,** stole, cloak, cape, mantle, scarf.

■ **under wraps** kept secret. **wrap someone/ thing up 1** (also **wrap up**) dress someone in or put on warm clothes. **2** bring a meeting or deal to a close.
□ **wrapper** noun.

wrasse /rass/ ▸ noun (plural **wrasse** or **wrasses**) a brightly coloured sea fish with thick lips and strong teeth.

wrath /roth/ ▸ noun extreme anger.

SYNONYMS **anger,** rage, temper, fury, outrage, spleen, resentment, (high) dudgeon, indignation.
ANTONYMS happiness.

□ **wrathful** adjective.

wreak ▸ verb **1** cause a lot of damage or harm. **2** take revenge on someone.

wreath ▸ noun (plural **wreaths**) **1** an arrangement of flowers or leaves fastened in a ring. **2** a curl or ring of smoke or cloud.

SYNONYMS **garland,** circlet, chaplet, crown, festoon, lei, ring, loop, circle.

wreathe ▸ verb (**wreathes, wreathing, wreathed**) **1** (**be wreathed**) be surrounded or encircled. **2** move with a curling motion.

SYNONYMS **1** *a pulpit wreathed in holly* **festoon,** garland, drape, cover, deck, decorate, ornament, adorn. **2** *blue smoke wreathed upwards* **spiral,** coil, loop, wind, curl, twist, snake.

wreck ▸ noun **1** the destruction of a ship at sea. **2** a ship destroyed at sea. **3** a building, vehicle, etc. that has been destroyed or badly damaged. **4** N. Amer. a road or rail crash. **5** a person in a very bad state.

SYNONYMS **1** *salvage teams landed on the wreck* **shipwreck,** sunken ship, hull.
2 *the wreck of a stolen car* **wreckage,** debris, ruins, remains, burnt-out shell.

▸ verb **1** destroy or badly damage. **2** spoil a plan. **3** cause a ship to sink or break up.

W

SYNONYMS **1** *he had wrecked her car* **destroy**, break, demolish, crash, smash up, write off; N. Amer. informal trash, total. **2** *the crisis wrecked his plans* **ruin**, spoil, disrupt, undo, put a stop to, frustrate, blight, crush, dash, destroy, scotch, shatter, devastate, sabotage; informal mess up, screw up, put paid to, stymie; Brit. informal scupper.

wreckage ▸ noun the remains of something that has been badly damaged.

wren ▸ noun **1** a very small bird with a cocked tail. **2** (in the UK) a member of the former Women's Royal Naval Service.

wrench ▸ verb **1** pull or twist something suddenly and violently. **2** twist and injure a part of the body.

SYNONYMS **1** *he wrenched the gun from her* **tug**, pull, jerk, wrest, heave, twist, force, prise; N. Amer. pry; informal yank. **2** *she wrenched her ankle* **sprain**, twist, turn, strain, rick, crick.

▸ noun **1** a sudden violent twist or pull. **2** a feeling of sadness on leaving a place or person. **3** an adjustable tool used for gripping and turning nuts or bolts.

SYNONYMS **1** *she felt a wrench on her shoulders* **tug**, pull, jerk, jolt, heave; informal yank. **2** *leaving was an immense wrench* **blow**, ache, trauma, pang. **3** *hold the piston with a wrench* **spanner**.

wrest ▸ verb **1** forcibly pull something from someone's grasp. **2** succeed in taking power or control from someone after a struggle.

wrestle ▸ verb (wrestles, wrestling, wrestled) **1** take part in a fight or contest that involves close grappling with your opponent. **2** struggle with a difficulty or problem. **3** struggle to move an object.

SYNONYMS **grapple**, fight, struggle, scuffle, tussle, brawl; informal scrap.

▸ noun **1** a wrestling bout or contest. **2** a hard struggle.
□ **wrestler** noun **wrestling** noun.

wretch ▸ noun **1** an unfortunate person. **2** informal an unpleasant person.

wretched ▸ adjective **1** in a very unhappy or unfortunate state. **2** of bad quality.

SYNONYMS **1** *I felt so wretched without you* **miserable**, unhappy, sad, heartbroken, grief-stricken, distressed, desolate, devastated, disconsolate, downcast, dejected, depressed, melancholy, forlorn. **2** *wretched living conditions* **harsh**, hard, grim, difficult, poor, pitiful, piteous, pathetic, tragic, miserable, bleak, cheerless, hopeless, sorry, sordid; informal crummy.
ANTONYMS cheerful, comfortable.

□ **wretchedly** adverb.

wriggle ▸ verb (wriggles, wriggling, wriggled) **1** twist and turn with quick short movements. **2** (**wriggle out of**) use excuses to avoid doing something.

SYNONYMS *she tried to hug him but he wriggled* **squirm**, writhe, wiggle, thresh, flounder, flail, twitch, twist and turn, snake, worm.

▸ noun a wriggling movement.
□ **wriggly** adjective.

wring ▸ verb (wrings, wringing, wrung) **1** squeeze and twist something to force water out of it. **2** twist and break an animal's neck. **3** squeeze someone's hand tightly. **4** (**wring something from** or **out of**) obtain something from someone with difficulty.
□ **wringer** noun.

wringing ▸ adjective very wet.

wrinkle ▸ noun a slight line or fold, especially in fabric or a person's skin.

SYNONYMS *fine wrinkles around her mouth* **crease**, fold, pucker, line, crinkle, furrow, ridge, groove; informal crow's feet.

▸ verb (wrinkles, wrinkling, wrinkled) make or become covered with wrinkles.

SYNONYMS *his coat tails wrinkled up* **crease**, pucker, gather, crinkle, crumple, rumple, ruck up, scrunch up.

□ **wrinkly** adjective.

wrist ▸ noun the joint connecting the hand with the lower part of the arm.

wristwatch ▸ noun a watch worn on a strap round the wrist.

writ¹ ▸ noun an official document from a court or other legal authority, ordering someone to do or not to do something.

writ² old-fashioned past participle of **WRITE**.
■ **writ large** in an obvious or exaggerated form.

write ▸ verb (writes, writing, wrote; past participle **written**) **1** mark letters, words, or other symbols on a surface with a pen, pencil, etc. **2** write and send a letter to someone. **3** compose a written or musical work. **4** fill out a cheque or similar document.

SYNONYMS **1** *he wrote her name in the book* **put in writing**, put down, jot down, note (down), take down, record, inscribe, sign, scribble, scrawl, pen, pencil. **2** *he promised to write* **correspond**, communicate, get in touch, keep in contact; informal drop someone a line. **3** *I wrote a poem* **compose**, draft, think up, formulate, compile, pen, dash off, produce.

■ **write something off 1** decide that something is useless or a failure. **2** decide

W

not to pursue a debt. **write-off** Brit. a vehicle that is too badly damaged to be repaired. **write-up** a newspaper review of a recent event, performance, etc.

writer ▸ noun a person who writes.

> SYNONYMS **author,** wordsmith; informal scribbler, scribe, pen-pusher, hack.

writhe /ryth/ ▸ verb (**writhes, writhing, writhed**) twist or squirm in pain or embarrassment.

writing ▸ noun **1** the activity or skill of writing. **2** a sequence of letters or symbols forming words. **3** (**writings**) books or other written works.

> SYNONYMS **1** *I can't read his writing* **handwriting,** hand, script, calligraphy, lettering, print, printing; informal scribble, scrawl. **2** *this fear did not show in her writing* **written work,** compositions, books, publications, papers, articles, essays, oeuvre.

wrong ▸ adjective **1** not correct or true; mistaken or in error. **2** unjust, dishonest, or immoral. **3** in a bad or abnormal condition.

> SYNONYMS **1** *the wrong answer* **incorrect,** mistaken, erroneous, inaccurate, inexact, imprecise; informal off beam, out. **2** *he knew he had said the wrong thing* **inappropriate,** unsuitable, ill-advised, ill-considered, ill-judged, unwise, infelicitous; informal out of order. **3** *I've done nothing wrong* **bad,** dishonest, illegal, unlawful, illicit, criminal, corrupt, unethical, immoral, wicked, sinful, iniquitous, nefarious, reprehensible; informal crooked. **4** *there's something wrong with the engine* **amiss,** awry, out of order, not right, faulty, defective.
> ANTONYMS right, correct, appropriate, legal.

▸ adverb **1** in a mistaken or unwelcome way or direction. **2** with an incorrect result.

> SYNONYMS *she guessed wrong* **incorrectly,** wrongly, inaccurately, erroneously, mistakenly.

▸ noun an unjust, dishonest, or immoral action.

> SYNONYMS **1** *the difference between right and wrong* **immorality,** sin, wickedness, evil, illegality, unlawfulness, crime, corruption, villainy, dishonesty, injustice, misconduct, transgression. **2** *an attempt to make up for past wrongs* **misdeed,** offence, injury, crime, transgression, sin, injustice, outrage, atrocity.
> ANTONYMS right.

▸ verb treat someone unfairly.

> SYNONYMS *she was determined to forget the man who had wronged her* **mistreat,** ill-use, ill-treat, do an injustice to, abuse, harm, hurt, injure.

■ **wrong-foot 1** (in a game) catch an opponent off balance. **2** place someone in a difficult situation by saying or doing something unexpected. **wrong-headed** having bad judgement.
□ **wrongly** adverb **wrongness** noun.

wrongdoer ▸ noun a person who commits illegal or dishonest acts.

> SYNONYMS **offender,** lawbreaker, criminal, felon, delinquent, villain, culprit, evil-doer, sinner, transgressor, malefactor, miscreant, rogue, scoundrel; informal crook, wrong 'un.

□ **wrongdoing** noun.

wrongful ▸ adjective not fair, just, or legal.
□ **wrongfully** adverb.

wrote past tense of WRITE.

wrought /rawt/ old-fashioned past and past participle of WORK.
▸ adjective **1** (of metals) beaten out or shaped by hammering. **2** made in a particular way: *well wrought.*
■ **wrought iron** tough iron suitable for forging or rolling.

wrung past and past participle of WRING.

wry ▸ adjective (**wryer, wryest** or **wrier, wriest**) **1** using dry, mocking humour. **2** (of a person's face) twisted into an expression of disgust, disappointment, or annoyance. **3** bending or twisted to one side.
□ **wryly** adverb.

wunderkind /vuun-der-kind/ ▸ noun a person who is very successful at a young age.

Wurlitzer /wer-lit-ser/ ▸ noun trademark a large pipe organ or electric organ.

WWI ▸ abbreviation World War I.

WWII ▸ abbreviation World War II.

WWW ▸ abbreviation World Wide Web.

Xx

X (or **x**) ▶ noun (plural **Xs** or **X's**) **1** the twenty-fourth letter of the alphabet. **2** an X-shaped written symbol, used to show that an answer is wrong, or to symbolize a kiss. **3** the Roman numeral for ten.
■ **X certificate** (in the past) a classification of a film as suitable for adults only. **X chromosome** a sex chromosome, two of which are normally present in female cells and one in male cells. **X-rated** pornographic or indecent. **X-ray 1** an electromagnetic wave of very short wavelength, which is able to pass through many solids and so make it possible to see into or through them. **2** an image of the internal structure of an object produced by passing X-rays through it.

xenon /zen-on/ ▶ noun an inert gaseous element, present in small amounts in the air.

xenophobia /zen-uh-foh-bi-uh/ ▶ noun dislike or fear of people from other countries.

xenophobic ▶ adjective relating to or affected by xenophobia.

SYNONYMS **jingoistic,** chauvinistic, flag-waving, nationalistic, isolationist, prejudiced, bigoted, intolerant.

Xerox /zeer-oks/ ▶ noun trademark **1** a process for copying documents using an electric charge and dry powder. **2** a copy made using such a process.
▶ verb (**xerox**) copy a document by such a process.

Xmas ▶ noun informal Christmas.

xylophone /zy-luh-fohn/ ▶ noun a musical instrument consisting of a row of bars which you hit with small hammers.

Yy

Y (or **y**) ▶ noun (plural **Ys** or **Y's**) the twenty-fifth letter of the alphabet.

■ **Y chromosome** a sex chromosome which is normally present only in male cells. **Y-fronts** Brit. trademark men's or boys' underpants with a seam at the front in the shape of an upside-down Y.

yacht /yot/ ▶ noun **1** a medium-sized sailing boat. **2** a boat with an engine, equipped for cruising.
□ **yachting** noun **yachtsman** noun (plural **yachtsmen**) **yachtswoman** noun (plural **yachtswomen**).

yahoo /yah-hoo/ ▶ noun informal a rude or bad-mannered person.

yak¹ ▶ noun a large ox with shaggy hair and large horns, found in Tibet and central Asia.

yak² (or **yack**) ▶ verb (**yaks, yakking, yakked**) informal talk continuously about something unimportant.

yam ▶ noun the tuber of a tropical plant, eaten as a vegetable.

yang ▶ noun (in Chinese philosophy) the active male force in the universe.

Yank ▶ noun informal an American.

yank informal ▶ verb pull quickly and hard.

SYNONYMS **jerk**, pull, tug, wrench.

▶ noun a sudden hard pull.

SYNONYMS **jerk**, pull, tug, wrench.

Yankee ▶ noun informal **1** an American. **2** US a person from New England or one of the northern states. **3** historical a Federal soldier in the Civil War.

yap ▶ verb (**yaps, yapping, yapped**) give a sharp, high-pitched bark.
▶ noun a sharp, high-pitched bark.

yard¹ ▶ noun **1** a unit of length equal to 3 feet (0.9144 metre). **2** a square or cubic yard. **3** a long piece of wood slung across a ship's mast for a sail to hang from.

yard² ▶ noun **1** Brit. a piece of enclosed ground next to a building. **2** an area of land used for a particular purpose. **3** N. Amer. the garden of a house.

yardarm ▶ noun either end of a ship's yard supporting a sail.

Yardie ▶ noun informal a member of a Jamaican gang of criminals.

yardstick ▶ noun a standard used for judging how good or successful something is.

yarmulke (or **yarmulka**) /yar-muul-kuh/ ▶ noun a skullcap worn by Jewish men.

yarn ▶ noun **1** thread used for knitting, weaving, or sewing. **2** informal a long story.

SYNONYMS **1 thread**, cotton, wool, fibre, filament. **2 story**, tale, saga; informal spiel, shaggy-dog story.

yashmak ▶ noun a veil concealing all of the face except the eyes, worn by some Muslim women.

yaw ▶ verb (of a moving ship or aircraft) turn unsteadily from side to side.
▶ noun a yawing movement.

yawn ▶ verb **1** open your mouth wide and take a deep breath, usually when tired or bored. **2** (**yawning**) wide open.

SYNONYMS (**yawning**) **gaping**, wide, cavernous, deep, huge, vast.

▶ noun an act of yawning.

yd ▶ abbreviation yard.

ye¹ plural of THOU.

ye² old use = THE.

yea ▶ adverb old use yes.

year ▶ noun **1** a period of 365 days (or 366 days in leap years) starting on 1 January. **2** a period of this length starting at a different point. **3** the time taken by the earth to go around the sun. **4** (**your years**) your age or time of life. **5** (**years**) informal a very long time. **6** a set of students who enter and leave a school or college at the same time.

yearbook ▶ noun a book published annually, giving details of the previous year's events.

yearling ▶ noun an animal between one and two years old.

yearly ▶ adjective & adverb happening or produced once a year or every year.

SYNONYMS **1** our yearly income **annual**. **2** there are about 250 cases yearly **annually**, once a year, per annum, each/every year.

y

yearn ▶ verb have a strong feeling of longing for something.

> SYNONYMS **long**, pine, crave, desire, want, wish, hanker, covet, hunger, thirst, ache; informal itch.

□ **yearning** noun & adjective.

yeast ▶ noun **1** a fungus which can convert sugar into alcohol and carbon dioxide. **2** a substance formed from this, used to make bread dough rise and to ferment beer and wine.

□ **yeasty** adjective.

yell ▶ noun a loud, sharp call or cry.

> SYNONYMS *a yell of rage* **shout**, cry, howl, scream, shriek, screech, yelp, squeal, roar.

▶ verb shout loudly.

> SYNONYMS *he yelled in agony* **shout**, cry out, howl, wail, scream, shriek, screech, yelp, squeal, roar, bawl.

yellow ▶ adjective **1** of the colour of egg yolks or ripe lemons. **2** informal cowardly.

> SYNONYMS **golden**, gold, blonde, fair, flaxen.

▶ noun a yellow colour.

▶ verb (of paper, fabric, etc.) become slightly yellow with age.

■ **yellow card** (in soccer) a yellow card shown by the referee to a player being cautioned. **yellow fever** a tropical disease that causes fever and jaundice and often death.

□ **yellowish** adjective.

yellowhammer ▶ noun a bird with a yellow head, neck, and breast.

yelp ▶ noun a short, sharp cry.

▶ verb give a yelp or yelps.

Yemeni /yem-uh-ni/ ▶ noun a person from Yemen.

▶ adjective relating to Yemen.

yen¹ ▶ noun (plural **yen**) the basic unit of money of Japan.

yen² ▶ noun informal a strong desire to have or do something.

yeoman /yoh-muhn/ ▶ noun (plural **yeomen**) (in the past) a man having his own house and small area of farming land.

■ **Yeoman of the Guard** a member of the British king or queen's ceremonial bodyguard.

yes ▶ exclamation **1** used to give a response in favour of something. **2** used to respond to someone who is talking to you.

> SYNONYMS **certainly**, very well, of course, by all means, sure, all right, absolutely, indeed, affirmative, agreed, roger; Scottish & N. English, aye; Nautical aye aye; informal yeah, yep, uh-huh, okay, OK; Brit. informal righto, righty-ho; N. Amer. informal surely.
> ANTONYMS no.

▶ noun (plural **yeses** or **yesses**) a decision or vote in favour of something.

■ **yes-man** a person who always agrees with people in authority.

yesterday ▶ adverb on the day before today.

▶ noun **1** the day before today. **2** the recent past.

yesteryear ▶ noun literary last year or the recent past.

yet ▶ adverb **1** up until now or then. **2** as soon as this. **3** from now into the future. **4** referring to something that will or may happen. **5** still; even. **6** in spite of that.

> SYNONYMS **1** *he hasn't made up his mind yet* **so far**, as yet, up to now, up till now. **2** *don't celebrate just yet* **(right) now**, at this time, already, so soon. **3** *yet more advice* **even**, still. **4** *he did nothing, yet he seemed happy* **nevertheless**, nonetheless, even so, but, however, still, notwithstanding, despite that, in spite of that, for all that, all the same, just the same, at the same time.

▶ conjunction but at the same time.

yeti ▶ noun a large hairy creature like a bear or a man, said to live in the highest part of the Himalayas.

yew ▶ noun an evergreen tree with poisonous red fruit.

Yiddish ▶ noun a language used by Jews from central and eastern Europe.

▶ adjective relating to Yiddish.

yield ▶ verb **1** produce or provide a natural or industrial product. **2** produce a result or financial gain. **3** give way to demands or pressure. **4** give up possession of. **5** give way under force or pressure.

> SYNONYMS **1** *such projects yield poor returns* **produce**, bear, give, provide, afford, return, bring in, earn, realize, generate, deliver, pay out. **2** *Duke was forced to yield* **surrender**, capitulate, submit, admit defeat, back down, give in. ANTONYMS withhold, resist.

▶ noun an amount or result yielded.

> SYNONYMS *we expected a higher yield* **profit**, gain, return, dividend, earnings.

> ✔ Remember, **i** before **e** except after **c**: y**ie**ld.

yin ▶ noun (in Chinese philosophy) the passive female presence in the universe.

yob (or **yobbo**) ▶ noun (plural **yobs** or **yobbos**) Brit. informal a rude and aggressive young man.

> SYNONYMS **lout**, thug, hooligan, tearaway, vandal, ruffian, troublemaker, hoodlum, rowdy; Austral. larrikin; informal tough, bruiser; Brit. informal lager lout; Scottish informal ned.

□ **yobbish** adjective.

yodel ▸ verb (yodels, yodelling, yodelled; US spelling yodels, yodeling, yodeled) sing or call in a style that alternates rapidly between a normal voice and a very high voice.
▸ noun a song or call of this type.
□ **yodeller** noun.

yoga ▸ noun a system involving breathing exercises and the holding of particular body positions, followed for fitness and relaxation and based on Hindu philosophy.
□ **yogic** adjective.

yogi ▸ noun (plural **yogis**) a person who is skilled in yoga.

yogurt (or **yoghurt** or **yoghourt**) ▸ noun a thick liquid food made from milk with bacteria added.

yoke ▸ noun 1 a piece of wood fastened over the necks of two animals and attached to a plough or cart in order for them to pull it. 2 a frame fitting over a person's neck and shoulders, used for carrying buckets or baskets. 3 something that limits freedom or is difficult to bear. 4 a part of a garment that fits over the shoulders and to which the main part of the garment is attached.
▸ verb (yokes, yoking, yoked) join together or attach to a yoke.

yokel ▸ noun an unsophisticated country person.

yolk ▸ noun the yellow part in the middle of an egg.

Yom Kippur /yom kip-**poor**/ ▸ noun an important day in the Jewish religion in which people pray and fast.

yon old use or dialect ▸ determiner & adverb that. ▸ pronoun that person or thing.

yonder old use or dialect ▸ adverb over there. ▸ determiner that or those.

yonks ▸ plural noun Brit. informal a very long time.

yore ▸ noun (**of yore**) literary in the past; long ago.

Yorkshire pudding ▸ noun an item of food made from baked batter, eaten with roast beef.

Yorkshire terrier ▸ noun a small breed of terrier with a long grey and brown coat.

you ▸ pronoun 1 used to refer to the person or people that the speaker is talking to. 2 used to refer to any person in general.

you'd ▸ short form 1 you had. 2 you would.

you'll ▸ short form 1 you will. 2 you shall.

young ▸ adjective (**younger**, **youngest**) 1 having lived or existed for only a short time. 2 relating to or characteristic of young people.

> SYNONYMS 1 *young people* **youthful**, juvenile, junior, adolescent, teenage. 2 *she's very young for her age* **immature**, childish, inexperienced, naive, green. 3 *a young industry* **fledgling**, developing, budding, in its infancy, emerging. ANTONYMS old, mature.

▸ plural noun young children or animals; offspring.

> SYNONYMS 1 *a robin feeding its young* **offspring**, progeny, family, babies, litter, brood. 2 *the young don't care nowadays* **young people**, children, boys and girls, youngsters, youth, the younger generation, juveniles, minors; informal kids.
> ANTONYMS old.

youngster ▸ noun a young person.

> SYNONYMS **child**, teenager, adolescent, youth, juvenile, minor, junior, boy, girl; Scottish & N. English lass, lassie; informal lad, kid, whippersnapper, teen.

your ▸ possessive determiner 1 belonging to or associated with the person or people that the speaker is talking to. 2 belonging to or associated with any person in general.

> ❗ Don't confuse **your** meaning 'belonging to you' (as in *let me talk to your daughter*) with the form **you're**, which is short for **you are** (as in *you're a good cook*).

you're ▸ short form you are.

yours ▸ possessive pronoun used to refer to something belonging to or associated with the person or people that the speaker is talking to.

> ✔ no apostrophe: **yours**.

yourself ▸ pronoun (plural **yourselves**) 1 used as the object of a verb or preposition when this is the same as the subject of the clause and the subject is the person or people being spoken to. 2 you personally.

youth ▸ noun (plural **youths**) 1 the period between childhood and adult age. 2 the qualities of energy, freshness, etc. associated with being young. 3 a young man. 4 young people.

> SYNONYMS 1 *he was a fine athlete in his youth* **early years**, teens, teenage years, adolescence, boyhood, girlhood, childhood, minority. 2 *local youths* **young man**, boy, juvenile, teenager, adolescent, junior, minor; informal lad, kid. 3 *the youth of the nation* **young people**, young, younger generation, next generation; informal kids.
> ANTONYMS adulthood, old age, elderly.

■ **youth club** a club where young people can meet and take part in various activities. **youth hostel** a place providing cheap overnight accommodation, especially for young people.

youthful ▸ adjective 1 young or seeming young. 2 characteristic of young people.

SYNONYMS **young**, boyish, girlish, fresh-faced, young-looking, spry, sprightly, vigorous, active.
ANTONYMS elderly.

□ **youthfully** adverb **youthfulness** noun.

you've ▸ short form you have.

yowl (*rhymes with* fowl) ▸ noun a loud wailing cry of pain or distress.
▸ verb make such a cry.

SYNONYMS **wail**, howl, yelp, shriek, scream, cry.

yo-yo ▸ noun (plural **yo-yos**) (trademark) a toy consisting of a pair of joined discs with a groove between them in which string is attached and wound, which can be spun down and up as the string unwinds and rewinds.
▸ verb (**yo-yoes**, **yo-yoing**, **yo-yoed**) move up and down repeatedly.

ytterbium /it-ter-bi-uhm/ ▸ noun a silvery-white metallic element.

yttrium /it-tri-uhm/ ▸ noun a greyish-white metallic element.

yucca ▸ noun a plant with long, stiff pointed leaves, native to the southern US and Mexico.

Yugoslav /yoo-guh-slahv/ ▸ noun a person from any of the states of the former Yugoslavia.
□ **Yugoslavian** noun & adjective.

Yule (or Yuletide) ▸ noun old use Christmas.

yummy ▸ adjective (**yummier**, **yummiest**) informal delicious.

yuppie (or yuppy) ▸ noun (plural **yuppies**) informal a young middle-class professional person who earns a lot of money.

y

Zz

Z (or **z**) ▸ noun (plural **Zs** or **Z's**) the twenty-sixth letter of the alphabet.

Zambian ▸ noun a person from Zambia.
▸ adjective relating to Zambia.

zany ▸ adjective (**zanier**, **zaniest**) amusingly unconventional or unusual.

> SYNONYMS **eccentric**, odd, unconventional, bizarre, weird, mad, crazy, comic, madcap, quirky, idiosyncratic; informal wacky, oddball, off the wall; Brit. informal daft; N. Amer. informal kooky, wacko.
> ANTONYMS conventional, sensible.

zap informal ▸ verb (**zaps**, **zapping**, **zapped**) **1** destroy completely. **2** move very fast. **3** use a remote control to change television channels.

zeal ▸ noun great energy and enthusiasm for a cause or aim.

> SYNONYMS **enthusiasm**, passion, ardour, fervour, fire, devotion, gusto, vigour, energy.
> ANTONYMS apathy.

zealot /zel-uht/ ▸ noun a person who follows a religion, cause, or policy very strictly and enthusiastically.
□ **zealotry** noun.

zealous /zel-uhss/ ▸ adjective showing great energy and enthusiasm for a cause or aim.
□ **zealously** adverb.

zebra ▸ noun an African wild horse with black and white stripes.
■ **zebra crossing** Brit. an area of road marked with broad white stripes, where pedestrians can cross.

zeitgeist /zyt-gysst/ ▸ noun the general spirit or mood of a particular period of history.

Zen ▸ noun a type of Buddhism that emphasizes the value of meditation and intuition.

zenith ▸ noun **1** the time at which someone or something is most powerful or successful. **2** the point in the sky directly overhead. **3** the highest point in the sky reached by the sun or moon.

zephyr ▸ noun literary a soft, gentle breeze.

Zeppelin ▸ noun a large German airship of the early 20th century.

zero ▸ cardinal number (plural **zeros**) **1** the figure 0; nought. **2** a temperature of 0°C (32°F), marking the freezing point of water. **3** a point on a scale of measurement from which a positive or negative quantity is reckoned.

> SYNONYMS **1** *the answer is zero* **nought**, nothing, nil, 0. **2** *there was absolutely zero I could do about it* **nothing (at all)**, nil, none; N. English nowt; informal zilch, not a dicky bird; Brit. informal damn all, not a sausage; N. Amer. informal zip, nada.

▸ verb (**zeroes**, **zeroing**, **zeroed**) (**zero in on**) take aim at or focus attention on.
■ **zero hour** the time at which a military operation or important event is set to begin. **zero tolerance** the policy of applying laws against antisocial behaviour very strictly.

zest ▸ noun **1** great enthusiasm and energy. **2** excitement or stimulation. **3** the outer coloured part of the peel of an orange or lemon.

zigzag ▸ noun a line or course having sharp alternate right and left turns.
▸ adjective & adverb veering to right and left alternately.
▸ verb (**zigzags**, **zigzagging**, **zigzagged**) move in a zigzag.

> SYNONYMS **twist**, meander, snake, wind, weave, swerve.

zilch ▸ pronoun informal nothing.

zillion ▸ cardinal number informal a very large number of people or things.
□ **zillionth** ordinal number.

Zimbabwean ▸ noun a person from Zimbabwe.
▸ adjective relating to Zimbabwe.

Zimmer frame ▸ noun trademark a metal frame that people use to help them walk.

zinc ▸ noun a silvery-white metallic element used in making brass and to coat iron and steel.

zing ▸ noun informal energy, enthusiasm, or liveliness.
□ **zingy** adjective.

z

Zionism ▸ noun a movement for the development of a Jewish nation in Israel.
□ **Zionist** noun & adjective.

zip ▸ noun **1** Brit. a fastener consisting of two flexible interlocking strips of metal or plastic, closed or opened by pulling a slide along them. **2** informal energy; liveliness.
▸ verb (**zips, zipping, zipped**) **1** fasten with a zip. **2** informal move quickly. **3** Computing compress a file so that it takes up less space.
■ **zip code** US a postcode.

zipper ▸ noun chiefly N. Amer. a zip fastener.

zippy ▸ adjective informal **1** speedy. **2** bright, fresh, or lively.

zircon ▸ noun a brown or semi-transparent mineral.

zirconium ▸ noun a hard silver-grey metallic element.

zit ▸ noun informal a spot on the skin.

zither /zi-*th*er/ ▸ noun a musical instrument with numerous strings stretched across a flat box, which you hold horizontally and play with your fingers and a plectrum.

zodiac ▸ noun an area in the sky in which the sun, moon, and planets appear to lie, divided by astrologers into twelve equal divisions or signs.
□ **zodiacal** /zuh-**dy**-uh-k'l/ adjective.

zombie ▸ noun **1** informal a person who seems to be only partly alive. **2** (in stories) a dead body that has been brought back to life by magic.

zone ▸ noun **1** an area that has particular characteristics or a particular use. **2** (also time zone) an area where a common standard time is used.

SYNONYMS **area,** sector, section, belt, stretch, region, territory, district, quarter, neighbourhood.

▸ verb (**zones, zoning, zoned**) divide something into zones.
□ **zonal** adjective.

zoo ▸ noun a place where wild animals are kept for study, conservation, or display to the public.

zookeeper ▸ noun a person employed to look after the animals in a zoo.

zoology ▸ noun **1** the scientific study of animals. **2** the animal life of a particular area or time.
□ **zoological** adjective **zoologist** noun.

zoom ▸ verb **1** move or travel very quickly. **2** (of a camera) change smoothly from a long shot to a close-up or vice versa.

SYNONYMS *he zoomed off* **hurry,** rush, dash, race, speed, sprint, career, shoot, hurtle, hare, fly; informal tear, belt; Brit. informal bomb.

■ **zoom lens** a lens allowing a camera to zoom.

zucchini /zuu-**kee**-ni/ ▸ noun (plural **zucchini** or **zucchinis**) N. Amer. a courgette.

Zulu ▸ noun **1** a member of a South African people. **2** the language of the Zulus.

zygote ▸ noun Biology a cell resulting from the joining of two gametes.

Wordfinder

Index

Index

Wordfinder

Animals

Amphibians

axolotl	fire	horned toad	natterjack	toad
bullfrog	salamander	marsh frog	newt	tree frog
cane toad	flying frog	midwife toad	salamander	waterdog
	frog	mud puppy	spadefoot	xenopus

Birds

adjutant bird	crossbill	griffon vulture	lyrebird	quail	stork
albatross	crow	grouse	macaw	rail	storm petrel
antbird	cuckoo	guillemot	magpie	raven	sunbird
Arctic tern	curlew	guineafowl	mallard	razorbill	swallow
auk	dabchick	gull	mandarin	red kite	swan
avocet	darter	gyrfalcon	duck	redpoll	swift
bald eagle	dipper	harrier	marabou stork	redshank	tawny owl
barnacle	diver	hawfinch	marsh harrier	redstart	teal
goose	dodo	hawk	martin	redwing	tern
barn owl	dotterel	hawk owl	meadowlark	reed bunting	thrush
bateleur eagle	dove	hedge	merlin	reed warbler	tit
Bewick's swan	duck	sparrow	mistle thrush	rhea	titmouse
bird of	dunlin	hen	moa	rhinoceros	toucan
paradise	dunnock	hen harrier	mockingbird	bird	treecreeper
bittern	eagle	heron	moorhen	ringdove	turkey
blackbird	eagle owl	herring gull	mute swan	ring ouzel	turkey vulture
blackcap	egret	hobby	mynah bird	roadrunner	turtle dove
black swan	eider duck	honeyguide	nighthawk	robin	vulture
bluebird	emperor	hooded crow	nightingale	rook	wagtail
blue tit	penguin	hoopoe	nightjar	ruddy duck	wallcreeper
booby	emu	hornbill	noddy	ruff	warbler
bowerbird	falcon	horned owl	nuthatch	sand martin	waxbill
brambling	fantail	house martin	ortolan	sandpiper	waxwing
broadbill	fieldfare	house	osprey	scops owl	weaver bird
brown owl	finch	sparrow	ostrich	screech owl	wheatear
budgerigar	flamingo	hummingbird	ouzel	sea eagle	whinchat
bullfinch	flycatcher	ibis	owl	seagull	whippoorwill
bunting	francolin	jackdaw	oystercatcher	secretary bird	whitethroat
bustard	frigate bird	jay	parakeet	shag	whooping
butcher-bird	fulmar	kestrel	parrot	shearwater	crane
buzzard	galah	kingfisher	partridge	shelduck	whydah
Canada goose	gannet	king penguin	peacock	shoebill	wigeon
canary	godwit	kite	peafowl	shoveler	willow
capercaillie	goldcrest	kittiwake	peewit	shrike	warbler
caracara	golden eagle	kiwi	pelican	siskin	woodchat
cassowary	goldfinch	kookaburra	penguin	skua	woodcock
chaffinch	goose	lammergeier	peregrine	skylark	woodlark
chicken	goshawk	lanner	falcon	snipe	woodpecker
chiffchaff	great auk	lapwing	petrel	snow bunting	wood pigeon
chough	great crested	lark	phalarope	snow goose	wren
coal tit	grebe	laughing	pheasant	snowy owl	wryneck
cockatiel	great tit	jackass	pigeon	song thrush	yellow-
cockatoo	grebe	linnet	pilot bird	sparrow	hammer
condor	green wood-	little grebe	pintail	sparrowhawk	
coot	pecker	little owl	pipit	spoonbill	
cormorant	greenfinch	long-tailed tit	plover	starling	
corncrake	greenshank	lorikeet	ptarmigan	stonechat	
crane	greylag goose	lovebird	puffin	stone curlew	

Butterflies and moths

Adonis blue	brimstone	cabbage	cinnabar	codlin/codling	copper
argus	brown	white	clearwing	moth	dagger
atlas moth	buff-tip	Camberwell	clouded	comma	death's head
birdwing	burnet	beauty	yellow	common	hawkmoth
blue	cabbage moth	chalkhill blue		heath	drinker

eggar | io moth | milkweed | papilionid | ringlet | tortrix
emerald | lackey | monarch | peacock | satyrid | tussock moth
emperor | lappet | morpho | butterfly | silk moth | underwing
ermine | leopard moth | Mother | peppered | silver Y | vapourer
fritillary | lobster moth | Shipton | moth | skipper | wall brown
gatekeeper | luna moth | mourning | plume moth | speckled | wax moth
goat moth | magpie moth | cloak | pug | wood | white admiral
grayling | marbled white | noctuid | purple | sulphur | white spot
gypsy moth | meadow | nymphalid | emperor | swallowtail | yellow-tail
hairstreak | brown | oak eggar | puss moth | swift |
hawkmoth | merveille du | old lady | pyralid | tiger moth |
heath | jour | painted lady | red admiral | tortoiseshell |

Crustaceans

acorn | fairy shrimp | hermit crab | land crab | Norway | spiny lobster
barnacle | fiddler crab | horseshoe | langouste | lobster | tiger prawn
barnacle | fish louse | crab | langoustine | prawn | woodlouse
crab | ghost crab | king crab | lobster | sandhopper |
crawfish | goose | king prawn | mitten crab | shrimp |
crayfish | barnacle | krill | | spider crab |

Dinosaurs

allosaurus | carnosaur | duck-billed | pliosaur | saurischian | triceratops
ankylosaur | coelurosaur | dinosaur | protoceratops | sauropod | tyrannosaurus
apatosaurus | deinonychus | hadrosaur | pteranodon | seismosaurus | velociraptor
brachiosaurus | diplodocus | iguanodon | pterodactyl | stegosaur |
brontosaurus | dromaeosaur | megalosaurus | raptor | theropod |

Fish

albacore | burbot | flathead | John Dory | pilotfish | sea trout
alewife | butterfly fish | flounder | kingfish | pipefish | shad
amberjack | butterfly ray | fluke | koi carp | piranha | shark
anchovy | carp | flying fish | labyrinth fish | plaice | shark-sucker
anemone fish | carpet shark | flying gurnard | lamprey | pollack | sheepshead
angelfish | catfish | frogfish | lanternfish | pomfret | shovelhead
angel shark | charr | garfish | leatherjacket | porbeagle | silverside
anglerfish | chimera | garpike | lemon sole | porcupine fish | skate
archerfish | chub | goatfish | ling | porgy | skipjack tuna
balloonfish | climbing | goby | loach | puffer fish | skipper
bandfish | perch | goldfish | lumpsucker | rabbitfish | smelt
barbel | clingfish | goosefish | lungfish | rainbow trout | smooth
barracouta | clownfish | gourami | mackerel | ray | hound
barracuda | coalfish | grayling | mako | redfish | snake
barramundi | cod | great white | manta | red mullet | mackerel
basking shark | coelacanth | shark | marlin | red snapper | snapper
bass | coley | grenadier | megamouth | ribbonfish | snipefish
beluga | conger eel | grey mullet | minnow | roach | sockeye
bitterling | crappie | grouper | molly | rock bass | salmon
blackfish | dab | grunion | monkfish | rockling | sole
bleak | dace | gudgeon | moonfish | rudd | sparling
blenny | damselfish | guitarfish | moray eel | ruffe | spearfish
blowfish | darter | gulper eel | mudfish | sailfish | sprat
bluefin | devil ray | gunnel | mudminnow | salmon | stargazer
bluefish | dogfish | guppy | mudskipper | salmon trout | stickleback
blue shark | dorado | gurnard | mullet | sand eel | stingray
boarfish | dory | haddock | needlefish | sandfish | stonefish
bonefish | Dover sole | hake | nurse hound | sand shark | sturgeon
bonito | dragonfish | halfbeak | nurse shark | sardine | sucker
bonnethead | eagle ray | halibut | oarfish | sawfish | sunfish
bowfin | eel | hammerhead | orfe | scad | surgeonfish
boxfish | eelpout | herring | parrotfish | scorpionfish | swordfish
bream | electric eel | hoki | perch | sea bass | swordtail
brill | electric ray | humpback | pickerel | sea bream | tench
brisling | fighting fish | salmon | pike | sea horse | tetra
brown trout | filefish | huss | pikeperch | sea perch | thornback
bullhead | flatfish | icefish | pilchard | sea robin | threadfin

Animals

thresher
tiger shark
tilapia
toadfish
tope

triggerfish
trout
tuna
tunny
turbot

walleye
weakfish
weever
whaler
whale shark

whitebait
whitefish
whiting
witch
wobbegong

wolf fish
wrasse
yellowfin
yellowtail
zander

Insects *see also* Butterflies and moths

alderfly
amazon ant
ant
ant lion
aphid
army ant
army worm
assassin bug
bark beetle
bedbug
bee
beetle
black ant
blackfly
blister beetle
blowfly
bluebottle
body louse
boll weevil
bombardier
  beetle
booklouse
borer
botfly
bulldog ant
bumblebee

bush cricket
butterfly
caddis fly
carpenter ant
carpenter bee
carpet beetle
carrion beetle
chafer
chigger
cicada
click beetle
cluster fly
cockchafer
cockroach
Colorado
  beetle
crab louse
crane fly
cricket
cuckoo bee
cuckoo wasp
daddy-long-
  legs
damselfly
darter

death-watch
  beetle
devil's coach-
  horse
dragonfly
driver ant
drone fly
dung beetle
dung fly
earwig
fire ant
firefly
flea
fly
froghopper
fruit fly
furniture
  beetle
gadfly
gall wasp
glow-worm
gnat
goliath beetle
grasshopper
greenbottle
greenfly

groundhopper
head louse
Hercules
  beetle
honey ant
honeybee
hornet
horsefly
housefly
hoverfly
jewel beetle
lacewing
ladybird
lantern fly
leafcutter ant
leafcutter bee
leafhopper
leaf miner
leatherjacket
locust
longhorn
  beetle
louse
mantis
mason bee
May bug

mayfly
meal beetle
mealy bug
midge
mining bee
mosquito
moth
oil beetle
pharaoh ant
phylloxera
pond skater
praying
  mantis
rhinoceros
  beetle
robber fly
sandfly
sawfly
scale insect
scarab
scorpion fly
sexton beetle
silverfish
springtail
stag beetle
stick insect

stink bug
stonefly
termite
thrips
thunderbug
thunderfly
treehopper
tsetse fly
velvet ant
warble fly
wasp
water beetle
water
  boatman
water
  scorpion
weevil
whirligig
white ant
whitefly
witchetty grub
woodwasp

Mammals *see also* Marsupials

aardvark
alpaca
angora
anteater
antelope
ape
armadillo
ass
aurochs
baboon
badger
baleen whale
Barbary ape
bat
beaked whale
bear
beaver
beluga
bison
black bear
blue whale
boar
bobcat
bottlenose
  dolphin
bottlenose
  whale
bowhead
  whale
brown bear
buffalo
bushbaby

camel
capuchin
  monkey
capybara
caracal
caribou
cat
chamois
cheetah
chimpanzee
chinchilla
chipmunk
civet
coati
colobus
colugo
cougar
cow
coyote
coypu
deer
dingo
dog
dolphin
donkey
dormouse
dromedary
duck-billed
  platypus
dugong
duiker
echidna

eland
elephant
elephant seal
elk
ermine
fallow deer
fennec
ferret
fin whale
flying fox
fox
fur seal
galago
gaur
gayal
gazelle
gemsbok
gerbil
gibbon
giraffe
gnu
goat
gopher
gorilla
grampus
grey seal
grizzly bear
groundhog
guinea pig
hamadryas
hamster

hanuman
  langur
hare
harp seal
hartebeest
hedgehog
hippo
hog
honey bear
hooded seal
horse
howler
  monkey
humpback
  whale
hyena
hyrax
ibex
impala
jackal
jaguar
jaguarundi
killer whale
kinkajou
Kodiak bear
kudu
langur
laughing
  hyena
lemming
lemur

leopard
leopard seal
lion
llama
loris
lynx
macaque
manatee
mandrill
margay
marmoset
marmot
marsupial
marten
meerkat
mink
minke whale
mole
mongoose
monkey
monk seal
moose
mouflon
mountain
  goat
mountain lion
mouse
mule
muntjac
musk deer
musk ox
narwhal

ocelot
okapi
onager
opossum
orang-utan
orca
oryx
otter
ox
panda
pangolin
panther
peccary
pig
pika
pilot whale
pine marten
pipistrelle
platypus
polar bear
polecat
porcupine
porpoise
possum
potto
prairie dog
proboscis
  monkey
puma
rabbit
raccoon
rat

Wordfinder

red deer	sea cow	sloth bear	squirrel	vervet monkey	wild boar
red panda	sea elephant	snow leopard	monkey	vole	wildcat
reindeer	seal	spectacled	stoat	walrus	wildebeest
rhesus	sea lion	bear	sun bear	wapiti	wisent
monkey	sei whale	sperm whale	tamarin	warthog	wolf
rhinoceros	serval	spider monkey	tapir	waterbuck	wolverine
right whale	sheep	spiny anteater	tarsier	water buffalo	woodchuck
roe deer	shrew	springbok	tiger	weasel	yak
rorqual	skunk	squirrel	toothed whale	whale	zebra
sable	sloth		vampire bat	white whale	zebu

Marsupials

antechinus	cuscus	kangaroo	planigale	Tasmanian	wombat
bandicoot	dasyure	koala	possum	devil	yapok
bettong	dibbler	mulgara	potoroo	Tasmanian	
bilby	dunnart	numbat	quokka	tiger	
brushtail	flying	opossum	quoll	thylacine	
brushtail	phalanger	pademelon	rat kangaroo	wallaby	
possum	glider	phalanger	ringtail	wallaroo	

Reptiles

adder	bushmaster	Egyptian	green turtle	mamba	slow-worm
alligator	caiman	cobra	hamadryad	moloch	smooth snake
anaconda	chameleon	fer de lance	hawksbill	monitor lizard	snake
asp	coachwhip	flying lizard	hognose	pit viper	taipan
axolotl	cobra	frilled lizard	snake	puff adder	terrapin
basilisk	colubrid	Gaboon viper	horned toad	python	tokay
bearded	constrictor	galliwasp	iguana	rat snake	tortoise
dragon	copperhead	garter snake	indigo snake	rattlesnake	tuatara
black mamba	coral snake	gecko	king cobra	reticulated	turtle
blind snake	corn snake	gharial	Komodo	python	viper
blindworm	crocodile	giant tortoise	dragon	rinkhals	water
boa	death adder	Gila monster	leatherback	sea snake	moccasin
constrictor	diamondback	glass lizard	lizard	sidewinder	water snake
boomslang	terrapin	grass snake	loggerhead	skink	whip snake
bull snake		green snake	turtle	slider	

Shellfish and other molluscs

abalone	cuttlefish	jewel box	oyster	sea butterfly	turret shell
angel wings	dog whelk	lamp shell	paper nautilus	sea hare	tusk shell
argonaut	dove shell	limpet	paua	sea slug	wedge shell
auger shell	duck mussel	mitre	pearl oyster	shipworm	wentletrap
cephalopod	edible snail	murex	periwinkle	slug	whelk
chiton	gaper	mussel	piddock	snail	winkle
clam	gastropod	nautilus	pteropod	softshell clam	
cockle	geoduck	nerite	quahog	squid	
conch	giant clam	nudibranch	ramshorn snail	teredo	
cone shell	harp shell	octopus	razor shell	tooth shell	
cowrie	helmet	ormer	scallop	triton	

Spiders and other arachnids

bird-eating	crab spider	itch mite	redback	sun spider	whip scorpion
spider	funnel-web	jigger	red spider	tarantula	wolf spider
black widow	spider	mite	mite	tick	
camel spider	harvestman	money spider	scorpion	trapdoor	
chigger	harvest mite	raft spider	spider mite	spider	

Male and female animals

Animal	Male	Female	Animal	Male	Female	Animal	Male	Female
antelope	buck	doe	camel	bull	cow	cougar	tom	lioness
badger	boar	sow	caribou	stag	doe	coyote	dog	bitch
bear	boar	sow	cat	tom	queen	deer	stag	doe
bobcat	tom	lioness	cattle	bull	cow	dog	dog	bitch
buffalo	bull	cow	chicken	cock	hen	donkey	jackass	jenny

Animals

Animal	Male	Female	Animal	Male	Female	Animal	Male	Female
duck	drake	duck	horse	stallion	mare	pig	boar	sow
elephant	bull	cow	impala	ram	ewe	rhinoceros	bull	cow
ferret	hob	gill	jackrabbit	buck	doe	seal	bull	cow
fish	cock	hen	kangaroo	buck	doe	sheep	ram	ewe
fox	fox	vixen	leopard	leopard	leopard-ess	swan	cob	pen
giraffe	bull	cow				tiger	tiger	tigress
goat	billy-goat	nanny-goat	lion	lion	lioness	weasel	boar	cow
			lobster	cock	hen	whale	bull	cow
goose	gander	goose	moose	bull	cow	wolf	dog	bitch
hare	buck	doe	peafowl	peacock	peahen	zebra	stallion	mare
hartebeest	bull	cow	pheasant	cock	hen			

Young animals

Young	Animal	Young	Animal	Young	Animal
calf	antelope/buffalo/ camel/cattle/ elephant/elk/ giraffe/hartebeest/ rhinoceros/seal/ whale	eyas	hawk	owlet	owl
		fawn	caribou/deer	parr	salmon
		filly	horse	peachick	peafowl
		foal	horse/zebra	pickerel	pike
		fry	fish	piglet	pig
		gilt	pig	porkling	pig
chick	chicken/hawk/ pheasant	gosling	goose	pup	dog/wolf/seal/rat
		joey	kangaroo/wallaby/ possum	puppy	dog/coyote
colt	horse			smolt	salmon
cub	badger/bear/fox/ leopard/lion/tiger/ walrus/wolf	kid	goat/roedeer	spiderling	spider
		kit	beaver/fox/weasel/ ferret/mink	squab	pigeon
				squeaker	pigeon
cygnet	swan	kitten	bobcat/cat/cougar/ rabbit/skunk	tadpole	frog/toad
duckling	duck			whelp	dog/wolf
eaglet	eagle	lamb	sheep		
elver	eel	leveret	hare		

Collective names for animals

shrewdness of **apes**
herd/pace of **asses**
troop of **baboons**
cete of **badgers**
sloth of **bears**
swarm/drift/hive/erst of **bees**
flock/flight/pod of **birds**
herd/gang/obstinacy of **buffalo**
bellowing of **bullfinches**
drove of **bullocks**
army of **caterpillars**
clowder/glaring of **cats**
herd/drove of **cattle**
brood/clutch/peep of **chickens**
chattering of **choughs**
rag/rake of **colts**
covert of **coots**
herd of **cranes**
bask of **crocodiles**
murder of **crows**
litter of **cubs**
herd of **curlew**
herd/mob of **deer**
pack/kennel of **dogs**
school of **dolphins**
trip of **dotterel** (type of plover)
flight/dole/piteousness of **doves**
paddling of **ducks** (on water)
safe of **ducks** (on land)
fling of **dunlins**
herd/parade of **elephants**
herd/gang of **elk**

busyness of **ferrets**
charm of **finches**
shoal/run of **fish**
swarm/cloud of **flies**
skulk of **foxes**
gaggle of **geese** (on land)
skein/team/wedge of **geese** (in flight)
herd of **giraffes**
cloud of **gnats**
flock/herd/trip of **goats**
band of **gorillas**
pack/covey of **grouse**
down/mute/husk of **hares**
cast of **hawks**
siege of **herons**
bloat of **hippopotami**
drove/string/stud/team of **horses**
pack/cry/kennel of **hounds**
flight/swarm of **insects**
fluther/smack of **jellyfish**
mob/troop of **kangaroos**
kindle/litter of **kittens**
desert of **lapwings**
bevy/exaltation of **larks**
leap/lepe of **leopards**
pride/sawt of **lions**
tiding of **magpies**
sord/suit of **mallard**
stud of **mares**
richesse of **martens**
labour of **moles**

troop of **monkeys**
span/barren of **mules**
watch of **nightingales**
parliament/stare of **owls**
yoke of **oxen**
pandemonium of **parrots**
covey of **partridges**
muster of **peacocks**
muster/parcel/rookery of **penguins**
bevy/head of **pheasants**
kit of **pigeons** (in flight)
litter/herd of **pigs**
congregation/stand/wing of **plovers**
rush/flight of **pochards**
pod/school/herd/turmoil of **porpoises**
covey of **ptarmigan**
litter of **pups**
bevy/drift of **quail**
bury of **rabbits**
string of **racehorses**
unkindness of **ravens**
crash of **rhinoceros**
bevy of **roe deer**
parliament/building/rookery of **rooks**
hill of **ruffs**
pod/herd/rookery of **seals**
flock/herd/trip/mob of **sheep**
dopping of **sheldrake**
wisp/walk of **snipe**

host of **sparrows**
murmuration of **starlings**
flight of **swallows**
game/herd of **swans** (on land)
wedge of **swans** (in flight)
drift/herd/sounder of **swine**
spring of **teal**
knot of **toads**
hover of **trout**

rafter of **turkeys**
bale/turn of **turtles**
bunch/knob of **waterfowl**
school/herd/pod/gam of
  whales
company/trip of **wigeon**
sounder of **wild boar**
dout/destruction of **wild cats**
team of **wild ducks** (in flight)

bunch/trip/plump/knob of
  wildfowl
pack/rout of **wolves**
fall of **woodcock**
descent of **woodpeckers**
herd of **wrens**
zeal of **zebras**

Many of these are fanciful or humorous terms which probably never had any real currency but have been popularized in books such as *Sports and Pastimes of England* (1801) by Joseph Strutt.

Art

Art schools, styles, and movements

abstract
  expressionism
Aesthetic
  Movement
Art Deco
Art Nouveau
Arts and Crafts
avant-garde
baroque
Beaux Arts
Blaue Reiter
Bloomsbury
  Group

classicism
conceptual art
constructivism
cubism
Dada
De Stijl
expressionism
fauvism
Florentine school
futurism
Grand Manner
Group of Seven
Impressionism

Jugendstil
magic realism
Mannerism
minimalism
modernism
naive art
naturalism
Nazarenes
neoclassicism
neo-
  Impressionism
neoplasticism
neo-realism

Neue Sachlichkeit
op art
performance art
photorealism
plein-air painting
pop art
post-
  Impressionism
postmodernism
Pre-Raphaelitism
primitive art
Purism
realism

Renaissance art
rococo
romanticism
socialist realism
social realism
Sturm und Drang
suprematism
surrealism
symbolism
tenebrism
ukiyo-e

Art techniques and media

acrylic
action
  painting
airbrushing
aquarelle
aquatint
batik
ceramics
cloisonné
collage
colour wash
Conté

distemper
divisionism
drawing
emulsion
enamel
encaustic
engraving
etching
finger-
  painting
fresco
frottage

gesso
glaze
gouache
grisaille
impasto
intaglio
kakemono
lino cut
lithography
marbling
marquetry
metalwork

mezzotint
miniature
montage
mosaic
mural
oil painting
pastel
photography
photogravure
photo-
  montage
pointillism

polychromy
screen
  printing
sculpture
scumbling
secco
silk-screen
  printing
sketching
stained glass
sumi-e
tachism

tapestry
tempera
wall painting
watercolour
wood carving
woodcut
wood
  engraving

Body

Human bones

ankle bone
anvil
backbone
breastbone
calcaneus
capitate
carpal
carpus
cheekbone
clavicle
collarbone
cranium

cuboid
cuneiform
  bone
ethmoid
femur
fibula
floating rib
frontal bone
hamate
hammer
heel bone
humerus

hyoid
ilium
incus
innominate
  bone
ischium
jawbone
kneecap
lacrimal
lunate bone
malleus
mandible

maxilla
metacarpal
metatarsal
navicular bone
occipital bone
palatine bone
parietal bone
patella
pelvis
phalanx
pisiform bone
pubis

rachis
radius
rib
ribcage
sacrum
scaphoid
scapula
shin bone
shoulder
  blade
skull
sphenoid

spinal column
spine
stapes
sternum
stirrup
talus
tarsal
tarsus
temporal
  bone
thigh bone
tibia

triquetral	vertebra	vertebral	zygomatic
ulna		column	bone

Organs of the body

anus	duodenum	ileum	mouth	skin	tonsil
appendix	ear	intestine	nose	spinal cord	trachea
bladder	eye	kidney	oesophagus	spleen	uterus
brain	gall bladder	larynx	ovary	stomach	vagina
breast	genitals	liver	pancreas	testicle	
colon	heart	lung	rectum	tongue	

Human teeth

bicuspid	eye tooth	molar	premolar	wisdom tooth
canine	incisor	permanent	primary tooth	
cuspid	milk tooth	tooth	tricuspid	

Parts of the ear

anvil	cochlea	hair cell	middle ear	stapes	vestibule
auditory canal	eardrum	hammer	organ of Corti	stirrup	
auditory nerve	Eustachian	incus	outer ear	tympanic	
auricle	tube	inner ear	pinna	membrane	

Parts of the eye

aqueous	conjunctiva	eyelid	lens	retina	vitreous
humour	cornea	fovea	limbus	rod	humour
blind spot	dilator muscle	iris	optic nerve	sclera	
choroid	eyeball	lacrimal	orbit	socket	
cone	eyelash	glands	pupil	tear glands	

Parts of the heart

aortic valve	mitral valve	pulmonary	vein	tricuspid valve	vena cava
atrium	myocardium	artery	semilunar	upper	ventricle
epicardium	pericardium	pulmonary	valve	chamber	

Clothing and Fabrics

Clothes

aloha shirt	boa	capri pants	crew neck	fichu	hipsters
anorak	board shorts	cardigan	crinoline	flak jacket	hoody/hoodie
apron	bodice	cargo pants	crop top	flannels	hose
ascot	body	carpenter	culottes	flares	hot pants
baggies	body stocking	trousers	cummerbund	fleece	housecoat
ballgown	bodysuit	catsuit	cut-offs	flying jacket	hula skirt
bandanna	body warmer	chador	cutaway	foulard	hunting jacket
bandeau	bolero	chaparajos	dashiki	frock coat	jacket
Barbour	bolo tie	chaps	denims	fustanella	jeans
(trademark)	bomber jacket	chemise	dhoti	gabardine/	jellaba
basque	bootlace tie	cheongsam	dinner jacket	gabardine	jerkin
bathing	bow tie	chinos	dirndl	gilet	jersey
costume	bra	churidars	divided skirt	glove	jibba
bedjacket	braces	cigarette	djellaba	gown	jilbab
bell-bottoms	breeches	pants	djibba	grandad shirt	jodhpurs
belt	Burberry	clamdiggers	dolman	greatcoat	jumper
Bermuda	(trademark)	coat	domino	guernsey	jumpsuit
shorts	burka/burkha/	coat dress	donkey jacket	gymslip	kaftan
bib	burqa	coatee	doublet	hacking jacket	kagoul
biker jacket	burnous	combat	dress	haik	kameez
bikini	bustier	trousers	dressing gown	halter neck	kecks
blazer	cagoule	cords	dress shirt	harem pants	kilt
bloomers	camisole	corduroys	ducks	hat	kimono
blouse	camiknickers	corset	duffel coat	hijab	knickers
blouson	cape	cravat	dungarees	hip-huggers	

knicker-
  bockers
leathers
lederhosen
leggings
leg warmers
leotard
loden
loincloth
loons
lumberjacket
lumberjack
  shirt
lungi
mac
macfarlane
mackintosh/
  macintosh
maillot
mandarin
  jacket
mantilla
mantle
mantlet
Mao jacket
mask
matinee coat
maxi
mess jacket
midi

mini
miniskirt
mitt
mitten
morning coat
muff
muffler
muumuu
neckerchief
Nehru jacket
nightdress
nightshirt
niqab
nor'wester
Norfolk jacket
obi
oilskins
overalls
overcoat
overtrousers
Oxford bags
palazzo pants
pantaloons
panties
pants
pantyhose
parka
pedal pushers
peignoir
pelisse

pencil skirt
peplum
petticoat
pinafore
pinafore dress
pinny
plastron
plus fours
polo neck
polo shirt
poncho
puffball skirt
pullover
pyjamas
raglan
rah-rah skirt
raincoat
redingote
reefer jacket
robe
roll-neck
ruff
sack dress
safari jacket
sailor suit
salopettes
salwar
Sam Browne
sari
sarong

sash
scarf
serape/sarape
shalwar
shawl
sheath dress
sheepskin
shell suit
shift
shirt
shirtwaister
shorts
shrug
skinny-rib
ski pants
skirt
slacks
slip
slipover
sloppy joe
smock
smoking
  jacket
sock
spencer
sports jacket
stirrup pants
stock
stocking
stole

string tie
suit
sundress
surcoat
surtout
sweater
sweatpants
sweatshirt
swimming
  costume
swimming
  trunks
swimsuit
swing coat
T-shirt
tabard
tailcoat
tank top
teddy
tee
tent dress
thong
tie
tights
tippet
toga
top
topcoat
toreador
  pants

tracksuit
trench coat
trews
trousers
trouser suit
trunks
tube dress
tunic
turtleneck
tutu
tux/tuxedo
tweeds
twinset
ulster
underpants
underskirt
veil
vest
V-neck
waistcoat
windcheater
woollens
wrap
yashmak
yukta

Footwear

ballet shoe
balmoral
boot
bootee
bovver boot
brogan
brogue
brothel
  creeper
buskin
carpet slipper
chappal
Chelsea boot

clog
court shoe
cowboy boot
Cuban heel
dap
deck shoe
Derby
desert boot
Dr Martens
  (trademark)
elevator shoe
espadrille
flip-flop

galosh
ghillie/gillie
gumboot
half-boot
Hessian boot
high heels
high-low
high-top
hobnail boot
jackboot
jelly shoe
kitten heel
lace-up

loafer
moccasin
moon boot
mukluk
mule
napoleon
overboot
overshoe
Oxford
patten
peep-toe
penny loafer
platform

plimsoll
pump
sabot
sandal
shoe
slingback
slip-on
slipper
sneaker
snow boot
snowshoe
step-in
stiletto

tap shoe
tennis shoe
top boot
track shoe
trainer
Turkish slipper
wader
walking boot
wedge
wellington
  boot
winkle-picker
zori

Headgear

Alice band
balaclava
balmoral
bandeau
baseball cap
beanie
bearskin
beaver hat
beret
biretta
boater
bobble hat
bonnet
bowler
busby
calash
cap

chaplet
circlet
cloche
cloth cap
cocked hat
coif
coolie hat
coronet
cowl
crash helmet
crown
deerstalker
derby
diadem
Dolly Varden
earmuffs
fedora

fez
flat cap
garland
glengarry
hairband
hard hat
headband
headscarf
headtie
helmet
high hat
hijab
homburg
hood
jester's cap
jockey cap
Juliet cap

keffiyeh
kepi
mantilla
mitre
mob cap
mortar board
opera hat
panama
peaked cap
picture hat
pillbox hat
pixie hat
poke bonnet
pork-pie hat
sailor hat
skullcap
slouch hat

snap-brim hat
snood
sola topi
sombrero
sou'wester
Stetson
  (trademark)
stocking cap
stovepipe hat
sun bonnet
sun hat
sun helmet
tam-o'-
  shanter
tarboosh
ten-gallon hat
tiara

top hat
topi
topper
toque
tricorne
trilby
triple crown
turban
veil
wideawake
wimple
wreath
zucchetto

Fabrics and fibres

acetate	chino	dupion	ikat	micromesh	polyester	tattersall
acrylic	chintz	elastane	jaconet	mohair	pongee	tatting
alpaca	ciré	faille	jacquard	moiré	poplin	terry
angora	cloqué	felt	jersey	moleskin	raffia	terylene
astrakhan	coconut	fishnet	jute	moquette	ramie	(trademark)
bafta	matting	flannel	kapok	moreen	rayon	ticking
baize	coir	flannelette	kemp	mousseline	rep	tiffany
barathea	cord	flax	Kendal	mungo	ripstop	toile
barkcloth	corduroy	fleece	Green	muslin	sackcloth	toile de
batiste	cotton	flock	kersey	nainsook	sacking	Jouy
Bedford	crêpe	foulard	kerseymere	nankeen	sailcloth	torchon
cord	crêpe de	frieze	khadi	needlecord	sarsenet	towelling
blanketing	Chine	fustian	khaki	net	sateen	tricot
bobbinet	crépon	gaberdine/	kikoi	Nottingham	satin	tulle
bobbin lace	cretonne	gabardine	lace	lace	satinette	tussore
bombazine	crewel	gauze	lambswool	nylon	saxony	tweed
Botany	crimplene	georgette	lamé	oakum	sea-island	twill
wool	(trademark)	gimp	lawn	oilcloth	cotton	Valen-
bouclé	crinoline	gingham	leathercloth	oilskin	seersucker	ciennes
broadcloth	crushed	Gore-tex	leatherette	organdie	serge	Velcro
brocade	velvet	(trademark)	(trademark)	organza	shahtoosh	(trademark)
buckram	cupro	gossamer	leno	organzine	sharkskin	velour
burlap	Dacron	grasscloth	Lincoln	Orlon	sheer	velvet
butter	(trademark)	grogram	green	(trademark)	Shetland	velveteen
muslin	damask	grosgrain	linen	ottoman	wool	vicuña
calico	denim	gros point	linsey-	paisley	shoddy	viscose
cambric	devoré	guipure	woolsey	panne	silk	Viyella
camel hair	dimity	haircloth	lint	velvet	sisal	(trademark)
candlewick	doeskin	Harris	lisle	pashmina	slub	voile
canvas	Donegal	tweed	loden	peau-de-	Spandex	waxcloth
cashmere	tweed	(trademark)	Lurex	soie	(trademark)	webbing
cavalry twill	drab	hemp	(trademark)	percale	spun silk	whipcord
challis	Dralon	herring-	Lycra	petersham	stockinet	wild silk
chambray	(trademark)	bone	(trademark)	pillow lace	suede	wincey
Chantilly	drill	hessian	madras	pilot cloth	surah	winceyette
lace	duchesse	holland	marocain	piqué	swansdown	wool
cheesecloth	lace	Honiton	marquisette	plaid	tabaret	worsted
chenille	duchesse	lace	matting	plush	taffeta	
cheviot	satin	hopsack	melton	plush velvet	tapestry	
chiffon	duffel	horsehair	merino	point lace	tarlatan	
chinchilla	dungaree	huckaback	microfibre	polycotton	tarpaulin	

Religious clothing

alb	clerical collar	dog collar	mitre	skullcap	tippet
amice	cope	frock	pallium	soutane	tunicle
biretta	cotta	Geneva bands	rochet	stole	wimple
cassock	cowl	habit	scapular	surplice	yarmulke
chasuble	dalmatic	hood	shovel hat	tallith	zucchetto

Drinks

Alcoholic drinks   *see also following lists*

absinthe	Armagnac	cherry brandy	fraise	kvass	ouzo
advocaat	arrack/arak	cider	framboise	liqueur	palm wine
aguardiente	bourbon	cognac	genever	manzanilla	pastis
alcopop	brandy	crème de	gin	maraschino	perry
amaretto	cachaca	cacao	ginger wine	marc	port
amontillado	Calvados	crème de	grappa	mead	poteen
anisette	cassis	menthe	Hollands	mescal	pulque
applejack	champagne	curaçao	kirsch	noyau	raki
aquavit	chartreuse	fino	kümmel	oloroso	ratafia

reposado	sake	scrumpy	slivovitz	triple sec	whisky
rye	sambuca	sherry	sloe gin	vermouth	
rum	schnapps	shochu	tequila	vodka	

Beers

ale	cask beer	India pale ale	mild	Pilsner/	shandy
barley wine	craft beer	(IPA)	milk stout	Pilsener	stout
bitter	gueuze	lager	pale ale	porter	wheat beer
bock	heavy	Lambic	Pils	Rauchbier	
brown ale	ice beer	light ale		real ale	

Wine and grape varieties

White wines and grapes

Aligoté	Grüner	Orvieto	Verduzzo	Cabernet	Meunier
Asti	Veltliner	Palomino	Vermentino	Sauvignon	Monte-
Auslese	Heuriger	Piesporter	Vernaccia	Cahors	pulciano
Barsac	Hock	Pinot Blanc	Vinho Verde	Chianti	Mourvèdre
Beerenauslese	Kabinett	Pinot Grigio	Viognier	Cinsault	Nebbiolo
Blanc de	Liebfraumilch	Pouilly-Fuissé	Viura	claret	Negroamoro
blancs	Lutomer	Pouilly-Fumé	Vouvray	Corvina	Nuits St
Bourgogne	Riesling	Retsina	Welschriesling	Côtes du	George
Blanc	Mâcon	Riesling	or Olasz	Rhône	Pauillac
Burgundy	Madeira	Rioja	Rizling or	Crozes-	Pinot Noir
Cava	Malvasia	sack	Laski Rizling	Hermitage	Pinotage
Chablis	Bianca	Sancerre		Dão	Pomerol
Champagne	Malvoisie	Saumur	**Red wines and grapes**	Faugères	Pommard
Chardonnay	Marsanne	Sauternes		Fitou	Rioja
Chenin Blanc	Meursault	Sauvignon	Barbaresco	Fleurie	Rofosco
Clairette	Minervois	Scheurebe	Barbera	Gaillac	Saint-Émilion
Colombard	Monbazillac	Sekt	Bardolino	Gamay	Saint-Estèphe
Crémant	Montrachet	Sémillon	Barolo	Gevrey-	Sangiovese
Eiswein	Morio-Muskat	Soave	Beaujolais	Chambertin	Shiraz/Syrah
Entre-Deux-	moscato	Spätlese	Beaune	Gigondas	Tempranillo
Mers	Moselle	Spumante	Blauer	Graves	Valdepeñas
Frascati	Müller-	Sylvaner	Portugieser	Grenache	Valpolicella
Gewürz-	Thurgau or	Tocai-Friulano	Bourgogne	Lambrusco	Zinfandel
traminer	Rivaner	Tokay	Rouge	Malbec	Zweigelt
Grenache	Muscadet	Traminer	Brouilly	Malvasia	or Blauer
Graves	Muscat Blanc	Trebbiano	Bull's Blood	Malvoisie	Zweigelt
	Muscat de	Trocken-	Burgundy	Rouge	
	Beaumes de	beeren-	Cabernet	Margaux	
	Venise	auslese	Franc	Médoc	
	Niersteiner	Verdicchio		Merlot	

Cocktails and mixed drinks

Bellini	cobbler	John Collins	old-fashioned	sex on the	toddy
B52	cosmopolitan	Kir	pina colada	beach	Tom Collins
Black Russian	Cuba libre	Kir Royale	pink gin	sidecar	whisky mac
black velvet	daiquiri	Long Island	planter's	Singapore	whisky sour
Bloody Mary	egg flip	iced tea	punch	sling	White Lady
blue lagoon	eggnog	mai tai	prairie oyster	slammer	White Russian
brandy	gimlet	manhattan	punch	snakebite	zombie
Alexander	gin sling	margarita	rattlesnake	snowball	
Bronx	grog	Martini	rum and black	sour	
Buck's Fizz	Harvey	(trademark)	sangria	spritzer	
caipirinha	Wallbanger	mint julep	screwdriver	tequila	
champagne	highball	mojito	sea breeze	slammer	
cocktail	Irish coffee	negroni		tequila sunrise	

Non-alcoholic drinks

barley water	cordial	horchata	milkshake	St Clements	tea
bitter lemon	cream soda	hot chocolate	mineral water	sarsaparilla	tonic water
cherryade	crush	Lassi	orangeade	seltzer water	
citron pressé	dandelion and	lemonade	orgeat	sherbet	
cocoa	burdock	limeade	prairie oyster	smoothie	
coffee	ginger ale	malted milk	pressé	soda water	
cola	ginger beer	maté	root beer	squash	

Teas

Assam	Darjeeling	herbal tea	lemon tea	peppermint	tisane
black tea	Earl Grey	iced tea	maté	tea	yerba maté
bohea	fruit tea	Indian	mint tea	pouchong	
camomile tea	green tea	Keemun	oolong	rooibos tea	
Ceylon	gunpowder	Lapsang	orange pekoe	rosehip tea	
China	tea	Souchong	pekoe	souchong	

Coffees

café au lait	caffè	decaffeinated	filter coffee	Irish coffee	mochaccino
café noir	macchiato	coffee	Gaelic coffee	latte	Turkish coffee
caffè latte	cappuccino	espresso	Greek coffee	mocha	

Food

Bread and bread rolls

bagel	brioche	farl	hoagie	petit pain	soda bread
baguette	bun	farmhouse	kaiser	pikelet	sourdough
bannock	chapatti	loaf	malt loaf	pitta	split tin
bap	ciabatta	flatbread	matzo	pone	stollen
bara brith	cob	focaccia	milk loaf	poppadom	
barmbrack	cornbread	French stick	muffin	pumpernickel	
barm cake	cottage loaf	fruit loaf	nan/naan	puri	
bloomer	crumpet	granary bread	panettone	roti	
bridge roll	damper	(trademark)	paratha	rye	

Cakes, biscuits, and desserts

angel cake	cabinet	dumpling	kulfi	plum pudding	stollen
angel food	pudding	Dundee cake	lady's finger	popover	streusel
cake	cassata	Eccles cake	langue de	pound cake	strudel
apfelstrudel	charlotte	eclair	chat	pretzel	suet pudding
apple	charlotte russe	egg custard	lardy cake	profiterole	summer
charlotte	cheesecake	Eve's pudding	layer cake	queen cake	pudding
apple pie	chocolate chip	fairy cake	macaroon	queen of	sundae
baba	clafoutis	fancy	Madeira cake	puddings	Swiss roll
baked Alaska	cobbler	flapjack	madeleine	ratafia	syllabub
Bakewell tart	compote	floating island	maid of	rice pudding	tart
baklava	cookie	Florentine	honour	rock cake	tarte Tatin
banana split	cracknel	flummery	marble cake	roly-poly	tartlet
Banbury cake	cream cracker	fool	marquise	rusk	tartufo
banoffi/	cream puff	fortune cookie	matzo	Sachertorte	tipsy cake
banoffee pie	crème brûlée	frangipane	meringue	sago pudding	tiramisu
Bath bun	crème caramel	fruit cocktail	milk pudding	Sally Lunn	torte
Battenberg	crêpe	fruit salad	millefeuille	saltine	treacle tart
beignet	crêpe Suzette	funnel cake	mince pie	sandwich	trifle
Berliner	crispbread	garibaldi	Mississippi	savarin	turnover
Black Forest	croquem-	gateau	mud pie	scone	tutti-frutti
gateau	bouche	gelato	mousse	seed cake	upside-down
blancmange	crumble	Genoa cake	mousseline	semolina	cake
bombe	crumpet	gingerbread	muffin	shoo-fly pie	Victoria
bourbon	cupcake	ginger nut	oatcake	shortbread	sponge
brack	custard cream	ginger snap	pancake	shortcake	waffle
brandy snap	custard pie	granita	panettone	simnel cake	water biscuit
bread	custard tart	halwa	panforte	singing hinny	water ice
pudding	Danish pastry	hasty pudding	parfait	sorbet	whip
bread-and-	death by	hokey-pokey	parkin	soufflé	yogurt
butter	chocolate	hot cross bun	pashka	sponge	yule log
pudding	devil's food	ice cream	pavlova	sponge	zabaglione
Brown Betty	cake	jelly	peach Melba	pudding	
brownie	digestive	junket	petit beurre	spotted dick	
bun	doughnut	Knickerbocker	petit four	steamed	
butterfly cake	drop scone	Glory	plum duff	pudding	

Wordfinder

Cheeses

asiago
Bel Paese
 (trademark)
blue vinny
Boursin
 (trademark)
Brie
Caerphilly
Camembert
cantal
Chaumes
Cheddar

Cheshire
chèvre
cottage
 cheese
cream cheese
crowdie/
 crowdy
curd cheese
Danish blue
Derby
Dolcelatte
 (trademark)

Double
 Gloucester
Dunlop
Edam
Emmental
feta/fetta
fontina
fromage blanc
fromage frais
Gloucester
Gorgonzola
Gouda

Gruyère
halloumi
havarti
Jarlsberg
 (trademark)
Lancashire
Leicester
Limburger
Manchego
mascarpone
Monterey Jack
mozzarella

Neufchâtel
paneer/panir
Parmesan
Parmigiano
 Reggiano
pecorino
Pont l'Évêque
Port Salut
provolone
quark
Red Leicester
ricotta

Romano
Roquefort
 (trademark)
sage Derby
scamorza
Stilton
taleggio
Tilsit
Wensleydale

Fruit

ackee
alligator pear
apple
apricot
Asian pear
avocado
bakeapple
banana
bilberry
blackberry
blackcurrant
blood orange
blueberry
boysenberry
breadfruit
bullace
cantaloupe
Cape
 gooseberry
carambola
cashew apple
chayote
checkerberry
cherimoya

cherry
cherry plum
Chinese
 gooseberry
citron
clementine
cloudberry
coconut
Costard
cowberry
crab apple
cranberry
currant
custard apple
damson
date
dewberry
durian
elderberry
feijoa
fig
galia melon
gooseberry
gourd

granadilla
grape
grapefruit
greengage
guava
honeydew
 melon
huckleberry
jackfruit
jamun
jujube
juneberry
kaki
kiwi fruit
kumquat
lemon
lime
lingonberry
loganberry
longan
loquat
lychee
mammee
mandarin

mango
mangosteen
maypop
medlar
melon
minneola
mulberry
muscat
musk melon
myrobalan
naseberry
nashi
navel orange
nectarine
Ogen melon
olive
orange
ortanique
papaya
partridgeberry
passion fruit
pawpaw
peach
pear

persimmon
physalis
pineapple
pippin
plantain
plum
pomegranate
pomelo
prickly pear
pumpkin
quince
rambutan
raspberry
redcurrant
roseapple
salmonberry
sapodilla
satsuma
sea grape
serviceberry
sharon fruit
sloe
sorb
soursop

star anise
star apple
starfruit
strawberry
sugar apple
sweetsop
tamarillo
tamarind
tangelo
tangerine
tayberry
tomatillo
tomato
Ugli fruit
 (trademark)
veitchberry
Victoria plum
watermelon
white currant
whortleberry
wineberry
youngberry

Herbs and spices

ajowan
allspice
angelica
anise
aniseed
asafoetida
balsam
basil
bay leaf
bergamot
black pepper
borage
camomile

caper
caraway
cardamom
cassia
cayenne
 pepper
chervil
chicory
chilli
chives
cilantro
cinnamon
clary

clove
coriander
cumin
curry powder
damiana
dill
dittany
dong quai
echinacea
fennel
fenugreek
feverfew
galangal

garam masala
garlic
ginger
ginseng
grains of
 Paradise
hyssop
juniper berry
lavender
lemon balm
lemon grass
lemon mint
lovage

mace
marjoram
milk thistle
mint
mustard
nutmeg
oregano
paprika
parsley
pepper
peppermint
rosemary
rue

saffron
sage
savory
sorrel
spearmint
St John's wort
sumac
sweet balm
sweet cicely
tarragon
thyme
turmeric
vanilla

Nuts

acorn
almond
areca nut
beechnut
betel nut
bitternut

Brazil nut
butternut
cashew
chestnut
cobnut
coco de mer

coconut
cola nut
conker
earthnut
filbert
groundnut

hazelnut
hickory nut
hognut
horse
 chestnut

macadamia
 nut
monkey nut
peanut
pecan
pine nut

piñon
pistachio
sweet
 chestnut
walnut

Pasta

agnolotti	conchiglie	linguine	pappardelle	rotini	tortellini
angel hair	ditalini	lumache	penne	spaghetti	tortelloni
bucatini	farfalle	macaroni	pipe	spaghettini	tortiglioni
cannelloni	farfalline	manicotti	radiatori	strozzapreti	trenette
capelli	fettuccine	noodles	ravioli	tagliatelle	vermicelli
capellini	fusilli	orecchiette	rigatoni	tagliolini	ziti
cappelletti	lasagne	orzo	rotelle	tortelli	

Sweets and confectionery

acid drop	chewing gum	Easter egg	jalebi	marshmallow	rock
aniseed ball	chocolate	fondant	jelly	marzipan	sherbet
barley sugar	chocolate	fruit drop	jelly baby	mint	sugared
bonbon	drop	fruit gum	jelly bean	nougat	almond
brittle	coconut ice	fruit pastille	jujube	pear drop	toffee
bullseye	comfit	fudge	Kendal mint	peppermint	toffee apple
butterscotch	cracknel	gobstopper	cake	peppermint	truffle
candy	crystallized	gulab jamun	laddu	cream	Turkish
candyfloss	fruit	gumdrop	liquorice	Pontefract	delight
caramel	dolly mixtures	halva	lollipop	cake	walnut whip
chew	dragée	humbug	lolly	praline	wine gum

Vegetables

ackee	butternut	cress	kidney bean	pea	spinach
acorn squash	squash	cucumber	kohlrabi	pepper	spinach beet
aduki/adzuki	cabbage	curly kale	lamb's lettuce	petits pois	spring greens
bean	calabrese	cush-cush	leek	pimento	spring onion
alfalfa	cannellini	custard	lentil	pimiento	squash
artichoke	bean	marrow	lettuce	pinto bean	string bean
arugula	capsicum	eggplant	lima bean	plantain	sugar pea
asparagus	cardoon	endive	lollo rosso	potato	sugar snap
aubergine	carrot	escarole	mache	pumpkin	pea
bamboo	cassava	fava bean	mangetout	puy lentil	swede
shoots	cauliflower	fennel	manioc	radicchio	sweetcorn
bean	cavolo nero	flageolet	marrow	radish	sweet pepper
beet	celeriac	French bean	marrowfat	red cabbage	sweet potato
beetroot	celery	garbanzo	pea	rocket	taro
black bean	chard	garden pea	mooli	romaine	tiger nut
black-eyed	chayote	garlic	mung bean	runner bean	tomato
bean	chervil	gherkin	mushroom	rutabaga	turnip
borlotti bean	chickpea	globe	mustard	salsify	vegetable
breadfruit	chicory	artichoke	oak leaf	samphire	spaghetti
broad bean	Chinese	gourd	lettuce	savoy cabbage	wasabi
broccoli	cabbage	greens	okra	scallion	water
Brussels	Chinese leaves	haricot bean	onion	scarlet runner	chestnut
sprout	corn on the	jalapeño	oyster plant	scorzonera	watercress
butter bean	cob	pepper	pak choi	sea kale	waxpod
butterhead	corn salad	Jerusalem	parsnip	shallot	yam
lettuce	cos lettuce	artichoke	pattypan	snow pea	zucchini
	courgette	kale	squash	soybean	

Wordfinder

Language and Literature

Literary schools, movements, and groups

Acmeism	Bloomsbury	Harlem	minimalism	post-	Sturm und
Aesthetic	Group	Renaissance	modernism	modernism	Drang
Movement	Cavalier poets	imagism	naturalism	primitivism	surrealism
Angry Young	classicism	Lake poets	neo-realism	realism	symbolism
Men	Dadaism	Liverpool	neoclassicism	romanticism	Vorticism
Augustans	expressionism	poets	Parnassians	social realism	
beat	futurism	magic realism	post-	socialist	
generation	Georgian	metaphysical	structuralism	realism	
	poets	poets		structuralism	

Poetry terms

alcaic verse	dimeter	free verse	Leonines	Petrarchan	spondee
alexandrine	distich	georgic	limerick	sonnet	terza rima
verse	disyllable	haiku	lyric	poem	tetrameter
anapaest	dithyramb	heptameter	macaronic	prothalamium	tribrach
aubade	doggerel	heroic couplet	verse	pyrrhic verse	trimeter
ballad	eclogue	heroic verse	monody	rondeau	triolet
ballade	elegiac	hexameter	nursery rhyme	roundel	triplet
blank verse	couplet	Horatian ode	ode	saga	trisyllable
choriambus	elegy	iambic	ottava rima	sapphics	trochaic verse
clerihew	epic	pentameter	paeon	satire	trochee
couplet	epigram	iambic verse	palinode	sestina	verse
dactyl	epithalamium	iambus	pastoral	sonnet	villanelle
dactylic verse	epode	idyll	pentameter	Spenserian	virelay
decasyllabic	epyllion	lay		stanza	

Types of drama

burlesque	docudrama	improvisation	miracle play	Noh
closet play	dumbshow	kabuki	monodrama	pantomime
comedy	duologue	kitchen-sink	morality play	passion play
comedy of	farce	drama	mummers'	teleplay
manners	Grand	masque	play	tragedy
commedia	Guignol	melodrama	mystery play	tragicomedy
dell'arte	Greek drama	mime	nativity play	two-hander

Types of fiction

Aga saga	comedy	folk tale	novelette	roman-fleuve	sword and
allegory	conte	ghost story	novella	saga	sorcery
antinovel	epic	gothic novel	parable	science fiction	thriller
Bildungs-	epistolary	graphic novel	picaresque	sci-fi	western
roman	novel	legend	novel	short story	whodunnit
black comedy	fable	mystery	police	spine-chiller	
blockbuster	fairy story	myth	procedural	stream of	
bodice-ripper	fairy tale	nouveau	policier	conscious-	
bonkbuster	fantasy	roman	roman-à-clef	ness	
chick lit	folk story	novel	romance		

Punctuation marks

accent	caret	ellipsis	inverted	quotation	stop
apostrophe	colon	em dash	comma	mark	stroke
asterisk	comma	en dash	obelus	rule	swung dash
asterism	dagger	exclamation	parenthesis	semicolon	virgule
backslash	dash	mark	period	solidus	
brace	diacritical	full stop	point	square	
bracket	mark	hyphen	question mark	bracket	

Phonetic alphabet

Alpha	Foxtrot	Kilo	Papa	Uniform	Zulu
Bravo	Golf	Lima	Quebec	Victor	
Charlie	Hotel	Mike	Romeo	Whisky	
Delta	India	November	Sierra	X-ray	
Echo	Juliet	Oscar	Tango	Yankee	

Medicine

Branches of medicine

Conventional	audiology	endocrinology	gynaecology	neurology	oncology
	cardiology	epidemiology	haematology	neuro-	ophthal-
allopathy	chiropody	gastro-	immunology	pathology	mology
anaesthesi-	dermatology	enterology	laryngology	neurosurgery	orthopaedics
ology	embryology	geriatrics	nephrology	obstetrics	orthotics

paediatrics
parasitology
pathology
pharmacology
physiotherapy
plastic surgery
proctology
prosthetics
psychiatry
psychosurgery
radiology
surgery

therapeutics
trichopathy
urology
venereology
veterinary
medicine

Alternative and complementary

acupressure
acupuncture

Alexander
technique
aromatherapy
Ayurveda
Bach flower
remedies
balneotherapy
Bates method
bioenergetics
bodywork
chiropractic
colour therapy

craniosacral
therapy
crystal
healing/
therapy
cupping
eurhythmics
faith healing
Feldenkrais
method
Gerson
therapy

herbalism
homeopathy
hydropathy
iridology
McTimoney
chiropractic
naturopathy
organo-
therapy
osteopathy
radionics
rebirthing

reflexology
reiki
Rolfing
shiatsu
thalasso-
therapy
zone therapy

Physical illnesses and conditions

acne
ague
Aids (acquired
immune
deficiency
syndrome)
allergy
alopecia
altitude
sickness
Alzheimer's
disease
anaemia
anaphylaxis
angina
ankylosing
spondylitis
ankylosis
anthrax
appendicitis
arc eye
arteriosclerosis
arthritis
asbestosis
asthma
ataxia
atherosclerosis
athlete's foot
avian flu
Bell's palsy
bends
beriberi
bilharzia
bird flu
blackwater
fever
blood
poisoning
botulism
Broca's
aphasia
bronchitis
brucellosis
bubonic
plague
Burkitt's
lymphoma
bursitis
cachexia
cancer
carcinoma
cardio-
myopathy
carditis

carpal tunnel
syndrome
(CTS)
cataract
cerebral palsy
chickenpox
cholera
chorea
chronic
fatigue syn-
drome (CFS)
cirrhosis
coeliac disease
colic
colitis
common cold
consumption
coronary heart
disease
cowpox
Creutzfeldt–
Jakob
disease (CJD)
Crohn's
disease
croup
crypto-
sporidiosis
cyanosis
cystic fibrosis
(CF)
cystitis
decompression
sickness
deep-vein
thrombosis
(DVT)
dengue
dermatitis
dermatosis
diabetes
diabetes
mellitus
diarrhoea
diphtheria
diverticular
disease
double
pneumonia
Down's
syndrome

Duchenne
muscular
dystrophy
(DMD)
Dupuytren's
contracture
dysentery
Ebola fever
eclampsia
economy-class
syndrome
eczema
elephantiasis
emphysema
encephalitis
endocarditis
endometriosis
endometritis
enteritis
epilepsy
ergotism
erysipelas
fetal alcohol
syndrome
fever
fibrositis
filariasis
flu
flux
food
poisoning
frozen
shoulder
gangrene
gastric flu
gastritis
gastro-
enteritis
German
measles
gigantism
gingivitis
glandular
fever
glaucoma
glue ear
glycaemia
goitre
gonorrhoea
gout
Gulf War
syndrome

Guillain–
Barré
syndrome
haemophilia
Hansen's
disease
hay fever
heat stroke
helminthiasis
hepatitis
A/B/C
hepatoma
hernia
herpes
herpes
simplex
hives
Hodgkin's
disease
hookworm
Huntington's
disease
hydrocephalus
hydrophobia
hypertension
hypo-
glycaemia
hypothermia
hypoxia
impetigo
infantile
paralysis
influenza
iritis
irritable bowel
syndrome
(IBS)
ischaemia
jaundice
Kaposi's
sarcoma
ketosis
kwashiorkor
laryngitis
Lassa fever
legionella
legionnaires'
disease
leishmaniasis
leprosy
leptospirosis
leukaemia
listeria
listeriosis

lupus
lupus vulgaris
Lyme disease
lymphoma
malaria
mastitis
measles
meningitis
motor neuron
disease
mountain
sickness
multiple
sclerosis
(MS)
mumps
muscular
dystrophy
myalgic
encephalo-
myelitis (ME)
narcolepsy
necrotizing
fasciitis
nephritis
neuropathy
new variant
Creutzfeldt–
Jakob
disease
(nvCJD)
non-
Hodgkin's
lymphoma
non-specific
urethritis
oedema
ophthalmia
orchitis
osteoarthritis
osteomyelitis
osteoporosis
pancreatitis
paratyphoid
Parkinson's
disease
parotitis
pellagra
pelvic
inflammatory
disease
pericarditis
peritonitis

pernicious
anaemia
pertussis
phlebitis
pink-eye
plague
pleurisy
pleuro-
pneumonia
pneumo-
coniosis
pneumo-
cystitis carinii
pneumonia
(PCP)
pneumonia
poliomyelitis
porphyria
prickly heat
pruritus
psittacosis
psoriasis
puerperal
fever
pulmonary
emphysema
pyaemia
pyrexia
quinsy
rabies
radiation
sickness
repetitive
strain injury
(RSI)
retinitis
retinopathy
rheumatic
fever
rheumatism
rheumatoid
arthritis
rhinitis
rickets
ringworm
roseola
rubella
St Vitus's
dance
salmonella
sarcoma
scabies
scarlet fever
schizophrenia

sciatica
scleritis
scleroderma
sclerosis
scrofula
scurvy
sepsis
septicaemia
severe acute
respiratory
syndrome
(SARS)
sexually

transmitted
disease (STD)
shingles
sick building
syndrome
(SBS)
sickle-cell
anaemia/
disease
silicosis
sinusitis
sleeping
sickness

smallpox
Spanish flu
spina bifida
spondylosis
strabismus
sudden infant
death
syndrome
(SIDS)
sunstroke
Sydenham's
chorea
synovitis

syphilis
tendinitis
tenosynovitis
tetanus
thrombosis
thrush
tonsillitis
Tourette's
syndrome
toxaemia
toxic shock
syndrome
toxocariasis

toxoplasmosis
trench foot
trichinosis
trypanosomia-
sis
tuberculosis
(TB)
typhoid
typhus
undulant fever
urethritis
urticaria
vaginismus

venereal
disease (VD)
viraemia
virus
vitiligo
Weil's disease
whooping
cough
yaws
yellow fever

Psychological illnesses and conditions

anorexia
nervosa
Asperger's
syndrome
attention
deficit
hyperactivity
disorder
(ADHD)
autism
bipolar
disorder

body
dysmorphic
disorder
bulimia
nervosa
catatonia
combat
fatigue
de Cleram-
bault's
syndrome
dementia
depression

dysphoria
dysthymia
eating
disorder
erotomania
false memory
syndrome
gender
dysphoria
hebephrenia
hyperactivity
hyperkinesis
hypomania

Korsakoff's
syndrome
manic
depression
megalomania
multiple-
personality
disorder
Munchausen's
syndrome
Munchausen's
syndrome by
proxy

obsessive–
compulsive
disorder
(OCD)
panic disorder
paramnesia
paranoia
paraphilia
pica
post-natal
depression

post-traumatic
stress
disorder
(PTSD)
psychosis
schizo-
affective
disorder
schizophrenia
seasonal
affective dis-
order (SAD)
shell shock

Types and forms of medication

abortifacient
alpha blocker
anaesthetic
analeptic
analgesic
anaphrodisiac
anodyne
anovulant
antacid
anthelmintic
antibacterial
antibiotic
anticoagulant
antidote
anti-emetic
antihistamine
anti-infective
anti-
inflammatory

antipruritic
antipsychotic
antipyretic
antiscorbutic
antiseptic
antispasmodic
antitussive
antiviral
anxiolytic
aperient
aphrodisiac
balsam
beta blocker
booster
cachet
calmative
caplet
capsule
carminative

contraceptive
convulsant
cream
curative
cure-all
decongestant
depressant
diaphoretic
digestive
dilator
diuretic
draught
drip
drops
ear drops
emetic
enema
euphoriant
evacuant

expectorant
eye drops
febrifuge
fungicide
gargle
germicide
hypodermic
inhalant
injectable
laxative
linctus
lotion
lozenge
mercurial
muscle
relaxant
narcotic
nasal spray
nebulizer

nervine
neuroleptic
nootropic
ointment
painkiller
palliative
pastille
pessary
pill
placebo
poultice
powder
preventive
prophylactic
psychotropic
relaxant
restorative
rub
salve

sedative
sleeping pill
soporific
spray
steroid
stimulant
stupefacient
sudorific
suppository
suppressant
tablet
tonic
tranquillizer
vasodilator
vermifuge

Phobias

Object of fear or dislike	Phobia	Object of fear or dislike	Phobia
air travel	aerophobia	body odour	bromidrosiphobia
American people and things	Americophobia	bridges	gephyrophobia
animals	zoophobia	bullets	ballistophobia
bacteria	bacteriophobia	cancer	carcinophobia
beards	pogonophobia	cats	ailurophobia
beating	mastigophobia	childbirth	tocophobia
bed	clinophobia	children	paedophobia
bees	apiphobia	Chinese people and things	Sinophobia
being buried alive	taphephobia	church	ecclesiophobia
birds	ornithophobia	clouds	nephophobia
blood	haemophobia	coitus	coitophobia
blushing	erythrophobia	cold	cheimaphobia

Object of fear or dislike	Phobia	Object of fear or dislike	Phobia
colour	chromophobia	illness	nosophobia
comets	cometophobia	imperfection	atelophobia
computers	cyberphobia	infinity	apeirophobia
constipation	prostasophobia	injury	traumatophobia
corpses	necrophobia	inoculation	trypanophobia/accinophobia
correspondence	epistolophobia	insanity	lyssophobia/maniphobia
crowds	demophobia/ochlophobia	insects	entomophobia
dampness	hygrophobia	insect stings	cnidophobia
darkness	scotophobia	Italian people	Italophobia
dawn	eosophobia	and things	
death	thanatophobia	itching	acarophobia
depth	bathophobia	jealousy	zelotypophobia
dirt	mysophobia	justice	dikephobia
disease	pathophobia/nosophobia	lakes	limnophobia
dogs	cynophobia	leprosy	leprophobia
dreams	oneirophobia	lice	pediculophobia
drink	potophobia	light	photophobia
drugs	pharmacophobia	lightning	astrapophobia
dust	koniophobia	lists	pinaciphobia/katastichophobia
electricity	electrophobia	loneliness	autophobia/ermitophobia
enclosed places	claustrophobia	machinery	mechanophobia
English people	Anglophobia	magic	rhabdophobia
and things		marriage	gamophobia
everything	panophobia/pantophobia	men	androphobia
eyes	ommetaphobia	metal	metallophobia
faeces	coprophobia	mice	musophobia
failure	kakorrhaphiaphobia	microbes	bacillophobia/
fatigue	kopophobia		microbiophobia
fear	phobophobia	mirrors	eisoptrophobia
feathers	pteronophobia	mites	acarophobia
fever	febriphobia	mobs	ochlophobia
fire	pyrophobia	money	chrematophobia
fish	ichthyophobia	motion	kinetophobia
flesh	selaphobia	music	musicophobia
floods	antlophobia	names	onomatophobia
flowers	anthophobia	narrowness	anginophobia
fog	homichlophobia	needles	belonephobia
food	cibophobia/sitophobia	new things	neophobia
foreigners	xenophobia	night	nyctophobia
freedom	eleutherophobia	nudity	gymnophobia
French people	Francophobia/	open places	agoraphobia
and things	Gallophobia	pain	algophobia
fur	doraphobia	parasites	parasitophobia
German people	Germanophobia	people	anthropophobia
and things	Teutophobia	philosophy	philosophobia
germs	bacteriophobia	pins	enetophobia
ghosts	phasmophobia	places	topophobia
giving birth	teratophobia	pleasure	hedonophobia
to monsters		poison	toxiphobia
glass	nelophobia	politics	politicophobia
God	theophobia	Pope	papaphobia
gold	chrysophobia/aurophobia	poverty	peniaphobia
hair	trichophobia	precipices	cremnophobia
heart disease	cardiophobia	priests	hierophobia
heat	thermophobia	punishment	poinephobia
heaven	uranophobia	rabies	hydrophobophobia
hell	hadephobia/stygiophobia	rail travel	siderodromophobia
heredity	patroiophobia	religious works	iconophobia
high buildings	batophobia	of art	
high places	acrophobia/hypsophobia	reptiles	batrachophobia
home	oikophobia	responsibility	hypegiaphobia
homosexuals	homophobia	ridicule	katagelophobia
horses	hippophobia	rivers	potamophobia
ice	cryophobia	robbers	harpaxophobia
ideas	ideophobia	ruin	atephobia
idleness	thassophobia		

Object of fear or dislike	Phobia	Object of fear or dislike	Phobia
Russian people and things	Russophobia	stealing	kleptophobia
saints	hagiophobia	string	linonophobia
Satan	Satanophobia	stuttering	lalophobia/laliophobia
scabies	scabiophobia	sun	heliophobia
Scottish people and things	Scotophobia	swallowing	phagophobia
		symmetry	symmetrophobia
sea	thalassophobia	taste	geumatophobia
sex	erotophobia	technology	technophobia
shadows	sciophobia	teeth	odontophobia
sharpness	acrophobia	telephone	telephonophobia
shock	hormephobia	thinking	phronemophobia
sin	hamartophobia	thirteen	triskaidekaphobia
skin disease	dermatosiophobia/ dermatopathophobia	thunder	brontophobia/ tonitrophobia
sleep	hypnophobia	time	chronophobia
slime	blennophobia	touch	haptophobia
small things	microphobia	travel	hodophobia
smell	olfactophobia	tuberculosis	phthisiophobia
smothering	pnigerophobia	tyrants	tyrannophobia
snakes	ophidiophobia	vehicles	ochophobia
snow	chionophobia	venereal disease	syphilophobia
solitude	eremophobia	voids	kenophobia
sound	acousticophobia	vomiting	emetophobia
sourness	acerophobia	water	hydrophobia
speech	lalophobia/laliophobia/ glossophobia/ phonophobia	waves	cymophobia
		weakness	asthenophobia
		wind	anemophobia
speed	tachophobia	women	gynophobia
spiders	arachnophobia	words	logophobia
standing	stasophobia	work	ergophobia
stars	siderophobia	worms	helminthophobia
		writing	graphophobia

Music and Dance

Musical genres

absolute music	chamber music	fusion	jump blues	pibroch	rocksteady
acid house	chant	gagaku	jungle	pogo	sakkie-sakkie
acid jazz	choral music	galant	klezmer	pop	salsa
acid rock	classical music	gangsta (rap)	Krautrock	popular music	serialism
alt.country	comic opera	garage	kwaito	programme music	sijo
ambient music	country	glam rock	kwela		ska
AOR	country and western	go-go	light opera	progressive	skiffle
bachata		gospel	marabi	psychedelic	soca
barbershop	country rock	Goth	mariachi	psychobilly	soukous
baroque	cumbia	grand opera	mbaqanga	punk	soul
barrelhouse	dancehall	grunge	mento	qawwali	surf
bel canto	death metal	gumbo	merengue	ragamuffin/ ragga	swing
benga	disco	hardcore	Motown		symphonic music
bebop	Dixieland	heavy metal	musique concrète	ragtime	
bhangra	doo-wop	highlife	New Age	rai	taarab
bluegrass	drum and bass	hip hop	New Romantic	ranchera	tasso
blues		honky-tonk	new wave	rap	techno
boogie-woogie	dub	house	norteño	rave	Tejano
bop	easy listening	indie	northern soul	reggae	Tex-Mex
breakbeat	electro	industrial	opera	reggaeton	thrash (metal)
Britpop	emo/emocore	jazz	opera buffa	rhythm and blues (R & B)	trad jazz
calypso	flamenco	jazz funk	opera seria	rock	trance
Cantopop	folk	jit	orbital	rockabilly	trip hop
	funk	jive	parang	rock and roll	
		juju			

twelve-note/	vocalese	world music
twelve-tone	western	zouk
music	swing	zydeco

Musical forms

air	concertino	gavotte	octet	rhapsody	solo
allemande	concerto	gigue	opera	ricercar/	sonata
anthem	concerto	glee	operetta	ricercare	sonatina
arabesque	grosso	gradual	oratorio	ritornello	song
aria	coronach	hornpipe	overture	romance	song cycle
arietta	courante	humoresque	partita	rondo	spiritual
arioso	dance	hymn	part-song	round	stomp
aubade	dead march	impromptu	paso doble	roundelay	strathspey
bagatelle	descant	interlude	passacaglia	rumba	study
ballad	dirge	intermezzo	passion	samba	suite
ballet	ditty	introit	pastoral	sarabande	symphonic
barcarole	duet	jig	pavane	scena	poem
berceuse	dumka	jingle	pibroch	scherzo	symphony
bourrée	duo	karanga	polka	schottische	terzetto
brindisi	ensemble	lament	polonaise	seguidilla	threnody
cabaletta	entr'acte	Lied	postlude	septet	thumri
calypso	entrée	lullaby	prelude	serenade	tiento
canon	étude	madrigal	psalm	serenata	toccata
canticle	fado	march	quadrille	setting	tone poem
canzone	fancy	mass	quartet	sextet	trio
canzonetta	fanfare	medley	quintet	shanty	variation
capriccio	fantasia	minuet	quodlibet	shuffle	verset
carol	fantasy	monody	rag	siciliano/	villanella/
catch	finale	motet	raga	siciliana	villanelle
cavatina	flourish	moto	rap	signature tune	voluntary
chaconne	foxtrot	perpetuo	recitative	sinfonia	waiata
chanson	frottola	movement	reel	sinfonia	
chant	fugato	musette	refrain	concertante	
chorale	fugue	nocturne	requiem	sinfonietta	
chorus	galop	nonet	reverie	Singspiel	

Musical instruments

accordion	chamber	flugelhorn	lyre	rattle	tambourine
acoustic guitar	organ	flute	mandola	rebec	tamburitza
aeolian harp	chitarrone	fortepiano	mandolin	recorder	tam-tam
alpenhorn	cimbalom	French horn	maraca	reed organ	temple block
althorn	citole	gamba	melodeon	reed pipe	tenor drum
American	cittern	glockenspiel	melodica	sackbut	tenor horn
organ	clarinet	gong	mouth organ	samisen	theorbo
autoharp	clarion	grand piano	oboe	santoor	thumb piano
bagpipes	clarsach	guitar	oboe d'amore	sarod	timpani
balalaika	claves	Hammond	ocarina	sarrusophone	tin whistle
banjo	clavichord	organ	ondes	saxhorn	tom-tom
barrel organ	clavier	(trademark)	martenot	saxophone	triangle
bass clarinet	conga drum	handbell	organ	serpent	triple harp
bass drum	contrabass	harmonica	oud	shawm	trombone
basset horn	contrabassoon	harmonium	pedal steel	side drum	trumpet
bass guitar	cor anglais	harp	guitar	sitar	tuba
bassoon	cornet	harpsichord	piano	slide guitar	tubular bell
bass tuba	cornetto	Hawaiian	piano	slide	ukulele/
bass viol	cymbal	guitar	accordion	trombone	ukelele
bell	didgeridoo	heckelphone	pianoforte	snare drum	upright piano
bombarde	double bass	helicon	pianola	sousaphone	vibraphone
bombardon	drum	hi-hat	piano organ	Spanish guitar	vihuela
bongos	dulcimer	horn	piccolo	spinet	viol
bouzouki	electric guitar	hurdy-gurdy	pipe	steel drum	viola
bugle	electric organ	Jew's harp	pipe organ	string bass	viola da
carillon	euphonium	kazoo	player piano	synthesizer	gamba
castanet	fiddle	kettledrum	portative	tabla	viola d'amore
celesta	fife	kick drum	organ	tabor	violin
cello	fipple flute	krummhorn	post horn	tambour	violoncello
Celtic harp	flageolet	lute	psaltery	tamboura	violone

Wordfinder

virginals	whistle	Wurlitzer	zither
Wagner tuba	wobbleboard	(trademark)	
Welsh harp		xylophone	

Types of singer

alto	castrato	countertenor	jongleur	opera singer	tenor
balladeer	choirboy	diva	Meistersinger	pop singer	treble
baritone	choirgirl	falsetto	mezzo	prima donna	troubadour
bass	chorister	folk singer	mezzo-	soloist	
basso	coloratura	gleeman	soprano	soprano	
profundo	contralto	Heldentenor	minstrel	spinto	

Dances and types of dancing

ballet	charleston	folk dance	lambada	Paul Jones	shuffle
ballroom	circle dance	formation	Lambeth Walk	pole dancing	skank
barn dance	clog dance	dancing	lap dancing	polka	slam dance
beguine	conga	foxtrot	limbo	polonaise	snake dance
belly dance	Cossack	galop	line dancing	quadrille	square dance
body popping	dance	gavotte	mambo	quickstep	stomp
bolero	cotillion	Gay Gordons	maypole	rain dance	strut
boogaloo	country dance	Highland fling	dance	reel	sun dance
boogie	cumbia	hoedown	mazurka	robotic	sword dance
bop	disco	hokey-cokey	minuet	dancing	tango
bossa nova	do-si-do	hornpipe	moonstomp	rock and roll	tap dance
Boston	ecossaise	hula-hula	moonwalk	ronde	turkey trot
break-dancing	eightsome	Irish jig	morris dance	round dance	twist
cakewalk	reel	Irish reel	mosh	roundelay	twosome reel
cancan	fan dance	jazz dance	old-time	rumba	two-step
carioca	fandango	jig	one-step	salsa	vogueing
ceroc	farruca	jitterbug	pas de deux	samba	waltz
cha-cha	flamenco	jive	paso doble	shake	war dance
cha-cha-cha	fling	jota	pas seul	shimmy	

Plants

Flowering plants and shrubs

Aaron's rod	aster	black-eyed	cactus	choisya	cotoneaster
abelia	astilbe	Susan	calceolaria	chokeberry	cottonweed
acacia	astrantia	blackthorn	calendula	cholla	cow parsley
acanthus	aubretia	bleeding heart	camellia	Christmas	cowslip
aconite	avens	bluebell	camomile	cactus	cranesbill
African daisy	azalea	bog asphodel	campanula	Christmas	creeping
African violet	balsam	bog rosemary	campion	rose	Jenny
agapanthus	baneberry	boneset	candytuft	chrysan-	crocus
agave	banksia	borage	canna lily	themum	crowfoot
agrimony	barberry	bougainvillea	Canterbury	cicely	crown
aloe	barrenwort	bramble	bell	cinchona	imperial
alstroemeria	bearberry	broom	Cape primrose	cinquefoil	crown of
alyssum	bedstraw	bryony	carnation	clarkia	thorns
amaranth	begonia	buckeye	catmint	clematis	cuckoo pint
amaryllis	belladonna	buddleia	cattleya	cloudberry	cuckooflower
anemone	bellflower	bugbane	ceanothus	clove pink	cyclamen
angelica	bergamot	bugle	celandine	clover	daffodil
angel's	betony	bugloss	centaury	cockscomb	dahlia
trumpet	bilberry	bulrush	chaffweed	coltsfoot	daisy
aquilegia	bindweed	burdock	chervil	columbine	damask rose
arabis	bird of	burnet	chickweed	comfrey	dandelion
arnica	paradise	busy Lizzie	chicory	coneflower	daphne
arrowgrass	flower	buttercup	chinaberry	convolvulus	deadly
arum lily	bird's-foot	butterfly bush	Chinese	coreopsis	nightshade
asphodel	trefoil	butterwort	lantern	cornflower	delphinium
aspidistra		cabbage rose	chives	corydalis	dianthus

dill
dittany
dock
dogbane
dog rose
dog violet
dropwort
duckweed
echinacea
edelweiss
eglantine
elder
evening
  primrose
eyebright
feverfew
figwort
firethorn
flax
fleabane
forget-me-not
forsythia
foxglove
frangipani
fraxinella
freesia
fritillary
fuchsia
furze
gaillardia
gardenia
gazania
gentian
geranium
gerbera
gillyflower
gladiolus
globeflower
glory-of-the-
  snow
gloxinia
goat's beard
golden rod
goldilocks
gorse
grape
  hyacinth
grass of
  Parnassus
groundsel
guelder rose
gypsophila
harebell

hawkbit
hawksbeard
hawkweed
hawthorn
heartsease
heather
hebe
helianthemum
helianthus
heliotrope
hellebore
helleborine
hemlock
herb
  Christopher
herb Paris
herb Robert
heuchera
hibiscus
hogweed
holly
hollyhock
honesty
honeysuckle
hop
hosta
hyacinth
hydrangea
ice plant
iris
jacaranda
Jack-by-the-
  hedge
Jacob's ladder
japonica
jasmine
jonquil
juneberry
kalanchoe
kalmia
kerria
kingcup
knapweed
knotgrass
laburnum
lady's mantle
lady's slipper
lady's smock
lady's tresses
larkspur
lavatera
lavender
lemon balm

leopard lily
lilac
lily
lily of the
  valley
lobelia
London pride
loosestrife
lords and
  ladies
lotus
lovage
love-in-a-mist
love-lies-
  bleeding
lungwort
lupin
madonna lily
magnolia
mahonia
mallow
mandrake
marguerite
marigold
marsh
  marigold
marshwort
may
mayflower
mayweed
meadow rue
meadow
  saffron
meadowsweet
Michaelmas
  daisy
mignonette
milfoil
milkwort
mimosa
mint
mistletoe
mock orange
monkey
  flower
monkshood
montbretia
moonflower
morning glory
motherwort
musk rose
myrtle
narcissus

nasturtium
nemesia
nettle
nicotiana
nigella
night-scented
  stock
nightshade
old man's
  beard
oleander
orchid
ox-eye daisy
oxlip
oyster plant
pansy
Parma violet
parsley
pasque flower
passion flower
pelargonium
pennyroyal
penstemon
peony
peppermint
periwinkle
petunia
peyote
pheasant's
  eye
phlox
pimpernel
pink
pitcher plant
plantain
plumbago
poinsettia
polyanthus
poppy
potentilla
prickly pear
prickly poppy
primrose
primula
privet
pulsatilla
pyracantha
pyrethrum
ragweed
ragwort
rampion
ramsons
rape

red-hot poker
rhododendron
rock rose
rose
rosebay
  willowherb
rose of Sharon
safflower
saguaro
St John's wort
salpiglossis
salvia
samphire
sandwort
saxifrage
scabious
scarlet
  pimpernel
scilla
sedum
shamrock
sheep's-bit
shrimp plant
skullcap
snapdragon
snow-in-
  summer
snowdrop
snowflake
soapwort
Solomon's
  seal
sorrel
sowthistle
speedwell
spider flower
spider plant
spiderwort
spikenard
spiraea
spurge
spurrey
squill
star of
  Bethlehem
starwort
stitchwort
stock
stonecrop
storksbill
strawflower
streptocarpus
sunflower

sweetbriar
sweet cicely
sweet pea
sweet rocket
sweet william
tansy
tea rose
teasel
thistle
thorn apple
thrift
tiger lily
toadflax
tormentil
tradescantia
traveller's joy
trefoil
tuberose
tulip
turnsole
valerian
Venus flytrap
verbena
veronica
vervain
vetch
viburnum
violet
viper's bugloss
wallflower
water lily
water violet
willowherb
winter jasmine
wintergreen
wintersweet
wisteria
witch hazel
wolfsbane
wood
  anemone
wood avens
woodruff
wood sorrel
woody
  nightshade
wormwood
yarrow
yerba buena
yucca
zinnia

Trees and shrubs

acacia
acer
ackee
alder
allspice
almond
angelica
anise
annatto
apple
apricot
araucaria
ash

aspen
avocado
azalea
balsa
balsam fir
bamboo
banksia
banyan
baobab
basswood
bay tree
beech
beefwood

bergamot
birch
blackthorn
bluegum
bodh tree
bog oak
bottlebrush
bottle tree
bo tree
box
box elder
breadfruit
bristlecone

pine
broom
buckeye
buckthorn
bullace
bur oak
butternut
cacao
calabash
camellia
camphor tree
candelabra
  tree

candleberry
candlenut
carambola
carob
cashew
cassava
cassia
casuarina
cedar
cherimoya
cherry
cherry laurel
cherry plum

chestnut
chinaberry
cinnamon
citron
clove
coco de mer
coconut palm
coffee
cola
coolibah
copper beech
coral tree
cork oak

coromandel	gum tree	laurel	monkey	pussy willow	stinkwood
cottonwood	handkerchief	lemon	puzzle	quassia	stone pine
crab apple	tree	Leyland	mountain ash	quince	storax
cryptomeria	hawthorn	cypress	mulberry	rain tree	sugar maple
curry leaf	hazel	leylandii	myrtle	rambutan	sumac
custard apple	hemlock fir	lilac	nectarine	redbud	sycamore
cypress	hickory	lime	Norway	red cedar	tallow tree
damson	holly	linden	spruce	redwood	tamarind
dawn	holly oak	liquidambar	nutmeg	rhodo-	tamarisk
redwood	holm oak	live oak	nux vomica	dendron	tangerine
dogwood	honey locust	locust	oak	robinia	tea
Douglas fir	honeysuckle	lodgepole	oleaster	roseapple	teak
dragon tree	hornbeam	pine	olive	rosewood	tea tree
ebony	horse	logwood	osier	rowan	thuja
elder	chestnut	Lombardy	pagoda tree	royal palm	tree of
elm	hydrangea	poplar	palm	rubber plant	heaven
eucalyptus	ilex	London plane	palmyra	rubber tree	trembling
euonymus	iroko	loquat	papaya	sallow	poplar
false acacia	ironbark	lychee	paper	sandalwood	tulip tree
fever tree	ironwood	macadamia	mulberry	sapele	tulipwood
ficus	jacaranda	macrocarpa	paperbark	sapodilla	umbrella tree
fig	jackfruit	madroño	pawpaw	sassafras	viburnum
filbert	jack pine	magnolia	pear	satinwood	walnut
fir	japonica	mahogany	pedunculate	schefflera	wattle
firethorn	jasmine	maidenhair	oak	Scots pine	weeping
flame tree	jojoba	tree	persimmon	senna	willow
frangipani	jujube	mandarin	pine	sequoia	wellingtonia
fuchsia	juniper	mango	piñon	service tree	whitebeam
gean	kalmia	mangosteen	pistachio	silver birch	willow
genipapo	kapok	mangrove	pitch pine	Sitka	witch hazel
ginkgo	kermes oak	maple	plane	slippery elm	wych elm
gorse	kola	mastic	plum	smoke tree	yew
grapefruit	kumquat	maté	pomegranate	soapberry	ylang-ylang
greengage	laburnum	may	pomelo	spindle	
guaiacum	lacquer tree	mimosa	poplar	spruce	
guava	larch	mirabelle	privet	star anise	

Mushrooms, toadstools, and other fungi

agaric	boletus	death cap	grisette	oyster	russula
amethyst	bracket	destroying	honey fungus	mushroom	shiitake
deceiver	fungus	angel	horn of plenty	parasol	sickener
armillaria	button	earthstar	horse	mushroom	stinkhorn
beefsteak	mushroom	ergot	mushroom	penny bun	straw
fungus	cep	fairies'	ink cap	polypore	mushroom
bird's-nest	champignon	bonnets	Jew's ear	porcini	tartufo
black bulgar	chanterelle	field	liberty cap	portobello	truffle
blewit	dead man's	mushroom	morel	puffball	
blusher	fingers	fly agaric	mousseron	reishi	

Science

Branches of science *see also* Branches of medicine

acoustics	biology	earth science	fluid	geophysics	marine
aerodynamics	botany	ecology	mechanics	glaciology	biology
agriscience	chemistry	economics	forensics	herpetology	mathematics
anatomy	climatology	electrical	genetic	histology	mechanics
anthropology	computer	engineering	engineering	holography	metallurgy
astronomy	science	electronics	genetics	hydro-	meteorology
astrophysics	cosmology	engineering	geochemistry	dynamics	microbiology
bacteriology	cryogenics	entomology	geography	hydrology	mineralogy
behavioural	cybernetics	ethnology	geology	hydrostatics	molecular
science	cytology	ethology	geomorph-	ichthyology	biology
biochemistry	dendrology	exobiology	ology	linguistics	mycology

natural	ocean-	particle	quantum	spectroscopy	zoo-
history	ography	physics	mechanics	statistics	geography
neuroscience	optics	petrology	radiology	stratigraphy	zoology
nuclear	ornithology	physics	robotics	taxonomy	zymurgy
chemistry	palaeobotany	physiography	seismology	tectonics	
nuclear	palaeon-	physiology	sociobiology	toxicology	
physics	tology	phytology	sociology	volcanology/	
	parasitology	psychiatry	soil science	vulcanology	

Chemical elements and symbols

Element	Symbol	Element	Symbol	Element	Symbol	Element	Symbol
actinium	Ac	einsteinium	Es	mendelevium	Md	rutherfordium	Rf
aluminium	Al	erbium	Er	mercury	Hg	samarium	Sm
americium	Am	europium	Eu	molybdenum	Mo	scandium	Sc
antimony	Sb	fermium	Fm	neodymium	Nd	seaborgium	Sg
argon	Ar	fluorine	F	neon	Ne	selenium	Se
arsenic	As	francium	Fr	neptunium	Np	silicon	Si
astatine	At	gadolinium	Gd	nickel	Ni	silver	Ag
barium	Ba	gallium	Ga	niobium	Nb	sodium	Na
berkelium	Bk	germanium	Ge	nitrogen	N	strontium	Sr
beryllium	Be	gold	Au	nobelium	No	sulphur	S
bismuth	Bi	hafnium	Hf	osmium	Os	tantalum	Ta
bohrium	Bh	hassium	Hs	oxygen	O	technetium	Tc
boron	B	helium	He	palladium	Pd	tellurium	Te
bromine	Br	holmium	Ho	phosphorus	P	terbium	Tb
cadmium	Cd	hydrogen	H	platinum	Pt	thallium	Tl
caesium	Cs	indium	In	plutonium	Pu	thorium	Th
calcium	Ca	iodine	I	polonium	Po	thulium	Tm
californium	Cf	iridium	Ir	potassium	K	tin	Sn
carbon	C	iron	Fe	praseodymium	Pr	titanium	Ti
cerium	Ce	krypton	Kr	promethium	Pm	tungsten	W
chlorine	Cl	lanthanum	La	protactinium	Pa	uranium	U
chromium	Cr	lawrencium	Lr	radium	Ra	vanadium	V
cobalt	Co	lead	Pb	radon	Rn	xenon	Xe
copper	Cu	lithium	Li	rhenium	Re	ytterbium	Yb
curium	Cm	lutetium	Lu	rhodium	Rh	yttrium	Y
darmstadtium	Ds	magnesium	Mg	roentgenium	Rg	zinc	Zn
dubnium	Db	manganese	Mn	rubidium	Rb	zirconium	Zr
dysprosium	Dy	meitnerium	Mt	ruthenium	Ru		

Rocks and minerals

agate	chalcedony	fire opal	jasper	onyx	sardonyx
alabaster	chalk	flint	lapis lazuli	oolite	schist
alexandrite	chert	fluorite	lava	opal	serpentine
almandine	chromite	fluorspar	limestone	orpiment	shale
amber	chrysolite	fool's gold	magnetite	pegmatite	slate
amethyst	chrysoprase	gabbro	malachite	peridot	smoky quartz
aquamarine	cinnabar	galena	manganite	peridotite	spinel
asbestos	cipolin	garnet	marble	phosphorite	steatite
balas ruby	citrine	girasol	marcasite	pitchblende	sunstone
baryte	coal	gneiss	marl	porphyry	talc
basalt	conglomerate	granite	mica	pumice	topaz
beryl	cornelian	graphite	mica schist	pyrites	tourmaline
bloodstone	corundum	greenstone	moonstone	pyrope	tuff
Blue John	cryolite	gypsum	moss agate	quartz	turquoise
borax	diamond	haematite	mudstone	quartzite	vermiculite
breccia	diorite	hornblende	muscovite	rag	zeolite
cairngorm	dolerite	hornfels	natron	rhyolite	zircon
calcite	dolomite	ironstone	nephrite	rock salt	
carbuncle	emerald	jacinth	obsidian	ruby	
carnelian	emery	jade	oil shale	sandstone	
cat's-eye	feldspar	jadeite	olivine	sapphire	

Subatomic particles

antiparticle	antiquark	baryon	electron	gluon	Higgs boson
antiproton	axion	boson	fermion	hadron	Higgs particle

hyperon	lambda	meson	neutron	pion	quark
kaon	particle	muon	nucleon	positron	tau particle
	lepton	neutrino	photon	proton	WIMP

Wordfinder

Sports and Games

Sports *see also following lists*

aerobatics	coarse fishing	gliding	match fishing	rounders	surfing
aerobics	coursing	greyhound	mountain	rowing	swimming
angling	cross-country	racing	biking	sailing	synchronized
aquaplaning	running	gymkhana	mountaineer-	scuba-diving	swimming
archery	curling	gymnastics	ing	sculling	three-day
athletics	cycle racing	hang-gliding	orienteering	sea fishing	eventing
badminton	cycling	harness racing	parachuting	shooting	tobogganing
ballooning	cyclo-cross	heli-skiing	paragliding	showjumping	trap shooting
base-jumping	darts	hiking	parapenting	skateboarding	trotting
beagling	dinghy racing	hockey	parasailing	skating	wakeboarding
BMX	diving	horse racing	parascending	skeet	walking
bobsleighing	downhill	hunting	pigeon racing	skiing	waterskiing
boxing	skiing	hydrospeed	pistol	skijoring	weightlifting
bullfighting	falconry	ice dancing	shooting	ski jumping	white-water
bungee	fencing	ice hockey	point-to-point	skin-diving	rafting
jumping	figure-skating	ice skating	potholing	skydiving	wild-water
caber tossing	fishing	jet-skiing	powerboat	slalom	racing
canoeing	flat racing	kabaddi	racing	snorkelling	wildfowling
canyoning	fly-fishing	kayaking	quoits	snowboarding	windsurfing
caving	fowling	kiteboarding	rafting	speed skating	wrestling
clay-pigeon	free skating	kitesurfing	rock climbing	spelunking	yachting
shooting	freestyling	langlauf	roller skating	sprinting	
climbing	game fishing	luge	rollerblading	steeplechasing	

Athletics events

biathlon	field event	hurdles	marathon	pole vault	tetrathlon
cross-country	half-marathon	javelin	middle-	relay race	track event
running	hammer	long jump	distance race	shot-put	triathlon
decathlon	heptathlon	long-distance	mile	sprint	triple jump
discus	high jump	race	pentathlon	steeplechase	tug of war

Martial arts and combat sports

aikido	fencing	judo	Krav Maga	sumo wrestling	ultimate
ba gua	hapkido	kalaripayattu	kung fu	tae kwon do	fighting
boxing	jeet kune do	karate	pa kua	t'ai chi chu'an	wing chun
budo	jousting	kendo	Shotokan	tang soo do	wrestling
capoeira	ju-jitsu	kick-boxing	Silat	Thai boxing	wushu

Motor sports

autocross	dirt-track	Formula One	Indycar	off-roading	speedway
cross-country	racing	go-karting	karting	rallycross	stock-car
demolition	drag racing	Grand Prix	motocross	rallying	racing
derby	enduro	hill-climbing	motorcycle	scrambling	trials
	F1	Indy	racing	sidecar racing	

Games *see also following lists*

Aunt Sally	cards	Chinese	equences	draughts	follow-my-
backgammon	catch	chequers	cops and	ducks and	leader
bagatelle	cat's cradle	Chinese	robbers	drakes	forfeits
battleships	charades	whispers	craps	dungeons and	frisbee
billiards	checkers	Cluedo	darts	dragons	(trademark)
bingo	chess	(trademark)	deck quoits	fantasy	go
blind man's	chicken	conkers	dice	football	halma
buff		conse-	dominoes	fivestones	hangman

hide-and-seek
hoopla
hopscotch
housey-housey
hunt the thimble
I spy
jacks
jackstraws
kabaddi
King of the Castle
kriegspiel
leapfrog
lotto
ludo
mah-jong
marbles
Monopoly (trademark)
murder in the dark
musical bumps
musical chairs
nim
noughts and crosses
pass the parcel
pat-a-cake
peekaboo
piggy in the middle
pinball
pitch-and-toss
poker dice
Poohsticks
pool
postman's knock
prisoner's base
quoits
ring-a-ring o' roses
roulette
sardines
Scrabble (trademark)
shove-halfpenny
shovelboard
Simon Says
snakes and ladders
snooker
solitaire
spillikins
spin the bottle
Subbuteo (trademark)
table football
tag
thimblerig
tic-tac-toe
tiddlywinks
tig
treasure hunt
Trivial Pursuit (trademark)
tug of war

Ball games

American football
Association Football
Australian Rules football
bandy
baseball
basketball
beach volleyball
billiards
boule/boules
bowling
bowls
Canadian football
clock golf
cricket
croquet
crown-green bowls
Eton fives
field hockey
five-a-side football
fives
flat-green bowls
football
French cricket
Gaelic football
goalball
golf
handball
hockey
hurling
jai alai
korfball
lacrosse
lawn tennis
mini rugby
netball
ninepins
paddleball
pelota
pétanque
polo
pool
rackets
racquetball
real tennis
rounders
rugby
Rugby fives
rugby league
rugby union
shinty
skittles
snooker
soccer
softball
squash
table tennis
tennis
tenpin bowling
volleyball
water polo

Card games

baccarat
beggar-my-neighbour
bezique
blackjack
Black Maria
Boston
brag
bridge
canasta
cheat
chemin de fer
cribbage
duplicate bridge
écarté
euchre
fan-tan
faro
gin rummy
happy families
loo
monte
nap
Newmarket
old maid
ombre
patience
pinochle
piquet
poker
pontoon
rouge et noir
rummy
skat
snap
solitaire
solo whist
stud poker
twenty-one
vingt-et-un
whist

Technology

Computing and Internet terms

acoustic coupler
agent
alias
applet
application
assembler
backup
bar-code reader
BASIC
baud
BIOS
bit
bitmap
blog
blogger
board
bookmark
boot
bot
browser
buffer
bug
bulletin board
bus
byte
cache
cache memory
card
CD-R
CD-ROM
CD-RW
central processing unit
chat room
chip
click
client
code
compact disc
computer
console
control unit
coprocessor
CPU
crash
crawler
cursor
daemon
data
debugger
desktop
dialler
dialog box
digital
digitizer
disk
disk drive
diskette
display
domain
domain name
DOS
dot-matrix printer
download
drive
DVD
DVD-R
DVD-ROM
DVD-RW
e-tailer
editor
email
emoticon
Ethernet
expansion card
expert system
FAQ
fax modem
file
filename
filter
firewall
firmware
flash memory
floppy disk
format
freeware
FTP
games console
gateway
GIF
gigabit
graphics card
groupware
hacker
hard disk
hard drive
hardware
home page
host
HTML
HTTP
hyperlink
hypertext
icon
in-box
information technology
inkjet printer
input
interactive
interface

Internet
service
provider
intranet
ISP
joystick
JPEG
keyboard
keypad
kilobyte
laptop
laser printer
light pen
log in
log out
loop
macro
mailer
malware
manager
megabyte
megapixel

memory
menu
microchip
micro-
computer
mini-
computer
modem
monitor
motherboard
mouse
mouse mat
navigator
Net
network
newsgroup
notebook
offline
online
optical disk
output
palmtop

parser
PC
PDA
PDF
phishing
plug-in
podcast
pop-up
port
portal
printed circuit
printed circuit
board
printer
printout
processor
program
RAM
random-
access
memory
read-only

memory
register
rollerball
ROM
routine
scanner
screen saver
script
search engine
sequencer
serial port
server
servlet
shareware
shell program
silicon chip
sniffer
software
sound card
spam
spellchecker
spider

spreadsheet
spyware
surf
talkboard
telnet
terminal
text editor
toggle
tool
toolbar
touch pad
touch screen
trackball
transistor
Trojan Horse
upload
URL
user interface
utility
vaccine
VDU
video card

viewscreen
virtual reality
virus
visual display
unit
wallpaper
Web
webcam
weblog
web page
website
wiki
word
processor
workstation
World Wide
Web
worm
XML
zip
zip file

Energy and fuels

acetylene
anthracite
atomic power
bio-diesel
biofuel
biogas
briquette
butane
Calor gas
(trademark)

chemical
energy
coal
coal gas
coke
derv
diesel
electricity
electro-
magnetic
energy

firewood
fossil fuel
fuel oil
fusion energy
gas
gasoline
geothermal
energy
heat
hydroelectric
power

hydrogen
kerosene
leaded petrol
light
lignite
methane
natural gas
nuclear power
oil
paraffin
peat

petrol
petroleum
propane
renewable
energy
solar energy
steam power
tidal power
turf
unleaded
petrol

water power
wave power
wind power
wood

Engines

aero engine
beam engine
diesel engine
donkey
engine
dynamo
electric motor
external-
combustion
engine

flat-four
engine
four-stroke
gas turbine
generator
heat engine
inboard
inline engine

internal-
combustion
engine
jet engine
linear motor
magneto
oil engine
outboard
petrol engine
piston engine

prop jet
pulse jet
radial engine
ramjet
rocket engine
rotary engine
scramjet
steam engine
steam turbine
straight-eight

transverse
engine
thruster
turbine
turbo diesel
turbofan
turbojet
turboprop
turboshaft

twin-cam
engine
two-stroke
V6
V8
V12

Tools

adze
air gun
Allen key
(trademark)
auger
awl
axe
bandsaw
beetle
bevel
billhook
blowlamp
blowtorch
bodkin
borer
bowsaw
brace

bradawl
burin
burnisher
burr
capstan lathe
centre bit
centre punch
chainsaw
chisel
chopper
circular saw
clamp
claw hammer
cleaver
compass saw
coping saw
cramp

cross peen/
pein
crowbar
cultivator
cutter
dibber
dibble
diestock
dovetailer
drill
edge tool
edging shears
edging tool
file
flail
float
fork

former
frame saw
fretsaw
froe
fuller
gimlet
glass cutter
graver
grinder
grouter
hack
hacksaw
hammer
hammer drill
hatchet
hedge clipper
hoe

hole saw
jack
jackhammer
jemmy
jigsaw
jointer
keyhole saw
knife
lathe
lawnmower
loppers
mallet
marlinspike
mattock
mortar board
nail punch
nailer

needle
nippers
padsaw
paint gun
panel saw
peen/pein
hammer
perforator
pestle
pick
pickaxe
pincers
pitchfork
plane
pliers
priest
pruning hook

punch	rule	scroll saw	socket	strickle	trowel
rake	sander	scythe	spanner	swage	tweezers
ram	sandpaper	secateurs	soldering iron	swingle	vice
rasp	saw	shears	spade	tenon saw	wedge
reamer	sawbench	shovel	spanner	tilt hammer	wheel brace
riddle	scarifier	sickle	spokeshave	tinsnips	whipsaw
ripsaw	scraper	slasher	square	torque	wire cutter
roller	screwdriver	sledge-	staple gun	wrench	wire stripper
roulette	screw tap	hammer	steam	trimmer	woodcarver
router	scribe		hammer	trip hammer	wrench

Units of measurement

acre	chain	furlong	kiloton	millilitre	rad
age	cord	gallon	kilovolt	millimetre	radian
air mile	coulomb	gauss	kilowatt	millisecond	rem
ampere	cubit	gigabit	kilowatt-hour	minim	rod
angstrom	cup	gigabyte	knot	minute	roentgen
astronomical	cupful	gigaflop	league	mole	rood
unit	curie	gigahertz	light year	month	scruple
atmosphere	cycle	gigawatt	line	nanometre	second
atomic mass	day	gill	link	nanosecond	siemens
unit	decade	grain	litre	nautical mile	sievert
bale	decalitre	gram	lumen	newton	span
bar	decametre	gray	lux	noggin	square
barrel	decibel	hand	Mach number	ohm	steradian
baud	decilitre	hectare	maxwell	ounce	stone
becquerel	decimetre	henry	megabyte	parsec	tablespoon
bel	degree	hertz	megaflop	pascal	teaspoon
bit	denier	hogshead	megahertz	peck	terabyte
brake	dessertspoon	horsepower	megaton	pennyweight	teraflop
horsepower	dioptre	hour	megavolt	perch	tesla
British thermal	drachm	hundred-	megawatt	period	therm
unit	dyne	weight	metre	pica	tog
bushel	electronvolt	inch	metric ton	pint	ton
byte	ell	joule	microgram	pipe	tonne
cable	epoch	kelvin	microlitre	point	troy ounce
calorie	erg	kilobyte	micrometre	poise	volt
candela	farad	kilocalorie	micron	pole	watt
carat	fathom	kilogram	microsecond	pound	weber
centigram	firkin	kilohertz	mile	quantum bit	week
centilitre	fluid drachm	kilojoule	millennium	quart	yard
centimetre	fluid ounce	kilolitre	millibar	quarter	year
century	foot	kilometre	milligram	quintal	

Wordfinder

Transport

Motor vehicles

all-terrain	bulldozer	dune buggy	hatchback	minelayer	personnel
vehicle	bus	dustcart	hearse	minicab	carrier
ambulance	cab	estate	heavy goods	moped	pickup
armoured car	cabriolet	fastback	vehicle	motorbike	public service
armoured	camper	fire engine	(HGV)	motor caravan	vehicle (PSV)
personnel	car	flatbed	horsebox	motorcycle	quad bike
carrier (APC)	charabanc	float	hot rod	multi-purpose	racing car
articulated	coach	forklift truck	Jeep	vehicle	ragtop
lorry	convertible	four-by-four	(trademark)	(MPV)	rally car
automobile	coupé	four-wheel	juggernaut	notchback	recreational
autorickshaw	dirt bike	drive (4WD)	kart	off-road	vehicle (RV)
battlebus	double-decker	go-kart	kit car	vehicle	removal van
beach buggy	bus	golf cart	limousine	off-roader	roadroller
Black Maria	dragster	gritter	lorry	omnibus	roadster
bowser	drophead	hackney cab	low-loader	pantechnicon	rover
(trademark)	DUKW	half-track	microcar	people carrier	runabout
buggy	dumper truck	hardtop	milk float		saloon

scooter
scrambler
sedan
shooting
  brake
snowcat
snowmobile

snowplough
soft top
sports car
sportster
sport utility
  vehicle (SUV)
station wagon

stock car
stretch limo
superbike
supercar
supermini
tank
tanker

taxi
taxicab
tourer
touring car
tow truck
tracklayer
tractor

trail bike
trailer
tram
transporter
trolleybus
troop carrier
truck

van
wagon/
  waggon
wrecker

Carriages and carts

barouche
brake
brougham
buggy
cab
cabriolet
caravan

carriole
chaise
chariot
clarence
coach
coach-and-
  four

coupé
covered
  wagon
curricle
dog cart
dray
droshky

fiacre
fly
gig
hackney
handcart
hansom
landau

ox cart
phaeton
postchaise
rickshaw
stagecoach
tilbury
trailer

trap
trishaw
tumbril
Victoria
wagon/
  waggon
wagonette

Trains and rolling stock

armoured
  train
bogie
boxcar
brake van
buffet car
bullet train
cable car
caboose
car
carriage

coach
couchette
diesel-electric
diesel
  locomotive
diesel multiple
  unit
dining car
double-header
electric train
engine

express
flatcar
freight train
goods train
goods wagon
guard's van
handcar
high-speed
  train
hopper
hospital train

locomotive
maglev
mail coach
mail train
metro
milk train
monorail
motor coach
observation
  car
pannier tank

passenger
  train
Pullman
railcar
restaurant car
saddle tank
shunter
sleeper
sleeping car
smokebox
smoker

steam
  locomotive
steam train
stopping train
subway train
tank engine
tender
TGV
underground
  train
wagon-lit

Ships and boats

airboat
aircraft carrier
amphibious
  assault ship
amphibious
  landing craft
auxiliary
barge
barque
barquentine
bateau
  mouche
bathyscaphe
bathysphere
battlecruiser
battleship
bireme
boatel
brig
brigantine
bulk carrier
bumboat
cabin cruiser
cable ship
caique
canal boat
canoe
capital ship
car ferry
caravel
cargo ship
carrack
catamaran
catboat
clipper

coal ship
coaler
coaster
cockleshell
collier
container ship
coracle
corvette
cruiser
cruise ship
cutter
destroyer
dhow
dinghy
diving bell
dory
dragon boat
dreadnought
dredger
drifter
dugout
E-boat
East Indiaman
factory ship
felucca
ferry
flag boat
flagship
flatboat
freighter
frigate
full-rigger
galleon
galley
galliot

gig
gondola
gulet
gunboat
helicopter
  carrier
hermaphro-
  dite brig
hospital ship
houseboat
hovercraft
hydrofoil
hydroplane
iceboat
ice-breaker
inboard
Indiaman
inflatable
  dinghy
ironclad
jetboat
jetfoil
jet ski
  (trademark)
jolly
junk
kayak
keelboat
ketch
landing craft
launch
liberty boat
lifeboat
life raft
lighter

lightship
liner
longboat
longship
lugger
mailboat
man-of-war
merchantman
merchant ship
minehunter
minelayer
minesweeper
monitor
monohull
motor boat
motor
  torpedo
  boat
motor yacht
multihull
narrowboat
oiler
oil tanker
outboard
outrigger
paddle boat
paddle
  steamer
pedal boat
pedalo
pilot boat
pink
pinnace
pirogue
pocket

battleship
pontoon
powerboat
pram
privateer
proa
punt
Q-ship
quinquereme
raft
RIB
rigger
riverboat
roll-on roll-off
rowing boat
rubber dinghy
safety boat
sailing boat
sailing ship
sampan
schooner
scow
scull
sealer
shallop
shell
ship of the
  line
showboat
side-wheeler
single-hander
skiff
skipjack
slaver
sloop

sloop of war
smack
speedboat
square-rigger
stake boat
steamboat
steamer
steamship
sternwheeler
submarine
submersible
supertanker
supply ship
tall ship
tanker
tender
torpedo boat
trader
training ship
tramp steamer
trawler
trimaran
trireme
troop carrier
troopship
tub
tugboat
U-boat
vaporetto
warship
water bus
water taxi
weekender
whaleboat
whaler

wherry	workboat	yacht
windjammer	xebec	yawl

Aircraft

airliner	dive bomber	gyrocopter	jetliner	ski-plane	troop carrier
airship	drone	gyroplane	jumbo jet	spaceplane	tug
autogiro	fighter	hang-glider	jump jet	spotter	turbofan
balloon	fighter-	helicopter	microlight	stealth	turbojet
biplane	bomber	hot-air	minelayer	bomber	turboprop
blimp	floatplane	balloon	monoplane	stealth fighter	warplane
bomber	flying boat	hydroplane	night fighter	swept-wing	water bomber
chopper	freighter	interceptor	paraglider	tanker	whirlybird
delta-wing	glider	jet	sailplane	towplane	widebody
dirigible	gunship	jet plane	seaplane	triplane	Zeppelin

War and Weapons

Weapons

A-bomb	buckshot	fragmentation	knife	petard	skean-dhu
air gun	cannon	bomb	knobkerrie	petrol bomb	sling
AK-47	cannonball	fragmentation	knuckleduster	pike	slug
anti-aircraft	car bomb	grenade	kris	pistol	slung shot
gun	carbine	fusil	kukri	plastic bullet	small arms
arquebus	case knife	fusion bomb	lance	plastic	small sword
Armalite	catapult	Gatling gun	landmine	explosive	Smith and
(trademark)	claymore	gelignite	lathi	Polaris	Wesson
arrow	club	grapeshot	Lee-Enfield	poleaxe	(trademark)
artillery	cluster bomb	grenade	letter bomb	pom-pom	smoke bomb
assault rifle	Colt	guided missile	Lewis gun	poniard	smooth-bore
assegai	(trademark)	gun	life preserver	pump-action	spear
atom/atomic	cordite	guncotton	limpet mine	shotgun	staff
bomb	cosh	gunpowder	longbow	quarterstaff	stave
automatic	crossbow	H-bomb	Luger	rapier	Sten gun
axe	cruise missile	halberd	(trademark)	revolver	stick
ballistic missile	cudgel	hand grenade	mace	rifle	stiletto
baseball bat	cutlass	handgun	machete	rocket	sub-machine
baton	dagger	harpoon	machine gun	rocket-	gun
baton round	daisy-cutter	harpoon gun	magnetic	propelled	switchblade
battleaxe	depth charge	harquebus	mine	grenade	sword
bayonet	derringer	hatchet	mail bomb	rubber bullet	swordstick
bazooka	dirk	high explosive	matchlock	sabre	tanto
bill	dirty bomb	horse pistol	Mauser	sawn-off	thirty-eight
birdshot	doodlebug	howitzer	(trademark)	shotgun	time bomb
blackjack	duelling pistol	hydrogen	Maxim gun	scimitar	tomahawk
blade	dumdum	bomb	Mills bomb	Scud	tommy gun
blowpipe	bullet	inter-	missile	semi-	torpedo
bludgeon	dynamite	continental	Molotov	automatic	tracer
blunderbuss	épée	ballistic	cocktail	Semtex	trebuchet
Bofors gun	Exocet	missile	mortar	sheath knife	trench mortar
bomb	express rifle	(ICBM)	musket	shell	Trident
boomerang	firebomb	incendiary	neutron bomb	shillelagh	truncheon
bowie knife	firelock	bomb	nuclear bomb	shotgun	Uzi
brass knuckles	flick knife	incendiary	nulla-nulla	sidearm	warhead
breech-loader	flintlock	device	panga	siege gun	Winchester
Bren gun	flying bomb	jackknife	parang	six-shooter	(trademark)
broadsword	forty-five	javelin	parcel bomb	sjambok	yataghan
Browning		Kalashnikov	pellet	skean	zip gun

Parts of a suit of armour

basinet	breastplate	casque	corselet	gauntlet	hauberk
beaver	brigandine	chain mail	coutere	gorget	helmet
bracer	burgonet	chausses	cuirass	greave	jambeau
brassard	camail	coif	cuisse	habergeon	lance rest

Wordfinder

mail	neck guard	plastron	rerebrace	solleret	ventail
morion	nosepiece	poleyn	sabaton	tasses	visor
nasal	pectoral	pouldron	sallet	vambrace	

Types of soldier

archer	conscript	gunner	legionnaire	pistoleer	sapper
artilleryman	cuirassier	halberdier	marine	point man	scout
beefeater	dragoon	havildar	mercenary	ranger	SEAL
blue helmet	drum major	hoplite	militiaman	ranker	sentinel
bowman	ensign	hussar	musketeer	recruit	sentry
cadet	evzone	infantryman	non-commis-	redcap	sepoy
cannoneer	foot soldier	irregular	sioned	redcoat	spearman
carabineer	freelance	janissary	officer (NCO)	regular	swordsman
cavalier	fusilier	klepht	officer	reservist	trooper
cavalryman	grenadier	knight	orderly	rifleman	yeoman
centurion	guardsman	lancer	paratrooper	sabreur	
commando	guerrilla	legionary	partisan	samurai	

Military ranks

British Army

Field Marshal
General
Lieutenant General
Major General
Brigadier
Colonel
Lieutenant Colonel
Major
Captain
Lieutenant
Second Lieutenant
Warrant Officer
Staff Sergeant
Sergeant
Corporal/Bombardier
Lance Corporal/Lance
  Bombardier
Private/Gunner

Royal Navy

Admiral of the Fleet
Admiral
Vice Admiral
Rear Admiral
Commodore

Captain
Commander
Lieutenant
  Commander
Lieutenant
Sub Lieutenant
Midshipman
Warrant Officer
Chief Petty Officer
Petty Officer
Leading Seaman
Able Seaman
Ordinary Seaman

Royal Air Force

Marshal of the Royal
  Air Force
Air Chief Marshal
Air Marshal
Air Vice-Marshal
Air Commodore
Group Captain
Wing Commander
Squadron Leader
Flight Lieutenant
Flying Officer

Pilot Officer
Acting Pilot Officer
Warrant Officer
Flight Sergeant
Sergeant
Senior Aircraftman/
  Aircraftwoman
Leading Aircraftman/
  Aircraftwoman
Aircraftman/
  Aircraftwoman

US Army and Air Force

Chief of Staff
General
Lieutenant General
Major General
Brigadier General
Colonel
Lieutenant Colonel
Major
Captain
First Lieutenant
Second Lieutenant
Warrant Officer

Sergeant
Corporal
Private First Class
Private

US Navy

Chief of Naval
  Operations
Fleet Admiral
Admiral
Vice Admiral
Rear Admiral
Captain
Commander
Lieutenant
  Commander
Lieutenant
Lieutenant junior grade
Ensign
Warrant Officer
Master Chief Petty
  Officer
Senior Chief Petty
  Officer
Petty Officer
Seaman

Wordfinder